Who Was Who in America®

Who Was Who in America®
with world notables

2009-2010
Volume XXI

MARQUIS
Who'sWho®

890 Mountain Avenue, Suite 300
New Providence, NJ 07974 U.S.A.
www.marquiswhoswho.com

Who Was Who in America®
Marquis Who's Who

For information, contact: Marquis Who's Who, 890 Mountain Avenue, Suite 300
                              New Providence, New Jersey 07974
                              1-800-473-7020; www.marquiswhoswho.com

WHO WAS WHO IN AMERICA is a registered trademark of Marquis Who's Who LLC.

International Standard Book Number	978-0-8379-0282-1	(23-Volume Set)
	978-0-8379-0279-1	(Volume XXI)
	978-0-8379-0280-7	(Index Volume)
	978-0-8379-0281-4	(Volume XXI & Index Volume)
International Standard Serial Number	0146-8081	

Table of Contents

Preface vi

Key to Information vii

Table of Abbreviations viii

Alphabetical Practices xv

Who Was Who in America Biographies 1

Preface

Marquis Who's Who is proud to present the 2009-2010 Edition of *Who Was Who in America*. This 21st edition features over 3,800 profiles of individuals who had previously been profiled in *Who's Who in America* and other Marquis Who's Who publications, whose deaths have been brought to our attention since the publication of the last edition of *Who Was Who in America*.

Among the notable Americans profiled in this volume are individuals as influential and diverse as George Steinbrenner, J.D. Salinger, Dennis Hopper, Art Linkletter, Tom Bosley, Lena Horne, Alexander Haig, Rue McClanahan, Ted Sorensen, and Marshall Nirenberg. The impact of these individuals during their lifetimes was enormous and their influence is certain to live on.

Of course, not every person profiled in this volume is a household name. These pages include the profiles of doctors, lawyers, entrepreneurs, researchers, inventors, and other prominent achievers.

The biographical information included in the profiles that follow was gathered in a variety of manners. In most cases, those listed had submitted their personal biographical details during their lifetime. In many cases, though, the information was collected independently by our research and editorial staffs, which use a wide assortment of tools to gather complete, accurate, and up-to-date information.

Who Was Who in America is an important component of the Marquis Who's Who family of publications. Along with *Who's Who in America* and *Who's Who in the World*, Marquis Who's Who also publishes a number of specialized and regionalized volumes. These include *Who's Who of American Women*, *Who's Who in American Law*, *Who's Who in Medicine and Healthcare*, and *Who's Who in the East*, to name a few.

It has been an honor to compile this edition of *Who Was Who in America*. It is our hope that the biographical profiles will do justice to the individuals memorialized on the pages that follow.

Key to Information

[1] **LINDELL, JAMES ELLIOT,** [2] literature educator; [3] b. Jacksonville, Fla., Sept. 27, 1947; [4] s. Elliot Walter and Tamara Lindell; [5] m. Colleen Marie, Apr. 28, 1969; [6] children: Richard, Matthew, Lucas, Samantha. [7] BA in English, Temple Univ., 1970, MA in English, 1972; PhD in English Lit., Univ. Chgo., 1976. [8] Cert. ESL 1972. [9] Assoc. prof. English Univ. Chgo., 197580, prof. 1980-1988, English dept. head 1989-2007; [10] mem. ESL Coalition, Teach for Tomorrow; bd. dir, Chgo. HS Scholarship Assn. [11] Contbr. articles to profl. jours. [12] vol. Red Cross, 1980-90. [13] Served to USMC, 1972-74. [14] Recipient Outstanding Tchr. award Univ. Chgo., 1990; grantee Teach for Tomorrow, 2000. [15] Fellow Assn. Tchrs. for ESL; mem. MADD, Am. Soc. ESL Tchrs. [16] Democrat. [17] Roman Catholic. [18] Achievements include the expansion of teaching English as a second language to European countries. [19] Avocations: swimming, reading, traveling. [20] Home: 1919 Greenridge Ln Chicago, IL 90921 [21] Office: Univ Chicago English Dept 707 Batsman Hall Chicago IL 90735 [22] Died Sept. 19, 2007.

KEY

[1]	Name
[2]	Occupation
[3]	Vital statistics
[4]	Parents
[5]	Marriage
[6]	Children
[7]	Education
[8]	Professional certifications
[9]	Career
[10]	Career-related
[11]	Writings and creative works
[12]	Civic and political activities
[13]	Military
[14]	Awards and fellowships
[15]	Professional and association memberships, clubs and lodges
[16]	Political affiliation
[17]	Religion
[18]	Achievements
[19]	Avocations
[20]	Home address
[21]	Office address
[22]	Death

Table of Abbreviations

The following is a list of some of the most frequently used Marquis abbreviations:

A

A Associate (used with academic degrees)
AA Associate in Arts
AAAL American Academy of Arts and Letters
AAAS American Association for the Advancement of Science
AACD American Association for Counseling and Development
AACN American Association of Critical Care Nurses
AAHA American Academy of Health Administrators
AAHP American Association of Hospital Planners
AAHPERD American Alliance for Health, Physical Education, Recreation, and Dance
AAS Associate of Applied Science
AASL American Association of School Librarians
AASPA American Association of School Personnel Administrators
AAU Amateur Athletic Union
AAUP American Association of University Professors
AAUW American Association of University Women
AB Arts, Bachelor of
AB Alberta
ABA American Bar Association
AC Air Corps
acad. academy
acct. accountant
acctg. accounting
ACDA Arms Control and Disarmament Agency
ACHA American College of Hospital Administrators
ACLS Advanced Cardiac Life Support
ACLU American Civil Liberties Union
ACOG American College of Ob-Gyn
ACP American College of Physicians
ACS American College of Surgeons
ADA American Dental Association
adj. adjunct, adjutant
adm. admiral
adminstr. administrator
adminstrn. administration
adminstrv. administrative

ADN Associate's Degree in Nursing
ADP Automatic Data Processing
adv. advocate, advisory
advt. advertising
AE Agricultural Engineer
AEC Atomic Energy Commission
aero. aeronautical, aeronautic
aerodyn. aerodynamic
AFB Air Force Base
AFTRA American Federation of Television and Radio Artists
agr. agriculture
agrl. agricultural
agt. agent
AGVA American Guild of Variety Artists
agy. agency
A&I Agricultural and Industrial
AIA American Institute of Architects
AIAA American Institute of Aeronautics and Astronautics
AIChE American Institute of Chemical Engineers
AICPA American Institute of Certified Public Accountants
AID Agency for International Development
AIDS Acquired Immune Deficiency Syndrome
AIEE American Institute of Electrical Engineers
AIME American Institute of Mining, Metallurgy, and Petroleum Engineers
AK Alaska
AL Alabama
ALA American Library Association
Ala. Alabama
alt. alternate
Alta. Alberta
A&M Agricultural and Mechanical
AM Arts, Master of
Am. American, America
AMA American Medical Association
amb. ambassador
AME African Methodist Episcopal
Amtrak National Railroad Passenger Corporation
AMVETS American Veterans
ANA American Nurses Association
anat. anatomical
ANCC American Nurses Credentialing Center

ann. annual
anthrop. anthropological
AP Associated Press
APA American Psychological Association
APHA American Public Health Association
APO Army Post Office
apptd. appointed
Apr. April
apt. apartment
AR Arkansas
ARC American Red Cross
arch. architect
archeol. archeological
archtl. architectural
Ariz. Arizona
Ark. Arkansas
ArtsD Arts, Doctor of
arty. artillery
AS Associate in Science, American Samoa
ASCAP American Society of Composers, Authors and Publishers
ASCD Association for Supervision and Curriculum Development
ASCE American Society of Civil Engineers
ASME American Society of Mechanical Engineers
ASPA American Society for Public Administration
ASPCA American Society for the Prevention of Cruelty to Animals
assn. association
assoc. associate
asst. assistant
ASTD American Society for Training and Development
ASTM American Society for Testing and Materials
astron. astronomical
astrophys. astrophysical
ATLA Association of Trial Lawyers of America
ATSC Air Technical Service Command
atty. attorney
Aug. August
aux. auxiliary
Ave. Avenue
AVMA American Veterinary Medical Association
AZ Arizona

B

B Bachelor
b. born
BA Bachelor of Arts
BAgr Bachelor of Agriculture
Balt. Baltimore
Bapt. Baptist
BArch Bachelor of Architecture
BAS Bachelor of Agricultural Science
BBA Bachelor of Business Administration
BBB Better Business Bureau
BC British Columbia
BCE Bachelor of Civil Engineering
BChir Bachelor of Surgery
BCL Bachelor of Civil Law
BCS Bachelor of Commercial Science
BD Bachelor of Divinity
bd. board
BE Bachelor of Education
BEE Bachelor of Electrical Engineering
BFA Bachelor of Fine Arts
bibl. biblical
bibliog. bibliographical
biog. biographical
biol. biological
BJ Bachelor of Journalism
Bklyn. Brooklyn
BL Bachelor of Letters
bldg. building
BLS Bachelor of Library Science
Blvd. Boulevard
BMI Broadcast Music, Inc.
bn. battalion
bot. botanical
BPE Bachelor of Physical Education
BPhil Bachelor of Philosophy
br. branch
BRE Bachelor of Religious Education
brig. gen. brigadier general
Brit. British
Bros. Brothers
BS Bachelor of Science
BSA Bachelor of Agricultural Science
BSBA Bachelor of Science in Business Administration
BSChemE Bachelor of Science in Chemical Engineering
BSD Bachelor of Didactic Science
BSEE Bachelor of Science in Electrical Engineering
BSN Bachelor of Science in Nursing
BST Bachelor of Sacred Theology
BTh Bachelor of Theology
bull. bulletin

bur. bureau
bus. business
BWI British West Indies

C

CA California
CAD-CAM Computer Aided Design–Computer Aided Model
Calif. California
Can. Canada, Canadian
CAP Civil Air Patrol
capt. captain
cardiol. cardiological
cardiovasc. cardiovascular
Cath. Catholic
cav. cavalry
CBI China, Burma, India Theatre of Operations
CC Community College
CCC Commodity Credit Corporation
CCNY City College of New York
CCRN Critical Care Registered Nurse
CCU Cardiac Care Unit
CD Civil Defense
CE Corps of Engineers, Civil Engineer
CEN Certified Emergency Nurse
CENTO Central Treaty Organization
CEO Chief Executive Officer
CERN European Organization of Nuclear Research
cert. certificate, certification, certified
CETA Comprehensive Employment Training Act
CFA Chartered Financial Analyst
CFL Canadian Football League
CFO Chief Financial Officer
CFP Certified Financial Planner
ch. church
ChD Doctor of Chemistry
chem. chemical
ChemE Chemical Engineer
ChFC Chartered Financial Consultant
Chgo. Chicago
chirurg., der surgeon
chmn. chairman
chpt. chapter
CIA Central Intelligence Agency
Cin. Cincinnati
cir. circle, circuit
CLE Continuing Legal Education
Cleve. Cleveland
climatol. climatological
clin. clinical
clk. clerk
CLU Chartered Life Underwriter
CM Master in Surgery
cmty. community

CO Colorado
Co. Company
COF Catholic Order of Foresters
C. of C. Chamber of Commerce
col. colonel
coll. college
Colo. Colorado
com. committee
comd. commanded
comdg. commanding
comdr. commander
comdt. commandant
comm. communications
commd. commissioned
comml. commercial
commn. commission
commr. commissioner
compt. comptroller
condr. conductor
conf. Conference
Congl. Congregational, Congressional
Conglist. Congregationalist
Conn. Connecticut
cons. consultant, consulting
consol. consolidated
constl. constitutional
constn. constitution
constrn. construction
contbd. contributed
contbg. contributing
contbn. contribution
contbr. contributor
contr. controller
Conv. Convention
COO Chief Operating Officer
coop. cooperative
coord. coordinator
corp. corporation, corporate
corr. correspondent, corresponding, correspondence
coun. council
CPA Certified Public Accountant
CPCU Chartered Property and Casualty Underwriter
CPH Certificate of Public Health
cpl. corporal
CPR Cardio-Pulmonary Resuscitation
CS Christian Science
CSB Bachelor of Christian Science
CT Connecticut
ct. court
ctr. center
ctrl. central

D

D Doctor
d. daughter of
DAgr Doctor of Agriculture
DAR Daughters of the American Revolution
dau. daughter

DAV Disabled American Veterans
DC District of Columbia
DCL Doctor of Civil Law
DCS Doctor of Commercial Science
DD Doctor of Divinity
DDS Doctor of Dental Surgery
DE Delaware
Dec. December
dec. deceased
def. defense
Del. Delaware
del. delegate, delegation
Dem. Democrat, Democratic
DEng Doctor of Engineering
denom. denomination, denominational
dep. deputy
dept. department
dermatol. dermatological
desc. descendant
devel. development, developmental
DFA Doctor of Fine Arts
DHL Doctor of Hebrew Literature
dir. director
dist. district
distbg. distributing
distbn. distribution
distbr. distributor
disting. distinguished
div. division, divinity, divorce
divsn. division
DLitt Doctor of Literature
DMD Doctor of Dental Medicine
DMS Doctor of Medical Science
DO Doctor of Osteopathy
docs. documents
DON Director of Nursing
DPH Diploma in Public Health
DPhil Doctor of Philosophy
DR Daughters of the Revolution
Dr. Drive, Doctor
DRE Doctor of Religious Education
DrPH Doctor of Public Health
DSc Doctor of Science
DSChemE Doctor of Science in Chemical Engineering
DSM Distinguished Service Medal
DST Doctor of Sacred Theology
DTM Doctor of Tropical Medicine
DVM Doctor of Veterinary Medicine
DVS Doctor of Veterinary Surgery

E

E East
ea. eastern
Eccles. Ecclesiastical
ecol. ecological
econ. economic
ECOSOC United Nations Economic and Social Council
ED Doctor of Engineering
ed. educated
EdB Bachelor of Education
EdD Doctor of Education
edit. edition
editl. editorial
EdM Master of Education
edn. education
ednl. educational
EDP Electronic Data Processing
EdS Specialist in Education
EE Electrical Engineer
EEC European Economic Community
EEG Electroencephalogram
EEO Equal Employment Opportunity
EEOC Equal Employment Opportunity Commission
EKG electrocardiogram
elec. electrical
electrochem. electrochemical
electrophys. electrophysical
elem. elementary
EM Engineer of Mines
EMT Emergency Medical Technician
ency. encyclopedia
Eng. England
engr. engineer
engring. engineering
entomol. entomological
environ. environmental
EPA Environmental Protection Agency
epidemiol. epidemiological
Episc. Episcopalian
ERA Equal Rights Amendment
ERDA Energy Research and Development Administration
ESEA Elementary and Secondary Education Act
ESL English as Second Language
ESSA Environmental Science Services Administration
ethnol. ethnological
ETO European Theatre of Operations
EU European Union
Evang. Evangelical
exam. examination, examining
Exch. Exchange
exec. executive
exhbn. exhibition
expdn. expedition
expn. exposition
expt. experiment
exptl. experimental
Expy. Expressway
Ext. Extension

F

FAA Federal Aviation Administration
FAO UN Food and Agriculture Organization
FBA Federal Bar Association
FBI Federal Bureau of Investigation
FCA Farm Credit Administration
FCC Federal Communications Commission
FCDA Federal Civil Defense Administration
FDA Food and Drug Administration
FDIA Federal Deposit Insurance Administration
FDIC Federal Deposit Insurance Corporation
FEA Federal Energy Administration
Feb. February
fed. federal
fedn. federation
FERC Federal Energy Regulatory Commission
fgn. foreign
FHA Federal Housing Administration
fin. financial, finance
FL Florida
Fl. Floor
Fla. Florida
FMC Federal Maritime Commission
FNP Family Nurse Practitioner
FOA Foreign Operations Administration
found. foundation
FPC Federal Power Commission
FPO Fleet Post Office
frat. fraternity
FRS Federal Reserve System
FSA Federal Security Agency
Ft. Fort
FTC Federal Trade Commission
Fwy. Freeway

G

GA, Ga. Georgia
GAO General Accounting Office
gastroent. gastroenterological
GATT General Agreement on Tariffs and Trade
GE General Electric Company
gen. general
geneal. genealogical
geog. geographic, geographical
geol. geological
geophys. geophysical

geriat. geriatrics
gerontol. gerontological
GHQ General Headquarters
gov. governor
govt. government
govtl. governmental
GPO Government Printing Office
grad. graduate, graduated
GSA General Services Administration
Gt. Great
GU Guam
gynecol. gynecological

H

hdqs. headquarters
HEW Department of Health, Education and Welfare
HHD Doctor of Humanities
HHFA Housing and Home Finance Agency
HHS Department of Health and Human Services
HI Hawaii
hist. historical, historic
HM Master of Humanities
homeo. homeopathic
hon. honorary, honorable
House of Dels. House of Delegates
House of Reps. House of Representatives
hort. horticultural
hosp. hospital
HS High School
HUD Department of Housing and Urban Development
Hwy. Highway
hydrog. hydrographic

I

IA Iowa
IAEA International Atomic Energy Agency
IBRD International Bank for Reconstruction and Development
ICA International Cooperation Administration
ICC Interstate Commerce Commission
ICCE International Council for Computers in Education
ICU Intensive Care Unit
ID Idaho
IEEE Institute of Electrical and Electronics Engineers
IFC International Finance Corporation
IL, Ill. Illinois
illus. illustrated
ILO International Labor Organization

IMF International Monetary Fund
IN Indiana
Inc. Incorporated
Ind. Indiana
ind. independent
Indpls. Indianapolis
indsl. industrial
inf. infantry
info. information
ins. insurance
insp. inspector
inst. institute
instl. institutional
instn. institution
instr. instructor
instrn. instruction
instrnl. instructional
internat. international
intro. introduction
IRE Institute of Radio Engineers
IRS Internal Revenue Service

J

JAG Judge Advocate General
JAGC Judge Advocate General Corps
Jan. January
Jaycees Junior Chamber of Commerce
JB Jurum Baccalaureus
JCB Juris Canoni Baccalaureus
JCD Juris Canonici Doctor, Juris Civilis Doctor
JCL Juris Canonici Licentiatus
JD Juris Doctor
jg. junior grade
jour. journal
jr. junior
JSD Juris Scientiae Doctor
JUD Juris Utriusque Doctor
jud. judicial

K

Kans. Kansas
KC Knights of Columbus
KS Kansas
KY, Ky. Kentucky

L

LA, La. Louisiana
LA Los Angeles
lab. laboratory
L.Am. Latin America
lang. language
laryngol. laryngological
LB Labrador
LDS Latter Day Saints
lectr. lecturer
legis. legislation, legislative
LHD Doctor of Humane Letters
LI Long Island
libr. librarian, library
lic. licensed, license

lit. literature
litig. litigation
LittB Bachelor of Letters
LittD Doctor of Letters
LLB Bachelor of Laws
LLD Doctor of Laws
LLM Master of Laws
Ln. Lane
LPGA Ladies Professional Golf Association
LPN Licensed Practical Nurse
lt. lieutenant
Ltd. Limited
Luth. Lutheran
LWV League of Women Voters

M

M Master
m. married
MA Master of Arts
MA Massachusetts
MADD Mothers Against Drunk Driving
mag. magazine
MAgr Master of Agriculture
maj. major
Man. Manitoba
Mar. March
MArch Master in Architecture
Mass. Massachusetts
math. mathematics, mathematical
MB Bachelor of Medicine, Manitoba
MBA Master of Business Administration
MC Medical Corps
MCE Master of Civil Engineering
mcht. merchant
mcpl. municipal
MCS Master of Commercial Science
MD Doctor of Medicine
MD, Md. Maryland
MDiv Master of Divinity
MDip Master in Diplomacy
mdse. merchandise
MDV Doctor of Veterinary Medicine
ME Mechanical Engineer
ME Maine
M.E.Ch. Methodist Episcopal Church
mech. mechanical
MEd. Master of Education
med. medical
MEE Master of Electrical Engineering
mem. member
meml. memorial
merc. mercantile
met. metropolitan
metall. metallurgical
MetE Metallurgical Engineer

meteorol. meteorological
Meth. Methodist
Mex. Mexico
MF Master of Forestry
MFA Master of Fine Arts
mfg. manufacturing
mfr. manufacturer
mgmt. management
mgr. manager
MHA Master of Hospital Administration
MI Military Intelligence, Michigan
Mich. Michigan
micros. microscopic
mid. middle
mil. military
Milw. Milwaukee
Min. Minister
mineral. mineralogical
Minn. Minnesota
MIS Management Information Systems
Miss. Mississippi
MIT Massachusetts Institute of Technology
mktg. marketing
ML Master of Laws
MLA Modern Language Association
MLitt Master of Literature, Master of Letters
MLS Master of Library Science
MME Master of Mechanical Engineering
MN Minnesota
mng. managing
MO, Mo. Missouri
moblzn. mobilization
Mont. Montana
MP Member of Parliament
MPA Master of Public Administration
MPE Master of Physical Education
MPH Master of Public Health
MPhil Master of Philosophy
MPL Master of Patent Law
Mpls. Minneapolis
MRE Master of Religious Education
MRI Magnetic Resonance Imaging
MS Master of Science
MSc Master of Science
MSChemE Master of Science in Chemical Engineering
MSEE Master of Science in Electrical Engineering
MSF Master of Science of Forestry
MSN Master of Science in Nursing
MST Master of Sacred Theology
MSW Master of Social Work
MT Montana

Mt. Mount
mus. museum, musical
MusB Bachelor of Music
MusD Doctor of Music
MusM Master of Music
mut. mutual
MVP Most Valuable Player
mycol. mycological

N

N North
NAACOG Nurses Association of the American College of Obstetricians and Gynecologists
NAACP National Association for the Advancement of Colored People
NACA National Advisory Committee for Aeronautics
NACDL National Association of Criminal Defense Lawyers
NACU National Association of Colleges and Universities
NAD National Academy of Design
NAE National Academy of Engineering, National Association of Educators
NAESP National Association of Elementary School Principals
NAFE National Association of Female Executives
N.Am. North America
NAM National Association of Manufacturers
NAMH National Association for Mental Health
NAPA National Association of Performing Artists
NARAS National Academy of Recording Arts and Sciences
NAREB National Association of Real Estate Boards
NARS National Archives and Record Service
NAS National Academy of Sciences
NASA National Aeronautics and Space Administration
NASP National Association of School Psychologists
NASW National Association of Social Workers
nat. national
NATAS National Academy of Television Arts and Sciences
NATO North Atlantic Treaty Organization
NB New Brunswick
NBA National Basketball Association
NC North Carolina
NCAA National College Athletic Association

NCCJ National Conference of Christians and Jews
ND North Dakota
NDEA National Defense Education Act
NE Nebraska
NE Northeast
NEA National Education Association
Nebr. Nebraska
NEH National Endowment for Humanities
neurol. neurological
Nev. Nevada
NF Newfoundland
NFL National Football League
Nfld. Newfoundland
NG National Guard
NH New Hampshire
NHL National Hockey League
NIH National Institutes of Health
NIMH National Institute of Mental Health
NJ New Jersey
NLRB National Labor Relations Board
NM, N.Mex. New Mexico
No. Northern
NOAA National Oceanographic and Atmospheric Administration
NORAD North America Air Defense
Nov. November
NOW National Organization for Women
nr. near
NRA National Rifle Association
NRC National Research Council
NS Nova Scotia
NSC National Security Council
NSF National Science Foundation
NSTA National Science Teachers Association
NSW New South Wales
nuc. nuclear
numis. numismatic
NV Nevada
NW Northwest
NWT Northwest Territories
NY New York
NYC New York City
NYU New York University
NZ New Zealand

O

ob-gyn obstetrics-gynecology
obs. observatory
obstet. obstetrical
occupl. occupational
oceanog. oceanographic
Oct. October
OD Doctor of Optometry

OECD Organization for Economic Cooperation and Development
OEEC Organization of European Economic Cooperation
OEO Office of Economic Opportunity
ofcl. official
OH Ohio
OK, Okla. Oklahoma
ON, Ont. Ontario
oper. operating
ophthal. ophthalmological
ops. operations
OR Oregon
orch. orchestra
Oreg. Oregon
orgn. organization
orgnl. organizational
ornithol. ornithological
orthop. orthopedic
OSHA Occupational Safety and Health Administration
OSRD Office of Scientific Research and Development
OSS Office of Strategic Services
osteo. osteopathic
otol. otological
otolaryn. otolaryngological

P

PA, Pa. Pennsylvania
paleontol. paleontological
path. pathological
pediat. pediatrics
PEI Prince Edward Island
PEN Poets, Playwrights, Editors, Essayists and Novelists
penol. penological
pers. personnel
PGA Professional Golfers' Association of America
PHA Public Housing Administration
pharm. pharmaceutical
PharmD Doctor of Pharmacy
PharmM Master of Pharmacy
PhB Bachelor of Philosophy
PhD Doctor of Philosophy
PhDChemE Doctor of Science in Chemical Engineering
PhM Master of Philosophy
Phila. Philadelphia
philharm. philharmonic
philol. philological
philos. philosophical
photog. photographic
phys. physical
physiol. physiological
Pitts. Pittsburgh
Pk. Park
Pky. Parkway
Pl. Place
Plz. Plaza

PO Post Office
polit. political
poly. polytechnic, polytechnical
PQ Province of Quebec
PR Puerto Rico
prep. preparatory
pres. president
Presbyn. Presbyterian
presdl. presidential
prin. principal
procs. proceedings
prod. produced
prodn. production
prodr. producer
prof. professor
profl. professional
prog. progressive
propr. proprietor
pros. prosecuting
pro tem. pro tempore
psychiat. psychiatric
psychol. psychological
PTA Parent-Teachers Association
ptnr. partner
PTO Pacific Theatre of Operations, Parent Teacher Organization
pub. publisher, publishing, published, public
publ. publication
pvt. private

Q

quar. quarterly
qm. quartermaster
Que. Quebec

R

radiol. radiological
RAF Royal Air Force
RCA Radio Corporation of America
RCAF Royal Canadian Air Force
Rd. Road
R&D Research & Development
REA Rural Electrification Administration
rec. recording
ref. reformed
regt. regiment
regtl. regimental
rehab. rehabilitation
rels. relations
Rep. Republican
rep. representative
Res. Reserve
ret. retired
Rev. Reverend
rev. review, revised
RFC Reconstruction Finance Corporation
RI Rhode Island
Rlwy. Railway

Rm. Room
RN Registered Nurse
roentgenol. roentgenological
ROTC Reserve Officers Training Corps
RR rural route, railroad
rsch. research
rschr. researcher
Rt. Route

S

S South
s. son
SAC Strategic Air Command
SAG Screen Actors Guild
S.Am. South America
san. sanitary
SAR Sons of the American Revolution
Sask. Saskatchewan
savs. savings
SB Bachelor of Science
SBA Small Business Administration
SC South Carolina
ScB Bachelor of Science
SCD Doctor of Commercial Science
ScD Doctor of Science
sch. school
sci. science, scientific
SCV Sons of Confederate Veterans
SD South Dakota
SE Southeast
SEC Securities and Exchange Commission
sec. secretary
sect. section
seismol. seismological
sem. seminary
Sept. September
s.g. senior grade
sgt. sergeant
SI Staten Island
SJ Society of Jesus
SJD Scientiae Juridicae Doctor
SK Saskatchewan
SM Master of Science
SNP Society of Nursing Professionals
So. Southern
soc. society
sociol. sociological
spkr. speaker
spl. special
splty. specialty
Sq. Square
SR Sons of the Revolution
sr. senior
SS Steamship
St. Saint, Street
sta. station

stats. statistics
statis. statistical
STB Bachelor of Sacred Theology
stblzn. stabilization
STD Doctor of Sacred Theology
std. standard
Ste. Suite
subs. subsidiary
SUNY State University of New York
supr. supervisor
supt. superintendent
surg. surgical
svc. service
SW Southwest
sys. system

T

Tb. tuberculosis
tchg. teaching
tchr. teacher
tech. technical, technology
technol. technological
tel. telephone
telecom. telecommunications
temp. temporary
Tenn. Tennessee
TESOL Teachers of English to Speakers of Other Languages
Tex. Texas
ThD Doctor of Theology
theol. theological
ThM Master of Theology
TN Tennessee
tng. training
topog. topographical
trans. transaction, transferred
transl. translation, translated
transp. transportation
treas. treasurer
TV television
twp. township
TX Texas
typog. typographical

U

U. University
UAW United Auto Workers

UCLA University of California at Los Angeles
UK United Kingdom
UN United Nations
UNESCO United Nations Educational, Scientific and Cultural Organization
UNICEF United Nations International Children's Emergency Fund
univ. university
UNRRA United Nations Relief and Rehabilitation Administration
UPI United Press International
urol. urological
US, USA United States of America
USAAF United States Army Air Force
USAF United States Air Force
USAFR United States Air Force Reserve
USAR United States Army Reserve
USCG United States Coast Guard
USCGR United States Coast Guard Reserve
USES United States Employment Service
USIA United States Information Agency
USMC United States Marine Corps
USMCR United States Marine Corps Reserve
USN United States Navy
USNG United States National Guard
USNR United States Naval Reserve
USO United Service Organizations
USPHS United States Public Health Service
USS United States Ship
USSR Union of the Soviet Socialist Republics
USTA United States Tennis Association
UT Utah

V

VA Veterans Administration
VA, Va. Virginia
vet. veteran, veterinary
VFW Veterans of Foreign Wars
VI Virgin Islands
vis. visiting
VISTA Volunteers in Service to America
vocat. vocational
vol. volunteer, volume
v.p. vice president
vs. versus
VT, Vt. Vermont

W

W West
WA, Wash. Washington (state)
WAC Women's Army Corps
WAVES Women's Reserve, US Naval Reserve
WCTU Women's Christian Temperance Union
we. western
WHO World Health Organization
WI Wisconsin, West Indies
Wis. Wisconsin
WV, W.Va. West Virginia
WY, Wyo. Wyoming

X, Y, Z

YK Yukon Territory
YMCA Young Men's Christian Association
YMHA Young Men's Hebrew Association
YM & YWHA Young Men's and Young Women's Hebrew Association
yr. year
YT Yukon Territory
YWCA Young Women's Christian Association

Alphabetical Practices

Names are arranged alphabetically according to the surnames, and under identical surnames according to the first given name. If both surname and first given name are identical, names are arranged alphabetically according to the second given name.

Surnames beginning with De, Des, Du, however capitalized or spaced, are recorded with the prefix preceding the surname and arranged alphabetically under the letter D.

Surnames beginning with Mac and Mc are arranged alphabetically under M.

Surnames beginning with Saint or St. appear after names that begin Sains, and are arranged according to the second part of the name, e.g., St. Clair before Saint Dennis.

Surnames beginning with Van, Von, or von are arranged alphabetically under the letter V.

Compound surnames are arranged according to the first member of the compound.

Many hyphenated Arabic names begin Al-, El-, or al-. These names are alphabetized according to each biographee's designation of last name. Thus Al-Bahar, Neta may be listed either under Al- or under Bahar, depending on the preference of the listee.

Also, Arabic names have a variety of possible spellings when transposed to English. Spelling of these names is always based on the practice of the biographee. Some biographees use a Western form of word order, while others prefer the Arabic word sequence.

Similarly, Asian names may have no comma between family and given names, but some biographees have chosen to add the comma. In each case, punctuation follows the preference of the biographee.

Parentheses used in connection with a name indicate which part of the full name is usually omitted in common usage. Hence, Chambers, E(lizabeth) Anne indicates that the first name, Elizabeth, is generally recorded as an initial. In such a case, the parentheses are ignored in alphabetizing and the name would be arranged as Chambers, Elizabeth Anne.

However, if the entire first name appears in parentheses, for example, Chambers, (Elizabeth) Anne, the first name is not commonly used, and the alphabetizing is therefore arranged as though the name were Chambers, Anne.

If the entire middle name is in parentheses, it is still used in alphabetical sorting. Hence, Belamy, Katherine (Lucille) would sort as Belamy, Katherine Lucille. The same occurs if the entire last name is in parentheses, e.g., (Brandenberg), Howard Keith would sort as Brandenberg, Howard Keith.

For visual clarification:

Smith, H(enry) George: Sorts as Smith, Henry George
Smith, (Henry) George: Sorts as Smith, George
Smith, Henry (George): Sorts as Smith, Henry George
(Smith), Henry George: Sorts as Smith, Henry George

Who Was Who in America®

AARON, MARVIN R., schools superintendent, consultant; b. NYC, Nov. 19, 1929; s. Jack R. and Elsie (Frisch) Aaron; m. Helen Aaron, June 29, 1950; children: Reid, Robin. BA, LI U., 1949; MA, CUNY, 1952, NYU, 1974; PhD, Southwestern U., 1983; LHD (hon.), London Inst. Rsch., 1974. Tchr. NYC Bd. Edn., 1950—56, sch. court coord., 1956—62, exec. asst., 1962—69; dep. supt. NYC Dist. 27 Queens Bd. Edn., 1969—74; supt., from 1974; mem. N.Y. State Adv. Commn. Tchr. Cert., 1983—84. Cons. Bank St. Coll. Consortium, from 1979; columnist, from 1978; radio announcer, TV prodr. Mem. Cmty. Planning Bd., Rockaway, NY, 1983—84; mem. exec. bd. Interfaith Coun, Queens, 1980—84, Bayswater Civic Assn., 1982—84; pres. NCCJ, Queens, 1982—84. Recipient numerous awards. Mem.: NY Exptl. Soc. Edn., Assn. NYC Supts. (treas. 1983), Lotos (NYC). Home: Far Rockaway, NY. Died Nov. 11, 2009.

ABBOTT, FRANK HARRY, lawyer; b. Lansdowne, Pa., May 6, 1919; s. Harry J. and Eva E. (LaGasse) A.; m. Elisabeth Dunigan, Jan. 29, 1943 (dec. 2006); children: Terence, Richard, Francis Harry Jr. B.E.E., Villanova U., 1941; JD, Temple U., 1949. Bar: Pa. 1950. Electronics engr. RCA, Camden, N.J., 1941-46; assoc. Schnader, Harrison, Segal & Lewis, Phila., 1949-59, ptnr., 1959-95, sr. counsel, 1995—2009. Served to lt. comdr. USNR, 1942-46, PTO Mem. ABA, Pa. Bar Assn., Phila. Bar Assn. Clubs: Merion Golf (Ardmore, Pa.); Lawyers, Union League (Phila.); Rehoboth Beach Country. Republican. Roman Catholic. Avocations: golf, shooting, tennis. Home: Rehoboth Beach, Del. Died Nov. 15, 2009.

ABBOTT, ISABELLA AIONA, retired biology educator; b. Hana, Maui, Hawaii, June 20, 1919; d. Loo Yuen and Annie Patseu (Chung) Aiona; m. Donald P. Abbott, Mar. 3, 1943 (dec.); 1 dau., Ann Kaiue Abbott. AB, U. Hawaii, 1941; MS, U. Mich., 1942; PhD, U. Calif., Berkeley, 1950. Prof. biology Stanford U., 1972-82; G.P. Wilder prof. botany U. Hawaii, 1978-98, G.P. Wilder emerita prof. botany, 1998—2010. Vis. rsch. biologist and tchr., Japan and Chile. Co-author: (with G.J. Hollenberg) Marine Algae of Calif., 1976, La'au Hawaii, traditional Hawaiian uses of plants, 1992; contbr. articles to profl. jours. Co-recipient NY Bot. Garden award for best book in botany, 1978; recipient Merit award Bot. Soc. America, 1995, G.M. Smith medal NAS, 1997, Spl. Award for Ethnobotany Wings WorldQuest Women of Discovery Awards, 2006, Lifetime Achievement award Hawaii Dept. Land & Natural Resources, 2008 Fellow AAAS; mem. Internat. Phycological Soc. (treas. 1964-68), Western Soc. Naturalists (sec. 1962-64, pres. 1977), Phycological Soc. Am., Bishop Mus. (bd. trustees), Hawaiian Bot. Soc. Died Oct. 28, 2010.

ABRAMS, MARY LOUISE, library director; b. NYC, Oct. 31, 1934; d. Clarence Joseph and Mary Eymard (Morrissey) Johnson; m. Sam Sottosanti, Feb. 6, 1960 (div. 1975); children: Sioux, William, Lisa, Robert, Margaret; m. Allan Gerald Abrams, July 18, 1985. BA, Marymount Coll., 1958; MLS, Columbia U., 1971. Libr. Johnson Libr., Hackensack, N.J., 1971-74; asst. dir. Englewood (N.J.) Libr., 1975-89; dir. Paramus (N.J.) Libr., from 1989. Pres. Bergen County Coop. Libr. System, Hackensack, N.J., 1991. Mem. Am. Libr. Assn., N.J. Libr. Assn. Roman Catholic. Home: Hackensack, NJ. Died Jan. 4, 2009.

ABRAMS, ROBERTA BUSKY, hospital administrator, nurse; b. Bklyn., Feb. 16, 1937; d. Albert H. and Gladys Busky; m. Robert L. Abrams, June 28, 1959 (div. 1977); children: Susan Abrams Federman, David B. BSN, U. Rochester, 1959; MA, Fairfield U., 1977. Asst. head nurse Jewish Hosp., Bklyn., 1959-60; instr. medicine/surgery Bklyn. Hosp., 1960-62, U. Rochester, N.Y., 1963-64; instr. ob-gyn Malden (Mass.) Hosp. Sch. Nursing, 1965-66; instr. prospective parents ARC, San Rafael, Calif., 1968-69; instr. ob-gyn SUNY, Farmingdale, 1970-71; instr. maternal/child health Stamford (Conn.) Hosp., 1971-75; clinician maternal/child health Lawrence Hosp., Bronxville, N.Y., 1975-78; asst. prof. nursing Ohio Wesleyan U., Delaware, 1981-84; dir. Elizabeth Blackwell Hosp. at Riverside Meth., Columbus, Ohio, 1978-86; dir. nursing Henry Ford Hosp., Detroit, 1986-87, assoc. adminstr. nursing, 1988-92. Sr. ptnr. Health Quad, Inc., 1997—; cons. maternal/child nursing currents Ross Labs., 1984-94; state coord. maternal/child health First Am. Home Care Co., 1994-95; dir. women's and children's health Arcadia Health Systems, 1995-96; lectr., cons. in field. Contbr. articles to profl. jours. Mem. LWV, Assn. for Women's Health, Obstetrics and Neonatal Nursing, Greater Detroit Orgn. Nurses Execs., Lamaze Internat., Sigma Theta Tau. Died Dec. 7, 2009.

ACKERMAN, HAROLD ARNOLD, federal judge; b. Newark, Feb. 15, 1928; Student, Seton Hall U., 1945-46, 48; LLB, Rutgers U., 1951. Bar: N.J. 1951. Adminstrv. asst. to Commr. of Labor and Industry, State of N.J., 1955-56; judge of compensation State of N.J., 1956-62, supervising judge of compensation, 1962-65; judge Union County Dist. Ct., 1965-70, presiding judge, 1966-70; judge Union County Ct., 1970-73, Superior Ct. law div., 1973-75, Superior Ct. Chancery div., 1975-79, US Dist. Ct., Dist. NJ, 1979—94, sr. judge, 1994—2009. Mem. Supreme Ct. Com. on Revision of Rules, 1967; chmn. Supreme Ct. Com. on County Dist. Cts., 1968; mem. faculty Nat. Jud. Coll., 1978 Sgt. U.S. Army, 1946-48. Recipient Disting. Alumni award Rutgers U. Sch. Law, 1980. Fellow ABA; mem. Order of Coif. Home: West Orange, NJ. Died Dec. 2, 2009.

ADAM, JOHN, JR., insurance company executive emeritus; b. Braintree, Mass., Dec. 14, 1914; s. John and Harriet E. (Hubley) A.; m. Ruth E. Maddock, Dec. 27, 1945. AB, Oberlin Coll., 1937; LL.D. (hon.), Clark U., 1974. Underwriter Glens Falls Ins. Co., 1938-39, mgr. inland marine dept., 1939-40; with Central Mut. Ins. Co., 1940-60, v.p., 1957-60, Worcester Mut. Ins. Co., 1960, pres., 1960-79; also dir. pres., dir. Hanover Ins. Cos., 1969-79, dir., 1979, pres. emeritus, from 1979; pres. Heald, Inc., 1979-87. Chmn. adv. com. Mich. Investment Fund, M.B.W. Venture Ptnrs. Author: More Sales for You, 1949, also articles. Chmn. Mass. Bd. Higher Edn., 1972-77; past pres. Greater Worcester Community Found. Mem. Worcester C. of C. (past pres., dir.), Worcester County Music Assn. (past pres.), C.P.C.U. Soc. (nat. pres. 1967, dir.), Worcester Econ. Club (past pres.), Boston Sales Execs. Club (past pres.) Home: Worcester, Mass. Died Feb. 5, 2009.

ADAMS, ALFRED HUGH, retired academic administrator; b. Punta Gorda, Fla., Mar. 8, 1928; s. Alfred and Irene (Gatewood) A.; m. Joyce Morgan, Nov. 10, 1954; children: Joy, Al, Paul; m. Lynda K. Long, Apr. 20, 1999. AA, U. Fla., 1948; BS, Fla. State U., 1950, MS, 1956, Ed.D., 1962; L.H.D., Fla. Atlantic U., 1972. Asst. coach varsity football Fla. State U., 1955-58, asst. dir. housing, instr. edn., 1958-62, asst. dean men, asst. prof. edn., 1962-64; supt. pub. instrn. Charlotte County, Fla., 1965-68; pres. Broward Community Coll., Ft. Lauderdale, Fla., 1968-87; exec. dir. Performing Arts Ctr. Authority, Ft. Lauderdale, 1987-88; pres. Broward Performing Arts Found., Ft. Lauderdale, 1990-91. Bd. dirs. Am. Council on Edn.; vis. lectr. in higher edn. Inst. Higher Edn., U. Fla., com. on internat. edn. relations, com. on mil-higher edn. relations; adv. com. Inst. Internat. Edn.; dir. Sun Bank/South Fla., N.A.; Vice chmn. Gov. Fla. Commn. Quality Edn., 1968-70; mem. Gov.'s Adv. Com. Edn., 1966-70; mem. regional council Southeastern Edn. Corp., 1966-69; mem. commn. adminstrv. affairs Am. Council on Edn., 1973; pres. Pub. Instns. Higher Learning in So. States, 1975; adv. com. Joint Coun. on Econ. Edn.; chmn. AACJC Internat./Intercultural Consortium, S.E. Fla. Ednl. Consortium; chmn. coun. pres. Fla. Cmty. Colls.; trustee South Fla. Edn. Center, Pub. Service TV Mem. editorial bd., Soc. for Coll. and Univ. Planning. Pres. United Way, 1973; bd. dirs. local chpt. ARC, 1971; bd. dirs. Opera Guild, Ft. Lauderdale, pres., 1983-85; bd. dirs. Coll. Consortium Internat. Studies; exec. dir. Performing Arts Ctr. Authority, Ft. Lauderdale; pres. Broward Performing Arts Found., Ft. Lauderdale. Comdr. USNR. Decorated knight Internat. Constantinian Order; recipient Liberty Bell award, 1975, Patriot award Freedoms Found., Disting. Alumnus award Fla. State U., A. Hugh Adams Coll. Gold Key. cert. of recognition Fla. Ho. of Reps., Disting Omicron Delta Kappa Alumnus of Yr., 1987; named Patriot Fla. Bicentennial Commn., Fla. State U. Sports Hall of Fame. Mem. Fla. Tchr. Edn. Adv. Council, Fla. Edn. Council Ethics Com. Sch. Adminstrs., Am. Assn. Sch. Adminstrs., Ft. Lauderdale C. of C. (v.p.), Profl. Practices Commn., Fla. Assn. Colls. and Univs. (pres. 1975), Naval Res. Assn., Res. Officers Assn., U.S. Naval Inst. (life), Broward Minutemen (pres.), Fla. Inter-agy. Law Enforcement Planning Council, Omicron Delta Kappa, Phi Theta Kappa. Clubs: Gulfstream Sailing, Fort Lauderdale; Tower (gov. 1985-86). Lodges: Kiwanis. Baptist. Died Aug. 23, 2010.

ADAMS, JAMES LOUIS, newspaper editor, retired; b. Cin., Sept. 4, 1928; s. James Brown and Flona (Godbey) A.; m. Phyllis Boehringer, July 16, 1955; children: Jeanne Kim Houck, Pamela Fay, Cheryl Lynn Adams, James Stewart. Grad., U. Cin., 1950; BA, Ohio State U., 1955. Reporter Elgin Courier News, Ill., 1955-56; city editor Wheaton Daily Jour., Ill., 1957-60; assoc. editor DuPage County News, Elmhurst, Ill., 1961-62; reporter, asst. met. editor Cin. Post, 1962-77, met. editor, 1977-83, assoc. editor, 1983-91, ret., 1991. Author: The Growing Church Lobby in Washington, 1970, Yankee Doodle Went to Church: The Righteous Revolution of 1776, 1989. Served with U.S. Army, 1950-52 Washington Journalism Ctr. fellow, 1967, Medill fellow Urban Journalism Ctr., 1973 Republican. Mem. Plymouth Brethren Ch. Avocations: reading, horseback riding, swimming. Home: Cincinnati, Ohio. Died Aug. 26, 2009.

ADAMS, JOHN, utility executive; b. Paget, Bermuda, Feb. 23, 1922; came to U.S., 1945; s. Henry Coolidge and Louise (Scarritt) A.; m. Ellen Noonan, Feb. 21, 1948; children: Ann Scarritt, Mary Minturn. BS, Columbia U. Sch. Bus., 1950. Chartered fin. analyst. Asst. to v.p. fin. West Penn Electric Co., NYC, 1950-57; fin. analyst Burns & Roe, Inc., NYC, 1957-58; asst. sec., asst. treas. Middle South Utilities, NYC, 1958-63; v.p. Kidder Peabody & Co. Inc., NYC, 1963-72; sr. v.p.-fin Allegheny Power System Inc., NYC, from 1972. Dir. West Penn Power Co., Monongahela Power Co., Potomac Edison Co., Ohio Valley Electric Co. Served with USN, 1944-46, PTO. Mem. N.Y. Soc. Sercurity Analysts Clubs: Rumson Country (N.J.), Seabright Beach (N.J.); Board Room (N.Y.C.). Republican. Home: Rumson, NJ. Died Jan. 5, 2010.

ADAMS, WESLEY P., JR., lawyer; b. NYC, Oct. 4, 1935; s. Wesley P. and Dorothy (Campbell) A.; m. Marcia Shaw, June 28, 1957 (div. 1972); m. Amelia Adams, Oct. 13, 1973; children: Denise, Catherine, wesley III, Jennifer. BA, Dartmouth Coll., 1957; JD, U. Va., 1960. Bar: Ky. 1960. Ptnr. Ogden, Robertson & Marshall, Louisville, 1960-82, Goldberg & Simpson, Louisville, 1982-91, Weber & Rose, Louisville, from 1991. Chair Legal Aid. Soc., Louisville, 1968-71; chair attys. divsn. Metro United Way, Louisville, 1966; precinct capt. Dem. Party, Louisville, 1960-66. Mem. ABA, Ky. Bar Assn. (Lawyers Helping Lawyers 1994-96), Louisville Bar Assn. (fed. practice com. 1972). Jewish. Avocations: tennis, gardening, working with alcoholics and homeless. Home: Prospect, Ky. Died May 4, 2010.

ADELBERG, EDWARD ALLEN, genetics educator; b. Cedarhurst, NY, Dec. 6, 1920; s. Max and Janet (Ehrlich) A.; m. Marion Sanders, Nov. 28, 1942; children: Michael G., David E., Arthur W. BS, Yale U., 1942, MS, 1947, PhD in Microbiology, 1949. Successively instr. to prof. microbiology U. Calif., Berkeley, 1949-60, chmn. dept. bacteriology, 1957-61; prof. microbiology Yale U., New Haven, Conn., 1961-74, chmn. dept., 1961-64, 70-72, dir. biol. scis., 1964-69, prof. human genetics, from 1974, dep. provost biomed. scis., from 1983. Cons. chem. rsch. divsn. Eli Lilly & Co., 1959-67, genetics br. NSF, 1971-74; chmn. bd. dirs. Med. Scis. Rsch. Ctr., Brandeis U., 1976-79. Author: (with Jawetz and Melnick) Review of Medical Microbiology, 1984, (with R.Y. Stanier and M. Doudoroff) The Microbial World, 1976; co-author: Medical Microbiology, 1989, Introduction to The Microbial World, 1979; editor-in-chief Bacteria Rev., 1967-70; contbr. articles on genetics to profl. jours. Maj. USAAF, 1942-46. Guggenheim fellow, 1956-57, 65-66. Fellow Am. Acad. Arts and Scis.; mem. NAS, Conn. Acad. Sci. and Engring. (mem. coun. 1978-81). Subspecialties in membrane biology, gene actions; rsch. using genetic and biochem. techniques to study structure-function relationships of mammalian membrane transport systems. Home: New Haven, Conn. Died Aug. 7, 2009.

ADELMAN, JANET ANN, English literature educator; b. Mt. Kisco, Jan. 28, 1941; d. Emanuel and Ceil (Greenfeld) A.; m. Robert Osserman, July 21, 1976; children: Brian, Stephen. BA, Smith Coll., 1962; postgrad., Oxford U., Eng., 1962-63; MA, PhD, Yale U., 1968. Prof. English lit. U. Calif., Berkeley, 1968—2010. Author: The Common Liar: An Essay on Antony and Cleopatra, 1973, Suffocating Mothers: Fantasies of Maternal Origin in Shakespeare, Hamlet to The Tempest, 1992; editor: Twentieth Century Interpretations of King Lear, 1978. Fellow Am. Coun. Learned Socs., 1976-77, Guggenheim Found., 1981-82. Mem. MLA, Shakespeare Assn. Am., San Francisco Psychoanalytic Inst. Home: Berkeley, Calif. Died Apr. 6, 2010.

ADLER, AARON, advertising agency executive; b. Chgo., Jan. 31, 1914; s. Abraham and Rachel A.; m. Alice Gamberg, Aug. 10, 1941; children: Michael L., Allan J., Jody R. Student bus., Northwestern U., 1932-36. Copywriter Salem N. Baskin Advt. Agy., Chgo., 1937-40, Gourfain Cobb Advt. Agy., Chgo., 1941-43; copywriter-account exec. William Hart Adler Advt. Agy., Chgo., 1946-49; copywriter, account exec. Olian Advt. Agy., Chgo., 1949-53; v.p. Gourfain-Loeff & Adler Advt. Agy., Chgo., 1953-66; exec. v.p., partner Stone & Adler Advt. Agy., Chgo., 1966-77, pres., 1977-80, Austin-Spencer Ltd., from 1992. Pres. Adler Corp., Chgo., 1966—; sec. Discovery House, mail order catalog co., Irvine, Calif., 1973-79; chmn. Bull. Atomic Scientists, Chgo., 1983-85, mem. exec. com., 1986-89; pres. The Archival Press Ltd., 1987-89. Pres. North Shore Sch. of Jewish Studies, Evanston, 1964-66; bd. dirs. Albert Einstein Peace Prize Found., 1980—; trustee Spertus Coll. Judaica, 1982. Served with M.C. U.S. Army, 1943-46. Mem. Direct Mail Mktg. Assn., Chgo. Assn. Direct Mktg. (Charles S. Downs Direct Marketer of Yr. award 1988), Chgo. Advt. Club, Sierra Club, Exec. Service Corps. Died Apr. 17, 2010.

ADLER, ROY DOUGLAS, consumer psychologist; b. Detroit, Sept. 9, 1943; s. Roy Alvin and Ruth Louise (Potz) A.; m. Cecilia Canales, Mar. 9, 1968; children: Douglas, Davidson. BA, Bucknell U., 1965; MA, Western Mich. U., 1971; MBA, Xavier U., 1973; PhD, U. Ala., 1982. Mktg. mgr. Procter & Gamble, Cin., 1969-71; cons. Levi Strauss & Co., Cin., 1972-75; assoc. prof. Xavier U., Cin., 1973-84; prof. Pepperdine U., Malibu, Calif., from 1984. Dir. Malibu Ctr. Consumer Trends, 1984—. Co-author: Marketing and Society, 1981, Marketing Megaworks, 1987. Chief pollster Springer for Gov., Ohio, 1982. Recipient Emmy award for Best Instructional Series, 1985; named Outstanding Faculty Mem., Pepperdine U., 1985, Fulbright scholar Univ. Nova, Lisbon,

Portugal, 1988. Mem. Acad. Mktg. Sci. (v.p. 1984—), Am. Mktg. Assn., Am. Psychol. Assn. Republican. Avocations: sailing, motor sports. Home: Newbury Park, Calif. Died Mar. 7, 2009.

AGRAWAL, KRISHNA CHANDRA, pharmacology educator; b. Calcutta, India, Mar. 15, 1937; naturalized; s. Prasadi Lal and Asarfi Devi (Agrawal) A.; m. Mani Agrawal, Dec. 2, 1960; children— Sunil, Lina, Nira BS in Pharmacy, Andhra U., Waltair, India, 1959, MS, 1960; PhD, U. Fla., 1965. Cert. in pharm. chemistry. Research assoc. dept. pharmacology Yale U. Sch. Medicine, New Haven, 1966-69, instr., 1969-70, asst. prof., 1970-76, assoc. prof., 1976; assoc. prof. dept. pharmacology Tulane U. Sch. Medicine, New Orleans, 1976-81, prof., 1981—2009, interim chmn., 1996-99, regents prof., chmn., 1999—2009. Cons. mem. Southeastern Cancer Study Group, 1980—85; mem. adv. com. on instnl. grants Am. Cancer Soc., 1980—85; mem. AIDS and Related Rsch. Rev. Group NIH, 1989—94, 1999—2002; mem. oncology merit rev. com. Vets. Adminstrn., 2002—04; exptl. therapeutics NIH, 2002—05. Conbr. articles to profl. jours.; patentee radiosensitizers for hypoxic tumor cells and compositions; novel AZT analogs. Grantee Nat. Cancer Inst., 1976-89, WHO, 1979-82, La. Bd. Regents, 1981-82, Nat. Inst. Allergy and Infectious Diseases, 1987-2009, US Dept. Def., 1994-96, Nat. Heart Lung and Blood Inst., 1997-2009. Fellow Am. Inst. Chemists; mem. Am. Chem. Soc., Am. Assn. Cancer Rsch., Internat. Soc. Antiviral Rsch., Internat. Soc. Heart Rsch., Radiation Rsch. Soc., Am. Soc. Pharmacology and Exptl. Therapeutics, Am. Soc. Hematology, Sigma Xi. Home: New Orleans, La. Died Dec. 12, 2009.

AHERN, RICHARD FAVOR, state legislator; b. Concord, NH, Aug. 21, 1912; s. William J. Jr. and Catherine (Favor) A.; m. Arlene M. Campbell, 1941 (dec. Aug. 1997); children: Richard C., Judith Fay (dec.). BS, U. N.H., 1934. Treas. Dem. Ward II Com., Manchester. Dep. collector Bur. Internal Revenue, 1943-52, agt., 1952-71, chief rev. staff, 1971-72, ret. Mem. Sigma Alpha Epsilon. Home: Concord, NH. Died Sept. 8, 2009.

AHNER, ALFRED FREDRICK, retired military officer; b. Huntington, Ind., Nov. 12, 1921; s. Ray C. and Kathryn (Stern) A.; m. Betty Young, May 3, 1944; children: Mark, Michael. BA, Ind. Central U., 1947; MS, Butler U., 1951. Joined Army N.G., 1947, advanced through grades to maj. gen., 1974; adj. gen. Ind. Army N.G., Indpls., 1960, 72-86. Chmn., Easter Seals, Ind., 1975-76. Served with U.S. Army, World War II, ETO. Mem. N.G. Assn. Ind. (pres. 1965-66), Adjs. Gen. Assn. U.S. (pres. 1979-80), Am. Legion. Home: Indianapolis, Ind. Died Sept. 21, 2010.

AJEMIAN, ROBERT MYRON, retired journalist; b. Boston, July 8, 1925; s. Shahin and Rose (Takvorian) A.; m. Ruth MacCrellish, Sept. 6, 1952 (div.); children: Robert, Katharine, Peter; m. Elizabeth Patterson, Nov. 27, 1959; children: David John, Andrew Howell. AB, Harvard U., 1948. Sportswriter Boston Evening Am., 1948-51; reporter Life mag., NYC, 1952-54; corr. TIME, Life mag., Denver, 1954-56; asst. nat. affairs editor Life mag., NYC, 1957-59; bur. chief Time-Life, Chgo., 1959-61; chief European bur. Life, Paris, 1961-63, polit. editor NYC, 1963-67, asst. mng. editor, 1968-72; corp. affairs Time, Inc., 1972-74; nat. polit. corr. TIME mag., 1974-77, Washington bur. chief, 1978-85, Boston bur. chief, 1985-92; ret. Served to lt. (j.g.) USNR, World War II, PTO. Mem. Sigma Delta Chi. Clubs: Harvard Lake Shore (Chgo.); Millbrook (N.Y.); Golf and Tennis, Fed. City, St. Botolph (Boston). Home: Boston, Mass. Died Sept. 24, 2010.

ALAIMO, ANTHONY A., federal judge; b. Sicily, Italy, Mar. 29, 1920; AB, Ohio No. U., 1940; JD, Emory U., 1948; D in Pub. Svc. (hon.), Coll. Coastal Ga., 2009. Bar: Ga. 1948, Ohio 1948. Assoc. Reuben A. Garland, 1949-51, 53-56; pvt. practice, Atlanta, 1967-63; ptnr. Highsmith, Highsmith, Alaimo & Knox, Brunswick, Ga., 1963-67, Cowart, Sapp, Alaimo & Gale, Brunswick, 1963-67, Alaimo, Taylor & Bishop, Brunswick, 1967-71; judge US Dist. Ct. (so. dist.) Ga., Brunswick, 1971—91, chief judge, 1976—90, sr. judge, 1991—2009. Died Dec. 30, 2009.

ALBRECHT, EDWARD DANIEL, metals manufacturing company executive; b. Kewanee, Ill., Feb. 11, 1937; s. Edward Albert and Mary Jane (Horner) A.; 1 child, Deborah J. BS in Metall. Engring., U. Ariz., Tucson, 1959, MS, 1961, PhD, 1964, MetE (hon.) in Metall. Engring., 1974. Registered profl. engr., Calif. Rsch. metallurgist Los Alamos Nat. Lab., 1959-61; sr. physicist, project mgr. U. Calif. Lawrence Radiation Lab., Livermore, 1964-71; founder, pres. Metall. Innovations Inc., Pleasanton, Calif., 1969-71; chmn. bd., 1971-73; gen. mgr. Buehler Ltd. & Adolph I. Buehler, Inc., Lake Bluff, Ill., 1972—76, v.p., 1973—76, pres., 1976—90; pres. bd. dirs. Buehler-Met AG, Basel, Switzerland, 1983-87; pres. Mowlem Tech. Inc., Lake Bluff, 1984-86; founder, pres., CEO Buehler Internat. Inc., 1985-90; chmn., 1988-91; chmn. emeritus, from 1991. Chmn. bd. Soiltest, Inc., Evanston, Ill., 1984-88, CPN Corp., Pacheco, Calif., 1984-89; bd. dirs. S.W. Steel, Inc., Tulsa, 1987-96, vice chmn., 1993-96, Gallery 10, Inc., Scottsdale, Ariz., 1988-94, Maxcor Mfg. Inc., Colorado springs, Colo., 1990-92, Nitrogen Ventures, Inc. (formerly Coal Gasification, Inc.), Scottsdale, 1986—, chmn. bd., 1986-87, 93—, Advanced Ceramics Rsch., Inc., Tucson, Ariz, chmn., 1997-2001; mem. indsl. adv. com. dept. materials sci. and engring. U. Wash., 1993-2002; mem. alumni and indsl. rels. com. dept. aerospace and mech. engring. U. Ariz., 1996-2001; mem. adv. bd. U. Ariz. engring. mgmt. program, 2002—08. Contbr. articles to profl. jours. Patentee in field. Bd. dirs. Danville Homeowners Assn., Calif., 1966-71, treas., 1969-71; bd. dirs. Lake Forest Acad.-Ferry Hall Prep Sch., Lake Forest, Ill., 1977-81; nat. adv. bd. Heard Mus. Native Am. Art and Culture, Phoenix, 1980-92, chmn., 1990-92, trustee, 1992-2004, mem. exec. com., 1993—2008, chmn. collections com., 1993-97, v.p., 1995-97, pres., 1997-2000, chmn. exec. com. 1997-2000, chmn. exec. search com., 1999, chmn. trustee com. 2000-01, chmn. bldg. and grounds com., 2000—08, hon. life trustee, 2005; trustee Millicent Rogers Mus., Taos, N.Mex., 1982-91, chmn. devel. com., 1983-85, hon. life trustee, 1993. Recipient Alumni Citizenship award U. Ariz., 1982, Disting. Alumni Centennial medallion, 1989, Alumni Assn. Centennial achievement award, 1998; NDEA fellow, 1959-62. Fellow Royal Micros Soc. Soc. Eng.; mem. Am. Soc. Metals (chmn. Tucson 1961, fellow, 1976, mem. coun. fellows 1997-2001, mem. editl. com. Jour. Materials Engring. and Performance 1988-2003, disting. life mem. 1989, mem. nominating com. 1998, mem. bd. trustees, 1999-2002); mem. Internat. Metallographic Soc. (v.p. 1971-73, 93-95, pres. 1973-75, 95-97, dir. 1975-81, 97-2000, chmn. gen. tech. meeting San Francisco 1969, Chgo. 1972, Brighton, Eng. 1980, Albuquerque 1985, Pres.'s award 1981, Henry Clifton Sorby award 1990), Deutsche Gesellschaft Materialkunde Inst., Chgo. Club, Onwentsia (Lake Forest, Ill.), Paradise Valley (Ariz.) Country Club, Quail Run (Santa Fe), Sigam Gamma Epsilon, Delta Upsilon. Home: Scottsdale, Ariz. Died Aug. 28, 2010.

ALDRICH, ANN, judge; b. Providence, June 28, 1927; d. Allie C. and Ethel M. (Carrier) A.; m. Chester Aldrich, 1960 (dec.); children: Martin, William; children by previous marriage: James, Allen; m. John H. McAllister III, 1986 (dec. May, 2004). BA cum laude, Columbia U., 1948; LLB cum laude, NYU, 1950, LLM, 1964, JSD, 1967. Bar: DC, NY 1952, Conn. 1966, Ohio 1973, US Supreme Ct. 1956. Rsch. asst. to mem. faculty NYU Sch. Law; atty. IBRD, 1952; atty., rsch. asst. Samuel Nakasian, Esq., Washington, 1952—53; gen. counsel's staff FCC, Washington, 1953—60; US del. to Internat. Radio Conf., Geneva, 1959; practicing atty. Darien, Conn., 1961—68; assoc. prof. law Cleve. State U., 1968—71, prof., 1971—80; judge US Dist. Ct. (no. dist.) Ohio, Cleve., from 1980. Instrn. com. Sixth Cir. Pattern Criminal Jury, from 1986. Mem. Fed. Bar Assn., Nat. Assn. of Women Judges, Fed. Communications Bar Assn., Fed. Judge Assn. Episcopalian. Died May 2, 2010.

ALEVIZOS, THEODORE G., lawyer, singer, author; b. Milw., Feb. 7, 1926; s. Gregory and Mary (Passaris) A.; m. Susan Thatcher Bamberger, May 6, 1960; children: Gregory, L. Richard, Theodore. Ph.B., Marquette U., 1950; postgrad., Juilliard Sch. Music, 1950-51; MS, Columbia U., 1957; JD, Suffolk U., 1966. Bar: Mass. 1974, Fed. 1975, U.S. Supreme Ct. 1980. Mem. sales staff McKesson & Robbins, Milw., 1952-56; asst. cataloger N.Y. U. Med. Library, NYC, 1956-57; asst. circulation librarian Widener Library, Harvard, 1957-61; asst. librarian Lamont Library, 1961-64, dir., 1964-74; mem. faculty Harvard U., 1966-74, lectr. modern Greek, 1969-73, lectr. voice, 1972-74, assoc. univ. librarian for pub. services, 1966-74; practiced in Boston, from 1974; ptnr. Alevizos & Alevizos, from 1978; faculty Suffolk U. Law Sch., 1986-93; instr. modern Greek, The Voice in Performance Cambridge Adult Center, 1972-86; nat. and internat. concertizing. Cons. MGM Records, Inc., 1965-71, Orgn. for Social and Tech. Innovation, Inc., Cambridge, 1968-70; mus. cons. Nat. Geographic, 1971-73; bd. dirs. Harvard Coop., 1973-74; mem. corp. Cambridge Ctr. Adult Edn.; faculty in entertainment and sports law Suffolk U. Law Sch., 1986—; mem. adv. coun. Ctr. for Greek Studies, U. Fla., Gainesville, 1995—. Author: Folksongs of Greece, 1968; legal columnist: Hellenic Chronicle, Boston, 1979—; Recordings include: Folksingers Round Harvard Square, 1959, Songs of Greece, 1960, Folksongs of Greece, 1961, Greek Folksongs, 1969, Poetry and Song, 1973, Traditional Songs and Dances of Greece and the Grecian Islands, 1978, A Greek Byzantine Christmas, 2000, A Greek Byzantine Easter, 2002; host WBCN-FM Boston, Greek Cult. Hour, 1965-67. Mem. Adv. Congress Cambridge Community TV; trustee Dexter Sch., 1976—, v.p. bd. trustees, 1980—. Served with USNR, 1944-46, PTO. Decorated Bronze Star.; Hon. assoc. Center for Neo-Hellenic Studies, U. Tex. at Austin, 1967— Mem. NARAS, Am., Mass., Boston Bar Assns., Mass. Acad. Trial Attys., ALA, Am. Folklore Soc., Modern Greek Studies Assn., Inst. Byzantine and Modern Greek Studies (hon.) Died Oct. 30, 2009.

ALEXANDER, JOHN DAVID, JR., retired academic administrator; b. Springfield, Tenn., Oct. 18, 1932; s. John David and Mary Agnes (McKinnon) A.; m. Catharine Coleman, Aug. 26, 1956; children: Catharine McKinnon, John David III, Julia Mary. BA, Southwestern at Memphis, 1953; student, Louisville Presbyn. Theol. Sem., 1953—54; PhD, Oxford U., Eng., 1957; LLD, U. So. Calif., Occidental Coll., 1970, Centre Coll. of Ky., 1971, Pepperdine U., 1991, Albertson Coll. Idaho, 1992; LHD, Loyola Marymount U., 1983; LittD, Rhodes Coll., 1986, Pomona Coll., 1996. Assoc. prof. San Francisco Theol. Sem., 1957-65; pres. Southwestern at Memphis, 1965-69, Pomona Coll., Claremont, Calif., 1969-91. Sec. Rhodes Scholarship Trust, 1981—98; mem. commn. liberal learning Assn. American Colleges, 1966—69, mem. commn. instl. affairs, 1971—74; mem. commn. colleges So. Assn. Colleges & Schools, 1966—69; mem. Nat. Commn. Acad. Tenure, 1971—72; bd. dirs. Children's Hosp., LA, 1994—2000, Wenner-Gren Found. for Anthrop. Rsch., 1995—2007; trustee Tchrs. Inst. and Annuity Assn., 1970—2002, Woodrow Wilson Nat. Fellowship Found., 1978—99, Webbs Schs., Calif., 1995—2004, Seaver Inst., 1992—2010, Fellows of Soc. Phi Beta Kappa, 1993—2010, v.p., 1998—2010; trustee Emeriti Retirement Health Care Inc., 2004—10; bd. overseers Huntington Libr., 1991—2010. Editor: The American Oxonian, 1997-2000, History of the American Rhodes Scholarships in History of Rhodes Trust, 2001, The Goddess Pomona, 2007. Pres. Am. Friends of Nat. Portrait Gallery (London) Found., from 2004. Decorated comdr. Order Brit. Empire; named Disting. Friend of Oxford U., 2000; Rhodes scholar, Oxford U., 1955—57. Fellow AAAS; mem. Soc. Religion Higher Edn., Phi Beta Kappa Alumni in So. Calif. (pres. 1974-76), Century Club, Calif. Club, Bohemian Club, Athenaeum (London) Phi Beta Kappa, Omicron Delta Kappa, Sigma Nu. Home: Claremont, Calif. Died July 25, 2010.

ALEXANDER, ROBERT JACKSON, economist, educator; b. Canton, Ohio, Nov. 26, 1918; s. Ralph S. and Ruth (Jackson) A.; m. Joan O. Powell, Mar. 26, 1949; children: Anthony, Margaret. BA, Columbia U., NYC, 1940, MA, 1941, PhD, 1950. Asst. economist Bd. Econ. Warfare, 1942, Office Inter-Am. Affairs, 1945—46; mem. faculty Rutgers U., from 1947, prof. econs., 1961—89, prof. emeritus, from 1989. Mem. Pres.-elect Kennedy's Latin Am. Task Force, 1960-61 Author 46 books including Juan Domingo Peron: A History, 1979, Romulo Betancourt and the Transformation of Venezuela, 1982, Bolivia: Past, Present and Future of Its Politics, 1982, Biographical Dictionary of Latin American and Caribbean Politics, 1988, Juscelino Kubitschek and the Development of Brazil, 1991, International Trotskyism 1929-85, 1991, The ABC Presidents, 1992, The Bolivarian Presidents, 1994, The Presidents of Central America, Mexico, Cuba and Hispaniola, 1995, Presidents, Prime Ministers and Governors of the English Speaking West Indies and Puerto Rico, 1997, The Anarchists in the Spanish Civil War, 1999, International Maoism in the Developing World, 1999, Hava de la Torre Man of the Millennium: His Life, Ideas and Continuing Relevance, 2001, A History of Organized Labor in Cuba, 2002, History of Organized Labor in Brazil, 2003, History of Organized Labor in Argentina in English Speaking West Indies, 2003, History of Organized Labor in Uruguay and Paraguay 2005 Nat. bd. League Indsl. Democracy, 1955—; nat. exec. com. Socialist Party-Social Dem. Fedn., 1957-66; bd. dirs. Rand Sch. Social Sci., 1951-56; exec. com. Open Door Student Exch., 1970-94. Decorated officer Order Condor of the Andes Bolivia Mem. Am. Econ. Assn., Latin Am. Studies Assn., Mid. Atlantic Coun. Latin Am. Studies (v.p. 1986-87, pres. 1987-88), Coun. Fgn. Rels., Interam. Assn. Democracy and Freedom (chmn. N.Am. com. 1970-87), Phi Gamma Delta. Home: Piscataway, NJ. Died Apr. 27, 2010.

ALEXANDER, SAMUEL CRAIGHEAD, anesthesiology educator; b. Upper Darby, Pa., May 3, 1930; s. Samuel Craighead and Laura (Duncan) A.; m. Betty Pyron, Aug. 3, 1951; children: Christian M. Alexander Libson, S. Craighead III, Baine B. Alexander Jackson. BS, Davidson Coll., 1951; MD, U. Pa., 1955. Diplomate American Bd. Anesthesiology. Intern Phila. Gen. Hosp., 1955-58; resident Hosp. Univ. Pa., 1960-62, fellow, 1962-64; med. officer in charge, sr. asst. surgeon USPHS Indian Hosp., Winslow, Ariz., 1956-58; instr. pharmacology U. Pa., Phila., 1958-60, instr. to assoc. prof. anesthesiology, 1960-69; prof. anesthesiology, chmn. dept. U. Conn., Hartford, 1969-71, U. Wis., Madison, 1971-90; assoc. dean for affiliate affairs Hahnemann U., Phila., 1991-92, vice provost for affiliate affairs, 1992—96. Vis. scientist Bispebjerg Hosp., Copenhagen, Denmark, 1968-69; chmn. bd. dirs. Affiliated Univ. Physicians, Madison, 1976-81, 87-90; founding pres. Univ. Care HMO, Madison, 1983-84; bd. dirs. Univ. Health Care, Inc., Madison; mem. adminstrv. bd. Coun. Acad. Socs. (chair-elect 1992), Assn. American Med. Colls.; pres. Soc. Acad. Anesthesia, chmn., 1981; founding pres. Assn. Anesthesia Program Dirs., 1986-87. Contbr. articles to profl. jours., book chpts. Deacon Bryn Mawr Presbyn. Ch., Pa., 1965-68; ruling elder and clk. session Covenant Presbyn. Ch., Madison, 1975-78. Recipient Career Devel. award USPHS, 1965-70; assoc. fellow in clin. pharmacology Pharm. Mfrs., 1959. Mem. Am. Soc. Anesthesiologists (chmn. coms.), Assn. Univ. Anesthetists, Am. Soc. Pharmacy and Exptl. Therapeutics, Madison Club. Democrat. Avocations: photography, travel. Home: Wayne, Pa. Died June 23, 2010.

ALLAN, WILLIAM ALEXANDER, editor; b. Turtle Creek, Pa., May 4, 1924; s. Alexander Malcolm and Isabel (Young) Allan; m. Rita McEvoy Allan, Mar. 17, 1951; children: William Alexander, Jeffrey, Marianne. Student, U. Va., 1943; BS in Physics and Journalism, U. Pitts., 1949. With McKeesport (Pa.) Daily News, 1947—51, Pitts. Press, from 1951, bus. and financial editor, 1963—70, features editor, 1970—80, roving editor, from 1980. Served with USAAF, 1943—45, ETO. Decorated Air medal Croix de Guerre, France; recipient Golden Quill award, Bus. Writing Pitts. Chpt. Sigma Delta Chi. Mem.: Press Club. Home: Pittsburgh, Pa. Died Apr. 21, 2009.

ALLEE, JOHN SELLIER, lawyer; b. NYC, May 23, 1932; s. John Percy and Alberta (Sellier) A.; m. Debra A. Cole, Mar. 7, 1964 (div. Feb. 1986); children— John Cole, David Sellier; m. Carol Tendler Morse, Apr. 19, 1986 BA, Wesleyan U., Conn., 1954; JD, Columbia U., 1960. Bar: N.Y. 1961. Assoc. Sullivan & Cromwell, NYC, 1961-65; asst. U.S. atty. U.S. Atty.'s Office, NYC, 1966-69; exec. asst. U.S. atty., So. Dist. N.Y., NYC, 1969-70; ptnr. Hughes Hubbard & Reed, NYC, from 1970. Author: Product Liability, 1984; decision editor Columbia Law Rev., 1959-60; contbr. articles to profl. jours. Served with U.S. Army, 1955-56 Mem. ABA, N.Y. State Bar Assn., Assn. Bar City N.Y. Democrat. Home: New York, NY. Died July 25, 2010.

ALLEN, DEDE (DOROTHEA CAROTHERS ALLEN), film editor; b. Cleve., Ohio, Dec. 3, 1925; d. Thomas Humphrey Cushing Allen & Dorothea S. Carthers; m. Stephen Fleischman; children: Ramey, Tom Editor: (short films) Endowing Your Future, 1957, It's Always Now, 1965, (films) Because of Eve, 1948, Terror from the Year 5000, 1958, Odds Against Tomorrow, 1959, The Hustler, 1961, America, America, 1963, Bonnie and Clyde, 1967, Rachel, Rachel, 1968, Alice's Restaurant, 1969, Little Big Man, 1970, Slaughterhouse Five, 1972, Visions of Eight, 1973, (with Richard Marks) Serpico, 1973, Dog Day Afternoon, 1975 (Academy award nomination best film editing 1975), (with Jerry Greenberg and Stephen Rotter) Night Moves, 1975, (with Greenberg and Rotter) The Missouri Breaks, 1976, Slap Shot, 1977, The Wiz, 1978, Harry and Son, 1984, (with Jeff Gourson) Mike's

Murder, 1984, The Breakfast Club, 1985, (with Angelo Corrao) Off Beat, 1986, (with Jim Miller) The Milagro Beanfield War, 1988, (with Miller) Let It Ride, 1989, (with Vivien Hillgrove Gilliam and William Scharf) Henry and June, 1990, (with Miller) The Addams Family, 1991, (with Curtis Lee Hanson) Wonder Boys, 2000, John Q, 2002, The Final Cut, 2004, Have Dreams, Will Travel, 2007, Fireflies in the Garden, 2008; prodn. asst.: (films) Story of a Woman, 1970; co-editor, co-exec. prodr.: (films) Reds, 1981 (Academy award nomination best film editing 1981). Died Apr. 17, 2010.

ALLEN, LEW, JR., retired military officer; b. Miami, Fla., Sept. 30, 1925; s. Lew and Zella (Holman) A.; m. Barbara Frink Hatch, Aug. 19, 1949; children: Barbara Allen Miller, Lew III, Marjorie Allen Dauster, Christie Allen Jameson, James Allen. BS, U.S. Mil. Acad., 1946; MS, U. Ill., 1952, PhD in Physics, 1954. Commd. 2d lt. USAAF, 1946; advanced through grades to gen. USAF, 1977, ret., 1982; physicist test div. AEC, Los Alamos, N.Mex., 1954-57; sci. advisor Air Force Spl. Weapons Lab., Kirtland, N.Mex., 1957-61; with Office Spl. Tech. US Dept. Def., Washington, 1961-65; from dir. spl. projects to dep. dir. adv. plans Air Force Space Program, 1965-72; dir. Nat. Security Agy., Ft. Meade, Md., 1973-77; comdr. Air Force Systems Command, 1977-78; vice chief of staff USAF, Washington, 1978, chief of staff, 1978-82; dir. Jet Propulsion Lab., Calif. Inst. Tech., Pasadena, Calif., 1982-90; chmn. Charles Stark Draper Laboratory, Boston, 1991-95. Mem. President's Fgn. Intelligence Advisory Bd., 1993—95. Decorated Def. D.S.M. with two clusters, Air Force D.S.M. with one cluster, Nat. Intelligence D.S.M., NASA D.S.M., Legion of Merit with two oak leaf clusters; recipient Robert H. Goddard Astronautics award Am. Inst. Aeronautics and Astronautics, 1995, Disting. Grad. award, Assn. of Graduates, 1999 Fellow AIAA (hon.), Am. Phys. Soc.; mem. Am. Geophys. Union, Nat. Acad. Engring., Coun. on Fgn. Rels., Sigma Xi, Sunset Club (L.A.), Alfalfa Club (Washington). Republican. Episcopalian. Avocations: ballooning, rafting. Home: Potomac Falls, Va. Died Jan. 4, 2010.

ALLEN, RICHARD CHARLES, naval officer; b. Rice Lake, Wis., Nov. 8, 1939; s. Everett Charles and Eleanor (Wall) A.; m. Margaret Perry Fricks, Nov. 9, 1963; 1 child, Laura Lee. BS in Engring. Sci., Navy Postgrad. Sch., Monterey, Calif., 1971. Commd. officer USN, 1960, advanced through grades to vice adm., 1988-94; comdg. officer Attack Squadron 85, 1975-77; comdr. Carrier Air Wing 6, 1979-80; comdg. officer USS Detroit (AOE-6), 1983-84, USS America (CV-66), 1985-87; comdr. Carrier Group 6, 1989-90; dir. assessment divsn. N-81 Office Naval Ops., Washington, 1992-93; comdr. Naval Air Force U.S. Atlantic Fleet, from 1994. A designer inflight refueling store night lighting system. Decorated Disting. Svc. medal Legion of Merit with 2 gold stars, Def. Superior Svc. medal; recipient John Paul Jones Inspirational Leadership award U.S. Navy League, 1986. Republican. Home: Norfolk, Va. Died May 24, 2009.

ALLIK, MICHAEL, manufacturing executive; b. NYC, Aug. 28, 1935; s. Michael and Alma (Busch) A.; m. Deborah Dixon, Jan. 2, 1983; children— William Michael, Timothy John, Ryan Andrew, Lauren Alexandra. BS, MIT, 1957; MBA, Harvard U., 1961. V.p. Kondu Corp., Erie, Pa., 1961-66; assoc. Booz, Allen & Hamilton, Cleve., 1966-69; gen. mgr. Textile Friction Group H.K. Porter, Pitts., 1969-71; gen. mgr. transformer div. Allis Chalmers, Pitts., 1971-75; exec. v.p. Mead Paper Group, Dayton, Ohio, 1975-78; sr. v.p. strategy and adminstrn. Mead Corp., Dayton, 1978-81; sr. v.p. fin. and adminstrn. Dart & Kraft, Inc., Northbrook, Ill., 1981-83, pres. Splty. Products Group, 1984-86; pres., chief oper. officer, dir. RTE Corp., Milw., 1986-89; pres. Premier Aluminum, Inc., Racine, Wis., 1989—2006. Ptnr. Harvest Capital Mgmt., Inc., Vero Beach, Fla.; mem. coun. Grad. Sch. Bus., U. Chgo., 1985-92. Pres. bd. trustees Victory Theatre, Dayton, 1980-81; bd. dirs. Chgo. Hort. Soc., 1982-86, Milw. Repertory Theater, 1991-93. Served to 1st lt. C.E. U.S. Army, 1957-59. Mem. Wis. Taxpayers Alliance (bd. dirs. 1987). Clubs: Chgo. Economic. Home: Vero Beach, Fla. Died Apr. 26, 2010.

ALLISON, DAVID C., state legislator; b. Pitts., July 8, 1924; m. Mary Elizabeth Allison; 3 children. BS, Rensselaer Poly., 1948, Wittenberg Coll., 1950. N.H. state rep. Dist. 7, Sullivan Dist. 10, from 1994; mem. com. and small bus. coms. N.H. Ho. of Reps., mem. judiciary and family law coms.; mem. Sullivan County Fin. Com., 1990-94, chmn., 1992-94; editor, writer. Sec. Sullivan County Dem., 1992-94, chmn., 1994—; mem. exec. com. N.H. Dem. Party, 1994—. Assoc. editor Bus. Week, 1951-56; tech. editor Time, Inc., 1956-61; sr. editor Internat. Sci. & Tech., 1961-68. Bd. dirs. Conn Valley Home Care, 1994—. Died Mar. 5, 2010.

ALLMAN, JAMES WILLIAM, radio station owner, engineer; b. Weston, W.Va., Mar. 28, 1946; s. F.W. Allman and Mary Elizabeth (Holloway) Allman McDaniel; m. Patricia Sue McKinney, July 1, 1978 (div. Nov. 1995). Grad. high sch., Lost Creek, W.Va. Electronic technician Bridgeport (W.Va.) TV, 1965-70; owner, electronic technician Allman's TV and Sound System, Lost Creek, W.Va., 1970-74; co-owner, electronic technician Allson Electronics, Anmoore, W.Va., 1974-77; studio engr., supr. Sta. WBOY-TV, Clarksburg, W.Va., 1975-79; studio engr. Sta. WDTV-TV, Weston, 1979-84; owner, chief engr. Allman Electronics Lab. Video Prodns., Clarksburg, 1978-91; operator, owner WOTR FM 96.3 Radio, Lost Creek, W.Va., from 1991. Studio maintenance WBOY-TV, Clarksburg, 1984—, Consol. Gas Transmission, Clarksburg, 1982—, design studio, 1982. Democrat. Avocations: electronics, antique cars. Died Jan. 27, 2009.

ALLRED, JOHN THOMPSON, lawyer; b. Mt. Airy, NC, June 6, 1929; s. Joe Henry and Irene (Thompson) A.; m. Helen Louise Landauer, Apr. 4, 1964; 1 child, John Thompson Jr. BS, U. N.C., 1951, JD with honors, 1959. Bar: N.C., U.S. Dist. Ct. (we., mid., and ea. dists.) N.C., U.S. Ct. Appeals (4th cir.), U.S. Supreme Ct. Assoc. Moore and Van Allen, Charlotte, N.C., 1959-64, from ptnr. to sr. ptnr., 1964-86; sr. ptnr., litig. Kilpatrick Stockton LLP, Charlotte, from 1986. Mem. N.C. Bd. Law Examiners, Raleigh, 1977-90, chmn., 1989-90. Editor N.C. Law Rev., 1958-59. Tchr. pub. speaking YMCA, Charlotte, 1964; exec. com. Thompson Children's Home, Charlotte, 1970-91; vestry Christ Episc. Ch., Charlotte, 1980. Lt. USNR, 1951-56. Fellow Am. Coll. Trial Lawyers, Am. Bar Found.; mem. ABA, N.C. Bar Assn. (patron), 4th Cir. Jud. Conf., 26th Jud. Dist. Bar Assn. (chmn. 1976). Democrat. Avocation: tennis. Home: Charlotte, NC. Died Mar. 4, 2009.

ALTER, DAVID, lawyer; b. Izka, Czechoslovakia, Oct. 31, 1923; came to U.S., 1929; s. Morris and Bertha Alter; m. Deborah King; children— Lisa, Amy BS, CCNY, 1947; LL.B., Harvard U., 1950. Bar: N.Y. 1950, U.S. Dist. Ct. (so. dist.) N.Y. 1953, U.S. Ct. Appeals (2d cir.) 1953, U.S. Dist. Ct. Conn. 1954, U.S. Ct. Appeals (4th cir.) 1957, U.S. Supreme Ct. 1962. Ptnr. Shea & Gould, NYC, 1979-89, Squadron, Ellenoff, Plesent & Lehrer, NYC, 1989-98; nat. counsel Screen Actors Guild, NYC, from 1998. Outside counsel Screen Actors Guild, 1966-98; trustee, mem. Fin. Com., Screen Actors Guild-Producers Pension & Health Plans, 1966-87, counsel 1987—. Pres. Hamlet of Seaview, Fire Island, N.Y., 1975-81; bd. dirs. Astoria Motion Picture and TV Ctr. Found., 1980-82, Am. Mus. of the Moving Image, 1983-86. Served with USAF, 1943-46. Mem. ABA, Assn. of Bar of City of N.Y., N.Y. State Bar Assn. Clubs: Harvard (N.Y.C.). Home: New York, NY. Died Aug. 27, 2009.

ALTHOFF, JAMES CORNELIUS, retail executive; b. Lansing, Iowa, Dec. 8, 1922; s. Henry Theodore and Anna Christine (Teeling) Althoff; m. Agnes Stroik, Oct. 17, 1945; children: Patricia Ann, Michael James. Pres. Ernies Wine and Liquor Corp., South San Francisco, 1964—72, Althoff Corp., Burlingame, Calif., from 1977. Pres. Prestige Investments; dir. Fortune's Almanac, San Francisco, Syndicated Bus. Corp. With USAAF, 1942—45, with USAF, 1951—53. Decorated D.F.C., Air medal with 5 oak leaf clusters. Mem.: Calif. Retail Liquor Dealers Assn. (pres. 1969—71), Nat. Liquor Stores Assn. (pres. 1973—75), St. Francis Yacht (San Francisco). Republican. Roman Catholic. Home: Menlo Park, Calif. Died May 22, 2009.

ALTSCHUL, MICHAEL, history educator; b. NYC, Sept. 29, 1936; s. Harry and Ethel (Brahinsky) A.; children: Jennifer, Emily. BA, NYU, 1957; PhD, Johns Hopkins U., 1962. Asst. prof. U. Mich., Ann Arbor, 1962-67; assoc. prof. Case Western Res. U., Cleve., 1967-77, prof. history, from 1977; vis. prof. Cleve. State U., 1972, 82; cons. Ednl. Testing Service, Princeton, N.J., 1982. Author: Baronial Family: Clares, 1965, Anglo-Norman England, 1969. Fulbright fellow (London), 1960-61; Am. Council Learned Socs. fellow, 1976; recipient Outstanding Teaching award Case Western Res. U., 1975 Fellow Royal Hist. Soc.; mem. Medieval Acad. Am. (adv. bd. 1979-82), Conf. Brit. Studies, Hasking Soc. Anglo-Norman Studies, Midwest Medieval Conf., Phi Beta Kappa Died July 8, 2010.

AMATO, ANTHONY J., director state aviation department; b. Phila., Jan. 18, 1937; AA, U. Md., 1964. Enlisted U.S. Army, 1953, rose through ranks to 1st sgt., resigned, 1978; svc. contractor U.S. Govt., 1980-86; flight instr. pvt. practice, Cheswold, Del., 1987-93; dir. aviation dept. transp. State of Del., Dover, from 1993. Mem. Nat. Assn. Aviation Officials, Nat. Bus. Assn., Inc. Died May 15, 2010.

AMBROSE, CHARLES CLARKE, investment banker; b. Tulsa, Sept. 21, 1924; s. Oliver Stephens and Maude May (Clarke) A.; m. Joan Aleen Johnston, June 1962; 1 child, Clarke Stephens. BChemE, Cornell U., 1948; MBA, Harvard U., 1950. First v.p. Drexel Burnham, NYC, 1950-73; exec. v.p., mng. dir. E.F. Hutton & Co., Inc., NYC, 1973-87; pres. Clarke Ambrose Corp., NYC, from 1987. Trustee The Stanley M. Isaacs Neighborhood Ctr., Inc. 2d lt. U.S. Army, 1943-45. Mem.: Union. Home: New York, NY. Died Mar. 22, 2009.

AMDAHL, DOUGLAS KENNETH, retired state supreme court justice; b. Mabel, Minn., Jan. 23, 1919; BBA, U. Minn., 1945; JD summa cum laude, William Mitchell Coll. Law, 1951, L.L.D. (hon.), 1987. Bar: Minn. 1951, Fed. Dist. Ct. 1952. Ptnr. Amdahl & Scott, Mpls., 1951-55; asst. county atty. Hennepin County, Minn., 1955-61; judge Mcpl. Ct., Mpls., 1961-62, Dist. Ct. 4th Dist., Minn., 1962-80, chief judge, 1973-75; assoc. justice Minn. Supreme Ct., 1980-81, chief justice, 1981-89; of counsel Rider, Bennett, Egan & Arundel, Mpls., 1989-99; ret. Asst. registrar, then registrar Mpls. Coll. Law, 1951-65; moot ct. instr. U. Minn.; faculty mem. and advisor Nat. Coll. State Judiciary; mem. Nat. Bd. Trial Advocacy; chmn. Nat. Ctr. for State Cts. Delay Reduction Adv. Com., 1986-88, Nat. Ctr. for State Cts. Coordinating Coun. on Life-Sustaining Decisionmaking by the Cts., 1989-93. Mem. ABA (chmn. com. on stds. of jud. adminstrn. 1987-96), Minn. Bar Assn., Hennepin County Bar Assn., Internat. Acad. Trial Judges, State Dist. Ct. Judges Assn. (pres. 1976-77), Conf. of Chief Judges (bd. dirs. 1987-88), Delta Theta Phi (assoc. justice supreme ct.). Home: Richfield, Minn. Died Aug. 24, 2010.

AMMERMAN, GALE RICHARD, organization executive, retired educator; b. Sullivan, Ind., Mar. 6, 1923; s. Lyman Sylvanious and Iva Mae Amerman; m. Jane Loretta Burke, Sept. 26, 1943; children: Kathleen, John, Joseph, Mark, Christopher. BS, Purdue U., 1950, MS, 1953, PhD, 1957. Asst. prof. Purdue U., Lafayette, Ind., 1958-60; dir. food rsch. Liby McNeill & Libby, Chgo., Ind., 1960-67; prof. food sci. Miss. State U., Starkville, 1967-85, dept. head, 1985-88, prof. emeritus, from 1990, mem. grad. coun., 1984-85; pres. Aliceville C. of C., from 1997. Author: Careers in Food Technology, 1975, Home Canning, 1978, An American Glider Pilot's Story, 2001; contbg. author: Channel Catfish Culture, 1985; contbr. over 125 articles on food sci. to profl. jours. Advisor to Pickens County Councillors Citizen of Yr., Aliceville, Ala., 1999. 1st lt. USAAF, 1941-45, ETO. Decorated Dutch Orange Lanyard The Netherlands; recipient Air medal (3). Fellow Inst. Food Technologists (chmn. Chgo. sect. 1964-65, pres. Magnolia sect. 1987-88, Calvert Willey award 1988); mem. Coun. for Agr. Sci. and Tech. (pres. 1985-86, bd. dirs. 1977-87), Phi Kappa Phi, Phi Tau Sigma (pres. 1984-85). Democrat. Roman Catholic. Achievements include patent for fish skinning process. Home: Aliceville, Ala. Died Apr. 21, 2009.

ANDERSEN, KENNETH JOSEPH, pharmaceutical company executive; b. Bklyn., Dec. 24, 1936; s. Conrad Joseph and Evelyn (Olsen) A.; m. Judith Gail Lamb, June 9, 1962; children: David J., Mark A. AA, Kendall Coll., 1956; BS, Davis & Elkins Coll., 1959; MS, Syracuse U., 1962, PhD, 1965. Assoc. chief biol. sci. Battelle Meml. Inst., Columbus, Ohio, 1965-72; assoc. dir. diagnostic svcs. Johnson & Johnson Internat., New Brunswick, N.J., 1972-73; dir. biol. rsch. Norwich (N.Y.)-Eaton Pharm. Inc., 1973-82; pres. Andersen Labs., Inc., Norwich, from 1982. Pres. South New Berlin Bd. Edn., 1984-85, Chenango Ednl. Opportunities, Norwich, 1988—; pres. Norwich Rotary Club, 1987-88. Fellow AAAS; mem. Am. Soc. Microbiology. Republican. Methodist. Avocation: raising registered beef cattle. Home: South New Berlin, NY. Died Feb. 27, 2010.

ANDERSON, EUGENE ROBERT, lawyer; b. Portland, Oreg., Oct. 24, 1927; s. Andrew E. and Ruth Beatrice (White) A.; m. Jenny Morgenthau, Nov. 8, 1986: children: Matthew, Martin. BS, UCLA, 1949; student, Oreg. State Coll., 1945; JD, Harvard U., 1952; LLM, NYU, 1960. Bar: N.Y. bar 1953, Mass., So. and Eastern dists. N.Y., Second Circuit, D.C. Circuit, U.S. Ct. Claims, U.S. Supreme Ct. bars 1953. Assoc. Chadbourne & Parke LLP, NYC, 1953-61, ptnr., 1965-69; asst. U.S. atty. (so. dist.) NY US Dept. Justice, Foley Square, 1961-65, chief civil div., 1963-65; ptnr. Anderson Kill & Olick, P.C., NYC, 1969—2010; asst. dist. atty. N.Y. County, 1977. Spl. hearing officer U.S. Dept. Justice, 1965-68; arbitrator Am. Arbitration Assn., 1965—, Small Claims Ct., 1970-76; mem. com. on trial practice and technique Second Circuit, 1967-73 Mem. N.Y.C. Mayor's Bus. Adv. Com., Mayor's Task Force Auto. Ins. Served with AUS, 1945-46. Mem. ABA, Fed. Bar Assn., Assn. Bar City N.Y., Police Athletic League (dir., gen. counsel). Died July 30, 2010.

ANDERSON, GEORGE HARDING, broadcasting company executive; b. Buffalo, Mar. 6, 1931; s. Gordon and Adeline (Harding) A.; m. Sandra Bradley, Aug. 24, 1957 (div. 1972); 1 child, Geoffrey Bradley; m. Barbara Rich Tisdale, Jan. 18, 1974. BA, Harvard U., 1954. With First Nat. Bank Boston, 1955-58, Randolph Assos., Wellesley, Mass., 1959-61; pres. Precision Products Co. Inc., Waltham, Mass., 1961-64; sales mgr. WBZ-TV, Boston, 1964-66; office mgr. Blair Radio, Boston, 1966-67; sales mgr. WHDH-TV, Boston, 1967-68; exec. v.p., dir. Guy Gannett Broadcasting Services, Sta. WGAN-AM-FM-TV, Portland, Maine, Sta. WHYN-AM-FM-TV, Springfield, Mass., Sta. WINZ-AM-FM, Miami, Fla., 1968-78; pres. Sta. KENS-TV, San Antonio, 1980-84; pres., chief operating officer Harte-Hanks TV Group, 1981-84; corp. v.p. Harte-Hanks Communications, 1981-84; pres. Broadcast div. Diversified Communications, 1985-91, ret., 1991. Dir. WTLV, Jacksonville, Fla., 1978-84, Maine Nat. Bank, Southworth Machine Co. Pres. Maine Audubon Soc., 1971, Portland Soc. Natural History, 1971; maj. Portland United Fund Dr., 1971, advance gifts chmn., 1972; co-chmn. fund dr. Edward Waters Coll., 1979; bd. dirs. Maine Cancer Soc., Jacksonville United Way, 1979—, San Antonio Red Cross, 1981—, vice chmn., 1983—, S.W. Tex. Blood Bank; bd. dirs. Camden Conf., 1993—; campaign chmn. N.E. Health Capital Campaign; N.E. Health Bd. Trustees, 1994-98; pres. trustees Camden Health Care Ctr., 1993-94, Camden Conf., 1994. Mem. Harvard Varsity Club, Owl Club, Camden Yacht Club, Megunticook Golf Club. Home: Falmouth, Maine. Died May 16, 2009.

ANDERSON, JOAN SCHEUERMANN, psychologist, educator; b. New Orleans, Mar. 17, 1933; d. Leonhard Naef and Margaret Scheuermann; m. Frank Clayton Anderson, Apr. 30, 1954; children: Frank Clayton III, Mollie Elise. BA, Sophie Newcomb Coll., 1954; PhD, U. Houston, 1969. Pvt. practice, Houston, from 1969; clin. assoc. prof. Baylor Coll. Medicine, Houston; chmn. Tex. Bd. Examiners Psychologists, 1982. Bd. dirs. Living Bank, from 1965, Children's World, 1970—75, Homes St. Mark, from 1977. Mem.: Houston Psychol. Assn. (pres. 1979), Tex. Psychol. Assn. (pres. 1977), Am. Psychol. Assn. Episcopalian. Home: Houston, Tex. Died June 26, 2009.

ANDERSON, RICHARD CHARLES, geology educator; b. Moline, Ill., Apr. 22, 1930; s. Edgar Oscar and Sarah Albertina (Olson) A.; m. Ethel Irene Cada, June 27, 1953; children: Eileen Ruth, Elizabeth Sarah, Penelope Cada. AB, Augustana Coll., Rock Island, Ill., 1952; SM, U. Chgo., 1953, PhD, 1955. Geologist Geophoto Svcs., Denver, 1955-57; from asst. prof. to prof. geology Augustana Coll., Rock Island, 1957-96; prof. emeritus, from 1996. Rsch. affiliate Ill. State Geol. Survey, Champaign, 1959—. Editor: Earth Interpreters, 1992; author reports. Recipient Neil Miner award Nat. Assn. Geology Tchrs., 1992. Fellow Geol. Soc. Am. (sect. co-chair 1990). Lutheran. Home: Champaign, Ill. Died Jan. 8, 2009.

ANDERSON, ROBERT THEODORE, music educator, organist; b. Chgo., Oct. 5, 1934; s. Albert Theodore and Lillian Gertrude (Chalbeck) A. B.Sacred Music, Ill. Wesleyan U., 1955; M.Sacred Music, Union Theol. Sem., NYC, 1957, D.Sacred Music, 1961. Mem. faculty So. Meth. U., from 1960, Univ. disting. prof. organ emeritus, from 1972, Meadows Found. disting. teaching prof., 1981-82. Organ cons., lectr., tchr. master classes. Author articles; composer anthems.

Fulbright grantee, 1957-59; named Distinguished Alumnus Ill. Wesleyan U., 1972 Mem. Am. Guild Organists, Internat. Bach Soc., Blue Key, Pi Kappa Lambda, Phi Mu Alpha, Phi Beta Phi. Methodist. Home: Honolulu, Hawaii. Died May 29, 2009.

ANDERSON, SPARKY (GEORGE LEE ANDERSON), retired professional baseball manager; b. Bridgewater, SD, Feb. 22, 1934; s. LeRoy Anderson; m. Carol Valle; children: George Jr., Shirlee Trece, Albert William. Second baseman Phila. Phillies, 1959, Toronto Maple Leafs, Internat. League, 1960—64, mgr., 1964, Rock Hill Cardinals, We. Carolinas League, 1965, St. Petersburg Cardinals, Fla. State League, 1966, Modesto Reds, Calif. League, 1967, Ashville Tourists, Calif. League, 1968; coach San Diego Padres, 1969—70; mgr. Cin. Reds, 1970-78, Detroit Tigers, 1979-95; announcer Anaheim Angels, Calif., 1997-98. Mgr. Nat. League All-Star Team, 1971, 73, 76, 77, Am. League All-Star Team 1985. Author: (with Dan Ewald) They Call Me Sparky, 1998; appeared in: (films) Tiger Town, 1983 Founder Caring Athletes Team for Children's and Henry Ford Hosp., 1987. Named Am. League Mgr. of Yr., 1984, 1987; named to Cin. Reds Hall of Fame, Cin. chpt. Baseball Writers Assn., 1999, Nat. Baseball Hall of Fame, 2000, Can. Baseball Hall of Fame, 2007. Achievements include first manager in Major League Baseball history to achieve 100 wins in a season in both the National League (Cincinnati Reds, 1970, 1975 & 1976) and the American League (Detroit Tigers, 1984); manager of World Series Championship winning Cincinnati Reds, 1975, 1976; Detroit Tigers, 1984; first manager in Major League Baseball histroy to win a World Series in both the National and American Leagues. Home: Thousand Oaks, Calif. Died Nov. 4, 2010.

ANDOLSEN, ALAN ANTHONY, management consultant; b. Cleve., Feb. 19, 1943; s. Lloyd Anthony and Helen Mae (Kozinski) A.; m. Barbara Hilkert, Jan. 20, 1968; children: Daniel, Ruth. AB magna cum laude, Borromeo Coll., 1964; MA, U. Dayton, 1967; postgrad., Vanderbilt U., 1967-69. Cert. mgmt. cons.; cert. records mgr. V.p. Bergamo East, Marcy, NY, 1969-71; dir. Met. Health Dept., Nashville, 1971-76; prin. Naremco Svc., Inc., NYC, 1976-79, v.p., 1979-86, pres., from 1986. Bd. dirs. Assn. Mgmt. Cons. Firms., N.Y.C. Editor: Management Consulting-A Model Course, 1989, 96; contbr. articles to profl. jours. Pres. Inst. Cert. Records Mgrs. Mem. Inst. Mgmt. Cons. (pres.), Assn. Records Mgrs. and Adminstrs., Assn. Image and Info. Mgmt., Am. Mensa Ltd. Roman Catholic. Avocations: music, bicycling, reading. Home: New York, NY. Died Jan. 24, 2010.

ANDREASSEN, POUL, business executive; b. Stubbekobing, Denmark, Feb. 18, 1928; s. Walther and Edith (Thulin) A.; m. Elsa Mogelbjerg Pedersen, Dec. 23, 1949; children: Lasse, Lise, Peter. Grad. in Machine Constrn. Engring., Kobenhavns Maskinteknikum, Copenhagen, 1951. Dir. Det Danske Rengorings Selskab, Copenhagen, 1962, mng. dir., 1962-72; pres., mng. dir. Internat. Service System, Charlottenlund, Denmark, from 1972. Chmn. ISS Internat. Service System Inc., N.Y.C., Storebaeltsforbindelsen A/S; vice chmn. Superfos A/S, Dk; bd. dirs. Privatbanken A-S, Cph., Politiken Found., Nat. Lab. RISØ, Dk, Meyers Parking Inc., N.Y. Bd. dirs. Egmont H. Petersen Found. Decorated Knight of Order of Dannebrog. Mem. Pres. Assn. Home: Charlottenlund, Denmark. Died Aug. 7, 2009.

ANDREOLI, THOMAS EUGENE, physician; b. Bronx, Jan. 9, 1935; BA cum laude, St. Vincent Coll., Latrobe, Pa, 1952—56; ScD (hon.), St. Vincent Coll., 1987; MD magna cum laude, Georgetown U., 1956—60; PhD (hon.), Univ. Paris, 1993; MD (hon.), Aristotle U., Thessaloniki, Greece, 2000, Semmelweis U., Budapest, Hungary, 2003. Diplomate: Am. Bd. Internal Medicine and subspecialty in nephrology. Intern, resident in medicine Duke U., Durham, NC, 1960-61, 64-65, assoc. prof. medicine and asst. prof. physiology, 1965-70; prof. medicine and physiology, dir. nephrology research and tng. center U. Ala. Sch. Medicine, Birmingham, 1970-78; prof., chmn. dept. internal medicine U. Tex. Med. Sch., Houston, 1979-87, Edward Randall III prof., chmn. dept. internal medicine, 1986-87; chief medicine Hermann Hosp., Houston, 1979-87; Nolan prof. and chmn. dept. internal medicine U. Ark. Coll. Medicine, Little Rock, 1988—2004, Disting. prof. dept. internal medicine, dept. physiology and biophysics, from 2004. Author: Disturbances in Body Fluid Osmolality, 1977; Physiology of Membrane Disorders, 1978, 86; Andreoli and Carpenters Cecil, Essentials of Medicine, 1986, 90, 93, 97, 2001, 04, 07; Molecular Biology of Membrane Transport Disorders, 1996; Editor Am. Jour. Physiology: Renal, Fluid and Electrolyte Physiology, 1976-83; Kidney Internat., 1984-97; assoc. editor Annual Rev. Physiology, 1977-83; Am. Jour. Medicine, 1979-86; mem. editorial bd. Jour. Clin. Investigation, 1976-81; Mineral and Electrolyte Metabolism, 1977-80, Tex. Health Letter; 1980-88, Seminars in Nephrology; 1980-92, Kidney Internat., 1981-85; Physiol. Revs., 1982-84. Recipient Louis Pasteur medal U. Louis Pasteur Strasbourg, France, 1995, Hume award Nat. Kidney Found., 1997, Making Lives Better award, 2004, Silver Plate award, Hungarian Kidney Found., 2006. Master ACP (Disting. Tchr. award 2000); fellow Royal Coll. Physicians, Edinburgh, London; mem. Assn. Am. Physicians, Assn. Profs. Medicine (Robert H. Williams Disting. Chair of Med. award, 1998), Am. Soc. Clin. Investigation, Am. Physiol. Soc. (Robert W Berliner award for excellence in Renal Physiology, 2000), Am. Soc. Nephrology (coun. 1988-95, pres. 1993-94, Homer W. Smith award 1995), Internat. Soc. Nephrology (hon., exec. com. 1985-2003, v.p. 1995-97, pres.-elect 1997-99, pres. 1999-2001). Died Apr. 14, 2009.

ANDREWS, ARCHIE MOULTON, retired federal official; b. Greenwich, Conn., July 29, 1919; s. Archie M. and Eleanor (Underwood) A.; m. Margaret Jane Jones, Mar. 3, 1944 (dec. Sept. 1977); children: Archie Moulton III, Peter Underwood, Duncan Trumbull; m. Nike Smith Middleton, Oct. 3, 1978 (dec. Mar. 1987); m. Dorothy Johnson Conley, Sept. 30, 1989. AB, Princeton U., 1941. Exec. trainee W.R. Grace & Co., 1941-42; econ. analyst State Dept., 1942-43; U.S. rep. blacklist com. Ministry Econ. Warfare, Am. embassy, London, 1943-45; with Dictograph Products, Inc., Danbury, Conn., 1946-63, pres., 1962-63; also dir.; pres. Acousticon-Dictograph Co. Ltd., Can., 1963, dir., 1958-63, Gen. Acoustics Ltd., Eng., 1950-63; dep. dir. Bur. Internat. Commerce, Dept. Commerce, 1964-69; dir. U.S. trade mission to N. Africa, 1966; comml. counsellor Am. embassy, London, 1970-75; dir. bus. services Office Internat. Affairs, HUD, Washington, 1976-77; dir. exporters service Office Export Adminstrn., Dept. Commerce, Washington, 1978-86; sr. policy analyst Office of Tech. and Policy Analysis, 1986-88, ret., 1988. Mem. SAR Clubs: Princeton (Washington and N.Y.C.); Pilgrims; Diplomatic and Consular Officers Ret. Home: Annapolis, Md. Died Jan. 3, 2010.

ANDREWS, CHARLES ROLLAND, library administrator; b. Scranton, Pa., July 5, 1930; s. Edgar W. and Margaret (Machenry) A.; m. Harriet Williams, Dec. 27, 1954 (dec. 1985); m. Dorothy Kramer, Dec. 10, 1988. BS in Edn., Bloomsburg U., 1954; MA in English Lit., U. Okla., 1959; MS in L.S., Case Western Res. U., 1964, PhD, 1967. Head reference dept. Cleve. Pub. Library, 1966-68, Case Western Res. Univ. Libraries, Cleve., 1968-69, librarian Freiberger Library, 1969-72, asst. dir. pub. services, 1972-74; univ. librarian Southeastern Mass. Univ. Library, North Dartmouth, 1974-76; dean library services Hofstra U. Library, Hempstead, NY, 1976-96, prof. emeritus, from 1997. Lectr. Hofstra U., U. Coll. Continuing Edn., 1997—. Editor: Reference Books for Small and Medium-Sized Libraries, 1973; contbr. articles, revs. to profl. jours. Bd. trustees Unitarian Universalist Congregation, Garden City, NY, 1998—2004, chair art exhibits com., 1999—2002, newsletter editor, 2000—06. Mem. ALA, Assn. Coll. and Rsch. Librs., Archons of Colophon, L.I. Libr. Resources Coun. (chair regional automation com. 1986-92, bd. trustees 1990-94), Am. Express (sr. adv. bd. mem. 1998-99). Democrat. Avocations: calligraphy, word processing, graphics. Died Nov. 17, 2009.

ANDREWS, EDWARD CLINTON, JR., pathologist, educator; b. Rockland, Maine, Jan. 9, 1925; married; five children. AB, Middlebury Coll., 1946, LLD (hon.), 1972; MD, Johns Hopkins U., 1951; DSc (hon.), U. Dakar, Senegal, 1973, Bowdoin Coll., 1986. Diplomate Am. Bd. Anatomical Pathology. Asst. in pathology Johns Hopkins U., Balt., 1951-52, instr. pathology, 1952-58; asst. pathologist John Hopkins Hosp., Balt., 1951-53, asst. resident pathology, 1953-55, resident pathology, 1955-56; assoc. prof. pathology U. Vt., Burlington, 1958-67, prof. pathology, from 1967, assoc. dean. Coll. Medicine, 1964-66, dean Coll. Medicine, 1966-70, pres., 1970-75, Maine Med. Ctr., Portland, from 1975. Chmn. bd. govs. W. Alton Jones Cell Sci. Ctr., Lake Placid, N.Y., 1970-72; regional dir.'s adv. com. Dept. Health, Edn. and Welfare, Boston, 1971; cons. div. physician and health profls. edn. NIH, Bethesda, Mass., 1971-72, Library Medicine, 1973, div. medicine Dept. Health, Edn. and Welfare, Health Resources Adminstrn., Bethesda, 1977; mem. Maine del. New Eng. Bd. Higher Edn., 1976-78, Maine Health Facilities Authority, Augusta, 1976-81, Maine Health Coordinating Council, Augusta, 1976-80, Adv. Com. on Med. Edn., Augusta, 1978-85; corporator Maine Savs. Bank, Portland, 1975-84; chmn. Sec. of Navy's Spl. Health Care Adv. Com., Washington, 1985; speaker in field; trustee, coprorator Med. Care. Devel., Inc. Augusta, 1978-80; trustee Med. Ctr. Hosp. Vt., 1970, Maine Med. Ctr., 1975; bd. dirs. Vt. Higher Edn. Council, Chittenden Trust Co., Burlington, Med. Mut. Ins. Co., Portland, Ventrex Ref. Lab., Portland. Contbr. articles to profl. jours. Chmn. adv. com. prgram for long-term care/chronic illness The Robert Wood Johnson Found., Princeton, N.J., 1979, cons., 1979; cons. on med. edn. and health care State Dept. and Agy. for Internat. Devel. to the Governmentof Pakistan, 1963-63; vis. com. gov.'s spl. commn. on edn. U. Maine, 1985-86; mem. Com. on Fgn. Relations, Portland, 1985; trustee Green Mountain Coll., Poultney, Vt., 1975-78, Ptnrs. of the Alliance, Honduras and Vt., 1966; bd. dirs. Vol. Budget Rev. Orgn., Augusta, 1980, North Yarmouth Acad., Maine, 1984-86Charles A. Dana Found. Inc., N.Y., 1976, Vol. Hosps. Am., Irving, Tex., 1985, New Eng. Council Inc., Boston, 1985. Mem. Am. Assn. Med. Coll. (council deans 1965-70), Maine Hosp. Assn. (trustee 1976-77, chmn. 1985-86, bd. dirs. 1983—), Am. Hosp. Assn. (council in fed. relations 1977-81, council patient care services 1984-86), Portland C. of C. (bd. dirs. 1981-85), Phi Beta Kappa. Died Feb. 19, 2010.

ANDREWS, IKE FRANKLIN, former United States Representative from North Carolina; b. Bonlee, NC, Sept. 2, 1925; s. Archie Franklin Andrews and Ina A. Dunlap; children: Alice Cecelia, Nina Patricia. Superior ct. solicitor, Dist. 10A, NC, 1961—64; bd. dirs. First Union Nat. Bank NC, Siler City, 1962—72; mem. NC State Senate, 1959—60, NC House of Reps., NC, 1967—72; chmn. Select New Chancellor Com., 1970—72; mem. US Congress from 4th NC Dist., 1973—85; ptnr. Edwards, Atwater & Andrews, 1992—2010. Served in US Army, 1943—45. Democrat. Baptist. Died May 10, 2010.

ANKERSON, ROBERT WILLIAM, management consultant; b. Mt. Vernon, NY, Sept. 23, 1933; s. Paul Gustav and Virginia (Roberts) A.; children: Robert William Jr., Samuel B. AB, Dartmouth Coll., 1955. Indsl. rels. asst. Texaco Inc., NYC, 1959-60; successively mktg. svcs. mgr., advt. sales rep., pub. affairs dir. Time Inc., NYC, 1960-73; sr. v.p. Devine, Baldwin and Assocs., NYC, 1973-75; v.p. and prin. Spencer Stuart and Assocs. Inc., NYC, 1975-80; sr. v.p. and dir. Billington, Fox and Ellis, Inc., NYC, 1980-82; sr. v.p. Haley Assocs. Inc., NYC, 1982-86; ptnr. Ward Howell Internat. Inc., NYC, 1986-93; pres. ConServ Inc., NYC, from 1993. With USNR, 1956-59. Home: East Quogue, NY. Died June 9, 2009.

ANSBACHER, CHARLES ALEXANDER, conductor; b. Providence, Oct. 5, 1942; s. Heinz L. and Rowena (Ripin) A.; m. Swanee Hunt, 1986; 1 son, Henry Lloyd. BA, Brown U., 1965; M.Music, U. Cin., 1968, D.MA, 1979. Nat. adv. bd. Avery Fisher awards music; mem. Colo. State Festival Council for Contennial-Bicentennial Commn., 1974-76; chmn. White House Fellows Regional Selection Com. Asst. condr., Kingsport (Tenn.) Symphony Orch., 1965-66, condr., mus. dir., Middletown (Ohio) Symphony Orch., 1967-70, Colorado Springs Symphony Orch., 1970-89, condr. laureate, Colorado Springs Symphony Orch., 1989-2010, conductor Boston Landmarks Orch., 2000-2010, conductor laureate, 2010; music dir., Rockefeller Found., Apprentice Musicians Program, Cin. Playhouse in Park, 1967, guest condr., Cin. Symphony Orch., Denver Symphony Orch., Frysk Orkest in Leeuwarden, Holland, Indpls. Symphony, Omaha Symphony, Ft. Worth Symphony, San Jose Symphony, Seoul Philharm., Young Musicians Symphony Orch. of London, 1985; condr., music dir., Young Artists Orch. Denver, 1980-84. White House fellow, 1976-77 Mem. Urban League Pike's Peak Region (treas.), Pike's Peak Musicians Assn. (v.p. 1974-76), Condrs. Guild of Am. Symphony Orch. League (chmn. 1979-81, pres. 1986—), Am. Symphony Orch. League (dir. 1979-81), Colo. Council Arts and Humanities (1978-84, chmn. 1987—), Colo. Pub. Edn. Partnership (1984—), Pub. Edn. Coalition of the Pikes Peak Region (co-pres. 1984—), Music Educators Nat. Conf., World Affairs Council Colorado Springs (pres. 1980-84, chmn. design constrn. subcom.), Pikes Peak Ctr. (founding bd. mem. charter fund), Conr.'s Guild, Inc. (pres. 1986—), Pub. Edn. Coalition Pikes Peak Region (bd. dirs. Colo. pub. edn. partnership, co-pres. 1985-86, chmn. design and constrn. subcom. Pikes Peak Ctr., founding bd. mem. charter fund). Clubs: Rotary, El Paso. Home: Denver, Colo. Died Sept. 12, 2010.

ANTHONY, CHARLES, JR., chemical engineer; b. Bloomfield, NJ, Oct. 14, 1921; s. Charles and Hannah Harriet (Johnson) Anthony; m. Alice Baxley Anthony, June 13, 1959; children: Eric Baxley, Stuart Brown. BChE, NYU, 1949; MBA cum laude, Fairleigh Dickinson U., 1962. Chief chemist Walter Kidde & Co., Belleville, NJ, 1946—59, mgr. materials & processes, 1959—66; mgr. product devel. M&T Chems., Inc., Rahway, NJ, 1966—70, corp. rsch. coord., 1970—72; rsch. dir. Booz-Allen & Hamilton, Florham Pk., NJ, 1972—75, v.p. NJ, 1972—75, 1975—80; pres. Case Cons. Labs., Whippany, NJ, from 1980. Treas., trustee Livingston Pub. Libr., 1971—76; mem. exec. com., bd. mgrs. West Essex YMCA, from 1978; bd. dirs. YMCA Oranges & West Essex, from 1983. Mem.: AAAS, Am. Arbitration Assn., Soc. Rsch. Adminstrs., Am. Electroplaters Soc., NY Acad. Scis., Am. Chem. Soc., Livingston Kiwanis. Republican. Congregationalist. Home: Maplewood, NJ. Died May 14, 2009.

ANTONELLI, LUIZ KUSTER, psychology educator; b. Sao Francisco de Assis, Brazil, Feb. 27, 1918; arrived in US, 1958; s. Pedro B. and Almerinda (Kuster) Antonelli. Student, State Tchrs. Coll., Cruz Alta, Brazil, 1935—37, U. Chile, 1947—48; BA, U. Rio Grande de Sul, 1949; postgrad., U. Denver, 1952, Inst. Practicing Psychotherapists, NYC, 1964, Ctr. Mental Health, 1968; MA, Columbia U., 1953, EdD, 1961. Pres. State Tchrs. Coll., Cachoeira do Sul, Brazil, 1943—50; supt. State of Rio Grande do Sul, 1953—54; prof., psychology Inst. Edn., Porto Alegre, Brazil, 1953—54; dean, students Aero. Inst. Tech. San Jose dos Campos, Sao Paulo, Brazil, 1955; dir. Inter-Am. Ctr. Pan Am. Union, Venezuela, 1956—58; counselor Bklyn. Coll., 1961; dir., divsn. gen. edn. Voorhees Tech. Inst., NYC, 1961—66; staff mem. Met. Ctr. Mental Health, NYC, 1963—64; mem., staff Postgrad. Ctr. Mental Health, 1964—68, staff, 1968—69; assoc. prof. Queen's Coll. City U. NY, from 1966, dir., counseling and guidance ctr., 1969—72, dir., master tng. program for urban sch. counselors, 1969—72, dir., peer counseling tng. program, 1976—78, coord. & supr., Family Counseling Program, from 1980; vis. prof. U. Brasilia, Brazil, 1981. Hon. chmn. Campaign Against Juvenile Delinquency, Venezuela. With Brazilian Army, 1938. Mem.: AAUP, NEA, AAAS, Am. Pers. and Guidance Assn., Am. Coll. Pers. Assn., Am. Ednl. Rsch. Assn., Am. Anthrop. Assn., Am. Psychol. Assn., Phi Delta Kappa, Kappa Delta Pi. Died Mar. 19, 2009.

APONE, CARL ANTHONY, journalist; b. Brownsville, Pa., July 9, 1923; s. Peter P. and Carmela (Puglia) A.; m. Kathleen King, Jan. 23, 1965; 1 child, Elizabeth. BA cum laude, U. Notre Dame, 1949; MA, Boston U., 1950. Dir. pub. rels., lectr. journalism and Am. lit. St. Mary's Coll., Notre Dame, Ind., 1950-53; staff writer UP, Detroit, 1953; city editor Brownsville Telegraph, 1953-57; staff writer Pitts. Sun- Telegraph, 1958-60; music editor Pitts. Press, 1960-89; mem. faculty journalism Duquesne U., 1967-72; free-lance writer, from 1950. Mem. St. Vincent DePaul Soc., 1963—. Served with inf. AUS, 1943-46. Recipient Golden Quill Journalism awards; Pa. Newspaper Pubs. Assn. awards. Home: Pittsburgh, Pa. Died Mar. 19, 2010.

APTER, DAVID ERNEST, political science and sociology professor; b. NYC, Dec. 18, 1924; s. Herman and Bella S. (Steinberg) A.; m. Eleanor Selwyn, Dec. 28, 1947; children: Emily Susan, Andrew Herman BA, Antioch Coll., 1950; MA, Princeton U., 1952, PhD, 1954; MA (hon.), Yale U., 1969. Asst. prof. Northwestern U., 1954-57; assoc. prof. U. Chgo., 1957-61; prof. U. Calif., Berkeley, 1961-69, dir. Inst. Internat. Studies, 1963-69; H.J. Heinz prof. comparative polit. and social devel. Yale U., New Haven, 1969—2000, dir. social sci. divsn., 1978-81, chmn. Dept. Sociology, 1997-99, sr. rsch. scientist, 2000—10. Chmn. Coun. African Studies Yale U., 1995-99; dir. legitimization of violence project UN Rsch. Inst. for Social Devel., Geneva, 1989-94; exec. sec. com. comparative study of new nations U. Chgo., 1957-61; vis. fellow All Souls Coll., Oxford U., Eng., 1967-68, St. Anthony's Coll., 1972, Inst. for Advanced Studies, Princeton, N.J., 1973, 74, Kyoto Am. seminar, 1979; Halevy prof. Found. Nat. des Scis.

Polit., Paris, 1981-82; vis. prof. U. Paris X, 1985; vis. fellow Magdalen Coll., Oxford U., spring 1988; fellow The Netherlands Inst. for Advanced Study, 1992; mem. Kennedy Task Force, Africa, 1957; Peace Corps dir. Ghana Tng. Program, 1961, 62; cons. Rand Corp., 1964-69, HUD, 1963, Coun. on Fgn. Relations, 1969-2010, State Dept. Adv. Com. for Africa, 1961-69; mem. U.S. Commn. for UNESCO, 1977-79. Author: Ghana in Transition, 1956; The Political Kingdom in Uganda, 1961; (with H. Eckstein) Comparative Politics, 1963; Ideology and Discontent, 1964; The Politics of Modernization, 1965; Some Conceptual Approaches to the Study of Modernization, 1968; (with C. Andrain) Contemporary Analytical Theory, 1972; Choice and the Politics of Allocation (Woodrow Wilson award Am. Polit. Sci. Assn), 1971; Political Change, 1973; Anarchism Today, 1973; Introduction to Political Analysis, 1977; (with L. Goodman) Multi-National Corporations and Social Change, 1977; (with Nagayo Sawa) Against the State, 1984, Rethinking Development, 1987; The New Realsim in Sub Saharas Africa, 1994; (with Carl Rosberg) Revolutionary Discourse in Mao's Republic, 1994; (with Tony Saich) Political Protest and Social Change, 1995, The Legitimization of Violence, 1997, Today's Past, 2002. Served with AUS, 1943-46 Fellow Social Sci. Rsch. Coun., Ghana, 1952-53, Ford Found., Uganda, 1955-56, Ctr. for Advanced Studies in Behavior Sci., 1957-59, Guggenheim Found., 1967-68, Fulbright Found., 1974, 79, Netherlands Inst. for Advanced Study, 1991-92; grantee Carnegie Found., 1955-60, Ford Found., 1967-71; recipient Dogan prize Internat. Social Sci. Coun., 2006. Fellow Am. Acad. Arts and Scis., Coun. on Fgn. Rels.; mem. Am. Polit. Sci. Assn., Internat. Polit. Sci. Assn. (pres. program com. 12th World Congress 1981), Century Assn. Club, Elizabethan Club. Democrat. Achievements include research in the politics of development, comparative theory, and case studies in violent protest in different regions of the world. Home: North Haven, Conn. Died May 4, 2010.

AQUILINO, DANIEL, banker; b. Needham, Mass., Feb. 4, 1924; s. Michael Aquilino and Anna (Bruno) A.; m. Theresa H. Barberio, Nov. 9, 1946; children: Donna Lee, Daniel C., Michael D. BS magna cum laude, Northeastern U., 1949; grad., Rutgers U., 1962. With Fed. Res. Bank Boston, 1949-85, exec. v.p., 1970-85, Bank of New Eng., Boston, 1985-89; cons. Boston, from 1990. Served with AUS, 1943-45. Recipient Sears B. Condit award Northeastern U., 1947, 49; recognition award Italian-Am. Soc., Inc., 1972. Home: Boston, Mass. Died Apr. 18, 2010.

ARANDA, MARY KATHRYN, state legislator; b. Nassawadox, Va., Sept. 28, 1945; d. John McCallister and Frances Esther (Mausteller) Copper; m. Ronald William Meyer, Dec. 28, 1965 (dec. June 1966); m. Rembert Aranda, Feb. 4, 1973; 1 child, Olivia Kathryn. BA, Goucher Coll., 1969. Jr. planner Balt. Regional Planning Coun., 1968-71; asst. planner edn. sect. N.Y.C. Dept. City Planning, 1971-74, assoc. dir. edn. and social svcs. sect., 1974-76; rep. Gen. Ct. State of N.H., Concord, 1993-96. Commr. Derry House and Devel. Authority, 1983-95; incorporator Alexander-Eastman Found., Derry and Concord, 1993-96; mem. Derry Planning Bd., 1984-88. Mem. Nat. Orgn. Women Legislators, Internat. Platform Assn. Republican. Avocations: sewing, gardening. Home: Nellysford, Va. Died Dec. 21, 2009.

ARCHER, DAVID HORACE, process engineer, consultant; b. Pitts., Jan. 20, 1928; s. Horace G. and Inez E. (Eichholtz) A.; m. M. Justine Garnic, July 29, 1950 (dec. Sept. 1973); children: Catherine M.I., Miriam. A. J. Archer McCann, Amy C.A.; m. Alice Ann Parsons, July 2, 1976; 1 child, Martha J. Knezovich. BS, Carnegie Mellon U., 1948; PhD, U. Del., 1953. Instr. chem. engring. U. Del., Newark, 1951-53; asst. prof. to assoc. prof. Carnegie Mellon U., Pitts., 1953-60, prof., from 1991; successively sr. engr., fellow engr., supr. engr., sect. mgr. R & D, dept. mgr., cons. engr. Westinghouse Electric, Pitts., 1960-91. Cons. Westinghouse Electric Corp., Pitts. Coke, Pa. Coke Tech., Pitts., 1954—, U.S. DOE, Caldon Inc., NAS-Nitrogen Oxides Panel, Washington. Co-contbr. numerous articles on process dynamics, optimization control, fuel cell power generation, fluidized bed combustion; holder 21 U.S. patents. Organist-choirmaster Mt. Zion Luth. Ch., Pitts., 1979—. Lt. U.S. Army, 1953-57. Mem. NAE, ASME, Am. Inst. Chem. Egrs., Am. Chem. Soc., Combustion Inst., Am. Soc. Engring. Edn. Republican. Lutheran. Home: Pittsburgh, Pa. Died June 24, 2010.

AREND, THOMAS EDWARD, advertising agency executive; b. Fremont, Ohio, Jan. 27, 1928; s. Chester E. and Betty Louise (Schmidt) A.; m. Judith Ann Carr, Dec. 9, 1961; children: Katherine, Thomas. BS, Northwestern U., 1951. TV producer NBC-TV, Cleve., 1951-53, Chgo., 1954-59; TV mgr. FCB Advt., Chgo., 1959-64, v.p. TV San Francisco, 1964-70, v.p. creative services Chgo., 1970-75, sr. v.p. corp. ops., from 1975. Dir. FCB Found., Chgo., 1981— Served with U.S. Army, 1946-48. Mem.: Bath and Tennis (Lake Bluff) (v.p. 1974-76); Internat. (Chgo.). Roman Catholic. Home: Pacific Palisades, Calif. Died Feb. 4, 2009.

AREY, WILLIAM GRIFFIN, JR., retired federal agency administrator; b. Shelby, NC, Feb. 18, 1918; s. William Griffin and Catherine (Roberts) A.; m. Louise Turner Craft, Mar. 7, 1942 (dec. 1988); children: William Griffin III, John G. C.; m. Jean Getman, July 13, 1991. AB, U. N.C., Chapel Hill, 1939. Pub., editor Cleveland Times Pub. Co., Shelby, 1941-48; pub. affairs officer US Dept. State, Bogota, Colombia, 1948-51, Panama, 1951-53; pub. rels. officer Panama Canal Co., Balboa Heights, C.Z., 1954-62; with US Travel Svc., US Dept. Commerce, Washington, 1963-76, dir. travel promotion, 1963-67, dep. dir., 1967-70, exec. officer, 1970-73, exec. dir., 1973-76; asst. exec. v.p. Nat. Trust Hist. Preservation, 1976-81, corp. sec., 1981-83, ret., 1987. 1st lt. USAAC, 1942-45. Recipient Silver medal US Dept. Commerce, 1973. Mem. Pub. Rels. Soc. Am., Internat. Union Ofcl. Travel Orgns. (v.p.), pacific Area Travel Assn. (dir.), Sigma Nu, Nat. Press Club, Cosmos, Rotary. Methodist. Home: Charlottesville, Va. Died Mar. 26, 2010.

ARGENTO, SAM J., state legislator; b. Oct. 23, 1942; married; 3 children. BA, W.Va. Inst. Tech., 1967. Sanitarian Nicholas County Health Dept.; mem. Dist. 35 W.Va. House of Delegates, 2004—10, asst. minority whip; mem. Govt. Orgn. Com., Agr. & Natural Resources Com., Const Revision Com. Democrat. Died Oct. 28, 2010.

ARGRAVES, HUGH OLIVER, poet, artist, playwright; b. Decatur, Ill., July 7, 1922; s. Wendell Oliver and Helen E. (Sax) A. Student, Beloit Coll., Wis., 1937. Retired. Author: Collected Poetry, 1960; contbr. poems to publs.; playwright: Osbert, 1978, The Great Depression, 1978, Greenwich Village, 1979, Hugh Oliver Argraves-Inferno, 1979, The Twenties, 1980, 2 One Act Plays, 1980, King Lear adaption, 1981, Skeleton Play, 1984, London Blitz-1941, 1984, Last Train to Berlin, 1985; 40-yr. retrospective Scuggi Gallery, Rockford, 1997; featured video The Great Depression; various group shows include Lynn Kottler Galleries, 1961, 66, Ahda Artz Galleries, N.Y.C., 1962-66, Ligoa Duncan Gallery, 1968; represented in permanent collection Mus. Modern Art, N.Y., Rockford Art Mus. Served with U.S. Army, 1943-46. Recipient Jessica Holt award, 1997. Republican. Presbyterian. Died June 23, 2010.

ARMERDING, HUDSON TAYLOR, retired college president, consultant; b. Albuquerque, June 21, 1918; s. Carl Armerding and Eva May Taylor; m. Miriam Lucile Bailey, Dec. 26, 1944 (dec. July 2006); children: Carreen, Taylor, Paul, Miriam, Jonathan. AB, Wheaton Coll., 1941; AM, Clark U., 1942; PhD, U. Chgo., 1948; DD (hon.), Gordon-Conwell Sem., 1972, Reformed Episcopal Sem., 1990; LLD (hon.), Houghton Coll., 1973; HumD (hon.), John Brown U., 1983; STD (hon.), Greenville Coll., 1976; LittD (hon.), Asbury Coll., 1977, Colo. Christian U., 2000. Prof. Wheaton Coll., Ill., 1946—48, 1961—82; provost Wheaton U., 1963—65, pres., 1965—82; prof. Gordon Coll., Wenham, Mass., 1948—49, 1950—61, dean, acting pres., 1950—61. V.p. Quarryville (Pa.) Presbyn. Retirement Cmty., 1982-99; min-at-large Officers Christian Fellowship, Englewood, Colo., 1979-2005; chmn. Site Acquisition Com., Batavia, Ill., 1975; pres. Nat. Assn. Evang., Wheaton, 1970-72; chmn. World Evang. Fellowship, Wheaton, 1974-80. Comdr. USN, 1942-46, USNR, 1946-66 Recipient Excellence in Leadership award Officers Christian Fellowship, 2001 Mem. Am. Legion, Mil. Officer Assn., Naval Inst Republican. Presbyterian. Avocations: travel, walking, camping, reading. Died Dec. 1, 2009.

ARMOUR, GEORGE PORTER, lawyer; b. Bryn Mawr, Pa., June 10, 1921; s. Charles Joseph and Florence (Eagle) A.; m. Isabel Blondet, Nov. 22, 1958; children: Luis O., Carlos O. BA, Temple U., 1943, JD, 1949. Bar: Pa. 1949, N.Y. 1969, Calif. 1975. Assoc. Bennett & Bricklin, Phila., 1949-59; atty. Atlantic Richfield Co., 1959-83; gen. atty. Phila., 1965-68; assoc. gen. counsel Phila., NYC, L.A., 1968-78; dep. gen. counsel LA, 1978-85; pvt. practice law, from 1983. Chmn. Internat. and Comparative Law Ctr., Southwestern Legal Found., Dallas, 1980-82. Mem. Assocs. Calif. Inst. Tech., 1981—; mem. Soc. of Fellows Huntington Libr. and Art Gallery, San Marino, Calif., 1982—. With USAAF, 1943-46. Mem. ABA, Calif. Bar Assn., Valley Hunt Club (Pasadena). Republican. Died July 19, 2009.

ARMSTRONG, CARL HINES, retired historic site director, former state official; b. DeKoven, Ky., May 1, 1926; s. Oral M. and Ethel M. (Wilson) A.; m. Ferrell Mann, May 16, 1947; children: Carla, Gayle, Dawn. Student, U. Evansville, Ind., 1945-47, Internat. Corr. Schs., 1947, Am. Inst. Banking, 1948-49, Butler U., 1959-61, Ind. U. Sch. Art, 1961-62, Christian Theol. Sem., from 1977, Louisville Presbyn. Sem., 1982-83, So. Bapt. theol. Sem., 1984-87. Bus. mgr. Dairy Service, Evansville, 1946-48; owner, operator Cardell Models, Evansville, 1959-69; bus. mgr. Children's Mus., Indpls., 1959-66; mus. specialist Ind. State Mus., Indpls., 1967-70, dir., 1970-82; dir. div. historic preservation Ind. Dept. Natural Resources, 1970-82; adminstr. Yellowwood Terr., from 1982. Com. mem. for feasibility study Central Exhibits Lab., U.S. Nat. Mus., Washington. Com. mem. Ind./Ky. Conf., United Ch. of Christ, 1971-72; lay minister United Ch. of Christ, 1975—, St. Mark's United Ch. of Christ, New Albany, Ind., 1985—; ordained United Ch. of Christ, 1987; bd. dirs. ch. mission interpretation div.Ind./Ky. Conf. UCC; min. St. Marks UCC, New Albany, 1989-90. Served with AUS, 1944. Mem. Am. Assn. Museums, Assn. Ind. Museums, Ind. State Mus. Soc. (exec. sec.), Midwest Museums Conf., Assn. for Preservation Tech., Assn. Sci. Mus. Dirs., Hoosier Homestead Commn., Ind. Am. Revolution Bicentennial Commn. Clubs: Masons, Order Eastern Star. Republican. Designer, Ind. State Mus. Master Plan and Complex, Gus Grisson Meml., Mitchell, Ind. Home: Columbus, Ind. Died Apr. 12, 2010.

ARMSTRONG, JAMES LOUDEN, III, retired lawyer; b. Miami, Fla., Jan. 7, 1932; s. James Louden and Jean Macrea (Cawley) A.; m. Mary Elizabeth McCall, Aug. 25, 1955; children: Patricia Payan, James L. IV. BA, Yale U., 1955, LLB, 1958. Bar: Fla. 1958, U.S. Dist. Ct. (so. dist.) Fla. 1958, U.S. Dist. Ct. (middle dist.) Fla. 1960, U.S. Dist. Ct. (no. dist.) Fla. 1964, U.S. Ct. Appeals (5th and 11th cir.) 1962, U.S. Supreme Ct. 1962. Assoc. Smathers & Thompson, Miami, 1958-64, ptnr., 1964-87, Kelley Drye & Warren LLP, Miami, 1987-95. Pres. Orange Bowl Com., Miami, 1976; co-chmn. Cmty. Partnership for Homeless, Inc., 1994—. Fellow Am. Coll. Trial Lawyers, Internat. Acad. Trial Lawyers; mem. Dade County bar Assn.(pres. 1972), Yale Club (pres. 1966). Republican. Presbyterian. Avocation: golf. Home: Coral Gables, Fla. Died Sept. 2, 2009.

ARMSTRONG, JOHN CHACE, industrial engineer, consultant; b. Rochester, NY, Nov. 25, 1918; s. George Simpson and Dorothy (Miller) A.; m. Helga Evensen, Dec. 28, 1950 (dec.); children: Karin A. Newhouse, Christine Armstrong, Elizabeth Anne Cook; m. Mary Helen Hurlimann, Mar. 4, 1977; stepchildren: Mary Ann, Lily and Susan A. Hurlimann. BA, Williams Coll., 1940; BS in Chem. Engring., NYU, 1942. Registered profl. engr., N.Y. Research chemist, indsl. engr. E.I. duPont de Nemours & Co., Niagara Falls, N.Y., 1942-46; cons. indsl. engr. Geo. S. Armstrong & Co., Inc., NYC, 1946-90, pres., 1946-90, also dir. Pres. Alumni Fedn., NYU, 1973-76, alumni trustee, 1977-81; chmn. Albert Gallatin Assocs., 1977-79. Mem. Williams Club (N.Y.C.), Riverside Yacht Club, Anglers' Club of N.Y., Round Hill Club (Greenwich, Conn.), Zeta Psi. Congregationalist. Home: Shelburne, Vt. Died Nov. 4, 2009.

ARNOLD, ARTHUR JOSEPH, writer, journalist; b. Kings Park, NY, Feb. 16, 1918; s. Gustave Arnold and Ellen Kenny; m. Margaret Dumas (div.); children: Joan, Conrad; m. Wilhelmina Staninger Arnold, Aug. 15, 1957 (dec.). Grad., Mt. Assumption Inst. H.S., Plattsburgh, NY. Former adjudicator VA, Newark; former jr. coll. instr. Cocoa, Fla.; former newspaper columnist, reporter, writer Plattsburgh Daily Rep. Author: Behold My Brother, 1963, A White Spring, 2000 (Book Fair award, 2000). Served with USN, 1942—45, PTO. Mem.: DAV. Democrat. Avocations: reading, writing, walking. Home: Titusville, Fla. Died Jan. 26, 2010.

ARNOLD, ERMA ARNETTA, automobile dealership executive; b. Danville, Va., Dec. 25, 1947; d. James Edward Arnold and Annie (Streat) Bailey. Student Va. Sem. and Coll., 1968-69; B.A. in Polit. Sci., Va. Union U., 1972; grad. Ford Motor Co. dealer devel. tng. program, 1985. Sales rep. Exxon Corp., Richmond, Va., 1973-75, Hunt-Wesson Foods, hdqrs. Fullerton, Calif., 1975-76; parts and service zone mgr. Ford Motor Co., Washington Dist., Falls Church, Va., 1976-85; dealer, trainee Dick Strauss Ford, Inc., Richmond, 1984-85; pres., chief exec. officer Waynesboro Sales and Service, Inc., Va., 1985—. Active Nat. Republican Party Com. Named Mgr. of Yr. Ford Motor Co., Richmond, 1977, 79. Mem. Nat. Automobile Dealers Assn., Va. Automobile Dealers Assn., Waynesboro Automobile Dealers Assn., Black Automobile Dealers Assn., Waynesboro C. of C., Waynesboro Bus. and Profl. Women's Club. Baptist. Avocations: restoring old cars and homes; tennis; sewing; cooking; crossword puzzles. Home: Waynesboro, Va. Died July 24, 2010.

ARNOLD, ROBERT GILBERT, retired chemist; b. Hartford, Conn., Dec. 25, 1923; s. John Adams and Gladys Lillian (Kerr) A.; m. Mary Alice Caruth, Dec. 27, 1947 BS in Chemistry, Yale U., 1944, PhD in Organic Chemistry, 1950. Research chemist E.I. DuPont de Nemours & Co., Inc., Wilmington, Del., 1949-81, supr., mgr. research dir., 1981-88. Served with U.S. Army, 1944-45 Home: Salem, NJ. Died Dec. 8, 2009.

ARNSDORF, MORTON FRANK, cardiologist, educator; b. Chgo., Aug. 7, 1940; s. Selmar N. and Irmgard C. (Steinmann) A.; m. Mary Hunter Tower, Dec. 26, 1963 (div. 1982); m. Rosemary Crowley, Dec. 27, 1986. BA magna cum laude, Harvard U., 1962; MD, Columbia U., 1966. Diplomate American Bd. Internal Medicine. House staff officer U. Chgo., 1966-69; fellow cardiology Columbia-Presbyn. Med. Ctr., NYC, 1969-71; asst. prof. medicine U. Chgo., 1973-79, assoc. prof., 1979-83, prof., 1983—2010, chief sect. cardiology, 1981-90. Mem. pharmacology study sect. NIH, 1981-84. Contbr. articles to profl. jours. Maj. USAF, 1971-73. Recipient Rsch. Career Devel. award NIH, 1976-81; rsch. grantee Chgo. Heart Assn., 1976-78, NIH, NIH Merit award Fellow ACP, Am. Coll. Cardiology (mem. editl. bd. JACC 1983-87, 90-2010, gov.-elect Ill. 1990-91, gov. Ill. 1991-94, pres. Ill. chpt. 1991-94, bd. gov. issues and concerns subcom. 1991-93, bd. gov. steering com. 1993-94, ad hoc com. quality assurance improvement initiative, sec. and trustee 1995, electrophysiology/electrocardiology/pacemaker com. 1994-2010); mem. Am. Heart Assn. (dir. 1981-83, chmn. exec. com. basic sci. coun. 1981-83, steering com. 1983-86, mem. rsch. program and evaluation com. 1989-91, assoc. editor circulation Rsch. 1986-91), Am. Heart Assn. Met. Chgo. (v.p. 1986, pres.-elect 1987-88, pres. 1988-89, bd. govs., chmn. rsch. coun. 1981, chmn. program coun. 1986-88), Am. Fedn. Clin. Rsch., Assn. Univ. Cardiologists, Ctrl. Soc. Clin. Rsch. (chmn. cardiovascular coun. 1986-87, sec.-treas. 1991-95), Assn. Profs. Cardiology (founding mem., bylaws com. 1989-90), Chgo. Cardiology Group (pres. 1990-92), Cardiac Electrophysiology Soc. (sec.-treas. 1984-86, pres. 1986-88). Clubs: Quadrangle. Died June 9, 2010.

ARON, BERNARD STEPHEN, oncologist; b. NYC, July 11, 1932; s. Mannie and Ruth (Baer) A.; m. Janice Levine, June 30, 1956; children: Melanie, Marc. BA, NYU, 1953, MD, 1957; Diploma in Med.-Radio Therapy, Christie Hosp., Manchester, Eng., 1961. Diplomate Am. Bd. Radiology, Am. Coll. Radiology. Intern Beth-El Hosp., Bklyn., 1957-58; resident in radiology Mt. Sinai Hosp., NYC, 1958-61; fellow Christie Hosp. and Holt Radium Inst., Manchester, Eng., 1962-63; clin. dir. Univ. Hosp. Downstate Med. Ctr., Bklyn., 1967-68; prof. clin. oncology U. Cin. Med. Ctr., 1973, 80-85, prof. radiology, from 1973, dir. div. radiation oncology, from 1976. Attending radiology therapist Children's Hosp. Med. Ctr., Cin., 1969—; attending radiologist Univ. Hosp., Cin., 1969—; cons. radiation therapy VA Med. Ctr., Cin., 1972. Contbr. 47 articles to profl. jours. Recipient Golden Apple award U. Cin. Coll. Medicine, 1971; fellow Am. Coll. Radiology, 1983. Mem. AMA, Am. Assn. Cancer Edn., Am. Soc. Therapeutic Radiology and Oncology, Am. Soc. Clin. Oncology, Am. Radium Soc. Home: Cincinnati, Ohio. Died July 16, 2010.

ARONSON, MILTON HOWARD, publishing executive, editor; b. Pitts., Nov. 24, 1918; s. Abraham and Anne Lea (Barbrow) A.; m. Cecily Miltar, Sept. 19, 1941; children: Nancy A. Aronson Gold, Robert S. BS in Physics, Carnegie Inst. Tech., 1939; MS in Math., George Washington U., 1946. Engr. U.S. Steel Corp., Clairton, Pa., 1939-42; physicist Naval Ordnance Lab., Washington, 1942-51; editor Instruments Pub. Co., Pitts., 1951-66; pub. Measurements and Data Corp., Pitts., from 1966. Lectr. chem. engring. Grad. Sch. U. Pitts, 1958-64; cons. tech. edn. Pitts Bd. Edn., 1957-66. Author 10 textbooks, over 100 profl. level courses on math., process control, electronics, physics, basic tech. concepts, measurements. With USNR, 1942-45. Mem. IEEE, Instrument Soc. Am., Measurements and Control Soc. Internat. (exec. sec.), Med. Electronics Soc. (exec. sec.), JWV, Sigma Xi, Delta Tau Delta, Tau Beta Pi Died May 29, 2009.

ARTHUR, JOHN MORRISON, retired utilities executive; b. Pitts., Aug. 17, 1922; s. Hugh Morrison and Anna Matilda (Crowe) A.; m. Sylvia Ann Martin, June 19, 1948; children: William Robert, John Martin, Andrew Scott. BEE, U. Pitts., 1944, MEE, 1947. With Duquesne Light Co., Pitts., 1944-87, asst. to chmn. bd. and pres., 1966-67, pres., 1967-68, chmn. bd., chief exec. officer, 1968-83, chmn. bd., pres., 1983-85, chmn. bd., 1986-87, ret., 1987. Trustee emeritus U. Pitts. With AUS, 1942-43. Mem. Duquesne Club, Montour Heights Country Club, Allegheny Country Club. Died Feb. 1, 2010.

ARY, T. S., federal official, geologist; b. Eldorado, Ill., Mar. 30, 1925; s. McKinley and Emma (Busby) A.; m. Martha K. Metz, Dec. 23, 1945; 1 child, David Metz. Student, Evansville Coll., Ind., 1942-43; BS in Mineral Sci., Stanford U., 1947. Registered geologist, Calif. Football, basketball, baseball coach Jacksonville (Fla.) Naval Air Sta., 1946-47; asst. football coach jr. varsity Stanford (Calif.) U., 1947-49; shift boss, asst. supt. Anaconda Copper Co., Butte, Mont., 1951-53; mining engr. Union Carbide Corp. (U.S. Vanadium Co.), Rifle, Colo., 1953-55, asst. mgr. exploration Grand Junction, Colo., 1955-57, mgr. domestic exploration, 1957-62; land mgr. Union Carbide Nuclear Co., NYC, 1962-67, v.p. mineral exploration mining and metals div., 1967-74; mgr. devel., v.p. mineral exploration Utah Internat. Inc., San Francisco, 1974-80; pres. mineral exploration, pres. resource div. Kerr-McGee Corp., Oklahoma City, 1980-87; dir. Bur. Mines U.S. Dept. Interior, Washington, 1988-93; chmn. Nat. Critical Materials Coun., 1989-93. Bd. dirs. Mineral Info. Inst., Denver; mem. Dept. State Adv. Com. to Task Force Com. of UN Law of the Sea, Washington, 1966-77, Internat. Atomic Energy Program Adv. Com., Vienna, Austria, 1970-75, Nat. Strategic Materials and Minerals Program Adv. Com., Washington, 1984-88; com. chmn. Am. Mining Congress, Washington, 1960-88; mem. minority staff Senate Energy and Natural Resource Com., 1993—. Assoc. editor, mem. editorial bd. Jour. Resource Mgmt. and Tech., 1982-88; author over 100 published articles on mineral resources, pub. lands mgmt., pub. land law, pub. policy, internat. bus. mgmt., fly fishing techniques, sports, religion. Sec.-treas. Lakehurst Homeowners Assn., Oklahoma City, 1983-88; dir. Last Frontier Coun. Boy Scouts Am., Oklahoma City, 1980-86; trustee Westminister Presbyterian Ch., Oklahoma City, 1984-87; telethon chmn. Oklahoma Soc. for Crippled Children, 1985-86; pres. Lido Isle Homeowners Assn., Foster City, Calif., 1978-80, sec. 1976-78; dir. Internat. Student Svcs. Internat. YMCA, N.Y.C., 1973-75, Sch. Bd. Dist. 51, Grand Junction, Colo., 1959-65; committeeman We. Colo. Boy Scout Coun., Grand Junction, Colo., 1960-64; dir. Grand Mesa Ski Corp., Grand Junction, 1960-65, pres. 1963-64; regional dir. Nat. Ski Patrol Assn., Denver, 1952-65; dir. Colo. Expenditure Coun., Denver, 1961-65, South Rocky Mountain Ski Assn., Denver, 1955-65, Butte (Mont.) Ski Club, 1952-53; active Boy Scouts Am., 1935-65. Lt. (j.g.) USN, 1943-47, ETO. Recipient Disting. Svc. award Rocky Mountain Coal Mining Inst., 1988, Disting. Svc. award Nat. Ind. Coal Operators, 1988, numerous athletic awards USN, AP, Nat. Coaches Assn., Nat. Athletic Scholastic Soc., 1938-48; named Outstanding Miner of Yr., Idaho Mining Assn., 1989; inducted into Am. Mining Hall of Fame, 1992; Paul Harris fellow Oklahoma City Rotary Internat. Club. Mem. Am. Inst. Profl. Geologists, Circum-Pacific Coun. Energy and Mineral Resources (program chmn. 1978-80), Am. Assn. Profl. Landmen, Wyo. Mining Assn. (Outstanding Man of Yr. 1991), Colo. Mining Assn. (Edn. Found. award 1990), N.W. Mining Assn. (Mining Man of Yr. 1988, Distg. Svc. award 1989), Calif. Mining Assn., N.Mex. Mining Assn. (Mining Man of Yr. 1988), Ariz. Mining Assn., AIME (sec., treas., vice-chmn., chm. 1955-65, Disting. Svc. award Wyo. sect. 1990, Pres. citation 1992, Robert Earll McConnell award 1993, Ben Dickenson III award 1994, Krumb Distg. Lctr. award 1994), Rocky Mountain Mineral Law Found., Mining Club of N.Y., Commonwealth Club of San Francisco, Forum on Fgn. Affairs (San Francisco), Nat. Assn. Mfrs. (chmn. natural resource com. 1985-87), Soc. Mining Engrs. Gem Found. (trustee), Sigma Nu. Republican. Avocations: bible studies, fly fishing, skiing, reading, rose competition. Home: Arlington, Va. Died Apr. 26, 2009.

ASHLER, PHILIP FREDERIC, international trade and development advisor; b. NYC, Oct. 15, 1914; s. Phillip and Charlotte (Barth) Ashler; m. Jane Porter, Mar. 4, 1942 (dec. 1968); children: Phillip Frederic, Robert Porter, Richard Harrison; m. Elise Barrett Duvall, June 21, 1969; stepchildren: Richard Edward Duvall, Jeffries Harding Duvall. BBA cum laude, St. Johns Coll., 1935; MBA, Harvard U., 1937; grad., Indsl. Coll. Armed Forces, 1956; ScD, Fla. Inst. Tech., 1969; LLD (hon.), U. West Fla., 1969; postgrad., U. Oxford, Eng., 1988, 89, 91. Enlisted USMCR, 1932; commd. ensign USN, 1938, advanced through grades to rear adm., 1959; served in D-Day at Normandy Invasion of France, Iwo Jima landings and Korea; dir. Office Small Bus., Dept. Def., Washington, 1948-49; mem. joint staff Joint Chiefs Staff, 1957-59; ret., 1959; dir. devel. Pensacola Jr. Coll., 1960-68; vice chancellor adminstrn. State Univ. System Fla., 1968-70, exec. vice chancellor, 1970-75; treas., ins. commr., fire marshal State of Fla., 1975-76, sec. of commerce, 1977-79; pres. Philip F. Ashler & Assos., Tallahassee, from 1979; chmn. bd. Cambridge Community Care, Inc., Tallahassee, 1981-86, Circle Seven Internat., Tampa, 1988-91. Mem. Fla. Edn. Coun., 1967—68; commr. Fla. Edn. Commn. States, 1967—68; mem. US Dept. Commerce Dist. Export Coun., 1978—92; chmn. bd. dirs. Fla. Internat. Vol. Corps., 1988—90, chmn. emeritus, from 2004; legis. adv. coun. So. Regional Edn. Bd., 1966—68; mem. Fla. Bd. Ind. Colls. and Univs., 1971—75, adv. coun. mil. edn., 1980—85; bd. adv. Ctr. Profl. Devel. Fla. State U., 1988—96; chmn. Fla. Civil Def. Adv. Coun., 1966—69; mem. Fla. Coun. Internat. Devel., 1973—92, vice chmn., 1979—80, chmn., 1980—82, chmn. emeritus, from 1990; mem. Select Coun. Post HS Edn., 1967—68; chmn. Fla. Med. Liability Ins. Commn., 1975—76, Fla. Task Force Auto and Workers Compensation, 1975—76; mem. Yugoslavia Adv. Coun., 1976—87, InterAm. Congress Psychology, Bogota, Colombia, 1974, NATO Advanced Sci. Inst., 1973; guest lectr. U. Belgrade, 1973; adv. econ. devel. to gov. Fla., 1977—78; mission leader Japan/S.E. US Assn., Tokyo, 1977; trustee Fla. Coun. Econ. Edn., 1979—81; svcs. policy adv. com. Office US Trade Rep. Exec. Office of Pres., Washington, 1980—85; mem. Republic of China/USA Econ. Coun., 1979—92. Chmn. bd. dirs. Fla. Heart Assn., 1969—71; bd. dirs., treas. Internat. Cardiology Found.; bd. dirs. Tallahassee Meml. Hosp., Easter Seal Soc., 1963—68; bd. dirs., mem. exec. com. Am. Heart Assn., 1971—77, Internat. Cardiology Fedn., Geneva, 1975—77; founding chmn. Tallahassee Symphony Orch., 1981—82; trustee So. Ctr. Internat. Studies, Atlanta, 1988—91; mem. adv. bd. Fla./China Inst., Miami, Fla., Fla./Japan Inst., Tampa, Fla./Brazil Inst.; mem. Fla. Ho. of Reps., 1963—68; lic. lay eucharistic min. Episc. Ch. Decorated Bronze Star with combat IV; recipient Korean Presdl. citation, French Medill du Jubile, Internat. Disting. Svc. award, Kiwanis Internat., 1965, Legis. award, St. Petersburg Times, 1967, Disting. Svc. award, Am. Heart Assn., 1965, 1971, Disting. Achievement award, 1975, Disting. Floridian award for Life Achievement, 2005. Mem.: S.E. US/Korea Econ. Coop. Coun. (bd. dirs.), Internat. C. of C. (US coun. 1979—87), Nat. Assn. Ins. Commrs. (vice chmn. exec. com. 1976), Fla. Med. Malpractice Joint Underwriting Assn. (chmn. bd. govs. 1975—76), US S.E./Japan Assn. (chmn. 1981—83), Econ. Club Fla. (chmn. 1987—90, chmn. emeritus from 1991), Govs. Club (bd. govs. 1989—93, v.p. fin. 1992—93, bd. govs. 1994—96, treas. 1996), Capital Tiger Bay Club (chmn. bd. dirs.), Rotary Internat. (proclaimed hon. mem.), Shriners, Masons (32 degree), Kappa Delta. Home: Tallahassee, Fla. Died Apr. 27, 2009.

ASHLEY, THOMAS WILLIAM LUDLOW, former United States Representative from Ohio; b. Toledo, Jan. 11, 1923; s. Meredith Ashley and Alida. A.; m. Margaret Sherman, 1955 (div.); children: Lise, William Meredith, Mark Michael; m. Kathleen Marie Lucey, 1967. With Toledo Publicity & Efficiency Commn., Ohio, 1948; dir. spl. project Radio Free Europe, 1952—53; mem. US Congress from 9th Ohio Dist., Ohio, 1955—81; chmn. US House Internat. Trade Subcommittee, 1967—74, US House Econ. Stabilization Subcommittee, 1974—76, US House Housing & Cmty. Devel. Subcommittee & Ad Hoc Energy Com., 1977—78, US House Merchant Marine & Fisheries Com., 1979—81. Democrat. Died June 15, 2010.

ATHEY, TYRAS SNOWDEN (BUNK ATHEY), retired state official; b. Burtonsville, Md., Mar. 30, 1927; m. Dorothy O'Lexey, 1951; children: Darlene, Bryan, Cathy. Mem. Dist. 32 Md. House of Delegates, 1966—93; chmn. Md. House Ways & Means Com., 1979—93; sec. of state State of Md., Annapolis, 1993—95. Delegate Democratic Nat. Convention, 1996; bd. dirs. Econ. Devel. Corp., 1999—2001. Served in USN, 1945—47. Died July 20, 2010.

ATKIN, GERALD CLIFFORD, advertising executive; b. Detroit, Jan. 19, 1936; Children: Derek, Cori. BS in Mktg., Wayne State U., 1958. Exec. J. Walter Thompson, Detroit, 1956-70; advt. mgr. Ford div. Ford Motor Co., Dearborn, Mich., 1970-73; account dir. McCann-Erickson, Inc., Sao Paolo, Brazil and Frankfurt, Fed. Republic Germany, 1973-81, exec. v.p. Detroit, from 1981. Promotional dir. United Way, Detroit, 1984. Mem. Am. Mgmt. Assn., Detroit Adcraft. Republican. Methodist. Home: Auburn Hills, Mich. Died Dec. 1, 2009.

ATKINS, HANNAH DIGGS, retired state official; b. Winston-Salem, NC, Nov. 1, 1923; d. James Thackeray and Mabel (Kennedy) Diggs; m. Charles Nathaniel Atkins, May 24, 1943 (dec. Dec. 1988); children: Edmund E., Charles N., Valerie Atkins Alexander; m. Everett Patton O'Neal, June 12, 1993 (div. Jan. 1996). BS, St. Augustine's Coll., 1943; BLS, U. Chgo., 1949; LHD (hon.), Benedict Coll., Columbia, SC; MPA, U. Okla., 1987; cert., Harvard U., 1987. Law libr. Okla. State Libr., Oklahoma City, 1959-68; mem. Okla. House of Reps., Oklahoma City, 1968-80, US Commn. to UNESCO, 1979-82; del. UN Gen. Assembly, 1980; asst. dir. Okla. Dept. Human Svcs., 1983-87; sec. of state State of Okla., Oklahoma City, 1987-91; adj. prof. polit. sci. U. Ctrl. Okla., Edmond, 1991-92, U. Okla., Norman, 1991-93, Okla. State U., Stillwater, 1991-93. Former nat. committeewoman Dem. Nat. Com.; pres., Okla. chpt. Am. Soc. Pub. Adminstrn.; bd. dirs. Women Execs. in State Govt., ACLU; former chmn. Okla. adv. com. U.S. Commn. on Civil Rights; bd. dirs. Nat. Women's Edn. Fund, Washington. Mem. AAUW (Kate Barnard award), Am. Soc. Pub. Adminstrn. (Advancing Excellence in Pub. Svc. 1989), Phi Beta Kappa, Alpha Kappa Alpha. Democrat. Episcopalian. Avocations: photography, reading, travel. Home: Washington, DC. Died June 17, 2010.

ATTAWAY, LEROY BANKS, magazine editor; b. Walterboro, SC, Sept. 16, 1937; s. LeRoy Banks and Claire Evangeline (Walker) A.; m. Jane Scott Brown, May 13, 1956 (div.); children— Dorothy Claire, Catherine Jane, LeRoy Banks III; m. Robyn Worth Gill, Apr. 24, 1982 Student, U. N.C., 1955-57. Reporter, photographer Beaufort Gazette, S.C., 1959-60; sports writer, asst. chief copy editor, Sunday editor News & Courier, Charleston, S.C., 1960-65; with pub. relations dept. Bell & Stanton, Atlanta, 1965; with corp. pub. relations dept. Olin Corp, NYC, 1965-68; writer Am. Sportsman/ABC-TV, NYC, 1968-69; writer, assoc. producer Harbinger Prodns., NYC, 1969-70; freelance writer, photographer numerous mags., 1970-78; assoc. editor Motor Boating & Sailing Mag., NYC, 1978-79, sr. editor, 1979-81; editor Boating Mag., NYC, 1981-86; editor in chief Yachting Mag., NYC, 1986-89. Recipient numerous awards for sports and feature writing and photography Mem. Writers Guild Am., Am. Soc. Mag. Editors. Episcopalian. Avocations: fishing; travel; music. Home: New York, NY. Died May 9, 2010.

AUBERGER, KENNETH JAMES, government official; b. Rochester, NY, Sept. 23, 1926; s. Joseph and Evelyn (McGinness) A.; m. Patricia Frances Sacco, Apr. 14, 1951. BBA, St. Bernadine-Siena Coll., 1950; JD, Am. U., 1959, MBA, 1961. Bar: D.C. bar 1960; C.P.A., Md. Accountant-auditor Carl Thomy & Co., Rochester, 1950-51, GAO, 1952-64; dep. gov., chief examiner Farm Credit Adminstrn., McLean, Va., 1965-82, dep. gov., chief of staff, from 1982, exec. asst. to gov., from 1984. Served with USNR, 1945-46, 51-52. Mem. Am., D.C. bar assns., Am. Inst. C.P.A.s, Md. Soc. C.P.A.s. Home: Rockville, Md. Died May 18, 2009.

AUBERT, EUGENE JAMES, laboratory administrator; b. North Bergen, NJ, Mar. 6, 1921; s. Charles Fernan and Agnes Catherine (Robertson) A.; m. Dorothy Marion Stephens, Nov. 7, 1942; children— Donald E., Patricia M., Aubert Kennedy, Allan C., Richard S. Student, Montclair State Coll., 1938-41; BS, NYU, 1946, MS, 1947; PhD, MIT, 1957. Br. chief meteorology lab. Air Force Cambridge Research Ctr., Bedford, Mass., 1951-60; v.p., dir. Travelers Research Ctr., Hartford, Conn., 1960-70; dir. internat. field year for Gt. Lakes NOAA, 1971-78, dir. Gt. Lakes Environ. Research Lab. Ann Arbor, Mich., from 1974. Author: The International Field Year for Great Lakes, 1981; contbr. articles to profl. jours. Served to lt. (j.g.) USN, 1942-46 Recipient Gold medal Dept. Commerce, 1973 Mem. AAAS, Am. Geophys. Union, Am. Meterol. Soc., Internat. Assn. Gt. Lake Research Methodist. Avocation: sailing. Home: Saint Leonard, Md. Died Mar. 6, 2009.

AUCHINCLOSS, LOUIS STANTON, writer; b. Lawrence, NY, Sept. 27, 1917; s. Joseph Howland and Priscilla (Stanton) A.; m. Adele Lawrence, Sept. 1957 (dec. 1991); children: John, Blake, Andrew. Student, Yale U., 1939; LLB, U. Va., 1941; LittD (hon.), NYU, 1974, Pace U., 1979, U. of the South, 1986. Bar: NY 1941. Assoc. Sullivan & Cromwell, 1941-51, Hawkins, Delafield & Wood, NYC, 1954-58, ptnr., 1958-86. Author: (novels) The Indifferent Children, 1947, Sybil, 1952, A Law for the Lion, 1953, The Great World and Timothy Colt, 1956, Venus in Sparta, 1958, Pursuit of the Prodigal, 1959, The House of Five Talents, 1960, Portrait in Brownstone, 1962, The Rector of Justice, 1964, The Embezzler, 1966, A World of Profit, 1968, I Came As a Thief, 1972, The Dark Lady, 1977, The Country Cousin, 1978, The House of the Prophet, 1980, The Cat and the King, 1981, Watchfires, 1982, Exit Lady Masham, 1983, The Book Class, 1984, Honorable Men, 1985, Diary of a Yuppie, 1986, The Golden Calves, 1988, Fellow Passengers: A Novel in Portraits, 1989, The Lady of Situations, 1991, Three Lives, 1993, The Education of Oscar Fairfax, 1995, Her Infinite Variety, 2000, The Scarlet Letters, 2003, East Side Story, 2004, East Side Story, 2004, The Headmaster's Dilemma, 2007 Last of the Old Guard, 2008; (collections) The Injustice Collectors, 1950, The Romantic Egoists, 1954, Powers of Attorney, 1963, Tales of Manhattan, 1967, Second Chance: Tales of Two Generations, 1970, The Partners, 1974, The Winthrop Covenant, 1976, Narcissa and Other Fables, 1982, Skinny Island: More Tales of Manhattan, 1987, False Gods, 1992, Tales of Yesteryear, 1994, The Collected Stories of Louis Aucincloss, 1994, The Atonement and Other Stories, 1997, The Anniversary and Other Stories, 1999, Manhattan Monologues, 2002, The Young Apollo and Other Stories, 2006, The Friends of Women and Other Stories, 2007; (nonfiction) Reflections of a Jacobite, 1961, Pioneers and Caretakers: A Study of Nine American Women Novelists, 1965, On Sister Carrie, 1968, Motiveless Malignity, 1969, Edith Wharton: A Woman in Her Time, 1972, Richelieu, 1972, A Writer's Capital, 1974, Reading Henry James, 1975, Life, Law and Letters: Essays and Sketches, 1979, Persons of Consequence: Queen Victoria and Her Circle, 1979, False Dawn: Women in the Age of the Sun King, 1985, The Vanderbilt Era: Profiles of a Gilded Age, 1989, Love Without Wings: Some Friendships in Literature and Politics, 1991, The Style's the Man: Reflection on Proust, Fitzgerald, Wharton, Vidal, and Others, 1994, The Man Behind the Book: Literary Profiles, 1996, Woodrow Wilson, 2000, Theodore Roosevelt (The American President Series), 2002 Trustee emeritus Josiah Macy, Jr., Found.; pres., Mus. City of N.Y., 1966-90; Lt. USNR, 1941-45. Recipient Nat. Medal of Arts, Nat. Endowment for the Arts, 2005; named a Living Landmark, NY Landmarks Conservancy, 2000. Mem. AAAL (pres. emeritus), Assn. Bar City N.Y., Century Assn. Episcopalian. Home: New York, NY. Died Jan. 26, 2010.

AUDETTE, ALBERT (SONNY) C., state legislator, retired utilities executive; b. Colchester, Vt., Feb. 19, 1932; m. Theresa Rochefort; 3 children. Public works dir., South Burlington, Vt., 1969—99; ret., 1999; mem. Dist. Chittenden-3-9 Vt. House of Reps., from 2000. Mem. Vt. Rail Coun., Chittenden MPO Tech. Adv. Com.; dir. City of South Burlington Emergency Mgmt., from 1973; state official Vt. Bowling Hall of Fame; vol. South Burlington Fire Dept.; first sec.-treas. Chittenden Solid Waste Dist.; mem. VLCT Transp. Com., 1984—99; state commr. Babe Ruth Baseball, 1990—95. With USAF, 1952—56. Mem.: Am. Pub. Works Assn., Vt. Mcpl. Assn. (founding mem., past pres.). Democrat. Roman Catholic. Home: South Burlington, Vt. Died Aug. 14, 2010.

AUERBACH, IRVING, chemist; b. Cleve., May 24, 1919; s. Jacob and Fannie (Rothmen) A.; m. Hertha Bienes, July 4, 1969. BS in Chemistry, Ohio State U., 1942, PhD in Chemistry, 1948. Research assoc. Case Western Res. U., Cleve., 1948-49, Cleve. Indsl. Research, 1949-51; mem. research staff Goodyr. Research, Akron, Ohio, 1951-57; mem. tech. staff Sandia Nat. Labs., Albuquerque, from 1957. Contbr. articles to profl. jours. Fellow AAAS (chmn. phys. scis. div. 1982-84), N.Mex. Acad. Scis. (pres. 1960-62), Am. Inst. Chemists; mem. Sigma Xi. Avocations: hiking, climbing, skiing, gardening. Home: Albuquerque, N.Mex. Died July 21, 2010.

AUST, JOE BRADLEY, surgeon, educator; b. Buffalo, Sept. 8, 1926; s. Joe Bradley and Edith (Derby) A.; m. Constance Ann MacMullin, June 18, 1949; children— Jay Bradley, Bonnie Jean, Barbara Ann, Linda Lee, Mary Louise, Tracey Roberta. MD, U. Buffalo, 1949; MS in Physiology, U. Minn., 1957, PhD in Surgery, 1958. Diplomate: Am. Bd. Surgery, Am. Bd. Thoracic Surgery. Intern U. Minn. Hosps., 1949-50, resident, 1950-58; scholar Am. Cancer Soc. U. Minn., 1957-62, mem. faculty, 1957-66, prof. surgery, 1964-66; prof. surgery, chmn. dept. U. Tex. Med. Sch., San Antonio, 1966-96, prof. dept. surgery, from 1996. Cons. Minn. State Prison, 1958-62, Anoka State Hosp., 1962-65, Brooke Army Med. Hosp., 1967—, Wilford Hall USAF Hosp., 1967—, Audie Murphy Meml. VA Hosp., 1973—; nat. cons. to surgeon gen. USAF, Washington, 1975-78 Served with M.C. USNR, 1950-52. Fellow ACS; mem. Am. Surg. Assn., Western Surg. Assn., So. Surg. Assn., Cen. Surg. Assn., Soc. U. Surgeons, Soc. Head and Neck Surgeons, Am. Assn. Cancer Rsch., Soc. Surg. Oncology, San Antonio Surgical Soc., Am. Assn. Cancer Edn., Halsted Soc., Soc. Clin. Oncology, Transplantation Soc., Sigma Xi, Alpha Omega Alpha, Phi Ch. Achievements include spl. research cancer immunity, regional cancer chemotherapy, shock, homotransplantation. Home: San Antonio, Tex. Died Mar. 17, 2010.

AUSTIN, FRANK HUTCHES, JR., aerospace physician, educator; b. Kerrville, Tex., 1924; m. Wilma Ord Austin (div.); 1 child, Robert (dec.); m. Anne Marie David (dec. 2008). MD, U. Tex., 1948. Intern Long Beach Naval Hosp.; resident in aerospace medicine U. Calif, Berkeley, 1960-63; assoc. clin. prof. sch medicine Wright State U.; flight air surgeon FAA, 1984—87. Recipient Louis H. Bauer Founders award Aerospace Medical Assn., 1985, Jeffries Med. Rsch. award AIAA., 1991. Home: Falls Church, Va. Died June 22, 2010.

AUSTIN, MAX EUGENE, horticulture educator; b. Pine Grove, Pa., July 17, 1933; s. Russell Lyle (dec.) and Hilda Havena (Hilkes) (dec.) A.; m. Eleanor Mae Fessenden, Aug. 29, 1953; children: Susan, Becky, Max Jr., Robin. BS in Landscape Design, U. R.I., 1955, MS in Pomology/Botany, 1960; PhD in Olericulture/Mech. Harvesting, Mich. State U., 1964. Jr. rsch. asst. U. R.I., Kingston, 1957-60; assoc. researcher Mich. State U., East Lansing, 1960-64, dist. hort. extension agt., 1964-65; asst. prof. horticulture Va. Poly. Inst. and State U., 1965-70, assoc. prof., 1970-72, U. Ga. Coastal Plain Experiment Sta., Tifton, 1972-79, prof., 1979-93, prof. emeritus, from 1993, head dept. horticulture Tifton, 1972-85. Acting head dept. horticulture Va. Poly. Inst. and State U., 1970-71; 1st Kagoshima (Japan) U. exch. prof. U. Ga., 1981; Blue Max cons. Contbr. numerous articles to profl. jours. 1st lt. inf. U.S. Army, 1955-57, Korea. Kagoshima U. fellow, 1990; grantee Va. Sweet Potato Commn., Va. Agrl. Found. Fellow Am. Soc. Hort. Sci. (pres. so. region 1985-86, v.p. internat. affairs div. 1991-92); mem. Ga. Hort. Soc. (bd. dirs. 1991-92), Internat. Soc. Hort. Sci., Internat. Soc. Tropical Root Crops, So. Assn. Agrl. Scientists, N.Am. Blueberry Coun. (rsch. com. 1989-95), Alpha Zeta, Gamma Sigma Delta, Phi Sigma, Sigma Xi, Phi Beta Delta. Episcopal. Achievements include production of Rabbiteye blueberries from breeding to post-harvest handling; release of 3 blueberry cultivars, Brightwell, Baldwin, and Georgiagem.; 1 rabbiteye blueberry cultivar named Austin. Home: Tifton, Ga. Died Dec. 31, 2009.

AUSTIN, SPENCER PETER, retired minister; b. Lone Wolf, Okla., Dec. 15, 1909; s. Otis Frank and Bertha Ethel (Sinclair) A.; m. Margaret Ellen Wolfinger, Dec. 15, 1932 (dec. Apr. 1968); children— Roy Frank, Jack Spencer, Margaret Anna; m. Kathleen B. Bailey, Dec. 30, 1969 (dec. June 1981); m. Kathleen B. Havens, Dec. 28, 1982. AB, Phillips U., 1931, MA, 1932, B.D., 1933, D.D., 1957; student, Boston U. Sch. Theology, 1943-45. Ordained to ministry Christian Ch. (Disciples of Christ), 1931; pastor in Cedardale and Tangier, Okla., 1929-33, Sayre, Okla., 1933-36, Mangum, Okla., 1937, Duncan, Okla., 1937-43, Everett, Mass., 1943-45; nat. dir. evangelism United Christian Missionary Soc., 1945-50, exec. resources dept., 1950-56; exec. Unified Promotion Christian Chs., 1957-74, chmn. com. relief appeals, 1957-63, adminstrv. sec. com. fraternal aid to Brit. chs., 1954-70; chmn. Week of Compassion com., 1963-76; pres. Christian Ch. Found., 1961-69. Trustee Nat. Christian Missionary Conv., 1957-69; exec. com. Council Christian Unity, 1957-82; mem. grad. sem. council Phillips U., 1962-70; denomination rep. Nat. Council Chs., 1950-72; also mem. exec. com. dept. stewardship and chmn. benevolence promotion com.; mem. exec. com. Ch. World Service, chmn., 1966-70; interim com. Council Agencies Christian Chs., 1952-68; pres. Ch. Finance Council, 1974-76; dir. spl. resources Christian Theol. Sem., 1976-82 Author: Evangelism, 1947. Mem. Disciples of Christ Hist. Soc. (life) Lodges: Rotary, Kiwanis (pres. Sayre 1936), Odd Fellow. Home: Carmel, Ind. Died Apr. 21, 2010.

AVALLE-ARCE, JUAN BAUTISTA, Spanish language educator; b. Buenos Aires, May 13, 1927; came to U.S., 1948; s. Juan B. and Maria Martina Avalle-Arce; m. Constance Marginot, Aug. 20, 1953 (dec. 1969); children: Juan Bautista, Maria Martina, Alejandro Alcantara; m. Diane Janet Pamp, Aug. 30, 1969 (div.); children: Maria la Real Alejandra, Fadrique Martín Manuel. AB, Harvard U., 1951, MA, 1952, PhD, 1955; LittD (hon.), U. Castilla-La Mancha, Spain. Tutor, Harvard U., 1953-55; asst. prof., then assoc. prof. Spanish, Ohio State U., 1955-62; prof. Spanish, Smith Coll., Northampton, Mass., 1962-66, Sophia Smith prof. Hispanic studies, 1966-69; William Rand Kenan, Jr. prof. Spanish, U. N.C., Chapel Hill, 1969-85; prof. Spanish U. Calif., Santa Barbara, from 1985, chmn. dept. Spanish and Portuguese, 1991-95, dir. Summer Inst. Hispanic Langs. and Culture, from 1991, José Miguel de Barandiarán prof. Basque studies, from 1993. Vis. scholar Univ. Ctr. Ga., 1972, lectr., 1961—, Univ. Ctr. Va., 1976; vis. prof. U. Salamanca, 1982, 84, 86, 88, U. Málagà, 1987, 90, 91, U. della Tuscia (Italy), 1988, Sophia U. (Japan), 1988, Kyoto U. Fgn. Affairs, 1988, U. Cuyo, U. Buenos Aires, 1989, Alcalá de Henares, 1995; vis. Hillyer Prof. Humanities U. Nev., Reno, 1996; Eccles scholar State U. Utah, 2003, Garner vis. scholar, 2003; PhD program evaluator N.Y. State Bd. Regents; cons. Coun. Grad. Schs. in U.s.; reader Nat. Humanities Ctr., Govt. Found. for 5th Centennial of Discovery of Am., Spain; cultural corr. Radio Nacional de España; ofcl. guest Euskadiko Erradio, Spain, 1988-89. Author: Conocimiento y vida en Cervantes, 1959, La novela pastoril española, 1959, 2d enlarged edit., 1974, La Galatea de Cervantes, 2 vols., 1961, 2d rev. edit., 1987, Gonzalo Fernández de Oviedo, 1962, 2d edit., 1989, El Inca Garcilaso en sus Comentarios, 1961, Deslindes cervantinos, 1961, Three Exemplary Novels, 1964, Bernal Francès y su Romance, 1966, El Persiles de Cervantes, 1969, Los entremeses de Cervantes, 1969, Don Juan Valera y Morsamor, 1970, El cronista Pedro de Escavias Una vida del Siglo XV, 1972, Suma cervantina, 1973, Narradores hispanoamericanos de hoy, 1973, Las Memorias de Gonzalo Fernández de Oviedo, 2 vols., 1974, El Peregrino en su patria de Lope de Vega, 1973, Nuevos deslindes cervantinos, 1974, Temas hispánicos medievales, 1975, Don Quijote como forma de vida, 1976, Dintorno de una època dorada, 1978, Cervantes, Don Quixote, annotated critical edit., 2 vols., 1978, rev. and enlarged edit., 1995, Cervantes, Novelas ejemplares, annotated edit., 3 vols., 1982, Lope de Vega, Las hazañas del Segundo David, 1984; La Galatea de Cervantes: 400 Años Despuès, 1985, Garci Rodriguez de Montalvo: Amadís de Gaula, 2 vols., 1985, Amadís de Gaula: El primitivo y el de Montalvo, 1991, Lecturas, 1987, Gonzalo Fernández de Oviedo, Batallas y quinquagenas, 1989, Garci Rodriguez de Montalvo Amadis de Gaula, 2 vols., 1991, Cancionero del Almirante don Fadrique Euriquez, 1993, Enciclopedia Cervantina, 1995, Poesía completa de Jorge de Montemayor, 1996, La épica colonial, 2000, Una obra olviera de Gonzalo Fernandez de Ovideo, 2003. Trustee Teutonic Order of the Levant, Marquès de la Lealtad. Recipient Bonsoms medal Spain, 1961; Guggenheim fellow, 1961; grantee Am. Coun. Learned Socs., 1965, 68; grantee NEH, 1968, 1978-80; grantee Am. Philos. Soc., 1961, 67; recipient Susan Anthony Potter Lit. prize, 1951; Centro Gallego Lit. prize, 1947; Diploma of Merit, Universitá delle Arti, Italy; named Grand Companion, Societé Internationale de la Noblesse Héréditaire. Sr. fellow Southeastern Inst. Medieval and Renaissance Studies; hon. fellow Soc. Spanish and Spanish Am. Studies; fellow Colegio Mayor Arzobispo D. Alonso de Fonseca of U. Salamanca; mem. MLA, Acad. Lit. Studies, Am. Acad. Rsch. Historians Medieval Spain, Academia Argentina de Letras, Anglo Am. Basque Studies Soc., Cervantes Soc. Am. (pres. 1979—), Ctr. for Medieval and Renaissance Studies, UCLA (assoc.), Soc. de Bibliofilos Espanoles, Modern Humanities Rsch. Assn., South Atlantic MLA, Asociación de Cervantistas (bd. mem.), Assn. Internac. de Hispanistas, Renaissance Soc. Am. (nat. del. to exec. coun. 1971), Real Sociedad Vascongada de Amigos del Pais, Centro de Estudios Jacobeos, Inst. d'Etudes Medievales, Inst. de Lit. Iberoamericana, Hispanic Soc. Am., Acad. Lit. Studies (charter), Mediaeval Acad. Am., Real Academia de Buenas Letras de Barcelona, Instituto Internacional de Literatura Iberoamericana, Sovereign Mil. Teutonic Order of the Levant (bailiff, knight grand cross, Grand Prior, Grand Priory of the U.S.), Harvard Club. Clubs: Triangle Hunt (Durham) (gentleman Whipper-in); U. N.C. Polo, Combined Training Events Assn. Died Dec. 25, 2009.

AVERELL, LOIS HATHAWAY, speech and language pathologist, audiologist; b. Boston, Apr. 8, 1917; d. Merle Leon and Mildred Hathaway (Allen) A. Diploma, Wheelock Coll., 1941; BS in Edn., Boston U., 1942, EdM, 1953, postgrad., 1963-65. Cert. tchr., Mass.; lic. speech-lang. pathologist, audiologist, Mass. Tchr. kindergarten Dana Hall Schs., Wellesley, Mass., 1942-44; head tchr., pre-sch. program Brimmer and May Sch., Boston, 1944-52; speech therapist United Cerebral Palsy of South Shore, Inc., Quincy, Mass., 1952-53; dir. speech and hearing Meeting St. Sch. Children's Rehab Ctr., Providence, 1953-57; head speech and hearing pathologist Children's Hosp. Med. Ctr., Boston, 1957-63; teaching fellow Boston U., 1963-64; dir. speech, hearing and cleft palate clinic North Shore Children's Hosp. Med. Ctr., Salem, Mass., 1966-76; speech pathologist, audiologist South Shore Mental Health Assn., Quincy, 1977-78; speech-alng. pathologist, audiologist Mayflower House Child Care Ctr., Plymouth, Mass., 1978-85; pvt. practice, from 1954. Mem. Am. Speech-Lang. and Hearing Assn. (dual cert. clin. competence), Mass. Speech and Hearing Assn., Am. Auditory Soc., Am. Assn. Clin. Counselors (diplomate, sec. 1968-75), Nat. Acad. Counselors and Family Therapists (life), Internat. Soc. for Augmentative and Alternative Communication, NE Communication Enhancement Group, Pi Lambda Theta, Alpha Sigma Alpha. Clubs: Women's Garden of Whitman (pres.). Lodges: Zonta (1st v.p. 1975-77 Salem club, pres. 1988-90). Republican. Baptist. Home: Hanson, Mass. Died Apr. 29, 2009.

AXINN, DONALD EVERETT, real estate investor and developer, poet, writer; b. NYC, July 13, 1929; s. Michael and Ann (Schneider) A. AB, Middlebury Coll., 1951, LittD (hon.), 1989; MA, Hofstra U., 1975, LLD (hon.), 1991; LittD (hon.), So. Vt. Coll., 1989; LHD (hon.), SUNY, Farmingdale, 1996; LHD (hon), Adelphi U., 2003. Founder, owner Donald E. Axinn Co., Jericho, LI, NY, from 1958; dir. Farrar, Straus & Giroux, Inc., NYC, 1971-94; assoc. dean Hofstra U. Liberal Arts and Scis., Hempstead, NY, 1971-72; also dir. Inst. Arts.; chmn., mem. Nassau County Fine Arts Commn., 1970-73; mem. Gov.'s Task Force on Cultural Life and Arts, from 1975. Trustee N.Y. Ocean Scis. Labs., Montauk, N.Y., 1969-71, Waldemar Cancer Rsch. Inst., Woodbury, N.Y., 1966-68, North Shore U. Hosp., 1980-91, N.Y. State Nature and Hist. Preserve Trust, 1978-83, Nassau County Mus., 1980-83; trustee Hofstra U., 1970, 72—, sec., 1973-74, vice chmn., 1974—; trustee emeritus The Nature Conservancy, 1990—, chmn. Long Island chpt., 1997—; bd. dirs. Pro Arte Symphony Orch., 1967-70, N.Y. Quar. Poetry Rev. Found., Inc., 1969—, Eglevsky Ballet Co., Outward Bound, Inc.; v.p. bd. dirs. Leukemia Soc.; treas. Interfaith Nutrition Network, 1984-85, bd. of trustees, Nassau Heritage, 2001-. Author: Sliding down the Wind, 1978, The Hawk's Dream and Other Poems, 1982, Against Gravity, 1986, The Colors of Infinity, 1990, Spin, 1992, Dawn Patrol, 1992, The Latest Illusion, 1995, The Ego Makers, 1998, Change as a Curved Equation, 2002, El Sueno de Halcon, 2003; prodr. film Spin, 2003 (L.I. Film Festival Prodrs. award 2005). Trustee Nassau Heritage, from 2001. Recipient archtl. design and community enhancement awards L.I. Assn. and Plainview C. of C., 1962-70, Brotherhood award NCCJ, 1977, Humanitarian award Am. Jewish Com., 1978, Interfaith Nutrition Network, 1989, hon. award Beta Gamma Sigma, 1978, L.I. Disting. Leadership award, 1979, Estabrook award Hofstra U., 1987; Tennessee Wiliams fellow in poetry Bread Loaf, 1979, Long Island Assn. Humanitarian of the Year award, 2003. Mem. PEN, Nat. Pilots Assn., Poets and Writers, Aircraft Owners and Pilots Assn., L.I. Early Fliers Club, Poetry Soc. Am. (bd. govs. 1987-95), Acad. of Am. Poets (bd. dirs. 1996—), L.I. Regional Econ. Devel. Coun., Poets House, Middlebury Coll. Alumni Assn. (v.p., adv. bd. 1978), Players Club (N.Y.C.), Sands Point Country Club (L.I.), Old Westbury Racquet Club (N.Y.), Delta Upsilon. Achievements include designing, developing Long Island Office Park, Engineers Hill Indsl. Parks, Montvale Office Park, The Ellipse at Garden City, Montvale III, Montvale IV, Meadow Hill Office Plz. Died Oct. 13, 2009.

AXINN, GEORGE HAROLD, rural sociology educator; b. Jamaica, NY, Feb. 1, 1926; s. Hyman and Celia (Schneider) A.; m. Nancy Kathryn Wigsten, Feb. 17, 1945; children: Catherine, Paul, Martha, William. BS, Cornell U., 1947; MS, U. Wis., 1952, PhD, 1958. Editorial asst. Cornell U. Geneva, N.Y., 1947; bull. editor U. Md., College Park, 1949; chmn. dept. rural communication U. Del., Newark, 1950; mem. faculty Mich. State U., East Lansing, from 1953, assoc. dir. coop. extension service, 1955-60; coordinator U. Nigeria program, 1961-65, prof. agrl. econs., 1970-85, prof. resource devel., 1985-95, prof. emeritus, from 1996, asst. dean internat. studies and programs, 1964-85; pres., exec. dir. Midwest Univs. Consortium for Internat. Activities, Inc., 1969-76, 1969-76. FAO rep. to Nepal, 1983-85, India and Bhutan, 1989-91; cons. World Bank, 1973-74, Ford Found., 1968, UNICEF, 1978, FAO, 1974, 87, 89, Govt. of India, 1988; vis. prof. Cornell U., Ithaca, N.Y., 1958-60, U. Ill., Urbana, 1969-70 Author: Modernizing World Agriculture: A Comparative Study of Agricultural Extension Education Systems, 1972, New Strategies for Rural Development, Rural Life Associates, 1978, FAO Guide Alternative Approaches to Agricultural Extension, 1988, Collaboration in International Rural Development - A Practitioner's Handbook (with Nancy W. Axinn), 1997; contbr. articles to various publs. Served with USNR, 1944-46. Recipient Outstanding Alumni award Cornell U. Coll. Agrl. and Life Sci., 1993; W.K. Kellogg Found. fellow, 1956-57. Home: Tucson, Ariz. Died Mar. 8, 2010.

AYISI, ERIC OKYERE, social anthropologist, educator; b. Mampong Akwapin, Ghana, Sept. 22, 1926; citizen of U.K.; came to U.S., 1974; s. Kofi and Mercy (Adebra) A.; B.Sc. in Sociol. and Anthropology, U. London, 1961, B.A. in Subs. Econs., 1960, Ph.D. in Social Change, 1965; m. Dorothy Evelyn Nayler, July 31, 1957; children— Kathleen Judith, Ruth Margaret Doddrell. Headmaster, Meth. Elem. Sch., Ghana, 1940-43; preacher Meth. Catechist, Ghana, 1943-45, Lagos, Nigeria, 1945-50; mem. faculty U. Ghana, 1965-74; Fulbright prof., curriculum cons. Ramapo, Mahwah, N.J., also Bloomfield (N.J.) Coll., 1972-73; disting. Fulbright lectr. humanities Dillard U., New Orleans, 1973-74; prof. religion and philosophy Fisk U., Nashville, 1973-74; vis. prof. Hampton (Va.) Inst. 1974-78; lectr. Christopher Newport Coll., Newport News, Va., 1979-81; vis. assoc. prof. anthropology Coll. William and Mary, Williamsburg, Va., 1980—, also asst. to provost; guest lectr. various colls., univs. Commr. of inquiry Nat. Liberation Council, Govt. Ghana, 1966-68; mem. nat. adv. com. Workers Brigade Ghana, 1966-72; mem. Ghana Meth. Conf., 1965—. NEH fellow, summer 1980. Mem. Ghana Sociol. Assn., Brit. Sociol. Assn., Internat. African Inst., U.K. African Studies Assn., Royal Anthrop. Inst., Internat. Polit. Sci. Assn., Current Anthropology (assoc.), Am. Acad. Polit. and Social Sci., Polit. Platform Assn. Author: An Introduction to the Study of African Culture, 3d edit., 1980; The Political Institutions of Akwapims, 1972; Kinship and Local Community of the Akwapims, 1972; also articles; research in African politics, Caribbean Basin. Home: Williamsburg, Va. Died June 14, 2010.

AYLESWORTH, JOHN BANSLEY, writer, television producer; b. Toronto, Ont., Can., Aug. 18, 1928; s. Fredrick Allen and Marie Thelma (Bansley) A.; (div.); children: Linda, Robert, John, Cynthia, William, Thomas. Writer The Perry Como Show, NYC, 1960-63; headwriter Judy Garland show ABC, LA, 1963-64; headwriter Hullabaloo NBC, NYC,

1965-66; headwriter Frank Sinatra - A Man and His Music CBS, LA, 1966; headwriter Kraft Music Hall NBC, NYC, 1967-68; producer, writer Jonathan Winters Show CBS, LA, 1968-69, creator, exec. producer Hee Haw L.A., Nashville, 1968-85; headwriter Julie Andrews Show, LA, 1972-73; cons. Dolly Parton Show ABC, LA, 1987-88. Author: Fee-Fi-Fo-Fum, 1961, THe Corn Was Green: The Inside Story of Hee-Haw, 2010; theatre musical: Durante, 1990, Palm Springs Confidential, 1998. Recipient Peabody award, 1967; named Man of Yr., Country Music Assn., 1970. Mem. Writers Guild America, Assn. TV and Radio Actors. Home: Palm Desert, Calif. Died July 28, 2010.

AYRES, STEPHEN MCCLINTOCK, physician, educator; b. Elizabeth, NJ, Oct. 29, 1929; s. Malcolm B. and Florence M. A.; m. Dolores Kobrick, June 11, 1955; children: Stephen (dec.), Elizabeth, Margaret. BA, Gettysburg Coll., 1951; MD, Cornell U., 1955. Intern N.Y. Hosp., NYC, 1955, resident, 1958-61; dir. cardio-pulmonary lab. St. Michael's Hosp., Newark, 1961-63, St. Vincent's Hosp. and Med. Ctr., NYC, 1963-73; physician-in-chief St. Vincent Hosp., Worcester, Mass., 1973-75; prof., chmn. dept. internal medicine St. Louis U. Med. Ctr., 1975-85; dean Med. Coll. Va., Richmond, 1985-93; dean emeritus, dir. office internat. health program Med. Coll. Va./Va. Commonwealth U., Richmond, from 1993. Author: Care of the Critically Ill, 3d edit., 1988; co-author: Textbook of Critical Care, 1988, Nutritional Support of the Critically Ill, 1988; editor: Major Issues in Critical Care Medicine, 1984; contbr. articles to profl. jours. Chmn. bd. Found. for Critical Care, 1985—. Served with M.C., U.S. Army, 1956-58. Fellow ACP, Am. Coll. Cardiology, Am. Coll. Chest Physicians; mem. Soc. Critical Care Medicine (pres. 1979-80), Am. Lung Assn., Assn. Am. Physicians, Am. Soc. Clin. Investigation. Died Sept. 12, 2009.

AZFAR, OMAR, economics professor; b. Islamabad, Pakistan, Nov. 19, 1968; Degree in philosophy, politics & economics, Oxford U., Eng., 1990; PhD in Economics, Columbia U., NYC, 1995. Assoc. prof. economics CUNY, NYC, 2006—07. Author: (book) Market-Augmenting Government. Died Jan. 21, 2009.

AZZOLINA, JOSEPH, retired state legislator; b. Newark, June 26, 1926; Student, Drew U.; BS, Holy Cross Coll., 1946; postgrad., NYU. Pres. Food Circus Supermarkets, Inc., Middletown, N.J.; chmn. bd. Foodtown, Capdebret, N.J.; mem. N.J. State Senate, 1972-73; mem. Dist. 13 N.J. State Assembly, 1966-71, 86-88, 91-2001. Chmn. N.J. State Rep. Conv., 1967. Capt. USN, ret. Named Man of Yr., Deborah Hosp., Italian Tribune News, St. Joseph's Coll., Legislator of Yr., Freeholder Assn., 1971. Mem. VFW, Am. Legion, Navy League, Middletown C. of C., Monmouth County Rep. Club, Lions. Died Apr. 15, 2010.

BABLADELIS, GEORGIA, retired psychology educator; b. Manistique, Mich., Jan. 30, 1931; d. Alexander and Panayota Babladelis. BA, U. Mich., 1953; MA, U. Calif., Berkeley, 1957; PhD, U. Colo., 1960. Sr. clin. psychologist Guidance Clinic, Ala. County Probation Dept., 1960-63; prof. psychology Calif. State U., Hayward, 1963-94, prof. emerita, from 1994. Cons. Calif. Sch. Profl. Psychology, Berkeley, 1979—; U.S. dir. rsch. UNESCO, 1979; lectr. in field. Author: The Study of Personality, 1985; co-author: The Shaping of Personality, 1967; editor Psychology of Women Quar., 1974-82, Computer Users Newsletter, 1984-87; contbr. articles to profl. jours. Chosen One of 100 Outstanding Women in Psychology, Divsn. 35 APA, 1992; grantee USPHS, NIMH, NSF, others, 1969-79. Fellow APA, The Psychology of Women Soc. (divsn. 35), The Soc. for Study of Societal Issues (divsn. 9). Avocations: writing, reading. Home: Manistique, Mich. Died May 28, 2009.

BACCINI, LAURANCE ELLIS, lawyer; b. Nov. 16, 1945; m. Christine Dianna Buccier, Dec. 30, 2004; children: Victoria Lauren Buccier, Giovanna Christina, Lauren Jean Buccier. BS, Drexel U., 1968; JD, Villanova U., 1971. Bar: Pa. 71, U.S. Dist. Ct. (ea. dist.) Pa. 73, U.S. Ct. Appeals (3d cir.) 79. Law clk. to chief judge U.S. Dist. Ct. (ea. dist.) Pa., 1971—73; assoc. Schnader, Harrison, Segal & Lewis, Phila., 1973—78, ptnr., 1979—91, mem. exec. com., 1990—91; ptnr. Wolf, Block, Schorr and Solis-Cohen, 1991—2002, Klehr, Harrison, Harvey, Branzburg & Ellers LLP, Phila., from 2002. Spkr., faculty mem. on labor law Practicing Law Inst., NYC; trustee Phila. Bar Found., from 1986; bd. dirs. Interest on Lawyers Inst. Acct. Bd. Author: NLRA Supervisor's Handbook; assoc. editor: albums. Recipient Drexel One Hundred honor award, 1992. Mem.: ABA (former chmn. and dir. young lawyers divsn. 1981—82, ho. of dels. from 1988, chmn. long-range planning com., fed. jud. standards com., mem. editl. bd. The Labor Lawyer, young lawyers divsn. fed. practice com., jud. conf. for 3d cir.), Greater Phila. C. of C. (bd. dirs. 1988), Pa. Bar Assn., Phila. Bar Assn. (commn. on jud. selection, retention and evaluation 1978—79, bd. govs. from 1978, chmn. 1982, ho. of dels. from 1983, vice chancellor 1986, chancellor-elect 1987, chancellor 1988, chmn. exec. com. young lawyers sect., chmn. long range planning com.). Died Oct. 20, 2009.

BACHLI, WILLARD CHARLES, insurance company executive; b. Chgo., Oct. 22, 1932; s. Ralph Willard Bachli and Evelyn Bachli Herr; m. Gerlinde Ertmude, Aug. 22, 1959; children: Willard C., Suzanne Tamera, Tiffany Heidi. AA in Engring., Wilson Jr. Coll.; BA in Polit. Sci., Am. Internat. Coll., Springfield, Mass., 1966; MBA in Bus., Western New Eng. Coll., 1969. CLU. Commd. 2d lt. USAF, 1954, advanced through grades to maj., 1967, ret., 1970; ind. life and health ins. broker Springfield, from 1970; real estate broker Tiffany Realty, Springfield, from 1978; gen. agt. West Mass. Ins. Agy., Springfield, from 1980; broker-dealer Bill Bachli Assocs., Inc, Springfield, from 1982. Prin. bus. start-up operation, Springfield, from 1970; mng. ptnr. Apco Assocs., Westfield, Mass., from 1980, Heritage Assocs, Westfield, 1981—84; mem. mng. bd. Empire One, Chicopee, Mass., from 1980; incorporator Bank of Western Mass. Mem.: Nat. Assn. Securities Dealers, Springfield Life Underwriters, Am. Soc. C.L.U.s. Republican. Home: Lake Worth, Fla. Died Mar. 28, 2010.

BACHRACH, LOUIS FABIAN, JR., portrait photographer; b. Newton, Mass., Apr. 9, 1917; s. Louis Fabian and Dorothy Deland (Keyes) B; m. Janice Rose Daugherty, Dec. 27, 1941 (dec. June 1988); children: Pamela Keyes, Gretchen Burdie, Louis Fabian III; m. Eleanor Fink Volk, Apr. 23, 1989. AB, Harvard U., 1939; MA in Italian Lit., Boston Coll., 1988. V.p. Bachrach, Inc., Watertown, Mass., 1950-76, treas., 1959, pres., 1976-84. Lt. USNR, 1942-45. Unitarian Universalist. Home: Newton, Mass. Died Feb. 26, 2010.

BACK, NATHAN, biochemist, pharmacologist, educator; b. Phila., Nov. 30, 1925; s. Joseph and Freda (Goldhirsh) B.; m. Toby D. Ticktin, June 17, 1951; children: Ephraim E., Aaron I., Adina, Rachel T., Sara D. BSc in Biochemistry, Pa. State U., 1948; MSc in Pharmacology, DSc in Pharmacology, Phil. Coll. Pharmacy & Sci., 1953. Pharmacists mate U.S. Navy Med. Corps, 1944-46; 1st lt. Israel Army Med. Corps, 1948-50; rsch. assoc. Wyeth Inst. Life Scis., 1950-52; cancer rsch. scientist dept. pharmacology Roswell Park Meml. Inst., Buffalo, 1955-58, sr. cancer rsch. scientist, 1958-61; rsch. fellow pharmacology Med. Sch. U. Buffalo, 1956-60, asst. prof., organizer, dir. pharmacology program Sch. Pharmacy, 1956-58, porf., assoc. prof., 1958-61; assoc. prof. pharmacology Sch. Pharmacy SUNY, Buffalo, 1961-63, chmn. dept. biochem. pharmacology, 1967-72; dir. pharmacology inst. Nat. Coun. Rsch., Jerusalem, 1969-71; sci. expert UN Devel. Pharmacology Inst. Project, Jerusalem, 1976-77; assoc. pharmacology Roswell Park Meml. Cancer Inst., Buffalo, from 1961; prof. biochem. pharmacology Grad. Sch. SUNY, Buffalo, from 1963, prof. biochem. pharmacology Health Scis. Faculty Sch. Pharmacy, from 1963. Cons. Battelle Meml. Inst., Ohio, Buffalo Gen. Hosp., Erie County Health Assn., Buffalo, Palestine Econ. Corp., N.Y., Nat. Coun. R & D, Israel, Roswell Park Meml. Inst., United Health Fund Buffalo, UNIDO-UNDP, Austria, WHO, Geneva. Author: Laboratory Manual in Pharmacology, 1958, 1964, Hypotensive Peptides, 1966, Bradykinin and Related Kinins-Cardiovascular, Biochemical and Neural Actions, 1970, Shock: Biochemical, Pharmacological and Clinical Aspects, 1972, Vasopeptides: Biochemistry, Pharmacology and Pathophysiology, 1972, Kinins: Pharmacodynamics and Biological Roles, 1976, Kinins III-Parts A and B, 1983; mem. editl. bd. Advances in Exptl. Medicine and Biology, Archives Internationales Pharmacodynamie et de Therapie, Circulatory Shock, Jour. Angiology, Jour. Medicine, Modern Methods in Pharmacology, Phar. Rsch. Progress Clin. & Biol. Rsch., West African Jour. Pharm. & Drug Rsch.; contbr. articles to profl. jours. Recipient E.K. Frey Basic Rsch. award, 1970; grantee NIH. Fellow AAAS, Am. Coll. Clin. Pharmacology, Internat. Hematology Soc., N.Y. Acad. Sci., Royal Soc. Medicine, Am. Biog. Inst. (rsch. bd. advisors); mem. Am. Assn. Cancer Rsch., Am. Chem. Soc. (medicinal chemistry divsn.), Am. Soc. Pharmacology & Exptl. Therapeutics, Am. Heart Assn. (coun. basic sci.), Internat. Congress Pharmacology, Internat. Inflammation Soc., Internat. Soc. Biochem. Pharmacology (founder), Internat. Soc. Hematology, Israel Soc. Pharmacology & Physiology, Italian Soc. Pharmacology, Kinin Club, Reticuloendothelial Soc., Shock, Soc. Exptl. Biology and Medicine, Sigma Xi. Avocations: photography, geneology, gymnastics. Died Mar. 1, 2009.

BADASH, LAWRENCE, science history educator; b. Bklyn., May 8, 1934; s. Joseph and Dorothy (Langa) B.; children: Lisa, Bruce. BS in Physics, Rensselaer Poly. Inst., 1956; PhD in History of Sci., Yale U., 1964. Instr. Yale. U., New Haven, 1964—65, research assoc., 1965-66; from asst. to assoc. prof. U. Calif., Santa Barbara, 1966-79, prof. history of sci., 1979—2002, prof. emeritus, from 2002. Dir. summer seminar on global security and arms control U. Calif., 1983, 86, energy rsch. group, 1992, pacific rim program mem., 1993-95; cons. Nuclear Age Peace Found., Santa Barbara, 1984-90. Author: Radioactivity in Am., 1979, Kapitza, Rutherford, and the Kremlin, 1985, Scientists and the Development of Nuclear Weapons, 1995, A Nuclear Winter's Tale: Science & Politics in the 1980s, 2009; editor: Rutherford and Boltwood, Letters on Radioactivity, 1969; Reminiscences of Los Alamos, 1943-45, 1980. Bd. dirs. Santa Barbara chpt. ACLU, 1971-86, 96—2008, pres., 1982-84, 96-98; nat. bd. dirs. Com. for a Sane Nuclear Policy, Washington, 1972-81; mem. Los Padres Search and Rescue Team, Santa Barbara, 1981-94. Lt. (j.g.) USN, 1956-59. Grantee, NSF, Cambridge, Eng., 1965-66, 69-72, 90-92, Am. Philos. Soc., New Zealand, 1979-80, Inst. on Global Conflict and Cooperation, Univ. Calif., 1983-87; J.S. Guggenheim fellow, 1984-85. Fellow AAAS (sect. mem. at large 1988-92), Am. Phys. Soc. (chmn. divsn. of history of physics 1988-89, exec. com. forum on physics and society 1991-93); mem. History of Sci. Soc. (founder West Coast chpt., chpt. bd. dirs. 1971-73, nat. coun. 1975-78). Democrat. Jewish. Avocation: backpacking. Home: Santa Barbara, Calif. Died Aug. 23, 2010.

BAERWALD, HANS H., retired political science professor; b. Tokyp, June 18, 1927; Ph.D in Polit. Sci., U. Calif. Berkeley. Asst. prof. govt. Miami U., Oxford, Ohio, 1956-61, assoc. prof., 1961-62; lectr. polit. sci. UCLA, 1962-65, assoc. prof., 1965-69, prof., 1969-91, prof. emeritus, 1992—2010. Served in US Army. Home: Pope Valley, Calif. Died June 2, 2010.

BAGGETT, MARY E., personnel executive; b. Kettering, Eng., Aug. 24, 1926; came to U.S., 1946; d. Robert Burgess and Kate Alice (Joy) Hulatt; m. L. C. Baggett; 1 child, Kay Davis; m. L. C. Baggett, Oct. 17, 1963. Student pub. schs., Bedford, Eng. Sec., timekeeper Coats & Clarks, Albany, Ga., 1948-57; personnel dir. Phoebe Putney Hosp., Albany, 1957—; cons. personnel dir. Ga. Hosp. Assn., Atlanta, 1961-66. Mem. Am. Hosp. Assn., Ga. Hosp. Assn., Albany Dougherty County Personnel Soc. Republican. Episcopalian. Avocations: gardening; cooking. Home: Albany, Ga. Died July 20, 2009.

BAHN, ARTHUR NATHANIEL, microbiologist, educator; b. Boston, Jan. 5, 1926; s. Benjamin Edward and Molly Sarah B.; m. Marna Jean Katz, Dec. 7, 1952; children— Lisa, Janice, Bruce; m. Barbara Ann Silverberg, Aug. 1, 1985. AB, Boston U., 1949; MA, U. Kans., 1950; PhD, U. Wis., 1956. Instr. Coll. Medicine U. Ill., 1956-58; asst. prof. Sch. Dentistry Northwestern U., 1958-60, assoc. prof. Sch. Medicine and Dentistry, 1960-70; prof. Sch. Dental Medicine So. Ill. U., Edwardsville, from 1970, chmn., dep. sect. microbiology, 1971-75, head sect. microbiology, from 1975. Cons. FDA, 1974-80, ADA, 1968—. Served with U.S. Army, 1943-45. Recipient Sr. Fulbright award Netherlands, 1977-78. Fellow AAAS; mem. Am. Soc. Microbiology, Internat. Assn. Dental Research. Home: Saint Louis, Mo. Died Oct. 22, 2009.

BAHR, NEIL EUGENE, real estate developer, consultant; b. Cleve., Sept. 17, 1925; s. Ernest Albert and Ethel Cecelia (Nageotte) Bahr; m. Anne Marie Laird, Jan. 18, 1947; children: Nancy, Michael, Thomas, Mark. Gen. mgr. R.A. Gall Realty Co., Cleve., 1954—59; v.p. sales Gen. Devel. Corp., Miami, Fla., 1960—62; v.p. mktg. Deltona Corp., Miami, 1962—66, exec. v.p., 1966—74; pres. Deltona Land and Investment Corp., Miami, from 1974. Chmn. bd. First Nat. Bank of Fla., Naples and Marco Island, from 1978. Bd. dirs. Fla. Installment Land Sales Bd., Tallahassee, from 1972. With USNR, 1943—46, PTO. Mem.: Riviera Country (bd. govs. 1979—81, 1983—84). Republican. Roman Cath. Home: Naples, Fla. Died Feb. 15, 2010.

BAILEY, JAMES (JIM BAILEY), lawyer, professional football team executive; b. Wilmington, Oreg., Aug. 21, 1946; m. Ann Bailey; children: Sarah, Jenny. Grad., Fla. State U.; JD, U. Mich. Assoc. Guren, Merritt, Sogg & Cohen, Cleve., 1971-76, ptnr., 1976; v.p., gen. counsel Cleve. Browns, NFL, 1978-84; exec. v.p. legal and adminstrn. Balt. Ravens, NFL, 1984-99; cons. San Diego, from 1999. Home: San Diego, Calif. Died Nov. 7, 2009.

BAINTON, DONALD J., diversified manufacturing company executive; b. NYC, May 3, 1931; s. William Lewis and Mildred J. (Dunne) B.; m. Aileen M. Demoulins, July 10, 1954; children: Kathryn C., Stephen L., Elizabeth A., William D. BA, Columbia U., 1952, postgrad., 1960. With Continental Group, Inc., 1954—67, gen. mgr. prodn. planning, 1967—68, gen. mgr. mfg. Ea. divsn., 1968—73, gen. mgr. Pacific divsn., 1973—74, gen. mgr. Ea. divsn., 1974—75; v.p., gen. mgr. ops. U.S. Metal, 1975—76; exec. v.p., gen. mgr. CCC-USA, 1976—78, corp. exec. v.p., pres. diversified ops., 1978—79; pres. Continental Can Co., 1979—81, Continental Packaging, 1981—83, exec. v.p., operating officer parent co., bd. dirs., 1979—83; chmn., CEO, dir. Viatech Inc., Syosset, NY, 1983—92, Continental Can Co., Inc., Boca Raton, Fla., from 1992. Bd. dirs. Viatech Inds., LLC. Bd. dirs. Columbia Coll. With USN, 1952-54, Korea. Mem. Inst. Applied Econs. (dir.), Milbrook Country Club (Greenwich, Conn.), Winged Foot Club (Mamaroneck, N.Y.), Union League Club (N.Y.C.), Royal Palm Yacht and Country Club (Boca Raton, Fla.). Republican. Roman Catholic. Died June 13, 2010.

BAIR, BRUCE BLYTHE, lawyer; b. St. Paul, May 26, 1928; s. Bruce B. and Emma N. (Stone) B.; m. Jane Lawler, July 19, 1952; children: Mary Jane, Thomas, Susan, Barbara, Patricia, James, Joan, Bruce, Jeffrey. BS, U. N.D., 1950, JD, 1952. Bar: ND 1952, US Dist. Ct. ND 1955, U.S. Ct. Appeals (8th cir.) 1971, US Supreme Ct. 1974. Assoc. Lord and Ulmer, Mandan, ND, 1955-57; ptnr. Bair, Bair, and Garrity, Mandan, 1957—2001, of counsel, from 2002. Spl. asst. atty. gen. ND Milk Mktg. Bd., 1967—; chmn. bd. Bank of Tioga, 1984-2003, also bd. dirs.; Rep. precinct committeeman, 1956-70, chmn. Morton County Rep. Com., 1958-62, mem. ND Rep. State Ctrl. Com., 1962-67; pres. sch. bd. St. Joseph's Cath. Ch., 1967-68; bd. dirs. Mandan Pub. Sch. Dist. #1, 1971-77; exec. com. Internat. Assn. Milk Control Agys., 1970-2000; bd. regents U. Mary, Bismarck, ND, 1984—. 1st lt. JAG Corps USAF, 1952-55. Mem.: ABA, ND Bar Assn., Am. Coll. Barristers (sr. counsel), Am. Legion, Elks. Roman Catholic. Home: Mandan, ND. Died Aug. 8, 2010.

BAIRD, CHARLES FITZ, retired mining and metals company executive; b. Southampton, NY, Sept. 4, 1922; s. George White and Julia (Fitz) B.; m. Norma Adele White, Sept. 13, 1947; children: Susan Baird Creyke, Stephen White, Charles Fitz, Nancy Baird Harwood. AB, Middlebury Coll., Vt., 1944; grad., Advanced Mgmt. Program, Harvard U., 1960; LLD, Bucknell U., 1976. With Std. Oil Co., NJ, 1948-65, dep. European fin. rep. London, 1955-58, asst. treas., 1958-62; dir. Esso Std. SA Française, 1962-65; asst. sec. for fin. mgmt. Dept. of Navy, 1966-67, undersec., 1967-69; v.p. fin. Inco Ltd., 1969-72, sr. v.p., 1972-76, vice-chmn., 1976-77, pres., 1977-80, chmn., CEO, 1980-87. Trustee Ctr. for Naval Analyses, 1990—2002, chmn., 1992—97; past trustee Logistics Mgmt. Inst.; mem. Pres.'s Commn. on Marine Sci., Engring. and Resources, 1967—69, Nat. Adv. Commn. on Ocean and Atmosphere, 1972—74. Trustee Marine Corps U. Found., 1993—2003, Bucknell U., 1969—93, chmn. bd. trustees, 1976—82; bd. advisers Naval War Coll., 1970—74. Served to capt. USMC, 1950—51, 1943-46. Mem. Coun. Fgn. Rels., Chevy Chase (Md.) Club, Maidstone Club (East Hampton, N.Y.), Bridgehampton Club (N.Y.). Home: Bethesda, Md. Died Dec. 26, 2009.

BAISLEY, ROBERT WILLIAM, music educator; b. New Haven, Apr. 5, 1923; s. Joseph V. and Mary (Bergin) B.; m. Jean Shanley, July 30, 1955; children: Joan Ann, Susan Jean, Elizabeth Veronica. Mus.B., Yale U., 1949; MA, Columbia U.,

1950. Tchr. Cherry Lawn Sch., Darien, Conn., 1950-51; dir. Neighborhood Music Sch., New Haven, 1951-56; asst. prof. piano, exec. officer Sch. Music Yale U., New Haven, 1956-65; prof. music Pa. State U., University Park, 1965-87, chmn. dept. music, 1965-79. Concert pianist in various concerts, recitals, radio and TV. Vol. United Fund, New Haven, 1951-65; rep. to Coun. of Social Agys., 1951-60; mem. adv. coun. Salvation Army, 1963-65; bd. dirs. Ctrl. Pa. Festival of Arts (pres. 1969-71). Served with AUS, 1942-45. Recipient cert. of merit Yale U., 1979 Mem. Coll. Music Soc., Yale U. Sch. Music Alumni Assn. (pres. 1979-82, 89-94, exec. com. 1977-97). Home: New York, NY. Died Mar. 7, 2009.

BAKER, A. HARVEY, psychology professor; life ptnr. Adela Oliver; children: Amy Anne, Jonah Marc. BA in Social Relations, Harvard Coll., Cambridge, Mass., 1958; MEd in Human Devel., Harvard Grad. Sch. Edn., 1960; PhD in Clin. and Exptl. Psychology, Clark U., Worcester, Mass., 1968. Lic. psychologist NY, 1974, mental health counselor NJ. Rsch. psychologist Ednl. Testing Svc., Princeton, NJ, 1969—74; prof. psychology Queens Coll., CUNY, Flushing, NY, from 1974. Contbr. articles to profl. jours. Home: Lawrenceville, NJ. Died June 6, 2010.

BAKER, AUGUSTUS L., JR., retired surgeon; b. Dover, NJ, May 1, 1915; s. Augustus L. and Ellene (Dodge) B.; m. Eleanor Jean Black, Apr. 24, 1948; children: Karen, Susan, Augustus III, Adrienne, Eric. AB, Princeton U., 1936; MD, NYU, 1940. Diplomate Am. Bd. Surgery. Intern Mountainside Hosp., Montclair, N.J., 1940-41; resident in surgery French Hosp., NYC, 1951-54; fellow in surgery Lahey Clinic, Boston, 1954-55; now ret., 1988. Alderman Town of Dover, 1956-60. With U.S. Army, 1941-47. Fellow ACS, Internat. Coll. Surgeons; mem. Med. Soc. N.J. (pres. 1980-81), Rotary Internat. (gov. dist. 4740 1987-88). Republican. Presyterian. Home: Hopatcong, NJ. Died May 26, 2010.

BAKER, C. EDWIN, law educator; b. 1947; BA, Stanford U., 1969; JD, Yale U., 1972. Asst. prof. U. Toledo, 1972-75, U. Oreg., Eugene, 1975-79, assoc. prof. law, 1979-81, prof. law, 1981-82, U. Pa., Phila., 1982—86, Nicholas F. Gallichio prof. law, 1986—2009. Fellow, vis. prof. Kennedy Sch. Govt., U. Tex., 1980, Harvard U., 1992-93, Cornell U., 1993; attny. ACLU, 1977-78. Author: Human Liberty and Freedom of Expression, 1989, Advertising and a Democratic Press, 1994; contbr. articles to law jours. Fellow Harvard U., Cambridge, Mass., 1974-75. Died Dec. 8, 2009.

BAKER, DAVID HIRAM, nutritionist, educator; b. DeKalb, Ill., Feb. 26, 1939; s. Vernon T. and Lucille M. (Severson) B.; m. Norraine A. Baker; children: Barbara G., Michael D., Susan G., Debora A., Luann C., Beth A. BS, U. Ill., 1961, MS, 1963, PhD, 1965. Sr. scientist Eli Lilly & Co., Greenfield, Ind., 1965-67; mem. faculty U. Ill., Champaign-Urbana, from 1967, prof. nutrition, dept. animal sci., nutritional biochemist, from 1974, dept. head, 1988-90. Author: Sulfur in Nonruminant Nutrition, 1977, Bioavailability of Nutrients for Animals, 1995; mem. editorial bd. Jour. Animal Sci., 1969-73, Jour. Nutrition, 1975-79, 89-99, Poultry Sci., 1978-84, Nutrition Revs., 1983-92; contbr. numerous articles to sci. jours. Chmn. bd. Champaign-Urbana Teen Challenge Drug Rehab. Program, 1977-80. Recipient Disting. Svc. award USDA, 1987; Univ. Scholar award, 1986; Nutrition Rsch. award, 1986; Am. Feed Mfrs., 1973; Merck award, 1977; Paul A. Funk award, 1977; H. H. Mitchell Tchg. award, 1979, 85; Broiler Rsch. award, 1983. Mem. NAS, Am. Soc. Animal Sci. (Young Scientist award 1971, Gustaf Bohstedt award 1985, Hoffman LaRoche award 1985, Morrison award 1994, Frontiers in Animal Nutrition award 2006, Charles A. Black award 2007), Poultry Sci. Assn., Am. Soc. Nutritional Sci. (Borden award 1986, Dannon award 2003), Fedn. Am. Socs. Exptl. Biology, Sigma Xi, Phi Kappa Phi, Alpha Zeta, Gamma Sigma Delta. Home: Urbana, Ill. Died Dec. 2, 2009.

BAKER, JOHN E., engineering executive; b. Portland, Oreg., Nov. 5, 1961; BS, U. Mo., Rolla, 1983. Registered profl. engr., Tex. Engr. City of Garland, Tex., dir. engring. dept. Tex., from 1996. Mem. Am. Soc. Civil Engrs., Nat. Soc. Profl. Engrs. Died Jan. 13, 2010.

BAKER, LLOYD HARVEY, retired lawyer; b. Sept. 17, 1927; s. George William and Marion (Souville) B.; m. Barbara I. Gustafson, Sept. 4, 1955; children: Laurie, Jeffrey. Student, Colgate U., 1945-48; LLB, NYU, 1951. Bar: N.Y. 1951, U.S. Dist. Ct. (so. and ea. dists.) N.Y. 1953, U.S. Ct. Appeals (2d cir.) 1970. Assoc. Milligan, Reilly, Lake & Schneider, Babylon, N.Y., 1952-53; staff Fgn. Claims Commn., Washington, 1954; spl. attorney windfall investigations FHA, Washington, 1955; asst. U.S. atty. for Ea. Dist. N.Y., 1955-59; sole practice Bayshore and Islip, N.Y., 1959-67; atty. Suffolk County (N.Y.) Legal Aid Soc., 1967-69; dep. chief civil div. U.S. Atty.'s Office for Ea. Dist. N.Y., 1969-74; asst. counsel met. region Penn Central R.R. and Conrail, NYC, 1975-81; ptnr. Bleakley, Platt, Remsen, Millham and Curran, NYC, 1982-87; asst. town atty. Town of Islip, N.Y., 1987-97, retired N.Y., from 1997. Mem. Suffolk County Republican Com., 1963-71. Episcopalian. Home: Ellicott City, Md. Died June 11, 2009.

BAKER, WALTER ARNOLD, lawyer; b. Columbia, Ky., Feb. 20, 1937; s. Herschel T. and Mattie B. (Barger) B.; m. Jane Stark Helm, Apr. 24, 1965; children: Thomas Herschel, Ann Tate. AB magna cum laude, Harvard U., 1958, LLB, 1961; LHD (hon.), Pikeville Coll., 2006. Assoc. Brown, Ardery, Todd & Dudley, Louisville, 1961-63; ptnr. Wilson, Baker, Herbert and Garmon, Glasgow, Ky., 1963-67; pvt. practice Glasgow, 1967-81 and from 83; asst. gen. counsel Office Sec. Def., Washington, 1981-83; justice Supreme Ct. of Ky., Frankfort, 1996. Rep. Ky. Ho. of Reps., 1968-71, senator State of Ky., 1972-81, 89-96; active Ky. Coun. on Postsecondary Edn., 1997-2008; pres. Ky. Hist. Soc., 2001-03; mem. Ky. Judicial Campaign Conduct Com., 2005. Lt. col. USAFR. Mem. Ky. Bar Assn., Barren County Bar Assn., Glasgow Rotary, Glasgow Golf and Country Club, Phi Beta Kappa. Republican. Episcopalian. Died May 24, 2010.

BAKER, WILLIAM DUNLAP, lawyer; b. St. Louis, June 17, 1932; s. Harold Griffith and Bernice (Kraft) B.; m. Kay Stokes, May 23, 1955; children: Mark William, Kathryn X., Beth Kristie, Frederick Martin. AB, Colgate U., 1954; JD, U. Calif., Berkeley, 1960. Bar: Calif. 1961, Ariz. 1961, U.S. Supreme Ct. 1969. Practice in, Coolidge, 1961, Florence, 1961-63, Phoenix, from 1963; law clk. Stokes & Moring, 1960; spl. investigator Office Pinal County Atty., 1960-61, dep. county atty., 1961-63; partner McBryde, Vincent, Brumage & Baker, 1961-63; assoc. atty. Rawlins, Ellis, Burrus & Kiewit, 1963-65, partner, 1965-81; pres., atty. Ellis & Baker, P.C., 1981-84, Ellis, Baker, Lynch, Clark & Porter P.C., 1984-86, Ellis, Baker, Clark & Porter, P.C., 1986-89, Ellis, Baker & Porter, P.C., 1989-92, Ellis Baker & Porter Ltd., Phoenix, 1992-95, Ellis, Baker & Porter, P.C., Phoenix, 1995-99, Ellis & Baker, P.C., from 1999. Referee Juvenile Ct. Maricopa County Superior Ct., 1966-85 Contbr. articles to profl. jours. Mem. Gov.'s Adv. Coun., Phoenix, 1969-71, Ariz. Environ. Planning Commn., 1974-75; bd. dirs. Agri-Bus. Coun., 1978—, sec., 1978-82; pub. mem. State Bd. Accountancy, 1995-03, sec., 1998-99, treas., 1999-00, pres., 2000-02, law com., 2004-09; mem. Nat. Assn. Bds. Accountancy, litig. com., 2001-03, nominating com., 2002-04; legal counsel Ariz. Com. Rep. Party, 1965-69, mem. exec. com., 1972-78; vice-chmn. Maricopa County Rep. Com., 1968-69, chmn., 1969-71; bd. dirs. San Pablo Home for Youth, 1964-72, pres., 1971; bd. dirs. Maricopa County chpt. Nat. Found. March of Dimes, 1966-71, campaign chmn., 1970; trustee St. Luke's Hosp., 1976-85, sec., 1978-82, chmn., 1982-85; bd. dirs. Luke's Men, 1971-80, pres., 1976-77; bd. dirs. Combined Health Resources, 1982-85, St. Luke's Health Sys., 1977-95, chmn., 1985-89; bd. dirs. St. Luke's Health Initiatives, 1995-2008, vice chair, 2000-02; bd. dirs., v.p. Ariz. Anglican Cursillo Movement, 1982-86, treas. 2005-06; Western dist. layman rep. Nat. Episcopal Cursillo Com., 1996-98; regional v.p. Colgate Alumni Corp., 1977-82; vice chancellor Episcopal Diocese Ariz., 1970-96, ch. atty, 1996-03; sr. warden Christ Ch. of Ascension, 1983-86, 2001-03, chancellor, 2004-2007; chancellor & sec. Christ Ch. Anglican, 2007-; bd. dirs. Ariz. Western Coun., Ltd., 2003-06; mem., chancellor Assn. Western Anglican Congregations, 2008-. Served to 1st lt. USAF, 1954-57. Mem. ABA, Nat. Water Resources Assn. (life, co-chmn. task force on reclamation law 1990-97, resolutions com. 1990-93, chmn. state caucus 1993—, mem. fed affairs com 2000-, chair water supply task force 2000—, Pres.'s award 1991), Ariz. Soc. CPAs (hon.), Ariz. Bar Assn., Calif. Bar Assn., State C. of C. (bd. dirs. 1988-92), Maricopa County Bar Assn., Flagstaff Golf Assn. (bd. dirs. 1992-93, 94-96, pres. 1994-95), Phoenix Country Club, Ariz. Srs. Golf Assn. (bd. dirs. 1990-, mem. chmn. 2005, sec., treas. 2006, v.p. 2007, pres. 2007-08), Sigma Chi, Phi Delta Phi. Anglican. Home: Phoenix, Ariz. Died May 3, 2010.

BALABANIAN, NORMAN, electrical engineering educator; b. New London, Conn., Aug. 13, 1922; s. Adam B. and Elizabeth (Seklemian) B.; m. Jean Tajerian, Aug. 16, 1947 (div. 1977); children: Karen J., Doris R., Gary N., Linda C.; m. 2d, Rosemary Lynch, Jan. 19, 1979. BSEE, Syracuse U., 1949, MSEE, 1951, PhD, 1954. From instr. to prof. Syracuse U., 1949-91, prof. emeritus, from 1991; mem. tech. staff Bell Labs., Murray Hill, N.J., 1956, IBM Devel. Lab, Poughkeepsie, N.Y., 1962; vis. prof. U. Calif., Berkeley, 1965-66; mem. UNESCO field staff Inst. Politecnico Nacional, Mexico City, 1969-70; Fulbright fellow U. Zagreb, Zagreb, Jugoslavia, 1974-75; acad. advisor Inst. Nat. d'Elec. et d'Elec., Boumerdes, Algeria, 1977-78; chmn. Dept. of Elec. & Computer Engring. Syracuse U., 1983-90. Vis. scholar MIT, 1990-95, Tufts U., 1990-95; courtesy prof. U. Fla., 1995—. Author: Network Synthesis, 1958, Fundamentals of Circuit Theory, 1961, Fourier Series, 1976, Ensenanza Programada en la Education Activa (in Spanish), 1974, Activne RC Mreze (in Serbo-Croatian), 1977, Electric Circuits, 1994; co-author: Linear Network Analysis, 1959, Electrical Network Theory, 1969, Electrical Science: Resistive Networks, 1970, Electrical Science: Dynamic Networks, 1973, Linear Network Theory, 1981, Digital Logic Design Principles, 2001; editor: Undergraduate Physics and Mathematics in Electrical Engineering, 1960, Electrical Engineering Education, 1961; editor (jour.) IEEE Transactions on Circuit Theory, 1963-65, (mag.) IEEE Technology and Society, 1979-86, 1993-95. Dist. commr. Dem. Party, Syracuse, N.Y., 1959-61; pres. Cen. N.Y. Civil Liberties Union, Syracuse, 1963-64, 79-80 (Civil Liberties award 1966); congl. candidate Liberal Party, People's Peace Party, Syracuse, N.Y., 1966. S/Sgt. Army AC, 1943-46. Recipient peace award Syracuse Peace Coun., 1966. Fellow AAAS, IEEE (life fellow, Centennial award 1984, Third Millenium medal 2000), IEEE Soc. Implications Tech. (v.p., pres. 1988-91); DK. mem. Am. Soc. for Engring. Edn. (life mem., pres. EE div. 1966-67), AAUP (pres. Syracuse U. chpt. 1964-65). Home: Gainesville, Fla. Died Dec. 14, 2009.

BALDWIN, GEORGE KOEHLER, retired retail executive; b. Cedar Rapids, Iowa, Nov. 17, 1919; s. Nathan and Ada Lillian (Koehler) B. BBA, State U. Iowa, 1942. From office mgr. to mgr. Wapsie Valley Creamery, Cedar Rapids, Iowa, 1946-60; treas., head payroll, accounts payable, sales audit dept. Armstrong's Inc., Cedar Rapids, 1960-87; also bd. dirs., treas. Armstrong's of Dubuque, Iowa, 1982-87; ret., 1987. Mem. adv. coun. Firstar Club, Firstar Bank, Cedar Rapids; theatre organist, 1961—. Composed and copyrighted for band Kinnick Stadium band march, 1992. Mem. Cedar Rapids Performing Arts Commn.; bd. dirs., pres. Cedar Rapids Cmty. Concert Assn., 1993—; pres. State U. of Iowa Concert Band, 1941-42; sec., treas., asst. conductor El Kahir Shrine Band of Cedar Rapids; bd. dirs. Cedar Rapids Stamp Club, 1997-00; chmn. adminstrv. bd. Trinity United Meth. Ch., 1987-92, usher & head usher and staff parish rels. com. chmn., ret. 2008; apptd. by mayor to Cedar Rapids Mcpl. Band Commn., 1994, vice chmn. 1998—; organist Paramount and Iowa theaters, Cedar Rapids, 1961-2008. With U.S. Army, 1942-46, ETO. Decorated Bronze Star medal, Knight comdr. Ct. Honor Ancient and Accepted Scottish Rite Bodies Masonry, 2005; named hon. Ky. Col.; George K. Baldwin day proclamation in his honor, Mayor of Cedar Rapids, Apr. 16, 1987. Mem. VFW, Cedar Rapids Consumer Credit Assn. (pres. 1968-69), Am. Theatre Organ Soc. (bd. dirs., treas. Cedar Rapids chpt. 1979-2006), Am. Legion, Rotary, Masons, Shriners (past pres. uniformed units), Rotary Svc. Club (chmn. fellowship com., sgt. of arms), State U. Iowa Pres.'s Club and Alumni Assn. (Gov.'s Vol. award, 2008). Methodist. Home: Cedar Rapids, Iowa. Died Dec. 26, 2009.

BALIO, JOHN PATRICK, judge; b. Utica, NY, Mar. 17, 1924; s. Anthony and Josephine (Dambro) Balio; m. Anne Comito, July 24, 1948; children: Joan Balio Uhlig, Karen Balio Clement, John R. Anthony. BA, Union Coll., 1946; LLB, Albany Law Sch., 1948, JD, 1968. Bar: NY 1949, NY (US Dist. Ct. (no. dist.)) 1949. Pvt. practice, Utica, 1949—73; asst. county atty. Oneida County, Utica, 1956—60, atty., 1960—62, family ct. judge, 1973—80; justice Town New Hartford, NY, 1970—73; judge NY State Supreme Ct., Utica, from 1980; assoc. justice, Fourth Dept. Appellate Divsn., from 1986. Pres. Oneida County Magistrates, 1973—74. Recipient Cert. of Appreciation, John E. Creedon Police Benevolent Assn., Utica, 1969, Comity Club Utica, 1979; named Hon. Erie Canaller, Rome C. of C., 1983. Fellow: NY Bar Found., Am. Bar Found.; mem.: Oneida County Bar Assn., NY State Bar Assn., NY State Magistrates Assn. (Disting. Jurist award 1996), ABA. Roman Catholic. Home: Naples, Fla. Died Jan. 30, 2010.

BALLARD, CLAUDE MARK, JR., real estate investment executive; b. Memphis, Sept. 27, 1929; s. Claude Mark and Elsie May (Miner) B.; m. Mary Theresa Birnbach, July 11, 1953; children: Karen Sue, Mary Melinda, Robyn Lisa. With Prudential Ins. Co. Am., 1948-69, v.p., regional treas. S.W. ops. Houston, 1967-73, sr. v.p. real estate investment dept. Newark, 1973-81; ptnr. Goldman Sachs & Co., NYC, from 1981. Bd. dirs. Am. Bldg. Maintenance Industries; chmn. Rockefeller Ctr. Properties; trustee Mut. Life Ins. Co. N.Y.; guest lectr. Cornell U., 1974-78, Mich. State U., 1975-80, NYU, 1975-80, Harvard U., 1976-92; chmn. Mortgage Inst., NYU; dir. ICM property Investors; chmn. Merit Equity Investors, 1976-92; mem. fin. com. Am. Hotel and Motel Assn. Contbr. articles to profl. jours.; mem. editorial bd. Corp. Design, Shopping Center World Mags. Chmn. Econ. Devel. Com., Houston, 1972-73; v.p., trustee Urban Land Inst., 1975—, mem. exec. com., 1977—, pres., 1983-85; pres., trustee Urban Land Research Found., Washington, 1977—; former chmn. bd. Real Estate Ctr. Wharton Grad. Sch., Phila., chmn. emeritus; mem. overseers vis. com. Grad. Sch. Urban Design, Harvard U.; former mem. HUD Council on Devel. Choices for 80's; bd. dirs. Greater N.Y. coun. Boy Scouts Am. Mem. Appraisal Inst., Internat. Coun. Shopping Ctrs., Nat. Urban Policy Roundtable, Am. Soc. Real Estate Counselors, Royal Instn. Chartered Surveyors (hon. mem.). Died Feb. 11, 2010.

BALYO, JOHN GABRIEL, minister, theology educator; b. Greenville, SC, Jan. 18, 1920; s. John Gabor and Etta (Groce) B.; m. Betty Louise Lindstrand, Oct. 14, 1945; 1 son, John Michael. Student, Atlanta Law Sch., 1937-40; LL.B., Valparaiso U., 1945; student, Goshen Coll., 1945-46; AB, Grace Theol. Sem., 1944, MDiv. magna cum laude, 1946; D.D., Grand Rapids Theol. Sem., 1960. Ordained to ministry Bible Bapt. Ch., 1950. Pastor, Three Oaks, Mich., 1942-45, Elkhart, Ind., 1945-46, Kokomo, Ind., 1946-53, Cedar Hill Bapt. Ch., Cleve., 1953-72; prof. Bible and practical theology Grand Rapids (Mich.) Bapt. Theol. Sem., 1972-80; chmn. council of ten Sunshine State Fellowship of Regular Bapt. Chs., Fla., 1980-81; pastor Sun Coast Bapt. Ch., New Port Richey, Fla., 1980-81; prof. theology and Bible Bapt. Bible Coll. and Sch. Theology, Clarks Summit, Pa., 1981-83; pres. Western Bapt. Coll., Salem, Oreg., 1983-91, chancellor, from 1991. Mem. gen. council Bapt. Mid-Mission, 1954-84, adminstrv. com., 1962-73, trustee, 1963-75, chmn. bd. trustees, 1968-75, chmn. council, 1966-68; mem. council 14 Gen. Assn. Regular Bapt. Chs., 1955-59, 60-64, sec. council, 1957-58, chmn. publs. com., 1956-60, 63-66, chmn. council 14, 1966-68, mem. finance com., 1968-69, publs. com., 1968-69, chmn. program com., 1968-69, chmn. edn. com., 1960-62, vice chmn. council, 1962-64, chmn., 1970-72, chmn. publs. com., 1972-73, chmn. council of 18, 1973-74, vice chmn. council of 18, 1983-86, chmn., 1986-87; exec. bd. dirs. Grand Rapids Bapt. Bible Coll. and Sem., 1961-72, chmn. curriculum com., 1963-66; missionary survey trips to, Europe and Africa, 1957-58, Ecuador, 1962, Peru, 1969, Brazil, 1975; bd. dirs. Hebrew Christian Soc., 1956-64; instr. pastor's seminar, Kiev, Ukraine, 1993; instr. Pacific Rim Grad. Sch. Theology, Seoul, Republic of Korea, 1994. Author: Sunday sch. material for Regular Bapt. Press; also booklet Creation and Evolution. Active gen. coun. Bapt. Mid. Missions, 1954-88. Mem. Oreg. Ind. Colls. Assn. (exec. com. Portland chpt. 1990-91). Home: Salem, Oreg. Died Apr. 18, 2009.

BANDER, MARTIN STANLEY, hospital administrator; b. Malden, Mass., Dec. 1, 1928; s. Samuel Joseph and Anna (Smith) B.; m. Kay Walker Boling. BS cum laude, Boston U., 1950. Edn. editor The Woonsocket (R.I.) Call, 1953-58, med. writer, 1958-66, Boston Herald, Traveler, Sunday Herald, Boston, 1966-68; med. editor Mass. Gen. Hosp., Boston, 1968-71, dir. news and pub. affairs, from 1971, dep. to the gen. dir., from 1974. Reviewer New England Jour. Medicine, Boston, 1970—; advisor Nat. T.V. programs, 1970—. Contbr. articles to profl. jours. With U.S. Army, 1951-53. Recipient Disting. Alumni award Coll. of Communication Boston U., 1988; numerous pub. rels. awards, 1970-77, 83, 85, 86, 90; Nat. Writing award AP, 1958, Cecil award Arthritis Found.,

1967. Mem. AAAS, Nat. Assn. for Sci. Writers, Am. Soc. for Hosp. Mktg. and Pub. Relations, Assn. Am. Med. Colls. Home: Rockport, Mass. Died Jan. 16, 2009.

BANKS, ROBERT SHERWOOD, lawyer; b. Newark, Mar. 28, 1934; s. Howard Douglas and Amelia Violet (Del Bagno) B.; m. Judith Lee Henry; children— Teri, William; children by previous marriage— Robert, Paul, Stephen, Roger, Gregory, Catherine. AB, Cornell U., 1956, LL.B., 1958. Bar: N.J. 1959, N.Y. 1968. Practice law, Newark, 1958-61; atty. E.I. duPont, Wilmington, Del., 1961-67; with Xerox Corp., Stamford, Conn., 1967-88, v.p., gen. counsel, 1975-88; sr. counsel Latham & Watkins, NYC, 1988-89; gen. counsel Keystone Holdings, 1989-92. Bd. dirs. Cornell U. Found.; mem. panel of mediators, neutral advisors Ctr. for Pub. Resources. Mem. adv. coun. Cornell Law Sch.; past trustee U.S. Supreme Ct. Hist. Soc.; past bd. dirs. Ctr. for Pub. Resources. Mem. ABA, N.Y. Bar Assn., Am. Arbitration Assn. (panel arbitrators), Am. Judicature Soc. (exec. com., bd. dirs., pres. 1989-91), Cornell Law Assn., Am. Corp. Counsel Assn. (bd. dirs., chmn. 1982-83), Atlantic Athletic Club. Home: Poway, Calif. Died Aug. 17, 2009.

BANNISTER, WALTER S., land development and housing company executive; b. Winnipeg, Man., Can., Dec. 24, 1922; s. Walter and Adeline Ellen B.; m. Margery Jean Anderson, June 12, 1942; children: Bruce, Judith, Eric, Neal. BS in Mining Engring, Mich. Technol. U., 1947. Various mine engring. mgmt. positions, 1947-63; v.p. prodn. Inland Cement Industries Ltd., 1963-70, pres., chief exec. officer, 1973-77; pres., gen. mgr. Argentine Portland Cement, Buenos Aires, 1970-73; exec. v.p. Genstar Ltd. (now Genstar Corp.), San Francisco, from 1977; pres. Genstar Devel. Inc., San Francisco, from 1978. Served to capt. Canadian Army, 1942-45. Mem. Assn. Profl. Engrs. Alta. Clubs: Engineers (San Francisco); Peninsula Golf and Country (San Mateo, Calif.). Died Mar. 20, 2009.

BANTLE, LOUIS FRANCIS, retired tobacco company executive; b. Bridgeport, Conn., Nov. 22, 1928; s. Louis A. and Marie E. (Daisenberger) B.; m. Virginia Clark, Jan. 20, 1961; children: Robert C., Terri Ann. BS, Syracuse U., NY, 1951. V.p. US Tobacco Co., Greenwich, Conn., 1966-73, chmn., pres., 1973-85, chmn., CEO, 1985-89, chmn., pres., CEO, 1989—93. Bd. dirs. US Tobacco Co., 1967-93 Mem. Statue of Liberty-Ellis Island Com.; trustee Syracuse U., Fairfield U. Served to capt. USMC, 1951-53; founder Internat. Inst. for Alcohol Edn. & Training, 1996-2010 Decorated Knight of the North Star Sweden, 1976; recipient Lettermen of Distinction award U. Syracuse, 1986, Regional Plan Assn. award, 1986; named to Hall of Fame, Nat. Assn. Tobacco Distbrs., 1980; recipient Good Scout award Greater N.Y. Couns. Boy Scouts America, 1988. Mem.: Winged Foot Golf Club, Wee Burn Country, Blind Brook Club. Republican. Roman Catholic. Home: Greenwich, Conn. Died Oct. 10, 2010.

BANTON, JAMES FOWLER, manufacturing executive; b. Chgo., May 29, 1937; s. Fowler Boyton and Margaret Collin (Gilruth) Banton; m. Susan Mary Abendroth, Sept. 1, 1966; children: James Andrew, Pembrook Collin, Bridget Gilruth. BS in Acctg., U. Ill., Champaign, 1959; MS in Engring., Ill. Inst. Tech., 1963. Mgr. project control Automatic Elec. Co. Subs. Gen. Telephone & Electronics, Northlake, Ill., 1961—64, program dir. ops. analysis, 1964—68; cons. mgr. Rexnord, Inc., Milw., 1968—79; v.p. ops. Agro Indsl. Group, Blount, Inc., Montgomery, Ala., 1979—81; pres. George A. Rolfes Co., Des Moines, from 1981. Dir. G.A. Rolfes Co., Rolfes Internat., Rolfes Can., LBI/Farmrite, Rolfes Agro S.A. de C.V.; lectr. U. Wis., 1966—72; guest lectr. Harvard U., 1973—76. Contbr. articles to profl. jours. Mem. Brookfield Parks & Recreation Commn., Wis., 1975—79, chmn., 1977—79; alderman Fourth Dist., Brookfield, 1978—79. With Army N.G., 1955—63. Mem.: Ops. Rsch. Soc. America (chmn. chpt. 1965—66, nat. publs. com. 1966—73, nat. meetings com. 1968—77, chmn. joint nat. meetings com. 1973—75, chmn. 1973—76, chmn. 43d nat. meeting), Inst. Mgmt. Scis. (chmn. Milw. chpt. 1965—66, nat. v.p. meetings 1977), Des Moines, Bohemian, Wakonda Country. Died Mar. 2, 2009.

BARAL, JACOB, dermatologist, pediatrician; b. Cracow, Poland, July 24, 1935; MBBS, U. Sydney, Australia, 1959. Diplomate Am. Bd. Dermatology, Am. Bd. Pediatrics. Jr. resident Bankstwon Dist. Hosp., Sydney, 1960-61; resident in pathology Royal Alexandra Hosp. for Children, Sydney, 1961-62; asst. resident in pediatrics The Babies' Hosp., Columbia Presbyn. Med. Ctr., NYC, 1962-64; med. dir. outpatient dept. Harlem Hosp., NYC, 1963; jr. rsch. fellow children's med. rsch. found. Royal Alexandra Hosp. for Children, Sydney, Australia, 1965-67; sr. resident in pediatrics, spl. fellow in pediatrics Roosevelt Hosp., NYC, 1976-77; dir. pediatric dermatology, fellow in dermatology Met. Hosp., NYC, 1977-79; fellow in dermatol. surgery NYU, NYC, 1980; clin. instr. pediatrics and dermatology Mt. Sinai Med. Sch., NYC, from 1980; asst. clin. prof. depts. pediatrics and dermatology Mt. Sinai Sch. Medicine, NYC, from 1987, asst. attending in dermatology and pediatrics, from 1987. Contbr. articles to profl. jours. Mem. Am. Acad. Dermatology, Am. Acad. Pediatrics, Am. Soc. Dermat. Surgery, Soc. Pediatric Dermatology, Dermatologic Soc. Greater N.Y., N.Y. County Med. Soc. Home: New York, NY. Died Apr. 30, 2010.

BARASCH, CLARENCE SYLVAN, lawyer; b. NYC, May 20, 1912; s. Morris and Bertha Lydia (Herschdorfer) B.; m. Naomi Bosniak, July 1, 1957; children: Lionel, Jonathan. AB, Columbia U., 1933, JD, 1935. Bar: N.Y. 1936, U.S. Dist. Ct. (so., ea. and no. dists.) N.Y. 1936, U.S. Ct. Appeals (2d cir.) 1936. Pvt. practice, NYC, 1935—. Lectr. law of real estate brokerage at various real estate bds.; faculty of N.Y. Real Estate Bd. on courses for lic. renewals required by the Dept. of State of N.Y.; chmn. Columbia U. Law Sch. Class of 1935 Ann. Fund 1965—, Columbia Coll. Class of 1933 Ann. Fund, 1977-79; decade chmn. Columbia Coll. Ann. Fund; outside counsel columns, N.Y. Law Jour., 1966-. Author: (with Elliot L. Biskind) The Law of Real Estate Brokers, 1969; also cumulative supplements, 1971-83; contbr. articles to profl. jours. Mentor Mt. Sinai Sch. Medicine, NYC, 2006-08; mem. adv. bd. to chaplain Columbia U., N.Y.C., 1950-70; dir. Columbia-Barnard Hillel and predecessor, 1946—; pres. Jewish Campus Life Fund, Inc. Columbia U., 1970-87. Capt. Signal Corps AUS, 1942-46. Recipient cert. of appreciation Columbia U., 1981, medal for conspicuous svc. Columbia U., 1984, Vital Svcs. award, Rt Hon Gordon Brown Prime Minister Great Britain, 2009, Svc. medal, Queen Elizabeth II. Chmn.: Columbia Law Sch., Stoneagers, 2007-, Mem. ABA, N.Y. State Bar Assn. (real property com.), N.Y. County Lawyers Assn. (com. on real estate brokerage matters), Real Estate Bd. N.Y. (mem. legis and law cms., 1970—, arbitration panel 1989—, rev. ann. Diary and Manual of the Real Estate Bd. of N.Y. and author of summary of real estate brokerage law and related legal matters 1991—), Am. Arbitration Assn. (arbitration panel 1986—), Men's Club (bd. dirs. 1972-80), Columbia U. Law Sch. Alumni Assn. (bd. dirs. 1985-89). Jewish. Home: New York, NY. Died Aug. 31, 2010.

BARBARO, ANTHONY JOSEPH, chemist, educator, patent cons; b. NYC, July 26, 1926; s. Salvatore Barbaro and Dina Baio; m. Rose Borrelli Barbaro, Sept. 9, 1951; children: Valerie Jean, Pamela Gail. BS, Wagner Coll., 1950; student, Bklyn. Law Sch., 1951—52, Am. U. Law Sch., 1957—58; MS, Western Conn. State U., 1972; diploma, Southern Conn. State U., 1978; NSF, Walter Reed Army Inst. Rsch., Washington, 1972, Am. U., Rensselaer Poly., 1978. Rsch. chemist chemotherapy Am. Cyanamid Co., Stamford, Conn., 1950—51; chemist Amsco, Carteret, NJ, 1952—53; petroleum engr. Swan-Finch Oil Co., Hackensack, NJ, 1953; dye chemist Pfister Chem. Co., Ridgefield, NJ, 1954—55; explosives chemist Naval Propellant Factory, Indian Head, Md., 1955; patent examiner US Patent Office, Washington, 1955—59; patent adviser Nopco Chem. Co., 1959—60; title examiner Home Title Co., White Plains, NY, 1960—65; criminal investigator Dept. Treasury, NYC, 1965—66; chemist NYC, 1966; tchr. biology Dover Plains HS, NY, 1967—75, coord. phys. sci., 1975—81; adj. prof. Westchester CC, Valhalla, NY, from 1981; tchr. NY Hall Sci., NYC, 1981; chemist US Mil. Acad., West Point, NY, from 1986. Item writer chemistry NY State Regents; radiol. officer O.E.D.S., NY. Translator: Chem. Abstracts. Fellow: Am. Inst. Chemists; mem.: Am. Chem. Soc., NY Acad. Sci., Phi Delta Kappa. Achievements include patents for amides preparation. Home: Cross River, NY. Died Apr. 15, 2009.

BARD, ELLEN MARIE, former state legislator, retired small business owner; b. Mpls., Jan. 11, 1949; d. James Donald and Elaine (Frank) B.; m. Robert George Stiratelli, 1973; 1 child, Allison. BA, Pomona Coll., 1971; MS, Boston U., 1972, MIT, 1980. Rsch. analyst Mass. Parole Bd., Boston, 1972-78; dir. market rsch. Bay Banks, Inc., Boston, 1978-79; rsch. assoc. Internat. Coal Refining Co., 1980-82; owner, founder Techlink Corp., Jenkintown, Pa., 1982—2000; mem. Dist. 153 Pa. House of Reps., Harrisburg, 1994—2004; ret., 2004. Writer, spkr., TV prodr., host Bard Means Business. Twp. commr., Abington, Pa., 1990-94; bd. dirs. Montgomery County Lands Trust; founder, bd. dirs. Earth Right; founder Abington Trails Adv. Com.; mem. coun. of pres.'s assocs. Manor Jr. Coll.; mem. adv. bd. Abington Coll., Pa. State U. Named Legislator of Yr., Pa. Tax Collectors Assn., 1996, Policymaker Yr., Penn Future, 2002, Legislator of Yr., Pa. Ortho. Soc., 2002; recipient Cmty. Svc. award Willow Grove C. of C., 1996, Friend of Edn. award Abington Sch. Dist. Republican. Died Oct. 28, 2009.

BARGE, JEAN MARIE, minister; b. Milw., Nov. 23, 1927; d. Charles B. and Genevieve (Schul) Wright; divorced; children: Lynn, Marc (dec.), Karl. BA, U. Rochester, 1949; MA, SUNY, Albany, 1953; MDiv, Luth. Sch. Theology, Phila., 1981. Ordained to ministry Luth. Ch., 1981. Pastor Holy Cross Luth. Ch., Farnham, N.Y., from 1981. 1st v.p. local chpt. LWV, Princeton, N.J., 1958-62; bd. dirs. Community Concern, Derby, N.Y., 1981—, Luth. Theol. Sem., Phila., 1983-86. Home: Farnham, NY. Died Feb. 26, 2010.

BARITZ, LOREN, history professor; b. Chgo., Dec. 26, 1928; s. Joseph Harry and Helen (Garland) B.; m. Phyllis L. Handelsman, Dec. 26, 1948; children: Tony, Joseph. BA, Roosevelt U., 1953; MA, U. Wis., 1954, PhD, 1956. Asst. prof. history Wesleyan U., Middletown, Conn., 1956-62; assoc. prof. Roosevelt U., Chgo., 1962-63; prof. U. Rochester, 1963-69, chmn. dept. history, 1964-67; leading prof. SUNY, Albany, 1969-71; exec. v.p. Empire State Coll., exec. dir. univ. commn. on purposes and priorities, 1975-76; from exec. v.p. to provost SUNY, 1971-79; dir. N.Y. Inst. Humanities; prof. history NYU, 1979-80; provost, vice chancellor for acad. affairs U. Mass., Amherst, 1980-83, prof. history, 1980-91, prof. emeritus, from 1991. Vis. lectr. U. Wis.-Madison, 1959-60; cultural cons. to UNESCO, Paris, 1968-71; mgmt. cons. Balykchy Inst. of Bus. and Law, Kyrgyzstan, 1997, 99, Slovak U. of Tech., Bratislava, Slovak Republic, 1997, Comenius U., Bratislava, 1998. Author: City on a Hill, 1964, Servants of Power, 1960, Sources of the American Mind, 2 vols., 1966, The Culture of the Twenties, 1970, The American Left, 1971, Backfire, 1985, 98, The Good Life, 1989. Co-chmn. policy coun. rsch. and svc. Assembly Univ. Goals, Am. Acad. Arts and Scis., 1969-70; del. Dem. Nat. Conv., 1968; bd. govs. chmn. com. on acad. affairs Haifa U., 1975-92; mem. exec. bd. Nat. Com. for Labor, Israel, 1984-94; mgmt. cons. Am. Stock Exchange, 1994-95, 97. Rsch. Tng. fellow Social Sci. Rsch. Coun., 1955-56, grantee, 1960; grantee Am. Council Learned Socs., 1963. Home: Sunderland, Mass. Died Dec. 31, 2009.

BARKER, NORMAN, JR., retired bank executive; b. San Diego, July 30, 1922; s. Norman and Grace (Bolger) B.; m. Sue Keefe, June 27, 1947 (div.); children: Peter, Timothy, Michael, Beth; m. Susan Woods, Nov. 14, 1987. BA, U. Chgo., 1947, MBA, 1953. Asst. cashier Harris Trust & Savs. Bank, Chgo., 1947-55; credit mgr. Am. Can Co., 1955-57; with First Interstate Bank of Calif., LA, 1957-86, pres., 1968-71, chmn. bd., CEO L.A., 1973-86, ret. LA, 1986. Bd. dirs. Carter Hawley Hale Stores, Inc., First Interstate Bank Calif., Pacific Am. Income Shares, Inc., Pacific Telesis Group, Southern Calif. Edison Co., Am. Health Properties, Inc., TCW Convertible Securities Fund Inc., First Exec. Corp., SPI Pharmaceuticals, Inc. Trustee Occidental Coll., U. Chgo., W.M. Keck Found., Los Angeles County Mus. Art; bd. overseers Henry E. Huntington Library. Lt. USNR, 1944-46, 50-52. Mem. Automobile Club So. Calif. (bd. dirs.), Delta Kappa Epsilon. Died Sept. 11, 2010.

BARLOW, ROBERT BROWN, JR., neuroscientist, educator; b. Trenton, July 31, 1939; s. Robert Brown and Mary Frances (Jones) B.; m. Patricia Ann Dreyer, June 17, 1961; children— Jill, Kim, Jack. BA, Bowdoin Coll., 1961; PhD, Rockefeller U., 1967. Research assoc. Am. Optical Co., Southbridge, Mass., 1960; investigator Marine Biol. Labs., Woods Hole, Mass., summers 1964, 71-73, 76—; asst. prof. Syracuse U., 1967-71, assoc. prof., 1971-77, prof., from 1977. Contbr. articles to profl. jours. Grantee NIH, 1971—, NSF, 1978— Mem. AAAS, Optical Soc. Am., Assn. Research in Vision and Ophthalmology, Soc. Neurosci., Sigma Xi (faculty research award 1979) Home: Jamesville, NY. Died Dec. 24, 2009.

BARNARD, KURT, marketing executive; b. Hamburg, Germany, Apr. 16, 1927; s. León and Senta (Künstlinger) Barnard-Jeserski; m. Wendy Holly Love, Dec. 9, 1979; 1 child, Lance Jonathan. Student, NYU, 1948, N.Y. State U., 1953; grad., New Sch. for Social Research, 1957. N.Y. corr. European and Japanese bus. publs., 1957-60; dir. Latin Am., Far Eastern pub. relations Anglo-Affiliated Corp., NYC, 1955-60; mktg. dir. Am. Research Merchandising Inst., Chgo., 1960-67; founding exec. dir. Internat. Mass Retail Assn., NYC, 1967-69; exec. v.p. Internat. Mass Retailing Assn., NYC, 1969-74, pres., 1974-76; exec. dir. Fedn. Apparel Mfrs., NYC, 1976-86; launched Barnard's Retail Cons. Group and Barnard's Retail Mktg. Report, 1984. Launched Barnard's Retail Cons. Group and Barnard's Retail Mktg. Report, 1984 (now Barnard's Retail Trend Report); cons. on wage-price freeze to dir. U.S. Office Emergency Preparedness, 1971-72; condr. retailing seminars in Europe, U.S.; frequent forecaster and commentator on retailing and consumer spending issues on TV, Radio, including McNeil-Lehrer Newshour, CBS Evening News, NBC's Today Show, ABC's Good Morning Am. show, CNN, CNNfn, CNBC, Wall Street Journal Radio, Nat. Pub. Radio; organizer Nat. Loss Prevention Coun., 1972, Store Thieves and Their Impact, A Study, 1973; named mem. U.S. Govt. Industry Sector Adv. Com., 1978; mem. U.S. Govt. Exporters Adv. Com., 1979; chmn. bd. N.Y. Internat. Fashion Fair, 1980; leader nat. campaign against fair trade laws. Author: Cargo of Death, 1966, An Untapped Source of Store Profits, 1974, Picture of a Tragedy, 1974, How Chains Succeed With Non-Foods, 1974, Can Supermarkets Capture Non-Food Sales?, 1974, In Retailing: Future Shock is Now, 1975, Guidelines to Effective Marketing Strategies for Self-Service Retailers, 1975; co-author: Mass Merchandisers Guide to Sales and Expense Reporting, 1969, Marketing: Key to Retail Prosperity, 1985; contbr. articles to mags. and profl. jours. Recipient Disting. Service award U.S.O., 1965, Am. Soc. Assn. Execs. award, 1965; commd. Ky. col., 1975; DuPont Co. grantee, 1971-75 Mem. Nat. Assn. Bus. Economists, Mus. Modern Art. Died Nov. 7, 2009.

BARNARD, WALTHER M., geosciences educator; b. Hartford, Conn., May 30, 1937; s. Walter Monroe and Florence Elzada (Wheeler) B. BS, Trinity Coll., 1959; AM, Dartmouth Coll., 1961; PhD, Pa. State U., 1965. Asst. prof. dept. geology/geosciences SUNY, Fredonia, 1964-70, assoc. prof., 1970-77, prof., from 1977, acting chairperson, 1986-87, 2006, chairperson, 1987-97. Mem. affiliate faculty U. Hawaii, Hilo, 1995—; dir. NSF undergrad. rsch. programs, summers, 1975-80. Recipient grant-in-aid Research Found. of SUNY, 1964, 66, 69, 72, faculty research fellowship, summers, 1966, 70, 73; research grantee Research Corp., 1965, U.S. Dept. Energy, 1975-77; Lake Erie Environ. Studies Research fellowship SUNY, Fredonia, summers, 1972-75, 78. Mem. AAAS, AAUP, Am. Geophys. Union, Am. Inst. Chemists, ASTM, Geochem. Soc., Geochem. Soc. Japan, Geol. Assn. Can., Geol. Soc. Am., Internat. Assn. Geochemistry and Cosmochemistry, Am. Meteorol. Soc., Nat. Earth Sci. Tchrs. Assn., Internat. Assn. Theoretical and Applied Limnology, mineral socs. Gt. Brit., Can., Am., Nat. Assn. Geology Tchrs., Internat. Assn. Gt. Lakes Research, N.Y. Acad. Scis., Soc. Applied Spectroscopy, Soc. Environ. Geochemistry and Health, Am. Chem. Soc., Am. Soc. Agronomy, Crop Sci. Soc. Am., Internat., Am., Can. socs. soil sci., Fedn. Am. Scientists, Nat. Sci. Tchrs. Assn., Soc. Coll. Sci. Tchrs., Nat. Ground Water Assn., Explorers Club, N.Y. State Geol. Assn. (pres. 1990), Sigma Xi. Author: Kaho'olawe, 1996; editor: Mauna Loa—A Source Book: Historical Eruptions and Exploration, From 1778-1907, Vol. 1, 1990, The Early HVO and Jaggar Yrs. (1912-40), Vol. 2, 1991, The Post-Jaggar Yrs. (1940-91), Vol. 3, 1992, Mauna Loa—A Potpourri of Anecdotes, 1996. Home: Fredonia, NY. Died Jan. 1, 2010.

BARNES, JOHN A., fast food company executive; b. Racine, Wis., Apr. 7, 1926; s. George K. and Katherine (Richter) B.; m. Ellen Rasmussen, Sept. 17, 1948; children— Allen, Susan, Janet BS, U. Wis., Madison. Food scientist Continental Can Co., Chgo., 1950-52; from food scientist to mgr. Pillsbury Co., Mpls., 1952-60, dir. food lab., 1960-70, McDonald Corp., Chgo., 1974-77; dir. research and devel. Burger King, Miami,

Fla., 1970-74, v.p. to sr. v.p., from 1977. Patentee dehydrated potato flake process, 1964 Served with USN, 1944-46 Fellow Inst. Food Technologists Republican. Lutheran. Died Jan. 26, 2009.

BARNES, THOMAS GARDEN, law educator; b. 1930; AB, Harvard U., 1952; DPhil, Oxford U., 1955. From asst. prof. to assoc. prof. Lycoming Coll., Williamsport, Pa., 1956-60; from lectr. to prof. history U. Calif., Berkeley, 1960—2010, humanities rsch. prof., 1971-72, prof. history & law, 1974—2006, co-chmn. Canadian studies program, 1982—2006, co-dir. Canadian studies program, 2006—10, emeritus prof. history and law, 2006—10. Dir. legal history project Am. Bar Found., 1965-86; com. mem. on ct. records 9th Cir. Ct. Author: Somerset 1625-1640: A County's Government During the Personal Rule, 1961, List and Index to Star Chamber Procs., James I, 3 vols., 1975, Lawes and Libertyes of Massachusetts, 1975, Hastings College of Law: The First Century, 1978; Shaping the Common Law" From Glanvill to Hale, 2008mem. editl. bd. Gryphon Legal Classics Libr.; editor Pub. Record Office. Huntington Libr. fellow, 1960, Am. Coun. Learned Socs. fellow, 1962-63, John Simon Guggenheim Found. fellow, 1970-71. Fellow Royal Hist. Soc.; mem. Selden Soc. (councillor, state corr.), Assn. Canadian Studies (pres. 2001-03, past pres., 2003-05). Died Mar. 9, 2010.

BARNESS, AMNON SHEMAYA, financial service executive; b. Israel, Oct. 16, 1924; s. Nahum and Lea (Muhlmann) B.; m. Caren Heller, 1978; children: Rena Barness Lahav, Dalia Barness Kempler, Daniel, Jordan. BA, Am. U. Cairo, 1947; MA, Syracuse U., 1950; PhD (hon.), Stonehill Coll., 1974. Pres. Trans-Internat. Mgmt. Corp., from 1976; founder, pres., chmn. bd. Daylin Inc. (now subs. W.R. Grace Co.); chmn. bd. Handy Dan Home Improvement Centers, Inc. (now subs. W.R. Grace Co.), Commerce, Calif., from 1972; gen. ptnr. Adam Assocs., Beverly Hills, Calif., from 1965; sr. ptnr. Adam Fin. Corp., from 1966; chmn. exec. com., dir. Pharma-Control Corp. (OTC), Englewood Cliffs, N.J., 1982-85. Bd. dirs. Serpro S.A., Unico Mortgage Bank, Tel Aviv, Israel, Bourguet de Clausade Traders, Paris, JOBA B.V., Amsterdam; spl. advisor Swiss Hotel Mgmt. Sch., Les Roches, Marbella, Spain. Founder, chmn. Fund Higher Edn.; founder, pres. Fund for Job Corp. Grads., 1965; gen. chmn. L.A. com., State of Israel Bonds campaign, 1968-71, 73-74; pres. Juvenile Opportunities Endeavor Found., 1974-75; v.p. Brandeis Inst., 1964-70; bd. dirs. Temple Sinai, Los Angeles, 1968-72; bd. govs. Weizman Inst. Sci., 1970—; Andean Pact countries rep. Mecaform, Paris, Am. Med. Internat., 1977-82; founder, bd. dirs. European Found. for Scis., Arts, and Culture, 1982-85; active Lyndon Johnson Youth Opportunity Campaign Coun., 1965. Decorated knight comdr. merit Equestrian Order, Holy Sepulcher of Jerusalem, Israel Prime Minister's medal, others; honored Inst. Pasteur-Weizmann, Paris, 1985; recipient award Army, Navy and Air Force of Ecuador, 1978; hon. fellow Tel-Aviv U., 1996. Home: Palm Beach, Fla. Died Dec. 12, 2009.

BARNETT, THOMAS BUCHANAN, physician, medical educator; b. Lewisburg, Tenn., May 27, 1919; s. William Lee and Erma (Halbert) B.; m. Anne Stone Daughtry, Sept. 20, 1944; children: William Buchanan, Richard Kirkpatrick, Susan Daughtry Barnett Norton. BA, U. Tenn., 1944; MD, U. Rochester, 1949. Diplomate Am. Bd. Internal Medicine. Instr. toxicology U. Rochester (N.Y.), 1945-47; instr. medicine U. N.C., Chapel Hill, 1952-54, head div. pulmonary medicine, 1954-75, asst. prof. medicine, 1954-58, assoc. prof. medicine, 1958-64, prof. medicine, 1964-90; Bonner Disting. prof. Bonner Found. U. N.C., 1981-90, prof. emeritus, from 1990. Attending physician, dir. pulmonary medicine N.C. Meml. Hosp. and Gravely Hosp., Chapel Hill, 1954-75; mem. U. N.C. Faculty Council Agenda Com., Chapel Hill, 1972-73; vis. scientist August Krogh Inst. U. Copenhagen, Denmark, 1975-76, 82-83; chmn. faculty com. advisor to Chancellor U. N.C., 1984. Contbr. articles to profl. jours. Active mem. various orgns. involved in conservation of natural resources, 1985—; bd. dirs. Bot. Garden Found., N.C., 1988-94, exec. com., 1991-94. Recipient Spl. Recognition award N.C. Bot. Garden and Found., 1991; Spl. Rsch. fellow NIH and Commonwealth Fund U. Copenhagen, Denmark, 1966-67. Fellow ACP; mem. Am. Physiol. Soc., Am. Clin. and Climatol. Assn., Southern Soc. for Clin. Investigation, Am. Thoracic Soc., N.C. Thoracic Soc. (Disting. Svc. award 1989). Democrat. Avocations: nature study, nature photography, travel, brick masonry. Home: Chapel Hill, NC. Died May 1, 2010.

BARNS, JUSTINE, state legislator; b. Wilkes-Barre, Pa., Feb. 2, 1925; m. Jonathan Barnes, 1943 (dec.); children: Duane, Scott. Mem. Mich. Ho. of Reps., from 1983. Chmn. sr. citizens and retirement com.; mem. edn. com., mem. legis. retirement and pub. health com.; vice chmn. govt. ops. and pensions com. Mem. Westland City Charter Commn., 1964-66, v.p. Wayne County, 1981-83; active Westland City Coun., 1966-83, Wayne-Ford Civic League, United Fund Drive. Named Citizen of Yr., Ford Motor Co., 1967, Woman of Yr., City of Westland, 1975, Legislator of Yr., Mich. Assn. Chiefs of Police, 1983, Leader of Yr., YMCA, 1989. Mem. Westland Bus. and Profl. Women, Westland C. of C., Rotary. Democrat. Died Mar. 4, 2010.

BARONNER, ROBERT FRANCIS, banker; b. Hollidaysburg, Pa., June 5, 1926; s. Lawrence H. and Elizabeth M. (Maher) B.; m. Jane C. Fickes, Feb. 21, 1952; children: Rebecca Ann, Elizabeth Jane, Robert F. BS in Bus. Adminstrn., St. Francis Coll., Loretto, Pa., 1950. Field rep. Gen. Motors Acceptance Corp., Altoona, Pa., 1950-51; asst. bank examiners Pa. Dept. Banking, Pitts., 1951-54; asst. br. mgr. People Union Bank and Trust Co., N.A., McKeesport, Pa., 1954-59; v.p. Peoples Union Bank and Trust Co., N.A., McKeesport, Pa., 1960-67, exec. v.p., 1967-69; sr. v.p. Union Nat. Bank of Pitts., 1969-70, Kanawha Valley Bank, N.A. (now named One Valley Bank N.A.), Charleston, W.Va., 1971-73, exec. v.p., 1973-75, pres., chief exec. officer, from 1975, One Valley Bancorp of W.Va. Inc., Charleston, from 1981. Chmn. One Valley Bancorp of W. Va.; bd. dirs. Fed. Res. Bank of Richmond. Trustee U. Charleston, 1979-82; pres. Fund for Arts, Charleston, 1982-83; chmn. bd. trustees Charleston Area Med. Ctr., 1982—; trustee Healthnet Inc., 1985—. Served with USN, 1944-46, PTO. Mem.: Rotary-Charleston. Home: Charleston, W.Va. Died May 19, 2010.

BARR, JAMES MILTON, business consultant; b. Columbus, Ohio, Apr. 10, 1936; s. Harold Jacob and Dorothy Irene (Bircher) B.; m. Rosalind Lenore Carfagno; children: Michelle Diane Haase, Anthony Charles, Andrew James, Jennifer Irene. BA, U. Notre Dame, 1958. Sales rep. Service Bur. Corp., Washington, 1961-65, sales mgr. Indpls., 1966-67, product mgr. NYC, 1967-68, group mgr. Rochester, N.Y., 1968-72; v.p. NLT Computer Services Inc., Blue Bell, Pa., 1972-77, sr. v.p. Nashville, 1977-82, Endata Inc., Nashville, 1982-85; exec. v.p. Murray Ohio Mfr. Co., Brentwood, Tenn., 1985-87; chief operating officer MicroBilt Corp., Atlanta, 1987-88. 1st v.p. March of Dimes, Nashville, 1987. Served to lt. U.S. Army, 1959-61. Mem. Am. Mgmt. Assn., Sales and Mktg. Execs., Notre Dame Alumni Assn. (bd. dirs. Nashvile chpt. 1987), Sierra Club (bd. dirs. 1987—). Republican. Roman Catholic. Home: Naples, Fla. Died Jan. 1, 2009.

BARRACLOUGH, CHARLES ARTHUR, retired endocrinologist, educator; b. Vineland, NJ, July 13, 1926; s. Charles A. and Martha (Romain) B.; m. Eleanor Pauline Kolakowski, June 28, 1952; children: Janet, Patricia. BS, St. Joseph's Coll., 1947; MS, Rutgers U., 1952, PhD, 1953. Asst. prof. UCLA, 1959-61; spl. rsch. fellow Cambridge (Eng.) U., 1961-62; assoc. prof. U. Md., Balt., 1962-65, prof. physiology, 1965-93, dir. Ctr. Studies Reproduction, 1985-93, dir. emeritus, prof. emeritus, from 1993. Reproduction biology study sec. NIH, Bethesda, 1967-69, 70-74. Contbr. over 125 articles to profl. jours., 25 chpts. to books. Recipient Rsch. award Soc. Study Reproduction, 1984, Carl Hartman award 1990. Fellow AAAS; mem. Endocrine Soc. (editorial bd. 1965-72), Soc. Neurosci., Soc. Exptl. Biology and Medicine (editorial bd. 1974-87), Am. Physiol. Soc. (editorial bd. 1979-83). Research on regulation by the brain of reproduction in females. Home: Levittown, Pa. Died Apr. 19, 2009.

BARRATT, MICHAEL SCOTT, architect; b. Elmhurst, Ill., Apr. 21, 1956; s. George Albert and Norma Jean (Travelute) B.; m. Carrie Joan Rebora, Apr. 27, 1985; 1 child, Anna Dorothy. BA in History of Architecture, U. Ill., 1982, BArch, 1982; MArch, Yale U., 1984. Architect Murphy/Jahn, Chgo., 1982, Edward Larrabee Barnes/John M.Y. Lee Archs., NYC, 1984-93, John M.Y. Lee/Michael Timchula Archs., NYC, 1993-94, Michael Scott Barratt Arch., NYC, 1994-95, Michael Scott Barratt Design Workshop, NYC, from 1994, HLW Internat., NYC, from 1995. Prin. works include Allen Libr., Seattle, Thurgood Marshall Fed. Judiciary Bldg., Washington. Mem. AIA. Home: New York, NY. Died Nov. 25, 2009.

BARRER, ROGER AARON, retail executive; b. NYC, June 5, 1926; s. Aaron and Eva (Dranow) B.; children— Richard, Robert. BS, NYU, 1948, MS, 1950. Pres. Alexander's Inc., NYC, from 1948, dir., from 1969. Served with USAAF, 1944-46, ETO Named Boy Scout of Yr., Boy Scouts Am., 1973 Avocations: tennis; horseback riding. Died Nov. 27, 2009.

BARRETO, EVANGELINA C., banker; b. Cuba, July 16, 1942; came to U.S., 1961; d. Evangelio and Consuelo (Hernandez) Jiminez; m. Francisco Barreto, July 24, 1961; children— Francisco III, Eva G. B.S., Havana U., Cuba, 1961; B.S., Barry U., Miami, Fla., 1984. Ops. officer Glendale Fed. Bank, Miami Lakes, Fla., 1979-80, br. mgr., Hialeah, Fla., 1980-81, asst. v.p., North Miami Beach, Fla., 1981-83, v.p., 1983—; lectr. Fla. U. Contbr. articles to newspapers and mags. Coordinator Glendale United Way, 1983-86; team capt. Dade County March of Dimes, 1983-86; dir. community adv. bd. Metro Police, North Dade, 1985-86; dir. St. Bernadette Ch., 1983-86. Named Future Bus. Leader of Am., Pompano Sch. Bd., 1980. Mem. North Dade C. of C. (v.p. 1985-86, recipient awards 1985, 86), Toastmasters (pres. 1982-84), Bankers Forum (chmn. 1983-86), South Fla. Soc. Br. Mgrs., Hialeah and North Miami Beach C. of C., Nat. Hispanic Assembly, PAC. Home: Fort Lauderdale, Fla. Died June 9, 2009.

BARRETT, ROGER WATSON, lawyer; b. Chgo., June 26, 1915; s. Oliver R. and Pauline S. B.; m. Nancy N. Braun, June 20, 1940; children— Victoria Barrett Bell, Holly, Oliver. AB, Princeton U., 1937; JD, Northwestern U., 1940. Bar: Ill. 1940. Mem. firm Poppenhusen, Johnson, Thompson & Raymond, Chgo., 1940-43; 45-50; charge documentary evidence Nuremberg Trial, 1944-45; regional counsel Econ. Stablzn. Agy., Chgo., 1951-52; ptnr. Mayer, Brown & Platt, Chgo., 1952-91, of counsel, from 1991. Life trustee Mus. Contemporary Art, Chgo. With AUS, 1943-45. Mem. ABA, Ill. Bar Assn., Chgo. Bar Assn., Am. Coll. Trial Lawyers, Indian Hill Club (Winnetka), Old Elm Club, Commonwealth Club (Chgo.), Caxton Club (Chgo.). Home: Palm Desert, Calif. Died Jan. 5, 2010.

BARRIE, JOHN PAUL, lawyer, educator; b. Burbank, Calif., Oct. 7, 1947; s. John and Virginia (Feagans) Barrie; m. Betsy Smith; children: Sean, Tyler. AB in Pol. Sci., UCLA, 1969; JD, U. Calif., San Francisco, 1972; LLM in Tax, NYU, 1973. Bar: Calif. 1972, DC 1975, Mo. 1977, NY 2001. Atty. advisor to judge U.S. Tax Ct., Washington, 1973-75; atty. office of gen. counsel Renegotiation Bd., Washington, 1975-77; assoc. Lewis & Rice, St. Louis, 1977-82, ptnr., 1982-86, Gallop, Johnson & Neuman, St. Louis, 1986-93, Bryan Cave L.L.P., St. Louis, 1993-98, Washington and NYC, from 1998. Adj. prof. Washington U. Sch. Law, St. Louis, 1979—99, Georgetown Law Ctr., from 1999, NY Law Sch., from 2006; past mem. IRS Dist. Dir.'s Liaison Group, Mo. Dept. Rev. Adv. Group, past chmn. Editor: Mo. Bar Ct. and CLE Bull.; editl. advisor Jour. Multistate Taxation; contbr. articles to profl. jours. Commr. Commn. Bot. Garden Subdistrict, St. Louis, 1989—99. Recipient Dir.'s award, IRS, 1993. Fellow: St. Louis Internat. Tax Group, St. Louis Corp. Tax Group (chmn.), St. Louis Tax Lawyers Group (past chmn.), Am. Coll. Tax Counsel, Exec. Inst. Advanced Study Washington U.; mem.: ABA (mem. coun. from 2007, tax sect., past chmn. com. govtl. submissions, past chmn. com. affiliated corps.), Nat. Assn. State Bar Tax Sects. (chmn. 1983—84), Bar Assn. Met. St. Louis (tax sect.), Am. Tax Policy Inst. (life; sponsor), NY Bar Assn. (tax sect.), DC Bar Assn. (tax sec., mem. steering com. from 2001, chmn. 2006—07), Calif. Bar Assn. (tax sect.), Mo. Bar Assn. (tax sect., past chmn. tax com., Pres.'s award 1983), NY Athletic Club, City Club (Washington), Noonday Club. Episcopalian. Home: New York, NY. Died Jan. 12, 2010.

BARRY, DONALD THOMAS (DON BARRY), writer; b. Newark, Apr. 29, 1927; s. Laurence A. and Margaret (Lynch) B.; m. Sylvia Gustavson, 1952; children: Laura, David, Patricia, Barbara, John, Susan, James. BS in Journalism, L.I. U., 1952; postgrad., Cornell U., 1981-82. Reporter Wellsville (N.Y.) Reporter, 1952; reporter, columnist Bradford (Pa.) Era, 1953-56; reporter Tonawanda News, North Tonawanda, N.Y., 1956-57; reporter, editor Buffalo Courier-Express, 1958-82; editor Buffalo Bus. Jour., 1984-85; freelance writer, playwright Buffalo, from 1986. Editor: Angler's Almanac, 1963; playwright The Pipsqueaks, 1996, Ladybug, 1996, Nightwater, 1996. With USN, 1944-46. Recipient numerous local, state and regional awards for journalism. Mem. Soc. Profl. Journalists, Dramatists Guild, Drama League, Authors League Am., Scriptores, Profl. Picture Framers Assn., Soc. Gilders, Am. Legion. Republican. Roman Catholic. Avocations: picture framing, photography, fishing. Died Jan. 8, 2009.

BARRY, GENE, actor; b. NYC, June 14, 1921; s. Martin and Eva Klass; m. Betty Claire Kalb, Oct. 22, 1944 (dec. Jan. 31, 2003); children: Michael Lewis, Fredric James, Elizabeth. Actor:(Broadway plays) Rosalinda, 1942, Movers, 1945, The Would Be Gentleman, Catherine Was Great, 1944, The Perfect Setup, 1962, La Cage Aux Folles (nominee Tony award), 1983; (films) The War of the Worlds, 1953, Soldier of Fortune, 1955, Thunder Road, 1958, Houston Story, 1958, China Gate, 1957, 27th Day, 1957, Maroc 7, 1968, War of the Worlds, 2005; (TV series) Bat Masterson, 1959-61, Burke's Law, 1963-66, 94-95, The Name of the Game, 1968-71, The Adventurer, 1972-73; (TV movies) Prescription Murder, 1968, Istanbul Express, 1968, Do You Take This Stranger, 1971, Aspen, 1977, A Cry for Love, 1980, The Girl, the Gold Watch and Dynamite, 1981, The Adventures of Nelly Bly, 1981, Perry Mason: The Case of the Lost Cove, 1987, Turn Back the Clock, 1989, The Gambler Returns: The Luck of the Draw, 1991, These Old Broads, 2001 Recipient Golden Globe award, 1964, ADL Man of Yr. award, 1986. Mem. Screen Actors Guild (past 1st v.p.) Home: Topanga, Calif. Died Dec. 9, 2009.

BARTLETT, ARTHUR EUGENE, real estate company executive; b. Glens Falls, NY, Nov. 26, 1933; s. Raymond Ernest and Thelma (Williams) Bartlett; m. Collette R. Bartlett, Jan. 9, 1955 (dec. 2002); 1 child, Stacy Lynn; m. Nancy Sanders Bartlett, Feb. 12, 2005. Sales mgr. Forest E. Olson, Inc., 1960-64; co-founder, v.p. Four Star Realty, Inc., Santa Ana, Calif., 1964-71, v.p., sec., 1964-71; founder, pres. Comps, Inc., Tustin, Calif., 1971-81; co-founder, chmn., pres., CEO Century 21 Real Estate Corp., Tustin, 1980—2010; pres. Larwin Sq. LLC Shopping Ctr, Tustin, 1979—2002. Chmn. bd. dirs. United Western Med. Ctrs., 1981—87. Mem.: Internat. Franchise Assn. (v.p., bd. dirs. 1975—80, Hall of Fame 1987), Camp Able, Hon. Deputy Sheriff Assn., Masons. Died Dec. 31, 2009.

BARTLETT, CLIFFORD ADAMS, JR., lawyer; b. NYC, Mar. 17, 1937; s. Clifford Adams and Frances (Burke) B.; m. Eileen Marie McCarthy; children: Elizabeth, Kathleen, Clifford III, Christopher, Charles, Eileen, Kevin, Jamison. BA, St. Francis Coll., NYC, 1959; JD, St. John's U., NYC, 1962. Bar: N.Y. 1963, U.S. Dist. Ct. (so. dist.) N.Y. 1964, U.S. Supreme Ct. 1966. Ptnr. Bartlett, McDonough, Bastone & Monaghan, Mineola, NY, from 1992. Mem. faculty Nassau Acad. Law, Mineola, N.Y. & N.Y.C., 1984—. Mem. ABA, N.Y. State Bar Assn., Nassau County Bar Assn., Nassau-Suffolk Trial Lawyers Assn., Suffolk County Bar Assn. Avocations: golf, skiing, swimming. Home: Upper Brookville, NY. Died Nov. 10, 2009.

BARTLEY, MATTHEW B., former insurance company executive; b. Oct. 28, 1956; BA, U. Pa.; MA, Yale U.; JD, Columbia U. Tax atty. Morgan, Lewis and Bockius, Phila.; v.p. taxes Engelhard Corp.; sr. internat. treasury and tax positions PepsiCo, Inc.; v.p., treas. Marsh & McLennan Companies, Inc., 2001—06, exec. v.p., CFO, 2006—08. Died Jan. 26, 2010.

BARTOLACCI, GUIDO JAMESS, retail company executive; b. Phillipsburg, NJ, May 20, 1929; s. Augusto and Elvira Bartolacci; m. Margaret Lesko, June 21, 1952. Vice-chmn., chief oper. officer Laneco, Inc., Palmer, Pa. Avocations: boating, bowling. Died Sept. 5, 2009.

BASHKOW, THEODORE ROBERT, electrical engineering consultant, former educator; b. St. Louis, Nov. 16, 1921; s. Maurice Louis and Caroline (Davidson) B.; m. Delphina Brownlee, Sept. 12, 1960; 1 stepdau., Lynn Michele. BS, Washington U., St. Louis, 1943; MS, Stanford U., 1947, PhD, 1950. Mem. tech. staff David Sarnoff Research Labs., RCA, 1950-52, Bell Telephone Labs., 1952-58; mem. faculty Columbia U., 1958-91, prof. elec. engring., 1967-79, prof.

computer sci., 1979-91, chmn. dept. elec. engring., 1968-71, mgr. Sch. Engring. Computing Center, 1961-64; ret., 1991. Cons. to industry, 1959—; dir. MSI Inc., Woodside, N.Y., 1961—; chmn. tech. program 1968 Spring Joint Computer Conf.; chmn. sci. sect. Internat. Fedn. Info. Processing Congress, 1965 Author articles, chpts. in books. Served to 1st lt. USAAF, 1943-45. Mem. Assn. Computing Machinery, IEEE, Profl. Group Circuit Theory and Electronic Computers. Home: Katonah, NY. Died Dec. 23, 2009.

BASKERVILLE, CHARLES ALEXANDER, geologist, educator; b. Jamaica, NY, Aug. 19, 1928; s. Charles H. and Annie M. (Allen) Baskerville; children: Mark Dana, Shawn Allison, Charles Morris, Thomas Marshall. BS, CCNY, 1953; MS, NYU, 1958, PhD, 1965. Cert. profl. geologist Maine. Asst. civil engr. N.Y. State Dept. Transp., Babylon, 1953-66; prof. engring. geology CUNY, NYC, 1966-79, dean sch. of gen. studies, 1970-79, prof. emeritus, from 1979; project rsch. geologist U.S. Geol. Survey, 1979-90; dept. chmn. Ctrl. Conn. State U., New Britain, 1992-94, prof. geology, 1990—2006; prof. emeritus, from 2006. Commonwealth vis. prof. George Mason U., Fairfax, Va., 1987-89; mem. U.S. Nat. Com. on Tunnelling Tech., NRC, chmn. subcom. on edn. and tng.; mem. Am. del Internat. Tunnelling Assn. to Internat. Colloquim of Tunnelling and Underground Works, Beijing, People's Republic of China, 1984; geol. cons. N.Y.C. Dept. Environ. Protection Water Tunnel #3; guest lectr. various colls., 1964—; geol. program evaluator for colls. seeking continued mid. states accreditation. Author numerous sci. papers. Mem. com. for minority participation in the geoscis. U.S. Dept. Interior, 1972-75; panelist Grad. Fellowship Program NRC; chmn. Minority Grad. Fellowship Program, 1979-80; mem. com. of visitors for edn. and human resources program divsn. earth scis. NSF, 1991; mem. N.Y. State Low Level Radioactive Waste Com. NAS, 1994-96. Recipient Founders Day award N.Y. U., 1966, 125th Anniversary medal The City Coll., 1973, award for excellence in engring. geology Nat. Consortium Black Profl. Devel., 1978, Recognition award Nat. Assn. Black Geologists and Geophysicists, 1998. Fellow Geol. Soc. Am. (sr., com. on minorities in geoscis., chmn. com. on coms. 1989), N.Y. Acad. Scis., Geol. Soc. Washington, Am. Inst. Profl. Geologists, Assn. Engring. Geologists (rep. to nat. bd. dirs. 1973-74, chmn. N.Y.-Phila. sect. 1973-74), Internat. Assn. Engring. Geology, Yellowstone-Bighorn Rsch. Assn., Sigma Xi. Home: Bronx, NY. Died Sept. 18, 2009.

BASSIN, JULES, foreign service officer; b. NYC, Apr. 16, 1914; s. Abe and Bessie (Brooks) B.; m. Beatrice M. Kellner, Dec. 25, 1938; children: Arthur Jay, Nelson Jay. BS, CCNY, 1936; JD, N.Y.U., 1938; student, Criminal Investigation Sch., U.S. Army, 1943, Security Intelligence Sch., 1944, Mil. Govt. Sch., U. Va., 1944, Far East Civil Affairs, Harvard, 1945; grad., Armed Forces Staff Coll., 1960. Bar: N.Y. bar 1939. Dir. law div. Gen. Hdqrs., Supreme Comdr. Allied Powers, Tokyo, Japan, 1945-51; legal attache Am. embassy, Tokyo, 1951-56; also spl. asst. to ambassador for politico-mil. affairs; spl. asst. to ambassador for mut. security affairs Am. Embassy, Karachi, 1956-59; State Dept. faculty adviser Armed Forces Staff Coll., Norfolk, Va., 1960-62; chief titles and rank br. Dept. State, 1962-63, chief functional assignments br., 1963-65, dir. functional personnel program, 1965-67, spl. asst. to dep. undersec. state for adminstrn., 1967-69, exec. sec. Bd. Fgn. Service, 1967-69; dep. rep. of U.S. to European office UN and other internat. orgns.; also dep. chief U.S. mission with personal rank of minister, Geneva, Switzerland, 1969-74; cons. on refugee and migration affairs Dept. State, from 1974; cons. USIA, 1975-76. Served from 2d lt. to col., Judge Adv. Gen. Corps. AUS, 1942-46; col. Res. Mem. Am. Fgn. Service Assn. Clubs: American Internat. (Geneva) (exec. com.). Home: Washington, DC. Died Jan. 23, 2009.

BATES, CAROL HENRY, musicologist, educator; b. Chgo., Aug. 31, 1944; d. Carl F.H. and Helga Irmgard (Bender) Henry; m. William Henry Bates, 1971; 1 child, Stephen Henry. MusB in Piano, Wheaton Coll., Ill., 1965; MusM in Musicology, Ind. U., 1968, PhD in Musicology, 1978. Asst. prof. Houghton Coll., NY, 1969—71. Vis. instr. U. West Fla., Pensacola, 1972; tchg. assoc. U. SC, Columbia, 1978—95; gen. editor Early Keyboard Jour., 2000—05. Editor: Elisabeth-Claude Jacquet de la Guerre: Pieces de clavecin, 1986, Triosonaten fur 2 Violinen und Basso Continue, 1993—95, Sonates pour le viollon et pour le clavecin, 1998—2002; contbr. articles to profl. jours. and publs., chapters to books. Fellowship, Ind. U., 1968—69, Rsch. grant, 1973, Travel grant, NEH, 1985, ACLS, 1988, Opening Presentation Art, Internat. Conf. Barque & Classical Music Durham, Eng., 1988. Mem.: Coll. Music Soc. (mem. Music Women Gender com. 1997—99), Southeastern Hist. Keyboard Soc. (exec. bd. 1987—88, sec. 1988—90, exec. bd. 1998—2001), Am. Musicological Soc. (sec. Southeast Chpt. 1989—90), Pi Kappa Lambda, Wheaton Coll. Scholastic Honor Soc. Home: Columbia, SC. Died Aug. 3, 2010.

BATHER, PAUL, state representative; b. June 30, 1947; MBA, U.Louisville; MSW, CUNY; degree in Liberal Arts, Fairfield U. Pres., CEO Bather Group; mem. Ky. Ho. of Reps., from 2000. Recipient Lena Coleman award, G.K. Offult/C. Eubank Tucker award, NAACP Freedom award, Stand UP award, NAACP Cmty Svc. award. Democrat. Home: San Antonio, Tex. Died Feb. 11, 2009.

BATTLE, WILLIAM ROBERT (BOB BATTLE), retired publishing executive; b. Nolensville, Tenn., Dec. 25, 1927; s. William Robert and Cleo (Smith) B.; m. Elizabeth Ogilvie, Dec. 23, 1948; children: Valerie Elizabeth Kienzle, William Robert III. Student, George Peabody Coll., 1946-49. Exec. offcl. Nashville Banner, 1943-98, police beat, county polit. beat, 1943-53, city editor, 1953-64, movie columnist, 1955-72, mng. editor, 1964-71, exec. editor, 1971-75, asst. to editor, 1975-78, regional editor, 1978-80, sr. editor, 1980-84, v.p., bus. editor, 1984-89, v.p., sr. bus. editor, 1989-98; staff writer Country Style mag., Livin Country. Columnist Williamson A.M., Tennessean; mem. exec. bd. Tenn. Dept. Agr. Agrl. Mus., 2002—06. Appeared as newspaperman in film Teacher's Pet, 1957, also in Country Music on Broadway, 1963; contbr. articles to profl. jours.; chpts. to books. Supt. gates and admissions Tenn. State Fair, 1953-64; pub. rels. chmn. Davidson County Coun. for Retarded Children, 1961-66; exec. bd. Mid. Tenn. coun. Boy Scouts Am.; active 4-H Club Found.; exec. bd. dirs., past sec. Nashville Boys Club, life bd. dirs.; bd. dirs. College Grove Sr. Enrichment Ctr., 2002-06; exec. coun. Coll. Grove Sr. Recreational Ctr., 2002-05; bd. dirs. Tenn. Agricultural Mus., 2002-05. Recipient Big Story award NBC-TV, 1956; named Man of Yr., 4-H Club, 1974, Man of Yr., Future Farmers Am., 1975, Silver Beaver award Boy Scouts Am., 1997; Robert Battle scholarship established in his honor Belmont U. Sch. Bus., By Opryland, U.S.A., 1989. Mem. Tenn. Press Assn., Nat. Screen Coun., Country Music Assn., Masons (33d deg., knights commdr. ct. of honor), Shriners (potentate 1976), Royal Order of Jesters (former dir.), Elks (former chmn. scholarship com.), Sigma Delta Chi (former chmn. scholarship com., former pres.). Methodist. Home: College Grove, Tenn. Died Jan. 22, 2010.

BAUER, DIETRICH CHARLES, retired medical educator; b. Elgin, Ill., July 1, 1931; s. Karl. E. and Martha (Dietrich) B.; m. Lois L. Reed, Nov. 13, 1954. Student, Lake Forest Coll., Ill., 1949-51; BS, U. Ill., 1954; MS, Mich. State U., 1957, PhD, 1959; postgrad., Case Western Res. U., Cleve., 1959-61. Rsch. asst. dept. microbiology Mich. State U., East Lansing, 1957-59; asst. prof. dept. microbiology and immunology Ind. U. Sch. Medicine, Indpls., 1961-65, acting chmn. dept., 1964-65, 81, assoc. prof., 1965-68, prof., 1968-96, chmn. dept. microbiology/immunology, 1981-96, prof. emeritus. Cons. Chas. Pfizer Co., 1968-71, John Wiley, Pub., 1979-80. Recipient Disting. Teaching award Ind. U., 1978, Faculty Colloquium on Excellence in Teaching award FACET, 1992. Mem. AAAS, Am. Soc. Microbiology, Am. Assn. Immunologists, Assn. Med. Sch. Microbiology and Immunology Chmn., Sigma Xi. Home: Egg Harbor, Wis. Died Aug. 7, 2010.

BAUM, JOHN, physician; b. NYC, June 2, 1927; s. Louis Israel and Lilian (Treitman) B.; m. Erna Rose Bailis, Jan. 28, 1950; children: Nina, Jane, Carl, Antonia, Theodore. BA, NYU, 1949, MD, 1954. Intern Baltimore City Hosp., 1954-55; resident in medicine Lenox Hill Hosp., NYC, 1955-56, VA Hosp., NYC, 1956-57; NIH clin. trainee N.Y.U.-Bellevue Hosp., 1957-58; NIH research fellow Rheumatism Research Unit, Taplow, Eng., 1958-59; asst. prof. medicine U. Tex. Southwestern Med. Sch., 1962-68; dir. arthritis clinic Parkland Meml. Hosp., Dallas, 1959-68, dir. med. clinics, 1965-67; co-dir. pediatric arthritis clinic Scottish Rite Hosp., Dallas, 1960-68; mem. faculty U. Rochester (N.Y.) Med. Sch., from 1968, prof. medicine pediatrics and rehab., 1972-93, prof. medicine emeritus, from 1993, chmn. rsch. subjects rev. bd., 1987-96, prof. orthopedics (rehabilitation), 1991-93, prof. pediatrics, from 1997. Vis. prof. rheumatology, hon. sr. rsch. fellow U. Birmingham, Eng., 1988-89; vis. prof. U. Kiev Med. Sch., 1995; dir. arthritis and clin. immunology unit Monroe Cmty. Hosp., 1968-93; dir. pediatric arthritis clinic Strong Meml. Hosp., 1970—; mem. drug efficacy panel NRC-NAS, 1960-65; mem. rsch. rev. bd. immunology VA, 1970-76; adv. panel U.S. Pharmacopeia, 1975—; coord. therapeutics U.S.-USSR Program Rheumatology, 1974—; mem. test com. for rheumatology Am. Bd. Internal Medicine, 1971-76; locum pediat. rheumatologist Princess Margaret Hosp. for Children, Perth, Australia, 1999-2000. Mem. editl. bd. Clin. Rheumatology (Brussels), Jour. Rheumatology (Can.), Japanese Rheumatology, 1984-93; contbr. articles to profl. jours., chpts. to books. Served with AUS, 1944-46. Recipient award of merit Rochester Acad. Medicine, 1999, Sr. Role Model award, 2000, Earl Brewer award, Am. Juvenile Arthritis Orgn., 2002; Fulbright scholar, 1958; clin. scholar rheumatology Arthritis Found., 1964-69. Mem. Am. Coll. Rheumatology (master 1993, coun. pediat. rheumatology 1975-80, 85-00), Heberden Soc., Am. Fedn. Clin. Rsch., Am. Soc. Human Genetics, Am. Assn. Immunologists, Reticuloendothelial Soc., So. Soc. Clin. Investigation, Tex. Rheumatism Assn., Brit. Soc. Rheumatology, Midlands Rheumatology Soc. (Eng.), Polish Rheumatol. Soc. (hon.), La Found. Rheum Argentina (Dr. Oswaldo Garcia Morteo int. sci. com. 1997—), Great Lakes Interurban Club, Sigma Xi. Died May 4, 2009.

BAUMEL, HERBERT, violinist, conductor; b. NYC, Sept. 30, 1919; s. Leon and Fannie (Beckerman) B; m. Rachael Bail, Oct. 17, 1949 (div. Nov. 1970); children: Susan, Samuel, Mary Elizabeth (dec.); m. Joan Patricia French, July 11, 1971. Student, Mannes Sch. Music, NYC, 1932-34; diploma, Curtis Inst. Music, Phila., 1937-42; postgrad., Santa Cecilia, Accademia Chigiana, Rome and Siena, 1954-56. Violinist, concertmaster, conductor with orchs., chamber groups, Broadway shows, jazz ensembles, ballets, operas worldwide, 1939—2010. Baumel-Booth-Smith Trio (1st racially integrated classical trio to tour deep south), 1968-71; Baumel-Booth Duo, 1968-96; violinist/storyteller, 1970—, co-dir., Baumel Assocs., Yonkers, N.Y., 1984-2010; judge Fulbright Nat. Screening Com., 1965-67; guest artist Sponsors' Concerts of Dallas Chamber Music Soc., 1991, Internat. Piano Archives U. Md., College Park, Beveridge Webster Celebration Concert, 1991; lectr. and violinist with Dr. Joan French Baumel, 1991—, Yonkers Pub. Libr., 1992, Greenburgh (N.Y.) Pub. Libr., 1992, Waverly Heights, Gladwyne, Pa., 1993, 94, 95, Alliance Francaise, Westchester, N.Y., 1993, 94, 95, 96, 1st Unitarian Soc. Westchester, 1994, Workmen's Circle Lodge, Sylvan Lake, N.Y., 1994, Thomas Paine/Huguenot/New Rochelle (N.Y.) Hist. Soc., 1995, 96, others; commentator All Things Considered, Nat. Pub. Radio, 1999-2010; contbr. (mag.) Opera News, 2000-10. Violinist Phila. Orch. with Ormandy, Toscanini, Walter, Monteux, Mitropoulos, Szell; first to play Samuel Barber's Violin Concerto with Curtis Symphony (Reiner), 1939 and Phila. Orch. (Ormandy); concert artist with: Stokowski, Stravinsky, Copland, Bernstein, Benny Goodman; concertmaster Phila. Opera, N.Y.C. Opera, N.Y.C. Ballet, Joe Bushkin Jazz Ensembles, (original Broadway musicals) New Girl in Town, Fiorello!, She Loves Me, Fiddler on the Roof, A Little Night Music, Rex, Dancin', also three Presdl. galas with Marilyn Monroe, Bill Cosby, Woody Allen, Jack Benny, Johnny Carson, Rudolph Nureyev, Margot Fonteyn; recs. with Heifetz, Horowitz, Rubinstein, Leonard Warren, Frank Sinatra, Edith Piaf, Tallulah Bankhead, many others; writer script and music ednl. audio-visual program The Art of Listening, 1972—; composer: Fiddlers Two, 1976, Caprice #48 1/2, 1978, Sentiment America, 1984, arranger Selections from Fiddler on the Roof, For Strings, 1971, 2001, 2008-09. Mem. adv. bd. Mark Brent Dolinsky Found., White Plains, N.Y., 1982-2010; played benefits for Westchester Assn. Retarded Citizens, 1982-2010, Coalition for the Homeless,Westchester County, N.Y., 1986-2010. Recipient Silver medal New York Music Week Assn., 1928, Gold medal New York Music Week Assn., 1929; 2-time Fulbright scholar to Rome, 1954-56; chosen for both Stokowski All-American Youth Orch. tours, S.Am., U.S., 1940, 41; chosen to organize, present and play concerts for U.S. Embassy and Cultural Offices in Rome and throughout Italy with Anna Moffo, Ezio Flagello, Ivan Davis, Gimi Beni, and in honor of Queen Elisabeth of Belgium, 1954-56, Phila. Drama Guild Lectr. Series, 1978. Mem. Am. Fedn. Musicians, Curtis Inst. of Music Alumni Assn., Phila. Orch. Retirees and Friends. Democrat. Jewish. Avocations: tennis, gardening, reading, photography, chess. Died Apr. 22, 2010.

BAYNE, DAVID COWAN, priest, educator, lawyer; b. Detroit, Jan. 11, 1918; s. David Cowan and Myrtle (Murray) B. AB, U. Detroit, 1939; LLB, Georgetown U., 1947, LLM, 1948; MA, Loyola U., Chgo., 1946, STL, 1953; SJD (grad. fellow), Yale, 1949; LLD (hon.), Creighton U., 1980. Bar: Fed. and D.C. 1948, Mich. 1960, Mo. 1963. Joined Soc. of Jesus, 1941; ordained priest Roman Catholic Ch., 1952; asst. prof. law U. Detroit, 1954-60; acting dean U. Detroit (Law Sch.), 1955-59, dean, 1959-60; research assoc. Nat. Jesuit Research Orgn., Inst. Social Order, St. Louis, 1960-63; vis. lectr. St. Louis U. Law Sch., 1960-63, prof. law, 1963-67; vis. prof. Mich. Law Sch., 1967, Inst. fur Auslandisches und Internationales Wirtschaftrecht, Frankfurt, 1967; prof. U. Iowa Coll. Law, Iowa City, 1967-88, prof. emeritus, from 1988. Vis. prof. U. Koln, Germany, 1970, 74 Author: Conscience, Obligation and the Law, 1966, 2d edit., 1988; The Philosophy of Corporate Control, 1986; editor legal materials; contbr. articles to profl. jours. Achievements include research in corp. law. Home: Toledo, Ohio. Died Apr. 8, 2009.

BAYNES, THOMAS EDWARD, JR., retired judge, lawyer, mediator, educator; b. NYC, Mar. 19, 1940; s. Thomas Edward and Ann Jane (Burke) B.; m. Maija Eva Kokko, Dec. 30, 1963; children: Cynthia Lynn, Barbara Ann. BBA, U. Ga., 1962; JD, Emory U., 1967, LLM, 1972, Yale U., 1973. Bar: Ga. 1968, U.S. Supreme Ct. 1971, Ct. of Mil. Appeals 1978, Fla. 1981. Dir. Legal Assistance to Inmates Program, Emory U., 1968-69; asst. dean, asst. prof. bus. law Ga. State U., 1969-72; acting regional dir. Nat. Ctr. for State Cts., Atlanta, 1973-74; prof. law and public adminstrn. Nova U. Law Ctr., Ft. Lauderdale, Fla., 1974-76, 77-81; jud. fellow U.S. Supreme Ct., 1976-77; speedy trial reporter U.S. Dist. Ct., So. Dist. Fla., 1977-81; ptnr. Peterson, Myers, Craig, Crews, Brandon & Mann, Lake Wales, Fla., 1981-87; U.S. bankruptcy judge for mid. dist. Fla. U.S. Bankruptcy Ct., Tampa, 1987—2005, chief bankruptcy judge, 2000—03; ret., 2005. State chmn., Ga., Nat. Council on Crime and Delinquency, 1971-72; legal counsel Reorgn. Study Commn. Ga., 1971-72 Author: (with W. Scott) Legal Aspects of Laboratory Medicine in Quality Assurance in Laboratory Management, 1978, Eminent Domain in Florida, 1979, Florida Mortgage Law, 1999, (with others) Supreme Court Justices, Illustrated Biographies, 1993; supplement editor Fla. Real Estate Law and Procedure, 1976; contbg. editor Norton Bankruptcy Law and Practice, 1995. Bd. dirs. F. Lee Moffitt Cancer Rsch Hosp., Tampa, 1989-94, 97—. Comdr. JAGC, USNR, 1960-80, ret. Sterling fellow Yale U. Law Sch., 1972-73; Harry J. Loman Found. rsch. fellow, 1979. Mem. Ga. Bar Assn., Fla. Bar Assn. (cert. cir. ct. and fed. ct. mediator and arbitrator), Am. Law Inst., Hillsborough Assn. Women Lawyers (bd. dirs. 2001-04), Fla. Acad. Profl. Mediators Inc., Supreme Ct. Hist. Soc., Am. Arbitration Assn., Nat. Adv. Com. for Bankruptcy, Ferguson-White Inn (pres. 1992-93, master), Omicron Delta Kappa. Home: Lake Wales, Fla. Died Dec. 16, 2009.

BEALL, CHARLES CLYDE, JR., bank executive; b. Oxford, Miss., Mar. 28, 1935; s. Charles Clyde and Jennie (Dale) B.; m. Ines Anne Watts, July 21, 1961; children: Charles Clyde III, Craig Alan. BBA, U. Miss., 1957, MBA, 1961. With Tex. Commerce Bank, Houston, from 1961, mgr. met. div., exec. v.p., mgr. banking dept., 1974-78, pres., from 1978, chmn., from 1983, also dir.; vice chmn. Tex. Commerce Bancshares Inc. (acquired by Chem. N.Y. Corp.), Houston, from 1983, also dir.; now cons. Served to 1st lt. USAF. Home: Houston, Tex. Died Feb. 7, 2010.

BEARDSLEY, ROBERT EUGENE, microbiologist, educator; b. Walton, NY, June 11, 1923; s. Harrison R. and Margaret (Sliter) B.; m. Philomena E. Pecora, Aug. 28, 1948; children: Luisa M., Margaret R., Robert E. BS, Manhattan Coll., 1950; AM, Columbia U., 1951, PhD, 1960. Instr. Manhattan Coll., 1951-54, asst. prof., 1954-58, asso. prof., 1958-68, prof., 1968-77; dir. Manhattan Coll. (Lab. Plant Morphogenesis), 1962-69, head dept. biology, 1969-77; prof. Iona Coll., New Rochelle, NY, 1977-89, prof. emeritus, from 1989, dean Sch. Arts and Sci., 1977-83. Vis. investigator Inst. Pasteur, Paris, 1966-67; co-chmn. Scientists Com. Radiation Info., 1960. Contbr. articles to profl. jours. Dist. comdr. U.S. Power

Squadrons, 1993. Served with AUS, 1943-46. Guggenheim fellow, 1966. Mem. APHA, Am. Soc. Microbiologists, AAAS, Sigma Xi, Epsilon Sigma Pi. Died Feb. 21, 2010.

BEASLEY, KENNETH LOWELL, university administrator, research administrator; b. Bedford, Ind., Sept. 16, 1930; s. Glen M. and Estella (Walls) Beasley; m. Betsy Turner, Nov. 22, 1953; children: Jonathan, Christopher, Timothy, Thomas. BA, Wabash Coll., 1952; M.A.T., Harvard U., 1953; PhD, Northwestern U., 1962. Assoc. dean grad sch. Northern Ill. U., DeKalb, 1966—72, asst. to pres., from 1972, Am. Coun. Edn., Washington, 1979—80; asst. to chancellor UCLA, 1969—70; exec. dir. Ctrl. States U., DeKalb, from 1972; advisor rsch. mgmt. NSF, Washington, 1973—74, Antarctic Rsch. Rev., 1974. Mem. commn. manpower and edn. Phi Delta Kappa, Bloomington, Ind., 1963—67. Author: The Administration of Sponsored Programs, 1982. Chmn. Task Force Governance Schs., Ill., 1972—74, govs. adv. com. Block Grants, from 1982; scout dir. Two Rivers Coun. Boy Scouts America, 1973—74. Served to cpl. US Army, 1953—55. Grantee, US Office Edn., 1966—67, NSF, 1972—75. Mem.: Nat. Coun. U. Rsch. Adminstrs. (regional pres. 1971—72), Soc. Rsch. Adminstrs. (pres. 1971—72, Excellence Rsch. Adminstrn. award 1978), Coun. Advancement and Support Edn., DeKalb C. of C. (v.p. from 1982). Avocations: skiing, camping. Home: Indianapolis, Ind. Died May 12, 2010.

BECHTLE, PERRY STEVENS, lawyer; b. Phila., Feb. 26, 1926; s. Charles R. Bechtle and Gladys (Kirchner) Warner; m. Mary Leigh, Dec. 27, 1948; children: Leigh, Marianne, Geoffrey, Christopher, Nina, Perry, Thaddeus. Student, St. Joseph Coll., 1946-48; JD, Temple U., 1951. Bar: Pa. 1951, U.S. Dist. Ct. (ea. dist.) Pa. 1952, U.S. Ct. Appeals (3rd cir.) 1955, U. S. Supreme Ct. 1963. Atty. Liberty Mutual Ins. Co., Phila., 1951-55; assoc., ptnr. Pepper, Hamilton & Sheetz, Phila., 1955-62; ptnr. Krusen, Evans & Burns, Phila., 1962-65; pvt. practice Phila., 1965-66; ptnr. Liebert, Harvey, Bechtle, Herting & Short, Phila., 1966-69, Cohen, Shapiro, Polisher, Shiekman & Cohen, Phila., 1969-77; sr. v.p., gen. counsel Gen. Accident Ins. Co., Phila., 1977-79; ptnr. LaBrum & Doak, Phila., from 1979. Lectr. at law Temple U. Sch. of Law: Federal Evidence 1977-78, Villanova Law Sch.: Trial Practice 1977-86. With USAF, 1944-45. Fellow Am. Coll. Trial Lawyers, Internat. Soc. Barristers, Internat. Acad. Trial Lawyers; mem. ABA, Pa. Bar Assn., Phila Bar Assn., Am. Bd. Trial Advocates, Internat. Assn. Def. Counsel, Phila. Assn. Def. Counsel, Union League, Overbrook Golf Club. Home: Norfolk, Va. Died May 9, 2010.

BECK, JAMES L., agricultural lending service executive; b. Badin, NC, July 6, 1933; s. Lytle Patrick and Thelma (Tadlock) Beck; m. Frances Riggins Beck, Aug. 25, 1950 (dec. 1972); children: Katherine Beck Smith, Charles P.; m. Peggy Jean Welch, June 7, 1972; children: Wesley L., Lisa G. Student, Wingate Coll., 1954—55; BS in Agronomy, NC State U., 1958. Br. mgr. Piedmont Prodn. Credit Assn., Monroe, NC, 1967—68; mgr. Fed. Land Bank Assn. of Monroe, 1968—70; pres. Fed. Land Bank Assn. of Winston-Salem, 1970—71, Farm Credit Service of Asheville, 1971—75; regional v.p. Farm Credit Banks of Columbia, SC, 1975—76; pres. Farm Credit Service of Lakeland, Fla., from 1976. Past dir. Lakeland Symphony Orch. With US Army, 1950—54. Mem.: Am. Soc. Agronomy, Wingate Lions Club, Rotary Club (past pres. and dir. Lakeland South), Lakeland Yacht and Country Club. Methodist. Home: Lakeland, Fla. Died Jan. 20, 2009.

BECKEL, CHARLES LEROY, physicist, educator; b. Phila., Feb. 7, 1928; s. Samuel Mercer and Katherine (Linsky) Beckel; m. Josephine Ann Beck, June 27, 1958; children: Amanda S., Sarah K., Timothy C., Andrea C. BS, U. Scranton, 1948; PhD, Johns Hopkins U., 1954. Asst. prof. physics Georgetown U., 1953-59, assoc. prof., 1959-64; rsch. staff mem. Inst. Def. Analyses, Arlington, Va., 1964-66; assoc. prof. U. N.Mex., Albuquerque, 1966-69, prof., 1969-94, prof. emeritus, from 1995, asst. dean, 1971-72, acting v.p. rsch., 1972-73, acting dir. Inst. Social R&D, 1972. Cons. Ballistics Rsch. Lab., Aberdeen Proving Ground, Md., 1955—57, Inst. Def. Analyses, 1962—64, 1966—69, Dikewood Corp., Albuquerque, 1967—72, Albuquerque, 1974—80, Albuquerque Urban Obs., 1969—71, U.S. ACDA, 1981—84; Fulbright lectr. U. Peshawar, Pakistan, 1957—58, Cheng Kung U., Tainan, Taiwan, 1963—64; vis. prof. theoretical chemistry Oxford U., 1973; vis. prof. chemistry and molecular scis. U. Sussex, England, 1987; phys. sci. officer U.S. Arms Control and Disarmament Agy., 1980—81; vis. prof. physics U. Scranton, 1995. Pres. Nat. Kidney Found. N.Mex Inc., 1968—72, del. trustee, 1972—73, 1976—80, mem. exec. com., 1974—80, 1983—86, v.p., 1982—83, trustee, 1987—93; bd. dirs. Nat. Capital Area Nat. Kidney Found., 1965—66, N.Mex Combined Health Appeal, 1972—73; mem. Navajo Sci. Com., 1975—82. Recipient Vol. award, Nat. Kidney Found. N.Mex, 1988, Frank J. O'Hara award for Disting. Achievement in Sci., U. Scranton Nat. Alumni Soc., 1988, award in solic state physics materials scis., U.S. Dept. Energy, 1988, Outstanding Tchg. award, Burlington No. Found., 1989. Mem.: Biolectromagnetics Soc., Am. Phys. Soc., Nat. Eagle Scout Assn. Died Aug. 13, 2009.

BECKER, ARNOLD GUSTAVE, manufacturing executive; b. Fond du Lac, Wis., May 4, 1920; s. John Henry and Ottilia Anna (Graf) Becker; m. Marilyn Linnea Johnson, July 19, 1952; children: Wendy, Bruce, Kurt, Mark. BA in Social studies, Wartburg Coll., 1942; diploma in Commerce, Northwestern U., 1949. Asst. personnel mgr. Goodman Mfg. Co., Chgo., 1948—49; mgr. labor rels. Continental Group, various locations, 1950—64; v.p. indsl. rels. Brockway Inc., from 1964. V.p. Glass Container Indsl. Rels. Coun., from 1979. Assoc. Grad. Sch. U. Pitts., 1977, N.Y. Sch. Indsl. and Labor Rels., Cornell U., 1978; trustee Maple Ave. Hosp., DuBois, Pa., from 1975. 1st lt. US Army, 1942—46. Republican. Lutheran. Home: Brockway, Pa. Died Oct. 4, 2009.

BECKER, CATHERINE HICKEY HANDY, retired librarian; b. Holyoke, Mass., May 10, 1932; d. Cornelius Joseph and Mary Agnes (Collins) Hickey; m. Wallace H. Handy, Nov. 1955 (dec. Nov. 1961); children: Cornelia and Roberta (twins), Mary; m. Bernhard H. Becker, Sept. 1992. BA, U. Mass., 1953; MS in LS, So. Conn. State Coll., 1965. Tchr. New Salem Acad., Mass., 1953-54, Londmeadow Jr. High Sch., Mass., 1954-56; libr. Wilson Jr. High Sch., Windsor, Conn., 1965-69; reference libr. Westfield State Coll., Mass., 1969-92, ret. Mass., 1992. Abstractor Libr. Currents, 1984-86. Vol. Noble Hosp., Westfield, 1977-80, LifeLink of S.W. Fla., 1996—, Venice Hosp., 1997—. Mem. AAUW, ALA (cert. sch. and acad. libr., reviewer RQ 1980-92, Choice 1984-92), Assn. Coll. and Rsch. Librs., New Eng. Libr. Assn., NEA, Mass. Tchrs. Assn., Mass. State Coll. Assn., U. Mass. Alumni Assn., Sigma Kappa. Roman Catholic. Avocations: reading, bicycling, birdwatching. Home: Venice, Fla. Died Jan. 10, 2009.

BEDOIT, WILLIAM CLARENCE, JR., chemicals executive; b. Chattanooga, Apr. 20, 1922; s. William Clarence and Cornelia Pyatt (Carter) Bedoit; m. Rebecca Irene Miller, July 4, 1943; children: William Clarence III, Thomas Miller. BS, U. Tenn., 1947, MS in Chemistry, 1948, PhD in Chemistry, 1950. Rsch. chemist Carbide & Carbon Chem., South Charleston, W.Va., 1950—52, Mallinckrodt Chem., St. Louis, 1952—54, Jefferson Chem. Co., Austin, Tex., 1954—57, mgr., market devel. dept., 1957—71; v.p. mktg. Martin Sweets Co., Louisville, 1971—73; pres. U.T.C. Inc., Louisville, 1973—84; cons. Union Carbide, 1984—85, part-time cons., from 1985. Contbr. articles to profl. publs. Capt. AC US Army, 1942—46. Mem.: Am. Inst. Chemists, Soc. Plastics Industry, Am. Chem. Soc., Comml. Devel. Assn., Alpha Chi Sigma. Republican. Methodist. Achievements include patents in field. Home: Louisville, Ky. Died May 13, 2010.

BEECHER, ROBERT WILLIAM, accounting company executive; b. Boston, Aug. 13, 1931; s. Leslie Dade and Ellen Frances (Duggan) B.; m. Myrna Joy MacClary, Mar. 19, 1955 (div. Dec. 1983); children— Joy A. Beecher Emerson, Gregory R., Joel T., Jennifer E., Pamela M.; m Georgina Marie Canty, July 11, 1984 BS summa cum laude, Boston U., 1957. C.P.A., N.Y., Mass. Acct. Peat, Marwick, Mitchell & Co., Boston and NYC, 1957-65, ptnr., mng. ptnr. White Plains, NY and Boston, 1965-81, vice chmn. Boston, 1981-84; dep. chmn. KPMG Peat Marwick (formerly Peat, Marwick, Mitchell & Co.), NYC, from 1984. Past corporator Mus. of Sci., Boston; past mem. bd. visitors Boston U.; past mem. Mass. Gen. Hosp., Boston, Mass. Fgn. Bus. Council; past treas. Newton-Wellesley Hosp., Wellesley, Mass.; past mem. bd. dirs. Boston Mcpl. Research Bur., Greater Boston C. of C. Served with U.S. Army, 1952-54 Korea Mem. Am. Inst. C.P.A.s, N.Y. State C.P.A.s, Mass. Soc. C.P.A.s, Nat. Assn. Accts., Beta Gama Sigma. Clubs: Board Room, Economic (N.Y.C.). Republican. Avocations: tennis; sailing; swimming. Home: New York, NY. Died May 4, 2009.

BEESON, JACK HAMILTON, composer, educator, writer; b. Muncie, Ind., July 15, 1921; children: Christopher Sigerist (dec. 1976), Miranda. Student, U. Rochester, Columbia U.; studied with, Béla Bartók; Mus D (hon.), Columbia U., 2002. Tchr. Juilliard Sch. Music; former chmn. dept. music, assoc. dir. opera workshop Columbia U., NYC, MacDowell prof. emeritus. Former sec. Alice M. Ditson Fund; former chmn. music publ. com. Columbia U. Press.; bd. dirs. Composers Recs., Inc., others. Author: (book) How Operas Are Created By Composers And Librettists: The Life of Jack Beeson, American Opera Composer; composer: (operas) Jonah, Hello Out There, The Sweet Bye and Bye, Lizzie Borden (commd. by Ford Found.), My Heart's in the Highlands (commd. by NET), Captain Jinks of the Horse Marines (commd. by Nat. Endowment of Arts), Dr. Heidegger's Fountain of Youth (commd. Nat. Arts Club), Cyrano, Sorry, Wrong Number, Practice in the Art of Elocution, (for orch.) Hymns and Dances, Symphony in A, Transformations, Interludes and Arias from Cyrano (for baritone and orchestra), Two Concert Arias (for soprano and orch.), (chamber music) Sonata for Viola and Piano, Interlude, Song, 4th and 5th Piano Sonatas, Two Diversions, Round and Round, Sonata Caronica for two alto recorders, Old Hundredth for Organ, (vocal works) Six Lyrics, Five Songs, Eldorado, Piazza Piece, Big Crash Out West, Indiana Homecoming, Margret's Garden Aria, To a Sinister Potato, (cycles) From a Watchtower, (bass-baritone and piano) Two by Betjeman and A Rupert Brooke Cycle, (for bass and piano) Three Viereck Songs, (countertenor and chamber ensemble) The Daring Young Man on the Flying Trapeze, (mezzosoprano and chamber ensemble) Ophelia Sings, (soprano, tenor and chamber ensemble) The Equilibrists, others, works for voice and string quartet, (choral works) Knots, Magicke Pieces, Epitaphs, In Praise of Singing, Summer Rounds and Canons, Four Gallows Songs. Recipient Rome prize, City of Rochester prize, Marc Blitstein Mus. Theatre award Nat. Inst. Arts and Letters, Gold medal for music Nat. Arts Club, 1976, Gt. Tchrs. award Columbia U., 1979, Alumni Achievement award U. Rochester, 1985, award for Lifetime Achievement award Nat. Opera Assn., 1998; Guggenheim fellow, Fulbright fellow to Italy. Mem. ASCAP (bd. dirs. 1991-95, award 2009), AAAL (treas., v.p. for music), Phi Beta Kappa. Died June 6, 2010.

BEGELL, WILLIAM, publisher; b. Wilno, Poland, May 18, 1928; came to U.S., 1947, naturalized, 1953; s. Ferdinand and Liza (Kowarski) Beigel; m. Esther Kessler, May 27, 1948; children: Frederick Paul (dec.), Alissa Maya (dec.). BChemE, CCNY, 1953; MChemE, Poly. Inst. Bklyn., 1958; postgrad., Columbia U., 1958-59; DSc, Acad. Sci. BSSR, Minsk, 1984. Engring. mgr. heat transfer research facility dept. chem. engring. Columbia U., 1953-59; co-founder, exec. v.p. Scripta Technica, Inc., Washington, 1959-74; founder, pres. Hemisphere Publishing Corp., Washington, 1974-91, Begell House, Inc., Pubs., NYC, from 1991; pres., chief scientist Byelocorp Sci., Inc., from 1991; dir. Supco Internat. Engring. Corp., Milan, from 1994. Lectr. pub. George Washington U., Washington, also NYU; cons. Heat Transfer Research Lab., Columbia U.; cons. in field. Editor 7 books; contbr. numerous articles on heat transfer to profl. jours.; patentee in field. Mem. nat. adv. bd. ctr. for the Book, Libr. of Congress; chmn. exec. coun. Profl. and Scholarly Pubs.; bd. dirs. Am. Fedn. for the Blind. Recipient Benjamin Gomez award book pub. divsn., Anti-Defamation League, 1984. Mem. AAAS, Am. Inst. Chem. Engrs., Am. Soc. for Engring. Edn., ASME (communications bd. Fellow, 1996, Disting. Svc. award 1992), Assn. Am. Publishers (dir.), NY Acad. Scis. (publs. bd.), Internat. Centre for Heat and Mass Transfer, Washington Book Publishers (founder), Am. Assn. Engring. Socs. Jewish. Home: New York, NY. Died July 4, 2009.

BEHREND, DONALD FRASER, academic administrator, educator; b. Manchester, Conn., Aug. 30, 1931; s. Sherwood Martin and Margaret (Fraser) B.; m. Joan Belcher, Nov. 9, 1957; children: Andrew Fraser, Eric Hemingway, David William. BS with honors and distinction, U. Conn., 1958, MS, 1960; PhD in Forest Zoology, SUNY, Syracuse, 1966. Forest game mgmt. specialist Ohio Dept. Natural Resources, Athens, 1960; res. asst. Coll. Forestry, SUNY, Newcomb, 1960-63, res. assoc., 1963-67; dir. Adirondack ecol. ctr. Coll. Environ. Science and Forestry, SUNY, Newcomb, 1968-73; acting dean grad. studies Syracuse, 1973-74; asst. v.p. research programs, exec. dir. Inst. Environ. Program Affairs, 1974-79; v.p. acad. affairs, prof., 1979-85; prof. emeritus, from 1987; asst. prof. wildlife mgmt. U. Maine, Orono, 1967-68; provost, v.p. acad. affairs U. Alaska Statewide System, Fairbanks, 1985-87, exec. v.p., provost, 1988; chancellor U. Alaska, Anchorage, 1988-94, chancellor emeritus, from 1994. Mem. patent policy bd. SUNY, 1983-85, chmn. Res. Found. com. acad. res. devel., 1984-85; chmn. 6-Yr. planning com. U. Alaska, 1985-86; bd. dirs. Commonwealth North, 1991-92, Alaska Internat. Ednl. Found., 1997; mem. selection com. Harry S. Truman Scholarship Found.; mem. Pres.'s Commn., NCAA, 1992-95; chmn. spl. com. on student athlete welfare access and equity, 1993-95; chmn. 20th Great Alaska Shootout, 1997. Contbr. numerous articles and papers to profl. jours. Mem. Newcomb Planning Bd., 1967-69; mem., pres. Bd. Edn. Newcomb Cent. Sch., 1967-73; chmn. governing bd. N.Y. Sea Grant Inst., 1984-85; trustee U. Ala. Found., 1990-94. Served with USN, 1950-54. Mem. Alaska Internat. Edn. Found. (bd. dirs. 1997—), Wildlife Soc., Soc. Am. Foresters, AAAS, Phi Kappa Phi (hon.), Sigma Xi, Gamma Sigma Delta, Sigma Lambda Alpha (hon.). Lodges: Rotary (bd. dirs. Fairbanks club 1985-86), Lions (bd. dirs. Newcomb club 1966-67). Avocations: reading, writing, photography, fly fishing, bagpiping. Home: Skaneateles, NY. Died July 25, 2010.

BEICHMAN, ARNOLD, political scientist, educator, writer; b. NYC, May 17, 1913; s. Solomon and Mary Beichman; mm. Doris Modry (div. 1946); m. Carroll Aikins, Oct. 9, 1950; children: Charles, Janine, John, Anthony (dec.). BA in Polit. Sci., MA in Polit. Sci., Columbia U., PhD in Polit. Sci., 1973. Assoc. prof., polit. scientist U. Mass., 1970-78; assoc. prof. polit. sci. U. B.C., 1974-75, U. Calgary, Alta., Can. Adj. prof. polit. sci. Georgetown U.; mem. editorial adv. bd., columnist Washington Times; vis. scholar Hoover Instn., 1982-2010, rsch. fellow, 1988-2010, Internat. Republican Inst. Observer, Ukraine Nat. Elections, 1998. Author: The "Other" State Department, 1969, Nine Lies About America, 1972, Herman Wouk: The Novelist as Social Historian, 1986; co-author: Yuri Andropov: New Challenge to the West, 1983, The Long Pretense: Soviet Treaty Diplomacy from Lenin to Gorbachev, 1991, Anti-American Myths: Their Causes and Consequences, 1993; editor: CNN's Cold War Documentary: Issues and Controversy, 2000; contbr. numerous articles to profl. jours. Founding mem. Consortium for the Study of Intelligence, Washington. Mem. Phila. Soc. (v.p.). Home: Naramata, Canada. Died Feb. 17, 2010.

BEISEL, DANIEL CUNNINGHAM, former newspaper publisher; b. Germantown, Pa., June 30, 1916; s. Fred Cornelius and Margaret Stewart (Cunningham) B.; children: Jane Ellen, Catherine E., Sarah T., Margaret A.; m. Lois Ann Bourgignon. Student, U. Mich., 1934-36. Traffic rep. Green Bay and Western R.R., 1938-42; with Green Bay (Wis.) Press-Gazette, 1946-80, pub., pres., 1965-80; dir. Green Bay Packers, Inc. Mem.: Oneida Golf and Riding, Delray Dunes Golf and Country, Delray Beach Club, Ocean Club Fla. Episcopalian. Home: Delray Beach, Fla. Died Oct. 31, 2009.

BELEW, JOE DUNCAN, banking association executive; b. Johnson City, Tenn., May 26, 1949; s. Henry Carr and Anne (Harrison) B.; m. Elaine Bunn, June 21, 1980; children: Anna, Duncan AB in Journalism, U. Ga., 1972. Press aide to Senator Herman Talmadge US Senator, Washington, 1972-75; exec. asst. to Rep. Doug Barnard US Congress, Washington, 1977-84; exec. v.p. Consumer Bankers Assn., Arlington, Va., 1984-87, pres., 1987—2009. Treas. Social Compact, 2000—08, vice chmn., 2008—09. Mem. Foundry United Methodist Church. Mem.: Am. Soc. Assn. Executives (mem. key industry advisory com.), Soc. Internat. Bus. Fellows. Democrat. Methodist. Home: Washington, DC. Died Jan. 7, 2009.

BELL, CARL JOSEPH, psychologist, consultant; b. Batchtown, Ill., July 22, 1922; s. Elbie Columbus and Minnie Louise (Cockrell) Bell; m. Grace Rita Glynn, Nov. 21, 1948; children: Christopher, Geraldine, Maureen. BS, Ill. State U., 1949, MS, 1950, postgrad., 1967. Lic. psychologist Fla. Maj. US Army, USAR, 1942—82; pvt. practice psychology Iowa, Ill., Ga., Fla., 1950—83; pres. Iowa Coun. Exceptional Children, Des Moines, 1953; co-founder Sheldered Workshop, Davenport, Iowa, 1956; pres. Mental Health Ctr.,

Bloomington, Ill., 1970; cons. Uganda, East Africa, from 1983. Author: Kindergarten Syllabus, 1967, Learning Disability, 1969; TV shows, Learning Disability, 1971. Mem.: APA, Res. Officers Assn. (pres. 1959), Iowa C. of C. (chmn. econs. course 1960—62), Kiwanis Lodge. Republican. Roman Catholic. Avocation: art. Died July 12, 2010.

BELL, ERNEST LORNE, III, retired lawyer; b. Boston, June 12, 1926; s. Ernest L. and Ellamay (Currier) B.; m. Margaret Van Nostrand Depue, Apr. 14, 1951 (dec. Oct. 1988); children: David E., Robin E., Roseanne Margaret; m. Sally Leavitt Cheney, Nov. 25, 1989. BA cum laude, Harvard Coll., 1949; JD, U. Mich., 1952. Bar: N.H. 1952, U.S. Supreme Ct. 1962. Pvt. practice, Keene, NH, 1952; ptnr. firm Bell & Falk, P.A., 1972-99; sole practice law Keene, NH, 1999—2003; ret., 2003. Author: An Initial View of Ultra as an American Weapon in World War II, Wings Over Keene. Mem. exec. bd. Daniel Webster coun. Boy Scouts Am., 1970-79, 93—; chmn. bd. advisers Colony House Mus., 1984-91; trustee Cheshire County Hist. Soc., 2004-09, Keene Pub. Libr., treas.; del. NH Constl. Conv., 1964, 74; mem. World War II Studies Assn.; mem. N.H. Aero. Commn., 1980-86. Recipient Silver Beaver award Fellow Am. Bar Found. (N.H. chair 1993-99); mem. ABA, N.H. Bar Assn (pres. 1978-79), N.H. Bar Found. (sec., bd. dirs. 1985-90, chmn. 1991-93), Cheshire County Bar Assn., Lawyer Pilots Bar Assn. (founding dir. 1962-68), Def. Rsch. Inst. (v.p. 1969-73, sec. 1973-76), Am. Kennel Club (del. 1979-81), Std. Schnauzer Club Am., Harvard Club (Boston). Anglican. Home: Keene, NH. Died Nov. 6, 2009.

BELL, GEORGE EDWIN, retired physician, insurance company executive; b. Canton, Ohio, Dec. 6, 1923; s. George Edwin and Florence Lea (Clark) B.; m. Evelyn Maxine Adams, Apr. 20, 1946; children: Richard, John, Jeffrey, David. Student, Wooster Coll., 1941-42, Yale U., 1943; MD, Ohio State U., 1947; postgrad., U. Pa., 1954-55. Am. Bd. Life Ins. Medicine. Intern Del. Hosp., Wilmington, 1947-48, resident in medicine, 1948-49; resident in pathology Aultman Hosp., Canton, Ohio, 1949-50; resident in medicine Ohio State U. Hosp., Columbus, 1955-56, asst. clin. prof. medicine, 1970-89; ltd. practice medicine Central Ohio Med. Group, Columbus, 1971-89; dir. med. service Columbus State Hosp., 1958-66, dir. research lab., 1966-69, med. dir., 1968-89; v.p. Nationwide Ins. Co., Columbus, 1980-89; chmn. dept. medicine Grant Hosp., Columbus, 1975-77. Cons. City of Columbus, 1989. Contbr. articles to profl. jours.; programmer computer programs for use in lab. office, 1967—; co-compiler first Chinese-English dictionary with an alphanumeric index; contbr. abstracts to med. jours. Advisor Columbus Pub. Health Nursing Dept., 1967-79; vol. physician Ecco Family Practice Clinic, 1970-74; bd. dirs. Columbus Council on Alcoholism, 1973-77, League Against Child Abuse, 1979-83, Recreation Unltd., 1985—; ad hoc data processing com. chmn. Columbus Acad. Medicine, 1980-81. Served as med. officer USAF, 1951-53. Fed., state, pvt. research grantee, 1958-59; recipient Vol. Services cert. Ohio Dept. Mental Health, 1981, Service plaques J.C. Penney Co., 1981, Service plaques Columbus Health and Life Claim Assn., 1983 Fellow ACP, Am. Life Ins. Med. Dirs. Assn.; mem. AMA, Am. Council Life Ins. (chmn. human resources com.), Acad. Medicine Columbus and Franklin County (history and archives com. 1982—), Midwestern Med. Dirs. Assn. (pres. 1985-86), Pres.'s Club, Kappa Mu Epsilon Home: Columbus, Ohio. Died Feb. 2, 2009.

BELL, JAMES THOMPSON, accountant, society executive; b. Mt. Vernon, NY, Jan. 5, 1932; s. Edwin Hines and Cecilia (Shea) B.; m. Elena Martinez; children: Julie, John, Jennifer. BS cum laude, Fordham U., 1958. C.P.A., N.Y. Auditor, cons. Arthur Young & Co., NYC, 1958-63; treas. Avis, Inc., Garden City, N.Y., 1963-69; assoc. J.H. Whitney & Co., NYC, 1969-74; exec. v.p. Clabir Corp., Greenwich, Conn., 1975-82; group v.p. fin. and adminstrn. Am. Cancer Soc., Inc., NYC, from 1982. Served with U.S. Army, 1952-54. Western Electric Co. scholar, 1957 Mem. Am. Inst. C.P.A.s. Republican. Roman Catholic. Home: Atlanta, Ga. Died Mar. 27, 2009.

BELL, PAUL A., state legislator; b. Algona, Iowa, Oct. 3, 1950; s. Alfred; m. Niki Bell; 2 children. BA, U. Northern Iowa, 1996. Police officer Newton Police Dept., Iowa, 1974—2005; mem. Dist. 41 (formerly Dist. 57th) Iowa House of Reps., 1993—2010. Mem.: Ill. DARE Officers Assn., Iowa DARE Officers Assn., Coun. State Govts., Nat. DARE Officers Assn., Iowa State Police Assn., Kiwanis. Democrat. Lutheran. Avocations: fishing, hunting, gardening. Home: Newton, Iowa. Died June 7, 2010.

BELL, ROBERT LAWRENCE, publisher; b. Everett, Mass., Feb. 21, 1919; BS with honors, Bowdoin Coll., 1942. Salesman Hallmark Greeting Cards, Boston, 1946-50; football scout Harvard Coll., 1947-50; sales trainer Rust Craft Greeting Cards, Boston, 1950-55; sales mgr. and v.p. Allied Pubs., Portland, Oreg., 1956-60; pres. Reliance Corp., Boston, 1960-68; pres., pub. Crescendo Pub. Co., Boston, 1968-80; pub. Bell Pubs. Co., Melrose, Mass., from 1980. Patentee digital timer, copyholder, domestic and internat. copyright work Desiderata, 1968— Hon. trustee Bridgton Acad., North Bridgton, Maine, 1976—; bd. dirs. Sapphire Shores Assn., Sarasota, Fla. Lt. USN, 1942-46, PTO. Mem. ASCAP, Small Pubs. Assn. (pres. 1976-78), Union Boat Club (Boston), Meadows Country Club, Bowdoin Club (pres.), UN Club. Home: Sarasota, Fla. Died Jan. 15, 2009.

BELL, ROUZEBERRY, dentist; b. Pitts., July 13, 1934; s. Rouzeberr and Velma (Pratt) Bell; m. Alice McGhee, Aug. 20, 1966; 1 child, Jeffrey Sanford; children: Cheryl Lynn, Karen Diane. BS in Pharmacy, U. Pitts., 1959; DDS, Howard U., 1970. Staff pharmacist U. Hosp. Cleve., 1959—66, Washington Hosp. Ctr., 1966—70; staff dentist Hough Norwood Family Care Ctr., 1971—76; anesthesiology fellow St. Lukes Hosp., 1971, dental intern, 1970—71; gen. practice dentistry Cleve. Heights, Ohio, from 1973; dental dir. K.W. Clement Family Health Care Ctr. Mem. Big Bros., Washington, 1966—70, Cleve., 1972—77. Served with USN, 1952—55. Mem.: Am. Soc. Hosp. Pharmacists, Buckeye State Dental Assn., Ohio Dental Assn., Nat. Dental Assn., Cleve. Dental Soc., Am. Soc. Dentistry Children, Forest City Dental Soc. Democrat. Avocations: photography, sports. Home: Cleveland, Ohio. Died June 28, 2010.

BELLAND, JOHN CLARKE, education educator; b. Chgo., Nov. 12, 1938; s. Robert Clarke and Ruth Elizabeth (Hare) B.; m. Elizabeth Ann Miller, Aug. 26, 1967; children: Charlotte Jane, Brian Robert. BA, Northwestern U., 1960; MS in Edn., No. Ill. U., 1967; PhD, Syracuse U., 1969. Tchr. Thornridge High Sch., Dolton, Ill., 1960-64; propr. Audiocraft, Chgo., 1964-67; rsch. asst., rsch. assoc. Syracuse (N.Y.) U., 1967-69; asst. prof. edn. U. N.C., Chapel Hill, 1969-70; from asst. prof. to prof. edn. Ohio State U., Columbus, from 1970, dir. Nat. Ctr. on Ednl. Media (Materials for Handicapped), 1991-92, program area coord., 1978-92 and from 93, sr. rschr. Ctr. for Collaborative Studies in Tchr. Edn., 1991-92. Assoc. editor Ednl. Broadcasting Rev., Columbus; editor Jour. Visual Literacy, Columbus, 1991—; speaker and presenter in field. Contbr. chpts. to books, articles to profl. jours. Mem. ctrl. com. Quality for Kids Edn., Worthington, Ohio. Mem. AAUP, Assn. for Ednl. Comm. and Tech., Internat. Visual Literacy Assn. (bd. dirs. 1990—), Ohio Ednl. Libr. Media Assn., Phi Delta Kappa. Home: Columbus, Ohio. Died Nov. 26, 2009.

BELLANGER, SERGE RENÉ, bank executive; b. Vimoutiers, France, Apr. 30, 1933; s. René Albert and Raymonde Maria (Renard) Bellanger. MBA, Paris Bus. Sch., 1957. With Citibank, 1966-73, mem. Paris br., 1966-69, world corp. rels. officer for Europe NYC, 1969-73, asst. v.p., 1969-71, v.p., 1972-73; sr. v.p., gen. mgr. Crédit Industriel et Commercial, NYC, 1974-79, exec. v.p., gen. mgr., from 1979; US gen. rep. CIC Group, NYC, from 1973, mem. exec. com., from 1998. Prof. banking French Banking Inst., 1961—64; mem. adv. com. French House Columbia U., from 1976, chmn., from 1996, mem. internat. adv. bd. Inst. Study Europe, from 2002; mem. Nat. Com. Fgn. Trade Advisors France, from 1978, exec. v.p. U.S. nat. com., 1985—93, bd. dirs. nat. com., 1987—2002, v.p. U.S. nat. com., 1992—93, mem. Paris exec. com., 1994—95; chmn. internat. banking course New Sch. Social Rsch., NYC, 1981—83; dir. Am. Ctr. Paris, 1985—93; mem. adv. com. Ctr. Study French Civilization and Culture NYU, NYC, 1988—2000; mem. adv. bd. French Inst. Culture and Tech. U. Pa., from 1992, chmn. adv. bd., 1992—95; mem. adv. bd. Lycée Francais, NY, from 2000; mem. Adv. Coun. French Abroad, 2000; mem. exec. com. Fedn. French Vets., from 2001; bd. dirs. Ubifrance, from 2002, French Ctr. Fgn. Trade, Banque Transatlantique, from 2002; pres. Grand Marnier Found., from 2004. With French Air Force, 1958—60. Decorated Algeria Commemorative medal, comdr. Legion of Honor, Nat. Order of Merit. Mem.: Bank Adminstrn. Inst. (mem. editl. bd. World Banking Mag. 1981—87, columnist Banker's Mag. 1986—96), NY Cotton Exch. (bd. dirs. fin. instrument exch. divsn. 1985—95), NY Futures Exch. (dir. 1980—87, chmn. fgn. exch. com. 1981—82), Banque de l'Union Européenne (bd. dirs. 1989—90), Assn. Promotion French Sci., Industry and Tech. (pres. 1986—91), Lyonnaise de Banque (bd. dirs. 1986—89), Inst. Internat. Bankers (trustee 1975—77, v.p. 1977—79, chmn. legis. and regulatory com. 1977—79, chmn. 1979—80), French Overseas Assn., European-Am. Bus. Coun. (bd. dirs. Washington from 1991), Food and Wine France (bd. dirs. 1983—93), NYC Partnership and C. of C. (ptnr. from 1991), Assn. French C. of C. and Industry Abroad (adminstr. from 1984, v.p. 1989—95, 1st v.p. 1995—99), NY C. of C. (mem. internat. bus. initiative 1994—95), French-Am. C. of C. (councillor 1973—74, mem. exec. com. 1974—80, v.p. 1980—82, exec. v.p. 1982—83, nat. pres. from 1983, pres. NY chpt. from 1983), European-Am. C. of C. (pres., CEO 1990—96, hon. chmn. from 1996), Automobile Club de France, River Club, Univ. Club. Home: New York, NY. Deceased.

BENDHEIM, ROBERT AUSTIN, textile executive; b. NYC, Aug. 5, 1916; s. Julius and Cora (Lowenstein) B.; children: Lynn, Kim; m. Judith G. Kew, Feb. 18, 1988. AB, Princeton U., 1937; postgrad., Harvard U. Bus. Sch., 1941-42; L.H.D. (hon.), Fordham U., 1966. Trainee Spartan Mills, Spartanburg, S.C., 1937-38; various positions with M. Lowenstein & Sons, Inc., 1938—, sec. and dir., 1946-47, v.p., 1947-59, exec. v.p., 1959-64, pres., 1964-71, chief exec. officer, 1970-85, chmn. bd., 1972-85, also dir. Trustee Mt. Sinai Hosp., N.Y.C., Fordham U.; mem. nat. campaign com. Princeton U.; bd. dirs. United Way N.Y.C.; mem. edn. com. N.Y.C. Partnership Served as lt. USNR, 1942-46. Mem.: Princeton, Century, Stanwich, Lyford Cay, Union League, Princeton, Century, Round Hill, Stanwich, Lyford Cay. Home: Greenwich, Conn. Died Aug. 21, 2009.

BENDINER, ROBERT, writer, editor; b. Pitts., Dec. 15, 1909; s. William and Lillian (Schwartz) B.; m. Kathryn Rosenberg, Dec. 24, 1934 (dec.); children: David, William (dec.), Margaret. Student, CCNY, 1928-33; LHD (hon.), L.I. U., 1994. Mng. editor The Nation, NYC, 1937-44, assoc. editor, 1946-50, free-lance writer, 1951-68, 78—. Lectr., program chmn. Wellesley Summer Inst. Social Progress, 1946-53; mem. faculty Salzburg Sem. in Am. Studies, 1956; vis. lectr. journalism Wesleyan U. (Conn.), 1983 Contbg. editor The Reporter, N.Y.C., 1956-60; U.S. corr. New Statesman, London, 1959-61; mem. editorial bd. N.Y. Times, 1969-77; author: The Riddle of the State Department, 1942, White House Fever, 1960, Obstacle Course on Capitol Hill, 1964, Just Around the Corner, 1967, The Politics of Schools, 1969, The Fall of the Wild, The Rise of the Zoo, 1981, TV documentary NBC White Paper, The Man in the Middle, The State Legislator, 1961. Served with AUS, 1944-45. Guggenheim fellow, 1962-63; grantee Carnegie Fund; recipient Benjamin Franklin Mag. award U. Ill., 1955, NEA award, 1960 Mem. Nat. Press Club. Clubs: Coffee House (N.Y.C.). Died Feb. 7, 2009.

BENEDICT, BURTON, retired museum director, anthropologist; b. Balt., May 20, 1923; s. Burton Eli Oppenheim and Helen Blanche (Deiches) B.; m. Marion MacColl Steuber, Sept. 23, 1950; children: Helen, Barbara MacVean AB cum laude, Harvard U., 1949; PhD, U. London, 1954. Sr. rsch. fellow Inst. Islamic Studies, McGill U., Montreal, Que., Can., 1954-55; sociol. rsch. officer Colonial Office, London and Mauritius, 1955-58; sr. lectr. social anthropology London Sch. Economics, 1958-68; prof. anthropology U. Calif., Berkeley, 1968-91, prof. emeritus, 1991—2010, chmn. dept. anthropolgy, 1970-71, dean social sciences, 1971-74, dir. Hearst Mus. Anthropology, 1989-94; dir. emeritus Hearst Mus. Anthropology, 1994—2010. Dir. U. Calif. Study Ctr. for U.K. and Ireland, London, 1986-88 Author: Indians in a Plural Society, 1961; author and editor: Problems of Smaller Territories, 1967, (with M. Benedict) Men, Women & Money in Seychelles, 1982, The Anthropology of World's Fairs, 1983; contbr. numerous articles to profl. jours. Trustee East Bay Zool. Soc. Sgt. USAF, 1942-46. Recipient Western Heritage award Nat. Cowboy Hall of Fame, 1984; rsch. fellow Colonial Office, 1955-58, 60, U. Calif., Berkeley, 1974-75; grantee NEH, 1981-83. Fellow Royal Anthrop. Inst. (mem. coun. 1962-65, 67-68, 86-89), Am. Anthrop. Assn.; mem. Assn. Social Anthropologists of Brit. Commonwealth, Athenaeum Club (London) Avocations: museums, the zoo, birdwatching, collecting postcards, world fairs. Home: Berkeley, Calif. Died Sept. 19, 2010.

BENESCH, WILLIAM MILTON, molecular physicist, atmospheric researcher, educator; b. Balt., Apr. 22, 1922; s. Jerome William and Blanche (Koshland) Benesch; m. Joan Sagner Benesch, June 1, 1946; children: Amy Joan, Sarah Elizabeth, Jane Margaret. BA, Lehigh U., 1942; MS, Johns Hopkins U., 1950, PhD, 1952. Asst. prof. U. Pitts., 1953—60; asst. prof. molecular physics U. Md., Coll. Pk., 1962—63, assoc. prof., 1964—66, prof., 1967—92, prof. emeritus, 1992—2010, dir. Inst. Molecular Physics, 1973—76; cons. Argonne Nat. Lab., Ill., 1978—80. Sgt. USAR, 1944—46. Fellow, Commn. Relief Belgium, Liege, 1952—53, Weizmann Inst., Rehovoth, Israel, 1960—62, Johns Hopkins U., Balt., 1977—2010. Fellow: Philosophical Soc. Washington, Washington Acad. Sci. (bd. mgrs. 1988—89, v.p. adminstrv. affairs 1989—90), Optical Soc. America (assoc. editor jour. 1978—84), American Phys. Soc.; mem.: Soc. Applied Spectroscopy, American Geophys. Union, Johns Hopkins U. Club (Balt.), Cosmos Club (Washington). Avocations: birdwatching, duplicate bridge, Bronze Life master. Home: Washington, DC. Died Sept. 17, 2010.

BENIGER, JAMES RALPH, communications educator, writer; b. Sheboygan, Wis., Dec. 16, 1946; s. Ralph Joseph and Charlotte Emma (Nitsch) B.; m. Kay Diane Ferdinandsen, Dec. 7, 1984. BA magna cum laude, Harvard U., 1969; MA in Sociology, U. Calif., Berkeley, 1973, MS in Statistics, 1974, PhD in Sociology, 1978. Lectr. U. Calif., Berkeley, 1976-77; instr. Princeton U., N.J., 1977-79, asst. prof., 1979-85; assoc. prof. Annenberg Sch. of Communications U. So. Calif., LA, 1985—2010. Editorial bd. Pub. Opinion Quar., Ann Arbor, Mich., 1982-87; bd. overseers Gen. Social Survey, U. Chgo., 1984-87; adv. coun. U.S. Congress Office of Tech. Assessment, 1991; assoc. editor Communication Rsch., L.A. Author: Trafficking in Drug Users, 1983, The Control Revolution, 1986 (Assn. of Am. Pubs. award 1987, N.Y. Times Book Rev., Notable Paperback award 1989). Named Samuel Lazero Meml. Lectr. Inst. for Sci. Info., Phila., 1988, Disting. Guest Contbr. Keio U., Tokyo, 1988; John Randolph Haynes and Dora Haynes Found. grantee Mem. aAAS, Am. Assn. Pub. Opinion Rsch. (sec., treas. 1988-90, chair 50th Anniversary Conf.), Am. Sociol. Assn. (program chmn. 1987-88), Internat. Comm. Assn., Am. Statis. Assn. Avocation: running. Home: Manhattan Beach, Calif. Died Apr. 12, 2010.

BENJAMIN, BRY, internist; b. NYC, Oct. 20, 1924; m. Marianne Benjamin. BS, Yale U., 1945; MD, Harvard Med. Sch., 1947. Diplomate Am. Bd. Internal Medicine. Intern Lenox Hill Hosp., NYC, 1947-48; resident Goldwater Meml. Hosp., NYC, 1948-50; fellow in psychosomatic medicine Cin. Gen. Hosp., 1950-51; resident in internal medicine SUNY, Bklyn., 1953-54; resident in comprehensive care Cornell U. Med. Coll., NYC, 1954-55; asst. clin. prof. medicine Cornell Univ. Med. Coll., NYC, from 1957. Asst. attending physician N.Y. Hosp., 1957—; assoc. attending physician Manhattan Eye, Ear and Throat Hosp., 1979—; attending physician Beth Israel Hosp., N.Y.C., 1995—; researcher human ecology study program Cornell U., 1955-63. Fellow Am. Coll. Physicians, N.Y. Acad. Medicine; mem. AAAS, AMA, Am. Soc. Internal Medicine, Am. Psychomatic Soc., Am. Geriatric Soc., Am. Pub. Health Assn., N.Y. Soc. Internal Medicine, N.Y. State Med. Soc., N.Y. Acad. Scis., Harvey Soc., Choice in Dying, N.Y. County Med. Soc. (managed care task force 1996—, pub. health com. 1975—), Alpha Omega Alpha. Home: New York, NY. Died Jan. 19, 2009.

BEN-MENACHEM, YORAM, radiologist, educator; b. Jerusalem, Sept. 1, 1934; came to U.S., 1969; s. Haim and Eva (Beisem) Ben-M.; m. Sylvia Tizes, Dec. 24, 1957; children: Tamir, Gadi, Drory. MD, Hebrew U., Jerusalem, 1960. Diplomate: Am. Bd. Radiology. Physician Israel Def. Forces, 1960-63; med. supt. Lilongwe (Malawi) Gen. Hosp., 1963-66; fellow in vascular radiology Thomas Jefferson U., Phila., 1969-72; prof. radiology U. Tex. Med. Sch., Houston, 1977-84, dir. vascular radiology, 1972-83; prof. radiology Baylor Coll. Medicine, Houston, 1985-87; prof. radiology, adj. prof. surgery U. Washington, Seattle, 1987-92; dir. dept. radiology Harborview Med. Ctr., Seattle, 1988-92; prof., vice chmn. dept. radiology U. Med. and Dentistry N.J., N.J. Med. Sch.,

Newark, from 1992; chief traumatologic radiology UMDNJ Univ. Hosp., Newark, from 1992. Rep. to Trauma Task Force of Joint Commn. on Accreditation Health Care Orgns., 1988—. Author: Angiography in Trauma: A Work Atlas, 1981; cons. editor Orthopedics Mem. Am. Soc. Emergency Radiology, Radiol. Soc. N.J., Am. Coll. Radiology, Radiol. Soc. N.Am., Soc. Cardiovasc. Intervention Radiology, Cardiovasc. Intervention Soc. Europe, Am. Roentgen Ray Soc., Internat. Wound Ballistics Assn. Jewish. Home: West Orange, NJ. Died July 12, 2009.

BENNETT, HARRY LOUIS, history professor; b. Ansonia, Conn., Dec. 22, 1923; s. Louis and Florence (Swole) B.; m. Claire Davis, July 2, 1949; 1 dau., Lisa Brierley. BA, Yale U., 1944, MA, 1948, PhD, 1954. Welfare investigator, Conn., 1950-51; mem. faculty Quinnipiac Coll., Hamden, Conn., from 1951, prof. history, dean coll., 1956-67, v.p. acad. affairs, 1967-69, 72-90, prof., chmn. history, 1969-72, provost, 1972-90, acting pres., 1978-79, provost emeritus, 1990, emeritus prof. history, from 1992. Sec.-treas. Conn. Conf. Community and Jr. Colls., 1955-62, v.p., 1962-64, pres., 1964-65; chmn. standing com. accreditation Conn. Council Higher Edn., 1964-65, vice chmn., 1985-86; chmn. Conn. Adv. Com. on Accreditation, 1986-88. 1st lt., inf. AUS, 1944-46, MTO. Mem. Am. Hist. Assn., Am. Cath. hist. Assn., New Eng. Hist. Assn., Orgn. Am. Historians, Assn. Study Conn. History, Conn. Hist. Soc., New Haven Colony Hist. Soc. Roman Catholic. Home: Milford, Conn. Died May 9, 2009.

BENNETT, JACK FRANKLIN, retired oil industry executive; b. Macon, Ga., Jan. 17, 1924; s. Andrew Jackson and Mary Eloise (Franklin) B.; m. Shirley Elizabeth Goodwin, Sept. 17, 1949 (dec. 2005); children: Jackson Goodwin, Philip Davies, Hugh Franklin, Elizabeth Fraser. BA, Yale U., 1944; MA, Harvard U., 1949, PhD, 1951. Negotiator Joint U.S.-U.K. Export Import Agy., Berlin, 1946—47; tchg. fellow fin. Harvard U., 1949—51; spl. asst. to adminstr. Tech. Assistance Program, US Dept. State, Washington, 1951—52; economist U.S. Mut. Security Agy., Washington, 1952—53; sr. economist Presdl. Commn. on Fgn. Econ. Policy, 1954; sr. fgn. exch. analyst Exxon Corp., NYC, 1955—58, dep. European fin. rep. London, 1958—60; treas. Esso. Petroleum Co., Ltd., London, 1960—61; asst. treas. Exxon Corp., NYC, 1961—65, mgr. gen. econs. dept., 1965—66, mgr. coordination and planning dept., 1966—67; gen. mgr. supply dept. Exxon Co., U.S.A., Houston, 1967—69; v.p., dir. Exxon Internat., NYC, 1969—71; dep. under sec. for monetary affairs US Dept. Treasury, Washington, 1971—74, under sec. for monetary affairs, 1974—75; sr. v.p. Exxon Corp., NYC, 1975—89. Dep. undersec. for monetary affairs US Dept. Treasury, Washington, 1971-74, under sec. for monetary affairs, 1974-75. Contbr. articles to profl. jours. Trustee Com. Econ. Devel. With USNR, 1943-46. Mem. Stanwich Club (Greenwich, Conn.), York Harbor Reading Rm. (Maine), Blind Brook Club, John's Island Club (Fla.). Republican. Died Apr. 25, 2010.

BENNETT, JAMES B., orthopedic surgeon; b. San Antonio, May 17, 1943; m. Margarita Bennett; children: James, Richard, Danielle. BA in Psychology, U. Okla., 1965; MD, U. Louisville, 1969; MBA, U. Houston, 1998. Cert. Am. Bd. Orthop. Surgery. Resident in gen. surgery U. Louisville Sch. Medicine, 1970—71; resident in orthop. surgery Upstate Med. Ctr., NY, 1971—74; hand fellowship La., 1975; chief hand surgery svc. Shriners Hosp., Houston, from 1984; chief of staff Tex. Orthop. Hosp., Houston, from 1995; clin. prof. orthop. surgery U. Tex. Med. Sch., from 1998; clin. prof. Baker Coll. Medicine. Program dir. Orthopedic Overseas, Peru, 1987—94. Contbr. over 50 articles to profl. jours., over 25 chpts. to books. Named Surgeon of Yr., Assn. Oper. Rm. Nurses, Houston, 2000. Mem.: AMA, ACS, Peruvian Plastic Surgery Elbow and Shoulder Soc., Tex. Med. Assn., Houston Orthop. Soc., Am. Shoulder and Elbow Surgeons, Am. Soc. for Surgery of Hand (Vol. Svc. award 2001), Am. Orthop. Assn., Am. Acad. Orthop. Surgeons. Home: Houston, Tex. Died July 15, 2010.

BENNETT, ROBERT MENZIES, retired gas pipeline company executive; b. Louisville, Oct. 24, 1926; s. Donald Menzies and Irene Marie (Schubring) B.; m. Elizabeth Lois Sherman, June 11, 1949; children: James, Elizabeth, Emily, Robert Jr. BEE, U. Louisville, 1950. Registered profl. engr., W.Va. Engr. Louisville Gas and Electric, 1950-55, Columbia Gas div. United Fuel Gas Co., Charleston, W.Va., 1955-61, supervisory engr., 1961-71; mgr. Columbia Gas W.Va., Charleston, 1971-73; dir. planning Columbia Gas Transmission Corp., Charleston, 1973-80, v.p. gas procurement, 1980-85, sr. v.p. mktg., 1985-87, pres., 1987-88, vice chmn., 1988-90, also bd. dirs.; co-owner Enerco Oil and Gas Corp., Charleston, from 1990. Served with U.S. Army, 1945-46, PTO. Mem. IEEE (chmn. W.Va. sect. 1972). Clubs: Kanawha Country. Lodges: Rotary. Republican. Episcopalian. Avocations: golf, hiking. Home: Charleston, W.Va. Died July 14, 2009.

BENNING, JOSEPH FRANCIS, JR., portfolio manager, financial analyst; b. Weehawken, NJ, Dec. 5, 1922; s. Joseph F. and Edith L. (Castelli) B.; m. Rita E. Kerlin, May 29, 1948; children: Joseph F. III, Robert E., James E., Barbara A. Busenbark. BS, St. Louis U., 1949; MBA, NYU, 1951. Chartered Fin. Analyst. V.p. Chemical Bank, NYC, 1951-84; pres. Citadel Advisors, Inc., Bay Head, N.J., from 1984. Mem. Consumers Adv. Coun., Jersey Cen. Power and Light, Morristown, N.J., 1986-88. T.Sgt. USAAF, 1943-45, ETO. Decorated Disting. Flying Cross, Air medal with 3 oak leaf clusters. Fellow Fin. Analysts Fedn.; mem. Inst. CFAs. Republican. Roman Catholic. Avocations: reading, travel. Home: Tinton Falls, NJ. Died Feb. 6, 2009.

BENSON, ROBERT ELLIOTT, investment banker, consultant; b. Bklyn., June 13, 1916; s. Philip Adolphus and Louise A. (Melville) B.; m. Elena Vittoria, June 13, 1942; children: Elena V. Benson Ganzenmuller, Christine L. Benson Pell, Robert Elliott, William M., David Philip. S.B., Mass. Inst. Tech., 1937; postgrad., Bklyn. Poly. Inst., 1938-39; MBA, Harvard, 1941; grad., Program for Execs., Carnegie Inst. Tech., 1957. Student engr. Consol. Edison Co. N.Y., Inc., NYC, 1937-39; security analyst City Bank Farmers Trust Co., NYC, 1940; asst. engr. L.I. Lighting Co., Mineola, N.Y., 1941-42; security analyst Equitable Life Assurance Soc. U.S., 1946, 2d v.p., 1956-60, v.p., 1960-66; exec. asst. to pres. Internat. Tel. & Tel. Corp., NYC, 1966, v.p., 1967-76; sr. cons. White, Weld & Co. Inc., NYC, 1976-78; v.p. Merrill Lynch, Pierce, Fenner & Smith Inc., 1978-85; sr. v.p., chief fin. officer Finacopro N.V., Curacão, Netherland Antilles and NYC, 1985-86; cons. Drexel Burnham Lambert Inc., 1986-90; cons. corp. fin. Locust Valley, N.Y., from 1990. Trustee, dir. Dime Savs. Bank of N.Y., 1963-88. Pres., trustee YWCA Retirement Fund, 1956-90; trustee, v.p. McAuley Water St. Mission; trustee, mayor, police commr. Village of Matinecock; vestryman, chmn. fin. com. St. John's of Lattingtown. Maj. AUS, 1942-46. Decorated Legion of Merit. Mem. Beaver Dam Winer Sports Club (Locust Valley), The Creek Club. Republican. Episcopalian. Died Apr. 18, 2009.

BENT, JOHN H., banker, conservator; b. Bklyn., July 6, 1926; s. John H. and Edna Josephine (Burke) B.; m. Helen Dorothy Reiss, Apr. 19, 1952 (dec. Apr. 1968); 1 child, Helen; m. Elaine Marie Dalton, Dec. 27, 1969; children— Judith, Jacquelyn, Sean Student cert., Am. Inst. Banking, NYC, 1947; grad. cert., Am. Inst. Banking, 1952. With Dime Savs. Bank N.Y., NYC, from 1947, v.p., gen. acctg. officer, 1979-82, sr. v.p., dir. fin. research, from 1982. Cons. taxes, 1950—; conservator, 1965—; EDP adviser, 1975— Republican. Roman Catholic. Home: Brooklyn, NY. Died Mar. 21, 2010.

BENTON, WILLIAM PETTIGREW, advertising agency executive; b. Laurinburg, NC, Nov. 4, 1923; s. William P. and Carlie (Austin) B.; m. Blanche Marilyn Lampke, June 26, 1948; children: Barbara, Mary Anne, Judy, Nancy. Student, U. N.C., 1946. With Ford Motor Co., Dearborn, Mich., 1947-84, v.p. mktg., 1971-73, v.p. parent co., gen. mgr. Lincoln-Mercury div., 1973-75, v.p. parent co., gen. mgr. Ford div., 1975-77, v.p. parent co., v.p. mktg. worldwide, 1981; v.p. sales Ford of Europe, 1977-81; dep. chmn. Brit. Car Group, Eng., 1984-86; chmn. Brit. Car Group Inc. U.S., 1984-86, Group Lotus Inc., 1985-86, Sandgate Corp., 1985-86; vice chmn. Wells, Rich, Greene/BDDP, Dearborn, 1986-96; exec. dir. Ogilvy & Mather, Dearborn, from 1997. Dir. automotive div. United Fund Campaign, Detroit, 1971. Gen. chmn. Meadowbrook Theatre and Music Festival, Oakland U., Rochester, Mich., 1972; bd. dirs. emeritus Sch. Bus. Adminstrn. Sponsors, Inc., Coll. William and Mary, 1976-86; bd. dirs. Marian H.S. Dads Club, 1973-76; mem. exec. com. Internat. Fedn. Multiple Sclerosis Worldwide, pres., 1985-93, pres. emeritus, 1994; bd. dirs. Beaumont Found., Ind. for Life, 1989-95. With USAAF, 1943-45. Decorated Bronze Star, Croix de Guerre (France). Mem. Advt. Coun. (bd. dirs. 1983-85), Detroit C. of C. (bd. dirs. 1983-84), Econ. Club Detroit, Bloomfield Hills Country Club, Lost Tree Club, Everglade Club, Palm Beach Yacht Club, Harry's Bar (London). Home: Bloomfield, Mich. Died Feb. 19, 2009.

BERES, WILLIAM PHILIP, physics educator; b. Peabody, Mass., Jan. 8, 1936; s. Solomon Alvin and Rachel (Cooper) B.; m. Mary J. Chinn, June 19, 1966; children: Deborah, Sharon, Ben David. BS, MIT, 1959, PhD, 1964. Physicist GCA Corp., 1964; rsch. assoc. U. Md., 1964-66; asst. prof. Duke U., Durham, N.C., 1966-69; assoc. prof. physics Wayne State U., Detroit, 1969-75, prof., from 1975, assoc. chmn. dept., 1991-99. Participant Latin Am. Sch. Physics, Mexico City, summer 1965; vis. prof. nuclear theory Lawrence Radiation Lab., Berkeley, Calif., summer 1967; Fulbright lectr. Hebrew U., Jerusalem, 1977-78. Contbr. numerous publs. to physics jours. Mem. Am. Phys. Soc., Am. Assn. Physics Tchrs. Died Feb. 19, 2009.

BERGENHEIM, ROBERT CARLTON, publisher, consultant; b. Boston, Jan. 19, 1924; s. Carl Olaf and Thyra Carolina (Branting) B.; m. Elizabeth Darling McKee, Aug. 30, 1948; children— Richard C., Carol E., Roger C., Robert C., Kristine E., Ronald C., Michael D. Student in journalism and bus. adminstrn. Boston U.; hon. degree in journalism, Suffolk U., 1978. Mgr., pub. Christian Sci. Pub. Soc., Boston, 1941-71; dir. newspapers McClatchy Papers, Sacramento, 1973-76; pub. Boston Herald, 1976-79; v.p. Boston U., 1979-81; pub., founder Boston Bus. Jour., 1980, Boston Bus. Mag., 1985, Providence Bus. News, 1986. Served with USN, 1943-46. Nieman fellow Harvard U., 1954. Avocations: photography; sailing; tennis. Home: Carlisle, Mass. Died June 5, 2010.

BERGERE, CARLETON MALLORY, contractor; b. Brookline, Mass., Apr. 4, 1919; s. Jason J. and Anna Lillian B.; m. Jean J. Pach, Oct. 1, 1950. Student, Burdett Bus. Coll., 1938, Babsons Sch. Bus., 1940. Self-employed contractor, Chgo., 1949-57; pres. Permanent Bldg. Supply Co., Inc., Chgo., 1957-62, Gt. No. Bldg. Products, Inc., Chgo., 1962-67, C.M. Bergere Co., Inc., Cgho., 1967-96, Carleton M. Bergere & Assocs., from 1996. Served with USN, 1944. Named Man of Yr., Profl. Remodelers Assn. Greater Chgo., 1978. Mem. Nat. Assn. Remodeling Industry (pres. Greater Chicagoland chpt., exec. dir., reg. v.p. 1991-95, Pres.'s award 1990, Profl. award 1992), Chgo. Assn. Commerce and Industry (indsl. devel. com.), Better Bus. Bur. Met. Chgo., Industry Trade Practice Com. on Home Improvment (chmn., bd. dirs. 1992—), Nat. Panel Consumer Arbitrators, Exec. Club (Chgo.). Died Aug. 3, 2010.

BERGMANN, ARTHUR M., writer, retired journalist, retired county official; b. NY, Nov. 24, 1927; s. Augustus H. Bergmann. BS in Polit. Sci. and Pub. Adminstrn., Empire State Coll., SUNY, Old Westbury, 1974; M in Pub. and Gen. Adminstrn., L.I.U., 1979. Cert. arbitrator. With N.Y. Herald Tribune, 1945-63; asst. news editor Riverhead News, 1949-50; Suffolk County (N.Y.) corr. for N.Y.C. newspapers, 1949-63; news editor Moriches (N.Y.) Tribune, 1950-51; mem. staff Newsday, 1951-71, Suffolk County polit. editor, columnist, 1965-71; chief dep. Suffolk County Exec., Hauppauge, NY, 1972-79. Chmn. Suffolk Criminal Justice Coordinating Coun., 1975-79, Arson Action Com.-Suffolk Arson Task Force, 1975-77, MTA Permanent Citizens Adv. Com., 1978-79; adv. coun. N.Y. State Crime Victims Compensation Bd., 1978-79; trustee Suffolk Acad. Medicine, 1974. Served with USAAF, 1946-47. Recipient Disting. Svc. award United Jewish Appeal, 1976; Pub. Adminstrn. award C. W. Post Coll., 1977; Disting. Svc. plaque L.I. Assn. Commerce & Industry, 1977; Exemplary Svc. award Empire State Coll., SUNY, 1981; nominated for Pulitzer prize (2). Mem. Acad. Polit. Sci., Soc. Silurians, Am. Legion, Pi Alpha Alpha. Died Sept. 17, 2009.

BERGMANN, PETER GEORGE, lawyer; b. NYC, July 1, 1949; s. Paul and Therese (Greenfield) B.; m. Kay Kirstine Gardiner, Oct. 13, 1991. BA, NYU, 1970; JD with honors, George Washington U., 1973. Law clk to Hon. James T. Foley U.S. Dist. Ct. (no. dist.) N.Y., Albany, 1973-74; ptnr. Cadwalader Wickersham & Taft, NYC, from 1974, chmn., Health Care & Not-for-Profit dept. Recipient Reverend Parks award St. Margaret's House, 1992, Lillian D. Wald award Visiting Nurse Service NY, 2007. Mem. ABA (past chmn. Regional Forum on Health Law), N.Y. State Bar Assn., Fed. Bar Council, N.Y. County Lawyers Assn. (past chmn. com. health svcs.), N.Y. Assn. Homes and Svcs. for Aging (gen. counsel), Am. Assn. Homes for Aging (chmn. legal com. 1998-2000). Home: New York, NY. Died Apr. 18, 2009.

BERKOVITZ, LEONARD DAVID, mathematician, educator; b. Chgo., Jan. 24, 1924; s. Judea and Esther (Trop) B.; m. Anna Whitehouse, June 18, 1953; children Dan M., Kenneth E. BS, U. Chgo., 1946, MS, 1948, PhD, 1951. AEC postdoctoral fellow Stanford U., Calif., 1951-52; rsch. fellow Calif. Inst. Tech., Pasadena, Calif., 1952-54; mathematician Rand Corp., Santa Monica, Calif., 1954-62; prof. math. Purdue U., West Lafayette, Ind., 1962—2003, head math. dept., 1975—80, acting head math dept., 1989—90, prof. emeritus West Lafayette, Ind., 2003—09. Author: Optimal Control Theory, 1974, Optimization and Convexity in Rn, 2002; mem. editl. bd. Soc. for Indsl. and Applied Math. Jour. on Control, 1970-89, Optimization Theory and Applications, 1983-2001, Jour. Math Analysis and Applications; mem. editl. com. Math. Reviews, Am. Math. Soc., 1985-92; contbr. articles to profl. jours. 1st Lt. USAAF, 1943-46. Mem.: Am. Math. Soc. Died Oct. 13, 2009.

BERKOWITZ, MONROE, economist, educator; b. Exeter, Pa., Mar. 9, 1919; s. Edward and Molly (Kaufman) B.; m. Shalvo Schwartz, Mar. 6, 1942; 1 son, Edward. AB, Ohio U., 1942; A.M., Columbia U., 1946, PhD, 1951. Assoc. economist NWLB, 1942-44; mem. faculty Rutgers U., from 1946, prof. econs., from 1960, chmn. dept. econs., prof. emeritus, from 1987. Mem. arbitration panels Am. Arbitration Assn., Fed. Mediation and Conciliation Service, N.Y.C. Office Collective Bargaining; cons. U.S. Dept. Labor, Social Security Adminstrn., Nat. Acad. Scis. Author: Public Policy Toward Disability, 1976, Economics of Accidents in New Zealand, 1979, Disability and the Labor Market, 1986, Permanent Disability Benefitss in Workers' Compensation, 1987. Mem. Nat. Acad. Arbitrators, Am. Econ. Assn., Indsl. Relations Research Assn., Phi Beta Kappa. Home: Naples, Fla. Died Nov. 15, 2009.

BERMAN, SIDNEY, psychiatrist; b. New Haven, Feb. 8, 1919; s. Benjamin and Pauline Muriel (Siegel) B.; m. Jenette Kelly, June 3, 1978; children: Robert Kelly, Barbara Kelly Titus, Leslie Jane Berman Oelsner. BA, Yale Coll., 1939; MD, Long Island Med. Coll., 1943. Diplomate Am. Bd. Psychiatry and Neurology. Intern, asst. resident in medicine and neurology Mt. Sinai Hosp., NYC, 1943-46, resident in neurology, 1943-46; resident staff in psychiatry Fairfield State Hosp., 1948, The Psychoanalytic Clinic for Tng. and Rsch., 1948-49; asst. chief neuropsychiatry VA Hosp., Newington, Conn., 1951-53, chief open psychiat. sect. neuropsychiat. svc. West Haven, Conn., 1953-54; pvt. practice New Haven, Conn., from 1949. Asst. clin. prof. psychiatry Yale Med. Sch., New Haven, 1952-71, assoc. clin. prof., 1971-96, lectr., 1996—; attending psychiatrist Yale-New Haven Med. Ctr., 1960-89, emeritus, 1989—, sr. staff, 1990—; staff psychiatrist Yale U. Health Svc., 1961-89; psychiat. cons. Conn. Alcohol and Drug Abuse Commn., 1984-91. Contbr. 12 articles to profl. jours. Asst. concert master New Haven Civic Symphony Orch., 1973-86; psychiatrist-in-charge Conn. Alcohol Commn. Bridgeport Alcohol Clinic, 1949-51 Capt. AUS, 1946-48. Sterling Meml. scholar Yale, 1935-39; Branford Coll. fellow, 1980—. Fellow Am. Psychiat. Assn. (life); mem. AMA, Conn. Med. Assn., Conn. Psychiat. Assn. (pres. 1957-58). Avocations: music, tennis, squash. Home: New Haven, Conn. Died Jan. 25, 2009.

BERMINGHAM, JOHN CORNELIUS, retired funeral home director; b. Wharton, NJ, Jan. 12, 1920; s. John A. and Anna (Heslin) Bermingham; m. Margaret Hogan, May 18, 1946; children: Ann C., John A. BFA, U. Notre Dame, 1942. Dir. Charter Fed. Savs. Bank, Randolph, NJ, from 1968. Exhibitions include NY Watercolor Soc. (award, 1995). Trustee Northwest Covenant Med. Ctr., Denville, NH, from 1994, SSM Health Care Ministry, Denville, NJ, from 1994. Served to 1st lt. US Army, 1942—46, 1950—52. Recipient Adolph and Clara Obrig prize, NAD, 1984, Cert. of Merit, 1982, Gold medal, Watercolor Acad. Artists, 1977. Mem.: Hudson Valley Art Assn. (pres.'s award 1982, Alvord award

1977, 1994, Coun. Am. Artists Soc. award 1984, Windsor Newton award 1985), NJ Water Color Soc. (pres. 1977—79, Silver medal 1977, 1988), Am. Watercolor Soc. (Edgar A. Whitney award 1981, C.S.F. medal 1989, Anne W. Glushien award 1993), Allied Artists America, Salmagundi Club. Roman Catholic. Home: Newtown, Conn. Died July 4, 2010.

BERNHARDT, DONALD JOHN, bank consultant; b. Bklyn., Feb. 25, 1937; s. Philip Graham and Mary Agnes (McVeigh) B.; m. Muriel Ann Kirk, Nov. 18, 1961; children: Donald Jr., Cory Ann, Kirk Graham. BA in Econs., St. John's U., Bklyn., 1970; postgrad. in internat. banking, U. Colo., 1973; postgrad. in internat. ops., Am. Inst. Banking, 1974. Credit analyst Bank of N.Y. (Empire Trust Co.), NYC, 1958-63; asst. dep. supt. N.Y. State Banking Dept., NYC, 1963-76; compt. Banco do Brasil S.A., NYC, 1976-83; v.p., mgr. Banque Brussel Lambert, NYC, 1983-85; dep. gen. mgr. Bank Dagang Negara, NYC, 1985-89; exec. v.p. Interbank of N.Y., 1989-91; Donald J. Bernhardt & Assoc. Bank Cons. With U.S. Army, 1956-58. Mem. Bank Adminstrn. Inst. (pres. 1984-86), Inst. Internat. Bankers (chmn. regulatory com. 1978-80, chmn. tax com. 1980-82, chmn. res. com. 1982-84). Avocations: reading, music, golf. Home: Valparaiso, Ind. Died June 15, 2009.

BERNSTEIN, JAY, pathologist, researcher, educator; b. NYC, May 14, 1927; s. Michael Kenneth and Frances (Kaufman) B.; m. Carol Irene Kritchman, Aug. 11, 1957; children: John Abel, Michael Kenneth. BA, Columbia U., 1948; MD, SUNY, Bklyn., 1952. Diplomate Am. Bd. Pathology. Asst. pathologist Children's Hosp. Mich., Detroit, 1956-58, assoc. pathologist, 1959, attending pathologist, 1960-62, cons. in lab. medicine, 1977—93, cons. emeritus, from 1993; attending pathologist Bronx Mcpl. Hosp. Ctr., NYC, 1962-68; asst. prof. pathology Albert Einstein Coll. Medicine, Bronx, N.Y., 1962-64, assoc. prof. pathology, 1964-68; chmn. dept. anatomic pathology William Beaumont Hosp., Royal Oak, Mich., 1969-90, dir. Rsch. Inst., 1983-98, assoc. med. dir., 1990-98, hon. consulting pathologist, from 1999; clin. prof. pathology Wayne State U. Sch. Medicine, Detroit, 1977—99. Chmn. sci. adv. bd. Nat. Kidney Found. Mich., 1986-88, nat. sci. adv. bd., 1976-82; sci. advisor Nat. Inst. Child Health, USPHS, 1976-81; profl. adv. bd. Nat. Tuberous Sclerosis Assn., 1990-93; clin. prof. health sci. Oakland U., Rochester, Mich., 1980-90; vis. prof. pathology Albert Einstein Coll. Medicine, Bronx, 1974-2001; com. on renal disease WHO; cons. pathologist Internat. Study of Kidney Diseases in Children, Lupus Study Group. Co-editor: Perspectives in Pediatric Pathology; past contbg. editor Jour. Pediatrics; past mem. editl. bd. Pediatric Nephrology; mem. editl. bd. Jour. Urologic Pathology; contbr. articles to profl. jours. With USN, 1945-46. Recipient Henry L. Barnett award Am. Acad. Pediats., 1997. Mem. AMA, Am. Soc. Investigative Pathology, Internat. Acad. Pathology (U.S.-Can. divsn.), Am. Soc. Clin. Pathologists, Soc. Pediatric Pathology (co-founder, past pres., Farber lectr. 1982, Spl. Disting. Colleague award 1987, 97), Am. Pediatric Soc., Am. Soc. Nephrology, Internat. Pediat. Nephrology Assn., Renal Pathology Soc. (past pres., Renal Pathology Founder award 1997), Am. Soc. Pediatric Nephrology (Founder's award 1999). Home: West Bloomfield, Mich. Died Feb. 26, 2009.

BERNSTEIN, SIDNEY, publishing company executive, lawyer; b. Bronx, NY, May 3, 1938; s. Meyer and Ethel (Sloop) B.; m. Joyce Elaine Blum, July 7, 1963 (div. 1979); children: Michael Louis, Sheryl Lyn; m. Andra Jane Schutz, June 6, 1982 (div. 1987). BA, Columbia U., 1960; JD, Cornell U., 1964. Bar: N.Y. 1966, U.S. Dist. Ct. (we. dist.) N.Y. 1966, U.S. Dist. Ct. (so. dist.) N.Y. 1978, U.S. Ct. Appeals (D.C. cir.) 1980, U.S. Supreme Ct. 1971. Jr. editor Lawyer's Coop. Pub. Co., Rochester, N.Y., 1964-65, asst. mng. editor, 1966-71, editor Case and Comment Mag., 1966-71; sr. mng. editor Matthew Bender & Co., NYC, 1971-75, asst. to pres., 1976-83; chief exec. officer, pres. Kluwer Law Book Pubs., Inc., NYC, 1984-89; counsel Tolmage, Peskin, Harris & Falick, NYC, 1989-90; v.p., pub. Thompson Pub. Group, Washington, NYC, from 1991. Mem. faculty Nat. Coll. Advocacy, 1977-83; mem. adj. faculty NYU Sch. Continuing Edn., 1980-81; assoc. pub. Lawyers Alert mag., 1990-91; cons. Law Press, Inc., Westport, Conn., 1990-91, Moran Pub. Co., 1990-91. Co-author: How To Write a Love Letter That Works, 1991; mem. editorial bd. Trial mag., 1982-83; mem. editorial adv. bd. Am. Criminal Law Rev., 1972-74; exec. editor Nat. Law Rev. Reporter, 1981-83; editor-in-chief Belli Soc. Internat. Law Jour., 1984-88; editor Jud. Rev. Damages, 1991, Criminal Defense Techniques, 6 vols., 1977-83; columnist Supreme Ct. Rev., Trial mag.; also articles. Mem. Roscoe Pound. Found.; adv. coun. Touro Law Sch., Huntington, N.Y.; pres. Belli Soc., 1985-86 Mem. ABA, Am. Law Inst., Am. Soc. Writers on Legal Subjects (past pres.), Assn. Trial Lawyers Am., Am. Judicature Soc., Trial Lawyers for Pub. Justice, Golda Meier Assn. (nat. v.p.), Vols. for Israel, Masons. Republican. Jewish. Home: New York, NY. Died Feb. 28, 2009.

BERNSTEIN, STANLEY ROBERT, financial consultant, mortgage broker and banker; b. Bklyn., July 9, 1921; s. Benjamin and Rose Bernstein; m. Elaine Tropp, June 1, 1946; children: David Allen, Harris Joshua. BS, NYU, 1942; LLB, Blackstone Sch. Law, Chgo., 1962. Owner Stan Burn Electronics, Bklyn., 1946-58; project and contract admin. RCA, Moorestown, N.J., 1958-62, project supr. legal dept., 1962-78; ops. mgr. N.B. Liebman Furniture, Cherry Hill, N.J., 1978-84; financing cons., mortgage banker Cherry Hill, from 1984; mortgage broker Internat. Rubber Techs., Global Tire Recylers, Delray Beach, Fla., from 1992; pres. AB Investments, Cherry Hill, Deerfield Beach, Fla., from 1993; sr. v.p. M.C. Group Inc., Marlton, N.J., from 1993. Vol. staff asst. State Atty., West Palm Beach, Fla., 1992-93; dir. Adult Victims of Domestic Abuse, Delray Beach, 1992-93; chair Nat. Victim's Rights Week, West Palm Beach, 1992-93; pub. rels. officer Fla. Atty. Gen.'s Srs. Against Crime Project, 1993—; campaign com. re-election H. James Saxton, Cherry Hill, 1992. Recipient Commendations Pres. Dwight Eisenhower, Pres. George Bush, Merit award Victim's Rights Coalition, 1992, listee Spl. Dir. Air Force Assn. ltd. 60,000 officers. Mem. Air Force Assn., Res. Officers Assn., Disabled Am. Vets., VFW, Am. Legion, Adam Smith Soc. (honoree), Phi Sigma Delta, Masons. Avocations: golf, bridge, travel. Home: Delray Beach, Fla. Died Nov. 25, 2009.

BERNSTINE, RICHARD LEE, obstetrician/gynecologist, educator; b. Phila., Jan. 8, 1925; s. J. Bernard and Rena (Berkowitz) B.; m. Joyce Tully, June 1, 1971. Student, St. Joseph's Coll., 1942-43, Villanova U., 1943-44; MD, Jefferson Med. Coll., 1948. Diplomate Am. Bd. Obstetrics & Gynecology. Intern Jefferson Med. Coll., Phila., 1948-50, instr. dept. obstetrics and gynecology, 1952-56, fellow in obstetrics and gynecology, 1954-56; enlisted USN, 1948, advanced through grades to capt., 1968; resident in obstetrics and gynecology U.S Naval Hosp., LI, N.Y., 1956-59, with obstetrics and gynecology staff Portsmouth, Va., 1959-62; sr. med. officer U.S. Naval Support Activity, London, 1962-65; force med. officer CINCUSNAVEUR, London, 1964-65; with clin. investigation dept. staff U.S. Naval Med. Research Inst. Nat. Med. Ctr., Bethesda, Md., 1965-70; with obstetrics and gynecology staff U.S. Naval Hosp., Bethesda, Md., 1966-70; retired USN, 1970; sr. research scientist Dept. Chemistry Am. U., Washington, 1970-73; head clin. specialties br. Research div. Bur. Medicine and Surgery USN, Washington, 1970-73; research scientist Health Care Study Ctr. Batelle Human Affairs Research Ctrs., Seattle, 1973-76; prof. obstetrics and genecology The Northeastern Ohio Univs. Coll. of Medicine, Rootstown, Ohio, from 1976; dir. edn. St. Elizabeth Hosp. Med. Ctr., Youngstown, Ohio, 1976-89. Author: (with others) Clinical Ultrasound in Obstetrics and Gynecology, 1978, Principles and Practice of Obstetrics and Perinatology, 1981, Ultrasound in Medicine and Biology, 1982, Operative Perinatology, Invasive Obstetric Techniques, 1984, Obstetrics/Gynecology: A Problem-Oriented Approach, 1985; contbg. editor Jour. of Clin. Ultrasound and scientific exhibits. Recipient Certificate of Merit AMA, 1956, 59, Bronze award AMA, Am. Acad. Pediatrics, 1971, Prize award Am. Coll. Obstetricians and Gynecologists, 1972. Mem. Am. Coll. Obstetrics and Gynecology (Prize award 1970), ACS, Am. Inst. Ultrasound in Medicine, Ohio State Med. Assn., Mahoning County Med. Soc., Nat. Bd. Med. Examiners. Home: Youngstown, Ohio. Died Mar. 15, 2009.

BERRIDGE, GEORGE BRADFORD, retired lawyer; b. Detroit, June 9, 1928; s. William Lloyd and Marjorie (George) B.; m. Mary Lee Robinson, July 6, 1957; children: George Bradford, Elizabeth A., Mary L., Robert L. AB, U. Mich., 1950, MBA, 1953, JD, 1954. Bar: N.Y. 1954. Assoc. Chadbourne & Parke, NYC, 1954-61; gen. atty., v.p. law Am. Airlines, Inc., NYC, 1961-71; sr. v.p., gen. counsel Americana Hotels, Inc., NYC, 1971-74, Nat. Westminster Bank U.S.A., NYC, 1975-89, Nat. Westminster Bancorp, NYC, 1989-93; ret., 1993. Contbr. articles to U. Mich. Law Rev. Served to lt. (j.g.) USN, 1951-53. Recipient Howard P. Coblentz prize U. Mich. Law Sch., 1954. Episcopalian. Home: Larchmont, NY. Died Aug. 2, 2009.

BERTELSEN, WILLIAM ROBERT, emergency care physician; b. Moline, Ill., May 20, 1920; s. John William and Cecilia Gertrude (Frey) B.; m. Alberta Carrol Menzel, Sept. 21, 1946; children: William D., Julia Sue, Janet Doris, Andrea Carol. BS, U. Ill., 1944; MD, U. Ill., Chgo., 1947. Project engr. exptl. dept. Mpls.-Moline Power Implement Co., 1940-42; intern St. Luke's Hosp., Chgo., 1947-48; resident in chest medicine Fitzsimons Army Hosp., Denver, 1953-55; pvt. practice Neponset, Ill., 1948-63; with Fitzsimons Army Hosp., Denver, 1953-55; pvt. practice Rock Island, Ill., 1963-69; emergency care physician, from 1973. Pres., chmn. Bertelsen, Inc., Neponset, 1960-94, v.p. R&D, dir., 1970-94, Aeromobile, Inc., Neponset, 1994—; lectr. Nat. Air and Space Mus. Smithsonian Instn., 1993. Lt. (j.g.) USN, 1947-48. Named Pioneer of Advanced Marine Vehicles Intersoc. Advanced Marine Vehicle Conf., 1989. Fellow AIAA (assoc.), Brit. Hovercraft Soc., Can. Aeronautics and Space Inst.; mem. AMA, Exptl. Aircraft Assn., Nat. Space Inst., U.S. Hovercraft Soc., Physicians for Social Responsibility, Sigma Xi. Achievements include first to fly man-carrying air cushion vehicle; invented arcopter VTOL aircraft, aeromobile air cushion vehicle, Gimbal fan air cushion vehicle, air cushion crawler tractor. Home: Rock Falls, Ill. Died July 16, 2009.

BERTON, JOHN ANDREW, mathematics educator; b. Villa Park, Ill., June 22, 1930; s. Phillip Lansdale and Kathryn (Henricksen) B.; m. Martha Kathleen Shoemaker, Aug. 23, 1952; children: John, Kathleen, David, Peter, Susan. Postgrad., Canterbury Coll., Danville, 1948-51, Ripon Coll., Wis., 1951-52; BA, U. of Ill., Urbana, 1955, PhD, 1964. Instr. Ind. State U., Terre Haute, Ind., 1959-60, asst. prof. of math., 1960-64; assoc prof. of math. Ripon Coll., Wis., 1964-67; prof. of math. Ohio Northern U., Ada, from 1967. Chmn. Hardin Co. Bd. Men Retardation and DD, Kenton, 1979-83; dist. Sct. chmn. Put-Han-Sen Area Council Boy Scouts of Am., Findlay, 1980--. Mem. Am. Math. Soc., Math. Assn. of Am., Nat. Council of Teachers of Math., Ass. for Computer Mach., Am. Assn. of U. Profs., Soc. for Indsl. and Applied Math., Lions Club (treas.), Masons (sec.) Episcopal. Home: Ottawa, Kans. Died Mar. 23, 2010.

BERUBEY, CAROLINE, electronic coil manufacturing company executive; b. East Longmeadow, Mass., June 10, 1923; d. Felice Anthony and Theresa (Belcamino) Costantini; m. Leroy Anthony Berubey, Dec. 16, 1943 (dec. Sept. 1981); 1 dau., Carole Anne Berubey Chapdelaine. Student pub. schs., Springfield, Mass. With Electronic Coils, Inc., Springfield, 1948—, v.p. adminstrn.; 1980—; notary pub. Mem. Springfield Bus. and Profl. Women (sec.). Home: Ludlow, Mass. Died July 22, 2009.

BERWIND, CHARLES GRAHAM, JR., retired manufacturing executive; b. Bryn Mawr, Pa., Nov. 13, 1928; s. Charles Graham Berwind; m. Joanne Berwind; children: Charles III, James, Jessica, Joanna. Diploma, U. Vt., 1951; MBA, Harvard U., 1953. Chmn., pres., CEO Berwind Corp., Phila., 1972—97, co-chmn., 1997—2006. Bd. dir. Phila. Orchestra. Served in USCG. Home: Bryn Mawr, Pa. Died Nov. 3, 2010.

BEVINGTON, EDMUND MILTON, electrical machinery manufacturing company executive; b. Nashville, Oct. 31, 1928; s. John Laurence and Mary (Halloran) B.; m. Elizabeth Anne Rickey, Sept. 8, 1951 (dec. June 1962); children: Milton, Rickey, Peter (dec.); m. Paula Maureen Lawton, Apr. 24, 1965; children: George, Mary-Laurence, Christian, Charles, Justin. Grad., Canterbury Sch., 1945; S.B. in Chem. Engring, Mass. Inst. Tech., 1949; MBA, Harvard, 1951. Plant supr. Dewey & Almy Chem. Co. (name changed to W.R. Grace Co., 1954), Cambridge, Mass., 1951-54, marketing research mgr., 1954-56; merchandising mgr. Westinghouse Electric Co., Staunton, Va., 1956-58, So. zone sales mgr. Atlanta, 1958-59; with The Trane Co., Atlanta and LaCrosse, Wis., from 1959, v.p., gen. mgr. consumer products div., 1969-70, exec. v.p., 1970-73; pres. Servidyne Systems, Inc., Atlanta, 1974—2002, Bevington & Co., Atlanta, 2002—07, Bevington Advisors, LLC, from 2008. Co-founder, prin. Bevington Advisors, LLC., Atlanta, 2008-; bd. dirs. AAA South. Mem. corp. devel. com. MIT, 1978—, bd. dirs. MIT Corp., 1985-91; chmn. Ga. Conservancy, 1989-92, bd. dirs.; bd. dirs. Atlanta coun. Boy Scouts Am., also v.p., 1989-90, pres., 1990-92; bd. dirs. So. region Boy Scouts Am.; pres. Metro Group, 1992-97; bd. dirs. Ga. Dept. Cmty. Affairs, 1988-92; bd. dirs. Flannery O'Connor-Andalusia Found, 2002. Mem. Pres.' Cir. of NAS, MIT Alumni Assn. (v.p. 1983-85, pres. 1985-86), Harvard Club, (NYC), Piedmont Driving Club (Atlanta), Tau Beta Pi, Sigma Alpha Epsilon. Home: Atlanta, Ga. Died May 20, 2010.

BEYER, GORDON ROBERT, retired ambassador; b. Chgo., Oct. 13, 1930; m. Mary Paine Winsor, Feb. 22, 1951; children: Theresa Gordon, Hugh Richard, Thomas Paine. AB, Harvard U.; MA, Northwestern U.; postgrad., Nat. War Coll., 1971-72. With Pres.'s Commn. on Vets.' Pensions (Bradley Commn.), 1956; commd. fgn. service officer US Dept. State, 1957; officer US Embassy, Bangkok, 1957-59, Washington, 1959-61, consul Yokohama, Japan, 1961-64, officer Somalia, consul Hargeisa, 1964-66, Mogadishu, 1966-67, dep. chief of mission Dar es Salaam, Tanzania, 1972-75; with US Dept. State, Washington, 1967-72, dep. dir. Egyptian desk, 1975-77, dir. Office East African Affairs, 1978-80, US amb. to Uganda Kampala, 1980-83; officer U.S. UN, 1977; with Nat. War Coll., 1983-85; pres. George C. Marshall Found., Lexington, Va., 1985-91. Bd. dirs. Dar es Salaam Internat. Sch., 1972-75, pres., 1974 Author: (monographs) Race and National Security, 1972, Can Low Intensity Conflict be Managed?, 1987, The Marshall Plan: A Contemporary View, 1989, America, Japan and the Atomic Bomb, 1993, The Who?, 1995. Chmn. Rockbridge County Dem. Com. 1st lt. USMC, 1953-55. Recipient meritorious honor awards US Dept. State, 1967, 75, 82. Mem. Am. Fgn. Service Assn., Cosmos Club (Washington), Harvard Club (N.Y.C.), Dacor Club (Washington). Home: Peterborough, NH. Died June 4, 2010.

BIBERMAN, LUCIEN MORTON, retired physicist; b. Phila., May 31, 1919; s. Lewis and Eva (Kerns) Biberman; m. Anne H. Wilner, Mar. 8, 1941 (dec. 1997); children: Leslie Biberman Gordon, Judith Biberman Robinson, Candace Biberman Evans; m. Virgina L. Hewitt, May 25, 2002. BS, Rensselaer Poly. Inst., 1940; postgrad., Harvard U., Cambridge, Mass., 1940-41, Stevens Inst., Hoboken, NJ, 1941-42. Phys. chemist Nairn Rsch. Labs., 1942-43; physicist in charge Mayport Magnetic Survey Area, Navy Dept., 1943-44; various positions from physicist in charge phys. measurements group to cons. Aviation Ordnance Dept. and Weapons Devel. Dept. Naval Ordnance Test Sta., 1944-57; assoc. dir. Labs. for Applied Scis. U. Chgo., 1957-63; rsch. staff rsch. and engring. support div. Inst. for Def. Analysis, Alexandria, Va., 1963-71, rsch. staff sci. and tech. div., 1972-96, emeritus, 1996—2010. Vis. prof. dept. elec. engring. U. R.I., 1971-72; fellow Mil. Sensing Symposium, 1999. Decorated citation U.S. Army Ctr. for Night Vision and Electro Optics; recipient Andrew J. Goodpaster award, 1989. Fellow: Washington Acad. of Sci. (Disting. Career in Sci. award), Soc. Photo-optical Instrumentation Engrs. (emeritus), Soc. Info. Display (emeritus), Optical Soc. Am. (emeritus), IEEE (life), Military Sensors Symposium, Infrared Info. Symposia. Died Mar. 28, 2010.

BICKERS, JAMES FRANKLIN, JR., management consultant; b. Bartlett, Tenn., Mar. 2, 1919; s. James Franklin and Kathryn Pauline (Diefenbach) B.; m. Emily Power, May 3, 1941; children— James Franklin, III, John P., Barbara L. B.F.A., U. Ill., 1941; grad. sr. exec. program, M.I.T., 1968. With R.R. Donnelley & Sons Co., Chgo., from 1951, v.p., then sr. v.p. gen. catalog sales div., 1969-75, group v.p. directories, 1975-81; group v.p. Digital Group R.R. Donnelley's Sons Co., from 1981. Served with AUS, 1941-45. Mem. Direct Mail/Mktg. Assn. (past dir.). Clubs: Tavern (Chgo.); Sunset Ridge Country, Dairymen's Country. Republican. Died Mar. 19, 2010.

BICKLEY, WILLIAM ELBERT, retired entomologist, editor; b. Knoxville, Tenn., Jan. 20, 1914; s. William Elbert and Lucretia Howe (Jordan) B.; m. Elizabeth Macgill, Apr. 5, 1941 (dec. 1997); children: Lucretia Bickley Pope, James Macgill, David Clarke, Edith Clarke Bickley Robb. B.S., U. Tenn., 1934, M.S., 1936; Ph.D., U. Md., 1940. Instr. entomology, U. Md., College Park, 1940-42; entomologist USPHS,

Norfolk, Va., 1942-46; asst. prof. biology U. Richmond, Va., 1946-49, assoc. prof., prof., dept. entomology, U. Md., College Park, 1949-78, head dept., 1956-71, prof. emeritus, 1978—2010; Editor Jour. Mosquito News, 1973-81; bibliography editor Jour. American Mosquito Control Assn., 1985-87; book review editor; Contbr. articles to sci. jours. Vol. researcher Walter Reed Biosystematics Unit, Smithsonian Instn. Mem. American Mosquito Control Assn., Entomol. Soc. Am., Entomol. Soc. Washington, Council of Biology Editors, Pest Sci. Soc. Washington, Washington Acad. Scis. Lodge: Rotary. Died Aug. 2, 2010.

BICKNESE, GUNTHER, German language educator, translator; b. Gutersloh, West Germany, Feb. 16, 1926; arrived in US, 1955; s. Ernst F. K. and Emma W. F. (Reinking) Bicknese; m. Gisela Marietta Eppe, Aug. 26, 1957; children: Karsten Mark E., Ralf. PhD, Philipps U., Marburg, W. Germany, 1953. Asst. prof. German, Southwestern U., Memphis, 1960—63; assoc. prof. Millersville State U., Pa., 1963—66; dir. Jr. Yr. in Marburg program, 1963—66; assoc. prof. Agnes Scott Coll., Decatur, Ga., 1963—70; prof. German, from 1970; chmn. dept., from 1969. Coord. European Study Tours. Author: Elementary German, 3d edit., 1976, Hier und Heute (German Reader), 1983, Travelog for young readers, 1957; translator: (novels) A Private Treason, 1981. Mem.: Am. Coun. Tchg. Fgn. Langs., Am. Assn. Tchrs. of German. Home: Suwanee, Ga. Died June 21, 2009.

BIDGOOD, BERKELEY CARRINGTON, tobacco corporation executive; b. Richmond, Va., Mar. 18, 1925; s. Charles Young and Mary (Carrington) B.; m. Harriett Bagardus Kirk, May 29, 1950; children: Ruth Kirk, Mary Taylor, Harriet Henley, Berkeley Carrington. Student, Williams Coll., Babson Bus. Inst., Boston. Trainee E.V. Webb Co., Kinston, N.C., 1949-54, Dibrell Bros., Inc., Danville, Va., 1954-61, asst. v.p., 1961-70, v.p., 1970-78, sr. v.p., from 1978, also dir. Dir. Am. Nat. Bank & Trust Co., Danville Bd. dirs. Danville YMCA, 1976-82. Served with USMC, 1943-46. Republican. Episcopalian. Home: Danville, Va. Died Jan. 3, 2009.

BIEGEL, JOHN EDWARD, retired industrial engineering educator; b. Eau Claire, Wis., Nov. 19, 1925; s. Otto Robert and Charlotte Mary (McGough) B.; m. Geraldine Elizabeth Lawrence, July 22, 1955 (div. Feb. 1978), remarried Nov. 22, 1986; children: Steven, N. Dale, Kurt. BS in Indsl. Engring., Mont. State U., 1948; MS in Engring. Sci., Stanford U., 1950; PhD in Solid State Sci., Syracuse U., 1972. Registered profl. engr., Fla. Instr. math. Mont. State U., Bozeman, 1948-49; instr., asst. prof. U. Ark., Fayetteville, 1950-52; engr. Ford Motor Co., Claycomo, Mo., 1952-53, Sandia Corp., Albuquerque, 1953-58; prof. Syracuse (N.Y.) U., 1958-78, Kans. State U., Manhattan, 1978-82; prof. indsl. engring. U. Ctrl. Fla., Orlando, 1982-98; ret., 1998. Rschr. in intelligent tchg. sys.; cons. IBM, Endicott, N.Y., 1980-81. Author: Production Control, 1963, 2d edit., 1971; inventor high strain rate tensile test device. With USNR, 1944-46, PTO. NSF sci. faculty fellow U. Calif., Berkeley, 1964-65. Mem. Inst. Indsl. Engrs. Avocation: woodworking. Home: Loveland, Colo. Died Jan. 20, 2010.

BIERMAN, GEORGE WILLIAM, retired food scientist; b. Cleve., Mar. 2, 1925; s. George Henry and Esther Josephine (Johnson) B.; m. Nyo Jeanne Iserloth; children: Cynthia, Barbara, Marsha, Jill, Wendy, Mindy, G. Steven, Chris. BS, Rutgers U., 1951; PhD, MIT, 1956. Technician R&D Am. Can Co., Maywood, Ill., 1943-45, Schering Corp., Bloomfield, NJ, 1947-48; tech. dir. Friend Bros., Inc., Malden, Mass., 1951-58; v.p. Herbert V. Shuster, Inc., Boston, 1958-75, pres. Quincy, Mass., 1975-89, vice chmn. bd., 1989-95, sr. scientist, 1995-96; tech. cons. Shuster Labs. Inc., 1996—98; ret., 1998. Sgt. U.S. Army, 1945-47. Mem.: Nat. Fisheries Inst. (smoked fish com. 1968—98), Inst. Food Technologists, Assn. Smoked Fish Processors (tech. dir. 1968—98). Presbyterian. Avocation: gardening. Home: Shrewsbury, Mass. Died June 9, 2009.

BIGELEISEN, JACOB, chemist, educator; b. Paterson, NJ, May 2, 1919; s. Harry and Ida (Slomowitz) Bigeleisen; m. Grace Alice Simon, Oct. 21, 1945; children: David M., Ira S., Paul E. AB, NYU, 1939; MS, Wash. State U., 1941; PhD, U. Calif., Berkeley, 1943. Rsch. scientist Manhattan Dist., Columbia, 1943-45; rsch. assoc. Ohio State U., Columbus, 1945-46; fellow Enrico Fermi Inst., U. Chgo., 1946-48; sr. chemist Brookhaven Nat. Lab., Upton, NY, 1948-68; prof. chemistry U. Rochester, NY, 1968-78, chmn. dept., 1970-75; Tracy H. Harris prof. U. Rochester (Coll. Arts and Scis.), 1973-78; v.p. research, dean grad. studies SUNY, Stony Brook, 1978-80, Leading prof. chemistry, 1978-89, Disting. prof., 1989, Disting. prof. emeritus, from 1989. Vis. prof. Cornell U., 1953; NSF sr. fellow, vis. prof. Eidgen Techn. Hochschule, Switzerland, 1962—63; chmn. Assembly Math. and Phys. Scis. NRC-Nat. Acad. Scis., 1976—80. Mem. editl. bd.: Jour. Phys. Chemistry, Jour. Chem. Physics. Trustee Sayville Jewish Ctr., 1954—68. Recipient Gilbert N. Lewis lectr., 1963, E. O. Lawrence award, 1964, Disting. Alumnus award, Wash. State U., 1983, Meliora award, Univ. Rochester, 1978; fellow John Simon Guggenheim, 1974—75. Fellow: AAAS, Am. Acad. Arts and Sci., Am. Chem. Soc. (Nuc. award 1958), Am. Phys. Soc.; mem.: Nat. Acad. Scis. (councilor 1982—85), Phi Lambda Upsilon, Sigma Xi, Phi Beta Kappa. Achievements include research in photochemistry in rigid media; isotopes; isotope separation; quantum statistics of gases; liquids and solids. Died Aug. 6, 2010.

BILANIUK, OLEKSA MYRON, physicist, researcher; b. Ukraine, Dec. 15, 1926; arrived in U.S., 1951, naturalized, 1957; s. Petro and Maria B.; m. Larissa T. Zubal, Nov. 14, 1964; children: Larissa, Laada. Student, U. Louvain, 1947—51; MS, U. Mich., 1953, MA, 1954, PhD, 1957; Dr. honoris causa (hon.), Nat. Univ. Lviv, Ukraine, 2002. Post-doctoral fellow U. Mich., 1957-58; rsch. assoc., asst. prof. U. Rochester, 1958-64; assoc. prof. physics Swarthmore (Pa.) Coll., 1964-70, prof., 1970-82, Swarthmore Centennial prof., from 1982. Vis. scientist Argentine Atomic Energy Commn., Buenos Aires, 1961-62, Institut de Physique Nucléaire, Orsay, France, spring 1980, Laboratori Nazionali di Frascati, Italy, spring 1984, U. Munich, fall 1988; vis. prof., cons. Delhi U., summer 1966, Shivaji U., Kolhapur, India, summer 1969, Faculté des Scis., Rabat, Morocco, spring 1978, Kiev U. Ukraine, spring 1994, Inst. Med. Radiology, Kharkiv, Ukraine, summer 1996; Fulbright prof. Lima, Peru, summer 1971, Kinshasa, Zaïre, fall 1975. NSF fellow Max Planck Inst., Heidelberg, Germany, 1967-68, Inst. Physique Nucléaire, Orsay, 1972; NAS exch. scientist Kiev, Ukrainian SSR, 1976, Spl. Recognisation medal, Ukraine Pres., 2007. Mem. Am. Phys. Soc., Nat. Acad. Scis. Ukraine, Ukrainian Acad. Arts and Scis. in U.S. (pres. 1998-2006), Schevchenko Sci. Soc. in U.S., European Phys. Soc., Société Française de Physique, Phi Beta Kappa, Sigma Xi. Achievements include research on nuclear structure; with Deshpande and Sudarshan challenged the view that Einstein's relativity precludes the possibility of existence of particles that travel faster than light, 1962. Home: Wallingford, Pa. Died Mar. 27, 2009.

BILDERBACK, GILBERT DEAN, printing company executive; b. Murphysboro, Ill., Dec. 9, 1935; s. Lester J. and Wanda M. (Berkbigler) Bilderback; m. Carolyn Janice Rench Bilderback, June 10, 1956; 1 child, Stephen E. BS, in Bus. So. Ill. U., 1962. Salesman Orchard Corp., St. Louis, 1957—66, dir. purchasing & traffic ops., from 1966. Mem. City Zoning Commn., Crestwood, Mo., 1984. Pres. Watson Elem. Sch. PTA, 1978—79; v.p. Truman Middle Sch. PTA, 1982—83; chmn. Troop 581 Gravois council Boy Scouts America, from 1982. Named Citizen of Yr., Crestwood-Sunset Hills C. of C., 1984. Mem.: Masons, Rotary (pres. 1984). Avocations: golf, travel. Home: Saint Louis, Mo. Died Oct. 15, 2009.

BILES, DONALD MCKAY, hotel executive; b. Phila., Nov. 2, 1922; s. Leslie Grant and Margaret Elizabeth (Batty) Biles; m. Eleanor Marie Milland, Sept. 13, 1947; children: Leslie Ann Biles Rode, Daniel Thomas, Robert Michael. BS in Hotel Adminstrn., Cornell U., 1952. With Skytop Lodges, Inc., Pa., from 1952, v.p., gen. mgr. Pa., 1968—74, pres., dir., gen. mgr. Pa., from 1974; also bd. dirs.; pres. Pocono Hotels Corp. Bd. dirs. Hotel Securities Corp.; instr. resort mgmt. Cornell U., Ithaca, NY, 1961—67. Trustee, mem. fin. com. Pocono Hosp., East Stroudsburg, Pa., 1974. With US Army, 1942—45, ETO. Decorated Bronze Star, Purple Heart. Mem.: Pa. Hotel-Motel Assn., Am. Hotel-Motel Assn. (exec. com., resort com.), Skytop Club (v.p. from 1974). Republican. Roman Catholic. Home: Skytop, Pa. Died Sept. 24, 2009.

BILLINGS, CHARLES EDGAR, physician; b. Boston, June 15, 1929; s. Charles Edgar and Elizabeth (Sanborn) B.; m. Lillian Elizabeth Wilson, Apr. 16, 1955; 1 dau., Lee Ellen Billings Kreinbihl. Student, Wesleyan U., 1947-49; MD, N.Y. U., 1953; M.Sc. (Link Found. fellow), Ohio State U., 1960. Diplomate: Am. Bd. Preventive Medicine. Instr. to prof. depts. preventive medicine and aviation Sch. Medicine Ohio State U., 1960-73, dir. div. environ. health Sch. Medicine, 1970-73, clin. prof. Sch. Medicine, 1973-83, prof. emeritus, from 1983; rsch. scientist integrated systems engring., from 1992. Med. officer NASA Ames Rsch. Ctr., Moffett Field, Calif., 1973-76; chief Aviation Safety Rsch. Office, 1976-80, asst. chief for rsch. Man-Vehicle Systems rsch. divsn., 1980-83, sr. scientist, 1983-91; chief scientist Ames Rsch. Ctr., 1991-92; cons. Beckett Aviation Corp., 1962-73; surgeon gen. U.S. Army, 1965-77, FAA, 1967-70, 75, 83; mem. NATO-AGARD Aerospace Med. Panel, 1980-86; assoc. advisor USAF Sci. Adv. Bd., 1978-90; mem. human factors adv. panel U.K. Civil Aviation Authority, 1999-2001; mem. aviation adv. bd. Ohio U., 2000-01. Author: Aviation Automation: The Search for a Human-Centered Approach, 1997; contbr. chpts. to books, numerous articles in field to med. jours. Served to maj. USAF, 1955-57. Recipient Air Traffic Svc. award FAA, 1969, Walter M. Boothby rsch. award, 1972, PATCO Air Safety award, 1979, Disting. Svc. award Flight Safety Found., 1979, John A. Tamisea award, 1980, Laura Taber Barbour Air Safety medal, 1981, Outstanding Leadership medal NASA, 1981, 90, Jeffries Aerospace Med. Rsch. medal AIAA, 1986, Lovelace award NASA Soc. Flight Surgeons, 1996, Forrest and Pamela Bird award Civil Aviation Med. Assn., 2001, Henry L. Taylor Founders award Aerospace Human Factors Assn, 2002; Ames Rsch. Ctr. fellow, 1989. Fellow AIAA (assoc.), Royal Aero. Soc., Aerospace Med. Assn. (pres. 1979-80); mem. AMA, Internat. Acad. Aviation and Space Medicine. Home: Columbus, Ohio. Died Aug. 30, 2010.

BINGHAM, CHARLES TIFFANY, JR., estate investment executive; b. Hartford, Conn., June 19, 1933; s. Charles Tiffany and Kathleen Watson (Howell) B.; m. Alice Berry Condon, June 28, 1958 (div. 1978); children— Eleanor Berry, Grace Bradlee, Charles Tiffany III; m. Ann Sanders Dickey, Aug., 1982. BA, Yale U., 1956. With Am. Snuff Co. (now Conwood Corp.), Memphis, 1960-78, regional sales mgr., 1967-70, asst. v.p., 1971-73, v.p. internat., 1973-78; exec. v.p. Memphis C. of C., 1979-84; engaged in real estate investments, 1985—. Dir. Conwood Corp., Data Communications Corp. Chmn. Regional Export Council, 1974-75, State of Tenn.-Japan S.E. Council, 1975, Tenn. Gov.'s Jobs Conf., 1979, Tenn. Film Commn., 1981, Memphis Pvt. Industry Council, 1980-84, Hands Across Am., Tenn., 1986; dir. ops. & devel. Am. Arts Alliance, 1989—. Served to capt. USMC, 1956-60. Episcopalian. Home: Washington, DC. Died Sept. 27, 2009.

BIRENBAUM, WILLIAM MARVIN, retired academic administrator; b. Macomb, Ill., July 18, 1923; s. Joseph and Rose (Whiteman) B.; m. Helen Bloch, Mar. 8, 1951; children: Susan (dec. 2008), Lauren Amy, Charles. Dr. Law, U. Chgo., 1949; L.H.D., Columbia Coll., Chgo., 1970. Dean students Univ. Coll., 1955-57. Dir. research, conf. bd. Asso. Research Councils, Ford Found. project study post-doctoral internat. ednl. exchanges, 1954-55; asst. v.p. Wayne State U., 1957-61; dean New Sch. Social Research, N.Y.C., 1961-64; v.p., provost Bklyn. Center, L.I. U., 1964-67; pres. Edn. Affiliate, Bedford-Stuyvesant Devel. & Services Corp., Bklyn, 1967-68, S.I. Community Coll., 1968-76; pres. Antioch U., 1976-85. Author: Overlive: Power, Poverty and the University, 1968, Something for Everybody is Not Enough: An Educator's Search for His Education, 1971; Contbg. author: Student Personnel Work in Urban Colleges. Cons. Austrian Ministry Edn., Vienna, 1969; higher edn. adviser Republic of Zambia, 1972; cons. U. Zambia, 1972; faculty Salzburg Seminar in Am. Studies, 1976; founder Nat. Student Assn., 1946-48; chmn. Mich. Cultural Commn., 1960-61; founder, original dir. Detroit Adventure, vol. assn. cultural instns., 1958-61; bd. adv. Bklyn. Acad. Music, Bklyn Inst. Arts and Scis; trustee Friends World Coll., Westbury, NY, Hasbro Childrens Found., 1985-99, Lit. Vols. NYC, 1986-98, Met. Coll. NY Mem. Chgo. Bar Assn., Delta Sigma. Home: Brooklyn, NY. Died Oct. 4, 2010.

BISHOP, DORIS JACKSON, retired government official; b. Rahway, N.J., June 26, 1927; d. Alfred Charles and Ella Mae (Snyder) Jackson; student Parsons Sch. Design, 1945, U. Nev., 1949, Coll. Charleston, 1971-72; m. Frank Davis Bishop (dec.). Statis. officer, mgmt. analyst Naval Supply Center, Charleston, S.C., 1958-73; dep. command EEO officer, Fed. Women's Program coordinator Naval Supply Systems Command, Washington, 1973-75; coordinator, dep. dir. EEO/Fed. Women's Program, Mil. Dist. Washington, U.S. Army, 1975-79; internal EEO program mgr. FHWA, Denver, 1979-80; regional EEO officer Nat. Park Service, Denver, 1980-85. Bd. dirs. Amberwick Homeowners Assn., 1980-82, Greenhouse Condominium, Alexandria, Va., 1977-79, Tibetan Found., Inc., 1984—. Served with USAF, 1951-53. Named Career Woman of Yr., Bus. and Profl. Women, Charleston, 1967; recipient Outstanding Performance awards, U.S. Navy, U.S. Army. Columnist, Alex Port Packet, weekly, 1977-79. Home: Golden, Colo. Died Aug. 15, 2010.

BISHOP, PAUL D., lawyer; b. Batavia, NY, Dec. 6, 1944; AB cum laude, Harvard U., 1966, JD cum laude, 1970. Bar: Mass. 1970. Atty. Mintz, Levin, Cohn, Ferris, Glovsky and Popeo, P.C., Boston. Fellow Am. Coll. Trust and Estate Counsel; mem. ABA, Mass. Bar Assn., Boston Bar Assn. (probate com. 1974—), Phi Beta Kappa. Died Jan. 16, 2009.

BISHOP, RICHARD WOODROW, lawyer, writer; b. Wayland, Mass., July 16, 1916; s. Warren Langmard and Edna Florella (Felch) Bishop; m. Ida Finch, Sept. 17, 1938; children: Richard L., Gregory F., Jill Rubalcaba. LLB, Boston U., 1938. Bar: Mass. 1938, Fed. 1940, U.S. Supreme Ct. 1946. Ptnr. Bishop, Ahern & Michienzi, Medford, Mass., 1938—87, of counsel, from 1987. Author: Stepping Stones to Light, 1954, From Kite to Kitty Hawk, 1956, Prima Facie Case 4 vols., from 1957. Vestry and clk. Grace Episcopal Ch., Medford; pres. Medford (Mass.) C. of C., 1965; trustee and clk. Lawrence Meml. Hosp.; trustee Hallmark Health, Melrose. Capt. JAG US Army, 1945—46. Mem.: Rotary (pres. Medford chpt. 1967). Republican. Episcopalian. Avocations: photography, stamp collecting/philately. Home: Stoneham, Mass. Died Feb. 13, 2009.

BISSELL, GEORGE ARTHUR, architect; b. L.A., Jan. 31, 1927; s. George Arthur and Ruby Zoe (Moore) B.; m. Laurene Conlon, Nov. 21, 1947; children: Teresa Ann, Thomas Conlon, William George, Robert Anthony, Mary Catherine. BArch, U. So. Calif., 1953. Registered architect, Calif. Ptnr. Bissell Co., Covina, Calif., 1953-57, Bissell & Durquette, A.I.A., Pasadena, Calif., 1957-61; owner George Bissell, A.I.A., Laguna Beach, Calif., 1961-65; ptnr. Riley & Bissell, A.I.A., Newport Beach, Calif., 1965-72; pres. Bissell/August, Inc., Newport Beach, 1972-83, Bissell Architects, Inc., Newport Beach, 1983—2010. Bd. dirs. Newport Ctr. Assn., 1973-78, Lido Isle Community Assn., Newport Beach, 1985-87, Hamilton Cove Assn., 1991-92. With U.S. Mcht. Marine, 1944-46. Fellow AIA (pres. Orange County chpt. 1975, Calif. coun. 1978, nat. bd. dirs. 1980-83, Progressive Arch. award 1974, Nat. AIA Honor award 1978, 98, Merit award Calif. Coun. 1988, AIA Calif. Coun. Lifetime Achievement award, 2000); mem. Newport Harbor Yacht Club, Lido Isle Yacht Club. Avocations: sailing, skiing, travel. Home: Newport Beach, Calif. Died Jan. 2, 2010.

BISSINGER, FREDERICK LEWIS, retired manufacturing executive; b. NYC, Jan. 11, 1911; s. Jacob Frederick and Rosel (Ensslin) B.; m. Julia E. Stork, Aug. 4, 1935 (dec. Dec. 1989); children: Frederick Louis, Elizabeth Julia; m. Barbara S. Simmonds, Dec. 4, 1993. ME, Stevens Inst. Tech., 1933, MS in Chemistry, 1936, DEng (hon.), 1973; JD, Fordham U., 1938. Bar: D.C. 1937, N.Y. 1939, Ohio 1943, U.S. Supreme Ct. 1943. Instr. chemistry Stevens Inst. Tech., Hoboken, NJ, 1933-36; assoc. Pennie, Davis, Marvin & Edmonds, NYC, 1936-42; counsel, bus. cons. Pennie, Davis, Marvin & Edmonds (name now Pennie & Edmonds), NYC, from 1976; with Indsl. Rayon Corp., Cleve., 1942-61, v.p. charge rsch., 1948-57, group v.p. mktg. and rsch., 1957-59, v.p., gen. mgr., 1959-60, pres., chief exec. officer, 1960-61; group v.p. Midland-Ross Corp., Cleve., 1961-62; v.p., dir., mem. exec. com. Stauffer Chem. Co., NYC, 1962-65; v.p. Allied Chem. Corp., NYC, 1965-66, exec. v.p., 1966-69, pres., chief oper. officer, 1969-74, vice chmn., 1974-76. Chmn. emeritus bd. trustees Steven Inst. Tech.; trustee emeritus Fordham U.; mem. N.Y. State Econ. Devel. Bd., 1975. Mem. AAAS, Am. Chem. Soc., Soc. of Chem. Industry (Am. sect.), Societe de Chimie Industrielle, Chemists Club, Sky Club, Sakonnet Golf Club, Met. Club, Sakonnet Point Club. Home: Chevy Chase, Md. Died Mar. 3, 2009.

BLACKMAN, SHERRY, mathematician, educator; b. Bklyn., July 27, 1937; d. Boris and Clara (Applefeld) Kunda; m. Sheldon Blackman, Sept. 15, 1957; children: Michael, Susan.

BA, Bklyn. Coll., 1957; MA, NYU, 1975, PhD, 1983. Lectr. Coll. S.I., NY, 1970—83, asst. prof., from 1983. Math text reviewer McGraw-Hill, NYC, 1975—80, John Wiley & Sons, NYC, 1976—80, Prentice Hall, NJ, from 1984, West Ednl. Pub. Co., from 1992, PWS Kent Pub. Co., from 1993; spl. reviewer Psychol. Reports, Missoula, Mont., from 1983. Author: Series in Mathematics Modules, 1973, Steps in Mathematics Modules, 1981; contbr. articles to profl. jours. Grantee, Coll. S.I., 1983, Aaron Diamond Found., 1989—90, Womens R & D Fund-CUNY, 1986. Mem.: Women Math. Edn., Assn. Women Sci., Assn. Women Math., Nat. Coun. Tchrs. Math., Math. Assn. Am. Home: Staten Island, NY. Died Apr. 15, 2009.

BLACKWELL, CECIL, science association executive; b. Enterprise, Miss., Oct. 29, 1924; s. George Dewey and Neely (Baggett) B.; m. Louise McLendon, May 27, 1944; children— Cecil Carl, Donna Lynn, Gregory Dale. BS, Miss. State U., 1951; MS, U. Md., 1955; postgrad., U. Ark., 1953-54. Asst. horticulturist Truck Crops Br. Expt. Sta., Crystal Springs, Miss., 1951; research asst. U. Md., College Park, 1951-52; instr., jr. horticulturist U. Ark., 1952-54; extension horticulturist U. Ga., 1954-56, head extension hort. dept., 1956-59; hort. editor Progressive Farmer, Birmingham, Ala., 1959-65; exec. dir. Am. Soc. Hort. Sci.; pub. Jour. Am. Soc. Hort. Sci., HortScience, St. Joseph, Mich., 1965-74, Mt. Vernon, Va., 1974-79, Alexandria, Va., 1979-88; exec. dir. emeritus Am. Soc. Hort. Sci., from 1989; cons., writer, from 1989. Author: (with L.A. Niven) Garden Book for the South, 1961. Served with USAAF, 1944-46. Decorated Air medal.; Gen. Edn. Bd. fellow Rockefeller Found., 1951-52 Fellow Am. Soc. Hort. Sci.; mem. AAAS, Internat. Soc. Hort Sci., Am. Inst. Biol. Scis., Royal Hort. Soc. (hon.), Alpha Zeta. Mem. Ch. of God. Died Apr. 30, 2010.

BLACKWELL, DAVID HAROLD, statistics educator; b. Centralia, Ill., Apr. 24, 1919; s. Grover and Mabel (Johnson) B.; m. Ann Madison, Dec. 27, 1944; children: Ann, Julia, David, Ruth, Grover, Vera, Hugo, Sara AB, U. Ill., 1938, A.M., 1939, PhD, 1941, D.Sc. (hon.), 1965, Mich. State U., 1967, Carnegie-Mellon U., 1981. Instr. stats. Southern U., 1942-43; instr. stats. Clark Coll., 1943-44; asst. prof. then prof. statistics Howard U., Washington, 1944—54, prof., U. Calif.-Berkeley, 1954—88, chmn. statistics dept., 1957—61, asst. dean Coll. Letters & Sciences, 1964—68; cons. The RAND Corp., 1948—50. Author: (with M.A. Girshick) Theory of Games and Statistical Decision, 1984 Recipient Von Neumann Theory prize Ops. Rsch. Soc. Am.- The Inst. Mgmt. Sci. Fellow Inst. Math. Stats. Am. Statis. Assn., Ops. Rsch. Soc. Am.-Inst. Mgmt. Scis. Home: Berkeley, Calif. Died July 8, 2010.

BLACKWOOD, TERRY WAYNE, accountant; b. Gary, Ind., Nov. 24, 1954; s. Hestle Brooks and Edna Ann Blackwood; m. Pamela E. Blackwood, Dec. 18, 1987; children: Nicole, Taylor. BS, U. Ala., Birmingham, 1977. CPA. Acct. Ernst & Ernst, Birmingham, 1977-79; acminstr. Carraway Meth. Med. Ctr., Birmingham, 1979-88; mgr. Coopers & Lybrand, Birmingham, 1988-91; CFO Broward Gen. Med. Ctr., Ft. Lauderdale, Fla., 1991-92, Coastal Healthcare Group, Durham, N.C., 1992-97, City of Hope Nat. Med. Ctr., Duarte, Calif., from 1997. Fellow Healthcare Fin. Mgmt. Assn. (Fullmer award 1997); mem. AICPA, Ala. Soc. CPAs, Pasadena Tournament of Roses. Avocations: internet, coaching soccer. Died Mar. 22, 2009.

BLAIR, BOWEN, investment banker; b. Bar Harbor, Maine, Aug. 4, 1918; s. William McCormick and Helen Haddock (Bowen) B.; m. Joan Halpine Smith, Dec. 9, 1950; children: Joan Bowen, Bowen. BA, Yale U., 1940; postgrad., Harvard U., 1940-41. With William Blair & Co., Chgo., from 1946, ptnr., from 1950. Trustee Art Inst. Chgo., Field Mus. Natural History, Chgo. Hist. Soc. Mem. Chgo. Club, Onwentsia Club, Shoreacres Club, Casino Club, Bath and Tennis Club (Palm Beach, Fla.). Home: Lake Forest, Ill. Died Sept. 11, 2009.

BLANCHARD, NINA, agent; b. Greenwich, Conn., July 21, 1928; d. John Dean and Mildred Eleanor (Weakley) Blanchard; m. Benjamin James Tomkins, May 28, 1950 (div.). Attended, El Camino Coll., 1948, Columbia U., 1950. Actress, L.A. and NYC, 1948—51; make-up artist NBC-TV, NYC, 1951—58; casting dir. NYC, 1954—55; talent agt., prin. Nina Blanchard Enterprises, Inc. & Nina Blanchard Agy., LA, 1961—2010. TV and film faculty UCLA Extension; vis. prof. Fla. State U.; lectr. in field; tchr. Burt Reynolds' Inst. for Theater Tng., from 1982. Author: How To Break Into Motion Pictures, Television, Commercials and Modeling, 1978; co-author (with Peter Barsocchini): The Look, 1995. Mem. adv. bd. Free Arts Clinic Abused Children, Hathaway Home for Children. Mem.: Com. 200, Women in Film, Acad. TV Arts and Scis., Assn. Talent Agts. (bd. dirs.). Died Feb. 7, 2010.

BLANDA, GEORGE FREDERICK, retired professional football player; b. Youngwood, Pa., Sept. 17, 1927; s. Michael and Mary (Durik) B.; m. Betty Harris, Dec. 17, 1949; children: George Jr., Leslie. BA in Edn., U. Ky., 1951. Quarterback, kicker Chgo. Bears, 1949, 1950—58, Baltimore Colts, 1950, Houston Oilers, 1960-66, Oakland Raiders, 1967-75. Recipient Bert Bell award, 1970; named All-American Football League (AFL), 1961—63, 1966—67, American Football League (AFL) MVP, AP, 1963, NFL All-Pro, 1967, 1970, 1973, Male Athlete of Yr., AP, 1970; named to The American Football League (AFL) All-Star Team, 1961—63, 1967, The Pro Football Hall of Fame, 1981, The U. Ky. Hall of Fame, 1998. Achievements include leading the Houston Oilers to 3 American League Football (AFL) Championships, 1960, 1961, 1967. Home: Oak Brook, Ill. Died Sept. 27, 2010.

BLANDER, MILTON, chemist; b. Bklyn., Nov. 1, 1927; s. Benjamin and Yetta (Schwartzman) B.; children: Benjamin, Alice, Kathryn, Daniel, Joshua. BS, CUNY, 1950; PhD, Yale U., 1953. Rsch. assoc. Cornell U., Ithaca, NY, 1953-55; chemist Oak Ridge (Tenn.) Nat. Lab., 1955-62; chemist, group leader Rockwell Internat. Sci. Ctr., Thousand Oaks, Calif., 1962-71; sr. chemist, group leader Argonne (Ill.) Nat. Lab., 1971-97; founder Quest Rsch., South Holland, Ill., from 1995. Recipient Materials Rsch. award U.S. Dept. Energy, 1984, Alexander von Humboldt award. Fellow AAAS, Meteoritical Soc.; mem. Metall. Soc., Am. Chem. Soc., Electrochem. Soc. (Max Bredig award 1987), Norwegian Acad. Tech. Scis. Died May 11, 2010.

BLANK, RAYMOND MICHAEL, management executive, author; b. Balt., Mar. 27, 1933; s. Benjamin and Bessie (Schreiber) B.; divorced; children: Paul Jeffrey, Jamie Allison, Adam Douglas, Peter Joshua. BA, U. Md., 1955; JD, U. Md., Balt., 1958. Founder No. Acceptance Corp. Credit Corp., Balt., 1958-68; cons. U.S. Agy. for Internat. Devel., Washington, 1965-70; adminstrv. v.p. Korvettes Dept. Store, NYC, 1969-74; dir. Spartan Industries, NYC, 1974-76, Arlen Properties, NYC, 1976-78; prin. R.M. Blank Assocs. Rsch., Balt., from 1978. Pres. Balt. Bullets, 1970-74; bd. dirs. Better Bus. Bur., N.Y.C., 1975-76. Author: Playing the Game: A Psychopolitical Strategy for Your Career, 1980. Bd. dirs. Ctr. Stage, Balt., 1976-80; cons. Gov.'s Commn. to Restructure Edn. in Md., Balt., 1989-70. Recipient Mktg. award Seklemian Com., 1966; named hon. permanent cons. to U.S. Agy. for Internat. Devel., 1970. Mem. Ctr. Club, Princeton Club (charter, N.Y.). Avocations: tennis, squash, golf, long-distance cycling, psychology. Died Aug. 10, 2009.

BLAUVELT, JOHN CLIFFORD, diversified consumer products company executive; b. Nyack, NY, Feb. 22, 1920; s. John Clifford and Henrietta Lane (Bower) B.; m. Laura Biddleman, July 29, 1944; children— Laura Lane Tabone, J. Clifford III. BS, Houghton Coll., 1940; postgrad., N. Tex. State Coll., 1940, N.Y. U., 1946-48. With Am. Cyanamid Co., Wayne, N.J., from 1940, various prodn. positions, 1940-69, corp. controller, 1969-71, pres. agrl. div., 1971-73, corp. v.p., 1973-75, sr. v.p., from 1975, also dir. Served to lt. USN, 1943-46. Home: Naples, Fla. Died Feb. 3, 2010.

BLAZEL, ROBERT PATRICK, sociology educator; b. Milw., July 18, 1942; s. Theodore L. and Katherine Jane (Flynn) B.; m. Mary K. Vollmer, July 10, 1965; children: John, Elizabeth, Edward, Jane. BA in Sociology, Quincy Coll., 1961-64; MSW, U. Wis., Milw., 1964-66; postgrad., Western Ill. U. Parole officer State of Wis., Milw., 1966-67; tchr. Milw. Vocat. Sch., 1967; prof. sociology Quincy (Ill.) Coll., from 1967. Founder Suicide Prevention Agy., Quincy, 1967-88; v.p. Home Ownership Assistance, Quincy, 1968-75, Family Svc., Quincy, 1986—; bd. dirs. Woodland Home, Quincy, 1980-85; past adj. prof. Washington U., St. Louis, St. Louis U., U. Mo. Bd. dirs. Cath. Charities, Quincy, 1975-77, Quincy Coll. Alumni Bd., 1987-90; pres. Quincy Mus. Natural History, 1985-87. Mem. Acad. Cert. Social Workers. Democrat. Roman Catholic. Avocations: wilderness canoeing, reading, travel, historic re-enactment. Home: Quincy, Ill. Died Sept. 12, 2009.

BLEILER, EVERETT FRANKLIN, writer, publishing company executive; b. Boston, Apr. 30, 1920; s. Joseph Eugene and Rose Caroline (Mayor) B.; m. Ellen Haas, May 12, 1956; children: Richard, John, Constance, Dorothy. AB cum laude, Harvard U., 1942; MA, U. Chgo., 1951; Diploma, U. Leiden, The Netherlands, 1952. Freelance writer, 1952-55; advt. mgr. Dover Publs., NYC, 1955-60, mng. dir., 1960-65, exec. v.p., 1965-78; editorial cons. Charles Scribners Sons, NYC, 1978-83. Author more than 60 books including The Checklist of Fantastic Literature, 1948, Essential Japanese Grammar, 1963, Best Tales of Hoffmann, 1967, Mother Goose's Melodies, 1970, Eight Dime Novels of the Victorian Period, 1974, Wagner, The Wehrwolf by G. W. M. Reynolds, 1975, Seventeenth Century Floral Engravings of Emanuel Sweerts, 1976, Richmond, Exploits of a Bow Street Runner, 1976, (under name Liberte E. LeVert) Prophecies and Enigmas of Nostradamus, 1979; A Treasury of Victorian Detective Stories, 1979, A Treasury of Victorian Ghost Stories, 1981, Science Fiction Writers, 1982, The Guide to Supernatural Fiction, 1983, Supernatural Fiction Writers, 1985, Science-Fiction: The Early Years, 1991, Science-Fiction: The Gernsback Years, 1998, Alice and the Snark, 2002, Magistrate Mai and the Invisible Murderer, 2006, Firegang, 2006, others; co-author: (with Wendell C. Bennett) Northwest Argentine Archeology, 1948, (with Guy Stern) Essential German Grammar, 1961. Sgt. U.S. Army, 1942-46. Recipient World Fantasy award World Fantasy Com., Providence, 1978, World Fantasy award (lifetime), London, 1988, Pilgrim award Sci. Fiction Rsch. Assn., 1984, Pres.'s award World Sci. Fiction Assn., 1986, Locus award for best non-fiction book, 1992, Living Legend award Internat. Horror Guild, 2004; named to N.J. Literary Hall of Fame, 1979; knight comdr. Order of Star, Realm of Redonda; Fulbright fellow, 1952. Democrat. Home: Interlaken, NY. Died June 13, 2010.

BLICKSILVER, EDITH, English language and literature educator; b. NYC, Jan. 6, 1926; d. Simon and Fanny Stettner; m. Jack Blicksilver, June 27, 1948; children: Paul, Diane, Robert. BA, Queens Coll., 1947; MA, Smith Coll., 1948. Lect. in history and English Smith Coll., Northampton, Mass., 1947-48; prof. of English So. State Tchrs. Coll., Sprinfield, S.D., 1953-54; instr. in English Northeastern U., Boston, 1962-63; assoc. prof. of English Ga. Inst. Tech., 1961-62, 63—. Author: The Ethnic American Women: Problems, Protests, Lifestyle, 5th expanded edit. 1994, Going Pro: The Georgia Tech. Basketball Story On and Off the Court, 1994. Grantee Ga. Inst. Tech.; winner Best Non-Fiction Book Award of Yr., Dixie Coun. of Authors and Journalists. Mem. AAUW (corp. rep., grantee), MLA (archivist), Multi-Ethnic Lit. Soc. U.S. (sec., past pres. Ga.-S.C. regional br.), Coll. English Assn. (past pres.). Home: Atlanta, Ga. Died Oct. 14, 2009.

BLOCK, ALAN JAY, physician, educator; b. Balt., Apr. 11, 1938; s. Michael and Sylvia (Rosenberg) B.; m. Linda Ray Crone, May 25, 1961; children: Margo Dee, Allison Lee. BA, Johns Hopkins U., 1958, MD, 1962. Intern, then resident Johns Hopkins Hosp., Balt., 1962-67, attending physician, 1967-70; instr. in medicine Johns Hopkins Med. Sch., Balt., 1967-69, asst. prof. medicine, 1969-70, U. Fla., Gainesville, 1970-73, asst. prof. anesthesiology, 1971-73, chief pulmonary div., 1973-95. Chief pulmonary sect. VA Med. Ctr., Gainesville, 1995—; assoc. prof. medicine U. Fla., 1973-75, prof. medicine, 1975—. Mem. edit. bd. Am. Rev. Respiratory Disease 1981-87; contbr. over 180 articles to profl. jours. Mem. senate U. Fla., 1976-78. Fellow Am. Coll. Chest Physicians (pres. 1987-88, editorial bd. jour., editor-in-chief Chest, 1993—); mem. Fla. Thoracic Soc. (pres. 1977-79, bd. dirs. 1973-76), Am. Thoracic Soc. (chmn. com. 1975-76, chmn. scientific assembly), Am. Fedn. Clin. Research, Assn. Pulmonary Program Dirs. (sec., treas. 1987—). Democrat. Jewish. Avocations: baseball, singing. Home: Gainesville, Fla. Died Dec. 5, 2009.

BLOEDE, LOUIS WILLIAM, seminary educator; b. Fond du Lac, Wis., Aug. 17, 1928; s. F. William and Amanda Marie (Klein) B.; m. Mary Trautmann, Nov. 12, 1955; children: Kirk, Paul. BA, North Ctrl. Coll., 1950; BDiv, Evang. Theol. Sem., 1953; DTh, Boston U., 1960. Ordained to ministry United Meth. Ch., 1953. Minister to students 1st Meth. Ch., Madison, Wis., 1951—53; pastor Grace United Meth. Ch., Wautoma, Wis., 1953—57, Ctr. United Meth. Ch., Saugus, Mass., 1958—60; founding pastor Peace United Meth. Ch., Green Bay, Wis., 1960—65; prof. worship Evang. Theol. Sem., Naperville, Ill., 1965—74; prof. parish ministry Iliff Sch. Theology, Denver, from 1974. Assoc. Inst. Gerontology U. Denver, 1976—84; bd. dirs. Widowed Persons Svc., Denver, from 1981; mem. bd. Ordained Ministry, Rocky Mountain Conf. United Meth. Ch., 1982—90; bd. dirs. Operation Nightwatch (street ministry), Denver, 1982—84. Author: Developing the New Congregation, 1965; contbr. sects. to books, articles, book revs. to publs. Bd. mgrs. Birch Homeowners Assn., Vail, Colo., 1983—89; v.p. Aspen Condominium Assn., Vail, from 1989. Fellow Inst. for Ecumenical and Cultural Rsch., Collegeville, Minn., 1970—71, Assn. Theol. Schs. rsch., 1977—78; scholar Hartman scholar, 1952—53. Fellow N.Am. Acad. Liturgy; mem. Assn. Theol. Field Edn. (steering com. 1979-81, 91-), Acad. Homiletics, Assn. Practical Theology, Field Edn. United Meth. Sem. (chmn. 1975-76), Dutch N.Am. Conf. on Practical Theology, YMCA Men's Club (pres. Green Bay 1964-65). Home: Denver, Colo. Died June 20, 2010.

BLOOM, MURRAY TEIGH, author; b. NYC, May 19, 1916; s. Louis I. and Anna (Teighblum) B.; m. Sydelle J. Cohen, Apr. 30, 1944; children: Ellen Susan Bloom Lubell, Amy Beth Bloom. BA, Columbia, 1937, MS, 1938. Reporter N.Y. Post, 1939; free-lance writer, from 1940. Founder, past trustee United Community Fund Great Neck, N.Y.; founder, past pres. Soc. Mag. Writers (now Am. Soc. Journalists and Authors); chmn. bd. trustees Llewellyn Miller Fund, 1988; corr. Stars & Stripes, Paris-Berlin, 1944-46; dept. head Sch. Journalism Biarritz-Am. U., 1945. Author: Money of Their Own, 1957, The Man Who Stole Portugal, 1966; play Leonora, 1966; The Trouble with Lawyers, 1969, Rogues to Riches, 1972, Lawyers, Clients and Ethics, 1974, The 13th Man, 1977; filmed as Last Embrace, 1979; The Brotherhood of Money, 1983, (play) The White Crow, 1984, Lifesize, 1990. Served with AUS, 1942-46. Recipient 50th Anniversary award Columbia U. Grad. Sch. Journalism, 1963, Career Achievement award Am. Soc. Journalists and Authors, 1995, Columbia Journalism Alumni award, 1996; named Outstanding Profl., Assn. for Edn. in Journalism and Mass Commn., 1994. Mem. Dramatists Guild of Authors League Am. Home: Fairfield, Conn. Died Feb. 10, 2009.

BLOUNT, ROBERT GRIER, retired pharmaceutical company executive; b. Newton, Mass., Nov. 30, 1938; s. Robert S. and Nathalie (Grier) B.; m. Betty E. Blount, 1960 (div. 1981); children: Robert Jr., Sharon, Stephen, Kristin; m. Joellen Fisher, Nov. 30, 1990. BSBA, Babson Coll., 1960. CPA, N.Y. Ptnr. Arthur Andersen & Co., NYC, 1960-74; v.p. fin. Am. Home Products Corp., NYC, 1974-83, sr. v.p. fin., 1983-87, exec. v.p., from 1987; sr. v.p. American Home Products Corp., NYC; also bd. dirs.; retired. Mem. N.Y. State Soc. C.P.A.s, Am. Inst. C.P.A.s Avocation: golf. Home: North Palm Beach, Fla. Died Jan. 26, 2010.

BLOUNT, ROBERT HADDOCK, management consultant, retired military officer; b. Miami, Fla., Dec. 8, 1922; s. Uriel and Aleve Sadie (Haddock) B.; m. Jeannette Mae Barclay, May 13, 1951 (dec. 1998); children: Barbara Mae, Jennifer. B.E.E., MIT, 1947; MS in Systems Engring, George Washington U., 1970; student, Naval War Coll., 1958-59. Commd. ensign USNR, 1946; transferred to U.S. Navy, 1947, advanced through grades to rear adm., 1973; comdr. submarines, service in MTO, PTO, Scotland, Panama; chief staff, aide to comdr. Submarine Flotilla 6, 1970-72; comdr. Naval Sta., Naval Base Charleston, SC, 1972-73; comdr. U.S. Naval Forces, So. Command; also comdt. 15th Naval Dist. Ft. Amador, C.Z., 1973-75; dir. undersea and strategic warfare div. Office Chief Naval Ops. Washington, 1975-77; dep. dir. research, devel., test and evaluation OPNAV, 1977-78; comdr. Operational Test and Evaluation Force, 1978-82, ret., 1982; pvt. industry cons., 1986-90; ret. Va. Ops. div. EDO Corp., 1990. Pres. C.Z. coun. Boy Scouts Am., 1974. Decorated D.S.M., Meritorious Service medal with star, Navy Expeditionary medal; recipient Scroll of Honor Navy League, 1974 Mem. Naval Submarine League, U.S. Naval Inst., Norfolk Yacht and Country Club, Rotary. Died May 4, 2009.

BLOUNT, STANLEY FREEMAN, marketing educator; b. Detroit, June 12, 1929; s. Harry Alfred and Thelma (Freeman) B.; m. Constance Parker, Aug. 30, 1957; children— Jeffrey Parker, Lori Maria. BA, Wayne State U., 1952, MA, 1959; PhD, Northwestern U., 1962. Account exec. Jam Handy Corp., Detroit, 1952-54; marketing mgr. Chrysler Corp., Detroit, 1954-58; instr. Northwestern U., 1961-62; asst. prof. U. Ill., 1962-63; assoc. prof. Kent State U., 1963-67; prof., dept. chmn. State U. N.Y. at Albany, from 1967, chmn. ednl. policies council, from 1970. Disting. vis. prof. U. of Americas, Mexico, 1966; dir. Femtec Inc.; exec. dir. U. Albany Found. Chmn. sub-com. legis. affairs N.Y. State affiliate Am. Heart Assn., 1974-99. Served with AUS, 1946-48. Named Outstanding Faculty Mem. Kent State U., 1964 Mem. Sigma Xi, Gamma Theta Upsilon. Clubs: Essayons, Audubon, Phalanx. Achievements include research on environment analysis and preception, digitized land use mapping, land use and resource mgmt. Home: Delmar, NY. Died Jan. 14, 2010.

BLUM, IRVING RONALD, lawyer; b. Phila., Mar. 3, 1935; s. William and Dorothy (Gaskin) Blum; m. Rochelle S. Klempner, June 17, 1956; children: Loren, Karen, Jill; 1 child, Jason. BA, Wayne State U., 1956; JD, Detroit Coll. Law, 1959. Bar: Mich. 1959, U.S. Dist. Ct. (ea. dist.) Mich. 1959, Detroit. Ptnr. Akerman, Kaplan & Blum, Detroit, 1959—62, Blum, Brady & Rosenberg, Detroit, 1962—82, Blum, Kobheim, Elkin & Blum, Southfield, from 1982. Mem.: Mich. Trial Lawyers, Trial Lawyers Am., 300 Club (bd. dirs.). Democrat. Jewish. Home: Palm Bch Gdns, Fla. Died Jan. 3, 2009.

BLUMBERG, GERALD, lawyer; b. NYC, July 25, 1911; s. Saul and Amelia (Abramowitz) B.; m. Rhoda Shapiro, Jan. 7, 1945; children: Lawrence, Rena, Alice, Leda. AB cum laude, Cornell U., 1931; JD cum laude, Harvard, 1934. Bar: Mass. 1934, N.Y. 1934. Pvt. practice, NYC, from 1934; mem. firm Gerald & Lawrence Blumberg LLP. Instr. econs. Cornell U., 1931; mem. Harvard Legal Aid Bur., 1934. Bd. dirs., v.p., exec. com. Am. Com. Weizmann Inst. Sci.; internat. bd. govs. Weizmann Inst. Sci., 1982—. Mem. ABA, N.Y. State, Westchester, Yorktown bar assns., Phi Beta Kappa, Phi Kappa Phi. Home: Yorktown Heights, NY. Died Jan. 23, 2009.

BLUMBERG, PETER STEVEN, manufacturing executive; b. Bklyn., Feb. 18, 1944; s. Howard G. and Lily G. (Goldberg) B.; m. Judith E. Pauly, Apr. 22, 1967; children: Anne Pauly, Matthew Edward, Heather Rebecca, Emily Jessica. BS, U. Va., 1967. Salesman Coll. House, Inc., Westbury, N.Y., 1967-71, sales mgr., 1971-76, gen. mgr., 1977-78; sec.-treas. Sch. Tchrs. Supply Corp., Westbury, N.Y., 1979-2000; pres., CEO College House, Richmond, Va., from 1979. Rsch. assoc. Fred Hutchinson Cancer Rsch. Ctr., Seattle, Sloan-Kettering Meml. Cancer Ctr.; active Nat. Right-to-work Legal Def. Found., United Jewish Appeal, World Jewish Congress, Leukemia Soc. Am., Coalition to Stop Gun Violence, Handgun Control, Inc., Leadership Coun. So. Poverty Law Ctr., Simon Wiesenthal Ctr. Holocaust Studies, Ams. Against Union Control of Govt., Jewish Chautaqucua Soc., Hebrew Immigrant Aid Soc.; charter supporter U.S. Holocaust Meml. Coun.; Jewish Cmty. Ctr. of Richmond. Mem. Nat. Assn. Coll. Stores, Screenprinting and Graphic Imaging Assn. Internat., U. Va. Alumni Assn. (life), Richmond Symphony, Hurrycanes Running Club, Richmond Road Runners, Equality Va., Parents and Friends Lesbians and Gays. Jewish. Home: Richmond, Va. Died Jan. 5, 2009.

BOARDMAN, EUNICE, retired music educator; b. Cordova, Ill., Jan. 27, 1926; d. George Hollister and Anna Bryson (Feaster) Boardman. B. Mus. Edn., Cornell Coll., 1947; M. Mus. Edn., Columbia U., 1951; Ed.D., U. Ill., 1963; DFA (hon.), Cornell Coll., 1995. Tchr. music pub. schs., Iowa, 1947-55; prof. music edn. Wichita State U., Kans., 1955-72; vis. prof. mus. edn. Normal State U., Ill., 1972-74, Roosevelt U., Chgo., 1974-75; prof. mus. edn. U. Wis., Madison, 1975-89, dir. Sch. Music, 1980-89; prof. music, dir. grad. program in music edn. U. Ill., Urbana, 1989-98; ret. Author: Musical Growth in Elementary School, 1963, 6th rev. edit., 1996, Exploring Music, 1966, 3d rev. edit., 1975, The Music Book, 1980, 2d rev. edit., 1984, Holt Music, 1987; editor: Dimensions of Musical Thinking, 1989, Dimensions of Musical Thinking: A Different Kind of Music, 2002, Up the Mississippi: A Journey of the Blues, 2002. Named to MENC Hall of Fame, 2004. Mem. Soc. Music Tchr. Edn. (chmn. 1984-86), Music Educators Nat. Conf. Avocations: reading, antiques. Home: Rock Island, Ill. Died May 5, 2009.

BOCK, JERRY (JERROLD LEWIS BOCK), composer; b. New Haven, Nov. 23, 1928; s. George Joseph and Rebecca (Alpert) B.; m. Patricia Faggen, May 28, 1950; children: George Albert, Portia Fane. Student, U. Wis., 1945-49, L.H.D. (hon.), 1985. Writer: score for high sch. mus. comedy My Dream, 1945; score for original coll. musical Big as Life, 1948; wrote: songs for TV show Admiral Broadway Revue, also Show of Shows, 1949-51; composer songs, Camp Tamiment, summers 1950, 51, 53; writer: continuity sketches Mel Torme show, CBS, 1951, 52; writing staff: Kate Smith Hour, 1953-54; writer: original songs for night club performers, including night club revue Confetti; wrote: songs for Wonders of Manhattan (hon. mention Cannes Film Festival 1956); composer: music for Broadway show Catch a Star, 1955, Mr. Wonderful, 1956, (collaborated with Sheldon Harnick on) The Body Beautiful, 1958, Fiorello, 1959 (Pulitzer prize, Drama Critics award, Antoinette Perry award), Tenderloin, 1960, She Loves Me, 1963, revival, 1990, Fiddler on the Roof, 1964, Silver Anniversary prodn. nat. tour, 1989-90, revival, 1990-91, 93, The Apple Tree, 1966, The Rothschilds, 1972, revival, 1990-91; London prodn. of She Loves Me, 1964, off-Broadway, 1982, Jerome Robbins Broadway, 1989; London prodn. of Fiddler on the Roof, 1964 (Tony award), Warsaw prodn., 1985, Fiorello, Goodspeed Opera House, summer 1985, (film) A Stranger Among Us, 1992; wrote series of children's songs now pub. under title Sing Something Special; also recorded album, N.Y. Bd. Edn., radio broadcasts; wrote music and lyrics for musicals, Children's Theatre Festival, U. Houston, 2000-03. Recipient 9 Tony awards Best Musical of Yr. Fiddler on the Roof, 1964, Johnny Mercer award Songwriters Hall of Fame, 1990, Olivier award Best Musical Revival for She Loves Me, 1994; named to Theatre Hall of Fame, 1990. Mem. Broadcast Music Inc. (adv. panel), Nat. Found. Advancement in Arts (endowment group). Died Nov. 3, 2010.

BODE, RICHARD ALBERT, retired financial executive; b. Oak Park, Ill., July 26, 1931; s. Charles John and Esther (Burgert) B.; m. Marjorie Ann Lane, July 28, 1962; children— Anne, Julie, John, Ellen, Mary Elizabeth. Student, Loras Coll., 1949-51; BSc, DePaul U., 1953; MBA, U. Detroit, 1960. CPA, Ill. With Baumann, Finney & Co. (pub. accountants), Chgo., 1953-56; staff accountant Nat. Tea Co., Chgo., 1956-58, divisional controller Detroit, 1958-62; asst. controller Eagle Food Centers, Rock Island, Ill., 1962-63; comptroller Brinks, Inc., Chgo., 1963-68, treas., 1968-69, v.p., treas., 1970-78; v.p. fin. DLM, Inc., Allen, Tex., 1978-89. Mem. Govt. Acctg. Stds. Adv. Coun., 1996-99. Mem. Village Hinsdale Plan Commn., 1969-75, Plano Bd. Adjustments, 1988-90; mem. Plano City Coun., 1990-2000, dep. mayor pro tem, 1995-96, mayor pro tem, 1996-97, 99-2000; sec.-treas. Allen Indsl. Found., 1983-88; bd. dirs. Plano Homeowners Coun., 1984-90, pres., 1987-88; mem. Regional Transp. Coun., 1993-2000; mem. adv. coun. Tex. Mcpl. Retirement Sys., 1996-2000; mem. Plano Econ. Devel. Bd., 1999-2000, Plano Sister City, Inc., 1994—2002, treas., 2000-02, Plano Heritage Commn., 2000-02; mem. leadership com. John Paul II H.S., 2000—03; bd. dirs. Hope's Door, 2000—, treas. 2001—. Mem. Ill. C.P.A. Soc. (dir. 1976-78) Home: Plano, Tex. Died May 1, 2009.

BODIAN, NAT G., author, lecturer; b. Newark, Feb. 12, 1921; s. Louis and Fannie (Gabot) B.; m. Ruth Naiman, June 28, 1947 (dec. Nov. 28, 2005); children: Mark, Lester. Student, Essex Jr. Coll., CCNY; grad., New Sch. for Social Research, 1947. Mgr. sales and promotion Baker & Taylor Co., Hillside, NJ, 1958-60; advt. promotion mgr. Rider Pub. Co., Hayden Book Co., NYC, 1960-62; mktg., promotion mgr. Am. Elsevier Pub. Co., NYC, 1963-71; mktg. dir. Transaction Books Rutgers U., New Brunswick, NJ, 1971-72, Crane Russak & Co., NYC, 1972-76; mktg. mgr. John Wiley & Sons., Inc. (Wiley-Sci-Tech. div.), NYC, 1976-88; founding mem., dir. Profl. Pubs. Mktg. Group, 1981. Guest lectr. Boston U., NYU, CUNY, Fairleigh Dickinson U., UCLA; WWII So. Atlantic correspondent Yank Mag.; editor various military base publs. Author: Book Marketing Handbook, Vol. 1, 1980, Vol. 2, 1983, How to Get the Most Out of Your Mailing Lists, 1982, Copywriter's Handbook, 1984, Encyclopedia of Mailing List Terminology and Techniques, 1986, Beyond Lead Generation: Merchandising Through Card Packs, 1986, The Publishers Direct Mail Handbook, 1987, Publishing Desk Reference: A Comprehensive Dictionary of Book and Jour. Marketing and Bookselling Practices and Techniques, 1988, How to Choose a Winning Title: A Guide for Writers, Editors and Publishers, 1988, NTC's Dictionary of Direct Mail and Mailing List Terminology and Techniques, 1990, Direct Marketing Rules of Thumb: 1000 Practical and Profitable Ideas, 1995, Portuguese updated edit., 1999, The Joy of Publishing: Fascinating Facts and Historic Origins About Books and Authors, Editors and Publishers, Bookmaking and Bookselling, 1996; contbr. to Trade Book Marketing, 1983, Book Publishing Career Directory, 1990, Internat. Ency. of Internat. Book Publishing, 1995, Book Marketing and Promotion: A Practical Handbook for Publishers in Developing Countries, 1999; Contributions in Various Conference Proceedings; columnist: COSMEP pub. newsletter, 1988-95; contbt. editor Against the Grain, Scholarly Pub. Today; contbr. articles and book revs. for nat. and internat. profl. jours. and trade publs. Found. mem., sec. NJ News Writers Assn., 1941; founding mem. Dorf Feature Svc./Newark Ledger/Star Ledger, 1938; founding mem., mem. steering com. Profl. Pubs. Mktg. Group, 1984-88. Served with USAAF, 1942-45, YANK Field Corr., 1943-45. Nominee AAP Curtis Benjamin award, 1984 and Pub. Hall of Fame, 1986; recipient Author's Citation, NJ Writers Conf., 1986, 87, 89. Home: Cranford, NJ. Died May 1, 2010.

BOGAD, ALICE ROSE, beverage company executive; b. Waterbury, Conn., July 26, 1922; d. Edward A. and Catherine A. (Wood) Rose; m. Alfred J. Bogad, Sept. 30, 1971; children by previous marriage: Nancy, Karen, Eric. Student CUNY Coll., 1943, U. Okla., 1944, Am. U., 1945. Propr., dir. Mid-Hudson Floor & Wall Co., Poughkeepsie, N.Y., 1948-51, Hudson Valley Welding and Supply, Poughkeepsie, 1951-55; propr. Colonial Knolls Devel. Co., 1955-65; asst. mgr. Dutchess County (N.Y.) Airport, 1965-68; propr. and mgr. Queen's Ransom Gallery, Poughkeepsie, 1967-71; sec., treas., dir. G.H. Ford Tea Co., Inc., Poughkeepsie, 1974—; guest lectr. on tea various schs. and community orgns., 1974—. Pres., Arlington High Sch. PTA, 1963-64; chmn. scholarship com. Arlington Sch. Dist., 1960-64; sec. to zoning bd. Town of Poughkeepsie, 1955-60, dep. zoning adminstr., 1971-73, chmn. Zoning Bd. Appeals, 1976-78; trustee Vassar Temple, 1979-87, chmn. membership, 1978-84; bd. dirs. Dutchess County (N.Y.) Arts Council, 1979-81, chmn. public funding com., 1979-80; mem. citizens' adv. com. Dutchess Community Coll. Served with WAVES, 1942-45. Recipient Life Member award PTA, N.Y. State, 1964, Outstanding Citizen award Dutchess County Bd. Legislators, 1981; named Woman of Yr., NYU Ctr. Food and Hotel Mgmt., 1987. Mem. Tea Assn. U.S. (assoc. bd. dirs. 1977-78, chmn. 1979). Culinary Inst. Am. (cons. 1975—, mem. corp. 1980—, chmn. fellows com.) Bus. and Profl. Women's Assn. Republican. Club: Zonta (sec. 1978-79). Contbr. articles on tea industry to bus. and trade jours. Home: Poughkeepsie, NY. Died Mar. 22, 2009.

BOGGS, ANDREW THOMPSON, III, retired association executive; b. Philipsburg, Pa., Aug. 11, 1920; s. Andrew Thompson and Eleanor (Wilson) B.; m. Marjorie Knepton Goodson, Dec. 21, 1961 BS in Chemistry, Norwich U., Northfield, Vt., 1947. Asst. to mgr. dir. Edison Elec. Inst., NYC, 1947-55; tech. sec. ASHRAE, NYC, 1955-61, assoc. sec., 1961-67, exec. dir., 1967-79, exec. v.p.-sec., 1979-81, Atlanta, 1981-85. Pres. Council of Engring. and Sci. Soc. Execs. 1982-83 Served to capt. U.S. Army, 1944-47; ETO Decorated Military Cross, Belgium, 1945. Fellow ASHRAE (hon., life) Clubs: Lords Valley Country (Pa.); Ansley Golf (Atlanta). Lodges: Masons. Republican. Avocations: music; golf; travel. Home: Hawley, Pa. Died Apr. 14, 2009.

BOH, IVAN, philosophy educator; b. Dolenji Lazi, Yugoslavia, Dec. 13, 1930; s. France and Marija (Mihelic) B.; m. Magda Kosnik, Aug. 30, 1957; children: Boris, Marko. BA, Ohio U., 1954; MA, Fordham U., 1956; PhD, U. Ottawa, Ont., Can., 1958. Instr. Clarke Coll., Dubuque, Iowa, 1957-59, asst. prof., 1959-62; vis. asst. prof. U. Iowa, 1962-63; Fulbright research fellow U. Munich, Germany, 1964-65; asso. prof. Mich. State U., 1966-69; prof. philosophy Ohio State U., Columbus, 1969-95, prof. emeritus, from 1995. Rsch. in Spanish librs., 1972-73; MUCIA exch. prof. Moscow State U., 1979-80; Fulbright sr. rsch. fellow U. Ljubljana (Yugoslavia), 1982-83; Irex and Fulbright sr. rsch. fellow U. Halle-Wittenberg, German Dem. Republic, and Jagiellonsky U. (Poland), 1986-87 Author: Epistemic Logic in the Later Middle Ages, 1993; contbr. articles to profl. jours. Recipient Evans Latin prize Ohio U., 1954. Mem. Am. Philos. Assn., Am. Catholic Philos. Assn., Medieval Acad. Am. Home: Dublin, Ohio. Died Sept. 11, 2009.

BOLDUC, ERNEST JOSEPH, management consultant, not-for-profit developer; b. Lawrence, Mass., June 11, 1924; s. Ernest Joseph and Ernestine (Mercier) B.; m. Grace Gaydis, June 23, 1945; children: Philip, Richard, Stephen. BS in M.E, Northeastern U., 1948. Cert. Assn. Exec. Market devel. rep. Kawneer Co., Boston and NYC, 1950-55; market devel. rep. Kaiser Aluminum, NYC, 1955-58; exec. sec. Com. Tool Steel Producers Am. Iron and Steel Inst., NYC, 1958-66; exec. dir. Nat. Council Paper Industry for Air and Stream Improvement, NYC, 1966-83; prin. EJB Assocs., Armonk, NY, from 1983. Lectr. in assn. mgmt., meeting planning; coord. program USAID for Mongolian C. of C. trade devel. delegation touring U.S., 1993; cons. to U.S. Dept. Commerce in Albania on assn. mgmt. project, 1995; cons. to World Environment Ctr. projects, Slovakia, Rumania, Bulgaria, Ukraine; cons. USAID-PEM Project, Haiti, 1998. Author: Curtain Wall Do's and Don'ts, 1955, Planning the Successful Meeting, 1959, The Art of Budgeting For Associations, 1980, The Three P's of Running Meetings, 1990; editor Tool Steel Trends, 1961-66. Vol. exec. Internat. Exec. Svc. Corps in Botswana, 1990, in Bulgaria, 1992; trustee No. Castle Hist. Soc., 1990-92; cons. to USAID Mission in Ghana, Africa on assn. mgmt. project, 1992; vol. advisor on assn. mgmt. related projects in Bulgaria for Citizens Democracy Corp in Bulgaria, 1995, Tblisi, Georgia, 1999; vol. speaker Am. Cancer Soc. on prostate cancer, 1998—; vol. advisor ACDI, VOCA and Ctr. for Internat. Pvt. Enterprise, 2001, Romania. Decorated Air medal with 3 oak leaf clusters; recipient Man of Yr. award N.Y. Producers Coun., 1955, W. Erwin Story citation Northeastern U., 1991, Vol. Recognition award Am. Cancer Soc., 1998. Mem. Am. Soc. Assn. Execs. (life; awards com. 1978-80, internat. com. 1992), N.Y. Soc. Assn. Execs. (life; dir. 1979-80, chmn. govt. rels. com. 1979-81, presdl. citation 1987, Disting. Svc. award 1993), Meeting Planners Internat. (bd. dirs. N.Y. chpt. 1979-80), Am. Arbitration Assn. (panel arbitrators). Home: Armonk, NY. Died Feb. 2, 2009.

BOLEN, CHARLES WARREN, university dean; b. West Frankfort, Ill., Sept. 27, 1923; s. William and Iva (Phillips) B.; m. Maxine Sheffler, Aug. 1, 1948; children: Ann, Jayne. B of Mus. Edn., Northwestern U., 1948; MusM, Eastman Sch. Music, 1950; PhD, Ind. U., 1954. Instr. music Ea. Ill. U., 1950-51; chmn. music dept. Ripon (Wis.) Coll., 1954-62; instr. flute Nat. Music Camp, summers 1954-62; dean Sch. Fine Arts, U. Mont., Missoula, 1962-70, Coll. Fine Arts, Ill. State U., Normal, 1970-88; dir. sr. profls. Acad. Srs., Mornings with the Profs., Normal, 1988-96. Contbr. articles to profl. jours. Chmn. Mont Arts Coun., 1965-70; mem. Pres.'s Adv. Coun. to Arts, Pres.'s Adv. Coun. to J.F. Kennedy Ctr. for Performing Arts, 1970; cons. Chancellor's Panel on Univ. Purposes, SUNY, 1970, Ednl. Mgmt. Svcs.; pres. Cen. Ill. Cultural Affairs Consortium, 1975-76. Recipient Ill. Treasure award Ill. Alliance for Ageing, 1993. Mem. Music Tchrs. Nat. Assn. (pres. East Cen. divsn. 1961-62, nat. v.p. states and divsns. 1962-65), Music Educators Nat. Conf., Am. Musicol. Soc., Internat. Coun. Fine Arts Deans (chmn. 1969-70), Fedn. Rocky Mountain States (mem. arts and humanities com. 1966-70), Assn. Western Univs. Home: Bloomington, Ill. Died July 14, 2010.

BOLINGER, JOHN C., JR., management consultant; b. Knoxville, Tenn., Feb. 12, 1922; s. John C. and Elsie (Burkhart) B.; m. Helen McCallie, Jan. 26, 1944; children: Janet Marie, John M., Robert B. BSBA, U. Tenn., 1943; MBA, Harvard U., 1947. Asst. sec. Lehigh Coal & Nav. Co., Phila., 1947-49, asst. to pres., 1949-50, v.p., 1950-54; asst. to pres. Mississippi River Corp., St. Louis, 1954-57; pres. East Tenn. Natural Gas Co., Knoxville, 1957-61; pres., dir. Houston Nat. Bank, 1961-63; exec. v.p., dir. Mississippi River Corp., St. Louis, 1963-67; pres. Mississippi River Transmission (subs.), 1964-67; mgmt. cons. Knoxville, from 1967. Pres. Tenn. Natural Resources (formerly Tenn. Natural Gas Lines), 1971-86, chmn., 1976-86; pres. Nashville Gas Co., 1972-82, chmn., 1976-86; vice-chmn. Piedmont Natural Gas Co., Charlotte, N.C., 1985-95; lectr. U. Tenn.; cons. in field. Served to capt. AUS, 1943-46. Decorated Bronze Star, Purple Heart, Croix de Guerre (France) Home: Knoxville, Tenn. Died Feb. 21, 2009.

BOLTZ, MARY ANN, aerospace materials and travel company executive; b. Far Rockaway, NY, Jan. 12, 1923; d. Thomas and Theresa (Domanico) Caparelli; m. William Emmett Boltz, (dec. Feb., 2008); children: Valerie Ann Boltz Austin, Beverly Theresa, Cynthia Marie Boltz O'Rourke. Publicist CBS, NYC, 1943-48; mgr. Coast-Line Internat. Distbrs. Ltd., Lindenhurst, NY, 1961-80, v.p., 1980-86, pres., 1987-90, CEO, from 1990; chief exec. officer Air Ship 'N Shore Travel, Woodmere, NY and Marco Island, Fla., from 1978; pres. ABOC Enterprises LLC, from 2003, owner, from 2003; pres. Mary A Boltz; v.p. Heather O'rourke. Pres. Bangor Realty, 1975. Formerly radio and TV editor local publs., writer Gotham Guide mag. Sec. Inwood Civic & Businessmen's Assn., 1952-64, pres., 1964-66, chmn. bd., 1967-68; pres. Lawrence Pub. Schs. System PTA, 1956-58; pres., life mem. Cen. Coun. PTA, 1958-60; founder Inwood Civic Scholarship Fund, 1964; v.p. Econ. Opportunity Coun., Inwood; fundraising bd. yearly ball St. Joachim Ch., Cedarhurst, NY; gift chmn. L.I. Bd. Boys Town of Italy; bd. dirs. Marco Island Cancer Fund Dr.; dir., promoter Marco Island Philharmonic Symphony; dir. polit. campaign William Sieffert, Oceanside, N.Y.; chmn. 30 yr. reunion Class of 41, 1971, 50 yr. reunion, 1991, 55th yr. Lawrence H.S. reunion Class of 1938-42; asst. chmn. 50 yr. reunion Class of 42, 1991, Lawrence H.S. 55th Reunion Class of 1941, 1996; fundraiser Stecker and Horowitz Sch. Music Dinner Com., 1978, Am. Bus. Women's Assn., Long Island charter chptr., Rockville Centre, N.Y., 1990-92, United Fund, Red Feather Ball, 1992 Recipient award Nassau Herald Newspaper, Cedarhurst, Inwood Civic Assn., PTA Life Membership award, 25 Yr. Silver Medallion Boys Town of Italy, gold medal, 1995, Citizen of Yr. Bronze Plaque award Inwood Civic Assn., 1996; named Woman of the Year Boys Town of Italy, 1997. Mem. Am. Bus. Women's Assn. (L.I. charter chpt.), Nissoquogue Golf Club, Sun 'N Surf Beach Club, Island Country Club (Marco Island, Fla.), Desert Mountain Country Club. Republican. Roman Catholic. Home: Auburn, Maine. Died Sept. 2009.

BOMBERGER, AUDREY SHELLEY, health facility administrator; b. June 12, 1942; Diploma in nursing, Reading Med. Ctr., 1963; BS in Edn., Millersville U., 1975; MS in Edn., Temple U., 1979; PhD in Health Adminstrn., Columbia-Pacific U., 1983. Enlisted U.S. Army, 1977, with Nurse Corps, 1977—99, ret. Col., 1999; dir. hosp. edn. and rsch. McKay-Dee Hosp., Ogden, Utah, 1984-87; dir. hosp. edn. Salinas (Calif.) Valley Meml. Hosp., 1987-91; owner Creative Health Svcs., Salinas, 1991-94; adminstr. profl. svcs. Al Hada Hosp., Tiaf, Saudi Arabia, 1994-95; dir. nursing Casa Serena Nursing Home, 1995-96; dir. quality mgmt., dir. profl. svcs. LifeCare Mgmt. Svcs., Dallas, 1996—99, clin. v.p. corp. offices, from 1999. Author: Radiation and Health: Disaster Planning, 1984; co-author: Disaster Planning, 1986, Medical/Surgical Nursing, 1982. Died Jan. 28, 2009.

BONDURANT, BYRON LEE, agricultural engineering educator; b. Lima, Ohio, Nov. 11, 1925; s. Earl Smith and Joy Koneta (Gesler) B.; m. Lovetta May Alexander, Feb. 28, 1944; children: Connie Jane Bondurant Jaycox, Richard Thayne, Cindy Lynn Bondurant Oxyer. Student, Case Inst. Tech., 1943-44, Rensselaer Poly. Inst., 1944; BS in Agrl. Engring., Ohio State U., 1949; MS in Civil Engring., U. Conn., 1953. Registered profl. eng., Maine, Ohio; registered surveyor, Maine. Dist. agrl. engr., western N.Y., N.Y. State Coll. Agr., Cornell U., 1949-50; instr. agrl. engring., extension agrl. engr., dept. agrl. engring. U. Conn., 1950-53; asso. prof. agronomy and agrl. engring., extension agrl. engr. dept. agronomy and agrl. engring. U. Del., 1953-54; prof. agrl. engring., head dept. U. Maine, 1954-64; prof. agrl. engring. Ohio State U., 1964-85; prof. emeritus Agrl. Engring. Ohio State U., from 1985. Also adviser to dean, later dean Coll. Agrl. Engring., Ludhiana, India, 1964-67, 69-71; vis. prof. agrl. engring. U. Nairobi, Kenya, 1974, Fulbright-Hays prof., 1979-80; project mgr. M.U.C.I.A., Mogadiscio, Somalia, 1976-78; curriculua advisor Irrigation Tng. Program, U.S. AID India, 1986-88. Fellow AAAS, Inst. Engrs. (India and Kenya), Indian Soc. Agrl. Engrs. (life), Am. Soc. Agrl. Engrs. (vice chmn. N. Atlantic sect. 1956-57, chmn. Acadia sect. 1961-62, sec.-treas. Ohio and Tri-State sect. 1983-84, dir. internat. div. 1980-82, Kishida Internat. award 1983); mem. AAUP, Soc. Internat. Devel. (life), Am. Soc. Engring. Edn. (chmn. agrl. engring. div.), Nat. Soc. Profl. Engrs., Maine Soc. Profl. Engrs. (pres. 1963), Sigma Xi, Sigma Pi Sigma, Tau Beta Pi, Gamma Sigma Delta, Epsilon Sigma Phi, Alpha Epsilon. Home: Soldotna, Alaska. Died Jan. 24, 2010.

BOOKATZ, SAMUEL, painter, sculptor; b. Phila., Oct. 3, 1910; s. Barnett and Ann (Cohen) B.; m. Helen Meyer, Oct. 12, 1963. Student, John Hunting Poly. Inst., 1928-31, Cleve. Mus. Inst. Art, 1931-35, Boston Mus. Sch. Art, 1935-37, Harvard U., 1935-37, London U., 1937—38, Grand Chaumiere, Paris, 1938, Collorossi, 1939, Am. Acad., Rome, 1938-41. Commd. officer U.S. Navy, advanced through grades to comdr., combat artist, ret., 1964. One man shows, group shows; represented: permanent collections Phillips Collection, Washington, Corcoran Gallery Art, Washington, Library of Congress, Washington, Smithsonian Instn., Washington, Norfolk Mus., Va., Cleve. Mus. Art, Am. Acad., Rome; White House artist (under Pres. Rosseveld Adminstrn.); portraits of Franklin D. Rossevelt, 1943, Mrs. Elinor Roosevelt, 1943, Joseph H. Hirshhorn, Hirshhorn Mus., Washington, 1983, Gov. of Pa. David L. Lawrence, 1964; author: Portrait of Pearl Buck, 1969. Inst. of Allendo fellow Mexico, 1954, Ford grantee, 1962. Recipient William Paige and Prix de Rome awards Boston Mus., 1987. Home: Vienna, Va. Died Nov. 16, 2009.

BOOTH, JOHN NICHOLLS, minister, writer, photographer; b. Meadville, Pa., Aug. 7, 1912; s. Sydney Scott and Margaret (Nicholls) B.; m. Edith Kriger, Oct. 1, 1941 (dec. Sept. 22, 1982); 1 child, Barbara Anne Booth Christie. BA, McMaster U., 1934; MDiv, Meadville/Lombard Theol. Sch., 1942; LittD, New Eng. Sch. Law, 1950. Ordained to ministry Unitarian Ch., 1942. Profl. magician, 1934-40; min. Unitarian Ch., Evanston, Ill., 1942-48, 1st Ch., Belmont, Mass., 1949-57, 2d Ch. (Now 1st Ch.), Boston, 1958-64, Unitarian Ch., Long Beach, Calif., 1964-71; interim pastor NYC, Gainesville, (Fla.), Detroit, 1971-73. Celebrity platform lectr. and performer on conjuring and mentalism, 1942-58; ministerial adviser to liberal students MIT, 1958-63; mem. books selection com. Gen. Theol. Library, Boston, 1960-63. Author: Super Magical Miracles, 1930, Magical Mentalism, 1931, Forging Ahead in Magic, 1939, Marvels of Mystery, 1941, The Quest for Preaching Power, 1943, Fabulous Destinations, 1950, Story of the Second Church in Boston, 1959, The John Booth Classics, 1975, Booths in History, 1982, Psychic Paradoxes, 1984, Wonders of Magic, 1986, Dramatic Magic, 1988, Creative World of Conjuring, 1990, Conjurians' Discoveries, 1992, The Fine Art of Hocus Pocus, 1995, Keys to Magic's Inner World, 1999, Extending Magic Beyond Credibility, 2001; contbr. articles to mags. and newspapers; photographer full length feature travel documentary films for TV, lecture platforms made in India, Africa, S.Am., Indonesia, South Seas, Himalayas; presented first color travelogue on TV in U.S. over NBC in N.Y.C., 1949; panel mem. radio program Churchmen Weigh The News, Boston, 1951-52; spl. corr. in Asia for Chgo. Sun-Times, 1948-49; by-line writer Boston Globe, 1954-66; producer, photographer motion pictures Heart of Africa, 1954, Golden Kingdoms of the Orient, 1957, Indonesia: Pacific Shangri La, 1957, Treasures of the Amazon, Ecuador and Peru, 1960, Adventurous Britain, 1962, South Seas Saga in Tahiti, Australia and New Guinea, summer 1966, The Amazing America of Will Rogers, 1970, Spotlight on Spain, 1975. Co-founder Japan Free Religious Assn., Tokyo, 1948; co-founder Mass. Meml. Soc., 1962, dir., 1962-64; organizer Meml. Soc. Alachua County (Fla.), 1972; pres. Long Beach Mental Health Assn., 1964-66; adv. coun. Fair Housing Found. Recipient John Nevil Maskelyne prize London Magic Cir., 1987; placed on former N.Y. Town Hall Travelogue Cinematographers Wall of Fame, 1967; named Disting. Alumnae Gallery of McMaster U.; lit. fellow Acad. Magical Arts, 1977, lifetime achievement fellow, 1990, masters fellow, 2001. Mem. Unitarian-Universalist Mins. Assn. (past dir.), Am. Unitarian Assn. (past com. chmn.), Unitarian Mins. Pacific S.W. Assn. (v.p.), Clergy Counseling Svc. So. Calif., Soc. Am. Magicians (inducted into Hall of Fame 1983), Magic Castle Hollywood, Internat. Brotherhood Magicians (hon. life), L.A. Adventurers Club (pres. 1983), Evanston (Ill.) Ministerial Assn. (pres. 1947-48). Achievements include having the first regularly scheduled TV series (Looking at Life) in U.S. by clergyperson, WBKB, Chgo., mid-1940s. Died Nov. 11, 2009.

BORDERS, WILLIAM DONALD, archbishop emeritus; b. Washington, Ind., Oct. 9, 1913; Attended, St. Meinrad Sem.; degree, Notre Dame Sem.; MS in Edn., U. Notre Dame, 1947. Ordained priest Diocese of New Orleans, 1940, assoc. pastor, 1940—43, 1946—48; asst. chaplain La. State U., 1948—57, asst. chaplain to chaplain, 1959—64; pastor Holy Family Ch., Port Allen, La., 1957—59; ordained bishop, 1968; rector St. Joseph Cathedral, Baton Rouge, 1964-68; bishop Diocese of Orlando, Fla., 1968-74; archbishop Archdiocese of Balt., 1974-89, archbishop emeritus, 1989—2010. With Chaplain Corps US Army, 1943—46. Roman Catholic. Home: Baltimore, Md. Died Apr. 19, 2010.

BOREN, WILLIAM MEREDITH, manufacturing executive; b. San Antonio, Oct. 23, 1924; s. Thomas Loyd and Verda (Locke) B.; m. Molly Brasfield Sarver, Dec. 3, 1976; children: Susan, Patricia, Janet, Jenny, Burton, Cliff. Student, Tex. A&M U., 1942-43, Rice U., 1943-44; BS in Mech. Engring., Tex. U., 1949. Vice pres., gen. mgr. Rolo Mfg. Co., Houston, 1949-54; mgr. sales engring. Black, Sivalls & Bryson, Houston, Oklahoma City, 1955-64; vice chmn., dir., mem. exec. com. Big Three Industries, Inc., Houston, from 1965; chmn. Bowen Tool Co., Houston. Bd. dirs. Engring. Adv. Coun., Tex. U.; dir. Air Liquide Am. Corp.; dir. Electric Reliability Coun. Tex. Inventor Classic Bridge game; screenwriter WWII movie Pegasus Bridge. Trustee S.W. Rsch. Inst., San Antonio; bd. dirs. Coun. Econ. Edn.; mem. chancellor's coun. U. Tex. Lt. (j.g.) USN, 1943-46. Named Disting. Grad. Engring. Dept., U. Tex., 1992. Mem. Internat. Oxygen Mfrs. Assn. (chmn.), French-Am. C. of C. (bd. dirs.), Tau Beta Pi, Pi Tau Sigma. Republican. Home: Houston, Tex. Died Mar. 15, 2010.

BOROD, RICHARD MELVIN, lawyer; b. Providence, May 11, 1933; s. Esmond S. and Lena H. Borod; m. A. Gail Cohen, Aug. 22, 1959. AB, Brown U., 1954; LLB, Yale U., 1962. Bar: R.I. 1962, U.S. Dist. Ct. R.I. 1963, U.S. Ct. Appeals (1st cir.) 1966, U.S. Supreme Ct. 1979. Assoc. Edwards & Angell, Providence, 1962-70, ptnr., 1970-97, of counsel, from 1997. Incorporator, 1st chmn. bd. R.I. Legal Svcs., Providence, 1969-72, bd. dirs., 1969-86. Vol. atty. R.I. Affiliate of ACLU, Providence, 1962—; trustee, officer Temple Beth El, Providence, 1986-93. With U.S. Army, 1956-59. Mem. ABA, fed. Bar Assn. (chmn. R.I. chpt. 1987-88), R.I. Bar Assn. Jewish. Avocations: tennis, biking, cross country skiing, classical guitar, duplicate bridge (acbl life master). Home: East Greenwich, RI. Died June 9, 2010.

BOROS, EUGENE JOSEPH, chemical company executive; b. Decatur, Ill, May 19, 1940; s. Eugene Joseph and Helen Louise B.; m. Nancy Lea Odum, aug. 28, 1960; children: Eric Eugene, Rohonda Lea. BS in Chemistry, U. Ill., 1962; PhD in Inorganic Chemistry, Iowa State U., 1966. Asst. prof. Wash. State U., Pullman, 1966-68; sr. chemist, project scientist, group leader, assoc. dir., dir. research and devel. dept. Union Carbide Corp., South Charleston, W.Va. and Research Triangle Park, N.C., from 1968, v.p. research and devel. Research Triangle Park. Contbr. articles to profl. jours.; patentee. Bd. mem. Youth Orch., Charleston, W.Va., 1980-81. Mem. Am. Chem. Soc., Phi Kappa Phi Clubs: Wildwood country (Raleigh). Presbyterian. Home: Raleigh, NC. Died Mar. 20, 2009.

BOSE, AJAY KUMAR, chemistry professor emeritus; b. Silchar, India, Feb. 12, 1925; arrived in US, 1947, naturalized, 2006; s. Abinash C. and Amita Kumari (Chanda) B.; m. Margaret Lois Logan, Sept. 13, 1950; children: Ryan, Ranjan, Indrani, Indira, Krishna, Rajendra. BS, U. Allahabad, India, 1944, MS, 1946; ScD, MIT, 1950; M in Engring. (hon.), Stevens Inst. Tech., Hoboken, NJ, 1963. Rsch. fellow Harvard U., Cambridge, Mass., 1950-51; lectr., then asst. prof. chemistry Indian Inst. Tech., Kharagpur, 1952-56; rsch. assoc. U. Pa., Phila., 1956-57; rsch. chemist Upjohn Co., Kalamazoo, 1957-59; assoc. prof. Stevens Inst. Tech., 1959-61, prof., 1961-83, George Meade Bond prof. chemistry, 1983-96, prof., 1996—2007; prof. emeritus, 2007. Founder, dir. Undergrad. Projects in Tech. and Medicine, 1971-2007; cons. various chem. cos. Mem. editl. bd. Jour. Heterocyclic Chemistry, 1980-83; contbr. over 350 articles to profl. jours.; patentee in field. Recipient Outstanding Achievement award Nat. Fedn. Indian Am. Assns., 1990, Ranbaxy Sci. Found. Rsch. award in Pharm. Scis., 1997, Nat. Catalyst award Chem. Mfrs. Assn., 1997, Presdl. award for excellence in sci., math. and engring. mentoring, 1999, Lifetime Achievement award, Indian Chem. Soc., 2006; named N.J. Prof. of Yr., Coun. for Advancement and Support of Edn. and Carnegie Found. for Advancement of Tchg., 1990. Fellow AAAS, Indian Nat. Sci. Acad.; mem. Am. Chem. Soc. (councillor 1964-70, Dreyfus award 1999), Sigma Xi. Avocation: popular sci. writing. Home: Easton, Pa. Died Feb. 12, 2010.

BOSE, NIRMAL KUMAR, electrical engineer, mathematics educator; b. Calcutta, West Bengal, India, Aug. 19, 1940; came to U.S., 1961; s. Dhruba Kumar and Roma (Guha) B.; m. Chandra Bose, June 8, 1969; children: Meenekshi, Enakshi. B.Tech., Indian Inst. Tech., Kharagpur, West Bengal, 1961; MS, Cornell U., 1963; PhD, Syracuse U., 1967. Asst. prof. U. Pitts., 1967-70, assoc. prof., 1970-76, prof., 1976-86; Singer prof. elec. engring. Pa. State U., University Park, 1986-91, HRB-Systems prof. elec. engring., from 1992; vis. assoc. prof. U. Calif., Berkeley, 1973-74. Cons. RCA, Meadowland, Pa., 1968-69; spl. lectr. Coll. of Steubenville, Ohio, 1968-70; vis. assoc. prof. Am. U. Beirut, 1971, U. Md., College Park, 1972; vis. fellow Princeton U., 1996; apptd. vis. prof. Israel Inst. Tech., 1996; UN expert in neural networks to instns. and ctrs., India, 1994-95; rschr. Japan Soc. for Promotion of Sci., 1998; Humboldt guest prof. Ruhr U., Bochum, Germany, 2000-03; invited sr. mem. Inst. Math. Scis., Nat. U. Singapore, 2003; invited lectr., rschr. Akita Prefectural U. Japan, 2005. Author: Applied Multidimensional Systems Theory, 1982, Digital Filters: Theory and Applications, 1985, rev. edit., 1993; co-author: Neural Network Fundammentals, 1996; editor: Multidimensional Systems: Theory and Application, 1979, Multidimensional Systems; Progress, Directions and Open Problems, 1985, 2nd edit., 2003; founding editor-in-chief Multidimensional Sys. and Signal Processing, 1990-; co-editor: Handbook of Statistics vol. on Signal Processing and Its Applications, 1993; assoc. editor Cirs., Sys., and Signal Processing Jour., IEEE Trans. of Cirs. and Sys., Jour. Franklin Inst.; adv. com. Internat. Jour. Smart Engring. Sys. Design. Recipient Invitational fellow for rsch. in Japan, Japan Soc. for Promotion of Sci., 1998, Charles H. Fetter Univ. Endowed fellow in elec. engring., 2001—04, Alexander von Humboldt Sr. U.S. Scientist Rsch. award, 1999. Fellow: IEEE (chmn. cirs. and systems tech. com. on edn. 1979—85, Merit award 2000, Circuits and Systems Soc. Edn. award 2007); mem.: Am. Soc. Elec. Engrs., AAAS, NY Acad. Scis., Am. Math. Soc., Sigma Xi. Hindu. Achievements include listed as 1st 15 influential engrs. in 2005 by Registry Pro. Avocations: table-tennis, stamp collecting/philately. Home: State College, Pa. Died Nov. 22, 2009.

BOSLEY, TOM, actor; b. Chgo., Oct. 1, 1927; s. Benjamin and Dora (Heyman) B.; m. Jean Eliot, Mar. 8, 1962 (dec. Apr. 1978); 1 child, Amy; m. Patricia Carr, Dec. 21, 1980. Student, De Paul U., 1946, Radio Inst. Chgo., 1947-48; studied with, Lee Strasberg, 1952. Actor: various roles TV programs Alice in Wonderland, 1953, Arsenic and Old Lace, 1962, Focus, 1961, Naked City, The Right Man, The Nurses, Law and Mr. Jones, Route 66, The Perry Como Show, The Dean Martin Show, Joanie Loves Chachi, The Rebels, Death Trap, Castaways on Gilligan's Island, Return of Mod Squad, For the Love of It, Jessie Owens Story, The Drew Carey Show, ER, Touched by an Angel, One Tree Hill; (TV films) Fatal Confession: A Father Dowling Mystery, 1987, The Love Boat, A Valentine Voyage, 1990; regular actor on TV shows Wait Til Your Father Gets Home, Murder She Wrote, 1984-87; (TV series) Happy Days, 1974-83, The Father Dowling Mysteries, 1989-92, the Parsley Garden, 1993, Legend of the Candy Cane, 2001, Mothers and Daughters, 2002, Returning Mickey Stern, 2002, Mary Christmas, 2002, Christmas at Water's Edge, 2004, The Fallen Ones, 2005, Hidden Places, 2006; (TV mini-series) The Bastard, 1978; narrator TV series That's Hollywood; voice in animated cartoon The Stingiest Man in Town; Broadway roles include: Fiorello, 1959 (Tony award for Best Featured Actor in a Musical, 1960), Nowhere to Go But Up, 1962, Natural Affection, 1963, A Murderer Among Us, 1964, The Education of H, Beauty and the Beast, 1994, Cabaret, 2002, On Golden Pond, 2006; actor: (films) Love with the Proper Stranger, 1963, The World of Henry Orient, 1964, Divorce American Style, 1967, The Secret War of Harry Frigg, 1968, Yours, Mine and Ours, 1968, To Find A Man, 1972, Mixed Company, 1974, Gus, 1976, O'Hara's Wife, 1982, Little Bigfoot 2: The Journey Home, 1997, Confession, 2005, Popstar, 2005, The Back-up Plan, 2010 Served with USNR, World War II. Recipient Antoinette Perry award for 1959-60 season as best actor in featured role of musical; Newspaper Guild of America Page One award and ANTA award for distinguished contbn. to theatre, 1960; N.Y. Drama

Critics award for performance in Fiorello, 1960; Festival of Leadership award Chgo.; Humanitarian award Performing Arts Theater of Handicapped, 1981; Tau award Sacred Heart Rehab. Hosp., Milw. Mem. Actors Equity Assn. (governing council 1961-69), AFTRA, Screen Actors Guild. Died Oct. 19, 2010.

BOSTON, LEONA, retired social services administrator; b. Joliet, Ill., Aug. 4, 1914; d. Dorie Philip and Margaret (Mitchell) Boston. Student, LaSalle Extension U., 1936-37, 46, Moody Bible Inst., 1939-40, U. Chgo., 1944-45. Tchr. Nat. Stenotype Sch., Chgo., 1937; stenotypist Rotary Internat., Evanston, Ill., 1937—44, sec. to comptroller, 1944—50, head personnel dept., 1950—65, exec. asst. to gen. sec., 1965—77, ret., 1977. Mem. exec. com. North Shore Festival Faith, Northfield, Ill., 1978. Bd. dirs. YWCA, Evanston, 1961—63; mem. Bus. and Profl. Women's Club, Evanston, 1965—80, chmn. fin. com., 1977—78; pres. Zonta, Evanston, 1970—71, membership com., 1976—78, chmn. membership com., 1976—78, historian, 1979—84, fin. com., 1985—89, 1993—2002, chmn. fin. com., 1987—89, 1994—2002, mem. club history and archives com., 1989—91, 1995—96, parliamentarian, 1991—92, membership com., 1993—94, intercity/internat. rels. com., 1993—94, 1998—2001; fin. sec. Winnetka (Ill.) Bible Ch., 1965—68, treas., 1979—80. Mem.: Zonta Club (v.p., chmn. program com. 1969—70), Bus. and Profl. Womens' Club (chmn. fin. com. 1977—78). Home: Schaumburg, Ill. Died Apr. 14, 2009.

BOUCEK, MARK MANSFIELD, pediatric cardiologist; b. Rochester, Minn., Apr. 29, 1949; BS, Fla. State U., Tallahassee, 1971; MD, U. Miami, 1977. Resident Vanderbilt U., Nashville, 1977-79; fellow U. Utah, Salt Lake City, 1979-81; asst. prof. pediats. U. Utah Coll. Medicine, Salt Lake City, 1981-88; assoc. prof. Loma Linda U. Sch. Medicine, Calif., 1988-92, prof. pediat. cardiology Calif.; prof. Children's Hosp. U. Colo., Denver, from 1992; dir. heart transplant program U. Colo. Sch. Medicine, Denver, 1992—2003, dir. pediats. cardiology, 1992—2001; dir. pediat. cardiology Joe DiMaggio Children's Hosp., from 2001. Vis. professorships at universities around the country; frequent participant and spkr. at internat. med. symposia. Co-author: Handbook of Cardiac Drugs-Basic Science and Clinical Aspects of Cardiovascular Pharmacology, 1992; assoc. editor Registry of Internat. Soc. for Heart and Lung Transplantation; contbr. several articles to profl. jours. and chapters to books. Grantee NIH, 1986, 87-90, 2001—, St. Jude Med. Ctr., 1987-88, Utah Heart Assn., 1984-88, Bugher Physician Scientist Tng. Program, 1990-97, HRSA, 2003—; cited frequently in America's Top Doctors. Fellow Am. Coll. Cardiology, Soc. for Cardiac Angiography and Intervention, Am. Acad. Pediats., Internat. Soc. for Heart and Lung Transplantation; mem. Am. Soc. Transplant Physicians (mem. pediatric com. 1996—, dir. pediatric transplantation 2003—, chair pediatric com. 2004—), United Network Organ Sharing (chair pediatric com. 1996—98, bd. dirs. 1998-2000), Pediatric Heart Transplant Working Group, Colo. Heart Assn. Avocations: running, diving. Died Feb. 27, 2009.

BOUCHER, WILLIAM PAUL, state legislator; b. Manchester, NH, Apr. 4, 1930; s. George E. and Violet (Rivard) B.; m. Eleanor McKinnon, 1952; children: William Patrick, Martin Paul. Student, U.S. Armed Forces Inst. N.H. state rep. Dist. 29, from 1971; mem. edn. com. N.H. Ho. of Reps., 1979-83, mem. fish and game com., state-fed. rels. com., mem. wildlife and marine resources com. Mem. Exec. Dept. and Adminstrn. and State-Fed. Rels. Com.; gunsmith, 1956-70. Chmn. Londonderry Sch. Bd., 1969-74; chmn. Rockingham County Del., 1977-78, 81-82; mem. Vocat. Rehab. Consumer Adv. Coun., Gov.'s Commn. for Handicapped, 1971—. Mem. Londonderry Fish and Game Club (dir.). Died Feb. 7, 2010.

BOUDREAU, LORRAINE JEANETTE, nursing researcher; b. W. Warwick, R.I., Aug. 24, 1943; d. Joseph Onesime and Beatrice Violet (Lecuivre) Boudreau; Diploma in Nursing, Roger Williams Gen. Hosp., 1964; B.S. in Nursing, U. Va., 1974; M.Nursing, UCLA, 1977. Nurse specialist in alcohol rehab. VA Med. Center, Sepulveda, Calif., 1974-78, coordinator community psychiatry program, 1978-80; asst. chief nurse VA Med. Center, Kerrville, Tex., 1980-84, nurse researcher, 1984—; asst. clin. prof. UCLA, 1978-79. Collaborator: Nurses in Vietnam: The Forgotten Veterans, 1987. Served with Nurse Corps, U.S. Army, 1965-71. Recipient Sustained Performance award, VA, 1979, 82; Comdr.'s Spl. Recognition, 6222d USAR Sch., 1980. Mem. Res. Officers Assn., Assn. Mil. Surgeons of U.S., Tex. Soc. Hosp. Nursing Adminstrs., Tex. Hosp. Assn., Nat. League for Nursing, others. Republican. Roman Catholic. Home: San Antonio, Tex. Died Jan. 19, 2010.

BOULDING, ELISE MARIE, sociologist, educator; b. Oslo, July 6, 1920; came to U.S., 1923, naturalized, 1929; d. Joseph and Birgit (Johnsen) Biorn-Hansen; m. Kenneth Boulding; Aug. 31, 1941; children: John Russell, Mark David, Christine Ann, Philip Daniel, William Frederic. BA, Douglass Coll., 1940; MS, Iowa State Coll., 1949; PhD, U. Mich., 1969. Rsch. assoc. Survey Rsch. Inst., U. Mich., 1957-58, Mental Health Rsch. Inst., 1959-60; rsch. devel. sec. Ctr for Rsch. on Conflict Resolution, 1960-63; prof. sociology, project dir. Inst. Behavioral Sci., U. Colo., Boulder, 1967-78; Montgomery vis. prof. Dartmouth Coll., 1978-79, chmn. dept. sociology, 1979-85, prof. emerita, 1985—2010; sec. gen. Internat. Peace Rsch. Assoc., 1989-91; pres. IPRA Found., 1992-96. Mem. program adv. council Human and Social Devel. Program, UN Univ., 1977-80; mem. governing council, 1980-86. Author: (with others) Handbook of International Data on Women, 1976, Bibliography on World Conflict and Peace, 1979, Social System of Planet Earth, 1980, Women and the Social Costs of Economic Development, 1981; author: The Underside of History: A View of Women Through Time, 1975, rev. edit., 1992, Women in Twentieth Century World, 1977, Children's Rights and the Wheel of Life, 1979, Building a Global Civic Culture: Education for an Interdependent World, 1988, 90, One Small Plot of Heaven, 1990, Cultures of Peace: The Hidden Side of History, 2000; (with Kenneth Boulding) The Future: Images and Processes, 1994; editor: Peace Culture and Society: Transnational Research and Dialogue with Clovis Brigagao and Kevin Clements (eds.), 1990; New Agendas for Peace Research: Conflict and Security Reexamined (ed.), 1992; Building Peace in the Middle East: Challenges for States and Civil Society, (ed.), 1993. Internat. chair Women's Internat. League for Peace and Freedom, 1967-70; mem. Exploratory Project on Conditions for Peace, 1984-90; mem. U.S. Commn. for UNESCO, 1978-84; mem. UNESCO Peace Prize jury, 1980-87; chair bd. Boulder Cmty. Parenting Ctr., 1988-92; bd. dirs. Am. Friends Svc. Com., 1990-94, Wayland MA Coun. on Aging, 1988-2000; councillor Interfaith Peace Coun., 1995—. Recipient Disting. Achievement award Douglass Coll., 1973, Ted. Lentz Peace award, 1976, Athena award, 1983, Nat. Women's Forum award, 1985, Inst. of Def., Disarmament, Peace and Democracy award, 1990, Jack Gore Meml. Peace award Denver Am. Friends Svc. Com., 1992, Global Citizen award Boston Rsch. Ctr., 1995, Peacemaker of Yr. award Rocky Mountain Peace and Justice Ctr., 1996, World Futures Studies Fedn. award, 1997, Jane Addams Peace Activist award Women's Internat. League for Peace and Freedom, 2000; named to Rutgers Hall of Disting. Alumni, 1994; Danforth fellow, 1965-67; named Peacemaker Elder, Nat. Conf. on Peacemaking and Conflict Resolution, 1999; chosen as one of 1000 Women for the Nobel Peace Prize, 2005. Mem. Am. Sociol. Assn. (Jessie Bernard award 1982, Peace and War sect. award 1994), Internat. Peace Rsch. Assn. (newsletter editor 1983-87), World Future Studies Fedn., Colo. Women's Forum. Mem. Soc. Of Friends. Home: Needham, Mass. Died June 24, 2010.

BOULGER, FRANCIS WILLIAM, metallurgical engineer; b. Mpls., June 19, 1913; s. Francis J. and Mary (Armstrong) B. Metall. Engr., U. Minn., 1934; MS (Battelle fellow), Ohio State U., 1937. With A.P., 1929-34; engr. Minn. Dept. Hwys., 1935-36; metallurgist Republic Steel Corp., Cleve., 1937; research metallurgist Battelle Meml. Inst., Columbus, Ohio, 1938-45, div. chief, 1945-67, sr. tech. advisor, 1967-85, ret. Cons. USAF; Materials Adv. Bd. OECD. Author: (with others) Forging Materials and Practices, 1968, Tri-Lingual Dictionary of Production Engineering, 1969, Forging Equipment, Materials and Practices, 1973; also over 150 tech. articles. Named Man of Yr. Columbus Tech. Council, 1966, Disting. Alumnus, Ohio State U., 1984; Gold medalist Soc. Mfg. Engrs., 1967; recipient Am. Machinist award, 1975 Fellow Am. Soc. Metals, Soc. Mfg. Engrs., ASME; mem. AIME (Hunt medal 1955), Nat. Acad. Engring., Internat. Inst. for Prodn. Research (hon. mem., past pres.), N. Am. Mfg. Research Instn. (co-founder), Internat. Cold Forging Group (co-founder), Sigma Xi. Roman Catholic. Home: Columbus, Ohio. Died Feb. 24, 2010.

BOURGEOIS, LOUISE, sculptor; b. Paris, Dec. 25, 1911; arrived in US, 1938, naturalized, 1953; m. Robert Goldwater, 1938 (dec. 1973); 3 children. Student, Sorbonne U., 1932-35; baccalaureate, Ecole des Beaux Arts, 1936-38; postgrad., Ecole du Louvre, 1936-37, Acad. Grande Chaumiere; D.F.A. (hon.), Yale U., 1977, Calif. Coll. Arts and Crafts, 1988, Moore Coll. Art, Mass. Coll. Art, 1983, Md. Art Inst., 1984, The New Sch., 1987. Instr. Md. Art Inst., Balt., 1984, New Sch. Social Rsch., NYC, 1987. One-woman shows include Norlyst Gallery, 1947, Peridot Gallery, 1949, 1950, 1953, Allan Frumkin Gallery, Chgo., 1953, White Art Mus., Cornell U., Ithaca, NY, 1959, Stable Gallery, 1964, Rose Fried Gallery, 1963, 112 Greene St., NYC, 1974, Xavier Fourcade Gallery, NYC, 1978-80, Max Hutchinson Gallery, NYC, 1980, Renaissance Soc., 1981, Mus. Modern Art, NYC, 1982, retrospective Contemporary Art Mus., Houston, 1983, Daniel Weinberg Gallery, LA, 1984, Robert Miller Gallery, 1982, 1984, 1987-89, 1991, Serpentine Gallery, London, 1985, Maeght-Lelong, Zurich, 1985, Paris, 1985, Taft Mus., Cin., 1987-89 (travelled to The Art Mus. at Fla. Internat. U., Miami, Fla., Laguna Gloria Art Mus., Austin, Tex., Gallery of Art, Washington U., St. Louis, Henry Art Gallery, Seattle, Everson Mus. Art, Syracuse, NY), Mus. Overholland, Amsterdam, The Netherlands, 1988, Dia Art Found., Bridgehampton, NY, retrospective Frankfurter Kunstverein, Frankfurt, Fed. Republic Germany, 1989 (travelled to Städtische Galerie im Lenbachhaus, Munich, 1990, Riverside Studios, London, 1990, Musée d'Art Contemporain, Lyon, 1990, Fondacion Tapies, Barcelona, Spain, Kunstmuseum, Berne, Switzerland, Kröller-Müller Mus., Otterlo, The Netherlands), Linda Cathcart Gallery, Santa Monica, Calif., 1990, Barbara Gross Gallerie, Munich, 1990, Karsten Schubert, London, 1990, Galerie Krinzinger, Vienna, 1990, Karsten Greve Gallery, Cologne, 1990, Ginny Williams Gallery, 1990, Monika Spruthe Galerie, Cologne, 1990, Robert Miller Gallery 1986, 1987, 1988, 1989, 1991, Galerie Lelong, Zurich, 1991 Parrish Art Mus., Southampton, NY, Ydessa Hendeles Found., Toronto, 1991, 1992, Milwaukee Art Mus., 1992, The Fabric Workshop, Phila., Galerie Karsten Greve, Paris, Linda Cathcart Gallery, Santa Monica, Calif., Second Floor, Reykjavik, Iceland, Tate Modern, London, 2000, Rockefeller Ctr., NYC, 2001, Guggenheim Mus., Bilbao, Spain, 2001, retrospective Inst. Contemporary Art, Boston, 2007, retrospective Tate Modern, London, 2007 (traveling: Ctr. Georges Pompidou, Paris, Guggenheim Mus., NYC, Mus. Contemporary Art, LA, Hirshhorn Mus. and Sculpture Garden, Washington); exhibited in numerous group shows, US, Europe including Sculpture Ctr., 1997, Jim Kempner Fine Art, 1997, Steinbaum Krauss Gallery, 1998, Mary Boone Gallery, 1998, Am. Craft Mus., 1998, Venice Biennale, 2007; represented in permanent collections Mus. Modern Art, NYC, Whitney Mus., Met. Mus. Art, Hirshorn Mus., Musée Nat. D'Art Moderne, Paris, RI Sch. Design, NYU, Albright-KnAustralian Nat. Gallery, Canberra, Musée d'Art Moderne, Paris, Mus. Fine Arts, Houston, Guggenheim Mus., NYC, Kunstmus. Bern, stmus. Lucerne, Albertina, Vienna, Mus. Modern Art, Vienna, Walker Art Ctr., Mpls., Storm King Art Ctr., Mountainville, NY, New Mus. Contemporary Art, NYC, DC Moore Gallery, NYC, Cheim & Read Gallery, NYC, Denver Art Mus., Colo.; appeared in Limited Edition Artists Books 1990; public works include installation sculpture (with Alan Wanzenberg) Hold Me Close, Hat Nopparat Nat. Pk., Thailand, 2007. Recipient Outstanding Achievement award Women's Caucus, 1980, Pres.'s Fellow award R.I. Sch. Design, 1984, Skowhegan medal sculpture Skowhegan (Maine) Sch. Painting, and Sculpture, Gold medal of honor Nat. Arts Club, 1987, Creative Arts Medal award Brandeis U., 1989, Grand Prix Nat. de Sculpture French Ministry of Culture, 1991, Nat. medal arts, 1999, Wolf prize in arts Wolf Found., Israel, 2003; recipient Lifetime Achievement award Coll. Art Assn., 1989, Internat. Sculpture Ctr., 1991; named Officer of Arts and Letters French Ministry of Culture, 1984. Fellow Am. Acad. Arts and Scis.; mem. Am. Acad. and Inst. Arts and Letters, Sculptors Guild, Am. Abstract Artists, Coll. Art Assn. (Disting. Artist award for lifetime achievement 1989). Home: New York, NY. Died May 31, 2010.

BOURJAILY, VANCE, novelist; b. Cleve., Sept. 17, 1922; s. Monte Ferris and Barbara (Webb) B.; m. Bettina Yensen, 1946 (div.); children: Anna (dec.), Philip, Robin; m. Yasmin Mogul, 1985; 1 child, Omar. AB, Bowdoin Coll., 1947, DLitt, 1993. Newspaperman, TV dramatist, playwright, lectr.; prof. U. Ariz., U. Iowa Writers Workshop, 1958-80; co-founder, editor Discovery, 1951-53; cultural mission to South America auspices US Dept. State, 1959, 73; Boyd prof. La. State U., Baton Rouge, 1985—2010. Disting. vis. prof. Oreg. State U., summer 1968; vis. prof. U. Ariz., 1977-78 Author: The End of My Life, 1947, The Hound of Earth, 1953, The Violated, 1958, Confessions of a Spent Youth, 1960, The Unnatural Enemy, 1963, The Man Who Knew Kennedy, 1967, Brill Among the Ruins, 1970, Country Matters, 1973, Now Playing at Canterbury, 1976, A Game Men Play, 1980, The Great Fake Book, 1987, Old Soldier: A Novel, 1990 co-author: (with Philip Bourjaily) Fishing By Mail: The Outdoor Life of a Father and Son, 1993. Mem. campaign staff Hughes for Senate, 1968. Served with Am. Field Service, 1942-44; Served with AUS, 1944-46. Recipient Academy Award in lit., American Academy of Arts and Letters, 1993. Home: San Rafael, Calif. Died Aug. 31, 2010.

BOURNE, HENRY CLARK, JR., electrical engineer, educator, retired academic administrator; b. Tarboro, NC, Dec. 31, 1921; s. Henry Clark and Marion (Alston) B.; m. Margaret Barr Thomas, Aug. 15, 1953; children: Katherine Wimberley, Henry Clark III, Thomas Franklin, Margaret Alston. S.B., MIT, 1947, S.M., 1948, Sc.D., 1952. Registered profl. engr., Calif., Tex. Asst. prof. Mass. Inst. Tech., 1952-54; asst. prof., then asso. prof. U. Calif. at, Berkeley, 1954-63; prof. elec. engring. Rice U., Houston, 1963-77, chmn. dept., 1963-74; sect. head engring. div. NSF, Washington, 1974-75, div. dir. engring., 1977-79; dep. asst. dir. Directorate Engring. and Applied Sci., 1979-81; v.p. for acad. affairs Ga. Inst. Tech., Atlanta, 1981-86, 87-88, acting pres., 1986-87, prof. elec. engring., 1988-92, prof. elec. engring. emeritus, from 1992. Cons. editor Harper & Row, N.Y.C., 1961-67; cons. elec. engring., 1952— Author tech. papers in field of magnetics. Served to 1st lt. C.E. AUS, 1943-46. Sci. Faculty fellow NSF, 1960-61; hon. research asso. Univ. Coll. London; Eng., 1961 Fellow IEEE, AAAS; mem. Am. Phys. Soc., Am. Soc. Engring. Edn., Sigma Xi, Tau Beta Pi, Eta Kappa Nu, Phi Kappa Phi, Omicron Delta Kappa, Beta Gamma Sigma, Delta Tau Delta. Episcopalian. Home: Winston Salem, NC. Died Mar. 25, 2010.

BOWDITCH, FREDERICK WISE, motor vehicle manufacturers association executive; b. Jamaica, L.I., NY, Nov. 17, 1921; s. Frederick Tryon and Eleanor (Wise) B.; m. Dorothy Vucic, June 17, 1944; children: Karalyn A., Dierdra E. BS in Mech. Engring, U. Ill., 1943; MS, Purdue U., 1948, PhD, 1951. Sr. research engr. fuels and lubricants Gen. Motors Research Labs., 1951-66; staff engr. emission control Gen. Motors Engring. Staff, 1966-68; dir. automotive emission control Gen. Motors Environmental Activities Staff, 1968-73, exec. asst. to v.p. vehicle emission matters Warren, Mich., 1973-80; v.p. tech. affairs div. Motor Vehicle Mfrs. Assn., 1980-91. Served to lt. (j.g.) USNR, 1943-46. Fellow Soc. Automotive Engrs. (vice chmn. automotive and air pollution com. 1971-72, Horning Meml. award 1952); mem. Air Pollution Control Assn. (dir. 1968-71), Automobile Mfrs. Assn. (past chmn. air quality com.), Orgn. Internat. des Constructeurs D'Automobile (chmn. tech. com. 1985-87), Engring. Soc. Detroit. Presbyterian (elder 1971-73). Club: Recess. Home: Wilmington, Del. Died Dec. 8, 2009.

BOWEN, PETER WILSON, medical collection agency administator, financial services executive; b. Evanston, Ill., Oct. 15, 1949; s. Oscar A. Jr. and Eileen (Wilson) B.; m. Cynthia Michele Prosser, July 22, 1990; 1 child, Audra Antoinette. BS in Fin., U. Ill., 1972; MBA, U. Iowa, 1975; M in Telecom., De Paul U., Chgo., 1989. Pres. Surf Collection Agy., Long Branch, N.J., from 1991. Recipient All Am. Swimmer award, 1967, State Champion Swimming award Ill., 1967. Republican. Episopalian. Avocations: scuba diving, gardening. Home: West Long Branch, NJ. Died Jan. 15, 2009.

BOWEN, ROBERT STEVENSON, diversified company executive; b. Chgo., Dec. 4, 1937; s. Earl McDonald and Helen T. (Stevenson) B.; m. Jane Carlson, Oct. 13, 1973; children: Thomas, Anne. AB, North Park Coll., Chgo., 1955; BS, Northwestern U., 1958; MBA, Harvard U., 1961; postgrad., U. Stockholm, (Sweden), 1963-64. Sr. planning mgr. Ford Motor Co., Dearborn, Mich., 1961-72; v.p. mktg. and internat. Zenith Radio Corp., Chgo., 1972-80; pres. sales and mktg. group Firestone Tire and Rubber Co., Brook Park, Ohio, 1980-84; pres., chief exec. officer Comnet Corp., Greenbelt, Md., from 1984; chmn., chief exec. officer Group I Software Inc., Greenbelt, from 1987. Chmn. bd. Zenith Time

S.A., LeLocle, Switzerland, 1974-78; bd. dirs. Ford Labs., Moonachie, N.J. Trustee Nat. 4-H Council, Chevy Chase, Md., 1980-84, Chesapeake Acad., Arnold, Md., 1987—. George F. Baker scholar Harvard Bus. Sch., 1960; Fulbright scholar, 1963-64 Home: Annapolis, Md. Died Nov. 18, 2009.

BOWEN, ZACK R., English language educator; b. Phila., Aug. 10, 1934; s. R. Zack and Mary (Upton) B.; m. Patricia Lingsch (div.); children: Zack, Daniel, Patricia; m. Lindsey Tucker. BA with honors, U. Pa., 1956; MA, Temple U., 1960; PhD, SUNY, Buffalo, 1964. Instr. Temple U., Phila., 1960; asst. prof. Fredonia (N.Y.) State Coll., 1960-64; asst. prof. to prof., dept. chmn. SUNY, Binghamton, 1964-76; prof., chmn. dept. English U. Del., Newark, 1976-86, U. Miami, Coral Gables, Fla., from 1986. Editor: British Literature Essay Series, 1982—, Irish Renaissance Annual, 1977-82; author several books including: Musical Allusions in the Works of James Joyce, 1974, A Companion to Joyce Studies, 1984, Ulysses as a Comic Novel, 1989; producer, dir. series of recorded interpretations of James Joyce's Ulysses, 1961-66; contbr. numerous articles to profl. jours. Recipient series grants SUNY Rsch. Found. Mem. James Joyce Soc. (pres. 1977-86), Internat. James Joyce Found. (trustee 1982—), Modern Lang. Assn., Assn. Depts. of English, South Atlantic Modern Lang. Assn., South Atlantic Assn. Dept. of English (exec. com. 1987—), Fla. Assn. Depts. of English. Democrat. Avocation: fishing. Home: Miami, Fla. Died Apr. 8, 2010.

BOWER, GWEN, legislative assistant; b. Blain, Pa., June 23, 1958; d. Clark William and Donna (Bratton) B. B.S. cum laude, East Stroudsburg U., 1980. Tchr., counselor New Life Youth and Family Services, Harleysville, Pa., 1981-82; program advisor Cumberland Perry Assn. Retarded Citizens, Carlisle, Pa., 1982-83; legis. asst. Senate of Pa., Harrisburg, 1983-85, dist. office mgr., 1985—; vol. Hetrick for Judge, Dauphin County, Pa., 1985, Spector for Senate, 1986. Author newsletter The Politicker, 1985. Chmn. Dauphin County Young Reps., 1985-86, sec., 1984; mem. Pa. State Young Reps., 1985, mem. exec. bd., 1986; water safety and CPR instr. ARC, Harrisburg, 1982-83; mem. Crossfire, Harrisburg, 1983—, chmn. citizenship com., 1986—. Mem. Rho Phi Alpha. Republican. Evangelical. Avocations: sports; cooking. Home: Harrisburg, Pa. Died Dec. 12, 2009.

BOWERS, GLENN LEE, retired professional society administrator; b. York, Pa., May 7, 1921; s. Elmer Frederick and Naomi Mae (Shellenberger) B.; m. Betty June Lehr, Apr. 21, 1943; children— Tina, Timothy BS, Pa. State U., 1946, MS, 1948. Wildlife biologist Pa. Game Commn., various locations, 1948-57, chief div. research Harrisburg, 1957-59, dep. exec. dir., 1959-65, exec. dir., 1965-82. Chmn. bd. dirs. Worldwide Furbearer Conf., Frostburg, Md., 1976-80 Contbr. articles to profl. jours. Served to capt. USMCR, 1942-45, PTO Recipient John Pearce Meml. award N.E. sect. Wildlife Soc., 1982; Nat. Wildlife Conservationist award Nat. Wildlife Fedn., 1982 Mem. Wildlife Soc., Internat. Assn. Fish and Wildlife Agys. (exec. com. 1972-80, pres. 1978-79, gen. counsel 1983-95, Seth Gordon award 1982), N.E. Assn. Fish and Wildlife Agys. (various offices, v.p., pres. 1965-82). Lodges: Masons. Republican. Methodist. Avocations: fishing, hunting. Home: Dillsburg, Pa. Died June 25, 2010.

BOWLES, JAMES L. (JIM BOWLES), oil industry executive; B in Mech. Engring., U. Ark., 1974. Joined Phillips Petroleum Co., 1974, supr. planning and budgeting Stavanger, Norway, 1976—81, with drilling and prodn. Houston, 1981—89, v.p. GPM Gas Corp., 1991—93, dep. mng. dir. Norway divsn., 1993—97, pres. America's divsn., 1997—2002; pres. ConocoPhillips Alaska, 2004—10. Bd. dir. KCS Energy; mem. E&P com. Am. Petroleum Inst.; mem. vis. com. Petroleum Engring. Dept. U. Tex. Mem.: Nat. Ocean Industries Assn. (mem. bd. dirs.). Died Feb. 13, 2010.

BOWMAN, HAZEL LOIS, retired English language educator; b. Plant City, Fla., Feb. 18, 1917; d. Joseph Monroe and Annie (Thoman) B. AB, Fla. State Coll. for Women, 1937; MA, U. Fla., 1948; postgrad., U. Md., 1961-65. Tchr. Lakeview HS, Winter Garden, Fla., 1939-40, Eagle Lake Sch., Fla., 1940-41; welfare visitor Fla. Welfare Bd., 1941-42; specialist U.S. Army Signal Corps, Arlington Hall, Va., 1942-43; recreation work, asst. procurement officer ARC, CBI Theater, 1943-46; lab. technician Am. Cyanamid Corp., Brewster, Fla., 1946-47; instr., asst. prof. gen. extension divsn. U. Fla., Fla. State U., 1948-51; freelance writer, editor, indexer NY, 1951-55, Fla., 1951—55; staff writer Tampa Morning Tribune, Fla., 1956; staff writer, telegraph editor Winter Haven News-Chief, Fla., 1956-57; registrar, admissions officer U. Tampa, 1957-59; coll. counselor Atlantic States, 1959-60; registrar, freshman advisor Towson State Tchrs. Coll., Balt., 1960-62; dir. student pers., guidance, admissions Harford Jr. Coll., Bel Air, Md., 1962-64; instr., asst. prof. English, journalism York Coll., Pa., 1965-69; tchr. S.W. Jr. HS, Lakeland, Fla., 1969-70; tchr. learning disabled Vanguard Sch., Lake Wales, Fla., 1970-82; libr. asst. Polk County Hist. and Geneal. Libr., Bartow, Fla., 1986-91. Editor Fla. Flambeau, FSCW, 1936-37, Tampa Altrusan, 1958-60, Polk County Hist. Calendar, 1986-90. Mem. Polk County Hist. Commn., 1992-99. Recipient Mayhall Music medal, 1933, Excellence in Cmty. Svc. award Nat. Soc. DAR, 1994, Outstanding Achievement award Fla. State Geneal. Soc., 2002. Mem.: AAUW (hon. 50 yr. life), Polk County Hist. Assn., Imperial Polk Geneal. Soc., Nat. Geneal. Soc., Mortar Board, Chi Delta Phi, Alpha Chi Alpha. Home: Tallahassee, Fla. Died Oct. 12, 2009.

BOWMAN, ROBERT STEPHEN, hydrology educator; b. Detroit, June 12, 1950; s. Ernest Paul and Lois Irene (Foote) B.; m. Karen Catherine Bailey, June 24, 1972; 1 child, Daniel Charles Bailey-Bowman. AB in Chemistry, U. Calif., Berkeley, 1972; PhD in Soil Chemistry, N.Mex. State U., 1982. Rsch. chemist Medi-Physics, Inc., Emeryville, Calif., 1972-76; rsch. asst. N.Mex. State U., Las Cruces, 1977-82; soil scientist U.S. Dept. Agr., Phoenix, 1982-87; prof. of hydrology N.Mex. Inst. of Mining and Tech., Socorro, N.Mex., from 1987. Cons. Socorro, 1987—. Contbr. articles to profl. jours.; assoc. editor: Jour. of Environmental Quality, 1990-96. Vol. firefighter Socorro County, 1988-99. Mem. Am. Geophys. Union, Am. Chem. Soc., Soil Sci. Soc. of Am. Home: Lemitar, N.Mex. Died June 6, 2009.

BOYAJIAN, LEVON ZAKAR, psychiatrist, administrator; b. NYC, Dec. 9, 1929; s. Apkar Zakar and Verkin (Nazarian) Boyajian; m. Gloria Zabel Hogrogian, June 2, 1956; children: Liza Lee, Zachary Levon. BA, Columbia Coll., 1951; MS, U. Ill., 1952; MD, Yale U., 1956. Diplomate Am. Bd. Psychiatry and Neurology. Intern in medicine Maimonides Hosp., Bklyn., 1956-57; resident in psychiatry Yale U. Sch. Medicine, 1957-60; asst. unit chief, then unit chief Hillside Hosp., Queens, NY, 1962—64; clin. dir., then acting dir. Lincoln Hosp. Mental Health Svcs., Bronx, N.Y., 1964-69; dir. clin. svcs. dept. psychiatry Cath. Med. Ctr. Bklyn. and Queens, 1969-71; mem. faculty divsn. cmty. and social psychiatry Columbia U., NYC, 1971-75; chmn. dept. psychiatry St. Joseph's Hosp. and Med. Ctr., Paterson, N.J., 1975-85, dir. Met. Paterson Cmty. Mental Health Ctr., 1977-80; acting med. dir. Mental Health Clinic of Ocean County, Toms River, N.J., 1985-86; acting med. dir., staff psychiatrist Richard Hall Cmty. Mental Health Ctr. of Somerset County, Bridgewater, NJ, 1986—88; staff psychiatrist Cmty. Mental Health Ctr. U. Medicine and Dentistry of N.J., Newark, 1989-91; med. chief adult outpatient, dept. psychiatry Elizabeth (N.J.) Gen. Med. Ctr., 1991-92; dir. med. ops., clin. dir. Greystone Park (N.J.) Psychiat. Hosp., 1993-94; staff psychiatrist Cmty. Ctrs. for Mental Health, Inc., Englewood and Dumont, N.J., 1995-97; clin. assoc. prof. psychiatry N.J. Med. Sch., Univ. Medicine and Dentistry of N.J., Newark, 1976-2001. Psychiat. cons. Altro Health and Rehab. Svcs., N.Y.C., 1965-71, Met. Life Ins. Co., N.Y.C., 1986-88, Prudential Life Ins. Co., Parsippany, N.J., 1988-89; instr. dept. psychiatry Albert Einstein Coll. Medicine, Yeshiva U., 1964-66, asst. prof., 1966-68, asst. clin. prof., 1968-69; asst. prof. clin. psychiatry, Columbia U., 1971-77; assoc. attending, attending psychiatrist Lincoln Hosp., 1964-69, Columbia Presbyn. Med. Ctr., N.Y.C., 1971-77; assoc. attending psychiatrist Cath. Med. Ctr. Bklyn. and Queens, 1969-71; chmn. dept. psychiatry St. Joseph's Hosp. and Med. Ctr., Paterson, 1975-85; presenter, panelist, spkr., moderator in field. Author: Hayots Badeevuh: Reminiscences of Armenian Life in New York City, 2004; contbr. articles to profl. jours. Lt. comdr. USNR, 1960—62. Fellow: North Jersey Psychiat. Assn. (coun. 1982—83, corr. sec. 1983—86), N.J. Hosp. Assn. (task force on patients discharged from state mental hosps. 1978, mental health com. 1978—84, co-chmn. 1984—85), N.J. Psychiat. Assn. (dist. br. com. on psychiat. units of gen. hosps. 1982—85), N.Y. Soc. Clin. Psychiatry (N.Y. County dist. br. com. on psychiatry and cmty. 1973—75), Am. Psychiat. Assn. (assoc. examiner 1972—73, commn. on certification in adminstrv. psychiatry 1974—79, assoc. examiner 1980, 1982, task force on prospective payment clin. adv. group 1984, task force on continuing edn. in adminstrn. for psychiatrists, com. on certification in adminstrv. psychiatry, disting. life fellow). Home: Englewood, NJ. Died Mar. 22, 2010.

BOYLE, JOHN EDWARD WHITEFORD, cultural organization administrator; b. Milw., Mar. 8, 1915; s. Herman Edward and Margaret Lauretta (Casey) B.; m. Renée Colin Kent, Feb. 2, 1950; children: Vanessa Whiteford Wayne, Christopher Whiteford, Andrea Heller, Alexandra Whiteford. PhB, Marquette U., 1937; postgrad., Harvard U., 1946-47, Inst. Franco-Iranien, 1959-60, U. Tehran, 1960-62, George Washington U., Georgetown U., UCLA; Doctorandus Lettres et Arts Persanes, Jungian Inst., Zurich, Switzerland, 1997. Journalist Hearst Mags., NYC, 1937, WISN, Milw., 1937-38, Milw. Jour., 1938-40; exec. CIA, Washington, L.A., Frankfurt am Main, Germany, 1947-58, Washington, 1964-67; dir. Am. Friends of the Middle East, Tehran, 1958-62, Tunis, Algeria, Libya, 1962-64, Whiteford Internat. Enterprise, Switzerland, 1967-72, France, 1972-74; fgn. corr. mag. Viewpoints, 1962-64, Middle East Mag., Beirut, Lebanon, 1963; pres. Fgn. Svcs. Rsch. Inst./Wheat Forders (press), Washington, 1974-99, pres. emeritus, from 1999, Internat. Acad. Ind. Schs. Cons. to embassies on edn., 1974—; cons. on edn. Shah of Iran, 1958-62; prof. Nat. U. Iran, 1960-62; co-founder in cooperation with Ministry of Ct., Iran. Author: Primers for the Age of Inner Space: I-Beyond the Present Prospect, 1977, II-The Indra Web, 1983, III-Graffiti on the Wall of Time (poetry), 1983, IV-Of the Same Root: Heaven, Earth and I, 1990, V-The Way of the Essentialist: Contra Sartres Existentialism, 1993, VI-The Unperceived Revolution: Cracking the Code of the Ultimate Enigma, 1997; VII-Structuring Private Spirituality: Essentialism*A Philosophy of the Presence, 2000. Campaign mgr. Roosevelt for Pres., No. Wis., 1940, John F. Kennedy for Pres., Iran, 1960; mem. Fulbright Commn., 1959-62; bd. dirs. Iran-Am. Soc., 1960-62, Pahlavi Found., Iran, 1959-62, Washington Humane Soc.; vol. Dem. Nat. Com., 1982. Served with USAAF, 1940-45. Recipient Prix Teilhard/Londres, 1982-83, Silver Poet award World of Poetry, 1990, Golden Poet award, 1992, Outstanding Alumni Scholar award Marquette U., 1991, 97, Editor's Choice award for Outstanding Achievemnt in Poetry Nat. Libr. Poetry, 1993. Mem. Acad. Ind. Scholars (pres.), Expt. in Internat. Living (hon. life), Essentialist Philos. Soc. (pres. 1991—), Homer Hon. Soc. Internat. Poets. Mem. Soc. Of Friends. Home: Portland, Maine. Died Apr. 18, 2010.

BOYLE, WILLIAM THOMAS, interior designer; b. Detroit, May 16, 1920; s. William Thomas and Sarah Ann (Sullivan) Boyle; m. Irene R. Boyle, Jan. 30, 1955. At, U. Detroit, 1944—45. Cert. kitchen designer. Owner, v.p. and interior designer St. Charles Co. of So. Calif., LA. Contbr. articles to profl. jours. With US Army, ETO. Mem.: Am. Soc. Interior Designers (cert. interior designer). Democrat. Roman Catholic. Home: Rosemead, Calif. Died Mar. 20, 2010.

BOYLES, JAMES KENNETH, retired banker; b. Louisville, Jan. 27, 1916; s. Forrest Lee and Florence (Glenn) B.; m. Hilda Margaret Rose, Sept. 13, 1940; children: Margaret, James, Douglas, Kevin. Student, Columbia U., Am. Inst. Banking, Rutgers U. With Guaranty Trust Co., NYC, 1933-37; loan officer Chem. Bank, NYC, 1937-50; exec. v.p. The Nat. State Bank, Elizabeth, N.J., 1950-83, dir., 1965-88. Trustee emeritus Union Coll., Cranford N.J. Served to 1st lt., inf., U.S. Army, 1942-46, ETO. Decorated Purple Heart. Mem. Robert Morris Assocs. (pres. 1963) Republican. Episcopalian. Home: Tampa, Fla. Died Nov. 18, 2009.

BRABHAM, LEWIS CORNELIUS, JR., (NEIL BRABHAM), engineering executive; b. Olar, SC, July 2, 1929; s. Lewis C. and Mildred (Cook) Brabham; m. Sylvia Bash Estes Brabham, Aug. 22, 1952; children: Edward, Mary Elizabeth. Student, U. SC, 1946—47. Registered profl. engr. Fla. Electronics and elec. engr. Dixie Radio Supply, Columbia, SC, 1952—55, DuKane Corp., St. Charles, Ill., 1955—58, Goddard Electronics, West Palm Beach, Fla., 1958—65, 1965—76; v.p., sec., ptnr. Brabham, Debay & Assocs., West Palm Beach, from 1976. Mem. West Palm Beach Bd. Adjustments & Appeals; past chmn. Fla. Hotel Motel Ad-Hoc Fire Code Com.; vice chmn. Fla. Bd. Bldg. Codes & Standards; chmn. Palm Beach County Fire Code Com. With USN, 1947—53. Mem.: Constrn. Specifications Inst. (past pres. Palm Beach County), Elec. Coun. Fla. (past pres. East Coast chpt.), Fla. Engring. Soc., Nat. Soc. Profl. Engrs. Democrat. Presbyterian. Home: River Ranch, Fla. Died Nov. 8, 2009.

BRACKETT, COLQUITT PRATER, JR., judge, lawyer; b. Norfolk, Va., Feb. 24, 1946; s. Colquitt Prater Sr. and Antoinette Gladys (Cacace) B.; 1 child, Susan Elizabeth Brackett Brooks. BS, U. Ga., 1966, MA, 1968, JD, 1973, LLM, 1976; travel mktg. profl. diploma, S.E. Tourism Soc. Mktg. Coll., 1999. Bar: Ga. 1973, U.S. Dist. Ct. (so. dist.) Ga. 1974, U.S. Dist. Ct. (mid. dist.) Ga. 1977, U.S. Supreme Ct. 1980, Tenn. 1987. Assoc. Surrett & CoCroft, Augusta, Ga., 1972-74; ptnr. Surrett & Brackett, Augusta, 1974-76; faculty Sch. Law, U. Ga., Athens, 1977-82; mng. ptnr. Brackett, Prince & Neufeld, Athens, 1982-90; adminstrv. law judge Ga. Dept. Med. Assistance, Athens, 1990-98. Hearing officer Ga. State Bd. Edn., 1979-91; v.p. Mus. Dolls & Gifts, Inc., Watkinsville, Ga., 1983—; pres. Bear Country Lodge and Conf. Ctr., Pigeon Forge, Tenn., 1996— Am. Toy Mus. Assoc., 2003-; chmn. bd. Adventures in Toy Land, 1999-00; exec. dir. Soc. Preservation of Am. Childhood Effects, 2002-; curator Toy Mus., Natural Bridge, Va., 2002-; bd. dirs. Va. Hospitality and Travel Assn., 2003-. Author: Court Administration, 1972; (monograph) The Security Inventors Protection Corporation and the Operations of SIPC, 1976; (musical play) Americanization of Mary Poppins, 1995. Pres. Athens/Clarke Mental Health Assn., 1985; chmn. bd. dirs. N.E. Ga. Mental Health Assn., 1989-90; officer of Election-Commonwealth of Va., 2002-04; bd. dirs. Coalition for The Blue Ridge Pkwy., 1994-00, Oconee Cultural Arts Found., 1995-97, Blue Ridge Pkwy. Assn., 1997-01. Fellow Paul Harris fellow, Buchanan Rotary Club; Nat. scholar, Phi Alpha Delta fraternity, 1973. Mem.: NRA, KC (4th deg.), ABA, Sevier County Bar Assn., Ga. Trial Lawyers Assn., Ga. Assn. Adminstrv. Law Judges (bd. dir. 1990—91), Ga. State Bar Assn., Blue Ridge/ Shenandoah Travel Mktg. Group (chmn. bd. from 2004), Blue Ridge Pkwy. Assn., Shenandoah Valley Travel Assn. (bd. dir. 2003—04), Internat. Platform Assn., S.E. Tourism Soc., Ea. Nat. Parks Assn., Soc. Am. Poets, 300 Club Roanoke, Magna Carta Barons, Cotillion Club Roanoke, Rotary Internat. (pres. elect 2004—05, pres. 2006—07, Paul Harris fellow), Phi Alpha Delta. Roman Catholic. Avocations: reading, music, golf, cross country skiing. Home: Sevierville, Tenn. Died Jan. 30, 2009.

BRADEN, WILLIAM EDWARD, retired trading company executive, consultant; b. Milw., Dec. 29, 1919; s. Armond Edward and Eve Ninette (Fuller) Braden; m. Sonoyo Matsuda, Jan. 23, 1950 (dec.); children: Amy, Sythe Edward, Robert Fuller, William Samuel; m. Margaret Peterson Bowen, Oct. 16, 1987; 1 child, Edward Norris Sr. 1 stepchild, Loring Fletcher. AB, Harvard U., 1941. Foreman Procter & Gamble Mfg. Co., Quincy, Mass., 1941—42; civilian employee War Dept., Changchun, Manchuria, 1946—47; pres. Pacific Projects Ltd., Tokyo, 1948—49, Taihei Boeki Co., Tokyo, 1955—80, chmn. bd., 1980—86; ret. Bd. dirs. Ferro Enamels (Japan) Ltd., Osaka, Nissan Ferro Organic Chem. Co., Ltd., Tokyo, Palace Housing Co., Ltd., Tokyo, Taiwan Longson Co. Ltd., Taipei; dir. Pacific Group Holdings, Inc., Honolulu. With AF USNR, 1943—45. Mem.: Pacific and Asian Affairs Coun. Honolulu (gov. 1984—90), Am. C. of C. in Japan, Am. Japan Soc., Asia Soc. N.Y.C., Japan Soc. N.Y.C., Chamber Music Soc. Hawaii (bd. dirs. 1984—90), Tokyo Am. Club, Harvard Club, Fgn. Corrs. Club (assoc.). Home: Kent, Conn. Died Nov. 6, 2009.

BRADFORD, JAMES C., JR., brokerage house executive; b. Nashville, July 25, 1933; s. James C. and Eleanor (Avent) B.; m. Lillian Frances Robertson, Nov., 1967; children: Jay, Bryan. BA, Princeton U., 1955. Trainee Lehman Bros., NYC, 1958; ptnr. J.C. Bradford & Co., Nashville, 1959-2000; sr. mng. dir. U.B.S. PaineWebber, Nashville, from 2001. Chmn. dist. com. Nat. Assn. Securities Dealers, Atlanta, 1970-73; dir. Securities Industry Assn., N.Y.C., 1972-75; gov. Am. Stock Exch., 1986-87; bd. dirs. N.Y. Stock Exch., 1987-93, Nat. Assn. Securities Dealers Regulation. Trustee Mongomery Bell Acad., Nashville, 1968—; pres. Nashville Symphony Assn., 1969-70; pres. bd. trustees Ensworth Sch., Nashville, 1988-89. 1st lt. USAF, 1955-57. Mem. Belle Meade Country Club (bd. dirs. 1987-89), Nat. Assn. of Securities (gov. Washington 1996). Republican. Episcopalian. Home: Nashville, Tenn. Died Mar. 8, 2010.

BRADFORD, WILLIAM HOLLIS, JR., lawyer; b. St. Petersburg, Fla., Feb. 11, 1937; s. William Hollis and Treva M. (Waymire) B.; m. Rebecca Mills, June 22, 1963 (div. 1969); children: Leslie, Stacey; m. Keith Ann McCausland, Jan. 23, 1999. AB, Duke U., 1959, JD, 1962; LLM, George Washington U., 1964. Bar: D.C. 1962, U.S. Supreme Ct. 1966, Md. 1972. Assoc. Hamel & Park, Washington, 1962-67, ptnr., 1967-88, Hopkins & Sutter, Washington, 1988-95; shareholder/officer Sanders, Schnabel, Brandenburg & Zimmerman, P.C., Washington, from 1995. Professorial lectr. George Washington U. Law Sch., 1991-97. Contbr. articles to Dem. View, 1983-93. Mem. Montgomery County Md. Dem. Cen. Com., Kensington, Md., 1974-86; vice-chair Md. State Dem. Cen. Com., Balt., 1982-83. Recipient Willis Smith prize Duke U., 1962. Mem. ABA, Md. State Bar Assn., D.C. Bar Assn., D.C. Estate Planning Council, Metropolitan Club, Order of Coif, Phi Beta Kappa. Unitarian Universalist. Avocations: photography, travel. Home: Key West, Fla. Died July 20, 2010.

BRADLEY, JOHN ANDREW, health facility administrator; b. Hammond, Ind., Aug. 3, 1930; s. Andrew C. and Florence (Wolfe) B.; m. Judith E. Salmi, June 1, 1955; children: John Michael, Kerry Kathleen, Kelly Ann. BS, Loras Coll., 1952; MHA, St. Louis U., 1955, PhD, 1962. Asst. adminstr. Incarnate Word Hosp., St. Louis, 1958-61; from assoc. adminstr. to adminstr. Santa Rosa Med. Ctr., San Antonio, 1961-69; from v.p. to sr. v.p. Am. Medicorp, Inc., San Antonio, 1969-78; with Am. Healthcare Mgmt., Dallas, 1978-89, pres., 1978-84, chmn., CEO, 1985-89, Chancellor Health Systems Inc., Dallas, from 1989. Capt. AUS, 1953-57. Home: Dallas, Tex. Died July 29, 2009.

BRADY, JOSEPH JOHN, marketing firm executive; b. Ossining, NY, Sept. 23, 1926; s. William and Kathryn Mary (Bell) B.; m. Barbara Kenney, Mar. 31, 1951; 1 son, Joseph John. BS, N.Y. U., 1949; grad. student, John Jay Grad. Center, Coll. City N.Y., 1968-69. Asst. v.p. econ. rsch. Nat. Indsl. Conf. Bd., NYC, 1952-63; v.p., gen. mgr. Benziger Bros., Inc. (ch. and sch. supply), NYC, 1963-67; pres. Hosp. Bur., Inc., Pleasantville, N.Y., 1967-77, ACME Inc., Assn. Mgmt. Cons. Firms, NYC, 1977-88; sr. cons. Fleming Assocs., Stamford, Conn., 1988-89; sr. market cons. Johnston Mktg. Group, Tarry Town, N.Y., from 1990. Mem. Westchester adv. bd. Chem. Bank, 1973-77 Commr. Westchester County Pky. Police, 1967-74; mem. Westchester Crime Control Planning Bd., 1968-74; exec. bd. Washington Irving council Boy Scouts Am., 1969-74; mem. Future Bus. Leaders Am.; adv. bd. N.Y. State Dept. Edn., 1974-77; Mem. devel. bd. Westchester Med. Center, 1973-74; mem. Bd. Edn., Ossining, N.Y., 1958-60. Served as officer USAF, 1951-52. Mem. Alpha Delta Sigma. Republican. Roman Catholic. Home: San Diego, Calif. Died May 11, 2010.

BRAKELEY, GEORGE ARCHIBALD, JR., fundraising consultant; b. Washington, Apr. 18, 1916; s. George Archibald and Lillian (Fay) B.; m. Roxana Byerly; children: George Archibald III, Deborah Fay, Joan Keller. BA, U. Pa., 1938. V.p., dir. John Price Jones Co., Inc. (fund-raising counsel), NYC; pres., treas. John Price Jones Co. (Can.), Ltd., 1950-52; chmn., CEO G.A. Brakeley & Co., Ltd., 1952-61, G.A. Brakeley & Co., Inc., LA, 1956-69; chmn., chief exec. officer Brakeley, John Price Jones Inc., 1972-83; chmn. Brakeley, John Price Jones, Inc., 1983-87, sr. cons., from 1987. Author: Tested Ways to Successful Fund Raising. Trustee Ctr. for the Study of the Presidency. Capt. C.E. AUS, WWII. Mem. Mayflower Soc., Anglers Club (N.Y.C.), Montreal Racket Club (hon.), Wee Burn Golf Club (Darien, Conn.), Royal Poinciana Golf Club (Naples, Fla.). Episcopalian. Died May 1, 2009.

BRAMWELL, HENRY, federal judge; b. Bklyn., Sept. 3, 1919; s. Henry Hall and Florence Elva (MacDonald) B.; m. Ishbel W. Brown, Jan. 29, 1966. LLB, Bklyn. Law Sch., 1948, LLD (hon.), 1979. Bar: N.Y. bar 1948. Asst. US atty. (ea. dist.) NY US Dept. Justice, Bklyn., 1953-61; assoc counsel NY State Rent Commn., 1961-63; judge N.Y. Civil Ct., NYC, Bklyn., 1966, 1969—75; asst. adminstrv. judge Kings County, Bklyn., 1974—75; judge US Dist. Ct. (ea. dist.) NY, Bklyn., 1975—87, sr. judge, 1987—2010. Mem. Community Mayors N.Y. State; trustee Bklyn. Law Sch., 1978-2010 Active Bklyn. Old Times Found., Inc. Served with AUS, 1942-44. Profiled in Black Judges on Justice, 1994. Mem. ABA, Nat. Bar Assn. (life), N.Y. State Bar Assn., Bklyn. Bar Assn. (trustee), Fed. Judges Assn. (founding mem.). Home: Brooklyn, NY. Died May 28, 2010.

BRANDON, WILLIAM CLINT, agribusiness consultant; b. Chancellor, Ala., Oct. 9, 1918; s. John W. and Bess (Broxson) B.; B.S. in Agr. with high honors, U. Fla., 1942, M.A., 1948; postgrad. Northwestern U., 1955-56, U. Mich., 1961, Harvard U., 1964; m. Ethel I. Pool, Aug. 23, 1963; children— Deborah Jean, Eric Bradley, Michael Clint, William Wade. Terr. mgr. Swift & Co., Miami, Fla., 1948-54, mgr. advt. and merchandising, Chgo., 1954-58, Midwest mktg. and ops. mgr., Cleve., 1958-59, dir. personnel, tng. and devel., Chgo., 1960-70; mgr. Sales and Mktg. Services Cons., Chgo., 1970-71; owner, pres. Agri-Bus. Tng. & Devel., Roswell, Ga., 1971—, Brandon Assos., Roswell, 1977—; exec. dir. Swift: Estech Reunion Assn., 1987—; cons. in field. Nat. pres. Danforth Found., 1942. Served with U.S. Army, 1942-47; mem. Res. Recipient Danforth Found. award, 1942; Fla. Blue Key Leadership award, 1976. Mem. Am. Feed Mfg. Assn. (cons. personnel devel.), Ga. Agri-Bus. Council, Nat. Speakers Assn., Ga. Speakers Assn. (dir.), Can. Feed Industry Assn. (cons. personnel devel.), Phi Gamma Delta (life, Loyal Fiji), Alpha Zeta (chancellor), Phi Eta Sigma, Phi Kappa Phi. Baptist. Author: Professional Selling in Agri-Business, 1972; Building and Developing Your Work Force, 1972; Motivation: Roots of Human Behavior, 1972, 80; Train-the-Trainer, 1977; Managerial Work Organization and Time Management in the Sales Territory, 1979; Closing Sales in Agri-Business, 1979; editor-in-chief U. Fla. Mag., 1941-42; contbr. numerous articles to profl. jours. Died May 17, 2010.

BRASH, SALLY MILLER, theater educator, playwright; b. Donora, Pa., Jan. 18, 1911; d. Mose and Rachel Leah (Kwass) Miller; m. J. Eugene, June 27, 1934 (dec. 1966); 1 child, Edward. BA, Chatam Coll., 1932; cert. in TV, U. Pa., 1949. Asst. prof. Harcum Jr. Coll., Bryn Mawr, Pa., from 1969. Dramatic dir. Children's Theatre, Phila., Stevens Sch., Phila., K.I. Temple, Phila., Forest Acres Camp, Fryeburg, Maine, Plays for Living, Phila., Penn Charter, Phila.; cons., presenter workshops Nat. Headstart, 1965-69, 87—; tchr. in creative drama various elem. and preschs. Author: Teaching Children Through Drama, 1988, (plays) If Books Could Talk, 1944, Five Tested Plays, 1944, Hanukah Pickets, 1945, The Magic Book Shop, 1946; dir. Plays For Living. Advisor Allen's Lane Art Ctr., Phila., Plays for Living, Family Svc. Avocations: theater, travel, music, swimming, reading. Home: Philadelphia, Pa. Died Aug. 11, 2009.

BRASS, WINSTON JOHN, protective services official; b. Vizagapatam, India, May 3, 1938; arrived in US, 1959, naturalized, 1966; s. Baden Anthony and Alice (Abraham) Brass; m. Pauline Marie Caronm, June 30, 1962; children: Renee, Denise, Andre, Elise, Yvonne, Dianne, Jeanette. Applied Sci., Kishwaukee Coll., Malta, Ill., 1978; degree, FBI Nat. Acad., 1976, So. Police Inst., U. Louisville, 1972. Patrolman Rochelle Police Dept., Ill., 1968—70; sgt., 1970—76; lt., 1974; chief of police, from 1974. Mem. adv. bd. Kishwaukee Coll. Law Enforcement, from 1980; mem. Ill Local Govtl. Law Enforcement Officers Tng. Bd., from 1986. Area coord. Blackhawk Area Boy Scouts Am., from 1982. Mem.: Internat. Assn. Chiefs Police, Ill. Assn. Chiefs of Police (pub. works com. 1980—82, legis. com. 1982—84). Republican. Roman Catholic. Home: Rochelle, Ill. Died July 10, 2009.

BREAZEALE, MACK ALFRED, research scientist, educator; b. Leona Mines, Va., Aug. 15, 1930; s. Carl Samuel and Maude Ella (Moore) Breazeale; m. Joanne Morton O'Dell, Oct. 4, 1952 (dec. Nov. 1989); children: Jennifer Lee, David Mark, William Carl; m. Louise Hanna Scott, Nov. 10, 1990. BA, Berea Coll., Ky., 1953; MS, U. Mo., Rolla, 1954, degree (hon.) in Physics, 2004; PhD, Mich. State U., East Lansing, 1957. Asst. rsch. prof. Mich. State U., 1957-62; assoc. prof. U. Tenn., 1962-67, prof. physics and astronomy, 1967—95; cons. solid state div. Oak Ridge Nat. Lab., 1962-71, cons. health and safety research div., 1985-87; cons. Naval Rsch. Labs., 1971-75; prin. investigator contracts Office Naval Rsch., AEC, 1963—95; disting. rsch. prof. U. Miss., from 1988; prin. scientist Nat. Ctr. for Phys. Acoustics, Miss., from 1988. Guest Inst. Basic Tech. Problems, Warsaw, Poland, 1972; vis. prof. Tech. U. of Denmark, 1977; guest U. Paris, 1977; mem. program com. Internat. Symposium on Nonlinear Acoustics, 1975, 76, 78, 81, 84, 87, 90, 93, 96, 99, 2002, 05, 08. Contbr. articles to profl. jours., chapters to books. Recipient U. Mo. Alumni Merit award, 1990; Fulbright rsch. fellow Tech. U., Stuttgart, Fed. Republic Germany, 1958-59; Fulbright travel grantee, 1977-78, NATO rsch. grantee, 1978-81, 92-2001, 2004-06, NSF US-Italy program grantee, 1982-86 Life fellow IEEE (adminstrv. com. ultrasonics, ferroelectrics and frequency control soc. 1987-89, program com. 1979—, pres. lectr., 1987, co-chair Atlanta Meeting Ultrasonics Symposium 2001, named Disting. Lectr. 1987-88, Achievement award, 2008); fellow Inst. Acoustics (UK), Acoustical Soc. Am. (assoc. editor Nonlinear Acoustics 1977-2001, Silver medal in phys. acoustics 1988); mem. AAUP, Acoustical Soc. Am., Am. Phys. Soc., Sigma Xi, Phi Kappa Phi, Sigma Pi Sigma. Died Sept. 14, 2009.

BREMER, ALFONSO M., neurosurgeon, neuro-oncologist; b. Mexico City, Aug. 3, 1939; came to U.S., 1966; s. Carlos and Guadalupe (Garcia) B.; m. Maria-Elena Montano, May 25, 1973; children: Maria-Elena, Rosanna Angelica, A. Michael. BS, U. Nacional Autonoma de Mexico, 1958, MD, 1965. Diplomate Am. Bd. Neurol. Surgery. Intern Deaconess Hosp., Buffalo, N.Y., 1966-67; resident Georgetown U. Hosps., Washington, 1967-72; cancer rsch. neurosurgeon I Roswell Park Meml. Inst., Buffalo, 1972-73, cancer rsch. neurosurgeon II, 1973-74, assoc. chief dept. neurosurgery, 1974-79; chief dept. neurosurgery U. Med. Ctr., Jacksonville, Fla., 1979-85; chief div. neurosurgery Meth. Med. Ctr., Jacksonville, 1986-92. Asst. rsch. prof. in exptl. pathology SUNY, Buffalo, 1972-79; rsch. prof. in exptl. pathology Niagara U., Niagara Falls, N.Y., 1972-79; prof. neurosurgery U. Fla., Jacksonville, 1979-85. Recipient Stroke Study grant Am. Heart Assn., 1973, 74, Yoshida-Yamagiwa Internat. Meml. Cancer Study grant Internat. Union Against Cancer, Osaka U., Japan, 1975. Fellow ACS, Stroke Coun.-Am. Heart Assn.; mem. Am. Assn. Neurol. Surgeons, Rsch. Soc. Neurol. Surgeons. Achievements include discovery that malignant secondary tumor of brain responded to intra-arterial chemotherapy. Home: Jacksonville, Fla. Died Jan. 27, 2009.

BRENNAN, FRANCIS PATRICK, banker; b. Somerville, Mass., Jan. 9, 1917; s. John Joseph and Bridget (Sullivan) B.; m. Mary J. Gilhooly, July 23, 1949; children: Mary Ann, Eileen, John, Thomas. AB cum laude, Boston Coll., 1939; postgrad., Bentley Coll. Accounting and Finance, 1941. Loan officer Reconstrn. Finance Corp., Boston, 1941-42, 46-53; exec. v.p. Mass. Bus. Devel. Corp., Boston, 1954-61; chmn., chief exec. officer Union Warren Savs. Bank, Boston, 1961-87; vice-chmn. Home Owners Savs. Bank (merger Union Warren Savs. Bank), Boston, 1987-90. Bd. dirs., trustee, chmn. audit com. Boston Co. Funds, Inc.; chmn., pres., treas. Laurel Mut. Funds, 1993—; bd. dirs., exec. and fin. coms., chmn. audit and salary com. Boston Mut. Life Ins. Co., chmn. Dreyfus/Laurel Mutual Funds. Former trustee vice chmn. exec. com., chmn. fin. com. Stonehill Coll.; chmn. Mass. Bus. Devel. Corp.; mem. Sidney Farber Cancer Inst., Boston; mem. Mass. Hist. Soc.; past bd. dirs. Boston Mcpl. Research Bur., Greater Boston Real Estate Bd., Boston met. chpt. ARC. 2d lt. AUS, 1942-45, ETO. Decorated Bronze Star. Mem. Savs. Banks Assn. Mass. (pres. 1972-73), Mass. Bankers Assn. (dir.-at-large), Greater Boston C. of C. (v.p., admitted to Acad. of Disting. Bostonians 1992), Algonquin Club (Boston), Clover Club (Boston), Winchester Country Club, Madison Sq. Garden Club, Knights of Malta, Knights of Holy Sepulchre. Roman Catholic. Home: Winchester, Mass. Died Apr. 4, 2010.

BRENTLINGER, WILLIAM BROCK, college dean; b. Flora, Ill., Aug. 21, 1926; s. Arthur Kenneth and Frances (Maxwell) B.; m. Barbara Jean Weir, Dec. 29, 1946; children: Gregory, Gary, Rebecca Anne, Garth, Barbara Sue. Student, Washington U., 1946-47; AB, Greenville Coll., 1950; MA, Ind. State U., 1951; PhD, U. Ill., 1959. Instr. speech Greenville Coll., 1951-59, chmn. dept., 1959-62, dean of coll., 1962-69, dean coll. fine arts and comm., 1969-92; interim pres. Lamar U., Beaumont, Tex., 1992-93, asst. to pres., from 1993. Cons. higher edn. Served with USNR, 1944-46. Recipient tchr. study award Danforth Found., 1957 Mem. Internat. Council Fine Arts Deans, Speech Communication Assn. Am., Tex. Speech Assn., Tex. Assn. Coll. Tchrs., Tex. Council Arts in Edn. (pres.), Phi Kappa Phi. Clubs: Rotary (Beaumont). Baptist. Home: Nederland, Tex. Died Feb. 19, 2009.

BRESNAHAN, RICHARD ANTHONY, retired army officer; b. Fitchburg, Mass., Nov. 14, 1924; Student, Colgate U., 1943; BS, U.S. Mil. Acad., 1946. Commd. 2d lt. U.S. Army, 1946, advanced through grades to maj. gen., 1973; instr. phys. edn. U.S. Mil. Acad., 1954-57; mem. staff and faculty Command and Gen. Staff Coll., Ft. Leavenworth, Kans., 1958-61; comdr. 1st Bn., 13th Inf., 8th Inf. div., Fed. Republic Germany, 1963-64; plans officer Hdqrs. Cen. Army Group, Fed. Republic Germany, 1964-65; with Office Dep. Chief of Staff for Personnel, then Office Army Chief of Staff, Washington, 1966-68; chief Force Devel. Div., Hdqrs. U.S. Army, Vietnam, 1968-69; comdr. 1st Brigade, 101st Airborne Div., Vietnam, 1969; dir. Far Ea. mil. studies, dept. mil. planning U.S. Army War Coll., Carlisle Barracks, Pa., 1969-70, chief of staff/sec. Coll., 1970-71; chief Strategic Plans and Policy div. Office Joint Chiefs of Staff, Washington, 1971-73; chief of staff 5th U.S. Army, Ft. Sam Houston, Tex., 1974-75; comdr. U.S. Army Readiness Region V, Ft. Sheridan, Ill., 1975-77; chief Jusmag, Greece, 1977-79; comdr. U.S. Army Readiness and Moblzn. Region VIII, Aurora, Colo., 1979-82; ret. U.S. Army, 1982. Bd. dirs., mem. exec. coun. Chgo. USO; mem. Denver Fed. Exec. Bd. Decorated Bronze Star, Silver Star, Legion of Merit with 3 oak leaf clusters, Air medal with 13 oak leaf clusters, Army Commendation medal with 2 oak leaf clusters, Combat Inf. Badge with star, Republic Vietnam Gallantry Cross with palm and oak leaf cluster Mem. Assn. U.S. Army, Denver Rotary. Roman Catholic. Home: Colorado Spgs, Colo. Died Apr. 25, 2009.

BREWER, MELVIN DUANE, educational consultant; b. Rochester, Pa., Mar. 6, 1913; s. Percy McPherson and Ida Viola (Noss) B.; m. Lila Margaret Scott, Nov. 28, 1940; children: Melvin Duane (dec.), Barbara Jo (Mrs. John T. Davis), Margaret Scott (Mrs. Robert Brower). Student, Geneva Coll., Beaver Falls, Pa., 1931-32; AB, Washington and Jefferson Coll., 1937, HHD (hon.), 1985. Served successively as alumni sec. dean freshmen, dir. admissions Washington and Jefferson Coll., 1937-44, asst. to pres., 1946-48; mem. staff Marts & Lundy, Inc., NYC, from 1948, v.p., sec., 1961-69, exec. v.p., treas., 1969-71, pres., from 1971, chmn., 1974-78, sr. cons., from 1978. Trustee Washington and Jefferson Coll. (life). Contbr. articles on ednl. adminstrn., fund raising to profl. jours. Bd. dirs. Nat. Soc. Prevention Blindness. Served to lt. (s.g.) USNR, 1944-46. Mem. Am. Assn. Fund Raising Counsel, Phi Kappa Psi. Republican. Presbyterian. Home: Columbus, Ohio. Died Feb. 25, 2009.

BREWER, NATHAN RONALD, veterinarian, consultant; b. Albany, NY, June 28, 1904; s. William and Rose (Johnson) B.; m. Jean Lees, Apr. 1, 1936; children: Maureen Pasik, Sandra Ginsberg, Jacquelyn Fechter. BS, Mich. State U., 1930, DVM, 1937; PhD in Physiology, U. Chgo., 1936; DSc (hon.), Chgo. Coll. Osteo. Medicine, 1977. Diplomate Am. Coll. Lab. Animal Medicine. Instr. pharmacology U. Ill., Chgo., 1935-36; veterinarian Detroit Bd. Health, 1937-38; prof. physiology Middlesex Vet. Sch., Waltham, Mass., 1938-39; pvt. practice Irvington (now Fremont), Calif., 1940-45; assoc. prof. physiology, dir. lab. animal facilities U. Chgo., 1945-69; pvt. cons. Chgo., 1969—2009. Contbr. articles to profl. jours. Named Man of Yr., Nat. Soc. Med. Rsch., 1956; recipient Arthur Brown award Delaware Valley Coll., 1983, Disting. Vet. Alumni award Mich. State U., 1997, Centennial award Del. Valley Coll., 1997, Rowsell award The Scientists Ctr. for Animal Welfare. Mem. Am. Assn. Lab. Animal Sci. (life, dist. svc. award 2000, pres. emeritus 2003), Am. Vet. Med. Assn. (chmn. various coms., Charles River award 1992, Animal Welfare award 2001), Nat. Acad. Sci. (chmn. parasitism com. 1953-58), Ill. State Vet. Med. Assn. (life), Chgo. Vet. Med. Assn. (life), Am. Physiol. Soc., Conf. Rsch. Workers in Animal Diseases, Ill. State Acad. Sci. (chmn. animals in rsch. com. 1968), Am. Assn. Lab. Animal Sci. (editor 1950-62, pres. 1950-55. editor emeritus, chmn. arrangements com. 1950-53, 59, 62, 66, Griffin award 1960, Ann. Nathan R. Brewer award established in his name 1994—), Nat. Acad. Sci. Inst. Lab. Animal Resources, Am. Coll. Lab. Animal Medicine (pres. 1957-59), Am. Soc. Vet. Physiologists and Pharmacologists, Am. Soc. Lab. Animal Practitioners (chmn. mgmt. practice com.), Ill. Acad. Vet. Practice. Avocation: chess. Died June 16, 2009.

BREWSTER, ROBERT CHARLES, diplomat, consultant; b. Beatrice, Nebr., May 31, 1921; s. Charles Lee and Lillian Asenath (French) B.; m. Mary Virginia Blackman, Feb. 22, 1951. Student, Grinnell Coll., 1939-41; AB, U. Wash., 1943; postgrad., U. Mex., 1946, George Washington U., 1947,

Columbia U., 1946-48. Fgn. affairs analyst State Dept., Washington, 1948-49, fgn. service officer, 1949-81; 3d sec. Am. Embassy, Managua, Nicaragua, 1949-51, 2d sec., 1951-52; vice consul Am. consulate gen. Stuttgart, Germany, 1952-55; policy briefing officer ICA, staff asst. to under sec. of state for econ. affairs, 1958, spl. asst. to under sec. of state, 1959-60; assigned Nat. War Coll., 1960-61; fgn. service insp., 1961-63; counselor Am. Embassy, Asuncion, Paraguay, 1964-66; dep. exec. dir. Bur. of European Affairs, 1966-67, exec. dir., 1967-69; dep. exec. sec. Dept. State, 1969-71, dir. personnel, 1971-73; amb. Ecuador, 1973-76; coord. for Law of Sea Dept. State, 1976, dep. asst. sec. for oceans and internat. environmental and sci. affairs, 1977-78, insp. gen., 1979-81, cons., 1981-89. Mem. D.C. Commn. on Aging, 1984-85; bd. dirs. Nat. Defense Univ. Found., 1984-87; mem. Com. on Research for Security of Future U.S. Embassy Bldgs. Nat. Acad. Scis., 1985-86. With USNR, 1943-46. Mem. Nat. War Coll. Alumni Assn. (pres. 1981-83), Foggy Bottom Assn. (v.p. 1984-85, pres. 1985-87), Diplomatic and Consular Officers Ret. Clubs: Cosmos (Washington). Home: Washington, DC. Died Dec. 20, 2009; Arlington National Cemetery.

BREWSTER, WILLIAM HAFNER, chemical company executive; b. Chicago, Ill., Sept. 27, 1922; s. George Ordway and Katherine Irene (Hennessey) B.; m. Nancy Lally, Jan. 9, 1945; children: William, Timothy, George, Nancy Jo, Mary Anne, Constance, Barbara. Student, DePaul U., Chgo., 1945-47; LL.B., Kent Coll. Law, Chgo., 1949. Bar: Ill. 1950, D.C. 1958. Vice-pres. employee relations Am. Can Co., Greenwich, Conn., 1967-75, Am. Can. Co., Washington, 1975-77; v.p. govt. liaison, v.p. adminstrn., corp. sec. M & T Chems., Inc., Woodbridge, N.J., from 1977; corporate sec. Ato Chem Inc., from 1985. Dir. Gerhardt Assocs., Tampa, Fla. Mem. adv. bd. visitors Mary Baldwin Coll., Staunton, Va., 1970-74; mem. adv. bd. visitors Sacred Heart U., Fairfield, Conn., 1973-75; dir. Urban League, Union County, N.J., 1977—; bd. dirs. Rahway Hosp., N.J., 1982-83; bd. regents Springhill Coll., Mobile, Ala. Served with USMC, 1942-45. Recipient disting. service award Gen. Services Adminstrn., Washington, 1965 Mem. ABA, Chem. Mfrs. Assn., Bus. Round Table (mem. labor relations com. 1964-67) Clubs: Colonia Country (N.J.) (dir. 1977—); Carrollwood Country (Tampa); Bent Tree Country (Sarasota, Fla.). Roman Catholic. Home: Westfield, NJ. Died Jan. 4, 2009.

BRIDGER, WAGNER H., psychiatrist, educator; b. NYC, Jan. 9, 1928; BA, NYU, 1946, MD, 1950. Diplomate Am. Bd. Psychiatry and Neurology. Intern U. Chgo., 1950-51; asst. resident psychiatry Bellevue Hosp., 1951-52; research fellow Pavlovian lab. Johns Hopkins Med. Sch., Balt., 1952-53; staff psychiatrist William Beaumont Army Hosp., 1953-54; resident psychiatrist River Crest Sanitarium, NYC, 1954-55, Bronx Mcpl. Hosp. Ctr. and Yeshiva U., 1955-56; research fellow dept. psychiatry, Yeshiva U., NYC, 1956-57, research instr., 1957-58, instr., 1958-60, asst. prof., 1960-65, assoc. prof., 1965-70, dir. research, 1965-82, prof., 1970-82, prof. neurosci., 1974-82, acting chmn., 1976-81; jr. psychiatrist Bronx Mcpl. Hosp. Ctr., 1956-57, asst. attending psychiatrist, 1958-65, assoc. attending psychiatrist, 1965-70, attending psychiatrist, 1970-82; chmn. dept. psychiatry, prof. psychiatry and pharmacology Med. Coll. Pa. at Ea. Pa. Psychiat. Inst., 1982-93, prof. psychiatry, from 1993. Vis. scientist Istituto Superiore di Sanita, Rome, 1969-70; vis. scholar psychology Harvard U., Cambridge, Mass., 1994-95, U. Calif., Berkeley, 1995; cons. Hastings Ctr.-Inst. of Soc., Ethics, and Life Scis.; investigator mental health career USPHS, 1958-63. Editor Biol. Psychiatry Jour., 1992. Recipient USPHS Research Sci. award, 1968-73. Fellow Am Psychiat. Assn., Am. Coll. Neuropsychopharmacology, Am. Coll. Psychiatrists; mem. Am. Psychpathological Assn. (council 1960), Group for Advancement of Psychiatry (com. pn psychopathology 1968-72), Pavlovian Soc. Am. (pres. 1968-69), Soc. Psychiat. Research (pres. 1970-71), Biol. Psychiatry (chmn. program com. IV World Congress 1984-85), Soc. Biol. Psychiatry (pres.-elect 1987-88, pres. 1988-89). Died Feb. 10, 2009.

BRIDGES, NORMAN VALETTE, college administrator; b. Newago County, Mich., Apr. 2, 1938; s. Guy Norman and Nellie (Ackley) P.; m. Janice Kay Stephey, Sept. 3, 1959; children: David, Jonathan, Daniel. BS, Bethel Coll., 1960; AM, U. Mich., 1964, PhD, 1970. Tchr. HS English Ind. Pub. Schs., 1960—62; tchr. jr. high sch. social studies Mich. Pub. Schs., 1962—63; dean students, prof., v.p. Bethel Coll., Mishawaka, Ind., 1966—76; pres. Barclay Coll., Haviland, Kans., 1976—85; v.p. u. rels. Friends U., Wichita, Kans., 1985—87, exec. v.p., 1987—89; pres. Bethel Coll., from 1989. Vice chmn. Kiowa County Meml. Hosp. Bd., Greensburg, Kans., from 1979. Mem.: Am. Assn. Bible Colls., Nat. Assn. Evangs., Rotary Club. Mem. Soc. Of Friends. Home: Mishawaka, Ind. Died Aug. 21, 2010.

BRIDGEWATER, CHARLES G., state legislator; b. Manchester, NH, Mar. 7, 1939; m. Nancy Bridgewater; 5 children. BS, Coll. Manchester, 1983; postgrad. Mem. exec. bd. Rep. City Com.; del. Rep. State Com.; chmn. Ward 8 Rep. com.; state rep. N.H. Ho. of Reps.; cons. quality assurance. Mem. Greater Manchester Jaycees (state dir.), U.S. Jaycees Daisy Shooting Edn. Program (internat. chmn. 1973), Greater Manchester Fedn. Chs. (vice chmn.). Home: Manchester, NH. Died Mar. 20, 2010.

BRINKER, THOMAS MICHAEL, retired finance company executive; b. Phila., Sept. 8, 1933; s. William Joseph and Elizabeth C. (Feeley) B.; m. Doris Marie Carlin, Oct. 11, 1958; children: Thomas Michael, James E., Joseph F., Diane M. Student, St. Joseph's U., U. Pa.; MS in Fin. Svcs., Am. Coll., 1980; DBA, Heed U., 1990; BA in Orgnl. Mgmt., Ea. Coll., 1991. Registered investment advisor; CLU, ChFC, CFP, AEP. With Ice Capades, 1951-52, 56; with Casa Carioca, Garmisch, Fed. Rep. Germany, 1954-56; profl. ice skating tchr. and mfrs. rep. Ridley Park, Pa., 1956-60; agt., div. mgr. Prudential Ins. Co., Phila., 1960-65; gen. agt. Mut. Trust Life Ins. Co., 1965-70; pres., founder Fringe Benefits Inc., Havertown, Pa., 1970—2008, Fin. Foresight Ltd., Havertown, Pa., 1983—2008. Adj. prof. Pa. State U., 1984—, St. Joseph's U., 1985—. Host: (radio) Financial Forum, Sta. WWDB-FM, 1982-90, Sta. WCZN-AM, 1990-91, daily report on fin. foresight Sta. WFLN-FM, 1992-, WCZN-AM, 1994-, children's fin. reports on Dr. Tom on Money Matters, WPWA-AM, 1994-, WWCN, Estero, Fla., 1997, others; co-host: (radio) Fin. Foresight, Sta. WFIL-AM, Phila., 1998-2000, WWDB-AM Phila., 2001-, WPEN-AM Phila., 2003-; author: HI, I'm Tom Brinker, You're on WWDB, 1987; columnist: Financially Yours, 1983-, Dollars and $ense, 1999-; ghostwriter: Nat. Assn. Life Underwriter's Fin. Fitness campaign, 1985; columnist Dollars and $ense, 1999-; contbr., author, condr. of seminars on fin. planning; contbr. articles to profl. jours. Pres., Delaware County Estate Planning Coun., 1979-80, Pipeline Inc., Springfield, Pa., 1970-71; dir. nat. coun. Invest-in-Am., 1986; bd. dirs. Pacific Advisors Fund, Inc., 1992—, Cypress Benefit Svcs., Inc., 1997—. Recipient Nat. Quality award Nat. Assn. Life Underwriters, 1966-2002, Nat. Sales Achievement award, 1970-2000, TransAmerica Fin. Advisors award, 2003. Mem. CLU, Delaware County Life Underwriters (pres. 1975-76, 82-83), Am. Coll. Life Underwriters, Nat. Assn. Life Underwriters, Internat. Platform Assn., Nat. Assn. Ins. and Fin. Advisors (inducted into Hall of Fame, 2003), Internat. Assn. Fin. Planners (v.p. Delaware Valley chpt. 1986-88, pres. 1989-, chmn. 1990-), Million Dollar Round Table (mem. Ct. of the Table 1986-, Top of the Table 1991, 93-95, Twenty-Five Million Dollar Internat. forum 1992-93), Lake Naomi Club (v.p., mem. bd. govs. 1982, pres. 1986), KC, Manor Club, Tom Brinker's Op. Christmas Baskets (pres.), Kingsport Club, Inc. (bd. dirs., treas. 1997-). Roman Catholic. Home: Pocono Pines, Pa. Died Feb. 11, 2010.

BRINKWORTH, DONALD A., lawyer; b. Shreve, Ohio, May 5, 1922; s. Arthur Sharon and Virginia Marie (Shoup) B.; m. Marjorie Marie Alexander, Sept. 22, 1951 (dec. 1999); children: Christine B. Pittman, Debra B. Leese, Donna B. Cullihan, Louise B. Snyder, Arthur A. Cert., Cambridge U., 1945; BA, Bethany Coll., 1946; JD, Capital U., 1951; postgra., U. Pitts., 1951-54. Bar: Ohio 1951, Pa. 1952, U.S. Dist. Ct. (we. dist.) Pa. 1952, U.S. Dist. Ct. (ea. dist.) Pa. 1970, U.S. Ct. Appeals (3d cir.) 1956, U.S. Supreme Ct. 1967. Law clk. to asst. gen counsel passenger service Pa. R.R., 1951-68; commerce counsel Pa. Cen. Transp. Co., 1968-76; v.p, gen. counsel Consol. Rail Corp., Phila., 1976-89; of counsel Schnader, Harrison, Segal & Lewis, Phila. Gen. counsel Am. Soc. of Traffic and Transp., Chgo. and Louisville, 1965-78, sec.-treas., Louisville, 1978-80, v.p., 1980-81. Staff sgt. artillery U.S. Army, 1943-46, ETO. Mem. ABA, Pa. Bar Assn., Phila. Bar Assn., Assn. Transp. Practitioners, Nat. Assn. R.R. Trial Counsel, Am. Soc. Transp. and Logistics (pres. 1981-82, chmn. bd. 1982-83), Edgeworth Club (v.p. Sewickley chpt. 1969), Broomall's Lake Country Club, Masons, Shriners. Republican. Presbyterian. Home: West Chester, Pa. Died Mar. 26, 2010.

BRINSON, GAY CRESWELL, JR., retired lawyer; b. Kingsville, Tex., June 13, 1925; s. Gay Creswell and Lelia (Wendelkin) B.; m. Bette Lee Butter, June 17, 1979; children from former marriage: Thomas Wade, Mary Kaye. Student, U. Ill., Chgo., 1947-48; BS, U. Houston, 1953, JD, 1957. Bar: Tex. 1957, U.S. Dist. Ct. (so. dist.) Tex. 1959, U.S. ct. Appeals (5th cir.) 1962 U.S. Dist. Ct. (ea. dist.) Tex. 1965, U.S. Supreme Ct. 1974; U.S. Dist. Ct. (no. dist.) Tex. 1990; diplomate Am. Bd. Trial Advocates, Am. Bd. Profl. Liability Attys. Spl. agt. FBI, Washington and Salt Lake City, 1957-59; trial atty. Liberty Mut. Ins. Co., Houston, 1959-62; assoc. Horace Brown, Houston, 1962-64, Vinson & Elkins, Houston, 1964-67, ptnr., 1967-91; of counsel McFall, Sherwood & Sheehy, Houston, 1992-2000. Lectr. U. Houston Coll. Law, 1964-65; mem. staff Tex. Coll. Trial Advocacy, Houston, 1978-86; prosecutor Harris County Grievance Com.-State Bar Tex., Houston, 1965-70 With AUS, 1943—46, ETO. Fellow Tex. Bar Found. (life); mem. Tex. Acad. Family Law Specialists (cert.), Tex. Assn. Def. Counsel, Tex. Bd. Legal Specialization (cert.), Fedn. Ins. Counsel, Nat. Bd. Trial Advocacy (cert.), Briar Club, St. Charles Bay Hunting Club, Phi Delta Phi. Home: Houston, Tex. Died May 1, 2010.

BRISLEY, CHESTER LAVOYEN, industrial engineer; b. Albion, Pa., Apr. 3, 1914; s. Voyen Francis and Nina May (Dearborn) B.; m. Eva Scott, June 19, 1932. Student, Gen. Motors Inst., 1936-39; BS, Youngstown State U., 1946; MS, Wayne State U., 1954, PhD, 1957. Indsl. engr. Packard Elec. div. Gen. Motors, Warren, Ohio, 1935-41; supr. indsl. engring. N.Am. Aviation, Dallas, 1942-44; mgr. indsl. engring. Wolverine Tube div. Calumet & Hecla, Inc., Detroit, 1946-58; asst. to dir. ops. Chance Vought Aircraft, Dallas, 1958-59; cons. A.T. Kearney, Chgo., 1960; mgr. indsl. engring. Allis Chalmers, Inc., Milw., 1961-62; mgr. mgmt. services Touche Ross C.P.A., NYC, 1963-64; prof. dept. engring. U. Wis., Milw., 1964-83, asso. chmn. dept. engring., 1964-83; prof. dept. indsl. engring. Calif. Poly. State U., San Luis Obispo, 1983-85; prof. dept. mech. engring. Marquette U., 1985-86; chmn. bus. edn. Edmundson Coll., 1986-87; prof. bus. adminstrn., 1987-90; dir. indsl. engring., 1990-92; prof. DeBusk Sch. Bus., 1992-94; dean, from 1995. Contbr. articles to profl. jours. Methods Time Measurement Assn. fellow, 1978 Fellow Inst. Indsl. Engrs. (past pres. Detroit and Milw. chpts., v.p. Region XI, exec. v.p. chpt. ops. 1983-85), Soc. Advancement Mgmt. (past pres. Detroit chpt.); mem. Methods Time Measurement Assn. (v.p. 1979-80), Nat. Soc. Profl. Engrs., Wis. Soc. Profl. Engrs. (pres. 1978-79), Engrs. and Scientists Milw. (pres. 1974-75), Milw. Council Engring. and Sci. Socs. (pres. 1975-76), Am. Soc. Engring. Edn. (chmn. continuing engring. studies div. 1972-73) Home: Cumberland Gap, Tenn. Died Dec. 9, 2009.

BRISTOL, RICHARD FREDRICK, veterinary medicine educator; b. Pontiac, Mich., Mar. 5, 1925; s. Glenand H. and Agnes Geraldine (Canuss) B. D.V.M., Mich. State U., 1951; MS in Pathology, Iowa State U., 1966. Gen. practice vet. medicine, Montfort, Wis., 1951-62, Merrill, Wis., 1970-74; asst.prof. Iowa State U., Ames, 1962-64, assoc. prof., 1966-68, prof., 1968-70; vis. lectr. U. Wis.-Platteville, 1958-62; prof. vet. sci. dept. U. Wis., Madison, 1974-81, prof. Sch. Vet. Medicine, from 1981, now assoc. dean clin. affairs. Recipient Pioneer Patron award U.-Wis.-Platteville, 1962; recipient Disting. Teaching award Iowa State U., 1966, Cardinal Key, 1967 Mem. AVMA, Am. Assn. Bovine Practitioners, Am. Assn. Vet. Clinicians, U.S. Animal Health Assn., Wis. Vet. Med. Assn. (pres. 1974 Wis. Vet. of Yr. award) Home: Waunakee, Wis. Died July 6, 2010.

BRODERICK, JOHN CARUTHERS, librarian, educator; b. Memphis, Sept. 6, 1926; s. John Patrick and Myrtle Vaughn (Newson) Broderick; m. Kathryn Price Lynch, Sept. 10, 1949; children: Kathryn Price, John Caruthers Jr. AB, Rhodes Coll., 1948; MA, U. N.C., 1949, PhD, 1953. Instr. English U. Tex., Austin, 1952—57; asst. prof. Wake Forest U., Winston-Salem, NC, 1957—58, assoc. prof., 1958—63, prof., 1963—65; with Libr. of Congress, Washington, 1964—88, specialist, 1964—65, asst. chief, 1965—74, chief manuscript divsn., 1975—79, asst. libr. rsch. svcs., 1979—88; ret., 1988. Adj. prof. English George Washington U., 1964—84; vis. prof. U. Va., 1959, U. N.C., 1968, Cath. U. Am., 1990—91. Author: Past Imperfect, Present Tense, 2000, Jason Wingate's Legacies, 2009; compiler Whitman the Poet, 1961; editor: The Journal of Henry David Thoreau, 1981—90; contbr. articles to profl. jours., Ency. of the Libr. of Congress; author: Jason Wingare's Ligacies, 2009. Mem. adv. com. U.S. Senate Hist. Office, 1974—78; mem. Nat. Hist. Publs. and Records Commn., 1978—82, Columbus Quincentennial Jubilee Commn., 1986—88. With US Army, 1945—46. Grantee, Danforth Found., 1960, Am. Coun. Learned Socs., 1962—63; fellow, Coun. Libr. Resources, 1971. Mem.: Omicron Delta Kappa, Sigma Alpha Epsilon. Home: Gaithersburg, Md. Died Jan. 4, 2010.

BRODEUR, ARMAND EDWARD, pediatric radiologist; b. Penacook, NH, Jan. 8, 1922; s. Felix and Patronyne Antoinette (Lavoie) B.; m. Gloria Marie Thompson, June 4, 1947; children: Armand Paul, Garrett Michael, Mark Stephen, Mariette Therese, Michelle Bernadette, Paul Francis. AB, St. Anselm Coll., 1945; MD, St. Louis U., 1947, M.Rd., 1952; LLD (hon.), St Anselm Coll., 1974. Intern St. Louis U. Hosps., 1947-48, resident in pediat., 1948-49; resident in radiology St. Louis U. Hosps. and St. Louis U. Grad. Sch., 1949-52; asst. dean. St. Louis Sch. Medicine, 1947, assoc. dean, 1950—52; instr. St. Louis U. Sch. Medicine, 1952-60, sr. instr., 1960-62, asst. prof., 1962-65, assoc. prof., 1965-70, prof. radiology, from 1970, chmn. dept. radiology, 1975-78, vice chmn. dept., 1978-88, prof. pediat., from 1979, prof. juvenile law, from 1979; pvt. practice specializing in pediat. radiology St. Louis, 1954-56; radiologist-in-chief Cardinal Glennon Meml. Hosp. for Children, St. Louis, 1956-88, Shriners Hosp. for Children, from 1988; assoc. v.p., bd. govs. Cardinal Glennon Children's Hosp., St. Louis. Lectr. and cons. in field; med. dir. radiography Sanford Brown Coll., 1996—. Radio show host Doctor to Doctor, Sta. KMOX-CBS, St. Louis; host weekly To Your Health; health reporter Sta. KMOV-TV, also Sta. WFUN-FM, Sta. KSIV-AM; TV host Sta. WCVB Channel 5, Boston; author: Radiologic Diagnosis in Infants and Children, 1965, Radiology of the Pediatric Elbow, 1980, Radiologic Pathology for Allied Health Professions, 1980, Child Maltreatment, 1993, also monographs; contbr. articles to profl. jours., numerous tchg. tapes. Bd. dirs. ARC, TB Soc., March of Dimes, 15 others. With U.S. Army, 1942-46, with USPHS, 1952-54. Decorated Knight Equestrian Order Holy Sepulchre Jerusalem; recipient Mo. Health Care Communicator of Yr. award, 1991, Welby award Nat. Acad. Radio and TV Health Communicators, Healthcare Leadership award Met. Hosp. St. Louis, 1994, numerous civic awards; Armand Brodeur Day proclaimed by City of St. Louis; named St. Paul Man of Yr., 1991; ann. lecture named in his honor dept. radiology St. Louis U. Sch. Medicine, 1998; named one of very few Top Radiologists in Am., 2002-03. Fellow Am. Coll. Radiology, Am. Acad. Pediat.; mem. AMA (Bronze medal, Golden Apple), Soc. Pediat. Radiology, Radio. Soc. N.Am., Nat. Assn. Med. Communicators (charter, co-founder, pres. 1987-88), Nat. Assn. Physician Broadcasters (founder, pres., Lifetime Achievement award), Sigma Xi, Alpha Omega Alpha, Alpha Sigma Nu, Phi Beta Kappa, Rho Kappa Sigma. Roman Catholic. Home: Saint Louis, Mo. Died Dec. 7, 2009.

BRODIE, HOWARD, artist; b. Oakland, Calif., Nov. 28, 1915; s. Edward and Anna (Zeller) B. Student, Art Inst. San Francisco, Art Student's League, NYC, U. Ghana, Accra; LHD (hon.), Acad. Art Coll., San Francisco, 1984. Mem. staff Life mag., Yank: the Army Weekly, Collier's, AP, CBS News, 1969-89; freelance artist, journalist, from 1990. Author: Howard Brodie: War Drawings, 1963, Drawing Fire, A Combat Artist At War, 1996; art journalist: (major wars) World War II, Korea, French Indo-China, Vietnam, (trials) Jack Ruby, Ray, Sirhan, My Lai, Charles Manson, Chicago Seven, Watergate, John Hinckley, Klaus Barbie in France, (famous people) John Wayne, Pres. Kennedy, James Jones; art at White House, 1946, 48; work represented in permanent collections Calif. Palace of Legion of Honor, San Francisco, Soc. Illustrators, N.Y., Libr. Congress, Washington, Air Force Acad., Colo.; prints, books: U.S. Army Infantry Mus., Ft. Benning, Ga., U.S. Army Mus., Presidio, Monterery, Oreg. Nat. Mil. Mus., The Hoover Instn. on War, Revolution and Peace, Anne S.K. Brown Mil. Collection Brown U. Libr., The Mus. of Books, Lenin Libr., Moscow, Gorky Sci. Libr., Moscow, Admiral Nimitz State Hist. Park, Tex., Henry E. Huntington Libr. (award), San Marina, New Britain Mus. Am. Art, Conn., West Point Libr., N.Y., Brown U. Libr., R.I.; commd. to draw The Contemporary Soldier in Action, Assn.

U.S. Army, 1999; guest on Merv Griffin Show, Charles Kuralt Sunday Morning program, Ted Koppel program, Night Line; featured Andy Rooney CBS Sunday Morning program, Nostagia Network, Dennis Wholey Am. Program; featured 1 out of 7 artists (PBS Documentary) They Drew Fire, 2000, (incompanion TV book) They Drew Fire, Combat Artists of World War II, 2000. Sgt., U.S. Army. Decorated Bronze Star; recipient honor medals Freedom Found., 1957, 58, 60, 61. Home: San Miguel, Calif. Died Sept. 19, 2010.

BRODNYAN, JOHN GEORGE, chemist; b. Phila., Nov. 29, 1929; s. John and Lillian (Sweeney) B.; m. Claire Catherine O'Donnell, June 9, 1956; children— James, Claire, Richard, Gerard. B.S. in Chemistry, Villanova U., 1952. Chemist, Franklin Inst., Phila., 1953-57, Rohm & Haas, Phila., 1957—. Democrat. Roman Catholic. Home: Philadelphia, Pa. Died Nov. 29, 2009.

BRODY, EUGENE BLOOR, psychiatrist, educator, editor; b. Columbia, Mo., June 17, 1921; s. Samuel and Sophie B.; m. Marian Holen, Sept. 23, 1944; children: Julie Anne, James Clarke (dec.), John Holen. AB, MA, U. Mo., 1941, DSc (hon.), 1991; MD, Harvard, 1944; grad., N.Y. Psychoanalytic Inst., 1957. Resident Yale Med. Sch., 1944-46, 48-49, from instr. to assoc. prof., 1949-57; prof. psychiatry U. Md. Sch. Medicine, Balt., 1957-76; chmn. dept., also dir. Inst. Psychiatry and Human Behavior, 1959-76, prof. psychiatry and human behavior, 1976-87, prof. emeritus, from 1987; sr. assoc. sch. of hygiene and pub. health Johns Hopkins U., from 1986. Vis. prof. U. Brazil, 1965-68, U. W.I., Kingston, Jamaica, 1972-75, U. Otago, New Zealand, 1981, James Cook U., No. Queensland, Australia, 1992; vis. prof. psychiatry Harvard Med. Sch., 1997-99; fellow Center for Advanced Studies in Behavioral Scis., Stanford, 1975-76, Inst. for Advanced Studies, Tel Aviv U., 1986; mem. adv. bd. Inst. Social Psychiatry, U. San Marcos, Peru, 1968-70; mem. nat. profl. adv. bd. psychiatry, psychology and neurology service VA, 1963-67; cons. WHO (Pan Am. Health Orgn. and Geneva, Switzerland), 1965-95; program dir. Interam. Mental Health Studies Program, 1967-69; mem. exec. bd. World Fedn. Mental Health, 1969-83, adminstrv. mem., 1972-74, mem.-at-large, 1979-81, pres., 1981-83, sec. gen., 1983-99, sr. cons., 1999—; mem. epidemiol. studies rev. com. NIMH, 1975-79, cons. clin. infant devel. program, 1979-81, hosp. rev. com., 1979-86, AIDS grant rev. com. 1987-92; mem. internat. adv. bd. Peruvian Nat. Inst. Mental Health, 1984-94, mem. editl. bd. jours., 1985-94; mem. adv. coun. Hogg Found., 1986-89; mem. sci. com. Internat. Social Sci. Coun., 1989, exec. com. 1989-91, 92-95; cons. UNESCO, 1986-93; sr. advisor Harvard Program Refugee Trauma, 1989-2004; cons. Balt. VA Med. Ctr., 1990-2004. Author: The Lost Ones, Social Forces and Mental Illness in Rio de Janeiro, 1973, Sex, Contraception and Motherhood in Jamaica, 1981, Psychoanalytic Knowledge, 1990, Biomedical Technology and Human Rights, 1993, The Search for Mental Health: A History and Memoir of WFMH, 1948-1997, 1998; editor: (with F.C. Redlich) Psychotherapy with Schizophrenics, 1952, (with R. Monroe and G. Klee) Psychiatric Epidemiology and Mental Health Planning, 1967, Minority Group Adolescents in the United States, 1968, Behavior in New Environments, 1970; cons. editor Jour. Nervous and Mental Disease, 1959-67, editor in chief, 1967—; adv. editor: Tice Med. Ency., 1967-80, Harper & Row Med. Ency., 1980-86; mem. editorial bd. Psychiatry Digest, 1967-71, Mental Hygiene, 1968-70, Social Psychiatry, 1970-81, Internat. Jour. Psychosomatic Obstetrics and Gynecology, 1984-92, Population and Environment, 1987-92; contbr. numerous articles to profl. jours. Chmn. adv. bd. Balt. chpt. Internat. Students Council, ARC, 1964-67; bd. dirs. Md. Partners of Alliance for Progress, 1965-66, Nat. Assn. Mental Health, 1964-66, mem. profl. adv. bd., 1967-71; mem. adv. bd. Inst. for Victims of Trauma, 1988-97; chiaf NP Svc. West Haven, Va., 1953-57. Served to capt. M.C. AUS, 1946-48. Fellow Am. Psychiat. Assn. (life; chmn. com. transcultural psychiatry 1966-68, rep. interam. council 1965-71, trustee 1968-71, chmn. task force family planning 1973-75, Human Rights award 1999), Am. Coll. Psychiatrists (charter), Am. Coll. Psychoanalysts (charter); mem. Assn. Behavioral Sci. and Med. Edn. (pres. 1981), Am. Psychoanalytic Assn. (life), Internat. psychoanalytic assns., Internat. Coll. Pediatrics (senate 1978-86), Internat. Assn. Psychosomatic Ob-Gyn (exec. bd. 1977-86), Peruvian Psychiat. Assn. (hon.), Peruvian Assn. Psychiatry, Neurology and Neurosurgery (hon.), Cosmos Club (Washington), 14 W. Hamilton St. Club (Balt.). Home: Baltimore, Md. Died Mar. 13, 2010.

BRODY, EUGENE DAVID, investment company executive; b. Bklyn., Feb. 6, 1931; s. Leon K. and Ruth (Parkoff) B.; m. Jacqueline Galloway, Apr. 5, 1959; children: Jessica, Leslie. BS, U. Pa., 1952; MBA, NYU, 1963. Gen. ptnr. A.W. Jones Assocs., NYC, 1965-70; v.p., bd. dirs. Downe Communications, NYC, 1970-74; chief exec. officer Founders Mut. Depositor Corp., Denver, 1970-74; pres. Beekman Capital, Inc., NYC, 1974—78; sr. v.p., ptnr. Oppenheimer & Co. Inc., NYC, 1978—86; mng. dir. Oppenheimer Capital, 1986-96; pres. Picanet, Inc., NYC, from 1997. Pub. Print Collectors Newsletter, 1971—96; trustee Manhattan Inst. for Policy Rsch., NYC. Author: Odds-On Investing, 1978. Lt. USNR, 1952-55. Mem. N.Y. Futures and Options Soc. (founding dir., pres. 1978-79), University Club N.Y.C., Stamford Yacht Club, East Hampton Tennis Club. Died Feb. 8, 2009.

BRODY, MARTIN, hotel executive; b. Newark, Aug. 8, 1921; s. Leo and Renee (Kransdorf) B.; m. Florence Gropper, Nov. 22, 1946; children: Marc, Renee. BA, Mich. State U., 1943. Pres. Indsl. Feeding Co., Newark, 1951-61; pres., dir. A.M. Capital Corp., NYC, 1961-71. Chmn. bd., dir. Waldorf System Inc., Boston, 1963-66, Restaurant Assocs., Inc., N.Y.C., 1964-66; chmn. bd., CEO Restaurant Assocs. Industries Inc., 1966-99; chmn. bd. St. Barnabas Corp.; dir. Jaclyn Inc., several Smith Barney mut. funds, Washington Nat. Life Ins. Co. of N.Y.; bd. dirs. Regional Planning Assn. Trustee St. Barnabas Med. Ctr.; bd. dirs. N.J. Transit Corp. Served to capt. AUS, 1943-45. Mem. Orange Lawn Tennis, Greenbrook Country (North Caldwell, N.J.), Boca Raton Hotel and Resort Club. Home: Livingston, NJ. Died Oct. 29, 2009.

BROGLE, RICHARD CHARLES, pharmaceutical company executive; b. Boston, July 12, 1927; s. Albert P. and Dorothy G. (Thompson) Brogle; m. Lucy F. Torrisi, Jan. 31, 1959; children: David, Nina, Kevin. SB in Biology, MIT, 1950, SM in BioChemistry, 1953, PhD in Food sci., 1960. Ptnr. Fuld & Brogle, Cambridge, Mass., 1956—60; chemist Am. Chicle Co., Long Island City, NY, 1960—66; dir. drug and cosmetic Warner-Lambert Co., Morris Plains, NJ, 1966—72, dir. clin. and regulatory, 1972—74, v.p. rsch. svcs. and quality assurance, 1974—77; v.p. lab. ops. Block Drug Co., Inc., Jersey City, 1978—83, v.p., dir. R&D, 1983—87; owner RCB Assocs., Montclair, NJ, from 1987. Contbr. articles to sci. jours. Mem. com. Boy Scouts Am., Montclair, 1977—82. Lt. US Army, 1951—52. Mem.: Non-prescription Durg Mfrs. Assn., Inst. Food Technologists, Am. Soc. Clin. Pharmacology and Therapeutics, MIT Alumni Club. Roman Catholic. Home: Montclair, NJ. Died Nov. 10, 2009.

BROMBERG, BARBARA SCHWARTZ, lawyer; b. Newark, Mar. 1, 1941; d. Louis and Ann (Shoolman) Wilner; m. Victor E. Schwartz, July 8, 1964 (div.); m. Robert S. Bromberg, Apr. 1, 1978. BA summa cum laude, U. Buffalo, 1962; LLB magna cum laude, Columbia U., 1965. Bar: N.Y., Ohio, U.S. Dist. Ct. (so. dist.) N.Y., U.S. Tax Ct., Ohio 1973, U.S. Ct. Appeals (6th cir.) 1988. Assoc. Rosenman, Colin, Kaye, Petschek, Freund and Emil, NYC, 1965-67; cons. Legal Research Group, Inc., Charlottesville, Va., 1970; legal editor The Michie Co., Charlottesville, 1970-71; assoc. Dinsmore, Shohl, Coates and Deupree, Cin., 1967-73; ptnr. Dinsmore, Shohl, Coats and Deupree, Cin., 1974-78, Benesch, Friedlander, Coplan & Aronoff, Cleve., 1978-81, Paxton and Seasongood, Cin., 1981-88; Thompson, Hine & Flory, from 1989. Lectr. ednl. instns., profl. meetings and numerous tax and estate planning forums; chmn. ctrl. region IRS Regional Counsel's Adv. Group, 1985-86, mem., 1993—. Columnist on taxation, legal publs.; contbr. articles to profl. publs.; editor: Columbia Law Review. Active Cin. Hist. Conservation Bd., 1982-90, Exempt Orgns. Adv. Group to Commr. IRS, 1988—. James Kent scholar, 1962-63, Harlan Fiske Stone Scholar 1963-64. Mem. ABA (taxation sect., spl. com. for study of legal edn., mem. ho. of dels.), Cin. Bar Assn. (chmn. taxation sect. 1975-76, exec. com. 1977-78, 82-84, treas. 1982-84, chmn. estate planning inst. 1984, Trustees' award 1996), Cin. Bar Found. (trustee, treas. 1990-92, pres. 1992-94), Assn. Bar City N.Y., Am. Hosp. Assn. (mem. task force on unrelated bus. income 1979-80), Nat. Health Lawyers Assn., Chi Omega. Avocations: reading, travel. Home: Cincinnati, Ohio. Died Jan. 30, 2009.

BROMFIELD, EDWARD, neurologist; b. Boston, May 2, 1951; MD, Harvard Med. Sch., 1983. Cert. Am Bd. Neurology and Psychiatry, 1989. Chief divsn. epilepsy and eeg Brigham and Women's Hosp., Boston, from 1996; assoc. prof. neurology Harvard Med. Sch., from 2004. Recipient Inspiration for a Cure award, Western Mass Epilepsy Com., 2000, Clin. Collaboration award, Brigham and Women's Physicians Orgn., 2004; named Co-Mentor of Yr., Ptnrs. Neurology Residency Program, 2005. Mem.: Epilepsy Found. Mass. and RI (pres. from 2001), Am. Epilepsy Assn. (assoc.; chair student and residency edn. com. 1996—2000, Cert. Appreciation 2000). Achievements include research in Epilepsy treatment. Home: Newtonville, Mass. Died May 10, 2009.

BRONSTEIN, ARTHUR J., linguistics educator; b. Balt., Mar. 15, 1914; s. Gershon and Bessie B.; m. Elsa Meltzer, May 15, 1941; children: Nancy Ellen, Abbot Alan. BA, CCNY, 1934; MA, Columbia U., 1936; PhD, NYU, 1949. Vis. scholar and rsch. assoc. in linguistics U. Calif., Berkeley, from 1987; prof. Queens Coll., NYC, 1938-67; Fulbright prof. U. Tel Aviv, (Israel), 1967-68, U. Trondheim, (Norway), 1979; prof. linguistics Lehman Coll. and Grad. Sch., CUNY, 1968-83, prof. emeritus, from 1983; exec. officer PhD program in speech and hearing scis. CUNY, 1969-72; exec. officer Ph.D. program in linguistics Grad. Sch., CUNY, 1981-83; cons. in field; with dept. linguistics U. Calif., Berkeley. Author: Pronunciation of American English, 1960, Essays in Honor of C.M. Wise, 1970, Biographical Dictionary of the Phonetic Sciences, 1977; project dir.: Dictionary of American English Pronunciation Served with Signal Corps and AGD USAAF, 1942-46. Fellow Am. Speech and Hearing Assn., Internat. Soc. Phonetic Scis., Dictionary Soc. N.Am., N.Y. Acad. Sci.; mem. MLA, Linguistics Soc. Am., Am. Dialect Soc., Internat. Phonetic Assn., Am. Assn. Phonetic Scis., Phi Beta Kappa. Home: Oakland, Calif. Died Jan. 5, 2010.

BROOKS, BARRY MICHAEL, lawyer; b. Chgo., Sept. 7, 1942; s. Samuel and Gail (Freedman) Brooks. AB, U. Chgo., 1963; JD, Northwestern U., 1966; LLM, John Marshall Law Sch., Chgo., 1967. Bar: Ill. 1967. Gen. counsel Scholl, Inc., Chgo., 1968—81; sole practice Chgo., from 1981. Contbr. articles, columns in newspapers. Mem.: Lawyers For Creative Arts, Decalogue Soc. Home: Chicago, Ill. Died May 8, 2009.

BROOKS, H. ALLEN, architectural educator, author; b. New Haven, Nov. 6, 1925; s. Harold Allen and Mildred (McNeill) B. BA, Dartmouth Coll., 1950; MA, Yale U., 1955; PhD, Northwestern U., 1957; D Engring. (hon.), Dalhousie U., 1984. Asst. prof. U. Ill., 1957-58; lectr. U. Toronto, 1958-61, asst. prof., 1961-64, assoc. prof., 1964-71, prof., 1971-86; vis. prof. Dartmouth Coll., 1969; Mellon chair Vassar Coll., 1970-71; vis. prof. Archtl. Assn., London, 1977-82, 2003. Author: The Prairie School: Frank Lloyd Wright and His Midwest Contemporaries, 1972 (recipient Alice Davis Hitchcock Book award 1973), Frank Lloyd Wright and the Prairie School, 1984, Le Corbusier's Formative Years: Charles-Edouard Jeanneret at La Chaux-de-Fonds, 1997 (Assn. Am. Pubs./Scholarly Pub. Divsn. Ann. award 1997); editor: Prairie School Architecture, 1975, Writings on Wright, 1981, The Le Corbusier Archive, 32 vols, 1982-85, Le Corbusier, 1987; editl. cons. Le Corbusier Sketchbooks, 1981-82; contbr. to numerous books and jours. With U.S. Army, 1946-47. Guggenheim Found. fellow, 1973-74; Can. Coun. fellow, 1975-76; Social Scis. and Humanities Rsch. Coun. Can. fellow, 1977-79, 83-85; Victoria U. fellow; receipent Wright Spirit award, Frank Llyod Wright Bldg. Conservency, 2002. Fellow Soc. Archtl. Historians; mem. Internat. Coun. Mus., Internat. Com. Monuments and Sites, Soc. Archtl. Historians U.S. (past pres., dir.), Soc. Archtl. Historians Gt. Britain, Soc. Study Architecture Can., Frank Lloyd Wright Bldg. Conservancy, Walter Burley Griffin Soc. Am. Died Aug. 8, 2010.

BROOKS, LORIMER PAGE, retired patent lawyer; b. Swampscott, Mass., May 11, 1917; s. William Lorimer and Maude (Page) B.; m. Arlene M. Cook, Nov. 9, 1941; children: Lorraine E. Brooks Phillips, Jr., Rosalind P. Brooks O'Malley. BS in elec. engring. with honors, Northeastern U., 1939; JD, Fordham U., 1948; postgrad., NYU Law Sch., 1951. Bar: N.Y. 1948, U.S. Dist. Ct. (so. dist.) N.Y. 1952, U.S. Dist. Ct. (ea. dist.) N.Y. 1957, U.S. Ct. Appeals (2d cir.) 1964, U.S. Dist. Ct. (we. dist.) N.Y. 1971, U.S. Supreme Ct. 1971, U.S. Ct. Appeals (fed. cir.) 1982. Patent agt. ITT, 1939-41, patent atty., 1945-50, Ward, Crosby, & Neal, NYC, 1950-54; ptnr. firm Ward, McElhannon, Brooks & Fitzpartrick, NYC, 1954-71, Brooks, Haidt, Haffner & Delahunty, NYC, 1971-98; ptnr. Norris McLaughlin & Marcus, PA, NYC, 1998—2004; ret. Rep. Nat. Council Patent Law Assns., 1976-77. Patentee in field. Sec. Westchester Park Citizens Assn., 1950-52, pres., 1952-54; dir. Westchester County Cerebral Palsy Assn., 1962-64; mem. Young Men's Republican Club Eastchester, N.Y., 1952-56. Served with AUS, 1941-45. Mem. Westchester County Bar Assn. (ethics com. 1978-86), N.Y. Patent Law Assn. (bd. govs. 1961-64, 74-78, chmn. subcom. practice and procedure in cts. 1961-62, chmn. com. ethics and grievances 1973-74, 1st v.p. 1974-75, pres. 1975-76, past pres. com. 1976—), IEEE, Aircraft Owners and Pilots Assn., Tau Beta Pi. Died Jan. 23, 2009.

BROOKSHIER, TOM (THOMAS JEFFERSON BROOKSHIER), retired sportscaster; b. Roswell, N.Mex., Dec. 16, 1931; s. Orville Brooks and Dola (Thornton) B.; m. Barbara J. Starrett, June 8, 1953; children: Linda K., Thomas J., Betsy J. BS, U. Colo., 1953. Defensive back Phila. Eagles, 1953-61; sportscaster Sta. WCAU-TV, Phila., 1958-77; analyst, play-by-play announcer NFL broadcasts CBS-TV Network, 1977—89. Writer weekly sports column Denver Post and Rocky Mountain News, 1957-61; co-host This Is The NFL, NFL Films, Inc., 1970-78; also syndicated series Sports Illustrated, 1976-77. Active Union League of Phila., World Affairs Council, Nat. Wildlife Soc. Served to 1st lt. USAF, 1954-56. Named to NFL All-Star Team Sporting News, 1959; named NFL All-Pro, 1959, 60, 61, U. Colo. Hall of Honor, 1973, Pa. Sports Hall of Fame, 1974, Pop Warner Hall of Fame, 1980; recipient Nat. Collegiate Athletic Assn. spl. recognition award, 1972, Bert Bell award, 1976, Sportscaster of Yr. award Nat. Sportscasters and Sportswriters, 1976, Main Line Jr. C. of C. award, 1965, humanitarian award Nat. Cystic Fibrosis Research Found., 1967, appreciation award Nat. Multiple Sclerosis Soc., 1975 Mem. NFL Alumni Assn. Clubs: Maxwell Football, Pop Warner Little Scholars, Fraternal Order Police. Republican. Died Jan. 29, 2010.

BROPHY, JERE EDWARD, education educator, researcher; b. Chgo., June 11, 1940; m. Arlene Sept. 21, 1963; children: Cheryl, Joseph. BS in Psychology, Loyola U., Chgo., 1962; MA in Human Devel., U. Chgo., 1965, PhD in Human Devel., 1967; Doctorate (hon.), U. Liege, 2004. Rsch. assoc., asst. prof. U. Chgo., 1967-68; from asst. to assoc. prof. U. Tex., Austin, 1968-76; staff devel. coord. S.W. Ednl. Devel. Lab., Austin, 1970-72; prof. Mich. State U., East Lansing, 1976-92, co-dir. Inst. for Rsch. on Tchg., 1981-93, univ. disting. prof., from 1993. Co-author: Teacher-Student Relationships: Causes and Consequences, 1974; editor (book series) Advances in Research on Teaching, 1989—. Fellow Ctr. for Advanced Study in the Behavioral Scis., 1994. Fellow: APA, Internat. Acad. Edn., Am. Psychol. Soc.; mem.: Nat. Soc. for the Study of Edn., Nat. Coun. for the Social Studies, Nat. Acad. Edn., Am. Ednl. Rsch. Assn. (Palmer O. Johnson award 1983, Presdl. citation 1995). Died Oct. 16, 2009.

BROTZEN, FRANZ RICHARD, materials scientist, educator; b. Berlin, July 4, 1915; arrived in U.S., 1941; s. Georg and Lena (Paculły) Brotzen; m. Frances Burke Ridgway, Jan. 31, 1950; children: Franz Ridgway, Julie Ridgway. BSMetE, Case Inst. Tech., 1950, MS, 1953, PhD, 1954. Salesman a Quimica Bayer Ltda., Rio de Janeiro, 1934-41; mfrs. rep. R.G. Le Tourneau, Inc., Longview, Tex., 1947-48; sr. rsch. assoc. Case Inst. Tech., Cleve., 1951-54; mem. faculty Rice U., Houston, from 1954, prof. materials sci., 1959—88, prof. emeritus, from 1988, dean engring., 1962-66, master Brown Coll., 1977-82. Vis. prof. Max Planck Inst., Stuttgart, Germany, 1960—61, Stuttgart, 1973—74, Fed. Poly. Inst., Zurich, Switzerland, 1966—67, U. Lausanne, Switzerland, 1981. Contbr. scientific papers to profl. jours. Chmn. Houston Contemporary Arts Assn., 1964—65. Served to 1st lt. US Army, 1942—46. Recipient Sr. Scientist award, West German Govt., 1973—74; Guggenheim fellow, 1960—61. Fellow: Am. Soc. Metals (chmn. Houston chpt. 1980—81); mem.: AIME, Soc. Engring. Sci., Am. Phys. Soc., Sigma Xi, Tau Beta Pi. Home: Houston, Tex. Died May 25, 2010.

BROUGHTON, JAMES WALTER, real estate development executive, consultant; b. Atlantic City, Dec. 16, 1946; s. Walter Lennie and Janet Caroline (Mossman) B.; m. Sharon Carter, Mar. 10, 1980; children: Jennifer Christine, Matthew James. Student, U. Colo., Colorado Springs, 1967-68, U. Md., 1968-70, U. Colo., Denver, 1972-73. Asst. regional sales dir.

Del E. Webb Corp., Denver, 1972-76; dir. mktg. Interval Internat., Miami, Fla., 1981-82; exec. dir. Time Sharing Inst., Miami, 1981-82; pres. J. Broughton, Inc., Miami, 1976-83, Spectrum Mktg. Group, Denver, 1983-84, Ocean Resourts Devel. Co., Ventura, Calif., 1984-85; sr. v.p. Fairfield Cmtys., Inc., Atlanta, 1985; chmn., pres., CEO, Lexes Enterprises, Inc., Las Vegas, Nev., from 1985. Bd. dirs. Consol. Resorts, Inc., PC Cons., Inc., Sea-Shore, Inc., Internat. Cruise and Excursion Gallery; pub. Time Sharing Ency., 1981, Time Sharing Ind. Rev., 1981. Contbr. articles to profl. jours. With USAF, 1964-71. Mem. Am. Resort Devel. Assn. (bd. dirs. 1985—, exec. com. 1988—, chmn. meetings coun. 1991—, resort devel. forum 1993—, treas. 1993—, recruitment award 1983, NTC svc. award 1987, Leader of Yr. award 1991, Industry Visionary Leader of Yr. award 1993), Nat. Time Sharing Coun. (chmn. 1984-86, bd. govs. 1984-92, recruitment award 1984), Interval Internat. (adv. bd. 1982-91), Urban Land Inst. (recreational devel. coun. 1993—). Republican. Died Jan. 16, 2009.

BROWN, DAVID, film producer, writer; b. NYC, July 28, 1916; s. Edward Fisher and Lillian (Baren) B.; m. Liberty LeGacy, Apr. 15, 1940 (div. 1951); 1 son, Bruce LeGacy; m. Wayne Clark, May 25, 1951 (div. 1957); m. Helen Gurley, Sept. 25, 1959. AB, Stanford U., 1936; MS, Columbia U., 1937. Apprentice San Francisco News and Wall St. Jour., 1936; night editor, asst. drama critic Fairchild Publs., 1937-39; editorial dir. Milk Research Council, 1939-40; assoc. editor Street & Smith Publs., 1940-43; assoc. editor, exec. editor, editor-in-chief Liberty mag., 1943-49; editorial dir. Nat. Edn. Campaign, A.M.A., 1949; assoc. editor, mng. editor Cosmopolitan mag., 1949-52; mng. editor, story editor, head scenario dept. 20th Century-Fox Film Corp. Studios, Beverly Hills, Calif., 1952-56, mem. studio exec. com., 1956-60, producer, 1960-62; v.p., dir. story operation 20th Century Fox Film Corp., Beverly Hills, Calif., 1964-69, exec. v.p. creative operations, 1969-70, dir., 1968-70; exec. v.p. creative operations, dir. Warner Brothers, 1971-72; ptnr. Zanuck/Brown Co., NYC, 1972-87; owner Manhattan Project Ltd., 1987—2010; pres. Island World, 1990-92; exec. story editor, head scenario dept., editorial v.p. New American Library World Lit., Inc., 1963-64. Final judge for best short story pub. in mags. Benjamin Franklin Mag. ann. awards, 1955-58. Author: Brown's Guide to Growing Gray, 1987, Let Me Entertain You, 1990, The Rest of Your Life is the Best of Your Life, 1991; Brown's Guide To The Good Life, 2006; contbr. Am. mag., Collier's, Harper's, Sat. Evening Post, Reader's Digest, Journalists in Action, 1963, others; editor: I Can Tell It Now, 1964, How I Got That Story, 1967; prodr.: (films) The Sugarland Express, 1974, The Eiger Sanction, 1975, Jaws, 1977, MacArthur, 1977, Jaws II, 1978, The Island, 1980, Neighbors, 1981, The Verdict, 1982, Target, 1985, Cocoon, 1985; exec. prodr.: Driving Miss Daisy, HBO Women and Men, 1 and 2, 1990, 1991, The Player, 1992, A Few Good Men, 1992, Watch It, 1993, The Cemetery Club, 1993, Canadian Bacon, 1994, Kiss The Girls, 1997, The Saint, 1997, Deep Impact, 1998, Angela's Ashes, 1999, Chocolat, 2000, Along Came a Spider, 2001; prodr.: (plays) A Few Good Men, 1989, TRU, The Cemetery Club, The Shawl, Mr. Goldwyn, Show Tune, Sweet Smell of Success, 2002, Vanilla, Dirty Rotten Scoundrels, 2005. Trustee com. on film Mus. Modern Art, N.Y.C. Served as 1st lt., M.I. AUS, World War II. Mem. Acad. Motion Picture Arts and Scis. (co-recipient Irving G. Thalberg Meml. award 1991), Producers Guild Am. (David O. Selznick Lifetime Achievement award 1993), Nat. Press Club (Washington), Coffee Ho. Club (N.Y.C.), Columbia U. Grad Sch. of Journalism, Players Club (N.Y.C.), Dutch Treat (N.Y.C.), Century Assn. (N.Y.C.), N.Y. Friars Club. Home: New York, NY. Died Feb. 1, 2010.

BROWN, EVERETT TRACY, electronics systems engineer, consultant; b. Staten Island, NY, Apr. 6, 1921; s. Tracy Allen and Alma Bell (Quick) B.; m. Violet Chalmers, June 5, 1942; children: Tracy Lynn, Alice, Judith. Student in Math, Physics, Wagner Coll., 1938-41; student in Elec. Engring., Va. Polytech. Inst., 1943-44, 46, UCLA Extension, 1956-59. Rsch. asst. Manhattan Project, NYC, 1945-46; methods engr. Hanovia Chem. & Mfg. Co., Newark, 1946-48; devel. project engr. Arma Corp., Bklyn., 1948-56; systems, project mgr. N.Am. Aviation, Downey, Calif., 1956-59, project mgr. Anaheim, Calif., 1959-62; program mgr. Rockwell Internat., Anaheim, 1962-73, dir. bus. devel. et al., 1973-81; cons. Santa Maria, Calif., from 1981. Grants writer Santa Maria (Calif.) Symphony Soc., Inc., 1984—. Mem. Elks (co-chmn. Gov. Rels. Com. Santa Maria 1989—). Died Jan. 6, 2009.

BROWN, JAMES LEHMON, chemical company executive; b. Detroit, Nov. 20, 1929; s. Abram Lehmon and Donnabelle (Chenoweth) Brown; m. Judith Marsh Sinclair, June 28, 1952; children: Kirk, Scott, Kim, Carrie, Elizabeth. AB, U. Mich., 1951, MBA, 1952. Propr. constrn. firm, Ann Arbor, Mich., 1955—58; sales mgr. Sinclair Mfg. Co., Toledo, 1958—64, pres., from 1964, chmn. bd., Sinclair Mfg. Assos., WGTE-TV-FM, 1980—84. Bd. dirs. 1st Nat. Bank Toledo; pres., bd. dirs. Solar Cells Inc., Toledo. Mem. Toledo Citizens Com. Effective Govt., 1971—72; pres. Toledo Area Govtl. Rsch. Assn., 1974—75; trustee Toledo Area Coun. Boy Scouts America, from 1971, U. Toledo Corp., from 1975, Toledo Chpt. ARC, 1977—79; exec. bd. mem. Toledo Area Coun. Boy Scouts America, from 1970, pres., from 1975. With US Army, 1952—55. Mem.: Toledo Club, Sigma Delta Chi, Theta Delta Chi, Phi Eta Sigma. Home: Scottsville, Va. Died Apr. 16, 2010.

BROWN, JOE LEROY, retired professional sports team executive; b. NYC, Sept. 1, 1918; s. Joseph Evan and Kathryn (McGraw) B.; m. Virginia Lee Newport, Sept. 24, 1940; children— Cynthia Lee, Don Evan Grad., Mercersburg Acad., 1937; student, UCLA, 1937-40. Mgr. Lubbock Baseball Club, Tex., 1939-40; pres. Waterloo Baseball Club, Iowa, 1941; publicity dir. Hollywood Baseball Club, Calif., 1946-47; spl. sports publicity Allied Artists Studio, 1948; gen. mgr. Zanesville Baseball Club, Ohio, 1949, Waco Baseball Club, Tex., 1950, New Orleans Baseball Club, 1951, pres., gen. mgr., 1952-54; scouting coordinator Pitts. Pirates, 1955, gen. mgr., 1956-76, spl. scout, 1977-85, exec. v.p., gen. mgr., 1985. Served to capt. USAAF, 1942-46 Mem. Zeta Psi Clubs: Duquesne, St. Clair Country, Pittsburgh Athletic. Died Aug. 16, 2010.

BROWN, JOHN EDWARD, textile company executive; b. NYC, Feb. 13, 1936; s. John Edward and Anne Marie (Douglas) B.; m. Barbara Ann Reiss, May 21, 1960; children: Kathleen, Michael, Douglas, Kevin. BA, Hofstra U., 1959. Salesman Riegle Textile, NYC, 1960-64; mgr. merchandising Greenwood Mills, NYC, 1964-72; v.p. M. Lowenstien, NYC, 1972-76, Texfi Industries, NYC, 1976-80; mgr. sales Burlington Industries, NYC, 1980-82; exec. v.p. Brucol Industries, NYC, 1982-83; v.p. Channel Textile Co., NYC, 1983-86, Lida Mfg. Co., NYC, 1986-88; v.p. mktg. and sales Ren Rob Fabrics, NYC, 1988-89; pres. Copensport, NYC, 1988-94, J.T.J. Repair, Amityville, N.Y., 1976-89; exec. v.p. mktg. and sales Cameron, Ind.; pres. Texfi Collections, from 1994, H.L.C. Collections, NYC, from 1996. Bd. dirs. St. Joseph's Cath. Youth Orgn., Kings Park, N.Y., 1974-85; capt. baseball team Hofstra U. Named Hofstra U. assoc., 1969-70. Mem. Am. Arbitration Assn. Democrat. Avocations: coaching, golf, tennis, softball. Home: Northport, NY. Died Aug. 0, 1984.

BROWN, JOHN PAIRMAN, religious organization administrator; b. Hanover, NH, May 16, 1923; s. Bancroft Huntington and Eleanor (Pairman) Brown; m. Dorothy Emily Waymouth, June 26, 1954; children: George Waymouth, Felicity Emily Brown McCarthy, Maryam Eleanor Brown Beros, David Pairman. BA summa cum laude, Dartmouth Coll., 1944; student, Harvard U., 1946—49, Gen. Theol. Sem., NYC, 1952; ThD, Union Theol. Sem., 1958. Ordained priest Episc. Ch., 1953, joint ministerial standing Christian Ch. (Disciples of Christ). Curate Grace Ch., Newark, 1952—54; tutor Gen. Theol. Sem., NYC, 1954—56; instr. Hobart Coll., Geneva, NY, 1956—58; assoc. prof. classics and ancient history Am. U., Beirut, 1958—65; prof. New Testament Ch. Divinity Sch. of the Pacific, 1965—68; editl. staff U. Calif. Press, 1968—70; staff Ecumenical Peace Inst., San Francisco, 1971—76; exec. dir. No. Calif. Ecumenical Coun., San Francisco, 1976—83. Rep. U.S. chs. and peace movement confs., Hanoi, 1967, Santiago, 76, Belfast; non-govtl. orgn. rep. Conf. Geneva and UN Spl. Session, 1982, Uppsala Ch. World Conf. and Moscow, 1983. Editor: The Witness, 1955—58, Sequoia, from 1980; author: The Displaced Person's Almanac, from 1961, The Lebanon and Phoenicia: Ancient Texts...The Forest, from 1969, The Liberated Zone, from 1969, Planet on Strike, from 1970, To a Sister on Laurel Drive, from 1972; contbr. articles to publs. in field. Active opposition to conscription during Vietnam War building B-1 Bomber, Livermore Nuclear Weapns Lab. With USAAF, 1944—46. Mem.: Nat. Assn. Ecumenical Staff, Soc. Bibl. Lit. Died Apr. 5, 2010.

BROWN, LESTER B., social worker, educator; b. Whitmire, SC, Jan. 11, 1943; s. William Barney and Minnie Eugenia (Vaughn) Brown. AB in Psychology, U. Chgo., 1969, AM in Social Work, 1971, PhD in Social Treatment, 1980. Sr. child care counselor, therapist Nicholas J. Pritzker Ctr. and Hosp., Chgo., 1964-68, 69; social worker I Ill. Dept. Children and Family Svcs., Chgo., 1967-70, social worker II, 1971; group homes social worker Jewish Children's Bur., Chgo., 1971-73; social worker, field instr. Jackson Park Hosp., Chgo., 1973, clin. dir., 1973-74, cons., 1975-77, SUNY, Albany, 1981, asst. prof. social work, chmn. undergrad. social welfare, 1981-86; prof. social worker Wayne State U., 1986-89; assoc. prof. social work Calif. State U., Long Beach, 1989-95, prof. social work, from 1995. Lectr. U. Wis., Milw., 1977—78, instr., 1978—80; lectr. U. Chgo., 1977—78; guest lectr. Boston Coll., 1981; cons., presenter in field. Author: (book) Two Spirit People: American Indian Lesbian Women and Gay Men, 1997, Gay Men and Aging, 1997, Brief Treatment and a New Look at the Task Centered Approach, 2003; contbr. articles to profl. jours., chapters to books; mem. editl. bd. Health Care Mgmt. Rev., 1981—84. Bd. dirs. Capital Dist. Travelers Aid Soc., 1983—86; condr. workshops ethnic sensitive work Pittsfield Sch. Dist., Mass., 1984; participant workshops mental health and child welfare; mem. com. Urban League. Grantee, SUNY, 1981, U.S. HHS, 1981, Sch. Social Welfare, 1982. Mem.: NASW, Coun. Social Work Edn., Acad. Cert. Social Workers. Democrat. Avocations: cooking, aerobics. Home: Long Beach, Calif. Died Feb. 16, 2009.

BROWN, LORRAINE A., literature educator; b. Grand Rapids, Mich., Apr. 3, 1929; d. Benjamin Franklin Dundas and Eva Elizabeth Campbell; m. William Liller; 1 child, Tamara Kay Liller. BA in English and Edn., U. Mich., 1952, MA, 1962; PhD, U. Md., 1968. From asst. prof. to prof. English George Mason U., from 1980. Home: Fairfax, Va. Died Feb. 27, 2010.

BROWN, MILTON PEERS, business administration educator; b. Yonkers, NY, Jan. 19, 1919; s. George Edwin and Linda Miriam (Schneider) B.; m. Joan Hawley, Aug. 25, 1945; children— Susan, Janet, Pamela. S.B. cum laude, Harvard U., 1940, MBA, 1942. Mem. faculty Harvard U. Bus. Sch., from 1942, prof. bus. adminstrn., from 1958, Lincoln Filene prof. retailing, from 1963; mgmt. cons., from 1950. Dir. Allied Stores Corp., Collins & Aikman Co., both N.Y.C., Dunkin Donuts, Randolph, Mass., Savogran Co., Norwood, Mass., Hollingsworth and Vose, Walpole, Mass., C.R. Bard Inc., Summit, N.J., High Voltage Engring. Co., Burlington, Mass.; mem. adv. com. Navy Resale System Office. Author: Operating Results of Multi-Unit Department Stores, 1961, Problems in Marketing, 3d edit, 1968; co-author: Strategy Problems in Mass Retailing and Wholesaling. Chmn., chief exec. officer, bd. dirs. Harvard Coop. Soc. Home: East Stoneham, Maine. Died Apr. 25, 2009.

BROWN, PAUL WILLIAM, evangelist, electronics executive; b. Niskayuna, NY, Aug. 29, 1948; s. Paul Walter and Esther Jean (West) B.; m. Susan Dianne Chapman, Mar. 17, 1954; children: David Paul, Charissa Joy. Grad. high sch., Schoharie, NY, 1966. Ordained to ministry Pentecostal Ch., 1975, 80. Prodn. specialist GE, Schenectady, N.Y., 1971-75; sr. pastor Mt. Zion Full Gospel Ch., Wellsboro, Pa., 1975-80; evangelist Oil and Wine Ministries, Canton, Pa., 1980-84; founder/pastor Bethel Family Worship Ctr., Mansfield, Pa., 1985-90; nat. sales mgr. Kingdom Tapes, Mansfield, 1985-90; gen. mgr. Nat. Cassette Svcs., Front Royal, Va., from 1990; founder/evangelist Commitment to Excellence, Front Royal, from 1990; pastor People's Ch., Manassas, Va., from 1991. Conf. speaker, cons. Nat. Cassette Svcs., 1990—; conf. speaker, dir. Commitment to Excellence, 1990—. Patentee in field. With U.S. Army, 1968-80, Vietnam. Mem. The Christian Outdoorsman (pres. 1988-90). Republican. Avocations: golf, fly tying, fly fishing, hunting. Home: Manassas, Va. Died Aug. 9, 2009.

BROWN, PHILLIP RAND, veterinarian, educator; b. Atlanta, Dec. 14, 1950; s. Hugh Denton and Sara (Phillips) B.; m. Beth Dockins, June 10, 1972 (div. Dec. 1985); m. Kathleen Marie Kalaher, Oct. 22, 1991. BS, U. Ga., 1971, DVM, 1975; MSc in Expt. Surgery, McGill U., Montreal, Can., 1980. Commd. capt., advanced through grades to lt. col. USAFR, 1981-97; veterinarian Roberts Animal Hosp., Hanover, Mass., 1975-77, Peninsula Vet. Clinic, Newport News, Va., 1977-78; resident in surgery, instr. sch. vet. medicine Tufts U., Boston, 1980-83; vet. surgeon South Shore Vet. Assocs., South Weymouth, Mass., 1983-85; vis. veterinarian sch. vet. medicine Cambridge (Eng.) U., 1985; asst., assoc. prof. Johns Hopkins U., Balt., from 1986; comdr. 175 Med. Squadron Air Nat. Guard, from 2003. Mem. Orthop. Rsch. Soc., Am. Vet. Med. Assn., Greater Balt. Vet. Med. Assn., Johns Hopkins Med. Surg. Soc. Avocation: sailing. Home: Loganville, Ga. Died Jan. 25, 2009.

BROWN, RICHARD MAURICE, physics and computer engineering educator; b. Cambridge, Mass., May 17, 1924; s. Irving Menzies and Vertene (Marsan) B.; m. Kathryn Margaret Doane, Sept. 15, 1946 (dec. 1961); children— Peter T., Alan W., Stephen H., Kathryn L.; m. Waynona Newcom, May 24, 1962 AB, Harvard U., 1944, MS, PhD, 1949. Asst. prof. physics Wash. State U., Pullman, 1949-55; asst. prof., then assoc. prof., prof. physics and elec. engring. U. Ill., Urbana, 1952-84, prof. emeritus, from 1984. Fellow Am. Phys. Soc.; mem. IEEE, Assn. Computing Machinery Home: Urbana, Ill. Died Aug. 22, 2009.

BROWN, ROBERT CHARLES, retired radiologist; b. Pottsville, Pa., Jan. 22, 1917; BS, Pa. State U., 1938; MD, Temple U., 1942. Diplomate Am. Bd. Radiology. Intern Nat. Naval Med. Ctr., Bethesda, Md., 1942-43; resident in radiology Phila. Gen. Hosp., 1951-54; chief dept. radiology Taylor Hosp., Ridley Park, Pa., 1954-55, St. Mary's Hosp., Phila., 1956-63, Riddle Meml. Hosp., Media, Pa., 1963-83, emeritus staff, from 1983. Died May 3, 2009.

BROWN, ROBERT DONALD, lawyer; b. Orange, NJ, Sept. 23, 1952; s. Francis Robert and Elizabeth Brown; children: William Robert, Daniel Thomas. BA, Clemson U., 1974; JD, Am. U., 1982. Bar: Fla. 1982, U.S. Dist. Ct. (so. and mid. dists.) Fla. 1982. Mktg. cons. New Eng. Tel. Co., Boston, 1977—79; econometrician Chesapeake & Potomac Tel. Co., Washington, 1979—81; atty. Blackwell Walker, P.A., Miami, Fla., 1982—94, Akerman Senterfitt & Eidson, Miami, 1994—96, Freidin & Brown, P.A., Miami, 1996—2005, Robert D. Brown, P.A., Miami, from 2005. Named one of Legal Elite, Fla. Trend Mag., 2004, 2005. Mem.: Dade County Trial Lawyers Assn. (bd. dirs. 1999—2004, editor newsletter 1999—2004). Died Jan. 11, 2010.

BROWN, SUSAN O'CONNOR, banker; b. Phila., Feb. 13, 1952; m. Michael J. Brown; children: Lindsay Kelso, Kevin Neil. BA, Rosemont Coll., 1974. Sr. v.p. 1st Pa. Bank, Phila., 1974-86; exec. v.p. Phila. Nat. Bank, from 1986. Mem. Robert Morris Assocs. Bd. dirs. Girl Scouts U.S., Greater Phila., 1986—, The People's Light & Theatre Co., Malvern, Pa., 1986—. Named an Outstanding Woman YWCA, 1985. Mem. Nat. Assn. Bank Women, Am. Bankers Assn., Consumer Bankers Assn., The Forum Exec. Women (v.p. 1989), Phila. Fin. Assn. Avocations: jazzercise, travel, reading, gardening. Home: Bryn Mawr, Pa. Died May 11, 2009.

BROWN, THOMAS B., investment executive, banker; b. NYC, July 29, 1927; s. Thomas B. and Ann (Lyons) B.; m. Barbara Hannon, Dec. 29, 1954; children— Thomas B., Michael P., Brian P., Brendan G., Erin M. BS, Hofstra U., 1951; postgrad., Rutgers U., 1966. Chartered fin. analyst. Examiner Fed. Res. Bank N.Y., NYC, 1951-56; v.p. Lincoln Rochester Trust Co., N.Y., 1956-76; sr. v.p. Shawmut Worcester County Bank, Mass., 1976-83; pres. One Fed. Asset Mgmt., 1983-87; sr. v.p. Shawmut Bank Boston, from 1983-87. Served with USN, 1945-47 Mem. Boston Soc. Security Analysts, Mass. Bankers Assn. (bd. dirs., chmn. trust exec. com. 1982-84) Republican. Roman Catholic. Home: Dover, Mass. Died Feb. 24, 2010.

BROWN, WILLIE B., state legislator; b. Anderson, SC, June 18, 1940; Grad., S.C. State Coll. Dist. 29 N.J. State Assembly, from 1974. Vice chmn. taxation com. N.J. State Assembly, 1974-76, majority whip, 1978-79, asst. majority leader, 1980-83, chmn. intergovt. rels. com., 1980—, sr. mem. appropriations com., 1980—, dep. speaker, 1984-85, dep. minority leader, 1986-87, minority leader, 1988-89, speaker pro tem,

1990-91. Chmn. N.J. State Legis. Black Caucus, 1983-85, regional dir.; U.S. rep. Nat. Conf. State Legis./Am. Coun. Young Polit. Leaders; co-founder, cons., adv. South Ward New Dem. Club. Mem. NAACP, Coun. State Govts., Masons. Died Jan. 5, 2009.

BROWNE, RAY, insurance agent, former United States Shadow Representative, DC; b. Washington, Dec. 8, 1938; s. Woodrow Lee and Mary Isabelle (Manning) B.; m. Barbara Lee Andrus, May 17, 1979; children: Ray II, Molly Lee. Student, U. Md., 1959-62. CLU; ChFC. Life ins. agt., gen. agt. Aetna Life & Casualty, Washington, Cleve., Charleston, W.Va., 1964-82; ins. broker The Browne Co., Washington, 1982—2010; shadow rep. from D.C. US House of Reps., Washington, 2001—07. Vis. lectr. John Carroll U., Cleve., 1972-77; speaker in field. Featured in documentary: Washington A Tale of Two Cities; contbr. polit. and bus. commentary to newspapers, articles to profl. jours. Adv. neighborhood commr. Washington Govt., 1989-90; mem. drug strategy team Washington Govt., 1989-90; vice chair Hurt Home Bd., Washington, 1987-89; candidate for City Coun., Washington, 1990; del Dem. Nat. Com., 2004; mediator Washington Superior Ct., 1985-88; mem. parish coun. Holy Trinity Cath. Ch., Washington, 2001-2004. With USN, 1956-58. Recipient Big Bros. and Big Sisters Merit award, 1990. Mem. Nat. Assn. Life Underwriters (dir. No. Va. 1964-66), Greater Washington Chpt. CLU (bd. dirs., sec., treas., v.p., pres. 1982-91), Million Dollar Roundtable (life), Mensa, U. Md. M Club, Alpha Tau Omega (Silver Circle award 1984). Democrat. Roman Catholic. Home: Washington, DC. Died Feb. 13, 2010.

BROWNING, CHAUNCEY H., JR., former state attorney general; b. Charleston, W.Va., Nov. 21, 1934; s. Chauncey H. and Evelyn (Mahone) B.; m. Patricia Ann Lewis; children: Chauncey Hoyt, III, Charles Preston, Steven Thomas. AB, W.Va. U., 1956, LL.B., 1958. Law clk. U.S. Dist. Ct. for So. Dist. W.Va., 1958; practice law Charleston, 1958-62; atty.-in-charge Legal Aid Soc. Kanawha and Putnam Counties, W.Va., 1959-60; commr. pub. instns. State of W.Va., 1962-68, atty. gen., 1969—85; pvt. law practice, 1985—2008. Mem. Nat. Commn. Rev. Antitrust Laws and Procedures; pres. Nat. Assn. Attys. Gen., 1978-79; del. to exec. com. Council of State Govts., permanent mem. exec. com. Editor: W.Va. Law Quar. Recipient Outstanding Public Servant award W.Va. State Bar Assn.-W.Va. Trial Lawyers Assn., 1978 Mem. Am., W.Va., Kanawha County bar assns., W.Va. State Bar, W.Va. Trial Lawyers Assn., Order of Coif, Phi Delta Phi, Kappa Sigma. Democrat. Died Dec. 31, 2009.

BROWNING, DON SPENCER, religious educator; b. Trenton, Mo., Jan. 13, 1934; s. Robert Watson and Nelle Juanita Browning; m. Carol LaVeta Browning, Sept. 28, 1958; children: Elizabeth Dell, Christopher Robert. AB, Ctrl. Meth. Coll., Fayette, Mo., 1956; DDiv, Ctr. Meth. Coll., Fayette, Mo., 1984; BD, U. Chgo., 1959, PhD, 1964; DDiv, Christian Theol. Sem., Indpls., 1990; DDiv (hon.), U. Glasgow, Scotland, 1998. Asst. prof. Phillips U., Enid, Okla., 1963-65; instr. Div. Sch. U. Chgo., 1965-66, asst. prof., 1966-69, assoc. prof., 1969-77, prof., 1977-79, Alexander Campbell prof. ethics and social sci., 1979—2010; co-prin. Investigation Templeton Found., New Sci. Virtue Project, 2009—10. Cadbury lectr. U. Birmingham, England, 1998; Woodruff prof. Emory U., 2001—03; Templeton lectr. Boston U., 2008. Author: Atonement and Psychotherapy, 1966, Generative Man: Society and Good Man in Philip Rieff, Norman Brown, Erich Fromm and Erik Erikson, 1973, The Moral Context of Pastoral Care, 1976, Pluralism and Personality: William James and Some Contemporary Cultures of Psychology, 1980, Religious Ethics and Pastoral Care, 1983, Religious Thought and the Modern Psychologies, 1987, 2d edit., 2004, A Fundamental Practical Theology, 1991; co-author: From Culture Wars to Common Ground: Religion and the American Family Debate, 1997, 2d edit., 2000, Reweaving the Social Tapestry: Toward a Public Philosophy and Policy of Families, 2001, Marriage and Modernization, 2003; sr. advisor (PBS documentary) Marriage--Just a Piece of Paper?; co-editor: Sex, Marriage and Family in the World Religions, 2006, Christian Ethics and the Moral Psychologies, 2006, Equality and the Family, 2007, American Religions and the Family, 2007, Children and Childhood in American Religions, 2009, Children and Childhood In World Religion, 2009, Reviving Christian Humanism: the new Conversation on Psychology, Psychotherapy, and Spirituality, 2010. Recipient Oskar Pfister award Am. Psychiat. Assn., 1999; Guggenheim fellow, 1975-76, fellow Inst. Religion in Age of Sci., 2003; Lilly Endowment grantee, 1991-97, 1997-2005, for Religion, Culture and Family Project, 1991-2003, grant Templeton Found., 2009-10. Home: Chicago, Ill. Died June 3, 2010.

BROWNLEE, WYATT CHINA, lawyer; b. Hodges, SC, Mar. 18, 1907; s. James W. and Elizabeth (Sanders) Brownlee; m. Emma M. Roundtree, Jan. 19, 1934; children: Wyatt C., Christopher. LLB, John Marhsall Sch. Law, 1944; LLD, Cleve. Marshall Law Sch., 1968. Bar: Ohio 1945, US Dist. Ct. (no. dist.) Ohio 1946, US Dist. Ct. (ea. dist.) Ohio 1946, US Supreme Ct. 1955. Asst. atty. gen., Cleve., 1964—74; asst. prosecutor, 1973—77. Asst. law dir., Cleve., 1975—77; referee Cleve. Mcpl. Ct., 1977—81; pvt. practice, Cleve., from 1981. Mem.: NAACP, Greater Cleve. Bar Assn. (meritorious svc. award 1970, 1972), Cuyahoga County Bar Assn., Norman Minor Bar Assn., Nat. Bar Assn. (jud. coun.), Assn. Trial Lawyers Am., Masons (former exalted ruler), Phi Beta Sigma. Home: Cleveland, Ohio. Died May 28, 2009.

BRUDNER, HARVEY JEROME, physicist; b. NYC, May 29, 1931; s. Joseph and Anna (Fiddelman) B.; m. Helen Gross, dec.18, 1963; children: Mae Ann, Terry Joseph, Jay Scott. BS in Engring. and Physics, NYU, 1952, MS, 1954, PhD, 1959; postgrad., U. Md., 1954-56, CCNY, 1958, Columbia U., 1959-61. Electronics engr. Bendix Corp., Teterboro, NJ, 1952; physicist U.S. Naval Ordnance Lab., White Oak, Md., 1953-54; sr. physicist Emerson Rsch. Labs., Washington, 1954-57; prin. physicist Emerson Radio, Jersey City, 1957-61; rsch. assoc. N.Y. U. Inst. Math. Scis., NYC, 1957-60; guest scientist Rockefeller Inst. for Med. Rsch., NYC, 1960-61; sr. rsch. assoc. Am. Can Co., Princeton (N.J.) Lab., 1964-67; v.p. R & D Westinghouse Learning Corp., NYC, 1967-71, pres., 1971-76; also dir.; mem. adminstrv. com. Westinghouse Electric Corp., Pitts., 1971-76; pres. Westinghouse Electric Corp. (Westinghouse Learning Group), 1971-76, H.J.B. Enterprises, NYC, from 1961, Med. Devel., Inc., NYC, 1962; dir. Ideal Sch. Supply Corp., Ednl. Products, Inc., Document Reading Svcs., Ltd., Linguaphone Inst. Ltd., Info. Synergy, Inc., Cambridge Learning Connection, Inc.; chmn. new devels. com. Project ARISTOTLE (Annual Rev. & Info. Symposium on Tech. of Tchg., Learning, Edn.) Nat. Security Indsl. Assn., 1966—72; acting dir. Gottscho Info. Center, Coll. Engring., Rutgers U.; prof. math., physics, dean sci. and tech. N.Y. Inst. Tech., 1962-64; instr. atomic physics N.Y. U., NYC, 1953-54. Cons. Nat. Inst. Edn., Mass. Inst. Tech., Rutgers U., Worcester Poly. Inst., Poly. Inst. N.Y., Nat. Inst. Community Devel., U.S. Ho. of Reps. Com. on Sci. and Tech.; with amateur radio K2EXN, 1953-57; mem. adv. com. Middlesex County Coll., 1966—, Paterson State Coll., 1975; mem. exec. planning com. tng. adv. sect. Nat. Security Indsl. Assn., 1966; nat. adv. bd. Am. Coll. in Jerusalem; dir. computers in edn. study Nat. Inst. Edn., 1979; bd. dirs. World Learning and Comms.; mem. Raritan Millstone Heritage Alliance, Inc., Somerset, N.J., 1998—, bd. dirs., 2006—. Editl. commentator Another Opinion, Sta. WCBS, N.Y.C., N.Y. Power Authority; author: Semiconductor Physics, 1954, College Technical Mathematics, 1967, Algebra and Trigonometry-A Programmed Course with Applications, 1971, On Fermat's Last Theorem, 1979, Fermat and The Missing Numbers, 1994, How the Babylonians Solved Numbered Triangle Problems 3600 Years Ago, 1998; columnist Light-On Series: Ednl. Tech. Mag., Source Data: Datamation Mag., Home News Tribune, 2006, 08; chmn. editl. adv. bd. Tech. Horizons in Edn. Jour.; participated Borough Highland Park March, 2005; commentator Rockefeller Ctr. Christmas Tree chosen from Suffern, N.Y., Sta. WOBM, 2004; centennial logo design stamp cacellation U.S. Postal Svc., 2005; centennial logo-design USPS Stamp Collection, 2005; contbr. articles to mags., jours., and newspapers. Mem. steering com. Project Program for Continuing Engring. Edn. DOE, NSF, Mcpl. Alliance Com., Highland Park, from 1990; capt. long-range planning com. Highland Park Sch. Bd.; trustee Ross Hall Heights Assn., 1966; chmn., pres. Joyce Kilmer Authority, New Brunswick, NJ, from 1986, Joyce Kilmer Centennial Commn., New Brunswick, 1986—2009; coord. WABC-TV News, NYC, Joyce Kilmer Trees, 1994; coord. program Fermat and Babylonian Rectangles, Sta. WCTC, 1994; apprd. to Mcppl. Alliance Against Drugs and Alcohol, 1990—99; apptd. to Middlesex County Mcpl. Alliance Network, from 1995; coord. Project DATE (Drugs, Alcohol, Tobacco, Education), Rutgers U. N.J. Forum, from 1995, Metlar-Bodine House Mus., Piscataway, NJ, 2003—09, New Brunswick Cmty. Bridge Project, 2001, Vets. Day Project, 2001; pres. Highland Park Centennial Commn., 2002—06; dir. cir. George Street Playhouse, New Brunswick, from 2002. Recipient cert. Americanism Vets. Alliance of Raritan Valley, 1992, award Kiwanis Internat., 1993, 2 Nobel Laureate speeches Sta. WCTC, 2003, speeches on Mayor Robert Wood Johnson, Highland Park, Triangles from Rectangles article, The Daily Targum, 2004, 2007, 2008; named Knight, Order of the Swan, 1996, New Brunswick Hist. Assn., 2003, Grand Marshall, Vets. Alliance Meml. Day Parade, 2004, Joyce Kilmer Magna Carta Day, Centennial Day 789 Yrs., 2004. Fellow IEEE (life, ednl. adminstrn. com., solar standards com., photovoltaic subcom.), mem., Am. Phys. Soc., Soc. Motion Picture and TV Engrs., Internat. Fedn. Med. Electronics, AAAS, Electronic Industries Assn. (edn. com.), Am. Ednl. Research Assn., Adult Edn. Assn. U.S.A., N.Y. Acad. Scis., Am. Mgmt. Assn. (ednl. adv. com.), Math. Assn. Am., Am. Soc. Tng. and Devel., Council Ams., Am. Judicature Soc., Am. Math. Soc., Am. Soc. Curriculum Devel., Knight, Order of the Swan, Sigma Xi, Sigma Pi Sigma, Tau Beta Pi. Clubs: Chemists (N.Y.C.); N.Y. Univ., The Midtown Exec. and Chemists' Club, N.Y.C., Toastmasters, Westinghouse SURE Home: Highland Park, NJ. Died Sept. 15, 2009.

BRUEGMAN, DONALD CHARLES, university administrator; b. Cin., Oct. 16, 1935; s. Peter Louis and Stella Mae (Biles) B.; m. Marlene Joy Erhardt; children: Kimberly, Stephanie. BBA, U. Cin., 1958; MS, U. Ill., 1963. Adminstrv. officer U. Cin., 1958-78; sr. v.p. Va. Commonwealth U., Richmond, from 1978. Speaker in field. Contbr. articles to profl. jours. Fundraiser YMCA, 1978—. Mem. Nat. Assn. Coll. and Univ. Bus. Officers, Richmond C. of C., Beta Gamma Sigma. Avocations: golf, jogging. Home: West Palm Beach, Fla. Died Dec. 4, 2009.

BRUNETTE, JOHN S., sales executive; b. Chgo., June 10, 1930; s. William B. and Mary Alice (Nolan) Brunette; m. Patricia Reese Brunette, Jan. 23, 1954; children: Steven, Cynthia, Gregory, Michael, William, Robert. Student, Northwestern U., 1957. Sales engr. Maxon Corp., Muncie, Ind., 1958—68; br. mgr. Detroit, 1968—75; gen. sales mgr. Muncie, 1975—79; v.p., from 1979; dir., Ind. Heating Equipment Assn. 1st lt. USAF, 1950—55, Rep. of Korea. Roman Catholic. Died Jan. 5, 2010.

BRUNNER, VERNON ANTHONY, marketing executive; b. Chgo., Aug. 9, 1940; s. Frank Anthony and Alfrieda (Eslinger) B.; divorced; children: Jack Daniel, Amanda Josephine; m. Sharon Ann Walschon, July 1, 1972; 1 child, Suzanne Marie. BS in Pharmacy, U. Wis., 1963. Registered pharmacist. Mgr. store Walgreen Co., Chgo., 1963-71, dist. mgr. Deerfield, Ill., 1971-75, dir. merchandising, 1975-77, dir. mktg., 1977-78, v.p. mktg., 1978-82, sr. v.p. mktg., 1982-90, exec. v.p. mktg., from 1990. Bd. dirs. Walgreen. Mem. Evans Scholar Alumni Assn. Roman Catholic. Home: Lake Forest, Ill. Died Apr. 1, 2009.

BRUNS, NICOLAUS, JR., retired agricultural products executive, lawyer, educator; b. NYC, Sept. 27, 1926; s. Nicolaus and Emily Marie (Hawkins) B.; m. Joan-Carol Littleton, Aug. 29, 1959; children: Nicolaus III, Gregory. BS, U. Miami, Fla., 1947; JD, Georgetown U., 1949, LL.M., 1952. Bar: D.C. 1950, Ill. 1965, U.S. Supreme Ct. 1965, N.Y. 1980. Spl. asst. U.S. Navy Dept., Washington, 1950-57; sr. trial atty. U.S. Dept. Justice, Washington, 1957-65; sr. atty. Internat. Minerals and Chem. Corp., Skokie, Ill., 1965-70, asst. gen. counsel, 1970-74, gen. counsel ops., 1974-79, v.p., sec., assoc. gen. counsel Northbrook, Ill., 1979-87; sr. v.p., sec., gen. counsel IMC Fertilizer Group Inc., Northbrook, Ill., 1987-90; antitrust policy coun. U.S. C. of C., Washington, 1981-90. Adj. prof. Loyola U., Chgo., 1980-81, Lake Forest Grad. Sch. Mgmt., Ill., 1981—2003; cert. arbitrator Am. Arbitration Assn., Fin. Industry Regulatory Authority, 1990-. Adminstrv. asst. to v.p. Boy Scouts Am., N.E. Ill. area, 1967, 80; pres. Fund for Perceptually Handicapped, Skokie, Ill., 1976, Concerned Help in Learning Devel., Highland Park, Ill., 1974-75. With U.S. Army, 1945-46. Mem. ABA (antitrust and securities com.), Chgo. Bar Assn., Fed. Bar Assn., Am. Soc. Corp. Secs. (bd. dirs. 1985-87, pres. Midwest region 1984), K.C. (past grand knight Washington coun.), Mich. Shore Club (Wilmette, Ill.), Harbour Ridge Club (Stuart, Fla.). Republican. Roman Catholic. Home: Palm City, Fla. Died May 11, 2009.

BRUNSVOLD, JOEL DEAN, retired state legislator; b. Mason City, Iowa, Feb. 26, 1942; s. Burnell Raymond and Esther Agusta (Geilendeld) B.; m. Barbara Louise Bashaw, Feb. 22, 1964; children: Timothy, Theodore. BA, Augustana Coll., 1964; student, Black Hawk Coll./We. Ill. U., 1969-71. Tchr. Sherrard (Ill.) Cmty. Unit # 200, 1969-83; mem. Ill. House of Reps., Rock Island, Ill., 1983—2003; dir. Ill. Dept. Natural Resources, 2003—05. Trustee, Milan, Ill., 1973-77, mayor, 1977-83. Mem. NEA, Ill. Edn. Assn., C. of C., Ducks Unlimited, Pheasants Forever, Phi Omega Phi. Democrat. Lutheran. Avocation: hunting. Home: Milan, Ill. Died Sept. 7, 2010.

BRUNT, MANLY YATES, JR., psychiatrist; b. Winston-Salem, NC, Nov. 7, 1926; s. Manly Yates and Jessie Corina (Evans) Brunt; m. Jacklyn Beatrice Bray, Dec. 2, 1961; children: Diane Strachan, William Bray, Douglas Evans, Kenneth Sherman. MD, Wake Forest U., 1948. Diplomate Am. Bd. Psychiatry and Neurology. Intern Grad. Hosp. U. Pa., 1949—50; exec. med. officer Inst. of Pa. Hosp., Phila., 1952—62, mem. sr. attending staff, 1968—2010; prin. investigator Behavior Rsch. Lab., 1957—61; mem. faculty U. Pa., 1953—68. Pres. Cmty. Nursing Bur. Met. Phila., 1961—64; bd. dirs. Main Line Health Care Group, Inc. Served with M.C. US Army, 1950—52. Mem.: AMA, Wake Forest U. Med. Alumni Assn., Phila. Coll. Physicians and Surgeons, Am. Psychoanalytic Assn., Am. Psychiat. Assn., Alpha Omega Alpha. Republican. Presbyterian. Died Aug. 4, 2010.

BRUTUS, DENNIS VINCENT, African literature, poetry and creative writing educator; b. Harare, Zimbabwe, Nov. 28, 1924; came to U.S., 1971; s. Francis Henry and Margaret Winifred (Bloemetjie) Brutus; m. May Jaggers, May 14, 1950; children: Jacinta, Marc, Julian, Antony, Justina, Cornelia, Gregory, Paula. BA in English, with distinction, U. Ft. Hare, South Africa, 1947; attended, U. Witwaterstrand, Johannesburg; LHD (hon.), Worcester State Coll., Mass., 1982, U. Mass., Amherst, 1984; LLD (hon.), Northeastern U., 1989. Tchr. public high schs., Port Elizabeth, 1948-61; journalist, 1960-61; dir. World Campaign for Release of South African Polit. Prisoners, London; mem. staff Internat. Def. and Aid Fund, London, 1966-71; prof. English Northwestern U., Evanston, Ill., 1971-85; Cornell prof. English lit. Swarthmore Coll., Pa., 1985; prof., chmn. dept. Black community edn. research and devel., prof. African Lit. and Writing U. Pitts., 1986-91. Bd. dirs. Moonstone, Inc.; vis. prof. English U. Denver, 1970; vis. prof. English, and African and Afro-Am. Studies Rsch. Ctr. U. Tex., Austin, 1974-75; vis. prof. Eng. Dept., Amherst Coll., 1982-83; vis. prof. African and African-Am. studies Dartmouth Coll., 1983; program dir. Program on African Writing in Africa and the Diaspora; lectr. Oxford Ctr. for Africa Studies, Internat. Summer Sch., 1990; Interport lectr. U. Pitts.; vis. fellow U. Durban, Westville, South Africa, 1992; Disting. vis. humanist, U. Colo., Boulder, 1992-93. Author: (poetry) Sirens, Knuckles, Boots, 1963, Letters to Martha, 1968, Poems from Algiers, Thoughts Abroad, 1970, A Simple Lust, 1972, Strains, 1975, China Poems, 1975, Stubborn Hope, 1978, Salutes and Censures, 1982, Airs and Tributes, 1989, African edit., 1988, Still the Sirens, 1993; contbr. poems to lit. jours.; mem. editorial bd. Africa Today, 1976—, Transition; guest editor: The Gar, 1978. Sec. S. African Sports Assn.; pres. S. African Non-Racial Olympic Com.; chmn. Internat. Campaign Against Racism in Sport; chmn. adv. bd. ARENA: The Inst. for Study of Sport and Social Analysis, U.S.; patron South African Coun. on Sport; founding mem. Troubadour Press; bd. dirs. So. Africa Media Ctr., African Arts Fund, Coun. Christians and Jews, Whistle-blowers Found.; chmn. Africa Network Recipient Chancellor's prize U. South Africa, 1947, Mbari award CCF, 1963, Freedom Writer's award Soc. Writers and Editors, 1975, Steve Biko award TransAfrica, 1985, First Outstanding Tchr. award Inst. for Policy Studies, 1987, Langston Hughes Medallion award CCNY, 1988, Paul Robeson award, 1989; key City of Sumter S.C., 1979 Fellow Internat. Poetry Soc.; mem. MLA, Union of Writers of African People (Ghana) (v.p., coord.), African Lit. Assn. U.S.A. (founding chmn., exec. com.), Exec. Nat. Writers Union, Congress S. African Writers (patron), Am. Poetry Centre (adv. bd.). Served 18 months as polit. prisoner in Robben Island Prison, South Africa, for opposition to apartheid, 1964-65. Became polit. asylee in U.S., 1983. Died Dec. 26, 2009.

BRUYNES, CEES, manufacturing executive; b. The Netherlands, Aug. 3, 1932; s. Arie and Petronella (Borst) B.; m. Elly Nagel, Feb. 1, 1963; children: Irene W., Jan Paul. Grad., Chr.

Lyceum, Arnhem, Netherlands, 1951. With N.V. Philips' Gloeilampenfabrieken, Netherlands, 1953-71; pres., chief exec. officer Philips Can., 1971-74; exec. v.p. N. Am. Philips Corp., NYC, 1975-78, pres., chief operating officer, from 1978, chief exec. officer, from 1981, chmn., 1985-88; chmn., pres., chief exec. officer Consol. Electronics Industries Corp., Stamford, Conn., from 1988. Served with Dutch Air Force, 1951-53. Mem.: Landmark (Stamford), Sky (N.Y.C.), Netherlands (N.Y.C.), Greenwich (Conn.) Country, Lyford Cay, Round Hill. Home: Greenwich, Conn. Died July 11, 2010.

BRYAN, COURTLANDT DIXON BARNES, author; b. NYC, Apr. 22, 1936; s. Joseph III and Katharine (Barnes) O'Hara; m. Phoebe Miller, Dec. 28, 1961 (div. Sept. 1966); children: J. St. George, Lansing Andolina; m. Judith Snyder, Dec. 21, 1967 (div. July 1978); 1 child, Amanda; m. Monique W. Simonds, Aug. 23, 1990 (dec.); m. Mairi Graham, 2007 Grad., Berkshire Sch., 1954; BA in English, Yale U., 1958. Writer-in-residence Colo. State U., winter 1967; vis. lectr. writers workshop U. Iowa, 1967-69; editor Monocle mag. Spl. cons. editorial matters Yale U., 1970; vis. prof. U. Wyo., 1975; adj. prof. Columbia U., 1976; fiction dir. Writers Community, N.Y.C.; English lectr. U. Va., 1983, Bard Coll., 1984. Author: P.S. Wilkinson, 1965 (Harper prize novel), The Great Dethriffe, 1970, Friendly Fire, 1976, The National Air and Space Museum, 1979, 2d rev. edit., 1988, Beautiful Women; Ugly Scenes, 1983. The National Geographic Society: One Hundred Years of Adventure and Discovery, 1987, 2d updated edit., 1997, Close Encounters of the Fourth Kind: Alien Abductions, UFOs and The Conference at MIT, 1995; also short stories, criticism, articles, polit. satire, introductions; represented anthologies; narration: Swedish film The Face of War, 1963. Served with AUS, 1958-60, 61-62. Fellow Nat. Endowment Arts, 1979, Guggenheim Found., 1986. Mem.: Yale. Home: Guilford, Conn. Died Dec. 15, 2009.

BRYANT, BETTY LOU, nursing educator; b. Parke County, Ind., Sept. 3, 1929; d. Odus A. and Latitia I. (Swaim) Ratcliff; Lic. Practical Nurse, Ivy Tech. Coll., 1972; B.S. Nursing, Ind. State U., 1980, MSN, 1985, postgrad., 1988; m. Bobby L. Bryant, Dec. 7, 1947; children: Taunnie Russell, Greg, Chris. Nurse's aide Ind. State Sanitorium, Rockville, Ind., 1968-70; Lic. Practical Nurse, Vermillion County Hosp., Clinton, Ind., 1972-79; asst. adminstr. Lee Alan Bryant Health Care Facility, Rockville, 1979-80, dir. nursing service, 1980-82; cons. gerontol. program Ind. State U. Sch. Nursing, Terre Haute, 1981-82, continuing edn. cons.-aging, 1981-82, asst. instr. anatomy, physiology, sci. dept. univ., 1979-80. Sec., Women's Soc. Christian Service, 1960-62; brownie leader Boy Scouts Am., 1961-62; leader Meth. Youth Fellowship, 1969-70, ch. camp counselor, 1968-70; precinct com. person Republican party, 1968-72, active Ind. state senator campaign, 1980-81; diabetes screener, 1979. Cert. nurse practitioner Am. Nurses Assn., 1986. Mem. Ind. Assn. Quality Assurance Profls., Central Ill. Soc. Health Edn. and Tng., Ind. State U. Alumni Assn., Ill. Nurses Assn., Ind. U. Alumni, AAUW, Am. Soc. Aging, Mid-Am. Congress on Aging. Died July 29, 2009.

BRYANT, CLIFTON DOW, sociologist, educator; b. Jackson, Miss., Dec. 25, 1932; s. Clifton Edward and Helen (Dow) B.; m. Nancy Ann Arrington, Sept. 13, 1953; m. Patty Maurine Watts, Feb. 1, 1957; children: Melinda Dow, Deborah Carol, Karen Diane, Clifton Dow II. Student, U. Miss., 1950-53, BA, 1956, MA, 1957; postgrad., U. N.C., Chapel Hill, 1957-58, La. State U., 1958-60, PhD, 1964. Vis. instr. dept. sociology and anthropology Pa. State U., summer, 1958; instr., rsch. assoc. dept. sociology and anthropology U. Ga., 1960-63; asst. prof., assoc. prof., chmn. dept. sociology and anthropology Millsaps Coll., Jackson, Miss., 1963-67; summer research participant, tng. and tech. project Oak Ridge Assn. Universities, summer 1967; prof., head dept. sociology and anthropology Western Ky. U., Bowling Green, Ky., 1967-72; prof. sociology Va. Poly. Inst. & State U., Blacksburg, 1972—2007, prof. emeritus, 2007—10, head dept. sociology Blacksburg, 1972-82. Vis. prof. Xavier U., Philippines, 1984-85; vis. prof., vis. rsch. scholar Miss. Alcohol Safety Edn. Program, Miss. State U., (summer), 1985; vis. Fulbright prof. dept. grad. inst. sociology Nat. Taiwan U., Taipei, Republic of China, 1987-88; vis. scientist U.S. Army summer faculty rsch. and engring. program, 1993; participant Fulbright-Hays Seminar Abroad program, Hungary, 1993, China, 1998. Author: Khaki-Collar Crime: Deviant Behavior in Military Context, 1979, Sexual Deviancy and Social Proscription, 1982; editor and contbr.: Deviant Behavior: Occupational and Organizational Bases, 1974, The Social Dimensions of Work, 1972, Sexual Deviancy in Social Context, 1977, Deviant Behavior: Readings in the Sociology of Norm Violations, 1990; editor-in-chief: The Encyclopedia of Criminology and deviant Behavior, 4 vols., 2001, Death and Dying: A Reference Handbook, 2 vols., 2003; co-editor, contbr.: Deviancy and the Family, 1973, The Rural Work Force: Nonagricultural Occupations in America, 1985; compiler: Handbook of Audio-Visual Resources to Accompany Social Problems Today, 1971; editor: Social Problems Today: Dilemmas and Dissensus, 1971; co-editor: Introductory Sociology: Selected Readings for the College Scene, 1970; editor in chief Deviant Behavior: An Interdisciplinary Jour., 1978-91; editor So. Sociologist, 1970-74; mem. editorial bd. Criminology: An Interdisciplinary Jour, 1978-91; chmn. editorial policy bd., founding editor-in-Chief Deviant Behavior: An Interdisciplinary Journal; chmn. editorial bd. Sociol. Symposium, 1968-80; assoc. editor Sociol. Forum, 1979-80, Sociol. Spectrum, 1981-85; mem. bd. adv. editors Sociol. Inquiry, 1981-85, assoc. editor, 1997—; bd. editors Society and Animals; assoc. editor spl. issue Marriage and Family Relations, fall 1982, Sociological Inquiry; contbr. chpts. to books, articles, book reviews to profl. publs. Served to 1st lt., M.P. U.S. Army, 1953-55. Recipient E. Gordon Ericksen Outstanding Grad. Faculty award sociology dept. Va. Poly. Inst. and State U., 1992, 93, spl. award for continuing contbn. to undergrad. tchg. enterprise, 1992, Undergraduate Tchg. Excellence award, 1995-96, 2001. Mem. Am. Sociol. Assn., Am. Soc. Criminology, So. Sociol. Soc. (pres. 1978-79, Disting. Book award 2001), Mid-South Sociol. Assn. (pres. 1981-82, Disting. Career award 1991), Rural Sociol. Soc., Soc. Anthropology of Work, Internat. Sociol. Assn., Inter-Univ. Seminar on Armed Forces and Society, So. Assn. Agr. Scientists, Omicron Delta Kappa, Phi Kappa Phi, Alpha Phi Omega, Alpha Kappa Delta, Pi Kappa Alpha, Phi Beta Delta. Presbyterian. Home: Blacksburg, Va. Died Sept. 13, 2010.

BRZEZINSKI-STEIN, KATHARINE ANNE, psychologist; b. Chgo., May 30, 1947; d. Casimir Frank and Anna Maria (Para) B. BA, So. Ill. U., 1970, MA, 1973; PhD, U. Nebr., 1981. Counselor So. Ill. U., Carbondale, 1972-73; psychologist James Madison U., Harrisonburg, Va., 1973-75, U. Nebr., Lincoln, 1975-85, Metro Employment & Rehab. Svc., St. Louis, 1985-90; program mgr. Ctr. for Cognitive Rehab. CCR, Good Samaritan Hosp., Puyallup, Wash., 1990-91; psychologist Greater Lakes Mental Health Found., Tacoma, Wash., from 1992. Psychologist Auburn and Enumclaw (Wash.) Psychol. Svcs., 1992—. Mem. com. Lincoln Regional Ctr. Human Rights, 1984-85; co-organizer Conf. for the Ministry in Human Sexuality, Lincoln, 1981-82, Fund Raiser for Lincoln Nuclear Freeze, 1984; state chmn. Wheat for Poland Appeal by Crop, Lincoln, 1982. Mem. APA, Am. Bd. Forensic Examiners. Avocations: spanish literature, sailing, swimming, home rehabilitation. Home: Tacoma, Wash. Died Jan. 21, 2009.

BUCCAFUSCO, JERRY JOSEPH, pharmacologist, educator; b. Jersey City, Aug. 20, 1949; s. Dominick A. and Rose N. B.; m. Regina N. Neilan, Dec. 22, 1973; children: Christopher, Martin. BS, St. Peter's Coll., 1971; MS, Canisius Coll., 1973; PhD, U. Medicine & Dentistry N.J., Newark, 1978. Postdoctoral fellow Roche Inst. Molecular Biology, Nutley, N.J., 1977-79; prof. pharmacology and toxicology Med. Coll. Ga., Augusta, from 1979, dir. animal behavioral ctr., Alzheimer's Rsch. Ctr., from 1979; rsch. pharmacologist VA Med. Ctr., Augusta, from 1985. Patentee in field. Mem. Am. Soc. Pharmacology & Exptl. Therapeutics, Soc. Neurosci., Behavioral Tocicology Soc., Sigma Xi. Home: Evans, Ga. Died Mar. 6, 2010.

BUCHANAN, HARRY WINTERS, III, chemical company executive; b. Bklyn., Nov. 9, 1923; s. Harry W. and Eugenie Marie (O'Brien) Buchanan; m. Barbara Combes, Oct. 30, 1951; children: Harry W., Bruce Stewart, Cathleen Joan, Virginia Gail, Brien Combes, Mary Ann. BS, Rensselaer Poly Inst., 1947; postgrad., MIT, 1956. Chem. engr. Metal & Thermit Corp., NYC, 1947—48, sales mgr., 1948—50, chem. sales. mgr., 1950—55, gen. sales mgr., 1955—60, v.p., 1960—61, exec. v.p., 1961—62, dir., 1962—63; group v.p. M & T Chems. Subs of Am. Can. Co., 1962—66; pres. Va. Chems., Inc., Portsmouth, Va., from 1966, CEO, from 1966, chmn. bd., from 1970. V.p. Celanese, from 1981; dir. United Va. Bankshares, Crompton & Knowles, NYC, Norfolk, Franklin & Danville Ry., Roanoke, Va. Bd. mem. assoc. U. Richmond, Va., from 1975; trustee U. Va., Colgate Darden Bus. Sch., from 1976, Va. Found. Ind. Colls., from 1978. With US Army, 1944—46. Mem.: Mfrs. Assn. (dir. 1970 1976, dir. 1980—84), Va. Mfrs. Assn. (chmn. 1976—77), Am. Electroplaters Soc., Am. Chem. Soc., Commonwealth Club, Sky Club, Pinnacle Club, Union League, Augusta Nat. Golf Club. Roman Catholic. Died Aug. 28, 2009.

BUCK, ALEXANDER KNAPP (WHIP BUCK), professional sports team executive; b. 1930; m. Sara Long, 1954; children: Alexander Jr., Norman. Attended, Lafayette Coll. Founder TDH; ltd. ptnr. Phila. Phillies, 1981—2010; cofounder Horizon Found., 1996. Trustee emeritus Medical Ctr. at Princeton. Served in USMC. Died Oct. 24, 2010.

BUCK, ALFRED ANDREAS, physician, epidemiologist; b. Hamburg, Germany, Mar. 9, 1921; came to U.S., 1958, naturalized, 1967; s. Heino C. and Antonie (Schwarz) B.; m. Kay A. Amann, Sept. 15, 1962; children: Suzanne Karen, Alfred Andreas. MD in Pharmacology, U. Hamburg, 1945; MPH, Johns Hopkins U., 1959, DrPH, 1961. Med. resident Univ. Hosp., Hamburg, 1945-52; physician, cons. Gen. Govt. Hosp., Makassar, Celebes, Indonesia, 1952- 55; head physician Red Cross Hosp., Pusan, Korea, 1955-58; mem. faculty Johns Hopkins U., Balt., from 1963, prof. epidemiology and internat. health, 1968-92, prof. immunology and infectious diseases, 1986-92, dir. div. bacteriology and mycology Sch. Hygiene, 1967-72, chmn. tropical medicine council, 1973-74, also research dir., geog. epidemiology group; dep. dir. Vector-Borne Disease Project, Arlington, Va.; adj. prof. immunology and infectious diseases Johns Hopkins U., Balt. Cons. AID, Ethiopia, 1962-64, West and Ctrl. Africa, 1971; mem. sr. staff WHO, Geneva, 1971-73, chief med. officer divsn. malaria and other parasitic diseases, 1974-78, chief rsch. coordination, epidemiology and tng. and sec. sci. working group for epidemiology, spl. program rsch. and tng. in tropical diseases; tropical medicine adv. Office of Health, Dept. State, AID, Washington, 1978-88; adj. prof. internat. health, molecular microbiology and immunology Johns Hopkins U., 1989-2003; adj. prof. tropical medicine Tulane U., 1988-99; vis. prof. Sch. of Medicine Ain Shams U., Cairo; vis. prof. Sch. of Medicine, Hannover, Germany, 1991-97; expert tropical medicine NIH/NIAID; resident scientist, Cairo; mem. Steering Coms. of Sci. Working Groups "Fieldmal" and "Epidemiology" of WHO, Geneva. Author books; contbr. articles in field; asso. editor: Tropenmedizin und Parasitologie. Recipient Meritorious Honor award Dept. State, 1980, Bernhard Nocht medal in tropical medicine, 1981, Meritorious Svc. award USAID, 1985, Superior Unit citation, 1991, AID/Dept. State Meritorious Svc. award, 1986, Spl. award DHHS/NIH, 1991, Donald Mackay medal in tropical medicine jointly Am. Soc. Tropical Medicine and Hygiene and Royal Soc. Tropical Medicine, 1995; hon. fellow in tropical medicine Faculty Liverpool Sch. Tropical Medicine, 1982. Fellow APHA, Am. Coll. Epidemiology; mem. Epidemiol. Rsch. Assn., Am. Soc. Tropical Medicine, Internat. Epidemiologic Soc., Am. Epidemiol. Soc., Tropical Medicine Assn. D.C., Delta Omega. Lutheran. Home: Mc Lean, Va. Died July 14, 2009.

BUCKLAND, CHARLES FRANCIS, forest products company executive; b. NYC, Nov. 3, 1920; s. Charles Richard and Frances (Walsh) B.; m. Doris A. Christensen, June 10, 1950; children: Gary, Deborah. BS in Civil Engring., U. Colo., 1948. Vice-pres. sales Jim Walter Corp., Tampa, Fla., 1964-66; v.p. mktg. Abitibi-Price Corp., Troy, Mich., 1966-72, pres., 1972-85, vice chmn., from 1985; group v.p. Abitibi-Price Inc., Toronto, 1982-85. Maj. USAAF, 1942-46, PTO. Mem.: Birmingham Country (Mich.) (dir. 1982-86). Home: Bloomfield Hills, Mich. Died May 21, 2009.

BUCKLEY, JOHN A., mayor; b. Detroit, Oct. 21, 1933; s. Charles F. and Edith L. B.; m. Helen E. Buckley, May 18, 1957; children: Brian, Patricia, Coleen, Denise, Diane, Patrick. PhB, U. Detroit, 1956; Profl. Designation in Contract Mgmt., Fla. Inst. Technology, 1968. Cert. prof. contract mgr. Nat. Contract Mgmt. Assn., 1975. Tech. writer, proposal coord. Chrysler Missile Divsn., Sterling Twp., Mich., 1956-61, contract coord. Melbourne, Fla., 1961-63; contract tech. mgr. NASA, Kennedy Space Ctr., 1963-94. City councilman City of Melbourne, 1986-96, mayor, 1996—. Recipient Norm Keller Disting. Svc. award Melbourne Jaycees, 1992. Mem. KC (state sec. 1985-86), Space Coast League of Cities (pres. 1994-95), Ancient Order of Hibernians, Elks, Honor Am. (pres. 1998-99), Nat. Space Club. Republican. Roman Catholic. Home: Melbourne, Fla. Died Feb. 19, 2009.

BUCKMAN, WILLIAM H. FISK, sales executive; b. Balt., Feb. 26, 1930; s. Samuel J. and Lena (Sunshine) B.; m. Norma K. Goldman, May 19, 1957; children: Steven, David, Karla. BA, John Hopkins U., Balt., 1951; MBA, Northwestern U., Evanston, Ill., 1962. Salesman Colgate Palmolive Co., Balt., 1951-59; advt. account exec. Lilienfeld & Co., Chgo., 1960-63, Earle Ludgin Co., Chgo., 1963-65, Young & Rubicam, Chgo., 1965-67; advt. exec. Leo Burnett Co., Chgo., 1967-69; pres. W.H. Buckman & Assocs., Inc., Northbrook, Ill., from 1969. Died June 20, 2009.

BUCKNER, KATHRYN TRIMBLE CURRENT, accountant, educator, administrator; b. Chariton, Iowa, June 18, 1926; d. Charles Ralston and Blanche Bernice (Cloe) Trimble; m. James Philip Current, Feb. 14, 1945 (dec. Feb. 1968); 1 child, James Philip; m. Newt M. Buckner, May 29, 1971. Student, Ball State Tchrs. Coll., 1948—49, Ind. U, 1958—59; BBA, Ga. State U., 1961; MBA, 1965, DBA, 1971. CPA Ga. Sec. various firms, Pensacola, Fla., 1943—45, Santa Ana, Calif., 1945—46; acct., office mgr. Thomas J. Marimon Auto Sales & Svc., Valparaiso, Ind., 1950—55, Boney & Mellette Dodge Auto Sales & Svc., Anaheim, Calif., 1955—56, acctg. jr. Woodrow Hulme, CPA, Ardmore, 1957—58, Ralph M. Braswell, CPA, Atlanta, 1956—57, 1959—61; acct., auditor, assoc. William T. Hankins, CPA, Atlanta, 1961—66; asst. prof. acctg. Ga. State U., Atlanta, 1966—74, assoc. prof., 1974—86, prof., 1986—98, emeritus prof., from 1998; dir. Master of Taxation program Sch. Accountancy, 1979—85. Lectr. in field; commr. Internal Revenue Roscoe Egger's Group. Author: Littleton's Contribution to the Theory of Accountancy, 1975; contbr. articles to profl. jours. Recipient Dean's key, Ga. State U., 1960, Faculty Appreciation award, 1975—76. Mem.: Am. Woman's Soc. CPA's Ga. Inc., Nat. Assn. Accts., Ga. Soc. CPA's (Silver Key award 1960, most valuable mem. 1975—76), Am. Woman's Soc. CPA's (nat. pres. 1983—84), Am. Soc. Women Accts. (pres. Atlanta chpt. 1964—65), Am. Inst. CPA's, Am. Acctg. Assn., Am. Acad. Acctg. Historians, Beta Alpha Psi (Appreciation award 1973), Phi Chi Theta (Scholarship Key award 1961), Crimson Key Honor Soc. Home: Palmetto, Ga. Died Mar. 7, 2010.

BUDIN, MORRIS, urban planning and statistics educator, consultant; b. Jersey City, N.J., July 17, 1920; s. Jacob and Bessie (Gordon) B.; m. Clara Ruttenberg, Sept. 25, 1947; children— David, Rachel. B.A., N.Y. U., 1941, M.P.A., 1947; Ph.D., New Sch., N.Y.C., 1954. Instr., Mohawk Coll., Utica, N.Y., 1947-48; assoc. prof. Utica Coll., N.Y., 1948-56; prof. Syracuse U., N.Y., 1956-64, SUNY-Binghamton, 1964—; econ. analyst U.S. Govt., AID, New Delhi, India, 1958-60; Indian Govt., New Delhi, 1962-64; cons. Johnson City Govt., N.Y. Author: (with others) Planning Under Regional Stagnation, 1981. Mem. Am. Assn. Geographers, Am. Econ. Assn., Am. Statistic Assn. Home: Vestal, NY. Died May 26, 2009.

BUECHNER, THOMAS SCHARMAN, artist, museum director, retired glass manufacturing company executive; b. Sept. 25, 1926; s. Thomas Scharman and Anne Evans (Lines) B.; m. Mary C. Hawkins, Sept. 15, 1949; children: Barbara Lines, Thomas Scharman, Matthew. Student, Princeton U., 1945, Ecole des Beaux Arts, Fontainebleau, 1946, Paris, 1947, Arts Students League, NYC, 1946-48, Institut voor Pictologie, Amsterdam, 1947; LittD, Elmira Coll., 2003. Designer Compañía de Fomento, San Juan, 1946; asst. display mgr. Met. Mus. Art, NYC, 1949-51, tchr., 1949-51; dir. Corning Mus. Glass, NY, 1951-60, 75-80, pres. NY, 1971-87; v.p., dir. cultural affairs Corning Glass Works, 1985-87, ret., 1987, cons., 1987—2010; faculty art sch. Bild-Werk, Fravenau, Germany, 1988—2010. Head dept. art Corning Community Coll., 1958-60; bd. dir. Bklyn. Mus.; chmn. Corning Glass Works Found., 1971-87; v.p. Steuben Glass, Corning, 1971-73, pres., 1973-82, chmn., 1982-85. Author: Glass Vessels in Dutch Painting of the 17th Century, 1952, Life and Work of Frederick Carder, 1952, Guide to the Collections of the Corning Museum of Glass, 1955, Guide to the Collections of the Brooklyn Museum, 1967, Norman Rockwell, Artist Illustrator, 1970, Arts of David Levine, 1979, Ogden Pleissner, 1984, How I Paint, 2000, Seeing A Life, 2007; portrait and landscape painter; one-man shows: Adler Gallery, N.Y.C., 1982, 84, Arnot Art Mus., 1985, 95, Heller Gallery, N.Y.c.,

1989, Gallery M, Lindau, Germany, 1989, Gallery Nakama, Tokyo, 1990, 93, 96, O.K. Harris Gallery, N.Y.C., Schloss Weissenstein, Regen, Germany, 1996, Melberg Gallery, Charlotte, N.C., 2002, Principle Gallery, Alexandria, Va., 2002, West End Gallery, Corning, N.Y., 2005; represented in permanent collections Met. Mus. Art, Nat. Mus. Am. Art, Smithsonian Inst., Bklyn. Mus., Lincoln Ctr., Herbert F. Johnson Mus. Cornell U., Musée des Arts Decoratifs, Lausanne, Switzerland, Renwick Mus., Smithsonian, Washington, Corning Mus. of Glass, Corning, N.Y., Elmira Coll. Trustee Tiffany Found., Pilchuck Sch., Corning Mus. Glass, Corning Glass Works Found., Rockwell Mus., Arnot Art Mus. Arts of the Southern Finger Lakes; pres. Rockwell Mus. 1982-87, trustee 1987-2010 Recipient Forsythia award Bklyn. Bot. Garden, 1971, Gari Melchers medal Am. Artist fellows, 1971, Lifetime Achievement Glass Art Soc., 2000. Mem. Bklyn. Inst. Arts and Sci. (trustee 1971-72, pres. 1971-72), Nat. Collection Fine Arts. (commr. 1972-91). Century Assn. Club, Knickerbocker Club, Elmira City Club. Episcopalian. Died June 13, 2010.

BUGGIE, FREDERICK DENMAN, management consultant; b. Toledo, Mar. 27, 1929; s. Horace and Loraine (Denman) B.; m. Betty Jo Chilcote, Sept. 7, 1951 (div. 1988); children: Martha Louise Buggie Kenney, John Chilcote Buggie; m. Debra Hingley, July 15, 1997. BA, Yale U., New Haven, Conn., 1956; MBA, George Washington U., Washington, DC, 1961. Cert. new product devel. profl. Product Devel. and Mgmt. Assn., 1988. Sales engr. Alcoa, Balt. and Phila., 1956-66; pres. Gt. Lakes Rsch. Inst., Erie, Pa., 1967-69; mktg. mgr. Technicon Instruments, Tarrytown, NY, 1969-71; program mgr. Innotech, Norwalk, Conn., 1971-74; pres. Inomation divsn. Van Dyck Corp., Westport, Conn., 1974-76; founder, CEO Strategic Innovations Internat., Inc., Lake Wylie, SC, from 1976. Pres. SII Strategic Innovations A.G., Zurich, Switzerland; founder, chmn. Strategic Innovations Internat. Ltd., Keele, Staffordshire, Eng., Strategic Innovations B.V., Rijswijk, The Netherlands; conf. leader, lectr.; adj. prof. various univs. Author: New Product Development Strategies, 1981; contbr. over 60 articles to trade mags., profl. jours. Pres. Assn. Corp. Growth, NY Chpt., 1979. Security svc. Russian translator USAF, 1950—54. Elected Fellow, Inst. Dirs., London. Mem. Comml. Devel. Mktg. Assn., Soc. Plastics Engrs., Product Devel. and Mgmt. Assn., Yale Club NYC. Avocations: rowing, backgammon. Died Jan. 5, 2009.

BUHROW, WILLIAM CARL, religious organization administrator; b. Cleve., Jan. 18, 1934; s. Philip John and Edith Rose (Leutz) B.; m. Carole Corinne Craven, Feb. 14, 1959; children: William Carl Jr., David Paul, Peter John, Carole Lynn. Diploma, Phila. Coll. Bible, 1954; BA, Wheaton Coll., Ill., 1956, MA, 1959. Ordained to ministry Gen. Assn. Regular Bapt. Chs., 1958. Asst. pastor (Hydewood Park Bapt. Ch.), N. Plainfield, NJ, 1959-63; with Continental Fed. Savs. & Loan Assn., Cleve., 1963-81, sr. v.p., 1971-75, pres., chief exec. officer, dir., 1975-81; chmn. bd. Security Savs. Mortgage Corp., Citizens Service Corp., New Market Corp., CFS Service Corp., 1975-81; trustee Credit Bur. Cleve., 1975-81, Bldg. Expositions, Inc., 1974-84; registered rep. IDS/Am. Express, Cleve., 1982-83; gen. credit mgr. Forest City Enterprises, Inc., Cleve., 1983-85; pres. Forest City Ins. Agy., Inc., Cleve., 1983-85; asst. v.p. Mellon Fin. Services Corp., Cleve., 1985-87; exec. adminstr. The Gospel Ho. Ch. and Evangelistic Ctr., Walton Hills, Ohio, from 1988. Trustee Bapt. Bible Coll. and Theol. Sem., Clarks Summit, Pa., 1977-90; vice chmn. bd. deacons Cedar Hill Bapt. Ch., Cleveland Heights, Ohio, 1981-87; trustee, sec. and treas. Gospel House Prison Ministry Found., 1992—. Mem. Christian Bus. Men's Com. Internat., Nat. Assn. Ch. Bus. Adminstrn. Baptist. Home: Lyndhurst, Ohio. Died May 4, 2010.

BULL, RICHARD SUTTON, JR., retired paper company executive, lawyer; b. Chgo., Jan. 21, 1926; s. Richard Sutton and Sara Rozet (Smith) B.; m. Lois Karna Werme, July 19, 1950; children: Lois Karna Bull Bouton, Sara Annette Bull Swiatlowski, Richard Sutton, Harry Calvin, Mary Ellen Frantz. BA, Yale U., 1948, JD, 1951; LLM, NYU, 1952. Bar: Ill. 1953, U.S. Supreme Ct. 1963. Instr. econs. Stone Coll., New Haven, 1950-51; atty. Swift & Co., 1952-57, Bradner Cen. Co., Chgo., 1957-91, pres., 1965-66, chmn. bd., chief exec. officer, 1966-91. Assoc. Northwestern U.; treas., bd. dirs. Clearview Farms; bd. dirs. Security Chgo. Corp., First Security Bank, Chgo. Mem. USS Abraham Lincoln Commissioning Com.; bd. dir. Civic and Arts Found., vice chmn., 1978--; v.p., bd. dirs. Chgo. Crime Commn., 1983--; bd. dirs. Met. Chgo. Air Force Community Coun.; mem. Coll. DuPage Adv. Coun.; mem. Exec. Svc. Corps.; deacon, elder Presby. Ch. With USNR, 1944-46. John Robinson fellow Food and Drug Inst. NYU, 1951-52. Mem. Chgo. Bar Assn., Chgo. Assn. Commerce and Industry (dir. 1973-87, gen. sec. 1980-81), Am. Arbitration Assn. (nat. panel arbitrators 1968—), Pres.'s Assn., Graphic Arts and Paper Assn. (pres. 1968-69), Edward Moss Martin Soc. (past pres.), Yale Club, Union League Chgo. (bd. dirs. 1980-83, sec. 1985-87), Chgo. Club, Econ. Club, Ruth Lake Country Club,. Khyble Bay Yacht Club (past commodore 1972-73, bd. govs. 1970—, Round Lake, Wis.). Home: Hinsdale, Ill. Died May 14, 2009.

BULLARD, TODD HUPP, political science researcher; b. Wheeling, W.Va., May 31, 1931; s. Luther Todd and Virginia (Netting) B.; m. Ella J. Rickey, June 6, 1953; children: Todd Whittam, Katharine Ann, Alice Elizabeth, Janice Louise, James Hupp. Student, Bethany Coll., W.Va., 1949-50; BA, W.Liberty State Coll., W.Va., 1953; MA, W.Va. U., 1956; PhD, U. Pitts., 1964. Dir. edn. W.Va. State Penitentiary, Moundsville, 1953; research asst. Bur. Govt. Research, W.Va. U., 1956- 57; asst. dir. W.Va. League Municipalities, 1956-57; asst. prof. polit. sci., dir. Falk program practical politics Bethany Coll., 1959-60; sr. research analyst Bur. Govt. Research, W.Va. U., 1960-61, dir. Parkersburg br., 1961-63; acad. dean Potomac State Coll. of univ., Keyser, 1963-64, pres., 1964-70; provost, v.p. acad. affairs Rochester (N.Y.) Inst. Tech., 1970-80; pres., prof. polit. sci. Bethany (W.Va.) Coll., 1980-88; scholar in residence Ctr. for Pub. Service U. Va., Charlottesville, from 1988. With north central, middle states and so. regional accrediting bodies; participant state studies of higher edn.; dir. Wheeling Dollar Bank, also health ins. cos. Author: (with E. R. Elkins) Manual of West Virgina Municipal Goverment, 1957, Labor and The Legislature, 1965; Contbr. articles to profl. jours. Bd. dirs. Boy Scouts Am., various community orgns. Mem. Am. Polit. Sci. Assn., W.Va. Assn. Coll. and Univ. Pres., Pi Sigma Alpha. Home: Charlottesville, Va. Died Jan. 1, 2009.

BUNDY, HOWARD, elementary school principal, language arts supervisor; b. Dix, Ill., Sept. 24, 1913; s. Raleigh Oran and Retha Pearl (Sanders); m. Frances 'Arlene Petrea, July 18, 1939; children: Michael, Vicky. BS, So. Ill. U., 1947, MS, 1964, U. Ill., 1949. Tchr. elem. rural one-room sch., Ill., 1934—38; prin., tchr. two-room sch. Walnut Hill, Ill., 1938—40, Centralia, Ill., 1940—43; prin. Centralia Elem. Sch., 1944—74; lang. arts supr., 1965—74; instr. McKendree Coll., Lebanon, Ill., 1952—62. Co-author: (book) History of Education in Centralia, 1949. Chmn. Marion County Draft Bd., Centralia, 1945, Kaskaskia Reading Coun. Organizer, 1960; co-chmn. community devel. program Centralia, 1962; chmn. Marion County Welfare Com., 1983. Named Outstanding Educator of So. Ill. U., 1963. Mem.: Phi Delta Kappa, Marion County Ret. Tchrs., Painters Union, Am. Legion, Ill. Ret. Tchrs. Assn. (life), Greenview Golf, Optimists. Republican. Elder 1st Christian Ch. Home: Centralia, Ill. Died Nov. 8, 2009.

BUNN, JOE MILLARD, retired agricultural engineering educator; b. Wayne County, NC, Jan. 20, 1932; s. Clarence S. and Zora S. (Woodall) B.; m. F. Marie Baker, June 26, 1955; children: Ronnie Joe, Kenneth Bruce. BS in Agrl. Engring., N.C. State Coll., 1955, MS in Agrl. Engring., 1957; PhD in Agrl. Engring. and Math., Iowa State U., 1960. Registered agrl. engr., Ky. 1963. From asst. prof. to assoc. prof. U. Ky., Lexington, 1960-78; engr. AID-Ky. Team, Khon Kean, Thailand, 1968-70; prof. Clemson (S.C.) U., 1978-97, chair agrl. and biol. engring. dept., 1995-97; ret., 1997. Contbr. tech. papers and chpts. in books in field. Mem. Meth. Ch. (Sunday sch. tchr. and bd. deacons), Lexington, Ky., 1965-78., Presbyn. Ch. (Sunday sch. tchr. and elder), Sandy Springs, S.C., 1979—. Grantee various pub. and pvt. agys. $1.5m for rsch. Fellow Am. Soc. Agrl. Engrs. (sec., vice chmn. various nat. state coms.); mem. Coun. Agr. Scis. Tech. Democrat. Presbyterian. Avocations: gardening, bowling. Home: Anderson, SC. Died Feb. 13, 2009.

BURBIDGE, GEOFFREY RONALD, astrophysicist, educator; b. Chipping Norton, Oxon, Eng., Sept. 24, 1925; s. Leslie and Eveline Burbidge; m. Margaret Peachey, 1948; 1 child, Sarah B.Sc. with spl. honors in Physics, Bristol U., 1946; PhD, U. Coll., London, 1951. Asst. lectr. U. Coll., London, 1950-51; Agassiz fellow Harvard, 1951-52; research fellow U. Chgo., 1952-53, Cavendish Lab., Cambridge, Eng., 1953-55; Carnegie fellow Mt. Wilson and Palomar Obs., Calif. Inst. Tech., 1955-57; asst. prof. dept. astronomy U. Chgo., 1957-58, assoc. prof., 1958-62, U. Calif. San Diego, La Jolla, 1962-63, prof. physics, 1963—83, 1988—2002; dir. Kitt Peak Nat. Observatory, Tucson, 1978-84. Phillips vis. prof. Harvard U., 1968; bd. dirs. Associated Univs. Research in Astronomy, 1971-74; trustee Associated Univs., Inc., 1973-82 Author: (with Margaret Burbidge) Quasi-Stellar Objects, 1967, (with F. Hoyle and J. Narlikar) A Different Approach to Cosmology, 2000; editor Ann. Rev. Astronomy and Astrophysics, 1973-2004; sci. editor Astrophys. Jour., 1996-02; contbr. articles to sci. jours. Recipient Jansky prize, Nat. Radio Astronomy Observatory, 1985, Vainu Bappu Meml award, Indian Nat. Acad. Sci., 1989, NAS award for Scientific Reviewing, 2007. Fellow Royal Soc. London, American Acad. Arts and Scis., Royal Astron. Soc. (recipient Gold medal 2005), American Phys. Soc., AAAS; mem. American Astron. Soc.(recipient Helen Warner prize, 1959), Internat. Astron. Union, Astron. Soc. Pacific (pres. 1974-76, Bruce medal 1999). Died Jan. 26, 2010.

BURCHMAN, LEONARD, retired federal official; b. NYC, Jan. 30, 1925; s. Hyman John-Hood and Edith (Speededy-Cohen) B.; m. Marilyn F. Burchman, June 11, 1950; children: Marc Harris, Corey Andrew BA, U. Denver, 1949; MA, Columbia U., 1950. Dir. press affairs N.Y. State Eisenhower presdl. campaign, 1951-52; info. officer-advance sec. labor US Dept. Labor, Washington and NYC, 1953-60, dir. integovtl. rels. Washington, 1971-78; pres. Medigard Chem. Corp., NYC, 1961; acting asst. sec., gen. sr. asst. sect. pub. affairs US Dept. Housing & Urban Devel. (HUD), Washington. Dir. labor rels. to U.S. Senator Kenneth Keating, N.Y., 1964; pub. affairs cons. to Gov. John Lodge of Conn., 1952; sr. advisor to Coretta Scott King; chmn. Martin Luther King Jr. Fed. Holiday Commn., 1985—, commr., 1989—, treas., 1989-92. Producer Office Mgmt. Budget/Nat. Sci. Found. film: Strengthening Intergovernmental Relations between Federal and State and Local Governments, 1976; journalist, creator (newspaper column) Scam Alert. Chmn. bd. Am. Heart Assn., Washington, 1981-83; pres. Found. for Study U.S. Cabinet, 1985-89; pres. J.R.L.W., Leisure World, Md., 1994-96; chmn. Found. to Interrupt Illegal Narcotics and Drugs To Children, 1989-2010; founding pres. Voice of the Elderly vote, 1997-2010, Hosp. Infusion Ctrs., US and Can., 2008-10; founder nat. Consumer Watch-Out, to protect sr. citizens against Scams and Frauds, 1988-2010; mem. Montgomery County (Md.) Commn. on Aging, 1997-2004, States Attys. Task Force on Elder Abuse, Md., 1997-2010 Recipient Disting. Svc. award Sec. US Dept. Housing & Urban Devel. (HUD). Mem.: DAV (life), Am. Legion (comdr. U.S. Dept. Labor Post). Died Mar. 28, 2010.

BURDETTE, BROOKS R., lawyer; b. Ga., Oct. 6, 1961; BA summa cum laude, Wofford Coll., SC, 1983; JD cum laude, Harvard Law Sch., 1986. Bar: NY 1987, registered: US Dist. Ct. (So. Dist.) NY 1987. Atty. Cravath, Swaine & Moore LLP, NYC; ptnr., pro bono dept. Schulte Roth & Zabel LLP, NYC. Dir. Harvard Legis. Rsch. Bur., 1985—86. Contbr. articles to profl. jour. Pres. Truman Scholars Assn.; v.p. Brainstorm Afterschool Inc.; trustee Harvard Law Sch. Alumni Assn., NYC. Harry Truman Scholar, Presdl. Scholar. Mem.: Fed. Bar Coun. (second cir. courts com.), NY County Lawyers Assn. (judiciary com.), ABA (co-chmn. trial evidence com.). Died May 13, 2009.

BURDINE, JOHN A., retired hospital administrator; b. Austin, Tex., Feb. 7, 1936; married; 3 children. BA, U. Tex., 1959; MD, U. Tex., Galveston, 1961. Diplomate Am. Be. Nuclear Medicine (orgnl. exam. com. 1971, chmn. certifyng exam. com. 1980-81, 81-82, editorial bd. Jour. Nuclear Medicine, 1973-81). Intern Med. Ctr. Ind. U., 1961-62; resident nuclear medicine, internal medicine U. Tex., Galveston, 1962-65; active med. staff St. Luke's Episcopal Hosp.-Tex. Children's Hosp., Houston, 1969-90; chief nuclear medicine svc. St. Luke's Episcopal Hosp.-Tex. Children's Hosp., Tex. Heart Inst., Houston, 1969-85; CEO, head adminstr. St. Luke's Episcopal Hosp., Houston, 1984-87, pres., chief exec. officer, 1986-91, vice chmn., CEO, bd. dirs., 1991-94, cons., 1995—2010. Asst. prof. dept. radiology Baylor Coll. Medicine, 1965-68, acting chmn. dept. radiology, 1968-71, chief nuclear medicine dept., 1965-95, assoc. prof. dept. radiology, 1968-74, prof. dept. radiology, 1974-2010, acting dir. sect. nuclear medicine dept. medicine, 1979-80, prof. dept. medicine, 1979-2010, mem. exec. faculty com., 1968-71, mem. com. human experimentation, 1969-71, chmn. radiosotope com., 1970-74, mem., 1966-82, other coms.; sec. Tex. Radiation Adv. Bd., 1981-86, exec. com., 1982-86, med. com., 1982-86, radioactive waste com., 1982-86, fee rules com., 1982-83; chmn. radioisotope com. Meth. Hosp., 1979-80, active med. staff, 1979-84, courtesy med. staff, acting med. dir. radioisotope lab., 1979-80; chief nuclear medicine sect. Harris County Hosp. Dist., 1965-83; mem. forward planning com. Tex. Med. Ctr.; trustee Tex. Heart Inst. Editorial bd. Cardiovascular Disease, 1974; contbr. book chpts., abstracts, papers. Bd. dirs. Houston Symphony Orch., 1987-88. Fellow Am. Coll. Nuclear Physicians (orgn. com. 1973-74, chmn. radioassay & radiopharmacy com. 1975-76, DOE speaker's bur. 1981-85), mem. AMA (rep. coun. nuclear medicine 1976-77), AAUP, Harris County Med. Assn., Tex. Med. Assn. (vice chmn. com. nuclear medicine 1968-71, chmn. 1971-78, others), Tex. Assn. Physicians in Nuclear Medicine, Soc. Nuclear Medicine (pres. 1982-83, southwestern chpt. trustee 1972-80, mem. numerous coms.), Phi Beta Kappa, Phi Eta Sigma, Alpha Epsilon Delta. Home: Houston, Tex. Died Apr. 12, 2010.

BURGESS, FRANKLIN DOUGLAS, retired federal judge; b. Eudora, Ark., Mar. 9, 1935; m. Treava Annette Whitted. BS in Engring., Gonzaga U., 1961, JD, 1966. Asst. city atty. City of Tacoma (Wash.), 1967-69; judge pro tem Mcpl. Ct. and Pierce County Dist. Ct., 1971-80; ptnr. Tanner & Burgess, Tacoma, 1971-76, Tanner, McGavick, Felker, Fleming, Burgess & Lazares, Tacoma, 1976-79, McGavick, Burgess, Heller & Foister, Tacoma, 1979-80; regional counsel US Dept. Housing & Urban Devel., Seattle, 1980-81; magistrate judge US Dist. Ct. (we. dist.) Wash., Tacoma, 1981—93, judge, 1994—2005, sr. judge, 2005—07. Resource person annual Nat. Black History Mo., Shiloh Bapt. Ch.; mem. Tacoma Urban League. Named NCAA All American, 1961, Gonzaga U. Hall of Fame Basketball, 1989. Mem. Wash. State Bar Assn., Pierce County Bar Assn., Loren Miller Bar Assn., Nat. Conf. U.S. Magistrate Judges, NAACP. Died Mar. 26, 2010.

BURKE, JOHN F(RANCIS), health care administrator; b. Bklyn., Dec. 10, 1942; s. Francis J. and Mary E. (Knight) B.; m. Geraldine Manning, Sept. 12, 1964; children: Timothy, Brendan, Sheila. BS, Siena Coll., Loudonville, NY, 1962; MPA, N.Y. State U., 1972; PhD, Clayton U., St. Louis, 1986. Cert. mental health adminstr.; cert. quality assurance profl. Systems analyst N.Y. State Dept. Health, Albany, 1968-72; accreditation specialist N.Y. State Office Mental Health, Albany, 1972-80; dir. quality assurance Capitol Dist. Psychiat. Ctr., Albany, 1980-86, adminstrv. dir., 1986-90, dep. dir., 1990-92; program dir. N.Y. State Office Mental Health, Albany, from 1992. Surveyor Joint Commn., Chgo., 1978—; spkr. workshops on mental health adminstrn., N.Y.C., Chgo., L.A., Houston, Miami, Phila., 1986-94. Contbr. articles to profl. jours. Maj. U.S. Army, 1964-68. Decorated Bronze Star medal, Meritorious Svc. medal, Army Commendation medal. Mem. Res. Officers Assn., Am. Legion, Nat. Assn. Mental Health Adminstrs. (treas. N.Y. State chpt. 1990-94, pres. 1994-96, Chpt. of Yr. award 1994-95), Nat. Assn. Quality Assurance Profls. Democrat. Roman Catholic. Avocations: skiing, sailing, golf. Home: Melbourne, Fla. Died Jan. 29, 2009.

BURKE, KEVIN T., film production company executive; b. Milw., Jan. 16, 1958; s. Walter J. and Aleatha (Luff) B. AA, Golden West Coll., 1979. Intern U.S. Senate Recording Studio, Washington, 1976; jr. engring. mgr. Rogers Cablesystem, Huntington Beach, Calif., 1980-81; dir. tech. services Karl/Lorimar Home Video, Costa Mesa, Calif., 1981-86, contract dir., producer, 1986-87; facilities mgr. Unreel Prodns., Costa Mesa, from 1987. Advisor CMX Editors Adv. Panel, Santa Clara, Calif., 1986-87. Dir., editor (home video) Exercise Shorts, 1986, The Jack LaLanne Way, 1985 (ranked 1st 1985); asst. producer The Jane Fonda Workout, 1985 (ranked 1st), Everyday With Richard Simmons, 1986. Dir. editor Hart Campaign, Calif., 1984. Recipient 2 Certs. Achievement, CMX Corp., 1986, Cert. Achievement, Ampex Corp., 1986. Mem. Internat. TV Assn. Democrat. Roman Catholic. Avocations: playing games, sailing, running. Home: Huntington Beach, Calif. Died Jan. 1, 2009.

BURKE, SOLOMON, singer, songwriter; b. Phila., Pa., Mar. 21, 1940; 21 children. Singer: (albums) Solomon Burke, 1962, Rock N Soul, 1962, I Wish I Knew, 1968, King Solomon, 1968, Proud Mary, 1969, Electronic Magnetism, 1972, King Heavy, 1972, I Have a Dream, 1974, Back to my Roots, 1975, Music to Make Love By, 1975, Lord We Need a Miracle, 1979, Sidewalks, Fences & Walls, 1979, Soul Alive!, 1985, A Change is Gonna Come, 1986, Homeland, 1990, Soul of the Blues, 1993, The Definition of Soul, 1997, We Need a Miracle, 1998, Soulman, 2002, Don't Give Up on Me, 2002 (Best Contemporary Blues Album, Grammy Awards, 2003), Make Do with What You Got, 2005, Nashville, 2006, Like a Fire, 2008, Nothing's Impossible, 2010, Hold On Tight, 2010, (songs) Cry To Me, 1962, Down in the Valley, 1962, Everybody Needs Somebody to Love, 1964. Named to The Rock and Roll Hall of Fame, 2001. Died Oct. 10, 2010.

BURKEY, LEE MELVILLE, SR., lawyer; b. Beach, ND, Mar. 21, 1914; s. Levi Melville and Mina Lou (Horner) B.; m. Lorraine Lillian Burghardt, June 11, 1938; 1 child, Lee Melville, III BA, U. Ill., 1936, MA, 1938; JD with honor, John Marshall Law Sch., 1943. Bar: Ill., 1944, U.S. Dist. Ct., 1947, U.S. Ct. Appeals, 1954, U.S. Supreme Ct.; 1983; cert. secondary tchr., Ill. Tchr. Princeton Twp. High Sch., Princeton, Ill., 1937-38, Thornton Twp. High Sch., Harvey, Ill., 1938-43; atty. Office of Solicitor, U.S. Dept. Labor, Chgo., 1944-51; ptnr. Asher, Gubbins & Segall and successor firms, Chgo., 1951-94; of counsel, from 1995. Lectr. bus. law Roosvelt Coll., Chgo., 1949—52. Contbr. numerous articles on lie detector evidence. Trustee, Village of La Grange, Ill., 1962-68, mayor, 1968-73, village atty., 1973-87; commr., pres. Northeastern Ill. Planning Commn., Chgo., 1969-73; mem. bd. dirs. United Ch. Christ, Bd. of Homeland Ministries, 1981-87; mem. exec. com. Cook County Coun. Govts., 1968-70; life mem. La Grange Area Hist. Soc.; bd. dirs. Better Bus. Bur. Met. Chgo., Inc., 1975-82, Plymouth Place, Inc., 1973-82; Brevet 2nd Lt. Ill. Nat. Guard, 1932. Recipient Disting. Alumnus award John Marshall Law Sch., 1973, Meritorious Svc. award Am. Legion Post 1941, 1974, Honor award LaGrange Area Hist. Soc., 1987. Fellow: Coll. Labor and Employment Lawyers. (charter); mem.: SAR (state pres. 1977, Good citizenship medal 1973, Patriot medal 1977), ABA (coun. sect. labor and employment law 1982—86, governance officer 1986—96), Chgo. Bar Assn., Ill. Bar Assn. (sr. counsellor 1994), United Empire Loyalists Assn. Can., La Grange Country Club, Masons, Order John Marshall. Mem. First Congl. Ch. Home: Brookfield, Ill. Died Oct. 16, 2009.

BURKHARDT, DOLORES ANN, library consultant; b. July 28, 1932; d. Frederick Christian and Emily (Detels) Burkhardt. BA, U. Conn., 1955; MS, So. Conn. State Coll., 1960; postgrad., Cen. Wash. State Coll., 1962, Columbia, from 1964; 6th yr. diploma, U. Conn., 1972. Asst. librarian So. Conn. State Coll. Libr., summers 1960,62; sch. libr. tchr. Farmington High Sch., Unionville, Conn., 1955-65; libr. cons., media specialist East Farms Sch., Farmington, Conn., 1967-70; sch. libr. coord. K-12 Durham-Middlefield, Conn., 1970-72; media specialist Regional Dist. 10, Burlington-Harwinton, Conn., 1972-78, ednl. media cons., from 1978. Instr. Boston U. Media Inst.; spl. cons. Conn. Dept. Edn., from 1965. Mem.: NEA, AAUW (sec. 1956—58), New Eng. Sch. Devel. Coun., Am. Assn. Sch. Librarians, Conn. Sch. Libr. Assn. (2d v.p. from 1965, chmn. standards com. 1970—72, chmn. sch. libr. devel., chmn., instructional materials selection policy com. Region 10), New Eng. Sch. Libr. Assn. (pres. 1969—70), Conn. Edn. Assn., Phi Delta Kappa. Lutheran. Died Jan. 6, 2009.

BURLING, WILLIAM JOHN, literature educator; b. Ladysmith, Wis., Jan. 27, 1949; s. Wesley and Patricia Burling; m. Brenda Jean Gunnes, Dec. 20, 1968 (div. Mar. 1, 1976); m. Debra Kay Drake, July 11, 1980; children: Amanda Nicole, Andrew Wayne. BS in Psychology, U. Wis., Eau Claire, 1972, MA in English, 1974; PhD, Pa. State U., 1985. Asst. prof. English Auburn (Ala.) U., 1985—89; prof. English S.W. Mo. State U., Springfield, from 1989. Author: The Colonial American Stage 1665-1774: A Documentary Calendar, Summer Theatre in London 1661-1820, and the Rise of the Haymarket Theatre, A Checklist of New Plays and Entertainments on the London Stage, 1700-1737; editor: The Plays of Colley Cibber. Mem.: Midwestern Am Soc. 18th Century Studies (pres. 2002), Springfield Astron. Soc. (pres. 2000—03). Home: Springfield, Mo. Died Mar. 7, 2009.

BURNETT, ANNICE JOHNSON, excavating company executive; b. Knoxville, Tenn., Jan. 8, 1924; d. Meno and May Elizabeth (Patty) Johnson; m. John Cecil Burnett, Sept. 5, 1950 (dec. May 1973); children— Capitola, Konda V., Karla J. Student pub. schs., Knoxville. Pres., Jay Burnett Co., Inc. Democrat. Baptist. Avocations: U. Tenn. football fan; traveling; bowling; camping; gardening. Home: Knoxville, Tenn. Died May 19, 2010.

BURNETT, JAMES EUGENE, JR., retired federal agency administrator; b. Little Rock, Sept. 20, 1947; s. James Eugene & Hazel (Baker) Burnett BA, JD, U. Ark. Bar: Ark. Ptnr. Burnett and Stripling, Clinton, Ark., 1973—2010; judge Van Buren County (Ark.) Juvenile Ct., 1973-79, City of Damascus, Ark., 1979-81; mem. Nat. Transp. Safety Bd. (NTSB), Washington, 1981—91, chmn., 1982—88. Spl. assoc. justice Supreme Ct. Ark. Named to The Space Tech. Hall of Fame, 1996. Mem. ABA, Ark. Bar Assn., Nat. Conf. Spl. Ct. Judges Republican. Died May 15, 2010.

BURNHAM, BRYSON PAINE, retired lawyer; b. Chgo., Oct. 11, 1917; s. Raymond and Patti (Paine) Burnham; m. Frances Katherine Burns, Feb. 8, 1941 (dec. Apr. 10, 2009); children: Janice Young, Stephanie Paine. BA, U. Chgo., 1938, JD, 1940. Bar: Ill. 1940, Colo. 1983. From assoc. to ptnr. Mayer, Brown & Platt, Chgo., 1940-83; of counsel Shand, McLachlan and Newbold, Durango, Colo., 1985-93; ret., 1993. Bd. dirs. Ft. Lewis Coll. Found., 1986—2002. Home: Durango, Colo. Died June 3, 2009.

BURNS, ALAN RAYMOND, operatic stage director; b. NYC, Apr. 27, 1936; s. Ward Raymond and Dorothy (Schwinzer) B.; m. Winifred Jenckes, Mar. 9, 1969; children: Vanessa, Raymond. Student, Adelphi Coll., 1955-57. 2nd asst. dir. MGM, Warner Bros., Columbia, United Artists, LA, 1969-84; adminstr. producers tng. program Dirs. Guild Am., NYC, 1978-83; prodn. asst. MGM, NYC, 1960-68; dir. Spottlo Opera, Seattle, 1970, Opera Theatre of N.J., Newark, from 1972. Mem. Dirs. Guild Am. Republican. Roman Catholic. Home: Hempstead, NY. Died Apr. 11, 2009.

BURRELL, CRAIG DONALD, physician, educator; b. Gravesend, Kent, Eng., July 5, 1926; came to U.S., 1960, naturalized, 1968; m. Mary Elizabeth Granger, 1960; children: Catherine, Sarah, Craig, Walter, David. MB, B of Surgery, U. N.Z., 1951; DSc (hon.), Ricker Coll., 1975; LLD (hon.), Union Coll., 1975. Rotating intern Wellington (N.Z.) Hosp., 1951-52; locum sr. house officer pediatrics Nottingham (Eng.) Children's Hosp., 1953; house physician gen. medicine and endocrinology Hammersmith Hosp. and Royal Postgrad. Med. Sch. Gt. Britain, London, 1954, sr. house officer endocrinology, 1954-56; registrar gen. medicine Royal Infirmary and Welsh Nat. Sch. Medicine, Cardiff, Wales, 1957-60; asst. prof. medicine and medicine in psychiatry Cornell U. Med. Sch., 1960-61; dir. clin. labs. Payne Whitney Psychiat. Clinic, 1960-61; with Sandoz Pharms., Inc., East Hanover, N.J., 1961-72, v.p. med. affairs, 1969-72; v.p., dir. external affairs Sandoz, Inc., East Hanover, 1973-85, Sandoz Corp., NYC, 1985-93. Asst. attending physician Cornell 2d Div., Bellevue Hosp., 1966-68; clin. asso. prof. medicine Coll. Medicine and Dentistry N.J., Newark, 1968—; clin. prof. dept. internat. health U. Calif.-San Diego Sch. Medicine, 1982—; participant numerous internat. profl. confs.; mem. tech. com. White House Conf. on Aging, 1980-81 Mem. editorial bd.: Internat Jour. of Addictions; editor: Drug Assessment in Ferment, 1976, Primary Health Care in Industrialized Nations, 1978, Second Colloquium in Biol. Scis., 1986, Medical Journalism, 1987; contbr. articles to profl. jours. V.p. mgr. Sandoz Found., 1967-93; vice chair Sandoz Found for Gerontological Rsch., 1990—; trustee Union Coll. of Ky.; bd. regents St. Peter's Coll., N.J. Fellow Am. Sch. Health Assn. (hon.), N.Y. Acad. Scis. (pres. 1984), Royal Soc. Medicine, Am. Sch. Health Assn. (hon.); mem. AMA, AAAS, Am. Coll. Clin. Pharmacology and Therapeutics, Endocrine Soc., European Soc. for Study Drug Toxicity, Sierra Club. Presbyterian (elder). Home: Shrewsbury, NJ. Died Nov. 20, 2009.

BURRELL, RICHARD LEE, footware company executive; b. Union City, Ohio, Feb. 19, 1933; s. Richard W. and Lola (Brierly) Burrell; m. Gretchen Haber, Aug. 12, 1954; children: Richard L., Paula K., Susan, Julie. BS, Miami U., Oxford, Ohio, 1955; MBA, Xavier U., 1965. With R.G. Barry Corp., Pickerington, Ohio, from 1966, v.p. fin., treas., sec., dir., from 1976. Dir. Lord, Sullivan, Yoder, Worthing, Ohio ZeeMed Svcs. Inc., Hilliard, Ohio. Cpl. US Army, 1955—57. Mem.: Fin. Execs. Inst. Lutheran. Home: Columbus, Ohio. Died Mar. 27, 2009.

BURRELL, VICTOR GREGORY, JR., marine scientist; b. Wilmington, NC, Sept. 12, 1925; s. Victor Gregory and Agnes Mildred (Townsend) B.; m. Katherine Stackley; Jan. 7, 1956; children: Cheri, Cathey, Charlene, Sarah. BS, Coll. Charleston, 1949; MA, Coll. William and Mary, 1968, PhD, 1972. Rsch. assoc. Va. Inst. Marine Sci., Gloucester Point, 1966-68, asst. marine scientist, 1968-70, assoc. marine scientist, 1970-72, S.C. Marine Resources Rsch. Inst., Charleston, 1972-73, assoc. marine scientist, asst. dir., 1973-74, sr. marine scientist, dir., 1974-91, dir. emeritus, from 1991. Contbr. numerous articles to profl. jours. With USN, 1943-46, PTO. Mem. Nat. Shell Fisheries Assn. (pres. 1982-83, hon. life mem. 1992), Estuarine Rsch. Fedn. (sec. 1975-77), Gulf and Caribbean Fisheries Inst., Southeastern Estuarine Rsch. Soc. (pres. 1986-88, hon. mem. 1990). Episcopalian. Died Dec. 20, 2009.

BURRIS, ROBERT HARZA, biochemist, educator; b. Brookings, SD, Apr. 13, 1914; s. Edward T. and Mabel T. (Harza) Burris; m. Katherine Irene Brusse, Sept. 12, 1945; children: Jean Carol, John Edward, Ellen Louise. BS, S.D. State Coll., 1936, D.Sc., 1966; MS, U. Wis., 1938, PhD, 1940. NRC fellow Columbia U., 1940—41; faculty U. Wis., Madison, from 1941, prof., 1951—84; chmn. biochemistry Coll. Agr., 1958—70, W.H. Peterson prof. biochemistry, 1976—84, prof. emeritus, 1984—2010. Recipient Charles Thom award, Soc. Indsl. Microbiology, 1977, Nat. Medal of Sci., 1980, Carty award, NAS, 1984, Wolf award in Agrl., Wolf Found., Israel, 1985; fellow Guggenheim Found., Cambridge U., 1954. Mem.: NAS, AAAS, Am. Soc. Plant Physiologists (pres. 1960, Stephen Hales award 1968, Charles Reid Barnes award 1977), Indian Nat. Sci. Acad. (fgn. assoc.), Am. Soc. Microbiology, Biochem. Soc., Am. Philos. Soc., Am. Soc. Biochemistry and Molecular Biology, Am. Chem. Soc. (Spencer award 1990). Home: Madison, Wis. Died May 11, 2010.

BURTON, DARRELL IRVIN, engineering executive; b. Ashtabula, Ohio, Sept. 21, 1926; s. George Irvin and Barbara Elizabeth (Streyle) B.; m. Lois Carol Warkentien, Apr. 14, 1951; children: Linda Jean Burton Clinton, Lisa Ann Burton Watts, Lori Elizabeth Burton Admokom. BS in Radio Engring., Chgo. Tech. Coll., 1954. R&D engr. Motorola, Inc., Chgo., 1951-60; devel. engr. Hallicrafters, Chgo., 1960-62; chief engr. TRW, Inc., Des Plaines, Ill., 1962-65; devel. engr. Warwick, Niles, Ill., 1965-68; systems mgr. Admiral Corp., Chgo., 1968-76; elec.-electronics lab. mgr. Montgomery Ward & Co., Chgo., 1976-82; staff engr. Wells-Gardner Electronics Corp., Chgo., 1982-85; sr. engr. Zenith Electronics Corp., Chgo., 1985-91, ret., 1991; pres. Burton Electronics Co., Elmhurst, Ill., from 1992. Tchr. electronics and math. Pres. Addison Homeowners Assn., 1958-60, v.p., 1960-62; mem. Addison Plan Commn., 1960-63; mem. bd. edn. Immanuel Luth. Sch., 1985-87, dir. audio/video ministry, 1973-98, ret., 1998, v.p., 1997, pres., 1998; elder Immanuel Luth. Ch., 1999-2002. Served with U.S. Navy, 1944, U.S. Mcht. Marine, 1945. Lutheran. Died June 8, 2009.

BURTON, JOHN CAMPBELL, accounting educator, former dean; b. NYC, Sept. 17, 1932; s. James Campbell and Barbara (French) B.; m. Jane Garnjost, Apr. 6, 1957; children: Eve Bradley, Bruce Campbell. BA, Haverford Coll., 1954; MBA, Columbia U., 1956, PhD, 1962. C.P.A., N.Y. Staff acct. Arthur Young & Co., NYC, 1956-60; prof. acctg. & fin. Grad. Sch. Bus. Columbia U., NYC, 1962-72, Ernst & Young prof. acctg. & fin., 1978—2002, dean Grad. Sch. Bus., 1982-88. Chief acct. SEC, Washington, 1972-76; dep. mayor fin., NYC, 1976-77; bd. dirs. Scholastic Inc.; dir., chmn. audit com. Commerce Clearing House Inc., 1979-95, First Pa. Corp.-First Pa. Bank, 1982-85; mem. adv. and valuation com. Warburg-Pincus Venture Capital Funds; mem. U.S. Comptroller Gen. Cons. Panel, 1978-95; bd. dirs. Accts. for Pub. Interest, 1978-85. Editor: Corporate Financial Reporting: Conflicts and Challenges, 1969, Corporate Financial Reporting: Ethical and Other Problems, 1972, (with Russell Palmer and Robert Kay) Handbook of Accounting and Auditing, 1981, The International World of Accounting: Challenges and Opportunities, 1981; co-mng. editor Acctg. Horizons, 1989-91; author: Accounting for Business Combinations, 1970, (with W.T. Porter) Auditing: A Conceptual Approach, 1971, and others; contbr. articles to profl. jours. Pres., trustee Millbrook Sch. (N.Y.), 1958-88; trustee ex officio Am. Assembly, 1982-88. Recipient Disting. Scholar award Hofstra U., 1975; Ford Found. fellow, 1961-62; Named to Acctg. Hall of Fame, 1997 Mem. AICPA (coun. 1980-83), Am. Acctg. Assn. (acad. v.p. 1980-82), Am. Fin. Assn., Am. Econ. Assn., Fin. Execs. Inst., Assn. Govtl. Accts., Nat. Assn. Securities Dealers (pub. gov. 1990-94), Met. Club (N.Y.C.), Lake Sunapee Yacht Club (N.H.). Clubs: Metropolitan (N.Y.C.); Lake Sunapee Yacht (N.H.). Home: New York, NY. Died May 16, 2010.

BUSKIRK, ELSWORTH ROBERT, physiologist, educator; b. Beloit, Wis., Aug. 11, 1925; s. Ellsworth Fred and Laura Ellen (Parman) B.; m. Mable Heen, Aug. 28, 1948; children: Laurel Ann Buskirk Wiegand, Kristine Janet Buskirk Hallett. Student, U. Wis., Madison, 1943; BA, St. Olaf Coll., Northfield, Minn., 1950; MA, U. Minn., Mpls., 1951, PhD, 1954. Lab. and tchg. asst. Lab. Physiol. Hygiene, U. Minn., 1951-53; rsch. fellow Life Inst. Med. Rsch. Fund, 1953-54; physiologist Environ. Rsch. Ctr., Natick, Mass., 1954-57, Nat. Inst. for Arthritis, Metabolic and Digestive Diseases, NIH, Bethesda, Md., 1957-63; prof. applied physiology Pa. State U., University Park, 1963-92, dir. Lab. Human Performance Rsch., 1963-92, Marie Underhill Noll prof. Human Performance, 1988-92, emeritus, from 1992. Mem. sci. adv. com. Pres.' Coun. on Phys. Fitness, 1959-61; mem. applied physiology study sect. divsn. rsch. grants NIH, 1964-68, 76-80; mem. com. on interplay of engring. with biology and medicine NAS-NAE, 1968-74, 82-88; mem. rsch. com. Pa. Heart Assn., 1970-73, 82-86, 87-89, 90-95; mem. Pa. Gov.'s Coun. on Phys. Fitness and Sports, 1978-82; mem. com. on mil. nutrition rsch. NAS/NRC, 1982-90; mem. clin. scis. study sect. divsn. rsch. grants NIH, 1989-92, spl. reviewer, 1992-99; mem. Def. Women's Rsch. Com. IOM, NAS-NRC, 1995. Sect. editor Jour. Applied Physiology, 1974-78, assoc. editor, 1978-84; co-editor Sci. and Medicine in Sports and Exercise, 1974, editor, 1973-75; editor-in-chief, 1984-88, cons., editor, 1989-94; mem. editl. bd. Physician and Sports Medicine, 1974-85, Jour. Cardiopulmonary Rehab., 1980-2000, Underseas and Hyperbaric Medicine, 1988-95, Am. Jour. Clin. Nutrition, 1982-92, Jour. Gerontology, 1982-92, Exptl. Gerontology, 1989-98; also over 250 articles on physiology, revs. to sci. jours. Bd. visitors Sargent Coll., Boston U., 1976-92; bd. dirs. Ctr. Cmty. Hosp., Pa., 1966-70, sec., 1971-72, v.p., 1973, pres., 1974-75. With US Army, 1943—46, with ETO, 1943—46, mem. 3rd Army commd. 2d lt. infantry, France, Germany. Recipient Disting. Alumni award St. Olaf Coll., 1969, U. Minn., 2006, Daggs Svc. award Am. Physiol. Soc., 2000; rsch. grantee NIH, 1963-92, U.S. Olympic Com., 1965-68, USAF, 1965-69, Pa. Dept. Health, 1966-67, Pa. Heart Assn., 1966, 76-80, NSF, 1968-70, Nat. Inst. Occupl. Safety and Health, 1969-74; NATO sr. fellow in sci., 1977; named to Athletic Hall of Fame, St. Olaf Coll., 2000. Mem. AAAS, AAPHERD, ASHRAE, Aerospace Med. Assn., Am. Acad. Phys. Edn., Am. Coll. Sports Medicine (citations 1973, 75, Honor award 1984, editl. award 1989, 93, Mid-Atlantic regional chpt. Svc. award 1991), Am. Inst. Nutrition, Am. Physiol. Soc. (pres. environ. and exercise sect. 1987-91, com. on coms. 1988-92, Honor award environ. exercise physiology sect. 1993, Daggs award 2002), Am. Heart Assn. (coun. on epidemiology), N.Y. Acad. Scis., NIH Alumni Assn., Pa. Heart Assn. (rsch. com. 1988-94), Am. Diabetes Assn., Coun. Biology Editors (Healthy Am. Fitness Leaders award 1992), Centre Hills Country Club; fellow Am. Soc. Nutrition. Lutheran. Home: State College, Pa. Died Mar. 28, 2010.

BUTLER, CONNIE MACK, Chemical company executive; b. NC, June 8, 1933; s. James Thomas and Pauline (West) Butler; m. Rachel Marie Sizemore, Oct. 28, 1932. BS in Bus. Adminstrn., Rollins Coll., 1955; S.B.A., U. N.C., 1973. Chemist, sales rep., gen. mgr. Naugatuck Chem. Co. (Conn.), 1958—62; dir. mktg., v.p. mktg. Copdymer Rubber and Chem. Co., Baton Rouge, 1962—69; gen. mgr. chem. div. Milliken & Co., Spartanburg, SC, 1970—78; dir. Petroleum Fermentations N.V., Amelia Island, Fla., from 1978; pres., CEO, dir. Petroferm USA, Amelia Island, from 1978; chmn. bd. Tamny Corp., Amelia Island, from 1978. Served with US Army, 1956—58. Mem.: Soc. Chem. Industry, Am. Chem. Soc., University (Jacksonville, Fla.), Chemists (N.Y.C.). Home: Fernandina Beach, Fla. Died Mar. 10, 2009.

BUTLER, EDWARD LEE, pastor, consultant; b. Frostproof, Fla., June 29, 1945; s. Willie and Lucinda (Hays) B.; m. Thelma Ruth Moore; children: Adina Zaneta, Edward Lee II. BA, Pacific States U., 1972; MDiv, Payne Theol. Sem., 1982. Ordained to ministry Episcopalian Ch., 1973. Pastor Bethel A.M.E. Ch., Mt. Union, Pa., 1973-74, St. Paul A.M.E. Ch., Uniontown, Pa., 1974-79, Quinn Chapel A.M.E. Ch., Wilmington, Ohio, 1979-82, Trinity A.M.E. Ch., Pitts., 1982-90, Ebenezer A.M.E. Ch., Aliquippa, Pa., from 1990. Mem. edn. com., cons. Interdenominational Social Action Alliance, Pitts., 1984—; part-time chaplain Pa. Coun. Chs., 1990—, Western Ctr. Mental Health Facility, Canonsburg, Pa., 1990—. Mem. council Am. Cancer Soc., Pitts., 1985-86; mem. adv. bd. Black Adoption Services, Pitts., 1987—; mem. publicity com. Black Polit. Enpowerment Project, Pitts., 1987—. Fellow Black Child Devel. Inst., Met. Crusade for Voters, Urban League; mem. NAACP. Lodges: Kiwanis (bd. dirs. Uptown Hill club 1986—). Democrat. Avocations: ping pong/table tennis, chess, gourmet cooking. Died June 17, 2009.

BUTLER, FREDERICK GEORGE, retired drug company executive; b. Greenwich, Conn., Mar. 25, 1919; s. Harold Nassau and Rosa (Rhinhart) Butler; m. Sarah Lou Allred Butler, Sept. 23, 1945 (dec.); children: Pamela Sue, Frederick Houston(dec.). AB, Middlebury Coll., Vt., 1941; MBA, Columbia U., 1947. CPA, N.Y. With Price Waterhouse & Co., 1941—42, 1947—49, McKesson & Robbins, Inc., NYC, 1949—63, asst. comptr., 1952—61, comptr., 1961—63; contr. Bristol-Myers Co., NYC, 1963—66, v.p., contr., 1966—69, v.p. ops., 1970—76; ret., 1976. Pioneered developement of bar code (compatible universal product code and nat. drug code) for supermarket automated checkout scanning and inventory control. Village mayor, Briarcliff Manor, N.Y., 1969-71. Served to comdr. USNR, 1942-46, 51-52. Mem. Fin. Execs. Inst., Pres.'s Club, Hillsdale (Mich.) Coll., Chi Psi. Methodist. Died Nov. 7, 2009.

BUTLER, IVORY ERNEST, JR., investment banker, accountant; b. Little Rock, June 17, 1928; s. Ivory Ernest and Vera Irene (Slaten) B.; m. Bobbie Jean Williams, Feb.11, 1955; children: Rebecca Jean, Ivory Ernest III, Craig Williams. BBA, Northwestern U., 1949. CPA, Ark. Acct. Russell Brown and Co., Little Rock, 1949-51, 1953-57; exec. v.p. Stephens Inc., Little Rock, from 1957. Pres. Bapt. Health Found., Little Rock, 1983-84, bd. dirs. 1976-86; bd. dirs. Ark. Theater Opera, 1980-84, Ind. Coll. Fund. Ark., 1990—; pres., bd. dirs. Parkway Village, 1986—; bd. dirs. cen. Ark. Radiation Therapy Inst., 1987—; adv. bd. YWCA. Methodist. Home: Little Rock, Ark. Died Dec. 17, 2009.

BUTLER, ROBERT LEONARD, retired sales executive; b. West Warwick, RI, Aug. 8, 1931; s. Leonard Thomas and Henrietta Marie (Theroux) B.; m. Rosemarie Ann D'Ambra, Nov. 5, 1955; children: Robert Arthur, David Paul. MS in Fin. Svcs., Am. Coll., 1982, MS in Mgmt., 1985. ChFC, CLU. With sales and dept. mgmt. Sears Roebuck & Co., Worcester, Mass., 1956-67; dir. investment, prodn., sales State Mut. Am., Worcester, 1976-86; asst. sec. SMA Life Assurance Co., Worcester, 1974-86; v.p. SMA Equities Inc., Worcester, 1976-86; sr. v.p. sales Phoenix Equity Planning Corp., Hartford, Conn., 1986-92. Spkr., workshop leader conf. Life Office Mgmt. Assn. Contbr. articles to ins. mags. Mem. Am. Soc. Life Underwriters, Am. Abritration Assn. (comml. arbitrator 1993), Internat. Assn. Fin. Planners, Ins. Affiliated Broker-Dealer Forum (chmn. 1978-81), Nat. Assn. Securities Dealers (mem. dist. bus. com., mem. ins. affiliated broker/dealer com. 1991-92), Limra Fin. Products and Svcs., KC. Roman Catholic. Avocations: golf, jogging, swimming, photography, sports cars. Home: Auburn, Mass. Died Mar. 16, 2010.

BUTLER, ROBERT NEIL, gerontologist, psychiatrist, writer, educator; b. NYC, Jan. 21, 1927; s. Fred and Easter (Dikeman) B.; m. Diane McLaughlin, Sept. 2, 1950; children: Ann Christine, Carole Melissa, Cynthia Lee; m. Myrna I. Lewis, May 17, 1975; 1 dau., Alexandra Nicole. BA, Columbia U., 1949, MD, 1953; degree (hon.), U. So. Calif., U. Gothenburg, Sweden. Intern St. Lukes Hosp., NYC, 1953-54; resident U. Calif. Langley Porter Clinic, 1954-55, NIMH, 1955-56, research psychiatrist, 1955-62; founder geriatric unit Chestnut Lodge, 1958, adminstr., 1958-59; research psychiatrist Washington Sch. Psychiatry, 1962-76; dir. Nat. Inst. on Aging, NIH, 1976-82; prof. geriatics and adult devel. Mt. Sinai Sch. Medicine, NYC, 1982—2010. Dir. Internat. Longevity Ctr., 1990-2010, pres., CEO, 1998-2010; mem. faculty George Washington U. Med. Sch., Washington, 1962-82, Howard U. Sch. Medicine; cons. NIMH, 1967-76, US Senate Spl. Com. on Aging. Author (with others): Human Aging, 1963; author: (with Myrna I. Lewis) Aging and Mental Health, 1973, 5th edit., 1998; author: Why Survive? Being Old in Amerca, 1975, reissue, 2002, Sex After Sixty, 1976; author: (with A. Bearn) The Aging Process, 1985; author: (with Herbert Gleason) Productive Aging, 1985; author: (with Myrna I. Lewis) Love and Sex After Forty, 1986; author: Modern Biological Theories of Aging, 1987, Human Aging Research, 1988, The Promise of Productive Aging, 1990, Who is Responsible for My Old Age?, 1993; author: (with Myrna I. Lewis) Love and Sex After Sixty, 3d edit., 1993; author: (with Jacob Brody) Delaying the Onset of Late-Life Dysfunction, 1995; author: (with Howard Fillit) Cognitive Decline, Strategies for Prevention, 1997; author: (with Claude Jasmin) Longevity and Quality of Life, 1999; author: (with Lawrence Grossman and Mia Oberlink) Life in an Older America, 1999; author: (with Myrna I. Lewis) The New Love and Sex After Sixty, 4th edit., 2002; editor: Geriatrics, 1986—2000; mem. editl. bd.: Jour. Geriatric Psychiatry. Sec. Nat. Ballet of Washington, 1962-75; chmn. DC Advisory Commn. on Aging, 1969-72; bd. dirs. Nat. Council on Aging, Mildred and Claude Pepper Found. Served with US Maritime Service, 1945-47. Recipient Pulitzer prize for gen. nonfiction, 1976, Leo Laks award, 1976; McIntyre award, 1977, Allied-Signal award, Gustav O. Lienhard award Inst. Medicine NAS, 1996, Heinz award, 2003; others. Fellow Am. Psychiat. Assn., American Geriatrics Soc. (founding mem.); mem. Group for Advancement Psychiatry (trustee 1974-76), Gerontol. Soc., Forum for Profls. and Execs. (founding) Clubs: Cosmos (Washington); Century (NYC). Home: New York, NY. Died July 5, 2010.

BUTLER, WILFORD ARTHUR, association executive; b. Grand Rapids, Mich., Apr. 17, 1937; s. Wilford A. and Dorothy (French) B. BA, Western Mich. U., 1961; MBA, Fla. Atlantic U., 1977. Dir. pub. relations Preferred Ins. Co., Grand Rapids, 1961-62; asst. to chmn. Delta Upsilon Fraternity, NYC, 1962, exec. sec. Indpls., 1963-74, exec. dir., 1974-86, Delta Upsilon Edml. Found., 1979-86; chmn. Interfraternity Inst., Ind. U., 1970-74; pres., chief exec. officer BCG Internat., Indpls., from 1987. Editor: Our Record, 1963-85; chief editorial advisor publ. Attracting, Organizing and Keeping Members, Am. Soc. Assn. Execs., 1989. Mem. steering com. Am. Coll. Fraternity Bicentennial, 1976-86, Midwest Ednl. Found., Inc., 1986-87; trustee, mem. exec. com. Mid-Am. Assn. Edn. Found., 1988—; bd. dirs. Greater Indpls. Republican Fin. Com., 1986-91; bd. dirs. Indpls. Conv. and Visitors Assn., 1983-91, coun. advisors, 1992—; trustee Columbian Hist. Found., 1985-88, Columbian Literary and Fine Arts Found, 198-88. Named Sagamore of the Wabash Mem. Am. Assn. Coll. Fraternities (past pres.), Fraternity Execs. Assn. (pres. 1976-86), Commn. on Fraternity Research (past treas.), Am. Soc. Assn. Execs. (adv. bd. communications sect. 1977-79, bd. dirs. 1983-86; vice chmn. cert. commn. 1989-91, chair 1991, chair cert. appeals com. 1992, mem. ann. mtg. adv. com. 1993, chair programs and projects com. ASAE Found. 1991-92, chair rsch. and edn. com., mem. exec. com. ASAE Found., adv. com. ann. meeting 1993, awards com. 1994, chair newsletter task force, 1994Key award 1983), Ind. Soc. Assn. Execs. (chmn. cert. study com. 1979-80, editor monthly newsletter Spotlight 1979-85, mem. exec. com. 1980-84, pres. 1983-84, mem. 1st com. 1986, chair 1991—, nominating com. 1987, chair ISAE Found. 1994), Delta Upsilon (editor quar. 1973-86) Clubs: Columbia (Indpls.) (sec., dir.). Died Dec. 13, 2009.

BUTLER, WILLIAM, IV, lawyer; b. West Chester, Pa., Nov. 2, 1937; s. William Butler III and Nell (Bleecker) Butler; m. Marilyn Gariepy Butler, June 22, 1963; children: William Scott, Glen Gariepy. AB with cum laude, Princeton U., 1959; JD, U. Pa., 1962. Bar: Pa. 1968. Ptnr. Butler & Butler, West Chester, 1962—73; asst. dist. atty. Chester County, Pa., 1968—70; ptnr. Klein, Elicker, Head & Butler, West Chester, 1974—76, Caine, DiPasqua, Edelson, Patterson & Butler, 1977—79, Crawford & Butler, West Chester, 1980—84, Butler, Van Alen Assocs., 1984—2010. Pvt. practice, West Chester; solicitor Chester County Bd. Health, 1965—67; mem. Voluntary Defender Assn., 1963—66; editor, case editor Chester County Law Reporter, 1968—73, 1979—81. Active United Way of Chester County, from 1973, gen. campaign chmn., 1977; mem. Delchester Lung Assn.; bd. dirs. Wilmington Opera Soc., Opera Del., from 1981; mem. choir & vestry Holy Trinity Episcopal Ch.; former chmn. Chester County Young Republicans, 1964—65. Mem.: ABA, Christian Legal Soc., Am. Judicature Soc., Pa. Trial Lawyers Assn., Chester County Bar Assn., Pa. Bar Assn., Hare Law (U. Pa.), U. Cottage (Princeton, NJ), Chester County Lions (bd. dirs. 1972—75). Died May 20, 2010.

BUTTERFIELD, JACK ARLINGTON, hockey league executive; b. Regina, Sask., Can., Aug. 1, 1919; came to U.S., 1945; s. Fred Gibson and Mary Elizabeth (Browning) B.; m. Nina Marie Combs, 1945; children: Fred, Ron. BSc, U. Alta., 1939. Gen. mgr. Springfield Indians, West Springfield, Mass., 1945-66; pres. American Hockey League, West Springfield, Mass., 1966—94, chmn., 1994—2010. Exec. dir. Melha Shrine Circus, Springfield Named to The Hockey Hall of Fame, Nat. Hockey League, 1980; recipient James C. Hendy Meml. award, 1971, 1984, Lester Patrick award, 1982, Thomas Ebright Meml. award, 1998 Mem. Masons, Shriners, Jesters. Home: Westfield, Mass. Died Oct. 16, 2010.

BYERLY, LEROY JAMES, psychiatrist, educator; b. Lykens, Pa., Sept. 20, 1931; m. Jane Shelley, June 16, 1956; children: Shelley, William, David. BS, Franklin and Marshall Coll., 1952; MD, Temple U., 1956. Diplomate Am. Bd. Psychiatry and Neurology. Intern U.S. Naval Hosp., LI, N.Y., 1956-57; resident U.S. Naval Hosp. and Ea. Pa. Psychiat. Inst., Phila., 1959-60; tng. in psychoanalysis Phila. Psychoanalytic Inst., 1962-70, mem. faculty, 1970; pvt. practice, Haddonfield, N.J., 1963-91, Marlton, N.J., from 1991. Mem. faculty Med. Coll. Pa., Phila., 1978-90, Jefferson Med. Coll., 1990-92; head sect. child psychoanalysis Med. Coll. N.J., Camden-Cooper Hosp., 1993—. Lt. M.C., USN, 1956-60. Fellow Am. Psychiat. Assn.; mem. AMA, Am. Psychoanalytic Assn., Phila. Psychoanalytic Soc. (pres. 1988-90), Tavistock Country Club, Union League (Phila.). Republican. Episcopalian. Home: Voorhees, NJ. Died Feb. 4, 2009.

BYNUM, GRETCHEN LUEPKE, geologist; b. Nov. 10, 1943; d. Gordon Maas and Janice (Campbell) Luepke; m. Robert Flournoy Bynum, Oct. 2, 1999. Student, U. Colo., 1962; BS cum laude, U. Ariz., Tucson, 1965, MS, 1967. Registered geologist, Oreg. Geol. field asst. U.S. Geol. Survey, Flagstaff, Ariz., 1964, geologist Pacific br. marine geology Menlo Park, Calif., 1967—99, emeritus geologist br. coastal and marine geology, from 1999. Project coord. Hist. Marine Geology Program US Geol. Survey; mem. US Congress Office Tech. Assessment Workshop Mining and Processing Placers of EEZ, 1986; contr. on placer deposits Circum Pacific Map Project on Offshore Mineral Deposits US Geol. Survey, 1996—99. Editor: Stability of Heavy Minerals in Sediments, Economic Analysis of Heavy Minerals in Sediments, book rev. Earth Scis. History, 1989—2002; contbr. articles on heavy-mineral analysis to publs. including, Circum Pacific Map Project on offshore mineral deposits, chapters to books. Fellow: Geol. Soc. Am. (Interdisciplinary Perspectives on the Hist. Earth Scis., Penrose Conf. 1994, Cordilleran sect. com. on geology and pub. policy 1998—2002, nominating com. History of Geology Divsn. 2000—02, com. chair 2002); mem.: Internat. Sedimantological Congress, Internat. Geological Congress, Internat. Marine Minerals Soc. (charter), Internat. Assn. Sedimentologists, History of the Earth Scis. Soc., Bay Area Mineralogists (chmn. 1979—80), Peninsula Geol. Soc., Ariz. Geol. Soc., Soc. Econ. Paleontologists and Mineralogists (chmn. com. librs. in developing countries 1988—91, mem. web com. 2007—08), Am. Geophys. Union, Geospeakers Toastmasters Club (charter, Competent Toastmaster 1995, Advanced Toastmaster-Bronze Level 2001, Silver Level 2006), Tau Beta Sigma, Sigma Xi. Home: Fremont, Calif. Died July 3, 2010.

BYRD, LLOYD GARLAND, retired civil engineer; b. Atlanta, May 6, 1923; s. Lloyd Porter and Gladys Ardee (Daniell) B.; m. Jeanne Mae Parkhurst, Jan. 23, 1943; children: Gary Daniell, Donna Jeanne, Jeffrey Alan, Julie Anne. BCE, Ohio State U., 1950. Staff engr. Ohio Dept. Hwys., Columbus, 1949-52; maintenence engr. Ohio Turnpike Commn., Berea, 1952-60; assoc. editor Pub. Works Publs., Ridgewood, NJ, 1960-63; ptnr. Byrd, Tallamy, MacDonald & Lewis, Falls Church, Va., 1963-72; sr. v.p., mgr. Byrd, Tallamy, MacDonald & Lewis div. Wilbur Smith & Assocs., Falls Church, 1972-84; interim dir. Strategic Hwy. Rsch. Program, Washington, 1984-86; pvt. practice Washington, 1986-99; ret. Chmn. group 3 coun. Transp. Rsch. Bd., Washington, 1972-76, chmn. overview com.; ex-officio governing bd. NRC, Washington, 1989-95; mem. bd. cons. Eno Found., Westport, Conn., 1986-89; mem. report rev. com. NRC, 1997—. Co-author: Street and Highway Maintenance Manual: American Public Works Association, 1985; assoc. editor: Handbook of Highway Engring., 1975; chmn. pub. affairs coun. Am. Assn. Engring. Socs., 1992. Chmn. Fairfax County Human Rights Commn., Va., 1978-79; pres. Fairfax County C. of C., 1975-76; bd. dirs. Hospice of Carolina Foothills, Inc., 2002-07. Recipient Disting. Alumnus award Ohio State U. Coll. Engring., 1978, Roy W. Crum award Transp. Rsch. Bd., Washington, 1986, P.D. McLean Meml. award Road Gang, Washington, 1989, Disting. Lectr. award, 1998, Transp. Rsch Bd. Fellow ASCE (pres. nat. capital sect. Washington 1976-77, nat. bd. dirs. N.Y.C. 1979-82, Wilbur S. Smith award 1985, Francis C. Turner Lecture award 1995); mem. NAE, Am. Pub. Works Assn., Univ. Club (Washington), Tryon (N.C.) Country Club, Rotary Club. Congregationalist. Avocations: golf, bridge. Home: Tryon, NC. Died Mar. 20, 2009.

BYRD, ROBERT CARLYLE, United States Senator from West Virginia; b. North Wilkesboro, NC, Nov. 20, 1917; s. Cornelius Sale and Ada (Kirby) Byrd; m. Erma Ora James, May 29, 1937 (dec. Mar. 25, 2006); children: Mona Carole Fatemi, Marjorie Ellen Moore. BA in Polit. Sci., Marshall U., Huntington, W.Va., 1994; JD cum laude, Am. U., Washington, 1963. Mem. W.Va. House of Reps., 1947-50, W.Va. State Senate, 1951-52, US Congress from 6th W.Va. Dist., 1953—59; US Senator from W.Va., 1959—2010; asst. majority leader (majority whip) US Senate, 1971—77, majority leader, 1977—81, 1987—89, minority leader, 1981-86, pres. pro tempore, 1989—95, 2001—03, 2007—10; chmn. US Senate Appropriations Com., 1989—94, 2007—09, ranking mem., 1995—2007. Author: The Senate, 1789-1989, 4 vols., 1989-94, The Senate of the Roman Republic: Addresses on the History of Roman Constitutionalism, 1995, Losing America: Confronting a Reckless and Arrogant Presidency, 2004, Robert C. Byrd: Child of the Appalachian Coalfields, 2005; contbr. articles to profl. jours. Recipient Disting. Svc award, Radio & TV News Dirs. Assn. 1986, Montgomery award, Nat. Guard Bur. 2000, Robert J. Collier award, Nat. Aeronautic Assn., 2001, Nat. Leadership award, Civil War Preservation Trust, 2002, Edmund S. Muskie Disting. Public Svc. award, Ctr. Nat. Policy, 2003, Freedom from Fear medal, Franklin & Eleanor Roosevelt Inst., 2003, Theodore Roosevelt-Woodrow Wilson award for civil svc., Am. Hist. Assn., 2004, Wellstone award, United Steelworkers America, 2004; named Most Influential Mem. in US Senate, US News & World Report Poll, 1979, Legislator of Yr., Nat. Coal Assn., 1986, West Virginian of Twentieth Century, W. Va. House Delegates, 2001. Mem.: Country Music Assn. (hon.), Masons. Democrat. Baptist. Achievements include holding the record for the longest period of service as a US Senator in 2006. Died June 28, 2010.

BYRNE, JOHN N., food company executive; b. Newark, May 21, 1925; s. Owen Francis and Rose (Daly) B.; m. Audrey Helmers; children: John W., Andrew J., Kathleen A., Steven T., Eileen R., Gregory F. BSME, Stevens Inst., 1949, MS in Indsl. Mgmt., 1954. Engr. Thomas J. Lipton Inc., Hoboken, N.J., 1948-54, plant mgr. Suffolk, Va., 1954-61, dir. engring. Englewood Cliffs, N.J., 1961-64, dir. production and Engring., 1964-67, asst. v.p. mfg., 1967-72, v.p. engring. and planning, 1972-77, v.p. gen. mgmt. group, 1977-84, sr. v.p., from 1984, also bd. dirs. V.p. Tidewater Devel. Council, Norfolk, Va., 1960. Served to 1st lt. USAF, 1943-45, ETO. Mem. Am. Soc. Mech. Engrs., Suffolk C. of C. (pres. 1958). Republican. Roman Catholic. Home: Hamilton Square, NJ. Died July 23, 2009.

BYRNES, CHRISTOPHER IAN, engineering educator; b. NYC, June 28, 1949; s. Richard Francis and Jeanne (Orchard) Byrnes; children: Kathleen, Alison, Christopher Jr.; m. Gwendolyn Renee Byrnes, Feb. 14, 2005. BS in Math., Manhattan Coll., 1971; MS in Math., U. Mass., 1973, PhD in Math., 1975; D of Tech. (hon.), Royal Inst. Tech., Stockholm, 1998. Registered profl. engr., Mo. Instr., dept. math. U. Utah, Salt Lake City, 1975-78; asst. prof., dept. math. and divsn. engring. and applied sciences Harvard U., Cambridge, Mass., 1978—82, assoc. prof., divsn. engring. and applied sciences, 1983—85; prof. engring. and of math., dept. electrical and computer engring. Ariz. State U., Tempe, 1984—89, grad. coll. disting. rsch. prof., 1988—89; prof. systems and controls, dept. systems sci. and math. Washington U., St. Louis, 1989—2005, prof. systems and controls, dept. electrical and systems engring., 2005—09, dir., Henry Edwin Sever Grad. Sch. Engring. and Applied Sci., 1991—2002, Edward H. and Florence G. Skinner prof. of systems sci. and math., 2000—09, Edward H. and Florence G. Skinner prof. of systems sci. and math. emeritus, 2009—10, chmn. dept. systems sci. and math, 1989—91, dean Sch. Engring. and Applied Sci., 1991—2006; rsch. prof. NC State U., 2009—10. Adj. prof., dept. optimization and system theory Royal Inst. Tech., Stockholm, 1986—90, vis. prof., 1985, Stockholm, 91, Stockholm, 2001, disting. vis. prof.; cons. Sci. Sys., Inc., Cambridge, 1980—84, Sys. Engring., Inc., Greenbelt, Md., 1986; sci. advisor Sherwood Davis & Geck, 1996—98; mem. technical adv. bd. Cernium Inc., 2002—07; regional dir. and chmn. adv. bd. for emerging technologies Midwest Bank Ctr., 2000—06; mem. NRC; bd. dirs., chmn. nominating and governance com. Belden Inc., 1995—2006; bd. dirs. Starnet, Inc., 1996—98, MinMax Technologies, Inc., 1997—99, chmn., 1998—99; chmn. bd. dir. Ctr. Emerging Techs., 1995—2004, chmn. emeritus, 2005—10; bd. dirs. Washington U. Tech. Associates, Inc (WUTA, Inc.), 1991—2004, pres., 1993—2003; mem. bus. adv. bd. Newberry Group Inc., 2002—10; Giovanni Prodi Chair in Nonlinear Analysis, U. vis. Chair U. Wuerzburg, 2009. Editor: (book series) Progress in Systems Control, 1988, Foundations of Systems and Control: Theory and Applications 1989-2002; Nonlinear Synthesis, 1991, 13 other books; contbr. numerous articles to profl. jours., book revs. Recipient Best Paper award, IFAC, 1993. Fellow: IEEE (Geroge Axelby award for Best Paper in Trans. Aut. Control 1991, George Axelby award for Best Paper in Trans. Aut. Control 2003, Hendrik W. Bode Lecture prize 2008), Soc. Indsl. Applied Math. (program com. 1986—89, W.T. and Idalia Reid prize 2005), Acad. Sciences of St. Louis (Fellows award 2001), Japan Soc. for Promotion Sci.; mem.: AIAA, AAAS, Regional Chamber for Growth Assn. (vice chmn. tech., chmn. Tech. Gateway Alliance 2000—03), Royal Swedish Acad. Engring. Sci. (fgn.), Am. Math. Soc., Pi Mu Epsilon, Tau Beta Pi, Sigma Xi. Avocations: cooking, fishing, travel. Died Feb. 11, 2010.

BYROM, FLETCHER LAUMAN, chemical manufacturing company executive; b. Cleve., July 13, 1918; s. Fletcher L. and Elizabeth (Collins) B.; m. Marie L. McIntyre, Feb. 17, 1945; children: Fletcher Lauman, Carol A. Byrom Conrad, Susan J. Byrom-Thomas. BS in Metallurgy, Pa. State U., State College, 1940; graduate Advanced Mgmt. Program, Harvard U., Cambridge, Mass., 1952. Sales engr. Am. Steel & Wire Co., Cleve., 1940-42; procurement and adminstrv. coord. Naval Ordnance Lab., also Bur. Ordnance and Research Planning Bd., Navy Dept., 1942-47; from asst. to gen. mgr. Tar Products divsn. Koppers Co., Inc., Pitts., 1947-82, pres., 1960—70, chmn., 1970—82; mgr. Micasu Tungsten LLC, from 2000. Mem. Pitts. br. Fed. Res. Bd. Cleve., 1962-68, chmn., 1966-68, N.Y. Stock Exch., 1980-86; mem. bd. govs. Com. Devel. Am. Capital, 1989-2004; bd. dirs. Purecycle Corp., 1988-2004, pres., bd. dirs. Micasu Corp. Bd. dirs. Allegheny Conf. on Cmty. Devel., v.p., 1970-83; chmn. Hershey Med. Ctr. Subcom., 1970-73; chmn. Pres.'s Export Coun., 1974-79, Pub. Edn. Fund, 1980-85; chmn. bd. trustees Presbyn.-Univ. Hosp., 1972-83, internat. 1975-80, Kiskiminetas Springs Sch., 1971-82; trustee Carnegie Mellon U., 1975-81, Allegheny Coll., 1969-79, Pa. State U., 1970-73; former trustee, Inst. Advanced Study, Inst. for Future Mem., Hudson Inst., Keystone Ctr.; trustee Conf. Bd., 1962-82, lifetime chancellor, 1968—; mem. pres.'s circle NAS, chmn., 1999-2000; trustee Com. for Econ. Devel., chmn. bd. dirs., 1978-84, lifetime trustee. Recipient Disting. Civilian Service award U.S. Navy Dept., Disting. Alumnus Pa. State U., David Ford McFarland award Pa. State U., 1979, Alumni Achievement award Harvard U. Bus. Sch., 1981, William Metcalf award West Pa. Engring. Soc., 1985; Woodrow Wilson Edn. Found. vis. fellow, Pa. State U. fellow. Mem. Pa. State U. Alumni Assn. (pres. 1965-66), Coun. Retired CEO's, Duquesne Club Pitts., Phi Kappa Psi. Presbyterian. Died July 23, 2009.

BYSTRYN, JEAN-CLAUDE, dermatologist, educator; b. Paris, May 8, 1938; arrived in U.S., 1949, naturalized, 1958; s. Iser and Sara Bystryn; m. Marcia Hammill, May 14, 1972; children: Anne, Alexander. BS, U. Chgo., 1958; MD, NYU, 1962. Diplomate Am. Bd. Dermatology, Am. Bd. Immunodermatopathology. Intern Montefiore Hosp., NYC, 1962-63, resident in medicine, 1963-64; resident in dermatology NYU Sch. Medicine, NYC, 1966-69, USPHS postgrad. tng. fellow in immunology, 1968-72, asst. prof. clin. dermatology, 1971—72, assoc. prof., 1976-84, prof., from 1984. Asst. dispensary physician Albany Med. Coll., 1964—66; asst. attending physician Univ. Hosp., NYC, from 1969; asst. vis. dermatologist Bellevue Hosp. Ctr., NYC, from 1969; dir. melanoma program NYU Kaplan Cancer Ctr., NYC; dir. Immunofluorescence Lab. NYU Med. Sch., NYC. Contbr. articles to profl. jours. Mem. adv. bd. Skin Cancer Found., Vitiligo Found.; chair, med. adv. bd. Nat. Alepecia Areata Found.; mem. adv. bd. Am. Skin Assn., Nat. Pemphigus Found. Lt. comdr. USPHS, 1964—66. Recipient Irma T. Hirschl Rsch. Career award, AOA; Ford Found. fellow, 1954—58, NIH grantee, from 1970. Mem.: N.Y. Dermatol. Soc. (dir.), Soc. Investigative Dermatology, Am. Assn. Cancer Rsch., Am. Assn. Immunologists, Am. Acad. Dermatology, Am. Dermatology Assn. Home: New York, NY. Died Aug. 19, 2010.

CAGGIANO, JOSEPH, retired advertising executive; b. NYC, Oct. 22, 1925; s. Daniel Joseph and Lucia (Gaudiosi) C.; m. Catherine Marie Gilmore, Aug. 28, 1948; children: Cathleen, Mary Yvonne. BBA, Pace Coll., 1953. Chief accountant Criterion Advt. Co., NYC, 1947-57; treas. Emerson Foote, Inc., NYC, 1957-67; became sr. v.p. Bozell & Jacobs, Inc. (now Bozell, Jacobs, Kenyon & Eckhardt Inc.), NYC, 1967, exec. v.p. finance and adminstrn. Omaha, 1971-91, vice chmn. bd., chief financial officer, 1991-97; vice chmn. bd. dirs. emeritus Bozell, Jacobs, Kenyon & Eckhart Inc., from 1991, ret., 1998. Bd. dirs. St. Mary's Coll., Omaha Zool. Soc. Served with USNR, 1943-46, ETO, PTO. Mem. N.Y. Credit and Financial Mgmt. Assn., Omaha Zool. Soc. (dir.) Home: Omaha, Nebr. Died July 11, 2009.

CALDWELL, RICHARD CLARK, banker; b. Ottawa, Ont., Can., July 28, 1944; came to U.S., 1945; s. Robert Ralston Chrisman and Patricia Ann (Clark) C.; m. Judith Ann Van Harn, Sept. 2, 1967; 1 child, Jennifer MacLean. AB, Kenyon Coll., 1967; MBA, Emory U., 1972. Officer Harris Bank, Chgo., 1976, asst. v.p., 1977-79, v.p., 1979-82, sr. v.p., group exec. instl. trust adminstrn., 1982-86, exec. v.p., trust dept. exec., from 1986; chmn. bd. dirs. Harris Investment Mgmt. Inc. Bd. dirs. Harris Trust Bank Ariz., Bank Montreal Investment Mgmt. Ltd., Harris Derivative Markets Inc. Treas. Travelers and Immigrants Aid, Chgo., 1982; bd. govs. Ill. Council on Econ. Edn.; trustee Hadley Sch. for Blind. Served to 1st lt. U.S. Army, 1968-71, Vietnam. Decorated Bronze Star with v-device, Air medal with v-device; recipient Phoenix award Atlanta Advt. Club, 1972 Mem. Beta Gamma Sigma Clubs: University, Economic (Chgo.), Commonwealth (Chgo.); Indian Hill (Winnetka, Ill.). Republican. Episcopalian. Home: Vero Beach, Fla. Died Feb. 19, 2010.

CALDWELL, WESLEY STUART, III, lawyer, lobbyist; b. Teaneck, NJ, June 3, 1946; s. Wesley S. Jr. and Helen Skrek C.; m. Theresa Hale, Apr. 20, 1970 (div. Jan. 1988); children: Ashley Hale, Ferris Elena; m. J.R. Dillenback, May 27, 1988. BA in Liberal Arts, Fairleigh Dickinson U., 1968; JD, Rutgers U., 1975. Bar: N.J. 1975, U.S. Dist. Ct. N.J. 1975, U.S. Supreme Ct. 1992. Dep. atty. gen. N.J. Atty. Gen.'s Office, Trenton, 1975-78; assoc. gen. counsel Prudential Reins. Co., Newark, 1978-79; v.p. Am. Ins. Assn., NYC, 1979-86; ptnr. LeBoeuf, Lamb, Greene & MacRae, Newark, 1986-95, Caldwell Megna & Brewster, Trenton, 1995-97, Caldwell Megna, Trenton, 1997—2001; ins. regulatory atty. Wesley S. Caldwell III Law Offices, Trenton, 2002—07. With U.S. Army, 1969-72. Mem. Hagner & Zohlman, LLC Cherry Hill, NJ, (OF Counsel 2008-); N.J. Bar Assn. (past chmn. ins. law sect.). Avocations: golf, pocket billiards. Died Jan. 22, 2009.

CALDWELL, WILLIAM GERALD, religion educator, minister; b. Atlanta, Jan. 21, 1934; s. George Wesley and Evelyn (Albright) C.; m. Emily Dianne Clemm, May 29, 1954; children: William Gerald, Janis Marie. BA, Samford U., 1954; MRE, Southwestern Bapt. Theol. Sem., Ft. Worth, 1956, DRE, 1963, EdD, 1972; PhD, Southwestern Bapt. Theol. Sem., 1994. Ordained to ministry So. Bapt. Conv., 1971. Min. edn. lst Bapt. Ch., Ferguson, Mo., 1959-63, Hunter Street Bapt. Ch., Birmingham, Ala., 1963-66, Cliff Temple Bapt. Ch., Dallas, 1966-69; prof. religious edn. Bapt. Bible Inst., Graceville, Fla., 1969-73; cons. adult work Bapt. Sunday Sch. Bd., Nashville, 1973-76; prof. adminstrn. Southwestern Bapt. Theol. Sem., from 1976. Author: Church Administration Handbook, Personnel Administration Guide; contbr. articles and curriculum materials to So. Bapt. periodicals. Mem. So. Bapt. Religious Edn. Assn., Bapt. Religious Edn. Assn. of S.W., Ea. Bapt. Religious Edn. Assn. (pres. 1974-75), Nat. Assn. Ch. Bus. Adminstrn., So. Bapt. Ch. Bus. Adminstrn. Assn., Ch. Mgmt. Hall of Fame. Died Mar. 2, 2009.

CALINESCU, MATEI ALEXE, literature educator; b. Bucharest, Romania, June 15, 1934; came to U.S., 1973, naturalized, 1981; s. Radu and Dora Maria (Vulcanescu) C.; m. Adriana Gane, Apr. 29, 1963; children: Irena, A. Matthew. MA in English, U. Bucharest, 1957; PhD in Comparative Lit., U. Cluj, Romania, 1972. Asst. prof. comparative lit. U. Bucharest, 1963-65, assoc. prof. comparative lit., 1965-72; vis. assoc. prof. comparative lit. Ind. U., Bloomington, 1973-75, assoc. prof. comparative lit. and west European studies, 1976-79, prof. comparative lit., from 1979, chair dept. comparative lit., 1996-98. Vis. fellow U. Chgo., 1988, Yale U., 1989. Author: Faces of Modernity: Avant-Garde, Decadence, Kitsch, 1977, Five Faces of Modernity: Modernism, Avant-Garde, Decadence, Kitsch, Postmodernism, 1987, Rereading, 1993, (with Ion Vianu) Amintiri in dialog, 1994, (with D.W. Fokkema) Exploring Postmodernism, 1990, others; contbr. numerous articles to profl. jours. Guggenheim fellowship, 1975-76, NEH Summer fellowship, 1991, Woodrow wilson Internat. Ctr. for Scholars fellowship, 1994-95. Home: Bloomington, Ind. Died June 24, 2009.

CALLAGHAN, FRANK D., state legislator; b. Rochester, NH, June 21, 1924; m. Dorothy A. Callaghan; 7 children. Grad. h.s. City councilman, Rochester, 1954-56; mem. dist. 15 N.H. Ho. of Reps., mem. wildlife and marine com. Mem. Sch. Bd., 1990—. Mem. KC (4th degree, faithful navigator 1967-68), Rochester Lodge Elks (exalted ruler 1961-62). Died July 27, 2009.

CALLIGAN, WILLIAM DENNIS, retired life insurance company executive; b. Hibbing, Minn., Mar. 21, 1925; s. Raymond George and Ann Matilda (Olson) C.; m. Aletha E. Cornelius, Dec. 21, 1949; children— Ann M., Timothy M. BA, Yankton Coll., SD, 1949. With NY Life Ins. Co., from 1953, dir. mass market products, 1963-77, v.p. pensions, 1977-87; ret., 1987. Mem. Internat. Found. Employee Benefit Plans, Inc. Served with USMC, World War II. Home: Wayne, Pa. Died July 7, 2009.

CALVERT, SAM J., JR., agricultural products executive; b. Port of Spain, Trinidad, W.I., Dec. 16, 1928; s. Sam James and Marion Leonore (Morse) C.; m. Peggy Ann Reeves, Apr. 16, 1955; children: Melanie Coley, Sam III, Gray. BBA, U. N.C., 1951. V.p. The Austin Co. Inc., Greeneville, Tenn., 1960-85, sr. v.p., 1985-88, exec. v.p., 1988-89, chmn. bd. Kinston, N.C., from 1989. Trustee Tusculum Coll., Greeneville, 1983-89. Mem. Tobacco Assn. U.S. (pres. (1990-91, chmn. exec. com. 1991-92). Republican. Episcopalian. Home: Greeneville, Tenn. Died May 16, 2010.

CAMBURN, MARVIN EDWIN, mathematician, educator; b. Stockbridge, Mich., Apr. 1, 1938; s. Burtis Harmon and Gertrude Lillian (Stephens) Camburn; m. Joyce Carol Weeman, June 7, 1959; children: Eric Marvin, Stephen Arthur. BA, Albion Coll., 1960; MA, U. Detroit, 1964; PhD, Mich. State U., 1971; postdoc., Harvard U., 1982. Tchr. math Pub. HS, Mich., NY, 1960—66; instr. Wayne State Coll., Nebr., 1966—68; assoc. prof. Mercyhurst Coll., Erie, Pa., 1971—78, chmn. dept. math., 1974—75, chmn. sci. divsn., 1975—77, corrd. instl. devel., 1976—78; dan faculty and instrn. Ill. Benedictine Coll., Lisle, from 1978; sec. Consortium West Suburban Colls., Lisle, 1979—80, from 1984; chmn. Acad. Adv. Panel, 1980—81; mem. exec. bd. Associated Colls. Chgo. Area, River Forest, Ill., 1979—84, treas., 1980—82, chmn., 1982—83. Contbr. articles to profl. jours. Fellowship, NSF, 1962—64, 1968, Tchg. fellowship, Mich. State U., 1969—71. Mem.: Lisle C. of C., Am. Coun. Acad. Deans, Am. Assn. Higher Edn., Math. Assn. America, Am. Math. Soc., Kappa Mu Epsilon. Home: Lisle, Ill. Died Jan. 3, 2009.

CAMP, OSCAR BAMBACE, health science association administrator; b. NYC, Aug. 23, 1920; s. Romolo and Angela (Bambace) Camponeschi; m. Leah Rosenblatt, Dec. 24, 1944 (div. Dec. 1975); children: Michael R., Mindy C. Tellez, Jonathon M. (dec.); m. Lorraine Papciak, May 17, 1980. BS, U. Md., 1941; MD, U. Md. Med. Coll., 1945; MS in Surgery, NYU Med. Coll., 1949. Diplomate Am. Bd. Surgery. Practice medicine specializing in surgery, Balt., 1952-77; pres. United Optical Ctr., Inc., Balt., 1964-83; sec., treas. Associated Pension and Welfare Adminstrn., Balt., 1971-79; pres. United Health Maintenance, Balt., 1972-76, also chmn. bd. Med. dir. Internat. Ladies Garment Workers Union Mid-Atlantic Region, Balt., 1956—, Seafarers Internat. Union, Balt., 1959—. Contbr. articles to profl. jours. Cons. Asian Am. Free Labor, Inst.-Agy. for Internat. Devel., 1974-76; chmn. Balt.-Genoa Sister City Com., Balt., 1985—; bd. dirs. Columbus 500, Balt., 1987—. Served as surgeon USPHS, 1946-48. Named Man of Yr. Histadrut, 1965, United Jewish Appeal, 1977. Fellow ACS, Internat. Coll. Surgeons, Southeastern Surgical Congress, Am. Bd. Abdominal Surgeons; mem. AMA, Am. Pub. Health Assn., Group Health Assn. of Am., Med. and Chirurgical Faculty of Md., Balt. City Med. Socs. Clubs: University (Balt.); Hillendale Country (Phoenix, Md.); St. Andrew's Country (Boca Raton, Fla.). Democrat. Avocations: golf, tennis, skiing. Died July 4, 2009.

CAMPBELL, ADDISON JAMES, JR., writer; b. Dilliner, Pa., Dec. 16, 1933; s. Addison James Campbell and Nora Lee (Marshall) Reynolds; m. Fumie Murashige, Oct. 13, 1962; 1 child, Gary Clark Campbell. Pres. Action Bolt Corp., Houston, 1965-72. Author: Nanci's World, Ukelele Lil of Lihue, The Object; co-author: Fumie Murashige Campbell, 1994; contbr. numerous articles and research papers to profl. jours. Sgt. USMC, 1952-55. Recipient recognition award for Adult Correction Officer for Island of Kauai, State of Hawaii, 1987, 88. Home: Kapaa, Hawaii. Died Jan. 2, 2009.

CAMPBELL, EDWIN DENTON, educational association administrator, consultant, accountant; b. Boston, June 25, 1927; s. William Edwin and Mildred (Altmiller) C.; m. Crystal Cousins, 1973; children: Geraldine, Linda, David, Sean, Jennifer. Grad., Bentley Coll., Boston, 1948; CAS, Harvard U., Cambridge, Mass., 1971; EdD, 1975. CPA, Mass. Mgr. Arthur Andersen & Co. CPAs, Boston, 1948-53; v.p. Lab. for Electronics, Inc., Boston, 1953-62, also dir.; exec. v.p. Itek Corp., Lexington, Mass., 1962-70, dir., 1962-83; pres. Edn. Devel. Ctr., Newton, Mass., 1971-76, trustee, 1971—2004; pres. Gulf Mgmt. Inst. div. Gulf Oil Corp., Boston, 1976-83; on loan as exec. v.p. Nat. Alliance of Bus., Washington, 1983-86; dean sch. bus. Adelphi U., Garden City, NY, 1986-87; trustee Ednl. Testing Svc., Princeton, NJ, 1983-87, v.p., 1987-89; exec. dir. Coalition of Essential Schs., Annenberg Inst. for Sch. Reform, Brown U., Providence, 1990-96; prin. Padanaram Assocs., Inc., 1996—2001. Interim exec. dir. Plimoth Plantation, 1997; bd. dirs. Artworks!, 1993-2003; mem. faculty Bentley Coll., Boston, 1956-58. Cons. editor: Change, 1980-98. Trustee Bentley Coll., 1963—, New Bedford Whaling Mus., 1996—2003, Friends Acad., 1996—2002, Ptnrs. in Edn., Inc., 1997-99; v.p. Mass. Assn. Mental Health, 1965-68, bd. dirs., 1962-73; mem. Mass Commn. Vocat. Rehab., 1966-68, Coll. Bd. Commn. on Pre-coll. Counseling, 1984-86; mem. vis. com. Harvard Sch. Edn., 1977-83; mem. fin. com. Town of Carlisle, Mass., 1965-68; trustee Boston Urban Found., 1969-75, Mass. Taxpayers Found., 1962-68, Fenn Sch., 1970-75, OSTI, Inc., 1971-76, Lesley Coll., 1972-76, Mass. Advocacy Ctr., 1975-76. Served with USMC, 1943-45, PTO. Mem. Assn. Industries Mass. (pres. 1967-69, now dir.), Harvard Club Boston, Cosmos Club Washington (D.C.), New Bedford Yacht Club. Home: Dartmouth, Mass. Died Aug. 14, 2009.

CAMPBELL, JAMES DOUGLAS, oil company executive; b. Cin., July 19, 1941; m. Nancy Duty; children: Mary, James. BA, Johns Hopkins U., 1963. Mktg. trainee, various sales and adminstrv. positions Standard Oil Co., Cleve., 1966-75; gen. mgr. wholesale BP Oil Co., Wilmington, Del., 1975; mktg., refinery planning mgr. BP Oil Co. subs. Standard Oil Co., Cleve., 1976, mgr. products., 1977-82, v.p. wholesale mktg., 1982-84, v.p. branded sales, 1984, v.p. refining, 1985, pres. chems. div., from 1986. Died May 21, 2009.

CAMPBELL, JOHN PALMER, lawyer; b. Utica, NY, Sept. 1, 1923; s. Samuel R. and Sophia (Doolittle) C.; m. Eleanor M. Seggerman, Aug. 27, 1949; children: Samuel R., Frederick B., Louisa D., Mary Camilla. AB, Harvard U., 1947; LLB, Columbia U., 1949. Bar: N.Y. 1950. Assoc. Reynolds, Rich-

WHO WAS WHO IN AMERICA 33 CAREY

ards & McCutcheon, NYC, 1949-50; asst. counsel com. to investigate crime in interstate commerce U.S. Senate, 1951; assoc. J.P. Morgan & Co. Inc., NYC, 1952, Curtis, Mallet-Prevost, Colt & Mosle, NYC, 1953-59, ptnr., from 1959. Dir. pvt. corps.; conservator, trustee Continental Vending Machine Corp., 1963-64. Mem. Nassau County (N.Y.) Rep. Com., 1952-57; del. Rep. Nat. Conv., 1976, 80, alt. del., 1984, 88; trustee Middlesex Sch., Concord, Mass., 1952-55, 57-72, Clarkson Coll. Tech., Potsdam, N.Y., 1969-79, 87—, Mus. Am. Indian, 1964-75. Capt. USAAF, 1942-46, ETO. Decorated Air medal. Mem. ABA, N.Y. State Bar Assn., Assn. of Bar of City of N.Y., Maine Bar Assn., D.C. Bar Assn., VFW. Republican. Episcopalian. Home: York, Maine. Died Mar. 10, 2009.

CAMSTER, BARON OF See WIEMANN, MARION JR.

CANADA, EUGENE (BUD CANADA), state senator; b. Hartshorne, Okla., June 6, 1925; 3 children. Student, U. Ark., Fayetteville. Mem. Ark. Ho. Reps., Little Rock, 1959-63, Ark. State Senate, Little Rock, from 1973, chmn. revenue and tax com., mem. Ark. Legis. Coun., mem. jt. budget com., budget hearings, mem. econ. and tax policy com., energy com., jt. budget com., mem. pub. retirement and social security programs com., mem. senate efficiency com., state agys. and govtl. affairs, others, pres. pro tempore, 1989-90. Pres. Mid-South Life Ins. Co., Deb Cancellation Sys. Inc. Former sheriff, Hot Springs, Ark. Mem. Masons Democrat. Baptist. Died Dec. 21, 2009.

CANDEE, BENJAMIN LEROY, JR., retired psychologist, educator; b. Syracuse, NY, May 24, 1921; s. Benjamin L. Sr. and Maude G. (Merrill) C.; m. Alice Kemeny Kohn, Jan. 8, 1951 (div. July 1958); m. Jean A. Carey, Dec. 24, 1960; children: William, Amy, Philip. BA, Cornell U., 1941; MS in Edn., Syracuse U., 1945; PhD, U. Nebr., 1955. Diplomate Am. Bd. Profl. Psychology. Ship's cattleman Brethren Svc. Com., 1946-47; ships purser US Lines, Inc., 1947-48; relief worker Am. Friends Svc. Com., 1949; area officer UN Relief and Works Agy. for Palestine Refugees, Acre, Israel, 1949-50; sch. psychologist Cleve. City Sch. Dist., Ohio, 1954-77, supr. psychol. svc. Ohio, 1977-87. Psychology instr. Cuyahoga C.C., Cleve., 1969-71, Cleve. (Ohio) State U., 1973-76; mem. testing com. Ohio Bd. Psychology, Columbus, 1975. Mem. War Resister's League, 1940—; activist, organizer Com. on Racial Equality, Syracuse, NY, 1941-42; conscientious objector fed. prison, Danbury, Conn., 1946; mem., clinic protector Nat. Abortion Rights League, Cleve., 1992-95. With Civilian Pub. Svc., 1943-45. Mem. ACLU, APA, Cleve. Psychol. Assn., Cleve. Assn. Sch. Psychologists, Psychologists for Social Responsibility, Planned Parenthood, Sierra Club. Avocations: reading, solving anacrostics, genealogy. Home: Shaker Heights, Ohio. Died Jan. 10, 2009.

CANNELL, STEPHEN JOSEPH, television writer, producer, director, actor; b. Los Angeles, Feb. 5, 1941; s. Joseph Knapp and Carolyn (Baker) C.; m. Marcia C. Finch, Aug. 8, 1964; children: Derek (dec.), Tawnia, Chelsea, Cody. BA, U. Oreg., 1964. CEO Stephen J. Cannell Prodns., 1979—2010. Creator, writer, producer (TV series) Rockford Files, 1974-80, creator, producer Baa-Baa Blacksheep, 1978, Richie Brockelman, 1978, The Duke, 1979, Stone, 1979, The Greatest American Hero, 1981-83, Henderson Monsters, 1980, Midnight Offerings, 1981, creator Baretta, 1976, producer The A-Team, 1983-86, Riptide, 1984-86, Wiseguy, 1987-90, Hardcastle and McCormmick, The Quest, Tenspeed and Brownshoe, Stingray, Hunter, 21 Jump Street, J.J. Starbuck, Booker, 1989, The Hat Squad, 1991, exec., supr. Disney presents the 100 Lives of Black Jack Savage, 1991, The Commish, 1991, Palace Guard, 1991, Street Justice, 1991, Cobra, 1993, Jake Lassiter: Justice on the Bayou, 1995, Marker, 1995, The Return of Hunter: Everyone Walks in L.A., 1995, Two, 1995, The Rockford Files: Crime and Punishment, Profit, 1996, The Rockford Files: Murder and Misdemeanors, 1997, actor Diagnosis Murder, 1997-99, Pacific Blue, 1999-2000, Castle, 2010, exec. prodr., writer (TV films) Hawaii-Five O, 1997, Hunter: Return to Justice, 2002, Hunter: Back in Force, 2003, actor Threshold, 2003, Ice Spiders, 2007, writer 24/24 Rule, 2007, prodr., writer (films) Dead Above Ground, 2002, It Waits, 2005, The Tooth Fairy, 2006, The A-Team, 2010, actor, The Contract, 2002, Half Past Dead, 2002, prodr. Deamon Hunter, 2005, Left in Darkness, 2006, The Garden, 2006, The Poker House, 2008, writer The Greatest American Hero: The Fan Series, 2009, author (Shane Scully series) The Devil's Workshop, 1999, Tin Collectors, 2000, Viking Funeral, 2001, Hollywood Tough, 2003, Vertical Coffin, 2004, Cold Hit, 2005, White Sister, 2006 Recipient Mystery Writers award, 1975; Emmy award, 1979, 80, 81 Mem. Writers Guild (4 awards), Producers Guild, Dirs. Guild. Episcopalian. Died Sept. 30, 2010.

CANTOR, GEORGE NATHAN, journalist; b. Detroit, June 14, 1941; s. Harold and Evelyn (Grossman) C.; m. Sheryl Joyce Bershad, Dec. 7, 1975; children: Jaime, Courtney. BA, Wayne State U., 1962. Reporter, editor Detroit Free Press, 1963-77; columnist Detroit News, from 1977; commentator WWJ-Radio, Detroit, 1981-90, WXYZ-TV, Detroit, 1982-90; editl. page writer Detroit News. Author: The Great Lakes Guidebook, 3 vols., 1978-80. Bd. dirs. Greater Detroit Area Hosp. Council, 1983. Recipient Malcolm Bingay Wayne State U., 1962; recipient Paul Tobenaw Meml. Columbia U., 1980, Disting. Achievement UPI, 1982 Mem. Phi Beta Kappa Jewish. Home: Southfield, Mich. Died Aug. 13, 2010.

CAPALBO, CARMEN, theater director, producer; b. Harrisburg, Pa., Nov. 1, 1925; s. Joseph and Concetta (Riggio) C.; m. Patricia McBride, July 9, 1950 (div. June 1961); children: Carla, Marco. Student, Yale Sch. Drama. Prodns. include: dir., co-prodr. (plays) Juno and the Paycock, Shadow and Substance, Dear Brutus, Awake and Sing!, The Threepenny Opera, The Potting Shed, A Moon for the Misbegotten, The Cave Dwellers, The Rise and Fall of the City of Mahagonny; dir. (opera) The Good Soldier Schweik, (plays) A Connecticut Yankee, Seidman and Son, The Strangers, Enter Solly Gold, Slowly, By Thy Hand Unfurled; original dir.: The Sign in Sidney Brustein's Window, The Chosen; also TV prodn. The Power and the Glory; story cons.: Studio One, 1951-52; cons. The Bronx: After the Fires, Conversation with Eddie, 1983; prodn. mgr. Emlyn Williams as Charles Dickens, 1952-53, Jean-Louis Barrault-Madeleine Renaud Co., 1952; dir., prodr., writer 200 radio plays. With US Army, 1944—45. Decorated Bronze Star, Purple Heart; recipient spl. Tony award 1956, Obie award 1956. Mem. League N.Y. Theatres, Dirs. Guild Am., Stage Dirs. and Choreographers Soc. (founding mem.), League OffBroadway Theatres (co-founder 1958, exec. bd. 1958-60), Royal Philatelic Soc. London. Died Mar. 14, 2010.

CAPELLE, KENNETH EARL, real executive executive; b. Fonddulac, Wis., May 25, 1938; s. Ira Richard and Aimee Cecelia (Dignin) Capelle. BA, U. Southern Fla., 1964; postgrad., Stetson U., 1966. Exec. trainee 1st Nat. Bank of Atlanta, 1966—68; mktg. rep. IBM, Atlanta, 1968—71; mgr. S.E. Divsn. Centurion Devel., Atlanta, 1973—77; v.p. Gallery Homes, Inc., Atlanta, 1978—83; pres. Transfer Location Corp., Dallas, from 1983. Mem. editl. com. Employee Relocation Coun., Washington, 1982—83. Contbr. articles to profl. jours. With USMC, 1957—60. Republican. Episcopalian. Home: Argyle, Tex. Died Jan. 21, 2010.

CAPICE, PHILIP CHARLES, retired broadcast executive; b. Bernardsville, NJ, June 24, 1931; s. Philip Joseph and Angelina Mary (Togno) C. BA, Dickinson Coll., 1952; M.F.A., Columbia U., 1954. Production supr., assoc. program dir. Benton & Bowles Inc., NYC, 1954-64, Vice pres. in charge program devel., 1965-69; dir. spl. programs CBS-TV Network, NYC, 1969-74; sr. v.p. creative affairs Lorimar Prodns., Burbank, Calif., 1974-78; pres. Lorimar TV, Burbank, Calif., 1978-79; ind. prodr. Lorimar Productions, Culver City, Calif., 1979—2009; pres., CEO Raven's Claw Productions, Los Angeles, Calif. Exec. producer: (TV series) The Blue Knight, 1975, Eight Is Enough, 1977-81, Hunter, 1977, Dallas, 1978-85, Flatbush, 1979; (TV mini-series) Studs Lonigan, 1979 A Man Called Intrepid, 1979; (TV movies) The Stranger Within, 1974, Bad Ronald, 1974, the Runaways, 1975, Hallmark Hall of Fame, 1975, Widow, 1976, Helter Skelter, 1976, Sybil, 1976 (Emmy Award, 1977), Peabody Award, 1977), Bunco, 1977, Green Eyes, 1977 (Peabody Award, 1978), Humanitas Prize, 1978), The Prince of Central Park, 1977, A Question of Guilt, 1978, Long Journey Back, 1978, Some Kind of Miracle, 1979 (Christopher Award), A Matter of Life and Death, 1981, Private Sessions, 1985 Trustee Dickinson Coll. Recipient Emmy award, 1977, Peabody award, 1977, 78, Disting. Alumni awrd for profl. achievements Dickinson Coll., 2003. Mem. Acad. TV Arts and Scis., The Caucus for Producers, Writers and Dirs, Producers-Writers Guild. Home: Los Angeles, Calif. Died Dec. 30, 2009.

CAPLIN, ARNOLD STEWART, recording company executive; b. NYC, May 8, 1929; s. Isadore Samuel and Lillian (Tanz) C.; m. Barbara Stein, June 29, 1950; children: Robert, Alan. Student, Sch. Visual Arts, 1966. Pres. Biograph Recrods, Inc., Chatham, N.Y., from 1964. Cons. Hist. Records, Chatham, 1964—; techr. Biograph and Hist. Records, Inc., Chatham, 1971—; advisor Record Industry Pers., N.Y.C. and Chatham, 1971—. Producer LP's including Bukka White, 1974 (Grammy 1974), Thad Jones, Mel Lewis, 1975 (Grammy 1976), Seasons of Peace, 1971 (Record of Yr. 1971, 72, 73); CD's including George Gershwin, 1988 (Indie 1989), Scott Joplin vol. 1 and vol 2, 1988 (Indie 1988), Thomas "Fats" Waller, 1988 (Indie 1989), James P Johnson, 1988 (Libr. Congress 1989), Three Shades of Blues, 1988 (Libr. Congress 1989), Benny Goodman, 1988. Pres., Bicentennial Celebration, Canaan, N.Y., 1976, Dem. Orgn., Canaan, 1976, 80. Recipient over 30 nominations in 25 yrs. for Grammy award, 1967-80. Fellow Nat. Acad. Recording Arts and Scis., Nat. Assn. Ind. Record Distributors and Mfrs., World Jazz Fedn.; mem. ASCAP, Broadcast Music, Inc. Avocations: fishing, painting, photgraphy, gardening, pruning. Home: Canaan, NY. Died Dec. 25, 2009.

CAPODILUPO, ELIZABETH JEANNE HATTON, public relations executive, writer; b. McRae, Ga., May 3, 1940; d. Lewis Irby and Essee Elizabeth (Parker) Hatton; m. Raphael S. Capodilupo, Jan. 21, 1967. Grad., Dale Carnegie Inst., 1976. Sec. A.R. Clark Acct., Fernandina Beach, Fla., 1958-59; statistician Yale New Haven Med. Ctr., 1959—60; receptionist, girl Friday Sta. WNDT-TV, NYC, 1960-62, Coy Hunt and Co., NYC, 1962-69; dir. pub. rels. Woodlawn Cemetery, 1969—98, historian, cmty. affairs coord., 1971-84, asst. to pres., 1984-99, dir. pub. rels., 1984; grad. asst. Dale Carnegie Inst., 1977-78. Editor, writer Woodlawn Cemetery Newsletter; rschr. Woodlawn Cemetery's Hall of Fame; contbr. articles to Collier Encyclopedia, 1985; contbr. articles to profl. jours. Chmn. ann. Adm. Farragut Honor Ceremony, Bronx, 1976—; founder, chmn. Toys for Needy Children, 1983-97; bd. dirs. Bronx Mus. Arts, v.p., 1983-84; pres. Bronx Coun. Arts, 1987-90, Network Orgn. Bronx Women, 1997-98; adv. bd. Salvation Army, 1985, Bronx Arts Ensemble, 1985; bd. mgrs. Bronx YMCA, 1985, vice-chmn., 1989—; bd. dirs. Bronx Urban League, 1985, Bronx Coun. on Arts, 1985, pres. 1987-90; active Bronx Landmarks Task Force, 1994—. Recipient award citation VFW, 1976, Voice of Democracy Program judge's citation, 1980, Disting. Community Svc. award N.Y.C. Council, II Leone di Sanmarco award Italian Heritage & Culture Com. Bronx, 1989, Lifetime Achievement Humanitarian award Bronx Coun. on Arts, 1999-2000; named Woman of Yr., YMCA, Bronx, 1986, Network Orgn. Bronx Women, 1986, Jeanne and Ray Capodilupo named as Mr. & Mrs. Bronx 1989-90 proclaimed by Borough Pres., named Pioneer of the Bronx, 1992, Citizen of Yr. Bronx Club, 1995; recipient cert. appreciation Dale Carnegie Inst., 1977, Outstanding Citizenship award Bronx N.E. Kiwanis Club, 1981, Service to Youth award YMCA of Bronx, 1983; recipient proclamation City Council of N.Y., Italian Heritage and Culture Com. of the Bronx, 1989; Outstanding Cemeterian award Am. Cemetery Assn., 1987-88; Citation of Merit Bronx Borough Pres.'s Office, 1988; Spl. Hons. for Outstanding Vol. Work Ladies Aux. Our Lady of Mercy Med. Ctr.; named Hon. Grand Marshall Bronx Columbus Day Parade, 1987-89, Bronx Meml. Day Parade, 1989; apptd. to commn. celebrating 350 yrs. of the Bronx by Borough Pres., recipient Pioneer award for Women's History Month for Outstanding Humanitarian Svcs., 1991, Lifetime Achievement award Bronx YMCA, 1999-2000, Role Model award Columbus Alliance, 2000; Jeanne Hatton Capodilupo Day proclaimed by Bronx Borough Presdl. Proclamation, 1999. Mem. Bronx County Hist. Soc., Bronx Coun. on the Arts (pres.), Network Orgn. Bronx Women (pres. 1997-99), Women in Communication, Bronx C. of C. (sec. 1988), YMCA (life mem.), NY Press Club, Italian Big Sisters Club, Women's City Club, Order Eastern Star. Methodist. Avocations: cooking, antiques, reading, dance, painting. Home: Yonkers, NY. Died July 28, 2009.

CAPON, EDWIN GOULD, retired religious organization administrator, minister; b. Boston, Apr. 1, 1924; s. Gould and Helen (Wood) C.; m. Norma Jean Wilcoxson (div. Jan. 1971); children: Peter Lawrence, Jonathan Edwin; m. Esther Constance Nicastro, Sept. 5, 1975. AB, Harvard U., 1947; STM, Andover-Newton Theol. Sem., 1949. Ordained to ministry Swedenborgian Ch., 1949. Min. Bridgewater (Mass.) New Ch., 1948-51, Elmwood (Mass.) New Ch., 1949-55, Detroit New Ch., Royal Oak, Mich., 1977-79; v.p. Swedenborg Sch. Religion, Cambridge, Mass., 1953-55, pres. Cambridge and Newton, Mass., 1955-77; pastor San Francisco Swedenborgian Ch., 1979-90; interim min. St. Paul Swedenborgian Ch., 1991-92, min., 1992-94; pres. The Swedenborgian Ch., Newton, 1992-98, chmn. coun. mins., 1956-67. Trustee Urbana (Ohio) U., 1966-80, 92-99; v.p. Mass. Coun. Chs. Mem. Swedenborgian Ch. Avocations: hiking, mountain climbing in new england. Home: Concord, Calif. Died Feb. 3, 2009.

CAPPS, CHARLES WILSON, JR., retired state legislator; b. Cleveland, Miss., Jan. 1, 1925; m. Allen Hobbs; 3 children. Mem. Miss. House of Reps., 1972—2005. Democrat. Methodist. Home: Cleveland, Miss. Died Dec. 25, 2009.

CARAVATT, PAUL JOSEPH, JR., communications executive; b. New Britain, Conn., Dec. 13, 1922; s. Paul Joseph and Bessie (Avery) C.; m. B. Laura Bennett, June 22, 1946; children— Cynthia Diane, Suzanne Laura. AB, Dartmouth, 1945, MBA, 1947. With Nat. Dairy Assn., 1947-49, Young & Rubicam, 1949-50; advt. mgr. Hunting and Fishing mag., 1950-52, Biow Co., 1952-56; v.p. Ogilvy, Benson & Mather, 1956-59; sr. v.p. Foote, Cone & Belding, 1960-64, LaRoche, McCaffrey & McCall (advt. agy.), NYC, 1964-66; pres. Carl Ally, Ind. (advt. agy.), NYC, 1966-67; chmn. bd., chief exec. officer Marschalk Co., Inc. (mem. Interpublic Group of Cos.), NYC, 1967-69; sr. v.p., dir. Interpub. Group Cos., NYC, 1970-72; pres., chief exec. officer, dir. Caravatt Communications, 1971-86, Newtel World Communications, NYC, 1971-86; pres., chief exec. officer Caravatt Mktg., Wilton, Conn., from 1986; pres. Caravatt Mktg. Group, from 1998. Exec. dir. Vision Fund, The Lighthouse, 1994—97. Mem. SAR, Spl. Interest Video Assn. (pres., exec. dir. 1988-97), Newcomen Soc., Univ. Club (N.Y.C.), Ednl. Found. of Spl. Interest Marketers and Prodrs. (pres. 1997—), Zeta Psi. Congregationalist. Home: Southbury, Conn. Died Apr. 3, 2009.

CARDWELL, DAVID EARL, lawyer; b. Bowling Green, Ky., Dec. 14, 1951; s. Emery Earl and Vera Mae (Reed) C.; m. Dagmar Reece Larsen, Sept. 8, 1973; children: Reece Elizabeth, Patrick John. BA with honors, U. Fla., 1973, JD, 1975. Bar: Fla. 1975, U.S. Dist. Ct. (no., so. and mid. dists.) Fla. 1977, D.C. 1978, U.S. Ct. Appeals (11th cir.) 1980. Dir. staff Fla. Ho. of Reps., Tallahassee, 1979; assoc. Hahn, Breathitt & Roberts, Lakeland, Fla., 1979-82; ptnr. Holland & Knight, Lakeland, 1982-91, Orlando, from 1991. City atty. City of Lakeland, 1979-82. Author: Elections and Ethics, 1980. Mem. ABA (bd. govs. 1992—, ho. of dels. 1991—, mem. commn. on non-dues revenue, chmn. urban, state and local govt. sect. 1990-91, mem. coun. of adminstrv. law sect. 1988-91, standing com. on election law 1989-92, task force on initiatives and refereda 1991-930, Fla. Bar (chmn. local govt. law sect. 1982, continuing legal edn. com. 1982-88), U. Fla. Nat. Alumni Assn. (pres. 1986-87), Nat. Assn. Bond Lawyers (lectr.). Home: Orlando, Fla. Died Nov. 18, 2009.

CAREY, BRUCE DOUGLAS, lawyer; b. Detroit, July 20, 1923; s. Frederick Arthur and Hazel Eleanor (Whited) C.; m. Catherine Dunwody McKinley, June 23, 1951; children: William M., Elizabeth M., Ann D. BA, U. Mich., 1947, JD, 1950. Bar: Mich. 1951. Practiced in, Detroit, from 1951; atty. Chrysler Corp., Detroit, 1950-55, Carey & Carey, Detroit, from 1955. Trustee Grosse Pointe Meml. Ch. Served as lt. (j.g.) USNR, 1943-46. Mem. ABA, Mich. Bar Assn., Detroit Bar Assn., Country Club Detroit. Presbyterian. Home: Grosse Pointe, Mich. Died Apr. 14, 2009.

CAREY, JOHN J., utilities executive; b. Massillon, Ohio, July 23, 1931; s. John Joseph and Mary A. (Foy) C.; m. Joyce Lorraine Bufalini; children: Lorraine, Barbara. BEE, U. Pitts., 1956. Elec. maintenance supr. J&L Steel Corp., Pitts., 1956-58, Duquesne Light Co., Pitts., 1958-66, station supt., 1966-79, dir. nuclear ops., 1979-81, v.p. then sr. v.p. nuclear ops., 1981-87, exec. v.p. ops., from 1987. Bd. dirs. Western Pa. chpt. Nat. Kidney Found., Pitts., 1984, The Med. Ctr., Beaver, Pa., 1986. Mem. Am. Nuclear Soc., Duquesne Club, Rivers Club. Republican. Roman Catholic. Home: Ambridge, Pa. Died June 9, 2009.

CAREY, JOHN LEO, lawyer; b. Morris, Ill., Oct. 1, 1920; s. John Leo and Loretta (Conley) C.; m. Rhea M. White, July 15, 1950; children: John Leo III, Daniel Hobart, Deborah M. BS, St. Ambrose Coll., Davenport, Ia., 1941; JD, Georgetown U., 1947, LLM, 1949. Bar: Ind. 1954, DC 1947, Ill. 1947. Legis. asst. Senator Scott W. Lucas, 1945-47; spl. atty. IRS, Washington, 1947-54; since practiced in South Bend; ptnr. Barnes & Thornburg, from 1954, now of counsel; law prof. taxation Notre Dame Law Sch., 1968-90. Trustee LaLumire Prep. Sch., Laporte, Ind. Served with USAAF, WW II; to lt. col. USAF, Korean War. Decorated D.F.C., Air medal. Mem. ABA (bd. govs. 1986-89, treas. 1990-93), Ind. Bar Assn. (pres. 1976-77), St. Joseph County Bar Assn., Signal Point Country Club, Quail Valley City Club. Home: Vero Beach, Fla. Died Jan. 16, 2009.

CAREY, SARAH COLLINS, lawyer; b. NYC, Aug. 12, 1938; d. Jerome Joseph and Susan (Atlee) Collins; m. James J. Carey, Aug. 28, 1962 (div. 1977); 1 child, Sasha; m. John D. Reilly, Jan. 27, 1979; children: Sarah Reilly, Katherine Reilly. BA, Radcliffe Coll., 1960; LLB, Georgetown U., 1965. Bar: D.C. 1966, U.S. Supreme Ct. 1977. Soviet specialist USIA/U.S. Dept. State, 1961-65; assoc. Arnold & Porter, Washington, 1965-68; asst. dir. Lawyers Com. for Civil Rights, Washington, 1968-73; ptnr. Heron, Burchette, Ruckert & Rothwell/predecessor firms, Washington, 1973-90; chair CIS Practice Steptoe and Johnson, Washington, 1990-99; chair CIS Practice, sr. ptnr. internat. Squire, Sanders & Dempsey, Washington, from 1999. Cons. Ford Found., 1975—83; bd. dirs. Yukos Oil Co., 2001—05, Akbars Bank, 2006—08. Bd. dirs. Acad. for Ednl. Devel., from 2004; chair bd. dirs. Eurasia Found., from 1994; bd. dirs. Russia-Am. Enterprise Fund, 1993—95, Def. Enterprise Fund, 1994—2001, Georgetown U. Sch. Law Inst. Pub. Representation, 1971—85, Am. Arbitration Assn., 1975—82, East Europe Found., Ukraine. Mem.: Internat. Women's Forum, Atlantic Coun., Coun. Fgn. Rels. Democrat. Home: Washington, DC. Died July 29, 2010.

CARFINE, KENNETH EDWARD, former federal agency administrator; b. Boston, 1949; m. Deborah J. Schmidt; children: Kenneth Jr., Gregory. BS in Acctg., U. Baltimore, 1971. Banking, cash mgmt., payments, check claims, govt.-wide acctg. positions US Dept. Treasury, 1973—2003, dep. asst. sec. for fiscal ops. & policy, 2003—07, asst. sec. for fiscal svc., 2007—09. Recipient Alexander Hamilton award, US Dept. Treasury, 2009. Home: Woodbine, Md. Died Apr. 23, 2010.

CARLIN, ANDREW CHARLES, lawyer; b. NYC, Feb. 3, 1932; s. Andrew James and Hazel (Ferraro) Carlin; m. Abbe E. Cooper, Dec. 19, 1982; 1 child, Erin Catherine. BA cum laude, St. John's U., 1953; JD, Harvard U., 1956. Bar: NY 1973. Mgr. pub. affairs Ciba-Geigy Corp., Ardsley, NY, 1971—77; sole practice Yonkers, NY, 1977—79; ptnr. Fusco & Carlin, Yonkers, from 1979. Mem. NY State Emergency Fin. Control Bd. of City of Yonkers, from 1984; pres. Yonkers Employment for Srs., Inc., 1981—84, Wainwright House, Inc., Rye, 1981—84. Trustee Yonkers Pub. Library, 1980—85. Mem.: Yonkers C. of C. (pres. 1983—84), Yonkers Lawyers Assn., Westchester Bar Assn., NY State Bar Assn., ABA. Republican. Roman Catholic. Died May 12, 2010.

CARLIN, HERBERT J., electrical engineering educator, researcher; b. NYC, May 1, 1917; s. Louis Aaron and Shirley (Salzman) C.; children: Seth Andrew, Elliot Michael; m. Mariann J. Hartmann, June 29, 1975 B.E.E., Columbia Coll., 1938, M.E.E., 1950; PhD in Elec. Engring., Poly. Inst. N.Y., 1947. Engr. Westinghouse Corp., Newark, 1940-45; from asst. to assoc. prof. Poly. Inst. Bklyn., 1945-60, prof., head electrophysics, 1960-66; J. Preston Levis prof. engring. Cornell U., Ithaca, NY, from 1966, dir. elec. engring., 1966-75. Mem. adv. panel Nat. Bur. Standards, Boulder, Colo., 1967-70; mem. rev. com. Lehigh U., Bethlehem, Pa., 1966-74, U. Pa., Phila., 1979-82; vis. prof. Ecole Normale Superieure, Paris, 1964-67, MIT, Boston, 1973-74; vis. scientist Nat. Ctr. for Telecommunications, Issy Les Moulineaux, France, 1979-80; vis. lectr. U. Genoa, Italy, summer 1973, U. London, Dec. 1979, The Technion, Haifa, Israel, Mar. 1980, Tianjin U., China, summer 1982, Univ. Coll., Dublin, Ireland, summer 1983, Polytech. of Turin, Italy, summer 1985, 91, Fed. Polytech., Lausanne, Switzerland, summer 1992. Co-author: Wideband Circuit Design, 1997. Fellow NSF, 1964; recipient Outstanding Achievement award U.S. Air Force, 1965 Fellow IEEE (chmn. profl. group on circuit theory 1955-56, Centennial medal 1985) Home: Walnut Creek, Calif. Died Feb. 9, 2009.

CARLSON, THEODORE JOSHUA, lawyer, retired utilities executive; b. Hartford, Conn., Jan. 4, 1919; s. John and Hulda (Larson) C.; m. Jacqueline L. Coburn, Apr. 25, 1953; children: Stephanie, Christopher J., Victoria, Antoinette. AB, Montclair State U., 1940; JD, Columbia U., 1948, AM, 1951; postgrad., U. Chgo., 1942. Bar: N.Y. 1948. Assoc. Gould & Wilkie, NYC, 1948-54, ptnr., 1954-96, sr. ptnr., 1970-96, of counsel, from 1997; dir. Central Hudson Gas & Electric Corp., Poughkeepsie, N.Y., 1968-89, chmn., prin. officer, 1975-89. Mem., chmn. fin. and audit com. N.Y. State Energy Rsch. Devel. Authority, 1980-88; dir. Empire State Electric Energy Rsch. Com., Edison Electric Inst., 1976-79; chmn. exec. com. Energy Assn. N.Y. State, 1976-77, 82-83, N.Y. Power Pool, 1977-78; dir., mem. exec. com. Mid-Hudson Pattern, Inc., Poughkeepsie, N.Y.; chmn. bd. dirs. Christian Herald Assn. and related cos., 1985-92. Author: A Design For Freedom. Pres. United Fund Rockville Centre, N.Y., 1966; chmn. adv. bd. Westchester County Salvation Army, 1977-80, State of N.Y., 1977-83; chmn. Greater N.Y. Adv. Bd., 1988-91; chmn. bd. trustees King's Coll., 1982-89. Capt. USAAF, 1942-46. Mem. ABA, N.Y. Bar Assn., Assn. of Bar of City of N.Y. (chmn. pub. utility sect. com. on post admissions-legal edn. 1970-73), Rotary (hon.). Died July 16, 2009.

CARLUCCIO, CHARLES GOLDHAMMER, physician; b. Hoboken, NJ, Mar. 8, 1926; s. Charles Goldhammer and Elsie (Visconte) C.; m. Rosaline Pizzino; children: Charles IV, Caroline Carluccio Canales. BS, St. Peters Coll., Jersey City, 1949; MD, U. Bologna, Italy, 1954. Diplomate Am. Bd. Psychiatry and Neurology. Rotating intern St. Michael's Hosp., Newark, 1954-55; gen. practice medicine Cliffside Park, N.J., 1955-58; resident in psychiatry Columbia Presbyn. Hosp., NYC, 1957-60, asst. psychiatrist Vanderbilt Clinic, 1971; pvt. practice psychiatry West New York, N.J., from 1960; exec. med. dir. Mt. Carmel Guild Child Guidance Inst., 1962; chief dept. psychiatry Meadowlands Med. Ctr., Secaucus, N.J., 1977; founder, med. dir. Ctr. for Treatment Stress Related Disorders, Ctr. for Treatment Headache of Holy Name Hosp., Teaneck, N.J., 1977. Contbr. articles to mags. and profl. jours. Mem. ACP (assoc.), Pan-Am. Med. Soc., N.J. Med. Soc., Am. Assn. for Study Headache, Nat. Headache Found. Died Mar. 15, 2010.

CARMICHAEL, LYNN PAUL, physician; b. Louisville, Sept. 15, 1928; s. Donald Palmer and Vivian Iris (Linler) C.; m. Joan Pauline Steinlight, June 26, 1954; children: John Kevin, Cynthia Gail, Jon Christian. Student, Ind. U., 1945-48; MD, U. Louisville, 1952. Diplomate Am. Bd. Family Practice. From intern to battalion surgeon U.S. Army, San Antonio, Korea, 1952-54; pvt. practice Mooresville, Ind., 1954-55; pvt. gen. practice Miami, from 1955. Fellow Harvard Med. Sch., Boston, 1953-54; faculty U. Miami, 1965-98; test com. Nat. Bd. Med. Examiners, 1976-79; residency rev. com. Accreditation Coun. for Grad. Med. Edn., Chgo., 1972-75; cons. Pub. Health Svc., Washington, 1976-90. Med. support ARC, Cuba, 1962, Medishare, Haiti, 1995. Decorated bronze star U.S. Army, 1953, Primary Care Achievement for Edn. Pew Found., 1996. Mem. AMA, Soc. Tchrs. Family Medicine (founding pres. 1967-70, founding editor 1978-83), Am. Acad. Gen. Practice, Inst. of Medicine Nat. Acad. Sci. (sr. membership 1995). Avocations: bicycling, swimming. Home: Tucson, Ariz. Died June 19, 2009.

CARNEY, THOMAS PATRICK, medical instruments company executive, researcher; b. Dubois, Pa., May 27, 1915; s. James Patrick and Margaret Elizabeth (Senard) Carney; m. Mary Elizabeth McGuire, Oct. 3, 1942; children: Thomas, Sheila, James, Janet. BS in Chem. Engring., Notre Dame U., 1937, LLD (hon.), 1969; MS, Pa. State U., 1939, PhD, 1941. Rsch. chemist Reilly Tar and Chem. Corp., Indpls., 1937—39, 1941—43, Eli Lilly & Co., Indpls., 1944—54, v.p., 1954—64; postdoc. fellow U. Wis., Madison, 1943—44; exec. v.p. G.D. Searle & Co., Skokie, Ill., 1964—74; chmn. exec. com. Nat. Patent Devel. Co., NYC, 1974—75; pres. Metatech Corp., Northbrook, Ill., 1976—86, dir., chmn., from 1986, Bioferm, Inc., Northbrook, from 1980. Bd. dirs. ImmunoGenetics, Vineland, NJ, TNI Pharms., Inc., Cistron Biotech., Bloomfield, NJ; cons. to sec. HEW, Washington. Author: Laboratory Fractional Distillation, 1949, Instant Evolution, 1980, False Profits, 1981; contbr. articles to profl. publs. Chmn. bd. trustees Barat Coll., 1970—80, U. Notre Dame, 1980—85. Recipient Disting. Svc. award, Assn. Cons. Chemists and Engrs., 1976, Ernest Stewart award, Coun. Advancement and Support Edn., 1982. Fellow: AAAS, Am. Inst. Chemists, Chem. Soc. London, NY Acad. Sci.; mem.: London Soc. Chem. Industry, Swiss Chem. Soc., Am. Chem. Soc. (divsn. chmn.), Phi Lambda Upsilon, Alpha Chi Sigma, Sigma Xi. Achievements include patents in field. Home: Lake Forest, Ill. Died Dec. 7, 2009.

CARNICERO, JORGE EMILIO, aeronautical engineer, transportation executive; b. Buenos Aires, July 17, 1921; arrived in US, 1942, naturalized, 1950; s. Alberto and Ana (Sulimeau) C.; m. Jacqueline Joanne Damman, Feb. 22, 1946; children— Jacqueline Denise, Jorge Jay. Student, U. LaPlata, Argentina, 1939—41, Rensselaer Poly. Inst., 1945. Chief engr. Dodero Airlines, Argentina, 1945, Flota Aerea Mercante, Argentina, 1945-46; v.p. Air Carrier Svc. Corp., Washington, 1946, exec. v.p., 1947-55, chmn. bd. dirs., dir., 1955-88; ret., 1988. Past chmn., bd. Dyncorp (formerly Calif. Ea. Aviation, then Dynalectron Corp.); pres., bd. dirs. Blue Cove, Inc., N.Y., Inter-Properties, Inc., Del., Trans-Am. Aero. Corp., Del., Round Hill Devel. Ltd., Jamaica. Bd. visitors Sch. Fgn. Service, Georgetown U., Washington; mem. council Rensselaer Poly. Inst., Troy, N.Y., mem. adv. bd. mech., aero. and mechanics dept. Fellow Royal Aero. Soc.; mem. Argentine-Am. C. of C. (bd. dirs.), Univ. Club, Met. Club, Congl. Country Club, Georgetown Club. Home: Washington, DC. Died Oct. 28, 2009.

CARONE, NICOLAS, artist; b. NYC, June 4, 1917; Student, Nat. Acad. of Design, Art Students League, Hans Hoffman Sch. Fine Arts, 1931—41. Founding mem. New York Studio School, Stable Gallery; tchr., painting Yale U., Columbia U., Brandeis U., Cornell U., Cooper Union, Sch. Visual Arts, Skowhegan Sch. Solo exhibitions, Lohin Geduld Gallery, Frumkin Gallery, Stable Gallery, Staempfli Gallery, group exhibitions, Mus. Modern Art, Rome, Brussel's World Fair, The Venice Biennale, The Tate Gallery, Guggenheim Mus., Mus. Modern Art, Nat. Acad. Design, Hunter Coll. Gallery, Baruch Coll. Gallery, Sewell Art Gallery Rice U., Rose Art Mus., Brandeis U., Ninth St. Show, Geitain Group, Japan, Represented in permanent collections, Whitney Mus., Mus. Am. Art, Hirschhorn Mus., Minn. Mus. Am. Art, Norton Mus. Art, Balt. Mus. Art. Recipient The Rome Prize, Andrew Carnegie prize, Nat. Acad. Mus.; named National Academician, 2001; grantee William Copely Grant, Childe Hassam Grant, NY State Coun. on Arts, Longview Found.; fellow Fullbright Fellowship. Died July 15, 2010.

CARPENTER, LIZ (ELIZABETH SUTHERLAND CARPENTER), journalist, writer, equal rights leader, lecturer; b. Salado, Tex., Sept. 1, 1920; d. Thomas Shelton and Mary Elizabeth (Robertson) Sutherland; m. Leslie Carpenter, June 17, 1944 (dec.); children: Scott Sutherland, Christy. BJ, U. Tex., 1942; PhD (hon.), Mt. Vernon Coll., Austin Coll. Reporter UP, Phila., 1944-45; propr. with husband of news bur. representing nat. newspapers Washington, 1945-61; exec. asst. to Vice Pres. Lyndon Johnson The White House, 1961-63, pres. sec., staff dir. to The First Lady, 1963-69; v.p. Hill & Knowlton, Inc., Washington, 1972-76; cons. LBJ Library, Austin, Tex.; asst. sec. for pub. affairs US Dept. Edn., 1980-81. Co-chmn. ERAmerica, 1976-81; dir. Nat. Wildflower Rsch. Ctr. Author: Ruffles and Flourishes, 1970, Getting Better All the Time, 1987, Unplanned Parenthood: Confessions of a Seventy-something Surrogate Mother, 1994, Start with a Laugh. An Insider's Guide To Making Speeches, Roasts, and Eulogies, 2000, Presidential Humor, 2006 Recipient Woman Year award in field of politics and pub. affairs Ladies Home Jour., 1977, Disting. Alumnae award U. Tex., 1974-75; named to Tex. Women's Hall Fame, 1985. Mem. Nat. Women's Polit. Caucus (founding mem. 1971), Women's Nat. Press (pres. 1954-55), Alpha Phi, Theta Sigma Phi (Nat. Headliners award 1962), Press Club (Washington), Headliners Club (Headliner award), Univ. Club (Austin). Died Mar. 20, 2010.

CARR, BEN WHEELER, sales executive; b. Knoxville, Tenn., Mar. 5, 1922; s. Hugh Patton and Mae (Wheeler) Carr; m. Allie Jones, Mar. 4, 1946; children: Ben W., Allen Patton. Student pub. schs., Harlan, Ky. With McComb Supply Co., Harlan, Ky., from 1941, salesman, 1950—76, v.p. sales, 1977—79, pres., 1980—85, chmn. bd., from 1986. With USMC, 1942—46, PTO. Mem.: C. of C., Harlan Country Club, United Comml. Travelers Club, Lions Lodge, Shriners Lodge, Masons Lodge. Republican. Baptist. Died June 29, 2010.

CARR, CHARLES LOUIS, retired religious organization administrator; b. Rockport, Ind., Sept. 9, 1930; s. Louis E. and Loris B. (Lindsey) C.; m. Shirley R. Cron, Nov. 15, 1950; children: Kathleen Carr Wright, Charles Stephen, Jeffrey Louis, David Wayne. Student, Ind. State U., 1949-50, So. Bapt. Theol. Sem., 1965-67; BS, Oakland City U., 1978, DD, 1994. Ordained to ministry Gen. Assn. Gen. Bapts., 1957. Pastor East Oolitic Gen. Bapt. Ch., Bedford, Ind., 1959-63, Mt. Zion Gen. Bapt. Ch., Indpls., 1963-65, Hunsinger Lane Gen. Bapt. Ch., Louisville, 1965-67; missionary to Saipan Mariana Islands, 1967-73; exec. dir. Gen. Bapt. Fgn. Mission Soc., Poplar Bluff, Mo., 1973-96; ret., 1996; pastor Wyatt United Meth Ch., from 1997, Dogwood United Meth Ch., from 1997; ret., 2005. Author: Seed, Soil and Seasons, 1988, Dancing Naked Before the Lord, 2008; contbr. articles to various publs. Home: Poplar Bluff, Mo. Died Nov. 2, 2009.

CARR, RUTH MARGARET, plastic surgeon; b. Waco, Tex., July 2, 1951; MD, U. Okla., 1977. Intern U. Okla. Med. Sch., Oklahoma City, 1977-78; resident U. Okla. Health Sci. Ctr., Oklahoma City, 1978-81, UCLA, 1981-83; plastic surgeon St. John's Hosp., from 1989. Clin. asst. prof. UCLA, 1983—, U. So. Calif., 1984-. Mem.: Bay Surgical Soc. (pres. 2004), Calif. Soc. Plastic Surgeons (parliamentarian 2004—05), Am. Soc. Plastic Surgeons. Died May 7, 2009.

CARRIER, WARREN PENDLETON, retired university chancellor, writer; b. Cheviot, Ohio, July 3, 1918; s. Burly Warren and Prudence (Alfrey) C.; m. Marjorie Jane Regan, Apr. 3, 1947 (dec.); 1 child, Gregory Paul; m. Judy Lynn Hall, June 14, 1973; 1 son, Ethan Alfrey. Student, Wabash Coll., 1938-40; AB, Miami U., Oxford, Ohio, 1942; MA, Harvard U., 1948; PhD, Occidental Coll., 1962. Asst. prof. English U. Iowa, 1949-52; assoc. prof. Bard Coll., 1953-57; lit. faculty Bennington, 1955-58; vis. prof. Sweet Briar (Va.) Coll., 1958-60; prof. Deep Springs (Calif.) Coll., 1960-62, Portland (Oreg.) State U., 1962-64; prof., chmn. English dept. U. Mont., Missoula, 1964-68; assoc. dean. prof. English and comparative lit., chmn. comparative lit. Livingston Coll., Rutgers U., 1968-69; dean Coll. Arts and Letters, San Diego State U., 1969-72; v.p. acad. affairs U. Bridgeport, Conn., 1972-75; chancellor U. Wis., Platteville, 1975-82. Author: The Hunt, 1952, Bay of the Damned, 1957, Toward Montebello, 1966, Leave Your Sugar for the Cold Morning, 1977, The Diver, 1986, Death of a Chancellor, 1986, An Honorable Spy, 1992, Murder at the Strawberry Festival, 1993, An Ordinary Man, 1997, Death of a Poet, 1999, Justice at Christmas, 1999, Risking the Wind, 1999, Coming to Terms, 2004; founder Quar. Rev. of Lit.; editor: Guide to World Literature, 1980; co-editor: Reading Modern Poetry, 1955, 68, Literature from the World, 1981; assoc. editor: Western Rev., 1949-51; contbr. articles, poems, revs. to lit. mags. Mem. Jud. Commn. Wis. Vol., Am. Field Service attached to Brit. Army, India-Burma, 1944-45. Recipient award for poetry Nat. Endowment for Arts, 1972; Colladay prize for poetry, 1986 Mem. Nat. Coun. Tchrs. English, Royal Soc. Arts, Wis. Acad. Arts and Scis., Phi Beta Kappa. Home: Washington, DC. Died Apr. 26, 2009.

CARROLL, ELIZABETH J., investment management consultant; b. Providence, Nov. 26, 1955; d. Robert Edward and Dorothy Mary (Desautels) Walker; m. Michael James Carroll, Feb. 12, 1978; children: Barton Joseph, Marina Jae, Morgan Joseph and Lydia Jae (twins). Student, U. R.I., 1976-77. Legal sec. Joseph B. Going, Esq., Newport, R.I., 1974-76; asst. adminstr. Forest Farm Health Care Ctr., Middletown, R.I., 1976-77; adminstrv. asst. Arboleda, Inc., Providence, 1977, treas., 1977-80; treas., gen. mgr. Third Beach Club, Middletown, 1986-94; treas. ABANCO Mgmt. Corp., Newport, 1980, v.p., treas., from 1980. Bus. mgr. 2d Story Theatre, Inc., Newport, 1978-84; cons. in field. Fundraiser Newport Co. Child & Family Svcs., 1982, various local charities; treas. van Bueren Charitable Found., 1989—; treas. Down Syndrome Soc. R.I., 1992-98, mem., 1992—. Named Career Woman of Yr., Bus. and Profl. Women of Newport Co., 1986. Mem. Newport Co. Bus. and Profl. Women (bd. dirs. 1984-87, treas. 1985-86). Democrat. Roman Catholic. Avocations: kite flying, camping, rubber stamping, needlecrafts. Home: Portsmouth, RI. Died Jan. 3, 2009.

CARROLL, HOLBERT NICHOLSON, political science educator; b. Charleroi, Pa., June 30, 1921; s. James Russell and Mary Leola (McDonough) C. AB, U. Pitts., 1943, MA, 1947; postgrad., Yale U., 1943-44; PhD, Harvard U., 1953. Faculty U. Pitts., 1946-48, 50—, prof. polit. sci., 1960-90, prof. emeritus, from 1990, chmn. dept., 1960-68; teaching fellow Harvard U., 1949-50. Cons. Brookings Instn., 1959 Author: The House of Representatives and Foreign Affairs, 1958, rev. edit., 1966, A Study of the Goverance of the University of Pittsburgh, 1972; contbr. chpt. to: The Congress and America's Future, 1965, rev. edit., 1973; book rev. editor: Am. Polit. Sci. Rev., 1979-81. Served with AUS, 1943-46, CBI. Mem. Am. Polit. Sci. Assn., Phi Beta Kappa, Omicron Delta Kappa. Died Mar. 11, 2010.

CARROLL, JOHN P., JR., lawyer; b. Bklyn., Sept. 19, 1924; AB, Cornell U., 1944; JD, Harvard U., 1949. Bar: N.Y. 1949. Sr. counsel Davis Polk & Wardwell, NYC. Mem. ABA, Assn. of Bar of City of N.Y. Died July 12, 2009.

CARROLL, THOMAS SYLVESTER, business executive; b. NYC, Oct. 1, 1919; s. Thomas Jeremiah and Johanna (Mulvihill) C.; m. Sidney Burke, Sept. 27, 1947 (div.); children: Jeffrey Burke, Thomas Jeremiah (dec.), James Francis, Matthew, Charles Laurence.; m. Caroline Wheelwright, May 30, 1981. AB cum laude, Catawba Coll., 1941; postgrad., MIT, 1941-42; MBA with distinction, Harvard U., 1947. Gen. mgr. mktg. services Lever Bros. Co., 1958-59, mktg. v.p., 1959-63, merchandising v.p., 1963-64, dir., from 1963, exec. v.p., 1964-67, pres., chief exec. officer, 1967-80, chmn. fin. com., 1980-83. Woodrow Wilson vis. fellow, 1986—. Police commr. City of New Canaan (Conn.), 1963-67; pres. Harvard Bus. Sch. Assn., 1973-74, mem. vis. com. Bus. Sch., 1975-81; bd. dirs. Assocs. Harvard Bus. Sch., 1975-83; trustee Mus. Modern Art, 1974—, Catawba Coll., 1967-88, Com. Econ. Devel.; bd. dirs. Internat. Exec. Service Corps., 1972-93, exec. v.p., 1980-82, pres., chief exec. officer, 1982-93. Served from cadet to lt. col. USAAF, 1941-46. Mem. Grocery Mfrs. Am. (chmn. 1978-80); mem. Conf. Bd. Clubs: Country of New Canaan; Racquet and Tennis, Economic (N.Y.C.) (dir. 1970-71); Metropolitan (Washington). Home: New Canaan, Conn. Died Feb. 1, 2010.

CARROLL, WILLIAM, retired English educator; b. Jan. 4, 1936; AB, Norfolk State U., 1965; MA, Temple U., 1967; PhD, U. N.C., 1978. Prof. Norfolk (Va.) State U., 1967-69, 73-99, prof. emeritus, from 1999; ret., 1999. Author: Songs, Scenes and Sentiments: Lyrical Works of Dr. Bill, 2003, The Untied Stats on American and Other Computer-assisted Writing Errors, 2005. Home: Virginia Beach, Va. Died Mar. 26, 2010.

CARSON, EDWARD MANSFIELD, retired bank executive; b. Tucson, Nov. 6, 1929; s. Ernest Lee and Earline M. (Mansfield) C.; m. Nadine Anne Severns, Dec. 13, 1952 (dec. 2007); children: Dawn, Tod. BSBA, Ariz. State U., 1951; grad. in banking, Rutgers U., 1963. With First Interstate Bank of Ariz., Phoenix, 1951-85, exec. v.p., 1969-72, chief adminstrv. officer, 1972-75, vice chmn., 1975-77, pres., CEO, 1977-85; pres. First Interstate Bancorp, L.A., 1985—90, chmn., CEO, 1990—95. Bd. dirs. Inspiration Resources Corp., Ramada Inns, Inc., First Interstate Bank of Oreg. Bd. fellows American Grad. Sch. Internat. Mgmt. Recipient Service award Ariz. State U. Alumni Assn., 1968; named to Ariz. State U. Alumni Assn. Hall of Fame, 1977. Mem. Assn. Res. City Bankers, Assn. Bank Holding Cos. (bd. dirs.). Clubs: Paradise Valley Country, Thunderbirds, Los Angeles Country, Calif.; Phoenix Country. Died Mar. 12, 2010.

CARSTENS, MARILYNN, freelance/self-employed music educator; b. Detroit, Feb. 24, 1930; d. Aldor John Carstens and Catherine Nettleton; m. Patrick Douglas Smiley, July 13, 1986; children: Joy Catherine, Carroll Lynn. BA, Holy Names U., Oakland, Calif., 1987, MA in Culture and Creation Spirituality, 1988; cert. in Level 1 Orff Schlwerk, Ariz. State U., Tempe, 1982; cert. in Level 2 Orff Schlwerk, U. Calif., Santa Cruz, 1983. Prin., owner Marilynn Carstens Music Studio, 1966—2006. Author (as Marilynn Thalman): Songs of Joy, 1963; author: Games & Activities for Improvisation, 1980, Games & Activities for Improvisation, revised, 2002. Dir. choir sch. Christ Luth. Ch., Clarendon, Calif. Mem.: Nat. Guild The Am. Coll. Musicians, The Am. Coll. Musicians, Music Tchrs. Assn. Calif. (chmn. improvisation 1978—2004, transitional chmn. 2005). Died Jan. 27, 2009.

CARSWELL, ROBERT DEAN, lawyer; b. Glasgow, Scotland, July 23, 1940; came to U.S., 1965; s. Robert and Helen Mary (Cowan) C.; m. Elizabeth Ann Turner, Sept. 7, 1967 (div.); children: Robbie, Ian, Lindsay; m. Gail Patterson Perez, Oct. 8, 1990. MA, U. Glasgow, 1962, LLB, 1965; postgrad., Cornell U., 1965-66. Assoc. Winthrop, Stimson, Putnam & Roberts, NYC, 1966; asst. McGrigor, Donald & Co., Glasgow and Edinburgh, Scotland, 1967-70, ptnr., 1971-79; v.p., internat. counsel Halliburton Logging Svcs., Inc. (formerly Gearhart Industries, Inc.), Ft. Worth, 1980-85, v.p., gen. counsel, 1985-89; atty. Internat. Legal Consultant, 1989-90; ptnr. McGrigor Donald, London, 1990-92. Internat. legal cons., 1992—. Contbr. articles to profl. jours. and chpts. to books. Fulbright Exch. fellow, 1965-66. Mem. ABA, Internat. Bar Assn., Law Soc. Scotland, Tex. Soaring Assn. Avocation: flying sailplanes. Died July 11, 2009.

CARTER, BRIAN ROBERT, judge; b. Paris, Nov. 10, 1925; s. David and Jeanne (Richmond) C.; m. Margaret Helen Schwarz, Feb. 14, 1958; children: Brian Robert, Scott David. BSEE, U. Iowa, 1950; postgrad., U. Kansas City, 1958; JD, Pepperdine U., 1969. Bar: Calif. 1970. Staff adviser Westinghouse Electric Corp., Pitts., 1952—54, promotion mgr. Kansas City, Mo., 1954—58, program mgr. Balt., 1958—62; dir. licensing electronics N.Am. Rockwell Corp., 1964—74; practice law Newport Beach, Calif., 1970—82, Santa Ana, Calif., 1970—82, San Diego, 1970—82; with Mcpl. Ct., Newport Beach, from 1982. Contbr. articles on yachting to various mags. With USNR, 1943—45, with USMCR, 1943—45. Decorated Purple Heart medal. Mem.: Iowa Alumni Assn. (named to Order Golden Hawk 1956), Orange County Bar, State Bar Calif., Bahia Corinthian Yacht Club, Masons, Beta Kappa Lambda (commodore 1972—73). Episcopalian. Home: Corona Del Mar, Calif. Died Apr. 14, 2010.

CARTER, DIXIE, actress; b. McLemoresville, Tenn., May 25, 1939; d. Halbert Leroy and Virginia Carter; m. Arthur Canter, 1967 (div. 1977); m. George Hearn, 1977 (div. 1979); m. Hal Holbrook, May 27, 1984. Student, U. Tenn., Southwestern U., Memphis; B in English, Memphis State U. Actress: (plays) The Winter's Tale, Oklahoma!, Kiss Me Kate, Carousel, 1960, The King and I; (Broadway plays) Sextet, 1974, Pal Joey, 1976, The Master Class, 1997, Thoroughly Modern Millie, 2004; off broadway Fathers and Sons, (Drama Desk nomination), Jesse and the Bandit Queen (Theatre World award), A Coupla White Chicks Sitting Around Talking, Buried Inside Extra; (TV series) One Life to Live, 1974, The Edge of Night, 1974-76, On Our Own, 1977-78, Out of the Blue, 1979, Filthy Rich, 1982-83, Diff'rent Strokes, 1984-85, Designing Women, 1986-93, Ladies Man, 1999, Family Law, 1999-2002, Desperate Housewives, 2006-07; (TV films) The Killing of Randy Webster, 1994, Gambler V: Playing for Keeps, 1994, Dazzle, 1994, Judith Krantz's Dazzle, 1995, Gone in the Night, 1996, Comfort and Joy, 2003; (Films) That Evening Sun, 2009; (instructional video) Dixie Carter's Unworkout, 1993; author: Trying to Get to Heaven: Opinions of a Tennessee Talker, 1996. Nominee Emmy award, 2007. Avocation: singing. Died Apr. 10, 2010.

CARTER, GEORGE HERBERT, psychiatrist, educator; b. Dobbs Ferry, N.Y., June 16, 1916; s. Franklin Jr. and Marion Phelps (Gutterson) C.; m. Shirley Chalmers, July 20, 1946; children— Richard Chalmers, David Warren. B.A., Williams Coll., 1938. M.D., Harvard U., 1943. Diplomate Am. Bd. Psychiatry and Neurology. Intern Mass. Gen. Hosp., Boston, 1943; resident in psychiatry Mass. Gen. Hosp.-Mass. Meml. Hosp., 1948-50; assoc. prof. dept. psychiatry Boston U., 1957—; dir. family therapy E.N. Rogers VA Hosp., Bedford, Mass., 1978—. Served to capt. AUS, 1944-46, ETO. Fellow (life) Am. Psychiat. Assn. Died Feb. 23, 2009.

CARTER, VIRGINIA MILNER, financial management executive; b. Atlanta, July 1, 1919; d. Willis Justus and Virginia Amanda (Cohen) Milner; B.A., Agnes Scott Coll., 1940; student Smith Coll., 1943, Radcliffe Coll., 1944, So. Meth. U., 1959-60, Wharton Bus. Sch., 1978; children— Alverson, Ida Richards (Mrs. Joseph N. Consola, Jr.), Virginia Seixas, Robert Milner. Dist. mgr. Prestige Silver Co., Atlanta, Charlotte, N.C. and Richmond, Va., 1947-58; agt. Ga. Internat. Life Ins. Co. and predecessor co., Atlanta, 1959-61, agy. dir., 1961-69, asst. corp. sec., 1965-69; v.p. Employee Benefit Plans, Rome, Ga., 1969; acct. exec. Planned Equity, Atlanta, 1971; v.p. Profl. Investment Counselors, Atlanta, 1970; div. mgr. Waddell & Reed, Atlanta, 1972-76; sr. v.p., nat. sales dir. A.L. Williams, Dulith, Dealer, Tucker, Ga., 1976—, also dir. A.L. Williams Corp.; former dir. Mario's Ristorantes, Inc., Nelco Enterprises. Bd. dirs. Atlanta YWCA, 1966-69; past pres. bd. trustees Covenant Presbyn. Ch. Served to lt. USNR, 1942-45. Mem. AAUW, LWV, Bus. and Profl. Women, Internat. Assn. Fin. Planners, DAR, Nat. Assn. Life Underwriters, Cert. Fin. Planners. Republican. Club: Dunwoody Country. Home: Duluth, Ga. Died June 18, 2010.

CARTER, WILLIAM ALLEN, accounting firm executive; b. Kokomo, Ind., Jan. 19, 1932; s. Virgil Glen and Edna Waneta (Edwards) C.; m. Carolyn Ann Miller, June 13, 1954; children: David, Matthew, Timothy, Joseph. BSBA, Ball State U., 1954. CPA, Ind., Calif. With Ernst & Whinney, from 1953, ptnr. in charge tax service Indpls., 1966-78, mng. ptnr. Indpls. office, 1978-84, mng. ptnr Ind. practice Indpls., 1984-86, vice-chmn., mng. ptnr. Western region Los Angeles, from 1986. Bd. dirs. Regional Inst. So. Calif., Los Angeles, Music Ctr. Oper. Com.; chmn. fin. com. Los Angeles 2000 Com.; gen. campaign chmn. L.A. Music Ctr., 1988-89, bd. govs., mem. exec. com.; mem. Commn. for Downtown, Inc., 1984-86, treas., dir., mem. exec. com. Served with U.S. Army, 1954-56. Named to Hall of Fame, Sch. Bus., Ball State U., 1980, named Alumnus of Yr., 1983; named Vol. of Yr., Fund Raising Council Ind., 1984. Mem. AICPAs (governing council 1970-71, 73-76, mem. tax div. 1973-75), Ind. Soc. CPAs (pres. 1970-71), Calif. C. of C. (bd. dirs.), Rotary, Regency Club, Lincoln Club, Calif. Club., Beta Gamma Sigma, Beta Gamma Psi. Republican. Methodist. Home: Indianapolis, Ind. Died Jan. 4, 2010.

CARTWRIGHT, HENRY ARTHUR, urologist; b. Detroit, June 27, 1946; s. Arthur and Thelma Lee (Black) Cartwright; m. Carol Susanne Major; children: Henry II, Michael. Student, U. Mich., 1966, MD, 1972; BS1968, Wayne State U. Diplomate Am. Bd. Urology. Intern Henry Ford Hosp., Detroit, 1972—73; gen. surgery resident U. Mich., Ann Arbor, 1973—75; urology resident Henry Ford Hosp., Detroit, 1975—78; urologist Harper-Grace Hosps., Detroit, from 1978, Hutzel Hosp., Detroit, 1978, Southwest Detroit Hosp., Detroit, from 1978; sec. Detroit Med. Soc., 1984. Maj. USNGR, 1972—80. Recipient Disting. Svc. award, Detroit Med. Soc., 1982. Fellow: ACS; mem.: Mich. State Med. Soc., Wayne County Med. Soc., Am. Urol. Assn. Avocations: boating, fishing, racquetball. Home: Southfield, Mich. Died June 6, 2010.

CARUTH, DONALD, state legislator; b. Princeton, W.Va., May 23, 1950; s. William B. and Elizabeth S. Caruth; m. Laura Caruth; stepchildren: Maria Boby, Andrea Boby, Christie Boby;children from previous marriage: Allison, Madison. BA, Concord Coll., Athens, W. Va.; JD, W.Va. U. Coll. Law. Atty. Athens Township, W.Va.; treas. New River Parkway Authority; regional supr., veteran's edn. and tng. W.Va. Dept. Edn.; mem. Dist. 25 W.Va. House of Delegates, Charleston, 2002—04; mem. Dist. 10 W.Va. State Senate, Charleston, 2004—10, minority leader, mem. Econ. Devel. Com., Govt. Orgn. Com., Interstate Cooperation Com., Judiciary Com. & Rules Com. Adj. prof. Concord Coll., Bluefield State Coll.; former exec. dir. W. Va. Career Coll., W. Va. Indsl. Coun. Bd. dirs. Athens Vol. Fire Dept., Athens Med. Ctr., Children's Home Soc. W. Va.; chmn.,. ch. coun. Concord United Meth. Ch. Named Legislator of Yr., W.Va. Bus. and Industry Coun., 2008. Mem.: Mercer County Bar Assn., W. Va. State Bar. Republican. Methodist. Died May 1, 2010.

CASCIO, RICHARD A., retail store executive; b. NYC, Nov. 9, 1932; s. Henry P. and Matilda (Dellanno) C.; m. Cheryl Rolls, Dec. 15, 1982; children from previous marriage: Richard A., Paul, Linda BA, St. Lawrence U., 1954. Buyer R.H. Macy, NYC, 1962-64, mdse. mgr, 1964-66, store mgr., 1966-74, sr. v.p. stores mgmt., 1974-79, J. L. Hudson Co., Detroit, 1979-84, exec. v.p. stores, 1984-85, exec. v.p., gen. mgr., from 1985; exec. v.p., dir. of stores Dayton Hudson Dept. Store Co., from 1985. Bd. dirs. Detroit Renaissance, Detroit, 1984—, New Detroit Inc., 1984—, Mich. Opera Theatre, Detroit, 1984—. Served with U.S. Army, 1954-55 Mem.: Detroit Athletic. Home: Franklin, Mich. Died Dec. 26, 2009.

CASE, EUGENE LAWRENCE, retired advertising executive; b. Knoxville, Tenn., Dec. 6, 1937; s. Harry Lawrence and Elinor Alice (Irish) C.; m. Mary Jane Austin, Apr. 30, 1959 (div. Mar. 1969); children: Christopher Lawrence, Alison Austin, Timothy Punch; m. Ilon Specht, Jan. 28, 1972 (div. 1983); 1 child, Brady Geronimo Specht; m. Sylvia Rodriguez, Sept. 10, 1994; 1 child, Billie Mitchell. Student, Cornell U., 1955-59. Copywriter J. Walter Thompson, 1961-62, Foote, Cone & Belding, 1963; asst. copy supr. Doyle, Dane, Bernbach, NYC, 1964; ptnr., creative dir. Jack Tinker & Partners, NYC, 1966-69; ptnr., founder Case & McGrath Inc., NYC, 1969—2002; founder Alamo Prodns., NYC, 1982—2002, Avenging Angels, 2002—10. Writer, co-producer: TV film Ohms. Home: New York, NY. Died Sept. 9, 2010.

CASS, RICHARD BRANNAN, pianist, music educator; b. Greenville, SC, May 3, 1931; m. Susan Bryan, Mar. 11, 1967. Student, Furman U., Chautauqua Inst., Ecole Normale de Musique de Paris. Concert pianist, from 1954. Prof. music U. Mo., Kansas City. European debut, Paris, 1954, N.Y.C. debut, Town Hall, 1957; tour with Detroit Symphony Orch., 1963; other recitals include Carnegie Hall, N.Y.C., Judson Hall, Tully Hall; albums include Prokofiev Concerto III, Beethoven Concerto III, Rachmaninoff Concerto II, Chopin Concerto II. Recipient Young Artists Auditions award Nat. Fedn. Music Clubs, 1953, Fulbright Prize award, 1954, 55; Fulbright scholar, 1953-54. Mem. Music Tchrs. Nat. Assn., Pi Kappa Lambda. Died Nov. 28, 2009.

CASSIDY, CARL EUGENE, physician; b. Salineville, Ohio, Dec. 4, 1924; s. Clifford J. and Dortha (Lance) Cassidy; m. Helen Ruth Skinner Collord, Dec. 21, 1961 (dec. 1975). AB, Kenyon Coll., Gambier, Ohio, 1946; MD, Western Res. U., Cleve., 1948. Intern Youngstown Hosp. Assn., Ohio, 1948—49; fellow in medicine Cleve. Clinic Found., 1951—54; rsch. fellow in endocrinology Pratt Clinic, New Eng. Med. Ctr. Hosps., Boston, 1954—56, asst. physician, 1956—67, sr. physician, 1968—72; physician-in-chief Baystate Med. Ctr., 1972—76; dir. Postgrad. Med. Inst., Boston, 1978—94; dir. rev. CME program New Eng. Jour. Medicine, Walthan, from 1994, emeritus dir. Asst. in medicine Tufts U. Sch. Medicine, 1954-56, clin. instr. medicine, 1956-58, instr., 1958-59, sr. instr., 1959-62, asst. prof., 1962-68, assoc. prof., 1968-73, clin. prof., 1973— Co-editor: Clinical Endocrinology II, 1968; contbr. articles to med. jours. Served with USNR, 1943-45; to lt. M.C. 1949-51. Mem. Mass. Med. Soc., Am. Thyroid Assn., Endocrine Soc., Longwood Cricket Club (Chestnut Hill, Mass.), Singing Beach Club (Manchester by the Sea, Mass.), Essex County Club (Manchester by the Sea). Home: Lynnfield, Mass. Died Dec. 11, 2009.

CASSIMATIS, EMANUEL ANDREW, judge; b. Pottsville, Pa., Dec. 2, 1926; s. Andrew Emanuel and Mary H. (Calopedis) Cassimatis; m. Thecla Karambelas, June 2, 1952; children: Mary Ann Maza, John E., Gregory E. BA, Dickinson Coll., 1949, LLB, 1951; LLD (hon.), York Coll., 1991. Bar: Pa. 1951. Pvt. practice, York, Pa., 1951—53, 1955—57; assoc. Kain, Kain & Kain, York, 1953—55; ptnr. Stock & Leader, York, 1957—78; judge Ct. Common Pleas, York, 1978—96, sr. judge, from 1996. Solicitor Springettesbury Twp., York, 1960—66, Sewer Authority, 1965—66, Wrightsville Borough, Pa., 1966—71, Mcpl. Authority, 1968—78, York Suburban Sch. Dist., 1970—77; faculty mem. Pa. Coll. Judiciary, 1981—83; pres. Pa. Conf. State Trial Judges, 1989—90, chmn. spl. projects com., 1980—82, ann. meeting com., 1984—85; pres. Juvenile Ct. Sect., 1988—89; mem. juvenile adv. com. Pa. Commn. Crime and Deliquency, from 1996; mem. Juvenile Ct. Judges' Commn., 1989—98, chmn., 1990—94; mem. Pa. three-judge breast implant cord. panel, from 1993. Co-chmn. steering com. York Cmty. Audit Human Rights, 1959; pres. United Way York County, 1964—65, Children's Growth and Devel. Clinic, 1974; bd. dirs. Capital Blue Cross, Harrisburg, Pa., 1970—79, Historic York, 1977—82. With US Army, 1945—46. Named Young Man of Yr., York Jr. C. of C., 1960, Vol. of Yr., Pilot Club, 1965. Mem.: CASA (hon. mem. supreme coun.), CASA. Greek Orthodox. Home: York, Pa. Died Nov. 4, 2009.

CASSTEVENS, FRANCES HARDING, medical researcher, genealogist; b. Winston-Salem, N.C., Sept. 9, 1936; d. Franklin Daniel Boone and Laura (Bowman) Harding; m. Gerald Royce Casstevens, Jan. 4, 1954; children— Gerald D., Caren J., Michael Lee, Tony Layne, Sandra K., Timothy T. Student Draughon's Bus. Sch., 1954-55, Surry Community

Coll., 1974-75; B.A. magna cum laude, U. N.C.-Greensboro, 1976, M.A., 1984. Clk.-typist McLean Trucking Co., Winston-Salem, 1956-58; postal clk. U.S. Post Office, Yadkinville, N.C., 1959-60; clk. Yadkin County Pub. Library, 1962-67; editorial asst. Bowman Gray Sch. Medicine, Wake Forest U., Winston-Salem, 1977-83, research asst., 1983—; ptnr. Casstevens Heraldic Arts, 1984—. Editor, author: Heritage of Yadkin County, 1981; author: (play) Retreat to Victory, 1976, Daniel Boone on the Yadkin, 1985; (poems) Beyond the Yadkin, The Battle of Shallow Ford, 1979; (geneal. history) The Descendants of Solomon Lineberry; Thomas Casteven: A Geneal. History, 1976. Leader 4-H Club, Yadkinville, 1970-72; pres. Yadkin County Hist. Soc., 1979-81, 85-88, v.p., 1985. Mem. DAR (regent Henry Hampton chpt. 1967-72). Republican. Methodist. Home: Yadkinville, NC. Died Sept. 16, 2009.

CASWELL, PAUL HADLEY, communications company executive; b. Dover, NH, Aug. 19, 1936; s. Gay E. and Gladys (Joy) C.; m. Barbara Ann Bradley, Jan. 7, 1967; children: Paul B., Philip C., Carolyn A. BS, U. N.H., 1960. With N.Y. Telephone, 1960-84; gen. plant mgr. Queens, 1973; asst. v.p. NYC, 1974-75; gen. mgr. tech. services, 1975-77; dep. dir. ops. City of N.Y., 1977-78; v.p. bus. services N.Y. Telephone, NYC, 1978-81; v.p. N.E. Region Bus. Services White Plains, 1981-85; dir. ops. dept. City of N.Y., 1977-78; v.p. materials mgmt. svcs. AT&T, Parsippany, N.J., from 1987. Served with USN, 1954-56. Mem.: Country Club of Darien (bd. govs. 1982-87, pres. 1985-87). Republican. Home: Rye Beach, NH. Died May 10, 2009.

CATALANO, EDUARDO FERNANDO, architect; b. Buenos Aires, Dec. 1, 1917; came to U.S., 1951; s. Fernando and Maria Catalano; divorced; Alejandrina, Adrian. Architect diploma, U. Buenos Aires, 1936-40; MArch, U. Pa., 1944, Harvard U., 1945. Prof. U. N.C., Raleigh, 1951-56, MIT, Cambridge, Mass., 1956-77; prin. Eduardo Catalano Architects and Engrs., Inc., Cambridge, 1951—2010. Author: Structures of Warped Surfaces, 1962, Eduardo Catalano Buildings and Projects, 1976, Structure and Geometry, 1986; prin. works include Peace Garden Nat. Meml., Washington. Recipient 3 1st prizes Nat. Archtl. Competitions; fellow U.S. Dept. States, Brit. Council, Fulbright Commn. for Exchange Scholars. Home: Cambridge, Mass. Died Jan. 28, 2010.

CATHEY, WILLIAM L., lawyer; b. Gastonia, NC, Oct. 2, 1947; BS, U. N.C., 1969; MA, Ctrl. Mich. U., 1974; JD magna cum laude, U. Mich., 1977. Bar: Calif. 1977. With Munger, Tolles & Olson, LA. Assoc. editor Mich. Law Review, 1975-76, mng. editor, 1976-77. Mem. ABA (corp., banking, bus. law sect.), State Bar Calif., L.A. County Bar Assn., Order of Coif, Beta Gamma Sigma. Died Oct. 17, 2009.

CAUHAPE, ELIZABETH BROADHURST, psychotherapist, author, social service administrator; b. Pontiac, Mich., June 1, 1923; d. James William and Esther (Crohn) Broadhurst; m. Thomas Wendell Waldrop, Feb. 20, 1945; children: Thomas Wendell II, Duncan William. BA, Cornell U., 1945; MS, San Jose State U., 1967; PhD, U. Calif.-San Francisco Med Ctr., 1980. Rsch. cons. OEO, Santa Clara County, Calif., 1965—67; mem. faculty San Jose State U., Calif., Ohlone Coll., Fremont, Calif., Hayward State U., Calif., 1967—81; pvt. practice psychotherapy Walnut Creek, Calif., 1970, Syracuse, NY; asst. dir. BALDCO, Inc., Berkeley, Calif., 1982—85; dir. Ctr. Adult Transition Studies. Author: Fresh Starts, Men and Women After Divorce, 1983. Recipient Tchr. of Yr. award Ohlone Coll. Student Coun., 1973, Nat. Insts. Child Health and Human Devel., Nat. Inst. Aging predoctoral rsch. fellow U. Calif.-San Francisco, 1974—77. Mem.: Calif. Assn. Marriage and Family Therapists, Cornell Club (NYC). Home: San Francisco, Calif. Died Mar. 3, 2009.

CAVIN, F. G., JR., bank executive; b. McKenzie, Tenn., Sept. 28, 1930; m. Sally Thornton; children: Virginia, Sarah, John, Carol. BS in Agr, U. Tenn., Martin. With Martin Bank, to 1968; exec. v.p. Farmers Exchange Bank (became affiliate First Amtenn Corp., holding co. 1973), Union City, Tenn., 1968-71, pres., 1971-74; exec. v.p. First Amtenn Corp., Nashville, 1974-76, vice chmn., 1979, pres., 1979; exec. v.p. in charge of banking adminstrn. First Am. Bank, First Amtenn Corp. lead bank, Nashville, 1976, vice chmn. bd., 1979; now vice chmn. First Am. Corp., Nashville. Chmn. Tenn. Indsl. Devel. Authority, 1972-78; chmn. adminstrv. bd. Brentwood United Methodist Ch. Mem.: Corinthian, Masons, Shriners. Died May 28, 2009.

CAZES, JACK, chemist, marketing consultant, editor; b. NYC, Feb. 2, 1934; s. Angel and Esther (Calderon) C.; m. Eleanor Harriet Schwartz, Mar. 25, 1961; 1 child, Larry Alan. BS in Chemistry, CCNY, 1955; MS in Organic Chemistry, NYU, 1962, PhD in Organic Chemistry, 1963. Sr. rsch. chemist Mobil Chem. Co., Edison, N.J., 1963-69; supervising chemist Mobil Oil Corp., Paulsboro, N.J., 1970-74; with Waters Assocs., Inc., Milford, Mass., 1974-81; v.p. Marcel Dekker, Inc., NYC, 1981-83, Elf Aquitaine, S.A., NYC, 1983-84, Varex Corp., Rockville, Md., 1984-87, Sanki Labs., Inc., Mt. Laurel, N.J., 1987-94, The Cazes Group, Inc., Coconut Creek, Fla., from 1994. Instr. Rutgers U., New Brunswick, N.J., 1963-69; lectr. Queens Coll., Flushing, N.Y., 1961-62; cons. various cos., 1959—. Editor-in-chief Jour. Liquid Chromatography, 1973—, Instrumentation Sci. & Tech., 1994—, numerous chromatographic sci. books; contbr. articles to profl. jours. With U.S. Army, 1955-57. Mem. Am. Chem. Soc. (prof. short course 1967-71), Sigma Xi. Jewish. Achievements include research on chromatography theory and applications. Home: Lady Lake, Fla. Died Feb. 16, 2010.

CELEBREZZE, FRANK D., chief justice Ohio Supreme Court; b. Cleve., Nov. 13, 1928; s. Frank D. and Mary (Delsander) C.; m. Mary Ann Armstrong, Jan. 20, 1949; children: Judith, Frank, Laura, David, Brian, Steven, Jeffrey, Keith, Matthew. Student, Ohio State U., 1948-50; BS, Baldwin-Wallace Coll., 1952; LLB, Cleve.-Marshall Coll. Law, 1956; LLD (hon.), Capital U., 1980, Ohio Coll. Podiatric Medicine, 1985. Bar: Ohio 1957. Began legal practice, Cleve., 1957; judge Ohio Ct. Common Pleas Cuyahoga County, 1964-72; justice Ohio Supreme Ct., 1972-78, chief justice, from 1978; mem. Ohio Senate, 1956-58. Served with U.S. Army, 1946-47. Recipient Jud. Service award Ohio Supreme Ct., 1972, Outstanding Alumnus award Cleve.-Marshall Coll. Law, 1973, Community Service award AFL-CIO, 1973, Disting. Citizen of Parma award, 1976, Unita Civic award of Youngstown, 1976, Man of Yr. award Greater Cin. UAW-CAP Council, 1986; named Man of Yr., Delta Theta Phi Law Frat., 1986. Mem. ABA, Inst. Jud. Adminstrn. of Bar Assn. Greater Cleve., Cuyahoga County Bar Assn., Cuyahoga County Joint Vets. Adminstrn. (past pres., past trustee), Cleve. YMCA, Catholic War Vets. Democrat. Roman Catholic. Died Mar. 21, 2010.

CEMBER, HERMAN, environmental health educator; b. Bklyn., Jan. 14, 1924; s. Arthur and Lilly (Shuster) C.; m. Sylvia L. Brudner, Dec. 5, 1943; children— Michael, Marilyn BS, CCNY, 1949; MS, U. Pitts., 1952, PhD, 1960. Diplomate Am. Acad. Environ. Engrs.; registered profl. engr., Ill.; cert. Am. Bd. Health Physics. Asst. prof., then assoc. prof. U. Pitts. Grad. Sch. Pub. Health, 1950-60; assoc. prof. U. Cin. Coll. Medicine, 1960-65; tech. expert in occupational health ILO, Geneva, 1961-62; vis. prof. Hadassah Med. Sch., Hebrew U., Jerusalem, 1972-73; prof. environ. health McCormick Sch. Engring. and Applied Sci., Northwestern U., Evanston, Ill., from 1964. Vis. prof. physics Stellenbosch U., 1983; cons. in field. Author: Introduction to Health Physics; contbr. articles on health physics to profl. jours. Fellow NRC, 1949-50, Fulbright Found., 1972-73 Fellow Am. Pub. Health Assn., Health Physics Soc. (Disting. Sci. Achievement award 1990); mem. AAAS, Am. Acad. Health Physics, Am. Indsl. Hygiene Assn., N.Y. Acad. Scis. Lodges: B'nai Brith. Jewish. Died Mar. 7, 2009.

CHABOT, ROBERT F., state legislator; b. Manchester, NH, Mar. 8, 1924; m. Cecile Chabot; 7 children. With plumbing and heating industry, 1986; rep. N.H. Ho. of Reps., Dist. 48, Concord. Mem. health, human svcs. and elderly affairs coms., N.H. Ho. of Reps.; former mem. Plumbers Examining Bd. Mem. United Plumbers Assn. Local 131. Died Mar. 10, 2009.

CHALMERS, E(DWIN) LAURENCE, JR., museum administrator; b. Wildwood, NJ, Mar. 24, 1928; s. Edwin Laurence and Carolyn (Smith) C.; children: Edwin Laurence III, Thomas Henry; m. Hani Kamp, 1973; 1 son, Timothy Blair. AB, Princeton U., 1948, MA, 1950, PhD, 1951. Instr. psychology Princeton, 1951-52; research psychologist USAF, Denver, 1952-53, 56-57; mem. faculty Fla. State U., 1957-69; prof. psychology, dean Fla. State U. (Coll. Arts and Scis.), 1964-66, v.p. acad. affairs, 1966-69; chancellor U. Kans., Lawrence, 1969-72; pres. Art Inst. Chgo., 1972-86, San Antonio Mus. Assn., 1987-93. Contbr. articles to profl. jours. Served to 1st lt. USAF, 1953-56. Mem. Phi Beta Kappa, Sigma Xi, Omicron Delta Kappa. Home: San Antonio, Tex. Died Nov. 24, 2009.

CHAMBERLAIN, THEODORE JOHNSTONE, psychologist, dean; b. Boston, Nov. 23, 1944; s. George Arthur and Mabel (Greene) Chamberlain; m. Liria Lee Bower Chamberlain, Aug. 26, 1967; children: Kristin Liria, Jennifer Joan. AB, Gordon Coll., 1967; MTS, Gordon-Conwell Theol. Sem., 1969; MEd, Boston Coll., 1971, PhD, 1979. Assoc. dean students Gordon Coll., Wenham, Mass., 1970—76; dean students Eastern Coll., St. Davids, Pa., 1976—78, v.p., dean students, from 1978; adj. prof. Eastern Baptist Theol. Sem., Phila., from 1982, Fuller Theol. Sem., Pasadena, Calif., from 1982; counselor St. Davids Counseling Assocs., from 1982; cons. Coun. Ind. Colls., Washington, from 1980. Mem.: Pa. Assn. Student Pers. Adminstrs. (treas. from 1983). Died May 22, 2010.

CHAMBERLAIN, WILLARD THOMAS, retired metal products executive; b. New Haven, Nov. 22, 1928; s. Thomas Huntington and Alice Irene (Daley) C.; m. Harriet Halbert Keck, Nov. 20, 1965; children: Huntington Wilson, Amy Thatcher. B.E., Yale U., 1950; postgrad., Ill. Inst. Tech., 1951-53. With Armour Research Found., Chgo., 1951-53; asst. to tech. mgr. Anaconda Brass div. Anaconda Corp., Waterbury, Conn., 1953-56, tech. supr., 1956-60, metall. mgr. Torrington, Conn., 1960-61, mgr. devel. Waterbury, 1961-62, lab. mgr., 1962-64, mgr. research-tech. ctr., 1964-67, mgr. Valley Mills, 1967, Ansonia, 1967-70, mgr. prodn. planning, 1970-71, v.p. mfg., 1971-72, exec. v.p. Brass div., 1972-74, pres., 1974-80, Anaconda Industries, 1980; sr. v.p. Atlantic Richfield Co., 1980-82; pres. Arco Metals Co., 1982-85; sr. v.p. corp. affairs Atlantic Richfield Co., 1985-87; sr. v.p. govt. and pub. affairs ARCO, 1987-89. Mem. So. Calif. bus. com. Econ. Literacy Council Adv. of Calif. Mem. exec. bd. Waterbury Republican Town Com., 1964-70; commr. Waterbury Bd. Fin., 1966-67, chmn. charter revision com., 1966-67; mem. exec. bd. Mattatuck council Boy Scouts Am., 1965-72, Waterbury Assn. for Retarded Children, 1965-66; co-chmn. Clergy-Industry Conf., 1965-66; campaign chmn. Valley United Fund, 1970-71; bd. dirs. United Way, Central Naugatuck Valley, 1974, The Banking Ctr., 1974-81, Western Conn. Indsl. Council, 1974-81, Calif. State U. Found., Found. for Am. Communications, Los Angeles Arts Council; trustee Calif. Mus. Found., Harvey Mudd Coll.; bd. trustees Greater Los Angeles Partnership for the Homeless; bd. dirs. L.A. Habitat for Humanity. Recipient Outstanding Civic Leader award, 1967. Mem. Copper Devel. Assn., Aluminum Assn. (dir.), Am. Soc. Metals, Yale Engring. Assn., Greater Waterbury C. of C. (bd. dirs. 1974), Alliance Aging Rsch. (bd. dirs.), Am. Petroleum Inst. (emerging issues task force), Brookings Instn. (coun. mem.), Calif. State U. Found. (bd. dirs., compensation planning com., chmn. investment com.), Calif. State U. Bus. Assocs., Constl. Rights Found. (bus. adv. coun.), Econ. Literacy Coun. Adv. Calif. (so. Calif. bus. com.), Found. Am. Communications (dir.), Hugh O'Brian Youth Found., Math. Engring. and Sci. Achievement (industry adv. bd.), Nat. Action Coun. for Minorities in Engring., Nat. Minority Supplier Devel. Coun. (bd. dirs.), Nat. Wetlands Policy Forum, Nat. Wildlife Fedn. (vice chmn. corp. conservation coun.), Vols. of Am., L.A., Town Hall, U.S. C. of C., World Affairs Coun., Univ. Club L.A., Yale Club, So. Calif. Presbyterian. Home: Riverside, Calif. Died Nov. 8, 2009.

CHAMBERLAND, BERTRAND LEO, chemist, educator; b. Manchester, NH, Mar. 17, 1934; s. Alfred Joseph and Albina (Dube) Chamberland; m. Eleanor Marie McCormack, May 15, 1965; children: Michael, Michelle, Laura. AB, St. Anselm's Coll., 1955; MS, Holy Cross Coll., 1956; PhD, U. Pa., 1960. Chemist Union Carbide, Parma, Ohio, 1956—57, DuPont Co., Wilmington, Del., 1960—69; prof. chemistry U. Conn., Storrs, from 1969. Cons. Giner Inc., Waltham, Mass., from 1982. Mem.: Am. Crystallographic Assn., Am. Ceramic Soc., Chem. Soc. London, Am. Chem. Soc., Alpha Chi Sigma, Phi Lambda Upsilon. Home: Tempe, Ariz. Died Mar. 10, 2010.

CHAMPION, PAUL HENRI, citrus grower, national trust examiner, bank examiner and field manager; b. Orlando, Fla., Dec. 24, 1945; s. Paul Henri and Marion Alice (Joyce) Champion. BS, U. West Fla., 1968; MBA, Stetson U., 1970. Asst. trust examiner Regional Adminstr. Nat. Banks, Atlanta, 1971—74, nat. trust examiner, 1974—78; examiner-in-charge Atlanta Trust Subregion, 1976, nat. bank examiner, from 1978; chmn. bd. Tuscawilla Properties, Inc., Leesburg, Fla., from 1974; tech. edn. specialist Comptroller of Currency, Washington, 1976—78; instr. mgmt. techniques Fed. Fin. Instns. Coun., from 1977. Recipient Spl. Achievement award, Dept. Treasury, 1978, Spl. Recognition award, Comptroller Currency, 1978, Cert. of Appreciation award, 1982. Mem.: Soc. Advancement Mgmt., Kingwood Country. Republican. Roman Catholic. Home: Thomasville, Ga. Died Jan. 26, 2010.

CHANCE, HENRY MARTYN, II, engineering executive; b. Pottsville, Pa., Jan. 16, 1912; s. Edwin M. and Eleanor (Kent) C.; m. Suzanne Sharpless, June 12, 1934 (dec. 1993); children: Edwin M. Suzanne, Barbara; m. Elizabeth Reese, Aug. 19, 1944; children: Steven K., James M., Henry Martyn III (dec. 1995), Mark Raymond. Grad., Haverford Sch., 1930; BS in Civil Engring., U. Pa., 1934, LL.D. (hon.), 1983. Registered profl. engr., 7 states. Chemist, assayer American Smelting & Refining Co., 1934-36; with United Engrs. & Constructors, Inc., Phila., 1936—77, pres., 1954-71, chmn., 1972-77, dir., cons., 1977—2010. Life trustee, mem. exec. bd. U. Pa., 1964-82, emeritus trustee, 1982—2010; pres. Haverford Sch., 1962-70, mem. bd., 1962-72, life dir., 1974—2010; bd. mgrs. emeritus Franklin Inst.; mem. bd. overseers U. Pa. Mus. Named Engr. of Year Del. Valley, 1964 Died July 27, 2010.

CHANDLER, LEROY, manufacturing executive; b. Charley, Ky., Mar. 10, 1918; s. John Henry and Nora (Hayes) Chandler; m. Ruth Burdelle, Oct. 10, 1936; children: James Edward, Carol Lee, Preston, Mabel Ruth Pillion. BA (hon.), U. Hard Knocks, Alderson Broadus Coll., U. W.Va., 1984. Salesman Chandlers Plywood Products Ins., Huntington, W.Va., 1952—77, pres., dir., from 1977; v.p., dir. Cabinet Supplier Co., 1977—7980. Mem.: Rotary Lodge (Kenova W.Va.). Republican. Home: Huntington, W.Va. Died Mar. 16, 2009.

CHANOCK, ROBERT MERRITT, pediatrician; b. Chgo., July 8, 1924; m. Catherine Elizabeth Osgood (dec. 2009); children: Foster (dec. 1980), Stephen BS, U. Chgo., 1945, MD, 1947, DSc (hon.), 1977. NRC fellow Children's Hosp., Cin., 1950—52; asst. prof. rsch. pediat. Coll. Medicine, U. Cin., 1954—56; asst. prof. epidemiology Sch. Hygiene and Pub. Health, Johns Hopkins U., 1956—57; surgeon USPHS, 1957—59, head respiratory viruses sect., 1959—61; chief lab. infectious diseases Nat. Inst. Allergy and Infectious Diseases, NIH, Bethesda, Md., 1968—2001. Nat. Found. Infantile Paralysis fellow, 1951—52; sr. rsch. fellow USPHS, 1956—57; virologist Children's Hosp. D.C., from 1957; mem. Internat. Nomenclature Com. Myxoviruses, 7th and 8th Internat. Microbiol. Congress, Armed Forces Epidemiology Bd., Com. Acute Respiratory Disease, 1960—62; assoc. mem. Com. Influenza, 1963—74; dir. Internat. Ref. Ctr. Lab. Mycroplasms, WHO, 1962; mem. Internat. Com. Nomenclature Bacteria, 1966; clin. prof. Georgetown U., 1970—71; mem. nominating com. NAS, 1979—80; mem. sci. rev. com. Scripps Clin. and Rsch. Found., 1986—89. Recipient E. Mead Johnson award pediatric rsch., 1964, Squibb Gorgas medal, Assn. Mil. Surgeons, 1972, Robert Koch medal, Fed. Republic of Germany, 1981, Virol prize, ICT Internat., 1990, Bristol-Myers Squibb award, Albert B. Sabin Gold medal. Mem. NAS, Soc. Pediat. Rsch., Am. Soc. Microbiology, Am. Epidemiol. Soc., Am. Epidemiology, Am. Pediat. Soc., Am. Soc. Clin. Investigation, Soc. Exptl. Biology and Medicine, Assn. Am. Physicians, Royal Danish Acad. Scis. (fgn. mem.). Died July 30, 2010.

CHAPLIK, ARNOLD SIDNEY, paper company executive; b. Indpls., Feb. 15, 1928; s. Sam and Dora (Simesman) C.; m. Carol A. Chaplik; children— Elaine Judy, Barbara Lynn Student, Ind. U. Successively office boy Capital Consol. Inc., Indpls., sales rep., mgr. sales, v.p., exec. v.p. Served as cpl. U.S. Army, 1952-54 Mem. Nat. Paper Trade Assn., Midwest Paper Assn. Clubs: Broadmoor Country (bd. dirs. 1980-82). Republican. Jewish. Home: Indianapolis, Ind. Died Mar. 29, 2009.

CHAPMAN, JOSEPH DUDLEY, obstetrician, gynecologist, author; b. Moline, Ill., Apr. 29, 1928; s. Joseph Dudley and Lillian Caroline (Pruder) Chapman; m. Mary Kay Sartini, June 1949 (div.); children: Mary Jo Tucker, Nancy Jo Robinson; m. Virginia Helene Milius, June 1958 (div.). BS, U. Ill.

and Roosevelt Coll., Chgo., 1950; DO, Coll. Osteo. Medicine and Surgery, 1953, DSc, 1963; MD, Calif. Coll. Medicine, 1962; PhD, Inst. Advanced Study Human Sexualtiy, 1986. Cert. Am. Osteo. Bd. Ob-Gyn. Intern, resident in ob-gyn. Still Coll. Hosp., Des Moines; practice medicine specializing in ob-gyn. North Madison, Ohio, from 1973; clin. prof. ob-gyn. Ohio U., from 1979; mem. faculty, acad. bd. Inst. Advanced Study Human Sexuality, San Francisco, from 1979; tv appearances Phil Donahue Show, Good Morning Am., The Last Word. Med. examiner FAA, comml. pilot. Author: (book) The Feminine Mind and Body, 1966, The Sexual Equation, 1977; contbr. chapters to books, articles to profl. jours. Active Boy Scouts America. Mem.: Am. Med. Writers Assn., Acad. Psychosomatic Medicine, Am. Coll. Osteo. Ob-Gyn., Am. Assn. Gynocol. Laparoscopists, Am. Fertility Soc. Lutheran. Home: Madison, Ohio. Died Apr. 3, 2009.

CHARD, NANCY I., state legislator; b. Point Pleasant, NJ, July 14, 1933; m. John T. Chard; 3 children. BA, Upsala Coll., 1955, MA, 1959. Mem. Vt. Ho. of Reps., 1989-94; mem., Windham County Vt. Senate, Montpelier, 1995—2003. Dir. Vt. State Colls. So. Vt. Edn. Ctr.; trustee Winston Prouty Ctr. Austine Sch. and Vt. Cmty. Found. Home: Brattleboro, Vt. Died Feb. 18, 2010.

CHARLES, BALLENGER EUGENE, power company executive; b. Sneads, Fla., July 5, 1923; s. Lee and Mattie Charles; m. Carolyn McDonald; children: Ballanger E. Jr., Terry L. AA, Chipola Jr. Coll., 1953; student, Internat. Corr. Sch., 1954—57. Metalsmith J.S. Walters, 1947—49; yard clk. A.C.L. RR, 1951—53; with Gulf Power Co., from 1953, plant supr., 1965—76, supr. ops., 1976—81, generating plant safety and tng. supr., from 1981. Chmn. Ala. and West Fla. Coun. Boy Scouts America; mem. Nat. Congress PTA, Fla. Sch. Bd. Assn., Apalachee Correctional Inst., Jackson County Bd. Pub. Instrn., Fla. Regional Corrections Adv. Coun. Ch.; past city councilman Sneads; past bd. dirs. Chipola Jr. Coll. With USN, World War II. Mem.: Chipola Jr. Coll. Alumni Assn., Sneads HS Alumni Assn., Masons Lodge. Methodist. Home: Sneads, Fla. Died Mar. 15, 2009.

CHARLES, CAROLYN STOWELL, counselor educator; b. Derby, Conn., Aug. 14, 1921; d. Austin Leavitt and Doris Carolyn (Hillery) S.; children: Elizabeth Charles Gomes, Kathryn Charles Zaugg. BA in Psychology, Fla. State U., 1943; MRE in Christian Edn., Presbyn. Sch. Christian Edn., 1946; MA in Student Pers., U. Ala., Tuscaloosa, 1970, PhD in Counseling, 1973. Asst. to mgr. pers. Ensign-Bickford Co., Simsbury, Conn., 1943-44; Missionary to Brazil, 1948-65; instr., counselor U. Hosp. Sch. Nursing, Birmingham, Ala., 1965-67; counselor New Careers Program, Birmingham, Ala., 1967-68; vocat. counselor Lawson State Community Coll., Birmingham, Ala., 1968-70; prof. counseling U. North Ala., Florence, 1972-88, prof. emerita, from 1988. Prayer ptnr. Overseas Missionary Fellowship. Mem. Am. Assn. Counseling and Devel., Mortar Bd., Chi Delta Phi, Kappa Delta Pi, Phi Kappa Phi. Republican. Baptist. Home: Chesapeake, Va. Died July 15, 2010.

CHARRON, HELENE KAY SHETLER, retired nursing educator; b. West Bloomfield, NY, Nov. 17, 1937; d. Ellis John and Helene Esther (Moore) Shetler; m. Ronald W. Charron, July 1964; children: Michele Gefell, Andrea Hagen. Diploma, Rochester State Hosp. Sch., NYC, 1958; BS in Nursing, U. Rochester, 1964, MS in Nursing Edn., 1965. Staff nurse Strong Meml. Hosp., Rochester, 1958-60; head nurse Monroe Community Hosp., Rochester, 1961-63; coord. psychiat. nursing Monroe CC, 1965—87; mental hygiene staff devel. specialist Rochester Psychiat. Ctr., 1982-83; chair dept. nursing Monroe CC, Rochester, 1987—96; ptnr. Initiatives in Nursing Edn., West Bloomfield, N.Y., from 1995. Writer numerous instructional computer programs, ancillaries, test banks, videotapes and games in field. Died Aug. 4, 2010.

CHASE, JAMES RICHARD, retired college president; b. Oxnard, Calif., Oct. 7, 1930; s. James Warren and Nina Marie (Fiscus) C.; m. Mary Corinne Sutherland, Dec. 16, 1950; children: Kenneth Richard, Jennifer Corinne. B. Theology, Biola Coll., 1951; BA, Pepperdine U., 1953, MA, 1954; PhD, Cornell U., 1961. Instr. Biola Coll., La Mirada, Calif., 1953-57, prof., chmn. dept. humanities, 1959-65, v.p. acad. affairs, 1965-70, pres., 1970-82, Wheaton (Ill.) Coll., 1982-93, pres. emeritus, from 1993. Teaching asst. Cornell Univ., Ithaca, N.Y., 1957-59; bd. dirs. World Christian Tng. Ctr., 1970-82; bd. dirs. Christian Coll. Coalition, 1977-79, chmn. bd., 1977-79; bd. dirs. Mission Aviation Fellowship, 1975-81, chmn. bd., 1978-81; bd. dirs. Western Coll. Assn., 1980-82 Mem. Nat. Assn. Ind. Colls. and Universities (dir. 1980), Assn. Ind. Calif. Colls. and Univs. (mem. exec. com. 1978-82), American Assn. Bible Colls. (dir. 1974-80), Nat. Assn. Intercollegiate Athletics (pres. adv. com. 1976-82), Nat. Assn. Evangelicals (exec. com. 1984-92), We. Assn. Schs. and Colls. (sr. commn. 1981-82), American Assn. Pres. Ind. Colls. and Univs. (dir. 1980-85, v.p. 1982-85), Speech Communication Assn., Christian Coll. Consortium (chmn. 1986), Coalition (chmn. 1976), Fedn. Ind. Ill. Colls. and Univs. (exec. com., chmn. bd. 1989-91). Baptist. Home: Carol Stream, Ill. Died Aug. 20, 2010.

CHASSIN, JAMESON LEWIS, retired surgeon; b. Maspeth, NY, Mar. 12, 1922; s. Isaac and Esther Chassin; m. Charlotte Eunice Cowan, Nov. 6, 1945; children: Mark Russell Gray, Pamela Sue, Robert Glenn, Richard Niles. BA, Harvard U., Cambridge, Mass., 1941; MD, Johns Hopkins U., Balt., 1945. Chmn. dept. of surgery N.Y. Hosp. of Queens, Flushing, 1960—93; prof. of clin. surgery NYU Med. Ctr., NYC, from 1965. Author: (textbook) Operative Strategy in General Surgery, (author) Chassin's Operative Strategy in General Surgery. Capt. med. unit, 1949—52. Home: New York, NY. Died Aug. 20, 2010.

CHAUDHARI, PRAVEEN, science administrator, materials physicist; b. Ludhiana, Punjab, India, Nov. 30, 1937; came to U.S., 1961; s. Hans Raj and Ved (Kumari) C.; m. Karin Romhild, June 13, 1964; children: Ashok, Pia. BS with honors, Indian Inst. Tech., Kharagpur, 1961; MS in Phys. Metallurgy, MIT, 1963, ScD in Phys. Metallurgy, 1966. Rsch. assoc. MIT, Cambridge, Mass., 1966; rsch. staff mem. IBM T.J. Watson Rsch. Ctr., Yorktown Heights, NY, 1966-70, mgr., 1970-80, dir. phys. scis., 1981-82, v.p. sci., dir. phys. scis., 1982-91, v.p. sci., tech. com., 1988-91, rsch. staff, 1991—2003; dir. Brookhaven Nat. Lab., Upton, NY, 2003—06. Exec. sec. Presdl. Com. on Super Conductivity, 1988; mem. Presdl. Commn. on Super Conductivity, 1989; chmn. U.S. Liaison Commn. to Internat. Union of Pure and Applied Physics; mem. com. on Physics for the Next Decade, sponsored by NRC/NAS, Nat. Critical Tech. panel; chmn. sci. coun. Internat. Ctr. for Theoretical Physics, Trieste, Italy; chmn. adv. coun. math. and phys. scis. NSF; mem. governing bd. NY State Inst. Superconductivity. Author of papers on mechanical properties and defects in crystalline solids, amorphous solids, quantum transport, superconductivity and magnetic monopoles and neutrino mass experiments. Recipient Harry C. Gatos prize MIT, 1994, Nat. Medal Tech., 1995, Excellence award US Pan Asian Amer. C. of C., Liebmann prize IEEE, 1992, George Pake award Am. Phys. Soc., 1987. Mem.: NAS (mem. governing bd. physics and astronomy), Am. Acad. Arts and Sci., Nat. Acad. Engring., Am. Inst. Physics (mem.-at-large governing bd.), NY Acad. Scis. (mem. governing bd.). Home: Briarcliff Manor, NY. Died Jan. 12, 2010.

CHECCHI, ARTHUR ALFRED, consulting company executive; b. Calais, Maine, Aug. 13, 1922; s. Attilio R. and Dina A. (Pisani) C.; B.A., U. Maine, 1944; postgrad. Harvard U., 1944-45; m. Josephine Anne Soldati, Nov. 30, 1946; children— Alfred A., Anne Marie, Lisa A., Joanne M. Various positions (Boston, Kansas City, Denver), then staff mem. Office of Commr., FDA, Washington, 1945-59; v.p. Checchi & Co., Washington, 1960-75; pres., chmn. bd. Arthur A. Checchi, Inc., Washington, 1975—. Mem. Assn. Food and Drug Ofcls., Inst. Food Technologists. Roman Catholic. Home: Silver Spring, Md. Died Jan. 14, 2009.

CHEEK, JAMES EDWARD, retired academic administrator; b. Roanoke Rapids, NC, Dec. 4, 1932; s. King Virgil and Lee Ella (Williams) C.; m. Celestine Juanita Williams, June 14, 1953; children: James Edward, Janet Elizabeth. BA, Shaw U., 1955, HHD, 1970; BD, Colgate Rochester Div. Sch., 1958, Mdiv; PhD, Drew U., 1962, LLD, 1971; LHD, Trinity Coll., 1970; LLD, A&T U., 1971, Del. State Coll., 1972; D honoris causa, L'Universite d'Etat d'Haiti, 1972; EdD, Providence Coll., 1972, N.Y. Inst. Tech., 1980, U. N.C., 1981; HHD, U. Md., 1975; DDiv, Bucknell U., 1975; LLD, N.Y. Inst. Tech., 1980, U. N.C., 1981; DHL, Duke U., 1982, Fisk U., 1984, Fla. Meml. Coll., 1986, Cen. State U., 1988; LLD, Tuskegee U., 1989; DHL, Adelphi U., 1989; LLD, Rider Coll., 1989. Teaching asst. hist. theology Drew Theol. Sch., Madison, N.J., 1959-60; instr. Western history Union Jr. Coll., Cranford, N.J., 1959-61; vis. instr. Christian history Upsala Coll., East Orange, N.J., summer 1960; asst. prof. N.T. and hist. theology Sch. Religion, Va. Union U., Richmond, 1961-63; pres. Shaw U., Raleigh, N.C., 1963-69, Howard U., Washington, 1969-89, pres. emeritus, 1989—2010. Mem. Pres.'s Commn. on Campus Unrest, 1970; spl. cons. to Pres. on Black Colls. and Univs., 1970; mem. ad hoc com. univ. and coll. presidents Citizens Exchange Corps Congress Internat. Edn. Citizens; mem. adv. bd. Colgate-Rochester Div. Sch.; mem. nat. adv. council Independent Found.; mem. nat. adv. council Minorities in Engring.; mem. adv. council Nat. Archives; mem. nat. coordinating council Drug Abuse, Edn. and Info., Inc.; mem. nat. adv. com. Nat. Council for Black Studies; hon. mem. Washington Cornaro Tercentenary Com.; mem. Nat. Com. for Full Employment, Mordecai Wyatt Johnson Meml. Fund; mem. Am. Found. for Negro Affairs; mem. task force for women's equity AAUW. Bd. editors: Black Forum, Inc.; hon. chmn. Jour. Religious Thought, bd. editorial assocs. Chmn. bd. trustees Fisk U., Benedict Coll., N.Y. Inst. Tech.; hon. trustee Choral Arts Soc. Washington, Fed. City Coun., United Way of Nat. Capital Area, Washington Ctr. for Met. Studies; hon. bd. trustees Inst. Internat. Edn.; mem. coll. adv. bd. Black Sports; mem. nat. adv. bd. Sch. Rev.; bd. advisors Close Up, Nat. Black Monitor, Speak Out; chmn. pres.'s bd. advisors on historically Black Colls. and Univs.; founder, pres. Nat. Orgn. African Ams.; bd. dirs. GEICO Corp. Recipient Presdl. Medal of Freedom, The White House, 1983; Colgate-Rochester grad. fellow, 1958; Lily Found. fellow, 1958-59, Rockefeller Doctoral fellow, 1960-61. Mem. Am. Acad. Religion AAUP, Am. Soc. Ch. History, Nat. Assn. Bibl. Instrs., Nat. Soc. Lit. and the Arts, Religious Research Assn., Soc. Bibl. Lit. and Exegesis, Nat. Assn. for Equal Opportunity in Higher Edn. (bd. dir.), Continental African C. of C. (bd. dir.), Alpha Theta Nu, Alpha Phi Alpha, Sigma Pi Sigma, Alpha Kappa Delta, Phi Beta Kappa, Omicron Kaqppa Upsilon, Phi Delta Kappa. Republican. Home: Greensboro, NC. Died Jan. 8, 2010.

CHENEY, LLOYD THEODORE, civil engineering educator; b. Buffalo, Nov. 11, 1917; s. William Bennett and Mary Walborga (Frey) C.; m. Lorraine Tyszko, Sept. 22, 1945; children: Anne L., Marcia L., Margaret L. BSCE, Syracuse U., 1938; MSCE, Lehigh U., 1940. Registered profl. engr., Mich. Instr. Case Sch. of Applied Sci., Cleve., 1940-43; stress engr. Fisher Body Div., Gen. Motors, Cleve., 1943-44; sr. engr. applied physics lab. Johns Hopkins U., Silver Spring, Md., 1944-45; asst. prof. civil engring. Cornell U., Ithaca, N.Y., 1945-48, Wayne U., Detroit, 1948-51; assoc. prof. civil engring. Wayne State U., Detroit, 1951-59, prof. civil engring., 1959-82, prof. emeritus, from 1982; vis. assoc. prof. U. Mich., Ann Arbor, 1953, 54, 57; vis. prof. U. Detroit, 1974. Structural engr. Giffels & Valet, L. Rossetti, Detroit, summer 1950, 51, 52, 54. Exam. cons. N.Y. State Civil Svc., Albany, 1950; spl. examiner Wayne County Civil Svc., Detroit, 1962. Recipient Commendation, Office of Scientific R & D, 1945, Naval Ordnance Devel. award, 1945; named Outstanding Civil Engr., ASCE, 1983. Fellow ASCE (dir. 1964, 67); mem. AAUP, Engring. Soc. Detroit (outstanding leadership award 1988-89, disting. svc. award 1991), Am. Concrete Inst., Am. Soc. for Engring. Edn. Roman Catholic. Home: Minneapolis, Minn. Died July 17, 2009.

CHENG, KUANG LU, chemist, educator; b. Yangchow, China, Sept. 14, 1915; came to U.S., 1947, naturalized, 1955; s. Fong Wu and Yi Ming (Chiang) C.; children: Meiling, Chiling, Hans Christian. PhD, U. Ill., 1951. Microchemist Comml. Solvents Corp., Terre Haute, Ind., 1952-53; instr. U. Conn., Storrs, 1953-55; engr. Westinghouse Electric Corp., Pitts., 1955-57; assoc. dir. research metals div. Kelsey Hayes Co., Utica, NY, 1957-59; mem. tech. staff RCA Labs., Princeton, NJ, 1959-66; prof. chemistry U. Mo., Kansas City, 1966-90, prof. emeritus, from 1990. Recipient Achievement award RCA, 1963, Benedetti-Pichler award Am. Microchem. Soc., 1989; N.T. Veatch award for Disting. rsch. and creative activity U. Mo., 1979; cert. of recognition U.S. Office of Naval Rsch., 1979, cert. of recognition Coll. Engring., Tex. A&M U., 1981; bd. trustees fellow U. Kansas City, 1984. Fellow AAAS, Chem. Soc. London; mem. Am. Chem. Soc. (Longtime Achievement award 2004, Revolutionary Rsch. Analytical and Surface Sci. award 2008), Electrochem. Soc., Soc. Applied Spectroscopy, Am. Inst. Physics. Achievements include development of ISE double capacitor theory, 1983; discovery of interfacial triple layer, 2001. Died Mar. 30, 2010.

CHERNIACK, NEIL STANLEY, pulmonologist, educator; b. Bklyn., May 28, 1931; s. Max and Rebecca (Roulnick) C.; m. Sandra Lebowitz, Dec. 31, 1954; children: Evan, Andrew, Emily. AB (hon.), Columbia U., 1952; MD, SUNY, 1956; MD (hon.), Karolinska Inst., Stockholm, Sweden, 1990; MA, U. Pa., 1972; degree (hon.), Karolinska U., 1991. Cert. Am. Bd. Internal Medicine, 1956. Intern U. Ill., Chgo., 1956-57, resident, 1957-58, 60-62; resident, fellow Columbia Presbyn. Hosp., NYC, 1962-64; practice medicine specializing in pulmonary disease Chgo., 1964-69, Phila., 1969-77, Cleve., 1977—95; asst. prof. medicine U. Ill., Chgo., 1964-68, assoc. prof., 1968-69, U. Pa., Phila., 1969-73, prof., 1973-77, Case Western Res. U., from 1977, chief pulmonary svc., 1977-89, prof. physiology, from 1982, assoc. dean, 1983-90, dean sch. medicine, v.p. med. affairs, 1990-95, vice chmn. div. gen. med. sci., 1986-90, vice chmn. dept. medicine, 1987-90; chief pulmonary svc., sr. attending physician Phila. Gen. Hosp., 1969-77; assoc. dir. pulmonary svc., attending physician U. Pa. Hosp., 1973-77, U. Hosps. of Cleve., Cleve. VA Med. Ctr.; vis. prof. Karolinska U., Stockholm, 1976-77, dir. clin. svc., 1995—2000; dir. of clin. svcs., acting chmn. dept. physiology & pharmacology U. Medicine & Dentistry N.J., Newark, 1995—97. External vis. com. Aga Khan U., Karachi, 1980—85; chmn. vis. com. neurosci. program Howard U., 1998—2005; pulmonary svc. Cherniack Med. Svc., Cleve., 2005—08. Mem. editl. bd.: Circulation Rsch., Am. Rev. Respiratory Disease, Chest; editor: Jour. Applied Physiology, Handbook of Physiology; assoc. editor: Jour. Lab. Clin. Medicine, Respiration Handbooks of Physiology, Respiration and Respiratory Medicine Revs. Capt. USAF, 1958—60, with USAF, 1960—62. Mem.: N.Y. Clin. Soc., Neurosci. Soc., Ctrl. Soc. Clin. Rsch., Biomed. Engring. Soc. (bd. dirs. 1984—87, councilor 1986), Biogengring. Soc., Am. Physiol. Soc., Am. Lung Assn., Am. Thoracic Soc. (councilor 1982), Am. Soc. Clin. Investigation, Am. Assn. Physicians, Morris County Art Assn., Soc. Columbia Grads., Beta Sigma Rho, Alpha Omega Alpha, Phi Beta Kappa. Jewish. Avocation: digital art. Home: Morris Plains, NJ. Died Oct. 21, 2009.

CHIESA, ROBERT L., lawyer; b. Denver, Mar. 31, 1931; AB, Dartmouth Coll., 1953; LLB, Boston U., 1960. Bar: N.H. 1960. Ptnr. Wadleigh, Starr, Peter, Dunn & Chiesa, Manchester, N.H. Mem. N.H. Supreme Ct. Com. of Judicial Conduct, 1981-88, The Defense Rsch. Inst., Inc. Fellow Am. Bar Found.; mem. ABA (mem., standing com. on fed. judicial improvements 1983-86, N.H. state del. 1983-88, chmn. spl. com. on civil rico 1985-86), Manchester Bar Assn. (pres. 1974-75, assn. del. to ABA 1979-83), Internat. Assn. Def. Counselors, No. New England Def. Counsel. Died Jan. 14, 2010.

CHIKLIS, CHARLES KOULIAS, chemist; b. Lowell, Mass., Nov. 30, 1933; s. Christy Charles and Sophie (Koulias) Chiklis; m. Joan Marie Desimone, June 23, 1956; children: Debora, Gregory, Cynthia. BS, Lowell Technol. Inst., 1955, MS, 1956, PhD, 1964. Scientist materials dept. rsch. divsn. AVCO-RAD, Lowell, 1962, group leader polymer and foamed materials lab., 1963—65; scientist polymer rsch. lab. Ctrl. Rsch. Labs., Polaroid Corp., Cambridge, Mass., 1965—67, group leader, 1967—73, asst. mgr., 1973—79, mgr., 1979—85, mgr. coatings and reagent rsch. lab., 1975—80, program mgr. intrinsically conductive polymers, from 1985; mem. U. Lowell Chemistry and Plastics Adv. Bd. Contbr. articles to sci. jours. Co-pres. Fiske Sch. PTA, Lexington, Mass., 1971—72; chmn. cub pack Minuteman Coun. Boy Scouts America, 1973—75; co-chmn. St. Brigid's Youth Group, 1976—77; mem. Lexington Bicentennial Town Band, from 1977. With USAF, 1956—59. Lowell Technol. Inst. Rsch. Found. fellowship, 1959—62, E.I. duPont de Nemours Rsch. fellowship, 1962. Mem.: NY Acad. Sci., Am. Chem. Soc., Elks Club, Delta Kappa Phi, Sigma Xi. Achievements include patents in field. Home: Lexington, Mass. Died Aug. 31, 2009.

CHILCOAT, RICHARD ALLEN, military officer, university president; b. Wilmerding, Pa., Sept. 16, 1938; s. Floyd Donald and Edna Bailey (Moles0 C.; m. Dixie Lowers, June 6, 1964; children: Michael, Sharon A. BS, U.S. Mil. Acad., 1964; MBA, Harvard U., 1974. Commd. 2d lt. US Army, 1964; speechwriter to Gen. John A. Wickham Jr., Office Chief of Staff, U.S. Army, Washington, 1984-87; comdr. Devil

Troop Brigade, 5th Inf. Divsn. US Army, Ft. Polk, La., 1987-89, chief of staff, 3d Inf. Divsn. Germany, 1989-90; exec. asst. to Gen. Colin L. Powell, Joint Chiefs of Staff, Washington, 1990-92; dep. comdg. gen. US Army Tng. Ctr., Ft. Jackson, SC, 1993-94; comdt. US Army War Coll., Carlisle Barracks, Pa., 1994-97; pres. Nat. Def. U., Washington, 1997—2000; lt. gen. US Army (ret.), 2000; dean, George Bush Sch. Govt. & Public Svc. Texas A&M Univ., College Station, from 2001. Decorated DSM, Legion of Merit, Bronze Star with oak leaf cluster, Air medals. Mem. Assn. of U.S. Army, U.S. Mil. Acad. Assn. of Grads. Avocations: tennis, golf. Died Mar. 16, 2010.

CHILDS, BARTON, retired physician, educator; b. Chgo., Feb. 29, 1916; s. Robert William and Katherine Sayles (Barton) Childs; m. Eloise L.B. MacKie, Mar. 29, 1950 (dec. 1980); children: Anne Lloyd, Lucy Barton; m. Ann E. Pulver, Dec. 1986. AB, Williams Coll., 1938; MD, Johns Hopkins, 1942. Successively intern, asst. resident, resident pediat. Johns Hopkins Hosp., 1942—43, 1946—48; research fellow Children's Hosp., Boston, 1948—49; Commonwealth Fund fellow Univ. Coll., London, 1952—53; mem. faculty Johns Hopkins Sch. Medicine, 1949—2010, prof. pediat., 1962—2000, prof. emeritus, 2000—10. Mem. cons. coms. NIH, 1959—63, 1963—67, 1967—69, 1970—74, from 1978. Capt. Med. Corps US Army, 1943—46. Recipient Rsch. Career award, NIH, 1962, Meade Johnson award pediat., 1959, Allen award human genetics, 1974, Howland award pediat., 1989; scholar John and Mary Markle, 1953—58, Grover F. Powers Disting., 1960—62. Mem.: Am. Acad. Arts and Scis., Inst. Medicine NAS, Genetics Soc. Am., Am. Soc. Human Genetics, Am. Acad. Pediat., Soc. Pediatric Rsch., Am. Pediatric Soc. Home: Baltimore, Md. Died Feb. 18, 2010.

CHILDS, JOHN FARNSWORTH, retired bank executive; b. NYC, Nov. 24, 1909; s. Albert Ewing and Amelia (McGraw) C.; m. Mary Elizabeth Cardozo, Apr. 21, 1950; 1 dau., Susan Elizabeth. BS, Trinity Coll., Hartford, Conn., 1931, MS, 1932; MBA, Harvard, 1933; LLB, Fordham U., 1946. Bar: N.Y. 1946. Analyst Dick & Merle-Smith, NYC, 1935-40; sr. v.p., head corporate services div. Irving Trust Co., NYC, 1941-74; sr. v.p. Kidder-Peabody Inc., 1974-94, Paine Webber Inc., NYC, 1994-97. Mem. tech. adv. com. on fin. Fed. Power Commn., 1973-74; adj. prof. Columbia Grad. Bus. Sch.; cons. in field. Author: Long-Term Financing, 1961, Profit Goals and Capital Management, 1968, Earnings Per Share and Management Decisions, 1971, Encyclopedia of Long Term Financing and Capital Management, 1976, Corporate Finance and Capital Management for the Chief Executive Officer and Directors, 1979; Contbr. articles to profl. publs. Past treas., trustee Lenox Sch.; bd. dirs. N.Y. Council on Econ. Edn.; past bd. dirs. Sch. Book Fair Inc., Fla. Power Corp. Served as lt. comdr. USNR, World War II. Mem. Am. Mgmt. Assn. (pres. coun., past dir.), Atomic-Indsl. Forum (past dir.), N.Y. Soc. Security Analysts, Pine Valley Golf Club (Clementin, N.J.). Home: Nantucket, Mass. Died Jan. 11, 2009.

CHINITZ, BENJAMIN, economics educator; b. NYC, Aug. 24, 1924; s. Abraham and Mollie (Resnick) C.; m. Ethel Kleinman; children: Adam, Michael. AB, Yeshiva U., 1945; AM in Econs., Brown U., 1951; PhD in Econs., Harvard U., 1956; degree egree (hon.), Yeshiva U., 1969. Mem. sr. staff N.Y. Met. Region Study Regional Plan Assn., Harvard U., NYC, 1956-59; prof., chair dept. econs., assoc. dir. ctr. regional econ. studies U. Pitts., 1959-65; dep. asst. sec. commerce for econ. devel. Washington, 1965-66; prof., chair dept. econs. Brown U., Providence, 1961-73; prof. econs., dir. ctr. for social analysis SUNY, Binghamton, 1973-81; dean coll. mgmt. sci. U. Mass., Lowell, 1982-87; dir. rsch. Lincoln Inst. of Land Policy, Cambridge, Mass., 1987-91; fellow A. Alfred Taubman Ctr. for State and Local Govt. John F. Kennedy Sch. of Govt., Harvard U., Cambridge, from 1992. Faculty assoc. Lincoln Inst. of Land Policy, Cambridge; vis. prof. coll. urban & pub. affairs Fla. Atlantic U., Ft. Lauderdale; vis. mem. faculty dept. urban studies, MIT, 1967; cons. State of Conn., 1961-64, Appalachian Regional Commn., 1963-65, Rand Corp., 1961, 64, 67, U.S. Coun. Econ. Advisors, 1966, The White House, 1970, Resources for The Future, 1970-71, U.S. Econ. Devel. Adminstrn., 1970-72, UN, 1970, 72, NAS, 1970-71, The Brookings Instn., 1972-74, The Ford Found., 1976, Abt Assocs., 1975-81. Author: Freight and The Metropolis, 1960, City and Suburb: The Economics of Metropolitan Growth, 1964, Cities, 1965, The Declining Northeast, 1977, Central City Economic Development, 1979; (with others) Essays in Regional Economics, 1971, Social Responsibility and the Business Predicament, 1974, The Urban Economy, 1976; coord. editor Urban Studies, 1980-92; contbr. articles to profl. jours. Fullbright Vis. scholar U. Glasgow, 1965. Mem. Regional Sci. Assn. (com. urban econs. 1967-75, pres. 1970, 90). Home: Newton L F, Mass. Died Mar. 30, 2009.

CHINKES, HY, management consultant, financial planner; b. Tighina, Roumania, Oct. 14, 1918; s. Max and Anna (Crausman) Chinkes; m. Sophie Jacobs, July 1942 (div. 1955); children: Joel David, Barbara Rebecca; m. Charlotte Flora Maisel, Sept. 11, 1956. Mfrs. rep. to various photog. cos., 1956—58; pres., founder Crown Camera, Atlanta, 1958—76; fin. planner Consol. Planning, Atlanta, from 1976; spl. place ops. supr. US Census Bur., Atlanta, 1980; pres., chief exec. officer Employment World, Atlanta, 1980—81; founder, chief exec. officer APD Fin. Services, Atlanta, from 1976; pres., founder Ind. Camera Stores, Atlanta, 1974—76. Pres. Atlanta City Salesman's Club, 1975; mem. White House Council Small Bus., 1978; founder, mem. bd. Jewish Vocat. Svcs., Atlanta, from 1962; house dist. chmn., mem. county exec. com. Democratic Party, Atlanta, from 1970; chmn. Devel. Authority Fulton County, Atlanta, 1976—82; mem. allocation panel; mem. United Way, Atlanta, from 1977. Treas. Service Corps Ret. Execs., Atlanta, from 1976. Mem.: Masons. Home: Lake Worth, Fla. Died Apr. 21, 2010.

CHITTICK, ELIZABETH LANCASTER, advocate; b. Bangor, Pa., Nov. 11, 1908; d. George and Flora Mae (Mann) Lancaster. Student, Columbia U., 1944—45, N.Y. Inst. Fin., 1950—51, Hunter Coll., 1952—56, Upper Iowa U., Fayette, 1976. Adminstrv. asst., chief clk U.S. Naval Air Stas., Seattle and Banana River, Fla., 1941—45; v.p. treas. W.A. Chittick & Co., Manila, 1945—52; real estate salesperson La Jolla, Calif., 1949; registered rep. Bache & Co., N.Y. Stock Exch., NYC, 1950—62, Shearson & Hamil, 1962—63, investment adviser, 1962—65; revenue officer IRS, NYC, 1965—72; pres. Nat. Woman's Party, Washington, 1971—89, Woman's Party Corp., 1978—91; commr. Washington Commn. on Status of Women, 1982—86; pres., adminstr. Sewall-Belmont House. Bd. dirs. Wexita Corp., N.Y.C., Pan Am. Liason Com. of Women's Orgns. Inc.; 1st v.p., bd. dirs. Nat. Coun. Women U.S. Lectr., TV and radio commentator on Equal Rights Amendment; author: Answers to Questions About the Equal Rights Amendment, 1973, 76. Mem. Coalition for Women in Internat. Devel., Internat. Women's Yr. Continuing Com., 1978-81, Women's Campaign Fund, Washington, 1975-80, Women's Nat. Rep. Club, N.Y.C., Women Govt. Rels., Washington; mem. U.S. com. of cooperation to Inter-Am. Commn. of Women, OAS, 1974-80; del. U.S. World Conf. of Internat. Women's Yr., Mexico City, 1975; mem. women's history ctr. task force Am. Revolution Bicentennial Adminstrn., 1973-76; mem. adv. com. U.S. Ctr. for Internat. Women's Yr., 1973-76; vice convenor com. on law and status of women Internat. Coun. of Women; chmn. UN Drive for war orphans and widows, Manila, 1949 Mem. Greater Washington Soc. Assn. Execs., Internat. Coun. Women (Paris), Nat. Fedn. Bus. and Profl. Women's Clubs, Gen. Fedn. Women's Clubs, Women's Press Club (N.Y.C.), Am. Newswomen's Club, Nat. Press Club, Order Eastern Star. Home: West Palm Beach, Fla. Died Apr. 16, 2009.

CHMIEL, CHESTER T., chemist, consultant; b. Lackawanna, NY, Feb. 26, 1926; m. Margaret Fox, Apr. 14, 1956; children: Stephanie, Catherine, Carolyn, Geraldine, Gregory. BS, Canisius Coll., 1949, MS, 1951; PhD, Cornell U., 1956; MBA, Mich. State U., 1972. Chemist Monsanto, Springfield, Mass., 1956-60, Uniroyal, Inc., Wayne, N.J., 1960-67, sect. mgr. Mishawaka, Ind., 1967-87; v.p. R & D Uniroyal Adhesives and Sealants Co., Mishawaka, 1987-92; pres. Chester T. Chmiel, Cons., Niles, Mich., from 1990. Contbr. articles to profl. jours. Republican. Roman Catholic. Achievements include 14 patents for adhesives. Home: Niles, Mich. Died Apr. 6, 2009.

CHRISTIAN, MAUREEN MAHER, clinical psychologist; b. Poughkeepsie, N.Y., Mar. 30, 1947; d. Thomas Francis and Linda Maher; B.A. (scholar), Trinity Coll., 1969; M.A., Am. U., 1971, Ph.D., 1979; m. James H. Christian, Aug. 8, 1970; 1 child, Justin Maher. Staff psychologist Youth Ctr. One, D.C. Dept. of Corrections, Lorton, Va., 1971-74, chief psychologist Youth Ctr. Two, 1974-80; clin. psychologist St. Elizabeth's Hosp., Washington, 1980-85, chief clin. psychologist, 1985-87; chief psychologist Acute Care Hosp. D.C. Commn. on Mental Health Services, 1987—. Cons., bd. dirs. Isaiah House, Washington, 1979-80; bd. dirs. Shadowalk Home Assn., Fairfax Sta., Va., 1981-84, v.p., 1982-84; mem. reorgn. research task force D.C. Mental Health Service, 1985—; mem. exec. bd. Boy Scouts Am., 1982—; mem. Hospitalwide Psychology Adv. Council, 1985—; chmn. O'Malley Inservice Edn. Com.; mem. utilization rev. com. St. Elizabeth's Hosp.; mem. bd. dirs. St. Elizabeth's Psychol. Assn.; mem. exec. bd. D.C. Psychol. Assn. Recipient award of excellence D.C. Dept. Corrections, 1979, 80, St. Elizabeth's Hosp., 1984. Mem. Am. Psychol. Assn., D.C. Psychol. Assn., Med. Soc. St. Elizabeth's Hosp., Psi. Chi, Phi Kappa Phi. Contbr. articles to profl. publs. Home: Fairfax Station, Va. Died June 28, 2009.

CHRISTO-JAVACHEFF, JEANNE-CLAUDE, art gallery owner; b. Morocco, June 13, 1935; d. Jacques Marie and Precilda Angela (Eton) de Guillebon; m. Christo Vladimirov Javacheff; 1 child, Cyril Christo. B.A. in Latin and Philosophy, U. Tunis, Paris, 1952. Dealer Christo's Works of Art, N.Y.C., curator, registrar, 1958—2009; Author articles. Recipient Keys of City, Rifle, Colo., 1972, Kansas City, Mo., 1978, Miami, Fla., 1983. Cited by Calif. Legislature for Running Fence sculpture, 1976. Mem. Mus. Modern Art, Project Studios One, Archtl. League, Internat. Ctr. Photography. Avocation: photography. Died Nov. 19, 2009.

CHRISTY, ARTHUR HILL, lawyer; b. Bklyn., July 25, 1923; s. Francis Taggart and Catherine Virginia (Damon) C.; m. Gloria Garvin Osborne, Feb. 14, 1980; children by previous marriage: Duncan Hill, Alexandra. AB, Yale U., 1945; LL.B., Columbia U., 1949. Bar: N.Y. 1950. Assoc. Baldwin, Todd & Lefferts, NYC, 1950-52; spl. asst. atty. gen. State of NY, NY, 1952-53, asst. atty. gen. NY, 1955; asst. U.S. atty. (so. dist.) US Dept. Justice, 1953-54, chief criminal divsn., 1955-57, chief asst. U.S. atty., 1957-58, US atty., 1958-59; chief prosecutor spl. asst. atty. gen. Saratoga and Columbia County Investigations, 1954-55; ptnr. Christy & Viener (and predecessors), NYC, 1959—2010. Spl. asst. to Gov. Rockefeller, 1959-61; apptd. 1st spl. prosecutor Under Ethics in Govt. Act of 1978 to investigate charges against White House Chief of Staff, 1979-80. Artist in scrimshaw. Trustee, vice chmn. Bklyn. Hosp., Cmty. Svc. Soc.; v.p., gen. counsel, mem. coun. N.Y. Heart Assn. Lt. USNR, 1944-46. Mem. ABA, N.Y. State Bar Assn., Fed. Bar Assn., Assn. Bar City N.Y. (chmn. exec. com. 1966-67, v.p. 1968-69), Am. Coll. Trial Lawyers, Century Assn., Rockefeller Luncheon Club, Univ. Club (N.Y.C.), Mastigouche Fish and Game Club (Que., Can.). Republican. Episcopalian. Home: New York, NY. Died Mar. 12, 2010.

CHU, JOHNSON CHIN SHENG, retired physician; b. Peiping, China, Sept. 25, 1918; arrived in U.S., 1948, naturalized, 1957; s. Harry S.P. and Florence (Young) Chu; m. Sylvia Cheng, June 11, 1949; children: Stephen, Timothy. MD, St. John's U., 1945. Intern Univ. Hosp., Shanghai, 1944-45; resident, research fellow NYU Hosp., 1948-50; resident physician in charge State Hosp. and Med. Ctr., Weston, W.Va., 1951-56; chief services, clin. dir. State Hosp., Logansport, Ind., 1957-84, ret., 1998. Active mem. Meml. Hosp., Logansport, Ind., 1968—. Contbr. articles to profl. jours. Fellow: Am. Coll. Chest Physicians, Am. Psychiat. Assn.; mem.: AAAS, AMA, Cass County Med. Soc., Ind. Med. Assn. Achievements include research in cardiology and pharmacology. Home: Monticello, Ind. Died Mar. 11, 2009.

CIALELLA, ROSEANN MARGARET, educational administrator; b. Bklyn., Oct. 9, 1947; d. Vincent James and Mary Rose (Cuoco) Internicola; m. Edward Charles Cialella, Feb. 27, 1971. BS, SUNY, Brockport, 1969; MEd, Rutgers U., 1977; EdD, Nova Southeastern U., Ft. Lauderdale, Fla., 1994. Cert. tchr., prin, supt. schs., N.J. Tchr. Penns Grove (N.J.) Bd. Edn., 1973-76, Gloucester County Vo-Tech, Sewell, N.J., 1976-78; prin. Mullica Twp. Bd. Edn., Elwood, N.J., 1978-79, Washington Twp. Bd. Edn., Sewell, 1979-84; supt. Berkeley Twp. Bd. Edn., Bayville, N.J., 1984-87, Merchantville (N.J.) Bd. Edn., 1987-89; supr. U. Pa., Phila., 1989-90; supt. schs. Estell Manor (N.J.) Bd. Edn., from 1990. Mem. prof. devel. com. N.J. State Dept. Edn., Trenton, 1992—. Charter mem. Estell Manor Cmty. Drug Alliance, 1990-93. Mem. AAUW, Am. Assn. Sch. Adminstrs., N.J. Assn. Sch. Adminstrs. (various coms.), Phi Delta Kappa. Avocations: golf, needlecrafts, reading, antiques, interior design. Home: Las Cruces, N.Mex. Died Feb. 7, 2009.

CIARDULLO, MARION DOROTHY, public relations specialist; b. Newport, R.I., Oct. 22, 1924; d. Benjamin and Fannie (Lack) Rudick; m. Michael Ciardullo, May 31, 1950; children— Robin Bruce, Frances Audrey. A.B., Hunter Coll., 1947; postgrad. Columbia U., 1950. Copywriter, gen. Asst. Vanguard Advt., N.Y.C., 1947-48; media specialist J. Walter Thompson, 1948-50; pub. relations coordinator Norden, United Technologies Corp., Norwalk, Conn., 1971-81; mgr. mktg. communications Safe Flight Instrument Corp., White Plains, N.Y., 1982-84; mgr. mktg. communications W.W. Gaertner Research, Inc., Norwalk, Conn., 1985-93. Contbr. articles to profl. jours. Mem. Aviation/Space Writers Assn., Pub. Relations Soc. Am., Fairfield County Pub. Relations Soc., Internat. Assn. Bus. Communicators, Women in Communication. Democrat. Jewish. Home: Syracuse, NY. Died Apr. 3, 2009.

CIMINO, JAMES ERNEST, physician; b. NYC, July 7, 1928; s. Ernest S. and Rose (Gorga) C.; m. Dorothy Hilary Naperkoski, June 5, 1954; children: James, Ernest, Christopher, Peter, Paul, Maria. Student, Syracuse U., 1946-48; AB, NYU, 1950, MD, 1954. Diplomate Am. Bd. Internal Medicine, Am. Bd. Nephrology. Intern, then resident E.J. Meyer Meml. Hosp., Buffalo, 1954-58; rsch. fellow in physiology U. Buffalo, 1957-58; internal medicine physician, dir. renal svc. VA Hosp., Bronx, N.Y., 1960-68; attending physician Calvary Hosp., Bronx, N.Y., from 1961, chief medicine, med. dir., 1963-80, co-med. dir., 1994, dir. Palliative Care Inst., from 1994. Cons. medicine St. Joseph's Hosp., Yonkers, N.Y., Holy Name Hosp., Teaneck, N.J., cons. medicine VA Hosp., Bronx, 1970-77, dir. hemodialysis unit, 1960-70; asst. clin. prof. medicine Mt. Sinai Sch. Medicine, N.Y.C., 1970-73; clin. prof. medicine N.Y. Med. Coll., 1980—; adj. prof., cons. nutrition NYU, 1972-93; cons. internal medicine N.Y.C. Dept. Health, 1971-74, also chmn. com. advanced cancer, 1971-74; mem. instnl. biohazards com. Albert Einstein Coll. Medicine, 1980-92. Mem. edit. bd. N.Y. Med. Quar.; mem. edit. review bd. Am. Jour. of Hospice and Palliative Care; contbr. articles to med. jours. Bd. dirs. N.Y.C. chpt. Am. Cancer Soc. With USAF, 1958-60. Recipient commendation VA, 1968, Ann. Merit award N.Y.C. Pub. Health Assn., 1979, 1st ann. Catherine McParlan Humanitarian award, 1980, Dialysis Pioneering award Nat. Kidney Disease Found., 1982, Il Leone di San Marco award in medicine, 1991; co-recipient Good Samaritan award Nat. Cath. Devel. Conf., 1981; included in The Best Drs. in N.Y., N.Y. Mag., 1996, Best Drs. in Am. North East Region Woodward White, 1996-97. Fellow ACP (Laureate award 1992); mem. AMA, Am. Heart Assn., Internat. Soc. Nephrology, Am. Soc. Nephrology, Am. Dietetic Assn. (Hon. Membership award 1995), Greater N.Y. Dietetic Assn. (hon.). Achievements include development of arterio-venous fistula in hemodialysis and pioneering work in field of palliative care for cancer patients and in the field of nutritional education. Died Feb. 11, 2010.

CLABAULT, ROBERT ALEXANDER, chemical company executive; b. Boston, Feb. 16, 1928; s. Wilfred Alexander and Eleanor Elizabeth (Cross) C.; m. Helen Gray Morrison, Feb. 16, 1952; children— David, Jeffrey BS in Chemistry, Tufts U., 1950; MBA with high distinction, Harvard U., 1954. Vice pres. W.R. Grace & Co., NYC, 1955-77, exec. v.p., dir., chief tech. officer, from 1978; pres. Mallinckrodt, Inc., St. Louis, 1977-78. Patentee in field Various town offices Town of Hingham, Mass., 1965-77; state committeeman Republican Party, Mass., 1968-72. Served with USAR, 1950-54 Bakers scholar Harvard U. Bus. Sch., 1954 Mem. Am. Chem. Soc., Soc. Chem. Industry (dir. 1979-82), Chem. Mfrs. Assn. (bd. dirs. 1975-77) Clubs: N.Y. Yacht, Hingham Yacht (commodore 1972-74). Congregationalist. Avocations: sailing; golf; tennis. Died May 12, 2010.

CLARK, ARTHUR JOSEPH, JR., mechanical engineer, retired electrical engineer; b. West Orange, NJ, June 10, 1921; s. Arthur Joseph and Marjorie May (Courter) Clark; m. Caroline Katherine Badgley, June 12, 1943; children: Arthur Joseph III, Durward S., David P. BSME, Cornell U., 1943; MS, Poly. Inst. Bklyn., 1948; MSEE, U. N.Mex., 1955.

Design engr. Ranger Aircraft Engines Co., Farmingdale, NY, 1943—46; sr. structures engr. propeller divsn. Curtis Wright Co., Caldwell, NJ, 1946—51; mgr. space isotope power dept. and aerospace nuc. safety dept. Sandia Labs., Albuquerque, 1951—71, mgr. environ. sys. test lab., 1971—79, mgr. mil. liaison dept., 1979—86; pres. Engring. Svcs. Cons. Firm, 1987; ret., 1986. Mem. faculty U. N.Mex, 1971—75; invited lectr. Am. Mgmt. Assn. Active local Boy Scouts Am., 1958—66; pres. Sandia Base Sch. PTA, 1960—61; chmn. fin. com. Albuquerque chpt. Am. Field Svc., 1964—66; chmn. Sandia Labs. divsn. U.S. Savs. Bond Dr., 1973—75. Recipient Order Arrow, Boy Scouts Am., 1961, Order St. Andrew, 1962, Scouters Key award, 1964, cert. Outstanding Svc., Sandia Base, 1964. Fellow: ASME (nat. v.p. 1975—79, past chmn. N.Mex sect.); mem.: IEEE (sr.), Cornell Engring. Soc., Four Hills Country Club, Kirtland Officers Club, Theta Xi. Home: Albuquerque, N.Mex. Died Mar. 19, 2010.

CLARK, BURTON ROBERT, sociologist, educator; b. Pleasantville, NJ, Sept. 6, 1921; s, Burton H. and Cornelia (Amole) C.; m. Adele Halitsky, Aug. 31, 1949; children: Philip Neil (dec.), Adrienne. BA, UCLA, 1949, PhD, 1954; Doctorate (hon.), U. Strathclyde, 1998, U. Turku, Finland, 2000. Asst. prof. sociology Stanford (Calif.) U., 1953-56; rsch. assoc., asst. prof. edn. Harvard U., 1956-58; assoc. prof., then prof. edn. and assoc. rsch. sociologist, then rsch. sociologist U. Calif., Berkeley, 1958-66; prof. sociology Yale U., 1966-80, chmn. dept., 1969-72, chmn. higher edn. rsch. group, 1973-80; Allan M. Cartter prof. higher edn. UCLA, 1980-91, prof. emeritus, 1991—2009. Author: Adult Education in Transition, 1956, The Open Door College, 1960, Educating the Expert Society, 1962, The Distinctive College, 1970, The Problems of American Education, 1975, Academic Power in Italy, 1977, The Higher Education System, 1983, The Academic Life, 1987, Places of Inquiry, 1995, Creating Entrepreneurial Universities, 1998, Sustaining Change in Universities, 2004, On Higher Education: Selected Writings, 1956-2006, 2008; co-author: Students and Colleges, 1972, Youth: Transition to Adulthood, 1973, Academic Power in the United States, 1976, Academic Power: Patterns of Authority in Seven National Systems of Higher Education, 1978; editor: Perspectives on Higher Education, 1984, The School and The University, 1985, The Academic Profession, 1987, The Research Foundations of Graduate education, 1993; co-senior editor: Encyclopedia of Higher Education, 1992. Served with AUS, 1942-46. Recipient Comenius medal UNESCO, 1998. Fellow Brit. Soc. for Rsch. in Higher Edn., AAAS, Am. Ednl. Rsch. Assn. (Am. Coll. Testing award 1979, Divsn. J. Disting. Rsch. award 1988, Outstanding Book award 1989); mem. Am. Sociol. Assn., Assn. Study Higher Edn. (pres. 1979-80, Rsch. Achievement award 1985, Howard Bowen Disting. Svc. award 1997), Nat. Acad. Edn. (v.p. 1989-93), Consortium Higher Edn. Rschrs., European Assn. for Instnl. Rsch. (disting. mem.) Home: Santa Monica, Calif. Died Oct. 28, 2009.

CLARK, CAROLYN LEIS, audiovisual specialist, video producer; b. Clairton, Pa., June 10, 1945; d. J. Clark and Aleda Marie (Blank) Leis; m. Richard M. Clark, 1965 (div. 1973); 1 son, Brian. Student Pa. State U., 1963-65; B.A. in Psychology with high honors, Rutgers U., 1972; cert. elem. edn. Kean Coll., 1974-75; postgrad. Hunter Coll., 1978. Art. therapist Rutkowski Sch., New Brunswick, N.J., 1968-69, tchr. emotionally impaired, 1969-73; asst. dir. Rutgers Motoric Devel. Program, 1971-74; edn. cons. AV Media Craftsman, Inc., N.Y.C., 1973, dir. creative services, 1974-79, v.p., 1980-82, pres., 1982—; audio visual cons., video producer J.C. Penney Co., N.Y.C., McGraw-Hill, Pinkerton's, Inc., N.Y.C., John Wiley & Sons, N.Y.C., 1979-84, others. Author, producer Consumer Edn., 1977-84; producer, dir. Mem. hon. bd. Jean Cocteau Theatre, N.Y.C., 1981-83; mem. Assn. for Help of Retarded Children, Friends of Disabled, 1980-87. Recipient George Washington award Freedoms Found. at Valley Forge, 1977, Consumer Edn. award, Silver award Internat. Film and TV Festival, 1977, Award of Merit Soc. Tech. Communications, 1983, 85, 86; Award of Achievement Internat. Audio Visual Competition, 1983, Award of Creative Excellence U.S. Indsl. Film Festival, 1985, Producer's award Am. Soc. for Indsl. Security, 1986. Mem. Nat. Assn. Female Execs., Wagner Internat. Soc., Screen Actors Guild, Rutgers Alumni Assn., LWV, Assn. for Research and Enlightenment (N.Y. coordinator 1986), Delta Zeta. Mem. Unity Ch. Died July 19, 2009.

CLARK, DONALD ROBERT, retired insurance company executive; b. Chgo., Jan. 19, 1924; s. Sherman Fred and Frieda (Grossklags) C.; m. Lora Marie Steiner, Aug. 11, 1945; children: Gregory Wayne, Sharon Louise. Student, Northwestern U., 1941-43, U. Wis., 1943-44. With Kemper Nat. Ins. Cos., 1941-89; ret., 1989. Exec. v.p., dir. Am. Mfrs. Mut. Ins. Co., Am. Motorists Ins. Co., Kemper Corp., Lumbermen's Mut Casualty Co.; former v.p., dir. Am. Protection Ins. Co., Economy Fire & Casualty Co., Fed. Kemper Ins. Co., Fed. Kemper Life Assurance Co., Fidelity Life Assn., Kemper Internat. Corp., Kemper Europe Reassurances, Belgium, Kemper S.A., Belgium, Kemper Ins. Co., Australia, Kemper Reins. Co., Long Grove, Ill.; former dir. Kemper Reins. Co. London Ltd., Kemper Fin. Services, Inc., Kemper Fin. Cos., Inc., Kemper Investors Life Ins. Co. Chgo. Contbr. to: Insurance Accounting Fire and Casualty, 2d edit, 1965, Property-Liability Insurance Accounting, 1974. Mem. Ins. Acctg. and Systems Assn. (pres. 1968-69), Fin. Execs. Inst. Lutheran (past chmn. congregation and fin. com.). Home: Prospect Heights, Ill. Died Apr. 23, 2010.

CLARK, JOSEPH ABEL, physicist; b. Lancaster, Pa., Jan. 14, 1939; s. Howard Edwin and Kathryn (Abel) C. BA in Physics, U. Notr Dame, 1960; MS in Mech. Engring., Cath. U. Am., 1967, PhD in Physics and Acoustics, 1969. From adj. assoc. prof. to adj. prof. Cath. U., Washington, 1973-82, adj. prof., 1982-89; physicist carderock divsn. Naval Surface Warfare Ctr., Bethesda, Md., from 1989. Vis. assoc. prof. U. Nat. Engring., Lima, Peru, 1977, Albert Einstein Coll. Medicine, Ye Shiva U., N.Y.C., 1979-85; physicist NIH, 1980; vis. scientist Ctr. Marine Biotech., U. Md., Balt., 1994—. With. USN, 1960-65. Rotary Internat. fellow, 1961-62, NDEA fellow Cath. U., 1965-68. Mem. AAAS, Acoustical Soc. Am. Roman Catholic. Achievements include patents for nearfield acoustic holography measurement system, method and system of mapping acoustic nearfield, far field acoustic radiation reduction. Home: Arlington, Va. Died Feb. 18, 2009.

CLARK, PAUL EDWARD, publishing executive; b. Metropolis, Ill., Mar. 7, 1941; s. Paul E. and Lillie Jean (Melcher) Clark. BA, Southern Ill. U., 1963, MA, 1965; MDiv, Northwestern U., 1970; DMus, Inst. Musical Rsch., London, 1973; PhD, U. Ill., 1978. Ordained to ministry Meth. Ch., 66. Staff accompanist The Story and White Sisters, 1959—62; staff accompanist voice faculty Southern Ill. U., Carbondale, 1961—65; pastor Stockland United Meth. Ch, 1966—70; minister of music First United Meth. Ch., Watseka, Ill., 1972—76; dir. choral activities Unit 3 Donovan schs., 1970—79; studio musician LA, from 1966; pres. Clark Music Pub. and Prodn., Watseka, from 1973; bus. mgr., transp. dir. Cmty. Unit 3 Schs., from 1980. Contbr. articles to profl. jours., columns in newspapers; composer: The Voice That Calls His Name, 1961, Jesus Dear Jesus, 1971, Spring Was But A Child, 1977, Country Living, 1976, Losing is the Hurting Side of Love, 1977, Use Me Lord, 1978, Come On In, 1978, All I Ask of You, 1979. Recipient Gospel Music Instrumentalist award, 1971, Ill. Chess Coach award, 1973; named Piano Tchr. of Yr., Southern Ill. U., 1970. Mem.: Broadcast Music Inc., Southern Ill. U. Alumni Assn., US Chess Fedn., Ill. Music Educators Assn., Music Educators Nat. Conf., Am. Fedn. Musicians, Am. Choral Dirs. Assn., Mu Alpha Theta, Phi Mu Alpha. Republican. Methodist. Home: Watseka, Ill. Died Apr. 25, 2010.

CLARK, SANDRA JEAN, humanities educator; b. Niagara Falls, NY, Mar. 28, 1942; d. Stanley LaVerne and Jean Elizabeth (Kelman) Stephens; m. Ronald Keith Clark, June 27, 1964; 1 child, Christopher Keith. BS in English, Anderson Coll., 1964; MA in English, Ball State U., 1967, PhD in Composition and Rhetoric, 1995. Cert. lang. arts tchr., Ind. English tchr. Highland H.S., Anderson, Ind., 1964-72; prof. English Anderson (Ind.) U., from 1975, writing program dir., from 1985. Founder, bd. dirs. Women's Alternatives, Anderson, 1977-85. Mem. Ind. Tchrs. of Writing (sec. 1986-88. v.p. 1995-96, pres. 1996-98). Mem. Ch. of God. Home: Anderson, Ind. Died Dec. 14, 2009.

CLARK, WILLIAM ALFRED, federal judge; b. Dayton, Ohio, Aug. 27, 1928; s. Webb Rufus and Dora Lee (Weddle) C.; m. Catherine C. Clark, Apr. 5, 1952; children: Mary Clark Youra, Jennifer Clark Kinder, Cynthia S., Andrea G. AB, U. Mich., 1950, JD, 1952. Bar: Ohio 1952, Mich. 1953. Pvt. practice, Dayton, 1954—57; assoc. Frank J. Svoboda, Dayton, 1957—73; ptnr. Legler, Lang & Kuhns, Dayton, 1973-82, Pickrel, Schaeffer & Ebeling, Dayton, 1982-85; judge so. dist. Ohio U.S. Bankruptcy Ct., Dayton, 1985-99, chief judge, 1993-99; apptd. recalled bankruptcy judge, from 1999. Judge Montgomery County Ct., Dayton, 1958-62; trial counsel in eminent domain Asst. Atty. Gen. Ohio, Dayton, 1963-70; tchr. bus. law Dayton chpt. Cert. Property and Casualty Underwriters, 1963-83; arbitrator Montgomery County Common Pleas Ct., Am. Arbitration Assn., Better Bus. Bur. Contbr. to Ohio Practice and Procedure Handbook, 1962. Lt. USAF, 1952-54. Named Alumnus of Yr., U. Mich. Club, Dayton, 1965. Mem. ABA, Ohio State Bar Assn. (chmn. eminent domain 1979-82), Dayton Bar Assn. (treas. 1964-65), Nat. Conf. Bankruptcy Judges, Lawyers Club. Republican. Avocations: tennis, other sports, reading, travel. Died Jan. 21, 2009.

CLARK, WILLIAM FRANCIS, JR., training manager; b. Elizabeth, NJ, Nov. 22, 1943; s. William Francis and Rose Elizabeth (Fisher) Clark; m. Patricia Ann Hodgins, June 1, 1971 (div.); m. Gail Peay Clark, Nov. 1, 1976. BA, Elon Coll., 1970; postgrad., Winthrop Coll., 1972. Sci. tchr., coach, Fort Mill, SC, 1970—72; area mgr. Internat. Harvester, Charlotte, NC, 1972—74; sales tng. instr., 1974—75; instr., developer, 1975—76; program coord., 1976—78; mgr. tng. edn. A.O. Smith Harvestore Products, Inc., Arlington Heights, Ill., from 1978. Mgr. sales and product tng. NAP Consumer Electronics Corp.; guest spkr. Nat. Agri-Mktg. Assn., Shawnee Mission, Kans., 1983. Mem.: ASTD, Mantread Agy., Am. Mgmt. Assn., Alpha Pi Delta. Presbyterian. Home: Suwanee, Ga. Died June 7, 2010.

CLARKE, ROBERT FLANDERS, librarian, administrator, retired public health service officer; b. Newport News, Va., June 20, 1932; s. Harrison Wheeler and Jessie Boggs (Flanders) Clarke; m. Haydee Garcia Caceres, Dec. 17, 1964; children: Emily Victoria, Valerie Alexandra. Student, USCG Acad., 1949—50; BS in Gen. Engring., US Naval Acad., 1954; MLS, Rutgers U., 1961; PhD, 1963; postgrad. in law, Am. U., 1974—76. Lic. libr. Va, NJ, NY. Commd. officer USPHS, 1962; advanced through grades to capt., 1974; systems analyst office of dir. Nat. Library Medicine, Bethesda, Md., 1963—64; dep. chief tech. svc. divsn. Nat. Lib. Medicine, Bethesda, Md., 1964—66; chief library svcs. Nat. Clearinghouse for Smoking and Health, Arlington, Va., 1966—68; spl. asst. to chief NIH Library, Bethesda, 1968—72; spl. asst. for biomed. commn. FDA, Rockville, Md., 1972—77; program chief mental lit. NIMH, Adelphi, Md., 1977—81; dir. foods libr. Ctr. for Food Safety FDA, Washington, 1982—84; cons. Kendrick & Co., ActMedia, Sci. Mgmt. Corp., 1985—86; dir. librs. John F. Kennedy Libr., Hialeah, Fla., from 1992. Cons. div. water supply pollution control USPHS, Arlington, 1965—66; office asst. Sec. Health Sci. Affairs, Washington, 1968, Parklawn Adv. Com., Washington, 1968—69. Contbr. book, directory, publs. in field., articles to profl. jours. Recipient Outstanding Service medal, USPHS, 1982, Commendation medal, 1969, Superior Service award, Alumni Assoc. award, USCG Acad., 1950; fellowship, Rutgers U., 1961. Fellow: Washington Acad. Scis.; mem.: ALA, Commd. Officers Assn., Spl. Librs. Assn., DC Librs. Assn., Med. Libr. Assn. Home: Miami, Fla. Died Feb. 22, 2009.

CLAUSEN, HUGH JOSEPH, retired army officer; b. Mobile, Ala., Dec. 25, 1926; s. Hugh Martin and Elizabeth Hazel (Orrell) C.; m. Betty Sue Richards, June 7, 1949; children: Melinda, Joseph. LL.B., U. Ala., 1950; grad., Advanced Mgmt. Program, Harvard U., 1970. Bar: Ala. 1950, U.S. Supreme Ct. 1959, U.S. Ct. Mil. Appeals 1959. Commd. 1st lt. U.S. Army, 1951, advanced through grades to maj. gen.; various assignments U.S. and Europe, 1951-62; asst. staff judge adv. (8th Army), Korea, 1962-64; judge adv. U.S. Disciplinary Barracks, Fort Leavenworth, Kans., 1964-66; instr. U.S. Army Command and Gen. Staff Coll., 1966-68; staff judge adv. 1st Inf. Div., Vietnam, 1968-69; assigned Office Legis. Liaison, Dept. Army, Washington, 1969-71; chief mil. justice div. Office JAG, 1971-72, exec. officer, 1972-73; staff judge adv. III Corps and Ft. Hood, Tex., 1973-76; chief judge U.S. Army Ct. Mil. Rev., Falls Church, Va., 1976-78; asst. judge adv. gen. for mil. law Dept. Army., 1978-79, asst. judge adv. gen., 1979-81, judge adv. gen., 1981-85. Vice pres. for adminstrn., sec. bd. trustees Clemson U., S.C., 1985-92, v.p. emeritus, 1992—. Decorated Disting. Service Medal, Bronze Star with 3 oak leaf clusters, Meritorious Service medal, Legion of Merit with oak leaf cluster, Air medal with oak leaf cluster, Army Commendation medal with oak leaf cluster; RVN Honor medal; RVN Gallantry Cross with palm; RVN Civic Action Honor medal with palm. Mem. Ala. Bar Assn., Phi Alpha Delta. Died May 7, 2009.

CLAWSON, JOHN ADDISON, investment company and retired chemicals executive; b. Monaco, Pa., June 4, 1922; s. Ralph S. and Elsie (Winnett) C.; m. Patricia Harmon, July 5, 1947; children: Christine Brandwie, Hunter Winnett. BS, Miami U., 1943, LLD, 1979; postgrad., Harvard U., 1968. Vice pres., nat. mgr. bus. and labor reports div. Prentice-Hall, NYC, 1948-55; with DuBois Chems. div. Chemed Corp., Cin., 1955-78, dist. mgr. NYC, 1955-60, regional mgr. Ea. div., 1960-64, divisional mgrs. v.p., 1964-66, exec. v.p., dir. sales, 1966-70, gen. mgr., 1968-70, pres., chief exec. officer, 1970-79, group exec., 1975-79; v.p. Chemed Corp., 1971-77, exec. v.p., 1978-79, ret., 1979. Chmn. Whitehall Mgmt. Corp., Cin.; bd. dirs. Suburban Fed. Savs. & Loan Assn. Trustee Providence Hosp., 1974-76; dean's assoc. Miami U., 1973—. Lt. (j.g.) USNR, 1943-46. Mem. Cin. C. of C. (city and county planning com. 1971-74), Soap and Detergent Assn. (vice-chmn. bd. 1971-73, chmn. bd., chief exec. officer 1974-75, mem. exec. com., bd. dirs. 1976-79), Delta Sigma Phi, Sigma Alpha Epsilon. Clubs: Queen City (Cin.), Kenwood Country (Cin.); John's Island (Fla.), Cat Cay, Ltd., Commodore (Bahamas). Presbyterian. Home: Vero Beach, Fla. Died June 14, 2010.

CLAY, CHARLES HORACE, railroad executive; b. Troy, Mont., Aug. 5, 1925; s. Charles Horace and Helen Ethel C.; m. Audrey Jorgenson, Mar. 17, 1951; children— John Sheldon, Janis Marie, Steven Charles. BBA, U. Minn., 1948, LL.B., 1950. Atty. Soo Line R.R. Co., Mpls., 1952-59, gen. atty., 1959-72, gen. freight traffic mgr., 1972-73, asst. to pres., 1973-77, v.p., 1977-78, exec. v.p., from 1978. Died Mar. 1, 2009.

CLAYBURGH, JILL, actress; b. NYC, Apr. 30, 1944; d. Albert Henry and Julia (Door) C.; m. David Rabe, Mar., 1979; children: Lily, Michael; 1 stepchild: Jason BA in Theater, Sarah Lawrence Coll., 1966. Mem., Charles Playhouse, Boston; stage appearances include The Sudden and Accidental Re-Education of Horse Johnson, 1968, The Rothschilds, 1970, Pippin, 1972, In the Boom Boom Room, Design for Living, 1984, A Naked Girl on the Appian Way, 2005 Barefoot in the Park, 2006, The Busy World Is Hushed, 2006, All My Sons, 2008; actress: (films) The Wedding Party, 1969, The Telephone Book, 1971, Portnoy's Complaint, 1972, The Thief Who Came to Dinner, 1973, The Terminal Man, 1974, Gable and Lombard, 1976, Silver Streak, 1976, Semi-Tough, 1977, An Unmarried Woman, 1978, Luna, 1979, Starting Over, 1979, It's My Turn, 1980, First Monday in October, 1981, I'm Dancing as Fast as I Can, 1982, Hannah K, 1983, In Our Hands, 1984, Where Are The Children, 1986, Shy People, 1987, Beyond the Ocean, 1990, Whispers in the Dark, 1992, Le Grand Pardon II, 1992, Rich in Love, 1993, Naked in New York, 1994, Fools Rush In, 1997, Going All the Way, 1997, Never Again, 2001, Vallen, 2001, Running with Scissors, 2006; (TV films) Snoop Sisters, 1972, The Art of Crime, 1975, Hustling, 1975, Griffin and Phoenix, 1976, Miles to Go..., 1986, Who Gets the Friends?, 1988, Fear Stalk, 1989, Unspeakable Acts, 1990, Reason for Living: The Jill Ireland Story, 1991, Trial: The Price of Passion, 1993, Firestorm: A Catastrophe in Oakland, 1993, For the Love of Nancy, 1994, Honor Thy Father and Mother: The True Story of the Menendez Brothers, 1994, The Face on the Milk Carton, 1995, When Innocence is Lost, 1997, Sins of the Mind, 1997, Crowned and Dangerous, 1998, My Little Assassin, 1999, Phenomenon II, 2003; (TV series) Dirty Sexy Money, 2007-09; (TV documentaries): Ask Me Anything: How to Talk to Kids About Sex, 1989; (TV appearances) Frasier, 1993, Ally McBeal, 1997, Trinity, 1998, Everything's Relative, 1999, Leap of Faith, 2002, The Practice, 2004, Nip/Tuck, 2004 Died Nov. 5, 2010.

CLEARY, JAMES ROY, lawyer; b. Springville, Ala., July 16, 1926; s. Bereman Leroy and Bertie (Jones) C.; m. Miriam Voncille James, Apr. 10, 1960; children: Johanna, Susan. BA, Birmingham-So. Coll., 1948; JD, Northwestern U., 1951. Bar: Ala. 1951, U.S. Supreme Ct. 1970. Practiced in, Huntsville, from 1956; atty. Dept. Army, Redstone Arsenal, 1951-55; mem. firm Cleary, Bailey & McDowell, from 1956. Named

Young Man of Year Huntsville, 1957 Mem. Jr. Chamber Internat. (life mem., senator). Clubs: Ala.-Miss. Dist. Optimists Internat. (past lt. gov.). Home: Huntsville, Ala. Died Feb. 15, 2010.

CLEARY, MARTIN JOSEPH, real estate company executive; b. NYC, July 27, 1935; s. Patrick Joseph and Kathleen Theresa (Costello) C.; m. Peggy Elizabeth McIntyre, June 22, 1957; children: Patrick Francis, Eileen Ann, Michael Thomas, Kathleen Marie, Maureen Elizabeth. BS, Fordham U., 1960; MBA, N.Y. U., 1963. With Tchrs. Ins. and Annuity Assn. and Coll. Retirement Equities Fund, NYC, 1953-81; pres. Richard E. Jacobs Group, Westlake, Ohio, 1981—2001, ret., 2001. Bd. dirs. Guardian Life Ins. Co., Lamson & Sessions, CBL & Assocs. Mem. Internat. Coun. Shopping Ctrs. (trustee 1980—, pres. 1983-84). Died Oct. 18, 2009.

CLEARY, THOMAS CHARLES, technology company executive; b. Chgo., Nov. 15, 1921; s. Thomas Harold and Mary Margaret (Russell) C.; m. Barbara Winnifred Johnson, Dec. 18, 1948; children: Thomas Robert, Margaret Mary Cleary Nurmia, Mary Ann Cleary Robitaille. BS in Mech. Engring., UCLA, 1949. Pres., gen. mgr. Whittaker Corp., Denver, 1950-63; dir. program mgmt. Litton Industries, Woodland Hills, Calif., 1963-65; asst. gen. mgr. Teledyne Sys., Inc., 1965-66; v.p., CEO Viking Industries, Chatsworth, Calif., 1966-67; v.p. Power Conversion, Inc., Long Beach, Calif., 1967-68; chmn. bd. dirs., mng. dir. TRW Electronic Comp. Co., Taiwan, Republic of China, 1968-69; pres., CEO Deutsch Relays, Inc., East Northport, NY, 1969-89, Struthers Dunn-Hi G, Pitman, NJ, 1989-91; chmn., CEO G&H Tech., Inc., Camarillo, Calif., from 1992. Author: Dynamic Management System, 1990, Management By Intent, 1991. Fundraiser Meml. Sloan-Kettering Cancer Ctr., N.Y., 1989—; mem. chancellor's assocs. UCLA, 1992—, mem. exec. com., dean's coun., sch. engring., 1992—; mem. bd. councillors UCLA Found., 1997. Capt. inf. U.S. Army, 1942-50, PTO. Named Entrepreneur of Yr. in mfg. Greater L.A. Area, 1997. Republican. Roman Catholic. Achievements include patents in the gyroscope and relay areas. Home: Gilbert, Ariz. Died Sept. 16, 2009.

CLEARY, TIMOTHY FINBAR, professional society administrator; b. Cork, Ireland, Sept. 30, 1925; s. John Francis and Nora (Riordan) C.; m. Patricia Agnes Hanley, June 21, 1947; children: Timothy F. X., Maureen P., Therese A., Richard S., Gail P., Eileen P. BS, Fordham U., 1955, JD, 1959. Bar: N.Y. 1959, D.C. 1980. Atty. N.Y.C. Police Dept., 1959-67; asst. counsel US Occupational Safety & Health Review Commn., U.S. Dept. Labor, Washington, 1967-71, chief counsel, 1971-73, mem., 1973-85, chmn., 1977—80; cons. in occupational safety and health, 1985—2010; exec. dir. Nat. Trust for Tng., Edn. & Rsch. in Constrn., 1987-1991; internal campaign contbn. administrator Internat. Brotherhood Elec. Workers. Chmn. U.S. Occupational Safety and Health Rev. Commn., Washington, 1977-81; mem. Adminstrv. Conf. U.S.; cert. arbitrator Nat. Mediation Bd.; lectr. labor law Practising Law Inst., U. Wis., Washington and Lee U., Cumberland Sch. Law, Ohio No. U., Brookings Instn., AFL-CIO Center for Labor Studies, Gompers-Murray Inst.Trade Assc., numerous others. Contbr. articles to profl. jours. Served with USN, 1943-45. Mem.: Friendly Sons St. Patrick, D.C. Died Feb. 6, 2010.

CLEMMER, DAN ORR, retired librarian; b. Etowah, Tenn., Dec. 28, 1938; s. Dan Orr and Nancy Elizabeth (Haney) C.; m. Elizabeth Louise Campbell, Aug. 25, 1962; children: Nancy Day, Helen, Stephen. BA, Davidson Coll., 1961; MA Teaching, Brown U., 1964; MS Libr. Svc., Columbia U., 1967. Intern Libr. of Congress, Washington, 1967-68, asst. head African-Asian exchange, 1968-70; asst. to librarian Smithsonian Inst. Libr., Washington, 1970-72, asst. chief access svc., 1972-73; chief, reader svcs. U.S. Dept. State Libr., Washington, 1973-92, chief librarian, 1992—2002; ret., 2002. Mem. Depository Libr. Coun., 1994-98. Contbr. articles to profl. jours. Mem. ALA (pres. Fed. Librs. Roundtable 1993-94, exec. bd. of Fed. Libr. and Info. Ctr. com.); mem. D.C. Libr. Assn. (pres. 1995-96). Home: Chevy Chase, Md. Died Apr. 5, 2010.

CLEMONS, WILLIAM RUSSELL, real estate company executive; b. Topsham, Maine, Mar. 14, 1917; s. Oscar William and Delia T. (Tripp) Clemons; m. Ada Yates, June 20, 1940; children: Anne Clemons Jones, William T., James A. Student, Columbia U., 1936—40. Foreman Todd-Bath Shipbldg. Corp., South Portland, Maine, 1943—47; asst. gen. mgr. Gen. Shipbldg. Corp., Balt., 1947—49; pres., owner New Eng. Reupolstering Co., Brunswick, Maine, 1949—58, Clemons Agy., Brunswick. Mem.: Merrymeeting Sportsmen Assn., Merrymeeting Bd. Realtors, Androscoggin Bd. Realtors, Maine State Bd. Realtors, Nat. Assn. Realtors, Blue Club, Bruns Club, Rotary Club (Brunswick), Shriner, Mason, Yates Lodge Perfection. Home: Harpswell, Maine. Died Oct. 22, 2009.

CLEVELAND, CLYDE, retired city official; b. Detroit, May 22, 1935; m. Mary; 1 child. Student, Wayne State U. Pub. aid worker City of Detroit, 1958, 60-64; supervisor cmty. svc. Mayor's Com. Human Resources Devel., Detroit, 1965-68; cmty. planner Inner City Bus. Improvement Forum, 1968-71; city councilman City of Detroit, 1974—2001; ret., 2001. Del. Dem. Nat. Conv., 1980; former vice chair Mich. State Dem. Party; co-campaign mgr. Jesse Jackson Victory in Mich., 1988; vice chair Southeastern Mich. Coun. Govts.; cmty. orgn. specialist New Detroit, Inc., 1971-73. Served in U.S. Army, Korea. Mem. NAACP, Elks, People's Cmty. & Civic League, Assn. Study Negro Life & History, Booker T. Washington Bus. Assn., Shriners, Masons. Baptist. Home: Detroit, Mich. Died June 3, 2009.

CLIFFORD, DONALD JOSEPH, newspaper publisher; b. Rutland, Vt., Jan. 23, 1925; s. John M. and Ethel LeClair C.; m. Helen Connell, Nov. 9, 1950; children— Stephen F., Thomas J., Martha L., Daniel J., Donald J., Sarah F. Pub. The Star, Oneonta, N.Y., 1968-74, The Record-Eagle, Traverse City, Mich., 1974-79; pres. The Standard Times Pub. Co.; pub. The Standard Times, Daily and Sunday, New Bedford, Mass., 1979-86; v.p. Ottaway Newspapers Inc., Campbell Hall, N.Y., 1987-88. Dir. Mechanics Exchange Savs. Bank, Oneonta, N.Y.; lectr. Am. Press Inst., 1959-61 Trustee Fox Hosp., Oneonta, Swain Sch. of Design, New Bedford; bd. dirs. SE Mass. Univ. Found., mem. New Bedford Indsl. Found. Served with USAF, 1942-45. Mem. Am. Newspaper Pubs. Assn., New Eng. Daily Newspaper Assn. Home: Peru, NY. Died Apr. 10, 2009.

CLIFFORD, MARGARET LOUISE, psychologist; b. Lakeland, Fla., Dec. 13, 1920; d. Thomas Saxon and Beatrice (Tillie) C.; m. Charles Robert Davis, Apr. 4, 1950; children: Daniel Thomas Davis, Kelly Owen Davis. BA in Edn., Chapman Coll., Orange, Calif., 1950; MS in Cons. & Sch. Psycho, San Diego State U., Calif., 1972; PhD Psychology, The Union Inst., Cin., 1976. Tchr. Elem. schs., Blythe, San Diego., Calif., 1950-68; columnist Daily Midway Driller, Taft, Calif., 1955; owner, operator Marge Davis Sch. Dance, Blythe, Calif., 1961-64; psychologist U.S. Peace Corps, Kingston, Jamaica, 1973-76, Apalachee Community Mental Health Ctr., Talahassee, Fla., 1977-80; coordinator of elderly services Beth Johnson Community Mental Health Ctr., Orlando, Fla., 1980-83; crisis support counselor Mental Health Services of Orange County, Orlando, 1983-88; supr. therapist Peace River Ctr. for Personal Devel., Bartow, Fla., 1988-89; therapist pvt. practice, Winter Garden, Fla., from 1989. Guest speaker Fla. So. Coll., Orlando, 1981-82, Rollins Coll., Winter Park, Fla. Organizer, bd. pres. Widowed Person Svc. Orange County, Orlando; bd. dirs. Coun. on Aging, sec., 1982-85; mem. adv. bd. Cmty. Care for the Elderly, Orange County, Fla., 1992-95. Mem. Fla. Coun. Community Mental Health (pres. 1978-81), Am. Psychol. Assn. Avocations: travel, scuba diving, drawing. Home: Pinellas Park, Fla. Died Jan. 16, 2009.

CLIFTON, LUCILLE THELMA, author; b. Depew, NY, June 27, 1936; d. Samuel Louis and Thelma (Moore) Sayles; m. Fred James Clifton, May 10, 1958 (dec. Nov. 1984); children: Sidney, Fredrica (dec. 2000), Channing (dec. 2004), Gillian, Graham, Alexia. Student, Howard U., 1953-55, Fredonia State Tchrs. Coll., NY, 1955; DL (hon.), Dartmouth Coll., 2005. Prof. literature & creative writing U. Calif., Santa Cruz, 1985-90; Dist. prof. humanities St. Mary's Coll. Md., 1990—2010, Hilda C. Landers endowed chair in liberal arts, 2000—10. Vis. prof. Columbia U., 1995—99. Poet-in-residence, Coppin State Coll., Balt., 1972-76, Jenny Moore vis. writer, George Washington U., 1982-83. Author: Good Times, 1969, Good News About The Earth, 1972, An Ordinary Woman, 1974, Generations: A Memoir, 1976, Two-Headed Woman, 1980, Sonora Beautiful, 1981, Next: New Poems, 1987, Good Woman: Poems and a Memoir, 1969-1980, 1987, Quilting: Poems, 1987-1990, 1991, The Book of Light, 1993, The Terrible Stories, 1996 Blessing the Boats: New and Collected Poems, 1988-2000, 2000 (Nat. Book awar for Poetry, 2000), Mercy, 2004, Voices, 2008; Everett Anderson books and other books for children; co-author: Free to Be You and Me, 1974 Named Poet Laureate, State of Md., 1979-85; recipient Discovery award Poetry Center, 1969, Ruth Lilly Poetry prize, 1987, Shelly Meml. award, 1991, Lannan Literrary award for Poetry, 1996, Ruth Lilly Poetry prize, 2007; YMHA grantee, 1969, Nat. Endowment Arts grantee, 1970, 72 Fellow Am. Acad. Arts and Scis.; mem. Authors League, Author Guild, P.E.N., Acad. Am. Poets (chancellor), Poetry Soc. Am. (bd. dirs., Lila Wallace/Reader's Digest award 1999). Home: Columbia, Md. Died Feb. 13, 2010.

CLINARD, MARSHALL BARRON, sociologist, educator; b. Boston, Nov. 12, 1911; s. Andrew Marshall and Gladys (Barron) C.; m. Ruth Blackburn, Aug. 28, 1937 (dec. Jan. 19, 1999); children: Marsha Clinard, Stephen Andrew; m. Arlen Runzler Westbrook, Jan. 15, 2002. BA, Stanford U., 1932, MA, 1934; PhD, U. Chgo., 1941; LLD (hon.), U. Lausanne, Switzerland, 1985. Instr. U. Iowa, 1937-41; chief criminal stats. U.S. Bur. Census, 1941-43; chief analysis report, enforcement dept. OPA, 1943-45; assoc. prof. Vanderbilt U., 1945-46; mem. faculty U. Wis., from 1946, prof. sociology, 1951-79, prof. emeritus, from 1979. Fulbright rsch. prof. U. Stockholm, 1954-55; vis. prof. Makerere U. Coll., Kampala, Uganda, 1968-69; cons. urban cmty. devel. Ford Found., India, 1958-60, 62-63; UN expert Asian Seminar Urban Cmty. Devel., Singapore, 1962; rapporteur 3rd UN Congress Prevention Crime and Treatment Offenders, Stockholm, 1965; panel expert 4th UN Congress, Kyoto, 1970; cons. 5th UN Congress, Geneva, 1975, Dept. Labor, 1966-67. Author: The Black Market: A Study of White Collar Crime, 1952; (with Robert F. Meier) Sociology of Deviant Behavior, 12th edit., 2004, 13th edit., 2008; editor, contbr.: Anomie and Deviant Behavior: A Discussion and Critique, 1964, Slums and Community Development: Experiments in Self-Help, 1966; (with Richard Quinney and John Wildeman) Criminal Behavior Systems: A Typology, 1967, 3d edit., 1994; (with Daniel J. Abbott) Crime in Developing Countries: A Comparative Perspective, 1973, Cities with Little Crime: The Case of Switzerland, 1978, Illegal Corporate Behavior, 1979; (with Peter C. Yeager) Corporate Crime, 1980, reprinted with new Intro., 2005, Corporate Ethics and Crime: The Role of Middle Management, 1983, Corporate Corruption: The Abuse of Power, 1990. Recipient Sutherland award Am. Soc. Criminology, 1970, Cressey award Assn. Cert. Fraud Examiners, 1994; NSF rsch. grantee, Switzerland, 1973, U.S. Dept. Justice grantee, 1977, 81. Mem. Soc. Study Social Problems (exec. com. 1959-60, 62-63, 65-67, pres. 1961-62), Midwest Sociol. Soc. (pres. 1965-66), Am. Sociol. Assn. (coun. mem. at large 1966-68) Home: Santa Fe, N.Mex. Died May 30, 2010.

CLINE, MARLIN GEORGE, agronomy educator; b. Bertha, Minn., Dec. 31, 1909; s. Sampson and Amy Elizabeth (Smith) C.; m. Agnes Irene Israelson, Aug. 17, 1936; children: Richard, Mary Cline Harris, Carol Cline Powers. BS, N.D. State U., 1935; PhD, Cornell U., 1942; DSc (hon.), Trinity Coll., Dublin, Ireland, 1965, N.D. State U., 1965. Jr. soil surveyor USDA, N.D., Hawaii, Tenn., 1935-38, asst. soil scientist Tenn., 1941-42, agt. Washington, 1942-54, 56-74; asst. prof. Cornell U., Ithaca, N.Y., 1942-43, assoc. prof., 1943-45, prof., 1945-74, prof. emeritus, from 1974. Cons. U.K. Colonial Office, Africa, 1949; soil scientist USGS Mil. Geology Unit, Washington, 1944-45; prof., cons. U. Philippines, Los Banos, 1954-56; cons. to USSR, USDA, 1958. Author: Soils of Hawaii, 1956; contbr. articles to profl. jours. Mem. Dryden (N.Y.) Sch. Bd., 1952-54. Recipient Cert. of Merit Soil Conservation Svc. USDA, 1974. Fellow AAAS, Soil Sci. Soc. Am.; mem. Am. Soc. Agronomy (hon.), N.Y. State Agrl. Soc. (Disting. Svc. Citation 1964). Democrat. Avocation: mineral collection. Home: Ithaca, NY. Died Jan. 9, 2009.

CLINE-DENNEY, DOROTHY MAY STAMMERJOHN, education educator, consultant; b. Boonville, Mo., Oct. 19, 1915; d. Benjmain Franklin and Lottie (Walther) Stammerjohn; m. Edward Wilburn Cline, Aug. 16, 1938 (dec. May 1962); children: Margaret Ann (Mrs. Rodger Orville Bell), Susan Elizabeth (Mrs. Gary Lee Burns), Dorothy Jean; m. Arthur Hugh Denney, July 11, 1998 (dec. Mar. 2006). Grad. nurse, U. Mo., 1937, BS in Edn., 1939, postgrad., 1966-67; MS, Ark. State U., 1964. Dir. Christian Coll. Infirmary, Columbia, Mo., 1936-37; asst. chief nursing svc. VA Hosp., Poplar Bluff, Mo., 1950-58; tchr.-in-charge staff State Tng. Ctr. No 4, Poplar Bluff, 1959-66, Dorothy S. Cline State Sch. #53, Boonville, 1967-85; instr. U. Mo., Columbia, 1973-74. Cons. for workshops for new tchrs., curriculum revision Mo. Dept. Edn. Mem. Butler County Council Retarded Children, 1959-66; v.p. Boonslick Assn. Retarded Children, 1969-72; sec.-treas. Mo. chpt. Am. Assn. on Mental Deficiency, 1973-75; bd. dirs. Unltd. Opportunities Sheltered Workshop. Mem. NEA, Mo. Tchrs. Assn., Am. Assn. on Mental Deficiency, Coun. for Exceptional Children, AAUW (v.p. Boonville br. 1968-70, 75-77), Mo. Writers Guild, Creative Writer's Group (pres. 1974—), Columbia Creative Writers Group, Eastern Center Poetry Soc., Laura Speed Elliott High Sch. Alumni Assn., Bus. and Profl. Women's Club, Smithsonian Assn., U. Mo. Alumni Assn., Ark. State U. Alumni Assn., PEO, Internat. Platform Soc., Friends Historic Boonville, Delta Kappa Gamma. Mem. Christian Ch. Died June 18, 2009.

CLINEFELTER, RUTH ELIZABETH WRIGHT, historian, educator; b. Akron, Ohio, Nov. 2, 1930; d. Cyril and Ruth Elizabeth (Dresher) Wright. BA, U. Akron, Ohio, 1952, MA, 1953; MLS, Kent State U., Kent, Ohio, 1956. Serial libr. U. Akron, Akron, Ohio, 1953-61, social sci. rsch. libr., 1961-76, humanities rsch. libr., 1977-83, social sci. humanities bibliographer, from 1983. Lectr. in gen. studies U. Akron, 1960, instr. bibliography, 1956-59, asst. prof. bibliography, 1959-77, assoc. prof. bibliography, 1977-84, prof. bibliography, 1984-99, prof. emeritus, 2000—; resource person NEH, Ohio; mem. joint study com. Am. History Rsch. in Ohio, Ohio Hist. Soc., 1969-70; mem. acad. affairs com. Ohio Faculty Senate, 1971-72; mem. hist. abstracts bibliographic svc. ABC Clio Users Bd., 1978-79. Contbr. articles to profl. jour. Trustee, Akron Area Women's History Project, Summit County Hist. Soc., 1997—, bd. mem. Humane Soc. Greater Akron, Nat. Trust for Hist. Preservation, Progress Through Preservation, 2004—. Recipient Pioneer award for contbns. to women Mortar Board, 1997; named Woman of the Yr., Akron Area NOW, 2001, Organizational Woman of the Yr., History Project, 1993, 1998 Mem. AAUP, Assn. for Bibliography of History, North Am. Conf. British Studies, Cascade Locks Park Assn.(bd. dirs., archives and history com.) Democrat. Episcopalian. Home: Akron, Ohio. Died Aug. 12, 2010.

CLINTON, MARIANN HANCOCK, educational association administrator; b. Dyersburg, Tenn., Dec. 7, 1933; d. John Bowen and Nell Maurine (Johnson) Hancock; m. Harry Everett Clinton, Aug. 25, 1956; children— Carol, John Everett. BMus, Cin. Conservatory Music, 1956; BS, U. Cin., 1956; MMus, Miami U., Oxford, Ohio, 1971. Tchr. music public schs., Hamilton County, Ohio, 1956-57; tchr. voice and piano Butler County, Ohio, from 1964; instr. music Miami U., 1972-75; exec. dir. Music Tchrs. Nat. Assn., Cin., 1977-86. Mng. dir. Am. Music Tchr., 1977-86. Mem. adminstrv. bd. Middletown (Ohio) 1st United Methodist Ch., 1968-72; bd. dirs. Friends of the Sorg Opera House; concert presenter Friends of Music of Charlotte County (Fla.). Mem. Music Educators Nat. Conf., Am. Ednl. Research Assn., Am. Soc. Assn. Execs., Nat. Fedn. Music Clubs, Pi Kappa Lambda, Kappa Delta Pi, Mu Phi Epsilon, Phi Mu. Republican. Home: Dublin, Ohio. Died Oct. 22, 2009.

CLOER, CARROLL MARTIN, textile company official; b. Patterson, NC, Jan. 29, 1926; s. Carl Elisha and Nancy Lois (Holder) Cloer; m. Rachel Tuttle, Oct. 2, 1954. BS in Textile Engring., N.C. State U., 1950; grad., Air War Coll. Supr. Hudson Mills Co. (N.C.), 1950—52; foreman Pacific Mills Co., Rhodhiss, N.C., 1953—58; quality control supr. Burlington Industries, Rhodhiss, 1959—61; quality control supt. Beaunit Fibers, Elizabethton, Tenn., 1961—68; assoc. prof. textiles Danville (Va.) CC, 1969—70; mfg. mgr. Virginia Mills Co., Swepsonville, 1970—71; quality control mgr. Firestone Fibers & Textiles Co., Gastonia, NC, 1971—83, sr. process engr., from 1983. Served with USAAF, 1944—45, maj. Res. ret. Decorated Air medal with 3 oak leaf clusters. Mem.: Mensa., ASTM, Am. Inventory and Prodn. Mgmt. Soc., Am. Soc. Quality Control (cert. quality engr.). Home: Lenoir, NC. Died Apr. 14, 2010.

CLOUD, DANIEL TUTTLE, pediatric surgeon, hospital administrator; b. Olathe, Kans., Aug. 18, 1925; s. Daniel Tuttle and Theresa (Adams) C.; m. Virginia Purgason, Feb. 14, 1952; children— Priscilla, Andrew, Lela Ann AB, Ill. Coll., 1946; BS in Medicine, U. Mo., 1946; MD, U. Ill., 1948. Diplomate Am. Bd. Surgery, Am. Bd. Pediatric Surgery. Resident in surgery St. Joseph's Hosp., U. Ill. Research and Ednl. Hosp., Chgo., 1949-50; resident in orthopedic surgery U.S. Naval Hosp., Oakland, Calif., 1951-52; resident in surgery St. Francis Hosp., Peoria, Ill., 1952-54; fellow in pediatric surgery Childrens Meml. Hosp., Chgo., 1954-55; practice medicine specializing in pediatric surgery Phoenix, from 1955; pres. Phoenix Children's Hosp., from 1983. Mem. Joint Commn. for Accreditation Hosps., 1974-83 Mem. editorial bd. Western Jour. Medicine. Contbr. articles to profl. jours. Served to lt. M.C., USNR, 1943-45, 50-52 Recipient Leslie B. Smith Medal award, 1972, Dr. Clarence Salsbury medal, 1973, Presdl. citation Assn. Tchrs. Preventive Medicine, 1982, Disting. Alumnus award U. Ill., 1982, Man of Year award State of Israel Maimonides, 1982 Fellow ACS, Am. Acad. Pediatrics; mem. AMA (trustee 1974-80, pres. 1981-82), Am. Pediatric Surg. Soc., Am. Coll. Chest Physicians, Assn. Mil. Surgeons U.S., Am. Coll. Angiology, Soc. for Surgery Alimentary Tract, Ariz. Med. Assn. (bd. dirs. 1964—, chmn. various coms.), Lilliputian Surg. Assn., S.W. Surg. Assn., Maricopa County Med. Soc., Phoenix Surg. Soc., Am. Coll. Physicians Execs. Republican. Episcopalian. Avocations: tennis; hunting; photography. Home: Phoenix, Ariz. Died July 6, 2010.

COBB, JAMES RICHARD, banker; b. Little Rock, Feb. 12, 1942; s. James Harvol and Elizabeth (Whitaker) C.; m. Virginia Stuart, July 4, 1965; children: William Claiborne, Cynthia Ruffin. BSBA, U. N.C., 1965. Mgr. Del. Coca—Cola, Wilmington, 1965-73; v.p. Mid-Atlantic Canners Assn., Hamburg, Pa., 1971-73, Comml. Nat. Bank, Little Rock, 1974-77, sr. v.p., 1977-78, exec. v.p., 1978-83; pres. Comml. Bankstock Inc., Little Rock, 1981-83; vice chmn. bd. First Comml. Bank N.A., 1983-89, First Comml. Corp., from 1984. Former pres., bd. dirs. Little Rock unit Am. Cancer Soc.; bd. dirs. Ark. div. Am. Cancer Soc., Central Ark. Radiation Therapy Inst., Pulaski Acad., Met. YMCA, Little Rock Port Authority, C.A.R.T.I. Found.; trustee Ark. Arts Ctr. Mem.: Little Rock Country, Little Rock Racquet. Home: Little Rock, Ark. Died Jan. 16, 2010.

COBLENTZ, WILLIAM KRAEMER, lawyer; b. San Francisco, July 28, 1922; s. Zach B. and Fritz (Levy) C.; m. Jean Berlin, Nov. 24, 1952; children: Wendy K., Andrew S. BA, U. Calif., Berkeley, 1943; LLB, Yale U., 1947. Bar: Calif. 1947. Ptnr. Coblentz, Cahen, McCabe and Breyer, San Francisco; mem. U. Calif. Bd. Regents, 1964-80, chmn., 1978—80. Adj. prof. Haas Sch. Mgmt., U. Calif., San Francisco; bd. dirs. McClatchy Newspapers, Koret Found., Pub. Policy Inst. Calif., U. Calif. Press. Contbr. articles to profl. jours., mags. Vis. fellow Wolfson Coll., Oxford U., 1981. Mem. Coun. on Fgn. Rels., ABA, Calif. Bar Assn., San Francisco Bar Assn., Assn. of Bar of City of N.Y., American Law Inst. Home: San Francisco, Calif. Died Sept. 13, 2010.

COCCHIA, NEAL, retired newspaper editor; b. NY, 1917; Copyboy Newark Sunday Call; various position including editorial writer, editorial page editor The Star-Ledger, Newark, 1939—95. Died Aug. 26, 2010.

COCHRAN, ROBERT GLENN, nuclear engineering educator; b. Indpls., July 12, 1919; s. Lucian Glenn and Daisy P. (Wachstetter) C.; m. Mary Olive Worland, Mar. 1945; 1 son, Robert Glenn. BA, Ind. U., 1948, MS, 1950; PhD, Pa. State U., 1957. Registered profl. engr. Physicist Ohio State Health Dept., 1950; physicist, group leader Oak Ridge Nat. Lab., 1950-55; dir. research reactor, asso. prof. Pa. State U., 1955-59; prof., head dept. nuclear engring. Tex. A&M U., College Station, 1959-83, prof., 1983-96, emeritus prof. for life, from 1996. Vis. prof. nuclear engring. Tex. A&M U., 1985—; cons. USAF, U.S. AEC, NRC. Author: (textbook) The Nuclear Fuel Cycle: Analysis and Management, 1989, revised edit., 1999; contbr. articles to profl. jours. and textbooks. Served with USNR, 1942-45. Fellow Am. Nuclear Soc.; mem. Am. Phys. Soc., Am. Soc. Engring. Edn. (life), Sigma Xi, Phi Kappa Phi. Lodges: Mason. Home: Caldwell, Tex. Died May 2, 2009.

COCKRELL, CLAUDE O'FLYNN, JR., oil executive; b. Memphis, May 10, 1937; s. Claude O'Flynn and Audrey (Roberts) C.; div.; children: Cana Lynn, Claude O'Flynn III, Valerie Paige. Student, Memphis State U., 1955, U. Miami, 1955-57. Pres. Shelby Paper Box Co., Memphis, 1952-56; pres.-owner Memphis Corrugated Container Co., Memphis, 1956-61; owner Cockrell Container Co., Memphis, 1961-81, Cockrell Comms. Corp., from 1981. Pres. West Corp., Memphis, 1971-77, West Prodns., Inc., 1977—, Great Am. Container Corp., 1975—, Nashville Corrugated Box Inc., 1975—, Photo Finish, Inc., 1978—, World Racing Network, 1982—; pres., owner Am. Divers, 1972—; pres. Cockrell Export Ltd., Nassau, Bahamas, 1979, Gulf Atlantic Seafood Corp., Halifax, N.S. and Goose Bay, Nfld., Can., 1973—, Secret Charters, Ft. Lauderdale, Fla., 1977, Spanish Cay (Bahamas) Island, 1984—, Cockrell Oil Corp., 1985—, West Aviation, Inc., Smyrna, Tenn., 1985—, Cockrell Oil Ltd., Nassau, Bahamas, 1985, U.S. Aviation Inc., 1992—, Noah's Ark Found., Inc., 1993—, West Prodns., Inc., 1994—, New Eastern Airlines, Inc., 1996—, Cara Corp., 1986—; pres., CEO Internat. Fin. Corp., Nashville, 2000, Global Recovery Group, Smyrna, Tenn., 2000, New Ea. Airlines Inc., Nashville, 1996, U.S. Aviation Inc., Nashville, 1994. State marshall Freedom Trail Found., Tenn., 1973—; head campaign George Wallace for Pres., Memphis and Tri-state area, 1968. Mem. Tenn. Thoroughbred Breeders and Racing Assn. (pres. 1977—), Moose, Pi Kappa Alpha. Presbyterian. Died Jan. 28, 2009.

COFFIN, FRANK MOREY, retired federal judge, former United States Representative from Maine; b. Lewiston, Maine, July 11, 1919; s. Herbert Rice and Ruth (Morey) Coffin; m. Ruth Ulrich, Dec. 19, 1942; children: Nancy, Douglas, Meredith, Susan. AB, Bates Coll., 1940, LLD, 1959; postgrad. indsl. adminstrn., Harvard U., 1943, LLB, 1947; LLD, Bates Coll., 1959, U. Maine, 1967, Bowdoin Coll., 1969; degree (hon.), Colby Coll., 1975. Bar: Maine 1947. Law clk. to fed. judge Dist. of Maine, 1947—49; engaged in practice Lewiston, 1947—52; with Verrill, Dana, Walker, Philbrick & Whitehouse, Portland, Maine, 1952—56; mem. US Congress from 2d Dist. Maine, 1957—61; mng. dir. Devel. Loan Fund, Dept. State, Washington, 1961; dep. adminstr. US Agy. for Internat. Devel. (USAID), 1961—64; U.S. rep. devel. assistance com. Orgn. Econ. Coop. & Devel. (OECD), 1964—65; judge US Ct. Appeals (1st cir.), 1965—89, chief judge, 1972—83, sr. judge, 1989—2006; chmn. com. jud. br. US Jud. Conf., 1984—90. Adj. prof. U. Maine Sch. Law, 1986—89. Author: Witness for Aid, 1964, The Ways of a Judge-Reflections from the Federal Appellate Bench, 1980, A Lexicon of Oral Advocacy, 1984, On Appeal, 1994. Emeritus Bates Coll.; dir. The Governance Inst., from 1987; mem. emeritus The Examiner; chair Maine Justice Action Group, 1996—2001. Lt. USNR, 1943—46. Recipient Edward J. Devitt Disting. Svc. to Justice award, 2001. Mem.: ABA (co-chmn. com. on loan forgiveness and repayment 2001—02), Am. Acad. Arts and Sci. Home: South Portland, Maine. Died Dec. 7, 2009.

COHAN, MARTIN, television producer, writer; b. San Francisco, July 4, 1932; m. Dawn Cohan; 4 children. BA, Stanford U., 1955. Creator, writer: (TV series) Silver Spoons, 1982-86, Who's the Boss, 1984-92; writer: (TV series) The Odd Coupole (2 episodes), 1971-72, The Mary Tyler Moore Show (8 episodes), 1971-73, The New Dick Van Dyke Show (1 episode), 1972, The Partidge Family (3 episodes), 1972, The Bob Newhart Show (6 episodes), 1972-74, All in the Family (1 episode), 1973, The Bob Crane Show (1 episode), 1975, Doc (1 episode), 1976, The Love Boat (1 episode), 1978, Flying High, 1978-79, Hello Larry (5 episodes), 1979, Diff'rent Strokes, 1979-84, The Upper Hand (4 episodes), 1993-95; (TV movies) The Fantastic World of D.C. Collins, 1984; exec. prodr.: (TV series) The Bob Newhart Show, 1973-74, Flying High (3 episodes), 1978, Diff'rent Strokes, 1979-85, Who's the Boss?, 1984-92 Recipient Writer's Guild America award, NAACP Image award. Died May 19, 2010.

COHEN, AARON, engineering professor, retired aerospace engineer; b. Tex., Jan. 31, 1931; s. Charles and Ida (Moloff) C.; m. Ruth Carolyn Goldberg, Feb. 7, 1953; children: Nancy Ann Santana, David Blair, Daniel Louis BS, Tex. A&M U., 1952; MS in Applied Math., Stevens Inst. Tech, 1958, D Engring. (hon.), 1982. Microwave tube design engr. RCA, Camden, N.J., 1954-58; sr. research engr. Gen. Dynamics, San Diego, 1958-62; mgr. Apollo command and service module lunar module guidance nav. and control NASA, Houston, 1962-70, mgr. command and service module project, 1970-72, mgr. shuttle orbiter project, 1972-82, dir. research and engring., 1982-86, dir. Johnson Space Ctr., 1986-93, acting dep. adminstr., 1992; Zachry prof. engring. Tex. A&M U., College Station, 1993—2010. Editor Astronautics sect. Marks Mechanical Engineer's Handbook, 9th edit.; contbr. articles to profl. jours. Vice chmn. engring. task force Target 2000 Tex. A&M U., College Station, 1981-83. Served to lt. C.E., U.S. Army, 1952-54, Korea Recipient Exceptional Service medal NASA, Houston, 1969, Disting. Service medal, 1973, 81, 88, 93, Goddard Meml. trophy, 1988; Presdl. Rank of Meritorious Exec., The White House, Washington, 1981, Presdl. Rank of Disting. Exec., 1982, 88; Named NASA Engr. of Yr., Washington, 1982, Engr. of Yr. Nat. Acad. Engring., 1988. Fellow Am. Astron. Soc. (W. Randolph Lovelace II award 1982), AIAA (Von Karman lectureship 1984, Von Braun award 1993, Hon. Fellow, 1995, Robert H. Goddard Astronautics award 1996); mem. NAE, ASME (medal 1984), AJAA, Tau Beta Pi. Jewish. Avocation: tennis. Home: College Station, Tex. Died Feb. 25, 2010.

COHEN, FREDERICK H., lawyer; b. Chgo., Feb. 28, 1965; BA in Fin., U. Ill., 1987; JD with honors, U. Chgo., 1990. Bar: Ill. 1990, US Dist. Ct. (no. dist. Ill.) 1991, US Ct. Appeals (7th cir.) 1991, US Supreme Ct. 2001. Prin. Goldberg, Kohn, Bell, Black, Rosenbloom & Moritz, Chgo. Adj. prof. Kent Coll. Law. Recipient Equal Justice award, Sargent Shriver Nat. Ctr. Poverty Law, 2004, Child Health Adv. of Yr. award, Acad. Pediat., 2005, Excellence in Pro Bono award, US Dist. Ct. (no. dist. Ill.), 2006; named Lawyer of Yr. for Taxpayers Against Fraud, 2007, Lawyer of Yr., Trial Lawyers for Pub. Justice, 2007; named one of The Nation's Top Litigators, The Nat. Law Jour., 2007. Died May 4, 2010.

COHEN, MARK STEVEN, public relations executive; b. Bklyn., Apr. 14, 1954; s. Hyman Robert and Miriam (Briendel) Cohen; married. BFA, Emerson Coll., 1977. Assoc. pub. relations dir. Prentice-Hall, Inc., NYC, 1978—81; dir. pub. rels. Franklin Watts, Inc., NYC, 1981—83, Am. Mgmt. Assn., NYC, 1984—87; acct. exec. Mount & Nadler Inc., from 1987. Contbr. columns in newspapers. Staff asst. Senator Edward Kennedy's Pre-Election Com., Boston, 1972; pres. Reagan's Re-election com., NY, 1984. Mem.: Publicity Club NY (bd. dirs. from 1984), Pubs. Publicity Assn., Am. Mgmt. Assn. (bd. dirs. 1984—87), Pub. Rels. Soc. America. Died Oct. 16, 2009.

COHEN, MELVIN STEPHEN, jewelry company executive; b. NYC, July 11, 1919; s. Harry and Sallie (Bodker) C.; m. Frances Mand, Sept. 25, 1942; children: Sallie (Mrs. Michael Goldwyn), Gwen Coleman (Mrs. Jerry Sroka). BS, NYU, 1940; MBA, Harvard, 1942. Dir. personnel A. Cohen & Sons Corp. (subsequently Cohen Hatfield Industries Inc., now MacAndrew & Forbes Group Inc.), NYC, 1943-47, dir. sales, 1947-59, pres., 1959-69, chmn. bd., 1969-80, chmn. exec. com., 1980-85, also treas., 1985-93. Cons. Fortunoff, 1985-94; bd. dirs. Maidenform Co., Rocket Box Co. Trustee, vice chmn. Dist. 65 Pension and Welfare Plan, 1946-92, vice chmn., 1980-93; chmn. exec. com. jewelry divsn. O.R.T. 1st lt. AUS, 1942-46. Mem. Am. Jewelry Distbrs. Assn. (exec. com. 1960-89, pres. 1960-62), Jewelry Industry Coun. (bd. dirs. 1970-83), Jewelry Vigilance Com. (bd. dirs. 1974-87, 1st v.p., treas. 1981-87), Internat. Golf Soc. (U.S. bd. dirs. 1985—), Glen Oaks Club (gov. 1977-90, treas. 1980, sec. 1981-89), 24 Karet Club (pres. 1975, bd. dirs. 1975-87, vice chmn. 1980, chmn. 1983-86), Ariz. Biltmore Club. Died Jan. 1, 2010.

COHEN, MORTON IRVING, physiology educator; b. NYC, July 11, 1923; s. Oscar and Bessie (Beller) C.; m. Priscilla J. Goettler, Dec. 16, 1958; children: Sibyl A., Eve L. BS, CCNY, 1942; AM, Columbia U., 1950, PhD, 1957. Instr. Albert Einstein Coll. Medicine, Bronx, N.Y., 1957-59, asst. prof., 1959-68, assoc. prof., 1968-73, prof. physiology, from 1973. With U.S. Army, 1945-46. Mem. Am. Physiol. Soc., Soc. Neurosci., European Neurosci. Assn. Home: Pelham, NY. Died June 1, 2010.

COHEN, SAUL G., chemist, educator; b. Boston, May 10, 1916; s. Barnet M. and Ida (Levine) C.; m. Doris E. Brewer, Nov. 27, 1941 (dec. July 1971); children— Jonathan Brewer, Elisabeth Jane; m. Anneliese F. Kissinger, June 1, 1973. AB summa cum laude, Harvard U., 1937, MA, 1938, PhD, 1940; ScD, Brandeis U., 1986. Research fellow Harvard, 1939-40, 41-43, instr., 1940-41; NRC fellow, lectr. U. Calif. at Los Angeles, 1943-44; research chemist Pitts. Plate Glass Co., 1944-45, Polaroid Corp., 1945-50, cons., 1950—98; with Brandeis U., from 1950, prof. chemistry, from 1952, Univ. prof., 1974-86, prof. emeritus, from 1986, chmn. Sch. Sci., 1950-55, dean faculty, 1955-59, chmn. dept. chemistry, 1959-66, 68-72; vis. prof. Havard Med. Sch., 1965, Hebrew U., Jerusalem, 1972. Contbr. articles on reaction mechanisms, free radicals, photochemistry, enzymology to profl. jours. Bd. overseers Harvard U., 1983-89; mem. Joint Com. on Appointments, 1984-89. Fulbright sr. scholar, 1958-59; Guggenheim fellow, 1958-59; Centennial medalist Harvard Grad. Sch. Arts and Scis., 1992. Fellow Am. Acad. Arts and Scis. (council), AAAS; mem. Am. Soc. Biol. Chemists, Am. Chem. Soc. (James F. Norris award 1972, trustee Northeastern sect. 1976-84), Chem. Soc. London, AAUP, Fedn. Am. Scientists, Phi Beta Kappa, Sigma Xi. Achievements include patents in polymers, hyroxylamines as photographic developers, heterocyclic silver solvents, dye-developers, diagnostic assays. Home: Lexington, Mass. Died Apr. 24, 2010.

COLE, BILL S., retired academic administrator; b. Stuart, Okla. m. Sondra Cole; children: Brent, Page, Rhys, Wade, Drew. AA, Eastern Okla. State Coll., 1957; BA in Edn., East Ctrl. U., 1959; MS in Natural Sci., U. Okla., 1965; EdD, Okla. State U., 1973. Biology tchr. Putnam City High Sch., 1959—64; science tchr. Purcell High Sch., 1965—67; chair Science Dept. El Reno Jr. Coll., 1967—75, asst. dean instruction, 1975—76, pres., 1976—89, East Ctrl. U., Ada, Okla., 1989—2006, pres. emeritus, 2006—10. Bd. dirs. ECU Foundation Inc., Ada Area United Way, Okla. Chamber of Commerce & Industry. Recipient Disting. Leadership award, Coun. of Opportunity in Edn., 2005; named to The Okla. Higher Edn. Hall of Fame, 1996, The Okla. Educators Hall of Fame, 2005. Mem.: Ada Sunrise Rotary Club. Died Mar. 10, 2010.

COLE, JONATHAN OTIS, psychiatrist; b. Boston, Aug. 16, 1925; s. Arthur Harrison and Anna (Steckel) C.; m. Kathleen Gleason, July 12, 1952; children: Jonathan Patrick, Joshua Peter. Student, Harvard Coll., 1942-43; MD, Cornell U., 1947. Intern Peter Bent Brigham Hosp., Boston, 1947-48; resident psychiatry Payne Whitney Clinic, NYC, 1948-51; profl. assoc. Nat. Acad. Scis., Washington, 1953-56; dir. psychopharmacology research br. NIMH, Chevy Chase, Md., 1956-67; supt. Boston State Hosp., 1967-73; prof. psychiatry Tufts Med. Sch., 1967-73; prof., chmn. dept. psychiatry Temple Med. Sch., 1973-74; psychiatrist McLean Hosp., Belmont, Mass., from 1974. Prof. psychiatry Harvard Med. Sch., Cambridge, Mass. Editor: Psychopharmacology: Problems in Evaluation; Contbr. numerous articles to sci. jours. Served with AUS, 1951-53. Fellow Am. Psychiat. Assn. Am. Coll. Neuropsychopharmacology, Collegium Internationale Neuro-Psychopharmacologicum; mem. Am. Psychopathol. Assn. Home: Cambridge, Mass. Died May 26, 2009.

COLE, JUNE ROBERTSON, psychotherapist; b. Dothan, Ala., Sept. 29, 1931; d. C. Pete and Mary (Danzey) Robertson; m. Robert Walker Jr. Cole, Feb. 11, 1956; children: Robert Pete, Mary Cathlyn. AA, Del Mar Coll., 1974; BA, Tex. A&I U., 1976; MA, Corpus Christi State U., 1978; postgrad., Fielding Inst., Santa Barbara, from 1985. Lic. marriage and family therapist, profl. counselor. Actress, singer Radio, Films, TV, Stage, 1933—55; rec. artist Gold Label Records, 1951—55; pres. Coastal Bend Security Co., Corpus Christi, 1969—71; dir. Reality Therapy Ctr., Corpus Christi, from 1975; co-dir. Counseling and Psychology Resource Ctr., Corpus Christi, 1984—97; pvt. practice psychotherapy, from 1976; mem. mental health staff Bayview Psychiatric Hosp., Corpus Christi, from 1986, Charter Psychiart. Hosp., Corpus Christi, from 1990; faculty Park Coll., Naval Air Sta., Corpus Christi, 1987—92. Bd. dirs. Coastal Bend Jazz Soc., 1978—79; presenter papers Post Traumatic Stress Disorder, Compatibility Psychotherapy & 12 Step Programs in alcohol, drug addictions. Mem.: APA, AACD, Internat. Inst. Reality Therapists, Coastal Bend Marriage and Family Therapists Assn., Tex. Mental Health Counselors Assn., Gulf Coast Assn. Counseling and Devel., Tex. Assn. Counseling and Devel., Nueces County Psychol. Assn., Corpus Christi Council Women, Internat. Assn. Group Psychotherapists, Tex. Psychol. Assn., Am. Assn. Behavior Therapists, Am. Assn. for Mental Health Counselors, NOW. Home: Crp Christi, Tex. Died Dec. 15, 2009.

COLE, KENNETH DUANE, architect; b. Ft. Wayne, Ind., Jan. 23, 1932; s. Wolford J. and Helen Francis (McDowell) Cole; m. Carolyn Lou Meyer, Apr. 25, 1953; children: David Brent, Denelle Hope, Diana Faith, Dawn Love. Student, Ft. Wayne Art Inst., 1950-51; BS in Architecture, U. Cin., 1957. Draftsman/intern Humbrecht Assocs., Ft. Wayne, 1957-58; ptnr., arch. Cole-Matott, Archs./Planners, Ft. Wayne, 1959-94, Cole & Cole Archs., Ft. Wayne, from 1995. Mem. adv. bd. Gen. Svcs. Adminstrn., Region 5, 1976, 78. Prin. works include Weisser Pk. Jr. HS, 1963, Brandt Hall, 1965, Bonsib Bldg., 1967, Lindley Elem. Sch., 1969, Young Elem. Sch., 1972, Study Elem. Sch., 1975, Old City Hall Renovation, 1978, Peoples Trust Bank Adminstrv. Svcs. Ctr., 1979, Cole Residence (Design award, 1988), Ossian Office Old 1st Nat. Bank, 1988, Perimeter Security Wall, Ind. State Prison. Bd. dirs. Ft. Wayne Art Inst., 1969—74, Izaak Walton League Am., Ft. Wayne, 1970—76, Arch, Inc., Ft. Wayne, 1975—77, Downtown Ft. Wayne Assn., 1977—82, Hist. Soc. Ft. Wayne and Allen County, 1982—88. Mem.: AIA (bd. dirs. No. INd. 1971—74, pres. 1974), Am. Arbitration Assn. (panel arbitrators 1980—96), Ft. Wayne Soc. Archs. (pres. 1970—71), Ind. Soc. Archs. (bd. dirs. 1973—76, sec. 1976, citation for remodeling Bonsib Bldg. 1978), Ft. Wayne C. of C. Lutheran. Home: New Haven, Ind. Died May 1, 2010.

COLE, ORLANDO TIMOTHY, cellist; b. Phila., Aug. 16, 1908; s. Lucius Sylvanus and Rosalia (Winkler) C.; m. Rosamonde Adams, Jan. 15, 1933 (dec. 1989); children: Timothy, Deborah, David. MusB, Curtis Inst. Music, 1932, MusD (hon.), 1986, New Sch. Music, 1986. Prof. cello New Sch. Music, Phila., Curtis Inst. Music. Cellist, Curtis String Quartet, 1927-81, concerts, throughout U.S., Europe, 1935-37, at, The White House, 1934, in, London for silver jubilee King George V, 1935. Recipient medal achievement Phila. Art Alliance, 1954, Tchr. of the Year award Am. String Tchrs. Assn., 1990. Home: Philadelphia, Pa. Died Jan. 25, 2010.

COLEMAN, EARL MAXWELL, publishing company executive; b. NYC, Jan. 9, 1916; s. Samuel Sidney and Rose (Ensleman) C.; m. Frances Louise Allan, Mar. 23, 1942 (div. Mar. 15, 1965); children: Allan Douglass, Dennis Scott; m. Ellen Schneid, Aug. 19, 1973. Student, NYU, 1933-34, CCNY, 1934-35, Columbia U., 1946. Founder, pres. Plenum Pub. Corp. (and predecessors), NYC, 1946-77, chmn. bd. dirs., 1960-77, cons., 1977—2009. Founder Earl M. Coleman Enterprises, Inc. (Pubs.), 1977-2009; pres. Nat. Pubs. The Black Hills Inc., 1984-89; cons. Prentice Hall Coll. div., 1989-90. Contbr. poems, short stories to mags.; author: A Stubborn Pine in a Stiff Wind, 2001 Served with USAAF, 1941-45. Mem. Info. Industry Assn. (bd. dirs. 1971—2009), Assn. Am. Publishers (exec. com. tech.-sci.-med. div. 1970—2009), Sci. Tech. Med. Publishers (Holland). Home: Somerset, NJ. Died Oct. 12, 2009.

COLEMAN, FRANCIS XAVIER, JR., investment banker; b. NYC, Dec. 9, 1930; s. Francis Xavier and Cecilia Estelle (Campion) C.; m. Agnes Catherine Lyons, June 20, 1953; children— Neil, Janice, Ellen, Denys, Francis X. III BS, N.Y.U., 1955. Ptnr. Goldman Sachs & Co., NYC, 1975-86, ltd. ptnr., from 1986. Trustee, Friends Acad., Locust Valley, N.Y., 1980—; mem. Cardinal's Com. of the Laity, Roman Catholic Ch., N.Y.C., 1982—; trustee Fordham Prep. Sch., N.Y.C., 1983-90. Named Man of Yr., Nat. Housing Conf., N.Y.C., 1983; decorated Knight of Malta, 1984 Mem. Mcpl. Bond Club N.Y., N.Y. Mcpl. Forum, Washington Mcpl. Forum Republican Roman Catholic Home: Glen Head, NY. Died Mar. 6, 2009.

COLEMAN, MALINA, law educator; b. Akron, Ohio, Sept. 23, 1954; d. Dorlan Oliver and Virginia (Dove) C. BS summa cum laude, Cen. State U., 1980; JD, Yale U., 1985. Bar: Pa. 1987. Law clerk to hon. Frederica Messiah-Jackson Ct. of Common Pleas, Phila.; assoc. Harper and Paul, Phila.; asst. prof. U. Akron Sch. Law, 1989-96, assoc. dean, assoc. prof. law, from 1996. Bd. dirs. Planned Parenthood, Summit County, Ohio, 1992-94, Western Reserve Girl Scouts, Akron, 1991-94, Boys & Girls Clubs Summit County, 2000—. Mem. ABA, Akron Barristers' Assn., Nat. Bar Assn. Home: Akron, Ohio. Died Oct. 25, 2009.

COLEMAN, ROBERT LEE, retired lawyer; b. Kansas City, Mo., June 14, 1929; s. William Houston and Edna Fay (Smith) C. B of Music Edn., Drake U., 1951; LLB, U. Mo., 1959. Bar: Mo. 1959, Fla. 1973. Law clk. to judge U.S. Dist. Ct. (we. dist.) Mo., Kansas City, 1959-60; assoc. Watson, Ess, Marshall & Enggas, Kansas City, 1960-66; asst. gen. counsel Gas Svc. Co., Kansas City, 1966-74; v.p., corp. counsel H & R Block, Inc., Kansas City, 1974-94; ret., 1994. With U.S. Army, 1955-57. Mem.: ABA. Died Aug. 25, 2009.

COLEMAN, SYLVIA ETHEL, biologist, researcher; b. Gainesville, Fla., Mar. 23, 1933; d. John Melton and Jessie Lee Coleman; m. Henry Carl Aldrich, Jan. 1, 1978. BS, U. Fla., 1955, MS, 1956, PhD, 1972. Grad. teaching asst. U. Fla., Gainesville, 1955—56; med. bacteriologist Mound Park Hosp., St. Petersburg, Fla., 1959—60; rsch. microbiologist Bay Pines VA Med. Ctr., St. Petersburg, 1960—67; rsch. biologist VA Med. Ctr., Gainesville, from 1972; grad. teaching asst. dept. microbiology U. Fla., Gainesville, 1967—71, electron microscopy technician, 1972, adj. asst. prof. microbiology, from 1976, adj. postdoctoral fellow dept. botany, 1979. Contbr. articles to profl. jours. Pres. u. br. North Fla. chpt. Nat. Multiple Sclerosis Soc., 1980—82. Mem.: NY Acad. Scis., Fla. Acad. Scis., S.E. Electron Microscopy Soc., Histochem. Soc., Electron Microscopy Soc. Am., Am. Assn. Pathologists, Am. Soc. Microbiology (Pres. award 1961), Am. Soc. Cell Biology, Alpha Lambda Delta, Sigma Xi (Annual award 1972). Democrat. Mem. Christian Ch. Home: Oak Park, Calif. Died June 25, 2009.

COLEMAN, THEO HOUGHTON, animal science educator; b. Millport, Ala., Oct. 25, 1921; s. Elbert W. and Blanche (Prater) C.; m. Maxine Ashcraft, May 19, 1949 BS, Auburn U., 1943, MS, 1948; PhD, Ohio State U., Columbus, 1953. Instr. Ohio State U., Columbus, 1951-52; owner, mgr. Comml. Poultry Farm, 1953-54; asst. prof. Mich. State U., East Lansing, 1955-57, assoc., 1957-63, prof., from 1963, acting chmn. poultry sci. dept., 1978-79, 80. Sect. editor Poultry Sci., 1979-82. Contbr. articles to profl. jours. Served to 1st lt. AUS, 1943-46 Decorated Bronze Star; recipient Poultry Sci. Teaching award Ralston Purina, 1966, Excellence in Service award Mich. State U. chpt. Alpha Zeta, 1976, Outstanding Faculty Mem. award Mich. State U. Sr. Class Council, 1984, award for Devotion to Poultry, Mich. Allied Poultry Industries, 1985 Fellow AAAS, Poultry Sci. Assn.; mem. Am. Genetic Assn., Genetics Soc. Am., Soc. Study Reprodn., World's Poultry Sci. Assn., Sigma Xi, Gamma Sigma Delta, Phi Kappa Phi, Phi Alpha Zeta Mem. Ch. of Christ. Died June 22, 2009.

COLEN, ALLYN R., engineer; b. Cleve., Jan. 19, 1920; s. Morry M. and Ann M. (Minsky) C.; m. Joy Rosalind Colen; children: Russell, Laurel. BSME, Ohio State U., 1949; BEd, Ariz. State U., 1967, MEd, 1970. Registered profl. engr. Ariz., Calif., Nev., N.Mex., Okla., Colo., Wash. Prin. ETC Engring., Phoenix, 1976-78; dir. engring. Enercom, Inc., Tempe, Ariz., 1978-81; engr. Airresearch, Inc., Phoenix, 1981-82; prin. A.R. Colen Engring., Phoenix, 1982-84; v.p. Johannessen & Girand Engrs., Phoenix, from 1984, Diversified Engring., Phoenix, from 1985. Chmn. Electric League, Phoenix, 1985, Energy Civic Program, Phoenix, 1982. Served to sgt. U.S. Army, 1941-45. Mem. ASHRAE, ASPE, Assn. Energy Engrs. (charter), Electric League Ariz. Jewish. Home: Scottsdale, Ariz. Died July 26, 2009.

COLLIAS, NICHOLAS ELIAS, zoology educator, ornithologist; b. Chicago Heights, Ill., July 19, 1914; s. Elias and Marina (Giatras) C.; m. Elsie Cole, Dec. 21, 1948; 1 child, Karen. BS, U. Chgo., 1937, PhD, 1942. Instr. biology Amherst Coll., Mass., 1946—47; instr. zoology U. Wis., Madison, 1947—51; wildlife biologist Wis. Conservation Dept., Madison, 1952—53; postdoctoral fellow Cornell U., Ithaca, NY, 1953—54; prof. zoology Ill. Coll., Jacksonville, 1954—58; from asst. prof. to prof. zoology UCLA, from 1958. Author: (with E. Collias) Evolution of Nest-building in the Weaverbirds, 1964, Nest Building and Bird Behavior, 1984; editor: External Construction by Animals, 1976. 1st lt. USAAC, 1943-46. Guggenheim fellow, 1962-63; NSF grantee, 1960-80. Fellow AAAS, Am. Ornithologists Union (Elliott Coues award 1980), Animal Behavior Soc. (Disting. Animal Behaviorist 2000); mem. Cooper Ornithol. Soc. (hon.), Wilson Ornithol. Soc. (Margaret Morse Nice medal 1997). Avocations: natural history, birding. Died Apr. 28, 2010.

COLLIN, RICHARD HARVEY, history educator; b. Phila., Mar. 4, 1932; s. Bernard Henry and Esther (Rubens) C.; m. Rima Drell Reck, Dec. 4, 1969. AB, Kenyon Coll., Gambier, Ohio, 1954; PhD, NYU, 1966. Asst. prof. history U. New Orleans, 1966-71, assoc. prof. history, 1971-85, prof. history, from 1985. Author: Theodore Roosevelt's Caribbean, 1990, Theodore Roosevelt, Culture, Diplomacy and Expansion, 1985, New Orleans Underground Gourmet, 1970; joint author: New Orleans Cookbook, 1975. Recipient Excellence in Teaching award, U. New Orleans Alumni Assn., 1985; Am. Philos. Soc. grantee, 1970, 88; U. New Orleans grantee 1985, 89; Penfield fellow, NYU, 1965. Mem. Lower Miss. Am. Studies Assn. (pres. 1971-87), So. Am. Studies Assn. (exec. bd. 1987—, v.p. 1991-93, pres. 1993-95), Am. Hist. Assn., Orgn. Am. Historians, Latin Am. Studies Assn., Soc. Historians of Am. Fgn. Rels. Died Jan. 20, 2010.

COLLINS, JOHN JOSEPH, JR., retired surgeon; b. Thomasville, Ga., Jan. 22, 1934; s. John Joseph and Frances (Ryan) C.; m. Mary Hogan Collins; children: Maureen, John III, Robert MD, St. Louis U., 1957. Intern Ohio State U. Hosp., 1957-58; jr. asst. resident in surgery St. Louis U. Hosps., 1958-59; NIH postdoctoral fellow Peter Bent Brigham Hosp., Boston, 1962-63, resident surgeon, 1963-66, jr. assoc. in surgery, 1968-70; fellow in thoracic surgery Peter Bent Brigham Hosp.-Mt. Auburn Hosp., Cambridge, Mass., 1966-68; rsch. fellow surgery Harvard U. Med. Sch., 1966-68, mem. faculty, 1969—99, prof. surgery, 1977—99. Chief div. thoracic and cardiac surgery Brigham and Women's Hosp., Boston, 1970-88, vice chmn. dept. surgery, 1988-99. Editor: Clinical Cardiology, 1979; mem. editorial bd. Am. Heart Jour., Chest. Officer M.C., USNR, 1959-61. Recipient Roche award St. Louis U., 1957, commr.'s spl. citation FDA, 1976, Purkinye medal Czechoslovak Med. Soc., 1978, St. Louis U. Sch. Medicine Alumni Merit award, 2002, Thomasville-Thomas County Pinnacle award, 2004 Fellow Am. Coll. Cardiology (Susan B. Cummings Humanitarian award 1975); mem. ACS, AMA, Assn. Thoracic Surgery, Soc. Thoracic Surgeons, Am. Surg. Assn., Am. Heart Assn., Soc. Internat. Chirurgie, Alpha Omega Alpha. Died Mar. 6, 2010.

COLLINS, JOYCE PLOEG, home health agency administrator, consultant; b. Grand Rapids, Mich., July 3, 1930; Postgrad., Calvin Coll., 1952, Grand Rapids Jr. Coll. RN Blodgett Hosp., 1951. Adminstrn. Med. Pers. Pool, Grand Rapids, 1972—84, v.p., from 1985; ptnr. Alpha Investments, Grand Rapids, from 1983; v.p. Comprehensive Home Svcs., Grand Rapids, from 1985; bd. dirs. Western Mich. Health Sys., Grand Rapids, from 1977, health expo steering com., 1982—84. Mem.: Am. Nurses Assn., Mich. Nurses Assn. (bd. dirs. from 1981), Grand Rapids Dist. Nurses (pres. 1978—82, Svc. award 1982). Republican. Avocation: reading. Home: Grand Rapids, Mich. Died July 30, 2009.

COLLINS, ROBERT ARNOLD, literature and language professor; b. Miami, Fla., Apr. 25, 1929; s. John William and Edna (Arnold) C.; m. Laura Virginia Roberts, June 3, 1960; 1 child, Judith. BA in English, U. Miami, Coral Gables, Fla., 1951; MA in English, U. Ky., 1960, PhD in English, 1968. Chair English Midway (Ky.) Jr. Coll., 1960-64; assoc. prof. English No. Ill. U., DeKalb, 1964-68, Morehead (Ky.) State U., 1968-69; from assoc. prof. to prof. English Fla. Atlantic U., Boca Raton, 1970—2005, prof. emeritus, from 2005. Founder, dir. Internat. Conf. on the Fantastic in the Arts, Ft. Lauderdale, Fla., 1980—. Author: Thomas Burnett Swann: A Critical Biography, 1980, Science Fiction and Fantasy Book Review Annual, 1987-91; editor: Scope of the Fantastic, 1985, Modes of the Fantastic, 1995, Festschrift: Lilith in a New Light, Ed. Lucas Harriman, 2008; editor Fantasy Rev., 1981-87; mng. editor Jour. of the Fantastic in the Arts, 1995—2003; contbr. articles to profl. jours. Recipient World Fantasy award World Fantasy Conv., New Haven, 1982, Balrog award Sword and Shield, 1982, 83. Home: Boca Raton, Fla. Died June 27, 2009.

COLLINS, WILLIAM F., JR., neurosurgery educator; b. New Haven, Jan. 20, 1924; MD, Yale U., 1947. Diplomate Am. Bd. Neurol. Surgery. Intern Barnes Hosp., St. Louis, 1947-49, asst. resident in neurosurgery, 1951-52, resident, 1952-53; fellow neurophysiology Washington U., 1953-54; instr. neurosurgery Western Res. U., Cleve., 1954-55, sr. instr., 1955-57, asst. prof., 1957-60, assoc. prof., 1960-63; prof., chmn. divsn. neurosurgery Med. Coll. Va., 1963-67; prof. Yale U., New Haven, chief sect. neurosurgery, 1963—86, chmn. dept. surgery, 1986-93, prof. neurosurgery emeritus, from 1994; clin. prof. neurosurgery U. Calif. Sch. Medicine, San Diego, from 1997. With M.C., U.S. Army, 1949-51. Died June 17, 2009.

COLLOM, PATRICIA ANNE, hospital administrator; b. N.Y.C., June 27, 1947; d. Edward J. and Elizabeth M. (Farrell) Kiernan; m. John A. Collom; 1 child, Kriste Ashley. Student Fordham U., 1984. Departmental mgr. NYU Med. Ctr., N.Y.C., 1972-76, adminstr., 1984—; spl. asst. to v.p. N.Y.C. Health and Hosp. Corp., 1976-78; asst. to dep. dir. Bellevue Hosp., N.Y.C., 1978-80; asst. to pres. S. Masuda, Inc., N.Y.C., 1980-82; departmental mgr. Beekman Downtown Hosp., N.Y.C., 1982-84. Mem. Nat. Assn. Female Execs., Am. Mgmt. Assn. Democrat. Roman Catholic. Avocations: painting; reading. Home: New York, NY. Died Jan. 15, 2009.

COLOMBARI, GIUSEPPE, steel company executive; b. Gemmano, Italy, Dec. 13, 1922; arrived in US, 59; s. Alfredo and Quinta (Mancini) Colombari; m. Margaret Jean Pelton, May 18, 1957; children: Thomas P., Michael J., Brian D. Degree, U. Bologna, Italy, 1946; postgrad. in Exec. Mgmt., Columbia U., 1960. Topographer to asst. gen. supt. Orinoco Mining Co. Subs. US Steel Corp., Venezuela, 1950—64; gen. mgr. to v.p. Navios Corp. Subs. US Steel, Bahamas, 1964—72; v.p. US Steel Internat., NYC, 1972—75, Pitts., 1972—75; pres. Navios Corp., Bahamas, 1975—76; v.p. resource devel. USX, Pitts., 1976—79, v.p., 1979—84, gen. mgr. ores, 1979—84, sr. v.p. related resources, 1984—87; pres. US Steel Internat. Inc., from 1988. Lt. Italian Army, 1940—44. Mem.: AIME, Am. Iron and Steel Inst., St. Clair Country Club (Pitts.), Duquesne Club. Roman Catholic. Home: Pittsburgh, Pa. Died Feb. 17, 2010.

COLTER, ELIZABETH ANN, nurse; b. Norristown, Pa., Jan. 26, 1931; d. Lewis J. and Nancy (Hardy) Coffey; m. Norman C. Colter, July 4, 1952 (div. Sept. 1979); children: Gregory, Marianne. Diploma, Sacred Heart Hosp., Allentown, Pa., 1951; AAS, Meramec CC, St. Louis, 1976; BS in Mgmt., Maryville Coll.; MA in Mgmt., Ctrl. Mich. U., 1983. Nurse Mercy Hosp., Jackson, Mich., 1954—56, Madigan Meml. Hosp., Houlton, Maine, 1956—59; staff nurse to asst. head nurse operating rm. Mercy Hosp., Jackson, 1959—69; staff nurse St. Lawrence Hosp., Lansing, Mich., 1969—70; nurse Barnes Hosp., St. Louis, 1970—80, head nurse operating rm., 1971—74, asst. dir. operating rm., 1974—80; dir. operating rms. U. Mich., Ann Arbor, 1980—87; mgr. critical care Aga Khan U. Hosp., Karachi, Pakistan, from 1987. Mem.: Am. Coll. Hosp. Adminstrs. (nominee), Assn. Operating Rm. Nurses (pres. St. Louis 1973—74), Phi Theta Kappa, Sigma Theta Tau. Democrat. Lutheran. Home: Florissant, Mo. Died Mar. 3, 2009.

COLTHUP, NORMAN BERTRAM, retired spectroscopist; b. Paris, July 6, 1924; BS, Antioch Coll., 1949; DS (hon.), Fisk U., 1974. Co-author: Introduction to Infrared and Raman Spectroscopy, 3d edit., 1990, The Handbook of Infrared and Raman Characteric Frequencies of Organic Molecules, 1991. Recipient Williams-Wright award, Coblentz Soc., 1979, Maurice Hasler award, 1999, Hon. Mem. award, Soc. Applied Spectroscopy, 2007 Home: New Canaan, Conn. Died June 9, 2009.

COLTMAN, JOHN WESLEY, physicist; b. Cleve., July 19, 1915; s. Robert White and Louise (Tyroler) C.; m. Charlotte Waters Beard, June 10, 1941; children: Sally Louise Condit, Nancy Jean Horner. BS in Physics, Case Inst. Tech., 1937; MS, U. Ill., 1939, PhD in Physics, 1941. Rsch. scientist Rsch. Labs. Westinghouse Electric Corp., Pitts., 1941—49, mgr. electronics and nuc. physics dept., 1949—60, assoc. dir. rsch. labs., 1960—64, dir. rsch. math. and radiation, 1964—69, dir. rsch. industry, def. and pub. sys., 1969—74, dir. rsch. and devel. planning, 1974—80. Mem. adv. group on electron devices Dept. Def., 1958-62; mem. Naval Intelligence Sci. Adv. Com., 1971-73, NRC Commn. on Human Resources, 1977-80; privately sponsored rschs. on acoustics of the flute. Contbr. articles to profl. jours. Recipient Longstreth medal Franklin Inst., 1960; Roentgen medal Remscheid, W. Ger., 1970; Gold medal Radiol. Soc. N.Am., 1982 Fellow Am. Phys. Soc., IEEE; mem. Nat. Acad. Engring., Am. Musical Instrument Soc. Presbyterian. Achievements include inventing x-ray image amplifier, universally used world-wide for fluoroscopy, and the scintillation counter. Home: Pittsburgh, Pa. Died Feb. 10, 2010.

COMPTON, OLIN RANDALL, consulting electrical engineer, researcher; b. Parsons, W.Va., Apr. 12, 1925; s. Troy William and Strauda Belle (Robinson) C.; m. Patricia Ruth Osborne, June 3, 1947; children: Patricia Randall, Olin Bryan, Lisa Adrienne, Barry Christopher. BSEE, W.Va. U., Morgantown, 1949; Cert., Advanced Sch. Electric Utility Engring., Pitts., 1961. Registered profl. engr., Va. Jr. engr. Va. Electric & Power Co., Richmond, 1949-56, asst. supt elec. equipment, 1956-59, supt. elect. equipment, 1959-64, asst. substa. engr., 1965-79, elec. systems coord., 1979-83, corp. engring. advisor, 1983-85, prin. engr., 1985-91; pvt. practice cons., elec. rsch. Richmond, from 1991. Chmn. C76 Am. Nat. Standards Inst., Washington, 1968-72, C29, 1983-86; U.S. expert on transformers Internat. Electrochem. Commn., Geneva, Switzerland, 1982-86, on insulators, 1986-89. Contbr. 60 articles to profl. jours. Dir. Ctrl. Va. Ednl. TV Group, Richmond, 1972-79; commr. Tuckahoe Little League, Richmond, 1972-80; dir. United Meth. Lay Tng. Sch., Richmond, 1973-79; Native Am. Ministries coord. Va. Conf. United Meth. Ch., 1995—; chmn. State Spl. Edn. Adv. Com., Richmond, 1976-79; constrn. chmn., 1995-97, bd. dirs. Richmond Metro Habitat for Humanity, Inc., 1995—. 2d lt. USAAF, 1943-47. Fellow IEEE (chmn. substa. com. 1976-78, chmn. transformer com. 1985-88, Disting Svc. awards, best paper prizes 1948, 89). Republican. Avocation: bible study. Died June 8, 2009.

CONARD, ALFRED FLETCHER, legal educator; b. Grinnell, Iowa, Nov. 30, 1911; s. Henry S. and Laetitia (Moon) C.; m. Georgia Murray, Aug. 7, 1939; children— Joy L., Deborah J. AB, Grinnell Coll., 1932, LL.D., 1971; postgrad., U. Iowa, 1932-34; LL.B., U. Pa., 1936; LL.M., Columbia, 1939, J.S.D., 1942. Bar: Pa. 1937, Mich. 1967. Practice in Phila., 1937-38; asst. prof. U. Kansas City (Mo.) Law Sch., 1939-42, acting dean, 1941-42; atty. OPA, 1942-43, Office Alien Property Custodian, 1945-46; asso. prof., then prof. law U. Ill. Law Sch., 1946-54; prof. law U. Mich. Law Sch., 1954-81, prof. emeritus, from 1981. Vis. prof. U. Tex., 1952, U. Colo., 1957, 84, U. Ariz., 1982, U. Calif., Berkeley, 1983, Pepperdine U., 1985-86, U. San Diego, 1989; vis. prof. Stetson U., 1990, vis. scholar, 1991-93; lectr. U. Istanbul, 1958-59, Luxembourg, 1959, Mex., 1963, Brussels, 1965, Salzburg, 1971, Saarbrucken U., 1988, 90; chmn. editorial adv. bd. Bobbs-Merrill Co., 1962-78; exec. com. Am. Assn. Law Schs., 1964-65, chmn. rsch. com., 1968-70, pres. 1971, chmn. bus. assns. sect., 1979. Author: Studies in Easements and Licenses, 1942, Cases on Business Organization, 3d edit., 1965, Automobile Accident Costs and Payments: Studies in the Economics of Injury Reparation, 1964, Corporations in Perspective, 1976, Enterprise Organization, 4th edit., 1987; editor-in-chief Am. Jour. Comparative Law, 1968-71; chief editor bus. and pvt. orgns.: Internat. Ency. Comparative Law, 1965-82; editorial adv. bd. Am. Bar Found. Rsch. Jour., 1976-86. Served OSS AUS, 1943-45. Decorated Purple Heart; Ordre des Chevaliers de la Couronne Belgium; recipient Kulp Meml. award Am. Risk & Ins. Assn., 1965; Guggenheim fellow, 1975 Mem. AAUP (chpt. pres. 1963-64), NRC, Am. Bar Assn. (exec. com. corp. law sect. 1967-71, com. on corp. laws 1974-80, com. on clin. legal edn. 1981-84), Internat. Acad. Comparative Law, State Bar Mich., Am. Law Inst., Law and Soc. Assn. (trustee 1968-75), Council on Law-Related Studies (trustee 1969-74), Phi Beta Kappa, Order of the Coif. Clubs: Rotarian (club pres. 1976-77). Mem. Soc. Of Friends. Home: Midland, Mich. Died Sept. 21, 2009.

CONDON, ROBERT VINCENT, JR., manufacturing company financial executive; b. Morristown, NJ, June 3, 1946; s. Robert Vincent Condon and Helen Margaret (Malley) Condon Murray; m. Vita Marie Rizzo, Oct. 18, 1969; children— Robert, Sean BA, Marist Coll., 1968; MBA, Fairleigh Dickinson U., 1976. C.P.A., N.J. Staff acct. J. H. Cohn & Co., Newark, 1972-78; mgr. budgeting Seton Co., Newark, 1978-80; mgr. internal auditing Gen. Felt Industries, Saddle Brook, N.J., 1980-82, v.p. fin., from 1982, chief fin. officer, from 1985. Served to sgt. U.S. Army, 1968-70. Home: Short Hills, NJ. Died June 10, 2010.

CONNOR, JOSEPH E., former international organization official; b. NYC, Aug. 23, 1931; s. Joseph E. Connor; m. Cornelia B. Camarata, Apr. 17, 1958 (dec. Oct. 11, 1983); children: Anthony, Cornelia, David; m. Sally Howard Johnson, Dec. 27, 1992. AB summa cum laude, U. Pitts.; MS in Bus., Columbia U.; DHL (honoris causa), Georgetown U., 1989. Joined Price Waterhouse & Co., NYC, 1956, ptnr., 1967-92, ptnr. in charge So. Calif., 1973-76, mng. ptnr. Western region LA, 1976-78, chmn. policy bd. U.S., 1978-88, chmn. World Firm, 1988-92, ret., 1992; disting. prof. bus. Georgetown U., 1992-94; under-sec. gen. UN, NYC, 1994—2002. Cons. fgn. direct investment program U.S. Dept. Commerce; project adv. rsch. study AICPA; lectr. in field.; mem. adv. coun. Columbia U. Grad. Sch. Bus.; bd. visitors U. Pitts. Grad. Sch. Bus., Georgetown U. Sch. Bus.; chmn. U.S. Coun. for Internat. Bus., 1987—; mem. Pres.'s Mgmt. Adv. Coun., Pres.'s Pvt. Sector Survey on Cost Control Contbr. articles to profl. lit. Trustee YMCA Greater N.Y.; bd. overseers Meml. Sloan Kettering Cancer Inst.; bd. dirs. Georgetown U., 1982-92; mem. coun. Brookings Instn. Served to 1st lt. U.S. Army, 1954-56. Mem. N.Y. State Soc. CPAs (chmn. internat. ops. com., mem. acctg. and auditing com., real estate acctg. com.), Calif. Soc. CPAs (legis. com.), Internat. C. of C. (exec. bd. 1989-94, pres. 1990-92), Met. Club (Washington), Links Club, Univ. Club. Home: New York, NY. Died May 6, 2009.

CONNOR, WILLIAM ELLIOTT, internist, educator; b. Pitts., Sept. 14, 1921; s. Frank E. and Edna S. (Felt) C.; m. Sonja Lee Newcomer, Sept. 19, 1969; children: Rodney William, Catherine Susan, James Elliott, Christopher French, Peter Malcolm. BA, U. Iowa, 1942, MD, 1950. Diplomate Am. Bd. Internal Medicine, Am. Bd. Nutrition, Am. Bd. Clin. Lipidology. Intern USPHS Hosp., San Francisco, 1950-51; resident in internal medicine San Joaquin Gen. Hosp., Stockton, Calif., 1951-52; practice medicine specializing in internal medicine Chico, Calif., 1952-54; resident in internal medicine VA Hosp., Iowa City, 1954-56; cons., 1967-75; mem. faculty U. Iowa Coll. Medicine, 1956-75, prof. internal medicine, 1967-75; acting dir., then dir. Clin. Research Center, 1967-75, dir. lipid-atherosclerosis sect., cardiovascular div., 1974-75. Vis. prof. Basic Sci. Med. Inst., Karachi, Pakistan, Ind. U., 1961-62, Baker Med. Rsch. Inst., Melbourne, Australia, 1982; vis. fellow clin. sci. Australian Nat. U., Canberra, 1970; prof. cardiology and metabolism-nutrition, dept. medicine, 1975-79, head sect. clin. nutrition, 1979-90, acting head, head div. endocrinology, metabolism and nutrition, 1984-90, prof. sect. clin. nutrition, 1990-2009, dir. lipid-atherosclerosis lab., assoc. dir. Clin. Rsch. Ctr., Oreg. Health Scis. U. Portland, 1975-94; chmn. heart and lung program project com. Contbr. numerous articles to med. jours.; editor Jour. Lab. and Clin. Medicine, 1970-73; mem. editorial bds., reviewer profl. jours. Mem. Johnson County (Iowa) Cen. Dem. Com., 1965-69; mem. nat. council Fellowship Reconciliation; nat., North Central and Pacific Northwest bds. Am. Friends Service Com. Served with AUS, 1943-46. Research fellow Am. Heart Assn., 1956-58; ACP traveling fellow Sir William Dunn Sch. Pathology, Oxford, Eng., 1960; recipient Career Devel. Research award Nat. Heart Inst., 1962-73, Discovery award Med. Research Found. Oreg. Mem. AAAS, ACP, AMA, AAUP (pres. U. Iowa chpt. 1968-69, pres. Oreg. Health Sci. U. chpt. 1978-79), Am. Diabetes Assn. (vice chmn. food and nutrition com. 1972-74), Am. Dietitic Assn. (hon.), Am. Fedn. Clin. Rsch., Am. Heart Assn. (chmn. coun. arteriosclerosis 1975-78, exec. com. coun. epidemiology 1967-70, exec. com. coun. cerebral vascular disease 1966-68, C. Lyman Duff meml. lectrue 1989), Am. Soc. Clin. Nutrition (pres. 1978), Nat. Acad. Sci. (food and nutrition bd. 1986-89), Am. Inst. Nutrition, Am. Oil Chemists Soc., Am. Physiol. Soc., Am. Soc. Clin. Investigation, Am. Soc. Study Arteriosclerosis, Assn. Am. Physicians, Ctrl. Soc. Clin. Rsch., Nutrition Soc., Soc. Exptl. Biology and Medicine (coun. 1971-72, pres. Iowa sect. 1971-72), Western Assn. Physicians, Western Soc. Clin. Rsch., Phi Beta Kappa, Sigma Xi, Alpha Omega Alpha. Achievements include research in nutrition, lipid metabolism, blood vessel diseases. Home: Portland, Oreg. Died Oct. 25, 2009.

CONNORS, THOMAS JOSEPH, retired pharmaceutical company executive; b. NYC, Dec. 29, 1924; s. Thomas Joseph and Mae (Healey) Connors; m. Helen Irean Conlin, Sept. 6, 1947; children: Doreen, Gail, Thomas, Nancy, Ronald, Lisa, Keith. BS, Holy Cross Coll., 1947; LLB, Fordham U., 1951. Bar: NY 51. Dir. Porta Sys. Corp., Syosset, NY; with Pfizer Inc., NYC, 1952—89, ops. v.p., 1983, exec. v.p. ops., 1984—89. Served to lt. (j.g.) USN, 1943—46. Mem.: NY Bar Assn., Erksine Lake Sailing Club (Ringwood, NJ), Plandome Assocs. Club (dir. 1984). Roman Catholic. Home: Plandome, NY. Died July 29, 2009.

CONRAD, PAUL FRANCIS, cartoonist; b. Cedar Rapids, Iowa, June 27, 1924; s. Robert H. and Florence G. (Lawler) C.; m. Barbara Kay King, Feb. 27, 1954; children: James, David, Carol, Elizabeth. BA, U. Iowa, 1950. Editorial cartoonist Denver Post, 1950-64, L.A. Times, 1964-93; cartoonist L.A. Times Syndicate, 1973-2000, Tribune Media Svcs., 2000—10. Richard M. Nixon chair Whittier Coll., 1977-78 Exhibited sculpture and cartoons LA County Mus. Art, 1979, Libr. of Congress, 1999; permanent collection Am. Treasures Libr. of Congress; author: The King and Us, 1974, Pro and Conrad, 1979, Drawn and Quartered, 1985, CONArtist: Thirty Years With The Los Angeles Times, 1993, Drawing The Line, 1999. Served with C.E. AUS, 1942-46, PTO. Recipient Editl. Cartoon award, Sigma Delta Chi, 1963, 1969, 1971, 1981—82, 1988, 1997, Pulitzer prize editl. cartooning, 1964, 1971, 1984, Overseas Press Club award, 1970, 1981, Journalism award, U. So. Calif., 1972, Robert F. Kennedy Journalism award 1st prize, 1985, 1990, 1992, 1993, Hugh M. Hefner 1st Amendment award, 1990, Lifetime Achievement award, Am. Assn. Editl. Cartoonists, 1998, Lifetime Pub. Svc. award, Edmund G. Brown Inst. Pub. Affairs, 2000; fellow sr. fellow, Sch. Pub. Policy and Social Rsch., UCLA, 2001—03. Fellow Soc. Profl. Journalists; mem. Phi Delta Theta. Democrat. Roman Catholic. Died Sept. 4, 2010.

CONTI, JAMES JOSEPH, retired chemical engineer, educator; b. Coraopolis, Pa., Nov. 2, 1930; s. James Joseph and Mary (Smrekar) Conti; m. Concetta Razziano, May 13, 1961; children: Lori Ann, James Robert. BChem Engring. summa cum laude, Poly. Inst. Bklyn., 1954, MChem Engring., 1956, D Chem. Engring., 1959. Sr. engr. Bettis atomic power divsn. Westinghouse Electric Corp., 1958—59; mem. faculty Polytech. U. N.Y., 1959—90, prof. chem. engring., 1965—90, chmn. dept., 1964—70, provost, 1970—78, v.p. ednl. devel., 1978—90; pres. Webb Inst. Naval Architecture, Glen Cove, NY, 1990—99, ret., 1999. Cons. in field. Contbr. articles to profl. jours.; patentee in field. Trustee Webb Inst. Naval Architecture, 1974—99. Fellow: AAAS, Am. Inst. Chemists; mem.: AIChE, Am. Soc. Engring. Edn., Omega Chi Epsilon, Phi Lambda Upsilon, Tau Beta Pi, Sigma Xi. Home: Bethpage, NY. Died Oct. 22, 2009.

CONWAY, JOSEPH P., lawyer; b. Mar. 3, 1930; Bar: N.Y. 1954. Mem. firm Cahill, Gordon & Reindel, NYC. Died Mar. 22, 2009.

COOGLE, JOSEPH MOORE, JR., management consultant, university educator; b. Louisville, Jan. 13, 1933; s. Joseph Moore and Dorothy Virginia (Miller) C.; m. Maryhelen Doty, Jan. 27, 1957; children: Suzanne Grace, Virginia Louise. BS, U. Ky., 1957; MBA, U. Chgo., 1958. Grocery products salesman Pillsbury Co., Mpls., 1958-59, with mktg. rsch. to sr. rsch. analyst, 1959-62, mktg. mgr., grocery products mktg. dept., 1962-65; account exec. Ketchum, MacLeod & Grove, Pitts., 1965-66, account supr., 1966-68, v.p., account mgr., 1968-70, v.p., dir. mktg., rsch. and media planning, 1970-72, sr. v.p., 1972-77, dir. ops. planning, 1975-77, dir. mktg. NYC, 1977-79, exec. v.p., 1978-79; pres. Ketchum Internat. Inc., Pitts., 1979-84; dir. Ketchum Comm. Inc., Pitts., 1979-90, exec. v.p. ops. and planning, 1984-86, exec. v.p. specialized svcs. group, 1986-88, exec. v.p., 1988-90; pres., mgmt. cons. Leadtime, Inc., Sewickley, Pa., 1991-92; prin. mgmt. cons. Coogle & Assocs., Sewickley, Pa., 1992-94, Annapolis, Md., from 1994. Adj. prof. mgmt. and mktg. Duquesne U., Pitts., Robert Morris Coll., Pitts., 1991-94; assoc. prof. mgmt. and mktg. grad. sch. U. Md., College Park, 1994—; bd. dirs. MCS, Inc. Bd. dirs., past pres. Pressley Ridge Schs., Md.; past founding pres., bd. dirs. Pressley Ridge Schs. Found.; past bd. dirs., vice chmn. Sewickley Valley Hosp.; past chmn., past bd. dirs. Three Rivers Shakespeare Festival; past pres., bd. dirs. Pitt. Dance Coun.; past bd. dirs. Sweetwater Art Ctr.; past bd. advisors Mon Valley Renaissance. With U.S. Army, 1953-55. Mem. Strategic Leadership Forum, Am. Mktg. Assn., Allegheny Country Club, Annapolis Yacht Club, Beta Gamma Sigma. Lutheran. Home: Annapolis, Md. Died Aug. 9, 2010.

COOK, GEORGE WALLACE FOSTER, retired lawyer, tree farmer; b. Shrewsbury, Vt., May 20, 1919; s. Edward Jay C. and Helen M. (Cook) Foster; m. Laicita Warburton Gregg, Sept. 21, 1947; children: Constance Cook Whitmer, David Wellington, Jonathan Foster, Timothy George, Heather Tiffany. AB, Middlebury Coll., 1940; LL.B., Columbia U., 1948; LL.M., Georgetown U., 1952. Bar: D.C. 1949, Vt. 1955. Counsel Dept. of Navy, Washington, 1948-55; pvt. practice Rutland, Vt., 1955-69; mem. Kinney & Cook, Rutland, Vt., 1955-63; U.S. atty. Dept. Justice, Rutland, Vt., 1969-78, 81-86; U.S. magistrate Adminstrv. Office U.S., Rutland, Vt., 1978-81. Mem. Vt. Senate, Montpelier, 1959-69 chmn. jud. com. 1963-69, pres. pro tem 1965-69; mem. platform com. Republican Nat. Conv., 1964; chmn. Vt. Constl. Revision Commn., 1967-69. Served to 2d lt. USAF, 1943-46. Mem. ABA, Vt. Bar Assn., Rutland County Bar Assn. Home: Rutland, Vt. Died Sept. 26, 2009.

COOK, WILLIAM HOWARD, architect; b. Evanston, Ill., Dec. 19, 1924; s. Clare Cyril and Matilda Hermine (Schuldt) C.; m. Nancy Ann Dean, Feb. 1, 1949(dec. July 24, 2009); children: Robert, Cynthia, James. BA, UCLA, 1947; BArch, U. Mich., 1952. Chief designer Fabrica de Muebles Camacho-Roldan, Bogota, Colombia, S.Am., 1949-52; assoc. architect Orus Eash, Traverse City, Mich., Ft. Wayne, Ind., 1952-60; ptnr. Cook & Swaim (architects), Tucson, 1961-68; project specialist in urban devel. Banco Interamericano de Desarrollo, Buenos Aires, Argentina, 1968-69; pres. Cain, Nelson, Wares, Cook and Assocs., architects, Tucson, 1969-82. Vis. lectr. architecture U. Ariz., 1980-89; coord. archtl. exch. with U. LaSalle, Mexico City, 1983, 85, 87, 89, 93. Served to lt. (j.g.) USNR, 1943-46. Fellow AIA (pres. So. Ariz. 1967); mem. Ariz. Soc. Architects (pres. 1970). Died July 24, 2009.

COOPER, CHARLES JASPER (JACK COOPER), lawyer, educator, civic and political activist; b. Tampa, Fla., Mar. 20, 1929; s. Harry Alva and Ruth (Smith) C.; m. Sally Ann Hill, Sept. 8, 1951; children: Carol, Douglas, Charles, Elizabeth, Kate. AB, Brown U., 1951; JD, Harvard U., 1954; PhD, Bryn Mawr Coll., 1967. Bar: Pa. 1955, Va. 1985. Assoc. counsel Montgomery, McCracken, Walker & Rhoads, Phila., 1954-55, Bellwoar, Rich & Mankas, Phila., 1956-60; lectr. polit. sci. Bryn Mawr Coll., Pa., 1961-63, U. Pa., Phila., 1964-67, asst. prof., 1967-68, vis. lectr., 1968-69; assoc. gen. counsel ARA Svcs., Inc., Phila., 1968-71; v.p., sec.-treas., dir. InterAx, Inc., Phila., 1971-72; pvt. practice Bryn Mawr, Pa., 1972-83; legal counsel for devel. Randolph-Macon Coll., Ashland, Va., 1984-87; devel. adminstr. Richmond Hill, Inc., Richmond, Va., 1989. Bd. dirs. Asten-Hill Mfg. Co., Asten-Hill, Ltd, 1951-68; mng. ptnr. Cooper Family Ptnrship., 1968—. Trustee, treas. Friends Cen. Sch., 1970-74, Ardmore Ave. Community Ctr., Soul Shack, 1975-81; chmn. Harold and Ida Hill Charitable Fund, 1969—; bd. mgrs., treas. Friends Pub. Corp., 1972-79; bd. dirs. Phoenix House, 1973-79, 80-83, Phila. Child Guidance Clinic, 1981-83; bd. dirs., treas. Va. League for Planned Parenthood Inc., 1988-91; bd. dirs., chmn. Assn. Va. Planned Parenthood, 1989-91; bd. dirs., corp. sec. Hand Workshop, Richmond, Va., 1989—; bd. dirs., treas. Family Support Ctr., 1976-79 Mem. Am. Polit. Sci. Assn., Am. Acad. Polit. and Social Sci., Ams. for Dem. Action (bd. dirs. S.E. Pa. 1955-83, nat. bd. dirs. 1967-88), Commonwealth Club, Capital Club, Bull and Bear Club, Phi Beta Kappa. Died Nov. 19, 2009.

COOPER, GEORGE ROBERT, electrical engineer, educator; b. Connersville, Ind., Nov. 29, 1921; s. William Russell and Margaret (Frederick) C.; m. Helen Elizabeth Conder, Nov. 23, 1949 (div. 1982); children: George Michael, David Russell, Susan Rachael, Ann Elizabeth, Steven Robert, Thomas Jonathan.; m. Elizabeth Jane Heald, Jan. 30, 1982. BS, Purdue U., 1943, MS, 1945, PhD, 1949. Instr. elec. engring. Purdue U., 1943-49, asst. prof., 1949-51, assoc. prof., 1951-55, prof., 1955-85. Cons. elec. engring. Fellow IEEE; mem. Am. Soc. Engring. Edn., Sigma Xi, Eta Kappa Nu, Tau Beta Pi, Sigma Pi Sigma. Patentee in field. Died June 8, 2010.

COOPER, GERALD RICE, clinical pathologist; b. Scranton, SC, Nov. 19, 1914; s. Robert McFadden and Viola Lavender Cooper; m. Lois Corrina Painter, Mar. 9, 1946; children: Annetta, Gerald Jr., Rodney. AB, Duke U., 1936, MA, 1938, PhD, 1939, MD, 1950. Cert. Am. Bd. Clin. Chemistry. Intern Atlanta VA Hosp., 1950-51, resident, 1951-52; rsch. assoc. Duke U. Sch. Medicine, Durham, NC, 1939-46; chief chemistry, hematology and pathology Ctrs. for Disease Control, Atlanta, 1952-72; rsch. med. officer Ctrs. for Disease Control, Nat. Ctr. Environ. Health, Atlanta, from 1973. Author (with others) books; contbr. articles to profl. jours. Col. USPHS. Decorated commendation medal, Superior Svc. award, Disting. Svc. medal, Asst. Sec. Health award for exceptional achievement; recipient Hektoen Silver medal AMA, 1954, Fulton County Med. Achievement award, 1954,

Billings Silver medal, 1956, Sigma Xi Rsch. award, 1997, Lifetime Sci. Achievement award CDC, 2002 Disting. Alumnus awrd Duke U. Sch. Medicine, 2004. Mem. Am. Assn. for Clin. Chemistry (pres. 1984, bd. dirs. 1975-77, chmn. bd. editors of selected methods 1967-80, bd. editors Clin. Chemistry jour. 1970-76, Fischer award 1975, Dade Internat. award 1975, N.J. Gerulat award 1979, SE Sect. Meritorious Svc. award 1989, Outstanding Contbn. Clin. Chemistry award 1992), Internat. Fedn. Clin. Chemistry (apolipoprotein expert panel 1985), Am. Soc. Clin. Pathologists (chmn. clin. chemistry coun. 1974, Continuing Edn. award 1967, 77). Methodist. Home: Atlanta, Ga. Died May 25, 2009.

COOPER, JAMES H., book publishing company executive, lawyer; b. Bklyn., May 20, 1929; s. James H. and Helen M. (Hofeditz) C.; m. Vera D. Duboy, May 28, 1958; children—James K., Jonathan S. AB, Columbia U., 1951, JD, 1957. Bar: N.Y. 1957, U.S. Supreme Ct. 1965. Sole practice, Millerton, N.Y., 1957-58; law editor Lawyers Coop. Pub. Co., Rochester, N.Y., 1958-63, mng. editor, editor-in-chief, 1973-78; legal adviser NASA, Washington, 1963-65; asst. mng. editor, editorial dir. Bancroft Whitney Co., San Francisco, 1965-73; pres. Shepard's-McGraw-Hill, Colorado Springs, Colo., 1978-85; exec. v.p. McGraw-Hill Book Co., NYC, from 1985. Past Bd. dirs. Colorado Springs Symphony, Colo. Opera Festival. Served to capt. USMC, 1951-54. Decorated Bronze Star medal. Mem. ABA, Assn. Trial Lawyers Am., Fed. Bar Assn. (bd. dirs. book industry study group), Am. Assn. Pubs. (exec. council profl. & scholarly pub.). Died Oct. 2, 2009.

COOPER, STEPHEN F., management consultant, film company executive; b. Gary, Ind., Oct. 23, 1946; married; 2 children. BS, Occidental Coll., 1968; MBA, U. Pa., 1970. CPA. Ptnr. Touche Ross; co-founder, ptnr. Zolfo Cooper LLC, 1985—2002; chmn. Kroll Zolfo Cooper, NYC, from 2002; interim CEO Malden Mills Industries; vice chmn., chief restructuring officer Laidlaw Inc.; interim CEO Family Golf Ctr.; interim CEO, chief restructuring officer Enron Corp., Houston, 2002; CEO Krispy Kreme Doughnuts Inc., Winston-Salem, NC, 2005—06, chief restructuring officer, 2006; chmn. Collins & Aikman Corp., Troy, Mich., from 2005; vice chmn. Metro-Goldwyn-Mayer Inc., L.A., Calif., from 2009, mem. Office of CEO, from 2009. Fellow: Am. Bankruptcy Inst.; mem.: Am. Inst. CPAs, NY State Soc. CPAs, Inst. Mgmt. Accountants, Turnaround Mgmt. Assn., Assn. Insolvency & Restructuring Advisors, Internat. Insolvency Inst. Died Feb. 1, 2009.

COOPER, WILL, brokerage house executive; b. Winnipeg, Man., Can., July 26, 1932; arrived in US, 1938; s. Arthur and Mary (Bass) Cooper; m. Phyllis Silverman, June 29, 1952; children: Steven Mitchell, Lynn Sheryl, Diane Karen, Lori Joy. BSA, Walton Coll.; MBA, U. Chgo. CPA Ill., Calif. Acct. A.A. Weiner & Co., Chgo., 1954—58; internal auditor Bell & Howell, Chgo., 1958—62; chief fin. officer Beverly Banking Group, Chgo., 1962—68; treas. Internat. Industries, LA, 1968—69; v.p., dir. corp. devel. Envirodyne, Inc., LA, 1969—78; pres., chmn. West Coast Bank, LA, 1978—84; pres. Select Financial Inc., LA, from 1984. Pres. community adv. coun. Encino Hosp., 1982—84; pres. U. Chgo. Bus. Sch. Alumni Assn. So. Calif, 1976; bd. dirs. LA Pops Orch., from 1982. Contbr. articles to profl. jours. With US Army, 1952—54. Mem.: Am. Inst. C.P.A.s, Encino C. of C. (pres. 1983). Home: Tarzana, Calif. Died July 15, 2010.

COPELAND, ERIC ALEXANDER, JR., diversified materials company executive; b. Gadsden, Ala., Mar. 16, 1936; s. Eric Alexander Sr. and Doris Evelyn (Walden) C.; m. Jo Ann Burke, Mar. 17, 1955; children: Eric Alexander III, Christopher Burke. BS in Acctg., U. Ala., 1960. CPA, Tenn. Audit mgr. Arthur Andersen & Co., Chattanooga, 1960-69; v.p., controller Imperial Carpets, Cartersville, Ga., 1969-74; treas. Bean Mech., Syracuse, N.Y., 1974-77; dir. audits Mead Corp., Dayton, Ohio, from 1977. Served with USN, 1952-55, Korea. Mem. Inst. Internal Auditors (pres. Dayton chpt. 1984). Republican. Lutheran. Avocations: flying, spectator sports, tennis. Home: Orange Beach, Ala. Died Apr. 1, 2009.

COPELAND, GEORGE FREDERICK, retired bearing company executive; b. St. Thomas, Ont., Can., May 15, 1923; came to U.S., 1955; s. Harley Anon and Irene Grace (Hepburn) (Sinclair) C.; m. Lillian Marie Roden, Dec. 8, 1945; children: Stephen George, Susan Irene, Richard Harley. Sr. matriculator, London South Collegiate, Canada, 1942; student, Queens U., Kingston, Ont., Can., 1943, Am. Inst. for Fgn. Trade, Phoenix, 1959, Harvard Bus. Sch., 1967. Div. indsl. engr. Timken Co., Canton, Ohio, 1957-58; pres. Timken Co. Brazil, Sao Paulo, 1959-66, Can. Timken Ltd., St. Thomas, 1966-73, Tyson Bearing Co., Glasgow, Ky., 1973-79; pres., chief exec. officer Brenco Inc., Petersburg, Va., 1980-85; ret., 1985. Pres. St. Thomas Bd. Trade; pres. St. Thomas Art Gallery. Recipient City of St. Thomas Dedicated Service to Community award, 1973; recipient award Soc. Advancement Mgmt., 1973 Mem. Am. Inst. Indsl. Engrs. (v.p. 1959-60 contbn. to indsl. engring. award) Clubs: Vista Plantation. Republican. Presbyterian. Home: Vero Beach, Fla. Died July 11, 2009.

CORCORAN, ROBERT J., former state supreme court justice; b. NYC, Jan. 20, 1934; BA, Iona Coll., 1954; JD, Fordham U., 1957; LLM, U. Va., 1982. Bar: N.Y. 1957, Ariz. 1960. Law practice, NYC, 1957-59, Phoenix, 1959-76; judge Superior Ct. Ariz., Maricopa County, 1976-81; judge divsn. 1 Ariz. Ct. Appeals, 1981-96; justice Supreme Ct. Ariz., 1996; ret., 1996. Editor Fordham Law Rev., 1956-57. Mem. ABA (jud. adminstrn. divsn.). State Bar Ariz. (civil practice and procedure com.), Maricopa County Bar Assn., Gamma Eta Gamma. Died July 27, 2010.

CORDA, MIKE, record company executive, composer; b. NYC, July 8, 1921; s. Jack and Rose (Riedler) C.; m. Helen Marie Wheeler, Dec. 7, 1952; children: Betty, Julie, Nikki. Student, N.Y. Coll. Music. Bassist Honolulu Symphony Orch., 1945-46; bassist Broadway prodn. Kiss Me Kate, NYC, 1948-51; songwriter various record cos., NYC, Los Angeles, from 1952; pres., producer, composer New Horizon Prodns., Las Vegas, Nev. Producer, dir. (rec.) Bluebirds Over the Mountain (Ersel Hickey), CBS Records, 1958; composer: The Green Years of Love, Let's Make the Most of a Beautiful Thing; composer, record producer for Mickey Rooney, Robert Goulet, Bill Haley and The Comets, Gloria Lynne, Joe Williams; composer, lyricist America I Love You So (read into Congl. Record 1995). Served with USMC, 1942-46. Mem. ASCAP. Died Feb. 13, 2010.

CORNELL, ROBERT WITHERSPOON, retired mechanical engineer; b. Orange, NJ, Aug. 16, 1925; s. Edward Shelton and Helen Lauretta (Lawrence) Cornell; m. Patricia Delight Plummer, June 24, 1950; children: Richard W., Delight W. Cornell Dobby, Elizabeth Cornell Wilkin, Roberta Shelton Wolfe. BSME, Yale U., New Haven, 1945, MSME, 1947, D in Engring., 1950. Registered profl. engr., Conn., N.Y. Instr. math. New Haven Jr. Coll., 1947-48; analytical engr. Pratt & Whitney Aircraft, East Hartford, 1947; with Hamilton Std., Windsor Locks, 1948—87, head stress analysis & vibration, 1961—63, chief applied mechanics and aerodynamics, 1963—87; instr. engring. Hillyer Coll., Hartford, 1955; pres. Cornell Cons., Hartford, 1973—2000, Cornell Enterprises, West Hartford, 1984—2000; ret., 2000. Adj. prof. Yale U., 1985, 90. Contbr. articles to profl. jours. Rep. state senatorial candidate 5th dist. State of Conn., 1988, 1994, state Rep. candidate 18th dist., 1990; bd. dirs., treas. Yale Sci. and Engring. Assn., 1969—2001, Conn. State Taxpayers Assn., Stratford, 1984—86; past pres., bd. dirs. West Hartford Taxpayers Assn., West Hartford, 1972—97, 2002—03; dir. Agawam Coun., 1993—99; mem. Svc. Corps. Ret. Execs., 1989—2002, chmn., 1998—2000. With USN, 1943—46. Fellow: ASME; mem.: Hartford Golf Club, Yale Club Hartford, Sigma Xi, Tau Beta Pi. Achievements include patents in field. Avocations: tennis, squash, jogging, swimming, gardening. Home: Bloomfield, Conn. Died Aug. 8, 2010.

CORSON, KEITH DANIEL, manufacturing executive; b. South Bend, Ind., Oct. 27, 1935; Student, Wichita State U., 1958-59. Mgmt. trainee Sears Roebuck & Co., Wichita, Kans., 1959-60; product mgr. Taylor Products div. Tecumseh Products, Inc., Elkhart, Ind., 1960-64; pres., chief ops. officer, coachmen Coachmen Industries, Middlebury, Ind., 1964-82; chief exec. officer Robertson's Dept. Stores, South Bend, 1982-83; pres., chief exec. officer Koszegi Products, Inc., South Bend, 1983-90; pres., chief oper. officer Coachman Industries, Elkhart, Ind., from 1990. Home: Granger, Ind. Died July 14, 2010.

CORTÉS, JULIO, language educator, educator; b. Bilbao, Spain, Jan. 23, 1924; came to the U.S., 1967; s. Antonio and María (Soroa) C.; m. Consuelo Colomer, Dec. 21, 1967; 1 child, Antonio. MA in Semitic Philology, U. Madrid, 1952, PhD, 1965. Dir. Hispanic Cultural Ctr., Damascus, Syria, 1956-60, 62-67; prof. Arabic and Spanish U. N.C., Chapel Hill, 1980—. Editor, translator El Coran, 1992, Al-Qur-an al-Hakim, 1992, Diccionario de Arabe Culto Moderno, 1996. Recipient Orden del Mérito Govt. of Spain, 1959. Mem. MLA, Am. Oriental Soc., Union Européenne des Arabisants et Islamisants, Ascn. Española de Orientalistas, Middle East Studies Assn., Am. Assn. Tchrs. Arabic, Linguistic Soc. Am. Roman Catholic. Avocation: reading. Home: Chapel Hill, NC. Died Apr. 13, 2009.

CORYELL, DONALD DAVID, retired professional football coach; b. Seattle, Oct. 17, 1924; m. Alisha Coryell (dec. 2008); children: Mike, Mindy. BA, U. Wash., 1950, MA, 1951. Asst. coach U. Wash., 1953-54; coach Wenatchee Valley Jr. Coll., 1955, Whittier Coll., 1957-59; asst. coach U. So. Calif., 1960; head coach San Diego State U., 1961-72, St. Louis Cardinals, 1973-77, San Diego Chargers, 1978—86. Named to The San Diego Chargers Hall of Fame, 1986, The Coll. Football Hall of Fame, 1999. Died July 1, 2010.

COSGRIFF, JAMES ARTHUR, physician; b. Lamberton, Minn., Mar. 18, 1924; s. James Arthur and Elsie Ann (Forster) C. BS summa cum laude, Coll. St. Thomas, 1944; MD, U. Minn., 1946. Intern St. Mary's Hosp., Duluth, Minn.; pvt. practice Olivia, Minn., from 1949. With USN, 1947-49. Fellow Am. Acad. Family Physicians; mem. Minn. Acad. Family Physicians (pres. 1963, Merit award 1964), Alpha Omega Alpha. Roman Catholic. Avocations: travel, photography, reading, music. Home: Olivia, Minn. Died Sept. 26, 2009.

COSTA, ERMINIO, pharmacologist, cell biologist, educator; b. Cagliari, Italy, Mar. 9, 1924; s. Oreste and Gigina (Murgia) Costa; divorced; children: Max, Robert Henry, Michael John; m. Ingeborg Hanbauer, July 13, 1973. MD, U. Cagliari, 1947, PhD in Pharmacology, 1953; PhD in Biol. Sci. (hon.), U. Cagliari, Italy, 1986; DSc (hon.), Georgetown U., 1992; MD (hon.), U. Tampere, Finland, 1992. Asst. prof., assoc. prof. U. Cagliari, 1948—54, prof. pharmacology, 1954—56; physician II, med. rsch. assn. Thudichum Psychology Rsch., Galesburg, Ill., 1956—60; vis. scientist NIH, Bethesda, Md., 1960—61; dep. chief lab. chem. pharmacology Nat. Heart Inst., Bethesda, 1961—63, head sect. clin. pharmacology, 1963—65; assoc. prof. pharmacology Columbia U., NYC, 1965—68; chief lab. preclin. pharmacology St. Elizabeth's Hosp., Washington, 1968—85; dir. Fidia-Georgetown Inst. for the Neuroscis. Georgetown U., Washington, 1985—94, from 1996; McDonnel vis. prof. neurology Washington U. Sch. Medicine, St. Louis, from 1994; sci. dir., prof. biochemistry in psychiatry U. Ill. at Chgo. Psychiat. Inst., from 1996. Editor Neuropharmacology, 1967, Advanced Biochem. Psychopharmacology, 1968, contbr. 915 articles to profl. jours. Recipient Bennet award and Gold medal, Soc. Biol. Psychiatry, 1990, Gold medal Fed. II Univ., Naples, 1990, Premio Fiuggi award, Fiuggi Rsch. Found., 1988. Mem.: NAS, Am. Soc. Biol. Chemistry and Molecular Biology, Am. Soc. Physiology, Am. Soc. Pharmacology and Exptl. Therapeutics, Academia Nazionale Lincei, Peripatetic Club, Cosmos Club. Home: Chevy Chase, Md. Died Nov. 28, 2009.

COSTANZA, MARGARET MIDGE, political consultant, public service administrator; b. Rochester, NY, Nov. 28, 1932; d. Philip Joseph and Concetta (Granata) C. LLD (hon.), Framingham State Coll., 1979. Exec. asst. to pres. John J. Petrossi Enterprises, Rochester, NY; asst. to Pres. for pub. liaison The White House, Washington, 1977—78; prof. polit. sci. San Diego State U., 2004—10. Speaker on human rights, fgn. policy, econs. various orgns. including John F. Kennedy Sch. Politics, Harvard U., Ford Hall Forum, Mass., The Econs. Club of Southwestern Mich., Inst. of Internal Auditors; exec. dir. Shirley Maclaine Enterprises, Los Angeles; v.p. Alan Landsburg Prodns. Talent coordinator, segment producer (TV series) America; spl. corr., segment producer (TV series) America Talks Back, Woody Fraser Prodns. Mem. exec. com. 22d Ward, 1959-64; mgr. Robert F. Kennedy Senatorial campaign, Monroe County, N.Y., 1964; vice-chmn. Monroe County Dem. com., 1966-70; mem. County Com., 1966-70, Dem. State Com., 1967-79; Dem. Nat. C, 1972-80, Rochester City Council, 1974-77 (1st woman to be elected); Dem. Congl. cand., 35th dist., N.Y., 1974; co-chairperson N.Y. State Carter campaign, 1975-76, N.Y. State Platform com., 1976; mem. com. Nat. Dem. Platform, 1976; del. Nat. Conv., 1976; pres. Nat. Coalition to End Pound Seizure, Los Angeles, 1988; bd. dirs. New Hope for Animals, Los Angeles, 1988. Democrat. Roman Catholic. Home: San Marcos, Calif. Died Mar. 23, 2010.

COSTELLO, RICHARD G., systems engineer, consultant; b. NYC, Apr. 16, 1938; s. William Joseph and Dorothy Costello; m. Trini Costello, Mar. 28, 1959; children: Carrie, Lisa, William. BEE, The Cooper Union, 1959; MSEE, NYU, 1960; PhD, U. Wis., 1966. Asst. rsch. scientist NYU, NYC, 1959-60; sys. engr. N.Am. Aviation, Anaheim, Calif., 1960-61; instr. U. Wis., Madison, 1962-66; designer Gilson Med. Electronics, Madison, 1963; sys. engr. Cornell Aero. Labs., Buffalo, 1966-67; prof. The Cooper Union, NYC, 1967-95, prof. emeritus, from 1995. Cons. Con Ed, N.Y.C., 1990—, U.S. DOJ, N.Y.C., 1996-97, Honneywell, N.Y.C., 1996-97; rsch. staff Consumers Union, N.Y.C., 1985; restoration staff Mus. Modern Art, N.Y.C., 1972; project dir. Elec. Power Rsch. Inst., 1988-90. Author: Digital Computing, 1982; prin. author: John Wiley Handbook of Electrical Engineering, 1986; contbr. articles to profl. jours. Pres. Whitehall Ter. Block Assn., N.Y.C., 1979-81; bd. dirs. WNCN Program Guild, Carnegie Hall, N.Y., 1980-81, Ft. Salonga Assn., 1999—. Grantee Emil Schweinburg Com., 1955, Ford Found., 1965, NSF, 1968, 93, 95. Mem. IEEE (sr., Computer Soc. chmn. 1977, Outstanding Advisor award 1993, Outstanding Rsch. Advisor award 1995), Eta Kappa Nu, Sigma Xi. Achievements include co-founder of cooperative research program in bioengineering with hospital for joint diseases. Home: Northport, NY. Died June 2, 2009.

COSTES, NICHOLAS CONSTANTINE, aerospace scientist, educator, retired government agency administrator; b. Athens, Greece, Sept. 20, 1926; came to U.S., 1948, naturalized, 1959; s. Constantine Nicholas and Anna (Papadopoulou) C.; m. Polytime Andros, Nov. 22, 1958; children: Constantine Nicholas, Anna Amalia, Christina Smaragtha. Diploma, Sci. Sch., Athens Coll., 1945; student, Athens Nat. Tech. U, 1945-48; AB, Darthmouth Coll., 1950, MSC.E. (George W. Davis scholar), 1951; A.M., M.E.N., Harvard U., 1962; MS, N.C. State U., 1955, PhD (Ford Found. fellow), 1965. Registered profl. engr., N.C., Ill. Teaching fellow dept. civil engring. N.C. State U., Raleigh, 1951-53, instr., 1962-63; materials engr. N.C. State Hwy. and Pub. Works Commn., Raleigh, 1953-56; research civil engr. U.S. Army Cold Regions Research and Engring. Lab., Hanover, NH, 1956-62; sr. research scientist space sci. lab Marshall Space Flight Center, NASA, Huntsville, Ala., 1965-98, team leader Apollo II Soil Mechanics Investigation Sci. Team, co-prin. investigator Apollo 12, 13 Lunar Geology Experiment, Apollo 14-17 Soil Mechanics Expt., from 1991, prin. investigator, co-investigator, project scientist Mechanics of Granular Materials Microgravity Expt., from 1991. Cons. geotech. engring., from 1965; adj. prof. U. Colo., Boulder, 1998. Contbr. articles and tech. reports to profl. jours. Recipient Dartmouth Soc. Engrs. prize, 1951; recipient NASA awards including cert. of appreciation, 1970, Group Achievement award Lunar Roving Vehicle Team, 1971, invention award, 1971, Astronauts' Silver Snoopy award, 1972, dirs. commendation achievement, 1973, Group Achievemnt award Flow Process Modeling Space Shuttle Main Engine, 1985, Group Achievement awards Environs Definition of Space Shuttle Solid Rocket Motor Team, Challenger Incident, 1986, Mechanics of Granular Materials (MGM) Microgravity Expt. Fellow ASCE (life, Norman medal 1972, chmn. program com. aerospace council 1973-75, exec. com. aerospace div. 1976-82, chmn. 1980-81, profl. coordination com. 1982—), AIAA (assoc. fellow, dir. Ala./Miss. sect. 1976-79, Outstanding Aerospace Engr. award 1976, Martin Schilling award 1979, Herman Oberth award 1998); mem. NSPE, AAAS, Am. Geophys. Union, Dartmouth Soc. Engrs., Soc. Harvard Engrs. and Scientists, Assn. Civil Engrs. Greece (hon.), N.Y. Acad. Scis., Am. Men and Women of Sci., Sigma Xi, Phi Kappa Phi, Chi Epsilon Greek Orthodox. Died Apr. 28, 2009.

COSTLOW, JOHN DEFOREST, zoology educator; b. Brookville, Pa., Jan. 28, 1927; s. John DeForest and Kathryn (Scott) C.; m. Ann O'Rourk, May 31, 1952 (div. May 1980); children: Jane T., Beth S.; m. Virginia Mason Herrman, Feb. 27, 1982. BS, Western Md. Coll., 1950; PhD, Duke U., 1956.

Research assoc. Duke U. Marine Lab., Beaufort, N.C., 1954-59, prof., dir., from 1968; asst. prof. zoology Duke U., Beaufort, 1959-65, assoc. prof., 1965-67; liaison scientist Office Naval Research, London, 1966-68; on leave Cambridge U., Eng. Contbr. numerous articles to sci. publs. Mayor Town of Beaufort, 1963-66; pres. Beaufort Hist. Assn., 1962-66, 68-70. Recipient numerous grants NSF; recipient numerous grants Dept. Energy, numerous grants NIH, numerous grants UNESCO, numerous grants Rockefeller Found. Republican. Episcopalian. Home: Beaufort, NC. Died Apr. 12, 2009.

COSTNER, CHARLES LYNN, retired civil engineer; b. Banner, Miss., Aug. 15, 1928; s. Charles Arthur and Clyde Margarite (Head) C.; m. Sara Lynn McGuire, May 26, 1951; 1 child, Jeffrey Lynn. BSCE, U. Miss., 1951, postgrad., 1955. Registered profl. engr., Miss. Engr. E.I. Dupont, Wilmington, Del., 1951-53, Farnsworth & Chambers, Baton Rouge, 1953—54, Ross E. Cox, Baton Rouge, 1955—65, Brown & Butler Cons. Engrs., Baton Rouge, 1965—83; pres., ptnr. Brown & Butler Inc., Baton Rouge, 1983—98; ret., 1998. Contbr. articles to mags. Airport Services Management, Ports 83, ASCE. With U.S. Army, 1946-48, Korea. Republican. Baptist. Home: Oxford, Miss. Died Nov. 15, 2009.

COSTRELL, LOUIS, physicist, researcher; b. Bangor, Maine, June 26, 1915; s. Solomon Nathan and Annie (Cohen) C.; m. Esther Klaiman, Apr. 11, 1942; children: James A., Daniel N., Robert M. BS, U. Maine, 1939; postgrad., U. Pitts., 1940-41; MS, U. Md., 1949. With Elliot Co., Ridgeway, Pa., 1940, Westinghouse Corp., East Pittsburgh, 1940-41, Bur. Ships, Dept. Navy, Washington, 1941-46; with Nat. Bur. Stds., Dept. Commerce, Washington, from 1946, chief radiation instrumentation sect., 1952-81, physicist Ctr. for Radiation Research Gaithersburg, Md., from 1981. Tech. adviser to U.S. Nat. Com. for Internat. Electrotech. Commn., 1962—; chmn. AEC Nuclear Instrument Modules Com. (now Dept. Energy Nat. Instrumentation Methods), 1964— Recipient Meritorious Svc. award Dept. Commerce, 1955, Disting. Svc. award, 1968, Spl. Svc. award, 1963, Edward Bennett Rosa award, 1979. Fellow IEEE (chmn. profl. group on nuclear sci. 1960-61, H. Diamond meml. award 1975, Nuclear and Plasma Sci. merit award 1975, Disting. Mem. award 1987), Nuclear and Plasma Sci. Soc. (Computer Applications in Nuclear and Plasma award 1993), Washington Acad. Sci.; mem. Am. Phys. Soc., Am. Nat. Stds. Inst. (chmn. com on radiation instruments 1960—), Tau Beta Pi, Phi Kappa Phi. Died June 8, 2009.

COTE, PATRICIA L., state legislator; b. Lynnfield Center, Mass., Apr. 20, 1926; m. Alfred J. Cote; 4 children. Grad. high sch., Wakefield, Mass. Mem. dist. 9 N.H. Ho. of Reps.; past mem. labor, industry and rehabilitative svcs. coms.; mem. mcpl. and county govt. com. Mem. bd. selectman, Danville, Mass., 1979—, chmn. 1985-89; past owner, attendant ambulance. PTA (past treas., pres.), 4-H. Home: Danville, NH. Died July 6, 2009.

COTMAN, ROBERT JOHN, food service company executive; b. Cleve., Oct. 31, 1945; s. John Earnest and Esther Marie (Fleischer) Cotman; m. Janet Christie Muhleman, Mar. 12, 1982 (div.); 1 child, John Phillip Muhleman. Student, U. Mich., 1963—67; BS, Ohio State U., 1973, MFA, 1978. Rsch. assoc. Ctr. Vocat. Edn., Columbus, Ohio, 1973—75; founder, pres. Group 243 Design, Inc., Ann Arbor, Mich., 1974—81; sr. v.p. Domino's Pizza, Inc., Ann Arbor, 1981—85, dir.; pres. Sponsers Report, Inc., from 1985; chmn. bd. Joyce Julius & Assocs. Inc., from 1985, Ashlar Devel., Inc., from 1986; dir. Visual Comm. Processes, Inc., Cubecraft Furniture Makers, Inc. Served with US Army, 1968—70. Decorated Commendation medal. Mem.: nn Arbor C. of C., Am. Inst. Graphic Artists, Sigma Nu. Home: Ann Arbor, Mich. Died May 28, 2010.

COTTINGHAM, WILLIAM BROOKS, university administrator; b. Chgo., Dec. 1, 1933; s. Ellis Brooks and Lillian Beverly (Nixon) C.; m. Gloria Dawn Smith, Sept. 12, 1975; children by previous marriage: Cynthia Mae, Cheryl Ann, Karen Jo. BSM.E., Purdue U., 1955, MSM.E., 1956, PhD, 1960. Mem. tech. staff Bell Telephone Labs., Whippany, N.J., 1960-63; asso. prof. Sch. of Mech. Engring. Purdue U., West Lafayette, Ind., 1963-66, prof., 1966-75; head sch. Sch. of Mech. Engring., Purdue U. (Mech. engring.), 1970-75; dean acad. affairs Gen. Motors Inst. (name changed to GMI Engring. and Mgmt. Inst. 1982), Flint, Mich., 1975-76; pres., from 1976. Founding partner, pres. TecTran, Inc., Lafayette, Ind., 1968-72; guest researcher Medisch Fysisch Inst., Utrecht, Netherlands, 1970 Author: (with P.W. McFadden) Physical Design of Electronic Systems, Vol. 4, 1970; patentee in field. Pres. bd. dirs. Lafayette Symphony Orchestra, 1969-70, bd. dirs., 1969-75; bd. dirs. Flint Inst. Music, 1975—. Mem. ASME, Soc. Automotive Engrs., Am. Phys. Soc. Am. Soc. Engring. Edn., Pi Tau Sigma, Sigma Xi, Tau Beta Pi. Clubs: Mason. Home: Flint, Mich. Died Sept. 29, 2009.

COTTON, EUGENE, lawyer; b. NYC, May 20, 1914; s. Jacob and Ida (Fundler) C.; m. Sylvia Glickstein, Jan. 21, 1940 (dec. 2008); children: Richard, Stephen Eric. B in Social Sci., CCNY, 1933; LLB, Columbia U., 1936. Bar: N.Y. 1936, Ill. 1947, U.S. Ct. Appeals (D.C., 1st, 5th, 7th, and 8th cirs.) 1947, U.S. Supreme Ct. 1942. Assoc. Szold & Brandwen, NYC, 1936-37; atty. N.Y. Labor Rels. Bd., NYC, 1937-41; spl. counsel FCC, Washington, 1941-42; asst. gen. counsel CIO, Washington, 1942-48; ptnr. Elson & Cotton, Chgo., 1948-50, Cotton, Watt, Jones & King, Chgo., 1951-94. Gen. counsel United Packinghouse Workers Am., 1948-68; gen. counsel packinghouse dept. Amalgamated Meat Cutters, Butcher Workmen Am., 1968-79 Served with USNR, 1943-45. Mem. Ill. and Chgo. Bar Assns. Clubs: City of Chgo. (gov., pres. 1966-68). Died Nov. 11, 2009.

COUDERT, VICTOR RAPHAEL, JR., marketing and sales executive; b. Dayton, Ohio, Mar. 8, 1926; s. Victor Raphael and Anita Marie (Ohmer) C.; m. Virginia Beach, Sept. 1, 1956; children: Anne, Victor III, Margaret, Catherine, Matthew, Paul, Lucy. AB in Econs., Yale U., 1946; postgrad., Stanford U., 1947-48; MBA, Harvard U., 1950. Sales trainee Hollingsworth & Whitney Co., Inc., Boston, 1950-52; salesman, exec. v.p. Montmorency Paper Co., NYC, 1952-73; pres. Coudert Assocs. Inc., Greenwich, Conn., from 1973; from v.p. to exec. v.p. and gen. mgr. Irving Forest Products, Inc., Greenwich, Conn., 1978-92; ret.; pres. United-Coudert, Inc., Pawtucket, R.I., from 1992. Published booklet on Soviet Union; contbr. articles to profl. jours. and newspapers. Chmn. Greenwich Bd. Ethics, 1977—; mem. fin. com. St. Mary Coun., 1986—, chmn., 1986-95; mem. Conn. Ethics Commn., 1984-85, Conn. Internat. Trade Coun., 1997—; bd. dirs. YMCA, 1975-81; trustee Sacred Heart U., 1975—, Convent Sacred Heart, Greenwich, 1985-92; trustee Fairfield Found., 1981—, pres., 1991-93. Lt. (j.g.) USN, 1943-47, PTO. Named Knight of Order of St. Gregory the Great, Pope John Paul II, 1988. Mem. Assn. Am. Woodpulp Importers (pres. 1970-71), Tech. Assn. Pulp and Paper Industry, Greenwich Horseneck Club, Harpoon Club, N.Y. Yacht Club, Indian Harbor Yacht Club, Am. Assn. of the Sovereign Mil. Order of Malta, Equestrian Order of the Holy Sepulchre of Jerusalem (Knight Commdr.) Republican. Roman Catholic. Avocations: yachting, travel. Home: Greenwich, Conn. Died Dec. 22, 2009.

COURT, JOHN CHRISTIAN, printing industry executive; b. Detroit, Feb. 2, 1942; s. Andrew Trawick and Aurelia (Browne) C. AB, Amherst Coll., 1964; MBA, Harvard U., 1967. Asst. to Henry Kissinger U.S. Dept. State, Washington, 1968-72; asst. adminstr. EPA, Washington, 1972-73; v.p. First Nat. Bank, Chgo., 1973-75, N-Ren Corp., Cin., from 1975; now pres., chief exec. officer Multi-Color Corp., Cin. Died Mar. 8, 2009.

COUTURE, JOSIE BALABAN, foundation director, insurance executive; b. Chgo., Dec. 10, 1922; m. Louis Couture, May 20, 1945 (div. 1948); 1 child, Dan B. Student, Tobias Matthay Sch. Pianoforte, London, Eng., 1938-39; studied with, Tobias Matthay; student, Yale U., 1939-40, Manhattan Sch. Music, 1940-42. Debut concert pianist Civic Theatre Chgo. Opera House, 1941; concert pianist live performances, radio, TV, 1941-50; entertainer USO tours; stockbroker N.Y. Stock Exch., 1955-60; ins. agt., broker, cons. NYC, from 1956; internat. pub. info. coord. Al-Anon Hdqs., NYC, 1970-76; founder, pres. TOVA (The Other Victims of Alcoholism, Inc.), NYC, from 1976. Lectr., speaker in field. Editor: Domino Quar., 1977—; past mem. editorial adv. bd. Alcoholism Digest, Labour-Mgmt. Alcoholism Jour.; contbr. articles to profl. jours. Liaison rep. nat. adv. coun. Nat. Inst. on Alcohol Abuse and Alcoholism U.S. Dept. Health and Human Svcs., Washington, 1977—; testified at senate hearings Women and Alcoholism, 1976, Impact Alcohol and Drug Abuse on Family Life, 1977, Comprehensive Alcohol Abuse and Alcoholism Prevention, Treatment, and Rehab. Act Amendments, 1979. Recipient New Pioneer award Office Women and Alcoholism Nat. Coun. Alcoholism Inc. and Women's Inst. Am. Univ., 1977; recognized in Congl. Record for New Nat. Orgn. TOVA, 1976. Died May 5, 2009.

COWEE, JOHN WIDMER, retired university chancellor; b. Wausau, Wis., Aug. 1, 1918; s. Charles Arthur and Hattie L. (Widmer) C.; m. Nancy Lee Pendleton, Dec. 22, 1973; children— John Widmer, Jeffrey Deane. BA, U. Wis.-Madison, 1947, MBA, 1948, PhD, 1950, LLB, 1956. Bar: Wis. Mem. faculty U. Calif.-Berkeley, 1954-66, prof. bus. adminstrn., 1960-66, chmn. dept., 1961-66, prof. law, 1954-66; dean Sch. Bus. Adminstrn., also Grad. Sch. Bus. Adminstrn. U. Calif., 1961-66; provost Marquette U., Milw., 1967-74, v.p. bus. and fin., 1966-67, prof. law and bus. adminstrn., 1966-76, exec. v.p. Med. Sch., 1967-69; prof. bus. adminstrn., prof. law U. Colo., Boulder, from 1976; chancellor health affairs U. Colo. Med. Center, 1976—85; ret., 1985. Trustee, asst. sec. Calif. Physicians Svc., 1959-66; mem. bd. govs. Internat. Ins. Seminars; bd. dirs. Calif.-Western States Life Ins. Co., Nordberg Mfg. Co., Milw., Marine Nat. Exch. Bank, Milw., Sta-Rite Industries, Milw.; chmn. policyowners exam. com. Northwestern Mut. Life Ins. Co., Milw., WICOR, Milw. Author studies, reports. Trustee Am. Conservatory Theatre Found., San Francisco, Univ. Sch., Milw., Davis Inst. Care and Study of Aging, Denver; bd. dirs. Marquette U. Sch. Medicine, Wis. Heart Assn.; adv. com. Lingnan Inst. Bus. Adminstrn., Chinese U., Hong Kong. Served with AUS, 1942-46. Decorated Bronze Star. Mem. ABA, Wis. Bar Assn., Internat. Assn. Ins. Law (co-founder Am. sect.), Internat. Ins. Seminars, Am. Assn. U. Adminstrs., Univl Club (Milw.), Denver Club. Clubs: University (Milw.); Denver. Home: Aurora, Colo. Died May 15, 2010.

COWLISHAW, MARY LOU, retired state legislator; b. Rockford, Ill., Feb. 20, 1932; d. Donald George and Mildred Corinne (Hayes) Miller; m. Wayne Arnold Cowlishaw, July 24, 1954; children: Beth Cowlishaw McDaniel, John, Paula Cowlishaw Rader. BS in Journalism, U. Ill., 1954; DHL, North Ctrl. Coll., 1999; DHL (hon.), Benedictine U., 2000. Mem. editorial staff Naperville (Ill.) Sun newspaper, 1977-83; mem. Ill. House of Reps., Springfield, 1983—2003, chmn. elem. and secondary edn. com., 1995—97, vice-chmn. pub. utilities com., 1995—2003, mem. joint House-Senate edn. reform oversight com., 1985—97; assoc. Ctr. for Govtl. Studies Northern Ill. U., 2003—10; adj. prof. North Ctrl. Coll., Naperville, Ill., 2003—10. Mem. Ill. Task Force on Sch. Fin., 1990-96; vice chmn. Ho. Rep. Campaign Com., 1990-2010; co-chair Ho. Rep. Policy Com., 1991-2003; chmn. edn. com. Nat. Conf. State Legislatures, 1993-97; mem. Joint Com. Adminstrv. Rules, 1992-2003; commr. Edn. Commn. of the States, 1995-2002; chair, Ill. Women's Agenda Task Force, 1994-2010; mem. Nat. Edn. Goals Panel, 1996-2010, bd. govs. Lincoln Series for Excellence in Pub. Svc., 1996-2010. Author: This Band's Been Here Quite a Spell, 1983; columnist Ill. Press Assn., 2003—. Mem. Naperville Dist. 203 Bd. Edn., 1972-83; co-chmn. Ill. Citizens Coun. on Sch. Problems, Springfield, 1985-2003. Recipient 1st pl. award Ill. Press Assn., 1981, commendation Naperville Jaycees, 1986, Golden Apple award Ill. Assn. Sch. Bds., 1988, 90, 92, 94, Outstanding Women Leaders of DuPage County award West Suburban YWCA, 1990, Activator award Ill. Farm Bur., 1996, 98, Bd. of Dirs. award Little Friends, Inc., 1998, Honor award Ill. Math. and Sci. Acad., 2002, Pub. Svc. award West Suburban Higher Edn. Consortium, 2002; named Best Legislator, Ill. Citizens for Better Care, 1985, Woman of Yr., Naperville AAUW, 1987, Best Legislator, Ill. Assn. Fire Chiefs, 1994, Outstanding Edn. Adv. Indian Prairie Sch. Dist. 204, 1994, Legislator of Yr., Ill. Assn. Pk. Dists., 1995; commr. Edn. Commn. of the States, 1994-2002; Mary Lou Cowlishaw Elem. Sch. named in her honor, 1997, Legislator of Yr., Ill. Assn. Mus., 1998. Mem. Am. Legis. Exch. Coun., Conf. Women Legislators, Nat. Fedn. Rep. Women, DAR, Naperville Rep. Women's Club (pres. 1994—). Methodist. Avocation: the violin. Home: Naperville, Ill. Died June 23, 2010.

COX, DAVE, state legislator; b. Holdenville, Okla., Feb. 20, 1938; m. Maggie Cox; children: Cathleen, Mary Margaret, Sarah. BA, U. San Diego, 1961; M in Sci. Adminstrn., Golden Gate U., 1986. Bd. supr. Sacramento County, Mcpl. Utility Dist. Bd.; mem. Dist. 5 Calif. State Assembly, 1999—2004, minority leader, 2002—04; mem. Dist. 1 Calif. State Senate, 2005—10, vice chmn. local govt. com., vice chmn. appropriations com., mem. banking, fin. and ins. com., energy, utilities and comm. com., health com. Mem.: Rotary Club. Republican. Episcopalian. Died July 13, 2010.

COX, DAVID A., rail transportation executive; b. Tipton, Ind., Feb. 21, 1936; BA, Purdue U. Chainman Nickel Plate R.R., Frankfort, Ind., 1956, rodman Brewster, Ohio, 1956-59, asst. structural engr. Cleve., 1959-62, draftsman, 1962-64, Norfolk and Western Rlwy., Cleve., 1964-65, real estate agt. Roanoke, Va., 1965-71, dir. real estate, 1971-82; dir. indsl. devel. Norfolk (Va.) So. Corp., 1982-90, asst. v.p. indsl. devel., 1990-95, v.p. properties, 1995-99, sr. v.p. properties and devel., from 1999. Dir. Forward Hampton Rds. Died Sept. 26, 2009.

COX, GENE SPRACHER, forestry educator; b. Norton, Va., Mar. 21, 1921; s. Dewitt Cam and Kathleen (Spracher) C.; m. Nell Ruth Jones, Jan. 19, 1946; children: Thomas, Alan. BS, Duke U., 1947, MS, 1948, PhD, 1953. Asst. prof. Stephen F. Austin State U., Nacogdoches, Tex., 1951-53; from asst. prof. to assoc. prof. U. Mont., Missoula, 1953-60; from assoc. prof. to prof. forestry U. Mo., Columbia, 1960-88, prof. emeritus, from 1988, assoc. dir., 1986-88. Vis. scientist NSF, 1969-71 Served with U.S. Army, 1942-45. Recipient Superior Teaching Gamma Sigma Delta, 1966; recipient Outstanding Teaching Standard Oil Found., 1969, Faculty Alumni U. Mo. Alumni Assn., 1981 Mem. Soc. Am. Foresters, Soil Sci. Soc. Am., Ecol. Soc. Am., Am. Soc. Agronomy, AAAS, Sigma Xi, Xi Sigma Phi, Gamma Sigma Delta Unitarian Universalist. Home: Ocean Springs, Miss. Died Jan. 22, 2009.

COX, WILLIAM ANDREW, cardiovascular thoracic surgeon; b. Columbus, Ga., Aug. 3, 1925; s. Virgil Augustus and Dale Jackson C.; m. Nina Recelle Hobby, Jan. 1, 1948; children: Constance Lynn Cox Rogers, Patricia Ann Cox Brown, William Robert, Janet Elaine Cox Sidewater. Student, Presbyn. Coll., Clinton, SC, 1942, Harvard U., Cambridge, Mass., 1944-45, Cornell U., Ithaca, NY, 1945; BS, Emory U., Atlanta, 1950, MD, 1954; MS in Surgery, Baylor U., Waco, Tex., 1961. Diplomate Am. Bd. Surgery, Am. Bd. Thoracic Surgery. Active duty USN, 1943-46; lt. (j.g.) USNR, 1946-54; commd. 1st lt. MC US Army, 1954, advanced through grades to col., 1969; intern Brooke Army Med. Ctr., San Antonio, 1954-55, resident gen. surgery, 1956-60; resident cardiovasc. thoracic surgery Walter Reed Army Med. Ctr., Washington, 1960-62, staff cardiothoracic surgeon, 1962; asst chief cardiothoracic surgery Letterman Gen. Hosp., San Francisco, 1962-65; performed first Star Edwards mitral valve replacement at Letterman Gen. Hosp. Presidio San Francisco, 1964; chief dept. surgery and cardiothoracic surgery 121 Evacuation Hosp, Seoul, Korea, 1965-66; cons. cardiothoracic surgery Korean Theatre, 1965-66; asst. chief cardiothoracic surgery Brooke Army Med Ctr., 1966-69, chief, 1969-73, performed first triple coronary artery bypass graft at Brooke Gen. Hosp. San Antonio, 1969, bd. dirs. thoracic surgery residency programs, 1966-73, ret., 1973. Brooke Tower, on call for Pres. Lyndon B. Johnson when he visited his Tex. Ranch, 1967-72; clin. prof. cardio-thoracic surgery U. Tex. Sch. Medicine, San Antonio, 1971—; practice specializing in cardiovasc. thoracic surgery, Corpus Christi, Tex., 1973-93; pvt. practice, 1973-93; cons. cardio-thoracic surgery Brooke Army Med. Ctr., San Antonio, 1977—; chief staff Meml. Med. Ctr., 1980; dir. disaster med. care region 3A Tex. State Dept. Health, 1973-88; mem. Coastal Bend Coun. Gov.'s Emergency Med. Svc. Commn., 1979-88; adv. bd. on congenital heart disease Tex. Dept. Health, 1980-88; participant joint confs. on cardiovasc. surgery and thoracic surgery Am. People Amb. Program, Leningrad, Moscow, Bucharest, Romania, Belgrade, Yugoslavia, Prague, Czechoslovakia, 1987; del. Vanderbilt U. Joint conf. vascular surgery Dublin, Ireland, Edinburgh, Scotland, London, 1986; participant joint confs. cardiovasc. surgery and thoracic surgery Am. Amb. People to People Program, Singapore, Kuala Lumpur, Malaysia, Hanoi, Vietnam, DaNang, Vietnam, Hue, Vietnam, Saigon, Vietnam, Hong Kong, 1992, People to People Am. Amb. Program, Eng., Scotland, Wales, 1996, 13th worldwide conf., Chester, England, 1998, 14th worldwide conf., Hong Kong, 2000, Denton A. Cooley Cardiovasc. Surgery Soc. mtg. Coeur d'Alene, Idaho, 2000; spkr. symposium Controversies in Cardiology, Dr. Willis Hurst, Holland Am. Lines Veendam, 1997; invited spkr. on open heart surgery 780 Bomb Squadron, Gainesville, 2001

Contbr. over 40 articles to profl. jours.; 4 profl. articles were selected for publication in the Yearbook of Surgery by editor Michael DeBakey. Ruling elder Presbyn. Ch., 1960—. Decorated Legion of Merit, Army Commendation medal; recipient A Prefix award Surgeon Gen. US Army, commendation Surgeon Gen. South Korea, commendation Eighth US Army Commdg. Gen. for Emergency Surgery on Adm. Blackburn US Negotiator for Peace, Pan mun jom, North Korea; named hon. citizen Phila. by Mayor Edward G. Rendell, 1995; recipient Tex. Med. Assn. Mem. Recognition 50 Yrs. award 1954-2004, 2004. Fellow Am. Coll. Chest Physicians (emeritus); mem. AMA, Soc. Thoracic Surgeons, Denton A. Coley Cardiovasc. Surgery Soc., Tex. Med. Assn. (del. conf. infectious diseases Bangkok, Hong Kong, Beijing, Shanghai, 1983), So. Thoracic Surgery Assn., Nueces County Med. Soc., Corpus Christi Surg. Soc., 38th Parallel Med. Soc., U.S. Power Squadron, People to People Internat., Internat. Platform, USN League (life), Ret. Officers Assn. (life), Navy Meml. Yacht Club (past commodore presidio San Francisco), T-Bar-M Racquet Club, Corpus Christi Country Club, Corpus Christi Athletic Club, Corpus Christi Town, Ft. Sam Houston Officers Club. Republican. Died Mar. 4, 2010.

CRAIG, CORNELIUS ABERNATHY, II, former insurance company executive, marketing and financial planning company executive; b. Nashville, Jan. 27, 1929; s. Edwin Wilson and Elizabeth (Wade) C.; m. Virginia Hubble Tipton, Apr. 24, 1954. BA, Vanderbilt U., 1951. With Nat. Life and Accident Ins. Co., Nashville, 1951-83, sr. v.p. sales and mktg., 1971-74, exec. v.p. mktg., 1974-77, sr. exec. v.p., 1977-80, chmn. bd., chief operating officer, 1980-82, pres., chief exec. officer, 1982-83, also dir.; chmn. bd., pres., chief operating officer, dir. Nat. Property Owners Ins. Co.; chmn. bd., chief operating officer, dir. NLT Mktg. Services, Inc., 1982-83; chmn., chief exec. officer Nat. Mktg. Services, Inc., Nashville, 1983-85, U.S. Fin. Services, Inc., Nashville, from 1983; chmn. bd. Money Concepts (Can.) Ltd., Toronto, from 1983. Dir Third Nat. Bank Nashville Mem. Nat. council Boy Scouts Am., 1968—; past pres. Middle Tenn. council, past pres. Area II.; trustee Episcopal High Sch., Alexandria, Va.; bd. govs., exec. com. St. Thomas Hosp. Devel. Bd. Recipient Silver Beaver award Boy Scouts Am., 1970, Silver Antelope award, 1980 Mem. Life Ins. Mktg. and Research Assn. (dir.; former chmn. combination companies com., former chmn. agy. officer round table; past chmn. ann. meeting com.), Underwriters Tng. Council (past mem. bd.), Life Insurers Conf. (past chmn.), Nashville C. of C. (past bd. govs. and exec. com.), Phi Delta Theta. Clubs: Belle Meade Country (Nashville); Sawgrass, Ponte Vedra (Fla.). Methodist. Home: Nashville, Tenn. Died June 9, 2009.

CRAIG, GEORGE ARTHUR, retired marketing and sales executive; b. Buffalo, July 22, 1923; s. Roy Vincent and Margaret (Connors) C.; m. Rittchell Marion Peterson, Aug. 27, 1949; children: Rittchell Anne, Scott Roy, Sandra Lynn. BA, Knox Coll., 1949; A.M.P., Harvard U., 1959. Commerce agt., gen. agt., dir. indsl. devel. Chgo. & Eastern Ill. R.R., Chgo., 1951-58, v.p. traffic, 1958-61; v.p. mktg. Tex. & Pacific R.R., Dallas, 1961-65; asst. v.p. sales Mo. Pacific R.R., St. Louis, 1965-77, v.p. Houston, 1977-82, sr. v.p. mktg., 1982-83; sr. v.p. mktg. and sales Union Pacific R.R., Omaha, 1983-87. Served with USAAF, 1942-45. Mem. Nat. Freight Transp. Assn., Nat. Def. Transp. Assn. Republican. Presbyterian. Home: Naples, Fla. Died Dec. 24, 2009.

CRAIG, JOHN GILBERT, JR., retired editor; b. Wilmington, Del., Apr. 13, 1933; s. John Gilbert and Ruth (Veasey) C.; m. Candace Best, June 27, 1981; children: Eliza, Landon, Peter, Emily Dutton. BA, Trinity Coll., Hartford, Conn., 1954; MA, Fletcher Sch. Internat. Law and Diplomacy, Medford, Mass., 1957. Mem. staff News-Jour. Co., Wilmington, Del., 1968-75, exec. editor, v.p., 1970-75; asst. to pubs. Pitts. Post-Gazette, 1976-77, editor, 1977—2003. Trustee Va. Theol. Sem., 1980—2010. With AUS, 1954-56. Mem. Am. Soc. Newspaper Editors, Alpha Delta Phi. Clubs: HYP, Fox Chapel Raquet. Democrat. Episcopalian. Home: Sewickley Heights, Pa. Died May 26, 2010.

CRAUGH, JOSEPH PATRICK, JR., insurance company executive, lawyer; b. Yonkers, NY, Oct. 21, 1934; s. Joseph Patrick and Lucille Maxine (Gruber) C.; m. Ellen Maria Roesser, Sept. 5, 1959; children: Joseph Patrick III, Elizabeth Anne. BS, Coll. of Holy Cross, 1956; LLB, Syracuse U., 1959. Bar: N.Y. 1961, N.H. 1971. Counsel Inter-County Title Guaranty Co., White Plains, N.Y., 1959-61; dist. claims mgr. Utica (N.Y.) Mut. Ins. Co., 1961-70; staff lawyer Nat. Grange Mut. Ins. Co., Keene, N.H., 1970-75, gen. counsel, v.p., bd. dirs., 1975-81; sr. v.p., govt. affairs counsel Harleysville (Pa.) Mut. Ins. Co., from 1981. Instr. profl. courses. Chmn. Cheshire County Republican Com., 1979. Mem. N.Y. State Bar Assn., N.H. Bar Assn., Internat. Assn. Def. Counsel, Am. Corp. Counsel Assn., Fedn. Ins. Counsel, Assn. CPCU, Am. Soc. Corp. Secs., Am. Arbitration Assn., K.C. Republican. Roman Catholic. Avocations: whitewater canoeing, baseball, conservative politics. Home: Lansdale, Pa. Died Sept. 3, 2009.

CRAWFORD, JAMES WELDON, psychiatrist, educator, administrator; b. Napoleon, Ohio, Oct. 27, 1927; s. Homer and Olga (Aderman) C.; m. Susan Young, July 5, 1955; 1 child, Robert James AB, Oberlin Coll., 1950; MD, U. Chgo., 1954, PhD, 1961. Intern Wayne County Hosp. and Infirmary, Eloise, Mich., 1954-55; resident Northwestern U., Chgo., 1958-59, Mt. Sinai Hosp./Chgo. Med. Sch., 1959-60; practice medicine specializing in occupational, individual and family psychiatry Chgo., from 1961. Mem. staff Rush St. Lukes-Presbyn. Med. Ctr.; clin. assoc. prof. dept. psychiatry Sch. of Medicine, U. Ill. at Chgo., 1970—; chair and assoc. prof. dept. psychiatry Ravenswood Hosp. Med. Ctr., 1973-79; chmn. J.W. Crawford Assocs., Inc., 1979-82; assoc. prof. depts. behavioral scis. and psychiatry Rush U. Med. Ctr. Contbr. articles to profl. jours. Bd. dirs. Pegasus Players, Chgo., 1978—96, chmn. bd. dirs., 1979-84; bd. dirs. Bach Soc., 1985-98; adv. Ill. Masonic Med. Ctr.; health adv. com. Cook County (Ill.) Commr., 2003—; del. to Russia and the Ukraine with People-to-People Internat., 1993, del. to Kenya, 1995, del. to China, 1998. NIH Inst. Neurol. Diseases postdoctoral fellow, 1955-59. Fellow Am. Psychiat. Assn. (life, dist. mem.), Am. Orthopsychiat. Assn.; mem. AAAS, Am. Soc. Psychoanalytic Physicians, Nat. Coalition Mental Health Profls. and Consumers, Ill. Coalition Mental Health Profls. and Consumers (steering com.), Ill. Psychiat. Soc., Chgo. Assn. for Psychoanalytic Psychology, Nat. Coun. on Family Rels., Rotary (com. mem. profl. rep.), Sigma Xi. Achievements include research in dendritic field and EEG; neuropsychology and neuroendocrinology, cocitation analysis of psychiatric field. Died Sept. 18, 2009.

CRAWFORD, JOHN WILLIAM, b. Buffalo, Nov. 24, 1930; s. John Hassall and Helen Susan (Albin) Crawford; m. Helen Marie Sihler, Feb. 6, 1955; 1 child, Carolyn Marie. Student, U. Mich., 1948—50; BS, U.S. Naval Acad., 1954. Sales mgr. Stellite divsn. Union Carbide Co., Kokomo, Ind., 1960—65; mgr. indsl. mktg. Eutectic Corp., Flushing, NY, 1965—67; v.p. mktg. Walbar, Inc., Peabody, Mass., 1967—71; v.p. sales Precision Castparts Corp., Portland, Oreg., 1972—80, sr. v.p., mktg. and internat. ops., from 1980. Lt. USN, 1950—60. Mem.: Am. Morgan Horse Assn. Died Sept. 10, 2009.

CRAYPO, CHARLES, labor economics professor; b. Jackson, Mich., Jan. 3, 1936; s. Norman Laverne and Ann Marie (Bogdan) C.; m. Mary Louise Vaclavik, Sept. 6, 1958; children: Jack, Carrie, Susan. BA in Econs., Mich. State U., 1959, MA in Econs., 1961, PhD in Econs., 1966. Asst. prof. econs. U. Maine, Orono, 1966-67; assoc. prof. Mich. State U., East Lansing, 1967-72, Pa. State U., University Park, 1972-78, U. Notre Dame, Ind., 1978-82, prof. Ind., 1984-2000, prof., chmn. dept. econs. Ind., 1984-93; prof. Cornell U., Ithaca, NY, 1982-84. Bd. dirs. Bus. Devel. Com., South Bend, Ind.; dir. Bur. Workers Edn., U. Maine, Orono, 1966-67, Higgins Labor Rsch. Ctr., U. Notre Dame, 1993; mem. acad. evaluating com. Labor Studies Ctr., Empire State Coll., SUNY, 1980; mem. labor studies dept. Ramapo Coll., 1981; mem. indsl. rels. dept. LeMoyne Coll., Syracuse, N.Y., 1983, Bur. of Labor Edn., U. Maine, Orono; external rev. mem. Divsn. Labor Studies Ind. U., 1998-99; mem. Labor Rsch. Adv. Coun., Bureau Labor Statistics, U.S. Dept. Labor, 2000; lectr. in field; expert witness. Author: Economics of Collective Bargaining, 1986, Grand Designs, 1993; mem. editl. bd., bus. mgr. Labor Studies Jour., 1976-80, chmn. editl. bd., 1980-85; mem. editl. bd. Contbns. to Labor Studies, 1989-97; internat. mem. editl. bd. Indsl. Rels. Jour., 1989-2002; contbr. articles to profl. jours. Mem. acad. adv. com. Divsn. Labor Studies Ind. U., 1978-82, 84-92, 95-96. Served with USMC, 1953-55. Recipient Lilly Endowment, 1992, D. Dority Labor Rsch. Fund, Ganey Rsch. award, 2002; grantee NEH, 1981, Rsch. grant, Dept. Commerce, 1984. Mem.: Indsl. Rels. Rsch. Assn. Home: Granger, Ind. Died Mar. 22, 2009.

CREECH, GLENWOOD LEWIS, academic administrator, educator; b. Middleburg, Ky., Dec. 31, 1920; s. Chester B. and Tennie (Estes) Creech; m. Martha Josephine Brooks, Apr. 4, 1942; children: Carolyn Ann, Walton Brooks. Student, Centre Coll., 1938; BS, U. Ky., 1941, MS, 1950; PhD, U. Wis., 1957. Tchr. Stanford (Ky.) High Sch., 1946—49; rsch. specialist U. Ky., Lexington, 1951—54, editor, 1954—56, prof., v.p., 1959—65; pres. Fla. Atlantic U., Boca Raton, 1973—83, prof. adminstrn., from 1973; vis. prof. Cornell U., 1958; cons. US Dept. State, US Dept. Agr.; bd. dirs. U. Ky. Devel. Coun., 1965—73, U. Ky. Athletics Assn., 1965—73, Spindletop Hall, Inc., Lexington, 1965—73, Children's Theatre, 1966—73, Living Arts and Sci., Ctr. Ctrl. Ky., 1966—73, Boca Raton YMCA, from 1975, Fla. Endowment Humanities, 1977—79; trustee St. Andrew's Sch., Boca Raton, 1975—77, Boca Raton Cmty. Hosp.; public trustee Miami Ednl. TV Sta., 1974—79; mem. Historic Boca Raton Preservation Bd. Commrs., 1975—78; bd. dirs. United Way Greater Boca Raton, pres., 1979—80, Fla. Assn. Colls. and Univs., 1980—81, Econ. Coun. Palm Beach County. With US Army, 1941—46. Recipient Disting. Svc. award, U. Ky. Alumni Assn., 1967; named Hall of Disting. Alumni, U. Ky., 1975. Mem.: Blue Key, Greater Boca Raton C. of C., Rotary (Boca Raton) (hon.), Phi Theta Kappa, Phi Kappa Phi, Delta Sigma Pi, Omicron Delta Kappa, Phi Delta Kappa. Died July 1, 2010.

CREECH, JOHN LEWIS, botanist, consultant; b. Woonsocket, RI, Jan. 17, 1920; s. Edward and Bessie (Faulkner) C.; m. Amy Elizabeth Wentzel, Feb. 14, 1942 (dec. Apr. 1984); children: Diane, Victoria, John; m. Elaine E. Godden Innes, July 10, 1984 (dec. July 2003). BS in Horticulture, U. R.I., 1941; MS in Horticulture, U. Mass., 1947; PhD in Botany, U. Md., 1953. Instr. horticulture U. Mass., Amherst, 1946-47; horticulturist Office Plant Exploration, Agrl. Rsch. Svc. USDA, 1947-50, asst. chief new crops rsch. br. Agrl. Rsch. Svc., 1958-66, chief br. Agrl. Rsch. Svc., 1966-72, scientist nat. program staff Agrl. Rsch. Svc., 1972-73; dir. U.S. Nat. Arboretum, Washington, 1973-80, N.C. Arboretum, 1987-88. Sr. adviser Internat. Bd. for Plant Genetic Resources; negotiator Bicentennial gift of Nat. Bonsai Collection from people of Japan; developer Nat. Herb Garden; program dir. for conservation of plant genetic materials Internat. Biol. Program, NAS; mem. panel FAO, 1966-74; preparer U.S. position paper for Stockholm Conf. on the Environment; adj. prof. biology U. N.C., Asheville; bd. dirs. N.C. Arboretum, Asheville, interim dir., 1986-87; U.S. judge Internat. Flower & Garden Expo, Japan, 1990; leader 9 plant expeditions Japan, China, Taiwan, USSR, Nepal, 1955-78; co-chmn. Genetic Resource Team, China, 1974; rev. nat. gen. resource program USDA, NAS, 1988-92; cons. Time-Life Books for Children, 1993; cons. in horticulture; leader hort. tours; mem. sci. & edn. com. Internat. Dendiology Soc. Author: The Bonsai Saga, 2001; co-author: Brocade Pillow, 1984, Garden Shrubs and Their Histories, 1992. Capt. U.S. Army, 1941-45, prisoner of war, ETO. Decorated Silver Star, Bronze Star; recipient Gold medal Scott Found., Gold medal Garden Club Am., Gold Seal medal Nat. Coun. State Garden Clubs, Thomas Roland medal Mass. Hort. Soc., Silver medal FAO-UN, Hort. medal Fedn. Garden Clubs N.Y., Norman J. Colman award Am. Nurserymans Assn., Hutchinson medal Chgo. Bot. Garden/Chgo. Hort. Soc., 1987, Gold medal and cert. of merit City of Kurume, Japan, 1988, Veitch Meml. medal Royal Hort. Soc., U.K., 1992, Award of Merit, Am. Assn. Bot. Gardens and Arb., 2000, Pres. award U. R.I., 2002, Disting. Svc. award Azalea Soc. Am., 2006; grantee Merrill Found., 1976, Nat. Geog. Soc., 1978, Japan Found., 1982; selected to give Morrison Meml. lecture. Mem. Am. Genetics Assn. (bd. dirs., Meyer medal), Am. Hort. Soc. (pres. 1954-56, profl. citation, Liberty Hyde Bailey medal 1989), Internat. Dendrology Soc. (v.p. 1989—), NC Arboretum (life, bd. dirs.), Sigma Xi, Phi Kappa Phi, Pi Alpha Xi. Republican. Episcopalian. Achievements include introduction of several plant varieties. Fax. Home: Orlando, Fla. Died Aug. 7, 2009.

CREWE, ALBERT VICTOR, physicist, researcher, artist; b. Bradford, Yorkshire, Eng., Feb. 18, 1927; came to U.S., 1955, naturalized, 1961. s. Wilfred and Edith Fish (Lawrence) C.; m. Doreen Blunsdon, Apr. 9, 1949; children: Jennifer, Sarah, Elizabeth, David. BS in Physics, U. Liverpool, Eng., 1947, PhD, 1951; degree (hon.), Lake Forest Coll., 1972, U. Mo., 1972, Elmhurst Coll., 1972, U.Liverpool, 2001. Asst. lectr. U. Liverpool, Eng., 1950-52, lectr., 1952-55; rsch. assoc. U. Chgo., 1955-56, asst. prof., 1956-58, assoc. prof., 1958-63; prof. dept. physics Enrico Fermi Inst., 1963-71, dean phys. scis. divsn., 1971-81; William Wrather Disting. Svc. prof. physics, 1958-61; emeritus, 1996—2009; dir. particle accelerator divsn. Argonne Nat. Lab., 1958-61, dir., 1961-66; pres. Orchid One Corp., 1987-90. Chmn. Chgo. Area R&D Coun. Recipient Outstanding Local Citizen in Field of Sci. award Chgo. Jr. Assn. Commerce and Industry, 1961; Outstanding New Citizen of Year award Citizenship Coun. Chgo., 1962; award for outstanding achievement in field of sci. Immigrant's Service League, 1962; Man of Year in Rsch. award Indsl. Rsch., Inc., 1970; Michelson medal Franklin Inst., 1977; Duddell medal Inst. of Physics, 1980. Fellow Am. Phys. Soc., Royal Microscopical Soc. (hon.), Chinese Electron Microscope Soc. (hon.); mem. NAS, Sci. Rsch. Soc. Am., Electron Microscopy Soc. Am. (Disting. Svc. award 1976), N.Y. Microscope Soc. (Abbe award 1979), Am. Acad. Arts and Scis., Palette and Chisel Acad. (artist mem.). Achievements include research on electron optics, design of electron microscopes, first images of single atoms. Home: Chesterton, Ind. Died Nov. 18, 2009.

CRIPPEN, RAYMOND CHARLES, chemist, consultant; b. Bklyn., Mar. 1, 1917; s. Charles H. and Betty B. (Brixner) C.; m. Helen L. Wolf, July 5, 1941; children: Lawrence J., Judith Ann Frisco. BS in Chemistry, Iowa State U., 1939; MSChemE, Johns Hopkins U., 1948; PhD in Analytical Chemistry, St. Thomas Inst., 1970. Chemist Allied Chem., Chgo., 1939-41; chemist, group leader E. I. dupont de Nemours & co., Ft. Madison, Iowa, 1941-45; cons. R&D Penniman and Browne, Inc., Balt., 1948-49; head of lab. Crippen Labs., Inc., Balt., 1949-61; group leader R&D Atlas Chem. Industries, Inc., Wilmington, Del., 1961-66; section head Stauffer Chem. Co., Silicones, Adrian, Mich., 1966-68; head methods devel. dept. Richardson-Merrell Co., Cin., 1968-70; instr. North Ky. State U., Highland Heights, 1970-75; pres. Crippen Labs., Inc., 1975-87; cons. Cecon Group, Inc., Wilmington, 1987-95; pres. Crippen Consulting Co., Hockessin, Del., 1995-98, Parkville, Md., from 1999. Mem. Tel-Tech Internat. Info Sci. Telephone Group. Author: ID of Organic Compounds, 1973, GC/LC Instr., Deriv. in ID Pollut., 1983, The Waste of Money (How to Avoid It), 1983; contbr. articles to profl. jours.; patentee in field. Inducted into Profl. and Exec. Hall of Fame, Orlando, Fla., 1967. Fellow Am. Inst. Chemists (cert. profl. com. pin 1983-87); mem. ASTM (com. mem. 1954—), Am. Chem. Soc. (editor/chemist Md. sect. 1949-61, asst. editor DelChem Bull. Del. sect. 1961-66), Soc. Appl. Spect. (chmn. 1964-65), Dickinson Theatre Organ Soc., St. Tropez Condo Owners Assn. Republican. Methodist. Achievements include patent for device for application to environment; development of Grecian Formula 16, Aspercreme, Charles Antell Hair Care Preparations, non-hazardous rodent control product. Died Feb. 5, 2009.

CRISPINO, JERRY L., judge; b. NYC, Apr. 17, 1930; s. Louis Crispino and Nina Fucci; m. Marguerite Probo; children: Nina, Louis. BA, Manhattan Coll., 1952; postgrad., NYU; LLB, Fordham U., 1955. Bar: N.Y. 1955, U.S. Supreme Ct. 1959. Adminstrv. asst. to U.S. Congressman Alfred E. Santangelo, 1962—63; assoc. counsel joint legis. com. Study N.Y. State Alcoholic Beverage Laws, 1964; mem. Cmty. Planning Bd. No. 11, 1965—67; arbitrator Am. Arbitration Assn., 1969—75; coun. mem. N.Y.C., 1975—91, chmn. health com., mem. com. pub. safety, 1st chmn. new land use com.; judge Supreme Ct. State of N.Y., from 1992. Dem. candidate State Senator 33d S.D., Bronx, 1968, 1970; dep. commr. City Dept. of Real Estate, 1974; mem. Bronx County Cath. Interracial Coun., Allerton Ave. Homeowners Assn.; past bd. dirs. Victory Day Care Ctr., Inc., Bronx Found. Sr. Citizens, Nat. Multiple Sclerosis Soc.; mem. Chester Civic Assn. With N.Y. N.G., 1955—58, maj. N.Y. N.G. Recipient Distng. Svc. Arbitrator award, Am. Arbitrator Assn., 1969, cert. Appreciation, U.S. Pres., 1972, Hon. citizenship, Boys Town Rome, 1978, Cmty. Support award, Decatur Dem. Club, 1980, Cmty. Svc. award, Woodlawn Taxpayers Assn., 1980, Winthrop Tenants Assn., 1983, Mindbulder Creative Arts Ctr., 1986, Cmty. Svc. & Support award, Edenwald/Gunhill Com. Ctr., 1983, Dedicated Svc. award, 1985, Distng. Leadership award, Alcoholism Coun. Greater N.Y., 1984, Svc. & Support to Youth award, Cmty. Sch. Bd. #11, 1987, others; named Legislator of the Yr., Evander Childs HS, 1984, Disting. Humanitarian, Am. Jewish Congress, 1984, Dedicated Svc. award, Boston Secor Tenants Assn., 1985. Fellow: No. Bronx

Dem. Club; mem.: NAACP (life), Colombia Lawyers Assn., Bronx County Bar Assn., N.Y. State Bar Assn., La Salle Alumni Assn., Fordham Law Sch. Alumni Assn., Columbus-Esca Alliance, Order Sons of Italy. Avocations: tennis, swimming, reading, politics. Died Mar. 20, 2009.

CRISSEY, JOHN THORNE, dermatologist, educator; b. Tonawanda, NY, July 19, 1924; s. Earl Guy and Sadie Kay (Harris) C.; m. Alice Jessamine Hogue, Jul. 30, 1949; children: Jennifer, Kaye, John Jr. MD, U. Buffalo, 1946. Diplomate Am. Bd. Dermatology and Syphilology. Assoc. prof. medicine U. Buffalo, 1952-64; clin. prof. medicine U. So. Calif. Sch. Medicine, Los Angeles, from 1964. Author: Classics in Clinical Dermatology, 1952 (Garrison-Morton Classic award 1952), The Dermatology and Syphilology of the 19th Century, 1981, Syphilis, 1984. Served to capt. U.S. Army, 1943-49. Recipient Gougerot prize for med. history Société de Dermatologie Gougerot, 1985. Fellow Am. Acad. Dermatology; mem. Am. Dermatological Assn. (gold award for scientific exhibit 1988), Sigma Xi Republican. Presbyterian. Avocations: musical composition, photography. Home: San Marino, Calif. Died Jan. 29, 2009.

CRITES, JOHN LEE, zoology educator; b. Wilmington, Ohio, July 10, 1923; s. Wilfred John and Mildred (Baker) C.; m. Phyllis Naomi Steelquist, July 21, 1946 (dec. Aug. 2004); children: Jill Ann, Robert Hilton B.Sc., U. Idaho, 1949, M.Sc., 1951; PhD, Ohio State U., 1956. Instr. dept. zoology Ohio State U., Columbus, 1955-59, asst. prof., 1959-63, assoc. prof., 1963-67, prof., from 1967, chmn. dept., from 1981. Assoc. dir. Put-In Bay, Ohio, 1970-80; cons. in biology AID-NSF Aligarh, India, 1964 Contbr. articles to profl. jours. Served with U.S. Army, 1942-45, PTO. Fellow Ohio Acad. Sci.; mem. Am. Soc. Parasitology (council), Wildlife Disease Assn., Helminthological Soc. Washington (editorial bd.), Sigma Xi Home: Columbus, Ohio. Died Jan. 9, 2010.

CROFT, WILLIAM CROSSWELL, corporate executive; b. Greenville, SC, Jan. 8, 1918; s. Edward S. and Mary (Crosswell) C.; m. Helen Barbara Engh, Mar. 7, 1942; children—William Crosswell, Mary Barbara, Douglas E., Helen W., Jean Ann. Student, The Citadel, 1935-36; BS, U.S. Naval Acad., 1940. Tech. supr. Anaconda Wire & Cable Co., Orange, Calif., 1946-48; gen. mgr. William J. Moran Co., Alhambra, Calif., 1948-50; works mgr. Pyle-Nat. Co., Chgo., 1950-52, v.p., 1953-54, exec. v.p., 1955, pres., 1955-76; chmn. Clements Nat. Co., Chgo., from 1976. Bd. dirs. Methode Electronics, Inc., United Trust Inc., Springfield, Mercury Fin. Co., Northbrook, Fla. Pres. Chgo. Crime Commn. Served from ensign to lt. comdr. USN, 1940-46. Mem. Chgo. President's Orgn., Ill. Mfrs. Assn. (past pres., dir.) Clubs: Union League (Chgo.), Chicago (Chgo.), Glen View (Chgo.), Mid-America (Chgo.). Home: Northbrook, Ill. Died Mar. 21, 2009.

CROMPTON, LOUIS WILLIAM, English literature educator; b. Port Colborne, Ont., Can., Apr. 5, 1925; came to U.S., 1955, naturalized, 1961; s. Clarence Lee and Mabel Elsie (Weber) C. BA, U. Toronto, 1947, MA, 1948; AM, U. Chgo., 1950, PhD, 1954. Lectr. math. U. B.C., 1948-49; lectr. English U. Toronto, 1953-55; asst. prof. U. Nebr., 1955-60, asso. prof., 1960-64, prof. English, 1964-88, prof. emeritus, from 1989. Vis. asst. prof. U. Chgo., 1959, U. Calif., Berkeley, 1961 Author: Shaw the Dramatist, 1969, Byron and Greek Love: Homophobia in 19th-Century England, 1985, Homosexuality and Civilization, 2003; mem. editorial bd. Shaw Rev, 1970-80, Annual of Bernard Shaw Studies, 1980-88; editor: Shaw Series in Bobbs-Merrill Library of Lit., 1969, Great Expectations (Dickens), 1964, Arms and the Man (Shaw), 1969, The Road to Equality (Shaw), 1971, The Great Composers (Shaw), 1978; editorial bd. series on homosexuality in lit., Arno Press, 1975, Jour. Homosexuality, 1977—. Recipient Christian Gauss award in lit. criticism Phi Beta Kappa, 1969, named Bonnie and Vern L. Bullough award Found. Sci. Study Sexuality, 2004. Home: El Cerrito, Calif. Died July 11, 2009.

CRONENWORTH, CHARLES DOUGLAS, manufacturing executive; b. Mohawk, Mich., Aug. 7, 1921; s. Jacob and Margaret (Therien) C.; m. Lorraine Evelyn DeBruyne, May 18, 1946; children: Carol, Linda, Mary, Charles. BSME, Mich. Tech. U., 1944. Registered profl. engr., Mich. Design engr. Chrysler Corp., Detroit, 1946-47; project engr. Gen. Foods, St. Clair, Mich., 1947-50; plant mgr. Diamond Crystal Salt Co., St. Clair, Mich., 1950-68, gen. mgr. prodn., 1968-75, pres., chief exec. officer, 1975-85, vice chmn., 1985-86; founder, pres. Mohawk Plastics, Marine City, Mich., from 1987. Bd. dirs. Comml. & Savs. Bank, St. Clair, Maritek Corp., Corpus Christi, Tex., Worldwide Protein Bahamas, Nassau, Diamond Crystal Salt, St. Clair, Seaway Fin. Corp., St. Clair; chmn. bd. dirs. Charles Corp., Marine City, Mich. Mem. chmn. Mich. Mineral Well Adv., Lansing, Mich., 1970-78; mayor City of St. Clair, 1962-63, councilman, 1955-58. Recipient Silver medal Mich. Tech. U., 1976 Mem. Mich. Soc. Profl. Engrs. (alt. dir. 1958-62), Nat. Soc. Profl. Engrs., Nat. Assn. Mfrs. (dir. 1980-86) Lodges: Rotary Internat. (St. Clair pres. 1979-80, St. Clair dir. 1976-82). Republican. Roman Catholic. Home: Saint Clair, Mich. Died May 2, 2009.

CROSBY, HARRY HERBERT, rhetoric educator; b. New England, ND, Apr. 18, 1919; s. Guy L. and Eva (McClellan) C.; m. Jean E. Boehner, Apr. 11, 1943 (dec. 1980); children: Stephen, April, Jeffrey, Rebecca.; m. Mary Alice Brennan, June 26, 1982; stepchildren: Haley, Maura, John. BA, U. Iowa, 1941, MA, 1947; PhD, Stanford U., 1953. Instr. U. Iowa, 1946-47, 50-51, asst. prof., 1951-58, writing supr., 1956-58; asst. instr. Stanford U., 1947-50; instr. San Jose State Coll., 1950; assoc. prof. Boston U., 1958-59, prof. rhetoric, 1959-85, chmn. divsn. comm. skills Coll. Basic Studies, 1958-65, chmn. divsn. rhetoric, 1966-85; dir. Writing Ctr. Harvard U., 1985. Dir. studies Pakistan Air Force Acad., Risalpur, West Pakistan, 1960-62; cons. USAF Acad., 1953-60. Author: A Wing and A Prayer, 1993; co-author: The McLuhan Explosion, 1968, College Writing, 1968, 2d edit., 1974, Just Rhetoric, 1971, The Shape of Thought, 1978, College Spelling, 1980, The Committed Writer, 1986. Mem. bd. aldermen City of Newton, Mass., 1970-73; pres. Newton Arts Ctr., 1979; sr. warden Grace Episcopal Ch., 1971-73. Lt. col. USAAF, 1942-45. Decorated Air medal, D.F.C. with two bronze oak leaf clusters, Bronze Star; Croix de Guerre (France). Mem. MLA, Nat. Coun. Tchrs. of English, Phi Eta Sigma (hon.). Home: Lovell, Maine. Died July 28, 2010.

CROSS, DEWAIN KINGSLEY, financial executive; b. Watertown, NY, Sept. 26, 1937; s. Kenneth Alden and Beverly Elizabeth (Hay) C.; m. Margaret Ann Waterhouse, May 1962 (div. Dec. 1978); children— Kenneth Alden, Judith Ellen, Richard Alan, Carol Marie; m. Kathleen Susan Rolfes, July 28, 1979 BBA, Clarkson U., 1961; grad. advanced mgmt. program, Harvard U., 1978. C.P.A., N.Y. Specialist fed. taxation Arthur Young & Co., Buffalo, 1961-66; mgr. taxation, dir. acctg. and taxation, asst. controller Cooper Industries, Inc., Houston, 1966-71, treas., 1971-72, v.p. fin., 1972-80, sr. v.p. fin., from 1980. Dir. Aviall, Inc., Dallas Mem. Am. Inst. C.P.A.s, N.Y. Soc. C.P.A.s, Machinery and Allied Products Inst. (fin. council) Clubs: Houston. Home: Houston, Tex. Died Aug. 24, 2009.

CROSS, THEODORE LAMONT, publisher, author; b. Newton, Mass., Feb. 12, 1924; s. Gorham Lamont and Margaret Moore (Warren) C.; m. Sheilah Burr Ross, Sept. 16, 1950 (div. 1972); children: Amanda Burr, Lisa Warren; m. Mary Warner, 1974. Grad., Deerfield Acad., 1942; AB, Amherst Coll., 1946; LLB, Harvard U., 1950. Bar: Mass. 1950, N.Y. 1953. With Hale and Dorr, Boston, 1950-52; chmn. bd., CEO Warren, Gorham & Lamont, Inc., 1980-83; chmn. Faulkner & Gray, Pubs., 1985-92, Hanover Pub., Inc., from 2010; editor in chief Bus. and Soc. Rev., 1971—2010; editor Jour. of Blacks in Higher Edn., 1993—2010. Cons. HEW, Fed. Office Econ. Opportunity, 1964-69; pub. gov. Am. Stock Exchange, 1972-77; bd. dirs. Inst. for Sci. Info., 1988-2010; lectr. on inner city econs. and minority econ. devel. Harvard, Cornell U., U. Va. Author: Black Capitalism: Strategy for Business in the Ghetto (McKinsey Found. book award 1969), (with Mary Cross) Behind the Great Wall, 1979, The Black Power Imperative, 1984, Birds of the Sea, Shore and Tundra, 1989; founder: Atomic Energy Law Jour., 1959; editor Harvard Law Rev., 1948-50. Trustee Amherst Coll., chmn. investment com., 1976-88; trustee Folger Shakespeare Libr., Princeton U. Press, Inst. Advanced Study, Nat. Humanities Ctr., John Simon Guggenheim Meml. Found.; mem. Coun. Fgn. Rels.; dir. Legal Def. Fund, NAACP, Century Assn., N.Y.C. With USNR, 1945-46. Mem. Coun. on Fgn. Rels. (treas.), Am. Philos. Soc. Home: Princeton, NJ. Died Feb. 28, 2010.

CROSS, WILLIAM HERBERT, protective services official; b. Salisbury, NC, Feb. 18, 1945; s. John Herbert and Margaret Ruth (Kestler) Cross; m. Linda Mariette Cauble, Mar. 7, 1969. Cert. fire control specialist. Stock mgr. Winn-Dixie Stores, Inc., Salisbury, 1963—67; fire control specialist Fire Dept., Salisbury, from 1967. Mem.: Clan Ferguson Soc. N.Am., Rowan County Fireman's Assn., NC State Fireman's Assn., Nat. Fire Protection Assn., NC Wildlife Fedn., Order of DeMolay Lodge (life). Republican. Methodist. Avocation: hunting. Home: Salisbury, NC. Died Jan. 29, 2009.

CROSSMAN, WILLIAM WHITTARD, retired wire cable and communications executive; b. Mineola, NY, Aug. 10, 1927; s. Homer Danforth and Emily May (Whittard) C.; m. Mary DeJesu, Dec. 6, 1952; children: William Whittard Jr., Lindsay Maria, Michael DeJesu. BS in Engring. Sci., U. Miami, 1949. West coast mgr., gen. mgr. HiTemp Wires div. Simplex Wire & Cable Co., 1955-69; pres. surprenant divsn. ITT Corp., 1969-74, pres. royal electric divsn. Pawtucket, RI, 1974-77, group gen. mgr. NYC, 1977-85, v.p., 1979-87, chmn. and group exec. comm. and info. svcs. Secaucus, NJ, 1985-88, sr. v.p., 1987-88, ret., 1988. With USNR, 1945-46, USAF, 1951. Mem.: San Remo Club, Owls Head Harbor Club. Republican. Episcopalian. Home: New Canaan, Conn. Died Feb. 28, 2009.

CROSSON, FREDERICK JAMES, retired dean, humanities educator; b. Belmar, NJ, Apr. 27, 1926; s. George Leon and Emily (Bennett) Crosson; m. Mary Patricia Burns, Sept. 5, 1953; children: Jessica, Christopher, Veronica, Benedict, Jennifer. BA, Cath. U. Am., 1949, MA, 1950; postgrad., U. Paris, 1951-52; PhD, U. Notre Dame, 1956. From instr. to assoc. prof. U. Notre Dame, Ind., 1953—66, prof., from 1966, O'Hara Disting. prof. philosophy, 1976-84, Cavanaugh Disting. prof. humanities, 1984—98, dean Coll. Arts and Letters, 1968-76. Author: (book) The Modeling of Mind, 1963, Philosophy and Cybernetics, 1967, Science and Contemporary Society, 1967; editor: Review of Politics, 1976—83. With USN, 1943—46. Mem.: North Ctrl. Assn. (exec. commr. 1984—89), Am. Cath. Philos. Assn. (pres. 1990—91), Am. Philos. Assn., Phi Beta Kappa (senator 1982—2000, v.p. 1994—97, pres. 1997—2000). Home: Notre Dame, Ind. Died Dec. 9, 2009.

CROWE, JAMES WILSON, university administrator, educator; b. Churubusco, Ind., June 27, 1934; s. James A. and Ruth Crowe; m. Barbara Jones; children: Michael James, Monica Sue Crowe Black. BS, Purdue U., 1959; MS, U. Fla., 1960; Dir. Degree, Ind. U., 1970, EdD, 1979. Grad. asst. in health and safety edn. U. Fla., Gainesville, 1959-60; health edn. tchr., coach, dir. driver edn. program Edinburg (Ind.) Cmty. H.S., 1960-65; dir. health and safety edn. Atterbury Job Corps Ctr., Columbus, Ind., 1965-66; asst. prof. applied health sci. Ind. U., Bloomington, 1966-80, assoc. prof. applied health sci., 1980-96; prof., from 1996; dir. Ctr. for Health and Safety Studies Ind. U., Bloomington, from 1992, co-dir. Inst. for Drug Abuse Prevention, from 1992, acting chair dept. applied health sci., 1992-93, chair dept. applied health sci., from 1993. Bd. dirs. Monroe County chpt. ARC, 1991-94. Recipient Svc. award ARC, 1986, 87, 88, 89, Instr. of Yr. award ARC, 1985, 87, 88, Outstanding Tchg. award Amoco, 1977. Mem. AAHPERD (v.p. cmty./safety divsn. Midwest dist. 1989-90), Am. Assn. Active Lifestyles and Fitness (bd. dirs. 1994—), Am. Driver and Traffic Edn. Assn. (Visions of Tomorrow award 1992), Am. Sch. Health Assn., Nat. Safety Coun. (mem.-at-large ednl. rsch. sect. 1993, cert. in recognition of outstanding contbn. 1994), Sch. and Cmty. Safety Soc. Am. (bd. dirs. 1991—, pres.-elect 1992-94, pres. 1994-96, past pres. 1996-98, scholar award 1996, C.P. Yost Disting. Svc. award 1998). Died Apr. 21, 2010.

CROWELL, ELDON HUBBARD, lawyer; b. Middletown, Conn., May 15, 1924; s. Eldon Lewis and Alice (Hubbard) Crowell. AB, Princeton U., 1948; LLB, U. Va., 1951. Bar: DC 1951, Conn. 1951, US Dist. Ct. DC 1951, US Ct. Appeals (D.C. cir.) 1951. Assoc. Cummings, Stanley et al Washington, 1951—52, ptnr., 1952—53, Sellers, Conner & Cuneo, Washington, 1953—70, Jones, Day, Reavis, Washington, 1970—79, Crowell & Moring LLP, Washington, 1979—90, sr. counsel, 1990—2010. Lectr. U. Va. Law Sch., Charlottesville, 1967—80; judge Adv. Gen. Sch., Charlottesville, from 1975, George Washington Nat. Law Sch, from 1975, Fed. Publs. Inc., Washington, from 1975. Contbr. articles to legal jours. Trustee Williston-Northampton Sch., Easthampton, Mass., 1965—75, Madeira Sch., Greenway, Va., 1970—75, Expt. Internat. Living, Putney, Vt., 1950—60; chmn. law firm div. United Way Campaign for Met. Washington, 1983—85; bd. dirs. City Lights Sch., Washington, Procurement Round Table, from 1993. Served with US Army, 1942—45. Fellow: Am. Bar Found.; mem.: ABA, Chevy Chase Club, Nat. Security Indsl. Assn., DC Bar Assn., Internat. Comparative Law Ctr. (bd. advisors), Nat. Contract Mgmt. Assn., Met. Club. Home: Washington, DC. Died May 23, 2010.

CROWELL, PETER O., former state legislator; b. Framingham, Mass., Oct. 1, 1944; divorced; 2 children. Grad., Mass. N.H. state rep., mem. resources, recreation and devel. coms. N.H. Ho. Reps.; dir. NE Lumber Mfr. Mem. New London Fire Dept.; lumberman. Home: New London, NH. Died Oct. 4, 2009.

CRYSTAL, BORIS, artist; b. nr. Warsaw, Poland, Dec. 25, 1931; came to U.S., 1968, naturalized, 1974; s. Shea and Bronislawa (Blumenfeld) C.; m. Dalia Gilad, Oct. 6, 1961; children: Julius S., Byron R. Student, Plocer's Sch. Fine Arts, 1962-63, Acad. Fine Arts Israel, 1963-64. One-man exhbns. include, Katz Art Gallery, Tel Aviv, 1964, Art Gallery 97, Tel Aviv, 1965-66, Journalist House Art Gallery, Tel Aviv, 1967, Lerner Art Gallery, N.Y.C., 1968, Herzl Inst., N.Y.C., 1969, Roerich Mus., N.Y.C., 1970, Crystal Art Gallery, N.Y.C., 1972-76, group exhbns. include, Katz Art Gallery, 1964-68, Mus. Israel, Tel Aviv, 1964-68, Lerner Art Gallery, 1968-76, Roerich Mus., 1968-76, Jewish Mus., N.Y.C., 1968-76, Mus. Modern Art, N.Y.C., 1968-76, LaGalerie Mouffe, Paris; represented in permanent collections, Katz Art Gallery, Mus. Israel, Art Gallery 97, Journalist House, Continental Gallery, Crown Art Gallery, Herzl Inst., Lerner Art Gallery, Roerich Mus., Jewish Mus., Mus. Modern Art. Recipient Gold medal Accademia Italia delle Arti e del Lavoro, 1980; Contbns. to Arts award Am. Biog. Inst., 1981 Mem. Artists Equity Assn. Home: Forest Hills, NY. Died Feb. 21, 2009.

CSIZMADIA, GAIL ROSA, retail executive, marketing professional, consultant; b. Bklyn., Sept. 21, 1957; d. Bela Kenneth and Ellinor Margrete (Finvag) Csizmadia. Student, Ohio State U., 1975. Store mgr. Beehive, Inc., North Olmsted, Ohio, 1974—79, v.p. ops., from 1979; cons. Collectors' Info. Bur., Winnetka, Ill., from 1982, Greenbook Soc., East Setauket, NY, from 1983; mem. exec. com. Gt. Northern Mall Mchts. Assn., North Olmsted, from 1983, v.p., from 1984. Recipient Highest Sales award, Gt. Northern Mall, 1983—85. Mem.: Royal Doulton, North Olmsted C. of C., Sebastian Miniatures Club, Precious Moments Club, Goebel Coll. Club. Republican. Lutheran. Home: Cleveland, Ohio. Died Aug. 9, 2010.

CUCULO, JOHN A., chemist, educator; b. Providence, June 23, 1924; s. John Joseph Paul and Carolina Cuculo; m. Eve Katherine Cortese, July 13, 1946; children: Cheryl Alison, Patricia Carol, Lauren Maria. ScB in Chemistry, Brown U., 1946; PhD in Chemistry, Duke U., 1950. Rsch. chemist E.I. DuPont de Nemours, Wilmington, Del., 1950—60, sr. rsch. chemist Kinston, NC, 1960—61, Richmond, Va., 1961—65, Wilmington, 1965—68; prof. dept. chemistry N.C. State U., Raleigh, NC, from 1968, Hoechst Celanese prof. emeritus, from 1995. Cons. in field. Contbr. articles to profl. jours., chpts. to books. Recipient The S. Smith Meml. medal, Brit. Fiber Soc., London, 1993, Decoration for Merits, Tech. U. Lodz, Poland, 1993. Mem.: Am. Chem. Soc., Sigma Xi. Roman Catholic. Achievements include patents for Stren fishing line; discovery of two new reactions of cellulose; new solvents for cellulose. Home: Raleigh, NC. Died Aug. 21, 2009.

CULP, ROBERT, actor; b. Oakland, Calif., Aug. 16, 1930; m. Elaybe Carroll (div.); m. Nancy Wilner, 1957 (div. 1967); children: Joseph, Joshua, Jason, Rachel; m. France Nuyen, December 9, 1967 (div. 1969); m. Sheila Sullivan, December 25, 1971 (div. 1976); m. Candace Faulkner, December 31, 1981; 1 child, Sammantha Hallie Student, Coll of Pacific, Washington U., St. Louis, San Francisco State Coll. Stage appearances include He Who Gets Slapped (Obie award), The Prescott Proposals, A Clearing In the Woods; actor: (films) PT 109, 1963, Sammy, 1963, The Raiders, 1964, Sunday in New York, 1964, Rhino!, 1964, Bob & Carol & Ted & Alice, 1969, Hannie Caulder, 1971, A Name for Evil, 1973, The Castaway Cowboy, 1974, Inside Out, 1975, Sky Riders, 1976, The Great Scout and Cathouse Thursday, 1976, Breaking Point, 1976,

Inside Out, 1976, Cry for Justice, 1977, Goldengirl, 1979, National Lampoon's Movie Madness, 1982, Turk 182, 1985, Big Bad Mama II, 1987, Silent Night, Deadly Night III, Better Watch Out!, 1989, Pucker Up and Bark Like a Dog, 1990, Timebomb, 1991, The Pelican Brief, 1993, Xtro 3: Watch the Skies, 1995, Panther, 1995, National Lampoon's Favorite Deadly Sins, 1995, Spy Hard, 1996, Most Wanted, 1997, Wanted, 1999, Unconditional Love, 1999, Farewell, My Love, 1999, Dark Summer, 2000, NewsBreak, 2000, Hunger, 2001, Farewell My Love, 2001, Blind Eye, 2003, The Almost Guys, 2004, Santa's Slay, 2005; actor, dir. (films): Hickey & Boggs, 1972; actor: (TV series) Trackdown, 1957-59, I Spy, 1965-68, The Greatest American Hero, 1981-83; (TV movies) The Movie Maker, 1964, The Hanged Man, 1964, See the Man Run, 1971, The Lie, 1973, A Cold Night's Death, 1973, Outrage, 1973, Give Me Liberty, 1974, Houston, We've Got a Problem, 1974, A Cry for Help, 1975, Strange Homecoming, 1974, Flood!, 1976, Spectre, 1977, Last of the Good Guys, 1978, Women in White, 1979, Hot Rod, 1979, The Dream Merchants, 1980, The Night the City Screamed, 1980, Killjoy, 1981, Though Shalt Not Kill, 1982, Her Life As a Man, 1984, Calendar Girl Murders, 1984, Brothers-in-Law, 1985, The Key to Rebecca, 1985, The Gladiator, 1986, The Blue Lightning, 1986, Combat High, 1986, What Price Victory, 1988, Voyage of Terror: The Achile Lauro Affair, 1990, Perry Mason: The Case of the Defiant Daughter, 1990, Murderous Vision, 1991, I Spy Returns, 1994, Favorite Deadly Sins, 1995, Mercenary, 1997, Big Guns Talk: The Story of the Western, 1997, Running Mates, 2000, Early Bird, 2005; (TV mini-series) From Sea to Shining Sea, 1974-75; (TV guest appearances) You Are There, 1953, Star Tonight, 1956, Playwrights '56, 1956, The United States Steel Hourb (3 episodes), 1956-58, Kraft Television Theatre, 1957, Robert Montgomery Presents, 1957, Alfred Hitchcock Presents, 1957, Zane Grey Theater (3 episodes), 1957-60, The DuPont Show with June Allyson, 1960, General Electric Theater, 1960, Tate, 1960, Johnny Ringo, 1960, The Chevy Mystery Show, 1960, Outlaws, 1960, The Westerner, 1960, Shirley Temple's Storybook, 1960, The Rifleman (2 episodes), 1960-62, Hennesey, 1961, Rawhide, 1961, The Detective Starring Robert Taylor, 1961, The Barbara Stanwyk Show, 1961, The Americans, 1961, 87th Precinct, 1961, Death Valley Days, 1961, Bonanza, 1961, Target: The Corruptors, 1961, Wagon Train, 1962, Cain's Hundred (2 episodes), 1962, Disneyland (2 episodes), 1962, Empire, 1963, Naked City, 1963, Insight, 1963, Combat, 1963, The Alfred Hitchcock Hour, 1963, The Outer Limits (3 episodes), 1963-64, Dr. Kildare (2 episodes), 1963-65, The Great Adventure, 1964, Bob Hope Presents the Chrysler Theatre, 1964, The Virginian, 1964, Ben Casey (2 episodes), 1964, The Man from U.N.C.L.E., 1964, Gunsmoke, 1964, Mr. Novak, 1965, Get Smart, 1968, ITV Saturday Night Theatre, 1970, The Name of the Game (2 episodes), 1970, Columbo (4 episodes), 1971-90 Shaft, 1973, Police Story (3 episodes), 1975-79, Greatest Heroes of the Bible, 1978, Mrs. Columbo, 1979, A Man Called Sloane, 1979, The Love Boat, 1980, Harcastle and McCormick, 1984, Murder, She Wrote, 1986, Hotel (2 episodes), 1986-87, Highway to Heaven, 1987, The Cosby Show, 1987, Matlock (2 episodes), 1987, Jake and the Fatman (2 episodes), 1987-91, Doctor Doctor, 1989, Who's the Boss?, 1989, The Golden Girls, 1990, Ray Bradbury Theatre, 1990, Dr. Quinn, Medicine Woman, 1993, Lonesome Dove: The Series (3 episodes, 1994, The Nanny, 1994, Wings, 1994, Walker, TexasRanger, 1995, Lois & Clark: The New Adventures of Superman (2 episodes), 1995, Burke's Law, 1995, Gargoyles (4 episodes), 1995-96, Everybody Loves Raymond (11 episodes), 1996-2004, Spy Game, 1997, Viper, 1997, Diagnosis Murder, 1997, Conan, 1998, Holding the Baby, 1998, Cosby, 1999, Chicago Hope, 2000, The Dead Zone, 2003, Robot Chicken, 2007; dir: (TV episodes) I Spy (1 episode), 1966, The Greatest American Hero (2 episodes), 1982-83. Died Mar. 24, 2010.

CULVER, ROBERT LONZO, JR., b. Hartselle, Ala., July 13, 1922; s. Robert Lonxo and Lelma Lee (Alford) Culver; m. Imogene Webb, Apr. 11, 1959; 1 child, Jeri Dawn. Grad., Anderson Airplane Sch., 1942, Alverson Bus. Coll., 1948; student, U. Ala., 1955—58. Assemblyman Glenn L. Martin Aircraft Corp., Middleriver, Md., 1942—44; sec. U.S. Steel Corp., Fairfield, Ala., 1948—71, mem. plant security, 1971—86; owner, propr. Westside Realty & Ins. Co., Birmingham, Ala., 1956—76; pres., CEO Bob Culver Realty, Inc., Birmingham, from 1976. Developer, property owner Hardee's of Forestdale, Inc., Quincy's Family Steak House of Forestdale, Inc. Mem. preservation forum Nat. Trust for Hist. Preservation. With US Army, 1944—46, with USAF, 1951—52. Recipient, Ins. Women of Birmingham, 1960; named Hon. Lt. Col., Ala. State Militia, 1965. Mem.: Birmingham Assn. Realtors, Ala. Assn. Realtors, Nat. Assn. Realtors, Nat. Assn. Real Estate Appraisers, Internat. Platform Assn., Forestdale C. of C. (charter), Masons (worshipful master Adamsville Lodge 1953—54), VFW. Democrat. Baptist. Home: Birmingham, Ala. Died July 7, 2010.

CUMMINS, HERMAN ZACHARY, physicist; b. Rochester, NY, Apr. 23, 1933; s. Louis H. and Rhoda Edith (Kitay) Kominz C.; m. Marsha Z. Hirsch, Aug. 18, 1963. BS, MS, Ohio State U., 1956; Diplome d'Etudes Superieures, U. Paris, 1957; PhD, Columbia U., 1963; D honoris causa, U. P. et M. Curie, 1999. Rsch. assoc. Columbia U., NYC, 1963-64; asst. prof. physics Johns Hopkins U., Balt., 1964-67, assoc. prof., 1967-69, prof., 1969-71; prof. physics NYU, 1971-73; disting. prof. physics City Coll., CUNY, 1973—2004, prof. emeritus, from 2004. Guggenheim fellow, 1984-85; Sloan fellow, 1969-72; recipient von Humboldt Sr. Rsch. award, 1998. Fellow Am. Phys. Soc., N.Y. Acad. Scis., Am. Assn. Adv. Sci.; mem. NAS, Am. Acad. Arts and Scis. Achievements include research in laser light scattering physics; phase transitions and critical phenomena; laser Doppler velocimetry; solid state and biophysics; liquid-glass transition; alloy solidification and pattern-forming instabilities. Died Apr. 21, 2010.

CUMMIS, CLIVE SANFORD, lawyer; b. Newark, Nov. 21, 1928; s. Joseph Jack and Lee (Berkie) C.; m. Ann Denburg, Mar. 24, 1956; children: Andrea, Deborah, Cynthia, Jessica. AB, Tulane U., 1949; JD, U. Pa., 1952; LL.M., N.Y. U., 1959. Bar: N.J. 1952. Law sec. Hon. Walter Freund, Appellate Div., Superior Ct., 1955-56; partner firm Cummis & Kroner, Newark, 1956-60; chief counsel County and Mcpl. Law Revision Commn., State of N.J., Newark, 1959-62; partner firm Schiff, Cummis & Kent, Newark, 1962-67, Cummis, Kent, Radin & Tischman, Newark, 1967-70; sr. v.p., dir. Cadence Industries, NYC, 1967-70; dir. Plume & Atwood Industries, Stamford, Conn., 1969-71; chmn., chmn. emeritus Sills Cummis & Gross, P.C., Newark, from 1970; exec. v.p. law and corp. affairs, sec. Park Place Entertainment corp., Las Vegas, Nev., 1999—2001; vice chmn. bd. dirs. Caesars Entertainment, Inc., Las Vegas, Nev., 2000—05. Dir. Essex County State Bank, Financial Resources Group; instr. Practising Law Inst. Chief counsel County and Mcpl. Revision Commn., 1959-62, N.J. Pub. Market Commn., 1961-63; counsel Bd. Edn. of South Orange and Maplewood, 1964-74, Town of Cedar Grove, 1966-70, Bd. Edn. of Dumont, 1968-72; mem. com. on rules and civil practice N.J. Supreme Ct., 1975-78. Assoc. editor NJ. Law Jour., 1961—. Trustee Newark Beth Israel Med. Ctr., 1965-75, Northfield YM-YWHA, 1968-70, U. Medicine and Dentistry NJ, 1980-84, Newark Mus., NJ Performing Arts Ctr., Blue Cross and Blue Shield NJ, 1983-93, Found. U. Medicine and Dentistry NJ, 1999—; gen. coun. NJ Turnpike Authority, 1990-94; commr., Turnpike Authority, NJ, 2008-; bd. overseers U. Pa. Law Sch., 1991-96; bd. govs. Daus. Israel Home for Aged, 1968-70; active NJ Commn. on Statue of Liberty; pres.'s coun. Tulane U., 1992—; pres. bd. dirs. Tulane Assocs., 1994-96; Pres.'s commn. on White House Fellows, 1993-2001; dir. NJ Regional Planning Assn., Horizon Found., NJ, 2004—, Flame of Charity Found., 2005—. Recipient 1st Ann. Judge Learned Hand award Am. Jewish Com., 1994, First Ann. Disting. Citizen award N.J. Med. Sch., 2002. Fellow Am. Bar Found.; mem. ABA, Am. Law Inst. (life, bd. dirs.), Am. Judicature Soc. (dir.), U. Pa. Law Sch. Alumni Soc. (pres.), NJ Bar Assn., Essex County Bar Assn., NY Athletic Club (NYC), Greenbrook County Club (North Caldwell, NJ), Stockbridge Golf Club (Mass.). Democrat. Jewish. Home: West Orange, NJ. Died Feb. 9, 2010.

CUNNINGHAM, AUSTIN, business consultant; b. Washington, Sept. 5, 1914; s. Austin and Clotilde (Mattingly) C.; m. Jacqueline Coder, Jan. 24, 1946; children: Kathryne, Amy, Austin III. Student, George Washington U., 1933-37; JD, U. Va., 1940, postgrad., 1946. Sales mgr. Ediphone div. Thomas A. Edison Inc., 1947-53; various exec. positions Magnavox Co., Chgo., 1953-61; pres. Product Specialties Inc. div. Sunbeam Corp., Chgo., 1963-69, Sunbeam Outdoor Co. div. Sunbeam Corp., Santee, S.C., 1969-76; pres., chief exec. officer Restaurant Assocs. Inc., Orangeburg, S.C., from 1976, A&J Inc., Orangeburg, from 1976, Quality Fish Inc., Orangeburg, from 1976. Bd. dirs. First Nat. Bank, Orangeburg. Chmn. budget com., trustee United Fund, Kenilworth, Ill., 1971-72; trustee Ravinia Festival Assn; chmn. Econ. Recovery Com., Orangeburg, 1983. Served to 1st lt. USAF, WW II. Recipient Presdl. Citation, Dept. Labor, Washington, 1984. Mem. Outdoor Power Equipment Inst. (trustee), Dickens Soc. (London), Orangeburg C. of C. (v.p. 1981-82), Newcomen Soc. Clubs: Orangeburg Country. Republican. Presbyterian. Home: Orangeburg, SC. Died Jan. 26, 2009.

CUNNINGHAM, SISTER MADONNA MARIE, retired academic administrator, nun; b. Trenton, NJ, Aug. 31, 1933; AB, Villanova U., 1961; MA, Fordham U., 1964, PhD, 1968. Joined Sisters of St. Francis, Roman Cath. Ch., 1953. Intern in psychology St. Elizabeth's Hosp., Washington, 1965-66; elem. tchr. Spokane, Wash., 1956-60, Elsmere, Del., 1956-60; dir. counseling, asst. prof. psychology Our Lady of Angels Coll., Aston, Pa., 1967-71, pres., assoc. prof., 1971-83. Lectr. Dept. Edn., St. Joseph's Coll., Phila., 1968-70; staff psychologist Phila. Archdiocesan Counseling Svc. for Religions, 1969-76. Trustee St. Joseph Hosp., Towson, Md., Archmere Acad., Claymont, Del., Franciscan Health System, Neumann Coll. Mem. Am. Psychol. Assn., Pa. Psychol. Assn., Psychologists Interested in Religious Issues, Sigma Xi. Died Jan. 20, 2010.

CURRENT, DAVID HARLAN, physicist; b. Connersville, Ind., July 26, 1941; s. Harlan Paul and Margaret Ruth (Risser) C.; m. Diane Ellen Heck, June 11, 1966; children: Michael David, Daniel Steven. BA, Carleton Coll., 1963; MS, Northwestern U., 1966; PhD, Mich. State U., 1971. Instr. Ctrl. Mich. U., Mt. Pleasant, Mich., 1966-71, asst. prof., 1971-75, assoc. prof., 1975-79, prof., from 1979. Vis. rsch. assoc. Argonne (Ill.) Nat. Lab, summers 1978-80. Contbr. articles to profl. jours. Recipient Teaching Equipment grant NSF, 1981, Rsch. professorship Ctrl. Mich. U., 1987, Rsch. grant NSF, 1992. Mem. Am. Phys. Soc., Am. Assn. Physics Tchrs., Soc. Sigma Xi. Home: Mount Pleasant, Mich. Died Dec. 30, 2009.

CURRIE, JAMES BRADFORD, aerospace consultant; b. Milw., Sept. 18, 1925; s. James Washburn and Lucille Bradford (Torrey) C.; m. Laura Betty Jensen; children by previous marriage: James S., Michael B. Student, U. Wis., 1946-48; BBA, U. Mich., 1958; grad., Indsl. Coll. Armed Forces, 1970. Joined U.S. Air Force, 1943, advanced through grades to maj. gen., 1977, 468 combat missions as pilot Korea and Vietnam; assigned to Japan and Korea, 1948-51; assigned to Air Research Devel. Command U.S. Air Force, 1952-57; served in France, 1958-62, India, Iran, Norway, Turkey, Zaire, 1962-64, Vietnam, 1964-65, Germany, 1966-69; assigned Hdqrs. U.S. Air Force, Washington, 1970-78, dir. programs, 1977-78; ret., 1979; cons. to aerospace industries, from 1979. Decorated D.S.M., D.F.C., Air medal with 12 oak leaf clusters, Legion of Merit, Bronze Star, others. Mem. Air Force Assn., Order Daedalions. Clubs: Army-Navy Country. Presbyterian. Died Sept. 20, 2009.

CURRY, BERNARD FRANCIS, former banker, consultant; b. NYC, Aug. 8, 1918; s. John F. and Mary F. (McKiernan) C.; m. Lorraine Vocco Kelly, Sept. 10, 1947; 1 child, Catherine V. AB, Coll. Holy Cross, 1939; JD, Columbia U., 1942. Bar: N.Y. 1946. Sec. to Surrogate Delehanty, New York County, 1946-47; assoc. Davis Polk Wardwell, Sunderl & Kendl, NYC, 1947-55; with Morgan Guaranty Trust Co. N.Y., NYC, 1955-84, sr. v.p., 1970-82; pres. Morgan Trust Co., Fla., 1982-84, dir. Fla., 1984-91, J.P. Morgan, Fla., from 1994. Adv. council Labor Dept., 1976-79. V.p., bd. dirs. Dom Mocquereau Found., N.Y.C., 1967-96; trustee W. Alton Jones Found., Flower Hosp., 1979-82, W. Alton Jones Cell Soc. Ctr., 1980-97, Harry I. Etelman Found., 1985—, Mary Alice Fortin Child Care Found.; bd. dirs. Ireland Am. Arts Exch., 1984-95, Young Broadcasting Inc., 1994—. With AUS, 1942-46. Mem. Assn. Bar City N.Y., Am. Bankers Assn. (pres. trust divsn. 1979-80) Clubs: Knight of Malta. Home: Palm Beach, Fla. Died Oct. 16, 2009.

CURTIN, DENNIS JAMES, medical supply company executive; b. NYC, July 29, 1947; s. James Vincent and Anne (Fischer) C.; m. Geraldine Ann Riva, June 30, 1973; children: Elizabeth, Margaret, Ann. BA in Econs., Iona Coll., 1969, MBA in Fin., 1972. Mgmt. trainee Fed. Res. Bank N.Y., NYC, 1969-71; various positions with, ending as plant mgr. Continental Group (Continental Can Co.), NYC, 1972-78; various positions with, ending as mgr. corp. acctg. Clairol div. Bristol Myers, NYC, 1978-83; v.p., chief fin. officer E-Z-EM Inc., Westbury, N.Y., from 1983. Bd. dirs. E-Z-EM Internat., St. Thomas, V.I., E-Z-EM Caribe, San Lorenzo, P.R., E-Z-EM Pa., Phila. Mem. Nat. Assn. Accts. Republican. Roman Catholic. Avocations: skiing, boating, reading. Home: Westhampton Beach, NY. Died July 3, 2010.

CURTIS, TONY (BERNARD SCHWARTZ), actor; b. NYC, June 3, 1925; s. Manuel and Helen (Klein) Schwartz; m. Janet Leigh, June 4, 1951 (div. 1963); children: Kelly, Jamie Lee; m. Christine Kaufmann, Feb. 8, 1963 (div. 1967); children: Alexandra, Allegra; m. Leslie Allen, Apr. 20, 1968 (div. 1982); children: Nicholas (dec. 1994), Benjamin; m. Andrea Savio, 1984 (div. 1992); m. Lisa Deutsch, Feb. 28, 1993 (div. 1994); m. Jill Vandenberg, Nov. 6, 1998. Student drama, New Sch. Social Rsch. Actor: (films) Criss Cross, 1948, City Across the River, 1949, Flesh and Fury, 1952, Houdini, 1953, Black Shield of Falworth, 1954, Six Bridges to Cross, 1955, So This is Paris, 1954, Trapeze, 1956, Mister Cory, 1957, Sweet Smell of Success, 1957, Midnight Story, 1957, The Vikings, 1958, Defiant Ones, 1958 (Acad. award nomination for best actor), Some Like It Hot, 1959, Perfect, Furlough, 1958, Spartacus, 1960, The Great Imposter, 1960, Pepe, 1960, The Outsider, 1961, Taras Bulba, 1962, Forty Pounds of Trouble, 1962, Paris When it Sizzles, 1964, The List of Adrian Messenger, 1963, Captain Newman, 1963, Wild and Wonderful, 1964, Sex and the Single Girl, 1964, Goodbye Charlie, 1964, The Great Race, 1965, Boeing, Boeing, 1965, Arriverderci, Baby, 1966, Not with My Wife, You Don't, 1966, Don't Make Waves, 1967, Boston Strangler, 1968, Lepke, 1975, The Bad News Bears Go to Japan, 1978, The Manitou, 1978, Sextette, 1978, Little Miss Marker, 1980, The Mirror Crack'd, 1980, Venom, 1982, Brainwaves, 1983, Insignificance, 1985, Club Life, 1986, The Last of Philip Banter, 1988, Midnight, 1989, Lobster Man from Mars, 1990, Prime Target, 1991, Center of the Web, 1992, Naked in New York, 1994, The Immortals, 1995, The Celluloid Closet, 1995, Louis & Frank, 1997, Brittle Glory, 1997, Alien X Factor, 1997, Stargames, 1998, Reflections of Evil, 2002, (voice only) The Blacksmith and the Carpenter, 2007, David & Fatima, 2008; (TV series) The Persuaders, 1971-72, McCoy, 1975-76, Vegas, 1978-81; (TV films) The Users, 1978, Moviola: The Scarlet O'Hara War, 1980, The Million Dollar Face, 1981, The Second Girl on the Right, 1985, Mafia Princess, 1986, Christmas in Connecticut, 1992; author: (novel) Kid Andrew Cody and Julie Sparrow, 1977, (with Barry Paris) Tony Curtis: An Autobiography, 1993, (with Peter Golenbock) American Prince: A Memoir, 2008 Served in USN, 1942—45. Recipient Golden Globe award World Film Favorite-Male, 1957, Most Popular Male Star award, Photoplay Awards, 1958, Bambi award, 1958, 1973, Golden Globe award World Film Favorite-Male, 1960, USA Film Festival Master Screen Artist award, 1992, Desert Palm Achievement award, Palm Springs Internat. Film Festival, 1995, "The General" Hon. award, Sitges - Catalonian Internat. Film Festival, 2000, Spl. David award, David di Donatello Awards, 2001, Golden Camera for Lifetime Achievement, Golden Camera, Germany, 2004, Lifetime Achievement award, Empire Awards, UK, 2006, Grand Prix Spl. des Amériques, Montéal World Film Festival, 2008. Died Sept. 29, 2010.

CUSANOVICH, MICHAEL ANTHONY, biochemist; b. LA, Mar. 2, 1942; s. Lucien Anthony and Elizabeth Ruth (McElroy) C.; m. Carol Owens Raiter, June 15, 1963 (div. May 1973); children: Kurt Michael, Carrie Elizabeth; m. Marilyn Jean Wainio Halonen, Mar. 31, 1980; 1 child, Darren Anthony. BS, U. of the Pacific, Stockton, Calif., 1963; PhD, U. Calif.-San Diego, La Jolla, 1967. Asst. prof. chemistry U. Ariz., Tucson, 1969-74, assoc. prof., 1974-79, prof. biochemistry, 1979—2005, Regents prof. biochemistry, from 2005, acting vice dean grad. coll., 1987-88, v.p. rsch., 1988-98, interim provost, 1992. Program dir. NSF, Washington, 1981-82; cons. Univ. Patents, Inc., Westport, Conn., 1983-88. Contbr. over 285 articles to profl. jours. Mem. Rep. Nat. Com, Washington, 1980—. Rsch. grantee NSF, 1970—, NIH, 1970—, NIH Career Devel. awardee, 1975-80. Republican. Avocations: tennis, golf, skiing, model building. Home: Tucson, Ariz. Died Apr. 12, 2010.

CUTLIP, RANDALL BROWER, retired psychologist, university president emeritus; b. Clarksburg, W.Va., Oct. 1, 1916; s. M.N. and Mildred (Brower) C.; m. Virginia White, Apr. 21, 1951; children: Raymond Bennett, Catherine Baumgarten. AB, Bethany Coll., 1940; cert. indsl. pers. mgmt., So. Meth.

U., 1944; MA, East Tex. U., 1949; EdD, U. Houston, 1953; LLD, Bethany Coll., 1965, Columbia Coll., 1980; LHD, Drury Coll., 1975; ScD, S.W. Bapt. U., 1978; LittD, William Woods U., 1981. Tchr. adminstr. Tex. pub. sch., 1947-50; dir. tchr. placement U. Houston, 1950-51, supr. counselling, 1951-53; dean students Atlantic Christian Coll., Wilson, NC, 1953-56, dean, 1956-58; dean personnel, dir. grad. divsn. Chapman U., Orange, Calif., 1958-60; pres. William Woods Coll., Fulton, Mo., 1960-81, pres. emeritus, from 1981; trustee William Woods U., Fulton, Mo., 1981-85 and from 92. Chmn. bd. dirs. Mo. Colls. Fund, 1973-75; chmn. Mid-Mo. Assn. Coll., 1972-76; bd. dir. Marina del Sol, bd. pres., 1985-90, 92-95. Mem. visitors' bd. Mo. Mil. Acad., 1966-70, chmn., 1968-72; trustee Schreiner Coll., Kerrville, Tex., 1983-92, Amy Shelton McNutt Charitable Trust, 1983—, Permanent Endowment Fund, 1987-96, Scholarship Found. and Res. Fund of Christian Ch., 1992-96, Christian Found., 1990—; bd. dir. Univ. of the Americas, 1984-96, exec. v.p., 1985-96; bd. dirs. Tex. State Aquarium, 1994, exec. com., 1994—, pres. 1998; elder emeritus Christian Ch., bd. dir., exec. com. Recipient McCubbin award, 1968, Delta Beta Xi award, 1959 Mem. Am. Pers. and Guidance Assn., Alpha Sigma Phi, Phi Delta Kappa, Kappa Delta Pi, Alpha Chi. Died May 21, 2010.

DACEY, KATHLEEN RYAN, lawyer, former federal judge; b. Boston; m. William A. Dacey (dec. Aug. 1986); 1 child, Mary Dacey White AB with honors, Emmanuel Coll., 1941; MS in L.S., Simmons Coll., 1942; JD, Northeastern U., 1945; postgrad., Boston U. Law Sch., 1945-46; LLD (hon.), Suffolk Law Sch., 1990, Emmanuel Coll., 1992. Bar: Mass. 1945, U.S. Supreme Ct. 1957. Law clk. to justices Mass. Supreme Jud. Ct., 1945-47; Practiced in Boston, 1947-75; asst. dist. atty. Suffolk County, Mass., 1971-72, Mass., 1971-72; auditor, master Commonwealth of Mass., Boston, 1972-75, Suffolk and Norfolk Counties, Mass., 1972-75; asst. atty. gen., chief civil bur. Mass. Dept. Atty. Gen., Boston, 1975-77; U.S. adminstrv. law judge Commonwealth of Mass., Boston, 1977-99; of counsel Cushing & Dolan P.C., Mass., from 1999; asst. dist. atty. Suffolk County, Mass., 1971-72. Mem. panel def. counsel for indigent persons U.S. Dist. Ct. Dist. Mass.; lectr., speaker in field Contbr. articles to profl. jours. Bd. dirs. Mission United Neighborhood Improvement Team, Boston; mem. Boston Sch. Com., 1945-46, chmn., 1946-47 Recipient Silver Shingle award Boston U. Sch. Law, 1980; named Alumnae Woman of Yr., Northeastern U. Law Sch. Assn., 1976 Mem. ABA (ho. of dels. 1982—, exec. com. conf. of adminstrv. law judges jud. adminstrn. divsn. 1987—), Internat. Bar Assn., Mass. Bar Assn., Boston Bar Assn., Norfolk Bar Lawyers Assn., Nat. Assn. Women Lawyers (pres.), Mass. Assn. Women Lawyers, Internat. Fedn. Women Lawyers, Boston U. Law Sch. Alumni Assn. (corr. sec. 1974-76), Boston U. Nat. Alumni Coun. Home: Milton, Mass. Died Apr. 5, 2010.

DADDARIO, EMILIO QUINCY, retired lawyer, former United States Representative from Connecticut; b. Newton Centre, Mass., Sept. 24, 1918; s. Attilio Dante and Julia (Ciovacco) D.; m. Berenice Mary Carbo, Oct. 20, 1940 (dec. 2007); children: Edward, Stephen, Richard. BA, Wesleyan U., 1939; LLB, U. Conn, 1942; DSc, Wesleyan U., 1967; LLD, Rensselaer Polytech. Inst., Troy, NY, 1967, Phila. Coll. Osteo. Medicine, 1976. Bar: Conn., Mass., D.C. Judge Middletown Mcpl. Ct., Conn., 1948-50; mem. US Congress from 1st Conn. Dist., 1959—71; dir. Office Tech. Assessment, Washington, 1973-77; mem. Wilkes, Artis, Hedrick & Lane, Washington, 1977-87. Vis. prof. MIT, Cambridge, 1970-71; co-chmn. ABA-AAAS Conf. of Lawyers and Scientists, Washington, 1976-88. Contbr. articles on sci. policy to profl. publs. Mayor, City of Middletown, Conn., 1946-48; mem. Commn. on Sci., Engring. and Pub. Policy, Nat. Acad. Scis., Washington; trustee Wesleyan U.; adv. bd. Georgetown U. Sch. of Nursing. Served to maj., inf. U.S. Army, 1942-45, 50-52, ETO, PTO, Korea. Decorated Legion of Merit; Medaglia D'Argento (Italy). Mem. Silver Anniversary All-Am. Football Team, 1964; recipient Ralph Coats Roe award ASME, 1974; honor award and medal Stevens Inst. Tech., 1975; Pub. Welfare award Nat. Acad. Scis., 1976; Disting. Svc. award Nat. Sci. Found., 1990, W.R. Grace award Am. Cham. Soc., 1992. Mem. ABA, AAAS (pres. 1977, chmn. 1978, chmn. governance com. 1989-90), Inst. Medicine (bd. health sci. policy 1991-97), D.C. Bar Assn., Oak Ridge Associated Univs. (bd. dirs. 1991-97), Nat. Acad. Sci. (com. nat. forum on sci. and tech. goals 1995), Vets of OSS. Clubs: Cosmos (Washington). Democrat. Roman Catholic. Home: Washington, DC. Died July 7, 2010.

DAENZER, BERNARD JOHN, insurance company executive, consultant; b. NYC, Jan. 15, 1916; s. Bernard Cornelius and Amelia Catherine (Heinze) D.; m. Valerie Antoinette Lee, June 8, 1941 (dec. Feb. 29, 2004); children: Peter, Jean Daenzer Aiken, John, Richard (dec.). AB, Fordham Coll., 1937, JD, 1942; LLD, Coll. Ins. NYC, 1981. Spl. agt. Loyalty Group, Westchester, NY, 1937-43; with Security-Conn. Group, 1943-57, exec. v.p., 1955-57; pres. Wohlreich & Anderson Ltd., Cranford, NJ, 1957-81. Dir. Alexander Howden Group Ltd., London, 1968-81; underwriter Lloyds of London, 1968-04; dir. emeritus RLI Corp., Peoria, Ill., 1972-07. Columnist: Weekly Underwriter, 1964-86; author 11 books, also other publs. and mystery stories. Trustee Loman Found., Malvern, Pa. Served with USNR, 1944-46. Mem.: Soc. Chartered Property and Casualty Underwriters, Coll. Ins. N.Y.C., Racquet Club, Card Sound Country Club, Ocean Reef Club. Republican. Roman Catholic. Home: Key Largo, Fla. Died Mar. 20, 2010.

DAHM, DOUGLAS BARRETT, b. Buffalo, Apr. 12, 1928; s. J. Earle and Beatrice (Peck) Dahm; m. Jay Goodall, Dec. 24, 1959; children: Doni Lee, Mark Barrett, Douglas Kurt. BSME, Northwestern U., 1950; postgrad. in engring. mgmt., George Washington U., 1958—63; M in Engring., SUNY Buffalo, 1964. Registered profl. engr., N.Y. Asst. chemist Bell & Howell, 1945—46; exec. trainee Caterpillar Tractor Co., Peoria, Ill., 1946—51; staff scientist Calspan Corp. (formerly Cornell Aero. Lab., Inc.), Buffalo, 1955—65; program mgr. Calspan Corp., Buffalo, 1965—70, head dept. environment, 1970—75; v.p. plans and programs Calspan Field Svcs., Buffalo, 1978—81, v.p. space programs, from 1981. Contbr. articles to profl. jours. With USAF, 1950—55. Decorated D.F.C., Bronze Star with V device, 3 Air medals. Mem.: AIAA (C31 com.), N.Y. Acad. Scis. (past pres. and dir.), Orgn. for Devel. Rsch. (dir. 1975—76), U.S. Environment and Resource Coun., Buffalo C. of C., Air Force Assn., Old Crows, Derby Tennis Club, New Concord Ski Club, Wanakah Country Club, Sigma Alpha Epsilon. Achievements include patents in field. Died Aug. 14, 2009.

DAIL, HILDA LEE, psychotherapist; b. Franklin Springs, Ga., Aug. 23, 1920; d. Ransom Harvey and Mattie (Gray) Lee; m. Francis Roderick Dail, Dec. 27, 1941; children: Janice Sylvia, Roderick Lee. BA, Piedmont Coll., 1941; PhD, The Union Inst., 1979. Cert. expressive therapist. Tchr. pub. schs., N.C., Tenn. and Ga., 1939-54; assoc. sec. Bd. of Missions, Methodist Ch., New York, 1954-60; dir. pub. rels. and tchr. Leonard Theol. Coll., Jabalpur, India, 1960-64; editor lit. Bd. of Missions, United Meth. Ch., NYC, 1964-70; exec. dir. Int. Found. Ewha Women's Univ., Seoul, Republic of Korea, 1970-71; dir. devel. Ch. Women United, 1971-73; dir. resources cen. nat. bd. YWCA, 1973-75; pres. Hilda Lee Dail & Assoc. Internat., NYC, 1975-83, Myrtle Beach, S.C., from 1983. Mem. adj. faculty Coastal Carolina U., Conway, 1981-95, Webster U., Myrtle Beach, 1981—; bd. dirs. Enablement Inc., Boston, 1975-89, Assn. Coop. Agys. Asian Women's Coll., 1971-85; founder, pres. Internat. Ctr. for Creativity and Consciousness, 1989—. Author: Decision and Destiny, 1957, Encounters Extraordinary, 1969, Let's Try a Workshop With Teen Women, 1974, The Lotus and the Pool, 1983, How to Create Your Own Career, 1989, 2d. edit. 1999. Dir. Citizens Against Spouse Abuse, Myrtle Beach, 1982-88, pres. Gotham Bus. and Prof. Women's Club, N.Y., 1978, dir. Green Chimney Sch., N.Y., 1978-83, v.p., Zonta Internat., N.Y., 1976-84. Fellow Nat. Expressive Therapy Assn. (speaker 1983-89); mem. ASTD (bd. dirs. 1972-89), Mental Health Assn. (bd. dirs., pres. 1988-89). Democrat. United Methodist. Avocations: theater, ballet, opera, travel. Died Feb. 22, 2009.

DALBERG, PAUL EVERETT, architect, planner, consultant; b. Chgo., Apr. 21, 1938; s. Garfield T. and Helen J. (Person) D.; m. Barbara B. Egr, Aug. 14, 1948; 1 child, Kimberly Dawn. AS, U. Nebr., Omaha, 1967. Registered architect, Ill., Wis. Architect The Salvation Army, Camplake, Wis., 1967-69, Thomas/Roche & Assocs., Camplake, 1969-70, O'Donnell/Wicklund/Pigozzi, Northbrook, Ill., 1970-71, Environment Seven Ltd., Chgo., 1971-79, John D. Hiltscher & Assocs., Chgo., 1979-83; cons. Assocs. Cons., Oak Park, Ill., from 1983. Program and devel. adv. Anchor No. 1, New World Christian Ministries. Served with U.S. Army, 1962-65. Mem. AIA, Ill. Chpt. Nat. Org. Minority Architects, Interfaith Forum on Religion, Art and Architecture, Am. Planning Assn., Am. Soc. Interiors, Designers (assoc.), Constrn. Specification Inst., NAACP, Nat. Trust for Hist. Preservation. Avocations: sports, nature, community services. Home: Janesville, Wis. Died June 19, 2010.

DALEY, MICHAEL LEO, electrical engineering educator; b. Brighton, Mass., May 16, 1942; s. James Joseph and Agnes (Halisey) D.; m. Carol Donna Place, Dec. 28, 1968; 1 child, Leah Diana. BSEE, U. Mass., 1968; MSEE, U. Rochester, 1970, PhD, 1973. Postdoctoral fellow Good Samaritan Hosp., Portland, Oreg., 1973-74; instr. Oreg. Health Sci. U., Portland, 1974-76, assoc., 1976-78, instr., 1978-79; asst. prof. U. Memphis, 1979-87, assoc. prof., 1988-95, prof. elec. engring., from 1995. Cons. Prentice Hall, Englewood Cliffs, N.J., 1993, 96. Contbr. over 50 articles to profl. publs. Sec. Citizens Planning Orgn., Portland, 1985-86. With USAF, 1960-64. Fellow Tenn. Acad. Sci. (pres. elect. 1996, pres. 1997); mem. IEEE (Outstanding Engr. award 1996, sr. mem.), Sigma Xi. Roman Catholic. Achievements include patents in field of ophthalmological, neurology and neurosurgical applications. Home: Germantown, Tenn. Died Feb. 8, 2010.

DALLOW, PHYLLIS FLORENCE, realtor; b. NJ, Nov. 17, 1924; d. Harry and Pauline (Isaacson) Lash; m. Theodore J. Dallow, July 30, 1944; children: Ellen Poor, Richard, Constance. Student, CCNY, 1944. V.p., relocation dir., chief real estate mgmt. dept. Theodore J. Dallow Inc., Farmingdale, NY, 1952—82; pres. Century 21 Dallow Realty, Inc., Levittown, NY, from 1982. Pres. Levittown South-North Wantagh Rep. Club, 1972—73; committeewoman Rep. Com., 1964—69. Recipient Hon. Svc. award, Mademoiselle Mag., 1944. Mem.: Internat. Real Estate Fedn., Inst. Real Estate Mgmt., Nat. Assn. Realtors, L.I. Bd. Realtors, Order Ea. Star. Home: Farmingdale, NY. Died May 27, 2010.

DALY, CHARLES PATRICK, publishing company executive; b. Bayonne, NJ, Dec. 14, 1930; s. Charles Edward and Catherine Agnes (McGuinness) D.; m. Barbara Dempsey, July 23, 1955 (div. 1977); children: Seton, Elise, Phyllis, Charles P. Jr., Shelagh; m. Jane Hocker, Oct. 29, 1978. BS, St. Peter's Coll., Jersey City, 1953. Account exec. Paul Klemptner & Co., NYC, 1964-66, R.A. Becker & Co., NYC, 1966; pub. RN Mag., Oradell, N.J., 1966-69, Med. Econs., Oradell, 1969-71; exec. v.p. Litton Pub. Co., Oradell, 1971-74, pres., 1974-75; v.p. Litton Industries Inc., Oradell, 1975-81; chmn., chief exec. officer Med. Econs. Co. Inc., Oradell, 1981-85; pres. chief exec. officer Internat. Thomson Bus. Info., Teaneck, N.J., 1985-90; adj. prof. New York U., N.Y., from 1990. Bd. dirs. Bus. Publs. Audit Inc., N.Y.C. Mem. Assn. Bus. Publs. (bd. dirs. 1974-81, 85-90, chmn. 1978-79), Balusrol Golf Club, Short Hills Club. Presbyterian. Avocation: golf. Home: Basking Ridge, NJ. Died July 25, 2009.

DALY, MARY F., feminist philosopher; b. Schenectady, NY, Oct. 16, 1928; AB, Coll. St. Rose, Albany, NY; AM, Cath. U.; STL, STD, PhD, U. Fribourg; PhD in Religion, U. Notre Dame. Assoc. prof. theology Boston Coll., 1967—99. Author: The Church and the Second Sex, 1968, 3rd rev. edit., 1985, Beyond God the Father: Toward a Philosophy of Women''s Liberation, 1973, 2nd edit. rev., 1985, Gyn/Ecology: The Metaethics of Radical Feminism, 1979, Pure Lust: Elemental Feminist Philosophy, 1984, Websters' New Intergalactic Wickedary of the English Language, 1987, Outercourse: The Bedazzling Voyage, Containing Recollections from My Logbook of a Radical Feminist Philosopher, 1993, Quintessence-...Realizing the Archaic Future: A Radical Elemental Feminist Manifesto, 1998, Amazing Grace: Recalling the Courage to Sin Big, 2006. Died Jan. 3, 2010.

DALY, WILLIAM GERALD, business executive; b. McKeesport, Pa., Sept. 13, 1924; s. William P. and Helen J. (McGowan) D.; m. Jean F. Wandrisco, June 24, 1950; 1 dau., Kathleen Jean. BS in Chem. Engring, Worcester Poly. Inst., 1946; BS in Indsl. Mgmt, Carnegie Mellon U., 1951; postgrad., Columbia U. Exec. Mgmt. Sch. Mfg. exec. Procter & Gamble, 1954-66; v.p. mfg. Heublein, Inc., Hartford, Conn., 1967-73; v.p. Riviana Foods, Inc., Houston, 1973-74; pres. Hills div. Riviana Foods, Topeka, 1974-80; pres. Gen. Plastics, Inc., Miami, Fla., 1980-82. Pres., owner BJ Restaurants, Inc., Key Largo, Fla., 1980—, WGD Assoc., Key Largo, 1979—; assoc. Bruckner Group Author: The Management Challenge, 1980. Served with USN, 1944-46, 52-54. Mem. Pet Food Inst. (dir.), Am. Pet Products Mfg. Assn. (dir.), C. of C. Clubs: Ocean Reef, Ocean Reef Yacht, Racquet at Ocean Reef. Republican. Roman Catholic. Died Oct. 6, 2009.

DANCIS, JOSEPH, pediatrics educator, researcher; b. NYC, Mar. 19, 1916; s. Abraham Goldberg and Sarah Dancis; m. Bernice Schrier, July 4, 1948; children: Andrew, Dale. AB, Columbia U., 1934; MD, St. Louis U., 1938. Intern Queens Gen. Hosp., N.Y., 1938-40; resident NYU-Bellevue Hosp., 1945-46; prof. pediatrics Sch. Medicine NYU, from 1960, chmn. dept. pediatrics, 1974-89. Cons. Nat. Inst. Child Health and Human Devel. NIH, 1971-78. Mem. edit. bds. sci. jours. Served to capt. Med. Service Corp. U.S. Army, 1941-45. John and Mary Markle scholar, 1956-61; NIH grantee, 1962-74; recipient nutrition studies award, Borden Co., 1966. Mem. Am. Pediatrics Soc. (council 1973-80, pres. 1983-84), Soc. Gynecol. Investigation (hon.), Alpha Omega Alpha. Home: New York, NY. Died Mar. 30, 2010.

DANIELS, GEORGE GOETZ, editor; b. Bklyn., Aug. 17, 1925; s. George Bryant and Katherine June (Goetz) D.; m. Doris Alden Billings, Dec. 19, 1965; 1 dau., Katherine Billings; children by previous marriage: Peter, Michael, Robert, Geoffrey. BA cum laude, Harvard U., 1949. Corr., Time mag., Detroit, 1949-50, contbg. editor, 1950-56, asso. editor, 1956-60, sr. editor, 1960-71; editor Time-Life Records, 1971-73; series editor Time-Life Books, 1973-82, exec. editor, from 1982. Served to 1st lt. USAAF, 1943-46. Mem. Am. Ornithologists Union, Am. Birding Assn. (dir.) Clubs: Harvard, Explorers, Bermuda Anglers. Home: Rockville, Md. Died July 7, 2010.

DANIELS, JANET VICTORIA, management analyst; b. Bay City, Mich., Apr. 19, 1943. A.A., Delta Coll., Mich., 1968; C.dA. U. Grenoble, France, 1969; B.S. cum laude, Mich. State U., 1971; M.S., So. Ill. U., 1975. Compliance officer U.S. Dept. Interior, Washington, 1972-77, program evaluation specialist Bur. Land Mgmt., 1978-79, spl. asst. Office of Asst. Sec., 1979-80, staff specialist for Alaska programs, 1980-81, mineral leasing specialist Bur. Land Mgmt., 1981-83; mgmt. analyst Nat. Park Service, Lakewood, Colo., 1984—; instr. Presdl. Classroom for Young Ams., 1976. Editor: Guide to Wind Cave National Park, 1984; author articles. Active Savs. Bonds campaigns. Mem. Nat. Trust Hist. Preservation (assoc.), Denver Art Mus. (assoc.), Historic Denver Soc., Natural History Assn. (life), Nat. Assn. Female Execs. Democrat. Avocations: sailing; golf; tennis; English saddle riding; antiques; gourmet cooking. Died Aug. 18, 2009.

DANIELS, ROBERT VINCENT, history professor, former state senator; b. Boston, Jan. 4, 1926; s. Robert Whiting and Helen Underwood (Hoyt) D.; m. Alice May Wendell, July 2, 1945; children: Robert H., Helen L. Turcotte, Irene L., Thomas L. AB, Harvard U., 1945, MA, 1947, PhD, 1951; LLD (hon.), U. Vt., 1994. Rsch. assoc. MIT, Cambridge, 1951-52; social sci. faculty Bennington (Vt.) Coll., 1952-53, 57-58; asst. prof. Slavic studies Ind. U., 1953-55; rsch. assoc. Columbia U., 1955-56; from asst. prof. history to prof. U. Vt., Burlington, 1956-88, prof. emeritus, 1988—2010, chmn. dept., 1964-69, dir. exptl. program, 1969-71; mem. Vt. Senate, 1973-82, asst. minority leader, 1977-80, minority leader, 1981-82. Chmn. Vt. Gov.'s Commn. Med. Care, 1974-75; mem. Vt. Health Policy Corp., 1977-80; mem. adv. com. on East Europe and USSR, Coun. on Internat. Exch. of Scholars, 1983-85; adv. coun. Ctr. for Internat. Polit. Studies, Rome, 1989-2010; mem. sister state com. Vt.-Karelia, 1991-2010, co-dir. self-govt. tng. program, 1993-94; dir. U. Vt. Petrozavodsk U. partnership program, 1994-95; mem. supervisory bd. Internat. Coop. Ctr. Karelian br. St. Petersburg Acad. Pub. Adminstrn. Author: The Conscience of the Revolution, 1960, Documentary History of Communism, 1960, rev. edit., 1993, The Nature of Communism, 1962, Studying History, 1966, Red October, 1967, The Russian Revolution, 1972, Fodor's Europe Talking, 1975, Russia-The Roots of Confrontation, 1985, Is Russia Reformable?, 1988, Year of the Heroic Guerrilla, 1989, Trotsky, Stalin and Socialism, 1992, The End of the Communist Revolution, 1993, Soviet Communism from Reform to Collapse, 1994, Russia's Transformation, 1997, The Fourth Revolution, 2005, The Rise and Fall of Communism in Russia, 2007; editor: The University of Vermont: The First Two Hundred Years, 1991. Mem. Chittenden County (Vt.) Dem. Com., 1959-2010; mem. Burlington City Dem. Com., 1965-2010; chmn. policy and planning platform com. Vt. Dem. Party, 1962-66, 69-73, 76-80, mem. exec. com., 1981-85; alt. Dem. Nat. Conv., 1968; mem. Dem. Platform Com., 1980; bd. visitors USAF Acad., 1965-67. Ensign USNR, 1944-46. U.S.-Soviet Cultural Exch. scholar U. Moscow, 1966, USSR Acad. Scis. scholar, 1976, 84, 88; NEH fellow, 1971-72, Guggenheim fellow, 1980-81, Kennan Inst. fellow, 1985. Fellow Vt. Acad. Arts and Scis.; mem. Am. Hist. Assn. (pres. conf. Slavic and East European history 1976-77), Am. Assn. Advancement Slavic Studies (bd. dirs. 1968-71, v.p. 1991, pres. 1992, chmn. com. on govt. affairs 1993-94, Disting. Contbns. award 2001), Can. Assn. Slavists, Authors' Guild, Vt. Hist. Soc. (trustee 1968-71), Vt. Coun. World Affairs, Norwich Ctr./Bridges for Peace (bd. dirs. 1988-94), Harvard Club Vt. (pres. 1974-75). Democrat. Home: Burlington, Vt. Died Mar. 28, 2010.

DANIELS, WORTH BAGLEY, JR., retired internist; b. NYC, Jan. 3, 1925; MD, Johns Hopkins U., 1948. From asst. med. rschr. to rschr. Balt. City Hosp., 1954-57; physician, assoc. prof. Johns Hopkins U., 1958-98; ret., 1998. Mem. AMA, ACP, Inst. Medicine-NAS, Am. Soc. Internal Medicine. Home: Baltimore, Md. Died July 9, 2009.

DANKO, JOSEPH CHRISTOPHER, metals engineer, university official; b. Homestead, Pa., Jan. 12, 1927; s. John and Anna Danko; m. Laverne Elizabeth Uramey, June 20, 1951; children: Christopher, Kimberly, Mark. BS in Metals Engring., Carnegie-Mellon U., 1951; MS in Metals Engring., Lehigh U., 1954, PhD in Metals Engring., 1955. Engr. GE Co., Schenectady, 1951-52, mgr. San Jose, Calif., 1964-78; instr. Lehigh U, Bethlehem, Pa., 1952-56; mgr. Westinghouse Electric Corp., Pitts., 1956-62; program mgr. Electric Power Rsch. Inst., Palo Alto, Calif., 1978-84, 1978-84; v.p. Am. Welding Inst., Knoxville, Tenn., 1984-86; dir. Ctr. for Materials Processing U. Tenn., Knoxville, from 1986; mem. corrosion adv. com. Electric Power Rsch. Inst., Palo Alto, Calif., 1974-78. Mem. tech. adv. com. MPC, N.Y.C., 1974-91; cons. Dupont Savannah River Lab., Aiken, S.C., 1986-91; cons. in field. Contbr. over 100 tech. papers to publs. Pres. Knoxville Dismas Project, Knoxville, 1987-89. Fellow Am. Soc. Metals; mem. AAAS, Nat. Assn. Corrosion Engrs., Am. Welding Soc., Am. Nuclear Soc. Achievements include patents in material processing; first demonstration of solar thermionic power system; first operation of nuclear thermionic thermoelectric device. Home: Vancouver, Wash. Died Aug. 20, 2009.

DANNENBERG, MARTIN ERNEST, retired insurance company executive; b. Balt., Nov. 5, 1915; s. Martin Ernest and Wilhelmina (Wilfson) D.; m. Esther Salzman, May 29, 1941 (dec. June 1989); children: Betsy, Richard; m. Margery Singer, Oct. 21, 1990; 1 child, Joan. Student, Johns Hopkins U., U. Balt. Law Sch. V.p. adminstrn., then sr. v.p., sec. Sun Life Ins. Co. America, 1966-76, vice chmn. bd., 1976-79, chmn. bd., 1979-87, chmn. emeritus, 1987—2010. Bd. dirs. Assoc. Placement and Guidance Bur., Balt. Urban Coalition, Balt. Goodwill Industries, Md. Life & Health Guaranty Assn., Balt. Choral Arts Soc., Sudden Infant Death Syndrome Inst., Levindale Geriat. Ctr. & Hosp.; mem. Mayor Balt. Adv. Com. Bus. Edn., Balt. County Phys. Fitness Commn., Md. Commn. Aging, Mayor Balt. Labor Market Adv. Commn.; assoc. gen. campaign chmn. United Way of Ctrl. Md.; exec. bd., v.p. Balt. coun. Boy Scouts Am.; v.p. Balt. City Coun. PTAs; exec. bd., v.p. N.W. Hosp. Ctr. With CIC, AUS, 1942-45, ETO. Decorated Bronze Star; named Disting. Citizen Md. Mem. Life Office Mgmt. Assn. (past chmn. combination co. com., systems and procedures council), Adminstrv. Mgmt. Soc. (past pres. Balt.), Life Insurers Conf., Nat. Assn. Life Cos., Am. Council Life Ins., Surburban Country Club, Center Club, Johns Hopkins Club. Home: Baltimore, Md. Died Aug. 18, 2010.

DARAZSDI, JAMES JOSEPH, food processing executive; b. Bethlehem, Pa., Feb. 13, 1949; s. George Edward and Anna (Venanzi) Darazsdi; m. Janet Beth Hughes, Aug. 29, 1970. BS, Fairleigh Dickinson U., 1971; MA, Goddard Coll., 1989; PhD, Union Inst., 1996. CPA Md., Va., cert. mgmt. acct. Sr. acct. Texaco, Inc., Atlanta, 1971—77; gen. acctg. mgr. Georgetown Tex. Steel, Beaumont, 1978—79; asst. corp. contr. Perdue, Inc., Salisbury, Md., 1980—81; v.p. fin. Rocco Enterprises, Harrisonburg, Va., 1982, exec. v.p., 1982—88; CEO, 1988. Bd. dirs. NBC. Bd. dirs. Bridgewater Coll., Elizabeth State U., James Madison U. Mem.: AICPA, Am. Mgmt. Assn., Exec. Planning Inst., Nat. Assn. Accts., Nat. Assn. Corp. Dirs., Va. Soc. CPAs. Home: Dudley, Mass. Died Nov. 17, 2009.

DARDEN, JOHN WALDON, III, small business owner; b. Conway, SC, Dec. 15, 1945; s. John Waldon and Hannah Ross (Smith) Darden; m. Susan Ann Wright, Nov. 18, 1971; children: Stuart L., Elizabeth Ross. BS in Bus., U. SC, 1969; student, Holland Sch. for Jewelers, 1976. Diamond cert. Gemological Inst. America, 1977. With Darden's Jewelers, from 1969, mgr. Lancaster, SC, 1969—73, Conway, SC, 1973—74, Myrtle Beach, SC, 1974—75; pres. Darden's Jewelers of Conway, Myrtle Beach, Lancaster, Georgetown, from 1975, Jewelry Outlet, Goldcrafters Outlet, Spartansburg, SC; master jeweler Holland Sch. for Jewelers; cons. Nat. Profl. Jewelers Inst. Housing commr. Conway Housing Authority; bd. dirs. Conway Downtown Coun. Mem.: Am. Gem Soc. (registered jeweler), Retail Jewelers America (coun. affiliated svcs.), SC Retail Jewelers Assn. (pres. 1975—77), Outlet Pk. Mchts. Assn. (pres.), SC Mchts. Assn. (past pres.), Conway C. of C., Lancaster Jaycees (bd. dirs., state dir., chmn., adminstrv. bd., fin. com.), Conway Lions Club (dir.), Lancaster Toastmasters Club. Democrat. Methodist. Home: Conway, SC. Died Apr. 16, 2010.

DARLING, ROBERT ENSIGN, JR., investment banker, consultant; b. Hartford, Conn., May 31, 1937; s. Robert Ensign and Virginia Kusterer (Young) Darling; m. Ardelle Darling; children: Elizabeth, Robert, Frederick. BA, Yale U., 1959; MA, Trinity Coll., 1968. Rsch. analyst Advest, Inc., Hartford, 1960—65; with Travelers' Ins. Co., Hartford, 1966—70; pres. Pinnacle Mountain Estates, Inc., Simsbury, Conn., 1971—82; sr. v.p. B.L. McTeague & Co., Simsbury, from 1972. Dir. Ensign Bickford Co., Simsbury Bank & Trust Co., No. Calif. Soccer, Ltd. Bd. trustees Bushnell Meml. Hall, from 1981, Hartford Symphony Orch., from 1970, Renbrook Sch., 1979—86, Roanoke Coll., from 1984. With US Army, 1960—61. Mem.: Univ. Club Misquamicut, Hartford Golf Club. Republican. Congregationalist. Home: Simsbury, Conn. Died Oct. 20, 2009.

DARROW, DEAN J., mechanical engineer, mineral leasing agent; b. Baraboo, Wis., Feb. 2, 1921; s. Harold A. and Lillian Agusta (Rodewald) Darrow; 1 child, Tobin Scott. Attended, St. Ambrose Coll., 1942; B.S.M.E., U. Wis., Madison, 1947; postgrad., UCLA, 1958. Registered profl. engr., Calif. Sr. test engr. Gen. Dynamics, San Diego, 1954—60; rsch. specialist Lockheed, Inc., Sunnyvale, Calif., 1960—62; Apollo project engr. Rockwell, Inc., Downey, Calif., 1963—68; cons. Land Use Planning, Spearfish, SD, 1968—73; securities rep. First Investors Corp., NYC, 1968—73; dir. Bellefish, Inc., Rapid City, SD, 1973—78; lease agt. Teledyne, Inc., Houston, 1978—82. Designer oilless cylinder air compressor, water cooled gas turbine. Contbr. articles to profl. jours. Dem. campaign leader, SD, 1967; survey leader SD, 1977. Mem.: AIAA, ASME (life), Elks Lodge. Unitarian Universalist. Avocations: golf, fishing, hunting. Died Jan. 2, 2009.

DAULT, RAYMOND ARTHUR, engineering educator; b. Muskegon, Mich., June 30, 1923; s. Joseph F. and Eloise M. (Grosselin) Dault; m. Joyce J. Martin, Oct. 19, 1946; 1 child, Suzanne Raye. AB, Mich. State U., 1950; MBA, Ind. U., 1969. Cert. food exec., hotel adminstr. Asst. reservation mgr. Bismarck Hotel, Chgo., 1950; asst. mgr. Ind. Meml. Union, Ind. U., Bloomington, 1950—53; mgr. Union Bldg. Med. Ctr., Indpls., 1953—70; assoc. prof. restaurant, hotel and instnl. mgmt. Ind.-Purdue U., Indpls., 1970—74, prof., from 1974, Frank E. Burley disting. prof. Sch. Engring. and Tech., from 1986; cons. Nat. Sanitation Found., Ann Arbor, 1970—72, Com. for a Quality Environ., 1970—73, Am. Hotel and Motel Assn., from 1968. Contbr. articles to profl. publs. Pres. Speedway (Ind.) Bd. Zoning Appeals, 1959—63; trustee Speedway Sch., 1988. With US Army, 1943—46. Recipient Keys award, NYC, 1968, New Orleans, 1968, Elizabethtown, Ky., 1968, 1968, Award, Oklahoma City, 1974, Indpls., 1974, Cleve., 1975, Cin., 1975, Louisville, 1975, South Bend, 1978, Hon. Order of Ky. Cols., Outstanding Faculty Mem. award, Purdue U. Sch. Engring. and Tech., Indpls., 1976, 1981, Key to City of Indpls.Key to City of Indpls., 1984; named Coll. and U. Food Operator of Yr., Internat. Foodservice Mfrs. Assn., 1970, Alumnus of Yr., Mich. State U. Sch. Hotel, Restaurant and Instnl. Mgmt., 1972, Hall of Fame civic category Civil Town of Speedway, 1978. Mem.: KC, Am. Legion, Mich. State U. Motel and Restaurant Alumni Assn. (pres. 1970—73), Assn. Coll. Unions Internat., Indpls. Hotel and Motel Assn. (exec. v.p.), Ind. Hotel and Motel Assn. (exec. v.p.), Nat. Restaurant Assn., Lions. Home: Indianapolis, Ind. Died Aug. 14, 2009.

DAVENPORT, ROBERT RALSEY, writer; b. Brookline, Mass., Apr. 30, 1950; s. Harry Augustus and Jean Ann (Yeager) D. BA, Middlebury Coll., 1972; JD, St. John's U., NYC, 1979; MBA, Harvard U., 1984; MFA in Screenwriting, UCLA, 1999. Bar: N.Y. 1980, Calif. 1988. Atty. U.S. Dept. Justice, Washington, 1979-81, Office Gen. Counsel Dept. Navy, Washington, 1981-82; creative exec. Twentieth Century-Fox Film Corp., LA, Calif., 1983, Columbia Broadcasting System, LA, 1984-85, Viacom Prodns., LA, 1986-87; dir. bus. affairs New World TV, LA, 1987-88; exec. v.p. Soaring Eagle Prodns., LA, 1988-89; pres. The Historic Trust, LA, from 1992. Author: The Davenport Genealogy, 1982, Hereditary Society Blue Book, 1992, 94, 95, 96, 97, 98, 99, 2000, Rich and Famous Baby Name Book, 1994, Pet Names of The Rich and Famous, 1995, The Celebrity Almanac, 1995, The Celebrity Birthday Book, 1996, Roots of the Rich and Famous, 1998. Lt. col. JAGC, U.S. Army; lt. USN. Mem. Soc. of Cincinnati (past pres. Calif. chpt.), DAV (life), Order of Indian Wars of U.S., Aztec Club of 1847, VFW (life), Mil. Order of the Purple Heart (life). Home: Los Angeles, Calif. Died July 1, 2010.

DAVENPORT, THOMAS IRA, lawyer, lobbyist; b. Kingston, Pa., Apr. 30, 1923; s. Stephen Ira and Alice May (Hopkins) D.; m. Dorothy Mae Christie, Nov. 11, 1923; children: Christie Lee Davenport Kauffman, Allison Ann Davenport Morrison, Barbara Dorothy. BA in Sci., Pa. State U., 1944, BS in Physics, 1947, MS in Physics, 1951; JD, George Washington U., 1955. Bar: Mich., U.S. Ct. Appeals (2d, 3d, Fed. cirs.). Physicist Mound Lab. AEC, Miamisburg, Ohio, 1947-49, Nat. Bur. Standards, Washington, 1951-55; patent counsel GE Rsch. Lab., Schenectady, N.Y., 1955-56, The Budd Co., Phila., 1956-72, corp. counsel Troy, Mich., 1972-84, v.p., gen. counsel, from 1984. Treas. citizenship com. The Budd Co., 1976—; dir. adv. com. Product Liability Coun., Detroit, 1989—, lobbyist 1980—, pres. N.Am. subcom. Author, co-author handbook, radio and TV scriptsob product liability; patentee in field. Active Lawyers for Civil Justice, Nat. Legal Ctr. for Pub. Interest. Lt (j.g.) USNR, 1944-46. Mem. Pa. Bar. Assn., Mich. Bar Assn., D.C. Bar Assn., Am. Corp. Coun. Assn. (founding dir.). Republican. Avocations: skiing, sailing, ballooning, radio control gliders. Home: Birmingham, Mich. Died Aug. 19, 2009.

DAVEY, LYCURGUS MICHAEL, neurosurgeon; b. NYC, Feb. 20, 1918; s. Michael Marco and Elizabeth (Delaveris) D.; m. Artemis Diana Pappas, June 7, 1942 (dec. Aug. 2003); children: Michael Dean, Elaine Anne, Elizabeth. BA, Yale U., 1939, MD, 1943. Diplomate Am. Bd. Neurol. Surgery, 1954. Surg. intern New Haven Hosp., 1943-44, asst. resident in surgery, 1946-50, William Harvey Cushing fellow, 1947-48, resident neurosurgeon, 1951-52; asst. resident in neurosurgery Hartford Hosp., 1950-51; clin. clk. Nat. Hosp., London, summer 1954; clin. instr. neurosurgery Yale U., 1952-60, asst. clin. prof., 1960-68, asso. clin. prof., 1968-77, clin. prof., from 1977. Assoc. fellow Trumbull Coll. Yale U., 1959—; cons. practice in neurosurgery New Haven, 1952-2002; emeritus staff Mid State Med. Ctr. (formerly Vets Meml. Med. Ctr.); emeritus Hosp. St. Raphael; hon. staff mem. Yale-New Haven Med. Ctr., 1952-01, pres. med. staff, 1971-72, assoc. sect. chief, 1954-91, emeritus, 1991-2001, hon. staff mem., 2002-; bd. dirs. Tex. Citrus Found. Editl. bd. historian Neurosurgery. Class sec. Yale U. Class of 1939, 1999—. Served to comdr. USNR, 1942-46, 52-54; capt. Res. ret. 1973. Fellow ACS, Internat. Coll. Surgeons; mem. AMA, Naval War Coll. Found., Inc. (life), U.S. Naval Inst. (life), Naval Res. Assn. (life), Navy League of U.S. (life), Conn. Med. Soc. (chmn. sect. on neurosurgery 1971-72), Conn. Soc. Neurol. Surgeons (hon. spkr. 2000), New Haven County Med. Soc. (pres. 1987), New Haven Med. Assn. (pres. 1972), Am. Assn. Neurol. Surgeons, New Eng. Neurosurg. Soc., Congress Neurol. Surgeons (mem. editl. bd., historian Neurosurgery 2001—, Disting. Svc. award 1966), Assn. Rsch. in Nervous and Mental Diseases, Soc. Med. Cons. to Armed Forces, Assn. Yale Alumni in Medicine (pres. 1995-97, Disting. Alumni Svc. award 1997, Peter Parker, M.D. Dean's medal 2003). Home: New Haven, Conn. Died June 15, 2009.

DAVIDSON, DAVID ROBERT, organist, conductor; b. Middletown, Ohio, Sept. 25, 1948; s. William R. and Florence L. Davidson; m. Judith Anne, Aug. 1, 1970; children: Christopher Allan, Jena Michelle. MusB, U. Cin., 1970. Band dir. West Clermont Pub. Schs., Ohio, 1970—75; band dir., supr. music Lebanon City Schs., Ohio, 1975—79; ch. musician Mt. Carmel Presbyn. Ch., 1975—79, Kennedy Heights Presbyn. Ch., 1975—79, Lebanon United Meth. Ch., 1975—79; minister music Northminster Presbyn. Ch., Cin., 1979—85, handbell, choral and ch. music clinician, 1979—85; dir. music Highland Park Presbyn. Ch., Dallas, from 1985; dir. Dallas Symphony Chorus, from 1993. Adj. instr. Handbells Perking Theol. Sem. So. Meth. U. Founder; mus. dir. Dallas Handbell Ensemble; chmn. worship and choral music com. Mem.: Am. Choral Dir.'s Assn., Am. Guild Organists, Choristers Guild, Presbyn. Assn. Musicians, Am. Guild English Handbell Ringers. Home: Dallas, Tex. Died Sept. 5, 2009.

DAVIDSON, FRED, III, manufacturing executive; b. Indpls., Oct. 3, 1941; s. Fred D. and Frances Louise (Lawler) Williams; m. Evelyn G. DeVane, July 30, 1966 (div. Sept. 1969); children: La Shavon, Freddia Gaynelle; m. Regenia Bridgeforth, Aug. 20, 1970. BA, Central State U., Wilberforce, Ohio, 1965; L.H.D. (hon.), Nat. U., Vista, Calif., 1983. White House intern Dept. Treasury, Washington, 1959-63; zone mgr. Ford Motor Co., Indpls., 1969-77; govt. account rep. Xerox Corp., Indpls., 1977-80; v.p. Metro Fin. Group Ltd., Chgo., 1980-81; dep. asst. sec. Dept. Navy, Washington, 1981-85; prin. Davidson and Assocs., Washington, 1985-88; dir. govt. sales Action Systems Techs., Inc., Indpls., from 1988; exec. recruiter R.E. Lowe Assocs., Indpls., from 1989. Bd. dirs. Greater Indpls. Housing Devel. Corp., 1978; pres. fin. bd. Washington Twp. (Ind.) Bd., 1979-81; trustee U.S. Naval Acad. Found., 1983—. Served to 1st lt. USMC, 1966-69, Vietnam; served to lt. col. USMCR, 1970—. Decorated Cross of Gallantry Vietnam, Naval order of the U.S., Army Commendation medal; recipient Meritorious Pub. Service award U.S. Dept. Transp. U.S. Coast Guard, Disting. Civilian Service award U.S. Navy; granted Knighthood, Sovreign Mil. Order of Temple of Jerusalem, Oslo. Mem. VFW, Marine Corps Res. Officers Assn., Montford Point Marine Assn. (pres. Indpls. chpt. 1977-78), Montford Point Marines Assn. (pres. Chgo. chpt. 1980-82), Res. Officers Assn., Naval Res. Assn., Am. Legion, Navy League of U.S., Ret.Officers Assn., Fleet Res. Assn., Naval Enlisted Res. Assn., Kappa Alpha Psi; life mem. NAACP (bd. dirs. 1975-77). Clubs: U.S. Senatorial. Lodges: Masons; Shriners. Republican. Methodist. Home: Indianapolis, Ind. Died June 22, 2009.

DAVIDSON, WILLIAM HAROLD, management consultant; b. Dayton, Ohio, Sept. 22, 1928; s. Oscar Roy and Anna Mary (Fisher) Davidson; m. Patricia Lucille Kernan, Apr. 23, 1949; children: Jill, Patricia, William Harold, Maribeth, Sally. BBA, U. Dayton, 1954; MBA, Ind. U., 1955. Dir. mgmt. devel. Chrysler Corp., Detroit, 1955—63; v.p. Booz, Allen & Hamilton, Chgo., 1963—67; pres. Davidson-Kernan Corp., Ft. Worth, from 1967, dir., Visa Travel, Inc.; tchr. U. Detroit, 1958—62; pres. Warren (Mich.) Bd. Edn., 1961—62. With USNR, 1948—52. Mem.: Ft. Worth Club, Rivercrest Country Club. Republican. Roman Catholic. Home: Fort Worth, Tex. Died May 18, 2009.

DAVIS, CLAYTON, writer, pilot, photographer; b. Portersville, Ala., Feb. 27, 1931; s. Horace Milton Davis and Agnes Zama Meadows; m. Irene Alice Brink, Apr. 8, 1952; children: Lynne, Keith Harold. AA in Math. and History, San Antonio Coll., 1966; BA in Russian and Russian Studies, Syracuse U., 1967; postgrad., U. Md., 1971-75. Cert. comml. pilot and airline transport pilot, Md. Enlisted USAF, 1947, advanced through grades to master sgt., 1966, ret., 1970; math. tchr. Anne Arundel County Schs., Annapolis, Md., 1970-77; pilot Met. Air Charter, Balt., 1977-89, dir. ops., 1981-87. Flight instr., Md. Author: Flying Secrets, 1992, Flying Stories, 1992, So, You Want to Be a Pilot, 1999, Kindness: A Little Drop of Water Cures Everything, 2002, Where Pheasants Sing: Life in South Dakota 1900-2000, 2002, Medical Miracle in Maryland, 2004, Amelia, Jet Pilot, 2005, Aviation: How and Why, 2007; contbg. editor Pvt. Pilot Mag.; contbr. to Redfield (SD) Press, Golden Times, SD, Severna Park Voice, Md., aviation mags., others. Founding mem. Md. Aviation Hist. Task Force. Recipient St. Ignatius Gold medal, Azov Acad., Russia, 2003. Mem. Nat. Writers Assn. (founder, pres. Balt.-Washington chpt. 1993). Republican. Lutheran. Avocations: photography, flying, gardening. Home: Severna Park, Md. Died Apr. 17, 2010.

DAVIS, DONALD WALTER, retired manufacturing company executive; b. Springfield, Mass., June 10, 1921; s. Donald Walter and Laura (Mansfield) D.; m. Mary Virginia Cooper, Aug. 2, 1947; children: Randall C., Deborah Davis Curtiss, Donald Walter III, Palmer R., Jennifer Davis Heard, Ruth AB, Pa. State U.; MBA, Harvard U. Various positions Stanley Works, New Britain, Conn., 1948-62, exec. v.p., 1962-66, pres., CEO, 1966-77, chmn. bd., 1977-89, CEO, 1977-87. Bd. dirs. NE Utilities, Berlin, Conn., Pitney Bowes, Inc., Stamford Conn., Allied-Signal Inc., Morristown, N.J. Bd. dirs. New Britain Gen. Hosp., Conn. Pub. TV, Nat. Captioning Inst., Nat. Inst. for Dispute Resolution; vice chmn. bd. regents U. Hartford. Lt. USN, 1943-46. Mem. NAM (vice chmn. 1986, chmn. 1987). Died Sept. 11, 2010.

DAVIS, DREXELL REED, retired state treasurer; b. Shelbyville, Ky., July 18, 1921; s. E. Forest and Myrtle Francis (Stacy) Davis; m. Sarah Lillis Davis, Oct. 15, 1947; children: Drexel R., Ann Lillis. Student, Georgetown Coll., 1940—42. Dep. clk. Ky.'s Ct. Appeals, 1948—52, 1956—63, clk., 1964—67; adminstrv. asst. Ky. Sec. State, Frankfort, 1952—56; dist. mgr. Investors Heritage Life Ins. Co., Frankfort, 1969—72; state treas. State of Ky., Frankfort, 1972—75, 1980—84, sec. state, 1975—79. Served with Signal Corps US Army, 1942—45. Mem.: VFW, Southeastern Nat. Treas.'s Assn. (chmn.), Shriners, Masons, Lions (dist. govt.), Am. Legion. Democrat. Died Dec. 16, 2009.

DAVIS, EDWARD BERTRAND, retired federal judge, lawyer; b. West Palm Beach, Fla., Feb. 10, 1933; s. Edward Bertrand and Mattie Mae (Walker) D.; m. Patricia Lee Klein, Apr. 5, 1958; children: Diana Lee Davis, Traci Russell, Edward Bertrand, III. JD, U. Fla., 1960; LLM in Taxation, N.Y. U., 1961. Bar: Fla. 1960. Pvt. practice, Miami, 1961-79; counsel High, Stack, Lazenby & Bender, 1978-79; U.S. dist. judge So. Dist. Fla., 1979-2000; shareholder Ackerman Senterfitt, Miami, 2000, chair state wide litig. practice. Served with AUS, 1953-55. Mem.: Fla. Bar Assn., Dade County Bar Assn. Home: Miami, Fla. Died May 24, 2010.

DAVIS, EDWARD M., information processing and business machine company executive; b. Apr. 5, 1927; BSEE, Carnegie Inst. Tech., 1955; MS, Calif. Inst. Tech., 1958; PhD, Stanford U., 1958. Mgr. solid logic tech. module devel., dir. memory devel, site mgr. East Fishkill office, divn. dir. sys. products IBM Corp., 1958—78, v.p. gen. tech. divsn., 1978—81, pres. gen. tech. divsn., 1981—82, corp. v.p., pres. gen. tech. divsn., 1982—83, v.p. mfg., 1983—85, v.p., pres. data sys. divsn. White Plains, NY, from 1985. Died July 29, 2010.

DAVIS, EDWARD SHIPPEN, lawyer; b. NYC, Jan. 23, 1932; s. Wendell and Lavinia (Riker) D.; m. Barbara Thompson, Sept. 13, 1980; children: Martha K., Edward Shippen Jr. (dec.). AB, Harvard U., 1954, LL.B., 1959. Bar: Conn. 1959, N.Y. 1960, D.C. 1973. Assoc. Hughes Hubbard & Reed LLP, NYC, 1959-66, ptnr., from 1967. Dir. Cognitronics Corp.; Hillenbrand Industries Inc. Author articles in field. Served with AUS, 1954-56. Mem. Am. Bar Assn., Conn. Bar Assn., Assn. Bar City N.Y., Century Club, Harvard (N.Y.C.) Club. Home: New York, NY. Died Aug. 28, 2009.

DAVIS, JAMES ALLEN, chemist; b. Glasgow, Ky., Oct. 17, 1940; s. James C. and Bernice (Allen) Davis. BSc, Western Ky. U., 1962; MSc, U. Akron, 1967. Rsch. asst. Goodyear Aerospace Co., Akron, Ohio, 1964—67; microbiologist Century Pharm. Labs., Metairie, La., 1967—68; adminstrv. microbiologist Baxter Labs., Kingstree, SC, 1968—69; sr. rsch. scientist Firestone Tire & Rubber Co., Akron, from 1969. Mem.: Am. Chem. Soc., Akron Rubber Group, Phi Sigma. Methodist. Achievements include patents for rubber to metal adhesion, tire compound devel. Avocations: coin collecting/numismatics, basketball, jogging, fishing, camping. Home: Westfield, Ind. Died June 8, 2009.

DAVIS, JON FRANCIS, psychologist; b. Milford Center, Ohio, Mar. 4, 1936; s. Francis Robert and Dorothy Mitchell D.; m. Mary Macauley June 26, 1968; 1 child Shiella Macauley. BS in Edn., Capital U., 1959; AM in Psychology, Ohio State U., 1961; PhD Psychology, Columbia U., 1968. Lic. psychologist N.Y., Ohio. Pvt. practice psychology, NYC and Columbus, Ohio, from 1968. Bd. dirs. Mills Ctr., Marysville, Ohio. Author: One Hundred Ways to Prepare Elephant, Diamonds Are Chilly in the Winter, Alvan Macauley Sr.: Automotive Leader and Pioneer, Packard Motor Car Company, The Mitchell Pioneers in Union County, 1799: Tea Time at Poshly Manor, Journal of an Usherette. Lt. U.S. Armu, 1957-59. Mem. Country Club Detroit, Grosse Pointe Club, Otswego Ski Club, Mill Reef Club, Scioto Country Club, University Club, Colony Club, Mus. Modern Art, Metro. Mus. Art., Nat. Soc. Sons and Daughters of Am. Colonists. Republican. Avocations: theater, fine arts. Died Jan. 1, 2009.

DAVIS, PERLEY E., state legislator; b. Colebrook, NH, Mar. 23, 1929; m. Janice Davis; 2 children. Student, Colebrook Acad., NH, Norwich U., 1951. Mem. dist. 1 N.H. Ho. of Reps., mem. environ. and agrl. com., sch. bus. adminstr., N.H. House Reps., ret. Republican. Home: Colebrook, NH. Died Feb. 21, 2010.

DAVIS, RALPH E., lawyer; b. Danville, Ill., Nov. 13, 1919; s. Mervin Francis and Florence Lucille (Dunbar) D.; m. Evelyn Esther Henne, June 28, 1947; children: Richard M., Judith A. Pomeranz. BS, U. Ill., 1942, LLD, 1943. Assoc. Hopkins & Sutter, Chgo., 1943-55, ptnr., 1956-86, of counsel, from 1987. Bd. dirs. Client Security Fund Bar Ill., Chgo. Contbr. numerous articles to profl. jours. Trustee Trinity Ch. North Shore, Wilmette, Ill., 1972—, pres., 1986-90; trustee U. Ill. YMCA, Champaign, 1973—, chmn., 1979-91. Mem. ABA, Ill. Bar Assn., Chgo. Bar Assn. (lawyer reference com. 1948-55, vice chmn. com. 1952-53, chmn. 1953-54, com. on inquiry 1958-67, chmn. com. on inquiry 1966-67), Law Club Chgo., Legal Club Chgo., Mid-Day Club, Mid-Am. Club. Republican. Methodist. Avocation: travel. Home: Evanston, Ill. Died Aug. 11, 2010.

DAVIS, RANSOM J., lawyer; b. Lansing, Mich., May 4, 1942; BA, Johns Hopkins U., 1964; LLB cum laude, Columbia U., 1967. Bar: Md. 1968, U.S. Dist. Ct. Md. 1969, U.S. Ct. Appeals (4th cir.) 1970, U.S. Tax Ct. 1976, U.S. Ct. Fed. Claims 1982, U.S. Ct. Appeals (D.C. cir.) 1988, U.S. Supreme Ct. 1989. Law clk. to Hon. Alexander Harvey II U.S. Dist. Ct. Md., 1967-68; asst. U.S. atty. Office U.S. Atty. Dist. Md., 1970-72; asst. atty. gen. Office Atty. Gen. State of Md., 1974-77; counsel to Md. Automobile Ins. Fund, 1977-79; atty. Whiteford, Taylor & Preston, Balt. Active Inquiry Com. to Atty. Grievance Commn. Md., 1979—. Mem. ABA, Md. State Bar Assn., Nat. Assn. Railroad Trial Counsel, Bar Assn. Balt. City (mem. exec. coun. 1976-78). Died Jan. 15, 2010.

DAVIS, RICHARD MALONE, economics professor; b. Hamilton, NY, June 2, 1918; s. Malone Crowell and Grace Edith (McQuade) Davis. AB, Colgate U., 1939; MA, Cornell U., 1941, PhD, 1949. From instr. to assoc. prof. econs. Lehigh U., Bethlehem, Pa., 1941-54; assoc. prof. econs. U. Oreg., Eugene, 1954-62, prof., 1962-83, prof. emeritus, from 1983. Contbr. articles to profl. jours. With US Army, 1942—45, CBI. Mem.: Phi Beta Kappa. Republican. Home: Rochester, NY. Died Mar. 13, 2010.

DAVIS, ROBERT EDWARD, retired communications educator; b. Wichita, Kans., Apr. 2, 1931; s. Edward Lorenzo and Dorrinda Belle (Packer) D.; m. Jacqueline Peggy Baas, Aug. 22, 1955 (div. 1979); children: Robert J., Sarah J., James E.; m. Martha Toni Merrill, Jan. 8, 1983. BA, U. No. Iowa, 1953; MA, U. Iowa, 1956, PhD, 1965. Instr. Grundy Ctr. (Iowa) High Sch., 1953-54; asst. to dir. radio and TV U. No. Iowa, Cedar Falls, 1954-58; lectr., instr. dept. speech and theatre Hunter Coll., NYC, 1961-63, 65-66; asst. prof. dept. speech U. Mich., Ann Arbor, 1966-69; from assoc. prof. to prof. and chmn. dept. cinema and photography So. Ill. U., Carbondale, 1969-74; prof. and chmn. Dept. Radio-TV-Film, U. Tex., Austin, 1974-87, John T. Jones Jr. Centennial prof. in communication, 1987-89, now emeritus and from 1989. Author: Response to Innovation, 1976; co-producer, dir. (film) Maple Sugar Farmer, 1973 (7 nat. and internat. awards); writer, performer, dir., producer over 1000 ednl. radio and tv programs; contbr. articles to profl. jours. Mem. Pacific Grove City Coun., 1990—98; mayor pro tem Pacific Grove, 1994—98; mem. Pacific Grove Planning Commn., from 1999, chair, 2005—07; bd. dirs. Heritage Soc. Pacific Grove, from 2001. Mem.: Pacific Grove Citizens Police Acad. Alumni Assn. (bd. dirs. from 2000, chmn. 2005—07). Republican. Methodist. Avocations: travel, photography. Home: Pacific Grove, Calif. Died Apr. 14, 2010.

DAVIS, ROBERT EDWARD, retired state supreme court chief justice; b. Topeka, Aug. 28, 1939; s. Thomas Homer and Emma Claire (Hund) D.; m. Jana Jones (dec.); children: Edward, Rachel, Patrick, Carolyn, Brian. BA in Polit. Sci., Creighton U., 1961; JD, Georgetown U., 1964. Bar: Kans. 1964, U.S. Dist. Ct. Kans. 1964, U.S. Tax Ct. 1974, U.S. Ct. Mil. Appeals 1965, U.S. Ct. Mil. Review, 1970, U.S. Ct. Appeals (10th cir.) 1974, U.S. Supreme Ct. 1982. Pvt. practice, Leavenworth, Kans., 1967-84; magistrate judge Leavenworth County, 1969-76, county atty., 1980-84, judge dist. ct., 1984-86; judge Kans. Ct. Appeals Jud. Br. Govt., Topeka, 1986-93; justice Kans. Supreme Ct., Topeka, 1993—2009, chief justice, 2009—10. Lectr. U. Kans. Law Sch., Lawrence, 1986-95. Capt. JAGC, U.S. Army, 1964-67, Korea. Mem. Am. Judges Assn., Kans. Bar Assn., Leavenworth County Bar Assn. (pres. 1977), Judge Hugh Means Am. Inn of Ct. Charter Orgn. Roman Catholic. Home: Leavenworth, Kans. Died Aug. 4, 2010.

DAVIS, ROBERT NASON, museum curator; b. Thomaston, Maine, May 16, 1938; s. Harlan Augustus Davis and Violet Page (McLean) Edwards. Assoc. liberal arts Famous Artist Sch., 1959; seismographic crew mem. Texaco, Hanesville, Va., 1961—62; artist, painter, interior designer Rockland, Maine, 1963—78; engr. Harbor Supply Co., Portland, Maine, 1979—80; curator, historian Shore Village Mus., Rockland, from 1981. Bd. dirs. Maine Lobster Festival, Rockland, from 1978; vol. worker WCBB-TV, Pub. Broadcasting Sta., Lewiston, Maine, from 1983; fellow Farnsworth Art Mus., Rockland. Contbr. articles to newspapers and mags. Served with USN, 1956—60. Recipient Appreciation award, Rockland City Coun., 1981, 1982, 1983, Knox County Bd. Commrs., 1985. Mem.: Maine Citizens Historic Preservation, Nat. Maritime Hist. Soc., Shore Village Hist. Soc. (bd. dirs. from 1983), Island Inst., Rockland Area C. of C., US Lighthouse Soc., Seven Seas Cruising Assn. (assoc.), Knox County Stamp Club (Rockland). Republican. Avocations: collecting stamps, collecting books, collecting antiques, art, music. Home: Rockland, Maine. Died Sept. 0, 1974.

DAVIS, ROBERT PAUL, retired physician, educator; b. Malden, Mass., July 3, 1926; s. Samuel and Sarah (Lemberg) D.; m. Ruby (Black), Sept. 5, 1953; children: Edward L., John R., Elizabeth A. BA cum laude (hon.), Harvard U., 1947, MD (hon.) magna cum laude, 1951, MA, 1955; MA ad eundem, Brown U., 1967. Diplomate: Am. Bd. Internal Medicine, sub splty. bd. nephrology. Intern Peter Bent Brigham Hosp., Boston, 1951—52, asst. medicine, 1952—55; jr. fellow Soc. of Fellows, Harvard, Boston, 1952—55; sr. asst. resident physician Peter Bent Brigham Hosp., Boston, 1955—56, chief resident physician, 1956—57; asst. medicine Harvard Med. Sch., Boston, 1956—57; asst. prof. medicine U. N.C., 1957—59; asst. vis. physician Bronx Mcpl. Hosp. Ctr., NY, 1959—65; asst. prof. medicine Albert Einstein Coll. Medicine, 1959—66; career scientist Health Rsch. Coun., NYC, 1962—67; assoc. vis. physician Bronx Mcpl. Hosp. Ctr., NY, 1966—67; assoc. prof. Albert Einstein Coll. Medicine, 1967; physician in chief Miriam Hosp., Providence, 1967—74; prof. med. sci. Brown U., 1967—84, chmn. sect. in medicine div. biol. and med. sci., 1971—74; dir. renal and metabolic diseases Miriam Hosp., Providence, 1974—79; prof. emeritus Brown U., 1984. Vis. scientist Ins. Biol. Chemistry of U. Copenhagen, 1965-66; past mem. corp. Butler Hosp., Jewish Family and Children's Svc.; mem. sci. adv. coun. N.E. Regional Kidney Program; vice chmn. R.I. Advisory Commn. Med. Care and Edn. Found.; chmn. med. adv. bd. R.I. Kidney Found.; past bd. dir. Associated Alumni Brown U.; mem. med. adv. bd. New Eng. sect. Am. Liver Found., 1986-90; trustee New Eng. Organ Bank, Boston, 1968-2006, treas., 1969-2006; pres. End Stage Renal Disease Coordinating Coun. Network 28, New Eng., 1978-79; dealer in rare and antiquarian books Gadshill. Assoc. editor: R.I. Med. Jour, 1971-80; contbr. articles to profl. journals; numerous book chapters in med. texts. Served as ensign USNR, 1944-46; as lt. (j.g.) M.C. 1951. Traveling fellow Commonwealth Fund, 1965-66; Willard O. Thompson meml. traveling scholar A.C.P., 1965 Mem. Am. Fedn. Clin. Rsch., Am. Soc. Transplantation (com. on intrathoracic organs 2003), Harvey Soc., Biophy. Soc., NY Acad. Medicine, Am. Heart Assn., NY Acad. Sci., Am. Soc. Cell Biology, Soc. Gen. Physiologists, Am. Physiol. Soc., Am. Soc. Artificial Internal Organs, Internat. Soc. Nephrology, Clin. Diabetes Assn. RI (pres. 1970-71), RI Med. Soc., Am. Soc. Nephrology, Am. Soc. Pediatric Nephrology, Soc. Health and Human Values, Am. Philos. Assn., Phi Beta Kappa, Sigma Xi, Grolier Club, John Russell Bartlett Soc. (pres. 1985-87), Ephemera Soc. Am., Dickens fellowship (pres. Greater Boston br. 2000-06), Antiquarian Booksellers Assn. Am., Internat. League Antiquarian Booksellers, Mass and RI Antiquarian Booksellers, Dickens Soc., Hakluyt Soc., Ticknor Soc.; fellow AAAS, ACP. Avocations: history of western civilization and medicine, classical music. Home: Providence, RI. Died June 3, 2010.

DAVIS, SHELTON HAROLD, social anthropologist; b. Pitts., Aug. 13, 1942; s. Robert Davis and Fannie Secher; m. Mary Clare Gubbins, July 20, 1979; children: Rebecca Anne, Peter Daniel. Student, London Sch. Econs., 1963—64; BA, Antioch Coll., 1965; PhD, Harvard U., 1970. Lectr. social anthropology Harvard U., Cambridge, Mass., 1971—73; founder and dir. Indigena, Inc., Berkeley, Calif., 1973—75, Anthropology Resource Ctr., Boston, 1975—84; sr. sociologist The World Bank, Washington, 1987—92, prin. sociologist social policy and resettlement divsn., environment dept., 1993—98, sector manager-L.Am. and Caribbean region, social devel. unit, 1998—2004; sr. fellow Ctr. for Latin American Studies, Edmund A. Walsh Sch. Fgn. Svc., Georgetown U., Washington, 2004—08. Bd. dirs. Plumsock Fund, South Woodstock, Vt.; adj. asst. prof. anthropology MIT, Cambridge, 1976—79, Boston U., 1979—82; adj. prof. Latin America studies program, Edmund A. Walsh Sch. Fgn. Svc. Georgetown U., Washington, 1992—2010; vis. lectr. social anthropology Fed. U. Rio de Janeiro, 1969—70; vis. scholar OAS Inter-American Commn. Human Rights, 1984—86. Author: Victims of the Miracle: Devel. and the Indians of Brazil, Land Rights and Indigenous Peoples: The Role of the OAS Inter-Am. Commn. on Human Rights, La Tierra de Nuestros Antepasados: Estudio de la Herencia y la Tenencia de la Tierra en el Altiplano de Guatemala; editor: Antropologia do Direito: Estudo Comparativo de Categorias de Divida e Contrato, (albums) Social Exclusion and Poverty Reduction in Latin America and the Caribbean Region; co-editor (with Estanislao Gacitua-Mario and Carlos Sojo): (joint pub. FLACSO Costa Rica and World Bank Latin Am. & Caribbean Region Social Devel. Unit) Desafios de Desarrollo Social en Centro America, 2004; contbr. articles to profl. jours. and monographs, chapters to books. Grantee, Am. Coun. Learned Socs. and Social Sci. Rsch. Coun., 1981, J. Roderick MacArthur Found., 1984—86, World Bank Rsch. Com., 1996—98, World Bank Learning and Leadership Ctr., 1996; fellow, NIMH, US Pub. Health Svc., 1965—69. Jewish. Avocations: walking, hiking, travel, visiting art museums, listening to jazz and latin music. Home: Falls Church, Va. Died May 27, 2010.

DAVIS, SPEAR JOHN (JACK DAVIS), retired school system administrator; b. Black Lick, Pa., Oct. 9, 1928; BS, Ind. U. of Pa., 1950, LLD (hon.), 1980; MA, George Washington U., 1955; DEd, Am. U., 1972. Sci. tchr. Arlington County (Va.) Pub. Schs., 1951-55, asst. prin., 1955-58; dir. Flint Hill Prep Sch., Oakton, Va., 1958-63; asst. prin., acting prin. Fort Hunt High Sch., Fairfax County, Va., 1963-66; area II supt. Fairfax County Pub. Schs., 1967-70, div. supt., 1970-79; supt. pub. instruction Commonwealth Va., Richmond, 1979—90. Contbr. articles to profl. jours. Bd. dirs. Fairfax Community Action Program, 1977-78, The Fairfax Symphony Orch., 1976-78, Jr. Achievement, 1972-75; adv. com. Voluntary Action Ctr., 1977-79; steering com. Virginians for Bonds, 1977; exec. bd. Ft. Belvoir Civilian-Military Adv. Council, 1972; adv. bd. The Memco Charitable and Scholarship Found.; scholarship final selection com. Continental Telephone Service Corp.; adv. council No. Va. Hotline; dist. nominatng com. Boy Scouts Am. Recipient Recognition award Richmond Area Reading Council, 1984, Paul Harris Fellow award Annandale Rotary, 1980, Service to Mankind award Sertoma of Richmond, 1980, Community Leadership award United Black Fund of Greater Washington, 1978, Recognition cert., Gov. Va., 1977, Appreciation cert. Council for Exceptional Children, 1976, Disting. Service award Assn. Practitioners Ednl. Adminstrn. George Washington U., 1975; named Ednl Adminstr. Yr., Va. Assn. Ednl. Secs., 1975, Educator Yr., Phi Delta Kappa Chpt. No. Va., 1974-75. Mem.

Nat. Edn. Assn. (life), Va. Edn. Assn., Am. Assn. Sch. Adminstrs. (audit com., supts. summer conf. planning com., 1978), Va. Assn. Sch. Adminstrs. (pres. 1977-78), Nat. Assn. Secondary Sch. Prins., Va. Sch. Bds. Assn., Nat. Fedn. Urban/Suburban Sch. Dists. (exec. com. 1975-79, orgnl. structure com. 1975-76), Washington Area Sch. Study Council, PTA (life), Coll. Entrance Exam Bd., No. Va. Ednl. TV Assn. (bd. dirs.), Cen. Va. Ednl. TV Corp. (bd. dirs.), No. Va. Ednl. Telecommunications Assn. (bd. dirs.), No. Va. Assn. Children with Learning Disabilities (profl. adv. bd. 1975-76), Ednl. Com. of the States, So. Regional Edn. Bd. (chmn., task force on higher edn. and schs.), S. Assn. Colls. and Schs., Va. Council of Higher Edn., Fairfax County C. of C. Clubs: The Fed. Schoolman's. Lodges: Masons (32d degree). Methodist. Died Nov. 22, 2009.

DAVISON, DANIEL POMEROY, retired banking executive; b. NYC, Jan. 30, 1925; s. F. Trubee and Dorothy (Peabody) D.; m. Catherine Cheremeteff, June 27, 1953; children: Daniel P. Jr., George P., Henry P. BA, Yale U., 1949; JD, Harvard U., 1952. Assoc. White & Case, NYC, 1952-55; exec. v.p. Morgan Bank, NYC, 1955-79; chmn., CEO U.S. Trust, NYC, 1979-90; chmn. Christie's, NYC, 1990-94, Burlington No. Sante Fe R.R., Fort Worth, 1996-97. Treas. Florence Gould Found., N.Y.C. Recipient Legion of Honor, France. Mem. Piping Rock Yacht Club, Seawanhaka Yacht Club. Republican. Episcopalian. Avocations: sailing, fishing, hunting. Home: Locust Valley, NY. Died Aug. 25, 2010.

DAVY, RONALD KENNETH, university administrator; b. Rochester, NY, Dec. 1, 1942; s. William Kenneth Davy and Doris Gertrude (McDonald) Nichols; m. Susan Lauretta Davy, Feb. 12, 1966; children: Elisabeth, Christopher. BA, George Wash. U., 1965; MBA, George Mason U., 1976. Cert. emergency med. technician, acct. Gen. With Bus. Svcs., Bethesda, Md., 1973—75; controller Metcor, Washington, 1975—76; asst. comptroller United Mine Workers Health-Retirement Fund, Washington, 1976—78; adminstr. George Wash. U., from 1978; faculty cons. Office Health Maintenance Orgn., Rockville, Md., 1981—82. Treas. Lakewinds Cluster Assn., Reston, Va., 1979—80, pres., 1981. Comdr. USNR, from 1965. Mem.: Reston Soccer Assn. (asst. soccer commr. 1976—77), Group Health Assn. Am. (lectr.). Home: Reston, Va. Died Nov. 30, 2009.

DAWSON, JOHN JOSEPH, lawyer; b. Binghamton, NY, Mar. 9, 1947; s. Joseph John and Cecilia (O'Neill) D. BA, Siena Coll., 1968; JD, U. Notre Dame, 1971. Bar: Ariz. 1971, Nev. 1991, Calif. 1993, D.C. 1994, N.Y. 1996. Nat. practice group chair, bankruptcy and creditors rights practice group Quarles & Brady LLP, Phoenix. Reporter local rules ct. U.S. Bankruptcy Ct. for Dist. Ariz.; atty. rep. U.S. Ct. Appeals (9th cir.), 1992-95 Co-author: Advanced Chapter 11 Bankruptcy, 1991. Fellow Ariz. Bar Found.; mem. State Bar Ariz. (chmn. bankruptcy sect. 1976-77, 80-81), Am. Bankruptcy Inst. Republican. Roman Catholic. Avocations: sports, reading, movies, travel, writing. Home: Phoenix, Ariz. Died Nov. 2009.

DAY, RICHARD PUTNAM, marketing professional, arbitrator, employee benefits consultant; b. Hartford, Conn., Feb. 13, 1930; s. Godfrey Malbone and Sheila (Wilson) D.; m. Patricia Ann Brady, Jan. 26, 1957; children: Richard Jr., Stephen, Thomas (dec.), Gregory, Katharine, Martha, Ward, Emily. Student, The Choate Sch., 1948; AB, Middlebury Coll., 1952. With group field sales Conn. Gen. Life Ins. Co., Hartford, Detroit, Toledo, Phoenix, 1952-61; dir. sales group Bankers Life Nebr. (name changed to Ameritas Life Ins. Corp.), Lincoln, 1961-73, v.p. group, 1973-87, exec. v.p. group, 1987-91, exec. v.p. bus. devel., 1991-93; prin. R.P. Day Consulting, Paradise Valley, Ariz., from 1993. Dir. Nat. Health Care Svcs., Jacksonville, Fla., 1985—95. Trustee, pres. bd. Madonna Profl. Care Ctr., Lincoln, 1970-80, trustee Lincoln Gen. Hosp., 1980. Lt. USN, 1952-56. Mem. VFW, Internat. Soc. Cert. Employee Benefit Specialists (bd. dirs. pres. governing coun., chmn. bd. 1986), Am. Soc. CLUs, Internat. Found. Employee Benefit Plans, Profl. Ins. Mass-Mktg. Assn., Mass-Mktg. Ins. Inst., Nat. Assn. Dental Plans, Am. Legion, Mil. Officers Assn., Country Club of Lincoln, Scottsdale Country Club, Blue Key Honor Soc., Phi Kappa Tau. Republican. Episcopalian. Avocation: golf. Home: Paradise Valley, Ariz. Died July 15, 2009.

DEALY, FRANCIS XAVIER, JR., publisher; b. NYC, June 23, 1938; s. Francis Xavier and Kathleen (Donovan) D.; m. Jane Elizabeth Sim, June 2, 1960 (div. Aug. 1972); children—Patrick, Brendan, Christopher; m. Ellen Joanna Fairbanks, June 23, 1984 BS, Mt. St. Mary's Coll., Emmintsburg, Md., 1960; postgrad., Harvard U., 1965-66. Pres. Shannon Communications, NYC, 1974-78; v.p., gen. mgr. Dow Jones & Co. Book Digest, NYC, 1978-83; pub. Tennis, N.Y. Times, NYC, 1983-84; v.p., pub. CBS, Inc., NYC, 1984-85, Family Media, NYC, from 1985. Bd. dirs. Tennis Found. N.Am., Palm Beach, Fla. Mem.: Town Tennis, Athletic (N.Y.C.). Avocations: writing; tennis; running; skiing; swimming. Died Aug. 10, 2009.

DEAN, JIMMY, meat processing company executive, entertainer; b. Plainview, Tex., Aug. 10, 1928; s. G. O. and Ruth (Taylor) D.; m. Donna L. Meade, Oct. 1991; children from previous marriage: Garry, Connie, Robert. Student public schs., Plainview. Pres. Jimmy Dean Meat Co., Plainview, Tex., 1969-72, chmn. bd. Dallas, 1972-91, Jimmy Dean Foods, Cordova, Tenn., from 1991. Entertainer, Washington area, 1948-57; host: Morning Show, CBS-TV, Washington, 1957, Jimmy Dean Show, NYC, 1958-59, Jimmy Dean Show, ABC-TV, 1963-65; appeared on: radio and TV show Town & Country Jamboree, 1950's; entertained, US Armed Forces, Caribbean, 1952, Europe, 1953, rec. artist, 1953—2010; records include Big Bad John, 1961 (Gold Record); IOU, 1976 (Gold Record), (author, with Donna Meade Dean) Thirty Years of Sausage, Fifty Years of Ham, 2004. Served with USAAF, 1946-48. Recipient Georgie award as outstanding performer in field of live entertainment for country music AGVA, 1972, Timmie award Touchdown Club, Washington, 1987; named to Hall of Fame Washington Area Music Assn., 1986. Mem. Actors' Equity Assn., AFTRA, Screen Actors Guild. Died June 13, 2010.

DEAN, SHARON LOU, information consultant; b. Ithaca, NY, Nov. 4, 1943; d. Kermit Lewis and Lila Lee (Moravia) D.; m. Richard Stephen Chrappa. BA, Keuka Coll., 1964; MA, Syracuse U., 1965; MLS, U. Wash., 1978, cert. in bus. adminstrn., 1981. Cert. profl. libr., Wash.; cert. secondary tchr., Wash., N.Y., Ariz. Supr. learning resource ctr. Mercer Island Sr. H.S., Wash., 1975-77; head libr. John F. Kennedy H.S., Seattle, 1977-81; sr. info. analyst Cigna Corp., Phila., 1982-83, mktg. cons., 1983-84, sys. mgr., 1984-86, bus. cons., 1986-90; pres. Corp. Fact Finders, from 1989. Author: Winning Marketing Techniques for Information Professionals, 1990, 2d edit., 1998; contbr. articles to profl. and bus. jours. Bd. dirs. Unitarian Ch., West Chester, Pa., 1984-85, 99—. Recipient State of Wash. Commendation award Gov., Sec. of State, 1976, Profl. Achievement award Keuka Coll., 1991. Mem. Spl. Librs. Assn., Assn. Ind. Info. Profls. Avocations: photography, reading, needlecrafts, travel. Died Jan. 29, 2010.

DE BEAUSSET, VALERY SERGEI, country development consultant; b. St. Petersburg, Russia, Feb. 13, 1915; s. Serge Nicolas and Anna (Petrova) de B.; B.S., Haverford Coll., 1938; postgrad. SUNY; m. Constance Lee Stanton, June 4, 1944; children— Constance, Lee Tyler, Valerie Stanton, Denise, Alexander Macomb. Project mgr. cons. team for econ. devel., Taiwan, 1948-58; dir. chem. engring. div. J.G. White Engring. Corp., N.Y., 1958-60; cons. devel. Mexico, Bolivia, El Salvador, Equador, Colombia, Venezuela, Costa Rica, 1960-67; adviser to pres. Central Am. Devel. Bank, 1967-74; cons. steel industry in Honduras, 1974-79; coordinator application of rural-appropriate techs. to country devel. AID-Govt. of Honduras, 1979—; lectr. in field. Mem. various vestries Episcopal Ch., 1963—; bd. dirs. Am. Sch., Honduras, 1969-72, Home for Abandoned Children, Honduras, 1972—. Served with USMCR, 1944-46. Decorated Order Brilliant Star (Taiwan, 1951-54). Mem. AAAS, Am. Inst. Chem. Engrs., Am. Chem. Soc. Clubs: Taiwan Golf (life); Costa Rican Golf and Country. Author: Industrial Development in Costa Rica. Home: Grosse Ile, Mich. Died Oct. 18, 2009.

DEBOLD, RICHARD CHARLES, writer; b. NYC, July 20, 1927; s. William John and Emma Anna DeBold; m. Marjorie Cope, Sept. 28, 1957; 1 child, William John. PhD, U. Calif., 1963. Prof. emeritus LI U., Bklyn., from 1968; pub. Higganum Hill Books, Higganum, Conn., from 1995. Author: (novels) The Banana Shooter, (essays) Winter. Trustee The Hartford Art Sch., West Hartford, Conn., 1966—2004. Lt. s.g. USN, 1950—53. James Rowland Angel Rsch. fellow, Yale U., 1957—58. Mem.: Acad. Am. Poets (assoc.). Roman Catholic. Avocation: sailing. Home: Higganum, Conn. Died June 29, 2010.

DEBUS, ALLEN GEORGE, historian, educator; b. Chgo., Aug. 16, 1926; s. George Walter William and Edna Pauline (Schwenneke) D.; m. Brunilda Lopez-Rodriguez, Aug. 25, 1951; children: Allen Anthony George, Richard William, Karl Edward. BS, Northwestern U., 1947; A.M., Ind. U., 1949; PhD, Harvard U., 1961; postgrad., U. Coll. London, 1959-60; D.Sc. h.c., Cath. U. Louvain, 1985. Research chemist Abbott Labs., North Chicago, Ill., 1951-56; asst. prof. U. Chgo., 1961-65, assoc. prof. history, 1965-68, prof., 1968-78, Morris Fishbein prof. history sci. and medicine, 1978-96, Morris Fishbein prof. emeritus, from 1996; dir. Morris Fishbein Ctr. for Study History Sci. and Medicine, 1971-77. Disting. vis. prof. Ariz. ctr. for medieval and renaissance studies Ariz. State U., 1984; vis. prof. Inst. Chemistry, U. São Paulo, Brazil, 1990; mem. internat. adv. com. Tel-Aviv U. The Cohn Inst. History and Philosophy of Sci. and Ideas, Ctr. for History and Philosophy of Sci. of Hebrew U. of Jerusalem; mem. internat. adv. bd. Annali dell'Istituto e Museo di Storia della Scienza di Firenze; cons. lit. and sci. curriculum Ga. Inst. Tech. Author: The English Paracelsians, 1965, 66, (with Robert P. Multhauf) Alchemy and Chemistry in the 17th Century, 1966, The Chemical Dream of the Renaissance, 1968, 2d edit., 1972, Science and Education in the 17th Century, 1970, (with Brian Rust) The Complete Entertainment Discography, 1973, 2d rev. edit., 1989, The Chemical Philosophy, 2 vols., 1977, 2d edit., 2002, Japanese transl., 1999, Man and Nature in the Renaissance, 1978, 15th rev. edit., 1995, Italian transl., 1982, Spanish transl., 1985, 86, 2d edit., 1995, Japanese transl., 1986, Chinese transl., 1988, 2000, Greek transl., 1997, Portuguese trans., 2002, Robert Fludd and His Philosophical Key, 1979; Science and History: A Chemist's Appraisal, 1984, Chinese tranl., 1999, Chemistry, Alchemy and the New Philosophy, 1550-1700, 1987, The French Paracelsians: The Chemical Challenge to Medical and Scientific Tradition in Early Modern France, 1991, 2002, Paracelso e la Tradizione Paracelsiana, 1996, Chemistry and Medical Debate: Van Helmont to Boerhaave, 2001, The Chemical Promise, 2006; editor: World Who's Who in Science from Antiquity to the Present, 1968, Science, Medicine and Society in the Renaissance, 2 vols, 1972, Medicine in Seventeenth-Century England, 1974; editor reprint: Theatrum Chemicum Britannicum (1652), 1967, John Dee's Mathematicall Praeface (1570), 1975; editor: (with Ingrid Merkel) Hermeticism and the Renaissance: Intellectual History and the Occult in Early Modern Europe, 1988, (with Michael T. Walton) Reading the Book of Nature: The Other Side of the Scientific Revolution, 1998, Alchemy and Early Modern Chemistry: Papers from Ambix, 2004; essayist: Festschrift: Experiencing Nature: Essays for Allen G. Debus (edited by Paul Theerman and Karen Parshall, 1997); mem. bd. adv. editors Physis Rivista internazionale de storia della scienza, Nuncius, The 16th Century Jour.; adv. editor: History of Science; hon. bd. editors Incognita; programmed 3 records released by Smithsonian Instn. Music of Victor Herbert, 1979; notes to CD releases by Archeophone-Bert Williams, Nora Bayes and Jack Norworth, 2003-04, Monarchs of Minstrelsy, 2006, Elsie Janis; contbr. articles to profl. jours.; patentee in field. Social Sci. Rsch. Coun. fellow, 1959-60; Fulbright fellow, 1959-60; Fels Found. fellow, 1960-61; Guggenheim fellow, 1966-67; overseas fellow Churchill Coll. Cambridge (Eng.) U., 1966-67, 69; mem. Inst. Advanced Study Princeton, N.J., 1972-73; NEH fellow Newberry Libr., Chgo., 1975-76; fellow Inst. for Rsch. in Humanities U. Wis., Madison, 1981-82, NEH, 1987, Folger Shakespeare Libr., Washington; rsch. grantee Am. Philos. Soc., 1961-62, Wellcome Trust, 1962, NIH, 1962-70, 74-75, 77-78, 92-97, NSF, 1961-63, 71-74, 80-83, Am. Coun. Learned Socs., 1966, 70, 71. Fellow AAAS (mem. electorate nominating com., sect. L 1974-77, chmn. com. 1974); mem. History of Sci. Soc. (council 1962-65, 87-90, program chmn. 1972, Pfizer award 1978, Sarton medal 1994, Disting. lectr. 1996), Soc. Study Alchemy and Early Chemistry (mem. council 1967—), Am. Assn. for History Medicine (program com. 1975), Brit. Soc. for History Sci., Internationale Paracelsus Gesellschaft, Am. Chem. Soc. (asso. mem. history of chemistry div., exec. com. 1969-72, Dexter award 1987), Soc. Med. History of Chgo. (sec.-treas. 1971-72, v.p. 1972-74, pres. 1974-76, mem. council), Académie Internat. d'Histoire de la Medecine, Société Internationale d'Histoire de la Medecine, Academie Internat. d'Histoire des Scis. (corr. 1971, membre effectif 1991), Am. Inst. History of Pharmacy (Edward Kremers award 1978, adv. panel hist. activity 1979-81, awards com. 1981—), Am. Soc. Reformation Research, Assn. Recorded Sound Collections., Midwest Junto for History of Sci. (pres. 1983-84), Academia das Ciencias de Lisboa. Home: Deerfield, Ill. Died Mar. 6, 2009.

DECAMINADA, JOSEPH PIO, retired insurance company executive; b. Gebo, Wyo., Oct. 17, 1935; s. Pio and Ida (Franch) Decaminada; m. Genevieve Caputo, Aug. 30, 1958; 1 child, Joseph. BA magna cum laude, St. Francis Coll., 1956; JD, St. John's U., 1959; postgrad., Harvard U., 1978-79. CPCU, CLU, chartered fin. cons. From corp. sec. to sr. v.p., sec. Atlantic Mut. Ins. Co., Centennial Ins. Co., NYC, 1971-86, exec. v.p., sec., 1986-96. Past chmn. bd. dirs. CPCU-Harry J. Loman Found., Motor Vehicle Accident Indemnification Corp., N.Y. Property Ins. Underwriting Assn., Ind. Fedn. N.Y. Contbr. articles to profl. jours. Bd. dirs., chmn. bd. Coll. Mt. St. Vincent, Riverdale, NY. Decorated Knight of Malta; recipient Brotherhood award, NCCJ, 1991; named named Ins. Man of Yr., Recovery Forum, 1978; Anglo-Am. fellow, B.D. Cooke & Ptnrs., Ltd., London, 1966. Mem. Soc. CPCU (nat. pres. 1984-85, Disting. Svc. award 1989, Eugene A. Toale Meml. award N.Y. chpt. 1974), Soc. CLU. Home: Scarsdale, NY. Died Mar. 21, 2010.

DECKER, CHARLES RICHARD, investment company executive, educator; b. Murphysboro, Ill., Mar. 13, 1937; s. Ernest George and Joyce Ellen (Gibson) D.; m. Jeanine Ann Cowell, June 6, 1959; children: Ann Marie Britt, Lynn Rochelle Lake, Charles Ernest BBA, U. Miss., 1959; MBA, Ind. U., 1962, EdD, 1968; cert., Harvard U., 1981. Cert. fin. planner, 1990. Asst. prof. Ill. State U., Normal, 1968-70, chmn. dept. bus. adminstrn., 1970-74; dean sch. bus. Millikin U., Decatur, Ill., 1974-80, provost, v.p., 1980-86, Grover M. Hermann prof. bus. policy, 1986-98; ptnr. Black Watch Investment Mgmt., from 2002. Investment mgr., bd. dirs. John Warner Fin. Svcs. Inc., 1996-2002. Contbr. articles to profl. jours. Bd. dirs. Decatur Civic Ctr., 1984-92, vice chmn., 1986-87, chmn., 1987-92; bd. dirs. United Way of Decatur and Macon County, 1984-87, Boys Club, Decatur, 1980-82; mem. exec. bd. Lincoln Trails Coun. Boy Scouts Am., 1988-93, SME chair, 1989-91, v.p., 1990-93. Mem. North Cent. Assn. Acad. Deans (pres. 1984-85), C. of C. (bd. dirs. 1976-79, v.p. 1979), Alpha Lambda Delta, Phi Delta Kappa, Phi Kappa Phi, Omicron Delta Kappa, Sigma Chi. Avocations: photography, tennis, bicycling. Home: Decatur, Ill. Died July 26, 2010.

DEEMS, RICHARD EMMET, magazine publisher; b. NYC, Jan. 19, 1913; s. Walter A. and Marie (Neufeld) D.; m. Jean S.; 1 child, Cynthia. LHD (hon.), Oglethorpe U., 1972. Propr. Interstate News Service, 1930-32; with circulation dept. New Yorker mag., 1932-33; circulation mgr. Esquire mag., 1933-39; with Harper's Bazaar, 1939-52, advt. mgr., 1947-52; v.p. charge advt. Hearst mags., 1952-55, exec. v.p., 1955-60, pres., 1960-76, chmn., 1976-78. Dir., mem. fin. and exec. coms. Hearst Corp.; dir. Nat. Mag. Co., London. Trustee William Randolph Hearst Found., The Hearst Found. Inc. Decorated knight Order of St. Martin, 1972 Mem. Mag. Pubs. Assn. (dir., Pub. of Yr. award 1979) Clubs: Bohemian (San Francisco), Everglades (Palm Beach, Fla.). Home: Palm Beach, Fla. Died May 4, 2009.

DEITZ, MERRITT SINGLETON, JR., judge; b. Wilmore, Ky., Jan. 6, 1936; s. Merritt S. and Irene Elizabeth (Wilder) Deitz; m. Sandra Tattershall Deitz, June 1961; m. Susan Langan Deitz, Oct. 22, 1978; children: Merritt Singleton III, Hillary Graham. BA in Journalism, U. Ky., 1961; LLB, George Washington U., 1965; LLM, U. Va., 1982. Bar: Ky. 65, US Dist. Ct. Ky. 65, US Supreme Ct. 76. Assoc. Wyatt Grafton & Sloss, Louisville, 1965—68; counsel to gov. Ky., 1968—69; commr. of econ. security Ky., 1969—71; pvt. practice Louisville, 1971—77; US bankruptcy judge Western Dist. Ky., Louisville, from 1977. Sgt. USMC, 1955—59. Mem.: Ky. Bar Assn., Pendennis Club, Sigma Delta Chi, Order of Coif. Republican. Episcopalian. Home: Louisville, Ky. Died Apr. 11, 2009.

DEKKER, GEORGE GILBERT, literature professor, writer, former academic administrator; b. Long Beach, Calif., Sept. 8, 1934; s. Gilbert J. and Laura (Barnes) D.; m. Linda Jo Bartholomew, Aug. 31, 1973; children by previous marriage: Anna Allegra, Clara Joy, Ruth Siobhan, Laura Daye. BA in

English, U. Calif.-Santa Barbara, 1955; MA in English, 1958; M.Litt., Cambridge U., Eng., 1961; PhD in English, U. Essex, Eng., 1967. Lectr. U. Wales, Swansea, 1962-64; lectr. in lit. U. Essex, 1964-69, reader in lit., 1969-72, dean Sch. Comparative Studies, 1969-71; assoc. prof. English Stanford U., Calif., 1972-74, prof., 1974—2001, prof. emeritus, from 2001, chmn. dept., 1978-81, 84-85, Joseph S. Atha prof. humanities, from 1988, dir. program in Am. Studies, 1988-91, assoc. dean grad. policy, 1993—96, 2000—02. Author: Sailing After Knowledge, 1963, James Fenimore Cooper the Novelist, 1967, Coleridge and the Literature of Sensibility, 1978, The American Historical Romance, 1987, The Fictions of Romantic Tourism, 2005, Touching Fire: A Forestry Memoir, 2008; editor: Donald Davie: The Responsibilities of Literature, 1983 Nat. Endowment Humanities fellow, 1977; Inst. Advanced Studies in Humanities fellow U. Edinburgh (Scotland), 1982; hon. fellow, Clare Hall Cambridge, 1997, Stanford Humanities Ctr., 1997. Mem. Am. Lit. Assn. Democrat. Home: Palo Alto, Calif. Died Feb. 25, 2010.

DELANEY, JOHN WHITE, lawyer; b. Springfield, Mass., Feb. 28, 1943; s. Frank T. and Emily (White) D.; m. Betsey Secor; children: Erin, Elizabeth. AB, Harvard U., 1964, JD, 1967. Bar: Mass. 1967, U.S. Dist. Ct. Mass. 1968. Staff asst. to U.S. senator Leverett Saltonstall, Washington, 1966; law clk. Mass. Superior Ct., Boston, 1967-68; asst. atty. gen. State of Mass., Boston, 1968-69; legis. asst. Gov. Commonwealth of Mass., Boston, 1969-73; asst. sec. consumer affairs and bus. regulation Commonwealth of Mass., 1973-76; exec. dir. Boston Mcpl. Rsch. Bur., 1976-80; dir. govt. and community affairs Bank of Boston, 1980-89; sr. ptnr. Hale and Dorr, Boston, 1989—2004; ptnr. Wilmer Cutler Pickering Hale and Dorr LLP, Boston, 2004—06; sr. counsel Wilmer Hale, Boston, 2007—08. Dir. New England Legal Found., Boston, 1986-2008. Dir. Robert F. Kennedy Action Corps, Boston, 1973-92, mem. adv. coun., 2006—; sec. Harvard Class of 1964, 1979-, Coordinating Com., Boston, 1984-87; trustee, mem. exec. com. Mass. Taxpayers Found., Boston, 1986—; dist. rep. Dedham Town Meeting, Mass., 1986—; trustee Boston Mcpl. Rsch. Bur., 1991—2009, Brain Sci. Found., 2005—; mem. adv. coun. The Trustees of Reservations, 1993-99, 2000-06, bd. dirs., 2006-; dir. Greater Boston C. of C., 1992—2009; pres. Friends of RFK Children's Action Corps, Inc., 1996-03; mem. Mass. IOLTA Com., 2004—. Fellow Mass. Hist. Soc.; mem. Boston Bar Assn. (mem. coun. 2003-06), Clover Club Boston (pres. 2006). Home: Dedham, Mass. Died July 30, 2010.

DELBRIDGE, NORMAN GEORGE, JR., army officer, civil engineer; b. Detroit, Jan. 4, 1928; s. Norman G. and Eleanor (Meyers) D.; m. Margaret McClure Drane, June 22, 1957; children— Norman Scott, David McClure BS, U.S. Mil. Acad., West Point, 1953; MS in Civil Engring., Iowa State U., Ames, 1957. Registered profl. civil engr. Served as enlisted man U.S. Army, 1946-47, active duty res. officer, 1947-49; commd. 2d lt. C.E. U.S. Army, 1953, advanced through grades to maj. gen., 1981, chief surveillance target acquisition OCRD Washington, 1969-72, dist. engr. Pitts. dist., 1972-75, div. engr. European div. Frankfurt, Fed. Republic Germany, 1976-78, div. engr. S. Pacific div. San Francisco, 1978-80, asst. chief engrs. Washington, 1980-84, dep. chief engrs., from 1984. Chmn. bd. engrs. for rivers and harbors, Washington, 1984—; pres. Calif. Debris Commn., San Francisco, 1978-80; mem. Coastal Engring. Research Bd., San Francisco, 1978-80 Author papers in field Recipient Profl. Achievement Citation in Engring. Iowa State U., 1985; Disting. Service medal, U.S. Govt., 1984 Mem. Soc. Am. Mil. Engrs. (post pres. 1973-74, 1979-80), Am. Pub. Works Assn. (bd. dirs. 1985—), Nat. Soc. Profl. Engrs., Permanent Nat. Assn. of Navigation Congresses, ASCE Avocations: philately; wood working. Home: Lovettsville, Va. Died July 30, 2010.

DELELLIS, JOSEPH, electrical engineer; b. Newton, Mass., Dec. 18, 1939; s. Giuseppe and Constance (Berghelli) deL.; m. Geraldine A. Desrosiers, Nov. 10, 1962; children— Daniel, Mellisa. B.S.E.E., Northeastern U., 1962, M.S.E.E., 1968. Engr. NSA, Ft. Meade, Mo., 1962-83; sr. engr. Raytheon, Sudbury, Mass., 1963-65; sr. engr. specialist GTE, Needham, Mass., 1966—. Patentee in field. Contbr. articles to profl. jours. Recipient CSD Superior Performance award GTE, 1985, Leslie Warner award GTE, 1976, 85, Navmat Reliability Maintenance award U.S. Navy, 1983. Mem. IEEE. Avocation: music. Home: Walpole, Mass. Died Mar. 27, 2010.

DEL GRECO, FRANCESCO, physician, educator; b. Italy, Aug. 23, 1923; came to U.S., 1951, naturalized, 1959; s. Gaetano and Gilda (Borga) del G.; 1 son, Paul. MD, U. Rome, 1946; postgrad., Northwestern U., 1959-61. Intern Univ. Hosp., Rome, 1946-50, resident, 1950-51; research fellow Cleve. Clinic, 1951-54, asst. staff, 1955-57; vol. asst., research fellow Postgrad. Med. Sch. U. London, St. Thomas Hosp., 1954-55; intern Passavant Meml. Hosp., Chgo., 1957-58, resident, 1958-60, attending staff, 1960-72, dir. Dialysis Ctr., 1958-93, dir. Clin. Research Ctr., 1961-81; attending staff VA Lakeside Med. Ctr., Chgo., from 1960, Northwestern Meml. Hosp., from 1972. Prof. medicine Med. Sch. Northwestern U., Chgo., 1967—, chief sect. nephrology-hypertension, 1973-85; med. adv. bd. Ill. Kidney Found., chmn., 1975-79; mem. cardiovascular-renal study sect. Nat. Heart Inst.-NIH, 1975-79; mem. renal disease adv. com. State of Ill., 1974— Danish Govt. scholar, 1951; Nat. Heart Inst. NIH fellow, 1952-53 Fellow ACP, AAAS; mem. Am. Heart Assn. (fellow coun. on circulation, coun. on high blood pressure rsch.); mem. Am. Physiol. Soc., Soc. Exptl. Biology and Medicine, Ctrl. Soc. Clin. Rsch., Am. Soc. Artificial Internal Orgns., Am. Soc. Nephrology, Am. Fedn. Clin. Rsch., Internat. Soc. Nephrology, Internat. Soc. Hypertension, Am. Soc. Transplant Physicians, Am. Soc. Hypertension. Home: Chicago, Ill. Died Jan. 17, 2010.

D'ELIA, DONALD JOHN, historian, educator; b. Jersey City, June 16, 1933; s. Anthony Bartholomew and Frances Marie (Santello) D.; m. Margaret Cingel, May 25, 1957; children: Keith, Gregory, Nancy, Anthony. BA, Rutgers U., 1956, MA, 1957; PhD, Pa. State U., 1965. Instr. Pa. State U., University Park, 1959-61; assoc. prof. social studies Bloomsburg (Pa.) State U., 1961-65; prof. history SUNY, New Paltz, from 1965. Lectr. Marist Coll., Poughkeepsie, N.Y., 1967, Dickinson Coll., Carlisle, Pa., 1968; adj. prof. NYU, 1983; ednl. cons. Friends of St. Maria Goretti USA, Maryknoll, N.Y., 1990—. Author: Dr. Benjamin Rush, 1974; co-author: Motion Towards Perfection, 1990, We Hold These Truths and More, 1993, The American Enlightenment, 1993 and others. Min. prefect St. Peter Damian Secular Franciscan Fraternity, New Paltz; hon. bd. dirs. Christopher Dawson Ctr. for the Study of Christian Culture, Renfrew, Ont., Can. 2d lt. U.S. Army, 1957. Recipient Citation for tchg. Gov. Mario Cuomo, N.Y., 1984. Mem. Soc. Cath. Social Scientists (co-chmn., bd. dirs. 1992—), Mid-Hudson Italian-Am. Cultural Found. (Man of Yr. award 1983), Assn. Italian-Am. Faculty SUNY (co-founder), KC. Roman Catholic. Avocations: chess, computers, travel, music. Home: New Paltz, NY. Died July 27, 2009.

DELIBES, CLAUDE BLANCHE, communications company executive; b. Paris, Sept. 20, 1932; came to U.S., 1940; naturalized, 1954; d. Andre Jean and Simone (Barou) Seligmann; m. Maurice Delibes, Dec. 31, 1961; 1 child by previous marriage, Roger Schwartz; 1 child, Jacqueline Delibes, 1954. B.A., Sorbonne U., Paris, 1953. Editor Fairchild Publications, N.Y.C., 1961-65; dir. pub. rels. West Point Pepperell Corp., N.Y.C., 1968-72; sr. account supr. The Siesel Co., N.Y.C., 1972-75; pres. Delibes Communications, Ltd., N.Y.C., 1975—. Mem. Women Execs. in Pub. Rels., Fashion Group, Internat. Furnishings and Design Assn. Died Mar. 14, 2010.

DELOACHE, WILLIAM REDDING, pediatrician; b. Camden, SC, Mar. 27, 1920; s. William Redding and Louise Blakeney (Zemp) DeL.; m. Bond Davis, Sept. 7, 1943; children: Frances D., William Redding Jr. Student, Furman U., Greenville, SC, 1937-38; BA, Vanderbilt U., 1941, MD, 1943. Diplomate Am. Bd. Pediatrics; lic. Tenn. Healing Arts.; cert. med. examiner, S.C. Intern pediatrics Vanderbilt Hosp., Nashville, 1944, resident pediatrics, 1947-48, N.C. Bapt. Hosp., Bowman Gray, Winston-Salem, 1948-49; pvt. practice Greenville, S.C., 1949-53; ptnr. Christie Pediatric Group, Greenville, 1953-72; dir. nurseries Greenville Hosp. Sys., 1972-77, dir. med. edn., 1977-82; assoc. exec. dir. Am. Bd. Pediatrics, Chapel Hill, N.C., 1982-87, ofcl. examiner, 1976-90. Assoc.,sr. assoc. Greenville Meml. Hosp., Greenville Hosp. Sys., 1994-92; mem. pediatric staff St. Francis Hosp., Greenville, 1949-92; assoc. prof. pediatrics Med. U. S.C., 1973-87; mem. bd. Vanderbilt U. Med. Ctr., Nashville, 1985-91, mem. adv. bd., 1991—. Contbr. articles to profl. jours. Elder Fourth Presbyn. Ch., Greenville. Capt. U.S. Army, 1944-46. Mem. AMA, Am. Acad. Pediatrics (career achievement award S.C. chpt. 1987), Greenville County Med. Soc. (pres. 1971), S.C. Med. Assn., So. Soc. Pediatric Rsch., So. Perinatal Assn., Greenville C. of C. (bd. mem.), Rotary Club (mem. bd. 1976—), Greenville Country Club, Poinsett Club. Avocations: woodworking, gardening, travel, tennis. Home: Greenville, SC. Died Mar. 4, 2009.

DE LORIMIER, ALFRED ALEXANDRE, retired pediatric surgeon; b. Washington, May 30, 1931; s. Alfred Alexandre and Emilie Blanche (Kidder) de L.; m. Sandra Marie Veano, Nov. 21, 1953; children: Robert Maurice, Sally Renee, Nancy Denise. BS, U. Calif., Berkeley, 1953; MD, U. Calif., San Francisco, 1956. Diplomate Am. Bd. Surgery. Intern San Joaquin Gen. Hosp., Stockton, Calif., 1956-57; resident in gen. surgery U. Calif., San Francisco, 1957-62; fellow in pediat. surgery Ohio State U., Columbus, 1962-64; asst. prof. surgery U. Calif., San Francisco, 1964-71, assoc. prof. surgery, 1971-80, prof. surgery, 1980-96, chief pediat. surg. divsn., 1965-88, Calif. Pacific Med. Ctr., San Francisco, 1994-96; ret., 1996. Owner de Lorimier Vineyards, 1974—. Maj. USAFR, 1966-71. Avocations: sailing, growing winery grapes. Home: Geyserville, Calif. Died Oct. 4, 2009.

DE LUTIS, DONALD CONSE, investment advisor, consultant; b. Rome, NY, Apr. 25, 1934; s. Conse R. and Mary D.; m. Ruth L.; 1 child, Dante. BS in Econs., Niagara U., 1956; MBA, Boston Coll., 1962. V.p. John Nuveen & Co., Inc., San Francisco, 1968-74; acct. exec. Dean Witter & Co., London, 1975-77; sr. investment officer Buffalo Savs. Bank, NY, 1978-80; exec. v.p. Robert Brown & Co., Inc., San Francisco, 1980-89, Capitol Corp. Asset mgmt., 1989-91; exec. v.p., dir. Pacific Securities, Inc., San Francisco, 1980—90; mng. dir. Coast Ptnrs. Securities, Inc., 1998-99; chmn. Orrell Capital Mgmt., Inc., 1991-98, from 2000. Commr. San Francisco Bay Conservation and Devel. Commn., 1983-93, State of Calif. Commn. Housing and Community Devel., 1974-77. Served with USAF, 1957-58. Republican. Roman Catholic. Home: San Francisco, Calif. Died July 3, 2010.

DELVALLE, HUGH MADURO, international trading executive; b. Yonkers, NY, Mar. 9, 1920; s. Kenneth and Eunice (Maduro) D.; m. June Ackerman, Dec. 26, 1949; children: Kenneth (dec.), Bruce, Margot. BS, Purdue U., 1940. Various positions Union Bag and Paper Corp., 1941-43, Motta's of Panama, 1943-45; mgr. Colon Import and Export Co. Ltd., Republic of Panama, 1945-50; mgr. import dept. W.R. Grace & Co., NYC, 1951-55; v.p. Internat. Ore and Fertilizer Corp., NYC, 1955-80, Occidental Chem. Corp., NYC, 1965-89; pres. Delchem Inc., Greenwich, Conn., 1980-85, Mamoreck, N.Y., 1986-91. Mem. Mexican C. of C. of U.S., ADIFAL (Mex.). Theta Chi (steward Purdue U. 1939-40). Died Jan. 25, 2009.

DEMETER, THOMAS MICHAEL, advertising executive; b. Flint, Mich., Jan. 14, 1949; s. John Charles and Alice Marie (Hatzenbuhler) D.; m. Nola Susanne May, May 29, 1970; children— Heather Lynne, Heidi Anne. Student Marquette U., 1967-69. Vice pres., creative dir. The Imagination Corp., Lansing, Mich., 1974-75; producer Glass Apple Music, Inc., Flint, Mich., 1976-77; creative dir. Counter Graphics Ltd., Flint, 1977-79; exec. art dir. Provandie and Chirurg Advt., Boston, 1980; v.p., creative dir. Schmullenberger and Nargassans, Boston, 1981-83; v.p., assoc. creative dir. Cosmopulos, Crowley and Daly, Boston, 1984—; cons. Artists Found., Boston, 1969—; cons. in field; commd. artist and illustrator. Writer-producer 3 part rock documentary Rocket Radio Hour, 1974, multi-media theatrical prodns. Equestrian Recess, Welcome Back to the Other Side. Contbr. articles, creative works to profl. jours. Recipient Hammermill award, 1979, 3 Hatch awards, 1981, Mytec award, 1983, Best TV Comml. of 1982 Internat. Newspaper Advt. and Mktg. Execs., 4 first place DESI awards, 1985, 4 N.Y. Art Dir. Show Certs. of Merit, 1985, 4 Am. Corp. Identity awards, 1985. Mem. New Eng. Broadcast Assn., Boston Advt. Club. Club: Silver Lake Ski (Mich.). Avocations: snow skiing; water skiing; surfing; tennis; music. Died Apr. 13, 2009.

DEMING, WILLIS RILEY, retired lawyer; b. Ada, Ohio, Nov. 28, 1914; s. Cliffe and Okla (Riley) D.; m. Dorothy Arline Hill, 1950 (div. 1971); children: Susan Elizabeth, Deborah Anne Gunst, David Riley; m. Constance S. Mori, 1971 (div. 1986); m. Olive Plunkett Rose, 1994 (dec. 1999). BA, Ohio State U., 1935, JD, 1938. Bar: Ohio 1938, Calif. 1947, D.C. 1957. Pvt. practice, Columbus, Ohio, 1938-39; casualty claim examiner Am. Surety Co., NYC, 1939-41; chief bds. and claims rev. br. San Francisco Port of Embarkation, 1946-47; atty. Treadwell and Laughlin, San Francisco, 1947-54, Brobeck, Phleger & Harrison, San Francisco, 1954-56, Washington, 1956-60; pvt. practice Washington, 1961-62; sr. v.p., gen. counsel Matson Nav. Co., San Francisco, 1962—71, 1974—92; v.p., sec., gen. counsel Alexander & Baldwin, Inc., Honolulu, 1968—74. Served to lt. col. AUS, 1941-46; col. U.S. Army, ret. Mem. ABA, State Bar Calif., Soc. for Asian Art (pres. 1995-97), Claremont Country Club (Oakland). Home: Oakland, Calif. Died Dec. 30, 2009.

DENENBERG, HERBERT SIDNEY, journalist, lawyer, educator, retired state official; b. Omaha, Nov. 20, 1929; s. David Aaron and Fannie (Rothenberg) Denenberg; m. Naomi N. Glushakow, June 22, 1958. BS, Johns Hopkins U., 1958; JD, Creighton U., 1954; LLM, Harvard U., 1959; PhD, U. Pa., 1962; LLD, Allentown Coll. St. Francis de Sales, 1989; LHD, Spring Garden Coll., 1992. CLU, CPCU. Mem. firm Denenberg & Denenberg, Omaha, 1954—55; asst. prof. ins. U. Iowa, Iowa City, 1962, Wharton Sch. Fin. and Commerce, U. Pa., 1962—65, assoc. prof., 1965—68, Harry J. Loman prof. ins., 1968—73; commr. ins. State of Pa., 1971—74; commr. Pa. Pub. Utility Commn., 1975; columnist Phila. Bull., 1975—79; consumer columnist Phila. Daily News, 1979—81, Phila. Jour., 1981—82, Del. County Daily and Sunday Times, 1987—90, Bucks County Courier Times, 1987—90, Pottstown Mercury, 1988—94, Burlington County Daily Times, 1987—90, Reading Eagle, from 1989, Doylestown Patriot, from 1991, Citizen's Choice of Wilkes-Barre, Pa., from 1992, Mainliner, 1992—94, Auto Insider, 1992—93, Collector's Guide, 1992—93, New Chester Jour., 1992—94, Del. County Bus. Monthly, 1993—96, Hellenic News, from 1993, 1994, Phoenixville, Phoenix, 1994—96, Eastern Poconos Cmty. News, from 1999; editor The Denenberg Report Orgn., from 1999; consumer and investigative reporter Adelphia Cable Update Cable Sys., 1999—2000, Sta. WCAU-TV (NBC), Phila., 1975—98; talk show host Sta. WCAU-AM CBS, Phila., 1976—80; consumer reporter WLVT-TV (PBS), 2001—10. Columnist Sales and Mktg. Mag., 1976—80, Ins. Monitor, Hyderalnd, India; regular on Real People NBC-TV, 1979—80; consumer reporter Nat. Pub. Radio, 1979; spl. counsel, rsch. dir. Pres.'s Nat. Adv. Panel on Ins. in Riot-Affected Areas., 1967—68; spl. adviser to Gov. Pa. on consumer affairs, 1974—75; assoc. dir. Wis. Ins. Laws Rev. Project, 1966—71; cons. Dept. Labor, 1965—68, Coop. Devel. Adminstrn., PR, 1967—68, John F. Kennedy Ctr., Washington, 1966—71, Small Bus. Adminstrn., 1968—71, Dept. Justice, 1969, FTC, 1968, Dept. Transp., 1969—70, State of Nev., 1969—71, Alaska Legislature, 1976, U.S. Commn. Civil Rights, 1977—78, Concerned Physicians for Patient Care; spl. cons. to Mayor Washington, 1968—69; mem. Bd. of Health Promotion and Disease Prevention of Inst. Medicine NAS, 1973—74, mem., from 1973; vis. prof. law Temple U.; adj. prof. ins., info. sci. and tech. Cabrini Coll., from 1999; rsch. fellow Sapio Inst. Interactive Learning, from 1999. Author (with others): (book) Risk and Insurance, 2d edit., 1973; author: (with Spencer L. Kimball) Insurance Government and Social Policy, 1969; author: (with J.R. Ferrari) Life Insurance and/or Mutual Funds, 1967; author: (with S.L. Kimball) Mass Marketing of Property and Liability Insurance, 1970; author: The Insurance Trap, 1972, Shopper's guide to Surgery, 1972, Shopper's Guide to Dentistry, 1973, Shopper's Guide to Insurance on Mobile Homes, 1973, A Citizens Bill of Hospital Rights, 1973, Shopper's guide to Bankruptcy, 1974, Shopper's guide Book, 1974, Herb Denenberg's Smart Shopper's Guide, 1980, Shopper's guide to Medical Equipment, 1990, A Consumer's Guide to Herbal Medicines, 1999, Guide to Selecting a Pharmacist, 1999; columnist, mem. editl. bd. Caveat Emptor, 1971—79; columnist: Phila. Evening Bulletin; mem. adv. bd. medicine and health newsletter The Dr.'s People, 1989—93. Mem. adminstrv. bd. S.S. Huebner Found., 1968—71; pres. Am. Risk and Ins. Assn., 1969—70; Dem. candidate U.S. Senate, 1974; bd. dirs. Consumers Union, 1973—76; bd. trustees Ctr. for Proper Medication Use, from 1994. 1st lt. JAGC US Army, 1955—58. Recipient awards for articles, Jour. Risk and Ins., Lambert award, 1972, Nat. Press Club award, 1976, 1977, 1980, 1984, 1988, Journalism award, Am. Osteo. Assn., 1976, Am. Chiropractors Assn., 1977—80, 1988, citation, Columbia U., Media award, ATLA, 1986, Enterprise Reporting award, Phila. Press Club, 1986, 1987, 1999, Pub. Svc. award, 1987, 1989, 1996, 1997, 1999, Best Feature award, 1995, 1996,

1997, Spot News award, 1999, award for lifetime achievement, 1998, Gov.'s Hwy. Safety award, State of Pa., 1997, Enterprise Reporting award, Pa. AP, 1988, Nat. Headliner award, 1987—88, 1990, 1992, 40 Emmy awards, Best TV Pub. Svc. award, Soc. Profl. Journalists, 1987, 1988, 1990, 1992, 1993, 1994, 1998, 1999, TV Feature award, 1989, 1994, 1995, 1996, 1997, 1998, TV Mag. Feature award, 1989, 1992, Best Media Criticism, 1990, 1993, Best Investigation, 1990, 1992, 1993, 1994, 1995, 1996, 1997, 1998, 1999, Best Health and Sci. Report, 1995—99, Breaking News award, 1998, Outstanding Media Consumer Svc. award, Consumer Fedn. Am., 1990, Sam Beber Disting. AZA Alumnus award, B'nai B'rith, 1990, Outstanding Citizen award, Firemen's Assn. Pa., 1991, Consumer of Yr. award, Pa. Assn. Weights and Measures, 1991, Phila. award integrity in journalism, 1988, Award of Excellence in legal reporting and analysis, Am. Bd. Trial Advocates, 1996, Award of Lifetime Achievement, Phila. Press Club, 1998, Award for Excellence in Legal Reporting and Analysis, Am. Bd. Trial Advocates, 1996, Phila. Press Club award for lifetime achievement, 1998, others, Am. Bd. Trial Advocates award, 1996; named to Phila. Press Club Hall of Fame, 1995. Mem.: ABA (life), Internat. Assn. Ins. Law (v.p. sci. sect. Am. chpt. 1967—71), Med. Soc. Access to Physicians (blue ribbon panel Phila. County from 1998), Am. Risk and Ins. Assn. (2nd v.p. 1967—68, bd. dirs. 1967—71, pres. 1969—70), Montgomery County Bar Assn., Pa. Bar Assn., Old Clunker Club (founder, pres. from 1982). Home: Saint Davids, Pa. Died Mar. 18, 2010.

DENIORD, RICHARD NEWNHAM, JR., surgeon; b. Buffalo, Mar. 6, 1925; s. Richard N. and Hollis (Hunt) deNiord; m. Nancy Perkins deNiord, Aug. 31, 1946 (div. 1977); children: Sally, Richard Newnham III, Holly, Lyman; m. Ruth Ann Schmitz, Apr. 6, 1979. BA, Yale U., 1948, MD, 1952. Diplomate Am. Bd. Surgery, Am. Bd. Thoracic Surgery. Intern Grace New Haven Med. Ctr., 1952—56. Resident in surgery Yale U. Med. Ctr., New Haven, 1952—56; resident in thoracic & cardiovasc. surgery U. Va. Hosp., Charlottesville, 1956—58; practice medicine specializing in thoracic & cardiovasc. surgery, Lynchburg, Va., 1958—76, Crookston, Minn., 1977—83, Wolfeboro, NH, from 1983; mem. staff Huggins Hosp., NH. Contbr. articles to profl. jours. 2d lt. USMCR, 1943—45. Fellow: ACS, So. Thoracic Soc., Thoracic Surgery Soc., Am. Assn. for Thoracic Surgery; mem.: Southeastern Surg. Soc. Republican. Presbyterian. Avocations: squash, tennis, writing. Home: Wolfeboro, NH. Died Apr. 30, 2010.

DE PAN, HARRY MCCARTHY, retired surgeon; b. Glens Falls, NY, July 13, 1923; Grad., Williams Coll., 1945; MD, Cornell U., 1947. Cert. surgeon, 1955. Intern Hartford Hosp., 1947-48, resident surgeon, 1948-49, 52-54, Hosp. Spl. Surgeons, NYC, 1949-50; resident thoracic surgeon Cedarcrest Hosp., Newington, Conn., 1958-59; sr. attending surgeon Glens Falls N.Y. Hosp. Mem. AMA, ACS, DAGS. Home: Queensbury, NY. Died May 26, 2010.

DEPRIEST, DOUGLAS JUNIOUS, statistician, scientific officer, lecturer; b. Sandston, Va., June 9, 1944; s. James Henry and Octavia (Christian) DePriest; m. Kerdene Mayo DePriest, Sept. 3, 1968; children: Marcia, Kraig, Delmar. BS, Hampton Inst., 1966; MS, U. Tenn., 1968; PhD, Am. U., 1976. Instr. Howard U., Washington, 1968—69; sci. officer Office Naval Rsch., Arlington, Va., from 1971; dep. for spl. programs, from 1984; lectr. Am. U., Washington, from 1979. Editor: Reliability in Acquisitions Process, 1983, Statistical Analysis of Weather Modification Experiments, 1980. Sec. YMCA, Fairfax, Va., 1983. With US Army, 1969—71. Recipient Outstanding Performance award, US Navy, 1979, Merit Pay Performance award, 1982, 1984. Fellow: AAAS; mem.: Biometrics Soc., Inst. Environ. Sci., Am. Statis. Assn., Beta Kappa Chi, Alpha Kappa Mu. Avocations: music, reading, sports. Home: Vienna, Va. Died Oct. 12, 2009.

DERICCO, LAWRENCE ALBERT, retired college president; b. Stockton, Calif., Jan. 28, 1923; s. Giulio and Agnes (Giovacchini) DeR.; m. Alma Mezzetta, June 19, 1949; 1 child, Lawrence Paul. BA, U. Pacific, Stockton, Calif., 1949, MA, 1971, LLD (hon.), 1987. Bank clk. Bank of Am., Stockton, 1942-43; prin. Castle Sch. Dist., San Joaquin County, Calif., 1950-53; dist. supt., prin. Waverly Sch. Dist., Stockton, 1953-63; bus. mgr. San Joaquin Delta Jr. Coll. Dist., Stockton, 1963-65, asst. supt., bus. mgr., 1965-77, v.p. mgmt. services, 1977-81; pres., supt. San Joaquin Delta Coll., 1981-87, pres. emeritus, from 1988. Mem. Workforce Investment Bd. With AUS, 1943-46, PTO. Mem. NEA, Calif. Tchrs. Assn., Native Sons of Golden West (past pres.), Phi Delta Kappa Home: Stockton, Calif. Died July 2, 2010.

DESVEAUX, JAMES JOSEPH, lawyer; b. Waterville, Maine, Oct. 12, 1944; s. Joseph W. and Imogene (Dyer) DesVeaux; m. Barbara L. Suess, Jan. 29, 1973; children: Nicole, Matthew. BBA, Western Ill. U., 1967; JD, DePaul U., 1976. Bar: Ill. 1976, US Dist. Ct. Ill. 1977. Claim rep., supr. Aetna Life & Casualty, Chgo., 1969—76, sr. atty, 1976—80, mng. atty., from 1980; pvt. practice Chgo., from 1976. Served with US Army, 1967—69. Mem.: ABA, Chgo. Bar Assn., Ill. State Bar Assn., Def. Rsch. Inst., Trial Lawyers Club. Republican. Roman Catholic. Home: Glen Ellyn, Ill. Died Jan. 15, 2009.

DETRE, THOMAS, psychiatrist, educator; b. Budapest, Hungary, May 17, 1924; came to U.S., 1953, naturalized, 1958; m. Katherine Maria Drechsler, Sept. 15, 1956; children: John Allan, Antony James. BA, Gymnasium of Piarist Fathers, Kecskemet, Hungary, 1942; postgrad., Horthy Miklos U. and Pazmany Peter U., Hungary, 1945-47; MD, Rome U., 1952. Diplomate: Am. Bd. Psychiatry and Neurology (assoc. examiner). Intern Morrisania City Hosp., NYC, 1953-54; resident in psychiatry Mt. Sinai Hosp., NYC, 1954-55, Yale U., 1955-57, chief resident, instr., 1957-58, instr., 1958-59, asst. prof., 1959-62; dir. psychiat. inpatient service Yale-New Haven Hosp., 1960-68, assoc. prof., 1962-70, asst. chief psychiatry div., 1965-68, psychiatrist in chief, 1968-73, prof., 1970-73; prof., chmn. dept. psychiatry U. Pitts., 1973-82, assoc. sr. vice chancellor, 1982-84, Disting. svc. prof. health sciences, 1982—2004, sr. v.p. health sciences, 1984-92, sr. vice chancellor for health scis., 1992-98, pres. med. and health care div., 1986-90, pres. med. ctr., 1990-92, emeritus dist. vice chancellor health sci., 2004—10, emeritus Disting. svc. prof. psychiatry, 2004—10; dir. Western Psychiat. Inst. and Clin. Western Psychiat. Inst. and Clin., 1973-94; exec. v.p. internat. and acad. programs, dir. internat. med. affairs UPMC Health Sys., Pitts., 1998—2002, med. dir. internat. programs, 2002—04. Mem. Nat. Adv. Mental Health Coun., NIH, 1994-97; pres. bd. regents Nat. Libr. Medicine, 2005. Author: (with H.G. Jarecki) Modern Psychiatric Treatment, 1971; contbr. chpts. to books. Fellow Am. Coll. Psychiatrists, Am. Coll. Neuropsychopharmacology (pres. 1994), Am. Psychiat. Assn. (life fellow); mem. Inst. Medicine, Collegium Internat. Neuropsychopharmacologicum. Home: Pittsburgh, Pa. Died Oct. 9, 2010.

DETWEILER, JOHN ADAM, physician; b. Pine Grove, Pa., Apr. 16, 1924; s. John A. and Bessie (Philips) D.; m. Elaine Wedemeyer, Sept. 6, 1946; children— Judith, Joan, Jeanne BS, Lebanon Valley Coll., 1948; MD, Tufts U., 1952. Diplomate Am. Bd. Internal Medicine. Intern St. Francis Hosp., Evanston, IL, 1952-53; med. resident Hines VA Hosp., Ill., 1953-56; practiced medicine specializing in internal medicine Arlington Heights, Ill.; chief of staff Northwest Community Hosp., Arlington Heights, 1965. Served with AUS, 1946-48 Fellow ACP; mem. Phi Rho Sigma. Home: Brooksville, Fla. Died Dec. 25, 2009.

DEUTSCH, WILLIAM EMIL, ophthalmology professor; b. Chgo., Mar. 31, 1926; s. Emil and Jeannette (Weil) D.; m. Natasha Sobotka, Dec. 23, 1951; children: Thomas A., Judith Deutsch Kornblatt, Susan E. BS, U. Ill., 1948, MD, 1950. Diplomate Am. Bd. Ophthalmology. Intern Michael Reese Hosp., Chgo., 1950-51; resident U. Ill., Chgo., 1951-53, clin. asst. prof. ophthalmology, from 1971; pvt. practice ophthalmology Chgo., from 1955; assoc. prof. ophthalmology Rush Med. Coll., Chgo., 1971-82, prof., chmn. dept., from 1982. Bd. mem. Ill. Soc. Prevention Blindness, Chgo., 1983—, Coun. Jewish Elderly, 1982—; tech. rev. bd. State of Ill., 1985—. Capt. USAF, 1953-55. Mem. Am. Acad. Ophthalmology (councilor 1988—), Assn. Rsch. in Vision and Ophthalmology, Assn. Univ. Profs. Ophthalmology, Ill. Assn. Ophthalmology (bd. dirs. 1979—), Chgo. Opthal. Soc. (coun. 1979-90, pres. 1982-83). Home: Evanston, Ill. Died July 15, 2009.

DEVINE, JAMES FRANCIS, state official, public relations professional; b. Rocky Mount, NC, Dec. 17, 1935; s. Joseph David and Cecilia Frances (Higgs) D.; m. Denorah A. Radford; children: James Francis Jr., Angela Adele. Student, Belmont Abbey Coll., NC, 1953-54, E. Carolina U., 1955, Internat. Corres. Schs., 1970. Account exec. advt. The News and Observer Pub. Co., Raleigh, N.C., 1966-70; dir. pub. affairs N.C. Dept. Agr., Raleigh, 19706. Pres. Longview Writers Inc., raleigh, 1991—. Editor: The Voice, 1966-76. Mem. N.C. Assn. Govt. Info. Officers (pres. 1974-75), N.C. Farm Writers and Broadcasters Assn. (pres. 1985-86), Capital City Civitan Club (pres. 1966-67, dist. lt. gov. 1964-65). Democrat. Roman Catholic. Avocations: fishing, fiction writing, hunting. Home: Raleigh, NC. Died July 10, 2010.

DEVINE, JAMES RICHARD, legal educator; b. Newark, Jan. 31, 1948; s. Richard Caryl and Lucy Mae (Babcock) D.; m. Sharon Ann Jungquist, May 25, 1971; children: Zachary James, Joshua Calvin, Noah Brooks. AB, Franklin & Marshall Coll., 1970; JD cum laude, Seton Hall U., 1975. Bar: N.J. 1975, Mo. 1983. Law sec. N.J. Superior Ct., Freehold, 1975-76; assoc. Madden & Holobinko, Middletown, N.J., 1976-80; assoc. prof. U. Mo., Columbia, 1980-84, prof. law, 1984-85, David Ross Hardy prof. law, from 1986; assoc. cir. judge Iron County, Mo., 1990. Sec. dist. ethics and fee commn. N.J. Superior Ct., Monmouth County, 1976-80; chmn. com. on lawyer advt. Mo. Supreme Ct., Jefferson City, 1982-84. Author: Materials on Lawyer Trust Accounting, 1984, Cases/Materials on Professional Responsibility, 1985, Missouri Civil Pleading, 1986, Missouri Jury Instructions, 1985, Problems in Insurance Law, 1989, Non-Jury Case Files for Trial Advocacy, 1991. Bd. dirs. Mid-Mo. Legal Svcs. Mem. Mo. Bar Assn., N.J. Bar Assn., Am. Judicature Soc., Order of Coif (pres. U. Mo. chpt. 1987-88). Home: Columbia, Mo. Died May 12, 2010.

DE VOS, GEORGE ALPHONSE, psychologist, anthropologist; b. Detroit, July 25, 1922; s. Medard Joseph and Marina Marie (Tack) De V.; m. Winifred Olsen, May 4, 1944 (div. 1974); m. Suzanne Lake, Nov. 18, 1974; children: Laurie, Susan, Eric, Michael. BA in Sociology, U. Chgo., 1946, MA in Anthropology, 1948, PhD in Psychology, 1951. Chief psychologist, dir. psychol. tng. Elgin (Ill.) State Hosp., 1951-53; asst. prof. psychology U. Mich., Ann Arbor, 1955-57; assoc. prof. social welfare U. Calif., Berkeley, 1957-63, prof. anthropology, 1963-91, prof. emeritus, 1991—2010. Vis. prof. U. Rome, 1975, U. Paris, 1979, Cath. U. Leuven, Belgium, 1986, U. Barcelona, 1992; exch. prof. U. Leningrad (now U. St. Petersburg), 1990; chmn. Ctr. for Japanese and Korean Studies U. Calif., 1965—91; cons. Family Planning Rsch., Korean Inst. Behavioral Scis., Seoul, Republic of Korea, 1970—71; rsch. assoc. Ecole des Hautes Etudes en Scis. Sociales, U. Paris, 1973—91; sr. cons. series prodn. The Japanese Film PBS, 1975; dir. NSF project The Korean Minority in Japan; cons. on Japanese culture Human Rels. Area File, New Haven, 1975—82; cons. Cultural Learning East-West Center, Hawaii, 1978—79. Author: 22 books, including Oasis and Casbah, 1960, Japan's Invisible Race, 1966, Socialization for Achievement, 1973, Ethnic Identity, 1975, 4th edit., 2006, Responses to Change, 1976, Koreans in Japan, 1981, Heritage of Endurance: Delinquency in Japan, 1984, Culture and Self, 1985, 1984, Religion and the Family in East Asia, 1986, Symbolic Analysis Cross Culturally: The Rorschach Test, 1989, Status Inequality, 1990, Social Cohesion and Alienation, 1992, Confucianism and The Family, 1998, Basic Dimensions in Conscious Thought, 2004, Cross Cultural Dimensions in Conscious Thought, 2004, Concluding Thoughts in Challenges to Japanese Education. Fulbright fellow, Nagoya, Japan, 1953-55, NIMH fellow French Min. Justice, 1963, NSF fellow UN Social Def. Rsch. Inst., Rome, 1972-73; Fulbright Sr. Rsch. Sch. Cath. U. Rio Grande do Sul, Brazil, 1992. Mem. APA (pres. Soc. for Psychol. Anthropology 1984-85), Assn. Asian Studies, Am. Anthropology Assn. Home: Oakland, Calif. Died July 9, 2010.

DE VRIES, MARGARET GARRITSEN, economist; b. Detroit, Feb. 11, 1922; d. John Edward and Margaret Florence (Ruggles) Garritsen; m. Barend A. de Vries, Apr. 5, 1952; children: Christine, Barton. BA in Econs. with honors, U. Mich., 1943; PhD in Econs., MIT, 1946. With IMF, Washington, 1946-87, sr. economist, 1949-52, asst. chief multiple currency pratices div., 1953-57, chief Far Eastern Div., 1957-59, econ. cons., 1963-73, historian, 1973-87. Professorial lectr. econs. George Washington U., 1946-49, 58-63 Author: The International Monetary Fund, 1966-71, The System Under Stress, 2 vols., 1977, The International Monetary Fund, 1972-78, Cooperation on Trial, 3 vols., 1985, The IMF in a Changing World, 1945-85, transl. into Chinese, 1986, Balance of Payments, Adjustment: The IMF Experience, 1945-86, transl. into Chinese, 1989, (with I.S. Friedman) Foreign Economic Policy of the United States in the Postwar, 1947, (with J.K. Horsefield) The International Monetary Fund, 1945-65, Twenty Years of International Monetary Cooperation, 3 vols., 1969; contbr. articles to profl. jours. Recipient Disting. Alumni award U. Mich., 1980, Cert. of Appreciation George Washington U., 1987, Outstanding Washington Woman Economist award, 1987; AAUW scholar, 1939-42; U. Mich. Univ. scholar, 1942; Phi Kappa Phi fellow, 1943; MIT fellow, 1943-46; Ford Found. grantee, 1959-62. Mem. Am. Econ. Assn. (CSWEP - Carolyn Shaw Bell award 2002), U. Mich. Alumni Assn., MIT Alumnae Assn., Phi Beta Kappa, Phi Kappa Phi. Mem. United Church of Christ. Home: Bethesda, Md. Died Dec. 18, 2009.

DEW, WILLIAM WALDO, JR., bishop; b. Newport, Ky., Dec. 14, 1935; s. William Waldo and Thelma (Dittus) D.; m. Mae Marie Eggers, Jan. 5, 1958; children: Linda Dew-Hiersoux, William, Marilyn. BA, Union Coll., Barbourville, Ky., 1957; MDiv, Drew Theol. Sch., 1961; PhD (hon.), Rust Coll., 1991, Union Coll., 1992. Ordained to ministry United Meth. Ch. as deacon, 1958, as elder, 1963. Pastor Springville (Calif.) United Meth. Ch., 1961-64, Lindsay (Calif.) United Meth. Ch., 1964-67, Meml. United Meth. Ch., Clovis, Calif., 1967-72, Epworth United Meth. Ch., Berkeley, Calif., 1972-79; dist. supt. Cen. Dist. Calif.-Nev. Annual Conf., Modesto, Calif., 1979-84; pastor San Ramon Valley United Meth. Ch., Alamo, Calif., 1984-88; bishop United Meth. Ch., Portland, Oreg., 1988-96, United Meth. Ch. Desert S.W. Conf., Phoenix, from 1996. Lectr. Pacific Sch. Religion, Berkeley, 1976-79. Trustee Willamette U., Salem, Oreg., 1988-96, Alaska Pacific U., Anchorage, 1988-96, Claremont Sch. Theology, 1996—. Paul Harris fellow Rotary Internat., 1988. Democrat. Avocations: fishing, golf, reading, travel. Home: Elk Grove, Calif. Died July 14, 2010.

DEWITT, EUGENE A. (GENE DEWITT), advertising agency executive; b. Norwalk, Conn., Feb. 3, 1943; s. Albert W. and Anna (Astrab) DeW.; m. Juliana Fera, July 31, 1965; 1 child, Katharine. AB magna cum laude, Tufts U., 1965. Media planner, buyer Dancer-Fitzgerald-Sample, Inc., NYC, 1965-66; broadcast buyer BBDO, Inc., NYC, 1966; asst. media dir. Ogilvy & Mather, Inc., NYC, 1966-71; exec. v.p., dir. media and bus. affairs Rosenfeld, Sirowitz & Lawson, Inc., NYC, 1971-77; sr. v.p., dir. media and network programming BBDO, Inc., NYC, 1978-79; exec. v.p., dir. U.S.A. media services McCann Erickson, Inc., 1979-84; founder, pres. DeWitt Media, Inc., 1984—2009; chmn., CEO Optimedia, 2000—02; pres., CEO Syndicated Network Television Assn., 2001—03. Seminar leader Assn. Nat. Advertisers. Mem. mktg. com. USIA. Mem. Advt. Research Found. (mem. media communications council) Home: New York, NY. Died Jan. 22, 2009.

DIAMOND, DOROTHY BLUM, writer, editor; b. NYC, Sept. 7, 1919; d. Asher and Lily (Williams) Blum; m. Walter H. Diamond, June 15, 1947. BA with highest honors, Wellesley Coll., 1940; MS (hon.), Columbia U., 1941; LLD (hon.), St. Thomas U., 2002; LLD, Thomas Jefferson Sch. Law, 2007. Reporter Newark Star-Ledger, 1941; assoc. editor Young Am. Mag., NYC, 1941—42; sr. editor, columnist Tide Mag., NYC, 1942—47, 1955—59. Columnist Printers Ink, NYC, 1959—61, Modern Floor Coverings, NYC, 1958—63. Author: Tax Havens of the World, 1974, Tax-Free Trade Zones of the World, 1976, International Tax Treaties of All Nations, 1976, Capital Formation and Investment Incentives Around the World, 1983, International Trust Laws and Analysis, 1994, One of a Kind: Learning The Secrets of World Leaders, 2005; contbr. articles to mags. and newspapers. Adv. bd. mem. Offshore Inst. Recipient Achievement award, Syracuse Sch. Mgmt., 2002. Mem.: Wellesley-in-Westchester Club (past bd. dirs.), Merchandising Execs. Club (award 1958), Phi Beta Kappa. Died May 15, 2010.

DICKEY, BERT GERMAN, III, political adviser; b. Memphis, Feb. 14, 1949; s. Bert German and Alta Baer (Coldren) Dickey; m. Penny Farrar Dickey, Mar. 22, 1976; children: Cal, B.G. AA, Wentworth Jr. Coll., 1969; BSE, U. Ark., 1973; BS, Inst. Politics & Govt., Little Rock, 1980; MBA, Ark. State U., 1988. Pres. B. G. Dickey Farms, Earle, Ark., 1973—84; trustee Fed. Bankruptcy Ct., Little Rock, 1981—85, polit.

adviser Earle, 1980—84. Commr. housing, Earle, 1983; dep. commr. state lands, Little Rock, 84; chmn. Dem. Exec. Com., Little Rock, 1978—84; mem. Ark. Dem. Com., 1978—84, Ark. Dem. Fin. Coun., 1978—84, Dem. Jud. Coun., 1978—84; mem. adv. bd. Young Dems., 1978—84, del., 1980; with Dem. Nat. Conv., NYC, 1980, 82, Dem. Conf., Phila., 1982. 2d lt. US Army, 1970—76. Mem.: Safari Club Internat. (pres. 1979—80). Methodist. Avocations: hunting, skiing, golf. Home: Little Rock, Ark. Died June 24, 2010.

DICKEY, JOHN PHILLIPS, finance company executive; b. Cleve., Oct. 23, 1938; s. Paul Smith and Annabelle (Phillips) Dickey; m. Patricia Ethel Temple, June 6, 1964; children: Barbara, Allison. BS, Purdue U., 1960. Asst. v.p. Coldwell Banker, San Jose, Calif., 1969—74; v.p. Bowest Corp., Menlo Park, Calif., 1974—78, McMorgan & Co., San Francisco, 1978—82; pres. Pension Fund Real Estate Investment Co., Los Altos, Calif., from 1981; exec. v.p. Guarantee Fin. Corp., Fresno, Calif., from 1982. Panelist Internat. Coun. Shopping Ctrs., San Francisco, 1982; cons. Internat. Found. Employee Benefit Plans, 1980—81. Served to lt. USN, 1962—65. Died June 2, 2010.

DICKINSON, JOSHUA CLIFTON, JR., museum director, educator; b. Tampa, Fla., Apr. 28, 1916; s. Joshua Clifton and Mary (Martin) D.; m. Lucy Jackson, Apr. 13, 1936 (wid. June 10, 1997); children: Joshua Clifton III, Martin Freeman, Susan Ellissa; m. Sarah Donnovin Hadley, Nov. 1, 1997. Student, U. Va., 1936-39, Cornell U., 1938; BS, U. Fla., 1940, MS, 1946, PhD, 1950. Faculty U. Fla., from 1946, asst. prof. biology, 1950-55, assoc. prof. biology, 1955, prof. zoology, 1973-79; curator Fla. State Mus. (name changed to Fla. Mus. of Natural History-U. Fla.), 1952-79, chmn. natural scis., 1953-60, acting dir., 1959-61, dir., 1961-79, dir. emeritus, from 1979. Vis. investigator Woods Hole Oceanographic Inst. Marine Biol. Lab., 1952; expdns. to, Honduras, 1946, Bahamas, 1958-62, 66-67, Jamaica, 1946, Baffin Island, 1955, Sombrero Island, 1964, Navassa Island, 1967, Turks and Caicos Islands, 1974. Contbr. articles to profl. jours. Chmn. Fla. Bd. Archives and History, 1967-69; mus. adv. panel Nat. Endowment for Arts, 1970-72, co-chmn., 1972-74; panelist fellowship program NSF, 1966-68; mem. Nat. Council on Arts, 1976-82, chmn. com. planning and policy; bd. dirs. Fla. Arts Celebration, 1984-92, vice chmn., 1985-86. Comdr. USCGR, 1942—46, ret. Grantee Nat. Park Service, 1954, NSF, 1955-57; Rsch. fellow Harvard U., 1951-52; recipient Disting. Alumnus award U. Fla., 1977, Presdl. Medallion U. Fla., 1979; Dickinson Hall named in his honor U. Fla. Mem. Am. Ornithologists Union, Am. Soc. Naturalists, Am. Assn. Museums (chmn. sci. mus. sect. 1961, mem. council 1964-70, sec. 1970), Am. Soc. Zoologists, Wilson Ornithol. Soc., Am. Assn. Sci. Mus. Dirs. (v.p. 1967-69), Assn. Systematic Collections (pres. 1972-75, bd. dir. 1974-76, chmn. membership com. 1976-79), Bahamas Nat. Trust, Assn. S.E. Biologists (sec. 1955-58), Fla. Acad. Scis. (chmn. biology sect. 1952, editor quar. jour. 1955-63), Conf. Dirs. Systematics Collections (pres. 1976-78), Fla. Audubon Soc. (bd. dir. 1958-64, 79-84), S.E. Museums Conf. (v.p. 1971-72, pres. 1972, James L. Shortt award 1987), Internat. Council Museums (exec. com. 1974-77), Am. Assn. Museums (vis. accreditation team 1973-75), Sigma Xi, Phi Sigma, Alpha Tau Omega. Democrat. Presbyterian. Home: Gainesville, Fla. Died Jan. 21, 2009.

DICKSON, DORIS ROSE, retired psychologist; b. Cleve., Dec. 7, 1922; adopted d. Herman and Lydia Kathryn (Smith) Lustig; divorced; children: Suzanne Joyce Germond, Terry Marc. BS, U. Toledo, 1958, MEd, 1963; PhD, Walden U., 1978. Lic. psychologist, Ohio. Psychologist Columbus (Ohio) Pub. Schs., 1957-89; pvt. practice psychology Columbus, 1980-89. Adj. prof. Union for Experimenting Colls. and Univs., Cin., 1988— Mem. Internat. Transactional Anaylsis Assn., Ohio Psychol. Assn., Nat. Sch. Psychol. Assn., Cen. Ohio Cons. Psychologists, Cen. Ohio Psychol. Assn., AAUW. Avocations: gardening, sewing, cooking, pets. Died Jan. 6, 2009.

DIDHAM, JAMES RICHARD, director; b. Canton, Ohio, Nov. 6, 1943; s. Robert Hewlitt and Elizabeth (Truscott) Didham; m. Cheryl Kay Hoffman, Aug. 12, 1967 (div. 1977); 1 child, Laural Lyn; m. Edieann B. Freeman, Sept. 3, 1978; 1 child, Robert James. BA, Baldwin-Wallace Coll., Berea, Ohio, 1965; MA, Kent State U., 1972; postgrad., U. Mich., 1975. Tchr. HS Strongsville Bd. Edn., Ohio, 1965—67; asst. prof. Spanish lit. & counselor Baldwin-Wallace Coll., 1967—70; dir. admissions Mt. Union Coll., Alliance, Ohio, 1970—73; asst. to pres. Findlay Coll., Ohio, 1975—81; mgmt. cons. Moody-Woodley Mgmt., Inc., Findlay, 1981—84; dir. corp. devel. Bowling Green State U., Ohio, from 1984. Author: La Augustia de la Ciudad en las Obras de Florencio Sanchez, 1972; co-author (with others): Changing Practices in Higher Education, 1976. V.p. Findlay Area Arts Coun., from 1984, Findlay Swim Bd., from 1984. Rsch. fellowship, Carnegie Coun., 1975. Mem.: Assn. Study Higher Edn., Planning Execs. Internat., Am. Assn. Higher Edn. Presbyterian. Avocations: racquetball, skiing, gardening, photography, classical music. Home: Findlay, Ohio. Died July 24, 2009.

DIECKE, FRIEDRICH PAUL JULIUS, physiologist, educator; b. Holzen, Germany, June 27, 1927; s. Walter Wilhelm and Emma S. D.; m. Elizabeth Bennett, Nov. 26, 1955; children— Dietrich W., Friedrich K. Doctor rer. nat. magna cum laude in Comparative Physiology, U. Wurzburg, 1953. Postdoctoral fellow UCLA, 1953-55; asst. U. Wurzburg, 1955-56; instr. U. Tenn. Coll. Medicine, 1956-57, asst. prof., 1957-59; vis. investigator Rockefeller Inst., 1959; assoc. prof. physiology George Washington U. Coll. Medicine, 1959-63; prof. U. Iowa Coll. Medicine, 1963-75, acting head dept. physiology, 1973-75; prof., chmn. dept. physiology Univ. Medicine and Dentistry of N.J., N.J. Med. Sch., Newark, from 1975. Mem. AAAS, Am. Physiol. Soc., Soc. Gen. Physiologists, Biophys. Soc., Soc. Neurosci., Assn. Chairmen Depts. Physiology, N.Y. Acad. Scis., Nat. Fulbright Screening Com., Sigma Xi. Home: Short Hills, NJ. Died Jan. 15, 2009.

DIEHL, HARRY ALFRED, chemist, genealogist; b. York, Pa., Mar. 2, 1923; s. Ralph Eugene and Anna (Danner) D.; m. Margaret Marie Ehrhart, June 28, 1945; children: Rodney Eugene, Diane Susan Foster, Lori Elaine Vogan, Brian Eric. BA, Gettysburg Coll., 1948; MS, Pa. State U., 1951; MEd, U. Del., 1976. Tchr. chemistry William Penn Sr. High Sch., York, Pa., 1948-50; rsch. chemist E.I. DuPont, Wilmington, Del., 1951-83; genealologist pvt. practice, Wilmington, Del., from 1977. Author: Ancestors and Descendants of Francis & Lucinda Cornbower, 1982, Diehl-Deal-Dill-Dale Families of America, Vol. I, 1989. Cub Scout leader Boy Scouts Am., Wilmington, 1958-65, asst. scoutmaster, 1970-82; trustee, elder Presbyn. Ch., Wilmington, 1957-62, 95-2002. Sgt. USAF, 1941-46. Mem. Pa. Genealogy Soc. (bd. dirs. 1983-84), Del. Genealogy Soc. (bd. dirs., pres. 1981-82), Genealogy Soc. South Ctrl. Pa. (pres. 1992-93), Md. Genealogy Soc., Masons. Avocations: mineralogy, history. Home: Phoenixville, Pa. Died July 20, 2010.

DIGANGI, FRANK EDWARD, academic administrator; b. West Rutland, Vt., Sept. 29, 1917; s. Leonard and Mary Grace (Zafonti) DiG.; m. Genevieve Frances Colignon, June 27, 1946; children: Ellen (Mrs. Philo David Hall), Janet (Mrs. W. Dale Greenwood). BS in Pharmacy, Rutgers U., 1940; MS, Western Res. U., 1942; PhD, U. Minn., 1948. Asst. prof. U. Minn. Coll. Pharmacy, 1948-52, asso. prof., 1952-57, prof. medicinal chemistry, from 1957, also asso. dean adminstrv. affairs. Author: Quantitative Pharmaceutical Analysis, 7th edit, 1977, The History of the Minnesota Pharmacists Association, 1883-1983, 2004; Contbr. articles to pharm. jours. Served with USNR, 1943-46, PTO. Recipient Alumni Assn. Disting. Pharmacist award, 1977, Faculty Recognition award Coll. of Pharmacy Alumni Soc., 1981, Lawrence and Delores M. Weaver medal, 1997. Mem. Am. Pharm. Assn., Minn. Pharm. Assn. (pres. 1971, chmn. bd. 1972-73, Pharmacist of Yr. award 1972, Harold R. Popp Meml. award 1979, hon. mem. 1994), Mpls. Soc. Profl. Pharmacists (hon.), AAUP, Am. Chem. Soc., Am. Assn. Colls. Pharmacy, Univ. Campus Club (Mpls.), Univ. Faculty Golf Club (Mpls., Gownin-Town Club (Mpls.), Sigma Xi, Phi Beta Phi, Phi Lambda Upsilon, Rho Chi. Home: Stamford, Conn. Died Mar. 2, 2010.

DIGEORGE, ANGELO MARIO, pediatric endocronologist; b. Phila., Apr. 15, 1921; s. Anthony and Amelia (Taraborrelli) D.; m. Natalie J. Picarello, May 5, 1951; children: Anthony M., Christopher D., Anita DiGeorge-Brister. BA, Temple U., Phila., 1943; MD, Temple U., 1946, MS in Pediats., 1953. Diplomate Am. Bd. Pediatrics with subspecialty in pediat. endocrinology. Rotating intern Temple U. Hosp., Phila., 1946-47, instr. pediats., 1953-58, asst. prof., 1958-61, assoc. prof., 1961-67, prof., 1967-91, prof. emeritus, from 1991. Attending endocrinologist St. Christopher Hosp. for Children, Phila., 1952-61, chief endocrinology and metabolism, 1961-89; cons. and lectr. U.S. Naval Hosp., Phila., 1967-80; asst. chief pediats. Phila. Gen. Hosp., 1956-66; mem. test com. Nat. Bd. Med. Examiners, Phila., 1974-80; dir. Clin. Rsch. Ctr., NIH, 1965-82. Author: Nelson Textbook Pediatrics, 1954-2000; contbr. over 200 articles to profl. jours.; editl. bd. Pediatrics, Jour. Pediatrics, others. Chmn. Diabetes in Youth Com., Phila., 1973-82; bd. govs. Camp Firefly for Diabetic Children, Phila., 1981-85; mem. Nat. Commn. for Orphan Diseases, Washington, 1986-89, Nat. Orgn. for Rare Diseases, 1993-99. Capt. U.S. Army, 1947-49. Recipient Award of Recognition, Cystic Fibrosis Found., 1958, Disting. Svc. award Phila. Endocrine Soc., 1973, Disting. Sci. award Temple U. Sch. Medicine, 1987; named to Phila. Pediat. Soc. Hall of Fame, 1996. Mem. AAAS, Am. Soc. Human Genetics, Endocrine Soc., Am. Pediat. Soc. Avocations: stamp collecting/philately, gardening, reading history and biography. Home: Philadelphia, Pa. Died Oct. 11, 2009.

DIGGS, WILLIAM EDWARD, Oil company executive; b. Fredricksburg, Va., July 1, 1931; s. Charles Douglas and Elizabeth (Macy) Diggs; m. Wauhilla Adkins, Mar. 9, 1957; children: Charles Edward, Charlotte Lynn, William Douglas. BSc in Geology, Va. Poly. Inst., 1953, MSc in Geology, 1955. Geologist Carter Oil Co., Ft. Smith, Ark., 1954—62; pvt. practice Ft. Smith, 1962—68; gen. mgr. Alliance Oil Devel., Melbourne, Australia, 1968—76; mgr. Bates Oil Co., Tulsa, 1977—79; v.p. exploration Heston Oil Co., Tulsa, 1979—83, ONEOK Exploration Co., Tulsa, from 1983. Mem. Australian Inst. Mining and Metallurgy, Melbourne, 1970—75. Mem.: Oklahoma City Geol. Soc., Tulsa Geol. Soc., Am. Assn. Petroleum Geologists (sec., House of Dels. 1985, cert.), Sigma Xi. Presbyterian. Home: Tulsa, Okla. Died Apr. 22, 2009.

DILJA, LUBLIN, diplomat; b. Elbasan, Albania, Oct. 10, 1957; m. Arbnora Dilja; 1 child. D in Edn. and Psycology, U. Tirana. Tchr. English, Peqin, Albania; univ. lectr. chair psychology and pedagogy Tirana U., Albania, 1984-87; chair dept. pedagogy and psychology U. Elbasan, Albania, 1987-91, vice rector, 1991-93; amb. to U.S. Govt. Albania, Washington, 1993-97. Died Feb. 1, 2009.

DILWORTH, ROBERT LEXOW, career military officer, educator; b. Chgo., Aug. 19, 1936; s. Robert Oliver and Linda Agnes (Lexow) D.; m. Doris Elthea Smith, Sept. 1, 1981; children by previous marriage: Alexa, Robert. BS in Advt., U. Fla., 1959; MS in Mil. Sci., U.S. Army Command and Gen. Staff Coll., 1971; MA in Pub. Adminstrn., U. Okla., 1975; MEd, EdD, Columbia U., 1993. Commd. 2nd lt. U.S. Army, 1959, advanced through grades to brig. gen., 1986, chief adminstrn. div. office chief of staff Washington, 1968-70, chief mgmt. analysis br. office chief of staff, 1971-75, chief of staff 2nd infantry div. Republic of Korea, 1975-76, chief mgmt. div. adj. gen. ctr. Washington, 1976-77, chief compt. div. Nat. Guard Bur., 1978-81, dep. comdr. 1st pers. command Schwetzingen, Fed. Republic of Germany, 1981-84, dir. resource mgmt. U.S. Mil. Acad. West Point, NY, 1984-86, adjutant gen. army Alexandria, Va., 1986-88, dep. chief of staff base ops. support tng./doctrine command Ft. Monroe, Va., 1988-91; assoc. prof. emeritus adult edn., human resource devel. Va. Commonwealth U., Richmond, 1993—2005. Guest lectr. Hungarian Mil. Acad., 1989. Contbr. articles to profl. jours. on action learning; author: (book) Fogs on War and Peace: A Mid Stream Analysis of World War III, 2008. Mem. ASPA (exec. com. mgmt. sci. and policy analysis sect. 1992-96), ASTD (chair nat. rsch. to practice com. 2000-2002), Acad. Human Resource Devel., Assn. U.S. Army, Mil. Officer Assn., Internat. Soc. Quality Govt. (nat. dir. 1992-93). Mem. Lds Ch. Avocation: writing for publication. Home: Gum Spring, Va. Died June 6, 2009.

DI NARDO, BRUNO, internaional lawyer; b. Gamberale, Chieti, Italy, Nov. 1, 1939; came to U.S., 1954; s. Francesco and Ida (Gizzi) Di N.; divorced; 1 son, Thomas. BA, Duquesne U., 1961; JD, Fordham U., 1964. Bar: Ill. 1969, N.Y. 1973. Jr. atty. Burroughs Corp., Detroit, 1969-71; corp. devel. mgr. Lever Bros., NYC, 1971-73; gen. counsel French Am. Banking Corp., NYC, from 1973; pres., owner Law Offices Di Nardo and Co, P.C., NYC, from 1978. Mem. N.Y. County Lawyers Assn. Republican. Died Sept. 28, 2009.

DINERMAN, MIRIAM, social work educator; b. NYC, Apr. 13, 1925; d. Abraham J. and Frances (Shostac) Goldforb; m. Harold Dinerman, June 12, 1951 (dec. June 1976); children: David, Ellen, Ruth. BA with honors, Swarthmore Coll., 1945; MSW, Columbia U., 1949, D of Social Welfare, 1972. Youth dir. Jewish Assn. for Neighborhood Ctrs., NYC, 1949-50, program dir., 1951-54; various social work part time positions, 1955-60; asst. prof. Rutgers U. Grad. Sch. Social Work, New Brunswick, NJ, 1961-72, assoc. prof., 1972-76, prof., 1976-99, asst. dean for acad. planning, 1973-75, assoc. dean, 1975-81, acting dean, 1978, chmn. health care sequence, mem. New Brunswick faculty coun., 1989-93, chair, 1991-92; dir. PhD program Rutgers U. Sch. Social Work, 1992-97, emerita, from 1999. Mem. grants rev. panel Office Human Devel. Svcs., HHS, 1986—90; cons. on health and social svcs. N.J. Legis. Task Force on 21st Century; mem. task force on std. of need N.J. Divsn. Econ. Assistance, 1989—91; manuscript rev. editor Longman's Press, Methuen Press; dir. Ctr. for Internat. and Comparative Social Work, 1977—99; adj. prof. Yeshiva U. Sch. Social Work, from 1999. Editor: Social Work Futures, 1983; mem. editl. bd. Affilia: Jour. Women and Social Work, 1985-94, 1995—, book rev. editor., 1995-00, editor-in-chief, 2000-06, mem. corp. bd., 2006-; contbr. articles to profl. jours., chpts. to books. Bd. dirs. Def. for Children Internat., 1980—88; steering com. Nat. Jobs for All Campaign, from 2005; bd. dirs. Friend to Advance Social Svc., 2006. Grantee NIMH, 1966-67, Rutgers U. Rsch. Coun. and Samuel Silberman Fund, 1979-80. Mem.: NJ AAUP (task force on health care policy), NASW (chpt. pres. 1984—86, nat. com. on nominations and leadership identification 1988—97, editl. com. 1991—95, steering com. polit. action for candidate election NYC chpt. from 1996, bd. dirs. NYC chpt. from 1999), Group for Advancement of Doctoral Edn. (sec. steering com. 1990—96), Coun. on Social Work Edn. (program planning com. 1984—89, ednl. policy and planning commn. 1989—94), Internat. Assn. Schs. Social Work (agt. 1988—95, bd. dirs.), Acad. Cert. Social Workers. Home: Pasadena, Calif. Died July 17, 2010.

DIPLACIDO, DONALD FRANK, chamber of commerce executive; b. Erie, Pa., Dec. 18, 1924; s. Alfonso and Stella (Mangin) DiPlacido; m. Irene Barbara Balgieski, June 19, 1954; 1 child, Susan DiPlacido Shickler. BS, Gannon Coll. Gen. mdse. mgr. Boston Store, Erie, Pa., 1945—74; store mgr. Joseph Horne Co., Erie, 1975—83; former exec. dir.; bd. incorporators St. Vincent Health Ctr., Erie, from 1983, Hamot Med. Ctr., Erie, from 1983, Gannon U., Erie, from 1985; mem. adv. bd. dirs. Arts Coun., Erie, from 1985; chmn. Pvt. Industry Coun., Erie, 1984—85; mem. adv. coun. Vocat. Tech. Edn., Erie, from 1985. Named Ad Man of Yr., Ad Club, 1985. Mem.: Probus Profl. Men's Assn., Erie, Rotary. Roman Catholic. Avocations: bicycling, bowling. Home: Erie, Pa. Died Apr. 3, 2010.

DISNER, ELIOT GORDON, lawyer; b. Detroit, Apr. 19, 1947; s. Jerry and Devora (Gordon) D.; m. Sandra Ferrari; children: Perrin, Seth, Madeleine. BA, U. Mich., 1969; JD, Harvard U., 1972. Bar: Mich. 1972, Calif. 1976, D.C. 1976. Legal asst. Office of the Gov. State of Wash., Olympia, 1970; legal asst. IBM Corp., Armonk, N.Y., 1971; gen. atty. FTC, Washington, 1972-74, atty., advisor, 1974-75; ptnr. Romney, Golant, et al, LA, 1976-84, Sullivan, McWilliams, et al, LA, 1984-86; of counsel Shapiro, Posell & Close, LA, 1988—96; ptnr. Cohen & Jessup, LLP, 1996—2002, Manatt, Phelps, Phillips, LLP, 2002—06, McGuireWoods LLP, LA, 2004—07, Van Etten Suzumoto & Becket LLP, LA; prin. Disner Law Corp., LA, from 2002. Mem. Bur. Nat. Affairs, L.A., 1984-89; mem. antitrust and trade regulation adv. bd. Bur. Nat. Affairs, 1984-1989; atty. rep. 9th Cir. Jud. Conf., 2003-06. Author: Antitrust Questions, Answers Law and Commentary, 1989, 3d edit., 2007; contbr. articles to profl. jours. Mem. Calif. Bar Assn. (chmn. antitrust and trade regulation sect., exec. com. 1986-2005), LA County Bar Assn. (antitrust sect., exec. com. 1977—, chmn. 1982-83), Am. Arbitration Assn. mediator and arbitrator), Am. Inn of Ct. (pres. bus. litig. So. Calif. chpt. 2001-2003). Avocations: travel, home repair. Home: Los Angeles, Calif. Died Apr. 4, 2009.

DISNEY, ROY EDWARD, retired entertainment company executive; b. L.A., Jan. 10, 1930; s. Roy Oliver and Edna (Francis) D.; m. Patricia Ann Dailey, Sept. 17, 1955 (div. Jan. 19, 2007); children: Roy Patrick, Susan Margaret, Abigail

Edna, Timothy John; m. Leslie DeMeuse, 2008 BA, Pomona Coll., 1951. Apprentice film editor Mark VII Prodns., Hollywood, 1942; guest relations exec. NBC, Hollywood, Calif., 1952; asst. film editor, cameraman prodn. asst., writer, producer Walt Disney Prodns., Burbank, Calif., 1954-77, dir., 1967—77; pres. Roy E. Disney Productions Inc., Burbank, Calif., 1978—2009; chmn. bd. dir. Shamrock Broadcasting Co., Hollywood, 1979—2009; founder, chmn. Shamrock Holdings Inc., Burbank, Calif., 1980—2009; chmn. Walt Disney Animation, 1984—2003; vice chmn. The Walt Disney Co., Burbank, Calif., 1984—2003, dir. emeritus, cons., 2005—09. Trustee Calif. Inst. of the Arts, Valencia, from 1967. Prodr.: (films) Pacific High, Mysteries of the Deep, 1959; exec. prodr.: (films) Cheetah, 1989, The Little Mermaid, 1989, Beauty and the Beast, 1991, The Lion King, 1994, Pocahontas, 1995, Fantasia 2000;(TV series) Walt Disney's Wonderful World of Color Bd. dirs. Big Bros. of Greater Los Angeles, U.S. com. UNICEF, Ronald McDonald House charities, chmn. emeritus, Peregrine Fund; mem. adv. bd. dirs. St. Joseph Med. Ctr., Burbank; mem. U.S. Naval Acad. Sailing Squadron, Annapolis, Md.; fellow U. Ky. Recipient Acad. award nomination for Mysteries of the Deep, Mort Walker award for Outstanding Contbn. to the Cartoon Industry, Boca Raton Internat. Mus. of Cartoon Art, 1997, Internat. Creative Achievement. award, Cinema Expo, 1997, Disney Legends award, 1998, Elizabeth Ann Seton award, Nat. Catholic Edn. Assn. 1999, Henry Bergh Humane award, ASPCA, 1999, Inaugural Environ. Leadership award, Audubon Soc. 2000, Lifetime Achievement in Animation, Santa Clarita Internat. Film Festival, 2002; named one of Forbes' Richest Americans, 2006. Mem. Dirs. Guild Am. West, Writers Guild Am. Clubs: 100, Confrerie des Chevaliers du Tastevin, St. Francis Yacht, Calif. Yacht, San Diego Yacht, Transpacific Yacht, Los Angeles Yacht. Republican. Died Dec. 16, 2009.

DITTES, JAMES EDWARD, psychology of religion educator; b. Cleve., Dec. 26, 1926; s. Mercein Edward and Mary (Freeman) D.; children: Lawrence William (dec.), Nancy Eleanor, Carolyn Ann, Joanne Frances; m. Anne Hebert Smith, Nov. 27, 1987. AB, Oberlin Coll., 1949; BD, Yale U., 1954, MS, 1955, PhD, 1958. Instr. Am. Sch., Talas, Turkey, 1950-52; ordained to ministry United Ch. Christ, 1954; mem. faculty Yale U., 1955—2002, prof. psychology of religion, 1967-84, prof. pastoral theology and psychology, 1984-2001, chmn. dept. religious studies, 1975-82, Squire prof. pastoral counseling, 2001—02. Chmn. Council on Grad. Studies in Religion in U.S. and Can., 1970-71 Author: The Church in the Way, 1967, Minister on the Spot, 1970, Bias and the Pious, 1973, When the People Say No, 1979, The Male Predicament, 1985, When Work Goes Sour, 1987, Men at Work, 1996, Driven by Hope, 1996, Pastoral Counseling, 1999, Re-Calling Ministry, 1999, (with Robert Menges) Psychological Studies of Clergymen, 1965, (with Donald Capps) The Hunger of the Heart, 1990. Served with USNR, 1945-46. Guggenheim fellow, 1965-66; Fulbright Research fellow Rome, 1965-66; sr. fellow NEH, 1972-73 Mem. Soc. Sci. Study of Religion (exec. sec. 1959-63, editor jour. 1966-71, pres. 1971-73) Died Aug. 24, 2009.

DIXON, DANIEL ROBERTS, JR., retired lawyer; b. Rocky Mount, NC, Feb. 22, 1911; s. Daniel Roberts and Ida Louise (Mason) D.; children: Daniel Roberts III, Carolyn Roy Dixon Dyess. AB, Coll. William and Mary, 1937; JD, Duke U., 1941; LLM in Taxation, NYU, 1951. CPA, N.C.; bar: N.C. Atty. Hamel, Park & Saunders, Washington, 1951-52; asst. prof. N.C. State U., Raleigh, 1954-76; pvt. practice Raleigh, from 1953. Author: Graphic Guide Fundamental Accounting; inventor building block; contbr. articles to profl. jours. Mem. Internat. Visitors Coun., Raleigh, N.C. Capt. U.S. Air Corps., 1942-46. Mem. Navy League of U.S. (judge advocate 1990-96), N.C. Triangle Coun., N.C. Bar Assn., Wake County Bar Assn., Phi Beta Kappa (pres. Wake County), Omicron Delta Epsilon. Avocations: carpentry, organist. Died Jan. 17, 2009.

DIXON, FRANK ALOYSIUS, JR., Oil company executive; b. Phila., Oct. 18, 1928; s. Frank Aloysius and Helen (Iversen) Dixon; m. Patricia Riley, Feb. 24, 1967. BA, Brown U., 1950. Pres. Pengo Petroleum Co., Houston. Bd. dirs. Okla. City Symphony, 1969, Alley Theatre Houston, 1969—72. Mem.: Chgo. Yacht Club, Tavern Club, Racquet Club, NY Doubles Club, Sleepy Hollow Country Club, Tex. Corinthian Yacht Club, River Oaks Country Club (Houston). Republican. Roman Catholic. Home: Houston, Tex. Died July 6, 2009.

DIXON, LOUIS FREDERICK, information sciences and telecommunications consulting executive; b. Wilkes-Barre, Pa., June 16, 1928; s. Jesse Guy and Elizabeth Mary (Garney) D.; m. Elaine Ray Dietterick, July 25, 1950; children: Pamela Elaine Dixon, Valerie Lynn (dec.), Jeffrey Louis. BS, U.S. Mil. Acad., 1950; MBA, Harvard U., 1956; postgrad., U. Heidelberg, Germany, 1957-59. Commd. lt. U.S. Army, 1950, advanced through grades to col.; dir. mgmt. info. and audio-visual systems U.S. Army War Coll., Carlisle Barracks, Pa., 1971-77; ret., 1977; asst. prof. math. and computer sci. Shippensburg U., Pa., 1978-80; pres. Applied Decision Systems, Inc., 1980-90; dir. Harrisburg ops. Mandex, Inc., Mechanicsburg, Pa., 1981-83; v.p. decision support systems Camp Hill, Pa., 1983-84; v.p. systems devel. group, 1984-85; v.p. info. systems group Springfield, Va., 1985-87. Co-author: Management Consulting, 1958. Chmn. long range planning com. Keystone Area coun. Boy Scouts Am., 1982-84, mem. exec. bd., 1977-91; adv. voun. Carlisle chpt. Order of Demolay, 1971-85; bd. dirs. Suntree Master Home Owners Assn., 1996-98; com. chmn. Boy Scouts Am., St. Pauls Anglican Ch. Decorated Legion of Merit with oak leaf cluster, Bronze Star with oak leaf cluster, Purple Heart with oak leaf cluster, Army Commendation medal; recipient Legion of Honor award Order of Demolay, 1951, Silver Beaver award Boy Scouts Am., 1977. Mem. Ret. Officers Assn. (Space Coast chpt.), Space Coast West Point Soc., Sojourners/Hereos, Masons, Elks. Republican. Home: Melbourne, Fla. Died Jan. 2, 2010.

DIXON, WILLIAM ROBERT, musician, educator; b. Nantucket, Mass., Oct. 5, 1925; s. William Robert and Louise Ann (Wade) D.; children: William, Claudia Gayle, William. Diploma, Hartnette Conservatory Music, 1951. Clk., internat. civil servant UN Secretariat, NYC, 1956-62; free lance musician, composer NYC, 1962-67; mem. faculty Columbia U. Tchrs. Coll., 1967-70; composer-in-residence George Washington U., Washington, 1967; dir. Conservatory of Univ. of the Streets, NYC, 1967-68; guest artist in residence Ohio State U., 1967; mem. faculty dept. dance Bennington (Vt.) Coll., 1968-95, chmn. dept. black music, 1973-86. Vis. prof. U. Wis., Madison, 1971-72; lectr. painting and music Mus. Modern Art, Verona, Italy, 1982, Palast, Nuremberg, Fed. Republic Germany, 1990; lectr. workshop on contemporary music Pori, Finland, 1991, Jerusalem, Tel Aviv, Israel, 1990; lectr. in Black Art Music Maison du Livre et du Son, Villeurbanne, France, 1994; tchr. Master Classes in Improvisation Ecole Nationale de Musique, Villeurbanne, France, 1994, Master Class Composition and Performance NYU, 1996; in residence Wesleyan U., 2005. Recs. include Archie Shepp-Bill Dixon Quartet, 1962, Bill Dixon 7-Tette, 1963, Intents and Purposes: The Bill Dixon Orchestra, 1967, For Franz, 1976, New Music, Second Wave, 1979, Bill Dixon in Italy, 2 vols., 1980, considerations 1 and 2 Bill Dixon, 1980, 82, November: 1981, 1982, Bill Dixon in the Labyrinth, 1983, Collection, 1985, Thoughts, 1986, Son of Sisyphus, 1990, Bill Dixon: Vade Mecum, 1994, Vade Mecum II, 1996, (6-CD set) Bill Dixon: Solo Trumpet, 1998, PAPYRUS vol. 1 and 2, compositions for trumpet, percussion & piano, 1999, Berlin Abbozzi, 2000; retrospective of music compositions 1963-91 by Radio Sta. WKCR, Columbia U., 1991-92; trumpet soloist Celebration Orchestra, Berlin, Germany, 1994; concert performance of original compositions Espace Tonkin, Villeurbanne, France, 1994, Teatro Colosseo, Rome, Italy, 1996, Nickelsdorf, Austria, 1997; new composition quintet performace Vision Festival, NYC, 2005, trio performance Pompidou Ctr., Paris, 2006; guest trumpet soloist in ensemble Que., Can., 2006; composed orch. piece Cologne (Germany) Radio Sta., 1998; performer new compositions Festival of New Music for Trumpet, 2004, Donaueschingen, Guiramers and Royal Festival Hall, London, 2004; exhbns. include Ferrari Gallery, Verona, Italy, 1982, Multimedia Contemporary Art Gallery, Brescia, Italy, 1982, Uferpalast, Nuremberg, Germany, 1990, Cite de la Musique, Paris, 2002, Columbia U., 2005, Sons d'Hiver Festival, 2006; lithograph exhbns. Villeurbanne, France, 1994, Chittenden Bank, Bennington, Vt., 1994-95, Skoto Gallery, N.Y.C., 1996, Rogue Art Gallery, 2006; retrospective of paintings 1968-91, So. Vt. Coll., 1991; author: L'Opera, (bio-discography by Ben Young) Dixonia, 1998; prodr. lithographs Union Regionale pour le Devel. de la Lithographie d'Art, Lyon, France, 1994; orchestral work Index, 2000; artist album cover, 2002; artist in residence Wesleyan U., 2005; orch. piece NY Vision Festival, 2007, (Lifetime Achievement award, 2007); soloist with Exploding Star Orch., Chgo., 2007, soloist, composer, 2009, Tapestries For Small Orch., 2009; recorded compositions: Entrances One, Entrances Two, Chgo., 2007; exhibited lithographs NY, Chgo., 2007. Mem. adv. com. New Eng. Found. of the Arts. Served with U.S. Army, 1944-46. Recipient Musician of Yr. Jazz Mag., 1976, Giancarlo Testini award best recordings, Discographical Society, Milan, 1981, Disting. Visitor in the Arts Middlebury Coll., 1986. Fellow Vt. Acad. Arts and Scis.; mem. Am. Fedn. Musicians, Duke Ellington Jazz Soc. (hon.) Died June 16, 2010.

DOAN, DAVID BENTLEY, geologist; b. State College, Pa., Jan. 9, 1926; s. Francis Janney and Josephine Cornelia (Bentley) D.; m. Phebe J. Reed, Oct. 27, 1954; children—Susan, Jean, Thomas, Patricia. B.S., Pa. State U., 1948, M.S., 1949. Registered geologist, cert. engring. geologist, Calif., diplomate Am. Inst. Profl. Geologists. Geologist U.S. Geol. Survey, Washington and Tokyo, 1949-62; ops. analyst Research Analysis Corp., McLean, Va., 1962-68; cons., Bethesda, Md., 1968-90; chief geologist Gold Lake Mines, Inc., Janesville, Wis., 1982—, pres., 1983-85; dir. Bobcat Properties, Fort Lauderdale, Fla., Augusta Gold Mines, Winnipeg, Man., Can.; chief pro tem br. Latin Am. and Can., Divsn. Internat. Minerals, U.S. Bur. of Mines, Washington; vis. lectr. U. Md., College Park, 1976-83. Author: The Influence of Terrain on Tactics and Strategy, 1959; Geology of Tinian, Mariana Islands, 1960; Geology of Miyako Archipelago, Ryukyu Islands, 1961; (with others) Geology of Guam, 1963. Served to lt. (j.g.) USN, 1943-46, PTO. Mem. Geol. Soc. Am., Am. Geophys. Union, Geol. Soc. Washington, Am. Assn. Petroleum Geologists, Soc. Petroleum Engrs., Explorers Club, Sigma Xi, Alpha Nu. Episcopalian. Avocations: soaring; scuba diving; composing. Died Mar. 27, 2010.

DOBAN, ROBERT CHARLES, glass company executive; b. Kenosha, Wis., Feb. 25, 1924; s. Charles and Mary D.; m. Eleanore Szatko, July 25, 1947; 1 son, Geoffrey Robert. BS, Yale U., 1949; PhD, U. Wis., 1952. Research chemist E.I. DuPont de Nemours & Co., Inc., Wilmington, Del., 1952-57, various research mgmt. positions, 1957-68, lab. dir., 1968-70, venture mgr., 1970-72, research dir., 1972-74; v.p. tech. services Owens-Corning Fiberglas Corp., Toledo, 1974-77, sr. v.p. sci. and tech., from 1978. Chmn. Ohio Diagnostics Corp.; dir. Sherwin-Williams Co., Cleve.; mem. bldg. research bd. NRC Trustee St. Vincent's Hosp. Med. Ctr.; bd.dirs. WGTE-TV-FM, pub. broadcasting, 1978—. Served to lt. USN, 1944-46. Mem. Am. Chem. Soc., AAAS, Indsl. Research Inst., Chem. Soc. (London). Clubs: Toledo, Belmont Country, Caranor Hunt and Polo; Internat. (Washington). Home: Perrysburg, Ohio. Died June 21, 2010.

DOCKRAY, GEORGE HENRY, editor, publisher; b. Phila., May 4, 1920; s. George L. and Mary (Finan) D.; m. Louise Stedman, Nov. 9, 1942 (dec. May 1970); children: Karen E., George Henry, Andrea; m. Audrey Laney Cochran, June 2, 1973. BS, Phila. Coll. Textiles and Sci., 1948. Textile research asso. Research Inst. Temple U., 1948-49; textile engr. Nat. Cotton Council Am., Washington, 1949-53; asso. editor Textile Industries, Atlanta, 1953-56, exec. editor, 1956-57, editor, 1957-68, editor-in-chief, 1968-79; pub. Textiles Panamericanos, Atlanta, 1978-83; group pub. Textile Group W.R.C. Pub. Co., Atlanta, 1983. Served with AUS, 1941-45. Mem. Fiber Soc., Textile Inst. (Eng.), Am. Assn. Textile Chemists and Colorists, Sigma Delta Chi, Delta Kappa Phi. Home: Atlanta, Ga. Died Jan. 10, 2010.

DODGE, PHILIP ROGERS, neurologist, educator; b. Beverly, Mass., Mar. 16, 1923; s. Israel R.; children: Susan, Judith. Student, U. N.H., 1941-43, Yale, 1943; MD, U. Rochester, 1948. Diplomate Am. Bd. Psychiatry and Neurology. Intern Strong Meml. Hosp., 1948-49; asst. resident neurology Boston City Hosp., 1949-50, resident, 1950, sr. resident, 1951-52; practice medicine, specializing in child neurology Boston, 1956-67, St. Louis, from 1967; teaching fellow neurology Harvard Med. Sch., 1950, 51-53, instr. neurology, 1956-58, assoc. in neurology, 1958-61, asst. prof., 1962-67; asst. neurologist Mass. Gen. Hosp., 1956-59, dir. pediatric neurology program, 1958-67, assoc. neurologist, 1959-63, neurologist, 1963-67, assoc. pediatrician, 1961-62, pediatrician, 1962-67; investigator Joseph P. Kennedy, Jr. Meml. Labs. for Study Mental Retardation, 1962-67; pediatric neurologist Boston Lying-In Hosp., 1961-67; cons. in neurology Walter E. Fernald State Sch. for Retarded Children, 1963-67; med. dir. St. Louis Children's Hosp., 1967-84, pediatrician-in-chief, 1967-86; assoc. neurologist Barnes Hosp., from 1967; chmn. Mallinckrodt Dept. Pediatrics, Washington U. Sch. Medicine, 1967-86, prof. pediatrics and neurology, 1967-93; prof. emeritus pediatrics and neurology Washington U. Sch. Medicine, from 1993; lectr. in pediatrics, 1993-99. Cons. collaborative project cerebral palsy Nat. Inst. Neurol. Diseases and Blindness, 1958; vis. scientist Cin. Rsch. Ctr., U. PR, 1965—66, hon. vis. prof. physiology, 1967; bd. dirs., chmn. rsch. adv. com. Mass. Soc. Prevention Cruelty to Children, 1961—67; mem. sci. rsch. adv. bd. Nat. Assn. Retarded Children, 1963—67; bd. dirs. Ctrl. Midwestern Regional Lab., Inc., 1968—70; mem. gen. clin. rsch. ctrs. adv. com. USPHS, 1971—74; chmn. Mo. Mental Health Commn., 1974—78; mem. nat. adv. child health and human devel. coun. NIH, 1974—77; chmn. panel neurol. disorders, devel., long-range program strategies NINCDS, 1977—79; panel chmn., consensus devel. conf. diagnosis and treatment Reye's Syndrome, 1981; vis. prof. pediat. and adolescent medicine Royal Postgrad. Med. Sch., U. London, from 1986; hon. vis. fellow dept. pathology U. Western Australia, Nedlands, 1986—87; vis. prof. neurology Columbia U. Coll. Physicians and Surgeons, NYC, 1987—88; spl. asst. to dir. mental retardation Nat. Inst. Child Health and Human Devel., NIH, Washington, 1987—88. Author (with others): Nutrition and the Developing Nervous System, 1975; mem. editl. bd. Jour. Devel. Medicine and Child Neurology, from 1965, Jour. Pediat., 1970—80, Pediatric Rsch., 1970—78, Current Problems in Pediat., 1969—84, Neurology, 1973—76; contbr. articles to profl. jours. Maj. M.C. US Army, 1950—56. Mem.: Assn. Med. Sch. Pediatric Dept. Chmn. (pres. 1975—77), St. Louis Soc. Neurol. Scis., Soc. Biol. Psychiatry, Soc. Pediatric Rsch., Assn. Rsch. Nervous and Mental Disease, Child Neurology Soc., Am. Neurol. Assn., Am. Acad. Neurology (past com. chmn.), Am. Pediatric Soc. (coun. 1972—78, chmn. coun. 1978—79), Alpha Omega Alpha. Home: Saint Louis, Mo. Died Aug. 30, 2009.

DOLAN, JAMES FRANCIS, lawyer; b. Orange, NJ, Jan. 5, 1930; s. Thomas and Edna (Monahan) D.; m. Rita Hughes, June 27, 1953; children: James E., Stephen T., Michael, Richard F. BS, Seton Hall U., 1950; LL.B., Columbia U., 1953. Bar: D.C. 1953, N.Y. 1957. Assoc. atty. Davis Polk & Wardwell, NYC, 1957-66, ptnr., from 1966. Served to lt. USN, 1953-57. Mem. ABA, N.Y. State Bar Assn., Assn. of Bar of City of N.Y. Clubs: Seminole Golf (North Palm Beach, Fla.). Home: Hobe Sound, Fla. Died Apr. 19, 2010.

DOLAN, KEVIN LEO, retired publishing company executive; b. Framingham, Mass., Oct. 16, 1937; s. Matthew L. and Helen N. (Flaherty) Dolan; m. Janet E. Duncan, Mar. 15, 1966; children: Kerry A., Tracy E. BS, Boston Coll., 1959; MBA, Columbia U., 1964. Various fin. staff positions Time Inc., NYC, 1964—70, gen. mgr. Books and Arts Assocs. divsn., 1971—72, asst. treas., 1972—74, asst. contr., 1974—78, v.p., 1982—88; sr. v.p. Time Inc. Book Co., NYC, 1989—91. Pres. Little Brown & Co., Boston, 1985—91. Trustee Huntington Theatre Co., from 1986, Bennington Coll., from 1987. 1st lt. US Army, 1959—63, Korea. Mem.: Assn. Am. Pubs. (bd. dirs. 1987—89). Home: Boston, Mass. Died Feb. 13, 2009.

DOMS, KEITH, retired library director; b. Endeavor, Wis., Apr. 24, 1920; s. Reinhard Edward and Lillian (Gohlke) D.; m. Margaret Ann Taylor, Apr. 1, 1944; children: Peter Edward, David Laurance. BA, U. Wis., 1942, B.L.S., 1947. City librarian Concord (N.H.) Pub. Library, 1947-51; dir. Grace A. Dow Meml. Library, Midland, Mich., 1951-56; asso. dir. Carnegie Library of Pitts., 1956-64, dir., 1964-69; pres., dir. Free Library of Phila., 1969-87; exec. dir. Urban Libraries Council, Philadelphia, 1987-93, ret., 1995. Cons. pub. library devel. programs and pub. library bldgs.; specialist, dir. library seminar for State Dept., Pakistan, 1964; pres. Pitts. Regional Library Center, 1967-69; Pa. del. to White House Conf. on Libraries and Info. Services, 1978 Contbr. articles to tech. lit. Pres. United Mental Health Services of Allegheny County, 1963-65, Pa. Home Teaching Soc., 1969-76, Union Library Catalogue Pa., 1974-75, Palinet/Union Library Catalogue, 1975-77; vice chmn. Gov.'s Council on Library Devel., 1968-76; mem. Pa. State Bd. Edn. and Council of Higher Edn., 1975—; trustee On Line Computer Library Center, 1982-88; bd. visitors Grad. Sch. Library and Information Scis., U. Pitts., 1968-87; mem. Museum Council; bd. dirs. Greater Phila. Cultural Alliance, 1972-75, Reading is Fundamental Found., 1971-72, Freedom to Read Found., 1970-73.

Served with AUS, 1942-46. Mem. ALA (mem. council 1960-63, exec. bd. 1963-67, v.p. 1970-71, pres. 1971-72, chmn. com. on freedom access to libraries 1966-68, coordinating com. on library services to disadvantaged 1968-70, pres. library adminstrn. div. 1963-64, Lippincott award 1982), Pa. Library Assn. (pres. 1961, Disting. Service award 1976), World Affairs Council Phila. (bd. 1969-73), Internat. Fedn. Library Assns. (dir. pub. library sect. 1978-81), Internat. Assn. 1972, City Libraries (pres. 1974-77), Spl. Library Assn., Community Leadership Seminar Assos. U. Pa., Beta Phi Mu (pres. 1962-64) Clubs: Pittsburgh Bibliophiles, Philobiblon, Franklin Inn (pres. 1978-81), Sci. & Arts (Germantown). Home: State College, Pa. Died Sept. 26, 2009.

DONAHOE, RITA LOUISE, real estate executive; b. Boston, Jan. 16, 1930; d. Franklin Augustine and Barbara Rita (Coyne) Bannister; m. Robert Francis Donahoe, June 15, 1957; children: Steven Francis, Christopher John. Student, Boston Coll., 1948-51. Asst. clk. Suffolk Superior Criminal Ct., Boston, 1948-57; v.p., treas. D&G Constrn. Co., Inc., Merrimack, N.H., 1964-68; broker Fisher Assocs., Nashua, N.H., 1968-71; propr. R. Donahoe Assocs., Bedford, N.H., 1971—. Mem. Nashua Bd. Realtors (v.p. 1975, pres. 1976, Realtor of Yr. 1977), Manchester Bd. Realtors, So. N.H. Multiple Listing Service (v.p. 1975—, award 1973), Greater Manchester Multiple Listing Service, Women's Council Realtors (chpt. pres. 1974), Nat. Assn. Realtors, N.H. Assn. Realtors (dir. exec. com. 1976—), Realtors Nat. Mktg. Inst. Died Nov. 4, 2009.

DONALDSON, PAUL RODERICK, judge; b. Shaker Heights, Ohio, Feb. 11, 1926; s. Ralph J. and Hilda Irene (Stump) Donaldson; m. Mignon Farkas, Dec. 26, 1948; children: Stephen Paul, Kristine Louise. Student, Wittenberg Coll., 1946—47, Northwestern U., 1952, John Carroll U., 1951—53; JD, Cleve. Marshall Law Sch., 1957. Bar: Ohio 1957. Mem. firm Donaldson and Menak, 1957—59; asst. dir. law Shaker Heights, 1957—73, dir. law, 1973—81; judge Shaker Heights Mcpl. Ct., from 1982; pvt. practice, 1961—81. Exec. dir. Shaker One Hundred, Inc., 1961—81. Mem.: ABA, Greater Cleve. Mcpl. Judges Assn., Ohio Mcpl. Judges Assn., Ohio Bar Assn. Episcopalian. Home: Scottsdale, Ariz. Died Dec. 16, 2009.

DONATUCCI, ROBERT C., state legislator; b. Phila., May 3, 1952; s. Yolanda Donatucci; m. Maria Patelmo; 2 children. BA, Temple U., 1974. Mem. Dist. 185 Pa. House of Reps., Pa., 1980—2010. Democrat. Died Nov. 9, 2010.

DONNELLY, JOSEPH THOMAS, JR., arson investigator; b. Somerville, Mass., Sept. 4, 1922; s. Joseph Thomas and Mabel (Grant) Donnelly; m. Doris Patricia Morrissey, Jan. 12, 1946; children: Robert Grant, Susan Marie, Paul James. With Medford (Mass.) Fire Dept., 1947—80, lt., 1961—68, capt., 1968—78, dept. chief in charge fire prevention and investigation, 1978—80; spl. agt. Arson Detection Specialists Inc., Boston, from 1980; fire cons. Tufts U., 1979; instr. fire and arson investigative courses. Served with USN, 1942—45, ETO. Mem.: Internat. Assn. Fire Fighters, Mass. Assn. Arson Investigators, Nat. Assn. Arson Investigators, Internat. Assn. Arson Investigators, Am. Soc. Safety Engrs. Home: Medford, Mass. Died Apr. 26, 2009.

DONNELLY, LLOYD W., consultant; b. Tillamook, Oreg., Mar. 15, 1927; s. Lloyd W. Sr. and Margaret Mary (Mulveny) D.; m. Marjorie L., Aug. 27, 1949; children: Kathleen Donnelly Tomlinson, Peter, Nancy, Mark. BSME, Tex. A&M U., 1951; MBA, Columbia U., 1980. Registered profl. engr., Tex., La., Miss., Mass. Engring. supr. Monsanto Corp., St. Louis, 1951-66; dir. engring. Geigy Chem. Co., Mobile, Ala., 1966-69; v.p., ptnr. So. Tech. Services, Mobile, 1969-71; sr. v.p. Daniel Constrn. Co., Greenville, S.C., 1971-82; pres. Wyher/Livsey Constrn. Co., Atlanta, 1982-84; sr. v.p. Dravo Corp., Pitts., 1984-87; prin. L.W. Donnelly Assocs., from 1987. Bd. dirs. Pulp & Paper Inst., N.C. State U., 1983—, World Tech. Ctr., Atlanta, 1982—. Mem. Marine Fisheries Adv. Com., Washington, 1987-90: flotilla comdr. USCG Aux. Ala. S. Coast. With USN, 1943-45, PTO. Mem. Gulf Shores C. of C., Dusquesne Club, Laurel Valley Club (Pitts.), Atlanta Country Club. Republican. Roman Catholic. Died May 21, 2009.

DONOHUE, ALFRED F., retired telecommunications supervisor; b. Bklyn., July 31, 1932; m. Mary Donohue; children: William, Margaret, Elizabeth, Daniel, Peter, Thomas, Matthew, Joan, Kathleen, Maryanne. Craftsman NY Telephone Co., 1956—69, supr., 1969—92; ret. Candidate, NY Dist. 9 US House of Representatives, 2002. Conservative. Roman Catholic. Died Oct. 5, 2009.

DORSETT, BURT, investment company executive; b. Chgo., Nov. 8, 1930; s. Burton and Della (Reader) D.; m. Judith Martin, Dec. 14, 1952 (div.); children: Mark, Deborah, Jeffrey, Cindy (dec.); m. Trixie Landsberger, Mar. 1, 1981. BA, Dartmouth Coll., 1953; MBA, Harvard U., 1959. Indsl. engr. E.I. duPont de Nemours, Seaford, Del., 1953-57; cons. Booz-Allen & Hamilton, NYC, 1959-62; v.p. U. Rochester, 1962-70; exec. v.p., trustee Coll. Retirement Equities Fund, NYC, 1970-79; chmn., pres. Westinghouse Pension Investment Corp., NYC, 1979-86, Dorsett-McCabe Capital Mgmt. Inc., 1987—2007. Chief investment officer Money Growth Inst., 1999-2002. Author: (with others) Epoxy Resins, Market Survey and Users Reference, 1959. Budget com. Cmty. Chest, Rochester, 1967-70; trustee Convalescent Hosp. for Children, Rochester, 1967-70, Hillside Children's Home, Rochester, 1968-70, Keuka Coll., N.Y., 1968-71; mem. com. Boys Club of N.Y.C., 1970-80; investment com. Am. Psychol. Assn., 1969-87. William J. Cook scholar, 1953. Mem. Dartmouth Club, Harvard Bus. Sch. Club, WeeBurn Country Club (Darrien, Conn.). Home: Naples, Fla. Died Apr. 26, 2009.

DOUCETTE, RICHARD F., state legislator; b. Edgartown, Mass., Dec. 23, 1918; m. Priscilla R. Doucette (dec.); 1 child. Grad. h.s., New Bedford. N.H. state rep. Dist. 17, 1987-92, Dist. 19, from 1995; mem. state inst. and housing com. N.H. Ho. of Reps., 1987-92, mem. corrections and criminal justice coms.; former chef. Food cons., Keene. Mem. Tanglewood Tenants Assn., pres., 1975-87. Mem. KC, N.E. Army Retiree Coun. (chmn. 1985-87, v.p. 1975-82), Assn. U.S. Army (adv. bd. dir. 1990—), Am. Legion. Died July 4, 2009.

DOUGLAS, JOHN WOOLMAN, lawyer; b. Phila., Aug. 15, 1921; s. Paul H. and Dorothy S. (Wolff) D.; m. Mary Evans St. John, July 14, 1945 (dec. 2007); children: Katherine D. Torrey, Peter R. AB, Princeton U., 1943; LLB, Yale U., 1948; DPhil, Oxford U., 1950. Bar: N.Y. 1948, D.C. 1953. Law clk. to Justice Harold H. Burton US Supreme Ct., 1951—52; asst. atty. gen. civil divsn. US Dept. Justice, 1963—66; ptnr. Covington & Burling LLP, Washington. Chmn. Carnegie Endowment for Internat. Peace, 1978-86. Served to lt. (j.g.) USNR, 1943-46, MTO, PTO. Trustee Deerfield Acad., 1972-77; co-chair Citizens for McGovern Com., 1972; chmn. Robert F. Kennedy Meml. Found., 1980-83. Rhodes scholar, 1948-50. Fellow American Coll. Trial Lawyers; mem. ABA, D.C. Bar Assn. (pres. 1974-75), Nat. Lawyers Com. for Civil Rights Under Law (co. chmn. 1969-71), Nat. Legal Aid and Defender Assn. (pres. 1970-71), Yale Law Sch. Assn. (pres. 1975-77). Democrat. Presbyterian. Home: Washington, DC. Died June 2, 2010.

DOWNING, JOANN ARLOWYN, non-profit association administrator; b. Detroit, Nov. 7, 1955; d. Kenneth Dale and Arlowyn Mary (Natche) D. BS with honors, Mich. State U., 1978. Program dir. level 1 YWCA of Metro Detroit, 1978, program dir. level 2, 1979; asst. camp dir. Fair Winds Girl Scout Coun., Flint, Mich., 1980, asst. camp dir. older girl program specialist, 1981-84, dir. The Timbers, 1985-94, dir. outdoor program and properties, from 1995. Prodr. radio show Sta. WFBE-FM, flint, 1985-96, Sta. WCBN-FM, Ann Arbor, Mich., 1994—. Mem. affirmative action leadership coun. Mich. Ho. of Reps., Lansing, 1995; vol. fundraiser Lana Pollack Campaign for U.S. Senate, Ann Arbor, 1994; bd. dirs. Washtenaw Rainbow Action Project, Ann Arbor, 1995; instr., instr. trainer ARC, 1975-95. Named one of Outstanding Young Women Am., 1987. Mem. Am. Camping Assn. (sec. Mich. sect. 1986-95, nominating com. 1983-84, v.p. for devel. 1984-85), NOW (sec. 1982-84, v.p. Flint chpt. 1991—), Kiwanis. Avocations: singing, jazz dancing, guitar, running, swimming, canoeing. Home: Flint, Mich. Died Jan. 7, 2009.

DOWNING, ROBERT ALLAN, lawyer; b. Kenosha, Wis., Jan. 6, 1929; s. Leo Vertin and Mayme C. (Kennedy) D.; m. JoAnn C. Cramton, Apr. 14, 1951 (div. Sept. 1977); children: Robert A., Kevin C., Tracey Downing Clark, Gregory E.; m. Joan Govan Reiter, Oct. 29, 1977; 1 child, Charles E. Reiter III. BS, U. Wis., 1950, JD, 1956. Bar: Wis. 1956, Ill. 1956, U.S. Supreme Ct. 1965. Assoc. Sidley & Austin, Chgo., 1956-64, ptnr., 1964-94, counsel, 1994-97, Ruff, Weidenaar & Reidy, Ltd., Chgo., from 1997. Trustee (life), former pres. Episcopal Charities and Cmty. Svcs., Chgo. Diocese. Served to lt. USN, 1950-53, Korea. Fellow Am. Coll. Trial Lawyers; mem. ABA, Soc. Trial Lawyers, Ill. Bar Assn., Chgo. Bar Assn., Wis. Bar Assn., 7th Cir. Bar Assn., Union League Club, Law Club, Legal Club, MidDay Club, Westmoreland Country Club. Republican. Episcopalian. Died May 4, 2009.

DOYLE, JOHN LAWRENCE, artist; b. Chgo., Mar. 14, 1939; s. John W. and Cecelia M. (Tarkowski) D.; children: Lynn, Sean, Morgan. BA, Sch. of Art Inst. Chgo., 1962; MA, No. Ill. U., 1967. Tchr. art Forest View High Sch., Arlington Heights, Ill., 1962-72; pres. Yancey Crafted Tile. Bd. dirs. Toe River Arts Coun., Yancey Libr., Amy Regional Libr. Sys., Yancey History Assn., Yancey Evening Sch. Program, Steering Com., Yancey Mus./Visitor Ctr. Project. One-man shows of prints and/or paintings include: Denver Natural History Mus., Natural Am. Indian Mus., Spokane, Wash., Allen Galleries, Milw., U. N.D., U. S.D., Black Gallery, Taos, N.Mex., Vanderbilt U., Nashville, Tenn., Johns Hopkins U., Balt., Jockey Club Gallery, Miami, Fla., New West Whitney Gallery Western Art, Cody, Wyo., Harvard Med. Library, Lesch Gallery, Mpls., Clev. Clinic, Mayo Clinic, MGM Grand, Las Vegas, Yale U. Hosp., Now and Then Gallery, N.Y.C., Fine Print Unltd., Miami, Grand Gallery, Nev., Galerie Une, Puerto Vallarta, Mex., Welnetz Studio, Wis., Gallery G, Wichita, all 1981; group shows, latest being: U. Miami, Fla., Tex. Tech U., Amarillo and Lubbock, U. Iowa Hosp. and Clinic, Loma Linda U., Calif., Art Resources, Denver, Hayden Hayes Gallery, Colorado Springs, Colo., Southwestern Gallery, Dallas, Nat. Library of Medicine, Bethesda, Md., Cornell Med. Coll., N.Y.C., Columbia U., N.Y.C., U. Kans., Harvard Law Library, Denver Nat. Hist. Mus., William Mitchell Law Sch., Mpls., United Bank of Austin, Tex., others, 1982-85, Inter Art, Nice, France, Loyola U. Sch. Law, New Orleans, Fine Arts Ltd., Miami, U. Dubuque, Iowa, Art Expo Los Angeles, Art Expo N.Y., Degan Bella Gallery, San Antonio, U. Ariz., Tempe, Midwest Mus. Am. Art, Ind., 1986, U. Ill., Chgo., 1987, R. Volid Gallery, Chgo., 1987, Royce Gallery, Denver, 1987, Denver Mus. Nat. History, 1987, No. Ill. U., DeKalb, 1987, Art Expo, N.Y.C., 1987, U. Ill. Chgo., 1988, R. Volip Gallery, Chgo., 1988, Ramses II Denver Mus., N.H., 1988, Royce Gallery, Denver, 1988, Hayden-Hayes Gallery, Colorado Springs, 1988, World Trade Ctr., Mpls.-St. Paul, 1988, Bergren Gallery, Rockford, Ill., 1988, Red Carpet Gallery, Minn., 1988, Yancey County Hist. Mus., N.C., 1988, Minn. World Trade Ctr., St. Paul, 1989, U. Ill., Champaign, 1989, U. Wis., Madison, 1989, Jean Stephen Gallery, Mpls., 1989, New West Cont. Art, Buffalo Bill Hist. Ctr., Cody, Wyo., 1990, White Thunder World Gallery, Milw., 1990, D. Ehrlein Gallery, Milw., 1990, Bank One, Milw., 1990, White Hart Gallery, Steamboat Springs, Colo., 1991, Suzanne Brown Gallery, Scottsdale, Ariz., 1991, Midwest Mus. Am. Art, Elkhart, Ind., 1991, Scripps Meml. Hosp. Schaetzel Ctr., La Jolla, Calif., 1991, Suzanne Brown Gallery, Scottsdale, Ariz., 1992, Walker Art Ctr., Asheville, N.C., 1992; represented in permanent collections: Library of Congress, Washington, Art Inst. Chgo., Indpls., Mus. Art, Carnegie Inst., Pitts., Norton Gallery of Art, West Palm Beach, Fla., Birmingham (Ala.) Mus. Art, Canton (Ohio) Art Inst., Columbus Mus. Fine Art, Columbus, Ohio, Fort Lauderdale (Fla.) Mus. Art, Miss. Art Mus., Whitney Gallery Western Art, Jackson, Nat. Gallery of Art, Washington, U. Mich., Ann Arbor, Savannah (Ga.) Coll. Art and Design, Scripps Meml. Hosp., La Jolla, Appalachian State U., Boon, NC, U. NC, Asheville, Dunedin (Fla.) Fine Arts. Bd. dirs. Family Violence Coalition Yancey County Vol. Coop, Toe River Arts Coun., Yancey Libr., Amy Regional Libr., Healthy Yancy; pres. Yancey History Assn.; sec., treas. Mus. Visitor Ctr. Project; chair subcom. Land Use Planning Commn.; mem. 21st century cmtys. action com. Yancey County Cultural Resource Commn., now pres.; chmn. Yancey Arts, Traditional Voices Com., Riddlefest Com., Internat. Biog. Ctr., Cambridge, Eng.; mem. Sch. Cir. Devel. Com. Recipient 21st Century award, Internat. Biog. Ctr., Cambridge, Eng., Hon. Mention Internat. Printmakers, 1971; George Brown Travelling fellow, 1962 Died Mar. 15, 2010.

DRAPER, JOHN CLAYTON, manufacturing executive; b. Boston, Oct. 2, 1945; s. Charles Stark and Ivy Hurd (Willard) D.; m. Sue Ellen Taylor, July 3, 1971; children: Kara Stark, Danielle Clayton. BA, Ohio Wesleyan U., 1967; JD, U. Cin., 1970. Bar: Mass. 1970. Pres. Pearce-Draper Assocs., Columbus, Ohio, 1970-72; v.p. Epicure Products, Inc., Newburyport, Mass., 1972-79; pres. Runtal N.Am., Inc., Ward Hill, Mass., 1980-89, vice-chmn., from 1990; chmn., chief exec. officer MRR Traders, Ltd., Allston, Mass. Bd. dirs. Snell Acoustics, Haverhill, Mass.; investment advisor. Mem. Mass. Bar Assn. Mem. United Ch. of Christ. Avocations: tennis, hiking. Home: Cary, NC. Died July 7, 2010.

DREW, JOHN JAY, electronics and automobile manufacturer executive; b. St. Paul, Feb. 21, 1925; s. Verne Marvin and Mary Elizabeth (Thorpe) D.; m. Regina E. Muysson, Sept. 2, 1977; 1 child, Donald Verne. BS, State U. Iowa, 1948. Chief inspector Ford Motor Co. Dallas Assembly Plant, 1950-65; gen. mgr. Odyssey Trailer Co., Magnolia, Ark., 1965-68; contracts divsn. mgr. Tex. Instruments, Dallas, 1968-90; pres. J.D.D. Inc., Plano, Tex., from 1997. Aviation cadet USN, 1943-45. Mem. Scottish Rite (32 Mason). Republican. Presbyterian. Avocations: golf, fishing, hunting. Home: Forney, Tex. Died Jan. 19, 2009.

DRIGGS, CHARLES MULFORD, lawyer; b. East Cleveland, Ohio, Jan. 26, 1924; s. Karl Holcomb and Lila Vandeveer (Wilson) D.; children: Ruth, Rachel, Carrie, Karl H., Charles M.; m. Ann Eileen Zargari, Oct. 25, 1991. BS, Yale U., 1947, JD, 1950. Bar: Ohio 1951. Assoc. Squire, Sanders & Dempsey, Cleve., 1950-64, ptnr., 1964-88, of counsel, 1988-91; pvt. practice civil law Cleve., 1991-95; prin. Driggs, Hogg, Daugherty & Del Zoppo Co., LPA, Willoughby Hills, Ohio, 1995. Pres. Bratenahl (Ohio) Sch. Bd., 1958—62; mem. adv. coun. Cleve. Ctr. for Theol. Edn., from 1978. Mem. ABA, Ohio Bar Assn., Lake County Bar Assn., Cleve. Bar Assn., Greater Cleve. Growth Assn., Cleve. Law Libr. Assn. (trustee 1977-91), Ct. Nisi Prius (judge 2000), Citizens League Greater Cleve., Geauga County Bar Assn., Phi Delta Phi, Tau Beta Pi, Phi Gamma Delta. Home: Kirtland, Ohio. Died Mar. 9, 2010.

DRISCOLL, JOHN GERARD, retired academic administrator; b. NYC, Apr. 17, 1933; s. John P. and Mary T. (Kennedy) D. BS in Physics, Iona Coll., 1954; MS, St. John's U., 1957; PhD in Theoretical Mathematics, Columbia U., 1969; DSc, Coll. New Rochelle, 1971. Tchr. elem. schs. Rice High Sch., 1956-57, St. Joseph Sch., Antigua, 1957-61, Power Meml. Sch., 1961-65; prof. math. Iona Coll., New Rochelle, NY, 1965—95, asst. to pres., 1969-71, pres., 1971—95; scholar-in-residence Hebrew U., Jerusalem, 1995—2010. Bd. dirs. Chase N.B.W. Bank, City Harvest, Inc., N.Y. Trustee St. Joseph's Sem. & Sch. Theology, Yonkers, N.Y.; bd. dirs. New Rochelle Hosp. Med. Ctr., Irish American Sports Found. Named to The Iona Coll. Hall of Fame, 1994. Mem. World Trade Inst. Died Sept. 21, 2010.

DRISCOLL, LEE FRANCIS, JR., retired lawyer; b. Phila., July 27, 1926; s. Leon F. and Helen (Carroll) D.; m. Phoebe Albert, Dec. 30, 1959; children— Lee Francis III, Patrick McGill, Phoebe Driscoll Fisher, Helen Louise. AB, U. Pa., 1949, LLB, 1953. Bar: Pa. 1954. Ret. Pres. Phila. United Way, 1980-82; Dem. candidate for U.S. Congress, 1962. Served with AUS, 1944-46, 50-51. Decorated Bronze Star. Mem. Union League (Phila.), Phila. Club. Roman Catholic. Home: Ambler, Pa. Died Mar. 28, 2009.

DROHAN, FRANCIS PIERCE, JR., optometrist; b. Jacksonville, Fla., July 31, 1922; s. Francis Pierce and Helene (Cook) Drohan; m. Elizabeth Hancock Drohan, May 4, 1952 (div. 1964); children: Cheryl Helene, Michael Pierce, Deidre Elaine, Lisa Marian. AA, Williams Coll., 1944; OD, No. Ill. Coll. Optometry, 1949. Pvt. practice, Jacksonville, Fla., from 1955. Lt. comdr. USNR, 1942—72. Recipient Will Wasson award, N.E. Fla. Soc. Prevention of Blindness, 1975. Fellow: Am. Acad. of Optometry; mem.: N.E. Fla. Optometric Assn. (past pres. 1956—57, 1971—72), Les Amis Du Vin, Jacksonville (dir. 1985), Lions (vice chmn. 1957). Republican. Roman Catholic. Died Apr. 17, 2010.

DROZDZIEL, MARION JOHN, aeronautical engineer; b. Dunkirk, NY, Dec. 21, 1924; s. Steven and Veronica (Wilk) D.; m. Rita L. Korwek, Aug. 30, 1952; 1 child, Eric A. BS in Aero. Engring., Tri State U., 1947, BSME, 1948; postgrad., Ohio State U., 1948, Niagara U., 1949-51, U. Buffalo, 1951-52. Stress analyst Curtiss Wright Corp., Columbus, Ohio, 1948; project engr. weight analysis Bell Aerospace

Textron, Buffalo, 1949-52, stress analyst, 1952-60, asst. supr. stress analysis, 1960-64, chief stress analysis propulsion, 1964-79, chief engr. stress and weights, 1979-84, staff scientist, 1984-85, cons. structures and fractures mechanics, from 1985. Del. Internat. Citizens Ambassador Program; active Buffalo Fine Arts Acad., N.Y. Acad. Scis.; mem. Tech. Socs. Coun. of the Niagara Frontier. With US Army, 1944—47. Recipient cert. of achievement NASA-Apollo, 1972, Wisdom award Wisdom Soc. for Advancement of Knowledge, Learning and Rsch. in Edn., 2000; cert. commendation U.K. NATO program, 1982; named to Wisdom Hall of Fame, Wisdom Soc. for Advancement of Knowledge, Learning and Rsch. in Edn., 2000. Mem. AAAS, AIAA (Mem. Chmn.'s award 1988-90, 92-93), Soc. Reliability Engrs. (bd. dir. 1998-), U.S. Naval Inst., Am. Space Found., Nat. Conservancy, Nat. Audubon Soc., Sierra Club, Am. Acad. Polit. and Social Sci., Acad. Polit. Sci., Union Concerned Scientists, Air Force Assn., Nat. Space Soc., Soc. Allied Weight Engrs., Planetary Soc., Am. Mgmt. Assn.,Bibl. Archeology Soc., Archeol. Inst. Am., Cousteau Soc., Smithsonian Assocs., Buffalo Audubon Soc., Bell Mgmt. Club, Natural History Mus., Internat. Hypersonic Rsch., Disabled Am. Vets, Kosciuszko Found., Polish Arts Club Buffalo, Exch. Club of Tonawandas (sec. 1996-98, bd. dir. 1999-2000), Nat. Exch. Club (Disting. Sec. award 1996-99). Republican. Roman Catholic. Achievements include development of criteria and methods of structural analysis extending analyses into the plastic and creep ranges for titanium and columbium rocket nozzle extensions; of criteria and methods of structural analysis for extendable rocket nozzle extensions, including rapid nozzle deployment involving plasticity; of methods of structural analysis for low strength, high ductility steels, aluminums, and teflons as positive expulsion devices for zero gravity application in propellant tanks including bellows, reversing heads, rolling diaphragms devices and collapsing or folding concepts; structural analysis on "X" series of aircraft, on Mercury, Gemini, and Apollo spacecraft reaction control and propulsion systems; structural and weight analysis of programs involving rocket engines, propulsion systems, aircraft, air cushion vehicles, surface-effect ships, laser systems avionics, airborne and ground antennae, Army tanks and fighting vehicles. Died Feb. 24, 2010.

DRUCKER, ROLF, audio-video engineering executive; b. Nuremberg, Ger., Sept. 15, 1926; came to U.S., 1941, naturalized, 1945; s. Benno and Erna (Engel) D.; student CCNY, 1950; m. Olga M. Lenk, Oct. 22, 1950; children: Jane L., Robert S., Alice S. Engr., Sta. WNYC, 1946-48; tech. dirs. Sta. ABC-TV, N.Y.C., 1948-77, v.p. ops. and engring. Sta. WNET-TV, N.Y.C., 1977-83; dir. electronic graphics ABC-TV, 1983-90; owner Audiovideo Engring. Co., Stuart, Fla., 1969—. Designed video effects keyer, 1951, automatic video delay line, 1967, video hum-stop coil, 1969; active in developing TV sender, Berlin, NOVA TV Network, Czech Republic. Served with U.S. Army, 1944-46. Recipient Emmy award Nat. Acad. TV Arts and Scis., Innsbruck, Austria, 1976. Home: Palm City, Fla. Died Apr. 12, 2009.

DRUM, SARA RUTH, nursing administrator; b. Evanston, Ill., Aug. 6, 1929; d. Raymond Borland and Ruth Armstrong (Pettit) D.; R.N., Ch. Home and Hosp. Sch. Nursing, 1955; postgrad. in gerontology and nursing adminstrn. U. Ariz., Weber State Coll., UCLA, U. So. Calif., U. Calif.-Northridge; Dir. nursing Colonial Convalescent Hosp., Santa Ana, 1967-68; supr. Rio Hondo Meml. Hosp., Downey, Calif., 1968-69; dir. nursing Intercommunity Convalescent Hosp., Norwalk, Calif., 1969-76, Southland Geriatric Ctr., Norwalk, 1976-85, Calif. Convalescent Hosp., Long Beach, 1985-86. Mem. assoc. degree nursing adv. com. Cerritos Coll.; adv. bd. baccalaureate degree nurse program Biola Coll.; mem. occupational adv. com. nursing Whittier Union High Sch. Dist. Democrat. Home: Anacortes, Wash. Died Aug. 20, 2009.

DUAL, PETER ALFRED, school system administrator, management consultant; b. Alexandria, Va., Jan. 27, 1946; s. Peter Lloyd and Averlee Lucritia (Coco) Dual; m. Toni Irene Nixon, Aug. 24, 1968; children: Nikki Averlee, Peter Aaron, Tony Ahmaad, Alfred Michael. AA, Lake Mich. Coll., 1966; BS, Western Mich. U., 1969, MA, 1971; PhD, Mich. State U., 1973; MPH, U. Tex.-Houston, 1975. Counselor Neighborhood Youth Corps., Benton Harbor, Mich., 1967—69; tchr. Benton Harbor, 1968—69, Battle Creek, Mich., 1969—70; adminstrv. asst. to dir. sch. cmty. rels. Kalamazoo Pub. Schs.; assoc. corm dir. Western Mich. U., Kalamazoo, 1970—71; counselor multi-ethnic counseling ctr. Mich. State U., East Lansing, 1971—72, asst. to ombudsman, 1971—73; asst. chmn. African and Afro-Am. Studes and Rsch. Ctr. U. Tex., Austin, 1973—74, asst. prof. cultural founds. and ethnic studies, 1973—75; assoc. dir. continuing edn., asst. prof. health behavior and health edn. U. Mich., Ann Arbor, 1975—78; dir., asst. to dean Grad. Sch. Pub. Health, 1978—80; acad. dean, prof. health svcs. adminstrn. Ea. Mich. U., Ypsilanti, 1980—83; acad. dean Coll. Health and Human Svcs., prof. pub. health San Diego State U., from 1983. Contbr. articles to profl. jours. Active Nat. Health Coun., 1979, Greater Detroit Area Hosp. Coun., 1982. Mem.: Mich. Pub. Health Assn., Adult Edn. Assn., NEA, Am. Soc. Allied Health Professions, Nat. Assn. Supervision and Curriculum Devel., Am. Assn. Higher Edn., Am. Pub. Health Assn., Am. Coun. Edn., Rotary Club. Died Aug. 11, 2010.

DUDLEY, CARL SAFFORD, religion educator; b. Balt., Oct. 27, 1932; s. Harold Jenkins and Margaret (Safford) D.; m. Shirley Sanford, June 18, 1955; children: Nathan, Rebecca, Andrew, Deborah, Steven. BA, Cornell U., 1954; postgrad., N.Y. Sch. Social Work, 1954-56; MDiv, Union Theol. Sem., 1959; D of Ministry, McCormick Theol. Sem., 1974. Social worker Manhattanville Community Ctr., NYC, 1954-56; asst. pastor 1st Presbyn. Ch., Buffalo, 1959-62; pastor Berea Presbyn. Ch., St. Louis, 1962-73; prof. McCormick Theol. Sem., Chgo., 1973-93, Hartford (Conn.) Seminary, from 1993. Exec. dir. Ctr. for Ch. and Community Ministries. Author: Making the Small Church Effective, 1978, Where Have All Our People Gone, 1979, Orientations to Faith, 1982; co-editor, co-author: Building Effective Ministry, 1983, Handbook for Congregational Studies, 1986, New Testament Tensions in the Contemporary Church, 1987, Developing Your Small Church's Potential, 1988, Carriers of Faith, 1991, Basic Steps toward Community Ministry, 1991, Energizing the Church, 1993. Commr. St. Louis Housing Authority, 1970-73; bd. dirs. Sch. Bd. 200, Oak Park, Ill., 1981-87. Mem. Religious Rsch. Assn. (exec. com. 1979-82, assoc. editor Religious Rsch. Rev. 1980-82), Soc. Sci. Study of Religion, Assn. Sociology of Religion. Died Apr. 22, 2009.

DUDLEY, GEORGE ELLSWORTH, lawyer; b. Earlington, Ky., July 14, 1922; s. Ralph Emerson and Camille (Lackey) D.; m. Barbara J. Muir, June 28, 1950 (dec. Feb. 1995); children: Bruce K., Camille Dudley McNutt, Nancy S., Elizabeth Dudley Stephens. BS in Commerce, U. Ky., 1947; JD, U. Mich., 1950. Bar: Ky. 1950, D.C. 1951, U.S. Dist. Ct. (we. dist.) Ky. 1962, U.S. Ct. Appeals (6th cir.) 1987. Assoc. Gordon, Gordon & Moore, Madisonville, Ky., 1950-51; pvt. practice law Louisville, 1952-59; ptnr. Brown, Ardery, Todd & Dudley, Louisville, 1959-72, Brown, Todd & Heyburn, Louisville, 1972-92, of counsel, from 1992, mem. mgmt. com., 1972-90, chmn., 1989-90. Pres. Ky. Easter Seal Soc., Louisville, 1971-72; treas. Ky. Dem. Party, Frankfort, 1971-74; bd. dirs. Alliant Adult Health Svcs., Louisville, 1976—; 1st v.p. Nat. Easter Seal Soc., Chgo., 1981. Capt. inf. U.S. Army, 1943-46, ETO; capt. JAGC, U.S. Army, 1951-52. Mem. ABA, Ky. Bar Assn., Louisville Bar Assn., U.S. 6th Cir. Jud. Conf. (life), Harmony Landing Country Club (pres. 1978-79), Barristers Soc., Omicron Delta Kappa. Presbyterian. Avocations: golf, tennis, travel, sports spectator. Home: Louisville, Ky. Died Sept. 25, 2009.

DUELL, ROBERT WILLIAM, agronomist; b. NYC, Feb. 24, 1929; s. Christopher J. and Minnie D. (Butterweck) D.; m. Gladys Sylvia Thorkildsen, Aug. 18, 1956; children: Elise, Kristin, Julie, Rodney. BA, U. Conn., 1950, MS, 1954; PhD, Rutgers U., 1957. Rsch. assoc. Farm Crops Dept. Rutgers U., New Brunswick, N.J., 1955-57, asst. rsch. specialist, 1957-61, assoc. rsch. specialist, 1961-65, assoc. rsch. prof. Soils and Crops Dept., from 1967; agronomist IRI Rsch. Inst., Rio de Janeiro, 1965-67. Cons. agronomist U.S. AID, 1977-88, U.S. Army C.E., 1988—. Contbr. articles to profl. jours. With U.S. Army, 1951-53. Mem. Am. Soc. Agronomy (chmn. C-5 div. 1980-81), Sigma Xi. Republican. Lutheran. Achievements include Fortress creeping red fescue; Banner chewings fescue; Reliant hard fescue; Spartan hard fescue; Roadside vegetation, landfill coverage. Home: Princeton, NJ. Died May 21, 2010.

DUENAS, CRISTOBAL CAMACHO, federal judge; b. Agana, Guam, Sept. 12, 1920; s. Jose Castro and Concepcion Martinez (Camacho) D.; m. Juanita Castro Calvo, May 8, 1954; children: Christopher, Therese, Vincent, Zerlina, Joanna, Richard, David. Student, Aquinas Coll., Grand Rapids, Mich., 1946-48; AB, U. Mich., 1950, JD, 1952. Bar: Guam 1952. Asst. atty. gen. Dept. of Law, Govt. of Guam, Agana, 1952-57; dir. dept. of Land Mgmt. Govt. Guam, Agana, 1957-60; judge Island Ct. of Guam, Agana, 1960-69, U.S. Dist. Ct. for Guam, Agana, from 1969, now chief judge. Mem. ABA, Guam Bar Assn. (v.p. 1966-67), Am. Judicature Soc. Clubs: K.C. Home: Agana, Guam. Died Feb. 14, 2010.

DUFF, ERNEST ARTHUR, political scientist, educator; b. Charlottesville, Va., Dec. 27, 1929; s. Ernest Ragland and Emma Ruth (Bennett) D.; m. Barbara Ellen Jones, Aug. 30, 1955; children: Ernest A. Jr., Melanie Duff Badesch, Cameron John, Valerie Duff-Strautmann. BA, U. Va., 1952, MA, 1957, PhD, 1964. Fgn. svc. officer Dept. of State, Havana, Cuba, 1957-60, Washington, 1960-62, Bogota, Colombia, 1962-63; prof. Randolph-Macon Woman's Coll., Lynchburg, Va., 1964-97, Charles Dana prof., 1986, prof. emeritus, from 1997. Spl. field rep. Rockefeller Found., Cali, Colombia, 1966-67; vis. Fulbright prof. U. Mexico, Mexico City, 1979-80. Author: Agrarian Reform in Colombia, 1968, Violence and Repression in Latin America, 1974, Leader and Party in Latin America, 1984; reviewer Choice mag. Am. Libr. Assn. Polit. analyst WSET-TV, Lynchburg, Va., 1987—. Lt. USN, 1952-55, Korea. NROTC scholar USN and U. Va., 1948-52; Helen Wessell fellow, U. Va., 1963-64, NEH fellow, Brown U., Providence, 1990. Mem. Latin Am. Studies Assn., So. Polit. Sci. Assn., Southeastern Coun. Latin Am. Studies, Va. Polit. Sci. Assn. Baptist. Avocations: tennis, gardening. Home: Lynchburg, Va. Died Apr. 17, 2009.

DUGAN, RICHARD D., investment banker; b. Plainfield, NJ, Aug. 31, 1948; s. Frank J. and Edythe S. (Schnabel) D.; m. Barbara S. Schaible, June 15, 1985; children: Christine A., Jennifer J. BSChemE, Lehigh U., 1970, MBA, 1972. Asst. treas. Gen. Motors Corp., NYC, 1972-84; prin. Morgan Stanley & Co. Inc., NYC, from 1984. Pres. Bay Point Harbour Assn., Point Pleasant, N.J., 1984-89. Mem. Internat. Game Fishing Assn. Republican. Episcopalian. Home: New York, NY. Died Dec. 26, 2009.

DUGAN, ROBERT PERRY, JR., retired minister, religious organization administrator; b. Morristown, NJ, Jan. 19, 1932; s. Robert P. and Marion Frances (Sahrbeck) D.; m. Marilyn I. Wertz, Aug. 8, 1953; children: Robert Perry III, Cheryl. AB, Wheaton Coll., 1953; MDiv, Fuller Theol. Sem., 1956; DD, Denver Conservative Bapt. Sem., 1985; LHD, Geneva Coll., 1985; LLD, Roberts Wesleyan Coll., 1990. Ordained to ministry Conservative Bapt. Assn. Am. 1957. Postgrad. teaching fellow in Hebrew Fuller Theol. Sem., 1954-57; minister of youth ch. Bloomfield, NJ, 1957-58; pastor Rochester, NH, 1959-63, Elmhurst, Ill., 1963-69, Trinity Baptist Ch., Wheat Ridge, Colo., 1970-75; chaplain Senate of State of Colo., 1974-75; pres. Conservative Baptist Assn. Am., 1973-76; v.p. Rockmont Coll., Lakewood, Colo., 1976-78; dir. Office of Pub. Affairs, Nat. Assn. Evangelicals, Washington, 1978-96; v.p. governmental affairs Nat. Assn. Evangelicals, Washington, 1996-98; ret., 1999. Bd. dirs. Denver Sem., chmn., 1998-2001; Staley disting. Christian scholar lectr., 1973, 82, 84, 86, 88, 94; participant Internat. Congress on World Evangelism, Lausanne, Switzerland, 1974. Author: Winning the New Civil War: Recapturing America's Values, 1991, Stand and Be Counted: A Washington Insider Tells How to Preserve America's Liberties for You and Your Children, 1995; editor monthly newsletter NAE Washington Insight, 1979-97. Candidate for U.S. Congress, 1976; mem. ethics adv. bd. USIA, 1982-84; bd. dirs. Justice Fellowship, 1983-91, Transformation Internat., 1987-91; bd. trustees Williamsburg Charter Found., 1988-89. Home: Rio Rancho, N.Mex. Died May 4, 2010.

DUNAYEVSKAYA, ALLA, radiologist; b. Odessa, USSR, July 25, 1920; came to U.S. 1982; d. Leo and Isabella (Feldman) Shmulyan; m. Victor Dunayevsky (dec. 1965); 1 child, Valery Dunaevsky. MD, Med. Inst. Rostov-Don, Russia, 1947. Resident in radiology Inst. for Qualification of Physicians, Leningrad, 1948; resident in roentgen diagnosis Roentgeno Radiol. Inst., Moskow, 1951, 53, 64; resident in radiol. diagnoses of cardiovascular diseases Acad. Med. Sci. of Surgery of Cardiovascular Diseases, Moscow, 1969; resident in radiol. diagnosis of bone and joint diseases Radiol. Inst. for Qualification of Physicians, Kiev, 1977; mgr. radiology Dist. Polyclinic, Murmansk, Russia, 1948-60; chief radiologist Council of Trade Union of Health Resorts of Latvien Rep., Russia, 1961-81; vol. Forbes Reg. Health Ctr., Pitts., 1982-85; rschr. in med. stats. and quality assurance, radiology dept. Forbes Regional Hosp./Forbes Health System, Pitts., from 1985. Cons. in field. Contbr. articles to profl. jours. Mem. Peace Links of Pa., Internat. Women's Club. Jewish. Avocations: stamp collecting/philately, walking, music, libraries, museums. Home: Monroeville, Pa. Died Mar. 29, 2010.

DUNBAR, WALLACE HUNTINGTON, manufacturing executive; b. NYC, Dec. 17, 1931; s. Duncan and Marion (Eaton) D.; m. Ellen Thomas, June 13, 1953; children: Wallace Huntington, Thomas, Martha, Laura, Sarah, Jonathan. AB, Denison U., 1953; MBA, Ind. U., 1954. Accountant Gen. Electric Co., NYC, 1954-55; with Thomas Industries, Inc., Louisville, 1957-81, v.p. fin., 1962-72, chmn. bd., chief exec. officer, 1972-79, cons., 1979-81; chmn. bd. Trojan Luggage Co., Memphis, from 1981. Bd. dirs. Banc One Ky. Corp., Louisville, Thomas Industries Inc. Bd. dirs. Honey Locust Found., 1959—, Dunbar Found., 1967—; trustee Denison U., Granville, Ohio. Served with AUS, 1955-57. Mem. Phi Delta Theta. Clubs: Harmony Landing Country. Lodges: Rotary. Home: Sanibel, Fla. Died Jan. 28, 2009.

DUNCAN, BUELL GARD, JR., banker; b. Orlando, Fla., July 31, 1928; s. Buell Gard and Elizabeth Phillips (Parks) D.; m. Patricia Ann Jones, Mar. 25, 1952; children: Buell Gard III, Patricia Ann, Allan Griffin, Nancy Elizabeth. BA, Emory U., 1950; postgrad., BMA Sch. Bank Mktg., 1959. With Sun First Nat. Bank (name now Sun Bank, N.A.), Orlando, from 1953; asst. cashier Sun First Nat. Bank, Orlando, 1956-60, asst. v.p., 1960-61, v.p., 1961-68, sr. v.p., 1968-72, exec. v.p., 1972-75, pres., 1975-76, chmn. bd., chief exec. officer, from 1977, also dir.; now chmn. Sun Banks Inc., Orlando, Sun Bank N.A., Orlando. Bd. dirs. Jacksonville br. Fed. Res. Bank Atlanta, Commonwealth Ins. Co. Bd. dirs. Fla. Coun. on Econ. Edn, Crummer Sch. Bus., Rollins Coll., U. Cen. Fla. Found.; adv. bd. U. Cen. Fla. Coll. Bus. Adminstrn.; bd. dirs. Indsl. Devel. Commn. Mid-Fla., Inc. Served with USAF, 1951-53. Mem. Fla. Bankers Assn., Bank Mktg. Assn. (pres. 1971-72), Fla. C. of C. (v.p. econ. devel., bd. dirs., immediate past pres., mem. exec. com.), Orlando C. of C. (pres. 1970-71), Fla. Blue Key, Phi Delta Theta. Clubs: Kiwanian. (Orlando), Country of Orlando (Orlando) (pres., dir.), Citrus (Orlando), Univ. (Orlando). Died Mar. 10, 2010.

DUNCAN, DAN L., energy executive; b. Jan. 2, 1933; s. James Duncan and Maggie Ray; m. Jan Duncan; children: Randa, Dannine; 1 child, Milane. Grad., Massey Bus. Coll.; student, South Tex. Coll. With Wanda Petroleum, 1957—69; prin. EPCO Inc., Houston, 1969—70, pres., 1970—79, CEO, 1970—95, chmn., 1979—2010, Enterprise Products GP, Houston, 1998—2010, Enterprise GP Holdings LP, Houston, 2005—10. Bd. trustees Baylor Med. Coll. With US Army. Recipient World Hunting Award Ring, Safari Club Internat., 1997, Internat. Hunting award, 1998, Weatherby Hunting and Conservation award, 1999, Conklin award, 2005; named one of Forbes 400: Richest Americans, 2005—09, World's Richest People, Forbes Mag., 2005—09. Died Mar. 28, 2010.

DUNKIN, R(EASON) THOMAS, dentist, dental educator; b. West Union, Ohio, Sept. 12, 1919; s. Clifton Ellis and Susie (Vane) Dunkin; m. Josephine Marie Cribari, Apr. 28, 1946; children: Deborah Ann Hubby, Janice Marie Wittman, Elizabeth Jane Patrick. DDS, Ohio State U., 1943, postgrad., 1947. Intern Cin. Gen. Hosp., 1944; gen. practice dentistry San Jose; staff mem. O'Connor Hosp., 1949—83; clin. prof. dept. periodontics, part-time U. Pacific Sch. Dentistry, San Francisco, from 1952; pres. Seal Records, from 1960; cons. Aquatec-Teledyne, 1967—72; pres. Santa Clara County Dental Rsch. Found., 1969—72. Contbr. chpt. to book, articles to profl. jours. Active San Jose Bd. Health, 1974—80, 1981—82; chmn. ctrl. sect. Santa Clara County United Way, 1982—83; bd. dirs. Adult and Child Guidance Clinic, 1951—55, pres. bd., 1953—55. With USN, 1942—46, capt. USNR, 1946—47. Fellow Internat. Coll. Dentists, Am. Coll. Dentists, Acad. Dentistry Internat., Coll. Applied Nutrition; mem. ADA, Calif. Dental Assn., Santa Clara Dental Soc. (sec.-treas. 1951-52, pres. 1953-54), Am. Acad. Periodontology, Western Soc. Periodontology, Calif. Acad. Periodontology (pres. 1955-56), Pierre Fauchard Acad. (No. Calif. chmn. 1975-80), Internat. Assn. Dental Rsch., Omicron Kappa Upsilon, San Jose Country Club, Sainte Claire Club, Tenn. Squire Club, Knights of Malta. Republican. Roman Catholic. Avocations: golf, golf club collecting, travel. Home: San Jose, Calif. Died Sept. 8, 2009.

DUNN, JOHN RAYMOND, JR., stockbroker; b. Pittsfield, Mass., Aug. 24, 1937; s. John Raymond and Margaret Mary (Coyne) D.; 1 child, John Raymond III. AB, Boston Coll., 1960. Ins. agt. John Hancock Ins. Co., Boston, 1964-67; dist. mgr. Nat. Life Ins. Co., Montpelier, Vt., 1967-74; gen. agt. United Life & Accident Ins. Co., Concord, NH, from 1974; stockbroker, regional mgr. Cornerstone Fin. Svcs., Inc., Boston, 1974-80; stockbroker, br. mgr. Weinrich, Zitzman, Whitehead Fin. Svcs., Inc., St. Louis, from 1980; pres. Dunn Assocs., Amherst, Mass., from 1965; br. mgr. Jefferson Pilot Securities Corp., from 1998. Field adv. mem. Pres. Adv. Coun. CFS-Div. Weinrich, Zitzman, Whitehead, Inc., 1982—; named to gen. agts. adv. com. Chubb Life Am./Chubb Securities Corp., 1988-89; dist. mgr. Chubb Securities Leaders' Club; lectr. in field. Author seminar: Let's Make Money; freelance writer Investment Dealer Digest, 1980; film prodr. Ernest Hemingway documentary. Dir. Parents and Tchrs. for Social Responsibility, Moretown, Vt., 1982-85. Mem. White Mountain Club (Club award 1984-92), Summit Club, Life U.S.A. Club, Chmns. Club., Pres. Club. Roman Catholic. Home: Amherst, Mass. Died June 12, 2009.

DUNNAN, WEAVER WHITE, retired lawyer; b. Paxton, Ill., Sept. 23, 1923; s. J. Wallace and Mabel (White) Dunnan; m. Diana Barrett Baldwin, Feb. 14, 1953; children: Bruce B., Douglas M., Donald S., Winifred B., John M. AB, Harvard U., 1947, LLB, 1949. Bar: DC 1951, US Supreme Ct. 1954, US Tax Ct. 1957, US Ct. Appeals (DC cir.) 1960. Law clk. US Ct. Appeals (2d Cir.), NYC, 1949—50; law clk. to Justice Felix Frankfurter US Supreme Ct., Washington, 1950—51; assoc. Covington & Burling LLP, Washington, 1951—60, ptnr., 1960—94, mem. mgmt. com., 1974—78. Bd. dirs. Beauvoir Sch., Nat. Cathedral, Washington, 1969—74; bd. govs. St. Albans Sch, Washington, 1974—80. Sgt. US Army, 1943—46, PTO. Decorated 2 Overseas Svc. Bars, Am. Campaign medal, Asiatic Pacific Theater ribbon with 3 bronze battle stars, Phillippine Liberation ribbon with 2 bronze stars. Mem.: ABA, Chevy Chase Club, Met. Club (Washington). Republican. Home: Bethesda, Md. Died June 29, 2010.

DUNNE, NANCY ANNE, retired social services administrator; b. Ionia, Mich., Aug. 5, 1929; d. Warner Kingsley and Hazel Fern (Alliason) McSween; m. James Robert, Oct. 28, 1952; children: James Robert Jr., Stephen Michael. BA, Albion Coll., Mich., 1951. Tchr. Oakdale Elem., Grand Rapids, Mich., 1951-53, Lakeside Sch., East Grand Rapids, Mich., 1953; clk. Office of Naval Rsch., Washington, 1954-55; dir. pub. rels. Diocesan Office Health and Social Svcs., Albany, NY, 1971-74; dir. vol. action dept. Coun. of Human Resources, Schenectady, NY, 1974-76; pers. asst. Am. Soc. Assn. Execs., Washington, 1977-78; adminstrv. asst. N.Y. Soc. Cons. Engrs., NYC, 1978-79, Assessment Designs, Inc., Orlando, Fla., 1980-82, Catholic Social Svcs., Orlando, Fla., 1982-84, ret., 1984. Active NY State Comm. Cultural Resources, Albany, 1970-73, Anna Maria Island Cmty. Ctr., 2000-01; bd. dirs. Coalition for the Homeless, Orlando, 1983-87; tutor Anna Maria Island Elem. Sch., Fla.; vol. Blake Hosp., Bradenton, Fla., 1999-2003, Imagine Manatee Task Force, Bradenton, 2003; 1st v.p. Performing arts Downtown Manatee County, Inc., 2003; tutor Anna Maria Island Elem. Sch., Manatee County Symphony Assn.(bd. dir. 2008-). Mem. AAUW (pres. Manatee County br. 2001-03, bd. dir. 2006-), Jr. League of Schenectady (Vol. of Yr. award 1965-66), Schenectady Symphony Orch. (pres. 1969-70), Ladies of Charity (pres. Albany chpt. 1970-72, pres. Orlando chpt. 1984-86, nat. pres. 1990-94, nat. bd. dirs. 2001-02, v.p. internat. 1990-94, bd. dirs. 1994-2000), Women's Club Anna Maria Island (1st v.p. 2004—, pres. 2005-06, rotary club fellowship award, 2003). Roman Catholic. Avocations: reading, travel, golf, bridge, entertaining friends. Home: Holmes Beach, Fla. Died Oct. 11, 2009.

DUNNING, LINDA SCHMIDT, medical education administrator, nurse; b. Farmville, Va., Jan. 29, 1952; d. Leroy Wheeler and Edith Elizabeth (Elliott) Schmidt; m. Frederick Graydon Dunning, Nov. 24, 1979; children— Meredith Lin, Allison Gray. Diploma with honors, Richmond Meml. Hosp. Sch. Nursing, 1973; BS in Pub. Adminstrn., St. Joseph's Coll., North Wyndam, Maine, 1987. Cert. occupational health nurse, nursing asst. Richmond Meml. Hosp., Va., 1971-73; staff nurse Philip Morris, U.S.A., Richmond, 1973-79, coordinator med. edn. programs, 1979-84, supr. med. edn. and supply, 1984—, chairperson developed health awareness and phys. fitness program, 1985. Recipient Service medal award ARC, 1985, 87. Mem. Capital Area Assn. Occupational Health Nurses (pres. 1979-81), Va. Assn. Occupational Health Nurses. Republican. Baptist. Avocations: volleyball; traveling; dancing. Died Nov. 10, 2009.

DUNNING, THOMAS E., former newspaper editor; b. Lamasco, Ky., Nov. 2, 1944; s. Floyd Bowman and Tylene Elizabeth (Garrett) D.; m. Judy Davis, Feb. 28, 1981; children: Thomas Matthew, William Davis. BA, U. Evansville, 1967. Sportwriter Evansville (Ind.) Press, 1962-67; city editor The Evansville Courier, 1970-76; Sunday editor The Knoxville (Tenn.) News-Sentinal, 1976-77; asst. mng. editor The Cin. Post, 1977-81, mng. editor, 1981-85; asst. mng. editor Scripps Howard News Svc., 1985-87; dep. mng. editor news Cin. Enquirer, 1987-90, mng. editor, 1990-93, night mng. editor, 1993-95; mng. editor Boston Bus. Jour., 1996-97; news editor The Patroit Ledger, Quincy, Mass., 1997-00. Bd. dirs. The Mental Health Assn., Cin., 1982, Leadership Cin., 1982-84; trustee Family Svcs. Cin. With USCG, 1967-70. Mem. AP Mng. Editors, Am. Soc. Newspaper Editors, Soc. Profl. Journalists, Nat. Press Club. Episcopalian. Home: Cincinnati, Ohio. Died Aug. 5, 2010.

DUPUIS, VICTOR LIONEL, retired curriculum and instruction educator; b. Chgo., Oct. 30, 1934; s. Edward G. and LaVerne Ann (Brown) D.; m. Mary Jean Miles, Aug. 11, 1956; children: Mary Catherine, Victor Edward, Elizabeth Ann. BS, Northwestern U., Evanston, Ill., 1956; MA, Am. U., DC, 1961; PhD, Purdue U., West Lafayette, Ind., 1965. Tchr. jr. high sch., Arlington, Va., 1956-61; tchr. Klondike Sch. Dist., West Lafayette, Ind., 1961-63, curriculum dir., 1962-63; grad. instr. Purdue U., West Lafayette, 1963—65; asst. prof. Pa. State U., University Park, 1967—70, assoc. prof. curriculum, 1970—74, prof., chmn. curriculum and supervision, 1974—91, prof. edn. curriculum and instrn., 1989-91, Waterbury prof. secondary edn., 1990-92, chmn. curriculum and suprvision, 1991, prof. emeritus curriculum and instrn., from 1992; CEO Dupuis Assocs., from 1985. Cons. to various pvt. and public schs., state depts. edn. Native Am. programs. Author: Resource Booklet and Overhead Transparency Masters for Foundation of American Education, 1966, (textbooks) Introductory Readings in the Foundation of American Education, 1966, An Introduction to the Foundations of American Education, 1969, 14th edit., 2008; author: (with others) Introduction to the Foundations of American Education, 1966; author: Foundation of American Education: Readings, 1969, 1985, Issues in Education, 1991, Resource Booklet: Foundations of American Education, 2002, video collection of articles in profl. jours. Chmn. Patton Twp. (Pa.) Park Bd., 1969-70, Patton Twp. Planning Commn., 1971-73; Democratic precinct committeeman Patton Twp., 1971-76, chmn., twp. supr., 1973-92. Served to 2d lt. inf. U.S. Army, 1957-59. Recipient Waterbury Chair honoree, Pa. State U., 1989—91. Mem. ASCD, Am. Ednl. Rsch. Assn., Nat. Staff Devel. Coun., Pa. Assn. Supervision and Curriculum Devel., Phi Delta Kappa. Home: State College, Pa. Died Aug. 17, 2009.

DURANT, ROBERT MARVIN, bandleader, record company executive; b. Detroit, July 21, 1922; s. Hamlet Harry and Irene Alvina (Schultz) D.; m. Loretta Marie Burchyett; children: Barbara Ann, Robert Raymond. Student, Detroit Inst. Tech., 1941. Pianist, arranger Louis Primo Orch., on tour, 1942-43, Sta. WWJ Studio Orch., Detroit, 1946, Sam Donohue Orch., NYC, 1946, Bob Durant Orch., Detroit, from 1957; bandleader Detroit Fedn. Musicians, from 1957; pres. R and L Records, Grosse Pointe Woods, Mich., from 1980. Ind. tchr. piano, Grosse Pointe Woods, 1951-86. Composer numerous popular, classical songs, 1956—; arranger various performers including Dorothy Lamour, Johnny Mathis, Lola Falana, Bobby Vinton, Danny Thomas, Kay Ballard, Harmonicats. With USN, 1943-46. Mem. Detroit Fedn. Musicians (v.p. 1982, exec. bd. 1973—), Detroit Orch. Leaders Assn. (pres. 1970), Am. Fedn. Musicians (del. convs. 1976-85, 88—), St. Clair Golf Club (Mich.). Lutheran. Avocations: golf, travel. Home: Grosse Pointe, Mich. Died Jan. 20, 2009.

DURBIN, DAVID P., lawyer; b. Detroit, Mar. 20, 1948; m. Anne Weitzel; children: Colleen, William, Katherine. BS in Foreign Svc., Georgetown U., 1970, JD, 1977. Bar: D.C. 1977, U.S. Dist. Ct. D.C. 1978, U.S. Ct. Appeals (4th cir.) 1979, U.S. Ct. Appeals (D.C. cir.) 1980, U.S. Dist. Ct. Md. 1983, U.S. Supreme Ct. 1984. Law clk. to Hon. George L. Hart, Jr. US Dist. Ct. D.C., 1977-78; assoc. Jordan, Coyne, Savits & Lopata, 1978—83, ptnr., 1983—2010. Mem. ABA, D.C. Bar, Bar Assn. D.C., D.C. Def. Lawyers Assn., The Counsellors, The Barristers. Died July 4, 2010.

DUROSE, STANLEY CHARLES, JR., retired insurance company executive; b. Joliet, MT, Oct. 26, 1923; s. Stanley Charles and Wilhelmena Amelia (Zwicky) DuR.; m. Lorraine Homan, May 27, 1977. BS, U. Wis., 1948. Various positions Wis. Dept. Ins., Madison, 1948-65; dep. commr. ins. State of Wis., Madison, 1965-69, commr. ins., 1969-75; v.p. govt. rels. Cuna Mut. Ins., Madison, 1976-80; sr. v.p. adminstrn. Cumis Ins. Soc., 1980-86, sr. v.p. reinsurance, 1986-88; dep. commr. of ins. State of Wis., 1989-91; ret., 1991. Contbr. articles to profl. publs. With USAF, 1943-45, 51-52. Mem. Casualty Actuarial Soc., Am. Acad. Actuaries. Home: Madison, Wis. Died Mar. 21, 2010.

DUTRO, JOHN THOMAS, JR., geologist, paleontologist; b. Columbus, Ohio, May 20, 1923; s. John Thomas and Dorothy Durstine (Smith) D.; m. Nancy Ann Pence, Jan. 2, 1948; children: Sarah Dutro Cormier, Christopher, Susan Dutro Hultman. BA, Oberlin Coll., 1948; MS, Yale U., 1950, PhD, 1953; DSc, Denison U., 1993. Geologist US Geol. Survey, 1948-94, chief paleontology & stratigraphy br., 1962-68, mem. geologic names com., 1962-83, emeritus scientist, 1994—2010. Vis. lectr. Am. U., 1957-59, George Washington U., 1962-63; mem. geology panel Bd. Civil Svc. Examiners, 1958-65; dir., field trip chmn. 9th Internat. Carboniferous Congress, 1979. Active area PTA, 1959-69, Boy Scouts Am., 1963-66, Fairlington Players, 1965-75. With Army Air Corps, 1943-46. Recipient Meritorious Svc. award US Dept. Interior, 1983, Disting. Svc. award, 1996; Sterling fellow, 1949. Fellow AAAS (sec. sect. E 1981-85, Pacific divsn. pres. 1996-97), Arctic Inst. N.Am., Geol. Soc. London, Geol. Soc. Am. (assoc. editor 1974-82); mem. Am. Geol. Inst. (vis. geoscientist 1961-67, bd. dirs., sec.-treas. 1965-71), Paleontol. Soc. (tech. editor 1991), Palaeontol. Assn., Paleontol. Rsch. Inst. (trustee 1986—, v.p. 1990-91, pres. 1992-94, recipient, Gilbert Harris Award, 2007), Internat. Paleontol. Assn., Paleontol. Soc. Washington (pres. 1955-56, 2003-04), Geol. Soc. Washington (sec. 1959-60, pres. 1978), Assn. Earth Sci. Editors (pres. 1989-90), Am. Polar Soc., Alaska Geol. Soc., Sigma Xi, Pick and Hammer Club, Cosmos Club, Yale Club (Washington). Democrat. Achievements include research in brachiopoda, Paleozoic biostratigraphy and biogeography of Arctic regions and western hemisphere, biostratigraphy of East Asia, and history of paleontology. Home: Washington, DC. Died June 13, 2010.

DYPSKI, CORNELL N., state legislator; b. Balt., Sept. 23, 1931; married; 1 child. Student, Balt. Poly. Inst., U. Balt. Adminstrv. officer Motor Vehicle Adminstrn.; senator Md. State Senate, 1975-83; mem. constl. and pub. law com.; mem. elec. laws task force; co-chmn. legis. com. on Port of Md.; del. Dist. 46 Md. State Delegation, from 1987, mem. judiciary com., from 1990, vice chmn. Balt. City Delegation, from 1991. Recipient Cmty. Svc. award United Charity Campaign. Home: Towson, Md. Died Jan. 20, 2009.

EAST, CHARLES DAVID, banker; b. Atlanta, Nov. 30, 1934; s. William David and Ann Mae (Carlton) E.; m. Mary Nell Reed, Nov. 20, 1962; children— Jill Leigh, David Scott, Brian Allen BS in Math. and Physics, Ga. State U., 1961; grad. cert., Rutgers U., 1971, Harvard U. Program for Mgmt. Devel., 1973. Tchr., coach Atlanta Bd. Edn., 1961-64; various auditing positions Fed. Res. Bank, Atlanta, 1964-69, asst. v.p., 1969-73, v.p., 1973-84, sr. v.p., comptroller, 1984-87; pres., chief exec. officer Rockdale Community Bank, Conyers, Ga., from 1988. Served with U.S. Army, 1954-56; Korea Mem. Am. Inst. Banking, Blue Key Nat. Honor Soc. (life-time mem.) Avocation: golf. Home: Conyers, Ga. Died June 13, 2010.

EASTHAM, WILLIAM KENNETH, chemical company executive; b. Mineola, NY, Dec. 30, 1917; s. William and Alice (Watson) E.; m. Dorothy Brush, Mar. 25, 1942 (dec. Dec. 1979); children: Gale Eastham Shadrick, Nancy Eastham Kaydo; m. Robin J. Ehrlich, Nov. 6, 1980. Student, Am. Inst. Banking, 1936-38, NYU, 1946-48; grad. Advanced Mgmt. Program, Harvard U., 1954. Teller Am. Bank for Savs., NYC, 1935-39; asst. advt. mgr. Whitehall Pharm. div. Am. Home Products Co., NYC, 1945-51; brand mgr. Soap div.; advt. mgr. Good Luck div.; advt. mgr. Pepsodent div. Lever Bros. Co., NYC, 1951-59; asst. to pres. Am. Home Products Co.; exec. v.p. div. Boyle Midway, 1959-64; v.p. div. household products S.C. Johnson & Son, Inc., Racine, Wis., 1964-67, exec. v.p. U.S. ops., 1967-71, exec. v.p. U.S. and European ops., 1971-72, pres., chief operating officer, 1972-79, pres., chief exec. officer, 1979-80, vice chmn., 1980-83, ret., 1983; dir., chmn. exec. com. Environ. Diagnostics, Inc., from 1985. Dir. Meredith Corp., Heritage Racine Corp., Kohler Co. Served with U.S. Army, 1940-45. Mem. C. of C. U.S. (dir.), Vets. of 7th Regt. Clubs: Racine Country, Burning Tree; Metropolitan (Washington). Home: North Garden, Va. Died May 9, 2010.

EASTMAN, DAN R., former state legislator; b. Mar. 12, 1946; m. Claudette Eastman. Former commr. Utah Dept. Transp.; former pres. Utah Auto Dealers Assn., Davis Dist. Bd. Edn.; mem. Dist. 23 Utah State Senate, 2001—08, majority whip, 2006. Republican. Died June 8, 2010.

EBELING, JOHN ALTMAN, trucking company executive; b. Green Bay, Wis., Aug. 4, 1937; s. John A. Ebeling and Kathleen (McCarey) Fowler; m. Jacqueline S. Thomson, Aug. 29, 1964; children: Mary Kathleen, Margaret Suzzane. BS, U. Wis., 1960; postgrad., U. Chgo. Grad. Sch. Mgmt., 1962-63; advanced mgmt. program, Harvard U. V.p. Consol. Freightways, Chgo., 1964-76; chmn. A.N.R. Freight Systems Inc., Denver, 1976-84; pres. Old Dominion Freight Line Inc., High Point, N.C., from 1985. Pres. Ill. Trucking Assn., Chgo., 1976-77; v.p. at large Am. Trucking Assn., Washington, 1977-84. Trustee Am. Trucking Assn. Found., Washington, 1977-84; bd. dirs. Kellog Sch., Northwestern U., Evanston, Ill., 1980-84. Republican. Episcopalian. Home: New London, NC. Died Oct. 10, 2009.

EBERT, PAUL ALLEN, surgeon, other: education; b. Columbus, Ohio, Aug. 11, 1932; m. Louise Joyce Parks, 1954; children: Leslie Ann, Michael Dean, Julie Ellen. BS, Ohio State U., 1954, MD, 1958. Diplomate Am. Bd. Surgery, Am. Bd. Thoracic Surgery. Intern in surgery Johns Hopkins Hosp., Balt., 1958—59, asst. resident surgeon, 1959—65, postdoctoral fellow Nat. Cancer Inst., 1962—63, chief resident, 1965—66; sr. asst. surgeon NIH, Bethesda, Md., 1960—62; asst. prof. surgery Duke U. Med. Ctr., Durham, NC, 1966—68, assoc. prof. surgery, 1968—71; prof., chmn. dept. surgery Cornell U. Med. Coll., NYC, 1971—75; surgeon in chief N.Y. Hosp., 1971—75; prof., chmn. dept. surgery U. Calif., San Francisco, 1975—86; dir. ACS, Chgo., 1986—98. Mem. editl. bd.: Am. Jour. Surgery, Annals Surgery, Cardiovascular Medicine, Internat. Dictionary Biology and Medicine, Surgery, Western Jour. Medicine; contbr. over 200 med. articles. With USPHS, 1960—62. Scholar Mead-Johnson scholar, ACS, 1964, Markle scholar, Duke U. Med. Ctr., 1967. Fellow: ACS, Royal Coll. Surgeons in Ireland (hon.), Royal Coll. Surgeons of Edinburgh (hon.); mem.: Soc. U. Surgeons (pres. 1975), Assn. for Acad. Surgery (pres. 1973), Am. Coll. Cardiology (pres. 1983—84), Am. Assn. Thoracic Surgery (pres. 1987—88), Alpha Omega Alpha. Home: Granite Bay, Calif. Died Apr. 21, 2009.

ECKENFELDER, WILLIAM WESLEY, JR., environmental engineer; b. NYC, Nov. 15, 1926; m. Kathy Hurley; children— Larry, Janice, Jennifer. BCE, Manhattan Coll., 1946; MS, Pa. State U., 1948; MCE, NYU, 1954; DSc (hon.), Manhattan Coll., 1990. Registered profl. engr., Tex. From instr. to assoc. prof. civil engring. Manhattan Coll., 1951-65; prof. civil engring. U. Tex., Austin, 1965-69; disting. prof. environ. and water resources engring. Vanderbilt U., 1970-89; also exec. dir. Center Environ. Quality Mgmt.; chmn. emeritus, sr. tech. dir. Eckenfelder, Inc., Nashville, from 1989. Chmn. bd. Aware Inc.; cons. in field. Author: Water Quality Management, 1980, Industrial Water Pollution Control, 2d edit., 1988; co-author: Water Pollution Control, 1970; contbr. articles to profl. publs. Recipient Indsl. Wastes medal Fedn. Sewage and Indsl. Waste Assn., 1957, Kenneth Allen award N.Y. State Sewage and Indsl. Waste Assn., 1957, SOCMA gold medal, 1974, Thomas Camp medal Water Pollution Control Fedn., 1981, Tadeuz Kosciuszko medal Tech. U. Kracow, Poland, 1989, Karl Imhoff-Pierre Koch medal Internat. Assn. Water Pollution Rsch. and Control, 1990, Gabriel Narutowicz medal Polish Govt., 1993; research fellow N.C. State Coll., 1947; research fellow Pa. State U., 1948 Fellow Instn. Pub. Health Engrs., Am. Inst. Chemists, Am. Soc. Engring. Edn.; mem. ASCE, Internat. Assn. Water Pollution Rsch. (hon.), Water Pollution Control Fedn. (hon.), Am. Chem. Soc., Am. Acad. Environ. Engrs. (diplomat), Instn. Pub. Health Engrs., Instn. Sewage Purification, N.Y. Acad. Scis., Sigma Xi, Chi Epsilon. Home: Nashville, Tenn. Died Mar. 28, 2010.

ECKSTEIN, JEROME, philosopher, retired educator; b. NYC, June 28, 1925; s. Marcus and Blanche (Wohlberg) E.; m. Kathleen Sharon Hoisington; 1 stepchild, Mari O'Donnell Midurski; children: Esther Schwartz, Sandra Bellehsen, Michael. Student, Rabbi Isaac Elchanan Theol. Sem., 1943-45; BA, Bklyn. Coll., 1949; postgrad., New Sch. Social Research, 1949-50; PhD, Columbia U., 1961. Buyer antique silverware Blanche Eckstein Silverware, Bklyn., 1945-53; dir. edn. and youth activities, various Hebrew congregations, 1950-61; lectr. philosophy CCNY, 1955-56, Bklyn. Coll., 1955-60; instr. contemporary civilization and philosophy Columbia U., NYC, 1960-63; asst. prof., then assoc. prof. philosophy, coordinator div. humanities Adelphi Suffolk Coll., Adelphi U., 1963-66; prof. philosophy of edn. SUNY-Albany, 1966-70, also first chmn. Judaic studies, 1970-74, prof. Judaic studies, 1970-97, prof. religious studies, 1990-97, prof. emeritus, from 1997. Participant Internat. Philosophy Yr., Brockport, N.Y., 1967, Conf. on Gerontology, U. Minn., 1978; vis. prof. philosophy Bar-Ilan U., Israel, 1978-79 Author: The Platonic Method: An Interpretation of the Dramatic-Philosophic Aspects of the Meno, 1968; The Deathday of Socrates, 1981, Metaphysical Drift: Love and Judaism, 1991, On Meanings or Life: Their Nature and Origin, 2002; contbr. articles to profl. jours. Fellow in logic CCNY, 1955-56; vis. scholar Va. Commonwealth U., Richmond, 1975; Am. Council Learned Socs. sr. fellow, 1973 Mem. Phi Beta Kappa Home: Bennington, Vt. Died May 8, 2009.

EDDY, DONALD DAVIS, language educator; b. Norfolk, Va., Apr. 19, 1929; s. Clarence Ford and Rebekah (Proctor Davis) E.; m. Edith Ann Quattlebaum, Dec. 20, 1954; children: Edith Evelyn, Elizabeth Nelson. BA, Dartmouth Coll., 1951; MA, PhD, U. Chgo.; MA (Munby fellow), Cambridge U., Eng., 1978. Prof. English Cornell U., Ithaca, NY, 1961-96, head dept. rare books univ. libr., 1968-89, prof. emeritus, from 1996. Works include A Bibliography of John Brown, 1971, Samuel Johnson: Book Reviewer in the Literary Magazine, 1979, Samuel Johnson, LL.D., 1983, Bibliography of Richard Hurd, 1999; editor John Brown, Essays on the Characteristics, 1969, Samuel Johnson and Periodical Literature, 16 vols., 1978-79, Sale Catalogues of the Librs. of Samuel Johnson, Hester Lynch Thrale (Mrs. Piozzi) and James Boswell, 1993. Served with USN, 1952-55. Mem. MLA, Bibliog. Soc., Oxford Bibliog. Soc., Cambridge Bibliog. Soc., Bibliog. Soc. Am., Bibliog. Soc. U. Va. Clubs: Grolier; Athenaeum (London); The Johnsonians. Episcopalian. Home: Oakland, Calif. Died Nov. 30, 2009.

EDELMAN, HARRY ROLLINGS, III, engineering and construction company executive; b. Pitts., Aug. 16, 1928; s. Harry Rollings, Jr. and Marian A. (Crooks) E.; m. Nancy Jane McCune, Aug. 26, 1950; children: Lisa E. Turbeville, Harry Rollings IV, John Reed, Amy E. Carrick. BS, U. Pitts., 1950. CEO, chmn. CCL-X Mgmt. Inc., Pitts., from 1993. Chmn. Heyl & Patterson, Inc., Heylpat Techs., Inc., Bridge & Crane Inspection, Inc., ForeTesting Labs., Inc. Author papers in engring., constrn., religion and mgmt. Past bd. dirs. Allegheny Health Edn. and Rsch. Found., Allegheny Gen. Hosp., Allegheny U. Med. Scis.; past pres. Christian Assn. S.W. Pa.; past chmn. Allegheny Neuropsychiat. Inst., Vocat. Rehab. Ctr. Allegheny County, Allegheny Singer Rsch. Inst., Med. Coll. Pa.; chmn. Presbyn. SeniorCare; past chmn. Allegheny U. Hosp. East; past moderator Pitts. Presbytery; pres. Presbyn. Scholarship Fund. With AUS, 1952-54. Recipient Regional Ecumenism award, 1985, Allegheny Disting. Svc. award, 1997. Mem. World Pres.'s Orgn., Duquesne Club, Pitts. Field Club, The Club at Seabrook Island. Died July 8, 2010.

EDEN, NORMAN NACHUM, insurance agent; b. Grodno, Poland, Sept. 27, 1920; came to U.S., 1938; s. Abraham Pinkus and Shytra (Rothenberg) Rajgrodski; m. Shulamit Gootman Eden, Dec. 19, 1943; 1 child, Avi Don. BA, U. Cin., 1947, MA, 1953. Asst. econ. rsch. Office of Prime Min., Israel, 1948-52; pres. NN Eden Agy., Cin., 1956-82, Midwest Exec. Ins. Agy., Cin., 1980-95. Lectr. Judaic Studies U. Cin., 1985. With U.S. Army, 1942-46. Democrat. Jewish. Avocations: travel, reading. Home: Philadelphia, Pa. Died Jan. 5, 2009.

EDGERTON, WINFIELD DOW, retired gynecologist; b. Caruthersville, Mo., Nov. 8, 1924; s. Winfield Dow and Anna Kathryn (Hale) E.; m. Rose Marie Cahill, June 24, 1945; 1 child, Winfield Dow Student, Central Coll., Fayette, Mo., 1942-44; MD, Washington U., St. Louis, 1947. Intern St. Luke's Hosp., St. Louis, 1947-48; resident Chgo. Lying-In Hosp., 1948-49, Free Hosp. for Women, Brookline, Mass., 1951, U.S. Naval Hosp., Chelsea, Mass., 1951-53; practice medicine specializing in obstetrics and gynecology Davenport, Iowa, 1955-87; clin. asst. prof. obstetrics and gynecology U. Iowa Coll. Medicine, 1971-78, clin. assoc. prof., 1979-82, clin. prof., from 1982; ret., 2000. Mem. staff, med. dir. Maternal Health Ctr. St. Luke's Hosp. (name changed to Edgerton Women's Health Ctr.), 1972-2000. Contbr. articles to med. jours. and texts Served to lt. M.C., USN, 1949-55 Fellow Am. Coll. Obstetricians and Gynecologists (past chmn. Iowa sect.), Royal Soc. Medicine; mem. Central Assn. Obstetricians and Gynecologists, Am. Fertility Soc., Am. Assn. Gynecologic Laparoscopists (past trustee), Gynecologic Laser Soc., AMA, Iowa Med. Soc., Scott County Med. Soc. (past pres.) Republican. Congregationalist. Home: Davenport, Iowa. Died Jan. 13, 2009.

EDSON, MARTHA JANET, banker; b. Troy, NY, Jan. 8, 1933; d. Wayne M. and Florence (Lewis) E. BS in Bus. Adminstrn., U. Vt., 1954. Personnel asst. Norton Co., Worcester, Mass., 1964-68; supr. employment Am. Sci. & Engring. Co., Cambridge, Mass., 1968-69; profl. recruiter Nat. Shawmut Bank, Boston, 1969-72; v.p. human resources Shawmut County Bank N.A., Cambridge, 1972-87, Shawmut Bank N.A., Boston, from 1987. Bd. dirs. Am. Cancer Soc., Boston, 1985-87. Mem. Internat. Assn. Personnel Women, Personnel Mgmt. Coun. (bd. dirs.). Republican. Congregationalist. Home: New York, NY. Died Jan. 8, 2009.

EDWARDS, JAMES CLIFFORD, finance company executive; b. Covington, Ky., June 27, 1930; s. Hubert and Elizabeth (Moore) E.; m. Judith Ann Bowker, Apr. 10, 1954; children: Karen, Thomas, Laura, James, Mary. BBA, U. Cin., 1955; MBA, U. Chgo., 1978. CPA Ohio. Audit staff/mgr. Arthur Andersen & Co., Cin., 1955—66; corp. v.p. fin. Bee Chem. Co., Lansing, Ill., 1966—85; exec. v.p. Allen Fin., Inc., Vero Beach, Fla.; vice chmn. Tioga Internat., Inc., Calument City, from 1989. Sec., treas., dir. Ru Van Inc., Evansville, Ind., Proform, Inc., Evansville, Ind., from 1990. Trustee Village of Olympia Fields, 1972; bd. dirs. Mfrs. Polit. Action Com., Chgo., 1984—85. Served USN, 1948—52. Mem. AICPA, Ill. Soc. CPA's, Fin. Execs. Inst., Internat. Assn. Fin. Planners, Ill. Mfrs. Assn. (chmn. tax com. 1984-85), Mfrs. Assn. Chgo. Heights and So. Suburbs (pres. 1981), Beta Gamma Sigma, Beta Alpha Psi. Republican. Baptist. Home: Orland Hills, Ill. Died May 22, 2010.

EDWARDS, JEROME, retired lawyer; b. NYC, July 5, 1912; s. Philip and Anna (Hollinger) E.; m. Mildred Kahn, Dec. 7, 1941 (dec.); children: Susan, Bruce (dec.). BS, NYU, 1931, JD, 1933. Bar: N.Y. State 1934, Calif. 1975. Asso. firm T.J. Lesser, 1934-36; pvt. practice NYC, 1936-42; sr. partner Phillips, Nizer, Benjamin, Krim & Ballon, NYC, 1942-62; v.p., gen. counsel 20th Century Fox Film Corp., NYC and Los Angeles, 1962-77; of counsel Kaplan, Livingston, Goodwin, Berkowitz & Selvin, Beverly Hills, Calif., 1977-81, Musick, Peeler & Garrett, Los Angeles, 1982-83, Phillips, Nizer, Benjamin, Krim & Ballon, Los Angeles, 1985-89. Mem. ABA, Am. Film Mktg. Assn. (arbitrator panel), Am. Arbitration Assn. (nat. pnel neutral arbitrators 1960-2000). Home: Tarzana, Calif. Died Mar. 13, 2009.

EDWARDS, WILLIAM EVERETT, dentist; b. Spartanburg, SC, Mar. 19, 1928; s. James Baxter and Cora (Stone) Edwards; m. Margaret Alice Carlton, July 28, 1951. BS, Wofford Coll., 1951; DDS, Emory U., 1965. Pvt. practice dentistry, Spartanburg. Mem. Spartanburg County Health Planning Commn., 1979—86. Fellow: Acad. Gen. Dentistry; mem.: Spartanburg County Dental Soc. (pres. 1979—80), SC Dental Assn., ADA, Sertoma Club (pres. Spartanburg 1983—84, chmn. bd. 1984—85, Exemplary Sertoman award 1987), Omicron Kappa Upsilon, Delta Sigma Delta. Avocation: golf. Home: Spartanburg, SC. Died Jan. 24, 2009.

EGGLESON, ROBERT AAKER, public relations executive; b. Stoughton, Wis., Nov. 18, 1928; s. Anon Odegard and Caroline (Aaker) Eggleson; m. Barbara Ann Krupnick, June 25, 1960; 1 child, Karen Jean. BA in English, Luther Coll., 1950. Newspaper reporter, Iowa, Minn., 1950—57; pub. rels. rep. Northwestern U., Evanston, Ill., 1957—59; divsn. publicist 3M Co., 1959—61; pub. rels. asst. Internat. Minerals & Chem. Co., 1961—62; asst. to dir. pub. affairs Champion Papers Inc., 1962—66; pub. rels. mgr. Welch Foods Inc., 1966—72; mfg. comm. mgr. Internat. Harvester Co., 1972—83; pres. Robert Eggleson-Comm., 1983; dir. pub. affairs Black Hawk Coll., Moline, Ill., from 1984. Mem. long range task force United Way of Rock Island-Scott Counties. With US Army, 1950—52. Mem.: Rock Island C. of C. (past dir.), Iowa-Ill. Pub. Rels. Coun., Rotary Club. Republican. Died Feb. 28, 2010.

EGORIN, MERRILL JON, physician; b. Balt., May 25, 1948; s. Nathan Anthony and Toba Rose (Rombro) E.; m. Karen Deborah Kantor, Aug. 6, 1969; children: Melanie Anne, Noah Michael. BA, Johns Hopkins U., 1969, MD, 1973. Intern Johns Hopkins Hosp., Balt., 1973-74, resident, 1974-75, instr. medicine, 1975-81, asst. prof. medicine, from 1981; clin. assoc. Balt. Cancer Rsch. Ctr./NCI, 1975-78, expert, 1978-81; asst. prof., dept. pharmacology U. Md. Sch. Medicine, Balt., 1982-83, assoc. prof., dept. pharmacology, 1983-90, prof. medicine, from 1990. Cons. Duke U. Bone Marrow Transplant, Durham, 1982; organizer workshop in field; advisor City of Hope Fellowship Tng., Duarte, Calif., 1992—. Editor-in-chief: Cancer Chemotherapy and Pharmacology jour., 1991—; assoc. editor: Cancer Rsch. jour., 1990—; bd. editl. advisors, Jour. Nat. Cancer Inst. With USPHS, 1975-78. Grantee in field. Fellow Am. Coll. Physicians; mem. Am. Assn. Cancer Rsch., Am. Soc. Clin. Oncology, Am. Soc. Pharmacology and Exptl. Therapeutics, Am. Soc. Clin. Pharmacology and Therapeutics, European Orgn. for Rsch. and Treatment of Cancer. Democrat. Jewish. Avocations: sailing, bicycling, lacrosse. Home: Pittsburgh, Pa. Died Aug. 7, 2010.

EHRE, MILTON, retired Slavic languages and literature educator; b. NYC, Apr. 15, 1933; s. Isaac and Sylvia (Weissberg) E.; m. Roberta Greene, June 9, 1963; children: Joelle, Julieanne. BA cum laude, CCNY, 1955; MA, Columbia U., 1966, PhD, 1970. Tchr. English N.Y.C. Bd. Edn., 1956-63; asst. prof. U. Chgo., 1967-72, assoc. prof., 1972-81, prof., 1981—2007; prof. emeritus dept. Slavic lang. and lit., 2007. Author: Oblomov and His Creator: The Life and Art of Ivan Goncharov, 1973, Isaac Babel, 1986; editor and translator The Theater of Nikolay Gogol, 1980; translator Chekhov for the Stage, 1992; mem. edtl. bd. Slavic and E. European Jour. Columbia U. Pres.'s fellow, 1964-66, Guggenheim fellow, 1975-76, Fulbright-Hays fellow, 1984, 90. Mem. Am. Assn. Advancement Slavic Studies, Am. Assn. Tchrs. Slavic and E. European Langs., Joseph Jefferson Awards Com. of Chgo. Jewish. Avocations: swimming, reading, theater, watching sports. Home: River Forest, Ill. Died June 30, 2009.

EICHELBERGER, ROBERT JOHN, retired government research and development administrator, consultant; b. Washington, Pa., Apr. 10, 1921; s. John Eugene and Dorothy Louise (Failinger) E.; m. Estella Ann Westcott, May 14, 1943; children: William J., Charles R., Sara Jane Eichelberger Yosua, Mary Ann Eichelberger Nals. AB, Washington and Jefferson Coll., 1942; MS, Carnegie Inst. Tech., 1948, PhD, 1954. Rsch. supr. Carnegie Inst. Tech., Pitts., 1943-55; chief detonation physics br. U.S. Army Ballistic Rsch. Labs., Aberdeen Proving Ground, Md., 1955-62, assoc. tech. dir. labs., 1962-67, dir. labs., 1967-86, ret., 1986; cons. Bel Air, Md., from 1986. Assoc. tech. dir. U.S. Army Armament R&D Command, 1976-80; lectr. in field. Contbr. articles to profl. jours. Recipient Disting. Civilian Svc. award Dept. Def., 1977, Exceptional Civilian Svc. award Dept. Army, 1971, R&D Achievement award, 1961, 71, Presdl. Meritorious Exec. award, 1982, Roger W. Jones award for exec. leadership Am. U., 1985, Clifford P. Gross award Am. Assn. Pub. Adminstrn., 1985, Comdr.'s award U.S. Army Materiel Command, 1986; Crozier prize Am. Def. Preparedness Agy., 1984; inductee U.S. Army Ordnance Hall of Fame, 1987. Mem. AAAS, Am. Phys. Soc., Nat. Coun. Advancement Rsch. (dir.), Soc. Natural Philosophy, Am. Def. Preparedness Assn. (cons.), Assn. U.S. Army, Combustion Inst., Internat. Ballistics Com. Democrat. Presbyterian. Home: Parkton, Md. Died Oct. 9, 2009.

EICHLER, BURTON LAWRENCE, lawyer; b. Newark, Mar. 11, 1933; s. Philip and Anna (Kessler) Eichler; children: Betsy, Peter, Thomas. BS, Ohio State U., 1954; LLB, Rutgers U., 1957. Bar: NJ 1958, NY 1983, US Dist. Ct. NJ 1958, US Ct. Appeals (3d cir.) 1981. Assoc., ptnr., predecessor Zucker, Brach & Eichler, 1958—59, ptnr., 1959—67, Eichler, Rosenberg & Silver, Newark, 1967—69, Brach, Eichler, Rosenberg, Silver, Newark, 1969—72, Brach, Eichler, Rosenberg, Silver, Bernstein & Hammer PA, East Orange, NJ, 1972—81, Brach, Eichler, Rosenberg, Silver, Bernstein, Hammer & Gladstone PC, Roseland, NJ, 1981—2003, Wolf Block Brach Eichler, Roseland, NJ, from 2003; chmn. dist. fee arbitration com. Essex County, from 2009. Dist. V-C mem. NJ Sup. Ct., 1983—86; pres., chmn. bd. Cerebral Palsy, North Jersy, 1967—69; bd. mem. Livingston, from 1965; mem. South Orange-Maplewood Bd. Edn., 1979—83, v.p., 1981—83; bd. dirs. YM-YWHA Met., West Orange, NJ, 1970—74, 1999—2002; former trustee Congregation B'nai Jeshurun, Short Hills; bd. dirs. Newark Beth Israel Med. Ctr. Recipient J.H. Cohn Outstanding Young Leadership award, Jewish Cmty. Fedn. Met. NJ, East Orange, 1961; named Outstanding Citizen, NJ Acad. Medicine, 1998, One of Best Lawyers, NJ, NJ Monthly; named one of Best Lawyers, America. Mem.: ABA, Am. Health Lawyers Assn., NJ Bar Assn., Eseex County Bar Assn. Home: Summit, NJ. Died Nov. 26, 2009.

EIN, MELVIN BENNETT, government official; b. Hammond, Ind., Apr. 2, 1932; s. David and Rose (Chayken) Ein; m. Connie Chong, Dec. 9, 1957; children: Esther, Deborah, Michael P., Ruth, Nathan S., Sarah. AB, Ind. U., 1955; BS, SUNY, 1976; MBA, Am. U., 1976. Cert. in material mgmt. Internat. Material Mgmt. Soc. Chief repair parts br. Engr. Sect. 8th. US Army, Seoul, Republic of Korea, 1958—63; regional adminstrv. svcs. Fed. Hwy. Adminstrn., Homewood, Ill., 1963—67; supply mgmt. officer US Fgn. Service, US Dept. State, AID, Am. Embassy, Vientiane, Laos, 1967—75; head material br. Naval Rsch. Lab., Washington, 1975—76; chief material br. FAA, Nat. Aviation Facilities Exptl. Ctr., Atlantic City, 1976—78, emergency preparedness officer, 1978—79; chief material mgmt. br. Dept. Transp., Washington, 1979—83. Lectr. in field. Served to 1st lt. US Army, 1955—58. Recipient Sustained Superior Performance award, Fed. Hwy. Adminstrn., 1965, HUG award, FAA, 1978. Mem.: Sigma Alpha Mu., Adminstrv. Mgmt. Soc. (adminstr. mgr), Nat. Property Mgmt. Assn. (profl. property mgr.), Internat. Material Mgmt. Soc., Toastmasters Club (Able award 1976). Democrat. Jewish. Home: Mays Landing, NJ. Died Oct. 26, 2009.

EISENMAN, TRUDY FOX, retired dermatologist; b. Chgo., Oct. 14, 1940; d. Nathan Henry and Bernice (Greenberg) Fox; m. Theodore S. Eisenman, Aug. 19, 1962 (div. 1985); children: Lawrence, Robert. Student, U. Ill. at Navy Pier, Chgo., 1958-60; MD, U. Ill., 1964. Diplomate Am. Bd. Dermatology. Rotating intern Milw. County Gen. Hosp., 1964-65, med. resident, 1965-66; resident in dermatology Northwestern U. Med. Sch., Chgo., 1970-73, instr., from 1973; practice medicine specializing in dermatology Chgo., 1973—98; attending dermatologist Louis A. Weiss Meml. Hosp., Chgo., 1973—98. Fellow Am. Acad. Dermatology; mem. AMA, Chgo. Dermatol. Soc., Am. Med. Women's Assn., Chgo. Med. Soc., Alpha Omega Alpha. Home: Tarpon Spgs, Fla. Died Mar. 20, 2009.

ELBEIN, ALAN DAVID, medical science educator; b. Lynn, Mass., Mar. 20, 1933; s. Gersh and Golda (Stryer) E.; m. Elaine J. Brooks, June 21, 1953; children: Steven Conrad, Bradley Martin, Richard Craig. AB, Clark U., 1954; MS, U. Ariz., 1956; PhD, Purdue U., 1960. Rsch. assoc. in biochemistry U. Mich. Med. Sch., Ann Arbor, 1960-63, U. Calif., Berkeley, 1963-64; from asst. prof. to assoc. prof. biology Rice U., Houston, 1964-69; prof. Health Sci. Ctr. U. Tex., San Antonio, 1969-90; prof., chmn. biochemistry dept. U. Ark. Med. Sci., Little Rock, from 1991. Mem. study sect. NSF, 1972-75, 99—, NIH, 1983-87, 93-97. Editor: Swainsonine; mem. editl. bd. Jour. Biol. Chemistry, Arch. Biochem. Biophysics, Plant Physiology, Glycobiology, Jour. Bacteriology,

Eur. Jour. Biochem.; contbr. articles to profl. jours., chapters to books. Disting. Faculty scholar U. Ark. Med. Scis., 1996-97. Mem. Am. Chem. Soc., Am. Soc. Plant Physiology, Am. Soc. Biol. Chem. and Molecular Biology. Jewish. Achievements include patents in field. Home: Little Rock, Ark. Died Nov. 30, 2009.

ELIEFF, LEWIS STEVEN, stockbroker; b. Sofia, Bulgaria, Aug. 2, 1929; s. Steven and Vera (Svetcoff) E.; m. Evanka Brown, May 25, 1958; children; Nancy Ann, Robert and Richard (twins). BBA, U. Mich., 1953, MBA, 1954. Statistician, tax acct. Gen. Motors Corp., Flint, Mich., 1954-60; stockbroker Roney & Co., Flint, 1960-73, ltd. ptnr., 1973-79, gen. ptnr., from 1979; stockbroker Raymond James & Assoc., St. Petersburg, Fla., from 1999. Tchr. stock market curriculum Flint Pub. Schs., 1960-68, Genesee County Community Coll., 1968-73, U. Mich. Extension and Grad. Study Ctr. Flint Campus, 1974—. Served with AUS, 1954-56. Mem.: U. Mich. Alumni Club and Assn., Genesee Valley Rotary. Home: Grand Blanc, Mich. Died Oct. 16, 2009.

ELINSON, HENRY DAVID, artist, language educator; b. Leningrad, USSR, Dec. 14, 1935; arrived in U.S., 1973; s. David Moses and Fraida Zelma (Ufa) Elinson; m. Ludmila Nicholas Tepina, Oct. 7, 1955; 1 child, Maria Henry. Attended, Herzen State Pedagogical U., Leningrad, 1954—57; BA, Pedagogical Inst., Novgorod, USSR, 1958; MA, Pedagogical Inst., Moscow, 1963. Cert. educator. Spl. edn. tchr. Leningrad Sch. Spl. Edn., 1961-64; supr. dept. speech therapy Psychoneurological Dispensary, Leningrad, 1964-73; instr. Russian lang. Yale U., New Haven, 1975-76, Def. Lang. Inst., Presidio of Monterey, Calif., 1976-94. One-man shows include Light and Motion Transmutation Galleries, N.Y.C., 1974, Thor Gallery, Louisville, 1974, Monterey Peninsula Art Mus., 1977, U. Calif. Nelson Gallery, Davis, 1978, Nahamkin Gallery, N.Y.C., 1978, Nahamkin Fine Arts, 1980, Gallery Paule Anglim, San Francisco, 1981, 1985, 1987, Gallery Puale Anglim, 1991, 1993, 1996, 1999, 2000, Dostoevsky's Mus., St. Petersburg, Russia, 1992, Mus. Art Santa Cruz, Calif., 1994, Duke U. Mus. Art, 1996, Mead Art Mus., 1998, Mus. Non Conformist Art, St. Petersburg, 2000, Russian Mus., 2002, exhibited in group shows at Ctrl. Exhbn. Hall St. Petersburg, 2004, Bklyn. Coll. Art Ctr., 1974, CUNY, 1974, Galleria II Punto, Genoa, Italy, 1975, New Art From Soviet Union, Washington, 1977, Gallery Hardy, Paris, 1978, Mus. Fine Art, San Francisco, 1979, Santa Cruz Mus. Fine Arts, 1994, V. Morlan Gallery Transylvania U., Lexington, Ky., 1995, Art Gallery, Adriondack CC, Queensbury, N.Y., 2002, A.P.E. Gallery, Northampton, Mass., 2003, others, Represented in permanent collections Mus. Fine Arts, San Francisco, Yale U. Art Gallery, Monterey Mus. Art, U. Calif. Art Mus., Berkeley, Bochum Mus., Germany, Check Point Charlie Mus., Berlin, State Russian Mus., Leningrad, Zimmerly Art Mus., Rutgers U., N.J., Duke U. Mus. Art, Mead Art Mus., Mus. St. Petersburg History, Mus. Non Conformist Art, State Hermitage, St. Petersburg, Visual Arts Gallery Adirondack CC, N.Y., A.P.E. Gallery, Northampton, Porto & Franco Art Pastor A Retrospective Art Works San Francisco, 2010. Mem. Underground Anti-Soviet Govt. Students' Orgn., 1957. Recipient Gold medal Art Achievement, City of Milan, 1975. Avocations: travel, writing. Home: Pacific Grove, Calif. Died Jan. 18, 2010.

EL-KHATIB, SHUKRI MUHAMMED, biochemist; b. Ein Yabroud, Ramallah, Palestine, Aug. 20, 1931; s. Muhammed Abdel Latif and Salmeh Sulaiman (Subih) El-K.; m. Joan Ann Sullivan,Apr. 10, 1960 (div.); children: Issam, Runda, Hala, Mona; m. Naheel Jaser Salameh, Aug. 8, 1991; 1 child, Muhammed Shukri. PhD, Tex. A&M, 1968. Instr. Baylor Coll. of Medicine, Houston, 1968-70; asst. prof. U. Tenn. Med. Sch., Memphis, 1970-73; assoc. prof. U. P.R. Med. Sch., San Juan, 1974-76; v.p. U. Cen. Del Caribe, Cayey, 1984-88, chmn., 1976-91, prof. Bayamon, from 1991. Cons. Lastra Ednl. Experts, San Juan, 1980. Author: Polytoxin and Tumor, 1976, Nutrition and Colon Cancer, 1983, 4th edit., 1986. Pres. Islamic Ctr. of P.R., Rio Piedras, 1985-90. Mem. N.Y. Acad. Sci., Sigma Xi. Republican. Muslim. Home: Bayamon, PR. Died Apr. 10, 2009.

ELLETT, ALAN SIDNEY, real estate developer; b. Seven Kings, Essex, Eng., Jan. 6, 1930; came to U.S., 1974, permanent resident, 1974; s. Sidney Walter and May (Fowler) E.; children: Denise, Michelle, Wayne. BSc in Bldg. Constrn., 1951, MBA. Mng. dir. Gilbert Ash Structures, 1960-68; dir., gen. mgr. Lyon Group (real estate), 1968-70; mng. dir. (pres.) Gilbert Ash Ltd., 1970-72; dir. Bovis Ltd.; chief exec. Bovis Property divsn. Audley Properties Ltd., 1972-74; chmn. bd. Forest City Dillon, Inc., 1974-88; exec. v.p., dir. Forest City Enterprises, Inc., Cleve., 1974-89; chmn. Forest City Rental Properties, 1982-89; chmn., pres. Forest City Comml. Constrn. Co., Inc., 1987-89; exec. v.p., COO Am. Malls Internat., Washington, 1997—2000; prin., owner Intercontinental Devel. and Investment Corp., Fla., from 1997. Contbr. articles to profl. jours. Fellow Inst. Builders, Inst. Dirs Mem. Conservative Party. Mem. Church of England. (London). Died Dec. 20, 2009.

ELLETT, JOHN SPEARS, II, retired taxation educator, accountant, lawyer; b. Richmond, Va., Sept. 17, 1923; s. Henry Guerrant and Elizabeth Firmstone (Maxwell) E.; m. Mary Ball Ruffin, Apr. 15, 1950; children: John, Mary Ball, Elizabeth, Martha, Henry. BA, U. Va., 1948, JD, 1957, MA, 1961; PhD, U. N.C., 1969. CPA, Va., La.; bar: Va. 1957. Lab. instr. U. Va., Charlottesville, 1953-58; instr. Washington and Lee U., 1958-60; asst. prof. U. Fla., 1967-71; assoc. prof. U. New Orleans, 1971-76, prof. taxation, 1976-94, prof. emeritus, from 1994. Trainee Va. Carolina Hardware Co., Richmond, 1948-51; acct. Equitable Life Assurance Soc., Richmond, 1951-52; staff acct. Musselman & Drysdale, Charlottesville, 1952-54; staff acct. R.M. Musselman, Charlottesville, 1957-58; mem. U. New Orleans Oil and Gas Acctg. Conf., 1973-92; bd. dirs., publicity chmn. U. New Orleans Energy Acctg. and Tax Conf., 1993-94, bd. dirs. publicity com.; pres. Maxwelton Farm and Timber Corp., 1994—; treas. U. New Orleans Estate Planning Seminar, 1975-78, lectr. continuing edn.; CPCU instr. New Orleans Ins. Inst., 1975-78. Author books; contbr. articles to profl. jours. Served with AUS, 1943-46. Mem. AICPA (40 yr. hon. mem. 2000—), Am. Acctg. Assn., Am. Assn. Atty.-CPAs (chmn. ptnrship. taxation continuing edn. com. 1989, ptnrship. taxation com. 1990, organized La. chpt., v.p. 1991-93), Va. Soc. CPAs, Soc. La. CPAs, Va. Bar Assn. (40 yr. hon. mem. 2000—). Democrat. Episcopalian. Home: Charlottesville, Va. Died Dec. 22, 2009.

ELLIOT, JEFFREY M., political science professor, department chairman; b. LA, June 14, 1947; s. Gene and Harriet (Sobsey) E. BA, U. So. Calif., 1969, MA, 1970; ArtsD in Govt., Claremont Grad. Sch., 1978; LittD (hon.), Shaw U., 1985; LLD (hon.), City U. L.A., 1986; cert. in grantsmanship, Grantsmanship Tng. Ctr., 1980; cert. in internat. trade and devel., N.C. Ctrl. U., 1995; cert. in conflict resolution, Ctr. for Peace Edn., 1997. Rsch. asst. U. So. Calif., 1969-70; instr. polit. sci. Glendale Coll., 1970-72, Cerritos Coll., 1970-72; asst. prof. history and polit. sci. U. Alaska-Anchorage C.C., 1973-74; asst. prof. history and polit. sci., dean curriculum Miami-Dade C.C., 1974-76; asst. prof. polit. sci. Va. Wesleyan Coll., Norfolk, 1978-79; sr. curriculum specialist Edn. Devel. Ctr., Newton, Mass., 1979-81; prof. polit. sci. NC Ctrl. U., from 1981, dept. chair. Disting. advisor fgn. affairs Congressman Mervyn M. Dymally (Dem. Calif.), 1985-94. Author: 150 books, including Keys to Economic Understanding, 1976, Science Fiction Voices, 1979, Literary Voices, 1980, Analytical Congressional Directory, 1981, Deathman Pass Me By: Two Years on Death Row, 1982, Tempest in a Teapot: The Falkland Islands War, 1983, Kindred Spirits, 1984, Black Voices in American Politics, 1985, Urban Society, 1985, The Presidential-Congressional Political Dictionary, 1985, Fidel Castro: Nothing Can Stop the Course of History, 1986, The State and Local Government Political Dictionary, 1986, The Third World, 1987, The Arms Control, Disarmament, and Military Security Dictionary, 1988, Dictionary of American Government, 1988, Fidel, 1988, Conversations with Maya Angelou, 1988, Voices of Zaire: Rhetoric or Reality?, 1990, Brown & Benchmark Reader in American Government, 1991, Brown and Benchmark Reader in International Relations, 1991, The Trilemma of World Oil Politics, 1991, Starclimber: The Autobiography of Raymond Z. Gallon, 1991, Adventures of a Free-Lancer: The Autobiography of Stanton A. Coblentz, 1991, The Work of Jack Dann: An Annotated Bibliography and Guide, 1991, The Work of George Zebrowski: An Annotated Bibliography and Guide, 1991, Brown & Benchmark Reader in American Government, 1992, Brown & Benchmark Reader in International Relations, 1992, The Third World, 1992, Into the Flames: The Life Story of a Righteous Gentile, 1992, After All These Years: Sam Moskowitz On His Science Fiction Career, 1992, The Encyclopedia of African-American Politics, 1994, The Work of Raymond Z. Gallun: An Annotated Bibliography and Guide, 1994, Fidel By Fidel, 1994, The African-American Historical Atlas, 1994, The Historical Dictionary of OPEC, 1995, The Dictionary of State and Local Government, 1995, The Historical Dictionary of the Third World, 1995, The Work of Pamela Sargent: An Annotated Bibliography and Guide, 1996, The Work of George Zebrowski: An Annotated Bibliography and Guide, 1996, The Work of Jack Dann: An Annotated Bibliography and Guide, 1997; contbr. 550 articles and revs. to profl. and popular jours.; contbg. editor Negro History Bull., 1976-80, West Coast Writers' Conspiracy, 1978-80, Trumphet of Conscience, 2000—. Mem. cmty. svcs. adv. coun. Miami (Fla.) Comty. Svcs., 1974-76; mem. Los Angeles Mayor's Adv. Com., 1971-72; speechwriter, rsch. asst., campaign strategist U.S. Sen. Howard W. Cannon of Nev., 1969—; cons. Calif. Clean Environment Act, 1970-72; commr. Human Rels. Commn., Durham, N.C., 1999—; co-chmn. Sister Cities Program, Durham, 1999—; bd. dirs. Justice Policy Ctr., Durham, 1999—, N.C. Student Rural Health Projec, 1999—. Recipient 100 literary and scholarly awards including Fair Enterprise Medallion award, 1965, Outstanding Polit. Sci. Scholar citation, 1970, Outstanding Tchr. award, 1971, Outstanding Am. Educator citation, 1975, Disting. Svc. Through Community Effort award, 1976, Outstanding Rsch. prize, 1987, 91, Disting. Scholarship award, 1987, Outstanding Rsch. Prize, 1991, Nancy Susan Reynolds award, 1991, Disting Svc. award Acad. Help Ctr., 1992, Gen. News, Election Analysis Associated Press award, 1993, Documentary Profile Cmty. TV award, 1994, Excellence award, Soc. Internat. Develop., 1995, meritorious contributions for Human and Civil Rights award, City of Durham, NC, 2002. Mem. AAUP, ASCD, Cmty. Coll. Social Sci. Assn. (dir. 1970-77, pres. 1975-77), So. Assn. Coll. and Sch. (accreditation team 1974-76), Am. Polit. Sci. Assn., Nat. Coun. for Social Studies, Rocky Mountain Social Sci. Assn., Soc. Internat. Devel. Coun. Fgn. Affairs, Internat. Studies Assn., Assn. Third World Studies, Am. Hist. Assn., Pi Sigma Alpha, Phi Delta Kappa. Home: Durham, NC. Died Dec. 12, 2009.

ELLIOTT, JAMES MARTIN, foundation administrator; b. Owensboro, Ky., Dec. 2, 1942; s. James Glenn and Margaret (Harris) E.; m. Jannette White, Sept. 10, 1966; children: Elizabeth, Alexandra, Andrew. BS, Ind. U., 1964, JD, 1969. Bar: Ky. 1969. Tchr. Owensboro Pub. Schs., 1964—66; assoc. law firm Wilson, Wilson & Plain, Owensboro, 1969—70; controller Ind. U. Found., Bloomington, 1970—75, v.p. fin., from 1975. Pres. Allways Travel; dir. Monroe County Bank, Bloomington, Voice Found., Monroe County Holding Co. Pres. Monroe County Heart Assn., Bloomington Cmty. Progress Coun. Mem. Am. Bar Assn., Ky. Bar Assn., Coun. for Advancement and Support of Edn., Bloomington Country Club (dir.), University Club N.Y.C., Indpls. Athletic Club. Methodist. Home: Bloomington, Ind. Died July 28, 2009.

ELLIS, HELEN CHARD, writer, former health agency executive; b. East Orange, N.J., Oct. 16, 1914; d. Claude Franklin and Harriet Correll (Wallen) Chard; m. Harlan Reed Ellis, Dec. 23, 1937; children— Reed Ellis, Karen Anne Ellis Stonesifer. Student, Wooster Coll., 1931-33, U. Fla.-Gainesville, 1966-67; B.S., Simmons Coll., 1936. Part-time editorial work U. Fla.-Gainesville, 1957-70; exec. dir. Birth Defects Found., Gainesville, 1970-79; freelance writer, 1982—; instr. community edn. program Santa Fe Jr. Coll., 1984-91. Compiler series of articles in Jour. of Teacher Edn., 1957-67; contbr. articles to mags. Mem., Fla. Gov.'s Alachua County Children's Commn., 1965-69, Alachua County Crime Victim Fund Rev. Com., 1979-83; bd. dirs. Dedicated Alternative Resources for Elderly, Inc. (DARE), 1992—, also treas. Recipient March of Dimes Service award, 1982, 83, AAUW Service award, 1983, Fla. Fedn. Women's Clubs Service award, 1983. Mem. Nat. League Am. Pen Women (pres. Gainesville br. 1978-84, Fla. pres. 1986-88), Women in Communications, Fla. Freelance Writer's Assn., AAUW (past pres.), Gainesville Fine Arts Assn. (1st v.p. 1980-82). Club: Gainesville Woman's (chmn. internat. affairs 1982-83, corr. sec. 1995-97). Home: Cedar Grove, NJ. Died June 1, 2009.

ELLIS, HERB (MITCHELL HERBERT ELLIS), jazz guitarist; b. Farmersville, Tex., Aug. 4, 1921; m. Patti Gahagan; 1 child, Kari. Student, North Tex. State Teachers Coll.; PhD (hon.), North Tex. Coll. of Music, 1997. Touring and Recording with (1945-2010) Oscar Peterson's Trio, Ray Brown, Joe Pass, Harry Edison, Freddie Green, Remo Palmier; (albums) Ellis in Wonderland, 1956, I Love John Frigo...He Swings, 1957, Nothing But the Blues, 1957, Herb Ellis Meets Jimmy Giuffre, 1959, THank You CHarlie Christian. 1960, The Midnight Roll, 1962, Pair to Draw to, Jazz/Concord, 1972, Seven, Come Eleven, 1973, Two for the Road, 1974, Soft Shoe, 1974, Hot Tracks, 1975, Hello Herbie, 1981, Doggin Around, 1988, Joe's Blues, 1998, Died Mar. 28, 2010.

ELLIS, JACK CLARE, theater arts educator; b. Joliet, Ill., July 9, 1922; s. Louis Nyle and Anna Louise (Cary) Ellis; m. Sue Carrol Scheffler, Apr. 26, 1987; children: David Hodges, Cameron Cary. Attended, Wabash Coll., 1943; MA, U. Chgo., 1948; EdD, Columbia U., 1955. Instr., English Western Mich. U., Kalamazoo, 1948—50; audio-visual specialist Citizenship Edn. Project, NYC, 1951—53; rsch. assoc. Film Coun. America, Evanston, Ill., 1953—56; asst. prof. to prof., film Northwestern U., Evanston, 1956—91, chmn., dept. radio-TV film, 1980—85, prof. emeritus, from 1991. Vis. asst. prof. theatre arts UCLA, 1959—60; mem. & US del. UNESCO Internat Meeting Tchg. Film and TV Appreciation, Oslo, Norway, 1962; mem. adv. com. Am. Coun. Edn., 1964—66; vis. assoc. prof. TV, motion pictures, radio NY U., 1965—66; prof. radio, TV and film U. Tex., Austin, 1972—73; mem. adv. film panel Ill. Arts Coun., 1970—72; dir. NEH Summer Seminar on History of Film, 1979—80. Author: A History of Film, 1979, rev. edit., 1985, 1990, 1995, John Grierson: A Guide to References and Resources, 1986, The Documentary Idea, 1989; co-editor: Cinema Examined, 1982; mem. bd. editl. advs. History of Am. Cinema Project, from 1980; editor: Cinema Jour., 1976—82; contbr. articles to profl. jours. With US Army, 1943—46. Mem.: Soc. Cinema Studies (pres., treas., councilman from 1959), Am. Fedn. Film Socs. (pres., chmn. bd. dirs., newsletter editor 1955—75). Home: Evanston, Ill. Died July 16, 2009.

ELLIS, WILLIAM GRENVILLE, academic administrator, management consultant; b. Teaneck, NJ, Nov. 29, 1940; s. Grenville Brigham and Vivian Lilian (Breeze) E.; m. Nancy Elizabeth Kempton, 1963; children: William Grenville, Bradford Graham. BS in Bus. Adminstrn., Babson Coll., 1962; MBA, Suffolk U., 1963; MEd, Westfield State Coll., 1965; EdD, Pa. State U., 1968; MS, Concordia U., 1991; MLE (Sears Roebuck Found. scholar), Harvard U., 1980; postgrad., U. Chgo., 1983, MIT, 1984, Harvard U., 1988-96. Asst. prof. bus. Rider U., 1968-69; div. dir., assoc. prof. Castleton (Vt.) State Coll., 1969-72; exec. v.p., prof. St. Joseph Coll. in Vt., Rutland, 1972-73; acad. v.p., dean grad. sch. Thomas Coll., Waterville, Maine, 1973-82; pres. Wayland Acad., Beaver Dam, Wis., 1982-95, New Eng. Coll., Henniker, N.H., 1995-97; dean Sch. Bus. and Legal Studies, Concordia U. Wis., Mequon, from 1997. Mem. adv. bd. CFX Bank, 1996-97; corporator 1st Consumers Savs., 1974-81, Maine Savs., 1981-82, BankOne, 1983-95. Author: The Analysis and Attainment of Economic Stability, 1963, The Relationship of Related Work Experience to the Teaching Success of Beginning Business Teachers, 1968, Marketing for Educational Administrators, 1991, A Gunner's Moon, 1997; contbr. numerous articles and abstracts to profl. jours. Trustee C.C. Vt., 1972-73, Marian Coll., 1988-91, Wayland Acad., 1982-95, New Eng. Coll., 1995-97; auditor Town of Castleton, 1969-71; pres. Kennebee Valley Youth Hockey, Augusta, Maine, 1975-77; pres. Beaver Dam C. of C., 1985, 86, Midwest Classic Athletic Conf., 1989, Wis. Assn. Ind. Schs., 1984-86; chair bd. dirs. Beaver Dam Cmty. Hosp., 1985-95; dir. North Ctrl. Assn. Colls. and Secondary Schs., 1991-94, Ind. Schs. Ctrl. States, 1991-95; dir. N.H. Coll. and Univ. Coun., 1995-97; dir. Ozaukee County Indsl. Devel. Corp., 2003-04, Internat. Assembly Collegiate Bus. Edn., 2004-. Recipient Cmty., Svc. award Rutland C. of C., 1973, Disting. Svc. citation Wayland Acad., 1995, Excellence in Edn. award Pa. State U., 2001; named Cons. of Yr., SBA, 1975, 77, Prof. of Yr. Concordia U. Wis., 1999. Mem. APA, Nat. Assn. Intercollegiate Athletics (cert. of merit 1979), Soc. for Advancement of Mgmt., Cum Laude Soc., Pheasant City Club, Rotary, Alpha Chi, Pi Omega Pi, Alpha Delta Sigma, Delta Pi Epsilon, Phi Delta Kappa. Home: Fox Point, Wis. Died Mar. 3, 2009.

ELLISON, LORIN BRUCE, management consultant; b. Chgo., Jan. 5, 1932; s. Edward L. and Bertha A. (Hoverson) E.; m. Beverley A. Burtar, July 24, 1953; children— Richard, Glen, Kirk, Kevin. BS in Bus. Adminstrn, Drake U., 1954.

CPA, Ill. Auditor Arthur Andersen & Co., Chgo., 1957-62; mem. corp. staff, divsn. contr. Interlake Steel Co., Chgo., 1962-65; v.p. fin., CFO, sec., divsn. pres. Tappan Co., Mansfield, Ohio, 1965-77; asso. cons. A.T. Kearney, Inc., Cleve., 1978-80; corp. contr., v.p. fin., CFO, v.p. bus. systems Bausch & Lomb, Rochester, NY, 1980-83; CFO, Design & Mfg. Corp., Willoughby, Ohio, 1984—95; CEO, chmn. bd. Wave Tek Inc., Mansfield, Ohio, 1984-87; pvt. practice mgmt. cons. Mansfield, from 1988; sr. v.p., CFO, Premier Salons Internat., Minnetonka, Minn., 1994-95; CFO. SRECO-Flexible, Inc., Marina Del Rey, Calif., 1996-98; exec. v.p., CFO, CRS Industries, Tampa, Fla., 1998-99; cons., from 2000. Mem. Fin. Execs. Inst. Home: Golden, Colo. Died Dec. 25, 2009.

ELLISON, ROBERT MUNROE, news correspondent; b. NYC, Sept. 22, 1942; s. Robert Alexander and Harriet Louise (Munroe) E.; m. Diane O'Reilly, Sept. 28, 1963 (div. July 1975); children: Robert, Michelle, Michael; m. Pamela Hathaway Crane, Aug. 27, 1986; 1 child: Angel BA, St. John's U., 1964. Tchr. jr. high sch. NYC. Bd. Edn., Jamaica, 1964-68; asst. program officer US Agy. for Internat. Devel. (USAID), Washington, 1968-78; reporter Sta. WOOK-FM, Washington, 1978-82; White House corr. American Urban Radio Network (formerly Sheridan Broadcasting), Washington, 1982—94; sr. v.p., media rels. Walls Communications, 1994—2007. Author: U.S. Radio Stations with African American Listeners, 1994. Mem. White House Corrs. Assn. (v.p. 1989-90, pres. 1990-91). Avocations: gardening, bicycling, reading. Home: Washington, DC. Died May 24, 2010.

ELLSWORTH, GARY GEORGE, lawyer; b. Hartford, Conn., Apr. 18, 1948; s. Elbert Thelus and Anita (Skarin) E.; m. Meredith Scott Spencer, Jan. 6, 1984 (div.); children: Spencer Thelus, Emma Lane. BA, Dartmouth Coll., 1970; JD, George Mason Sch. Law, 1976. Bar: D.C. 1976. Sole practice, Washington, 1976-77; counsel to Congressman Joe Skubitz US House of Reps., Washington, 1977; minority counsel US House Interior & Insular Affairs Com., Washington, 1977-81; dep. chief counsel US Senate Energy & Natural Resources Com., Washington, 1981-84; chief counsel US Senate, Washington, 1984-87, chief counsel to minority, 1987—99; lobbyist US Enrichment Corp., 1999—2003; pvt. cons., 2003—10. Served as lt. USN, 1970-73, Vietnam Mem. D.C. Bar Assn. Republican. Methodist. Home: Arlington, Va. Died July 16, 2010.

ELMORE, D. PAGE, state legislator; b. Nassawadox, Va., May 31, 1939; m. Carolyn Elmore; 3 children. Attended, U. Richmond. Owner & CEO Shore Disposal Inc., 1965—98; treas. Accomack County, Va., 1968—76; mem. Dist. 38A Md. House of Delegates, 2003—10. Mem.: Somerset Rep. Club, Wicomico Rep. Club, Salisbury-Wicomico C of C., Salisburg U. Found., Mid-Delmarva YMCA. Republican. Died June 26, 2010.

ELMORE, WALTER A., electrical engineer, consultant; b. Bartlett, Tenn., Oct. 2, 1925; s. Walter Alcorn and Lucile (Tapp) E.; m. Jane Ann Huey, June 3, 1950; children: Robin, Jamie, Laura. BSEE, U. Tenn., 1949. Registered profl. engr., Fla. Mgr. cons. engring. sect. Protective Relay div. Westinghouse Elec. Corp., Newark, 1951-79, Protective Relay div. ABB Power T & D Co., Coral Springs, Fla., 1979-89; mgr. cons. engring. sect. protective relay divsn. ABB Power T&D Co., Coral Springs, Fla., 1989-94, cons. engr. high voltage protection, 1994-96, ret., 1996. Author: (with others) Applied Protective Relaying, 1976, Protective Relaying Theory and Application, 1994, Pilot Protective Relaying, 1999. Fellow IEEE (chmn. IEEE/PES tech. coun. 1988-89, Gold medal for engring. excellence 1989); mem. NAE, Tau Beta Pi, Eta Kappa Nu, Phi Kappa Phi. Republican. Home: Blue Ridge, Va. Died Jan. 20, 2010.

EL-NAGGAR, AHMED SAMI, civil engineering educator, laboratory and global engineering executive; b. Egypt, Dec. 18, 1926; s. Ahmed Mohammad and Sanya (Hefny) El-Naggar; m. Janet Eileen Spinn, May 26, 1956; children: Tarik, Rhonda, Jilanne, Kareem. BCE, U. Cairo, 1948; MCE, U. Calif., Berkeley, 1951; PhD in Environ. Engring., Purdue U., 1956. Registered profl. engr., Egypt, Ind., Ill. Asst. lectr. Engring. Coll., Cairo, 1949—50; tchg. asst. U. Calif., 1951—53; constrn. engr. C.E. US Army, San Francisco, 1952—56; asst. prof. environ. engring. U. Alexandria, 1956; rsch. assoc. Purdue U., 1956—59; design engr. Clyde E. Williams & Assocs., 1959—60; prof. environ. and civil engring. Valparaiso U., Ind., from 1960; pres. Northern Labs. and Engring., Inc., from 1978. Cons. Met. San. Dist. Greater Chgo.; vis. prof. High Inst. Pub. Health, Alexandria, 1957—58, Ains Shams U., Cairo, 1958. Contbr. articles to profl. jours. Recipient Egyptian Govt. award, 1948; San. Engring. fellowship, WHO, 1958, NSF grantee, 1962—64, 1966—68, 1974, 1977—79. Mem.: AAAS, ASCE, Valparaiso C. of C., Am. Water Resources Assn., Ind. Water Pollution Control Assn. (pres. 1970—71, Outstanding Paper award 1965), Ind. Water Pollution Control Fedn., Water Pollution Control Fedn., Am. Acad. Environ. Engrs., Am. Pub. Works Assn., Am. Water Works Assn., Am. Soc. Engring. Edn., Kiwanis Lodge (pres. Valparaiso 1969—70), Tau Beta Pi, Mu San, Chi Epsilon, Sigma Xi. Achievements include patents for biological reactor. Home: Valparaiso, Ind. Died July 18, 2009.

EMBER, MELVIN LAWRENCE, anthropologist, educator; b. NYC, Jan. 13, 1933; s. Martin William and Ida F. (Trebuchovskaya) E.; m. Irma Stalberg, July 11, 1954 (div. Jan. 1970); children: Matthew, Rachel; m. Carol Lee Ruchlis, Mar. 21, 1970; children: Katherine, Julie. BA, Columbia Coll., 1953; PhD, Yale U., 1958. Postdoctoral fellow Yale U., New Haven, 1958-59; rsch. anthropologist NIH, Bethesda, Md., 1959-63; from asst. to assoc. prof. anthropology Antioch Coll., Yellow Springs, Ohio, 1963-67; assoc. prof. Hunter Coll., CUNY, 1967-70, prof., 1971-87; pres. Human Rels. Area Files, Inc., Yale U., New Haven, from 1987. Chmn. dept. anthropology Hunter Coll., CUNY, 1968-73, exec. officer PhD program in anthropology Grad. Sch., 1973-75. Co-author: Anthropology, 1973, Cultural Anthropology, 1973, 12th edit., 2007, Marriage, Family and Kinship, 1983, Human Evolution & Culture, 6th Edit., 2009, Sex, Gender and Kinship: A Cross-Cultural Perspective, 1997, Cross-Cultural Research Methods, 2001, 2nd edit., 2009, Human Culture, 2009; co-editor: Portraits of Culture, 1998, Research Frontiers in Anthropology, 1998, Cross-Cultural Research for Social Science, 1998, Encyclopedia of Cultural Anthropology, 1996, American Immigrant Cultures: Builders of a Nation, 1997, Cultures of the World, 1999, Countries and Their Cultures, 2001, Encyclopedia of Prehistory, 2001—02, Encyclopedia of Urban Cultures, 2002, Archaeology: Original Readings in Method and Practice, 2002, Physical Anthropology: Original Readings in Method and Practice, 2002, Encyclopedia of Sex and Gender, 2004, Encyclopedia of Medical Anthropology, 2004, Encyclopedia of Diasporas, 2005; editor: Cross-Cultural Rsch.: The Jour. of Comparative Social Sci., from 1982. Fellow AAAS, Am. Anthrop. Assn.; mem. Soc. for Cross-Cultural Rsch. (pres. 1981-82). Home: Hamden, Conn. Died Sept. 7, 2009.

EMERY, ALDEN HAYES, JR., chemical engineer, educator; b. Pitts., May 2, 1925; s. Alden Hayes and Dorothy (Radde) E.; m. Verna Elizabeth Murphy, Mar. 1, 1952; children— Janice Elaine, Gregg Alden. BS, Pa. State U., 1947; MS, Mass. Inst. Tech., 1949; PhD, U. Ill., 1955. Chem. engr. E.I. duPont de Nemours & Co., Wilmington, Del., 1949-52; asst. prof. Sch. Chem. Engring., Purdue U., Lafayette, Ind., 1954-58, asso. prof., 1958-64, prof., from 1964. Served with USNR, 1944-45. Fulbright scholar, 1967 Mem. Am. Inst. Chem. Engrs., Am. Chem. Soc. Home: West Lafayette, Ind. Died Feb. 7, 2009.

EMIL, ARTHUR D., lawyer; b. NYC, Dec. 29, 1924; s. Allan D'lugasch and Kate Silverman Emil; m. Jane Allen Emil, Sept. 15, 1948 (dec. 1973); children: David A., Jennie, Suzanne Emil Pleskunas; m. Lydia Moffat, July 6, 1976. BE, Yale U., 1945; LLB, Columbia U., 1950. Bar: N.Y. 1950, U.S. Dist. Ct. (so. dist.) N.Y. 1950, U.S. Ct. Appeals (2d cir.) 1950. Trial atty. Cahill, Gordon, Reindel & Ohl, NYC, 1950-52, U.S. Dept. Justice, Washington, 1952-53; assoc. McLaughlin & Fougner, NYC, 1953-55, Arthur D. Emil, NYC, 1955-60, Emil & Kobrin, NYC, 1960-70, 77-79, Emil, Kobrin, Klein & Garbus, NYC, 1970-77, Surrey & Morse, NYC, 1979-86, Jones, Day, Reavis & Pogue, NYC, 1986-93, Kramer, Levin, Naftalis & Frankel LLP, NYC, 1994—2003, Cohen Tauber Spievack and Wagner LLP, NYC, from 2003. Co-chmn. fin. com. Gov. Hugh Carey re-election campaign, N.Y., 1977-78. Lt. (j.g.) USNR, 1943-46, ETO, NATOUSA. Home: New York, NY. Died July 2010.

EMISON, JAMES HENRY, corporate financial executive; b. Vincennes, Ind., Feb. 5, 1926; s. John Wesley and Mary Irene (Hogue) E.; m. Eileen Patricia Sullivan, Sept. 11, 1948; children: James W., David L., Mark R., Susan P. AB, DePauw U., 1947; MBA, Harvard U., 1950. With Uniroyal Inc., 1950—62, plant controller Chicopee, Mass., 1962—64, info. ctr. dir. Allen Park, Mich., 1964—69; fin. v.p. Uniroyal Ltd., Toronto, Ont., Canada, 1973—76; div. controller Uniroyal Inc., Naugatuck, Conn., 1977—78, corp. controller Middlebury, Conn., 1980—84, exec. dir. fin. svcs., from 1984. Mem. Middlebury Econ. Devel. Commn., 1984. With USN, 1944—46. Mem.: Fin. Execs. Inst. Republican. Congregationalist. Home: Middlebury, Conn. Died Aug. 30, 2009.

ENFIELD, KURT FERDINAND, retired business machine retail company executive; b. Frankfurt, Germany, July 23, 1921; s. Henry and Alice (Bluethental) E.; came to U.S., 1939, naturalized, 1944; children: Gwen, Jill, Richard. Grad. Buxton Coll., Eng., 1937; Partner, Enfield's Camera Shop, Miami Beach, Fla., 1939-63; pres. Enfield's Bus. Products Co., Miami, 1955-85. Served with AUS, 1944-46. Decorated Bronze Star. Mem. Miami Beach C. of C., Bus. Products Council Assn. (pres. 1972-73), Nat. Microfilm Assn., Internat. Word Processing Assn. Democrat. Jewish. Clubs: Bayshore Service (pres. 1980-81), Tiger Bay Polit., Standard, Jockey, B'nai B'rith, U. Miami Founders; Club du Chateau (France). Died Apr. 11, 2009.

ENGEL, WALBURGA See VON RAFFLER-ENGEL, WALBURGA

ENGELBRECHT, RUDOLF, electrical engineering educator; b. Atlanta, Apr. 18, 1928; s. Walter and Dorothea Engelbrecht; m. Christel M. Kluth, Sept. 10, 1050; children: Richard, Rolf, Erika. BS, Ga. Inst. Tech., 1951, MSEE, 1953; PhD in Elec. Engring., Oreg. State U., 1979. Mem. tech. staff Bell Labs., Whippany, N.J., 1953—60, supr. Murray Hill, N.J., 1961—63, dept. head, 1964—69; dir. RCA Tech. Ctr., Somerville, N.J., 1970—72; group leader RCA Labs., Zurich, Switzerland, 1972—77; assoc. prof. Oreg. State U., Corvallis, 1977—93. Co-author: Microwave Devices, 1969; contbr. articles to profl. jours. Named to Oreg. State U. Engring. Hall of Fame, 1998. Fellow: IEEE (life Centennial award 1984, Third Millennium medal 2000); mem.: Sigma Xi. Achievements include patents in field. Home: Champaign, Ill. Died May 1, 2009.

ENGELER, WILLIAM ERNEST, retired physicist; b. Bklyn., Nov. 13, 1928; s. William Ernest and Marguerite E.; m. Marilyn Ann McKee, Nov. 26, 1955; children: William R., Amy K., Elizabeth A., Mary P. BS, Poly. Inst. Bklyn., 1951; MS, Syracuse U., 1958, PhD, 1961. Physicist GE, Schenectady, N.Y., 1951-52, Syracuse, N.Y., 1952-55, GE Corp. R&D Ctr., Schenectady, 1961-95; ret., 1995. Author, co-author 111 patents, 1953-92; contbr. articles to profl. jours., chpts. to books. With U.S. Army, 1955-56. Coolidge fellow GE, 1979. Fellow IEEE; mem. Am. Phys. Soc., Edison Club (Rexford, N.Y.). Avocations: woodworking, golf. Home: Rexford, NY. Died May 13, 2010.

ENGELMANN, RICHARD HENRY, electrical engineering educator, consultant; b. Cin., Jan. 6, 1923; s. Carl A. and Bertha (Leberecht) E.; m. Doris Rullman, Aug. 23, 1947; children: Karen, Richard. BS, U.S. Naval Acad., 1944; MS, U. Cin., 1949. Registered profl. engr., Ohio. Instr. elec. engring. U. Cin., 1948-51, from asst. prof. to prof., 1952-88, head dept. elec. engring., 1967-79, assoc. dean engring., 1981-86, prof., assoc. dean emeritus, from 1988. Guest prof. Bengal Engring. Coll., Howrah, India, 1963-64; coord. advanced course in mfg. Gen. Electric Aircraft Engine Bus. Group, Evendale, Ohio, 1981-86. Author: Static and Rotating Electromagnetic Devices, 1982; co-editor: Handbook of Electric Motors, 1995; co-author: Design of Devices and Systems, 1997. Lt. U.S. Navy, 1944-46, 51-52. Mem. IEEE (life sr. mem.), Am. Soc. for Engring. Edn. (life), Tesla Meml. Soc. (hon. mem. ad vitam). Achievements include 8 patents. Home: Cincinnati, Ohio. Died Aug. 11, 2010.

ENGELSON, JOYCE, editor, publishing company executive; b. NYC; d. David M. and Marion M. (Abrams) E.; m. Norman Keifetz, Jan. 1960; children— Brom Daniel, Amanda Sara. Student, Smith Coll.; BA cum laude, Barnard Coll., 1950; postgrad., N.Y. Sch. Social Work, Columbia U., 1950-51. Editorial asst. Viking Press, NYC, 1951-52; free-lance writer, editor, 1952-54; editor Abelard-Schuman Ltd., NYC, 1954-59, Dial Press subsidiary Dell Pub. Co., Inc., NYC, 1959-76, sr. editor, 1964-76, exec. editor, 1974-76; editor-in-chief Richard Marek Publishers, Inc. subs. G.P Putnam's, NYC, 1977-81, St. Martins Press-Richard Marek, NYC, from 1981; editor-in-chief, v.p. E.P. Dutton, NYC, from 1985. Author: Mountain of Villainy, 1960; co-author: The Silent Slain, 1959; contbr. short stories to mags.; mem. editorial bd. Barnard Alumnae Mag., 1977-80 Chmn. Nancy Bloch award com. Downtown Community Sch., N.Y.C., 1964-68; mem. pub. com. Friends of N.Y. Public Library, 1981—. Mem. Phi Beta Kappa Home: New York, NY. Died Dec. 25, 2009.

ENGLISH, NICHOLAS CONOVER, lawyer; b. Elizabeth, NJ, Apr. 12, 1912; s. Conover and Sara Elizabeth (Jones) E.; m. Agnes N. Perry, Mar. 18, 1939 (div. 1947); children— Henry H. P., Ann Whitall (Mrs. Edward J. Wardwell); m. Eleanor Morss, May 1, 1948; children— Priscilla English Vincent, Sara (dec.), Sherman, Eleanor English Folta. Grad., Pingry Sch., 1929; AB magna cum laude, Princeton, 1934; LL.B., Harvard, 1937. Bar: N.J. 1937. Since practiced in, Newark; partner firm McCarter & English, 1947-77, of counsel, from 1978. Bd. dirs. Summit (N.J.) YMCA, 1950-57, pres., 1953-55; bd. dirs. Newark YMWCA, also pres.; chmn. exec. com. Ctrl. Atlantic Area YMCA, 1957-63; mem. nat. coun. YMCA, 1954, 58-81, v.p., 1959-60, mem. nat. bd., 1960-71, 73-81, vice chmn., 1969-71, treas., 1977-81; trustee N.J. Nat. Land Trust, 1983-93, Kent Place Sch., 1959—, pres., 1961-72, Pingry Sch., 1954-73; bd. dirs. Nat. Legal Aid Assn., 1953-56. Lt. USNR, 1943—45. Mem. ABA (ho. of dels. 1957-58), N.J. Bar Assn., Essex County Bar Assn., Am. Bible Soc. (bd. trustees 1964-93, sr. trustee 1993—), Am. Law Inst. Congregationalist. Home: Hightstown, NJ. Died Jan. 11, 2010.

ENOWITCH, BENNETT IRVING, psychiatrist, consultant; b. Middletown, Conn., Feb. 17, 1934; s. Elliot H. and Anne (Chester) E.; m. Elisa Cohen, July 14, 1965; children: Schalleen J., Boris I. BA, Wesleyan U., 1955, MALS in Comparative Lit., 1987; MPH, Yale U., 1959; MD, Basel U., Switzerland, 1965, Geneva U., 1966; MA in German Lit., U. Conn., 1987, postgrad., 1972. Diplomat Am. Bd. Psychiatry and Neurology, Am. Bd. Quality Assurance and Utilization Physicians. Pvt. practice, Hartford, Conn., from 1969; cons. CIGNA, Hartford, 1973-94, Conn. HMO, Pathwise HMO, Concentra Healthcare, Meriden, Conn., 1997, Health Care Inc, N. Haven, Conn., from 1989, Blue Cross-Blue Shield, Meriden, from 1989, Rocky Hill (Conn.) Sch. System, 1985-89, Rocky Hill Vets. Hosp., from 1988. Attending psychiatrist Day-Kimball Hosp., Putnam, Conn., 1996—. With U.S. Army, 1956-57, Washington. Fellow Am. Psychiat. Assn.; mem. Phi Beta Phi. Avocation: german literature. Home: West Hartford, Conn. Died Jan. 6, 2009.

EPPES, WILLIAM DAVID, arts and humanities advocate; s. Talmadge DeWitt and Annie Lou (McCord) E AB, Coll. of William and Mary, 1939; BS in LS, Vanderbilt U., 1940; student, U. Manchester, Eng., 1950, Columbia U., 1950; MA, NYU, 1959; student, U. Durham, Eng., 1987. Reference asst. George Washington U., 1944—48, Calif. State U., San Francisco, 1948—49; head, stack personnel Butler Libr. Columbia U., NYC, 1954-58; assoc. prof. Kean State Coll., Union, NJ, 1958-61; asst. libr. Cooper Union, NYC, 1961-70. Founder Film Classics League, St. Petersburg, Fla., 1950; co-founder Backstage Gallery, St. Petersburg Jr. Coll., 1950, Littlebury Eppes Meml. Libr., Westover Ch., Va.; adv. bd. Coral Gables (Fla.) Hist. Preservation Bd. Rev., 1979-81; trustee Greenwich Village Trust for Hist. Preservation, Inc., 1980, pres., 1980-84, 1984-90; cons. Hist. Buckingham (Va.) Inc., 1987—; hon. commr. Eleanor Roosevelt Monument Fund, Inc., N.Y.C Author: The Empire Theatre (1893-1953), 1978, Gertrude Michael-A Star of the Golden Age of Hollywood, 1985, Montgomery (Ala.) Theatre 1822-1985, 1986, The House Off Main Street, A Chronicle of the McCord-Eppes Family; contbr. articles to mags. and hist. jours. Bd. dirs. St. Petersburg Symphony Orch., 1950-54; exec. bd. Assn. Village Homeowners, N.Y.C., 1969-82, Assocs. of Earl Gregg Swem Libr., Coll. of William and Mary, 1973-86; benefactor Jonathon Daniels Sch., Keene, N.H., 1998, Apple Hill Chamber Orch., Sullivan, N.H., 1998, Keene State U., 1999—; benefactor, hist. cons. Redfern Performing Arts Ctr. Keene (N.H.) State U., 2000—; pres. coun. Va. Hist. Soc., 1982; profl. advisor McLeod Plantation, Sea Island Hist. Soc., SC. Mem.

Theater Hist. Soc. (rsch. and reference com. 1977-81), Author's Guild, Inc., W&M Choir, Va. Hist. Soc. (pres.'s coun. 1993—, exec. coun. 1995), Sea Island Hist. Soc. (profl. adv. bd. 2000) Episcopalian. Home: Keene, NH. Died Aug. 2009.

EPSTEIN, HERBERT, construction executive, architect; b. Bklyn., Dec. 30, 1922; s. Samuel and Estelle (Ladden) Georky; m. Bernice Train, Sept. 11, 1945; children: Janet Jones, Irving Joel, Mark Alan. Student, Pratt Inst., Bklyn., 1940-41, Inst. Design and Constrn., 1948-51. Registered architect, N.Y., N.J., Conn., Fla. Archtl. draftsman Kelly, Syska & Hennessy, NYC, 1942, Skidmore, Owings & Merrill, NYC, 1945-48, Fellheimer & Wagner, NYC, 1948, Adolph Goldberg, Bklyn., 1948-51; asst. job capt. York & Sawyer, NYC, 1951-52; assoc., ptnr. Goldberg/Epstein Assocs., Bklyn., 1952-57; pres., chmn. Epstein/Greenfield/Sawicki Architects, P.C., Bklyn., 1957-85; chmn. E/G Constrn. Services, Ltd., NYC, from 1983. Trustee Helen Keller Services for the Blind, Bklyn., 1987—, Borough Hall Restoration Com., Bklyn., 1987—. Served with U.S. Army, 1942-45, ETO. Fellow AIA (nat. v.p. 1976-78, Edward C. Kemper award 1980); mem. N.Y. State Assn. Architects (pres. 1970-71), Bklyn Chpt. AIA (pres. 1959-61), Architects Council N.Y.C. (pres. 1967-70), N.Y. Soc. Architects (pres. 1965-67), N.E. Chpt. Ranger Battalions Assn. World War II (chpt. pres. 1987, nat. pres. 1988-89—). Lodges: Masons (master 1969). Avocations: computers, reading, swimming, walking. Home: Delray Beach, Fla. Died Mar. 8, 2009.

EPSTEIN, JEREMY G., lawyer; b. Chgo., Sept. 28, 1946; s. Joseph and Gayola (Goldman) E.; m. Amy Kallman, Sept. 15, 1968; children: Joshua, Abigail. BA summa cum laude, Columbia U., 1967; BA, Cambridge U., Eng., 1969, MA, 1973; JD, Yale U., 1972. Bar: N.Y. 1973. Law clk. to judge Arnold Bauman U.S. Dist. Ct. (so. dist.) N.Y., 1972-74; asst. U.S. atty. So. Dist. N.Y., 1974-78; ptnr. Shearman & Sterling, NYC, from 1982. Vol. Lawyers for the Arts; bd. dirs. Fund for Modern Cts, City Bar Fund, Inc. Fellow Am. Coll. Trial Lawyers, Phi Beta Kappa. Died July 22, 2009.

ERHART, CHARLES HUNTINGTON, JR., diversified company executive; b. NYC, July 31, 1925; s. Charles Huntington and Katherine (Kent) E.; m. Sylvia Montgomery, June 24, 1948; children— Victoria, Margaret, David, Stephen, Julia Grad., Groton Sch., 1944; BA, Yale U., 1949. With W.R. Grace & Co., from 1950, asst. treas., 1955-63, v.p. charge adminstrv. controls, 1963-68, exec. v.p., chief fin. officer, mem. appropriations com., 1968-81, vice chmn., chief adminstrv. officer, 1981-86, chmn. exec. com., 1986-89, pres., from 1989. Bd. dir. Chemed Corp., Cin., Omnicare Inc., Nat. Med. Care, Taco Villa, Inc., Roto Rooter, Inc., Nat. Sanitary Supply Co., Inc., Nat. Life Ins. Co. Bd. dirs. Leake and Watts Childrens Home, N.Y.C., Evergreens Cemetery, N.Y.C.; trustee Groton Sch., Mass. Mem. Newcomen Soc., Beta Theta Pi Clubs: Racquet and Tennis, Church, N.Y. Yacht (N.Y.C.); Northeast Harbor Fleet. Died Jan. 16, 2009.

ERICKSON, WILLIAM HURT, retired state supreme court justice; b. Denver, May 11, 1924; s. Arthur Xavier and Virginia (Hurt) E.; m. Doris Rogers, Dec. 24, 1953; children: Barbara Ann, Virginia Lee, Stephen Arthur, William Taylor. Degree in petroleum engring., Colo. Sch. Mines, 1947; student, U. Mich., 1949; LLB, U. Va., 1950; PhD in Engring. (hon.), Colo. Sch. of Mines, 2002. Bar: Colo. 1951. Pvt. practice, Denver; justice Colo. Supreme Ct., 1971-96, chief justice, 1983-86; faculty NYU Appellate Judges Sch., 1972-85. Mem. exec. Commn. on Accreditation of Law Enforcement Agys., 1980-83; chmn. Pres.'s Nat. Commn. for Rev. of Fed. and State Laws Relating to Wiretapping and Electronic Surveillance, 1976. Chmn. Erickson Commn., 1997, Limitations on use Deadly Force by Police; chmn. gov.'s Columbine Rev. Commn., 1999-2001. With USAAF, 1943. Recipient Disting. Achievement medal Colo. Sch. Mines, 1990. Fellow Internat. Acad. Trial Lawyers (former sec.), Am. Coll. Trial Lawyers (state chmn. 1970), Am. Bar Found. (chmn. 1985), Internat. Soc. Barristers (pres. 1971); mem. ABA, (bd. govs. 1975-79, former chmn. com. on standards criminal justice, former chmn. coun. criminal law sect., former chmn. com. to implement standards criminal justice, mem. long-range planning com., action com. to reduce ct. cost and delay), Colo. Bar Assn. (award of merit 1989), Denver Bar Assn. (past pres., trustee), Am. Law Inst. (coun. 1973—), Practising Law Inst. (nat. adv. coun., bd. govs. Colo.), Freedoms Found. at Valley Forge (nat. coun. trustees, 1986—), Order of Coif, Scribes (pres. 1978). Home: San Diego, Calif. Died Jan. 13, 2010.

ERICSON, CURTIS RICHARD, radio station executive; b. Bradford, Pa., June 24, 1949; s. Webster Curtis Ericson and Jean Olive (Edwards) Ericson Graham; m. Karen Ann Kautz, Aug. 18, 1973; children— Michael Richard, Todd Charles. A.S., Fla. Jr. Coll., 1974. Clk. typist Gator Freightway, Jacksonville, Fla., 1973-75; tri-loader operator Sears, Roebuck and Co., Jacksonville, 1975-77; advt. salesman Marion Daily Republican Newspaper, Marion, Ill., 1977-79; prin., pres. Radio Services of Wellsville, Inc., 1979-90, doing bus. as Sta. WLSV. Treas., Belmont Fire Co., 1985-87. Served with USAF, 1968-72. Mem. Wellsville C. of C. (bd. dirs.), Am. Legion. Clubs: Bradford (Pa.); Wellsville Country. Lodges: Lions, Elks, Moose. Home: Palm Bch Gdns, Fla. Died July 5, 2009.

ERICSON, JONATHON EDWARD, environmental health science educator, researcher; b. Bronx, NY, May 22, 1942; s. Erling and Ruth Cecila E.; m. Glenda Prince Ericson, Dec. 19, 1987; 1 child, Hana Christine; 1 child from previous marriage, Burke Evan. AB in Exploration Geophysics, UCLA, 1970, MA in Anthropology, 1973, PhD in Anthropology, 1977. Conservation chemist L.A. County Mus. Art, 1976-78; assoc. prof. dept. anthropology Harvard U., Cambridge, Mass., 1978-83; asst. prof. program in social ecology U. Calif., Irvine, 1983-85, assoc. prof. Dept. Environ. analysis and Design, 1985-91, assoc. prof. dept. anthropology, 1987-91, prof. depts. environ analysis and design, anthropology, 1991, prof. Soc. Ecology, Cmty. and Environ. Medicine. Chair Irvine divsn. edn. abroad com. U. Calif., Irvine, 1991-94; cons. NASA-Ames, Moffett Field, Calif., 1983, Keith Co./Irvine Co., 1988-93; designer Ctr. for Archaeol. Rsch. and Devel., Harvard U., 1978-80. Co-editor: Exchange Systems in Prehistory, 1977, Contexts of Prehistorical Exchange, 1982, Prehistoric Quarries and Lithic Production, 1984, American Southwest and Mesoamerica: Systems of Prehistoric Exchange, 1993, Prehistoric Exchange Systems in North America, 1994. Mem. Orange County Quincentenary Com., 1988-93; v.p. Mus. Natural History and Sci., Aliso Viejo, Calif., 1988-91; asst. scout master Boy Scouts Am., Dana Point, Calif., 1990-95. Fulbright Hayes scholar, 1980, 91; NASA fellow, 1983; NSF grantee, 1984-86. Fellow Sigma Xi (chpt. pres. 1995-96); mem. AAAS, Soc. Am. Archaeology, U.S. Systems in Space (regent), Soc. Archaeol. Scis. (pres. 1981-82). Episcopalian. Home: San Juan Capistrano, Calif. Died June 22, 2009.

ERNST, EDWARD WILLIS, retired electrical engineering educator; b. Great Falls, Mont., Aug. 28, 1924; s. Paul Wilson and Grace Vio (Woodmore) E.; m. Helen Kitty Todd, Jan. 29, 1950 (dec. Mar. 1975); children: Deborah Kitty, Thomas Edward (dec.); m. Margaret Frances Patton, Sept. 13, 1975 (dec. Feb. 2002); children: Alan Harmon, Ruth Margaret, Betty Carol; m. Barbara Allen Moye, Apr. 26, 2003. BSEE, U. Ill., 1949, MSEE, 1950, PhD in Elec. Engring., 1955. Rsch. engr. GE, Syracuse, NY, 1955, Stewart-Warner, Chgo., 1955-58; assoc. prof. U. Ill., Urbana, 1958-68, prof., 1968-89, assoc. head elec. engring., 1970-85, assoc. dean engring., 1985-89; Allied-Signal prof. engring. U. S.C., Columbia, 1990-2000, disting. emeritus engring. prof., 2000; ret., 2000. Program dir. NSF, Washington, 1987-90; chmn. Engring. Accreditation Commn., Accreditation Bd. for Engring. Tech., N.Y.C., 1985-86, pres., 1989-90. Pres. Mckinley Found., Champaign, Ill. 1968-72. Recipient Linton Grinter award Accreditation Bd. Engring. and Tech., 1992. Fellow IEEE (v.p. 1981-82, Centennial medal 1984, EAB Meritorious Achievement award in accreditation activities 1985), AAAS, Accreditation Bd. for Engring. Tech., Internat. Engring. Consortium (bd. dirs.), Am. Soc. for Engring. Edn. (editor Jour. Engring. Edn. 1992-96). Presbyterian. Avocations: photography, reading. Home: Belleville, Ill. Deceased.

ESCH, MARVIN L., former congressman, public affairs consultant; b. Flinton, Pa., Aug. 4, 1927; m. Olga Jurich; children: Emily, Leo, Thomas. AB in Polit. Sci, U. Mich., 1950, MA, 1951, PhD, 1957. Prof. Wayne State U.; also cons. U. Mich.-Wayne State U. Inst. Labor and Indsl. Relations, 1951-64; mem. Mich. Ho. of Reps., 1965-66, US Congress from 2d Dist. Mich., 1967—77; dir. pub. affairs U.S. Steel Corp., Washington, 1977-80; dir. programs and seminars Am. Enterprise Inst., Washington, 1981—87. Rep. candidate for US Senate from Mich., 1976. Emeritus trustee John F. Kennedy Ctr. the Performing Arts. Served with U.S. Army, U.S. Maritime Service, World War II. Republican. Died June 19, 2010.

ESPOSITO, RONALD ANDREW, psychologist; b. Chgo., Jan. 26, 1934; s. Andrew R. and Mary M. (Villani) Esposito; m. Marilyn K. Erickson Esposito, Oct. 5, 1963; children: Andrew, Laura. BA, MS, Southern Ill. U., 1960; PhD, Mich. State U., 1968. Asst. prof. counselor edn. Kent State U., Ohio, 1966—69; coord. Career Edn., RI Coll., 1969—77; founder Career Devel. & Psychol. Svcs., Pawtucke, RI, 1977—91, pres., dir., from 1977; grad. faculty rehab. counseling dept. Assumption Coll., from 1976; clin. assoc. Am. Geriatric Health Svcs. Inc., from 1991; pediat. med. staff St. Joseph Hosp., Providence, 1974—91; appointed psychologist Psychiat. Unit, 1987—91. Pres. Saylesville Sch. PTA, 1972—74, Saylesville Highland Assn., 1974—76; chmn. Lincoln Mental Health Assn., 1974; incorporator, dir. Northern R.I. Mental Health Clinic, 1975—80. Contbr. articles to profl. jours. Served with US Army, 1956—58. Grantee, US Office Edn., 1974—77. Mem.: RI Mental Health Counselors Assn. (pres. 1985—88), Am. Personnel & Guidance Assn. (del. 1972—76, senator 1977—81), RI Pers. & Guidance Assn. (pres. 1974—76), Kappa Delta Pi, Phi Delta Kappa. Home: Lincoln, RI. Died Aug. 19, 2009.

ESSENE, ERIC JOHN, geology educator; b. Berkeley, Calif., Apr. 26, 1939; s. Frank J. Rieva (Blazek) E.; m. Gail Elizabeth Bensman, July 7, 1963 (div. 1981); children: Michelle, Karen; m. Joyce Margaret Budai, Sept. 21, 1985; children: Adam, Zachary. BS, MIT, 1961; PhD, U. Calif., Berkeley, 1967. Rsch. fellow Cambridge Univ., 1966-68, Australian Nat. U., Canberra, 1968-70; asst. prof. U. Mich., Ann Arbor, 1970-76, assoc. prof., 1976-80, prof., from 1980. Author: Reviews in Mineralogy 10, 1982, Reviews in Mineralogy 11, 1983; contbr. chpts. to books. Recipient Univ. Mich. 1st Sokol award for outstanding rsch. program. Fellow Am. Mineral. Soc., Am. Geophys. Union. Avocations: fishing, reading. Home: Ann Arbor, Mich. Died May 20, 2010.

ETTRE, LESLIE STEPHEN, chemist; b. Szombathely, Hungary, Sept. 16, 1922; came to U.S., 1958, naturalized, 1965; s. Stephen and Mary Therese (Dunay) E.; m. Kitty Polonyi, May 16, 1953; 1 child, Julie Suzanne. Diploma Chem. Engring, U. Tech. Scis., Hungary, 1945, D.Tech. Scis. Chemist G. Richter Pharm. Works, Budapest, Hungary, 1946-49; rsch. chemist Rsch. Inst. for Heavy Chem. Industries, Veszprem, Hungary, 1949-51, head tech. office, 1951-53; sr. lectr. chemistry U. Veszprem, 1951-53; head indsl. dept. Research Inst. for Plastics Industry, Budapest, 1953-56; chemist Lurgi Cos., Frankfurt, Fed. Republic Germany, 1957-58; applications chemist Perkin-Elmer Corp., Norwalk, Conn., 1958-60, product specialist, 1960-62, chief applications chemist, 1962-68, sr. staff scientist, 1972-87, sr. scientist, 1987-90. Exec. editor Ency. Indsl. Chem. Analysis John Wiley & Sons, N.Y.C., 1968-72; rsch. assoc. dept. engring. and applied scis. Yale U., New Haven, 1977-78, adj. prof., 1989-95, rsch. affiliate, 1995—2004; adj. prof. U. Houston, 1978-88; chmn. various symposia on chromatography, intermittantly, 1972-93; co-chmn. Summer Symposium on Analytical Chemistry Miami U., Oxford, Ohio, 1973; lectr. in U.S., Can., Europe, Asia, Africa, Australia; participant lecture tours of Chromatography Coun. of Acad. Scis., USSR, 1976, 78, 79, 80, 81, 86, 88, Estonian Acad. Scis., 1979-81, Chinese Acad. Scis., 1980, 85, 87, Georgian Acad. Sci., 1981. Recipient Commemorative Chromatography medal Acad. Scis., USSR, 1978, M.S. Tswett award, 1978, L.S. Palmer award Minn. Chromatography Forum, 1980, A.J.P. Martin award Brit. Chromatography Discussion Group, 1982, Outstanding Svc. award Western Carolinas Chromatography Discussion Group, 1987, M.J.E. Golay award Internat. Symposium on Capillary Chromatography, 1992, Jubilee award, 1998, Golden Diploma U. Tech. Scis., Budapest, 1995, Diamond Diploma, 2005, Dimick award Pitts. Conf. on Analytical Chemistry and Applied Spectroscopy, 1998, Cs Horvath award Conn. Separations Sci. Coun., 2001. Fellow Am. Inst. Chemists; mem. ASTM (chmn. subcom. rsch. com. E-19, 1966-70, subcom. on nomenclature of com. E-19, 1970-73), Am. Chem. Soc. (award in chromatography 1985), Chromatography Soc. (exec. com. 1982-89), N.Y. Acad. Scis., Internat. Union Pure and Applied Chemistry (nomenclature com. 1981-91), Hungarian Chem. Soc. (hon.; Heureka award 2001). Died June 1, 2010.

EVAN, WILLIAM MARTIN, sociologist, educator; b. Ostrow, Poland, Dec. 17, 1922; BA, U. Pa., 1946; PhD, Cornell U., 1954. Instr. sociology Princeton U., 1954-56; asst. prof. Columbia U., 1956-59; research sociologist Bell Telephone Labs., Murray Hill, NJ, 1959-62; assoc. prof. sociology and mgmt. MIT, 1962-66; prof. U. Pa., Phila., from 1966. Ford vis. prof. sociology Grad. Sch. Bus., U. Chgo., 1971-72; vis. fellow Wolfson Coll., U. Oxford, 1978-79; cons.in field Author: (with others) Preventing World War III, 1962, Law and Sociology, 1962, Organizational Experiments, 1971, Interorganizational Relations, 1976, Organization Theory, 1976, Frontiers in Organization and Management, 1980, The Sociology of Law, 1980, Knowledge and Power in a Global Society, 1981, The Arms Race and Nuclear War, 1987, Social Structure and Law, 1990, Organization Theory: Research and Design, 1993, (with Ved P. Nanda) Nuclear Proliferation and the Legality of Nuclear Weapons, 1995, (with Mark Manion, in Chinese) Minding the Machines: Preventing Technological Disasters, 2002, War and Peace In An Age of Terrorism, 2005. Social Sci. Rsch. Coun. tng. fellow, 1951-52, Fulbright fellow, 1952-53; Russell Sage Found. resident, 1956-58. Fellow AAAS; mem. Am. Sociol. Assn., Internat. Sociol. Assn., Internat. Inst. Mgmt. Scis., Law and Soc. Assn., Internat. Studies Assn., Fulbright Assn., U. Pa. Faculty Club, Phila. Art Alliance. Home: Swarthmore, Pa. Died Dec. 25, 2009.

EVANS, FRANK EDWARD, former United States Representative from Colorado; b. Pueblo, Colo., Sept. 6, 1923; s. Frank Edward and Mildred Hoag Evans; m. Eleanor Trefz, 1952; children: Peter, Susan, Frances, Charles. BA, U. Denver, 1948; LLB, U. Denver Law Sch., 1950. Mem. Colo. House of Reps., Colo., 1961—65, US Congress from 3rd Colo. Dist., Colo., 1965—79. Served in USN, 1943—46. Democrat. Presbyterian. Home: Pueblo, Colo. Died June 8, 2010.

EVANS, JOHN, sugar company executive, lawyer; b. Jan. 13, 1932; m. Julia Shields. AB, U. Va., 1953; LL.B., George Washington U., 1958, LL.M., 1959. Bar: D.C. 1958, Colo. 1961, Calif. 1972. Sr. v.p., sec. Holly Sugar Corp., Colorado Springs, Colo., 1961-72, gen. counsel, from 1981, also bd. dirs. Sec., gen. counsel Imperial Holly Corp., Sugar Land, Tex.; bd. dirs. HSC Export Corp. div. Holly Sugar Corp., Colo. Springs. Member Order of Coif Died Sept. 2, 2009.

EVANS, ROBERT WARD WILLARD, psychiatrist, psychoanalyst; b. Lynchburg, Va., Aug. 7, 1914; s. Robert Gold and Jennie Willis (Canada) E. BS, Va. Mil. Inst., 1935; MD, U. Va., 1939; postgrad., Washington U., St. Louis, 1940-42, Columbia U., 1948-49; postgrad. in child psychoanalysis, Anna Freud Ctr. London, 1970-74. Diplomate Am. Bd. Psychiatry and Neurology. Intern in internal medicine Hosp. of U. Va., 1939-40; resident in psychiatry and child psychiatry Psychiat. Inst., Columbia U. and Kings County Hosp., N.Y., 1948-51; pvt. practice N.Y., 1951-70, New Haven, from 1974; prin. child psychiatrist St. Vincent's Hosp., NYC, 1963-65; attending physician in pediatrice Yale-New Haven Hosp., from 1974; clin. prof. psychiatry Child Study Ctr. Yale U., New Haven, from 1974. Instr. in cytology Washington U., 1940-42; assoc. in psychiatry Columbia U., N.Y.C., 1951-70; dir. Children's Day Treatment Ctr. and Sch., N.Y., 1965-70; cons. Superior Ct. for Juvenile Matters, New Haven, 1974— Contbr. articles to profl. publs. Lt. col. Med. Corps, U.S. Army, 1942-48. Decorated Legion of Merit. Mem. Am. Psychiat. Assn., Am. Acad. Child Psychiatry, Assn. for Child Psychoanalysis, Western New Eng. Psychoanalytic Soc. and Inst., Conn. Coun. Child Psychiatrists, Med. Soc. of County of N.Y., New Haven Colony Hist. Soc., Univ. Club. Episcopalian. Home: North Branford, Conn. Died May 13, 2010.

EVANS, ROGER, lawyer; b. Syracuse, NY, Apr. 18, 1951; s. David Longfellow and Louise Maude (Crawford) Evans; children: Jonathan Longfellow, Gillian Crawford, Catherine Leigh, Skylar Elizabeth. AB, Cornell U., 1974; postgrad., Columbia U., 1976-77; JD, Harvard U., 1977. Bar: Ohio 1977, U.S. Dist. Ct. (no. dist.) Ohio 1978, Tex. 1981, U.S. Dist. Ct. (no. dist.) Tex. 1981, U.S. Dist. Ct. (so. dist.) Tex. 1997, U.S. Ct. Appeals (5th, 6th and 11th cirs.) 1981, U.S. Ct. Appeals (10th cir.) 1982, U.S. Tax Ct. 1989, U.S. Dist. Ct. (we. and ea. dists.) Tex. 1998. Assoc. Jones, Day, Reavis & Pogue, Cleve., 1977-81, Dallas, 1981-84; ptnr. Shank, Irwin & Conant, Dallas, 1985, Gardner, Carton & Douglas, Dallas,

1986-88, Vinson & Elkins, Dallas, 1988-91; pvt. practice Dallas, 1991-2001; ptnr. Mathis & Donheiser, Dallas, from 2001. Gen. counsel Equest, Inc., Dallas, 1986—88; instr. trial advocacy, instr. law and econs. So. Meth. U. Sch. Law; instr. labor law Baylor U.; faculty Nat. Inst. Trial Advocacy. Author: Old Buck, 2006. Gen. counsel, bd. dirs. Freedom Ride Found., Dallas, 1985-86; cmty. svcs. bd. mgmt. YMCA, 1990-92; bd. dirs. Legal Svcs. Corp. North Tex., 1991-92; adv. bd. dirs. Providence Christian Sch. Tex., Inc., 1995-2000. Recipient Advocacy award, Dallas Epilepsy Assn., 1995. Mem. Tex. Bar Assn., Dallas Bar Assn., Cornell U. Alumni Assn. (class pres. 1984-89), Harvard U. Law Sch. Alumni Assn. No. Ohio (sec. 1978-81), Harvard Club. Died Aug. 14, 2009.

EVERETT, ROBERT GEORGE, food company executive; b. Binghamton, NY, Mar. 15, 1931; s. Robert L. and Madeline E.; m. Betty J. Whitten, Sept. 9, 1950; children: Elizabeth, Karen, Robert, Thomas. BS in Accounting, Harpur Coll., 1953; MBA, Cornell U., 1955. Various financial positions up to div. controller, corporate dir. financial planning IBM, 1955-69; exec. v.p. Great Western United Corp., Denver, 1969-72, pres., 1972-75; exec. v.p. Fisher Foods, Inc., Beford Heights, Ohio, 1977-79, vice chmn. bd., chief fin. officer, 1979-84, pres., 1981-84; exec. v.p. Lifestyle Restaurants, Inc., from 1984. Served with USNR, 1949-54. Mem. Fin. Execs. Inst. Clubs: Larchmont Shore, Larchmont Yacht. Home: Larchmont, NY. Died Feb. 12, 2010.

EVERITT, CHARLES BELL, publishing executive; b. NYC, May 24, 1935; s. C. Raymond and Helen (Goetzmann) E.; m. Susan Hannah Goetz, Nov. 6, 1965; 1 child, Timothy Spencer. BA, Yale U. Asst. news editor Pubs.' Weekly, NYC, 1960-63; mng. editor Little, Brown & Co., Boston, 1963-70, dir. pub. rels., 1971-74, assoc. editor, 1974-77; treas., founder World Paper, Boston, 1977-79; pres. Glove Pequot Press, Inc., Boston, from 1979; also bd. dirs. Editor: The Tavern at 100, over 150 others; contbr. articles to profl. publs. Mem. Siasconset Casino Assn., Essex County Club (past gov.), Tavern Club (bd. dirs.). Democrat. Avocations: reading, ski racing, tennis. Home: Manchester, Mass. Died July 11, 2010.

EVERITT, GEORGE BAIN, retired banker; b. Forest Hills, L.I., NY, Apr. 21, 1914; s. George B. and Lois E. (Richter) E.; m. Barbara Taylor, Mar. 25, 1944; children: Lois V., Margaret M. (Mrs. Manfred Gerling), Emily A., Elizabeth S. Caldwell. BA, Duke, 1936. With Sears, Roebuck & Co., 1936; with Merchandise Nat. Bank of Chgo., 1936-88, asst. v.p., 1941-49, dir., 1946-88, v.p., 1949-60, pres., 1960-65, chmn. bd., 1965-88, ret. Sec. Hadley Sch. for Blind, Winnetka, Ill., 1950-64, v.p., 1964—. Served with USNR, 1942-46. Mem. North Side Bankers Assn. (past pres.) Home: Chanhassen, Minn. Died Oct. 11, 2009.

EVERY, RUSSEL B., business executive; b. Bridgewater, Mich., Oct. 13, 1924; s. William Ward and Ola M. (Bennet) E.; m. Marion J. Olson, May 12, 1945; children— Gloria, David, William. Student, Cleary Coll. With Midland-Ross Corp., 1969-76, v.p., gen. mgr. frame div., group v.p. automotive, until 1976; co-organizer Midland Steel Products Co., Cleve., 1976; with Midsco, Inc. (merged into Lamson & Sessions Co.), Lakewood, Ohio, chmn., pres. Cleve., from 1979, pres., chief operating officer, 1984-88; chmn., chief exec. officer Lamson & Sessions Co., Cleve., from 1988, chmn. bd. Bd. dirs. Bearings, Inc. Trustee Fairview Gen. Hosp., YMCA; div. chairperson United Way Campaign; mem. Bus. Roundtable No. Ohio; pres.'s coun. Machinery and Allied Products Inst. With USN. Mem. Am. Mgmt. Assn., Ohio Mfrs. Assn., Ohio C. of C., Greater Cleve. Growth Assn., Presidents Assn., Soc. Automotive Engrs., U.S. C. of C., Union Club, Pepper Pike (Ohio) Country Club. Home: Osprey, Fla. Died Jan. 4, 2010.

EVITT, WILLIAM ROBERT, emeritus geology educator; b. Balt., Dec. 9, 1923; s. Raymond W. and Elsa (Schwarz) E.; m. Gisela Cloos, July 29, 1950; children: Eric R., Steven D., Glenn M. AB, Johns Hopkins, 1942; PhD, 1950. Instr. U. Rochester, 1948- 51, asst. prof. geology, 1951-55, asso. prof., 1955-56, acting chmn. dept. geology, 1955-56; sr. research geologist Jersey Prodn. Research Co., Tulsa, 1956-59, research assoc., 1959-62; vis. prof. Stanford U., 1961, prof. geology, 1962-85, emeritus prof., from 1986. Vis. sr. research scientist Continental Shelf Inst., Oslo, 1976 Served to capt. USAF, 1943-46. Decorated Bronze Star. Fellow Calif. Acad. Scis., Geol. Soc. Am.; mem. Am. Assn. Stratigraphic Palynologists (Sci. Excellence award 1982, hon. mem. 1989), Paleontol. Soc. (editor 1953-56, v.p. 1957) Home: Palo Alto, Calif. Died Mar. 22, 2009.

FA'ARMAN, ALFRED, engineer, applied physicist; b. NY, Nov. 29, 1917; s. Isidor and Becky (Mendelssohn) Pfaffarmann; m. Mildred Maisel, 1942 (div. 1969); children; David S., Lawrence M. BA in Physics cum laude, Bklyn. Coll., 1939; PhD in Physics, NYU, 1955. Registered profl. engr., Calif.; registered patent agt. Rsch. contract adminstr. Office Naval Rsch., NYC, 1946-49; rsch. assoc. physics dept. NYU, NYC, 1949-55; mem. tech. staff Hughes Rsch. Labs., LA, 1955-71; patent engr. Lawrence Radiation Lab., Livermore, Calif., 1972-74; cons. applied physics and engring. Applied Physics Cons., Castro Valley, Calif., from 1975. Info. sys. coord., telecom. Calif. Pub. Utilities Commn., San Francisco, 1980—; part-time lectr. UCLA, 1955-66. Author: Electronic Components in Radiation Environments: Designers Handbook, 1968; contbr. articles to profl. and tech. jours. 1st lt. U.S. Army, 1943-46. Recipient Founders Day award, NYU, 1958. Mem. Am. Phys. Soc., Am. Assn. Physics Tchrs., Propylaea, Sigma Xi. Home: Oakland, Calif. Died Jan. 17, 2009.

FABIETTI, VICTOR ARMANDO, accountant; b. Roccamorice, Abruzzi, Italy, June 18, 1920; came to U.S., 1930; s. Agostino and Maria C. (Pietrangelo) F.; m. Alda Lorraine Santini, Sept. 13, 1952; twin daughters, 1 son. Student, Camden Comml. Coll., NJ, 1947-49. CPA, N.J. Owner V.A. Fabietti & Co. CPAs, Atlantic City, N.J., 1958-90; chmn. Premium Fed. Savs. Bank, Gibbsboro, N.J., from 1987, also bd. dirs., 1987-91. Bd. dirs. Atlantic Nat. Bank, Atlantic City, 1970-82. Mem. congl. staff Thomas C. McGrath, 1978; comdr. Richard S. Somers Soc., Atlantic City, 1988. Sgt. maj. U.S. Army, 1942-46, ETO. Decorated Bronze Medals, Croix de Guerre (France). Fellow N.J. Soc. CPAs; mem. AICP, AICPA Divsn. for CPA Firms, Phila. Estate Planning Coun. Republican. Roman Catholic. Avocations: walking, cooking, writing, reading. Home: Margate City, NJ. Died Jan. 13, 2009.

FABRICAND, BURTON PAUL, physicist, researcher; b. NYC, Nov. 22, 1923; s. Irving Kermit and Frances (Sobler) F.; m. Heather C. North, Dec. 15, 1972; children by previous marriage: Nicole Diane, Lorraine Stewart. AB, Columbia U., 1947, A.M., 1949, PhD, 1953. Project engr. Philco Corp., Phila., 1952-54; lectr., research asso. U. Pa., 1954-56; sr. research scientist Columbia Hudson Labs., Dobbs Ferry, NY, 1957-69; prof. physics Pratt Inst., Bklyn., 1969-92, prof. emeritus, from 1992; mng. ptnr. Fabricand Assocs., from 1970. Cons. Moore Sch. Elec. Engring., U. Pa., 1954-60, Indsl. Electronic Hardware Corp., N.Y.C., 1960-64; investment mgr. Beating the Street Fund, 1996—; bd. dirs. Murphey, Marseilles, Smith & Nammack, N.Y.C. Author: Horse Sense: A New and Rigorous Application of Mathematical Methods to Successful Betting at the Track, 1965, Beating the Street, 1969, Horse Sense: Updated and Expanded Edition, 1976, The Science of Winning: A Random Walk on the Road to Riches, 1979, Abolish the Income Tax: A New and Rigorous Inquiry into the Wealth of Nations, 1986, Symmetry in Free Markets in Symmetry—Unifying Human Understanding, 1989, The Science of Winning: A Random Walk Along the Road to Investment Riches, 1996, 2002, American History Through the Eyes of Modern Chaos Theory, 2007; contbr. numerous articles on atomic and nuclear physics and oceanography. Served U.S. Army, 1942-46. Mem. Am. Phys. Soc., Sigma Xi. Home: New Milford, Conn. Died May 5, 2009.

FAIRCHILD, RAYMOND EUGENE, oil industry executive; b. Bowling Green, Ohio, June 25, 1923; s. Ira Ethalbert and Bessie Louise (Gearhart) F.; m. Eleanor Faith Vaughan, Sept. 1, 1973. BS, Ohio U., 1948; MS, U. Mo., 1950. Dist. geologist Pan Am. Prodn. Co., Houston, 1950-56; gulf coast divsn. exploration mgr. Pan Handle Eastern subs., Houston, 1956-72; mayor City of Hunter Creek, Tex., 1967-71; exploration mgr. A.P. Moller, Copenhagen, 1973-80; v.p. Hunt Oil Co., Dallas, 1980, former sr. v.p. internat. exploration, ret., 1988. Pres., dir. Mayfair Petroleum Inc., Mayfair Petroleum Corp., Mayfair Environ. Svcs., 1990—. Alderman, City of Hunter Creek, 1962-67; commr. Spring Br. Fire Dept., 1962. Fellow Geol. Soc. London, Am. Assn. Petroleum Geologists; mem. Petroleum Exploration Soc. Gt. Britain, Dansk Geologisk Forening, Gulf Coast Assn. Geol. Socs., Houston Geol. Soc., Dallas Geol. Soc., East Tex. Geol. Soc., Assn. Internat. Petroleum Negotiators, Dallas Petroleum Club. Died Mar. 11, 2009.

FALCONIERI, JOHN VINCENT, university administrator; b. N.Y.C., Feb. 17, 1920; s. Thomas and Catherine (Alessi) F.; m. Diana Nan Reynol, June 11, 1948; children: Thomas, Jonathan, David, Andrea. BA, U. Mich., 1941, MA, 1946, PhD, 1951. Instr. U. Mich., Ann Arbor, 1951-52; asst. prof. Bowling Green State U., Ohio, 1952-58; assoc. prof. Western Res. U., Cleve., 1958-64; prof. SUNY-Albany, 1964-71; dir. Am. U. Rome, Italy, 1979-89. Author: Commedia dell'Arte en Españ a, 1956; Gabriel del Corral, Valladolid, 1968. Contbr. numerous articles to various publs. Sgt. U.S. Army, 1942-46. Newberry Library grantee, 1958; Fulbright scholar, Spain, 1962. Mem. Philos. Soc. Am. Died Jan. 15, 2009.

FALVEY, PATRICK JOSEPH, lawyer; b. Yonkers, NY, June 29, 1927; s. Patrick J. Falvey and Nora Rowley Falvey; m. Eileen Ryan, June 29, 1963; 1 child, Patrick James. Student, Iona Coll., 1944—47; JD cum laude, St. John's U., Jamaica, NY, 1950. Bar: N.Y. 1951, U.S. Supreme Ct. 1972. Law asst. Port Authority of N.Y. and N.J., 1951, atty., 1951-65, chief condemnation and litigation, 1965-67, asst. gen. counsel, 1967-72, gen. counsel, 1972-91, gen. counsel, asst. exec. dir., 1979-87, dep. exec. dir., 1987-91, spl. counsel, from 1991. Advisor U.S. del. to UN Com. on Internat. Trade Law, U.S. State Dept. Pvt. Trade Law; advisor to U.S. del. UN diplomatic confs. on treaty on liability of ops. of transport terminals, N.Y. County Lawyers Assn., 1992—. With USN, 1945-46. Recipient Howard S. Cullman Disting. Svc. medal Port Authority of N.Y. and N.J., 1982, 91; Loftus award and Trustee's Honoree Iona Coll., 1982. Fellow Am. Bar Found.; mem. ABA (chmn. urban state and local govt. law sect. 1983-84, vice-chmn. model procurement code project 1979—, sect. del. 1987-90, Award for Lifetime Achievement in Local Law 2000), Assn. Bar City N.Y., N.Y. County Lawyers Assn. (chmn.), Internat. Assn. Ports and Harbors (hon., legal counsellors, arbitrator, mediator trade and comml. matters, cons. transp. and trade studies). Died Dec. 23, 2009.

FAN, CHANG-YUN, retired physics educator; b. Nantong, Jiangsu, Peoples Republic of China, Jan. 7, 1918; came to U.S., 1947; s. Li-Zhaun and Sze-Shue (Chen) F.; m. Tsung-Ying Teng, Sept. 29, 1950; children: Paula, Anna, Michael. BA, Cen. U., Nanjing, Peoples Republic of China, 1941; MA, U. Chgo., 1950, PhD, 1952. Rsch. assoc. dept. astronomy and astrophysics U. Chgo., Williams Bay, Wis., 1952-57; asst. prof. U. Ark., Fayetteville, 1957-58; sr. physicist, rsch. assoc., prof. U. Chgo., 1958-67; prof. physics U. Ariz., Tucson, 1967-88, prof. emeritus, from 1988. Grantee AEC, 1968-72, NSF, 1971-78, NASA, 1969—. Fellow Am. Phys. Soc.; mem. Am. Geophys. Union. Achievements include development of laboratory experiments on atomic collisions related to auroral excitation, on molecular composition of cosmic dust particles, searching for the origin of life; development of space experiment to measure energetic particles; research on 33P nuclide, new O2 band in auroral emission, high energy electrons near the earth's bow shock, H and He isotopes and anomalous component in primary cosmic radiation, partially stripped ions in solar cosmic rays, 27-day solar recurrent events, Lamb Shift in 6Li2 plus and 16 O2 plus. Home: Tucson, Ariz. Died Jan. 21, 2009.

FANG, JOONG, philosopher, mathematician, educator; b. Piongyang, Korea, Mar. 30, 1923; arrived in U.S., 1948, naturalized, 1962; s. Gabiong and Igab (Kim) Fang; children: Eva Maria, Guido Andreas. Student, Chuo U., Tokyo, 1939-41; BS, Coll. Tech. Seoul, Korea, 1944; MA, Yale U., 1950; PhD, U. Mainz, Germany, 1957. Asst. prof. math. Jinhae Coll., also U. Pusan, Republic of Korea, 1945-48, Valparaiso (Ind.) U., 1958-59, St. John's U., 1959-61, U. Alaska, 1961-62; assoc. prof. No. Ill. U., 1963-67; prof. math. and philosophy Memphis State U., 1967-73; prof. philosophy Old Dominion U., Norfolk, Va., 1974-90, prof. emeritus, 1990. Vis. prof. U. Münster, Germany, 1971. Author: (book) Das Antinomienproblem, 1957, Abstract Algebra, 1963, Kant-Interpretation, I, 1967, Numbers Racket: The Aftermath of the "New Math", 1968, Towards a Philosophy of Modern Mathematics, I, Bourbaki, 1970, II, Hilbert, 1970, Mathematicians from Antiquity to Today, I, 1972, Sociology of Mathematics and Mathematicians, 1975, The Illusory Infinite: A Theology of Mathematics, 1976, Logic Today, Basics and Beyond, 1979, Linguistic Sense of the Japanese (in Japanese), 1984, Kant and Mathematics Today, 1997, Learning, East and West, 2002, Docta Ignorantia, 2003, Ecrasez l'Infame!, 2004; editor: Philosophia Mathematica, 1964—92. Mem.: Am. Philos. Assn., Am. Math. Soc. Died Feb. 16, 2010.

FANTA, PAUL EDWARD, chemist, educator; b. Chgo., July 24, 1921; s. Joseph and Marie (Zitnik) F.; m. LaVergne Danek, Sept. 3, 1949; children: David, John. BS, U. Ill., 1942; PhD, U. Rochester, 1946. Postdoctoral research fellow U. Rochester, 1946-47; instr. Harvard U., 1947-48; mem. faculty Ill. Inst. Tech., 1948—84, prof. chemistry, 1961-84, prof. emeritus, 1984—2010. Exchange scholar Czechoslovak Acad. Sci., Prague, 1963-64, Soviet Acad. Sci., Moscow, 1970-71 Contbr. articles to profl. jours. NSF fellow Imperial Coll., London, Eng., 1956-57 Mem. Am. Chem. Soc., Sigma Xi, Phi Lambda Upsilon. Home: Oak Park, Ill. Died May 3, 2010.

FARBER, MILTON, research chemist; b. N.Y.C., Mar. 11, 1923; s. Max and Lillie (Falkson) F.; m. Cyrille June Solomon, May 31, 1953; children— William M., Abby N., Donald J. B.S. in Chemistry, CUNY, 1942; A.M. in Chemistry, Columbia U., 1947, Ph.D., 1950. Research assoc. Cornell U. Med. Coll., N.Y.C., 1950-54; group leader United Merchants Labs., N.Y.C., 1954-57; research assoc. elastomers and new products group Uniroyal, Inc., Naugatuck, Conn., 1957—. Patentee. Chmn. Bethany Dem. Town Com., 1982-84. Served to cpl. U.S. Army, 1943-46. Mem. Am. Chem. Soc., Sigma Xi, (chmn. Uniroyal chpt., Middlebury, Conn., 1972-73, program chmn. 1966—). Avocations: cross-country skiing; downhill skiing; jogging; gardening; theater. Home: Cheshire, Conn. Died Feb. 17, 2010.

FARLEY, ANDREW NEWELL, lawyer, consultant; b. Brownsville, Pa., Oct. 31, 1934; s. Andrew Polycarp and Sarah Theresa (Landymore) F.; m. Marta Olha Pisetska, May 5, 1963; children— Andrew Daniel, Mark Landymore. AB, Washington and Jefferson Coll., 1956; MPA, U. Pitts., 1962, JD, 1961; diploma, U.S. Army Command and Gen. Staff Coll., 1972, Indsl. Coll. Armed Forces, 1967; grad., U.S. Army War Coll., 1976. Bar: Pa. 1962, U.S. Supreme Ct. 1965. Assoc. Reed Smith Shaw & McClay, Pitts., 1961-65, ptnr., 1966-91; cons. Pitts., from 1992. Bd. dirs. Corp. Devel. USAM Mid-Atlantic and Ohio; mng. dir. USAM-Nat., 1992—; Am. Arbitration Assn. Nat. Panel Comml. Disputes, 1995—; mediator JAMS-Endispute, 1996—; sec.-treas. Internat. Acad. Mediators, 1996-2000; lectr. in fed. jurisprudence and adminstrv. law U. Pitts.; adminstrv. asst. Pa. Atty. Gen., 1959; counsel to Pa. Constl. Conv., 1968; mem. Pa. Atty. Gen.'s Task Force on Adminstrn., 1970; mem. faculty Pa. Bar Inst. Bus. Lawyer Inst., 1999—. Assoc. editor Pitts Legal Jour., 1963— (mem. exec. com.); contbr. articles to profl. jours. Bd. dirs. Ind. Sch. Chmn. Assn., World Affairs Coun., Pitts., Pitts. Opera, 1986-95; sec., bd. dirs. Found. for Calif. U. Pa.,; mem. adv. bd. Western Pa. Advanced Tech. Ctr., Internat. Resuscitation Rsch. Ctr., U. Pitts. Med. Sch., Mon Valley Renaissance; mem. bd. visitors U. Pitts. Grad. Sch. Pub. and Internat. Affairs; trustee Thiel Coll., 1989-95. Brig. gen. U.S. Army. Decorated Meritorious Svc. medals Dept. Def. and US Army, Army Commendation medals; recipient Gubernatorial citation, Commonwealth of Pa., 1978, Omicron Delta Kappa award, 1960, Ukrainian award, 2006, Mayoral citation, 2006; named Mon Valley Renaissance MVP, 1987; Nat. Def. Transp. Assn. fellow, 1956. Mem. Internat. Acad. Mediators, Pa. Bar Assn. (chmn. sect. internat. law, bd. editors, jud. adminstrn. com., statewide computer com. for the cts., alternative dispute resolution com.), In-house Coun. Com., Allegheny County Bar Assn. (fee determination com.), Am. Law Inst., Nat. Health Lawyers Assn., Am. Arbitration Assn., Soc. for Profls. in Dispute Resolution, Assn. U.S. Army (pres. Ft. Pitt chpt., pres. Pa.), Sr. Army Res. Comdrs. Assn. (exec. com.), Pitts. Athletic Assn., Duquesne Club, Pa. State Grange, Masons. Died May 3, 2009.

FARLEY, JOSEPH MCCONNELL, lawyer; b. Birmingham, Ala., Oct. 6, 1927; s. John G. and Lynne (McConnell) F.; m. Sheila Shirley, Oct. 1, 1958 (dec. July 1978); children: Joseph McConnell, Thomas Gager, Mary Lynne. Student, Birmingham-So. Coll., 1944—45; BSME, Princeton U., 1948; postgrad., U. Ala., 1948—49; LLB, Harvard U., 1952, Tuskegee U., 2005; LHD (hon.), Judson Coll., 1974; LLD (hon.), U. Ala. at Birmingham, 1983. Bar: Ala. 1952. Served with USNR, 1948—63, ret.; assoc. Martin, Turner, Blakey & Bouldin, Birmingham, 1952-57; ptnr. successor firm Martin,

Balch, Bingham & Hawthorne, 1957-65; exec. v.p., dir. Ala. Power Co., 1965-69, pres., dir., 1969-89; v.p. So. Electric Generating Co., 1970-74, pres., dir., 1974-89; exec. v.p., corp. counsel So. Co., 1991-92, exec. v.p. nuclear, bd. dirs., 1989-90; pres., CEO So. Nuclear Oper. Co., Birmingham, 1990-91, bd. dirs., 1970—92, bd. mem. Birmingham, 1990—92, chmn., CEO, 1991-92, also bd. dirs.; of counsel Balch & Bingham, LLP, Birmingham, from 1993. Mem. exec. bd. Southeastern Electric Reliability Coun., 1980-86, chmn., 1974-76; bd. dirs. Edison Electric Inst.; bd. dirs. Southeastern Electric Exch., pres., 1984; adv. dir. So. Co., 1992-97. Mem. Jefferson County Republican Exec. Com., 1953-65; counsel, mem. Ala. Rep. Com., 1962-65; permanent chmn. Ala. Rep. Conv., 1962; alternate del. Rep. Nat. Conv., 1956; bd. dirs. Ala. Bus. Hall of Fame; chmn. bd. trustees So. Rsch. Inst., 1970-99; trustee Tuskegee U., 1981-2002; trustee Children's Hosp. Birmingham, pres. bd. trustees 1983-85; mem. Pres.'s Cabinet U. Ala.-Tuscaloosa; bd. visitors U. Ala. Sch. Commerce, chmn., 1991-93. Mem. ABA, NAM (bd. dirs. 1987-92), Ala. Bar Assn., Birmingham Bar Assn., Inst. Nuclear Power Ops. (bd. dirs. 1982-89, chmn. 1987-89), U.S. Coun. for Energy Awareness (bd. dirs. 1985-92), Am. Nuclear Energy Coun. (chmn. bd. dirs. 1987-92), Newcomen Soc. N.Am., Birmingham Country Club, Shoal Creek Club, The Club, Mountain Brook Club, Summit Club, Rotary, Phi Beta Kappa, Kappa Alpha, Tau Beta Pi, Beta Gamma Sigma (hon.). Episcopalian. Died May 2010.

FARRAR, AILI R., cartographic draftsperson; b. Chester, Vt., Sept. 21, 1925; d. Erland Fabian and Amanda Matilda (Kangas) Raitanen; m. Arthur Paul Farrar, Nov. 1, 1943; children: Ronald, Russel, Roger, Reginald. Student, C.C. of Vt. Working supr. The Nat. Survey, Chester, Vt., from 1951; real estate broker Aili Farrar Real Estate, Chester, from 1972; Vt. state legislator, 1989-96. Mem. Chester Planning Commn., H.S. Bd.; mem. legal commn. Vt. Farm Bur., 1997. Mem. Windsor County Farm Bureau (trustee 1991-95, auditor 1995-97), Chester Historical Soc. (pres. 1996-97), Chester Review Club (co-pres.). Democrat. Lutheran. Home: Chester, Vt. Died July 1, 2009.

FARRINGTON, WILLIAM ERNEST, art and design educator, calligrapher; b. Nappanee, Ind., Apr. 15, 1932; s. Lloyd Maxwell Farrington and Marie Anna Krauter; m. Susanne Gail Fried, Mar. 16, 1940; children: Adam Ernest, Berry Elizabeth. BFA, Ball State U., 1955; cert. in fine arts, The Cooper Union, NYC, 1963; MFA, Pratt Inst., Bklyn., 1968. Designer of kitchens Mutschler Bros., Inc., Nappanee, 1950-52; assoc. gallery dir. Ball State U. Art Gallery, Muncie, Ind., 1952-55, 58-59; asst. mgr. Weyhe Gallery, NYC, 1959-63; art dir. Germaine Monteil, NYC, 1965-67; prof. fine arts and graphic design N.Y. Inst. Tech., NYC, 1965-67, Old Westbury, from 1968. Artist-in-residence, Gulf & Western, Altos de Chavon, La Romana, Dominican Republic, 1983. Dir. Sea Cliff (N.Y.) Civic Assn., 1970-77. With U.S. Army, 1956-58, Germany. Recipient Horrt Meml. Purchase award, Ft. Lauderdale (Fla.) Art Ctr., 1961, White Cap Cmty. Svc. award Sea Cliff Civic Assn., 1972, Distinctive Svc. in Edn. award N.Y. Club Printing Ho. Craftsmen, 1989. Mem. AAUP, Assn. Calligraphic Arts, Island Scribes (founder All L.I. Calligraphers Show 1993—, exhibits chair 1990-97), Suffolk Scribes (pres. 1990-94), Soc. Scribes, Ltd. (N.Y.C.; dir. Young Calligraphers Competition 1988-94, dir. 1980-90), Bow Valley Calligraphers Guild (Alta., Can.). Democrat. Unitarian-Universalist. Avocations: bicycling, canoeing and kayaking, camping, hiking, cross country skiing. Home: Hamilton, NY. Died Feb. 4, 2009.

FASANELLA, ROCKO MICHAEL, ophthalmologist; b. Trenton, NJ, Aug. 4, 1916; MD, Yale U., 1943; postgrad. in Ophthalmology, U. Pa., 1946-47, Lancaster Course Ophthalmology, 1947-48. Intern Grace-Comty. Hosp., New Haven, Conn., 1943-44, asst. resident in ophthalmology, 1948-49, resident in ophthalmology, 1949-50; rotating intern Mercer Hosp., Trenton, N.J., 1946-47; cons. St. Raphael's Hosp., New Haven, Conn., 1950, Waterbury (Conn.) Hosp., 1950; staff mem. Windham Comty. Meml. Hosp., 1950, instr., 1950-51, chief ophthalmology sect., 1951-61; assoc. clin. prof. ophthalmology Yale U., New Haven, 1961-86. Cons. Office of Hearings and Appeals, Social Security Adminstrn., Washington Editor: (books) Management of Complications in Eye Surgery, 1st edit., 1957, 2d edit., 1965, Eye Surgery--Innovations and Trends, Pitfalls and Complications, 1977, Modern Advances in Cataract Surgery, Chemical Zonulysis in Cataract Surgery, 1965; contbr. numerous articles to profl. jours. Capt. med. corps Army U.S., 1944-46. Assoc. fellow Ezra Stiles Coll. Fellow AMA (life), Am. Assn. Ophthalmologists and Otolaryngologists; mem. Soc. Francaise d' Ophthal., Soc. Americana de Oft, Pan Am. Ophthal. Found., Glaucoma Soc. Eng., Opthal. Soc., Castroviejo Soc.-Inst. Barraquer-SES (charter), Am. Soc. Ophthalmic, Plastic and Reconstructive Surgery (charter F., Carribean Ophthal. Soc. (founder), Oxford Ophthalmol. Congress, Am. Acad. Ophthalmology and Otolaryngology, Pan. Am. Acad. Ophthalmology and Otolaryngology, Pan Pacific Soc. Ophthalmology, N.Y. Soc. for Clin. Ophthalmology, New Haven Med. Soc., New Haven Med. Assn., New Haven County Med. Assn., Conn. State Med. Soc. Home: Scituate, Mass. Died Feb. 11, 2009.

FASI, FRANK FRANCIS, former mayor; b. East Hartford, Conn., Aug. 27, 1920; m. Florence Ohama (div.); children: Toni, Cappy, Francesca, Carl, Paul; m. Joyce Kono; children: Gina, Gioia, Charles, Frank, David, Salvador. BS, Trinity Coll., Hartford, 1942. Mem. Hawaii Senate, 1959; mayor City and County of Honolulu, 1969—84, 1984—94; owner Property & Bus., Honolulu, 1995. Mem. Dem. Nat. Com. for Hawaii, 1952-56; del. 2d Constl. Conv., 1968; mem.-at-large Honolulu City Coun., 1965-69; non-partisan candidate for Mayor of Honolulu, 2000. Served to capt. USMCR., 1941-44 Mem. Pacific-Asian Congress Municipalities (founder, past pres., exec. dir.), VFW (former comdr. Hawaii dept.), AFTRA (past v.p.). Republican. Home: Honolulu, Hawaii. Died Feb. 3, 2010.

FATELEY, WILLIAM GENE, chemist, educator, inventor; b. Franklin, Ind., May 17, 1929; s. Nolan William and Georgia (Scott) F.; m. Wanda Lee Glover, Sept. 1, 1953; children: Leslie Kaye, W. Scott, Kevin L., Jonathan H., Robin L. AB, Franklin Coll., Ind., 1951, DSc (hon.), 1965; postgrad., Northwestern U., Evanston, Ill., 1951—53, U. Minn., 1956—57; PhD, Kans. State U., Manhattan, 1956. Head phys. measurement Dow Chem. Co., Williamsburg, Va., 1958—60; fellow Mellon Inst., Pitts., 1960—62, head sci. rels., 1962—64, asst. to pres., 1964—67, sr. fellow in ind. rsch., 1965—72, asst. to v.p. for rsch., 1967—72; prof. chemistry Carnegie-Mellon U., Pitts., 1970—72; prof., head dept. chemistry Kans. State U., 1972—79, Univ. Disting. prof., from 1989; vis. prof. chem. dept. U. Tokyo, 1973, 1981; pres. D.O.M. Assocs. Internat., from 1979, 3LC, Inc., 1999. Dir. Pitts. Conf. on Analytical Chemistry and Applied Spectroscopy, 1964-65, pres., 1970-71; editor Jour. Applied Spectroscopy, 1974-94, Raman Newsletter, also fin. chmn., steering com. for interferometry; pres., CEO Three LC, Inc., 1999; bd. dirs., co-founder Plain Sight Sys.; vis. prof. dept. chemistry Tokyo U., 1972, 79, 81; vis. prof. U. Ariz., 1997, 99, Yale U., 2002-03. Author: Infrared and Raman Selection Rules, 1973, Characteristic Raman Frequencies, 1974, Fundamentals in General Chemistry, 1983, Handbook on Characteristic Infrared and Raman Frequencies, 1991, Silence or Fiction 10% Rosedog Books, 2008, also numerous sci. papers.; contbr. articles to profl. jours. Chmn. SAFEGUARD com. U.S. Army, 1999. Recipient Coblentz award for outstanding contbn. to molecular spectroscopy Coblenta Soc., 1965, Spectroscopy award Pitts. Conf. Analytical Chemistry and Applied Spectroscopy, 1976, H.H. King award, 1979, U.S. EPA citation for excellence in atmospheric measurements, 1993, Near Infrared award Ea. Analytical Symposium, 1995, Hassler awrd Pitts. Conf., 2000; named 1st outstanding grad. in chemistry Kans. State U., 1964, Most Disting. Alumni, Franklin Coll., 2008. Fellow Optical Soc. Am., Coblentz Soc. (hon.); mem. Am. Chem. Soc. (pres. phys.-inorganic sect. Pitts. 1969-70), Soc. Applied Spectroscopy (hon. mem., Disting. Svc. award 1987, Gold medal 1987, T.H.E. award in Sci. 1987), Phi Beta Kappa, Sigma Xi (award in rsch. 1991), Sigma Alpha Epsilon, Phi Lambda Epsilon, Pi Mu Epsilon. Home: Green Valley, Ariz. Died July 30, 2009.

FEDER, ALLAN APPEL, retired food products executive; b. Chgo., Aug. 6, 1931; s. Tobias M. and Belle (Appel) F.; m. Joan Feldman, Nov. 19, 1961; children: Steven, Michael, Lisa, Valerie. BS, Syracuse U., 1952; MBA, U. Pa., 1953. With Topps Chewing Gum, Inc., Duryea, Pa., 1965-70; gen. ops. mgr., v.p. mfg. Life Savers subs. Squibb Corp., NYC, 1970-72, exec. v.p. Dobbs Life Savers subs., 1972-73; pres. Dobbs Houses, Inc., Memphis, 1973-76; pres. mfg. group, also corp. sr. exec. v.p. and dir. Gt. Atlantic & Pacific Tea Co. Inc., Montvale, N.J., 1976-82; mgmt. cons., from 1982; pres., CEO Vitarroz Corp., 1988-96, dir., 1988-2000, vice chmn., CEO, 1996-2000; also bd. dirs. Bd. dirs. Edward Don & Co., The Topps Co.; ind. cons. Bd. dirs., mem. exec. com. Fla. West Coast Symphony Orch.; bd. dirs., v.p. Sarasota-Manatee Jewish Fedn.; bd. dirs. Sarasota-Manatee Jewish Cmty. Ctr., Jewish Housing Coun. Home: Osprey, Fla. Died Feb. 22, 2009.

FEHR, KENNETH MANBECK, retired computer company executive; b. Schuylkill Haven, Pa., Feb. 21, 1927; s. Theodore E. and Eva (Manbeck) F.; m. Jean Alice Greenawalt, June 28, 1952; children: K. Craig, Karen Jean, K. Todd. BS, Pa. State U., State College, 1951; MBA, U. Pitts., 1953. With U.S. Steel Corp., 1951-62, div. controller, 1962; controller Interlake Steel Corp., Chgo., 1962-68; v.p. fin. Hallicrafters Co., 1968-71, E.W. Bliss Co., Salem, Ohio, 1971-74; treas. Alliance Machine Co., Ohio, 1974-86; pres. I.M.S. Corp., Hudson, Ohio, 1986-90, Fehr & Greenawalt Investments, Salem, Ohio, from 1990, Salem Security Storage, LLC, 2002—05. Bd. dirs. Fegreen Inc.; night sch. tchr. U. Pitts., 1956—57. Treas. Salem Renaissance. With USNR, 1945—46. Mem.: Nat. Assn. Accts., Fin. Execs. Inst., Salem Hist. Soc., Salem Preservation Soc., Salem-Golf Club, Kiwanis (chpt. pres.), Masons. Home: Salem, Ohio. Died June 25, 2009.

FEIN, STANLEY, art director; b. N.Y.C., Dec. 21, 1919; s. Joseph M. and Helen (Friedfeld) F.; children— Saul Harold, Barbara Ruth. Student Parsons Sch. Design, 1950. Tchr. Pratt Inst. Evening Sch., Bklyn., 1956-58; art and creative dir. Doremus & Co., N.Y.C., 1958-70, Pesin Sydney Bernard, N.Y.C., 1970—; Phoenix Gallery dir., N.Y.C., 1960-69. Represented in permanent collections NYU, Bank of N.Y.; one-man shows include Phoenix Gallery. Served with U.S. Army, 1942-45, ETO. Recipient 1st prize Wall St. Art Assn., 1960; Cert. of Merit, N.Y. Art Dirs. Club., 1956, 65, Soc. Illustrators, 1970, 71. Home: Brooklyn, NY. Died Nov. 1, 2009.

FEINBERG, JULIUS ARTHUR, judge; b. Newark, Mar. 15, 1915; s. Lewis and Mary (Simon) Feinberg. Studen, Dana Coll., 1934; LLB, Rutgers U., 1937. Bar: NJ 1939. Pvt. practice, Newark, 1946—64; ptnr. Mylod & Feinberg, Bloomfield, NJ, 1964—72; judge NJ County Ct., Essex County, Newark, 1972—77, Superior Ct., Newark, 1977—85, from 1986, dep. atty. gen., 1955—59; asst. prosecutor Essex County, 1959—64; observer McClellan Commn. Hearings Organized Crime, 1959; lectr. criminal trial practice. Chmn. ARC, Newark, 1965—68; trustee Jewish Cmty. Fedn., 1971, Congregation Beth El, South Orange, NJ, from 1984. Mem.: Essex County Bar Assn., NJ Bar Assn., Bloomfield Lawyers Club, Lions (Newark) (pres. 1952). Home: South Orange, NJ. Died Sept. 16, 2009.

FEINSTEIN, NATHAN B., lawyer; b. Phila., Nov. 13, 1929; s. Oscar and Donia (Weiner) F.; m. Joanne S. Polk, Jan. 5, 1959; children: Elliot Abraham, Michael Joel. BA in Polit. Sci., Pa. State U., 1951; LLB, Yale U., 1954. Bar: Pa. 1955, Md. 1988, D.C. 1988, U.S. Ct. Appeals (3d and 4th cirs.), U.S. Supreme Ct. 1981. Law clk. to Hon. T. McKean Chidsey Pa. Supreme Ct., Phila., 1956-57; assoc., ptnr. Cohen, Shapiro, Polisher, Sheikman and Cohen, Phila., 1957-83; ptnr. Dilworth, Paxson, Kalish and Kauffman, Phila., 1984-87, Piper & Marbury LLP, Washington, 1987-2000, ptnr. emeritus, from 2000, Piper Marbury Rudnick & Wolfe LLP, Washington, from 2001. With US Army, 1954—56. Fellow: ABA (chair bus. bankruptcy com. 1989—93, chair joint com. on bankruptcy ct. structure 1993—97), Am. Coll. Bankruptcy; mem.: Phila. Bar Assn. (chair profl. guidance com. 1980—81), D.C. Bar Assn., Md. Bar Assn., Pa. Bar Assn. (chair com. on legal ethics and profl. responsibility 1983—84). Democrat. Jewish. Home: Baltimore, Md. Died May 31, 2009.

FEIT, EUGENE P., lawyer; b. NYC, Jan. 16, 1948; children: Daniel, Salena. BA, CCNY, 1969; JD, U. Calif., 1972. Bar: Calif. 1973, N.Y. 1974. Assoc. Shearman & Stirling, NYC, 1972-75, Arthur Dry & Kalish, NYC, 1975-81, ptnr., 1981-84; litigation counsel Uniroyal Inc., Middlebury, Conn., 1984-85; assoc. Herzfeld & Rubin, P.C., NYC, 1985-88, ptnr., from 1989. Pres., bd. trustees Croton Free Libr., Croton-on-Hudson, N.Y., 1983-85. Recipient Leading Def. Verdict awrd ABA, 1988. Mem. N.Y. State Bar Assn. (ho. of dels. 1980-84), Calif. State Bar, Assn. Bar City N.Y. (chair com. state legislation 1975-80, mem. com. on product liaility 1985-88). Avocations: history, skiing, sailing. Died Aug. 19, 2010.

FELABOM, LOREN WAYNE, SR., college administrator, consultant; b. Mishawaka, Ind., July 9, 1933; s. Alden Merrit and Ida May (Airgood) Felabom; m. Kathleen Jeanette Anderson, Sept. 7, 1952; children: Loren, Kathleen, Pamela, Julie. BSBA, Ind. U.-South Bend, 1968; MBA, Mich. State U., 1973; cert. in data processing and computers, IBM, Dept. Def. Cert. vocat. tchr. Ind. Instr., programmer South Bend Comml. Sch., 1963—67; supr. adminstrv. svcs. Bendix Corp., South Bend, 1952—60, 1967—74; bus. mgr. Miami Christian Coll., 1974—78; controller Mercy Coll., Detroit, 1978—79; assoc. dean bus. affairs Prince George's Cmty. Coll., Largo, Md., 1979—82; v.p. for adminstr. Cochise Coll., Douglas, Ariz., from 1983. Deacon First Bapt. Ch., Mishawaka, 1968—72; cons. Capitol Bapt. Ch., Largo, 1982; chmn., deacon First Bapt. Ch., Bisbee, Ariz., 1984—85, deacon ch. fin. com., from 1989. With USNR, 1951—59. Mem.: Ariz. Assn. Cmty. Coll. Adminstrn. (treas. 1986—88), Ariz. Assn. Coll., Bus. Ofcls. (sec. 1984—85, v.p. 1985—86, pres. 1986—87, treas. 1986—88), Nat. Assn. Colls. and Univ. Bus. Officers. Republican. Died Apr. 11, 2009.

FELD, MICHAEL STEPHEN, physics professor; b. NYC, Nov. 11, 1940; s. Albert and Lillian R. Norwalk; m. Alison M. Hearn; children: David A., Jonathan R., Alexandra A. SB in Humanities and Sci., MIT, 1963, SM in Physics, 1963; PhD in Physics, M.I.T., 1967. Postdoctoral fellow MIT, Cambridge, 1967-68, asst. prof., 1968-73, assoc. prof., 1973-79, prof. physics, from 1979, dir. George R. Harrison Spectroscopy Lab., from 1976, dir. Laser Research Ctr., from 1979; dir. Laser Biomed. Research Ctr., from 1985. Co-editor: Fundamental and Applied Laser Physics, 1973, Coherent Nonlinear Optics, 1980. Alfred P. Sloan rsch. fellow, 1973; recipient Disting. Svc. award MIT Minority Cmty., 1980, Gordon Y. Billard award, 1982, Thompson award Spectrochimica Acta, 1991, Vinci d'Excellence, France, 1995, Disting. Baltzer Colloquim spkr. Princeton U., 1996, Lamb medal Physics of Quantum Electronics Soc., 2003. Fellow: AAAS, Am. Optical Soc., Am. Phys. Soc., Am. Soc. Laser Medicine and Surgery (bd. dirs.), Sigma Xi. Died Apr. 10, 2010.

FELDMAN, ARNOLD, radiological physicist; b. Allentown, Pa., Apr. 12, 1924; s. Herman and Lillian (Krakusin) F.; m. Adele Eskind, Mar. 25, 1945 (div. 1972); children: Helen (dec.), Ethan; m. Sybil Frances Quinlan, Nov. 8, 1973. BS, Pa. State U., 1944; MS, Calif. Inst. Tech., 1948; PhD, U. Colo., Denver, 1960. Cert. radiol. physics Am. Bd. Radiology. Rsch. asst. S.A.M. Labs. (Manhattan Dist. Project), NYC, 1944; physics asst. Mayo Clinic, Rochester, Minn., 1948-51; faculty radiology dept. U. Colo. Med. Sch., Denver, 1951-64; cons., staff mem. Mayo Clinic, Rochester, 1964-68; faculty radiol. dept. Washington U. Sch. Medicine, St. Louis, 1968-73; radiol. physicist Midwest Radiation Therapy Cons., Ltd., Peoria, Ill., from 1973. Vis. scientist Radiol. Physics Ctr., Houston, 1973; mem., chmn. Radiologic Tech. Accreditation Bd., Ill. Dept. Nuclear Safety, Springfield, Ill., 1985-86; mem. task group Joint Commn. on Accreditation of Hosps., Chgo., 1986-87. Contbr. articles to profl. jours. Bd. dirs. Peoria (Ill.) chpt. ACLU, pres., 1985-87; mem. Manhattan Dist. Project at N.Y. and Los Alamos, N.Mex. With U.S. Army, 1944-46. Fellow Am. Coll. Radiology, 1956, Am. Assn. Physicists in Medicine, 1989, spl. fellow Nat. Cancer Inst., 1962-63; recipient Annual Merit award Chgo. Assn. Technological Socs., 1991. Mem. Peoria Optimist Club, B'nai B'rith. Democrat. Jewish. Achievements include rsch. in cobalt-60 dose calibration; in energy determination for electron-beam calibration; in measurement of electron-beam energy with R-P film; in compensation for tissue inhomogeneity in Co-60 teletherapy. Home: Peoria, Ill. Died Jan. 23, 2009.

FELLERS, RAYMOND, retired publisher; b. Bklyn., Nov. 6, 1923; s. Jack and Sylvia (Sperber) F.; m. Ellen Bogner, June 19, 1948; children: Jill, Alison. BA, George Washington U., 1950; MA, Seton Hall U., 1956; PhD, New Sch. for Social Rsch., 1972. Sales mgr. Duart Film Labs., Inc., NYC, 1956-70; founder, pres. Univ. Press Am., Washington; asst. adj. prof. polit sci. CUNY, 1960-76, St. John's U., from 1976; asst.

adj. prof. politics, sociology Touro Coll., from 1974. Author: Readings in Political and Social Control, 1973. With USAF, 1943-46, CBI. Mem. Am. Polit. Sci. Assn. Democrat. Died Dec. 12, 2009.

FENDERSON, ALBION PRENTICE, marketing executive; b. Wilkinsburg, Pa., Apr. 21, 1914; s. Albion P. and Elizabeth J. (Harris) Fenderson; m. Lynne Gage, Mar. 21, 1975; children: Jeremy, Kelley, Christopher. At Carnegie Inst. Tech., 1934—36; BS, George Washington U., 1941. Dir. coll. orgns. Am. Liberty League, 1934—46; mgr. rsch. and statistics Distilled Spirits Inst, 1936—41; asst. to dir. alcohol divsn. War Prodn. Bd., 1941—42; chief alcohol procurement and storage Def. Supplies Corp., 1942—43; asst. to pres. Fleischman Distilling Co., 1944, Publicker Industries, 1944—51; v.p. United Distillers, 1951—52; exec. v.p. E & J Gallo Winery, Modesto, Calif., from 1952. Mem.: Beta Theta Pi, Tau Beta Pi, Omicron Delta Kappa. Home: Modesto, Calif. Died May 23, 2010.

FENNINGER, LEONARD DAVIS, medical educator, consultant; b. Hampton, Va., Oct. 3, 1917; s. Laurence and Natalie Ayers (Bourne) F.; m. Jane Thomas, Mar. 20, 1943; children: David McClure, Anne Randolph. AB, Princeton U., 1938; MD, U. Rochester, 1943. Diplomate: Am. Bd. Internal Medicine. Asso. dean, prof. health services, chmn. dept., prof. medicine U. Rochester; also physician, med. dir. Strong Meml. Hosp., 1961-67; dir. Bur. Health Manpower, USPHS, 1967-69; asso. dir. health manpower NIH, 1969-73; dir. dept. grad. med. edn. AMA, Chgo., 1973-76, group v.p. med. edn., 1976-80, v.p. med. edn. and sci. policy, 1981-84; lectr. in medicine Northwestern U. Med. Sch., Chgo., from 1985; attending physician emeritus Northwestern Meml. Hosp., Chgo. Home: Evanston, Ill. Died Sept. 10, 2009.

FENSTER, MARVIN, lawyer, retail executive; b. Bklyn., Jan. 19, 1918; s. Isaac and Anna (Greenman) Fenster; m. Louise Rapoport, Nov. 13, 1953; children: Julie, Mark. BA, Cornell U., 1938; LLB, Columbia U., 1941. Bar: NY 42. Assoc. Lauterstein, Spiller, Bergerman & Dannett, NYC, 1941—42, 1946—48; atty., asst. gen. atty. R.H. Macy & Co., Inc., NYC, 1948—60, sr. v.p., gen. counsel, sec., 1960—84, sr. v.p. spl. counsel, sec., 1984—87, dir., sr. v.p., spl. counsel, sec, from 1987; pres., dir. Macy's Bank, from 1981; sr. v.p., sec. Macy Credit Corp., NYC, 1961—86, pres., dir., CEO, from 1986; pres., CEO Macy Receivables Funding Corp., NYC, from 1989. 1st lt. US Army, 1943—46. Mem.: Harmonie Club, Am. Coll. Real Estate Lawyers, Assn. of Bar, Beach Point Club, Phi Epsilon Pi. Jewish. Home: New York, NY. Died Aug. 6, 2009.

FERGUSON, NORMAN K., JR., state legislator; b. Boston, May 6, 1933; m. Barbara; four children. AS, Burdett Coll., 1957. Commissioner Oxford County, Maine, 1968-94; mem. Maine Senate, Augusta, from 1994. Mem. Am. Legion, NRA, Elks, Concord Coalition. Home: Hanover, Maine. Died Feb. 22, 2010.

FERGUSON, STANLEY C., stockbroker; b. Louisa, Ky., Dec. 28, 1947; s. Harold Conard and Rebecca Maxine (Richey) F.; m. Jo Ann Tyson, Dec. 20, 1975; children: Foster Clay, Lee Ward. BA in History/Polit. sci., Morehead State U., 1971; postgrad. in bus. adminstrn., U. Ky., 1974—76. With Bache, Lexington, 1975—76, Frontier-Kemper Constrn., Ashland, Ky., 1976—79; br. office mgr., stockbroker, v.p. J.C. Bradford & Co., Ashland, from 1979. Magistrate, Dist. 2 Lawrence County, Ky., 1980—81; vice chmn. Lawrence County Housing Authority, 1982—83; mem. Boyd County C. of C.; Repub. youth chmn. Lawrence County, Ky., 1978—80. With USMC, 1971—74, maj. USMCR, 1976—83. Named hon. Ky. Col. Mem.: Lexington Fin. Assn., Ashland Bus. Assn., Marine Corps Res. Officers Assn., Jaycees (chpt. pres. 1978—79). Republican. Baptist. Home: Louisa, Ky. Died Nov. 17, 2009.

FERGUSON, THOMAS HUGH, retired publishing executive; b. Bronx, NY, June 25, 1936; m. Helen Walsh Ferguson; children: Gregory, Donna, Nora, Cynthia, Thomas, Christopher. Grad., St. John's U., 1960; grad. studies, NYU. Clk. American Brands; salesman Berol; mgr. John H. Breck shampoo divsn. Cyanamid; v.p. mktg. Parade mag., 1972—77, pres., 1977—79; pres., gen. mgr. The Washington Post, 1979—95. Died Nov. 3, 2010.

FERNS, CHESTER KIPP, JR., geologist; b. Trenton, NJ, Aug. 24, 1930; s. Chester Kipp and Easter (Watson) Ferns; m. Dolores Feeler Ferns, Oct. 19, 1952; children: Donna Dee, Rebecca Kipp. BS in Mining Engring, Petroleum Geology Option, U. Mo., Rolla, 1952. With Cities Service Oil Co., 1953—80; dist. devel. geologist Coastal Oil & Gas Corp. (name formerly ANR Prodn. Co.), Jackson, Miss., 1980—82, dist. exploration mgr., 1982—84, regional exploration mgr., 1984—85, dist. exploration mgr., from 1986. Sec.-treas. Mornin' Lord Ministries, Inc., Jackson, from 1977; arbitrator Better Bus. Bur., Jackson, 1985. Cpl. US Army, 1953—55. Mem.: Miss. Geol. Soc. (pres. 1984—85), Gulf Coast Assn. Geol. Socs. (del. 1984—85), Am. Assn. Petroleum Geologists (del. 1982—85, from 1987), Toastmasters Club (Jackson) (pres. 1980—81, area gov. 1986—87). Republican. Baptist. Avocations: photography, basketball, football. Home: Jackson, Miss. Died Apr. 6, 2009.

FERRIGNO, DANIEL JOSEPH, JR., internist; b. Bronx, NY, Jan. 23, 1933; s. Daniel J. and Serena (Natarelli) F.; m. Patricia Bettencourt, Feb. 14, 1975; children: Shireen, Janine. AB, NYU, 1954; MD, SUNY, Downstate Bronx, 1960. Intern Bklyn. VA Hosp., 1961-62; resident in internal medicine Bklyn. Jewish Hosp., 1962-64; gen. practice internal medicine Sacramento, Calif., from 1966. Med. dir. CAREUnit (adult and adolescent), Starting Point Adolescent, Smokenders Internat., Sacramento; assoc. corp. med. dir. CompCare, Irvine; assoc. clin. prof. med., U. Calif. Med. Sch., Davis, 1975—. Bd. advisors Mercy Hosp. Found., Sacramento, 1975—. Served to capt. USAF, 1964-66. Mem. AMA, Calif. Med. Assn., Am. Soc. Internal Medicine, AMA for Alcoholism and Other Drug Dependencies, Nat. Council Alcoholism. Republican. Avocations: flying, photography, snow and water skiing. Home: Winton, Calif. Died Nov. 10, 2009.

FETRIDGE, BONNIE-JEAN CLARK, civic volunteer; b. Chgo., Feb. 3, 1915; d. Sheldon and Bonnie (Carrington) Clark; m. William Harrison Fetridge, June 27, 1941; children: Blakely (Mrs. Harvey H. Bundy III), Clark Worthington. Student, Girls Latin Sch., Chgo., The Masters Sch., Dobbs Ferry, NY, Finch Coll., NYC. Bd. dirs. region VII com. Girl Scouts U.S.A., 1939-43, nat. program com., 1966-69, nat. adv. bd., 1972-85, internat. commr.'s adv. panel, 1973-76, Nat. Juliette Low Birthplace Com., 1966-69; bd. dirs. Girl Scouts Chgo., 1936-51, 59-69, sec., 1936-38, v.p., 1946-49, 61-65, chmn. Juliette Low world friendship com., 1959-67, 71-72; mem. Friends Our Cabana Com. World Assn. Girl Guides and Girl Scouts, Cuernavaca, Mexico, 1969—, vice chmn., 1982-87; founder, pres. Olave Baden-Powell Soc. of World Assn. Girl Guides and Girl Scouts, London, 1984-93, bd. dirs., 1984—, hon. assoc., 1987; asst. sec. Dartnell Corp, Chgo., 1981-91, sec., 1991-98, bd. dirs. 1989-98; vice chmn. Dartnell Found., 1990-2000, Ravenswood Found., 2001—; bd. dirs. Jr. League of Chgo., 1937-40, Vis. Nurse Assn. Chgo., 1951-58, 61-63, asst. treas., 1962-63; women's bd. dirs. Children's meml. Hosp., 1946-50; v.p. parents coun. Latin Sch. Chgo., 1952-54, bd. dirs. alumni assn., 1964-69; Fidelitas Soc., 1979, 96; mem. women's bd. U.S.O., 1965-75, treas., 1969-71, v.p., 1971-73; mem. women's svc. bd. Chgo. Area coun. Boy Scouts Am., 1964-70, mem. nat. exploring com., 1973-76; staff aide and ARC Motor Corps, World War II. Recipient Citation of Merit Sta. WAIT, Chgo., 1971, Juliette Low World Friendship medal Girl Scouts U.S.A., 1989; 1st recipient Medal of Recognition World Assn.Girl Guides and Girl Scouts, London, 1993; Baden-Powell fellow World Scout Found., Geneva, 1983. Mem. Nat. Soc. Colonial Dames Am. (life, Ill. bd. mgrs. 1962-65, 69-76, 78-82, v.p. 1970-72, corr. sec. 1978-80, 1st v.p. 1980-84, state chmn. geneal. info. svcs. com. 1972-76, corr. sec. 1978-80, hist. activities com. 1979-83, mus. house com. 1980-83, house gov. 1981-82), Chgo. Dobbs Alumnae Assn. (past pres.), Nat. Soc. DAR, Conn. Soc. Genealogists, New Eng. Hist. Geneal. Soc., N.Y. Geneal. and Biog. Soc., Newberry Libr. Assocs., Chgo. Hist. Soc. (life), Casino Club, The Racquet Club Chgo., Onwentsia Club, Union League Club. Republican. Episcopalian. Home: Chicago, Ill. Died Jan. 17, 2009.

FETTERLY, FREDERICK ANTHONY, public relations and advertising executive; b. Rutherford, NJ, Jan. 5, 1930; s. Frederick Anthony and Ruth (Farnham) F.; m. Jane Ann Sholts, Sept. 1, 1960 (div. June 1978); children: Frederick Anthony III, Mark Andrew. BA, Upsala Coll., 1975; MS, Columbia U., 1959. Reporter, regional editor The Record, Hackensack, N.J., 1957—59; exec. city editor The Post-Times, West Palm Beach, Fla., 1960—65; owner Fred A. Fetterly & Assocs., West Palm Beach, from 1965. With USAF, 1951—55. Mem.: Pub. Rels. Soc. Am. (bd. dirs. Gulfstream chpt. 1980—84). Republican. Presbyterian. Home: Ryl Palm Bch, Fla. Died Feb. 8, 2009.

FICKERT, KURT JON, writer, retired language educator; b. Pausa, Saxony, Germany, Dec. 19, 1920; came to U.S., 1926; s. Kurt Alfred and Martha Elsa (Searchinger) F.; m. Madlyn Barbara Janda, Aug. 6, 1946; children: Linda Mosbacher, Jon, Chris. AB, Hofstra U., 1941; MA, NYU, 1947, PhD, 1952. Instr., then asst. prof. Hofstra U., Hempstead, N.Y., 1948-53; asst. prof. Fla. State U., Tallahassee, 1953-54, Kans. State U., Ft. Hays, 1954-56; assoc. prof., then prof. Wittenberg U., Springfield, Ohio, 1956-86, ret., 1986. Chairperson dept. langs. Wittenberg U., 1969-75. Author: To Heaven and Back, 1972, Hermann Hesse's Quest, 1978, Kafka's Doubles, 1979, Signs and Portents, 1980, Franz Kafka: Life, Work, Criticism, 1987, Neither Left Nor Right, 1987, End of a Mission, 1993, Dialogue with the Reader, 1996; contbr. articles and poetry to lit. publs. Fullbright grantee, Germany, 1957, NEH grantee, U. Calif., Irvine, 1981; Fickert Lang. award established in his honor Wittenberg U., 1986. Lutheran. Home: Springfield, Ohio. Died Mar. 20, 2010.

FIELD, ROBERT EUGENE, mechanical engineer, educator, consultant, researcher; b. Davenport, Iowa, July 14, 1946; s. Carl Ludgwig Field and Geraldine Gladis (Stahl) Weeks; m. Wanda M. Osborn, June 8, 1968; 1 child, Juliet M. BSME, Bradley U., 1968; MSME, Rensselaer Poly. Inst., 1972; PhD, Purdue U., 1989. Registered profl. engr., Ill., Fla. Sr. engr. Pratt & Whitney Comml. Products Div., East Hartford, Conn., 1968-74; mgr. rsch. and exploration Rockwell Internat., Admiral Appliance Group, Galesburg, Ill., 1974-77; project engr. govt. products div. Pratt & Whitney, West Palm Beach, Fla., 1977-91; asst. prof. No. Ill. U., DeKalb, Ill., from 1991. Instr. Fla. Engring. Edn. Delivery System, Gainesville, 1983-85. Contbr. articles to profl. jours. Recipient David Ross summer grant Purdue U., 1986. Mem. ASME. Achievements include patents in field of gas turbine cooling, high temperature structures cooling, research in gas/steam turbine design, radiation heat transfer in semitransparent materials. Home: Frazeysburg, Ohio. Died Feb. 1, 2010.

FIFKOVA, EVA, behavioral neuroscience educator; b. Prague, Czechoslovakia, May 21, 1932; came to U.S., 1968; d. Ivan and Maria Fifka. MD, Charles U., Prague, 1957; PhD, Inst. Physiology Czechoslovakia Acad. Scis., Prague, 1963. Lectr. Charles U., 1954-60; mem. staff Czechosolvakia Acad. Scis., 1960-68; research assoc. Calif. Inst. Tech., Pasadena, 1968-74; asst. prof. behavioral neurosci. U. Colo., Boulder, 1974-75, assoc. prof., 1975-78, prof., from 1978. Mem. neurobiology adv. panel NSF, Washington, 1982-85; alcohol biomed. rsch. rev. com. Nat. Inst. Alcohol Abuse and Alcoholism, 1988-89; mem. neurology study sect. NIH, 1990-94; mem. rev. bd. Bionat. Sci. Found., 1992—. Contbr. numerous articles to profl. jours. U. Colo. Faculty fellow, Boulder, 1979, 84; research grantee Nat. Inst. Aging, Bethesda, Md., 1984—, Nat. Inst. Alcohol, 1983—, Nat. Inst. Mental Health, 1988—. Mem. AAAS, Am. Physiol. Soc., Soc. Neurosci., Am. Assn. Anatomists, Electron Microscopy Soc. Am., Inst. Brain Rsch. Orgn. Clubs: Cajal (Denver). Home: Boulder, Colo. Died Feb. 1, 2010.

FILES, WILMER ROBERT, manufacturing executive; b. Phila., Oct. 7, 1931; s. Wilmer Robert and Mary (Ryan) F.; m. Patricia Alice Culhane, Apr. 24, 1953; children: Christine, Bryan. BS in Econs., U. Pa., 1953. Various positions Gen. Electric Co., Schenectady, 1953-60, Phila., 1960-61, Cin., 1961-65; chief fin. officer Nat. Enterprises Inc. (formerly Nat. Homes Corp.), Lafayette, Ind., from 1965. Mem. Fin. Execs. Inst. Clubs: Lafayette Country (pres. 1980-81). Roman Catholic. Home: Lafayette, Ind. Died July 31, 2010.

FIMRITE, RONALD DWAINE, retired sports journalist; b. Healdsburg, Calif., Jan. 6, 1931; s. Lester Thomas and Mildred Gladys (Ransom) F.; m. Joan Von Briesen, May 4, 1957 (div. 1970); children: Deborah, Peter; m. Mary Blake Green, Aug. 22, 1970 (div. 1977); m. Linda Fimrite (dec. 2009) BA, U. Calif.-Berkeley, 1952. In pub. relations So. Pacific Co., 1954; reporter, columnist Berkeley Gazette, Calif., 1955-59, San Francisco Chronicle, 1959-71; sr. writer Sports Illustrated, NYC, 1971—2005. Author: The World Series: A History of Baseball's Fall Classic, Birth of a Fan, The Square: The Story of a Saloon. Home: San Francisco, Calif. Died Apr. 30, 2010.

FINEDORE, WILLIAM FRANCIS, SR., manufacturing executive; b. Grand Rapids, Mich., Apr. 11, 1923; s. William and Clara Finedore; m. Grace M. Brush, Apr. 28, 1952; children: William F., Thomas E., James G., Nancy C., Jeffrey P. With mech. div. Kraft Foods, Morton Grove, Ill., 1945—62; from apprentice sheetmetal layout to leadman Dover divsn. Groen Mfg. Co., Elk Grove, Ill., 1962—72; foreman to supt. custom divsn. Leedal Inc., Chgo., 1972—77; plant mgr. Bloomfield Indsl. Divsn. Beatrice Foods, Chgo., 1977—78; dir. mfg., supt. custom divsn. Elkay Mfg. Co., Broadview, Ill., from 1978. With USMC, 1942—45. Recipient Ill. Swimming Assn. Swimming and Diving Ofcls. award, 1981, North Suburban YMCA Swim Coach award, 1973. Mem.: Keymen's (pres. execs. Elkay Mfg. Co.), Mfg. Mgrs. Assn. (past pres.), Boat Owners Assn. US, Nat. Rifle Assn., Nat. Skeet Shooting Assn., Harbor Lite Yacht Club, Gt. Lakes Cruising Club, Northbrook Sports Club. Republican. Roman Catholic. Home: Northbrook, Ill. Died Mar. 20, 2010.

FINKENSTAEDT, ELIZABETH, archaeologist, educator; b. Rockford, Ill., Aug. 13, 1930; d. Kimball Lawrence and Artena (Phillips) Finkenstaedt. AB, Wellesley Coll., 1952; MA, U. Mich., 1955; student, U. Utrecht Netherlands, 1960—61, student, 1962—63; PhD, Harvard U., 1963. Instr. U. Oreg., 1959—60, 1961—62; asst. prof. Mount Holyoke Coll., South Hadley, Mass., 1965—70; assoc. prof. U. Ky., Lexington, from 1970; asst. registrar Agora, Athens, Greece; excavator Idalion, Cyprus, Pollensa, Majorca; osteologist Ky. Indian excavations. Contbr. articles to profl jours. Frank L. Weill fellow, 1968, Sachs fellow, 1960—61. Mem.: AAAS, Soc. Field Archaeologists, Am. Research Ctr. Egypt, Phi Beta Kappa. Republican. Episcopalian. Home: Lexington, Ky. Died Nov. 7, 2009.

FINNIE, IAIN, mechanical engineer, educator; b. Hong Kong, July 18, 1928; s. John and Jessie Ferguson (Mackenzie) F.; m. Joan Elizabeth Roth, July 28, 1969; 1 dau., Shauna. BS with honors, U. Glasgow, 1949; MS, MIT, 1951, M.E., 1952, Sc.D., 1954; D.Sc. (hon.), U. Glasgow, 1974. With Shell Devel. Co., 1954-61, engr., to 1961; mem. faculty dept. mech. engring. U. Calif., Berkeley, from 1961, prof., 1963—92. Vis. prof. Cath. U. Chile, 1965, Ecole Polytechnique, Lausanne, Switzerland, 1976, 87. Author: Creep of Engineering Materials, 1959; contbr. articles to profl. jours. Guggenheim Found. fellow, 1967-68 Mem. Nat. Acad. Engring., ASME (hon., Nadai award 1982). Home: Berkeley, Calif. Died Dec. 19, 2009.

FIORENTINO, LEON FRANCIS, holding company executive; b. LaSalle, Ill., Feb. 22, 1925; s. Anton and Ann (Gatto) F.; m. Patricia C. Brady, Oct. 29, 1949; 1 child: Susan Ann. BS, Loyola U. Cert. internal auditor Ill. Asst. controller McGraw Edison, Elgin, Ill., 1962—78, asst. to pres., 1978—79; v.p. fin. Seebury Corp., Chgo., 1979—81; pres., CEO Bermico Co., West Bend, Wis., 1974—78, chmn. exec. com., dir., 1974—78; cons. pvt. practice, Boca Raton, Fla., 1980; v.p. fin., treas. Chgo. Milw. Corp., 1980—95; v.p. fin., treas., sec. Hearland Ptnrs., 1990—95; v.p., dir. Des Moines Union Ry. Co., 1986—88; pres. Minn. Transp. Rw. Co., 1986—96; v.p. fin., sec., treas. Heartlanc Tech. Inc., from 1998. V.p. fin. sec., treas., dir. P.G. Design Elec. Inc. Home: Oak Brook, Ill. Died June 23, 2010.

FIORITO, EDWARD GERALD, lawyer; b. Irvington, NJ, Oct. 20, 1936; s. Edward and Emma (DePascale) F.; m. Charlotte H. Longo (widowed 2-3-2004); children: Jeanne C., Kathryn M., Thomas E., Lynn M., Patricia A. BSEE, Rutgers U., 1958; JD, Georgetown U., 1963. Bar: U.S. Patent and Trademark Office 1960, Va. 1963, N.Y. 1964, Mich. 1970, Ohio 1975, Tex. 1984. Patent staff atty. IBM, Armonk, NY, 1958-69; v.p. patent and comml. relations Energy Conversion Devices, Troy, Mich., 1969-71; mng. patent prosecution Burroughs Corp., Detroit, 1971-75; gen. patent counsel B.F. Goodrich Corp., Akron, Ohio, 1975-83; dir. patents and licensing Dresser Industries, Inc., Dallas, 1983-93. Alt. mem. Dept. Commerce Adv. Commn. on Patent Law Reform, 1991-92; spl. master, arbitrator, neutral evaluator, expert providing opinion testimony in intellectual property litigation,

1986—; U.S. del. to World Intellectual Property Orgn. Diplomatic Conf., 1991. Bd. dirs. Akron's House Extending Aid on Drugs, 1976. Mem. ABA (chmn. sci. and tech. sect. 1984-85, chair intellectual property law sect. 2000-2001), IEEE, Tex. Bar Assn. (chmn. intellectual property law sect. 1990-91), Internat. Assn. for Protection Indsl. Property (exec. bd. 1989—), Assn. Corp. Patent Counsel (exec. com. 1982-84), Tau Beta Pi. Roman Catholic. Avocations: music, flying. Home: Pemberville, Ohio. Died Apr. 27, 2009.

FIPPINGER, RONALD ALAN, trade association executive, trade show producer; b. Melrose Park, Ill., June 1, 1942; s. Arthur William and Helen Anna (Hohensee) F.; m. Carol Marie McElroy, June 23, 1962; children: Lisa Marie, Peter Brian. Student, Inst. for Mgmt., Ill. Benedictine Coll., 1972-76. Cert. assn. exec.; cert. exposition mgr. Adminstrv. asst. Nat. Housewares Mfrs. Assn., Chgo., 1966-79, mng. dir., 1979-86; group show dir. HouseWorld Expo, produced by Interface Group, 1986-88; dir. merchandising Genie Corp. subs. R.R. Donnelly, 1985-86; pres. RF Internat., 1989-90; exec. v.p. Svc.Master, Bus. Cleaning Svc., from 1989; v.p. mktg. and ops. Show Mgmt. & Svcs., Inc., from 1990. V.p. Ill. Inst. Diving, Glen Ellyn, 1960-73 Pres. Lombard Hist. Soc., Ill., 1975-78; dir. Congress of Ill. State Hist. Socs. and Mus., Springfield Ill, 1976; dir. Lombard Hist. Commn., Ill., 1978—, chmn., 1989—; chpt. pres. City of Hope Recipient Chmn.'s award Japan External Trade Orgn., 1986. Mem. Profl. Assn. Diving Instrs. (master instr.), Am. Soc. Assn. Execs., Nat. Assn. Expn. Mgrs., Internat. Trade Assn. Greater Chgo., Trade Show Bur., Union Des Foires Internationales (Paris) Clubs: Merchants and Mfrs. (Chgo.) (dir. 1979-89, treas. 1985-89); Housewares (Chgo.); Housewares of N.Y. (N.Y.C.); Internat. Pot and Kettle. Home: Castle Rock, Colo. Died Apr. 23, 2009.

FISCHER, IRENE KAMINKA, geodesist, researcher, retired mathematician; b. Vienna, July 27, 1907; came to U.S., 1941; d. Armand and Clara (Loewy) Kaminka; m. Eric Fischer, Dec. 21, 1930 (dec. 1985); children: Gay A., Michael M.J. MA, U. Vienna/Vienna Inst. Tech., 1931; postgrad., U. Va., Georgetown U., 1950-57; D. in Engring., U. Karlsruhe/Tech. Inst., Karlsruhe, Fed. Republic Germany, 1975. Tchr. secondary schs., Vienna, 1931-38; tchr. secondary schs. and colls. Washington, D.C., Mass., N.Y., Mass, 1941-45; rschr. MIT, Cambridge, Mass., 1942-44; rsch. geodesist Army Map Svc., Def. Mapping Agy., Washington, 1952-77. Author: Geometry, 1965, Basic Geodesy, 1972, The Geoid--What's That?, 1973, Geodesy-What's That?, 1988; contbr. hundreds of articles to profl. jours. Recipient medals Dept. Army, 1957, 66, 67, Dept. Def., 1967, Def. Mapping Agy., 1971, Nat. Civil Svc. League Career award, 1976; named Fed. Retiree of Yr. Nat. Assn. Retired Fed. Employees, 1978. Fellow Am. Geophys. Union, Internat. Assn. Geodesy (sec. sect. V 1963-71, chmn. study groups 1963-75); mem. Nat. Acad. Engring. Home: Brighton, Mass. Died Oct. 22, 2009.

FISH, EDWARD ANTHONY, JR., construction company executive; b. Boston, June 13, 1933; s. Joseph Nicholas and Evelyn Irene (O'Mally) F.; m. Gretchen Fish; children: Karen, Edward Anthony, John, Kevin, Melissa, Matthew, Michael. BA magna cum laude in Econs, U. N.H., 1957. With Peabody Constrn. Co., Inc., Braintree, Mass., from 1957; v.p., 1962-65; pres., from 1965; owner Peabody Constrn. Co., Inc., Peabody Properties, Inc., Edward A. Fish Assocs., Inc. Bd. dirs. Cardinal Cushing Sch., 1978-80; life mem. bd. dirs. Family Counseling and Guidance Centers; hon. dir. Handi-Kids.; trustee Meadowbrook Sch. Served with AUS, 1952-54, Korea. Mem.: 100. Home: Weston, Mass. Died June 15, 2010.

FISHBEIN, MARTIN, psychologist, educator; b. NYC, Mar. 2, 1936; s. Sydney and Gloria (Nadelstein) F.; m. Deborah Louise Kaplan, Dec. 26, 1959. AB, Reed Coll., Portland, Oreg., 1957; PhD, UCLA, 1961. Mem. faculty U. Ill., Urbana, 1961—97, prof. psychology, 1970—97, head social-orgnl.-indsl. div., 1979-87, also rsch. prof. Inst. Comms. Rsch., 1970—97, exec. com. Survey Rsch. Lab., 1964-72, 81-86, assoc. mem. Ctr. Advanced Studies, 1974-75, 88-89, prof. emeritus, 1997—2009; Disting. prof. comm. Annenberg Sch. for Comm., U. Pa., 1997—2009; dir. health comm. area Annenberg Pub. Policy Ctr., 1997—2009; dir. theory and methods core Ctr. of Excellence in Cancer Comm. Rsch., U. Pa., 2003—08. Vis. scholar London Sch. Econs. and Polit. Sci., 1967-68, 74-75; cons. NIMH AIDS Rsch. Program, 1988-89, mem. AIDS adv. subcom., 1987-90, Nat. Acad. Scis., Bd. Behavioral, Cognitive and Sensory Scis., 2006-; guest rschr. CDC, 1992-97, acting chief behavioral intervention and rsch. br. divsn. STD prevention, 1994-95. Author: (with Steiner) Current Studies in Social Psychology, 1965, Readings in Attitude Theory and Measurement, 1967, (with Ajzen) Belief, Attitude, Intention and Behavior: An Introduction to Theory and Research, 1975, Progress in Social Psychology, vol. 1, 1980, (with Ajzen) Understanding Attitudes and Predicting Social Behavior, 1980, (with Goldberg and Middlestadt) Social Marketing, 1997,(with Jordan Kunkel and Manganello) Media Messages and Public Health, 2009; contbr. articles to profl. jours. Guggenheim fellow, 1967-68; inducted into Am. Mktg. Assn. Attitude Rsch. Hall of Fame, 1981, recipient Paul D. Converse award for disting. contbns. to theory and sci. in mktg., 1981, Spl. Recognition award Nat. Assn. Recording Merchandisers, 1982, Internat. prize Interam. Psychol. Soc., 1987, Charles C. Shepard award for Sci. Excellence, CDC, 1999, Mayhew Derryberry award for Outstanding Contbns. to Health Edn., Health Promotion and Health Comm. Rsch. and Theory, APHA, 2003, John P. McGovern award for health promotion U. Tex., 2005, Disting. Sci. contbn. award Soc. for Consumer Psychology, 1995. Fellow APA, Soc. Consumer Psychology (pres. 1991-92), Am. Psychol. Soc.; mem. APHA, Nat. Comm. Assn., Am. Sociol. Assn., Psychonomic Soc., Interam. Psychol. Soc. (pres. 1993-95), Internat. Comm. Assn., Nat. Comm. Assn., AIDS Impact (internat. bd. dirs. 1992—). Home: Philadelphia, Pa. Died Nov. 27, 2009.

FISHER, ANN, nurse; b. Queens, NY, Nov. 25, 1937; d. Joseph and Florence (French) Schneider; m. Leroy Fisher, Sept. 17, 1978. Grad., Jersey City Med. Ctr., 1958. RN, N.J.; cert. pediatric nurse practitioner. From staff nurse to head nurse Bergen Pines County Hosp., Paramus, N.J.; supr. Southern Ocean County Hosp., Manahawkin, N.J.; head nurse, med., surg. William B. Kessler Meml. Hosp., Hammonton, N.J., staff nurse, pediatrics. Home: Deland, Fla. Died Jan. 11, 2009.

FISHER, HOWARD NORTON, radio broadcast executive; b. Dec. 16, 1928; s. Jacob and Adele (Gershon) Fisher; m. Edith Reimer, Jan. 8, 1950; children: Jody, Richard; m. Sylvia Ruth Guenther, Feb. 14, 1971; children: Debra, Cyndi, Tamra. Student, Northwestern U., 1948, Columbia U., 1949. Radio announcer, sportscaster, newscaster Sta. WHOT, South Bend, Ind., 1950, Sta. WASK, Lafayette, Ind., 1951—53, Sta. WARL, Arlington, Va., 1953, Washington, 1953; with sales and mgmt. Sta. WLSE, Wallace, NC, 1953—56, Sta. KFMA, Davenport, Iowa, 1956—61, Sta. WEEF, Highland Pk., Ill., 1961—65, Sta. WPRO, Riverside, Calif., from 1965, pres., gen. mgr., from 1970, Stas. KPRD and KZNA, Barstow, Calif., from 1981; founder Media One Advt. Agy., Riverside, Calif., from 1983. News and spl. reporter Voice of Am., Washington, 1954; co-owner Am. Race Broadcasters subs. Am. Radio Broadcasters, exec. prodr. Past pres. Am. Cancer Soc.; bd. dirs. Salvation Army, ARC; bd. dirs. Loma Linda Faculty U. Calif., Riverside; adv. com. Riverside City Coll. Recipient various awards, Calif. State Senate, Calif. State Legislature. Mem.: Greater Riverside C. of C. (past pres.), Inland Empire Broadcasters Assn. (past pres.), So. Calif. Broadcasters Assn. (bd. dirs.), Rotary. Home: Riverside, Calif. Died Mar. 11, 2010.

FISHER, JAMES LEE, lawyer; b. Akron, Ohio, Apr. 10, 1944; s. James Lee and Maxine (Sumner) Fisher; m. Nancy Lorenz, Dec. 20, 1980. BSCE, U. Akron, 1968, JD, 1971. Bar: Ohio 1971. Staff atty. Brunswick Mgmt. Co., Akron, 1972-77; prin. James L. Fisher Co., L.P.A., Akron, 1977-88, Buckingham, Doolittle & Burroughs, Akron, from 1988. City planner City of Akron, 1968—71, cmty. devel. atty., 1971—73; mem. Metro Regional Transit Authority Bd., from 1992; sec.-treas. Summit County Planning Commn., 1978—99. Mem.: ABA, Ohio Planning Conf., Am. Planning Assn., Home Builders Assn., Akron Bar Assn., Ohio Bar Assn., Copley Lions (pres. 1982). Republican. Mem. United Ch. Of Christ. Home: Akron, Ohio. Died Sept. 14, 2009.

FISHER, JOHN COURTNEY, surgical physicist, consultant; b. Wilkinsburg, Pa., Apr. 19, 1922; s. Edwin Henry and Elizabeth (Walden) F.; m. Patricia Kingsbury, Nov. 26, 1942; children: Carolyn Fisher Ellis, John Courtney, Stephen Kingsbury; m. Jane Clauss, July 7, 1976. B.S., Harvard U., 1942, M.S., 1947, Sc.D., 1952. Teaching fellow Harvard U., 1942-52; sonar engr. Submarine Signal Co., Boston, 1945-46; dir. electromech. engring. Calidyne Co., Winchester, Mass., 1952-55; dir. devel. privately funded research project, Maynard, Mass., 1955-60; chmn., treas. Am. Dynamics Corp., Cambridge, Mass., 1960-68; northeastern regional sales mgr. Princeton Applied Research Corp., N.J., 1968-72, cons. in sci. instrumentation, Weston, Mass., 1972—; dir. med. devel. Cavitron Lasersonics div., Stamford, Conn., 1976-81; mem. surg. staff St. Barnabas Med. Center, Livingston, N.J., 1980—; founding mem., sec.-treas. Am. Bd. Laser Surgery, 1984—, pres., 1993—; vis. assoc. prof. laser medicine and surgery U. Cin., 1985; mem. consulting staff St. Luke's Med. Ctr., Milw., 1987-92; sci. advisor transmyocardial revascularization project Seton Med. Ctr., Daly City, Calif., 1988—. Contbr. articles to profl. jours. Patentee in field. Mem. Weston Planning Bd., 1974-80. Fellow Am. Soc. Laser Medicine and Surgery; mem. Internat. Soc. Laser Surgery, ASME, IEEE, AAAS, Gynecologic Laser Soc., Midwest Biolaser Inst., N.Y. Acad. Scis., Internat. Soc. Cosmetic Laser Surgeons, Sigma Xi. Home: Bradenton, Fla. Died Feb. 26, 2010.

FISHER, ROBERT WILSON, geologist, consultant; b. Chgo., May 11, 1931; s. Clyde and Mary Hannah (Robb) Fisher; m. Martha Sue Johnson, Apr. 5, 1952 (div. 1976); children: Thomas R., Richard W., Andrew D., David C.; m. Lauren Huddleston, Apr. 5, 1976. BS, U. Ill, Urbana, 1953; MS, U. Ill, Urban, 1956. Cert. geologist, geol. scientist. Rsch. analyst Ill. Geol. Survey, Champaign, Ill., 1955—56; project geologist Amoco Prodn. Co., New Orleans, 1956—64; chief geologist Estate William G. Helis, 1964—81; v.p. Lynx Exploration Co., Denver, 1981—83; pres. Bradden Exploration Co., 1983—86; founder, chmn. Fisher Energy Group, from 1986. Map compiler Geol. Map of Ill., 1967. Author: The Fisher Report, 1986—89, Energy and the Environment; co-author: Visual Estimates of Grain Size Distribution in Some Chester Sandstones, 1959; contbr. articles to prol. jours. Served to 1st lt. US Army, 1953—55. Mem.: Sight Savers Internat. (adv. bd.), Soc. Ind. Earth Scientists, Ind. Petroleum Assn. Am. (econ. policy com., spkrs. bur.), Internat. Transactional Analysis Assn. (advanced), Rocky Mountain Assn. Geologists, Am. Inst. Profl. Geologist, Am. Assn. Petroleum Geologists. Home: Boulder, Colo. Died Mar. 17, 2009.

FISHER, STANLEY, psychologist; b. NYC, June 7, 1927; s. Nathan and Fanny (Rosenthal) F.; m. May Wechsler, Nov. 25, 1951 (div. 1976); children: Paul G., Julia A.; m. Esther M. Margolis, Aug. 19, 1979. BS, CUNY, 1949, PhD, 1977; MSW, Columbia U., 1952. Cer. psychologist, N.Y. Asst. mgr. Recording and Stat Corp., NYC, 1957-63; dir. system programming Univac, NYC, 1963-65; cons. TBS, NYC, 1965-66; dir. corp. systems CCC, NYC, 1966-67; dep. chief internat. computing ctr. UN, NYC, 1967-68; research assoc. psychology and computer sci. CUNY, NYC, 1968-74; assoc. research sci. Columbia U., NYC, from 1974; pvt. practice NYC, from 1978. Lectr. in surgery Mt. Sinai Sch. Medicine, N.Y.C., 1984-88; vis. assoc. in surgery Albert Einstein Coll. Medicine, N.Y.C., 1983-91; cons. to numerous orgns. including Am. Heart Assn., N.Y. Hosp., U. P.R. Author: Discovering the Power of Self-Hypnosis, 1991; contbr. numerous articles to profl. jours. Active Heart Info. Services N.Y. Heart Assn. With USN, 1945-46. CUNY fellow, 1949-51. Mem. Am. Psychol. Assn., Am. Soc. Clin. Hypnosis, Soc. for Clin. and Experimental Hypnosis, Assn. for Computer Machinery, Psychoanalytic Soc. Jewish. Avocations: tennis, swimming, computers, reading. Died Jan. 20, 2009.

FISHMAN, ALFRED PAUL, physician; b. NYC, Sept. 24, 1918; s. Isaac Fishman and Anne (Tinter) Fishman; m. Linda Fishman, Oct. 7, 1984; children: Mark, Jay, Hannah Rae. AB, U. Mich., 1938, MS, 1939; MD, U. Louisville, 1943; MA (hon.), U. Pa., 1971. Diplomate Am. Bd. Internal Medicine, Nat. Bd. Med. Examiners. Intern Jewish Hosp., Bklyn., 1943—44; Dazian Found. fellow pathology Mount Sinai Hosp., NYC, 1946—47, asst. resident, resident medicine, 1947—48; Dazian Found. fellow cardiovascular physiology Michael Reese Hosp., Chgo., 1948—49; American Heart Assn. rsch. fellow Bellevue Hosp., NYC, 1949—50, established investigator American Heart Assn. cardiopulmonary lab., 1951—55; American Heart Assn. rsch. fellow in physiology Harvard U., Boston, 1950—51; instr. physiology NYU, NYC, 1951—53; assoc. in medicine Columbia Coll. Physicians and Surgeons, NYC, 1953—55, asst. prof., 1955—58, assoc. prof., 1958—66; prof. medicine U. Chgo., 1966—69; dir. Inst. and Divsn. Cardiovasc. Disease Michael Reese Hosp., Chgo., 1966—69; prof. medicine U. Pa., Phila., 1969—72, William Maul Measey prof. medicine, 1972—2010, assoc. dean Sch. Medicine, 1969—76, dir. cardiovasc.-pulmonary divsn., 1969—90, chmn. dept. rehab. medicine, 1990—97, mem. coun. grad. med. edn., 1992—93, assoc. dean program devel., 1998—99, sr. assoc. dean program devel., 1999—2010. Dir. Robinette Found., Clin. Cardiovascular Rsch. Ctr., U. Pa. Med. Ctr., 1969—82; mem. steering com. dept. chmn. U. Pa. Med. Ctr., 1992, coun. on grad. med. edn., 1992—93; dir. Specialized Center of Rsch. (Lung), 1973—81; sr. attending physician Phila. Gen. Hosp., 1970—78; physician Mass. Gen. Hosp., 1979; cons. to chancellor U. Mo., Kansas City, 1973—78; vis. prof. Harvard U., 1970, Oxford (Eng.) U., 1972, Washington U., St. Louis, 1973, Johns Hopkins U., 1974, Ben Gurion U., 1975, Emory U., Atlanta, 1976, U. Porto Alegra, Brazilia, Brazil, 1976, U. Zurich, Switzerland, 1978, Duke U., 1986, U. N.C., 1986; vis. scientist for NIH to Peking, China, 1980, to USSR, 1985; cons. Exec. Office Pres., 1961—69, U. Athens, Greece, 1980; mem. WHO Expert Panel, Geneva, 1973—76, Nat. Adv. Heart and Lung Council, NIH, 1968—71, 1979—83, Steering Com. of Dept. Chmn U. Pa. Med. Ctr., 1992, Coun. on Grad. Med. Edn. U. Pa. Med. Ctr., 1992—93; coun. mem. Coll. Physicians of Phila., 1993—2006, bd. govs., 2006; chmn. Gov.'s Com. for Rsch. on Respiratory Diseases in Coal Miners, 1974—90, Internat. Conf. on Lung, Titisee, Germany, 1976, Florence, Italy, 84, Prague, Czech Republic, 86, Prague, 89, NIH Conf. Proliferative & Obliterative Vascular Disease; chair steering com. Nat. Emphysema Treatment Trial, from 1996; U.S. chief del. Internat. Union of Physiol. Scis., Helsinki, Finland, 1989; cons. N.Y. State Bd. Health, 1987—91, Cleve. Found., from 1984; vis. com. Case Western Res. Sch. Medicine, Cleve., from 1989, Rsch Inst., Lankenau Hosp., Phila., 1990; chmn. Scientific Edn. Partnership U. Mo-U. Kans.-Merrill Dow, 1989—2001. Editor (with D.W. Richards): Circulation of The Blood-Men and Ideas, 1964; editor: (with H.H. Hecht) The Pulmonary Circulation and Interstitial Space, 1969; editor: Handbooks of Respiratory Physiology, Am. Physiol. Soc., 1967—72, 1979—87, Physiology in Medicine, New Eng. Jour. Medicine, 1969—79, Jour. Applied Physiology, 1981—89, 1989—99; editor: (with D.W. Richards) Circulation of the Blood Men and Ideas, 1982; editor: Merck Manual, 1972—80, Ann. Rev. Physiology, 1977—81, Heart Failure, 1979; editor: (with E. M. Renkin) Pulmonary Edema, 1979; editor: Pulmonary Diseases and Disorders, 1979, 2d edit., 1988, Classics in Biology and Medicine, 1989—97, The Pulmonary Circulation: Normal and Abnormal, 1990;: 3d edit., 1998, Pulmonary Rehabilitation, 1994, Fishman's Pulmonary Diseases and Disorders, 3rd edit., from 1998, Fishman's Manual of Pulmonary Diseases and Disorders, 2002; contbr. articles to profl. jours.; reviewer Health Care Financing Adminstrn., 1995—97, Washington Adv. Group, from 2000. Bd. dirs. Polachek Found., Phila. Zool. Soc.; mem. Kansas City Life Scis. Inst., 2000—01. Recipient Disting. Alumni award, U. Louisville, 1984, Disting. award in nephrology, A.N. Richards, 1998. Fellow: ACP, Royal Coll. Physicians, Am. Coll. Chest Physicians (hon.); mem.: AAAS, NAS (com. on sci., edn. and pub. policy 1987—90, policy bd. complementary/alternative medicine 2003), Am. Thoracic Soc. (Trudeau medal 2001), Heart Assn. Southeastern Pa. (bd. dirs.), Coll. of Physicians of Phila. (coun. from 1993, governance com. 2006, pres. 1996—97), N.Y. County Med. Soc., Nat. Space Biomed. Rsch. Inst. (bd. dirs. from 1999), Health Care Financing Adminstrn. (mem. lung transplant ctr. rev. com. from 1996, NIH-HCFA nat. emphysema treatment trial from 1996, chair steering com.), Am. Coll. Cardiology (A.N. Richards Disting. Achievement award 1997), Fedn. Am. Socs. for Exptl. Biology (exec. bd. 1983—85), Internat. Union Physiol. Scis. (U.S. Nat. Com. 1982—89, chmn. 1986—89), N.Y. Heart Assn. (pres. 1965—67), Am. Heart Assn. (chmn. coun. on cardiopulmonary disease 1972—74, rsch. coun. 1974—79, sci. pub. com. 1986—88, bd. dirs. 1988—92, chmn. 1988—94, sci. adv. com. 1992—98, founder, Disting. Achievement award 1980, Merit award 1989, Gold Heart award 1992, Sr. Rsch. award 2003), Assn. Am. Physicians, Royal Soc. Medicine (London), Am. Acad. Arts and Scis., Am. Soc. Clin. Investigation, Am. Physiol. Soc. (chmn. publs. bd. 1974—81, pres. 1983, chmn. centennial celebration com. 1985—87, editor handbook 1986, Ray G. Daggs award 2004, Trudeau medal 2005), Inst.

Medicine of NAS (chmn. health scis. bd. 1990—95, com. on social and ethical impact of advances in biomedicine 1992—94, com. on use of CAM by the pub. from 2004), Interurban Clin. Club, Alpha Omega Alpha. Home: Philadelphia, Pa. Died Oct. 6, 2010.

FISHWICK, JOHN PALMER, retired lawyer, railroad executive; b. Roanoke, Va., Sept. 29, 1916; s. William and Nellie (Cross) F.; m. Blair Wiley, Jan. 4, 1941 (dec. June 1987); children: Ellen Blair (Mrs. Guyman Martin III), Anne Palmer (Mrs. Wesley Posvar), John Palmer Jr.; m. Doreen Allton, Nov. 17, 1989. AB, Roanoke Coll., 1937, DHL (hon.), 1971; LL.B., Harvard U., 1940; DL (hon.), Washington & Lee Univ., 2000. Bar: Va. 1939. Assoc. Cravath, Swaine & Moore, NYC, 1940-42; asst. to gen. solicitor N. & W. Ry., Roanoke, Va., 1945-47, asst. gen. solicitor, 1947-51, asst. gen. counsel, 1951-54, gen. solicitor, 1954-56, gen. counsel, 1956-58, v.p., gen. counsel, 1958-59, v.p. law, 1959-63, sr. v.p., 1963-70, pres., CEO, 1970-80, chmn., CEO, 1980-81; ptnr. Windels, Marx, Davies & Ives, NYC, 1981-84; of counsel Fishwick, Jones and Glenn, Roanoke, Va., 1984-95; ret. Chmn., CEO Erie Lackawanna Ry. Co., 1968-70; pres., CEO, Del. & Hudson Ry. Co., 1968-70; pres., dir. Dereco, Inc., 1968-81; chmn. investment com., bd. dirs. Norfolk So. Corp., 1981-89. Trustee Roanoke Coll., 1964-72; trustee Va. Theol. Sem.; former chancellor Diocese S.W. Va.; former bd. dirs. Va. Found. Humanities; former trustee Va. Mus. Fine Arts, Richmond. Served as lt. comdr. USNR, 1942—45. Mem. Met. Club (Washington). Episcopalian. Home: Roanoke, Va. Died Aug. 9, 2010.

FISK, GEORGE WILLIAM, retired container corporation executive, lawyer; b. Bklyn, Aug. 24, 1919; s. Willaim Millard and Georgia Leona (Winans) F.; m. Dorothy Lee Bowles, May 8, 1943; children: Robert William, Virginia Lee Fisk Dunphy, Margaret Grace Fisk Genvert. AB, Colgate U., 1940; LL.B., Columbia U., 1948. Bar: N.Y. 1948, Pa. 1956, Ill. 1979. Assoc. Hubbell and Davis, NYC, 1948-50; atty. Allied Corp., NYC, 1950-55; assoc. gen. counsel Mobil Oil Corp., Phila., N.Y.C., 1955-79; gen. counsel Container Corp. Am., Chgo., 1979-84. Served to maj. AUS, 1941-46, ETO. Decorated Bronze Star Mem.: Burning Tree (Greenwich, Conn.). Republican. Congregationalist. Home: Salisbury, Md. Died Oct. 8, 2009.

FITCH, COY DEAN, internist, educator; b. Marthaville, La., Oct. 5, 1934; s. Raymond E. and Joey (Youngblood) F.; m. Rachel Farr, Mar. 31, 1956; children: Julia Anne, Jaquelyn Kay. BS, U. Ark., 1956, MS, MD, U. Ark., 1958. Diplomate Am. Bd. Internal Medicine and Endocrinology. Intern U. Ark. Sch. Medicine, 1958—59, resident, 1959—62, instr. biochemistry, 1959—62, asst. prof. medicine and biochemistry, 1962—66, dir. honors med. student rsch. program, 1965—67, asso. prof., 1966—67; practice medicine, specializing in internal medicine Little Rock, 1962—67; asso. prof. internal medicine and biochemistry St. Louis U. Sch. Medicine, 1967—73, prof. internal medicine, from 1973, prof. biochemistry, from 1976, head sect. metabolism, 1969—76, dir. div. endocrinology and metabolism, 1977—85; practice medicine, specializing in internal medicine St. Louis, from 1969; chief med. service St. Louis U. Hosps., 1976—77, vice-chmn. dept. internal medicine, 1983—85, acting chmn. dept. internal medicine, 1985—88, chmn. dept. internal medicine, 1988—2000; chief med. svc. St. Louis VA Med. Ctr., from 2005. Dir. Diabetic Clinic, U. Ark. Med. Ctr., 1962-67, head sect. metabolism and endocrinology, 1966-67; mem. nutrition study sect. div. research grants NIH, 1967-71 Assoc. editor: Nutrition Revs., 1964; contbr. articles to profl. jours. Served from capt. to lt. col., M.C. AUS, 1967-69. Recipient Lederle Med. Faculty award, 1966-67; Russell M. Wilder-Nat. Vitamin Found. fellow, 1959-62. Master ACP (gov. Mo. chpt. 1995-99); mem. Am. Inst. Nutrition, Am. Soc. Biol. Chemists, Ctrl. Soc. Clin. Rsch., Phi Beta Kappa. Deceased.

FITCHEN, ALLEN NELSON, publisher; b. Syracuse, Aug. 8, 1936; s. John Frederick and Mary (Nelson) F. III; m. Jane Cady, June 13, 1959 (div. Feb. 1986); children— Anne Wheeler, Christopher Hardy, William Mills; m. Shirley Bergen, May 23, 1991. BA in English cum laude, Amherst Coll., 1958; MA in English, Cornell, 1960. Coll. traveler Macmillan Co., NYC, 1960-62, editor, 1962-67; humanities editor U. Chgo. Press, 1968-82, sr. editor, 1971-82; dir. U. Wis. Press, 1982-98, ret., 1998. Mem.: Psi Upsilon. Home: Madison, Wis. Died Dec. 25, 2009.

FITZGERALD, GERALD FRANCIS, retired banker; b. Chgo., July 6, 1925; s. John J. and Olivia (Trader) F.; m. Marjorie Webb Gosselin, Sept. 10, 1949; children: Gerald Francis Jr., James Gosselin, Thomas Gosselin, Julie Ann Fitzgerald Schauer, Peter Gosselin. BS in Commerce, Northwestern U., 1949. Salesman Premier Printing Co., 1949-53; founder, ptnr. Fitzgerald & Cooke (now Hill and Knowlton, Inc. div. J. Walter Thompson), 1953-60, v.p., 1960-64; chmn. Lake Villa Trust & Savs. Bank, 1961-69, Palatine Nat. Bank, 1961-87, Suburban Nat. Bank of Palatine, Suburban Bank of Hoffman-Schaumburg, Suburban Bank of Cary-Grove, Suburban Bank of Rolling Meadows, Suburban Bank of Barrington, Suburban Bank of Bartlett, 1964-90; pres. Suburban Bancorp, Inc., Palatine, 1982-90, chmn., 1982-94, Southern Colo. Bank Holding Co., 1991—2010, Citizens Bank of Pagosa Springs, 1991-94. Cons. American Del. to NATO CCMS, Brussels, 1976; former chmn. Suburban Computer Svcs. Corp., Palatine; lectr. in banking field. Contbr. articles to profl. jours. Bd. dirs., past pres. Inverness Assn.; mem. Chgo. Coun. of Fgn. Rels.; cons. Portsmouth, R.I. Abbey Sch., 1978-80; life trustee Newberry Libr.; mem. John Evans Club, Northwestern U. Sgt. U.S. Army, 1944-46, ETO. Mem. Ill. Thoroughbred Owners and Breeders Found., Nat. Assn. of State Racing Commrs., Newcomen Soc., Max McGraw's Wildlife Found., Chgo. Athletic Assn., Inverness Golf Club, Safari Internat. Club, Caxton Club, Delta Upsilon. Avocations: travel, opera, rare books, photography, hunting. Home: Barrington, Ill. Died Oct. 30, 2010.

FITZGERALD, RITA LOUISE, author, former educator; b. Boston, Feb. 8, 1925; d. Joseph Patrick and Agnes (Coyne) Howley; grad. Boston Tchrs. Coll., 1947; postgrad. U. Calif., Berkeley, 1971-74, Hayward State U., 1974, U. Calif., Santa Clara, 1972, St. Mary's of Notre Dame, Belmont, Calif., 1975, San Jose State U., 1967-68; m. John Gerald Fitzgerald, Aug. 9, 1947 (dec.); children— John Joseph, Robert Vincent. Tchr., Boston Public Schs., 1947-56, Richmond (Calif.) Unified Sch. Dist., 1956-76, ret., 1976; West Coast rep. Louise Downey McNamara and Assocs., Quincy, Mass., 1979—; asso. author edn. div. World Almanac, Cleve., 1980—; tutor; ednl. cons., scholarship advisor, public speaker, reading asso. Marlborough Sch., London, 1975-76. Active Mt. Diablo Hosp. Vols. Assn., Mt. Diablo Hosp. Found. Assn., Roundtree Homeowners Assn., Concord High Sch. Boosters Club. Served with USN, 1945-46. Cert. in hosp. ministry tng.; reading specialist and elem. edn. lifetime teaching credentials, Mass., Calif. Life mem. NEA, Calif. Tchrs. Assn.; mem. Fairmede Tchrs. Assn., Boston Tchrs. Coll. Alumnae Assn., U. Calif. Alumnae Assn., AAUW, Internat. Assn. Childhood Edn., Internat. Platform Assn. Democrat. Roman Catholic. Author: Amanda Panda, 1981 (ednl. program); author 9 books on phonics, numbers, vocabulary, art. Died May 25, 2009.

FITZPATRICK, CHRISTINE MORRIS, retired legal administrator, former television executive; b. Steubenville, Ohio, June 10, 1920; d. Roy Elwood and Ruby Lorena (Mason) Morris; m. T. Mallary Fitzpatrick, Dec. 19, 1942; 1 child, Thomas Mallary III. Student, U. Chgo., 1943—44, U. Ga., 1945—46; BA, Roosevelt U., 1947; postgrad., Trinity Coll., Hartford, Conn., 1970. Assoc. dir. Joint Human Rels. Project, Chgo., 1965—66; tchr. English Austin Sch. Girls, Hartford, 1966—70; promotion coord. Conn. Pub. TV, Hartford, 1971—72, dir. cmty. rels., 1972—73, v.p., 1973—77; pub. rels. & affairs cons. Commonwealth Edison Co., Chgo., 1977—79; dir. spl. events Chgo. Pub. TV, 1979—84; v.p. Fitzpatrick Group, Inc., Chgo., 1986—88; adminstrv. dir. Fitzpatrick Law Offices, 1988—94, 1997—99, Fitzpatrick Eilenberg & Zivian, 1994—96, 2200 Ventures LLC, Chgo., 1999—2002; v.p. Pub. Rels. Clinic Chgo., 1980—81; ret., 2002. Bd. advisers Greater Hartford Mag., 1975—77; bd. dirs. World Affairs Ctr., Hartford, 1975—77; mem. adv. coun. Am. Revolution Bicentennial Commn., Conn., 1975—77. Mem.: LWV (Chgo. chpt. pres. 1962—64, Hartford chpt. v.p. 1971—73), Am. Women Radio and TV (New Eng. chpt. pres. 1976—77), Pub. Rels. Soc. America (dir. Conn. valley chpt. 1976—77). Home: Chicago, Ill. Died Jan. 27, 2009.

FLAHERTY, MICHAEL D., state legislator; b. Medford, Mass., July 7, 1934; m. Paula Barra; children: Colleen, Kevin, Keith. BS, Boston Coll., 1956; MBA, U. Vt., 1971. City councilman, South Burlington, Vt., from 1972; mem., mem. civic adv. com. Burlington Airport commn.; mem. Gov. Kunin's Commn. on Burlington State Rep. Bd. trustees Channel 17 Munic Channel. Home: S Burlington, Vt. Died Jan. 19, 2009.

FLANNAGAN, WILLIAM HAMILTON, hospital executive; b. Trevillians, Va., Sept. 14, 1920; s. Henry Alexander and Hanna Mae (Hamilton) F.; m. Kathryn Elizabeth Middleton, June 22, 1942; children— William Hamilton, Patricia Lyle Flannagan Sarver and John Michael (twins) BS, Hampden-Sydney Coll., Va., 1940, LL.D. (hon.), 1976. Asst. librarian Library of Congress, Washington, 1940-43; dir. hosp. service McGuire VA Hosp., Richmond, Va., 1946-49; adminstr. Bur. Hosps. and Nursing Home Services Va. Dept. of Health, Richmond, 1949-51; adminstr. Franklin Meml. Hosp., Rocky Mount, Va., 1951-54; pres. Roanoke Meml. Hosps., Va., from 1954. Past mem. Gov.'s Comm. on Va. Health Services Cost Rev.; dir. Va. Regional Med. Programs; past dir. The Hosp. Bur.; past mem. Blue Cross of Southwest Va. Bd., Va. Mental Health Study Commn.; past mem. exec. com. Roanoke Valley Regional Health Services Council; past pres. Carolinas-Virginias Hosp. Assn.; past pres. Roanoke Area Hosp. Council; past trustee Burrell Meml. Hosp., Roanoke; past mem. Gov.'s Adv. Hosp. Council; past vice chmn. Gov.'s Med. Facilities Commn.; dir. Colonial Am. Nat. Bank; mem., former chmn. adv. bd. So. Div. Brs.; pres. Roanoke Hosps. Found., Commonwealth Health Services Co., Roanoke Meml. Services Corp., RMH Air, Ltd., Syndicated Collection Agy. Ltd., Emerald Property Mgmt., Inc., Burrell Health Care Ctr. Corp., Health East, Inc., Healthcare Interiors, Inc., The House of Care of Southwest Va. Mem. adv. council, past bd. dirs. YMCA. Served to 1st lt. Med. Adminstrv. Corps, U.S. Army, 1943-46. Named one of ten Most Prominent Men in Roanoke area, 1977; recipient Resolution of Appreciation Va. Hosp. Assn., 1978; honoree Brotherhood Citation Dinner NCCJ, 1980; Chili Cookoff Champion of Va., 1980; named One of Dozen Who Made a Difference in Building Roanoke, 1982. Fellow Am. Coll. Hosp. Adminstrs. (past regent, spl. recognition award 1983), Royal Soc. Health (Great Britain); mem. Roanoke Hosp. Assn. (pres.), Southeastern Hosp. Conf. (bd. dirs., past chmn.), Va. Hosp. Assn. (past pres.), Am. Hosp. Assn., Nat. Council of Community Hosps. (mem. liaison com. to Congress), Hosp. Fin. Mgmt., Va. Council on Health and Med. Care. Presbyterian. Home: Roanoke, Va. Died May 4, 2010.

FLANNERY, GEORGE PERRY, lawyer; b. Mpls., Sept. 30, 1922; s. Henry Clay and Marcia (Beebe) F.; m. Mary Dutoit, 1946; m. Anne Montgomery, July 28, 1951; 1 child, Susan Flannery Breuer. BS, Harvard U., 1946, LLB, 1948. Bar: N.Y. 1948, Minn. 1951. Assoc. Wickes, Reddell, Blommer, Jacobi & McGuire, NYC, 1949-50; from assoc. to ptnr. Dorsey & Whitney, Mpls., 1951-87, of counsel, from 1988. Bd. dirs. FluiDyne Engring. Corp., Mpls. Bd. dirs. Legal Aid Soc. Minn., Mpls., 1966-72. Served with U.S. Army, 1943-46, CBI. Mem.: Minneapolis (Mpls.), Minikahda, Ruta Baga Inst. (pres. 1965—). Democrat. Presbyterian. Avocations: tennis, gardening. Home: Minneapolis, Minn. Died June 20, 2010.

FLAUM, MARSHALL ALLEN, television producer, writer, director; b. Bklyn. s. Mayer and Ethel (Lamkay) P.; m. Gita Faye Miller; children: Erica, Seth Baruch. BA, U. Iowa, 1948; DFA (hon.), So. Ill. U., Edwardsville, 1974. Story editor, writer, assoc. producer TV series for 20th Century, 1957-62; prodr., writer, dir. TV specials for Wolper Productions, 1962-65; founder Flaum-Grinberg Prodns., 1966; v.p. Metromedia Producers Corp., 1968-76; pres. Marshall Flaum Productions, Inc., 1976—2010. Prodr., writer, dir.: (TV specials) Day of Infamy, 1963, Hollywood: The Great Stars, 1963, The Yanks Are Coming, 1964, Battle of Britain, 1964, Berlin: Kaiser to Kruschev, 1964, Let My People Go: The Story of Israel, 1965 (Ohio State award, George Foster Peabody award), Miss Goodall and the Wild Chimpanzees, 1966 (Edinburgh Festival award), Bogart, 1967 (Melbourne Festival award) Hollywood: The Selznick Years, 1969 (Silver Lion award Venice film Festival), The Time of Man, 1969 (Silver Hugo award Chgo. Internat. Festival), Yabba Dabba Doo! The Happy World of Hanna-Barbera, 1977, Bing Crosby: His Life and Legend, 1978 (Christopher award), Playboy's 25th Anniversary Celebration, 1979, A Bing Crosby Christmas...Like the Ones We Used to Know, 1979, Bob Hope's Texaco Star Theatre, Life's Most Embarrassing Moments, 1984, Portrait of Dorothy Stratten, 1985, A Yabba Dabba Doo Celebration, 50 Yrs. of Hanna Barbera, 1989, Arts and Entertainment's Ancient Mysteries, 1996, Celebrate the Century, 1998-99, The Desilu Story, 1999-2000; prodr., writer TV spls. Killy Le Champion, 1969; exec. prodr., co-writer: (TV series) Undersea World of Jacques Cousteau, 1970-76, Jane Goodall and The World of Animal Behavior, 1972-76, The Wild Dogs of Africa, 1973 (Emmy award best documentary, Chgo. Internat. Festival Gold Hugo award), Baboons of Gombe, 1974, Hyena, 1975, Lions of Serengeti, 1976; prodr. Am. Film Inst. Salute to Bette Davis, 1977; prodr., co-writer (with others): TV spls. Ripley's Believe It or Not, 1982, Bob Hope's Who Makes the World Laugh, 1983. Recipient Emmy award as best documentary for A Sound of Dolphins, 1972, The Unsinkable Sea Otter, 1972, George Foster Peabody award for TV spls. for Miss Goodall and The Wild Chimpanzees, 1966, Monte Carlo Internat. TV Festival Golden Nymph award for TV spl. The Yanks are Coming, 1964, Silver medal Atlanta Film Festival for Wild Dogs of Africa, 1973, Octopus, Octopus, 1972, Chgo. Internat. Film Festival Silver Hugo award for Tragedy of the Red Salmon, 1971, Oscar nomination sfor best documentary feature for The Yanks Are Coming, 1964, Let My People Go, 1966, Golden Globe nomination for The Fogotten Mermaids, 1972, Writers Guild of Am. nomination for The Time of Man, 1969, 16 Emmy award nominations. Mem. Writers Guild Am., Dirs. Guild Am., Acad. Motion Picture Arts and Scis., Acad. TV Arts and Scis. Died Oct. 1, 2010.

FLEDDERJOHN, KARL ROSS, manufacturing executive; b. Indpls., Aug. 28, 1935; s. Riley Bartel and Virginia Louise (Saalmiller) F.; m. Mary Ann Hilligoss, Apr. 5, 1953; children: Deborah Westley, Diane Luke, Dan, Laura Fledderjohn Nichols. BSME, Gen. Motors Inst., Flint, Mich., 1958; MBA, Butler U., 1966. Engr. Allison div. Gen. Motors, Indpls., 1957-69; sr. project engr. Garrett Turbine Engine Co., Phoenix, Ariz., 1970-83; devel. specialist, asst. project engr., chief engr. fan and jet engines Garrett Pneumatic Systems Divsn., Tempe, Ariz., 1983-88; dir. engring., asst. divsn. mgr., v.p., div. mgr. Allied Signal Aerospace Co., Torrance, Calif., from 1988, pres. Airesearch Group, pres. sector staff, pres. equipment and controls group. Avocations: golf, music, sports cars, spectator sports. Home: Scottsdale, Ariz. Died Oct. 6, 2009.

FLEISCHAUER, EMIL A., JR., insurance executive; b. Colby, Wis., Apr. 4, 1927; s. Emil A. F.; m. Mary A. Fleischauer; children: Vicki, Alan, Missy, Kirk, Mark. BBA, U. Wis., 1949, JD, 1951. Bar: Wis. Various legal positions Sentry Ins., Stevens Point, Wis., 1958-81, v.p., gen. counsel, 1981-84, gen. counsel, v.p. legal and G.A., 1984-87, v.p., gen. counsel, corp. sec., from 1987; also bd. dirs. Sentry Ins. and subs. Bd. dirs. Wis. Ins. Alliance, Madison. Pres. Village of Park Ridge, Wis., 1981—. Mem. ABA, State Bar Wis. Home: Stevens Point, Wis. Died Jan. 10, 2010.

FLEISCHER, RICHARD CHRISTOPHER, accountant, educator; b. Paterson, NJ, Oct. 22, 1948; s. Adolph R. and Margaret Mary (Christensen) F.; m. Patricia Anita Reed, July 21, 1973; children: Richard Christopher, Lauren Marie. BA in Acctg., William Paterson Coll., 1975; BA in History, Canisius Coll., 1970. CPA, NJ Credit mgr. Sherwin Williams Co., Union, NJ, 1970-72; comml. lending officer Greater Jersey Bancorp, West Paterson, 1972-75; staff acct. Fox & Co., CPAs, Paterson, NJ, 1975-77; sr. acct. Stephen P. Radics & Co., CPAs, Haledon, NJ, 1977-79; chief fin. officer Bergen State Bank, Bergenfield, NJ, 1979-83; propr. Richard C. Fleischer, CPA, Pompton Lakes, NJ, 1983—; adj. prof. acctg. William Paterson Coll., 1980—. Mem. sch. bd. St. Mary's Roman Cath. Sch., Pompton Lakes, 1983-85; trustee, treas., coach Pompton Lakes Little League, 1980—; coach St. Mary's HS Basketball, 1982—. Fellow NJ Soc. CPAs; mem. Am. Inst. CPAs, Inst. Mgmt. Accts., Nat. Soc. Pub. Accts. Lodge: Elks. Home: Pompton Lakes, NJ. Died Apr. 27, 2010.

FLEISCHMAN, ALBERT SIDNEY (SID FLEISCHMAN), writer; b. Bklyn., Mar. 16, 1920; s. Reuben and Sadie (Solomon) F.; m. Beth Elaine Taylor, Jan. 25, 1942 (dec. 1993); children: Jane, Paul, Anne. BA, San Diego State Coll., 1949. Newspaper reporter San Diego Daily Jour., 1949-50; freelance screenwriter. Lectr. fiction writing UCLA. Author: (children's books) Mr. Mysterious & Company, 1962, By the Great Horn Spoon!, 1963, The Ghost in the Noonday Sun, 1965, Chancy and the Grand Rascal, 1966, McBroom and the Great Race, 1970, Longbeard the Wizard, 1970, Jingo Django, 1971, Kate's Secret Riddle Book, 1977, Me and the Man on the Moon-Eyed Horse, 1977, Jim Bridger's Alarm Clock and Other Tall Tales, 1978, Humbug Mountain, 1978, McBroom and the Beanstalk, 1978, The Hey Hey Man, 1979, McBroom and the Great Race, 1980, The Bloodhound Gang in the Case of the Cackling Ghost, 1981, The Bloodhound Gang in the Case of the Flying Clock, 1981, The Bloodhound Gang in the Case of the Princess Tomorrow, 1981, The Bloodhound Gang in the Case of the Secret Message, 1981, The Bloodhound Gang in the Case of the 264-Pound Burglar, 1982, McBroom's Zoo, 1982, McBroom's Ear, 1982, McBroom and the Big Wind, 1982, The Bloodhound Gang's Secret Code Book, 1983, McBroom's Almanac, 1984, The Whipping Boy, 1986 (John Newbery medal, 1987), The Scarebird, 1988, The Midnight Horse, 1990, Jim Ugly, 1992, Here Comes McBroom, 1992, McBroom's Wonderful One-Acre Farm, 1992, The 13th Floor, 1995, The Abracadabra Kid, 1996, A Writer's Life, 1996, Mr. Mysterious & Company, 1997, Chancy and the Grand Rascal, 1997, The Ghost on Saturday Night, 1997, Bandit's Moon, 1998, McBroom's Ghost, 1998, McBroom Tells the Truth, 1998, McBroom the Rainmaker, 1999, McBroom Tells a Lie, 1999, A Carnival of Animals, 2000, Bo and Mzzz Mad, 2001, Disappearing Act, 2003, The Giant Rat of Sumatra, 2005, Escape! The Story of the Great Houdini, 2006, The White Elephant, 2006; (screenplays) Blood Alley, 1955, Goodbye, My Lady, 1956, Lafayette Escadrille, 1958, The Deadly Companions, 1973, Scalawag, 1973, Prince Brat and the Whipping Boy, 1995. Served with USNR, 1941-45. Recipient Spur award Western Writers Am., Commonwealth Club award, Lewis Carrol Shelf award, Mark Twain award, Calif. Young Reader award, John and Patricia Beatty award. Mem. Writers Guild Am., Authors Guild, Soc. Children's Book Writers and Illustrators. Democrat. Jewish. Died Mar. 17, 2010.

FLEISCHMANN, ERNEST MARTIN, performing arts executive, consultant; b. Frankfurt, Germany, Dec. 7, 1924; came to U.S., 1969; s. Gustav and Antonia (Koch) F.; children: Stephanie, Martin, Jessica. B of Commerce, U. Cape Town, South Africa, 1950, MusB, 1954; postgrad., South African Coll. Music, 1954-56; MusD (hon.), Cleve. Inst. Music, 1987. Gen mgr. London Symphony Orch., 1959-67; dir. Europe CBS Masterworks, 1967-69; exec. v.p., mng. dir. LA Philharm. Assn. & Hollywood Bowl, 1969-98; artistic cons. LA Philharm. Assn., from 1998; pres. Fleischmann Arts, Internat. Arts Mgmt. Cons. Svc., 1998—2010. Mem. French Govt. Commn. Reform of Paris Opera, 1967-68; steering com. U.S. nat. commn. UNESCO Conf. Future of Arts, 1975; artistic dir. Ojai Festival, 1998-2003; bd. counselors U. So. Calif. Thornton Sch. Music; bd. dirs. Monday Evening Concerts,; hon. lifetime dir. LA Philharm. bd. of visitors Columbia Sch. for Performing Arts; bd dirs. Masika Angelica. Debut as condr. Johannesburg (Republic of South Africa) Symphony Orch., 1942; asst. condr. South African Nat. Opera, 1948-51, Cape Town U. Opera, 1950-54; condr. South African Coll. Music Choir, 1950-52, Labia Grand Opera Co., Cape Town, 1953-55; music organizer Van Riebeeck Festival Cape Town, 1952; dir. music and drama Johannesburg Festival, 1956; contbr. to music publs. Decorated officier Ordre des Arts et Lettres (France), comdrs. cross Order of Merit (Germany), knight 1st class Order of the White Rose (Finland); recipient award of Merit, L.A. Jr. C. of C., John Steinway award, Friends of Music award, Disting. Arts Leadership award U. So. Calif., 1989, L.A. Honors award, L.A. Arts Coun., 1989, Live Music award Am. Fedn. Musicians Local 47, 1991, Disting. Authors/Artists award U. Judaism, 1994, Treasures of L.A. award, Ctrl. City Assn. L.A., 1996, Los Amigos de Los Angeles award, L.A. Conv. and Vis. Bur., 1996; honored Mayor and City Coun. as First Living Cultural Treasure of L.A., 1998, Gold Baton award Am. Symphony Orch. League, 1999. Mem. Assn. Calif. Symphony Orchs., L.A. Philharm. Assn. (bd. dirs. 1984—), Salzburg Seminar/Alberto Vilar Conf. on Orch. Mgmt. (co-chmn. 2002). Died June 13, 2010.

FLETCHER, DOUGLAS BADEN, investment company executive; b. Pleasant Ridge, Mich., Mar. 25, 1925; s. Ernest H. and Gladys (Marthan) F.; m. Sally Wittenberg, Sept. 9, 1950; children: David, Christopher, James, Jonathan. BA, Princeton, 1949. Security analyst Walston & Co., NYC, 1949-53; mem. underwriting dept. Blyth & Co., Los Angeles, 1953-62; chmn. bd., chief exec. officer First Pacific Advisors, Inc., Los Angeles, 1962-83, Angeles Corp., 1968-83, Source Capital, Inc., Los Angeles, 1968-82; chmn. FPA Paramount Mut. Fund, Inc., LA, 1978-84; ptnr. Newport Ptnrs., from 1982. Bd. dirs., vice chmn. Bank of Am., Group of Mut. Funds; bd. dirs. TIS Mortgage Investment Co., San Francisco; chmn. bd. Fletcher Capital Advisors Inc., Newport Beach, 1991—. Trustee Claremont McKenna Coll. (Calif.), 1969—. With AUS, 1943-46. Mem. Inst. Chartered Fin. Analysts, L.A. Soc. Fin. Analysts (pres. 1960-61) Clubs: Princeton of So. Calif. (L.A.) (pres. 1962-64), Newport Harbor Yacht Club (Newport Beach, Calif.). Died June 13, 2009.

FLINT, BENNY, architect, real estate developer, consultant; b. Miami Beach, Fla., May 6, 1954; s. Israel and Frida (Lelental) Flint. Grad., U. Haifa, Israel, 1973; BArch, U. Miami, 1978; grad. in Real Estate Course, 1982. Project coord. Superconstrucciones, Bogota, Colombia, 1978—79, 9 Island Ave., Miami Beach, 1980—81; designer, ptnr. Architectum, Inc., Miami Beach, from 1981, v.p., from 1985; real estate developer F.G.F. Corp., Miami Beach, from 1981, pres., from 1985, B. Flint & Assocs., Haim, Flint & Assocs., from 1985. Contbr. chapters to books, articles to profl. jours. Recipient award, Miami Design Preservation League Art Deco, 1982—85, South Fla., Interior Design Guild, 1985. Mem.: Am. Soc. Interior Design (assoc.), Hebraica Club (Miami), Miami Beach Jaycees Club, Archtl. Club (Miami). Republican. Jewish. Home: Miami, Fla. Died Aug. 28, 2010.

FLINT, JERRY (YEHUDI MEYER FLINT), writer; b. Detroit, June 20, 1931; BA in Journalism, Wayne State U., 1953. Journalist, Chgo./Detroit burs. The Wall St. Jour., 1956-57, The NY Times, NYC, 1967-73; Washington bur. chief/asst. mng. editor/sr. editor Forbes mag., NYC, 1973—2010, columnist Backseat Driver, 1996—2010. Auto columnist, N.Y.C., 1996-2010; columnist Ward's Auto World, Detroit, 1996-2010; automotive commentator, CNNFN, N.Y., 1996-2010 Author: The Dream Machine: The Golden Age of American Automobiles, 1946-1965, 1997. Served in US Army. Recipient Gerald Loeb award, 2003. Home: New York, NY. Died Aug. 7, 2010.

FLOOR, RICHARD EARL, lawyer; b. Lynn, Mass., Aug. 3, 1940; s. Albert C. and Blanche (Goldthwait) F.; m. Elizabeth Wilson, Apr. 19, 1969; children: Amy, Lucy, Rebecca. AB, Fairfield U., 1962; JD, Harvard Law Sch., 1965. Bar: Mass. 1965, N.Y. 2001. Law clk. to Hon. C.P. O'Sullivan U.S. Ct. Appeals (6th cir.), 1965-66; assoc. Goodwin, Procter & Hoar, Boston, 1966-74; ptnr. Goodwin Procter LLP (formerly Goodwin, Procter & Hoar), Boston, from 1974; mem. mgmt. com. & exec. com. Goodwin, Procter & Hoar, Boston, 1987-93; mem. mgmt. com., co-chair corp. dept. Goodwin Procter LLP, Boston. Lectr. Harvard Bus. Sch., Cambridge, 1988-92; bd. dirs. Affiliated Mgrs. Group, Inc., New Am. High Income Fund, NYSE; mem. supervisory bd. Lyondell-Basell S.A. Contbr. articles to profl. jours. Co-chmn. reverse investment com. internat. trade adv. bd. Commonwealth Mass., 1994; organizer Inst. Mgmt. Edn. Thailand; trustee Regis Coll., Wellesley, Mass., 1990-97, 99-2007; chmn. Harvard Ctr. Eating Disorders, 2000-01. Mem. ABA, Boston Bar Assn. Home: Belmont, Mass. Died Feb. 18, 2010.

FLOWER, JOSEPH REYNOLDS, administrative executive; b. Indpls., Mar. 1, 1913; s. J. Roswell and Alice Marie (Reynolds) F.; m. Mary Jane Carpenter, June 6, 1940; children: Joseph Reynolds, Mary Alice, Paul William. Diploma, Cen. Bible Coll., Springfield, Mo., 1934. Ordained to ministry Assemblies of God Ch., 1934. Pastor chs. in Pa., N.Y., Maine, Mass., 1934-54; supt. N.Y. Dist. Assembly of God, 1954-75; mem. gen presbytery Gen. Coun., Springfield, from 1953, mem. exec. presbtery, from 1966, gen. sec., from 1976. Bd. dirs. Valley Forge Christian Coll., Phoenixville, Pa., Cen. Bible Coll., 1965-73, 1983-90, Assemblies of God Theol. Sem., Springfield, 1973-91, Evangel Coll., Springfield, 1979-87. Home: Springfield, Mo. Died Mar. 29, 2010.

FLOYD, JOHN B., JR., surgeon, educator; b. Louisville, Sept. 18, 1917; s. John B. and Barbara Lois (Lanahan) Floyd; m. Margaret Feeback Floyd; 1 child, Michael Feeback. AB, U. Ky., 1938; MD, U. Louisville, 1941; MS, Tulane U., 1949. Diplomate Am. Bd. Surgery. Intern St. Elizabeth Hosp., Covington, Ky.; jr. asst. resident in medicine City Hosp., Louisville, 1942—43; resident in surgery Lexington (Ky.) Clinic and Ochsner Found., 1943—48; individual practice medicine specializing in surgery Lexington Ky., 1949—86; clin. instr. vol. faculty U. Ky. Med. Ctr., from 1967; ret. Contbr. articles to profl. jours. Pres. sr. class U. of Louisville Sch. Medicine, 1940—41. Maj. MC USAF, 1955. Recipient Distinguished Service award, Ky. div. Am. Cancer Soc., 1950, Am. Cancer Soc., 1967. Mem.: ACS, Filson Club, So. Med. Assn., Ky. Hist. Soc., Ky. Med. Assn., Fayette County Med. Soc., Ky. Surg. Soc., Lexington Surg. Soc., Southeastern Surg. Congress, Filson Club, Lafayette Club. Democrat. Episcopalian. Died July 0, 1990.

FLUKE, LYLA SCHRAM (MRS. JOHN M. (LYLA) FLUKE SR.), publisher; b. Maddock, ND; d. Olaf John and Anne Marie (Rodberg) Schram; m. John M. Fluke, June 5, 1937 (dec. 2002); children: Virginia Fluke Gabelein, John M. Jr., David Lynd. BS in Zoology and Physiology, U. Wash., Seattle, 1934, diploma tchg., 1935. H.S. tchr., 1935-37; tutor Seattle schs., 1980-84; pub. Portage Quar. mag. Hist. Soc. Seattle and King County, 1980-84. Hon. chmn. nanotech. rsch. U. Wash., 2000, hon. chmn. campaign, from 2006. Contbr. articles to profl. jours. Co-founder N.W. chpt. Myasthenia Gravis Found., 1953, Wash. Tech. Ctr., 1996, pres., 1960-66; obtained N.W. artifacts for Navy destroyer Tender Puget Sound., 1966; mem. Seattle Mayor's Com. for Seattle Beautiful, 1962; sponsor Seattle World's Fair, 1962; charter and founding mem. Seattle Youth Symphony Aux., 1974; benefactor U. Wash., 1982-01, sponsor first chair mfg., U Wash., 1982, nat. chmn. ann. giving campaign, 1983-84; benefactor Cascade Symphony, Salvation Army, Sterling Cir. Stanford U., MIT, 1984, Seattle Symphony, 1982-2002, Wash. State Hist. Soc., Pacific Arts Coun., Pacific Sci. Ctr., 2003-04, Twenty-Twelve Club, 1962-2002; mem. condr.'s club Seattle Symphony, 1978-; mem. U. Wash. Campaign Exec. Com., 2003-04, hon. mem. Campaign Com. NSF Grant to Nat. Nanotechnology Infrastructure Network, 1984; hon. exec. com. on nanotech. U. Wash. Coll. Engring., 2003-; benefactor Seattle Symphony, 2004, U. Wash., 2004; mem. Seattle Beautification Com., 1965-68. Recipient Crystal plaque Coll. Engring. U. Wash., 2002, Framed document Pres. US; fellow Seattle Pacific U., 1972; named Father of Electronics in Wash. State, Gov. John Spellman, 1983; honored by Repub. Nat. Com. Eisenhower Commn., 2006. Mem. IEEE Aux. (chpt. charter mem., pres. 1970-73), Wash. Trust Hist. Preservation, Nat. Trust for Hist. Preservation, N.W. Ornamental Hort. Soc. (benefactor, life, hon.), Nat. Assn. Parliamentarians (charter mem., pres. N.W. unit 1961-64), Wash. Parliamentarians Assn. (charter), Seattle C. of C. (women's divsn. 1965-66), Seattle Symphony Women's Assn. (life, charter, sec. 1982-84, pres. 1985-87), Hist. Soc. Seattle and King County (exec. com. 1975-78, pres. women's mus. league 1975-79, pres. Moritz Thomsen Guild of Hist. Soc., 1978-80, 84-87), Highlands Orthopedic Guild (life), Wash. State Hist. Soc., Antiquarian Soc. (v.p. 1986-88, pres. 1988-90, hon. mem. John Fluke Mfg. Co. 20 Year Club 1987—), Rainier Club, Seattle Golf Club, U. Wash. Pres.'s Club, Twenty-Twelve Club, Pacific Sci. Ctr, Seattle. Republican. Lutheran. Achievements include sponsorship of the Fluke Chair in Coll. of Engring. U Wash. Home: Seattle, Wash. Died Jan. 15, 2010.

FOCHT, THEODORE HAROLD, lawyer, educator; b. Reading, Pa., Aug. 20, 1934; s. Harold Edwin and Ruth Naomi (Boyer) Focht; m. Joyce Gundy, Aug. 11, 1956; children: David Scott, Eric Steven. AB in Philosophy, Franklin and Marshall Coll., 1956; JD, Coll. of William and Mary, 1959. Bar: Va. 1959. Tchg. assoc. Columbia U. Sch. Law, NYC, 1959—60; atty. Office of Gen. Counsel SEC, NYC, 1960—61, legal asst. to Commr. Washington, 1961—63; mem. faculty U. Conn. Sch. Law, Hartford, 1963—71, leave of absence, 1969—71; spl. counsel securities legislation, Interstate and Fgn. Commerce Com. US House of Reps., Washington, 1969—71; gen. counsel Securities Investor Protection Corp., Washington, 1971—94, pres., 1984—94. Adj. prof. law American U. Sch. Law, Washington, 1979—84; mem. Fla. State Comptroller's Task Force on Regulatory DeCoupling, 1995; sr. mgr. World Bank Russian Fedn., Moscow, 1995—97, Tunisia, 1995. Mem.: Va. State Bar, Phi Beta Kappa. Home: New Port Richey, Fla. Died Apr. 22, 2010.

FODERARO, ANTHONY HAROLDE, nuclear engineering educator; b. Scranton, Pa., Apr. 3, 1926; s. Edward and Myrtha (Bachman) F.; m. Rita Lacey, May 4, 1953; children—Anthony, John, Diana. BS in Physics, U. Scranton, 1950; PhD in Physics, U. Pitts., 1955. Supervisory scientist Westinghouse Atomic Power Div., Pitts., 1954-56; sr. nuclear physicist Gen. Motors Research, Warren, Mich., 1956-60; assoc. prof. nuclear engring. Pa. State U., University Park, 1960-63, prof., 1963-88; prof. emeritus, from 1989. Cons. on radiation protection govt. and industry. Author: The Elements of Neutron Interaction Theory, 1971, The Photon Shielding Manual, 1976; co-author: The Reactor Shielding Design Manual, 1956, The Engineering Compendium on Radiation Shielding, 1968; contbr. articles to publs. in field. Served with US Army, 1943—46. Home: State College, Pa. Died Dec. 13, 2009.

FOGARTY, WILLIAM EUGENE, manufacturing executive; b. NYC, July 4, 1931; s. William Leo and Gertrude Eliose (Costello) Fogarty; m. Nancy Ellen Meehan, Sept. 15, 1956; children: Nancy, Kathleen, William, Terence. BS in Physics, Fairfield U., 1957; MBA, U. Conn., 1977. Project engr. A.W. Haydon Co., Waterbury, Conn., 1957—63, sales engr., 1963—65; applications engr. Veeder Root Co., Hartford, 1965—69, asst. sales and mktg. mgr. instrument div., 1969—70, tech. coordinator Internat. div., from 1978; exec. asst. to commr. State of Conn. Dept. Children and Youth Services, Hartford, 1971—78; chmn., Wolcott (Conn.) Town Council, 1969—73, councilman, 1965—73. Mem. Wolcott Republican Town Com., from 1962, chmn., 1978—86. Served with USMC, 1951—54. Mem.: VFW (comdr. Wolcott post 1963—64), Wolcott C. of C. (pres. 1968—69), Wolcott Jaycees (charter mem., dir. 1962—63). Republican. Roman Catholic. Home: Waterbury, Conn. Died Oct. 10, 2009.

FOGIEL, MAX, publishing executive; b. Magdeburg, Germany, Aug. 29, 1929; came to U.S., 1940; s. Abram and Sara (Pergericht) F. BME, Cooper Union U., NYC, 1952; MME, Poly. Inst., Bklyn., 1954; PhD in Elec. Engring., Tech. U., Munich, Germany, 1965. Bar: U.S. Patent Office, 1958; registered profl. engr., N.Y., N.J. Sr. engr. Ford Instrument, Long Island City, NY, 1952-56, Control Instrument, Bklyn., 1956-59; rsch. engr. Loral Electronics, Bronx, NY, 1959-61; project engr. RCA, NYC, 1961-64; pres., CEO, Rsch. & Edn. Assn., Piscataway, NJ, 1964—2004, dir. engring. seminars, 1964-66. Instr. in elec. engring. N.J. Inst. Tech., 1965-66. Author: Microelectronics, 1968, 1973, Life Insurance, 1972, Beauty Care, 1993, AIDS and HIV, 1995, Handbook of Electrical Engineering, 1996, Handbook of Chemical Engineering, 1998, Handbook of Mechanical Engineering, 1998; editor: 41 Problem Solvers, from 1973, Energy Technology, vol. I and II, 1975, Pollution Control, vol. I and II, 1978, Calculus Textbook, 2002, series bus. and math. 57 books, 1999; pub. H.S. and coll. study guides and handbooks in sci. and tech.; editor: Basic Electronics, 2003, (test preparation books for) No Child Left Behind series, 2003; contbr. articles in NY Times and newspapers. Achievements include patents in field. Avocation: painting. Home: Highland Park, NJ. Died Dec. 3, 2009.

FOLEY, PATRICK JOSEPH, lawyer; b. NYC, Oct. 2, 1930; s. John and Anne (Sheehan) F.; m. Ann Tubman; children: Maura, John. BA, Iona Coll., 1957; JD, N.Y. Law Sch., 1961. Bar: N.Y. 1961, U.S. Dist. Ct. (so., no., ea. and we. dists.) N.Y., U.S. Tax Ct., U.S. Ct. Customs, U.S. Ct. Claims, U.S. Ct. Appeals (2d cir.), U.S. Supreme Ct. Asst. underwriter Atlantic Mutual, NYC, 1958-60; acct. exec. Hagedorn and Co., NYC, 1960-62; with Am. Internat. Group, Inc. and subs. cos., NYC, from 1963; now v.p., assoc. gen. counsel Am. Internat. Group, Inc., NYC, sr. v.p., gen. counsel all domestic brokerage cos. of. Recipient Outstanding Young Ins. Man award, 1965. Mem. ABA (sect. corp. banking and bus. law), N.Y. State Bar Assn. (ins. law sect.), Westchester County Bar Assn., N.Y. State Trial Lawyers Assn., Am. Judges Assn., Ins. Fedn. of N.Y. (bd. dirs.), Ins. Fedn. Pa. (bd. dirs.), N.Y. Ins. Exchange (chmn. security fund), N.Y. State Ins. Assn. (bd. dirs.), Downtown Assn., India House, Gaelic Soc. N.Y., Friendly Sons of St. Patrick, Players Club, N.Y. Athletic Club, Univ. Club Albany, Elks, K.C., Knights of Malta, Phi Delta Phi. Republican. Roman Catholic. Home: Lake Worth, Fla. Died Oct. 21, 2009.

FOOT, PHILIPPA RUTH, philosophy educator; b. Owston Ferry, Eng., Oct. 3, 1920; came to U.S., 1975; d. William Sydney Bence and Esther (Cleveland) Bosanquet; m. Michael Richard Daniell Foot, June 21, 1945 (div. 1960). BA, Oxford U., Eng., 1942; MA, Oxford U., 1946. Lectr. Somerville Coll., Oxford, Eng., 1947-50, fellow, tutor, 1950-69, vice-prin., 1967-69, sr. rsch. fellow, 1970-88; prof. philosophy UCLA, 1974—2010, Griffin prof., 1988—2010. Editor: Theories of

Ethics, 1967; author: Virtues and Vices, 1978, Natural Goodness, 2001; contbr. numerous articles to philos. jours. Fellow Brit. Acad., American Acad. Arts & Sciences Social Democrat. Died Oct. 3, 2010.

FORD, ALMA REGINA, retired union official, educator; b. Owings, W.Va., Oct. 4, 1939; d. Charles Feathers and Pearl (Costello) Ford. AB, Fairmont State Coll., 1960; MA, W.Va. U., 1964, Ball State U., 1984; postgrad., Sorbonne. Cert. counselor. Tchr., Ohio, 1961—78, W.Va., 1961—78, Turkey, 1961—78, England, 1961—78, France, 1961—78, Italy, 1961—78, Germany, 1961—78; v.p., dep. rep. Dept. Def. Dependents Schs.-Europe; negotiator Overseas Fedn. Tchrs., 1978—80; tchr. Zweibrucken, Germany, from 1980, counselor, 1997; ret., 1999. Recipient Sustained Superior/Performance award, Dept. Army, 1972—76, Exceptional Performance award, 1984; NDEA fellow, 1968. Mem.: LWV, AARP, AAUW, Marion County Ret. Tchrs. Assn., W.Va. Sheriff's Assn., Overseas Fedn. Tchrs., Am. Fedn. Tchrs., Speech Assn. Am., Nat. Assn. Ret. People, Nat. Coun. Tchrs. English, Nat. Assn. Ret. Fed. Employees, Zweibrucken Alumnus Assn., Fairmont State Coll. Alumnus Assn., Ret. Eagles Club, W.Va. Travelers Club, Moose, Elks, Eagles Ladies Aux., Am. Legion Ladies Aux., VFW Ladies Aux., Alpha Psi Omega, Phi Delta Kappa. Died July 15, 2009.

FORD, DEXTER, retired insurance company executive; b. Utica, NY, Nov. 18, 1917; s. David E. and Anna Mae (Dexter) F.; m. Jean Brand McGowan, Nov. 1, 1944; children: David K., Dexter T., Nancy E. BS, St. Lawrence U., 1939. With Aetna Life & Casualty Co., Hartford, Conn., 1946—80, v.p. mktg., 1968-76, v.p. personal ins. dept., 1976-80. Chmn. bd. mgmt. YMCA, 1978-80. Served to lt. (s.g.) USNR, 1941-45. Recipient St. Lawrence U. Alumni citation, 1978 Mem. St. Lawrence U. Alumni Assn. (pres. 1974-75) Congregationalist (chmn. bd. trustees 1970). Home: Saratoga Springs, NY. Died Sept. 1, 2010.

FORD, ROGER JULIAN, SR., clergyman; b. Esmont, Va., Oct. 2, 1934; s. Fleming Vaughn and Frances Catherine (Copeland) Ford; m. Velma Lee Gray, Mar. 1, 1958; children: Lori Nadine, Francine, Robin, Wendy, Roger Julian. DD with honor, Va. Sem. & Coll., 1985. Pastor Chestnut Grove Baptist Ch., Esmont, Va., 1962—70, Mt. Zion Bapt. Ch., Greenwood, Va., 1963—69, Wake Forest Bapt. Ch., Slate Hill, Va., 1969—74, Mt. Sinai Bapt. Ch., Madison Heights, Va., from 1971. Exec. dir. Monticello Cmty. Action Agy., Charlottesville, Va., 1970—74, Opportunity Industrialized Ctr., Lynchburg, Va., 1968—80; manpower dir. Total Action Against Poverty, Roanoke, 1974—78; mgr. Ebonaire Ch. Supply, Madison Heights, from 1980. Pres. Va. State Conf. NAACP, 1978—80; co-chmn. Amherst County Br. NAACP, 1975—78, from 1980, Amherst County Dem. Party, 1980—82. Sgt. USMC, 1954—58. Recipient Cmty. Achievement award, Lynchburg Nationwide Ins. Co., 1980; named Minister of Yr. Community Advancement and Achievement Movement, 1977, Leader of Yr., Amherst County NAACP, 1979. Mem.: Odd Fellows. Home: Madison Heights, Va. Died June 10, 2010.

FORDHAM, SHELDON LEROY, retired dean, physical education educator; b. Walnut, Ill., June 1, 1919; s. Lafe L. and Alta (Miller) F.; m. Margaret Bischof, Jan. 18, 1945; 1 dau., Barbara Fordham Lubbers. BS, U. Ill., 1941, MS, 1949; EdD, Mich. State U., 1963. Tchr. pub. schs., Ill., 1945-47; mem. faculty U. Ill., Chgo. Circle, 1947-89; prof. phys. edn., dean U. Ill., Chgo. Circle (Coll. Phys. Edn. and Recreation), 1963-89. Cons. in field. Co author: Physical Education and Sports: An Introduction to Alternative Careers, 1978. Pres. scholarship bd. Evergreen Park (Ill.) High Sch., 1963-66. Served with USNR, 1942-45. Mem. AAHPER, Assn. Research, Adminstrn., Profl. Councils and Socs., Nat. Assn. Phys. Edn. in Higher Edn., Nat. Coll. Phys. Edn., Assn. Men (pres. 1974), Ill. Assn. Profl. Preparation in Health, Phys. Edn. and Recreation (pres. 1965) Died Apr. 12, 2010.

FORNOFF, FRANK J(UNIOR), retired chemistry educator, consultant; b. Mt. Carmel, Ill., Mar. 29, 1914; s. Frank and Ada (Arnold) F. AB, U. Ill., 1936; MS, Ohio State U., 1937, PhD, 1939. Asst. prof. Lehigh U., Bethlehem, Pa., 1942-44; chem. engr. Western Electric Co., NYC, 1944-45; asst. prof. chemistry Lehigh U., 1945-47, assoc. prof., 1947-53, Kans. State U., Manhattan, 1953-56; lectr. Rutgers U., New Brunswick, N.J., 1956-84; sr. examiner Ednl. Testing Svc., Princeton, N.J., 1956-93, group head, 1956-83. Editor AP Chemistry newsletter, 1976-90; contbr. articles to profl. jours. Active Boy Scouts Am., Princeton, 1957-93. NRC fellow U. Calif., Berkeley, 1939-40; Procter and Gamble fellow Ohio State U., 1938-39. Mem. AAAS, Am. Chem. Soc. (chmn. local sect. assn. publs. 1960-70), Am. Soc. Engring. Edn., Nat. Sci. Tchrs. Assn., Nat. Council Measurements in Edn., N.J. Acad. Sci., N.Y. Acad. Sci. Methodist. Home: Mount Carmel, Ill. Died May 16, 2010.

FORRESTER, MAUREEN KATHERINE STEWART, contralto; b. Montreal, Que., Can., July 25, 1930; d. Thomas and Mae (Arnold) F.; m. Eugene J. Kash, July 1954 (div. 1976); children: Paula, Gina, Daniel, Linda, Susanna. Student of, Sally Martin, Frank Rowe, Bernard Diamant; MusD (hon.), St. George William U., St. Mary's U., Toronto U., McMaster U., Victoria U., Bishop's U., York U., Western U., Mt. Allison U., Wilfred Pelletier U. Debut in Can., 1953, at Town Hall, N.Y.C., 1956; appearances with major orchs. and festivals throughout world; created roles: Orfeo in Orfeo, Madame de la Hattiere in Cendrillon, Klytemestra in Elektra, Witch in Hansel and Gretel, Mme de Croissy in Dialogues des Carmelites, Herodias in Salome, others; rec. artist: RCA Victor, Decca, Westminster, Philips, Columbia, DGG, Vanguard. Decorated companion Order of Can.; recipient Molson prize. Died June 16, 2010.

FORROW, BRIAN DEREK, lawyer; b. NYC, Feb. 6, 1927; s. Frederick George and Doris (Williams) F.; m. Eleanor Reid, Mar. 8, 1952; children: Lisa Coggins, Brian Lachlan, Catherine Frances, Derek Skylstead. AB, Princeton U., 1947; JD, Harvard U., 1950. Bar: N.Y. 1950, Conn. 1967, U.S. Supreme Ct. 1954. From assoc. to ptnr. Cahill, Gordon, Sonnett, Reindel & Ohl (and predecessors), 1950-68; v.p., gen. counsel Allied Chem. Corp., 1968-85, dir., 1969-85; sr. v.p., gen. counsel Allied-Signal Inc., 1985-92; pvt. practice, Greenwich, Conn., from 1992; of counsel Whitman Breed Abbott & Morgan, 1992-94. Bd. dirs. Union Tex. Petroleum, 1985-92. Contbr. articles to profl. publs. Mem. Greenwich Representative Town Meeting, 1993—; vestryman, former sr. warden, former diocesan rep., Episcopal Ch. Served to 1st lt. USAF, 1951-53. Mem. ABA, Am. Law Inst., Conn. Bar Assn., N.Y. State Bar Assn., Assn. Bar City of N.Y. (past chmn. com. corp. law depts.), Assn. Gen. Counsel, Am. Arbitration Assn. (bd. dirs. 1987-97), Corp. Bar Assn. Westchester-Fairfield (past pres., bd. dirs. 1986-91), Am. Corp. Counsel Assn. (bd. dirs. 1987-89), Assn. Corp. Counsel N.J. (past pres.), Indian Harbor Yacht Club (past bd. dirs.), Harvard Club N.Y., Ret. Men's Assn. Greenwich Conn. (officer, dir. 2003—). Republican. Died Aug. 4, 2010.

FORSTER, ARNOLD, lawyer, author; b. NYC, June 25, 1912; s. Hyman Lawrence and Dorothy (Turits) Fastenberg; m. May Kasner, Sept. 29, 1940 (dec. 2005); children: Stuart William (dec. 1991), Janie Forster Berman. LLB, St. John's U., 1935. Bar: N.Y. 1935, U.S. Supreme Ct. 1949. Gen. practice law, 1935-40; dir. law dept. Anti-Defamation League of B'nai Brith, 1940-46; assoc. dir. Anti-Defamation League of B'nai B'rith, 1946-78, gen. counsel, 1946—2003; of counsel Shea & Gould, NYC, 1979-94, Baer Marks and Upham, NYC, 1994—2010. Police justice N.Y. State, 1954-57 Author: Anti-Semitism in the United States, 1947, A Measure of Freedom, 1950, The Troublemakers, 1952, Cross-Currents, 1956, Some of My Best Friends, 1962, Danger on the Right, 1964, (with B.R. Epstein) Report on the Ku Klux Klan, 1965, Report on the John Birch Society, 1966, Radical Right: Report on the John Birch Society and Its Allies, 1967, Report From Israel, 1969, The New Anti-Semitism, 1974, Square One, 1988, Stubs-A Letter to His Children, 1994; author (TV/radio) Dateline Israel, 1967-83 Mem. bd. edn., New Rochelle, N.Y., 1962-66. Recipient Emmy award for film Avenue of the Just, 1980, Emmy award for film Zubin and the I.P.O., 1983 Home: New Rochelle, NY. Died Mar. 7, 2010.

FORSYTHE, JOHN, actor; b. Penn's Grove, NJ, Jan. 29, 1918; s. Samuel Jeremiah and Blanche Materson (Blohm) Freund; m. Parker McCormick (div.); m. Julie Warren (dec. Aug. 1994); children: Dall, Page, Brooke. Student, U. N.C., also N.Y. Actor's Studio. Radio announcer Bklyn. Dodgers, 1938-40. Actor: (films) Destination Tokyo, 1944, Captive City, 1952, Escape from Fort Bravo, 1953, It Happens Every Thursday, 1953, The Glass Web, 1954, Everything But the Truth, 1956, Kitten With a Whip, 1956, Trouble with Harry, 1956, Ambassador's Daughter, 1956, Madame X, 1966, In Cold Blood, 1968, Topaz, 1969, Happy Ending, 1970, And Justice for All, 1979, Scrooged, 1988, Stan and George's New Life, 1992, Chalie's Angels (voice only), 2000, Charlie's Angels II: Full Throttle (voice only), 2003; on tour with play Mr. Roberts, then on Broadway, later dir. City Center (N.Y.) revival, 1956; Broadway play Teahouse of the August Moon, 1953-56, Weekend, 1968, The Caine Mutiny Court Martial, 1971; (TV series) Bachelor Father, 1957-62, The John Forsythe Show, 1965-66, To Rome With Love, 1971, World of Survival, 1970-82, Charlie's Angels (voice only), 1976-81, Dynasty, 1981-89, The Powers That Be, 1991-92; (TV movies) See How They Run, 1964, Shadow of the Land, 1968, Murder Once Removed, 1971, The Letters, 1973, Lisa- Bright and Dark, 1973, Cry Panic, 1974, The Healers, 1974, Terror on the 40th Floor, 1974, The Deadly Tower, 1975, Cruise Into Terror, 1978, Amelia Earhart, 1976, Tail Gunner Joe, 1977, Never Con a Killer, 1977, The Users, 1978, With This Ring, 1978, A Time of Miracle, 1980, Sizzle, 1981, Mysterious Two, 1982, On Fire, 1987, Opposites Attract, 1990, Dynasty: The Reunion, 1991; host sports show Hollywood Park Feature Race, 1971-74. Recipient two Golden Globe awards. Avocation: tennis. Died Apr. 1, 2010.

FORTENBERRY, DELORES B., dean; b. McComb, MS, Jan. 31, 1933; d. Isaac and Maude Elma (Carmel) Brown; m. John Prowell, Jan. 22, 1956 (div. 1960); children: Dennis A. Prowell, Stevie G. Prowell; m. Fred D. Fortenberry, Dec. 3, 1971. BS, Jackson State U., 1963; MA, Ball State U., 1974, EdD, 1988. Sci. & math. tchr. McComb (Ms.) Pub. Schs., 1962-65; sci. tchr. Chgo. Pub. Schs., 1965-68; sci., art tchr. E. Chgo. Pub. Sch., Ind., 1968-80; sci. tchr. Ball State U. Lab Sch., Muncie, IL, 1980-81; sci., math. tchr., gen. edn. E. Chgo. Pub. Sch., Ind., 1981-89, dean, from 1989. Pres. Dist. Sci. Fair com., McComb, Miss., 1964-65; nat. chairperson Pike County Agrl. H.S. Alumni, Chgo., 1991-2000, Pike County Agrl. H.S. scholarship fund; chmn. sci. com. Nat. Alliance Black Sch. Educators, Washington, Chgo. Alliance Black Sch. Educators, 1984-86. Fellow NSF, 1963-64, Ball State U., 1980-81; sabbatical leave E. Chgo. Pub. Sch., 1980-81. Mem. AAUW, Nat. Alliance Black Sch. Educators, Chgo. Alliance Black Sch. Educators (certificate 1986), Afro-Am. History Club (chairperson 1999-2000), Pike County Agrl. H.S. Alumni (nat. chairperson 1991-2000, recipient plaques 1992-94, 96-98), Am. Fedn. Tchrs., Nat. Sci. Tchrs. Assn., Hoosier Assn. Sci. Tchrs., Assn. Supervision and Curriculum Devel., Kappa Delta Pi, Gamma Phi Delta (basilieus, 1968-73), Phi Delta Kappa. Avocations: reading, travel, collecting recipes, collecting black history materials, sports. Home: Glenwood, Ill. Died Jan. 30, 2010.

FORTH, STUART, librarian; b. Manistee, Mich., Aug. 13, 1923; s. Wade Stuart and Nan (Rumans) F.; m. Pearl Elizabeth Brown, Dec. 24, 1951. BA, U. Mich., 1949, MLS, 1950; PhD in History, U. Wash., 1961. Catalog librarian Oreg. State U., Corvallis, 1950-52, adminstrv. asst. to dir. libraries, 1952-54; reference librarian Seattle Pub. Library, 1954-59; undergrad. librarian U. Kans., Lawrence, 1959-61, assoc. dir. libraries, 1961-65; dir. libraries U. Ky., Lexington, 1965-73, prof. library sci., 1966-73, v.p. for student affairs, 1968-70; dean, univ. libraries Pa. State U., University Park, 1973-88, dean emeritus, from 1988. Teaching fellow history U. Wash., 1954-55, 57-58; instr. dept. Western Civilization U. Kans., 1960-65; Pres. Reagan appointee to adv. com. White House Conf. on Libr. and Info. Svcs., 1989—. Staff sgt. USAAF, 1942-45, PTO. Mem. ALA (past chmn./mem. various coms.) AAUP (pres. U. Kans. chpt. 1965), Assn. Coll. and Rsch. Librs., Assn. Rsch. Librs. (mem. or chair various coms.), Rsch. Librs. Group, Inc. (bd. govs. 1974-82, 84-86), Am. Hist. Assn., Orgn. Am. Historians, Manuscript Soc., Bibliog. Soc. Am., Pacific N.W. Libr. Assn. (sec. 1953-54), Kans. Libr. Assn. (chmn. coll. and univ. libr. sect. 1963-64), Pa. Libr. Assn. (pres. 1979-81). Anglican. Avocations: architectual history, reading, music. Home: State College, Pa. Died July 31, 2010.

FOSTER, DAVID RAMSEY, soap company executive; b. London, May 24, 1920; (parents Am. citizens); s. Robert Bagley and Josephine (Ramsey) F.; m. Anne Firth, Aug. 2, 1957 (dec. June 1994); children: Sarah, Victoria; m. Alexandra Chang, May 24, 1996. Student in econs., Gonville and Caius Coll., Cambridge (Eng.) U., 1938. With Colgate-Palmolive Co. and affiliates, 1946-79; v.p., gen. mgr. Europe Colgate-Palmolive Internat., 1961-65, v.p., gen. mgr. household products divsn. parent co. NYC, 1965-68, exec. v.p., 1968-70, pres., 1970-75, CEO, 1971-79, chmn., 1975-79. Author: Wings Over the Sea, 1990. Trustee Woman's Sport Found. Served to lt. comdr. Royal Naval Vol. Res., 1940-46. Decorated Disting. Svc. Order, D.S.C. with bar, Mentioned in Despatches (2); recipient Victor award City of Hope, 1974, Herbert Hoover Meml. award, 1976, Adam award, 1977, Harriman award Boys Club N.Y., 1977, Charter award St. Francis Coll., 1978, Walter Hagen award, 1978, Patty Berg award, 1986, Commr.'s award LPGA, 1995. Mem. Soc. Mayflower Descs., Hawks Club (Cambridge U.), Royal Ancient Golf Club (St. Andrews, Scotland), Royal Cinque Ports Golf Club (life), Sunningdale Golf Club, Sankaty Head Golf Club, Racquet and Tennis Club (N.Y.C.), Mission Hills Country Club, Bally Bunion Golf Club (life). Home: Vincentown, NJ. Died June 4, 2010.

FOSTER, MARCIA WILLIAMS, national account manager; b. Mobile, Ala., Sept. 28, 1950; d. D.V. and Erma Ganelle (Deese) Williams; m. Ronald Stewart Foster, Aug. 21, 1971 (div. Nov. 1987), remarried Sept. 1, 1990; children: Michael Stewart, Susan Genelle. Student, Spring Hill Coll., 1968-71; cert. gen. ins., Ins. Inst. Am., 1983. Cert. ins. profl., ins. counselor. Ins. sec., receptionist Millette & Assocs. Inc., Pascagoula, Miss., 1973-74; personal lines rep. Ross-King-Walker, Inc., Pascagoula, 1974-76; personal lines customer svc. Kennedy Ins. Agy., Inc., San Jose, Calif., 1978-79, Baumhauer-Croom Ins., Inc., Mobile, 1976-78, underwriting sec., asst. to pres., 1980-82; adminstrv. asst. to pres. Lyon Fry Cadden Ins. Agy., Inc., Mobile, 1982-94; account mgr., nat. accounts Willis Corroon Corp. of Mobile, Mobile, Ala., from 1994. Vol. Cystic Fibrosis Found., Mobile, 1985-90, Mathews City Park, Ranger Babe Ruth, Mobile, 1989—. Named Ala. State Ins. Woman of Yr., Ala. Ind. Ins. Agts., 1985. Mem. Ins. Women of Mobile (ednl. course instr. 1987—, pres. 1986-87, Presdl. Svc. award 1984, Mobile Ins. Woman of Yr. 1985, Anna S. Loding Meml. award 1990), Nat. Assn. Ins. Women Internat. (chmn. Ala. state conf. 1992, asst. region III dir. 1986-87, mem. Ala. coun.), Soc. Cert. Ins. Counselors (cert.). Episcopalian. Avocations: catamaran sailing, reading. Home: Mobile, Ala. Died July 15, 2009.

FOSTER, RICHARD, former state legislator; b. Nome, Alaska, Aug. 9, 1946; m. Cathy Foster; children: Neal, Jimmy, Myria, Justin, Tiffany, Richard, Nathan, Ramsey, Chandler. BBA, U. Alaska, Fairbanks, 1964—68. Former vice chmn. Cmty. & Regional Affairs Com.; former mem. Resources Com., Spl. Com. Mil. & Vet. Affairs, Bush Caucus; former bd. mem. Nome Cmty. Ctr., Norton Sound Health Corp., Northwest Cmty. Coll.; state rep. Dist. 23 Alaska, 1988—92; state rep. Dist. 38, 1992—2002; state rep. Dist. 39, 2003—09; majority whip, 1991—2009. Capt. US Army. Decorated Vietnam Svc. medal, Bronze Star medal, Commendation medal. Mem.: Pioneer Igloo No 1, Rotary, Lions Club. Democrat. Died Oct. 13, 2009.

FOWLER, JOSEPH CLYDE, JR., protective services official; b. Knoxville, Tenn., Jan. 22, 1927; s. Joseph Clyde and Elizabeth (Baker) F.; m. Wanda Sue Carroll, Aug. 4, 1956; 2 children. Student, U. Tenn., 1946-47, Bob James Jr. Coll., 1947, FBI Nat. Acad., 1967. Various positions Knoxville Police Dept., 1959-65, detective, sgt., lt. juvenile bur., 1965-70, asst. chief police, 1970-78, chief of police, 1979-82; pres. Ctrl. Comm. & Elecs., 1982-90; sheriff Knox County (Tenn.) Sheriff's Dept., 1990-94; warden Tenn. Dept. Corrections, Knoxville, from 1994; U.S. Marshall Ea. Tenn., from 1994. With USN, 1945-46, res., 1959-63. Mem. Kiwanis, Vestal Boys Club, Knoxville Lodge 769, Scottish Rite, Kerbala, Mystic Shriners, Am. Legion, FOP, Phi Gamma Delta. Methodist. Avocations: boating, horseback riding, swimming. Home: Knoxville, Tenn. Died Feb. 7, 2009.

FOWLKES, MARTHA RICHMOND, sociology educator, researcher, consultant; b. Boston, May 6, 1940; d. David and Mary (Warren) Richmond; children— Lisa Bladen, Anne Bladen, Abigail Fowlkes, Margaret Fowlkes. A.B. magna cum laude, Smith Coll., 1961; M.A., London Sch. Econs. and Polit. Sci., 1965; Ph.D. with distinction, U. Mass.-Amherst, 1977. Med. sociologist Regional Med. Program, Memphis, 1970; researcher evaluator Northampton State Hosp., Mass., 1970-71; assoc. dean student affairs, 1978-80; dir. alumnae research Smith Coll., Northampton, 1980—, assoc. prof. pub. policy,

1980—; cons. in field. Author: Behind Every Successful Man: Wives of Medicine and Academe, 1980; also monographs and articles. Trustee Northampton State Hosp., 1975-78. Recipient Woodrow Wilson fellow, 1975-76; Nat. Research Service award NIMH, 1975-76. Mem. Am. Sociol. Assn., Eastern Sociol. Assn., Phi Beta Kappa. Democrat. Avocations: gardening; camping. Home: Northampton, Mass. Died Mar. 17, 2009.

FOX, CARROLL LAWSON, electric utility executive; b. Sevierville, Tenn., June 23, 1925; s. Grady Bascom and Aura (Lawson) F.; m. Mildred Grace Perryman, Sept. 1, 1951; children: Lawson Alan, Shauna Carol Fox Oden. B.E.E., U. Tenn., 1944. Registered profl. engr., Tenn. With Elec. Power Bd. Chattanooga, from 1947, engr. substa. design, 1947-64, asst. sec., 1964-66, sec.-comptroller, 1966-72, sec.-treas., 1972-88, asst. gen. mgr., from 1989. Co-founder Employee Credit Union, pres., 1954-64 Active United Fund. Served with USNR, 1944-46. Mem.: Rotarian. Baptist. Home: Loudon, Tenn. Died Mar. 7, 2009.

FOX, JACK JAY, chemist, educator; b. NYC, Dec. 21, 1916; s. Samuel and Celia (Stern) F.; m. Ruth C. Inabu, June 13, 1939; children: Dolores M. Emspak, John Reed. AB, U. Colo., 1939, PhD, 1950. With Sloan-Kettering Inst. for Cancer Research, NYC, 1952-88, mem. emeritus, from 1988; head Lab. Organic Chemistry, prof. biochemistry Cornell U. Grad. Sch. Med. Scis., NYC, from 1958. Recipient Alfred P. Sloan award cancer rsch., 1956, C.S. Hudson award in carbohydrate chemistry Am. Chem. Soc., 1977, Pap award for sci. achievement, 1983, Norlin award U. Colo. Alumni Assn., 1984; NRC fellow, 1950-52; postdoctoral fellow Free U. Brussels, 1950-52; Damon Runyon Meml. Fund fellow, 1952-54. Mem. Am. Chem. Soc., Westchester Chem. Soc., Am. Soc. Biol. Chemists, Am. Assn. Cancer Rsch., Am. Soc. Antiviral Rsch., Sigma Xi. Achievements include research, numerous publs. on design, synthesis and structural elucidation of anticancer and antiviral agts., specific syntheses of compounds related to nucleic acid components, carbohydrate and heterocyclic chemistry. E-mail: jackfx252. Died Nov. 22, 2009.

FOX, JAMES HAROLD, JR., superintendent of schools; b. Washington, Nov. 30, 1941; s. James Harold and Evelyn Gertrude (Joness) F.; m. Marian Claire Cavender, Jan. 24, 1973; children: Dutch, Michael. BS, U. Va., 1963; MA, George Washington U., 1967, EdD, 1971. Tchr., coach Great Mills High Sch., St. Marys County, Md., 1963-66; asst. prin. Esperanza Jr. High Sch., St. Marys County, 1966-69; assoc. prin. Wakefield High Sch., Arlington, Va., 1969-71; prin. George Mason Middle/High Sch., Falls Church, Va., 1971-73; asst. supt. Kirkwood R-7 Schs., St. Louis, 1973-77; supt. Mansfield (Ohio) City Schs., 1977-80, Sarasota (Fla.) County Schs., 1980-85, Fulton County Schs., Atlanta, from 1985. Cons. in field. Contbr. articles to profl. jours. Mem., bd. dirs. Boy Scouts Am., Atlanta, 1987—; mem. Atlanta Com. for Olympic Games Edn. Recipient Disting. Svc. award Project Care, 1979, Outstanding Svc. award Sarasota Jaycees, 1985; named Ga. Sch. Supt. of Yr., 1992, Exec. Educator 100, 1993. Mem. Am. Assn. Sch. Adminstrs., Ga. Sch. Supts. Assn. (bd. dirs. 1987—), Atlanta Metro Assn. (chmn. 1987, 93), Nat. Mid. Sch. Assn. (pres. 1978), Greater North Fulton C. of C. (bd. dirs.), South Fulton C. of C. (bd. dirs.), Kiwanis, Phi Delta Kappa. Avocations: power boating, skiing, growing roses. Home: Austin, Tex. Died Feb. 9, 2010.

FOX, RAYMOND GRAHAM, educational technologist; b. Portland, Oreg., May 31, 1923; s. George Raymond and Georgia Dorothy (Beckman) Fox; m. Harriet Carolyn Minchin Fox, Apr. 17, 1948; children: Susan, Christine, Ellen, Laura, John. BS, Rensselaer Poly. Inst., 1943. Salesman IBM Corp., NYC, 1946—48, br. mgr., 1949—56, sys. mgr., 1957—65, edn. sys. devel. mgr., 1965—76; chmn. bd. Learning Tech. Inst., Warrenton, from 1975. Mem. Va. Coun. Deaf, 1978—84, chmn., 1980—83; mem. Sec. Navy Adv. Bd. Edn. & Tng., 1972—77; cons. tech. Va. Legis. Adv. Com. Handicapped, 1970; mem. Nat. Def. Exec. Res., 1970—83, mem. emeritus, from 1983. Served with USNR, 1943—46. Mem.: Nat. Security Indsl. Assn. (chmn. tng. group 1974—76), Soc. Applied Learning Tech. (pres. from 1972), Moorings (Vero Beach, Fla.), Columbia Country (Chevy Chase, Md.), Fauquier (Warrenton) (pres. 1993—94), Army & Navy (Washington). Anglican. Achievements include patents for interactive multimedia instruction delivery system. Home: Warrenton, Va. Died Oct. 5, 2009.

FOX, ROBERTA FULTON, lawyer, state legislator; b. Phila., Nov. 25, 1943; d. Robert Fulton and Irmgard Fox; m. Mike Gold; 1 stepchild, Shari Anna Gold. BA, U. Fla., 1964, JD, 1967. Admitted to Fla. bar, 1968; mem. Govt. Rsch. Coun., Miami-Dade C. of C., 1964—65; staff Goldin & Jones, Gainesville, Fla., 1968; atty. Legal Svcs., Greater Miami, 1970—72; pvt. practice Miami, Fla., 1972—93; ptnr. firm Gold & Fox, P.A., from 1972; mem. Fla. House Reps., 1976—82, Fla. Senate, 1982—86; bd. dirs. Sunshine Jr. Food Stores, Inc.; mem. Gov.'s Commn. on Marriage and the Family Unit, 1974—76; chairperson Dade County Women's Polit. Caucus, 1971—74, NOW Legal Def. and Edn. Fund., 1978—82; mem. Gov.'s task force battered women's syndrome, from 1990; hon. bd. dirs. Girls Clubs Greater Miami. Recipient Outstanding State Legislator award, 1979, Gov.'s award, 1980. Mem.: U. Fla. Law Ctr. Assn., U. Fla. Law Ctr. Assn., Fla. Bar Assn., Fla. Women Lawyers Assn., Bus. and Profl. Women. Home: Miami, Fla. Died Aug. 9, 2009.

FRAKER, WILLIAM A., cinematographer, director; b. L.A., Sept. 29, 1923; m. Denise Fraker; 1 stepchild, Baron. BA, U. So. Calif. Camera operator: (films) Father Goose, 1964, The Wild Seed, 1965, Morituri, 1965, The Professionals, 1966; cinematographer: (films) Forbid Them Not, 1961, Fade In, 1967, Games, 1967, The Fox, 1967, The President's Analyst, 1967, Rosemary's Baby, 1968 (Academy award nomination best cinematography 1968), Bullitt, 1968, Paint Your Wagon, 1969, The Day of the Dolphin, 1973, Coonskin, 1974, Aloha, Bobby and Rose, 1975, Rancho Deluxe, 1975, (with Haskell Wexler and Bill Butler) One Flew Over the Cuckoo's Nest, 1975, Gator, 1976, The Killer Inside Me, 1976, Lipstick, 1976, Exorcist II: The Heretic, 1977, (with others) Close Encounters of the Third Kind, 1977, Looking for Mr. Goodbar, 1977 (Academy award nomination best cinematography 1977), Heaven Can Wait, 1978 (Academy award nomination best cinematography 1978), American Hot Wax, 1978, 1941, 1979 (Academy award nomination best cinematography 1979), Old Boyfriends, 1979, Divine Madness, 1980, The Hollywood Knights, 1980, Sharkey's Machine, 1981, The Best Little Whorehouse in Texas, 1982, Wargames, 1983 (Academy award nomination best cinematography 1983), Irreconcilable Differences, 1984, Protocol, 1984, Fever Pitch, 1985, Murphy's Romance, 1985 (Academy award nomination best cinematography 1985), Spacecamp, 1986, Baby Boom, 1987, Burglar, 1987, An Innocent Man, 1989, Chances Are, 1989, The Freshman, 1990, Honeymoon in Vegas, 1992, Memoirs of an Invisible Man, 1992, Tombstone, 1994, There Goes My Baby, 1994, Street Fighter, 1994, Father of the Bride II, 1995, The Island of Dr. Moreau, 1996, Vegas Vacation, 1997, The Rules of Engagement, 2000, Town and Country, 2001, Walking Up in Reno, 2002; (TV movies) Death in Small Doses, 1995; (TV series) Frank's Place, 1987; dir. (films) Monte Walsh, 1970, A Reflection of Fear, 1973, The Legend of the Lone Ranger, 1981; (TV episodes) J.J. Starbuck, 1987, Unsub, 1989, Wiseguy (6 episodes), 1988-90, The Flash, 1991, Walker, Texas Ranger, 1993 Mem. Dirs. Guild America, American Society Cinematographers (Lifetime Achievement award, 2000) Died June 1, 2010.

FRANCK, CAROL EICHERT, healthcare association administrator; b. Lebanon, Pa., Dec. 12, 1937; d. Ralph F. and Mary Ellen (Beigh) Eichert; m. Michael, May 29, 1965; children: Michele, Lauren, Rebecca, Jennifer. BS, Cornell N.Y.Hosp. Sch. Nursing, 1960; MS, U. Calif., 1962; student, Tchrs. Coll., 1970; postgrad., Mich. State U., 1978. Staff nurse Cornell N.Y. Hosp., NYC, 1960-61, instr., asst. prof., 1962-68; asst. prof., leadership and mgmt. Coll. Nursing, Mich. State U., 1971-75, dir., undergrad. nursing program, 1978-82; dir. govt. affairs Mich. Nurses Assn., East Lansing, 1984-86, exec. dir. Okemos, from 1986. Invited participant, Inst. on Care of The Dying-Yale, New Haven, Conn., 1963; advisory comm. Drop In Day Ctr.-Handicapped, Mich., 1980-81. Adv. commn. Mich. Hosp. Orgn., Lansing, 1979-80; moderator Edgewood United Ch., East Lansing, 1983-84; adv. commn. Gov. Health Care Cost Mgmt. Team, Mich., 1989, State Health Planning Coun., 1991, Mich. Nursing Home Reimbursement Adv. Com.; trustee Olivet (Mich.) Coll., 1993—. Mem. Mich. Nurses Assn., Sigma Theta Tau, Phi Delta Kappa, Phi Kappa Phi. Avocation: travel. Home: Warwick, NY. Died Jan. 24, 2009.

FRANK, VICTOR H., JR., international financial consultant; b. Apr. 4, 1927; married; three children. BA, Yale U., 1950, LLB, 1953; LLM in Taxation, NYU, 1960. Pvt. practice law, NYC and Phila., 1953-66; tax counsel CPC Internat., Englewood Cliffs, N.J., 1966-73, v.p. fin., adminstrn. Best Foods div., 1973-77, v.p. diversified unit ops., 1977-79, spl. asst. to chief exec. officer, 1979-82, v.p. for info. resources, 1982-85, v.p. for govt. relations, 1986-87; U.S. dir., amb. Asian Devel. Bank, Manila, 1987-93; with Trinity Internat. Ptnrs., Washington, from 1993. Former mem. Nat. Adv. Bd. to U.S. Sec. Edn. on Internat. Programs; bd. dirs. Bus. Alliance Vietnamese Edn. Contbr. articles to Harvard Bus. Rev., Asian Wall St. Jour., Internat. Herald Tribune. Discus thrower 1948 U.S. Olympic Track and Field team. With USN, 1945-46. Home: Englewood, NJ. Died Apr. 6, 2010.

FRANKE, RICHARD HERBERT, business educator; b. Washington, Dec. 19, 1937; s. Herbert A. and Edna L. (Mathisen) F.; m. Elke Koerner, Dec. 23, 1963; children: Martin, Andrea, Erik. Student, U. Goettingen, 1956-57; BS in Chem. Engring., Cornell U., 1960; postgrad., U. Hamburg, 1963-64; MBA, U. Pitts., 1965; PhD in Mgmt., U. Rochester, 1974. Prodn. engr. in petrochems. field Union Carbide Internat. Co., Texas City and Victoria, Tex., 1960-62, Sircusa, Italy, 1962-63; research and mktg. research engr. St. Joseph Lead Co., Monaca, Pa., 1966-67; research asst. Mgmt. Research Ctr. U. Rochester (N.Y.), 1968-72; research fellow Nat. Acad. Scis., Belgrade, Yugoslavia, 1972-73; asst. prof. Sch. Bus. Adminstrn. U. Wis.-Milw., 1973-78; assoc. prof. Worcester Poly Inst., Mass., 1978-83; prof. Sellinger Sch. Bus. and Mgmt. Loyola Coll., Balt., from 1983. Contbr. articles to various publs. McMullen scholar, 1955-59; Nansen House-Cornell scholar, 1956-57; U. Pitts. fellow, 1964-65; U. Rochester fellow, 1968-72; Nat. Acad. Scis. grantee, 1972-73; Japan Found. grantee, 1979-80; nsf grantee, 1979-82 Mem. APA, AAAS, Acad. Mgmt., Am. Sociol. Assn., Strategic Mgmt. Soc. Home: Baltimore, Md. Died Sept. 1, 2009.

FRANKEL, JACK, pediatrician, allergist; b. NYC, Sept. 9, 1920; s. Max H. and Fanny F. Frankel; m. Irene J. Kittredge, Apr. 18, 1948; children: Barbara Meg, Judith Ann, Richard Harris, Carolyn, Joan Ellen. BS, Tulane U., 1941, MD, 1945. Diplomate Am. Bd. of Pediat. Intern Queens Gen. Hosp., Jamaica, NY, 1945-46; resident in pediat. and contagious diseases, 1948-50; pediatrician, allergist Manatee Family Physicians, Bradenton, Fla., from 1993; allergist, immunologist LIJ Hosp., New Hyde Park, 1974-77. Asst. prof. clin. pediatrics and allergy SUNY, Stony Brook, 1955-75, NYU, 1970-75; cons. Blake Meml. Hosp., Bradenton, Fla., 1970—, Manatee Meml. Hosp., Bradenton, 1977—. Capt. M.C. US Army, 1946—48. Fellow Am. Acad. Pediat., Am. Coll. Allergy. Jewish. Avocations: tennis, jogging. Home: Easthampton, Mass. Died Nov. 2, 2009.

FRANKENSTEIN, CURT, artist; b. Hannover, Germany, Mar. 11, 1922; came to U.S., 1947; m. Renate Solmitz, July 25, 1959. Cert., Am. Acad. Art, Chgo., 1947-50; postgrad., Art Inst. Chgo., 1950-53, Otis Art Inst., Los Angeles, 1953-54. Pvt. practice painting, printmaking, Chgo., from 1954. Represented in permanent collections Ill. State Mus., Union League Club Chgo. Recipient 1st prize painting Ill. State Fair, Springfield, 1967, Mcpl. Art league prize Art Inst. Chgo., 1963, Purchase award Minn. Mus. Art, Mpls., 1980, award of excellence Mcpl. Art League Chgo., 1998. Mem. Am. Union League Civic and Arts Found., Print Consortium, Chgo. Artists Coalition, Am. Jewish Arts Club. Died Jan. 4, 2009.

FRANKLIN, GEORGE ALVIS, industrial relations executive; b. Leominster, Mass., Oct. 26, 1918; s. George A. and Edith M. (Tranter) Franklin; m. Jennie Robertson, Aug. 1, 1942 (dec. Nov. 1977); children: George A., Malcolm G.; m. Shirley T. Nordfors; children: Deborah N. Weiss, Steven G. Nordfors, Jeffrey A. Nordfors. BS, NYU, 1942, MBA, 1948. Dir. pers. Automatic Switch Co., Florham Park, NJ, 1951—57, dir. indsl. rels., 1957—58, dir. indsl. rels, asst. sec., 1958—76, v.p. indsl. rels., 1976—81, v.p. indsl. rels., sec., from 1981. Trustee, chmn. Employees Security Fund Elec. Products Industries, Flushing, NY, from 1955; mem. exec. com. Pvt. Indsl. Coun., Morristown, NJ, from 1983; state vice chmn. Employers Legis. Com., Trenton, NJ, 1963—65, 1975—77; trustee, chmn. New Jobs, Trenton, from 1978. Capt. Signal Corps, 1942—46, ETO, PTO. Mem.: N.J. Bus and Industry Assn. (chmn. indsl. rels. and employment security from 1971), N.J. Pers. Assn. (chmn. 1962—63), Nat. Elec. Mfrs. Assn. (chmn. indsl. rels. com. from 1972), Am. Soc. Pers. Adminstrn., Am. Soc. Engring., Am. Mgmt. Assn., 200 Club Morris County, N.J., Shriners, Masons, Rotary Madison, N.J. (pres. from 1951). Methodist. Home: Morristown, NJ. Died Oct. 26, 2009.

FRANKLIN, JACK T., photographer; b. May 7, 1922; Attended, U. Oahu, Hawaii, U.S. Signal Photo Corps Ctr., Astoria, Long Island, Theater Art Inst. Photographer: (newspapers and mags.) Phila. Tribunem Germantown Courier, Johnson Publs., North City Free Press, Sepia Mag., Philly Talk, Logan Times, Nicetonian, North Penn Chat, Tioga News, Oakdale Treaty, Citizens Voice, Citizens Times, Penn Treaty Gazette, Scoop/USA, Nite-Life, Afro-American (yearbooks) Cheney State Coll., Temple U., Lincoln U., Berean Inst., William Penn H.S., others (organizations) NAACP, Sickle Cell Anemia Found., Am. Found. Negro Affairs, others (beauty and fashion) Ebony Fashion Fair, Miss Ebony, Miss AmeriColor, Black Teenage America (individual contracts) Sen. Herbert Arlene, Nat King Cole, Ella Fitzgerald, Sen. Freeman Hankins, Lionell Hampton, Chuck Jackson, George Kirby, Congressman Robert N.C. Nix, Jr. and Sr., Sen. Schweiker, Sen. Hugh Scott, Rev. Dr. Leon Sullivan, numerous others, Phila. Black Expo, 1971, 72, (freelance) Lyndon Baines Johnson Inaugural, Civil Rights Marches of Martin Luther King Jr., (2) Marches on Washington for Civil Rights Movement, Selma to Montgomery March of Martin Luther King Jr., others. With Army Signal Corpe, 1943-46. Recipient Candid Culture Photography Competition award Pa. Heritage Affairs Commn., 1989. Died Sept. 20, 2009.

FRANKLIN, LORETTA WOODS, mechanical contracting company executive; b. Clay County, Ky., Mar. 14, 1927; d. Robert and Ethel (Asher) Woods; m. Denver L. Franklin, May 6, 1956; children— John A., Darlene L. Vice pres. Delta Mech., Fairfield, Ohio, 1961—, pres., 1977—, chmn. bd., 1985—; v.p. Mo. Pipeline, Fairfield, 1965-77, pres., 1977-85, chmn. bd., 1985—. Mem. Am. Sub-Contractors Assn., Women in Constrn., Mech. Contractors Assn., Am. Arbitration Assn., Women Owned Bus. Assn., Ohio Women Entrepreneurs, Hamilton C. of C., Fairfield C. of C. Baptist. Avocations: golf; fishing. Home: Hamilton, Ohio. Died Dec. 12, 2009.

FRANKS, ROBERT DOUGLAS (BOB FRANKS), former United States Representative from New Jersey; b. Hackensack, NJ, Sept. 21, 1951; s. Norman A. and June Evans F. BA, Depauw U., 1973; JD, So. Methodist U., 1976. Exec. dir. People for Bateman, 1977; cons. Jim Courter for Congress Com., 1978; v.p. Med Data Inc., 1978-80; co-owner County News, 1980-83; cons. Tom Kean for Gov. Com., 1981; mem. Dist. 22 NJ State Assembly, Trenton, 1979-93; mem. US Congresses from 7th NJ Dist., 1993-2001; pres. Healthcare Institute of NJ, 2001—10. Bd. dirs. Intrenet.; mgmt. cons. in field; founder CREO; mem. Econ. Steering Com., 1980, Com. on Energy and Nat. Resources, 1981-83, Com. on State Govt., Civil Svc., Elections, Pensions and Vet. Affairs, 1981-85, N.J. State Pension Study Commn., 1982, Com. Revenue, Finance and Appropriations, 1984-93, State and Local Expenditure and Revenue Policy Commn., 1985-93, Waste Mgmt. Planning and Recycling Com., 1990-91; chmn. Task Force to Reform Congress Redistricting Process, 1982, N.J. Coalition for Regulatory Efficiency, 1985-93, Republican Policy Com., 1990-91, N.J. State Rep. Party, 1988-92; campaign mgr. Congressman Jim Courter, 1982, Congressman Dean Gallo, 1984; assembly liaison Rep. Majority. 1985. Bd. mgrs. Children's Specialized Hosp., Mountainside, N.J., 1980; mem. long range planning com. Overlook Hosp., Summit, N.J., 1982; mem. domestic task force Hands Across Am., 1986; mem. N.J. Jaycees. Named Legislator of Yr. Nat. Rep. Legislators Assn., 1986. Republican. Died Apr. 9, 2010.

FRANTZ, ANDREW GIBSON, endocrinologist, educator, dean; b. NYC, May 22, 1930; s. Angus Macdonald and Virginia (Kneeland) F. AB magna cum laude, Harvard U., 1951; MD, Columbia U., 1955. Intern Presbyn. Hosp., NYC, 1955-56, resident in medicine, 1956-58; fellow in endocrinology Columbia U., NYC, 1958-60, asst. prof. medicine, 1966-68, assoc. prof., 1968-73, prof., from 1973, chief divsn. endocrinology, 1971-87; chmn. admissions com., assoc. dean for admissions Columbia U. (Coll. Physicians and Surgeons), from 1981. Assoc. in medicine Harvard U., 1962-66; asst. in medicine Mass. Gen. Hosp., Boston, 1962-66; mem. staff Presbyn. Hosp., N.Y.C.; mem. med. adv. bd. Nat. Pituitary Agy., 1970-73; established investigator Am. Heart Assn., 1968-73 Contbr. articles on prolactin and other pituitary hormones and functions to med. and sci. jours.; mem. editorial bd.: Jour. Clin. Endocrinology and Metabolism, 1971-76; assoc. editor: Metabolism, 1969—. Served to lt. comdr. USNR, 1960-62. Recipient Silver Medal Coll. Physicians and Surgeons, Columbia U., 1981, Alumni Fedn. medal Columbia U., 1984, Disting. Tchr. award, Coll. Physicians and Surgeons, Columbia U., 1989. Mem. AAAS, Endocrine Soc., Assn. Am. Physicians, Am. Soc. Clin. Investigation, Internat. Soc. for Neuroendocrinology, Harvey Soc., Practitioners Soc. (pres. 1993-2000), Charaka Club, Am. Fedn. Med. Rsch., N.Y. Acad. Scis., N.Y. Acad. Medicine, Union Club, Century Assn. (N.Y.C.), P and S Alumni Assn. (pres. 1991-93), Alpha Omega Alpha. Episcopalian. Home: New York, NY. Died June 18, 2010.

FRANZMANN, ALBERT WILHELM, wildlife veterinarian, consultant; b. Hamilton, Ohio, July 19, 1930; s. Wilhelm Heinreich and Louise Marie (Schlichter) F.; m. Donna Marie Grueser, Dec. 13, 1953; children: Karl Wilhelm, Louise Ann. DVM, Ohio State U., 1954; PhD, U. Idaho, 1971. Diplomate Am. Coll. Zool. Medicine (hon.). Veterinarian Tiffin (Ohio) Animal Hosp., 1956-59; gen. practice vet. medicine Hamilton, 1959-68; NDEA rsch. fellow U. Idaho, Moscow, 1968-71; wildlife cons. F-2 Wildlife Cons., Moscow, 1971-72; dir. Kenai Moose Rsch. Ctr. Alaska Dept. Fish and Game, Soldotna, 1972-87; cons. AWF Profl. Svcs. Affil. assoc. prof., U. Alaska, Fairbanks, 1972-87; bd. dirs. Internat. Wildlife Vet. Svc. Inc., Laramie, Wyo., Hamilton Tool co., Bd. of Game State of Alaska, Alaska Outdoor Coun., Challenger Learning Ctr. Alaska, N. Am. Moose Found. Contbr. over 100 articles to profl. jours., 15 chpts. to books. Bd. dirs. N.Am. Moose Found. Capt. USAF, 1954-56. Named Disting. Moose Biologist, N.Am. Moose Conf., Prince George, B.C., Can.,1983; named to U. Idaho Hall of Fame., 2004; recipient Disting. Alumnus award Ohio State U. Coll. Vet. Medicine, Lifetime Conservation award Kenai Penisula chpt. Safari Club Internat., 2001. Mem. AVMA, Am. Assn. Wildlife Veterinarians (pres. 1979-81), Wildlife Disease Assn. (council 1980-81, Emeritus award 1996), Am. Assn. Zoo Veterinarians, Am. Coll. Zool. Medicine (hon. diplomate), The Wildlife Soc. (cert. wildlife biologist, Einarsen award N.W. sect.), Phi Zeta, Xi Sigma Pi. Lodges: Elks. Republican. Avocations: golf, gardening, travel. Died Feb. 13, 2009.

FRAPRIE, FRANK, health facility administrator; b. New Britain, Conn., Nov. 9, 1931; s. Raymond Tripp and Hazel Aline (Dohrenwend) F.; m. Ernestine Viola Moseley, Aug. 21, 1953; children; Frank Jr., Mark Raymond, Scott Alan. BS in Biology & Chemistry, Rensselaer Polytech Inst., 1953; MS in Hosp. Adminstrn., U. Iowa, 1957. Adminstrv. resident New Britain (Conn.) Gen. Hosp., 1956-58, adminstrv. asst., 1958-65, personnel dir., 1958-61, asst. dir., 1965-74, v.p. ops., 1974-82, sr. v.p., COO, 1982-91; v.p., sec. CenConn Health Corp., New Britain, from 1982; mgmt. cons. New Britain Gen. Hosp. & Ctrl. Conn. Health Alliance, from 1991. V.p. CenConn. Svcs., Inc., New Britain, 1982-91; pres. Newmed, Inc., New Britain, 1988—. Dir. exec. com. MidConn. Bank, Kensington, 1981-97; golf coach Conn. Spl. Olympics, Kensington, 1990—; dir., trustee New Britain Inst., 1995—; dir., exec. com. Mcpl. Econ. Devel. Agy., New Britain, 1983-97. With U.S. Army Med. Corps, 1953-55. Mem. Am. Coll. Health Care Execs., Am. Hosp. Assn., Shuttle Meadow Country Club (pres. 1994-1995, com. chmn. 1978—). Republican. Congregationalist. Avocations: golf, travel. Home: Farmington, Conn. Died Jan. 7, 2009.

FRAZETTA, FRANK, artist; b. Bklyn., Feb. 9, 1928; m. Eleanor Kelly, 1956 (dec. 2009); children: Alfonso Frank, William, Heidi, Holly. Student, Bklyn. Acad. Fine Arts. Former asst. to Michael Falanga; former artist numerous comic book houses including Baily, Pines, Fawcett, National, Eastern Color, Hillman, Avon, Western; artist syndicated comic strip Johnny Comet (later titled Ace McCoy), 1952-53; ghosted syndicated comic strip Flash Gordon comic strip, 1953; past asst. syndicated comic strip Al Capp; mem. staff syndicated comic strip L'il Abner comic strip; freelance illustrator syndicated comic strip, 1960—; artist publicity posters for movies, record album jackets, book covers including Writers of the Future, vols. 3 and 4 (L. Ron Hubbard), 1987, 88; author: Frank Frazetta, the Living Legend, 1980, (pencil drawings) Arcanum Book, 1994, Pillow Book, 1994; created characters for animated feature Fire and Ice, 1983; creator Death Dealer character painted on Army airplanes and tanks and Boeing helicopters; appeared in (documentaries) Frank Frazetta: Painting with Fire, 1996 Recipient Hugo award, 1966 Mem. Nat. Cartoonists Soc. Died May 10, 2010.

FREDENBURG, DAVID MARSHALL, SR., data processing executive, consultant, system designer; b. Fargo, N.D., Apr. 16, 1932; s. David Ralph and Mary Elizabeth (Davies) F.; m. Audrey Frances Brown, Apr. 11, 1959; children: David Marshall Jr., Dane Michael, Debra Michelle. B.S.E.E., U. Wash., 1954. Mem. tech. staff reliability Aerospace Corp., El Segundo, Calif., 1965-69; mgr. project control Computer Scis., Corp., El Segundo, 1969-73; mgr. product assurance data systems Lear Siegier, Grand Rapids, Mich., 1973-80, Northrop DSD, Rolling Meadows, Ill., 1980-83, Simmonds Precision, Vergennes, Vt., 1983—, also project leader, cons.; cons. Nat. Ski Patrol, Denver; ind. product assurance cons., Torrance, Calif., 1968-73. Contbr. articles to profl. publs. Nat. adviser Nat. Ski Patrol System, Denver, 1959-65, regional officer, Wash., Colo., Calif. and Mich., 1954-82. Named Outstanding Ski Patroller, 1978, also recipient 3 Gold Star Service awards Nat. Ski Patrol System, 1955, 64, 82; named Outstanding Profl. Engr. Northrop Def. System Div., 1982. Mem. Astron. Soc. (v.p. 1955-58), Hunting Beach C. of C. (chmn. polit. action 1970-73), Huntington Beach C. of C. (v.p. 1971-75). Republican. Baptist. Lodge: Rotary. Home: Charlotte, Vt. Died May 30, 2010.

FREDERICK, JERRELL LEE, recording, film sound executive; b. Muncie, Ind., Jan. 7, 1930; s. Henry Charles and Hilda L. (Young) F. BSEE, U. Mich., 1953. Pres., chief engr. Frederick Rec. Co., Midland, Mich., 1953-60; freelance re-rec. mixer Germany, 1960-65; freelance location rec. engr. throughout U.S., 1965-66; freelance location film mixer, 1966-67; v.p., chief engr. Spl. Recs., Inc., Detroit, 1967-85, re-rec. film mixer, 1970-85; pres., chief engr. Motion Picture Sound, Inc., Detroit, 1986. Guest lectr. various colls. and univs., Midwest and Can., 1970—. Re-rec. mixer: (indsl. film) Seat Belts Save Lives, (radio, TV, internat. film) The Game (Bronze award 1973), A Country Fair (Golden Eagle award 1975,), Africa: Dry Edge of Disaster Atlanta Internat. Film Festival 1976). Recipient Growth award Soc. Motion Picture and TV Engrs., 1981, Bronze Medallion, N.Y. Internat. Film Festival, 1981, Spl. award Detroit Communications Community, 1987, Oscar award nomination for Young at Heart, Acad. Motion Picture Arts and Scis., 1987, Emmy award, 1987, Telly award G.M.-Fisher Guide Div., 1988. Mem. Audio Engring. Soc., Soc. Motion Picture and TV Engrs., Detroit Producers Assn. (Lifetime Achievement award 1994). Lodges: Masons. (32 o). Republican. Presbyterian. Avocations: concerts, films. Home: Warren, Mich. Died July 11, 2010.

FREDERICK, LAURENCE DAVIS, retired surgeon; b. Omaha, Nebr., May 8, 1922; BS, U. Ill., 1942; MD, Ill. Med. Ctr., 1945. Diplomate Am. Bd. Surgery. Intern U. Ill. Rsch.-Edn. Hosp., Chgo., 1945-46; resident in surgery Columbia VA Hosp., 1948-51; mem. staff Piedmont Med. Ctr., Rock Hill, S.C.; ret., 1987. Fellow ACS, Internat. Coll. Surgeons; mem. AMA. Home: Chapel Hill, NC. Died Dec. 23, 2009.

FREDERICK, VIRGINIA FIESTER, retired state legislator; b. Rock Island, Ill., Dec. 24, 1916; d. John Henry and Myrtle (Montgomery) Heise; m. C. Donnan Fiester (dec. 1975); children: Sheryl Fiester Ross, Alan R., James D.; m. Kenneth Jacob Frederick, 1978 (dec.). BA, U. Iowa, 1938; postgrad., Lake Forest Coll., 1942-43, LLD, 1994, MLS, 1999. Freelance fashion designer, Lake Forest, Ill., 1952-78; pres. Mid American China Exch., Kenilworth, Ill., 1978-81; mem. Ill. House of Reps., Springfield, 1979-95, asst. minority leader, 1990-95. Alderman first ward, Lake Forest, 1974-78; del. World Food Conf., Rome, 1974; subcom. pensions and employment Ill. Commn. on Status of Women, 1976-79; co-chair Conf. Women Legislators, 1982-85; bd. dirs. Lake Forest Coll., 1995-98, Lake Forest Symphony Guild; city supr. City of Lake Forest, 1995-98. Named Chgo. Area Women of Achievement, Internat. Orgn. Women Execs., 1978; recipient Lottie Holman O'Neal award, 1980, Jane Addams award, 1982, Outstanding Legislator award Ill. Hosp. Assn., 1986, VFW Svc. award, 1988, Joyce Fitzgerald Meml. award, 1988, Susan B. Anthony Legislator of Yr. award, 1989, Delta Kappa Gamma award, 1991, Outstanding Legislator award, 1995, Svcs. for Srs. award, Ill. Dept. Aging, 1991, Ethics in Politics award, Rep. Womens's Club, 1992, Woman of Achievement award YWCA North Eastern Ill., 1994, Ill. Women in Govt. award, 1994, Lifetime Achievement award Equip for Equality, 1999. Mem. LWV (local pres. 1958-60, state dir. 1969-75, nat. com. 1975-76), AAUW (local pres. 1968-70, state pres. 1975-77, state dir. 1963-69, nat. com. 1967-69, Legislator of Yr. 1993), UN Assn. (bd. dirs.), Chgo. Assn. Commerce and Industry (bd. dirs.). Home: Lake Forest, Ill. Died May 30, 2010.

FREED, CHARLES, engineering consultant, researcher; b. Budapest, Hungary, Mar. 21, 1926; came to U.S., 1949; s. Erno and Ernestine (Duschnitz) F.; m. Florence Joan Wallach, Apr. 16, 1956; children: Lisa Ernestine, Josie Anne. BEE, NYU, 1952; SM, MIT, 1954, EE, 1958. Registered profl. engr., Mass. Rsch. asst. MIT, Cambridge, Mass., 1952-55, mem. staff, 1955-58; sr. engr., dept. head Raytheon, Waltham, Mass., 1958-62; mem. staff Lincoln Lab., Lexington, Mass., 1962-78, sr. staff mem., 1978-94, cons., from 1994. Lectr. dept. elec. engring. and computer sci. MIT, Cambridge, 1969-99. Contbr. over 60 articles to profl. jours. Fellow IEEE, Mil. Sensing Symposia; mem. Tau Beta Pi, Eta Kappa Nu, Sigma Xi. Achievements include patent in field. Home: Lincoln, Mass. Died Aug. 4, 2010.

FREED, DANIEL JOSEF, law educator; b. New York, May 12, 1927; s. Jules L. and Sara (Lobel) F.; m. Judith Darrow, June 30, 1967; children: Peter Jacob, Emily Sara;children from previous marriage: Jonathan Michael, Amy. BS, Yale U., 1948, LLB, 1951; LLD (hon.), New England Coll., 1994. Bar: N.Y. 1952, D.C. 1953, U.S. Supreme Ct. 1955; Justice of the Peace, Guilford, Vt, 2005. Atty.-investigator, preparedness subcom., com. on armed svcs., U.S. Senate, Washington, 1951-52; assoc. Ford, Bergson, Adams & Borkland, Washington, 1952-59; sr. trial atty. Antitrust divsn. US Dept. Justice, Washington, 1959-64, assoc. dir. Office Criminal Justice, 1964—68, dir., 1968-69; prof. law and its adminstrn. Yale U., New Haven, 1969-75, clin. prof., 1975-94, clin. prof. emeritus, profl. lectr. in law, 1994—2010. Dir. clin. program law Yale U., 1969-72, dir. Daniel and Florence Guggenheim program in criminal justice, 1972-87, dir. criminal sentencing program, 1988-96. Co-author: (with Patricia M. Wald) Bail in the United States: 1964, publ.1964; editor (periodical) Fed. Sentencing Reporter; contbr. articles to profl. jours. Trustee Vera Inst. Justice, NY, from 1970; pres. Yale Law Sch. Assn. Washington, 1968. With USN, 1945—46. Recipient Glenn R. Winters award Am. Judges Assn., 1992. Democrat. Jewish. Avocations: metal sculpture, swimming. Home: Guilford, Vt. Died Jan. 17, 2010.

FREEDMAN, MICHAEL LEONARD, geriatrician, educator; b. Newark, Dec. 12, 1937; s. David Hyman and Alice Ella (Zwain) F.; m. Cora Ruth Singer, June 24, 1962; children: Lawrence Andrew, Deborah Lynn. AB with honors, Colgate U., 1959; MD cum laude, Tufts U., 1963. Diplomate Am. Bd. Internal Medicine, Am. Bd. Hematology, Am. Bd. Geriatric Medicine. Intern, then resident NYU/Bellevue Med. Ctrs., 1963-65, 68-69; rsch. assoc. lab physiology to staff investigator Nat. Cancer Inst., NIH, Bethesda, Md., 1965-68; asst. prof. NYU Med. Ctr., 1969-74, assoc. prof., 1974-77, prof., from 1977, firm chief, dir. geriatrics, from 1979; Diane and Arthur Belfer prof. geriatric medicine NYU, from 1987. Cons. CBS, Inc., Bristol Meyers Corp., Kimberly-Clark Corp., Pfizer Corp., Nutrasweet Corp., Citicorp. Editor: Hematology in the Elderly, 1985; contbr. over 200 articles to profl. jours. Lt. comdr. USPHS, 1965-68. NIH rsch. grantee, 1969—; recipient Wholeness of Life award Hosp. Chaplaincy, 1988; named one of the Heroes of Bellevue, 1987. Fellow ACP, Am. Geriatrics Soc. (com. chmn. 1985—), Am. Soc. Hematology, Gerontol. Soc. Am. (com. chmn. 1984—); mem. Am. Soc. Clin. Investigation, Am. Soc. Hematology, AAAS, Am. Fed. Aging Rsch. (founder, mem. nat. adv. coun.), Alpha Omega Alpha. Democrat. Jewish. Avocations: photography, travel, tennis. Home: Scarsdale, NY. Died Feb. 16, 2010.

FREEH, EDWARD JAMES, chemical engineer; b. Pleasant Valley, Pa., Sept. 18, 1925; s. Charles Michael and Catherine (Jamann) F.; m. Vivian Marie Igel, Sept. 27, 1952; children— Edward James, Gerard, Vincent, George, Marianne. B. Chem. Engring, U. Dayton, 1948; MS, MIT, 1950; PhD, Ohio State U., 1958. Process engr. du Pont Co., Seaford, Del., 1950-52; staff U. Dayton Research Inst., 1952-55, asso. dir., 1959-62; instr. Ohio State U., 1955-58, prof. chem. engring., 1968-75; v.p. tech. Duval Corp., Tucson, 1975-86. Staff Indsl. Nucleonics Corp., Columbus, 1958-59; prof. U. Ariz., 1962-68; adj. prof. chem. engring. U. Ariz., 1985—; v.p. EXD Assoc., Cons., 1986-87. Mem. Ariz. Solar Energy Commn., 1980-87. Served with USNR, 1943-45. Mem. Am. Chem. Soc., AIChE, Instrument Soc. Am. Research in application of computers to mineral processing. Home: Munds Park, Ariz. Died Sept. 16, 2009.

FREEMAN, JACK LEROY, prosthodontist; b. Mansfield, Ohio, May 21, 1935; s. William Alexander and Viola Elizabeth (Bailey) F.; m. Joyce Rae Moody, Nov. 4, 1960; children: Tracy Lynn, Laura Jean. Grad., Ohio State U., 1955, DDS, 1959. Gen. practice dentistry, Mansfield, 1961-79; practice dentistry specializing in prosthodontics, from 1979. Elected mem. Mansfield Charter Commn., 1983-84. Served to lt. USN, 1959-61. Proclamation of Appreciation award City of Mansfield, 1976. Mem. ADA, Cen. Ohio Dental Soc., Mansfield Dental Soc. (pres. 1969-70), Amvets, Ohio State U. Alumnae Assn., Psi Omega, Kappa Sigma. Lodges: Elks. Republican. Congregationalist. Avocations: sailing, gourmet cooking. Home: West Chester, Ohio. Died Jan. 2, 2009.

FREEMAN, SAMUEL RALPH, financial executive, lawyer; b. NYC, Sept. 2, 1929; s. Benjamin S. and Ethel S. (Salit) F.; m. Joyce Siegel, Dec. 21, 1958; children: Laura, Susan, Carol. LL.B., Bklyn. Law Sch., 1951. Bar: N.Y. 1951, Colo. 1954. Asst. atty. gen., Colo., 1955-58; ptnr. Van Cise, Freeman, Tooley & McClearn, Denver, 1959-72; v.p., gen. counsel Rio Grande Industries, Inc., Denver, 1973-89, Denver Rio Grande Western RR Co., Denver, 1973-89; vice chmn. Concord, Denver, 1989-92, cons., from 1993; asst. to chancellor U. Denver, from 1993. Mem. bd. arbitrators NASD; bd. dirs. FirstConcord Acceptance Corp.; mem. urban transp. adv. com. Dept. Transp., 1969-74; ind. sec. adv. com. on energy Dept. Commerce, 1986—; mem. exec. com. Interstate Oil Compact, 1976-86, 1st vice chmn., 1985; chmn. Colo. Oil and Gas Conservation Commn., 1974-85; judge adv. Colo. N.G., 1954-63. Mem. ABA, Am. Arbitration Assn. Jewish. Home: Denver, Colo. Died Aug. 28, 2009.

FREIMARK, ROBERT (BOB FREIMARK), artist; b. Doster, Mich., Jan. 27, 1922; s. Alvin O. and Nora (Shinaver) F.; m. Mary Carvin (dec.); 1 child, Matisse Jon; m. Lillian Tihlarik (dec. 2005); 1 child, Christine Gay. B.E., U. Toledo, 1950; M.F.A., Cranbrook Acad. Art, 1951. Prof. art emeritus San Jose State U., 1964-86; W.I.C.H.E. prof. Soledad State Prison, 1967. Established artist in residence program Yosemite Nat. Park,1984-85, Fire Clay and Tile, Aromas, Calif., 1998; artist in residence Museo Regla, Cuba, 2000, Ferencsik Janos Zeneskola, L. Balaton, Hungary, 2002; panelist SECOLAS S.E. conf. Latin Am. Studies, Vera Cruz, Mex., NC U., Santa Domingo. Guest artist Harvard U., 1972-73; first Am. to make tapestries in Art Protis technique at Atelier Vlnena, Brno, Czechoslovakia.; contbr. to profl. publs.; One-man shows include Northamerican Cultural Inst., Mexico City, 1963, Minn. Inst. Arts, Toledo Mus. Art, Salpeter Gallery, Morris Gallery, NYC, Des Moines Art Ctr., Santa Barbara Mus., Moravska Mus., Czechoslovakia, Brunel U., London, Amerika Haus, Munich, Stuttgart, Regensburg, Joslyn Ctr. for Arts, Torrance, Calif, Stanford U., San Jose (Calif.) Mus. Art, Triton Mus., Santa Clara, Calif., Guatemalteco, Guatemala City, Dum Umeni Brno, CSFR, Strahov Closter, Prague, 1990, Walter Bischoff Gallery, Stuttgart, 1990, Kunstler aus den USA, Kunsthaus Ostbayern and Amerika Haus, Stuttgart, 1991, Max Planck Inst., Munich, The Gag Theatre, Prague, 1992, Haus Wiegand, Munich, 1993, San Jose State U., 1964, 1967-68, 1981, 1994, Viva!, Tokyo, 1994, Gallery Q, Sacramento, 1997, Parish Gallery, DC, 1997, 02, Barton Gallery, Sacramento, 1997, 2002-03, 05; Galeria Galiano Havana, 1998, Galerie Weber, Viechtach, Germany, 1998, Point Gall., Brno, Czech Rep., 1998, Galerie Divadlo, Uherske Hradiste, C.R., 1998, Marco Polo Galleries, Carmel, Calif., 2001, Colton Hall Mus., Monterey, Calif., 2002, Hart Galleries, Palm Desert, Calif., 2003, Morgan Hill Cmty. Cultural Ctr., 2004, Mexican Heritage Plz., San Jose, 2007, Quilts & Textiles, 2007; exhibited in group shows at Art Inst. Chgo., 1952, Pa. Acad. Fine Arts, 1953 (Lambert Fund prize), Detroit Inst. Arts, 1950, 56, Mich. State U., 1956 (Purchase award), N.A.D., 1956, Boston Print Symposium, 1997, Portland Art Mus., Oreg., 1997 (Purchase award), Honolulu Acad. Art, 1998, Internat. Graphic Triennial, Krakow, Poland, 1998, Internat. Small Engraving Salon, Florean Mus., Romania, Art Expo, NYC, 2000, Internat. Woodprint Assn., Kyoto, Japan, 1999, Bklyn. Mus. (Purchase award), Mus. Modern Art, Michael Stone Collection, DC, Contempo Collection, Tokyo, Havana Bienale, 2000, others; exhbn. 50 States toured, European Mus., 1970-71; represented in collections including Pa. Acad. Fine Art, Boston Mus. Fine Arts, Fogg Mus., Butler Inst. Am. Art, Ford Motor Co., South Bend Art Assn., Joslyn Art Mus., Seattle Art Mus., Ga. Mus., Huntington Gallery, Des Moines Art Center, Smithsonian Instn., Libr. Congress, LA County Art Inst., Brit. Mus., Nat. Gallery, Prague, Birmingham (Eng.) Mus., Moravske Mus., Brno, Czechoslovakia, Bibliotheque Nationale, Paris, Harn Mus., Gainsville, Fla., Portland Mus. Art (over 500 prints), Nat. Mus., Washington, Natl. Mus. Cuba, La Habana, Nat. Mus. Costa Rica, San Jose, Nat. Mus. Egypt, Cairo, Mus. Arte Contemporaneo, Bahia Blanca, Mus. Genaro Perez, Cordoba, Mus. de Bellas Artes, Cordoba, Argentina, Mus. Guayasamin, Quito, Ecuador, Mus. Nat., Panama City, Panama, others; tapestries in pub. and pvt. collections including Mus. of Quilts and Textiles, San Jose, Calif.,History San Jose, created tapestry representing U.S. for Olympic Games, Moscow, 1980, Parish Gallery, Washington, Triad Gallery, Seal Rock, Oreg., Haus Wiegand, Munich, Art Foundry Gallery, Sacramento, Greg Barlon Gallery, Sacramento, Hart Gallery, Palm Desert and Carmel, Calif.; prodr. video documentary: Arte Cubano (Contemporary Art and Culture in Cuba, 1999, 2000, 1st award, San Francisco Throwback Film Festival, Los Desaparecidos--The Disappeared Ones, 2003 (Freedom award Dahlonega Film Festival, also Best Documentary Short and Best of Show, Accolade Competition, Best Documentary Spl. Gold statuette, World Fest, Houston, Dirs. Citation award Black Maria Film Festival 2006, 20 Internat. Festivals); guest artist Joslyn Meml. Mus., 1961, instr. painting and drawing, Ohio U., 1955-59, artist in residence, Des Moines Art Center, 1959-63, dir., Crystal Lake Art Ctr., Frankfort, Mich., (1955-57), guest lectr.,one man show, Columbia U., 1963; guest artist Riverside Art Ctr., 1964, Agora Vienna, Austria, 1994, MuseoGuayasamin, Quito, Ecuador, 2002; curated exhibit Stuttgart, 1993; founder Bob & Lil Freimark Collection Portland Art Mus.; artist in residence MuseoRegla, Cuba, 2002, Lake Balaton, Hungary, 2002; Am. corollary to Dakar Bienale, 5 works, Senegal, 2002, Art Workshop, Dakar, others; contbr. to craft and fibre publs. With Western Interstate Commn. Higher Edn., Soledad State Prison, 1967. Coxwain USN, 1939—46, Pacific. Recipient 2d award for oil Northwest Territorial exhibit, 1954, Roulet medal Toledo Mus. Art, 1957, 1st award Print Exhbn., 1958, purchase award Midwest Biennial and Northwest Printmakers, Jurors award Berkeley Art Ctr, 1996; Calif. State Coll. Sys. spl. creative leave edit. serigraphs; elected to New Talent in U.S.A., 1957; Ohio U. rsch. grantee, 1958-59, Ford Found. grantee, 1965; Western Interstate Commn. for Higher Edn. grantee, 1967, San Jose State Coll. Found. grantee, 1966, 67, 68, 69, 70, 71, 85; designated ofcl. U.S. Bicentennial Exhbn. Amerika Hausen, Fed. Republic Germany, 1976. Independent. Avocations: hunting, fishing, reading, films, cooking. Home: Morgan Hill, Calif. Died Feb. 18, 2010.

FREUND, ROBERT DAVID, data processing executive; b. Bklyn., Mar. 7, 1946; s. Walter James and Muriel B. (Kadish) Freund. BS, NY U., 1967; MBA, CCNY, 1969. Cert. in computer programming, in data processing. Computer ops. supr. Forbes Inc., NYC, 1967—69; sys. analyst Avon Products Inc., NYC, 1971—73; mgr. computer programming Martin Marietta Corp., NYC, 1973—74; dir. data processing Citibank NA, Upper Manhattan Region, NYC, 1975—81; prin. Schilo Co. Inc., NYC, 1981—82; pres., chmn. bd. Preferred Computer Trading Corp., Sparta, NJ. Served with US Army, 1969—71, Vietnam. Decorated Bronze Star, Nat. Def. Svc. medal. Mem.: Assn. Inst. Cert. Computer Profls. (charter mem.), Assn. Computer Ops. Mgrs. (charter mem.), Mu Gamma Tau. Home: Forest Hills, NY. Died June 16, 2009.

FREY, DONALD NELSON, industrial engineer, educator, retired manufacturing executive; b. St. Louis, Mar. 13, 1923; m. Helen-Kay Eberley, Feb. 14, 2003; children: Donald Nelson, Judith Kingsley(dec.), Margaret Bente, Catherine, Christopher, Elizabeth. Student, Mich. State Coll., 1940—42; BS, U. Mich., 1947, MS, 1949, PhD, 1950, DSc (hon.), 1965; DSc, U. Mo., Rolla, 1966. Instr. metall. engring. U. Mich., 1949—50, asst. prof. chem. and metall. engring., 1950—51; rsch. engr. Babcock & Wilcox Tube Co., Beaver Falls, Pa., 1951; various rsch. positions Ford Motor Co. (Ford div.), 1951—57, various engring. positions, 1958—61, product planning mgr., 1961—62, asst. gen. mgr., 1962—65, gen. mgr. original Mustang auto, 1965—68, co. v.p. for product devel., 1965—67; pres. Gen. Cable Corp., NYC, 1968—71, Bell & Howell Co., Chgo., 1973—81, chmn., CEO, 1971—88; prof. of indsl. engring. & mgmt. sci. Northwestern U., Evanston, Ill., 1988—2008. Mem. exec. bd. World Bank, Washington; bd. dirs. Cin. Milacron, Clark Equipment Co., Packer Engring., My Own Meals, Hyatt Corp., Springs Industries, Quintar, 20th Century Fox Corp.; co-chair Japan study multinats. NRC, 1992—94; surveyor World Bank, Poland, 1990. Co-chmn. Gov.'s Commn. of Sci. and Industry, Ill., from 1988; exec. bd. mem. World Bank, 2003. With US Army, 1942—46. Recipient Nat. Medal of Tech., The White House, 1990; named Young Engr. of Yr., Engring. Soc. Detroit, 1953, Outstanding Alumni, U. Mich. Coll. Engring., 1957, Outstanding Young Man of the Yr., Detroit Jr. Bd. of Commerce, 1958, Man of the Yr., Weizmann Inst., 1988; Inaugural fellow, INFORMS, 2002. Fellow: INFORMS, AAAS; mem.: ASME, Coun. on Fgn. Rels., Detroit Engring. Soc. (pres., bd. dirs. 1962—65), Soc. Automotive Engrs. (vice chmn. Detroit 1958, Russell Springer award 1956), Nat. Acad. Engring. (mem. coun. 1972), Am. Soc. Metals, Am. Inst. Mining and Metall. Engrs. (chmn. Detroit chpt. 1954, chmn., editor Nat. Symposium on Sheet Steels 1956), Econ. Club, Saddle and Cycle Club, Chgo. Club, Hundred Club Cook County, Chgo. Commonwealth Club, Phi Delta Theta, Tau Beta Pi, Phi Kappa Phi, Sigma Xi. Achievements include established Margaret and Muir Frey Prize for innovation in engring., Northwestern Univ., 2002; Clara McKitrick Prize for Design in engring., Northwestern Univ., 2004. Home: Evanston, Ill. Died Mar. 5, 2010.

FRICKEY, PHILIP PAUL, law educator; b. Oberlin, Kans., June 29, 1953; s. Carl Lewis and Doreen Lydia (Nitsch) F.; m. Mary Ann Bernard, May 7, 1983; children: Alexander, Elizabeth. BA in Polit. Sci. with distinction, U. Kans., 1975; JD magna cum laude, U. Mich., 1978. Bar: D.C. 1980. Law clk. to Judge John Minor Wisdom U.S. Ct. Appeals (5th cir.), New Orleans, 1978-79; law clk. to Justice Thurgood Marshall U.S. Supreme Ct., Washington, 1979-80; assoc. Shea & Gardner, Washington, 1981-83; from assoc. prof. law to prof. U. Minn. Law Sch., Mpls., 1983—91, Faegre and Benson prof. law, 1991—98, Irving Younger prof. law, 1998—2000; Richard W. Jennings prof. law U. Calif., Berkeley, 2000—10. Vis. assoc. prof. law U. Kans. Law Sch., Lawrence, 1980; vis. prof. law Harvard U. Law Sch., Cambridge, Mass., 1996. Author (with Daniel A. Farber): Law and Public Choice: A Critical Introduction, 1991; author: (with William N. Eskridge Jr. and Elizabeth Garrett) Cases and Materials on Legislation: Statutes and the Creation of Public Policy, 2001; author: (with Daniel A. Farber and William N. Eskridge Jr.) Cases and Materials on Constitutional Law: Themes for the Constitution's Third Century, 2003; author: others; co-editor: Issues in Legal Scholarship, 2002—10; contbr. articles to profl. jours. Mem.: Am. Acad. Arts and Scis., Am. Law Inst., Order of Coif, Phi Beta Kappa. Died July 11, 2010.

FRIDAY, GILBERT ANTHONY, JR., pediatrician; b. Pitts., Apr. 16, 1930; s. Gilbert Anthony and Susan Dorothy (Kumer) F.; m. Christina Cecilia McShane, Sept. 12, 1959; children: Martin, Peter, Martha, Timothy, Amy, Anne, Robert. BS, Bucknell U., 1952; MD, Temple U., 1956. Diplomate Nat. Bd. Med. Examiners. Rotating intern Phila. Gen. Hosp., 1956-57; pediatric resident Children's Hosp. of Phila., 1960-62, Children's Hosp. of Pitts., 1962-63, asst. med. dir. ops., 1963-66, preceptorship in allergy/immunology, 1962-67; clin. instr. to asst. prof. U. Pitts., 1963-87, clin. assoc. prof., 1987, prof. pediatrics, 1987—2001, clin. prof., from 2001. Chmn. bd. dirs. Pa. Blue Shield, Camp Hill, 1992-96. Contbr. articles to profl. jours., chpts. to books. Lt. comdr. USN MC, 1956-66. Wyeth Pediatric scholar. Fellow Am. Coll. Allergy, Asthma, and Immunology, Am. Acad. Allery, Asthma, and Immunology, Am. Acad. Pediats.; mem. AMA, Allegheny County Med. Soc. (pres. 1987), Pa. Med. Soc., Pa. Allergy Soc. (pres. 1975), Alpha Omega Alpha. Republican. Roman Catholic. Avocations: boating, fishing. Home: Pittsburgh, Pa. Died Oct. 22, 2009.

FRIEDEN, BERNARD JOEL, urban studies educator; b. NYC, Aug. 11, 1930; s. George and Jean (Harris) F.; m. Elaine Leibowitz, Nov. 23, 1958; 1 child, Deborah Susan. BA, Cornell U., 1951; MA, Pa. State U., 1953; MCP, MIT, 1957, PhD, 1962. Asst. prof. urban studies and planning MIT, Cambridge, 1961-65, assoc. prof., 1965-69, prof., from 1969, Ford prof. urban devel., from 1989, assoc. dean architecture and planning, from 1993; dir. rsch. Ctr. for Real Estate Devel., mem. faculty com. Ctr. for Real Estate, Cambridge, 1985-87; chmn. faculty MIT, 1987-89; dir. MIT-Harvard U. Joint Center for Urban Studies, 1971-75, mem. exec. com., 1975-82. Cons. HUD, 1966-68, DOD, 1994—; staff Pres. Johnson's Task Force Urban Problems, 1965; mem. Pres. Nixon's Task Force Urban Problems, 1968, The White House Task Force Model Cities, 1969, Pres. Carter's Urban Policy Adv. Com., 1977-80; vis. scholar U. Calif., Berkeley, 1990-91, 96. Author: The Future of Old Neighborhoods, 1964, Metropolitan America, 1966, (with Robert Morris) Urban Planning and Social Policy, 1968, (with William W. Nash) Shaping an Urban Future, 1969, (with Marshall Kaplan) The Politics of Neglect, 1975, 77, (with Wayne E. Anderson and Michael J. Murphy) Managing Human Services, 1977, The Environmental Protection Hustle, 1979, (with Lynne B. Sagalyn) Downtown, Inc., 1989; editor: Jour. Am. Inst. Planners, 1962-65; contbr. to various books and encys. Bd. dirs. Citizens Housing and Planning Assn., 1966-75. Served with AUS, 1952-54. Guggenheim fellow, U. Calif., Berkeley, 1975—76, rsch. fellow, Urban Land Inst., 1978—89, sr. fellow, 1989—98, CMI fellow, Cambridge (Eng.) U., 2001—02, Life fellow, Clare Hall, Cambridge U. Mem. Am. Inst. Cert. Planners, Am. Planning Assn. Jewish. Home: Chestnut Hill, Mass. Died Sept. 9, 2009.

FRIEDMAN, MENDEL, construction company executive; b. Apr. 30, 1924; s. Hyman and Mamye (Dupkin) F.; m. Phyllis Trabish: Children: Roberta, Nancy, Gary, John, Marc, Carla Knoll. Student, Pa. State U. With Jolly Co. Inc., Balt., now pres., chief exec. officer. Trustee Nat. Jewish Hosp., Denver, 1981—; bd. dirs. Mt. Washington Pediatric Hosp., Balt., 1981—, Deafness Rsch Found. Chmn. Mayor's Ball, City Balt., 1983; fundraiser Ann. Scholar Athlete Awards, Balt., 1978—. Named Man of Yr., Nat. Jewish Hosp., Balt., 1985. Mem. Am. Technion Soc. (Balt. chpt. bd. dirs.), Nat. Trust Hist. Preservation, Johns Hopkins Club, N.Y. Road Runners Club. Avocations: marathons (10), patron arts, humanitarian, wine connoisseur, reading. Died Apr. 26, 2010.

FRIEDMAN, ORRIE MAX, biotechnology company executive; b. Grenfell, Sask., Can., June 6, 1915; s. Jack and Gertrude (Shulman) F.; m. Marcia Gordon, Sept. 8, 1950 (div. Aug. 1957); 1 child, Mark David; m. Laurel E. Leeder, Jan. 2, 1959; children: Gertrude Jane, Hugh Robert. BSc, U. Man., 1935; BSc in Chemistry, McGill U., 1941, PhD, 1944. Asst. prof. chemistry Harvard U. Med. Sch., Boston, 1952-53; asst. prof., prof., adj. res. prof. Brandeis U., Waltham, Mass., 1953-70; pres., sci. dir. Collaborative Rsch. Inc., Bedford, Mass., 1962-82, chmn. bd., from 1982, CEO, 1986-93. Pres. Grenfell Devel. Corp., 1994—; mem. com. on innovation SBA, 1973-75; mem. corp. Sidney Farber Cancer Inst., Boston, Mus. Sci., Boston; bd. govs. Dana Farber Cancer Inst., Technion, Israel Inst. Tech., Haifa; trustee Barnett Inst. Northeast U., Boston, Beth Israel Hosp., Boston; pres. GrenPharma LLC, 2000; sr. vis. scientist, Brandeis U., 2000—. Recipient many rsch. grants various U.S. Govt. Agys. Fellow AAAS; mem. Am. Chem. Soc., Am. Assn. Cancer Rsch., N.Y. Acad. Sci., Sigma Xi. Home: Brookline, Mass. Died June 28, 2009.

FROEHLICH, LAURENCE ALAN, lawyer; b. Syracuse, NY, Feb. 3, 1951; s. Fritz Edgar and Eileen (Karch) F.; m. Rochelle M. Gutman; children: Jason Nathaniel, Robin Gayle, Stephen Micah, Justin Mark. BA, Yale U., 1973; MSc, London Sch. Econ. and Polit. Sci., 1974; JD, George Washington U., 1977; student, Fed. Exec. Inst., 1988. Bar: N.J. 1977, U.S. Dist. Ct. N.J. 1977, D.C. 1979, U.S. Dist. Ct. D.C. 1979. Atty.-advisor HEW, Washington, 1977-79; counsel to insp. gen. USDA, Washington, 1979-84, chief counsel to insp. gen., 1984-90; gen. coun. to insp. gen. FDIC, Washington, from 1990. Chmn. Coun. of Counsels to the Insp. Gen., Washington, 1981-87; adj. lectr. Fed. Law Enforcement Tng. Ctr., Brunswick, Ga., 1980—, Legal Edn. Inst. Dept. Justice, Washington, 1987—, Inspectors Gen. Auditor Tng. Inst., Ft. Belvoir, Va., 1994—. County del. Gaithersburg (Md.) Elem. Sch. PTA, 1987, Forest Oak Mid. Sch. PTA, 1995—; pres. Goshen Elem. Sch. PTA, Gaithersburg, 1988-90; trustee Congregation Kehilat Shalom, Gaithersburg, 1988-91. Recipient Pub. Svc. award GSA, Washington, 1983, Outstanding leadership award GSA, Washington, 1986, Cert. appreciation Am. Soc. Access Profls., Washington, 1985, 89, Leadership award Coun. Counsels to Inspector Gen., 1996.! Mem. ABA (chmn. pub. advocates and pub. representation com., sect. adminstrv. law and regulatory practice 1991-92). Avocations: reading, stamp collecting/philately, music, the outdoors. Home: Gaithersburg, Md. Died July 15, 2010.

FRUEH, BARTLEY RICHARD, surgeon; b. Cleve., Sept. 1, 1937; s. Lloyd Walter and Elizabeth Virginia (Scott) F.; m. Frances Olive Beach, June 10, 1961 (div. Dec. 1976); children: Bartley Christopher, Dylan Beach (dec.), Walter Terry; m. Frances Mallet-Prevost Gaston Sargent, Dec. 31, 1976 (div. Oct. 1997); stepchildren: Eric Winslow Sargent, Laura Elizabeth Sargent; m. Cheryl Lynn Terpening, June 1, 2002; 1 stepchild, Cherilyn Marie Smith. BChemE, Cornell U., 1960; MD, Columbia Coll. Phys./Surgeons, 1964; MS Ophthalmology, U. Mich., 1970. Diplomate Am. Bd. Ophthalmology. Surg. intern N.C. Meml. Hosp., Chapel Hill, N.C., 1964-65; resident in ophthalmology U. Mich., Ann Arbor, 1967-70; fellow eye plastic surgery Alston Callahan, Birmingham, Ala., 1970; asst. prof. ophthalmology, eye plastic surgery U. Mo., Columbia, 1971-72, asst. clin. prof. ophthalmology eye plastic surgery, 1972-76, assoc. clin. prof. ophthalmology eye plastic surgery, 1976-79; pvt. practice, ophthalmology Columbia, 1972-79; assoc. prof. ophthalmology, eye plastic and orbital surgery U. Mich., Ann Arbor, 1979-86, prof. ophthalmology, from 1986. Cons. med. staff U. Mo. Med. Ctr., Columbia, 1971-79, Meml. Hosp., Jefferson City, 1971-73, Boone County Hosp., Columbia, 1972-79, Harry S. Truman Meml. Vet.'s Hosp., Columbia, 1971-79; med. staff Columbia Regional Hosp., Columbia, 1974-79, U. Mich. Med. Ctr., 1979—, VA Med. Ctr., 1979—; hon. guest spkr. Royal Australian Coll. Ophthalmology, 1995, Peter Rogers lectr., 1999, Bruce Frolick lectr. 2003; lectr. in field. Author: Transactions, American Ophthalmological Society, 1984; editor/author: Surgery of the Eye, 1988; editl. bd.: Ophthalmic Surgery, 1980-87, Am. Acad. Ophthalmology Clin. Modules, 1983-86, Ophthalmic Plastic and Reconstructive Surgery, 1984-98, Orbit; contbr. articles to profl. jours./publs., books in field. Capt. USAF, 1965-67, Taiwan. Grantee in field. Fellow Am. Acad. Ophthalmology (Wendell Hughes lectr. 1993, Sr. Honor award 1990); mem. Am. Soc. Ophthal. Plastic and Reconstructive Surgery (sec. 1973-74, pres. 1976), Am. Ophthalmol. Soc., Orbital Soc., Australasian Soc. Ophthalmic Plastic Surgeons (hon.), European Soc. Ophthal. Plastic and Reconstructive Surgeons (hon.). Avocations: pocket billiards, model t fords and old morgans, wine, violin. Died Feb. 16, 2010.

FRUITT, RONALD L., university administrator; b. Wabash, Ind., Feb. 25, 1937; m. Phyllis Ross, June 14, 1959; children: Mark Allen, David Lee, Nancy Ann, Steven Robert. BS in Agrl. Econs., Purdue U., 1959, MS in Counseling & Pers. Svcs., 1967. Mgmt. trainee Sears Roebuck & Co., Ft. Wayne, Ind., 1960-61; asst. residence hall mgr.-in-tng. Purdue U., West Lafayette, Ind., 1961-66, mgr. Wiley Hall, 1966-71, asst. dir. residence halls, student programs & counseling, 1971-81, dir. residence halls, 1981-83, v.p. for housing & food svcs., from 1983. Mem. Univ. Drug Com., 1972-79, Univ. Orientation Com., 1971-81, Pres'. Coun., Lafayette Home Hosp. Fair Com.; co-chair Univ. Health Coun., 1977-80; pres. United Way, 1991; past chmn. Ind. area coun. Boy's Club Am.; chmn. Purdue United Way Campaign, 1988; bd. dirs. Greater Lafayette United Way, Ind. State Fair Sch. for Boys, 1971-72. Mem. Greater Lafayette C. of C., U.S. Trotting Assn., John Purdue Coaches Club, Old Masters, Purdue Reamer Club, Tomahawk, Sire-Purdue Glee Club, Elks, Iron Key, Omicron Delta Kappa, Alpha Phi Omega. Avocations: work, golf, gardening, sports, travel, race horses. Home: West Lafayette, Ind. Died Mar. 18, 2009.

FRY, WILLIAM ALLEN, literature educator; b. Greenville, Ohio, Dec. 2, 1932; s. Walter Leonard and Grace Lucille (Moore) Fry; m. Lura Jane McGarvey, June 6, 1953; children: Rebecca Lynne, Deborah Anne, Cynthia Lou, Katherine Joy. BA, Wheaton Coll., Ill., 1955; MA, Columbia U., 1966, PhD, 1973. Prof. English, Nyack Coll., NY, 1963—78, Taylor U., Upland, Ind., from 1978. Contbg. editor Alliance Witness,

Nyack, 1983. Mem.: Conf. Christianity and Lit., Midwest Modern Lang. Assn., Nat. Coun. Tchrs. English, Phi Delta Kappa. Avocation: travel. Home: Orange Park, Fla. Died May 6, 2009.

FUHRER, ARTHUR K., lawyer; b. NYC, Oct. 19, 1926; s. Isidore and Toby (Schorr) Fuhrer; m. Lenore R. Lewis; children: Laura A., Robert A., David A. LLB, Bklyn. Law Sch., 1949; postgrad., NYU Sch. Law, 1951—52. Bar: NY 1950, US Dist Ct. (so. dist.) NY 1951, US Supreme Ct. 1977. Assoc. firm Sargoy & Stein, NYC, 1951—52; firm Andrew D. Weinberger, 1952—54; lawyer William Morris Agy., Inc., 1954—75; v.p., 1975—95; of counsel Frankfurt, Garbus, Klein & Selz, from 1995; co-chmn. Television & Motion Picture Seminar Practicing Law Inst., 1973. Contbr. articles to profl. jours. Home: Garden City, NY. Died May 23, 2010.

FUHRMAN, ROBERT ALEXANDER, retired aerospace transportation executive; b. Detroit, Feb. 23, 1925; s. Alexander A. and Elva (Brown) F.; m. Nan McCormick (dec. 1988); m. Nancy Richards BS, U. Mich., 1945; MS, U. Md., 1952; postgrad., U. Calif., San Diego, 1958; Exec. Mgmt. Program, Stanford Bus. Sch., 1964. Project engr. Naval Air Test Ctr., Patuxent River, Md., 1946-53; chief tech. engring. Ryan Aero. Co., San Diego, 1953-58; mgr. Polaris, 1958-64; chief engr. MSD, 1964-66; v.p., asst. gen. mgr. missile systems div. Lockheed Missiles & Space Co., Sunnyvale, Calif., 1966-68, v.p., gen. mgr., 1969, v.p., 1973-76, pres., 1976-83, chmn., 1979-91; v.p. Lockheed Corp., Burbank, Calif., 1969-76, group pres. Missiles, Space & Electronics System, 1983-85, pres., COO Calabasas, Calif., 1986-88, vice chmn., COO, 1980-90; pres. Lockheed Ga. Co., Marietta, 1970-71, Lockheed Calif. Co., Burbank, 1971-73. Bd. dirs. Charles Stark Draper Lab., Inc.; mem. Fleet Ballistic Missile Steering Task Group, 1966-70, Def. Sci. Bd. Mem. adv. coun. Sch. Engring., Stanford U.; mem. adv. bd. Coll. Engring., U. Mich. With USNR, 1944-46. Recipient Silver Knight award Nat. Mgmt. Assn., 1969, John J. Montgomery award San Diego Aerospace Mus., 1964, Disting. Citizen award Boy Scouts Am., 1983, Eminent Engr. award Tau Beta Pi, 1983; named to Mich. Aviation Hall of Fame, 1991. Fellow AIAA (hon., pres., Von Karman award 1978), Royal Aero. Soc., Soc. Mfg. Engrs. (award 1973, Donald C. Burnham award 1983); mem. NAE, Am. Astron. Soc. (sr.), Nat. Aero Assn., Navy League Soc. (life), Air Force Assn., Assn. U.S. Army, Soc. Am. Value Engrs. (hon.), Santa Clara County Mfrs. Group (past chmn.), Burning Tree Club (Bethesda, Md.), Carmel Valley Country Club (Calif.), Monterey Peninsula County Club (Pebble Beach, Calif.), Beta Gamma Sigma. Died Nov. 21, 2009.

FUKUYAMA, KIMIE, medical educator; b. Tokyo, Dec. 11, 1927; came to U.S., 1956; MD, Tokyo Women's Med. Coll., 1949, PhD, 1963; MS, U. Mich., 1958. Resident dermatology Tokyo Med. Coll., 1950-55; asst. prof. Tokyo Women's Med. Coll., 1961-64; lectr. U. Calif., San Francisco, 1965-67, asst. prof. in residence, 1967-72, assoc. prof. in residence, 1972-78, prof. in residence, from 1978, vice chmn., from 1980, dir. postgrad. tng., from 1976. Mem. Am. Acad. Dermatology (life), Japanese Assn. for Dermatology (hon.), Soc. for Investigative Dermatology (patron). Died Mar. 16, 2010.

FULKERSON, SUE ELLEN, poet; b. Zanesville, Ohio, Dec. 14, 1943; d. Arthur Amos and Helen Marie Bryan; m. Larry Dean Fulkerson, Apr. 5, 1968; children: Rebecca, Matthew. BA in Social Work, Valparaiso U., Ind., 1966. Probation officer Muskingum County Juvenile Ct., Zanesville, Ohio, 1966—67; caseworker Muskingum County Welfare Dept., Zanesville, 1967—68; social worker Franklin County Children Svcs., Columbus, Ohio, 1968—70; income maint. worker Muskingum County Welfare Dept., Zanesville, 1977—80; foster care coord. Muskingum County Children Svcs., Zanesville, 1980—81; social worker ODC Nursing Home, Zanesville, 1987—88; ret., 1988. Actor: (of poems); author: (book of poetry) Poems for Life's Seasons, 1999, (poems) A Poet's Note to an Artist, 2003, One Summer Day, 2003, Earth's Princess of Light, 2003, Heaven, 2004. Vol. Assisted Living Cmty., Zanesville; mem. Rep. Nat. Com., 2000—05, Trinity Luth. Ch. Recipient Editors Choice award for poem Autumn, Nat. Libr. Poetry, 1993, Editor's Choice award for poem Summer's Farewell, 1997, Editor's Choice award for outstanding achievement in poetry for poem The Autumn Leaves, 2002, Poetry Cert. of Recognition, Famous Poet Soc., 2001, Editor's Choice award outstanding achievement in poetry for poem One Summer Day, Internat. Libr. Poetry, 2003. Mem.: Acad. Am. Poets, Gideons Internat. (sec. 1985—99). Avocations: reading, making bookmarks, photography. Home: Zanesville, Ohio. Died Jan. 3, 2009.

FULLER, MARK ADIN, JR., forest products company executive; b. Cin., Jan. 1, 1933; s. Mark Adin and Ellen Dudley (Webb) F.; m. Julia Dula Van Patten, June 9, 1956; children: Mark Adin, Ellen McClain, Mallory McKnight. BA, Princeton U., 1954. With Champion Internat. Corp., Stamford, Conn., from 1957, v.p. sales, 1971-79, v.p., gen. mgr., 1979-80, exec. v.p., from 1980. Bd. trustees Xavier U. La., New Orleans; trustee New Canaan (Conn.) Nature Ctr. With USN, 1954-57. Mem. Am. Forest and Paper Assn., Muirfield Village Golf Club, Country Club of New Canaan. Home: Vlg Of Golf, Fla. Died Sept. 5, 2009.

FULLER, THEODORE, retired insurance executive; b. Yonkers, NY, Dec. 7, 1918; s. Clarence Wendel and Mary Edgar (Denniston) F. AB cum laude, Princeton U., NJ, 1941; LLB, Columbia U., NYC, 1948. Bar: N.Y. 1948. With Savs. Bank Life Ins. Fund, NYC, 1948-83, exec. v.p., 1964-65, pres., 1965-83. Former mem. N.Y. State Adv. Bd. Life Ins.; cons. Svc. Corps Ret. Execs. Comdr. USNR, World War II, Korea. Mem. Assn. of Bar of City of N.Y., Princeton Club, Univ. Glee Club, Indian Harbor Yacht Club, Retired Men's Assn. (former pres.), Ea. Packard Club, Antique Automobile Club Am., Classic Car Club Am. (former bd. dirs.), Rolls Royce Owners Club, Pierce Arrow Club, Sound Investments Club. Home: Greenwich, Conn. Died June 20, 2009.

FULLERTON, WILLIAM DEAN, health policy consultant, health educator; b. Mars, Pa., Dec. 9, 1927; s. Dean and June (Steele) F.; m. Julia Cordelia Cooper, Nov. 14, 1958; children: Catherine, Scott, James, Dirk. BA, U. Rochester, 1951. Div. chief Social Security Adminstrn., Balt., 1960-66; specialist Library of Congress, Washington, 1966-70; staff health policy US House Ways & Means Com., Washington, 1970-76; dep. adminstr. Health Care Fin. Adminstrn., Washington, 1977-78; prin. Health Policy Alternatives Inc., Washington, 1978—89. Adj. prof. U. N.C., Chapel Hill, 1982—89; mem. Fed. Prospective Payment Assessment Commn. Contbr. articles to profl. jours. Served with U.S. Army, 1945-47. Recipient Ralph D. McGill award in govt. U. Rochester, 1951; recipient Superior Service award HEW, 1966, 67, 78 Mem. Inst. Medicine Democrat. Home: Tavares, Fla. Died June 12, 2010.

FULLMER, DANIEL WARREN, former psychologist, educator; b. Spoon River, Ill., Dec. 12, 1922; s. Daniel Floyd and Sarah Louisa (Essex) F.; m. Janet Satomi Saito, June 1980; children: Daniel William, Mark Warren. BS, Western Ill. U., 1947, MS, 1952; PhD, U. Denver, 1955. Post-doctoral intern psychiat. div. U. Oreg. Med. Sch., 1958-61; mem. faculty U. Oreg., 1955-66; prof. psychology Oreg. System of Higher Edn., 1958-66; faculty Coll. Edn. U. Hawaii, Honolulu, 1966-95, retired, 1995, prof. emeritus, from 1974; pvt. practice psychol. counseling. Cons. psychologist Grambling State U., 1960-81; founder Free-Family Counseling Ctrs., Portland, Oreg., 1959-66, Honolulu, 1966-74; co-founder Child and Family Counseling Ctr., Waianae, Oahu, Hawaii, Kilohana United Meth. Ch., Oahu, 1992, v.p., sec., 1992; pres. Human Resources Devel. Ctr., Inc., 1974—; chmn. Hawaii State Bd. to License Psychologists, 1973-78. Author: Counseling: Group Theory & System, 2d. edit., 1978, The Family Therapy Dictionary Text, 1991, MANABU, Diagnosis and Treatment of a Japanese Boy with a Visual Anomaly, 1991; co-author: Principles of Guidance, 2d. edit., 1977; author (counselor/cons. training manuals) Counseling: Content and Process, 1964, Family Consultation Therapy, 1968, The School Counselor-Consultant, 1972, Family Therapy as the Rites of Passage, 1998; editor: Bulletin, Oreg. Coop Testing Service, 1955-57, Hawaii P&G Jour., 1970-76; assoc. editor: Educational Perspectives, U. Hawaii Coll. Edn. Served with USNR, 1944-46. Recipient Francis E. Clark award Hawaii Pers. Guidance Assn., 1972, Thomas Jefferson award for Outstanding Pub. Svc., 1993; named Hall of Fame Grambling State U., 1987. Mem. Am. Psychol. Assn., Am. Counseling Assn. (Nancy C. Wimmer award 1963), Masons. Methodist. Died Feb. 20, 2009.

FULLMER, DAVID R., lawyer; b. Cleve., June 8, 1931; AB, Denison U., 1953; JD, Ohio State U., 1956. Bar: Ohio 1956. Ptnr. Baker & Hostetler, Cleve. Died Aug. 7, 2010.

GABRIEL, RONALD LEE, management consultant; b. Bklyn., Nov. 8, 1941; s. Louis and Hazel H. (Peller) Gabriel. BS, U. NC, 1963; MBA, 1966; PhD, Am. U., 1974. Staff asst. The Hopp Press, Inc., NYC, 1958—62; statis. analyst Census Bur., 1964—65; mkt. rsch. analyst Benton & Bowles Advt., NYC, 1966—67, Warner Lambert Co., Morris Plains, NJ, 1967—68; econ. statistician Dept. Navy, Washington, 1970—75; personnel mgr. GSA, Washington, 1975—80, supervisory program analyst, 1980—86, human resources mgmt. cons., 1986—95; lectr. bus. stats. U. NC, 1964—65; pres., CEO Gabriel & Assocs., from 1995; adj. prof. U. Md., 1996; cons. Postal Svc. Mgmt. Inst., 1973—75; mem. Presdl. Inaugural Com., 1964—65, 1976—77, Carter-Mondale Transition Group, 1976—77; mem. spl. task force Pres.'s Reorgn. Project, 1977—78; mem. Clinton-Gore Inaugural Com., 1992—93, 1996—97; founder Cooperstown South Baseball Mus., Chevy Chase, Md., Bklyn. Dodger Fan Club. Recipient Superior Achievement award, US Postal Svc., 1972, Exceptional Svc. award, US Govt., 1994; named to Bklyn. Dodger Hall of Fame, 1984. Mem.: Phi Beta Kappa, Beta Gamma Sigma, U. N.C. Alumni Assn., Am. U. Alumni Assn., Soc. Am. Baseball Rsch. (v.p. 1989—91), Am. Soc. Tng. & Devel., Assn. MBA Execs., Am. Statis Assn., Am. Mktg. Assn., Internat. Mgmt. Coun. (chpt. exec. v.p. 1978—79, chpt. pres. 1979—81, sec. eastern region 1983—84, vice-chairperson nat. capital area 1981—82), Internat. Personnel Mgmt. Assn. (Chairperson's award 1980, Profl. Writers award 1986), Am. Soc. Public Adminstrn. (life; exec. coun.). Democrat. Jewish. Died June 13, 2009.

GABRIELSON, IRA WILSON, physician, educator; b. NYC, Nov. 27, 1922; s. Benjamin and Lily (Baran) G.; m. Mary Putnam Oliver, Sept. 4, 1948; children: Deborah Anne, David Dwight, Hugh Wilson, Carl Oliver. BA, Columbia U., 1944, MD, 1949; MPH, Johns Hopkins U., 1959. Diplomate: Am. Bd. Pediatrics, Nat. Bd. Med. Examiners. Adminstrv. asst., asst. dir. Johns Hopkins Hosp., 1953-57; dir. community program retarded children New Haven, 1959-61; asst. attending pediatrician Yale-New Haven Community Hosp., 1959-68; asst. prof. public health Yale, 1961-68, exec. officer dept. epidemiology and public health, 1962-67; clin. prof. U. Calif., Berkeley, 1968-71; prof., chmn. dept. community and preventive medicine Med. Coll. Pa., 1971-89, prof. pediatrics, 1987-90, prof. emeritus, from 1990. Adj. prof., exec. dir. physician asst. program Springfield (Mass.) Coll., 1994-97; cons. in field. Editor Medicine Looks at the Humanities, 1987. With AUS. Fellow Nat. Found., 1958 Fellow Am. Acad. Pediatrics, Am. Public Health Assn., Coll. Physicians Phila. (pub. health com. 1976-90); mem. Phila. Pediatric Soc. (chmn. sch. health com. 1983-90), Sigma Xi, Delta Omega. Clubs: Appalachian Mountain (Boston). Avocations: photography, hiking. Died Jan. 18, 2010.

GABY, DANIEL M., advertising executive; b. Scranton, Pa., Nov. 22, 1933; s. Simon and Frieda (Golnick) Gaby; m. Corrine Moore, Feb. 19, 1983; 1 child, Corrine Faith; children: Lisa, Suzanne, Keith, Vanessa. BS, Rutgers U., 1956. Pres. Keyes Martin & Co., Springfield, NJ, from 1957. Dir. SFM Corp., Plainfield, NJ, Compu-Health, Edison, Keyes Martin & Co., Springfield. Author: A Marriage of Convenience, 1960, Election Campaign Handbook, 1976, Non-Profit Organization Handbook, 1980. Chmn. New Dem. Coalition N.J., Trenton, 1969, Dem. Policy Coun., 1970—72, N.J. Citizens for Gov. Byrne, Union, 1973. With US Army, 1957—62. Mem.: N.J. Coun. Advt. (bd. dir. from 1983), Greater Newark C. of C. (bd. dir. from 1981), N.J. Soc. Prevent Blindness (bd. dir. from 1980), Rutgers Found. (bd. dir. from 1982), Regional Planning Assn. (bd. dir. from 1982). Jewish. Home: West Orange, NJ. Died Dec. 10, 2009.

GAFFNEY, THOMAS, retired banker; b. San Francisco, Sept. 22, 1915; s. John and Hannah (Doherty) G.; m. Claire Bastian, Dec. 15, 1945. Cert., Am. Inst. Banking, 1940. Bank insp. Bank of Am., 1935-50; asst. cashier First Nat. Trust and Savs. Assn., Santa Barbara, Calif., 1950-51; asst. cashier, asst sec. Oakland Central Bank, Calif., 1951-53; chief insp. Transamerica Corp., San Francisco, 1953-55; v.p., auditor First Western Bank, San Francisco, 1955-61; v.p. New First Western Bank, Los Angeles, 1961-74; v.p. and auditor Lloyds Bank Calif., Los Angeles, 1974-80; ret., 1980. Pres. Golden Gate chpt. Bank Adminstrn Inst., San Francisco, 1961, nat. bd. dirs., 1965-67, gen. chmn. conv., L.A., 1967, speaker bank convs., nationwide; chmn. crime deterrant com. Calif. Bankers Assn., 1977-79; banking cons., 1980—. Ad hoc com. to study and recommend controls on all city depts. City of LA, 1977—. Mem.: Elks (bd. dir. Locker Room 67 club San Francisco 1960). Home: Dana Point, Calif. Died Apr. 29, 2009.

GAIGE, FREDERICK HUGHES, university administrator; b. Quincy, Mass., Mar. 4, 1937; s. William Clement and Beatrice Emily (Farrell) G.; m. Austra Ozols, June 23, 1962; children— Karina Alexandra, Amity Weller. BA, Oberlin Coll., 1959; MAT., Brown U., 1962; PhD, U. Pa., 1970. Tutor history Wilson Coll., U. Bombay, 1961-63; grad. research historian Inst. Internat. Studies, U. Calif., Berkeley, 1968-69; instr., asst. prof. Davidson Coll., 1969-74; v.p. for profl. devel. Kansas City Regional Council for Higher Edn., Kansas City, Mo., 1974-77; dean Coll. Arts and Scis. Fairleigh Dickinson U., Madison, N.J., 1977-84; campus exec. officer Berks Campus Pa. State U., Reading, from 1984. Fulbright lectr. Nepal, 1983. Author: Search for National Unity in Nepal, 1975. NDEA fellow, 1964-66; Fulbright-Hays fellow, 1966-67 Mem. Nepal Studies Assn. (founding mem.), So. Atlantic States Assn. for African and Asian Studies, Profl. and Organizational Devel. Network in Higher Edn. Home: Reading, Pa. Died Aug. 25, 2009.

GAINER, GLEN BERTRAM, JR., state official; b. Parkersburg, W. Va., July 4, 1927; s. Glen B. and Nettie E. Gainer; m. Sally Jo Padgett, Oct. 31, 1955; children: Beth Lynn Criss, Glen B. III. AB, Marietta Coll., 1959; student, Glenville State Coll., 1947—48, Muskingum Coll., 1948—49; postgrad., W.Va. U., 1961—63. Tchr., coach Pub. Schs., Parkersburg, 1960—69; mayor City of Parkersburg, 1969—71; auditor State of W.Va., Charleston, from 1976. Served with USN, 1945—47. Democrat. Died Sept. 8, 2009.

GAISER, EDWIN DURANT, materials company executive; b. Finleyville, Pa., May 13, 1919; s. Vance D. and Lorena G. (Covert) Gaiser; m. Priscila Marcene Olson, Nov. 1, 1944; 1 child, Jan Elaine. At, Augustana Coll., Sioux Falls, SD, 1946—47. Field engr. Consolidated Coal Co., Pitts., 1940—42; supt. and mgr. Quinn Constrn. Co., Rapid City, SD, 1947—59; pres. and gen. mgr. Hills Materials Co./ Northwestern Engring. Co, 1959—87; dir. Hills Materials Co., 1971—87; chmn. and commr. S.D. State Cement Plant, from 1978. Chmn. C. of C. Indsl. Devel., Rapid City, SD, 1966—68; pres. Fairyland Park Found., 1976—77; bd. dir. Children's Aid, Mitchell, 1969—74. Mem.: S.D. Ready Mix Concrete Assn., S.D. Mining Assn. (dir. 1982—90), S.D. Associated Gen. Contractors (pres. 1974), Rotary (chpt. pres. 1982—83), Arrowhead County Club, Am. Legion, Elks. Home: Rapid City, SD. Died Apr. 16, 2009.

GAITHER, WILLIAM SAMUEL, civil engineering executive, consultant; b. Lafayette, Ind., Dec. 3, 1932; s. William Marcius and Susan Frances (Kirkpatrick) G.; m. Robin Cornwall McGraw, Aug. 1, 1959; 1 dau., Sarah Curwen. Student, Purdue U., 1950—51; BS in Civil Engring, Rose Poly. Inst., 1956; M. Sci. Engring. (Arthur Le Grand Doty fellow), Princeton, 1962, MA (Ford Found. fellow), 1963, PhD (Ford Found. fellow), 1964. Registered profl. engr., Del., Penn. Engr. Dravo Corp. (marine constrn.), Pitts., 1956-60; supt. Myer Corp., Neenah, Wis., 1960-61; supervising engr., pipeline divsn. Bechtel Corp., San Francisco, 1965-67; assoc. prof. coastal engring. dept. U. Fla. at Gainesville, 1964-65; mem. faculty U. Del. at Newark, 1967-84, assoc. prof. civil engring., 1967-70, prof. civil engring., 1970; prof., dean U. Del. at Newark (Coll. Marine Studies), 1970-84, also dir. sea grant coll. program; pres., prof., trustee Drexel U., Phila., 1984-87, Weston Inst., West Chester, Pa., 1988-93; Inner City Consortium, Inc., 1993-94; owner Gaither & Assocs., Tucson, from 1993. Trustee Mut. Assurance Co., 1985-96; mem. marine bd. NRC, 1975-81; chmn. Gov.'s Oil Transp. Study Com., 1971-73; mem. Gov.'s Task Force Marine and Coastal Affairs, 1970-72, Gov.'s Coun. Sci. and Tech., Del., 1970-72; bd. dirs. Roy F. Weston, Inc., 1974-91, vice chmn., 1988-91; bd. dirs. Phila. Electric Co., 1985-89; mem. ocean affairs adv. com. U.S. Dept. State; mem. Commn. on the Future, Rose-Hulman Inst. Tech., 1991-93; mem. Cyberfab.net. LLC, 1999—. Chmn. adv. coun. dept. civil engring. Princeton U., 1973-84; bd. dirs. University City Sci. Ctr., 1984-93, Penjurdel Coun., 1984-2000, Ednl. Found. of Chester County,

1989-92; pres., dir. Soc. John Gaither Desc., Inc., 1984-87; port warden Phila. Maritime Mus., 1987-93; founding dir., sec. Internat. Consciousness Rsch. Labs., 1996—; vestryman Ch. St. Andrew and St. Monica, 1987-93, chmn. fin. com. 1991-96; bd. dirs., mem. exec. com. Phila. H.S. Acads., Inc., 1988-93; chmn. bd. govs. Environ. Tech. Acad., 1988-93; prin. sponsor Delaware Valley Sci. Fairs, 1990-93. Pvt. U.S. Army, 1953. Recipient Disting. Achievement award Rose Poly. Inst., 1975, Disting. citizenship award News Jour. Papers, Del., 1975, Norman Sollenberger award Princeton U., 1983; named to Lambda Chi Alpha Alumni Hall of Fame, 1996; named hon. citizen of Lewes, Del., 1980. Fellow: ASCE (chmn. offshore policy com. 1979—84); mem.: Nat. Water Rsch. Inst. (rsch.adv. bd. 1991—2002), Acad. Sci. Phila. (bd. dirs. 1989—92), Sea Grant Program Instns. (pres. 1973—74), Del. Acad. Scis. (pres. 1971—72), Ariz. Sr. Acad., Cosmos Club. Died Sept. 11, 2009.

GALE, THOMAS MARTIN, retired dean; b. Green Bay, Wis., May 16, 1926; s. Thomas Griswold and Carrie (Danz) G.; m. Mary Margaret Hardman, May 28, 1960; children—Thomas Hardman, John Martin. BA, U. Calif., Berkeley, 1949, MA, 1950; PhD, U. Pa., 1958. Dean Coll. Arts & Sciences N.Mex. State U., 1971-91, acting provost, 2001, Regents prof. emeritus, 2006—10, bd. dirs. Acad. for Learning in Retirement, 1991—2010. With Border Books Festival, 1996-2000. Chmn. N.Mex. Humanities Coun., NEH, 1972-77; chmn. Las Cruces Am. 2000 Task Force, 1991-98; vice-chmn. N.Mex. Commn. on Higher Edn., 1997-99; pres. bd. dirs. N.Mex. State U. Found., 2001-03., bd. dirs. Las Cruces Pub. Sch. Found., 2002-06; With AUS, 1944-46. Social Sci. Rsch. fellow, 1952-53, 53-54; Huntington Libr. fellow, 1959; Fulbright fellow Peru, 1960; recipient N.Mex. Disting. Svc. award, 2002. Mem. Phi Beta Kappa, Phi Alpha Theta. Clubs: Rotarian. Home: Las Cruces, N.Mex. Died July 1, 2010.

GALLAGHER, DENNIS HUGH, television and film writer, producer, director; b. Chgo., May 2, 1936; s. Frederick Hugh and Mildred Agnes (Buescher) Gallagher. Student, Wright Coll., 1954—56, Ill. Inst. Tech., 1956—57; BSc in Physics, U. Ariz., 1966. Dir. Noble Planetarium and Obs., Ft. Worth Mus. Sci. and History, 1960—64; planetarium dir. Man. Mus. Man and Nature, Winnipeg, Canada, 1966—70; pres. Omnitheatre Ltd., Winnipeg, 1970—72, Gallagher & Assocs., Chgo., 1972—78, Internat. Travel Theatres, Chgo., 1978—81, Galaxy Prodns. Ltd., Chgo., 1981—95, Marine Labs., Chgo., from 1995. Mem. faculty, astronomy, civil engring. U. Man., 1967—68, cons. edn., theater, from 1967. Author: North American Planetariums, 1966, Planetariums of the World, 1969; contbr. articles to profl. jours.; author (producer, dir.): (multi-media road show) The Beginning & End of the World, 1972. Served with USAR, 1959—65. Mem.: Chicagoland Marine Aquarium Soc. (founder, pres. from 1995), Marine Aquarium Socs. N.Am. (v.p. 1995—97, pres. 1997—98), Chgo. Film Coun., Assn. Multi-Image, Internat. TV Assn., Am. Soc. Tng. and Devel., Nat. Acad. TV Arts and Scis., Am. Astron. Soc., Internat. Coun. Planetarium Execs., Planetarium Assn. Can. (founding pres. 1968—69). Home: Saint Paul, Minn. Died June 5, 2009.

GALLAGHER, JOSEPH FRANCIS, marketing executive; b. NYC, May 15, 1926; s. Joseph O'Neil and Nora (Shea) G.; m. Anne Decker, June 17, 1950; children: June, Virginia, Aline. Student, U. Va., 1947-50. Advanced to pres., dir. Erwin Wasey, Inc., Los Angeles, 1968-80; pres. JFG, Inc., Oildale, Calif., from 1981. Served with USNR, 1944-46. Mem. Phi Gamma Delta, Delta Sigma Rho. Home: Santa Monica, Calif. Died Aug. 31, 2009.

GALLAGHER, RICHARD ALLEN, construction executive, consultant, surveyor; b. NYC, Aug. 4, 1929; s. Joseph Edward and Mary Agnes (Bedard) Gallagher; m. Margaret Elizabeth Reeves; children: Frank Robert, Bruce Stephen. At, Fairleigh Dickenson U. Registered land surveyor, N.Y., N.J., Ga., Fla. Chief surveyor Adler & Assoc., Tappan, NY, 1966—68; surveyor Azolina Engring., Paramus, NJ, 1968—70; surveying supr. Bent Tree Co., Jasper, Ga., 1970—72; resident engr. Balswin & Cranston, Augusta, 1972—77; dir. Big Canoe Co., 1977—78, v.p., from 1978. Cons. archtl. control, Big Canoe, Ga., from 1974. Advisor Pickens Area Vocat. Tech. Sch., Jasper, Ga., 1972, North Ga. Area Planning and Devel. Commn., Dalton, 1974; bd. sec. The Chapel Christian Acad., Jasper, 1983; bd. dir. Property Owners Assn., Big Canoe, Condominium Assn. With USN, 1951—55, Korea. Mem.: DAV. Republican. Mem. Assembly Of God Ch. Home: Jasper, Ga. Died Mar. 14, 2009.

GALLAGHER, WILLIAM, administrative executive; b. Brownsville, Pa., Feb. 27, 1932; s. Edward W. and DeLellis S. (Shannon) G.; m. Nancy Cottom, Oct. 12, 1963; children: T. Scott, Nancy Ann. BS, Duquesne U., 1953. Ptnr. Am. Personnel Co., LA, 1957-59; mgr. profl. recruiting Raytheon Co., Waltham, Mass., 1959-65; asst. dir. OEO Exec. Office Pres., Washington, 1965-66; employment mgr. Imperial Chem. Industry U.S., Inc., Wilmington, Del., 1966-74, gen. mgr. adminstrv. svcs., from 1974. Bd. dir. F.T. Andrews, Inc., Georgetown Investment Trust Inc., Doman Helicopters Inc. Bd. dirs. Southeastern Pa. Heart Assn., 1973—, chmn., 1976-88. With U.S. Army, 1953-56. Recipient Outstanding Vol. award Southeastern Pa. Heart Assn., 1974. Mem. Employment Mgmt. Assn. (founder pres. 1972, dir., sr. adviser), Adminstrv. Mgmt. Assn., Nat. Assn. Fleet Adminstr., Nat. Passenger Travel Assn., Concord Country Club, Radley Run Country Club, Elks. Died Aug. 27, 2010.

GALSTON, CLARENCE ELKUS, lawyer; b. Cedarhurst, NY, June 5, 1909; s. Clarence G. and Estelle (Elkus) G.; m. Constance Matthiessen, May 18, 1937 (div. 1952); children: Virginia (Mrs. John J. Walsh, Jr.), John Wood, Linda Jane (Mrs. Richard J. Fates); m. Nina Moore Shields, Feb. 17, 1955; 1 stepson, William Shields III. AB magna cum laude, Harvard, 1930; LL.B., 1933. Bar: N.Y. bar 1933. Asso., then mem. firm Spence, Hotchkiss, Parker & Duryee, NYC, 1933-42, 45- 47. Pres., CEO Motor Haulage Co., N.Y.C., 1947-55; v.p. U.S. Trucking Corp., N.Y.C., 1955-59; trustee Welfare and Pension Funds of N.Y.C. Trucking Industry, Local 807, 1948-68; v.p., gen. counsel, sec. then exec. v.p. Tchrs. Ins. and Annuity Assn. Am., also Coll. Retirement Equities Fund, N.Y.C., 1960-73; bd. dirs. Am. Centurian Life Assurance Co., First Fortis Life Ins. Co.; exec. v.p. Assn. N.Y. State Life Ins. Cos., N.Y.C., 1974-77. Served from 1st lt. to col. USAAF, 1942-45; col. USAFR (ret.). Decorated Legion of Merit. Fellow Am. Bar Found.; mem. Am. Bar Assn., Bar Assn. City N.Y. (treas. 1978-82), Assn. Life Ins. Counsel. Clubs: Ausable (pres. 1986-88), Cold Spring Harbor Beach (pres. 1962-64); Winter (Huntington, N.Y.); Harvard (N.Y.C.); Piping Rock; Dedham Country and Polo; U.S. Srs. Golf Assn. Republican. Home: Ipswich, Mass. Died Oct. 27, 2009.

GANGEL, KENNETH OTTO, seminary professor; b. Paterson, NJ, June 14, 1935; s. Otto John and Rose Marie (Schneider) G.; m. Elizabeth Blackburn, Sept. 1, 1956; children: Jeffrey Scott, Julie Lynn. BA in Bus. Adminstrn, Taylor U., 1957; M.Div. cum laude, Grace Theol. Sem., 1960; MA in Christian Edn, Fuller Summer Sem., 1960; S.T.M., Concordia Sem., 1963; PhD in Coll. Adminstrn, U. Mo.-Kansas City, 1969; postgrad. in coll. finance, Fla. State U., 1973. Ordained to ministry Christian and Missionary Alliance; mem. faculty Calvary Bible Coll., Kansas City, Mo., 1960-70, dir. Christian service, 1960-63, registrar, 1963-66, acad. dean, 1966-69, acad. v.p., 1969-70; adminstrv. asst. for acad. affairs Kansas City (Mo.) Regional Council for Higher Edn., 1968-69; prof., dir. Sch. Christian Edn., Trinity Evang. Div. Sch., Deerfield, Ill., 1970-74; pres. Miami (Fla.) Christian Coll., 1974-82; prof., chmn. dept. Christian edn. Dallas Theol. Sem., from 1982, v.p. for acad. affairs, acad. dean, sr. prof. Christian edn., from 1992. Speaker, lectr. to numerous chs., schs., seminars throughout U.S. and fgn. countries, 1960— Author: Understanding Teaching, 1968; biography of Walter L. Wilson Beloved Physician, 1970; Leadership for Church Education, 1970, The Family First, 1972, So You Want To Be A Leader!, 1973, Between Christian Parent and Child, 1974, Competent To Lead, 1974, 24 Ways to Improve Your Teaching, 1974, You and Your Spiritual Gifts, 1975, Thus Spake Qoheleth, 1983, Unwrap Your Spiritual Gifts, 1983, Toward a Harmony of Faith and Learning, 1983, Christian Education: Its History and Philosophy, 1983, Christian Education Handbook, 1985, Building a Christian Family, 1987, Personal Growth Bible Studies: Acts, 1987, Personal Growth Bible Studies: I and II Timothy, 1987, Matthew, 1988, The Christian Educator's Handbook on Teaching, 1988, Feeding and Leading, 1989, (Accent on Truth Bible Study Series) Learning to Be the Church, Gorwing in Grace and Godliness, 1992, Rejoicing in Faith and Freedom, 1993, Communication and Conflict Management in Churches and Christian Organizaitons, 1993, The Christian Educator's Handbook on Adult Education, 1993, Volunteers for Today's Church, 1993; Contbg. editor: Jour. Psychology and Theology, Theology Annual; research editor: Christian Edn. Today; contbr. numerous articles to ch. publs. Bd. dirs. LeTourneau Found., Scripture Press Ministries, Evang. Tchr. Tng. Assn. Named Distinguished Alumnus of Year Grace Theol. Sem., 1973, Alumni Achievement award U. Mo. at Kansas City, 1975; Chamber of Achievement award Taylor U., 1976; Am. Assn. Theol. Schs. postdoctoral research grantee, 1972-73 Mem. NEA, Am. Assn. Higher Edn., Nat. Christian Sch. Edn. Assn., Nat. Assn. Evangelicals, Nat. Assn. Profs. Christian Edn. (past pres., 1st v.p., bd. dirs.). Died June 18, 2009.

GANS, CARL, zoologist, educator; b. Hamburg, Germany, Sept. 7, 1923; came to U.S., 1939, naturalized, 1945; s. Samuel S. and Else Hubertine (Leeser) G.; m. Kyoko Andow, Nov. 18, 1961 (dec. Dec. 1999). BME, NYU, 1944; MS, Columbia U., 1950; PhD in Biology, Harvard U., 1957; PhD (hon.), U. Antwerpen, Belgium, 1985. Contract and svc. engr. Babcock & Wilcox Co., 1947-55; from asst. prof. to prof. biology, chmn. dept. biology SUNY, Buffalo, 1958-71; prof. zoology U. Mich., Ann Arbor, 1971-98, chmn. dept., 1971-75, prof. emeritus MI, from 1998. Adj. prof. zoology U. Tex., Austin; rsch. assoc. Carnegie Mus., 1953—, Am. Mus. Natural History, 1958—; prof. lab. comparative anatomy Nat. Mus. Natural History, Paris, 1985, assoc., 1989—; guest prof. biology U. Antwerpen, 1985-86; sec., bd. dirs. Zool. Soc. Buffalo, 1961-71; mem. adv. coun. Detroit Zool. Pk., 1973-90; cons. in field; vis. prof. univs. and colls.; rsch. assoc. Mus. Zool. Kans., 1982—. Author: Biomechanics, 1974, Reptiles of the World, 1975; co-author: Photographic Atlas of Shark Anatomy, 1964, Electromyography for Experimentalists, 1986; gen. editor Biology of the Reptilia, 19 vols., 1969-91; editor Jour. Morphology, 1968-95. Internat. adv. coun. Nat. Collections Natural History Hebrew U., Jerusalem, 1997—. Served with AUS, 1944-47. Guggenheim fellow, 1953, 77; NSF predoctoral fellow, 1956-57; postdoctoral fellow U. Fla., Gainesville, 1957-58; grantee NSF, NIH; recipient Gold medal Royal Zool. Soc., Antwerpen, 1985 Fellow N.Y. Zool. Soc., Zool. Soc. London, AAAS, Animal Behavior Soc., Zool. Soc. India, Acad. Zoology India; mem. Am. Soc. Zoologists (pres. 1977), ASME, Soc. Study Evolution (v.p. 1971), Am. Soc. Ichthyology and Herpetology (gov. 1961, 70, 76, pres. 1979), Am. Inst. Biol. Scis. (gov. bd. 1975-78), Soc. Study Amphibians and Reptiles (pres. 1983), Am. Assn. Anatomists, Soc. Exptl. Biology, Am. Physiol. Soc., Senckenberg. Naturforsch. Gesellschaft (corr.). Achievements include 1 U.S. patent and 1 German patent. Home: Teaneck, NJ. Died Nov. 30, 2009.

GANS, MANFRED, chemical engineer; b. Borken, Germany, Apr. 27, 1922; came to U.S., 1950; s. Moritz and Else (Fraenkel) G.; m. Anita Lamm, July 17, 1948 (dec. Jan. 1991); children: Aviva Ruth, Daniel Jon. BSc with honors, U. Manchester, Eng., 1950; SM in Chem. Engring., MIT, 1951. Process engr. Sci. Design Co., NYC, 1951-55, mgr. pilot plant, 1955-57, chief operator, then asst. v.p. ops., 1957-70, v.p. process, project operation, 1970-79, sr. v.p. tech., 1971-85; pres. Tech. Evaluation and Devel. Assn., Inc., Hoboken, NJ, 1985—2010. Cons. devel. program UN, N.Y. and Vienna, Austria; lectr. in field. Co-author: Chemical Plant, 1966. Pres. B'nai Brith, Leonia, N.J., 1970, Cong. Sons of Israel, Leonia, 1985-87; nat. bd. dirs. O.R.T. Jewish vocat. ednl. orgn., N.Y.C.; Capt. Brit. Commandos, 1940-46. Decorated Orange Cross, Dutch Govt., 1946. Fellow AICE (award in chem. engring. practice 1993). Avocations: tennis, running, skiing, swimming in the ocean, classical music. Home: Fort Lee, NJ. Died Sept. 19, 2010.

GARABEDIAN, PAUL ROESEL, mathematics professor; b. Cin., Aug. 2, 1927; s. Carl A. and Margaret (Roesel) G.; m. Gladys Rappaport, Oct. 22, 1949 (div. 1963); m. Lynnel Marg, Dec. 31, 1966; children: Emily, Catherine. AB, Brown U., 1946; A.M., Harvard U., 1947, PhD, 1948. Asst. prof. math. U. Calif.-Berkeley, 1949-50; asst. prof. Stanford U., Calif., 1950-52, assoc. prof., 1952-56, prof. math., 1956-59, Courant Inst. Math. Sciences, NYU, 1959—2010, dir. divsn. computational fluid dynamics, 1978—2010; dir. Courant Math. & Computing Lab., 1972—78. Mem. editl. bd. Internat. Jour. Computational Fluid Dynamics, Applicable Analysis, Internat. Jour. Computational and Applied Math.; contbr. articles to profl. jours. NRC fellow, 1948-49, Sloan Found. fellow, 1961-63, Guggenheim fellow, 1966, 81-82, Fairchild Disting. scholar Calif. Inst. Tech., 1975; recipient Pub. Service Group Achievement award NASA, 1976, Boris Pregal award N.Y. Acad. Scis., 1980. Fellow Am. Phys. Soc.; mem. NAS (Applied Math. and Numerical Analysis prize 1998), Am. Acad. Arts and Scis., Am. Math. Soc. (Birkhoff prize 1983), Soc. Indsl. and Applied Math. (von Karman prize 1989). Died May 13, 2010.

GARANT, CAROL ANN, management consultant; b. Fall River, Mass., Dec. 17, 1945; d. Joseph and Stella (Dobek) G. BSN, U. Pa., 1969; MSN, Yale U., 1973; MBA, Boston Coll., 1983. Instr. Mass. Gen. Hosp., Boston, 1969-70; staff nurse Hosp. St. Raphael, New Haven, Conn., 1971-72; nstr. VA Hosp., Boston, Conn., 1973-74; cons. New Eng. Deaconess Hosp., Boston, Conn., 1974-84, Hillary O'Shea Assocs., NYC and Boston, Conn., from 1985. Adj. lectr. grad. mgmt. program The Newport Coll.; strategic planner and lobbyist, founding mem. Nurses United for Reimbursement of Services, Boston, 1975-79; adj. instr. mktg. Grad. Div. Salve Regina Coll., Newport, R.I., 1987—. Author, producer, dir. audio-visual presentation; contbr. articles to profl. jours. NIMH traineeship, 1970-73, Insts. of Health traineeship, 1967-69. Mem. Am. Mktg. Assn. (research com. writer 1983—), Fall River Ctr. City Bus. Assn. (exec. dir.), Am. Psychomatic Soc., Assn. Yale Alumni (univ. investments com., club membership com.), Sigma Theta Tau. Clubs: Penn (bd. dirs. 1974-78), Yale Bd. (dir. 1979-80) (Boston). Democrat. Roman Catholic. Avocations: squash, sailing, historic preservation, music. Died Jan. 25, 2009.

GARBER, CHARNA JANICE, wholesale shoe company executive; b. Lynn, Mass., Apr. 21, 1937; d. Saul William and Lena (Kline) Chalek; m. William Garber, Oct. 11, 1956; children— Holly Jeske, Ellise Garber. Student, U. N.H., 1960, 61, 62, Am. Inst. Banking, Lynn, Mass., 1954, 55. Mgr. customer services The Rochester Banks (N.H.), 1964-66; bus. mgr. computer dept. MIT, 1973-78; line builder, fashion coordinator Cole-Haan Footwear, 1978-80; sales rep. Internor Trade, N.Y.C., 1980-82; pres. C. G. Assocs. Inc., N.Y.C., 1982—; sec.-treas., owner N.E. Fashion Shoe Show, N.Y.C., 1976—; pres. d'Rossana Shoes. Bd. dirs. Dollars for Scholars, Mass., N.H., 1960-66. Mem. 210 Assn., Boot and Shoe Travelers Assn., Nat. Shoe Travelers Assn., Footwear and Accessories Council, NOW. Democrat. Jewish. Club: Hadassah. Home: New York, NY. Died Apr. 25, 2010.

GARDNER, BURDETT HARMON, English language educator; b. Ashland, Maine, Aug. 14, 1917; s. Wesley Isaiah and Addie Vince (Nevers) G.; m. Rachel Margaret Cohen, Jan. 8, 1964 (dec. Apr. 3, 2010); children: Benjamin, Daniel. Student, Colby Coll., 1935-36, La. State U., 1937-39; BA, Boston U., 1940; MA, Harvard, 1946, PhD (Univ. fellow), 1954. Instr. English U. Minn., 1947-48, U. Idaho, 1949-50, Fla. State U., 1950, Ga. Inst. Tech., 1950-52; asst. prof. English Heidelberg U., 1954-55, Elmira Coll., 1956-60; asso. prof. English Bloomsburg State Coll., 1961-62; asso. prof. English, chmn. dept. Park Coll., Parkville, Mo., 1962-63; prof. English, chmn. dept. Ky.-Wesleyan Coll., Owensboro, 1963-64; prof. English Monmouth Coll., West Long Branch, N.J., from 1964, chmn. dept., 1965-71. Lectr. English Harvard, 1955-56 Author: The Lesbian Imagination (Victorian Style): A Psychological and Critical Study of "Vernon Lee", 1987. Served with Signal Intelligence AUS, 1942-46. Mem. MLA, The English Inst. Home: West Long Branch, NJ. Died Apr. 3, 2010.

GARDNER, HOWARD ALAN, travel company executive, writer, editor; b. Rockford, Ill., June 24, 1920; s. Ellis Ralph and Leanor (Roseman) Gardner; m. Marjorie Ruth Klein, Sept. 29, 1945; children: Jill, Jeffrey. BA, U. Mich., 1941. With advt. dept. Chgo. Tribune, 1941-43; mgr. promotion dept. Esquire mag., 1943-46; advt. mgr. Mrs. Klein's Food Products Co., 1946-48; pres. Sales-Aide Svc. Co., 1948-56, Gardner & Stein, 1956-59, Gardner, Stein & Frank, Inc., Chgo., 1959-83, Fun-derful World, Chgo., from 1983. Mem.: Nat. Geog. Soc., Am. Geog. Soc., Confrerie de la Chaine des Rotisseurs (Bailli Honoraire, grand comdr., Pres.'s medal of honor), Travel Industry Assn. Am., Mid-Am. Club, Internat. Club, Travelers' Century Club, Phi Beta Kappa. Died Aug. 5, 2009.

GARDNER, MARTIN, writer; b. Tulsa, Okla., Oct. 21, 1914; s. James Henry and Willie (Spiers) G.; m. Charlotte Greenwald, Oct. 17, 1952 (dec. 2000); children: James Emmett, Thomas Owen. BA, U. Chgo., 1936; PhD (hon.), Bucknell U., 1978, Furman Univ., 1994. Freelance writer. Author 70 books including Mathematics, Magic, and Mystery, Aha Insight, Aha Gotcha, Perplexing Puzzles and Tantalizing Teasers, Space Puzzles, Codes, Ciphers and Secret Writing, The Annotated Snark, The Snark Puzzle Book, Fads and Fallacies, Logic Machines and Diagrams, Annotated Alice, More Annotated Alice, The Whys of a Philosophical Scrivener, Gardner's Whys and Wherefores, The New Age, Order and Surprise, The No-Sided Professor, The Annotated Casey at the Bat, The Annotated Night Before Christmas, On the Wild Side, The New Ambidextrous Universe, The Relativity Explosion, The Sacred Beetle, Science: Good, Bad and Bogus, The Night Is Large, Weird Water and Fuzzy Logic, Visitors From Oz, The Flight of Peter Fromm, Sixteen Collections of Scientific American Columns on Mathematics. With USN, 1942-46. Recipient Profl. Achievement award U. Chgo., 1971, Annual award Acad. of Magic Arts, Calif., 1975, Annual U.S. Steel Found. prize for sci. writing Am. Inst. Physics, 1983, Steele prize for math. writing, AMS, 1987, David Hilbert Annual Internat. award for math writing, 1992, Communication award Jt. Policy Bd for math., 1994, Forum award Am. Phys. Soc., 1997. Fellow Am. Acad. Arts and Scis.; mem. Am. Math. Soc., Math. Assn. Am. (hon. life), Com. for Sci. Investigation of Paranormal, Lewis Carroll Soc., Internat. Wizard of Oz Club. Died May 22, 2010.

GARDNER, RUSSELL MENESE, lawyer; b. High Point, NC, July 14, 1920; s. Joseph Hayes and Clara Emma-Lee (Flynn) G.; m. Joyce Thresher, Mar. 7, 1946; children: Winthrop G., Page Stansbury, June Thresher. AB, Duke U., 1942, JD, 1948. Bar: Fla. 1948, U.S. Ct. Appeals (5th cir.) 1949, U.S. Tax Ct. 1949, U.S. Supreme Ct. 1985. Ptnr. McCune, Hiaasen, Crum, Gardner & Duke and predecessor firms, Ft. Lauderdale, Fla., 1948-90, Gunster, Yoakley, & Stewart, from 1990. Bd. govs. Shepard Broad Law Ctr. Nova S.E. U. Trustee Mus. of Art, Inc., Ft. Lauderdale, pres., 1964-67; bd. dirs. Stranahan House, Inc., 1981—, pres., 1983-85; bd. dirs. Ft. Lauderdale Hist. Soc., 1962—, pres. 1975-85, pres. emeritus, 1985—; mem. estate planning council Duke U. Sch. Law; bd. dirs., vice chmn. Broward Performing Arts Found., Inc., 1985—. Served to lt. USNR, 1943-49. Fellow Am. Coll. Trust and Estate Counsel; mem. ABA (real property, probate, trust sect.), Am. Judicature Soc., Fla. Bar Assn. (probate, guardianship rules com. 1978-2002, probate law com.), Broward County Bar Assn. (estate planning council), Coral Ridge Country Club, Lauderdale Yacht Club, Tower Club. Republican. Presbyterian. Died Mar. 27, 2009.

GARDNER, THOMAS F., lawyer; b. NYC, May 19, 1945; BS, Ill. Wesleyan U., 1966; JD, U. Ill., 1969. Bar: Ill. 1969. Mem. Jones, Day, Reavis & Pogue, Chgo. Mem. Order of Coif. Died May 16, 2009.

GARDNER, VERNON EVERETT, consultant engineer; b. Alkabo, ND, Dec. 7, 1913; s. Timothy William and Julia Olgina (Hillestad) Gardner; m. Elizabeth Ann Hunt, Mar. 25, 1950. Student, ND Sch. Forestry, 1934—35; BS in Elec. Engring., U. ND, 1938; postgrad., U. Pitts., 1940. Elec. engr. Continental Motors Corp., Muskegon, Mich., 1938—39; instr. elec. engring. U. ND, 1939; elec. engr. Westinghouse Electric Corp., East Pitts., 1940; elec. electrochem. and reliability engr. Dept. Navy, Wash., 1941—74; reliability engr. Tensor Industries, Inc., Arlington, 1975—78, Columbia Research Corp., Arlington, 1978—79. Mem. joint bd. on sci. and engring. edn. contact mem. St. James Sch., Falls Ch., 1970—93, St. Anthony's Sch., Falls Ch., 1983—89. Recipient Superior Performance award, Dept. Navy, 1963, Golden Svc. award, ND Sch. Forestry, 1986. Mem.: IEEE, AAAS, Phi Theta Kappa, Tau Beta Pi, Sigma Xi, DC Coun. Engring. and Archtl. Socs., Assn. Scientists and Engrs. Dept. Navy, Electrochem. Soc., Washington Figure Skating, Arts of Washington, Elks. Unitarian. Died Jan. 6, 2010.

GARMEZY, NORMAN, psychology educator; b. NYC, June 18, 1918; s. Isadore and Laura (Weiss) G.; m. Edith Linick, Aug. 8, 1945; children: Kathy, Andrew, Lawrence. BBA, CCNY, 1939; MA, Columbia U., 1940; PhD in Clin. Psychology, State U. Iowa, 1950. From asst. prof. to prof. psychology Duke U., Durham, N.C., 1950-60; prof. U. Minn., Mpls., 1961-88, prof. emeritus psychology, from 1989; clin. prof. psychiatry dept. U. Rochester (N.Y.) Sch. Medicine, 1969-79. Vis. prof. U. Copenhagen, 1965-66, Cornell U., 1969-70; vis. colleague Inst. Psychiatry, Maudsley Hosp., London, 1975-76; vis. prof. psychiatry Stanford U. Med. Sch., 1979-80; mem. com. on schizophrenia rsch. Scottish Rite, Boston, 1968-82; cons. NIMH, also past mem. grants com.; mem. task force on rsch. Presdl. Commn. on Mental Health, 1977-78; bd. dirs. Founds. Fund for Rsch. in Psychiatry, 1976-82; mem. overall sci. adv. com. to health program McArthur Found., chmn. rsch. network on risk and protective factors in major mental disorders, 1983-88, network on successful aging, network on successful adolescence. Author: (with G. Kimble and E. Zigler) Principles of General Psychology, 2nd to 6th edit., 1984, (with R.J. Haggerty, Lonnie Sherrod and Michael Rutter) Stress, Risk and Resilience in Children and Adolescents, 1994; editor: (with Rutter) Stress, Coping and Development in Children, 1983; mem. internat. adv. editorial bd. Schizophrenia Bull., 1974—, Psychol. Medicine, 1976-92; corr. editor Jour. Child Psychology and Psychiatry, 1975-85, editorial bd., 1986-92; adv. editor McGraw-Hill Book Co., 1969-85, Ann. Rev. Psychology, 1982-86. Served with U.S. Army, 1943-45. Recipient Gold medal Am. Psychol. Found., 1989, Lifetime Rsch. Career award NIMH, 1962-88, Disting. Grad. award in Psychology, U. Iowa, 1986, Lifetime Contbns. award Soc. for Rsch. in Psychopathology, 1987, Pres.'s medal Baruch Sch. CUNY, 1988; co-recipient Stanley Dean award for basic rsch. in schizophrenia, 1967; fellow Ctr. for Advanced Studies in Behavioral Scis., Palo Alto, Calif., 1979-80. Fellow AAAS, APA (pres. divsn. clin. psychology 1977-78, Disting. Contbns. award 1988, G. Stanley Hall award 1992), Am. Acad. Arts and Scis., Am. Psychopath. Assn., Am. Orthopsychiat. Assn. (Ittelson Rsch. award 1986); mem. AAUP, Psychonomic Soc., Soc. Rsch. in Child Devel. (Disting. Sci. Contbn. award 1995), Assn. Advancement Psychology (chmn. bd. trustees 1977-78), Inst. Medicine, Cosmos Club (Washington). Home: Nashville, Tenn. Died Nov. 21, 2009.

GARMISE, DAVID BRUCE, otolaryngologist, educator; b. NYC, Mar. 1, 1935; AB in History, U. N.C., 1956, MD, 1960. Intern Beth Israel Hosp., NYC, 1960-61; resident gen. surgery Bronx VA Hosp., 1961-62, resident ear, nose and throat, 1962-65; pvt. practice Ruhway, N.J., 1967-92; chief Ear Nose and Throat dept. The Rahway Hosp., 1969-92; med. dir. Hospice for the Low County, Hilton Head Island, SC, 1993—2001; ret. Assoc. clin. prof. NJCMD-Rutgers, 1972-92. Capt. U.S. Army, 1965-67. Fellow Am. Acad. Otolaryngology-Head and Neck Surgery. Died Jan. 21, 2009.

GARNER, MARY JANE, cosmetics company executive; b. Terre Haute, Ind., Oct. 6, 1916; d. Thomas Law and Myra (Short) Kemp; m. William Stanley Garner, Jan. 11, 1941 (div. Nov. 1965); 1 child, William Stanley. Student, Lindenwood Coll. Women, 1935, John Heron Art Sch., 1936—38, Ind. U., 1967; Grad., Parsons Sch. Design, 1940, UNC, 1972. Model made-to-order dept. Bergdorft Goodman, NYC, 1940—41; asst. buyer Crystal Rm., Indpls., 1965—66; proof cons. fact St. Louis, 1968—69; pres. & founder Mary Jane Garner Cosmetics, Mary Jane Garner Cosmetics, NC, from 1985. Sec. Chapel Hill Hist. Soc., 1973—74, bd. dirs., 1973—75; mem. NC Bicentennial Com., 1974—78, Chapel Hill Bicentenial Commn., 1974—76; co-chmn. Holshouser Gov., Orange County, NC, 1972; rep. precinct chmn. Chapel Hill, 1972; rep. precinct registrar, 1973—75; pres. Rep. Women's Club, Chapel Hill, 1973—74; chmn. state conv. NC Fedn. Rep. Women, 1974, bicentennial chmn., 1974—76, legis. chmn., 1976—77, area v.p., 1978—80, pub. rels. chmn., 1981—83, mem. credentials com. nat. conv., 1980; mem. US Senate Minority Leader's Citizens Adv. Com., 1974—76; mem. nat. adv. bd. Am. Security Coun., 1978—79; mem. bldg. com. NC Rep. Hdqrs., 1978; mem. Nat. Presdl. Adv. Commn., from 1989. Recipient Cert. of Appreciation, Am. Revolution Bicentenial, 1976, Spl. Recognition award, Am. Security Coun., 1979, Achievement award, Pres. Reagan, 1982; named Most Improved Golfer, Golf Digest Mag., 1978. Mem.: Chapel Hill Country Club (bd. govs. 1975—76). Home: Indianapolis, Ind. Died Mar. 24, 2009.

GARRETT, HOWARD LEON, lawyer; b. Tampa, Fla., July 7, 1929; s. Herbert and Frances (Adams) Garrett; m. Marie Leonora Garcia Garrett, Dec. 10, 1950; children: Gloria Susan, Howardene Gay, Leslie Marie. AA, U. Fla., 1947, LLB, 1949, JD, 1967. Bar: Fla. 1949, US Dist. Ct. (so. dist.) Fla. 1950, US Ct. Appeals (5th cir.) 1950, US Supreme Ct. 1983; cert. cir. civil mediator. Ptnr. Sells & Garrett, 1949—53, Garrett & Garrett, P.A. Firm, Tampa, Fla., from 1953; assoc. city judge Tampa, 1965; chmn. Code Enforcement Bd., 1980—84. Served with USAR, 1948—52. Mem.: Hills County Bar Assn., Hills County Criminal Def. Lawyers, Lawyer-Pilot Bar Assn., Palma Ceia Golf & Country Club. Democrat. Died Feb. 2, 2009.

GARRISON, JOSEPH MARION, JR., British and American literature educator, consultant; b. Columbia, Mo., July 25, 1934; s. Joseph Marion and Evelyn (Hawkins) Garrison; m. Virginia Bumgardner Garrison, July 18, 1958 (div. 1979); children: Alan Fletcher, Kathryn Paige; m. Ann Dexter Herron Garrison, Aug. 27, 1980 (div. 1988). BA, Davidson Coll., 1956; MA, Duke U., 1957, PhD, 1961. Instr. English Coll. William & Mary, Williamsburg, Va., 1960—62; assoc. prof. English St. Andrews Presbyn. Coll., Laurinburg, NC, 1962—65, Mary Baldwin Coll., Staunton, Va., 1965—70, prof., from 1970, chmn. dept., from 1982; cons. Va. Poets-in-Pre-Schs., from 1975, Va. Secondary Schs., from 1978, Va. Pvt. Schs., from 1978. Project dir. Va. Found. Humanities & Pub. Policy, from 1982. Contbr. articles to profl. jours. Recipient Louise McNeill Peace prize, Morris Harvey Publs., 1972. Mem.: Poets and Writers. Democrat. Presbyterian. Avocations: guitar, woodworking. Home: Staunton, Va. Died May 9, 2010.

GARSTANG, ROY HENRY, astrophysicist, educator; b. Southport, Eng., Sept. 18, 1925; came to U.S., 1964; s. Percy Brocklehurst and Eunice (Gledhill) G.; m. Ann Clemence Hawk, Aug. 11, 1959; children: Jennifer Katherine, Susan Veronica. BA, U. Cambridge, 1946, MA, 1950, PhD, 1954, Sc.D., 1983. Research assoc. U. Chgo., 1951-52; lectr. astronomy U. Coll., London, 1952-60; reader astronomy U. London, 1960-64, asst. dir. Obs., 1959-64; prof. astrophysics U. Colo., Boulder, 1964-94, chair faculty assembly, 1988-89, prof. emeritus, from 1994; chmn. Joint Inst. for Lab. Astrophysics, 1966-67. Cons. Nat. Bur. Standards, 1964—73, Internat. Commn. Illumination, from 1990; v.p. commn. 14 Internat. Astron. Union, 1970—73, pres., 1973—76; Erskine vis. fellow U. Canterbury, New Zealand, 1971; vis. prof. U. Calif., Santa Cruz, 1971. Editor: Observatory, 1953-60; Contbr. numerous articles to tech. jours. Recipient Excellence in Svc. award, U. Colo., 1990. Fellow Am. Phys. Soc., AAAS, Optical Soc. Am., Brit. Inst. Physics, Royal Astron. Soc.; mem. Am. Astron. Soc., Royal Soc. Scis. Liege (Belgium). Achievements include rsch. on atomic physics and astrophys. applications; calculation of atomic transition probabilities, atomic spectra in very high magnetic fields and magnetic white dwarf stars; modelling of light pollution. Home: Boulder, Colo. Died Nov. 1, 2009.

GARVER, ROBERT VERNON, retired research physicist; b. Mpls., June 2, 1932; s. Walter Burdette and Daveda Margaret (Hansen) G.; m. Shirley Marie Phillips, June 15, 1957; children: Debra, Douglas, Daniel, Mary, Jennifer. BS, U. Md., 1956; M.E.A., George Washington U., 1968. Physicist Harry Diamond Labs., Washington, 1956-69, supervisory physicist, 1969-89. Program mgr. Army High Power Microwave Hardening Tech., 1982-89; cons. Weinschel Engring., Gaithersburg, Md., 1970-75; chmn. electromagnetic effects subcom. DoD VHSIC Qualification Com., 1981-89; pvt. cons., 1989-95; sr. engr. Xeta Internat. Corp., Crystal City, Va., 1990-95; cons. Envisioneering, Inc., Dahlgren, Va., 2000-05; developer Leap Flight Tech., The Garver Product Co., 2000-. Author: Microwave Diode Control Devices, 1976; inventor Microwave Diode Switch; patentee in field. Elder Presbyn. Ch., Germantown, Md., 1975. Served with U.S. Army, 1953-54. Fellow: IEEE (editor Jour. Solid State Cirs. 1969—73, mem. nat. adminstrv. com. profl. group microwave theory and techniques); mem.: Toastmasters. Republican. Died Aug. 16, 2010.

GATES, DARYL FRANCIS, retired police chief; b. Aug. 30, 1926; m. Wanda Hawkins (div. 1968); m. Sima Lalich (div. 1994). BS in Pub. Adminstrn., U. So. Calif., also postgrad. in Pub. Adminstrn. With L.A. Police Dept., 1949—52, sergeant, 1955—59, lt., 1959-63, capt., 1963-65, comdr., 1965-68, dep. chief, 1968-69, asst. chief, 1969-78, chief, 1978-92. Author: Chief: My Life in the LAPD, 1992. Bd. councilors U. So. Calif. Inst. Saftey and Systems Mgmt.; bd. dirs. YMCA, Los Angeles; mem. Children's Village Adv. Bd. Served in USN, 1943—45. Mem. Calif. Peace Officers Assn., Internat. police Assn., Calif. Police Chief Assn., Internat. Assn. Chiefs of Police, Women's Peace Officers Assn. Calif., Los Angeles C. of C. Lodges: Rotary. Home: Dana Point, Calif. Died Apr. 16, 2010.

GATES, JOANNE FERRY, counselor; b. NYC, Oct. 7, 1924; d. Joseph Rutherford and Constance (Riker) Ferry; m. Richard Judson Gates, Sept. 7, 1946; children: Pamela, Cynthia, Suzanne, Rebecca. BA, Conn. Coll., 1946; MA in Counseling, St. Josephs Coll., 1981; DHL (hon.), Centenary Coll., 1987. Mem. exec. bd. Jr. Leaghe Hartford, Conn., 1957-64; bd. dirs. Inst. of Living, 1968-69; counselor Counseling Ctr./Hartford Coll. for Women, 1981-92; bd. dirs. Hartford Symphony, 1973-76, aux. v.p. nominating chmn., 1977; with Greater Hartford Campus Ministry, from 1981, West Hartford Pastoral Counseling Ctr., 1985. Sec. Smith Gates Corp., Farmington, Conn. Trustee Children's Mus. Hartford, 1970-73, West Hartford Sch. Music, 1962-83, Hartford Coll. for Women, U. Hartford, 1997—; trustee Centenary Coll. for Women, N.J., 1968-86, trustee emeritus, 1986—, hon. chmn. capital campaign; pres. Jodik Found., 1977—; deacon 1st Ch. of Christ Congregational, 1977-79, tchr. religious edn., 1952-72, pres. women's guild, 1969-70; co-chmn. music and arts festival Trinity Coll., 1975; vol. Hartford Hosp., 1949-55, Meals on Wheels, 1977-80; v.p. women's bd., trustee, corporator Hartford Sem., 1978—; mem. alumnae exec. bd. Capital fund drives Northfield (Mass.) Mt. Herman Sch.; class agt. ann. fund Conn. Coll. Mem. Conn. Coll. Alumnae Assn., Northfield Mt. Herman Sch. Alumnae Assn., Seed and Weed Carden Cub, Stonington Country Club, Musical of Hartford Club, Watch Hill Yacht Club, Town and County Club of Hartford. Republican. Home: Granby, Conn. Died Feb. 25, 2010.

GATHRIGHT, JOHN BYRON, JR., colon and rectal surgeon, educator; b. Oxford, Miss., Sept. 29, 1933; s. J. Byron Sr. and Connie (Love) G.; m. Barbara Cooper, Sept. 19, 1959; children: John Byron III, Lin, John Miles, Peter C. BS, U. Miss., 1955; MD, Northwestern U., 1957. Diplomate Am. Bd. Colon and Rectal Surgery (pres. 1989-90), Am. Bd. Surgery. Intern Charity Hosp., New Orleans, 1957-58, resident in gen. surgery, 1958-62; fellow in colon & rectal surgery Alton Ochsner Med. Found., New Orleans, 1962-63; mem. staff So. Bapt. Hosp., New Orleans, 1963-69, Ochsner Found. Hosp., New Orleans, 1969-97, chmn. colon and rectal surgery dept.; clin. prof. surgery Tulane U., New Orleans, from 1991. Vis. surgeon So. La. Med. Ctr., Houma, 1977-97; trustee, exec. com., bd. dirs. Alton Ochsner Med. Found., 1980-97. Assoc. editor Diseases of the Colon and Rectum, 1977-93, Perspectives in Colon and Rectal Surgery, 1987-97, Colon and Rectal Surgery Outlook, 1987-97; mem. bd. editors Current Concepts in Gastroenterology, 1980-89. Fellow ACS (grad. edn. com. 1981-89, Am. Soc. Colon and Rectal Surgeons (pres. 1989-90), Soc. Coloproctology of Eng. and Ireland (hon.), Internat. Soc. Univ. Colon and Rectal Surgeons (sec. 1990-2002), Mex. Soc. Colon and Rectal Surgeons (hon.). Republican. Presbyterian. Avocations: boating, photography. Home: New Orleans, La. Died Aug. 28, 2010.

GAULDIN, MICHAEL GLEN, former federal agency administrator; b. Mena, Ark., Nov. 13, 1954; s. Harold Glen and Fairy Ella (Fitzgerald) G.; m. Jane Catherine Harrison, Dec. 28, 1974; children: Amanda, Patrick, John, Elizabeth. Grad. mil. journalism, Defense Info. Sch., Ft. Be Harrison, Ind., 1975; BJ, U. Ark., 1981. Mil. journalist 4th Infantry Div., Ft. Carson, Colo., 1975-77; reporter Rogers (Ark.) Daily News, 1979-80; wire editor The Springdale (Ark.) News, 1981-84; polit. cartoonist Syndicated Old Timer Art Works, Ark., 1982-84; reporter Russellville (Ark.) Courier News, 1984; asst. dir. info. U. Ark., Fayetteville, 1984-86; press sec. to Gov. Bill Clinton State of Ark., Little Rock, 1987-92; dir. pub. & consumer affairs US Dept. Energy, Washington, 1993-95; asst. to the Sec., dir. Office of Comm. US Dept. Interior, Washington, 1995—2001, dir. public affairs Office Surface Mining Reclamation & Enforcement, 2001—07, public affairs officer US Geological Survey, 2007—10. With U.S. Army, 1974-77. Recipient Thomas Jefferson award Dept. of Def., 1977, Spot News Reporting award Ark. Assoc. Press Mng. Editors, 1979; names Cartoonist of Yr., Ark. Press Assn., 1983. Democrat. Home: Alexandria, Va. Died July 22, 2010.

GAVIN, JOSEPH GLEASON, JR., management consultant, retired aerospace transportation executive; b. Somerville, Mass., Sept. 18, 1920; s. Joseph Gleason and Elizabeth (Tay) G.; m. Dorothy Dunklee, Sept. 1943; children: Joseph Gleason III, Tay Anne (Mrs. Peter B. Erickson) (dec. 1998), Donald Lewis. BS, MS in Aeros., MIT, 1942. With Grumman Aerospace Corp., Bethpage, N.Y., from 1946, chief missile & space engr., 1957-62, v.p., 1962-70; dir. Grumman Aerospace Corp. (Lunar Module program), 1953-72, sr. v.p., 1970-72, pres., 1972-76, chmn. bd., 1973-76; pres., COO Grumman Corp., Bethpage, 1976-85, chmn. exec. com., 1985, ret., 1985. Bd. dirs. European American Banking Corp., Charles Stark Draper Lab., Inc., Pine St. Fund; mem. energy research adv. bd. Dept. Energy. Mem. corp. vis. com. dept. aeros. and astronautics MIT, mem. exec. com. MIT Corp., 1985-2010, life mem., 1988-2010; former pres. Harborfields Bd. Edn., Central Sch. Dist. 6, Huntington, N.Y., 1960-64; chmn. United Fund, 1978; trustee Huntington Hosp., Poly. Inst. N.Y.; mem. policy adv. com., adv. panel on fusion energy US Dept. Def.; mem. com. on advanced space based high power techs. NRC. Served with USNR, 1942-46. Recipient Leadership award C.W. Post Coll. of L.I. U.; Distinguished Pub. Service medal NASA, 1971 Fellow AIAA (past pres.), American Astronautical Soc.; mem. Aerospace Industries Assn., Nat. Acad. Engring., Internat. Acad. Astronautics. Home: Amherst, Mass. Died Oct. 31, 2010.

GEBBER, GERARD LINCOLN, pharmacology and physiology educator; b. NYC, Feb. 12, 1939; s. Harry and Esther (Chernick) G.; m. Sandra Rosoff, Dec. 29, 1961; children: Audrey Joan, Elliott John. BS, L.I. U., 1960; PhD, U. Mich., 1964. Postdoctoral fellow U. Pa., Phila., 1964-65; instr. Tulane U., New Orleans, 1965-66; asst. prof. Mich. State U., East Lansing, 1966-70, assoc. prof., 1970-75, prof. dept. pharmacology, from 1975, prof. dept. physiology, from 1982. Contbr. articles to profl. jours., chpts. to books. Recipient Merit award NIH, 1988—. Mem. AAAS, IEEE, Engring. in Medicine and Biology Soc., Am. Physiol. Soc., Am. Soc. Pharmacology and Exptl. Therapeutics, Can. Physiol. Soc., Internat. Brain Rsch. Orgn., Soc. Neurosci. Home: East Lansing, Mich. Died Apr. 9, 2009.

GEBHART, BENJAMIN ISAAC, mechanical engineer, educator; b. Cin., July 2, 1923; s. William Isaac and Lillian Margaret (Grosch) G.; children: Raissa Mae, Lorna Doone. BSE, U. Mich., 1948, MSE, 1950; PhD, Cornell U., 1954; BA, U. Pa., 1980. Registered profl. engr., N.Y. Instr. U. Mich., Ann Arbor, 1949-50; from instr. to prof. Cornell U., Ithaca, N.Y., 1951-75; leading prof. SUNY, Buffalo, 1975-80; Samuel Landis Gabel prof. mech. engring. U. Pa., Phila., from 1980. Vis. prof. Oreg. State U., Corvallis, 1973-74, Ecole Des Mines, Nancy, France, 1988, U. Calif., Berkeley, 1966-67; prof. naval sea systems command Naval Postgrad. Sch., Monterey, Calif., 1980-81. Author: Heat Transfer, 1961, 2d revised edit., 1971; Buoyancy Induced Floor and Transport, 1988; Heat Conduction and Mass Diffusion, 1993; contbr. numerous articles to profl. jours. With USMC, 1942-45, PTO. Grantee NSF, 1958—. Fellow ASME (life, Heat Transfer Meml. award 1972, Freeman scholar 1978), Tau Beta Pi, Phi Kappa Phi, Phi Eta Sigma, Sigma Xi; mem. AAAS. Home: Glenmoore, Pa. Died Oct. 18, 2009.

GEEHR, RICHARD STOCKWELL, history educator; b. New Brunswick, NJ, May 6, 1938; s. Richard Lewis and Katherine Frances (Stockwell) G.; m. Gerda Josepha Kalchschmid, Sept. 9, 1961. BA, Middlebury Coll., 1960; MA, Columbia U., 1965; PhD, U. Mass., 1973. Chmn. admissions and fin. aid, group leader Expt. in Internat. Living, Putney, Vt., 1964-67; instr. Windham Coll., Putney, 1966-67, Keene (N.H.) State Coll., 1966-67, Mark Hopkins Coll., Brattleboro, Vt., 1967-68, Greenfield (Mass.) C.C., 1967-68; teaching asst. U. Mass., Amherst, 1967-73; instr. history Lake Michigan Coll., Benton Harbor, Mich., 1973-74; asst. prof. St. Mary's Coll. Md., St. Mary's City, 1975-76; prof. history Bentley Coll., Waltham, Mass., from 1977. Cons. Nat. Ctr. for Jewish Film, Brandeis U., Waltham, 1980—, Facing History and Ourselves, Brookline, Mass., 1982—. Author: The Approach of Cultural Fascism, 1973, Karl Lueger Mayor of Fin de Siècle Vienna, 1990; editor: Soviet History and Film, 1980, The Papers of Dr. Karl Lueger, 1982, Letters from the Doomed, 1992. 1st lt. Q.M.C., U.S. Army, 1960-63. Named Coll. Tchr. of Yr., Bentley Coll., 1984, 94, Advisor of Yr., 1989, Scholar of Yr., 1992, B'nai B'rith Educator of Yr., 1995; Fulbright fellow Vienna, Austria, 1969, 76, 85; grantee NEH, 1974, 75, Littauer grantee, 1988. Mem. Nat. Assn. Armenian Studies and Rsch., Internat. Robert Musil Gesellschaft, Historians' Film Com. Home: Brattleboro, Vt. Died Jan. 2, 2009.

GEHRKE, CHARLES WILLIAM, biochemistry professor; b. NYC, July 18, 1917; s. Henry Edward and Louise (Mader) G.; m. Virginia Dorothy Horcher, Dec. 25, 1941; children: Charles William (dec.), Jon Craig, Susan Gay. BA in Biochemistry, Ohio State U., 1939, BS in Edn, 1941, MS in Biochemistry and Bacteriology, 1941, PhD in Agrl. Biochemistry, 1947. Prof., head dept. chemistry Missouri Valley Coll., Marshall, Mo., 1942-49; instr. agrl. chemistry Ohio State U., Columbus, 1945-46; assoc. prof. agrl. chemistry U. Mo., Columbia, 1949-54, prof. biochemistry, 1954-87, prof. emeritus and from 1987, mgr. Expt. Sta. Chem. Labs., 1954-87, dir. interdisciplinary chromatography Mass Spectrometry Facility, 1982-87; founder, chmn. bd. dirs. Bioscis. and Tech. Internat., Inc., 1992. Founder, chmn. bd. dirs. Analytical Biochemistry Labs., Columbia, 1968-92, dir., 1992—; USA co-chmn. colloquium on A Lunar-Based Chem. Analysis Lab., 1989, 93; co-investigator lunar samples NASA, 1969-75; lectr., Russia, 1972, 74, 90, Japan, China, Taiwan, The Philippines, Hong Kong, 1982, 87, France, Germany, Eng., Norway, Sweden, Switzerland, Italy, Egypt, 1986, 89. Author: 75 Years of Chromatography--A Historical Dialogue, 1979, (book chpt.) Quantitation of Amino Acids and Amines by Chromatography, 2005, Milestones in Chromatography, 2006; author, editor: Amino Acid Analysis by Gas Chromatography, 3 vols., 1987, Chromatography and Modification of Nucleosides, 3 vols., 1990, A Lunar-Based Chemical Analysis Laboratory, 1993, A Lunar-Based Analytical Laboratory, 1997, Chromatography a Century of Discovery, 2001; mem. editl. bd. Jour. Chromatographic Sci., Jour. Chromatography; contbr. chpts. to books, more than 270 articles to sci. jours. Recipient Faculty Alumni Gold medal award U. Mo., 1975, Chromatography Meml. medal Sci. Council on Chromatography of USSR Acad. Scis., 1980, Ohio State Alumni Profl. Achievement award, 2001; Ohio State Outstanding scholar, 1996. Fellow Am. Inst. Chemists, Assn. Ofcl. Analytical Chemists (Harvey W. Wiley award 1971, chmn. Magruder standard sample subcom. 1958-79, bd. dirs., mem. editl. bd. 1979-82, pres.-elect 1983, pres. centennial yr. 1984); mem. AAAS, Am. Soc. Biol. Chemists, Am. Chem. Soc. (pres. Mo. sect. 1958-59, 78-79, Spencer award 1979, Midwest Chemist award 1986, Dal Nogare award in chromatography 1995, U. Mo. Faculty Retiree of Yr. award 1993, Nat. Am. Chem. Soc. Sci. and Tech. award 1999, Nat. Am. Chem. Soc. Chromatography award 2000), Am. Dairy Sci. Assn. (chmn. com. on protein nomenclature 1961-62), Fedn. Am. Socs. Exptl. Biology, Internat. Soc. Study of Origin of Life, N.Y. Acad. Sci., Cosmopolitan Luncheon Club (chmn. Diabetes Ctr. adv. com. 1976—), Diabetes Ctr., Sigma Xi. Home: Saint Paul, Minn. Died Feb. 11, 2009.

GELBOIN, HARRY VICTOR, biochemistry educator, researcher; b. Chgo., Dec. 21, 1929; s. Herman and Eva (Jurkowsky) Gelboin; m. Stella Bezansky, June 19, 1951; m. Marlena Maisels, Apr. 1, 1962; children: Michele Ida, Lisa Rebecca, Sharon Anna, Tamara Rachel. BA in Chemistry, U. Ill., 1951; MS in Biochemistry and Oncology, U. Wis., 1956, PhD in Biochemistry and Oncology, 1958; DSc (hon.), U. Inonu, Malatya, Turkey, 1999. Devel. chemist U.S. Rubber Co., Chgo., 1952-54; rsch. asst. McArdle Meml. Lab. for Cancer Rsch., U. Wis., 1954-58; biochemist lab. cellular pharmacology NIMH, 1958-60, biochemist lab. clin. sci., 1960-61; supervisory biochemist chemistry sect., diagnostic rsch. br. Nat. Cancer Inst., 1962-64, head chemistry sect., carcinogenesis studies br., 1964-66, chief lab. molecular carcinogenesis, div. cancer etiology, 1966—99; adj. prof. Georgetown U., 1974-78. Bd. dirs. Internat. Soc. Polycyclic Aromatic Com.; keynote spkr. carcinogenesis Gordon Res. Conf., 1965; Franz Bielschowsky meml. lectr., Dunedin, New Zealand, 66; Smith Kline French hon. lectr. U. Fla., 1974, U. Mich., 1976; hon. lectr. Israel Cancer Soc. and U. Tel Aviv, Israel, 1983; keynote lectr. Internat. Conf. Carcinogenesis, Alghero, Italy, 1986; Nakasone hon. lectr. Japan Found. Promotion Sci., Tokyo and Osaka, Japan, 1989; keynote speaker U.S. organizer and co-chmn. Princess Takamatsu Cancer Symposium, Tokyo, 1990; vis. prof. Hebrew U., Jerusalem, 1985—86, 2000; plenary lectr. Glinos Found., Athens, 1996; cons. drug metabolism, toxicology and drug discovery; domestic and fgn. spkr. in field. Editor 8 profl. books; assoc. editor Cancer Rsch., 1968-79, 83-87, mem. editl. adv. bd., 1965-67; assoc. editor Biochem. Toxicology, 1984-2010; mem. editl. bd. Chemico-Biol. Interactions, 1969-75, Archives Biochemistry and Biophysics, 1969-76, Life Scis., 1976, Environ. Health Scis., 1976-78; contbr. and co-contbr. over 420 sci. papers to med. publs.; editor/co-editor 10 books, 8 patents. Recipient Superior Svc. award NIH, 1970, Claude Bernard award U. Montreal, 1970, New Horizons award Radiol. Soc. N.Am., 1970, Merit awards Sr. Sci. Svc. NIH, 1983, 85, EEO award NIH, 1989 Fellow: Amer. Coll. Clin. Pharmacol.; mem.: Internat. Soc. for Study Xenobiotics, Internat. Soc. for Preventive Oncology, Am. Soc. for Pharmacology and Exptl. Therapeutics, Am. Soc. Biol. Chemists, Am. Cancer Soc. (adv. com. on carcinogenesis, mem. coun. from 1975), Am. Assn. for Cancer Rsch., AAAS. Achievements include discovery of mechanism of carcinogenesis and cytochrome P450; microsomal P450 activation of chemicals to forms binding to proteins and DNA; describing the activation system for the initial stages of mutagenesis and carcinogenesis, activation for Ames mutagen detection system; development of isolation of specific inhibitory and immunoblotting monoclonal antibodies to each of human cytochrome P450 enzymes, system analyzing drug and xenobiotic metabolism for reduction of drug toxicity; drug discovery; patents in field. Home: Chevy Chase, Md. Died Apr. 13, 2010.

GELINAS, WILLIAM PAUL, association executive; b. Bklyn., Aug. 30, 1930; s. William Joseph and Catherine (Rae) G.; m. Rita Ann Zielinski, May 1, 1954. BS in Bus. Adminstrn, U. Hartford, Conn., 1958; MA in Adminstrn. and Supervision, Central Mich. U., 1975; M.P.A., Nova U., Fla., 1976, D.P.A., 1980. With Am. Heritage Agy., West Hartford, Conn., from 1954, chmn. bd., from 1980. Exec. sec. Am. Assn. Profl. Bridal Cons.'s, West Hartford, 1962—; dir. Heritage Gen. Contractors, Guaranty Bank & Trust Co. Justice of peace, West Hartford, 1960-66, chmn. dist. com., mem. town com., 1960-66. Served to col. U.S. Army, 1956-75. Mem. Am. Soc. Public Adminstrn., Res. Officers Assn. Republican. Roman Catholic. Home: Rutherford, NJ. Died Dec. 30, 2009.

GELLER, JANICE GRACE CLACK, nurse; b. Auburn, Ga., Feb. 25, 1938; d. Erby Ralph and Jewell Grace (Maughon) Clack; m. Joseph Jerome Geller, Dec. 23, 1973; 1 child, Elizabeth Joanne. Student, LaGrange Coll., 1955-57; BS in Nursing, Emory U., 1960; MS, Rutgers U., 1962. Nat. cert. group psychotherapist; cert. clin. nurse specialist. Psychiat. staff nurse dept. psychiatry Emory U., Atlanta, 1960; nurse educator Ill. State Psychiat. Inst., Chgo., 1961; clin. specialist in mental retardation nursing Northville, Mich., 1962; faculty Coll. Nursing Rutgers U., Newark, 1962-63, faculty Advanced Program in Psychiat. Nursing, 1964-66; faculty Coll. Nursing U. Mich., Ann Arbor, 1963-64; faculty, Teheran (Iran) Coll. for Women, 1967-69; clin. specialist psychiat. nursing Roosevelt Hosp., NYC, 1969-70; faculty, guest lectr. Columbia U., NYC, 1969-70; supr. Dept. Psychiat. Nursing Mt. Sinai Hosp., NYC, 1970-72; pvt. practice psychotherapy NYC, 1972-77, Ridgewood, N.J., 1977-96. Faculty, curriculum coord. in psychiat. nursing William Alanson White Inst. Psychiatry, Psychoanalysis and Psychology, N.Y.C., 1974-84; mem. U.S. del. of Community and Mental Health Nurses to People's Republic of China, 1983. Contbr. articles to profl. jours.; editorial bd. Perspectives in Psychiat. Care, 1971-74, 78-84; author: (with Anita Marie Werner) Instruments for Study of Nurse-Patient Interaction, 1964. Mem. Bergen County Rep. Com., 1989. Recipient 10th Anniversary award Outstanding Clin. Specialist in psychiat.-mental health nursing in N.J., Soc. Cert. Clin. Specialists, 1982; Fed. Govt. grantee as career tchr. in psychiat. nursing, Rutgers U., 1962-63; cert. psychiat. nurse and clin. specialist, N.J., N.Y. Mem. AAAS, ANA (various certs.), N.C. Nurses Assn., Soc. Cert. Clin. Specialists in Psychiat. Nursing (chmn.), Coun. Specialists in Psychiat./Mental Health Nursing, Am. Group Psychotherapy Assn. (cert. group psychotherapist), Am. Assn. Mental Deficiency, World Fedn. Mental Health, Sigma Theta Tau. Home: Chapel Hill, NC. Died Jan. 31, 2009.

GELLMAN, ISAIAH, environmental consultant; b. Akron, Ohio, Feb. 19, 1928; s. Meyer and Pearl (Milker) F.; m. Lola Malkis, Dec. 27, 1947; children: Paula, Judith. B in Chem. Engring., CCNY, 1947; MS, Rutgers U., 1950, PhD, 1952. Rsch. assoc. Rutgers U., 1948-52; process engr. Abbott Labs., 1952-56; with Nat. Coun. Paper Industry for Air and Stream Improvement Inc., NYC, from 1956, tech. dir., 1969-77, exec. v.p., 1977-87, pres., 1987-95; environ. cons. Gellman Assocs., NYC, from 1995. Lectr. Johns Hopkins U., 1961-65 NIH fellow, 1948-52 Fellow TAPPI; mem. Sigma Xi. Home: New York, NY. Died Dec. 10, 2009.

GELLMAN, YALE H., lawyer; b. Yonkers, NY, Sept. 16, 1934; s. Abraham and Ray (Goldstein) G.; m. Estelle Sheila Klittnick, Aug. 23, 1964; children: Douglas Zane, Russell Marc, Beth Margot. BA, NYU, 1954; JD, Harvard U., 1957. Bar: N.Y. 1958, Fla. 1978, D.C. 1980. Assoc. Hall, Casey, Dickler, Howley & Brady, Inst. for Bus. Planning, NYC, 1958-61, Marshall, Bratter, Greene, Allison & Tucker, NYC, 1961-62, Dreyer & Traub, NYC, 1962-65, Proskauer, Rose, Goetz & Mendelsohn, NYC, 1965-71, ptnr., 1971-93. Lectr. Practicing Law Inst. Mem. ABA, Internat. Bar Assn. (vice chmn. real property com. 1989-92), N.Y. State Bar Assn. (lectr.), Assn. of Bar of City of N.Y., Nassau County Bar Assn. Home: Elkins Park, Pa. Died Jan. 24, 2009.

GENDELL, GERALD STANLEIGH, retired public relations executive; b. Stamford, Conn., June 14, 1929; s. Irving and Henrietta (Lund) G.; m. s. Marion F. Belvin, July 28, 1952; children: Carin Gaye, Danna Joyce, Adrian Leigh, Jeffrey Lund, David Blake, Marc Steven, Bradley Howard. BS, NYU, 1949. With Procter & Gamble Co., Cin., 1954-91, dir. community affairs and contbns., 1976-80, mgr. external affairs divsn., 1980, mgr. pub. affairs div., 1981—91, also pres., trustee Procter & Gamble Fund. Trustee Glen Manor Home, 1978-80, Queen City Housing Corp., Cin., 1981-89, Cin. Local Initiative Support Corp., The Spire Found., Jewish Fedn. So. Ariz.; vice chmn. bd. trustees Jewish Hosp. of Cin.; bd. dirs., trustee Nat. Coun. on Econ. Edn., 1985-91; mem. met. adv. coun. U. Cin.; mem. adv. coun. George Mason U. Sch. Law, 1988-91; mem. Cin. Mayor's Com. on Econ. Devel.; chmn. Found. for Pub. Affairs; mem. bd. overseers Hebrew Union Coll.; pres. Jewish Cmty. Found. of So. Ariz.; bd. dirs. Jewish Fedn. of So. Ariz., Ariz. Jewish Post. 1st lt. U.S. Army, 1950-53. Mem. Pub. Affairs Coun. Am. (bd. dirs. 1981-91, chmn. 1988-89), Greater Cin. C. of C. (vice chmn., mem. exec. com. 1981-87), Conf. Bd., Bankers Club (bd. govs. 1988-93). Home: Atlanta, Ga. Died June 29, 2009.

GENOVA, ANTHONY CHARLES, philosophy educator; b. Chgo., Aug. 2, 1929; s. Anthony Paul and Marguerite (Finney) G.; m. Veronica Barton; 1 child, Pamela. Ph.B., U. Chgo., 1957, BA, 1958, MA cum laude, 1958, PhD, 1965. Lectr. philosophy U. Chgo., 1959-62; instr. Roosevelt U., Chgo., 1959-61, Ill. Inst. Tech., Chgo., 1962; prof., chmn. dept. philosophy Wichita State U., Kans., 1962-72; prof., chmn. dept. U. Kans., Lawrence, from 1972. Lectr. in field; mem. Woodrow Wilson Fellowship Found. selection com., 1966-72; mem. nat. election com. Fulbright grants, 1987—. Contbr. articles to profl. jours. NEH fellow, 1968, Council for Philos. Studies fellow, 1968; grantee, Ford Found., 1958-59, Am. Philos. Soc., (2), 1970, 72; others Mem. Am. Philos. Assn., Southwestern Philos. Soc. (pres. 1983-84), Mountain Plains Philos. Soc., Colloquium for Social Philosophy Home: Lawrence, Kans. Died Mar. 22, 2010.

GEORGAS, JOHN WILLIAM, beverage manufacturing company executive; b. Freeport, NY, Jan. 14, 1928; s. William and Helen J. (Laricos) G.; m. Tarsi Babis, Apr. 24, 1955; children— William John, Gregory Evan, Laura Michelle BBA, Syracuse U.; MBA, Hofstra U. Mem. sales and mktg. staff Gen. Foods Corp., White Plains, N.Y., 1951-62; sr. v.p. J. Walter Thompson Co., Chgo., 1962-74; formerly sr. v.p. Coca-Cola Co., Atlanta, from 1974; now pres. Coca-Cola Export Corp., Atlanta, from 1989. Mem. Japan-Am. Soc. Ga., U.S. Nat. Commn. for Pacific Econ. Cooperation, U.S.-Asian Ctr. Tech. Exchange, U.S.-Korea Soc., Sch. Advanced Internat. Studies (bd. dirs.), Philippine Am. C. of C. Greek Orthodox. Home: New York, NY. Died Nov. 21, 2009.

GEORGE, FRED W., lawyer; b. Roanoke, Va., Oct. 2, 1949; BA, Va. Polytech. Inst. and State U., 1972; JD, Georgetown U., 1976, MLT, 1979. Bar: Va. 1976, D.C. 1977, Pa. 1978. With Eckert Seamans Cherin & Mellott, Pitts. Mem. ABA. Died June 12, 2009.

GERBER, CHRISTINE NINER, health center executive; b. Washington, Oct. 29, 1936; d. Paul Joseph and Anna M. (Wright) Niner; children: Thomas, Daniel, Anne. AB, Dunbarton of Holy Cross, 1958; MA, Ohio State U., 1982, PhD, 1985. Tchr./counselor Holy Cross High Sch., Rockville, Md.,

1958-63; acct., mgr. Estate-Trust, Columbus, 1972-80; counselor Maryhaven, Inc., Columbus, 1980-81; exec. dir. Brookwood Recovery Ctr., Columbus, Ohio, 1982—; lectr., cons. in field. Bd. dirs. Maryhaven, 1980-83, Tri-Christian Ctr., 1982-84, others. Mem. Women in Communication, Ohio Assn. Alcohol and Other Drug Counselors, Nat. Assn. Alcoholism Counselors, Nat. Council on Alcoholism. Democrat. Roman Catholic. Home: Powell, Ohio. Died Jan. 10, 2010.

GERDES, WILLIAM F., III, civil engineer; b. Quincy, Ill., Feb. 22, 1934; s. Clarence A. and Octavia L. (Lec) G.; m. Barbara A. Gates, May 25, 1936; children: Laura, William D., Parker. BSCE, U. Ill., 1957. Pres. Michelmann Steel Co., Quincy, Ill., from 1957. Mem., pres. Quincy Sch. Bd., 1975-82; bd. pub. works City of Quincy, 1986-92. Fellow ASCE; mem. ISPE (v.p. 1997-98), NSPE. Died Jan. 6, 2009.

GERDS, GRETCHEN DOROTHEA, retired publishing executive; b. Nutley, NJ, Feb. 26, 1924; d. Fritz and Margareta (Plank) G. LittB, Rutgers U., 1946. Reporter, feature writer Herald News, Passaic and Clifton, N.J., 1946-50; dir. pub. relations Am. Nurses' Assn., NYC, 1950-54; feature editor Am. Jour. Nursing, NYC, 1956-62, mng. editor, 1962-82; v.p., editorial dir. Am. Jour. Nursing Co., NYC, from 1982. Author: Steve and the Burro's Secret; contbr. articles to profl. jours. Mem. Am. Mgmt. Assn., Sigma Delta Chi. Home: Lincoln Park, NJ. Died Jan. 31, 2009.

GERHARD, EARL ROBERT, dean, chemical engineering educator; b. Louisville, Aug. 9, 1922; m. Phylys Krebs, June 14, 1947; children: Earl William, Barbara, Mary Kathryn, Robert, David. B in Chem. Engring., U. Louisville, 1943, M in Chem. Engring., 1947; PhD, U. Ill., 1953. Registered profl. engr., Ky. Chem. engr. Shell Oil Co., Norco, La., 1943-44; asst. prof. chem. engring. U. Louisville, 1951-54, assoc. prof. chem. engring., 1954-62, prof. chem. engring., from 1962, chmn. chem. engring. dept., 1969-73, assoc. dean acad., 1973-80, dean speed sch., from 1980. Mem. Ky. Energy Adv. Bd., Ky. Bd. Registration for Profl. Engrs. Author: Opportunities for Chemical Engineering Careers, 1979; contbr. articles to profl. jours. Served with U.S. Army, 1944-46, World War II. Mem. Am. Chem. Soc., Am. Soc. Engring. Edn., Am. Inst. Chem. Engrs., Nat. Soc. for Profl. Engrs., Theta Tau, Sigma Xi, Tau Beta Pi, Phi Kappa Phia, Omicron Delta Kappa. Home: Louisville, Ky. Died May 18, 2010.

GERNERT, WILLIAM EDGAR, other: real estate, director; b. Bowling Green, Ohio, May 21, 1917; s. William Henry and Lillian Leon (Forrest) Gernert; m. Mary Alice Hawley, May 30, 1942; children: William Edgar III, Deborah Janssen, Peggy Lane, Mary Beth Emry. BA, Bowling Green State U., 1938; BS in Civil Engring., US Mil. Acad., 1942; MBA, Ohio State U., 1948; grad., Indsl. Coll. Armed Forces, 1962. Commd. Col. US Air Force, 1955, advanced through grades to brig. gen., 1967; B-24 squadron comdr. Pacific Theater, 1944—45; chief advanced planning Armed Forces Nuclear Weapons Progra, Albuquerque, 1951—53; dir. rsch. and devel. Def. Atomic Support Agy., N.Mex., 1962—63; dir. nuclear safety US Air Force, Kirtland AFB, N.Mex., 1965—67, ret., 1970; self-employed broker and real estate appraiser Colo. Springs, Colo., from 1972; info. sys. mgr. Front Range Enterprises, from 1982; dir. Ctrl. Bank Colo. Springs; instr. real estate fin. and real estate appraising U. Colo., Colo. Springs, 1974—81. Decorated Legion Merit 3 clusters, Air medal 4 clusters, DFC, Purple Heart. Mem.: Nat. Assn. Rev. Appraisers (sr.), East Side Rotary (Colo. Springs) (past pres.). Died Sept. 20, 2009.

GERRITY, EDWARD JOSEPH, JR., communications executive; b. Scranton, Pa., Jan. 3, 1924; s. Edward Joseph and Helen T. (Walton) Gerrity; m. Katharine Casey Gerrity, Sept. 22, 1957; children: Katharine, Edward Joseph III. BS, U. Scranton, 1946; MS, Columbia U., 1948. Exec. v.p. ITT Corp., NYC, 1958—85; bus. cons. Ned Gerrity Assocs., Inc., Port Chester, from 1985. Sr. cons. Janes & Clark Advt., Port Chester, from 1987; bd. dirs. Norstar Bank, NYC. 2d lt. US Army, 1942—45, ETO. Decorated Silver Star, Bronze Star with cluster. Died June 2, 2009.

GERVAIS, JOSEPH FERNAND, investor; b. Madawaska, Maine, Jan. 15, 1931; s. Levite and Delia (Ringuette) Gervais; m. Juanita Shirley MacLean, May 9, 1953; children: Ken J., Steven M., William G., Carl R. Enlisted USAF, ret., 1980; mgr. Kachina Investment Club, Tucson, from 1977. Treas. Tucson Toros Booster Club, from 1980. Decorated Legion of Merit, Bronze Star. Mem.: DAV, Ret. Officers Assn., U.S. Army Warrant Officer Assn. Republican. Roman Catholic. Died July 2, 2009.

GERWIN, BRENDA ISEN, research biochemist; b. Boston, May 2, 1939; d. Maurice Joshua and Jeannette (Hershon) Isen; m. Robert David Gerwin, Dec. 18, 1960; children: David, Daniel, Joel. BA, Radcliffe Coll., 1960; PhD, U. Chgo., 1964. Instr. biochemistry Rockefeller U., NYC, 1964-66, Case-Western Res. U., Cleve., 1966-69; biochemist molecular anatomy program Oak Ridge Nat. Lab., Rockville, Md., 1969-71; sr. staff fellow Nat. Cancer Inst. NIH, Bethesda, Md., 1971-73, chemist Lab. of Tumor Virus Genetics, Nat. Cancer Inst., 1973-81, chemist Lab. of Molecular Oncology, Nat. Cancer Inst., 1981-83, rsch. chemist Lab. Human Carcinogenesis, Nat. Cancer Inst., from 1983. Treas. Internat. Mesothelioma Interest Group. Contbr. articles to profl. jours. Mem. AAAS, Am. Soc. Biochemistry and Molecular Biology, Am. Soc. Microbiology, Sigma Xi. Jewish. Avocations: backpacking, handcrafts, study and teaching of jewish culture. Home: Berkeley, Calif. Died June 8, 2009.

GESSELL, JOHN MAURICE, minister, educator; b. St. Paul, June 17, 1920; s. Leo Lancien and Mabel Asenath (Wing) Gessell. BA, Yale U., 1942, BD, 1949, PhD, 1960. Ordained priest Episcopal Ch., 1951. Rector Emmanuel Episcopal Ch., Nottoway Parish, Va., 1951—53; assoc. rector Grace Ch., Salem, Mass., 1953—61; prof. Christian edn. U. South Sch. Theology, Sewanee, Tenn., 1961—63, asst. prof. pastoral theology, 1963—74, prof. Christian ethics, 1974—84, prof. emeritus, from 1984. Pres. Multi-County Comprehensive Mental Health Ctr., Tullahoma, Tenn., 1972—74. Author: Grace and Obedience, 2002; editor: St. Luke's Jour. Theology, 1976—90; contbr. articles to profl. jours. Founder, exec. dir. Cumberland Ctr. for Justice and Peace; nat. exec. com. Episcopal Pace Fellowship; bd. dirs. Absalom Jones Theol. Inst., Atlanta, Mid-South Career Devel. Ctr., Nashville; Bd. dirs., pres. Sewanee Civic Assn. and Cmty. Chest, 1967—68. Dwight fellow, Yale U., 1949—50, Coll. of Preachers fellow, Washington, 1953. Mem.: AAUP, Am. Assn. Theol. Schs. (faculty fellow 1967—68), Am. Soc. Christian Ethics, Phi Beta Kappa. Home: Sewanee, Tenn. Died June 30, 2009.

GETTIG, MARTIN WINTHROP, retired mechanical engineer; b. South Bend, Ind., Nov. 8, 1939; s. Joseph H. and Esther (Scheppele) G.; m. Nancy Caroline Buchannan, June 25, 1960 (dec. 1965). Student, Pa. State U., 1957-60 and from 89. Process engr. Gettig Tech. Inc., Spring Mills, Pa., 1960-88. Inventor ultralight non-solid state miniature ignition systems for model aircraft employing small two cycle spark ignition engines. Staff sgt. Pa. N.G., 1961-67. Mem.: NRA, Acad. Model Awronautics, Soc. Antique Modelers and Model Airplanes, Model Engine Collectors Assn., Delta Phi. Republican. Lutheran. Home: Boalsburg, Pa. Died Jan. 31, 2010.

GEUTHER, RUSSELL LAWRENCE, investment company executive, consultant; b. Highland, Ill., Oct. 18, 1934; s. Milton Carl and Hilda (Garms) Geuther. At, Mo. Valley Coll., 1952—53; BS in Polit. Sci., So. Ill. U., 1963. Cert. assn. mgmt. U. Mich., 1969. Dist. exec. Boy Scouts Am., Bloomington Ill. and Lake Geneva, Wis., 1955—60; exec. dir. Carbondale C. of C., 1960—61; mgr. membership dept. ABA, Chgo., 1963—66; cons. Charles R. Feldstein & Co., Inc., Chgo., Calif., 1966—68; v.p. Found. for Human Ecology, Park Ridge, 1968—69, Greater Cleve. Growth Assn., 1968—73; sr. v.p. and mgr. pub. fin. McDonald & Co., Cleve., from 1973. Trustee Village of Matteson, Ill., 1965—69, chmn. fin., pub. works and ordinance coms., vice chmn. planning com.; mem. Bay Village (Ohio) Sch. Bd., 1979—84; bd. govs. Celeste High Speed Rail Task Force. With US Army, 1955. Mem.: Pub. Securities Assn. (legis. com.), Vermillion Yacht Club. Republican. Presbyterian. Home: Cleveland, Ohio. Died Mar. 29, 2009.

GIAQUINTA, BENJAMIN E., state representative; b. Brockton, Mass., Nov. 8, 1922; married; 6 children. Grad., La. State U., 1953. With Wehrly Realtors; state rep. dist. 80 Ind. Ho. of Reps., Indpls., from 1996, health and medicaid subcom. chmn., ways and means com., mem. cts. and criminal code, and pub. policy, ethics and vets affairs coms. Mem. adv. bd. Wayne Twp., Ind., 1986—90. Mem.: Southside Bus. Group, Ft. Wayne Area Assn. Realtors (govtl. issues com.), Am. Inst. Parliamentarians, Allen County Load Closers Assn., C. of C., One Summit Club 5254, Toastmasters Internat., Am. Legion Post 296. Died July 11, 2010.

GIBBONS, JAMES T. (JAMES THOMAS GIBBONS), bank executive; b. Bloomfield, NJ, June 2, 1922; s. Peter D. and Alice M. (Higham) Gibbons; m. Geraldine M. Clifford, June 1, 1946; children: James T. Jr., Constance, F. Clifford. At, Knox Coll., Galesburg, Ill., 1943, at, 1946—48; LLB, NYU, 1950; post grad., Rutgers U., 1958—60. Asst. v.p. 1st Nat. Bank Jersey City, 1950—60; v.p. Md. Nat. Bank, Easton, 1960—62; pres. and CEO Peoples Nat. Bank of Central Jersey, Piscataway, NJ, from 1963. With US Army, 1942—46, ETO. Mem.: Rotary. Roman Catholic. Home: Princeton, NJ. Died May 12, 2010.

GIBBONS, ROBERT PHILIP, management consultant, director; m. Mary Jane M. Jamieson, June 12, 1965; children: Laura Ann, Robert John. BSME, Stevens Inst. Tech., 1955; MS in Indsl. Mgmt., Purdue U., 1959. Ptnr. Touche Ross Co., NYC, 1959—74; v.p., gen. mgr. Carborundum Co., Niagara Falls, NY, 1975—78, Main Hurdman, NYC, 1978—84, Zolfo, Cooper & Co., NYC, 1984—86; ptnr. Gibbons, Quintero & Co., NYC, 1986—90, Gibbons & Co,., Tenafly, NJ, from 1990. Apptd. trustee U.S. Trustee and U.S. Bankruptcy Ct. Contbr. Am. Mgmt. Assn. Mgmt. Handbook, 1970. Bd. dirs., chmn. audit com., compensation com. Weldotron Corp., 1974—91. With US Army, 1956—58. Mem.: Turnaround Mgmt. Assn., Am. Bankruptcy Inst., Inst. Mgmt. Cons. (cert.), Am. Prodn. and Inventory Control Soc. (cert.). Deceased.

GIDUZ, ROLAND, journalist; b. Fall River, Mass., July 24, 1925; s. Hugo and Edith May (Baker) G.; children: William Roland, Robert Baker, Thomas Tracy. AB in Journalism, U. N.C., 1948; MS in Journalism, Columbia U., 1949; postgra., Harvard U., 1959; postgrad., Ga. Inst. Tech., 1979. Editor Chapel Hill (N.C.) News Leader, 1954-59, News of Orange County, Chapel Hill, 1960-66, Gen. Alumni Assn., U. N.C., Chapel Hill, 1966-81; news dir. Sta. WCHL, Chapel Hill, 1981-82; dir. pub. affairs Village Cos., Chapel Hill, 1982-96. Columnist Chapel Hill newspaper, 1952-82; owner, pub. The Triangle Pointer Mag., Chapel Hill, 1960-77; cable TV show host/producer Chapel Hill Almanac, 1982—. Author: Who's Gonna Cover 'Em Up?, 1985. Alderman, mayor pro-tem Town of chapel Hill, 1957-69; pres. Friends of chapel Hill Libr., 1975; chmn. cmty. bd. Hillhaven Convalescent Home, 1984; sec. Arts Ctr., 1988-89; trustee Preservation Soc., 1986-97, chmn., 1997—Pub. Sch. Found., 1988-92. Served with U.S. Army, 1943-45, ETO. Named Young Man of Yr. Chapel Hill Jaycees, 1960, Citizen of Yr. Sons Am. Revolution, 1969, Sertoma, 1976; recipient Silver Beaver award Boy Scouts Am., 1977. Mem. Harvard U. Alumni Assn. (regional dir. 1995-98), N.C. Train Host Assn. (editor 1995—). Clubs: Toastmasters, Rotary (pres. local club 1971). Lodges: Masons. Democrat. Presbyterian. Avocations: backpacking, jogging, racquetball. Home: Chapel Hill, NC. Died Jan. 23, 2009.

GIL, PETER PAUL, management educator, consultant; b. Havana, Cuba, Dec. 7, 1922; came to U.S., 1923; s. Peter Paul and Julia Cancio (Heredia) Fumagalli; m. Anita Maxwell, June 20, 1949 (dec. Feb. 1976); Karen, Andrew, Geneve; m. 2d Karin Enebuske, Apr. 15, 1977; stepchildren: William, Mary and John Trelease. AB cum laude, Harvard U., 1949, MBA, 1951; PhD magna cum laude, U. Geneva, Switzerland, 1963. Asst. dir. tng. and research Aluminium, Ltd., Montreal, Que., Can., 1951-56; asst. dir., prof. Internat. Mgmt. Inst., Geneva, 1956-62; assoc. dean, sr. lectr. Sloan Sch. Mgmt. MIT, Cambridge, 1962-82, hon. Alfred P. Sloan fellow, 1983; dean, prof. mgmt. Clark U., Worcester, Mass., from 1982. Affiliate prof. Worcester Poly. Inst.; hon. dir European Mgmt. Forum, Geneva, 1974—; dir. Standby Fund (Cowen), N.Y.C., Mechanics Bank (Multi-Fin. Bank Corp.) Incorporator Worcester Art Mus., 1983—; chmn. bd. trustees Cambridge City Hosp., 1980-82; mem. Cambridge Health Policy Bd., 1979-82; bd. dirs. Internat. Artists Series, Worcester, 1982—, Worcester Bus. Devel. Corp., Central Mass. chpt. ARC; mem. NCCJ; mem. adv. bd. U. Barcelona Faculty of Engring., Spain, 1972; trustee Meml. Hosp. Holding Co.; exec. com. Inter-Am. U. Council Econ. and Social Devel., 1985—. Served to 2d lt. Q.M.C. U.S. Army, 1942-45, ETO. Mem. U.S. Council Fgn. Relations, Internat. Univ. Contact, Acad. Mgmt. Clubs: MIT Faculty (exec. com. 1963-65), Hasty Pudding Inst. Home: New Castle, NH. Died Mar. 4, 2010.

GILBERT, ALLAN ARTHUR, retired manufacturing executive; b. Chgo., Jan. 7, 1925; s. Allan T. and Elizabeth (Boyce) G.; m. Gwendolyn M. Moore, June 24, 1950 (dec. June, 2004); children: Debora D. and Elizabeth (twins), Allan M.; m. Elizabeth Clark, 1990; children: Tyler Clark, Allan Moore II. Buyer Carson Pirie Scott & Co., Chgo., 1949-55; v.p. George Fry & Assocs., Chgo., 1956-65; v.p. mktg. Chamberlain Mfg. Corp., Elmhurst, Ill., 1966-68; v.p. Lester B. Knight & Assocs., Chgo., 1968-75; v.p. manpower devel. Emerson Electric Co., St. Louis, 1975-92, cons., 1992-2000. Asst. prof. Roosevelt U., 1951-52. Mem. Gov.'s Adv. Council, Ill., 1969-70; fund raiser Ill. Republicans., 1966-67. Lt. (j.g.) USNR, 1944-46. Mem. Soc. Colonial Wars (dep. gov. Mo.), Univ. Club of Chgo., Princeton Club, Harvard Bus. Sch. Club. Home: Cortlandt Manor, NY. Died Mar. 25, 2009.

GILBERT, RUBY, state legislator; b. Dec. 19, 1929; m. Booker Gilbert. Mem. Dist. 89 Kans. House of Reps., 1991—2004. Died Feb. 28, 2010.

GILBERT, THOMAS MARTIN, former government official, consultant; b. Elkmont, Ala., May 7, 1927; s. Van Buren and Mary Daly (McWilliams) Gilbert. AB, Athens State Coll., 1949. Mem. staff Senator Lister Hill, Washington, 1949—53; adminstrv. asst. Rep. Armistead Selden, Washington, 1953—69, Rep. George W. Andrews, 1969—71, Rep. Elizabeth Andrews, 1972—73, Rep. Marjorie Holt, 1973; cons. Grocery Mfrs. Am., Inc., Washington, from 1973. With USN, 1945—46. Episcopalian. Avocations: theater, books and programs collector. Home: Elkmont, Ala. Died Oct. 8, 2009.

GILBERTSON, OSWALD IRVING, marketing executive; b. Bklyn., Mar. 23, 1927; s. Olaf and Ingeborg Gabrielsen (Aase) Gilbertson; m. Magnhild Hompland, Sept. 11, 1954; children: Erik Olaf, Jan Ivar. Cert. electrotechnician, Sorlandets Tekniske Skole, Norway, 1947; BSEE, Stockholms Tekniska Inst., 1956. Registered profl. engr., Vt. Planning engr. test equipment design and devel. Western Electric Co., Inc., Kearny, N.J., 1957-61, planning engr. new prodn., 1963-67, engring. supr. test equipment, 63-67, engring. supr. submarine repeaters and equalizers, 1967-69; engring. mgr. comm. cables ITT Corp., Oslo, Norway, 1969-71; mktg. mgr. for ITT's Norwegian co. Std. Telefon og Kabelfabrik A/S (STK), 1971-87, STK factory rep., 1987-89, Alcatel Kabel Norge AS Factory rep., 1989-92, Alcatel Can. Wire Inc. Factory rep., 1992-95; divsn. mgr. Eswa Heating Sys., Inc., 1980-87, pres., 1987-89. Author: Electrical Cables for Power and Signal Transmission, 2000, Sånn va dae då i Kvinesdal, 1999, Visions, 2006, Visjoner, 2006. With AUS, 1948-52. Named Hon. Norwegian Consul, 1981-2004; apptd. Knight 1st Class Norwegian Order Merit, 1989. Mem. IEEE, Norwegian Soc. Profl. Engrs., Soc. Norwegian Am. Engrs., Sons of Norway. Achievements include patents in field. Died Oct. 30, 2009.

GILCHREST, THORNTON CHARLES, retired association executive; b. Chgo., Sept. 1, 1931; s. Charles Jewett Gilchrest and Patricia (Thornton) Thornton; m. Barbara Dibbern, June 8, 1952; children: Margaret Mary, James Thornton. BS in Journalism, U. Ill., 1953. Cert. tchr. Ill. Tchr. pub. high sch., West Chicago, Ill., 1957; exec. dir. Plumbing-Heating-Cooling Info. Bur., Chgo., 1958-64; asst. to pres. A.Y. McDonald Mfg. Co., Dubuque, Iowa, 1964-68; exec. dir. Am. Supply Assn., Chgo., 1968-77, exec. v.p., 1977-82, Nat. Safety Coun., Chgo., 1982-83, pres., 1983-95; chmn. Internat. Safety Coun., Chgo., 1992-95. Pres. Nat. Safety Coun. Found. for Safety and Health, 1986-95. Bd. dirs. Prevent Blindness Am., 1993. With USN, 1953-55. Mem. Am. Soc. Assn. Execs., Chgo. Soc. Assn. Execs. Methodist. Home: Northbrook, Ill. Died Nov. 15, 2009.

GILGORE, SHELDON GERALD, retired pharmaceutical company executive; b. Phila., Feb. 13, 1932; s. Harry S. and Ida (Pinkenson) G.; m. Irma Helene Swartz, Sept. 30, 1956; children: Lance, Laurence, Lloyd. BS in Biology, Villanova U., 1952; MD, Jefferson Med. Coll., 1956. Intern and resident in internal medicine Thomas Jefferson U., Phila., 1956-61; instr. medicine, asst. attending physician Jefferson Med. Coll., Phila., 1961-63; clin. asst. physician medicine and endocrinology St. Vincent's Hosp., Phila., 1964; assoc. dir. clin.

research Pfizer Pharms., NYC, 1963-65, dir. clin. pharmacology, 1965-66, dir. clin. research, 1966-69, v.p., med. dir., 1969-71, pres., 1971-86; chmn., pres., CEO G.D. Searle & Co., Skokie, Ill., 1986—95. Bd. dirs. Evanston Hosp. Corp., Nat. Mus. Health and Medicine Found.; chmn. Pharm. Mfrs. Assn. Found, Inc; mem. Pres.' Council Meml. Sloan-Kettering Cancer Ctr., N.Y.C.; bd. dirs. Chgo. Lyric Opera; chmn. bd. dirs. Conn. Grand Opera Co., Stamford. Mem. ABA, Pharm. Mfrs. Assn., American Coll. Clin. Pharmacology and Chemotherapy, Am. Fedn. Clin. Rsch, American Diabetes Assn., N.Y. Acad. Sciences Avocations: squash, opera, classical music. Home: Naples, Fla. Died Feb. 12, 2010.

GILL, GEORGE NORMAN, newspaper publishing company executive; b. Indpls., Aug. 11, 1934; s. George E. and Urith (Dailey) G.; m. Kay Baldwin, Dec. 28, 1957; children— Norman A., George B. AB, Ind. U., 1957. Reporter Richmond (Va.) News Leader, 1957-60; copy editor, reporter, acting Sunday editor, city editor, mng. editor Courier-Jour., Louisville, 1960-74; v.p., gen. mgr. Courier-Jour. and Louisville Times Co., 1974-79, sr. v.p. corp. affairs, 1979-80, pres., chief exec. officer, 1981-86. Chief exec. officer affiliates Standard Gravure Corp., WHAS, Inc., 1981-86; pres., pub. Courier-Jour. and Louisville Times Co., 1986-93. Served with USNR, 1954-56. Recipient Picture Editors award Nat. Press Photographers Assn., 1965 Mem. Am. Soc. Newspaper Editors, Asso. Press Mng. Editors, Alpha Tau Omega, Sigma Delta Chi. Home: Pewee Valley, Ky. Died Apr. 10, 2010.

GILL, RICHARD THOMAS, opera singer, economic analyst; b. Long Branch, NJ, Nov. 30, 1927; s. Thomas Grant and Myrtle (Sickles) G.; m. Betty Bjornson, Jan. 6, 1950; children: Thomas Grandon, Peter Severin, Geoffrey Karl. AB, Harvard U., 1948, PhD in Econs, 1956; postgrad., Oxford U., Eng., 1948-49. Lectr. economics Harvard U., 1963-71. Author: Economics and the Public Interest, 5th edit., 1991, Our Changing Population, 1992, Posterity Lost, 1997, others; TV commentator Economics USA (Annenberg/CPB project), 1985-92; debuts in N.Y.C. Opera, 1971, Met. Opera, 1973, Houston Grand Opera, 1972, Chgo. Lyric Opera, 1976, N.Y. Philharm., 1977; appeared at Edinburgh Festival, 1976; soloist numerous opera cos. and symphonies in U.S. and abroad. Served with inf. U.S. Army, 1946-47. Henry fellow, 1948-49; recipient Atlantic Monthly First Short Story prize, 1954 Mem. American Economics Assn. Died Oct. 25, 2010.

GILLESPIE, ELSIE JULIANNA, business executive; b. Phila., Sept. 24, 1912; d. Julius Adelbert and Martha Amanda (Brunner) Kinderman; 1 child, Edward R. Buckalew. Student, Pub. Schs., Phila. With menu and purchasing depts. Lintons Restaurants, Phila., 1930—42; cashier, mgr. accounts payable J.E. Caldwell Co., Phila., 1949—74; owner Gillespie Apts., cean City, NJ, from 1974; sec. Tourist Devel. Commn., from 1982. Mem.: C. of C. (Ocean City) (dir. 1982—85, chmn. com. 1983), Guest and Apt. House Assn. (Ocean City) (pres. 1982—84). Republican. Presbyterian. Died Jan. 23, 2009.

GILLMER, THOMAS CHARLES, retired naval architect; b. July 17, 1911; s. Derr Oscar and Hazel May (Voit) G.; m. Anna May Derge, June 5, 1937; children: Christina Gesell Gillmer Erdmann, Charles Voit; m. Ruth N. Morgan, 1999. BS, U.S. Naval Acad., 1935; postgrad., Case Western Res. U., 1946, Johns Hopkins U., 1946. Commd. ensign USN, 1935, advanced through grades to lt. (j.g.), 1939, lt. comdr., 1944-46; mem. faculty U.S. Naval Acad., Annapolis, Md., 1946-68, prof., dir. Naval Arch., 1961-68, chmn. naval engring. dept., 1963-68; pvt. practice naval arch. Annapolis, 1968-2000; ret., 2000. Mem. panel experts FAO, UN, Rome, 1963-66; cons. to Navy Dept. Restoration USS Constitution, 1991—. Author: Construction and Stability of Naval Ships, 1959, Modern Ship Design, 1970, 2d edit., 1975, Working Water Craft, 1972, 2d edit., 1994, Chesapeake Sloops, 1981, Introduction to Naval Architecture, 1982, The Story of Baltimore Clippers, 1991, Old Ironsides, Rise, Decline, and Resurrection of USS Constitution, 1993; designer PRIDE of Balt., 1976-77, Lady Maryland, 1985, PRIDE of Balt. II, 1987-88, A History of Working Watercraft of the Western World, 1994; contbr. articles to profl. jours. and papers to profl. confs.; designer Kalmar nickel replica ship of Del., 1998; patentee in field. Mem. bd. govs. Chesapeake Bay Maritime Mus., 1981-91, emeritus, 1995, curatorial chmn., 1989-91. Recipient 1st Maritime Preservation award Chesapeake Bay Maritime Mus., 1992, Robert G. Albion/James Monroe award for maritime history Nat. Maritime Hist. Soc., N.Y.C., 1995. Mem. AAUP, Soc. Naval Archs. and Marine Engrs. (award for individual efforts to further body of knowledge 1988), Am. Soc. Naval Engrs., Soc. Nautical Rsch., PRIDE of Balt. (ops. com. 1979—), Hellenic Inst. Nautical Archaeology Athens (Bronze medal 1985), Annapolis Yacht Club, de Voile Club (France), New Providence Club. Home: Annapolis, Md. Died Dec. 16, 2009.

GILMAN, JOHN JOSEPH, research scientist; b. St. Paul, Dec. 22, 1925; s. Alexander Falk and Florence Grace (Colby) G.; m. Pauline Marie Harms, June 17, 1950 (div. Dec. 1968); children: Pamela Ann, Gregory George, Cheryl Elizabeth; m. Gretchen Marie Sutter, June 12, 1976; 1 son, Brian Alexander. BS, Ill. Inst. Tech., 1946, MS, 1948; PhD, Columbia, 1952. Research metallurgist Gen. Electric Co., Schenectady, 1952-60; prof. engring. Brown U., Providence, 1960-63; prof. physics and metallurgy U. Ill., Urbana, 1963-68; dir. Materials Research Center Allied Chem. Corp., Morristown, N.J., 1968-78; dir. Corp. Devel. Center, 1978-80; mgr. corp. research Amoco Co. (Ind.), Naperville, Ill., 1980-85; assoc. dir. Lawrence Berkeley Lab./U. Calif., Calif., 1985-87; sr. scientist Lawrence Berkeley Lab., Calif., 1987-93; adj. prof. UCLA, from 1993. Author: Micromechanics of Flow in Solids, 1969, Inventivity-The Art and Science of Research Management, 1992, Electronic Basis of the Strength of Materials, 2003; editor: The Art and Science of Growing Crystals, 1963, Fracture of Solids (with D.C. Drucker), 1963, Atomic and Electronic Structures of Metals, 1967, Metallic Glasses, 1973, Energetic Materials, 1993; editl. bd. Jour. Applied Physics, 1969-72; contbg. editor Materials Tech., 1994-99; contbr. over 325 papers, articles to tech. jours. Served as Ensign USNR, 1943-46. Recipient Mathewson gold medal Am. Inst. Metal Engrs., 1959, Disting. Service award Alumni Assn. Ill. Inst. Tech., 1962, Application to Practice award, 1985. Fellow AAAS, Am. Phys. Soc., The Materials Soc., Am. Soc. for Metals (Campbell lectr. 1966); mem. Nat. Acad. Engring., Phi Kappa Phi, Tau Beta Pi. Home: Newton, NJ. Died Sept. 10, 2009.

GILMORE, HORACE WELDON, former federal judge; b. Columbus, Ohio, Apr. 4, 1918; s. Charles Thomas and Lucille (Weldon) G.; m. Mary Hays, June 20, 1942; children— Lindsay Gilmore Feinberg. AB, U. Mich., 1939, JD, 1942. Bar: Mich. bar 1946. Law clk. U.S. Ct. Appeals, 1946-47; practiced in Detroit, 1947-51; spl. asst. U.S. atty., Detroit, 1951-52; mem. Mich. Bd. Tax Appeals, 1954; dep. atty. gen. State of Mich., 1955-56; circuit judge 3d Jud. Circuit, Detroit, 1956-80; judge U.S. Dist. Ct. (ea. dist.) Mich., from 1980, now sr. judge Detroit. Adj. prof. law Wayne State U. Law Sch., 1966-82; lectr. law U. Mich. Law Sch., 1969-90; faculty Nat. Coll. State Judiciary, 1966-83; mem. Mich. Jud. Tenure Commn., 1969-76; chmn. Mich. Com. to Revise Criminal Code, 1965-82, Mich. Com. to Revise Criminal Procedure, 1971-79; trustee Inst. for Ct. Mgmt. Author: Michigan Civil Procedure Before Trial, 2d edit, 1975; contbr. numerous articles to legal jours. Served with USNR, 1942-46. Mem. ABA, State Bar Mich., Am. Judicature Soc., Am. Law Inst., Nat. Conf. State Trial Judges. Home: Grosse Pointe, Mich. Died Jan. 25, 2010.

GIMBEL, R. NICHOLAS, lawyer; b. Phila., July 25, 1951; m. Martha Morse; children: Martha, Anne. BA magna cum laude, Yale U., 1973; JD, U. Chgo., 1976. Bar: Ill. 1976, Mass. 1979, D.C. 1980, N.Y. 1984, Pa. 1987. Law clk. to Hon. Collins J. Seitz US Ct. Appeals (3d Cir.), 1976-77; atty. Office Gen. Counsel Securities & Exch. Commn. (SEC), 1978-80; asst. U.S. atty. (so. dist.) NY US Dept. Justice, 1980-84; ptnr. Klett, Lieber, Rooney & Schorling, Phila., 1984—2002, McCarter English, Phila., 2002—09. Lectr. Rutgers U. Sch. Law, 2003—05. Mem. ABA, Am. Law Inst., Phila. Bar Assn. (mem. fed. ct. com.). Died Nov. 19, 2009.

GINEPRA, ALFRED LEON, JR., public relations executive, educator; b. Boston, Mass., July 30, 1933; s. Alfred Leon and Ruth Dorothy (Burns) Ginepra; m. Joan Marie Mariner, June 27, 1959; children: Joanne Ruth, Lawrence Paul. AB, Columbia U., 1955, postgrad., 1955—56, MBA, 1963; postgrad., Stanford U., 1958—59, UCLA, 1969—70; DEd, Calif. Internat. U., 1977. Analyst Dun & Bradstreet, Inc., 1959—61; editor E. I. duPont de Nemours & Co., 1963; govtl. affairs rep. Gen. Tel. Co., 1963—69; put. rels. supr. Carnation Co., LA, 1969—78; pub. rels. mgr. Korean Airlines, 1978—79; pub. rels. dir. USO, 1979—86; v.p. Mktg. Americoia, from 1986; pres. LA Mktg. Advt. Pub. Rels., from 1986. Asst. prof. Calif. State U., Northridge, 1975; sr. lectr. UCLA, from 1973; lectr. Pacific States U., from 1980; prof. Calif. Internat. U., from 1979. Bd. dirs., mem. exec. com. Am. Heart Assn., LA ARC. With US Army, 1956—58. Named All-Am. Scholastic Football Player, 1954; named to Columbia Coll. Centennial All-Star Football Team 1870-1970. Mem.: NAM, LA Pub. Affairs Officers Assn., LA Soc. Pub. Rels. Counselors (pres. 1976), Pub. Rels. Soc. Am., Toastmasters, LA Area C. of C., So. Calif. Rugby Union and Alumni Assn. (pres., founder 1984), Calif. C. of C., Northridge Hosp. Found. (pres. 1974), UCLA Pub. Rels. Club, LA Rugby and Old Blue Club, Columbia U. Club, Olympic Club, Century City, N.Y. Rugby Club (life), Shriners, Masons (32 degree). Died Feb. 2, 2010.

GINSBERG, ROBERT IZHAK, mail order company executive; b. Tel Aviv, July 7, 1933 (parents Am. citizens); s. Sidney Samuel and Ella (Bach) G.; m. Ilene E. Shapiro, July 2, 1959; children— Jennifer, Elizabeth, Seth. B.A., Antioch Coll., 1955; postgrad. Cornell U., 1955-56. Mgr. products Cadillac Pub. Co., N.Y.C., 1960-68; asst. pub. Xerox Ednl. Pubs., Middletown, Conn., 1968-72; dir. mktg. Fuller and Dees Pubs., Montgomery, Ala., 1972-73; dir. mktg., v.p. Carol Wright Sales Inc., Stamford, Conn., 1973-86, exec. v.p., chief operating officer, 1987—, also bd. dirs.Contbr. articles to trade mags. Treas. Congregation for Humanistic Judaism, Westport, Conn.; trustee St. John's Community Found., Stamford, Conn. Served with U.S. Army, 1956-58. Mem. Direct Mktg. Assn., New Eng. Mail Order Assn., New Eng. Direct Mktg. Assn., Direct Mktg. Idea Exchange, Pacific Mail Order Assn. (bd. dirs. Hong Kong chpt. 1987—). Jewish. Club: Sprite Island Yacht (East Norwalk, Conn.) (bd. dirs. 1982-84), Repulse Bay Yacht (Hong Kong). Avocations: sailing, amateur clarinetist. Home: Norwalk, Conn. Died Aug. 16, 2010.

GINSBURG, MARTIN DAVID, lawyer, educator; b. NYC, June 10, 1932; s. Morris and Evelyn (Bayer) Ginsburg; m. Ruth Bader, June 23, 1954; children: Jane, James. AB, Cornell U., 1953; JD, Harvard U., 1958; LLD (hon.), Lewis and Clark Coll., 1992, Wheaton Coll., 1997. Bar: N.Y. 1959, D.C. 1980. Practiced in N.Y.C., 1959-79; mem. firm Weil, Gotshal & Manges, NYC, 1963-79; of counsel firm Fried, Frank, Harris, Shriver and Jacobson, Washington, 1980—2010; Charles Keller Beekman prof. law Columbia U. Law Sch., NYC, 1979-80; prof. law Georgetown U. Law Center, Washington, 1980—2010; lectr. U. Leiden, The Netherlands, 1982; lectr. Salzburg Seminar Austria, 1984; mem. tax divsn adv. group US Dept. Justice, 1980-81; mem. adv. group to Commr. Internal Revenue, 1978-80; mem. adv. bd. U. Calif. Securities Regulation Inst., 1973-91. Adj. prof. law NYU, 1967—79; vis. prof. law Stanford U., Calif., 1978, Harvard U., Cambridge, Mass., 1986, U. Chgo., 1990, NYU, 1993; cons. joint com. on taxation U.S. Congress, 1979—80, acad. advisor, 2000—01; chmn. tax adv. bd. Commerce Clearing House, 1982—94; mem. bd. advisors NYU/IRS Continuing Profl. Edn. Program, 1983—88, co-chmn., 1986—88; sub coun. on capital allocation, co-chmn. taxation expert group Competitiveness Policy Coun., 1993—95; chmn. tax adv. bd. Little, Brown, 1994—96; bd. dirs. Millennium Chems., Inc., 1996—2003, Chgo. Classical Rec. Found.; lectr. various tax insts.; Mandella Inst. Disting. Vis. lectr. U. Witwatersrand, South Africa, 2006. Co-author, editor Tax Consequences of Investments, 1969; spl. editor: Structuring Venture Capital, Private Equity, and Entrepreneurial Transactions, 2009; co-author: Mergers, Acquisitions, and Buyouts, 2009; contbr. articles to legal jours. Mem. vis. com. Harvard Law Sch., 1994—98. 1st lt. arty. US Army, 1954—56. Recipient Chair named in his honor, Georgetown U. Law Ctr., 1986, Marshall-Wythe Medallion, Coll. of William and Mary Sch. Law, 1996, Outstanding Achievement award, Tax Soc. NYU, 1993, Vicenial medal, Georgetown U., 2000, Disting. Svc. award, ABA section of Taxation, 2006. Fellow: Am. Bar Found. (bd. dirs. 2000—03), Am. Coll. Tax Counsel; mem.: ABA (mem. com. corp. taxation, tax sect. from 1973, chmn. com. simplification 1979—81, mem. tax sect. coun. 1984—87, tax systems task force 1995—97), Assn. Bar City N.Y. (chmn. com. taxation 1977—79, mem. audit com. 1980—81), N.Y. State Bar Assn. (mem. tax sect. exec. com. from 1969, chmn. tax sect. 1975, ho. of dels. 1976—77), Am. Law Inst. (cons. Fed. Income Tax Project 1974—93). Home: Washington, DC. Died June 27, 2010.

GITTELL, MARILYN, political scientist, educator; b. NYC, Apr. 3, 1931; d. Julius and Rose (Meyerson) Jacobs; m. Irwin Gittell, Aug. 20, 1950 (dec. 2005); children: Amy, Ross. BA, Bklyn. Coll., 1952; MPA, NY U., 1953, PhD, 1960. Instr. polit. sci. Queens Coll., CUNY, 1960—62, asst. prof., 1960—62, assoc. prof., 1965—67, prof., 1967—71, prof. urban studies, 1971—73; dir. Inst. Cmty. Studies, 1967—73, chmn. dept. urban studies, 1971—73; prof. polit. sci. Bklyn. Coll., CU, 1973—78, asst. v.p. and assoc. provost, 1973—78; prof. polit. sci. CUNY, 1978—2010. Cons. NJ Dept. Higher Edn., Ford Found., Nat. Inst. Edn. Author: Local Control in Education, 1972; co-author (with Fantini): Decentralization: Achieving Reform, 1973; author: School Boards and School Policy, 1973; co-author (with Cook and Mack): City Life: A Documentary History of the American City, 1973; author: What Was It Like: When Your Grandparents Were Your Age, 1976, Limits to Participation: The Decline of Community Organizations, 1980, State Politics and the New Federalism, 1986. Mem. White House Conf. Children and Youth, 1970, Queens Lay Advocate Svc., from 1972; mem. cmty. com. Met. Mus. Art, from 1971; mem. assoc. task force on manpower US Dept. Labor, 1970—74; Mem. adv. bd. PR Rsch. Ctr., Washington, 1972. Mem.: Phi Beta Kappa. Home: New York, NY. Died Feb. 26, 2010.

GIUTTARI, THEODORE RICHARD, lawyer; b. Jersey City, Feb. 4, 1931; s. Anthony and Giovanna (Santamaria) Giuttari; m. Maria Elena Domingo, Feb. 25, 1973; children: Joanna, Melissa, Jennifer. BA, Fordham U., 1952, LLB, 1958; MIA, Columbia U., 1954, MA in Polit. Sci., 1958, PhD in Polit. Sci., 1969. Bar: NY 1958, NJ 1959, US Dist. Ct. (so. dist.) NY 1958, US Dist. Ct. NJ 1959. Assoc. Bigham Englar Jones & Houston, NYC, 1963—69; internat. counsel Norwich Internat., NYC, 1969—73; internat. atty. Am. Home Products Corp., NYC, from 1973. Author: American Law of Sovereign Immunity, 1970. Mem.: Internat. Law Assn. (hon. sec.-treas. Am. br. 1970—73, mem. exec. com. from 1973). Home: Jersey City, NJ. Died Aug. 30, 2010.

GLAD, BETTY, political scientist, educator; b. Salt Lake City, Sept. 27, 1927; d. Harluf Anderson and Edna Janette (Geertsen) G.; m. Irving T. Diamond, Sept., 1954 (div. Jan. 1957). BS magna cum laude, U. Utah, 1949; PhD, U. Chgo., 1962. Instr. Mt. Holyoke Coll., 1958-59; lectr., instr. Bklyn. Coll., 1960-64; from asst. prof. to assoc. prof. U. Ill., Urbana, 1964-72, prof., 1973-89, dept. head, 1972-73; prof. U. S.C., Columbia, 1989-93, Caroline disting. prof., 1993-95, Olin D. Johnston prof., 1995—2008; Johnston prof. emeritus, from 2008. Mem. hist. adv. com. U.S. Dept. State, Washington, 1990-95; rev. panelist NEH, Washington, 1980-83; chair Midwest Univs. Seminar in U.S. Fgn. Policy, 1972. Author: Charles Evans Hughes and the Illusion of Innocence, 1966, Jimmy Carter: In Search of the Great White House, 1980, Key Pittman: Tragedy of a Senate Insider, 1985, An Outsider In The White House: Jimmy Carter, His Advisor & The Making of US Foreign Policy, 2009; editor, contrbr. Psychological Dimension of War, 1990, The Russian Transformation, 1999, Striking First, 2004; mem. numerous editl. bds., 1968-73; contbr. articles to profl. jours.; appeared on numerous TV and radio shows. Nat. Pub. Svc. fellow, 1952, Kappa Kappa Gamma nat. fellow, 1952, Disting. Alumnus award Coll. of Behavioral and Social Scis., U. Utah, 2007. Mem. Internat. Soc. for Polit. Psychology (pres. 1993-94, Harold Lasswell award 1997), Am. Polit. Sci. Assn. (treas. 1978-79, v.p. 1994-95, pres. Presidency Rsch. Group 1989-90, Mentor of Distinction award 1989, Women's Caucus, Frank Goodnow award 2000), U. Utah Beehive Soc., Mortar Bd., Phi Beta Kappa (women's caucus). Democrat. Unitarian Universalist. Avocations: jazz, piano, dance, theater, travel. Home: Columbia, SC. Died Aug. 5, 2010.

GLASSNER, MARTIN IRA, geography educator; b. Plainfield, NJ, July 7, 1932; s. Samuel and Augusta (Lerner) G.; m. Renée Gewirtzman, June 19, 1955; children: Karen Aline, Aleta Bonny, Cindy Miriam. BA in Geography and Polit. Sci., Syracuse U., 1953, postgrad., 1953, U. Wis., 1953-54, George Williams Coll., 1957; MA in Geography and Polit. Sci., Calif. State U., Fullerton, 1964; postgrad., U. Am., Mexico, 1965; PhD in Internat. Rels., Claremont Grad. Sch., 1968. Fgn. svc. officer U.S. Dept. State, various locations, 1958-63; lectr. polit. sci. Chapman Coll., Orange, Calif., 1964-65; asst. prof. social sci. Calif. State Poly. Coll., Pomona, 1965-67; asst. prof. polit. sci. U. Puget Sound, Tacoma, Wash., 1967-68;

from asst. prof. to prof. geography So. Conn. State U., New Haven, from 1968, acting chmn. dept. geography, 1970, coord. Latin Am. Studies program, 1975-77, coord. Marine Studies program, 1981-92, chmn. dept. geography, 1982-94, Univ. prof. geography, 1993-95, prof. emeritus, from 1995. Bd. dirs. Conn. State U. Rsch. Found., 1986-89; vis. sr. lectr. geography U. Haifa, Israel, 1971-72; lectr. polit. sci. U. New Haven, West Haven, 1973-75; advisor to Govt. of Nepal under UN Devel. Program, summer 1976; cons. UN Devel. Program, mission to various countries, summer 1979, winter 1984, summer 1990; mem. group of experts on land-locked states UN Conf. on Trade and Devel., 1984; vis. prof. Universidad de Atacama, Chile, 1985, Yellow River U., China, 1989; lectr. in field. Author: Access to the Sea for Developing Land-Locked States, 1970, Systematic Political Geography, 3d edit., 1980, 4th edit., 1988, Bibliography on Land-Locked States, 1980, 2d edit., 1986, 3d edit., 1991, 4th edit., 1995, Neptune's Domain: A Political Geography of the Sea, 1990, Political Geography, 1992, 2d edit., 1996; editor: Global Resources: Challenges of Interdependence, 1983; co-editor (with Nikos Papakakis) The International Law of the Sea and Marine Affairs: A Bibliography, 1984; contbr. articles, book revs. to jours. With U.S. Army. Mem. Internat. Studies Assn., Assn. Am. Geographers (mem. Marine Geography Specialty Group and Polit. Geography Specialty Group 1974—, bd. dirs. Polit. Geography Specialty Group 1986-88, 95—), Itnernat. Law Assn. (mem. com. on land-locked states 1975-84, com. on Antarctica 1983-91), Am. Soc. Internat. Law, Conf. Latin Americanist Geographers (bd. dirs. 1977-80, com. on membership and nominations 1979-82), Acad. Coun. on UN System, Internat. Geog. Union. Avocations: collecting stamps, maps, folklore, flags. Home: Hamden, Conn. Died Aug. 21, 2010.

GLENN, JAMES FRANCIS, urologist, educator; b. Lexington, Ky., May 10, 1928; s. Cambridge Francis and Martha (Morrow) G.; children: Cambridge Francis II, Sara Brooke, Nancy Carrick, James Morrison Woodworth; m. Gay Elste Darsie, Jan. 11, 2002. Student (Yale Regional scholar), Univ. Sch., Lexington, 1946; BA in Gen. Sci. (Bausch and Lomb Nat. Sci. scholar), U. Rochester, 1949; MD, Duke U., 1952; DSc, U. Ky., 1998, Transylvania U., 2004. Diplomate Am. Bd. Urology (mem.), Nat. Bd. Med. Examiners. Intern Peter Bent Brigham Hosp., Boston, 1952-54; asst. resident urology Duke U. Med. Ctr., 1956-58, resident, 1958-59; instr. urology Duke U., 1958-59, prof., chief div. urology, 1963-80; asst. prof. Yale U., 1959-61; assoc. prof. Bowman Gray Sch. Medicine, Wake Forest Coll., 1961-63; practice medicine specializing in urology New Haven, 1959-61, Winston-Salem, N.C., 1961-63, Durham, N.C., 1963-80; prof. surgery, dean Med. Sch., Emory U., 1980-83; pres. Mt. Sinai Med. Ctr., 1983-87; prof. surgery U. Ky. Coll. Medicine, Lexington, from 1987; CEO Markey Cancer Ctr., 1989-93; chief staff Univ. Hosp., Lexington, 1993-95, chmn. dept. surgery, 1996-97. Sci. dir. Coun. for Tobacco Rsch. U.S.A., 1987-91, chmn. bd., 1991—. Contbg. author: Renal Neoplasia, 1967, Urodynamics, 1971, Textbook of Surgery, 1972, Plastic and Reconstructive Surgery of The Genital Area, 1973, Current Operative Urology, 1975, Campbell's Urology, 1977; author, editor: Diagnostic Urology, 1964, Ureteral Reflux in Children, 1966, Urologic Surgery, 1969, rev. edit., 1975, 84, 90; contbr. numerous articles to profl. jours. Capt. M.C., USAF, 1954-56. Mem. Am. Assn. Genitourinary Surgeons (pres. 1992-93, hon. 1998), Am. Surg. Assn., ACS, AMA (sec. sect. urology 1972-73, chmn. 1975-77), Assn. Am. Med. Colls., Internat. Urol Soc. (v.p. 1985-91, pres. 1991-94), Clin. Soc. Genito-Urinary Surgeons (pres. 1990-91), N.Y. Acad. Medicine, Soc. Pediatric Urology (pres. 1972-73), Soc. Pelvic Surgeons (pres. 1980-81), Soc. Univ. Surgeons, Soc. Univ. Urologists (pres. 1971-72), Royal Coll. Surgeons (hon. fellow 1987), German Urol. Assn. (hon.), Australasian Urologic Soc. (hon.), Brit. Assn. Urologic Surgeons (hon.) Died June 10, 2009.

GLICK, JANE MILLS, retired biomedical researcher; b. Memphis, Nov. 26, 1943; d. Albert Axtell Jr. and Mary Louise (Baynes) Mills; m. John Harrison Glick, May 25, 1968; children: Katherine Anne, Sarah Stewart. AB, Randolph-Macon Woman's Coll., 1965; PhD, Columbia U., 1971. Postdoctoral trainee NIH, Bethesda, Md., 1971-73; postdoctoral fellow Sch. of Medicine Stanford (Calif.) U., 1973-74; rsch. asst. prof. biochemistry Sch. Dental Medicine U. Pa., Phila., 1974-77; asst. prof. biochemistry Med. Coll. Pa., Phila., 1977-82, assoc. prof. biochemistry, 1982-90, prof. biochemistry, 1990-94; sr. rsch. investigator Inst. Human Gene Therapy Sch. Medicine U. Pa., 1994—2002, faculty adminstr. cell and molecular biology group, 2002—08. Mem. metabolism study sect. NIH, 1993—97; adj. assoc. prof. Sch. Medicine U. Pa., 1996—2008. Assoc. editor: Jour. Lipid Rsch., 1985-86, mem. editorial bd., 1987-99; contbr. articles to profl. jours. Trustee Episcopal Acad., Merion, Pa., 1989-95, Swarthmore Presbyn. Ch., 1995-97, pres. 1997. Recipient Rsch. Svc. award NIH, 1975-77, Young Investigator award, 1980-83, Teaching award Lindback Found., 1985. Mem. AAAS, AAUP (sec. 1990-92), Arteriosclerosis Coun. Am. Heart Assn. (program com. 1990-93), Am. Soc. for Biochemistry and Molecular Biology, Am. Soc. for Human Genetics, Phi Beta Kappa, Sigma Xi. Presbyterian. Home: Swarthmore, Pa. Died Nov. 15, 2009.

GOAR, ROBERT JEFFERSON, classical languages educator; b. Houston, May 20, 1932; s. Everett Logan and Josephine Eleise (Hailey) G.; m. Mary Elizabeth Hocken, July 17, 1965 (div. Oct. 1977); children: Colin Ramsay, Dudley Clive. AB, Harvard Coll., 1954; AM, Harvard U., 1958, PhD, 1968. Instr. in classics and English UN Internat. Sch., NYC, 1964-66; prof. classical langs. U. Mass., Amherst, from 1968. Author: Cicero and the State Religion, 1972, The Legend of Cato Uticensis, 1987; contbr. articles to profl. jours. Vol. Hospice of Hampshire County, Northampton, Mass., 1989-92, Cooley Dickinson Hosp., Northampton, 1987—. Served in U.S. Army, 1954-56. Grantee Am. Philos. Soc., 1982-83. Democrat. Roman Catholic. Avocations: films, mountain climbing, travel. Home: Hadley, Mass. Died July 10, 2010.

GODBOLD, JOHN COOPER, federal judge; b. Coy, Ala., Mar. 24, 1920; s. Edwin Condie and Elsie (Williamson) Godbold; m. Elizabeth Showalter, July 18, 1942; children: Susan, Richard, John C., Cornelia. BS, Auburn U., 1940; JD, Harvard U., 1948; LLD (hon.), Samford U., 1981, Auburn U., 1988, Stetson U., 1994. Bar: Ala. 1948. With firm Richard T. Rives, Montgomery, Ala., 1948-49; ptnr. Rives & Godbold, 1949-51, Godbold & Hobbs and successor firms, 1951-66; cir. judge US Ct. Appeals (5th cir.), 1966-81, chief judge, 1981, US Ct. Appeals (11th cir.), 1981-86, sr. judge, 1987—2009; dir. Fed. Jud. Ctr., Washington, 1987-90; prof. law Cumberland Sch. Law, Samford U., 1990—2009. Mem. Fed. Jud. Ctr. Bd., 1976—81. With field arty. US Army, 1941—46. Mem.: FBA, ABA, Montgomery County Bar Assn., Ala. Bar Assn., Phi Kappa Phi, Omicron Delta Kappa, Alpha Tau Omega. Episcopalian. Home: Montgomery, Ala. Died Dec. 22, 2009.

GODCHAUX, WALTER, III, biochemistry educator, researcher; b. New Orleans, Apr. 15, 1939; s. Walter Jr. and Susan (Shaw) G.; m. Martha E. Miller, June 10, 1960 (div. 1988); 1 child, Louise R. SB, MIT, 1960, PhD, 1965. Tchg. asst. dept. biology MIT, Cambridge, 1960-62, NSF grad. fellow, 1961-64; postdoctoral fellow dept. chemistry U. Oreg., 1965-67; postdoctoral fellow dept. microbiology Yale U., New Haven, 1967-70; asst. prof. dept. biology Amherst (Mass.) Coll., 1970-77, rsch. assoc., 1977-79; rsch. assoc. in biol. scis. U. Conn., Storrs, 1979-83, assoc. prof. in residence molecular and cell biology, from 1984, prof. in residence. Presenter in field, 1965—. Mem. editl. bd. Jour. Microbiol. Methods; contbr. articles to sci. jours. Mem. com. on bicycle safety Town of Amherst, 1980-87. Grantee USPHS, 1964-65, NIH, 1970-72; postdoctoral fellow USPHS, 1965-67. Mem. Am. Soc. for Biochemistry and Molecular Biology, Am. Soc. for Microbiology, Sigma Xi. Avocations: computers, fishing, carpentry. Home: Mansfield Center, Conn. Died July 14, 2009.

GODKINS, THOMAS REGIS, university administrator; b. Pitts., Jan. 5, 1944; s. Regis and Ellen K. Godkins; m. Lois Weihiemer Godkins, Dec. 26, 1968; children: T. Scott, Heather O'Shea. Student, Youngstown (Ohio) State U., 1965—66. Physician assistant program Duke U., 1967—69; BS U. Okla., 1974, MPH, 1983; physician's asst. dept. internal medicine and cardiology Mayo Clinic, 1969—72; assoc. dir. physician's assoc. program U. Okla., Oklahoma City Health Scis. Ctr., 1972—81; asst. prof. Coll. Medicine, 1974—77, assoc. prof., from 1977; asst. to provost for adminstrv. affairs U. Okla., from 1981, dir. capital planning, from 1986; staff physician's asst. VA Med. Ctr., Oklahoma City, 1972—87. Contbr. articles to book, articles to profl. jours.; manuscript reviewer Med. Care, 1978—84, mem. editorial bd., 1980—84. Served with USN, 1961—65. Mem.: Am. Pub. Health Assn. Home: Edmond, Okla. Died June 28, 2010.

GODSEY, JOHN DREW, retired minister, theology educator emeritus; b. Bristol, Tenn., Oct. 10, 1922; s. William Clinton and Mary Lynn (Coma) Godsey; m. Emalee Caldwell, June 26, 1943 (dec. Oct. 1993); children: Emalee Lynn Godsey Murphy, John Drew Jr., Suzanne Godsey Douglas, Gretchen Godsey Brownley; m. Cozette Hapney Barker, Sept. 23, 1995. BS, Va. Poly. Inst. and State U., 1947; BD, Drew U., 1953; D.Theol., U. Basel, Switzerland, 1960. Ordained to ministry United Meth. Ch., 1952. Instr. systematic theology, asst. dean Drew U., Madison, N.J., 1956-59, asst. prof., 1959-64, assoc. prof., 1964-66, prof., 1966-68; prof., assoc. dean Wesley Theol. Sem., Washington, 1968-71, prof. systematic theology, 1971-88, emeritus prof., 1988—2010. Author: The Theology of dietrich Bonhoeffer, 1960, Karl Barth's Table Talk, 1963, Preface to Bonhoeffer, 1965, Introduction and Epilogue to Karl Barth's How I Changed My Mind, 1966, The Promise of H. Richard Niebuhr, 1970; co-editor: Ethical Responsibility: Bonhoeffer's Legacy to the Churches, 1981, Dietrich Bonhoeffer, Discipleship, 2000. Mem. Montgomery County Fair Housing Assn., Md. With US Army, 1943—46. Recipient Disting. Svc. Alumni award, Drew U. Theol. Alumni Assn., 1995; Faculty fellow, Am. Assn. Theol. Schs., 1964—65, Fulbright scholar, U. Goettingen, Germany, 1964—65. Mem.: Am.'s Registry Outstanding Profls., New Haven Theol. Discussion Group, Karl Barth Soc. N.Am., Internat. Bonhoeffer Soc. (editor newsletter 1989—92), Bibl. Theologians, Am. Theol. Soc. (pres. 1985—86), Am. Acad. Religion, Common Cause, Alpha Zeta, Phi Kappa Phi, Omicron Delta Kappa. Democrat. Home: Gaithersburg, Md. Died Oct. 12, 2010.

GODWIN, JAMES BECKHAM, retired landscape architect; b. Richmond, Va, Nov. 17, 1918; s. James Bunyan and Carrie (Beckham) G.; m. Rebecca Maude Cade, Feb. 5, 1949 BS, N.C. State U., 1950. Assoc. R.D. Tillson & Assocs., High Point, N.C., 1950-55; ptnr. Godwin & Bell, Raleigh, N.C., 1955-61; pres. James B. Godwin & Assocs., Inc., Raleigh, N.C., from 1961. Pres., Gov.'s Beautification Com., Raleigh, 1967-69; bd. dirs. Keep N.C. Beautiful, Raleigh, 1971—; bd. visitors Louisburg (n.C.) Coll., 1971-80; chmn. travel com. N.C. Art Soc., Raleigh, 1983-84. Served to capt. U.S. Army, 1941-46, PTO Decorated Purple Heart, Bronze Star. Fellow Am. Soc. Landscape Architects (trustee 1966-72). Democrat. Methodist. Avocations: reading, history, gardening, travel. Died May 10, 2009.

GOEBEL, WILLIAM MATHERS, lawyer; b. Jacksonville, Ill., Nov. 5, 1922; s. William George and Elizabeth (Mathers) G.; m. Barbara Leeper, Mar. 10, 1944; children: William Mathers, Helen Elizabeth. AB, Ill. Coll., 1946; JD, U. Mich., 1948. Bar: Ill. 1949. Practice in, Carmi, 1949-59; partner Conger, Elliott, Goebel & Elliott, 1949-59; asst. gen. counsel Ill. Agrl. Assn. (and affiliated cos.), 1959-64; partner Dunn, Goebel, Ulbrich, Morel & Hundman, 1964-89, of counsel, 1989-96; lectr. dept. ednl. adminstrn. Ill. State U. Instr. Ill. Wesleyan U. Contbr. to: U. Ill. Law Forum, 1962. Mem. Ill. Citizens Com. for Uniform Comml. Code; mem. Ill. Sch. Problems Commn., 1965-69; bd. dirs. Bloomington-Normal Symphony Soc., 1967-73; trustee Brokaw Hosp., Normal, Ill., 1964-69; sec. bd. trustees, mem. exec. com. Ill. Wesleyan U., Bloomington, 1964-94. Served with AUS, World War II. Fellow Am. Bar Found., Ill. Bar Found.; mem. Am. Judicature Soc., ABA, Ill. Bar Assn. (past council chmn. comml. banking and bankruptcy law sect., mem. fed. judiciary appointments com. 1976-80), McLean County Bar Assn. (pres. 1983-84) Clubs: Bloomington Country. Lodges: Rotary. Democrat. Presbyterian. Home: Bloomington, Ill. Died Feb. 5, 2009.

GOETTE, RICHARD A., lawyer; b. Rochester, NY, Dec. 22, 1948; BA, Lawrence U., 1971; JD, Southwestern U., 1975. Bar: Calif. 1975, D.C. 1980. Ptnr. Baker & Hostetler, LA. Mem. ABA, State Bar Calif., Maritime Law Assn. U.S. Died July 29, 2010.

GOFORTH, CAROLYN MAE, artist; b. Toledo, June 7, 1931; d. Herbert Ernest John and Frieda Elsie (Reeck) Graves; m. John William Goforth, Dec. 27, 1952; children: David J., Cynthia L. Goforth Sawyer, Mark W., Laurie A. Goforth Hullinger. BS in Edn., Bowling Green State U., 1953, MA, 1977. Cert. tchr., Ohio. Art tchr. Columbus (Ohio) Pub. Schs., 1953-55, Toledo Pub. Schs., 1955-86; mgr. and co-owner Prestige Studio and Gallery, Toledo, from 1988. Art judge, 1980—. Exhibited watercolors in group shows: Toledo Mus. Art, Grandpa's Jug, 1988; First Nat. Bank, Garden Forms, 1986 (3rd place); Athena, Winter, 1987 (1st place), Specturm, Oak Creek Canyon, 1987 (Best of Show). V.p. Providence Luth. Ch. Women, 1992; mem. com. to select outstanding arts grad. Bowling Green State U., 1992—. Nominated to top 25 grads., Bowling Green State U., 1989; named Art Tchr. of Yr., Gov. award, Ohio, 1981, Outstanding Tchr., Toledo Pub. Schs., 1981; recipient award of Honor State Art Exhibit, 1989. Mem. Nat. League Am. Pen Women (art exhibit award of honor 1989), Ohio League Am. Pen Women (treas. N.W. br. 1990), Toledo League Am. Pen Women, Ladies Oriental Shrine of N.Am., Athena, Spectrum (bd. dirs. 1986-88), Friends of Photography (edn. com. 1988-90), Toledo Artist Club, Nat. Women in Arts. Home: Toledo, Ohio. Died Aug. 17, 2010.

GOLDBERG, IRA BARRY, physical chemist; b. Bklyn., Apr. 10, 1943; s. Murray M. and Esther R. (Lederman) Goldberg; m. Susan Marilyn Winterstein, Dec. 17, 1966; children: Elizabeth, Adam, Rachel. AB, Adelphi U., 1964; PhD, U. Minn., 1969. Rsch. fellow U. Tex., Austin, 1969—71; mem. tech. staff Rockwell Sci. Ctr., Thousand Oaks, Calif., from 1971. Contbr. articles to profl. jours. Pres. Temple Etz Chaim, Thousand Oaks. Mem.: Soc. Magnetic Resonance (regional chpt. pres. 1980—82), Am. Chem. Soc., Am. Phys. Soc., Sigma Xi. Jewish. Achievements include patents in field; research in microwave and magnetic properites and characterization. Home: Thousand Oaks, Calif. Died Jan. 13, 2010.

GOLDBERG, IVAN D., microbiologist, educator; b. Phila., May 13, 1934; s. Max and Frances Goldberg; m. Noveta McCracken, July 27, 1979; children— Micki, Judy, Lisa; stepchildren— Nick, Vikki Russell AB, U. Pa., 1956; PhD, U. Ill., 1961. Postdoctoral fellow Rutgers U., 1961-62; postdoctoral Oreg. State U., 1962-63; NRC postdoctoral research assoc. U.S. Army Biol. Labs., Frederick, Md., 1963-65, microbial geneticist, 1965-71; assoc. prof. dept. microbiology U. Kans. Sch. Medicine, Kansas City, 1971-77, prof., from 1977. Contbr. articles to profl. jours. NIH grantee; recipient Leroy D. Fothergill Sci. award, 1970 Mem. Am. Soc. Microbiology (pres. Mo. Valley br. 1974), Sigma Xi Democrat. Jewish. Home: Shawnee Mission, Kans. Died Apr. 29, 2009.

GOLDBERG, LEONARD MARVIN, lawyer; b. Jersey City, Mar. 21, 1937; s. Jack Geddy and Ida Reva (Steinberg) G.; m. Susan Lee Horstein, Aug. 7, 1960; children: Mark Jay, Philip Seth. AB magna cum laude, Tufts U., 1957; JD magna cum laude, Harvard U., 1960. 010Bar: N.J. 1960, U.S. Tax Ct. 1964, N.Y. 1966. Trial atty. tax divsn. Dept. Justice, Washington, 1960-64; assoc. Roberts & Holland, NYC, 1964-70; ptnr. Clapp & Eisenberg, Newark, 1970-79; sr. ptnr. Goldberg, Mufson & Spar (formerly Goldberg & Stark), West Orange, NJ, from 1979. Lectr. Practicing Law Inst., ABA Taxation Soc., ABA Ctr. for Continuing Edn., N.J. Inst. CLE, Tenn. Fed. Tax Inst., Fairleigh Dickinson U. Tax Inst., Seton Hall U. Tax Inst., Estate Planning Couns.; N.J. del. to lawyers' liaison com. Mid-Atlantic region IRS, 1973-76. chmn. West Orange pub. edn. com., 1976-77, mem. Am. Jewish Com.; co-chmn. lawyers div., trustee Met. N.J. State of Israel Bonds, 1989-92; v.p., trustee Congl. Oheb Shalom, So. Orange, N.J., 1990-92; trustee Cong. Agudath Israel, Caldwell, N.J., 2000—; treas. Jewish Edn. Assn., 2003—; pres. Oheb Shalom Hebrew Free Loan Soc., 1990-96. Fellow Am. Coll. Trust and Estate Counsel; mem. (exec. counc., 1969—) ABA, N.J. Bar Assn. (chmn. taxation sect. 1973-75, chmn. small law firms comm. taxation sect.), N.Y. State Bar Assn., Essex County Bar Assn. (chmn. tax com. 1988-89), Estate Planning Coun. No. N.J., Internat. Assn. Jewish Lawyers and Jurists. Contbr. articles to profl. jours. Contbr. articles to profl. jours. Home: Livingston, NJ. Died Jan. 6, 2009.

GOLDBERG, ROBERT MYRON, corporate financial executive; b. Bklyn., Jan. 27, 1937; s. Alexander and Edith (Kirchmar) Goldberg; m. Jane Anne Wowk Goldberg, Oct. 26, 1968; 1 child, Jennifer Jane. Student, U. RI, 1956—61. Mgr. Albarn Corp., Providence, 1960—65; with Old Stone Bank, Providence, from 1966, sys. officer, sr. project leader, 1970—74, asst. v.p., mgr. computer programming, 1974—80; v.p., mgr. Corp. Mgmt. Info. Ctr., 1981, End-User Computing, 1987, Corp. Info. Ctr., from 1981; cons. in field; tchr. course sys. planning and design, 1978—81. Bd. dirs. United Cerebral Palsy RI, 1978—81, from 1984, chmn. ops. ann. telethon, from 1982, pres. RI chpt., from 1986; vice chmn. bus. adv. coun. Warwick Voc-Tech. Sch., RI, from 1976; chmn. West Warwick Vocat. Tech. Coun, 1983—87. Mem.: Data Processing Mgmt. Assn. Home: Coventry, RI. Died Aug. 26, 2009.

GOLDBERGER, ARTHUR STANLEY, economics professor; b. NYC, Nov. 20, 1930; s. David M. and Martha (Greenwald) G.; m. Iefke Engelsman, Aug. 19, 1957; children: Nina Judith, Nicholas Bernard. BS, N.Y.U., 1951; MA, U. Mich., 1952, PhD, 1958. Acting asst. prof. econs. Stanford U., 1956-59; assoc. prof. econs. U. Wis., 1960- 63, prof., 1963-70, H.M. Groves prof., 1970-79, Vilas research prof., 1979-98, prof. emeritus, from 1998. Vis. prof. Center Planning and Econ. Rsch., Athens, Greece, 1964-65, U. Hawaii, 1969, 71, Stanford U., 1990, 96, 2000; Keynes vis. prof. U. Essex, 1968-69. Author: (with L.R. Klein) An Econometric Model of the United States, 1929-52, 1955, Impact Multipliers and Dynamic Properties, 1959, Econometric Theory, 1964, Topics in Regression Analysis, 1968, Functional Form and Utility, 1987, A Course in Econometrics, 1991, Introductory Econometrics, 1998; editor: (with O.D. Duncan) Structural Equation Models in the Social Sciences, 1973, (with D.J. Aigner) Latent Variables in Socioeconomic Models, 1976; Assoc. editor: Jour. Econometrics, 1973-77; bd. editors: Am. Econ. Rev, 1964-66, Jour. Econ. Lit, 1975-77. Fulbright fellow Netherlands Sch. Econs., 1955-56, 59-60; fellow Ctr. for Advanced Study in Behavioral Scis., Stanford, 1976-77, 80-81; Guggenheim fellow Stanford U., 1972-73, 85. Fellow Am. Statis. Assn., Econometric Soc. (council 1975-80, 82-87); mem. Am. Econ. Assn. (Disting. fellow 1988), Nat. Acad. Scis., Royal Netherlands Acad. Scis. Home: Madison, Wis. Died Dec. 11, 2009.

GOLDEN, THOMAS M., federal judge; b. Pottsville, Pa., Nov. 1, 1947; BA, Pa. State U., 1969; JD, Dickinson Sch. Law, 1972. Mng. ptnr. Golden Masano Bradley, 1972—2006; judge US Dist. Ct. (Ea. dist.) Pa., Phila., from 2006. Mem. adv. bd. Nat. Penn Bank. Mem. adv. bd. Jesuit Ctr. for Spirtual Growth. Fellow: Pa. Bar Found.; mem.: Pa. Bar Assn. (pres. 2003—04, pres.-elect, House of Dels., zone 2 gov., vice chair editl. com., chair client and cmty. rels. com., task force for quality of life/balance, task force on entities and ops., Spl. Achievement award 2000), Berks County Bar Assn. (dir. 1990—93, pres. 1992), Berks County Golf Assn. (past pres.). Died July 31, 2010.

GOLDFARB, BERNARD SANFORD, lawyer; b. Cleve., Apr. 15, 1917; s. Harry and Esther (Lenson) Goldfarb; m. Barbara Brofman Goldfarb, Jan. 4, 1966; children: Meredith Stacy, Lauren Beth. AB, Case Western Res. U., 1938, JD, 1940. Bar: Ohio 1940. Since practiced in, Cleve.; sr. ptnr. firm Goldfarb & Reznick, 1967-95; pvt. practice Cleve., from 1997. Spl. counsel to atty. gen. Ohio, 1950, 1971—74; mem. Ohio Commn. Uniform Traffic Rules, 1973—80. Contbr. articles to profl. jours. With USAAF, 1942—45. Mem.: ABA, Cuyahoga County Bar Assn., Greater Cleve. Bar Assn., Ohio Bar Assn. Home: Pepper Pike, Ohio. Died July 25, 2009.

GOLDFIELD, ALFRED SHERMAN, lawyer; b. Hartford, Conn., July 5, 1939; s. Max and Anne (Gersten) Goldfield; m. Joan M. Strassburger Goldfield, Feb. 11, 1971; children: Amanda, Alexis. BA, Yale Coll., 1961; JD, Columbia U., 1964. Bar: NY 1964, US Dist. Ct. (so. and ea. dists.) NY 1966, US Supreme Ct. 1970, Fla. 1974. Ptnr. Greenfield Stein & Senior LLP, NYC. Pres. Manhattan Theatre Club, 1973—75, dir., from 1973; sec., treas., dir. Ensemble Studio Theatre; mem. Manhattan Cmty. Bd. No. 8, from 1981; sec., dir. NY Found. Sr. Citizens Inc., from 1981. Mem.: ABA, Assn. Bar City NY, NY State Bar Assn., India House, Grollier, Elizabethan, Yale Club NYC. Died Nov. 4, 2009.

GOLDHABER, GERSON, astrophysicist, researcher; b. Chemnitz, Germany, Feb. 20, 1924; came to US, 1948, naturalized, 1953; s. Charles and Ethel (Frisch) G.; m. Judith Margoshes, May 30, 1969; children: Amos Nathaniel, Michaela Shally, Shaya Alexandra M.Sc., Hebrew U., Jerusalem, 1947; PhD, U. Wis., 1950; PhD honoris causus, U. Stockholm, 1986. Instr. Columbia U., NYC, 1950-53; acting asst. prof. physics U. Calif.-Berkeley, 1953-54, asst. prof., 1954-58, assoc. prof., 1958-63, prof. physics, 1963-92, prof. physics emeritus, 1992—2010, Miller research prof. Miller Inst. Basic Sci., 1958-59, 75-76, 84-85, prof. Grad. Sch., 1994—2010; Morris Loeb lectr. in physics Harvard U., 1976-77. Co-author (with R.N. Cahn): (textbook) The Experimental Foundations of Particle Physics, 1988; co-author:, 2009. Named Calif. Scientist of Yr., 1977, Sci. Assoc., CERN, 1986. Gruber prize in Cosmology, 2007; Ford Found. fellow CERN, 1960-61; Guggenheim fellow CERN, 1972-73. Fellow Am. Phys. Soc. (Panofsky prize 1991), Sigma Xi; mem. Am. Astron. Soc., Royal Swedish Acad. Sci. (fgn.), Nat. Acad. Sci. Achievements include discovery of the antiproton annihilation process; Bose-Einstein nature of Pions; J/Psi and Psion spectroscopy; charmed Mesons; dark energy. Avocations: drawing, painting. Died July 19, 2010.

GOLDING, WILLIAM M., former state representative; b. Manchester, NH, Apr. 16, 1928; m. Rosalyn L. Golding, 1953; four children, six stepchildren. BS, USN Postgrad. Sch., 1961; postgrad., Coll. Holy Cross, Worcester, Mass., USN War Coll., 1962. Commd. USN, 1946, advanced through grades to comdr., ret., 1967; Rep. rep. N.H. Ho. Reps., 1996-98; energy officer N.H., 1992; sec. Manchester Rep. Com. N.H. Ho. Reps., 1994-98, 2d vice-chmn. Manchester Rep. Com., 1997-99. Active Concord Cmty. Players, N.H., Mus. N.H. Hist. Mem. Navy League (sec., 1986, treas. 1987-96). Roman Catholic. Home: Manchester, NH. Died May 31, 2009.

GOLDMAN, ALAN JOSEPH, mathematician, educator; b. NYC, Mar. 2, 1932; married; 1 child. BA, Bklyn. Coll., 1952; MA, Princeton U., 1954, PhD in Math., 1956. Instr. Princeton U., 1955-56; mathematician Nat. Bur. Standards, 1956-61, chief ops. rschr., 1961-79, dep. chief. Applied Math Divsn., 1968-78; prof. math. sci. Johns Hopkins U., 1979—99, prof. math. sci. emeritus, 1999—2010. Lectr. Am. U., 1956-57, Cath. U., 1957-63; mathematician Nat. Inst. Stanards and Tech., 1979—. Recipient US Dept. Commerce Gold Medal, 1976. Mem. NAE, Math Assn. Am., Am. Math. Soc.Inst. Ops. Rsch. and Mgmt. Sci., Sigma Xi. Died Feb. 13, 2010.

GOLDMANN, MORTON AARON, cardiologist, educator; b. Chgo., July 11, 1924; s. Harry Ascher and Frieda (Cohon) G.; m. Doris-Jane Tumpeer, July 18, 1951; children: Deborah, Jory, Erica, Leslie BS, U. Ill., 1943, MD, 1946. Diplomate Am. Bd. Internal Medicine. Intern Cook County Hosp., Chgo., 1946-47, resident physician, 1949-52, practice medicine specializing in internal medicine and cardiology Skokie, Ill., 1952—2003, trustee emeritus, from 2003; chief of medicine Rush North Shore Med. Ctr. (formerly Skokie Valley Hosp.), 1964-65, also trustee, 1968—2002, trustee emeritus, from 2002, pres. med. staff, 1968-69, attending physician, med. dir. heart sta. and cardiac rehab. unit, 1973-96, bd. dirs., from 1970; former attending physician Ill. Rsch. Hosp.; former assoc. prof. Abraham Lincoln Sch. Medicine, U. Ill., Chgo.; prof. Cook County Grad. Sch. Medicine. Pres. Heart Assn. North Cook County, 1978-81, North Suburban Assn. Health Resources, 1974-77 Contbr. numerous articles to profl. jours. Capt. M.C., AUS, 1947-49, PTO Fellow ACP, Inst. Medicine Chgo., Am. Coll. Cardiology; mem. AMA, Am. Soc. Internal Medicine, Am. Heart Assn., Ill. Med. Soc., Chgo. Med. Soc., Chgo. Heart Assn. (bd. govs., bd. dirs. 1978-87, bd. trustees 1979-83). Died Aug. 23, 2009.

GOLDSCHMIDT, WALTER ROCHS, anthropologist; b. San Antonio, Feb. 24, 1913; s. Hermann and Gretchen (Rochs) G.; m. Beatrice Lucia Gale, May 27, 1937 (dec.); children: Karl Gale (dec.), Mark Stefan. BA, U. Tex., 1933, MA, 1935; PhD, U. Calif., Berkeley, 1942. Social scientist Bur. Agrl. Econs., 1940-46; mem. faculty UCLA, from 1946, prof. anthropology, 1956—2010, chmn. dept., 1964-69, prof. anthropology & psychiatry, 1970-83, prof. emeritus, 1983—2010. Vis. lectr. Stanford, 1945, U. Calif., Berkeley, 1949, Harvard, 1950 Dir. radio program: Ways of Mankind, 1951- 53, Culture and Ecology in E. Africa, 1960-68. Spl. editor: World of Man Series, Aldine Pub. Co., 1966-75. Author: Small Business and the Community, 1946, As You Sow, 1947, 2nd edit., 1978, Nomlaki Ethnography, 1951, Ways to Justice, 1953, Man's Way, 1959, Exploring the Ways of Mankind, 1960, 3rd edit., 1977, Comparative Functionalism, 1966, Sebei Law, 1967, Kambuya's Cattle, The Legacy of an African Herdsman, 1968, On Being an Anthropologist, 1970, Culture and Behavior of the Sebei, 1976, The Sebei: A Study in Cultural Adaptation, 1986; The Human Career: The Self in The Symbolic World, 1990, The Bridge to Humanity: How Affect Hunger Trumps the Selfish Gene, 2006; co-author: Haa Aaní, Our Land: Tlingit and Haida Land Rights and Use, 1998; editor: The U.S. and Africa, rev, 1963, French edit., 1965, The Anthropology of Franz Boas, 1959, (with H. Hoijer) The Social Anthropology of Latin America, 1970, The Uses of Anthropology, 1979, Anthropology and Public Policy: A Dialogue, 1986, Am. Anthropologist, 1956-59; founding editor: Ethos, 1972-79. Fulbright scholar U.K., 1953; grantee Social Sci. Rsch. Coun., 1953, Wenner-Gren. Found., 1953; NSF postdoctoral fellow, 1964-65, fellow Center Advanced Study Behavioral Scis., 1964-65, sr. sci. fellow NIMH, 1970-75; disting. lectr. U. Indonesia, 1993. Fellow Am. Anthrop. Assn. (pres. 1975-76, Dist. Svc. award 1994), African Studies Assn. (founding, bd. dirs. 1957-60); mem. Southwestern Anthrop. Assn. (pres. 1950-51), Am. Ethnol. Soc. (pres. 1969-70), Phi Beta Kappa, Sigma Xi. Home: Pasadena, Calif. Died Sept. 1, 2010.

GOLDSMITH, STEPHEN ERNEST, lawyer; b. NYC, Dec. 25, 1944; s. Ernest and Charlotte Caroline Marie (Krohn) Goldsmith. BA, Marietta Coll., 1968; JD, Okla. City U., 1976. Bar: Hawaii 1977, US Dist. Ct. Hawaii 1977, US Ct. Appeals (9th cir.) 1977. Assoc. atty. James Krueger Atty. Law, Wailuku, Hawaii, 1977—81; pvt. practice Wailuku, from 1981, Maui, from 1981. Bd. dirs. Maui Philharmonic Soc., 1984—85. Mem.: Western Trial Lawyers (past pres. 1994—95, bd. mem. from 1996), Consumer Lawyers Hawaii (bd. dirs. from 1995), Maui County Bar Assn. (bd. dirs. 1984, adminstrv. v.p., pres. 1986—87), Hawaii Bar Assn., Assn. Plaintiff Lawyers Hawaii (bd. dirs. 1988—89), Assn. Trial Lawyers America (state del. 1984—93), Phi Delta Phi. Home: Makawao, Hawaii. Died June 8, 2009.

GOLDSTEIN, BERNARD, metal recycling, transportation and casino executive; b. Rock Island, Ill., Feb. 5, 1929; s. Morris and Fannie (Borenstein) G.; m. Irene Alter, Dec. 18, 1949; children: Jeffrey, Robert, Kathy, Richard. BA, U. Ill., 1949, LLB, 1951. Bar: Iowa 1951. With Alter Co., Bettendorf, Iowa, from 1951, chmn. bd., from 1979, Isle of Capri Casinos, Inc., St. Louis, from 1992, CEO, 1997—2008. Bd. vis. U. Ill. Coll. Law, 2005—08. Pres. Quad City Jewish Fedn., 1975; mem. U. Ill. Coll. Law Bd. Visitors. Recipient Ernst and Young Entrepreneur of the Yr. award, 1999, Rivers Hall of Fame Achievement award, 1999, Simon Wiesenthal Disting. Cmty. award, Compass award, Passenger Vessel Assn., Outstanding Bus. Leader award, Jewish Fedn. South Palm Beach County, Jerusalem medal, State of Israel Bonds, Disting. Alumnus award, U. Ill. Coll. Law Bd. Visitors, Lifetime Achievement award, Inst. Scrap Recycling Industries, 2008; named Top Performing Gaming CEO of the Yr., Am. Gaming Assn., 2001; named to Hall of Fame, 2008. Jewish. Home: Boca Raton, Fla. Died July 5, 2009.

GOLDSTEIN, ELLIOTT, retired lawyer, director; b. Atlanta, Oct. 23, 1915; s. Max Fullmore and Sarah Ray (London) G.; m. Harriet Weinberg, Oct. 24, 1942 (dec. Dec. 2004); children: Lillian, Ellen. Student, Ga. Sch. Tech., 1932—33; BS, U. Ga., 1936; LLB, Yale U., 1939. Bar: Ga. 1938, D.C. 1977. Asso. firm Little, Powell, Reid & Goldstein, Atlanta, 1939-40; partner firm Atlanta, 1946—77, Washington, 1977—80, Atlanta, from 1980. Spl. counsel com. on standards ofcl. conduct U.S. Ho. of Reps., 1978; mem. legal adv. com. N.Y. Stock Exchange, 1982-85. Author: Counselling the Board of Directors in its Structure, Functions and Compensation, 1985, Georgia Corporation Law and Practice, 1989; contbr. articles to profl. jours. Hon. v.p. Am. Jewish Com.; chmn. Atlanta Hist. Soc., 1990-94. Lt. col. F.A., U.S. Army, 1941-46, ETO. Decorated Bronze Star with V. Fellow ABA Found.; mem. ABA (chmn. com. corp. laws 1979-84, chmn. ad hoc com. ALI Corp. governance project 1982-86, mem. coun. sect. corp. banking and bus. law 1983-86, sr. del. ho. of dels. 1986-94), Am. Law Inst., Ga. Bar Assn., Atlanta Bar Assn., Lawyers Club Atlanta, Commerce Club, Standard Club, Kiwanis Club. Democrat. Home: Atlanta, Ga. Died Sept. 10, 2009.

GOLDSTEIN, HELEN HAFT, writer; b. Albany, Dec. 7, 1921; d. Harry and Clara (Duchen) Haft; m. Irving S. Goldstein, Dec. 16, 1945; children: Ardath Goldstein Weaver, Darra Goldstein Crawford, Jared Haft. AB, Rutgers U., 1943; MSW, Boston U., 1948; MEd, U. Pitts., 1962. Chief psychiat. social worker Brazos County Counseling Svc., Bryan, Tex., 1968—71; dir. social work program W.H. Trentman Mental Health Ctr., Raleigh, NC, 1972—77; dir. social work extension program dept. sociology NC State U., Raleigh, 1977—80; columnist Family Forum, Cary (N.C.) News, from 1974; columnist Kids' Cuisine, Raleigh Times, from 1981; pvt. practise. Author: Kids' Cuisine, 1983, Recipes from Rufus, 1983; editor: Cleaner Times, from 1987. Bd. dirs. N.C. Conf. for Social Svc., 1981—83, YWCA of Wake County, NC, 1982—83; mem. N.C. Legis. Commn. on Med. Cost Containment, 1983—85; mem. adv. bd. Wake County Council on Aging; active sr. citizens adv. com. Town of Cary, 1991—93. Lt. USNR, 1944—46. Named NC Mother of Yr., 1982. Fellow: Am. Orthopsychiat. Assn.; mem.: Am. Pub. Health Assn., Nat. Assn. Social Workers (pres. N.C. chpt. 1981—83), Cary Women's (sec. 1982—84), NC State U. Women's (v.p.). Died Feb. 12, 2010.

GOLLER, NORMAN JAMES, financial executive; b. Milw., Dec. 15, 1930; s. John Adam and Katherine (Von Weber) G.; m. Trudy Barbara Butenhoff, May 8, 1964; children: Daniel, Michael, Christopher, John, Mary Clare. BS in Acctg., Marquette U., 1957; MBA, U. Wis., 1970. CPA, Wis. Acct. Caterpillar Tractor Co., Peoria, Ill., 1957-58; asst. contr. The Journal Co., Milw., 1958-65; contr. Douglas Motors Corp., Milw., 1965-66; successively asst. contr., contr., v.p., chief fin. officer Grede Foundries Inc., Milw., from 1966. Bd. dirs. Roberts Foundry Co., Greenwood, S.C., Grede New Castle (Ind.) Inc., Grede Perm Cast, Inc., Cynthiana, Ky. 1st lt. U.S. Army 1951-53, Korea. Mem. Fin. Execs. Inst. (officer, bd. dirs.), Western Racquet Club (bd. dirs. 1989—). Republican. Roman Catholic. Avocations: tennis, civil war buff, boating. Home: Elm Grove, Wis. Died May 7, 2010.

GONZALEZ, OSWALDO, import/export firm executive; b. Matanzas, Cuba, Dec. 26, 1932; s. Estanislao and Felicita (Rodriquez) G.; came to U.S., 1965, naturalized, 1974; J.D., Havana U., 1959; m. Teresa, Nov. 8, 1950; children—Teresita, Osualdo. Admitted to Havana (Cuba) bar, 1959; pres. Silver Paint Co., Havana, 1954-62, Concreseal Co., Havana, 1957-62, Estrella de Plata, Havana, 1957-62, Argon Trading Co., Havana, 1959-62; pres. Comput Income Inc., Union City, N.J., 1969—; internat. advisor bus. financing in Latin Am. countries. Mem. Cuban Lawyers Assn. Roman Catholic. Clubs: Latin Am. Press of N.Y. (founder), UN Lions. Author: Murallas de Silencio, 1961. Research in art field. Died Dec. 27, 2009.

GOODE, RICHARD BENJAMIN, economist, educator; b. Ft. Worth, July 31, 1916; s. Flavius M. and Laura Nell (Carson) G.; m. Liesel Gottscho, June 23, 1943 (dec. May 2002). AB, Baylor U., 1937; MA, U. Ky., 1939; PhD, U. Wis., 1947. Economist U.S. Bur. Budget, 1941-45, Treasury Dept., 1945-47; asst. prof. econs. U. Chgo., 1947-51; with IMF, Washington, 1951-59, 65-81, dir. fiscal affairs dept., 1965-81; mem. staff Brookings Instn., Washington, 1959-65, guest scholar, 1981-87; professorial lectr. Sch. Advanced Internat. Studies, Johns Hopkins U., 1981-88. Cons. Treasury Dept., 1947-51, UN, 1950, World Bank, 1964. Author: The Corporation Income Tax, 1951; The Individual Income Tax, 1964, rev. edit., 1976; Government Finance in Developing Countries, 1984; Economic Assistance to Developing Countries through the IMF, 1985. Editor Nat. Tax Jour, 1948-51. Mem. Am. Econ. Assn., Royal Econ. Soc., Nat. Tax Assn. (Holland medal for contbns. to study and practice of pub. fin. 1997), Internat. Inst. Pub. Fin., Cosmos Club. Home: Washington, DC. Died July 18, 2010.

GOODELL, WARREN FRANKLIN, retired academic administrator; b. Champaign, Ill., May 10, 1924; s. Warren Franklin and Dorothy Newell (Talbot) G.; m. Suzanne Vassamillet, Aug. 25, 1946; children— Warren Emile, Kenneth Franklin. BS in Engring. Physics, U. Ill., 1944; MA in Physics, Columbia, 1947, PhD in Physics, 1951. Mem. staff Radiation Lab., MIT, 1944-46; assoc. dir. Nevis Cyclotron Lab., Columbia U., NYC, 1951-64, assoc. dir. Office Projects and Grants, 1964-67, v.p. adminstrn., 1967-72; v.p., dean Pleasantville Campus Pace U. (N.Y.), 1972-77; dir. planning Mercy Coll., 1977-87, ret. Trustee Columbia U. Press, 1967-72; dir. Yale-Columbia So. Obs., Inc. Mem. Bd. Edn., Irvington, N.Y., 1957-67. Mem. Nat. Assn. Coll. and U. Bus.

Officers (com. govt. relations 1968-72), Sigma Xi, Phi Kappa Phi, Tau Beta Pi, Beta Theta Pi. Republican. Methodist. Home: Fort Myers, Fla. Died June 28, 2010.

GOODENDAY, KENNETH BENJAMIN, marketing educator; b. London, July 28, 1930; s. Alexander and Minnie (Saunders) Goodenday; m. Lucy Sherman Goodenday, Aug. 31, 1958. BA in English Lit., U. Calif.-Berkeley, 1972, MBA in Fin. Eastern Mich. U., 1977. Product planning mgr. Burlington Industries, NYC, 1953—63, Ernst Ties, San Francisco, 1965—68; ops. mgr. Paragon Resources, Warren, Mich., 1978—80. Adj. prof. mktg. Eastern Mich. U., Ypsilanti, 1980—84, U. Toledo, 1984—89, 1993—96, Ea. Mich. U., 1990—93; ret., 1996. Home: Swanton, Ohio. Died July 1, 2010.

GOODGOLD, JOSEPH, physician, educator; b. NYC, Mar. 21, 1920; s. Ben and Celia (Berr) G.; m. Mildred Simons, May 2, 1942; children: Ellen (Mrs. Daniel Frohwirth), Shelley. BS, Bklyn. Coll., 1942; MD, Middlesex U., 1945. Diplomate: Am. Bd. Phys. Medicine and Rehab., Am. Bd. Electrodiagnostic Medicine. Intern Beth-El Hosp., Brookdale, Bklyn., 1945-46, asst. resident in medicine, 1946-47; fellow Inst. Rehab. Medicine, NYU, Bellevue Med. Ctr., 1953-54, Howard A. Rusk prof. rehab. research, 1975-84; chmn. dept. rehab. medicine NYU Sch. Medicine, 1884-89; cons.-lectr. postgrad. div. N.Y. U. Sch. Medicine (Sch. of Edn.), 1956-89; dir. Electrodiagnostic Service, N.Y. U. Med. Ctr., 1957-89, dir. rehab. med. services, 1981-89. Attending physician dept. rehab. medicine Univ. Hosp., 1960; cons. Brookdale Hosp. Ctr., Manhattan VA Hosp., Morristown Meml. Hosp. Contbr. articles to med. jours. Mem. med. adv. bd. Muscular Dystrophy Assn.; cons. HEW, Social Security Adminstrn., N.Y. State Dept. Vocat. Rehab. Served with M.C. AUS, 1951-53. Fellow Am. Coll. Cardiology, A.C.P., N.Y. Acad. Medicine, N.Y. Acad. Sci.; mem. Am. Assn. Electromyography and Electrodiagnosis (pres. 1966-67), A.M.A., Am. Congress Rehab. Medicine, Am. Rheumatism Assn., Am. Acad. Phys. Medicine and Rehab. (Frank Krusen award 1985), Am. Assn. Acad. Physiatrists (pres. 1973-74), Med. Soc. Kings County. Clubs: Lords Valley Country; University (N.Y.C.). Died Aug. 29, 2009.

GOODHEW, HOWARD RALPH, JR., wholesale executive; b. Manitowoc, Wis., Aug. 28, 1923; m. Marie Walter Goodhew; 5 children. Grad., HS. Credit mgr., br. store supr. Ridge Co., Inc., South Bend, Ind., 1940—46; sec., 1946—56; pres., 1956—86; chmn. bd. dirs., from 1986. Supt. South Bend Water Works, 1964—66, South Bend Utilities, 1966—68; bd. dirs. Nat. Bank & Trust Co., South Bend, 1st Interstate Bank, Ind.; sec., dir. H.J. Schrader Co., 1963—69, Grunow Authorized Svc., Inc., 1966—69; pres. St. Joe Sales Co., 1949—55, P.B.M. Inc., 1968—79; chmn. bd. St. Joe Distbg. Co., from 1984; pres. HRG Inc., from 1980; pres., chmn. bd., nat. pronto dir. Distbrs. Assn., from 1991. Mem. South Bend Crime Commn., from 1974; pres. Better Bus. Bur. South Bend-Mishawaka, 1961—62, 1974—75; mem. adv. bd. Adrian Coll. Found., 1958—75; deacon 1st Presbyn. Ch., South Bend, 1963—66, trustee, 1967—76; bd. dirs. United Cmty. Svcs. St. Joseph County, Inc., 1966—70; mem. bd. mgrs. cmty. planning div. United Cmty. Svc., 1965—70; bd. dirs. Meml. Hosp. South Bend, 1969; chmn. bldg. com., 1960—72; bd. dirs. South Bend Cmty. Sch. Corp., 1969—73, pres., 1971—72; mem. Ind. Wage Adjustment Bd., 1969—74; fin. chmn. Ind. Rep. 3d Dist., 1964—70, South Bend City Rep. Com., 1963, 1967, St. Joseph County Rep. Com., 1964—65, 1970; mem. St. Joseph County Rep. Adv. Bd., from 1964; mayor South Bend, 1963; dir., chmn. bd. dirs. Nat. Pronto, from 1984; v.p. South Bend Urban Enterprise Assocs., from 1986; chmn. Local Property Tax Control Bd. Ind. State, 1981—91; pres. South Bend Mid. Schs. Bldg. Corp., from 1974, South Bend Pub. Libr. Leasing Corp., from 1981, Brethern Care South Bend, Inc., 1974—83, St. Joseph County Parks Found., 1991. With US Army, World War II. Decorated Bronze Star; recipient GEORGE award, Mishawaka Enterprise-Record Newspaper, 1975, Sagamore of the Wabash award, Ind. Govs., 1976, 1984, Rotary Cmty. Svc. award, 1983. Mem.: South Bend-Mishawaka Area C. of C. (dir. 1968—84, v.p. 1970—82), Distbrs. Inst., South Gateway Improvement Assn. (pres. from 1984), Automotive Svc. Industries Assn., Rotary. Home: South Bend, Ind. Died Dec. 9, 2009.

GOODING, JUDSON, writer; b. Rochester, Minn., Oct. 12, 1926; s. Arthur Faitoute and Frances (Judson) G.; m. Françoise Ridoux, June 21, 1952; children: Amélie, Timothy. Grad. with honors, Yale U., 1948; diplome d'Études Françaises, U. Paris, 1950. Staff writer Dept. Army, Hdqrs. EUCOM, Germany, 1950-52; script writer Affiliated Film Producers, NYC, 1952-53; news writer WCCO-CBS, Mpls., 1953; reporter Mpls. Tribune, 1953-57, Life mag., NYC, 1957-60, fgn. corr. Paris, 1960-62, Time mag., Paris, 1962-65; chief of bur. Time-Life News Service, San Francisco, 1966-68; edn. editor Time mag., NYC, 1968-69; assoc. editor Fortune mag., 1969-73; v.p. Urban Research Corp.; also editor Trend Report, Chgo., 1973-75; mng. partner Trend Analysis Assocs., from 1975; exec. editor Next Mag., NYC, 1979-81, contbg. editor, 1981-82; counselor for pub. affairs U.S. Permanent Del. to UNESCO, 1982-84. Vis. lectr. in journalism U. Paris, Ecole Nationale d'Administration, also Togo, Kenya, Zaire, Senegal and Nigeria; writing cons. UN, Ford Found., Am. Assembly, also corps.; vis. lectr. in journalism, Barbados, Grenada, Dominica, Haiti and Martinique Author: The Job Revolution, 1972; contbr. to: American Dreams, The Environment, The Hippies, The Survival Equation, The Failure of Success; Contbr. articles to popular mags. and profl. jours. Bd. patrons Wilson Ctr., Faribault, Minn.; mem. program com. Internat. Found. for Cultural Cooperation, Courchevel, France; trustee Friends of John Jay Homestead, Walpole Hist. Soc., Walpole Pub. Libr. Served with USNR, 1944-46. Recipient 1st place award U. Mo. Sch. Journalism Penney-Mo., 1980, hon. certificate Program Mgmt. Devel. Harvard U. Grad. Sch., Disting. Alumnus award Middlesex Sch., 1994. Mem. Inst. Current World Affairs (elected), Common Cause, World Future Soc., Nat. Trust Hist. Preservation, Am. Soc. Journalists and Authors, Mensa. Clubs: Elizabethan (New Haven); Century Assn. (N.Y.C.), Yale (N.Y.C.); Bedford Bicycle Polo (founder, co-capt.); Polo de Paris, The Travellers (Paris). Home: Keene, NH. Died June 12, 2009.

GOODMAN, MAX A., retired law educator; b. Chgo., May 24, 1924; s. Sam and Nettie (Abramowitz) G.; m. Marlyene Monkarsh, June 2, 1946; children: Jan M., Lauren A. Packard, Melanie Murez. AA, Herzl Jr. Coll., 1943; student, Northwestern U., 1946—47; JD, Loyola U., 1948; LLD (hon.), Southwestern U. Sch. Law, 2000. Bar: Calif. 1948; cert. family law specialist, 1980, 85, 90. Pvt. practice, L.A., 1948-53; ptnr. Goodman, Hirschberg & King, L.A., 1953-81; prof. Southwestern U. Sch. Law, L.A., 1966—2006, prof. emeritus in residence, 2006—09. Lectr. Calif. Continuing Edn. of the Bar, 1971—90. Contbr. articles to profl. jours. Served to cpl. U.S. Army, 1943-45. Mem. ABA (chmn. law sch. curriculum com. family law sect. 1987-88, family law sect. 1987-88, 97-98), State Bar Calif. (del. conf. dels. 1972, 80-87, 91, exec. com. family law sect. 1981-85), Los Angeles County Bar Assn. (chmn. family law sect. 1971-72, editor family law handbook 1974-89). Avocation: bridge. Home: Los Angeles, Calif. Died Dec. 31, 2009.

GOODNOUGH, ROBERT ARTHUR, artist; b. Cortland, NY, Oct. 23, 1917; s. Leo J. and Hariett (Summers) G.; m. Miko Goodnough; children: Kathleen, Philip BFA, Syracuse U., 1940; MA, NYU, 1950; student, New Sch. for Social Research, 1949, Ozenfant Sch. Art, 1950-51, Hoffman Sch. Art, 1951. Instr. painting NYU, 1953, Fieldston Sch., Riverdale, NY, 1953-60, Cornell U., 1960. Contbr. articles to nat. mags.; one-man shows: Tibor de Nagy Gallery, NYC, Andre Emmerich Gallery, NYC, Nina Freudenheim Gallery, Bklyn.; work exhibited in permanent collections: Albright Art Gallery, Buffalo, Art Inst. Chgo., Mus. Modern Art, NYC, Whitney Mus., NYC, NYU Mus., RI Sch. Design Mus., NC Mus. Art, also pvt. collections. Served with US Army, 1941-45. Recipient award Art Inst. Chgo., 1962; Guggenheim fellow, 1972 Died Oct. 2, 2010.

GOODSTEIN, EDWARD MARC, communications executive; b. Bklyn., Feb. 11, 1947; s. Seymour and Shirley Mae (Sklar) Goodstein; m. Phyllis Diamond, Dec. 10, 1975; children: Craig Jackson, Dana Michelle. BS in Bus. Adminstrn., Boston Coll., 1969. Salesman Anixter-Telewire, Jamaica, NY, 1969—72; v.p. TW Comm. Corp., Gt. Neck, NY, 1972—82, pres., from 1982. Bd. dirs. TeleWire Supply Corp., Farmingdale, NY, from 1978. Mem.: IEEE, Clearmeadow Pistol (Levittown, N.Y.). Republican. Jewish. Died Sept. 7, 2009.

GOODY, JOAN EDELMAN, architect; d. Beril and Sylvia (Feldman) Edelman; m. Marvin E. Goody, Dec. 18, 1960 (dec. 1980); m. Peter H. Davison, Aug. 11, 1984 (dec. 2004). BA, Cornell U.; MArch, Harvard U. Prin. Goody, Clancy & Assocs., Inc., Boston. Asst. prof., design critic Harvard U., Cambridge, Mass., 1973-80, Eliot Noyes vis. critic, 1985; faculty Mayors Inst. for Design, 1989—; lectr. in field. Mem. Boston Landmarks Commn., 1976-87; chair Boston Civic Design Commn., 1994-2005, chair vis. com. to Harvard GSD, 2007-; bd. dirs. Historic Boston, MIT Mus. Fellow AIA (design awards), Boston Soc. Archs. (award of honor 2005), Boston Archtl. Ctr. (hon.), Saturday Club, Tavern Club. Died Sept. 8, 2009.

GOODY, MICHAEL CHRISTOPHER, aerospace engineer; b. Washington, July 7, 1969; s. Joseph Conrad and Sandra Kaye (Kidd) G. AS in Math., Computer Sci., Engring., No. Va. C.C., 1991; BS in Physics, Aerospace Engring., Va. Poly. Inst. and State U., 1994. Engr.-in-tng., Va. Grad. asst. Va. Poly. and State U., Blacksburg, from 1994. Mem. AIAA, Soc. Physics Students, Sigma Gamma Tau, Phi Theta Kappa. Roman Catholic. Avocations: paddling, softball, golf. Home: Chantilly, Va. Died Jan. 20, 2009.

GOOTT, DANIEL, economist; b. NYC, Apr. 23, 1919; s. Hyman and Min (Novak) G.; m. Sylvia Blousman, Aug. 29, 1940; children: Alan F., Eugene M. BSS, CCNY, 1940; postgrad., Columbia U., 1940-41; diploma, Grad. Sch. Internat. Studies, Geneva, 1946. Assoc. chief labor rels. br. War Prodn. Bd., 1942-43; spl. asst. internat. labor affairs to under sec. state US Dept. State, Washington, 1955—60, dep. coord. internat. labor affairs, 1961-62; 1st sec., labor attache US Embassy, Paris, 1962-65; chief spl. profl. affairs to dep. sec. US Dept. State, Washington, 1965—68. Labor and UN advisor Bur. European Affairs; mem. U.S. del. 7th spl. and 30th regular sessions UN Gen. Assembly, 1975; mem. U.S. delegations to ann. confs. of UN Spl. Agy., ILO, Geneva, 1955-60; pvt. cons. internat. labor and bus. affairs, 1980. With AUS, 1943-46. Decorated Bronze Star. Mem. Am. Econ. Assn., Indsl. Rels. Rsch. Assn., Am. Fgn. Svc. Assn., Am. Acad. Polit. and Social Sci., Am. Club. Home: Silver Spring, Md. Died Apr. 4, 2010.

GORDON, HARRY EDWARD, safety engineer; b. Moca, Dominican Republic, Nov. 2, 1924; arrived in US, 1934, naturalized, 1943; s. Charles and Grace (Pichardo) Gordon; m. Patricia A. Moyers, Nov. 19, 1977; children: Bruce, Nancy. BS in Indsl. Engring., NYU, 1951. Cert. safety profl. Supervising safety engr. Zurich Ins. Co., NYC, 1948—65, Gt. Am. Ins. Co., San Juan, 1965; supt. safety engr. Aerospace Divsn. Pan America, Cape Kennedy, Fla., 1965—66; cons. Risk Control, Inc., NYC, 1966—72; v.p. Group VII Svcs., Miami, 1972—84; mgr. loss control Johnson and Higgins, Miami, from 1984. Mem. Orange Bowl, Staging Com., Miami, from 1974. Sgt. US Army, 1943—45, ETO. Mem.: Am. Soc. Safety Engrs. (cert., profl., cons., sec. risk mgmt. ins. divsn.), Masons Lodge, Pk. Lodge. Avocations: boating, golf. Home: Miami, Fla. Died Sept. 2, 2009.

GORDON, LAWRENCE BARRY, manufacturing company executive; b. Paterson, N.J., Jan. 28, 1934; s. Simon and Molly (Blender) G.; m. Bayla E. Gann, Oct. 28, 1956 (div. Apr. 1979); children— Jeffrey S., Robert B.; m. Elizabeth Hope Levine, Jan. 1, 1982; stepchildren— Melissa, Jason. Student U. R.I., 1951-53; B.S. in Communications, Boston U., 1956. Dir. public relations Babson Coll., Wellesley, Mass., 1956-59; pres. Crown Cut Products, Pawtucket, R.I., 1959—. Mem. Nat. Rifle Assn., Tau Mu Epsilon. Republican. Jewish. Clubs: Sportsmen's. Avocations: Hunting; fishing; horseback riding; boating. Home: North Scituate, RI. Died Jan. 20, 2009.

GORDON, LINCOLN, economist, former ambassador; b. NYC, Sept. 10, 1913; s. Bernard and Dorothy (Lerned) Gordon; m. Allison Wright, June 25, 1937 (dec. 1987); children: Anne, Robert W., Hugh, Amy. AB, Harvard, 1933; DPhil (Rhodes scholar), Oxford U., Eng., 1936; LLD, Fairleigh Dickinson U., 1965, Columbia, 1967, Rutgers U., 1967, U. Md., 1968, Wash. Coll., 1968, U. Del., 1969; LHD, Loyola Coll., Balt., 1968. Instr., faculty instr. govt. Harvard U., 1936-41, William Ziegler prof. internat. econ. relations, 1955-61; research technician water, energy resources U.S. Nat. Resources Planning Bd., Washington, 1939-1940; mem. staff requirements com. W.P.B., 1942-45, program vice chmn., 1945; dir. bur. reconversion priorities Civilian Prodn. Adminstrn., 1945-46; assoc. prof. bus. Harvard U., 1946-47, prof. govt. and adminstrn., 1947-50; cons. U.S. Rep. UN AEC, 1946, Army and Navy Munitions Bd., Dept. of State, 1947, ECA, 1948; North Atlantic Council Com. of Three on non-mil. aspects of NATO, 1956; dir. program div. Office ECA, spl. rep. in Europe US Dept. State, 1949-50; econ. adviser to spl. asst. to Pres. The White Houae, 1950-51; asst. dir. Office of Mut. Security, 1951-52; chief Marshall Aid mission and minister econ. affairs in Am. Embassy in London, 1952-55; US amb. to Brazil US Dept. State, 1961-66, asst. sec. state for inter-American affairs, 1966-67; pres. Johns Hopkins U., Balt., 1967-71; vis. prof. polit. economy Sch. Advanced Internat. Studies, Washington, 1971-72; fellow Woodrow Wilson Internat. Center for Scholars, 1972-75; sr. fellow Resources for Future, Washington, 1975-80; mem. sr. rev. panel CIA, 1980-82, nat. intelligence officer-at-large, 1982-83. Author: The Public Corporation in Great Britain, 1938; author: (with M. Fainsod) Government and the American Economy, 1941; author: Fuel and Power in Industrial Location and National Policy, Nat. Resources Planning Bd., 1942, Representation of the U.S. Abroad (in part), 1956; author: (with Engelbert L. Grommers) United States Manufacturing Investment in Brazil, 1961; author: A New Deal for Latin America, 1963, Growth Policies and the International Order, 1979; author: (with Joy Dunkerley and others) Energy Strategies for Developing Nations, 1981; author: (with J.F. Brown and others) Eroding Empire: Western Relations with Eastern Europe, 1987; author: (with T. Stanley) Integrating Economic and Security Factors in East-West Relations, 1988; author: Brazil's Second Chance: En Route Toward the First World, 2001; editor: International Stability and Progress: U.S. Interests and Instruments, 1957, From Marshall Plan to Global Interdependence, 1978. Hon. trustee Com. Econ. Devel.; bd. dirs. Atlantic Coun. US. Decorated Grand Cross Order Quetzal Guatemala, Order Cruzeiro do Sul Brazil. Fellow: Am. Acad. Arts and Scis.; mem.: Royal Econ. Soc., Internat. Inst. Strategic Studies, Am. Polit. Sci. Assn., Coun. Fgn. Rels., Cosmos Club Washington, Phi Beta Kappa. Home: Mitchellville, Md. Died Dec. 19, 2009.

GORDON, MARCIA LAURA, psychiatrist; b. Lynn, Mass., Oct. 13, 1925; d. Jacob and Rebecca (Portnoy) G.; children: Mark D., Julie D., Susan R. AB, Radcliffe Coll., 1946; MD, Harvard Med. Sch., 1949. Diplomate Am. Bd. Psychiatry and Neurology. Intern U. Ill. Rsch. and Ednl. Hosps., Chgo., 1949-50; resident in pscyhiatry Boston State Hosp., 1950-51; fellow in psychiatry Beth Israel Hosp., Boston, 1951-52, Judge Baker Child Guidance Clinic & Children's Med. Ctr., Boston, 1952-53; staff Mass. Dept. Pub. Health, Quincy, Mass., 1953-54, Community Clinic Mass. Mental Health Ctr., Boston, 1955-56; instr. dept. psychiatry U. Miami Sch. Medicine, 1956-57, asst. prof., 1957-58; chief psychiat. outpatient svcs. Jackson Meml. Hosp. Psychiat. Inst., Miami, 1957-58; clin. asst. prof. U. Miami Sch. Medicine, 1958-79; staff, acting dir. Dade County Child Guidance Clinic, Miami, 1957-60; psychiat. cons. Sunland Ctr., Miami, 1975-78; sr. fellow U. Miami, 1976-77; dir. child psychiatric consultation-liaison svcs. U. Miami Sch. Medicine, 1977-79; psychiatrist pvt. practice Pinellas County, Fla., from 1980. Regional bd. mem. Anti-Defamation League of West Fla., Tampa, 1989-93; com. Tampa Bay Region Campaign for the Third Century of Harvard Medicine, 1990. Fellow Am. Orthopsychiat. Assn.; mem. Am. Psychiat. Assn., Fla. Psychiat. Assn., Am. Arbitration Assn., Pinellas County Psychiat. Assn. (pres. 1982-83, exec. bd. 1983-85), Fla. Med. Assn., Am. Med. Women's Assn. (pres. Suncoast br. 1982-83), B'nai B'rith (unit # 2603), Phi Beta Kappa. Jewish. Avocations: poetry, low calorie cooking. Died Jan. 5, 2009.

GORDON, MARK, actor, theater director, educator; b. NYC, May 19, 1926; s. Jacob and Sarah (Benin) G.; m. Barbara Glenn, Oct. 13, 1955; 1 child, Keith. Student, Theater Sch. Dramatic Arts, NYC, 1946-47, Actors Lab., Los Angeles, 1947-50, Am. Theater Wing, NYC, 1950-54, Drama Lab., 1954-55. Workshop dir., actor Compass Players, Chgo., 1955-56; ind. theatrical and film actor, 1955—2010; ind. theatrical dir., 1969—2010. Andrew Mellon guest prof. theater Carnegie-Mellon Univ., Pitts., 1969-70, Columbia Univ., N.Y.C., 1970-71, High Sch. Performing Arts, N.Y.C., 1970-72, Finch Coll., N.Y.C.; head M.B.K. Prodns., N.Y.C., 1982-2010 Playwight: (with others) Glorious Age, 1975; actor numerous Broadway prodns. including Desire Under the Elms, Of Mice and Men, Mr. Roberts, The Devils, off-Broadway prodns. include The Iceman Cometh, The Man Who Never Died...Joe Hill, TV appearances include Mary Tyler Moore, Hawaii 5-O, Kojack, Dick Van Dyke, Ed, Law and Order; film appearances include Take the Money and Run, 1969, Don't Drink the Water, 1969, A New Leaf, 1971, Sleeper, 1973, The Nickel Ride, 1974, Ninth Configuration, 1980; dir. Broadway prodn.: Before You Go (named Best Comedy Dir. on Broadway 1969), off-Broadway prodns. for Los Angeles Actors Theater, Carnegie Recital Hall, Playwrites Horizon, participating dir. Actors Studio; dir. numerous TV commls. Recipient numerous Andy awards, Clio nominations, Contribution to Comedy in Chgo. medal Univ. Chgo.; Rockefeller grantee Ctr. Opera of Mpls., 1963-64; scholar Am. Theater Wing. Mem. AAUP, AFTRA, Dirs. Guild Am., Screen Actors Guild, Actors Equity Assn., Nat. Acad. TV Arts and Scis., Soc. Stage Dirs. and Choreographers. Avocations: violin, scuba diving, photography. Home: New York, NY. Died Aug. 12, 2010.

GORDON, MYRON L., federal judge; b. Kenosha, Wis., Feb. 11, 1918; m. Peggy Gordon, Aug. 16, 1942 (dec. Mar. 1973); children: Wendy, John, Polly; m. Myra Gordon, Mar. 30, 1979. BA, MA, U. Wis., 1939; LLB, Harvard U., 1942. Judge U.S. Ct. Appeals, Milw., 1951-62, Wis. State Supreme Ct., Madison, 1966-67, U.S. Dist. Ct., Milw., from 1967; now sr. judge. Died Nov. 3, 2009.

GORDON, WILLIAM EDWIN, physicist, electrical engineer, academic administrator, educator; b. Paterson, NJ, Jan. 8, 1918; s. William and Mary (Scott) G.; m. Elva Freile, June 22, 1941 (dec. Feb. 2002); children: Larry Scott, Nancy Lynn; m. Elizabeth Bolgiano, Aug. 31, 2003. BA, Montclair State Coll., NJ, 1939, MA, 1942; MS, NYU, 1946; PhD, Cornell U., Ithaca, NY, 1953. Registered profl. engr., Tex. Cons. radio engr. Stromberg Carlson G.E. Airforce, NAVY, ARCO, from 1950; assoc. prof. Cornell U., 1953-59, prof., 1959-65; Walter R. Read prof. engring. Arecibo Ionospheric Obs., PR, 1965; prof. elec. engring. and space physics and astronomy Rice U., Houston, 1966-86, dean engring. and sci., 1966-75, dean Sch. Natural Scis., 1975-80, provost, v.p., 1980-86, disting. prof. emeritus, 1986—2010; fgn. sec. NAS, 1986-90. Conceived, directed design and early operation of Arecibo Obs. and 1000 foot antenna, 1960-65 (named Milestone in Elec. Engring. and Landmark in Mech. Engring. 2001); chmn. bd. trustees Upper Atmosphere Rsch. Corp., 1971, 73-78, Univ. Corp. for Atmospheric Rsch., 1979-81, 86-89, 91-92; trustee Cornell U., 1976-80; adv. bd. Arecibo Obs., 1977-80, 90-93; cons. in field. Bd. dirs. Taping for the Blind, Houston, 1994-2002. Capt. USAAF, 1942-46. Recipient Balth. Vander Pol award for disting. rsch. in radio sci., 1966; 50th Anniversary medal Am. Meteorol. Soc., 1969, Arktowski medal, 1984, Arecibo Telescope award, 2001; Guggenheim fellow, 1972-73. Fellow IEEE (chmn. profl. group on antennas and propagation 1964-65), Am. Geophys. Union; mem. AAAS, NAS, NAE, Am. Acad. Arts and Scis., Internat. Sci. Radio Union (v.p. 1975-81, pres. 1981-84, hon. pres. 1990-2010), Internat. Coun. Sci. Unions (v.p. 1988-93), Am. Meteorology Soc., Philos. Soc. Tex., Cosmos Club, Sigma Xi, Tau Beta Pi, Kappa Delta Pi, Sigma Kappa Nu, Phi Kappa Phi. Achievements include research in radio scattering. Home: Ithaca, NY. Died Feb. 16, 2010.

GOSS, MARY E. WEBER, sociology educator; b. Chgo., May 8, 1926; m. Albert E. Goss, 1945; 1 son, Charles. BA in Sociology with distinction (Univ. Merit scholar 1946-47, Chi Omega Sociology prize 1947), U. Iowa, 1947, MA, 1948; PhD (Gilder fellow 1951-52), Columbia U., 1959. Rsch. asst. U. Iowa, 1947-48, Amherst Coll., 1949; instr. Smith Coll., 1949-50, U. Mass., 1950-51, 55-56, adj. mem. grad. faculty, 1961-66; rsch. assoc. Bur. Applied Social Rsch., Columbia U., 1952-53; cons. sociology, mem. rsch. staff, rsch. coord. N.Y. Hosp.-Cornell U. Med. Center, NYC, 1957-66; mem. faculty dept. medicine Cornell U. Med. Coll., 1959-72, prof. sociology in pub. health, 1973-92, prof. emerita, from 1992. Author: Physicians in Bureaucracy, 1980; also numerous articles; editor: Jour. Health and Social Behavior, 1976-78; co-editor: Comprehensive Medical Care and Teaching: A Report on the N.Y. Hospital-Cornell Medical Center Program, 1967; mem. editorial bd. profl. jours. Fellow APHA, N.Y. Acad. Medicine; mem. AAAS, AAUP, Am. Sociol. Assn., Assn. Tchrs. Preventive Medicine, Acad. Health, Internat. Sociol. Assn., Ea. Sociol. Soc., Phi Beta Kappa, Sigma Xi. Home: Piscataway, NJ. Died June 23, 2010.

GOTTIER, RICHARD CHALMERS, retired computer company executive; b. Columbus, Ohio, Oct. 12, 1918; s. Chalmers M. and Grace (Eisnaugle) G.; m. Mary S. Hiatt, Nov. 13, 1965; children: Barbara, Diane, Richard Chalmers, Penny. BS in Bus. Adminstrn, Ohio State U., 1939; postgrad., Northwestern U. Grad. Sch. Bus., 1969. Spl. agt. FBI, Washington, 1940-51; with RCA, Indpls., 1951-59; dir. Magnavox Co., Ft. Wayne, Ind., 1959-70; sr. v.p. Control Data Corp., Mpls., 1970-80; chmn., gen. ptnr. Minn. Seed Capital, Inc., 1980-97. Home: Plymouth, Minn. Died July 20, 2009.

GOULD, HAROLD, actor; b. Schenectady, NY, Dec. 10, 1923; m. Lea Shampanier, Aug. 1950; children: Deborah, Joshua David, Lowell Seth. BA, SUNY, Albany, 1947; MA, Cornell U., 1948, PhD, 1953. Asst. prof. drama Randolph Macon Woman's Coll., 1953-56, U. Calif., Riverside, 1956-60. Films include Two for the Seesaw, Harper, Inside Daisy Clover, Marnie, The Arrangement, The Lawyer, Where Does It Hurt?, The Sting, 1973, The Strongest Man in the World, Gus, The Big Bus, Love and Death, 1975, The Front Page, 1976, Silent Movie, 1976, The One and Only, Seems Like Old Times, 1977, Romero, Killer, Patch Adams, My Giant; TV appearances include Columbo, L.A. Law, The Virginian, The Twilight Zone, Perry Mason, The Fugitive, Get Smart, Hogan's Heroes, The Big Valley, The Wild, Wild West, The F.B.I., Mission Impossible, I Dream of Jeannie, Cannon, The Rockford Files, Felicity, The Outer Limits, Lois & Clark: The New Adventures of Superman, The Long Hot Summer, Washington-Behind Closed Doors, Soap, Love Boat, Feather and Father, Rhoda (Emmy nomination), Gunsmoke, Petrocelli, Lou Grant, Double Solitaire, Streets of San Francisco, Hawaii Five-O, Mary Tyler Moore Show, The 11th Victim, Aunt Mary, Police Story (Emmy nomination), Man in the Santa Claus Suit, Insight/Holy Moses, The Gambler, Moviola (Emmy nomination), King Crab, Never Too Late, St. Elsewhere, Mrs. Delafield Wants to Marry (Emmy nomination), Night Court, Dallas, Empty Nest, The Golden Girls, Midnight Caller, Ray Bradbury Theatre (Emmy nomination and ACE award 1989), The Sunset Gang, Touched by an Angel, For Hope; appeared in Broadway plays including Fools, 1980, Grown Ups, 1982, Artist Descending a Staircase, 1989, Mixed Emotions, 1993, and others; also appeared in other plays including King Lear, 1958, Rhinoceros, 1962, Much Ado About Nothing, 1958, Merchant of Venice, 1964, Troilus and Cressida, 1958, JB, 1965, Seidman and Son, 1964, Once in a Lifetime, 1975, The Miser, 1968, The Devils, 1967, The Birthday Party, 1986, House of Blue Leaves, 1971, The Price, The World of Ray Bradbury, 1964, Life with Father, 1982, Skin of Our Teeth, 1982, I'm Not Rappaport, 1985, Through Roses, 1987, I Never Sang for My Father, 1988, one man show Freud, 1990, Love Letters, 1990, King Lear, 1992, Incommunicado, 1993 (L.A. Drama Critics award 1994), Old Business, 1995-95, The Tempest, 1995, Substance of Fire, 1996, Death of a Salesman, 1997; off-Broadway appearance in Increased Difficulty of Concentration (Obie award), 1969. Recipient Centennial Alumnus award SUNY Albany, Nat. Assn. State Univs. and Land-Grant Colls., 1987. Died Sept. 11, 2010.

GOULD, ROBERT L., air transportation executive, pilot; b. Bklyn., Mar. 10, 1938; s. James Frederick and Ethel (MacLean) G.; m. Susan Ellen Work, Sept. 21, 1960 (div. 1972); children: Kristen, Katherine, Kimberly; m. Pamela Jean Balser, Mar. 24, 1973; children: James, Laura, Emily, Amy. BA in Econs., Yale U., 1965. Capt. line pilot Pan Am World Airways Inc., NYC, from 1965, dir. employee stock ownership plan, 1982-85, bd. dirs., 1982-85, exec. adminstr. to vice-chmn., 1986-87, sr. v.p. airline/strategic planning, 1987-88, sr. v.p. ops., 1988-90; pres. Ea. Airlines, Miami, Fla., from 1990. Head of pilot union Pan Am World Airways Inc., 1982-85. Capt. USMC, 1959-63. Recipient Humanities award Queens Coun. Mayors, 1990. Republican. Presbyterian. Home: Redding, Conn. Died Mar. 6, 2009.

GRABOWSKI, CHESTER ADAM, financial executive; b. Chgo., Jan. 8, 1946; s. Chester Aloysius and Stella Marie (Wzorek) G.; m. Janice Arleen Zielinski, June 28, 1969 BS in Chem. Engring., Ill. Inst. Tech., 1967, MBA, 1969. Chem. engr. Nalco Chem. Co., Chgo., 1968-72; asst. treas. Assoc. Corp. N.Am., South Bend, Ind., 1972-75; treas. Ponderosa System Inc., Dayton, Ohio, 1975-78; v.p. fin. Wis. Steel Corp., Chgo., 1978-80; v.p. fin., chief fin. officer Goldblatt Bros., Inc., Chgo., 1980-84, Costain Holdings Inc., Chgo., from 1984, also dir. Chmn. bd. Westmont Mining Inc. Active Lupus Erythematosis Soc., Chgo., 1978—; bd. dirs. Nathan Goldblatt Cancer Found., 1980-84, Willowbrook Community Assn., Crete, Ill., 1982— Mem. Fin. Execs. Inst. Clubs: Union League (Chgo.). Avocations: outdoor sports; music. Home: Romeoville, Ill. Died Jan. 25, 2009.

GRACEY, DOUGLAS ROBERT, internist, pulmonologist, physiologist, educator; b. Ft. Dodge, Iowa, Aug. 7, 1936; s. Warren Robert and Areta Mary (Thompson) G.; m. Edith Ann Haas, Dec. 23, 1961; children— Laura, Douglas Robert BA, Coe Coll., 1958; MD, Northwestern U., 1962; MS, U. Minn., 1968. Diplomate Am. Bd. Internal Medicine. Intern Cook County Hosp., Chgo., 1962-63; resident Mayo Grad. Sch. Medicine, 1963-66, 68-69; asst. prof. medicine Northwestern U. Med. Sch., 1969-75; assoc. prof. medicine Mayo Med. Sch., Rochester, Minn., 1975-83, prof., from 1983, vice chmn. pulmonary div., 1982-87; vice chmn. for practice dept. medicine Mayo Clinic, Rochester, 1983-93, dir. critical care medicine div., 1985-89, chmn. revenue systems com., 1993—2005, chmn. divsn. pulmonary and critical care medicine. Author: (with W.W. Addington) Tuberculosis, 1972, Flying Lessons, Ambulances and orther Air Force Vignettes, 2000; editor: Pulmonary Diseases in the Adult, 1981; contbr. articles to profl. jours. Trustee Coe Coll., 1976-92. Capt. USAF, 1966—68. Decorated USAF Commendation Medal; Am. Thoracic Soc. tng. fellow, 1968-69. Fellow ACP, Am. Coll. Chest Physicians; mem. Nat. Assn. Med. Direction Respiratory Care (past pres.), Masons, Shriners. Republican. Presbyterian. Died June 21, 2010.

GRADY, JOHN EDWARD, JR., publisher, entrepreneur; b. Boston, June 15, 1935; s. John Edward and Catherine Agnes (Connolly) Grady; m. Susanna Fenhagen, 1985; children: John Edward III, Robert Emmet McDonnell, Douglas Anderson. BA, Harvard U., 1956, MBA, 1965. Acct. exec. Merrill Lynch, Pierce, Fenner & Smith, NYC, 1960—63; sr. assoc. Cresap, McCormick and Paget, NYC, 1965—69; v.p. Investment Mgmt. and Rsch., Inc., St. Petersburg, Fla., 1969—70; v.p. fin., treas. Suncoast Highland Corp., Clearwater, Fla., 1970—74, v.p. fin. ops., sec. treas., 1974—76, dir.; v.p. corp. fin. Raymond James & Assocs., Inc., St. Petersburg, Fla., 1976—82; pub. Art Product News, from 1982; pres. Grady Pub. Co., from 1982, In-Art Pub. Co., from 1982. Regional chmn. Harvard Bus. Sch. Fund, 1971—73; mem. pres.'s roundtable Eckerd Coll., 1971—81; trustee Canterbury Sch. Fla., St. Petersburg, 1973—79, treas., 1974—75, chmn., 1975—76; mem. com. social svc. allocations City of St. Petersburg, 1978; bd. dirs. The Fla. Orch., St. Petersburg, Tampa, 1979—82; mem. com. Harvard Clubs Assn. Harvard Alumni, 1980—84, mem. com. on schs. and scholarships, 1980—86; mem. Tampa Bay Area Com. on Fgn. Rels., 1979—84, Com. of 100, 1984—88. Lt. USNR, 1956—60. Mem.: Fla. Mag. Assn. (bd. dirs. from 1987, treas. from 1989), Rotary, St. Petersburg Yacht Club, Harvard West Coast Club (St. Petersburg-Tampa) (pres. 1976—78, chmn. schs. and scholarships com. from 1976), Harvard Bus. Sch. West Coast Club (dir. 1976—86, pres. 1983—84). Home: Tampa, Fla. Died Feb. 26, 2010.

GRAEBNER, NORMAN ARTHUR, historian, educator; b. Kingman, Kans., Oct. 19, 1915; s. Rudolph William and Helen (Brauer) G.; m. Laura Edna Baum, Aug. 30, 1941; m. Jane Shannon, Jan. 3, 1998 (dec. 2002); m. Mary Moon, July 2, 2004. BS, Milw. State Tchrs. Coll., 1939; MA, U. Okla., 1940; PhD, U. Chgo., 1949; LittD, Albright Coll., 1976; MA, Oxford U., 1978; DHL (hon.), U. Pitts., 1981, Valparaiso U., 1981, Ea. Ill. U., 1986, U. Wis., Milw., 1997; DHL, Averett U., 2003; D of Pedagogy, Marshall U., 1993. Asst. prof. Okla. Coll. for Women, 1942—43, 1946—47; from asst. prof. to prof. Iowa State Coll., 1948—56; prof. history U. Ill., Urbana, 1956—67, chmn. dept. history, 1961—63; Edward R. Stettinius prof. modern American history U. Va., 1967—82, Randolph P. Compton prof., Miller Ctr. Pub. Affairs, 1982—2010. Vis. prof. Stanford U., 1952-53, summers 1959, 72, U. Colo., summer 1968, Concordia Tchrs. Coll., summer 1971, US Mil. Acad., West Point, NY, 1981-82, Beloit Coll., spring 1987, Va. Mil. Inst., fall 1987, Coll. of William and Mary, spring 1988, Marshall U., spring 1989; Commonwealth Fund lectr. U. Coll., London, 1958; Fulbright lectr. U. Queensland, Brisbane, Australia, 1963, U. Sydney, Australia, 1983, U. Heidelberg, Germany, 1998-99; disting. vis. prof. history Pa. State U., 1975-76; Harmsworth prof. Am. history Oxford U., 1978-79; Phi Beta Kappa vis. scholar, 1981-82; Thomas Jefferson vis. scholar Downing Coll., Cambridge U., 1985; disting. vis. prof. Nat. War Coll., 1994-95. Author: Empire on the Pacific, 1955, The New Isolationism, 1956, Cold War Diplomacy, 1962, rev. edit., 1977, The Age of Global Power, 1979, America As a World Power: A Realist Appraisal from Wilson to Reagan, 1984, Foundations of American Foreign Policy: A Realist Appraisal from Franklin to McKinley, 1985, A Twentieth-Century Odyssey: Memoir of a Life in Academe, 2002; co-author: A History of the United States, 2 vols, 1970, A History of the American People, 1970, 2d edit., 1975, Recent United States History, 1972, Reagan, Bush, Gorbachev, 2008; Editor: The Enduring Lincoln, 1959, Politics and the Crisis of 1860, 1961, An Uncertain Tradition: American Secretaries of State in the Twentieth Century, 1961, The Cold War: A Conflict of Ideology and Power, 1963, rev. edit., 1976, Ideas and Diplomacy, 1964, Manifest Destiny, 1968, Nationalism and Communism in Asia: The American Response, 1977, Freedom in America: A 200-Year Perspective, 1977, American Diplomatic History before 1900, 1978; Traditions and Values: American Diplomacy, 1790-1865, 1985, 1865-1945, 1985; The National Security: Its Theory and Practice, 1945-1960, 1986; contbr. articles to hist. jours. Dir. bicentennial program Pa. State U., 1975-76. Served to 1st lt. US Army, 1943-46. Recipient Thomas Jefferson award, U. Va., 1985, Excellence award, 2006. Mem. Am., So. hist. assns., Orgn. American Historians, Soc. American Historians, Soc. Historians America, Fgn. Rels. (pres. 1972), American Acad. Arts and Scis., Mass. Hist. Soc., Phi Beta Kappa. Home: Charlottesville, Va. Died May 10, 2010.

GRAFF, JOHN FREDERIC, insurance company executive; b. Highland Pk., Ill., Dec. 1, 1933; s. Karl Von and Bernice Mildred (Mattes) Graff; m. Mary Lynn Bjerke, Sept. 5, 1981; children: Barbara Lynn, Karen Sue stepchildren: Charlene, Ericka. BA in Econs., DePauw U., 1955. Registered health underwriter Nat. Assn. Health Underwriters, CLU. Agt. Provident Mut. Life Ins. Co., Chgo., 1958—61; mem. mgmt. devel. program Phila., 1961—62; agy. mgr. Chgo., 1962—73; owner, propr. John F. Graff & Assocs., Chgo., from 1973; pres. United Corp. of Am., Inc., from 1973, Ill. Bus. Corp., from 1976. Contbr. articles to trade mags. Past officer New Trier Republican Orgn.; charter mem., pres. Greater Chgo. Ins. Coun. City of Hope, 1980—84; past chmn. Village Party, Wilmette, Ill. Lt. j.g. USN, 1955—58. Named Ins. Man of Yr., City of Hope, 1978. Mem.: Chgo. Gen. Agts. and Mgrs. Assn., Chgo. Assn. Health Underwriters (dir. from 1975, Edward H. O'Connor Disting. Svc. award 1977), Ill. Life Underwriters Assn. (pres. 1977—78), Chgo. Chpt. C.L.U.s (pres. 1976—77, Huebner Scholar-Disting. Svc. award 1979), Chgo. Assn. Life Underwriters (pres. 1975—76, Disting. Svc. award 1979), Chgo. Estate Planning Coun., Nat. Assn. Life Underwriters, Westmoreland Country Club, Univ. Club (Chgo.). Republican. Methodist. Home: Wilmette, Ill. Died June 5, 2010.

GRAHAM, BRUCE JOHN, architect; b. La Cumbre, Bogota, Colombia, Dec. 1, 1925; s. Charles Stewart and Angélica (Gómez de la Torre) G. (parents U.S. citizens); m. Jane Johanna Abend, Sept. 1, 1960 (dec. 2004); children: George, Lisa, Mara B.F.A., B.Arch., U. Pa, 1949. Ptnr. Skidmore, Owings & Merrill, Chgo., 1949-89, Graham & Graham, Hobe Sound, Fla., 1990—2010. Hon. prof. U. Nacional Federico Villareal, Peru, 1980; Noyes prof. Harvard U., 1985; vis. prof. U. Nebr., 1989. Chmn. bd. overseers Sch. Fine Arts, U. Pa., 1981-91, trustee, 1981—2010; bd. dirs. Temple Hoyne Buell Ctr., Columbia U., N.Y.C., 1984-89; pres. Chgo. Central Area Com., 1980-90; bd. dirs. Chgo. Council on Fgn. Relations, Chgo., 1983-90; mem. Urban Land Inst.; mem. adv. bd. govs. Urban Land Research Found.; mem. mem. com. on visual arts U. Chgo., 1982-92; pres. Chgo. Inst. Architecture and Urbanism, 1989-92. Recipient numerous awards for architecture. Fellow AIA; mem. Royal Inst. Brit. Architects, Royal Archtl. Inst. Can., Inst. Urbanism and Planning Peru (hon.) Clubs: Chicago, Commercial (Chgo.). Home: Hobe Sound, Fla. Died Mar. 6, 2010.

GRANDY, LEONARD A., education educator; b. NJ, June 1, 1916; m. Marjorie; children: Michael, Russell, James, Leslyn. BS, N.J. State U.; MA, Tchrs. Coll., Columbia U., 1949; EdD, U. So. Calif., 1959. Tchr., dept. chmn. public schs., N.J., 1941-42, 46-49; tchr. math. and drafting Whittier (Calif.) Union High Sch. Dist., 1949-51, asst. supt. bus., 1951-63, asst. supt., 1962-63; asst. supt., v.p. Rio Hondo Coll., 1963-76; supt., pres. Rio Hondo Community Coll. Dist., Whittier, 1976-81; cons. Rio Hondo C.C. Dist., Whittier, from 1984; adj. prof. Whittier Coll., 1981-84. Mem. pres.'s adv. com. Calif. State U., Pepperdine U. Contbr.: articles to Calif. Sch. Bds. Jour., Coll. Mgmt. Bd. dirs. YMCA Women's Center, Whittier. Served to lt. USN, 1942-46. Mem. Chief Exec. Officers Assn. of Calif. Community Colls., founders com., Assn. Chief Bus. Ofcls. (pres. 1974-75), dir. (1973-74), Assn. Calif. Community Coll. Adminstrs. (founders com., dir.) Republican. Episcopalian. Home: Lake Forest, Calif. Died Feb. 14, 2010.

GRANEY, MICHAEL PROCTOR, lawyer; b. Ashland, Ky., June 2, 1943; s. Mike Latelle and Irene (Sparks) G.; children: Noelle, Michael W. BA, Duke U., 1965; JD, Ohio State U., 1968. Bar: Ohio 1968, D.C. 1976, U.S. Supreme Ct. 1976. Assoc. Porter, Stanley, Treffinger & Platt, Columbus, Ohio, 1968-74; ptnr. Porter, Stanley, Platt & Arthur, Columbus, 1974-80, Simpson, Thacher & Bartlett, Columbus, from 1980. Mem. ABA, D.C. Bar Assn., Ohio Bar Assn., Columbus Bar Assn. Home: Powell, Ohio. Died June 16, 2009.

GRANGER, HARVEY, JR., retired manufacturing executive; b. Savannah, Ga., Sept. 9, 1928; s. Harvey and Marion (Rauers) G.; m. Barbara Brandt, Sept. 8, 1951; children: Harvey, Matthew Brandt, Barbara James. B in Indsl. Engring., Ga. Inst. Tech, 1951. Indsl. engr. Union Camp Paper Co., Savannah, 1950-56, Great Dane Trailers, Savannah, 1956-61, plant mgr., 1961-71, v.p. mfg., 1971-78, exec. v.p., chief operating officer, 1978-84, pres., chief exec. officer, 1984-91; cons. Savannah, 1992-96; ret., 1996. City adv. bd. dirs. Nations Bank, Savannah, 1979-95. Mem. adv. bd. Sch. Engring. Ga. Inst. Tech., 1985-91; mem. bd. trustees St. Joseph's Hosp., Savannah, 1988-97, vice-chmn. 1995, chmn. 1996-97; chmn. bd. trustees St. Joseph's-Candler Health Sys., Savannah, 1997-2000, vice chmn., 2000—03; dir. vol. trustees Not-For-Profit Hosps., Washington, 1995—2003, mem. exec. com., 1997, sec., 1998, vice chmn., 1999—2003. With USN, 1945-47. Mem. Truck Trailer Mfrs. Assn. (chmn. 1986-87). Clubs: Oglethorpe (Savannah) (pres. 1984-85), Savannah Golf. Avocations: golf, fishing. Home: Savannah, Ga. Died Sept. 10, 2009.

GRANT, ALBERT, physician, consultant; b. Balt., Feb. 17, 1919; s. Samuel and Rebecca (White) Gubnitsky; m. Sara Jane Lebowitz, Apr. 30, 1946; children: Samuel, Frederic, Jonathan, Keith. BS, U. Md., 1940, MD, 1943. Diplomate Am. Bd. Internal Medicine. Intern Lincoln Hosp., NYC, 1943—44; resident, medicine Luth. Hosp., Balt., VA Hosp., Louisville; pvt. practice Balt., 1949—61; cons. Social Security Disability Program, Balt., from 1958; med. cons. B&O, C&O RR, Balt., 1961—70; dir., cardiac rehab. program Sinai Hosp., Balt., 1970—84. Co-author: (booklet) Vocational Rehabilitation in Stroke, 1972; contbr. articles to profl. jours. Served to capt. M.C. US Army, 1944—46. Fellow: ACP; mem.: Am. Heart Assn. (Md. affiliate subcom., Cardiac Rehab.). Democrat. Jewish. Avocation: boating. Home: Boynton Beach, Fla. Died Feb. 5, 2009.

GRANZEIER, ROBERT WILLIAM, human services administrator; b. Cleve., Sept. 25, 1929; s. Phil and Elizabeth (Weisbarth) Hynes; m. Loudeen Mary Rant, Oct. 12, 1957; 1 child, Mary Beth A. Farmer. BA, Mich. State U., 1952. Exec. mgmt. trainee Sears Roebuck & Co., Saginaw, Mich., Chgo., 1954—59; sales mgr. Ctrl. Soya Co., Ft. Wayne, Ind., 1959—67; mgmt. exec. Ill. Dept. Rehab., Springfield, 1967—80, cabinet office dir., 1980—84; mgmt. exec. Ill. Dept. Mental Health, Springfield, from 1984. Cons. instr. Southern Ill. U. Rehab. Inst., Carbondale, 1974; faculty Valpar Corp., Tucson, 1979—80; cons. San Diego State U. Rehab. Inst., 1982; commr. Commn. Cert. Work Adjustment and Vocat. Evaluation Specialists, Washington, 1982—84; vice chmn. facilities com. Coun. State Adminstrn. Vocat. Rehab., Washington, 1982—84; instr. Sangamon State U., Springfield, 1983; bd. dirs. Electronic Industries Found., Washington, 1983; mem. nat. adv. Menninger Found., Topeka, from 1983. 1st lt. US Army, 1952—54, Korea. Recipient Cmty. Svc. award, Chgo. Lighthouse Blind, 1982, Disting. Svc. award, Electronic Industries Found., Washington, 1983, Spl. Recognition award, Commn. Accreditation Rehab. Facilities, Chgo., 1983. Mem.: VFW, Nat. Rehab. Assn., Elks Lodge. Avocations: fishing, stein collecting. Home: Springfield, Ill. Died June 15, 2010.

GRAVENSTEIN, JOACHIM STEFAN, anesthesiologist, educator; b. Berlin, Jan. 25, 1925; came to U.S., 1952, naturalized, 1959; m. Alix Trutschler, Aug. 27, 1949; children— Nikolaus, Alix, Frederike, Stefan, Ruprecht, Dietrich, Constanze, Katharina. MD, U. Bonn, Germany, 1951, Harvard, 1958; MD (hon.), U. Graz, Austria, 1988. Resident and staff appointments anesthesia Mass. Gen. Hosp., 1952-58; fellow, tchr. Harvard Med. Sch., 1952-58; chief anesthesiology Coll. Medicine, U. Fla., 1958-69; prof. anesthesiology, chmn. dept. Case Western Res. Med. Sch., 1969-79; grad. research prof. Coll. Medicine, U. Fla., Gainesville, 1979-96, prof. emeritus, from 1996. Mem. Am. Soc. Anesthesiology. Home: Gainesville, Fla. Died Jan. 16, 2009.

GRAVER, LAWRENCE STANLEY, language educator; b. NYC, Dec. 6, 1931; s. Louis and Rose (Pearlstein) G.; m. Suzanne Levy, Jan. 28, 1960; children: Ruth, Elizabeth. BA, CCNY, 1954; MA, U. Calif., Berkeley, 1959, PhD, 1961. Asst. prof. English UCLA, 1961-64, Williams Coll., Williamstown, Mass., 1964-67, assoc. prof. English, 1967-72, prof. English, from 1972, William R. Kenan, Jr. prof. English, 1977-81, John H. Roberts prof. English, 1981-97, Roberts prof. emeritus English, from 1997. Author: Conrad's Short Fiction, 1969, Carson McCullers, 1969; editor: Mastering the Film, 1977, Samuel Beckett, 1979, (Landmarks of World Lit. series) Waiting for Godot, 1989, 2d edit., 2004, An Obsession With Anne Frank: Meyer Levin and the Diary, 1995; asst. editor: Columbia Companion to the Twentieth Century American Short Story, 2001. Served with U.S. Army, 1954-56. NEH fellow, 1980-81. Mem. MLA, AAUP. Democrat. Home: Williamstown, Mass. Died Feb. 28, 2010.

GRAVES, PETER, actor; b. Mpls., Mar. 18, 1926; s. Rolf C. and Ruth E. (Duesler) Aurness; m. Joan E. Endress, Dec. 16, 1950; children: Kelly Jean, Claudia King, Amanda Lee. Student, U. Minn., 1949. Actor: (TV series) Fury, 1955-60, Whiplash, 1960-61, Court Martial, 1965-66, Mission Impossible, 1966-73 (Golden Globe award Best Actor in a TV Series Drama, 1971), New Mission: Impossible, 1988-90, 7th Heaven, 1997-2007; (TV miniseries) The Winds of War, 1983, War and Rembrance, 1988; (films) Winning Your Wings, 1942, Rogue Rover, 1950, Up Front, 1951, Fort Defiance, 1951, Angels in the Outfield, 1951, The Congregation, 1952, Red Planet Mars, 1952, Stalag 17, 1953, War Paint, 1953, East of Suamatra, 1953, Beneath the 12-Mile Reef, 1953, Killers From Space, 1954 The Yellow Tomahawk, 1954, The Raid, 1954, Black Tuesday, 1954, Court Martial of Billy Marshall, 1955, Robbers Roost, 1955, Witchita, 1955, The Long Gray Line, 1955, The Night of the Hunter, 1955, The Naked Street, 1955, Fort Yuma, 1955, It Conquered the World, 1956, Hold Back the Night, 1956, Canyon River, 1956, Beginning of the End, 1957, Death in Small Doses, 1957, Wolf Larsen, 1958, A Stranger in My Arms, 1959, A Rage to Live, 1965, Texas Across the River, 1966, Sergeant Ryker, 1968, The Ballad of Josie, 1968, The Five-Man Army, 1968, Missile X, 1978, High Seas Hijack, 1978, The Survival Run, 1979, The Clonus Horror, 1979, Airplane!, 1980, The Guns and the Fury, 1981, Airplane II: The Sequel, 1982, Savannah Smiles, 1982, Number One With a Bullet, 1986, Adams Family Values, 1993, The House on Haunted Hill, 1999, Men in Black II, 2002; (TV films) Las Vegas Beat, 1961, Valley of Mystery, 1967, Call to Danger, 1973, The President's Plane Is Missing, 1973, Scream of the Wolf, 1974, The Underground Man, 1974, Where Have All the People Gone?, 1974, Dead Man on the Run, 1975, SST: Death Flight, 1977, The Gift of the Magi, 1978, The Rebels, 1979, Death Car on the Freeway, 1979, The Memory of Eve Ryker, 1980, Three Hundred Miles for Stephanie, 1981, Best of Friends, 1981, If It's Tuesday, It Still Must Be Belgium, 1987, These Old Broads, 2001, With You In Spirit, 2003; (TV guest appearances) Gruen Guild Playhouse, 1952, Where's Raymond?, 1953, Schlitz Playhouse of Stars, 1953, The Pepsi-Cola Playhouse (2 episodes), 1953-54 Fireside Theatre (4 episodes), 1953-55, Biff Baker, U.S.A., 1954, Studio 57, 1954, Hallmark Hall of Fame (2 episodes), 1954-55, TV Reader's Digest, 1955, Studio One, 1956, Matinee Theatre, 1956, Celebrity Playhouse, 1956, Cavalcade of America, 1956, The Millionaire, 1956, Lux Video Theatre, 1957, Climax! (2 episodes) 1957-58, Cimarron City, 1959, Route 66 (2 episodes), 1962, The Alfred Hitchcock Hour, 1963, Kraft Suspense Theatre (2 episodes), 1963, The Farmer's Daughter, 1964, The Virginian, 1964, The Great Adventure (2 episodes), 1964, The Eye Creature, 1965, Laredo, 1966, Branded (2 episodes) 1966, Run For Your Life, 1966, Daniel Boone, 1966, Disneyland (3 episodes), 1966-78, 12 O'Clock High, 1967, The F.B.I., 1967, The Invaders, 1967, The Red Skelton Show, 1969, Fantasy Island (5 episodes), 1978-83, The Love Boat (4 episodes), 1978-87, Buck Rogers in the 25th Century, 1979, Matt and Jenny, 1980, Simon & Simon, 1981, Murder, She Wrote, 1984, Hammer House of Mystery & Suspense, 1985, Life With Lucy, 1986, The Golden Girls, 1991, Burke's Law, 1995, The Angry Beavers, 1998, Diagnosis Murder, 1999, House M.D., 2005, Minoriteam, 2006, Cold Case, 2006, American Dad!, 2007; host/narrator: Discover! The World of Science, 1985-90, A & E Biography 1987-2010 Hon. Calif. chmn. American Cancer Soc., 1968, hon. nat. crusade chmn., 1974; celebrity chmn. Arthritis Found., 1990-91. With USAAF. Recipient Outstanding Achievement award, U. Minn., 1968. Mem. Phi Kappa Psi. Died Mar. 14, 2010.

GRAVING, RICHARD JOHN, law educator; b. Duluth, Minn., Aug. 24, 1929; s. Lawrence Richard and Laura Magdalene (Loucks) G.; m. Florence Sara Semel; children: Daniel, Sarah. BA, U. Minn., 1950; JD, Harvard U., 1953; postgrad., Nat. U. Mex., 1964-66. Bar: Minn. 1953, N.Y. 1956, U.S. Dist. Ct. (so. dist.) N.Y. 1956, Pa. 1968, U.S. Dist. Ct. (we. dist.) Pa. 1968, Tex. 1982, U.S. Dist. Ct. (so. dist.) Tex. 1982. Assoc. Reid & Priest, NYC, 1955-61, Mexico City, 1961-66; v.p. American & Fgn. Power Co., Inc., Mexico City, 1966-68; atty. Gulf Oil Corp., Pitts., 1968-69, Madrid, 1969-73, London, 1973-80, Houston, 1980—82; pvt. practice London, 1982—84; prof. law South Tex. Coll., Houston, 1983—2010; prof. Bush Grad. Sch. Tex. A&M U., Coll. Sta., 2001—05. With U.S. Army, 1953-55. Mem. Am. Soc. Internat. Law. Home: Houston, Tex. Died Apr. 19, 2010.

GRAY, ARTHUR, JR., investment counselor; b. NYC, Dec. 21, 1922; s. Arthur and Beatriz (Lerner) G.; m. Adele Hall, Dec. 1944 (div. 1954); children— Michael H., Kathleen W., John M., Wendy L.; m. Betty Johnson; children— Lydia B., Elisabeth C. Asso. Student, Lawrenceville School, NJ, 1937-40, Mass. Inst. Tech., 1941-42. With Kuhn, Loeb & Co., 1945-53; pres. Michael Myerberg Prodns., 1953-57; exec. v.p., dir. A.M. Kidder & Co., Inc., 1957-59; sr. partner Gray & Co.; mem. N.Y. Stock Exchange, 1959-75; 1st v.p. Mitchell, Hutchins; chmn. Tallasi Mgmt. Co., NYC, 1975-80; mng. dir. Dreman Gray & Embry, 1981-83; pres., chief exec. officer Dreyfus Personal Mgmt., 1984-93; mng. dir. Cowen Asset Mgmt., NYC, 1993-99; sr. mng. dir. Carret & Co., NYC, from 1999. Bd. dirs. Seventh Generation, Inc., GeneLabs, Inc. Pres. bd. Speech and Hearing Inst., 1970-74; chmn. spl. events Citizens for Eisenhower-Nixon, 1952; trustee Am. Mus. Natural History; pres. Lerner-Gray Found.; bd. dirs. ICD Internat. Ctr. for Disabled, Smithsonian Nat. Mus. of Natural History; trustee Woodlwan Cemetery. Served to 1st lt. US-AAF, 1942-45. Decorated D.F.C., Air medal with 4 oak leaf clusters. Mem. Am. Arbitration Assn. (dir.), Sigma Alpha Epsilon. Presbyn. (trustee). Clubs: Union, University (N.Y.C.). Home: Haverhill, NH. Died Dec. 14, 2009.

GRAY, ARTHUR EVERETT, utility company executive; b. Collinsville, Ill., Jan. 21, 1931; s. Arthur and Irene Sylvetta (Fletcher) G.; m. Margaret Helen Fuhrman, May 2, 1959; 1 child, Peggy Ellen BS in Acctg., U. Ill., Urbana, 1952. Asst. sec. Ill. Power Co., Decatur, Ill., 1968-71, mgr. acctg., asst. sec., 1971-73, controller, asst. sec., 1973-74, v.p., 1979-81, v.p., sec., from 1981. Served to cpl. U.S. Army, 1952-54; Korea Mem. Met. Decatur C. of C., Ill. State C. of C. Republican. Methodist. Home: Decatur, Ill. Died Oct. 19, 2009.

GRAY, CHARLES AUGUSTUS, banker; b. Syracuse, NY, Sept. 16, 1928; s. Charles William and Elizabeth Marie (Koch) G. Cert., Am. Inst. Banking, 1958, Sch. Bank Adminstrn., 1961. Cert. internal auditor. With Mchts. Nat. Bank & Trust Co. of Syracuse, 1946-77, auditor, 1959-77, v.p., 1970-77; N.Y. State dir. Bank Adminstrn. Inst., 1970-72; regional auditor cen. N.Y. region Irving Bank Corp., 1977-82, v.p. cen. N.Y. region, 1982-89. Author: A History of Brantingham, 2000. Treas. Upper N.Y. Synod, Luth. Ch. in Am., 1966-87, Upstate N.Y. Synod, Evang. Luth. Ch. in Am., 1988-2002, Meml. Masonic Temple Corp., 1996—, Luth. Found. Upstate N.Y., 1977-78, bd. dirs., 1980—; pres. Interfrat. Alumni Coun., Syracuse U., 1980-83; treas. N.Y. State Coun. Deliberation, 1997—. Mem. Bank Adminstrn. Inst. (pres. central N.Y. chpt. 1970-72), Inst. Internal Auditors (treas. cen. N.Y. chpt. 1974-76, pres. 1985-86), Lions (pres. local club 1973-75), Masons, Shriners. Republican. Died Mar. 3, 2010.

GRAY, JOHN BULLARD, manufacturing executive; b. Boston, Oct. 9, 1927; s. Francis Calley and Helen Rotch (Bullard) G.; m. Virginia Hamilton Tripp, June 25, 1949; children: John Bullard, David M., Lucinda M. AB, Harvard U., 1949, MBA, 1951. Gen. mgr. Dennison Mfg. Co., Framingham, Mass., 1962-74, sr. v.p., 1974-79, exec. v.p., 1979-86, pres., chief operating officer, from 1986, also dir. Bd. dirs. EG&G, Inc., Wellesley, Mass., State St. Bank, Boston, Liberty Mut. Ins. Cos., Boston. Selectman, Town of Dover, Mass., 1960-64. Served with USMC, 1945-46 Mem.: Dedham Country (Mass.) (pres. 1979-81). Home: Dover, Mass. Died June 14, 2010.

GRAY, KATHERINE WILSON, newspaper editor; b. Sumter, SC, Aug. 23, 1940; d. Thomas III and Suzanne Barden (Winstead) Wilson; m. Kermit S. King (div. 1980); children: Suzanne E., John D.; m. Robert Faulkner Gray II, July 14, 1990. AB in Journalism cum laude, U. N.C., 1961. Reporter Charlotte (N.C.) Observer, 1961-62; advt. and news copywriter Sta. WWOK-FM, Charlotte, 1962-63; advt. copywriter Belk, Charlotte, 1963-64; asst. dir. pub. rels. Winthrop Coll., Rock Hill, S.C., 1964-67; exec. women's editor The State and Columbia (S.C.) Record, 1968-69, reporter, 1979-84; assoc. editl. page editor Columbia Record, 1984-87, editl. page editor, 1987-88; assoc. editl. page editor The State, Columbia, from 1988. Bd. dirs. Greater Columbia Fighting Back Task Force against Alcohol and Drug Abuse, 1990—, Columbia Commn. Children and Youth, 1992-95. Recipient Blue Cross-Blue Shield award, 1981, Media Person of Yr. award Animal Protection League, 1989; Tribute to Women in Industry honoree YWCA Midlands, 1991. Mem. Nat. Fedn. Press Women (award 1992), Nat. Conf. Editl. Writers, Media Women S.C. (award, Media Woman of Yr. 1987), S.C. Press Assn. (10 awards 1980-94), Columbia Media Club, Summit Club, Phi Beta Kappa, Kappa Tau Alpha. Home: Columbia, SC. Died Jan. 16, 2009.

GRAY, MARGARET EDNA, nursing educator, department chairman, dean; b. Norfolk, Va., June 11, 1931; d. William E. and Margaret E. (Smith) G. Diploma Norfolk Gen. Hosp., Sch. Nursing, 1952; BSN, Columbia U., 1956; MS, U. Md., 1966; EdD, Va. Poly. Inst. and State U., 1980. Staff nurse Norfolk Gen. Hosp., 1952-55, asst. night supr., 1953-54, instr. med.-surg. nursing, 1956-58, Riverside Hosp. Sch. Nursing, Newport News, Va., 1958-64; ednl. dir. Va. Bd. Nursing, Richmond, 1965-69; coord. health technology Va. Dept. CC, Richmond, 1969—72; assoc. prof. nursing, dir. nursing program Va. Appalachian Tricoll., Abingdon, 1972-78; grad. rsch. asst. Va. Poly. Inst. and State U., Blacksburg, 1979; mem. adj. faculty outreach grad. program U. Va. Sch. Nursing, Charlottesville, 1977-79, asst. prof. nursing grad. program, 1980-82; chmn. dept. nursing Va. State U., Petersburg, 1982-87; prof., dean sch. nursing Ga. Southwestern Coll., Americus, 1988-96; ret., 1996. Cons. nursing programs various c.cs. in Va., from 1969; mem. adv. com. ARC Health Systems Agy., Va., 1977—78, Tenn., 1977—78; mem. Rosalyn Carter Inst. tng. com. Contbr. articles on health care edn. to profl. publ. Mem. human rights com. Southside Tng. Ctr. and mem. adv. com. allied health programs John Tyler C.C., Chester, Va. Recipient Woman of Achievement award Americus/Sumter County Bus. and Profl. Women, 1989-90; pres. Americus/Sumter County BPW, 1993-94. Mem. ANA, Nat. League Nursing, Ga. League Nursing, Ga. Nurses Assn. (cabinet on continuing edn.), Ga. Southwestern Coll. Honor Soc., Sigma Theta Tau Internat. (charter mem. Mu Pi chpt., Lifetime Achievement award 1996). Presbyterian. Home: Chesapeake, Va. Died Mar. 1, 2010.

GRAY, PHILIP HOWARD, former psychologist, writer, educator; b. Cape Rosier, Maine, July 4, 1926; s. Asa and Bernice (Lawrence) G.; m. Iris McKinney, Dec. 31, 1954; children: Cindelyn Gray Eberts, Howard. MA, U. Chgo., 1958; PhD, U. Wash., 1960. Asst. prof. dept. psychology Mont. State U., Bozeman, 1960—65, assoc. prof., 1965—75, prof., 1975—92; ret., 1992. Vis. prof. U. Man., Winnipeg, Can., 1968-70, U. N.H., 1965, U. Mont., 1967, 74, Tufts U., 1968, U. Conn., 1971; pres. Mont. Psychol. Assn., 1968-70 (helped write Mont. licensing law for psychologists); chmn. Mont. Bd. Psychologist Examiners, 1972-74; spkr. sci. and geneal. meetings on ancestry of U.S. presidents; presenter, instr. grad. course on serial killers and the psychopathology of murder; founder Badger Press of Mont., 1998. Organizer folk art exhbns. Mont. and Maine, 1972-79; author: The Comparative Analysis of Behavior, 1966, (with F.L. Ruch and N. Warren) Working with Psychology, 1963, A Directory of Eskimo Artists in Sculpture and Prints, 1974, The Science That Lost Its Mind, 1985, Penobscot Pioneers vol. 1, 1992, vol. 2, 1992, vol. 3, 1993, vol. 4, 1994, vol. 5, 1995, vol. 6, 1996, Mean Streets and Dark Deeds: The He-Man's Guide to Mysteries, 1998, Ghoulies and Ghosties and Long-leggety Beasties: Imprinting Theory Linking Serial Killers, Child Assassins, Molesters, Homosexuality, Feminism and Day Care, 1998, Egoteria of a Psychologist: Poetry, Letters, Memos from Nether Montana, 2001, Classic Inuit Artists: A Critique and Directory of 500 Eminent Artists in Sculpture and Prints, 2006; contbr. numerous articles on behavior to psychol. jours.; contbr. poetry to lit. jours; pub. military articles; contbr. articles to mil. jours. With US Army, 1944—46. Decorated EAME medal Ctrl. Europe and Rhineland Campaigns, Victory medal WWII, Presdl. Unit citation, Ardennes-Alsace Army Occupation medal, Meritorious Unit Commendation; recipient numerous rsch. grants. Fellow: APA, AAAS, Internat. Soc. Rsch. on Aggression, Am. Psychol. Soc.; mem.: SAR (trustee 1989, v.p. Sourdough chpt. 1990, pres. 1991—2006, v.p. gen. intermountain dist. 1997—98, pres. state soc. 1998—99, trustee from 2001, v.p. gen. intermountain dist. 2003—04, 2007—08), NRA (life), Order of the Crown of Charlemagne, Gallatin County Geneal. Soc. (charter, pres. 1991—93), Nat. Geneal. Soc., 78th Divsn. Vets. Assn. (life), Vets. of the Battle of the Bulge WWII (life), New Eng. Hist. Geneal. Soc., Deer Isle-Stonington Hist. Soc., Flagon and Trencher, Order Descs. Colonial Physicians and Chirugiens, Internat. Soc. Human Ethology, Descs. Illegitimate Sons and Daus. of Kings of Britain, Bozeman Rifle and Pistol Club. Republican. Avocations: collecting folk art, first and signed editions of novels, pistol shooting. Home: Bozeman, Mont. Died Nov. 18, 2009.

GREEN, CHARLES ADAM, retired education educator, psychologist; b. Detroit, Mich., Oct. 17, 1927; s. Fred Green and Charlena Cragwall; m. Marilyn Anderson Anderson, Aug. 22, 1987; m. Mildred Saphronia Wilson, Jan. 4, 1957 (div. May 23, 1975); children: Iris Denise Diop, Robin Charles. BA, U. of Mich., 1952; MEd, Wayne State U., 1957, PhD, 1974. Diplomate Am. Coll. Forensic Examiners; lic. psychologist Mich. Tchr. Detroit Bd. of Edn., 1954—58; dir. of spl. edn. Northville (Mich.) State Hosp., 1958—62; sch. psychologist Detroit Bd. of Edn., 1962—68, rsch. assoc., 1968—2001. Pres. Met. Cmty. Housing Devel. Orgn., Detroit, from 1995. Contbr. articles to profl. jours. Chmn., Thunder Bird dist. Boys Scouts of Am., Detroit, 1973—75; chairperson The Westsider Orgn., Detroit, 2000—03; bd. chmn. Highland Park (Mich.) YMCA, 1981—85. Pvt. USAF, 1945—46. Recipient Ability is Ageless award, Operation Able of Mich. Fellow: Am. Assn. on Mental Deficiency; mem.: APA, Phi Delta Kappa. Liberal. Avocations: boating, photography, travel, writing. Home: Detroit, Mich. Died Jan. 6, 2010.

GREEN, LEON W(ILLIAM), mathematics educator; b. Passaic, NJ, Dec. 12, 1925; m. M.G. Benson, Feb. 10, 1956 (dec.); children— Sarah, Eric; m. Jill J. Smith, Apr. 22, 1983 AB, Harvard U., 1948; MA, Yale U., 1949, PhD, 1952. Instr. Princeton U., N.J., 1952-53; instr. math. U. Minn., Mpls., 1953-54, asst. prof., 1954-59, assoc. prof., 1959-63, prof., from 1963. Vis. prof. U. Calif.-San Diego, 1971-72, U. N.C., 1987; exch. prof. U. Paris, 1969. Author: (with others) Flows on Homogeneous Spaces, 1963; contbr. articles to profl. jours. U. Warwick fellow, Eng., 1969 Mem. Am. Math. Soc., Math. Assn. Am., Phi Beta Kappa, Sigma Xi Died Aug. 17, 2009.

GREEN, RICHARD JAMES, aerospace engineer; b. Newark, Apr. 15, 1928; s. John and Alice Margaret (Murdoch) G.; m. Patricia Agnes Higgins, Oct. 7, 1957; children: John, Alice, Richard, Patricia. BS in Biology, Holy Cross Coll., 1949; MS in Physics, Fordham U., 1955; grad. advanced mgmt. program, Harvard U., 1977. Engr. Pratt & Whitney Aircraft, E. Hartford, Conn., 1955-57; R & D engr. Mobil Oil, Paulsboro, N.J., 1957-61; exec. tech. asst. NASA, Washington, 1962-66, mgr. Apollo Lunar Surface Expt. Program, 1966-70; exec. asst. NSF, Washington, 1970-72, dep. asst. dir. rsch. applications, 1972-79, asst. dir. Sci., Tech., and Internat. Affairs Directorate, 1982-89, dir. rsch. facilities office, 1989-91; assoc. dir. Fed. Emergency Mgmt. Agy. (FEMA), Washington, 1979-81; pres. Green Associates Science, Tech. and Internat. Cons., Washington, 1996—2010. Chmn., vice chmn. U.S.-Israel Binat. Sci. Found., Washington, Jerusalem, 1982-90; sr. tech. advisor Tech. Adminstrn., U.S. Dept. Commerce, 1991-92; rsch. prof., dir. spl. projects Colo. Sch. Mines, Golden, 1991-94; dir. spl. programs U. Wyo., Laramie, 1994-95; spl. asst. U. Md. Sys. Adminstrn., 1995-96. Organizer, pres. Penn-Branch Citizen's Assn., Washington, 1963-70; com. chmn. Boy Scouts Am., Washington, 1969-76. Maj. USAF, 1950-54, 1961-62. Recipient Exceptional Sci. Achievement medal NASA, 1969, Commendation award AEC, 1970, Meritorious Svc. award NSF, 1974, U.S. Presdl. Meritorious Svc. award, 1986 Mem. AAAS, Cosmos Club. Roman Catholic. Home: Washington, DC. Died Aug. 4, 2010.

GREEN, ROBERT WAYNE, financial manager, accounting educator; b. NYC, July 2, 1945; s. Donald Edward and Theresa M. (McGuire) G.; m. Carolyn Elvira Casertano, June 17, 1967; children: Mindy Ann, Robert W. Jr. AAS in Acctg., Manhattan Community Coll., 1967; BBA in Acctg., Pace U., 1970. Cert. mgmt. acct., U.S. and Can. Chief acct. Ebasco Svcs. Inc., NYC, 1971-74, mgr. fin. analysis, 1981-87, assst. treas., mgr. fin. planning and analysis, 1987-89; mgr. fin. Ebasco Svcs. of Can. Ltd., Toronto, 1974-76, controller, 1976-77; sec.-treas. Ebastec Lavalin Inc., Toronto, 1977-81; v.p., treas., chief fin. officer Am. Internat. Contractors Inc., from 1989. Asst prof. Pace U., N.Y.C., 1983—. Mem. Inst. Cert. Mgmt. Accts., Controllers Coun., Nat. Assn. Accts. (former dir. CMA programs N.Y. chpt.), Soc. Mgmt. Accts. Alta, Am. Acctg. Assn., Pace U. N.Y. Undergrad. Alumni Assn. (bd. dirs. 1986), Fin. Execs. Inst., Nat. Corp. Cash Mgmt. Assn. Republican. Roman Catholic. Avocations: camping, fishing, swimming, tennis, woodworking. Home: Whiting, NJ. Died Apr. 18, 2009.

GREENBAUM, MAURICE COLEMAN, lawyer; b. Detroit, Apr. 3, 1918; s. Henry and Eva (Klayman) G.; m. Beatrice Wiener, June 28, 1942. BA, Wayne State U., 1938; JD, U. Mich., 1941; LLM, NYU, 1947. Bar: Mich. 1941, N.Y. 1947, Conn. 1948. Assoc. Herman H. Copelon, New Haven, 1948—50, Greenbaum, Wolff & Ernst, NYC, 1950—54, ptnr., 1955—82, Katten, Muchin, Rosenman LLP (formerly Rosenman & Colin, LLP), NYC, 1982—91, counsel, from 1991. Mem. vis. com. Rosenstiel Sch. Marine and Atmospheric Sci.; mem. adv. com. Great Neck Sr. Citizen Ctr.; mem. adv. com. Helen Merrill Fund; bd. dirs. Humanity in Action, Rosenstiel Found., World Rehab. Fund. Co-author: Estate Tax Techniques; grad. editor Tax Law Rev., 1946-47. Village Justice, Kings Point, N.Y., 1985—; assoc. trustee North Shore U. Hosp., Manhasset, N.Y.; bd. trustees N.Y. Found., 1967-83. Served to maj. U.S. Army, 1941-45. Democrat. Jewish. Home: Kings Point, NY. Died Oct. 22, 2009.

GREENBERG, ALLAN DAVID, actuary; b. Winnipeg, Man., Can., Mar. 20, 1945; came to U.S., 1973; s. Ted Isaac and Esther Marlene (Essers) G.; m. Lois Ann Scheer, Dec. 28, 1975; children: James, Sarah. BS, U. Man., 1966, postgrad., 1967. Actuary Prudential Ins. Co., Newark, 1967-76; cons. Coopers & Lybrand, NYC, 1976-78, Peat Marwick & Mitchell Co., NYC, 1978-81; chief actuary, v.p. Geneve Capital Group, Inc., NYC, from 1981, also bd. dirs. Fellow Soc. Actuaries (program com.); mem. Am. Acad. Actuaries. Clubs: Actuaries of N.Y. Jewish. Home: Greenwich, Conn. Died Jan. 11, 2009.

GREENBERG, DAVID BERNARD, chemical engineering educator; b. Norfolk, Va., Nov. 2, 1928; s. Abraham David and Ida (Frenkil) G.; m. Helen Muriel Levine, Aug. 15, 1959 (div. Aug. 1980); children: Lisa, Jan, Jill BS in Chem. Engring., Carnegie Inst. Tech., 1952; MS in Chem. Engring., Johns Hopkins U., 1959; PhD, La. State U., 1964. Registered profl. engr., La. Process engr. U.S. Indsl. Chem. Co., Balt., 1952-55; project engr. FMC Corp., Balt., 1955-56; asst. prof. U.S. Naval Acad., Annapolis, Md., 1958-61; from instr. to prof. La. State U., Baton Rouge, 1961-74; prof. chem. engring. U. Cin., from 1974, head dept., 1974-81, prof. emeritus, 2007. Program dir. engring. divsn. NSF, Washington, 1972-73, chem. and thermal scis. divsn., 1989-90; sr. scientist Chem. Sys. Lab., Dept. Army, Edgewood, Md., 1981-83; cons. Burk & Assocs., New Orleans, 1970-78; lectr. cosmology and math. Inst. for Learning in Retirement, U. Cin. Coll. Continuing Edn., 2001—. Contbr. numerous articles on chem. engring. to profl. jours. Mem. Cin. Mayor's Energy Task Force, 1981—. Served to lt. USNR, 1947-52 Esso rsch. fellow, 1964-65, NSF fellow, 1961 Fellow Am. Soc. for Laser Medicine and Surgery; mem. Am. Inst. Chem. Engrs., Am. Chem. Soc., Am. Soc. for Engring. Edn., Sigma Xi, Tau Beta Pi, Phi Lambda Upsilon. Jewish. Home: Cincinnati, Ohio. Died July 25, 2010.

GREENBERG, ROBERT MILTON, retired psychiatrist; b. Silver Spring, Md., Oct. 24, 1916; s. Joseph and Rae (Levin) G.; m. Johanna Falleti, July 30, 1942 (dec. 1970); children: Roberta Rae, Harold Ellis; m. Jean Mildred Halpern, June 18, 1972; step-children: Susan, Elaine, Jill. AB, George Washington U., 1937, MD, 1941. Diplomate Am. Bd. Psychiatry and Neurology, Nat. Bd. Med. Examiners. Intern Sibley Meml. Hosp., Washington, 1941-42; resident, staff physician VA Hosp., Coatesville, Pa., 1946-51; pvt. practice psychiatry Chevy Chase, Md., 1951-93. Faculty to assoc. clin. prof. psychiatry George Washington U., 1951-87; chief psychiatric cons. Hebrew Home of Greater Washington, 1951-81. Contbr. articles to medico-legal jour. Trauma. Lt. comdr. USNR, 1942-46. Fellow Am. Soc. Psychoanalytic Physicians (pres. 1968-69), Am. Psychiat. Assn. (life); mem. AMA, Wash. Psychiat. Soc., Am. Coll. Psychiatrists (emeritus), Jewish War Vets. (founder and trustee Silver Spring chpt.). Democrat. Jewish. Avocations: travel, reading, antiques. Home: Chevy Chase, Md. Died Mar. 7, 2009.

GREENE, MARCIA SLACUM, editor; b. Balt., Sept. 27, 1952; m. Jackie Greene. Bachelor's degree, James Madison U., Harrisonburg, Va., 1974; Bachelor's degree in Journalism, U. Md., 1976. Taught English Prince Edward Pub. Schools; with Phila. Inquirer, St. Petersburg Times, Fla.; joined Washington Post, Washington, 1983, city desk editor, 2004, asst. dist. editor, politics & govt., city editor, 2006—09. Nieman Fellowship, Harvard U., 1990. Mem.: Nat. Assn. of Black Journalists. Died Jan. 4, 2010.

GREENFIELD, NORMAN SAMUEL, psychologist, educator; b. NYC, June 2, 1923; s. Max and Dorothy (Hertz) G.; m. Marjorie Hanson Klein, May 17, 1969; children— Ellen Beth, Jennifer Ann, Susan Emery. BA, NYU, 1948; MA, U. Calif., Berkeley, 1951, PhD, 1953. Fellow med. psychology Langley Porter Clinic, U. Calif. Med. Center, 1949-50; VA Mental Health Clinic trainee San Francisco, 1950-53; instr. clin. psychology U. Oreg. Med. Sch., 1953-54; from asst. prof. to prof. psychiatry U. Wis. Med. Sch., Madison, 1954—2005, emeritus prof. psychiatry, from 2006; assoc. dir. Wis. Psychiat. Inst., U. Wis. Ctr. for Health Scis., 1961-74. Emeritus prof. psychiatry, 1991—. Co-editor: The New Hospital Psychiatry, Handbook of Psychophysiology, Psychoanalysis and Current Biological Thought; contbr. articles to profl. jours. Served with USAAF, 1943-46. Mem. AAUP, Am. Psychol. Assn., Soc. Psychophysiol. Rsch., Am. Psychosomatic Soc. Died June 10, 2009.

GREENSPAN, DONALD, mathematician, educator; b. NYC, Jan. 24, 1928; BS, NYU, 1948; MS, U. Wis., 1949; PhD, U. Md., 1956. Instr. U. Md., 1948-56; research engr. Hughes Aircraft Co., 1956-57; asst. prof. Purdue U., 1957-61, asso. prof., 1961-62; permanent mem. U. Wis. Math. Research Center, Madison, 1962-68; prof. computer scis., cons. to U. Wis. Computing Center, 1965-78; prof. math. U. Tex., from 1978. Lectr. Am. Math. Assn., 1963-64, U. Mich. Summer Conf., 1964; referee NRC, NSF. Author: Theory and Solution of Ordinary Differential Equations, 1960, Introduction to Partial Differential Equations, 1961, 2d edit., 2000, Introductory Numerical Analysis of Elliptic Boundary Value Problems, 1965, Introduction to Calculus, 1968, Lectures on the Numerical Solutions of Linear, Singular, and Nonlinear Differential Equations, 1968, Introduction to Numerical Analysis and Application, 1970, Discrete Models, 1973, Discrete Numerical Methods in Physics and Engineering, 1974, Arithmetic Applied Mathematics, 1980, Computer-Oriented Mathematical Physics, 1981, (with U. Bulgarelli and V. Casulli) Pressure Methods for the Numerical Solution of Free Surface Fluid Flow, 1984, (with V. Casulli) Numerical Analysis for Applied Mathematics, Science and Engineering, 1988, Quasimolecular Modelling, 1991, Particle Modeling, 1997, A Science Handbook for Musicians, Entrepreneurs and Candidates for Public Office, 2002, N-Body Problems and Models, 2004, Molecular and Particle Modellng of Laminar and Turbulent Flows, 2005, Numerical Solution of Ordinary Differential Equations for Classical, Relativistic and Nano Systems, 2005; editor: Numerical Solutions of Nonlinear Differential Equations, 1966, (with Pal Rosza) Numerical Methods, 1988, 2d rev. edit., 1991; editl. bd. Jour. Computers and Math. with Applications, Systems Analysis-Modelling-Simulation, CDC Handbook of Fluid Dynamics; contbr. articles to profl. jours. Active Common Cause, NAACP. Mem. ACLU, Am. Math. Soc., Am. Phys. Soc., Assn. Computing Machinery, Ams. for Dem. Action. Died May 2, 2010.

GREENSPAN, MICHAEL ALAN, lawyer; b. Bklyn., Dec. 16, 1940; s. Abe and Leona (Peckerar) G.; m. Heather Gold, Aug. 2, 1964; children: Lisa, David. BA, Cornell U., 1962; LLB, Columbia U., 1965. Bar: N.Y. 1965, D.C. 1968. Assoc. Melrod Redman & Gartlan, Washington, 1969; asst. sec., sr. atty. Bd. Govs. Fed. Res. System, Washington, 1969-73; ptnr. Metzger, Noble, Schwarz & Kempler, Washington, 1973-78, Noble, Greenspan & Austin, Washington, 1978-82, Thompson Mitchell, Washington, 1982-96, Thompson Coburn, Washington, from 1996. Adj. prof. U. Balt. Law Sch., 1998—. Author: (with others) Direct Investment and Development in the U.S., 1978; contbr. articles to profl. jours. Trustee Temple Emanuel, Kensington, Md., 1986-88; prin. Coun. for Excellence in Govt., Washington, 1990—. With U.S. Army, 1966-68. Mem. ABA (chmn. com. on fin. markets & instns. sect. antitrust law), Fed. Bar Assn. (coun. banking law com.). Republican. Jewish. Avocations: chess, sign lang., photography, performing. Home: Rockville, Md. Died Jan. 22, 2009.

GREENSPAN, STANLEY IRA, psychiatrist; b. NYC, June 1, 1941; m. Nancy Thorndike; children: Elizabeth, Jake, Sarah. BA cum laude, Harvard U., 1962; MD, Yale U., 1966. Intern SUNY Upstate Med. Ctr., Syracuse, 1966; resident in psychiatry Psychiat. Inst., Columbia Presbyn. Med. Ctr., NYC, 1967; fellowship in adolescent and child psychiatry Hillcrest Children's Ctr., Children's Hosp. Nat. Med. Ctr., 1969; cons. to student health George Washington U., 1969; clin. practice child/adult psychiatry and psychoanalysis, 1970—2010; clin. prof. psychiatry, behavioral sci. and pediatrics George Washington U. Med. Sch., 1982—2010. Rsch. psychiatrist Lab. Psychology, NIMH, 1970, Mental Health Study Ctr., NIMH, 1972-74, asst. chief, 1974, acting chief, 1974-75, chief, 1975-82; dir. Clin. INfant Devel. Program, NIMH, 1975-82; chief Clin. Infant Devel. Rsch. Unit, Lab. Psychology and Psychopathology, IRP, NIMH, 1982-84; chief Clin. Infant/Child Devel. Rsch. Ctr., DMCH, HRSA and NIMH, 1984-86; founder Nat. Ctr. for Clin. Infant Programs, pres. 1975-84, chmn. diagnostic classification com.; others. Editorial bd.: Jour. American Psychoanalytic Assn., Jour. Preventive Psychiatry, Jour. Psychoanalytic Inquiry, Infant Mental Health Jour., Jour. Psychotherapy Practice and Rsch.; author, editor of monographs and books; contbr. chpts. to books and articles to profl. jours. Past mem. Surgeon Gen.' Task Force on Infant Mortality; past regional v.p. World Assn. for Infant Psychiatry and Allied Disciplines. Recipient Edward A. Strecker award for outstanding contbrs. to Am. psychiatry, Pub. Health Svc. Spl. Recognition award, Heintz Hartman prize for contbrs. to psychoanalysis. Fellow Am. Psychiat. Assn. (Ittleson prize for outstanding contbrns. to child psychiatry rsch.); mem. Am. Psychoanalytic Assn. (chmn. com. on program liaison, cert. in adult, child and adolscent psychoanalysis 1979), Am. Coll. Psychiatry, Am. Coll. Psychoanalysis. Died Apr. 27, 2010.

GREENWALD, JOHN EDWARD, publishing executive, journalist, artist; b. NYC, Oct. 28, 1942; s. Herbert and Carrie (Weisberg) G.; m. Rita Lynn Lipman, May 16, 1987. BA, Syracuse U., 1963. Copy boy N.Y. Post, NYC, 1963-64; assoc. editor Air Force Times, Washington, 1967-70; editor The Times Mag., Washington, 1970-80; editorial dir. Jour. Newspapers, Inc. (Fairfax Jour., Arlington Jour., Alexandria Jour., Prince George's Jour., Prince William Jour., Montgomery Jour.), Springfield, Va., 1980-90; editor Am. Legion Mag., Indpls., 1991-94; asst. mng. editor/Sunday & Spl. Projects The Sun, Lowell, Mass., 1994-98; entertainment columnist Waterbury (Conn.) Republican-Am., 2000—10; free-lance writer, from 1999; arts writer Lowell (Mass.) Sun, 2002—10. Film reviewer Times Jour. Co., Springfield, Va., 1967-85. Exhibitions include Nude 2002, Lexington (Ky.) Art League, La Boniche, Whistler House Mus. of Art, 2002, 2003, Higher Ground, 2003, Arts League of Lowell, 2005, 2007, Prescott St. Gallery, Lowell, Mass., 2005. Coord. Lowell Cultural Roundtable, 1998-2009; mem. Arts League of Lowell, 2003-; served with U.S. Army, 1964-67. Died Aug. 3, 2010.

GREER, MELVIN, medical educator; b. NYC, Oct. 14, 1929; s. Aaron and Ceil (Cohen) Jefkel; m. Arline Ebert, Dec. 16, 1951; children: Jonathan, Richard, Alison, David. BA magna cum laude, NYU, 1950, MD, 1954. Intern, resident Bellevue Hosp., NYC, 1954-56; fellow N.Y. Neurol. Inst., Columbia, 1958-61; prof., chmn. dept. neurology U. Fla. Coll. Medicine, Gainesville, 1963-2000. Cons. NIH, 1971—, Fla. Div. Corrections, 1971—; lectr., cons. Navy Dept.; prof. dept. neurol. dept. psychiatry, dept. pediatrics, U. Fla. Coll. Medicine; endowed professorship neurology U. Fla. Coll. Medicine, Gainesville, 1991—; prof. emeritus, dept. Neurology, U. Fla. Coll. Medicine, 2007-, courtesy prof. dept. Psychiatry and Pediat., 2007-, Hon. Alummus U. Fla. 2008 Author: Mass Spectrometry of Biologically Important Aromatic Acids, 1969, Differential Diagnosis of Neurological Diseases, 1977; also articles.; Editorial bd.: Neurology, Geriatics, 1968—. Served to lt. comdr. USNR, 1956-58. Recipient Medallion award Columbia U., 1968, Hippocratic award U. Fla., 1970, Outstanding Clin. Tchr. award, 1975, 79, Hon. Alumnus U. Fla., 2008; NIH grantee, 1962-71 Fellow Am. Acad. Neurology (councillor, sec.-treas. 1977-81, pres.-elect 1983-85, pres. 1985-87), Am. Acad. Pediatrics; mem. Am. Neurol. Assn. (councillor), Soc. Pediatric Research, Am. Pediatric Soc., Phi Beta Kappa, Alpha Omega Alpha. Died May 19, 2010.

GREGG, PAUL CHARLES, occupational health medical officer; b. NYC, Mar. 8, 1925; s. Benjamin Paul and Catherine Jane (Fales) Gregg; m. Ann Taylor Garner, June 11, 1949 (dec. Sept. 1982); children: Paul Charles, Patricia Ann Florek, Janice Taylor Wilkins, Michael Benjamin, Elizabeth Lucette; m. Mildred Louise Hatcher, Apr. 6, 1983. BS, Union Coll., 1947; MD, Johns Hopkins U., 1951, MPH, 1967. Diplomate Am. Bd. Preventive Medicine. With US Navy, 1943, served in Pacific, 1943—44, commd. lt (j.g.), 1951, served active duty, 1951—53, 1962—80, advanced through grades to capt., 1968; intern US Naval Hosp., St. Albans, NY, 1951—52; pvt. practice Levittown, Pa., 1953—62; sr. med. officer USS Essex, 1962—64; asst. dir., tng. Naval Aerospace Med. Inst., Pensacola, Fla., 1964—66, resident, aerospace medicine, 1967—69; sr. med. officer Naval Air Sta., Corpus Christi, Tex.; med. officer Chief Naval Aviation Advanced Tng., 1969—71; commdg. officer Naval Hosp., Naval Regional Med. Ctr., New Orleans, 1976—78, US Naval Hosp., PR, 1978—80; med. officer 2nd Marine Air Wing, Marine Air Bases, East Cherry Point, NC, 1971—73; dep. commdg. officer Naval Aerospace and Regional Med. Ctr., Pensacola, 1974—76; ret., 1980; occupl. health med. officer Naval Air Sta., Pensacola, from 1981. Assoc. clin. prof. Tulane U., 1976—78, U. PR, 1978—80. Fellow: Am. Coll. Preventive Medicine, Aerospace Med. Assn. (assoc.); mem.: AMA, Johns Hopkins Med. Surg. Assn., Assn. Mil. Surgeons, Bucks County Med. Soc. (Pa.), Phi Chi, Phi Delta Theta. Home: Pensacola, Fla. Died Jan. 6, 2009.

GREGORY, ARTHUR ROBERT, toxicologist, oncologist; b. Binghamton, NY, Oct. 19, 1925; s. Arthur Matthewson and Jennie Etta (Barth) Gregory; m. Frances Louise Farnsworth, Dec. 3, 1978; children: Kathleen, Patrick, Brian, James, Jennifer, Joseph, Ann, Arthur, Austin, Lynn, Jane, Steven, Paulette, Stuart, Susanne, Troy. AB, Cornell U., 1949; B in Med. Sci., Albany Med. Coll., 1952; PhD, U NC, 1965. Diplomate Am. Bd. Toxicology. Tchr. Secondary Sch., 1952—54; faculty mem. U. Calif., Riverside, 1966—68, Roswell Pk. Meml. Inst., Buffalo, 1971—72, Buffalo Med. Coll., 1972—75; dir. toxicology lab. NASA, Houston, 1968—71; toxicologist Nat. Inst. Occupational Safety and Health, 1976—80; sr. scientist Consumer Product Safety Commn., Washington, 1980—87, prin. scientist combustion engring., 1987—88; prin. scientist SRA Techs., 1988—89. Contbr. articles to profl. jours. Mem. Internat. Soc. Philos. Enquiry, 1981; state advisor US Congl. Adv. Com., 1983. With USNR, 1943—45. Fellow, NIH, 1965—66. Fellow: NY Acad. Scis.; mem.: Interagy. Testing Commn. Toxic Substances, Am. Conf. Govt. Indsl. Hygienists, Soc. Risk Analysis, Am. Assn. Clin. Toxicologists, Assn. Govt. Toxicologists, Am. Indsl. Hygiene Assn., Am. Coll. Toxicology (pres. specialty sect. risk mgmt.), Soc. Toxicology, Sigma Xi. Home: Sterling, Va. Died Dec. 11, 2009.

GREINER, WILLIAM ROBERT, retired academic administrator; b. Meriden, Conn., June 9, 1934; s. William Robert and Dolores (Quinn) G.; m. Carol A. Morrissey, Aug. 24, 1957; children: Kevin Thomas, Terrence Alan, Daniel Robert, Susan Lynn. BA, Wesleyan U., Conn., 1956; MA in Econs., Yale U., 1959, JD, 1960, LLM, 1966. Bar: Conn. 1961, N.Y. 1973. Asst. prof. Sch. Bus., U. Wash., 1960—64, assoc. prof., 1964—67, Sch. Law, SUNY, Buffalo, 1967—69, prof., from 1969, assoc. provost, 1970—74, assoc. dean, 1975—80; assoc. v.p. acad. affairs SUNY, Buffalo, 1980—83, interim v.p. acad. affairs, 1983—84, provost, 1984—91, pres., 1991—2003. Cons. in field. Author: (with Harold J. Berman) Nature and Functions of Law, 1966, 72, 80, 96; contbr. articles to profl. jours. Home: Buffalo, NY. Died Dec. 19, 2009.

GRENFELL, RAYMOND FREDERIC, physician, researcher; b. West Bridgewater, Pa., Nov. 23, 1917; s. Elisha Raymond and Pearl (Bolland) G.; m. Maude Byrnes Chisholm, Aug. 19, 1944; children: Raymond Frederic, Milton Wilfred, James Byrnes, Robert Chisholm. B.S., U. Pitts., 1939, M.D., 1941. Intern Western Pa. Hosp., Pitts., 1941-42; practice medicine specializing in internal medicine, Jackson, 1946-79, practice medicine specializing in diagnosis and treatment of hypertension, 1979—; mem. staffs River Oaks East, Miss. Bapt. Hosp.; clin. instr. U. Miss. Med. Sch., Jackson, 1955-59, clin. asst. prof. medicine, 1959—, vis. teaching physician, 1977—, head hypertension clinic, 1956-79. Pres. Jackson Symphony Orch. Assn., 1961, Duling PTA, Jackson, 1963; deacon First Baptist Ch., Jackson, 1960—. Served to maj. U.S. Army, 1942-46. Recipient bronze medal Am. Heart Assn., 1963, silver medal, 1965. gov. Am. Coll. Angiology, 1979-86; Am. Coll. Chest Physicians; mem. Am. Soc. Clin. Pharmacology and Therapeutics (dir. 1968, v.p. 1976), Am. Fedn. Clin. Rsch., So. Med. Assn. (councilor 1968-73), Miss. Heart Assn. (pres. 1964-65), Am. Soc. Hypertension, Country Club, Univ. Club (gov. 1974-89). Republican. Home: Jackson, Miss. Died Apr. 5, 2010.

GRENVILLE, GEORGE, film editor; b. NYC, Feb. 22, 1920; m. Claire Bernstein, June 25, 1944; children: Larry Neal, Tony Deanne. BA, U. So. Calif., 1942. Pres. Am. Cinema Editors, West Hollywood, Calif., from 1989. Editor films The Happy Ending, 1970, Dollars, 1972, Bite The Bullet, 1973, Executive Action, 1974, Looking For Mr. Goodbar, 1977, Tom Horn, 1979, Purple Heart, 1983, Iron Eagle, 1985, Judgment. 1989. Died Feb. 12, 2009.

GRESHAM, JOHN KENNETH, state legislator; b. Drew, Miss., May 12, 1930; m. Betty Jo Overstreet. Student, U. Miss., U. Southern Miss. Mem. Miss. Senate; ins. agt.; real estate broker; health care exec. Bd. dirs. Trinity Meth. Ch., S. Washington County Hosp. Mem.: VFW, Greenville C. of C., Am. Legion, Delta Coun., Farm Bur. Democrat. Home: Greenville, Miss. Died Feb. 2, 2009.

GRESSMAN, EUGENE, lawyer; b. Lansing, Mich., Apr. 18, 1917; s. William Albert and Bess Beulah (Nagle) G.; m. Nan Alice Kirby, Aug. 6, 1944 (dec. May 2004); children: William, Margot and Nancy (twins), Eric. AB, U. Mich., 1938, JD with distinction, 1940; LLD, Seton Hall U., 1994. Bar: Mich. 1940, U.S. Supreme Ct. 1945, D.C. 1948, Md. 1959. Atty. SEC, Washington, 1940-43; law clk. to Justice Frank Murphy, U.S. Supreme Ct., 1943-48; ptnr. firm Van Arkel, Kaiser, Gressman, Rosenberg & Driesen, Washington, 1948-77, of counsel, 1977-81, Bredhoff & Kaiser, Washington, 1981-84, Brand & Frulla, Washington, 1984—2005. Spl. counsel US House of Reps., 1976-84; William Rand Kenan Jr. prof. law U. N.C., Chapel Hill, 1977-87, prof. emeritus, 1987-2010; disting. vis. prof. Fordham U. Law Sch., 1982-83, 1987-88; Disting. vis. prof. Seton Hall U. Law Sch., 1987-94; vis. prof. law Ohio State U., 1967, Mich. Law Sch., 1969, George Washington U., 1971-77, Ind. U., 1976, Cath. U. Am., 1977; judge Appeals Tax Ct. Montgomery County, Md., 1959-62; chmn. rules com. U.S. Ct. Appeals for 4th Cir., 1984-89. Author: Supreme Court Practice, 9th edit., 2007; (with Charles A. Wright and others) Federal Practice and Procedure: Jurisdiction, vol. 16, 1977; (with David Crump and David Day) Cases and Materials on Constitutional Law, 1989, 4th edit., 2002; contbr. articles to profl. jours. Fellow Am. Acad. Appellate Lawyers (hon.); mem. ABA, Fed. Bar Assn., D.C. Bar, Am. Law Inst. (life), Am. Judicature Soc., Order of the Coif, Order of Barristers, Phi Beta Kappa, Delta Theta Pi (Lifetime Achievement award). Home: Chapel Hill, NC. Died Jan. 21, 2010.

GRIFFIN, ANDREW STEVEN, urologist; b. Rocky Mount, SC, Nov. 8, 1956; s. Freddie Morton and Gretchen Jones Griffin; m. Anita Gertrude Paslack, Aug. 4, 1979; children: Andrew, Ashley. BA, Wake Forest U., Winston Salem, NC, 1979; MD, Bowman Gray Sch. Medicine, Winston Salem, 1983. Diplomate Am. Bd. Urology. Urologist Candina Urol. Assocs., Winston Salem, from 1988; pres. med. staff Med. Pk. Hosp., Winston Salem, 1997—98, Forsyth Med. Ctr., Winston Salem, 2005—06. Mem.: NC Med. Soc., Am. Urol. Assn. Avocations: race cars, motorcycling. Died Apr. 3, 2010.

GRIFFIN, MARY FRANCES, retired media consultant; b. Cross Hill, SC, Aug. 24, 1925; d. James and Rosa Lee (Carter) G. BA, Benedict Coll., 1947; postgrad., S.C. State Coll., 1948—51, Atlanta U., 1953, Va. State Coll., 1961; MLS, Ind. U., 1957. Tchr., libr. Johnston Tng. Sch., Edgefield County Sch. Dist., SC, 1947—51; libr. Lee County Sch. Dist., Dennis H.S., Bishopville, SC, 1951—52, Greenville County Sch. Dist., SC, 1952—66; libr. cons. S.C. Dept. Edn., Columbia, 1966—87; ret., 1987. Vis. tchr. U. S.C., 1977. Bd. dirs. Greater Columbia Lit. Coun.; mem. Richland County unit Assault on Illiteracy. Recipient Cert. of Living the Legacy award Nat. Coun. Negro Women, 1980. Mem. ALA, Assn. Ednl. Comms. and Tech., S.C. Assn. Curriculum Devel., AAUW (pres. Columbia br. 1978-80), Southeastern Libr. Assn. (sec. 1979-80), S.C. Libr. Assn. (sec. 1979), S.C. Assn. Sch. Librarians, Nat. Assn. State Ednl. and Media Pers. Baptist. Home: Laurens, SC. Died June 16, 2009.

GRIGGY, KENNETH JOSEPH, food company executive; b. Suffield, Ohio, Mar. 7, 1934; s. Edward F. and Margaret M. (Rothermel) G.; m. Janice Marie Doetzel, July 30, 1960; children: Jill, Matthew, Mark, Jennifer. BA, Athenaeum of Ohio, 1956; M.Ed., Xavier U., 1961. With Am. Heart Assn., Cin., 1960-61, Mead Johnson & Co., Evansville, Ind., 1962-64; v.p., dir. consumer product group Ralston Purina Co., St. Louis, 1964-73; pres., dir. domestic ops. Riviana Foods, Inc., Houston, 1973-75; chmn. bd., chief exec. officer Wilson Foods Corp., Oklahoma City, 1975-88; chmn., chief exec. officer G M Assocs., Inc., Oklahoma City, 1989-91; pres., chief exec. officer Golf USA Inc., Oklahoma City, Okla., from 1991. With U.S. Army, 1959-60. Mem. Oklahoma City Golf and Country. Home: Oklahoma City, Okla. Died July 21, 2010.

GRIMES, HOWARD RAY, management consultant; b. Manilla, Iowa, July 24, 1918; s. Ray Herb and Sarah Alice (Saunders) G.; m. Nancy Palmer, Nov. 17, 1993; children from previous marriage: Patricia, Susan, Nancy, Sarah, Laura. Student, U. Wis., Madison, 1939; BA, Grinnell Coll., Iowa, 1940. With Aetna Life & Casualty Co., 1940-82, field supr., regional mgr. Boston, 1950-74, regional dir., v.p., 1974—82; mgmt. cons., 1983-95; chmn. Benefit Svcs. Inc., 1968-93. Bd. dirs. Waterville Co. Inc. Served with USAAF, 1942-45. Sports-Illustrated Silver Anniversary All-Am. Mem. Weston Golf Club (Mass.), Bald Peak Colony Club (NH), The Moorings Club (Fla.), Harvard Club (Boston). Home: Vero Beach, Fla. Died Nov. 17, 2009.

GRIMLEY, JOSEPH FRANCIS, retail company executive; b. New Brunswick, NJ, Jan. 30, 1941; s. Joseph Francis and Wilhelmina ((Lauber Fritz)) Grimley; m. Christina Stratton, May 5, 1962. Student, St. Peters Coll., 1973—78. With Endicott Johnson Corp., Johnson City, NY, from 1961, dist. mgr. NY, Pa., NJ, 1972—79, ops. mgr. East Coast, 1979—86, regional sales mgr., 1986—87, west coast sales mgr., from 1987. With AUS, 1966—68. Decorated Bronze Star, Air medal, Purple Heart. Mem.: DAV, Tri Cities Opera Guild, Nat. Rifle Assn., Broome County Sportsmen's Assn. Republican. Home: Oceanport, NJ. Died June 23, 2010.

GRIMM, REINHOLD, humanities educator; b. Nuremberg, Germany, May 21, 1931; s. Eugen and Anna (Käser) G.; m. Anneliese E. Schmidt, Sept. 25, 1954; 1 dau., Ruth Sabine. Student, U. Erlangen, 1951—56, PhD, 1956; student, U. Colo., 1952—53; DHC (hon.), Georgetown U., 1988. Faculty German lit. U. Erlangen, Germany, 1957—61, U. Frankfurt, Germany, 1961—67; vis. prof. Columbia, N.Y.U., 1967, U. Va., 1978; Alexander Hohlfeld prof. German U. Wis., Madison, 1967—80, Vilas prof. comparative lit. and German, 1980—90; Presdl. prof. German and comparative lit. U. Calif., Riverside, 1990—92, prof., 1992—97, disting. prof., 1997—2003, prof. emeritus, from 2003. Mem. Inst. for Rsch. in Humanities, U. Wis., 1981. Author: Nach dem Naturalismus: Essays zur modernen Dramatik, 1978, Von der Armut und vom Regen: Rilkes Antwort auf die soziale Frage, 1981, Love, Lust and Rebellion: New Approaches to Georg Büchner, 1985, Echo and Disguise: Studies in German and Comparative Literature, 1989, Versuche zur europäischen Literatur, 1994, Felix Pollak as Self-Translator, 2002, Bertolt Brecht: La estructura de su obra, 2004, Fielding's Tom Jones and the European Novel since Antiquity, 2005, Pictorial Conversations: On Margot Scharpenberg's Iconic Poetry, 2006, Die Erweiterung des Kontinents: Brechts "Dreigroschenoper" in Nigeria und der Türkei, 2007; translator: Hans Magnus Enzensberger, Lighter than Air: Moral Poems, 2000, (with I. Hunt) German Twentieth Century Poetry, 2001, Thus and Not Otherwise: Poems by Günter Kunert with Translations and Commentaries by Reinhold Grimm, 2003, Magic Hoods: Selected Prose Poems by Walter Helmut Fritz, 2005, others; editor: Monatshefte, 1979-90, German Quar., 1991-94, Deutsche Romantheorien, 2d edit., 1974, Deutsche Dramentheorien, 3d edit., 1981, Bertolt Brecht, Poetry and Prose, 2003, others; co-editor: Basis, 1970-80, Brecht Yearbook, 1971-81, others; contbr. articles to profl. jours. Recipient Förderungspreis der Stadt Nürnberg, 1964; Guggenheim fellow, 1969-70; Hilldale award, 1988, Elisabeth Fraser de-Bussy Prose prize, 2002, Emeritus award U. Riverside, 2008-09 Mem. Am. Assn. Tchrs. German (hon., pres. 1974-75), Gottfried-Ben-Gesellschaft (hons.), PEN. Home: Riverside, Calif. Died Mar. 5, 2009.

GRINKER, JOEL A., public health educator; b. Chgo., Nov. 4, 1939; s. Bertram H. and Adele J. (Langfelder) G. BA, Wellesley U., 1961; PhD, NYU, 1967. Lic. psychologist. Postdoctoral fellow Rockefeller U., NYC, 1964-69; asst. prof., then assoc. prof. rockefeller U., NYC, 1969-83; prof. human nutrition Sch. Pub. Health U. Mich., Ann Arbor, from 1984, mem. Ctr. Human Growth and Nutrition, from 1984. Vis. scientist Jean Mager USDA/HNRC Tufts Med. Sch., Boston. Mem. NAS. Home: New York, NY. Died June 8, 2010.

GRISMORE, JOHN RICHARD, retired jeweler, watchmaker; b. Corydon, Iowa, Oct. 21, 1924; s. John Arthur and Jennie Gertrude (Bussey) Grismore; m. Virginia Lynn Rice, Dec. 30, 1947; children: John Richard Jr., Carol Lynn. Student, Bradley U., 1946—48. Lic. watchmaker. Ptnr. Grismore Jewelry, Centerville, Iowa, 1952—88; ret., 1988. Author poetry & short stories. Pres. Cmty. Club, Seymour, Iowa, 1956. With US Army, 1943—46, ETO. Methodist. Avocations: poetry, genealogy, astronomy, archaeology, anthropology. Home: Centerville, Iowa. Died June 10, 2009.

GRODSKY, JAMIE ANNE, law educator; b. San Francisco; d. Gerold Morton and Kayla Deane (Wolfe) G. BA in Human Biology/Natural Scis. and History with distinction, Stanford U., 1977; MA, U. Calif., Berkeley, 1986; JD, Stanford Law Sch., 1992. Ednl. dir. Oceanic Soc., San Francisco, 1979-81; rsch. asst. Woods Hole (Mass.) Oceanographic Inst., 1983; analyst Office Tech. Assessment US Congress, Washington, 1984-89; counsel US House Natural Resources Com., Washington, 1993—95, US Senate Judiciary Com., Washington, 1995-97; jud. clk. with chief judge US Ct. Appeals (9th cir.), 1997-98; sr. advisor to the gen. counsel EPA, Washington, 1999—2001; assoc. prof. law U. Minn. Law Sch., Mpls., 2001—05, George Washington U. Law Sch., Washington, 2005—10. Articles editor Stanford Law Rev.; contbr. articles to profl. jours. Trustee Desert Rsch. Inst. Found. Mem.: D.C. Bar Assn., Calif. Bar Assn., Supreme Ct. Bar Assn. Home: Washington, DC. Died May 22, 2010.

GROSS, EGON MILLER, manufacturing executive, lawyer; b. Hachenburg, Westphalia, Fed. Republic Germany, Feb. 12, 1934; came to U.S., 1951; s. Albert and Martha (Giehl) G.; m. Fillis Schaffner, Dec. 28, 1955; children: Stephen M., James M., David M. AB, JD, U. Mich., 1958. Bar: Pa. 1959, U.S. Dist. Ct. (we. dist.) Pa. 1961, U.S. Supreme Ct. 1961. Atty. Orinoco Mining Co., Caracas, Venezuela, 1959-60; attorney U.S. Steel Corp., Pitts., 1958-61, dir. fgn. mfg., 1962-75; pres., chief exec. officer ISG Pa. Corp., Pitts., 1976-79; pres., chief exec. officer, dir. Buderus Corp., Atlanta, 1979-88; pres., chief exec. officer Mgmt. Svcs. Internat., Atlanta, from 1988. Dir. ARI Valve Corp., Marietta, Ga., 1988—, Dickow Pump Co., Marietta, 1988—. Chmn., bd. suprs. highest elected mcpl. office, McMurray, Pa., 1972-76. Leckie Law Sch. scholar U. Mich., 1954-58, RCA fellow,

1958. Mem. Am. Arbitration Assn., Duquesne Club, The Georgian Club, Willow Springs Country Club. Republican. Avocations: reading, gardening, golf. Home: Roswell, Ga. Died Jan. 13, 2009.

GROSSMAN, DAVID WILLIAM, publishing executive; b. NYC, July 17, 1930; s. Charles and Rose Grossman; m. Marilyn Klein, Feb. 2, 1952; children: Barbara Ruth, Stephen Michael, Jeffrey Alan. Direct response mgr. Esquire, Inc., NYC, 1957—61, Redbook mag., 1962—66, McCall's, 1967—76; pres. Am. Media Assocs., 1976—81; circulation dir. Sheet Music Mag., Katonah, NY, from 1981. With US Army, 1952—54, Republic of Korea. Mem.: Phi Beta Kappa. Jewish. Home: Somers, NY. Died Dec. 6, 2009.

GROVER, CHARLES WYMAN, diplomat; b. Waltham, Mass., July 24, 1928; s. Eugene Sears and Louise (Wyman) G.; m. Janet Hilma Halsten, Aug. 25, 1957; children: Marisa, Charles, Michael, Ellen. BA, Antioch Coll., 1951; MA, U. Oreg., 1953; postgrad. in Latin Am. studies, Tulane U., 1965-66; postgrad., Stanford U., 1970-71. Joined fgn. service Dept. State, 1956; consul Medellin, Columbia, 1971-73; dep. exec. dir. Bur. Latin Am. Affairs, Dept. State, Washington, 1973-75, personnel officer, 1975-78; dep. chief of mission Santiago, Chile, 1978-82; consul gen. Guavaquil, Ecuador, from 1982. Served as cpl. U.S. Army, 1953-55. Mem. Am. Fgn. Service Assn., New Eng. Historic Geneal. Soc. Home: Hampstead, NH. Died Feb. 26, 2009.

GROVER, NORMAN LAMOTTE, theologian, philosopher; b. Topeka, Feb. 9, 1928; s. LaMotte and Virginia Grace (Alspach) G.; m. Anne Stottler, June 24, 1950; children: Jennifer Jean, Peter Neal, Rebecca Louise Grover Verna, Sandra Christine Grover Mason. B. Mech. Engring., Rensselaer Poly. Inst., 1948; B.D., Yale, 1951, S.T.M., 1952, PhD, 1957. Mem. faculty, chaplain Hollins (Va.) Coll., 1954-57, asst. prof. religion, 1956-57; ordained to ministry Presbyn. Ch., 1952; head dept. philosophy and religion Va. Poly. Inst. and State U., 1957-75, prof. philosophy and religion, 1961-83, prof. religion, 1983-91, prof. emeritus, from 1991. Adj. prof. Ctr. for Study Sci. in Soc., 1983-86, guest lectr. computer sci., 2005; mem. supervising com. So. leadership tng. project Fund for Republic, 1955-56; assoc. Danforth Found., 1958—, sr. assoc., 1962—, chmn. Va., N.C. and S.C. conf., 1962; psychotherapeutic counsellor Blacksburg Community Counselling Center, 1962-65 Bd. dirs. YMCA at Va. Tech. (Gold Triangle award 1962); bd. dirs. United Campus Ministries of Blacksburg, 1986-95; mem. Blacksburg Master Chorale and Va. Tech. Concert Choir Concert Tour in Berlin, Poland, Czech Republic, Salzburg, 1992, Germany, Austria, Czech Republic, 1995, England, Scotland, 2003; concert under Robert Shaw, 1998; study trip to Costa Rica, Nicaragua, El Salvador and Guatemala Presbyn. Ch. U.S.A. Presbytery of Peaks Partnership with CEDEPCA, 1989, 91; mem. Habitat for Humanity, New River Valley chpt., Montgomery County Race Rels. Work Group, Ecumenical Alliance of New River Valley; mem. local convening com. Interfaith Social Concerns Network, 1999—; mem. Montgomery County Dem. Com., 2004—; mem. Unified Coalition for Am. Indian Conerns. Danforth Found. grantee, 1967—69. Mem.: AARP (co-chaplain Blacksburg, Va. chpt.), ACLU, NAACP (life; exec. bd. Montgomery, Floyd, Radford br. from 1999, Mountain Climber award 2000, Martin Luther King Jr. Cmty. Svc. award 2006, Nannie B. Hairston Cmty. Svc. award 2006), AAUP (sec.-treas. chpt. 1959—60, v.p. chpt. 1960—61, pres. Va. Poly. Inst. and State U. chpt. 1961—62, sec.-treas. chpt. 1977—80, v.p. chpt. 1980—81, pres. Va. Poly. Inst. and State U. chpt. 1981—82, v.p. chpt. 1992—94), Ctr. for Theology and the Natural Scis., Am. Acad. Religion (chmn. SE region theology/philosophy religion sect. 1983—85, citizen amb. team to Ukraine and Russia 1993, China 1994, Yale U. alumni schs. com. from 1997, Yale Divinity Sch. reunion com. from 2006), So. Soc. Philosophy and Psychology, Va. Philos. Assn. (pres. 1969), People to People Internat. (Am. People amb. del. to India, Nepal and Tibet 1996, China 2000), Wilderness Soc., Smithsonian Assocs., Sierra Club, Bread for the World, Coalition for Justice in Ctrl. Am. (bd. dirs., v.p. 1990—94), Amnesty Internat., So. Poverty Law Ctr. (Wall Tolerance Honoree). Avocations: walking, singing. Home: Blacksburg, Va. Died June 15, 2010.

GROWT, JOHN CHARLES, personnel manager; b. LaCrosse, Wis., Mar. 4, 1930; s. Glenn Nichols and Fern Esther (Schroeder) Growt; m. Mary Frances Van Laanen, July 12, 1952; children: James, Tracy, Thomas, Katherine. BA, Ripon Coll., Wis., 1951. V.p. Green Bay Drop Forge Co., Wis., 1953—79; ptnr. Temporary Employment Svc., Green Bay, 1979—84; exec. dir. C. of C., De Pere, Wis., 1985—85; mayor City of De Pere, 1966—70; aslerman, 1961—66; mem. Gov.'s Fox River Locks Task Force, Appleton, Wis., 1982—84; field rep. Equitable Reserve Assn., Neenah, Wis., 1985—88; personnel mgr. Badger Wood Products, from 1988. Treas. De Pere Hist. Soc.; sec. adv. bd. Salvation Army. With USMC, 1951—53. Mem.: De Pere C. of C. (named Citizen of Yr. 1970), Wis. C. of C. Execs., Oneida Golf and Riding (Green Bay) (pres. 1974), Rotary (De Pere) (Roses for Living award 1966), Kiwanis (past pres.). Republican. Roman Catholic. Home: De Pere, Wis. Died Apr. 10, 2010.

GRUBE, DICK DEWAYNE, museum director; b. Punxsutawney, Pa., Feb. 9, 1933; s. E. Norman and Margaret F. Grube; m. Deanna A. Cook, Dec. 13, 1958; children: Elizabeth, Margaret, Jennifer. BS, Troy U., 1969. Commd. 2d lt. U.S. Army, 1952, advanced through grades to Lt. Col., ret., 1973; dir. Nat. Infantry Mus., from 1972. Chmn. Hist. Chattachoochee Commn., Eufala, Ala., 1978-79. Recipient award Gov. of Ga., 1991. Mem. Mil. Order World Wars (comdr.). Episcopalian. Home: Columbus, Ga. Died Mar. 29, 2010.

GRUNES, DAVID LEON, research soil scientist, educator, editor; b. Paterson, NJ, June 29, 1921; s. Jacob and Gussie (Griggs) G.; m. Willa Freeman Grunes, June 26, 1949; children— Lee Alan, Mitchell Ray, Rima Louise BS, Rutgers U., 1944; PhD, U. Calif., 1951. With USDA, 1950-96, tech. assistance expert to Internat. Atomic Energy Agy., UN, 1963-64, rsch. soil scientist Ithaca, NY, 1964-96; assoc. prof. crop and soil scis. Cornell U., Ithaca, 1967-76, prof., 1976-97; collaborator USDA, Ithaca, from 1996. Cons. editor soils, agr. McGraw-Hill Ency., Sci. and Tech., 1965-88. Contbr. chpts. to books, articles to profl. jours. Served with U.S. Army, 1944-45 Recipient Rsch. award USDA, 1959, 82, 89, 92, Am. Soc. Agronomy (Northeastern chpt.), 1988. Fellow AAAS, Am. Inst. Chemists, Am. Soc. Agronomy, Soil Sci. Soc. Am.; mem. Internat. Soc. Soil Sci., Council for Agrl. Sci. and Tech., Sigma Xi Home: Ithaca, NY. Died Apr. 19, 2009.

GUBSER, PETER ANTON, political scientist, writer, educator; b. Tulsa, May 9, 1941; s. Eugene Herbert and Mary (Douglass) G.; m. Annie Yeni-Komshian, Aug. 15, 1969; children: Sasha Mary-Helen, Christi Valerie. BA, Yale U., 1964; MA, Am. U. Beirut, 1966; PhD, Oxford U., Eng., 1970. Rsch. fellow U. Manchester, Eng., 1970-72; assoc. rsch. scientist American Institutes for Rsch., Washington, 1972-74; asst. rep. Ford Found., Beirut, 1974-77; pres. American Near East Refugee Aid, Washington, 1977—2007. Bd. dirs. Internat. Svc. Agencies, Washington, Interaction Wash., Internat. Coll., Beirut, Nat. Coun. on U.S.-Arab Rels., Washington, Found. for Mid. East Peace, Washington, Global Devel. Forum, Amman, Jordan; adj. prof. Georgetown U., Washington, 1995-2003, with Healing Across the Divides MA, American Friends UNRWA, Wash.; lectr. various govt. and non-govt. instns., 1977-2010. Author: Politics and Change at Karak, Jordan, 1973, Jordan: Crossroads of Middle East Events, 1983, Historical Dictionary of Hashemite Kingdom of Jordan, 1991, Saladin: Empire and Holy war, 2010. Mem. Somerset (Md.) Town Coun., 1994—2004, Montgomery County Adv. Bd., from 2004. Mem.: Washington Inst. Fgn. Affairs, Middle East Studies Assn., Middle East Inst., Am. Polit. Sci. Assn., Cosmos Club, Order of the Hosp. of St. John of Jerusalem. Democrat. Mem. Christian Ch. Avocations: hiking, reading, travel. Home: Chevy Chase, Md. Died Sept. 2, 2010.

GUCCIONE, BOB (ROBERT CHARLES JOSEP GUCCIONE), publishing executive, painter; b. Bklyn., Dec. 17, 1930; s. Anthony and Nina G.; m. Lilyann Becker, 1949 (div.); 1 child, Tonia; m. Muriel Hudson, 1966 (div. 1979); children: Bob Jr., Nina, Anthony, Nick; m. Kathy Keeton, Jan. 17, 1988 (dec. Sept. 19, 1997); m. April Dawn Warren, 2006 Chmn., CEO Penthouse Internat., Inc., 1965—2003; chmn. Gen. Media International Inc., 1988—2003. Pub. Viva mag., 1973-78, Omni mag., 1978-95 Artist, 1948-55, 92-2010; several gallery exhibits and museum shows, 1992-93; prodr: (films) Caligula, 1979; exec. prodr.: (TV shows) Omni: The New Frontier, Omni: Visions of Tomorrow Achievements include starting the magazine Penthouse in 1965 in England and brought to America in 1969. Avocations: collecting art, mostly impressionist, some old masters. Died Oct. 20, 2010.

GUERTIN, ROBERT POWELL, physics professor, dean; b. Trenton, NJ, July 5, 1939; s. Alfred N. and Rhoda (Thomas) G.; m. Margaret Eipper, Aug. 13, 1966 (div. 1999); children: Lynn Frances, Laura Thomas. BS, Trinity Coll., 1961; MA, Wesleyan U., 1963; PhD, U. Rochester, 1969. Asst. prof. physics Tufts U., Medford, Mass., 1968-75, assoc. prof., 1975-83, prof., from 1983, dean Grad. Sch. Arts and Scis., 1985-96, dean Grad. Sch. Rsch. and Profl. Edn., 1994-96. Bd. govs. Univ. Press New England, Hanover, N.H., 1985-96, chmn., 1986-87, 93-94; vis. scientist Nat. High Magnetic Field Lab., Fla., 1996—. Editor books on crystalline electric fields and anomalous rare earth magnetic effects, 1980, 83, 90, 94; contbr. articles to profl. jours. Mem. Lucretia Crocker adv. council Commonwealth Mass., 1986—; bd. dirs. N.E. Assn. Grad. Schs. NSF and NIH rsch. award, 1972-90. Mem. Am. Phys. Soc. (mem. various coms. 1968—). Unitarian Universalist. Avocations: piano, swimming. Home: Boston, Mass. Died June 12, 2009.

GUIDO, MICHAEL ANTHONY, evangelist; b. Lorain, Ohio, Jan. 30, 1915; s. Mike and Julia (DePalma) G.; m. Audrey Forehand, Nov. 25, 1943. Student, Moody Bible Inst., Chgo., 1933-35. Ordained to ministry So. Bapt. Conv., 1939. Min. youth and music lst Presbyn. Ch., Sebring, Fla., 1936-38, lst Bapt. Ch., Lake Charles, La., 1939; evangelist Moody Bible Inst., 1940-50; founder, pres., speaker Guido Evangelistic Assn., Metter, Ga., from 1950. Writer, speaker daily telecast A Seed from the Sower, 1972—, daily broadcaster The Sower, A Seed from the Sower, Seeds from the Sower 25, 1957—. Author: (autobiography) Seeds from the Sower, 1990, rev. edit., 1998, Treasury of Illustrations, 1999; editor Sowing and Reaping mag., 1957—; daily newspaper columnist Seeds from the Sower, 1957—. Named Alumnus of Yr., Moody Bible Inst., 1982, Citizen of Yr., Kiwanis Club, Metter, 1982. Baptist. Interstate bridge named in honor of Michael A. Guido, 1998. Home: Metter, Ga. Died Feb. 21, 2009.

GUILFORD, HARRY GARRETT, biology educator; b. Madison, Wis., June 20, 1923; s. Harry Morrill and Irene Garrett Guilford; m. Vivian Grace Bull Guilford, June 16, 1948; children: Joan Ellen, Susan Marie. PhB, U. Wis., 1944, PhM, 1945, PhD, 1949. Grad. asst. U. Wis., Madison, 1944—49; assoc. prof. Mercer U., Macon, Ga., 1949—50; asst. prof. biology U. Wis., Green Bay, 1950—56, assoc. prof., 1956—63, prof., from 1963, chmn. dept. human biology, 1980—84. Contbr. articles to profl. jours. Mem.: Wis. Acad. Sci. Arts & Letters, Am. Microscopical Soc., Soc. Protozoology, Am. Soc. Parasitologists, Sigma Xi. Congregationalist. Avocations: photography, hiking. Home: Green Bay, Wis. Died Feb. 4, 2009.

GUINEE, VINCENT F., medical epidemiologist; b. NYC, June 3, 1933; s. Florence V. Guinee; married, Mar. 12, 1983. BS, Fordham U., 1955; MD, Cornell U., 1959; MPH, Harvard U., 1966. Bd. cert. preventive medicine; lic. physician, Tex., N.Y. Intern St. Vincent's Hosp., NYC, 1959-60, resident, 1960-61, from asst. to assoc. attending physician, 1968-72, attending physician, 1973-75, cons., from 1976; resident Bellevue and Meml. Hosp., NYC, 1964-65, N.Y.C. Health Dept., 1966-67; clin. asst. dept. pediatrics Belleville Hosp., 1968-75; from clin. instr. to clin. asst. prof. dept. pediatrics NYU Med. Sch., 1968-75; assoc. prof. M.D. Anderson Cancer Ctr., Houston, 1974-92, prof., 1992; prof. epidemiology U. Tex. Sch. Pub. Health, from 1975; course dir., assoc. prof. internal medicine course dir., prof. internal medicine, Houston, 1987-95. Dir. immunization program N.Y.C. Dept. Health, 1966-71, dir. bur. preventable diseases, 1968-71, hearing officer, asst. commr. program rev. and devel., 1972-74; me. audit com. M.D. Anderson Cancer Ctr., med. info. needs com., rsch. com., chmn. edn. com., 1976-77, exec. com. of med. staff; chmn. dept. patient studies U. Tex. M.D. Anderson Cancer Ctr., 1974-95; cons. tng. br. Nat. Ctr. Disease Control, 1965-71, John A. Hartford Found., 1972, Moscow Cancer Rsch. Ctr., 1979, Roswell Park Meml. Inst., 1979, Am. Joint Com. for Cancer Staging and End Results Reporting, 1977-87, Netherlands Cancer Inst., 1979, 81, Nat. Cancer Inst., 1979-81, Nat. Inst. Oncology, Budapest, 1981, ACS, 1991-95; examiner Am. Bd. Preventive Medicine, 1972-76; mem. data monitoring com. Harvard Sch. Pub. Health, 1991—, infections com. St. Vincent's Hosp., 1968-74, N.Y.C. Prison Health Care Com., 1972-73, com. on lead poisoning Nat. Rsch. Coun., 1973, Centralized Cancer Patient Data Sys., 1977-84, numerous others. Reviewer: (jours.) Lancet, Sci., Yerabook of cancer, Cancer, Am. Jour. Medicine, Tex. Medicine, Head and Neck; cons. editor Cancer Bull.; contbr. articles to med. jours., chpts. to books. Chmn. Fordham U. Coun., 1973-75; night mayor N.Y.C., 1968-74. Lt. comdr., maj. USPHS, 1961-64. Fellow ACP (joint com. nat. data resources 1974-76), APHA, Am. Coll. Cardiology (assoc.); mem. AMA (jour. reviewer), Internat. Soc. Pharmacoepidemiology, Am. Coll. Epidemiology, Am. Soc. Clin. Oncology, Am. Fedn. Clin. Rsch., S.W. Sci. Forum, Tex. Med. Assn., N.Y. Acad. Scis., N.Y. State Med. Soc., N.Y. County Med. Soc. (pub. health com. 1968-74, infant mortality com. 1973-74), Harris County Med. Soc. (pub. health com. 1989—), Sigma Xi. Died July 12, 2010.

GUINN, KENNY CARROLL (KENNETH CARROLL GUINN), former Governor of Nevada; b. Garland, Ark., Aug. 24, 1936; m. Dema Guinn, July 7, 1956; children: Jeff, Steve. BA, Calif. State U., Fresno, 1959, MA, 1965; EdD, Utah State U., 1970. Supt. Clark County Sch. Dist., 1969—78; v.p. adminstrn. Nev. Savs. and Loan Assn. (PriMerit Bank), 1978-80; pres., COO Nev. Savs. & Loan Assn. (PriMerit Bank), 1980-85, CEO, 1985-92; pres. Southwest Gas Corp., 1987-88, chmn., CEO, 1988-93; interim pres. U. Nev., Las Vegas, 1994—95; gov. State of Nev., Carson City, 1999—2007. Bd. dirs. MGM Mirage, 2007—10. Republican. Episcopalian. Home: Las Vegas, Nev. Died July 22, 2010.

GUNDLACH, ROBERT WILLIAM, retired physicist; b. Buffalo, Sept. 7, 1926; s. Emanuel G. and Helen (Fuchs) G.; m. Audrey Jean Baker, Jan. 27, 1928; children: Gregory E., Eric R., Kurt B. BA in Physics, U. Buffalo, 1949, postgrad., 1949-51. Teaching asst. physics U. Buffalo, 1949-51; physicist Durez Plastics & Chems., North Tonawanda, NY, 1951-52; project leader Xerox Corp. (then Haloid Co.), Rochester, NY, 1952-55, sr. project leader, 1955-57, rsch. assoc., 1957-59; sr. rsch. assoc. Haloid-Xerox Corp., Rochester, 1959-61; sr. scientist Xerox Corp., Rochester, 1961-63, prin. scientist, 1963-66, rsch. fellow, 1966-78, sr. rsch. fellow, 1978-95, cons., 1995—2010. Contbr.: Xerography and Related Processes, 1965, Inventors at Work; 156 patents related to xerographic copying and printing; contbr. articles to profl. jours. Named to Nat. Inventors Hall of Fame, 2005; recipient Inventor of Yr. award Rochester Patent Law Assn., 1974, C.F. Furnas Meml. award U. Buffalo, 1992, Johann Gutenberg prize Soc. Info. Display, 1993. Mem. Electrostats. Soc. Am. (pres., sr. advisor 1971-94), Imaging Sci. and Tech. (Kosar Meml. award 1976, Vis. Lectr. award 1985, Carlson Meml. award 1986, Fellowship award 1991, Hon. mem. 1999), elected to Nat. Acad. of Engring., 1994. Mem. Soc. Of Friends. Avocations: skiing, canoe camping, birding, windsurfing, inventing. Home: Victor, NY. Died Aug. 18, 2010.

GUNN, WENDELL LAVELLE, insurance company executive; b. Stonewall, Miss., Sept. 14, 1932; s. Christopher Clayburn and Lorena (Logan) G.; m. Roberta Anne Ashmore, Mar. 14, 1959; children: Leslie, Katherine. BS in Acctg., Fla. State U., 1958. Actuarial cons. State of Fla. Dept. Ins., Tallahassee, 1957-59; asst. sec.-treas. Ind. Life & Accident, Jacksonville, Fla., 1959-65; v.p. United Educators Life Ins., Miami, Fla., 1965; controller, asst. sec. Ky. Cen. Life Ins., Lexington, 1965-72; v.p. Mobile Home Industries, Tallahassee, 1972-73; sr. v.p., sec.-treas. Ky. Cen. Life Ins., Lexington, from 1973. Charter mem. U. Ky. Sch. Accountancy Adv. Council, Lexington, 1987—; treas., trustee Lexington Pub. Library, 1986—; mem. indsl. revenue bond rev. com. Lexington-Fayette Urban County, 1984—; chmn. Fayette County Rep. Party, Lexington, 1984-86. Served with USN, 1950-53. Mem. Fin. Execs. Inst. (bd. dirs. 1986—), Am. Council Life Ins. (state v.p. 1982—). Republican. Methodist. Avocations: golf, reading. Home: Dunedin, Fla. Died Feb. 24, 2009.

GUSTKE, ARTHUR NORMAN, judge, lawyer; b. Parkersburg, W.Va., Nov. 1, 1928; s. Walter F. and Freda (Meyer) Gustke; m. Mary Jo Radcliffe, Aug. 9, 1959; children: David, James, Beth. BA, W.Va. U., 1953; JD, 1956. Bar: W.Va. 1956, W.Va. (US Dist. Ct. (no. and so. dist.)) 1956, (US Ct. Appeals (4th cir.)) 1974. Lawyer W.Va. Tax Dept., Charleston, 1956—58; assoc. Hiteshew, Cather & Renner, Parkersburg,

1959—62; mcpl. judge City of Parkersburg, 1963—65; ptnr. Hardman & Gustke, Parkersburg, 1965—74; circuit judge State of W.Va., Parkersburg, from 1975. Guest lectr. W.Va. Jud. Assn., Parkersburg Cmty. Coll. Pres. Mid-Ohio Valley United Fund, Parkersburg, 1982—83; bd. dirs. Parkersburg Cmty. Coll. Found., from 1976. With US Army, 1946—49. Recipient Disting. Svc. award, Parkersburg Jaycees, 1962; named Citizen of Yr., 1979. Mem.: Wood County Bar Assn., W.Va. Bar Assn., W.Va. Jud. Assn. (treas). Republican. Lutheran. Home: Parkersburg, W.Va. Died Sept. 27, 2009.

GUYKER, WILLIAM CHARLES, JR., electrical engineer, researcher; b. Donora, Pa., Aug. 21, 1933; s. William Charles C. and Mary Kurylak (Guyker); m. Alice Jane Burns, June 26, 1971; 1 dau., Patricia Lynn. BSEE, MIT, 1959. Registered profl. engr., Pa. Various engring. positions, 1959-68; with Allegheny Power Service Corp., Greensburg, Pa., 1968—85, prin. engr. research and devel., 1985-90, prin. engr., engring. group, 1990-91, mgr. R&D, 1991-96, cons. R&D, 1996-99, corp. rsch. dir., 1999—2002; mgr. EPRI Tech. Transfer, 1982—2002; EE. coord. Advanced Power and Electronics Rsch. Ctr., 2002—05. Adj. prof. West Va. U., Morgantown; lectr. U. Pitts., 1970—2002; accreditor Accreditation Bd. for Engring. and Tech., N.Y.C., 1977—; cons., 1996—. Contbr. articles to profl. jours. Mem. West Pa. Sustainable Energy Fund Bd. Served with US Army, 1952-55. Recipient Lifetime Achievement award, EPRI Environment Sector. Fellow IEEE (life, chmn. Pitts. sect. 1973-74 Power, Group award, Centennial medal 1984, Energy prize); mem. Am. Mgmt. Assn., AAAS, Elks., USDA-Nat. Biomass Initiative (biomass R & D tech. adv. com. mem.). Achievements include research in engring.; construction pioneering developments of transmission tech., mining, power plant work, customer applications, multiple system control and comm. application; expertise in Acid Rain, Global Warming, EMF, Power Quality, and other issues developed at sites and with engineering and regulatory requirements. Home: Greensburg, Pa. Died Sept. 29, 2009.

GUYON, JOHN CARL, retired academic administrator; b. Washington, Pa., Oct. 16, 1931; s. Carl Alexander and Sara Myrle (Bumgarner) G.; m. Elizabeth Joyce Smith, Nov. 12, 1955; children: Cynthia Joan, John Carl, II. BA, Washington and Jefferson Coll., 1953; MS, Toledo U., 1958; PhD, Purdue U., 1961. Mem. faculty U. Mo., 1961—71, prof. chemistry, chmn. dept., 1970—71, Memphis State U., 1971—74; dean Coll. Sci., So. Ill. U., Carbondale, 1974—75, Coll. Sci., So. Ill. U. (Grad. Sch.), assoc. v.p. research, 1976—80, v.p. acad. affairs and research, 1980; pres. So. Ill. U., 1987—95, chancellor, 1996—97. Author: Aanlytical Chemistry, 1965, Qualitative Analysis, 1966, Solution Equilbria, 1969; also articles, abstracts.; Gen. editor: Instrumental Methods of Analysis. With AUS, 1954—56. Eli Lilly Co. fellow, 1959-61; Owens Ill. Co. fellow, 1958; Jesse W. Lazear scholar, 1953 Mem. Am. Chem. Soc., AAAS, Phi Beta Kappa, Sigma Xi, Phi, Lambda Upsilon. Home: Carbondale, Ill. Died Mar. 17, 2010.

GWILLIM, RUSSELL ADAMS, manufacturing executive; b. Passaic, NJ, May 4, 1922; m. Elda E. Gwillim; children: Joanne, Linda, Cynthia. BS, MIT, 1948. Sales engr. CR Industries, Elgin, Ill., 1948-58, gen. sales mgr., 1958-64, v.p. mktg., 1964-65, exec. v.p., 1965-69, pres., 1969-84; chmn. bd. Safety-Kleen Corp., Elgin, 1974-90, chmn. emeritus, from 1990. Bd. dirs. Safety-Kleen Corp., Elgin. Chmn. United Way of Elgin, 1980; bd. dirs. Elgin Assn. Commerce, 1978, Ill. C. of C., 1979; mem. adv. bd. St. Joseph Hosp., Elgin, 1984. Served with U.S. Army, 1942-46, PTO. Mem.: Butler Country (Oak Brook, Ill.); Medinah Country (Itasca, Ill.) (bd. dirs. 1976—). Presbyterian. Avocation: golf. Home: Hilton Head Island, SC. Died Sept. 15, 2009.

GWINN, ROBERT P., retired publishing executive; b. Anderson, Ind., June 30, 1907; s. Marshall and Margaret (Cather) G.; m. Nancy Flanders, Jan. 20, 1942 (dec. 1989); 1 child, Richard Herbert. PhB, U. Chgo., 1929. With Sunbeam Corp., Chgo., 1936-51, gen. sales mgr. elec. appliance div., 1951-52, v.p., dir., 1952-55, pres., chief exec. officer, 1955-71, chmn. bd., chief exec. officer, 1971-82, also bd. dirs.; chmn. bd., chief exec. officer Ency. Britannica, Inc., Chgo., 1973-93, chmn. emeritus, from 1993. Chmn. bd., CEO Titan Oil Co., Riverside; bd. dirs. Continental Assurance Co., Continental Casualty Co., CNA/Fin. Corp., Inst. for Philos. Rsch., Alberto-Culver Corp. Trustee Chgo. Zool. Soc., U. Chgo.; mem. Citizens Adv. Com., Chgo.; bd. fellows Harvard Med. Sch., James Madison Coun., Libr. of Congress. Mem. Soc. Chgo., Internat. Food and Wine Soc. Chgo., Mid. Am. Club, Elec. Mfrs. Club (hon.), Comml. Club Chgo., Casino Club, Execs. Club, Bird Key Yacht Club, Riverside Golf Club, U. Chgo. Club, Alpha Sigma Phi. Home: Riverside, Ill. Died Dec. 10, 2009.

HAAS, BARBARA DOLORES, public relations executive, marketing educator; b. Pitts., Sept. 1, 1940; d. Edward Howard and Bertha Dolores (Estel) Yunk; m. Norbert James Haas, July 21, 1962; children: Susan, Craig, Cynthia. BA in Journalism, Pa. State U., 1962; MS, LaRoche Coll., 1984. Coord. publs. Quaker Valley Schs., Sewickley, Pa., 1972—80; pres. Wordcrafters, Inc., Pitts., 1980—82; dir. pub. affairs West Penn Hosp., Pitts., 1982—85; v.p. pub. rels. Equibank, Pitts., 1985—87; sr. v.p. mktg. Gainer Bank, Merrillville, Ind., 1986—92; group v.p. consumer svcs. No. Ind. Pub. Svc. Co., Merrillville, from 1992. Capital campaign chmn. The Caring Peace; bd. dirs. N.W. Ind. Symphony; Lake Are United Way. Recipient MacEachren award, Nat. Hosp. Assn., 1985. Mem.: Exec. Women's Coun., Women in Comm. Inc. (nat. pres. 1979—80, Georgina MacDougal Davis award 1982), Pub. Rels. Soc. Am., Internat. Assn. Bus. Communicators (Golden Quill award 1985). Avocation: tennis. Home: Valparaiso, Ind. Died Sept. 23, 2009.

HAAS, VALERIE S., classicist, educator; b. NYC, Apr. 5, 1918; d. Ignatz and Flora (Stein) Haas. BA in Latin, Hunter Coll., 1944; at, Columbia U., 1945—47; MA in Latin, U. Wash., Seattle, 1968. Substitute tchr. Brearley Sch., NYC, 1945—47; tchr. Latin Army Post Sch. Schofield, Oahu, Hawaii, 1947—48, Iolani Sch., Honolulu, 1950—54, Dept. Edn., 1955—57, Iolani Sch., 1957—63, Misawa H.S., Misawa Air Base, Japan, 1963—64, U. Hawaii, Honolulu, 1964—69, Leeward Cmty. Coll., 1968—71, Iolani Sch., from 1971. Mem. exec. com. Cmty. Scholarship Program, Honolulu, from 1972; editor Iolani Sch Bull., from 1979. Mem.: Vergilian Soc. (scholarship award 1972), Calif. Classical Assn., Am. Classical League. Home: Honolulu, Hawaii. Died Jan. 12, 2010.

HACK, MAURICE CHARLES, JR., dentist; b. Indpls., Jan. 7, 1935; s. Maurice Charles and Cornelia Gurtrude (Hirsch) Hack; m. Barbara Ann Moore, Nov. 25, 1970; children: Patricia, Paul. DDS, Loyola U., 1959. With Pub. Health Svc., Oslo, 1963—64; gen. practice dentistry Las Vegas, from 1964. To lt. comdr. USNR, 1959—62. Named hon. Ky. Col.; Mosby scholar, Loyola U., 1959. Mem.: Internat. Analgesia Soc., Pierre Fachard Acad., Acad. Gen. Dentistry, Clark County Dental Assn., Nev. Dental Assn., Am. Dental Assn., Blue Key, Desert Inn Country Club, Xi Psi Phi, Sigma Chi. Democrat. Roman Catholic. Home: Henderson, Nev. Died June 18, 2010.

HADGE, JAMES, printing company executive; b. Shalefa, Lebanon, Feb. 11, 1931; arrived in U.S., 1932; s. Leon and Martha (Maloof) Hadge; m. Joesphine Alice Pacillo, Oct. 11, 1953; children: Robert, Doreen, Richard, Deborah, Denise. Student, Northeastern U., 1949—50, Boston U., 1950—51. With Henry Sawyer, Boston, 1948—54; prin. Hadge Printing Co., Boston, 1954—57; plant supt. Fine Impressions, Brookline, Mass., 1957—60; v.p. Farnsworth Press, Boston, 1960—69; prin. Intergraphics, Arlington, Mass., 1969—71; pres. Goodway Graphics, Burlington, Mass., from 1971. Mem.: Boston Club of Printing House Craftsmen (dir.). Roman Catholic. Died Sept. 29, 2009.

HAGUE, RICHARD NORRIS, architect; b. Chgo., Aug. 4, 1934; s. Howard B. and Harriet (Jones) Hague; m. Gail L. Elwell, Mar. 24, 1960; children: Jonathan Norris, Mark Richard. BA in Architecture, U. Ill., 1959. Prin. Richard N. Hague, River Forest, Ill., 1961—63; with, v.p., pres., dir. Hague-Richards Assocs. Ltd., Chgo., 1964—91; mng. prin. LSH/Hague-Richards Assocs.; with Loebl, Schlossman and Hackl, Inc., from 1992. Mem. Frank Lloyd Wright Home and Studio Adv. Bd., Oak Pk., 1983, Mus. Broadcast Comms., Chgo., Nat. Assn. Realtors, Chgo. Mem.: AIA, Chgo. Archtl. Found., Nat. Coun. Archtl. Registration Bds., Oak Pk. Country Club, Alpha Rho Chi. Home: Fennville, Mich. Died Mar. 8, 2010.

HAGUE, WILLIAM EDWARD, writer; b. Duquesne, Pa., Feb. 2, 1919; s. William Edward and Edith H.; m. Margaret Cleland Anderson, July 22, 1950 (div.). AB, Princeton U., 1940; postgrad., U. Pitts. Sch. Law, 1940-41. Assoc. editor Tide mag., 1947-49; promotion dir. Living for Young Homemakers mag., 1949-50, copy editor, 1951-54, mng. editor, 1954-61; editor Living's Guide to Home Planning mag., 1958-61; with Conde Nast Publs., NYC; sr. editor House & Garden, 1961; editor-in-chief House & Garden Guides, 1962-72; asst. account exec. Fitzgerald Advt. Agy., New Orleans, 1950-51. Author: How to Decorate With Color, 1964, What You Should Know About Furniture, 1965, Planning Your Vacation Home, 1968, Plan Your Baths for Beauty and Efficiency, 1969, Plan The Kitchen That Suits You, 1969, Making The Most of The One-Room Apartment, 1969, Your Vacation House, How To Plan It, 1972, Doubleday's Complete Basic Book of Home Decorating, 1976, Know Your America, California, 1978, Remodel, Don't Move, 1981, The New Complete Basic Book of Home Decorating, 1983; editor: Country Kitchens and Baths, 1987; contbg. editor: Reader's Digest's Household Hints, 1987, Tumbleweed, A Book of Poems, 2006. Lt. USNR, 1942—46. Recipient Dorothy Dawe award for disting. journalistic coverage in home furnishings field, 1969 Mem.: Princeton Triangle Club. Home: New York, NY. Died May 2, 2010.

HAHN, LLOYD EDWARD, gas company executive; b. Buffalo, Jan. 5, 1925; s. Edwin Louis and Fanny Amelia (Schuchardt) H.; m. Sylvia Anna Hahn, June 14, 1948; children: Judith Lynn, Jeffrey Edwin, Douglas Lloyd. B in Mech. Engring., Cornell U., 1949. Various engring. positions Iroquois Gas Corp., Buffalo, 1949-55; asst. supt. Iriquois Gas Corp., Buffalo, 1955-58, supt. dist., 1958-63, gen. supt., 1963-72, v.p., 1972-74, Nat. Fuel Gas Dist. Corp., Buffalo, from 1974. Chmn., mem. adv. com. N.Y. Gas Ops., Buffalo, 1977—. Pres., mem. Gateway United Meth. Youth Ctr., Williamsville, N.Y., 1972-84; chmn., mem. Beechwood-Blocher Homes, Getzville, N.Y., 1980—. Recipient Silver Beaver award Boy Scouts Am., 1970. Mem. Soc. Gas Operators (pres. 1981-82). Lodges: Masons (master Hiram lodge 1969). Republican. Home: Buffalo, NY. Died Mar. 17, 2010.

HAIG, ALEXANDER MEIGS, JR., former United States Secretary of State, retired military officer; b. Phila., Dec. 2, 1924; s. Alexander Meigs and Regina Anne (Murphy) H.; m. Patricia Antoinette Fox, May 24, 1950; children: Alexander P., Brian F., Barbara E. Student, U. Notre Dame, 1943; BS, U.S. Mil. Acad., 1947; MA, Georgetown U., 1961; grad., Naval War Coll., 1960, Army War Coll., 1966; grad. hon. law degree, Niagara U.; LL.D. (hon.), U. Utah. Commd. 2d lt. US Army, 1947, advanced through grades to gen., 1973, staff officer Office Chief of Staff for Ops., 1962-64, mil. asst. to sec. of army, 1964; dep. spl. asst. to sec. & dep. sec. US Dept. Def., 1964-65; bn. and brigade comdr. 1st Inf. Divsn. US Army, Vietnam, 1966-67; regtl. comdr., dep. comdt. US Mil. Acad., 1967-69; mil. asst. to asst. to Pres. for nat. security affairs NSC, Washington, 1969-70, dep. asst. to pres., 1970-73; vice chief of staff US Army, Washington, 1973; chief of staff to Pres. The White House, 1973-74; comdr.-in-chief US European Command (EUCOM), 1974-79; supreme allied comdr. Europe Supreme Headquarters Allied Powers Europe (SHAPE), 1974-79; ret., 1979; pres., COO United Technologies Corp., Hartford, Conn., 1979-81; sec. US Dept. State, Washington, 1981-82. Chmn., pres. Worldwide Associates, Inc., 1984 Author: Caveat: Realism, Reagan and Foreign Policy, 1984, Inner Circles: How America Changed the World, A Memoir, 1992; TV host (weekly program) World Bus. Rev. Decorated D.S.C., Silver Star with oak leaf cluster, Legion of Merit with 2 oak leaf clusters, D.F.C. with 2 oak leaf clusters, Bronze Star with oak leaf cluster, Air medal with 23 oak leaf clusters, Army Commendation medal, Purple Heart U.S.; Nat. Order 5th Class; Gallantry Cross with palm; Civil Actions Honor medal 1st Class; grand officer Nat. Order of Vietnam, Republic of Vietnam; medal of King Abdel-Aziz Saudi Arabia; grand cross Order of Merit Fed. Republic Germany; recipient Disting. Svc. medal Dept. of Def.; Disting. Svc. medal U.S. Army; Man of Yr. award Air Force Assn.; James Forrestal Meml. award, Disting. Grad. award Assn. Grads. West Point. Mem. Soc. of 1st Divsn. Home: Mc Lean, Va. Died Feb. 20, 2010.

HAILE, LEROY YELLOTT, JR., real estate broker, tree farmer; b. Towson, Md., Feb. 6, 1929; s. LeRoy Yellott and Rachel Lillian (Stabler) Haile; m. Felicity Fletcher, June 8, 1957; children: LeRoy Yellott, Rachel Naomi. BS, Hampden-Sydney Coll., 1959. Pres. LeRoy Y. Haile, Inc., Towson, Md., from 1954. Bd. dirs. Towson Bus. Assn., Gunpowder Youth Camps, 1985—86; chmn. Towson 4th of July Parade, 1978. With USN, 1951—54. Mem.: Greater Balt. Bd. Realtors, Balt. County Appraisers Soc., Balt. County Hist. Soc. (pres. 1981—82), Kiwanis (past pres. Towson club). Democrat. Methodist. Home: Baltimore, Md. Died July 30, 2009.

HAIMAN, IRWIN SANFORD, lawyer; b. Cleve., Mar. 19, 1916; s. Alfred W. and Stella H. (Weiss) H.; m. Jeanne D. Jaffee, Mar. 8, 1942; children: Karen H. Schenkel, Susan L. Bensoussan. BA, Western Res. U., 1937; LL.B., Cleve. Marshall Law Sch., 1941; JD, Cleve. State U., 1969. Bar: Ohio 1941, U.S. Ct. Appeals (6th cir.) 1961, U.S. Supreme Ct. 1961. Asst. to pres. Tremco Mfg. Co., Cleve., 1936-42; house counsel William Edwards Co., Cleve., 1947-48; pvt. practice Cleve., 1948-68; ptnr. firm Garber, Simon, Haiman, Gutfeld, Friedman & Jacobs, 1968-80; ptnr. McCarthy, Lebit, Crystal & Haiman, from 1981. Lectr. in speech Western Res. U., 1948-70; dir. Washington Fed. Savs. and Loan Assn.; asst. law dir., prosecutor City of Lyndhurst, Ohio, 1965-79, law dir., 1979-84. Trustee Montefiore Home, Cleve., 1974-88 (life trustee 1988—)—, East End Neighborhood House, 1962-68; councilman City of South Euclid, 1948-54, pres., 1952-54; pres. Young People's Congregation, Fairmount Temple, 1951-52; sec., trustee Surburban Temple, 1962-65, trustee, 1983—, pres., 1984-87; chmn. speakers div., bd. dirs. Cleve. chpt. ARC, 1959-62; chmn. speaker and film div. Cleve. United Appeal, 1961-62; chmn. speakers div. Jewish Welfare Fund Cleve., 1973-79. Served as 1st lt. AUS, 1943-47. Mem. Ohio, Cleve. bar assns., Assn. Trial Lawyers Am., Zeta Beta Tau. Clubs: Oakwood Country, Lake Forest Country (pres. 1971-72, 75-79). Home: Cleveland, Ohio. Died Apr. 20, 2010.

HAINES, WILLIAM JOSEPH, retired pharmaceutical executive; b. Crawfordsville, Ind., Sept. 26, 1919; s. Burt and Lala R. (Luster) Haines; m. Wilma M. Hester, June 6, 1993; 2 children, Paula Sue Haines Curtis-Burn, Eric J. AB summa cum laude, Wabash Coll., 1940, DSc (hon.), 1970; PhD, U. Ill., 1943; grad. exec. program in bus. adminstrn., Columbia Bus. Sch., 1965. Rsch. biochemist Upjohn Co., Kalamazoo, 1943-50, head dept. endocrinology rsch., 1950-54; tech. dir. Armour Labs., Kankakee, Ill., 1954-58; v.p. dir. rsch. Ortho Pharm. Corp., Raritan, NJ, 1958-65, exec. v.p., 1965-67; vice chmn. Johnson & Johnson Internat., 1967-69; dir., mem. exec. com. Johnson & Johnson, New Brunswick, NJ, 1969-79, v.p. corp. office sci. and tech., 1979-82; pres. Bucks-Tech Assocs., Inc., Doylestown, Pa., from 1982. Chmn. sci. adv. com. Alliance Internat. Health Care Trust, 1983-87; former dir. Quidel Corp., La Jolla, Calif.; invited lectr. Laurentian Hormone Conf., 1952, Gordon Rsch. Conf., 1952. Contbr. numerous sci. articles to profl. jours., including pioneer paper on human requirement for essential amino acids, 1942. One of initial investigators to identify essential amino acids for human nutrition; patentee biosynthesis of adrenal cortex hormones, paper chromatography and automatic partition column chromatography of steroids. Trustee Wabash Coll., 1972-93, trustee emeritus, 1993—; trustee Hood Coll., 1975-87, vice chmn. bd., 1982-87, trustee emeritus, 1989—; Joslin Diabetes Found. Inc., Boston, 1974-79; elder Thompson Meml. Presbyn. Ch., New Hope, Pa. Recipient William E. Upjohn prize and medal, 1952, Alumni Merit award Nat. Assn. Wabash Men, 1973. Fellow AAAS, Am. Inst. Chemists; mem. Am. Chem. Soc. (med. cheistry div.), N.Y. Acad. Scis., Endocrine Soc., Am. Soc. Biol. Chemists, Soc. Chem. Industry (former chmn. Am. sect.), Pharm. Mfrs. Assn. (former chmn. R&D sec.), Assn. Rsch. Dirs., Indsl. Rsch. Inst., (dir. emeritus), N.J. Acad. Scis., Soc. Exptl. Biology and Medicine, Pacific Coast Fertility Soc., Am. Fertility Soc., Internat. Soc. Rsch. in Biology Reproduction (charter), Am. Inst. Mgmt. (exec. council), Am. Mgmt. Assn., Am. Found. Pharm. Edn. (Century Club), Ind. Covered Bridge Soc., Sons of Ind. (N.Y.C. chpt.), Chemists Club (N.Y.C.), Masons, Elks, Kiwanis (emeritus), Lake Naomi Club, Phi Beta Kappa, Phi Lambda Upsilon, Phi Kappa Phi, Sigma Xi, Alpha Chi Sigma. Republican. Home: Doylestown, Pa. Died Feb. 10, 2010.

HALE, JACK K., mathematics educator, research center administrator; b. Dudley, Ky., Oct. 3, 1928; s. James Marion and Cora Lee (Kelly) H.; m. Hazel Reynolds. BA in Math., Berea Coll., 1949; PhD in Math., Purdue U., 1953; DSc (hon.), Rijksuniveriteit-Gent, Belgium, 1983; doctor honoris causa, Stuttgart U., Federal Republic of Germany, 1988, Tech.

U. Lisbon, 1991, Rostoch U., Federal Rep. Germany, 1999, Clark U., 2000. Instr. Purdue U., West Lafayette, Ind., 1949-54; with Sandia Corp., Albuquerque, 1954-57, Remington-Rand Univac, St. Paul, 1957-58, Rsch. Inst. for Advanced Study, Balt., 1958-64; prof. div. applied math. Brown U., Providence, 1964-89, chmn., 1973-76; Regents' prof. Ga. Inst. Tech., Atlanta, 1988-98, dir. Ctr. for Dynamical Systems and Nonlinear Studies, 1989-98, regents prof. emeritus, from 1998. Author: Oscillations in Nonlinear Systems, 1963, Functional Differential Equations, 1977, Ordinary Differential Equations, 1978, Methods of Bifurcate Theory, 1982, Introduction to Infinite Dimensional Dynamic Systems, 1984, Asymptotic Behavior of Dissip. Systems, 1988, Dynamics and Bifurcation, 1992, Introduction to Functional Differential Equations, 1993; editor in chief Jour. Differential Equations, 1981—. Recipient Chauvenet prize Math. Assn. Am., 1965; Guggeheim fellow, 1979-80; disting. alumnus, Purdue, U., Berea Coll. Fellow Royal Soc. Edinburgh (hon.), Brazilian Acad. Sci. (corr.); mem. Polish Acad. Sci. (fgn.), Am. Math. Soc., Am. Acad. Mechanics, Brazilian Math. Soc. Home: Atlanta, Ga. Died Dec. 9, 2009.

HALEY, GEORGE BROCK, JR., retired lawyer; b. Atlanta, Feb. 9, 1926; s. George Brock and Naomi Esther (Alverson) H.; m. Marjorie Elizabeth Griffiths, June 24, 1950; children: Susan Haley Brumfield, Katherine Haley Herman, George Brock III, Victor Pearse. AB, Harvard U., 1948, LLB, 1951. Bar: Ga. 1951, D.C. 1976. Assoc. Kilpatrick & Cody (name changed to Kilpatrick Stockton), Atlanta, 1951-60, ptnr., 1960-93, of counsel, from 1994; ret. Mem. Ga. Gov.'s Jud. Process Rev. Commn., Atlanta, 1988-89; trustee Frances Wood Wilson Found. Staff sgt. AUS, 1944-46, MTO. Mem. ABA(life), State Bar Ga., Atlanta Bar Assn., Atlanta Lawyers Club, Capital City Club. Methodist. Avocations: boating, travel. Home: Atlanta, Ga. Died Jan. 31, 2010.

HALL, GEORGE ROBERT, economist; b. Pasadena, Sept. 30, 1930; s. George Jay and Anna Elizabeth (Turnbull) H.; m. Florence Ann Fray, Dec. 20, 1960; children: Elizabeth, Margaret, Andrew, George J. BA, Claremont McKenna Coll., 1951; MA, Harvard U., 1953, PhD, 1960. Asst. prof. U. Va., Charlottesville, 1959-63; economist Fed. Res. Sys., Washington, 1963-64; sr. economist Rand Corp., Santa Monica, Calif., 1964-73; dep. asst. sec. def. Dept. Def., Washington, 1974-76; sr. staff advisor Office of the Pres., Washington, 1976-77; commr. Fed. Energy Regulatory Commn., Washington, 1977-81; v.p. Charles River Assocs., Boston, 1981-87; cons. Putnam Hayes & Bartlett, Inc., Washington, 1987—2001; sr. cons. Charles River Assocs., Washington, from 2001. Home: Falls Church, Va. Died Apr. 8, 2010.

HALLMAN, RICHARD DOUGLAS, biology educator; b. Kitchener, Ont., Can., Aug. 11, 1951; came to U.S., 1977; s. Kenneth Franklin and Lillian Mary (Perschbacher) H.; m. Diane Brower, Jan. 8, 1978. BA in Psychology, Waterloo U., Can., 1974; MA in Biol. Sci., Hunter Coll., 1987. Lab. technician Ont. Water Resources Commn., Toronto, Can., 1970, 71; tech. asst. U. Göttingen (Fed. Republic of Germany), 1971-72; child care worker Whitby (Can.) Psychiat. Hosp., 1975-77; survey technician Lovell-Belcher Surveyors, NYC, 1977-81; math. and sci. tchr. Jr. High Sch. 123, Bronx, N.Y., 1981-83; biology tchr. Forest Hills High Sch., Queens, N.Y., from 1983. Curriculum developer Forest Hills High Sch., Queens, 1984-88. Recipient City of Waterloo scholarship, 1968, Govt. Ont. scholarship, 1969; N.Y. State Regents fellow, 1985, Am. Soc. Biochemistry and Molecular Biology fellow, 1991. Mem. N.Y. Biology Tchrs. Assn., Alumni Assn. Hunter Coll. Avocations: computer programming, piano, bonsai, aquaria. Home: Brooklyn, NY. Died Jan. 23, 2009.

HAM, NORMAN DOUGLAS, aeronautical engineer, educator; b. Toronto, Ont., Can., Sept. 30, 1929; came to U.S., 1954, naturalized, 1963; s. Norman Herbert and Eileen Anna H.; m. Margaret Kathryn Appleby, May 23, 1953; children—Marilyn, Kathryn, Joslin. BASc., U. Toronto, 1951; S.M., M.I.T., 1952, Aero.E., 1957, Sc.D., 1968. Registered profl. engr., Mass. Engr. Avro Aircraft Co., Toronto, 1949-53; sr. engr. Fairey Aviation Co., London, 1953-54; project engr. Doman Helicopter Corp., Danbury, Conn., 1954-56; research engr., project leader M.I.T., Cambridge, 1956-60; project engr. Kaman Aircraft Corp., Bloomfield, Conn., 1960-61; prof. dept. aeros. M.I.T., Cambridge, from 1961. Recipient Cierva Meml. prize Helicopter Assn. Gt. Britain, 1953; cert. AIAA, 1972; Army Research Office grantee, 1964-74; Naval Air Systems Command grantee, 1969-78; NASA grantee, 1968—Mem. Am. Helicopter Soc., U.S. Curling Assn. Clubs: Canadian (Boston). Inventor helicopter individual-blade control system. Home: Brookline, Mass. Died Feb. 13, 2010.

HAMALL, THOMAS KENNY, assn. exec. b. Evanston, Ill., July 21, 1932; s. Thomas Eugene and Margaret Katherine (Kenny) H.; m. Barbara Ann O'Brien, Nov. 23, 1957; children— Mary, Eileen, Annette, Rosemary, Claire, Kenneth. Student, U. Miami, 1950-53, Columbia U., 1957-59. Edn. dir. Am. Cancer Soc., Miami, Fla., 1953-56, program coordinator med. affairs NYC, 1956-59, exec. dir. Omaha, 1959-61, Elizabeth, N.J., 1962-64; dir. pub. relations fund raising N.J. Assn. Mental Health, 1963-64; dir. devel. Preventive Medicine Inst. Strang Clinic, NYC, 1964-67; dir. devel. and pub. affairs N.J. Coll. Medicine and Dentistry, Newark, 1967-70; corporate dir. civic affairs Borden, Inc., Columbus, Ohio, 1970-74; pres. Borden Found., 1970-74; fellow in met. governance and fin., dir. communications design center Acad. for Contemporary Problems, Columbus, 1974-75; exec. v.p. Atlanta C. of C., from 1975. Pub. Atlanta mag., 1975-78; mem. adv. bd. Bus. Atlanta mag.; dir. Nat. Minority Supplier Devel. Council; lectr. in field. Mem. adv. bd. Corp. Policy Center, Grad. Sch. Bus., Emory U.; bd. dirs. Lenbrook Found.; mem. adv. bd. Internat. Bus. Inst., Grad. Sch. Bus., Atlanta U. Served with USNR, 1950-53. Fellow George Internat. Bus. Inst.; mem. Am. C. of C. Execs. (dir., past chmn. met. council), Nat. Assn. Fund Raisers, Ga. Indsl. Developers Assn. (pres., dir.), Ga. C. of C. Execs. (dir.), So. Assn. C. of C. Execs., Atlanta Regional Commn. Roman Catholic. Died Apr. 29, 2010.

HAMILTON, CAROLINE ALICE (CARRIE HAMILTON), real estate broker; b. Columbus, Ohio, Jan. 13, 1928; d. Herbert Samuel and Mabel Ione (Tussing) Erwin; m. Mark Justin Hamilton, July 1, 1947; children— Kimberly Hamilton Turner, Karolyn Hamilton Landon, Mark Jay. Grad. Realtor's Inst., 1979. Cert. residential specialist. Real estate salesman Barstow Realty Co. (Calif.), 1966-68, real estate broker, 1968-76; owner, broker Hamilton Realty Better Homes and Gardens, Barstow, 1976—. Pres. Rep. Women's Club, Barstow, 1966-67; chmn. United Fund, Barstow, 1978; 2d v.p. Barstow Devel. Corp., 1983. Mem. Barstow Bd. Realtors (dir. 1970-77, 77—, pres. 1970, 80), Calif. Assn. Realtors (dir. 1969-71, 79-80), Barstow C. of C. (dir. 1976—, chmn. legis. com. 1981—, pres. 1980). Republican. Home: Barstow, Calif. Died May 25, 2010.

HAMILTON, JERALD, musician; b. Wichita, Kans., Mar. 19, 1927; s. Robert James and Lillie May (Rishel) H.; m. Phyllis Jean Searle, Sept. 8, 1954; children: Barbara Helen Maxey, Elizabeth Sarah Hamilton, Catharine Sandra Roelfs. MusB, U. Kans., Lawrence, 1948, MusM, 1950; postgrad., Royal Sch. Ch. Music, Croydon, Eng., summer 1955, Union Theol. Sem. Sch. Sacred Music, NYC, summer 1960; studies with, Laurel Everette Anderson, Andre Marchal, Catharine Crozier, Gustav Leonhardt. From instr. to asst. prof. organ and theory Washburn U., Topeka, 1949-59; dir. Washburn Singers and Choir, 1955-59; asst. prof. organ, dir. univ. singers and chorus Ohio U., Athens, 1959-60; asst. prof. organ and ch. music U. Tex., Austin, 1960-63; lectr. ch. music Episcopal Theol. Sem. S.W., Austin, 1961-63; mem. faculty U. Ill., Urbana-Champaign, 1963-88, prof. music, 1967-88, prof. emeritus, from 1988; organist, choirmaster Trinity Ch., Lawrence, Kans., 1945—49, Grace Cathedral, Topeka, 1949—59, St. David's Ch., Austin, 1960—63, St. John the Divine, Champaign, 1963—88, St. John's Cathedral, Albuquerque, 1988-93, organist-choirmaster emeritus, from 1994. Mem., chmn. commn. ch. music Episc. Diocese Kans., 1951-59; mem. bishop's commn. ch. music Episc. Diocese of Springfield, 1978-80, 82-88; concert organist, 1955-96. Author (with Marilou Kratzenstein) Four Centuries of Organ Music, Detroit Studies in Music Bibliography No. 51, 1984. Fulbright scholar, 1954-55. Mem. Assn. Anglican Musicians, Omicron Delta Kappa, Pi Kappa Lambda, Phi Mu Alpha. Episcopalian. Home: Edgewood, N.Mex. Died Nov. 1, 2009.

HAMILTON, SAMUEL D., federal agency administrator, biologist; b. 1955; m. Becky Arthur; children: Sam Jr., Clay. BS in Biology, Miss. State U., 1977. Youth conservation corps employee Noxubee Nat. Wildlife Refuge US Fish & Wildlife Svc., US Dept. Interior, Starkville, Miss., sr. biologist, mgr., spl. asst. to dir. & dep. dir. Washington, Tex. state adminstr. Austin, asst. regional dir. ecol. services SE region Atlanta, geog. asst. regional dir. Area II, dir. SE region Atlanta, 1997—2009, dir. Washington, 2009—10. Recipient Water Conservationist of Yr. Award, Ala. Wildlife Fedn., 1986. Died Oct. 20, 2010.

HAMILTON, WILLIAM T., English educator, former academic administrator; b. Ft. Dodge, Iowa, Sept. 6, 1939; s. William Levant Hamilton and Janey (Storer) Smith; m. Margaret Stewart Mims, Dec. 22, 1959; children: Jenny Stewart, Ann Claire, Amy Rebecca. BA in English, U. Wash., 1961; MA in English, U. Md., 1963; PhD in English, U. Minn., 1970. Park ranger Great Smoky Mountains Nat. Park, Tenn., 1961-62; instr. English Otterbein Coll., Westerville, Ohio, 1963-65, Coll. of St. Thomas, St. Paul, 1967-68; assoc. prof. Otterbein Coll., Westerville, 1968-70, chmn. English dept., 1970-73, dir. faculty devel., 1975-83, chmn. dept. Integrated Studies, 1973-81, dean of faculty, prof. English, 1981-83; v.p., dean of faculty Davis & Elkins Coll., Elkins, W.Va., 1983-86; v.p. acad. affairs Western State Coll., Gunnison, Colo., 1986-87, interim pres., 1987, pres., 1987-90; prof. English Met. State Coll., Denver, from 1991. Cons. in faculty Austin Coll., Sherman, Tex., 1979; project leader Ohio Council for Humanities, Ohio, 1982; chmn. Davis & Elkins team Lilly Endowment Workshop, Colorado Springs, Colo., 1986, chmn. Western State Coll. team, 1987. Rsch. fellow U. Minn., 1968, NEH fellow Mich. State U., 1978, sr. fellow Am. Assn. State Colls. and Univs., 1990-91. Home: Denver, Colo. Died July 5, 2009.

HAMLIN, KENNETH ELDRED, JR., retired pharmaceutical company executive; b. Balt., Mar. 27, 1917; s. Kenneth Eldred and Julia (Gallup) H.; m. Janet Hoy, June 18, 1941; children: Kathleen Ann, Kenneth Thomas. BS, U. Md., 1938, PhD, 1941. Research assoc. U. Ill., Urbana, 1941-42; instr. U. Md., 1942-43; research chemist, asst. head organic research, head organic research, asst. dir. chem. research Abbott Labs., North Chicago, Ill., 1943-61, dir. research, 1961-66; v.p. research and devel. Cutter Labs., Inc., Berkeley, Calif., 1966-73, v.p. research and quality assurance, 1973-74, sr. v.p. sci. ops., 1974-81, vice chmn. bd. dirs., 1980-81, dir., 1968-81. Vol. tchr. gen. sci., computer sci. Author: (with Jenkins, Hartung, Hamlin and Data) The Chemistry of Organic Medicinal Products, 1957. Mem. Am. Pharm. Assn., Am. Chem. Soc., AAAS, Sigma Xi, Rho Chi, Alpha Chi Sigma. Republican. Died Aug. 14, 2009.

HAMM, GEORGE FRANCIS, retired academic administrator; b. Rapid City, SD, June 26, 1931; s. Michael and Mae E. (Howard) H.; m. Jane Sigler, Aug. 29, 1958; children: Jean Marie, Gregory F., Robert Joseph (dec.), Daniel George (dec.) BA, S.D. State U., 1953; MA, U. Wyo., 1958, PhD, 1961; LHD (hon.), Tex. Coll., 1997. Asst. prof. Ariz. State U., 1962-63, dean students, 1963-69, v.p. student affairs, 1969-81; prof. psychology U. Tex., Tyler, 1981—98, pres., 1981—98, pres. emeritus, 2003—10. Mem. academic planning com. Inst. for Advanced Strategic & Polit. Planning, Jerusalem, Israel, 1985 Chmn. internat. bd. Sister Cities Internat., Washington; bd. dirs. E. Tex. Hosp. Found., Tyler, 1982; bd. dirs. Fiesta Bowl, Tempe, Ariz., 1978-81; bd. trustees St. Edwards U., Austin, Tex., 1982-87. Served with U.S. Infantry, 1954-56. Named Outstanding Young Man Yr. Jr. C. of C., Ariz., 1964; recipient Highest Civilian award U.S. Air Force, 1967; Disting. Alumnus award S.D. State U., 1983, Univ. Centennial Medallion, Ariz. State U., 1986; Southwestern Internat. Bus. fellow, 1987. Mem. Tex. Assn. of Atlantic Council, American Assn. State Colls. and Univs., Nat. Assn. State Univ. and Land Grant Colls. (exec. com. 1979-81, chmn. council on student affairs 1976-78), Phi Kappa Phi, Omicron Delta Kappa, Psi Chi Roman Catholic. Home: Tyler, Tex. Died Oct. 10, 2010.

HAMMEN, CARL SCHLEE, zoology educator; b. Newark, Aug. 26, 1923; s. Roy Merrill and Bertha Ida (Schlee) H.; m. Edna Ruth Graham, 1949 (div. 1961); children: Charles Scott, Carol Graham; m. Susan Chandler Lum, Oct. 13, 1962; children: Ralph (dec.), John, Elizabeth. BA, St. John's Coll., Annapolis, Md., 1947; MA, Columbia U., 1949; MS in Biol. Scis., U. Chgo., 1952; PhD in Zoology and Biochemistry, Duke U., 1958. Instr. biology and chemistry Mitchell Coll., Statesville, N.C., 1949-51; prof. biology and math. Cedarville (Ohio) Coll., 1952-53; biologist VA Hosp., Martinsburg, W.Va., 1953-54, Army Chem. Ctr., Edgewood, Md., 1954-56; assoc. prof. biology Newark State Coll., Union, N.J., 1958-60, Adelphi Coll., Garden City, N.Y., 1960-63; assoc. prof. zoology U. R.I., Kingston, 1963-71, prof. zoology, from 1971. Author: (book) Elementary Quantitative Biology, 1972, German translation, 1975, Japanese translation, 1976, Marine Invertebrates: Comparative Physiology, 1980; contbr. 49 tech. papers and rev. articles to profl. publs. Lt. (j.g.) USN, 1943-46, PTO. Rsch. grantee (3 instns.) NSF, 1959-66, U. R.I. rsch. com., 1972, 79; Noyes Found. fellow U. Chgo., 1952; NSF postdoctoral fellow Duke U. Marine Lab., 1959, 63; Fulbright scholar, Morocco, 1984. Mem. Am. Physiol. Soc., Am. Soc. Zoologists, Sigma Xi. Avocation: running. Died July 28, 2010.

HAMMER, ALFRED EMIL, artist, educator; b. New Haven, Jan. 11, 1925; s. Forrester L. and Eugenie (Bauer-Enquist) H.; m. Marian Valle, Aug. 14, 1948; children: Alfred Emil, Paul Forrester, Eric Valdemar, Eugenie Bauer; m. Jeanne Baker, Dec. 18, 1966; children: Stephen Drake, Rosamond Swan. BFA, R.I. Sch. Design, 1950, Yale U., 1951, MFA, 1952. From instr. to assoc. prof. painting and drawing R.I. Sch. Design, Providence, 1952-69, chmn. grad. studies, 1958-60, dean students, 1960-61; dean Cleve. Inst. Art, 1969-74; dir., prof. Sch. Art, U. Man., Winnipeg, Can., 1974-82; dir. Pacific N.W. Coll. Art, Portland, Oreg., 1982-83; prof. Hartford Art Sch., U. Hartford, Conn., 1983-88, dean Conn., 1983-86; freelance artist, from 1988. Exhibited in group shows R.I. Ann. (1st prize award 1952), Providence Art Club Ann. (1st prize award 1953, 54, 55, 57), Newport Ann. (1st prize 1959), Boston Arts Festival, 1958, Shippee Gallery, N.Y.C., 1985, Joseloft Gallery U. Hartford, 1992, Conn. Watercolor Soc. (prize 1992, 97), New Britain Mus. Am. Art (1st prize for watercolor 1988); one-man shows include U. Maine, 1954, U. Man., 1980, Thomas Gallery, 1980, Melnyschenko Gallery, Winnipeg, 1981, Movie House Studio Gallery, Millerton, N.Y., 1992; represented in collections Agnes Gund, Jr. C. of C., Nat. Mus. Israel, R.I. Sch. Design Mus., Portland Art Mus., Conn. Bank and Trust Co., N.E. Savs., Hartford, Corp. Hdqrs. Otis Elevator Corp., Farmington, Conn., Bank of New Eng., Boston, Shawmut Bank, Hartford, Aenta Ins., Hartford, Govt. of Man., Gov.'s Coll. of Conn. Artists; represented in book Prize Winning Artists, 1960. Mem. Conn. Watercolor Soc., Lyme Art Assn. Home: Clifton, Va. Died Oct. 13, 2009.

HAMMER, FRANK JORGEN, psychologist, consultant; b. Appleton, Wis., Jan. 19, 1918; s. Frank Joseph and Marie (Rasmussen) Hammer; m. Joyce Frances Waldhaus, Apr. 7, 1968; children: Mark, Laurel, Dan, Frank, Aaron, Michelle, Matthew; m. Emily Sue Speed, Apr. 9, 1983; 1 child, Melanie Marie. BA, Lawrence U., Appleton, Wis., 1942; PhD, U. Chgo., 1952. Lic. psychologist Wash. Chief psychologist Madigan Army Hosp., 1952—55, Cmty. Psychiat. Clinic, Seattle, 1955—64; pvt. practice cons. psychology Seattle, Mountlake Terr., Wash., from 1964. Cons. Everett Ctr. Youth Svcs., Seattle Police Dept., King County Juvenile Ct., Valley Gen. Hosp., Snohomish County Family and Juvenile Cts., Seattle Sch. Dist.; clin. instr. U. Wash. Med. Sch. Chmn., bd. dirs. Source Found. Mentally Retarded Children; mem. Snohomish County Bd. Freeholders, 1968—69; mayor Mountlake Terr., 1960—64; bd. dirs. Snohomish County Alcoholism, Mental Health Svcs. Lt. col. US Army, 1942—55. Recipient football scholarship, Lawrence U., 1938—42. Mem.: Assn. Labor-Mgmt. Adminstrs. and Cons. Alcoholism, Am. Group Psychotherapy Assn., Western Psychol. Assn., APA, Wash. State Psychol. Assn., Mace, Beta Theta Pi, Sigma Xi. Died Mar. 22, 2010.

HAMMOND, ROBERT MORRIS, educator, author; b. NYC, Dec. 29, 1920; s. John Farnsworth and Hazel Marguerite (Morris) H.; m. Marguerite Masius, June 12, 1943; children: Roberta Masius, Charles Edward. BA, U. Rochester, 1942; MA, Yale U., 1947, PhD, 1952. Instr. French U. Ariz., Tucson, 1950-53, asst. prof., 1953-63, assoc. prof., 1963-67; prof. French Harvard U., 1965-66; vis. prof. French lit. and cinema Wells Coll., Aurora, N.Y., 1967-68; prof. French lit. and cinema, also chmn. internat. communications and culture dept. SUNY, Cortland, 1968-77, mem. faculty, 1968-88. Author: plays Solitaire, 1960, The Nursery, 1965, Beirut 75, 1976; Translator: plays by Pascal Vrebos Yalta 2000, 1976, Sade-Sack, 1980, Cocteau Reflects for Me; I Reflect for Him, 1984; editor: Deux Films Francais, 1966, Creative French, 1969, Beauty and the Beast (Jean Cocteau), 1970; curator Hammond Collection of French Film Scripts, Fales Libr., N.Y.

Univ., 1983—; contbr. articles on French cinema, teaching fgn. lang. by film to profl. jours. With USAAF, 1942-46. Fulbright fellow; also French govt. fellow, 1950; U. Ariz. rsch. grantee, 1966-67; N.Y. State rsch. grantee, 1971; Nat. Endowment for Humanities grantee for devel. interdisciplinary approach to study cinema, 1970-72. Mem. Dramatists Guild. Died Apr. 16, 2009.

HAMRICK, JOSEPH THOMAS, mechanical engineer, aerospace company executive; b. Carrollton, Ga., Mar. 20, 1921; s. James Mayfield and Mattie Almon (Gaston) H.; m. Dorothy Elizabeth Jones, June 19, 1948; children: Jane Elizabeth Hamrick Kneisley, Nancy Ann Hamrick Buchanan, Thomas Mayfield. B.m.E., Ga. Inst. Tech., 1946, MSm.E., 1948. Aero. rsch. scientist NACA, Cleve., 1948-55; chief rsch. engr. Thompson Ramo Wooldridge, Euclid, Ohio, 1955-61; pres. Aerospace Rsch. Corp., Roanoke, Va., from 1961. Pres. Cogeneration of Tenn., inc., Red Boiling Springs. Contbr. articles to profl. jours. Pres. North Franklin County Pub. Park, Inc. Served to 1st lt. USAAF, 1943-46; PTO. Recipient Tech. Achievement award Dept. Energy, 1984; Dept. of Energy grantee, 1978-91; NSF grantee, 1980; named Engring. Hall Fame, Ga. Inst. Tech., 2001. Mem. ASME. Republican. Unitarian Universalist. Subspecialties: Biomass (energy science and technology); Combustion processes. Current work: Rsch. on fueling gas turbines with wood, operation of 4000 Hp gas turbine with wood fuel. Patentee in field. Home: Roanoke, Va. Died Apr. 21, 2009.

HAN, YINGSHI, medical educator, researcher; b. Taian City, Shandong, China, Oct. 20, 1933; came to U.S., 1987; d. Zilu Han and Dailing Fu; m. Xiang-pu Wang; children: Han Wang, Jun Wang, Gang Wang. MD, Shandong Med. Coll., Jinan, 1955. Faculty and rschr. Hunan Med. U., Changsha, China, from 1955, assoc. prof., 1979-85, prof., from 1986; vis. prof. Cornell Med. Coll., NYC, 1987-89; investigator The Rockefeller U., NYC, 1989, Mt. Sinai Med. Ctr./CUNY, from 1989. Contbr. articles to profl. jours. Recipient Ministry of Health award for nasopharyngeal cancer rsch., 1984, for cadmium nephrotoxicity rsch., 1988, Hunan Province award for heavy metal renal damage rsch., 1993, for nephrotoxicity rsch., 1992; rsch. grantee Ministry of Health, China, 1979, 85, NSF, 1985, 90. Mem. Chinese Med. Assn., Anatomy Assn. China (chmn. or councilor Hunan br. 1970-87). Home: Eastchester, NY. Died Dec. 18, 2009.

HANCE, DARWOOD B., retired radiologist; b. Thief River Falls, Minn., Feb. 29, 1932; s. Alphie N. and Nora J. Hance; m. Helene M. Hance, Jan. 2, 1999; children: Joseph, Jeffrey, Julie, Richard, Kristina, Derek. Student, U. Miami, 1950-53; MD, U. Tenn., Memphis, 1956. Diplomate Am. Bd. Radiology, Am. Bd. Nuclear Medicine. Intern City of Detroit Receiving Hosp., 1956-57; resident in radiology Wayne State U., Detroit, 1957-60; chief of radiology 32d USAF Hosp., Minot, N.D., 1960-62, St. Jude Hosp., Memphis, 1962-63, Reid Meml. Hosp., Richmond, Ind., 1963-68, Kern Med Ctr., Bakersfield, Calif., 1968-83, Greater Bakersfield Meml. Hosp., 1968-97; fellow in neuroradiology UCLA, 1977, fellow in ultrasound, 1985, vis. assoc. prof.; radiologist UCLA Med. Ctr., 1997—2006; ret., 2006. Capt. USAF, 1956-62. Fellow: Coop. of Am. Physicians (pres. 1985—2005), Am. Coll. Radiology (counselor 1974—76), Am. Coll. Nuc. Medicine (pres. 1987, chmn. bd. 1991—2001, Gold medal 1999). Roman Catholic. Avocations: sailing, swimming. Died Mar. 3, 2009.

HANDLEY, JEAN M., telephone company executive; b. Manchester, Conn., Aug. 28, 1926; d. Francis P. and Margaret (Ivers) Handley. BA, Conn. Coll., 1948; MA, Northwestern U., 1949. Pub. rels. asst. So. New Eng. Tel. Co., New Haven, 1960, advt. and employee info. staff, 1960—66, dist. mgr., 1966—72, gen. info. mgr., 1973—75, v.p. pub. rels., 1978—84, v.p. pers. and corp. rels., from 1984; dist. mgr. AT&T, NYC, 1972—73, press rels. dir., 1976—78. Vice chmn. Sci. Park Devel. Corp., New Haven; chmn. bd. Conn. Coll., New London; vice chmn. Conn. Pub. Expenditure Council, Hartford; bd. dirs. New Haven Symphony Orch.; assoc. fellow Calhoun Coll., Yale U. Recipient Women in Leadership award, YWCA of New Haven, 1979, Greater New Haven C. of C. Cmty. Leadership award, 1984, Women Achievers award, YWCA of N.Y., 1984. Mem.: Am. Women in Radio and TV, Women in Commns., Inc., Pub. Rels. Soc. N.Y., Pub. Rels. Soc. Am. Home: Guilford, Conn. Died Jan. 26, 2010.

HANDY, ROBERT MAXWELL, lawyer; b. Buffalo, Apr. 1, 1931; s. John Abner and Yvonne Fernande (Blaise) H.; m. Berniece Emily Reist, July 2, 1955; children: Mary, Robert, David. BS, Trinity Coll., 1953; MS, Northwestern U., 1958, PhD, 1962; JD, Ariz. State U., 1984. New product devel. research mgr. Westinghouse Electric Co., Pitts., 1961-69; product mgr. Semiconductor div. Motorola, Inc., Phoenix, 1969-72, corp. dir. research, 1972-75; exec. dir. Ariz. Solar Energy Research Commn., 1975-76; dir. bus. and tech. planning Integrated Circuits div. Motorola, Inc., Mesa, Ariz., 1976-80, sr. patent counsel Phoenix, 1980-88, group patent counsel, 1988-94; intellectual property counsel Ea. Europe, Mid. East, and Africa Motorola GmbH, Weisbaden, Germany, 1995-98; pvt. practice Gilbert, Ariz., 1999—2002; patent atty. Ingrassia Fisher & Lorenz, Scottsdale, Ariz., from 2002. Fgn. expert instr. Quingdao U., China, 2001-02; instr. Carnegie Mellon U., 1967. Served to lt. (j.g.) USNR, 1954-57. Royall A. Cabell fellow, 1959-60 Mem.: IEEE, Phi Beta Kappa. Died Aug. 12, 2009.

HANEMANN, JOHN H., commodity exchange executive; b. NYC, Aug. 30, 1943; s. Paul A. and Lillian (Blumberg) H.; m. Stephanie D. Haneman, Nov. 14, 1967; children: Jonathan S., Gene P. Student, CUNY, 1962-63. Mgr. order room Orvis Bros., NYC, 1967-69; clk., broker Felix J. Forlenza & Co., NYC, 1969-80; sr. ptnr. Hanemann Commodities, NYC, 1980-82, Prestige Metals Tng. Co., NYC, from 1982. Bd. dirs. Comex, N.Y.C., 1979—, pres., 1988-89. Avocations: fishing, reading, skiing. Died Aug. 26, 2009.

HANNA, PAUL JOHNSTON, banker; b. Cannonsburg, Pa., Sept. 26, 1915; s. George J. and Ethel (Lyon) H.; m. Grace M. Gillen, June 22, 1946; children: Paul Johnston II, Lee E. BS, U. Pitts., 1939; postgrad., Rutgers U., 1950, Dartmouth Grad. Sch. Credit and Financial Mgmt., 1955. With Citizen's Trust Co., Canonsburg, 1939-41; sr. v.p. nat. div. Mfrs. Hanover Trust Co., NYC, 1946-72; exec. v.p. Mfrs. Hanover Corp., 1972-78, mem. adv. bd., from 1978; vice chmn. GEICO Corp., 1978-82, dir., vice chmn. investment com., 1982-86. Dir. United Jersey Banks, a; Holding Co., Princeton, N.J., Govt. Employees Fin. Services Co. Md., Banner Life Ins. Co., United Jersey Bank N.W. and Hackensack, N.J., Richard Blackman & Co.; chmn. Govt. Employees Fin. Corp., 1976-86, Firemen's Fund Mortgage Group; vice chmn. Govt. Employees Ins. Co., 1978-82; AVEMCO Corp., 1980, Resolute Reins. Co., 1981-86 Trustee, former chmn. bd. trustees Rider Coll. Served to lt. col. AUS, 1941-45. Decorated Bronze Star Belgian Croix de Guerre, Presdl. citation. Presbyn. (elder). Clubs: Baltusrol Golf (Springfield, N.J.) (gov., pres.); Columbia Golf (Chevy Chase, Md.); Links (N.Y.C.); Burning Tree Golf (Va.); Ocean Reef (Key Largo, Fla.); Card Sound Golf (Fla.), Harbor Course (Fla.) (v.p.). Home: Summit, NJ. Died Feb. 26, 2009.

HANNAH, BARRY (HOWARD BARRY HANNAH), writer; b. Meridian, Miss., Apr. 23, 1942; s. William Edward and Elizabeth (King) H.; m. Susan Varas, Mar. 29, 1986; children: Po, Edward, Lee. BA, Miss. Coll., 1964; MA, U. Ark., 1966, MFA, 1967. Assoc. prof. Clemson (S.C.) U., 1969-74; writer in residence U. Ala., Tuscaloosa, 1974-79, Middlebury (Vt.) Coll., 1972-73, Iowa U., Iowa City, 1981, Mont. U., Missoula, 1982-83, U. Miss., Oxford, 1984—2010. Author: Geronimo Rex, 1972, Night Watchmen, 1974, Airships, 1978, Ray, 1980, The Tennis Handsome, 1983, Power and Light, 1983, Captain Maximus, 1986, Hey Jack!, 1987, Boomerang, 1989, Never Die, 1991, Bats Out of Hell, 1993, High Lonesome, 1996, Yonder Stands Your Orphan, 2001, Sick Soldier at Your Door, 2010 Pres. Oxford Humane Soc., 1988-89. Recipient Fiction award AAAS, 1978, Guggenheim award, 1983, Miss. Gov.'s award in the Arts, 1986, Award in Fiction, Miss. Inst. Arts and Letters, 1994, PEN/Malamud award, 2003 Mem. Oxford Humane Soc. Democrat. Baptist. Avocations: playing the trumpet, fishing. Home: Oxford, Miss. Died Mar. 1, 2010.

HANNENBERG, VERA LOSEV, educational administrator; b. NYC, Dec. 9, 1923; d. Saul and Gussie (Gerstein) Losev; m. Sidney Hyman Hannenberg, Oct. 7, 1945 (dec.); children: Alexander A., Leo R.W. BA cum laude, Bklyn. Coll., 1944, MS in Edn., 1972; Cert., NYU, 1976. Lic. sch. adminstr. N.Y. Coord. occupational planning N.Y.C. Bd. Edn., 1972-76, dir. planning, evaluation and rsch./occupational edn., 1977-80, dir. Office Occupational Edn., from 1980. Supr. remedial reading Manpower Devel. Tng. Program, N.Y.C. Bd. Edn., 1966-71; mem. N.Y. State Coun. on Vocat. Edn., 1987—. Contbr. articles to profl. jours. Named Disting. Vocat. Educator of the Yr. N.Y. State Edn. Dept., 1989; recipient Disting. Svc. Plaque, U.S. Job Corps, Washington, 1985, 90. Mem. Am. Vocat. Assn., Nat. Assn. Local Adminstrs. in Vocat. Edn., N.Y. State Occupational Edn./Adminstrn. Assn. Home: Great Neck, NY. Died Jan. 15, 2009.

HANRAHAN, DONALD EUGENE, publisher; b. Chgo., Feb. 6, 1929; s. Charles Patrick and Ella (Bordwardt) H.; div. Oct. 1979; children— David Eugene, Eric Bradley, Christine Marie, Deborah Ann. B.S., Loyola U., 1952; postgrad. Northwestern U., 1953-54. Account mgr. Hearst, Chgo., 1953-55; with advt. sales dept. Fawcett, Chgo., 1955-58, mgr. advt., San Francisco, 1958-60, Western mgr., 1960-63, assoc. Midwestern mgr., 1963-65; v.p., dir. advt. Playboy Publs., Chgo., N.Y.C., 1965-76; pub. Sport mag., N.Y.C., 1976-78, cons., pub., exec. v.p., 1980—. Lutheran. Home: New York, NY. Died Feb. 8, 2010.

HANSEN, ARTHUR GENE, former academic administrator, consultant; b. Sturgeon Bay, Wis., Feb. 28, 1925; s. Henry A. and Ruth (Anderson) H. BSEE, Purdue U., 1946, MS in Math., 1948, DEng (hon.), 1971; PhD in Math., Case Inst. Tech., 1958; DSc (hon.), Ind. U., 1982. Rsch. scientist NASA, 1948-49, 50-58; tchr. U. Md., 1949-50; sect. head Cornell Aero. Lab., Buffalo, 1958-59; faculty mech. engring. U. Mich., 1959-66; dean Ga. Inst. Tech., 1966-69, pres., 1969-71, Purdue U., 1971-82; chancellor Tex. A&M U. System, 1982-86; dir. rsch. Hudson Inst., 1987-88. Prof. mech. engring. Tuskegee Inst., 1965; sr. rsch. engr. Douglas Aircraft Co., 1964; cons. to industry, 1961-70; chmn. bd. Corp. for Edn. Tech., 1992-94; chmn. Atlanta Civic Design Commn., 1968-79, Ga. Sci. and Tech. Commn., 1968-71, Ga. Ocean Sci. Ctr. of Atlantic Commn., Atlanta, 1968-71; adv. coun. Skidaway Oceanographic Inst. for Univ. System Ga., 1968-71; pres. Ind. Conf. Higher Edn., 1975; chmn. com. on minorities in engring. NRC, 1974-76; energy rsch. adv. bd. Dept. Energy; chmn. adv. coun. Electric Power Rsch. Inst., 1973-79; chmn. bd. Ind. State Symphony Soc., 1989-91. Author: Similarity Analyses of Boundary Value Problems in Engineering, 1964, Fluid Mechanics, 1967. Chmn. bd. visitors Air U., 1974-77; bd. visitors Air Force Inst. Tech., 1987-89; trustee Nat. Fund Minority Engring. Students, 1980-81; mem. acad. adv. bd. U.S. Naval Acad., 1975-79; past chmn. Tex. Com. Employer Support of Guard and Res., Tex. Sci. and Tech. Coun.; chmn. Ind. Commn. for Higher Edn., 1994—; bd. dirs. CUNY Rsch. Found., 1994-97. With USMCR, 1943-46. Recipient Leather medal Sigma Delta Chi, Disting. Svc. medal Dept. Def., 1985; named Ind. Engr. of Yr., 1979, Purdue Disting. Alumnus, 1979. Fellow AAAS; mem. NAE, Gas Rsch. Inst. (chmn. adv. coun. 1976-79), Sigma Xi, Eta Kappa Nu, Pi Tau Sigma, Tau Beta Pi, Phi Kappa Phi, Omicron Delta Kappa, Phi Eta Sigma, Kappa Kappa Psi. Home: Zionsville, Ind. Died July 5, 2010.

HANSEN, BARBARA L., retired English educator; b. Indpls., Sept. 27, 1935; d. Joseph Martin and Ruth Edna Hansen. BS in Edn., Ball State U., 1963, MA in English, 1964, PhD in English, 1971. Grad. tchr. Ball State U., Muncie, Ind., 1963-64, instr. English, 1964-67, doctoral fellow, 1967-68, instr. English, 1969-72; asst. prof. English U. Cin., 1972-78, assoc. prof. English, 1978-90, prof. English, 1990—2002; ret., 2002. Author: Picking Up the Pieces: Healing Ourselves After Personal Loss, 1991, rev. edit., 1993, The Strength Within: Cultivate Habits of Wholeness, Hope, and Joy, 2000, The Strength Within: A Practical Guide to Finding True Joy, 2002, The Strength Within, 2003; co-author: (with Rebecca McDaniel) Developing Sentence Skills, 1990, Simplified Sentence Skills, 1997; contbr. articles to profl. jours. Recipient Outstanding Handicapped Student award Venture Club, 1962, Midwest Handicapped Profl. Woman of Yr. award Pres.'s Com. for the Handicapped, 1972. Home: Maineville, Ohio. Died July 1, 2009.

HANSEN, CARL R., management consultant, county official; b. Chgo., May 2, 1926; s. Carl M. and Anna C. (Roge) Hansen; m. Christia Marie Loeser, Dec. 31, 1952; 1 child, Lothar. MBA, U. Chgo., 1954. Dir. mkt. rsch. Kitchens of Sara Lee, Deerfield, Ill., Earle Ludgin & Co., Chgo.; svc. v.p. Mkt. Rsch. Corp. Am., 1956—67; pres. Chgo. Associates, Inc., 1967—2010. Chmn. Ill. adv. coun. SBA, 1973—74; exec. com. Ill. Gov.'s Adv. Coun., 1969—72; resident officer U.S. High Commn., Germany, 1949—52; chmn. Viking Ship Restoration Com.; mem. Cook County Bd. Commissioners, 1970, 1974—2010, chmn. legis. com., adminstrn. com.; active American Scandinavian Found.; vice chmn. Rep. Ctrl. Com. Cook County; chmn. Cook County Young Reps., 1957—58, 12th Congl. Dist. Rep. Orgn., 1971—74, 1978—82, Suburban Rep. Orgn., 1974—78, 1982—86; del. Rep. Nat. Conv., 1968, 1984, 1992, Rep. State Conv., 1962—96; committeeman Elk Grove Twp. Rep., 1962—2002; pres. John Ericsson Rep. League of Ill., 1975—76; Rep. presdl. elector State of Ill., 1972; bd. dir. Nat. Assn. Counties. 1st lt. US Army, 1948, maj. USAR. Mem.: VFW, Planning Forum, Nat. Assn. Counties, Am. Statis. Assn., Am. Mktg. Assn., Swedish Am. Hist. Soc., Dania Soc., Chgo. Hist. Soc., Lions, Am. Legion, Res. Officers Assn., Shriners, Masons, Sons of Norway. Home: Mount Prospect, Ill. Died Feb. 2, 2010.

HANSEN, GROVER J., savings and loan association executive; b. Chgo., Sept. 29, 1923; s. Aage and Johanne (Rasmussen) H.; m. Geraldine Jones, Oct. 9, 1965; children: Michael E., Debra E., Denyse A., Robert H., Charles R. BS in Edn, No. Ill. U., DeKalb, 1949; MBA, U. Chgo., 1956; grad., Advanced Mgmt. Program, Harvard U., 1970. Exec. sec., ednl. dir. Am. Inst. Banking, 1951-61; asst. dir. banking edn. com. Am. Bankers Assn., 1961-62; gen. mgr. Produce Reporter Co., Wheaton, Ill., 1962-66; with First Fed. Savs. and Loan Assn., Chgo., from 1966, sr. v.p., 1967-71, pres., chief adminstrv. officer, dir., from 1971, pres., chief operating officer, 1976-83, pres., mng. officer, from 1983. Dir. First Savs. Corp., Lawyers Title Ins. Corp., First Fed. Savs. of Chgo. Found., Life of Va., Investors Mortgage Ins. Co., Western Employers Ins., Ill. Power Co.; chmn. bd. Savs. Place, Inc., Appraisal Services, Inc., First Fed. Agy.; pres., dir. First Savs. Investment Corp.; chmn. bd., chmn. exec. com., dir. Chgo. Area Renewal Effort Service Corp., 1972-76 Bd. dirs. Mid-Am. chpt. ARC, 1973-83, chmn., 1979-81; trustee Met. Crusade Mercy, 1976-79, chief crusader bus. and profl. div., 1976-80; chief crusader United Way/Crusade of Mercy, 1981-82; chmn. bd. Center Religion and Psychtherapy, Chgo., 1971-78; bd. dirs. Chgo. Theol. Sem., 1973-75, bd. assos., 1980—; chmn. devel. subcom. Cook County Econ. Devel. Adv. Com., 1977-79; bd. govs. Glenwood Sch. Boys, 1974—; bd. dirs. Ingalls Meml. Hosp., 1973-78; governing mem. Chgo. Symphony Orch., 1980—; mem. Cook County R.E. Tax Study Commn., 1977-79; vice chmn. spl. gifts campaign Chgo. YMCA, 1973-75; gen. fund dr. chmn. Chgo. Jr. Achievement, 1976. Served to lt. USAAF, 1942-45. Recipient Medal of Merit award from mayor of Chgo., 1976; Distinguished Service award Kiwanis Internat., 1977; Most Distinguished Alumni award No. Ill. U., 1977 Mem. Fed. Savs. and Loan Council Ill. (dir. 1977-79), Cook County Ins. Savs. Assns., Am. Inst. Banking (life), Am. Savs. and Loan Inst., Newcomen Soc. N.Am. Clubs: Union League (Chgo.) (dir. 1973-80, 1st v.p. 1977-78, pres. 1978-80), Econ. (Chgo.), Harvard Bus. Sch. (Chgo.). Died Aug. 14, 2009.

HANSEN, RICHARD W., retired foundation executive; b. Detroit, Oct. 4, 1919; s. Richard W. and Madeline Loba (Dickenson) H.; m. Jo Anne Huffman, Aug. 14, 1968. BA, Wayne State U., Detroit, 1940. With Prentice-Hall Pub. Co., Engelwood Cliffs, N.J., 1946-64, asst. v.p., exec. editor, 1958-64; pres. Dickenson Pub. Co., Los Angeles, 1964-72, dir., from 1965; exec. dir. Ednl. Found. Am., Woodland Hills, Calif., from 1972. Pres. So. Calif. Assn. for Philanthropy, 1983-84; chief fiscal officer Los Angeles County High Sch. for the Arts Found., 1984—. Served with AUS, 1941-46. Died Nov. 9, 2009.

HANSON, PEGGY ANN, neurologist, educator; b. Perth Amboy, NJ, Oct. 22, 1920; d. Charles Walter and Elizabeth D. (Brown) H.; children: Thomas J. Chambers, Patricia A.R. Chambers-Webb. BA, Manhattanville U., 1941; MD, Johns Hopkins U., 1944. Diplomate Am. Bd. Psychiatry and Neurology, Am. Bd. Pediatrics. Resident pediatrics Johns Hopkins Hosp., Balt., 1948; assoc. pediatrics Johns Hopkins U., Balt., 1950-60; resident neurology U. Pa. Hosp., Phila., 1967, asst. in neurology, 1968-70; prof. neurology and pediatrics Albany (N.Y.) Med. Coll., 1970-84, Georgetown U. Hosp., Washington, from 1984. Contbr. articles to profl. jours., chpt. to book.

Recipient award Muscular Dystrophy Assn. Mem. Am. Assn. Neurology, Child Neurology, Internat. Child Neurology Assn. Home: Gibson Island, Md. Died Jan. 23, 2009.

HARBERT, BILL LEBOLD, retired construction corporation executive; b. Indianola, Miss., July 21, 1923; s. John Murdock and Mae (Schooling) H.; m. Mary Joyce Patrick, June 28, 1952; children: Anne Harbert Moulton, Elizabeth Harbert Cornay, Billy L., Jr. BS, Auburn U., 1948; Advanced Mgmt. Program, Harvard U., 1966. Lic. profl. engr. and land surveyor, Ala. Exec. v.p. Harbert Constrn. Corp., Birmingham, Ala., 1948-79, pres., 1979-81; pres., COO Harbert Internat., Inc., Birmingham, 1981-90, vice-chmn., 1990-91, pres., chmn. bd., 1991-98; pres., chmn. bd. dirs. Bill Harbert Internat. Constrn., Inc., from 1992, chmn., CEO, 1998-99; ret., 1999. Trustee, co-chmn. Laborers Nat. Pension Fund, Dallas, 1968-2001; bd. dirs. U. Ala. Health Svc. Found., Birmingham, 1983-95, Met. Devel. Bd. of Birmingham, 1980-83, AMI Brookwood Med. Ctr., 1990—, Internat. Pipe Line Contractors Assn., 1980, 88, 93-94, 98, 2d v.p., 1999-2000, Comprehensive Cancer Ctr.-U. Ala., Birmingham, 1999-2000, SouthTrust Corp., 1979-1996. Sgt. U.S. Army, 1943-46. Mem. Birmingham Area C. of C., Vestavia Country Club (pres. 1971), Riverchase Country Club (pres. 1980). Methodist. Home: Birmingham, Ala. Died June 27, 2010.

HARDIN, CLIFFORD MORRIS, retired academic administrator, former United States Secretary of Agriculture; b. Knightstown, Ind., Oct. 9, 1915; s. James Alvin and Mabel (Macy) H.; m. Martha Love Wood, June 28, 1939; children: Susan Carol (Mrs. L.W. Wood), Clifford Wood, Cynthia (Mrs. Robert Milligan), Nancy Ann (Mrs. Douglas L. Rogers), James. BS, Purdue U., 1937, MS, 1939, PhD, 1941, DSc (hon.), 1952; Farm Found. scholar, U. Chgo., 1939-40; LLD, Creighton U., 1956, Ill. State U., 1973; Dr. honoris causa, Nat. U. Colombia, 1968; DSc, Mich. State U., 1969, N.D. State U., 1969, U. Nebr., 1978, Okla. Christian Coll., 1979. Instr. U. Wis., 1941-42, asst. prof. agrl. econs., 1942-44; assoc. prof. agrl. econs. Mich. State Coll., 1944-46, prof., chmn. agrl. econs. dept., 1946-48, dir. expt. sta., 1949-53, dean agr., 1953-54; chancellor U. Nebr., 1954-69; sec. USDA, Washington, 1969-71; vice chmn. bd., dir. Ralston Purina Co., St. Louis, 1971-80; dir. Center for Study of Am. Bus., Washington U., St. Louis, 1981-83, scholar-in-residence, 1983-85; cons., dir. Stifel, Nicolaus & Co., St. Louis, 1980-87. Bd. dirs. Gallup, Inc., Lincoln, Nebr., 1980-99; bd. dirs. Omaha br. Fed. Res. Bank of Kansas City, 1961-67, chmn., 1962-67. Editor: Overcoming World Hunger, 1969. Trustee Rockefeller Found., 1961-69, 72-81, Winrock, Internat., Morrilton, Ark., 1984-94, American Assembly, U. Nebr. Found.; mem. Pres.'s Com. to Stregthen Security Free World, 1963. Mem. Assn. State Univs. and Land-Grant Colls. (pres. 1960, chmn. exec. com. 1961). Home: Lincoln, Nebr. Died Apr. 4, 2010.

HARDY, ERNEST EDWARD, academic official, consultant; b. Hollis, NH, June 30, 1923; s. Harold Elwin and Estelle (Woodin) Hardy; m. Jane Elizabeth Little, Sept. 3, 1955; children: Edward, Robert. BS, Cornell U., 1953, MS, 1959, PhD, 1969; diploma, Oxford U., 1956. With family agrl. bus., Hollis, NH, 1941—49; fieldman Bird's Eye Gen. Foods Co., Rochester, NY, 1949—54; rsch. aide Cornell U., Ithaca, NY, 1957—65, rsch. assoc., 1965—71, sr. rsch. assoc., 1971—77; mem. NY State Land Use Com., 1972—85; sr. ext. assoc., dir. Resource Info. Lab., 1977—85, mem. grad. faculty; sr. cons. EPA, 1986; cons. The World Bank, 1987—91. Contbr. articles to profl. jours. Mem.: NY Acad. Scis., Am. Fedn. Music, Soil Conservation Soc. America, Am. Foresters, Am. Oxonians, Am. Soc. Photogrammetry (state office 1979—81), Epsilon Sigma Phi, Sigma Xi. Republican. Congregational. Achievements include development of a program for Geography Information System. Avocation: music. Home: Ithaca, NY. Died July 3, 2010.

HARDY, ROLLAND LEE, engineering educator; b. Carthage, Ill., May 2, 1920; s. William Bryan Hardy and Gladys Lenelle Timberlake; m. Dorinne Harriet DeKrey, Aug. 16, 1953 (div. Nov. 1988); children: Rosalin, Timothy, Melinda; m. Betty jean Devore, Oct. 24, 1990. BS in Gen. Sci., U. Ill., 1947; BSCE, U. Mo., 1950; DEng, U. Karlsruhe, Germany, 1963. Cert. profl. engr., Mo., Iowa; cert. profl. surveyor, Mo., Iowa. Topographic engr. U.S. Geol. Survey, Rolla, Mo., 1947-51; geodetic engr. U.S. Army Map Svc., Washington, 1951-52; project engr. U.S. Army Engr. R&D Lab., Ft. Belvoir, Va., 1952-56; asst. prof. George Washington U., Washington, 1956-58; hwy. engr. U.S. Bureau Pub. Rds., Washington, 1958-59; geodetic engr. adv. Agy. Internat. Devel., Khartoum, Sudan, 1959-61; gen. engr. Mapping, Charting, Geodesy Directorate Def. Intelligence Agy., Arlington, Va., 1963-67; prof. Iowa State U., Ames, 1967-88; sr. scientist in geodesy Nat. Rsch. Coun. Nat. Acad. Sci., Washington, 1977; adj. rsch. prof. dept. oceanography Naval Post Grad. Sch., Monterey, Calif., 1984; emeritus prof. Iowa State U., 1988; pres. Internat. Inst. Sci. and Tech., Bogalusa, La., from 1991. Recipient Ark. Traveler award Gov. Ark., 1971, Excellence award Soc. Land Surveyors, Iowa, 1985, recognition award Royal Thai Survey Dept. Supreme Cmd. HQ, Bangkok, Thailand, 1988. Fellow Am. Congress on Surverying and Mapping (life, Earle Fennell award 1986), Am. Soc. Civil Engrs.; mem. Am. Soc. Photogrammetry and Remote Sensing (emeritus), Am. Geophysical Union, Am. Legion, Moose Lodge. Avocations: mathematics, harmonica, keyboard, walking. Died Mar. 25, 2009.

HARE, LINDA P., educational administrator; b. Nashville, June 10, 1948; d. Hulit H. and Juanita Elizabeth Paskett; m. George C. Hill; children: Nicole, Brian. BA, Nashville, 1969; MS, Ind. U., 1974; Ed D, Tenn. State U., 1984. English tchr. Gary Cmty. Sch. Corp., Ind., 1969-80, Sumner Co. Schs., Gallatin, Tenn., 1981-83; adj. instr. Tenn. State U., Nashville, 1980-84; v.p. Meharry Med. Coll., Nashville, 1983-95, Middle Tenn. State U., Murfreesboro, from 1995. Bd. dirs. Cumberland Mus., Nashville, 1990—98; v.p. 100 Black Women, Nashville, 1994—99; adv. bd. Nashville Pub. TV, 1999; sec. bd. dirs. Leadership Nashville Alumni, from 1998. Recipient Adult Achiever Yr., YMCA, Nashville, 1994. Mem. Coun. Advancement and Support Edn. (dist. III bd. dirs. 1999—, internat. commn. philanthropy 1995-98), Rotary. Died Jan. 6, 2009.

HARGRAVE, IRVIN PHILIP HENRY, JR., reinsurance company executive; b. Glen Cove, N.Y., Nov. 17, 1935; s. Irvin Philip Henry and M. Grace (Delany) H.; m. Rosemarie Anna Kraus, Apr. 28, 1962; children— Laura M., Margaret G., Philip J., David M. B.S., Mt. St. Mary's Coll., Emmitsburg, Md., 1957. Spl. agt. Ins. Co. N.Am., Phila., 1957-64; property facultative reins. underwriter Gen. Reins. Corp., N.Y.C., 1964-72, asst. sec., Hartford, Conn., 1972-79, asst. v.p., 1979-82, 2d v.p., 1982—. Roman Catholic. Avocations: golf; piano; guitar; choral and solo singing. Home: Simsbury, Conn. Died Aug. 2, 2009.

HARGREAVES, GEORGE HENRY, civil and agricultural engineer, researcher; b. Chico, Calif., Apr. 2, 1916; s. Carey and Luella May (Raymond) H.; m. Elizabeth Ann Gardner, Aug. 9, 1941 (dec. Dec. 1947); 1 child, Margaret Ann Hargreaves Stolpmann; m. Sara Etna Romero, Jan 6, 1951; children: Mark Romero, Sonia Maria Hargreaves Hart, George Leo. BS in Soils, U. Calif., Berkeley, 1939; BSCE, U. Wyo., 1943. Civil engr. U.S. Bur. Reclamation, Sacramento, 1946-48; reclamation engr. U.S. Army C.E., Greece, 1948-49; engr. AID, Greece, Peru, Haiti, Philippines, Brazil and Colombia, 1950-68; chief civil engr. engring. br. Natural Resources divsn. Inter-Am. Geodetic Survey, Ft. Clayton, 1968-70; rsch. engr. in irrigation Utah State. U., Logan, 1970-86; rsch. Internat. Irrigation Ctr., 1980-86, rsch. prof. emeritus, from 1986. Author: World Water for Agriculture, 1977; co-author: Irrigation Fundamentals, 1998, Fundamentos Del Riego, 2000; contbr. numerous articles to profl. jours. Lt. (j.g.) USNR, 1943-46, PTO. Recipient Royce J. Tipton award, 1997. Fellow: ASCE; mem.: Internat. Commn. Irrigation and Drainage (chmn. U.S. Com. on crops and water use 1992—96, drainage and flood control 1999—2003, chmn. U.S. com. on history of irrigation), Am. Soc. Agrl. Engrs. (chmn. Rocky Mountain sect. 1974). Achievements include development of methodology used by the International Water Management Institute in the IWMI World Water and Climate Atlas, providing worldwide climate data and an index of rainfall adequacy for agricultural production. Home: Logan, Utah. Died Sept. 2009.

HARKINS, CRAIG, management consultant; b. Boston, May 1, 1936; s. Edwin Craig and Shirley Nadine (Pike) H.; m. Betty Letitia Hester, June 17, 1961 (div. 1985); children: Daniel, Sean, Lance; m. Donna Marie Hamlin, Sept. 1, 1990; 1 child Angelika. BA, Colby Coll., Waterville, Maine, 1958; MA, NYU, 1959; Profl. Dipl., Columbia U., NYC, 1963; PhD, Rensselaer Poly. Inst., Troy, NY, 1978. Computer operator Pacific Mutual, LA, 1957; reporter Evening Independent, St. Petersburg, Fla., 1960-61; pub. rels. mgr. IBM, N.Y./Calif, 1961-82; mgmt. cons. Hamlin Harkins Ltd., San Jose, from 1982. Co-editor: Guide to Writing Better Technical Papers, 1982; contbr. numerous articles to profl. jours. Sec. Hudson River Sloop Restoration, Poughkeepsie, N.Y., 1972-76; communications/mktg. com. United Way, Santa Clara, Calif., 1981—; mem. mktg. com. San Jose Cleve. Ballet, 1991—. With USMCR, 1961-66. Mem. Internat. Communication Assn., Peninsula Mktg. Assn., Soc. for Tech. Communication (bd. dirs. 1980-81), IEEE Profl. Communications Soc. (sec. 1977-80). Democrat. Roman Catholic. Avocations: gardening, swimming, poetry, hockey. Home: San Jose, Calif. Died Mar. 17, 2009.

HARLAN, LOUIS RUDOLPH, history educator, writer; b. West Point, Miss., July 13, 1922; s. Allen Dorset and Isabel (Knaffl) H.; m. Sadie Morton, Sept. 6, 1947; children: Louis Knaffl, Benjamin Wailes BA, Emory U., 1943; MA, Vanderbilt U., 1948; PhD, Johns Hopkins U., 1955. From asst. to assoc. prof. East Tex. State Coll., 1950-59; from assoc. prof. to prof. U. Cin., 1959-66; prof. history U. Md., College Park, 1966-84, Disting. prof. history, 1984-92, prof. emeritus, 1992—2010. Mem. Nat. Hist. Publs. and Records Commn., 1984-88. Author: Separate and Unequal: Public School Campaigns and Racism in the Southern Seaport States, 1901-1915, 1958, Booker T. Washington: The Making of a Black Leader, 1856-1901, 1972 (Bancroft award, 1973), Booker T. Washington: The Wizard of Tuskegee, 1901-1915, 1983 (Beveridge award, Bancroft award, Pulitzer Prize 1984), All at Sea: Coming of Age in World War II, 1996; editor: Booker T. Washington Papers, 14 vol. series, 1972-89. Bd. dirs. ACLU, Cin., 1963-66, Montgomery County, Md., 1967-72. Lt. (j.g.) USN, 1943-46; ETO, PTO. Fellow Am. Coun. of Learned Socs., 1962, Guggenheim Found., 1975, Inst. Advanced Study in Behavioral Scis., 1980, award for disting. svc. in documentary preservation and publ. Nat. Hist. Publs. and Records Commn., 1991. Fellow Soc. Am. Historians; mem. Am. Hist. Assn. (pres. 1989), So. Hist. Assn. (exec. bd. 1983-85, pres. 1989-90), Assn. for Documentary Editing (Julian P. Boyd award 1989), Assn. Study Afro-Am. Life and History (exec. bd. 1968-75), Orgn. Am. Historians (pres. 1989-90), Phi Beta Kappa, Phi Kappa Phi. Democrat. Avocations: tennis; swimming. Died Jan. 22, 2010.

HARLAN, NORMAN RALPH, construction executive; b. Dayton, Ohio, Dec. 21, 1914; s. Joseph and Anna (Kaplan) H.; m. Thelma Katz, Sept. 4, 1955; children: Leslie, Todd. Indsl. Engring. degree, U. Cin., 1937. Chmn. Am. Constrn. Corp., Dayton, 1949, Harlan, Inc., realtors. Mem. Dayton Real Estate Bd., Ohio Real Estate Assn., Nat. Assn. Real Estate Bds., C. of C., Pi Lambda Phi. Home: Kettering, Ohio. Died June 7, 2009.

HARPER, CARMELA ROSE, direct marketing company executive; b. N.Y.C.; d. Antonio and Assunta (Grenci) Vergara; m. Rondel H. Harper, May 8, 1947 (dec.). Student Coll. New Rochelle, 1936-38. Auditor, Liberty Mut. Ins. Co., N.Y.C., 1947-50; pres., chief exec. officer The Kleid Co. Inc., N.Y.C., 1950-95. Author: Mailing List Strategies, 1986; contbr. articles to profl. jours. Named to Direct Mktg. Hall of Fame, 1985. Mem. Direct Mktg. Assn. (bd. dirs., chmn. 1981-82). Roman Catholic. Avocations: investments, animals, children, old people's and ednl. causes, swimming. Home: Hartsdale, NY. Died Feb. 4, 2010.

HARPER, EMERY WALTER, lawyer; b. Hackensack, NJ, Feb. 25, 1936; s. Walter Van Saun and Dorothy Charlotte (Schmidt) H.; m. Judith Van Nest Hover, Sept. 9, 1961 (div. 1991); 1 child, Caroline Curry BA cum laude, Amherst Coll., 1958; LLB, Yale U., 1961. Bar: N.Y. 1962. Assoc. Lord Day & Lord, Barrett Smith, NYC, 1961-69, ptnr., 1970-93, Schnader, Harrison, Segal & Lewis, NYC, 1993—96, chmn. internat. maritime group, 1993-95; pres. Harper Cons., Inc., NYC, from 1997; of counsel Inman Deming LLP, 1998—2003, Law Offices Harry A. Inman, from 2003. Bd. dirs. The Shipping Network, Inc.; bd. dirs., founding mem. The Admiralty/Fin. Forum, Inc.; lectr. on maritime law Dalian, PRC, 1984; advisor U.S. del. to joint working group on liens and mortgages Internat. Maritime Orgn., 1st, 2d, 5th and 6th sessions UN Conf. on Trade and Devel., 1986-89; lectr. on admiralty and maritime financing; lectr. on ship fin. topics, Mex., Panama, Chile, Thailand, 1993-95; course dir. practice and techniques Financing Marine Assets and Ops., N.Y., 1995; organizer, pres. Am. Corps. in Coastwise Trade; participant U.S. Delegation to IMO/UNCTAD Joint Diplomatic Conf. on Maritime Liens and Mortgages, Geneva, 1993; cons. Inman Deming Internat., LLC, Washington, 1998—2003; del. to diplomatic conf. arrest of ships Internat. C. of C., 1999. Co-author: Essays on Maritime Liens and Mortgages and on Arrest of Ships, 1985; contbr. articles to profl. publs. Trustee The Gateway Sch., N.Y., 1975-83; deacon Brick Presbyn. Ch., 1970-76, elder, 1976-82, trustee, corp. sec., 1982-88; mem. legal adv. com. Liberian Shipowners Coun., 1988-2000; chmn. Subcom. on Liberian Maritime Law Revision, 1993-99; chmn. Marshall Islands Roundtable, 1999-2001; mem. Seatransport com. U.S. Coun. for Internat. Bus., 1987-91; dir. Cmty. Living Corp. Found., Inc., 2002—; bd. dirs. CLC Found., Inc., 2002—. With USAFR, 1961-67. Mem. ABA (chmn. admiralty and maritime law com., sect. internat. law, sect. dispute resolution), Assn. of Bar of City of N.Y. (mem. admiralty com. 1974-80, 90-93, 98-2000, chmn. 1977-80), Maritime Law Assn. (founding chmn. com. on Marine financing 1978—), Com. Maritime Internat. (internat. subcom. on maritime liens and mortgages), Marine Soc. City of NY, N.Y. Amherst Alumni Assn. (pres. 1975-77), Pilgrims Soc., Union Club. Deceased.

HARPER, PHYLLIS HAWKINS, journalist; b. Fawn Grove, Miss., Oct. 6, 1933; d. Edward Clinton and Mittie (Leslie) Hawkins; m. James Leverne Harper, Dec. 23, 1954 (div. May 1970); children— Lynn, Laurie, Leslie, Jamie, Beth Anne. Student Itawamba Jr. Coll., 1951-53, U. Miss., 1953-54. Proofreader, N.E. Miss. Daily Jour., Tupelo, 1969-72, reporter, 1972-77, feature editor, 1977—, speaker/lectr., 1977—; tchr. Tupelo City Schs., 1970-72. Bd. dirs. Tupelo Artists Guild, 1982—; co-chmn. March of Dimes Teamwalk, Lee County, Miss., 1984. Recipient Outstanding Pub. Service award St. Jude Children's Hosp., Memphis, 1979, Outstanding Service award Salvation Army of Tupelo-Lee County, 1982, 83, Battered Boot award March of Dimes, 1982; named Woman of Distinction, Altrusa Club, Tupelo, 1982; Service to God and Man award West Point Civitan Club, 1982; hon. dep. sheriff Lee County. Mem. Miss. Press Assn., Itawamba Hist. Soc. (Service award 1983), Tupelo Museum Assn., Community Devel. Found. Presbyterian. Home: Tupelo, Miss. Died Feb. 12, 2009.

HARR, ALMA ELIZABETH TAGLIABUE, nursing educator; b. Glen Cove, NY, Apr. 11, 1927; d. Frederick Edwin and Lillian T. (Spittel) Tagliabue; (widowed 1981); m. Kenneth E. Harr, Nov. 21, 1962; 1 child, Kendal Elizabeth; stepchildren: Rose Marie Torreano, Kathleen Dobson. Student, Renssalaer Poly. Inst., 1947; RN, N.Y. Hosp. Sch. Nursing, 1950; BSN, Cornell U., 1950; MA, Columbia U., 1955; cert. in maternal nutrition, U. N.C., 1982. Cert. pub. health nurse, sch. nurse tchr., childbirth educator. Asst. head nurse Cornell U.-N.Y. Hosp., NYC, 1950-51, head nurse, 1951-52; asst. DON, dir. nursing and patient edn. Trudeau Sanitorium, N.Y., 1952-54; instr. Bklyn. Coll., 1955-63, lectr., 1963-65, asst. divsn. chmn. dept. nursing, 1961-65; assoc. prof. Nassau Community Coll., Garden City, N.Y., 1965-69, prof., 1969-91, prof. emerita, from 1991. Contbr. articles to profl. jours. Mem. nurses adv. com. March of Dimes, 1969-91, chmn. nurses adv. com., 1981-88, mem. profl. com., 1981-88. Mem. ANA, Am. Soc. Psychoprophylactic Obstetrics, Nassau Community Coll. Fedn. Tchrs., Nat. League Nursing, Pi Lambda Theta, Kappa Delta Pi, Sigma Theta Tau. Republican. Episcopalian. Avocations: reading, swimming, walking, knitting, needlepoint, crocheting. Home: Fort Myers, Fla. Died Jan. 4, 2009.

HARRIGAN, ANTHONY HART, author; b. NYC, Oct. 27, 1925; s. Anthony Hart and Elizabeth Elliott (Hutson) H.; m. Elizabeth McP. Ravenel, Aug. 16, 1950; children: Anthony Hart, Elizabeth Chardon, Elliott McP., Mary Ravenel. Student, Bard Coll., Kenyon Coll., Gambier, Ohio, U. Va. Reporter Virginian-Pilot, Norfolk, 1953-55, Charleston (S.C.) News & Courier, assoc. editor, 1957-70; exec. v.p. U.S. Indsl. Coun., Nashville, 1970-78, pres., 1978-90. Pres. U.S. Bus. and Indsl. Coun. Ednl. Found., 1978-90; trustee, rsch. fellow Nat. Humanities Inst.; lectr. Harvard U., Nat. War Coll., Vanderbilt U., U. Colo.; past mem. rsch. com. S.C. Commn. Higher Edn. Author: Ten Poets Anthology, 1947, The Editor and the Republic, 1952, Red Star Over Africa, 1964, The New

Republic, 1965, Defense Against Total Attack, 1966, A Guide to the War in Vietnam, 1965, American Perspectives, 1974, American Perspectives II, 1977; co-author: The Indian Ocean and the Threat to the West, 1976, The Southern Oceans and the Security of the Free World, 1978, Putting America First, 1987, American Economic Pre-eminence, 1989; co-author or editor other works, 1978; editl. adv. bd. Modern Age, 1955—; author newspaper column, 1970-90, also numerous articles in nat. jours. Trustee Nat. Humanities Inst. Served with USMCR, World War II. Recipient Mil. Rev. award U.S. Army Command and Gen. Staff Coll., 1965; grantee Relm Found., 1966, Wilbur Found., 1992, 95, Earhart Found., 1993. Mem. Soc. Colonial Wars in S.C., Carolina Yacht Club. Anglican. Died May 28, 2010.

HARRIMAN, RICHARD LEE, performing arts administrator, educator; b. Independence, Mo., Sept. 10, 1932; s. Walter S. and M. Eloise (Faulkner) Harriman. AB, William Jewell Coll., 1953, LittD (hon.), 1983; MA, Stanford U., 1959. Instr., asst. prof. English U. Dubuque, Iowa, 1960—62; asst. prof. English William Jewell Coll., Liberty, Mo., 1962, acting head English dept., 1965—69, dir. fine arts program, 1965—2003, assoc. prof., from 1966. Artistic dir. Harriman-Jewel Series, Liberty, from 2003. Treas. Kansas City Arts Coun., 1980, sec, 1981, Kansas City Am. Arts Festival, 1988—89. With AUS, 1953—55. Woodrow Wilson fellow, 1957. Mem.: AAUP, MLA, Assn. Performing Arts Presenters (nat. exec. bd. 1975—78), Shakespeare Assn. Am., Internat. Soc. Performing Arts, Alpha Psi Omega, Sigma Tau Delta, Lambda Chi Alpha. Methodist. Home: Liberty, Mo. Died July 15, 2010.

HARRIS, BARBARA NELSON, librarian; b. Bridgeport, Conn., May 12, 1924; d. Carl Alexander and Helen Ella (Bodie) Nelson; m. John Donald Harris, July 12, 1946; children: John, Ralph, Lisa, Todd, Heather. Student, Jr. Coll. Conn., Bridgeport, 1942-43; cert., Audio-Visual Inst. for Effective Communication, Bloomington, Ind., 1976; cert. pub. relations for libraries and info. service, Simmons Coll., 1978. Circulation and reference asst. Groton (Conn.) Pub. Library, 1964-68, head adult services, 1969-72; reference asst. pub. relations Waterford (Conn.) Pub. Library, 1976—; mem. Groton Pub. Library Bd., 1976-77. Co-author: Reflexions in an Herb Garden, 1981. Sec. New London (Conn.) YWCA, 1970-71; pres. LWV Groton, 1976-77, Friends of Groton Pub. Library, 1975-76. Served with WAVES, USN, 1944-46. Mem. ALA, Conn. Library Assn. (chmn. publicity com. 1980-81, head pub. relations sect. 1981-82, treas. 1983-86), New Eng. Library Assn. Democrat. Unitarian. Home: Groton, Conn. Died Mar. 22, 2010.

HARRIS, EDWARD DAY, JR., physician; b. Phila., July 7, 1937; children: Ned, Tom, Chandler. AB, Dartmouth Coll., 1958, grad. with honors, 1960; MD cum laude, Harvard U., 1962. Diplomate Am. Bd. Internal Medicine and Rheumatology (chmn. subsplty. bd. in rheumatology 1986-88). Intern Mass. Gen. Hosp., Boston, 1962-63, asst. resident, 1963-64, sr. resident, 1966-67, clin. research fellow arthritis unit, 1967-69; asst. prof. Harvard Med. Sch., Boston, 1970; from asst. prof. to prof. Dartmouth Med. Sch., Hanover, NH, 1970-83, Eugene W. Leonard prof., 1979-83, chief connective tissue disease sect., 1970-83; mem. staff Mary Hitchcock Meml. Hosp., 1970-83; chief med. service Middlesex Gen. U. Hosp., New Brunswick, NJ, from 1983; asst. prof. Harvard U. Med. Sch., Boston, 1970; prof., chmn. medicine U. Medicine and Dentistry N.J.-Rutgers U. Med. Sch., New Brunswick, 1983-88; Arthur L. Bloomfield prof. medicine Stanford U. Sch. Medicine, 1988-95, chmn. dept. medicine, 1988-95, George DeForest Barnett prof. medicine, 1988—2003, George DeForest Barnett prof. medicine emeritus, from 2003; acad. sec. to Stanford U., 2002—07. Chief med. svc. Stanford U. Hosp., 1988-95; dir. Ctr. for Musculoskeletal Diseases, Stanford, 1996-99, emeritus, 2003—; pres. med. staff, Stanford U. Hosp., 1997-99; med. dir. Internat. Med. Svc., 1997—2002. Master: ACP (gov. No. Calif. chpt. from 2000), Am. Coll. Rheumatism (numerous coms. from 1967, pres. 1985—86, Dist. Rheumatism award 2004); fellow: Royal Soc. Medicine; mem.: Alpha Omega Alpha (exec. sec. from 1997, editor The Pharos from 1997). Home: Stanford, Calif. Died May 21, 2010.

HARRIS, JAMES GEORGE, JR., social services administrator, consultant; b. Cuthbert, Ga., Oct. 27, 1931; s. James George and Eunice (Mitchner) Harris; m. Lydia Rodriguez, Aug. 7, 1997; children: Peter, Robin, Freda, Maria, Madalene, Raymon, Frances. BS, U. Hartford, 1958. State social worker, Hartford, Conn., 1960—64; asst. dir. Conn. Office Econ. Opportunity, Hartford, 1965—66; spl. asst. and state civil rights coord. Conn. Gov. John Dempsey, Hartford, 1966—70; exec. dir. Cmty. Renewal Team Greater Hartford, 1970—82; commr. Conn. Dept. Human Resources, 1983—87, Hartford Commn. Aging; mem. state legis. com. AARP, Capitol City Task Force; cons. Data Inst., Expand Assocs., Silver Spring, Md., from 1987; bd. dirs. Lillian Johnson-Tomas Roderiguez Tutorial Program, Hartford, from 1994. Sec. Conn. Assn. Community Action, 1975—76, pres., 1976—78. With USAF, 1950—54. Mem.: New Eng. Cmty. Action Program Assn. (pres. 1978—80, chmn. 1981—82, New Eng. v.p. 1978), Knights of Peter Claver (St. Benedict coun. 311 fin. sec. 1994, Grand knight 1994—95), Com. 20 Club, High Noon Club, Alpha Phi Alpha. Democrat. Roman Catholic. Died Aug. 28, 2009.

HARRIS, WILLIAM BURLEIGH, geologist, educator; b. Norfolk, Va., July 2, 1943; s. Roy Solomon and Emily (Kasey) Harris; m. Sharon Jones, Aug. 25, 1965; children: Daniel Wyatt, Timothy Roy. BS in Geology, Campbell U., 1966; MS in Geology, W.Va. U., 1968; PhD in Geology, U. NC, Chapel Hill, 1975. Petroleum geologist Texaco, Inc., Tulsa, 0638—1970; econ. geologist Va. Div. Mineral Resources, Charlottesville, 1970—72; asst. prof. geology U. NC, Wilmington, 1976—81, assoc. prof., 1981—82; rsch. specialist Exxon Prodn. Rsch. Co., Houston, 1982—83; prof. geology U. NC, Wilmington, from 1984; cons. ARCO Oil and Gas, 1985—89, Westinghouse Savannah River Lab., from 1989, US Army Corps. Engrs., from 1992. Contbr. articles to profl. jours. NC Bd. Sci. and Tech. grant, 1976—77. Mem.: Sigma Gamma Epsilon, Sigma Xi, Southeastern Geol. Soc., Soc. Econ. Paleontologists and Mineralogists, Geol. Soc. Am., Carolina Geol. Soc. Presbyterian. Home: Wilmington, NC. Died Sept. 1, 2009.

HARRISON, FRED FRANCIS, other: manufacturing; b. NYC, Aug. 31, 1928; s. John Edmond and Anna (Schaefer) H.; m. Claire Marie Klueber, Dec. 27, 1952; children: Dennis, Katherine, Robert, Joseph, Francine, Therese, Edward, Elizabeth, John. BBA, Iona Coll., 1951; postgrad., Fordham U., Grad. Sch. Bus. Adminstrn., NYU, 1953—54. Collection corr. CIT Corp., NYC, 1953—54, new bus. rep., 1955, new bus. mgr., 1956—62, dist. sales mgr., 1963—65, sales mgr., 1966—67, div. head, asst. v.p. Detroit, 1968—72, div. head, v.p. NYC, 1973—76, v.p. comml. fin., 1977, v.p. mktg., sales devel., from 1977. Nat. health care cons. Author: Salesman's Handbook, 1980, 1983. Exec. bd. St. Elizabeth Ann Seton Ch., Schrub Oak, NY, 1966—67; com. chmn. St. Thomas More Ch., Troy, Mich., 1968—72; mem. parish coun. fin. com. St. Patrick's Ch., Yorktown, NY, 1974; scoutmaster Bronx coun. Boy Scouts Am. With US Army, 1951—53. Mem.: Material Handling Equipment Distbrs. Assn., Food Processing Equipment & Supply Assn., Healthcare Fin. Mgmt. Assn., Cath. Hosp. Assn. Roman Catholic. Home: Wharton, NJ. Died Apr. 1, 2010.

HARRISON, TIMOTHY STONE, surgery and physiology educator; b. Kodaikanal, S. India, July 13, 1927; (parents U.S. citizens); came to U.S., 1939; s. Paul Wilberforce and Regina (Robbe) H. m. Eliza Middleton Cope, July 1, 1961; children—Abigail DeNormandie, Emily Cope. AB, Hope Coll., Holland, Mich., 1949; MD, Johns Hopkins U., 1953. Intern, then resident in surgery Johns Hopkins Hosp., Balt., 1953-56; resident in surgery Mass. Gen. Hosp., Boston, 1956-59; spl. research fellow in physiology Karolinska Inst., Stockholm, 1959-60; asst. prof., then assoc. prof. surgery U. Mich. Med. Sch., 1962-68, prof., 1971-75; prof. surgery, chmn. dept. Am. U., Beirut, 1968-71; prof. surgery and physiology Milton S. Hershey (Pa.) Med. Center, Pa. State U. Med. Sch., from 1975. Vis. prof. surgery Aga Khan U., Karachi, Pakistan, 1985-87; cons. surgeon Ministry of Health, Sultanate of Oman, 1990-93. Sr. author: Surgical Disorders of the Adrenal Gland: Physiologic Background and Treatment, 1975, Surgery For All, 1992. Served with USNR and USMCR, 1945-47. Grantee NIH, 1963— Mem. Endocrine Soc., Am. Surg. Assn., Soc. Clin. Surgery, Soc. U. Surgeons, Am. Physiol. Soc., Halsted Soc., James IV Assn. Surgeons. Episcopalian. (elder). Home: Rumford, RI. Died July 21, 2010.

HARRISON, WILLIAM FLOYD NATHANIEL, obstetrician-gynecologist; b. Conway, Ark., Sept. 8, 1935; s. Benjamin G. and Mattie Evelyn (Powell) H.; m. Betty Arlene Waggoner, June 20, 1960; children: Amanda Lynn, Benjamin G. III, Rebecca Irene. BA, U. Ark., 1963, MD, 1968. Cert. in ob-gyn. Intern, resident U. Hosp., Little Rock, 1968-72; with Washington Regional Hosp., Fayetteville, Ark., Springdale Meml. Hosp., Ark.; clin. asst. prof. ob-gyn. U. Ark. Coll. Medicine. Mem. ACOG, American Fertility Soc., American Assn. Gynecol. Laparoscopists, Nat. Abortion Found. Democrat. Methodist. Home: Fayetteville, Ark. Died Sept. 24, 2010.

HARSHA, WILLIAM HOWARD, JR., former United States Representative from Ohio; b. Portsmouth, Ohio, Jan. 1, 1921; m. Rosemary Spellerberg; children: Bill, Mark, Bruce, Brian. AB, Kenyon Coll., 1943; LLB, Western Reserve U., 1947. Asst. city solicitor, Portsmouth, Ohio, 1947—51; prosecutor Scioto County, Ohio, 1951—55; mem. US Congress from Ohio, 1961—81; cons. Washington, 1981—86. Contbr. articles to profl. jours. Served in USMC, 1942—44. Recipient Disting. Svc. award, Nat. Limestone Inst., Am. Constl. Action, Honor award, Freedom Found., 1st Internat. Road Safety award, Eng. Min. Transp., London. Mem.: YMCA, Elks, Bus. & Prof. Men's Club, Exchange Club (former exalted ruler), Mason. Republican. Presbyterian. Died Oct. 11, 2010.

HART, DAVID WILLIAM, bank executive, lawyer; b. Albion, Pa., Feb. 6, 1921; s. William Lynn and Ruth Elizabeth (Lavely) H.; m. Jean Frances McCarthy, Apr. 4, 1942; children: Gordon William, Marilyn Jean. BS cum laude, Ohio State U., 1948, MA, JD, Ohio State U., 1950. Bar: Ohio 1950, N.Y. 1957. Pvt. practice law, asso. law firm Fuller, Harrington & Seney, Toledo, 1950-51; atty. Gen. Electric Co., Schenectady, 1951-60; asst. sec., atty. White Motor Corp., Cleve., 1960-68; sec., dir. White Motor Credit Corp., 1962-68; pres. White Motor Internat. (S.A.), Cleve., 1970-71; v.p., gen. counsel Nat. City Bank, Cleve., 1971-80, sr. vice-pres., gen. counsel, from 1980. V.p., gen. counsel, sec. Nat. City Corp., Cleve., 1973-80, sr. v.p., gen. counsel, sec., 1980— Served with AUS, 1942-46. Mem. Greater Cleve. Growth Assn., Phi Delta Phi, Beta Gamma Sigma, Beta Alpha Psi. Clubs: Canterbury Golf (past dir.), Union. Died Jan. 1, 2009.

HART, JAMES HARLAN, retired emergency medicine physician; b. Hamilton County, Ill., Dec. 16, 1934; s. Gleason and Elizabeth Jane (Smith) Hart; m. Sharon Lenore Darr, Sept. 20, 1937; m. Lora Rae Barnett, May 9, 1955; children: Shane, Kyle, Raelene. BS, Southwestern State U., Weatherford, Okla., 1963; MD, Okla. U., 1968. Clin. assoc. prof. U. Ill. Med. Sch., Urbana; intern Mercy Hosp., Okla. City, 1968—69; resident, ob-gyn. St. Anthony Hosp., Okla. City, 1969—72; pvt. practice Woodriver, Ill., 1972—77, Lincoln, Ill., 1977—80; emergency medicine physician St. Elizabeth Hosp., Danville, Ill., 1980—89; med. dir., emergency svc., 1980—89; emergency medicine physician Danville, Ill., 1980—89; med. dir., urgent care clinic Cmty. Hosp., Williamsport, Ind., 1989—92; med. dir., emergency med. technicians program, 1989; dir., emergency med. dept. Williamsport Cmty. Hosp., 1991; ret., 1994. With US Army, 1957—59. Mem.: AMA, Vermillion County Med. Soc., Warren County Ind. Med. Soc., Ind. State Med. Soc., Ill. State Med. Soc., Am. Coll. Emergency Physicians. Republican. Home: Williamsport, Ind. Died Mar. 20, 2010.

HART, THOMAS R., Romance language educator; b. Raleigh, NC, Jan. 10, 1925; s. Thomas Roy and Mary (Medlin) H.; m. Margaret Alice Fulton, June 30, 1945; children: John Fulton, Katherine Anne. BA, Yale U., 1948, PhD, 1952. Instr. Amherst Coll., Mass., 1952-53, Harvard U., Cambridge, Mass., 1953-55; asst. prof. Johns Hopkins, Balt., 1955-60; assoc. prof. Emory U., Atlanta, 1960-64; prof. Romance langs. U. Oreg., Eugene, from 1964, prof. comparative lit., 1989-90, prof. emeritus, from 1990. Vis. prof. Oxford U., winter 1986. Editor: Jour. Comparative Literature, Gil Vicente: Obras dramaticas castellanas, 1962, Gil Vicente: Farces and Festival Plays, 1972, Cervantes and Ariosto: Renewing Fiction, 1989. Fulbright research grantee, 1950-51, Madrid, 1966-67; NEH fellow, 1985-86, Camargo Found. fellow, France, 1990. Mem. Associacion Internacional de Hispanistas Home: Eugene, Oreg. Died Jan. 17, 2010.

HARTMANN, ROBERT ELLIOTT, retired manufacturing executive; b. Bklyn., Apr. 10, 1926; s. James and Edna Mae (Schroeder) H.; m. Anne Marie Mongiello, Feb. 15, 1948; children: Barbara Hartmann Kaszor, Donna Hartmann Dow. BS, Miami U., Oxford, Ohio, 1946. CPA, N.Y. Acct. Price, Waterhouse & Co., NYC, 1948-57; mgr. fin. acctg. Air Products & Chems., Allentown, Pa., 1957-58; v.p. Alpha Portland Cement Co. divsn. Alpha Portland Industries, Inc., Easton, Pa., 1958-82. Sec. Slattery Group, Inc. (formely Alpha Portland Industries, Inc.), Easton, 1962-89; sec., treas. Energy and Resource Recovery Corp., until 1982; sec., treas., dir. H.O.H. Corp., until 1982; past pres. Moravian Book Shop, Inc. Bd. dirs. Bethlehem Area Moravians. Served to lt. Supply Corps USNR, World War II. Mem. Inst. Mgmt. Accts. (pres. Lehigh Valley chpt. 1973-74), Financial Execs. Inst. (treas. N.E. Pa. chpt. 1972-74), Am. Inst. C.P.A.s. Mem. Moravian Ch. Home: Bethlehem, Pa. Died Feb. 20, 2010.

HARTNETT, MAURICE A., III, former state supreme court justice; b. Dover, Del., Jan. 20, 1927; s. Maurice and Anna Louise (Morris) H.; m. Elizabeth Anne Hutchinson, Aug. 21, 1965; 1 child, Anne Elizabeth. Student, Washington Coll.-Chestertown, Md., 1946-47; BS, U. Del.-Newark, 1951; postgrad., Georgetown U., 1951; JD, George Washington U., 1954; EdM, U. Del., 1956. Bar: Del. 1954, U.S. Dist. Ct. Del. 1957, U.S. Supreme Ct. 1959. Pvt. practice law, Dover, Del., 1955-76; exec. dir. Del. Legis. Ref. bur., Dover, 1961-69; vice chancellor Del. Ct. Chancery, Dover, 1976-94; justice Del. Supreme Ct., 1994—2000. Code revisor Del. Rev. Code Commn., 1961-72; commr. Nat. Conf. Com. Uniform State Laws, Chgo., 1962—, sec., exec. com., 1977-83; chmn. State Tax Appeal Bd., Wilmington, Del., 1973-76. Served with U.S. Army, 1945-46. Mem. ABA, Del. Bar Assn., Kent County Bar Assn. (pres. 1974), Am. Law Inst. Democrat. Home: Dover, Del. Died May 11, 2009.

HARTZHEIM, WAYNE ARTHUR, insurance company executive; b. Appleton, Wis., May 11, 1928; s. Arthur Michael and Emma Marie (Brux) Hartzheim; m. Marilyn Jean Farley, June 28, 1952; children: Susan, Jane, Thomas, William. BS, Marquette U., 1952; postgrad. in advanced sales mgmt., Mich. State U., 1959; AMP, Harvard, 1980. Claims adjuster and examiner, chief adjuster Sentry Ins. Mut. Co., Milw, 1952—56, sales rep, 1956—59, sales mgr. Mpls., 1959—66, casualty specialist Stevens Point, Wis., 1966—67, br. mgr. Morristown, NJ, v.p. spl accounts Stevens Point, 1978—80, v.p. sales, 1979—80, exec. v.p. ins. ops., from 1982. V.p. Sentry Life Ins. Co., Syracuse, NY, 1967—68, pres., 1968—78, Patriot Gen. Life Ins. Co., Concord, Mass., 1977—78; exec. v.p. Sentry Ctr. West, Scottsdale, Ariz., 1980—82. Dir. Dairyland Ins. Co., Great Southwest Fire Ins. Co., Middlesex Ins. Co., Parker Services, Inc., Patriot Gen. Ins. Co., Sentry Cash. Mgmt. Fund, Sentry Fin. Services Corp., Sentry Fund, Inc., Sentry Indemnity Co., Sentry Life Ins. Co. of N.Y., Great Southwest Surplus Lines Ins. Co.; pres. Sentry Cash Mgmt. Fund, Sentry Fund, Inc., Sentry Indemnity Co., Great Southwest Fire Ins. Co., Great Southwest Surplus Lines Ins. Co., Dairyland Ins. Co.; chmn. bd. Parker Services, Inc., Sentry Cash Mgmt. Fund, Sentry Fund. Mem.: Ins. Rev. Com. (issues rev. Com.), Alliance of Am. Insurers (mktg. mgmt. com.), Harvard Alumni (Wis. assn.), K.C., Kiwanis. Roman Cath. Home: Stevens Point, Wis. Died Aug. 13, 2010.

HARVEY, CHARLES ALBERT, JR., lawyer; b. Beverly, Mass., Sept. 28, 1949; s. Charles A. and Phyllis B. (O'Rourke) H.; m. Whitney Ann Neville, Sept. 21, 1985; children: John Whitney, Charlotte Baird. AB, Assumption Coll., 1971; JD, U. Maine, 1974. Bar: Maine 1974, Mass. 1974, U.S. Supreme Ct. 1979. Assoc. Verrill & Dana, Portland, Maine, 1974-79, ptnr., 1979-95, Harvey & Frank, Portland, from 1995. Assoc. chief counsel President's Commn. on Accident at Three Mile Island, Washington, 1979; mem. adv. com. on civil rules Maine Supreme Jud. Ct., 1978-91, chmn. adv. com. on cameras in trial cts., 1991-93, cons. on civil rules, 1996—, chmn. adv. com. on civil rules, 1987-91; chmn. adv. com. on local rules U.S. Dist. Ct. Maine, 1985—, mem. civil justice adv. com., 1992-97; chmn. Maine Gov.'s Select Com. on Jud. Appointments, 1987-91; mem. Senator Olympia J. Snowe's adv. com. on appointment of U.S. Dist. Judge, U.S. Atty. and U.S. Marshal, 2001-02; chmn. grievance commn. Maine Bd. Overseers of the Bar, 1996-97. Contbr. articles to profl. jours. Trustee Portland Sympnony Orch., 1980-89, pres., 1987-89, adv. trustee, 1989—; trustee Portland Stage Co., 1984-87, adv. trustee, 1987—; trustee Waynflete Sch., 1990-96; adv. trustee Maine Childrens Mus., 1992-1999, Maine Vol. Lawyers for the Arts, 1994-1999. Fellow Portland Mus. of Art, 1993—. Fellow Am. Coll. Trial Lawyers, Maine Bar Found.; mem. Am. Law Inst. Republican. Died Feb. 18, 2009.

HARVEY, FRED, retail executive; b. Boston, Aug. 20, 1932; s. Fred and Dorothea (Sprague) H.; m. Shirley Bondurant Moore, July 1956 (div. 1983); children: Fred, Charles K., Amy. BA in Econs., Vanderbilt U., 1954. Pres. Burk & Co., Nashville, 1956—57; mgr. basement mdse. Harvey's Dept. Store, Nashville, 1957—60, pres., from 1960. Dir. Third Nat. Bank, Nashville, from 1974. Mem. adv. bd. Middle Tenn. Coun. Boy Scouts Am., Nashville; former chmn. Nashville Meml. Hosp.; former mem. Met. Nashville Parking and Traffic Commn. Lt. USN, 1954—56, Pacific. Named Retailer of Yr., Nashville Real Estate Bd., 1964, Outstanding Young Man, Nashville Jaycees, 1966, Boss of Yr., Am. Bus. Women's Assn./Nashville, 1966. Mem.: Nat. Retail Mchts. Assn. (bd. dirs., state dir. Tenn.), The Honors Course (Ooltewah, Tenn.), Belle Meade Country Club Nashville, Metro Club N.Y. Home: Nashville, Tenn. Died Dec. 29, 2009.

HARVEY, JOSEPH PAUL, JR., orthopedist, educator; b. Youngstown, Ohio, Feb. 28, 1922; s. Joseph Paul and Mary Justinian (Collins) H.; m. Martha Elizabeth Toole, Apr. 12, 1958; children: Maryalice, Martha Jane, Frances Susan, Helen Lucy, Laura Andre. Student, Dartmouth Coll., 1939—42; MD, Harvard U., 1945. Diplomate Nat. Bd. Med. Examiners. Intern Peter Bent Brigham Hosp., Boston, 1945-46; resident Univ. Hosp., Cleve., 1951-53, Hosp. Spl. Surgery, NYC, 1953-54; instr. orthopedics Cornell Med. Coll., NYC, 1954-62; mem. faculty Sch. Medicine, U. So. Calif., Los Angeles, 1962-92; prof. orthopedic surgery U. So. Calif., 1966-92, prof. emeritus, from 1992; chmn. sect. orthopedics Keck Sch. Medicine, U. So. Calif., 1964-78. Dir. dept. orthopedics U. So. Calif.-LA County Med. Ctr., 1964-79, staff, 1979— Editor-in-chief: Contemporary Orthopedics, 1978-96. Served to capt. AUS, 1946-48. Exchange orthopedic fellow Royal Acad. Hosp., Upsala, Sweden, 1957. Fellow Western Orthop. Assn., Am. Acad. Orthop. Surgery, A.C.S., Am. Soc. Testing Materials; mem. AMA, Calif. Med. Assn., Los Angeles County Med. Assn., Am. Rheumatism Assn., Am. Orthop. Assn., Internat. Soc. Orthopedics and Traumatology. Home: Pasadena, Calif. Died Dec. 7, 2010.

HARVEY, WALTER H., lawyer, treasurer; b. Rye, NY, Feb. 5, 1944; s. William H. and Kathryn (Detweiller) H.; m. Jeanne Ann Lazorchak, Sept. 14, 1966; children: Evan Hughes, Dayna Price. BA, Lehigh U., 1966; JD, Fordham U., 1969; MBA, NYU, 1971, LLM in Taxation, 1975. Bar: N.Y. 1969; CPA, N.Y. Sr. tax acct. Ernst & Ernst, NYC, 1968-71; tax mgr. Loral Corp., NYC, 1971-73, SCM Corp., NYC, 1973-76; dir. taxes Hertz Corp., NYC, 1976-80; v.p., treas. Zale Corp., Dallas, from 1980. Mem. adv. com. Dallas County Treas., 1987. Mem. ABA, Am. Inst. CPA's, Nat. Assn. Corp. Treas., Tax Execs. Inst. Clubs: Brookhaven Country (Dallas). Republican. Episcopalian. Avocations: golf, tennis, bridge. Home: Dallas, Tex. Died Jan. 9, 2010.

HARVILL, H. DOYLE, newspaper publisher; b. Keysville, Fla., July 11, 1929; Grad., U. Tex. Printer St. Petersburg Times; composing room foreman Texarkana Gazette; copy desk, reporter, city editor, mng. editor Tampa Times; exec. editor Greenville News; v.p., pub. The Advertiser Co. Multimedia Inc.; v.p., exec. editor The Tampa Tribune, 1986-90, pub., chmn., from 1990. Past chmn. Community Found. Greater Tampa, Inc., bd. dirs. U. Tampa. With USMC, 1948-52. Mem. Soc. Profl. Journalist, Assoc. Press Mng. Editors, Am. Soc. Newspaper Editors, Fla. Soc. Newspaper Editors, S.C. Press Assn., Ala. Press Assn., So. Newspaper Pub. Assn. (bd. dirs.), Greater Tampa C. of C. (bd. govs.). Died Dec. 17, 2009.

HARWELL, WILLIAM EARNEST (ERNIE HARWELL), retired commentator; b. Washington, Ga., Jan. 25, 1918; s. Davis Gray Harwell; m. Lula Tankersley, Aug. 30, 1941; children: William Earnest, Jr., Gray Neville, Julie, Carolyn. AB, Emory U., 1940; LittD (hon.), Adrian Coll., 1985; LHD (hon.), No. Mich. Coll., 1990; dr. humane letters, LLD, U. Mich., 2008. Pres. Erine Harwell Found.; Sports dir. Sta. WSB, Atlanta, 1940-43; announcer Atlanta Crackers, 1946-48, Bklyn. Dodgers, 1948-49, N.Y. Giants, 1950-53, Balt. Orioles, 1954-59, Detroit Tigers, 1960—91, 1993—2002; ret., 2002. Announcer All-Star games, World Series, NBC, CBS Radio, pro football Balt. Colts, N.Y. Giants; broadcaster Master's golf tournament, NBC, 1942, 46. Author: Tuned to Baseball, 1985, Diamond Gems, 1991, The Babe Signed My Shoe, 1994, Stories From My Life in Baseball, 2001, Life After Baseball, 2004, Ernie Harwell's Audio Scrapbook, 2006, Breaking 90, 2007; composer songs including I Don't Know Any Better, Move over Babe, Only a Fool, One-Room World, One Dream, Sing Every Song. With USMC, 1942—46. Recipient Lowell Thomas Broadcast award, 1985, Alvin Foon award Mich. Jewish Sports Hall of Fame, 1988, 90, Big Mac award Detroit News, 1989, Golden Compass award Campfire Inc., 1989, Life Directions Enrichment award, 1989, Nat. Lifetime Nat. Achievement award March of Dimes, 1991, Joe Louis award, 1991, Ken Hubbs Meml. award, 1991, Stanley Kresge award, 1994, U. Detroit Jesuit Magis award, 1995; named Most Durable Baseball Announcer, Guinness Book Records, 2003-07; named to Baseball Hall of Fame, Cooperstown, 1981, Mich. Sports Hall of Fame, Emory U. Hall of Fame, Nat. Sportscasters and Sportswriters Hall of Fame, Am. Sportscasters Hall of Fame, Catch Hall of Fame, Ga. Broadcasters Hall of Fame, Nat. Radio Hall of Fame, 1998, SAE Leadership Hall of Fame, 2001, Ga. Sports Hall of Fame, 2008; named one of The Top 50 Sportscasters Am. Sportscasters Assn., 2009. Mem.: ASCAP, Sigma Alpha Epsilon. Died May 4, 2010.

HARWOOD, STANLEY, retired judge, lawyer, arbitrator, mediator; b. NYC, June 23, 1926; s. Benjamin and Hannah (Schwartz) H.; m. Deborah Weinerman, June 18, 1950 (dec. 1995); children: Richard, Ellen Harwood Jacobs, Michael, Jonathan; m. Cathleen Hamilton, May 25, 1997. AB, Columbia U., 1949, LLB, 1952. Bar: N.Y. 1954, U.S. Dist. Ct. (ea. and so. dists.) N.Y. 1956, U.S. Supreme Ct. 1960. Atty. Dept. of Navy, Washington, 1952—53; assoc. Benjamin Harwood, Bklyn., 1953—56; pvt. practice Levittown, NY, 1956—61; law clk. to justice N.Y. Supreme Ct., Mineola, 1961—65, justice, 1982—92, judge appellate divsn., 1987—92; ptnr. Mishkin, Miner, Harwood & Semel, Mineola, 1965—69, Shayne, Dachs, Stanisci & Harwood, Mineola, 1969—81, Bower & Gardner, NYC, 1992—94; counsel Jaspan, Schlesinger, from 1994. Mem. N.Y. State Assembly, 1966-72; chmn. Nassau County Dem. Com., 1973-81; commr. elections Nassau County Bd. Elections, 1976-81; bd. dirs. Nat. Conf. Christians and Jews, 1993-98. With USNR, 1944-46, U.S. Merchant Marines. Mem. N.Y. State Bar Assn., Nassau County Bar Assn. (chmn. cts. com. 1971-73, chmn. pro bono com. 1988-90, bd. dirs. 1997-2000, Nassau-Suffolk Law Svs. Committment to Justice medal 2002), Mill River Club. Jewish. Home: Centerport, NY. Died Aug. 20, 2010.

HASKELL, PETER ABRAHAM, actor, director; b. Boston, Oct. 15, 1934; s. Norman Abraham and Rose Veronica (Golden) H.; m. Ann Compton, Feb. 27, 1960 (div. 1974); m. Dianne Tolmich, Oct. 26, 1974; children: Audra Rosemary, Jason Abraham. BA, Harvard U., 1962; student, N.Y. Law Sch., 1982-83. Actor (plays) The Love Nest, 1963, The Seagull, 1979, A Rich Full Life, 1985, Jenny, 2002, One Step Over, 2006, A Couple of Horses Asses, 2006, Leash on Life, 2006, (films) Finnegans Wake, 1965, Legend of Earl Durand, 1972, Christina, 1974, Forty Days of Musa Dagh, 1982, Riding the Edge, 1987, Child's Play II, 1990, Child's Play III, 1991, Robot Wars, 1993; (TV series) Bracken's World, NBC, 1969-71, Rich Man Poor Man, Book II, ABC, 1976-77, Ryan's Hope, ABC, 1982-83, Search for Tomorrow, NBC, 1983-85, Rituals, Metromedia, 1985, The Law and Harry McGraw, CBS, 1987-88; (TV films) Love, Hate, Love, 1970, The Eyes of Charles Sand, 1972, Mandrake, 1977, The Cracker Factory, 1979, Christine Cromwell, 1990, Columbo, 1991, Maid for Each Other, 1992, Faces of Deception, 1993, Never Talk to Strangers, 1997; dir. (plays) Nightgames, 2000, Mrs. Warren's Profession, 2004, What are Friends For, 2006, The Wedding Night, 2006, Mark on Society, 2007, Back In The Day, 2008. Active duty 11th and 101st Airborne Divsn. US Army, 1954—56, with USAR, 1956—62. Mem. SAG, AFTRA, Actors Equity. Democrat. Avocations: photography, skiing. Home: Northridge, Calif. Died Apr. 12, 2010.

HASSELL, JOYCE BARNETT, state legislator; b. Baldwyn, Miss., Mar. 14, 1932; married. BS, Blue Mountain Coll.; M, U. Memphis. Mem. Tenn. State Legis. Republican. Baptist. Home: Memphis, Tenn. Died Dec. 7, 2009.

HASSID, SAMI, architect, educator; b. Cairo, Apr. 19, 1912; came to U.S., 1957, naturalized, 1962; s. Joseph S. and Isabelle (Israel) H.; m. Juliette Mizrahi, June 29, 1941; children: Fred, Muriel. Diploma in Architecture with distinction, Sch. Engring., Giza, Egypt, 1932; BA in Architecture with honors, U. London, Eng., 1935; M.Arch., U. Cairo, 1943; PhD in Architecture, Harvard U., 1956. Tchr. Alexandria (Egypt) Tech. Sch., 1932-34; successively tchr., lectr., asst. prof. U. Cairo, 1934-56; prof. architectural theory and design U. Ein-Shams, Cairo, 1957; mem. faculty U. Calif., Berkeley, from 1957, prof. architecture, 1964-79, prof. emeritus, from 1979; also assoc. dean U. Calif. (Coll. Environ. Design), 1977-83, faculty asst. to vice-chancellor for campus planning, 1980-85, dir. campus planning office, 1983-84; archtl. practice Cairo, 1932-57, Berkeley, 1957-85; from draftsman to sr. designer office Ali Labib Gabr (architect), Cairo, 1935-47; ptnr. Sami Hassid and Youssef Shafik, Cairo, 1947-57, Hassid and Kelemen, Berkeley, 1963-65. Author: The Sultan's Turrets, 1939, Architectural Construction Details, 1954, Development and Application of a System for Recording Critical Evaluations of Architectural Works, 1964, Architectural Education U.S.A, 1967, (with others) Innovations in Housing Design and Construction Techniques as Applied to Low-Cost Housing, 1969, Surface Materials in Architecture, 1970, Doctoral Studies in Architecture, 1971, Methods for the Development of Shipboard Habitability Design Criteria, 1974, Fire Safety in Buildings, A Course Offering Package, 1976, (with others) The Berkeley Campus Space Plan, 21 publs., 1981-83; Proc. Workshop on Seismic Upgrading of Existing Bldgs., NSF, 1982; prin. works include Hill House; student hostel, Am. U. Cairo, 1952. Commr. Calif. Bd. Archtl. Examiners, 1961-71. Fulbright grantee, 1954-56; recipient First prize Al-Chams Competition, Cairo, 1947, First prize San Francisco AIA Hdqrs. Competition, 1963 Fellow AIA; mem. Bldg. Research Inst., Assn. Collegiate Schs. Architecture. Democrat. Jewish (trustee temple; v.p. East Bay synagogue council 1970-71). Home: Walnut Creek, Calif. Deceased.

HATFIELD, ROBERT CARLETON, retired education educator, consultant; b. Plainwell, Mich., June 26, 1929; s. Carleton K. and Mildred I. (Galer) H.; m. Patricia G. Sharkofsky, July 7, 1950; children: Judith G. Hurst Hatfield, Susan L. BS in Agr., Mich. State U., 1950, tchr. cert., 1954, MA in Vocat. Agrl. Edn., 1960; EdD in Edn. and Curriculum, Wayne State U., 1968. Cert. tchr., Mich. Self-employed, 1950-53; tchr. vocat. agr. and adult edn. Marcellus (Mich.) Pub. Schs., 1954-59; tchr. social studies and adult edn., dept. chmn. Fraser (Mich.) Pub. Schs., 1959-66; instr. Detroit Area Tchr. Edn. Ctr., Mich. State U., 1967, dir. student teaching and elem. intern program, 1967-70, dir. Lansing Suburban Area Tchr. Edn. Ctr., 1971-79, chmn. div. student teaching and profl. devel. East Lansing, 1979-81, prof. dept. tchr. edn., 1981-92, prof. emeritus, from 1992. Presenter in field. Contbr. articles to profl. jours., chpts. to books. Grantee U.S. Office Edn. and Mich. State U., 1970-72, Mich. Dept. Edn., 1975-76, 1989-90, univ. rsch. grantee, 1974-75, 1984-85. Mem. ASCD, Phi Delta Kappa. Avocations: photography, archaeology. Home: Morgantown, W.Va. Died Feb. 27, 2010.

HATTEN, WILLIAM SEWARD, manufacturing executive, consultant; b. Chgo., Apr. 7, 1917; s. William Seward and Margaret (Ahearn) H.; m. Marjorie Popp, Dec. 29, 1939; 1 dau., Patricia Marie (Mrs. Dudley D. Pendleton III) BA, Lawrence Coll., 1939; MBA, Northwestern U., 1944; PhD, Kennedy-Western U., 2000. Indsl. engr. Sears, Roebuck & Co., 1940-43; mgr. control div. Chgo. Ordnance Dist., 1943-45; owner Eskimo Ice Cream Co., Tucson, 1945-50; gen. mgr. Utica Knitting Co., NY, 1950-54; cons. Worden & Risberg, Phila., 1954-64; pres., chief exec. officer, dir. Clayton Mark & Co., Evanston, Ill., 1964-67; chmn. bd. Ken-Ray Brass Products, Inc., Vermont, Ill., 1964-67; pres., chief exec. officer, dir. Harper-Wyman Co., Hinsdale, Ill., 1967-69; exec. v.p. Warner Electric Brake & Clutch Co., Beloit, Wis., 1969-72; group v.p. engines and generators Kohler Co., Wis., 1973—80; pres. Hatten & Assocs., Lakeland, Fla., from 1980. Mem. Am. Ordance Assn., Northwestern U. Grad. Bus. Alumni Assn., Lone Palm Golf Club (Lakeland, Fla.), Lakeland Yacht and Country Club (Lakeland, Fla.), Union League (Chgo.), Phi Delta Theta. Episcopalian. Home: Birmingham, Ala. Died Nov. 5, 2009.

HATTON, GLENN IRWIN, neuroscientist, educator; b. Chgo, Dec. 12, 1934; s. Irwin Alfred and Anita Hatton; m. Patricia Joann Hatton, Sept. 4, 1931; children: James Daniel, William Graham, Christopher Jay, Jennifer Kay, Tracey Elisabeth. BA, North Ctrl. Coll., 1960; MA, U. Ill., 1962, PhD, 1964. Asst. prof., assoc. prof., prof. Mich. State U., East Lansing, 1965-91; prof., chair U. Calif., Riverside, from 1992. Contbr. numerous articles to profl. jour. Fellow NIH, 1982, Guggenheim Fellow, 1989; recipient Javits Neurosci. Investigator award NINDS, 1985, 93. Fellow AAAS; mem. Assn. Neurosci. Dept. and Programs (pres. 1994-95), Am. Physiol. Soc., Am. Assn. Anatomists, Soc. Neurosci. Avocations: music, travel, wine tasting. Home: Riverside, Calif. Died Jan. 16, 2009.

HAUPT, ANDREA MOORE, psychologist, therapist; b. Princeton, NJ, Aug. 1, 1943; d. Frank Leslie and Lucille M. (Kipp) Moore; m. Raymond E. Haupt, Aug. 19, 1978. BA in Liberal Arts and Chemistry, SUNY, Binghamton, 1965; ABD in Biochemistry, U. Pa., 1967; MEd in Ednl. Psychology, Temple U., 1972, PhD in Counseling Psychology, 1990. Lic. psychologist. Caseworker Dept. Pub. Assistance, Phila., 1967-69; mental health worker Phila. State Hosp., 1969-72; counselor Horizon House, Phila., 1972-74; psychologist Jefferson Cmty. Mental Health Ctr., Phila., 1974-84; pvt. practice Phila., 1984—98. Consulting psychologist Grad. Hosp. Dept. Psychiatry, Phila., 1990—96; consulting psychol. examiner City of Phila., from 1990; bd. dirs. Women Therapist's Network, 1993—96. Juried mem. Phila. Watercolor Soc., 1982—. Recipient N.Y. Regents scholar, 1961-65; NIH fellow U. Pa., 1965-67, Univ. fellow Temple U., 1984-86. Fellow: Pa. Psychol. Assn.; mem.: APA. Avocations: gardening, pets, writing, travel, watercolor. Died Jan. 2, 2009.

HAUSE, ROBERT LUKE, music educator, conductor; b. Shelby, Nc, Dec. 12, 1935; s. Robert Luke and Lucille Morehead Hause; m. Karen Nelle McCann, Sept. 28, 1939; children: Eric Mathew, Jonathan Michael; 1 child, Evan Robert. M.M., U. of Mich., Ann Arbor, Michigan, 1954—60. Prof. Stetson U., DeLand, Fla., 1962—67, East Carolina U., Greenville, NC, 1967—98; asst. dean Sch. of Music,East Carolina U., Greenville, NC. Composer: (violin sonatina) Sonatina for Violin and Piano, (chaconne for string orchestra) Chaconne in E Minor, Buxtehude/Hause. Nat. pres. Phi Mu Alpha Sinfonia Frat., Evansville, Ind., 1991—94. Grantee Scholarship grant, Liberace Found., 2001 - 2003. Mem.: United State Power Squadron (pubilic rels. from 2002). D-Liberal. Avocation: boating. Home: Greenville, NC. Died Feb. 4, 2010.

HAUSNER, JOHN HERMAN, retired judge; b. Detroit, Oct. 31, 1932; s. John E. and Anna (Mudrak) Hausner; m. Alice R. Kieltyka, Aug. 22, 1959. PhB cum laude, U. Detroit, 1954, MA, 1957, JD summa cum laude, 1966. Bar: Mich. 1967, US Ct. Appeals (6th cir.) 1968, US Supreme Ct. 1971, US Tax Ct. 1976, US Ct. Claims 1976, US Ct. Mil. Appeals 1976. Tchr. Detroit Pub. Schs., 1954, 56-59; tchg. fellow U. Cin., 1959-61; instr. U. Detroit, 1961-74; pvt. practice Detroit, 1967-69; asst. US atty., 1969-73; chief asst. US atty. Ea. Dist. Mich., 1973-76; judge 3rd Jud. Cir. Mich., Wayne County, 1976-94; ret., 1994. Lectr. law sch.; faculty adviser Nat. Jud. Coll., 1978—79. Author: Sebastian, The Essence of My Soul, 1982, 2007, 2008, Janosik, We Remember, 2008; contbr. articles to profl. jours. With US Army, 1954—56. Mem.: State Bar Mich., Fed. Bar Assn. (mem. exec. bd. Detroit chpt. 1976—82), Mich. Ret. Judges Assn., Blue Key, Alpha Sigma Mu. Republican. Home: Saint Clair Shores, Mich. Died May 24, 2010.

HAVILAND, BANCROFT DAWLEY, lawyer; b. Yonkers, NY, May 13, 1925; s. Harold Bancroft and Dorothy (Dawley) H.; m. Dorothy MacFarland, Oct. 30, 1945; children: Lucy, William, Thomas, Amy. BA in Polit. Sci., U. Pa., 1947, LLB, 1949. Bar: N.Y. 1951, Pa. 1952. Gowen teaching fellow U. Pa. Law Sch., Phila., 1949-50; assoc. Donovan, Leisure, Newton & Irvine, NYC, 1950-51, Schnader, Harrison, Segal & Lewis, NYC, 1951-61, ptnr., 1961-90, ret., 1991. Trustee Westtown (Pa.) Friends' Sch., 1960-94, Media-Providence (Pa.) Friends' Sch., 1960-95; chmn. Westtown Sch. Com., 1988-93; commr. Rose Tree Soccer Club, Media, 1971-98, Aston Twp., Pa., 1954-61; justice of peace Middletown Twp., Pa., 1963-65. Lt. (j.g.) USN, 1943-45, PTO. Mem. ABA, Pa. Bar Assn., Phila.

Bar Assn., Am. Judicature Soc., Order of Coif Lodges: Lions. Democrat. Mem. Soc. Of Friends. Avocations: woodworking, reading, gardening. Home: Kennett Square, Pa. Died Apr. 13, 2009.

HAVOC, JUNE, actress; b. Vancouver, BC, Can., Nov. 8, 1916; came to U.S., 1916; d. John Olaf and Rose (Thompson) Hovick; m. William Spier, Dec. 22 (dec. 1973); 1 daughter, April Hyde (dec. 1998) Artistic dir. New Orleans Repertory Theatre, 1969-71. Film appearances include Baby June, 1918; vaudeville appearances, 1918 (as Dainty Jane) The Darling of Vaudeville, registered U.S. Patent Office; headliner: Keith-Orpheum Circuit, 1923-25; actress 22 Broadway shows including Pal Joey, 1941, Sadie Thompson, 1944, That Ryan Girl, 1945, Dinner at Eight, 1966, Habeas Corpus, 1975, Annie, 1982; Sweeney Todd on tour, 1982, The Old Lady's Guide to Survival, 1994-95, Do Not Go Gentle; actress: (films) My Sister Eileen, 1942, Gentlemen's Agreement, 1947, Intrigue, 1947, When My Baby Smiles at Me, 1948, Lady Possessed, 1952, Hello, Frisco, Hello, The Iron Curtain, Chicago Deadline, Can't Stop the Music, A Return to Salem's Lot, 1987; creator, dir.: one-woman show An Unexpected Evening with June Havoc or Baby Remembers, 1983; (TV guest appearances) Murder, She Wrote; toured Eng. in The Gift, 1987; author: Early Havoc, 1959, More Havoc, 1980; play Marathon '33, 1963. Active in animal welfare orgns. Mem. Actors Equity Assn., Screen Actors Guild, Am. Fedn. TV and Radio Artists, Dramatists Guild, Authors Guild. Home: Stamford, Conn. Died Mar. 28, 2010.

HAWES, BESS LOMAX, retired folklorist; b. Austin, Tex., Dec. 21, 1921; m. Baldwin Hawes; children: Corey, Naomi, Nicholas. BA in Sociology, Bryn Mawr U., 1941; MA, U. Calif., 1970; PhD (hon.), Kenyon Coll., 1994, U. N.C., 1995. With music divsn. N.Y. Pub. Libr.; prof. anthropology Calif. State U., Northridge, 1963—74, Smithsonian Instn., 1974—76; dir. Folk Arts Program Nat. Endowment for Arts, 1977—92; ret., 1992. Author: Step It Down: Games, Plays, Songs, and Stories from the Afro-American Heritage, 1987, Sing It Pretty: A Memoir, 2008. Recipient Nat. Medal of Arts, The White House, 1993. Died Nov. 27, 2009.

HAWK, DONALD LEE, banker; b. Massillon, Ohio, Jan. 22, 1947; s. Elroy L. and Mary C. Hawk; m. Margaret Crary; 1 child from previous marriage, Brian P. BS, Ohio State U., 1970. Acting ctr. dir. Columbus (Ohio) Bus. U., 1970-73; asst. to v.p. personnel Baxter Travenol Labs., Inc., Deerfield, Ill., 1973-78; v.p. programs Ctr. for Creative Leadership, Greensboro, N.C., 1978-81; exec. v.p. Tex. Commerce Bancshares, Inc., Houston, from 1981. Bd. dirs. Tex. Commerce Bank, San Antonio, McAllen, Tex., Brownsville, Tex. Contbr. articles to profl. jours. Chmn. fellow adv. com. Coll. Bus. Adminstrn. A&M U., College Station, Tex.; bd. dirs. Houston Job Tng. Partnership Coun., Houston. Mem. Acad. of Mgmt., Am. Psychol. Assn., Houston Club. Avocations: fresh-water fishing, travel, reading. Home: Houston, Tex. Died June 19, 2009.

HAWKE, ROBERT DOUGLAS, state legislator; b. Gardner, Mass., July 20, 1932; s. Arthur Eugene Hawke and Gladys Emma (Waite) Sorton; m. Nancy Marie Moschetti, July 20, 1958; children: Linda, Cynthia, Heather, Dean, Mark. BA, Northeastern U., 1954; LLB, Boston U., 1956; MA, Fitchburg State U., 1970. Cert. tchr., Mass. Tchr. Murdock High Sch., Winchendon, Mass., 1956-66, Gardner (Mass.) High Sch., 1966-90; mem. Mass. Ho. of Reps., Boston, 1990-97. Trustee Heywood Hosp., Gardner, 1981-97, Gardner Mus., 1980-83, Baldwinville Nursing Home, templeton, Mass.; mem. So. Gardner Hist. Soc., 1984—; adv. bd. Mt. Wachusett C.C., Gardner, 1968-81; chmn. Gardner Rep. Com., Rep. City Com., 1966-76; area campaign coord. Reagan Com., North Ctrl. Mass., 1980-84; councillor at large to Gardner City Coun., 2001-04; pres. Consortium of New Eng. Cmty. Art Mus., 1999-2002. Named Citizen of Yr. Grange of Gardner, 1993, So. Gardner Hist. Soc., 1993, Legislator of Yr. award Worcester County League of Sportmen's Clubs, 1996. Mem. Nat. Rep. Legis. Assn., Nat. Conf. State Legislators, Polish Am. Citizens Club, Account Exec. for Greater Gardner C. of C., Eagles. Republican. Baptist. Avocations: reading, tennis, softball. Home: Gardner, Mass. Died Feb. 4, 2009.

HAWKINS, EDWARD J., retired lawyer; b. Fall River, Mass., June 24, 1927; s. Edward Jackson and Harriet (Sherman) H.; m. Janet Schwerdt; children: Daniel, George, Robert, Harriet. Grad., Phillips Acad., Andover, Mass., 1945; AB summa cum laude, Princeton U., 1950; LLB magna cum laude, Harvard U., 1953. Bar: Ohio 1954, D.C. 1990. Assoc., ptnr. Squire, Sanders & Dempsey, Cleve., 1953-78, ptnr. Cleve. and Washington, 1982-96, counsel, 1997-99; ret., 2000. Chief tax counsel U.S. Senate Fin. Com., Washington, 1979-80, minority tax counsel, 1981; gen. chmn. Cleve. Tax Inst., 1969. Contbr. articles to profl. jours. With U.S. Army, 1945-46. Mem. ABA (vice chmn. govt. rels. tax sect. 1987-89), D.C. Bar Assn., Phillips Acad. Alumni Assn. (alumni coun. 1967-70), Quadrangle Club. Democrat. Home: Keswick, Va. Died Jan. 15, 2010.

HAWKINS, LAWRENCE CHARLES, management consultant, educator; b. Greenville County, SC, Mar. 20, 1919; s. Wayman and Etta (Brockman) H.; m. Earline Thompson, Apr. 29, 1943; children: Lawrence Charles Jr., Wendell Earl. BA, U. Cin., 1941, BEd, 1942, MEd, 1951, EdD, 1970; AA (hon.), Wilmington Coll., 1979; LittD (hon.), Cin. Tech. and CC; LHD (hon.), Mt. St. Joseph Coll. Cert. sch. supt. Ohio. Elem./secondary tchr. Cin. Pub. Schs., 1945-52, sch. prin./dir., 1952-67, asst. supt., 1967-69; dean U. Cin., 1969-75, v.p., 1975-77, sr. v.p., 1977-83; vis. asst. prof. Eastern Mich. U., Ypsilanti, summers 1955-60; mem. Cincinnatus Assn., 1971-87. Vice chair Student Loan Funding Corp., 1982-98; mem. cmty. rels. panel Cin. Mayors, 1979—, others; cons. US Dept. Justice, Dept. Edn.; bd. dirs. We. and So. Fin. Group. Bd. dirs. exec. com. Ohio Citizens Coun. Health and Welfare, 1966-73; vice chair Ohio Valley Regional Med. Program, 1972-77, bd. trustees Cmty. Chest and Coun. Cin. Area Inc., 1970-72; bd. dirs. Wilmington Coll., Ohio, 1980-90, Bethesda Hosp., Cin., 1980-90; trustee Children's Home of Cin., 1978-90, Coll. Mt. St. Joseph, 1989-93; pres., CEO Omni-Man, Inc., 1981-96; bd. dirs. emeritus Nat. Underground R.R. Freedom Ctr., 1994-98; owner The L.C.H. Resource; vice chmn. Greater Cin. TV Ednl. Found., WCET-TV, 1983; co-chmn. Cin. area NCCJ 1980-87; nat. bd. dirs. Inroads, 1982-87; bd. trustees Knowledge Works Found., 1999-2002. Served to lt. USAAF, 1943-45 (an original Tuskegee Airman). Recipient award of Merit, Cin. Area United Appeal, 1955, 73, cert. Pres.'s Coun. on Youth Opportunity, 1968, City Cin., 1968, Disting. Svc. citation Greater Cin. NCCJ, 1988; named Great Living Cincinnatian, Greater Cin. C. of C., 1989. Mem. NEA (life), ASCD, Am. Assn. Sch. Adminstrs. (conv., Golden Eagles Lifetime Achievement award 1998), Nat. Congress Parents and Tchrs. (hon. life; chmn. com.), Phi Delta Kappa, Kappa Delta Pi, Kappa Alpha Psi, Sigma Pi Phi. Home: Cincinnati, Ohio. Died Apr. 4, 2009.

HAWKINS, PAULA, former United States Senator from Florida; b. Salt Lake City, Jan. 24, 1927; m. Walter Eugene Hawkins; children: Genean, Kevin Brent, Kelley Ann. Student, Utah State U., 1944-47, HHD (hon.), 1982; PhD (hon.), Nova U., St. Thomas Villa Nova, Bethune-Cookman, 1986, Rollins Coll., 1990. Dir. Southeast First Nat. Bank, Maitland, Fla., 1972-76, Rural Telephone Bank Bd., 1972—78; del. Rep. Nat. Conv., Miami, 1968, 72, 76, 80, 84, 88, 92, mem. rules com., 1972, co-chmn. rules com., 1980, co-chmn. platform com., 1984; bd. dirs. Fla. Fedn. Rep. Women, from 1968; mem. Fla. Pub. Svc. Commn., Tallahasee, 1972—79, chmn., 1977—79; mem. Rep. Nat. Com. for Fla., 1968-87, mem. Rule 29 Com., 1973-75; US Senator from Fla., 1981-87; chmn. US Senate Family & Child Subcommittee, 1982-86, US Senate Drug Enforcement Caucus, 1981-87; apptd. chmn. Nat. Commn. on Responsibilities for Financing Post Secondary, 1990-92; pres. Paula Hawkins and Associates, Winter Park, Fla., 1988—2009. V.p. Air Fla., 1979-80; bd. dirs. Philip Crosby Assocs., Alexander Proudfoot; del. UN Narcotic Conv., Austria, 1987, Spain, 1993, N.Y.C., 1994. Author: Children at Risk, My Fight Against Child Abuse: A Personal Story and a Public Plea, 1986. Charter mem. bd. dirs. Fla. Americans Constl. Action Com. of 100, 1966-68, sec.-treas., 1966-68; mem. Fla. Gov.'s Commn. Status Women, 1968-71; mem. Pres.'s Commn. White House Fellowships, 1975; bd. dirs. Freedom Found.; del. UN Narcotic Conv., Seville, Spain, 1993; U.S. del. UN Conv., N.Y.C. Recipient citation for service Fla. Rep. Party, 1966-67, Award for Legis. Work Child Fund Inc, 1982, Israel Peace medal, 1983, Tree of Life award Jewish Nat. Found, 1985, Nat. Mother of Yr. award, 1984, Grandmother of Yr.award, 1985, Albert Einstein Good Govt. award, 1986, Good Govt. award Maitland Jaycees, 1976, Outstanding award Am. Acad, Pediatricians, 1986; named Guardian of Small Bus. Nat. Fedn. Ind. Bus., 1982, 83, 84, 86, Rep. Woman of Yr. N.Y. Women's Nat. Rep. Club, 1981, Outstanding Woman of Utah, 1985, Outstanding Woman of Yr. in Govt. Orlando C. of C., 1977, Woman of Yr., KC, 1973; named to The Fla. Women's Hall of Fame, 2000 Mem. Maitland C. of C. (chmn. congl. action com. 1967) Mem. Ch. Jesus Christ of Latter-day Saints (pres. Relief Soc., Orlando Stake 1960-64. Club: Capitol Hill (Washington), Interlaken Country (Winter Pk.). Died Dec. 3, 2009.

HAWORTH, DANIEL THOMAS, emeritus chemistry professor; b. Fond du Lac, Wis., June 27, 1928; s. Arthur Valentine and Mary Lena (Wattawa) H.; m. Mary Hormuth, Dec. 27, 1952 (dec. Nov. 2, 2008); children: Daniel G., M. Judith, Steven T. BS, U. Wis., Oshkosh, 1950; MS, Marquette U., 1952; student, Oak Ridge Sch. Reactor Tech., 1952; PhD, St. Louis U., 1959. Nuclear chemist Bur. of Ships, Washington, 1952-53; rsch. chemist All-Chalmer Mfg. Co., Milw., 1958-60; instr. chemistry Marquette U., Milw., 1955, from asst. prof. to assoc. prof., 1960-68, prof., from 1968. Vis. prof. chemistry U. Wis.-Milw., 2001—02. Contbr. numerous articles to profl. jours.; patentee in field. Served as cpl. U.S. Army, 1953-55. Recipient Pere Marquette award for tchg. excellence Marquette U., 1971, Nicolos Salgo Outstanding Tchr. Soc. award, 1971, Milw. Sect. award, Am. Chem. Soc. Mem. Am. Chem. Soc. (emeritus), N.Y. Acad. Scis., Wis. Acad. Arts/Scis./Letters, Sigma Xi (emeritus). Roman Catholic. Avocation: stamp collecting/philately. Home: Milwaukee, Wis. Died July 6, 2009.

HAXO, FRANCIS THEODORE, marine biologist; b. Grand Forks, ND, Mar. 9, 1921; s. Henry Emile and Florence (Shull) H.; m. Judith Morgan McLaughlin, Apr. 15, 1961; children: John Frederick, Barbara, Philip, Francis Theodore, Aileen. BA, U. N.D., 1941; PhD, Stanford U., 1947. Teaching, research asst. Stanford U., 1941-44, acting instr., 1943; research asst. Calif. Inst. Tech., 1946; research asso. Hopkins Marine Sta., Pacific Grove, Calif., 1946-47; from instr. to asst. prof. plant physiology Johns Hopkins U., 1947-52; mem. faculty U. Calif. Scripps Inst. Oceanography, La Jolla, 1952-88, prof. biology, 1963-88; prof. emeritus, from 1988; chmn. marine biology dept. U. Calif. Scripps Inst. Oceanography, 1960-65, chmn. marine biology research div., 1960-77; instr. marine botany Marine Biol. Lab., Woods Hole, Mass., 1949-52, 70. Vis. faculty botany U. Calif. at Berkeley, 1957, U. Wash. Marine Lab., Friday Harbor, 1963 Abraham Rosenberg fellow Stanford U., 1945. Fellow AAAS, San Diego Zool. Soc.; mem. Am. Soc. Photobiology, Phycological Soc. Am., Western Soc. Naturalists, Internat. Phycological Soc., Phi Beta Kappa, Sigma Xi. Achievements include spl. rsch. photosynthesis, plant pigments, physiology of algae. Home: La Jolla, Calif. Died June 10, 2010.

HAYAKAWA, KAN-ICHI, retired food scientist; b. Shibukawa, Gumma, Japan, Aug. 12, 1931; arrived in U.S., 1961, naturalized, 1974; s. Chyogoro and Kin (Hayakawa) H.; m. Setsuko Maekawa, Feb. 18, 1967. BS, Tokyo U. Fisheries, 1955; PhD, Rutgers U., 1964. Rsch. fellow Canners' Assn. Japan, 1955—60; asst. prof. food sci. Rutgers U., New Brunswick, NJ, 1964—70, assoc. prof. food sci., 1970—77, prof. food engring., 1977—82, Disting. prof. food engring., 1982—99, prof. emeritus, from 1999. Cons. to food processing cos.; organizer, chmn., participant NSF sponsored U.S.-Japan Coop. Conf., Tokyo, 1979; lectr. Industry R&D Inst. and Nat. Taiwan U., 1982, Wuxi Inst. Light Industry, China, 1986, Tokyo U. Fisheries, 1992. Co-editor: Heat Sterilization of Food, 1983; contbr. articles to books, profl. jours. and encys.; developer new math methods for predicting safety of food processes; found theoretical and exptl. theorems on heat and mass transfer in biol. material with or without strain--stress formation. Rsch. grantee USPHS, 1966-73, Nabisco Found., 1975-76, NSF, 1981-82, travel grantee NSF, 1972, Rutgers Rsch. Found., 1977, rsch. grantee Advanced Food Tech. Ctr., 1985-89, John von Neumann Nat. Supercomputer Ctr., 1989-90, Pitts. Nat. Supercomputer Ctrs., NSF, 1990-97, Cray Rsch. Inc., 1993-95, U.S. Army Natick R & D Ctr., 1992-94, USDA, 1994-98. Fellow Inst. Food Technologists; mem. ASHRAE (life, chmn. tech. com. on thermophys. property values of food 1981-85, mem. com. 1981-96). Home: Honolulu, Hawaii. Died May 15, 2009.

HAYES, AILISH MAIRE, pediatrician; b. Limerick, Ireland, Feb. 1, 1951; arrived in U.S., 1984; d. Richard F. and Christina Beatrice (McDonald) H.; m. Haig Oghigian, Sept. 8, 1984 (div.). Grad., Univ. Coll., Dublin, Ireland, 1974, diploma in child health, 1976, diploma in obstetrics, 1978; MB, BCh, BAO, Nat. Univ. Ireland, Dublin, 1974. Bd. cert. in genetics. Intern in surgery Mater Miseriacordia Hosp., Dublin, Ireland, 1974-75; resident in pediatrics Children's Hosp., Crumlin, Dublin, 1975-77; fellow in neonatology Nat. Maternity Hosp., Dublin, Ireland, 1977-80; sr. resident in pediatrics Toronto Sick Children's Hosp., 1980-81; fellow in genetics Montreal Children's Hosp., 1981-84; instr. in pediatrics Med. Sch., Harvard U., Boston, from 1984; pediatrician Revere Pediatric Assocs., from 1993; asst. in pediatrics Mass. Gen. Hosp., Boston, 1990-93. Former attending physician Children's Hosp., Boston, Brigham and Women's Hosp., Boston, Beth Israel Hosp., Boston; cons. Nat. Birth Defects Ctr., Boston, 1986—; cons. in teratology Mass. Gen. Hosp., Boston, 1987-90; cons. pediatrics and genetics Retina Assocs., Boston, 1991-92; cons. Prenatal Diagnostic Ctr., Boston, 1994—; lectr. Harvard U. Med. Sch., Boston, 1989-91; presenter in field. Fellow Royal Coll. Physicians (fellow 1982), Royal Coll. Physicians. Home: Marblehead, Mass. Died Nov. 4, 2009.

HAYES, ARTHUR HULL, JR., physician, clinical pharmacology educator, medical school dean, business executive, consultant; b. Highland Park, Mich., July 18, 1933; s. Arthur Hull and Florence Margaret (Gruber) Hayes; m. Barbara Anne Carey, July 16, 1960; children: Arthur Hull III, Elizabeth, Katherine. AB magna cum laude, U. Santa Clara, 1955, D (hon.) in Pub. Svc., 1980; MA, Oxford U., 1957; postgrad., Georgetown U., 1957—60; MD, Cornell U., 1964; LLD (hon.), St. John's U., 1983; DSc (hon.), NY Med. Coll., 1983. Diplomate Am. Bd. Clin. Pharmacology. Intern in medicine NY Hosp., NYC, 1964—65, resident in cardiology, 1967—68; assoc. prof. pharmacology, asst. prof. medicine, assoc. dean Cornell U. Med. Coll., NYC, 1968—72; prof. pharmacology and medicine, chief div. clin. pharmacology Pa. State Coll. Medicine, Hershey (Pa.) Med. Center, 1972—81; commr. US FDA, Rockville, Md., 1981—83; provost, dean NY Med. Coll., 1983—86, prof. medicine, pharmacology and community and preventive medicine, 1983—99; pres., CEO EM Pharmaceuticals, Inc., Hawthorne, NY, 1986—90, MediSci. Associates, Inc., New Rochelle, NY, 1991—2006; clin. prof. medicine and pharmacology Pa. State U. Coll. Medicine, 1981—2004. Trustee US Pharmacopeial Conv., 1980—81, from 1985, pres., 1985—90; bd. dirs. Cadbury-Schweppes, Stamford, Conn., Synergen, Inc., Denver, Myriad Genetics, Inc., Salt Lake City, Food and Drug Law Inst., Washington, NaPro Bio Therapeutics, Inc., Premier Rsch. Worldwide, Tapestry, Inc., Celgene, from 1995, mem. audit com. bd. dirs.; chmn. Coun. Family Health, NYC, Medic Alert Found., Inc., Turlock, Calif., 1991—93; prin. Ctr. Excellence in Govt. Contbr. articles to profl. jours.; editl. bd. Rational Drug Therapy, Clin. Pharmacology and Therapeutics, Med. Advt. News, Jour. Clin. Pharmacology, Today's Therapeutic Trends, Pharmaceutical Medicine, Prescriber's Newsletter, World Pharm. Report. Permanent deacon Roman Cath. Ch.; bd. dirs. Peace Found., NYC; bd. regents Santa Clara (Calif.) U.; mem. bd. overseers L.I. U. Coll. Pharmacy. Capt. med. corps US Army, 1965—67. Decorated Knight of Holy Sepulchre (comdr.); recipient Foch medal, Govt. France, 1953, Nobili medal, U. Santa Clara, 1955, Good Physician award, Cornell Med. Coll., 1964, Faculty Devel. award, Pharm. Mfrs. Assn. Found., 1968, Bronze medallion seal award, DHHS, 1982, Disting. Pub. Svc. award, 1983, Founders Day award, Lebanon Valley Coll., 1983, Henry Elliot Disting. Svc. Clin. Pharmacology award; fellow Danforth, 1955, NIH, 1960—62; scholar Rhodes, 1955. Fellow: ACP, Am. Acad. Pharm. Physicians, Acad. Pharm. Scis., Am. Coll. Chest Physicians, Royal Soc. Medicine, NY Acad. Medicine, Am. Soc. Clin. Pharmacology and Therapy (Henry Elliot Disting. Svc. Clin. Pharacology award 1993), Am. Coll. Cardiology, Coll. Physicians Phila.; mem.: AMA, Assn. Am. Med. Colls. (coun. of deans., con. acad. socs.), Med. Soc. State of N.Y., Harvey Soc., N.Y. Acad. Scis., Am. Pharm. Assn. (hon.), Am. Fedn. Clin. Rsch., Am. Soc. Clin. Pharmacology and Therapeutics (pres. 1980—81), Am. Soc. Pharmacology and Exptl. Therapeutics, Knights of Malta, KC, Alpha Omega Alpha, Sigma Xi, Phi Beta Kappa, Alpha Omega Alpha. Roman Catholic. Home: Oxford, Conn. Died Feb. 11, 2010.

HAYES, WILLIAM CHARLES, retired editor, consultant; b. Jersey City, Apr. 17, 1926; s. John James and Helena Sophia (Janecki) H.; m. Lilliam Antoinette Wehr, Apr. 16, 1955 (div. Aug. 1979); children: William Allen, Thomas Baker; m. Ann

Theresa Coppola, Jan. 2, 1982. BS in Naval Engring., Brown U., 1946, BSME cum laude, 1947; MSME, Harvard U., 1949. Engr. Pub. Svc. Electric & Gas Co., Newark, 1949-53, underground engr. Jersey City, 1953-61, div. engr. Secaucus, N.J., 1963-68; transmission/distbn. editor Elec. World Mag., NYC, 1968-72, editor-in-chief, 1972-92. Bd. dirs. Casazza, Schultz, Assocs., Washington; mem. adv. bd. Elec. Utility Ctr. for Mgmt. & Supervisory Devel., Salt Lake City, 1988—; host cable TV program Invest Am., 1978, 80. Writer over 400 editorials, over 50 spl. reports; editor hundreds of articles; pub. ann. industry forecasts; ann. contbr. sect. on electric utilities for McGraw-Hill Yearbook of Science and Technology. Charter mem. ARC Blood Bank, Englewood, N.J., 1957—; elder Presbyn. Ch., Englewood, 1961—. 2d lt. USMC, 1944-47. Named to Hon. Order Ky. Cols. Sr. mem. IEEE (chair pub. rels. 1973-79); mem. Am. Nuclear Soc., Conf. High-Voltage Electric Systems (exec. com. 1965-93, tech. com. 1975-93), Am. Power Conf. (industry com. 1975-93), Internat. Conf. Distbn. Systems (U.S. com. 1990—), World Energy Conf. (U.S. nat. com., bd. dirs. 1974-82), Am. Bus. Press (editorial bd. 1976-78), Tau Beta Pi. Republican. Died June 9, 2009.

HAYSBERT, RAYMOND VICTOR, retired food company executive; b. Cin., Jan. 19, 1920; s. William and Emma (Walton) H.; m. Carol Evelyn Roberts, Dec. 25, 1945; children: Raymond V., Reginald, Nikita Michelle, Brian Robert. BS cum laude, Cen. State U.; BS in Math. cum laude, Wilberforce U.; BS in Mech. Engring., U. Cin.; postgrad., Johns Hopkins U. From powerplant laborer to engr. Dept. Water, City of Cin.; waiter Mariemont Inn; mgr. VA Housing Authority, Wilberforce (Ohio) Coll. Bookstore; instr. Ctrl. State U., Morgan State Coll.; acct. Bayless & Son Constrn.; ptnr. Johns & Haysbert Acctg. Svcs.; exec. v.p. Parks Sausage Co., Balt., pres., CEO. Bd. dirs. Bell Atlantic Corp., Equitable Bancorp., C&P Telephone Co. of Md., 1611 Corp.; adv. bd. Advance Fed. Savings & Loan, Harbor Bank of Md., Security Am. Svcs., Inc.; pres. DoRayte Corp., Fed. Res. Bank of Richmond; civilian aide Sec. of Army of Md.; chmn., pres., dir. Forum Caterers, Inc.; v.p., dir. D.H. Lloyd Ins. of Md. Bd. dirs. Jr. Achievement of Met. Balt., ARC, Balt. Coun. on Fgn. Affairs, Commn. on Urban Devel., United Appeal, Health & Welfare Coun., Boy Scouts of Am.-Balt., Balt. Area Coun. on Alcoholism, Community Chest of Balt.; v.p., dir. United fund of Cen. Md.; sec., dir. Great Balt. Com.; adv. bd. Sch. Bus. Coppin State Coll., U. Balt., Va. State U., Morgan State U.; bd. dirs. Coun. on Econ. Edn. in Md.; trustee bd. Wilberforce U.; 1st found. chmn. bd. Sojourner Douglas Coll. With U.S. Army, 1941-4 Recipient Founders awards Ctrl. State U. Alumni Assn., Berkeley Burrell award Nat. Bus. League, Irving Blum award United Fund of Md., Man of Yr. award Balt. Mktg. Assn., Ideal Citizen award Transcendental Meditation Soc., Man of Yr. award Sml. Businessman's League of Balt., Dow Jones Entrepenuer award; named Nat. Minority Entrepreneur of Yr. Nat. Minority Mfr. (U.S.) Min. Bus. Devel. Agy., 1991, Hall of Fame Balt. Bus.; honored for dedicated svc. Resolution in Md. Senate, for Outstanding Svc. U.S. Dept. HUD, others. Lutheran. Home: Baltimore, Md. Died May 24, 2010.

HEALEY, JAMES STEWART, library science educator; b. Chgo., July 14, 1931; s. James Alfred and Bernice (Stewart) H.; m. Beate M. Barlas, Feb. 16, 1990; children by previous marriage: James F., Siobhan E., Kathleen E. AB, Stonehill Coll., 1955; MS, Simmons Coll., 1958; D.Library Sci., Columbia U., 1973. Reference asst. Boston Pub. Library, 1955-56; librarian Stoneham, Mass., 1956-61; city librarian New Bedford, Mass., 1961-67; chief div. library extension services Dept. State Library Services of R.I., Providence, 1967-68; assoc. prof. U. R.I., 1968-75; prof., dir. Sch. Library Sci., U. Okla., Norman, 1975-82; prof., dir. Sch. Libr. and Info. Scis. San Jose State U., 1985-93, prof., 1993-95, prof. emeritus, from 1995. Cons. to pub. and spl. libraries Author: John E. Fogarty, 1974 U.S. Title IIB fellow, 1969-70 Home: Bethesda, Md. Died July 20, 2009.

HEALY, NICHOLAS JOSEPH, retired lawyer; b. NYC, Jan. 4, 1910; s. Nicholas Joseph and Frances Cecilia (McCarthy) H.; m. Margaret Marie Ferry, Mar. 29, 1937; children: Nicholas, Margaret Healy Parker, Rosemary Healy Bell, Mary Louise Healy White, Donall, Kathleen Healy Hamon. AB, Holy Cross Coll., 1931; JD, Harvard U., 1934. Bar: N.Y. 1935, U.S. Supreme Ct. 1949. Pvt. practice, NYC, 1935—42; mem. Healy & Baillie (and predecessor firms), from 1948. Spl. asst. to atty. gen. U.S., 1945-48; tchr. admiralty law NYU Sch. Law, 1947-86, adj. prof., 1960-86; Niels F. Johnsen vis. prof. maritime law Tulane Maritime Law Ctr., 1986; vis. prof. maritime law Shanghai Maritime Inst. (now Shanghai Maritime U.), 1981, 86, 88. Contbr. chpts. to Ann. Survey Am. Law, 1948-87; author: (with Sprague) Cases on Admiralty, 1950; (with Currie) Cases and Materials on Admiralty, 1965; (with Sharpe) Cases and Materials on Admiralty, 1974, 3rd edit., 1998; (with Sweeney) The Law of Marine Collision, 1998; editor: Jour. Maritime Law and Commerce, 1980-90, mem. editl. bd., 1969-79, 91—; assoc. editor: American Maritime Cases; mem. scientific bd. Il Dirittimo Marittimo; contbr. to Ency. Brit. Chmn. USCG Adv. Panel on Rules of the Road, 1966-72; mem. permanent adv. bd. Tulane Admiralty Law Inst. Lt. (s.g.) USNR, 1942-45. Fellow Am. Coll. Trial Lawyers; mem. ABA (ho. of dels. 1964-66), N.Y. State Bar Assn., Assn. of Bar of City of N.Y., N.Y. County Lawyers Assn., Maritime Law Assn. U.S. (pres. 1964-66), Assn. Average Adjusters U.S. (chmn. 1959-60), Com. Maritime Internat. (exec. coun. 1972-79, v.p. 1985-91, hon. v.p. 1991—), Ibero-Am. Inst. Maritime Law (hon.). Died May 20, 2009.

HEANEY, GERALD WILLIAM, retired federal judge; b. Goodhue, Minn., Jan. 29, 1918; s. William J. and Johanna (Ryan) H.; m. Eleanor R. Schmitt, Dec. 1, 1945; children: William M., Carol J. Student, St. Thomas Coll., 1935—37; BSL, U. Minn., 1939, LLB, 1941, LLD for Pub. Svc., 2001. Bar: Minn. 1941. Atty. securities divsn. Minn. Dept. Commerce, 1941—42; atty. Lewis. Hammer, Heaney, Weyl & Halverson, Duluth, 1946—66; judge US Ct. Appeals (8th cir.), 1966—88, sr. judge, 1988—2006. Bd. regents U. Minn., 1964—65; Mem. Dem. Nat. Com. from Minn., 1955. Capt. AUS, 1942—46. Decorated Silver Star, Bronze Star. Mem.: ABA, American Judicature Soc., Minn. Bar Assn. Dfl. Roman Catholic. Died June 22, 2010.

HEARD, ARTHUR BERNARD, lawyer; b. Cleve., Oct. 26, 1924; s. Gus and Henri (Chambliss) H.; m. Marion Elizabeth Dennis, Mar. 3, 1945; 1 child, Martin Bernard. Cert. in acctg., Fenn Coll., Cleve. State U., 1959; JD, Cleve. Marshall Coll. Law, 1963. Bar: Ohio 1963. Teller, bookkeeper Quincy Savs. & Loan Co., Cleve., 1953-60, corporate sec., mng. officer, 1960-75, pres., mng. officer, 1975-76; practice in Cleve., from 1976. Mem. Cleve. Zoning Bd. Appeals, 1974—; dir. Office Equal Opportunity, Bd. Commrs. Cuyahoga County, 1983-85; dep. clk., referee Probate Ct. of Cuyahoga County, 1985—; v.p. Cleve. CSC, 1970-74; treas. Greater Cleve. Growth Corp., 1972—; pres. bd. trustees Cleve. Pub. Library; trustee Cath. Charities. Served with USMCR, 1943-46. Recipient Outstanding Alumnus award Cleve. Marshall Law Coll., 1964, Interracial Justice award Cath. Interracial Council, 1975 Mem. Cuyahoga County Bar Assn., Savs. and Loan Accounting Soc., Cath. Lawyers Guild (treas. 1975—) Republican. Roman Catholic (eucharistic minister). Club: KC (4 deg.). Home: Cleveland, Ohio. Died Mar. 19, 2009.

HEAVNER, ROBERT OWEN, finance company executive; b. Akron, Ohio, Nov. 20, 1941; s. Clarence Owen and Lena (Coburn) H.; m. Elaine Louise Conrad, July 3, 1964; children: Jocelyn, Kristin, Amanda. BS, USAF Acad., 1963; MA in Econs., Georgetown, 1964; PhD in Bus., Econs., Stanford U., 1976. Commd. 2d lt. USAF, 1959, advanced through ranks to col., 1980; asst. to dir. OMB, Office of the Pres., USAF, Washington, 1977-79; speech writer Chief of Staff, USAF, Washington, 1979-80; asst. dep. ops. 81st TFW, USAF, Bentwaters, Eng., 1980-81, resource mgr., 1981-82; dir. plans Europe USAF, Ramstein, Fed. Republic Germany, 1982-83, ret., 1983; prof. Westmont Coll., Santa Barbara, Calif., 1983-88; pres. Heavner & Assoc., Santa Barbara, 1984-88; sr. v.p. Calif. Thrift and Loan, Santa Barbara, 1988-91, exec. v.p., from 1991. Chmn. bd. KSB, Inc., Bakersfield, Calif., 1985—, Presentek, Inc., Santa Barbara, 1987—. Decorated Silver Star, Legion of Merit, Disting. Flying Cross with oak leaf cluster. Home: Santa Barbara, Calif. Died Apr. 12, 2009.

HEBB, MALCOLM HAYDEN, physicist; b. Marquette, Mich., July 21, 1910; s. Thomas Carlyle and Evelyn Shewell (Hayden) H.; m. Marion Elizabeth Evers, May 8, 1943. BA, U. B.C., 1931, D.Sc. (hon.), 1963; postgrad., U. Wis., 1931-34; PhD, Harvard, 1936. Instr. physics Harvard, 1936-37; Harvard Sheldon travelling fellow to U. Utrecht, 1937-38; instr. physics Duke, 1938-42; anti-submarine devices Harvard Underwater Sound Lab., Nat. Def. Research Com., 1942-45; physicist research lab. Sharples Corp., 1945-49; research asso. Gen. Electric Co., 1949-51, mgr. gen. physics research dept., 1951-68, physicist, 1968-75. Vis. com. physics Tufts U., 1967; mem. council Harvard Found., 1958-63; vis. com. elec. engring. Princeton, 1959-71 Recipient Gov. Gen. Medal B.C., 1931 Fellow Am. Phys. Soc.; mem. Netherlands Phys. Soc., Sigma Xi. Clubs: Mohawk, Mohawk Golf. Home: Eustis, Fla. Died Aug. 11, 2009.

HECHT, LEE, software company executive; b. Phila., May 11, 1942; s. Hymen Nathan and Anne Rosalee (Brodsky) H.; 1 dau., Kimberley Kenney. MS in Physics, U. Chgo., 1965, MBA (NDEA fellow), 1969. Teaching asst. physics, research asst. U. Chgo., lectr. physics, 1966-67; applied maths. U. Chgo. (Sch. Bus.), 1967-69, policy studies, 1973-80; chmn., pres., chief exec. officer Phoenix-Hecht Inc. (computer services co.), Chgo., 1968-75, dir., 1968-76; pres., chief exec. officer Phoenix-Hecht Cash Mgmt. Services Inc., Chgo., 1973-75, chmn. bd., 1973-76; pres., chief exec. officer, chmn. Kenwood-Pacific Corp., San Francisco, 1973-82; dir. Holloway Mgmt. Group, Ltd., Chgo., 1973-82, chmn., 1976-82, Kenwood Group, San Francisco, 1977-82; chief exec. officer Teknowledge, Inc., Palo Alto, Calif., 1981-88, chmn., 1982-88; pres., chief exec. officer Middlefield Group Inc., 1981-91, Middlefield Capital Corp., 1981-86; dir. Digital Pathways Inc., Palo Alto, Calif., 1976-82, 89, chmn., 1994-96, Kenwood Group Inc., 1978-82; dir. Cimflex Teknowledge Corp., 1989-91; chmn., pres., chief exec. officer Modernsoft., Inc., Palo Alto, 1989-97; mng. ptnr. Salent LLC, from 1997. Vis. lectr. bus. adminstrn. U. Calif., Berkeley, 1975-77; vis. lectr. mgmt. Stanford U., 1976; v.p. Nat. Vidiograph Inc. (motion picture prodn.), Berkeley, 1975-77; dir. U.S. Home Corp., Houston, 1985-86. Mem. Econ. Died Jan. 19, 2009.

HECKEL, RICHARD WAYNE, metallurgical engineering educator; b. Pitts., Jan. 25, 1934; s. Ralph Clyde and Esther Vera (Zoerb) H.; m. Peggy Ann Simmons, Jan. 3, 1959 (dec. Apr. 1998); children: Scott Alan, Laura Ann Rowe. BS in Metall. Engring., Carnegie Mellon, 1955, MS, 1958, PhD, 1959. Sr. rsch. metallurgist E.I. duPont de Nemours & Co., Wilmington, Del., 1959—63; prof. metall. engring. Drexel U., Phila., 1963—71; head dept. materials sci. and engring. Carnegie Mellon, Pitts., 1971—76; prof. materials sci. and engring. Mich. Tech. U., Houghton, 1976—96, prof. emeritus, from 1996; tech. dir., owner Engring. Trends, Houghton, from 2000. Commr. at large Engring. Workforce Commn., 1997—, founder, tech. dir. Engring. Trends (e-commerce). Contbr. articles to profl. jours. Served as 1st lt. Ordnance Corps, U.S. Army, 1959-60. Recipient Lindback Teaching award Drexel U., 1968; Research award Mich. Tech. U., 1985 Fellow ASM Internat. (life; Bradley Stoughton Young Tchr. of Metallurgy award 1969, Phila. Ednl. Achievement award 1967); mem. The Metals, Minerals and Materials Soc., Am. Welding Soc. (Adams Meml. mem. 1966), Am. Soc. Engring. Edn., Sigma Xi, Omicron Delta Kappa, Tau Beta Pi, Phi Kappa Phi, Alpha Sigma Mu. Died May 25, 2010.

HECKERT, RICHARD EDWIN, retired chemical company executive; b. Oxford, Ohio, Jan. 13, 1924; s. John W. and Winifred E. (Yahn) H.; m. Barbara Kennedy, 1945; children: Alex Y., Andra Heckert Rudershausen. BA, Miami U., Ohio, 1944; MS in Organic Chemistry, U. Ill., 1947, PhD in Organic Chemistry, 1949. With E.I. DuPont de Nemours & Co., from 1949, research chemist Wilmington, Del., 1949-54, from supr. cellophane research and devel. lab. film dept. to asst. mgr. lab. Richmond, Va., 1954-57, tech. supt. cellophane plant, 1957-58, Clinton, Iowa, 1958-59, plant mgr. Circleville, Ohio, 1959-63, dir. supporting research and devel. Wilmington, 1963-65, asst. gen. mgr. film dept., 1965-67, asst. gen. mgr. plastics dept., 1967-69, gen. mgr. fabrics and finishes dept., 1969-72, v.p., 1972-73, sr. v.p., dir., 1973-81, pres., 1981-85, vice chmn., COO, 1981-85, dep. chmn., 1985-86, chmn., CEO, 1986-89. Contbr. articles on cyanocarbon chemistry to sci. jours.; patentee in field. Pres. Longwood Gardens, Inc., trustee; dean's assoc. bus. adv. coun. Miami U. Sch. Bus. Adminstrn.; chmn. bd. trustees Carnegie Instn. of Washington: trustee Del. Coun. on Econ. Edn., Found. Nat. Action Coun. for Minorities in Eng.; mem. Nat. Bd. for Profl. Teaching Standards; bd. govs. Nature Conservancy; mem. fin. com. of Joint Coun. on Econs. Edn. With U.S. Army, 1944-46. Mem. AAAS, NAM (bd. dirs.), Am. Chem. Soc. Clubs: Pine Valley Golf, Wilmington, Vicmead Hunt. Died Jan. 3, 2010.

HEDGEPETH, CHESTER MELVIN, JR., university dean; b. Richmond, Va., Oct. 28, 1937; s. Chester M. Sr. and Ethel (Carter) H.; m. Thelma Washington, Aug. 16, 1969; 1 child, Chester III. BA, Blackburn Coll., 1960; MA, Wesleyan U., 1966; EdD, Harvard U., 1977. Tchr. English Maggie L. Walker High Sch., Richmond, 1960-65; instr. English Va. Union U., Richmond, 1965-68, Coll. St. Thomas, St. Paul, 1969-70, Macalester Coll., Mpls., 1970-71; asst. prof. English Va. Union U., Richmond, 1972-75, Va. Commonwealth U., Richmond, 1978-83; dean arts and sci. U. Md. Ea. Shore, Princess Anne, Md., from 1983. Author: Theories of Social Action in Black Literature, 1968, 20th Century Afro-American Writers and Artists, 1991; sr. editor Md. Rev., 1986—. Trustee bd. Wicomico Presbyn. Ch., 1986-89. Grantee NEH, 1971, Va. Found. Humanities, 1978, Md. Humanities Coun., 1988. Mem. Phi Delta Kappa, Sigma Pi Phi. Avocations: photography, biking. Home: Salisbury, Md. Died Aug. 25, 2009.

HEDRICK, DAVID WARRINGTON, lawyer; b. Jacksonville, Fla., Oct. 25, 1917; s. Frederic Cleveland and Edith (Warrington) Hedrick; m. June Nicholson, Apr. 23, 1949 (div. 1991); children: John Warrington, Stephen Brian; m. Sherra M. Hedrick, Jan. 31, 1992. BA with honors, U. Fla., 1940, JD with honors, 1947. Bar: Fla. 1947, US Supreme Ct. 1962. Capt. US Army, ETO, 1941—46; served to col. USAR, 1946—67; assoc., LeRoy B. Giles, 1947—52; ptnr. Giles, Hedrick & Robinson, Orlando, Fla., 1953—92, David W. Hedrick Atty., from 1992. Dir. First Fed. Savs. and Loan Assn., 1963—79, Indsl. Devel. Commn. Mid-Fla., 1978—79; pres. Attys. Title Svcs., 1963—64, Sharaconcept Inc., from 1987; dir. & sec. Comint Corp., 1966—84. Bd. dirs. Holiday Hosp. Orlando, 1966—69; legal counsel & bd. dirs. Ctrl. Fla. Coun. Boy Scouts America, from 1970; pres. Orange County Human Planning Coun., 1973—75, bd. dirs., 1973—89, mem., Orlando Mayor's Interracial Adv. Commn., 1967; chmn. United Appeal Dr. Orange County, Fla., 1967, pres., 1970, chmn. bd. dirs., 1971, chmn., social planning com., 1973—76, legal counsel, from 1975; chancellor Diocese Ctrl. Fla., Orlando, 1970—90. Decorated Bronze Star, Belgian Fourragere; recipient Disting. Eagle Scout award, Boy Scouts America, 1972, Silver Beaver award, 1976. Mem.: VFW, ABA, Am. Judicature Soc., Fla. Bar, Orange County Bar Assn. (pres. 1959—60, past pres. coun. from 1976), Res. Officers Assn., Fla. Blue Key, Assn. US Army, Am. Legion, Kiwanis North Orlando Club, River Club (Jacksonville), Country Orlando Club, U. Club (Orlando), Alpha Tau Omega, Phi Delta Phi, Phi Kappa Phi. Democrat. Episcopalian. Home: Orlando, Fla. Died Mar. 16, 2010.

HEEKE, DENNIS HENRY, state legislator; b. DuBois, Ind., Sept. 9, 1927; s. Theodore C. and Clara (Theising) H.; m. Leola Mae Schuler, May, 1950; children: Terrence, Garret, Bruce, Brian. Grad. high sch., DuBois, 1946. State rep. Ind. Legislature, from 1964. Chmn. Dem. Caucus, Ind., 1972—. Roman Catholic. Home: Dubois, Ind. Died Aug. 14, 2009.

HEFFNER, WILLIAM JOSEPH, investment executive; b. Balt., Dec. 6, 1928; BS, Johns Hopkins U., 1961; JD, U. Balt., 1967. V.p. Merc. Safe Deposit & Trust Co., Balt., 1965-74; pres. Redwood Capital Mgmt., Balt., 1974-86, Mt. Vernon Assocs. Inc., Balt., from 1986. Bd. dirs. Triangle Industries, Am. Nat. Can. Mem. Nat. Economists, Fin. Analysts Fedn., Indsl. Relations Council. Clubs: Balt. Country, Center Club. Home: Baltimore, Md. Died Mar. 27, 2009.

HEFNER, JAMES HOMER, superintendent of schools; b. Ellijay, Ga., Oct. 18, 1932; s. Jeffie Homer and Essie (Reece) H.; m. Esther Joyce Ralston, Feb. 7, 1953; 1 child, Rhonda. BS in Edn., North Ga. Coll., 1954; MA in Edn., Western Carolina u., 1961; edn. specialist grad., Ga. State U., 1979. Cert. Edn. Specialist in Edn. Asminstrn. Tchr./counselor Gilmer County Bd. Edn., Ellijay, Ga., 1957-69; coord. student svcs. Pickens Area Vocat.-Tech. Sch., Jasper, Ga., 1969-79; vocat. adminstr. Gilmer County Bd. Edn., Ellijay, 1979-84; supt. schs. Gilmer County Sch. System, Ellijay, from 1985. Cons. U.S. Office Career Edn., Washington, 1976, Vocat. Career Devel. Ctr. Ga. State U., Atlanta, 1980-88; pres. Guidance Div. Ga. Vocat. Assn., 1978-79; mem. Adv. Coun. on Vocat. Edn., Atlanta, 1977-86. Pres. Ellijay Jr. C. of C., 1964; chmn. Gilmer County Health Adv. Com., 1969-70, Bd.

dirs. Apple Valley Rehab. Ctr., 1968-79, Gilber County Bd. Health, 1987-91; bd. dirs. Gilmer County Heart Assn., 1980-91. Recipient Cert. of Appreciation Commn. on Occupational Edn. Inst., Atlanta, 1980; named Outstanding Heart vol. Gilmer Co. Heart Assn., Ellijay, 1984. Mem. Ga. Assn. Ednl. Leaders, North Ga. Regional Ednl. Svc. Agcy. (chmn., 1988—), Ga. Assn. Sch. Supts., Ninth Dist. Sch. Supts., Cartecay Optimist Club (bd. dirs., 1987-90), Ellijay Lions Club, Rotary Club of Gilmer County. Baptist. Avocations: fishing, travel. Died May 18, 2010.

HEFTEL, CECIL LANDAU, former United States Representative from Hawaii; b. Cook County, Ill., Sept. 30, 1924; m. Joyce Glasmann; children: Cathi, Lani, Peggy, Susan, Christopher, Terry, Richard. BS, Ariz. State U., 1951; postgrad., U. Utah, N.Y. U. Pres. Heftel Broadcasting Co., 1986—2010; mem. US Congress from 1st Hawaii Dist., 1977—86. Author: End Legalized Bribery: An Ex-Congressman's Proposal to Clean Up Congress, 1998. Active March of Dimes. Mem. Am. Legion. Clubs: Elks, Eagles, Shriners. Democrat. Lds Church. Died Feb. 5, 2010.

HEGELMANN, JULIUS, retired pharmacy educator; b. NYC, Oct. 19, 1921; s. Julius and Augusta (Schubert) H.; m. Marjorie Scallon, May 30, 1943; children: Marjorie Ann (Mrs. Jay Wohl), Jill Marie (Mrs. F. Menshel). BS in Pharmacy, Rutgers U., 1943. Prodn. mgr. EB Bilhuber Inc., 1939-50; v.p., sales mgr., dir. Knoll Pharm. Co., 1950-62; with Hegelmann & Bartolone Inc., NYC, 1962-70, chmn. bd., 1962-70; pres. J. Hegelmann Assos., Inc., Franklin Lakes, N.J., 1970-73; asst. prof., dir. pharm. extension services Rutgers U., New Brunswick, N.J., 1973-78, asso. prof., 1978-85, prof. emeritus, from 1985. Exec. sec. Rutgers Nat. Pharm. Conf., 1973-85 Author: The Evolution of Knoll Pharmaceutical Company 1904-1975, The 75th Anniversary, The George Merck Legacy. Pres. Orange (N.J.) C. of C., 1956; trustee Franklin Lakes Library; mem. Franklin Lakes Bd. Adjustment, 1973-82. Served with AUS, 1943-46, ETO; 1st lt. Res. Fellow Am. Soc. Cons. Pharm.; mem. Am. Mgmt. Assn., Am. Pharm. Assn., Pharm. Advt. Club, Am. Assn. Colls. Pharmacy, Am. Inst. History of Pharmacy, N.J. Acad. Cons. Pharm., Delta Sigma Theta, Rho Chi. Clubs: Rotarian (pres. Orange 1956). Home: Franklin Lakes, NJ. Died July 11, 2010.

HEGYELI, RUTH INGEBORG ELISABETH JOHNSSON, pathologist, federal official; b. Aug. 14, 1931; came to U.S., 1963; d. John Alfred and Elsa Ingeborg (Sjogren) Johnsson; m. Andrew Francis Hegyeli, July 2, 1966 (dec. June 1982). BA in Scis., U. Toronto, 1958, MD, 1962. Intern Toronto Gen. Hosp., 1962-63; rsch. assoc. Nobel Laureates Albert Szent Györgyi, Weeds Hole, Mass., 1963—65; rsch. pathologist Battelle Meml. Inst., Columbus, Ohio, 1965—67, sr. rsch. pathologist, 1967-69; med. officer Nat. Heart and Lung Inst., 1969-73; chief program devel. and evaluation Nat. Heart, Lung and Blood Inst., Bethesda, Md., 1973-76, acting dir. office program planning, 1975-76, asst. dir. internat. rels., 1976-86, assoc. dir. internat. rels., 1986—2005. Mem. sci. adv. bd. Giovanni Lorenzini Found., Inc., NYC., Milan, from 1982. Coord. editor: Jour. Soviet Rsch. in Cardiovasc. Diseases, 1979-86; editor: Christopher Columbus Commemorative Book on Discovering New Worlds in Medicine, 1992, Internat. Position Paper: Women's Health and Menopause, A Comprehensive Approach, 2002, also 11 sci. books; contbr. poetry to nat. and internat. anthologies. Mem. nat. adv. bd. Nat. Mus. Women in Arts. Recipient German Friendship award, German Ministry Rsch. and Tech., 1988, Nicolaus Copernicus medal, Academica Medica, 1988, Superior Svc. award, HEW, 1975, DHHS, 1991, Outstanding Achievement award in Poetry, 2003, Internat. Peace prize, 2004, Exemplary Svc. award, Surgeon Gen., 2005, Fogarty Scholar Gold medal, 2005; named Hon. Mem. Eagle Tribe of Haida Indians, Queen Charlotte Islands, B.C., Can., 1961; named to, Internat. Poetry Hall of Fame, 1997. Fellow Acad. Medicine, Toronto; mem. Soc. Geriatric Cardiology (founding mem.), Am. Soc. Artificial Internat. Organs, N.Y. Acad. Scis., Acad. Am. Poets, Internat. Soc. Poets, World Literary Acad., Fed. Exec. Alumni Assn. Republican. Avocations: poetry, writing, art, music, travel. Home: Gaithersburg, Md. Died June 1, 2009.

HEIGHT, DOROTHY, retired foundation administrator; b. Richmond, Va., Mar. 24, 1912; d. James Edward and Fannie (Burroughs) Height. BA, MA, NYU. Mem. nat. staff YWCA of the U.S.A., 33 yrs.; caseworker NYC Welfare Dept., 1934; dir. Ctr. Racial Justice YWCA of the U.S.A., 1946; nat. pres. Nat. Coun. Negro Women Inc., 1957—97, pres. emeritus, 1998—2010. With Dept. Def. Adv. Com. Women, 1952—55; mem. N.Y. State Social Welfare Bd., 1958—68; bd. govs. ARC, 1964—70; pres.'s com. Employment Handicapped; mem. ad hoc com. Pub. Welfare Dept. Health Edn. and Welfare; dir. Ctr. Racial Justice YMCA. Author: Open Wide the Freedom Gate, 2003. Pres. Nat. Coun. Negro Women; hon. mem. nat. bd. dirs. YWCA of USA. Recipient Disting. Svc. award, Nat. Conf. Social Welafre, 1971, William L. Dawson award, 1974, Citizens Medal award, 1989, Camille Cosby World Children award, 1990, Amb. award, YWCA of the USA, 1993, Presdl. Medal of Freedom, The White House, 1994, Congl. Gold Medal, 2004; named one of The 100 Most Influential Black Americans, Ebony mag., 2006; named to The Power 150, 2008. Died Apr. 20, 2010.

HEINE, RICHARD WALTER, metallurgical engineer; b. Detroit, July 22, 1918; s. Walter G. R. and Lisette H.; m. Mary Arlene Conklin, Mar. 30, 1940; children: Sally Lee, Robert Walter. BSCh.E., Wayne State U., 1940; MS in Metall. Engring, U. Wis., 1948. Instr. Gen. Motors Inst., Flint, Mich., 1940-43, 46-47; instr. U. Wis., Madison, 1947-48, asst. prof. metall. engring., 1948-54, asso. prof., 1955-62, prof., from 1962, chmn. dept. metall. engring., 1964-74; asso. dir. Engring. Expt. Sta., 1974-76. Cons. to industry. Author: Principles of Metal Casting, 1965; contbr. numerous articles on metal casting processes to profl. publs. Served to lt. Ordnance Corps USN, 1943-46, PTO. Recipient C.H. Jennings award Am. Welding Soc., 1976, Ragnar E. Ohnstad award Coll. Engring., U. Wis., 1979, award excellence Iron Castings Soc., 1983. Fellow ASM, Am. Soc. for Metal Internat.; mem. AIME (C.W. Briggs award 1975), Am. Inst. Chem. Engrs., Am. Foundrymen's Soc. (Mac Fadden Golf medal 1966, Silver Anniversary Best Paper award 1983, 85, 89, Best Paper award Engring. div. 1987, H.F. Taylor award 1993). Home: Madison, Wis. Died May 17, 2009.

HEINEMAN, FREDERICK K. (FRED HEINEMAN), former United States Representative from North Carolina; b. New York, NY, Dec. 28, 1929; m. Linda Heineman; 6 children. BBA in Mgmt., St. Francis Coll., 1970; M in Criminal Justice, John Jay Coll., 1975. From patrolman to dep. chief insp. N.Y.C. Police Dept., 1955-79; chief of police City of Raleigh, N.C., 1979-94; mem. US Congress from 4th NC dist., 1995—97. Active Triangle Challenge in Support of DARE, Wake County Child Protection Team, North Carolinians Against Race and Religious Violence. With USMC, 1951-54. Mem. Nat. Exec. Inst., N.C. Assn. Chiefs of Police, N.C. Police Execs. Assn., Internat. Assn. Chiefs of Police. Republican. Lutheran. Died Mar. 20, 2010.

HEINEMAN, NATALIE, civic worker; b. Chgo., Ill., Mar. 16, 1913; m. Ben Heineman; children: Martha, Ben Jr. Formerly med. social worker, Chgo.; bd. dirs. Child Welfare League Am., 1960-86, pres., 1971-74, now hon. life mem.; chmn. citizens com. Ill. Adoption Svc., 1959-71; bd. dirs. Chgo. Child Care Soc., 1959-97, pres., 1967-71, now hon. life mem.; mem. citizens' com. Juvenile Ct. of Cook County, 1984-95. Bd. dirs. Children and Family Justice Ctr., Northwestern U. Sch. Law, 1991-96; mem. women's bd. Field Mus. Natural History, U. Chgo., Northwestern U.; vis. com. U. Chgo. Sch. Social Svc., 1956-91. Bd. dirs. United Way Met. Chgo., 1975-86, United Way America, 1974-80, Erikson Inst. for Advanced Study Child Devel., 1966-88. Died Feb. 28, 2010.

HEINICKE, RALPH MARTIN, science administrator, consultant; b. Hickory, NC, Sept. 3, 1914; s. Martin John and Lydia Sophia (Kurth) H.; m. Sarah Anne Hall, July 31, 1944; 1 child, Mark. BS, Cornell U., 1936; PhD, U. Minn., St. Paul, 1950. Agr. chemist Shell Oil Co., NYC, 1939-43; tech. advisor Jintan-Dolph, Osaka, Japan, 1962-86; assoc. faculty U. Hawaii, Honolulu, 1950-86; chemist Pineapple Rsch. Inst., Honolulu, 1950-55; dir. rsch. Dole Co., Honolulu, 1955-72; v.p. Biol. Control Systems, Honolulu, 1981-86; pres. Biotech. Resources Inc., Clarksville, Ind., 1990-94; cons. Morinda, Inc., 1996. Cons. various drug cos., 1972—; cons. on the xeronine-sys. Inventor, patentee on xeronine; inventor, patentee on nerve toxin insecticide, proxeronine, proxerinonase. Master sgt. U.S. Army, 1942-45, CBI. Democrat. Avocations: music, writing, philosophy. Home: Louisville, Ky. Died Nov. 26, 2009.

HEISER, CHARLES BIXLER, JR., botany educator; b. Cynthiana, Ind., Oct. 5, 1920; s. Charles Bixler and Inez (Metcalf) H.; m. Dorothy Gaebler, Aug. 19, 1944; children—Lynn Marie, Cynthia Ann, Charles Bixler III, Leslie Nosier Dakins. AB, Washington U., St. Louis, 1943, MA, 1944; PhD, U. Calif., Berkeley, 1947. Instr. Washington U., St. Louis, 1944-45; assoc. botany U. Calif. at Davis, 1946-47; mem. faculty Ind. U., Bloomington, 1947—86, prof. botany, 1957—86, Disting. prof., 1979-86, disting. prof. emeritus, from 1986. Author: Nightshades, The Paradoxical Plants, 1969, Seed to Civilization, The Story of Man's Food, 1973, The Sunflower, 1976, The Gourd Book, 1979, Of Plants and People, 1985, Weeds in my Garden, 2003, Wheat in my Garden, 2006. Guggenheim fellow, 1953; NSF Sr. Postdoctoral fellow, 1962; recipient Pustovoit award Internat. Sunflower Assn., 1985. Mem. Am. Soc. Plant Taxonomists (pres. 1967, Asa Gray award 1988, Raven Outreach award 2002), Bot. Soc. Am. (Merit award 1972, pres. 1980), Soc. Study Evolution (pres. 1974), Soc. Econ. Botany (pres. 1978, Disting. Econ. Botanist 1984), Nat. Acad. Scis., Phi Beta Kappa, Sigma Xi. Achievements include research and numerous publications on systematics flowering plants, natural and artificial hybridization, origin cultivated plants. Home: Bloomington, Ind. Died June 11, 2010.

HEIZER, EDGAR FRANCIS, JR., venture capitalist; b. Detroit, Sept. 23, 1929; s. Edgar Francis and Grace Adelia (Smith) H.; m. Molly Bradley Hunt, June 17, 1952; children: Linda Heizer Seaman, Molly Hunt, Edgar Francis III. BS, Northwestern U., 1951; JD, Yale U., 1954. Bar: Ill. 1954; CPA, Ill. Mem. audit and tax staff Arthur Andersen & Co., Chgo., 1954-56; fin. analyst Kidder, Peabody & Co., Chgo., 1956-58; mgmt. cons. Booz, Allen & Hamilton, Chgo., 1958-62; asst. treas., mgr. venture capital divsn. Allstate Ins. Co., Northbrook, Ill., 1962-69; chmn., founder, CEO Heizer Corp., a venture capital & bus. devel. co., Chgo., 1969-85; venture capitalist Tucker's Town, Bermuda, from 1985; dir. Chesapeake Energy Corp., Material Sciences Corp., Elk Grove, Ill. Bd. dirs. Needham & Co., N.Y., Material Sci. Corp., Elk Grove Village, Ill., Manus Health Systems Inc., Lake Forest, Ill., Chesapeake Energy Corp., Oklahoma City, Okla.; mem. adv. bd. Kellogg Sch. Mgmt., Northwestern U.; chmn. Heizer Ctr. for Entrepreneurship at Kellogg Sch. Mgmt. Chmn. task force on capital formation for White House Conf. on Small Bus., 1978-80. Mem. Nat. Venture Capital Assn. (founder, 1st pres., chmn.), Nat. Assn. Small Bus. Investment Cos., Delta Upsilon (chmn. bd. dirs. 1985-88, chmn. ednl. found. 1990-98). Clubs: Chgo. Curling, Shoreacres, Econ. of Chgo., Coral Beach and Tennis, Mid-Ocean; Riddells Bay Golf (Bermuda). Republican. Presbyterian. Home: Tuckers Town, Bermuda. Died Dec. 3, 2009.

HEKIMIAN, NORRIS CARROLL, retired electrical engineer; b. Washington, Jan. 14, 1926; s. Nejib and Louise Marie (Von Andrian) H.; m. Joan Elizabeth Scovall, June 15, 1955; 1 stepson, Allen Mark Knechtel; children: Joan Allison, Christopher David, Catherine Louise. BSE.E., George Washington U., 1949; MS, U. Md., 1951, PhD, 1969. Registered profl. engr., Md. Radio engr. Nat. Bur. Standards, Washington, 1949-54; br. chief Nat. Security Agy., Ft. Meade, Md., 1954-61; asst. dir. research and devel. Page Communications Engrs., Inc., Washington, 1961-68; founder, pres. Hekimian Labs., Inc., Rockville, Md., 1968-81, CEO Gaithersburg, Md., 1981-82. Cons. Boggs & Hekimian, Kensington, Md., 1953-60 Contbr. articles to mags., chpts. in books; holder 24 patents. Dir. Corp. for Tech. Tng., Montgomery County, Md., 1983—; engring. alumni bd. dirs. George Washington Enging. Alumni Assn., 1969-79; alumni trustee George Washington U., 1986—. Served to pvt. USAAF, 1944-45. Recipient Alumni Achievement award George Washington U., 1976 Fellow IEEE (Patron award 1979, mem. exec. com. Washington sect. 1968-78); mem. Sigma Tau, Eta Kappa Nu Clubs: Lakewood Country (Rockville). Republican. Unitarian Universalist. Home: Potomac, Md. Died June 10, 2010.

HELFRECHT, GARY FREDERICK, electronics executive; b. Newark, June 11, 1947; s. William John and May Ruth (Roudolf) H.; m. Susan Jean Leadbetter, July 1, 1967; children: Kristin, Jessica, Courtney. BA, Davis and Elkins Coll., 1969. Mgr. gen. mdse. H & P House Furnishing Co., Fairlawn, N.J., 1969-75; mng. dir. E. Yuen (U.S.A.) Ltd., NYC, 1975-78; v.p. ops. Wall Trading Co., Central Islip, N.Y., 1978-84; dir. internat. sales Carpenter Packaging Co., Richmond, Va., 1984-88, gen. mgr., 1988-90; exec. v.p., chief exec. officer Nimbus Records Inc., Charlottesville, Va., from 1990. Mem. Charlottesville C. of C. Republican. Avocations: golf, reading, music. Home: Richmond, Va. Died Aug. 21, 2010.

HELM, FREDERICK, dermatology educator; b. Reichenberg, Czechoslovakia, July 19, 1926; came to U.S., 1960; naturalized, 1969; s. Friedrich and Mathilde (Bayer) H.; m. Juta; children: Jutta M., Klaus F., Thomas N. Preclin. exam., U. Erlangen, Fed. Republic of Germany, 1949; MD, U. Graz, Austria, 1955. Diplomate Am. Bd. Dermatology, Am. Bd. Dermatopathology. Rotating intern City Hosp., Vienna, Austria, 1955-56, 1955-56; resident dept. dermatology U. Graz, Vienna, Austria, 1956-57; resident, lectr. asst. I Dermatology Clinic, U. Vienna, Austria, 1957-60; resident, teaching fellow in dermatology and syphilology, dept. dermatology Tufts U., Boston City Hosp., Boston Dispensary, Boston, 1961-62; resident Roswell Pk. Meml. Inst., Buffalo, 1962-63; resident dept. internal medicine Deaconess Hosp., Buffalo, 1964; cancer rsch. dermatologist (part-time), dept. dermatology Roswell Pk. Meml. Inst., Buffalo, 1963-81, prof. emeritus dermatology, 1981-89, prof. emeritus, 1989; chmn. dept. dermatology SUNY, Buffalo, 1983-89. Dir. dermatology Buffalo Gen. Hosp., 1983-89, Erie County Med. Ctr., 1983-89, U. Dermatopathology Lab., SUNY at Buffalo Affiliated Hosps., 1983; attending physician VA Hosp., Buffalo, 1983—; cons. Children's Hosp. of Buffalo, VA Med. Ctr., Roswell Pk. Meml. Inst., 1981—, Brook Meml. Hosp., Dunkirk, N.Y., West Seneca (N.Y.) Developmental Ctr. Author or co-author 89 published articles in dermatology field. With German army, 1943-46. Recipient recognition as tchr. Am. Acad. Family Physicians, 1976. Fellow Soc. Investigative Dermatology, Am. Acad. Dermatology, AMA, ACP, Royal Coll. Physicians of Can., Am. Soc. Laser Medicine and Surgery, Buffalo Acad. Medicine, N.Y. State Soc. Dermatology, Can. Dermatol. Assn., Am. Soc. Dermatol. Surgery; mem. Austrian Med. Assn., Coll. Physicians and Surgeons Man., Can., Med. Coun. Can., N.Y. State Med. Soc., Buffalo-Rochester Dermatol. Soc. (pres. 1974-75), Osterreichische Dermatologische Gesellschaft, Internat. Soc. Tropical Dermatology, Am. Soc. Dermatopathology. Roman Catholic. Home: Buffalo, NY. Died May 7, 2009.

HELSON, HENRY BERGE, publisher, retired educator; b. Lawrence, Kan., June 2, 1927; s. Harry and Lida G. (Anderson) H.; m. Ravenna W. Mathews, June 12, 1954; children—David M., Ravenna A., Harold E. AB, Harvard U., 1947, PhD, 1950. Lectr. U. Uppsala, Sweden, 1950-51; instr., then asst. prof. math. Yale, 1951-55; mem. faculty U. Calif. at Berkeley, from 1955, prof. math.; retired, 1993. Vis. prof. Swedish univs., spring 1962, U. Paris, Orsay, France, 1966-67, U. Sci. and Tech., Kumasi, Ghana, spring 1969, U. du Languedoc, Montpellier, France, 1971-72, Marseille, France, fall 1976; vis. prof. Indian Statis. Inst., Calcutta, spring 1980; lectr. St. Mary's Coll. of Calif., 2001-02. Author: Invariant Subspaces, 1964, Harmonic Analysis, 1983, The Spectral Theorem, 1986, Linear Algebra, 1990, Honors Calculus, 1992, Calculus and Probability, 1998, Dirichlet Series, 2005. Mem. Soc. Friends; treas. Friends Com. on Legis. Calif., 1989-95. Sheldon Traveling fellow, Warsaw and Wroclaw, Poland, 1947—48. Home: Berkeley, Calif. Died Jan. 10, 2010.

HELSTAD, ORRIN L., lawyer, educator; b. Ettrick, Wis., Feb. 9, 1922; s. Albert J. and Martha H. (Gimse) H.; m. Charlotte Dart Ankeney, June 26, 1954. Student, U. Wis., La Crosse, 1940-42; BS, U. Wis., Madison, 1948, LL.B., 1950. Bar: Wis. 1950. Research assoc. Wis. Legis. Council, 1950-61; assoc. prof. law U. Wis., Madison, 1961-65, prof., 1965-85; assoc. dean U. Wis. (Sch. Law), 1972-75, acting dean, 1975-76, dean, 1976-83, dean emeritus, from 1985, prof. emeritus, from 1985. Mem. consumer advisory council Wis. Dept. Agr., 1970-72; vice chmn. Wis. Supreme Ct. com. on the State bar, 1977; mem. Fed. Jud. Nominating Commn. Western Dist. Wis., 1979-83 Contbr. articles to law revs.; co-author, editor: Wisconsin Uniform Comml. Code Handbook, 1965, 1971. Recipient Disting. Svc. award Wis. Law Alumni Assn., 1991. Fellow Am. Bar Found.; mem. State Bar Wis., ABA (council sect. on local govt. law 1975-79), Wis. Bar Assn., Dane County Bar Assn., Am. Judicature Soc. Unitarian Universalist. Home: Madison, Wis. Died Dec. 11, 2009.

HEMPHILL, JAMES CALVIN, JR., architect; b. Greenwood, SC, July 25, 1920; s. James Calvin and Millwee (Davis) H.; m. Patricia Williams, May 31, 1943; children—James C., John A. BS in Architecture, Clemson U., 1942. Structural research engr. Glenn L. Martin Aircraft Co., 1942-44; structural research engr. NASA, 1944-45; draftsman Robert & Co., architects and engrs., Atlanta, 1945-46; architect James C. Hemphill, Sr., architect, Greenwood, N.C., 1947-52; prin. assoc. A.G. Odell, Jr. & Assocs., Charlotte, N.C., 1952-70; prin. James C. Hemphill, Jr., architect, Charlotte and Greenwood, 1970-74; owner Hemphill Assocs., Charlotte, from 1974. Vis. lectr. Clemson U., 1964-66; pres. N.C. Bd. Architecture, 1975; pres. Charlotte Mecklenburg Environ. Quality Council, 1971; mem. Charlotte Tree Commn., 1973-75. Archtl. works include; Carolina Motor Club Corp. Hdqrs., Strom Thurman Fed. Bldg., U.S. Courthouse, Columbia, S.C., Range Control Bldg., Ft. Bragg, N.C. Fellow AIA (pres. N.C. 1967, chmn. nat. specification com. 1963-65, chmn. nat. document rev. bd. 1966), Constrn. Specifications Inst. (past nat. bd. dirs.), Greenwood Jr. C. of C. (past pres.) Clubs: Civitan (pres. 1986—); Myers Park Country; Charlotte City. Presbyterian. Avocations: tennis. Home: Charlotte, NC. Died Apr. 5, 2009.

HENKEL, DAVID SEABURY, retired lawyer; b. Chatham, Va., Sept. 6, 1913; s. David Socrates and Elizabeth Wood (Vaughan) Henkel; m. Charlotte Eliot Henkel; m. Helen Snow Henkel, July 30, 1954; children: Charlotte, David Seabury Jr. BA, U. Richmond, 1933; LLB, U. Va., 1936. Bar: Va. 1935, NY 1937, US. Ct. Appeals (2d cir.) 1964, US Dist. Ct. (ea. dist.) NY 1964, US Supreme Ct. 1964. Ptnr. Sullivan & Cromwell, NYC, from 1936; ret.; dir. USLIFE Corp., The Gen. Tire & Rubber Co. 1st lt. US Army, 1944—46. Mem.: ABA, Am. Law Inst., NY State Bar Assn., NY County Lawyers Assn., Assn. Bar City NY. Died Sept. 16, 2009.

HENKIN, LOUIS, law educator; b. Russia, Nov. 11, 1917; came to U.S., 1923, naturalized, 1930; s. Yoseph Elia and Frieda Rebecca (Kreindel) H.; m. Alice Barbara Hartman, June 19, 1960; children: Joshua, David, Daniel. AB, Yeshiva Coll., 1937; DHL (hon.), Yeshiva U., 1963; LLB, Harvard U., 1940; LLD, Columbia U., 1995; JD (hon.), Bklyn. Law Sch., 1997; LLD (hon.), Jewish Theol. Sem., 2003. Bar: N.Y. 1941, U.S. Supreme Ct. 1947. Law clk. to Judge Learned Hand, 1940-41; law clk. to Justice Frankfurter, 1946-47; cons. legal dept. UN, 1947-48; with US Dept. State, 1945-46, 48-57; U.S. rep. UN Com. Refugees and Stateless Persons, 1950; adviser U.S. del. UN Econ. and Social Coun., 1950, UN Gen. Assembly, 1950-53, Geneva Conf. on Korea, 1954; assoc. dir. Legis. Drafting Rsch. Fund, lectr. law Columbia U., 1956-57; prof. law U. Pa., 1958-62; prof. internat. law and diplomacy, prof. law Columbia U., 1962, mem. Inst. War and Peace Studies, from 1962, Hamilton Fish prof. internat. law and diplomacy, 1963-78, Harlan Fiske Stone prof. constl. law, 1978-79, univ. prof., 1979-88, univ. prof. emeritus and spl. svc. prof., 1988—2010; co-dir. Ctr. for Study of Human Rights, 1978-86, chmn. of directorate, 1986—2010. U.S. mem. Permanent Ct. Arbitration, 1963-69; adviser U.S. Del. UN Conf. on Law of the Sea, 1972-80; adv. panel on internat. law US Dept. State, 1975-80, 93-2010; human rights com. U.S. Commn. for UNESCO, 1977-80, Internat. Covenant Civil and Polit. Rights, 1999-2002; Carnegie lectr. Hague Acad. Internat. Law, 1965; Frankel lectr. U. Houston, 1969; Gottesman lectr. Yeshiva U., 1975; Lockhart lectr. U. Minn. Law Sch., 1976; Francis Biddle lectr. Harvard Law Sch., 1978; lectr. Columbia U., 1979; Sherrill lectr. Yale U. Law Sch., 1981; Jefferson lectr. U. Pa. Law Sch., 1983; Irvine lectr. Cornell U., 1986; disting. lectr. Coll. Physicians and Surgeons, Columbia U., 1988; Solf lectr. Judge Adv. Gen.'s Sch., 1988; Cooley lectr. U. Mich. Law Sch., 1988; White lectr. La. State U., 1989; prin. lectr. The Hague Acad. Internat. Law, 1989; Blaine Sloane lectr. Pace U. Law Sch., 1991; Gerber lectr. U. Md. Law Sch., 1991; Nathanson lectr. law sch. U. San Diego, 1994; Sibley lectr. U. Ga. Law Sch., 1994; Brandeis lectr. Israel Acad. Sciences and Humanities, 1994; Phi Kappa Phi lectr., James Madison U., 1996, Doris & A. Leo Levin lectr. Bar Ilan U., Israel, 1996; cons. to govt., pres. U.S. Inst. Human Rights, 1970-93, Robert L. Levine lectr. Fordham Law Sch.; chief reporter Am. Law Inst., Restatement of the Law (3d), Fgn. Rels. Law of the U.S., 1979-87; bd. dirs. Lawyers Com. Human Rights, Immigration and Refugee Svcs. America, v.p., 1994-2010; pres. American Soc. Internat. Law, 1992-94; vis. prof. law U. Pa., 1957-58; mem. human rights com. Internat. Covenant Civil and Polit. Rights, 2000-02. Author: Arms Control and Inspection in American Law, 1958, The Berlin Crisis and the United Nations, 1959, Disarmament: The Lawyer's Interests, 1964, Law for the Sea's Mineral Resources, 1968, Foreign Affairs and the Constitution, 1972, 2nd edit., 1996, The Rights of Man Today, 1978, How Nations Behave: Law and Foreign Policy, 2nd edit., 1979; (with others) Human Rights in Contemporary China, 1986, Right v. Might: International Law and the Use of Force, 1989, 2nd edit., 1991, The Age of Rights, 1990, Constitutionalism, Democracy and Foreign Affairs, 1990, International Law: Politics and Values, 1995; editor: Arms Control: Issues for the Public, 1961, (with others) Transnational Law in a Changing Society, 1972, World Politics and the Jewish Condition, 1972, The International Bill of Rights: The International Covenant of Civil and Political Rights, 1981; (with others) International Law: Cases and Materials, 3d edit., 1993, 4th edit., 2001, Constitutionalism and Rights: The Influence of the United States Constitution Abroad, 1989, Foreign Affairs and the U.S. Constitution, 1990, Human Rights: Cases and Materials, 1999; bd. editors: American Jour. Internat. Law, 1967-2010, co-editor-in-chief, 1978-84; bd editors Ocean Devel. and Internat. Law Jour., 1973-2010, Jerusalem Jour. Internat. Relations, 1976-2010; contbr. articles to profl. jours. Served with AUS, 1941-45. Decorated Silver Star; recipient Law Alumni Medal of Excellence Columbia U. Sch. Law, 1982, Friedmann Meml. award Columbia Soc. Internat. law, 1986, Hudson medal American Soc. Internat. Law, 1995, Leadership in Human Rights award Columbia Human Rights Law Rev., 1995, Human Rights award Lawyers Com. for Human Rights, 1995, Outstanding Rsch. in Law & Govt. award Fellows of American Bar Found., 1997, Stefan Riesenfeld award U. Calif., 2003; Guggenheim fellow, 1979-80; Festschrift (Liber Amicorum): Politics, Values and Functions, Internat. Law in the 21st Century, Essays on Internat. Law in his honor, 1997, Louis Henkin Professorship in Human and Constitutional Rights established in his honor Columbia Law Sch., 1999. Fellow Am. Acad. Arts and Scis.; mem. Coun. Fgn. Rels., American Soc. Internat. Law (v.p. 1975-76, 88-90, pres. 1992-94, hon. v.p. 1994-2010, Goler T. Butcher medal for outstanding contbn. to internat. human rights law 2001), Internat. Law Assn. (v.p. American branch, 1973-2010), American Soc. Polit. and Legal Philosophy (pres. 1985-87), Inst. de Droit Internat., American Polit. Sci. Assn., Internat. Assn. Constl. Law (v.p. 1982-95, hon. pres. 1995-2010), U.S. Assn. Constl. Law (hon. pres. 1997-2010), American Philos. Soc. (Henry M. Phillips prize in jurisprudence 2000). Home: New York, NY. Died Oct. 14, 2010.

HENNION, REEVE LAWRENCE, communications executive; b. Ventura, Calif., Dec. 7, 1941; s. Tom Reeve and Evelyn Edna (Henry) H.; m. Carolyn Laird, Sept. 12, 1964; children: Jeffrey Reeve, Douglas Laird. BA, Stanford U., 1963, MA, 1965. Reporter Tulare (Calif.) Advance-Register, 1960-62; reporter UPI, San Francisco, 1963-66, mgr. Fresno, Calif., 1966-68, regional exec. Los Angeles, 1968-69, mgr. Honolulu, 1969-72, San Francisco, 1972-75, Calif. editor, 1975-77, gen. news editor, 1977-81, bus. mgr., 1981-83, v.p., gen. mgr. Pacific div., 1983-85; v.p., gen. mgr. Calif.-Oreg. Broadcasting, Inc., 1985-86; pres. Viatech Inc., 1986-92; propr. Buncom Ranch; pres. Keypoint Svcs. Internat., Inc., Medford, Oreg., 1992—2002; interim exec. dir. Rogue Valley Coun. of Govts., 1998. Editor: The Modoc Country, 1971, Buncom: Crossroads Station, 1995. Chmn. Calif. Freedom of Info. Com., 1983-84; chair Jackson County Planning Commn.; mayor of Buncom, Oreg.; pres. Buncom Hist. Soc.; active Rogue C.C. Found. Bd. Mem. Am. Planning Assn., Delta Kappa Epsilon. Home: Jacksonville, Oreg. Died July 9, 2009.

HENRIKSEN, MELVIN, mathematician, educator; b. NYC, Feb. 23, 1927; s. Kaj and Helen (Kahn) Henriksen; m. Lillian Viola Hill, July 23, 1946 (div. 1964); children: Susan, Richard, Thomas; m. Louise Levitas, June 12, 1964 (dec. Oct. 1997). BS, Coll. City N.Y., 1948; MS, U. Wis., 1949, PhD in Math, 1951. Asst. math., then instr. extension div. U. Wis., 1948-51; asst. prof. U. Ala., 1951-52; from instr. to prof. math. Purdue U., 1952-65; prof. math., head dept. Case Inst. Tech., 1965-68; research assoc. U. Calif. at Berkeley, 1968-69; prof., chmn. math. dept. Harvey Mudd Coll., 1969-72, prof., 1972-97, prof. emeritus, from 1997. Mem. Inst. Advanced Study, Princeton, 1956-57, 63-64; vis. prof. Wayne State U., 1960-61; rsch. assoc. U. Man., Winnipeg, Can., 1975-76; vis. prof. Wesleyan U., Middletown, Conn., 1978-79, 82-83, 86-87, 93-94. Author: (with Milton Lees) Single Variable Calculus, 1970; assoc. editor: Algebra Universalis, 1993—2008, Topology Atlas, 1996-2002, Topological Commentary, 1996-2002; mem. editl. bd. Functiones et Approximatio Commentario Mathematici, 2001-06; author articles on algebra, rings of functions, gen. topology. Sloan fellow, 1956—58. Mem. Am. Math. Soc., Math. Assn. Am. (assoc. editor Am. Math. monthly 1988-91, assoc. editor Algebra Universalis 1993-2008). Home: Claremont, Calif. Died Oct. 15, 2009.

HENRY, EDWARD FRANK, retired data processing executive; b. East Cleveland, Ohio, Mar. 18, 1923; s. Edward Emerson and Mildred Adelia (Kulow) H.; m. Nicole Annette Peth, June 18, 1977. BBA, Dyke Coll., 1948; postgrad., Case Western Reserve U., 1949, Cleve. Inst. Music, 1972. Internal auditor E.F. Hauserman Co., 1948-51; sales and radio announcer Sta. WSRS, 1951; office mgr. Frank C. Grismer Co., 1951-52, Broadway Buick Co., 1952-55; sec., treas. Commerce Ford Sales Co., 1955-65; nat. mgr. Auto Acctg. divsn. United Data Processing Co., Cin., 1966-68; v.p. Auto Data Sys. Co., Cleve., 1968-70; pres. Profl. Mgmt. Computer Sys., Inc., Cleve., 1970—2003, Profl. Mgmt. Computer Sys. Became Internat., 1999—2003, ComputerEASE, Small Bus. Computer Ctrs. divsn. Profl. Mgmt. Computer Sys., Inc., 1985—2003, VideoEASE CompuAIDE Computerized Video Rental Sys. divsn. Profl. Mgmt. Computer Systems, Inc., 1987-89; pres. CompuPRINT divsn. Profl. Mgmt. Computer Sys., Inc., 1995—2003, pres. TravelEASE divsn., 1996—2002; ret., 2007. Drum maj., musician Wurlitzer Marching Band, Cleve., 1939—42, The Ed Henry Dance Band, 1939—42; with USAF Marching Band, Kearns, Utah, 1943; dramatic dir., actor Euclid Little Theatres, Jewish Cmty. Ctr.; actor Cleve. Playhouse, 1961—63; dramatic dir., actor various other theatres; exec. artistic dir. NorthCoast Cultural Ctr., from 1989. Contbr. photography, Travel Agents Internat. mag., 1990 (hon. mention, 1990); prodr., dir. (Jesters) (plays) National Book of the Play Acapulco, Mexico, 1985, nat. prodr., dir. (Jesters) Nat. Book of the Play Reno, from 1988, Bally's Celebrity Rm., Las Vegas, 1989—96, Hyatt Regency O'Hare, 1998, Millennium, 2000, Nat. Book of the Play Bally's Las Vegas. Charter pres. No. Ohio Coun. Little Theatre, 1954—56; founder, artistic and mng. dir. Exptl. Theatre, Cleve., 1959—63; bd. dirs. Cleve. Philharm. Orch., 1972—74, Cleve. Jazz Orch., 1991—2006, Cleve. Opera League, Back on Board, 2002. 1st lt. USAF, 1943—46, PTO, capt. USAF, 1946—58, capt. USAFR, 1995. Decorated Bronze Star with 3 oak leaf clusters; recipient Best Photos & Photographers award, Internat. Libr. Photography, Owings Mills, Md., 2007; named and featured in publ. book Showtime in Cleveland: The Rise of A Regional Theater Center (John Vacha). Mem.: APA, Internat. Lib. Photography (Top Six Best Photos and Photographers 2007), Res. Officers Assn., Internat. Soc. Photographers (Silver award bowl 2006, Bronze Commemorative award 2006), Associated Photographers Internat., Internat. Platform Assn., Am. Soc. Profl. Cons., Nat. Assn. Profl. Cons., Data Processing Mgmt. Assn., Mil. Order World Wars (comdr. Cleve. chpt. 1994—95, dept. comdr. State of Ohio from 2001, adjutant from 2001, nat. staff mem. from 2003), Inst. Mgmt. Accts., Am. Mgmt. Assn., Air Force Assn. (life), Art Inst. Chgo., Cleve. Mus. Art, Mayfield Area C. of C., Ky. Cols., Nat. Assn. Met. Mus. Art of N.Y., Rotary, Hermit Club, Acacia Country Club, Univ. Club, Deep Springs Trout Club, Cleve. Grays Club, Jesters (dramatic dir. from 1971, dir. 1981, impresario 1984—99, impresario emertus 2000, Cleve. Ct. # 14, SOBIB, Kachina, dir. emeritus 2007), Grotto, Cuyahoga County Meml. Lodge (worshipful master 1993—94), Heroes of '76 (comdr. Cleve. 1977), KT, VFW, Am. Legion, Masons (60 yr. honor 2004, hon. 33d degree), Sojourners (Nat. President's cert. 1977—78, pres. Cleve. chpt. #23 1978), DeMolay (master Cleve. chpt. 1942, Legion of Honor 1970), Scottish Rite (dramatic dir. from 1967, thrice potent master 1982—84, class named in his hon. 1994), Shriners (dramatic dir. 1968—88), Phi Kappa Gamma (charter pres., past nat. pres.). Republican. Presbyterian. Home: Gates Mills, Ohio. Died Oct. 19, 2009.

HENRY, JOHN BERNARD, pathologist, educator, academic administrator; b. Elmira, NY, Apr. 26, 1928; m. Georgette Boughton, June 10, 1953; children: Maureen Anne, Julie Patricia, William Bernard, Paul Bernard, John Bernard, Thomas David. AB, Cornell U., 1951; MD, U. Rochester, 1955. Diplomate: Am. Bd. Pathology (v.p. 1974-75, 76-79, pres. 1976-78, trustee). Intern ward med. service Barnes Hosp., St. Louis, 1955-56; resident pathology Presbyn. Hosp., NYC, 1956-58, New Eng. Deaconess Hosp., Boston, 1958-60; trainee Nat. Cancer Inst., NIH, 1958-60; clin. pathologist, chmn. clin. lab. com., dir. Blood Bank and Clin. Labs. Teaching Hosp. and Clinic, U. Fla., 1960-64; asst. medicine Washington U. Sch. Medicine, St. Louis, 1955-56; asst. pathology, then instr. pathology Columbia Coll. Phys. and Surg., 1956-58; teaching fellow pathology Harvard U. Med. Sch., 1959-60; asst. prof., then asso. prof. pathology U. Fla. Coll. Medicine, 1960-64; prof. pathology Coll. Medicine; dir. clin. pathology SUNY, Upstate, Syracuse, 1964-79; dean Coll. Health Related Professions SUNY Upstate Med Ctr., 1971-77; dean, prof. pathology Georgetown U. Sch. Medicine, Washington, 1979-84; pres. SUNY Upstate Med. U., Syracuse, 1985-92, prof. pathology, past pres., from 1992. Author numerous articles on chemistry, med. edn. and immunopathology field. Bd. dirs. FACT, 1985-90. With USN, 1946-48, capt. USNR, 1967-95. Recipient S.C. Dyke Founder award Assn. Clin. Pathologists, 1979. Fellow Coll. Am. Pathologist, Am. Soc. Clin. Pathologists (bd. dirs. 1974-82, pres. 1980-81, Distinguished Serv. Clin. Pathology award 1993), Am. Coll. Physician Execs.; mem. AMA, AAAS, Am. Blood Commn. (pres. 1978-80), Am. Assn. Blood Banks (pres.), Am. Assn. Clin. Chemists, Assn. Am. Med. Colls., Am. Assn. Pathologists, Am. Soc. Histocompatibility and Immunogenetics, Internat. Soc. Blood Transfusion, Soc. Med. Consultants to Armed Forces, Med. Soc. D.C. (exec. bd. 1982-84), CAP (chmn. future tech. com. 1985-92, bd. dirs. council on edn. and pubs. 1986-92), Onondaga Med. Soc. (bd. dirs.), Alpha Omega Alpha. Died Apr. 10, 2009.

HENSON, RAY DAVID, law educator, consultant; b. Johnston City, Ill., July 24, 1924; s. Ray David and Lucile (Bell) Henson. BS, U. Ill., 1947, JD, 1949. Bar: Ill. 1950, U.S. Supreme Ct. 1960. Assoc. CNA Fin. Corp., Chgo., 1952-70; prof. law Wayne State U., 1970-75, Hastings Sch. Law, U. Calif., San Francisco, 1975—95, prof. emeritus, from 1995. Author: Landmarks of Law, 1960, Secured Transactions, 1973, 2d edit., 1979, Documents of Title, 1983, 2d edit., 1990, The Law of Sales, 1985, others; editor: The Business Lawyer, 1967-68; contbr. numerous articles to law revs. Mem. legal adv. com. N.Y. Stock Exch., 1971-75. Served with USAAC, 1943-46. Mem. Am. Law Inst. (life), ABA (chmn. bus. law sect. 1969-70, adv. bd. jour. 1974-80, chmn. uniform comml. code com.), Ill. Bar Assn. (chmn. corp. banking and bus. law sect. 1963-65, chmn. uniform comml. code com.), Chgo. Bar Assn. (chmn. uniform comml. code com.). Home: San Francisco, Calif. Died Mar. 7, 2009.

HERBERT, CHARLES EMMET, architect; b. Chgo., Oct. 16, 1925; s. Frank Arthur and Ella (St. Germain) H.; m. Adrienne Rickerd, Dec. 27, 1950; children: Jeffrey, Christopher, Peter (dec.), Timothy, Matthew, Charles II. BArch, Iowa State U., 1951. Registered architect. Intern architect John Flad & Assocs., Madison, Wis., 1953-57; ptnr. Karl Keffer Assocs., Atherton Dean Herbert, Des Moines, 1957-61; pres. Charles Herbert & Assocs., Des Moines, 1961-87, Herbert Lewis Kruse Blunck, Des Moines, from 1987. Trustee, sec. Des Moines Art Ctr., 1968-80, v.p., pres., 1982—; bd. govs. Iowa State U., Ames, 1985—. Served with USNR, 1944-47. Recipient Profl. Achievement Citiation Iowa State U., 1975, Christian Petersen Design award Iowa State U., 1985. Fellow AIA (juror nat. awards 1979, juror design awards, 40 design awards Cen. States region, 57 design awards Iowa chpt.). Clubs: Wakonda (bd. dirs. 1973-76), Des Moines. Republican. Episcopalian. Home: Des Moines, Iowa. Died Apr. 24, 2010.

HERGERT, LOUIS GEORGE, JR., computer company executive; b. Bridgeville, Pa., Nov. 16, 1927; s. Louis George and Irma (Delphus) H.; m. Donna Sue Kephart, June 9, 1956; children: Louis George III, Paul Donald. BS in Mil. Engring., U.S. Mil. Acad., West Point, NY, 1950; MA in Bus. Stats., U. Ala., Tuscaloosa, 1962. Commd. 2d lt. U.S. Army, 1950, advanced through grades to col., ret., 1975; from staff v.p. to group sr. v.p. Sci. Applications Internat. Corp., Huntsville, Ala., from 1975. Pres. West Point Soc. of the Tenn. Valley, 1976—. Mem. Assn. U.S. Army, Flint Farm Club (pres. 1986—). Republican. Roman Catholic. Avocations: hunting, golf. Home: Huntsville, Ala. Died Sept. 11, 2009.

HERMANN, PHILIP J., lawyer; b. Cleve., Sept. 17, 1916; s. Isadore and Gazella (Gross) H.; m. Cecilia Alexander, Dec. 28, 1945; children: Gary, Ann. Student, Hiram Coll., 1935-37; BA, Ohio State U., 1939; JD, Western Res. U., 1942. Bar: Ohio 1942. With Hermann Cahn & Schneider and predecessors, Cleve., 1946-86. Founder, former chmn. bd. Jury Verdict Rsch., Cleve.; pres. Legal Info. Pubs. Author: 1956, Better Settlements Through Leverage, 1965, Do You Need a Lawyer?, 1980, Better, Earlier Settlements through Economic Leverage, 1989, Injured? How to Get All the Money You Deserve, 1990, The 96 Billion Dollar Game: You are Losing, 1993, How to Select Competent Cost-effective Legal Counsel, 1993, Profit With the Right Lawyer, I Was Raised by a St. Bernard, 2003; contbr. articles to profl. jours. Served to lt. comdr. USNR, 1942-46, PTO. Mem. ABA (past vice chmn. casualty law com., past chmn. use of modern tech. com.), Ohio Bar Assn. (past chmn. ins. com., past chmn. fed. ct. com., past mem. ho. of dels.), Cleve. Bar Assn. (past chmn. membership com.), Am. Law Firm Assn. (past chmn. bd.), Fedn. Ins. Counsel. Died July 16, 2009.

HERMANN, THOMAS GEORGE, lawyer; b. Cleve., June 15, 1935; s. George James and Elizabeth Virginia (Kreckel) Hermann. AB, John Carroll U., Cleve., 1963; JD, Cleve. State U., 1969. Bar: Ohio 1969, US Dist. Ct. (no. dist.) Ohio 1970, US Ct. Appeals (6th cir.) 1971, NY 1986, US Dist. Ct. (so. dist.) NY 1986, US Dist. Ct.(ea. dist) Mich. 1993. Atty. Legal Aid Soc. Cleve., 1969—70; assoc. Squire, Sanders & Dempsey, Cleve., 1970—79; dir. Toxic Tort Def. Group, from 1980; lectr. seminars Cleve. Advocacy Inst., life mem. 8th jud. conf., 1987—95; mem. com. ct. tech. Ohio Supreme Ct., 1988—94. Served with USAR, 1954—57. Recipient Merit Svc. award, Bar Assn. Greater Cleve., 1981—82, Project award, ABA-AMA, 1982, Exceptional Performance award, Def. Rsch. Inst., 1982. Mem.: ABA (chmn. law office tech. com. 1982—88, chmn. tech. legal practive & jud. sys. divsn. 1988—92, sec. 1994—95, vice-chair from 1995, sect. sci. & tech.), Cleve. Assn. Civil Trial Attys. (pres. 1981—82), Cuyahoga County Bar Assn., Bar Assn. Greater Cleve. (chmn. med.-legal com., chmn. group travel com.). Died Apr. 18, 2010.

HERMANN, WILLIAM HENRY, retired hospital administrator, consultant; b. Hillsboro, Ill., Apr. 6, 1924; s. Fred William and Mearle Hermann (Reinecke) H.; m. Loretta Pfister, July 28, 1956; children— Karen Elise, Diane Ellen. BA, U. Mo., 1951; MS, Yale U., 1953. With Arabian-Am. Oil Co., Dhahran, Saudi Arabia, 1953-58; adminstr. Dhahran Health Ctr., 1956-58; mem. staff Touro Infirmary, New Orleans, 1958-67, dir., 1962-64, exec. dir., 1965-66; coordinator program in hosp. adminstrn. Tulane U. Med. Sch., 1965-68; sr. v.p. Mary I. Bassett Hosp. and Clinics, Cooperstown, N.Y., 1968-90, ret. sr. vp. and now cons., from 1990. Cons. The Clark Found., N.Y.C., 1990—; adj. asst. prof. pub. health and adminstrv. medicine Columbia U. Sch. Medicine; bd. dirs. Cmty. Health Plan, Latham, N.Y.C., 1986-90, Valley Health Svcs., Herkeimer, N.Y. Pres. Templeton Found., Cooperstown; bd. dirs. Clara Welch Thanksgiving Home, Cooperstown, 1975—, Fernleigh Found., N.Y.C., Hospice Inc., Oneonta, N.Y.; vestryman Episcopal Ch. With M.C., USNR, 1945-47. Mem. Am. Coll. Hosp. Adminstrs. (life), Yale Club (N.Y.C.), Pi Kappa Alpha (life). Home: Keene, NH. Died Oct. 20, 2009.

HERRING, BRUCE E., engineering educator; b. Fremont, Ohio, Sept. 6, 1934; s. Harold W. and Eloise E. (Hanson) H.; m. Nancy Jane Kelly, June 9, 1955; children: Melanie Jane Herring Smith, Rylan Bruce. B Indsl. Engring., Ohio State U., 1958; MSME, N.Mex. State U., 1963; PhD, Okla. State U., 1972. Asst. prof. indsl. engring. Auburn (Ala.) U., 1965-73, assoc. prof., 1973-87, prof. indsl. and mfg. engring., 1987-94, prof. emeritus indsl. engring., 1994; ret., 1994. Prof. computer sci. Tuskegee (Ala.) U., 1980-84; cons. various computer applications, 1972—. Author: Project Management Simulator, 1972. Mem. City Coun., Auburn, 1972-76; asst. scoutmaster Boy Scouts Am., Auburn, 1974—; bd. dirs. Auburn Mus. Soc., 1976-92. NSF sci. faculty fellow, 1970; named Outstanding Instr. Indsl. Engring. Student Engring. Coun., Auburn U., 1969-70, 88-89, 92-93, Birdsong laureate, 1994. Mem. Am. Inst. Indsl. Engrs., Soc. Computer Simulation. Achievements include development of Ala. Resources Info. System and several other info. systems for state of Ala. and industry. Home: Auburn, Ala. Died June 28, 2010.

HERRMANN, DANIEL ALFRED, retail drug store chain executive; b. Rochester, NY, Sept. 10, 1930; s. Alfred Jospeh and Josephine J. (Wecker) H.; children: Michael, Susan. BS in Pharmacy, U. Buffalo, 1952. Registered pharmacist, N.Y., Mich. Pharmacist, store mgr. Miller Drug Co., Buffalo, 1952-61; v.p. Fay's Drug Co., Syracuse, N.Y., 1961-76, pres., from 1976. Bd. dirs. Syracuse Chiefs Baseball Team, 1979—, sec., 1985—; vice chmn. Hiawatha council boy Scouts Am., Syracuse, 1982-83, pres., 1985. Mem. Affiliated Drug Stores Inc. (chmn. 1982-83), Nat. Assn. Chain Drug Stores, Better Bus. Bur. Central N.Y. (chmn. 1978-81) Clubs: Cavalry Country. Republican. Presbyterian. Home: Syracuse, NY. Died Jan. 19, 2010.

HERSHBERGER, ROBERT DEAN, manufacturing executive; b. Canton, Ohio, Oct. 15, 1934; s. Lloyd George and Cora Ann (Hosttler) H.; m. Barbara Boyd, Aug. 15, 1958 (div. 1968); children: Robert, Debra, Barbara; m. Renee McClahra, Mar. 18, 1969 (dec.); children: Jeffrey, Jennifer. BS, Morris Harvey U., 1956; postgrad., U. Mich., 1970—72. Dept. mgr. Goodyear Aerospace Co., Akron, Ohio, 1965—69; prodn. mgr. Ohio Match Co., Wadsworth, 1969—73; plant engr. New Systems Inc., Petersburg, Va., 1973—75; asst. plant mgr. Faultless Rubber Co., Ashland, Ohio, 1975—80; v.p. mfg. Polytechniques Inc., Solon, Ohio, from 1980. Patentee variable speed drive, mold cleaning agt. Mem. Wadsworth C. of C. Mem.: Airplane Owners and Pilots Assn., Ohio Pilots Assn., Elks Club, Masons. Republican. Lutheran. Home: Canton, Ohio. Died Jan. 19, 2009.

HERSHER, KURT BERNARD, building materials executive; b. Fed. Republic Germany, Apr. 4, 1928; came to U.S., 1938; naturalized, 1943; s. Bernard and Elsa (Muenzer) H.; m. Claire Elovitz, Jan. 29, 1956 (div. Mar. 1970); children: Wayne, Terry, Karen; m. Edith Doby, Nov. 1, 1975. BS in Indsl. Engring., Bradley U., 1951. Chief ops. officer Stevenson (Conn.) Lumber Co., 1954-68; pres. chief exec. officer Stelco Industries, Inc., Stevenson, 1968—; pres. Truss-Tech Inc.; dir., co-founder Builders Supply Credit Bur., Bridgeport, 1960-72; bd. dirs. Westport Bank & Trust, Westport Bancorp. Mem. bd. of assocs. U. of Bridgeport, U. Bridgeport Law Sch.; mem. bd. regents Sacred Heart U.; bd. dirs. UJA. With Signal Corps, AUS, 1951-53. Mem. Am. Inst. Indsl. Engrs., Northeast Retail Lumbermens Assn., Fairfield County Home Builders Assn., Monroe (Conn.) C. of C. Home: Easton, Conn. Died Aug. 2, 2009.

HERSTEIN, BARRY STUART, industrial designer; b. Bklyn., Aug. 14, 1942; s. Jesse and Clara H.; B. Indsl. Design, Pratt Inst., Bklyn., 1964; m. Claire Berg, Jan. 23, 1966; children— Robert, James. Product designer Emerson Elec. Co., Prescott, Ariz., 1964-65; dir. research and devel. Emenee Industries, Flushing, N.Y., 1965-69; v.p. research and devel. Buddy L Corp., N.Y.C., 1969-86; v.p. Herstein/Schecterson Inc., N.Y.C., 1986—; lectr. Pratt Phoenix Sch., New Sch. Social Research. Recipient Clio Mag. award, 1979; Creativity award Art Direction Mag., 1979, 80, 87; Addy award, 1980; Potlatch Corp. award, 1981; Mead Paper award, 1981. Mem. Toy Mfrs. Assn., Indsl. Designers Soc. Am. Home: Ringwood, NJ. Died Oct. 1, 2009.

HERZOG, ARTHUR, III, author; b. NYC, Apr. 6, 1927; s. Arthur Jr. and Elizabeth Lindsay (Dayton) H.; 1 son by previous marriage, Matthew Lennox. Student, U. Ariz., 1945-46; BA, Stanford U., 1950; MA, Columbia U., 1956. Editor Fawcett Publs., 1957-59. Cons. Peace Corps, 1967-68; polit. cons., 1969-71; bd. dirs. Leslie Mandel Enterprises, Mandel Airplane Funding and Leasing Co. Author: (with others) Smoking and the Public Interest, 1963, The War-Peace Establishment, 1965, The Church Trap, 1968, McCarthy for President, 1969, The B.S. Factor, 1973, The Swarm, 1974, Earthsound, 1975, Orca, 1977, Heat, 1977, rev. edit., 1989, IQ 83, 1978, Make Us Happy, 1978, Glad to be Here, 1979, Aries Rising, 1981, The Craving, 1982, L.S.I.T.T., 1983, Vesco-From Wall Street to Castro's Cuba, The Rise, Fall and Exile of the King of White Collar Crime, 1987, Takeover, 1987 (formerly L.S.I.T.T.), The Woodchipper Murder, 1989, Seventeen Days: The Katie Beers Story, 1993, How to Write Almost Anything Better and Faster, 1995, Body Parts, 2001, Imortalon, 2003, The Village Buyers, 2003, Icetopia, 2004, The Town That Moved to Mexico, 2004, Murder in Our Town, 2007, (almost all works transl. and published in Hungary); Group shows: The Third State, 2005, Beyond Sci-Fi, 2008; contbr. articles profl. jours. Campaign mgr. Oreg., nat. pub. rels. dir. Eugene McCarthy Presdl. Campaign, 1968; founder New Democratic Coalition, N.Y. and nationally, 1968-69, Lexington Dem. Club, 1974. With USNR, 1944-45. Mem.: PEN, Authors League, Authors Guild, Pigeon Point Club Tobago. Died May 26, 2010.

HERZOG, HAROLD KENNETH, insurance company executive; b. NYC, Feb. 13, 1924; s. Phillip and Lillian (Kronick) H.; m. Elizabeth Ann Huffaker, Dec. 15, 1944. BS, N.Y. U., 1953, MBA, 1959. Acct. N.Y. Life Ins. Co., NYC, 1941-51, fin. analyst, 1952-62, asst. v.p., 1962-66, 2d v.p., 1966-72, v.p. investment dept., 1972-80, sr. v.p. in charge investments, 1980-83, sr. v.p. in charge real estate, 1983-86, sr. v.p. corp. planning, 1986-88; corp. dir. Holly Hill Fruit Products, Davenport, Fla. Bd. dirs. Revco Drug Stores, Twinsburg, Ohio, Sargasso Mut. Ins. Co., Hamilton Bermuda, Med. Liability Mut. Ins. Co. N.Y. Served with U.S. Army, 1943-46. Home: New Canaan, Conn. Died July 17, 2010.

HESELDEN, JOHN EDWARD, communications executive; b. Syracuse, NY, Apr. 11, 1920; s. Thomas M. and Blanche E. (Gaffey) H.; m. Ethel Quackenbush, June 6, 1942; children— Barbara Heselden Smith, Nancy Heselden Kantarian, Carol (dec.) AB, Syracuse U., 1940, M.P.A., 1942. Personnel asst. Atlantic Refining Co., Phila., 1946-47; asst. to exec. sec. N.Y. State Pubs. Assn., Syracuse, 1947-53; advt. dir. Geneva Daily Times, N.Y., 1953-55; corp. staff positions Gannett Corp., Rochester, N.Y., 1955-63, 66-68; pub. Plainfield Courier-News, N.J., 1964-65; gen. mgr. Gannett Rochester Newspapers, 1970-71; v.p. personnel Gannett Co., Inc., Rochester, 1972-74, sr. v.p. staff and services, 1975-78, sr. v.p. mktg., 1978-79, sr. v.p. and pres. newspaper div., 1979—, also dir.; dir. Newspaper Advt. Bur., from 1978. Trustee, Frank E. Gannett Newspaper Found., 1967—, N.Y. State Newspapers Found., 1977—, Rochester Inst. Tech., 1979—, Rochester Mus. and Sci. Ctr., 1980—. Served from 2d lt. to maj. USAAF, 1942-46; to lt. col. Res. (ret.) Mem. N.Y. State Pubs. Assn. (pres. 1977), Phi Beta Kappa, Sigma Delta Chi, Sigma Phi Epsilon Clubs: Country of Rochester, Oak Hill Country (Rochester). Presbyterian. Home: Towson, Md. Died Apr. 1, 2009.

HESLING, DONALD MILLS, consulting engineer; b. Dubuque, Iowa, Nov. 3, 1914; s. Francis J. and Mae L. (Mills) H.; m. Rheata E. Peterson, Apr. 2, 1945; children: Donald, Christine, Mary, Carol, Joanne, Terry, Judy, David, Debra, Patrice, Daniel, Dennis, Thomas. Student, Muskegon Community Coll., Mich., 1934-36, U. Mich., 1936-37. With Sealed Power Corp., Muskegon, from 1946, mgr. mfg. engring., then v.p. mfg. engring., 1952-57, v.p. research engring., 1957-80; cons. engr., from 1980. Contbr. articles to profl. jours. Mem. IEEE, AIM, Am. Mgmt. Assn., Am. Ordnance Assn., Nat. Bus. Aircraft Assn., Soc. Automotive Engrs., Serra Internat. Roman Catholic. Home: Lansing, Mich. Died Apr. 16, 2009.

HESSON, PAUL ANTHONY, architect; b. Luck, Wis., Sept. 4, 1923; s. Lynn James and Clara Ann (Paulson) Hesson; m. Margaret June Lovaas, Apr. 6, 1942; children: Kathi Lyn Hesson Curtis, Paula Diane Hesson Dove. BArch, U. Minn., 1949. Registered arch. Tex., La., Okla. Intern architect Perry Crosier Assoc., Mpls., 1950—51, Hal Fridlund Assoc., 1951—52; arch. Cerf Ross Assoc., San Antonio, 1952—53; ptnr. Hesson & May Assoc., 1953—83; pres. Hesson, Andrew, Sotomayor, San Antonio, from 1983. Dir. Comml. Nat. Bank. Bd. dirs. North San Antonio C. of C., from 1981. Cpl. USAAF, 1942—45. Mem.: AIA, Tex. Bd. Archtl. Examiners, Nat. Coun. Archtl. Registration Bds., Greater San Antonio C. of C., Petroleum Club, San Antonio Country Club, Kiwanis Lodge. Republican. Avocations: flying, travel, golf. Home: San Antonio, Tex. Died Apr. 30, 2010.

HIBBARD, WALTER ROLLO, JR., retired engineering educator; b. Bridgeport, Conn., Jan. 20, 1918; s. Walter R. and Helen S. (Kenworthy) H.; m. Charlotte H. Tracy, Mar. 21, 1942 (dec. 1970); children: Douglas, Lawrence, Diana; m. Louise A. Brembeck, Jan. 29, 1972. AB, Wesleyan U., 1939; DEng, Yale U., 1942; LLD (hon.), Mich. Tech. U., 1968; DEng (hon.), Mont. Coll. Mineral Scis. and Tech., 1970. Asst., then assoc. prof. Yale U., New Haven, 1946-51; rsch. assoc., then mgr. metallurgy and ceramics GE Rsch. Lab., Schenectady, NY, 1951-65; dir. U.S. Bur. Mines, Washington, 1965-68; v.p. Owens Corning Fiberglas Corp., 1968-74; prof. engring. Va. Poly Inst. and State U., Blacksburg, 1974-87, prof. emeritus, from 1987. Dir. Va. Ctr. for Coal and Energy Research, Blacksburg, 1977-87. Contbr. numerous articles to profl. publs. Lt. comdr. USNR, 1942-46. Recipient Yale U. Engring. Alumni award, 1955, Wesleyan U. Disting. Alumnus award, 1979. Mem. AIME (R.W. Raymond award 1950, J. Douglas medal 1969, Mineral Econs. award 1983), Nat. Acad. Engring., Am. Soc. Metals, Am. Ceramic Soc. Home: Saint Augustine, Fla. Died Feb. 24, 2010.

HIBEL, BERNARD, financial consultant, former apparel company executive; b. NYC, Dec. 22, 1916; s. Jacob and Leah (Singer) H.; m. Annette; children: Laurel, Karen, Miriam; adopted children: Michael Weiser, Scott Weiser, John Weiser. BBA magna cum laude, St. John's U., 1937. C.P.A. Mng. exec. charge contract termination Cleve. Ordnance Dist., 1945-46; mng. acct. Bernard M. Joffe & Co., NYC, 1946-48, Aronson & Oresman (C.P.A.s.), NYC, 1948-55; exec. v.p. Kayser-Roth Corp., NYC, 1975-81, also dir.; cons., from 1982. Tchr. acctg. Bklyn. Coll., U.S. Army. Bd. dirs. Miss Universe Beauty Pageant. With AUS, 1943-45. Decorated Bronze Star Mem. Am. Inst. C.P.A.s, N.Y. State Soc. C.P.A.s. Home: New York, NY. Died Sept. 20, 2009.

HICKEL, WALTER JOSEPH, retired investment company executive, foundation administrator, former United States Secretary of the Interior, former governor of Alaska; b. Claflin, Kans., Aug. 18, 1919; s. Robert A. and Emma (Zecha) H.; m. Janice Cannon, Sept. 22, 1941 (dec. Aug. 1943); 1 child, Theodore; m. Ermalee Strutz, Nov. 22, 1945; children: Ted, Robert, Walter Jr., Jack, Joseph, Karl. DEng (hon.), Stevens Inst. Tech., 1970, Mich. Tech. U., 1973; LLD (hon.), St. Mary of Plains Coll., 1970, St. Martin's Coll., 1971, U. Md., Adelphi U., 1971, U. San Diego, 1972, Rensselaer Poly. Inst., 1973, U. Alaska, 1976, Alaska Pacific U., 1991, Benedictine Coll., Kans., 2003; D in Pub. Adminstrn. (hon.), Willamette U., 1971. Founder Hickel Investment Co., Anchorage, 1947—2007; gov. State of Alaska, Alaska, 1966—68, 1990—94; sec. US Dept. Interior, 1969-70; founder Inst. of the North, from 1995; sec. gen. The Northern Forum with Arctic and Sub-Arctic Regional Govts., 1994. Nominated for pres. at Rep. Nat. Convention, 1968, del., 68, 72, 76; founder Commonwealth North, 1979; co-founder Yukon Pacific Corp. Author: Who Owns America?, 1971, Crisis in the Commons: The Alaska Solution, 2002; contbr. articles to newspapers. Mem. Rep. Nat. Com., 1954-64; bd. dirs. Salk Inst., 1972-79, NASA Adv. Coun. Exploration Task Force, 1989-91; USAR amb. representing Alaska. Named Alaskan of Year, 1969, Man of Yr. Ripon Soc., 1970; recipient DeSmet medal Gonzaga U., 1969, Horatio Alger award, Am. Schools & Colleges Assn., 1972, Grand Cordon of the Order of Sacred Treasure award, His Imperial Majesty the Emperor of Japan, 1988. Mem. Pioneers of Alaska, Equestrian Order Holy Sepulchre, KC. Democrat. Roman Catholic. Home: Anchorage, Alaska. Died May 7, 2010.

HICKLER, ROGER BALDWIN, physician, cardiologist, educator; b. Medford, Mass., Oct. 26, 1925; s. Walter Rol and Rosalie Baldwin (Dunlap) H.; m. Dorothy Masterton, July 27, 1974; children— Luisa, Mathew, Sarah, Samuel. Student, M.I.T., 1943-45; MD, Harvard U., 1949. Diplomate: Am. Bd. Internal Medicine. Intern Peter Bent Brigham Hosp., Boston, 1949-50, resident, 1952-54; practice medicine, specializing in internal medicine Worcester, Mass., from 1971; dir. hypertension unit Peter Bent Brigham Hosp., 1961-69; chief of medicine Framingham Union Hosp., 1969-71; prof., chmn. dept. medicine U. Mass. Med. Sch., 1971-77; Lamar Soutter Disting. prof. medicine, dir. unit for study of aging Med. Center, from 1977. Contbr. articles to med. jours. Served with USNR, 1950-52. Recipient Research Career award NIH, 1961-66; investigator Howard Hughes Med. Inst., 1966-69 Fellow A.C.P., Am. Coll. Cardiology; mem. Am. Soc. Clin. Investigation, Am. Heart Assn. (adv. bd. Council for High Blood Pressure Research), Nat. Hypertension Council (adv. council) Unitarian Universalist. Home: Lunenburg, Mass. Died Mar. 2, 2010.

HICKOK, ROBERT LYMAN, JR., electrophysics educator; b. Feb. 25, 1929; s. Robert Lyman and Nellie (Williams) Hickok; m. Rose Marie Kapusta, June 12, 1949; children:

Robert, Susan, Sandra. BS, Rensselaer Poly. Inst., 1951; MA, Dartmouth Coll., 1953; PhD, Rensselaer Poly. Inst., 1956. Postdoc. fellow Yale U., 1956—58; rsch. physicist Mobil R & D Corp., 1958—60, sr. rsch. physicist, 1960—65, rsch. assoc., 1965—71; assoc. prof. electrophysics Rensselaer Poly. Inst., Troy, NY, 1971—74, prof., 1974—93, prof. emeritus, from 1994. Fellow: IEEE, Am Phys. Soc.; mem.: U. Fusion Assn. Home: Potomac, Md. Died Apr. 15, 2009.

HIGGINS, ANNE VOLZ, presidential assistant; b. NYC, Oct. 7, 1939; m. George B. Higgins, 1968 (dec. 2003) BA, George Washington U., 1974. Exec. sec. Office of Richard Nixon, NYC, 1965-69; staff asst. to Pres. The White House; dep. dir. corr., dir. Office of Presdl. Corr., Washington, 1969-77; mem. ad hoc Com. in Def. of Life, Washington, 1977-78, 79-80; exec. dir. Americans for Constl. Conv., Washington, 1978-79; spl. asst. to pres. for correspondence The White House, Washington, 1981—88; co-founder Higgins & Associates, 1988—2010. Died Aug. 12, 2010.

HIGGINS, SISTER THERESE, literature educator, former college president; b. Winthrop, Mass., Sept. 29, 1925; d. James C. and Margaret M. (Lennon) Higgins. AB cum laude, Regis Coll., 1947; MA, Boston Coll., 1959, DHL, 1993; PhD, U. Wis., 1963; DHL, Emmanuel Coll., 1977, Lesley Coll., 1991; postgrad. in lit. and theology, Harvard U., 1965-66; LLD (hon.), Northeastern U., 1982, Bentley Coll., 1992, Regis Coll., 1994. Joined Congregation of Sisters of St. Joseph, Roman Cath. Ch., 1947; asst. prof. English, Regis Coll., Weston, Mass., 1963-65, asst. prof., 1965-67, assoc. prof. English lit., from 1968, pres., 1974-92, also trustee, v.p. devel., 2003—05; cons., 1995—2010. Book reviewer Boston Globe, 1965—2010. Trustee Waltham (Mass.) Hosp., 1978—85, Cardinal Spellman Philatelic Mus., 1976—92; mem. Mass. Gov.'s Commn. on Status Women, 1977—79. U. Wis. rsch. grantee Eng. Mem. Nat. Cath. Ednl. Assn., AAUW, MLA, AAUP, Assn. Ind. Colls. and Univs. Mass. (exec. com.), New Eng. Colls. Fund, NEASC (commn.). Died Feb. 21, 2010.

HIGGINS, WILLIAM ROBERT, college administrator; b. Gaffney, SC, Jan. 28, 1938; s. James Thomas and Willie Davis Higgins; m. Eva Poythress, Sept. 3, 1966; children: Mirabeau B.L., Randle W. BA, U. S.C., 1959, MA, 1967; PhD, Duke U., 1970. Assoc. prof. Murray (Ky.) State U., 1968-75; producer, dir. History in TV, Balt., 1975-77; dir. ops. Coun. of Original 13 States, Alexandria, Va., 1977-83; pres. Southeastern U., Washington, from 1984. Author: American Revolution in the South, 1979. Recipient Program Devel. award NEH, 1977-80, Pub. Media award, 1975-77, Sr. Fellow award, 1973-74, Vis. Fellow award Johns Hopkins U., 1975-77, Fellow in Humanities award IBM, 1966-67. Episcopal. Home: Baltimore, Md. Died Feb. 18, 2010.

HIGGINSON, JOHN, retired career officer; b. St. Louis, Oct. 24, 1932; s. John and Clara Elizabeth (Lindemann) H.; married; children: Robert, Mark, Patrick, Paul. BA, St. Mary's U., 1954; BS, Naval Postgrad. Sch., 1966; MS, George Washington U., 1968. Ensign USN, advanced through grades to Rear Adm., ret.; comdr. Helicopter Anti-submarine Squadron 2, 1973-74, Helicopter Anti-submarine Squadron 10, 1976-78, USS Inchon, 1979-80, Amphibious Squadron 7, 1981-83, Amphibious Group 3, 1985, Naval Surface Group, Long Beach, 1986, ret., 1990-92; pres. Long Beach C. of C. Prof. mgmt. Naval War Coll., Newport, R.I. Co-author: Sea and Air, The Marine Environment, 1968, 2nd. edit., 1973. Bd. dirs. United Way, LA, Long Beach Symphony, Long Beach Youth Activities, DARE, Inc., Leadership Long Beach, St. Mary's Med. Ctr.; trustee Long Beach City Coll. Found.; dir. Internat. City Theater, Arts Coun. for Long Beach; exec. bd. Long Beach coun. Boy Scouts of Am.; trustee The Pacific; exec. coun. Industry-Edn. Coun. Calif.; former chmn. LA Combined Fed. Campaign; pres., CEO Am. Gold Star Manor Charitable Trust, 1993-2008. Mem. Navy Helicopter Assn. (former pres.), Fed. Exec. Bd. (former chmn.), Rotary (commr. Calif., mem. Vets. Meml. Commn.), Housing Opportunities Program for Elderly, (pres., 2007-). Home: Long Beach, Calif. Died Jan. 12, 2010.

HIGHSMITH, HUGH PURCELL, retail executive; b. Flat Rock, Ill., June 22, 1914; s. Harry Johnson and Fannye Ellen (Purcell) H.; m. Doris Mary Morter, Apr. 15, 1944; children: William M., Duncan J., Ralph Tod. BS, Ind. U., 1936. Account exec. Western Advt. Agy., Racine, Wis., 1938—45; pres. Nat. Agrl. Supply Co., Ft. Atkinson, Wis., 1946—56; editor, pub. Farmer's Digest, Ft. Atkinson, 1956—68; pres. Highsmith Co., Ft. Atkinson, 1956—87, Rolamech Co., Inc., Scottsdale, Ariz., from 1978; chmn. Highsmith Co., from 1987. Recipient Cmty. Svc. award, Ft. Atkinson C. of C., 1975, Outstanding Work in Local History award, State Hist. Soc. of Wis., 1980. Republican. Episcopalian. Home: Fort Atkinson, Wis. Died June 7, 2009.

HILL, DOUGLAS FRANKLIN, rubber company executive; b. Aurora, Ill., Jan. 20, 1933; s. Wayne W. and Edna C. (Browning) H.; m. Shirley M. Ellis, Aug. 3, 1956; children: Geoffry, Mark, Monique. BS, Am. Grad. Sch. Internat. Mgmt., Glendale, Ariz., 1958, Ariz. State U., 1957; postgrad., Stanford U., 1975. Pres. Goodyear Mexico, Mexico City, 1971-74; regional dir. Goodyear Internat. Corp., Akron, Ohio, 1974-79, v.p., 1979-80, exec. v.p., from 1980; v.p. Goodyear Tire & Rubber, Akron, from 1980. Served to cpl. U.S. Army, 1953-54, ETO. Mem.: Fairlawn Country (Akron). Republican. Methodist. Home: Akron, Ohio. Died June 10, 2010.

HILL, HAROLD NELSON, JR., lawyer; b. Houston, Apr. 26, 1930; s. Harold Nelson and Emolyn Eloise (Geeslin) H.; m. Betty Jane Fell, Aug. 16, 1952; children: Douglas, Nancy. BS in Commerce, Washington and Lee U., Lexington, Va., 1952; PhD, Washington & Lee U., 1981; LL.B., Emory U., 1957, PhD, 1986. Bar: Ga. 1957. Assoc., then partner firm Gambrell, Harlan, Russell, Moye & Richardson, 1957-66; asst. atty. gen. Ga., 1966-68; exec. asst. atty. gen., 1968-72; partner firm Jones, Bird & Howell, 1972-74; assoc. justice Supreme Ct. Ga., 1975-82, chief justice, 1982-86; ptnr. Hurt, Richardson, Garner, Todd & Cadenhead, Atlanta, 1986-92, Judicial Resolutions Inc., Atlanta, 1993-94; of counsel Long, Aldridge & Norman, Atlanta, 1994-95. Author: History of the Supreme Court of Georgia, 1946-1996, 2005. Served with AUS, 1952-54. Fellow Am. Bar Found.; Mem. Am. Law Inst., State Bar Ga., Lawyers Club Atlanta, Old War Horse Lawyers Club. Methodist. Home: Atlanta, Ga. Died July 5, 2010.

HILL, PHILIP BONNER, lawyer; b. Charleston, W.Va., May 1, 1931; AB, Princeton U., 1952; LLB, W.Va. U., 1957. Bar: W.Va. 1957, Iowa 1965. Assoc. Dayton, Campbell & Love, Charleston, 1957—61; ptnr. Porter, Hill, Thomas, Williams & Hubbard, Charleston, 1961—65; v.p. Thomas & Hill, Charleston, 1961—65; assoc. counsel Equitable Life Ins. Co. of Iowa, Des Moines, 1965—68, counsel, 1968—75; ptnr. Riemenschneider, Hanes & Hill, Des Moines, 1975—79, Austin & Gaudineer, Des Moines, 1979—82, Snyder & Hassig, Sistersville and New Martinsville, W.Va., 1982—96, of counsel, 1997—99, Bowles Rice McDavid Graff & Love, LLP, Martinsburg, W.Va., from 2000. Mem. staff W.Va. Law Rev., 1955-57; contbr. articles to profl. jours. Lt. USNR, 1952—54. Fellow W.Va. Bar Found.; mem. ABA (exec. coun. young lawyers sect. 1966-67), W.Va. State Bar (chmn. jr. bar sect. 1961-62, bd. govs. 1989-92), W.Va. Bar Assn. (pres. 1998-99), Iowa State Bar Assn., Assn. Life Ins. Counsel, Am. Judicature Soc., Phi Delta Phi. Home: Shepherdstown, W.Va. Died Nov. 19, 2009.

HILL, WILMER BAILEY, administrative law judge; b. Washington, May 18, 1928; s. Wilmer A. and Matilda F. (Nabor) H.; m. Joan C. Brunelle, June 24, 1967; children: Stuart Michael, Stephen Mark. AB, Dartmouth Coll., 1950; LL.B., JD, Georgetown U., 1953. Bar: D.C. 1956. Sec.-treas., dir. Ames, Hill & Ames, Washington, 1955-81; sole practice Washington, 1981-86; sr. adminstrv. law judge Social Security Adminstrn., Portland, Oreg., from 1986. Vice-pres. Brookdale Citizens Assn., 1975-76. Served with AUS, 1953-55. Mem. Fed. Adminstrn. Law Judges Conf., Assn. Adminstrn. Law Judges, Transp. Lawyers Assn. (pres. 1984-85), Sigma Phi Epsilon, Delta Theta Phi. Clubs: Portland Golf. Republican. Methodist. Home: Beaverton, Oreg. Died Mar. 21, 2010.

HILTS, EARL T., lawyer, government official, educator; b. Ilion, NY, Mar. 31, 1946; stepson Leon Thomas and Gertrude Annette (Daly) Butler; m. Mae Hwa Kim, Apr. 13, 1973; children: Troy Alan, Kimberly Michelle. BS, St. Lawrence U., 1967; JD, Albany Law Sch., 1970. Bar: NY 1972. Gen. atty.-advisor Dept. Army Watervliet Arsenal, N.Y., 1978-80, supervisory atty.-advisor N.Y., 1980-99; ret., 1999; pvt. practice, from 1999. Adj. prof. Schnectady C.C., 1985—, St. Rose Coll., 1999—. Catechism instr. St. Mary's Ch., 1990-92; pee wee football coach, wrestling coach Shenendehowa Sch., 1983-87; little league coach West Crescent Halfmoon Baseball League, 1980-90. Capt. JAGC, U.S. Army, 1972-76. Scholar St. Lawrence U., 1963-67, Albany Law Sch., 1967-70. Mem. N.Y. State Bar Assn., Am. Legion, Pi Mu Epsilon. Republican. Roman Catholic. Died Jan. 27, 2010.

HINKLE, BENNY STEWART, food company executive; b. Blackstar, Ky., May 5, 1942; s. Everett Discel and Mabel Bell (Young) Hinkle; m. Marlene Mary Reichert, July 12, 1966; 1 child, Dawn Michelle. AS, Sinclair Coll., 1967. Cert. comml. pilot Burnside Ott Aviation Sch., Ft. Lauderdale, 67. With Dayton Tire & Rubber, Ohio, 1964—67; pilot Burnside-Ott, Ft. Lauderdale, 1967—69; pilot, ins. sales pilot, ins. sales CUNA Mut. Ins., Madison, Wis., 1969—81; pres. L. J. Products Co., Dayton, from 1981; cons. L. J. Products, Dayton, from 1981. With USAF, 1960—64. Home: Vandalia, Ohio. Died Mar. 25, 2010.

HINOTE, SAMUEL IRA, agricultural company executive; b. Robertsdale, Ala., Aug. 28, 1942; s. Ira NMI and Elodia (Phillips) H.; m. Ann Reinard Alford, June 29, 1968; children: Samuel Clinton, Amy Elizabeth, David Michael. BS, Auburn U., 1965, MS, 1967. Market analyst Con Agra, Inc., Omaha, 1967-69, dir. econ. rsch., 1969-73, gen. mgr. fish products ops., 1970-80; CEO Delta Pride Catfish, Inc., Indianola, Miss., 1980-90; ptnr. Plantation Fisheries, Isola, Miss., 1982, Bayou Fisheries, Choctaw, Miss., from 1983; CEO Hinote Enterprises, Inc., Montrose, Ala., 1990—2010. Dir., mem. exec. com. Peoples Bank of Delta, Indianola, 1986-92, Delta Pride Cathfish Inc., 1980-90; dir. Fishbelt Feeds Inc., Moorhead, Miss., 1990-93, Catfish Farmers Am., Indianola, 1980—, Gt. Am. Foods Corp., Ore City, Tex., 1985-89. Mem. bi-racial com. City of Indianola, 1987-92; mem. adv. bd. Auburn U. Sch. Agr. With USAFR, 1967-73. Mem. Nat. Fish and Seafood Promotional Coun. (vice chmn. 1990-92), Indianola C. of C. (v.p. 1987-88, pres. 1988-89), Rotary (dir. 1987-88). Republican. Baptist. Avocations: hunting, gardening. Home: Montrose, Ala. Died Mar. 6, 2010.

HINSON, DERL JASON, utilities executive; b. Loris, SC, Feb. 2, 1933; s. Ambrose Trenton and Lois (Cox) H.; m. Angelyn Grainger; Angelyn Rene, Penelope Denise. BS in agr. econs., Clemson U., 1959. Staff asst. Pee Dee Electric Co-op, Inc., Darlington, S.C., 1960-67; Gainesville dist. mgr. Jackson Electric Membership Cooperative, Jefferson, Ga., 1967-69; gen. mgr. Morgan County Rural Electric Membership Cooperative, Martinsville, Ind., 1969-74, Lumbee River Electric Membership Cooperative, Red Springs, N.C., 1974-82; v.p. Federated Rural Electric Ins. Corp., Overland Park, Kan., 1983; gen. mgr. 4-County Electric Power Assn., Columbus, Miss., 1983-88; exec. v.p. Ga. Electric Membership Corp. (GEMC), Atlanta, from 1988. Bd. dirs. Ga. Agr. Coun., Co-op Devel. Fedn., Ga. Electrification Coun. Rural Elec. Mgmt. Devel. Coun. Mem. Ga. C. of C. (bd. dirs.), Masons, Rotary. Avocation: golf. Home: Loris, SC. Died Jan. 11, 2009.

HIRSCH, ELEANOR GULBIS, author, editor; b. Chgo., Nov. 26, 1923; d. Christian and Alvine Katherine (Bauman) Gulbis; B.A. in English, U. Ill., 1946; m. Fred W. Hirsch, Apr. 6, 1951; children— Leslie Kathleen, Melanie Ann. With Scott, Foresman and Co., Chgo., 1947-66, project editor, 1961-66; directing editor Ency. Brit. Ednl. Corp., Chgo., 1966-67; mng. editor Lyons and Carnahan, Chgo., 1967-73; editorial dir. Rand McNally, Skokie, Ill., 1973-75; exec. editor Holt, Rinehart and Winston, N.Y.C., 1975-77; editorial v.p. Scott, Foreman & Co., Glenview, Ill., 1977-78; v.p., dir. reading Ginn and Co., Lexington, Mass., 1978-80; author, ednl. cons., 1980—; author: The Principal's Resource, A Handbook, 1982; exec. editor monthly newsletter Principal's Principles, 1982—. Mem. devel. com. Chgo. Met. YWCA, 1981—; adv. bd. Youngperson. Honoree, Salute to Women in Bus., YWCA. Mem. Acad. Women Achievers (charter), Internat. Reading Assn., Nat. Assn. Elem. Sch. Prins., Assn. Supervision and Curriculum Devel., Nat. Council Tchrs. English. Unitarian. Died Aug. 18, 2009.

HIRSCH, ROBERT BRUCE, lawyer; b. Newark, Mar. 28, 1926; s. Henry Beryl and Sophie (Heller) H.; m. Rosalyn M. Marinoff, Dec. 26, 1948 (dec. 2009); children: Noah, Alene, Andrea, Carolyn, Henry. LL.B., George Washington U., 1950. Bar: D.C. 1950. Assoc. Arent, Fox, Kintner Plotkin & Kahn, Washington, 1950-57, ptnr., 1957—97, sr. ptnr., 1997—2010. Bd. dirs. Washington Sch. Psychiatry, Patrons Capital affiliate American Heart Assn.; exec. com. Greater Washington Jewish Cmty. Found.; chair adv. bd. George Washington Law Sch. With USAAF, 1944-46, ETO. Recipient Judge Learned Hand award, American Jewish Com., 2001. Democrat. Avocations: tennis; reading; grandparenting. Home: Washington, DC. Died Mar. 13, 2010.

HIRSCH, STANLEY, engineer; b. NYC, Jan. 22, 1926; s. Charles and Bessie (Reisman) H.; m. Suzanne Hakner, Apr. 6, 1952; children: Richard, Laurie. BAE, NYU, 1948; MBA, Hofsra U., 1963. Mgr. engring. sect. Fairchild Camera & Instrument Co., Syosset, NY, 1955—67; dir. engring. Bulova Watch Co., NYC, 1967—70; pres. Loric Devel. Corp., Hicksville, NY, 1970—74; dir. engring. Standard Motor Products, Inc., Long Island City, NY, from 1974. Patentee in field (4). With USAF, 1944—45. Recipient State scholar, 1952. Mem.: Soc. Automotive Engrs. Republican. Jewish. Died Mar. 6, 2010.

HIRSH, IRA JEAN, retired psychology professor; b. NYC, Feb. 22, 1922; s. Ellis Victor and Ida (Bernstein) H.; m. Shirley Helene Kyle, Mar. 21, 1943; children: Eloise, Richard, Elizabeth, Donald. AB, N.Y. Coll. for Tchrs., 1942; A.M., Northwestern U., 1943; MA, Harvard, 1947, PhD, 1948. Research asst. psycho-acoustic lab. Harvard, Cambridge, Mass., 1946-47; research fellow Harvard U., 1947-51; with Central Inst. for Deaf, St. Louis, 1951—58, asst dir. research, 1958-65, dir., 1965-83, 1992-94; mem. faculty or adminstrn. Washington U., St. Louis, 1951-92, prof. psychology, 1961-92, dean faculty arts and sciences, 1969-73, Mallinckrodt Disting. Univ. prof., 1984-92, prof. emeritus, 1992—2010, chmn. psychology dept., 1983-87. Vis. prof. U. Paris, 1962-63, U. Tsukuba, Japan, 1982; U.S. del Internat. Standards Orgn., 1962-76; mem. Internat. Acoustics Commn., 1969-75; chmn. behavioral scis. and edn. NRC, 1982-87. Author: The Measurement of Hearing, 1952; Contbr. articles to profl. jours. Served with USAAF, 1943-45; Served with AUS, 1945-46. Recipient Biennial award, 1956, Gold medal, 1992 Acoustical Soc. Am., Assn. Honors Am. Speech and Hearing Assn., 1968 Fellow Acoustical Soc. Am. (pres. 1967-68, gold medal 1992), Am. Psychol. Assn., Am. Speech and Hearing Assn. (exec. council 1958-61, 65-68); mem. NAS. Home: Chatham, NY. Died Jan. 12, 2010.

HIRSH, ROBERT LEE, management consultant; b. Bklyn., June 3, 1923; s. Harry L. and Tilly Hirsh; m. Marian Metzger, June 16, 1973; 1 child, Bonny L. Henderson. AA, Valley Forge Mil. Jr. Coll., 1943. Pres. R.L. Hirsh Assocs., Ltd., Bay Shore, NY, from 1956. Editl. cons.: Physicians Mgmt. Mag., 1966—72, Med. World News, 1969—72, Doctors Fin., 1971—72, Med. Econs. Mag., from 1965; editor: Systems for Managing Your Practice, from 1975, Practice Plan, from 1978, Starting Practice in Ob/Gyn, from 1978, OPHLINE, from 1978, Guideline for Starting a Practice in Anesthesiology, 1981, Starting Your Pediatric Practice, 1982, Building Your Orthopedic Practice, 1983, Starting Your Surgical Practice, 1984; contbr. articles to Econs. Mag., tapes to Med. Econs. Cassette Tape Svc., 1974. Civil def. adminstr. Islip Town, Suffolk County, 1953—57; founder, trustee Suffolk County Hearing Ctr., from 1966; mem. Suffolk County County Cmty. Coun., from 1966; campaign chmn. Bay Shore/Brightwaters United Fund, 1966—68, pres., 1969—70; adv. coun. South Side Hosp., from 1976; treas. Sinai Reform Temple, 1962—63. 1st lt. Med. Adminstrv. Corps, 1943—52. Recipient proclamation Robert L. Hirsch Day June 4, Suffolk County Execs., Suffolk County Legis., Town of Islip, 1983. Mem. Med.-Dental Hosp. Burs. Am. (cert., pres. 1978, Mauk and Helrung award 1977, 78), Soc. Profl. Mgmt. Cons. (exec. v.p. 1970), Soc. Profl. Bus. Cons., Internat. Cons. Found., Nat. Secs. Assn. (hon. life, Boss of Yr. award 1966). Republican. Jewish. Home: Key Largo, Fla. Died Aug. 19, 2009.

HOBEN, WILLIAM JOSEPH, dean; b. Hardinsburg, Ky., May 19, 1927; s. William Joseph and Maud H. (Smith) Hoben. BS, U. Dayton, 1950; MBA, Xavier U., 1960. CPA Ohio. Sr. acct. David E. Flagel & Co., Dayton, Ohio, 1952—57; asst. prof. U. Dayton, 1957—59, assoc. prof., asst. dean, 1959—62, acting dean, 1962—63; dean Sch. Bus. Adminstrn., from 1963. Dir. Catholic Telegraph Register, MAP, Inc., Tech., Inc. Pres. and chmn. bd. Teach Fund, Inc., 1960; bd. dirs. SW Ohio chpt. NCCJ, from 1965; trustee Sinclair CC, 1974—80. With USNR, World War II, Korean. Mem.: Ohio Inst. CPAs (dir., com. chmn. Dayton 1960), Columbus C. of C., Dayton C. of C., Am. Mgmt. Assn., Inst.

Internat. Auditors, Ohio Bus. Tchrs. Assn., Nat. Bus. Tchrs. Assn., Nat. Assn. Accts., Rotary (Dayton) Club, Bicycle Club, Racquet Club, Alpha Kappa Psi. Roman Catholic. Died Dec. 2, 2009.

HOCH, RICHARD CLARK, chemical company executive; b. Nazareth, Pa., Oct. 22, 1925; s. Elwood Charles and Nellie Mae (Eichman) H.; m. Edith Lorraine Stowell, June 23, 1951; children: Richard Clark, Pamela Ann. BS in Chemistry, Lehigh U., 1950; attended, Babson Inst. Tech. dir., v.p. Endura Corp., Quakertown, Pa., 1950—59; with W.R. Grace & Co., from 1959; rsch. mgr. Polyfibron div. Endura Products, Quakertown, 1959—62; rsch. mgr. synthetic leather Polyfibron div. Battery Separators and Automotive Products div., Cambridge, Mass., 1962—66; gen. mgr. Endura Products, Quakertown, from 1968, v.p. Polyfibron div., from 1968. Patentee in field. Pres. Quakertown Jaycees, 1954; v.p. Upper Bucks C. of C., 1960—61, Quakertown Planning Commn., 1960—61; bd. dirs. Quakertown Cmty. Hosp., 1969—78, v.p., 1973—78. With AUS, 1943—46. Decorated Purple Heart. Republican. Methodist. Home: Daytona Beach, Fla. Died Feb. 2, 2010.

HOCHMUTH, FRANK WILLIAM, engineer executive, consultant; b. Staunton, Ill., June 11, 1917; s. John C. Hochmuth and Johanna Novak; m. Frances Viola Fraser, July 20, 1946; children: Carol Susan, Patricia JoAnne. BSME, U. Ill., 1941. Registered profl. engr. Maine, Con. Tech. rep. Combustion Engring. Inc., U.S. and Can., 1941-44, design engr. NYC, 1945-47, chief engr. paper, 1948-59, mgr. pulp and paper Windsor, Conn., 1960-68; dir. engring. Combustion Engring. Ltd., Montreal, Que., Can., 1969-75, v.p. engring., 1975-77; pres. Consulting Svcs., Hudson, Que., 1978-79, Holden, Maine, from 1980. Mem. Black Liquor Recovery Boiler Com., 1952-78. Holder 24 U.S. patents. Fellow ASME; mem. NSPE, Tech. Assn. Pulp and Paper Industry, Can. Pulp and Paper Assn. Republican. Avocations: travel, gardening, wood working, mechanical models, fishing. Home: Orono, Maine. Died Aug. 5, 2009.

HOCHSTEIN, PAUL, biochemist; b. NYC, Feb. 7, 1926; s. Samuel and Ida (Leshan) Hochstein; m. Gianna Smith, Mar. 9, 1956; children: Miles, Evon. BS, Rutgers U., 1950; MS, U. Md., 1952, PhD, 1954; PhD (hon.), U. Stockholm, 1986. Postdoc. fellow Nat. Cancer Inst., 1954—57; rsch. assoc. Columbia U., 1957—63; assoc. prof. Duke U., Durham, NC, 1963—69; prof., pharmacology. U. Southern Calif., LA, 1969—80, prof., toxicology and biochemistry, 1980—93, dir., Inst. Toxicology, 1980—93, assoc. dean, 1981—93, disting. prof. emeritus, from 1993. Contbr. articles to sci. profl. jours. With US Army, 1943—46. Recipient Rsch. Career award, NIH, 1965—69. Fellow: The Oxygen Soc.; mem.: Soc. Gen. Physiologists, Am. Soc. Pharmacology and Exptl. Therapeutics, Soc. Toxicology, Am. Soc. Biol. Chemists. Home: Cambria, Calif. Died June 12, 2010.

HODDY, GEORGE WARREN, electric company executive, electrical engineer; b. Columbus, Ohio, Mar. 7, 1905; s. Arthur H. and Mary E. (Lutz) H.; m. Lois L. Mitchell, May 30, 1947; children: John, Peter, Matthew, Elizabeth Hoddy Howe, Rebekah Hoddy Smith, Melissa Hoddy. BEE, Ohio State U., 1926, MEE, 1932; LHD (hon.), Baker Coll., 1991. Elec. engr. Day-Fan Electric Co., Dayton, Ohio, 1926-29, Robbins & Myers, Inc., Springfield, Ohio, 1929-31; chief engr. Pioneer divsn. Master Electric Co., Dayton, 1932-34; v.p., gen. mgr. Redmond Co., Inc., Owosso, Mich., 1934-41; founder, pres., CEO Universal Electric Co., Owosso, 1942-71, chmn. bd. dirs., dir. internat. rels., 1971-79, vice chmn., 1979-85; chmn. Universal Electric Ltd., Gainsboroguh, Eng., 1974-82; chmn., bd. dirs. Am. Universal Electric Ltd., New Delhi, 1962-92; vice chmn., bd. dirs. Intertherm, Inc., 1972-74, chmn., 1974-84; owner, pres. Fiji Marina, LA, 1968-76; pres., bd. dirs. Ventrola Mfg. Co., Owosso, 1968-76. Founder, pres., chmn. Team 21, Inc., 1995—. Patentee in field. Bd. dirs. Mich. Accident Fund, 1945-61, Owosso Cmty. Concert Assn., 1946-53, Shiawassee United Way, 1956-59, Shiawassee County Mental Health Bd., 1963-67, United Cerebral Palsy Assn., 1963-65; trustee Meml. Hosp., Owosso, 1948-84, pres. 1954-58; chmn. Owosso Charter Rev. Commn., 1956-57, Owosso Citizens Savs. Bonds, 1971-80; mem. Owosso Pub. Sch. Bd., 1957-76, pres., 1975-76; trustee Flint Osteo. Hosp., 1985-90, A.M. Bentley Found., Owosso, 1986—; trustee Baker Coll., Flint, Mich., 1985—; regent Baker Coll. of Owosso, 1987—, chmn., 1993—; bd. dirs., pres. Shiawassee Found., 1973-77; trustee, chmn. Shiawassee County Bldg. Authority Comm., Corunna, Mich., 1986-95; mem. Tall Pine cou. Boy Scouts Am., 1942—, dist. chmn., 1954-58, mem. adv. bd., 1954—; trustee Oak Hill Cemetary Co., 1997—. 2nd lt. U.S. Army, 1931-36. Recipient Silver Beaver award Boy Scouts Am., 1958, Disting. Alumnus award Coll. Engring., Ohio State U., 1970, Alumni Citizenship award Ohio State U., 1975, Paul Harris fellow Rotary, 1997; others. Mem. NAM, Mich. Mfrs. Assn., U.S. C. of C., Owosso Corunna Area C. of C. (bd. dirs. 1948-61, adv. bd. 1961-78), Ohio State U. Alumni Assn., Newcomen Soc., Shriners, Masons, Sigma Xi, Tau Beta Pi, Pi Mu Epsilon, Eta Kappa Nu, Lambda Chi Alpha. Congregationalist. Home: Owosso, Mich. Died June 13, 2010.

HOENICKE, EDWARD HENRY, lawyer, corporate executive; b. Chgo., Apr. 12, 1930; s. Edward Albert and Henrietta Christina (Hameister) Hameister; m. Janice Armande Gravel Hoenicke, Aug. 14, 1954; children: Jeanne E., Anne L. AB, Cornell U., 1950; JD, U. Mich., 1956. Bar: NY 1956. Assoc. Cravath, Swaine & Moore, NYC, 1956—59; divsn. counsel Olin Corp., NYC, 1959—68; v.p., gen. counsel Beechnut Inc., NYC, 1968—69; pres. Beechnut Lifesavers Internat., NYC, 1969—76; v.p., asst. gen. counsel Squibb Corp., NYC, 1976—77; sr. v.p., gen. counsel UAL Inc., United Airlines Inc., Elk Grove Village, Ill., from 1977. Bd. dirs. Care Inc., from 1971. With USAF, 1951—53. Mem.: ABA, Bronxville Field Club (NY), Exmoor Country Club (Highland Pk., Ill.). Died June 13, 2010.

HOFFMAN, DANIEL STEVEN, lawyer, educator; b. NYC, May 4, 1931; s. Lawrence Hoffman and Juliette (Marbes) Ostrov; m. Beverly Mae Swenson, Dec. 4, 1954; children: Lisa Hoffman Ciancio, Tracy Hoffman Cockriel, Robin Hoffman Black. BA, U. Colo., 1951; LLB, U. Denver, 1958. Bar: Colo. 1958. Assoc., then ptnr. Fugate, Mitchem, Hoffman, Denver, 1951—55; mgr. of safety City and County of Denver, 1963—65; ptnr. Kripke, Hoffman, Carrigan, Denver, 1965—70, Hoffman, McDermott, Hoffman, Denver, 1970—78; of counsel Hoffman & McDermott, Denver, 1978—84; mem. Holme Roberts & Owen, LLC, Denver, 1984—94; dean Coll. Law, U. Denver, 1978—84, dean emeritus, prof. emeritus, from 1984; ptnr. McKenna & Cuneo LLP, Denver, 1994—2000, Hoffman Reilly Pozner & Williamson LLP, from 2000. Chmn., mem. Merit Screening Com. for Bankruptcy Judges, Denver, 1979—84; chmn. subcom. Dist. Atty.'s Crime Adv. Commn., Denver, from 1984; chmn. Senator Wirth's jud. nomination rev. com., Cong. DeGette's jud. nomination rev. com.; mem. jud. ethics adv. com. Colo. Supreme Ct., from 2004. Contbr. chpts. to books Mem. Rocky Mountain region Anti-Defamation League, Denver, 1985; bd. dirs. Colo. chpt. Am. Jewish Com., 1985, Legal Ctr., Denver, 1985—; mem. adv. com. Samaritan Shelter, Denver, 1985; chmn. Rocky Flats Blue Ribbon Citizens Com., Denver, 1980-83; mem. bd. visitors J. Reuben Clark Law Sch. Brigham Young U., 1986-88. With USAF, 1951-55. Recipient Am. Jewish Com. Nat. Judge Learned Hand award, 1993, Humanitarian award Rocky Mountain chpt. Anti-Defamation League, 1984, Alumni of Yr. award U. Denver Coll. Law, 1997, Lifetime Achievement award Colo. Trial Lawyers Assn., 2001. Fellow: Am. Bar Found., Colo. Bar. Found., Am. Coll. Trial Lawyers (state chmn. 1975—76), Internat. Soc. Barristers; mem.: Am. Judicature Soc. (bd. dirs. 1977—81), Assn. Trial Lawyers Am. (nat. com. mem. 1962—63), Colo. Trial Lawyers Assn. (pres. 1961—62, Lifetime Achievement award 2001), Colo. Bar. Assn. (pres. 1976—77, Young Lawyer of Yr. award 1965), Order of Coif (hon.). Democrat. Jewish. Avocation: tennis. Home: Greenwood Village, Colo. Died Sept. 1, 2009.

HOFFMAN, OSCAR ALLEN, retired forest products company executive; b. Newark, Feb. 4, 1920; s. Ernest Benjamin and Edith Marie (Myers) H.; m. Carolyn Ruth Layman, May 10, 1947 (div.); children: Peter Miles, Jared Mark; m. Geri McReynolds, Aug. 21, 1956. AB, Drew U., 1943; MS, Syracuse U., 1945; PhD, Stanford U., 1948; postgrad., U.S. Naval War Coll., 1953. Sect. leader MIT-Naval Ops. rsch. group, Washington, 1948-54; mgr. ops. rsch. AMF, Greenwich, Conn., 1954-58; v.p., spl. asst. to pres. Champion Internat. Corp., Stamford, Conn., 1958-85; commr. fin. City of Stamford, 1978—82. Chief ops. research Turkish Gen. Staff, Ankara, summer 1956 Episcopalian. Home: Ellicott City, Md. Died Apr. 10, 2010.

HOFFMANN, ROBERT SHAW, museum administrator, educator; b. Evanston, Ill., Mar. 2, 1929; s. Robert Charles and Dorothy Elizabeth (Shaw) H.; m. Sally Ann Monson, June 17, 1951; children: Karl Robert, John Frederick, David Randolf, Brenna Elizabeth. BS, Utah State U., 1950; MA, U. Calif., Berkeley, 1954, PhD, 1955; DS (hon.), Utah State U., 1988. From instr. to prof. U. Mont., Missoula, 1955-68; prof., curator U. Kans., Lawrence, 1968-86, Summerfield Disting. prof., 1982; dir. Nat. Mus. Natural History, Washington, 1986-87; asst. sec. for rsch. Smithsonian Instn., Washington, 1988-92, asst. sec. sci., 1992-94, provost, 1994-95; acting dir. Nat. Air & Space Mus., Washington, 1995-96; sr. scientist Nat. Mus. Natural History, Washington, 1996—2003, sr. scientist emeritus, 2003—10. Gis. fellow Nat. Mus. Natural History, Washington, 1975-76; mem. U.S. Nat. Com. for INQUA, NAS, 1970-82, sec.-treas., 1972-74, vice chmn., 1974-77, chmn., 1977-82, mem. adv. com. on USSR and Ea. Europe, 1970-75, mem. com. on Yellowstone Grizzlies, 1973-74, mem. ad hoc com. discussion group on US-USSR sci. policies, 1973; mem. mountain habitats com. Internat. Union for Conservation of Nature and Natural Resources, 1971-2010; mem. organizing com. First Internat. Theriological Congress, Moscow, 1974, mem. presidium, 1974-78; mem. Insectivore group, 1987-2010, Lagomorph Group, 1990-2010, Species Survival Commn.; mem. Soviet Union and Ea. Europe area com. Coun. Internat. Exch. Scholars, 1985-90; co-chair high latitude directorate U.S. Nat. Com. for Man and Biosphere, 1989-92; mem. com. on monographs and classification Systematics Agenda 2000, 1991; mem. adv. com. Internat. Sci. Found., 1992-94, chair biology III panel, 1993-94; mem. biodiversity working group of China Coun. for Internat. Cooperation in Environment and Devel., 1997-2010; co-chair planning com. Smithsonian-Am. Inst. Biol. Sci. "Challenges for the New Millenium" conf.; cons. Faisalabad U., Pakistan, 1971-2010; adviser Inst. Arctic and Alpine Rsch., Boulder, Colo., 1980-2010, Quaternary Rsch. Ctr., Seattle, 1981-2010, and numerous others; rsch. assoc. Mus., Tex. Tech U., 1998-2010. Co-author: Mammals in Kansas, 1981, Mammals of the Northern Great Plains, 1983; coord., contbr. Mammal Species of the World, 1982, 93; also articles. NAS fellow, 1963-64; NSF grantee, 1957-87, and numerous other grants; recipient 30 Yr. medal U.S.-USSR Interacad. Exch., 1989. Fellow AAAS; mem. Internat. Coun. Mus. (mem. exec. coun. 1995-98, mem. ethics com. 1998-00, U.S. Nat. Com. (bd. dirs. 1990-01), Am. Assn. Mus., Am. Assn. Quarternary Rsch., Am. Soc. Mammalogists (bd. dirs., chmn. com. internat. rels. 1964-68, 72-78, 1st v.p. 1973-78, pres. 1981-82), Brit. Mammal Soc., Ecol. Soc. Am., Internat. Assn. Ecology, Internat. Mountain Soc., Soc. Systematic Biology (pres. 1988-89), Xerces Soc. (bd. dirs.), Acta Zoologica Sinica (edit. bd. 1990-2010), Acta Theriologica Sinica (editl. bd. 1993-2010), Russian Acad. Natural Scis. (fgn.), All-Union Theriological Soc. (hon.), Sigma Xi, Phi Kappa Phi, Phi Sigma. Avocations: birdwatching, hiking, skiing, travel. Home: Bethesda, Md. Died Apr. 6, 2010.

HOGG, DAVID CLARENCE, physicist; b. Vanguard, Sask., Can., Sept. 5, 1921; came to U.S., 1953, naturalized, 1964; s. Francis Sandison and Frances Katherine (Gadsby) H.; m. Jean E. MacMillan, Feb. 15, 1947; children— David Randal, Rebecca Jean. BSc, U. We. Ont., 1949; MSc, McGill U., 1951, PhD, 1953. With Bell Telephone Labs., 1953—77, head atmospheric physics rsch., 1966—72, head antenna and propagation rsch. Holmdel, NJ, 1972—77; chief environ. radiometry wave propagation lab. Environ. Rsch. Lab., NOAA, Boulder, Colo., 1977—83, chief radio meteorology wave propagation lab., 1983—86; lectr., adj. prof. U. Colo., from 1984, lectr. ECE dept, from 1989; sr. scientist Colo. Inst. Rsch. Environ. Scis., U. Colo., 1986—89. Research, numerous publs. on microwaves, optics, satellite communications and remote sensing; patentee microwave antennas; composer vocal, choral, strings and piano classical music. Served with Can. Army, 1940-45. Recipient Silver medal U.S. Dept. Commerce, 1983, Composer's award Colo. Music Educators Assn., 1992. Fellow IEEE (founder Jersey Coast sect., Disting. Achievement award 1984); mem. NAE, Union Radio Scientifique Internat., Am. Music Ctr. Episcopalian. Died Aug. 9, 2009.

HOLDEN, DAVID MORGAN, medical educator; b. Bronx, NY, Jan. 29, 1938; s. James Francis and Lois (Morgan) H.; m. Carolyn Cleaves Chadbourne, Dec. 20, 1959 (div. Nov. 1971); children: David Chadbourne, James Morgan, Katherine Van-Tassel; m. Susan Elizabeth Garner, Dec. 23, 1971 (div. Mar. 1985); 1 child, Hannah Garner; 1 adopted child, Erin Elizabeth; m. Carol Ann Battaglia, Apr. 12, 1985. BS, Tufts U., 1959; MD, Yale U., 1963. Diplomate Am. Bd. Pediatrics, Nat. Bd. Med. Examiners, Am. Bd. Family Practice. Intern in pediatrics Yale New Haven Med. Ctr., 1963-64; resident in pediatrics Babies Hosp. Columbia Presbyn. Med. Ctr., NYC, 1964-66; med. epidemiologist Ctr. Disease Control USPHS, Atlanta and Manila, 1966-69; clin. instr. Emory U. Sch. Medicine, Atlanta, 1969-73; assoc. prof. family medicine U. N.D. Med. Sch., Minot, 1973-75; prof. family medicine, asst. dean Coll. Human Medicine U. Wyo., Laramie, 1976-77; prof. family medicine Coll. Human Medicine Mich. State U., East Lansing, 1977-80, asst. dean coll. human medicine, 1977-80; prof. family medicine, pediatrics sch. medicine U. Kans., Wichita, 1980-83; prof., chmn. dept. family medicine SUNY Sch. Medicine, Buffalo, 1983-93; prof. family medicine SUNY Downstate Sch. Medicine, Bklyn., from 1993; dir. ambulatory care L.I. Coll. Hosp., Bklyn., 1993-94, chmn. family practice, from 1993. Dir. N.W. N.D. Area Health Edn. Ctr., Minot, 1973-75; residency rev. com. Family Practice, 1991-98, chmn., 1994-98. Contbr. articles to profl. jours; chpts. to books. Fellow Am. Acad. Pediatrics, Am. Acad. Family Physicians; Soc. Tchrs. Family Medicine, County chpt. Am. Acad. Family Physicians, N.Y. chpt. Am. Acad. Family Physicians. Republican. Episcopalian. Avocations: reading, biking, walking. Home: Ridgefield, Conn. Died Sept. 18, 2009.

HOLLAND, BURT S., statistics educator, consultant; b. Bklyn., Dec. 4, 1945; s. Samuel J. and Bernice S. (Sanders) H.; m. Margaret Robin Mondros, Mar. 15, 1975; children: Irene, Andrew, Benjamin. BA, Binghamton U., NY, 1966; MS, N.C. State U., 1968, PhD, 1970. Asst. prof. statistics Temple U., Phila., 1970-76, assoc. prof., 1976-91, prof., 1991—2010, chairperson Dept. Stats., 1991-96. Cons. in field; chairperson Collegial Assembly Temple U. Sch. Bus & Mgmt., 1989-90; reviewer in field. Co-author: Statistical Analysis and Data Display, 2004; contbr. articles to profl. jours. Grad. trainee grantee Nat. Sci. Found., 1966-69; Regent's Coll. scholar N.Y. State Dept. Edn., 1962-66. Fellow Am. Stats. Assn.; mem. Biometric Soc., Inst. Math. Stats. Achievements include development of new procedures for simultaneous inference. Home: Huntingdon Valley, Pa. Died June 21, 2010.

HOLLAND, JOHN MADISON, retired family practice physician; b. Holden, W.Va., Oct. 7, 1927; s. Ophia I. and Lou V. (Elliott) H.; m. Mary Louise Bourne, Sept. 2, 1950; children— David, Stephen, Nancy BS, Eastern Ky. State U., Richmond, 1949; MD, U. Louisville, 1952. Diplomate Am. Bd. Family Practice, Am. Bd. Hospice and Palliative Medicine. Intern St. Joseph Infirmary, Louisville, 1952-53; gen. practice family medicine Physicians Group, Springfield, Ill., 1955-80; med. dir. St. John's Hosp., Springfield, 1971-94, St. John's Hospice, 1995—2010; clin. prof. family practice So. Ill. U., Springfield, from 1978. Served to capt. USAF, 1953-55 Mem. Am. Acad. Family Physicians, Am. Acad. Hospice/Palliative Medicine. Baptist. Home: Springfield, Ill. Died Aug. 24, 2010; St. John's Hospice.

HOLLAND, NANCY HINKLE, physician; b. Paris, Ky., July 10, 1921; d. Charles Thomas and Sue Clay (Buncker) Hinkle; m. Charles Phillip Holland, July 3, 1961. BS, U. Denver, 1949; MD, U. Louisville, 1954. Asst. prof. pediatrics U. Cin., 1962-64, U. Ky., 1964-67, assoc. prof. pediatrics, 1967-72, prof. pediatrics, from 1972; resident Cin. Childrens Hosp., 1955-57, fellow in immunology, 1957-60. Bd. dirs. Nat. Sub-bd. Pediatric Nephrology, 1976-82. Contbr. articles to profl. jours. Bd. dirs. Hendle Contracting Corp., Paris, 1960—. 2d lt. U.S. Army, 1643-45. Mem. Am. Acad. Pediatrics, Am. Soc. Pediatric Nephrology, Am. Pediatric Soc., Internat. Soc. Nephrology, Soc. Pediatric Rsch. Avocations: farming, horse breeding. Home: Stamping Ground, Ky. Died Mar. 7, 2010.

HOLLEY, EDWARD GAILON, library science educator, former university dean; b. Pulaski, Tenn., Nov. 26, 1927; s. Abe Brown and Maxie Elizabeth (Bass) H.; m. Robbie (Bobbie Lee) Gault, June 19, 1954; children: Gailon Boyd,

Edward Jens, Beth Alison, Amy Lin Holley. BA magna cum laude, David Lipscomb Coll., Nashville, 1949; MA, George Peabody Coll., 1951; PhD, U. Ill., 1961. Asst. libr. David Lipscomb Coll., 1949-51; mem. staff U. Ill., 1951-62, libr. edn., philosophy and psychology libr., 1957-62; dir. librs. U. Houston, 1962-72; dean Sch. Libr. Sci. Sch. Library Sci., U. N.C. at Chapel Hill, 1972-85, prof., 1985-89, William Rand Kenan, Jr. prof., 1989-95; prof. emeritus U. N.C. at Chapel Hill, from 1996. Vis. lectr. U. Wis., Madison, summer 1968; vis. prof. North Tex. State U., summer 1970, UCLA, fall 1986; mem. adv. coun. libr. resources U.S. Office Edn., 1968-71; cons. various librs. Tex., Ill., S.C. bd. higher edn., NEH, U.S. Dept. Edn. Author: Charles Evans, American Bibliographer, 1963, Raking the Historic Coals, 1967, (with Don Hendricks) Resources of Texas Libraries, 1968, ALA at 100, 1976, Resources of South Carolina Libraries, 1976; co-author: The Library Services and Construction Act, 1983; contbr. articles to profl. jours. Trustee Disciples of Christ Hist. Soc., 1973-85; mem. governing bd. U. N.C. Press, 1975-95, chmn., 1989-93; trustee OLC, Inc., 1985-94, chmn., 1989-92. Lt. USNR, 1953-56. Coun. on Libr. Resources fellow, 1971. Mem. ALA (pres. 1974-75, chmn. pub. bd. 1972-73, Scarecrow Press award 1964, Melvil Dewey medal 1983, Lippincott award 1987), Assn. for Libr. and Info. Sci. Assn. (Profl. Edn. award 1998), Tex. Libr. Assn. (pres. 1971), Southea. Libr. Assn. (Rothrock award 1992), N.C. Libr. Assn. (Disting. Svc. award 1995), Assn. Coll. and Rsch. Librs. (editor monographs 1969-72, Rsch. Libr. of Yr. award 1988), Spl. Librs. Assn. (hon.), Phi Kappa Phi, Kappa Delta Pi, Beta Phi Mu (pres. 1984-86, award 1991, Alise award 1998). Democrat. Mem. Ch. of Christ. Home: Durham, NC. Died Feb. 18, 2010.

HOLLIMAN, DAN CLARK, biology educator; b. Birmingham, Ala., Aug. 25, 1932; s. Murray and Kathleen (Hyde) H.; m. Mary Agnes Brooks, July 26, 1958; 1 child, Diane Carol. BS, U. Ala., 1957, MS, 1959, PhD, 1963. Prof. biology Birmingham (Ala.)-So. Coll., from 1961. Contbr. articles to profl. jours. Mem. The Wildlife Soc., Sigma Xi. Democrat. Presbyterian. Home: Birmingham, Ala. Died Feb. 19, 2009.

HOLLINSHEAD, MAY BLOCK, anatomist, educator; b. NYC, Nov. 28, 1913; d. Abraham and Pauline (Markle) Block; m. Merrill Taylor Hollinshead, May 10, 1942 (dec. 1994); 1 child, Richard Clark. AB, Hunter Coll., 1936; PhD, Columbia U., 1951. Rsch. asst. Vanderbilt U. Sch. Medicine, Nashville, 1942; lab. asst. Stat. Hosp./Army Air Field, Amarillo Shepard Field, Tex., 1943; asst. in anatomy Bowman Gray Sch. Medicine/U. N.C. Med. Sch., Winston-Salem/Chapel Hill, N.C., 1943, U. So. Calif. Sch. Medicine, LA, 1945, Columbia U. Coll. of Physicians and Surgeons, NYC, 1949-51; instr. in anatomy NYU Coll of Medicine, NYC, 1951-56; asst. prof. anatomy Seton Hall Coll. Medicine and Dentistry, Jersey City, N.J., 1956-61; assoc. prof. anatomy N.J. Coll. Medicine and Dentistry, Jersey City/Newark, 1961-72; prof. anatomy U. of Medicine and Dentistry, N.J. Med. Sch., Newark, 1972-90; retired, 1990. Contbr. articles to profl. jours.; contbg. author to books in field. Recipient grant-in-aid Columbia U., 1941, Curtis Scholarship, 1948; named Woman of the Yr., Am. Med. Womens's Assn. (br. 4, N.J.), 1979. Mem. AAAS, Am. Assn. Anatomists, CAJAL Club, Union of Concerned Scientists, NOW, Nat. Women's Health Network, Gray Panthers of No. N.J. (chair), N.J. Peace Action, Amnesty Internat., Sigma Xi. Avocations: reading, classical music, swimming. Died July 4, 2010.

HOLLOWAY, EDWARD GRAHAM, investment company executive; b. Miami, Fla., Apr. 26, 1930; s. Imla Cresson and Cleo B. (Prothro) Holloway; m. Carolyn Ann Green, Nov. 22, 1956; children: Imla Graham(dec.), Valerie L. Haughland, Gregory Scott. BA, U. N.C., 1952. Pres. No. Am. Investors, Atlanta, 1960—64, Am. Funds Distributors, LA, 1964—88, chmn. bd. dirs., from 1988; dir. Capital Group, from 1983; with Capital Rsch. Mgmt., from 1981, Am. Funds Distrobutors, from 1973. Bd. dirs. Am. Funds Svc. Co. Trustee Ark. Coll., Batesville, from 1979, acting pres., from 1988; bd. dirs. Am. Funds Svc. Co., from 1985. Sgt. US Army, 1950—52. Mem.: Internat. Assn. Fin. Planners, Coll. Fin. Planning (chmn. bd. trustees 1978—79), Bent Tree Country Club (Dallas). Republican. Episcopalian. Home: Georgetown, Tex. Died Oct. 5, 2009.

HOLM, DONALD GODFREY, utility company executive; b. Chgo., Aug. 19, 1927; s. Godfrey F. and Adeline (Carlson) H.; m. Geraldine Sliger, Sept. 5, 1949; children: Carol, Mark, John. BBA, Northwestern U., 1949; MBA, U. Chgo., 1961. Asst. treas. Peoples Energy Corp., Chgo., 1971-74, asst. sec., 1974-75, asst. treas., asst. sec., 1975-81, v.p., sec., treas., 1981-87, v.p., controller, sec., treas., 1987-89; ret. Bd. dirs. ARC Mid-Am. chpt., Chgo. Served to sgt. U.S. Army, 1952-54. Mem. Am. Soc. Corp. Secs., Am. Gas Assn. Presbyterian. Home: Lake Villa, Ill. Died Mar. 28, 2009.

HOLM, JEANNE MARJORIE, writer, retired military officer; b. Portland, Oreg., June 23, 1921; d. John E. and Marjorie (Hammond) H. BA, Lewis and Clark Coll., 1956. Commd. 2d lt. U.S. Army, 1943; transferred to USAF, 1948, advanced through grades to maj. gen., 1973; chief manpower and mgmt. Hdqrs. Allied Air Forces Southern Europe, Naples, Italy, 1957-61; congl. liaison officer, directorate manpower and orgn. Hdqrs USAF, Washington, 1961-65; dir. Women in the Air Force, 1965-73, Sec. Air Force Pers. Coun., Washington, 1973-75; ret., 1975; cons. Def. Manpower Commn., Washington, 1975, Undersec. Air Force, Washington, 1979-81. Spl. asst. to Pres., 1976-77; advisor United Services Life Ins. Co., Washington; lectr. on manpower and women in mil., Presideo Press, Novato, Calif. Author: Women in the Military: An Unfinished Revolution, 1982, rev. edit., 1992; Editor, co-author: In Defense of a Nation: Servicewomen in World War II, 1997; contbr. Encyclopedia of the American Military, 1994; contbr. articles to profl. jours. Chair adv. com. women vets. VA, Washington, 1986-88; adv. com. USCG Acad., 1983-89; dir. U.S. com. for UN Fund for Women; trustee Air Force Aid Soc., 1988-96, Air Force Hist. Found.; mem. nat. adv. com. Women in Mil. Svc. Meml. Found.; mem. hon. coun. Vietnam Women's Meml. Project. Decorated DSM with oak leaf cluster, Legion of Merit, medal for Human Action (Berlin Airlift), Nat. Def. Svc. medal with bronze star; recipient Disting. Achievement award, Alumni Assn. Lewis and Clark Coll., Eugene Zuckert Leadership award, Arnold Air Soc., citation of honor, Air Force Assn., Living Legacy award, Women's Internat. Ctr., 1985, Sen. Margaret Chase Smith Leadership awrad, Women in Mil. Svc. Meml. Found., 1998, Internat. Hall of Fame award, Internat. Women's Forum, 1992; named Woman of Yr. in Govt. and Diplomacy, Ladies Home Jour., 1975; named to Nat. Women's Hall of Fame, Seneca Falls, N.Y., 2000. Mem.: Exec. Women in Govt. (founder, 1st chair), Ret. Officers Assn., Air Force Assn. (Lifetime Achievement award 2003). Home: Edgewater, Md. Died Feb. 15, 2010.

HOLMES, GEORGE MILTON, state legislator; b. Mt Airy, NC, June 20, 1929; s. John William and Thelma Elizabeth Dobie Holmes; m. Barbara Ann Ireland, 1956; 1 child, Jennifer Leigh. Pres. W. N. Ireland Ins. Agy.; mem. Dist. 41 NC House of Reps., NC, 1975—79, 1979—2003, mem. Dist. 92, 2003—09, minority party joint caucus leader, 1983—84, minority whip, 1981—82, co-chmn. Appropriation Com., 1995—98. Mem.: Oasis Temple, Shriners, Yadkin Masonic Lodge 162. Republican. Baptist. Died Dec. 31, 2009.

HOLMES, RALPH W., manufacturing executive; b. Charleston, W.Va., June 14, 1930; s. Otho Oliver and Alda Ernestine (Bain) H.; m. Janet Gay Harrison; children: Kimberly, Ralph, Mark. BS in History, U. Charleston, 1960. With McJunkin Corp., Charleston, from 1955, mgr. nat. accounts, 1972-74, sales mgr., 1974-78, regional mgr., 1978-82, corp. sales mgr., 1982-84, sr. corp. v.p., from 1984. Coach high sch. boys Emmanuel Bapt. Ch.; active Boy Scouts Am., Charleston; fund raiser U. Charleston; pres. U. Charleston Athletic Club, 1983-85. With USN, 1951-55. Mem. Masons. Republican. Avocations: golf, tennis. Died July 7, 2009.

HOLT, BERTHA MERRILL, retired state legislator; b. Eufaula, Ala., Aug. 16, 1916; d. William Hoadley and Bertha Harden (Moore) Merrill; m. Winfield Clary Holt, Mar. 14, 1942 (dec. 2003); children: Harriet Wharton Holt Whitley, William Merrill, Winfield Jefferson. AB, Agnes Scott Coll., 1938; LLD (hon.), Agnes Scott Coll., Decatur, Ga., 2007; postgrad., U. NC Law Sch., 1939-40; LLB, U. Ala., 1941; grad., Sch. Creative Leadership, Greensboro, NC, 1992; PhD in Humane letters (hon.), Agnes Scott Coll., 2007. Bar: Ala. 1941. With US Dept. Treasury, Washington, 1941-42, US Dept. Interior, Washington, 1942-43. Mem. N.C. House of Reps. from 22d Dist., 1975-80, 25th Dist., 1980-94, chmn. select com. govtl. ethics, 1979-80, chmn. constl. amendments com., 1981, 83, mem. joint commn. govtl. ops., 1982-88, chmn. appropriation com. justice and pub. safety, 1985-88, co-chair House appropriation sub-com. transp., 1991-92, co-chair appropriation sub-com. Justice and Pub. Safety, 1993-94. Pres., Dem. Women of Alamance, 1962, chmn. hdqrs., 1964, 68; mem. NC Dem. Exec. Com., 1964-75, 95-2010; pres. Episcopal Ch. Women, 1968; mem. coun. NC Episcopal Diocese, 1972-74, 84-87, 95-98; chmn. budget com. 1987; chmn. fin. dept., 1973-75, parish grant com., 1973-80, mem. standing com., 1975-78; mem. Episcopal Diocese Eccles. Ct., 1998-2002; vestry mem. Ch. of Holy Comforter, 2005-07, mem. bd. NC coun. of Chs., 2005-10; chmn. Alamance County Social Svcs. Bd., 1970; mem. N.C. Bd. Sci. and Tech., 1979-83; chair Legis. Women's Caucus, 1991-94; past bd. dirs. Hospice NC; bd. dirs. State Coun. Social Legis., pres. SCSL 1996-97, State Conf. Social Work, NC Epilepsy Assn., NC Pub. Sch. Forum, 1989, U. NC Sch. Pub. Health Adv. Bd., Salvation Army Alamance County, NC, Nursing Found., 1989, Epilepsy Found., 1989; bd. Alternatives for Status Offenders Burlington, NC, Sch. Pub. Health Adv. Bd.; bd. dirs. NC ACLU, Partnership For Children NC, 1993-98; mem. Alamance County Home Health ADv. Bd., 2005-06; bd. dirs. Ctrl. Carolina Planned Parenthood. Recipient Outstanding Alumna award Agnes Scott Coll., 1978, Legis. award for svc. to elderly Non-Profit Rest Home Assn., 1985, health, 1986, ARC, 1987, Faith Active in Pub. Affairs award NC Coun. of Chs., 1987, Ellen B. Winston award State Coun. For Social Legis., 1989, NC Disting. Women's award in gov., 1991, Disting. Svc. award Alamance County, 1992, Chi Omega award Women in Leadership, 1st ann. Hallie Ruth Allen Dem. Women award Alamance County, 1992, Disting. Svc. award Chi Omega, 1996, Svc. award Triennial Conv., Episcopal Ch. Women of US, 1997, Outstanding Alumna award U. NC, Chapel Hill, 1998, Gwyneth B. Davis award NC Assn. Women Attys., 1998, Outstanding Svc. award NC Assn. Women Attys., 1998, Disting. Alumna award U. NC,Chapel Hill, 1999, AAUW award for Edn. and Equity for Women and Girls, 2004, Lifetime Achievement 200 award Alamance County Dem. Party, 2004, Award for Outstanding Svc., NC Sr. Dems., 2005, NC Dem. Women Trail Blazers award, 2008, ACLU Frank Porter Graham award, 2009, Joitumcveil Smith award, 2010, others; named One of 5 Disting. Women of NC (Govt.), 1991; named Bertha B. Holt award in her honor NC Bar Juvenile Justice Sect., first recipient, 2004; named Bertha B. Holt Legislative Courage and Leadership award in her honor Planned Parenthood Ctrl. NC, first recipient, 2007; honored as Legis. and Scholar award Jeannette Rankin Assn. NC Women, 2005.women Mem. AAUW, NOW, N.C. Women's Forums, Law Alumni Assn. U. N.C. Chapel Hill (bd. dirs. 1978-81, 1994-99), N.C. Bar Assn. (bd. dirs. sr. lawyers sect., constnl. rights sect. 1998-04, 05, juvenile justice and children's rights 1999-, chair 2002-03, John McNeil Smith award, 2010), English Speaking Union, N.C. Hist. Soc., Soc. Wine Educators, Les Amis du Vin, Pi Beta Phi, Phi Kappa Gamma, Delta Kappa Gamma, Phi Theta Kappa, Century Club. Home: Burlington, NC. Died June 18, 2010.

HOLT, TERRY WAYNE, car rental company executive; b. Columbia, Ind., Oct. 14, 1954; s. Hint F. and Myrtle G. (Crumley) H.; m. Deborah K. Love, Jan. 26, 1973; children: Jason, Kelly, Jon, Katie. Student Columbia (Tenn.) State Community Coll., 1973-74, U. Tenn., 1974-76, Akron U., 1985; asst. mgr. 1st Mark Fin., Louisville, 1976-77; office mgr. Agy. Rent-A-Car, Nashville, 1977-81, dist. mgr. Solon, Ohio, 1981-83, regional dir., 1983-85, v.p. ops., 1985-88, exec. v.p., 1988-89, pres., from 1989. Republican. Mem. Ch. of Christ. Avocations: boating, antiques. Home: Bradenton, Fla. Died Apr. 22, 2010.

HOLTZMAN, ABRAHAM, retired political science professor; b. Detroit, Nov. 3, 1921; s. Morris and Rebecca Holtzman; m. Sylvia Hochfield, Dec. 16, 1947; children: Joshua Peter, Adam Paul, Seth Matthew. BA, UCLA, 1943, MA, 1947, Harvard U., 1950, PhD, 1952. Tchg. asst. UCLA, 1945—47; tchg. fellow Harvard U., 1950—52; instr. Dartmouth Coll., 1952—53; asst. to chmn. Dem. Nat. Com., Washington, 1954; prof. polit. sci. NC State U., Raleigh, 1955—2010. Author: Interest Groups and Lobbying, 1966, Legislative Liaison: Executive Leadership in Congress, 1970, American Government, Ideals and Reality, 1980, 1984; contbr. articles to profl. jours. Mem. NC Gov.'s Coordinating Com. Aging, 1960, Labor Force Devel. Coun., 1978—79, Pvt. Industry Coun., 1979—80, Conf. Aging, 1981; grant co-dir. The Constitution: Continuity and Conflict, NEH, 1983—87. Named Disting. Classroom Tchr., NC State U., Raleigh, 1959—60, 1964—65, Outstanding Tchr., 1965—66, 1971—72, Alumni Disting. Prof., 1974—77. Mem.: AAUP, Nat. Com. Effective Congress, Am. Profs. Peace Mid. East, Southern Polit. Sci. Assn. (mem. exec. coun. 1980—83), NC Polit. Sci. Assn., Am. Polit. Sci. Assn. Home: Raleigh, NC. Died Jan. 18, 2010.

HOLVECK, ELEANORE, philosophy educator; b. Pitts., Oct. 22, 1942; d. Alexander Walkowski and Anna Kuprewicz; m. John Holveck, Aug. 10, 1966. BA, Duquesne U., 1964; MA, U. N.C., 1966, PhD, 1970. Assoc. prof. Duquesne U., Pitts., from 1967, chair dept. philosophy, from 1990. Contbr. articles to profl. publs. Chancelor's scholar, 1964-65; NDEA fellow, 1965-67. Mem. Am. Philos. Assn., Soc. Phenomenology and Existential Philosophy, Simone de Beauvoir Soc., Sartre Soc. N.Am. Home: Pittsburgh, Pa. Died Jan. 24, 2009.

HOMZE, EDWARD LEE, historian, educator; b. Canton, Ohio, Oct. 13, 1930; s. John F. and Mary A. (Granchi) H.; div.; children: Eric John, Heidi A. BA, Bowling Green State U., 1952, MA, 1953; PhD, Pa. State U., 1963. Prof. Emporia (Kans.) State U., 1961-65; prof. history U. Nebr., Lincoln, from 1965. Prof. strategy Naval War Coll., Newport, R.I., 1975-76; mem. USAF Hist. Adv. Com., 1979-83; mem. Fulbright Nat. Selection Bd. for Germany, 1989—. Author: Foreign Labor in Nazi Germany, 1967, Arming the Luftwaffe, 1976, German Military Aviation, 1984. 1st lt. USAF, 1953-56. Mem. Am. Hist. Assn., German Studies Assn. (sec.-treas. 1989-91). Democrat. Roman Catholic. Avocations: tennis, skiing. Home: Reno, Nev. Died Feb. 18, 2009.

HONEY, AVON R., state legislator; Former tchr. North Scotlandville Elem. Sch.; adminstr., edn. talent search Southern U., Baton Rouge, 1983; mem. Edn. Com., Environment Com.; state rep., spl. election, Dist. 63 La., 2002. Democrat. Died Feb. 12, 2010.

HONEY, RICHARD DAVID, psychology educator; b. Millcreek Twp., Pa., Dec. 24, 1927; s. Bennett Vincent and Eleanor Violet (Will) H. AB, Transylvania Coll., 1957; PhD, U. Chgo., 1962. Prof. psychology, clin. psychologist Transylvania U., Lexington, Ky., 1964-91. Sr. psychologist Psychiat. Inst., Municipal Ct., Chgo., 1961, prin. psychologist, 1962-64; Clin. cons. VA Hosp. Served with AUS, 1952-54, Korea. Woodrow Wilson fellow, Danforth fellow; named to Hon. Order of Ky. Cols. Mem. APA, Sigma Xi, Psi Chi, Phi Kappa Tau, Omicron Delta Kappa (Lampas Cir.). Home: Gerry, NY. Died May 3, 2010.

HONEYSTEIN, KARL, lawyer, media specialist; b. NYC, Jan. 10, 1932; s. Herman and Claire (Rosen) H.; m. Buzz Halliday, Sept. 14, 1965 (div. Dec. 1978); 1 child, Gail; m. Shauna Wood Trabert, Jan. 24, 1995. BA, Yale U., New Haven, Conn., 1953; JD, Columbia U., NYC, 1959. Bar: NY 1959. Assoc. Greenbaum, Wolff & Ernst, NYC, 1959-62; v.p. Ashley Famous Agy., NYC, 1962-69, Internat. Famous Agy., NYC, 1969-71; exec. v.p. The Sy Fischer Co., NYC and L.A., 1971-80; exec. v.p., chief operating officer The Taft Entertainment Co., L.A., 1980-88; pres. K.H. Strategy Corp., L.A., from 1988. Dir. Rhythm & Hues, Inc.; lectr. law Bklyn. Law Sch., NYC, 1973-75; mem. adv. group Wood Warren, Investment Bankers. Served to lt. j.g. USNR, 1953-56 Mem.: Internat. Acad. TV Arts and Scis., Friars Club. Home: Beverly Hills, Calif. Died July 30, 2009.

HOOKS, BENJAMIN LAWSON, civil rights advocate, retired civil rights association executive; b. Memphis, Jan. 31, 1925; s. Robert B. Hooks Sr. & Bessie (White) H.; m. Frances Dancy Hooks, March 21, 1951; 1 child: Patricia Gray Student, LeMoyne Coll., Memphis, 1941-43, Howard U., 1943-44; JD, DePaul U., Chgo., 1948; LL.D. (hon.), Howard U., 1975, Wilberforce U., 1976, Central State U., 1976. Bar: Tenn. 1948. Individual practice law, Memphis, 1949-65, 68-72; asst. pub. defender City of Memphis, 1961-64; judge Div. IV Criminal Ct. of Shelby County, 1966-68; ordained to ministry Baptist Ch., 1956; pastor Middle Bapt. Ch., Memphis, 1956-64, Greater New Mt. Moriah Bapt. Ch., Detroit, 1964-72; co-founder, v.p., dir. Mut. Fed. Savs. & Loan Assn., Memphis, 1955-69; commr. FCC, Washington, 1972-78; exec. dir. NAACP, NYC, 1977-93; sr. v.p. The Chapman Co., Memphis, 1993; prof. social justice Fisk U., 1993—2002. Disting. adj. prof. polit. sci. U. Memphis. Producer, host: television program Conversations in Black and White; co-producer: television program Forty Percent Speaks; panelist: television program What Is Your Faith. Bd. dirs. Memphis and Shelby Human Relations Com.; mem. Martin Luther King Fed. Holiday Commn.; pres. Nat. Civil Rights Mus., Memphis. Served with AUS, World War II. Recipient: Masons Man of Yr. award, 1964, Lincoln League award, 1965, Optimist Club of Am. award, 1966, Regional Baptist Convention award, Gold Medal Achievement award, 1972, Spingarn award NAACP, 1986, Presdl. Medal of Freedom, The White House, 2007; named to The Internat. Civil Rights Hall of Fame, 2008 Mem. ABA, Nat. Bar Assn., Tenn. Bar Assn., So. Christian Conf., Tenn. Coun. Human Rels., Omega Psi Phi Fraternity Home: Memphis, Tenn. Died Apr. 15, 2010.

HOOPER, JOHN ALLEN, retired banker; b. Danbury, Conn., Dec. 9, 1922; s. Kenneth Malcolm and Grace Lillian (Jardon) H.; m. Susanne Leona Sipperly, Nov. 27, 1948; children: Judith Elaine, John Nash. BBA, U. Mich., 1947, MBA, 1948. With Chase Manhattan Bank, NYC, 1948-85, exec. v.p., 1972-83, sr. v.p., 1964-71, mem. mgmt. com., 1975-85, vice-chmn. bd., 1983-85; chmn. bd., chief exec. officer Bank of the Commonwealth, Detroit, 1971-72. Served with AUS, 1943-46. Decorated Army Commendation medal; named Man of Year, Inst. Human Relations, 1974 Mem. Patterson Club, Wilderness Country Club, Royal Poinciana Golf Club. Home: Ashford, Conn. Died July 31, 2009.

HOPPER, DENNIS, actor, writer, photographer, film director; b. Dodge City, Kans., May 17, 1936; s. Jay and Marjorie Hopper; m. Brooke Hayward, 1961 (div. 1969); 1 child, Marin; m. Michelle Phillips, Oct. 31, 1970 (div. Nov. 8, 1970); m. Doria Halprin, 1972 (div. 1976); 1 child: Ruthana; m. Katherine LaNasa, June 17, 1989 (div. April 1992); 1 child, Henry Lee.; m. Victoria Duffy, Apr. 13, 1996 (separated 2010); 1 child, Galen Actor: (films): Rebel Without a Cause, 1955, Jagged Edge, 1955, I Died A Thousand Times, 1955, Giant, 1956, The Steel Jungle, 1956, Story of Mankind, 1957, Gunfight at the O.K. Corral, 1957, From Hell to Texas, 1958, The Youngland, 1959, Key Witness, 1960, Night Tide, 1963, The Sons of Katie Elder, 1965, Queen of Blood, 1966, The Trip, 1967, Glory Stompers, 1967, Hang 'Em High, 1968, Cool Hand Luke, 1967, True Grit, 1969, Easy Rider, 1969, The Last Movie, 1971, Kid Blue, 1973, Hex, 1973, The Sky is Falling, 1975, Mad Dog Morgan, 1976, Tracks, 1976, American Friend, 1978, Apocalypse Now, 1979, Wild Times, 1980, Out of the Blue, 1980, King of the Mountain, 1981, Renacer, 1981, Human Highway, 1981, Rumble Fish, 1983, The Osterman Weekend, 1983, Slagskämpen, 1984, My Science Project, 1985, O.C. & Stiggs, 1985, White Star, 1985, The Texas Chainsaw Massacre Part 2, 1986, Blue Velvet, 1986 (Montreal World Film Festival award 1986), Hoosiers, 1986, River's Edge, 1987, Black Widow, 1987, Pick-up Artist, 1987, Straight to Hell, 1987, Riders of the Storm, 1988, Let it Rock, 1988, Blood Red, 1989, Flashback, 1990, Motion & Emotion, 1990, Chattahoochie, 1990, Superstar: Life and Times of Andy Warhol, 1990, Backtrack, 1991, Sunset Heat, 1991, Schneeweißrosenrot, 1991, Indian Runner, 1991, Hearts of Darkness, 1991, Paris Trout, 1991, Eye of the Storm, 1991, Super Mario Brothers, 1993, Boiling Point, 1993, True Romance, 1993, Red Rock West, 1993, Speed, 1994, Chasers, 1994, Waterworld, 1995, Search and Destroy, 1995, Carried Away, 1996, Last Days of Frankie the Fly, 1996, Cannes Man, 1996, Basquiat, 1996, Top of the World, 1997, Road Ends, 1997, Good Life, 1997, Star Truckers, 1997, Blackout, 1997, Tycus, 1998, Meet the Deedles, 1998, Sources, 1999, Lured Innocence, 1999, Justice, 1999, Jesus' Son, 1999, Bad City Blues, 1999, EdTV, 1999, Straight Shooter, 1999, Spreading Ground, 2000, Luck of the Draw, 2000, Held for Ransom, 2000, Choke, 2000, Ticker, 2001, Knockaround Guys, 2001, L.A.P.D.: To Protect and to Serve, 2001, Unspeakable, 2002, Leo, 2002, The Keeper, 2003, Out of Season, 2004, House of 9, 2004, Americano, 2005, The Crow: Wicked Prayer, 2005, Land of the Dead, 2005, (narrator) Inside Deep Throat, 2005, Sleepwalking, 2008, Elegy, 2008, Swing Vote, 2008, Palermo Shooting, 2008, Hell Ride, 2008, (voice) Alpha and Omega, 2010; writer, dir. Easy Rider 1969 (Cannes Film Festival Best New Dir. award 1969), The Last Movie, 1971, Out of the Blue, 1980, Chasers, 1994, Colors, 1988, The Hot Spot, 1990, Paris Trout, 1991, Double Crossed, 1991, Sunset Heat, 1992, Nails, 1992; (TV movies) The Heart of Justice, 1993, Samson and Delilah, 1996, Marlon Brando: The Wild One, 1996, The Last Days of Frankie the Fly, 1996, Jason and the Argonauts, 2000, Firestarter 2: Rekindled, 2002, The Piano Player, 2002, The Groovenians (voice), 2002, Suspense, 2003, Last Ride, 2004; (TV series) Flatland, 2002, E-Ring, 2005-2006, Crash, 2008; appeared in: (documentaries) James Dean-The First American Teenager, 1975, Easy Riders, Raging Bulls: How the Sex, Drugs and Rock 'N' Roll Generation Saved Hollywood, 2003, A Decade Under the Influence, 2003; exhibited photographs at Fort Worth Art Mus., Denver Art Mus., Wichita Art Mus., Cochran Art Mus., Spileto Mus., Parco Gallery, Tokyo, Osaka, Kumatomo, Japan; author: (photographic book) Out of the Sixties, 1986. Recipient Best Film award Venice Film Festival, 1971, Best Film award Cannes Film Festival, 1980; named Comdr. France's National Order Arts & Letters, 2008 Died May 29, 2010.

HORNE, LENA, singer; b. Bklyn., June 30, 1917; m. Lennie Hayton, Dec. 1947 (dec. 1971); children: Gail Lumet Buckley, Terry Jones. Degree (hon.), Howard U., Spelman Coll., Yale U. Dancer, Cotton Club, 1934; toured, recorded with Noble Sissle Orch., 1935-36, Charlie Barnet's Band, 1940-41; became cafe soc. singer; starred in: motion pictures Cabin in the Sky, Stormy Weather, Death of a Gunfighter, Thousands Cheer, I Dood It, Swing Fever, Broadway Rhythm, Two Girls and a Sailor, Ziegfield Follies, Panama Hattie, Till the Clouds Roll By, Words & Music, Duchess of Idaho, Meet Me in Las Vegas, others; singer popular music; TV appearances include spl. Harry and Lena, 1970, series Cosby Show, Sanford and Son; theatrical appearances in Dance with Your Gods, Blackbird, The Lady & Her Music, 1984; albums: Lena Goes Latin, 1987, Stormy Weather, The Men in My Life, 1989, Greatest Hits, 1992, At Long Last Lena, 1992, Best of Lena Horne, 1993, We'll Be Together Again, 1994, Lena Horne Christmas, 1995, Lena Sings Hollywood, 1996, Whispering, 1996, Lena Soul, 1996, More Than You Know, 1997, Being Myself, 1998; author: (with Richard Schickel) Lena, 1965. Recipient Page One award N.Y. Newspaper Guild, Lifetime Achievement award Ebony Mag., Antoinette Perry Spl. award, 1981, Spingarn award NAACP, 1983, Kennedy Ctr. honor for lifetime contributions to the arts, 1984, Paul Robeson award Actor's Equity, 1985, Pied Piper award ASCAP, 1987, 2 Grammy awards; named to Black Filmmakers Hall of Fame. Died May 9, 2010.

HORNSBY, ROGER ALLEN, classics educator; b. Nye, Wis., Aug. 8, 1926; s. Huntley Burton and Lucile James; m. Jessie Lynn Gillespie, June 8, 1960. AB magna cum laude, Adelbert Coll. Western Res. U., 1949; A.M., Princeton U., 1951, PhD, 1952. Instr. classics U. Iowa, Iowa City, 1954-59, asst. prof., 1959-62, asso. prof., 1962-67, prof., 1967-91, chmn. dept., 1966-81, prof. emeritus Iowa City, from 1991; chief reader advance placment Latin IV Ednl. Testing Service, 1965-69. Vis. prof. Trinity Coll., 1967, UCLA, 1976, Georgetown U., 1992; Whichard Disting. prof. East Carolina U., 1997-98. Author: Reading Latin Poetry, 1967, Patterns of Action in the Aeneid, 1970; Contbr. articles on Latin poetry to profl. jours. Mem. council Am. Acad. in Rome, 1974. Served with AUS, 1952-54. Old Gold Research fellow, 1963; sr. fellow U. Iowa, 1983; resident Am. Acad. Rome, 1983. Fellow Am. Coun. Learned Socs. (del. 1984-2000); mem. Am. Philol. Assn. (bd. dirs. 1974-77), Classical Assn. Mid. W. and S. (pres. 1968-69), Archeol. Inst. Am. (pres. Iowa chpt. 1966-67, 84-86), Am. Numis. Soc. (coun. 1973—, 2d 1984—2000), Am. Acad. Rome (trustee 1990-92), Virgilian Soc. (trustee 1991-93). Died Oct. 26, 2009.

HOROWITZ, BEN, retired health facility administrator; b. Bklyn., Mar. 19, 1914; s. Saul and Sonia (Meringoff) H.; m. Beverly Lichtman, Feb. 14, 1952; children: Zachary, Jody. BA, Bklyn. Coll., 1940; LLB, St. Lawrence U., 1940; postgrad., New Sch. Social Rsch., 1942. Bar: N.Y. 1941. Dir. N.Y. Fedn. Jewish Philanthropies, 1940-45; assoc., ea. regional dir. City of Hope, 1945-50, nat. exec. sec., 1950-53, exec. dir., 1953-85. Bd. dirs. Beckman Rsch. Inst. Mem. Gov.'s Task Force on Flood Relief, 1969-74; bd. dirs., v.p. Hope for Hearing Found., UCLA, 1972-96; bd. dirs. Forte Found., 1987-92, Ch. Temple Housing Corp., 1988-93, Leo Baeck Temple, 1964-67, 86-89, Westwood Property Owners Assn., 1991—. Recipient Spirit of Life award, 1970, Gallery of Achievement award, 1974, Profl. of Yr. award So. Calif. chpt. Nat. Sco. Fundraisers, 1977; Ben Horowitz chair in rsch. established at City of Hope, 1981; city street named in his honor, 1986. Jewish. Formulated the role of City of Hope as pilot center in medicine, science and humanitarianism, 1959. Home: Los Angeles, Calif. Died Oct. 2, 2010.

HORSBURGH, ROBERT LAURIE, entomologist; b. Coronach, Sask., Can., June 23, 1931; came to U.S., 1974; s. Minno Spencer and Helen (Louise) H.; m. Norma Jean Hodge; children: Karn Irene, Robert Scott, Sandra Lynn. BS, McGill U., Montreal, Can., 1956; MS, Pa. State U., State Coll., 1968, PhD, 1969. Entomologist Nova Scotia Dept. Agr., Kentville, N.S., Can., 1956-66, 1970-74, Va. Polytech. Inst., Steeles Tavern, Va., 1974-81; ctr. dir., entomologist Alson H. Smith Jr. Rsch. & Ext. Ctr. Va. Poly. Inst. and State U., Winchester, from 1981. Named Outstanding Extension Entomologist, Entomol. Soc. Am., 1983. Mem. Entomol. Soc. Can. Presbyterian. Home: Stephens City, Va. Died Mar. 8, 2009.

HORTON, JARED CHURCHILL, retired diversified financial services company metal products executive; b. Greenwich, Conn., Oct. 8, 1924; s. Frederic Jared and Marcelene (Churchill) H.; m. Pauline Elizabeth Finn, June 14, 1947; children: Janette Elizabeth Hall, Cynthia Joan Carpenter, Allison Jane, Juliana Ruth. Student, Yale U., 1942; grad., Packard Jr. Coll., 1948. With PM Industries, Stamford, Conn., 1948-54; with Alleghany Corp., NYC, 1954-88, treas., 1956-88, sec., 1959-61, 63-88, v.p., 1967-88. Served to 1st lt. AUS, 1942-46. Episcopalian. Home: Greenwich, Conn. Died Jan. 19, 2010.

HOTCHKISS, BILL, author, educator; b. New London, Conn., Oct. 17, 1936; s. William H. and Merle B. (Stambaugh) H. BA in English, U. Calif., Berkeley, 1959; MA in English, San Francisco State U., 1960; MFA in Creative Writing, U. Oreg., 1964, DA in English, 1971, PhD in English, 1974. Tchr. English Colfax H.S., 1960-62; instr. English Sierra Coll., Rocklin, Calif., 1963-79, 84-85, prof. English, from 1988; instr. English Shasta Coll., 1980-81, Rogue C.C., 1985-88, 90. Author: Last Bear McCain, 2004, (textbook) Tilting at Windmills, 1966; (novels) The Medicine Calf, 1981, reissue, 1987, Crow Warriors, 1981, Soldier Wolf, 1982, Ammahabas, 1983, Spirit Mountain, 1984, Mountain Lamb, 1985, People of the Sacred Oak, 1986, Fire Woman, 1987, Dance of the Coyote, To Fell the Giants, 1991, Sierra Santa Cruz, 1992, Yosemite, 1995, (poetry) Steephollow Poems, 1966, The Graces of Fire, 1974, Fever in the Earth, 1977, Climb To The High Country, 1978, Middle Fork Canyon, 1979, Great Upheaval, 1990, Who Drinks the Wine, 2000, I Hear the Coyote, 2003, others, (criticism) Jeffers: The Sivaistic Vision, 1975, Poet from the San Joaquin, 1978; author numerous poems; co-author: Shoshone Thunder, 1983, Pawnee Medicine, 1983, McLaffertys, 1986, Desert Moon, 1987; (handbook) Sancho's Guide to Uncommon Literacy, 1990, 3rd edit., 1995; editor: Sierra Jour., 1965-78, 88-90, 95-96, 2003, 06-07, 08-; editor, book designer, printer, publ. Blue Oak Press; book designer, text editor Castle Peak Edits., 1966—; co-editor: Perspectives on William Everson, 1992, William Everson's The Residual Years, 1997, The Integral Years, 2000, Jeffers, The Double Axe, 1977; typesetter, book design adv. Dustbooks, Quintessence, Story Line, Blue Oak Press, Castle Peak Edits.; contbr. to programmed instructional software, filmstrips. Home: Cedar Ridge, Calif. Died May 18, 2010.

HOTELLING, HAROLD, economics professor, lawyer; b. NYC, Dec. 26, 1945; s. Harold and Susanna Porter (Edmondson) H.; m. Barbara M. Anthony, May 4, 1974; children: Harold, George, James, Claire, Charles. AB, Columbia U., 1966; JD, U. N.C., 1972; MA, Duke U., 1975, PhD, 1982. Bar: N.C. 1973. Legal advisor U. N.C., Chapel Hill, 1972-73; instr. bus. law U. Ky., Lexington, 1977-79, asst. prof., 1980-84; asst. prof. dept. econs. Oakland U., Rochester, Mich., 1984-89; assoc. prof. econs. Lawrence Technol. U., Southfield, Mich., from 1989, chmn. dept. humanities social scis. and comm., 1994-99. Contbr. articles to profl. jours. Lt. j.g. USNR, 1968—70. Episcopalian. Home: Rochester Hills, Mich. Died Dec. 29, 2009.

HOTES, ELIZABETH ANN, heavy equipment and land development company executive; b. Birmingham, Ala., Oct. 4, 1918; d. Richard and Florence (Ford) Oswald; m. Douglas N. Hotes; children— Richard, Elizabeth, John, Florence, Douglas. Student Hollins Coll., 1937-39, Phila. Sch. Indsl. Art, 1939-40, Art Inst., Chgo., 1941. Engring. draftsman Coast and Geodetic Survey, Washington, 1941-44; cartographer Aero Service, Phila., 1946-48; draftsman, artist C.E., Anchorage, 1968-71; sec., treas. T.E.R.R.A., Inc., Anchorage, 1971—; dir. Amstan, Inc., Anchorage, 1971-87, pres., 1980—; pres. Alaska Contracting Co. Inc., Anchorage. Home: Anchorage, Alaska. Died Aug. 9, 2010.

HOUCK, BECKY ANN, biology professor; d. J. A. and Mary Helen Abildskov; m. James Houck; 1 child, Clayton James. BS, U. Utah, Salt Lake City, 1972; PhD, U. Hawaii, Honolulu, 1977. Prof. biology U. Portland, Oreg., from 1978. Named Outstanding First Yr. Student Adv., Nat. Resource Ctr., 1999, Outstanding Prof. Yr., Oreg. Acad. Sci., 2000, Oreg. Prof. Yr., Carnegie Found., 2001. Achievements include research in octopus and fruit bat behavior. Died Sept. 2009.

HOUSER, JAMES HOWELL, chemical company executive; b. Milroy, Pa., Sept. 28, 1931; s. J. Lester and A. Adaleena (Treaster) H.; m. Sara Alice Graybill, July 25, 1956; children— James H., Patricia L., David B. BS in Chemistry, Dickinson Coll., 1953; MS in Indsl. Adminstrn, Carnegie-Mellon U., 1959. Sales rep. Koppers Co., Inc., 1959-63; sales rep. Pennwalt Corp., 1963-66, regional sales mgr. Phila., 1966-69, product mgr., 1969-73, dept. mgr., 1973-81; pres. Pennwalt Corp. (Fluorochems. div.), from 1981. Chmn. United Way, 1978-80. Served with U.S. Navy, 1953-56. Mem.: Whitford Country. Republican. Presbyterian. Home: West Chester, Pa. Died June 19, 2010.

HOUSER, JON PETER, chiropractor; b. Bklyn., Aug. 27, 1929; s. Floyd Malachi and Dolly (Samish) Houser; m. Donna R. Youngberg, Dec. 28, 1968; children: Jon Peter, Jennifer Rae, Joi Lynn, Jessica Ruth, Tania Marina. Student, Purdue U., 1953—55; D in Chiropractics, Lincoln Chiropractic Coll., 1956. Diplomate Nat. Chiropractic Bd. Extern Spears Chiropractic Hosp., Denver, 1956—57; dir. Palmer Chiropractic Clinic, Harvey, Ill., from 1957; co-dir. Oak Forest Chiropractic Clinic, Ill., from 1981; mem., sec. chiropractic staff Janse Chiropractic Ctr., 1982—84, mem., exec. rev. bd. Exec. bd. trustees Nat. Coll. Chiropractic, 1982—84, planning and devel. com., 1983—84, coun. alumni affairs and devel., 1983—85, pres.'s adv. panel, 1983—84, chmn., student liaison com., 1983—85. With USAF, 1948—52. Mem.: VFW, Coun. Roentgenology, Nat. Coll. Chiropractic Alumni Assn. (pres., dir. from 1983), Lincoln Chiropractic Coll. Alumni Assn. (pres., dir.), Am. Acupuncture Soc., Am., Ill., Chgo. Chiropractic Socs. (pres.), Shriners Club, Masons Club, Am. Legion (life; post comdr. 1979—85). Home: Park Forest, Ill. Died July 3, 2010.

HOVDESVEN, ARNE, lawyer; b. Hagerstown, Md., May 17, 1928; s. E. Arne and Florence (Lesher) H.; m. Helen Murray, Nov. 5, 1988; children from previous marriage: Steven, Eric, Susan. BA, North Tex. State Coll., Denton, 1947; JD, U. Mich., Ann Arbor, 1956. Bar: N.Y. 1957, U.S. Dist. Ct. (so. dist.) N.Y. 1959, U.S. Ct. Appeals (2d cir.) 1958. Indsl. relations specialist Allis-Chalmers Mfg. Co., Milw., 1947-50; assoc. Shearman & Sterling, NYC, 1956-65, ptnr., 1965-91, of counsel, from 1992. 1st. lt. U.S. Army, 1950-53. Mem. ABA (com. on corp. practice), N.Y. State Bar Assn. (chmn. bus. banking and corp. law sect. 1984-85), Assn. Bar City of N.Y. Clubs: Sleepy Hollow Country (Scarborough, N.Y.). Episcopalian. Home: Wilmington, NC. Died Mar. 12, 2009.

HOVING, THOMAS, museum director, consultant, writer; b. NYC, Jan. 15, 1931; s. Walter and Mary (Osgood Field) H.; m. Nancy Melissa Bell, Oct. 3, 1953; 1 dau., Petrea Bell. BA, Princeton U., 1953, MFA, 1958, PhD, 1959, HHD (hon.), 1968; LHD (hon.), Hofstra U., 1966; LLD (hon.), Pratt Inst., 1967; DFA (hon.), NYU, 1968; LittD (hon.), Middlebury Coll., 1968. Staff Medieval Met. Mus. Art and The Cloisters, 1959-65, curator, 1965-66; commr. NYC Dept. Parks, NYC, 1966-67; adminstr. NYC Dept. Recreation & Cultural Affairs, 1967; dir. Met. Mus. Art, 1967-77; museum and cultural affairs cons. firm Hoving Associates, Inc., NYC, 1977—2009; pres. spl. mus. exhibitions The Planning Corp., 1983-91; arts and entertainment corr. ABC-TV show 20/20, 1978-84; editor Connoisseur mag., 1981-91. Author: Guide to the Cloisters, 1964, The Chase, The Capture, 1975, Kuerners and Olsons; exhbn. catalogue, 1976, Two Worlds of Andrew Wyeth: A Conversation with Andrew Wyeth, 1978, Tutankhamun, The Untold Story, 1978, King of the Confessors, 1981, Masterpiece, 1986, Discovery, 1989, Making the Mummies Dance: Inside the Metropolitan Museum of Art, 1993, Andrew Wyeth: Autobiography, 1995, False Impressions, The Search for Big Time Art Fakes, 1996, Greatest Works of Art of Western

Civilization, 1997, Art for Dummies, 1999, The Art of Dan Namingha, 2000, American Gothic, 2005, Master Pieces, The Curators' Game, 2005; contbr. articles on art, parks and recreation to profl. publs., mags. and newspapers; art commentator Artnet. Com, 2008-09. Past trustee Inst. Fine Arts NYU. Lt. USMC, 1953-55. Decorated knight Legion of Honor France; recipient Bronze medal Citizens Budget Com., 1966, Cue mag. award, 1966, Disting. Achievement award Advt. Club America, 1966, Disting. Contbn. award Park Assn. N.Y.C., 1967, Elsie de Wolfe award American Inst. Interior Designers, 1967, Woodrow Wilson award Princeton U., 1977 Mem. AIA (hon.) Died Dec. 10, 2009.

HOWARD, ALLEN RICHMOND, JR., corporate executive; b. San Francisco, Dec. 15, 1920; s. Allen Richmond and Elizabeth Mead (Coates) Howard; m. Carlotte Greenfield, Mar. 7, 1953; children: Charles F., Allen Richmond III, Derek G. Student, Brown U., 1940—41; BS, U.S. Naval Acad., 1944. Registered profl. engr., Pa. Commd. ensign USN, 1944, advanced through grades to lt. comdr., 1954, assigned to USS Lake Champlain, USS San Diego, various aircraft squadrons and air stas., ret., 1954; with Singer Mfg. Co., Bridgeport, Conn., 1954—55, Thalheimer & Wertz, Architects and Engrs., 1955—58; pres. McCullough Howard & Co., Phila., 1959—69, Williard Inc., Jenkintown, 1969—79; chmn. Greenfield Co., Phila., 1980—82, mgmt. cons., 1982—87; pres. Quaker City Internat., Inc., 1987—89; mem. Pa. Aeros. Com., 1957—62. Mem.: Harbour Ridge Yacht and Country Club (Stuart, Fla.), Overbrook Golf Club (Bryn Mawr, Pa.), Mid Ocean Club (Bermuda), N.J. Golf Club, Pine Valley Club, Sunnybrook Golf Club (Plymouth Meeting, Pa.). Episcopalian. Died Oct. 8, 2009.

HOWARD, GODFREY G., state legislator; b. Montreal, Que., Can., Sept. 18, 1924; AB, Harvard U., 1950; postgrad., Northeastern U.; MBA, Columbia U. Ret. incorporator No. N.H. Found.; mem. dist. 10 N.H. Ho. of Reps., Concord. Mem. Tuftonboro planning bd., Lake Winnipesaukee Watershed project; mem. sci. tech. and energy com. N.H. Ho. of Reps. Dir. Spaulding Youth Ctr. Mem. Tuftonboro Assn. (pres.). Republican. Home: Mirror Lake, NH. Died Sept. 4, 2009.

HOWARD, LEE MILTON, international health consultant; b. India, Nov. 9, 1922; s. John A. and Grace Mary (Lemen) H.; m. Maxwell C. Croft, June 22, 1946; children: Regan Ellis, Christine Baker, Kirk Anderson, Gene Reid. B.Sc., Baylor U., 1945; MD, Johns Hopkins U., 1947, M.P.H., 1958, Dr.P.H., 1959. Diplomate: Am. Bd. Preventive Medicine. Med. and surg. resident Church Home Hosp., Balt., 1947-50; mem. med. staff Clough Meml. Hosp., Ongole, Andhra, India, 1950-53; dir. Victoria Meml. Hosp., Warangal, Andhra, India, 1953-56; physician Med. Care Clinic, Johns Hopkins Hosp., 1957; U.S. adviser on malaria Philippines, 1960-62; U.S. regional malaria adviser Far East AID, 1962-64; chief malaria br. health div. AID, Washington, 1964-66; dep. dir. health svc. Office Tech. Coop. and Rsch., 1966-67, dir., 1967, Office Health, Devel. Support Bur., 1967-80; mem. expert co. on malaria WHO, 1966-79, chmn. com., 1970, adviser parasitic diseases, 1970; mem. U.S. del. World Health Assembly, 1969-79, WHO cons. on resource moblzn., 1979-81. AID devel. fellow, 1979-80; vis. asso. prof. parasitology Inst. Hygiene, U. Philippines, 1960—; vis. lectr. Johns Hopkins U. Sch. Pub. Health, Harvard Sch. Pub. Health, Yale U., Boston U., Tulane U.; lectr. Takemi Sympoisum, U. Tokyo, 1988; vis. fellow Inst. Devel. Studies, U. Sussex, 1979; mem. U.S. del., PAHO directing coun.; chief office resource mblzn. PAHO, 1981-82, office of external affairs, 1982-87; cons. to AID, WHO, World Bank, 1987—; sec., mem. exec. com. Gorgas Meml. Inst., 1972; mem. U.S. Sr. Exec. Svc. Recipient Superior Honor award AID, 1974, Disting. Career Svc. award AID, 1987, Disting. Alumnus award Baylor U., 2001; rsch. fellow U.S. Armed Forces Epidemiol. Bd., 1958-59. Fellow Am. Pub. Health Assn., Royal Soc. Tropical Medicine and Hygiene; mem. Am. Soc. Tropical Medicine and Hygiene, Philippine Pub. Health Assn., Johns Hopkins U. Sch. Pub. Health Soc. Alumni (pres. 1984-85), Soc. Scholars (Johns Hopkins U.), Nat. Coun. Internat. Health (charter mem.), Diplomatic and Consular Officers Ret., Cosmos Club (Washington). Home: Catonsville, Md. Died Apr. 28, 2009.

HOWELL, DEBORAH, editor; b. San Antonio, Jan. 15, 1941; m. Nicholas D. Coleman, 1975 (dec. 1981); C. Peter Magrath, 1988; 8 stepchildren. Grad., U. Tex., 1962. City editor The Mpls. Star, 1975—79; editor St. Paul Pioneer Press, 1979—90; chief Washington bur., editor Newhouse News Svc., 1990—2005; ombudsman The Washington Post, 2005—08. Adv. bd. Univ. Tex. Coll. Comm. Died Jan. 1, 2010.

HOY, CYRUS HENRY, language professional, educator; b. St. Marys, W.Va., Feb. 26, 1926; s. Albert Pierce and Marie Dorothy (West) H. BA, U. Va., 1950, MA, 1951, PhD, 1954. Instr. English U. Va., 1954-56; asst. prof. Vanderbilt U., 1956-60, asso. prof., 1960-64; prof. English U. Rochester, N.Y., 1964-76, John B. Trevor prof. English and comparative lit. N.Y., 1976-94, John B. Trevor prof. emeritus N.Y., from 1994, chmn. dept. English N.Y., 1984-88. Author: The Hyacinth Room, An Investigation Into the Nature of Comedy, Tragedy, and Tragicomedy, 1964; author: intro., notes and commentaries to The Dramatic Works of Thomas Dekker, 4 vols., 1980; mem. editl. bd. Shakespeare Quar., 1968-90, Medieval and Renaissance Drama, 1980-92; gen. editor: Regents Renaissance Drama Series, 1964-76; co-editor Dramatic Works in the Beaumont and Fletcher Canon, Vol. 1, 1966, Vol. 2, 1970, Vol. 3, 1976, Vol. 4, 1979, Vol. 5, 1982, Vol. 6, 1984, Vol. 7, 1989, Vol. 8, 1992, Vol. 9, 1994, Vol. 10, 1996; contbr. articles to profl. jours. Fulbright scholar, 1952-53; Guggenheim fellow, 1962-63 Democrat. Presbyterian. Home: Rochester, NY. Died Apr. 27, 2010.

HOY, MARY CAMILLA, retired French linguist, educator; b. Clinton, SC, Jan. 3, 1925; d. William Edwin and Mabel Elizabeth (George) H. AB magna cum laude, U. S.C., 1943, MA, 1944; postgrad., U. Paris, 1946-47; PhD, Bryn Mawr Coll., 1954. Instr. French and Spanish Sweet Briar Coll., 1948-50, St. Mary's Coll., Raleigh, N.C., 1952-59; asst. prof. French Birmingham So. Coll. (Ala.), 1959-61, assoc. prof., 1961-66; assoc. prof. French East Carolina U., 1966-67; chmn. dept. fgn. langs Greensboro (N.C.) Coll., 1967-82; chmn. div. humanities Greensboro Coll. (N.C.), 1982-84, Moore prof. French and Spanish, 1985—89, prof. emerita, 1989—2010. French Govt. fellow, 1946-47; fellow Bryn Mawr Coll., 1944-46 Mem. Am. Modern Lang. Assn., S. Atlantic Modern Lang. Assn., Am. Assn. Tchrs. French, Am. Assn. Tchrs. Spanish and Portuguese (sec. N.C. chpt. 1982-84), AAUW (corp. del. Greensboro Coll.), Nature Conservancy, Phi Beta Kappa, Alpha Chi (regional pres. 1984-86). Republican. Episcopalian. Home: Ashland, Ky. Died July 28, 2010.

HOYER, DAVID RALPH, oil company executive; b. Phila., Aug. 12, 1931; s. Ralph W. and Clara Barton (Patterson) H.; m. Sandra; children: David, Ann, Richard. BS, U. Del., 1953. Vice pres. refining Gulf Oil Co., Houston, 1972-75, v.p. supply and transp., 1975; pres. Warren Petroleum Co. div. Gulf Oil Corp., Tulsa, 1976-77, Gulf Oil Co.-Internat., London, 1977-82; pres. Warren Petroleum div. Chevron U.S.A., Inc., Tulsa, 1983-87; sr. v.p. mfg., supply & mktg. Chevron U.S.A. Inc., San Francisco, 1987-91; pres. Chevron U.S.A. Products Co., San Francisco, from 1992. Mem. bd. govs. San Francisco Symphony; mem. corp. ann. support Fine Arts Mus. San Francisco; mem. corp. adv. com. Nat. Coun. of La Raza. Methodist. Died Feb. 18, 2009.

HRUBY, NORBERT JOSEPH, former college president, educational consultant, playwright; b. Cicero, Ill., Feb. 4, 1918; s. Thomas John and Marie Frances (Rychtik) H.; m. Dolores Marie Smith, June 19, 1943; children: Michael G., Monica M., Patricia A. PhB, Loyola U., Chgo., 1939, MA, 1941; postgrad. drama, Yale, 1946-47; PhD, Loyola U., Chgo., 1951; LittD (hon.), Hope Coll., Mich., 1985; ArtsD (hon.), Kendall Coll. Art & Design, 1990; DHL (hon.), Aquinas Coll., 1992. Instr. English Loyola U., Chgo., 1947-48; asst. dean Coll. Commerce, 1948-51, dir. pub. info., 1951-55; dir. radio and TV U. Chgo., 1955-58; assoc. dean Univ. Coll., 1958-62; v.p. Mundelein Coll., Chgo., 1962-69; pres. Aquinas Coll., Grand Rapids, Mich., 1969-86, adj. prof., from 1986; interim pres. Kendall Coll. Art and Design, 1989. Ednl. cons., dir. coll. self-studies, 1966-70; cons. communications Am. Mut. Ins. Alliance, 1960-70; co-planner in founding Chgo. Ednl. TV Assn. channel WTTW, 1951-54; assoc. dir. Court Theatre, Chgo., 1957-62; pub. relations cons. Forest Preserve Dist., Cook County, Ill., 1958-62; mem. Nat. Adv. Council on Adult Edn., 1973-75; examiner North Central Assn. Colls. and Secondary Schs., 1972-86. Dir.: Faustus, 1957, The Cenci, 1958, Francesca da Rimini, 1959, Six Characters in Search of an Author, 1961; producer, dir., author radio and TV series, Loyola U., U. Chgo., 1951-58; Author: Survival Kit for Invisible Colleges, 1973, 2d edit., 1980; contbr.: chpts. to New Directions series, 18 plays staged. Officer Grand Rapids Area Council Chs.; pres. Grand Rapids Area Center for Ecumenism, 1972-74; bd. dirs. Grand Rapids Symphony, Grand Rapids Civic Theatre, 1973-74, Greater Grand Rapids Housing Corp., 1971-74, Hope Rehab. Network, 1987—; pres. Grand Rapids Council for Humanities, 1988—. Served to capt. AUS, 1942-46. Recipient 5 nat. awards for network and syndicated radio series prodns. U. Chgo., 1956-58, Bishop Haas Social Justice award, 1985; named one of 100 Most Effective Pres., Exxon Edn. Found., 1986. Mem. Assn. Cath. Colls. and Univs. (bd. dirs. 1971-80, chmn. 1976-78), Nat. Assn. Ind. Colls. and Univs. (bd. dirs. 1983-86), Blue Key, Alpha Sigma Nu, Pi Gamma Mu. Roman Catholic. Home: Grand Rapids, Mich. Died May 18, 2010.

HSIE, ABRAHAM W., biomedical sciences educator; b. Hsinwu, Tauyuan, Taiwan, Mar. 3, 1940; came to U.S., 1963; s. Yuntsai and Lanmei (Drum) H.; m. Mayphoon Hsu, July 14, 1963; children: Marvin Suchin, Dora Yuchin Hsie-Hilty. BS, Nat. Taiwan U., Taipei, 1962; MA, Ind. U., 1965, PhD, 1968. Instr. U. Colo. Med. Ctr., Denver, 1969-71, asst. prof., 1971-72; group leader Oak Ridge Nat. Lab., 1972-86; lectr. U. Tenn., Oak Ridge, 1972-76, prof., 1976-86; prof., assoc. dir. environ. toxicology, med. br. U. Tex., Galveston, from 1986. Disting. vis. scientist U.S. EPA, Washington. Author: (with others) Banbury Report II: Quantitative Mammalian Cell Mutagenesis, 1979; contbr. 150 articles to profl. jours. 2d lt. Republic of China Air Force, 1962-63. Recipient Disting. Alumni Svc. award Ind. U., 1980. Fellow Japan Soc. Sci.; mem. Am. Assn. Cancer Rsch., Am. Soc. Biology Chemists and Molecular Biologists, Environ. Mutagen Soc., Radiation Rsch. Soc., Soc. Toxicology, Soc. Chinese Bioscientist in Am., Houston Hakka Chinese Assn. (1st v.p. 1993). Democrat. Achievements include discovery of adenosine 3',5'-phosphate-mediated reversed transformation of Chinese hamster ovary (CHO) cells and establishment of roles of cyclic nucleotides in carcinogenesis; development of a mutational assay at the hypoxanthine-quanine phosphoribosyltransferase (hprt) locus in CHO cells and a polymerase chain reationbased molecular analysis procedure at this locus in CHO cells for studies of quantitative and molecular mammalian cell mutagenesis. Home: Galveston, Tex. Died Apr. 10, 2010.

HUBBARD, JAMES MITCHELL, accounting firm executive; b. Montgomery, Ala., May 7, 1943; s. Lawrence Thornton and Mary Elizabeth (Crumpton) H. BS in Acctg, U. Ala., 1966, postgrad., 1978-80. Internal auditor Vanity Fair Mill, Monroeville, Ala., 1966-68; staff acct. Arthur Young & Co., Birmingham, Ala., Charlotte, N.C., 1968-72; controller Constrn., Fin., Mgmt. Corp., Charlottesville, Va., 1972-73; audit mgr., adminstrv. mgr., treas. Motion Industries, Inc., Birmingham, Ala., 1973-80, dir. corp. purchasing and distbn., 1980-83; ptnr. Snow Stewart Hubbard & Cade, C.P.A.s, 1983-85; pres. Jim Hubbard & Assocs., Inc., from 1985. Mem. Am. Inst. C.P.A.s. Home: Birmingham, Ala. Died May 25, 2009.

HUBE, RICHARD W., JR, (RICK HUBE), state legislator; b. Hartford, Conn., Jan. 31, 1947; State rep. Windham Dist. 4 Vt. House of Reps., 1999—2002, state rep. Dist. 1, 2003—09; small bus. owner; dir. Stratton Winhall Found., Stratton Arts Festival; trustee Chapel Of Snows; founder Hube Inc., 1990—2009. Recipient Legislative Svc. award, Vt. League of Cities & Towns, 2008. Republican. Died Dec. 21, 2009.

HUCHRA, JOHN PETER, astronomer, educator; b. Jersey City, Dec. 23, 1948; s. Mieczyslaw Piotr and Helen Ann Huchra; m. Rebecca M. Henderson; 1 child, Harry Matthew. BS, MIT, 1970; PhD, Calif. Inst. Tech., 1976. Ctr. fellow Ctr. Astrophysics, Cambridge, Mass., 1976-78; astronomer Smithsonian Astrophys. Obs., Cambridge, Mass., 1978-89, sr. astronomer, 1989—2005; lectr. dept. astronomy Harvard U., Cambridge, Mass., 1979-84, prof. dept. astronomy, 1984—2002, Robert O. and Holly Thomis Doyle prof. cosmology, 2002—10, vice-provost rsch. policy, 2005—06, sr. adv. to provost on rsch. policy; assoc. dir. Ctr. for Astrophysics, Cambridge, Mass., 1989—98; dir. Fred Lawrence Whipple Observatory, 1994-98. Mem. coun. Space Telescope Sci. Inst., Balt., 1987-95, 2007-10; chmn. working group on galaxy radial velocities Internat. Astron. Union, Paris, 1988-2010; chmn. large astron. data base working group NASA/IPAC, Washington, 1988-92, Astrophysics subcom. NASA, 2007-10; mem. astronomy and astrophysics survey Optical Panel, NAS, NRC, 1989-90; adv. bd. and vis. com. Arecibo Obs., Ithaca, NY, 1989-92; users com. Cerro Tololo Inter-Am. Obs., La Serena, Chile, 1989-91; vis. com. ESO, 1993-97; mem. NRC Com. on Astronomy and Astrophysics, 1994-2001, co-chmn. 1997-2001; mem. AURA, bd. dirs., 1995-2004, chair, 2001-04; mem. NRC bd. on physics and astronomy, 1997-2003, chair, 2000-03; chair NOAO Future Directions Com., 1998-99; vis. prof. Cambridge U., 2003-10; mem. math. and phys. sci. adv. com. NSF, 2003-07; lectr. in field. Contbr. chapters to books to profl. jours. Rsch. grantee, NASA, 1979-2010, Smithsonian Instn., 1980, NSF, 1984-89, 99-2010 Fellow AAAS (Newcomb Cleve. award 1990), American Phys. Soc. AIP (pub. policy com. 1988-95); mem. NAS, Am. Acad. Arts and Scis., Am. Astron. Soc. (pub. bd. chmn., 1986-88, councillor 1998-2001, sci. editor Astrophys. Jour. 1998-2003, pres.-elect, 2007-08, pres. 2008-10, past pres. 2010), Royal Astron. Soc., Astron. Soc. of the Pacific, Am. Phys. Soc. Astrophysics Divsn. (exec. com. 1996-97), Nat. Environ. Leadership Coun., Wilderness Soc., Nat. Audubon Soc., Mass. Audubon Soc., Union of Concerned Scientists, Nature Conservancy, Trustees of Reservations, Appalachian Trail Conf., Am. Contract Bridge League, Greenpeace, Green Mtn. Club, Appalachian Mtn. Club, Sierra Club, Sigma Xi, Gamma Nu. Achievements include discovery of Comet Huchra, of nearest gravitational lens; revision of cosmic distance scale; completion of first and second Center for Astrophysics Redshift Survey; measurement of infall of our Milky Way Galaxy into the Virgo Cluster; discovery of Great Wall of galaxies, 2 Micron All Sky Survey. Died Oct. 8, 2010.

HUDSON, RICHARD L., retired adult education educator, minister; b. Watertown, NY, Dec. 1, 1920; s. M. A. and M. (D.) Hudson; m. Beatrice Evalin Olson, Apr. 23, 1955; 2 children. AB, Syracuse U., 1944, PhD, 1970; BD, Yale U., 1947, STM, 1950. Ordained to ministry United Meth. Ch., 1945. Asst. min. Rome (NY) Meth. Ch., 1946-48, Meth. Ch., Parish, NY, 1950-54; commentator Religion Makes News, Sta. WSYR, Syracuse, NY; dir. pub. rels. Syracuse Area United Meth. Ch., 1954-56; min. Meth. Ch., Carthage, NY, 1956-58; Cokesbury fellow, grad. asst. Syracuse U., 1958-61; mem. faculty Wyoming Sem., Kingston, Pa., 1961-64, New Eng. Coll., Henniker, NH, 1964-83, prof., 1971-83, prof. emeritus, from 1983, dean humanities, 1970-71. Adj. prof. history Post Coll., Waterbury, Conn., 1985—91, Quinnipiac Coll., Hamden, Conn., 1987—97. Author: A Burden for Souls, 1950, A Student's Guide to the New Testament, 1963, The Challenge of Dissent, 1970; editor: The Only Henniker on Earth, 1980. Chmn. Henniker HIst. Soc., 1976—83; docent Canterbury Shaker Village, 1975—83, New Haven Colony Hist. Soc., 1984—93, bd. dirs., 1988—90. Mem.: Nat. Assn. Scholars, Mayflower Soc., Tabard, Tau Theta Upsilon, Theta Chi Beta. Died July 10, 2009.

HUENING, WALTER CARL, JR., retired consulting application engineer; b. Boston, Feb. 10, 1923; s. Walter Carl and Gladys (Whittemore) H.; m. Margaret Laurence McGeary, Aug. 5, 1944 (dec. 1986); children: Peter Carl, Susan Laurence Huening Locke; m. Elizabeth Ann Young Wright, Apr. 9, 1988. BSEE magna cum laude, Tufts U., 1944. Registered profl. engr., N.Y., Ohio. Instr. elec. engring. Tufts U., Medford, Mass., 1946-48; distbn. engr. plant engring. dept. GE, Lynn, Mass., 1948-50, application engr. indsl. power engring. Schenectady, NY, 1952-56, product planner protective devices dept. Plainville, Conn., 1956-58, design engr. vacuum cleaner dept. Cleve., 1958-59, application engr. comml. and mcpl. dept. Schenectady, 1960-62, application engr. steel mill, 1962-68, cons. application engr. indsl. power engring., 1968-89; ret., 1989. Mem. U.S. nat. com. Internat. Electrotech. Commn., tech. advisor on Tech. Com. 73 matters, 1972-89. Contbr. tech. papers to jours. and chpts. to books; patentee vacuum cleaner latch. Lt. comdr. USNR, 1944-46, 50-52, ret. Fellow IEEE (life, R. H. Kaufmann award 1988, Indsl. and Comml. Power Systems Dept. Achievement award 1989, prizes for papers 1970, 82); mem. Tau Beta Pi. Independent. Avocations: photography, collecting recorded traditional jazz music. Home: Lawrenceville, Ga. Died Aug. 29, 2009.

HUG, ARTHUR, JR., banker; b. Far Rockaway, NY, Dec. 17, 1922; s. Arthur and Jennie (Blick) H.; m. Julia Fowler. BBA, Hofstra U., 1953. Vice pres. Security Nat. Bank, Huntington, N.Y., 1956-59; exec. v.p. Nat. Bank N.Am., West

Hempstead, N.Y., 1959-68; pres. L.I. Trust Co., Garden City, N.Y., 1968-74, chmn. bd., pres., chief exec. officer, 1974-79, chmn. bd., chief exec. officer, 1979-83, chmn. bd., from 1983. Chmn. bd., pres., chief exec. officer LITCO Bancorp. of N.Y., Inc., Garden City, 1974-84; chmn. bd., chief exec. officer N.Am. Bancorp Inc., Garden City, 1985— Mem. Banking and Monetary Policy Commn., U.S. Chamber of Commerce, 1965-69, N.Y. State Assembly Adv. Subcom. on Econ. Devel., 1970-72; Chmn. council SUNY, Old Westbury, 1971-74; mem. Nassau County (N.Y.) Reapportionment Commn., 1975. Served with USNR, 1942-46. Mem. N.Y. State Bankers Asson., Am. Bankers Assn., Ind. Bankers Asson. N.Y. (exec. comm. 1978, Co-chmn. legislative comm., dir. 1974-75), L.I. Bankers Asson. (director 1968, treas. 1968, v.p. 1969, pres. 1970), Pres.'s Assn. Died July 12, 2010.

HUGHES, ALLEN, music critic; b. Brownsburg, Ind., Dec. 28, 1921; s. Maurice McKinley and Bess (Collyer) H.; m. Marian Nina Berklich, Mar. 28, 1964. Student, George Washington U., 1940-42; BA, U. Mich., 1946, B.Mus., 1947; postgrad., N.Y. U., 1948-50. Lectr. music Toledo Mus. Art, 1946-47; asst. editor, critic Musical America, 1950-53; freelance writer Paris, 1953-55; music critic N.Y. Herald Tribune, 1955-60; mem. music faculty Bklyn. Coll., 1958-60; music critic N.Y. Times, 1960-61, asst. dance critic, 1961-62, dance critic, 1962-65, music critic, 1965-86. Columnist Chamber Music mag., 1998—2002. Served to lt. (j.g.) USNR, 1943-46. Died Nov. 16, 2009.

HUGHES, BLAKE, retired professional society administrator, retired publishing executive; b. NYC, June 24, 1914; s. Ferdinand Holme and Ines (de Cordova) H.; m. Betty Jean Wolf, Aug. 26, 1951; children: Diane Elizabeth, Brian Blake. Degre de civilisation, Sorbonne U., Paris, 1935; AB summa cum laude, Dartmouth Coll., 1936; postgrad., Columbia U., 1936-37. Salesman Edward B. Smith & Co., Smith, Barney & Co., investment bankers, NYC, 1936-38, N.Y. Life Ins. Co., 1939-40; promotion mgr. Engring. News Record, Constrn. Methods, McGraw-Hill Inc., NYC, 1947-50; promotion mgr., dir. mktg. Archtl. Record F.W. Dodge Corp., NYC, 1951-61; assoc. pub. Archtl. Record McGraw-Hill Inc., NYC, 1961-68, pub. Archtl. Record, 1968-80, pub. House & Home, 1976-77; pres. Internat. Inst. for Architecture, Washington, 1978-81. Author: (novels) A Lifetime's Too Short, 2002, (short stories) Good Job, 2001, Loves and Consequences, 2005, Collected Poems, 2005. Trustee Unity (Maine) Coll., 1965-75; pres. Internat. Archtl. Found., 1973-78; bd. dirs. Nat. Home Improvement Coun., 1976-77. Lt. USNR, 1940-45. Decorated Order of Fatherland War (Russia). Mem. Union Internat. Architects (archtl. critics com. 1978-80), Appalachian Housing Inst. (bd. dirs.), Charleston Artist Guild (pres. 1990-91), English Speaking Union (pres. Charleston chpt. 1995-96), Carolina Yacht Club, Phi Beta Kappa, Delta Sigma Rho. Home: Charleston, SC. Died June 11, 2009.

HUGHS, RICHARD EARL, business school dean; b. Rochester, NY, Jan. 2, 1936; s. Earl Leaman and Frances Rose H.; m. Gretchen Markwardt, Mar. 31, 1959; children— Mark Allen, Grant Evan. BS in Physics, U. Rochester, 1957; MS in Math, Purdue U., 1959, PhD, 1962. Systems analyst Sandia Corp., Albuquerque, 1962-64; asst. prof. Carleton Coll., 1964-66; pres. Math. Service Assos., Inc., Edwardsville, Ill., 1966-69; asso. prof. applied math. and info. systems So. Ill. U., 1966-69; sr. cons. Cresap, McCormick & Paget, Inc., 1968-70; assoc. dean Grad. Sch. Bus. Adminstr., NYU, 1970-77; dean Coll. Bus. Adminstrn., U. Nev., Reno, 1977-84; v.p. corp. affairs Sierra Pacific Resources, Reno, 1984-90; dean Sch. Bus. SUNY, Albany, from 1990. Bd. dirs. Bonnel Growth Fund, Childs Geriatric Mgmt. Svcs. Corp, ARC Regional Blood Svcs., N.Y., Pa. bd.; bd. dirs., chmn. Citizens Pvt. Enterprise, 1986-89; com. on edn. C. of C. and Industry N.Y.C., 1970-74; adv. com. Medgar Evers Coll., CUNY, 1971-74; NSF rsch. fellow Purdue U., 1958-60. Mem. deferred compensation com. State of Nev., 1978-84, Nev. Gov.'s Commn. on Econ. Diversification, 1981-83, State of Nev. Trade Mission to Japan, South Korea, Hong Kong and China, 1986; cmty. liaison com. IRS, 1991—; mem. bus. adv. coun. Mental Health Assn. in N.Y. State Inc.; bd. dirs. Albany Bus. Maintenance Orgn. Mem. Assn. Corp. Growth, Western Assn. Collegiate Schs. Bus. (bd. dirs. 1977-84), Mid Atlantic Assn. Colls. Bus. Adminstrn. (exec. com. 1990—), Albany-Colonie Regional C. of C. (bd. dirs. 1991-95), Rotary (bd. dirs. 1989-90), Sigma Xi, Beta Gamma Sigma. Home: Reno, Nev. Died Apr. 28, 2010.

HULET, ERVIN KENNETH, retired nuclear chemist; b. Baker, Oreg., May 7, 1926; s. Frank E. and Marjorie (Suiter) H.; m. Betty Jo Gardner, Sept. 10, 1949 (dec. Jan. 1992); children: Carri, Randall Gardner. BS, Stanford U., 1949; PhD, U. Calif., Berkeley, 1953. AEC grad. student U. Calif. Radiation Lab., Berkeley, 1949-53; research chemist nuclear chemistry div. Lawrence Livermore Nat. Lab., Livermore, Calif., 1953-66, group leader, 1966-91, ret., active emeritus, from 1991. Achievements include discovery of divalent oxidation state in actinide elements; co-discovery of symmetric fission in actinides. Served with USNR, 1944-46. Fulbright scholar Norway; Welch Found. lectr., 1990; recipient Am. Chem. Soc. award for Nuc. Chemistry, 1994. Fellow AAAS, Am. Inst. Chemists (chmn. Golden Gate chpt. 1992); mem. Am. Chem. Soc. (chmn. divsn. nuclear chemistry and tech. 1987, award in nuclear chemistry 1994), Am. Phys. Soc. Achievements include co-discovery of Element 106; discovery of bimodel fission. Home: Diablo, Calif. Died June 29, 2010.

HUMPHREY, JOSEPH ANTHONY CHRISTIE, mechanical engineering educator; b. London, Jan. 15, 1948; came to U.S., 1977; s. Joseph A. and Madelaine I. (Curran) H.; m. Vivienne Mooney, Aug. 24, 1970 (div. Jan. 1992); children: Luisa, Fiona, Katie; m. Sarah E. Davis, Mar. 6, 1993. Diploma in chem. engring., Instituto Quimico De Sarria, Barcelona, Spain, 1970; MASChemE, U. Toronto, Ont., Can., 1973; PhDME, Imperial Coll. Sci. and Tech., London, 1977. Rsch. staff dept. mech. aerospace engring. Princeton (N.J.) U., 1977-78; asst. prof. mech. engring. U. Calif., Berkeley, 1978-83, assoc. prof., 1983-88, prof., from 1988, vice chmn., 1989-91. Harrison prof. mech. engring. U. Liverpool, 1987-88. Adv. editor Internat. Jour. Heat and Fluid Flow, 1988—; assoc. editor Jour. Fluid Engring., 1991—, Advances in Info. Storage Systems, 1990; contbr. numerous articles to profl. jours. Fulbright fellow, 1984. Mem. ASME, AAAS, Am. Phys. Soc., Brit. Arachnological Soc., Inst. Quimico de Sarria, Soc. Engring. Sci. (bd. dirs. 1991—), Coun. for Internat. Exch. of Scholars (bd. dirs., com. S.W. Europe 1990—), Pi Tau Sigma, Sigma Chi. Avocations: swimming, reading, classical music. Home: Ivy, Va. Died Mar. 1, 2010.

HUMPHREY, SAMUEL STOCKWELL, town official, physicist; b. Canton Center, Conn., Apr. 25, 1923; s. Harold William and A. Genevieve (Stockwell) H.; m. Mary Elizabeth Mills, Feb. 4, 1945; children: Warren Mills, Kenneth Stockwell, Marianne Ruth. BS, U. Conn., 1948; MA, Wesleyan U., Middletown, Conn., 1950; postgrad., U. Utah, 1961-63. Enlisted USAF, 1942, advanced through grades to lt. col., 1966, ret., 1971; physicist Wesleyan U., 1948-51; cons. physicist Canton, Conn., 1971-74; tchr. physics Canton (Conn.) High Schs., 1973-74, real estate broker, 1975-93; first selectman Town of Canton, 1983-87, selectman, 1989-91, mem. bd. fin., from 1997; mgr. Cherry Brook Farm LLC. Dir. Conn. Conf. Municipalities, Conn. Interlocal Risk Mgmt. Agys. (CIRMA), 1987; bd. dirs. Sundown Ski Patrol, Inc.; mem. policy bd. and exec. com. Capitol Region Coun. of Govts., 1983-87; cons. physicist RCA, Burlington, Mass., 1971-74, Martin Marietta, Orlando, Fla., 1971-72; co-founder Simsbury (Conn.) Bank & Trust Co.; researcher in field. Author, editor numerous studies and reports. Trustee, treas. 1st Congl. Ch., Canton Ctr., 1972-85; chmn. Hist. Dist. Commn., Canton, 1972-80, Mcpl. Bd. Fin., Canton, 1975-83, 97—; justice of peace State of Conn., 1974—. Recipient numerous awards and decorations USAF and Philippines; Wesleyan U. fellow, 1948-50. Mem. Optical Soc. Am. (emeritus), Air Force Assn., Conn. Christmas Tree Growers Assn. (bd. dirs. 1984-90, v.p. 1990, pres. 1992-95), New Eng. Christmas Tree Assn. (dir. 1990—), Selman Field Hist. Assn. La. (dir. 2005—), Hanscom Flying Club (Bedford, Mass., pres. 1955-59), Skiesta Club (pres. 1964-68), Sigma Xi (assoc.), Sigma Pi Sigma. Republican. Mem. United Ch. of Christ. Avocation: ski patrol. Home: Canton Center, Conn. Died July 10, 2009.

HUMPHREY, WATTS SHERMAN, information technology executive, writer; b. Battle Creek, Mich., July 4, 1927; s. Watts Sherman Humphrey and Katharine (Strong) Osborne; m. Barbara Fallon, May 22, 1954; children: Katharine Pickman, Lisa Fish, Sarah DeCamello, Watts Jr., Peter, Erica Jarrett, Christopher. BS in Physics, U. Chgo., 1949, MBA, 1951; MS in Physics, Ill. Inst. Tech., 1950; PhD in Software Engring. (hon.), Embry Riddle Aero. U., 1998. Electronics engr. Fermi Inst. U. Chgo., 1949-51, dir. sci. pers. Chgo. Midway Lab., 1951-53; mgr. computing devel. Sylvania Electric Products, Natick, Mass., 1953-59; instr. computer design Northeastern U., Boston, 1956-59; with IBM, White Plains, NY, 1959-86, mgr. teleprocessing systems devel., 1959-64, dir. systems application engring., Armonk, N.Y., 1964-65, dir. time sharing systems, White Plains, 1965-66, dir. programming, 1966-68, v.p. tech. devel., Armonk, 1968-70, dir. Endicott (N.Y.) Labs., 1970-72, dir. policy devel., Armonk, 1972-79, dir. tech. assessment, White Plains, 1979-83, dir. programming quality and process, Poughkeepsie, N.Y., 1983-86; dir. software process program Software Engring. Inst. Carnegie Mellon U., Pitts., 1986-91, fellow, from 1991. Chmn. adv. bd. IBM Systems Rsch. Inst., N.Y.C., 1973-82. Author: Switching Circuits with Computer Applications, 1958, Managing for Innovation, Leading Technical People, 1987, Managing the Software Process, 1989, A Discipline for Software Engineering, 1995, Managing Technical People, Innovation, Teamwork and the Software Process, 1997, Introduction to the Personal Software Process, 1997, Introduction to the Team Software Process, 1999, Winning with Software: an Executive Strategy, 2002, PSP: A Self-Improvement Process for Software Engineers, 2005, TSP: Leading a Development Team, 2006, TSP: Coaching Development Teams, 2006; co-author (with W.R. Thomas): Reflections on Management: How to Manage Your Software Projects, Your Teams, Your Boss, and Yourself, 2010; contbr. numerous articles to profl. jours.; (mem. editl. bd.) Jour. Sys. and Software, 1988-96, Software Process, Improvement and Practice, 1996-, Empirical Software Engring., 1996-. Bd. examiners Malcolm Baldridge Nat. Quality Award, 1991; sci. adv. com. Std. System Ctr. USAF, 1989-92. With USN, 1944-46. Recipient Aerospace Software Engineering award American Inst. of Aeronautics & Astronautics, 1993, Boeing award for Leadership & Innovation in Software Process Improvement, 2000, Nat. Medal of Tech. The White House, 2003, Profl. Achievement award Ill. Inst. Tech. Alumni Assn., 2010. Fellow IEEE (editorial bds. Spectrum 1982-83, The Institute 1982-83, reviewer Software 1984, Computer 1984, IBM System Jour. 1989), Assn. for Computing Machinery, Inst. for Radio Engrs. (chmn. computer sect. 1959). Democrat. Achievements include patents in field. Avocations: running, piano, bridge. Home: Sarasota, Fla. Died Oct. 28, 2010.

HUNT, ALBERT BARKER, textile company executive; b. Santa Barbara, Calif., Jan. 22, 1910; Student, Stanford U., 1932, Harvard U. Sch. Bus. Adminstrn., 1934. Pres., treas. Rivett, Inc., Boston, until 1967; chmn. bd. Fieldcrest Mills Inc., Eden, N.C., 1980-83, Amoskeag Co., Boston. Bd. dirs. Bangor & Aroostook R.R. Co. Died Dec. 6, 2009.

HUNT, JAMES L., lawyer; b. Chgo., Oct. 20, 1942; BA magna cum laude, DePauw U., 1964; JD, Northwestern U., 1967. Bar: Calif. 1967. Atty. McCutchen, Doyle, Brown & Enersen, San Francisco, 1967, ptnr., chmn. firm, 1988—91, 1999—2001, chmn. litig. dept., 1991—95; ptnr. Bingham McCutchen LLP, San Francisco, from 2001, chmn. litig. practice group. Atty. rep. 9th Cir. Jud. Conf., 1991-94; bd. dirs. The Lurie Co.; trustee The Lurie Found. Assoc. editor: Northwestern U. Law Rev., 1966-67. Bd. dirs. San Francisco Giants; bd. visitors Northwestern U. Law Sch., 1989—. Named a No. Calif. Super Lawyer, Law & Politics & SF Mag., 2004. Mem. Am. Coll. Trial Lawyers, Phi Beta Kappa, Order Coif. Died Mar. 29, 2010.

HUNT, RICHARD VINCENT, architectural designer; b. Gloucester, Mass., Nov. 30, 1923; s. John Henry and Mildred Janet (Johnson) H.; student Northeastern U., 1948; B.S., Wentworth Inst. Tech., 1951; m. Alice M. McCollum, May 12, 1947; children— Eileen Jane, Richard Vere, Alison Joan, John Henry, Alan Drew. With John H. Hunt & Son Inc., Gloucester, Mass., 1951—, estimator and project mgr., 1957-62, pres., owner, chief designer, 1962—; incorporator Cape Ann Savs. Bank. Mem. Gloucester Planning Bd., 1955-65, chmn., 1960-65; chmn. Gloucester Bldg. Code Bd. Appeals, 1975—; incorporator Addison Gilbert Hosp.; past chmn. bd. trustees Health & Wellfare Fund; trustee Gloucester Lyceum and Library, Seacoast Health Systems. Served with USNR, 1942-46; ETO, PTO. Mem. Am. Soc. Profl. Cons., Boston Soc. Architects, Contractors and Builders Assn. Cape Ann, Nat. Trust Hist. Preservation, Nat. Maritime Hist. Trust, Bostonian Soc. Republican. Clubs: Algonquin of Boston, Masons. Died Mar. 1, 2009.

HUNTER, ROBERT NELSON, real estate financing and investment executive; b. Palmer, Mass., June 5, 1930; m. Elizabeth Angell, Sept. 11, 1954; children: Robert N. Jr., Thomas A. BA, Trinity Coll., 1952; MBA, U. Mich., 1956. Real estate analyst Conn. Mut. Life Ins. Co., Hartford, 1956-59, mgr., 1959-63, officer, 1963-72, asst. v.p., 1972-77, v.p., 1981-89, sr. v.p., 1987-89; pres. Jefferson Capital Advisers, Hartford, from 1989. Bd. dirs. Capitol Housing Corp., Hartford, Lyman Farms Inc., Middlefield, Conn., Southport Fin. Corp. Served to 1st lt. USAF, 1952-54. Recipient Trinity Alumni medal Trinity Coll., Hartford, 1983. Mem. Am. Inst. Real Estate Appraisers (pres. Conn. chpt. 1965), Mortgage Bankers Assn. Am. (bd. govs.). Home: Captiva, Fla. Died June 16, 2009.

HUNTER, WALTER RAYMOND, physician; b. Bloomington, Ind., Aug. 2, 1953; s. Richard Raymond and Cecile Ruth (Rogers) H. AB, Ind. U., 1974; MD, Ind. U., Indpls., 1978. Diplomate Am. Bd. Internal Medicine. Intern internal medicine Youngstown (Ohio) Hosp. Assn., 1978-81, chief resident, 1981-82; internist, chief medicine King Khahid Mil. City Hosp., Saudi Arabia, 1982-83; internist PruCare/Health First Med. Group, Memphis, 1983-85, Lerwick Clinic, St. Louis, 1986, Littleton (Colo.) Clinic, 1987-89; pvt. practice Denver, from 1989. Mem. Archdiocesan AIDS Task Force, Denver, 1991—; advisor Archdiocesan Hospice of Peace, Denver, 1992; chmn. ethics com. Mercy Med. Ctr., Denver, 1990—; clin. instr. U. Colo. Sch. Medicine, Denver, 1990—; advisor pastoral care dept. St. Thomas Sem., Denver, 1991—. Columnist The 12 Step Times, 1989—; mem., contbg. editor Partners Mag. Choir mem. St. John's Cathedral Choir, Denver, 1987-92; mem., actor Main St. Players, Littleton, Colo., 1992. Mem. AMA, ACP, Am. Soc. Internal Medicine, Am. Soc. Law, Medicine and Ethics, Nat. Hospice Orgn., Soc. for Health and Human Values, The Hastings Ctr., Kennedy Inst. Ethics. Roman Catholic. Avocations: piano, theater, singing, golf. Home: Myrtle Beach, SC. Died Mar. 20, 2009.

HURLEY, ANN MARIE, municipal official; b. N.Y.C., July 13, 1925; d. Timothy Charles and Mary Frances (Lacey) O'Neill; ed. N.Y.C. public schs., bus. courses and seminars; m. John D. Hurley, Jr., Aug. 24, 1947; children— John Edward, Patty Ann Hurley McGovern. Clk., bookkeeping supr. Guaranty Trust Co., N.Y.C., 1942-47; bookkeeping supr. Continental Bank & Trust Co., N.Y.C., 1947-48, N.Y. Trust Co., N.Y.C., 1948-49; head bookkeeper, prin. clk., dep. receiver of taxes Town of Huntington, N.Y., 1960-67, receiver of taxes, 1967—; spl. com. revision Suffolk County Tax Act, mem. Blue Ribbon com. to revise Suffolk County Tax Act, 1982; mem. adv. bd. N.Y. State Community Affairs. Pres. Heatherwood Civic Assn., South Huntington Democratic Club; exec. bd. Suffolk County Dem. Party; Dem. zone leader, Huntington Station, N.Y.; committeeperson Dem. Party, 1960—; mem. Spl. Com. on Women's Issues, 1983—; parish council St. Elizabeth Roman Catholic Ch.; grand marshal Huntington ann. St. Patrick's Day Parade, 1976; bd. dirs. ARC; mem. adv. bd. Immaculate Conception Seminary; mem. Cancer Care, Deborah Hosp. Found.; chmn. fundraising Paulist Fathers. Named Woman of Yr., Nassau and Suffolk Bus. and Profl. Women's Clubs, 1983; recipient Clara Barton award Red Cross, 1988. Mem. N.Y. State Receivers and Collectors of Taxes Assn. (v.p. 1979-82, pres. 1982), Suffolk County Receivers of Taxes Assn. (pres. 1969-83). Club: Soroptimist (Grand Pres. Huntington chpt. 1977-80, bd. dirs., Woman of Distinction 1987). Home: Huntington Station, NY. Died Mar. 13, 2009.

HURST, KENNETH THURSTON, publisher; b. London, Apr. 3, 1923; came to U.S., 1947, naturalized, 1953; s. Ralph Thurston and Karen (Tottrup) H.; m. Joan Gee Dec. 10, 1994; children: Lincoln, Brian, Maria Therese. Student pvt. schs. Account exec. Hutzler Advt. Agy., Dayton, Ohio, 1948-53; advt. and promotion mgr. McGraw-Hill Book Co., NYC, 1953-58; advt. and publicity mgr. Hawthorn Books, Inc., NYC, 1958-61; gen. mgr. Prentice-Hall of India Pvt. Ltd., New Delhi, 1961-63; v.p., gen. mgr. Prentice-Hall Internat., Inc., Englewood Cliffs, N.J., 1963-70, exec. v.p., 1970, now pres. Dir. Internat. Book Distbr., Ltd., Prentice-Hall S.E. Asia Ltd., Prentice-Hall India Ltd.; State Dept. adviser to Brazil and Burma; adviser AID Mission to Turkey, 1964, Morocco, 1965; cons. U.S. Info. Agy., U. N.C., U. Scranton, SUNY, MIT, Faculty Folio mag.; lectr. State Dept. Program Bur.,

NYU, Rockland Community Coll., U. Scranton, Drew U., Wagner Coll., Lake Forest (Ill.) Coll., Olivet (Mich.) Coll., Rosemont Coll., Pa., Oberlin Coll., Ohio, Corning Coll., N.Y., U. Cen. Fla., U. So. Fla., Edison C.C., Pepperdine Coll., Calif., Chestnut Hill (Pa.) Coll., Spearfish Coll., S.D., Rockpoint Colony, Cornell U., Stanford U., Russell Sage Coll., Fla. State U.; faculty ann. pubs. seminar; co-chmn. Internat. Sports Awards, 1982, Pub. Hall of Fame, 1984; mem. policy bd. Ctr. for the Book; chmn. Books Across the Sea. Co-author: Books for National Growth, 1965, Indian Publishing Since Independence, 1980, American Books Abroad, 1986, Spiritual Insights for Daily Living, 1986; author: Live Life First Class, 1985, Paul Brunton: A Personal View, 1988, Living the Good Life, 1989; contbr. articles to profl. jours. Mem. Spiritual Adv. Coun., Elizabeth Kubler-Ross Ctr.; mem. com. to balance budget Ctr. Applied Rsch. in Edn., Internat. Inst. Integral Scis.; trustee Valley Cottage Free Libr.; chmn., mem. nat. exec. coun. Spiritual Frontiers Fellowship; chmn. N.Y. Easter Seal dr., 1983, Paul Brunton Philosophic Found.; bd. dirs. Ctr. for Positive Living; pres., bd. dirs. Collier County Friends of Libr. Assn.; mem. Lee County Libr. Adv. Bd.; v.p. Las Vistas Assn. With Fleet Air Arm Royal Navy, 1942-47. Recipient Presdl. E award and E Star, Pub. Hall of Fame. Mem. Asia Soc., St. John's Old Boys' Assn., Assn. Am. Pubs. (chmn. internat. div., chmn. del. to India 1979, 84, to Thailand 1981), Am. Mgmt. Assn., Inst. Bus. Planning, Mensa, Acad. Religion (trustee), Inst. Near-Death Studies (bd. dirs.), Circumnavigators Club, Forum Club (bd. dirs.), Eng. Speaking Union (bd. dirs.), Internat. Club Fla., Overseas Press Club, Fla. Coun. Humanities, Neapolitan Club, Boston Athletic Club, Publishers Club, Englewood Club (gov.), Rotary (bd. dirs.). Republican. Episcopalian. Died Apr. 29, 2009.

HURT, JAMES RIGGINS, English language educator; b. Ashland, Ky., May 22, 1934; s. Joe and Martha Clay (Riggins) H.; m. Phyllis Tilton, June 5, 1958; children: Christopher, Ross, Matthew. AB, U. Ky., 1956, MA, 1957; PhD, Ind. U., 1965. Asst. prof. Ind. U., Kokomo, 1963-66; asst. prof. U. Ill., Urbana-Champaign, 1966-69, asso. prof., 1969-73, prof. English, from 1973. Author: Aelfric, 1972, Catiline's Dream, 1972, Film and Theatre, 1974, Writing Illinois, 1992, (play) Abraham Lincoln Walks at Midnight, 1980; co-editor: Literature of the Western World, 1984. Served with U.S. Army, 1957-59. Fellow Ill. Ctr. Advanced Study, 1979-80, 86-87. Mem. MLA, Ill. State Hist. Soc. Home: Champaign, Ill. Died June 16, 2010.

HURVICH, LEO MAURICE, experimental psychologist, educator, vision researcher; b. Malden, Mass., Sept. 11, 1910; s. Julius Solomon and Celia (Chikinsky) Hurvich; m. Dorothea Jameson, Oct. 23, 1948 (dec. 1998). BA, Harvard U., 1932, MA, 1934, PhD, 1936; MA (hon.), U. Pa., 1972; DSc (hon.), SUNY, 1989. Asst. dept. psychology Harvard U., Cambridge, Mass., 1936-37, instr. psychology, 1937-40; researcher Grad. Sch. Bus. Adminstrn., Harvard U., Boston, 1940-47; research psychologist Eastman-Kodak Co., Rochester, N.Y., 1947-57; prof. psychology, chmn. Washington Square Coll., NYU, 1957-62; prof. U. Pa., Phila., 1962-79, prof. emeritus, from 1979, mem. Inst. Neurol. Scis., from 1962, mem. Inst. for Rsch. in Cognitive Sci., 1990—2000. Vis. prof. Ctr. Visual Sci. U. Rochester, NY, 1974; adv. mem. vision com. NRC-NAS, Washington; mem. rsch. adv. com. Lighthouse Internat.; fellow Ctr. Advanced Study in Behavioral Scis., Stanford, Calif., 1981—82; mem. vis. com. MIT, 1977—83. Author: Color Vision, 1981, (with D. Jameson) The Perception of Brightness and Darkness, 1966; editor: (with D. Jameson) Visual Psychophysics-Handbook of Sensory Physiology, 1972; assoc. editor: Jour. Optical Soc. Am., 1980-84; topical editor color vision Color Rsch. and Application, 1992-94; contbr. articles to profl. jours. Mem. NRC-NAS com. on U.S. currency study, 1984-86. Recipient Howard Crosby Warren award Soc. Exptl. Psychologists, 1971, Deane B. Judd-AIC award Association Internationale de la Couleur, 1985, fellow John Simon Guggenheim Found., 1964-65, Hermann von Helmholtz award Cognitive Neurosci. Inst.,1987. Fellow: Am. Acad. Arts & Scis., Am. Psychol. Soc. (William James Fellow), Am. Psychol. Assn. (del. inter soc. color coun. 1955—82, Disting. Sci. Contbr. award 1972), NY Acad. Scis., Optical Soc. Am. (Edgar D. Tillyer medal 1982); mem.: Vision Sci. Soc., Rsch. Group in Color Vision Deficiencies, Inter-Soc. Color Coun. (I.H. Godlove award 1973), Internat. Brain Rsch. Orgn. (contbr. to Ency. of Neurosci. on Color Vision Deficiencies), Soc. Neurosci., Psychonomic Soc., Nat. Acad. Scis., Ea. Psychol. Assn., Sigma Xi, Phi Beta Kappa. Home: New York, NY. Died Apr. 25, 2009.

HUSK, G. RONALD, chemist; b. Waynesburg, Pa., Oct. 19, 1937; s. Woodrow W. and Freda (Wells) Husk. BS summa cum laude, Waynesburg Coll., 1959; MS in Chemistry, U. Mich., 1961, PhD, 1964. Rsch. assoc. U. Wis., Madison, 1964—66; asst. prof. Villanova U., Pa., 1966—71; chief organic chemistry br. Army Rsch. Office, Durham, NC, 1971—73; chief chemistry br. US Army European Rsch. Office, London, 1973—77; chief organic and polymer chemistry br. Army Rsch. Office, Rsch. Triangle Park, 1977—84, chief chem. synthesis and polymer chemistry, from 1986; vis. rsch. assoc. prof. U. NC, Chapel Hill, 1977—84; sec. Army Fellowship, 1984—85; vis. scientist U. Tex., Austin, 1984—86; adj. prof. Southwest Tex. State U., 1984—86; scientist in residence Durham Sch. Sys., 1982—83; adj. prof. NC State U., from 1990. Contbr. articles to sci. jours. Mem.: AAAS, Am. Inst. Chemists, Am. Chem. Soc., Sigma Xi. Died Jan. 0, 1993.

HUSSEY, WARD MACLEAN, retired federal official; b. Providence, Mar. 13, 1920; s. Charles Ward and Agnes (Shaw) H.; m. Anne Hutchinson (div.); children: Thomas Ward, Carolyn Anne Hussey Bourdow, Wendy Ellen Hussey Addison. AB, Harvard U., 1940, LLB, 1946; MA, Columbia U., 1944. Bar: D.C. 1946. With Office Legis. Counsel, US House of Reps., Washington, 1946-89, dep. legis. counsel, 1970-72, legis. counsel, 1972-89; adviser to fgn. governments on tax reform, 1989—2009. Co-author: Basic World Tax Code, 1992, rev. edit., 1996. With USNR, 1942-46. Fellow Harvard Internat. Tax Program (sr.). Home: Alexandria, Va. Died Nov. 16, 2009.

HUSTING, PETER MARDEN, advertising consultant; b. Bronxville, NY, Mar. 28, 1935; s. Charles Ottomar and Jane Alice (Marden) H.; m. Carolyn Riddle, Mar. 26, 1960; children: Jennifer, Gretchen, Charles Ottomar; m. Myrna Diaz, May 11, 1996. BS, U. Wis., 1957; grad., Advanced Mgmt. Program, Harvard U., 1974. Sales rep. Crown Zellerbach Corp., San Francisco, 1958-59; media analyst Leo Burnett Co., Chgo., 1959-61, time buyer, 1961-62, asst. account exec., 1962-63, account exec., 1963-68, v.p., account supr., 1968-72, sr. v.p., account dir., 1972-79, group exec., 1979-86, exec. v.p., 1979-92, dir. human relations internat., 1986-92, also bd. dirs., ret., 1992; pres. Husting Enterprises, Chgo., from 1993. Dir. Columbian Mutual Life Ins. Co., Harley-Davidson Customer Funding Corp. Trustee Shedd Aquarium Soc., Chgo., 1980-94, hon. life trustee, 1995—; bd. dirs. Chgo. Better Govt. Assn., 1976-92, Leadership Coun. Met. Open Cmtys., Chgo., 1980-86, Lyric Opera Guild, 1971-78, Chgo. Forum, 1969-76. Served with AUS, 1958. Mem.: Indian Hill (Winnetka) (bd. govs. 1975-79), The Valley Club (Montecito, Calif.), Coral Casino Club (Santa Barbara). Avocations: flying, swimming, hunting, trekking, golf. Died June 4, 2009.

HUTCHINSON, FREDERICK EDWARD, retired academic administrator; b. Atkinson, Maine, June 1, 1930; s. Malcolm Eugene and Gertrude (Sargeant) H.; m. Dione Kendall Williams, Sept. 6, 1952; children: Juliana, Karen. BS, U. Maine, 1953, MS, 1958; PhD, Pa. State U., 1966. Mem. faculty dept. plant and soil scis. U. Maine at Orono, 1953-72, prof. soil sci., 1967-72, chmn. dept., 1971-72, dean Coll. Life Scis. and Agr., dir. expt. sta., 1972-75, v.p. for research and pub. service, 1975-80, 81-82, acting v.p. acad. affairs, 1980-81; exec. dir. Bd. for Internat. Food and Agr. Devel., 1982-85; dir. Ohio Agr. Research and Devel. Ctr., 1985-86; v.p. for agrl. adminstrn. Ohio State U., Columbus, 1986-89, provost, v.p. acad. affairs, 1989-90, sr. v.p., provost, 1990-92; pres. U. Maine, 1992—97. Mem. bd. govs. ICRISAT, Hydrebad, India, 1978-82; bd. govs. CIAT, Cali, Columbia, chmn. bd. govs., 1988-90. Mem. editorial bd. Jour. Higher Edn. Chmn. bldg. fund dr. U. Maine, 1973-75; mem. adv. bd. Maine Rural Environ. Conservation Program, 1974-78, commn. on missions N.W. United Meth. Ch., Columbus; chmn. joint research com. AID, 1977-80; pres. ARI, 1988; trustee Maine Coast Meml. Hosp., 1998-2006; chmn. bd. trstees Maine Coast Healthcare Found., 2003-08; With AUS, 1948-49. Alumni fellow Pa. State U., 1992. Fellow AAAS, Am. Inst. Chemists, Soil Conservation Soc. Am.; mem. Am. Soc. Agronomy (Outstanding Tchr. award N.E. chpt. 1971), Agrl. Research Inst. (pres. 1988-89), Soil Sci. Soc., Assn. Theol. Schs. (com. on accrediting), Audubon Soc., Sigma Xi, Phi Kappa Phi, Alpha Zeta. Methodist (chmn. ch. bldg. com. 1967-73). Died Apr. 7, 2010.

HUTCHISON, JAMES DONALD, state agency administrator; b. Columbus, Ohio, Nov. 15, 1932; s. Harold Warren and Valerie Helen (Jarnot) H.; m. Brenda Mae Ruth, Apr. 28, 1962; children: Caroline, Jamie, Adrianne, Shannon. Student, Niagara U., 1956-58, U. Buffalo, 1958-61. Technician Carborundum Co., Niagara Falls, N.Y., 1956-57; inspector Retail Credit Co., Atlanta, 1957-62; investigator N.Y. State Dept. Labor, Albany, 1962-88; adminstr., analyst N.Y. State Dept. Social Svcs., Albany, from 1968. Bd. dirs. Lay Budget Com. East Green Bush Schs., N.Y., 1972-76; mem. Empire State Regatta Com., 1987-94. With USCG, 1950-53, U.S. Army, 1953-56. Mem. BPOE (esq. 1988-89), Elks (esq. 1988-89). Republican. Roman Catholic. Avocations: rowing, tennis. Home: Rensselaer, NY. Died Jan. 11, 2009.

HUTTON, EDWARD LUKE, retired medical products executive; b. Bedford, Ind., May 5, 1919; s. Fred and Margaret (Drehobl) H.; m. Kathryn Jane Alexander; children Edward Alexander, Thomas Charles, Jennie Hutton Jacoby. BS with distinction, Ind. U., 1940, MS with distinction, 1941; LLD (hon.), Ind. U., Cumberland Coll., 1992. Dep. dir. Joint Export Import Agy. (USUK), Berlin, 1946-48; v.p. World Commerce Corp., 1948-51; asst. v.p. W.R. Grace & Co., 1951-53, cons., 1960-65, exec. v.p., gen. mgr. Dubois Chems. div., 1965-66, group exec. Specialty Products Group and v.p., 1966-68, exec. v.p., 1968-71; cons. internat. trade and fin., 1953-58; fin. v.p., exec. v.p. Ward Industries, 1958-59; pres., CEO Chemed Corp., Cin., 1970—93, chmn., 1993—2004, non-exec. chmn., from 2004; chmn. Omnicare, Inc., Cin., 1981—2003, non-exec. chmn., 2003—08, chmn. emeritus, from 2008. Chmn. bd. dirs. Nat. San. Supply Co., 1983-97; E. Hutton Internat. scholarship program establisher, Ind. U., 2003; bldg. funder, Hutton Sch. Bus., Cumberland Coll., Williamsburg, Ky., 2004. Co-chmn. Pres.'s Pvt. Sector Survey on Cost Control, exec. com., subcom.; former trustee Millikin U., 1973-84. 1st lt., U.S. Army, 1945-47. Recipient Disting. Alumni Svc. award Ind. U., 1987. Mem. AAUP (governing bd. dirs. 1958—), Econ. Club, Princeton Club, Univ. Club, Queen City Club, Bankers Club. Home: Cincinnati, Ohio. Died Mar. 3, 2009.

HUTTON, JAMES MORGAN, III, investment banker; b. Detroit, Aug. 18, 1927; s. James Morgan, Jr. and Marianne (Wurlitzer) H.; m. Virginia Palfrey, Dec. 17, 1954; children—Marianne D. Hutton Felch, Sarah J., James P. Grad., Hill Sch., 1945, Dartmouth Coll., 1950. Salesman New Eng. Mut. Life Ins. Co., 1950-51; with W.E. Hutton & Co., NYC, 1951-74, partner, 1958-64, mng. partner, 1964-74, W.E. Hutton & Co. (merged into Thomson McKinnon Securities, Inc.), 1974; exec. v.p. Thomson McKinnon Securities, Inc., 1974-89, Thomson McKinnon Securities Inc. (merged into Prudential-Bache Securities, Inc.), from 1989. Served with USNR, 1945-46. Mem. Psi Upsilon. Clubs: Apawamis, Am. Yacht (Rye); Nantucket (Mass.) Yacht.). Home: Rye, NY. Died July 25, 2010.

HYDZIK, MICHAEL JAMES, retired hotel executive, consultant; b. Elmira, NY, Nov. 4, 1950; s. William and Anna Ruth (Baker) H. AAS, Corning CC, NY, 1970, SUNY, Delhi, 1975; BS, Lehigh U., 1975. Restaurant mgr. Holiday Inn, Horseheads, N.Y., 1974-76; banquet mgr. Am. Inn Town House, Rochester, N.Y., 1976-77; asst. food and beverage mgr. The Hotel Syracuse, Syracuse, N.Y., 1977-78; dir. catering The Am. Rochester, 1978-79; restaurant mgr. The Changing Scene, Rochester, 1979-81; dir. restaurants E.J. Delmonte Corp., Rochester, 1981-84; dir. food and beverage Sheraton U. Inn, Syracuse, 1984-86; exec. v.p. ops. The Thousand Islands Club, Alexandria Bay, N.Y., 1986-88; v.p. food and beverage The Lodge of Woodcliff, Fairport, N.Y., 1988-92; dir. food and beverage The Univ. Club of Rochester, 1992-94; gen. mgr. Richardson's Canal House Inn, Oliver Lands Inn Bed & Breakfast, Pittsford, N.Y., 1994-97; dir. food and beverage Four Points by Sheraton, Rochester, N.Y., 1997-99; ret., 1999. Mem. N.Y. State Wine & Grape Found., Penn-Yann, N.Y., Save the River, Clayton, N.Y. N.Y. State Wine Found. scholar, 1972. Mem. N.Y. State Restaurant Assn., Thousand Islands Club Yacht Club. Avocation: cooking. Died Jan. 19, 2009.

HYMES, DELL HATHAWAY, anthropologist, educator; b. Portland, Oreg., June 7, 1927; s. Howard Hathaway and Dorothy (Bowman) H.; m. Virginia Margaret Dosch, Apr. 10, 1954; 1 adopted child, Robert Paul; children: Alison Bowman, Kenneth Dell; 1 stepchild, Vicki (Mrs. David Unruh). BA, Reed Coll., 1950; MA, Ind. U., 1953, PhD, 1955; postgrad., UCLA, 1954-55; degree (hon.), U. Turino, Italy, 2002, U. Mass., Amherst, 2005. From instr. to asst. prof. Harvard U., 1955-60; from assoc. prof. to prof. U. Calif., Berkeley, 1960—65; prof. anthropology U. Pa., 1965-72, prof. folklore and linguistics, 1972-88, prof. sociology, 1974-88, prof. edn., 1975-88, dean Grad. Sch. Edn., 1975-87; prof. anthropology and English U. Va., 1987-90, Commonwealth prof. anthropology, 1990-98, Commonwealth prof. English, 1990-98, prof. emeritus, 1998—2009. Bd. dirs. Social Sci. Rsch. Coun., 1965-67, 69-70, 71-72. Author: Language in Culture and Society, 1964, The Use of Computers in Anthropology, 1965, Studies in Southwestern Ethnolinguistics, 1967, Pidginization and Creolization of Languages, 1971, Reinventing Anthropology, 1972, Foundations in Sociolinguistics, 1974, Soziolinguistik, 1980, Language in Education, 1980, In Vain I Tried to Tell You, 1981, (with John Fought) American Structuralism, 1981, Essays in the History of Linguistic Anthropology, 1983, Vers la Competence de Communication, 1984, Ethnography, Linguistics, Narrative Inequality, 1996, Now I Know Only So Far, 2003; assoc. editor: Jour. History Behavioral Scis., 1966-93, Am. Jour. Sociology, 1977-80, Jour. Pragmatics, 1977-2009; contbg. editor: Alcheringa, 1973-80, Theory and Society, 1976-96; editor: Language in Society, 1972-92; poetry editor Anthropology and Humanism, 2003-05; editl. bd.: New World Studies U. Va. Trustee Ctr. for Applied Linguistics, 1973-78. With AUS, 1945-47. Fellow Ctr. Advanced Study Behavioral Scis., 1957-58, Fellow Clare Hall, Cambridge, Eng., Guggenheim fellow, 1969-70, Nat. Endowment for Humanities sr. fellow, 1972-73. Fellow Am. Acad. Arts and Scis., Am. Folklore Soc. (pres. 1973-74), Brit. Acad.; mem. Am. Anthrop. Assn. (exec. bd. 1968-70, pres. 1983), Am. Assn. Applied Linguistics (pres. 1986), Linguistic Soc. Am. (exec. bd. 1967-69, pres. 1982), Coun. on Anthropology and Edn. (pres. 1978), Consortium Social Sci. Assns. (pres. 1984-85), Folklore Fellows Finland. Home: Charlottesville, Va. Died Nov. 13, 2009.

HYMES, NORMA, internist; b. NYC, July 20, 1949; d. Richard and Ellen (Posner) H.; m. Vincent M. Esposito, Nov. 1978 (div.); 1 child, Richard Hymes-Esposito. BS, Oberlin Coll., 1971; MD, Mt. Sinai, 1975. Diplomate Bd. of Internal Medicine. Intern, resident Maimonides Med. Ctr., Bklyn., 1975-78; internist Manhattan Health Plan, NYC, 1978-81, Manhattan Med Group, P.C., NYC, 1981-92, N.Y. Med. Group, P.C., 1992-2000, Continuum Health, 2000—01; pvt. practice, from 2001. Mgr. The Colonnade Condominium, N.Y.C., 1982-85; trustee N.Y. Soc. For Ethical Culture, N.Y.C., 1989-93, 96-2001. Mem. ACP, Am. Med. Women's Assn. Home: New York, NY. Died July 4, 2010.

ILARDI, VINCENT, historian, educator; b. Newark, May 15, 1925; s. Vincent and Filippa (Giannazzo) I.; m. Antoinette Ficarra, Dec. 26, 1952; 1 child, Vincent Michael. AB, Rutgers U., 1952; AM, Harvard U., 1953, PhD, 1958. Instr. Carnegie Inst. Tech., Pitts., 1956-57, U. Mass., Amherst, 1957—59, asst. prof. history, 1960—61, assoc. prof. history, 1961—68, prof. history, 1969—95, prof. emeritus, from 1995. Vis. rsch. scholar Yale U., New Haven, 1990-93, vis. prof. history, 1993-2000 Author: (with P.M. Kendall) Dispatches With Related Documents of Milanese Ambassadors in France and Burgundy, 1450-1461, 2 vols., 1970-71, Vol. 3, 1466, 1981, Studies in Italian Renaissance Diplomatic History, 1986, Renaissance Vision From Spectacles to Telescopes, 2007. Bayard Cutting fellow, 1953, Emerton fellow, 1954, 55-56, Faculty of Arts and Scis. fellow, 1954, Fulbright Rsch. scholar, 1959-60, Am. Philos. Soc. Rsch. grantee, 1960-63, Rockefeller Found. Rsch. grantee, 1961-63, Rockefeller Found. Internat. Rels. Rsch. grantee, 1963-64, Guggenheim fellow, 1970-71, NEH grantee, 1976-85, Nat. Italian Am. Foun. grantee, 1985. Home: Pittsfield, Mass. Died Jan. 6, 2009.

IMMEL, VINCENT CLARE, retired law educator; b. Gibsonburg, Ohio, Mar. 15, 1920; s. Joseph C. and Rosa F. (Bauer) I. Student, U. Toledo, 1937-38; BS, Bowling Green State U., 1941; JD, U. Mich., 1948. Bar: Ohio 1949, U.S. Supreme Ct. 1960, Mo. 1962. Mem. faculty Ohio No. U. Law

Sch., 1948-58, prof. law, 1957-58; mem. faculty St. Louis U. Law Sch., 1958—2004, asso. prof. law, 1958-61, prof. law, 1961-90, prof. emeritus, from 1990, asst. dean, 1959-62, dean, 1962-69. Vis. prof. law U. Ga., 1979-80, U. Liverpool, Eng., 1982-83, McGeorge Sch. Law, 1991-92, Roger Williams U. Sch. Law, 1994-95; mem. contracts com. multi-state bar exam., 1972-2000. Contbr. articles to legal jours. Mem. exec. com. St. Louis Civil Liberties Com.; bd. dirs. Little Symphony Assn., Legal Aid Soc. City and County St. Louis, St. Louis Symphony Soc. Served to lt. AUS, 1942-46. Decorated Bronze Star. Fellow Am. Bar Found.; mem. Am., Ohio, Mo. bar assns., Am. Judicature Soc., Bar Assn. St. Louis, Am. Law Inst., K.C., Phi Beta Kappa, Phi Alpha Delta, Phi Kappa Theta, Kappa Mu Epsilon, Kappa Delta Pi, Pi Kappa Delta. Home: Saint Louis, Mo. Died Nov. 26, 2009.

IMPERIALI, BEATRICE, financial and corporate communications executive; b. Naples, Italy, Apr. 6, 1957; d. Gian Luca and Luisa (Asquer) I. BA magna cum laude, Boston Coll., 1980; MA, Johns Hopkins U., 1982. Assoc. Greenwich (Conn.) Assocs., 1982-83; v.p. Bankers Trust Co., NYC, 1983-89; sr. v.p. Ruder-Finn, Inc., NYC, from 1990. Del. Commn. of European Communities Press and Info. Service, Washington, 1981; del. Commn. European Communities to the UN, N.Y.C., 1979. Avocations: reading, travel, languages. Home: New York, NY. Died July 4, 2010.

INGBAR, MARY LEE, economist; b. NYC, May 18, 1926; d. Lee Adam Gimbel and Edward C. and Ruth (Prince) Mack; m. Sidney H. Ingbar, May 28, 1950; children: David H., Eric E., Jonathan. SB in Econs. cum laude, Radcliffe Coll., 1946, AM in Econs., 1948, PhD in Econs., 1953; MPH cum laude, Harvard, 1956. Corrector dept. econs. Harvard U., 1949-50, Tufts U., 1949; rsch. assoc. Grad. Sch. Pub. Adminstrn. Harvard U., Cambridge, Mass., 1961-66; assoc. prof. health econs. in residence U. Calif., San Francisco, 1972-75; prin. rsch. assoc. in preventive and social medicine Harvard Med. Sch., Boston, 1976—80, prin. rsch. assoc. in social medicine and health policy, 1980-85, prin. assoc. in social medicine and health policy, from 1985; prof. family and community medicine U. Mass. Med. Sch., Worcester, 1977-82. Prin. rsch. assoc. in medicine, Beth Israel Hosp., Boston, 1976-88; vis. prof. health econs. The Amos Tuck Sch. of Bus. Adminstrn. at Dartmouth Coll. and Dartmouth Med. Sch., 1976-77; project dir. Innovative Methods of Pricing Ambulatory Care Treatment for Patients with Hypertension/U.S. Dept. Health Human Svcs. grant, 1980-82; cons. various cos. including WaterTest Corp., Manchester, N.H., 1982-88, Software Craftsmen, Inc., Boston, 1982-84; bd. dirs. WaterTest Corp.; pres. IFF, Inc., 1989—; lectr. in field, others. Editorial bd. Medical Care Jour., 1977-79; contbr. chpts. to books, articles to profl. jours. Overseer Peter Bent Brigham Hosp., 1976-84; trustee Brigham and Women's Hosp., 1984-86. Fellow: APHA (chmn. med. care sect. 1978—79, governing coun. 1974—76, 1985—88, 1991—93); mem.: AAAS, N.Y. Acad. Scis., Internat. Health Econs. Assn., Assn. Univ. Programs in Health Adminstrn., Assn. Tchrs. of Preventive Medicine, Am. Assn. World Health, Inst. Ops. Rsch. and Mgmt. Scis., Mass. Pub. Health Assn., Acad. Health, Am. Hosp. Assn., Am. Econ. Assn., Am. Med. Informatics, Phi Beta Kappa (Iota chpt. of Mass.). Died Sept. 18, 2009.

INGERSOLL, ROBERT STEPHEN, retired ambassador; b. Galesburg, Ill., Jan. 28, 1914; s. Roy Claire and Lulu May (Hinchliff) I.; m. Coralyn Eleanor Reid, Sept. 17, 1938 (dec. 2001); children: Coralyn Eleanor, Nancy, Joan (dec.), Gail, Elizabeth. Grad., Phillips Acad., 1933; BS, Yale U., 1937. With Armco Steel Corp., 1937-39, Ingersoll Steel & Disc div. (later Ingersoll Products div.), 1939-41, 42-54; pres. Ingersoll Products div., 1950-54; adminstrv. v.p. Borg-Warner Corp., 1953-56, pres., 1956-61, chmn., 1961-72, CEO, 1958-72; with Central Rsch. Lab., 1941-42; US amb. to Japan US Dept. State, Tokyo, 1972-73, asst. sec. for East Asian affairs Washington, 1974, dep. sec., 1974-76. Pres. Winnetka (Ill.) Sch. Bd., 1957-63; dep. chmn., life bd. trustees U. Chgo.; trustee Smith Coll., 1966-71, Aspen Inst. Humanistic Studies, Calif. Inst. Tech.; past bd. dirs. Johnson Found., Trilateral Commn. N.Am.; past mem. coun. Yale U.; past mem. adv. coun. Caterpillar Asia Pacific; past vice-chmn. Pacific adv. coun. United Techs. Nat. Park Found. Mem. Japan Soc. (chmn. N.Y.C. chpt. 1978-85), Chgo. Coun. Fgn. Rels., Coun. Fgn. Rels. N.Y.C., Indian Hill Club, Chgo. Club, Econ. Club (Chgo.), Comml. Club. Died Aug. 22, 2010.

INGRAM, MARY ELLEN, town official; b. Bryson City, N.C., Oct. 8, 1931; d. John Wright Higdon and Mary Ellen (Crisp) Higdon Christopher; m. Herbert Dewitt Ingram, Jr., June 6, 1953; children— Melanie, DeWitt. Student George Washington U., 1950-53. Cert. mcpl. clk. Sec., librarian U.S. Govt., Washington, Alaska and Taiwan, 1950-63; sec. Frank Briscoe Co., Leesburg, Va., 1971-75; town clk. Town of Herndon, Va., 1975—; sec. The White House, Washington, 1977-78. Active Loudoun County Republican Women, 1975—, Episcopal Women, St. James Ch., Leesburg, Va., 1974—. Mem. Bus. and Profl. Women (Woman of Yr. 1981), DAR, Internat. Inst. Mcpl. Clks., Va. Mcpl. Clks. Assn. Home: Leesburg, Va. Died Apr. 26, 2009.

INGWERSEN, NIELS, Scandinavian literature and folklore educator; b. Horsens, Denmark, May 18, 1935; came to U.S., 1965; s. Hans Henrik and Karen (Bach) I.; m. Faith Charlene Sloniger, June 3, 1965. Cand. mag., U. Copenhagen, 1963. From asst. to assoc. prof. U. Wis., Madison, 1965-73, prof., from 1973. Vis. prof. U. Aarhus, Denmark, 1978-79, UCLA, 1983. Editor: (anthology) Seventeen Danish Poets, 1981; co-author: Quests for a Promised Land, 1984; co-editor Scandinavian Studies, 1985-90, Wis. Introduction to Scandinavia, 1982—. Mem. Soc. for Advancement of Scandinavian Study (pres. 1969-71), Danish Rsch. Acad. Home: Madison, Wis. Died Nov. 14, 2009.

INKELES, ALEX, sociology educator; b. Bklyn., Mar. 4, 1920; s. Meyer and Ray (Gewer) K.; m. Bernadette Mary Kane, Jan. 31, 1942; 1 child, Ann Elizabeth BA, Cornell U., 1941; postgrad., Washington Sch. Psychiatry, 1943-46; MA, Cornell U., 1946; PhD, Columbia U., 1949; AM (hon.), Harvard U., 1957; student, Boston Psychoanalytic Inst., 1957-59; prof. (hon.), Faculdade Candido Mendez, Rio de Janerio, 1969, Faculdade Candido Mendez, 2002. Social sci. research analyst Dept. State and OSS, 1942-46; cons. program evaluation br., internat. broadcasting div. Dept. State, 1949-51; instr. social relations Harvard U., Cambridge, Mass., 1948, lectr., 1948-57, prof. sociology, 1957-71, dir. studies social rels. Russian Rsch. Ctr., dir. studies social aspects econ. devel. Ctr. Internat. Affairs, 1963-71, rsch. assoc., 1971-79; Margaret Jacks prof. edn., prof. sociology Stanford U., Calif., 1971-78, prof. sociology, 1978-90; sr. fellow Hoover Inst., from 1978; prof. emeritus, from 1990. Mem. exec. com. behavioral sci. div. NRC, 1968-75; lectr. Nihon U., Japan, 1985. Author: Public Opinion in Soviet Russia, 1950 (Kappa Tau Alpha award 1950, Grant Squires prize Columbia 1955); with R. Bauer, C. Kluckhohn) How the Soviet System Works, 1956, (with R. Bauer) The Soviet Citizen, 1959, Soviet Society (edited with H.K. Geiger), 1961, What is Sociology?, 1964, Readings on Modern Sociology, 1965, Social Change in Soviet Russia, 1968, (with D.H. Smith) Becoming Modern, 1974 (Hadley Cantril award 1974), Exploring Individual Modernity, 1983; editor: (with Masamichi Sasaki) Comparing Nations and Cultures, 1996, National Character: A Psychosocial Perspective, 1997, One World Emerging? Convergence and Divergence in Industrial Societies, 1998; editor-in-chief Ann. Rev. Sociology, 1971-79; editl. cons. Internat. Rev. Cross Cultural Studies; editl. bd. Ethos, Jour. Soc. Psychol. Anthropology, 1978; editor Founds. Modern Sociology Series; adv. editor in sociology to Little, Brown & Co.; contbr. articles to profl. jours. Recipient Cooley Mead award for Disting. Contbn. in Social Psychology, 1982; fellow Ctr. Advanced Study Behavioral Sci., 1955, Founds. Fund Research Psychiatry, 1957-60, Social Scis. Research Council, 1959, Russell Sage Found., 1966, 85, Fulbright Found., 1977, Guggenheim Found., 1978, Bernard van Leer Jerusalem Found., 1979, Rockefeller Found., 1982, Eisenhower Assn., Taiwan, 1984; NAS Disting. Scholar Exchange, China, 1983; grantee Internat. Rsch. and Exchs. Bd., 1989, NSF, 1989. Fellow AAAS (co-chmn. western ctr. 1984-87, chmn. Talcott Parsons award com. 1988-93), Am. Philos. Soc., APA; mem. NIMH, Nat. Inst. Aging (monitoring com. health retirement survey 1990—), Nat. Acad. Scis. (corr. human rights com. 1986-88, mem. com. on scholarly comms. with People's Republic of China, chmn. panel on social sci. and humanities, NRC panel on issues in democratization 1991-92), Am. Sociol. Soc. (coun. 1961-664, v.p. 1975-76), Ea. Sociol. Soc. (pres. 1961-62), World Assn. Pub. Opinion Rsch., Am. Assn. Pub. Opinion Rsch., Inter-Am. Soc. Psychology, Sociol. Rsch. Assn. (exec. com. 1975-79, pres. 1979), Soc. for Study Social Problems. Home: Palo Alto, Calif. Died July 9, 2010.

INOS, RITA HOCOG, retired school system administrator; b. Songsong, Rota, Northern Mariana Islands, May 12, 1954; m. Cristobal Songao Inos; children: Denise Lorraine, Ana Blossom. BA in Liberal Arts, U. Hawaii, 1979; MA in Sch. Adminstrn. and Supervision, San Jose State U., 1983; EdD in Ednl. Planning, Policy and Adminstrn, USC, 1993. Dir. programs & services Pacific Resources for Edn. & Learning (PREL), 1990—94, dep. dir., 1994—98, chair bd. dirs., 2004—06; commr. Northern Mariana Islands Pub. Sch. System, Saipan, 2002—06. Chairperson Northern Marianas Coll. Bd. Regents, 2006—08. Republican. Died Aug. 10, 2009.

IRELAND, HERBERT ORIN, retired engineering educator; b. Buckley, Ill., June 12, 1919; s. Harvey Glenn and Anna Estella (Perkinson) I.; m. Mary Leota Austin, Mar. 1, 1941; children: Orin Lee, Marin Fae, Jeanne Lu. BS, U. Ill., 1941, MS, 1947, PhD, 1955. From research asst. to prof. civil engring. U. Ill., Urbana, 1946-79, emeritus, from 1979. Cons. soil mechanics and found. engring., 1946—. Contbr.: sect. to Structural Engineering Handbook, 1968; also articles profl. jours. Served from 2d lt. to maj., C.E. AUS, 1941-46. Fellow Am. Soc. C.E., Geol. Soc. Am.; mem. Am. Ry. Engring. Assn., Sigma Xi, Tau Beta Pi, Chi Epsilon. Methodist. Home: Gilman, Ill. Died June 3, 2010.

IRVINE, PHYLLIS ELEANOR, nursing educator, administrator; b. Germantown, Ohio, July 14, 1940; m. Richard James Irvine, Feb. 15, 1964; children: Mark, Rick. BSN, Ohio State U., 1962, MSN, 1979, PhD, 1981; MS, Miami U., Oxford, Ohio, 1966. Staff nurse VA Ctr., Dayton, Ohio, 1962-66; mem. nursing faculty Miami Valley Hosp. Sch. Nursing, Dayton, 1968-78; teaching asst., lectr. Ohio State U., Columbus, 1979-82; assoc. prof. Ohio U., Athens, 1982-83; prof., dir. N.E. La. U., Monroe, 1984-88; prof., dir. sch. nursing Ball State U., Muncie, Ind., from 1988. Reviewer Health Edn. Jour., Reston, Va., 1987; contbr. articles to profl. jours. Mem. Mayor's Commn. on Needs of Women, La., 1984-88; 1st v.p., bd. dirs. United Way of Ouachita, La., 1986-88. Mem. ANA, Ind. Nurses Assn., Ind. Coun. Deans and Dirs. of Nursing Edn. (pres. 1992-98), Internat. Coun. Women's Health Issues (bd. dirs. 1986-92, 98-2000), Assn. for the Advancement Health Edn., Sigma Theta Tau. Home: Lafayette, Ind. Died Nov. 11, 2009.

IRVING, ROBERT CHURCHILL, retired quality assurance professional, manufacturing company executive; b. Waltham, Mass., Sept. 15, 1928; s. Frederick Charles and Emily Alvina (Churchill) I.; children: Robert F., John W. AS, Franklin Inst. of Boston, 1965; cert. of profl. achievement, Northeastern U., 1975. Sr. draftsman Mason-Neilan, Boston, 1948-54; mgr. design svcs. Kinney Vacuum Co., Gen. Signal Corp., Boston, 1955-69; mgr. engring. svcs. Sturtevant div. Westinghouse Electric Corp., Hyde Park, Mass., 1969-81, supr. quality assurance, 1981-84; mgr. engring. svcs. Am. Davidson, Inc., Hyde Park, Mass., 1984-87, mgr. quality control, 1987-89; mgr. quality assurance Howden Sirocco, Inc., 1989-94; ret., 1994. Served with U.S. Army, 1946-48. Mem. Am. Soc. for Quality Control, Am. Legion. Home: Brockton, Mass. Died Mar. 18, 2010.

ISAACS, RICHARD B., investigative and protective services professional; b. Evanston, Ill., Nov. 12, 1942; s. Harry Columbus and Natalie I.; m. Catherine Anne Nicodemo, Oct. 25, 1980 (div. 1994). BA, NYU, 1964; MA, Columbia U., 1975. Cert. CPP. V.p. Blackstone & West, Inc., Phila., 1967-69; indsl. photographer NYC, 1970-76; programmer STSC, Inc., NYC, 1976-81; pres. Blackstone & West, Inc., NYC, 1981-89; prin., sr. v.p. The Lubrinco Group, Inc., NYC, 1989-2001. Dir. ASR Instrs. Coun., Arlington, Tex., 1983-2001. Author: (book) The Seven Steps to Personal Safety, 1993, rev. 1998; editor: The Bus. Security e-Jour., 1998-2001; others. Vol. Peace Corps, Colombia, 1964-66. Mem. Am. Soc. Law Enforcement Trainers (mem. security com. 1999-2001), Tactical Response Assn., Soc. Competitive Intelligence Profls., Internat. Assn. Counterterroism and Security Profls. Avocations: poetry, translating, flying, 50-meter free pistol, Aikido. Home: New York, NY. Died Apr. 30, 2010.

ISBAN, ROBERT CHARLES, bank executive, accountant; b. Endicott, NY, July 21, 1926; s. Charles S. and Gladys (Lawton) I.; m. Marjorie B. Davis, Jan. 31, 1948. BS, Syracuse U., 1949; MBA, NYU, 1954; postgrad., Rutgers U., 1961; A.M.P., Harvard U., 1969. C.P.A., N.Y. Acct. R.G. Rankin & Co., NYC, 1949-55, Price Waterhouse, Washington, 1955-56; asst. controller Hanover Bank, NYC, 1956-70; controller Mfrs. Hanover Trust, NYC, 1970-77, exec. v.p., from 1977. Trustee St. Joseph's Coll., 1975. Mem. Bank Adminstrn. Inst. (chmn. 1984-85), Fin. Exec. Inst. Republican. Roman Catholic. Home: Osprey, Fla. Died Apr. 3, 2010.

ISON, EUNICE, artist; b. Wis., June 18, 1911; d. William Charles and Drucilla (Bowman) Duff; children; Noreen R. Cook, L. Ison Jr., Kathy Latini, Linda Bennett. Certificate of completion, Sch. for Blind, Ft. Myers, Fla., 1997. Exhbns. include one-man shows: Suzy Gy Gallery, Ft. Meyers, 1998, The SoCo Gallery, A Gallery SyZyGy/2000; profiled in mag. Expressions WGCU Pub. Broadcasting, 2002. Home: Fort Myers, Fla. Died Jan. 9, 2009.

ISTOK, CHRISTINE MARKWARD, retired executive director social service agency, consultant; b. Washington, July 5, 1947; d. George Albert and Mary Ruth (Stalcup) Markward; m. Donald Phillip O'Sullivan, June 27, 1985. Sec. Gas Distributors Info. Svc., Washington, 1966-70; adminstr. asst. Nat. Airlines, Washington, 1970-71; office mgr. Tire Industry Safety Coun., Washington, 1971-75; pres. Type-Right Exec. Sec. Svc., Washington, Pitts., 1976-91; exec. dir. Eastside Cmty. Ministry, Zanesville, Ohio, 1991—2001. Chair FEMA Emergency Bd., Muskingum, Morgan and Perry Counties, Ohio, 1994-97, 99-2000; chair United Way Exec. Dirs. Coun., 1994-97, United Way agy. relations com. 2000-03, allocations com. 2002-04; v.p. Muskingum County Hunger Network, Zanesville, 1993-99. Author: Write a Good Resume, 1976. Mem. task force Literacy Coun., 1993—2000; mem. steering com. Muskingum County Operation Feed, 1992—99; trustee Disability Network of Ohio-Solidarity, from 2001; mem Zanesville City Sch. Bldg. Adv. Coun., Ohio, 2001—03; v.p. Muskingum County Women's Rep. Club, 1994, sec., 1995; mem. Downtown Clergy Assn., from 1992, pres., 1995—96; bd. dirs. Human Care Ministry, Ohio dist. Luth. Ch., Mo. Synod, PRO-Muskingum, 1995—2000; commr. Mo. Synod Luths. to Commn. on Religion in Appalachia, 1996—98; chair human care bd. Trinity Evang. Luth. Ch., from 2003; bd. dirs. Muskingum County Women's Coalition, 1994—97, Families and Children First Coun., 1995—2000, Interfaith Response to Ohio Disaster, 1988—91, Luth. Social Svcs. Emergency Assistance Com., 1998—99, Muskingum County Family Adv. Team, 2000—01. Recipient Cert. of Achievement for Mil. Family Support, U.S. Army, 1991, Excellence in Cmty. Svc. award Aid Assn. Luths., 1993, Excellence in Cmty. Svc. award Muskingum County DAR, 1994, Positive Action award, NOW, 1997, YWCA Woman of Achievement award, 1997, Americanism award VFW, 1992, Cmty. Involvement award Richvale Grange, 1997, Cmty. Citizen award State of Ohio Grange, 2000; named Outstanding Cmty. Vol. Zanesville Daybreak Rotary Club, 1997. Mem.: Nat. Multiple Sclerosis Soc. (program com. Buckeye chpt. 2001—04), Muskingum County Respiratory Assn. (bd. dirs. from 2001, sec., bd. dirs. from 2003), Disability Network Ohio Solidarity (trustee from 2001), Richvale Grange, Kiwanis (Zanesville chpt. bd. dirs. 1997—99, spiritual aims com. chair Dist. 18 of Ohio 1998—99). Avocations: creative writing, music. Home: South Bend, Ind. Died Feb. 24, 2010.

ITANO, HARVEY AKIO, biochemistry educator; b. Sacramento, Nov. 3, 1920; s. Masao and Sumako (Nakahara) I.; m. Rose Nakako Sakemi, Nov. 5, 1949; children: Wayne Masao, Glenn Harvey, David George. BS, U. Calif., Berkeley, 1942; MD, St. Louis U., 1945; PhD, Calif. Inst. Tech., 1950; DSc (hon.), St. Louis U., 1987. Intern City of Detroit Receiving Hosp., 1945-46; commd. officer USPHS, Bethesda, Md., 1950-70, advanced through grades to chief, sect. on chem. genetics, Nat. Inst. Arthritis and Metabolic Diseases, NIH, 1962-70, mem. hematology study sect., NIH, 1959-63, research fellow then sr. research fellow, Calif. Inst. Tech. Pasadena, 1950-54; prof. Dept. Pathology U. Calif. San Diego, La Jolla, 1970-88, prof. emeritus, 1988—2010. Vis. prof. Osaka (Japan) U., 1961-62, U. Chgo., 1965, U. Calif., San Francsico, 1967; cons. sickle cell anemia, mem. hematology study sect. 1953-63, various sickle cell anemia rev. coms., 1970-81, NIH, Bethesda. Editor: (with Linus Pauling) Molecular Structure and Biological Specificity, 1957; contbr. articles to profl. jours. George Minot lectr., AMA, 1955; Japan Soc. for Promotion of Sci. fellow, Okayama U., 1983-84; recipient Martin Luther King Jr. award Southern Christian Leadership Conf., 1972 Mem. NAS, Am. Acad. Arts and Scis.,

Am. Chem. Soc. (Eli Lilly award in Biol. Chemistry 1954), Am. Soc. Biochemistry and Molecular Biology, Am. Soc. Hematology, Internat. Soc. Hematology, Phi Beta Kappa, Sigma Xi, Alpha Omega Alpha. Home: La Jolla, Calif. Died May 8, 2010.

IVEY, REEF CHALLANCE, II, lawyer; b. Wadesboro, NC, Jan. 26, 1943; s. Reef Challance and Ethel (Rivers) Ivey; m. Linda Bauer, Oct. 10, 1981; 1 child, Reef Challance III 1 stepchild, Meredith Coleman. BA, NC State U., 1965, JD, 1968. Bar: NC 1968, NY 1969, Ill. 1976, US Supreme Ct. 1982, Okla. 1982. Adminstrv. asst. Mfrs. Hanover Trust Co., NYC, 1968—69; assoc. counsel Dairylea Coop., Inc., NYC, 1969—71; asst. dist. atty. NY County, NYC, 1971—73; atty. PepsiCo Inc., Purchase, NY, 1973—74; corp. counsel Wilson Sporting Goods Co., River Grove, Ill., 1974—76; area counsel Pepsico Internat., Purchase, 1976—80, v.p. world trade, 1980—81; v.p., gen. counsel and sec. Wilson Foods Corp., Okla. City, 1981—83, sr. v.p., from 1983, pres. internat. divsn., from 1983. Mem.: ABA, Okla. Bar Assn., Ill. Bar Assn., NY Bar Assn., NC Bar Assn., Quail Golf and Country Club (Okla. City), Stanwich Club (Greenwich, Conn.), Rockaway Hunting Club (Cedarhust, NY), Kiwanis Club. Home: Oklahoma City, Okla. Died Mar. 5, 2009.

IZARD, JOHN, lawyer; b. Hartford, Conn., Mar. 4, 1923; s. John and Elizabeth (Andrews) I.; m. Mary Bailey, apr. 16, 1955; children: Sarah Izard Pariseau, John Jr., David Bailey. BS, Yale U., 1945; LLB, U. Va., 1949. Bar: Ga. 1950. Assoc. King & Spalding, Atlanta, 1949-52, ptnr., 1952—91. Mem. Adminstrv. Conf. U.S., Washington, 1978—82. Author, pub.: A Traveler's Table, 2002; editor-in-chief Va. Law Rev., 1948; contbr. articles to legal periodicals. Mem. Nat. Com. To Study Antitrust Laws and Procedures, Washington, 1978; trustee Episcopal Media Ctr., Atlanta, 1988—2004, chmn., 1992-96; trustee U. Va. Law Sch. Found., Charlottesville, 1974-97, Alliance for Christian Media, Atlanta, 2004—; founding chmn. Sr. Citizens Svcs. of Met. Atlanta, 1967. Lt. (j.g.) USNR, 1944-46, PTO. Mem. ABA (chmn. antitrust sect. 1974-75), Ga. Bar Assn. (chmn. antitrust sect. 1969-71), Atlanta Legal Aid Soc. (pres. 1960), Lawyers Club Atlanta, Capital City Club (bd. dirs. 1976-79), Peachtree Golf Club, Piedmont Driving Club. Democrat. Episcopalian. Home: Atlanta, Ga. Died July 10, 2009.

JACHE, ALBERT WILLIAM, retired chemistry professor, academic administrator, research scientist; b. Manchester, NH, Nov. 5, 1924; s. William Frederick and Esther (Ruemely) J.; m. Lucy Ellen Hauslein, June 14, 1948; children: Ann Gail, Ellen Ruth, Philip William, Heidi Verena. BS, U. N.H., 1948, MS, 1950; PhD, U. Wash., 1952. Sr. chemist Air Reduction Co., Murray Hill, NJ, 1952-53; rsch. assoc. dept. physics Duke U., 1953-55; asst. prof. dept. chemistry Tex. A&M U., College Station, 1955-58, assoc. prof., 1958-61; cons. Ozark Mahoning Co., Tulsa, 1960-61, assoc. rsch. dir., 1961-64; sr. rsch. assoc. Olin Mathieson Chem. Corp. (now Olin Corp.), New Haven, 1964-67, sect. mgr., 1965-67, cons., 1967-75; prof. chemistry Marquette U., Milw., 1967-90, prof. emeritus, 1970—2008, chmn. chem. dept., 1967-72, dean Grad. Sch., 1972-77, assoc. acad. v.p. for health scis., 1974-77, assoc. v.p.-acad. affairs, 1977-85; scientist-in-residence Argonne (Ill.) Nat. Lab., 1985-86, scientist, 1991-96, temporary appointment, 1991-96; with ChemLab, 2000—08. Program coordination com. Med. Center S.E. Wis.; lectr. U. Tulsa, 1963-64, New Haven Coll., 1967; cons. Allied Chem. Corp., 1977-78, 2000-; salt panel com. remediation buried and tank wastes NAS/NRC, 1996-97. Trustee Milw. Sci. Ednl. Found.; pres. Milw. Sci. Ednl. Trust, 1973—; trustee Argonne Univs. Assn., 1977-80; chmn. Assn. Grad. Schs. in Cath. Univs., 1973-75; mem. AUA nuclear engring. edn. com. U. Chgo, 1977-89, chmn., 1984, sec., 1989; double bass player River Cities Symphony Orch., 1997-2001, Evergreen Comty. Orch., 1994-07, Evergreen String Ensemble, 1994-2000, Marietta Chamber Orch., 1994-97. With AUS, 1942-46. Fellow AAAS (Sr. Scientists and Engrs. Am.), Am. Inst. Chemists; mem. Am. Chem. Soc. (chmn.-elect, program chmn. div. fluorine chemistry 1981, chmn. div. fluorine chemistry 1982), Sigma Xi, Omicron Kappa Upsilon, Alpha Sigma Nu. Achievements include research and numerous patents in the area of inorganic fluorine chemistry with emphasis on anhydrous hydrogen fluoride as a solvent or reaction medium and Hypofluorite chemistry. Died May 3, 2010.

JACKMAN, ROBERT WILLIAM, political science educator; b. Oamaru, New Zealand, Oct. 31, 1946; came to U.S., 1968; s. David Spalding and Helen Agnes Jackman; m. Mary Ruth Jackman, Sept. 10, 1968; children: Rachael, Saul. BA, U. Auckland, New Zealand, 1968; MA, U. Wis., 1970, PhD, 1972. Asst. prof. to prof. Mich. State U., East Lansing, 1972-89; prof. U. Calif., Davis, from 1989. Author: Politics and Social Equality, 1975, Power Without Force, 1993; co-author: Class Awareness in the U.S., 1983. Guggenheim fellowship John S. Guggenheim Found., 1980, fellowship Ctr. for Advanced Study, 1986-87. Home: Davis, Calif. Died Oct. 8, 2009.

JACKSON, ALTHEA, nun, writer, retired bookstore executive; b. Taunton, Mass., June 27, 1922; d. Harold Robinson Hall and Jeannette (Cahoon) Tingwall; m. John E. Jackson, June 15, 1945 (dec. Aug. 1974); children: Jean, Paul. BA, Middlebury Coll., 1944; MS, Simmons Coll., 1965. Cert. profl. libr. Libr., Mass., 1959—74; propr. Agape Bible & Book Store, St. Augustine, Fla., 1982—88. Mem.: ALA (life). Roman Catholic. Home: Denton, Tex. Died Feb. 7, 2009.

JACKSON, DAVID ALONZO, retired newspaper editor; b. Litchfield, Ill., Oct. 7, 1924; s. David Winchester and Maude Abbot (McEwen) J.; m. Mina Jean Miller, Feb. 18, 1950 (dec. July 1998); children: Anne, David M., Jennifer E., Jeffrey A.; m. Martha Ann McHenry Cassity, Aug. 1, 1999. Student, Tex. A&M U., 1943, Pasadena Jr. Coll., Calif., 1943; BA, Ill. Coll., 1949. Apprentice printer Litchfield News-Herald, 1946, mgr. classified advt., 1949-58, advt. mgr., 1958-74, editor, 1974-89; columnist Break Time, 1979—2006, ret., 2006. Mem. Montgomery County Bd., 1994-2004; past mem. Litchfield Postal Adv. Com.; trustee Litchfield Carnegie Pub. Libr., 1957-95, pres. 1959-92, 93-95; v.p., sec. Lewis and Clark Libr. Sys., Edwardsville, Ill., 1965-71, 77-83, 86; chmn. Litchfield Fire and Police Commn., 1985-95; bd. dirs. Bottomley-Ruffing-Schalk Baseball Mus., 1997-2002; dir. Corr Cemetery, Carlinville, Ill., 2003-04; former pres. Elmwood Cemetery, Litchfield. With Corps Mil. Police US Army, 1943—46, with Corps Mil. Police US Army, 1951. Recipient Dedicated Leadership plaque Ill. Coll., 1984, Disting. Citizen award, Ill. Coll., 1986, County Master Citizen award Montgomery County Fair Bd., 1987, Spl. Mayoral award City of Litchfield, 1987, Civic Activities award Litchfield Rotary Club, 1987, Statesman of the Yr., Litchfield C. of C., 1990, Studs Terkel Humanities Svc. award, Ill. Humanities Coun., 2000.; named to So. Ill. U. Journalism Hall of Fame, 1996, Mem. Ill. Hist. Soc., Montgomery County Geneal. Soc. (charter; pres. 1990-91, 92-95), Ill. Coll. Alumni Assn. (sec. 1977-83, nat. pres. 1984), Ill. Geneal. Soc., Macoupin County (Ill.) Geneal. Soc., Iredell County (N.C.) Geneal. Soc., VFW, Moose, Am. Legion (editor, Litchfield sesquicentennial history book com.). Republican. Methodist. Home: Litchfield, Ill. Died May 1, 2010.

JACKSON, DAVID GORDON, religious organization administrator; b. Derby, NY, Nov. 5, 1936; s. Peter Thomas and Sarah (Staubitz) J. BS, SUNY, Buffalo, 1960; MDiv, Huntington Coll. Theol. Sem., 1964. Ordained elder Ch. of the United Brethren in Christ, 1969. Dir. youth work Ch. United Brethren in Christ, Huntington, Ind., 1966-73, adminstrv. asst., treas., 1973-79; exec. sec., treas. Internat. Soc. Christian Endeavor, Columbus, Ohio, 1979-84, exec. dir., from 1981, World's Christian Endeavor Union, Columbus, from 1984. Adj. lectr. U. Calif. San Francisco, 1980—, asst. clin. prof., 1986—. Died Dec. 9, 2009.

JACKSON, DONNA CARDAMONE, retired music educator; b. Utica, NY, Nov. 16, 1937; d. Angelo Joseph and Mary Christine Cardamone; m. David Lee Jackson, May 24, 1977; 1 child, Anna Lee. BA magna cum laude, Wells Coll., Aurora, NY, 1959; MA, Harvard U., 1964, PhD, 1972. Prof. music U. Minn., Mpls., 1969—2007, ret., 2007. Mem. editl. bd. Jour. Am. Musicological Soc., Phil., 1995—98. Author: (book) The Canzone Villanesca alla Napolitana, 1981; editor: Adrian Willaert and His Cir., 1978, Orlando di Lasso: Canzoni Villanesche, 1991; co-author (with James Haar): Giovanthomaso Cimello: The Collected Secular Works, 2001, The Canzona Villanesca alla Napolitana, Variorum Collected Studies Series, 2008; editor: The Canzone Villanesca alla Napolitana: Social Cultural and Historical Contexts, 2008. Recipient Fulbright award, US Govt., Bologna, Italy, 1966—67; grantee, Am. Coun. of Learned Societies. Mem.: Phi Beta Kappa. Avocations: gardening, golf. Home: Falcon Heights, Minn. Died Oct. 2009.

JACKSON, EDWIN ATLEE, retired physicist, educator; b. Lyons, NY, Apr. 18, 1931; s. Frederick Wolcott and Helen Jean (Carroll) J.; m. Cynthia Ann Gregg; children: Eric Hugh, Mark Wolcott. BS in Physics, Syracuse U., NY, 1953, MS in Physics, 1955, PhD in Physics, 1958. Asst. lectr. Brandeis U., Waltham, Mass., 1957—58; postdoctoral Airforce Cambridge Rsch. Ctr., Bedford, Mass., 1958—59; rsch. staff Princeton U., NJ, 1959—61; asst. prof. U. Ill., Urbana, 1961—64, assoc. prof., 1964—77, physics prof., 1977—98, prof. emeritus, from 1998. Dir. ctr. for complex systems rsch. Beckman Inst. U. Ill., Urbana, 1989-98; vis. faculty FOM-Inst. Voor Plasma Fysica, Jutphaas, The Netherlands, 1967-68; vis. staff Los Alamos Sci. Lab., N.Mex., 1971; vis. prof. Chalmers U., Göteberg, Sweden, 1984; JIFT prof. Nagoya U., Japan, 1984; core rschr. Santa Fe Inst., 1992-98. Author: Equilibrium Statistical Mechanics, 1968, Perspectives of Nonlinear Dynamics, vol. 1, 1989, vol. 2, 1990, Japanese transl., 1994, Exploring Nature's Dynamics, 2001; contbr. more than 80 articles to profl. jours. Fellow Am. Phys. Soc. Home: Austin, Tex. Died Mar. 9, 2010.

JACKSON, J(OHN) DAVID, physicist, researcher; b. London, Ont., Can., Jan. 19, 1925; arrived in US, 1957, naturalized, 1988; s. Walter David and Lillian Margaret Jackson; m. Barbara Cook, June 26, 1949; children: Ian, Nan, Maureen, Mark. BS in Physics and Math., U. Western Ont., 1946, DSc (hon.), 1989; PhD in Physics, MIT, 1949. Rsch. assoc. dept. physics MIT, Cambridge, 1949; from asst. prof. to assoc. prof. math. McGill U., Montreal, Que., Canada, 1950-57; from assoc. prof. to prof. physics U. Ill., Urbana, 1957-67; prof. U. Calif., Berkeley, 1967-92, dept. chair, 1978-81, prof. emeritus, from 1993. Vis. fellow Cambridge (Eng.) U., 1970; acting head theory group Fermilab, Batavia, Ill., 1972-73; head physics divsn. Lawrence Berkeley Lab., 1982-84; dep. dir. SSC Cen. Design Group, Berkeley, 1985-87; vis. sr. rsch. fellow Oxford (Eng.) U., 1988-89; mem. vis. com. Argonne Nat. Lab., CERN, SSC Lab., Stanford Linear Accelerator Ctr., others. Author: Physics of Elementary Particles, 1958, Classical Electrodynamics, 1962, rev. edit., 1975, 3d edit., 1998, Mathematics for Quantum Mechanics, 1962, reprinted 2006; also contbr. numerous articles to profl. publications; editor Ann. Rev. Nuclear and Particle Sci., 1977-93 J. S. Guggenheim Found. fellow, 1956-57, Ford Found. fellow, 1963-64. Fellow Am. Phys. Soc.; mem. NAS (elected 1990), Am. Acad. Arts and Scis. (elected 1989), ACLU (life). Avocations: hiking, swimming, scientific bibliophily. Home: Berkeley, Calif. Died May 20, 2010.

JACKSON, VICTOR LOUIS, retired naturalist; b. Thanh-Hoa, Annam, Vietnam, July 2, 1933; s. Richmond Merrill and Hazel Irene (Peebles) J.; m. Lois Annetta Scott, Apr. 4, 1959 (div. Oct. 1991); children: Nathan Ray, Sharon Ruth (Jackson) Maxwell. BS, Wheaton Coll., (Ill.), 1955. Sub-dist. ranger Natchez Trace Pkwy., Collinwood, Tenn., 1958-61; park naturalist Gt. Smoky Mountains Nat. Park, Gatlinburg, Tenn., 1961-63; chief park naturalist Organ Pipe Cactus Nat. Monument, Ajo., Ariz., 1963-66; asst. chief naturalist Grand Teton Nat. Park, Moose, Wyo., 1966-73; chief park naturalist Zion Nat. Park, Springdale, Utah, 1973-88; assn. coordinator Zion Natural History Assn., Springdale, 1973-88; ret. Springdale, 1988. Author, photographer: Discover Zion, 1978, in pictures, Zion, The Continuing Story, 1989; editor: Plants of Zion, 1976, Zion Adventure Guide, 1978, Pipe Spring and the Arizona Strip, 1984, The Sculpturing of Zion, 1984, Zion Album, A Nostalgic History of Zion Canyon, 1986, Hiking in Zion National Park: The Trails, 1988, Exploring the Backcountry of Zion National Park: Off-Trail Routes, 1988, Zion National Park: Towers of Stone, 1988. Bd. dirs. So. Utah Folklife Festival, 1976-88, God's Refuge, Inc., Dewey, Ariz., 1998-99; vol. naturalist Zion Nat. Pk., 1988-91, Prescott Pines Bapt. Camp, Prescott, Ariz., 1992—; naturalist Prescott Nat. Forest Interpretive Vol. Corps, 1996-98. Capt. Signal Corps U.S. Army, 1955-57. Named Outstanding Interpreter of Yr. in Nat. Park Service, Nat. Parks and Conservation Assn., 1982; recipient Freeman Tilden award, 1982 Republican. Baptist. Home: Sandy, Oreg. Died Oct. 25, 2009.

JACKSON, WILLIE LEE, guidance counselor; b. Waynesboro, Ga., Apr. 1, 1945; s. J.D. and Annabell (Holmes) J. BA, Hope Coll., Holland, Mich., 1969; MA, Princeton Sem., 1971; EdM, Rutgers U., 1975; MA, Columbia U., 1989. Dorm counselor Rutgers Coll., New Brunswick, N.J., 1971-74; coll. counselor Livinston Coll., New Brunswick, 1974-83; high sch. counselor N.Y.C. Bd. Edn., from 1988. Mem. AACD. Avocations: tennis, golf, basketball. Home: New York, NY. Died Jan. 14, 2009.

JACOBS, CHARLES ROBINSON, newspaper publisher; b. Chgo., Dec. 10, 1918; s. Charles Robinson and Amy (Orton) J.; m. Patricia Ann Patterson, Mar. 19, 1942; children: Randall Woodruff, Sheldon Truesdale, William Orton. Student, U. Va., 1939-41. Pub. Meredith (N.H.) News, 1945-50; editor-pub. Wauseon (Ohio) Republican, 1950-56; mem. advt. staff Bradenton (Fla.) Herald, 1956-58; editor, pub. Daily Leader, Brookhaven, Miss., 1958-97, editor emeritus, from 1997. Chmn. Indsl. Devel. Found., Brookhaven, 1984, Brookhaven Pub. Housing Authority, 1985-90; coach Little League Baseball, 1975-81, Peewee Basketball, 1978-81. Served with USCG, 1941-45. Named Soap Box Man of Yr. Brookhaven C. of C., 1968, King Harvest Ball, Krewe of Ceres, 1978. Mem. Miss. Press Assn. (bd. dirs. 1970-75, 80-85), So. Newspaper Pub. Assn., Brookhaven Lincoln C. of C. (bd. dirs.). Clubs: Brookhaven Country; Sarasota (Fla.) Yacht. Lodges: Kiwanis. Republican. Methodist. Avocations: antique furniture, woodworking, furniture reproductions, tennis, boating, genealogy. Home: Brookhaven, Miss. Died Feb. 24, 2010.

JACOBS, IRA, electrical engineering educator, former telecommunications company executive; b. Bklyn., Jan. 3, 1931; s. Nathan and Leah (Pincheff) J.; m. Irene Rosalie Schuman, May 20, 1956; children— Phillip, Mona, Nancy BS, CCNY, 1950; MS, Purdue U., 1952, PhD, 1955. Teaching and research asst. Purdue U., West Lafayette, Ind., 1950-55; mem. tech. staff Bell Labs., Whippany, N.J., 1955-60, supr., 1960-62, dept. head, 1962-67, Holmdel, N.J., 1967-69, dir. devel., 1969-87; prof. elec. engring. Va. Poly Inst., Blacksburg, from 1987. Cons. Inst. for Def. Analyses, Washington, 1964, 66; lectr. in field Pres. bd. dirs. Little Silver Bd. Edn., N.J., 1971-77; v.p. bd. trustees Congregation B'nai Israel, Rumson, N.J., 1978-87; pres. Blacksburg Jewish Community Ctr., 1989-90. Purdue Research Found. fellow, 1952 Fellow IEEE; mem. Optical Soc. Am., Phi Beta Kappa, Sigma Pi Sigma (pres. Purdue chpt. 1953-54) Home: Blacksburg, Va. Died Aug. 11, 2010.

JACOBS, MARY LEE, lawyer; b. Pitts., June 29, 1950; d. George and Mary Jane (Swinderman) Jacobs. BA in History, Wellesley Coll., 1972; JD, Boston U., 1974. BAr: Mass. 1975, U.S. Dist. Ct. Mass. 1976, U.S. Ct. Appeals (1st cir.) 1978, U.S. Supreme Ct. 1981. Gen. counsel Tufts U., Medford, Mass., from 1984. Mem. ABA, Boston Bar Assn., Nat. Assn. Coll. and Univ. Attys. Home: Concord, Mass. Died Apr. 30, 2010.

JACOBSON, ARENT JOHN, lawyer; b. Chgo., Feb. 17, 1925; s. Arent and Mary (Campbell) Jacobson; m. Barbara Lucille Feidt, Oct. 15, 1949 (dec. 1975); children: Jenny, Linda, Gary, Jim, Tim, Kurt. AA, Wright Jr. coll., Chgo., 1946; LLB, DePaul U., 1948. Bar: Ill. 1949. Sr. trial counsel Zurich Ins. Co., Chgo., 1950—67; assoc. trial lawyer Ross and East, Chgo., 1967—68; pvt. practice Chgo., 1968—73, 1977—89; ptnr. Jacobson & Miller, Chgo., 1973—75, McBreen, Tobin & Jacobson, Chgo., 1975—77; sr. counsel Margolis & Velasco, Chgo., from 1989. Hearing officer U.S. Dept. Justice, Ill., State Med. Ctr. Commn., Chgo.; guest lectr. Ill. State Bar, Assn. Casaulty and Surity, Northwestern U. Law Sch.; instr. law Zurich Ins. Co. Contbr.: articles to legal jours. Precinct capt. New Trier Rep. Orgn., 1958—68; mem. Glencoe Caucus Com., 1984—85. Mem.: Ill. Def. Counsel, Chgo. Bar Assn., Ill. State Bar Assn., Ill. Trial Lawyers Assn., Soc. Trial Lawyers, Am. Arbitration Assn. (arbitrator), Nordic Law Club (past pres.), North Shore Regional Rose Soc. Cook County (past pres.), Botanical Gardens. Roman Catholic. Home: Chicago, Ill. Died July 20, 2009.

JACOBSON, IRVING, lawyer; b. Dayton, Ohio, June 22, 1926; s. Nathan and Bernice (Bloom) J.; m. Sandra, July 31, 1955; 1 child, Bonnie Nancy AB, Harvard U., 1948, LL.B. cum laude, 1952. Bar: N.Y. 1953. Atty. RCA Corp., NYC, 1952-53; assoc. Szold & Brandwen, NYC, 1953-58, Shea & Gould, NYC, 1958-61, ptnr., from 1961. Editor Harvard Law Rev., 1950-52 Served with U.S. Army, 1945-46 Mem. ABA, Assn. Bar of City of N.Y., N.Y. State Bar Assn., Phi Beta

Kappa Independent Republican. Jewish. Club: Harvard of N.Y.C. Avocations: opera and symphonic recordings. Home: White Plains, NY. Died July 3, 2010.

JACOBSON, RUTH ANNETTE KRAUSÉ, public relations counselor; b. Watertown, NY, June 30, 1925; d. Thomas M.R. and Ruth E. (Parmelee) Krausé; married; 1 child, Anne Heyliger Jacobson Nunno. Grad., Medill Sch. Journalism, Northwestern U., 1947; postgrad., U. Chgo., Northwestern U., Washington U. Guest editor Mademoiselle mag., NYC, 1945; with Howard G. Mayer & Assocs., Chgo., 1947-48; Midwest area rep. CARE, Inc., Chgo., 1948-50; account exec. Harshe-Rotman and Druck, Chgo., 1950-51; free-lance pub. relations counselor, 1955-57; pub. relations counselor Fleishman-Hillard, Inc., St. Louis, 1957-68, dir. spl. events, from 1968, sr. ptnr., from 1971. Bd. dirs. Forum for Contemporary Art, Chatillon-DeMenil House Found., chmn. pub. relations com.; bd. dirs. Vanderschmidt's Secretarial Sch., chmn. mktg. com.; bd. dirs. St. Louis Conservatory and Schs. for the Arts, chmn. communications com.; chmn. Commerce mag. com. St. Louis Regional Commerce Growth Assn.; bd. dirs. VP Fair Found., Women's Soc. of Washington U.; mem. pres.'s adv. cabinet Greater St. Louis council Girl Scouts U.S.A.; dir. emeritus Downtown St. Louis; bd. govs., chmn. pub. relations com. Assn. Churchill Fellows Winston Churchill Meml. and Library in U.S., Westminster Coll., Fulton, Mo.; pres. Mo. Bapt. Hosp.; mem. adv. Council YWCA; mem. adv. com. Experience St. Louis. Recipient Ann. Signal award St. Louis Sentinel, 1983, Leader Lunch Spl. award YWCA, 1983; named one of Ten Women of Achievement in St. Louis Sta. KMOX and The Suburban Journal's newspaper. Mem. Pub. Relations Soc. Am. (past sec. St. Louis chpt.), St. Louis Soc. Blind (past bd. dirs), Landmarks Assn. St. Louis (counselor-at-large to bd. dirs. on pub. relations 1976-77), Women in Communications (Mentor award 1986), St. Louis Forum, Internat. Women's Forum, Mo. Women's Forum, Mo. Hist. Soc. (past bd. trustees), St. Louis Symphony Soc., Friends of St. Louis Art Mus., St. Croix Landmarks Soc., Nat. Trust for Historic Preservation, Vis. Nurse Assn. (past bd. dirs.). Episcopalian. Home: Saint Louis, Mo. Died Mar. 9, 2010.

JACOBSON, SHELDON, emergency medicine physician, medical administrator; b. Sept. 3, 1938; m. Diana Brody. BS, CCNY, 1960; MD, Albert Einstein Coll. Medicine, 1964. Dir. emergency svc., attending physician Bronx (N.Y.) Mcpl. Hosp. Ctr., 1970-79; dir. Non-Appointment Ctr., dir. Inst. Emergency Medicine Albert Einstein Coll. Medicine, Bronx, 1974-79, assoc. dir. emergency medicine, 1975-79; dir. emergency svc., med. dir. Hosp. Univ. Pa., Phila., 1979—92; chmn. emergency medicine Mt. Sinai Sch. Medicine, NYC, from 1994, sr. attending physician, from 1995. Assoc. prof. surgery and medicine U. Pa., Phila., 1979—. Author: Dysrhthmias Diagnosis and Self Assessment Workbook, 1987; author: (with others) Airway Obstruction, 1989. Fellow: Am. Coll. Emergency Physicians, Am. Acad. Emergency Medicine; mem.: AMA, Phi Beta Kappa, Wilderness Med. Soc., Phila. Emergency Physicians Soc., Soc. Tchrs. Emergency Medicine, Soc. Acad. Emergency Medicine, Alpha Omega Alpha. Home: Nyack, NY. Died June 30, 2009.

JAFFE, MELVIN, security firm executive; b. NYC, May 20, 1919; s. Benjamin and Zelda (Karp) J.; m. Muriel Hamptman, June 9, 1941 (dec. Mar. 1984); children: Marcy, Meredith; m. Suzanne MacMillan, Jan. 20, 1985; children: Cynthia Johnson, Katie Marsico. BS in Edn., Bucknell U., 1940. Pres. Benjamin jaffe & Son Inc., Bklyn., 1946-68; sr. v.p. investments Morgan Stanley Dean Witter Reynolds, Garden City, NY, from 1969. Pres. Lions Internat., Blkyn., 1965. Staff sgt. U.S. Army, 1942-45, ETO. Mem. Am. Legion (Post 304), Masons. Jewish. Home: Garden City, NY. Died Mar. 23, 2010.

JAHSMAN, WILLIAM EDWARD, mechanical engineer; b. Detroit, May 13, 1926; s. William Edward and Eleanor Isabel (Blanchard) J.; m. Nona Marie Simi, June 20, 1949; children— William Edward, III, Hendrick Edwin, Amy Luise. B.Engring. Physics, Cornell U., 1951; MS in Engring. Mechanics, Stanford U., 1953, PhD in Engring. Mechanics, 1954. Research asso. Oak Ridge Nat. Lab., summer, 1950; engr. Boeing Airplane Co., Seattle, summer 1951, Gen. Electric Co. Knolls Atomic Power Lab., Schenectady, 1954-55, supr., 1955, mech. specialist, 1955-56; research scientist Lockheed Palo Alto Research Lab., Calif., 1956-61, staff scientist, 1961-64, mgr., 1964-65, cons. scientist, 1965-67; prof. mech. engring. U. Colo., Boulder, 1967-80, chmn. dept. mech. engring., 1974-80; mgr. assembly quality assurance Intel Corp., Santa Clara, Calif., 1980-83, mgr. package tech., 1983-86, mgr. customer interface, from 1986. Lectr. dept. aeros. and astronautics Stanford U., 1961-67; liaison scientist Office Naval Research, London br., 1969-70; vis. prof. Oxford (Eng.) U., 1979 Contbr. numerous articles on solid and fluid mechanics to profl. jours. Served with USN, 1944-46. U. Colo. at Boulder Council on Research and Creative Work faculty fellow, 1979; NSF grantee, 1970-73, 73-76 Mem. ASME, Am. Soc. Engring. Edn., Am. Acad. Mechanics (charter), Assn. Chairmen Depts. Mechanics, U.S. Nat. Metric Assn. Died June 2, 2010.

JAKLITSCH, JOSEPH JOHN, JR., technical publications consultant; b. Bklyn., Mar. 28, 1919; s. Joseph John and Josefa (Stonitsch) Jaklitsch; m. Eleanor Mulligan, May 29, 1948; children: Gary, Diane. BS, Pratt Inst., 1940. With planning dept. Brewster Aero. Corp., NYC, 1940—41; test engr. ordnance dept. US Army, 1941—44, editor, 1944—45; tech. editor ASME, NYC, 1945—50; assoc. editor, 1950—55; acting editor, 1956; editor Mech. Engring. also Trans. ASME, 1957—81; editorial adv. com. Engrs. Joint Coun., 1960—64; cons. editor Crowell-Collier Ednl. Corp., 1960—64; spl. cons. Barnhart World Book Dictionary, 1964—68; cons. editor-at-large Marcel-Dekker, Inc., from 1980; cons. editor Sheridan Printing Co., Inc., from 1983. Contbg. editor Am. Year Book, 1946—50, Collier's Year Book, 1951—59; assoc. editor Applied Mechanics Revs., 1948—56; info. com. Engrs. Joint Coun., 1964—68, Profl. Devel. Adv. Coun., Pratt Inst. Sch. Engring., 1976—80. Fellow: ASME (Outstanding Leadership in Engring. award 1968); mem.: Martin Downs Country (Palm City, Fla.), Walkill Country (Franklin, NJ), Tamarack Assn. (NJ), NY Bus. Press Editors. Home: Maricopa, Ariz. Died July 1, 2010.

JALBERT, LAWRENCE EDWARD, sales executive; b. San Diego, Dec. 1, 1943; s. Llewellyn Edward and Alice (Wood) Jalbert; m. Cheryl Anne Morrison Jalbert, May 11, 1985; children: Shannon Rea, Leigh Erica. Student, Old Dominion U., Norfolk, Va., 1964—65. Lic. profl. diver Fla. With Crofton Divers, Norfolk, Va., 1963—68; sales mgr. Cardinal Signs, Norfolk, 1968—73; owner, mgr. Window Displays, Ltd., Virginia Beach, Va., 1968—74; sales mgr. Monroe Transfers & Storage Co., Norfolk, 1973—74; ter. sales mgr. Johnson Wax Co., Racine, Wis., from 1974, cons. advt. & infection control, diving tchr., from 1963. Bd. dirs Va. Beach Civic League. Author: Hosp. Infection Control, 1979. Fellow: Worldwide Innopro; mem.: Smithfield Flyers, Va. Beach Divers, Edgar Cayce Found. Republican. Avocations: photography, diving, flying, canoeing, hiking. Died June 7, 2009.

JAMES, HERMAN DELANO, retired academic administrator; b. St. Thomas, V.I., Feb. 25, 1943; s. Henry and Frances (Smith) J.; m. Marie Nannie Gray, Feb. 25, 1964; children: Renee, Sybil, Sidney BS, Tuskegee Inst., 1965; MA, St. John's U., NYC, 1967; PhD, U. Pitts., 1972; LLD (hon.), Tuskagee U., 1996. Asst. prof. U. Mass., Boston, 1973-78, assoc. provost, 1975-77, asst. chancellor, 1977-78; vice provost Calif. State U.-Northridge, 1978-82; v.p. Glassboro State Coll., 1982-84; pres. Rowan U. (formerly Glassboro State Coll.), Glassboro, NJ, 1984-98, pres. emeritus, Disting. prof., 1998—2010. Bd. dirs. Mid. States Assn., S. Jersey Industries. Contbr. articles to profl. jours. Bd. dirs. Gloucester County (N.J.) United Way NIH fellow, 1968-71; recipient Outstanding Achiever award Boston YMCA, 1977, Outstanding Contbr. award Nat. Ctr. for Deafness, 1982, Civic award Cherry Hill Minority Civic Assn., N.J., 1985; Tosney award, Amer. Assn. of Univ. Admin., 1994. Mem. American Assn. Higher Edn., American Sociol. Assn., N.J. C. of C. (bd. dirs.). Avocation: basketball. Home: Kirkwood Voorhees, NJ. Died Oct. 2, 2010.

JAMES, THOMAS NAUM, cardiologist, educator; b. Amory, Miss., Oct. 24, 1925; s. Naum and Kata J.; m. Gleaves Elizabeth Tynes, June 22, 1948; children: Thomas Mark, Terrence Fenner, Peter Naum. BS, Tulane U., 1946, MD, 1949. Diplomate Am. Bd. Internal Medicine (mem. bd. govs. 1982-88), Bd. Cardiovasc. Diseases (bd. dirs. 1972-78). Intern Henry Ford Hosp., Detroit, 1949-50, resident in internal medicine and cardiology, 1950-53, staff, 1959-68; instr. medicine Tulane U., New Orleans, 1955-58, asst. prof., 1959; prof. medicine U. Ala. Med. Ctr., Birmingham, 1968-87, prof. pathology, 1968-73, assoc. prof. physiology and biophysics, 1969-73, dir. Cardiovasc. Rsch. and Tng. Ctr., 1970-77, chmn. dept. medicine, dir. divsn. cardiovasc. disease, 1973-81, Mary Gertrude Waters prof. cardiology, 1976-87, Disting. prof., 1981-87; prof. medicine, prof. pathology U. Tex. Med. Br., Galveston, 1987—2004, pres., 1987-97, dir. WHO Cardiovasc. Ctr., 1988-98, Thomas N. and Gleaves T. James Disting. chair cardiology, 1997—2004. U. Tex. Med. Br., Galveston, 1997—; physician-in-chief U. Ala. Hosps., 1973-81; mem. adv. coun. Nat. Heart Lung and Blood Inst., 1975-79; pres. 10th World Congress Cardiology, 1986; mem. cardiology del. invited by Chinese Med. Assn. to China, 1978; Campbell orator Queens U., Belfast, No. Ireland, 1982; Mikamo lectr. Japan Circulation Soc., 1982; Sir Thomas Lewis lectr. Brit. Cardiac Soc., 1983, Einthoven lectr. U. Leiden, The Netherlands, 1993, Bailey K. Ashford lectr. U. P.R., 1995; hon. lectr. U. Padua, 1998. Author: Anatomy of the Coronary Arteries, 1961, The Etiology of Myocardial Infarction, 1963; Mem. editl. bd. Circulation, 1966-83, Am. Jour. Cardiology, 1968-82, Am. Heart Jour, 1976-79; contbr. articles to profl. jours. Capt. M.C. U.S. Army, 1953-55. Recipient Sesquicentennial Medal of Honor Paul Tulane Coll. Tulane U., 1997, 50-year Lifetime Achievement award Tulane Med. Alumni Assn., 1999, James B. Herrick award Am. Heart Assn., 1999, Disting. Achievement award Soc. Cardiovasc. Pathology, 2005. Fellow ACP (gov. Ala. 1975-79, master 1983); mem. AMA, Am. Clin. and Climatological Assn. (v.p. 1992-93, councillor 1992-93), Assn. Am. Physicians, Am. Soc. Clin. Investigation, Assn. Univ. Cardiologists (pres. 1978-79), Am. Heart Assn. (pres. 1979-80, Herrick award Coun. on Clin. Cardiology 1999), Am. Coll. Cardiology (v.p. 1970-71, trustee 1970-71, 76-81, First Disting. Scientist award 1982, chmn. publs. com. 1994-97), Am. Soc. Pharmacology and Exptl. Therapeutics, Soc. Exptl. Biology of Medicine, Am. Coll. Chest Physicians, Ctrl. Soc. Clin. Rsch., Internat. Soc. and Fedn. Cardiology (pres. 1983-84), WHO (expert adv. panel on cardiovasc. diseases 1988-97), So. Soc. Clin. Investigation, Am. Fedn. Clin. Rsch., Ala. Acad. Honor. Philos. Soc. Tex., Cosmos Club, Mountain Brook Club, Galveston Arty. Club, Phi Beta Kappa, Sigma Xi, Omicron Delta Kappa, Alpha Omega Alpha, Alpha Tau Omega, Phi Chi. Presbyterian. Died Sept. 11, 2010.

JAPENGA, JACK WALLACE, radiologist; b. Chgo., June 22, 1928; s. Jacob Martin and Theresa Alberta (Jaax) J.; Ph.B., U. Chgo., 1949, M.D., 1953; m. Laurena Booker, Nov. 1, 1952; children— William Martin, Ann Theresa, Charles Albert, Diana. Intern, USPHS Hosp., San Francisco, 1953-54; resident in radiology U. Chgo., 1956-59; practice medicine specializing in radiology, Covina, Calif., 1959—, also med. seminar dir.; mem. staffs Magan Med. Clinic, Covina, Calif., San Dimas (Calif.) Community Hosp. (hon.), Foothill Presbyn. Hosp., Glendora, Glendora Community Hosp.; chmn. pub. health commn. County of Los Angeles, 1975-81. Served with USPHS, 1953-56. Mem. Am., Calif. (ho. of dels., mem. polit. action com.), Los Angeles County (pres. Foothill Dist.) med. assns., Am. Coll. Radiology Am. Fedn. Physicians and Dentists (pres. Calif. council), Glendora Radiol. Assn. Inc. (past pres.; dir.), Am. Thermographic Soc. Republican. Home: Covina, Calif. Died May 21, 2010.

JAQUITH, RICHARD HERBERT, chemistry professor, retired academic administrator; b. Newton, Mass., Mar. 31, 1919; s. Milo W. and Helen F. (Evans) J.; m. E. Louise Bottum, Apr. 4, 1942 (dec. 1995); children: Nancy L., Richard L. (dec. 2009), David A. (dec. 2009), Robert E., Randall W. BS, U. Mass., 1940, MS, 1942; PhD, Mich. State U., 1955. Instr. chemistry U. Conn., 1942-47; asst. prof. Colby Coll., 1947-54; mem. faculty U. Md., 1954—87, prof. chemistry, 1965—87, asst. vice chancellor for acad. affairs, 1973—87. Served with USNR, 1944-46, 50. Mem. Sigma Xi, Alpha Phi Omega, Phi Kappa Phi, Omicron Delta Kappa. Home: Greenbelt, Md. Died Apr. 5, 2010.

JARZYK, SUSAN, publishing company editor; b. Trenton, NJ, Dec. 11, 1952; d. William Henry Jarzyk and Loretta Mae (Murl) Episcapo; m. Michael Belluomo, June 11, 1975 (div. Dec. 1985). Student, Broadcasting Acad., Washington, 1971, Sch. Visual Arts, NYC, 1977. Lic. FCC operator. Radio announcer Sta. WOUR-Radio, Sta. WMBO-WRLX-Radio, Utica and Auburn, N.Y., 1970-73; comml. photographer Studio One, San Francisco, 1973-75; dep. dir. Hearst Internat. mags., NYC, 1975-84; mgr. Books Direct King Features Syndicate, NYC, 1984-85, acquisitions editor and sales rep. N. Am., from 1987; acquisitions editor News Am./Times of London Syndicates, NYC, 1985-87. Mem. News Women's Club N.Y. (speaker). Roman Catholic. Home: New York, NY. Died Feb. 25, 2009.

JAY, DAVID JAKUBOWICZ, management consultant; b. Dec. 7, 1925; came to U.S., 1938, naturalized, 1944. s. Mendel and Gladys Gitta (Zalc) Jakubowicz; m. Shirley Anne Shapiro, Sept. 7, 1947; children: Melvin Maurice, Evelyn Deborah. BS, Wayne State U., 1948; MS, U. Mich., 1949, postgrad., 1956-57, U. Cin., 1951-53, MIT, 1957. Registered profl. engr., Calif., Mich., Ohio. Supr. man-made diamonds GE Corp., Detroit, 1951-56; instr. U. Detroit, 1948-51; asst. to v.p. engring. Ford Motor Co., Dearborn, Mich., 1956-63; project mgr. Apollo environ. control radiators N.Am. Rockwell, Downey, Calif., 1963-68; staff to v.p. corp. planning Aerospace Corp., El Segundo, Calif., 1968-70; founder, pres. PBM Sys. Inc., 1970-83; pres. Cal-Best Hydrofarms Coop., Los Alamitos, 1972-77, Inkmarks Corp., 1989—95. Cons. in field. Patentee in air supported ground vehicle, others. Pres. Cmty. Design Corp., Los Alamitos, 1971-75; bronze life master Am. Contract Bridge League. With USNR, 1944-46. Fellow Inst. Advancement Engring.; mem. Art Stamp and Stencil Dealers Assn. (pres. 1993-95), Inst. Mgmt. Sci. (chmn. 1961-62), Western Greenhouse Vegetable Growers Assn. (sec.-treas. 1972-75), Tau Beta Pi. Jewish. Home: Santa Ana, Calif. Died Feb. 18, 2009.

JEFFERSON, DENISE, dance school director; b. Chgo., Nov. 1, 1944; Studied ballet with Edna L. McRae; BA, Wheaton Coll., PhD (hon.), 2000; MA, NYU. Co-founder, co-dir. Chgo. Dance Ctr.; tchr. dance U. Ill., Chgo.; with Pearl Lang Dance Co.; mem. dance faculty Sch. Arts NYU, Alvin Ailey Dance Ctr., 1975—80; dir. Alvin Ailey American Dance Ctr. Scholarship program, 1980-84, Alvin Ailey Dance Sch., 1984—2010. Remedial writing tchr. Seek program Hunter Coll.; developed modern dance program Benedict Coll.; guest tchr. U.S., internat.; mem. internat. team dance profls. Dutch govt. to evaluate Dance acads. in Holland, 1990; adjudicator Arts Recognition, Talent Search Confederation Nat. de Danse, Fedn. Interprofl. de la danse, 1992. Mem. adv. bd. Profl. Children's Sch.; mem. adv. com. dance dept. U. Okla.; trustee Elisa Monte Dance Co. Grantee Nat. Endowment Arts and Humanities; scholar Martha Graham Sch. Contemporary Dance. Mem. Nat. Assn. Schs. Dance (bd. dirs. 1989-91, program evaluator, mem. commn. accredation), N.Y. State Coun. Arts (dance panel, appeal panel). Died July 16, 2010.

JEFFRIES, JAMES RICHARD, dean, education consultant, speaker; b. Glasgow, Ky., Jan. 23, 1940; s. Delmar Clayborn and Annie Laverne (Medley) Jeffries; m. Betty Joyce Meece, Apr. 3, 1959; children: Melody Logan, Timothy, Jamie Ann Coomer, Richard, Robert, Philip, Stephen. AB, Lexington Baptist Coll., 1975; MA, Morehead State U., 1976; MHE, 1977; MRE, Lexington Baptist Coll., 1978; DD, 1981. Cert. ordained Gospel minister. With Cin. Gas and Electric Co., 1958—67; pastor Emmanuel Baptist Ch., Winchester, Ky., 1967—70, Fincastle Baptist Ch., Ohio, 1970—74; Bapt. missionary Eastern, Ky., 1974—76; instr. Lexington Baptist Coll., from 1979. Author: (book) A Brief Bible Survey, 1980; co-editor: A Study Guide: Term Papers, Reports and Theses, 1981. With USAF, 1956—61, NG. Mem.: Nat. Audio-Visual Assn., Ky. Assn. Collegiate Registrars and Admissions Officers, Assn. Bus. Adminstrs. Christian Colls. Home: Lexington, Ky. Died May 16, 2009.

JELINEK, FREDERICK, electrical engineer, educator; b. Prague, Czechoslovakia, Nov. 18, 1932; arrived in U.S., 1949, naturalized, 1955; s. William and Trudy (Kocmanek) J.; m. Milena Tobolova, Feb. 4, 1961; children: Hannah, William. BS, MIT, 1956, MS, 1958, PhD, 1962; DS Math. and Physics (hon.), Charles U., Prague, 2001. Instr. MIT, Cambridge, 1959-62; lectr. Harvard U., Cambridge, 1962; asst. prof. Cornell U., Sch. Elec. Engring., Ithaca, NY, 1962-66, assoc. prof., 1966-72, prof., 1972-74; vis. scientist MIT, Lincoln Lab., 1964, 65, IBM, 1968-69; sr. mgr. continuous speech recognition IBM, T.J. Watson Research Center, Yorktown Heights, NY, 1972-93; prof., dir. Ctr. Lang. and Speech Processing Whiting Sch. Engring. Johns Hopkins U., Balt., 1993—2010, Julian Sinclair Smith prof. Author: Probabilistic Information Theory, 1968, Statistical Methods for Speech Recognition, 1998; contbr. articles to profl. jours. Chmn.

Liberal Party, Ithaca, NY, 1970-72, mem. state exec. com., 1971-73. Recipient Outstanding Achievement in the Field of Speech Comm. European Speech Comm. Assn., 2000; named One of top 100 innovators in speech recognition by Tech. Mag., 1981. Fellow IEEE (life; pres. Info. Theory Group 1977, bd. govs. 1970-79, 81-86, Info. Theory Group best paper award 1971, Soc. award Signal Processing Soc. 1998, Golden Jubilee Paper award Info. Theory Soc. 1998, Third Millennium medal 2000, Computer, Speech and Lang. paper award 2002); mem. NAE. Home: Baltimore, Md. Died Sept. 14, 2010.

JELLINEK, GEORGE, retired broadcast executive, music educator, writer; b. Budapest, Hungary, Dec. 22, 1919; came to U.S., 1941; s. Daniel and Jolan Jellinek; m. Hedy Dicker, July 29, 1942; 1 child, Nancy Berezin. Student, Lafayette Coll., 1943; MusD (hon.), L.I. U., 1984. Dir. program services SESAC, Inc., NYC, 1955-64; rec. dir. Muzak, Inc., NYC, 1964-68; music dir. Sta. WQXR, NYC, 1968-84; asst. prof. music NYU, NYC, 1976-91; ret. Author: Callas, Portrait of a Prima Donna, 1960, 2d edit. 1986, The Magic Chair, 1966, The Scarlet Mill, 1968, History Through the Opera Glass, 1994, My Road and The Vocal Scene, 2007; contbg. editor: Stereo Rev. mag., 1958-74, Ovation mag., 1974-88; contbr. articles to the N.Y. Times, Musical America, The Opera Quar.; host (radio show) The Vocal Scene, 1969-2004. Trustee emeritus Bagby Found. Served to 1st lt. M.I., U.S. Army, 1942-46. Recipient Maj. Armstrong Broadcast award, 1978, Ohio State award, 1978, Gabriel award, 1982, George Washington award Am. Hungarian Found., 1986, Gold medal Internat. Radio Festival, 1995, Grammy award, 1996. Mem. ASCAP, AFTRA. Died Jan. 16, 2010.

JENKINS, MARGARET AIKENS, educational administrator; b. Lexington, Miss., May 14, 1925; d. Joel Bryant and Marie C. (Threadgill) Melton; m. Daniel Armstrong, May 21, 1944 (div. 1950); children: Marie Cynthia, Marsha Rochelle; m. Gabe Aikens, June 29, 1954 (div. 1962); m. Herbert Jenkins, May 21, 1966. Student, Chgo. Conservatory of Music, 1959, Moody Bible Inst., Chgo., 1959, Calif. State U.-Northridge, 1984; HHD (hon.), Payne Acad., 1984, Pentecostal Bible Coll., 1988, So. Calif. Sch. Ministry, 1990, Liberty U., 1990—. Clk., U.S. Signal Corps, Chgo., 1944, Cuneo Press, Chgo., 1948-52, Ford Aircraft, Chgo., 1952-58, Corps of Engrs., Chgo., 1958-64; progress control clk. Def. Contract Adminstrn. Service Region, Los Angeles, 1966-73; founder, adminstr. Celeste Scott Christian Sch., Inglewood, Calif., 1976—; founder, pres. Mary Celeste Scott Meml. Found., Inc., Inglewood, 1973—; pub., writer, founder Magoll Records, Chgo., 1958-64, M&M Aikens Music, 1957—; mem. Inglewood Coalition Against Drugs, 1987—; radio broadcast Look and Live Sta. KTYM, Inglewood, Calif., 1986—; Mayor of Inglewood Ann. Prayer Breakfast Com., 1988. Recipient Cert. Appreciation, Mayor of Inglewood, 1984, Mayor of Los Angeles, 1980, State Senator, 1975, State Rep., 1976, Congressional Cert. of Appreciation, 1993, Appreciation award A.F.M. Westbury Congregation South Africa, 1993; named Woman of Yr., Los Angeles Sentinel, 1982, Inglewood C. of C., 1982, Presdl. Commemorative Honor Roll, 1991, Outstanding Christian Woman of Faith World Won for Christ Ministries, Englewood, Calif., 1993. Mem. Broadcast Music Inc., Am. Fedn. TV and Radio Artists, Nat. Assn. Pentecostal Women and Men Inc. Avocations: religion, writing and recording music, education. Died Mar. 6, 2009.

JENKINS, MARGARET BUNTING, human resources executive; b. Warsaw, Va., Aug. 3, 1935; d. John and Irma (Cookman) Bunting; children: Sydney, Jr., Terry L. Student, Coll. William and Mary, 1952, AA in Bus. Adminstrn., 1973; AA in Human Resources Mgmt., Christopher Newport U.; BA in Human Resource Devel., St. Leo Coll., 1979; M in Adminstrn., George Washington U., 1982; PhD in Human Resources Mgmt., Columbia Pacific U., 1986. Rehab. counselor, tchr. York County Schs., Yorktown, Va.; mgr. Waterfront Constrn. Co., Seafood Corp., Seaford, Va., 1960—72; labor rels. specialist Naval Weapons Sta., Yorktown, 1974—77, staffing specialist, 1977—78, position classification specialist, supr. shipbuilding, conversion and repair Newport News, Va., 1978-81, supr. pers. mgmt. specialist, supr. shipbuilding, conversion and repair, 1981—90, pers. mgmt. specialist Yorktown and Cheatham, Va., 1990—94. Bd. dirs. various health orgns.; owner Jenkins Consulting. Author: Organizational Impact on Human Behavior, 1996; (poetry) Heron Haven Reflections, 1996; poetry published in Mists of Enchantment, 1995, Treasured Poems of America, 1996, Poets of the 90's, A Celebration of Poets, Showcase Edit., 1998, 99, The Best Poems of Poets award 2001; featured in: Cancer Has Its Privileges, Stories of Hope and Laughter (Christine K. Clifford), 2002 (Best Poets award 2002, 03, 04, 05, 06, 07, 08 Internat. Poetry award 2003, 04, 05, 08, 09). Decorated Meritorious Civilian Svc. award USN Supvr. Shipbuilding, Conversion and Repair, 3 Navy commendations; recipient award Newport News, 1990, Alumni medallion Coll. William and Mary, 1994-2000. Mem.: Nat. Ptnr. Assn., Nat. Women's History Mus., Wilderness Soc. (charter mem.), Chesapeake Writers Assn., Classification and Compensation Soc. (pres. 1984), Soc. for Human Resource Mgmt., Long Ridge Writers Group, Nature Conservancy, Audubon Soc., 4-Alumni Assn., Internat. Soc. of Poets (Disting. mem. 1996, 2005, 2006), Toastmasters Internat. (pres. 1985—87, various offices, award), Sezford Womens Club, Sierra Club, Fedn. Women's Clubs. Methodist. Avocations: art, writing, crafts. Home: Seaford, Va. Died Feb. 9, 2010.

JENNINGS, DAVID VINCENT, JR., judge; b. Milw., Feb. 10, 1921; s. David V. and Mary (Hanrahan) Jennings; m. Mary Johnston, Sept. 7, 1946 (div. Nov. 1974); children: Maureen, David, Kathleen, Sheila, Robert, Ellen, Therese, Steven, Colleen, Janet, Bridget; m. Margaret R. Horan, July 26, 1985. AB, Holy Cross Coll., 1943; LLB, Marquette U., 1948. Bar: Wis. 1948, US Dist. Ct. (ea. dist.) Wis. 1948, US Ct. Appeals (7th cir.) 1951, US Supreme Ct. 1955. Pvt. practice, Milw., 1948—66; judge Cir. Ct., Milw., from 1966. Served as lt. USNR, 1942—46, PTO. Mem.: ABA, Milw. County Bar Assn., Ozaukee County Bar Assn., Wis. Bar Assn., Wis. Club, Milw. Hunt Club (dir., treas.), Mill Creek Hunt Club (Lake Forest, Ill.) (pres., chmn. bd.). Roman Catholic. Home: Naples, Fla. Died Aug. 3, 2010.

JENSEN, BURL CHARLES, geologist; b. LaGrange Park, Ill., Dec. 6, 1937; s. James Burl and Margaret (Collins) Jensen; m. Betty Ann Rakich, May 14, 1972; children: Eric B., Christoffer P. BS in Geology, U. Idaho, 1961. Geologist, mining engr. Freeman United, Chgo., 1963—75; gen. supt. ops. Colowyo Coal Co., Meeker, Colo., from 1975. With US Army, 1962—63. Mem.: Rocky Mountain Coal Mining Inst., AIME. Republican. Died May 23, 2009.

JENSEN, HERLUF MATTHIAS, retired bishop; b. Cordova, Nebr., July 12, 1923; s. Alfred and Milda Hanna (Schmidt) J.; m. Dorthea Lund, July 3, 1948; children: Tezanne, Lance, Cynthia, Peter, Roslind AB, Harvard U., 1949; MA, U. Minn., 1951; M.Div., Union Theol. Sem., 1964; DD (honoris causa), Grand View Coll., 1989; DLitt (honoris causa), Upsala Coll., 1990. Ordained to ministry Lutheran Ch. in Am., 1968, consecrated bishop, 1978. Pres. Luth. Student Assn. in America, Chgo., 1951-53; exec. sec. United Student Christian Coun., NYC, 1954-59; gen. sec. Nat. Student Christian Fedn., NYC, 1959-62; lay staff ofcl. Bd. Social Ministry, Luth. Church in America, 1963-68; pastor St. Matthew Luth. Church, Moorestown, NJ, 1968-78; bishop N.J. Synod Lutheran Church in America (merged into Evang. Luth. Church in America 1988), 1978—91. Pres. Coalition of Religious Leaders, N.J., 1983-85. Pres. Human Relations Council, East Brunswick, N.J., 1965-68; trustee Neighborhood House, New Brunswick, 1965-68, Luth. Theol. Sem., Phila., 1975-91, Upsala Coll., East Orange, N.J., 1978-90. Served with U.S. Army, 1943-46, ETO. Decorated Purple Heart; recipient Disting. Service award Human Relations Council, 1968 Mem. Liturgical Soc. America, Luth. Human Relations Assn. America, Luth. Soc. for Worship, Music & the Arts Democrat. Home: Moorestown, NJ. Died Oct. 14, 2010.

JENSEN, WALTER EDWARD, retired lawyer, educator; b. Chgo., Ill., Oct. 20, 1937; AB, U. Colo., 1959; JD, Ind. U., 1962, MBA, 1964; PhD, Duke U., 1972. Bar: Ind. 1962, Ill. 1962, DC 1963, US Tax Ct. 1982, US Supreme Ct. 1967. Asst. prof. bus. law U. Colo., Boulder, 1958—62; assoc. prof. Colo. State U., 1964—66, U. Conn., Storrs, 1966—67, Ill. State U., 1970—72; prof. bus. adminstrn. Va. Poly. Inst. & State U., 1972; prof. fin., ins. & law, 1972—2005; prof. emeritus, 2005. With Inst. Advanced Legal Studies, U. London, 1983—84; ret.; prof. US Air Force Grad. Mgmt. Program, Europe, 1977—78, 1983—85; vis. lectr. pub. internat. law U. Istanbul, 1988, Roberts Coll. U. Bosporous, Istanbul, Uludag U., Turkey, 1988; rschr. U. London Inst. Advanced Legal Studies, London Sch. Econs. & Inst. Commonwealth Studies, 1969, 1971—74, 1976; ford found. rsch. fellow Ind. U., 1963—64; faculty rsch. fellow in econs. U. Tex., 1968; Bell Telephone fellow in econs. regulated pub. utilities U. Chgo., 1965; staff editor Am. Bus Law Jour., from 1973; vice chmn. assoc. editor for adminstrv. law sect. young lawyers Barrister (Law Notes), 1975—83; staff editor Bus. Law Rev., from 1975. Contbr. articles to profl. publs. Recipient Dissertation Travel award, Duke U. Grad. Sch., 1968; fellowship, Ind. U., 1963, 1974. Mem.: ABA, Am. Bus. Law Assn., Am. Judicature Soc., Am. Soc. Internat. Law, Am. Polit. sci. Assn., Ind. Bar Assn., Ill. Bar Assn., DC Bar Assn., Beta Gamma Sigma, Pi Kappa Alpha, Pi Gamma Mu, Phi Alpha Delta, Alpha Kappa Psi. Home: Lakewood, Colo. Died June 28, 2009.

JENSH, RONALD PAUL, retired anatomist; b. NYC, June 14, 1938; s. Werner G. and Dorothy (Hensle) J.; m. Ruth Eleanor Dobson, Aug. 18, 1962 (dec. 2004); children: Victoria Lynn, Elizabeth Whitney BA, Bucknell U., 1960, MA, 1962; PhD, Jefferson Med. Coll., 1966. From instr. anatomy to prof. Thomas Jefferson U., Phila., 1966—68, prof. anatomy, 1982—2004, course coord. histology, 1988—2004, emeritus, 2004—10. Staff Op. Concern Inc., Cherry Hill, N.J., 1970-72; cons. reproductive biology Bio-Search Inc., Argus Rsch. Lab. Inc., Ortho Rsch. Found. Contbr. articles to sci. jours.; author: Lifelines, 2002, Epiphany, 2007 Task force com. on comm. S. Jersey Methodist Conf., 1974-80; chmn. Learning Resources Ctr., Haddonfield United Meth. Ch., NJ, 1976-79. Recipient Christian R. and Mary F. Lindback Found. Disting. Teaching award, 1978, Disting. Alumnus award, 1985, Faculty Achievement award Burlington Northern Found., 1989, Jefferson Med. Coll. Portrait, 1994, Award for Disting. Alumnus in a Chosen Profession, Bucknell U., 1997. Mem. AAAS, Am. Soc. Zoologists, N.Y. Acad. Scis., Teratology Soc. (treas. 1989-92), Behavioral Teratology Soc. (pres. 1985-86), Am. Assn. Anatomists, Soc. Am. Mus. Natural History, Inst. Social Ethics and Life Scis., Jefferson Med. Coll. Alumni Assn. (hon. life), Phi Beta Kappa, Sigma Xi, Psi Chi, Phi Sigma. Home: Haddonfield, NJ. Died Jan. 20, 2010.

JENTZ, GAYLORD ADAIR, law educator; b. Beloit, Wis., Aug. 7, 1931; s. Merlyn Adair and Delva (Mullen) Jentz; m. JoAnn Mary Hornung, Aug. 6, 1955; children: Katherine Ann, Gary Adair, Loretta Ann, Rory Adair. BA, U. Wis., 1953, JD, 1957, MBA, 1958. Bar: Wis. 1957. Pvt. practice law, Madison, 1957-58; from asst. prof. to assoc. prof. bus. law U. Okla., 1958-65; assoc. prof. U. Tex., Austin, 1965-68, prof., 1968-98, Herbert D. Kelleher prof. bus. law, 1982-98, prof. emeritus, from 1998, chmn. gen. bus. dept., 1968-74, 80-86. From vis. instr. to vis. prof. U. Wis. Law Sch., Wis., 1957—65. Author (with others): Texas Uniform Commercial Code, 1967; author: rev. edit., 1975; author: (with others) Business Law Text and Cases, 1968, Business Law Text, 1978, Legal Environment of Business, 1989, Texas Family Law, 7th edit., 1992, Business Law Today-Alternate Essentials Edition, 4th edit., 1997, Fundamentals of Business Law, 8th edit., 2010, Fundamentals of Business Law, Excerpted Cases, 2nd edit., 2010, West's Business Law: Alternate Edition, 10th edit., 2007, Business Law: Text and Cases, 11th edit., 2009, Law for E-Commerce, 2002, West's Business Law-Extended Case Approach, 2d edit., 2006, Business Law Today-Interactive Text, 7th edit., 2006, Business Law Today-Comprehensive Edition, 8th edit., 2010, Business Law Today-The Essentials, 8th edit., 2008, Business Law Today-Standard Edition, 8th edit., 2008, Essentials of the Legal Environment. 2nd edit., 2008; dep. editor: Social Sci. Quar., 1966—82, mem. editl. bd.:, 1982—94, editor-in-chief: Am. Bus. Law Jour., 1969—74, adv. editor:, from 1974. With US Army, 1953—55. Recipient Outstanding Tchr. award, U. Tex. Coll. Bus., 1967, Jack G. Taylor Tchg. Excellence award, 1971, 1989, Joe D. Beasley Grad. Tchg. Excellence award, 1978, CBA Found. Adv. Coun. award, 1979, Grad. Bus. Coun. Outstanding Grad. Bus. Prof. award, 1980, James C. Scorboro Meml. award for outstanding leadership in banking edn., Colo. Grad. Sch. Banking, 1983, Utmost Outstanding Prof. award, 1989, CBA award for excellence in edn., 1994, Banking Leadership award, Western States Sch. Banking, 1995, Civitatis award, U. Tex., 1997; named to CBA Hall of Fame, 1999. Mem.: So. Bus. Law Assn. (pres. 1967), Wis. Bar Assn., Tex. Assn. Coll. Tchrs. (pres. Austin chpt. 1967—68, mem. exec. com. 1979—80, state pres. 1971—72), Acad. Legal Studies Bus. (pres. 1971—72, mem. exec. com. 1989—94), Am. Arbitration Assn. (nat. panel 1966—96), Southwestern Fedn. Adminstrv. Disciples (v.p. 1979—80, pres. 1980—81), Phi Kappa Phi (pres. 1983—84), Omicron Delta Kappa. Home: Austin, Tex. Died Nov. 2009.

JERNIGAN, MARIAN SUE, fashion merchandising educator; b. Chattanooga, Dec. 18, 1940; d. John Marion and Coye M. (Cunningham) Hayes; m. G. William Jernigan, Dec. 22, 1969. BS, Purdue U., 1962, MS, 1964, PhD, 1968. Exec. trainee Hutzler Bros. Co., Balt., 1963-64; dept. mgr. L.S. Ayres & Co., Lafayette, Ind., 1964-65; instr. Purdue U., W. Lafayette, Ind., 1965-66; asst. prof. La. State U., Baton Rouge, 1968-73; assoc. prof. Fla. State U., Tallahassee, 1973-76, N. Tex. State U., Denton, 1976-83, acting dir., 1980-83; prof. fashion merchandising Tex. Woman's U., Denton, from 1983. Mem. exec. com. Tex. Coun. Faculty Governance Orgns., 1992-96. Co-author: Merchandising Mathematics for Retailing, 1984, 2d edit., 1992, Fashion Merchandising and Marketing, 1990. Pres. Internat. Toastmistress, Lewisville, Tex., 1983. Mem. Fashion Group Internat., Internat. Textile and Apparel Assn., Am. Collegiate Retailing Assn., Am. Assn. Family and Consumer Scis., Costume Soc. Am., Tex. Assn. Family and Consumer Scis. (divsn. sec., divsn. chair), Delta Kappa Gamma, Alpha Lambda Delta, Omicron Nu, Phi Kappa Phi, Phi Upsilon Omicron, Zeta Tau Alpha (advisor student chpts.). Methodist. Home: Metairie, La. Died July 13, 2009.

JEUCK, JOHN EDWARD, business educator; b. Chgo., Oct. 17, 1916; s. John S. and Lila E. (Burke) J. AB, U. Chgo., 1937, MBA, 1938, PhD, 1949; MA (hon.), Harvard U. Instr. marketing, dir. placement, sch. bus. Miami U., 1940-41; instr. marketing, sch. bus. U. Chgo., 1946-47, asst. prof., 1947-50, asso. prof. marketing, asso. dir. exec. program, 1950-52, prof. marketing, dean sch. bus., dir. exec. program, 1952-55; prof. bus. adminstrn. Harvard Grad. Sch Bus. Adminstrn., 1955-58; cons. in mgmt. edn. European Productivity Agy., 1956-57; bus. cons., from 1950; Robert Law prof. bus. adminstrn. U. Chgo., 1958-87, emeritus, from 1987. Bd. dirs. Midway Airlines; trustee, bd. dirs. various Dean Witter funds, 1987—. Author: (with Boris Emmet) Catalogues and Counters, A History of Sears, Roebuck and Company, 1950; Co-editor: Readings in Market Organization and Price Policy, 1952; Editorial bd.: Jour. Marketing, 1951-61; Contbr. articles to profl. jours. Served as lt. USNR, 1942-46. Mem. Beta Gamma Sigma. Clubs: Quadrangle (Chgo.), University (Chgo.), Economic (Chgo.), Tavern (Chgo.). Roman Catholic. Home: Chicago, Ill. Died Dec. 18, 2009.

JOB OF HARTFORD, Bishop See OSACKY, JOHN

JOFFE, ROBERT DAVID, lawyer; b. NYC, May 26, 1943; s. Joseph and Bertha (Pashkovsky) Joffe; m. Virginia Ryan, June 20, 1981; stepchildren: Elizabeth DeHaas, Ryan DeHaas;children from previous marriage: Katherine, David. AB, Harvard U., 1964, JD, 1967. Bar: NY 1970, US Dist. Ct. (so. and ea. dists.) NY 1971, US Ct. Appeals (2d cir.) 1972, US Supreme Ct. 1973. Ford Found. fellow Maxwell Sch. Africa Pub. Svc., Malawi, 1967—69; state counsel, 1968—69; assoc. Cravath, Swaine & Moore LLP, NYC, 1969—75, ptnr., 1975—2010, dep. presiding ptnr., 1998, presiding ptnr., 1999—2006. Bd. dirs. Romanian American Enterpise Fund, 1994—2003. Chair Harvard Law Sch. Nat. Fund, 1995—97, dean's adv. bd., 1997—2009; bd. dirs. Jericho Project, 1985—97, Human Rights First, 1988—2010, vice chmn., 2005—10; bd. dirs. After Sch. Corp., 2001—10, chmn., 2006—10; bd. trustees Met. Mus. Art, 2006—10, chmn. legal com., 2007—10, mem. exec. com, 2007—10, mem. search com., 2008, mem. fin. com., 2009—10, mem. vis. com., dept. photographs, 2007—10, mem. compensation com. Recipient Disting. Leadership Recognition award for helping secure passage of Civil Rights Act of 1991, Lawyers Com. Civil Rights, 1992, Learned Hand award, American Jewish Com., 2004, John J. McCloy award, Fund for Modern Courts, 2005, Servant Justice award, Legal Aid Soc., 2006, Lifetime Achievement award, The American Lawyer mag., 2010; named one of The 100 Most Influential Lawyers, The Nat. Law Jour., 2006. Mem.: ABA, NY State Jud. Screening Commn., Coun. Fgn. Rels., Assn. Bar City N.Y. (chmn. trade regulation com. 1980—83, mem. exec. com. 1995—99, nominating com. 2001—02, chmn. task force jud. selection 2003, v.p. 2003—04, chmn. task force jud. selection 2006, chmn. nominating com. 2008), N.Y. Bar Assn., Human Rights Watch/Africa (mem. adv. com.), Century Assn. Club, Harvard Club. Home: New York, NY. Died Jan. 28, 2010.

JOHANNESSEN, LEIF BERTRAM, orthodontist, psychotherapist; b. Oslo, Aug. 25, 1925; came to U.S., 1945; s. Jens W. and Bernthine (Aspevold) J.; m. Berit Hem, Mar. 27, 1947; children: Erik B., Lars, Nils H., Ingrid K., Sigrid L. Examen Artium in Psychology, Hegdehaugen Coll., Oslo, 1944; DMD, Tufts U., 1949. DMD Mass., Calif., Maine, N.H., Norway. Dir. dental health Norway Pub. Health Svc., Tromsdalen, Norway, 1949-50; intern Forsyth Dental Ctr., Boston, 1951-52; Lt., Norwegian Dental Svc. Norway Royal Navy, Horten, Norway, 1950-51; vis. pedodontist Perkins Sch. for Blind, Watertown, Mass., 1952-60; pvt. practice orthdontist, psychotherapist Needham, Mass., 1952-80; rsch. assoc. Harvard U. Sch. Dental Medicine, Boston, 1957-60; pvt. practice orthdontist, psychotherapist Wakefield, N.H., from 1983. Contbr. articles to profl. jours. Chief fundraiser New Eng. Lutheran Ch., 1965, Boy Scouts Am., Needham, Mass., 1964. Capt. USPHS Dental Corps, 1953-55, Korea. Mem. ADA, Norumbega Lodge Sons of Norway (charter), Omicron Kappa Upsilon. Republican. Lutheran, Congregational. Avocations: organ playing, choir singing, farming organic vegetables. Died Apr. 4, 2009.

JOHNSON, ALBERT WILLIAM, mortgage banker, real estate broker; b. Raleigh, NC, June 25, 1919; s. William Thompson and Evie (Barnes) J.; m. Margaret Hayes, Oct. 25, 1945; children: Albert William II, Brian Allen, Douglass Stevens. BS in Commerce, U. N.C., 1940; postgrad., Mich. State U., 1964. Cert. mortgage banker, real estate financier, real estate appraiser. Enlisted cadet USAF, 1940, advanced through grades to col., honorably discharged, 1955, asst. judge advocate gen. Gen. Staff of Hdqrs. 14th Command Orlando, Fla., war plans officer Gen. Staff Hdqrs. Tactical Air Command Langley Field, Va.; war plans officer Gen. Staff NATO Hdqrs., Paris; NATO war plans officer Sec. of Air Force Office Pentagon, Washington; co-founder, real estate broker, mortgage banker Dobson & Johnson, Nashville, from 1955, chmn., CEO. Chmn., CEO Albert William Johnson Ins. Co., Inc., Met. Land Corp., Fed. Title and Securities Corp., Dobson & Johnson Capital Corp., Outdoor Resorts of Am.;dir. Fidelity Investment & Bond Corp.; past trustee N.Y. Stock Exch. listed real Estate Investment Trust, Am. Century Mortgage Investors. Life mem. bd. trustees Scarritt Coll. for Christian Workers, Nashville, chmn. exec., investment, and bus. affairs coms.; life mem. bd. trustees Winchendon (Mass.) Sch. Boys; past dir. Mid. Tenn. Heart Assn.; patron Cheekwood Hort. Soc.; past dir. Internat. Com. on Fgn. Rels.; assoc. Grad. Sch. Bus., Vanderbilt U. Decorated Disting. Svc. medal, Paris, DFC with one oak leaf cluster, Air medal with six oak leaf clusters, Purple Heart; recipient The Freedom medal (highest U.S. Civilian Decoration). Mem. Nat. Soc. Real Estate Fin. (past pres., chmn. bd. govs., Disting. fellow of mortgage banking 1964), Mortgage Banking Assn. Am., Nat. Assn. Cert. Mortgage Bankers (past pres., chmn. bd.), Nashville Mortgage Bankers Assn. (bd. dirs., past pres.), Cert. Real Estate Appraisers Assn. (dir.), Mortgage Bankers Assn. Am. (vice chair exec. com.), Tenn. Mortgage Bankers Assn. (past pres.), Nashville Bd. Realtors (past dir.), Nat. Assn. Real Estate Bds., Tenn. Bd. Realtors, Nashville Bd. Realtors, Nashville Home Builders Assn., Nashville Apt. Owners and Developers Assn., Nat. Soc. Real Estate Fin. (chmn. bd. govs. 1983-91, bd. govs. 1983-92), C. of C. of U.S., Nashville C. of C., Alumni Assn. U. N.C. (life), Nashville Rotary Club, Belle Meade Country Club, Cumberland Club, Univ. Club (life), N.Y. Athletic Club (life), The N.Y. World Trade Ctr. Windows of the World, Doubles Club (N.Y.C.), Everglades Club, Bath and Tennis Club, Palm Beach Yacht Club, Club Colette, Pres.'s Club (Palm Beach, Fla.). Phi Kappa Sigma. Presbyterian. Home: Nashville, Tenn. Died Dec. 16, 2009.

JOHNSON, BARBARA ELAINE SPEARS, retired education educator; b. Chgo., May 24, 1932; d. William Everett and Sadie Mae (Fennoy) Spears; m. John Gilbert Johnson, July 29, 1967 (dec. Jan. 1985); children: Steven W., Jeri-Lynn Johnson Jackson. AB, U. Chgo., 1952; EdB, Chgo. Tchrs. Coll., 1954; EdM, Loyola U., Chgo., 1967; EdS, U. Ill., Urbana, 1982; MSEd in Counseling, Chgo. State U., 1986. Tchr. Chgo. Pub. Schs., 1954-64, counselor, 1964-70; evening tchr. Chgo. Pub. High Schs., 1964-66; dir. resource skills City Colls. of Chgo., 1970-84, dir. audio visual, 1985-86, coordinator academic support ctr., 1986-87, prof. acad. support, 1988-93, prof. emeritus, from 1993. Faculty coun. City Colls. of Chgo., v.p. 1989-90, pres. 1990-91. Coordinator food ministry Cosmopolitan Community Ch., Chgo., 1983-90. Recipient Dedication to Youth award McCosh Sch. Council, 1985, citations of recognition Ill. Community Coll. Bd., 1982, 84. Fellow Ill. Com. Black Concerns in Higher Edn. (plaque 1984); mem. AARP (exec. bd. 1997-2004, v.p. 2000), Ill. C.C. Faculty Assn. (life, exec. bd 1979—, pres. 1981-82, plaque 1982), Ill. Assn. Personalized Learning Programs (exec. bd., treas. 1975-85, Outstanding Contbn. award 1985), U. Ill. Mothers Assn. (chair 1977-81), Ill. C.C. Annuitants Assn. (exec. bd. dirs. 1993—, pres. 1995-97), Alpha Kappa Alpha (50 yr. mem. award 2002) Home: Chicago, Ill. Died Sept. 10, 2009.

JOHNSON, CARL E., retired obstetrician-gynecologist, consultant; b. Chgo., Nov. 13, 1919; s. Carl J. and Gerda Johnson; m. Irene Poczik, July 9, 1946; children: Carolyn, Gail, Carl. BS, Wheaton Coll., 1942; MD, Northwestern U., 1946; MS, U. Minn., 1951. Cert. ob-gyn., 1954, recert., 1980. Intern Cook County Hosp., Chgo., 1945-46; med. corps USNR, Rochester, Minn., 1946-48; fellow in ob-gyn. Mayo Found., Rochester, Minn., 1948-52; staff ob-gyn Mayo Clinic St. Mary's Hosp. and Meth. Hosp., Rochester, Minn., 1952—88; assoc. prof. ob-gyn Mayo Med. Sch. Fellow ACOG, ACS; mem. AMA, Ctrl. Assn. Ob-Gyn., Am. Fertility Soc., Rotary. Died Mar. 6, 2010.

JOHNSON, CHARLES M., chemical company executive, lawyer; b. Jefferson, Iowa, Nov. 3, 1934; s. Charles M. Oblinger and Jane (Henderson) Johnson; m. Barbara Jane Quinn, Aug. 30, 1958 (dec. Nov. 1980); children— Susan, Nancy, Laura BA, Yale U., 1956, LL.B., 1959; LL.M., NYU, 1969. Bar: N.Y. Assoc. Lord, Day & Lord, NYC, 1963-68; asst. sec., atty. Stauffer Chem. Co., Westport, Conn., 1968-77, corp. sec., from 1977. Served with JAGC, U.S. Army, 1960-63 Mem. Am. Soc. Corp. Secs., Westchester-Fairfield Corp. Counsel Assn. Republican. Roman Catholic. Home: Westport, Conn. Died July 12, 2010.

JOHNSON, CHARLES WARREN, sales executive; b. Elkhart, Ind., June 9, 1935; s. Warren E. and Kathryn (Cart) Johnson; m. Norine Carroll Goode, Aug. 23, 1958; children: Cammarie, Kathryn Carroll, Margaret Ellen. AB, DePauw U., 1957; MBA, Ind. U., 1959. With Scott Paper Co., Shaker Heights, Ohio, 1959—68, dist. mgr. sales, 1965—68; nat. sales mgr. Brilliant Seafoods Inc., Boston, 1968—70, v.p. mktg., 1970—75, sr. v.p., 1975—78, chief exec. officer, 1978—80; sr. v.p., dir. ops. Barclay Brown & Kavanagh, Hingham, Mass., from 1981; v.p. sales mktg. Treasure Isle Inc., Tampa, Fla.; dir. CTA Corp. Bd. dirs. incorporator Ctr. Creative Arts, Medfield, Mass., from 1968; bd. dirs. fin. chmn. Life Experience Sch., Sherborn, Mass.; v.p. Kennedy assocs. Kennedy Meml. Hosp. Mem.: Nat. Fisheries Inst., Am. Mktg. Assn., Nat., Midwest, Eastern Frozen Food Assns., Carrollwood Golf and Tennis Club (Tampa), Racquet Club (Miami Beach), Milton Hoosic Country Club, Delta Tau Delta. Home: Chelsea, Mass. Died Feb. 1, 2010.

JOHNSON, CLIFFORD R., retired retail executive, consultant; b. Chgo., Aug. 19, 1923; m. Mitzi Delich, Sept. 9, 1949; children: Susan, Glenn, Jeanne, Robert. BS, Northwestern U., 1947; postgrad., U. Chgo., 1963-64; grad., Advanced Mgmt. Program, Harvard U., 1973. With Jewel Cos., Inc., 1949-86, exec. v.p., from 1973. Bd. dirs. Mercury Fin. Co. Home: Arlington Heights, Ill. Died July 9, 2009.

JOHNSON, DAVID ALLEN, vocalist, minister, lyricist, investment advisor; b. Indpls., Dec. 15, 1954; s. Eugene Robert and Vivian Claire (Moon) J. BA in English, Ind. U., 1977; cert., Columbia Sch. of Broadcasting, 1985. Ordained to ministry United Christian Ch., 1996. Founder, pres. Worldwide Assn. Disabled Entrepreneurs, Indpls., from 1993. Founder Global Access and Info. Network (GAIN), L.L.C., DAJ Consulting Co.; wealth mgmt. exec. Singer, songwriter gospel and love songs; contbr. poems and articles to various publs.; concert promoter in field. Named 2000 Poet of the Yr., Famous Poets Soc. Mem. Mensa, Internat.-Nat. Ctr. for Creativity, Toastmasters (pres. 2000-01—). Republican. Avocations: reading, writing, biblical research, basketball. Died Apr. 17, 2010.

JOHNSON, DORCAS MARIA, actress; b. Jamaica, NY, Feb. 21, 1965; d. Colin Oliver Allen and Iris Elizabeth Johnson. BS in Performance Studies, Northwestern U., 1987; MFA in Acting, DePaul U., 1994. Actor, writer, prodr., founder dogwood prodns., Jamaica, from 1997. Actor, writer Glakk Luv..., Chgo., 1994; actor Merchant of Venice, Goodman Theater, Chgo., Royal Shakespeare, London, Thalia, Hamburg, Germany, Bobigny-MC 93, Paris, 1994, Two Weeks, Twice a Year, George St. Playhouse, New Brunswick, TYA, N.J., 1995, for colored girls, New Fed. Theater, N.Y.C., NBTF, N.C., Tribeca Performing Arts Ctr., N.Y.C., Fordsburg's Finest, Market Theater, Johannesburg, South Africa, 1998, (TV show) New York Undercover, 1996; actor, writer, prodr. ugli wmn, N.Y.C., 1997. Democrat. Avocation: gardening. Home: Rego Park, NY. Died Jan. 27, 2009.

JOHNSON, EVANGELINE CAROLYN, accountant; b. Carteret, N.J., Feb. 16, 1925; d. William Douglas and Fannie Page (Howard) Dewberry; A.A.S. in Bus. Adminstrn., Camden County Coll., 1974; B.S. in Bus. Adminstrn. summa cum laude, Glassboro State Coll., 1982; m. Lonnie E. Johnson, Oct. 11, 1947; children— Lonnie, Anita, Enoch, Marcelia. Asst. underwriter Ins. Co. N.Am., Phila., 1966-68; faculty sec. English dept. Camden County Coll., Blackwood, N.J., 1968-74, purchasing agt., 1975-81; acct. Ins. Co. N.Am., Phila., 1981-82; auditor Navy Audit Service, Washington, 1983—; lectr. in field. Troop leader Girl Scouts U.S.A., Lawnside, N.J.; mem. scholarship com. Kaighn Ave. Baptist Ch. Mem. Am. Mgmt. Assn., Minister Wives Assn. So. N.J., NAACP, Colored Women's Civic Assn., Nat. Acctg. Assn., AAUW, Lawnside Master Choral Soc. Club: Lawnside Scholarship. Home: Lawnside, NJ. Died Apr. 24, 2009.

JOHNSON, HOWARD WESLEY, retired academic administrator, finance company executive; b. Chgo., July 2, 1922; s. Albert H. and Laura (Hansen) J.; m. Elizabeth J. Weed, Feb. 18, 1950; children: Stephen Andrew, Laura Ann, Bruce Howard. BA, Central Coll., Chgo., 1943; MA, U. Chgo., 1947; cert., Glasgow U., Scotland, 1946; LLD (hon.), Harvard U., U. Miami, 1966, U. Mass., 1969, Oklahoma City U., 1970, U. Cin., 1973, Babson Coll., 1978; ScD (hon.), Lowell Tech. Inst., Tufts U., Bryant Coll., 1967; LHD (hon.), Northea. U., 1966, Roosevelt U., 1969; LittD (hon.), Clarkson Coll. Tech., 1973. From asst. to assoc. prof., dir. mgmt. rsch. U. Chgo., 1948-51, 53-55; asst. to v.p. pers. adminstrn. Gen. Mills, Inc., 1952-53; assoc. prof., dir. exec. programs, assoc. dean Sloan Sch. Mgmt., MIT, 1955-59, prof., dean, 1959-66; pres. MIT, 1966-71; chmn. MIT Corp., 1971-83, hon. chmn., 1983-90, life mem., 1983-97, life mem. emeritus, 1997—2009. Exec. v.p. Federated Dept. Stores, 1966; chmn. Fed. Res. Bank Boston, 1968-69; trustee Putnam Funds, 1961-71; mem. Pres.'s Adv. Com. on Labor-Mgmt. Policy, 1966-68; chmn. Environ. Studies Bd. NAS-NAE, 1973-75; mem. sci. adv. com. Mass. Gen. Hosp., 1968-70; mem. Nat. Manpower Adv. Com., 1967-69, Nat. Commn. on Productivity, 1970-72; trustee Com. Econ. Devel., 1968-71, Wellesley Coll., 1968-86, trustee emeritus 1986-2009; trustee Radcliffe Coll., 1973-79; hon. trustee Aspen Inst. for Humanistic Studies, Inst. Deaf Analyses, 1971-79; mem. corp. Woods Hole (Mass) Oceanog. Instn. Author: Holding the Center: Memoirs of a Life in Higher Education, 1999. Trustee WGBH Ednl. Found., 1966-71, Henry Francis du Pont Winterthur Mus., 1984-87, Dibner Inst., 1992-97; mem. corp. Mus. Sci., Boston; overseer Boston Symphony Orch, 1968-72; mem.-at-large Boy Scouts Am.; pres. Boston Mus. Fine Arts, 1975-80, trustee 1971-72, chmn. bd. overseers, 1980-83, chmn. exec. com., 1983-87, hon. life trustee 1992-2009; trustee Alfred P. Sloan Found., 1982-95, chmn. bd. 1988-95; bd. dirs. Nat. Arts Stablzn. Found., 1983-87, Museo de Arte de Ponce, 1983-87. With AUS, 1943-46. Recipient Alumni medal U. Chgo., 1970, Gyorgy Kepes Fellowship prize MIT, 1999. Fellow AAAS, Am. Acad. Arts and Scis.; mem. Coun. Fgn. Rels., Am. Philos. Soc., Nat. Acad. Scis. (Pres.'s Circle), Nat. Acad. Engring. (Pres.'s Cir.), Inst. of Medicine (Pres.'s Cir.), Century Assn. (N.Y.C.), Comml. Club (Boston), Tavern Club (Boston), St. Botolph Club (Boston), Phi Gamma Delta. Died Dec. 12, 2009.

JOHNSON, JAMES DOUGLAS (JIM JOHNSON), lawyer, retired state supreme court justice; b. Crossett, Ark., Aug. 20, 1924; s. Thomas William and Maudie Myrtle (Long) J.; m. Virginia Morris, Dec. 21, 1947; children: Mark Douglas, John David and Joseph Daniel (twins). LL.B., Cumberland U., 1947. Bar: Ark. 1948. Pvt. law practice, Crosset, 1948-58, Little Rock, 1966—2010; mem. Dist. 22 Ark. State Senate, 1950-54; assoc. justice Supreme Ct. Ark., 1958-66. Served with USMCR, World War II. Mem. Ark. Jud. Council, Lamda Chi Alpha. Republican. Christian Scientist. Died Feb. 13, 2010.

JOHNSON, JOHN ROBERT, petroleum company executive; b. Omaha, Apr. 17, 1936; s. Robert William and Hazel Marguerite (White) J.;m. Margaret Elizabeth Roberts, June 20, 1959; children: Robert Harle, Martha Elizabeth. BS, Davidson Coll., 1958. With Johnson Oil Co. Inc., Morristown, Tenn., from 1961, pres., from 1963. Dir. Lakeway Pubs., First Vantage Bank Tenn.; appointed Tenn. Petroleum Underground Storage Tank Bd., 1991-97. Magistrate, Hamblen County Ct., 1968-78, chmn., 1971-72; pres. Hamblen County United Fund, 1969; pres. Great Smoky Mountain Coun. Boy Scouts Am., 1977-78, 86; dir. Youth Emergency Shelter; trustee Lakeway Regional Hosp.; mayor Morristown, 1977-87, 91-95, 99—; mem. Tenn. Adv. Commn. on Intergovtl. Rels., 1987-95; Tenn. state svc. coun. ARC. Lt. U.S. Army, 1958-61. Recipient Disting. Svc. award Morristown Jr. C. of C., 1966; named Tenn. Mayor of Yr., Tenn. Mcpl. League, 1983. Mem. Morristown C. of C. (pres. 1976, dir.), Tenn. Oil Marketers Assn., Rotary (pres. 1997-98). Democrat. Episcopalian. Home: Morristown, Tenn. Died Dec. 28, 2009.

JOHNSON, JOHN WILLIAM, JR., business advisor; b. St. Petersburg, Fla., Dec. 10, 1932; s. John William and Elizabeth (Lowitz) J.; m. Cecelia Lynn Wescott, Feb. 6, 1960; children: William Wescott, James Robert, Gayle McCrimmon. AB, Wesleyan U., Middletown, Conn., 1954; postgrad., NYU, 1958-59. With Benton and Bowles, Inc., NYC, 1958-82, v.p., account supr., 1963-70, sr. v.p., mgmt. supr., 1970-82, adminstr. profit sharing plan, 1969-82, dir., 1977-82; with Webb, Johnson Assocs., NYC, 1982—2002, founder, former pres., 1982-95, mng. dir., 1995-2000, sr. mng. dir., 2000—02; co-founder, mng. dir. Johnson & Norinsky Assocs., from 2002. Mem. Scarsdale Planning Bd., 1984-88, Scarsdale Non-Partisan Jud. Qualifications Com., 1987-92, Scarsdale Bd. Ethics, 1995-2000; pres. Rainsford House Assn., N.Y.C., 1964-66, bd. dirs., 1962-70; bd. mgrs. Jacob Riis Settlement, 1963-89; bd. dirs. St. Christopher's Inc., 1965-2000, hon. bd. dirs., 2000—05; mem. parents steering com. Coll. William and Mary, 1987-91; warden Ch. St. James the Less, Scarsdale, 1993-95, Fin. & Invest Com, 2001-; trustee Healthcare Chaplaincy, 1999-2005. Pilot USNR, 1954-58 Decorated China Def. Ribbon; co-honoree Scarsdale Hist. Soc. award, 1996. Mem. Winged Foot Golf Club, Union League Club, Harbour Ridge Club. Home: New Rochelle, NY. Died Apr. 11, 2009.

JOHNSON, JOSEPH EGGLESTON, III, physician, educator; b. Elberton, Ga., Sept. 17, 1930; s. Joseph Eggleston Jr. and Marie (Williams) J.; m. Judith H. Kemp, Jan. 21, 1956; children: Joseph Eggleston IV, Judith Ann, Julie Marie. BA cum laude, Vanderbilt U., 1951, MD, 1954. Diplomate Am. Bd. Internal Medicine (bd. govs. 1977-83, exec. com. 1981-83), Am. Bd. Allergy and Immunology. Intern Johns Hopkins Hosp., Balt., 1954-55, resident, 1957-61, physician, 1961-66; mem. faculty Johns Hopkins Med. Sch., Balt., 1961-66, asst. dean, 1963-66; chief infectious diseases U. Fla. Coll. Medicine, Gainsville, 1966-72, assoc. dean, 1970-72; prof., chmn. dept. Bowman Gray Sch. Medicine, Winston-Salem, N.C., 1972-85; chief med. service N.C. Baptist Hosp., mem. residency rev. com. internal medicine, 1978-83, chmn. residency rev. com. internal medicine, 1983-85; dean Med. Sch., prof. medicine U. Mich., Ann Arbor, 1985-90, prof. internal medicine, 1985-93; accreditation commn. on grad. med. edn., 1988-93; interim exec. v.p. American Coll. Physicians, Phila., 1994-95. Adj. prof. of medicine U. Pa., 1994-2010 Contbr. articles to profl. jours. Served to lt. USNR, 1955-57. John and Mary R. Markle scholar, 1962-67; Mead-Johnson postgrad. scholar, 1960-61 Fellow ACP (sci. program com. 1979-85, chmn. sci. program com. 1982-85, chmn. elect bd. govs. 1985, chmn. bd. govs., bd. regents 1985-93, gov.-elect N.C. 1981-82, gov. N.C. 1982-86, treas. 1991-93, interim exec. v.p. 1994-95), Am. Acad. Allergy, Royal Soc. Medicine (travelling fellow 1970-71); mem. AMA (chmn. Med. Sch. sect. 1990-91, alternate del. 1996-2003), Internat. Soc. Internal Medicine (pres. 2000-02), Am. Fedn. Clin. Rsch., Assn. Am. Physicians, Infectious Diseases Soc. Am., Soc. Exptl. Biology and Medicine, N.Y. Acad. Scis., Am. Assn. Immunologists, So. Soc. Clin. Investigation, Am. Soc. for Microbiology, Assn. Profs. Medicine (sec.-treas. 1978-81, pres.-elect 1981-82, pres. 1982-83), Am. Clin. and Climatol. Assn., Société Française de la Tuberculose et des Maladies Respiratoires, Assn. Program Dirs. in Internal Medicine (exec. coun. 1980-83), Assn. Am. Med. Colls. (exec. coun. 1983-85), Coun. Acad. Socs. (adminstrv. bd. 1978-85), Federated Coun. for Internal Medicine (vice chmn. 1981-82, chmn. 1982-83), Johns Hopkins Soc. Scholars, Phi Beta Kappa, Sigma Alpha Epsilon, Phi Chi, Omicron Delta Kappa, Alpha Omega Alpha. Home: Ponte Vedra, Fla. Died Apr. 19, 2010.

JOHNSON, KEITH, Jamaican ambassador to US; b. Spanish Town, St. Catherine, Jamaica, July 29, 1921; s. Septimus A. and Emily Johnson; m. Pamela B. Rodgers; children: Hope, Marie. Grad., Kingston Coll., Jamaica, 1937; Postgrad. in demography, Columbia U., 1950—51. With Jamaica Civil Svc., 1939—48, statistician, 1942—48; rsch. asst. Bur. Applied Social Rsch., Columbia U., 1948—49; profl. trainee various positions to social affairs officer, UN population br., dept. social and econ. affairs UN, 1967—73; formerly consul gen. Jamaica in US; Jamaica's permanent rep. to UN, 1967—73; non-resident ambassador to Republic of Argentina, 1969—73; ambassador to W.Ger., Luxembourg and Netherlands, 1973—81; non-resident ambassador to Israel, 1975—81; non-resident ambassador to Holy See, 1980—85; ambassador to US Washington, from 1981; permanent rep. to OAS, from 1981. Chmn. prep. com., rapporteur-gen. UN Conf. Human Environ. Decorated Comdr. Order of Distinction Jamaica, Grand Cross Germany, Luxembourg, Order of Pius IX, Vatican; recipient Jamaica Ind. medal, 1963, Internat. Rels. award, US and City Coll. Chpt. West Indian Students Assn., 1963, Human Rels. award, West Indian Cultural Soc., Boston, 1965, Humanitarian award, West Indian Celebration Com., 1966, Franklin Mint Peace medal, 1967, Grand marshall award, Martin Luther King Jr. Meml. Day Parade, 1968, Order of Jamaica, 1983. Mem.: West Indian Students Assn. (pres. 1954—57, chmn. adv. com. from 1958), Soc. Fgn. Consuls, Inst. Sci. Study Population, 369th Vets.' Assn. (hon.). Died Oct. 1, 2009.

JOHNSON, LAMONT, JR., film director; b. Stockton, Calif., Sept. 20, 1922; s. Lamont and Ruth (Fairchild) Johnson; m. Toni Merrill, 1945 (dec. 2009). Student, UCLA. Dir. 2 operas Los Angeles Philharm., 1964; founder, dir. Profl. Theater Group UCLA. Dir.: (films) Thin Ice, 1961, A Covenant with Death, 1966, Kona Coast, 1968, The Mackenzie Break, 1970, A Gunfight, 1971, The Groundstar Conspiracy, 1972, You'll Like My Mother, 1972, The Last American Hero, 1973, Visit to a Chief's Son, 1974, Lipstick, 1976, One on One, 1977, Somebody Killed Her Husband, 1978, Cattle Annie and Little Britches, 1981, Spacehunter: Adventures in the Forbidden Zone, 1983, (TV films) Deadlock, 1969, My Sweet Charlie, 1970, That Certain Summer, 1972, The Execution of Private Slovik, 1974, Fear on Trial, 1975, Paul's Case, 1979, Off the Minnesota Strip, 1980, Crisis at Central High, 1981, Escape From Iran: The Canadian Caper, 1981, Dangerous Company, 1982, Life of the Party: The Story of Beatrice, 1982, Ernie Kovacs: Between the Laughter, 1984, Unnatural Causes, 1986, Gore Vidal's Lincoln, 1988 (Emmy award), Voices Within: The Lives of Trudi Chase, 1990, Crash Landing: The Rescue of Flight 232, 1992, The Broken Chain, 1993, The Man Next Door, 1996, All the Winters That Have Been, 1997; (TV mini-series) The Kennedys of Massachusetts, 1990; (TV episodes) Felicity, 2000 Mem. Directors Guild America Died Oct. 24, 2010.

JOHNSON, LESTER FREDRICK, artist; b. Mpls., Jan. 27, 1919; s. Edwin August and Helma Marie (Holmes) J.; m. Josephine Valenti, Feb. 12, 1949; children: Leslie Maria, Anthony Edwin. Student, Mpls. Art Inst., 1939-41, St. Paul Art Sch., 1939-41, Art Inst. Chgo., 1943. Prof. painting Yale U., 1964—89, dir. studies Grad. Painting Program, 1969—74. Mem. Milford (Conn.) Fine Arts Council, 1972-73; mem. art adv. com. Housatonic Community Coll., Stratford, Conn., 1969-87 One-man shows, Zabriskie Gallery, N.Y.C., Martha Jackson Gallery, N.Y.C., Donald Morris, Detroit, Walter Moos Gallery, N.Y.C., Toronto, Can., David Barnett Gallery, Milw., Mpls. Art Inst., Dayton Art Inst., Fort Worth Art Inst., Yale Univ. Mus., Gimpel Fils Gallery, London, Gimpel Hanover Gallery, Zurich, Switzerland, Westmoreland Mus. Art. Greenburg, Pa. (traveling), Augustana Coll. Centennial Hall Gallery, Pa. Acad. Fine Arts, Newport Harbor Art Mus., Edward Thorpe Gallery, N.Y.C., Gimpel-Weitzenhofer Gallery, N.Y.C., Peter Findley Gallery, N.Y.C., Denise Dade' Gallery, N.Y.C., Joseph Rickards Gallery, N.Y.C., Jim Goodman Gallery, N.Y.C.; exhibited in numerous group shows; represented in permanent collections, Albright Knox Mus., Dayton Art Inst., Met. Mus. Art, N.Y.C., Mus. Modern Art, New Sch. for Social Research, Phoenix Art Mus., U. Nebr., Walker Art Mus. Recipient Creative Arts award Brandeis U., 1978, Jimmy Ernest award in art Am. Acad. Arts and Letters, 2003; Trumbull Coll. fellow, 1996—; Guggenheim fellow, 1973. Mem. Nat. Acad. Design (coun.), Am. Acad. Letters. Home: Southampton, NY. Died May 30, 2010.

JOHNSON, MARY ELIZABETH, musician, educator; b. Tyler, Tex., Mar. 29, 1933; d. Robert Edward and Mamie Oberia (Walters) Spaulding; m. George Devereaux Johnson, Mar. 31, 1955; children: Bradford D., Robin Elizabeth. BFA, So. Meth. U., 1955; pvt. studies with Bomar Cramer, Dallas, 1964—69. Music tchr. Dallas Country Day Sch., 1955; tchr. Dayton Pub. Schs., Ohio, 1956—57; pvt. tchr. piano Dallas, from 1962; profl. accompanist, from 1985; duo-pianist, from 1965; sponsor, tchr. creative and performing arts program Dallas Ind. Sch. Dist., 1981—82, 1983, 1984. Sponsor Jr. Melodie and Jr. Harmonie; pianist mem. String Quintette des Amies, 2008-. Named to Hall of Fame, Am. Coll. Musicians, 1981. Mem. Nat. Guild Piano Tchrs. (cert., named to honor roll 1971, chmn. auditions Dallas 2007-10), Tex. Fedn. Music Clubs (historian 1974-76, state chmn. music svc. in cmty. 1971-73, dist. jr. counselor 1971-78, dist. chmn. music svc. in cmty. 1971-78, rec. sec. 5th dist. 1975-76, 1st v.p. 1977-78, jr. festival chmn. 1977-80, dist chmn. Jr. Gold Cup awards 1980, 84, 85, 86, 87, 88, asst. chmn. North Dallas divsn. 5th dist. jr. festival 1981-82), Music Tchrs. Nat. Assn., Jr. Pianists Guild Dallas (chmn. jr. recitals 1983, chmn. sr. recitals 1984, treas. 2003-2005), Tex. Music Tchrs. Assn., Dallas Music Tchrs. Assn., Van Katwijk Club (tchr. mem.), Music Study Club Dallas (chmn. piano program 1981-82), Dallas Fedn. Music Clubs (del. 1969-78, 1st v.p. 1977), Daus. Republic Tex. (1st v.p. Bonham chpt. 1975-76), Melodie Club (pres. 1969-71, 2d v.p. 1977-78, 2007-, 1st programs v.p. 2003-06, 2009-, choral accompanist 2005-, counselor jr. club, historian, press sec. 1981-82, 1st v.p. 2003-2004, 2004—), Kalista Club (yearbook chmn. 1983-2000, v.p. 1984-85, pres. 1986-87), Park Cities Club, Tower Club, Melodie Club (v.p. program ch. 2009-), Kermis Club, Rondo-Carrousel Club, Trippers Club, Steinway Hall's Ptnrs. in Performance, Alpha Delta Pi, Mu Phi Epsilon (patron). Methodist. Home: Dallas, Tex. Died Jan. 20, 2010.

JOHNSON, MILLARD WALLACE, JR., mathematics and engineering professor; b. Racine, Wis., Feb. 1, 1928; s. Millard Wallace and Marian Manilla (Rittman) J.; m. Ruth Pugh Gifford, Dec. 26, 1953; children: Millard Wallace III, Jeannette Marian Brooks, Charles Gifford, Peter Allen. BS in Applied Math. and Mechanics, U. Wis., Madison, 1952, MS, 1953; PhD in Math, MIT, Cambridge, 1957. Rsch. asst. MIT, 1953-57, lectr., 1957-58; mem. staff Math. Rsch. Ctr. U. Wis., Madison, 1958-94, prof. mechanics, 1958-63, prof. mechanics and math., 1964-94, mem. staff Rheology Rsch. Ctr., from 1970, mem. Engine Rsch. Ctr., from 1985, prof. emeritus math. and engrng.-physics depts., from 1994. Contbr. articles to profl. jours. Adv. bd. Internat. Math. and Statis. Librs. (IMSL), 1971-92. With USN, 1946-48. Fellow ASME; mem. Soc. Rheology, Soc. Indsl. and Applied Math., Am. Acad. Mechanics, Brit. Soc. Rheology, Wis. Acad. Scis., Arts and Letters, Phi Beta Kappa. Home: Madison, Wis. Died Feb. 20, 2009.

JOHNSON, ROBERT BRITTEN, geology educator; b. Cortland, NY, Sept. 24, 1924; s. William and Christine (Hofer) J.; m. Garnet Marion Brown, Aug. 30, 1947; children: Robert Britten, Richard Karl, Elizabeth Anne. Student, Wheaton Coll., Ill., 1942-43, 46-47; AB summa cum laude, Syracuse U., NY, 1949, MS, 1950; PhD, U. Ill., Champaign-Urbana, 1964. Asst. geologist Ill. Geol. Survey, 1951-54; asst. prof. geology Syracuse U., 1954-55; sr. geologist and geophysicist C.A. Bays & Asso., Urbana, Ill., 1955-56; from asst. prof. to prof. engrng. geology Purdue U., 1956-66, head, engrng. geology dept., 1964-66; prof. geology DePauw U., 1966-67, head, dept. geology, 1966-67; prof. geology Colo. State U., 1967-88, acting chmn. dept. geology, 1968, chmn. dept., 1969-73, prof. in charge geology programs, dept. earth resources, 1973-77, acting head dept. earth resources, 1979-81, prof. emeritus, from 1988; regional geophysicist U.S. Bur. of Reclamation, 1967-76; geologist U.S. Geol. Survey, 1976-88. Cons. in field, 1957—; instr. Elderhostel programs, 1991-2000. Active local Boy Scouts Am., 4-H Club, Sci. Fair, dist. schs.; VITA vol. Served with USAAF, 1943-46. Fellow Geol. Soc. Am. (sr. fellow, E.B. Burwell Jr. Meml. award 1989), Assn. Engrng. Geologists (Claire P. Holdredge Outstanding Publ. award 1990), Phi Beta Kappa. Republican. Home: Fort Collins, Colo. Died Sept. 21, 2009.

JOHNSON, WALTER KLINE, civil engineer; b. Mpls., Aug. 28, 1923; s. Horace Edward and Ida Axelina (Kline) J.; m. Geneva Lorraine Olson, Sept. 2, 1950; children: Kristine Idelle, Karen Margaret, Konstance Louise. BCE, U. Minn., 1948, MS, 1951, PhD, 1963. Registered profl. engr., Minn. With Greeley and Hansen, Chgo., 1948-49, Infilco, Inc., Tucson, 1951-52, Toltz, King, Duvall, Anderson & Assocs., St. Paul, 1952-55; faculty U. Minn., Mpls., from 1955, assoc. prof. civil engrng., 1965-74, prof., 1974-75; dir. planning Met. Waste Control Commn., St. Paul, 1975-89; mgmt. cons. in environ. engrng. St. Paul, from 1989. Patentee wastewater sampler. Capt. USAAF, 1943-46. EPA rsch. fellow Brit. Water Pollution Rsch. Lab., 1971. Fellow ASCE (pres. N.W. sect. 1972-73), Am. Water Works Assn., Cen. State Water Environment Assn.; mem. Am. Acad. Environ. Engrs. (diplomate). Lutheran. Achievements include rsch. on biol. waste water treatment, sludge bulking, nitrogen removal by denitrification. Home: Minneapolis, Minn. Died Dec. 22, 2009.

JOHNSON, WALTER WILLIAM, library director; b. Grand Rapids, Mich., Oct. 21, 1925; s. Carl and Dewey (Vander Mass) Johnson; m. Marcelon Cadeaux Matteson, Apr. 9, 1948; children: Koe Johnson-Orneles, Brook, Camille, Leigh, Stacy Ferl, Chad. BA, Mich. State U., 1949, MA in Art, 1950; MS in LS, U. So. Calif., 1957. Tchr. art Poly. H.S., Long Beach, Calif., 1950—51, Artesia (Calif.) H.S., 1952—53; libr. Calif. State U., Long Beach, 1956—58; dir. Huntington Beach Libr., Calif., from 1958. Sec. to Allied Arts Bd.; liaison to Allied Arts Assn. Former pres. Orange Coast Unitarian-Universalist Ch. Served with inf. AUS, 1944—45. Decorated Bronze star, Purple Heart. Mem.: ALA, Calif. Libr. Assn., Pub. Libr. Execs. So. Calif., Orange County Libr. Assn. (past pres.), Pub. Adminstrs. Orange County (past pres.), Rotary. Died May 19, 2010.

JONAS, JAN HANZEL, academic administrator; b. Barberton, Ohio, Oct. 6, 1942; d. George Frank and Grace Naomi (Carillon) Jonas; m. Stephen Jonas, June 19, 1966. BA, Ohio State U., 1964; MS, Ind. U., 1966, Ed.D, 1974. Assoc. dir. U. Wis., Madison, 1966—69; head counselor Ind. U., Bloomington, 1969—71; asst. to exec. vice chancellor Cuyahoga CC, Cleve., 1976—79, dir. program devel., 1979—81; dean of instrn Parma, 1981—84; provost, v.p., Warrensville Twp., Ohio, from 1984. Cons., evaluator North Central Assn., Chgo., from 1982. Mem.: Am. Assn. Women in Community and Jr. Colls., Am. Assn. Higher Edn., Phi Beta Kappa. Avocations: sailing, reading, travel. Died May 13, 2010.

JONES, ALLEN, JR., lawyer; b. Washington, May 24, 1930; s. Allen Sr. and Gladys May (Bunch) J.; m. Gloria Jean Clyma, Nov. 29, 1952 (div. June 1989); children: Victoria, Jennifer, Matthew; m. Cheryl B. Crook, Aug. 11, 1991. BA, Mich. State U., 1952; JD, Georgetown U., 1957. Bar: D.C. 1957, U.S. Supreme Ct. 1961, Md. 1962. Sales rep. Ethyl Corp., Salt Lake City, 1952; sr. atty. Wilkes Artis Chartered, Washington, 1957-2000; of counsel Hamilton and Hamilton, LLP, Washington, from 2001. Mem. exec. com., treas. Coun. for Ct. Excellence, Washington, 1988-98; mem. D.C. study devel. coun. Mich. State U., 1999—. Mem. Civil Delay Reduction Task Force, Washington, 1988-92; co-founder Washington Lawyers Against Drugs, 1986-87; mediator Superior Ct. of D.C., 1986—; vice chmn. Children's Hosp. Found., Washington, 1988-92; chmn. Children's Hosp. Telethon, Washington, 1988-89; v.p. Rotary Found. Washington, 2001, pres., 2002. Mem. ABA (Ho. of Dels. D.C. chpt. 1986-87), D.C. Bar Assn. (pres. 1986-87, pres. rsch. found. 1984-85), The Barristers (pres. 1982-83), Lawyers Club, The Counsellors, Jud. Conf. of D.C., Rotary Club Washington (pres.-elect 1997, pres. 1998-99). Republican. Lutheran. Avocations: golf, biking, hiking. Home: Stevensville, Md. Died Nov. 28, 2009.

JONES, BEVERLY ANN MILLER, nursing administrator, retired patient services administrator; b. Bklyn., July 14, 1927; d. Hayman Edward and Eleanor Virginia (Doyle) Miller; m. Kenneth Lonzo Jones, Sept. 5, 1953 (dec.); children: Steven Kenneth, Lonnie Cord. BSN, Adelphi U., 1949. Chief nurse regional blood program ARC, NYC, 1951-54; asst. dir., acting DON M.D. Anderson Hosp. and Tumor Inst., Houston, 1954-55; asst. DON Sibley Meml. Hosp., Washington, 1959-61; assoc. dir. nursing svc. Anne Arundel Gen. Hosp., Annapolis, Md., 1966-70; asst. adminstr. nursing Alexandria Hosp., Va., 1972-73; v.p. patient care svc. Longmont United Hosp., Colo., 1977-93; pvt. cons., 1993-99; ret. Instr. ARC, 1953-57, chmn. nurse enrollment com. D.C. chpt., 1959-61; mem. adv. bd. Boulder Valley Vo.-Tech. Health Occupations Program, 1977-80; del. nursing adminstrs. good will trip to Poland, Hungary, Sweden and Eng., 1980. Contbr. articles to profl. jours. Mem.-at-large exec. com. nursing svc. adminstrs. sect. Md. Nurses' Assn., 1966-69; bd. dir. Meals on Wheels, Longmont, 1978-80, Longmont Coalition for Women in Crisis, Applewood Living Ctr., Longmont; mem. utilization com. Boulder (Colo.) Hospice, 1979-83; mem. task force on nat. commn. on nursing Colo. Hosp. Assn., 1982, mem. coun. labor rels., 1982-87; mem. U. Colo. Task Force on Nursing, 1990; vol. Champs program St. Vrain Valley Sch. Dist., 1986—, Prestige Plus program Longmont United Hosp., 1999—. Named Outstanding Vol. of Yr., St. Vrain Valley Sch. Dist., 1986—2004. Mem. Am. Orgn. Nurse Exec. (chmn. com. membership svc. and promotions, nominee recognition of excellence in nursing adminstrn.), Colo. Soc. Nurse Exec. (dir. 1978-80, 84-86, pres. 1980-81, mem. com. on nominations 1985-86, Outstanding Vol. of Yr. 2002). Home: Lyons, Colo. Died Dec. 25, 2009.

JONES, BRANSON COLTRANE, textile executive; b. Concord, NC, Aug. 15, 1927; s. Robert Eldridge and Mariam Elizabeth (Coltrane) J.; m. Joan Marcelle Simpson, Oct. 28, 1949; children— Joan Marcelle, Elisa Coltrane BS in Commerce and Bus., Presbyterian Coll., Clinton, SC, 1949. Trainee Cannon Mills Co., Kannapolis, N.C., 1949-52, acct. DecFab div. Concord, 1952-67, asst. v.p. DecFab div., 1967-76, v.p. Kannapolis, 1979-82, exec. v.p., from 1982; exec. v.p. then pres. Wiscassett Mills Co., Albermarle, N.C., 1976-79. Chmn. bd. First Charter Bank Chmn. bd. trustees Cabarrus County Library, Kannapolis, 1984—; trustee Catawba Coll., Salisbury, N.C., Pfeiffer Coll., Misenheimer, N.C.; bd. visitors Presbyn. Coll., Clinton. Served with USN, 1945-46 Mem. Am. Textile Mfrs. Inst. Inc. Democrat. Methodist. Avocation: golf. Died Jan. 31, 2010.

JONES, CHARLES W., labor union executive; b. Gary, Ind., Apr. 29, 1923; s. Charles Browning and Inez (Teegarden) J.; m. Ursula M. Wilden, Aug. 25, 1950; children: Charles Alan, Newton Browning, Donna Ruth, Doris Ursula. Grad. high sch., Gary. Boilermaker various constrn. contractors; organizer, then staff rep., rsch. & edn. dir., internat. v.p. Internat. Brotherhood of Boilermakers, Iron Ship Builders, Blacksmiths, Forgers and Helpers, Kansas City, Kans., now internat. pres.; ret. Chmn. bd. dirs. BB&T Co.; v.p. bldg. constrn. trades dept., v.p. metal trade dept. AFL-CIO. Died Apr. 5, 2010.

JONES, CLARENCE WHITEHEAD, bank and trust company executive; b. Columbia, SC, Oct. 13, 1933; s. Clarence W. and Arizona (Waites) J.; m. Carole Joanne Medlin, June 13, 1959; children: Kenneth, Scott, Leah. BS in Acctg., U. S.C., 1955. Agt. Liberty Life Ins. Co., Columbia, 1955-56; mgr. Universal C.I.T. Credit Corp., various locations, 1958-71; adminstr. 1st Nat. Bank S.C., Columbia, 1971-84; dep. adminstr. S.C. Nat. Bank, Columbia, 1984-86; sr. v.p., adminstr. consumer credit div. 1st Citizens Bank & Trust Co., Columbia, from 1986. Coach Little League Baseball,Columbia, 1970-71, Pee Wee League Football, Columbia, 1972-73. With U.S. Army, 1956-58. Republican. Baptist. Avocation: sports. Home: Columbia, SC. Died Jan. 12, 2009.

JONES, DOUGLAS EPPS, natural history museum director; b. Tuscaloosa, Ala., May 28, 1930; s. Walter Bryan and Hazel Lucile (Phelps) J.; m. Bonnie A. Cook, June 4, 1955; children: Susan, Elizabeth, Walter B. II. BS in Geology, U. Ala., 1952; MS in Geology, La. State U., 1956, PhD in Geology, 1959. Research geologist La. Geol. Survey, Baton Rouge, 1954-58; asst. prof. geology U. Ala., Tuscaloosa, 1958-61, assoc. prof., 1961-66, prof., 1966-98, dean Coll. Arts & Scis., 1968-84, dean univ. libraries, 1984-86, acad. v.p., 1988-90; dir. Ala. Mus. Natural History U. Ala. Mus., Tuscaloosa, 1986-98, ret. Served to 1st lt. U.S. Army, 1952-54. Mem. Kiwanis, Sigma Xi. Presbyterian. Avocations: antique gun collecting, hunting, fishing. Home: Tuscaloosa, Ala. Died Apr. 2, 2010.

JONES, EILEEN MARGARET, computer programmer; b. Quincy, Mass., Nov. 28, 1956; d. James Michael and Mary Virginia (Keating) Conley; m. Donald Patrick McCall, Aug. 19, 1979 (div. 1982); 1 child, Jaclyn Melissa McCall Jones; m.

Gregory Tapply Jones, July 27, 1985; 1 child, Lindsay Anna. B.A. in French, Assumption Coll., 1978; student U. Nice, France, 1976-77. Cert. programmer. Flight attendant Capitol Airways, Jamaica, N.Y., 1978-80; interpreter Mass. Gen. Hosp., Boston, 1981-82; programmer Honeywell Info., Waltham, Mass., 1982-83; programmer/analyst Dynamics Research Corp., Wilmington, Mass., 1984, Digital Equipment Corp., Maynard, Mass., 1984-85; project leader Gen. Electric, Fort Wayne, Ind., 1986-87. Mem. Mass. Businessman's Assn., Nat. Assn. Female Execs., AAUW. Episcopalian. Avocations: sewing; skiing; boating. Home: Wiscasset, Maine. Died Feb. 21, 2010.

JONES, GREYDON G., real estate development executive; b. Warsaw, NY, Feb. 16, 1926; s. Onias S. and Dorothy M. (Goetz) J.; m. Janis R. Anderson, June 21, 1946; children: Carrell Jones Tysver, Melodee K. Jones Hyslop. Student, Syracuse U., 1943-44, Ohio State U., 1944-45, Tex. A&M U., 1945; B.C.S., Auerswald Bus. U., 1949. C.P.A., Wash. Partner V.L. Maxfield & Co., Seattle, 1949-57; prin. Haskins & Sells, Seattle, 1958-68; v.p., treas. Weisfield's, Inc., Seattle, 1968-75; chief financial officer Roland and Roland, Inc., Gig Harbor, Wash., from 1975. Served with AUS, 1943-46. Mem. Wash. Soc. C.P.A.s, Am. Inst. C.P.A.s, Fin. Execs. Inst. Home: Bothell, Wash. Died Apr. 11, 2010.

JONES, JANE HARDY, psychologist, administrator, educator; b. St. Louis, May 9, 1927; d. Charles Merton and Lois (Lavery) Hardy; m. John Robert Jones, Aug. 24, 1947; children: Leslie Kathleen, Robert Hardy. BA, U. Colo., 1947; MEd, Auburn U., 1965, EdD, 1967. Lic. psychologist, Hawaii. Tchr. Arvada (Colo.) H.S., 1947-51, Warwick (Va.) H.S., 1951-52; Dept. of Army editor Transp. Sch., U.S. Army, Ft. Eustis, Va., 1952-54; tchr. Giessen (Germany) H.S., 1962-63; psychologist U. Hawaii, Honolulu, 1967-85, asst. dir. and coord. tng., 1985-94; pvt. practice Ctr. for Psychol. Svcs., Honolulu, from 1970. Author: Intimacy and Type, 1998, also articles. Fellow Am. Coll. Forensic Examiners (life; diplomate); mem. NEA (life), APA (life), Hawaii Psychol. Assn. (life; treas. 1978-79), Assn. for Psychol. Type (prs. Pacific chpt. 1979-83), Internat. Coun. Psychologists (life), Phi Beta Kappa. Christian. Avocations: reading, swimming, computers, writing. Home: Honolulu, Hawaii. Died Jan. 13, 2009.

JONES, JENNIFER, actress; b. Tulsa, Mar. 21, 1919; d. Philip R. and Flora Mae (Suber) Isley; m. Robert Walker, Jan. 2, 1939 (div. June 20, 1945); children: Robert Hudson, Michael Ross; m. David O. Selznick, July 13, 1949 (dec. June 22, 1965); 1 child, Mary Jennifer (dec. May 11, 1976); m. Norton Simon, May 30, 1971 (dec. June 1, 1993) Student, pub. schs., Dallas, Monte Cassino Jr. Coll., Northwestern U., Am. Acad. Dramatic Arts. Actress: (films) New Frontier, 1939, The Streets of New York, 1939, Dick Tracy's G-Men, 1939, The Song of Bernadette, 1943 (Acad. award for Best Actress, 1944, Golden Globe award for Best Actress, 1944), Since You Went Away, 1944, Love Letters, 1945, American Creed, 1946, Cluny Brown, 1946, Duel in the Sun, 1946, Portrait of Jennie, 1948, We Were Strangers, 1949, Madame Bovary, 1949, Gone to Earth, 1950, Wild Heart, 1952, Carrie, 1952, Ruby Gentry, 1952, Indiscretion of an American Wife, 1953, Beat the Devil, 1953, Love is a Many-Splendored Thing, 1955, Good Morning, Miss Dove, 1955, The Man in the Gray Flannel Suit, 1956, The Barretts of Wimpole Street, 1957, A Farewell to Arms, 1957, Tender Is The Night, 1962, The Idol, 1966, Angel, Angel Down We Go, 1969, The Towering Inferno, 1974; (stage appearances) Country Girl, 1966 Pres. Norton Simon Mus., Pasadena, Calif., 1989-2009 Winged Victory award France, 1948; Triunfo award Spain, 1953; Film Critics Award Japan, 1953; First Ann. Audience award, 1955; winner Nat. Critics Poll, 1955; award Stars and Stripes citation for war work ARC; medal and citation for work at front during Korean War. Died Dec. 17, 2009.

JONES, KENNETH JAMES, educator; b. Cambridge, Mass., Sept. 15, 1946; s. Kenneth James and Amy Teresa (Chamberlain) J.; m. Priscilla Pitt, June 11, 1966; children— Prudence, Kendrick, Krister S.B., MIT, 1956; MA, Harvard U., 1957, Ed.D. in Psychol. Measurement, 1966. Asst. prof. Harvard U., Cambridge, Mass., 1966-67; prof. Brandeis U., Waltham, Mass., from 1968. Author computer software Harvard Computer Ctr. fellow, 1963 Fellow AAAS; mem. Am. Statis Assn. Republican. Congregationalist. Home: Dover, Mass. Died July 3, 2010.

JONES, LAWRENCE NEALE, retired dean, minister; b. Moundsville, W.Va., Apr. 24, 1921; s. Eugene Wayman and Rosa (Bruce) J.; m. Mary Ellen Cooley, Mar. 29, 1945 (dec. Aug. 2003); children: Mary Lynn, Rodney Bruce. B.Ed., W. Va. State Coll., 1942, LL.D., 1965; MA, U. Chgo., 1948; B.D., Oberlin Grad. Sch., 1956; PhD, Yale U., 1961; LL.D., Jewish Theol. Sem., 1971. Ordained to ministry United Ch. Christ, 1956; student Christian Movement Middle Atlantic Region, 1957-60; dean chapel Fisk U., 1960-65; dean students Union Theol. Sem., NYC, 1965-71; prof. Union Theol. Sem. (Afro-Am. ch. history), 1970; dean Union Theol. Sem., 1971-74, acting pres., 1970; dean Sch. Div. Howard U., Washington, 1975-91, ret., 1991. Pres. Civil Rights Coordinating Council, Nashville, 1963-64 Bd. dirs. Sheltering Arms and Children's Svc., 1970-75, Inst. Social and Religious Studies Jewish Sem., United Ch. Bd. for World Ministries, 1969-75; bd. dirs., sec. exec. com. Assn. Theol. Schs., U.S. and Can.; chmn. exec. com. Fund for Theol. Edn., 1978-2009. With AUS, 1943-46, 47-53. Rockefeller Doctoral grantee; Lucy Monroe scholar; Rosenwald scholar; Am. Assn. Theol. Schs. Study grantee. Mem. Am. Ch. History Soc., Am. Acad. Religion, Soc. Study Black Religion (pres. 1973-75), Nat. Com. Black Churchmen. Home: Silver Spring, Md. Died Dec. 7, 2009.

JONES, MARY GARDINER, lawyer, consumer products company executive, educator; b. NYC, Dec. 10, 1920; d. Charles Herbert and Anna Livingston (Short) Jones. BA, Wellesley Coll., 1943; JD, Yale U., 1948. Bar: N.Y. 1949. Intern tchr. George Sch., Newtown, Pa., 1943—44; rsch. analyst, rsch. and analysis br. Internat. Law sect. OSS, Washington, 1944—46; assoc. Donovan, Leisure, Newton and Irvine, NYC, 1948—53, Webster, Sheffield, Fleischmann, Hitchcock & Chrystie, NYC, 1961—64; trial atty. antitrust divsn. US Dept. Justice, NYC, 1953—61; commr. FTC, Washington, 1964—73; prof. Coll. Commerce and Bus. Adminstrn. and Coll. Law U. Ill., Urbana, 1973—75; v.p. for consumer affairs Western Union Telegraph Co., Washington, 1975—82; founder, pres. Consumer Interest Rsch. Inst., Washington, 1983—2001. Mem. com. on sci. and tech. Fed. Coun. Sci. and Tech., non-trustee mem. rsch. and policy com.; mem. bd. Coun. Econ. Priorities, 1976—84; mem. Pres.'s Panel on Antitrust Laws, 1977—78. Bd. editors Jour. Consumer Affairs, editl. rev. bd. Jour. Consumer Interest; contbr. articles to profl. jours.; author: Tearing Down Walls: A Woman's Triump, 2008. Pres. Mental Health Assn., Washington, 1998—2004, mem. bd., 1982—2004, from 2005; trustee Colgate U., 1966—80, Wellesley Coll., 1971—89; nat. adv. coun. Hampshire Coll. Mem.: AAUW (2d v.p. Washington br. 1968—69, adv. coun.), Nat. Inst. Dental Health (institutinal review bd. 2003—05), Yale Law Sch. Assn. (v.p. D.C. 1969—70, exec. com. 1971—76), Am. Arbitration Assn., Assn. Bar City of N.Y., Internat. Law Assn., Fed. Bar Assn. Home: Washington, DC. Died Dec. 23, 2009.

JONES, NANCY THOMPSON, voice educator; b. Humansville, Mo., Oct. 31, 1938; d. Guy Hill and Noveta Luelle (Brown) Thompson; m. Russell Ransom Jones, June 23, 1962; children: Beverly, Steven. MusB, Coll. Conservatory of Music, Cin., 1960; MS, Pitts. State U., Kans., 1962. Pvt. voice tchr., Kans., from 1959, Mo.; adj. prof. voice Baker U., Baldwin, Kans., 1967-70, Park Coll., Parkville, Mo., 1971-73, St. Mary Coll., Leavenworth, Kans., 1973-76, William Jewell Coll., Liberty, Mo., 1976-86; prof. voice Ctrl. Meth. Coll., Fayette, Mo., from 1987, dir. opera workshop, from 1987, interdisciplinary specialist in value-centered curriculum, from 1991. Part time educator Pittsburg State U., 1973-90. Performer numerous recitals, 1958—, also recordings; vocalist with Kansas City Lyric Opera, 1967-92. Mem. choir United Meth. Ch., Marshfield, 1987-94; spokesperson Ellis-Fischel Cancer Ctr., Columbia, Mo., 1993—. Curators' faculty scholar Curators of Ctrl. Meth. Coll., 1992-94; faculty grantee William Jewell Coll., 1980; recipient Barrows award for European Study, Geraldine Barrows, 1977. Mem. Am. Guild Musical Artists, Actors' Equity Assn., Music Educators' Nat. Conf., Mo. Music Educators Assn., Coll. Music Soc., Phi Beta Arts Fraternity (v.p. 1989—), Mu Phi Epsilon. Avocations: opera, church activities. Home: Rocheport, Mo. Died May 22, 2010.

JONES, NAPOLEON A., JR., federal judge; b. Hodge, La., Aug. 25, 1940; BA, San Diego State U., 1962, MSW, 1967; JD, U. San Diego, 1971. Legal intern, staff atty. Calif. Rural Legal Assistance, Modesto, Calif., 1971-73; staff atty. Defenders, Inc., San Diego, 1973-75; ptnr. Jones, Cazares, Adler & Lopez, San Diego, 1975-77; judge San Diego Mcpl. Ct., 1977-82, San Diego Superior Ct., 1982-94, US Dist. Ct. (so. dist.) Calif., San Diego, 1994—2007, sr. judge, 2007—09. Mem. San Diego County Indigent Def. Policy Bd. Bd. visitors Sch. Social Work San Diego State U.; active Valencia Park Elem. Sch. Mem. San Diego County Bar Assn., Earl B. Gilliam Bar Assn., San Diego Bar Found., Nat. Bar Assn., Calif. Bar Assn., Calif. Black Attys. Assn., Nat. Assn. Women Judges, Masons, Sigma Pi Phi, Kappa Alpha Psi. Died Dec. 12, 2009.

JONES, ROBERT B., state legislator; b. Jeffersonville, Ga., Apr. 22, 1944; m. Calli Baskerville; children: Michelle, Kenneth, Robert Jr., Jahim, Hari, Jahdal. Former mayor, Kalamazoo; former rsch. chemist Ft. Valley State U.; chem. prodn. supr. Pharmacia & Upjohn; mem. Dist. 60 Mich. House of Reps., 2007—10; mem. Tax Policy Com., 2007—10. Recipient NAACP Humanitarian award, 2003. Mem.: Urban Core Mayors (former co-chair), Mich. Mcpl. League (former v.p.), Mich. Econ. Devel. Corp. (former exec. bd.), Kalamazoo Cmty. Devel. Block Grant Adv. Bd. (former chair), Nat. Brownfield Assn. (former Mich. pres.), United Way (vol.), Alpha Phi Alpha Frat. (former SW Mich. dir.). Democrat. Baptist. Died Oct. 17, 2010.

JONES, TRACEY KIRK, JR., retired minister, educator; b. Boston, Mar. 16, 1917; s. Tracey Kirk and Marion (Flowers) J.; m. Martha Clayton, Sept. 12, 1942 (dec. June 1975); children: Judith Grace Watson, Tracey Kirk Jones, III, Deborah Anita Jones Breitenbach; m. Junia K. Moss, July 1, 1978. BA, D.D., Ohio Wesleyan U.; B.D., Yale Div. Sch., 1942. Ordained to ministry Meth. Church, 1945; missionary Meth. Ch., China, 1946-50, Malaya, 1952-55, exec. bd. mission, 1955; exec. sec. S.E. Asia, 1955-62; assoc. gen. sec. div. world missions, 1962-64; assoc. gen. sec. world div., 1964-68; gen. sec. bd. missions, 1968-72; gen. sec. bd. global ministries, 1972-80. Adj. prof. Drew Theol. Sch., Madison, N.J., 1980-89; mem. governing bd. Nat. Coun. Chs., 1st v.p., 1978-80. Author: Our Mission Today, 1963. Home: Sarasota, Fla. Died Dec. 16, 2009.

JONES, WALTON LINTON, internist, retired government agency administrator; b. McCaysville, Ga., Dec. 4, 1918; s. Walton Linton and Pearl Josephine (Gilliam) J.; m. Caroline Wells Schachte, June 5, 1943; children— Walton Linton III, Francis Stephen, Kathleen Caroline BS, Emory U., 1939, MD, 1942. Diplomate Am. Bd. Preventive Medicine. Commd. lt. (j.g.) U.S. Navy, 1942, advanced through grades to capt., 1956; rotating intern U.S. Naval Hosp., Charleston, SC, 1942-43, aerospace medicine, 1944; flight surgeon USMC Aircraft Squadrons, 1944-47; head aero. med. safety Navy Dept., 1947-53; sr. med. officer U.S.S. Randolph, 1953-55; dir. aero. med. ops. and equipment Bur. Medicine and Surgery, Navy Dept., 1955-64; dir. biotech. and human research div. NASA, 1964-66; ret. U.S. Navy, 1966; civilian dir. biotech and human research div. NASA, Washington, 1966-70, dep., dir. life scis., 1970-75, dir. occupational medicine, 1975-82, dir. occupational health, 1982-85; cons. aerospace medicine, from 1985. Mem. exec. com. hearing and bioacoustics Nat. Acad. Scis., 1964-85, chmn., 1970, mem. exec. com. on vision, 1964-85; Kober lectr. Georgetown U., 1968 Leader, mem. com. Nat. Capital Area council Boy Scouts Am., Falls Church, Va., 1956-64 Decorated Legion of Merit; recipient Exceptional Service medal NASA, 1979, Outstanding Leadership medal NASA, 1985. Fellow Aerospace Medicine Assn. (Bauer award 1970, pres. 1980), AIAA (assoc., recipient John Jeffries award 1970), Royal Soc. Health; mem. Internat. Astronatics Acad., Assn. Mil. Surgeons (Founders award 1956), Internat. Acad. Aerospace Medicine. Home: Fort Myers, Fla. Died May 5, 2010.

JONES, WILLIAM KENNETH, law educator; b. NYC, Sept. 1, 1930; s. William Arthur and and Mary (Cody) J.; m. Cecile Patricia Flower, June 7, 1952; children— Deborah Ann, Patricia Lynn, John William. AB, Columbia, 1952, LLB, 1954. Bar: N.Y. bar 1955, Ohio bar 1957. Law clk. to U.S. Supreme Ct. Justice Tom C. Clark, 1954-55; atty. Dept. Air Force, 1955-56; asso. firm Jones, Day, Cockley & Reavis, Cleve., 1956-59; mem. faculty Columbia, from 1959; prof. law, 1962-72; James Dohr prof., 1972-75; Milton Handler prof., 1975-91; Charles Evans Hughes prof., from 1991. Pub. service commr., N.Y. State, 1970-74; Cons. Am. Law Inst., 1959; research dir. com. licenses and authorizations Adminstrv. Conf. U.S., 1961-62 Author: Regulated Industries, 1967, 2d edit., 1976, Electronic Mass Media, 1976, 2d edit., 1979. Served to 1st lt. USAF, 1955-56. Died July 28, 2009.

JORDAN, BETTY SUE, retired special education educator; b. Lafayette, Tenn., Sept. 4, 1920; d. Aubrey Lee and Geneva (Freeman) West; m. Bill Jordan, Oct. 22, 1950; 1 child, L. Nicha. Student, David Lipscomb Coll., 1939-41; BS, U. Tenn., 1943; registered dietitian, Duke U. Hosp., 1945; MEd, Clemson U., 1973. Dietitian U. Ala., Tuscaloosa, 1945-46, Duke U., Durham, N.C., 1946-48, Stetson U., DeLand, Fla., 1948-50, Furman U., Greenville, S.C., 1950-52; elem. tchr. Greenville County Schs., S.C., 1952-66, tchr. orthopedically handicapped S.C., 1966-85. With Shriners Hosp. for Crippled Children Sch. Pres. Robert Morris S.S. class U. Meth. Ch., 1992, pres. Susanna Wesley S.S. Class, 2003—. Named Outstanding Judge, Carolina Dist. Rose Soc., 2001. Mem. NEA, Assn. Childhood Edn. (treas. 1980-85), United Daus. Confederacy (pres. Greenville chpt. 1978-99), Greenville Woman's Club (exec. bd. 1991-94), Lake Forest Garden Club (pres. 1970-71, 77-79, 80-81, historian 1981-87, 1st v.p. 1991-92, Woman of Yr. awards 1991, 91, Rachel McKaughan Horticulture award 1992, 94, 95, Lois Russel Arrangement award 1993-95), Greater Greenville Rose Soc. (pres. 1983-84, bronze medal 1996), Am. Rose Soc. (accredited rose judge 1986, rose arrangement judge, cons., Rosarian, Outstanding Judge Carolina dist. 2003, Bronze Hon. medal 2004), Clarice Wilson Garden Club (pres. 1987-89, Woman of Yr. 1991, 2003, Award for Arrangements, Bette Jackson award 1997, Canal Ins. award 1999, Lena Whatley Wallace award 1999, Clarice Townsend Wilson award), Greenville Garden Club (recipient Past Pres.'s Silver Punch Bowl 1998-99, Hall of Fame cert. 2000, Mary Griffith Stevens award, Horticulture Achievement award 2003, Cert. Appreciation, others), Delta Kappa Gamma (pres. Tau chpt. 1976-78, state chmn. comm. 1979-81, state chmn. rsch. 1983-85, leadership/mgmt. seminar Austin, Tex. 1989), Kappa Kappa Iota (state pres. 1972-73, conclave pres. 1983-85). Avocations: collecting antiques, growing roses, flower arranging. Home: Greenville, SC. Died Jan. 19, 2009.

JORDAN, MICHAEL HUGH, retired information technology executive; b. Kansas City, Mo., June 15, 1936; m. Kathryn Hiett, Apr. 8, 1961 (div.); children: Kathryn, Stephen; m. Hilary Cecil, Mar. 4, 2000. BSChemE, Yale U., 1957; MSChemE, Princeton U., 1959. Cons., prin. McKinsey & Co., Toronto, London and Cleve., 1964—74; dir. fin. planning PepsiCo, Purchase, NY, 1974—76, sr. v.p. planning and devel., 1976—77; sr. v.p. mfg. ops. Frito-Lay divsn. PepsiCo Internat., Dallas, 1977—82, pres., CEO Frito-Lay divsn., 1983—85; pres. PepsiCo Foods Internat., 1982—83; exec. v.p., CFO PepsiCo Inc., Purchase, 1985—86, pres., 1986; pres., CEO PepsiCo Worldwide, Dallas, 1987—92; ptnr. Clayton, Dubilier and Rice, NYC, 1992—93; chmn., CEO Westinghouse Electric Corp./CBS, Pitts., 1993—98; ptnr. Beta Capital Group LLC; gen. ptnr. Global Asset Capital, LLC; chmn., CEO Electronic Data Systems Corp., Plano, Tex., 2003—07, chmn., 2007, chmn. emeritus, strategic adv., 2008—10. Bd. dirs. Aetna, eOriginal Inc.; chmn. Nat. Fgn. Trade Coun.; trustee Brookings Instn. Bd. dirs., former chmn. United Negro Coll. Fund, from 1986; bd. dirs. Ctr. for Excellence in Edn., Washington, 1988—92; mem., former chmn. US -Japan Bus. Coun.; mem. Bus. Coun.; mem. bd. trustees US Coun. for Internat. Bus.; mem. Bus. Roundtable; dir. Viventures. With USN. Recipient cert. nuclear engring., Bettis Labs. Atomic Power Labs., Pitts. Died May 25, 2010.

JORDAN, ROBERT ELIJAH, III, lawyer; b. South Boston, Va., June 20, 1936; s. Robert Elijah and Lucy (Webb) Jordan; children: Janet Elizabeth, Jennifer Anne, Robert Elijah IV, Maggie Shay. SB, MIT, 1958; JD magna cum laude, Harvard U., 1961. Bar: DC 1962, Va. 1964, Calif. 1998. Spl. asst. civil rights Office Sec. Def., Washington, 1963-64; asst. U.S. atty. for D.C., 1964-65; exec. asst. for enforcement Office Sec. Treasury, 1965-67; dep. gen. counsel Dept. Army, 1967, acting gen. counsel, 1967-68; gen. counsel of Army, spl. asst. for civil functions to Sec. Army, 1968-71; ptnr. Steptoe & Johnson, Washington, 1971—2008, mng. ptnr., 1988-90. Mem. bd. cert. US Cir. Cts. Appeals Cir. Execs., 1987—88;

pres. Langley Sch., 1981—82; mem. civil pro bono com. US Dist. Ct., 1991—92. Contbr. articles to profl. jours. Bd. dirs. Washington Humane Soc., 2000—03. Served to 1st lt. US Army, 1961—63. Recipient Karl Taylor Compton award, 1958, Arthur S.Flemming award, 1970, award for Exceptional Civilian Svc., US Dept. Army, 1971; Sloan Found. scholar, Edward J. Noble Found. fellow. Mem.: Atlantic Coun. (bd. dirs. 1993—2001, mem. exec. com. 1994—2001, chmn. nominating com. 1997—2001), DC Bar Found. (pres. 1993—94, 1997—98), Calif. State Bar, DC Bar (chmn. ethics com. 1978—83, mem. spl. com. model rules profl. conduct 1983—89, pres. 1987—88), Va. State Bar, Tau Kappa Alpha, Tau Beta Pi. Democrat. Home: Sarasota, Fla. Died May 14, 2010.

JOSEFF, JOAN CASTLE, manufacturing executive; b. Alta., Can., Aug. 12, 1912; naturalized, US, 1945; d. Edgar W. and Lottie (Coates) Castle; 1 child, Jeffrey Rene. BA in Psychology, UCLA. With Joseff-Hollywood, jewelry manufacture and rental and aircraft components and missiles Burbank, Calif., 1939—2010, chmn. bd., pres., sec.-treas. Active Burbank Salary Task Force, 1979—2010, LA County Earthquake Fact-Finding Commn., 1981—2010; bd. dirs. San Fernando Valley Area Chpt. Am. Cancer Soc.; treas. Genesis Energy Sys. Inc., 1993—2010; mem. Rep. Cen. Com.; del. Rep. Nat. Conv., 1980, 84, 88, 92, 96, 2000; active Beautiful People Award Com. Honoring John Wayne Carcer Clinic; with Gov. Wilson Barber and Cosmotology Bd., Pres. Clinton Selective Svc. Sys. TV, CBS This Morning, Australia This Morning, Am. Movie Channel. Recipient Women in Achievement award, Soroptomist Internat., 1988, award, Rep. Congl. Com., 2004, Bus. Woman of Yr. award, Nat. Rep. Congl. Com., 2004. Mem.: NFRW Conv. (chmn., Gala 2040 Mems. 2007), St. Joseph Hosp. (with oral history 2006), LA County Fedn. Rep. Women (scholarship chmn.), Calif. Fedn. Rep. Women (chaplain, Americanism chmn. southern divsn., regent chmn., Women Achievement award 1988), Nat. Fedn. Rep. (voting mem., program chair from 1994, bylaws chair from 1998), Toluca Lake Property Owners Assn. (treas. from 1992), North Hollywood Rep. Women (pres. 1981—82, parliamentarian), Calif. Rep. Women (bd. dir., treas. 1986—90), Nat. Fedn. Rep. Women (bd. dir., Caring for Am. award 1986), Women Motion Picture Industry (life; hon. mem.). Home: Toluca Lake, Calif. Died Mar. 24, 2010.

JOSEPH, FREDERICK HAROLD, retired investment banker; b. Boston, Apr. 22, 1937; s. Edward M. and Sarah (Mostowitz) J.; children from previous marriage: Melissa, Melinda, Amy, Tommi Beth, Mark Joseph; m. Linn Anderson BA, Harvard, 1959, MBA, 1963. With E.F. Hutton Co., NYC, 1963-70, Shearson Hamill Co., NYC, 1970-74, Drexel Burnham Lambert Inc., NYC, 1974-90, vice chmn., CEO, 1985-90; pres. Drexel Burnham Lambert Group, 1987-90; adv. DBL Liquidating Trust, NYC, 1991-93; chmn. Clovebrook Capital Corp., NYC, 1994-98; sr. adv., mng. dir. ING Barings LLC, NYC, 1998—2001; co-founder, mng. dir. Morgan Joseph & Co. Inc., NYC, 2001—09. Bd. dirs. American Biltrite Inc., 1997—2009, Watsco Inc., 2003—09. With USNR, 1959-61. Died Nov. 27, 2009.

JOSEPH, HARRIET, retired English literature educator; b. Montreal, Mar. 14, 1919; came to U.S., 1944; d. Samuel and Hanna Mai (Brown) Bloomfield; m. Edward D. Joseph, Aug. 16, 1942; children: Leila Muriel, Alan Pinto, Brian Daniel. BA, McGill U., Montreal, Que., 1941; MA, Bryn Mawr Coll., 1942. Instr. to assoc. prof. English lit. Pace U., Pleasantville, N.Y., 1966-81, prof., 1981-96; ret. Author: Shakespeare's Son-in-Law: Man & Physician, 1964; contbr. articles on Eng. litr. to jours. Active LWV, Scarsdale, N.Y. Mem. MLA, Internat. Shakespeare Assn., Shakespeare Assn. Am., Am. Jewish Congress, Women's Am. Orgn. for Rehab. Through Tng., Author's League, AAUW. Avocations: swimming, art, biking. Died July 14, 2009.

JOSLIN, STUART LORIN, retired psychiatrist; b. Springfield, Mass., May 1, 1916; s. Lorin Lee and Florence (Mellen) Joslin; m. Dorothy Dennett (dec. Nov. 1988); children: Ellen Johnck, Nancy Fritz, Ernst Laurent. BA, Wesleyan Coll., Middletown, Conn., 1937; MS, Yale U., 1939, MD, 1943. Diplomate Am. Bd. Psychiatry and Neurology. Intern Yale U., New Haven, 1943-44; resident Johns Hopkins U., Balt., 1944-45, N.Y. Hosp., 1945; pvt. practice Fairfield, Conn., 1946-99; ret., 1999. Psychiatrist Yale Dept. Psychiatry, New Haven, 1966-68, Yale Child Study Ctr., New Haven, 1968-70. Lt. (j.g.) USN, 1945-47. Mem. Am. Psychiat. Assn., Am. Acad. Child and Adolescent Psychiatry. Democrat. Congregationalist. Home: North Adams, Mass. Died Jan. 25, 2009.

JOSSEM, EDMUND LEONARD, physics educator; b. Camden, NJ, May 19, 1919; BS, CCNY, 1938; MS, Cornell U., 1940—42, PhD in physics, 1950. Asst prof. Cornell U., 1946—50, assoc. prof., 1950—52, chmn Dept. Physics, 1967—80; prof. physics Ohio State U., 1964—89, prof. emeritus, from 1989. Exec. sec. Cmty. Coll. Physics, 1963—65, chmn., 1966—71, mem. commn. on coll. physics; mem. Nat. Adv. Coun. Edn. Profl. Devel., 1967—70; bd. dirs. Mich.-Ohio Edn. Lab., 1967—69; hon. bd. Internat. Conf. X-ray and Atomic Inner Shell Physics, 1981—82; mem. sci. staff Advanced Divsn. Lost Alamos, 1942—47; mem. com. tchg. sci. Internat. Coun. Sci. Unions; cons. World Bank-Chinese U. Devel. Project, China; hon. prof. physics Beijing (China) Normal U. Fellow: AAAS; mem.: Am. Assn. Physics Tchrs. (v.p. 1971—72, pres. 1973—74, chmn. com. tchr. preparation from 2002, Phillips award 1985, Oersted award 1994), Am. Physics Soc., Sigma Xi. Home: Columbus, Ohio. Died Aug. 29, 2009.

JOYCE, RAYMOND M. H., state legislator; b. Holyoke, Mass., Mar. 11, 1928; s. Raymond Michael and Katherine (Courtney) J.; m. Betty Ann Keating, Sept. 17, 1955; children: R. Michael, David, Brendan, Patrick, Timothy. BS, Coll. of Holy Cross, 1951. CPCU. Trainee, spl. agt. Phoenix Ins. Co., Hartford, Conn., 1953-57; tchr. Moody Sch. Commerce, New Britain, Conn., 1957-69; ins. agt. Raymond Joyce Ins. Agy., New Britain, 1957-93; mem. Conn. Ho. of Reps., Hartford, from 1979. Mem. New Britain Dem. Town Com., 1972-79. Sgt. USMC, 1951-53. Roman Catholic. Avocations: piano, tennis, art. Died Mar. 12, 2009.

JOYNER, FLOYD TALMAGE, JR., life insurance company executive; b. Richmond, Va., July 5, 1927; s. Floyd Talmage and Irene (Rogers) J.; m. Sarah Gene Hart, Aug. 18, 1951; children— Debra Joyner Geisel, Sarah Joyner Hall. AB, Coll. William and Mary, 1949. Examiner Bur. Ins. State Corp. Commn. of Va., 1949-59, chief, audit sect., 1959-60; asst. controller Fidelity Bankers Life Ins. Co., Richmond, Va., 1960-62, treas., 1962-68, sr. v.p., treas., 1968-74, sr. v.p., chief fin. officer, 1974-76, sr. v.p., sec., chief fin. officer, from 1976. Served with USN, 1945-47 Fellow Life Mgmt. Inst. Clubs: Bull and Bear, Richmond Country (Richmond). Baptist. Home: Richmond, Va. Died May 14, 2009.

JUDD, O'DEAN P., physicist; b. Austin, Minn., May 26, 1937; MS in Physics, UCLA, 1961, PhD in Physics, 1968. Staff physicist and project dir. Hughes Rsch. Lab., Malibu, Calif., 1959-67; postdoctoral fellow UCLA Dept. Physics, 1968-69; researcher Hughes Rsch. Lab., Malibu, Calif., 1969-72; researcher, group leader Los Alamos (N.Mex.) Nat. Lab., 1972-81, chief scientist for def. rsch. and applications, 1981-87, energy and environ. chief scientist, lab. fellow, 1990-93, ind. tech. advisor and cons., from 1995; chief scientist Strategic Def. Initiative Orgn., Washington, 1987-90; nat. intelligence officer for sci. and tech. Nat. Intelligence Coun., Washington, 1993-94. Mem. numerous govt. coms. related to sci. and tech., def. and nat. security policy; adj. prof. physics U. N.Mex., Albuquerque; mem. sci. adv. bd. USAF, 1999-2003. Patentee in sci. and tech.; contbr. numerous articles to sci. and def.-related jours. Fellow IEEE, AAAS, Los Alamos Nat. Lab. Inst. Advanced Engring.; mem. Am. Phys. Soc. Deceased.

JUDGE, MARGARET ANN, nurse, nursing administrator; b. Simpson, Pa., Sept. 3, 1933; d. Grant Edward and Mary E. (Newcombe) Bishop; m. Joseph M. Judge, June 29, 1957; children— Ann E., Joseph, Thomas A., II, Carolyn M., Mary Catherine. Diploma in Nursing St. Joseph Hosp., 1954; B.S. in Pub. Sch. Nursing, Millersville State Coll., 1975; M.S. in Edn., Temple U., 1977; M.S. in Nursing, U. Del., 1984. Registered nurse, Pa., Del. Operating nurse Phila., Gen. Hosp., 1954-55, head nurse operating room, 1955-56; head nurse operating room Bryn Mawr Hosp., Pa., 1956-57; dir. inservice edn. Lancaster Gen. Hosp., Pa., 1974-77, dir. nursing sch., 1977—, v.p. nursing, 1983—. HEW grant, scholar, 1982. Mem. Am. Nursing Soc., Am. Orgn. Nurse Execs., Assembly Hosp. Schs. Nursing, Pa. Soc. Nurse Adminstrs., Operating Room Nurses Assn. (pres. Southeast Pa. 1973-74), Pa. Nurses Assn. (sec. dist. 16 1978-79), MidAtlantic Nurses Assn. (dir. 1982-84), Pa. Hosp. Assn. (governing councilor 1984—). Roman Catholic. Home: Millersville, Pa. Died May 30, 2010.

JUDY, BERNARD FRANCIS, retired newspaper editor; b. Grove City, Pa., Mar. 20, 1920; s. Francis Xavier and Catherine Veronica (Toomey) J.; m. Jane Elizabeth Urey, Apr. 3, 1945; children— Kathleen, Cynthia, Jill, Mark. BS in Commerce, Grove City Coll., 1941; AB in Econs, Washington and Lee U., Lexington, Va., 1947; MS in Journalism, Columbia, 1948. Mem. staff Toledo Blade, 1948-89, assoc. editor, 1969-73, editor, 1973-85, editor-in-chief, 1985-89; ret., 1989. V.p., dir. Toledo Blade Co. Served with USAAF, 1942-44; CIC AUS, 1945. Mem. Am. Soc. Newspaper Editors, Phi Beta Kappa, Sigma Delta Chi. Roman Catholic. Home: Toledo, Ohio. Died June 30, 2010.

JUILLERAT, ERNEST EMANUEL, JR., safety engineer; b. Portland, Ind., Dec. 2, 1921; s. Ernest Emanuel and Anna Liza Etta (Stanley) Juillerat; m. Mary Frances Knakal Juillerat, Nov. 18, 1945; children: Martha Grace, Mary Anne Juillerat Koepfler. BBA, Capitol City Coll., 1951; postgrad., W.Va. State Coll., 1959—61. With Union Carbide Corp. Inst., W.Va., 1947—61; mgr. fire analysis dept. Nat. Fire Protection Assn., Boston, 1961—70; asst. exec. dir. Nat. Sch. Bds. Assn., 1971—73; asst. dir. safety and fire protection dept. pub. safety Northwestern U., Evanston, Ill., from 1973; cons. in field; lectr. in field. Bd. dirs. Bel Canto Found., from 1979, Northwestern Libr. Coun., from 1972. Author: Campus Fire Safety, 1978; contbr. articles to profl. jours. Served with USCG, 1942—46, PTO. Decorated Silver Star. Mem.: Am. Legion, US Naval Inst., Campus Safety Assn., Nat. Safety Coun., Nat. Fire Protection Assn., Am. Soc. Safety Engrs., Shriners, Masons. Republican. Presbyterian. Home: Skokie, Ill. Died Jan. 27, 2009.

JULIAN, BROOKS PATTON, former banker; b. Mt. Sterling, Ohio, Oct. 7, 1917; s. Earl R. and Stella L. (Brooks) J.; m. Helen McCoy, Feb. 7, 1942 (dec. 1987); children: Kathryn Julian Goldberg, Constance Julian Glickman, Jeanne. BS, Ohio State U., 1940; grad., U. Wis. Sch. Banking, 1954. Asst. cashier Ohio Nat. Bank, Columbus, 1951-53, asst. v.p., 1953-56, v.p., 1956-68, exec. v.p., 1970-76; v.p. BancOhio Corp., 1968-70; pres. BancOhio/Ohio Nat. Bank, 1976-79, chief exec. officer, 1979; sr. v.p. BancOhio Corp., 1977-82; pres. BancOhio Nat. Bank, 1979-82, also dir. Dir. Scioto Investment Co. Trustee Grant Med. Ctr., 1972—, Episcopal Retirement Homes, Inc.; bd. dirs. Franklin County unit Am. Cancer Soc.; adv. bd. Whetstone Convalescent Center. Served to capt. Mil. Intelligence AUS, 1941-45; lt. col. Res. ret. Mem.: University, Columbus Country, Ohio Automobile (trustee 1964—). Republican. Episcopalian. Home: Columbus, Ohio. Died May 31, 2009.

JUNGELS, ELEANOR ELIZABETH, county official; b. Aurora, Ill., Jan. 29, 1922; d. Peter William and Marie Anna (Koerfer) J. Grad. high sch., Aurora. Chief clk. bd. of rev. Kane County, Ill., 1938-39, clk.-typist, recorder, 1940-43, supr. tract index, 1943-72, chief dep. recorder, 1952-72, elected recorder, 1972—. Mem. St. Anne's Soc. St. Nicholas Roman Catholic Ch.; bd. dirs. Aurora Hist. Soc., 1972—; rec. sec. Kane County Republican Central Com., 1982-84. Named Woman of Yr. in Professions YWCA, 1984., Woman of Yr. Dundee Twp. Rep. Women, 1986. Mem. Aurora Bus. and Profl. Women (pres. 1985-87), Ill. Assn. County Ofcls., Ill. Assn. County Clks. and Recorders (legis. com. 1981-87), Clks. and Recorders of No. Ill. (pres. 1979-80, Pres. Plaque), Internat. Assn. County Ofcls., Nat. Assn. County Recorders and Clks., St. Cecilia Evening Music Club (pres. 1954-55). Home: Aurora, Ill. Died Aug. 2, 2009.

KABAKER, RICHARD ZOHN, lawyer; b. Chgo., Feb. 22, 1935; s. Herman A. and Eve (Horwitz) Kabaker; m. Patricia Lee Florsheim, Sept. 18, 1964; children: Douglas J., Nancy L. BA, U. Mich., 1956, JD, 1959. Bar: Ill. 59, US Dist. Ct. Ill. 60, Ohio 69, Wis. 73, US Supreme Ct. 78. Assoc. McDermott, Will & Emery, Chgo., 1960—69, Jones, Day, Cockley & Reavis, Cleve., 1969—71; assoc. prof. law. U. Detroit, 1971—72; asst. prof. U. Wis., Madison, 1972—77; ptnr. Murphy & Desmond, Madison, 1977—88, Lee, Kilkelly, Paulson & Kabaker, Madison, from 1988. Author: Wisconsin Estate Planning, 1984; contbr. articles to profl. jours.; editor: Will and Trust Forms, 1981. Smongeski Rsch. fellowship, U. Wis., 1976. Fellow: Am. Law Inst., Am. Coll. Trust and Estate Counsel; mem.: ABA (vice chmn. com. on tax regulations and legis. joint tenancy 1981—84, chmn. com. on creditors rights in estates and trusts 1986—88), State Bar Wis. (chmn. com. on estate tax apportionment 1983—86, sec. taxation), Internat. Acad. Estate and Trust Law, Rotary, Madison Club. Died Jan. 29, 2009.

KAHN, SUSAN, artist; b. NYC, Aug. 26, 1924; d. Jesse B. and Jenny Carol (Peshkin) Cohen; m. Joseph Kahn, Sept. 15, 1946 (dec.); m. Richard Rosenkranz, Feb. 1, 1981. Grad., Parsons Sch. Design, 1945; student, Moses Soyer, 1950-57. Subject of: book Susan Kahn, with an essay by Lincoln Rothschild, 1980; One-woman shows include Sagittarius Gallery, 1960, A.C.A., Galleries, 1964, 68, 71, 76, 80, Charles B. Goddard Art Center, Ardmore, Okla., 1973, Albrecht Gallery Mus. Art, St. Joseph, Mo., 1974, NY Cultural Center, NYC, 1974, St. Peter's Coll., Jersey City, 1978, Heidi Neuhoff Gallery, NYC, 1989, Sindin Galleries, 1996; exhibited in group shows Audubon Artists, NYC, Nat. Acad., NYC, Springfield (Mass.) Mus., City Center, NYC, A.C.A., Galleries, NYC, Nat. Arts Club, NYC, Butler Inst., Youngstown, Ohio, Islip Art Mus., East Islip. NY, 1989, Fine Arts Mus. of S., Mobile, Ala., 1989, Chatanooga Regional History Mus, 1989, Longview (Tex.) Mus. Art, 1990, Monroe Ctr. Arts, Hoboken, NJ, 2007; represented in permanent collections, Tyler (Tex.) Mus., St. Lawrence U. Mus., Canton, NY, Fairleigh Dickinson U. Mus., Rutherford, NJ, Syracuse U. Mus., Sheldon Swope Gallery, Terre Haute, Ind., Montclair (NJ) Mus. Fine Arts, Butler Inst. Am. Art, Youngstown, Ohio, Reading (Pa.) Mus., Albrecht Gallery Mus. Art, St. Joseph(Mo.), Cedar Rapids (Iowa) Art Center, NY Cultural Center, NYC, Edwin A. Ulrich Mus., Wichita, Kans., Wichita State U., Johns Hopkins Sch. Advanced Internat. Studies, Washington, Joslyn Mus., Omaha, U. Wyo., Laramie. Recipient Knickerbocker prize for best religious painting, 1956; Edith Lehman award Nat. Assn. Women Artists, 1958; Simmons award, 1961; Knickerbocker Artists award, 1961; Nat. Arts Club award, 1967; Knickerbocker Medal of Honor, 1964; Famous Artists Sch. award, 1967 Mem. Nat. Assn. Women Artists (Anne Barnett Meml. prize 1981, Solveig Stromsoe Palmer Meml. award 1987, Dorothy Schweitzer award 1990,Audrey Hope Shirk Meml. award 2006), Artists Equity, Met. Mus., Mus. Modern Art, Nat. Assn. Women Artists. Home: New York, NY. Died Sept. 20, 2010.

KAHT, JOSEPH EDWARD, banker, lawyer; b. Bklyn., Feb. 4, 1928; s. Joseph Martin and Isabelle (Stewart) K.; m. Rose Perazzo, Apr. 24, 1954; 1 child, Jo Ann. Student, St. Francis Coll., 1946-48; LL.B., N.Y. Law Sch., 1952. Bar: N.Y. 1953, U.S. Supreme Ct. 1961, D.C. 1978. Assoc. atty. Dewey, Ballantine, Bushby, Palmer & Wood, NYC, 1952-61; house counsel Irwin, Wolfson, NYC, 1961-63; asst. v.p., atty. Dry Dock Savs. Bank, 1963-67, v.p., atty., 1967-69, sr. v.p., gen. counsel, 1970-82; v.p., assoc. gen. counsel Anchor Savs. Bank, 1983-86, v.p., dep. gen. counsel, asst. sec., from 1986. Lectr. real estate Practising Law Inst., 1965—; assoc. Finley, Kumble, Wagner, Heine, Underberg & Casey, 1982-83; mem. adv. bd. Security Title & Guaranty Co., N.Y.C., 1961— Mem. adv. bd. Little Village Sch. Fellow Am. Coll Mortgage Attys.; mem. ABA (com. on econs. and real estate, real property and probate sect., com. mut. savs. banks), N.Y. State Bar Assn., N.Y. County Bar Assn., Catholic Lawyers Guild, Mortgage Bankers Assn. Am. (com. on income producing property), Nat. Assn. Mut. Savs. Banks (mortgage investments) Clubs: Hempstead (N.Y.) Golf. Home: Lake Worth, Fla. Died Apr. 8, 2010.

KAISER, ROBERT LEE, retired engineering executive; b. Louisville, June 28, 1935; s. Harlan K. and LaVerne (Peterson) K.; m. Margaret Siler; children: Robin Lee, Robert Lee. Student, U. Louisville, 1953—54, U. Ky., 1958—61; BSME, Ashbourne U., 1977, MSME, 1979. Registered profl. engr., Fla., Ky., 1965. Draftsman, designer E.R. Ronald & Assocs., Louisville, 1953-54, Thompson-Kissell Co., 1954-56; estimator, engr. George Pridemore & Son, Lexington, Ky., 1956-58; designer, engr., supr. Frankel & Curtis, Lexington, 1958-61; engr. Hugh Dillehay & Assocs., 1961-65; owenr, engr., operator K-Svc., Inc., 1965-74; project engr. Mason & Hanger, Silas Mason Co., Inc., 1974-77; v.p. Webb-Dillehay Design Group, 1977-81; pres. Kaiser-Taulbee Assocs., Inc., Lexington, Louisville, Orlando, Fla., ret., 2000. Past chmn., pres. and bd. dirs. Opportunity Workshop Lexington; vis. lectr. mech. engring. and Coll. Architecture, U. Ky.; mem., past chmn. Ky. State Bd. of Registration for Engrs, and Land Surveyors, Ky. Task Force to Develop New Engring. and Surveying Laws; charter commn. merger Lexington-Fayette County govts.; mem. Ky. Airport Zoning Comsn., mem. Gov.'s Task Force on Ednl. Constrn. Criteria; past trustee, chmn. Humana Hosp., Lexington, Aviation Mus. Ky. Chmn. storm water task force Lake County Water Authority, Fla.; mem. Harris Chain of Lake Restoration Coun.; mem., chmn. adv. com. Cmty. Redevelopment Adminstrn., Tavares, Fla. Mem. ASME, NSPE (life), ASHRAE (past pres. local chpt.), Ky. Soc. Profl. Engrs. (life), Fla. Engring. Soc., Rotary Club Mt. Dora (pres. 2007-08). Episcopalian. Home: Tavares, Fla. Died Jan. 20, 2010.

KALLEN, DAVID JOHNSON, clinical sociologist, educator; b. Danbury, Conn., July 21, 1929; s. Horace Meier and Rachel (Oatman) K.; m. Suzanne Libby, Feb. 1, 1952 (div. July 1985); children: Hugh Anthony, Benjamin Thomas, Nina Elizabeth; m. Sandra Ames Greenwood, Apr. 25, 1992. BA, Cornell U., 1951; MA, U. Mich., 1953, PhD, 1958. Rsch. asst. U. Mich., Ann Arbor, 1951-54, rsch. assoc., 1954-57; rsch. dir. Health & Welfare Coun. Balt. Area, Balt., 1957-62; health sci. adminstr. NIH, Bethesda, Md., 1962-70; assoc. prof. Mich. State U., East Lansing, 1970-74, prof., 1974—2000, prof. emeritus, from 2000. Bd. dirs. Sci. Analysis Corp., San Francisco. Editor: (jour.) Clin. Sociology Rev., 1985-91. Mem. APA, Sociol. Practice Assn. (cert. clin. sociologist, Award of Merit 1986, pres. 1993-96, Rubert Ezra Park Lifetime Achievement award 2000), Am. Sociol. Assn. (com. chair 1990-93, Lifetime Achievement award Sociol. Practice sect. 1992), Soc. for Study of Social Problems (com. chair). Democrat. Jewish. Home: Grand Ledge, Mich. Died Apr. 20, 2009.

KALLERES, MICHAEL PETER, career officer; b. Gary, Ind., June 28, 1939; s. Peter Michael and Tula (Panos) K.; m. Georgine Maria Karras, Sept. 4, 1966; children, Deme, Peter. INDM in Engring., Purdue U., 1962; MS in Indsl. Adminstrn., George Washington U., 1971; disting. grad., Naval War Coll., 1971, Nat. Def. U., 1980. Commd. ensign USN, 1962, advanced through grades to vice adm., 1990; comdg. officer USS Dewey, Charleston, S.C., 1976-78; dir. Exec. Leadership Tng., Washington, 1978-79; comdr. DESRON 24, Mayport, Fla., 1980-81, DESRON 8, Mayport, Fla., 1981-83; dep. dir. fin. planning USN, Washington, 1983-85, dir. personal policy, 1985-86; comdr. Carrier Battle Group 12, Mayport, 1986-88; dir. fin. planning USN, Washington, 1988-90; comdr. 2d Fleet, Atlantic Ocean, 1990-92, Mil. Sea Lift Command, Washington, 1992-94; pres. Global Assocs. Ltd., TSG, Falls Church, Va., from 1994. Mem. Nat. Def. Sci. Bd. for Strategic Mobility, 1995—. Elected mem. Nat. Bd. of the Salvation Army, 1996—. Recipient Mil. Man. of Yr. award Axios Orgn., L.A., 1988, St. Andrew's medal Greek Orthodox Chs. N. and S.Am., 1988, Leadership award Hellenic Inst., 1993; named Purdue Old Masters Man of Yr., Purdue U., 1991, Mil. Man of Yr., Pan Hellenic Assn., 1991, Archon Greek Orthodox Ch., 1993. Mem. lPurdue Alumni Assn., George Washington U. Alumni Assn. (graduation speaker 1990). Avocations: collecting naval hats, classic fountain pens, letter writing. Home: Jacksonville, Fla. Died July 18, 2010.

KAMINSKI, EDWARD JOZEF, pathologist, toxicologist educator; b. Torun, Poland, Mar. 24, 1926; came to U.S., 1956; m. Krystyna Karpinski, Sept. 15, 1951; children: Norbert E., Yvonne K. PhB, Northwestern U., Evanston, Ill., 1960, PhD, 1964. Diplomate Am. Bd. Toxicology. Rsch. technologist U. Edinburg, Scotland, 1946-51, Royal Cancer Hosp./U. London, 1951-53; med. technologist Mt. Sinai Hosp., Toronto, Can., 1953-56; rsch. technologist Northwestern U., Chgo., 1956-60, lectr. in chemistry, 1963-67, prof. pathology, 1964-95, prof. emeritus, from 1996. Cons. in toxicology Indsl./Bio-Test Labs, Northbrook, Ill., 1964-79, various legal cases, 1980—. Editorial bd. BioMaterial Med. Devices Internat. Jour., 1973-89; contbr. 80 articles to profl. jours./abstracts. Bd. mem. Niles Twp. High Sch. Dist. 219, Skokie, Ill., 1974-78. Mem. Soc. Toxicology (pres. midwest regional chpt. 1982-83), Polish Inst. Arts and Scis. Am., Am. Chem. Soc., Omicron Kappa Upsilon, Sigma Xi. Home: Morton Grove, Ill. Died Oct. 6, 2009.

KANABROCKI, EUGENE LADISLAUS, chemist; b. Chgo., Apr. 18, 1922; s. Paul and Jeanette (Tyrala) Kanabrocki; m. Rose Marie Spata, Nov. 5, 1950; children: Joseph, Paul. BS in Chemistry, DePaul U., 1948; MS in Chemistry, Loyola U., Chgo., 1969; DSc in Chronobiochemistry, Jagiellonian U., Krakow, Poland, 1983. Registered chemist Nat. Registry Clin. Chemistry. Clin. chemist Bethesda Hosp., Chgo., 1971—73, VA Hosp., Hines, Ill., 1946—71, rsch. chemist, from 1984; chemist regional lab. US Customs Svc., Chgo., 1973—83. Dir. Cardiovascular Lab., Evergreen Pk., Ill., 1977—78; cons. chemist Edward Hosp., Naperville, Ill., 1981—85. Contbr. articles to profl. jours. With US Army, 1943—46, ETO, col. USAR. Decorated Meritorious Svc. medal; WHO grantee, 1970. Mem.: Health Physics Soc., Am. Chem. Soc., Sigma Xi. Roman Catholic. Home: Melrose Park, Ill. Died Apr. 23, 2009.

KANTER, ARNOLD LEE, international business consultant, policy analyst; b. Chgo., Feb. 27, 1945; s. Norton and Mary Kanter; m. Anne Strassman, June 28, 1969; children: Clare Megan, Noah Charles. AB, U. Mich., 1966; MPhil in Polit. Sci., Yale U., 1969, PhD in Polit. Sci., 1975. Rsch. fellow, asst. The Brookings Instn., Washington, 1969-71; instr. Ohio State U., Columbus, 1971-72; asst. prof., rsch. assoc. U. Mich., Ann Arbor, 1972-77; spl. asst. to dir. Bur. Politico-Mil. Affairs, US Dept. State, Washington, 1977-78, dep. dir. Office Systems Analysis, 1978-81, dir. Office Policy Analysis, 1981-83, prin. dep. asst. sec., 1984-85; assoc. program dir. internat. security and def. policy The RAND Corp., Santa Monica, Calif., 1985-86, program dir. nat. security strategies, 1986-87, sr. rsch. staff, 1987-89; spl. asst. to Pres., sr. dir. for arms control and def. policy NSC, Washington, 1989-91; dep. to under sec. for polit. affairs US Dept. State, 1983-84, under sec. for polit affairs Washington, 1991-93; sr. fellow The RAND Corp., Washington, 1993—2010, The Forum for Internat. Policy, 1993—2010; prin., founding mem. The Scowcroft Group, 1994—2010. Author: Defense Politics: A Budgetary Perspective, 1979; co-author: Bureaucratic Politics and Foreign Policy, 1974; co-editor: Readings in American Foreign Policy, 1973; contbr. numerous articles to profl. jours. Mem. Coun. on Fgn. Rels., Internat. Inst. Strategic Studies, Phi Beta Kappa. Home: Mc Lean, Va. Died Apr. 10, 2010.

KANZLER, WALTER WILHELM, biomedical educator; b. Jersey City, Sept. 17, 1938; s. George Hess and Martha (Strasser) K. BA, Montclair State Coll., 1960, MA, 1963, Marshall U., 1964; PhD, U. Cin., 1972. Cert. counselor, N.J. Tchr. biology Union City (N.J.) High Schs., 1960-65; asst. prof. Trenton State Coll., 1965-66; instr. Wagner Coll., SI, N.Y., 1966-72, asst. prof., 1972-76, assoc. prof., 1976-84, prof., from 1984. Adj. prof. St. John's U., S.I., 1989, St. Peter's Coll., Jersey City, 1990—; cons. Scientist's Ctr. Animal Welfare, Washington, 1981—; sr. rsch. assoc. Nat. Ctr. for Biomed. Ethics, Drew U., 1976. Author: Phermones and Trail Making in Ants. Fellow NASA, 1969-70, NSF, U. Calif., 1971; grantee NSF-Am. Mus. Natural History, N.Y.C., 1994. Mem. AAAS, Nat. Wildlife Fedn., Animal Behavior Soc., Sigma Xi, Beta Beta Beta. Avocations: lithography, photography. Home: Jersey City, NJ. Died June 26, 2009.

KAPLAN, BENJAMIN, retired judge; b. NYC, Apr. 9, 1911; s. Morris and Mary (Berman) K.; m. Felicia Lamport, Apr. 16, 1942 (dec. 1999); children: James L., Nancy L. Mansbach. AB, CCNY, 1929; LL.B., Columbia, 1933; LL.D., Suffolk U., 1974, Harvard U., 1981, Northeastern U., 1981. Bar: N.Y. 1934, Mass. 1950. Assoc., then mem. firm Greenbaum, Wolff & Ernst, NYC, 1933-42, 46; vis. prof. law Harvard Law Sch., 1947, prof. law, 1948—72, Royall prof. law, 1961-72, prof. emeritus, 1972—2010; assoc. justice Supreme Jud. Ct. Mass., 1972-81; judge Mass. Appeals Ct., 1983—2005. Reporter to adv. com. on civil rules Jud. Conf. U.S., 1960-66, mem., 1966-70; co-reporter restatement (2d) of judgments to American Law Inst., 1970-73 Served to lt. col. AUS, 1942-46. Mem. Am. Law Inst., Assn. Bar City of N.Y., Phi Beta Kappa. Achievements include assisting Justice Jackson on Nuremberg Trial, 1945. Home: Cambridge, Mass. Died Aug. 18, 2010.

KAPLAN, HAROLD, editor, former foreign service officer; b. Newark, July 29, 1918; s. Samuel and Celia K.; m. Celia Scop, Nov. 18, 1938; children— Leslie, Roger Francis, Lionel Philip. BA, U. Ill., 1938, MA, 1941. Instr. U. Chgo., 1941; Fgn. service officer, various posts Europe, North Africa, Asia, 1952-67; dep. asst. sec. state, 1967-68; counselor NATO mission, 1968; mem. del. Vietnam Peace Talks, 1968-69; ret., 1969; v.p. Bendix Corp., 1972-78; editor-in-chief GEO mag., NYC, 1978-82; sec.-treas., editorial bd. In the Pub. Interest, from 1982; now editorial cons. NYC and Paris. Author: novella The Mohammedans, 1943; novel The Plenipotentaries, 1950, The Spirit and The Bride, 1952; translator: novel Raymond Queneau's Loin De Rueil (pub. as The Skin of Dreams), 1950; mem. editorial bd. In the Nat. Interest; contbr. numerous articles to mags. Mem. Council Fgn. Relations, Inst. Ednl. Affairs, Century Assn., Centre int. de Formation europeene (France). Jewish. Died Oct. 18, 2009.

KAPLAN, JEROME I., physics educator; b. NYC, July 28, 1926; s. George Kaplan and Hannah Cohen; m. Ann Ruth Maslow, Dec. 17, 1965; 1 child, Jean Maslow. BS in Math., U. Mich., 1950; PhD in Physics, U. Calif., Berkeley, 1954. Researcher NRL, Washington, 1954-59; postdoctoral fellow Brandeis U., Waltham, Mass., 1995-62; assoc. prof. rsch. Brown U., Providence, 1963-67; researcher Battelle Inst., Columbus, Ohio, 1967-73; prof. Ind. U.-Purdue U., Indpls., from 1973. Fulbright lectr. Salisbur, South Rhodesia, 1962-63. Author: (chpt.) Electron Spin Relaxation in Liquids, 1972, (with others) Physical Basis for Heterogeneous Catalysts, 1985; co-author: NMR of Chemically exchanging Systems, 1980. Mem. Indpls. Nuclear Freeze, 1986-89. Louis Lipsky fellow Weizmann Inst., 1956-57, Mem. Am. Phys. Soc. Achievements include patents in NMR Imaging; research in NMR chemcial exchange, non-linear pulses from lasers, gas about a neutron star, non-exponential chemical exchange. Home: Indianapolis, Ind. Died Aug. 10, 2010.

KAPLAN, SEYMOUR H., allergist, immunologist, pediatrician; b. NYC, Sept. 28, 1924; Student, NYU, 1942-45; MD, U. Health Scis., 1950. Diplomate Am. Bd. Allergy and Immunology, Am. Bd. Pediats. Intern Harlem Hosp., NYC, 1949-50; resident pediats. Coney Is. Hosp., NYC, 1950-51, Maimonides Hosp., NYC, 1951, Beth-El Hosp., NYC, 1953-54; attending physician allergy, pediats. N. Shore U. Hosp., Manhasset, N.Y., from 1955, Long Is. (N.Y.) Jewish Med. Ctr., New Hyde Park, from 1955; pvt. practice, from 1955. Fellow Am. Acad. Allergy and Immunology, Am. Acad. Pediats., Am. Coll. Allergy and Immunology. Died Mar. 9, 2009.

KAPPY, WILLIAM FRED, secondary school educator; b. Cleve., Oct. 26, 1919; s. William Ernest and Lena Maria (Scherler) Kappy; children: William John, Amy Lyn Douglass. Grad, Kent State U., 1969. Pipe welder Standard Oil Co., 1939—65; tchr. welding Thomas Edison HS, 1964—70, Martin Luther King HS, 1970—79; vocat. welding instr. East Tech. Sch., Cleve., from 1980. Tchr. adult edn. Manpower Tng. Ctr., 1967—75, Cuahoga Valley Joint Vocat. Sch., 1981—83; cons. welding, 1965—80. Served with USAF, 1942—47, PTO. Mem.: Am. Vocat. Assn., Am. Welding Soc., Iota Lambda Sigma. Died Jan. 17, 2009.

KARACAN, ISMET, psychiatrist, educator; b. Istanbul, Turkey, July 23, 1927; BS, U. Istanbul, 1948, MD, 1953; DSC in Medicine, SUNY Downstate Med. Ctr., 1965. Cert. Turkish Bd. Neuropsychiatry, Am. Bd. Psychiatry and Neurology. Rsch. Ctr. Baylor Coll. Medicine, Tex. Med. Ctr., Houston, from 1973; assoc. chief staff rsch. & devel., dir. Sleep Rsch. Lab. VA Med. Ctr., Houston, from 1973. Recipient Nathaniel Kleitman prize Assn. Sleep Disorders Ctrs., 1981. Fellow Am. Psychiat. Assn., Am. Coll. Physicians; mem. AMA, AAAS, Sleep Rsch. Soc. (pres. 1976-79), N.Y. Acad. Sci., Am. Coll. Neuropsychopharmacol., Brit. Assn. Psychopharmacol. Achievements include rsch. in phychological and physiological mechanisms of male impotence, neurophysiological and biochemical mechanisms responsible for male erectile failure, pharmacology of human sleep. Died June 30, 2009.

KARESH, JANICE LEHRER, special education consultant; b. NYC, May 22, 1924; d. Maxwell and lillian (Cohen) Lehrer; m. Irwin Karesh, June 15, 1947 (dec. 1959); children: Sara, Hyman, Ann, Charles. BS in Pre-Medicine, Rutgers U., 1945; MA in Psychol. Counseling, NYU, 1946. Tchr. algebra Chicora H.S., Charleston, S.C., 1946-47; tchr. math. Charleston H.S., 1963; tchr. gifted Addleston Hebrew Acad., Charleston, 1963-64; tchr. physics, biology Rivers H.S., Charleston, 1964-65; cons. spl. edn. S.C Dept. Mental Retardation, Charleston, 1966-69; dir. spl. svcs. Beaufort (S.C.) Sch. Dist., 1969-89; ind. cons. spl. edn. Charleston, from 1989. Vol. advocate guardian at litem, Family Ct., S.C., 1990—; mem. exec. com. Charleston Democratic Party, 1994—. Mem. LWV (past bd. dirs.), Nat. Coun. Jewish Women (pres. 1951, past bd. dirs.), Coun. for Exceptional Children, Poetry Soc. of S.C., Douglass Alumnae Assn. (v.p. 1995—). Democrat. Jewish. Avocations: needlepoint, writing poetry and essays, child advocacy issues. Home: Charleston, SC. Died Jan. 5, 2009.

KARGMAN, MARIE WITKIN, marriage and family therapist; b. Chgo., Aug. 28, 1914; d. Joseph and Clara (Zucker) Witkin; m. Max Kargman, 1935; children: Donna, William, Robert. JD, DePaul U., 1936; MA, Radcliffe Coll., 1951. Pub. defender Boys' Court, Chgo., 1936-37; ptnr. Kargman & Kargman, 1937-44, Boston, 1953-54, pvt. practice marriage counselor, family mediator, from 1953. Chmn. gov.'s council on home and family, Commonwealth of Mass., Boston, 1966-76. Author: How to Manage a Marriage, 1985; contbr. articles to profl. jours. Mem. Assn. of Practicing Sociologists (cited outstanding contbr.), Nat. Council on Family Relations, DePaul U. Law Sch. Alumni Assn. Avocations: tennis, tv appearances, golf. Home: Boston, Mass. Died Jan. 11, 2009.

KARKUT, ANN LOUISE, publisher; b. Bellwood, Ill., June 30, 1924; d. Walter Karkut and Anna (Jacobs) Knippenberg Karkut; m. Edward Karkut Karkut, Mar. 20, 1943; children: Patricia, Edward, Stanley, Susan, Christopher. Attending, LaSalle U. Asst. editor Lockport Herald, Ill., 1960—63; editor, 1963—69; asst. editor Naperville Sun, Ill., 1969—70; editor Joliet Cir., 1970, Pointer Publs., Riverdale, Ill., 1970—72; asst. editor Lisle Sun, Ill., 1972—74, Big Farmer Mag., Frankfort, Ill., 1974—81. Sec. Homer Fire Dept. Aux., 1962, Dist. 92 Band Parents, 1967; mem. Homer Rep. Precinct Com., from 1976, Homer Twp. clk., from 1981; bd. dirs. Will County Hist. Soc. Mem.: Ill. Press Women's Assn., Ill. Fedn. Bus. & Profl. Women's Clubs Found. (dir. Dist. 5), Ill. Bus. & Profl. Women's Club (bull. editor 1983—84), Lockport Bus. & Profl. Women's Club (charter mem., past pres., Woman of Yr. 1979), Waa-Shee Riders (pres.). Roman Catholic. Home: Lockport, Ill. Died Aug. 21, 2009.

KARL, BARRY DEAN, historian, educator; b. Louisville, July 24, 1927; s. Aaron and Anne (Simons) K.; m. Alice Hideko Woodard, June 14, 1957; children: Elisabeth Mead, Sarah Anne. BA, U. Louisville, 1949; MA, U. Chgo., 1951; PhD, Harvard U., 1961. Assoc. editor for humanities and history U. Chgo. Press, 1951-55; exec. sec. to com. on gen. edn. Harvard U., 1959-61; asst. prof. history Washington U., St. Louis, 1962-63, prof., 1963-68, Brown U., Providence, 1968-71; prof. Am. history U. Chgo., from 1971, Norman and Edna Freehling prof., 1977-96, Norman and Edna Freehling prof. emeritus, from 1996; William Henry Bloomberg prof. philanthropy Harvard U., 1998-90; chmn. dept. history U. Chgo., 1976-79. Lectr. Jefferson Meml., U. Calif., Berkeley, 1991. Author: Executive Reorganization and Reform in the New Deal, 1963, Presiential Planning and Social Science Research, 1969, Charles E. Merriam and the Study of Politics, 1974, Public Administration and American History, 1976 (Frederick Mosher award), Executive Reorganization and Presidential Power, 1978, (with Stanley N. Katz) The American Private Philantrophic Foundation and the Public Sphere 1890-1930, 1981, The Citizen and the Scholar: Ships That Crash in the Night, 1982, Corporate Philantrophy: Historical Background, 1982, The Uneasy State: The U.S. from 1915-1945, 1983, Lo, The Poor Volunteer, 1984 (with Stanley Katz) Foundations and Ruling Class Elites, 1987, The American Bureaucrat, 1987, Constitution and Central Planning, 1989, Legislatures and Bureaucracy, 1994, Foundations and Public Policy, 1995, Volunteers and Professionals, 1996, Foundations and the Federal Government, 1998, Foundations and Government, 1999. Co-recipient Faculty prize Harvard U. Press, 1962-63; Charles Warren Ctr. fellow Harvard U., 1965; Hauser Sr. Rsch. scholar, 1990—. Mem. Orgn. Am. Historians. Died July 7, 2010.

KARL, NELSON GEORGE, judge; b. Cleve., Aug. 1, 1926; s. Abe and Ida Karl; m. Alice Lillian Einstein, May 28, 1950; children: Joanne, Michael, Louis. BA, Western Res. U., 1949; JD with cum laude, Cleve. Marshall Law Sch., 1953. Bar: Ohio 1953, US Dist. Ct. (no. and ea. dists.) Ohio 1955, US Ct. Appeals (6th cir.) 1958, US Supreme Ct. 1973. Pvt. practice, Cleve., 1953—55, 1962—71, 1978—81; ptnr. Blum, Brover, Goldish & Karl, Cleve., 1955—62, Rudd, Karl, Sheerer, Lybarger & Campbell, Co., L.P.A., 1971—77; adminstrv. law judge Social Security Adminstrn., Cleve., from 1981. Gen. counsel Ohio Civil Liberties Union, 1960—66, 1975—81; instr. in bus. law Cuyahoga CC, 1965—72. Bd. dirs. Ohio Teamsters Credit Union; chmn. ACLU of Greater Cleve., 1976—77. With USN, 1944—46. Home: Cleveland, Ohio. Died Sept. 2, 2009.

KASDORF, DONALD LEE, retired manufacturing company executive; b. Chgo., July 13, 1929; s. Harry Ernst and Frances Lillian (Granquist) K.; m. Carol Jean Gaebel, July 21, 1951; children— Leslie Lynne, Donna Lee. BSBA, Northwestern U., 1960. Corp. controller Wells Mfg. Co., 1955-62; div. controller Lamb Industries, Milw., 1962-63; corp. controller Abbott Labs., North Chicago, Ill., 1963-71; sr. v.p. fin., treas. Modine Mfg. Co., Racine, Wis., 1971-86. Mem. Racine Environ. Com.; chmn. adv. bd. Salvation Army, Racine, 1977-86. Served with U.S. Army, 1951-53. Mem. Fin. Execs. Inst., Nat. Assn. Accountants, Am. Mgmt. Assn. Clubs: Racine Country. Home: Racine, Wis. Died Jan. 18, 2010.

KASTEN, RICHARD JOHN, accountant; b. Chgo., July 4, 1938; s. Victor and Margaret Dorothy (Madertz) K.; m. Karen Linet' Weindorf, June 23, 1962; 1 child, Kent Lane. BS in Mktg. Rsch., U. Ill., 1960, M in Commerce, 1962. CPA, Ill. Staff acct. Ernst & Ernst, Chgo., 1962-63, advanced staff acct., 1963-64, sr. acct., 1964-65, sr. cons., 1965-67, supr., 1967-68, mgr., 1968-72, ptnr., 1972-80; vice-chmn. cons. services Ernst & Whinney, Cleve., 1980-85, regional dir. mgmt. cons. svcs. Chgo., 1985-86, mng. ptnr. midwest cons., 1986-88, ptnr. in charge healthcare Great Lakes region, 1988-89; pres. Kasten Industries, Inc., Inverness, Ill., from 1989, Redmore Products Co., Palatine, Ill., from 1990. Chmn. fin. com. St. Joseph's Hosp., Chgo., 1978-80; active Gov. Walker's Com. on Health, Chgo., 1977. Sgt. USNG, 1962-68. Mem. AICPA (exec. com. mgmt. adv. svcs. 1981-84), Anderson com. 1983-86), Ill. CPA Soc., Hosp. Fin. Mgmt. Assn., Chgo. Club, Inverness Golf Club (fin. com. 1979-80). Republican. Lutheran. Avocations: golf, physical fitness, reading. Home: Palatine, Ill. Died Dec. 23, 2009.

KASTLER, BERNARD ZANE, retired energy executive; b. Billings, Mont., Oct. 30, 1920; s. B.Z. and Elsie (Grossman) K.; m. Donna Irene Endicott, July 24, 1948; children: Lynn, Kerry Sue. Student, U. Colo., 1940-41; LL.B. summa cum laude, U. Utah, 1949. Bar: Utah 1949, Mont. 1948, U.S. Supreme Ct., also fed. cts. Pvt. law practice, Salt Lake City, 1949-52; atty. Mountain Fuel Supply Co., Salt Lake City, 1952—58, sec., asst. treas., gen. counsel, 1958-68, v.p. fin., treas., 1968-72, pres., chief adminstrv. officer, 1972-74, 76-82, CEO, 1974-82, chmn. bd., 1976—85. Chmn. bd. Entrada Industries Inc., Mountain Fuel Resources, Inc., Wexpro Co., Celsius Energy Co., Interstate Brick Co., Interstate Land Corp.; dir. Albertson's, Inc., Bonneville Internat. Corp., Intermountain Health Care, Inc., 1st Security Corp.; mem., chmn. Rocky Mountain regional council Conf. Bd.; mem. Utah Ho. of Reps., 1963-66 Contbr. articles to profl. jours. Bd. dirs. Mountain States Legal Found.; moderator Nat. Assn. Congl. Christian Chs., 1955; trustee Westminster Coll.; co-chmn. NCCJ; mem. Latter-day Saints Hosp.-Deseret Found.; trustee Youth Tobacco Adv. Council; mem. exec. adv. com. Jr. Achievement Greater Salt Lake. Served with USNR, World War II. Mem. ABA, Utah Bar Assn., Salt Lake County Bar Assn., Mont. Bar Assn., Fed. Power Bar Assn., Ind. Natural Gas Assn., Salt Lake City C. of C. (gov. 1967-78, pres. 1977-78), U. Utah Alumni Assn., Pacific Coast Gas Assn. (chmn. 1980), Am. Gas Assn. (past dir.), Rocky Mountain Oil and Gas Assn. (past dir. and mem. operating and exec. coms.), Zion Natural History Assn. (dir.), Hon. Cols. Corp., Order of Coif, Phi Kappa Phi, Phi Delta Phi Congregationalist (former deacon and trustee). Lodges: Masons; Kiwanis. Died Nov. 22, 2009.

KASTNER, ELLIOTT, film producer; b. NYC, Jan. 7, 1930; m. Tessa Kennedy (div.); stepchildren: Cassian Elwes, Damian Elwes, Cary Elwes. Prodr.: (films) Bus Riley's Back in Town, 1965, Harper, 1966, Kaleidoscope, 1966, The Bobo, 1967, Sol Madrid, 1968, Sweet November, 1968, Where Eagles Dare, 1968, THe Night of the Following Day, 1968, Man on Horseback, 1969, Lauhgter in the Dark, 1969, Michael Kohlhaas, 1969, The Walking Stick, 1970, The Devil's Widow, 1970, A Severed Head, 1970, When Eight Bells Toll, 1971, Villain, 1971, The Nightcomers, 1971, X, Y, & Zee, 1971, Fear Is the Key, 1972, Count Your Bullets, 1972, Cry for Me, Billy, 1972, The Long Goodbye, 1973, Jeremy, 1973, Cops & Robbers, 1973, Face to the Wind, 1974, 11 Harrow House, 1974, 92 in the Shade, 1975, Dogpound Shuffle, 1975, Rancho Deluxe, 1975, Farewell, My Lovely, 1975, Breakheart Pass, 1976, Russian Roulette, 1975, The Missouri Breaks, 1976, Swashbuckler, 1976, The Stick-Up, 1977, Equus, 1977, Black Joy, 1977, The Big Sleep, 1978, Absolution, 1978, A Little Night Music, 1978, The Medusa Touch, 1978, Yesterday's Hero, 1979, ffolkes, 1979, Goldengirl, 1979, The First Deadly Sin, 1980, Death Valley, 1982, Man, Woman & Child, 1983, Garbo Talks, 1984, Oxford Blues, 1984, Nomads, 1986, Heat, 1986, Angel Heart, 1987, White of the Eye, 1987, Zombie High, 1987, Zits, 1988, Never on Tuesday, 1988, Jack's Back, 1988, The Blob, 1998, A Chorus of Disapproval, 1989, Homeboy, 1990, The Last Party, 1993, Frank and Jesse, 1994, Love Is All There Is, 1996, Sweet November, 2001, Opa!, 2005, The Madman's Tale, 2009; (TV movies) Mr. Horn, 1979 Died June 30, 2010.

KATCHER, AVRUM L., pediatrician; b. Phila., Aug. 28, 1925; s. William and Anna (Cahan) K.; m. Estelle Sklar, Nov. 4, 1957; children: Ruth, Susan, Eva, Daniel. Student, Pa. State Coll., 1942-44; MD, Johns Hopkins U., 1948. Intern Johns Hopkins Hosp., Balt., 1948-49; resident, fellow in pediatrics Mt. Sinai Hosp., NYC, 1949-52; asst. prof. clin. pediatrics U. Pa. and Childrens Hosp., Phila., 1955-59; dir. pediatrics Hunterdon Med. Ctr., Flemington, N.J., 1959-87. Prof. clin. pediatrics Robert Wood Johnson Med. Sch., New Brunswick, N.J., 1975—. Contbr. articles to profl. jours. Founder Hunterdon Occupational Tng. Ctr., 1972; active N.J. Com. Humanities, New Brunswick, 1984-90. Capt. U.S. Army, 1952-55. Fellow Am. Acad. Pediat. (chmn. N.J. chpt. 1975-78, com. child disabilities 1984-90, Diagnostic and Statis. Manual for Primary Care in Children work group, sr. sect. exec. com. 1997—); mem. AAAS. Home: Flemington, NJ. Died June 4, 2010.

KATSAKIORES, GEORGE NICHOLAS, state legislator, retired food service executive; b. Derry, NH, Dec. 11, 1924; s. Nicholas G. and Agorista (Siatravinos) K.; m. Lucille Brunelle, Nov. 11, 1963 (div. July 1980); children: Sheila, Glen, Greg, Karen, Gary; m. Phyllis M. Harrie, Oct. 9, 1983 Grad., U. NH. Owner White's Restaurant, Derry, 1948—88, ret., 1988; mem. Derry Dist. 5 NH House of Reps., 1982—2010, chair Transp. Com., 1982—91, chmn. emeritus, 1991. Dir. Derry Devel. and Preservation Corp.; vice chmn. Airport Access Hwy. Task Force, Manchester, N.H.; mem. transp. task force Am. Legis. Exch. Coun., Washington, 1984—; apptd. to N.H. Integrated Trans. and R.R. Coun., 1985—, Internat. Hellenic Union, 2004- Dir. Derry Devel. and Preservation Corp.; vice chmn. Airport Access Hwy. Task Force, Manchester, NH; mem. transp. task force Am. Legis. Exch. Coun., Washington, from 1984; apptd. to NH Integrated Transp. and RR Coun., from 1985, Internat. Hellenic Union, from 2004; dir. NE Corridor Initiative, Boston, Greater Derry/Saleit Transp. Coun., Nutfield Sr. Devel. Corp., Cmty. Alliance Regional Transp.; mem. Rockingham County Com., Brentwood, NH, from 1998; chmn. Rock City Del., 1999—2004, Rep. Nat. Party, NH Rep. Com., from 1982; bd. dirs. Cmty. Alliance for Regional Transp. Cpl. med. corps US Army, 1943—45, ETO. Recipient Ahepa Nat. Svc. award, 2008; Inducted into Pinkerton Acad. Hall of Fame, 1999 Mem. VFW (Post 1617), AARP, Nat. Coun. State Legislators (trans-com.), N.H. Transp. and Hwy. Users Coalition, N.H. R.R. Revitalization Assn., Internat. Hellenic Union, Am. Legion, Hoodkroft County Club (Derry) Greek Orthodox. Avocations: golf, politics, gardening. Died Feb. 1, 2010.

KATZ, LEON, retired packaging company executive; b. Springfield, Mass., Aug. 27, 1921; s. Frederick and Sarah (Kirsner) K.; m. Blossom Shirley Zeidman, June 8, 1947; children: Stanley G., Barbara D., Nancy L. BS, Trinity Coll., 1944; PhD in Organic Chemistry, U. Ill., 1947. With GAF Corp., 1953-70; v.p. research and devel.; exec. v.p. Rockwood Industries, 1970-72; v.p. comml. devel. Polychrome Corp., 1972-73; v.p. research and devel. packaging div. Am. Can Co., 1973-80, v.p. gen. mgr. recovery systems and research and devel. fiber, 1980-82; sr. v.p. corp. research and devel. James River Corp., Norwalk, Conn., 1982-85, v.p. corp. tech., 1985-89, cons., from 1989. Patentee in field; contbr. articles to profl. jours. Served with AUS, 1943-44. Named to Hall of Fame Packaging, 1992. Mem. Am. Chem. Soc., AAAS, Sigma Xi, Pi Mu Epsilon, Phi Lambda Upsilon. Died Feb. 13, 2010.

KATZ, MARVIN, federal judge; b. Phila., Nov. 22, 1930; m. Relli Eisenberg; 1 child, Robert. BA, U. Pa., 1951; LL.B., Yale U., 1954. Law clk. to Hon. Francis X. McClanaghan Ct. Common Pleas, 1959—60; pvt. law practice, 1954-77; asst. to the commr. IRS, 1977-81; assoc. Mesirov, Gelman, Jaffe, Cramer & Jamieson, Phila., 1981-83; judge US Dist. Ct. (ea. dist.) Pa., Phila., 1983-97, sr. judge, 1997—2010. Died Oct. 12, 2010.

KAUFFMAN, JOHN THOMAS, utility executive; b. Weehawken, NJ, Aug. 17, 1926; s. William Carl and Frances E. K.; m. Julia A. Crouch, Aug. 19, 1949; children: Anne E. Kauffman Zayaitz, Janet L. BS in Marine Engring, U.S. Mcht. Marine Acad., 1946; BS in Mech. Engring, Purdue U., 1950. Test engr. Pa. Water & Power Co. (merger with Pa. Power & Light Co. 1960), Holtwood, 1950-52, various engring. positions, 1952-60; asst. plant betterment engr. Pa. Power & Light Co., Allentown, 1960-64, constrn. supt.-elec. and structural, 1964-70, supt. generation, 1970-73, asst. v.p. system power and engring., 1973-74, v.p. system power and engring., 1974-78, exec. v.p. ops., 1978-89, exec. v.p., chief exec. officer, 1989-90, chmn., pres., chief exec. officer, 1990-91, chmn., chief exec. officer, from 1991. Bd. dirs. Assn. Edison Illuminating Cos. Active Pennsylvanians for Effective Govt., Harrisburg, 1990—; mem. adv. com. Minsi Trails Coun. Boy Scouts Am., Allentown; bd. dirs. U.S. Coun. Energy Awareness, Washington, 1990—, Am. Nuclear Energy Coun., Washington, 1990—, U.S. Chamber's Ctr. for Workforce Preparation and Quality Edn., Washington, 1990—, Pa. 2000, Lehigh Valley 2000, Bus.-Edn. Partnership, Lehigh Valley Partnership, Quality Valley-USA, Lehigh Valley Bus. Conf. on Health Care; mem. Conf. Bd., N.Y.C.; bd. dirs. Hillside Sch. for Learning Disabled Children, pres.' adv. bd. Good Shepherd Home. Mem. ASME, Pa. Electric Assn. (past chmn.), Pa. Chamber Bus. and Industry (bd. dirs. 1990—), Pa. Bus. Roundtable (bd. dirs. 1990—), The Nature Conservancy (bd. dirs. Ea. Pa. chpt. 1990—), Pa. Soc. Clubs: N.E. River Yacht; Brookside Country (Allentown). Home: Oxford, Pa. Died Feb. 28, 2010.

KAUFMAN, IRVING, retired engineering educator; b. Geinsheim, Germany, Jan. 11, 1925; came to US., 1938, naturalized, 1945; s. Albert and Hedwig Kaufmann; m. Ruby Lee Dordek, Sept. 10, 1950; children— Eve Deborah, Sharon Anne, Julie Ellen. BE, Vanderbilt U., 1945; MS, U. Ill., 1949, PhD, 1957. Engr. RCA Victor, Indpls., Ind. and Camden, NJ, 1945-48; instr., research assoc. U. Ill., Urbana, 1949-56; sr. mem. tech. staff Ramo-Wooldridge & Space Tech. Labs., Calif., 1957-64; prof. engring. Ariz. State U., 1965-94, ret., 1994; founder, dir. Solid State Research Lab., 1968-78. Collaborator Los Alamos Nat. Lab., 1989, 91; vis. scientist Consiglio Nazionale delle Ricerche, Italy, 1973-74; vis. prof. U. Auckland, N.Z., 1974; liaison scientist U.S. Office Naval Rsch., London, 1978-80; lectr. and cons. elec. engring. Contbr. articles to profl. jours. and encys.; patentee in field. Recipient Disting. Research award Ariz. State U. Grad. Coll., 1986-87; Sr. Fulbright research fellow Italy, 1964-65, 73-74, Am. Soc. for Engring. Edn./Naval Rsch. Lab. fellow, 1988. Fellow IEEE (life, Phoenix sect. leadership award 1994); mem. Electromagnetics Acad., Gold Key (hon.), Sigma Xi, Tau Beta Pi, Eta Kappa Nu, Pi Mu Epsilon. Jewish. Home: Tempe, Ariz. Died July 14, 2010.

KAYSEN, CARL, economics professor; b. Phila., Mar. 5, 1920; s. Samuel and Elizabeth (Resnick) K.; m. Annette Neutra, Sept. 13, 1940 (dec. 1990); children: Susanna, Laura; m. Ruth Butler, 1994. AB, U. Pa., 1940; PhD, Harvard U., 1954. Rschr. Nat. Bur. Econ. Rsch., 1940-42; economist OSS, 1942; mem. faculty Harvard U., 1950—66; jr. fellow Harvard U. (Soc. Fellows), 1947-50, asst. prof. economics, 1950-55, assoc. prof., 1955-57, prof., 1957-66, Lucius N. Littauer prof. polit. economy, 1964-66; assoc. dean Harvard U. (Grad. Sch. Public Adminstrn.), 1960-66; dir. Inst. Advanced Study, Princeton, NJ, 1966-76, prof., 1966-77; David W. Skinner prof. polit. economy MIT, 1977-90, dir. program in sci., tech. and soc., 1981-87, prof. emeritus, 1990—2010. Clk. to Judge C. E. Wyzanski, US Dist. C., 1950-52; dep. spl. asst. to Pres. Kennedy for nat. security affairs, 1961-63; mem. Carnegie Commn. on Higher Edn.; vice chmn., dir. rsch. Sloan Commn. on Govt. and Higher Edn.; faculty lectr. London Sch. Econs., 1956; Haynes lectr. Calif. Inst. Tech., 1966; Stafford Little lectr. Princeton U., 1968; Oliver W. Holmes lectr. Harvard Law Sch., 1969; Paley lectr. Hebrew U., Jerusalem, 1970; Godkin lectr. Harvard U., 1976; Bernard Brodie lectr., UCLA, 1994. Hon. Life trustee U. Pa. Served to capt. air intelligence AUS, 1942-45. Fulbright scholar London Sch. Econs., 1955-56; Guggenheim fellow, 1955-56; Ford Found. fellow Greece, 1959-60 Mem. Am. Philos. Soc., Am. Acad. Arts and Scis., Phi Beta Kappa. Clubs: Century (NYC). Home: Cambridge, Mass. Died Feb. 8, 2010.

KAZAN, BENJAMIN, electrical engineer, researcher; b. NYC, May 8, 1917; s. Abraham Eli and Esther (Bookbinder) K.; m. Gerda B. Mosse, Nov. 4, 1988; 1 child from previous marriage, David Louis. BS in Physics, Calif. Inst. Tech., 1938; MA in Physics, Columbia U., 1940; PhD in Physics, Tech. U. Munich, 1961. Radio engr. Dept. Def., Ft. Monmouth, NJ, 1940-50; nrsch. engr. RCA Labs., Princeton, NJ, 1950-58; head solid state display group Hughes Rsch. Lab., Malibu, Calif., 1958-61; head imaging sect. Electro-Optical Sys., Pasadena, Calif., 1961-68; head exploratory display group T.J. Watson Rsch. Ctr., Yorktown Heights, NY, 1968-74; prin. scientist Xerox Rsch. Ctr., Palo Alto, Calif., 1974-85; cons. display and imaging tech., from 1985. Cons. Advisory Group Electron Devices, Dept. Def., 1973-82; adj. prof. U. R.I., Kingston, 1970-74. Author: (with others) Storage Tubes, 1952, Electronic Image Storage, 1968; editor: Advances in Image Storage, 1968, Advances in Image Pickup and Display series, 1972-84; assoc. editor Advances in Imaging and electron Physics series, 1984—; contbr. articles to profl. jours., patentee in field. Recipient silver medal Am. Roentgen Ray Soc., 1957. Fellow IEEE (assoc. editor Jour. Electron Devices 1979-83), Soc. Info. Display (editor jour. 1974-78); mem. Am. Phys. Soc., Sigma Xi, Tau Beta Pi. Home: Los Gatos, Calif. Died Jan. 24, 2009.

KEARNEY, DENNIS FERRELL, English language educator; b. Chattanooga, Tenn., Feb. 18, 1959; s. Ferrell Frank and Barbara (Ann) K.; m. Lori Denise Poteat, Mar. 7, 1980 (div. 1989); children: Colleen Mist, Phillip Adam, Christopher Julien; m. Maryse Danielle Francoise Bonaventure, June 29, 1991. BA, Tenn. Temple U., 1983; MA, Mid. Tenn. State U., 1986; PhD, U. Miss., 1990. Instr. U. Miss., Oxford, 1990-91; asst. prof. English Lindsey Wilson Coll., Columbia, Ky., from 1991. Author: Clarus Saga: An Edition and Translation, 1991, various short stories. Mem. MLA. Avocations: reading, guitar, sports, travel. Died Dec. 19, 2009.

KEARNEY, JOSEPH LAURENCE, retired athletic conference administrator; b. Pitts., Apr. 28, 1927; s. Joseph L. and Iva M. (Nikirk) K.; m. Dorothea Hurst, May 13, 1950; children: Jan Marie, Kevin Robert, Erin Lynn, Shawn Alane, Robin James. BA, Seattle Pacific U., 1952, LLD, 1979; MA, San Jose State U., 1964; EdD, U. Wash., 1970. Tchr., coach Paradise (Calif.) H.S., 1952-53; asst. basketball coach U. Wash., 1953-54, athletic dir., assoc. dir., 1964-76; coach, tchr. Sunnyside (Wash.) H.S., 1954-57; prin., coach Onalaska (Wash.) H.S., 1957-61; prin. Tumwater (Wash.) H.S., 1961-63; asst. dir. Wash. H.S. Activities Assn., 1963-64; athletic dir. intercollegiate athletics Mich. State U., East Lansing, 1976-80, Ariz. State U., Tempe, 1980; commr. Western Athletic Conf., Denver, 1990—94. Hon. chmn. Holiday Bowl, 1994, commr. emeritus, 1994-2010 Pres. Cmty. Devel. Assn., 1957-61; bd. dirs. U.S. Olympic Com., 1985-94, chmn. games preparation com., 1985-2001. With USN, 1945—47. Recipient Disting. Svc. award Mich. Assn. Professions, 1979, Citation for Disting. Svc. Colo. Sports Hall of Fame, U.S. Olympic Com. Order of Olympic Shield, 1996; named to Paradise HS Athletic Hall of Fame, Calif., 2007. Mem. Nat. Football Found. (ct. of honors com., Western Regional Leadership award 1999), NCAA, Nat. Assn. Collegiate Dirs. Athletics (Corbett award 1991, Adminstr. Excellence award), Collegiate Commrs. Assn. (pres., award of Merit 1998), Am. Football Assn. (Commrs. award 1996, Athletic Dir.'s award 1998). Home: Tucson, Ariz. Died May 5, 2010.

KEATON, WILLIAM THOMAS, academic administrator, pastor; b. England, Ark., Aug. 29, 1921; m. Theresa Simpson, July 29, 1946; children: Sherrye Ann, William II, Bernard, Denise, Edwin, Karen, Renwick, Zelda, Aloysius. AA, Ark. Bapt. Coll., 1940-42; BA, U. Ark., 1948; MA, Columbia U., 1951. Supt. Howard County Sch. Dist. #38, Mineral Springs, Ark., 1951-56, East Side Sch. Dist., Menifee, Ark., 1956-61; prin. Quachita County High Sch., Bearden, Ark., 1961-68, Peake High Sch., Arkadelphia, Ark., 1968-70; coord. state programs Ark. Dept. Edn., Little Rock, 1970-85; pres. Ark. Baptist Coll., Little Rock, from 1985. Vis. prof. Ala. State U., 1972; researcher Office of Edn., Washington, 1973; state insvc. coord. Region VI-AR, staff devel. specialist, Little Rock, 1970-85; staff assoc. adult edn. U. Tex., Austin, 1967-70, Lafayette, La., 1972; pastor Greater Mt. Zion Bapt. Ch., Ashdown, Ark., 1951-72, Greater Pleasant Hill Bapt. Ch.,

Arkadelphia, Ark., 1972-79, Canaan Missionary Bapt. Ch., Little Rock, 1979—; mem. pres. adv. bd. dirs. Historically Black Colls. and U., 1989. Mem. NCCJ, NEA (life), NAACP (life), Ark. Edn. Assn., Ark. Adult Edn. Assn. (pres. 1969-70), Union Dist. Assn. (dean 1980—), Nat. Assn. Pub. Continuing Edn., Nat. Assn. Equal Opportunity Higher Edn. (sec. 1988-93, bd. dirs. 1989), Masons, Alpha Phi Alpha, Phi Delta Kappa. Democrat. Baptist. Home: Little Rock, Ark. Died Feb. 26, 2010.

KEBABIAN, PAUL BLAKESLEE, retired librarian; b. Watch Hill, RI, July 24, 1917; s. John Couzu and Edith Jennie (Blakeslee) K.; m. Justine Richardson, Nov. 21, 1942; children: Jean Edith, Ann Ruth, Helen Jane; m. Johanna Thomas, Jan. 27, 1995. BA, Yale U., 1938; BS, Columbia U., 1948. Cataloger, supr. exchanges Yale U. Library, New Haven, 1939-42, 46-47; chief cataloger preparation div. N.Y. Pub. Library, 1949-61, 62-63; Ford Found. program specialist Library of U. Baghdad, Iraq, 1961-62; asso. dir. libraries U. Fla., Gainesville, 1963-66; dir. libraries U. Vt., Burlington, 1966-82. Assoc. prof. library sci. U. Fla., 1963-66; cons. in field. Author: American Woodworking Tools, 1978; co-editor, contbr.: Tools and Technologies— America's Wooden Age, 1979; contbr. articles to profl. jours. Served with USAAF, 1942-46. Mem. ALA, Assn. Coll. and Research Libraries, Midwest Tool Collectors Assn., Early Am. Industries Assn. (past pres., dir. 1970-82, editor 1982-84, contbr. Chronicle), Vt. Hist. Soc., Antique Crafts and Tools in Vermont (past pres., editor 1973-88), N.Eng. Tool Collectors Assn. (editor 1988-95). Democrat. Home: Jamesville, NY. Died Oct. 12, 2009.

KECK, JAMES COLLYER, retired physicist; b. NYC, June 11, 1924; s. Charles and Anne (Collyer) K.; m. Margaret Ramsey, Sept. 6, 1947; children: Robert Lyon, Patricia Anne. BA, Cornell U., 1947, PhD, 1951. Research asst. Cornell U., 1951-52; sr. research fellow Calif. Inst. Tech., 1952-55; prin. scientist Avco-Everett Research Lab., Everett, Mass., 1955-65, dep. dir., 1960-64; Ford prof. engring. MIT, Cambridge, 1965-89, prof. emeritus, 1989—2010. Served with AUS, 1944-46. Fellow Am. Acad. Sci., Nat. Acad. Engring.; mem. Am. Phys. Soc., Combustion Inst., Phi Beta Kappa, Sigma Xi, Phi Kappa Phi. Achievements include research on high energy photonuclear reactions, theory of chem. reaction rates, high temperature gas dynamics, combustion, air pollution, thermodynamics, thermionics. Home: Andover, Mass. Died Aug. 9, 2010.

KEE, THOMAS JOHN, III, army officer; b. Everette, Mass., July 30, 1955; s. Thomas John, Jr. and Carol Ann (Falconer) K. BS in Engring., U.S. Mil. Acad., 1979; student U.S. Army Flight Sch., 1980. 2d lt. U.S. Army, 1979, advanced through grades to capt., 1983; helicopter platoon leader, Korea, 1980-81, Fort Belvoir, Va., 1982-83; brigade ops. and intelligence officer Davison Aviation Command, Fort Belvoir, 1983-84, exec. officer, fixed wing platoon leader, fixed wing ops. officer, 1984-85; comdr. HHD 70th Transp. Bn.; army rep. Hearst Senate Youth Found., 1983, White House Social Aid, 1984. Mem. Army Aviation Assn. Am. Avocations: competitive sailing, scuba, flying, gourmet cuisine. Died Mar. 6, 2010.

KEENER, RICHARD NORRIS, office furniture manufacturing executive; b. Lancaster, Pa., Aug. 17, 1928; s. Irvin L. and Hilda W. (Buckley) Keener; m. Doris Ann Holthaus Keener, Sept. 30, 1950; children: Alan, Mark, Kevin, Lynne, David, Richard. BS, U. Wis., 1950. Div. mgr. Am. Seating Co., Grand Rapids, Mich., 1955—69, dir. mktg. rsch., 1969—73, v.p. corp. devel., 1973—78, pres. internat., 1978—82; pres., dir. mgr. interior sys. divsn. Interiors Internat. Inc., Grand Rapids, 1983—86. Co-owner, pres., chief exec. officer Keener-Blodee, Inc., Holland, Mich., from 1987. Mem.: Am Mgmt. Assn. Home: Grand Rapids, Mich. Died Nov. 24, 2009.

KEIL, ROBERT MATTHES, retired chemical company executive; b. Bloomefield, NJ, Apr. 5, 1926; s. Wiiliam August and Myra (Maguire) K.; m. Betty Jane Apgar, May 3, 1952; children: Barbara Lynn, Nancy Lee. BS, Syracuse U., 1948. Gen. mgr. olefin plastics Dow Chem. U.S.A., Midland, Mich., 1969-76, v.p. consumer goods and services, 1976-78, v.p. mktg., 1978-79, exec. v.p., 1979-80; fin. v.p. Dow Chem. Co., Midland, Mich., 1980-82, exec. v.p., from 1982, also bd. dirs. Bd. dirs. Midland, Comerica Bank, Detroit; chmn. Dow Chem. Que. Ltd., 1978-82. Pres. Midland Community Ctr., 1976-77, trustee. Lt. U.S. Army, 1943-46, 51-52. Home: Midland, Mich. Died Mar. 2, 2010.

KEIM, BETTY LOU, actress, literary consulant; b. Malden, Mass., Sept. 27, 1938; d. Buster and Dorothy Clair (Tracy) Keim; m. Warren Berlinger, Feb. 18, 1960; children: Lisa, David, Edward, Elizabeth. Grad., Lodge Acad., NYC, 1956. Appeared in films These Wilder Years, 1956, Teenage Rebel, 1956, Wayward Bus, 1957, Some Came Running, 1958; appeared on Broadway in Strange Fruit, Rip Van Winkle, Crime and Punishment, Texas Lil Darlin, The Remarkable Mr. Pennypacker, Roomful of Roses; appeared on TV in Omnibus, Playhouse 90, Alcoa Hour, Philco PlayHouse; appeared in TV series My Son Jeep, The Deputy. Assoc. Aid Project LA, 1984-97; life mem., vol. Actors Fund of Am. Recipinet Motion Picture award Calif. Women's Club, 1956, Filmdoms Famous Five award Film Daily Critics, 1956, Laurel award, 1956. Home: Chatsworth, Calif. Died Jan. 27, 2010.

KEIM, BRIAN T., lawyer; b. West Chester, Pa., Mar. 22, 1943; m. Catharine Keim; children: Todd, John, Laura. BA, Yale U., 1965; LLB, U. Pa., 1968. Bar: D.C. 1969, Pa. 1970. Law clk. US Tax Ct., Washington, 1968—70; atty. Ballard Spahr Andrews & Ingersoll, Phila., 1970—77, Frankfurt, Salt Lake City, Washington DC, 1980—98; sr. v.p., gen. counsel Barber Oil Corp., 1977—80; v.p., gen. counsel LWB Refractories Co., York, Pa., 1998—2009. Trustee Meadowbrook Sch., 1980—94, pres., 1986—90; chmn. bd. Artman Lutheran Home, 1992—99; chmn., bd. Liberty Lutheran Services, 2001—05; council mem. St. Paul's Lutheran Church, 2005—10, v.p., 2005—09, pres., 2009—10. Mem.: ABA, Phila. Bar Assn., Pa. Bar Assn., American Rhododendron Soc. (pres. Greater Phila. Chapter 1989—94). Lutheran. Died Aug. 26, 2010.

KELLER, BRIAN DAVID, marine ecologist; b. Boston, Apr. 26, 1948; s. William John and Rosemary (Kelsey) K.; m. Geryld Louise Johnson, June 1970 (div. 1975); m. Fiona Coralie Wilmot, May 17, 1986. BS, Mich. State U., 1970; PhD, Johns Hopkins U., 1976. Rsch. oceanographer Scripps Inst. Oceanography, La Jolla, Calif., 1976-79; rsch. assoc. Yale U., New Haven, 1980-84; acting head, rsch. fellow Discovery Bay Marine Lab., Jamaica, 1984-86; project mgr. Smithsonian Tropical Rsch. Inst., Panama, 1987-94; exec. dir. Ecol. Soc. Am., Washington, from 1994. Contbr. articles to profl. jours.; editor tech. reports. Grantee Sigma Xi, 1973-75, Geol. Soc. Am., 1973. Mem. AAAS, Ecol. Soc. Am., Soc. Conservation Biology, Am. Inst. Biol. Sci., Am. Soc. Assn. Execs., Coun. Engring. and Sci. Soc. Execs. Home: Marathon, Fla. Died Mar. 10, 2010.

KELLER, EDWARD CLARENCE, JR., foundation executive, ecologist, statistician, geneticist, educator; b. Freehold, NJ, Oct. 8, 1932; s. Edward Clarence and Pauline (Van Sickle) K.; children: Edward Clarence III, Kim Lorie. BSc, Pa. State U., 1956, MSc, 1959, PhD, 1961; ScD, Salem Coll., 1978. Faculty Pa. State U., 1956-61, NIH fellow, 1959-60; NIH fellow, research assoc. U. N.C. med. Sch., 1961-64; assoc. prof. U. Md., College Park, 1964-67; mgr. data systems and biostatistics biol. systems div. NUS Corp., Hawthorne, Calif., 1967-68; prof. biology W.Va. U., Morgantown, 1968-74, chmn. dept. biology, 1969-74; v.p. Ecometrics, Inc., Morgantown, 1973-85. Vis. prof. sci. edn. U. Md., 1980; cons. various industry groups, various govtl. agys.; sec. Found. for Sci. and Disability, 1977-86, v.p., 1988-90, pres., 1990-92; sci. edn. adv. com. NSF, 1985-87, equal opportunity in sci. com., 1988-92, mem. NSF task force disabled persons in sci. and engring., 1990-91, expert on disabled persons in sci. and engring., 1991-92; dir. of many NSF programs for youth with disabilities; chmn. adv. bd. spl. edn. NSTA, 1989-94, mem. adv. bd. on spl. edn., 1988—. Co-author books and lab. manuals; contbr. articles to profl. jours.; reviewer fed. agys. and sci. jours. Mem. AAAS, Nat. Sci. Tchrs. Assn., Am. Statis. Assn., W.Va. Acad. Sci. (pres. 1977-78, editor procs. 1980-94, Nat. Found. alumnus of yr. 1965), Found. for Sci. and Disability (sec. 1975-90, pres. 1991-92, treas. 1993—, editor newsletter), Sci. Assn. Disabled Persons (v.p. 1995-97), Sigma Xi, Gamma Sigma Delta, Phi Epsilon Phi, Phi Sigma, Beta Beta Beta. Home: Morgantown, W.Va. Died Mar. 18, 2010.

KELLER, ELIOT AARON, broadcast executive; b. Davenport, Iowa, June 11, 1947; s. Norman Edward and Millie (Morris) Keller; m. Sandra Kay McGrew, July 3, 1970; 1 child, Nicole. BA, U. Iowa, 1970; MS, San Diego State U., 1976. Corr. Sta. WHO-AM-FM-TV, Des Moines, 1969-70; newsman Sta. WSUI-AM, Iowa City, 1968-70; newsman, corr. Sta. WHBF-AM-FM-TV, Rock Island, Ill., 1969; newsman Sta. WOC-AM-FM-TV, Davenport, Iowa, 1970; freelance newsman and photographer Iowa City, 1969-77; pres., bd. dirs. mem. KZIA, Inc. (formerly KRNA, Inc. and Communicators, Inc.), Cedar Rapids, from 1971, treas., 2003—09; gen. mgr. Sta. KRNA FM, Iowa City, 1974-98, Sta. KQCR FM, Cedar Rapids, 1994-95, Sta. KXMX FM, 1995—98, Sta. KZIA-FM, from 1998, Sta. KGYM-AM, from 2006. Dir. KZIA, Inc. (formerly KRNA, Inc. and Communicators, Inc.), Cedar Rapids, Iowa; adj. instr. dept. comm. studies U. Iowa, Iowa City, 1983, 84; mem. adv. bd. dept. comm. arts Wartburg Coll., Waverly, from 2001; mem. prof. adv. bd. Sch. Journalism and Mass Comm. U. Iowa, from 2002. Recipient Hall of Fame, Iowa Broadcasters Assn., 2009; named Corridorian of Yr., Assess Iowa, Ceder Rapids, Iowa, 2009, Broadcaster of Yr., Iowa Broadcasters Assn., 2001; named to Hall of Fame, 2004. Mem.: Iowa City Area C. of C. (chmn. local govt. task force 1981, chmn. transp. subcom. 2000—05, vice chmn. 2004—05, chmn. legis. coun. 2005—09, named Vol. of Yr. 2004), Iowa Assn. R.R. Passengers (chmn. excursion from 1988), R.R. Passenger Car Alliance, Mid-Continent Rlwy. Hist. Soc. (bd. dir. 2000—03). Jewish. Home: Iowa City, Iowa. Died Dec. 28, 2009.

KELLER, JOHN MILTON, gynecologist, obstetrician, educator; b. Phila., Jan. 12, 1922; s. Frederick E. and Ruth (Lock) Keller; m. Ruth C. Stranford Keller, Apr. 28, 1929; children: John Frederick, Brian Keith. BA, W. Va. U., 1943; MD, Jefferson Med. Coll., 1946. Diplomate Am. Bd. Ob-Gyn. Resident ob-gyn. St. John's Hosp., Bklyn., 1951—54; clin. fellow Am. Cancer Soc., SUNY, Bklyn., 1954—55; attending obstetrician gynecologist Williston, ND, 1955—62, Geisinger Med. Ctr., Danville, Pa., 1962—69; assoc. prof. Abraham Lincoln Sch. Med., U. Ill., Chgo., 1969—70, U. Health Scis., Chgo. Med. Sch., 1971—74; prof. u. health scis. Chgo. Med. Sch., 1974—80; assoc. clin prof. Peoria Sch. Medicine, U. Ill., from 1982; clin. prof. Creighton U. Sch. Medicine, 1983—90; attending chief ob-gyn. Fairbury (Ill.) Hosp., 1980—84; sr. attending Colposcopy Clinic, St. Francis Hosp., Peoria, 1981—84; attending ob-gyn. mem. St. Elizabeth Hosp., Bryan Meml. Hosp., Nebr., from 1984; obstetrician-gynecologist Health Am., Lincoln, from 1984. With MC US Army, 1947—49. Geisinger Med. Ctr. grantee, 1968, grant, 1971—72. Mem.: AMA, ACS, Lancaster County Med. Soc., Nebr. Med. Soc., Chgo. Gynecol. Soc., Am. Inst. Ultrasound Medicine, Am. Soc. Colposcopy, Am. Coll. Ob-Gyn, Shriner, Masons (32 degree). Republican. Lutheran. Home: Naples, Fla. Died Aug. 18, 2010.

KELLEY, JOHN JOSEPH, JR., lawyer; b. Cleve., June 17, 1936; s. John Joseph and Helen (Meier) K.; m. Gloria Hill, June 20, 1959; children: John Joseph III, Scott MacDonald, Christopher Taft, Megan Meredith. BS cum laude in Commerce, Ohio U., 1958; LL.B., Case Western Res. U., 1960. Bar: Ohio bar 1960. Clk. firm Walter & Haverfield, Cleve., 1957-60; assoc. Walter, Haverfield, Buescher & Chockley, Cleve., 1960-66, partner, 1967-72; chief exec. officer Fleischmann Enterprises, Cin., 1972-77; pvt. practice law Cin., 1977-87; ptnr. Kohnen & Patton, Cin., from 1988. Chmn. bd. Basic Packaging Systems, Inc., 1982-87; dir. Orgamac Leasing Ltd; pres. Naples Devel. Inc., 1974-87, Yankee Leasing Co. Mem. Lakewood (Ohio) City Council, 1965-72, pres., 1972; mem. exec. com. Cuyahoga County (Ohio) Republican Central Com., 1965-72; mem. Hamilton County (Ohio) Rep. Policy Com.; Ohio chmn. Robert Taft, Jr. Senate Campaign Com., 1970, 76; bd. govs. Case Western Res. U., 1961, 84-87. Mem. ABA, Assn. Ohio Commodores, Ohio State Bar Assn., Cin. Bar Assn., Cin. Country Club, Queen City Club (Cin.), Wyndemere Country Club (Naples). Home: Cincinnati, Ohio. Died Mar. 18, 2010.

KELLISON, JAMES BRUCE, lawyer; b. Richmond, Va., June 18, 1922; s. John Ray and Clara (Cato) K.; m. Audrey Cresswell, May 5, 1962; children: Bruce, Jr., Elizabeth, Julia. BA, U. Richmond, 1943; JD, George Washington U., 1948. Bar: D.C. 1948. Ptnr. Hogan & Hartson LLP, Washington, 1954-73, Altmann Kellison & Siegler, Washington, 1973-83; pvt. practice Washington, 1983—2007. Mem. adv. com. on rules of probate procedure Superior Ct., 1972-94. Pres., bd. trustees Louise Home, 1971-2010; trustee, Columbia Lighthouse for the Blind, 1969-76; trustee Audubon Naturalist Soc., 1968-71. Served with USNR, 1943-45. Fellow Am. Coll. Trust and Estate Counsel; mem. Am., D.C. bar assns., Omicron Delta Kappa, Lambda Chi Alpha, Phi Delta Phi. Clubs: Metropolitan (Washington), Barristers (Washington), St. Albans Tennis (Washington); Chevy Chase (Md.); Lawyers (Washington). Republican. Home: Seattle, Wash. Died Mar. 16, 2010.

KELLMAN, JOSEPH, small business owner; b. Chgo., Jan. 7, 1920; s. Jacob and Celia (Weinstein) K.; m. Marjorie Lewin, June 6, 1941 (div. May 1983, dec.); children: Jack, Celia (dec.), Richard; m. Lou Ann Hancock, June 16, 1983. Grad., Plamondon Primary Sch., Chgo., 1934; EdD (hon.), Nat. Coll. Edn., Chgo., 1989. Owner The Globe Group, Chgo., 1953—97. Founder Better Boys Found., Chgo., 1961, Corp./Community Schs. Am., Chgo., 1988; bd. dirs. Spl. Children's Charities, Chgo., 1989—. Mem. Businessmen for Profl. Interest (bd. dirs.), Nat. Glass Assn., Auto Glass Industry Coun., B'nai B'rith. Democrat. Jewish. Home: Chicago, Ill. Died Jan. 7, 2010.

KELLOGG, RALPH HENDERSON, physiologist, educator; b. New London, Conn., June 7, 1920; s. Edwin Henry and Constance Louise (Henderson) K. BA, U. Rochester, NYC, 1940, MD, 1943; PhD, Harvard U., 1953. Intern Univ. Hosps., Cleve., 1944; investigator physiology U.S. Naval Med. Rsch. Inst., Bethesda, Md., 1946; teaching fellow physiology Harvard Med. Sch., Boston, 1946-47, instr., 1947-53; asst. prof. physiology U. Calif., Berkeley, 1953-58, San Francisco, 1958-59, assoc. prof., 1959-65, prof., 1965-90, prof. emeritus, from 1990, lectr. history of health scis., 1978-90, acting chmn. physiology, 1966-70; acting chmn. history of health scis. U. Calif.-San Francisco, 1984-85. Mem. physiology study sect. NIH, 1966-70; physiology test com. Nat. Bd. Med. Examiners, 1966-73, chmn., 1969-73; com. respiration nomenclature Internat. Union Physiol. Scis., 1970-77, commn. respiratory physiology, 1975-81; editorial com. U. Calif. Press, 1972-76 Physiology editor: Stedman's Med. Dictionary, 1972-89; joint editorial bd.: Am. Jour. Physiology and Jour. Applied Physiology, 1962-66; editorial bd.: Jour. Applied Physiology, 1977-79; contbr. articles to profl. publs.; contbg. author books on physiology of saline and urea diuresis, respiration, high-altitude acclimatization, history of physiology. Served with M.C., USNR, 1943-46. Sr. rsch. fellow Harvard U., 1962-63; vis. fellow Corpus Christi Coll. Univ. Lab. Physiology, Oxford (Eng.) U., 1970-71; vis. scientist Laboratoire de Physiologie Respiratoire, Centre National de la Recherche Scientifique, Strasbourg, France, 1977; NIH rsch. grantee, 1962-76 Mem. AAAS, Am. Physiol. Soc., AAUP, Am. Assn. History of Medicine, History of Sci. Soc., Phi Beta Kappa, Sigma Xi, Alpha Omega Alpha. Clubs: Roxburghe, Harvard. Home: San Francisco, Calif. Died Oct. 22, 2009.

KELLS, RICHARD B., lawyer; b. Providence, Sept. 10, 1953; s. Richard B. and Ann M. (Pate) K. BS, Cen. Conn. State U., 1975; JD, Oklahoma City U., 1977; LLM, NYU, 1979. Bar: Okla., 1978; CPA, Okla. Assoc. Speck Philbin Fleig Trudgeon & Lutz, Oklahoma City, 1979-82, Andrews Davis et al, Oklahoma City, from 1982. Adj. instr. Oklahoma City U. Law Sch., 1980-85; instr. Okla. Soc. CPA's, 1980—, Okla. Bar Rev., 1982—. Contbr. articles to profl. jours. Mem.: KC. Republican. Home: Oklahoma City, Okla. Died Mar. 6, 2010.

KELLY, DONALD PHILIP, entrepreneur; b. Chgo., Feb. 24, 1922; s. Thomas Nicholas and Ethel M. (Healy) K.; m. Byrd M. Sullivan, Oct. 25, 1952; children: Patrick, Laura, Thomas. Student, Loyola U., Chgo., 1953-54, De Paul U., 1954-55, Harvard U., 1965. Mgr. tabulating United Ins. Co. Am., 1946-51; mgr. data processing A.B. Wrisley Co., 1951-53, Swift & Co., 1953-65, asst. controller, 1965-67, controller, 1967-68, v.p. corporate devel., controller, 1968-70, fin. v.p., dir., 1970-73, Esmark, Inc., Chgo., 1973, pres., COO, 1973-77, pres., CEO, 1977-82, chmn., pres., CEO, 1982-84; pres. Kelly, Briggs & Assocs., Inc., Chgo., 1984-86; chmn. Beatrice Co., Chgo., 1986-88; chmn., CEO E-II Holdings Inc., Chgo., 1987-88; pres., CEO D.P. Kelly & Associates,L.P., Oak Brook, 1988—2010; chmn., pres., CEO Envirodyne Industries Inc., 1989-96. With USNR, 1942-46. Mem. Chgo. Club. Died Mar. 18, 2010.

KELLY, JAMES P., lawyer; b. Boston, July 19, 1943; AB, Harvard U., 1965; JD, U. Mich., 1968. Bar: R.I. 1968, Mass. 1985. Mem. Edwards & Angell, Providence. Mem. R.I. Bar Assn. Died June 5, 2010.

KELLY, JOHN VINCENT, state legislator; b. Jersey City, July 11, 1926; s. Joseph and Mary (Silvestri) K.; m. Elizabeth Mell, 1954; children: Regina, Joseph, John, Renee. Grad., St. Peters Coll., 1951. Former mayor City of Nutley, N.J.; state assemblyman dist. 30 N.J., 1982-84; state assemblyman dist. 36 N.J., from 1986. Supr. acctg. dept. Peat, Marwick, Mitchell & Co., 1951-62; pres. Nutley Savs. & Loan Assn., 1962—. Active Nutley Sr. Citizens Housing Com., March of Dimes, exec. com. Recipient Citizen award Vet. Coun., 1978, Svc. award ARC, 1979, Outstanding Citizen award Amvets N.J., 1979, award Elks Lodge 1290, 1980, Citizenship award Hospice Ins. Essex County, 1983. Mem. Am. Legion, Optimists, Third Half Club, Nat. Assn. State Savs. & Loan Assns. Home: Nutley, NJ. Died Oct. 30, 2009.

KELLY, RICHARD JAMES, accounting company executive; b. Yonkers, N.Y., May 4, 1934; s. John J. and Margaret (Smyth) K.; BS, CCNY, 1955; m. Elaine Hubbard, Aug. 4, 1956; children: Richard James, Christopher Scott. Partner, Peat Marwick Main (name formerly KMG Main Hurdman), Stamford, Conn., 1967—. Bd. dirs. Stamford Found. CPA, N.Y., Conn., Fellow Hong Kong Soc. Chartered Accts.; mem. N.Y. State Soc. CPAs Conn. Soc. CPAs, Am. Inst. CPAs, Nat. Assn. Accts. Clubs: Landmark, Woodway Country. Author: The Advertising Budget: Preparation, Administration, Control, 1967. Cons. editor Jour. of Accountancy, 1972. Died Sept. 26, 2009.

KELLY, RICHARD SMITH, judge; b. Chgo., Jan. 18, 1925; s. Frank Brazzil and Adelaide (Smith) K.; m. Nancy G. Gibbons, Aug. 26, 1950; children: Richard Smith, Mark F., David G., Peter M., Anne M., John T., Paul T. BA, U. Mich., 1948; JD, Northwestern U., 1951. Bar: Ill. 1951. Ptnr. Springer, Bergstrom & Crowe, Chgo., 1951-55; assoc. McDermott, Will & Emery, Chgo., 1955-60; atty. Container Corp. Am., Chgo., 1960-67, asst. gen. counsel, 1967-69, gen. counsel, 1969-71, v.p., gen. counsel, 1971-77, sr. v.p., gen. counsel, 1977-83, bd. dirs., 1975-83; ptnr. Keck, Mahin & Cate, Chgo., 1983-84; assoc. judge Cir. Ct. of Cook County, Chgo., from 1984. Sec., asst. gen. counsel Marcor Inc., Chgo., 1968-71; sec., gen. counsel, 1971-78. With AUS, 1943-46. Mem. ABA, Ill. Bar Assn., Chgo. Bar Assn., Law Club, Mich. Shores Club, Econ. Club. Died May 14, 2009.

KELLY, TIMOTHY MICHAEL, magazine publisher; b. Cleve., Aug. 17, 1938; s. William Edward and Catherine Rita (Toolis) K.; m. Marcia Kathleen Hurd, Dec. 29, 1962; children: Kimberly, Shannon, Michael. Degree in Naval Sci., US Naval Acad., 1961. Aviator USN, 1961-68; dist. sales mgr. Rosemont Engring., 1968-69; regional mgr. Research & Development Mag., Cleve., 1969-79, sales mgr. Barrington, Ill., 1979-81, assoc. pub., 1981-83, v.p., pub., 1983-90, Plant Engring., Des Plaines, Ill., 1990-95, Cons.-Specifying Engr., Des Plaines, from 1995. Home: Naperville, Ill. Died Dec. 12, 2009.

KELMAN, ARTHUR, plant pathologist, educator; b. Providence, Dec. 11, 1918; s. Philip and Minnie (Kollin) K.; m. Helen Moore Parker, June 22, 1949; 1 child, Philip Joseph. BS, U. R.I., 1941, DSc (hon.), 1977; MS, N.C. State U., 1946; PhD, 1949. Faculty N.C. State U., Raleigh, 1948-65, prof., 1957-65, W.N. Reynolds distinguished prof. plant pathology, 1961-65, univ. dist. scholar, from 1990; chmn. dept. plant pathology U. Wis., Madison, 1965-75, L.R. Jones Disting. prof., 1975-89, prof. bacteriology, 1977-89, WARF Sr. Disting. Rsch. prof., 1984-89; chief scientist Competitive Grants Program Nat. Rsch. Initiative, Coop. State Rsch. Svc., USDA, 1991-93. Vis. investigator Rockefeller Inst., 1953-54; chmn. div. biol. sci. Assembly Life Sci. NRC, 1980-82, chmn. bd. basic biology, Commn. Life Scis., 1984-85 Author: The Bacterial Wilt Caused by Pseudomonas solanacearum, 1953. Served with AUS, 1942-45. NSF sr. postdoctoral fellow Cambridge (Eng.) U., 1971-72; recipient E.C. Stakman award, 1987. Fellow AAAS, Am. Acad. Arts and Scis., Am. Phytopath. Soc. (chmn. sourcebook com., councilor-at-large, v.p. 1965-66, pres. 1966-67, award of distinction 1983), Am. Acad. Microbiology; mem. NAS (coun. 1986-89, chmn. sect. applied biology 1981-83, chmn. class VI Applied biology and agrl. scis., 1988-91), Internat. Soc. Plant Pathology (v.p. 1968-73, pres. 1973-78), Soc. Gen. Microbiology, Am. Soc. Microbiology, Am. Inst. Biol. Sci., Phytopathol. Soc Japan (hon.), Sigma Xi, Alpha Zeta, Gamma Sigma Delta, Phi Kappa Phi, Phi Sigma, Xi Sigma Pi. Home: Fort Lee, NJ. Died June 29, 2009.

KELSEY, HARRY FRANKLIN, JR., academic administrator; b. Ft. Wayne, Ind., July 16, 1926; s. Harry Franklin Sr. and Mabel Ida (Dunkle) K.; m. Lyn Rose Thomas, Aug. 24, 1970 (div. 1972). MBA, Ind. U., 1975, D.Bus.Adminstrn., 1976. Pres. Kelsey Enterprises, Los Angeles, 1960-64; exec. Bonsib Pub. Relations, Ft. Wayne, Ind., 1964-66; pres. Ren, Inc., Indpls., 1966-73; dir. Babcock Ctr. Wake Forest U., Winston-Salem, N.C., 1976-79; dean Coll. of Bus. Jacksonville (Fla.) U., 1979-83; dean Sch. of Bus. Calif. State U., Bakersfield, 1983-88; resident dean St. Leo's Coll., Key West, Fla., from 1988; grad. advisor Troy State U., NAS, Key West, Fla., from 1990. Chmn. bd. dirs. Kern Econ. Devel. Corp., Bakersfield, 1987-88. Served to capt. USAF, 1958-62. Mem. Kegley Inst. Ethics (bd. dirs. Bakersfield chpt. 1987-88), Dorian Soc. (bd. dirs. Bakersfield chpt. 1984-88), Pub. Rels. Soc. Am. (cert.), Beta Gamma Sigma, Sigma Iota Epsilon. Republican. Presbyterian. Died Feb. 12, 2010.

KELSO, JOHN HODGSON, retired federal agency administrator; b. Iowa City, June 16, 1925; s. Edward Lewis and Eliza (Hodgson) K.; m. Marian Louise Towers, Aug. 22, 1948; 1 child, John T. BA, State U. Iowa, 1949, MA, 1950. Occupational research analyst Bur. Naval Personnel, Dept. Navy, Washington, 1951-55; orgn. and methods examiner Agr. Research Services, Dept. Agr., Washington, 1955-57; mgmt. analyst mgmt. adv. br. Bur. State Services, USPHS, HEW, Washington, 1957-58, chief survey group, 1958-60, chief mgmt. adv. br., 1960-62, asst. exec. officer, 1962-66; exec. officer USPHS, Bethesda, Md., 1966-68; asso. adminstr. mgmt. Health Services and Mental Health Adminstrn., 1968-73; dir. office regional operations USPHS, Office Asst. Sec. for Health, HEW, 1973-76; dep. adminstr. Health Services Adminstrn., 1976-81, acting adminstr., 1981-82; dep. adminstr. Health Resources and Services Adminstrn., 1982-94, acting adminstr., 1985-86, 88-89. Cons. United Network for Organ Sharing, Richmond, Va., 1994-2006. Served with AUS, 1943-46. Recipient Superior Svc. award USPHS, 1969, Disting. Svc. award US Dept. Health Edn. & Welfare (HEW), 1972, Presdl. Meritorious Rank award 1983, Disting. Presdl. Rank award 1989, Surgeon Gen.'s medallion, 1989. Mem. Sigma Alpha Epsilon. Methodist. Home: Alexandria, Va. Died Oct. 9, 2010.

KEMPER, WALKER WARDER, JR., dentist, educator; b. Indpls., Aug. 26, 1924; s. Walker Warder Sr. and Margaret Louise (Mast) Kemper; m. Janet Morene Cottingham, June 10, 1950 (div. Oct. 1973); children: Walker Warder III, Todd Geller; m. Stephanie Ann Brean, June 24, 1978; stepchildren: Jeffrey L., Michael L., Scott L. BS, Butler U., 1949; DDS, Ind. U., 1953, MSc in Dentistry, 1965. Clin. instr. Ind. U., Indpls., 1953—65; pvt. practice Indpls., from 1953; mem. Ind. State Bd. Dental Examiners, 1971—77; dental dir. Marquette Manor Retirement Home, Indpls., from 1975; chief dental sect., exec. com. St. Vincent Hosp. and Health Care Ctr., 1976—86; faculty practitioner Ind. U., 1979—94. Peerview Inc. Ind. Active mem. Ind. U. Century Club, Indpls., from 1968, Butler U. Pres.'s Club, 1966; bd. dirs. Little Red Door Cancer Soc., 1970—74, Paul Coble Post, Am. Legio; chmn. Boys State, 1978—79. Sgt. USAF, 1943—46. Decorated Bronze Star, Air medal with 2 oak leaf clusters. Mem.: ADA (life), Adult Firecrafter, Safari Club Internat. (pres., Ind. chapt. 1982—83), East Africa Hunters Assn., Pierre Fauchard Acad., Am. Coll. Prosthodontics, Am. Acad. Dental Medicine, Am. Acad. Crown and Bridge, Indpls. Dist. Dental Assn. (pres., Honor Dentist of Yr. 1988), Ind. State Dental Assn., John F. Johnston Soc. (exec. com. 1977—86, pres. 1982), Game Conservation Internat. (life Game Coin), Am. Coll. Dentists (life; pres. Ind. sect. 1988—89), Columbia Club (Indpls.)., Meridian Hills Country Club, Psi Omega, Omicron Kappa Upsilon (Dental hon award), Phi Delta Theta. Avocations: hunting, fishing, scuba diving, swimming, golf. Home: Brownsburg, Ind. Died Apr. 18, 2010.

KENDALL, PAUL E., former state representative; b. Hanover, NH, Aug. 2, 1930; m. Barbara Patenaude; two children. Grad., Vt. Sch. Agr., 1950. State rep. Vt. Ho. of Reps., 1996-98. Mem. Vt. Trails and Greenways Coun., Woodstock Bd. Civil Authority. Mem. Green Mountain Horse Assn., S. Woodstock Fire Protective Assn. Died July 6, 2010.

KENDALL, WILLIAM FORREST, physicist; b. Clarksburg, W.Va., Apr. 2, 1936; s. Forrest O. and Yvonne O. (Quinet) K.; m. Elaine Ellen Reinhardt, May 26, 1973. AB, W.Va. U., 1958; MS in Health Physics, U. N.C., 1966, PhD in Med. Physics, 1973. Cert. Am. Bd. Health Physics, cert. diagnostic and therapeutic physics Am. Bd. Radiology. Commd. 2d lt. U.S. Army, 1960, advanced through grades to lt. col., ret., 1981; med. physicist Meth. Hosps. Dallas, 1981-94, Ariz. Oncology Svcs., Phoenix, from 1994. Mem. Am. Assn. Physicists in Medicine, Health Physics Soc., Am. Coll. Radiology. Republican. Methodist. Avocations: woodworking, photography. Home: Fayetteville, NC. Died Jan. 12, 2009.

KENDRICK, JOHN WHITEFIELD, economist, educator, consultant; b. NYC, July 27, 1917; s. Benjamin Burks and Elizabeth W.W. (Shields) K.; m. Maxine Fillyaw; children: Bonnie Elizabeth, Karen Johanna, John Burks. AB, U. N.C., 1937, MA, 1939; PhD, George Washington U., 1955. Economist Nat. Resources Planning Bd., Washington, 1941-43, US Dept. Commerce, Washington, 1946-53, chief economist, 1976-77; sr. staff mem. Nat. Bur. Econ. Rsch., NYC, 1953-56, part-time, 56-78; prof. economics George Washington U., Washington, 1956-88, prof. emeritus, 1988—2009. Univ. prof. U. Conn., Storrs, 1964-66; vis. prof. Georgetown U., UCLA, Stanford U., U. Hawaii, Simon Fraser U., v.p. for econ. rsch. The Conf. Bd., N.Y.C., 1972-73, part-time, 1973-76; dir., trustee Pioneer Mut. Funds, Boston, 1961-2000; bd. dirs. Am. Productivity and Quality Ctr., Houston, 1977-2009; cons. AT&T, 1964-83, Office Mgmt. and Budget, NSF, GAO, other cos. and govt. agys.; mem. Conf. on Rsch. in Income and Wealth, chmn. 1963-64; adj. scholar Am. Enterprise Inst., 1980-86. Author: Productivity Trends in the United States, 1961 (Pres. Kennedy Libr. award 1962), (with Daniel Creamer) Measuring Company Productivity: Handbook with Case Studies, 1961, rev. edit., 1965, Economic Accounts and Their Uses, 1972, The Formation and Stocks of Total Capital, 1976 (also Russian trans.), Improving Company Productivity, 1977, (with E. Grossman) Productivity in the United States: Trends and Cycles, 1980, (with John B. Kendrick) Personal Productivity, 1988 (trans. in Korean and Japanese), other books; editor 6 conf. vols.; mem. editl. bds. Rev. of Income and Wealth, Bus. Econs.; contbr. over 150 articles to profl. jours. 1st lt. A.C., U.S. Army, 1943-45; served with U.S. Strategic Bombing Survey, 1945-46, ETO. Recipient Graham Dodd award for article Fin. Analysts Jour., 1962, Abramson award for article in Bus. Econs. jour., 1987. Fellow Am. Statis. Assn., Nat. Assn. Bus. Economists; mem. Am. Econ. Assn., So. Econ. Assn. (pres. 1982-83), Nat. Economists Club (pres. 1975-76, chmn. bd. 1976-77), World Acad. Productivity Sci., Atlantic Econ. Soc. (disting. assoc., pres. 1992-93), George Washington U. Club, Phi Beta Kappa. Unitarian-Universalist. Avocations: swimming, walking, reading, tv talk shows. Home: Falls Church, Va. Died Nov. 17, 2009.

KENNEDY, CHRISTINA KAY, microbiologist, director, biology professor; b. Dayton, Nov. 24, 1945; d. David Thomas and Arlene Beatty Kennedy; m. Paul David Calvert (div.); 1 child, Meredith Emily Kennedy Calvert. BA with high honors, Northeastern U., Boston, 1967; PhD, MIT, Cambridge, 1972. Rsch. assoc. Dept. of Biology, Sussex U., 1972-73; prin. scientific officer Agr. and Food Rsch. Coun., Brighton, Sussex, England, 1972—91; prof. dept. plant pathology and microbiology U. Ariz., Tucson, from 1992. Advisor, New Delhi, 1983; internat. adv. bd. nitrogen fixation Pasteur Inst., Paris, from 1995; editor Ferns Microbiology Jour., 1998—2003, Jour. of Bacteriology, Washington, 2000—05; program dir. Nat. Sci. Found, Arlington, Va., 2004—06. Author: Ann. Review Microbiology, 1987; contbr. articles to profl. jours. Named Outstanding Tchr., U. Ariz., 1995; grantee, USDA, 1992—2002, NSF, 1997—2002; Commonwealth fellow, The Royal Soc., 1978. Mem.: AAAS, Am. Soc. Microbiology (editl. bd. 2000—04), Nat. Mus. Women in Arts, Kennedy Ctr. Arts, Tucson Mus. Art, Ariz. Sonoran Mus. Achievements include research in field of genetics of nitrogen fixing bacteria. Avocation: travel. Home: Redwood City, Calif. Died Mar. 26, 2009.

KENNEDY, DONALD DAVIDSON, JR., retired insurance company executive; b. Philadelphia, Pa., 1931; m. Barbara Kennedy; children: Elizabeth, Susan, Donald III. BA in Sociology, Princeton U., Princton, NJ, 1953; JD, U. Pa., Phila., 1960. Atty. Ballard Spahr Law Firm, 1960—63; gen. counsel National Libery, 1971—91; pres. Providian Life & Health Ins. Co., Valley Forge, Pa. Mem.: Hole-in-the-Wall Golf Club (pres. 2000—01), Gulph Mills Golf Club (pres. 1988—90). Home: Naples, Fla. Died July 3, 2010.

KENNEDY, LEROY ERRETT, retired insurance executive; b. Nortonville, Ky., Mar. 13, 1924; s. Albert Roy and Bessie Mae (Oldham) K.; m. Lois Helen Carroll, Aug. 9, 1946 (div. July 1979); children: Karen Ruth Kennedy Howick, Martha Ann. AB, Louisville U., 1949; JD, Stetson U., 1951. Bar: Fla. 1951, Ky. 1951. Claim rep. State Farm Mut. Ins. Co., Mayfield, Ky., 1951-53; regional claim mgr. Allstate Ins. Co., Jackson, Miss., 1953-59; home office claim mgr. Gen. Mut. Ins., Birmingham, Ala., 1959-61; v.p. Celina Ins. Group, Ohio, 1961-69, Northwestern Nat. Inc. Co., Milw., 1969-81; pres. Northwestern Nat. Ins. Co., Milw., 1981-86, ret., 1986; bd. chmn. DePaul Rehab. Hosp., Milw., from 1986. Bd. dirs. DePaul Hosp., 1983, Milw. County Social Services, 1987—, Skylight Theater, 1987—. Served to 1st lt. U.S. Army, 1943-56, ETO. Mem. Central Claim Execs. Assn. (pres. 1974-75), Ohio Ins. Info. Service (trustee 1962-69), Def. Research Inst., Internat. Assn. Ins. Counsel, Fedn. Ins. Counsel, ABA Clubs: Milw. Athletic. Home: Milwaukee, Wis. Died Mar. 28, 2009.

KENNEY, FRANK DEMING, lawyer; b. Chgo., Feb. 20, 1921; s. Joseph Aloysius and Mary Edith (Deming) K.; m. Virginia Stuart Banning, Feb. 12, 1944 (dec. 2010); children: Claudia Kenney Carpenter, Pamela Kenney Voetberg, Sarah Kenney Swanson, Stuart Deming Kenney AB, U. Chgo., 1948, JD, 1949. Bar: Ill. 1948, U.S. Dist. Ct. (no. dist.) Ill. 1949. Assoc. J.O. Brown, Chgo., 1948-49; assoc., ptnr. Winston & Strawn, and predecessors, Chgo., 1949-92, ret., 1992. 1st lt. AUS, 1942-46, CBI, PTO. Mem. ABA, Ill. Bar Assn., Chgo. Bar Assn. (chmn. real property law com. 1982-83), Lawyers Club Chgo., Fox River Valley Hunt Club, Quadrangle Club, Nat. Beagle Club Am. (bd. dirs. 1981-92), Spring Creek Basset Hunt Club (master 1977-93, chmn. bd., 1993-98, hon. chmn. bd. 1998-2002, hon. master 2002-10), Kappa Sigma (nat. housing fin. commr. for U.S. and Can., 1959-91). Republican. Roman Catholic. Died Sept. 8, 2010.

KENT, JOE, state legislator; b. Vicksburg, Miss., Jan. 22, 1938; m. Becky; children: Kevin, Joe. Student, Miss. Jr. Coll., Memphis State U. Mem. Tenn. State Legis. Republican. Methodist. Home: Old Hickory, Tenn. Died Feb. 9, 2010.

KEPPLER, JAMES GEORGE, nuclear regulation administrator; b. Syracuse, NY, Mar. 19, 1934; s. Harold George and Genevieve Velma (Parrott) Keppler; m. Marietta Estelle Farrell, Oct. 6, 1956; children: James R., Timothy J., Melinda J. BS in Physics, LeMoyne Coll., 1956. Reactor physicist Gen. Electric Co., Cin., 1956—61, San Jose, Calif., 1961—65; reactor insp. AEC, Chgo., 1965—67, br. chief Bethesda, Md., 1967—73; regional dir. US Nuc. Regulation Commn., Chgo., 1973—81, regional adminstr., from 1981. Recipient Presdl. Meritorious award, Washington, 1982, Equal Employment Opportunity award, US NRC, 1986. Roman Catholic. Avocation: golf. Died May 19, 2010.

KERSHMAN, HARVEY ALLEN, business executive; b. Balt., July 19, 1939; s. Abraham and Marion (Shear) K.; m. Debra Hurwitz, June 17, 1962 (div. 1979); children— Lauri, Randi. B.S., U. Balt., 1960, LL.B., 1963. Pres. Freestate Receivables, Owings Mills, Md., 1972—. Served to sgt. U.S. Army, 1959-60. Mem. Hosp. Credit Assn., Hosp. Fin. Mgmt., Md. C. of C., Southwest Petroleum Credit Assn., Am. Collecters Assn. Democrat. Jewish. Clubs: Tri-Fed, Race Pace. Avocations: triathlon; photography; automobiles; music; raising donkeys. Home: Owings Mills, Md. Died Nov. 19, 2009.

KESSLER, RICHARD HOWARD, physician; b. Paterson, NJ, Dec. 15, 1923; s. Mitchell Richard and Rae (Levin) K.; m. Marian Judith Singer, May 14, 1944; children— William Samuel, Peter Bernard, John Robert. BS, Rutgers U., 1948; MD, N.Y. U., 1952. From instr. to asso. prof. Cornell U. Med. Sch., 1955-68; prof. Northwestern U. Med. Sch., Chgo., 1968-77; also asso. dean; cons. physician Northwestern Meml. Hosp., 1972-77; sr. v.p. profl. and acad. affairs Michael Reese Hosp., 1977-83, attending physician, 1977-83; prof. medicine Pritzker Sch. Medicine, U. Chgo., 1978-83; acting dir. medicine Beth Israel Med. Ctr., 1983-84; dir. acad. affairs Hosp. Joint Disease Orthopedic Inst., from 1984; prof. medicine Mt. Sinai Sch. Medicine, from 1984; attending physician N.Y. Hosp., 1965-68, VA Research Hosp., Chgo., 1968-71. Cons. health econs. Nat. Bur. Econ. Research; cons. edn. service VA, Washington. Cons. editor: Ency. Brit, 1973-79; contbr. articles to profl. jours. Vice pres. Kidney Found. Ill., 1974-77; bd. dirs. Cook County Grad. Sch. Medicine; mem. exec. com. Anti-Defamation League of B'nai B'rith, Ill. Regional Med. Program, 1972-77; commr. Health and Hosp.

Governing Com. of Cook County, 1974-76, Health Systems Agy., City of Chgo., 1980—; mem. exec. com. Ill. Cancer Council, 1981—. Served with AUS, 1942-46. Life Ins. Med. Research fellow, 1955-56; sr. fellow Nathan Hofheimer Found., 1957-62; Fellow Hastings Inst. Soc.; Fellow Ethics and Life Scis.; Fellow A.C.P. Mem. Am. Physiol. Soc., Am., Internat. socs. nephrology, Harvey Soc., Central Soc. for Clin. Research, Am., Ill., Chgo. heart assns., Am. Soc. Clin. Pharmacology and Therapeutics (editorial bd. 1966-83), Hosp. Research and Ednl. Trust (editorial bd. 1975-78), AAAS, Alpha Omega Alpha. Home: Sarasota, Fla. Died Jan. 11, 2010.

KETTEL, EDWARD JOSEPH, retired oil industry executive; b. NYC, Sept. 13, 1925; s. Harold J. and Evelyn M. (Melbourne) K.; m. Janet M. Johnson, Nov. 27, 1952; children: Dorothy A., David A. Student, St. John's U., 1943; BA, St. Francis Coll., 1949; MA, Columbia U., 1953. Ins. mgr. Arabian Am. Oil Co., 1950-56, Ethyl Corp., 1956—63, Sinclair Oil, 1963—65; asst. treas. Atlantic Richfield Co., LA, 1965-85, Chevron Corp., San Francisco, 1985-94; expert witness, from 1994. Chmn. bd. Oil Ins., Ltd.; pres. Greater Pacific, Ltd.; dir. Am. S.S. Owners Mut. Protection and Indemnity Assn., Inc., Internat. Tanker Indemnity Assn., Ltd. With inf. AUS, 1943-46. Decorated Purple Heart with oak leaf cluster. Mem. Am. Petroleum Inst., Mfrs. Chem. Assn., Nat. Fire Protection Assn., Risk and Ins. Mgmt. Soc., N.Y. Athletic Club, L.A. Athletic Club, Palos Verdes Country Club, Ocean Colony Golf Club, Westhampton Beach Yacht Squadron Ltd. Died July 5, 2010.

KEYES, ROBERT W., physicist, researcher; b. Chgo., Dec. 2, 1921; s. Lee P. and Katherine K.; m. Sophie Skadorwa, June 4, 1966; children— Andrew, Claire. BS, U. Chgo., 1942, MS, 1949, PhD, 1953. With Argonne Nat. Lab., 1946-50; staff mem. Westinghouse Research Lab., Pitts., 1953-60; mem. research staff IBM Research Lab., Yorktown Heights, NY, from 1960. Vis. physicist Am. Phys. Soc. Vis. Indsl. Physicists Program, 1974-75, 77; vice chmn. Gordon Conf. on High Pressure Physics, 1970; chmn. Gordon Conf. on Chemistry and Physics of Microstructure Fabrication, 1976, Nat. Materials Adv. Bd. (ad hoc com. on ion implantation as a new surface treatment tech.), 1978, Internat. Conf. Heavily Doped Semiconductors, 1984; mem. Nat. Acad. Scis.-NAE-NRC evaluation panel Nat. Bur. Standards, 1970-73; cons. physics survey com., mem. statis. data panel Nat. Acad. Sci.-NRC Council Physics Survey Com., 1972; mem. data and info. panel Nat. Acad. Sci.-NRC Com. on Survey of Materials Sci. and Engring., 1974; Girling Watson vis. prof. elec. engring. U. Sydney, Fall 1996. Author: Physics of VLSI Systems, 1987; assoc. editor Revs. Modern Physics, 1976-95; corr.: Comments on Solid State Physics, 1970-85. With USN, 1944—46. Recipient Outstanding Contbn. award IBM, 1963, Disting. Svc. award Saw Mill River Audubon Soc., 2008. Fellow Am. Phys. Soc. (chmn. com. applications of physics 1976-78), IEEE (life, chmn. subcom. cultural and sci. relations 1976, mem. del. to USSR 1975, W.R.G. Baker prize 1976, awards bd. 1984, Sigma Xi, Phi Beta Kappa. Achievements include invention of epitaxially strained field effect transitor. Home: Ossining, NY. Died Apr. 5, 2010.

KHAN, MOHAMMED ABDUL QUDDUS, biology professor; b. Kaimgunj, India, Mar. 15, 1939; s. Mohammed Hanif and Maryam (Khan) Khan; m. Anwarun Nisa Khan, Apr. 8, 1954; children: Sarah, Samreen, Yaseen. BS, Karachi U., Pakistan, 1957, MS, 1959; PhD, U. Western Ont., London, 1964; MD, U. Autonoma de Ciudad Juarez, Mex., 1984. Postdoc. fellow NC State U., Raleigh, 1965—67, Oreg. State U., Corvallis, 1967—68, Rutgers U., NB, NJ, 1968—69; mem. faculty U. Ill., Chgo., from 1969, assoc. prof., 1969—74, prof. biology, from 1974; vis. scientist NIH, Rsch. Triangle Pk., NC, 1975—76; vis. chemist EPA, Corvallis, Oreg., 1980. Editor in chief Jour. Biochem. Toxicology, from 1986. Editor: Pesticides in Aquatic Environments, 1977; co-editor: Survival in Toxic Environments, 1976, Pesticide and Xenobiotics in Aquatic Organisms, 1979, Toxicology of Halogenated Hydrocarbons, 1980. Rsch. grantee, USPHS, NIH, 1972, 1977. Mem.: AAAS, Soc. Toxicology, Entomol. Soc. America, Am. Chem. Soc., Sigma Xi. Democrat. Islam. Avocations: poetry, writing. Home: Bartlett, Ill. Died June 21, 2010.

KIBLER, DAVID BURKE, III, lawyer; b. Lakeland, Fla., Feb. 5, 1924; s. David Burke, Jr. and Bessie (Dew) K.; m. Nell Idalene Bryant, Sept. 26, 1945 (wid. Sept. 1996); children: David Burke IV, Thomas Bryant, Jacquelyn, Nancy Dew. BA cum laude, U. Fla., 1947, JD, 1949; LLD (hon.), Flagler Coll., 1983, Fla. So. Coll., 1986; LHD (hon.), St. Leo Coll., 1970, Fla. State U., 1990. Bar: Fla. 1949. Since practiced in, Lakeland; ptnr., chmn. Holland & Knight and predecessor, 1964-94, chmn. emeritus, from 1995. Chmn., dir. Kibler Agrl. Corp.; atty. Fla. Citrus Com., 1961-65. Past pres., bd. dirs., exec. com., Lakeland United Fund; mem. Fla. Bd. Regents, 1967-76, chmn., 1969-72; past chmn. Fla. Council 100; mem., chmn. Fla. Postsecondary Edn. Com.; chmn. Fla. Postsecondary Edn. Planning Commn.; bd. dirs. U. South Fla. Found.; bd. dirs. Bok Tower Found.; pres., bd. dirs. U. Fla. Found; mem. Gov.'s High Speed Rail Commn., Gov.'s Unitary Tax Commn., Orange Bowl Com.; chmn. Lakeland Com. of 100. Served to 1st lt. AUS, 1943-46, ETO. Decorated Bronze Star with V, Purple Heart with oak leaf cluster; inducted to Tampa Bay Bus. Hall of Fame, 1992. Mem. Am., 10th Jud. Circuit bar assns., Am. Judicature Soc., Southeastern Legal Found. (legal adv. bd.), Am. Law Inst., Fla. Bar, Am. Legion, Fla. Blue Key, Alpha Tau Omega, Phi Delta Phi. Clubs: Lakeland Yacht and Country, Lone Palm Golf (Lakeland), Grasslands Golf and Country (chmn. bd.), Univ. (Tampa, Fla.). Lodges: Elks. Democrat. Presbyterian. Home: Lakeland, Fla. Died Dec. 13, 2009.

KICKLIGHTER, CLOIS EARL, academic administrator; b. Plant City, Fla., June 18, 1939; s. James A. and Elizabeth M. (Grooms) K.; m. Joan M. Cheatham, Aug. 8, 1964; children: Bradley, Cynthia. BS, U. Fla., 1962; MS, Ind. State U., 1963; EdD, U. Md., 1966. Instr. U. Md., College Park, 1963-66; prof. Ea. Mich. U., Ypsilanti, 1966-83; dean Ind. State U., Terre Haute, from 1983. Cons. Goodheart-Willcox Co., Tinley Park, Ill., 1983—, bd. dirs.; mem. mfg. com. Corp. for Sci. and Tech., Indpls., 1985—; bd. dirs. Goodheart-Willcox. Author: Architecture: Residential Drawing and Design, 1972, rev. edit., 1995, Masonry: Brick, Block and Stone, 1977, rev. edit., 1996, Crafts, 1980, Residential Housing, 1986, rev. edit., 1998, Modern Woodworking, 1986, rev. edit. 1995, Drafting for Industry, 1995. Mem. Ind. Adv. Coun. for Econ. Devel., Indpls., 1985-90, Alliance for Growth and Progress, Terre Haute, 1987-89, Gov. Orr's Task Force on Mktg. Edn. and Tng. Internationally, 1988, Gov. Bayh's Adv. Counsel on Long-Range Tech. Strategy for the State of Ind., 1989; chmn. Corp. for Sci. and Tech. Com. on Indsl. Products and Processes, 1989; bd. dirs. Sci. and Tech. Mus. Terre Haute, 1986-89. Grantee, Corp. for Sci. and Tech., 1984. Mem. Nat. Assn. Indsl. Tech. (pres. 1986-87, chmn. bd. dirs. 1988-89, cons. 1988—, chmn. nat. bd. accreditation 1997, Chuck Keith award 1992, Outstanding Region Dir. award 1981, Exemplary Svc. award 1989), Soc. Mfg. Engrs., Antique Automobile Club. Am. (Hershey, Pa.), Phi Kappa Phi, Phi Delta Kappa, Epsilon Pi Tau (citation 1992). Avocations: antique auto restoration, antique furniture collecting. Home: Naples, Fla. Died Mar. 5, 2010.

KIELTY, JOHN LAWRENCE, III, search company executive; b. NYC, June 24, 1943; s. John L. and Patricia (Heagen) K.; m. Arlene J. Colandrea, Apr. 19, 1945 (div.); children: John, Keith, Brian. BS in Acctg., L.I. U., 1965. CPA. Dir. human resources Price Waterhouse, NYC, 1964-80; chmn. Earley Kielty & Assocs., NYC, from 1980. Mem. AICPA, N.Y. State Soc. CPAs, Rep. Club. Roman Catholic. Home: Keansburg, NJ. Died Jan. 21, 2010.

KIERNAN, OWEN BURNS, educational consultant; b. Randolph, Mass., Mar. 9, 1914; s. Thomas Francis and Elizabeth (Burns) K.; m. Esther Harriet Thorley, July 13, 1940; children: Joan Ann, Nancy Elizabeth, John Albert. BS, Bridgewater Coll., Mass., 1935; M.Ed., Boston U., 1940, Sc.D. (hon.), 1968; Ed.D., Harvard U., 1950; L.H.D. (hon.), Lesley Coll., 1956; LL.D., Northeastern U., 1961; Litt.D. (hon.), Stonehill Coll., 1965; Ped.D. (hon.), R.I. Coll., 1966. Prin. Henry T. Wing High Sch., Sandwich, Mass., 1938-44; supt. schs. Wayland and Sudbury, Mass., 1944-51, Milton, 1951-57; commr. edn. State of Mass., 1957-68; exec. dir. Nat. Assn. Secondary Sch. Prins., 1969-79; dir. sch. div. McManis Assos., Inc., 1980-82; cons. Washington, from 1983. Past chmn. Mass. Bd. Edn., Mass. Bd. Vocat. Edn.; corp. mem. MIT Trustee U. Mass.; trustee Lowell Tech. Inst., Mus. Fine Arts, Mus. Sci. Boston, Boston U.; bd. dirs. Atlantic Council U.S.; chmn. edn. com. Atlantic Treaty Assn., 1968-72; gov. bd. Atlantic Info. Centre for Tchrs., London, 1968-76; exec. com. U.S. People-to-People Program. Mem. Am. Assn. Sch. Adminstrs., New Eng., Mass. supts. assns., State Sch. Officers (pres. 1967), Phi Delta Kappa. Home: Centerville, Mass. Died Jan. 5, 2010.

KIESLING, LYNNWOOD ALLEN, hardware sales professional; b. Lansing, Mich., May 11, 1951; s. Donald Linwood and Leola Lairain (Cummings) K.; divorced. Student, Grahan Sch. for Cattlemen, Garnett, Kans., 1972. Dairy farmer, Morrice, Mich., 1961-86; livestock breeder Curtiss Candy, Morrice, Mich., 1969-72; technician Am. Breeder, DeForest, Wis., 1972-80; crop farmer Morrice, 1984-87; hardware clk. Meijer Stores, Okemos, Mich., from 1987. Named one of Outstanding Young Men U.S. Jaycees, 1982. Mem. United Food Workers (community rels. 1991-92, active ballot club 1992, phone bank 1988), Future Farmers Am. (alumni pres. Perry, Mich. chpt. 1972-80, state sec. East Lansing, Mich. chpt. 1981, Hon. Farmer 1972), Smithsonian Inst. (assoc.). Democrat. Avocations: flower gardening, reading. Home: Lansing, Mich. Died Jan. 8, 2009.

KILGORE, DONALD GIBSON, JR., pathologist; b. Dallas, Nov. 21, 1927; s. Donald Gibson and Gladys (Watson) K.; m. Jean Upchurch Augur, Aug. 23, 1952; children: Michael Augur, Stephen Bassett, Phillip Arthur, Geoffrey Scott, Sharon Louise. Student, So. Meth. U., 1943-45; MD Southwestern Med. Coll., U. Tex., Dallas, 1949. Diplomate Am. Bd. Pathology, Am. Bd. Dermatopathology, Am. Bd. Blood Banking; notary pub. Intern Parkland Meml. Hosp., Dallas, 1949—50; resident in pathology Charity Hosp. La., New Orleans, 1950—54, asst. pathologist, 1952—54; pathologist Greenville (S.C.) Hosp. Sys., from 1956, dir. labs., 1985—96, Greenville Meml. Hosp., 1972—96. Cons. pathologist St. Francis Hosp., from 1963, Shriners Hosp., Greenville, from 1963, Easley Baptist Hosp.; vis. lectr. Clemson U., from 1963; asst. prof. pathology Med. U. S.C., from 1968; pres. Pathology Assocs. of Greenville, 1983—96. Deacon Westminster Presbyn. Ch., 1961, ruling elder, 1969, trustee, from 2001; mem. bd. govs. S.C. Patient Compensation Fund, 1977—2001; bd. govs. Roper Mountain Sci. Ctr., 2001—07. Capt. M.C. USAFR, 1954—56. Recipient Disting. Svc. award S.C. Hosp. Assn., 1976; awarded Order of The Palmetto by S.C. Gov. David M. Beasley, 1996. Fellow: Am. Soc. Dermatopathology, Am. Soc. Clin. Pathologists (councilor S.C. 1959—62), Coll. Am. Pathologists (life; assemblyman S.C. 1968—71); mem.: AMA (life; ho. of dels. 1978—94), Greater Greenville C. of C. (pres. ednl. task force 1965—70, elected trustee sch. dist. of Greenville County 1970—90), S.C. Soc. Pathologists (pres. 1969—72), S.C. Inst. Med. Edn. and Rsch. (pres. 1974—80), Nat. Assn. Med. Examiners, Greenville County Dental Soc. (life), Am. Assn. Blood Banks (life; adv. coun. 1962—67, insp. committeeman Southeast dist. 1965—2001), Am. Numismatic Assn. (life), Am. Coll. Nuc. Medicine, Am. Soc. Cytology, S.C. Med. Assn. (exec. coun. 1969—76, pres. 1974—75, exec. coun. 1978—94, A.H. Robins award for Outstanding Cmty. Svc. 1985), So. Med. Assn., Soc. Med. Friends of Wine, Epicurean Assn. of Am. (selection com.), Confrerie de la Chaine des Rotisseurs (bailli and echanson de l'ordre mondial, Greenville chpt.), Clan Douglas Soc. N.Am., Ltd. (life), Richard III Soc. (co-chmn. Am. 1966—75), Hist. Greenville Found. (exec. com. 1994—2001, pres. 1998—2000), S.W. R.R. Hist. Soc., S.C. Gov.'s Task Force on Hist. Preservation and Heritage Tourism, Roper Mountain Sci. Ctr. Assn. (bd. dirs. 2001—07), Brit. Museum Soc., U.S. Power Squadron, Confrerie des Chevaliers du Tastevin (chevalier Atlanta chpt.), S.C. Hist. Soc. (life), Tex. State Hist. Assn. (life), Thomas Wolfe Soc. (life), Medieval Acad. Am. (life), Archeol. Inst. Am. (life), Brookgreen Gardens Found. (life), Friends of Tewkesbury Abbey (life), Canterbury Cathedral Trust in Am. (life), Assn. Friends of Lincoln Cathedral (life), Am. Numis. Soc. (life), Soc. Ancient Numismatics (life), Royal Numis. Soc. (life), S.C. Numis. Assn. (life), Mensa (life), S.C. Congress Parents and Tchrs. (life), Greenville County Hist. Soc. (life), Preservation Soc. of Charleston (life), Wine Acad. Am. (life), Les Amis du Vin (life), Clan MacDuff Soc. Am. (life; exec. coun. 1980—2000), So. Meth. U. Alumni Assn. (life), Highland Park H.S. Alumni Assn. (life), Am. Wine Soc. (life), Blue Ridge Numis. Assn. (life), Am. Numis. Assn. (life), Confrerie de Les Grapilleurs du Beaujolais (chevalier), St. Andrews Soc. Upper S.C. (bd. govs. 1991—93), L'Academie de Gastronomie Brillat-Savarin des Etats-Unis (founding mem.), Soc. Wine Educators, Soc. Med. Friends of Wine, Piedmont Econ. Club, Poinsett Club (life), Commerce Club (life), Greenville Country Club (life), Chandon Club, Thirty-Nine Club (pres. 1981—82), Torch Club (pres. 1964—65), Rotary (Paul Harris fellow 1988), Phi Chi, Phi Eta Sigma. Democrat. Home: Greenville, SC. Died Mar. 8, 2010.

KILLIAN, EDWARD JAMES, retired pediatrician; b. Bklyn., Nov. 14, 1927; s. Edward James and Helen Marie K.; m. Henriette Marian Killian, 1957; children: Christopher Edward, Bryan Alfred, Paul Matthew. BS, St. John's Coll., 1950; MD, SUNY, 1954. Diplomat Am. Bd. Pediatrics, Nat. Bd. Med. Examiners; lic. physician, N.Y. Intern Bklyn. Hosp., 1954-55, resident, 1955-57, attending pediatrician, 1959-61, Southside Hosp., Bayshore, NY, 1961-93, Good Samaritan Hosp., West Islip, NY, 1961-93, ret., 1994. Capt. USAF Med. Corps, 1957-59. Fellow Am. Acad. Pediatrics; mem. AMA, Med. Soc. State N.Y. (life), Suffolk County Med. Soc. (life), Suffolk Pediatric Soc. (emeritus). Avocations: swimming, hiking, gardening. Home: Woodstock, Vt. Died Jan. 3, 2009.

KILLPATRICK, JAMES CARL, newspaper editor, journalist; b. Hillsboro, Ill., Nov. 25, 1931; s. Carl Leon and Wanna (Sears) K.; m. Frances Eleanor Van Cleave, Oct. 17, 1959; children: Amy Ruth, Patrick Emerson. Student, U. Ill., 1949-50, So. Ill. U., 1954-55. News editor So. Illinoisan, Carbondale, 1956-61; night city editor, news editor Comml. Appeal, Memphis, 1961-71; sr. corr. Reuters News Service, NYC, 1972-74; chief bureaus, sr. editor U.S. News and World Report, Washington, 1974-87; press sec. Senator Paul Simon, 1987-88; mng. editor The Jour. Newspapers (5 suburban dailies), Washington, from 1989. Co-author: (with Frances Killpatrick) The Winning Edge, 1989, rev. edit., 1991. Served with CIC, U.S. Army, 1952-54. Presbyterian. Home: Alexandria, Va. Died Jan. 14, 2009.

KILPATRICK, JAMES JACKSON, JR., retired columnist, retired writer; b. Oklahoma City, Nov. 1, 1920; s. James Jackson and Alma Mia (Hawley) K.; m. Marie Louise Pietri, Sept. 21, 1942 (dec. May 1997); children: Michael Sean, Christopher Hawley, Kevin Pietri; m. Marianne Means, June 19, 1998. BJ, U. Mo., 1941. Reporter Richmond (Va.) News Leader, 1941-49, chief editorial writer, 1949-51, editor, 1951-67; writer nat. syndicated columns, TV commentator. Author: The Sovereign States: Notes of a Citizen of Virginia, 1957, The Smut Peddlers, 1960, The Southern Case for School Segregation, 1962, The Foxes' Union, 1977, (with Eugene J. McCarthy) A Political Bestiary, 1978, (with William Bake) The American South: Four Seasons of the Land, 1980, The American South: Towns and Cities, 1982, The Writer's Art, 1984, The Ear is Human, 1985, A Bestiary of Bridge, 1986, Fine Print - Reflections on the Writing Art, 1993; editor: We the States, 1964; co-editor: The Lasting South, 1957. Vice chmn. Va. Com. on Constl. Govt., 1962-68; chmn. Va. Magna Carta Com., 1965; trustee Thomas Jefferson Ctr. for Protection of Free Expression, 1990—2004, Supreme Ct. Hist. Soc., 1987-2010 Recipient medal of honor for distinguished service in journalism U. Mo., 1953; ann. award for editorial writing Sigma Delta Chi, 1954; William Allen White award U. Kans., 1979; Carr Van Anda award Ohio U., 1987; named to Okla. Hall of Fame, 1978 Fellow Soc. Profl. Journalists; mem. Nat. Conf. Editorial Writers (chmn. 1955-56), Black-Eyed Pea Soc. Am. (No. 1 Pea pro tem 1965—), Gridiron Club. Whig. Episcopalian. Home: Washington, DC. Died Aug. 15, 2010.

KIMBRELL, ODELL CULP, JR., internist; b. Spartanburg, SC, May 2, 1927; s. Odell Culp and Leona (Nicholas) K.; m. Etta Lou; children from former marriage: Odell Culp III, Cynthia Anne. AB, Duke U., 1947; MD, U. Pa., 1951. Diplomate: Am. Bd. Internal Medicine, Am. Bd. Life Ins. Medicine. Intern Med. Coll. Va., Richmond, 1951-52, resident in internal medicine, 1954-56; sr. resident in internal medicine VA Hosp., Phila., 1956-57; practice medicine specializing in internal medicine and endocrinology Gallipolis, Ohio, 1957-60, Raleigh, NC, 1960-93; practice ins. medicine, from 1967; mem. hon. staff Wake Med. Ctr.; clin. prof. medicine U.N.C. Med. Sch., 1970-90. Med. dir., cons. Pa. Life Ins. Co., from 1998. Contbr. articles to med. jours. Bd. dirs. Wake County Hosp. System Inc., Raleigh, 1971-81, sec., 1973-74, chmn., 1974-76; bd. dirs. Wake Health Facilities and Service Inc., 1975-81, pres., 1975-76; chmn. Wake County Heart Fund, 1961; deacon Hudson Meml. Presbyn. Ch., Raleigh, 1971-73. Served with USAF, 1952-54. Fellow ACP; mem. AMA, N.C. Med. Soc., Wake County Med Soc., Am. Soc. Internal Medicine, N.C. Soc. Internal Medicine, Am. Acad. Ins. Med., Mid-Atlantic Med. Dirs. Club (pres. 1979-80, 92). Home: Raleigh, NC. Died Aug. 13, 2010.

KIMEN, THOMAS W., JR., banker; b. Detroit, Aug. 23, 1936; s. Thomas W. and Aira (Maki) K.; m. Gail Carmichael, Oct. 6, 1962; children— Thomas W., Amy McLean BA, Mich. State U.; MBA, U. Mich. With No. Trust Co., Chgo., v.p., 1968-72, sr. v.p., from 1981; pres. Security Trust Co., Miami, Fla., 1972-81; chmn. bd. Security Trust, Sarasota, Fla., 1977-82, Naples, Fla., 1978-82, Palm Beach, Fla., 1979-82. Trustee Central DuPage Hosp., Winfield, Ill. Home: Green Lake, Wis. Died Sept. 14, 2009.

KINCAID, OWINGS WILSON, physician, radiology educator, consultant; b. Owingsville, Ky., May 6, 1921; s. Reuben Walton and Sara Elizabeth (Crooks) K.; m. Harriet Elizabeth Bonney, Sept. 16, 1944; children— Sarah Bonney, Linda Marie, Elizabeth Owings. Student, Morehead State U., 1939-43, D.Sc. (hon.), 1978; MD, U. Louisville, 1946; postgrad., Vanderbilt U., 1950-52; MS, U. Minn., 1955. Diplomate Am. Bd. Radiology. Intern St. Joseph Infirmary, Louisville, 1946-47, resident in medicine, 1947-48; resident in internal medicine Vanderbilt U., 1950-52, asst. instr. medicine, 1951-52; fellow in radiology Mayo Clinic-Mayo Found., Rochester, Minn., 1952-55; mem. staff Mayo Clinic, Rochester, from 1955, co-dir. Cardiovascular Lab., 1960-71. Cons. diagnostic radiology Mayo Clinic, 1956—; prof. radiology Mayo Med. Sch., Rochester, 1973—; prof. Grad. Sch. Medicine, U. Minn., Mpls., 1973-81; cons. Alaska Native and Arctic Health Svc. and Alaska Heart Assn., 1964-69. Author: Renal Angiography, 1966; An Atlas of Vascular Rings and Related Malformations of the Aortic Arch System, 1964; mem. adv. editorial bd. Jour. Radiology, 1969-74; mem. editorial bd. Jour. Clin. Medicine, 1970-74; editorial con. Jour. Chest, 1971-74; contbr. 125 articles to profl. jours. Served to capt. M.C., USAF, 1948-50. Recipient Billings Gold medal AMA, 1968; Gold medal award Am. Acad. Pediatrics, 1968. Fellow Am. Coll. Radiology; mem. Am. Coll. Cardiology (gov.'s award 1970), Radiol. Soc. N.Am. (v.p. 1975), Am. Roentgen Ray Soc., Rocky Mountain Radiol. Soc. (hon.), Minn. Radiol. Soc. (pres. 1974), Tex. Radiol. Soc. (hon.), Zumbro Valley Med. Soc., Minn. Med. Assn., Sigma Xi. Presbyterian. Home: Rochester, Minn. Died Nov. 28, 2009.

KING, LOUIS BLAIR, minister; b. Dec. 31, 1925; m. Freya Synnestvedt; children: Khary Allen, Steven, Alan C., Janne Odhner, Cedric, Bronwin Cooper, Aileen Synnestvedt, Blair, Wendy Walter, Kristin Bibler, Dag. P., Bradley, John Cairn, Tamar. BA, U. Pa.; BTh, Acad. of New Ch.; postgrad., Acad. of New Ch. Theol. Sch. Ordained to ministry Gen. Ch. in Can., 1951. Min. Sharon Ch., Chgo., 1952, pastor, 1952-54, Pitts. Soc., 1955-62; pastor, headmaster ch. sch. Immanuel Ch., Glenview, Ill., 1963-72; asst. bishop Gen. Ch., 1973-75, bishop, gen. pastor, from 1976; pastor Bryn Athyn Ch., 1976-80; dean Bryn Athyn (Pa.) Ch., 1973; exec. v.p. Acad. Corp., Bryn Athyn, 1974, pres., 1975, chancellor, from 1976. Vis. pastor South Ohio Circle, 1954, Erie Circle, Pa., 1960, North Ohio Circle, 1961; pres. Midwestern Acad., 1963-72; pres. Gen. Ch. in Can., 1976—, Gen. Ch. Internat., Inc., 1976—. With U.S. Army, 1944. Mem. Rotary. Avocations: golf, fishing, playing violin. Home: Bryn Athyn, Pa. Died June 21, 2010.

KING, MARY FRANCES GOOCH, nursing executive; b. Fredericksburg, Va., Dec. 28, 1925; d. Mercer Ray and Agnes Moncure (Brooks) Gooch; m. Robert Patrick King, Mar. 29, 1945; 1 child, Agnes Ann King Norris. Diploma in nursing, Sibley Meml. Hosp., 1945; BS in Psychology, Old Dominion Coll., 1965; MEd, Va. Poly. Inst. and State U., 1970, Ed.D., 1976. RN. Vol. sch. nurse Navy Dependents Sch., Naples, Italy, 1961-64; instr. nursing Norfolk (Va.) City Schs., 1965-69; coordinator nursing Kapiolani Community Coll., Honolulu, 1970-72; supr. vocat. edn. State Dept. Edn., Richmond, Va., 1972-74; coordinator health occupations Richmond Pub. Schs., 1975-77; dir. nursing Bremerton Kitsap Health Dept., Wash., 1978—; 2d v.p. Hawaii League Nursing, Honolulu, 1971-72; cons. Maui (Hawaii) Community Coll., 1971; co. dir. health edn. curriculum project Va. Poly. Inst. and State U., Blacksburg, 1974-76; bd. dirs. Wash. Assn. Home Health Agys., 1979. Author: (with others) On the Health Scene, 1976. V.p. Kitsap Community Action Program, Bremerton, 1985; bd. dirs. Kitsap Council Aging, Bremerton, 1979, Human Resources, Bremerton, 1980, Kitsap Paratransit; bd. dirs., 2d v.p. United Way Kitsap County; adv. council Foster Grandparents, Bremerton, 1980; mem. bishop's com. St. Antony's Episcopal Ch., Silverdale, Wash. Dept. Edn. fellow 1974. Mem. Va. Assn. Vocat. Indsl. Clubs Am. (hon. life), Am. Nurses Assn., Wash. State Nurses Assn., Am. Pub. Health Assn., Wash. State Pub. Health Assn. Avocations: sewing, spinning, tole painting. Home: Nome, Alaska. Died Mar. 30, 2009.

KING, NINA DAVIS, journalist; b. Coco Solo, Panama, May 7, 1941; d. James White and Ruth (Steele) Davis. BA in French, U. NC, 1963, MA in Comparative Lit. (Chancellors fellow), 1967; PhD in English, Wayne State U., 1973. Lectr. Queens Coll., 1970-73; copy editor Newsday, LI, N.Y., 1973-76, asst. news editor, 1976-77, asst. book rev. editor, 1977-79, book rev. editor, 1979-88; book editor The Washington Post, 1988-99. Author: (with R. Winks) Crimes of the Scene: A Mystery Novel Guide for the International Traveler, 1997. Mem. Nat. Book Critics Circle, Phi Beta Kappa. Died May 6, 2010.

KING, PETER JOSEPH, JR., retired gas company executive; b. Concord, NH, Aug. 5, 1921; s. Peter Joseph and Helen (Hallinan) K.; m. Louise Lynch, Sept. 11, 1948; children: Anne, Peter BS, Georgetown U., 1942; LL.B., Harvard U., 1948, postgrad. Advanced Mgmt. Program, 1966. Bar: N.H. 1949, Mass. 1950, Colo. 1973. Practice law, N.H., 1948-51; with AEC, 1952-53, Colo. Interstate Gas Co., Colorado Springs, 1953-86, pres., chief operating officer, dir., 1977-85, vice chmn., 1985-86, also bd. dirs. Bd. dirs. Myron Stratton Home, Colorado Springs, 1974-93; mem. Colo. Transp. Commn., 1987-95, chmn., 1991-92. 1st lt. AUS, 1942-45, 51-52. Mem. Garden of the Gods Club, El Paso Club. Roman Catholic. Home: Woodland Park, Colo. Died Jan. 7, 2009.

KING, THOMAS H., publishing executive; b. Bklyn., Sept. 2, 1934; s. John B. and Helen (Holdridge) K.; m. Marthena Marrin, Aug. 23, 1959; children— John, Michael, Paul BS in Bus. Adminstrn., Syracuse U., 1956. Pub. McGraw-Hill Pub. Co., NYC, 1956-78., v.p. mfg., 1978-79, group v.p., 1979-81; pres. Am. Bus. Press, NYC, 1981-85; pub., v.p. High Tech. Mag., NYC, 1985-87; pres. Webb Pub. Co., St. Paul, 1988-89; pres., chief exec. officer Schnell Pub. Co., NYC, from 1990. Dir. Advt. Council, N.Y.C., Bus. Press Edn. Found., N.Y.C. Served with U.S. Army, 1956-62. Mem. Bus. Profl. Advt. Assn. Clubs: Woodway Country (Darien, Conn.); Pine Valley Country (N.J.). Roman Catholic. Avocations: golf; fishing; travel. Home: Stamford, Conn. Died Apr. 9, 2009.

KING, THOMAS JOSEPH, chief of police; b. Manchester, NH, June 15, 1922; s. Thomas and Bridget (O'Malley) King; m. Barbara Lee; children: Linda, Coleen, Barbara, Colin, John, Christopher. AS in Criminal Justice, St. Anselm's Coll., 1973. Patrolman Manchester Police, NH, 1950—58, sgt., 1958—64, lt., 1964—67, capt., 1967—69, dep. chief, 1969—74, chief of police, from 1975. With USN, 1943—46. Mem.: NH Assn. Chiefs Police, New Eng. Assn. Chiefs Police, Internat. Assn. Chiefs Police, Rotary Lodge. Democrat. Roman Catholic. Home: Manchester, NH. Died May 15, 2010.

KINGSBURY, READ AUSTIN, retired journalist; b. Lanesboro, Pa., Nov. 6, 1925; s. Hale and Esther (Austin) K.; m. Barbara Brown, Sept. 6, 1951 (div. 1976); children— Laura, Glenn, Elaine; m. Neva S. Flaherty, Dec. 24, 1985. BA, Western Res. U., 1949. Reporter-editor Republican-Courier, Findlay, Ohio, 1952-53; reporter Dispatch, Columbus, Ohio, 1953-58; reporter, city editor Times-Union, Rochester, N.Y., 1958-74, editorial page editor, 1974-87; sr. editor Times-Union and Dem. Chronicle, Rochester, 1987-91. Bd. dirs. Block Island Conservancy, 1993—. Served with USN, 1945-47, U.S. Army, 1950-52 Mem. Nat. Conf. Editorial Writers (dir. 1979-81), Adirondack Mountain Club. Avocations: sailing; skiing; hiking. Home: Brewster, Mass. Died May 11, 2010.

KINGSLEY, WALTER INGALLS, television executive; b. NYC, Oct. 20, 1923; s. Samuel and Esther (Schenker) K.; m. Betty Jane Bower, Oct. 14, 1944; children: Samuel John, James Oliver, Thomas Andrew; m. Patricia Ratchford, Apr. 1, 1966; 1 child, Janis Susan; m. Jeanene Foster, Mar. 3, 1979. Grad., Phillips Andover Acad., 1942; BA, Amherst Coll., 1947. Sales exec. Cowles Broadcasting Co., Boston, 1948-50; gen. sales mgr. Ziv TV, NYC and L.A., 1950-58; pres. Ind. TV Corp. (I.T.C.), NYC, 1958-62; exec. v.p. Wolper Prodns., Metromedia Producers Corp. div. Metromedia, NYC, 1966-72; pres. Kingsley Co., 1972-94, Am. Film Inst., 1983-94. Faculty Interracial Coun. for Bus. Opportunity, N.Y.C. Co-founder, bd. dirs. Big Bros. Greater L.A.; bd. dirs. Big Bros./Big Sisters Am.; trustee Windward Sch.; vice chmn. UCLA Ctr. on Aging. With AUS, 1943-46. Home: Portland, Oreg. Died Feb. 6, 2010.

KINTALA, CHANDRA MOHANRAO, computer scientist; b. Berhampur, India, July 22, 1948; came to U.S., 1974; s. Kumaraswamy and Drowpadi (Jammula) K.; M.Tech. in Elec. Engring., I.I.T., Kanpur, India, 1973; Ph.D. in Computer Sci., Pa. State U., 1977; m. Bharati Vysyaju, Aug. 18, 1977; children— Sreelata, Kumar Swamy. Asst. prof. U. So. Calif., Los Angeles, 1977-80; mem. tech. staff Bell Labs., Murray Hill, N.J., 1980-83, supr., 1984—; adj. prof. Stevens Inst. Tech.; cons. Control Data Corp., 1979-80. Mem. Assn. for Computing Machinery, IEEE, Computer Soc. India, Sigma Xi, Phi Kappa Phi. Inventor concept of restricted nondeterminism, 1976; contbr. articles in computational complexity, formal and programming langs., database systems and software engrng. to profl. jours. Home: Plainfield, NJ. Died Nov. 5, 2009.

KIPP, HENRY WILLIAM, forester, range conservationist; b. Pitts., Dec. 14, 1930; s. Harold Ambrose and Margarita (Boettger) Kipp; m. Elaine Jane Maki, June 22, 1962; children: Thomas J., Laurie A. BA in History, Trinity Coll., Hartford, Conn., 1954; postgrad., U. Pitts., 1956, Duke U., 1958; BS in Forestry, U. Idaho, 1960; MRA, U. Mont., 1972. Forestry technician Bur. Land Mgmt., 1960; forester Idaho Dept. Lands, 1961, Blackfeet Reservation, Bur. Indian Affairs, 1962—63, Timber Sales and Forest Devel. Flathead Reservation, 1963—68, in-charge, forest disease control program, 1968; supervisory natural resources specialist Rocky Boy's Reservation, Mont., 1968—83; natural resources mgr. Jicarilla Apache Reservation, Dulce, N.Mex., 1983—85; natural resources specialist Divsn. Water and Land Resources, Washington, from 1985. Lectr., natural resources Northern Mont. Coll., 1973—83; with Project '80 Extension, Water Studies Commns.; tchr. Triangle Youth Conservation Camps; participant, preparation forest history Rocky Boy's Reservation Hist. Rsch. Assocs., Missoula, Mont.; tree farmer. Contbr. articles to profl. jours. Participant Havre C. of C., Chippewa-Cree Tribe Winter Outdoor Recreation Devel., Bear Paw Ski Bowl, Mont., 1975—80, Mont., 1976—83; ruling elder First Presbyn. Ch., Havre, Mont., 1972—80. Decorated Letter Commendation Senator Len B. Jordan Idaho; recipient 5-Yr. Safety award, Bur. Indian Affairs, 1973, Havre C. of C. award, 1974; named Senator John Melcher, Mont., 1981. Mem.: Smithsonian Assocs., Soc. Am. Foresters, Soc. Range Mgmt. (chmn., Northern N.Mex. chpt. 1984—85), Am. Mus. Natural History (assoc.), Delta Tau Delta. Republican. Presbyterian. Home: Olympia, Wash. Died June 29, 2009.

KIRK, JAMES ROBERT, research development and quality assurance executive; b. DuBois, Pa., Oct. 30, 1941; s. Joseph James and Vinetta Helen (Fromm) K.; m. Elaine Gralton, Jan. 5, 1963 (div. July 1985); children: Leanne, James Joseph, John Daniel; m. Paulette DeJong, Sept. 15, 1985. BS in Biology, Holy Cross Coll., 1964; MS in Food Sci., Mich. State U., 1966, PhD, 1971. Asst. prof. Mich. State U., East Lansing, 1971-74, assoc. prof., 1974-78, prof., 1978; prof., chmn. dept. food sci. and human nutrition U. Fla., Gainesville, 1978-83; corp. v.p. R & D, Campbell Soup Co., Camden, N.J., 1983-91, corp. sr. v.p. R & D and quality assurance, from 1991; exec. v.p. Campbell Inst. Research and Tech., Camden, 1983-88, pres., from 1988; dir. Nat. Nutrition Consortium, 1979-83. Chmn. food nutrition conf. Gordon Rsch. Conf., 1982; mem. food nutrition bd. Nat. Acad. Scis., 1982-87. Contbr. over 100 articles to profl. jours. Recipient Future Leader award Nutrition Found., 1977. Fellow Inst. Food Technologists (Babcock Hart award 1983; exec. com. 1983-86); mem. Am. Soc. Agrl. Engrs., Research and Devel. Assn., Am. Chem. Soc. Avocations: tennis, photography, golf. Died June 7, 2010.

KIRLEY, MARION RACHEL, psychoanalyst, psychotherapist; b. Winthrop, Mass., Aug. 7, 1934; d. Patrick Francis and Hazel Elizabeth (Cody) K. BS in Nursing, Boston Coll., 1959, MS in Nursing, 1967, EdD, 1980. Diplomate Am. Bd. Med. Psychotherapists; cert. psychotherapist, clin. nurse specialist. Staff nurse Mass. Gen. Hosp., Boston, 1959-61, supr. operating room, 1961-63, psychiat. nurse clinician, 1969-74; instr. Mt. Auburn Hosp., Cambridge, Mass., 1963-65; nursing care coord. Danvers (Mass.) State Hosp., 1967-69; inst. Salem (Mass.) State Coll., 1976; nurse clinician San Francisco Gen. Hosp., 1981; asst. psychoanalyst Karen Horney Clinic, NYC, 1981-86, Soloman Carter Fuller Mental Health Ctr. Crisis Intervention, Boston, 1987-89; pvt. practice psychoanalysis Boston, 1987, NYC, 1989; pvt. practice Am. Inst. Psychoanalysis Psychotherapy Program, NYC, 1989. Mem. faculty Am. Inst. Psychoanalysis, 1989. Served to capt. USAF, 1969—74. Mem. Assn. Advancement Psychoanalysis (sec.), Am. Nursing Assn. (cert.), Am. Nurses Council Psychiat. Mental Health Nursing, Mass. Nurses Assn., Am. Inst. Psychoanalysis (cert.). Roman Catholic. Home: Salem, NH. Died Jan. 4, 2009.

KIRSCHENBAUM, ARTHUR SAMUEL, federal government education analyst; b. N.Y.C., Oct. 10, 1932; s. Edward and Ether (Oestriecher) K.; m. Athalie Frasier Solloway, Apr. 27, 1985; stepchildren: Barbara, Marcia, Debra. BBA, CCNY, 1959. Ednl. program analyst U.S. Dept. Edn., Washington, 1966—; conv. panelist Assn. Edn. and Communications Tech., Washington, 1972-74, Nat. Assn. Ednl. Broadcasters, Washington, 1973-75; del. Md. Gov.'s Conf. on Libraries and Info. Services, 1978. Mem. editorial bd. Pub. Library quar., 1978-82. Pres. Bowie Citizens Assn. (Md.), 1971; mem. Prince George Meml. Library Bd., Hyattsville, Md., 1973-78, chmn., 1977; parliamentarian, mem. Bowie Health Ctr., 1974-78; bd. dirs. Life Experiences Activities Program of Greater Washington, Inc., 1984-87; Active Friends Arlington County Lib., 1986—. Served with AUS, 1953-55. Mem. ALA (adv. bd. Office of Library Outreach 1973—), Am. Library Trustees Assn. (regional v.p. 1978-82, chmn. intellectual freedom com. 1976-77, resolutions com. 1987—, co-chmn. spl. outreach com. 1981-87, action devel. com. 1981—), Pub. Library Assn. (chmn. sub task force of pub. library heritage task force 1983-85), Assn. Specialized and Cooperative Library Agencies (Decade of Disabled Persons Com. 1984—), Mu Gamma Tau. Club: Can. Washington. Lodge: B'nai B'rith (pres. Chesapeake lodge 1978-79). Home: Edmonds, Wash. Died July 14, 2009.

KIRSHENBAUM, HOWARD DAVID, internist; b. Bklyn., 1948; s. Isidore and Lucy Kirshenbaum; m. Elaine B. Jaffe; children: Jennifer, Daniel. MD, Harvard Med. Sch., 1974. Cert. internal medicine 1977, cardiovasc. diseases, 1979. Intern Peter Bent Brigham Hosp., Boston, 1974-75, resident medicine, 1975-76; fellow rsch. cardiology Mass. Gen. Hosp., Boston, 1976-79; asst. prof. U. Mass. Med. Sch., from 1979; exec. dir. of med. affairs U. Mass. Health Sys.-Marlborough Hosp., 1997—2010. Fellow American Coll. Cardiology. Died May 26, 2010.

KIRSHNER, NORMAN, pharmacologist, educator, researcher; b. Wilkes-Barre, Pa., Sept. 21, 1923; s. Samuel and Marie (Frank) K.; m. Annette Grossman, Feb. 14, 1962; children: Naomi Lynn, Susan Laura, Miriam Amy. BS, U. Scranton, 1947; MS, Pa. State U., 1951, PhD, 1952. Asst. prof. biochemistry Duke U., 1957-66, assoc. prof., 1966-70, prof., from 1970, chmn. dept. pharmacology, 1977-88, prof. emeritus, from 1993. Mem. study sect. NSF, NIH, Washington; cons. Roche Inst., Nutley, N.J. Contbr. numerous articles to profl. jours.; editor: Molecular Pharmacology, 1978-82. Served with U.S. Army, 1943-45, ETO, PTO. NIH grantee, 1957—; NSF grantee Mem. Am. Soc. Biol. Chemists, Am. Soc. Pharmacology and Exptl. Therapeutics, Am. Soc. Neurochemistry Democrat. Jewish. Died June 27, 2010.

KISSELL, DON R., state legislator; Mem. dist. 17 Mo. Ho. of Reps. Died Mar. 15, 2010.

KIZER, JOHN OSCAR, lawyer; b. Wheeling, W.Va., Mar. 6, 1913; s. Edwin O. and Laura E. (Dennis) K.; m. Lillian Taylor Cart, Sept. 15, 1934; children: Nora Kizer Bell, Stephen. AB, W.Va. U., 1934, LLB, 1936. Bar: W.Va. 1936. Dir. safety responsibility dept. W.Va. Rd. Commn., 1936-39; assoc. Clark, Woodroe & Butts, Charleston, W.Va., 1939; ptnr. Campbell, Love, Woodroe & Kizer and predecessor firms, Charleston, 1939-75, Love, Wise, Robinson & Woodroe, Charleston, 1976-83, Love, Wise & Woodroe, Charleston, 1983-89, Kay, Casto, Chaney, Love & Wise, Charleston, from 1989. Gen. receiver Cir. Ct. Kanawha County, 1953-98; dir. emeritus Charleston Nat. Bank. Bd. dirs., past pres., co-incorporator Children's Mus., Charleston; co-incorporator Sunrise Found.; bd. dirs. Daywood Found. Recipient Spl. Achievement award for Pub. Svc. W.Va. U. Coll. of Law, 1991, W.Va. Bar Assn. Lifetime Achievement award, 1998. Mem. ABA, W.Va. Bar Assn., W.Va. State Bar (chmn. com.

legis. 1960-71, mem. com. legal ethics, 1964-84, chmn. 1968-84), Berry Hills Country Club, Delta Tau Delta. Presbyterian. Home: Macon, Ga. Died Apr. 8, 2009.

KLEIMAN, DEVRA GAIL, zoologist, park research scientist; b. NYC, Nov. 15, 1942; BS in Biopsychology, U. Chgo., 1964; PhD in Zoology, U. London, 1969. Rsch. asst. Wellcome Inst. Comparative Physiology, Zool. Soc. London, 1965-69; NIMH postdoctoral fellow Inst. Animal Behavior, Rutgers U., N.J., 1970-71; rsch. assoc. Smithsonian Instn., 1970-72; reproduction zoologist Nat. Zool. Pk., Smithsonian Instn., Washington, 1972-79, acting head dept. zool. rsch., 1979-81, head dept. zool. rsch., 1981-96, acting asst. dir. animal programs, 1983-84, asst. dir. rsch. ednl. activities, 1984-85, asst. dir. rsch., 1985-96, sr. rsch. scientist, 1997-2001; dir. conservation planning Conservation Internat., Washington, 2001—10. Adj. asst. prof. dept. Psychology George Washington U., 1974-77; adj. asst. prof. dept. Zoology U. Md., 1979-84, adj. prof., 1984-2010; studbook keeper International Studbook for Leontopithecus rosalia, 1974-84; grant reviewer NIMH, 1977, 81, NSF, 1978, 79; adj. prof. Biology George Mason U., Fairfax, Va., 1980-82; U.S. del. com. Internat. Ethological Conf., 1980-86; mem. bd. fellowships and grants Smithsonian Instn., 1982-84, chair rsch. policy com., 1984-86; mem. species survival plan mgmt. com. L. r. chrysomelas, 1985-2010, L. r. chrysopygus, 1986-2010; scientific adv. com. Jersey Wildlife Preservation Trust, 1986-2010; co-studbook keeper Giant Panda Ailuropoda melanoleuca, 1988-96; chair species survival plan giant panda, 1993-96; ad hoc reviewer behavioral and neuroscis. studies sect. NIH, 1988; adv. bd. program on zoos Sta. WQED, 1990; presenter numerous confs. Mem. editorial bd. International Zoo Yearbook, 1977-2010, Carnivore, 1977-81, Zoo Biology, 1982-99; consulting editor American Jour. Primatology, 1983-91; chief editor Wild Mammals in Captivity, 1983-96; field editor Jour. Soc. conservation Biology, 1986-2010; contbr. articles to profl. jours. Bd. dirs. Scientists Ctr. Animal Welfare, 1984-86; trustee Dian Fossey Gorilla Fund, 1990-95. Recipient Women in Sci. and Engring. award NSF, 1987, award for Disting. Achievement Soc. Conservation Biology, 1988, Outstanding Svc. award Am. Zoo and Aquarium Assn., 1993. Fellow AAAS, Animal Behavior Soc. (sec. 1977-80, pres. 1983-2010); mem. Am. Assn. Zool. Pks. and Aquariums (species coord., internal mgmt. com. L. r. rosalia, species survival plan subcom. 1986-90, vice chair Giant Panda task force 1988-92, chair 1992-93, mem New World Primate TAG, Cheetah SSP, Brazil FIG, Reintro. adv. group, rsch. coord. group 1991-2010, chair behavior and husbandry adv. group 1992-93), World Conservation Union (mem. SSC primate specialist group 1983-2010, SSC reintro./specialist group 1988-2010, vice-chair primates 1989-2010), Consortium Aquariums, Univs. and Zoos (adv. com. 1986-2010), Internat. Soc. Endangered Cats (rsch. adv. bd. 1988-91), Sigma Xi. Died Apr. 29, 2010.

KLEIN, BURTON HAROLD, economics educator; b. Mpls., Oct. 16, 1917; s. Joseph Harry and Ethel Anna (Figen) K.; m. Cecelia Katz, Jan. 29, 1955; children— Roger, Jon, Margaret Ann. BA, Harvard Coll., 1940, PhD, 1953. Staff mem. Council Econ. Advisors, Washington, 1948-52; with Rand Corp., Santa Monica, Calif., 1952-67, head econs. dept., 1963-67; spl. asst. to Sec. Def., Washington, 1963-65; prof. econs. Calif. Inst. Tech., Pasadena, from 1967. Vis. prof. Harvard U., 1961, Hebrew Univ., Jerusalem, 1963, M.I.T., 1981 Author: Germany's Economic Preparations for War, 1956, Dynamic Economics, 1977, Wages, Prices, and Business Cycles, 1983. Served with A.C. U.S. Army, 1942-46. Recipient David Wells Prize Harvard U., 1953. Mem.; Phi Beta Kappa. Jewish. Home: Santa Barbara, Calif. Died Feb. 12, 2010.

KLEIN, LEONARD ROBERT, government official; b. Erie, Pa., Sept. 8, 1938; s. Robert George and Mary Elizabeth (Logan) K.; m. Ruth Ann O'Neil, Dec. 9, 1967 (div. May 1991); children: Kristen Ann, Martin Leonard. BS in Indsl. Mgmt., Gannon U., Erie, 1960. Mgmt. intern Pa. Civil Svc. Commn., Harrisburg, 1960-62; staffing specialist Naval Supply Depot, Mechanicsburg, Pa., 1962-63; joy analyst Naval Propellant Plant, Indian Head, Md., 1963-66; chief job analyst Naval Med. Ctr., Bethesda, Md., 1966-67; job analyst Navy Dept., Washington, 1967-69; regional coord. Navy Office of Manpower, Balliston, Va., 1969-72; pers. dir. Naval Oceanographic Office, Suitland, Md., 1972-74, Naval Surface Weapons Ctr., Dahlgren, Va., 1974-80; dir. staffing and pay U.S. Navy Dept., Washington, 1980-83, 85-86; pers. dir. Navy Material Command, Washington, 1983-85; dep. assoc. U.S. Office Pers. Mgmt., Washington, 1986-89, assoc. dir., from 1989. Mgmt. intern Pa. Civil Svc. Commn., Harrisburg, 1960-62; staffing specialist Naval Supply Depot, Mechanicsburg, Pa., 1962-63; job analyst Naval Propellant Plant, Indian Head, Md., 1963-66; chief job analyst Naval Med. Ctr., Bethesda, Md., 1966-67. Recipient Meritorious Svc. medal Navy Dept., 1981, Superior Svc. medal, 1985; named Meritorious Exec. Pres. Reagan, 1988, Disting. Exec. Pres. Clinton, 1993. Died Feb. 7, 2009.

KLEIN, MARTIN HERBERT, pharmaceutical company executive; b. N.Y.C., June 11, 1917; s. Harry and Lillian (Rogick) K.; m. Mimi Gilbert, May 16, 1943; children— Allan S., Jodi H. B.S., CCNY, 1938. Salesman Premo Pharm. Labs., South Hackensack, N.J., 1946-70; v.p., gen. mgr. Spencer Mead Inc., Valley Stream, N.Y., 1970-79; v.p. sales Premo Pharm. Labs., South Hackensack, 1979-80; sales mgr. Vitarine Co., Springfield Gardens, N.Y., 1980-83, Pvt. Formulation Inc., Edison, N.J., 1983-86; nat. dir. sales, Inwood Labs., Inc., 1986—. Served to 1st lt. USAF, 1942-46. Democrat. Avocation: copper embossing. Home: Bellmore, NY. Died Apr. 5, 2010.

KLEIN, MARTIN SAMUEL, management consultant; b. NYC, Dec. 8, 1932; s. David and Dorothy (Manheim) K.; m. Elizabeth Jann Perks, Dec. 19, 1964 (dec. Aug. 1994); children: Sarah Madeline, Dorothy Ann. AB, Harvard U., 1954, MBA, 1962. V.p. United Rsch., Cambridge, Mass., 1962-69, Boston Cons. Group, 1969-73; pres. Instnl. Strategy Assocs., Belmont, Mass., 1973—2005. Cons. Brookings Instn., Washington, 1963-64. Author: (with others) Impact of Transportation on Development, 1964, Combining Public Health Nursing Agencies, 1964; contbr. articles to profl. jours. Bd. dirs. Vis. Nurse Assn., Boston, 1972-82, Harvard Cmty. Health Plan, Boston, 1978-93; vice chmn. Harvard Cmty. Health Plan Found., 1986-93, Cambridge Ctr. for Adult Edn., 1983-85; sec.-treas. Ctr. for Effective Philanthropy, Cambridge, 1982-98; trustee Mt. Auburn Hosp., Cambridge, 1995-2006, overseer, 1994—; trustee Big Sister Assn. Greater Boston, 1996-99, Walter E. Fernald Corp., 2005—; counselor to bd. trustees Aga Khan U., Karachi, 1993-2002. Sr. fellow Cheswick Ctr., 1980—, trustee; Harvard Coll. scholar, 1954, Fulbright scholar, Australia, 1954-55, George F. Baker scholar Harvard Bus. Sch., 1962. Mem. Am. Hosp. Assn. (com. on governance 1998-2001), Mass. Hosp. Assn. (trustee adv. coun. 2002-06), Harvard Club (N.Y.C. and Boston), Belmont Hill Club (treas. 1979-80), Harvard Travellers Club (Boston), Kirribilli Club (Sydney, Australia). Jewish. Home: Duxbury, Mass. Died May 4, 2009.

KLEIN, STANLEY JOSEPH, industrial engineering consultant; b. Rochester, NY, Nov. 17, 1916; s. Benjamin and Ethel (Cohen) K.; m. Rosalind Glazer, Aug. 30, 1940; children: Penelope, Abby, Andrew. BS in Mech. Engring., U. Rochester, 1939. Registered profl. engr., N.Y.; accredited Bd. Cert. Safety Profls., Nat. Coun. Engring. Examiners. Design engr. Electromatic div. IBM Corp., Rochester, 1939-44, Eastman Kodak Co., Rochester, 1944-46; chief engr. LeRoy (N.Y.) Machine Co., 1947-58; dir. safety, mgr. product devel. plastics div. Nat. Distillers Corp., Macedon, N.Y., 1958-62; indsl. engring. cons., owner S.J. Klein Assocs., Rochester, from 1962. Safety cons. UN Indsl. Devel. Orgn., Vienna, Austria, 1974, 76, 84. Author: How to Avoid Products Liability-Management Guide, 1980. Past pres. Rochester Safety Council; mem. citizen's adv. bd. Monroe County Legis. Pub. Works Com.; vol. exec. Internat. Exec. Service Corps. Mem. ASME, NSPE (past chmn. forensic engrs. com.), Am. Soc. Safety Engrs. (past pres), Human Factors Soc. Home: Milwaukee, Wis. Died Jan. 16, 2009.

KLEMM, RICHARD HENRY, retired investment company executive; b. NYC, Aug. 10, 1931; s. Richard F. and Sophie (Leymann) K.; m. June Christ, Feb. 21, 1954; children: Janet, Lynda, Richard. BSCE, Bucknell U., 1953; MBA in Econs., NYU, 1964. Fin. planner N.Y. Tel., NYC, 1956-65; div. mgr. AT&T Corp., NYC, 1965-81; v.p. GTE Investment Mgmt. Corp., Stamford, Conn., 1981-85; exec. v.p. Warburg, Pincus Counsellors, NYC, 1985-98; v.p. E.M. Warburg, Pincus & Co., NYC, 1987-98, ret., 1998. Prin. Boxwood Inns, Akron, Pa., 1991—, ExecuServ, Akron, 1985—; vice chair Akron Water/Sewer Authority, 1996—; bd. dirs. Ridge Oak, Inc., Basking Ridge, N.J., sec.-treas., 1990, v.p. 1991. Bd. dirs. Pa. Dutch Conv. and Vis. Bur., Lancaster, 1995—. Mem. Ephrata (Pa.) C. of C. Republican. Episcopalian. Home: Willow Street, Pa. Died Jan. 11, 2009.

KLEMMER, WERNER EDWARD, banker; b. Boston, June 2, 1923; s. August William and Hilda Augusta (Ehrmann) K.; m. Louise Martin, June 28, 1947; children— Lisa Klemmer Vallieres, Lynne Klemmer Husby BA, Brown U., 1944. Loan interviewer Nat. City Bank, NYC, 1946-49; pres., chmn. Franklin Bank, Paterson, N.J., 1949-80; chmn., chief exec. officer Northeastern Bank, Paramus, N.J., 1980-83; chmn. bd. Horizon Bank, Morristown, N.J., from 1983. Dir. Horizon Bancorp, Morristown Councilman, Borough of Paramus, 1953-58; bd. taxation Bergen County, Hackensack, N.J., 1961-67. Served to lt. (j.g.) USN, 1943-46; ETO, PTO Mem.: Ridgewood Country (Paramus); Hamilton (treas. 1970-74) (Paterson). Avocations: golf, tennis. Home: Vineyard Havn, Mass. Died June 28, 2009.

KLETZSCH, CHARLES FREDERICK, composer; b. Milw., Apr. 4, 1926; s. Gustav Adolph and Elizabeth (Schroeder) K. BA, Harvard U., 1951, MA, 1953. Composer in residence Dunster House Library Dunster House, Cambridge, Mass, from 1953. Composer instrumental, vocal and operatic chamber music. Avocation: swimming. Home: Lexington, Mass. Died Jan. 15, 2009.

KLIMAN, SYLVIA STERN, communications executive; b. Boston, July 16, 1934; d. Edward I. and Bernice Stern; m. Allan Kliman, June 24, 1956; children: Gilbert Harrow, Douglas Hartley. AB, Vassar Coll., 1956. Editl. asst. Harvard Law Sch. profs., Cambridge, Mass., 1956-58; editor Vassar Micellany News, Poughkeepsie, N.Y., 1953-56; editor, founder Park Parent, Brookline, Mass., 1968-73; pres. Sylvia S. Kliman Real Estate Brokerage, Brookline, from 1971. Pres. Dunewind Films, 1979—, creative cons. for feature films & TV, 1977—. Vol. Mass. ARC blood program, 1970-73; polit. speechwriter, 1960—; mem. Barn Gallery, Ogunquit Mus. of Art, Friends of Vassar Art Gallery; trustee Park Sch., Brookline, 1970-73; bd. friends Peter Bent Brigham Hosp., 1970-75; bd. dirs. Spl. Com. to Restore Ogunquit Dunes, 1975—. Mem. Park Sch. Parents Assn. (pres. 1968-70), Norfolk Dist. Med. Soc. Womens Aux., Boston Mus. Fine Arts, Vassar Club (bd. dirs.), Coll. Club. Unitarian. Home: Brookline, Mass. Died Jan. 1, 2010.

KLIMCZAK, ERNEST JOSEPH, paper company executive; b. Chgo., Aug. 3, 1924; s. John and Angeline (Niadek) K.; m. Bernice Owsiany, May 15, 1965. BS, Ill. Inst. Tech., 1945; MBA, U. Chgo., 1958, diploma exec. program, 1959. Registered profl. engr., Ill. With Ahlberg Bearing Co., Chgo., 1943-58, v.p., gen. mgr., dir., 1955-58; exec. v.p., dir. Braden Winch Co., Tulsa, 1958; gen. mgr. Arrow Gear Co., Tulsa, 1958-59; v.p. Motor Products Corp., Detroit, 1959-60; pres., dir. Allied/Egry Bus. Systems Co., Dayton, Ohio, 1960-64; Egry Continuous Forms, Ltd., Toronto, Ont., Can., 1960-64; pres. Allied Paper Corp., Chgo., 1964-73; v.p. SCM Corp., Kalamazoo, from 1973; pres. Allied Paper Inc., from 1964. Died Mar. 24, 2010.

KLIMES, CYRIL STEFAN, construction company executive; b. Piestany, Czechoslovakia, Jan. 18, 1935; came to U.S., 1960; s. Jozef and Maria Anna (Bartek) K.; m. Gladys Leticia Arancibia, May 26, 1933; children: Brigitte Anna, Michelle Tamara, Charlotte Corine, Yvette Elke. BS in Constrn. Engring., Universidad Santa Maria, Valparaiso, Chile, 1960; BS in Indls. Mgmt., Lawrence Inst. Tech., 1972. Jr. estimator Walbridge Aldinger Co., Livonia, Mich., 1960-62, estimator, 1962-64, project mgr., 1964-66, v.p. engring. and estimating, 1966-73, sr. v.p., from 1973. Mem. Engring. Soc. Detroit, Am. Mgmt. Assn. Clubs: Chilean Mich. (adv., treas. 1984). Avocation: soccer. Died July 16, 2009.

KLINE, RAYMOND ADAM, professional organization executive; b. New Ringgold, Pa., Sept. 14, 1926; s. Raymond Adam and Helen Marie (Herb) K.; m. Jeanelle Batley, Apr. 26, 1958; children— Robin Jeanelle, Raymond Ashley. AB, Lebanon Valley Coll., 1950, LLD (hon.), 1990; LLB, George Washington U., 1957, JD (hon.), 1982. Bar: DC 1958. Mgmt. analyst Army Missile Command, Huntsville, Ala., 1958-61; chief mgmt. devel. office Marshall Space Flight Ctr., Huntsville, 1961-66; asst. assoc. adminstr. for systems mgmt. NASA Hdqrs., Washington, 1967-75, asst. adminstr. instl. mgmt., 1975-77, assoc. adminstr. mgmt. ops, 1977-79; dep. adminstr. GSA, 1979-84, acting adminstr., 1981, 1984-85; pres. Nat. Acad. Pub. Adminstrn., 1985-92. Instr. in polit. sci. U. Ala., 1958-63 Trustee The Kerr Found., Inc., Okla. City, Okla., 1993-2010. Served with US Army, 1944-46, 50-51. Mem. D.C. Bar, Phi Delta Phi, Pi Gamma Mu. Home: Rockville, Md. Died Apr. 14, 2010.

KLINMAN, NORMAN RALPH, immunologist, medical educator; b. Phila., Mar. 23, 1937; s. William and Miriam (Ralph) K.; m. Linda A. Sherman, June 18, 1978; children— Andrew, Douglas, Theodore, Matthew AB, Haverford Coll., Pa., 1958; MD, Jefferson Med. Coll., Phila., 1962; PhD (Helen Hay Whitney Found. research fellow 1963-66), U. Pa., 1965. Fellow in immunology U. Pa. Med. Sch., 1962-66, Weizman Inst., Tel Aviv, 1966-67, Nat. Inst. Med. Research, London, 1967-68; mem. faculty U. Pa. Med. Sch., 1968-78, prof. pathology, 1975-78; prof. dept. immunology The Scripps Rsch. Inst., La Jolla, Calif., from 1978. Adj. prof. U. Calif., San Diego; cons. NIH, 1975-78; mem. sci. adv. bd. Hybritech, 1981-86, Baxter, 1985—; mem. NIH Aging Rev. Com., 1982-85, I UIS Nomenclature Com., 1983-87; mem. fellowship screening com. ACS, Calif. div., 1983-85. Author articles in field, chpts. in books; assoc. editor: Immunochemistry, 1970-74, Jour. Immunology, 1972-76, Developmental and Comparative Immunology, 1982-86, Jour. Molecular and Cellular Immunology, 1983—, Internat. Revs. of Immunology, 1984—, Jour. Exptl. Zoology, 1985-87, Aging: Immunological and Infectious Diseases, 1987-95; adv. editor: Jour. Exptl. Medicine; editor: B Lymphocytes in the Immune Response. Am. Cancer Soc. research scholar, 1966-68; recipient USPHS Career Devel. award, 1970-75, Parke-Davis award, 1976, NIH Merit award 1987. Mem. Am. Assn. Immunologists, Am. Assn. Exptl. Pathologists, Gerontology Soc. Am., Internat. Soc. Developmental and Comparative Immunology Home: La Jolla, Calif. Died May 4, 2010.

KLIPHARDT, RAYMOND A., engineering educator; b. Chgo., Mar. 18, 1917; s. Adolph Lewis and Hortense Marietta (Brandt) K.; m. Rhoda Joan Anderson, May 5, 1945; children: Janis Kliphardt Emery, Judith Kliphardt Ecklund, Jill Kliphardt White, Joan Kliphardt Quinn, Jennifer Kliphardt Miller. BS, Ill. Inst. Tech., Chgo., 1938, MS, 1948. Instr. North Park Coll., Chgo., 1938-43; asst. prof. Northwestern U., Evanston, Ill., 1945-51, assoc. prof., 1952-63, prof. engring. scis., 1964-87, prof. emeritus, from 1987, dir. U. Khartoum project, 1964-68, dir. focus program, 1975-78, chmn. engring. scis. and applied maths. dept., 1978-87. Cons. applied maths. div. Argonne Nat. Lab., Lemont, Ill., 1962-63; cons. on patent litigation Kirkland and Ellis, Chgo., 1976-77. Author: Analytical Graphics, 1957; Program Design in Fortran IV, 1970. Mem. bd. edn. Morton Grove, Ill., 1952-55, Niles Twp., Ill., 1957-58. Served as ensign USNR, 1943-45. Recipient Western Electric Fund award for excellence in instrn. of engring. students, Am. Soc. Engring. Edn., 1967. Home: Lombard, Ill. Died May 23, 2009.

KLOPMAN, WILLIAM ALLEN, manufacturing executive; b. NYC, Aug. 23, 1921; s. William and Hazel Alice (Wolfe) K.; m. Anne Lyon, Dec. 28, 1944; children: William A. Jr., Peter H., Linda A., Betsy L., James, Thomas S. BA, Williams Coll., 1943. Apprentice Burlington Industries, NYC, 1946-47; pres. Klopman Mills, Inc., NYC, 1960-69; group v.p. Burlington Industries, NYC, 1972-74, pres./dir., 1974-76, chief exec. officer, 1976-86. Bd. dirs. N.C. Nat. Bank, Charlotte. Trustee N.C. State U.; pres. HoHoKus (N.J.) Sch. Bd., 1968-74. Lt. (j.g.) USN, 1942-46, PTO, MTO. Decorated Bronze Star; recipient Frank L. Geise textile award Phila. Coll. Textile Sci., Samuel Slater Disting. Svc. award Am. Textile Inst., 1986. Mem. Am. Textile Mfg. Inst. (pres. 1982), Soc. of Fiber Sci. and Tech. Republican. Episcopalian. Avocations: fly fishing, golf, tennis, photography. Home: Greensboro, NC. Died July 25, 2010.

KLOSKA, RONALD FRANK, manufacturing executive; b. Grand Rapids, Mich., Oct. 24, 1933; s. Frank B. and Catherine (Hilaski) K.; m. Mary F. Minick, Sept. 7, 1957; children: Kathleen Ann, Elizabeth Marie, Ronald Francis, Mary Josephine, Carolyn Louise. Student, St. Joseph Sem., Grand Rapids, Mich., 1947-53; PhB, U. Montreal, Que., Can., 1955; MBA, U. Mich., 1957. Staff acct. Coopers & Lybrand, Niles, Mich., 1957, staff to sr. acct., 1960—63; treas. Skyline Corp., Elkhart, Ind., 1963, v.p., treas., 1964—67, exec. v.p. fin., 1967—74, pres., 1974—85, pres., chief ops. officer, 1985—91, vice chmn., chief adminstrn. officer, 1991—94, vice chmn., chief adminstrn. officer, sec., 1994—95, vice chmn., dep. CEO, chief adminstrn. officer, 1995—98, vice chmn., CEO, chief adminstrn. officer, 1998—2001, dir., cons., from 2001. With US Army, 1957—60. Mem. Mich. Soc. CPAs, Ind. Soc. CPAs, South Bend Country Club. Roman Catholic. Home: South Bend, Ind. Died May 16, 2009.

KLUGE, JOHN WERNER, retired broadcast executive; b. Chemnitz, Germany, Sept. 21, 1914; s. Fritz Kluge and Gertrude Donj; m. Theodora Thomson, 1946 (div.); m. Yolanda Zucco, 1969 (div.); children: Samantha, Joseph; m. Patricia Rose Gay, 1981 (div. 1991); 1 child, John Werner II; m. Maria Tussi. Student, Wayne U.; BA, Columbia, 1937. Vice pres., sales mgr. Otten Bros., Inc., Detroit, 1937-41; pres., dir. radio sta. WGAY, Silver Spring, Md., 1946-59, St. Louis Broadcasting Corp., Brentwood, Mo., 1953-58, Pitts. Broadcasting Co., 1954-59; pres., treas., dir. Capitol Broadcasting Co., Nashville, 1954-59, Asso. Broadcasters, Inc., Ft. Worth-Dallas, 1957-59; partner Western N.Y. Broadcasting Co., Buffalo, 1957-60; pres., dir. Washington Planagraph Co., 1956-60, Mid.-Fla. Radio Corp., Orlando, 1952-59; treas., dir. Mid-Fla. Television Corp., 1957-60; owner Kluge Investment Co., Washington, 1956-60; partner Nashton Properties, Nashville, 1954-60, Texworth Investment Co., Ft. Worth, 1957-60; chmn. bd. Seaboard Service System, Inc., 1957-58; chm. bd., pres., CEO Metromedia Inc., Secaucus, NJ, 1959-86; former gen. ptnr., chm. bd., pres., CEO Metromedia Co.; now pres., chmn. bd. Benale Holdings Corp., Dallas; also chmn., dir. LDDS Comm., Jackson, Miss.; investor, operator NY/NJ Metro Stars, Secaucus, NJ, 1995. Pres. New Eng. Fritos, Boston, 1947—55, NY Inst. Dietetics, NYC, 1953—60; chmn. bd., pres., dir. Metromedia, Inc., NYC, Bear Stearns Co., Inc.; chmn. bd., treas., dir. Kluge, Finkelstein & Co., Balt.; chmn. bd., treas. Tri-Suburban Broadcasting Corp., Washington, Kluge & Co., Belding Hemingway Co., Inc.; chmn. bd., pres., treas. Silver City Sales Co., Washington; bd. dirs. Marriott-Hot Shoppes, Inc., Chock Full O' Nuts Corp., Nat. Bank Md., Waldorf Astoria Corp., Just One Break, Inc., Belding Heminway Co., Inc.; mem. adv. coun. Mfrs. Hanover Trust Co.; mem. Washington Bd. Trade. Trustee Strang Clinic Miliken U.; bd. govs. NY Coll. Osteo. Medicine; v.p., bd. dirs. United Cerebral Palsy Rsch. & Ednl. Found., from 1972; bd. dirs. Brand Names Found., Inc., Shubert Found. Served as capt. US Army, 1941—45. Named one of The World's Richest People, Forbes Mag., 1999—2010, Forbes 400: Richest Americans, Forbes mag., 1999—2010. Mem.: Nat. Sugar Brokers Assn., Advt. Coun. NYC, Grocery Mfrs. Reps. Washington, Nat. Assn. Radio & TV Broadcasters, Advt. Club Washington, Grocery Wheels Washington, Washington Food Brokers Assn. (pres. 1958), Nat. Food Brokers Assn., NYC Met. Club, Nat. Capital Skeet &Trap Club, Washington Army Navy. Died Sept. 8, 2010.

KNAKE, ELLERY LOUIS, weed science educator; b. Gibson City, Ill., Aug. 26, 1927; s. Louis Franz and Wilhelmina Dorthea (Behrens) K.; m. Colleen Mary Wilken, June 23, 1951; children: Gary Louis, Kim Paul. BS, U. Ill., 1949, MS (Wright fellow), 1950, PhD, 1960; weed stomper degree (hon.), Oreg. State U.; Future Farmers of Am. state farmer degree. Tchr. vocat. agr. Barrington (Ill.) Consol. High Sch., 1950-56; instr. vocat. agr. service U. Ill., Urbana, 1956-60, asst. prof. weed sci. dept. agronomy, 1960-64, assoc. prof., 1964-69, prof., 1969-95, prof. dept. crop scis., from 1995. UNDP cons., Yugoslavia, 1976; participant East-West Ctr. Confs., Honolulu, 1976-77, 1st Internat. Weed Control Congress, Australia, 1992, People to People Agronomy Del., People's Republic of China, 1983. Editor Weeds Today mag., 1978-82; assoc. editor Agronomy Jour., 1976-78; mem. editorial bd. Meister Pub. Co., 1988—; contbr. articles to profl. jours. Mem. Order of Arrow, Boy Scouts Am.; mem. Marching Illini Football Band, 1945. With AUS, 1945-46. Recipient Ciba-Geigy award for outstanding contbns. to agr., 1972, Educator award Midwest Agr. Chem. Assn., 1975, Funk award Coll. Agr., U. Ill., 1978, Superior Svc. award U.S. Dept. Agr., 1983, Sustained Excellence award Ill. Coop. Ext. Svc., 1983, Good Nabor Alumnus award Nabor House Fraternity, 1983. Fellow Am. Soc. Agronomy (best article award Crops. and Soils mag. 1967, ext. edn. award 1978), Weed Sci. Soc. Am. (v.p. 1972, pres.-elect 1973, pres., chmn. bd. 1974, bd. dirs. 1986-88, Outstanding Ext. Worker award 1972, editl. bd. Herbicide Handbook); mem. North Cen. Weed Control Conf. (hon., 2d v.p. 1969, 1st v.p. 1970, pres. 1971, bd. dirs. 1985-88), Crop Sci. Soc. Am., Am. Agrl. Editors Assn., Internat. Weed Sci. Soc., Intersoc. Consortium Plant Protection, Iroquois County Hist. Soc. (charter life), Soc. Chem. Industry (Pest Mgmt. in Soybean Conf. London 1992), Coun. for Agrl. Sci. and Tech. (bd. dirs. 1984-93), Am. Legion, KC (3d degree), Sigma Xi, Phi Eta Sigma, Alpha Tau Alpha, Alpha Zeta, Phi Kappa Phi, Gamma Sigma Delta, Epsilon Sigma Phi, Nabor House (bd. dirs. 1951-52, v.p. 1955-57, pres. 1958-60). Roman Catholic. Home: Urbana, Ill. Died Mar. 1, 2009.

KNAPP, BETTINA LIEBOWITZ, literature educator; b. NYC, May 9, 1926; d. David and Emily (Gresser) Liebowitz; m. Russell S. Knapp, Aug. 28, 1949; children: Albert, Charles. BA, Barnard Coll., 1947; MA, Columbia U., 1949, PhD, 1956; cert., Sorbonne, 1947. Lectr. Columbia U., 1952-60; prof. Hunter Coll., from 1961, Grad. Center CUNY, from 1961. Lectr. in field. Author numerous books including: Louis Jouvet, Man of the Theatre, 1957, That Was Yvette. A Biography of Yvette Guilbert, 1964, Aristide Bruant, A Biography, 1968, Jean Genet, 1968, Jean Cocteau. A Critical Study of his Writings, 1970, Georges Duhamel. A Critical Study of his Writings, 1972, Off-Stage Voices, 1975, Dream and Image, 1977, Maurice Maeterlinck, Fernand Crommelynck, 1978, Anais Nin, 1978, The Prometheus Syndrome, 1979, Gerard de Nerval The Mystic's Dilemma, 1980, Emile Zola, 1980, Theatre and Alchemy, 1980, Sacha Guitry, 1981, Paul Claudel, 1982, The Lewis Mumford/David Liebovitz Letters 1923-1968, 1983, Archetypes, Dance, and the Writer, 1984, Andrée Chedid, 1984, A Jungian Approach to Literature, 1984, Edgar Allan Poe, 1984, Word/Image/Psyche, 1985, French Theatre, 1918-1939, 1985, Stephen Crane, 1987, Women in Twentieth-Century Literature: A Jungian View, 1987, Archetype, Architecture and the Writer, 1986, The Reign of the French Theatrical Director: 1887-1924, 1988, Music, Archetype, and the Writer: A Jungian View, 1988, Liliane Atlan, 1988, Machine, Metaphor, and the Writer, 1989, Emily Dickinson, 1989, Gertrude Stein, 1990; contbr. articles to profl. jours. Guggenheim fellow, 1973-74; Am. Philos. Soc. grantee, 1975-76; recipient Alliance Française medal, 1948, Shuster award, 1981. Jewish. Died Aug. 27, 2010.

KNAPP, DAVID CURTIS, retired academic administrator; b. Syracuse, NY, Nov. 13, 1927; s. Clifford Raymond and Alma Isobel (Curtis) K.; m. Rita Kyllikki Roschier, Aug. 31, 1964; children: Karl M., Eric J. AB, Syracuse U., 1947; MA, U. Chgo., 1948, PhD, 1953; LLD (hon.), U. N.H., 1978, Emerson Coll., 1989; LHD (hon.), Northeastern U., 1986; LLD, U. Mass., 1990. Asst. prof. to prof. govt. U. N.H., 1953-62, dean Coll. Liberal Arts, 1961-62; asso. dir. Study of Am. Colls. of Agr., College Park, Md., 1963-65; dir. Inst. of Coll. and Univ. Adminstrs. Am. Council on Edn., 1965-68; dean N.Y. State Coll. Human Ecology Cornell U., Ithaca, N.Y., 1968-74, provost, 1974-78; pres. U. Mass., 1978-90, pres. emeritus, Ralph Waldo Emerson prof., 1990—2010. Author: (with C.E. Kellogg) The College of Agriculture: Science in the Public Service, 1964. Served with U.S. Army, 1950-52. Decorated Order of Rising Sun (Japan); Fulbright rsch. scholar, Finland, 1959-60; Bullard fellow Harvard U. Grad. Sch. Pub. Adminstrn., 1962-63. Mem. Am. Polit. Sci. Assn., Am. Soc. for Pub. Adminstrn., Phi Beta Kappa. Home: Concord, Mass. Died Apr. 13, 2010.

KNAPP, ELIZABETH MARGARET, college registrar; b. Kalamazoo, Mich., Dec. 24, 1923; d. Charles Merriam and Evelyn (Osborn) K. B.A., MacMurray Coll., 1945. Sec. bldg. and endowment fund Bennett Coll., Millbrook, N.Y., 1946-52, dir. of residence, 1952-60, assoc. dir. internat. studies program, 1960-73, asst. to dean, 1970-73, registrar, 1973-78; registrar Bradford Coll., Mass., 1978—. Recipient Greek prize MacMurray Coll., 1944-45. Mem. Am. Assn. Collegiate Registrars and Admissions Officers, New Eng. Assn. Collegiate Registrars and Admissions Officers, D.A.R. Republican. Episcopalian. Avocations: travel, sewing, reading. Home: Haverhill, Mass. Died June 17, 2010.

KNAPP, PETER OSBORN, banker; b. Lexington, Ky., Aug. 13, 1930; s. Charles M. and Evelyn (Osborn) K.; m. Barbara Elizabeth Curtis, June 11, 1957; children: Curtis Merriam, Elizabeth Knapp Morris. AB, Kenyon Coll., Gambier, Ohio, 1952; MBA, Wharton Sch., Phila., 1959. Trainee First Pa. Bank, Phila., 1957-59; v.p. Cen. Trust Co., Cin., 1959-69; mgr. fin. and adminstrn. Distronics Corp., Cherry Hill, N.J., 1969-71; v.p. Provident Bank, Cin., 1971-75; sr. v.p. Soc. Bank, N.A., Dayton, Ohio, 1975-89, exec. v.p. credit adminstr., from 1990; regional exec. v.p. Soc. Nat. Bank, from 1992. Chmn. Met. YMCA, Dayton, 1987-89, exec. com. Ohio Found. Ind. Coll. Inc., Columbus, 1984—, St. Leonard Ctr., Dayton, 1985-88, St. Mary Devel. Corp., 1991—. Mem. Robert Morris Assocs. (pres. Ohio Valley chpt. 1966), Dayton Country Club. Republican. Episcopalian. Avocation: swimming. Home: Hilton Head, SC. Died Feb. 8, 2009.

KNICKERBOCKER, DANIEL CANDEE, JR., legal educator; b. Glen Ridge, NJ, Apr. 16, 1919; s. Daniel Candee and Elizabeth Eleanor (Hadley) K.; m. Helaine Joyce Blutman, Mar. 23, 1951; children: Daniel Candee III, Mallory Jane. AB, Syracuse U., 1940; JD with distinction, Cornell U., 1950; postgrad., Harvard U., 1940-41, postgrad. Sch. Bus. Adminstrn., 1969. Bar: N.Y. 1951, U.S. Supreme Ct. 1959, Mass. 1964. Acct., Bethlehem Steel Co., 1942-47; assoc. Carter, Ledyard & Milburn, NYC, 1950-58, Skadden, Arps, Slate, Meagher & Flom, NYC, 1958-60, McCanliss & Early, NYC, 1961-63; tax counsel John Hancock Mut. Life Ins. Co., Boston, 1963-66, counsel, 1966-70, v.p. and counsel, 1970-83, sr. v.p., gen solicitor, 1983-84; prof. law Seton Hall U. Sch Law, Newark, 1984-90, prof. emeritus, from 1990; vis. prof. law N.Y. Law Sch., from 1990. Lectr. law Cornell U., 1959-60; grad. tax program Boston U., 1965, 66, 67, 81, 82, U. Conn., 1979-80; mem. Tax Mgmt. Adv. Bd. on Estates, Trusts and Gifts, 1972—. Editor-in-chief Cornell Law Quar., 1949-50; author Fiduciary Responsibility under ERISA, 1991, supplement 1992, 94, 95, 96; contbr. articles to profl. jours. Pres. South Brooklyn Neighborhood Houses, 1962-63, New Eng. Home for Little Wanderers, 1973-76; bd. dirs. Family Counseling and Guidance Centers, Boston, 1974-84, hon. dir. for life, 1985—, v.p., 1979-80, pres., 1980-83. Fellow Am. Coll. Tax Counsel; mem. Am. Law Inst. (life), ABA (sec. coun. real property, probate and trust law 1983-89), Assn. Bar City N.Y. (mem. employee benefits com. 1991-94, 95—), Assn. Life Ins. Counsel (chmn. tax sect. 1982-84), Cornell Law Assn. (exec. com. 1959-62), AAUP, Soc. Am. Law Tchrs., Order of Coif, Phi Kappa Phi, Psi Upsilon. Democrat. Episcopalian. Home: Brooklyn, NY. Died May 17, 2010.

KNISEL, RUSSELL H., banker; b. Englewood, NJ, June 18, 1933; s. Adolph C. and Elsie (Vieght) K.; m. Diane Taylor, June 18, 1955; children: Susan, Kimberly, Sally, Russell H. BA, Wesleyan U., Middletown, Conn., 1955; postgrad., Harvard Grad. Sch. Bus., 1963. Pension mgr. Conn. Gen. Life Ins. Co., 1955-58; with Marine Midland Bank, NYC, 1958-78, sr. v.p., 1968-74, exec. v.p., 1974-76, group exec. v.p., 1976-78; vice chmn. Conn. Nat. Bank, from 1978. Dir. Miller Co., Chase Packaging Corp. Trustee Conn. Trust Historic Preservation, Stamford Health Corp. Mem. Assn. Res. City Bankers, Wesleyan Alumni Assn., Southwestern Area Commerce Assn. (dir.) Clubs: Wee Burn Country (Darien) (dir.); Landmark (dir.); Hartford. Home: Darien, Conn. Died Apr. 30, 2010.

KNOBEL, ROLAND JEFFERSON, health adminstration educator; b. NYC, Feb. 23, 1923; m. Mary Jo Kishler Knobel, Feb. 23, 1946; children: Cathy, Bradley. BA, Miami U., 1946; MA in Econs., George Washington U., 1966; PhD, U. Mich., 1970. Commd. ensign USN, 1945, advanced through grades to comdr., ret., 1966; prof. Ga. State U., Atlanta, 1970-85; prof. emeritus, 1986; prof. Emory U., Atlanta, from 1975. Contbr. articles to profl. jours. Mem. Hemlock (bd. trustees 1991-95), Meml. Soc. Ga. (pres. 1993—). Avocation: painting. Home: Atlanta, Ga. Died Aug. 16, 2010.

KNOX, BERNARD MACGREGOR WALKER, retired classics educator; b. Bradford, Eng., Nov. 24, 1914; came to U.S., 1939, naturalized, 1943; s. Bernard and Rowena (Walker) K.; m. Betty Baur, Apr. 12, 1939; 1 child, Bernard MacGregor Baur. BA, St. John's Coll., U. Cambridge, Eng., 1936; PhD, Yale U., 1948, L.H.D., 1983; MA (hon.), Harvard U., 1962; Litt.D., Princeton U., 1964; L.H.D., George Washington U., 1977, Georgetown U., 1988; L.H.D. (hon.), U. Mich., 1985. Mem. faculty Yale U., 1947-61, prof. classics, 1959-61; dir. Center Hellenic Studies, Washington, 1961-85; Sather lectr. U. Calif., Berkeley, 1963; Martin lectr. Oberlin Coll., 1981; West lectr. Stanford U., 1984; Nellie Wallace lectr. Oxford U., 1975. Author: Oedipus at Thebes, 1957, Oedipus the King, 1959, The Heroic Temper: Studies in Sophoclean Tragedy, 1964, Word and Action: Essays on the Ancient Theater, 1979, Essays Ancient and Modern, 1989, The Oldest Dead White European Males and Other Reflections on the Classics, 1993, Backing into the Future: The Classical Tradition and Its Renewal, 1994; also articles; author, actor ednl. films on Oedipus of Sophocles; asst. editor, contbr. Cambridge History of Classical Literature, 1985; editor The Norton Book of Classical Literature, 1993. Served to capt. AUS, 1942-45, ETO. Decorated Bronze Star with cluster, Croix de Guerre (France), Comdr. Order of Phoenix (Greece); recipient award for lit. Nat. Inst. Arts and Letters, 1967, George Nathan award for dramatic criticism, 1978, Spielvogel-Diamonstein award PEN, 1990, Frankel prize NEH, 1990; Guggenheim fellow, 1956-57; NEH Jefferson lectr., 1992. Mem. American Philosophical Assn. (pres. 1980, Medal Disting. Svc. 1996), Am. Acad. Arts and Scis., Philos. Soc. Am. (Jefferson medal 2004), Brit. Acad. (corr.) Clubs: Cosmos (award 1979) (Washington). Died July 22, 2010.

KOCH, ROBERT BRUCE, former healthcare administration executive; b. Cin., Sept. 26, 1927; s. George Frederick and Lysle Gladys (Drake) Koch; m. Jane Boyd Vinsonhaler, June 16, 1951; children: John Woodson, Thomas Lawson. BA, U. Cin., 1950; AMP, Harvard U., 1964. Actuary Union Ctrl. Life, Cin., 1950—60; dir., electronic data processing John Hancock Ins. Co., Boston, 1960—67, v.p., 1967—81; exec. v.p. Hancock Dikewood Svcs., Albuquerque, 1982—84, dir. With US Army, 1946—47. Fellow: Soc. Actuaries; mem.: Am. Acad. Actuaries, Vokes Theatre Club (pres. 1970—72), Phi Delta Theta. Republican. Home: Albuquerque, N.Mex. Died Aug. 12, 2009.

KOCH, ROBERT HARRY, astronomer, educator; b. York, Pa., Dec. 19, 1929; s. Harry Jacob and Veronica Cecelia (Jamison) K.; m. Joanne C. Underwood, July 4, 1959; children: Thomas R., James E., Elizabeth G., Patricia R. BS in Mathematics, U. Pa., 1951; MS in Astronomy, U. Ariz., 1957; PhD in Astronomy, U. Pa., 1959. Instr. Amherst Coll., Mt. Holyoke Coll., Amherst, Mass., 1959-60; asst. prof. Amherst Coll., 1960-65; assoc. prof. U. Mass., Amherst, 1965-66, U. N.Mex., Albuquerque, 1966-67, U. Pa., Phila., 1967-69, prof. astronomy, 1969—96, chmn. dept. astronomy, 1969—73, dir. Flower & Cook Observatory, 1989—94. Co-author: Realm of Interacting Binary Stars, 1991; author procs. NATO Advanced Study Inst., 1990. 1st lt. U.S. Army, 1951-53. Recipient Gold medal Korean Space Sci. Soc., 1990. Mem. American Astron. Soc. (invited lectr. 1967), Internat. Astron. Union (commn. 42 pres. 1988-91). Home: Ardmore, Pa. Died Oct. 11, 2010.

KOEHLER, GEORGE APPLEGATE, broadcasting company executive; b. Phila., July 23, 1921; s. Herbert Jacques and Mildred Warrington (Applegate) K.; m. Jane Marie Caputi, Feb. 20, 1944; children: Eric George, Gary Stephen. BA, U. Pa., 1942. Various positions WFIL Stas., Phila., 1945-55; sta. mgr. WFIL Radio and TV, 1955-68; gen. mgr. radio and TV div. Triangle Pubs., Inc., Phila., 1968-72; pres. Gateway Communications, Inc., Cherry Hill, N.J., 1970-84, vice chmn. bd, 1985—2001. Mem. planning com. Phila. Commn. on Human Rels., 1957; mem. Adv. Com. on Naval Affairs, 1968-70; pub. rels. chmn. United Fund, 1965. Trustee Meth. Hosp., Phila., 1962-97, Salem County C.C., 1996-98; com. commn. United Meth. Ch., 1980-84; bd. dirs. Pennington (N.J.) Sch., 1973-80; elder Presbyn. Ch., 1992-2000. Capt. USAAF, 1942-45. Decorated D.F.C., Air medal with 3 oak leaf clusters; recipient Distinguished Service award Chapel of 4 Chaplains, 1969; named Man of Yr. TV and Radio Advt. Club, Phila., 1971; Broadcast Pioneer of Yr. Delaware Valley chpt. Broadcast Pioneers. Mem.: Relilgion in Am. Life (bd. dirs. 1986—87, inducted Phila. Broadcasting Hall of Fame 1994), Assn. Maximum Svc. Telecasters (bd. dirs. from 1976, sec.-treas. 1980—83, chmn. 1984—85, chmn. emeritus 1986), ABC-TV Affiliates Assn. (adv. bd. 1967—71, chmn. 1970—71), Pa. Assn. Broadcasters (pres. 1958—59), Union League Club (Phila.), Union League Club, Rotary (pres. 1960), Alpha Delta Sigma. Republican. Died July 5, 2009.

KOENIG, HERMAN EDWARD, retired electrical engineering educator; b. Marissa, Ill., Dec. 12, 1924; s. Herman Christopher and Clara Cristena Koenig; m. Ruth Janet Parett, June 12, 1949; children: Bruce E., Roger L., Steven R. BS, U. Ill., 1947, MS, 1949, PhD, 1953. Engr. Delco Products div. GM, Dayton, Ohio, 1948-49; vis. asst. prof. MIT, Cambridge, 1954-55; asst. prof. U. Ill., Champaign/Urbana, 1955-56; assoc. prof. elec. engring. Mich. State U., East Lansing, 1956-59, prof. elec. engring. and systems sci., Coll. Engring., 1959-95, prof. emeritus, 1995—2010, dir. systems sci. program, 1966-68, chmn. dept., 1968-76, dir. Ecosystems Design and Mgmt. Program, 1971-78, dir. Ctr. Environ. Quality, Office V.P. Rsch. and Grad. Studies, 1976-81, dir. industry assistance, 1982-84, asst. v.p. rsch. svcs. and industry assistance, 1984-95. Mem. Gov.'s Coun. Jobs, Econ. Devel., Lansing, Mich., 1982-84; bd. dirs. Mich. Tech. Coun., Ann Arbor, 1983— Author: Electromechanical System, 1961,

Analysis of Discrete Physics, 1967; contbr. over 60 articles to profl. jours. Recipient Disting. Faculty award Mich. State U., 1968; grantee NSF, GE, DuPont Co., Mich. Dept. Commerce, 1956-86. Fellow IEEE, AAAS, Sigma Xi; mem. Mich. State U. Faculty Club. Lutheran. Avocation: farming. Home: Okemos, Mich. Died July 31, 2010.

KOEPKE, WULF, retired humanities educator; b. Luebeck, Germany, Sept. 24, 1928; came to U.S. 1965; s. Otto and Emma (Jahnke) K.; m. Monique Lehmann-Lukas, June 8, 1953; children: Niels, Detlev, Rebekka, Jens. Student, U. Hamburg, Germany, 1949, U. Freiburg, 1949-51, U. Paris, 1951-52; PhD, U. Freiburg, Germany, 1955. Lectr. U. Singapore, 1955-59; head divsn. Goethe Inst., Munich, Germany, 1959-65; assoc. prof. U. Ill., Chgo., 1965-68, Rice U., Houston, 1968-71, Tex. A&M U., College Station, 1971-73, prof., 1973-91, disting. prof. humanities, 1991-95, disting. prof. humanities emeritus, from 1995. Author: Understanding Max Frisch, 1971, Erfolglosigkeit, 1977, Lion Feuchtwanger, 1983, J.G. Herder, 1987. Recipient Jean Peal medal Jean Paul Soc., Bayreuth, 1960. Mem. MLA, German Studies Assn. (pres. 1982-84), Am. Soc. Eighteenth Century Studies, Internat. Herder Soc. (pres. 1985-90). Home: Roslindale, Mass. Died May 14, 2010.

KOEPPE, OWEN JOHN, university provost; b. Cedar Grove, Wis., May 29, 1926; s. Edwin Walter and Elizabeth Mary (Renskers) K.; m. JoAnn E. Moessner, June 14, 1950; children: John F., Robert A., Barbara A. AB, Hope Coll., 1949; MS, U. Ill., 1951, PhD, 1953. Successively asst. prof., assoc. prof., prof. U. Mo.-Columbia, to 1980, chmn. biochemistry dept., 1968-73, provost acad. affairs, 1973-80; provost Kans. State U., Manhattan, from 1980. Served with USNR, 1944-46. Mem. Am. Chem. Soc., Am. Soc. Biol. Chemists, Sigma Xi Presbyterian. Home: Columbia, Mo. Died Jan. 28, 2010.

KOEPPL, JOHN, lawyer; b. Milw., Aug. 15, 1941; BA, Marquette Univ., 1964, JD, 1967. Bar: Wis. 1967, U.S. Dist. Ct. (we. dist.) Wis. 1967, U.S. Tax Ct. 1967, U.S. Ct. of Appeals (7th cir.) 1973, U.S. Dist. Ct. (ea. dist.) Wis. 1974, U.S. Supreme Ct. 1976. Lawyer Stafford, Rosenbaum, Rieser & Hanson, Madison, 1967-88, DeWitt Ross & Stevens, S.C., Madison, from 1988. Editor: Wisconsin Environmental Law Handbook. Died June 4, 2010.

KOFF, GAIL JOANNE, lawyer; b. NYC, May 15, 1945; d. Murray and Sylvia Joan (Winer) Koff; m. Ralph Brill, Oct. 8, 1978 (div. 1998); children: Micah, Loren, Wade. BA, U. Calif., Berkeley, 1967; JD, George Washington U., 1970. Asst. to dir. Tng. and Demonstration Program, Legal Services Program, Washington, 1969—71; assoc. Gasperini & Savage, NYC, 1972—76, Skadden, Arps, Slate, Meagher & Flom, NYC, 1976—78; founder, ptnr. Jacoby & Meyers, NYC, from 1978, exec. v.p., 1982—2010. Lectr. in field. Editor: Legal Delivery Systems, 1977; author: Jacoby & Meyers Practical Guide to Everyday Law, 1985, Jacoby & Meyers Guide to Divorce, 1991. Chmn. Cmty. Action Legal Svcs., NYC, 1979—81; mem. Com. 200. Mem.: NY Bar Assn., Assn. Bar City (NY) (chmn. com. legal assistance 1976—79, exec. com. 1979—83, com. chmn.). Jewish. Home: Cold Spring, NY. Died Aug. 31, 2010.

KOHL, BENJAMIN GIBBS, historian, educator; b. Middletown, Del., Oct. 26, 1938; s. Victor Philip and Catherine B. (Carpenter) K.; m. Judith Ann Cleek, Jan. 2, 1961; children: Benjamin Gibbs, Laura Ann Kohl Ball. AB with honors, Bowdoin Coll., 1960; MA, U. Del., 1962; PhD, Johns Hopkins U., 1968. Adj. instr. Franklin and Marshall Coll., Lancaster, Pa., 1961-62; instr. history Johns Hopkins U., Balt., 1965-66, Vassar Coll., Poughkeepsie, NY, 1966-68, asst. prof., 1968-74, assoc. prof., 1974-81, prof., 1981-2001, chmn. dept. history, 1979-82, 88, 1993-96, Andrew W. Mellon prof. of humanities, 1994-2001, prof. emeritus, from 2001. Pres. Am. Friends of Warburg Inst., NYC, 1994-96; adv. bd. Renaissance Studies, 1988-2008; pres., Hedgelawn Found., Worton, Md., 2003—. Author: Renaissance Humanism, Bibliography of Materials in English, 1985, Padua Under the Carrara, 1998, The Records of the Venetian Senate on disk 1335-1400, 2000, Culture and Politics in Early Renaissance Padua, 2001; co-author: (with A.A. Smith), Major Problems in the History of the Italian Renaissance, 1995, (with A. Mozzatto and M. O'Connoll) Rulers of Venice, 1332-1524, 2009; co-editor: (with R.G. Witt) The Earthly Republic, 1978; co-editor Centennial Directory of the American Academy in Rome, 1995, Weyer on Witchcraft, 1998; contbr. more than 30 scholarly essays and more than 50 books revs. on medieval and Renaissance history to profl. jours Historian City of Poughkeepsie, 1971—77; sec. planning commn. Betterton, Md., from 2005; bd. visitors and govs. Washington Coll., Chestertown, Md., from 2006. Fulbright fellow, Padua, Italy, 1964-65; Am. Acad. fellow, Rome, 1970-71; Delmas fellow, Venice, 1978, Mellon Found. Emeritus fellow, 2006-09. Fellow Royal Hist. Soc.; mem. AAUP (pres. chpt. 1987-89, 95-98), Medieval Acad. Am. (life), Renaissance Soc. Am. (life), Am. Hist. Assn. (life), Hist. Soc. Kent County (Chestertown, Md.) (pres. 2010-). Democrat. Episcopalian. Avocations: reading, walking, gardening. Home: Betterton, Md. Died June 10, 2010.

KOHN, ALAN ROBERT, psychologist; b. Albany, N.Y., Aug. 7, 1928; s. Maurice Jacob and Lillian Ruth (Milstein) K.; B.S. (coll. scholar), Union Coll., 1950; M.S., SUNY, Oneonta, 1956; M.A., U. Ill., 1959, Ph.D., 1961; children— Marcy Joy, Gary Paul, Ellen Phyllis. Psychology trainee VA Hosp., Albany, N.Y., 1961-62, asst. dir. day treatment center, 1962-64, counseling psychologist, 1964-66, chief, counseling psychology sect., 1966-70; dir. psychol. services N.Y. State Drug Abuse Commn., Albany, 1970-76; pvt. practice psychology, Albany, 1976—. Served with U.S. Army, 1951-53. USPHS fellow, 1960-61. Mem. Am. Psychol. Assn. Lodge: B'nai B'rith. Died May 10, 2010.

KOHN, SHALOM L., lawyer; b. Nov. 18, 1949; s. Pincus and Helen (Roth) K.; m. Barbara Segal, June 30, 1974; children: David, Jeremy, Daniel. BS in Acctg. summa cum laude, CUNY, 1970; JD magna cum laude, Harvard U., 1974, MBA, 1974. Bar: Ill. 1975, U.S. Dist. Ct. (no. dist.) Ill. 1975, U.S. Ct. Appeals (7th cir.) 1976, U.S. Supreme Ct. 1980, N.Y. 1988, U.S. Dist. Ct. (so. dist.) N.Y. 1988, others. Law clk. to chief judge US Ct. Appeals (2d cir.), NYC, 1974-75; assoc. Sidley Austin LLP, Chgo., 1975-80, ptnr., from 1980. Exec. com. Adv. Coun. Religious Rights in Eastern Europe and Soviet Union, Washington, 1984-86; bd. dirs. Brisk Rabbinical Coll., Chgo. Contbr. articles to profl. jours. Mem. ABA, Chgo. Bar Assn. Home: Evanston, Ill. Died May 30, 2010.

KOHN, WILLIAM IRWIN, lawyer; b. Bronx, NY, June 27, 1951; s. Arthur Oscar and Frances (Hoffman) K.; m. Karen Mindlin, Aug. 29, 1974; children: Shira, Kinneret, Asher. Student, U. Del., 1969—71; BA with honors, U. Cin., 1973; JD, Ohio State U., 1976. Bar: Ohio 1976, US Dist. Ct. (no. and so. dists.) Ohio 1976, Ind. 1982, US Dist. Ct. (no. and so. dists.) Ind. 1982, DC 1992, US Supreme Ct., 1992, Ill. 1994, US Dist. Ct. (no., ctrl., and so. dists.) Ill., NY 2006, US Dist. Ct. (so. dist.) NY 2007; cert. Bus. Bankruptcy Law Am. Bankruptcy Bd. Cert. Ptnr. Krugliak, Wilkins, Griffith & Dougherty, Canton, Ohio, 1976-82, Barnes & Thornburg, Chgo., 1982—2001, Sachnoff & Weaver Ltd., Chgo., 2002, Schiff Harden LLP, Chgo., 2002—06, Benesch Friedlander Coplan & Aronoff, LLP, Cleve., from 2006. Adj. prof. law U. Notre Dame, Ind., 1984—90; bd. dirs. Ctr. for Disability and Elder Law, 2006. Author: West's Indiana Business Forms, West's Indiana Uniform Commercial Code Forms; contbr. articles to profl. jours. Bd. dirs. Family Svcs., South Bend, 1985—94, Jewish Fedn., Highland Park United Way, Jewish Family and Cmty. Svcs., 2000—05. Recipient Excellence in Pub. Interest Svc. award, US Dist. Ct. (no. dist.) Ill. and Fed. Bar Assn., 2006; named Vol. of Yr., Ctr. for Disability and Elder Law, 2006. Mem. ABA (bus. bankruptcy subcom.), Am. Bankruptcy Inst. (insolvency sect.), Ill. Bar Assn., Chgo. Bar Assn., Comml. Law League, Am. Bd. Certification (treas.). Home: Pepper Pike, Ohio. Died Feb. 24, 2010.

KOLAKOWSKI, DIANA JEAN, economic development director; b. Detroit, Aug. 28, 1943; d. Leo and Genevieve (Bosh) Zyskowski; m. William Francis Kolakowski, Jr., Oct. 22, 1966; children: Wiliam Francis III, John. BS, U. Detroit, Mich., 1965. Lab. asst. chemistry dept. U. Detroit, 1961-65; rsch. chemist Detroit Inst. Cancer Rsch., Mich. Cancer Found., 1965-70; substitute tchr. Warren (Mich.) Consol. Schs., 1979-81; Commr. Macomb County, Mt. Clemens, Mich., 1983—2006; vice chmn. Macomb County Bd. Commrs., Mt. Clemens, 1993-95, chmn., 1995-97; econ. devel. dir. City of Warren, from 2006. Dir. S.E. Mich. Transp. Authority, Detroit, 1983—85; trustee Macomb County Ret. System, Mt. Clemens, 1988—91, 1992—95, 2003—06; del. S.E. Mich. Coun. Govts., Detroit, 1987—2006, vice chmn., 1995—99, chmn., 1999—2000, Regional Transit Coord. Coun., 1995—97; bd. dirs. Creating a Healthier Macomb, 1996—2001, Macomb Bar Found., 1996—2006. Contbr. articles to sci. jours. Trustee Myasthenia Gravis Found., Southfield, Mich., 1964-71; dir. Otsikita coun. Girl Scouts Am., 1995-96; mem., sec. Sterling Heights (Mich.) Bd. Zoning Appeals, 1978-83; mem. Macomb County Dem. Exec. Com., Mt. Clemens, 1982—, 10th and 12th Dem. Congl. Dist. Exec. Com., Warren, 1982—, del. 1996 Dem. Nat. Conv.; mem. behavioral medicine adv. coun. St. Joseph Hosp., Warren Cmty. Chorus Recipient Leadership award, Cath. Social Svcs. Macomb, 1997, Polish Pride award, Polish Am. Citizens for Equity, 1997, Excellence in County Govt. award, 1997, Regional Ambassador award, S.E. Mich. Coun. Govt., 2005; named Woman of Distinction, Macomb County Girl Scouts U.S.A., 1996, Woman of Yr., Am. Fedn. State, County and Mcpl. Employees 411, 2004; GM scholar, U. Detroit, 1961—65. Mem.: Warren Hist. Soc., Polish Am. Congress, Alpha Sigma Nu. Roman Catholic. Avocations: singing, piano, crossword and jigsaw puzzles. Home: Troy, Mich. Died June 30, 2009.

KOLIBACHUK, JOHN FILIMON, steamship company executive; b. Plainfield, NJ, Oct. 29, 1925; s. Filimon and Anastasia (Cymbalak) K.; m. Tressie Howard, June 22, 1948; children— David John, Debra Jane, Dana Jean. BS, Rutgers U., 1947; MBA, N.Y. U., 1951. Staff accountant Price Waterhouse & Co., NYC, 1947-57; subsidy analyst U.S. Lines, Inc., NYC, 1957-66, asst. comptroller, 1966-71, comptroller, 1971-74, v.p., comptroller, 1974-79, v.p., fin. coordinator Cranford, N.J., 1979-81, dir. regulatory acctg., from 1981. Sec. Dunellen (N.J.) Bd. Edn., 1955-61, mem., 1961-76. Served with USNR, 1943-46. Mem. Am. Inst. C.P.A.'s, Assn. Water Transp. Accounting Officers (pres. 1978-79) Home: Warren, NJ. Died Aug. 29, 2009.

KOLYER, JOHN MCNAUGHTON, materials scientist, retired chemist; b. East Williston, NY, June 30, 1933; s. John and Mildred (McNaughton) K.; children: Scott McNaughton, Paul Franklin, Craig David, Jeffrey John. BA, Hofstra U., 1955; PhD, U. Pa., 1960. Technician Olin-Mathieson Chem. Corp., Port Washington, NY, 1955-56; rsch. chemist FMC Corp., Princeton, NJ, 1960-62; tech. supr. Allied Chem. Corp., Morriston, NJ, 1964-71; mem. tech. staff Rockwell Internat., Anaheim, Calif., 1973-96; scientist, engr. Boeing Co., Anaheim, 1997—2006; ret. Author: many technical articles and works of fiction and verse; patentee in field; author: Engaged to be Dead, 2004. Mem.: NY Acad. Scis., Soc. Advancement Materials Processing and Engring., Am. Chem. Soc., Phi Lambda Upsilon, Kappa Mu Epsilon, Sigma Kappa Alpha. Died Jan. 6, 2010.

KOMACK, ROY LEONARD, investment advisor; b. Weehawken, NJ, Dec. 2, 1941; s. Sam and Min (Kregstein) K.; m. Constance Kugel (div. Feb. 22, 1977); 1 child, Andrew; m. Lauren Jacobs, Aug. 1, 1982. BS, Mass. Inst. Tech., 1963, MS, 1964; MBA, Boston U., 1969. CFP. Tech. staff United Carr Inc., Cambridge, Mass., 1964-70; mgr. profl. products Bose Corp., Framingham, Mass., 1970-87; mgr. engring. automation Bytex Corp., Westborough, Mass., 1988-94; pres. Komack Mgmt. Svcs., Inc., Natick, Mass., from 1989. Mem. Inst. CFPs, Nat. Assn. Personal Fin. Advisors, Am. Assn. Individual Investors. Avocations: skiing, music, running, sailing. Home: Natick, Mass. Died Jan. 6, 2009.

KONDRUP, JOHN THOMAS, retired research scientist; b. NYC, May 24, 1925; s. James John and Anna Kondrup; m. Anna Rabinowitz (div.); children: Bella, David, Gloria, James; m. June B. Graham, May 15, 1976. BS, MS. Dir., oper., mgr. Acasian Resume & Writing, Baton Rouge, 1982—99; sales rep., cashier Wal-Mart, Zachary, La., 1999—2006; ret., 2006. With USN, 1943—59. Independent. Home: Jackson, La. Died Jan. 16, 2009.

KOONS, LAWRENCE FRANKLIN, chemistry educator; b. Columbus, Ohio, Sept. 14, 1927; m. Benjamin Franklin and Ruth Elizabeth (Betsch) K.; m. Dorothy Helen Baesmann, Sept. 5, 1952 (dec. Dec. 1982); m. Helen Curtis Campbell, Mar. 30, 1991. BS in Chemistry, Ohio State U., 1949, PhD in Chemistry, 1956. Police chemist City of Columbus, 1952-56; instr. to asst. prof. DePaul U., Chgo., 1956-59; asst. prof. to prof. Tuskegee (Ala.) Inst., from 1959. Fulbright lectr. U. Dakar, Senegal, 1977-78; cons. Inst. at U. of Allahabad, Burdwan and Lucknow, 1965-67; abstractor of Russian articles Chem. Abstracts, 1960-87. Editor, translator: The Troubadours, 1965. Mem. AAAS, CAP, Am. Chem. Soc. (sect. chmn. 1972-73), Aircraft Owners and Pilots Assn., Sigma Xi. Home: Tuskegee Institute, Ala. Died Apr. 1, 2009.

KOPIDAKIS, EMMANUEL G., general surgeon; b. Iraklion, Crete, Greece, Apr. 15, 1931; s. George and Victoria K.; m. Marianna; children: George, Thomas. MD, Athens U. Med. Sch., 1956. Diplomate Am. Bd. Surgery. Dir. surgery Evangelismos Hosp., Iraklion, 1965-68; surgeon John F. Kennedy Med. Ctr., Edison, N.Y., from 1968. Med. officer Greek Army, 1957-59. Avocation: painting. Died Jan. 30, 2010.

KOPPELMAN, CHAIM, artist, educator; b. Bklyn., Nov. 17, 1920; s. Samuel and Sadie (Mondlin) K.; m. Dorothy Myers, Feb. 13, 1943; 1 child, Ann. Student, Bklyn. Coll., 1938, Am. Artists Sch., 1939; student Aesthetic Realism, with Eli Siegel, 1940-78; student, Art Coll. Western Eng., Bristol, 1944, Ecole des Beaux-Arts, Rheims, 1945, Art Students League, 1946, Amedée Ozenfant Sch., 1946-49; student Aesthetic Realism, with Ellen Reiss, from 1978. Art instr. N.Y. U., 1947-55, N.Y. State U., New Paltz, 1952-58; instr. Sch. Visual Arts, NYC, from 1959. Cons. Aesthetic Realism Found., N.Y.C., 1971— Author: This is the Way I See Aesthetic Realism, 1969; illustrator: Damned Welcome, Aesthetic Realism Maxims (by Eli Siegel), 1972; contbr. articles to profl. jours.; Bibliographies of his work The Indignant Eye (Ralph Shikes), 1969, The New Humanism (Barry Schwartz), 1974, The Art of the Print (Fritz Eichenberg), 1976, American Prints and Printmakers (Una Johnson), 1980, Hilla Rebay: In Search of the Spirit in Art (Joan Lukach), 1983; one man shows include Asso. Am. Artists Gallery, 1973, Terrain Gallery, N.Y.C., 1974, 83, Warwick (Eng.) Gallery, 1975, Merida Rapp Graphics, Louisville, 1985, Print Club, Phila., Beatrice Conde Gallery, 2000, others; group shows include Purdue U., 1972, Utah State U., 1972, Arte Fiera, Bologna, 1978, NAD, N.Y.C., 1983, Print Club, Phila., 1988, Alternative Mus., N.Y.C., 1988, Art Mus., Bogota, 1996; represented in permanent collections Victoria and Albert Mus., London, Mus. Fine Arts, Caracas, Venezuela, Mus. Modern Art, N.Y.C., Met. Mus. Art, N.Y.C., Library of Congress, Washington, Los Angeles County Mus. Art, Phila. Mus. Art, Guggenheim Mus., others; sculptor Eli Siegel Meml., Druid Hill Park, Balt., 2002. Served with USAF, 1942-45. Decorated Bronze Star; recipient N.Y. State Creative Artists Pub. Svc. award, 1976, prize Soc. Am. Graphic Artists, Fabri prize Nat. Acad. Ann., 1989, Cook prize, 1998, Lifetime Achievement award Soc. Am. Graphic Artists, 2004, Peace Tower award Whitney Biennial, 2006; Louis Comfort Tiffany grantee, 1956, 59, Documenta II, Kassel, 1961. Mem. Nat. Acad. Design. Home: New York, NY. Died Dec. 9, 2009.

KORCHYNSKY, MICHAEL, metallurgical engineer; b. Kiev, Ukraine, Apr. 11, 1918; arrived in U.S., 1950, naturalized, 1956; s. Michael and Jadwiga (Zdanowicz) K.; m. Taisija Lapin, Nov. 22, 1951; children: Michael, Marina, Roksana Dipl. Ing. in Metals Tech., Tech. U. Lviv, 1942. Lectr. Tech. U. Lviv, 1942-44; chief engr. C.E., U.S. Army, Germany, 1945-50; rsch. metallurgist Union Carbide Co., Niagara Falls, NY, 1951-61; rsch. supr. Jones & Laughlin Steel Corp., Pitts., 1962-68, dir. product rsch., 1969-72; dir. alloy devel. metals divsn. Union Carbide Co., NYC, 1973-77, Pitts., 1978-86; cons., prin. Korchynsky and Assocs., Pitts., from 1986. Metall. cons. Strategic Minerals Corp.-STRATCOR, from 1986; lectr. Niagara U., 1957—58; keynote spkr. internat. confs., Sanya, Hainan, China, 2005, Ekaterinburg, Russia, 06, Kolkata, India, 07, Ranchi, India, 08. Recipient Achievement award, Vanadium Internat. Tech. Com., 2003, China Fgn. Specialist award, Govt. of China, 2004, Leadership award, Ctr. for Tech. Studies and Rsch., San Sebastian, Spain, 2005, Materials Sci. medal, Krakow U., 2003; Sr. fellow, Union Carbide, 1979. Fellow Am. Soc. Metals Internat. (Andrew Carnegie lectr. 1973, W.H. Eisenman medal 1984, F.C. Bain award 1986); mem. AIME (Howe meml. lectr. 1983, Robert Earll McConnell engring. achievement award 1991) Iron and Steel Soc., SAE Internat., Am. Iron and Steel Inst. (medalist), Acad. Engring. Scis. of Ukraine, Ukrainian Technol. Soc., Polish Metall. Assn. (hon.). Achievements include patents for alloy design and processing tech. of a family of micro-alloyed high-strength low alloy steel; research in advances in metallurgy of high strength steels. Home: Bethel Park, Pa. Died Aug. 5, 2010.

KORMAN, NATHANIEL IRVING, research and development company executive; b. Providence, Feb. 23, 1916; s. William and Tillie (Jacobs) K.; m. Ruth C. Kaplan, Apr. 6, 1941; children: Michael, Robert. BS summa cum laude,

Worcester Poly. Inst., 1937; MS (Coffin fellow), MIT, 1938; PhD, U. Pa., 1958. Dir. advance mil. systems RCA Corp., 1958-67. Chmn. radar panel U.S. R&D Bd., 1948-56; lectr. U. Pa. Evening Grad. Sch., 1967-68; cons. in field Color Sci., 1968-83; pres. Ventures R&D Group. Author: The Evolution of Human Society, 1998; patentee in field. Mem. Citizens Com. for Better Schs., Moorestown, N.J., 1958. Recipient Merit award RCA, 1951. Fellow IEEE; mem. Sigma Xi. Home: Albuquerque, N.Mex. Died Feb. 11, 2010.

KORSCHOT, BENJAMIN CALVIN, retired investment company executive; b. LaFayette, Ind., Mar. 22, 1921; s. Benjamin G. and Myrtle P. (Goodman) K.; m. Marian Marie Schelle, Oct. 31, 1941; children: Barbara E. Korschot Haehlen, Lynne D. Korschot Gooding, John Calvin. BS, Purdue U., 1942; MBA, U. Chgo., 1947. V.p. No. Trust Co., Chgo., 1947-64; sr. v.p. St. Louis Union Trust Co., 1964-73; exec. v.p. Waddell and Reed Co., Kansas City, Mo., 1973-74, pres., 1974-79, vice-chmn. bd., 1979-85; pres. Waddell & Reed Investment Mgmt. Co., 1985-86; chmn. bd. Waddell & Reed Asset Mgmt. Co., 1973-86, retired, 1986. Pres. United Group of Mut. Funds, Inc., Kansas City, Mo., 1974-85, chmn., 1985-86; vice-chmn. Roosevelt Fin. Group, St. Louis, 1968-91, chmn. adv. bd., 1991-92; treas. Helping Hand of Goodwill Industries, 1993-95, chmn. investment com., 1995-2004; bd. dirs. Mo. United Meth. Found., 1995-2004, chmn. investment com., 2001-2004; chmn. bd. govs. Investment Co. Inst., 1980-82; chmn. bd. Fin. Analyst Fedn., 1978-79. Contbr. articles on investment fin. to profl. publs.; author autobiography, 1997. Mem. Civic Coun. Greater Kansas City, Mo., 1974-85; chmn. fin. com. ARC Retirement Sys., 1986-87. With USN, 1942-45, 50-52. Mem. Inst. CFAs, Fin. Execs. Inst., Kansas City Soc. Fin. Analysts, Lakewood Oaks Golf Club. Republican. Home: Lees Summit, Mo. Died July 12, 2010.

KOSSANYI, MARIA, broadcasting company executive; b. Budapest, Hungary, Feb. 19, 1926; came to U.S., 1951; d. Oszkar and Stephanie (Hovany) Monostory; m. Anthony Krasznai, Sept. 20, 1944 (div. 1971); children: Maria-Athena, Csilla, Patricia; m. Miklos Kossànyi, Jan. 9, 1973; 1 child, Attila. Diploma, U. Budapest. Mgr. Slenderella Internat., Cleve., 1954-58; hungarian program dir. Sta. WZAK, Cleve., 1963-77; gen. mgr. Nationality Broadcasting Network, Cleve., from 1977. Cons. Deutsche Welle, Köln, Fed. Republic Germany, 1977—, RAI Italian Broadcasting, 1979—, Swiss Radio Internat., Bern, Switzerland, 1982—, Hungarian Radio-TV, 1963. Exec. producer (video) Slovenia, 1964, Hello Cleveland, 1988, Hungary, 1984, Budapest, 1989. Bd. dirs. Heritage Club, Washington, 1967, All Nation Found., Cleve., 1984; hon. co-chmn. Ohio Celebrates Liberty, Columbus, 1986. Recipient Gov.'s award, 1973, U.S. Congress award, 1982, U.S. Marin award, 1986, various internat. awards. Avocations: swimming, boating, travel, gardening. Home: Cleveland, Ohio. Died Aug. 15, 2010.

KOSTER, ELAINE, publishing executive; b. NYC, 1940; m. Bill Koster; 1 child, Elizabeth. BA, Barnard Coll., 1962. Pres., pub. Dutton Signet, NYC; founder Elaine Koster Literary Agy., LLC, NYC, 1998—2010. Died Aug. 10, 2010.

KOTZ, SAMUEL, statistician, educator, translator, editor; b. Harbin, China, Aug. 28, 1930; s. Boris and Guta (Kahana) K.; m. Roselyn Greenwald, Aug. 6, 1963; children: Tamar Ann, Harold David, Pauline Esther. MSc with honors, Hebrew U., Jerusalem, 1956; PhD, Cornell U., 1960; Dr. honoris causa, U. Athens, 1995, Harbin Inst. Tech., 1984, Bowling Green State U., 1997. Rschr. Israel Meteorol. Svc., 1954-58; lectr. Bar-Ilan U., Israel, 1960-62; postdoctoral Ford fellow U. NC, 1962-63; assoc. prof. U. Toronto, 1963-67; prof. math. Temple U., 1967-79; prof. stats. U. Md., College Park, 1979-97, disting. scholar-tchr., 1984-85. Disting. vis. prof. Bucknell U., 1977, Guelph (Can.) U., 1987; hon. prof. Harbin Inst. Tech., 1987; Eugene Lukacs disting. rsch. prof. Bowling Green (Ohio) State U., 1992; vis. prof. U. Luleå, Sweden, 1993, 95, Hong Kong U., 1994, U. Copenhagen, summer 1996, U. South Brittany, Vannes, France, 1998; vis. prof. econs. and fin. St. Petersburg (Russia) U., summer 1995; vis. rschr. Internat. Statis. Inst., The Hague, summer 1996, U. Paul Sabatier, Toulouse, France, summer 1998, U. York, Eng., 1999, U. Salford, Eng., 1999, 2000, Athens U. Econs., 1999, U. Lund, Sweden, 2000; vis. sr. rsch. scholar George Washington U., 1997-2010, U. Trento, Italy, summers, 2001, 02, U. Padua, 2002, U. Bologna, 2002. Author, editor 30 books, 4 Russian-English profl. dictionaries, over 135 rsch. papers; translator 18 books; co-editor-in-chief: Encyclopedia of Statistical Sci., 9 vols. and supplement, 1982-89, editor-in-chief up-date vols. 1-3, 1994-98, 2d edit., 16 vols., 2005; co-editor: Breakthroughs in Statistics, 3 vol., 1995-98; editor: Leading Statistical Personalities, 1997; co-author: Process Capability Indices, 1993, 98, Applied Bayesian Statistics (in Chinese), 2000, 2d edit., 2001, Extreme Value Distributions, 2000, 3d edit., 2005, Correlation and Dependence, 2001, Laplace Distributions and Applications, 2001, Strength-Stress Models, 2003, Statistical Size Distributions in Economics, 2003, Multivariate T-distributions and Applications, 2004, Beyond Beta, 2005, Handbook of Capability Indices, 2006; mem. editl. bd. Jour. Quality Rsch. and Tech.; coord. editor AIEE Transactions; editor-in-chief: Quality Management and Control. Served with Israeli Army, 1950-52. Fellow Am. Statis. Assn., Inst. Math. Stat., Royal Statis. Soc., Washington Acad. Sci. (hon.); mem. Internat. Statis. Inst. (elected mem.). Home: Silver Spring, Md. Died Mar. 16, 2010.

KOURIDES, PETER THEOLOGOS, lawyer; b. Istanbul, Turkey, July 24, 1910; arrived in US, 1912, naturalized, 1931; s. Theologos and Zafiro (Gurlides) Kourides; m. Anna E. Spetseris, Aug. 4, 1938; children: Ione A., P. Nicholas. BA, Columbia, 1931, JD, 1933; HHD (hon.), Hellenic Coll., 1985. Bar: NY 1933. Mem. firm Seward, Raphael & Kourides, NYC, from 1935; gen. counsel Greek Archdiocese N.Am. and S.Am., 1938-96; trustee Hellenic Cathedral City NY, 1938-98; trustee, counsel St. Basil's Acad., Garrison, NY, 1946-97, United Greek Orthodox Charities, 1965-70; counsel World Conf. Religion Peace, 1970-82, Consultate Gen. Greece, NYC, 1963-90. Rep. at enthronement of Athenagoras I Greek Archdiocese of N.Am. and S.Am., Istanbul, 1949. Author: The Evolution of the Greek Orthodox Church in America and Its Current Problems, 1959, The Centennial History of the Archdiocesan Cathedral of the Holy Trinity, 1992. Nat. v.p. Order of Ahepa, 1960; counsel Columbia U. Cancer Clinic, Greece, 1965—70; mem. gen. bd. Nat. Coun. Chs., 1960—82, v.p., 1969—72; del. 3d Assembly World Coun. Chs., New Delhi, 1961, del. 4th Assembly Uppsala, Sweden, 1968, del. 5th Assembly Nairobi, Kenya, 1975, mem. internat. affairs com., 1968—74; del. World Conf. Religion on Peace, Kyoto, 1971; trustee Hellenic Coll., Brookline, Mass., 1968—97. Decorated grand comdr. Knights of Holy Sepulchre Jerusalem, Golden Cross Order of Phoenix King Constantine II of Greece, Titular Archon Megas Nomophylax Ecumenical Patriarchate of Ea. Orthodox Ch. Mem.: ABA, Am. Judicature Soc., Consular Law Soc., NY Bar Assn., Columbia Alumni Assn., Hellenic Am. C. of C. (dir., counsel from 1955). Home: Forest Hills, NY. Died Feb. 16, 2010.

KOVACEVICH, CHRISTOPHER, bishop; b. Galveston, Tex., Dec. 25, 1928; s. Petar B. and Rista (Vujacic) K.; children: Petar V., Paul V., Valerie Kovacevich Backo, Velimir V. BD, St. Sava Sem., 1949; BA, U. Pitts., 1954, MLitt, 1957; M Divinity, Holy Sch. Theology, 1978; postgrad., Chgo. Theol. Sem., 1974-78. Ordained deacon/priest, 1951; consecrated bishop, 1978. Pastor St. Nicholas Serbian Orthodox Ch., Johnstown, Pa., 1951-54, St. Sava Serbian Orthodox Ch., Pitts., 1954-62, St. Archangel Michael Serbian Orthodox Ch., Chgo., 1962-78; bishop Serbian Orthodox Diocese Eastern Am. and Can. (now 2 separate dioceses), Edgeworth-Sewickley, Pa., 1978-85; bishop of Met. Midwestern America Diocese Serbian Orthodox Church - U.S.A., 1991—2010. Various positions Dept. Edn., Eccles. Ct., Diocesan Council, pastorates; Orthodox chaplain four univs., Pitts., Va Hosps., Pitts.; mem. governing bd. Nat. Council Chs. of Christ in USA; mem. Dialogue Commn. Orthodox/Roman Cath. Bishops in USA. Author manual for Serbian Orthodox Ch. Camps, 1960; co-author 50th anniversary history St. Archangel Michael Ch., 1976; co-editor Diocesan Jour. U.S.A., Can., chronical Shadeland Monastery history. Mem. Pitts. Bicentennial Com. Mem. World Council Chs. Avocation: golf. Died Aug. 18, 2010.

KOVAL, CHARLES FRANCIS, entomologist, agricultural administrator, educator; b. Ashland, Wis., May 10, 1938; s. George F. and Katherine (Brozovic) K.; m. Patricia L. Riley, Aug. 24, 1957; children: Michael, Daniel, Mary Louise. BA, Northland Coll., 1960; MS, U. Wis., 1963, PhD, 1966. Instr. entomology U. Wis., Madison, 1965-66, asst. prof., 1966-69, assoc. prof., 1969-73, prof., from 1973, dir. agrl. rsch. stas., 1980-83, dean coop. extension svc., assoc. dir., 1983-87, chmn. dept., 1987-90, ext. entomologist, 1965-95; prof. emeritus, from 1995. Home: Madison, Wis. Died Aug. 3, 2009.

KOVNER, ABRAHAM, steel construction consulting company executive; b. N.Y.C., Jan. 13, 1919; s. Benjamin and Anna (Chalkin) K.; student N.Y. Naval Shipyard Apprentice Sch., 1940-43, Pratt Inst., 1941-43, N.Y. U., 1946-47, Pace U., 1966-67; m. Sarah Lederman, Nov. 19, 1938; children—Mark, Nancy. Planner, estimator N.Y. Naval Shipyard, Bklyn., 1940-50; sr. steel insp. N.Y.C. Dept. Public Works, 1950-61; chief engr. Classon Welding, Bklyn., 1961-62; pres., chief engr. M.K.B. Industries, Bklyn., 1962-66; marine designer M. Rosenblatt & Son., N.Y.C., 1966-67; pres. A. Kovner Assos., N.Y.C., 1967—; adj. assoc. prof. NYU Real Estate Inst. Maj. N.Y.C. Aux. Police, 1950-66. Recipient cert. of merit N.Y. State Conservation Dept., 1955; cert. of public service State of N.Y., 1958, cert. of merit, 1963; 1958; award of merit Office of CD, 1960; cert. constrn. estimator. Mem. Am. Soc. Profl. Estimators, Am. Soc. Naval Engrs., Am. Def. Preparedness Assn., Am. Welding Soc., ASTM, Soc. Naval Architects and Marine Engrs., U.S. Naval Inst., Nat. Rifle Assn. Contbr. articles to profl. jours. Home: New York, NY. Died Mar. 25, 2010.

KOWALOFF, DOROTHY RUBIN, retired lawyer; b. NYC, May 8, 1917; d. Saul and Fannie (Romanoff) Roberts; m. Meyer Kowaloff, Mar. 18, 1945 (dec.); children: Arthur, Nina. BA, NYU, 1938; LLB, Columbia U., 1940. Bar: (N.Y.). Sole practice, NYC, 1941-50; pres. Rokor Corp., 1950-67; atty., corp. counsel office Dept. Law, City of N.Y., 1967-86. Mem.: N.Y. State Women's Bar Assn., Women's Bar Assn. City N.Y. Home: New York, NY. Died Mar. 3, 2010.

KOZYRIS, PHAEDON JOHN, law educator, consultant; b. Thessaloniki, Greece, Jan. 2, 1932; came to U.S., 1954, naturalized, 1960; S. John and Marika (Metaxotou) K.; m. Stella Doulis, Sept. 9, 1956 (div. 1978); children— Maria, Kynthia; m. Litsa Spyropoulou, Nov. 5, 1978 JD, U. Thessaloniki, Greece, 1954; M. Comparative Law, U. Chgo., 1955; JD, Cornell U., 1960; S.JD, U. Pa., 1984. Bar: N.Y. 1961, Ohio 1973. Assoc. Cahill, Gordon, Reindel & Ohl, NYC, 1960-69; prof. law Ohio State U., Columbus, from 1969. Vis. prof. law Duke U., Durham, N.C., 1971-72, U. Tex., Austin, 1978 Contbr. articles on corp., internat. and conflicts law to many law revs. Fulbright grantee U. Chgo., 1954-55, U. Thessaloniki, 1980 Mem. Am. Soc. Internat. Law, Am. Soc. Study Comparative Law (bd. dirs., bd. editors), League Ohio Law Schs. (pres. 1985-86), Order of Coif, Phi Kappa Phi. Home: Columbus, Ohio. Died Feb. 10, 2010.

KRABBENHOFT, KENNETH LESTER, radiologist, educator; b. Sabula, Iowa, Jan. 7, 1923; s. Lester Henry and Bessie Grant (Thompson) K.; m. Gloria Darlene Eriksen, June 17, 1944; children: Kenneth Lester, Douglas Harold, Karen Ann Krabbenhoft Caumartin. BA, State U. Iowa, 1943, MD, 1946. Diplomate: Am. Bd. Radiology. Intern Harper Hosp., Detroit, 1946-47, resident in radiology, 1949-52, assoc. radiologist, 1952-57, radiologist, from 1957; practice medicine specializing in radiology Birmingham, Mich., from 1957; prof., chmn. dept. radiology Wayne State U., Detroit, 1969-84; chief radiology Detroit Receiving Hosp.-Univ. Health Center, 1980-84. Cons. radiologist VA Hosp., Allen Park, Mich., Children's Hosp. Mich., Crittenton Gen. Hosp., Herman Kiefer Hosp., Nat. Cancer Inst.; mem. Nat. Cancer Adv. bd., 1970-73; pres. Affiliated Radiologists, Inc., Detroit, 1973-85, Detroit Gen. Hosp. Rsch. Corp., 1974-82; mem. Environ. Radiation Exposure Adv. Com., 1975-78; trustee Am. Bd. Radiology, 1971-93, sec., exec. dir., 1981-93, assoc. exec. dir., 1993-95; treas. Am. Bd. Med. Specialists, 1981-85; alt. del. Internat. Congress Radiology. Cons. editor: Am. Jour. Roentgenology, 1975-81. Served to lt. (j.g.), M.C. USNR, 1947-49. Recipient Disting. Alumnus award M.D. Anderson Cancer Ctr., 1988; Nat. Cancer Inst. grantee, 1971-75; Nat. Cancer Inst. Specialized Cancer Center grantee, 1973-75. Fellow Am. Coll. Radiology (Gold medal 1989); mem. Detroit Acad. Medicine, Detroit Med. Club, AMA (vice chmn. sect. council 1969-71), Mich., Wayne county med. socs., Mich. Radiol. Soc. (pres. 1969-70), Am. Radium Soc., Am. Roentgen Ray Soc. (Silver medal 1962, Gold medal 1983), AAAS, Radiol. Soc. N.Am., Chicago Radiol. Soc. (hon., Gold medal 1992), Inter-Am. Coll. Radiology, Friends of Detroit Public Library, Founders Soc. Detroit Inst. Art, State Hist. Soc. Iowa, Mich. Hist. Soc., Lost Lakes Woods Assn., Sigma Xi, Alpha Omega Alpha. Clubs: Masons. Achievements include exhibited portable radioactive istopes for radiography at Smithsonian Inst., 1964-67. Died Feb. 1, 2010.

KRAFT, IRVIN ALAN, retired psychiatrist; b. Huntington, W.Va., Nov. 20, 1921; m. Shirley Goldin, July 4, 1951; children: Karen Kraft Pennebaker, Joanna Kraft Katz, Elizabeth Kraft Schmachtenberger, Mark. BS, NYU, 1943, MD, 1949. Diplomate Am. Bd. Psychiatry and Neurology, Am. Bd. Child Psychiatry. Chief psychiatry Tex. Children's Hosp., Houston, 1958-65; prof. mental health U. Tex. Sch. Pub. Health, Houston, 1975-91; emeritus prof. mental health U. Tex., Houston, from 1991; assoc. clin. prof. pediatrics Baylor Coll. Medicine, Houston, 1977—2009, clin. prof. psychiatry, 1977—2009, U. Tex. Sch. Medicine, Houston, Galveston. Med. dir. Tex. Inst. Family Psychiatry, Houston, 1964-79; dir. Houston Heart Assn., 1969-70; med. dir. Adult Adolescent Rehab. Ctr., Houston, 1982-85; chmn. subcom. Mental Health Needs Coun., Houston, 1988-89. Author: (with others) Adolescent Group Psychotherapy, 1989, Bibliography of Child and Adolescent Psychiatry, 1990; co-editor: Child Group Psychotherapy: Future Tense, 1986; mem. editorial bd. Jour. Child and Adolescent Group Therapy, 1989—. Mem. drug prevention com. High Sch. for Health Professions, Houston, 1989-90; mem. Tex. House Rep. Com. on Edn., 1974. N.Y. Acad. Scis. fellow, 1971—; recipient Gold award Am. Acad. Pediatrics, 1969, cert. of award Am. Group Psychotheraphy Assn., 1970. Fellow Am. Acad. Child and Adolescent Psychiatry (life), Am. Group Psychotherapy Assn. (life), Am. Acad. Psychoanalysis (life), Am. Psychiat. Assn. (life), Houston Group Psychotherapy Soc. (life), Southwestern Group Psychotherapy Soc. (life), Houston Psychiat. Soc. (life), Tex. Soc. Psychiat. Physicians (life), Tex. Soc. of Child and Adolescent Psychiatry (life), Am. Orthopsychiatry Assn. (life). Home: Houston, Tex. Died May 30, 2010.

KRAMER, DANIEL CALEB, political scientist, educator; b. Chgo., Sept. 23, 1934; s. Samuel N. and Mildred (Tokarsky) K.; m. Clare Richenda Lee, Aug. 20, 1960; children: Tamsyn, Bruce, Elspeth. BA, Kenyon Coll., 1955; LLB, Harvard U., 1959; PhD, U. Pa., 1964. Asst. prof. polit. sci. U. Ill., Urbana, 1964-67; asst.-assoc. prof. polit. sci. CUNY, SI, 1967-84, prof. polit. sci., from 1985. Author: Participatory Democracy, 1972, Comparative Civil Rights and Liberties, 1982, State Venture Capital and Private Enterprise: the Case of the U.K. Nat. Enterprise Board, 1988; contbr. articles to profl. jours. Mem. Dem. Com., S.I., 1970, 80, 87—, N.Y.C. Community Bd. 1, S.I., 1980. Fulbright fellow, 1955-56, 1984-85. Mem. Am. Polit. Sci. Assn., Law and Soc. Assn., NE Polit. Sci. Assn., N.Y. State Polit. Sci. Assn. (exec. com. 1983-84), S.I. Dem. Assn. (v.p. 1979, sec. 1982). Jewish. Avocations: reading, swimming, walking. Home: Staten Island, NY. Died Mar. 11, 2010.

KRAMISH, ARNOLD, physicist, historian, writer; b. Denver, June 6, 1923; m. Vivian Ruth Raker, Aug. 19, 1952; children: Pamela, Robert. BS, U. Denver, 1945; A.M., Harvard U., 1947. With Manhattan Project, 1944-46, AEC, 1946-51; sr. staff mem. Rand Corp., Santa Monica, Calif., 1951-68; v.p. Inst. for the Future, Washington, 1968-70; sci. attache U.S. Mission to UNESCO, Paris, 1970-73; counselor for sci. and tech. affairs U.S. Mission to OECD, Paris, 1974-76; sci. research R & D Assocs., Arlington, Va., 1976-81; ind. tech. cons., 1981—2010; tech. dir. White House Study preliminary to Strategic Def. Initiative, 1981—84; advisor to under sec for policy US Dept. Def., 1984—91; assoc. Global Bus. Access Ltd., 1991—2010. Prof. UCLA, 1965-66, London Sch. Economics, 1967-68; adj. prof. internat. studies U. Miami, Fla., 1969; fellow Woodrow Wilson Internat. Ctr. for Scholars, 1982-83; Rockefeller scholar, Bellagio, Italy, 1984; pres. Tech. Analysis Internat., 1983-2010 Author: Atomic Energy for Your Business, 1956, Atomic Energy in the Soviet Union, 1959, The Peaceful Atom in Foreign Policy, 1963, The Future of Non-Nuclear Nations, 1970, The Griffin, 1986; also numerous articles, book chpts.; patentee nuclear radiometer. Sci. advisor European Cmty., 1960-62. With AUS, 1943-46. Carnegie fellow Coun. on Fgn. Rels., 1958-59; John Simon Guggenheim fellow, 1966-67; Rsch. fellow Inst. for Strategic Studies, London, 1966-67; Sr. fellow Global Access Inst., 1994-2010 Mem. PEN, Authors Guild. Died June 15, 2010.

KRANE, STEVEN CHARLES, lawyer; b. Far Rockaway, NY, Jan. 20, 1957; s. Harry and Gloria Krane; m. Faith Krane, Oct. 1, 1983; children: Elizabeth, Cameron. BA in Polit. Sci. with honors, Stony Brook U., NY, 1978; JD, NYU, 1981. Bar: NY 1982, US Dist. Ct. (so., no. and ea. dists.) NY 1982, US Ct. Appeals (1st, 2d, 3d, 6th and DC cirs.) 1987, US Supreme

Ct. 1987; cert. serve as chief judge, assoc. judge, Commn. Jud. Nomination, 2007. Law clk. to Assoc. Judge Judith S. Kaye NY Ct. Appeals, NYC and Albany, 1984-85; assoc. Proskauer Rose LLP, 1981—84, 1985—89, ptnr. NYC, 1989—2010, gen. counsel, 2009—10. Chair law firm practice group Proskauer Rose LLP, 2004-10, chair com. profl. stds., 2001-10, ethics ptnr., 1990-2009; lectr. law Columbia U. Sch. Law, NYC, 1989-92; vis. prof. Ga. Inst. Tech., 1994-96; departmental disciplinary com. Appellate divsn. 1st Jud. dept. Supreme Ct. NY, 1996-99, spl. trial counsel, 1991-93, Appellate divsn. 2d Jud. dept.; mem. grievance com. 9th Jud. Dist. NY, spl. referee, 2006-10; US Dist. Ct., So. Dist. NY, (chair, grievance panel, 1995-2001). Editor articles, NYU Jour. Internat. Law and Politics, 1980-81. Bd. dirs. John Jay Homestead, Katonah, NY, from 2007; subcom. chair ind. jud. election qualification commn. 1st jud. dist., from 2007. Securities Inst. NYU fellow, 1980-81; recipient Vol. Counsel award Legal Aid Soc., 1984, Legal Aid Soc. Pro Bono Svc. award, 2006, inducted George W. Hewlett HS Alumni Hall Fame, 2004. Fellow Am. Bar Found. (chmn. NY state), NY Bar Found. (dir. 2004-08); mem. ABA (standing com. ethics & profl. responsibility 2004-06, chmn. 2006-08, Gramm-Leach-Bliley task force 2002-08, ho. dels. 2000-10, liaison task force on atty.-client privilege 2005-10, mem. com. transnat. legal practice 2006-10, adv. task force internat. trade in legal svcs. 2006-10, co-chair, task force outsourcing legal svcs. 2008-10, mem. task force on FTC Red Flag Rules 2009-10, bd. govs. 2009-10), NY Bar Assn. (com. on stds. of atty. conduct, chmn. 1999-2010, com. on profl. ethics 1990-94, spl. com. to rev. the code of profl. responsibility 1992-95, chmn. 1995-99, vice chair spl. com. on future of profession 1997-2000, ho. dels. 1996-2010, com. on mass disaster response 1997-2003, com. on multidisciplinary practice and legal profession 1998-99, exec. com. 1998-2003, mem.-at-large, exec. com. 1998-2000, spl. com. on law gov. firm structure and ops., vice chair 1999-2003, chair, spl. com. on multidisciplinary practice, 2003-06, pres. 2001-02, pres. com. on access to justice, co-chair 2000-01, co-chair spl. com. to rev. atty. fee regulation, 2003-05, spl. assn. ho. com. chair 2000-05, vice chair sect. internat. law and practice 2003-08, exec. vice chair 2008-09, chair spl. com. on cross-border legal practice 2004-10, spl. com. for student loan assistance for public interest 2005-10, chair-elect 2009-), Assn. of Bar of City of NY (com. on profl. and jud. ethics 1990-93, chmn. 1993-96, sec. 1985-88, com. on profl. responsibility, chmn. subcom. provision legal svcs. 1985-88, com. on fed. cts. 1996-99, chmn. del. to NY State Bar Assn. ho. dels. 1997-98, Thurgood Marshall award for death row inmate representation 1998, internat. security affairs 2001-03), Am. Law Inst., NY State Jud. Inst. Professionalism in Law (mem. 2005-07, co-chair 2007-09, mem. 2009-10), Federalist Soc. (profl. responsibility practice group exec. com. 1999-2003, sr. advisor 2003-10), Hist. Soc. Cts. of State of NY (trustee 2001), Phi Beta Kappa, Pi Sigma Alpha. Republican. Avocations: military history, meteorology, Boston Red Sox baseball. Home: Bedford, NY. Died June 22, 2010.

KRASNANSKY, MARVIN L., public relations company executive; b. Bklyn., Feb. 18, 1930; s. Isadore and Anna (Zuckerman) K.; m. Johanne Wehner, Oct. 9, 1954; children—Melanie, William, Timothy BA in Journalism, Pa. State U. Vice pres. corp. communications Batten, Barton, Durstine, and Osborne, Internat., NYC, 1972-73; pres. Corp. Info. Ctr., NYC, 1973-74; v.p. corp. communications Becton Dickinson, Paramus, N.J., 1974-79; v.p. corp. relations McKesson Corp., San Francisco, from 1979. Bd. dirs. San Francisco Zool. Soc., Pa. State U. Devel. Council, University Park, Calif. State Parks Found. Mem. Nat. Investors Rels. Inst. (A.R. Roalman 1986), Soc. Profl. Journalists. Home: Sonoma, Calif. Died Mar. 8, 2010.

KREBS, EDWIN GERHARD, biochemistry educator; b. Lansing, Iowa, June 6, 1918; s. William Carl and Louise Helena (Stegeman) K.; m. Virginia Frech, Mar. 10, 1945; children: Sally, Robert, Martha. AB in Chemistry, U. Ill., 1940; MD, Washington U., St. Louis, 1943; DSc (hon.), U. Geneva, 1979; degree (hon.), Med. Coll. Ohio, 1993; DSc (hon.), U. Ind., 1993; doctorate (hon.), U. Nat. De Cuyo, 1993; DSc (hon.), U. Ill., 1995, Washington U., St. Louis, 1995. Intern, asst. resident Barnes Hosp., St. Louis, 1944-45; rsch. fellow biol. chemistry Wash. U., St. Louis, 1946-48; prof., chmn. dept. biol. chemistry Sch. Medicine U. Calif., Davis, 1968-76; from asst. prof. to prof. biochemistry U. Wash., Seattle, 1948-66, prof., chmn. dept. pharmacology, 1977-83, prof. biochemistry & pharmacology, 1984-91, emeritus prof., biochemistry and pharmacology, 1991—2009; investigator, sr. investigator Howard Hughes Med. Inst., Seattle, 1983-90, sr. investigator emeritus, 1991—2009. Mem. Phys. Chemistry Study Sect. NIH, 1963-68, Biochemistry Test Com. Nat. Bd. Med. Examiners, 1968-71, rsch. com. Am. Heart Assn., 1970-74, bd. sci. counselors Nat. Inst. Arthritis, Metabolism and Digestive Diseases, NIH, 1979-84, Internat. Bd. Rev., Alberta Heritage Found. for Med. Rsch., 1986, external adv. com. Weis Ctr. for Rsch., 1987-91; mem. subgroup interconvertible enzymes IUB Spl. Interest Group Metabolic Regulation; internat. adv. bd. Advances in Second Messenger Phosphoprotein Rsch.; external adv. com. Cell Therapeutics Inc., Seattle; adv. bd. Kinetek, Vancouver, B.C. Mem. editorial bd. Jour. Biol. Chemistry, 1965-70; mem. editorial adv. bd. Biochemistry, 1971-76; mem. editorial and adv. bd. Molecular Pharmacology, 1972-77; assoc. editor Jour. Biol. Chemistry, 1971-93; mem. internat. adv. bd. Advances in Cyclic Nucleotide Rsch.; editorial advisor Molecular and Cellular Biochemistry Recipient Gairdner Found. award, Toronto, 1978, J.J. Berzelius lectureship, Karolinska Institutet, 1982, George W. Thorn award for sci. excellence, 1983, Sir Frederick Hopkins Meml. lectureship, London, 1984, Rsch. Achievement award Am. Heart Assn., Anaheim, Calif., 1987, 3M Life Scis. award FASEB, New Orleans, 1989, Albert Lasker Basic Med. Rsch. award, 1989, CIBA-GEIGY-Drew award Drew U., 1991, Steven C. Beering award, Ind. U., 1991, Welch award in chemistry Welch Found., 1991, Louisa Gross Horwitz award Columbia U., 1989, Alumni Achievement award Coll. Liberal Arts and Scis. U. Ill., 1992, Nobel prize in physiology or medicine, 1992, Kaul Found. award for excellence, 1996; John Simon Guggenheim fellow, 1959, 66. Mem. NAS, Am. Soc. Biol. Chemists (pres. 1986, ednl. affairs com. 1965-68, councillor 1975-78), Am. Acad. Arts and Scis., Am. Soc. Pharmacology and Exptl. Therapeutics. Achievements include life-long study of the protein phosphorylation process. Home: Seattle, Wash. Died Dec. 21, 2009.

KREIDER, JOHN WESLEY, medical educator; b. Phila., Mar. 24, 1937; s. Wesley Johnson and Angeline (Scafidi) K.; m. Kathleen Anne Porter, June 1, 1963; children: Eric, Ted. AB, LaSalle U., 1959; MD, U. Pa., 1963. Resident Yale U., New Haven, 1963-64; resident, postdoctoral fellow U. Pa., 1964-68; from asst. prof. to prof. Pa. State U., Hershey, 1968-98. Chief divsn. exptl. pathology, dir. Jake Gittlen Cancer Rsch. Inst. Hershey Med. Ctr.; cons. biotech. firms. Mem. AMA, Pa. Med. Soc. Avocations: model railroads, wood carving. Home: Palmyra, Pa. Died Jan. 29, 2010.

KRENZLER, ALVIN IRVING, retired federal judge; b. Chgo., Apr. 8, 1921; AB, Case Western Res. U., 1946, LLB, 1948; LL.M., Georgetown U., 1963. Bar: Ohio 1948. Assoc. Jappe & Jappe, 1948-52; atty. Benesch, Friedlander, Coplan & Aronoff, 1958-59, Williams, Krenzler, Bartunek & Welf, 1960, Gottfried, Ginsberg, Guren & Merritt, 1963-68; judge Cuyahoga County Ct. Common Pleas, Ohio, 1968-70, Ohio Ct. Appeals, Cleve., 1970-81, US Dist. Ct. (northern dist.) Ohio, Cleve., 1981—92, sr. judge, 1992. Counsel, dir. Ohio Narcotics Investigation, 1953-55; asst. atty. gen. State of Ohio, 1951-56; trial atty. office chief counsel IRS, Washington, 1960-63 Chmn. Cuyahoga County Bd. Mental Retardation, 1967-70; trustee Cleve. State U., 1967-70, Mt. Sinai Hosp., Cleve., 1973-82; chmn. Ohio Criminal Justice Supervisory Commn., 1975-83. With USN, 1942-45. Mem. ABA, Greater Cleve. Bar Assn., Cuyahoga County Bar Assn., Fed. Bar. Assn. Home: Bonita Springs, Fla. Died Sept. 16, 2010.

KREPS, JUANITA MORRIS, retired economics professor, former United States Secretary of Commerce; b. Lynch, Ky., Jan. 11, 1921; d. Elmer M. and Cenia (Blair) Morris; m. Clifton H. Kreps, Jr., Aug. 11, 1944 (dec. Aug. 23, 2000); children: Sarah, Laura, Clifton. AB, Berea Coll., 1942; MA, Duke U., 1944; PhD, 1948; LLD (hon.), Bryant Coll., 1972, U. N.C. at Chapel Hill, 1973, Tulane U., Colgate U., 1980, Trinity Coll., 1981, U. Rochester, Grove City Coll., 1984, Davidson Coll., 1990, Lenoir-Rhyne Coll., 1991, U. Notre Dame, 1992, Duke U., 1993; LittD (hon.), Cornell Coll., 1973, Western Md. Coll., 1982; LHD (hon.), Denison U., 1973, U. Ky., Queens Coll., St. Lawrence U., 1975, Wheaton Coll., 1976, Claremont Grad. Sch., Berea Coll., 1979. Instr. economics Denison U., 1945-46, asst. prof., 1948-50; mem. faculty Duke U., 1955-77, assoc. prof., 1962-68, prof. economics, 1968-77, James B. Duke prof., 1972-77, James B. Duke prof. emerita, 1979—2010, asst. provost, 1969-72, v.p., 1973-77, v.p. emerita, 1979—2010; sec. US Dept. Commerce, 1977-79. Mem. adv. com. Congl. Commn. for the Future of Worker Mgmt. Rels., Secs. of Commerce and Labor, 1993-94. Author: (with C.E. Ferguson) Principles of Economics, 2d rev. edit, 1965, Lifetime Allocation of Work and Income, 1971, Sex in the Marketplace: American Women at Work, 1971, Women and the American Economy, 1976; co-author: (with Richard Perlman and Gerald Somers) Contemporary Labor Economics, 1973; Editor: Employment, Income and Retirement Problems of the Aged, 1963, Technology, Manpower and Retirement Policy, 1966, Sex, Age and Work, 1975. Bd. dirs. Am. Coun. on Germany, Rsch. Triangle Found., Ednl. Testing Svc., 1972-77; mem. Nat. Manpower Policy Task Force; trustee Berea Coll., 1972-78, 80-98, Duke Endowment, 1979—, Nat. Humanities Ctr., 1983-86, U. N.C., Wilmington, 1993-2001, Humrro, 1980-83, Coun. Fgn. Rels., 1983-89, Kenan Inst. Pvt. Enterprise of U. N.C., Chapel Hill, 1995—; pres. bd. overseers Tchrs. Ins. and Annuity Assn., 1992-96; bd. dirs. TIAA, 1968-72, 85-96, Coll. Retirement Equities Fund, 1972-77. Named to Presl. Commn. on Nat. Agenda for the 80's, 1979; recipient N.C. Pub. Svc. award, 1976, Stephen Wise award, 1978, Woman of Yr. award Ladies Home Jour., 1978, Duke U. Alumni award, 1983, Haskins award Coll. Bus. and Pub. Adminstrn., NYU, 1984, First Corp. Governance award Nat. Assn. Corp. Dirs., 1987, Dir.'s Choice Leadership award Nat. Women's Econ. Alliance Found., 1987, Disting. Meritorious Svc. medal Duke U. Alumni, 1987. Fellow Gerontol. Soc. (v.p. 1971-72), Am. Acad. Arts and Scis.; mem. AAUP, AAUW (Achievement award 1981), Am. Econ. Assn. (v.p. 1983-84), So. Econ. Assn. (pres. 1975-76), Indsl. Rels. Rsch. Assn. (exec. com.). Home: Durham, NC. Died July 5, 2010.

KRESS, ALBERT OTTO, JR., polymer chemist; b. Cullman, Ala., June 15, 1950; s. Albert Otto and Odell Pearl (Norris) K.; m. Ruth Jeanette Beach, Dec. 30, 1972 (div. Aug. 1978); children: Adrian Konrad, Katyna Ileana; m. Roby Lynn Rice, Apr. 14, 1984 (div. Oct. 1998); 1 child, Ashley Alan Rice Kress. BS, U. Montevallo, 1972; PhD, U. Ala., 1979. Rsch. scientist Hercules Chem. Corp., Wilmington, N.C., 1979-83; rsch. assoc. Clemson (S.C.) U., 1983-84; assoc. prof. U. Montevallo, Ala., 1984-86; rsch. assoc. U. So. Miss., Hattiesburg, 1986-88; sr. scientist Schering-Plough HealthCare Products Corp., Memphis, 1988-99, Urethane Specialist Cons., Cleveland, Tenn., from 1999. Contbr. articles to Jour. Organic Chemistry, Dissertation Abstracts Internat. B., Jour. Chem. Soc., Jour. Applied Polymer Sci. Recipient Dean's scholarship U. Ala., 1975. Mem. AAAS, Soc. Plastics Industry, Soc. Plastics Engrs., Am. Chem. Soc., Moose. Republican. Lutheran. Died Jan. 13, 2009.

KRIESBERG, IRVING, painter; b. Chgo., Mar. 13, 1919; s. Max and Bessie (Turner) K.; m. Ruth Miller, Apr. 5, 1921 (div. 1973); children: Nell, Matthias; m. Barbara Nimri Aziz, Dec. 2, 1974 (div.); m. Felice K. Shea BFA, Sch. of Art Inst. Chgo., 1941; MA, NYU, 1972. Tchr. Yale U. Grad. Sch., 1962-71; dir. state-wide honors studio program SUNY, 1972-77; tchr. painting Columbia U. Grad. Sch., 1977-79; tchr. painting and ceramics La. State U. Grad. Sch., 1980; Beaumont prof. painting Washington U., St. Louis, 1982; instr. terra-cotta, vis. artist Skidmore Coll., 1989; vis. artist painting Vt. Studio Sch., 1989; instr. sculpture Appalachian Ctr. for Crafts, 1992. Conductor lectrs. and workshops throughout the U.S. and India. Author: Looking at Pictures, 1955, Art, The Visual Experience, 1965, Working with Color, 1987; one-man shows at Guggenheim Mus., 1972, Fairweather-Hardin, Chgo., 1979, Dintenfass Gallery, N.Y.C., 1980-82, Everson Mus., Syracuse, N.Y., 1980, Rose Mus., Brandeis, 1980, Washington U. Art Mus., St. Louis, 1982, Graham Modern Gallery, N.Y.C., 1985, Montclair (N.J.) Art Mus., 1986; represented in permanent collections at Balt. Mus. Art, Cin. Mus. Art, Mus. Modern Art, N.Y.C., Whitney Mus., N.Y.C., Corcoran Gallery, Washington, Rose Mus., Brandeis, Nat. Gallery Am. Art, Washington, Rep. Peter Findlay Gall, N.Y.C. Recipient awards Ford Found., 1965, Fulbright, 1965-66, N.Y. State, 1974, 78, 91, NEA, 1984, Guggenheim, 1976. Mem. NAD (academician, 1994-) Home: New York, NY. Died Nov. 11, 2009.

KRISTOF, LADIS KRIS DONABED, political scientist, writer; b. Cernauti, Romania, Nov. 26, 1918; came to U.S., 1952, naturalized, 1957; s. Witold and Maria (Zawadzki) Krzysztofowicz; m. Jane McWilliams, Dec. 29, 1956; 1 son, Nicholas. Student, U. Poznan, Poland, 1937-39; BA, Reed Coll., Portland, Oreg., 1955; MA, U. Chgo., 1956, PhD, 1969. Regional exec. dir., Sovromlemn, Romania, 1948; sales mgr. Centre du Livre Suisse, Paris, France, 1951-52; lectr. U. Chgo., 1958-59; assoc. dir. Inter-Univ. Project History Menshevism, NYC, 1959-62; mem. faculty dept. polit. sci. Temple U., 1962-64; research fellow Hoover Instn., Stanford U., 1964-67; faculty polit. sci. U. Santa Clara, 1967-68; asso. Studies Communist System, Stanford, 1968-69; mem. faculty polit. sci. U. Waterloo, Ont., Can., 1969-71; prof. polit. sci. Portland (Oreg.) State U., 1971-89, prof. emeritus, from 1990. Vis. prof. U. Wroclaw, Poland, 1990, U. Iasi, Romania, 1991, U. Punjab, India, 1992, U. Bucharest, Romania, 2004. Author: The Nature of Frontiers and Boundaries, 1959, The Origins and Evolution of Geopolitics, 1960, The Russian Image of Russia, 1967, The Geopolitical Contours of the Post-Cold War World, 1992; also articles in Romania; co-author, co-editor: Revolution and Politics in Russia, 1972. Active Internat. YMCA Center, Paris, 1950-52, NAACP, Chgo., 1957-59, Amnesty Internat., Portland, 1975—. Served with Corps Engrs. Romanian Army, 1940-45. Fulbright scholar Romania, 1971, 84 Mem. Am. Polit. Sci. Assn., Assn. Am. Geographers, Am. Assn. for Advancement of Slavic Studies, Internat. Polit. Sci. Assn., Western Slavic Assn. (pres. 1988-90), Am.-Romanian Acad. Arts and Scis. (v.p. 1995-00). Home: Yamhill, Oreg. Died June 15, 2010.

KROLL, ARTHUR HERBERT, lawyer, educator, writer; b. NYC, Dec. 2, 1939; s. Abraham and Sylvia Kroll; m. Lois Handmacher, June, 1964; children: Douglas, Pamela. BA, Cornell U., 1961; LLB cum laude, St. John's U., 1965; LLM in Taxation, NYU, 1969. Assoc. Patterson, Belknap, Webb & Tyler, NYC, 1965-72, ptnr., 1972-90, Pryor, Cashman, Sherman & Flynn, NYC, 1990-95; CEO KST Cons. Group, Inc.; prof. Baruch U. Adj. prof. law U. Miami, NYU, Baruch Sch. Bus.; mem. adv. bd. Bur. Nat. Affairs Tax Mgmt., Inc., Practising Law Inst. Tax Adv. Bd., U. Miami Inst. Estate Planning, Bus. Laws, Inc.; mem. adv. com. NYU Ann. Inst. on Fed. Taxation; lectr. in field Author: Executive Compensation, 3 vols., Compensating Executives; monthly newsletter Family Bus. Profl.; contbg. editor Exec. Mag.; mem. bd. contbg. editors and advisers Corporate Taxation; mem. editl. adv. bd. Jour. Compensation and Benefits; contbr. articles to profl. jours. Home: Scarsdale, NY. Died Feb. 15, 2010.

KROUSE, SUSAN APPLEGATE, museum curator; b. Detroit, July 1, 1955; d. John D. and Carol Edith (Summers) Applegate; m. Ned Allan Krouse, Aug. 19, 1978. AB, Ind. U., 1976, MA, 1981. Acting curator I.U. Mus., Bloomington, Ind., 1978—79; curator New Hanover County Mus., Wilmington, NC, 1981—86; tchg. asst. U. Wis., Milw., from 1986. Mem.: Am. Assn. Anthropology. Home: Milwaukee, Wis. Died July 12, 2010.

KRUGER, GUSTAV OTTO, JR., retired oral surgeon, educator, department chairman; b. NYC, Sept. 28, 1916; s. Gustav Otto and Anna Charlotte (Mellquist) K.; m. Helyn E. Hollingsworth, Apr. 12, 1947; children: Deborah Ann (Mrs. M. Henry King III), Tristram Coffin, Abigail Hollingsworth Imus. BS, George Washington U., 1938, AM, 1939; DDS, Georgetown U., 1939, ScD (hon.), 1977. Diplomate Am. Bd. Oral and Maxillofacial Surgery (pres. 1964). Intern Johns Hopkins Hosp., 1939-40; fellow Mayo Found., 1940-42, 45-48; mem. faculty Georgetown U. Sch. Dentistry and Grad. Sch., 1948-87, prof. oral surgery, chmn. dept., 1948-87, prof. emeritus, from 1987, assoc. dean, 1966-82; ret., 1987. Chief dental dept. Georgetown U. Hosp., Washington, 1948-82; cons. VA hosps., Martinsburg, W.Va. and Washington, U.S. Naval Hosp., Bethesda, D.C. Gen. Hosp., Washington; cons. to Pres.'s physician, 1960-64; cons. Walter Reed Army Med. Ctr.; mem. cancer tng. com. Nat. Cancer Inst., USPHS, 1967-71, chmn., 1969-71. Author: Textbook of Oral and Maxillofacial Surgery, 1959, 6th edit., 1984; contbr. articles to profl. jours. Capt. Dental Corps AUS, 1942-45, CBI, PTO. Recipient Arnold K. Maislen award N.Y. U., 1970; Simon P. Hullihen award W.Va. Soc. Oral Surgeons and W.Va. Med. Ctr., 1980; named Man of Year Georgetown U. Alumni Assn., 1961, Disting. Svc. award, 1992. Fellow AAAS, Am. Coll. Dentists (chmn. D.C. sect. 1969-71, Disting. Svc. award 2002), Internat. Coll. Dentists (chmn. D.C. sect. 1967-70); mem. ADA (chmn. oral surgery sect. 1961, mem. rev. commn. on advanced edn. in oral surgery 1965-71, chmn. commn. 1969-71), D.C. Dental Soc. (pres. 1960, Sterling V. Mead award 1989), Am. Assn. Oral and Maxillofacial Surgeons (program chmn. 1961, 79th Ann. Meeting dedication 1997), Middle Atlantic Soc. Oral and Maxillofacial Surgeons (pres. 1952), Am. Assn. Dental Schs., Am. Acad. Oral Pathology, Am. Acad. Oral and Maxillofacial Radiology, Internat. Assn. Dental Research, Am. Coll. Oral and Maxillofacial Surgeons

(Harry Archer award 1992), Wash. Dental Study Club (pres. 1993), Kiwanis (co-chmn. orthop. com. 1971-86), Xi Psi Phi, Sigma Gamma Epsilon, Omicron Kappa Upsilon. Home: Bethesda, Md. Died July 5, 2010.

KRUGER, PAUL, nuclear civil engineering educator; b. Jersey City, June 7, 1925; s. Louis and Sarah (Jacobs) K.; m. Claudia Mathis, May 19, 1972; children: Sharon, Kenneth, Louis. BS, MIT, 1950; PhD, U. Chgo., 1954. Registered profl. engr., Pa. Rsch. physicist GM, Detroit, 1954-55; mgr. dept. chemistry Nuclear Sci. and Engring. Corp., Pitts., 1955-60; v.p. Hazleton Nuclear Sci. Corp., Palo Alto, Calif., 1960-62; prof. nuc. civil engring. Stanford (Calif.) U., 1962-87, prof. emeritus, from 1987. Cons. Elec. Power Rsch. Inst., Palo Alto, 1975-95, Los Alamos (N.Mex.) Nat. Lab., 1985-98. Author: Principles of Activation Analysis, 1973, Geothermal Energy, 1972, Alternative Energy Resources, 2006. 1st lt. USAF, 1943-46, PTO. Recipient achievement cert. U.S. Energy R & D Adminstrn., 1975. Fellow Am. Nuclear Soc.; mem. ASCE (divsn. chmn. 1978-79), Nat. Hydrogen Assn.(hon.). Home: Stanford, Calif. Died Sept. 17, 2010.

KRUGLIK, MEYER, psychiatrist; b. NYC, Nov. 3, 1914; s. Max and Sarah (Fratkin) Kruglik; m. Gertrude Barbara Ginsburg, Feb. 6, 1938; children: Michael, Gerald, Sally Kruglik Bauer, Martin. Bs, U. Ill., 1936; MD, 1969. Intern Univ. Hosp., Cook County Hosp., 1938—41; resident Va., 1942—47; practice medicine specializing in psychiatry Chgo., from 1947. Mem. faculty Chgo. Med. Sch., 1948—58; cons. Ill. Dept. Corrections, from 1947. Capt US Army, 1942—46. Mem.: AMA, Ill. Med. Soc., Chgo. Med. Soc., Ill. Psychiat. Soc. (life), Am. Psychiat. Assn. (life). Home: Glenview, Ill. Died May 9, 2010.

KRUTENAT, ROBERT ALFRED, electronics engineer; b. Batavia, NY, Nov. 16, 1930; s. Carl Alfred and Doris (Baldeck) Krutenat; m. Dolores Marie Ortega, June 7, 1952; children: Robert, Christina, Joseph, John. AA, Ventura Coll., 1964; BSEE, U. So. Calif., 1964. Electronic technician USN Missile Test Ctr., Point Mugu, Calif., 1953—54; data analyst Bendix Corp., 1954—56; electronic tech. staff engr. U. So. Calif. Wind Tunnel, 1956—58, US Naval Civil Engring. Lab., Port Hueneme, Calif., 1958—65; asst. chief engr. Rothenbuhler Engring., Sedro Woolley, Wash., 1965—69; sr. staff asst. US Navy Undersea Warfare Engring. Sta., Keyport, from 1969; cons. Notward Found., Port Ludlow, from 1978. Mem. Wash. Sch. Dirs. Assn., 1976; bd. dirs. Sch. Dist. #49, Jefferson County, Wash., 1975—77. Mem. Evangel. Free Ch. Am. With USN, 1948—53. Mem.: IEEE. Republican. Achievements include patents for in field. Home: Port Ludlow, Wash. Died Aug. 12, 2009.

KUCERA, HENRY, linguistics educator; b. Trebarov, Czechoslovakia, Feb. 15, 1925; arrived in U.S., 1949, naturalized, 1953; s. Jindrich and Marie (Kral) K.; m. Jacqueline M. Fortin, Oct. 6, 1951; children: Thomas Henry, Edward James. MA, Charles U., Prague, Czechoslovakia, 1947, PhDr, 1991; PhD, Harvard U., 1952; MA ad eundem, Brown U., 1958; DSc (hon.), Bucknell U., 1984; PhilD (hon.), Masaryk U., Brno, Czechoslovakia, 1990. Asst. prof. fgn. langs. U. Fla., 1952-55; from mem. faculty to prof. Brown U., 1955—90, prof. emeritus, from 1990; mem. Ctr. for Cognitive Sci., 1977-85, exec. com., 1980-86; mem. Ctr. for Neural Studies, 1973-90, exec. com., 1977-90; dir. Inst. for Cognitive and Neural Research, 1981-88. Fellow Russian Rsch. Ctr., Harvard U., 1952, 79-87, rsch. assoc. Slavic dept., 1977-79; rsch assoc. MIT, 1960-63; vis. prof. U. Mich., 1967, U. Calif. at Berkeley, 1969; vis. scholar U. Vienna, 1968-69; pres. Lang. Software Systems, Inc., 1982-2001. Author: The Phonology of Czech, 1961, (with W.N. Francis) Computational Analysis of Present-Day American English, 1967, (with G. Monroe) A Comparative Quantitative Phonology of Russian, Czech and German, 1968, Computers in Linguistics and in Literary Studies, 1975, (with K. Trnka) Time in Language, 1975, (with W.N. Francis) Frequency Analysis of English Usage, 1982; also linguistic and lit. articles.; Editor: American Contributions to the Sixth International Congress of Slavists, 1968. Bd. dirs. Internat. Inst. Providence, 1960-67; bd. adminstrn. Howard Found., 1977-95; mem. R.I. Com. for Humanities, 1986-90. Ford fellow, 1954-55; Howard Found. fellow, 1960-61; Guggenheim fellow, 1960-61; sr. fellow NEH, 1968-69; Am. Council Learned Socs. fellow, 1969-70 Hon. fellow Linguistic Soc. of Czech Acad. Scis.; mem. MLA, Linguistic Soc. Am., Czechoslovak Soc. Arts and Scis. in Am. (v.p. 1980-82), Prague Linguistic Circle (hon.), Phi Beta Kappa. Died Feb. 17, 2010.

KUCHEMAN, CLARK ARTHUR, philosophy and religious studies educator; b. Akron, Ohio, Feb. 7, 1931; s. Merlin Carlyle and Lucile (Clark) K.; m. Melody Elaine Frazer, Nov. 15, 1986. BA, U. Akron, 1952; BD, Meadville Theol. Sch., 1955; MA in Econs., U. Chgo., 1959, PhD, 1965. Instr., then asst. prof. U. Chgo., 1961-67; prof. Claremont (Calif.) McKenna Coll., from 1967, Claremont Grad. Sch., from 1967. Co-author: Belief and Ethics, 1978, Creative Interchange, 1982, Economic Life, 1988; contbg. editor: The Life of Choice, 1978; contbr. articles to profl. jours. 1st lt. USAF, 1955—57. Mem. Am. Acad. Religion, Hegel Soc. Am., N.Am. Soc. for Social Philosophy. Democrat. Home: Riverside, Calif. Died Dec. 27, 2009.

KUEMPEL, EDMUND, state legislator; b. Nov. 29, 1942; m. Roberta Blumberg; children: Margaret Brady, John. BA in Bus., Tex. Luth. Coll., Seguin, Tex. Salesman Structural Metals, Inc., 1964; mem. Dist. 46 Tex. House of Reps., 1983—90, mem. Dist. 45, 1991—2000, mem. Dist. 44, 2001—10. Recipient Rep. of Year, Assoc. Builders & Contractors of Tex., 1985, Blue & Gold award, Future Farmers of America, 1985, Legislator of Year, Tex. Pub. Employees Assn., 1987, Environ. award, Lower Colorado River Authority, 1988, Better Life award, Tex. Health Care Assn., 1989, Legislature Leadership award, Tex. C. of C., 1992, Career Achievement Award, 1994, Leader Excellence award, Free Mktg. Com., 1993, Man of Year award, Tex. Co. Agr. Agt. Assn., 1997, Disting. Svc. award, Voct. Agr. Tchr Assn., Golden Flame award, Voct. Home Econ. Tchr. Assn. Tex. Mem.: Seguin & Guadalupe Co. C. of C. (former mem.). Republican. Lutheran. Died Nov. 4, 2010.

KUESEL, THOMAS ROBERT, civil engineer; b. Richmond Hill, NY, July 30, 1926; s. Henry N. and Marie D. (Butt) K.; m. Lucia Elodia Fisher, Jan. 31, 1959; children— Robert Livingston, William Baldwin B. Engring. with highest honors, Yale U., 1946, M. Engring., 1947. With Parsons, Brinckerhoff, Quade & Douglas, 1947-90, project mgr. San Francisco, 1967-68, ptnr., sr. v.p. NYC, 1968-83, chmn. bd., dir., 1983-90; cons. engr., from 1990; vice chmn. OECD Tunneling Conf., Washington, 1970; mem U.S. Nat. Com. on Tunneling Tech., 1972-74. Chmn. Geotech. bd. NRC, 1988-89. Contbr. 60 articles to profl. jours.; designer more than 120 bridges, 135 tunnels and numerous other structures in 36 states and 20 fgn. countries, most recent L.A. Metro, 1982-98, Geo Coleman Bridge Replacement, Yorktown, Va., 1991-95, Boston Ctrl. Artery and Harbor Tunnel, 1994—, Boston Ocean Outfall Tunnel, 1988-90, Cumberland Gap Tunnel, Ky. and Tenn., 1986-90, Jamuna River Bridge, Bangladesh, 1985-95, Trans Koolau Tunnel, Hawaii, 1985-90, Ft. McHenry Tunnel, Balt., 1978-85, Rogers Pass Rwy. Tunnel, B.C., 1981-85, Glenwood Canyon Tunnel, Colo., 1981-88, subways Boston, N.Y., Balt., Wash., Atlanta, Pitts., San Francisco, Seattle, L.A., Caracas, Singapore and Taipei. Fellow: ASCE; mem.: Nat. Acad. Engring., Yale Club N.Y.C., Yale Sci. and Engring. Assn., Am. Underground Constrn. Assn. (hon.), Wee Burn Club, The Moles, Tau Beta Pi. Died Feb. 17, 2010.

KUHLMANN, FRED L., retired professional sports team executive; b. St. Louis, Apr. 24, 1916; s. Fred A and Meta (Borrenpohl) K.; m. Mildred E. Southworth, July 11, 1941; children: Marilyn Kuhlmann Brickler, F. Mark. AB, JD, Washington U., 1938; LLM, Columbia U., 1942. Bar: Mo. 1938. Ptnr. Stolar, Kuhlmann, Heitzmann & Eder, 1956-67; gen. counsel Anheuser-Busch Inc., St. Louis, 1967-70, v.p., gen. counsel, 1971-74, sr. v.p. adminstrn. & services, 1974-77, exec. v.p., 1977-84; pres., CEO St. Louis Cardinals Baseball Team, 1984-91. Bd. dirs. Civic Ctr. Corp., St. Louis Nat. Baseball Club, Inc.; mem. devel. bd. St. Luke's Health Corp. Mem. ABA, Mo. Bar Assn., St. Louis Bar Assn., Order of the Coif, Phi Beta Kappa. Clubs: St. Louis, Bellerive Country. Home: Saint Louis, Mo. Died Apr. 3, 2010.

KUHN, ALBIN OWINGS, agronomist, retired academic administrator; b. Woodbine, Md., Jan. 31, 1916; s. Howard Schloenacher and Clara May (Owings) K.; m. Ella Elizabeth Cissel, Nov. 23, 1938; children: Philip Howard, Joseph Albin, Roger Cissel, Albin Owings, Lois Ellen. BS, U. Md., 1938, MS, 1940, PhD, 1948; postgrad., U. Wis., 1947. Agronomic extension work U. Md., 1939-44, assoc. prof. agronomy, 1946-48, prof. agronomy, 1948—82, head dept., 1948-55, asst. pres., 1955-58, exec. v.p., 1958-65, v.p. Balt. campuses, 1965-67, chancellor Balt. campuses, 1967-71; chancellor U. Md. at Balt., 1971-82; exec. v.p. U. Md., 1979-82. Bd. dirs. Hosp. Cost Analysis Service, Inc.; trustee, pres., v.p., sec. Md. Hosp. Service, Inc.; Mem. Md. Hosp. Commn., 1964-67, vice chmn., 1966-67; mem. Gov.'s Com. on Rehab., 1965-67, Commn. Modernization Exec. Br. Md. Govt., 1966-67; mem. gov.'s adv. council to State's Inter-agy. Com. for Comprehensive Health Planning, 1968-69; mem. Balt. Urban Coalition, 1967-69; pres. Md. Assn. Higher Edn., 1968-69. Served with USNR, 1944-46, PTO. Fellow Am. Soc. Agronomy (pres. Northeastern br. 1954); mem. Assn. Acad. Health Centers (dir. 1972—), Northeastern Weed Control Conf. (pres. 1954), Sigma Xi, Alpha Zeta, Omicron Delta Kappa, Phi Kappa Phi, Alpha Gamma Rho, Pi Sigma Alpha. Died Mar. 24, 2010.

KUHN, LESLIE ALVIN, cardiologist; b. S. Fallsburg, NY, May 10, 1924; Student, Harvard U., Cambridge, Mass., 1946; MD, SUNY, Downstate, 1948. Diplomate Am. Bd. Internal Medicine, Am. Bd. Cardiovascular Diseases. Intern Mt. Sinai Hosp., NYC, 1948-49, resident medicine, 1951-52, fellow cardiology, 1952-53, attending cons., from 1974; resident medicine Boston City Hosp., 1949-51; clin. prof. medicine Mt. Sinai Sch. Medicine, NYC, from 1974; pvt. practice. Cons. cardiologist Bronx VA Hosp. Editor-in-chief: Mt. Sinai Jour. Medicine. Fellow Am. Coll. Cardiology, ACP; mem. Am. Fedn. Clin. Rsch., AHA, AMA. Died July 10, 2009.

KUMMLER, RALPH H., chemical engineer, educator, dean; b. Jersey City, Nov. 1, 1940; m. Jean Evelyn Helge, Aug. 25, 1962; children: Randolph Henry, Bradley Rolf, Jeffrey Ralf. BSChemE, Rensselaer Poly. Inst., 1962; PhD, Johns Hopkins U., 1966. Chem. engr. GE Space Scientist Lab., Valley Forge, Pa., 1965—69; assoc. prof. chem. engring. Wayne State U., Detroit, 1970—75, prof., from 1975, chmn. dept., 1974—93, dir. hazardous waste mgmt. programs, 1986—2006, assoc. dean rsch., 1997—2001, interim dean, 2001—04, dean, from 2004. Contbr. articles to publs. Bd. dirs., past pres. Kirkwood Lake Assn. Fellow: Engr. Soc. Detroit (bd. dirs. from 2008, Young Engr. of Yr. award 1975, Gold award 1990, Disting. Svc. award 1994, Horace Rackham Humanitarian award 1999, Disting. Svc. award 2004), Am. Inst. Chemists; mem.: AIChE (past pres. Detroit chpt.), Svc. award 1981, Chem. Engr. of Yr. award 1981), Mich. Air and Waste Mgmt. Assn. (past pres., Waste Mgmt. award 2002), Tau Beta Pi, Sigma Xi. Achievements include co-patentee in chem. innovations. Died Dec. 7, 2009.

KUNDU, MUKUL RANJAN, physics and astronomy professor; b. Calcutta, India, Feb. 10, 1930; came to U.S., 1959; s. Makhan Lal and Monoroma K.; m. Sept. 9, 1958; children: Krishna, Rina, Sanjit. BS (with first class honors), U. Calcutta, India, 1949, MS, 1951; DSc, U. Paris, 1957. Assoc. prof. Cornell U., Ithaca, NY, 1962-65, Tata Inst. Fund Rsch., Bombay, 1965-68; prof. U. Md., College Park, from 1968, dir. astronomy, 1978-85. Editor: Radio Physics of the Sun, 1980, Unstable Current Systems and Plasma Instabilities in Astrophysics, 1984, Energetic Phenomena on the Sun, 1989; author: Solar Radio Astronomy, 1965; mem. editorial bd. Solar Physics, 1967—. Named Nat. Acad. Sci. fellow, 1967, 74-75, 86, U.S. Sr. Scientist awardee Humbolt Found., 1978, Am. Phys. Soc. fellow, 1989. Fellow Am. Phys. Soc.; mem. Am. Astron. Soc., Am. Geophys. Union, Internat. Astron. Union, Internat. Union Radio Sci. Home: Silver Spring, Md. Died June 16, 2010.

KUNTZ, MARION LUCILE LEATHERS, classicist, historian, educator; b. Atlanta, Sept. 6, 1924; d. Otto Asa and Lucile (Parks) Leathers; m. Paul G. Kuntz, Nov. 26, 1970; children by previous marriage: Charles, Otto Alan (Daniels). BA, Agnes Scott Coll., 1945; MA, Emory U., 1964, PhD, 1969. Lectr. Latin Lovett Sch., Atlanta, 1963-66; from mem. faculty to prof. Ga. State U., 1966—75, Regents' Prof., from 1975, chmn. dept. fgn. langs., 1975-84, Fuller E. Callaway prof., from 1984, rsch. prof., from 1984, reagents prof. emeritus, 2005. Author: Colloquium of the Seven About Secrets of the Sublime of Jean Bodin, 1975, second edit., 2008, Guillaume Postel, Prophet of the Restitution of All Things: His Life and Thought, 1981, Jacob's Ladder and the Tree of Life: Concepts of Hierarchy and the Great Chain of Being, 1987, Postello, Venezia e Il Suo Mondo, 1988, Venice, Myth and Utopian Thought, 1999, The Anointment of Dionisio: Prophecy and Politics in Renaissance Italy, 2002; second printing of Colloquium of the Seven about Secrets of the Sublime, 2008; also scholarly articles; mem. editl. bd. Library of Renaissance Humanism. V.p. acad. affairs Am.-Hellenic Found.; patron Atlanta Opera. Named Latin Tchr. of Yr. State Ga., 1965; Am. Classical League scholar, 1966, Gladys Krieble Delmas scholar, 1991; Am. Coun. Learned Socs. grantee, 1970, 73, 76, 81, 87, 90; recipient Alumni Disting. Prof. award Ga. State U., 1994, medal for excellence in Renaissance studies Pres. of Coun. Gen., Tours, France, 1995, Disting. Career Alumna award Agnes Scott Coll., 1995 Master: Soc. Values in Higher Edn., Philosophy and Religion; mem.: The Renaissance Soc. Am. (trustee from 2003), Société des Hautes Etudes de la renaissance, Am. Cath. Hist. Assn., Classical Assn. Midwest and South (Semple award 1965), Am. Philol. Assn., Archaeol. Inst. Am., Soc. di Philosophique Medievale, Soc. Medieval and Renaissance Philosophy (exec. bd. 1988—90), Medieval Acad. Soc. de Culture Europèenne, Soc. des Seizièmistes, Soc. Christian Philosophers (exec. bd. from 1987), Internat. Soc. Neo-Latin Studies, Internat. Soc. Neo-Platonic Studies, Am. Hist. Assn., Am. Soc. Ch. History, Am. Cath. Philos. Assn., Am. Soc. Aesthetics, Renaissance Soc. Am. (coun. 1994—97, trustee from 2003), The Abbeville Inst. Southern Culture, Am. Acad. Rome (sec.-treas. 1970—74), The Atlanta Opera, Michael C. Carlos Mus. (patron), The Atlanta Symphony, Friends of the Warburg Inst., Atlanta Hist. Soc., Italia Nostra, Fondazione Ambiente Italiana, Am. Friends Vatican Libr. Patron Arts in Vatican Mus., Coun. Amici di Biblioteca Nazionale di San Marco, Italian Cultural Soc., Nat. Trust Hist. Preservation, High Mus. of Art, World Monuments Fund, Druid Hills Civitan Club, The Commerce Club, Omicron Delta Kappa, Phi Kappa Phi, Phi Beta Kappa. Roman Catholic. Home: Atlanta, Ga. Died July 10, 2010.

KURTZ, ANTHONY DAVID, physicist; b. NYC, May 3, 1929; s. Jacob Kurtz and Claire Juscow; m. Nora Morcos, May 27, 1985; 1 child, Sandria; m. Margery Geilich, Apr. 3, 1955 (div. May 1985); children: Jennifer Kurtz Unger, John. BS in Physics, MIT, 1951, MS in Physics, 1952, ScD in Phys. Metallurgy, 1955. Staff mem. semiconductor physics Lincoln Lab., 1952—55; project mgr. diffused device rsch. Clevite Transistor Products, 1955—56; dir. semiconductor applied rsch. Mpls.-Honeywell Regulatory Co., 1956—59; dir. R&D, sr. scientist, CEO Kulite Semiconductor Products, Inc., Leonia, NJ, from 1959. Adj. prof. dept. mech. engring. Columbia U., NYC, from 2002. Contbr. articles to profl. jours. Recipient I R 100 for miniature semiconductor pressure transducer, Indsl. Rsch. Inc., 1968, Si Fluor Tech. award, Instrument Soc. Am., 1978; named to N.J. Inventors Congress and Hall of Fame, State N.J., 1991. Achievements include patents in field; invention of MEMS technology. Home: Saddle River, NJ. Died Feb. 2010.

KUSHNICK, THEODORE, retired pediatrics educator; b. Bklyn., Mar. 29, 1925; s. Elias and Fae (Feinstein) K.; m. Judith Frances Barr, Apr. 12, 1949; children: Eric B., William B., Steven B. BS, Ohio State U., 1944, MS, 1947; MD, Harvard U., 1951. Diplomate Am. Bd. Pediatrics, Am. Bd. Med. Genetics. Intern Boston City Hosp., 1951-52; resident in pediatrics Children's Hosp. Med. Ctr., Boston, 1952-55; resident in psychology Boston State, 1953-54; fellow in pediatrics med. ctr. Harvard U., Boston, 1955; asst. prof. pediatrics Seton Hall Coll. Medicine, Jersey City, 1959-63; assoc. prof. pediatrics N.J. Coll. Medicine, Newark, 1963-69; prof. pediatrics N.J. Med. Sch., Newark, 1969-79, dir. genetics, 1960-79; prof. pediatrics and dir. genetics E. Carolina U. Sch. Medicine, Greenville, N.C., from 1979; now staff mem. Pitt County Med. Ctr., Greenville, N.C.; ret. Cons. in field to numerous hosps.; adv. com. Southeastern Regional Genetics Group, 1984—. Contbr. over 73 articles to profl. jours., book revs., chpts. to books. Pres. Union County TB and Health League, Elizabeth, N.J., 1958-67; chmn. bd. trustees Woodbridge (N.J.) State Sch. for Retarded, 1965-79; scoutmaster Boy Scouts Am., Linden, N.J., 1962-68, physician, 1969-79; bd. dirs. ARC/PC, Greenville, N.C., 1987—. Lt. (j.g.) USNR, 1944-46; PTO. Med. Svc. grantee, NF-MOD, Newark, 1974-79; Genetic Svc. grantee, Dept. Human Resources, Raleigh, 1980—. Mem. Am. Acad. Pediatrics (charter genetics sect.), Am. Assn. Human Genetics, AMA, N.C. Med. Soc., N.C. Pediatric Soc., So. Soc. Pediatric Rsch., Nat. Tay Sachs and Allied Diseases Assn. (adv. com.), N.C. Med. Genetics Assn., N.J. Human Genetics Assn. Phi Beta Kappa, Sigma Xi. Jewish. Avocations: flying, fishing, golf, space exploration by proxy. Home: Franklin, Maine. Died May 1, 2010.

KUSS, RICHARD L., oil company executive; b. Springfield, Ohio, Jan. 4, 1923; s. Peter John and Frances Leone (Rizer) Kuss Lent; m. Barbara Deer, July 8, 1944; children: Carolyn

Kuss Patterson, Paul R., Gregory R., Philip D. BA, Wittenberg U., 1945, L.H.D., 1979; postgrad. in bus. adminstrn., Harvard U., 1944-45. Sales mgr. Bonded Oil, Springfield, 1946-49, v.p., 1949-67, pres., 1967-83, Kuss Petroleum Co., Springfield, from 1983, Emro Mktg. Co., Springfield, 1976-83; dir. Stocker & Sitler Oil Co., Heath, Ohio, 1969-93; chmn. bd. Merchants and Mechanics Fed. Savs. and Loan Assn., Springfield, 1978-91; dir. Credit Life Cos., Inc., Springfield, from 1985. Vice chmn. bd. Wittenberg U., Springfield, 1972-84, nat. chmn. Campaign for Wittenberg, 1978-82, bd. dirs., 1968-87, dir. emeritus, 1988—; assoc. chmn., mem. campaign adv. com. United Way Springfield, 1974-75, co-chmn. leadership giving div., Clark and Champaign Counties, 1985; chmn. $14.4 million campaign Clark Civic Ctr., 1988-93, 1,500 seats in auditorium which has been named in honor Mr. and Mrs. Kuss; laureate of Jr. Achievement Bus. Hall of Fame, 1991. Lt. (j.g.) USN, 1943-46, PTO. Recipient Marts & Lundy award, 1971; recipient Silver Knight of Mgmt. award Springfield chpt. Nat. Mgmt. Assn., 1979, medal of Honor Wittenberg U., 1983, Exceptional Achievement award council for Advancement and Support Edn., 1983, resolution for Outstanding Ohio Citizen Ohio Senate, 1983; named to Ohio Found. Ind. Colls. Hall of Excellence, 1993. Mem. Am. Petroleum Inst. (bd. dirs. 1968— cert. appreciation, life mem. gen. com. mktg. 1986—), Am. Petroleum Inst. (lifetime mem. bd. dirs. 1983—), Nat. Oil Jobbers Council (chmn. planning com., treas., v.p. cert. appreciation), 25 Yr. Club of Petroleum Industry, Ohio Petroleum Marketers Assn. (pres., dir. Distng. Service award), Ohio Found. Ind. Colls. (dir. 1972-86), Springfield Area C. of C. (v.p., dir.), Springfield Jaycees (pres.) Clubs: Country (Springfield) (pres.), Univ. (Springfield) (pres.), Van Dyke (Springfield) (pres.); Muirfield Village Golf, Coral Ridge Country, Zanesfield Rod & Gun (bd. dirs. 1990-93). Lodges: Rotary (Springfield). Republican. Presbyterian. Home: Springfield, Ohio. Died Aug. 9, 2010.

KUTCHER, FRANK EDWARD, JR., printing company executive; b. Teaneck, NJ, Dec. 20, 1927; s. Frank Edward Sr. and Helen Marie (Crowley) K.; m. Elizabeth Vespaziani, Jan. 19, 1952; children— Kenneth, Karen, Kristin BS cum laude, Fairleigh Dickinson U., 1953. Mgmt. cons. Peat, Marwick, Mitchell & Co., Inc., 1961-63; controller Celanese Plastics Co., 1963-65, Pfister Chem. Co., Ridgefield, N.J., 1965-67; v.p. fin. Litton Industries, NYC, 1967-70; v.p., controller McCall Pub. Co.-Norton Simon, Inc., NYC, 1970-73; pres. Foote & Davies-Lincoln, Nebr., from 1978; chmn., pres., chief exec. officer FDI Holdings, Inc., Doraville, from 1985. Served with USN, 1945-46 Mem. Graphics Arts Tech. Found. (bd. dirs. 1982—), Fin. Execs. Inst., Nat. Assn. Accts., Mensa Clubs: Atlanta Athletic, Commerce (Atlanta); Atrium (N.Y.C.). Home: Alpharetta, Ga. Died June 1, 2009.

KUYPER, FRANCES IRENE, cake decorator, educator; b. Harvey, Ill., June 26, 1918; d. John August William and Lovie DeVal (Smith) Schultz; m. Frank Kuyper, Aug. 17, 1947; 1 child, Carol Jean. Student Afleck Art Studio Sch. of Design, Cin., 1947; diploma Aaron Bros., Buena Park, Calif., 1969; master cake decorator Wilton Sch., 1974. Entertainer show bus. Sister Team, E. of Miss. River, 1935-46; home bus. of personalized cakes, Compton, Calif., 1950-55; head decorator bakeries, Los Angeles, 1955-74; tchr. coordinator Wilton Enterprises, Chgo., 1974-79; owner Cake Lady Services, Anaheim, Calif., 1979—, Pasadena, 1979—; founder Mini Cake Mus., 1994; cons. in field; cons. Baskin Robbins, 1980—; condr. classes in Australia, Indonesia, Tokyo, Can., Singapore, England, others; lectr., Kuala Lumpur, Malaysia, Osaka and Japan, 1986. Author Plaid Enterprises; Norcross, Ga., 1983-85; demonstrator Parrish's Cake Supplies, Los Angeles, 1956-86; instr. Cake Lady Services, Pasadena, 1979-86. Author: How to Air Brush on Cake, 1979; Craft Book-Stencil-A-Cake, 1983, Star Spangled speakers, 1982, others; also video tapes; elder, chair mission evangelism com. Michilinda Presbyn Ch. Goodwill ambassador Internat. Cake Exploration Société World, 1977, bd. dirs., 1982, v.p., 1983, internat. liaison, 1984. Inducted in Internat. Cake Decorators Hall of Fame, 1985; recipient Key to cities of Sulphur and Lafayette, La., 1983; hon. citizen City of Houston. Mem. Calif. Cake Club (hon. advisor, organized 3 C's), Soc. Craft Designers, Demonstrators, Golden Voice chpt. Nat. Speakers Assn. Republican. Clubs: Assn. of Ret. Persons, Nat. Assn. Letter Carriers, Calif. Cake Club (organizer). Avocations: crafts; music; arts. Home: Pasadena, Calif. Died July 15, 2010.

LABOURDETTE, PEDRO JUAN, financial executive; b. Havana, Cuba, Feb. 3, 1945; came to U.S., 1960; s. Pedro Bernardo and Margarita (Sastre) L.; m. Beverly Sue Munves, Nov. 22, 1975; children— Peter William, Rafael Steven. B.S. in Acctg., U. Md., 1970. Supr., C.P.A. firm, Washington, 1971-75; sr. internal auditor Marriott Corp., Bethesda, Md., 1975-76, controller for Brazil, 1977-79, regional controller S.Am. and Africa, 1979-81, dir. internat. costing, 1981-83, dir. internat. fin., 1983-84, internat. div. controller 1984—; dir. Marriott Brazil, 1977-81, Marriott Argentina, 1979-81, Marriott J.V., 1979-81. Mem. Am. Inst. Pub. Accts., Md. State Bd. Pub. Accts. Republican. Roman Catholic. Home: Potomac, Md. Died Mar. 19, 2009.

LABRIOLA, ALBERT CHRISTY, language professional, educator; b. Pitts., Oct. 22, 1939; s. Albert P. and Christine M. (Zullo) L.; m. Regina Ann Helzlsouer, June 18, 1966; children: Michael A. and Regina A. BEd, Duquesne U., Pitts., 1961; M in Teaching, Columbia U., 1962; MA, U. Va., 1963, PhD, 1966. Asst. prof. English Coll. William and Mary, Williamsburg, Va., 1968-70, Duquesne U., 1970-72, assoc. prof. English, 1972-76, prof. English, from 1976. Coeditor: Eyes Fast Fixt: Current Perspectives in Milton Methodology, 1975, Milton's Legacy in the Arts, 1988. Served to capt. US Army, 1966-68, U.S.A., Vietnam. Mem. The Milton Soc. Am. (sec. 1974—). Roman Catholic. Home: Pittsburgh, Pa. Died Mar. 11, 2009.

LACY, ALEXANDER SHELTON, retired lawyer; b. South Boston, Va., Aug. 18, 1921; s. Cecil Baker and Lura Elizabeth (Byram) L.; m. Carol Jemison, Aug. 8, 1952; children: John Blakeway, Joan Elizabeth Chancey, Alexander Shelton. BS in Chemistry, U. Ala., 1943; LLB, U. Va., 1949. Bar: Ala. 1949, U.S. Ct. Appeals (5th, 11th and D.C. cirs.) 1981, U.S. Supreme Ct. 1979. Assoc. Bradley, Arant, Rose & White, Birmingham, Ala., 1949-54; with Ala. Gas Corp., Birmingham, 1954-86; v.p., asst. sec., atty. Ala. Gas Corp./Energen Corp., 1969-86; v.p., sec., atty. Ala. Gas Corp., 1974-86; with Patrick and Lacy, Birmingham, 1986-96, ret., 1996. Pres., chmn. bd. Birmingham Symphony Assn., 1964-67; chmn. Birmingham-Jefferson Civic Center Authority, 1965-71. Served with USN, 1943-46. Mem. ABA, Ala. Bar Assn. (chmn. energy law com. 1984-86), Birmingham Bar Assn., Am. Gas Assn. (chmn. legal sect. 1983-85), Fed. Energy Bar Assn., Fed. Bar Assn., Am. Judicature Soc., Mountain Brook Club, Phi Gamma Delta, Phi Delta Phi. Episcopalian. Home: Birmingham, Ala. Died Feb. 4, 2010.

LADEN, BEN ELLIS, economist, writer; b. Savannah, Ga., Mar. 4, 1942; s. Bernard and Fannie Rachel (Cooper) L.; m. Susan Sherman, Aug. 16, 1964; children: Francine, Jonathan, Paul. AB, Princeton U., 1963; PhD, Johns Hopkins U., 1969. Asst. prof. econs. Ohio State U., 1967-71; economist Fed. Res. Bd., 1971-74; v.p., chief economist T. Rowe Price Assocs., Balt., 1974-87; dir. fin. instns. regulation staff HUD, Washington, 1990-94; pres. Bel Assocs., Washington, from 1994. Sr. adjunct scholar Hudson Inst., 2001. Author: Economic Trend, 1974-87; also articles. Fellow Nat. Assn. Bus. Economists (dir. 1981-87, pres. 1984-85); mem. Am. Econs. Assn. Jewish. Home: Washington, DC. Died Jan. 20, 2009.

LADERMAN, CAROL C., anthropologist, educator; b. Bklyn., Oct. 25, 1932; d. Philip and Sylvia (Sugarman) Ciavati; m. Gabriel Laderman, Feb. 12, 1953; children: Raphael, Michael. BA with honors, Hunter Coll., 1972; MA, Columbia U., 1975, PhD with distinction, 1979. Vis. lectr. Yale U., New Haven, 1980-82; asst. prof. Fordham U., Bronx, 1982-88, assoc. prof., 1988-90; prof. anthropology City Coll.-CUNY, NYC, from 1990, chmn. dept., 1990—96, 1999—2002; evaluator applications John Simon Guggenheim Meml. Found., 1994—2004. External assessor Acad. of Malay Studies, U. Malaya. Author: Wives and Midwives, 1983, Taming the Wind of Desire, 1991, Main Peteri: Malay Shamanism, 1991; editor: Techniques of Healing in Southeast Asia, 1988, The Performance of Healing, 1996; mem. editl. bd. Anthropology and Humanism. Cons. N.Am. Conf. on Ethiopian Jewry, N.Y.C. Social Sci. Rsch. Coun. fellow, 1975-78, John Simon Guggenheim fellow, 1987-88; NEH grantee, 1982-85, 87-90; Resident scholar Rockefeller Found., 1989; Rsch. grant, CUNY, 1991, 1993, 2001, 2003—; Fordham U. fellow, 1989-1990, 1984, 1985, NIMH fellow, 1975-1978, Danforth fellow, 1972-1975, 1978. Mem. Am. Anthropol. Assn., Am. Ethnological Assn., Soc. for Med. Anthropology, Coun. on Nutritional Anthropology (exec. bd. 1985-89), Internat. Assn. for Study of Traditional Asian Medicine (sec.-gen. 1992-96). Avocations: music, art. Home: New York, NY. Died July 6, 2010.

LAESSIG, RONALD HAROLD, preventive medicine and pathology educator, state official; b. Marshfield, Wis., Apr. 4, 1940; s. Harold John and Ella Louise L.; m. Joan Margaret Spreda, Jan. 29, 1966; 1 child, Elizabeth Susan. BS, U. Wis., Stevens Point, 1962; PhD, U. Wis., 1965. Cert. chem. chemist Nat. Registry Cert. Chemists, 1968. Jr. faculty Princeton (N.J.) U., 1966; chief clin. chemistry Wis. State Lab. Hygiene, Madison, 1966-80, dir., 1980—2007, emeritus dir., 2007; asst. prof. preventive medicine U. Wis., Madison, 1966-72, assoc. prof., 1972-76, prof., 1976—2007, emeritus prof., 2007, prof. pathology, from 1980. Cons. Ctrs. Disease Control, Atlanta, bd. sci. counselors Nat. Ctr. Environ. Health Ga., 2004-; dir. Nat. Com. for Clin. Lab. Stds., Villanova, Pa., 1977-80; chmn. invitro diagnostic products adv. com. FDA, 1974-75; mem. rev. com. Nat. Bur. Stds., 1983-86; legis. coun., State of Wis., 2003-04; chair Pub. Health Adv. Com., Wis., 2003-05, mem. 1998-. Mem. editl. bd. Analytical Chemistry, 1970-76, Health Lab. Sci., 1970-76, Med. Electronics, 1970-80; contbr. articles to profl. jours. Mem. State of Wis. Tech. Com. Alcohol and Traffic Safety, 1970-88; mem. adv. com. Newbon Screening, Wis. Recipient Excellence in Advocacy award, March of Dimes, 2004, APHL, Gold Std. for Pub. Health Excellence award, 2004; Sloan Found. grantee, 1966; recipient numerous grants. Mem. APHA (Difco award 1974), Am. Assn. Clin. Chemistry (chmn. safety com. 1984-86, bd. dirs. 1986-89, Natelson award 1989, Contbns. Svc. to Profession award 1990, Reiner award 1998, Eiler award 1999), Am. Soc. for Med. Tech., Nat. Com. Clin. Lab. Stds. (pres. 1980-82, bd. dirs. 1984-87), Assn. Pub. Health Labs. (chmn. environ. health com. 2001-04, Gold Std. Pub. Health Excellence award 2004), Nat. Ctr. Environ. Health/CDC (bd. counselors 2004-07), Sigma Xi. Avocation: woodworking. Home: Madison, Wis. Died Mar. 29, 2009.

LAGEDROST, HUGH LEROY, architect; b. Dayton, Ohio, June 9, 1923; s. Fred and Kathryn (Geran) Lagedrost; m. Jo Ann Elde, Dec. 17, 1983; children: Reed, Susan, Scott, Jill, Kelly, Holly, Eric, Hugh II. PhD, Hamilton State U., 1953. Head engr. Monsanto Chem., 1945—47; chief arch. Brown & Assoc., Dayton, 1947—54, Great Southwest Devel., San Antonio, 1956—72; arch. Assoc. Archs., San Antonio, from 1972. Real estate insp. Nat. Assn. Realtors, Boerne, Tex., from 1982; real estate appraiser Tex. Assn. Realtors, from 1984. Prin. works include Down to Earth Homes; author: Teach Them Early, 1984. Mem. Nat. Coun. Archtl. Registration, San Antonio, from 1985. Recipient Best Arch. Design award, Gt. SW Devel. Corp., 1980. Mem.: AIA, Am. Inst. Real Estate Appraisers, Mercator Internat. Club (Dayton), Rotary Lodge (bd. dirs. 1973). Republican. Avocations: flying, art, cartooning. Died Jan. 8, 2009.

LAHR, JOHN CLARK, geophysicist; b. Indpls., Nov. 11, 1944; s. Paul H. and Irene (Mahannah) Lahr; m. Karen Olson, Dec. 16, 1966 (div. 1977); children: Taya M., Nils B.; m. Janice Henderson, Aug. 19, 1978. BS in Physics, Renssalaer Poly. Inst., 1966; MS in Seismology, Columbia U., 1971, PhD in Seismology, 1975. Geophysicist U.S. Geol. Survey, Menlo Park, Calif., 1971—75, project chief Alaska seismic studies, from 1975. Contbr.: articles to profl. jours. Fellow, Columbia U. faculty, 1970. Mem.: Seismol. Soc. Am., Am. Geophys. Union. Democrat. Unitarian-Universalist. Home: Tacoma, Wash. Died Mar. 17, 2009.

LAMAR, WILLIAM FRED, chaplain, educator; b. Birmingham, Ala., Jan. 4, 1934; s. William Fred Sr. and Everette (Kelley) L.; m. Roberta Anton, Sept. 17, 1955 (dec.); 1 child, Jonathan Frederick; m. Martha Anne Lee, June 7, 1986. BA, U. Ala., 1954; BD, Vanderbilt U., 1957; PhD, St. Louis U., 1972; D Min., Eden Theol. Sem., 1974; grad., Spanish Lang. Sch., Antigua, Guatemala, 1993. Minister United Meth. Ch., Bynum, Ala., 1959-61, Fultondale, Ala., 1961-65; campus minister U. Mo., Rolla, 1965-74; chaplain, prof., dir. overseas missions DePauw U., Greencastle, Ind., 1974-97; dir. United Meth. Com. on Relief Vol. Programs, Travnik, Bosnia, 1996-98. Advisor overseas vol. program United Meth. Ch. Ind., Indpls., 1980-88; mem. Eli Lilly Found. study on the future of the ministry, 1989-91; cons. internat. vol. programs United Theol. Sem., Vanderbilt U. Div. Sch. and Westminster Coll., Oxford U., 1989-93; bd. dirs. Ecumenical Ventures, The Philippines, China; adj. prof. Eckerd Coll., 2001-02; adj. prof. Eckerd Coll. Author: (book) Role of the College Chaplain at the Church-Related College, 1984; designer electric utility computer programs, 1979-85. Vice chmn. County Welfare Bd., Rolla; bd. dirs. Sr. Vol. Program Action, Greencastle, 1977-80. Served to 1st lt. U.S. Army, 1957-59. Recipient Award of Honor, Ind. Gov's. Voluntary Action, 1976, Cross of Jerusalem, Episcopal Diocese of Guatemala, 1979, Cross of St. Francis, Inst. de Asuntos Culturales del Peru, 1982, 587th Point of Light award Pres. George Bush, 1991, Vol. award Ind. Nature Conservancy, 1993; Danforth fellow, 1971-72. Fellow Ctr. Spiritual Life, Eckerd Coll.; mem. Nat. Campus Ministry Assn. (chmn. sci. and ethics network), Nat. Assn. Coll. Chaplains, Assn. Religion in Intellectual Life, Assn. Coll. and U. Religious Advisors (nat. program chair 1993; bd. dirs. Ind. office campus ministry 1988-98), Acad. Sr. Profls. (Eckerd Coll.). Died Jan. 13, 2010.

LAMB, RONALD M., convenience stores executive; Store mgr. Casey' Gen. Stores, Inc., v.p., 1976-88, pres., CEO Ankeny, Iowa, 1988—2006, chmn., 2006—10. Died June 11, 2010.

LAMBDIN, WILLIAM CHARLES, manufacturing executive; b. Elkhart, Ind., June 18, 1943; s. Cecil Curtis and Dorothy May (Markel) Lambdin; m. Ann Kathleen Miller, Aug. 25, 1944; children: Laura Ann, Thad Philip, Amanda Ruth. BSIM, Purdue U., 1968. Sales engr. Gen. Electric Co., York, Pa., 1969—72; mgr. strategy devel. Ft. Wayne, Ind., 1972—76; nat. acctg. exec. Grand Rapids, Mich., 1976—78; mgr. sales and internat. Holland, Mich., 1978—83; mgr. programs Tyler, Tex., 1983—87; mgr. strategic account, from 1987. Adviser GATT Negotiations, NYC, 1972—74. Recipient Pub. Svcs. award, Am. Radio Relay League, West Hartford, Conn., 1966, Recognition award, Purdue U., 1968, Best. Bus. Planner award, Gen. Electric Co., 1972, Holt Mktg. award, 1977, GE Quest for Quality award, 1984—85. Mem.: Elfun Soc., Hollytree Country. Republican. Baptist. Home: Nashville, Tenn. Died June 19, 2009.

LAMBERSON, DONALD LESLIE, air force officer; b. Dublin, Ind., May 5, 1931; m. Carolyn Milam; children— Steven Edward, Deborah Sue Archer, Linda Jean B.Chem. Engring., Purdue U., 1949; M.Nuclear Engring., Air Force Inst. Tech., 1961, D.Aerospace Engring., 1969. Commd. 2d lt. U.S. Air Force, 1954, advanced through grades to maj. gen., 1982; nuclear weapons research officer Air Force Weapons Lab., Kirtland AFB, N.Mex., 1961-65, head high energy laser program, 1969-72, chief Advanced Radiation Tech. Office, 1972-78; dep. for devel. and acquisition conventional armament Armament Devel. and Test Ctr., Eglin AFB, Fla., 1978-79, armament div. Air Force Systems Command, Eglin AFB, Fla., 1979-82; dep. asst. for directed energy weapons Office Under Sec. Def. for Research and Engring., Washington, 1982-83; asst. dep. chief of staff for research, devel. and acquisition Hdqrs. U.S. Air Force, Washington, from 1983. Decorated Disting. Service medal, Legion of Merit Home: Niceville, Fla. Died Mar. 17, 2009.

LAMBERT, CARL FREDERICK (NICK LAMBERT), risk management consultant; b. Kans. City, Mo., Sept. 29, 1932; s. Carl Frederick and Genevieve Elizabeth (Corbin) Lambert. Student, U. Va., 1950—53. Commd., 2d lt. USAF, 1956, advanced through grades to maj., 1967; life ins. salesman and mgr., regional dist. mgr. Equitable Life Assurance Soc., Lakeland, Fla., 1968—72; v.p. Consol. Investors Life Assurance Co., Coral Gables, Fla., 1972—76; mgr. safety and compliance Hannah Marine Corp., Lemont, Ill., 1977—82; mgr. loss control-loss prevention Canonie, Inc., Muskegon, Mich., 1982—85; pres. Cons. Risk Mgmt. Svc., Muskegon, from 1985. Mem.: Midwest Watercolor Soc., Am. Soc. Marine Artists. Home: Naples, Fla. Died Dec. 19, 2009.

LAMONT, FREDERICK FRANCIS, JR., public relations and marketing consultant; b. Trenton, NJ, May 7, 1927; s. Frederick Francis and Helen Elizabeth (Westenburger) L.; m. Mary Louise Kingsbury, Oct. 3, 1959; children: Catherine Ann Lamont McDonald, Frederick Francis III, Sarah Kingsbury. AB, Harvard U., 1948, MBA, 1951; Assoc. Econs., London Sch. Econs., 1966. Research editor New Yorker mag., 1949-51; producer-dir. ABC-TV, 1951-55; radio-TV account exec. Compton Advt. Inc., NYC, 1955-63; mktg. dir. So. Ariz. Bank & Trust Co., Tucson, 1963-67; v.p., mgr. Bozell & Jacobs, Phoenix, 1967-69; v.p., dir. fin. relations Aztec Mining Corp., Denver, 1969-71; v.p. N.W. Ayer & Son, Inc., 1971-73;

ind. cons., from 1973. Cons. I. Orrin Spellman Co., Lamont-Bruno Assocs. Dir. radio-TV Nat. Assn. Retarded Children, 1961-63; v.p., chmn. Ariz. Civic Theatre, 1965-67; sub-deacon St. Matthew's Ch., Pennington, N.J.; bd. dirs. Family Service Assn. Am. Served with A.C., USNR, 1944-46. Fellow Pub. Rels. Soc. Am. (diplomate), Harvard Club, Players Club (N.Y.C.), Garrick Club (London), Old Pueblo Club (Tucson), Red-Headed League (N.J.), Top Road Assn. Home: Cincinnati, Ohio. Died Mar. 27, 2009.

LANCASTER, LIONEL GLOVER, construction executive; b. Grosse Pointe Shores, Mich., May 12, 1920; s. William John and Edith (Allor) Lancaster; m. Lois Jean Wherle; children: Lionel G., Jeffery B., Patrick, DAniel, Cathy, Tara, Gary. Student, U. Detroit, 1939—41; BCE, U. N.Mex., 1950. Registered profl. engr., Ariz., N.Mex., W.Va., Alta., Can. Project mgr. constrn. Apollo V Launch Facilities, NASA, Cape Kennedy, Fla., 1955—58; pres. L.G. Lancaster & Assocs., Tucson, 1962—68; constrn. mgr. Trans Mountain Canadian Pipeline, Vancouver, B.C., Canada, 1964—67; exec. v.p. ops., dir. Simpson Industries, Allied Engring. Co., South Gate, Ga., 1968—70; cons. engr. Leslie C. Gates & Assocs., Bechley, W.Va., 1970—72; v.p. design and constrn. Big Sky Montana, Inc., Big Sky, from 1972; owner Lancaster Cos., Phoenix. Dir. Beacon Steel; mgmt. cons. to constrn. industry. With USAF, 1941—45. Decorated Silver Star, D.F.C., Air medal with four oak leaf clusters; recipient Merit award, Intercontinental Ballistic Missile Site Devel. USAF, 1964. Mem.: NSPE, Soc. Am. Mil. Engrs., Chi Epsilon. Republican. Roman Catholic. Home: Scottsdale, Ariz. Died Nov. 1, 2009.

LANDER, BERNARD, academic administrator, sociologist, clergyman; b. NYC, June 17, 1915; s. David and Goldie L. Lander; m. Sara Rebecca Shragowitz, Nov. 1, 1948 (dec. 1995); children: Esther, Hannah, Debra, Daniel. BA, Yeshiva Coll., 1936; LHD (hon.), Yeshiva U., 1969; MA, Columbia U., 1943, PhD, 1949. Ordained rabbi, 1938. Rabbi Beth Jacob Congregation, Balt., 1939-44; assoc. dir. NYC Mayor's Com. Unity, 1944—50; lectr. Columbia U., NYC, 1948-49; prof. Hunter Coll., CUNY, 1949—70; dean Bernard Revel Grad. Sch., Yeshiva U., NYC, 1954—69; pres. Touro Coll., NYC, 1970—2010. Cons. Md. Com. Juvenile Delinquency, 1941-43, Youth Bd., 1950-54, Ctr. Study Man, U. Notre Dame, South Bend, Ind., 1965-70; mem. Pres.'s Adv. Coun. Juvenile Delinquency and Crime, 1961-63; dir. Nat. Study on Juvenile Delinquency and Crime, U. Notre Dame, 1965-70. Author: Toward an Understanding of Juvenile Delinquency, 1958; also numerous articles on sociology. V.p. Union of Orthodox Jewish Congregations of Am., N.Y.C.; co-founder Yeshiva Dov Revel; founder Bar-Ilan U., 1950-; cons. US Pres. Mem. Am. Sociol. Assn., Rabbinical Council Am. Home: Forest Hills, NY. Died Feb. 8, 2010.

LANDERS, SANDRA JEAN, retail company executive; b. Roanoke, Va., July 15, 1937; d. James Lilburn and Dorothy Ellen (Newman) Blankenship; m. Brenton Sylvester Mongan, July 3, 1974 (div. 1982); 1 child; m. Julian Miller Landers, Jr. Attending, Va. So. U., 1957. Med. sec. Lewis Gale Hosp., Roanoke, 1961—67; owner, operator Mystic Sea Hotel, Myrtle Beach, SC, 1974—77, Poindexter Hotel, Myrtle Beach, 1974—77, Sheraton by-the-Sea, Jekyll Island, Ga., 1978—80. Owner, pres. Cassandra's Ltd, Roanoke, from 1978, Cassandra's Carousel, from 1983. Bd. dirs. Recreation Dept., Roanoke, 1971—72; pres. Va.'s Jr. Miss Pageant, 1961—76. Recipient Am.'s Jr. Miss State Pageant award, 1973. Mem.: Bus. Women of America (bd. dirs. 1982—83), Roanoke Jr. Woman's (v.p. 1968—73). Republican. Baptist. Home: Charlotte, NC. Died Aug. 25, 2009.

LANE, KENNETH EDWIN, retired advertising agency executive; b. Orange, NJ, Sept. 30, 1928; s. Clarence Edwin and Erma Catherine (Kinser) L.; children by previous marriage— Kenneth, Laura, Linda, Katherine; m. Susan Spafford Zimmer, Sept. 13, 1980; stepchildren— Todd and Margaret Zimmer. BA, U. Chgo., 1947, MA, 1950. Mgr. media Toni div. Gillette Co., 1953-63; media dir. MacParland-Aveyard Co., 1963-64; assoc. media dir. Leo Burnett Co., Chgo., 1964-71, mgr. media dept., 1971-75, sr. v.p. media services, 1975-84. Bd. dirs. Traffic Audit Bur. Maj. USAR, ret. Mem. Am. Assn. Advt. Agys., Media Dirs. Council., Phi Beta Kappa Home: Chicago, Ill. Died Jan. 27, 2009.

LANE, LAURENCE WILLIAM, JR., (BILL LANE), retired ambassador, publisher; b. Des Moines, Nov. 7, 1919; s. Laurence William and Ruth (Bell) L.; m. Donna Jean Gimbel, Apr. 16, 1955; children: Sharon Louise, Robert Laurence, Brenda Ruth. Student, Pomona Coll., 1938-40, LLD (hon.), 1976; BJ, Stanford U., 1942; DHL (hon.), Hawaii Loa Coll., 1991. Chmn. bd. Lane Pub. Co.; pub. Sunset Mag., Sunset Books and Sunset Films; US amb. to Australia & Nauru US Dept. State, 1985-89. Bd. dirs. Calif. Water Svc. Co., Crown Zellerbach Corp., Pacific Gas and Electric Co.; bd. dirs. Time Inc.; bd. dirs. Oreg. Coast Aquarium, Internat. Bd. Advice, ANZ Bank; U.S. amb. and commr. Gen. Worlds Fair, Japan, 1975-76; hon. fellow Coll. Notre Dame, 1974. Former mem. adv. bd. Sec. Interior's Bd. Nat. Parks; mem. adv. coun. Grad. Sch. Bus., Stanford U., SRI; mem. Pres.'s Nat. Productivity Adv. Com.; mem. Pacific Basin Econ. Coun.; former bd. dirs. Pacific Forum, CSI, Nat. Parks Found.; vol. The Nat. Ctr.; mem. bd. overseers Hoover Instn. War, Revolution and Peace; mem. exec. com. Ctr. for Australian Studies, U. Tex., Austin. Lt. USNR, World War II, PTO. Decorated officer Order of Australia; recipient Conservation Svc. award Sec. Interior; Theodore and Conrad Wirth award NPF, 1994; Wiliam Penn Mott Jr. Conservationist of Yr. award NPCA, 1995; named hon. prof. journalism Stanford U. Mem. Newcomen Soc. N.Am., Pacific Asia Travel Assn. (life mem., chmn. 1980-81), Coun. of Am. Ambs., Los Rancheros Vistadores, Advt. Club San Francisco, No. Calif. Alumni Assn., Bohemian Club, Pacific Union, Men's Garden Club L.A., Alpha Delta Sigma. Republican. Presbyterian. Home: Menlo Park, Calif. Died July 31, 2010.

LANE, MARY B., education educator, writer; b. Edwardsville, Mich., Mar. 7, 1911; d. Hugh Dunning Beauchamp and Carrie Scott; m. Howard Lane, July 16, 1958 (dec.); children: Jay Howard, Mary Kelley. BS, Kirksville State U., 1930; MA, Northwestern U., 1945; EdD, N.Y. Coll., 1950. Lifetime cert. tchr. Calif. Tchr., LaPlata, Mo., 1930—39, Webster Groves, Mo., 1939—45; adminstrv. asst. Pub. Sch. Bd. Edn., Webster Groves, 1945—48, Mpls., 1948—50; asst. to supt. pub. sch. Pasadena, Calif., 1950—53; prof. U. Fla., N.Y. U., U. Calif. & San Francisco State U., 1950—72, San Francisco State U., 1999; dir. Head Start, Oakland, Calif., 2002. Spkr. in field, Can., South Africa; dir. bay area Head Start, 1966, nat. cons., 1967—75; project dir. nurseries NIMH, 1965—70; dir. Oakland Parent Child Ctr., 1977—87. Co-author (with Howard Lane): Human Relations in Teaching, 1955, Understanding Human Development, 1959; editor: On Educating Human Beings, 1964; contbr. articles to profl. jours. Home: San Francisco, Calif. Died Apr. 26, 2010.

LANE, NEIL A(RDEN), automotive executive, consultant; b. Ft. Wayne, Ind., Aug. 3, 1931; s. Wilburg M. and Esther V. (Grable) Lane; m. Doris I. Lytle, Aug. 7, 1954; children: Jeffrey, David, Scott, Sarah. BS, Ind. U., 1953. Dir. nat. sales Canteen Corp., Chgo., 1961—67; dir. mktg. Walker Mfg. Co., Racine, Wis., 1967—72; pres., chief exec. officer Mechanex Corp., Englewood, Colo., 1972—81, Solaron Corp., Englewood, 1981—83; owner Lane Enterprises, Inc., Littleton, Colo., from 1981. With USNR, 1949. Mem.: Heavy Duty Forum (bd. dirs 1979—81). Republican. Home: Littleton, Colo. Died Feb. 3, 2009.

LANE, NEWTON ALEXANDER, retired lawyer; b. Boston, June 16, 1915; s. Samuel B. and Eva (Robbins) L. AB, Harvard U., 1936, JD, 1939. Bar: Mass. 1939. Ptnr. emeritus Lane Altman & Owens, Boston. Served with AUS, 1942-46. Mem. Phi Beta Kappa. Home: Newton, Mass. Died Mar. 6, 2009.

LANES, SELMA GORDON, critic, writer, editor; b. Boston, Mar. 13, 1929; d. Jacob and Lily (Whiteman) Gordon; m. Jerrold B. Lanes, Nov. 21, 1959 (div. Mar. 1970); children: Andrew Oliver, Matthew Gordon. BA, Smith Coll., 1950; MS in Journalism, Columbia, 1954. Asst. to publicity dir. Little Brown & Co., Boston, 1950—51; assoc. editor Focus Mag., NYC, 1951—53; travel page editor Boston Globe, 1953; spl. editorial asst., rschr. Look Mag., 1956—60; children's entertainment editor Show Mag., 1961—63; critic children's books Book World (NY Herald-Tribune, later World Jour. Tribune, Wash. Post and Chgo. Tribune), 1965—71, NY Times Book Rev., from 1966. Articles editor Parents Mag., 1971—74; editor-in-chief Parents Mag. Press, 1974—78; editl. dir. Western Pub. Co.; cons. Penguin Books, 1967, Starstream Books, 1980—81; lectr. New Sch./Parsons Sch. Design, 1975—77, Del. Art Mus., 1979, Simmons Coll., 1988; dir. Schiller-Wapner Galleries, 1983—84; freelance writer, from 1984. Author: Amy Loves Good-byes, 1966, The Curiosity Book, 1968, Down the Rabbit Hole, A critical work for adults on children's literature, 1971, paperback, 1976, The Art of Maurice Sendak, 1980, Through the Looking Glass, 2004, selector-adapter: A Child's First Book of Nursery Tales, 1983, Windows of Gold, 1989; co-author: Lillian Gish: An Actor's Life for Me!, 1987. Judge Children's Spring Book Festival, 1970; dir., 1972; judge NY Times Ten Best Illus. Children's Books, 1973, 1979—80; trustee Fund for Art Investment, NYC. Mem.: Phi Beta Kappa. Died Apr. 8, 2009.

LANEY, ELIZABETH CARDWELL, free-lance photojournalist; b. Bluefield, W.Va., Aug. 19, 1912; d. Alexander Drake Cardwell and Harriet Louise (Parker) Martin; m. Luther Hubbard Laney, Apr. 6, 1941; 1 son, Charles. Student St. Paul Normal Coll., 1930-31, Franklin U., Ohio State U., Bliss Bus. Sch., Columbus Bus. Coll., St. Mary of the Springs, Ill. Wesleyan Coll., Columbus Tech. Inst., Ohio Dominican Coll., Capital U.; cert. Poro Sch. Cosmetology, 1941. Stenographer, U.S. Govt., Dayton, Ohio, 1941-43; cosmetician, mgr., owner Laney Beauty Salon, Columbus, Ohio, 1945-50; sec., auditor City of Columbus, 1950-75; spl. feature contbg. writer The Ohio State Sentinel, 1960-62, Call and Post Newspaper (syndicated), 1967—, photojournalist, 1977—; editor Ohio Bapt. Jour. Ohio Bapt. Gen. Conv., 1984—. Author: (poetry) Poetry in Prayer, 1977. Editor Centennial Jour., 1969; 100 Years, Shiloh Baptist Church History, 1974. Composer numerous hymns. Ch. sch. tchr., dir. pub. relations Shiloh Bapt. Ch., 1970—, Sunday Sch. sec., treas., founder Gleaners class; dir. pub. relations Eastern Union Missionary Bapt. Assn., Eastern Union Assembly Ground, Eastern Union Bapt. Coll., Ohio Bapt. Gen. Conv., 1983; sec. bd. trustees Eastern Union Bapt. Coll.; mem. Eastern Union Assembly Ground; publicity chmn. Christian Women's Workshop; active mem. Urban League, Urban League Guild, Women's Service Bd. Grant Hosp. (life), Ch. Women United (life), Ohio Bapt. Women's Conv. (life); founder, organizer Triangle Civic Assn., 1945; sec. Eastgate Garden/Civic Assn., 1955-57. Named Woman of Yr., Shiloh Bapt. Ch., 1962, 71, 75; recipient Cert. of Honor, Mayor Tom Moody, 1975, Cert. of Honor, Columbus City Council, 1975; 1st, 2nd, 3rd prize certs. Columbus Writers Guild, 1965-70; 1st, 2nd, 3rd place ribbons Golden Hobby Show, 1979-81; numerous ribbons, prizes Ohio Dominican Coll., 1980-81; selected as guest photojournalist Israel Journalist, Jerusalem Post Newspaper; 1 of 5 selected for Equal Opportunity Day, Columbus Call and Post Newspaper, 1962; recipient Mayor's award for vol. service, 1984; named WCKX Citizen of Week, 1987; cited for Civic and Community service Columbus Urban League Guild, 1987. Mem. Women in Communications, Nat. Assn. Colored Women's Clubs, Eta Phi Beta (named chpt. Black Woman of Yr. 1983). Republican. Lodge: Order Eastern Star. Avocations: music; arts; writing; photography; travel. Home: Columbus, Ohio. Died Dec. 24, 2009.

LANG, MABEL LOUISE, retired classics educator; b. Utica, NY, Nov. 12, 1917; d. Louis Bernard and Katherine (Werdge) L. BA, Cornell U., 1939; MA, Bryn Mawr Coll., 1940, PhD, 1943; Litt.D., Coll. Holy Cross, 1975, Colgate U., 1978; L.H.D., Hamilton Coll. Mem. faculty Bryn Mawr Coll., 1943-91, successively instr., asst. prof., 1943-50, assoc. prof., 1950-59, prof. Greek, 1959-88, prof. emerita, 1988—2010, chmn. dept., 1960-88, acting dean coll. 2d semester, 1958-59, 60-61; chmn. mng. com. American Sch. Classical Studies, Athens, 1975-80, chmn. admissions and fellowship com., 1966-72; Blegen disting. rsch. prof. semester I Vassar Coll., 1976-77; Martin classical lectr. Oberlin Coll., 1982. Co-author: Athenian Agora Measures and Tokens; author: Palace of Nestor Frescoes, 1969, Athenian Agora Graffiti and Dipinti, 1976; Herodotean Narrative and Discourse, 1984, Athenian Agor Ostraka, 1990; contbr. articles profl. jours. Guggenheim fellow, 1953-54; Fulbright fellow Greece, 1959-60 Mem. Am. Philos. Soc., Am. Acad. Arts and Scis., German Archaeol. Inst., Am. Philol. Assn., Soc. Promotion Hellenic Studies (Eng.), Classical Assn. (Eng.). Home: Bryn Mawr, Pa. Died July 21, 2010.

LANGE, ANDREW E., cosmologist, astronomer, physicist, educator; b. Urbana, Ill., July 23, 1957; 3 children. BA, Princeton U., 1980; PhD, U. Calif., Berkeley, 1987. Vis. assoc. Calif. Inst. Tech., 1993—94, prof., 1994—2001, Marvin L. Goldberger prof. physics, Observational Cosmology Group, 2001—10, chair, divsn. physics, math. & astronomy, 2008—10. Sr. rsch. scientist NASA Jet Propulsion Lab., 2006. Recipient Dan David prize in Astrophysics, 2009; co-recipient Balzan prizein Observational Astronomy & Astrophysics, 2006; named Calif. Scientist Yr., Calif. Sci. Ctr., 2003; Leverhulme Fellow. Mem.: APS, AAAS, NAS. Achievements include expert in structure and geometry of very early universe and in measurement of irregularities in cosmic microwave background radiation; principal investigator of the project "BOOMERanG" (Ballon Observations of Millimetric Extragalactic Radiation and Geophysics) in 1998. Died Jan. 22, 2010.

LANGE, KLAUS ROBERT, chemist; b. Berlin, Jan. 15, 1930; came to U.S., 1948; s. Horst and Gertrud (Rabinowitz) L.; m. Sylvia Pollack, June 17, 1951; children: Stephen Mark, Karen Judith. AB, U. Pa., 1952; MS, U. Del., 1954, PhD, 1956. Research chemist Atlantic Refining Co., Phila., 1955-59; sr. research chemist, lab mgr. Phila. Quartz Co., 1959-69; lab. mgr. Betz Labs., Trevose, Pa., 1969-75; lab. mgr., tech. dir., research dir, sr. research adv. Quaker Chem. Corp., Conshohocken, Pa., from 1975. Author: 19 scientific publications; patentee in field. V.P. Congregation Beth Chaim, Feasterville, Pa. Named Matheson Corp. fellow, 1953-55. Fellow Am. Inst. of Chemistry; mem. Am. Chem. Soc., Tech. Assn. of the Pulp and Paper Industry, Iron and Steel Inst. Democrat. Jewish. Avocations: sailing, photography, stamp collecting/philately. Home: Huntingdon Valley, Pa. Died Aug. 24, 2009.

LANGER, RAY FRITZ, retired insurance executive; b. Manchester, NH, Apr. 29, 1921; s. Fritz Bruno and Clara (Lindh) L.; m. Myrtle Elaine Sargent, May 23, 1942; 1 child, Barry Frederick. Cert., U. N.H., 1940. Chief statistician N.H. Ins. Co., Manchester, 1942-71; chief statistician, asst. sec. N.H. & Am. Internat. Group, Manchester, 1972-84, asst. sec., 1984-91; cons. N.H. Group, Manchester. Dir. Suncook Bank, 1979—83. Selectman Town of Hooksett, N.H., 1970-78, councilor, 1988-91, state rep., 1993-05; pres. Hooksett-ites Sr. Citizens, 1993-97; vol. VA Hosp., 2005-. Capt. USAF, 1943-46, PTO, 1955-57, Korea, ret. 1981. Mem. Soc. Ins. Accts. (past pres.), Am. Legion. Republican. Methodist. Avocations: hunting, fly fishing, painting. Home: East Montpelier, Vt. Died Sept. 12, 2009.

LANGFORD, JOHN WILLIAM, logistics and systems engineer, educator; b. Carrollton, Ky., Dec. 9, 1932; s. Audley Delbert and Marguerite Bland (Campbell) L.; m. Margery Ann Staley, Jan. 24, 1955; children: Mary Elizabeth, Margaret Carole, Dirk William. BS in Indsl. Engring., Ga. Inst. Tech., 1954; MS in Logistics Mgmt., Air Force Inst. Tech., Dayton, Ohio, 1965. Cert. profl. logistician, engr., Va. Commd. lt. U.S. Air Force, 1955, advanced through grades to lt. col., 1980; planning officer U.S. So. Command, Panama Canal Zone, 1968-71; asst. for logistics Hdqrs., U.S. Air Force, Pentagon, 1973-75; advisor to Shah of Iran, Imperial Command Staff, Tehran, 1976-78; ret., 1980; cons. in mgmt., Dept. Energy, Washington, 1980-82; mgr. marine svcs. U.S. Navy, ERC Internat., Vienna, Va., 1982—; cons. edn. Dept. Def., Washington, 1983—; sr. assoc. Bus. Mgmt. Rsch., Arlington, Va., 1980—; prof. logistics engring. Fla. Inst. Tech., Melbourne, 1983—, George Mason U., Fairfax, Va., 1983—. Author: Air University Report: Defense Contract Profits, 1965; Air War College Report: Brazil Air Force Logistics, 1975; Author, editor series on logistics and systems engring. Soc. of Logistics Engrs. newsletter, 1983—; author, seminar Compendium of Quantitative Logistics Mathematical Methodologies, Third Internat. Logistics Congress, Florence, Italy, 1987, Fifth Internat. Logistics Congress, London, 1989, tutorial workshop compendium on Reliability, Maintainability, Availability. Decorated Air Force Commendation medal, Joint Service Commendation medal Dept. Def., Meritorious Service medal. Mem. Smithsonian Instn. (assoc.), Nat. Trust Hist. Preservation (Capital region assoc.), Am. Film Inst., Nat. Contract Mgmt. Assn., Inst. Indsl, Engrs., Soc. Logistics Engrs. (Forrest Waller award, tech. vice-chmn. 1987—), Ret. Officers Assn., U.S. Naval Inst. Republican. Club: Westwood Country (Vienna) Lodges: Masons, Scottish Rites. Avocations: numismatics, military history, foreign languages, golf, scuba diving. Home: Vienna, Va. Died Mar. 22, 2009.

LANGRALL, HARRISON MORTON, JR., internist; b. Balt., Mar. 24, 1922; s. Harrison Morton and Hazel Lucille (Clarke) L.; m. Mary Ann Saviano; children: Lucille Clarke, Kate Kidwell, Hazel Marie Langrall. BA, Johns Hopkins U., 1949; MD, U. Md., 1953; MS in Medicine, U. Minn. Mayo Found., 1958. Lic. physician Ind., Md., Minn., N.J., Pa. Rotating internship Winchester (Va.) Meml. Hosp., 1953-54; fellow internal medicine Mayo Found., Mayo Clinic, Rochester, Minn., 1954-66; pvt. practice in internal medicine, endocrinology The Davis Clinic, Marion, Ind., 1957-66; attending staff Marion (Ind.) Gen. Hosp., 1964-66, chief of medicine, 1966-77; assoc. med. dir. Hoffmann LaRoche, Inc., Nutley, N.J., 1966-77; v.p., med. rsch. Sandoz, Inc., East Hanover, N.J., 1977-82; pres. Langrall Assocs., Inc., Paoli, Pa., 1982-92; v.p. med. rsch. Photofrin Med., Inc., Buffalo, 1984-85, Great Valley Pharms., Inc., Paoli, from 1992. Clin. instr. in medicine Ind. U. Sch. of Medicine, Marion County Gen. Hosp., Indpls., 1957-66. Contbr. articles to profl. jours. 1st lt. Med. Adm. Corps., U.S. Army, 1942-46. Recipient Physician's Recognition award, 1982, 85, 88, 91, 94. Fellow Am. Coll. Clin. Pharmacology; mem. AMA, N.J. Acad. Medicine, Chester County Med. Soc., Pa. State Med. Soc. Home: Paoli, Pa. Died Feb. 26, 2009.

LANGWIG, JOHN EDWARD, retired wood science educator; b. Albany, NY, Mar. 5, 1924; s. Frank Irving and Arlene Stone (Dugan) L.; m. Margaret Jacquelyn Kirk, Aug. 31, 1946; 1 dau., Nancy Ann Langwig Davis. BS, U. Mich., 1948; MS, Coll. of Forestry, SUNY, Syracuse, 1968, PhD, 1971. Asst. to supt. Widdicomb Furniture Co., Grand Rapids, Mich., 1948-50; salesman John B. Hauf Furniture, Inc., Albany, NY, 1950-51; asst. mgr. furniture dept. Montgomery Ward Co., Menands, NY, 1951-52; office mgr. U.S. Plywood Corp., Syracuse, 1952-65; instr. wood products engring. SUNY Coll. Forestry, Syracuse, 1969-70; asst. prof. wood sci. Okla. State U., Stillwater, 1971-74, prof., head dept. forestry, 1974-81, prof. wood sci., wood products extension specialist, 1982-86, mem. faculty council, 1983-86; mem. Gov.'s Com. on Forest Practices, 1975-77. Contbr. articles to profl. jours. Served with AUS, 1943-45. NSF fellow, 1966-68 Mem. Soc. Am. Foresters, TAPPI, Forest Products Research Soc. (regional bd. dirs. 1983-89, regional rep. to nat. exec. bd. 1983-86), Soc. Wood Sci. and Tech., Okla. Acad. Sci., Okla. Forestry Assn. (bd. dirs. 1982-83), Council Forestry Sch. Execs., Sigma Xi, Xi Sigma Pi., Gamma Sigma Delta, Alpha Zeta, Phi Kappa Phi. Episcopalian. Home: Stillwater, Okla. Died Apr. 4, 2010.

LANHAM, CHARLES WARREN, retired lawyer; b. Cumberland, Md., Jan. 18, 1922; s. Charles Warren and Mary Shaw (Rawlings) Lanham; m. Nora Olivia Sherertz, Dec. 6, 1944; children: Charles Lamar, Eleanor Kathryn Lanham Bartley, Ann Elizabeth Lanham Cardwell. BS in in Mech. Engring., Duke U., 1943; JD, Georgetown U., 1951. Bar: DC 1951, (US Dist. Ct.) 1951, (US Ct. Appeals (D.C. cir.)) 1951, (US Ct. Customs and Patent Appeals) 1951. Patent examiner US Patent Office, Washington, 1946—63, primary examiner, 1963—65, supervisory primary examiner, 1965—79. Master Boy Scouts America, Silver Spring, Md., 1951—61; lay leader Good Shepherd Meth. Ch., Silver Spring, 1951—54, Glenmont Meth. Ch., Wheaton, Md., 1963—71; del. Balt. Ann. Conf., Meth. Ch., 1977—79; active mem. Fla. Guardian Ad Litem Program. Served to lt. USN, 1944—46, PTO. Recipient Bronze medal, US Dept. Commerce, 1975. Mem.: Washington Patent Lawyers Club (treas. 1952), Patent Office Soc. (exec. com. mem. 1965). Republican. Home: Summerville, SC. Died June 17, 2009.

LANSDALE, BRUCE MCKAY, educational administrator; b. Worcester, Mass., Feb. 11, 1925; s. Herbert Parker and Marjorie Middleton (McKay) L.; m. Elizabeth Joan Krihak, Jan. 22, 1949; children: David Parker, Jeffrey Dexter, Christine Kellog, Michael Lee. BS, U. Rochester, 1945; MS in Agrl. Edn, Cornell U., 1949. Chief interpreter Allied Mission for Greek Plebescite, Greece, 1946; vol. worker Am. Farm Sch., Thessaloniki, Greece, 1947, asst. dir., 1953-55, dir., pres., from 1955. Fulbright tchr., Greece, 1949-53 Cons. World Council Chs.; cons. Tanzanian Ministry Agr. and AID, 1981; bd. dirs. Fulbright program for Greece.; Bd. dirs. Pinewood Sch., Thessaloniki Sch. Blind, Thessaloniki Tb Assn.; Mem. Eisenhower Fellowhip Com.— Greece. Served with USNR, 1946-52. Decorated Order of George I Greece; recipient (with wife) Disting. Alumni award U. Rochester, 1977 Mem. Modern Greek Lang. Assn., Greek Friends of Farmer Assn., Thessaloniki YMCA, Phi Beta Kappa, Tau Beta Pi Clubs: Rotary (Thessaloniki), Yacht (Thessaloniki). Presbyterian. Home: Thessaloniki, Greece. Died Feb. 2, 2009.

LAPPLE, JUDITH A., music educator, director; b. Rochster, NY, Oct. 23, 1953; d. Carl L. and Josephine Rose Genovese; m. William Martin Kaschak, Oct. 23, 1999; children: Jennifer Jean, Megan Marie, Alexandra Molly, Jacquie Lynn. BM, Eastman Sch. Music, Rochester, 1975; MM, NE La. U., Monroe, 1977. Dir. and founder Summer Woodwind Camp, Fairfax, Va., 1994—2008; prof. flute George Mason U., Fairfax, from 1994. Musician: (tchg., mentoring) Creating the Winning Flute Section (Outstanding tchr. award, 2004). Mem.: MTNA. Home: Leesburg, Va. Died Aug. 10, 2010.

LAQUEUR, MARIA, educational association administrator; b. San Francisco, Sept. 25, 1942; d. Gert Ludwig and Mary Alice (Murphy) L.; m. William Gerald Hamm, Feb. 12, 1983. BA German, Am. Univ., 1965, MA German/Linguistics, 1968; MPA, U. of No. Colo., 1978. German lang. cataloger Libr. of Congress, Washington, 1965-70, assoc. catalog editor, 1970-76, asst. dir. NUC proj., 1976-81; assoc. pub. Bemrose UK, Ltd., London, 1981-85; exec. dir. Assoc. of Part-time Profls., Falls Church, Va., from 1988. Author: Flexible Work Options: A Selected Bibliography, 1990; co-author: Breaking Out of 9 to 5, 1994. Fellow U.S. Office Edn., 1967. Home: Weems, Va. Died July 23, 2009.

LARDY, HENRY ARNOLD, biochemistry professor; b. Roslyn, SD, Aug. 19, 1917; s. Nicholas and Elizabeth (Gebetsreiter) L.; m. Annrita Dresselhuys, Jan. 21, 1943; children; Nicholas, Diana, Jeffrey, Michael. BS, S.D. State U., 1939, DSc (hon.), 1979; MS, U. Wis., 1941, PhD, 1943. Asst. prof. U. Wis., Madison, 1945-47, assoc. prof., 1947-50, prof., 1950-88, Vilas prof. biol. sciences, 1966-88, prof. emeritus, 1988—2010. Henry Lardy annual lectr. S.D. State U., Brookings, 1985. Mem. editl. bd. Archives Biochemistry and Biophysics, 1957-60, Jour. Biol. Chemistry, 1958-64, 80-85, Biochem. Preparations, Methods of Biochem. Analysis, Biochemistry, 1962-73, 75-81; contbr. over 475 articles to profl. jours. Pres. Citizens vs McCarthy, Wis., 1950. Recipient Neuberg medal Am. Soc. European Chemists, 1956, Wolf prize in agr., Wolf Found., Israel, 1981, Nat. award Agrl. Excellence, 1982. Fellow Wis. Acad. Arts and Scis.; mem. Am. Chem. Soc. (chmn. biol. divsn. 1958, Paul-Lewis Labs. award 1949), Am. Soc. Biol. Chemists (pres. 1964, William Rose award 1988), Am. Acad. Arts and Scis. (Amory prize 1984), Am. Philos. Soc., Am. Diabetes Assn., Nat. Acad. Scis., Biochem. Soc. Great Britain, Harvey Soc., Soc. for Study of Reprodn. (Carl Hartman award 1984), The Endocrine Soc., Japanese Biochem. Soc. (hon.), Golden Retriever Club Am. (pres. 1964). Democrat. Achievements include patents for steroid compounds and lab. apparatus. Home: Madison, Wis. Died Aug. 4, 2010.

LARSEN, JEFFREY CLARENCE, banker; b. Montclair, NJ, Oct. 11, 1942; s. Clarence Melia and Hannah (Dunn) L.; m. Barbara Jean Ricker, Sept. 10, 1976; children: Julie Dane, David. MBA, Pepperdine U., 1982. Exec. v.p. Security Pacific Fin. Corp., San Diego, Calif., 1979-83; sr. v.p. Bank of Montreal, Toronto, 1983-84; exec. v.p. Crocker Nat. Bank, San Francisco, 1984-86; pres. Mellon Fin. Services Corp., Oak Brook, Ill., 1986-87, Barclay's Am./Fin. Inc., Charlotte, N.C., from 1987. Mem. Nat. Second Mortgage Assn. Republican. Home: Wellfleet, Mass. Died Mar. 24, 2009.

LASKER, MORRIS EDWARD, federal judge; b. Hartsdale, NY, July 17, 1917; m. Helen M. Schubach; 4 children. BA magna cum laude, Harvard U., 1938; LLB, JD, Yale U., 1941. Bar: NY 1941. Atty. Nat. Def. Com., US Senate, 1941-42, Battle, Fowler, Jaffin & Kheel, 1946-68; judge US Dist. Ct. (so. dist.) NY, 1968—83, 1983—2009. Contbr. articles to profl. jours. Hon. trustee, bd. dirs. Vera Inst. Justice. Maj. US Army, 1942-46. Recipient Learned Hand medal Fed. Bar Coun., Edward Weinfeld award NY County Lawyers Assn. Mem. ABA, Assn. of Bar of City of NY (exec. com. 1985-89). Avocations: gardening, reading, history. Died Dec. 25, 2009; Cambridge, Mass.

LATHEM, EDWARD CONNERY, librarian, editor, educator; b. Littleton, NH, Dec. 15, 1926; s. Belton Gilreath and Myrtie Etta (Connery) L.; m. E. Elizabeth French, Nov. 27, 1957. AB, Dartmouth Coll., 1951; MS, Columbia U., 1952; D.Phil., Oxford U., 1961. With library Dartmouth Coll., 1952-78, librarian, 1968-78, dean of libraries, 1973-78, Bezaleel Woodward fellow, from 1978, couns. to pres., from 1982; officer, dir. Stinehour Press Inc., 1958-77, Plymouth Cheese Corp., from 1959, N. Country Pub. Co., 1970-78, Vt. Provisioners Inc., 1972-82, Meriden-Stinehour Inc., 1977-95; co-pub. Coös County Democrat, 1970-78; fence viewer Hanover, N.H., from 1962; adv. editor Dodd, Mead & Co., 1974-84. Corp. mem. Hanover Improvement Soc., 1971—; trustee N.H. Hist. Soc., 1956-76, Howe Libr., Hanover, 1967-87, Dr. Seuss Found., 1985—, William L. Bryant Found., 1986—; pres. Assn. Rsch. Lib.rs., 1976-77. Organizer microfilm edit. Papers of Daniel Webster, 1971; initiator Univ. Press of New Eng; editor and compiler: numerous books including (with Hyde Cox) Selected Prose of Robert Frost, 1966, Interviews with Robert Frost, 1966, (with Lawrance Thompson) Robert Frost and the Lawrence, Mass. High Sch. Bulletin, 1966, Your Son, Calvin Coolidge, 1968, The Poetry of Robert Frost, 1969, A Concordance to the Poetry of Robert Frost, 1971, (with Lawrance Thompson) Robert Frost: Poetry and Prose, 1972, Calvin Coolidge Says, 1972, Chronological Tables of American Newspapers 1690-1820, 1972, Robert Frost 100, 1974, 76 United Statesiana, 1976, North of Boston Poems (R. Frost), 1977, Thirteen Colonial Americana, 1977, The Dartmouth Experience (John Sloan Dickey), 1977, American Libraries as Centers of Scholarship, 1978, Robert Frost: A Biography (Lawrance Thompson and R.H. Winnick), 1981, (with Hyde Cox) Prose Jottings of Robert Frost, 1982, Stories of Life: North and South (Erskine Caldwell), 1983, Rudolph Ruzicka: Speaking Reminiscently, 1986, On the Teaching of Creative Writing (Wallace Stegner), 1989, A Vermont 14, 1992, Robert Frost: Seasons, 1992, On the Teaching and Writing of History (Bernard Bailyn), 1994. Mem. Phi Beta Kappa. Clubs: Century, Dartmouth (N.Y.C.); St. Botolph (Boston). Home: Hanover, NH. Died May 15, 2009.

LAUER, PETER BIRCHMORE, association administrator, consultant; b. Chgo., Aug. 18, 1947; s. John Birchmore and Barbara (Varty) L; m. Rebecca Franklin Ratz, Oct. 8, 1977; 1 child, Margaret Elizabeth. A.A., Kemper Jr. Coll., Boonville, Mo., 1967; B.A., U. Miss., 1971. Counselor, Boys Town, Omaha, 1971-72; salesman St. Charles Mfg., Houston, 1972-73; field dir. Congl. campaign, Geneva, Ill., 1973-75; asst. dir. AMPAC, Chgo., 1975-80, exec. dir., Washington, 1980—; lectr. George Washington U., Washington, 1982—. Dir. City Club of Chgo., 1979-81. Served to sgt. USAR, 1971-78. Mem. Am. Assn. Med. Soc. Execs., Am. Assn. Polit. Cons. (bd. dirs. 1984—), Am. Soc. Assn. Execs. (mem. polit. action com. 1982-87, com. chmn. 1985—), Nat. Assn. Bus. Polit. Action Coms. (bd. dirs. 1987—), Phi Kappa Tau, Order of Omega. Republican. Episcopalian. Avocations: golf; travel; reading. Home: Geneva, Ill. Died Feb. 24, 2010.

LAUFER, IGOR, radiologist; b. Humene, Czechoslovakia, Aug. 6, 1944; came to U.S., 1976; s. Henry and Sara (Mittleman) L.; m. Bernice H. Grafstein, May 28, 1967; children: Miriam, Jacob. B.Sc., U. Toronto, 1966, MD, 1967. Intern New Mt. Sinai Hosp., Toronto, 1967-68; resident Toronto Western Hosp., 1968-69, Beth Israel Hosp., Boston, 1969-72; mem. active staff dept. radiology McMaster U. Med. Center, Hamilton, Ont., Can., 1972-76, lectr. radiology, 1972-74, asst. prof., 1974-76; chief radiology dept. U. Pa. Hosp., Phila., 1976—97, residency training program dir., 1993—2000, residency selection dir., 1999—2004; assoc. prof. radiology U. Pa., 1976-80, prof., 1980—2010. Chief sect. gastrointestinal radiology Hosp. U. Pa., Phila., 1976 Author: Double Contrast Gastrointestinal Radiology With Endoscopic Correlation, 1979, 2d edit., 1992; author, editor Textbook Gastrointestinal Radiology, 1994; assoc. editor: Gastrointestinal Radiology, 1978—. Fellow Royal Coll. Physicians and Surgeons Can., Coll. Physicians Phila.; mem. Soc. Gastrointestinal Radiologists (pres. 1985, Cannon medal 1989), American Roentgen Ray Soc. (Outstanding Educator award, 2005), American Gastroenterology Assn., Radiol. Soc. North America, Canadian Assn. Radiology, Canadian Med. Assn., Pacific N.W. Radiol. Soc. (hon.), New Eng. Roentgen Ray Soc., N.S. Assn. Radiologists (hon.), Ont. Med. Assn., Toronto Radiol. Soc. (hon.), Phila. Roentgen Ray Soc. Jewish. Home: Bala Cynwyd, Pa. Died Sept. 14, 2010.

LAUFMAN, HAROLD, surgeon, consultant; b. Milw., Jan. 6, 1912; s. Jacob and Sophia (Peters) L.; m. Marilyn Joselit, 1940 (dec. 1963); children: Dionne Joselit Laufman Weigert, Laurien Laufman Kogut; m. June Friend Moses, 1980 (dec. 1999). BS, U. Chgo., 1932; MD, Rush Med. Coll., Chgo., 1937; MS in Surgery, Northwestern U., Chgo., 1946, PhD, 1948. Diplomate Am. Bd. Surgery, Am. Bd. Vascular Surgery. Intern Michael Reese Hosp., Chgo., 1936-39; fellow in gen. surgery St. Marks Hosp., London, Northwestern U. Med. Sch., Cook County Hosp., Hines VA Hosp., 1939-46; attending surgeon Michael Reese Hosp., 1940-53; mem. faculty Northwestern U., 1941-65, Grunow prof. experimental surgery, 1964; from clin. asst. to prof., attending surgeon Passavant Meml. Hosp., Chgo., 1953-65; prof. surgery, history of medicine Albert Einstein Coll. Medicine, NYC, 1965-81, prof. emeritus, from 1982; dir. Inst. Surg. Studies, Montefiore Hosp. and Med. Ctr., Bronx, NY, 1965-81; pvt. practice gen. and vascular surgery Chgo., 1941-65, NYC, 1965-82; ret. professorial lectr. surgery Mt. Sinai Sch. Medicine, NYC, 1979-83, emeritus, 1983—2010; attending surgeon Mt. Sinai Hosp., NYC, 1979-83. Cons., lectr. in field; chmn. FDA Classification Panel Gen. and Plastic Surgery Devices, 1975-78; pres. Harold Laufman Assocs., Inc., 1977-2003, sr. ptnr., 1988-2004. Author: (with S.W. Banks) Surgical Exposures of the Extremities, 1953, 2d edit., 1986, (with R.B. Erichson) Hematologic Problems in Surgery, 1970, Hospital Special Care Facilities, 1981, The Veins, 1986, One Man's Century with Pen, Brush, Fiddle and Scalpel, 2007; editor Chgo. Medicine, 1959-63; contbg. editor Modern Medicine, 1965-70; chmn. editl. bd. Diagnostica, 1974-79; mem. editl. bd. Med. Devices, 1969-80, Tech. for Surgery, 1976-86, Surgery, Gynecology and Obstetrics, 1974-92, Infection Control, 1980-88, Med. Instrumentation, 1972-83, Med. Rsch. Engring., 1972-79; contbr. articles to sci. publs. Chmn. bd. dirs. NY Chamber Soloists, 1974-80, Chamber Music Conf. and Composers Forum of the East, 1975-91, pres., 1987-90. Capt. to maj. head of surg. team, 16th Evac. Hosp. 5th army USMC, 1942—46, North Africa, Sicily, Italy. Recipient James IV Traveling Professorship in Surgery, Israel, Vienna and Moscow, 1963, Disting. Alumnus award, Rush Med. Coll., 1993, U. Chgo. divsn. Biol. Svcs., 1999. Fellow: ACS, Am. Surg. Assn.; mem.: Surg. Infection Soc. (councillor 1980—84, founding mem.), Soc. Surgery Alimentary Tract (founding mem.), Internat. Cardiovasc. Soc., Soc. Vascular Surgery, NY Surg. Soc., Ctrl. Surg. Assn., Western Surg. Assn., Societe Internationale de Chirurgie, Am. Med. Writers Assn. (pres. 1968—69, Harold Swanberg award 1969), Am. Assn. Healthcare Cons., Assn. Advancement Med. Instrumentation (pres. 1974—75, chmn. bd. 1976—77), Harmonie Club (NYC), Alpha Omega Alpha, Sigma Xi, Zeta Beta Tau. Died May 3, 2010.

LAUN, LOUIS FREDERICK, government official; b. Battle Creek, Mich., May 19, 1920; s. Louis Frederick and Roena (Graves) L.; m. Margaret West, Jan. 25, 1947; children: Nancy, Kathryn Webb, Margaret. BA, Yale U., 1942. Asst. advt. mgr. Bates Fabrics, Inc., NYC, 1946-48; asst. to pres., indsl. and public relations Bates Mfg. Co., Lewiston, Maine, 1948-55; advt. dir. Burlington Industries, NYC, 1955-57; gen. merchandising mgr. Celanese Fibers Co., NYC, 1957-60, v.p., dir. mktg., 1960-63, exec. v.p. mktg., 1963-64; pres. Celanese Fibers Mktg. Co. div. Celanese Corp., 1964-71, also v.p. corp., 1964-71; asso. adminstr. ops. SBA, Washington, 1973, dep. adminstr., 1973-77; pres. Am. Paper Inst., NYC, 1977-86; asst. Sec. Commerce for Internat. Econ. Policy Dept. of Commerce, Washington, 1986-89, exec. br. commr., H elsinki Commn. on Security and Cooperation in Europe, 1988-89; cons. Nat. Exec. Svc. Corp, 1989—2001. U.S. pulp and paper rep. food and agrl. orgns. UN; bd. dirs. Overseas Pvt. Investment Corp., Noranda Aluminum, Inc.; exec. br. mem. Commn. on Security and Cooperation in Europe (Helsinki Commn.); vol. cons. Nat. Exec. Svc. Corps, 1989-2001. Bd. dirs. N.Y. Bd. Trade, Better Bus. Bur. N.Y., Alliance to Save Energy, Bus. Adv. Com. on Fed. Reports; bd. dirs., mem. exec. com. The Grace Commn. on Govt. Waste; indsl. asst. to chmn. Opportunities Industrialization Ctrs. Am.; nat. adv. coun. SBA; chmn. Rep. Industry Workshop program; field dir. Com. for Re-election of Pres., 1972; trustee Taft Sch.; mem. exec. com. President's Pvt. Sector Survey on Cost Control; chmn. Kids to Kids Internat., 1999; bd. dirs. New Castle Hist. Soc., 1999-2001, Edwin Gould Svcs. for Families and Children, 1997-2001, United Way of No. Westchester, 1998-2001. Lt. col. USMC, 1942-46. Decorated Bronze Star; recipient Human Rights award Anti-Defamation League, 1968; Achievement award Textile Vets. Assn., 1970; named Young Man of Yr. Lewiston-Auburn C. of C., 1953, Man of Yr. Textile Salesman Assn., 1970, Man of Yr. Fabric Salesmen's Guild, 1971; Gold medal for disting. service SBA, Citation Merit Taft Sch., 1988. Mem. Color Assn. U.S. (sec.), Man-Made Fiber Producers Assn. (chmn. 1967-69), Yale Club (N.Y.C.), Sleepy Hollow Country Club (Scarborough, N.Y.), Met. Club (Washington), Mid-Ocean Club (Bermuda). Died May 21, 2010.

LAUR, WILLIAM EDWARD, retired dermatologist; b. Saginaw, Mich., Nov. 17, 1919; s. Vertner Linton and Ruth Gae (Eyre) L.; m. Mary Elizabeth Kirby, Dec. 31, 1943; children: Eric, Edward, John, J. Michael. BS, Mercer U., Macon, Ga., 1941; MD, U. Mich., 1943; MS in Medicine, Wayne State U., Detroit, 1949. Diplomate Am. Bd. Dermatology. Intern John Sealy Hosp., Galveston, Tex., 1943;

resident Wayne State U., 1946-49; pvt. practice Amarillo, Tex., 1949-70; pres. High Plains Dermatology Ctr., P.A., Amarillo, 1975—90; ret., 1990. Cons. VA, USAF, 1952-90; assoc. prof. Tex. Tech. Health Sci. Ctr., Amarillo, 1965-90. Contbr. articles to profl. jours. including Archives of Dermatology, Internat. Jour. Dermatology, Cutis, So. Med. Jour., Jour. Am. Acad. Dermatology, Panhandle Med. Soc. Bull., Urologic and Cutaneous Rev. Dir. Moon Watch, NASA, Amarillo, 1956. Capt. U.S. Army, 1944-46, ETO. Fellow Am. Acad. Dermatology; mem. AMA, Tex. Med. Assn., Noah Worcester Dermatol. Soc., Potter Randall County Med. Soc. (pres. 1964), Alpha Tau Omega, Alpha Chi. Avocations: cooking, bridge, computers. Home: Amarillo, Tex. Died Apr. 20, 2010.

LAW, DAVID HILLIS, physician; b. Milw., July 24, 1927; s. David Hillis Law III and Hazel Janice (May) Young; m. Patricia Bicking Thornton, Sept. 14, 1949 (dec. 2005); children: Linda Clark, Wendy, David, Kimberly Rankin, Cassandra. BA, Cornell U., 1950, MD, 1954. Resident in internal medicine Cornell U. Med. Coll., NYC, 1954-57, fellow in gastroenterology, 1957-59; dir. personnel health svcs. N.Y. Hosp., Cornell Med. Ctr., NYC, 1959-60; asst. prof. medicine, chief gastroenterology Vanderbilt U. Med. Coll., Nashville, 1960-69; prof., vice chmn. dept. medicine U. New Mex. Sch. Med., Albuquerque, 1969-85; chief med. svcs. Vets. Adminstrn. Med. Ctr., 1969-85; dir. med. svcs. Vets. Adminstrn. Ctrl. Office, Washington, 1985-86, dep. asst. chief med. dir. for clin. svcs., 1986-89, asst. chief med. dir. clin. affairs, 1989-91, acting dep. assoc. chief med. dir. for hosp.-based svcs., 1991-95, assoc. dep. chief med. dir. for clin. program, 1993-95, acting chief patient care officer, 1995-96; assoc. chief of staff for edn. Bay Pines Med. Ctr., Fla., 1996—2002; prof. internal medicine U. South Fla., from 1998; cons. Health Care Exec. Devel., from 2003. Human rsch. com. Los Alamos (N.Mex.) Sci. Lab., 1972-80; sabbatical dept. clin. physiology Karolinska Inst., Stockholm, 1980; officer N.Mex. Nutrition Improvement Program, 1970-75; sub-com. chmn. U.S. Pharmacopeia Commn. on Revision, 1975-80. Editor, Parenteral Nutrition; mem. editorial bd., Am. Jour. Digestive Diseases, 1968-74; rev. numerous med. jours.; contbr. articles to numeous profl. jours. Bd. dirs., officer Albuquerque Friends of Music, 1975-85; active Nat. Digestive Disease Adv. Bd., 1989-95, Interdepartmental Digestive Disease Coordinating Com.; pres. Bay Pines Edn. Found., Inc., 2001, bd. dirs., 2003-05. With U.S. Army, 1945-46. Named Tchr. and Attending Physician of Yr. Dept. Medicine House Staff, 1985. Fellow ACP (gov. 1989-96); mem. AMA (lectr.), Western Assn. Physicians, Western Soc. Clin. Rsch., Am. Gastroenterol. Assn., Am. Inst. Nutrition, Alpha Omega Alpha. Republican. Presbyterian. Avocation: hot air ballooning. Home: Baton Rouge, La. Died Aug. 22, 2009.

LAWRENCE, ANDREA MEAD, county official, recreational land use consultant; b. Rutland, Vt., Apr. 19, 1932; d. Bradford Belcher and Janet Brocket (Ross) Mead; m. David Lawrence, Mar. 31, 1951 (div. 1969); children: Cortlandt Bradford, Matthew David, Deirdre Bario, Leslie Peace, Quentin Andrea. Student pub. schs., Rutland. Competitive skier, 1942-56; mem. U.S. Olympic Alpine Team, 1948, 52, 56; winner gold medals for slalom and giant slalom Internat. Olympics, 1952; 1st in downhill, slalom and giant slalom N.Am. Championships, 1953; winner downhill, slalom and giant slalom Am. Internat. Races, Stowe, Vt., 1952, 53, 54; Nat. Alpine champion in downhill, slalom and combined events, 1949, 52, 55; Nat. Alpine giant slalom chamption, 1953, 55; mem. Mono County Bd. Suprs., Mammoth Lake, Calif., from 1982, vice chmn., 1983, 85, chmn., 1986. Mem. Gt. Basin Unified Air Pollution Control Dist., Local Agy. Formation Commn., Mono County Hist. Records Commn., Ea. Sierra Com., Econ. Devel. Steering Com., Interagy. Com. on Owens Valley and Wildlife, Inyo-Mono Fish and Game Adv. Commn., Mono County Mental Health Adv. Bd., Long Valley Volcanic Hazards Adv. Coun., Mono County Housing Authority; spl. cons., ski resort cons. Allan O'Connor & Assocs., 1974-77, Wallace, McHarg, Roberts, Todd & Assocs., 1974-77, June Mountain Devel. Corp., 1974. Author: (with Sara Burnaby) A Practice of Mountains, 1980. Mem. Aspen (Colo.) Bd. Adjustment and Planning Commn., 1963-64; founder Friends of Mammoth, 1971-75; a founder Mammoth Adv. Coun., 1972-76; mem. Mono County Grand Jury, 1973; mem. citizens working group for long range plans for allocation winter sports resources in Inyo Nat. Forest, U.S. Forest Svc.; mem. Citizen's Com. To Rev. U.S. Forest Svc. Practices in Calif., 1979. Named to New Eng. Hall of Fame, 1952, Helms Hall of Fame, 1953, Ski Hall of Fame, 1958; recipient Athlete of Yr. award Helms Found. and Sportfolio mag., 1947, Am. Ski Trophy, 1950; inducted into Women's Sports Found. Hall of Fame, 1983; on cover Time mag., Jan. 21, 1952. Mem. Nat. Assn. Counties (pub. lands steering com.), County Suprs. Assn. Calif. (housing, land use and transp. com., transp. task force subcom.), So. Calif. Regional Assn. County Suprs., Mountain Counties Water Resources Assn., Sacramento-Mother Lode Regional Assn. County Suprs. Democrat. Avocations: cross country skiing, backpacking, hiking, photography, reading. Home: Mammoth Lakes, Calif. Died Mar. 31, 2009.

LAWRENCE, BARBARA CORELL, insurance company director, real estate investor; b. Binghamton, NY, Nov. 19, 1927; d. Archibald G. and Helen (Smith) C.; m. Albert Lawrence, June 28, 1950; children: David C., Janet H., Elizabeth A. BS, Cornell U., 1949. Tchr., Johnson City, N.Y., 1949-50, Schenectady, N.Y., 1957-58; prop. owner, mgr. Lawrence Props., Schenectady, from 1955. Bd. dirs., sec. United Community Ins. Co., N.Y.C., Lawrence Ins. Group, Albany, N.Y., Lawrence Agy. Corp., Albany, Lawrence Group, Inc., Schenectady, Senate Ins. Co. Ariz.; dir. Northeast Savings. Founder Lawrence Inst.; mem. Jr. League; elder, First Reformed Ch., chmn. Chanel Guild; mem. women's aux. Schenectady Boys and Girls Club, The Schenectady Found.; bd. dirs. Ind. Living in the Capital Dist., Schenectady County Humane Soc.; patron Saratoga Performing Arts Ctr.; trustee Ellis Hosp., Proctor's Guild; co-chair Schenectady 300th Anniversary; trustee Union Coll.; patroon of Schenectady; mem. Regents Select Commn. on Disabilities, Met. Opera Assn.; bd. dirs. Adirondack Conservancy. Recipient Julliet Lowe Woman of Achievement award Mohawk Pathways Girl Scout Coun., 1990. Mem. Schenectady Panhellenic Assn. (past pres.), Delta Gamma, PEO Sisterhood, Garden Club Schenectady, Gardeners Wookshop, Cornell Club of the Capital Dist. and N.Y.C., Northern Lake George Yacht Club, Mohawk Golf Club. Avocations stitchery, flower arranging. Home: Schenectady, NY. Died Oct. 15, 2009.

LEACH, JAMES LINDSAY, mechanical engineering educator; b. Lawrenceville, Ill., Apr. 9, 1918; s. James Gard and Nellie Irene (Biesecker) L.; m. Mary Jane Zipprodt, Oct. 13, 1945; children— James Lindsay, Charles, Robert, Janet Sue. BS, U. N.Mex., 1942; MS, U. Ill., 1949; PhD, Ill. State U., 1974. Mem. faculty U. Ill., Urbana, from 1946, assoc. prof. mech. engring., 1949-53, prof., from 1953. Mech. engr. foundry div. Gen. Motors, Danville, Ill., 1949-51; engr. Tex. Co. Lawrenceville, 1946-47; cons. in field; vis. prof. Indian Inst. Tech., Kharagpur, 1960-61, Summer Sch. for Engring. Tchrs. India, New Delhi, summer, 1964—, Bengal Engring. Coll., Calcutta, 1964, U. Wis., New Delhi, summer 1965, Thermal Fabircation Inst., Coimbatore, India, summers, 1966-67, Survey Tech. Edn., Kenya Vista, 1971, Evaluation and Tng. Tech. Edn. Tchrs., 1972; cons. Acad. Ednl. Devel. and Ministry Transport, Iran, 1976 Author: (with others) Manufacturing Processes and Materials for Engineers, 2d. edit, 1969; contbr. (with others) articles to profl. jours. Served to lt. col. USAAF, 1943-45. Recipient citation Am. Soc. Die Casting Engrs., 1975 Mem. ASME, Am. Soc. Mil. Engrs., Am. Soc. Petroleum Engrs., Nat. Soc. Engring. Edn., Nat. Soc. Profl. Engrs., Sci. Research Soc. Am., Fedn. Am. Scientists, Am. Foundrymen's Soc. (bd. dirs. Central Ill. chpt. 1960—, svc. citation 1968), Pi Tau Sigma, Tau Beta Pi, Sigma Tau. Home: Flat Rock, Ill. Died Aug. 4, 2010.

LEADER, MORTON, banker, financial advisor; b. NYC, May 10, 1928; s. Harry and Eva (Keller) L.; m. Adele Fox, Dec. 1, 1951; children: Emily, Jamie. BBA, CCNY, 1950. Credit mgr., v.p, sr. v.p. United Mcht. and Mfrs. United Factors Corp., NYC, 1951-79; v.p., sr. v.p., exec. v.p. Republic Nat. Bank/Republic Factors, NYC, from 1979. Bd. dirs. N.Y. Credit & Fin. Mgmt. Mem. Met. Mus. Art, N.Y.C., United Jewish Appeal/Fedn. Jewish Philanthropists, Am. Jewish Congress. Mem. B'nai B'rith (bd. dirs. 1979-80). Democrat. Jewish. Avocations: golf, tennis. Home: Jamesburg, NJ. Died Aug. 22, 2010.

LEAL, LUIS, literature educator, writer; b. Linares, Mexico, Sept. 17, 1907; m. Gladys Leal (dec.); children: Luis(dec.), Antonio. BS in Spanish, Northwestern U., 1940; MS in Spanish, U. Chgo., 1941, PhD in Spanish & Italian, 1950. Prof. Spanish U. Ill. at Urbana-Champaign; prof. Chicano studies U. Calif. Berkeley, 1976—2004, Luis Leal Endowed Chair in Chicano Studies, 1995—97. Mem. Jurado de Letras de Oro, Mex.; lectr. in field. Author: A Brief HIstory of the Mexican Short Story, 1956; Pub. more than 40 anthologies and critical works on Spanish-American lit.; mem. editl. bd. several publs.; contbr. numerous articles and essays to profl. publs. Am. for U.S.-Mex. lit. rels. Served in US Army. Luis Leal Endowed Chair in Chicago Studies established in his honor U. Calif., Santa Barbara; recipient Disting. Scholar award, Nat. Assn. Chicano Studies, 1988, Águila Azteca medal Pres. of Mex., Carlos de Salinas de Gotari, 1991, Nat. Hamanities Medal, The White House, 1997, Died Jan. 25, 2010.

LEBARON, FRANCIS NEWTON, retired biochemistry educator; b. Framingham, Mass., July 26, 1922; s. Paul Burrows and Dorothy (Lamson) LeB.; m. Margaret Lenore Shaw, July 8, 1953 (dec. May 11, 2009); 1 child, Geoffrey Shaw. BS, MIT, 1944; MA, Boston U., 1948; PhD, Harvard U., 1951. Assoc. biochemist McLean Hosp., Belmont, Mass., 1957-64; assoc. biol. chemist Harvard U. Med. Sch., 1959-64; assoc. prof. biochemistry U. N.Mex. Med. Sch., 1964-69, prof., 1969-83, chmn. dept., 1971-78, chmn. ad hoc nutrition planning commn., 1969. Vis. scholar MIT, 1974-75. Mem. editl. bd.: Jour. Neurochemistry, 1965-74; contbr. articles to profl. jours. Served with USNR, 1943-46. Mem. Am. Chem. Soc., Biochem. Soc. (London), Am. Soc. Biol. Chemists, AAAS, Internat. Soc. Neurochemistry, Am. Soc. Neurochemistry (pres. 1969-71), Theta Delta Chi. Home: Yarmouth Port, Mass. Died Nov. 2, 2009.

LEBOS, LEO, JR., actuary; b. Asheville, NC, Mar. 15, 1942; s. Leo and Mary Elizabeth (Mosley) Lebos Hubbard; m. Sherrell Agnes Varnell, Apr. 22, 1962; children: Leo III, Tracy Elizabeth. Actuarial student Interstate Life Ins. Co., Chattanooga, 1963-72; actuary Gr. Commonwealth, Dallas, 1972-73; asst. v.p. Interstate Life Ins. Co., Chattanooga, 1973-77; v.p., actuary Gulf Life Ins. Co., Jacksonville, Fla., 1977-80, sr. v.p., actuary, from 1981. Dir. Interstate Fire Ins. Co., Chattanooga, Fin. Computer Services, Jacksonville; chmn. bd. Fla. Guaranty Fund, Tallahassee, 1981—, State Comprehensive Health Assn., Tallahassee, 1983— Fellow Soc. Actuaries; mem. Am. Acad. Actuaries, Internat. Actuarial Assn., Southeastern Actuaries Club (exec. com. 1983—) Home: Orange Park, Fla. Died June 30, 2009.

LEBOWITZ, CATHARINE KOCH, state legislator; b. Winchester, Mass., June 30, 1915; d. William John and Carolyn Sophia (Kistinger) Koch; m. Murray Lebowitz, Sept. 21, 1971 (dec. Oct. 1978). Student, Northwestern U., 1948-49, Boston Coll., 1949-52; degree (hon.), Ea. Main Tech. Coll., 2003. Sec. ERA, Bangor, Augusta, Maine, 1935-38, WPA, Portland, Maine, 1938-42; pers. officer, exec. sec. USN, Portland, 1942-47; exec. sec. Clark Babbitt, Boston, 1947-48; adminstrv. asst. Moore Bus. Forms, Boston, 1948-52; apt. mgr., wholesale appliance divsn. Coffin-Wimple Inc., 1952-62; clk. U.S. Dist. Ct. Bangor (no. dist.), 1962-79; sec. Portland Credit Bur., 1980-86; mem. Bangor City Coun., 1985-87, Maine State Legislature, 1982-92. Bd. dirs. Eastern Transp., 1989—94; mem. Bus. Adv. Coun., from 1991; active Program Rev. Subcom., from 1991; mem. adv. coun. Ea. Maine Tech. Coll., from 1992; bd. dirs. Rural Health Ctrs. Maine, Inc., 1992—99; chair, adv. bd., Gala decorating com. Maine Ctr. for Arts, U. Maine, 1992—2003. Sec. Symphony Women, Bangor, 1964—84; bd. dirs. Opera House Com., 1978—94; legis. com. United Way of Penobscot Valley, 1988—93, bd. dirs., 1993—99; adv. com. Maine Devel. Found., 1988—90; adv. bd. Aftercare, Cmty. Health & Counseling Svc., 1992; planning bd. St. Joseph Hosp., 1987—92; dir., v.p. St. Joseph Hosp. Aux., 1994—99, Maine Ctr. Arts Adv. Bd., 1994—2002; apptr. by gov. Maine Commn. Cmty. Svc., 1996—2002; mem. Bangor City Hosp. Aux., 1988—99; bd. dirs. Penobscot Theater, 1990; accredited Beauty Pageant judge, from 1986; mem. Eastern Main Commn. Cmty Svc., 1996; del. Rep. Nat. Conv., 1984, 1988. Recipient Civilian Meritorious Svc. award USN, Portland, Maine, 1946, Paul Bunyan award, C. of C., 1997, Cmty. Spirit award Sr. Star recognition Merrill Merchants Bank Bangor, 1999; named Hon. Alumnus Secretarial Sci., Husson Coll., 1980, Ea. Main Tech. Coll. Champion award, 2002. Mem.: Ea. Maine Med. Ctr. Aux., Ret. Fed. Employees (v.p. from 1994, pres. 1996), Newcomb Soc., Penobscot County Reps., Bangor C. of C. (mem. comsumer rels. coun., 1981-90, gov. affairs com. from 1996, coord. 150th ann. prodn. Music Man 1994), Bangor Dist. Nursing Assn. (corp. mem. at large), Credit Women Bangor (sec. 1965—67), Nat. Assn. Ret. Fed. Employees (v.p. bd. dirs. from 1993, sec. 1994), Credit Profls. Bangor Cmty. Theater (treas. 1973—98), Credit Women Internat. (treas. 1975—77), Penobscot County Ext. Svc. (hon.; bd. dirs. from 1995), Main Art N.G. (hon.), Maine N.G. Assn. (hon.), Bangor Hist. Soc. (bd. dirs. from 1993, exec. bd. sec. 1994—99, pres. 1999—2002), U. Maine Maine Masque Theater (judge 1983—90), Mgmt. Club, Bangor City Rep. Club (bd. dirs., treas. 1993—97), Penobscot County Rep. Women's Club (sec. 1979), Zonta Club (pres. Bangor 1962—64, 1980—82, v.p. 1994, adv. bd. Maine migrant health program from 2001, cooperator cmty. health and counseling svcs. from 2001, Outstanding Leader 1991). Home: Bangor, Maine. Died Apr. 26, 2010.

LEBRETON, MARIETTA M., history professor; d. Guy Joseph and Marietta Schneidau LeBreton. BS, La. State U., 1958, MA, 1961, PhD, 1969. Instr. social sci. Northwestern State U., Natchitoches, La., 1963—65, asst. prof. history, 1965—70, assoc. prof. history, 1970—73, prof. history, from 1973, head dept. history, 1980—83. Vis. asst. prof. history Tulane U., New Orleans, 1968—70. Author: Northwestern State University: A History, 1985; contbr. chapters to books, articles to profl. jours. Mem. pastoral coun. Holy Cross Ch., Natchitoches, 2003—05. Recipient Frank Gipson trophy, DAR, 1976, Outstanding Tchr. award, Northwestern State U., 1990; fellow, Nat. Trust for Hist. Preservation, 1960. Mem.: La. Preservative Alliance, Assn. for Preservation Hist. Natchitoches, No. La. Hist. Assn. (bd. dirs. 1970—73), La. Hist. Assn. (bd. dirs. 1970—72, 1977—80, 1983). Avocations: travel, gardening. Died Mar. 2009.

LECKLITNER, MYRON LYNN, nuclear physician; b. Canton, Ohio, June 16, 1942; s. Myron Devoy and Margaret (Koon) Lecklitner; m. Carol Vance, Sept. 1979; 1 child, Tonja Ann. BS in Acctg. and Economics, Pa. State U., 1964; BS in Chemistry and Biology, U. Ala., 1970, MD, 1974. Diplomate Am. Bd. Nuc. Medicine. Intern Lloyd Noland Hosp., Birmingham, Ala., 1974—75, resident, internal medicine, 1975—77; fellow, nuc. medicine and ultrasound U. Ala., Birmingham, 1977—79; asst. prof. U. Tex., San Antonio, 1979—83; assoc. prof. U. South Ala., Mobile, 1983—86, prof., from 1986. Dir., diagnostic imaging divsn. & sr. scientist U. South Ala. Cancer Ctr., from 1984; vis. prof. U. Nuevo Leon, Mex., 1983, U. Oxford, England, 1985, 88, Royal Postgrad. Sch. Med. U. London, 1985. Contbr. chapters to books, articles to profl. jours. Served to capt. US Army, 1964—67. Decorated Bronze Star medal, Army Commendation medal, Air medal. Fellow: Am. Coll. Nuc. Physicians (treas. 1988—90, vice chmn., membership com. 1985—87, exec. com. 1985—90, bd. Regents 1985—90, chmn., fin. com. 1986—88, chmn., publs. com. 1994—96); mem.: Soc. Nuc. Medicine (bus. advisors group from 1990, socioeconomics com. from 1991), Am. Coll. Radiology (nuc. med. mktg. com. from 1992), Ala. Soc. Nuc. Medicine (pres. 1985—86, trustee, SE chpt. from 1988, chmn., govt. affairs com.). Home: Mobile, Ala. Died Jan. 1, 2010.

LEDBETTER, STEWART MANEE, financial consultant, state government official; b. NYC, Nov. 9, 1932; s. John Nelson and Gladys Stewart (Manee) Ledbetter; m. Sheila Barbara Tynan Ledbetter, June 18, 1959; children: Stewart Manee, John Patton. BA, Rollins Coll., 1955; MBA, Stanford, 1957; postgrad, Columbia, 1960—61; grad, Realtors Inst., Concord, NH, 1974. V.p. 1st Nat. City Bank, NYC, 1961—71; pres. Real Estate Assos. Vt., Manchester, 1971—83, chmn., from 1983; with Thomson McKinnon Securities Inc., from 1983. Pres. Ledbetter Properties Inc., Dorset, Vt., 1972—76, Investment Assos. So. Vt., Manchester, 1971—80, South Ctrl. Vt. Bd. Realtors, 1975; commr. banking & ins., Vt.; chmn. Vt. Housing Fin. Agy., Vt. Home Mortgage Guaranty Bd.; commr. Vt. State Housing Authority; mem. Gov.'s Coun. Econ. Advisors. Rep. candidate US Senate, 1980, 1982; mem. Vt. Retirement Bd.; trustee Vt. State Tchrs. Retirement Sys. 1st lt. Fin. Corps US Army, 1957—60. Mem.: Internat. Assn. Fin. Planning, Conf. State Bank Suprs. (vice chmn. dist. 1), Nat. Assn. Ins. Commrs. (chmn. zone 1), Nat. Assn. Realtors, Vt. Assn. Realtors (dir.). Home: Manchester, Vt. Died Nov. 5, 2009.

LEDERER, WILLIAM JULIUS, author; b. NYC, Mar. 31, 1912; s. William J. and Paula (Franken) L.; m. Ethel Hackett, Apr. 21, 1940 (div. Jan. 1965); children: Brian, Jonathan, Bruce; m. Corinne Edwards Lewis, July 1965 (div. May 1976). BS, U.S. Naval Acad., 1936; A Nieman fellow, Harvard U., 1950-51. Enlisted USN, 1930, commd. ensign, 1936, advanced through grades to capt., 1952, ret., 1958; Far East corr. Reader's Digest, 1958-63; lectr. colls. and univs., from 1949. Author in residence, Harvard U., 1966-67; Author: All the Ship's at Sea, 1950, The Last Cruise, 1950, Spare Time Article Writing for Money, 1953, Ensign O'Toole and Me, 1957, A Nation of Sheep, 1961, Timothy's Song, 1965, Pink Jade, 1966, (with Eugene Burdick) The Ugly American, 1958, Sarkhan, 1965, Our Own Worst Enemy, 1967, (with Don D. Jackson) The Mirages of Marriage, 1968, (with Joe Pete Wilson) Complete Cross-Country Skiing and Ski Touring, 1970, (with others) Marriage for and Against, Marital Choices, A Happy Book of Happy Stories, I, Giorghos, 1984, Creating a Good Relationship, 1984. Mem. Signet Soc., Authors Guild, Acad. Orthomolecular Psychiatry, European Acad. Preventive Medicine, Internat. Acad. Preventive Medicine, Internat. Coll. Applied Nutrition, Lotos Club, Trap Door Spiders Club, Harvard Faculty Club, Sigma Delta Chi. Home: Baltimore, Md. Died Dec. 5, 2009.

LEDOGAR, STEPHEN JOSEPH, retired diplomat; b. NYC, Sept. 14, 1929; s. Edward & Margaret Ledogar; m. Marcia Hubert, Sept. 16, 1967; children: Lucy, Charles. BS, Fordham U., 1954, LLB, 1958. Bar: N.Y. 1959. Surety claims atty. Chubb & Son, NYC, 1954-59; with Fgn. Svc., 1959-97, ret., 1997; press spokesman, U.S. del. Vietnam Peace Talks, Paris, 1967-72; with U.S. Mission to NATO, 1973-76; spl. asst. to under sec. US Dept. State, 1976-77; dir. Office of NATO Affairs, 1977-80; mem. State Dept. Senior Seminar, 1980-81; dep. chief of mission U.S. Mission to NATO, Brussels, 1981-87; amb., U.S. rep. European Conventional Stabilility Negotiations and Mutual and Balanced Force Reductions Talks, 1987-89; amb. and head U.S. Del. to Negotiations on Conventional Armed Forces in Europe, 1989; amb. and U.S. rep. Conference on Disarmament, 1989-97; prin. U.S. negotiator of chem. weapons convention, 1993; prin. U.S. negotiator Comprehensive Nuclear Test Ban Treaty, 1996. Lt. USN, 1949-52, USNR, 1954-60 (Naval Aviator). Died May 3, 2010.

LEDWIDGE, PATRICK JOSEPH, lawyer; b. Detroit, Mar. 17, 1928; s. Patrick Liam and Mary Josephine (Hooley) L.; m. Rosemary Lahey Mervenne, Aug. 3, 1974; stepchildren: Anne Marie, Mary Clare, John, David, Sara. AB, Coll. Holy Cross, 1949; JD, U. Mich., 1952. Bar: Mich. 1952. Assoc. firm Dickinson, Wright, Moon, Van Dusen & Freeman, Detroit, 1956-63; mem. Dickinson Wright PLLC, Bloomfield Hills, Mich., from 1964. Served to lt. j.g. U.S. Navy, 1952-55. Mem. Mich. Bar Assn., Detroit Bar Assn., Am. Law Inst. Clubs: Detroit Athletic, Detroit Golf. Roman Catholic. Deceased.

LEE, CHEN HSI, retired structural engineer; b. Shanghai, China, Oct. 26, 1923; came to U.S., 1948, naturalized, 1962; s. Kung and Teh-Ling (Yu) L.; BS, Chiao-Tung U., Shanghai, 1947; MS, U. Mich., 1950; m. Stella T., Nov. 19, 1955; 1 child, Grace T. Registered profl. engr., N.Y. Prin. structural designer J.G. White Engring Corp., N.Y.C., 1950-63; aerospace stress analyst Grumman Aerospace Corp., Bethpage, N.Y., 1963-78, stress and fatigue structure engr., 1978-90; ret., 1990. Recipient Apollo Achievement award NASA, 1969, Lunar Module Structure Sci. award Grumman Aerospace Corp., 1969. Assoc. fellow: AIAA (L.I. sect. council man, pub., sec. L.I. sect., editor L.I. sect. Flier, chmn. L.I. sect. 1987-88), N.Y. Profl. Engrs. Soc., Alpha Lambda. Club: Toastmasters Internat. Home: Plainview, NY. Died June 9, 2009.

LEE, DAN M., retired state supreme court chief justice; b. Petal, Miss., Apr. 19, 1926; s. Buford Aaron and Pherbia Ann (Camp) L.; m. Peggy Jo Daniel, Nov. 27, 1947 (dec. 1952); 1 child, Sheron Lee Anderson; m. Mary Alice Gray, Sept. 30, 1956; 1 child, Dan Jr. Attended, U. So. Miss., 1946; LLB, Jackson Sch. Law, 1949; JD, Miss. Coll., 1970. Bar: Miss. 1948. Ptnr. Franklin & Lee, Jackson, Miss., 1948-54, Lee, Moore and Countiss, Jackson, Miss., 1954-71; county judge Hinds County, 1971-77; cir. judge Hinds-Yazoo Counties, 1977-82; assoc. justice Miss. Supreme Ct., Jackson, 1982-87, presiding justice, 1987-95, chief justice, 1995-98; ret., 1998; of counsel Dogan & Wilkinson, PLLC, Jackson, 1999. With U.S. Naval Aviation, 1944-46. Mem. ABA, Hinds County Bar Assn., Miss. State Bar Assn., Aircraft Owners and Pilots Assn., Am. Legion, VFW, Kiwanis Internat. Baptist. Home: Brandon, Miss. Died May 9, 2010.

LEE, DEBORA ANN, elementary school educator, reading specialist; b. Beckley, W. Va., May 2, 1958; d. David Lavon and Edith (Graham) L. AB in Bus. Adminstrn., Beckley Coll., 1978; AB in Arts, Beckley Coll., W.Va., 1982; BS, Concord Coll., 1984; MA, U. W. VA., 1990. Cert. tchr. elem. edn. 1-8, reading specialist k-12, adult. Sec. United Mine Workers Assn., Mullens, W. Va., 1978; receptionist, sec. Ashland Fin., Mullens, 1978-79; tchr. Wyoming County Bd. Edn., Pineville, W. Va., from 1984. Mem. NEA, W. Va. Edn. Assn., Internat. Reading Assn., W. Va. State Reading Coun., Wyoming County Reading Coun. (charter, pres. 1990), Kappa Delta Pi. Democrat. Baptist. Avocations: reading, cooking, needlepoint, music, travel. Home: Mullens, W.Va. Died Jan. 9, 2009.

LEE, ELIZABETH BOBBITT, architect; b. Lumberton, NC, July 9, 1928; d. William Osborne and Catharine Wilder (Bobbitt) Lee. Student, Salem Coll., 1945—47; BArch with honors, NC State Coll., 1952. Registered arch., NC, 1955, SC, 1964. Assoc. William Coleman Arch., Kinston, NC, 1952—55, Skidmore, Owens & Merrill, NYC, 1955—56; prin. Elizabeth B. Lee FAIA Arch., Lumberton, NC, 1956—73, from 1982; sr. ptnr. Lee & Thompson Archs., Lumberton, 1973—82. Bd. dirs. Robeson Little Theatre, Lumberton, 1977—80, NC Dance Theatre, Winston-Salem, 1980—85, Robeson County Cmty. Concerts, Lumberton, 1980—87; trustee NC State U., Raleigh, 1983—92, mem., bd. endowment, from 1993. Recipient Recognition award, Randolph E. Dumont Design Program, 1970, Disting. Alumna award, Salem Coll., 1989. Fellow: AIA (nat. dir. 1983—85, officeholder, NC chpt. 1959, v.p. 1978, pres. 1979, bd. dirs. 1980, pres., eastern sect. NC chpt. 1975, bd. dirs., South Atlantic Regional Coun. 1977—79); mem.: NC State Alumni Assn. (bd. dirs. 1982—85, chmn., Robeson county chpt.), Lumberton Jr. Svc. League (pres. 1968), NC Archtl. Found. (pres. 1982—83), NC Design Found., Robeson County Heart Assn. (pres. 1970), Jr. League (pres., Lumberton chpt. 1968), Phi Kappa Phi. Democrat. Presbyterian. Home: Lumberton, NC. Died Feb. 2, 2010.

LEE, HOWARD DOUGLAS, academic administrator; b. Louisville, Ky., Mar. 15, 1943; s. Howard W. and Margaret (Davidson) L.; m. Margaret Easley, Nov. 20, 1965; children: Gregory Davidson, Elizabeth Anna. BA in English, U. Richmond, 1964; ThM, Southeastern Seminary, Wake Forest, NC, 1968; PhD in Religion, U. Iowa, Iowa City, 1971. Prof. religion, devel. dir. Va. Intermont Coll., Bristol, 1971-73; dir. univ. relations Wake Forest (N.C.) U., 1973-78; v.p. devel. Stetson U., DeLand, Fla., 1978-80, v.p. planning and devel., 1980-83, exec. v.p., 1984-86, pres.-elect, 1986-87, pres., 1987—2009. Contbr. articles to profl. jours. Founding dir. Atlantic Ctr. for Arts, New Smyrna Beach, Fla., 1978—; chmn. DeLand C. of C., 1994; chair Volusia Vision Com., 1994-96. Mem. So. Assn. Colls. and Schs. (exec. coun. 1993-94), Rotary, Deland Country Club, Omicron Delta Kappa. Avocations: running, golf, wood carving, woodworking/antiques, reading. Home: Deland, Fla. Died Aug. 25, 2009.

LEE, JUNE WARREN, dentist; b. Boston, Feb. 24, 1952; d. Earl Arnold and Rosemary Regina (Leary) Warren; m. William Lee, July 25, 1976; children: Jaime Michelle, Daniel William. BA, Brandeis U., 1973; DDS, Georgetown U., 1977; student, U.S. Dental Inst., 1985-87. Pvt. practice, Boston, from 1977. Mem. Dorchester Bd. of Trade, from 2000. Active Pierce Mid. Sch. PTO, 1997-2000, Cunningham Sch. PTO, Milton, Mass., 1987-97, Parent-Adv. Coun., Collicot Elem. Sch., Milton, 1986-87; dental instr. Cunningham Sch., 1987-97; dental screening Healthworks, Neponset Health Ctr., Boston, 1981-84; bd. dirs. Delta Dental Plan Mass., 1995-2001, Delta Dental Found. Mass., 1995-2001; vol. Dentist for SmileLine On-Line, 2001-02, Masons Child Identification Program, 2000-2005. Master Acad. Gen. Dentistry (coun. ann. meetings and internat. confs. 1993-98, 2002-, chmn. 1998 local arrangements com., past pres. New Eng. Mastertrack program, pres. Mass. chpt. 1998-2001, past chmn. editl. rev. bd. Audiodent, coun. constn. and bylaws and jud. procedures 2001-02, region one dir. 2003—); fellow Am. Coll. Dentists, Internat. Coll. Dentists, Acad. Dentistry Internat.; mem. ADA, Mass. Dental Soc. (allied profl. liaison com. 1998-99, 2000-01, amb. 2000), Yankee Dental Congress (mem. steering com. 1998-2001, 2004—, chmn. steering com. 2005-06, chmn. ednl. continuum 2005—, gen. chmn. 2003-04, co-chmn. social and cultural com., 2001, co-chmn. sci. com., 1998, co-chmn. gen. arrangements, 1996, allied sci. co-chmn. 1994), South Shore Dist. Dental Soc. (chmn.-elect 1991, chmn. 1992, chmn. program com. 1995-96), Am. Orthodontic Soc., Am. Assn. for Functional Orthodontics (master 2005), Am. Assn. Women Dentists (sec. 1987, v.p. 1988, pres. 1990, A.T. Cross Co. Women of Achievement award 1985, bd. dirs., treas. Gillette Hayden Meml. Found. 1996-2000, Lucy Hobbs Taylor award 2004), Women's Dental Soc. Mass. (sec. 1978, v.p. 1979-81, pres. 1981-83, advisor to bd. 2003—), Mass. Dentists Interested in Legislation, Chestnut Hill Rsch. Study Club. Roman Catholic. Avocations: travel, genealogy, reading, writing, celtic music. Home: Milton, Mass. Died Apr. 4, 2010.

LEE, LAURENCE RAYMOND, retired pharmaceutical company executive; b. Chgo., Feb. 3, 1928; s. Victor L. and Evelyn (Plumhoff) L.; m. Barbara E. Rogers, Jan. 28, 1956; children: Justin, David. PhB, U. Chgo., 1946, JD, 1951. Bar: Ill. 1951. Assoc. Miller, Gorham, Wescott & Adams, Chgo., 1951-55; atty. Abbott Labs., North Chicago, Ill., 1955-63, v.p., sec., gen. counsel, 1963-81, sr. v.p., sec., 1981-88, ret., 1988. Bd. dirs., v.p. Clara Abbott Found., 1981—; trustee Village Lak Bluff, Ill., 1989—, Lake Forest Coll., 1991—. With U.S. Army, 1946-48. Home: Lake Bluff, Ill. Died Jan. 7, 2010.

LEE, MILDRED SCHIFF, art consultant, art gallery executive; b. Columbus, Ohio, Apr. 4, 1920; d. Robert W. and Rebecca (Lurie) Schiff; B.A., U. Wis., 1941; m. Herbert C. Lee, Oct. 21, 1941; children— Thomas H., Richard S., Jonathan. Owner, operator Lee Gallery, Belmont, Mass., 1970—; mem. art bd. overseers Brandeis U., 1963-72; mem. visitors com. Mus. Fine Arts, 1973-77; chmn. Com. to Rescue Italian Art, 1967; art history tchr. Belmont Hill Sch., 1965-68; modern art lectr. Adult Edn. Groups, 1960-68; co-chmn. art exhbns. and sales, bd. dirs. Friends of Art, Boston U., 1960-61; mem. council of friends, mem. acquisition com. Decordova and Dana Mus.; charge outdoor art exhbns. and music festivals Cape Cod Conservatory Music and Art, 1958-59. Pres., Friends of Rose Art Mus.; sec. bd. dirs. Assn. of Art of Music; bd. dirs. Boston U. Youth Symphony Orch., New Arts Orch., Young Audiences, Am. Jewish Com., Jewish Family and Childrens Service, League Women Voters of Brookline; trustee, adviser music com. Belmont Community Center; trustee womens com., Belmont area chmn. Combined Jewish Appeal; mem. womens com. Brandeis U., leader art study groups, mem. Extended Ednl. Program for Women; bd. overseers Met. Center. Clubs: Belmont Country, Belmont Hill. Home: Belmont, Mass. Died May 7, 2009.

LEE, PALI JAE, retired librarian, writer; b. Nov. 26, 1925; d. Jonathan Everett Wheeler and Ona Katherine (Grunder) Stead; m. Richard H.W. Lee, Apr. 7, 1945 (div. 1978); children: Catherine Lani Honcoop, Karin Elizabeth Robinson, Ona G., Laurie Brett, Robin Louise Halbert; m. John K. Willis, 1979 (dec. 1994). Student, U. Hawaii, 1944-46, Mich. State U., East Lansing, 1961-64. Cataloguer and processor US Army Air Force, 1945-46; with US Weather Bur. Film Library, New Orleans, 1948-50, FBI, Wright-Patterson AFB, Dayton, Ohio, 1952, Ohio Wholesale Winedealers, Columbus, Ohio, 1956-58, Coll. Engring., Ohio State U., Columbus, 1959; writer tech. manual Annie Whittenmeyer Home, Davenport, Iowa, 1960; with Grand Rapids Pub. Libr., Mich., 1961-62; dir. Waterford Twp. Librs., Mich., 1962-64; acquisition librarian Pontiac Pub. Librs., Mich., 1965-71, dir. East Side br. Mich., 1971-73; rsch. asst. dept. anthropology Bishop Mus., Honolulu, 1975-83; pub. Night Rainbow Pub., Honolulu, from 1984. Author: HIstory of Wine Growing in America, 1952, House Parenting at its Best, 1960, Mary Dyer, Child of Light, 1973, Giant: Pictorial History of the Human Colossus, 1973, History of Change: Kaneohe Bay Area, 1976, English edit., 1983, Tales of the Night Rainbow, 1981, rev. edit., 1988, Mo'olelo O Na Pohukaina, 1983, Ka Ipu Kukui, 1994, Ho'opono, 1999, rev. edit., 2007, Remembrance: The History of a Family, 2003; contbr. articles to profl. jours. Chmn. Oakland County br. Multiple Sclerosis Soc., 1972-73, co-chmn. Pontiac com. of Mich. area bd., 1972-73; sec. Ohana o Kokua, 1979-83, Paia-Willis Ohana, 1982-91, Ohana Kame'ekua, 1988-91; bd. dirs. Detroit Multiple Sclerosis Soc., 1971; mem. Mich. area bd. Am. Friends Svc. com., 1961-69; mem. consumer adv. bd. Libr. for Blind and Physically Handicapped, Honolulu, 1997—, bd. dirs. 1999—; pres. Blind 55 plus Hawaii Ctr. for Ind. Living, 1990-94, pres., 1995-96; pres. Honolulu chpt. Nat. Fedn. of Blind, 1991-93, 1st v.p. #93 state affiliate, 1991-93, editor Na Na Maka Aloha newsletter, 1990-94 Recipient Mother of the Yr. award Quad City Bus. Men, 1960, Bowl of Light award Cmty. Hawaii, 1989. Mem. Soc. Friends, Talking Book Readers Club (1st v.p. Hawaii chpt. 1994-95, pres., 1996, corr. sec. 2000-05), Hahamenalima Club (chmn. youth outreach com.), Peace and Social Concerns Soc. Friends (corr. dinajor, peace sub com.). Home: Honolulu, Hawaii. Died Mar. 22, 2009.

LEECH, NOYES ELWOOD, lawyer, educator; b. Ambler, Pa., Aug. 1, 1921; m. Louise Ann Gallagher, Apr. 19, 1954; children: Katharine, Gwyneth. AB, U. Pa., 1943, JD, 1948. Bar: Pa. 1949. Assoc. Dechert, Price & Rhoads (and predecessors), Phila., 1948-49, 51-53; mem. faculty law sch. U. Pa., Phila., 1949-57, prof., 1957-78, Ferdinand Wakeman Hubbell prof. law, 1978-85, William A. Schnader prof. law, 1985-86, prof. emeritus, from 1986. Co-author: The International Legal System, 3d edit., 1988; gen. editor: Jour. Comparative Bus. and Capital Market Law, 1978-86. Mem. Order of Coif, Phi Beta Kappa. Home: Philadelphia, Pa. Died July 1, 2010.

LEECH, SPENCER JENNINGS, JR., information services company information services company executive, communications consultant; b. Greenwich, Conn., Apr. 5, 1938; s. Spencer Jennings and Emilie T. (Lesher) Leech; m. Alice Turner Michalak Leech, Apr. 22, 1961 (div. 1981); children: Spencer Jennings III, Elizabeth T., Susanne A.; m. Nancy D. Lewis Leech, June 7, 1982. Applied sci. rep. IBM, Washington, 1960—64, project mgr. NYC, 1964—68, nat. acct. dir., 1968—77; cons. Pacific Basin Countries, 1967—80; cons., pres. Orion Assocs. Ltd., Honolulu, 1980—84; pres. Home Vue Hawaii Inc., Honolulu, 1983; dir. Pacific Telecomm. Coun., Honolulu, from 1981, Intelect, Inc., Honolulu. Mem.: Royal N.Z. Yacht Squadron Club (Auckland), Cruising Club (NYC). Home: Honolulu, Hawaii. Died July 3, 2010.

LEEPA, ALLEN, artist, educator; b. NYC, Jan. 9, 1919; s. Harvey and Esther (Gentle) L. Student (scholar), The New Bauhaus Sch., 1937-38; scholar, Hans Hofmann Sch., 1938-39; BS, Columbia U., 1942, MA (scholar), 1948, Ed.D., 1960. Art instr. Hull Sch., Chgo., 1937-38, Bklyn. Art Ctr., 1939-40, 99, Met. Mus., NYC, 1940-41, St. Marks Center, NYC, 1941-42; draftsman Acrotorque Co., Conn., 1942, Glen Martin Aircraft, NYC, 1942-44; prof. art Mich. State U., 1945-84, ret. prof. emeritus. Mem. Leepa Gallery of Fine Art, Tarpon Springs, Fla., 1987-90. Author: The Challenge of Modern Art, 1949, 95, Abraham Rattner, 1974; contbr.: (anthologies) The New Art, 1966, 68, The Humanitites in Contemporary Life, 1960, Minimal Art; art editor: The Centennial Rev. Arts and Scis. Jour., 1959-62; one man shows Artists Gallery, N.Y.C., 1953, La Cours D'Ingres, Paris, 1961, Artists Mart, Detroit, 1969, Duke U., 1981; group shows include Mus. Modern Art, N.Y.C., 1953, VII Bienal, São Paulo, Brazil, 1963, Prado Mus., Madrid, Spain, 1956, Detroit Inst. Arts, 1948, 50, 56, 80, Pa. Acad. Fine Arts, 1951, 63; represented in permanent collections Mich. State U., Grand Rapids (Mich.) Mus., South Bend (Ind.) Mus.; lifetime work Tampa Mus. Fine Art, Leepa/Rattner Mus. Fine Arts St. Petersburg (Fla.) Jr. Coll. Fulbright award to Paris, 1950-51; Ford Found. grantee Brazil, 1970; recipient numerous prizes for paintings including: 1st prize statewide mural competition, Mich., 1983; 1st prize abstract painting Guild Hall Mus., East Hampton, N.Y., 1985 Mem. Mich. Acad. Arts, Scis., Letters. Died June 26, 2009.

LEES, JAMES EDWARD, health science facility administrator; b. Cleve., Dec. 11, 1939; s. Thomas Murray and Marian Lees; m. Charlotte Anderson, 1964; children: Allison Marie, Shannon Anderson. BA, Kenyon Coll., 1962; cert. advanced mgmt. program, Case Western Res. U., 1972, MBA, 1981; cert. health systems mgmt. program, Harvard U., 1975. Rsch. adminstr. Cleve. Clinic Found., 1964-69, adminstrv. asst. div. pathology, 1967-69, adminstrv. asst. bd. govs., 1969-70, dir. clinic adminstrn., 1970-71, acting dir. personnel, 1974, exec. sec. bd. govs., 1972-79, assoc. dir. ops., 1979-80, dir. ops., 1980-89, chief adminstrv. officer, from 1980, North Beach Hosp., from 1990. Insp. Accreditation Assn. for Ambulatory Health Care, Skokie, Ill., 1979—; pres., bd. trustees Calcilex Corp., Cleve., 1985—; clin. asst. prof. U. Pitts., 1983-85; instr. Capital U., Columbus, Ohio, 1984; vis. com. Frances Payne Bolton Sch. Nursing, Cleve., 1982—; corp. bd. mem. Community Dialysis Ctr., Cleve., 1978-79; bd. trustees Organ Recovery Inc., Cleve., 1984-87; mem. exec. com. No. Ohio Red Cross Blood Program, Cleve., 1967-69, planning com. Met. Health Planning Assn., Cleve., 1978-79. Mem., grad. Leadership Cleve./Greater Cleve. Growth Assn., 1978; bd. dirs. Conv. Bur. Greater Cleve., 1978-80. Fellow Am. Coll. Med. Group Administrators (examiner 1980); mem. Am. Group Practice Assn., Greater Cleve. Hosp. Assn. (exec. com.) Avocation: horticulture. Home: Cleveland, Ohio. Died Sept. 4, 2009.

LEFRAK, JOSEPH SAUL, lawyer, accountant; b. NYC, Sept. 23, 1930; s. Paul B. and Elizabeth (Iken) L.; m. Susan Siskind, Sept. 14, 1952; children: Babette C., Mark P. (dec.) Student, NYU, 1948-52; BS, Bklyn. Law Sch., JD, 1955. Cert. CFP; Bar: N.Y. 1955, Fla. 1978, U.S. Supreme Ct. 1960. Practice law, NYC and Palm Beach, Fla.; partner firm Winter & Lefrak, C.P.A.s, NYC, 1959-66, Blackman, Lefrak & Blackman, C.P.A.s, NYC, 1966-72; ptnr. law firm Lefrak & Holman P.C., NYC, West Palm Beach, Fla., from 1966. Trustee, past pres. Congregation Rodeph Sholom, N.Y.C. Mem. ABA, N.Y. State Bar Assn., Fla. Bar Assn., Am. Inst. CPA's, N.Y. Soc. CPA's, Fla. Soc. CPA's, Am. Assn. Atty. CPA's, N.Y. Assn. Atty. CPA's, Union Am. Hebrew Congregations (bd. dirs.). Clubs: City Athletic, Friars, Mamaroneck, Yacht (N.Y.) (commodore 1981-83). Home: New York, NY. Died Aug. 26, 2009.

LEHMAN, WILLIAM LEWIS, other: manufacturing; b. Pemberville, Ohio, Aug. 3, 1936; s. Ernest Henry and Opal Lavern (Milnor) Lehman; m. Mary Sylvia Owens, Jan. 22, 1956; children: Daniel L., Paul H., Thomas J. BS in Sales and Sales Mgmt., Bowling Green State U., Ohio, 1961. Salesman Kimberly Clark Corp., Columbus, Ohio, 1961—63, IBM Corp., Columbus, 1963—64, Ortho Diagnostics, Ohio, Ind., W.Va, Ky., 1965—67, Spectra Biologicals, Ohio, Ind., W.Va., Ky., 1967—70; v.p., dir. purchasing Gamma Biologicals, Inc., Houston, 1970—85; corporate v.p. Diagnostics Internat., Inc., Conroe, Tex. Sgt. USMC, 1954—57. Mem.: Beta Gamma Sigma. Republican. Methodist. Home: Cypress, Tex. Died May 18, 2010.

LEHNHART, ROBERT EARL, international studies educator; b. LA, Nov. 4, 1932; s. Howard Clinton and Anne Romaine (Killian) L.; m. Mary Lou Barth, June 30, 1956; children: Kathleen, Gary, Ron. BA, Bryan Coll., 1954; grad., Flight and Mechanics Inst., 1958; MA, Johns Hopkins U., 1995. Dir. internat. ops. Mission Aviation Fellowship, Fullerton, Calif., 1959-73; mktg. mgr. mfrs. and real estate cos., Orange, Calif., 1973-78; gen. mgr. Orange County Athletic Clubs, 1978-81; dir. emergency relief & devel. Mission Aviation Fellowship, Redlands, Calif., 1981-84; founder, pres., CEO Air Serv Internat., Redlands, 1984-94. Fellow Case Method Inst. Assn. Case Tchg. Presbyterian. Home: Lake Forest, Calif. Died Aug. 17, 2009.

LEHRER, ROBERT NATHANIEL, retired engineering educator, executive, consultant; b. Sandusky, Ohio, Jan. 17, 1922; s. Henry William and Margaret (Boyd) L.; m. Patricia Lee Martin, July 7, 1945; children— Joan Elizabeth. BS in Mech. Engrng. with distinction, Purdue U., 1945, MS, 1947, PhD, 1949; student engrng., Midshipman Sch., 1945. Registered profl. engr., Ga. Research asst., instr. Purdue U., 1946-49; asst. prof. indsl. engrng. Oreg. State Coll., 1949-50; assoc. prof. indsl. engrng., research assoc. Ga. Inst. Tech., 1950-54, prof. indsl. engrng., research assoc., 1954-58; prof. indsl. engrng., chmn. dept. Technol. Inst., Northwestern U., 1958-63; prof., assoc. dir. Sch. Indsl. Engrng., Ga. Inst. Tech., Atlanta, 1963-66; dir. Sch. Indsl. and Systems Engrng., 1966-78, prof., 1978-81, prof. emeritus, dir. emeritus, from 1981. Assoc., vis. sr. adv. Am. Productivity Ctr., 1978-79; cons., 1950—; mem. Nat. Acad. Scis. panel to Indonesia, 1971. Author: Work Simplification: Creative Thinking About Work Problems, 1957, The Management of Improvement: Concepts, Organization and Strategy, 1965, Participative Productivity and Quality of Work Life, 1982, White Collar Productivity, 1983; editor-in-chief: Jour. Indsl. Engrng, 1953-61, exec. editor, 1961-62; cons. editor textbook series Reinhold Pub. Corp., 1960-67; contbr. articles to tech. jours. Adv. bd. mil. personnel supplies NRC, 1965-68; mem. nat. research council Am. Acad. Scis., 1965-68; expert indsl. engrng. UNESCO, Mexico, 1962-63; mem. adv. bd. dept. indsl. engrng. Coll. Engrng., Clemson U., 1984-90. Served with USNR, 1943-46. Designated Disting. Alumnus, Purdue U., 1964; recipient Frank and Lillian Gilbreath Indsl. Engrng. award Inst. Indsl. Engrs., 1987. Fellow Am. Inst. Indsl. Engrs. (Outstanding Indsl. engr. in Southeast 1957, v.p. publs. 1960-62), AAAS; mem. Sigma Xi, Tau Beta Pi, Phi Kappa Phi, Alpha Pi Mu, Pi Tau Sigma, Phi Delta Theta. Episcopalian. Home: Atlanta, Ga. Died Jan. 25, 2010.

LEIBLUM, SANDRA RISA, psychology educator; b. Bklyn., Aug. 18, 1943; m.; 1 child, Jonathan Kassen. AB, Bklyn. Coll. CUNY, 1965; MA, U. Ill., 1968, PhD, 1971. Staff mem. U. Ill. Psychol. Clinic, Urbana, 1967-68; adult clin. pschology intern Worcester (Mass.) Youth Guidance Ctr., 1968-69, child clin. psychology intern, 1969-70; postdoctoral fellow U. Colo. Med. Ctr., Denver, 1971-72; grad. psychology faculty Rutgers U., New Brunswick, N.J., from 1972; prof. clin. ob-gyn. U. Medicine and Dentistry N.J. Robert Wood Johnson Med. Sch., New Brunswick, 1984—2007, prof. clin. psychiatry Piscataway, N.J., from 1988; pvt. practice Bridgewater, Mass., from 2008. Con. Neighborhood Youth Corps, Worcester, 1968-69; co-dir. sexual counseling svc., UMDNJ Robert Wood Johnson Med. Sch., 1972—, dir. internship in clin./community psychology, 1988—. Co-editor: Sexual Desire Disorders, 1988, Principles and Practices of Sex Therapy --update 90s, 1989 (Guilford, 2007); author: How to Do Psychotherapy and How to Evaluate It; co-author: Getting the Sex You Want: A woman's guide to becoming proud, passionate and pleased in bed (Crowne, 2002); contbr. articles to profl. jours. Mem. APA, Soc. Sex Therapy and Rsch. (pres. 1991, Masters & Johnson Lifetime Achievement award), Am. Assn. for Sex Educators, Counselors and Therapists (award), N.J. Psychol. Assn., Am. Soc. Psychosomatic Ob-Gyn., Internat. Acad. Sex Rsch. Achievements include first president of the International Society for the Study of Women's Sexual Health. Home: Bridgewater, NJ. Died Jan. 28, 2010.

LEMBERGER, AUGUST PAUL, university dean, pharmacy educator; b. Milw., Jan. 25, 1926; s. Max N. and Celia (Gehl) L.; m. Charlyne A. Young, June 30, 1947; children: Michael, Mary, Thomas, Terrence, Ann, Kathryn, Peter. BS, U. Wis., 1948, PhD, 1952. Sr. chemist Merck & Co., Inc., Rahway, N.J., 1952-53; asst. prof. U. Wis. Sch. Pharmacy, 1953-57, asso. prof., 1957-63, prof. pharmacy, 1963-69; prof. pharmacy, dean U. Ill. Coll. Pharmacy, Chgo., 1969-80, U. Wis.-Madison Sch. Pharmacy, 1980-91, ret., 1991. Sec. Wis. Pharmacy Internship Bd., 1965-69; conf. dir. Nat. Indsl. Pharm. Research Conf., 1966-69; mem. Am. Council on Pharm. Edn., 1978-84, v.p., 1980-84 Served to 1st lt. AUS, 1944-46. Recipient Kiekhofer Meml. Teaching award U. Wis., 1957, citation of merit, 1977, Disting. Pharmacist award Wis. Pharm. Assn., 1969, Higuchi Lecture award Acad. Pharm. Sci. and Tech., Japan, 1989, Pres.' award Wis. Soc. Hosp. Pharmacists, 1991, Alumnus of Yr. award Pharmacy Alumni Assn., 1991. Fellow AAAS, Am. Found. for Pharm. Edn. (Disting. Svc. Profile award 1990), Acad. Pharm. Scis., Am. Assn. Pharm. Scientists; mem. Am. Soc. Hosp. Pharmacists, Am. Assn. Colls. Pharmacy (past com. chmn., exec. com. 1971-74, chmn. coun. deans 1975-77, chmn. sect. tchrs. of pharmacy Conf. Tchrs., hon. pres. 1993-94), Acad. Pharm. Scis. (v.p. 1976-77, pres. 1983-84), Am. Pharm. Assn. (mem. jud. bd. 1976-79, trustee 1985-88, treas. 1989-90, hon. pres. 1996-97), Wis. Pharm. Assn., Sigma Xi, Rho Chi (v.p. 1979-81, pres. 1981-83). Home: Madison, Wis. Died Feb. 16, 2010.

LENOIR, WILLIAM BENJAMIN, retired astronaut; b. Miami, Fla., Mar. 14, 1939; s. Samuel S. Lenoir; m. Elizabeth Lenoir, 1964; children: William Benjamin, Samantha. SB, MIT, 1961, SM, 1962, PhD, 1965. Asst. elec. engr. MIT, Cambridge, 1962-64, instr., 1964-65, asst. prof., 1965-67, Ford fellow engrng., 1965-66; scientist-astronaut Johnson Space Ctr. NASA, Houston, 1967-84, mission specialist, 5th Mission of Columbia, 1982, assoc. adminstr. for space flight, 1989—92; with Booz Allen & Hamilton, Inc., Arlington, Va., 1984—89, v.p. applied systems divsn., 1992—2010. Recipient Exceptional Svc. medal, NASA, 1974, Space Flight medal, 1982. Mem. AAAS, Am. Geophys. Union Died Aug. 28, 2010.

LENZ, ROBERT WILLIAM, polymer chemistry educator; b. NYC, Apr. 28, 1926; s. Henry B. and Olga A. (Grote) L.; m. Madeleine Leblanc, June 6, 1953; children: Kathleen, Douglas, Cynthia, Suzanne. BSChemE, Lehigh U., 1949; PhD, SUNY, Syracuse, 1956. Rsch. chemist Chicopee Mfg. Co., Chicopee Falls, Mass., 1951-53, Dow Chem. Co., Midland, Mich., 1955-61, Framingham, Mass., 1961-63; asst. dir. FRL Inc., Dedham, Mass., 1963-66; prof. U. Mass., Amherst, 1996-95, prof. emeritus, from 1995. Cons. many cos. in the chem. industry, 1966—; dist. faculty lectr. U. Mass., 1994. Author: Organic Chemistry of Synthetic High Polymers, 1967; assoc. editor Macromolecules, 1982-94, editor-in-chief, 1995—; contbr. over 375 articles to publs. Mem. adv. bd. Petroleum Rsch. Fund, 1989-93, Greve Found., N.Y.C., 1988-94; bd. dirs. Cult Awareness Network, Chgo., 1989-91. Recipient Sr. Humboldt prize, Humboldt Found., Bonn, Fed. Republic of Germany, 1979, Polymer Chemistry award Am. Chem. Soc., 1992, Outstanding Contbns. to Polymer Chemistry award Soc. of Polymer Sci. Japan, 1995; faculty fellow U. Mass., 1984. Achievements include 16 patents in field. Home: Amherst, Mass. Died July 2, 2010.

LEON, DENNIS, sculptor; b. London, July 27, 1933; came to U.S., 1951, naturalized, 1956; s. Ralph and Rebecca (Stone) L.; m. Joan Schaefer, Mar. 20, 1964 (div.); children: Ann, Susan; m. Christin Ann Nelson, 1985. BFA, Temple U., 1956, BS in Edn, 1956, MFA, 1957; Doctor (hon.), Calif. Coll. Arts and Crafts, 1993. Head dept. fine arts Phila. Coll. Art, 1965-67, chmn. dept. sculpture, 1967-70; prof. sculpture Calif. Coll. Arts and Crafts, Oakland, 1972-93, prof. emeritus, from 1993. Exhibited in numerous one-man shows including Kraushaar Gallery, N.Y.C., 1966, 68, 70, Hansen Fuller Goldeen Gallery, 1985, San Francisco, 1977, 79, 81-82, 84-85, Galleria D'Arte del Cavallino, Venice, Italy, 1978, San Jose Mus. Art, 1981, Jewish Mus. San Francisco, 1986, Goldeen Gallery, L.A., 1988, 89, 90, 92, Calif. State U., Fresno, 1990, Chemeketa Coll., Salem, Oreg., 1991, Anne Reid Gallery, Ketchum, Idaho, 1991, Cheryl Haines Gallery, San Francisco, 1991, 93, Butters Gallery, Portland, Oreg., 1991, Dorthy Goldeen Gallery, Santa Monica, Calif., 1991, Anne Reed Gallery, Ketchum, Idaho, 1991, Chemeketa Coll. Sale, 1991; exhibited in group shows including U. Calif. at Davis, 1974, Phila. Mus. Art, 1976, San Francisco Mus. Art, 1977, Newport Harbor Mus., 1981, Oakland (Calif.) Mus., 1989, Hudson River Mus. N.Y., 1990; represented in permanent collections Phila. Mus. Art, Oakland Mus. Art, San Francisco Mus. Modern Art, Storm King Art Ctr., N.Y., Bank of Ams., Phillip Morris Collection, Corcoran Mus. Art., Rutgers Archive; work commd. by Chevron Oil Co., 1986. Cons. La. State Bd. Regents, 1980. Served with U.S. Army, 1957-59. Recipient Nat. Inst. Arts and Letters award, 1967; fellow Guggenheim Found., 1967, Macdowell Found., 1981, Djerassi Found., 1983-84; grantee San Francisco Mus. Modern Art, 1978, Nat. Endowment for Arts, 1979. Home: Oakland, Calif. Deceased.

LEONARD, HERMAN, photographer; b. Allentown, Pa., 1923; BFA, Ohio U., 1947; apprentice to master photographer Yousuf Karsh, Ottawa, 1947—48; MS in photography (hon.), Brooks Inst. Photography, Santa Barbara, Calif., 1995. Independent photographer, from 1949; personal photographer to Marlon Brando, 1956; European photographer Playboy, Paris; founder Herman Leonard Jazz Archive, 2007—10. Represented in permanent collections Smithsonian Inst., Washington, Jazz at Lincoln Ctr., NYC, Ogden Mus. Southern Art, LA, George Eastman House, NY; author: The Eye of Jazz, 1985, Jazz Memories, 1995, Jazz, Giants, and Journeys: The Photography of Herman Leonard, 2006. Anesthetist 13th Mountain Med. Bn. US Army, 1943—45, Burma. Recipient Milt Hinton award for Excellence in Jazz Photography, Jazz Photographer's Assn., 1999, Excellence in Photography award, Jazz Journalists Assn., 2000, Lifetime Achievement award, Downbeat mag., 2004, Lucie award for Achievement in Portraiture, Internat. Photography Awards, 2008. Died Aug. 14, 2010.

LEONARD, LAWRENCE LE ROY, JR., family counselor, clergyman; b. Bklyn., Nov. 28, 1943; s. Lawrence Le Roy and Elizabeth (Schell) L.; B.A., Pacific Coll., 1972; postgrad. Columbia U., 1975; D.D., Universal Life Ch., 1979, Ph.D., 1980; D.Metaphysics, 1981. Asst. to asso. dir. Fresh Air Fund, N.Y.C., 1973-74; ordained to ministry Universal Life Ch., 1972; family counselor Agy. Child Devel., Human Resources Adminstrn., N.Y.C., 1974-77; regional supr., legal services specialist Day Care Council N.Y., 1977-78; pvt. practice family counseling, St. Albans, N.Y., 1974—; pres. Paper Talk Counseling Service; former chmn. bd. trustees St. Albans Congregation Universal Life Ch.; program coordinator N.Y.C. Community Centers; condr. leadership seminars for Day Care Center dirs. Producer, dir. S.E. Queens Youth Programs; pres. Positive Praise Award Program; mem. Jamaica Polit. Action League; community liaison Neighborhood Council Services; producer Children's Creative Arts Festival, 1975; scoutmaster Neighborhood Services council Boy Scouts Am., 1974; nat. bd. adv. Am. Biog. Inst. Served with USMC, 1963-69. Recipient honors for USO show, French Consul, Marseilles, France, 1965; cert. family counselor Human Resources Adminstrn.; cert. comml. photographer; holder black belt in martial arts. Mem. Nat. Assn. Edn. of Young Children, Day Care Council N.Y., Smithsonian Inst., Nat. Geog. Soc., Martinist Order (asso.), Internat. Platform Assn., Assn. Research and Enlightenment, Planetary Citizens. Club: Rosicrucian Order (10 deg.). Inventor painting instrument; editor, pub. Axis mag., 1968; co-dir. Actors Quarters, San Diego, 1968; art works exhibited Southwestern Coll., Calif., 1970, Lynn Kottler Galleries, N.Y.C., 1971; profl. flutist, composer; author: Self-Mastery, 1982. Died June 5, 2009.

LEONE, IDA ALBA, retired plant pathology educator; b. Elizabeth, NJ, Apr. 28, 1922; d. Joseph and Josephine (Aprigliano) L. BS, N.J. Coll. for Women, 1944; MS, Rutgers U., 1946. Rsch. asst. Cook Coll., Rutgers U., New Brunswick, N.J., 1946-61, asst. rsch. specialist, 1961-71, assoc. rsch. prof. plant pathology, 1971-76, rsch. prof. I, 1976-86, prof. II, 1986-88, prof. II emerita, from 1988. Expert witness N.Y. State Dept. Environ. Conservation, Albany, 1975-76; mem. siting com. Atlantic Electric Co., Atlantic City, 1979; mem. rsch. adv. com. Lake Erie Generating Sta., Niagara Mohawk Power Corp., Syracuse, N.Y., 1985-88 Contbr. over 175 articles to sci. jours., chpts. to books. Mem. Rahway (N.J.) Air Pollution Commn., 1970-80; commr. Cen. Jersey Air Pollution Control Agy., Woodbridge, N.J., 1970-80; trustee Amateur Astronomers, Inc., Cranford, N.J., 1984-86, St. John the Apostle Ch., Linden, N.J., 1985—, choir mem., 1964, trustee fin. com., 1985; vol. N.J. Coalition for the Homeless, 1990—, St. Joseph Civic Ctr. Soup Kitchen, Elizabeth, 1990—. Recipient AMITA award Nat. Italian-Am. Found., 1966, Disting. Prof. award Rutgers U., 1987; scholar State of N.J., 1940-44. Mem. Am. Soc. Plant Physiologists, Am. Phytopath. Soc., Air and Waste Mgmt. Soc. (chmn. ecology com. 1986-88), N.J. Jr. Acad. Sci. (bd. dirs. 1988—, dir. 1990—), Audubon Soc., Douglas Soc. (elected). Roman Catholic. Avocations: travel, music, reading, amateur astronomy, volunteering. Home: Westfield, NJ. Died Apr. 18, 2009.

LESLIE, HENRY ARTHUR, lawyer, retired bank executive; b. Troy, Ala., Oct. 15, 1921; s. James B. and Alice (Minchener) L.; m. Anita Doyle, Apr. 5, 1943; children: Anita Lucinda Leslie Bagby, Henry Arthur Jr. BS, U. Ala., 1942, JD, 1948; JSD, Yale U., 1959; grad., Rutgers U., 1964. Bar: Ala. 1948. Asst. prof. bus. law U. Ala., 1948-50, 52-54; prof., asst. dean U. Ala. Sch. Law, 1954-59; v.p. trust officer Birmingham Trust Nat. Bank, 1959-64; sr. v.p., trust officer Union Bank & Trust Co., Montgomery, Ala., 1964-73, sr. v.p., sr. loan officer, 1973-76, exec. v.p., 1976-78, pres. CEO, 1978-91, bd. dirs.; ret., 1991; pvt. practice Montgomery, from 1991. Mem. Ala. Oil and Gas Bd., 1984-85. Pres. Downtown Unltd., 1983-84; mem. Ala. Bd. Bar Examiners, 1973-78, bd. dirs. YMCA, 1992—; mem., vice-chmn. Ala. Jud. Campaign Oversight Com., 1999-2001; mem. Bus. Com. Arts, 2003—. With US Army, WWII, with USAR, retired as ltd. col. JAGC Res., 1970. Decorated Bronze Star for heroic svc. in France. Mem. ABA, Ala. Bar Assn., Montgomery Bar Assn. (Liberty Bell award 1989), Ala. Ind. Bankers (chmn. 1983-84), Ala. Bankers Assn. (trust div. pres. 1963-65), Ind. Bankers Assn. Am. (dir. 1983-90), Ala. World Affairs Coun. (past pres.), Farrah Order Jurisprudence (pres. 1973), Order of Coif Alumni, Montgomery C. of C. (dir. 1983-84, pres. 1987-88), Maxwell Officers Club, Montgomery Country Club, Regional Kiwanis Club, Delta Sigma Pi, Phi Delta Phi, Omicron Delta Kappa, Pi Kappa Phi. Episcopalian (past sr. warden). Home: Montgomery, Ala. Died June 26, 2009.

LESTZ, GERALD SAMUEL, author, editor, publisher; b. Lancaster, Pa., Mar. 29, 1914; s. Jacob Louis and Fannie (Simon) L.; m. Edith Allport, Aug. 2, 1944 (dec. 1957); children— Michael E., Linda Lestz Weidman; m. Margaret E. Gordon, Apr. 24, 1958; stepchildren— Rien Boebel (dec.), Robert G. Dana. B.S., Wharton Sch., U. Pa., 1935. Reporter, Lancaster Ind., Pa., 1935-37, Lancaster New Era, 1937-41; columnist, editorial writer Lancaster New Era, 1946-79; editor Baer's Agrl. Almanac, Lancaster, 1948—; editor, pub. Stemgas Pub. Co., Lancaster, 1975—, Strasburg Weekly News (Pa.), 1986—, ptnr. Barr-Hurst Book Shop, 1987—. Author various books on history of Lancaster, Amish culture. pres. Heritage Ctr. Mus.; past pres. Lancaster Summer Arts Festival; past pres. Demuth Found., Lancaster; active Gov.'s Adv. Council Library Devel., Harrisburg, 1980-84. Served with USAAF, 1942-46. Recipient Connie award Soc. Am. Travel Writers, 1979; Mayor's Red Rose award Mayor Wohlsen, Lancaster, 1979; various news awards. Mem. Pa. Guild Craftsmen (past state pres.). Republican. Jewish. Clubs: Hamilton, Montana. Home: Lancaster, Pa. Died Sept. 15, 2009.

LEUKART, RICHARD HENRY, II, lawyer; b. Detroit, Mar. 15, 1942; s. Richard Henry and Marjorie Ruth (Smith) Leukart; m. Barbara Joan Gottfried, Oct. 7, 1977; children: Elisabeth, Jennifer, Kathleen, Richard Henry III, Brian. AB,

Dartmouth Coll., 1964, Amos Tuck Sch. Bus., 1964; JD, U. Mich., 1967. Bar: Ohio 1967. Ptnr. Baker & Hostetler, Cleve., from 1967; chair Firmwide Employment Law and Employee Benefits Group, from 1995. Bd. trustees Hudson Heritage Assn., 1984—88. Alfred P. Sloan Found. scholar, 1960—62, Daniel Webster scholar, 1963—64. Mem.: ABA, County Club of Hudson (trustee from 1996), Cleve. Bar Assn., Ohio Bar Assn., Union Club of Cleve. Republican. Presbyterian. Home: Hudson, Ohio. Died May 2, 2010.

LEVIE, HOWARD S(IDNEY), lawyer, educator; b. Wolverine, Mich., Dec. 19, 1907; s. J. Walter and Mina (Goldfarb) L.; m. S. Blanche Krim, July 24, 1934 AB, Cornell U., 1928, JD, 1930; LL.M., George Washington U., 1957. Bar: N.Y. 1931, Mo. 1965, U.S. Dist. Ct. (ea. dist.) N.Y. 1934, U.S. Dist. Ct. (so. dist.) N.Y. 1935, U.S. Supreme Ct. 1947, U.S. Ct. Appeals (D.C. cir.) 1949, U.S. Ct. Mil. Appeals 1953. Assoc. Weit & Goldman, NYC, 1931-42; with JAGC, U.S. Army, 1942, advanced through grades to col., 1954; staff officer UN Command Armistice Del., Korea, 1951-52; chief internat. affairs div. Office of JAG, 1954-58; legal adviser U.S. European Command, Paris, 1959-61; ret., 1963; prof. law St. Louis U., 1962—72, prof. emeritus, from 1972; prof. U.S. Naval War Coll., Newport, RI, 1972—73, Charles H. Stockton prof. internat. law, 1972—73; instr. internat. law Salve Regina Coll., Newport, RI, 1984-88. Adj. prof. Naval War Coll., 1991—. Author: Prisoners of War in International Armed Conflict (Internat. Soc. for Mil. Law and the Law of War Ciardi prize 1982), 1979, Documents on Prisoners of War, 1980, Protection of War Victims, 4 vols., 1979-81, The Status of Gibraltar, 1983, The Code of International Armed Conflict, 1986, The Law of Non-International Armed Conflict, 1987, The Law of War and Neutrality: A Selected English-Language Bibliography, 1988, Mine Warfare at Sea, 1992, Terrorism in War: The Law of War Crimes, 1993; editor vols. 7-12: Terrorism: Documents of International and Local Control, 1997, Levie on the Law of War, 1998. Decorated Legion of Merit, Bronze Star; grantee Ctr. for Advanced Rsch., Naval War Coll., 1980-82, U.S. Inst. Peace, 1991; Howard S. Levie Mil. Chair of Operational Law established by U.S. Naval War Coll., 1994; recipient Outstanding Civilian Svc. medal Dept. of the Army, 1995; named Disting. Mem. of Judge Advocate Gen.'s Corps Regiment, 1995, The Col. Howard S. Levie Libr., established at the Army Judge Advocate's School is named in his honor. Mem. ABA, Am. Soc. Internat. Law (exec. coun. 1969-70), Internat. Law Assn., Ret. Army Judge Advs. Assn., Internat. Soc. for Mil. Law and Law of War, Phi Beta Kappa. Home: Newton Center, Mass. Died Apr. 19, 2009.

LEVIN, RICHARD LOUIS, retired language educator; b. Buffalo, Aug. 31, 1922; s. Bernard and Meta (Block) Levin; m. Muriel Abrams, June 22, 1952; children: David, Daniel. BA, U. Chgo., 1943, MA, 1947, PhD, 1957. Mem. faculty U. Chgo., 1949-57, asst. prof. English, 1953-57; prof. English, SUNY, Stony Brook, from 1957, acting chmn. English dept., 1960-63, 65-66, ret., 1994. Mem. adv. bd. World Ctr. Shakespeare Studies; mem. acad. adv. coun. Shakespeare Globe Ctr.; Fulbright lectr., 1984—85. Editor: Tragedy: Plays, Theory and Criticism, 1960, The Question of Socrates, 1961, Tragedy Alternate, 1965, Michaelmas Term (Thomas Middleton), 1966, The Multiple Plot in English Renaissance Drama, 1971, New Readings vs. Old Plays: Recent Trends in the Reinterpretation of English Renaissance Drama, 1979, Looking for an Argument: Critical Encounters with the New Approaches to the Criticism of Shakespeare and His Contemporaries, 2003. Served to lt. (j.g.) USNR, 1943—46, ETO. Recipient Explicator award, 1971; fellow, Am. Coun. Learned Socs., 1963—64; Rsch. fellow, SUNY, 1961, 1965—68, 1971, 1973, Faculty Exch. scholar, NEH Sr. fellow, 1974, Guggenheim fellow, 1978—79, Nat. Humanities Ctr. fellow, 1987—88. Mem.: MLA (mem. adv. com. publs., mem. del. assembly), Medieval and Renaissance Drama Soc. (mem. coun.), Shakespeare Assn. Am. (trustee), Internat. Shakespeare Assn., Columbia U. Shakespeare Seminar, Joseph Crabtree Found. Democrat. Jewish. Home: Melville, NY. Died Oct. 30, 2009.

LEVINE, DAVID, artist; b. Bklyn., Dec. 20, 1926; s. Harry and Lena Levine; children: Matthew, Eve. BFA, Temple U. Tyler Sch. Art, Phila., 1949; BS in Edn, Temple U., 1949; student, Hans Hoffman Sch. Paintings, 1950, Pratt Inst., NYC. Illustrator, caricaturist NY Rev. of Books, 1963—2006; numerous other works featured in Esquire. NY Times, Washington Post, Rolling Stone, Sports Illustrated, New York Mag., TIME, Newsweek, The New Yorker, The Nation, Playboy. One-man shows Forum Gallery, NYC, 1966-, Ga. Mus. Art, 1968, Calif. Palace Legion of Honor, 1968-69, 71-72, 83, Wesleyan U., 1970, Bklyn. Mus., 1971, Princeton U., 1972, Galerie Yves Lambert, Paris, 1972, Yale U., 1973, Hirshhorn Mus. and Sculpture Garden, Washington, 1976, Galerie Claude Bernard, 1979, Phillips Gallery, 1980, Pierpont Morgan Library, 1981, Santa Fe East Gallery, 1983, Ash Molean Mus., Meredith Long, Houston, 1984; represented by Forum Gallery; author: The Man From M.A.L.I.C.E., 1966, Pens and Needles, 1969, No Known Survivors, 1970, The Arts of David Levine, 1978, Aesop's Fables. Served with US Army, 1945—46. Recipient Tiffany award, 1955, Isaac N. Maynard prize, 1958, Julius Halligarten prize, 1960, Thomas B. Clark prize, 1962, George Polk award, 1965, Childe Hassam Purchase prize 1972, Benjamin Altman prize, 1973, Gold medal for Graphic Work, Am. Acad. Inst. Arts and Letters, 1992, Thomas Nast award, 1995; Guggenheim fellow, 1967. Mem.: AAAL. Died Dec. 29, 2009.

LEVINE, IRVING STANLEY, lawyer; b. Cleve., Nov. 26, 1928; s. Albert Eli and Sadelle B. (Neff) Brass Levine; m. Joan Kandell, Mar. 21, 1959 (div. 1964); m. Elaine R. Martz, Oct. 3, 1964; children— Kenneth, Robert, Tina, Alan BA, Hobart Coll.; LL.B. cum laude, U. Miami, 1954, JD cum laude, 1967. Bar: Fla., 1955. Pres. Levine, Reckson & Geiger P.A. and predecessors, Miami, 1955-82; ptnr. Blank, Rome, Comisky & McCauley, Miami, 1982-86, Levine & Partners P.A. (formerly Levine & Geiger, P.A.), Miami, 1987—2010. Chmn., bd. dirs. Comml. Trust Bancorp, Inc.; sec., bd. dirs. Airco Plating Co., Miami Bd. dirs. Miami Design Preservation League, sec. Concert Assn. of Fla., Inc., chmn. 1987-91, dir. 1987-91; trustee Mt. Sinai Med. Ctr.; sec., co-chmn. laws com., 1985; mem. Dade County Coun. Arts and Scis., 1982, 83, Dade County Performing Arts. Coun., 1984-86; v.p., bd. dirs. South Fla. Arts Ctr.; bd. dirs. Temple Beth Sholom, 1986-91; bd. dirs. Miami City Ballet, 1986-92, Fla. Food Recovery Project; v.p., bd. dirs. Infants In Need, Inc.; mem. City of Miami Beach Community Benefit Com. for Performing Arts, 1987-92; mem. Miami Beach Vis. & Conv. Authority; mem. Dade County Performing Arts Ctr. Trust; bd. dirs. Advantage Children, Inc. Recipient Outstanding Forrest Steward of the Yr. award, 2009. Mem. ABA, Fla. Bar Assn., U. Miami Alumni Assn., Greater Miami C. of C. (trustee 1983-85), Phi Delta Phi Avocations: golf; boating. Home: Miami, Fla. Died Sept. 20, 2010.

LEVINE, JACK, artist; b. Boston, Jan. 3, 1915; s. Samuel Mayer and Mary (Grinker) L.; widowed; 1 child, Susanna Levine Fisher. AFD, Colby Coll., Waterville, Maine, 1956. One-man shows include Downtown Gallery, N.Y.C., 1938, Artists, 1942, Mus. Modern Art, N.Y.C., 1943; exhibited in group shows at Jeu de Paume, Paris, 1938, Carnegie Internat. exhbns., 1938-40, Artists for Victory, Met. Mus., N.Y.C., 1942, retrospective at Jewish Mus., N.Y.C., 1978-79, Bklyn. Mus., 1999; represented in permanent collections Mus. Modern Art, Met. Mus. Art, N.Y.C., William Hayes Foggs Mus., Harvard U., Addison Gallery, Andover, Mass., Mus. Vatican, D.C. Moore Gallery, N.Y., DeYoung Mus., San Francisco. With AUS, 1942-45. Mem. American Acad. Arts and Letters (pres., chancellor), Inst. Arts and Letters (pres. 1993), Nat. Acad. Design, Century Club. Home: New York, NY. Died Nov. 8, 2010.

LEVINE, PETER HUGHES, physician, health facility administrator; b. Everett, Mass., Nov. 13, 1938; s. Louis and Helen (Hughes) L.; m. Catherine Brooks Holst, Aug. 26, 1962; children: Thomas H., William H., James L. BS, Tufts U., 1960; MD, Tufts U., Boston, 1964. Diplomate Am. Bd. Internal Medicine, Am. Bd. Hematology. Hematology fellow Tufts - N.E. Med. Ctr., Boston, 1967-69; hematologist Andrews AFB Referral Hosp., Washington, 1969-71; dir. blood coagulation lab. and hemophilia ctr. Tufts - N.E. Med. Ctr., Boston, 1971-75; chmn. dept. medicine Worcester (Mass.) Meml. Hosp., 1975-90, dir. Blood Rsch. Lab., 1975-98; pres., CEO Meml. Health Care, Worcester, 1990-98, U. Mass. Meml. Health Care, Worcester, Mass., from 1998. Asst. prof. medicine Tufts U. Sch. Medicine, Boston, 1971-75; prof. medicine U. Mass. Med. Sch., Worcester, 1975—. Contbr.over 168 articles to med. jours., 135 published abstracts in area of hematology. Med. dir. Nat. Hemophilia Found., N.Y.C., 1983-87; pres. Worcester County Music Assn., 1989-92; trustee Worcester Poly. Inst., 1990—, Mass. Biotech. Rsch. Inst., 1990—, Worcester Bus. Devel. Com., 1992—, United Way Ctrl. Mass., 1993—; trustee and exec. com. mem. Mass. Hosp. Assn., 1992—; trustee Alpha Beta Biotech., Inc., 1996—. Maj. USAF, 1969-71. Recipient Disting. Tchr. award Tufts U. Sch. Medicine, Boston, 1973, 75, Outstanding Med. Educator, U. Mass. Med. Sch., Worcester, 1981, 85, 86, 88, 89, 91, House Staff Disting. Tchr., Worcester Meml. Hosp., 1980, 87, 88, Murray Thelin Award for Rsch. Nat. Hemophilia Found., 1987, Worcester Citizen of Yr. award, 1998, NCCJ/Accord award, 1998. Fellow ACP; mem. Am. Soc. Hematology, Am. Fedn. Clin. Rsch. Achievements include patents on method for cure of hemophilia by gene therapy; development of model program for home therapy of hemophilia; research on production and effects of leukocyte-generated oxidants, and omega-3 fatty acids on prostanoids, and platelet and leukocyte function. Home: Worcester, Mass. Died Dec. 15, 2009.

LEVINE, SANFORD HAROLD, lawyer; b. Troy, NY, Mar. 13, 1938; s. Louis and Reba (Semegren) L.; m. Margaret R. Appelbaum, Oct. 29, 1967; children: Jessica Sara, Abby Miriam. AB, Syracuse U., 1959, JD, 1961. Bar: NY 1961, US Dist. Ct. (no. dist.) NY 1961, US Dist. Ct. (we. dist.) NY 1979, US Dist. Ct. (ea. and so. dists.) NY 1980, US Ct. Appeals (2d cir.) 1962, US Supreme Ct. 1967. Law asst. to assoc. judge NY Ct. Appeals, Albany and to justice NY Supreme Ct., 1962-66, NY Ct. Appeals, Albany, 1964; asst. counsel NY State Temporary commn. on Constl. Conv., NYC, 1966-67; assoc. counsel SUNY System, Albany, 1967-70, dep. univ. counsel, 1970-78, acting counsel, 1970-71, acting univ. counsel, 1978-79, univ. counsel, vice chancellor legal affairs, 1979-97, prof. Sch. of Edn., dir. program in edn. and law, 1997—2007. Adj. prof. Sch. of Edn. SUNY, Albany, 1992—97, Albany, 2007—09; mem. paralegal curriculum adv. com. Schenectady County Community Coll., 1975—2009. Editl. bd. Syracuse U. Law Rev., 1960-61; editl. adv. bd. Jour. Coll. and Univ. Law, 1977-81. Fellow Am. Bar Found., NY Bar Found., State Acad. for Pub. Adminstrn.; mem. ABA (ho. dels. 1987-89), NY State Bar Assn., Albany County Bar Assn., Nat. Assn. Coll. and Univ. Attys. (exec. bd. 1979-82, bd. dirs. 1982-89, pres. 1986-87), Am. Soc. Pub. Adminstrn. Home: Schenectady, NY. Died Nov. 18, 2009.

LEVINSON, JOHN MILTON, obstetrician, gynecologist; b. Atlantic City, Aug. 17, 1927; m. Elizabeth Carl Bell; children: Patricia Anne, John Carl, Mark Jay. BA, Lafayette Coll., Easton, Pa., 1949; MD, Thomas Jefferson U., 1953. Diplomate Am. Bd. Ob-Gyn. Intern Atlantic City Hosp., 1953-54; Am. Cancer Soc. clin. fellow Jefferson Med. Coll. Hosp., Phila., 1954-55; resident in ob-gyn. Del. Hosp., Wilmington, 1955-57; pvt. practice ob-gyn. Wilmington, 1957-85; prof. dept. ob-gyn. Jefferson Med. Coll., Thomas Jefferson U., Phila., hon. clin. prof., from 1990; sr. attending physician emeritus Med. Ctr. Del., Wilmington, from 1986; attending chief dept. ob-gyn. St. Francis Hosp., Wilmington, chief emeritus, 1986-92. Founder, pres. Aid for Internat. Medicine, Inc., 1966—; med. dir., chief surgeon Quark Expeditions, 1991-95; cons. Riverside Hosp., 1972-86, Wilmington Pa. Blue Shield, 1982—: cons. gynecology U.S. VA, 1974-85; founding mem., treas., bd. dirs. Physicians Health Svcs., Del., Ltd., 1985-87; vis. prof., cons., ship's surgeons, practicing physician various orgns. in Africa, Antarctica, Arctic regions, Ctrl. Am., Europe, S.E. Asia, S.W. Asia, 1963—; lectr. in field; internat. med. cons. to Sen. Edward M. Kennedy, 1967—; chmn. Antarctic expdns. study group to advise NSF, 1992-93; co-chmn. Com. for Safety in Arctic and Antarctic Frontier Expeditions, 1992-93. Author: Shorebirds: The Birds, the Hunters, the Decoys, 1991, Safe Passage Questioned: Medical Care and Safety for the Polar Tourist, 1998, Advanced First Aid Afloat, 2000; assoc. prodr. 3 films on explorer Ernest Shackleton; contbr. articles to profl. jours., chpts. to books. Bd. dirs. Del. com. Project H.O.P.E., 1965-75, ARC, 1968-70, Charles A. Lindbergh Fund, Inc., 1985-90; trustee Blue Cross/Blue Shield Del., Inc., 1968-86, Brandywine Coll., 1972-77; bd. dirs. Nat. Assn. Blue Shield Plans, 1971-77; mem adv. com. Trinity Alcohol and Drug Program, 1978-85; mem. Del. Gov.'s Commn. on Health Care Cost Mgmt., 1985-87; bd. dirs. founding mem. World Affairs Coun. Wilmington Inc, v.p., 1981-86; pres. Rockland Mills Cmty. Assn., 1992-94; mem. bd. advisors World Sportsmen Ctr., Orlando, 1997—, With USN, 1945-47; col. M.C., USAFR, 1984-87. Recipient Brandywine award Brandywine Coll., 1968, cert. of appreciation for med. svcs. Ministry of Health, Republic of Vietnam, 1963-66, commendation Pres. of U.S., 1971, The Eisenhower award People to People Internat., 1986, Commemorative medal Charles A. Lindbergh Fund, 1987, Phila. Explorers award 1987, Citation for Outstanding Contbn. to People of Del., Med. Soc. Del., 1992. Fellow Am. Coll. Ob.-Gyn., Royal Geog. Soc. London; mem. AMA, Am. Assn. Gyn. Laporoscopists (founding, bd. dirs.), Del. Obstetric Soc. (pres. 1980-82), Phila. Obstetric Soc., Med. Soc. Del. (Citation of Merit award 1992), New Castle County Med. Soc., Soc. Ob-Gyn. Vietnam (hon.), Ducks Unltd. (sponsor, mem. Del. com. 1980-92), Explorers Club (fellow 1966—, chmn. Phila. chpt. 1983-85, bd. dirs. 1981-88, pres. N.Y.C. 1985-87), Univ. and Whist Club Wilmington (life, bd. govs. 1961-64), Rotary (bd. dirs. local club 1991-93), Theta Chi (pres. 1945) Phi Beta Pi (pres. 1952), Kappa Beta Phi (pres. 1952). Avocations: hunting, polar history, sailing, carving bird decoys. Died Oct. 4, 2009.

LEVIS, ALLEN, marketing consultant; b. Chgo., Feb. 2, 1917; s. Samuel and Jennie (Finkelstein) Levitetz; m. Elaine Herst Levis, Mar. 6, 1943; children: William H., Laurence A. BA, U. Ill., 1940. Exec. v.p. Herst-Allen Co., Chgo., 1949—59; pres. Gen. Nutrients Co., 1960—62, Ford Labs., Inc., NYC, 1962—64, Allen Levis Orgn., Inc., Northfield, Ill., from 1965. Guest lectr. Cornell U. Food Industry Mgmt. Program. Author: General Merchandise in Food Stores: A Marketing Guide, 1981. Pres. Congregation Solel, Highland Pk., Ill., 1961—62; bd. dirs. Jewish Vocat. Svc., 1959—60. With US Army, 1942—45, ETO. Mem.: Am. Rsch. Mdse. Inst. (pres. 1951—55). Home: Winnetka, Ill. Died Dec. 13, 2009.

LEVITT, JAREN, real estate company officer; b. NYC, Mar. 19, 1946; s. Seymour and Harriet (Finorsky) L.; children: Jaden, Janna; m. Theresa Julyun Kim, Oct. 16, 1995. BS in Psychology and Biology, Syracuse U., 1965; MS in Clin. Psychology, U. Tex., 1967; PhD in Clin. Psychology, UCLA, 1974. Spl. asst Mayor's Office, NYC, 1968-71, Pres. U.S., Washington, 1971; pres. Med. Cons. Internat., Woodland Hills, Calif., 1973-78; mktg. dir. vacation planning Playboy Internat., McAffe, N.J., 1978-80; regional mktg. dir. Gen. Devel. Co., Miami, Fla., 1981-88, asst. v.p., 1988, v.p. Cen. Region and Far East Norridge, Ill., 1988-90, pres. Am. Real Estate Devel. Corp. Fla.; pres. Global Acquisition and Devel. Corp., 1990-95, Stone Trend Internat., Inc., Sarasota, from 1995, owner, RoadWarriorTrading.com. Cons. substance abuse projects to bus. and fgn. govts., 1968-78. Contbr. articles to profl. jours. Mem. Heritage Found. Republican. Jewish. Avocations: scuba, skiing, sky-diving, tennis, flying. Home: Sarasota, Fla. Died June 27, 2009.

LEVITT, NORMAN JAY, mathematician; b. NYC, Aug. 27, 1943; s. Saul and Molly (Gershin) L.; m. Renee Greene; two children. BA, Harvard Coll., 1963; MA, Princeton U., 1965, PhD, 1967. Instr. Courant Inst., NYC, 1967-69; from asst. prof. to prof. Rutgers U., New Brunswick, N.J., from 1969. Vis. scholar Aarhus U., Denmark, 1972; vis. prof. Stanford U., Palo Alto, Calif., 1976-77, U. B.C., Vancouver, 1981. Author: Grassmanians and Gauss Maps in Piecewise Linear Topology, 1989, Prometheus Bedeviled, 1999; co-author: Higher Superstition, 1994; co-editor: Algebraic & Geometric Topology, 1985, The Flight from Science and Reason, 1996. Home: New York, NY. Died Oct. 24, 2009.

LEVY, MARK IRVING, lawyer; b. Chgo., June 28, 1949; s. Kenneth Warren and Arleen (Langhaus) L.; m. Judith Jarrell Levy, Sept. 8, 1979; children: Elizabeth Sara, Mitchell Bennett. BA summa cum laude with distinction, Yale U., New Haven, 1971; JD, Yale U., New Haven, Conn., 1975. Bar: DC 1976, US Dist. Ct. D.C. 1977, US Supreme Ct. 1980, Ill. 1986, US Ct. Appeals (DC Cir.) 1990, US Ct. Appeals (6th, 7th and 8th Cirs.) 1990, US Tax Ct. 1990, US Ct. Appeals (9th Cir.) 1993, US Ct. Appeals (2d, 4th and 10th Cirs.) 1994, US Ct. Appeals (3d, 5th, 11th and Fed. Cirs.) 1996, US Ct. Appeals (1st Cir.) 2000, US Ct. Claims 2007. Law clk. Judge Gerhard A. Gesell, Washington, 1975-76; assoc. Covington & Burling, Washington, 1976-79, 81-83; asst. to solicitor gen. US Dept. Justice, Washington, 1979-81, 83-86; ptnr. Mayer, Brown & Platt, Chgo., 1987-93; dep. asst. atty. gen. (Appellate) Civil Divsn. US Dept. Justice, Washington, 1993-95; ptnr. Howrey & Simon, Washington, 1995—2003; of counsel Kilpatrick Stockton LLP, 2004—09. Adj. faculty, appellate sem. U. Va. Sch. Law, 1999-2002, 2004-09; mem. adv. com. fed. rules of appellate procedure, former mem. adv comm. on procedures DC Cir. Exec. editor Yale Law Jour., 1974-75; columnist Nat. Law Jour. Recipient Israel H. Peres prize Yale Law Sch., 1975, Super Lawyers Law Diagram 3000 Leading Lawyers America; named one of Best Lawyers in America, America's Leading Lawyers Bus. Chambers USA. Fellow

Am. Acad. Appellate Lawyers; mem. Yale Law Sch. Alumni Assn. (former treas., exec. com. mem. 1987-90), Edward Coke Appellate Am. Inn of Ct. (master), Phi Beta Kappa (fellow). Home: Bethesda, Md. Died Apr. 30, 2009.

LEVY, MARTIN BERYL, physical therapist, rehabilitation consultant; b. NYC, June 17, 1927; s. William Harold and Ethel Marie (Ament) L.; m. Helen E. Lipkin, June 6, 1954; children: Elizabeth, Patricia. BS, NYU, 1951, MA, 1956. Lic. phys. therapist, Ohio. Staff therapist Inst. Phys. Medicine and Rehab., NYC, 1955; for pvt. physician Cedarhurst, L.I., N.Y., 1956; coord. rehab. Drake Meml. Hosp., Cin., 1957-83; dir. rehab. Cmty. Multi-care Ctr., Fairfield, Ohio, 1983-86, Quality Health Care Inc., Cin., 1986-99, Clinfton Villa, Cin., 1986-94; ret., 1999. Phys. therapy cons., mem. adv. com. home health svcs. Cin. Health Dept. 2d lt. USAF, 1952-53. Mem. Am. Phys. Therapy Assn. Jewish. Home: Cincinnati, Ohio. Died Feb. 11, 2010.

LEVY, MICHAEL B., lawyer; b. NYC, Sept. 15, 1942; BEE, CUNY, 1965; JD cum laude, NYU, 1968. Bar: N.Y. 1968. With Robinson Silverman Pearce Aronsohn & Berman, NYC. Editor: NYU Law Review, 1967-68. Pomeroy scholar. Mem. Assn. of Bar of City of N.Y., Order of Coif. Died Oct. 28, 2009.

LEWIS, ANDREA ELEN, editor; b. Detroit, June 4, 1957; d. Frank Joe and Mae (Shaw) L. BS, Ea. Mich. U., 1982. Arts and entertainment editor Plexus: West Coast Women's Press, Oakland, Calif., 1984-88; rsch. editor Mother Jones mag., San Francisco, 1990-92; editl. asst. Harper Collins Pubs., San Francisco, 1992-94; sr. editor Third Force mag., Oakland, from 1992; assoc. editor Pacific News Svc., San Francisco, 1996—2000; writer NBCi.com, San Francisco, from 1997. Mem. adv. bd. Nat. Radio Project, 1996—. Contbg. writer: The Black Women's Health Book, 1990, Beyond Identity Politics, 1996; contbg. artist (CD rec. project) Bob Ostertag's Fear No Love, 1995; commentator (radio broadcasting) Pacifica Radio, 1995, 96, 97; co-host/prodr. The Morning Show KPFA Radio, Berkeley, Calif., 2000-. Chorus mem. San Francisco Symphony Chorus, 1987—, sect. leader, alto, 1991, 92, 93, 95, 99, mem. artistic adv. com., 1995, 96, 98, 99; mem. planning com., panelist, spkr. Media and Democracy Congress, San Francisco, 1996; fellow Vallecitos Mountain Refuge, N.Mex., 1998. Recipient Merit award Local Music Series, 2001, Nat. Fedn. Cmty. Broadcasters Golden Reel awards, 2001. Mem. NARAS (Grammy awards for best choral recording 1992, 95). Avocations: massage therapist, musician, golfer, outdoor activities. Home: Ocala, Fla. Died Nov. 15, 2009.

LEWIS, CHARLES EDWIN, epidemiologist, educator; b. Kansas City, Dec. 28, 1928; s. Claude Herbert and Maudie Friels (Holaday) Lewis; m. Mary Ann Gurera, Dec. 27, 1963; children: Kevin Neil(dec.), David Bradford, Matthew Clinton, Karen Carleen. Student, U. Kans., 1948—49; MD, Harvard, 1953; MS, U. Cin., 1957, ScD, 1959. Diplomate Am. Bd. Preventive Medicine (Occupl. Medicine). Intern, resident U. Kans. Hosp., 1953—54; trainee USPHS, 1956—58; fellow occupational health Eastman Kodak Co., 1958—59; asst. clin. prof. epidemiology Baylor U. Sch. Medicine, 1960—61; asso. prof. medicine U. Kans. Med. Sch., 1961—62, prof., chmn. dept. preventive medicine, 1962—69; coordinator Kan. Regional Med. Program, 1967—69; prof. social medicine Harvard Med. Sch., 1969—70; prof. pub. health, head div. health adminstrn. UCLA Med. Sch., 1970—72, prof. medicine, div. head, 1972—90, head div. preventive and occupational medicine, 1991—93; dir. Health Services Rsch. Ctr., 1991—93, UCLA Ctr. Health Promotion and Disease Prevention, 1991—93; chair acad. senate UCLA, 1995—96. Cons. Getty Trust, Walt Disney Prodns.; mem. Nat. Bd. Med. Examiners, 1964—68, 1968—83, Jt. Commn. on Accreditation Health Care Orgns., 1989—95; mem. health svcs. rsch. study sect. USPHS, 1968—76; vis. scholar Annenberg Sch. Comm., U. So. Calif., 1980—81; mem. adv. bd. Hosp. Rsch. and Edn. Trust, 1972—75. Contbr. articles to profl. jours. Capt. USAF, 1954—56. Recipient Ginsberg prize medicine, U. Kans., 1954, Glasier award, Soc. Gen. Internal Medicine, 1988. Master: ACP (regent 1988—94, Rosenthal award 1980, Laureate award So. Calif. III 1994); fellow: APHA, Acad. Occupl. Medicine; mem.: Am. Assn. Physicians, Assn. Tchrs. Preventive Medicine (pres. coun. 1977—80), Internat. Epidemiology Soc. Home: Los Angeles, Calif. Died Jan. 27, 2010.

LEWIS, CHARLES LEONARD, psychologist; b. Wellsville, Ohio, Jan. 6, 1926; s. Cleo L. and Charlotte (Hahn) L.; m. Charlotte J. Wynn, Sept. 8, 1948 (dec. Mar. 1987); children: Stephen C., Janet J., Judith A.; m. Jane E. McCormick, Oct. 1, 1988. BS in Edn. with honors, Ohio U., 1949; MA, U. Minn., 1953, PhD, 1955. Asst. dean of men Ohio U., 1948-50; assoc. dir. activities U. Minn., 1950-55; dean student affairs, assoc. prof. psychology U. N.D., 1955-62; exec. dean, assoc. prof. ednl. psychology U. Tenn., 1962-67; v.p. student affairs Pa. State U., 1967-72; exec. dir. Am. Personnel and Guidance Assn., Washington, 1972-74, exec. v.p., 1974-83, exec. v.p. emeritus, from 1984; pres. Charles L. Lewis & Assocs., Annandale, Va., 1983-85, Chuck Lewis et al, Lancaster, Pa., from 1985. Guest prof. U. Md., 1973; mem. Nat. Adv. Com. for Devel. Guidance Components-Career Edn., 1972-76. Founding editor Jour. Coll. Students Pers., 1958-64; mem. editl. bd. Pers. and Guidance Jour., 1954-57. Mem. Pres.'s Com. for Handicapped, 1972-80; bd. dirs. Ctr. Cmty. Hosps., Bellefonte, Pa. With U.S. Army, 1944-47. Recipient George Hill Disting. Alumni award, Ohio U., 1981; named Outstanding Alumnus, Coll. Edn. Ohio U., 1988. Mem.: AAUP, APA, Willow Valley Computer Sig. (pres. 1999—2001), Ohio U. Alumni Soc. and Friends Coll. Edn. (coun. 1985—92, bd. dirs. 1986—92), Coun. Advancement of Stds. (bd. dirs.), Am. Assn. Univ. Adminstrs. (dir. 1973), Am. Pers. and Guidance Assn. (dir. 1967—70), Nat. Assn. Woman Deans and Counselors, Nat. Assn. Student Pers. Adminstrs., Am. Coll. Pers. Assn. (pres. 1968—69, honoree Diamond Anniversary 1999, Lifetime Achievement award 2001), Am. Assn. Higher Edn., Psi Chi, Chi Sigma Iota (founding dir. 1984—90), Beta Theta Pi, Kappa Delta Pi. Episcopalian. Home: Lancaster, Pa. Died Feb. 6, 2010.

LEWIS, DIANE, entrepreneur; b. Chgo., Jan. 24, 1936; d. George W. and Kathryn (McKinnen) W.; divorced; children: William Brosius, Dwight Scott. Student, U. Ill., Chgo., 1953-57. Exec. officer, founding dir. Interviewing Technicians, Inc., Chgo., 1959-69, Interviewing Dynamics, Inc., Chgo., Atlanta and Houston, from 1969, London, from 1980; cons. IDI Profl. Recruitment, Inc., Chgo., from 1988, Indyna Pub. & Pub. Rels., Inc., Chgo., from 1988, Internat. Cons., Inc., Chgo., from 1978; owner I.D. Mgmt., Chgo., from 1981. Lectr., pub. speaker TV. Authors: Insider's Guide to Finding the Right Job, 1987, Equal to the Challenge, 1988. Speaker Inner Cir. Rep. Com. Job Seminars, U.S. & Can., 1984—. Trustee Adv. Bd. City Univ. Mem. Am. Mgmt. Assn., Ill. Employment Assn., Aircraft Owners & Pilots Assn., Equal to the Challenge Assn. (pres., founder 1988—). Avocations: gourmet cooking, aerobics, english horseback riding. Died Nov. 21, 2009.

LEWIS, JOHN PRIOR, economist, educator; b. Albany, NY, Mar. 18, 1921; s. Leon Ray and Grace (Prior) L.; m. June Estelle Ryan, July 12, 1946 (dec. 2009); children: Betsy Prior, Sally Eastman, Amanda Barnum (dec. 2008) Student, St. Andrews U., Scotland, 1939-40; AB, Union Coll., Schenectady, 1941; M.Pub. Adminstrn., Harvard, 1943, PhD in Polit. Economy and Govt, 1950; D.C.L., Union Coll., 1970. Instr., asst. prof. econs. and govt. Union Coll., Schenectady, 1946-50; mem. staff, asst. to chmn. Council Econ. Advisers, Exec. Office of the Pres., Washington, 1950-53; cons. UN Korean Reconstrn. Agy., Pusan, Korea, 1953; assoc. prof. Ind. U., 1953-56, prof. bus. econs. and pub. policy, 1956-64, disting. service prof. bus. econs. and pub. policy, 1964, chmn. dept., 1961-63; mem. Council Econ. Advisers, Exec. Office of Pres., Washington, 1963-64; minister-dir. USAID mission to India, 1964-69; dean Woodrow Wilson Sch. Pub. Affairs, 1969-74; prof. economics & internat. affairs Princeton U., 1969-91, prof. emeritus, 1991—2010; on leave as chmn. devel. assistance com. OECD, Paris, 1979-81, as DAC chmn. ann. OECD vols. on devel. cooperation, 1979-81; sr. advisor Overseas Devel. Coun., 1981—99. Sr. staff mem. in India Brookings Instn., Washington, 1959-60; mem. UN Com. on Devel. Planning, 1970-83, rapporteur, 1972-78 Author: Business Conditions Analysis, 1959, 2d edit., (with R.C. Turner), 1967, Quiet Crisis in India: Economic Development and American Policy, 1962, (with Ishan Kapur) The World Bank, Multilateral Aid, and the 1970's, 1973, (with V. Kallab) U.S. Foreign Policy and the Third World, 1983, Development Strategies Reconsidered, 1986, Strengthening the Poor, 1988, India's Political Economy, 1995, (with Devesh Kapur and Richard Webb) The World Bank: Its First Half Century, 1997, The Goliath Problem: The Wages of Hegemony, 2004, Development Corporation, 2006. Served to lt. USNR, 1943-46, PTO. Home: Lawrenceville, NJ. Died May 19, 2010.

LEWIS, THOMAS SKIPWITH, insurance and engineering company executive; b. Bluefield, W.Va., Nov. 21, 1936; s. Thomas Sidney and Frances Glendora (Pasley) L.; m. Jane Elizabeth Townsend, Aug. 4, 1962; children: Kathleen Townsend, Glenn Skipwith. BEE, Va. Poly. Inst., 1958; MEE, U. Va., 1964, ScD, 1967. Registered profl. engr., Conn., Mass. Microwave engr. Air Am. div. Westinghouse, Balt., 1959-62; inst. elec. engring. U. Va., Charlottesville, 1962-67; sr. research engr. United Aircraft Research Labs., East Hartford, Conn., 1967-70; assoc. prof. U. Hartford, West Hartford, Conn., 1970-71, dean engring., 1971-81; asst. v.p. Hartford (Conn.) Steam Boiler Inspection & Ins. Co., 1981-83, v.p., 1983-85, sr. v.p., from 1985. Bd. dirs. Materials Property Council, N.Y.C. Contbr. articles to profl. jours.; patentee in field. Trustee David Chase Found., Hartford, 1985-87. Served to 2d lt. U.S. Army, 1960-61. Named Young Engr. of Yr., Conn. Soc. Profl. Engrs., 1972. Mem. IEEE (sr.), Am. Soc. Engring. Edn., Nat. Soc. Profl. Engrs. Democrat. Avocations: cooking, tropical fish. Home: Hebron, Conn. Died Oct. 10, 2009.

LICHTERMAN, HARVEY S., lawyer; b. Chgo., July 29, 1940; s. Leo and Laura (Levin) L.; m. Barbara Sue Bertman, Nov. 19, 1967; children: Larry, Holly. BA, U. Mich., 1962; JD cum laude, Harvard U., 1965. Bar: Ill. 1965, U.S. Dist. Ct. (no. dist.) Ill. Assoc. Lord, Bissell & Brook, Chgo., 1965-72, ptnr., from 1973, mng. ptnr., chmn. exec. com., 1986-90. Mem. ABA, Ill. State Bar Assn., Chgo. Bar Assn., Phi Beta Kappa. Died Apr. 27, 2009.

LICHTWARD, FRED, headmaster; b. St. Paul, Apr. 27, 1950; s. Fred Whitmore and Violet (Hunter) L.; m. Deborah Ann Schultz, Jan. 13, 1973; 1 child, Fred. BS, Mercy Coll., Dobbs Ferry, NY, 1973; MA, U. North Fla., Jacksonville, 1974; EdS, U. Fla., 1979; EdD, U. Sarasota, 1981. Cert. in spl. edn., elem. edn., ednl. adminstrn., Fla. Tchr. Nassau County Schs., Fernandina Beach, Fla., 1974-79; headmaster St. Andrew's Episc. Sch., Jacksonville, 1979-82, Assumption Sch., Jacksonville, 1982-87; exec. dir. Hope Haven Children's Clinic, Jacksonville, 1987-90; headmaster Arlington Country Day Sch., Jacksonville, from 1990. Author ednl. games Games for Remediation, 1975; contbr. articles to ednl. jours. Bd. dirs. YMCA, Jacksonville, 1984-86; pres., bd. dirs., umpire Assumption Athletic Assn., Jacksonville, 1988-90; bd. dirs. Southside Youth Athletic Assn., Jacksonville, 1984-87, Arlington Child Devel. Ctr., Jacksonville, 1990-92; vol. coach YMCA, Arlington, 1984—. Named Tchr. of Yr., West Jacksonville Jaycees, 1974, Vol. of Yr., YMCA, Jacksonville, 1984; U. North Fla. grad. fellow, 1973. Avocations: reading, walking, tutoring. Home: Jacksonville, Fla. Died Jan. 18, 2009.

LIDDLE, ERNEST VICTOR, university dean, librarian; b. Enniskillen, No. Ireland, June 10, 1923; came to U.S., 1951; s. George Edwin and Mini (McCormack) L.; m. Grace Edith MacMurchy, Sept. 21, 1957; children: David Ernest, Philip Victor. BA, Edinburgh U., Scotland, 1951; BD, Asbury Theol. Sem., Wilmore, Ky., 1952, ThM, 1954; ThD, No. Bapt. Theol. Sem., Lombard, Ill., 1956; MA, Bucknell U., 1960; MS, Drexel U., 1966. Ordained to ministry Bapt. Ch., 1955. Undergrad. libr. U. Pa., Phila.; dir. libr. Seattle Pacific U., Palm Beach Atlantic U., West Palm Beach, Fla.; acquisitions libr. Western Ill. U., Macomb; dean libr. Liberty U., Lynchburg, Va., from 1979. Editor asst. Watchman-Examiner, 1956-57; contbr. numerous articles to profl. jours. Baptist. Avocation: world travel. Home: Port Saint Lucie, Fla. Died Jan. 18, 2009.

LIFKA, MARY LAURANNE, history professor; b. Oak Pk., Ill., Oct. 31, 1937; d. Aloysius William and Loretta Catherine (Juric) Lifka. BA, Mundelein Coll., 1960; MA, Loyola U., LA, 1965; PhD, U. Mich., 1974; postdoc. student, London U., 1975. Cert. tchr. Prof. history Mundelein Coll., Chgo., 1976—84, coord. acad. computer, 1983—84; prof. history Coll. St. Teresa, Winona, Minn., 1984—89, Lewis U., Romeoville, Ill., from 1989. Chief reader in history Ednl. Testing Svc., Princeton, NJ, 1980—84; cons. world history project Longman, Inc., from 1983; cons. in European history Coll. Bd., Evanston, Ill., from 1983. Contbr. articles to publs. Recipient Br. Miguel Febres Cordero award, 1998. Mem.: Ednl. Testing Svc. Devel. Com. History, Am. Hist. Assn. Democrat. Roman Catholic. Home: Dubuque, Iowa. Died Oct. 16, 2009.

LIGHT, JEROME ELLIOTT, dentist; b. Bklyn., Jan. 9, 1928; s. Harry and Sara (Altman) L.; m. Margery Ruth Jacobs, Aug. 10, 1951; children: Douglas, Jonathan. AB, NYU, 1950; DDS, Columbia U., 1955. Gen. practice dentistry, Armonk, N.Y. Pres., Byram Hills Scholarship Fund, Armonk, 1962. Served to cpl. U.S. Army, 1946-48. Mem. 9th Dist. Dental Soc. (peer rev. com. 1985—), No. Westchester Dental Study Group (pres. 1968-69). Jewish. Lodge: Lions (sec. 1959). Avocations: skiing, tennis, sailing. Home: Armonk, NY. Died Nov. 29, 2009.

LILEY, PETER EDWARD, retired engineering educator; b. Barnstaple, North Devon, Eng., Apr. 22, 1927; came to U.S., 1957; s. Stanley E. and Rosa (Ellery) L.; m. Elaine Elizabeth Kull, Aug. 16, 1963; children: Elizabeth Ellen, Rebecca Ann. BSc, U. London, 1951, PhD in Physics, 1957, DIC, 1957. With Brit. Oxygen Engring., London, 1955-57; asst. prof. mech. engring. Purdue U., West Lafayette, Ind., 1957-61, assoc. prof., 1961-72; assoc. sr. researcher Thermophys. Properties Research Ctr., Purdue U., West Lafayette, Ind., 1961-72, prof. mech. engring., 1972-98; sr. rschr. Ctr. for Info. and Numerical Data Analysis and Synthesis, Purdue U., West Lafayette, Ind., 1972-92; ret., 1997. Cons. in field. Author: Sect. 2 Perry's Chemical Engineers Handbook, 7th edit., 1997; author: (with Hartnett et al.) Handbook of Heat Transfer Fundamentals, 2d edit., 1985; author: (with others) Marks Mechanical Engineers Handbook, 11 edit., 2006, Schaums 2000 Solved Problems in Mechanical Engineering Thermodynamics, 1995, Kutz Mechanical Engineers Handbook, 3d edit., 2006; co-author: Steam and Gas Tables with Computer Equations, 1985, Thermal Conductivity of Nonmetallic Liquids and Gases, 1970;: Properties of Nonmetallic Fluid Elements, 1981, Properties of Inorganic and Organic Fluids, 1988; editor, mem. editl. bd. Internat. Jour. Thermophysics, 1980—86; contbr. chpts. to handbooks in field, articles to profl. jours.; reviewer profl. jours. Served with Royal Corps Signals, Brit. Army, 1945-48. Lutheran. Home: Lafayette, Ind. Died Apr. 23, 2009.

LILLEY, JAMES RODERICK, think-tank executive, former ambassador; b. Tsingtao, China, Jan. 15, 1928; s. Frank Walder and Inez (Bush) L.; m. Sally Booth, May 1, 1954; children: Douglas, Michael, Jeffrey. BA, Yale U., 1951; MA, George Washington U., 1972. Fgn. affairs officer US Dept. State, various East Asian posts, 1958-75, dep. asst. sec. for East Asian affairs Washington, 1985-86; nat. intelligence officer CIA, Washington, 1975-78; sr. East Asian specialist NSC, Washington, 1981; dir. Am. Inst. in Taiwan, Taipei, 1982-84; US amb. to Republic of Korea US Dept. State, Seoul, Republic of Korea, 1986-89, US amb. to China Beijing, 1989-91; asst. sec. US Dept. Def., Washington, 1991-93; sr. resident fellow Am. Enterprise Inst. (AEI), Washington, 1993—2009. Cons. Hunt/Sedco Oil Co., Dallas, 1979-81, United Techs., Hartford, Ct., 1979-80, Otis Elevator, Farmington, Ct., 1984-85, Westinghouse, Balt., 1984. Author: Beyond MFN, 1994, (with Jeffrey Lilley) China Hands, 2004 With U.S. Army, 1946-47; 1st lt. USAFR, 1950-67. Recipient Disting. Intelligence medal, CIA, 1979, Kang Hua medal Republic of Korea. Mem. Met. Club (Washington), Royal Bangkok Sports Club. Republican. Home: Washington, DC. Died Nov. 12, 2009.

LILLEY, ROBERT FRANCIS, textile company executive; b. Mass., May 29, 1939; s. John F. and Helen M. (Mahoney) L.; m. Nancy C. Latshaw, Aug. 4, 1962; children: Robert, Michael, Kathleen. BS, Northeastern U., 1962; MBA, Boston Coll., 1967; grad. advanced mgmt. program, Harvard U., 1977. Systems analyst Raytheon Co., 1962-64; with Am. Thread Co., Stamford, Conn., 1964-82, gen. corp. controller, 1975-78, v.p., sec., treas., 1978-79, pres., chief exec. officer, 1979-82, chmn. bd., 1980-82; owner, pres. William Unger & Co., NYC, from 1982. Mem. nat. council Northeastern U. Home: Trumbull, Conn. Died Aug. 18, 2010.

LILLIENSTEIN, MAXWELL JULIUS, lawyer; b. Bklyn., Dec. 18, 1927; s. Benjamin and Lillian (Camporeale) L.; m. Janet Newman, June 23, 1951; children: Steven, Robert, Carol. B. Social Scis. cum laude, CCNY, 1949; JD, Columbia U., 1952. Bar: N.Y. 1952. Ptnr. Friedberg, Blue & Rich, NYC, 1958-63, Rich, Lillienstein, Krinsly, Dorman & Hochhauser, NYC, 1963-90; counsel Cooperman, Levitt & Winikoff, NYC, from 1991; mng. ptnr. Maxwell Assocs., 1982-87; gen. counsel Am. Booksellers Assn. Pres. Maxwell Fund, 1967-72; bd. dirs. numerous corps.; investment adviser; lit. agt.; atty. in many maj. 1st Amendment cases. Contbr. numerous articles to mags. and newspapers. Pres. Ardsley (N.Y.) Democratic Club, Westchester County, 1966-67, mem. exec. bd., 1966-70, Westchester County Dem. committeeman, 1968-82; trustee Village of Ardsley, 1968-71, village atty., 1971-79; Chmn. Ardsley (N.Y.) Library Com., 1967-68; co-founder Ardsley Pub. Library, 1970; mem. Ardsley Narcotics Guidance Council, 1971-78. Served with AC AUS, 1946-47. Mem. Am. Booksellers Found. for Free Expression (bd. dirs.), Nat. Coalition Against Censorship (bd. dirs.) Media Coalition (bd. dirs.). Died May 13, 2010.

LIMATO, EDWARD FRANK, talent agent; b. Mt. Vernon, NY, July 10, 1936; s. Frank and Angelina (Lacerra) L. Grad. high sch., Mt. Vernon. With IFA (formerly Ashley Famous Agency), NYC, 1966—78; sr. exec. William Morris Agy. Inc., L.A., 1978—88; with Internat. Creative Mgmt., 1988—2007, talent agt. NYC, L.A., co-pres., 1999—2007; sr. v.p. William Morris Agy. Inc., Beverly Hills, 2007—09, William Morris Endeavor Entertainment, LLC, 2009—10. Bd. dirs. Abercrombie & Fitch Co., 2003—10, Motion Picture and TV Fund, L.A. Conservancy, American Cinematheque. Mem. Acad. Motion Picture Arts & Scis. (assoc.). Republican. Roman Catholic. Died July 3, 2010.

LINCOLN, ABBEY (ANNA MARIE WOOLRIDGE, AMINATA MOSEKA), jazz singer, actress; b. Chicago, IL, Aug. 6, 1930; m. Max Roach, 1962 (div. 1970). Singer: (albums) Affair: A Story of a Girl in Love, 1956, That's Him, 1957, It's Magic, 1958, Abbey is Blue, 1959, We Insist!: Freedom Now Suite, 1960, Straight Ahead, 1961, It's Time, 1962, People in Me, 1979, Golden Lady, 1981, Talking to the Sun, 1984, Abbey Sings Billie, 1987, The World is Falling Down (with Stan Getz), 1990, You Gotta Pay the Band, 1991, Abbey Sings Billie, Volume 2, 1992, Devil's Got Your Tongue, 1993, Talking To The Sun, 1993, Lincoln on Paris, 1993, When There Is Love (with Hank Jones), 1992, A Turtle's Dream, 1994, Painted Lady: In Paris, 1995, Who Used to Dance, 1996, Wholly Earth, 1998, Over the Years, 2000, It's Me, 2003, Abbey Sings Abbey, 2007; actress: (films) The Girl Can't Help It, 1956, Nothing But a Man, 1964, For the Love of Ivy, 1968, A Short Walk to Daylight, 1972, Mo' Better Blues, 1990; (TV appearances) The Name of the Game, 1968, Mission: Impossible, 1971, On Being Black, 1971, Marcus Welby M.D., 1974, All in the Family, 1978; (TV movies) Short Walk to Daylight, 1972, Abbey Lincoln: You Gotta Pay the Band, 1993; writer, dir., prodr.: (plays) A Pig in a Poke, 1975. Inducted into Black Filmakers Hall of Fame, 1975; recipient Jazz Masters award NEA, 2003 Died Aug. 14, 2010.

LINDBLADE, ERIC N., former state legislator; b. Orange, Mass., Oct. 17, 1916; m. Brenda Lindblade; 6 children. AB, MA, Tufts U., 1940; MA, B in Sacred Theology, Harvard U., 1943. Clergyman; rep. N.H. Ho. of Reps., Manchester. Vice chmn. N.H. Zoning Bd., 1978—, chmn. State Com. on Mental Health, 1987-88; mem. commmerce, small bus., consumer affairs, and econ. devel. coms., N.H. Ho. of Reps. Mem. Rotary (pres. 1980). Died May 28, 2010.

LINDE, EDWARD H., real estate manager; b. Bklyn., June 22, 1941; s. Irving and Dorothy Linde; m. Joyce Goldfine, 1962; children: Douglas, Karen. BS in Civil Engring., MIT, 1962; MBA, Harvard Bus. Sch., 1964. V.p., sr. project mgr. Cabot, Cabot & Forbes; co-founder Boston Properties Inc., 1970—2010, pres., CEO, 1997—2007, CEO, 2007—10. Dir. Jobs State Mass.; exec. com. Nat. Assn. Real Estate Investment Trusts. Chmn. bd. trustees Boston Symphony Orchestra, 2005—10; chmn. Board Beth-Israel Hospital, 1989—91; mem. M.I.T. Corp., 1990—95. Mem.: AAAS, Real Estate Round Table (mem. bd. dir.). Died Jan. 10, 2010.

LINDEMAN, BARD E(DWARD), magazine editor; b. NYC, Sept. 28, 1928; s. Edward A. and Martha (Quitzau) L.; m. Adele Lindeman, May 6, 1955 (dec. Sept. 1971); children: Leslie, Paul, Janet; m. Jan Still, Dec. 18, 1982. BA in English, Middlebury Coll., 1950. Newsman AP, Dallas and NYC, 1953-54; reporter, writer World Telegram & The Sun, NYC, 1954-62; contbg. writer Sat. Evening Post, NYC, 1962-66; editor-in-chief Today's Health mag., Chgo., 1970-75; med. writer Miami (Fla.) Herald, 1975-78; health editor Family Circle mag., NYC, 1982-83; editor 50 Plus mag., NYC, from 1983. Author: The Twins Who Found Each Other, 1969; co-author: (with James B. Donovan) Strangers on a Bridge, 1964. Dir. communications Am. Lung Assn., N.Y.C., 1980-81; sci. editor Nat. Multiple Sclerosis Soc., 1979-80. Recipient Best Newspaper Series Polk award, 1956, Best Mag. Article award Nat. Arthritis Found., 1971, 75, Best News Feature award Fla. Heart Assn., 1987. Home: Stone Mountain, Ga. Died Dec. 2, 2009.

LINDEN, HENRY ROBERT, chemical engineer, researcher; b. Vienna, Feb. 21, 1922; arrived in US, 1939, naturalized, 1945; s. Fred and Edith (Lermer) Linden; m. Natalie Govedarica, 1967; children from previous marriage: Robert, Debra. BS, Ga. Inst. Tech., Atlanta, 1944; MChemE, Poly. U., 1947; PhD, Ill. Inst. Tech., Chgo., 1952. Chem. engr. Socony Vacuum Labs., 1944-47; with Inst. Gas Tech., 1947-78, various rsch. mgmt. positions, 1947-61, dir., 1961-69, exec. v.p., dir., 1969-74, pres., trustee, 1974-78; various acad. appointments Ill. Inst. Tech., Chgo., 1954-86, Frank W. Gunsaulus Disting. Prof. chem. engring., 1987-90, McGraw prof. energy and power engring. and mgmt., from 1990, interim pres., CEO, 1989-90, interim chmn., CEO Ill. Inst. Tech. Rsch. Inst., 1989-90; COO GDC, Inc., Chgo., 1965-73; CEO Gas Devel. Corp. subs. Inst. Gas Tech., Chgo., 1973-78, also bd. dirs.; pres., dir. Gas Rsch. Inst., Chgo., 1976-87, exec. advisor, 1987-2000. Contbr. articles to profl. jours. Recipient award of merit oper. sect., Am. Gas Assn., 1956, Disting. Svc. award, 1974, Gas. Industry Rsch. award, 1982, R & D award, Nat. Energy Resources Orgn., 1986, Homer H. Lowry award for excellence in fossil energy rsch., U.S. Dept. Energy, 1991, award, U.S. Energy Assn., 1993, Walton Clark medal, Franklin Inst., 1972, Bunsen-Pettenkofer-Ehrentafel medal, Deutscher Verein des Gas und Wasserfaches, 1978, Lifetime Achievement award, Energy Daily Jour., 1996, Alumni medal, Ill. Inst. Tech., 1995; named to Hall of Fame, 1982, Engring. Hall of Fame, Ga. Tech., 1996. Fellow: AAAS, AIChE (Ernest W. Thiele award 2000), Inst. Energy; mem.: Am. Chem. Soc. (chmn. divsn. fuel chemistry 1967, councilor 1969—77, H.H. Storch award), So. Gas Assn. (hon.), NAE. Achievements include patents for fuel technology. Home: Chicago, Ill. Died Sept. 2009.

LINDEN, THEODORE ANTHONY, computer science researcher; b. Cleve., June 25, 1938; s. Anton and Frances Mary (Ott) L.; m. Betty J. Gevatoff, Jan. 18, 1969; children: Jennifer Fran, Gregory David. BA, Loyola U., Chgo., 1961; MA, Yeshiva U., 1965, PhD, 1968. Asst. prof. Fordham Univ., Bronx, N.Y., 1967-69; prin. scientist U.S. Dept. of Defense, Washington, 1970-74, Nat. Bur. Standards, Gaithersburg, Md., 1974-78; dept. mgr. Xerox Corp., Palo Alto, Calif., 1978-84; prog. mgr. Advanced Decision Systems, Mountain View, Calif., from 1984. Contbr. articles to profl. jours. Fellow NSF, 1963-68, Kent Fellowship, Danforth Found., St. Louis, 1963. Mem. IEEE, Assn. Computing Machinery, Am. Assn. Artificial Intelligence (prog. com. 1989-90). Home: Palo Alto, Calif. Died Jan. 20, 2009.

LINDENBAUM, S(EYMOUR) J(OSEPH), physicist; b. NYC, Feb. 3, 1925; s. Morris and Anne Lindenbaum; m. Leda Isaacs, June 29, 1958. AB, Princeton U., 1945; MA, Columbia U., 1949, PhD, 1951. With Brookhaven Nat. Lab., Upton, NY, 1951-96, sr. physicist, 1963-96, sr. physicist emeritus, from 1996, group leader high energy physics research group, 1954-89; vis. prof. U. Rochester, 1958-59; Mark W. Zemansky chair in physics CCNY, 1970-95, Mark Zemansky prof. emeritus of physics, from 1995. Cons. Centre de Etudes Nucleaire de Saclay, France, 1957, CERN, Geneva, 1962; head CCNY Experimental High Energy and Nuclear Physics Rsch. Group, 1970—; dep. for sci. affairs ERDA, 1976-77 Author: Particle Interaction Physics at High Energies, 1973; scriptwriter, narrator, sci. prodr. (multi-screen, audio-visual slide show) Atom Smashing, Atom Smashers: Fifty Years, Smithsonian Instn. Exhibit, 1977; contbr. articles to profl. jours. Fellow Am. Phys. Soc.; mem. NY Acad. Scis., AAAS. Achievements include discovering nucleon isobars dominated high energy particles interactions, isobar model; inventor on line computer technique in scientific experiments; proved experimentally that Einstein's special theory of relativity was correct down to subnuclear distances one hundredth the radius of a proton; discovered the glueball states predicted by quantum chromodynamics. Home: Rock Hill, NY. Died Aug. 17, 2009.

LINDSAY, DAVID BREED, JR., aircraft company executive, former editor and publisher; b. Fayetteville, NC, Dec. 25, 1922; s. David Breed and Helen Carter (Dodson) L.; m. Elizabeth Hotchkiss Girvin, June 19, 1944; children: David G.B., Robert A., Ann C., Edward H. BS, Purdue U., 1947. Reporter/photographer Marion (Ind.) Chronicle, 1947-48; editor, gen. mgr. Sarasota (Fla.) Herald Tribune, 1948-55, editor, pres., 1955-82; pres. Cavalier Aircraft Corp., 1955-70, Lindair, Inc., from 1971. Designer, test pilot Enforcer Aircraft; cons. Piper Aircraft Corp. Founder, trustee New Coll., Sarasota, 1950-75. Served with U.S. Army, 1943-46. Decorated Army Commendation medal. Mem. Am. Newspaper Pubs. Assn. (dir.), Am. Newspaper Pubs. Assn. Found. (pres.), Inter Am. Press Assn. (dir.), Soc. Exptl. Test Pilots., Sigma Delta Chi Clubs: Met. (Washington); Old Capital (Monterey, Calif.). Episcopalian. Inventor various aircraft systems, including Enforcer Aircraft. Died July 2, 2009.

LING, CHUNG-MEI, pharmaceutical executive; b. Wen-Ling, Zhejiang, China, May 5, 1931; came to U.S., 1960; s. Hsin-Sao Ling and San-Mei Juan; m. Jeanine Wu; children: Dori, Shawn, Ellen, Katelin. BS, Nat. Taiwan U., 1958; MS, Ill. Inst. Tech., 1962, PhD, 1965. Head virology lab. Abbott Labs., North Chicago, Ill., 1968-81, rsch. fellow, 1978-84, mgr. rsch. and devel., 1981-84; founder, chmn. bd. dirs., chief sci. officer Gen. Biologicals Corp., Hsinchu, Taiwan, 1984-88, hon. chmn. bd., from 1991; prof. Nat. Tsing-Hua U., Hsinchu, 1991-93. Asst. prof. Ill. Inst. Tech., Chgo., 1965-68; sci. specialist Nat. Inst. Preventative Medicine, Taipei, Taiwan, 1984-85; dir. biosci. rsch. ctr. KangLing Biotech. Corp., Hsinchu, 1988—. Contbr. articles to profl. jours. Fellow Am. Acad. Microbiology; mem. Am. Soc. Biol. Chemists, Am. Clin. Chem., Sigma Xi. Achievements include invention of hepatitis B diagnostics; therapeutics and various health products; patents in field. Avocations: sight-seeing, singing, interior design. Died Jan. 13, 2009.

LINGENFELTER, KENNETH ALBERT, protective services official; b. Chgo., Aug. 8, 1944; s. Albert Luther and Mary Barbara (Ocwieja) Lingenfelter; m. Carol Lynn Tong, (div. 1975); 1 child, Adam; m. Linda Diane Brewer; children: Ryan, Ashley. AA, North Fla. Jr. Coll., Madison, 1965; student, Fla. State U., 1965-66. Cert. Police Standards Commn., Fla. Detective, vice Jacksonville (Fla.) Sheriff's Office, 1974-76 and from 83, detective, burglary, 1976-77, detective, intelligence, 1977-79, detective, narcotics, 1979-83. Swat negotiator, Jacksonville Sheriff's Office, 1988—, critical incident counselor, 1989—; lectr. hostage situations in a med. setting. Asst. editor coll. newspaper 1964, mil. newspaper 1965; author Shrine newspaper 1981-84. Youth leader St. David's Episcopal Ch., Jacksonville, 1981-84, ch. counselor, 1986—; lay dir. Happening of Fla., North Fla., 1984-88; Little League coach, Lake Lucina Youth Assn., Jacksonville, 1981-87; dir. div. of youth ministry Episcopal Diocese of Fla. Mem. Mason (ambassador Shrine 1983—), Scottish Rite 32 degree, Chi Delta Tau (co-founder, charter mem., 1st sec. Madison chpt.). Republican. Avocations: running, swimming, bicycling, rappeling, moutain climbing. Home: Jacksonville, Fla. Died Jan. 21, 2009.

LINHART, JOSEPH WAYLAND, retired cardiologist, educational administrator; b. NYC, Feb. 7, 1933; s. Joseph and Myrla Watson (Wayland) L.; m. Marilyn Adele Voight, Sept. 1, 1956; children: Joseph, Mary-Ellen, Richard, Jennifer, Donna-Lisa, Daria. BS, George Washington U., 1954, MD, 1958. Diplomate Am. Bd. Internal Medicine with subspecialty in cardiovascular diseases. Intern Washington Hosp. Ctr., 1958-59; resident George Washington U. Hosp., Washington, 1959-60, Duke U. Hosp., Durham, NC, 1961, fellow, 1960, 62-63, Nat. Heart Inst./Johns Hopkins Hosp., Bethesda/Balt., Md., 1963-64; asst. prof. medicine U. Fla., Gainesville, 1964-67; clin. assoc. prof. U. Miami, Fla., 1967-68; assoc. prof. medicine U. Tex., San Antonio, 1968-71; prof., dir. cardiology Hahnemann Med. Coll., Phila., 1971-75; prof., chmn. dept. medicine Chgo. Med. Sch., 1975-79, Oral Roberts U., Tulsa, 1979-83; prof. medicine U. South Fla., Tampa, 1983-92; prof., regional chmn. medicine Tex. Tech. U., Odessa, 1992-93; prof. medicine La. State U., Shreveport, 1993-97; chief med. svc. VA Med. Ctr., Shreveport, 1993-97, acting chief of staff, 1996-97; ret., 1997. Cons. in cardiology and med./legal questions. Contbr. articles to profl. jours.; author 4 books. Mem. med. adv. com. YMCA, Niles, Ill., 1976-79; bd. govs. Phila. Heart Assn., 1972-75; mem. rsch. coun. Okla. Heart Assn., Tulsa, 1980-83. Fellow ACP, Am. Coll. Cardiology; mem. AAAS, Planetary Soc., Nat. Space Soc., Astron. Soc. of Pacific, Alpha Omega Alpha. Republican. Avocations: astronomy, history, model building, organ playing, music. Home: Saint Petersburg, Fla. Died Mar. 28, 2010.

LINIHAN, MARTIN G., lawyer; b. Buffalo, Dec. 18, 1940; BA, Hamilton Coll., 1963; BEE, Rensselaer Poly. Inst., 1965; JD with honors, George Washington U., 1968. Ptnr. Hodgson, Russ, Andrews, Woods & Goodyear, Buffalo. Mem. Am. Intellectual Property Law Assn., Niagara Frontier Patent Law Assn., Eta Kappa Nu. Died Mar. 1, 2010.

LINK, ARTHUR ALBERT, Former United States Representative from North Dakota; b. Alexander, ND, May 24, 1914; m. Grace Johnson, 1939; 6 children. Mem. Randolph Township Bd., McKenzie Co. Welfare Bd., ND House of Reps., ND, 1947—71; chmn. ND State Advisor Coun. Vocat. Edn., 1969—71; mem. US Congress from 2nd ND Dist., ND, 1971—73; gov. State of ND, 1973—81, Centennial Com., ND, 1985—90. Mem. Randolph Township Bd., 1942—72, Randolph Sch. Bd., 1945—63, McKenzie County Welfare Bd., 1948—69. Recipient Nat. Future Farmers America award, 1974, Agriculturist of Yr. award, Saddle & Sirloin Club, NCak State U., 1981, ND State U. Outstanding Agr. award, 1992, ND State U. Outstanding Bus award, 1992, Liberty Bell award, 1981. Mem.: ND State Bar Assn. (founding mem.), Kiwanis, Ekls, Nat. Cowboy Hall of Fame, PTA, Lions, Williston U. Ctr. Found. Democrat. Lutheran. Home: Bismarck, ND. Died June 1, 2010.

LINKE, RUTH ANNA, home economist; b. N.Y.C., Aug. 26, 1926; d. George and Elsie (Schmidt) Renz; B.S., N.Y.U., 1946, Ph.D., 1957; M.A., Columbia U., 1947; m. William F. Linke, Apr. 14, 1949; children— William, Robert Christopher, Jennifer Ann. Instr. part time N.Y. U., Tchrs. Coll., Columbia U., Hunter Coll., Lehman Coll., 1950-64; asst. prof. dept. home econs. and nutrition N.Y. U., 1973-76, assoc. prof., 1976—, acting chmn. dept., 1974-75, dep. chmn., 1979—. Mem. Bd. Edn. Stamford (Conn.), 1962-71, pres., 1964-65, 68-69; mem. urban edn. com. Conn. Assn. Bds. of Edn., 1966-70; mem. Conn. State Advisory Com. for Ednl. Profl. Devel. Act, 1966-70. Mem. Am., N.Y. State (dir., v.p. 1982-84, treas. dist. 5 1977-79, dist. pres. 1980-81) home econs. assns., Coll. Tchrs. Household Equipment (membership com. 1979-80), Assn. Home Econs. Tchrs. N.Y.C., Elec. Women's Round Table, Am. Assn. Housing Educators, Am. Vocat. Assn., N.Y. State Home Econs. Tchrs. Assn., AAUW, Omicron Nu, Pi Lambda Theta. Contbr. articles to profl. jours. Home: Stamford, Conn. Died Feb. 8, 2009.

LINKLETTER, ARTHUR GORDON, radio and television broadcaster; b. Moose Jaw, Sask., Can., July 17, 1912; s. Fulton John and Mary (Metzler) L.; m. Lois Foerster, Nov. 25, 1935; children: Jack (dec. 2007), Dawn, Robert (dec. 1980), Sharon, Diane (dec. 1969). AB, San Diego State Coll., 1934. Program dir. Sta. KGB, San Diego, 1934; program dir. Calif. Internat. Expn., San Diego, 1935; radio dir. Tex. Centennial Expn., Dallas, 1936; San Francisco World's Fair, 1937-39; pres. Linkletter Prodns.; ptnr., co-owner John Guedel Radio Prodns. Chmn. bd. Linkletter Enterprises; owner Art Linkletter Oil Enterprises. Author: theme spectacle Cavalcade of Golden West, 1940; author and co-producer: theme spectacle Cavalcade of Am, 1941; writer, producer, star in West Coast radio shows, 1940-55; former star, writer: People Are Funny, NBC-TV and radio, Art Linkletter's House Party, CBS-TV and radio; Author: People Are Funny, 1953, Kids Say The Darndest Things, 1957, The Secret World of Kids, 1959, Confessions of a Happy Man, 1961, Kids Still Say The Darndest Things, 1961, A Child's Garden of Misinformation, 1965, I Wish I'd Said That, 1968, Linkletter Down Under, 1969, Oops, 1969, Drugs at My Door Step, 1973, Women Are My Favorite People, 1974, How to be a Super Salesman, 1974, Yes, You Can!, 1979, I Didn't Do It Alone, 1979, Public Speaking for Private People, 1980, Linkletter on Dynamic Selling, 1982, Old Age is not for Sissies, 1988; co-host (with Bill Cosby) series Kids Say the Darnedest Things, 1998-2000; lectr. convs. and univs. Nat. bd. dirs. Goodwill Industries; commr. gen. to U.S. Exhibit at Brisbane Expo 88, Australia, 1987; commr. gen. to rank of U.S. amb. to The 200th Anniversary Celebration, Australia, 1987—; bd. regents Pepperdine U.; chmn. bd. Ctr. on Aging, UCLA; chmn. bd. French Found. for Alzheimers Rsch., Solargenix; pres. USA-Next (sr.). Recipient numerous awards. Mem.: United Srs. Assn. (pres.). Died May 26, 2010.

LINTZ, ROBERT CARROLL, retired financial holding company executive; b. Cin., Oct. 2, 1933; s. Frank George and Carolyn Martha (Dickhaus) Lintz; m. Mary Agnes Mott, Feb.

1, 1964 (dec.); children: Lesa, Robert, Laura, Michael. BBA, U. Cin., 1956. Staff accountant Alexander Grant, Cin., 1958—60; dist. mgr. Uniroyal, Memphis, 1960—65; v.p. Am. Fin. Corp., Cin., 1965—2002; dir. Rapid-American Corp., McGregor Corp., Faberge Inc., NYC, H.R.T. Industries Inc., LA, Fisher Foods Inc., Cleve., Am. Agronomics, Tampa, Fla. Trustee St. Francis-St. George Hosp., Cin., 1974—81. Served to capt. US Army, 1956—58, 1961—62. Republican. Roman Catholic. Home: Cincinnati, Ohio. Died Jan. 26, 2010.

LINZ, GERHARD DAVID, psychologist, consultant; b. Waltershausen, Thuringia, Germany, Jan. 5, 1927; came to U.S., 1936; s. Leopold and Rita (Nussbaum) L.; m. Frances Ann Pierson; children: Christopher, Michael, Stephanie, Peter. B in Elec. Engring. with honors, Ga. Inst. Tech., 1948, MS, 1949; BDiv, Episcopal Theol. Sem. S.W., Austin, Tex., 1956; PhD, U. Tex., Austin, 1980. Diplomate Am. Bd. Profl. Psychology, Counseling Psychology. Rsch. engr. RCA Labs., Princeton, N.J., 1949-51; rsch. engr., Engring. Experiment Sta. Ga. Tech., Atlanta, 1951-53; rsch. engr., Def. Rsch. Lab. U. Tex., Austin, 1953-56; vicar All Saints Episcopal Ch., Warner Robins, Ga., 1956-59; assoc. rector Christ Ch. Episcopal, Macon, Ga., 1959; Episcopal chaplain U. Tex., Austin, 1960-66; asst. prof. Counseling Ctr. Mich. State U., East Lansing, 1966-70; from assoc. prof. to prof., assoc. dir. Counseling Ctr. Ga. State U., Atlanta, 1970-93, Alumni Disting. prof., 1984; pvt. practice Decatur, Ga., from 1971. Mem. dept. Christian Edn., Episcopal Diocese of Atlanta, 1957-59; bd. dirs. Inst. for Marital and Family Therapy, Atlanta. Author: Novice Notes-An Introduction to Cryptanalysis, 1990; contbr. articles to profl. jours. Chaplain Civitan Club, Warner Robins, Ga., 1958-59. With U.S. Army, 1945-46, ATO. Mem. Assn. Counseling Ctr. Tng. Agts. (v.p. 1979-85), Am. Psychol. Assn., Soc. for Clin. and Exptl. Hypnosis, Southeastern Psychol. Assn., Ga. Psychol. Assn., Ga. Coll. Pers. Assn. Episcopalian. Avocations: cryptography, bridge, photography, computers. Died Jan. 27, 2009.

LITMAN, JACK THEODORE, lawyer; b. NYC, July 26, 1943; s. Charles Louis and Sarah G. (Hornblas) L.; m. Helena Dunica, Aug. 25, 1968; children: Sacha F., Benjamin S. BA, Cornell U., 1964; LLB, Harvard U., 1967; diploma, Inst. Criminology, Paris, 1968. Bar: NY 1968, US Dist. Ct. (so. and ea. dists. NY) 1973, US Ct. Appeals (2nd cir.) 1973, US Supreme Ct. 1975. Asst. dist. atty. NY County (Manhattan) Dist. Attorney's Office, NYC, 1968-74, sr. trial asst., dep. chief Homicide Bur., 1968—74; sr. ptnr. Litman, Asche, & Gioiella, LLP, NYC, 1974—2010. Adj. prof. law NYU, 1970-93; lectr. in field. Editor: Criminal Trial Advocacy, 1975; contbr. articles to profl. jours. Fulbright scholar, 1967-68; named NY Super Lawyer, 2006, 2007, 2008. Mem. NY State Bar Assn. (mem. exec. com. criminal justice sect., named Outstanding Practitioner of Yr. 1986), Assn. of Bar of City of NY (mem. com. criminal courts and law procedure 1975-78), NY Criminal Bar Assn. (pres. 1987-89, bd. dirs.), NACDL (bd. dirs.), NY State Assn. Criminal Def. Lawyers (bd. dirs., pres. 1990-91) Democrat. Jewish. Avocations: chess, movies, sports, number theory. Died Jan. 23, 2010.

LITTAUER, RAPHAEL M., retired physics and nuclear science educator; b. Leipzig, Germany, Nov. 28, 1925; naturalized US citizen. m. 1950; 2 children. MA, Cambridge U., PhD in Physics, 1950. Asst. physics Cambridge U., Eng., 1947-50; rsch. assoc. in nuclear physics Cornell U., Ithaca, N.Y., 1950-54, rsch. assoc. prof. physics, 1955-63, rsch. prof., 1963-65, prof. physics, nuclear studies, from 1965, chmn. dept., 1974-77. Rsch. assoc. nuclear physics Synchrotron Lab. GE, 1954-55. Mem. Am. Phys. Soc. (Robert R. Wilson prize for Achievement in the Physics of Particle Acceleration, 1995). Died Oct. 19, 2009.

LITTLE, CHARLES EDWARD, mathematics educator, university administrator; b. Kansas City, Kans., Apr. 18, 1926; s. Clarence A. and Anna Lu (Brown) L.; m. Janet R. Thompson, June 18, 1947; children: Steven, Jennifer, Timothy. AB, U. Kans.-Lawrence, 1948; MS, Ft. Hays Kans. State U., 1955; Ed.D., U. No. Colo., 1964. Tchr., adminstr. Burdett pub. schs., Kans., 1951-61; instr. math. U. No. Colo., Greeley, 1961-64; asst. prof. math. No. Ariz. U., Flagstaff, 1964-65, assoc. prof., 1965-68, prof., 1968-90, prof. emeritus, from 1990, chmn. dept. math. Flagstaff, 1967-70, dean Coll. Arts and Sci., 1974-84. Mem. adv. com. Ariz. State Bd. Edn. math., 1986-87, com. on essential skills for math., 1987; dir. Math Tchr. Retng. Program, 1987-89; adv. commn. textbook, math selection Ariz. State Bd Edn. Author: Mathematics for Liberal Arts, 1965, Programmed Instruction, 1967, Basic Concepts of Mathematics, 1967. Bd. dirs. Flagstaff Federated Ch., 1967, Univ. Heights Corp., Flagstaff, 1969—, pres., 1969-76; mem. Flagstaff City Coun., 1974-78; chmn. City of Flagstaff Water Commn., 1978-90; mem. City of Flagstaff Housing Authority Commn., 1987—; bd. dirs. Flagstaff Housing Corp., 1985—. Mem. Math. Assn. Am., Nat. Council Tchrs. Math., Phi Kappa Phi, Phi Delta Kappa, Kappa Mu Epsilon, Lambda Sigma Tau Home: Flagstaff, Ariz. Died Apr. 21, 2009.

LITTLE, GEORGE DANIEL, clergyman; b. St. Louis, Dec. 18, 1929; s. Henry and Agathe Cox (Daniel) L.; m. Joan Phillips McCafferty, Aug. 22, 1953; children: Deborah Phillips, Cynthia McCafferty (dec.), Alice Annette, Daniel Ross, Benjamin Henry. AB, Princeton U., 1951; MDiv, McCormick Theol. Sem., Chgo., 1954; LLD (hon.), Huron Coll., 1977. Ordained to ministry Presbyn. Ch., 1954; pastor East London Group Ministry, Presbyn. Ch. Eng., 1954-56, Friendship Presbyn. Ch., Pitts., 1956-62; assoc. dir. dept. urban ch., planning assoc. Bd. Nat. Missions, United Presbyterian Ch. U.S.A., NYC, 1962-72; assoc. for budgeting Gen. Assembly Mission Council, 1973-76, exec. dir. council, 1976-84; pastor First Presbyn. Ch., Ithaca, NY, 1984-93; interim pres. McCormick Theol. Sem., Chgo., 1993-94; pastor-in-residence Village Presbyn. Ch., Prairie Village, Kans., 1995-96, Westminster Presbyn. Ch., Mpls., 1997-99, 2002; ret., 1999. Presbyterian. Home: Madison, Wis. Died Nov. 16, 2009.

LITTLE, JAMES DAVID, lawyer; b. Laurinburg, NC, Mar. 9, 1944; s. James A. and Lucille (Quick) Little. BA in Polit. Sci., U. NC, Chapel Hill, 1966; JD, 1972. Bar: NC 1972, US Dist. Ct. (ea. dist.) NC 1974, US Ct. Appeals (4th cir.) 1978, US Supreme Ct. 1979, US Ct. Mil. Appeals 1980. Asst. dist. atty. Dist. Atty.'s Office, Fayetteville, NC, 1972—73; chief pub. defender Pub. Defender's Office, Fayetteville, 1974—76; ptnr. law firm Singleton, Murray, Harlow & Little and Predecessor Firm, Fayetteville, 1976—80, ptnr., 1980—82; chief counsel NC Utilities Commn. Pub. Staff, Raleigh, from 1983. Cons. NC Bar Assn., 1974—76, Nat. Ctr. Def., 1975—79; dir. NC Legal Svcs. Corp., Raleigh, 1976—82. Legal cons. Cumberland County Assn. Indian People, 1975—80; mem. NC Criminal Code Commn., 1979—82. Mem.: ABA, NC State Bar Assn., NC Bar Assn., NC Acad. Trial Lawyers. Democrat. Presbyterian. Home: Raleigh, NC. Died Mar. 18, 2010.

LITTLE, JOSEPH ALEXANDER, pediatrician; b. Bessemer, Ala., Mar. 16, 1918; s. Joseph Alexander and Kathleen W. (Vann) L.; m. Sarah Goodpasture, Aug. 2, 1941; children—Sarah Marsh, Susan McLaughlin, Joseph Alexander. AB, Vanderbilt U., 1940, MD, 1943. Intern Vanderbilt Univ. Hosp., Nashville, 1943, 46-47; resident Children's Hosp., Cin., 1947-48; practice medicine, specializing in pediatrics Cin., 1948-49, Louisville, 1949-62, Nashville, 1962-70, Shreveport, La., 1970-84. Pediatrician-in-chief Children's Hosp. Louisville, 1956-62; instr. pediatrics U. Cin. Sch. Medicine, 1948-49; asst. to prof. U. Louisville Sch. Medicine, 1949-62; assoc. prof. pediatrics Vanderbilt U. Sch. Medicine, 1962-70; prof., head dept. pediatrics La. State U. Med. Center Sch. Medicine, 1970-83. Pres. Caddo-Bossier Day Care Assn., 1972-74. Mem. Am. Acad. Pediatrics (chmn. Ky. 1959-62), Am. Pediatric Soc., Am. Heart Assn. (pres. La. 1979-80), Alpha Omega Alpha, Omicron Delta Kappa. Clubs: Episcopalian. Home: Sewanee, Tenn. Died Nov. 3, 2009.

LITTLE, WILLIAM FREDERICK, academic administrator; b. Hickory, NC, Nov. 11, 1929; s. William H. and Mary Elvira (Sheely) L.; m. Dell Hoyle, July 19, 1958; 1 child, Teresa Dell Marcellin-Little. BS, Lenoir Rhyne Coll., 1950; MA, U. N.C., 1952, PhD, 1954. Instr. Reed Coll., Portland, Ore., 1955-56; prof. U. N.C., Chapel Hill, from 1977. Chmn. dept. chemistry U. N.C., Chapel Hill, 1965-70, vice chancellor devel. & pub. svc., 1973-78, interim provost & vice chancellor acad. affairs, 1991-92, v.p. acad. affairs, sr. v.p., 1992—; chmn. exec. com. Rsch. Triangle Found., Rsch. Triangle Park, N.C., 1987—, corp. sec., 1990—; chmn. exec. com. Rsch. Triangle Inst., 1968-77; pres. Triangle Univs. Ctr. for Advanced Studies, Inc., 1982-87. Trustee Lenoir Rhyne Coll., Hickory, N.C., 1960-63, devel. bd., 1967-73; mem. N.C. Bd. Sci. & Tech., 1963-78. Mem. Am. Chem. Soc. (chmn. N.C. sect. 1965), Order of the Golden Fleece, Sigma Xi. Home: Chapel Hill, NC. Died Feb. 27, 2009.

LITWACK, ARLENE DEBRA, psychotherapist, psychoanalyst, educator, consultant; b. Brookline, Mass., July 18, 1945; d. Hyman and Bessie Litwack. BA cum laude, Boston U., 1967; MS, Columbia U., 1969; postgrad., Ctr. for Mental Health, NYC, 1981; psychoanalyst cert., Inst. for Psychoanalytic Tng. and Rsch., 1993. Caseworker Pride Treatment Ctr., Douglaston, NY, 1969—73, supr., 1973—78, sr. worker, 1978—80; pvt. practice psychotherapy and psychoanalysis NYC, from 1980. Mem. faculty Inst. for Mental Health Edn., Englewood, NJ, 1983—89; clin. cons. NY Spaulding for Children, 1989; bd. dirs. child therapy dept. LI Consultation Ctr., Rego Park, NY, 1980—85; faculty workshop leader Human Svcs. Workshops, NYC; adj. faculty Fordham U., from 1991; mem. faculty, supr., chair object rels. Psychoanalytic Study Ctr., from 1991, exec. com.; cons. 9/11 recovery program ARC, 2003—05. Contbr. articles to profl. jours. Mem.: NASW, NY State Soc. Clin. Social Workers (presenter workshops on grief from 1999). Home: New York, NY. Died Feb. 18, 2009.

LITZ, JAMES CHARLES, artist; b. Buffalo, Sept. 17, 1948; s. Thomas Edward and Barbara A. (Thiell) L.; m. Beverly Jean Gast. Grad. high sch., Cheektowaga, NY. Truck driver, 1970-76; employee gas sta., 1976-82; artist, from 1982. Prin. works represented in numerous permanent collections including Musee d'Art Naif de Lile de France, Am. Folk Art Mus., N.Y.C., Buffalo and Erie County N.Y. State Hist. Soc., Benjamans Art Gallery, Buffalo, Vern Steins Fine Arts Gallery, Williamsville, N.Y., The Gov.'s Mansion, Albany, N.Y., Mingei Internat. World Folk Art Mus., La Jolla, Calif., Burchfield Art Mus. Ctr., Buffalo, Fenimore House Farmers Mus., Cooperstown, N.Y., Cooperstown Art Assn.; exhibited in group shows including N.Y.C. World Famous Art Exposition, 1989, Albright-Knox Art Gallery, N.Y.C., 1988, Ea. Ill. U., 1988, Midwest Mus. Am. Art, Elkhart, Ind., 1988, Wright Mus. Art, Beloit, Wis., 1987; Cin. Mus. Art, 1986. With U.S. Army, 1968-69. Mem. Burchfield (N.Y.) Art Ctr. Home: Buffalo, NY. Died Nov. 24, 2009.

LIVINGSTON, J. STERLING, management consultant, educator; b. Salt Lake City, June 7, 1916; s. Julius Edward and Lucille (Scott) L.; m. Ruth Elizabeth Flume, Feb. 6, 1943; children: Lucille Scott, Sterling Christopher, Matthew Steele, Florence Ruth. BBA cum laude, U. So. Calif., 1938; MBA, Harvard U., 1940, D.C.S., 1948. Research asst. Grad. Sch. Bus. Administrn., Harvard U., 1940, asst. prof., 1946-48, assoc. prof., 1948-50, prof., 1956-71; spl. asst. to asst. atty. gen. Thurman Arnold; cons. to chmn. WPB, 1941-42; dir. Harbridge House, Inc. (mgmt. cons.), 1949-63, pres., 1949-61, chmn., 1961-63; pres., dir. Mgmt. Systems Corp., Cambridge, 1960-65; mng. partner Peat, Marwick, Livingston & Co., 1965-67; pres. Sterling Inst., Washington, 1967-86, chmn., 1987—2010; pres. Tech. Fund P.R., Inc., 1961-65; v.p., treas. pres. Mining Research Corp., 1951-57, dir., 1951-57. Author: (with R.T. Davis) Cases in Sales Management; contbr. (with R.T. Davis) articles to profl. jours. Served as comdr. Supply Corps USNR, 1942-46. Recipient Ann. Merit award Armed Forces Mgmt. Assn., 1962; McKinsey award Harvard Bus. Rev., 1971 Mem. Phi Kappa Tau. Clubs: Harvard (N.Y.C.); Harvard Bus. Sch. (Washington and S.Fla.). Home: Miami, Fla. Died Feb. 14, 2010.

LIVINGSTON, RUTH, actress; b. New Haven, Mar. 25, 1927; d. Alan V. and Theresa A. (Kieffer) L.; m. Leslie Barrett, June 19, 1977. BA in Speech, U. Mich.; trainee, Am. Theatre Wing, studied with Uta Hagen, William Bell. Appeared in (stage prodns.) A Streetcar Named Desire, 1960, 67, A Shot in the Dark, Henry IV, Arsenic and Old Lace, 1966, The Odd Couple, 1968, Romeo and Juliet, Tartuffe, 1977, On Golden Pond, 1978, (film) The Group, 1963, (TV) As the World Turns, All My Children. Mem. Actors' Equity Assn., AFTRA. Home: New York, NY. Died Mar. 2, 2010.

LLEWELLYN, JAMES BRUCE, retired food products executive; b. Harlem, NY, July 16, 1927; s. Charles and Vanessa Llewellyn; m. Jacqueline Brown; children: Lisa, Alexandra; m. Shahara Ahmad; 1 child, Jaylaan. Grad., City Coll. NY, 1955; JD, NYU Law Sch., 1960. Liquor store owner, Harlem, NY, 1952—56; student asst. Dist. Attorney's Office NY County, 1958—60; ptnr. Evans Burger & Llewellyn, 1962—65; acting pres. Freedom Nat. Bank; pres. Fedco Food Stores, 1969—84, Overseas Private Investment Corp. (OPIC), 1978—80; chmn., CEO Phila. Coca-Cola Bottling Co. Served in US Army, 1941—46. Died Apr. 7, 2010.

LLOYD, JOHN H., wholesale food company executive; b. Atlanta, May 30, 1921; s. John H. and Margaret (Harris) L.; m. Harriet Rogers; 1 child, John Van. Student, Ga. State U. V.p. Colonial Stores Inc., Columbia, S.C., 1939-72; exec. v.p. Fleming Foods, Geneva, Ala., 1972-79, v.p. Columbia, 1979-85; pres. Wetterau Foods Inc., Charleston, S.C., from 1985. Republican. Baptist. Home: Summerville, SC. Died May 25, 2009.

LO, ARTHUR WU-NIEN, engineering educator; b. Shanghai, May 21, 1916; came to U.S., 1945, naturalized, 1957; s. Liang-Kan and Shou-Pan (Heng) L.; m. Elizabeth H. Shen, Aug. 24, 1950; children: Katherine E., James A. BS, Yenching U., 1938; MA, Oberlin Coll., 1946; PhD, U. Ill., 1949. Mem. tech. staff RCA Research Labs., 1951-60; mgr. advanced devel., data systems div. IBM Corp., 1960-62, mgr. exploratory devel., components div., 1962-64; prof. elec. engring. Princeton U., 1964-86, prof. emeritus, from 1986. Cons. in field, 1964—, spl. research digital electronics and computer systems. Author: Transistor Electronics, 1955, Introduction to Digital Electronics, 1967; also papers in field; patentee in field. Fellow IEEE; mem. Sigma Xi, Eta Kappa Nu, Pi Mu Epsilon. Home: Hightstown, NJ. Died Feb. 25, 2010.

LOBEL, CHARLES IRVING, physician; b. Phila., Nov. 9, 1921; s. Maurice and Dora (Barnett) L.; m. Julia Valentine Skellchock, June 12, 1955; children: Meredith Anne Lobel-Angel. AA, San Jose State U., 1948; student, Stanford U., 1948-49; MD, U. So. Calif., 1954. Physician Permanente Med. Group, Inc., South San Francisco, 1954-65; physician, courtesy staff Chope Cmty. Hosp., San Mateo, Calif., 1965-89, Sequoia Hosp., Redwood City, Calif., 1965-94; physician Permanente Med. Group, Inc., Redwood City, Calif., 1965-95. Clin. prof. emeritus of medicine divsn. rheumatology Stanford U. Sch. Medicine, from 1965; chief profl. edn. Kaiser Found. Hosp., Redwood City, 1968—80, rehab. coord., 1968—80, pres. med. staff, 1968—70; mem. Calif. Med. Assn. Staff Survey Com., San Francisco, 1970—90; mem. 4th dist. Bd. Med. Quality Assurance State Calif., 1979—84; faculty physician Samaritan House Med. Clinic, San Mateo, Calif., from 1997. 1st Lt. U.S. Army, 1942-46. Decorated Combat Infantry Badge, Bronze Star, Presdl. Unit citation, 3 Battle Stars. Fellow Am. Acad. Family Physicians, Am. Coll. Rheumatology; mem. AMA, AAAS, San Mateo County Med. Soc. (bd. dirs. 1975-78), Calif. Med. Soc. (alt. del. 1979-83), N.Y. Acad. Scis., Am. Heart Assn., Royal Soc. of Med., Med. Friends of Wine, Arthritis Found. No. Calif., Phi Delta Epsilon. Avocations: music, theater, literature, travel, gourmet cooking. Home: Hillsborough, Calif. Died Jan. 13, 2009.

LOCATELLI, PAUL LEO, academic administrator; b. Santa Cruz, Calif., Sept. 16, 1938; s. Vincent Dino and Marie Josephine (Piccone) L. BS in Acctg., Santa Clara U., 1961; MDiv, Jesuit Sch. Theology, 1974; DBA, U. So. Calif., 1971. CPA, Calif.; ordained priest Roman Cath. Ch., 1974. Prof. acctg. Santa Clara (Calif.) U., 1974-86, assoc. dean Bus. Sch., 1976—78, acad. v.p., 1978—86, pres., 1988—2008, chancellor, 2008—10. Mem. Silicon Valley Leadership Group, Cath. Relief Svcs.; trustee Jesuit Sch. Theology, Berkeley. Mem. acad. adv. bd. Panetta Inst.; mem. internat. com. Jesuit Higher Edn.; sec. higher edn. Soc. Jesus. Recipient Pro Ecclesia et Pontifice, 2002, Spirit of Silicon Valley Lifetime Achievement award, Silicon Valley Leadership Group. Mem. Calif. Soc. CPAs (Disting. Prof. of the Yr. award 1994), Assn. Jesuit Colls. and Univs., Commonwealth Club Silicon Valley. Democrat. Died July 12, 2010.

LOCKARD, THOMAS SWIFT, JR., communications executive; b. Columbia, Pa., Aug. 12, 1924; s. Thomas Swift and Bertha Mary (Jewell) L.; m. Blanche Galbraith Miller, June 12, 1955; children: Christianne Jewel, Rebecca Galbraith, Katherine Rossiter. BA in Econs., Franklin and Marshall Coll., 1950. Assoc. sales dir. N.Y. Mag., 1967-72; v.p. mktg. Mag. Pubs. Assn., NYC, 1972-74; v.p., assoc. pub. Saturday Review, NYC, 1974-76; dir. mktg. Petersen Pub., NYC, 1976-77; v.p., assoc. pub. New West Mag., Beverly Hills, Calif., 1978-80; dir. spl. mag. projects Knapp Communications Corp.; nat. sales mgr. UPI. Lectr. pub. procedures Radcliffe Coll.; lectr. U. Soc. Calif. Mem. Montclair (N.J.) Bd. Edn., 1969-71. Lt. comdr. USNR, 1943-46, 50-53. Mem. Advt. Club Los Angeles, Mag. Pubs. Assn., Western Pub. Assn. (dir.), Los Angeles Club, Ironwood Country Club (Palm Desert, Calif.). Republican. Died June 6, 2009.

LOEBEL, KURT, musician, educator; b. Vienna, Dec. 19, 1921; came to U.S., 1939; s. Rudolph and Margarete (Schoenfeld) L.; m. Ingrid Moor, Nov. 18, 1945; 1 child, David. MusB, Cleve. Inst. Music, 1951, MusM, 1952. Mem. 1st violin sect. Dallas Symphony, 1945-47, Cleve. Orch., from 1947; 1st violinist Symphonia Quartet, Cleve., 1960-70. Mem. faculty Cleve. Inst. Music, 1952—, mem. string quartet 1952-62, Blossom Festival Sch., 1968—; 1st violinist Symphonia Quartet, 1960-70. Contbr. articles to profl. jours. Bd. dirs. Ams. Dem. Action, Am. Jewish Com.; mem. Fairmount Temple Soc. Action Com., Cleve. Served with U.S. Army, 1943-45, ETO. Democrat. Jewish. Avocations: writing, social action, liberal causes. Died Oct. 18, 2009.

LOEBL, BURTON B., lawyer; b. Bklyn., Apr. 19, 1925; s. Richard and Blanche (Broudy) Loebl; m. Jocelyn Helene Planick, July 8, 1951 (div.); 1 child, Lauren Wynne. Attended, U. Miami, 1946—49, JD, 1949. Bar: Fla. 1949, U.S. Dist. Ct. (so. dist.) Fla. 1951, U.S. Dist. Ct. (mid. dist.) Fla. 1960, U.S. Ct. Appeals (5th cir.) 1963, U.S. Ct. Appeals (11th cir.) 1981. Sole practice, Miami Beach, 1949—60, North Miami Beach, 1960—69; pub. utilities counsel City of North Miami Beach, 1969—74, from 1978, city atty., 1969—74, 1978, assoc. mcpl. judge, 1975; town atty. Surfside, Fla., 1975—76; spl. counsel Pembroke Pines, Fla., from 1975; sole practice North Miami Beach, from 1974. Contbr.: chpts. to books, articles to profl. jours. Bd. dirs. North Miami Beach C. of C., from 1968. Served US Army, 1943—46. Recipient awards, Italian Am. Club, North Dade Bar Assn., N.Y. Club of Fla., Small Bus. Com. U.S. Congress, City of North Miami Beach. Mem.: Union Internationale des Avocats, North Dade Bar Assn., Fla. Bar Assn., ABA, Rotary Club, Shriners, Masons. Democrat. Jewish. Home: Miami, Fla. Died Mar. 28, 2010.

LOESER, HANS FERDINAND, lawyer; b. Kassel, Germany, Sept. 28, 1920; s. Max and Cecilia H. (Erlanger) Loeser; m. Herta Lewent, Dec. 14, 1944; children: Helen, Harris M., H. Thomas. Student, CCNY, 1940—42, U. Pa., 1942—43; LLB magna cum laude, Harvard U., 1950. Bar: Mass. 1950, U.S. Supreme Ct. 1968. Assoc. Foley, Hoag & Eliot, Boston, 1950—55, ptnr., from 1956. Hon. consul-gen. Republic of Senegal, 1970—85; former mem. Mass. Bd. Bar Overseers; trustee Vineyard Open Land Found., Martha's Vineyard, Mass.; mem. exec. com., nat. bd. Lawyers' Com. for Civil Rights Under Law; steering com., past chmn. Lawyers Com. for Civil Rights Under Law of Boston Bar Assn.; founder, dir., treas. Lawyers Alliance for World Security, Washington. Corporator Mt. Auburn Hosp., Cambridge, Mass. Capt. US Army, 1942—46. Decorated Bronze Star, Purple Heart; hon. fellow, U. Pa. Law Sch., 1978—79. Fellow: Mass. Bar Found., Am. Bar Found.; mem.: ABA, Boston Bar Assn., Mass. Bar Assn., Cambridge Club. Died May 15, 2010.

LOFTUS, ROBERT EARL, cataract and ocular implant surgery consultant; b. Belvedere, Ill., Aug. 5, 1922; s. Frederick Charles and Bertha Belle (Allen) Loftus; m. Marjorie Lucille Miller, June 30, 1945; children: Steven Robert, Charles Webber, David Kendall, Barbara Dianne. BS, Lawrence Coll., Appleton, Wis., 1944; PhD, U. Chgo., 1947; LittD, U. Barcelona, 1977. Midwest regional mgr. Warren-Teed Co., Mpls., 1950—64; eastern divisional mgr. Wesley-Jessen, Chgo., 1964—72; dir. ednl. services House of Vision, Chgo., 1972—74, Cavitron Surg. Sys., Atlanta, 1974—79; asst. to pres. Intermedica/Intraocular, Inc., Pasadena, Calif., 1979—86, Pharmacia Ophthalmics, from 1986. Cons. Charing Cross Med. Ctr., London, 1975—79, Lucknow Med. Ctr., India, 1978, Goethe U., Frankfurt, Germany, 1977, Soc. Ophthalmology, Rio de Janiero, 1983. With US Army, 1943. Recipient Citations award, Lions Club, 1976—77, award, Soc. Venezuelan Opthalmology, 1983. Mem.: Phi Kappa Tau, Halum-Arnold Eye Found., Am. Coll. Ophthalm. Surgeons. Republican. Died Feb. 17, 2009.

LOMBARDO, EUGENE VINCENT, advertising executive; b. NYC, Aug. 20, 1938; s. Michaelangelo and Maria (Di Gaetano) Lombardo; m. Carol Josephine Marrale, Aug. 28, 1968. Majored in bus. adminstrn., N.Y.C. Community Coll., 1957—59; grad. in mil. sci., Empire State Mil. Acad., 1965, U.S. Army Command and Gen. Staff Coll., 1977, Nat. Def. U., 1979; grad. nat. issues program, U.S. Army War Coll., 1986; BS in Bus. Comm., SUNY, 1987. Cert. bus. communicator. Pres., promoter Eugene V. Lombardo Enterprises, Ltd., Bklyn., 1959—61, 1964—65; accounts exec., mgr. Addressograph-Multigraph Corp., NYC, 1965—69; commd. officer USAR, 1965, advanced through grades to col., 1988; chief pub. affairs hdqrs. 77th USAR Command, Ft. Totten, Queens, NY, 1981—87; div. chief. for pub. edn. Civil Affairs Command, 1987—89; apptd. dep. chief staff for info. mgmt. 77th USAR Command; ea. regional advt. mgr. ASHRAE Jour., NYC, 1969—74; N.Y. mgr., advt. exec. IEEE Spectrum Mag., NYC, 1974. Dist. capt., county committeeman Democratic Party Orgn. of Richmond County, SI, NY, 1973. With U.S. Army, 1962—64. Decorated Meritorious Service Medal with four oak leaf clusters. Mem.: Am. Legion, Res. Officers Assn. U.S., Bus. and Profl. Advt. Assn. N.Y., Italian Club of S.I. (pub. rels. dir. 1973—77, Man of Yr. award 1977), Advertising (N.Y.C.). Roman Cath. Home: Staten Island, NY. Died Apr. 9, 2010.

LONG, CARL FERDINAND, retired engineering educator; b. NYC, Aug. 6, 1928; s. Carl and Marie Victoria (Wellnitz) L.; m. Joanna Margarida Tavares, July 23, 1955; children: Carl Ferdinand, Barbara Anne. S.B., MIT, 1950, S.M., 1952; D.Eng., Yale U., 1964; A.M. (hon.), Dartmouth Coll., 1971. Registered profl. engr., N.H. Instr. Thayer Sch. Engring., Dartmouth Coll., Hanover, N.H., 1954-57, asst. prof., 1957-64, assoc. prof., 1964-70, prof., 1970-94, assoc. dean, 1970, dean, 1972-84, dean emeritus, from 1984; prof. emeritus, from 1994; dir. Cook Design Ctr. Thayer Sch. Engring., Dartmouth Coll., 1984-94. Engr. Western Electric Co., Alaska, 1956-57; v.p. ops., dir. Controlled Enivronment, 1975-81; pres., dir. Q-S Oxygern Processes, Inc., 1979-84; N.H. Water Supply and Pollution Control Com., U.S. Army Small Arms Systems Agy.; mem. New Eng. Constrn. Edn. Adv. Coun., 1971-74; mem. adv. com. U.S. Patenta and Trademark Office, 1975-79; mem. ad hoc vis. com. Engrs. Coun. for Profl. Devel., 1973-81; pres., dir. Roan of Thayer, Inc., 1986-93; bd. dirs. Micro Tool Co., Inc., Micro Weighing Systems, Inc., 1986-91, Roan Ventures, Inc., 1987-91; pres., dir. Hanover Water Works Co., 1989-97. Mem. Hanover Town Planning Bd., 1963-75, chmn., 1966-74; trustee Mt. Washington Obs., 1975-92; bd. dirs. Eastman Community Assn., 1977-80; mem. corp. Mary Hitchcock Meml. Hosp., 1974—. NSF Sci. Faculty fellow, 1961-62; recipient Robert Fletcher award Thayer Sch. of Engring., 1985, Fellow Members awd., Am. Soc. for Engineering Education, 1992. Fellow AAAS, ASCE, Am. Soc. Engring. Edn. (chmn. New Eng. sect. 1977-78, chmn. council of sects. Zone 1, dir. 1981-83); mem. Sigma Xi, Chi Epsilon, Tau Beta Pi. Republican. Baptist. Home: Hanover, NH. Died Feb. 25, 2010.

LONG, CLARENCE WILLIAM, accountant; b. Hartford City, Ind., Apr. 17, 1917; s. Adam and Alice (Weschke) L.; m. Mildred Bernhardt, Aug. 8, 1940; children: William Randall, David John, Bruce Allen. BS, Ind. U., 1939. With Ernst & Young, Indpls., 1939-78, ptnr., 1953-78, ret., 1978. Mem. econ. exec. com. Gov. Ind., 1968-73. Mem. nat. budget and consultation com. United Way of Am., 1968-70; bd. dirs. United Fund Greater Indpls., 1966—, treas., 1968—; bd. dirs. Jr. Achievement, Ind., 1966-67; mem. exec. com. Nat. Jr. Achievement, 1966-67; mem. fin. com. Indpls. Hosp. Devel. Assn., 1966-67; trustee Ind. U., 1975-84; trustee Art Assn. Indpls., pres., 1977-86; mem. adv. com. to dir. NIH, 1986-92. Mem. Am. Inst. C.P.A.'s (council 1959-62), Ind. Assn. C.P.A.'s, Nat. Assn. Accountants, Ind. C. of C. (dir.), Delta Chi, Beta Alpha Psi, Alpha Kappa Psi. Clubs: Woodstock (Indpls.) (dir. 1958-60), Columbia (Indpls.) (dir. 1971-77, pres. 1976), Royal Poinciana Golf Club (Naples, Fla.). Republican. Lutheran. Home: Indianapolis, Ind. Died July 4, 2009.

LONG, GERALD H. (JERRY LONG), retired tobacco company executive; b. Mineola, NY, 1928; m. Marieanne Long. Grad., Adelphi U., 1952; postgrad., NYU, 1962. With R.J. Reynolds Tobacco Co., Winston-Salem, NC, 1969—88, exec. v.p., mem. exec. com., 1979-81, pres., COO, 1981-84; chmn., CEO R.J. Reynolds Tobacco USA, Winston-Salem, NC, 1984—88. Bd. dirs. RJR/Nabisco. Home: Clennons, NC. Died Nov. 3, 2010.

LONG, JAMES EDWARD, educational administrator; b. Balt., Dec. 25, 1933; s. John T. and Helen R. (Sweeney) L.; m. Elizabeth James Lacey, Nov. 26, 1959; children: James Jr., William, Mary, Peter. BS in Math., Loyola Coll., Balt., 1955; MA in Math., Bowdoin Coll., 1966; MA in Theology, St. Mary's Sem. and Univ., 1976. Cert. math. tchr., prin., Md. Engr. Martin Co., Middle River, Md., 1955-56, computer specialist, 1958-59; math. and sci. tchr. Balt. County Sch. System, Towson, Md., 1959-61; math. tchr., lacrosse coach Moses Brown Sch., Providence, 1962-64; head math. dept. John Carroll Sch., Bel Air, Md., 1964-72, vice prin., from 1972, lacrosse coach, 1964-68. With U.S. Army, 1956-58. Lawrence Cardinal scholar Ecumenical Inst. St. Mary's U., 1974. Mem. Archdiocesan Assn. of Secondary Sch. Adminstrs. (treas. 1965-70, pres. 1970-71, 85-86). Democrat. Roman Catholic. Avocations: swimming, racquetball, lacrosse. Home: Bel Air, Md. Died Jan. 1, 2009.

LONGENECKER, JOHN BENDER, biochemist, nutritionist, educator; b. Salunga, Pa., July 8, 1930; married, 1954; 2 children. BS, Franklin & Marshall Coll., 1952; MS, U. Tex., 1954, PhD in Biochemistry, 1956. Rsch. biochemist EI du Pont de Nemours & Co., Inc., Del., 1956-61; group leader Mead Johnson & Co., Ind., 1961-64; prof. nutrition, head divsn. U. Tex., Austin, from 1964. Grantee USPHS, 1964-71, Allied Health Fellow grantee, 1969-74. Mem. Am. Chem. Soc., Am. Inst. Nutrition, N.Y. Acad. Sci. Achievements include research on interrelationships among nutrients; in vivo plasma amino acid studies to evaluate protein and amino acid nutrition; nutritional status studies. Died Nov. 16, 2009.

LORD, ROY ALVIN, retired publisher; b. Middletown, Ohio, July 2, 1918; s. Arthur Edwin and Mary Marie (Bell) L.; m. Elizabeth Frances Powell, Nov. 1, 1941; children— Thomas A., Frances A., William F. BA, Ohio Wesleyan U., 1941; postgrad., Harvard U. Bus. Sch., 1962. With advt. sales Time Inc., NYC and Chgo., 1946-55, upper midwest mgr. advt. sales Mpls., 1955-62, nat. advt. sales mgr. NYC, 1963-68; pres. ML&A Inc., NYC, 1968-73; v.p. In-Store Publs., NYC, 1973-74; pres. The Weekend Co., Inc., 1974-76; pub. A.D. Publs., Inc., NYC, from 1976. Bd. dirs. Minn. Orchestral Assn., 1957-62; Minn. state chmn. Crusade for Freedom, 1960-62. Served with AC U.S. Army, 1942-45. Presbyterian. Home: Tucson, Ariz. Died Jan. 24, 2009.

LORINCZ, ALLAN LEVENTE, dermatologist, educator; b. Chgo., Oct. 31, 1924; s. Frank C. and Theresa (Csore) L.; m. Lillian Irene Tatter, Feb. 2, 1952 (dec. 1996); children: Donald, Linda, Alice. BS, U. Chgo., 1945, MD, 1947. Intern U. Chgo. Hosps., 1947-48; resident U. Chgo. Hospitals, 1948-51; mem. faculty U. Chgo. Med. Sch., 1951—2006, prof. dermatology, 1967—2006, head dermatology sect., 1960-91. Chief dept. dermatology Walter Reed Army Inst. Rsch., Washington, 1954-56; nat. cons. in dermatology Surgeon Gen. of USAF, 1962-65; spl. cons. USPHS, 1961-64; mem. com. on cutaneous system NRC, 1962-68. Mem. Chgo. Dermatol. Soc. (pres. 1963), Phi Beta Kappa, Sigma Xi, Alpha Omega Alpha. Research in physiology and biochemistry of skin, cutaneous fungous diseases, acne, psoriasis. Home: Oak Lawn, Ill. Died Sept. 7, 2010.

LORING, ARTHUR DENNIS, lawyer; b. Newark, Dec. 15, 1930; s. Arthur Francis and Dorothy C. (Judge) Loring; m. Madalaine Vita LoCrasto Loring, Nov. 10, 1973; children: Mark, Margaret Ann, Arthur, David, Matthew, Patricia stepchildren: Pamela Campbell, John Misso, Ribert Misso. AB, Seton Hall U., 1953, JD, 1959. Bar: NJ 1960, US Dist. Ct. NJ 1960. Asst. sec., closing officer NJ Realty Title Ins. Co., Newark, 1956—62; sole practice Hazlet, NJ, Middletown, NJ, 1963—83; gen. counsel Stavola Group, Tinton Falls, NJ, from 1983; dir. Sandawood Corp., Middletown. Pres. Better Govt. League, Hazlet, 1966—68. Served to 1st lt. US Army, 1953—56. Recipient Comml. Law award, Lawyers Coop. Pub. Co., 1959. Mem.: ABA, NJ Bar Assn. Home: Middletown, NJ. Died Aug. 6, 2010.

LOSEFF, LEV LIFSCHUTZ, Russian educator; b. Leningrad, USSR, June 15, 1937; came to U.S., 1976. s. Vladimir Lifschultz and Assia Genkina; m. Nina P Mokhov, Apr. 20, 1959; children: Dimitry, Marie. MA in Philology, U. Leningrad, USSR, 1959; PhD, U. Mich., 1981. Journalist The Sakhalin Oil-Worker Newspaper, Okha-in-Sakhalin, 1959-60; free-lance writer Leningrad, 1961-62; editor Kostyor Mag., Leningrad, 1962-75; part-time editor Ardis Pub. House, Ann Arbor, Mich., 1976-78; vis. prof. Mich. State U., East Lansing, 1978-79; from instr. to prof. Dartmouth Coll., Hanover, N.H., from 1979, prof., from 1992. Author: On the Beneficence of Censorship: Aesopian Language in Modern Russian Literature, 1984,(essays) Eats, 1984, (poems) A Miraculous Raid, 1985, A Privy Councillor, 1988; editor: Mikhail Bulgakov, Notes on the Cuffs, 1981, Nikolay Oleynikov, Ironic, 1982, Brodsky's Poetics, 1986, Norwich Symposia on Russian Literature and Culture, (Boris Pasternak), 1991, (with Valentina Polukhina) Brodsky's Poetics and Aesthetics, 1990; contbr. articles to profl. jours. Book review broadcasts, Voice of Am. Russian Svc., 1979—, Radio Liberty, BBC, Radio France. Mem. Am. Assn. Advancement of Slavic Studies, Am. Assn. Tchrs East European and Slavic Lang. Died May 6, 2009.

LOTZ, AILEEN ROBERTS, government consultant, author, photographer, travel consultant; b. Orange, NJ, Dec. 11, 1924; d. Paul R. and Aileen (Jeandron) Roberts; children: Alexandra Virginia, David William. BA, U. Miami, 1971. Exec. dir. Miami Beach Taxpayers Assn., 1954-60, Govt. Rsch. Coun., Miami, Fla., 1960-66; sr. adminstrv. asst. to mgr. Dade County, Miami, 1966-72; dir. Dade County Dept. Human Resources, 1975-82; cons. to local govt., 1982-90. Author: Metropolitan Dade County: Two-Tier Government in Action, 1984, Birding Around the World, 1987, Birding Around the Year, 1989; contbr. articles to profl. jours. Candidate Fla. H o. of Reps., 1974. Mem. N.Am. Nature Photography Assn. (charter dir.), Zool. Soc. of Fla. (exec. dir. 1983-84), The Explorers Club. Democrat. Home: Las Cruces, N.Mex. Died Mar. 7, 2009.

LOUX, NORMAN LANDIS, psychiatrist; b. Souderton, Pa., June 27, 1919; s. Abram Clemmer and Martha Wasser (Landis) L.; m. Esther Elizabeth Brunk, June 4, 1941; children— Philip Michael, Elizabeth Ann, Peter David. Student, Eastern Mennonite Coll., 1940-42; BA, Goshen Coll., 1943; MD, Hahnemann Med. Coll., 1946; postgrad., Yale, 1950-51. Intern Hahnemann Hosp., Phila., 1947; gen. practice medicine Souderton, 1947-48; psychiat. resident Butler Hosp., Providence, 1949-50, chief service, clin. dir., asst. supt., 1951-55; founder Penn Found. Mental Health, Inc., Sellersville, Pa., 1955, med. dir., 1955-80; chief Psychiat. Svc. Grand View Hosp., Sellersville, 1955-80, pres. med. staff, 1963-64; exec. com., joint conf. com. Mem. Gov.'s Adv. Com. for Mental Health and Mental Retardation, 1955-80. Mem. Pa. State Bd. Pub. Welfare, 1971-85. Bd. dirs. Dock Woods Retirement Community, 1989—, Adult Communities Total Svcs. Inc., 1990—. Co-recipient Earl D. Bond award, 1964; recipient Achievement award Souderton Lions Cub, 1963, Community Svc. award B'nai B'rith, 1976, citation for achievements Mennonite Med. Assn., 1978; dept. of psychiatry Grand View Hosp. rededicated in his name, 1992. Fellow Am. Psychiat. Assn., A.C.P., Pa. Psychiat. Soc., Am. Coll. Psychiatrists; mem. AMA, Pa., Bucks County med. socs., Group for Advancement Psychiatry, Southeastern Mental Health Assn., Acad. Religion and Mental Health. Mem. Mennonite Ch. Home: Lansdale, Pa. Died May 20, 2010.

LOVE, BEN HOWARD, retired organization executive; b. Trenton, Tenn., Sept. 26, 1930; s. Ben Drane and (Whitehead) Virginia; m. Ann Claire Hugo, Mar. 4, 1933; children: Ben H. Jr., Phillip H.(dec.), Leigh Anne, Mark E. BS, Lambuth Coll., 1955, HHD (hon.), 1986; Dr. Philanthropy (hon.), Pepperdine U., 1987; LHD (hon.), Montclair State U., 1991. With Boy Scouts Am., from 1955, dist. exec. Jackson, Tenn., 1955-60, scout exec. Delta area council, Clarksdale, Miss., 1960-64, dir. Nat. coun. North Brunswick, NJ, 1964—68, scout exec. Longhorn coun. Ft. Worth, 1968—71, scout exec. Sam Houston coun. Houston, 1971—73, dir. Northeast region Dayton, NJ, 1973—85, chief scout exec. Nat. coun. Irving, Tex., 1985—93. Bd. dirs. AIG Valic I, Valic II; ret., 2008. Served with U.S. Army, 1951-52. Recipient Gold medal SAR, Bronze Wolf award World Scout Orgn. Republican. Presbyterian. Avocations: tennis, golf, swimming, reading, spectator sports. Home: Cedar Park, Tex. Died July 31, 2010.

LOVELADY, STEVEN M., newspaper editor; b. Morganfield, Ky., July 2, 1943; s. Talmage C. and Virginia Dell (Fortenberry) L.; m. Linda R. Higgins, June 18, 1965 (div. Apr. 1979); children: Stephanie, Sara; m. Ann Judith Kolson, Apr. 30, 1979 B.J., U. Mo., 1965. Midwest corr. Wall Street Jour., Chgo., 1965-66, West Coast corr. Los Angeles, 1966-69, Page 1 editor NYC, 1969-72; asst. mng. editor Phila. Inquirer, 1972-75, assoc. mng. editor, 1975-80, assoc. exec. editor, 1980-91, mng. editor, 1991—96; editor-at-large Time Inc., 1996—2004; mng. editor Columbia Journalism Rev. Daily, NYC, 2004—06. Directed Pulitzer prize-winning news coverage, 1977, 79, 85, 87, 88, 89; Pulitzer prize juror, 1989, 90; seminar leader Poynter Inst., St. Petersburg, Fla., 1981, 82, 85, 87. Active Center City Phila. Residents Assn. Mem. AP Mng. Editors Avocation: breeding and racing thoroughbred horses. Home: New York, NY. Died Jan. 15, 2010.

LOVETT, RADFORD DOW, marine terminal real estate and investment company executive; b. Jacksonville, Fla., Sept. 6, 1933; s. William Radford And Agnes (Dow) L.; m. Katharine R. Howe, June 25, 1955 (dec. Jan. 1991); children: Katharine, William Radford, Philip, Lauren; m. Susan Wylie Rogers, June 16, 1995; children: Nick, Peter, Teddy Rogers. With Merrill Lynch, Pierce, Fenner & Smith Inc., NYC, 1958-78; mng. dir. Capital Markets Group, 1975-78; pres. Piggly Wiggly Corp., Jacksonville, Fla., 1978-82; chmn. bd. Commodores Pt. Terminal Corp., Jacksonville, from 1978. Chmn. Southcoast Capital Mgmt. Corp., Jacksonville, 1995—; bd. dirs. Wachovia Corp., Fla. Rock Industries Inc., Patriot Transp., Inc., Winn-Dixie Stores, Inc. Trustee Drew U., 1976-79, St. Vincent's Found., Jacksonville Zool. Soc. Lt. F.A. U.S. Army, 1955-57. Mem. Coastal Conservation Assn. Fla. (bd. dirs.). Episcopalian. Died July 4, 2010.

LOVINGER, SOPHIE LEHNER, child psychologist; b. NYC, Jan. 15, 1932; d. Nathaniel Harris and Anne (Rosen) Lehner; m. Robert Jay Lovinger, June 18, 1957; children: David Fredrick, Mark Andrew. BA, Bklyn. Coll., 1954; MS, City Coll., NYC, 1959; PhD, NYU, 1967. Diplomate in clin child psychology Am. Bd. Profl. Pschology. Sr. clin. psychologist Bklyn. State Hosp., 1960-61; grad. fellow NYU, NYC, 1964—67; psychotherapy trainee Jamaica (N.Y.) Ctr., 1964-67; asst. prof. Hofstra U., Hempstead, N.Y., 1967-70; prof. Cen. Mich. U., Mt. Pleasant, 1970-98; psychotherapist, psychoanalyst Mt. Pleasant, Mich., 1970—98, Charleston, SC, 1999—2010. Author: Learning Disabilities and Games, 1978, Language-Learning Disabilities, 1991, Child Treatment from Intake Interview to Termination, 1998; contbr. articles to profl. jours. Fellow: APA, Am. Acad. Clin. Psychology; mem.: Nat. Register Health Svc. Providers. Home: Charleston, SC. Died Mar. 23, 2010.

LOW, JOHN T. C., lawyer; b. NYC, Nov. 20, 1918; s. James and Charlotte (Manning) L.; m. Virginia Ball Kull; 1 dau., Virginia Nichols. AB, Colgate U.; JD, Columbia. Bar: Miss., N.Y., Ky. With firm Davis, Polk & Wardwell, NYC, 1942-45; law asst. to Gov. T. Dewey, Albany, N.Y., 1945-47; with firm Dewey Ballantine, NYC, 1947-57; ptnr. Low & Furby, Jackson, Miss., from 1957. Lectr. law Pace Coll., N.Y.C. Contbr. articles on taxation to profl. jours. Mem. Nat. Assn. Bond Lawyers, Am., Miss., Hinds County bar assns. Clubs: Jackson Country, Univ. Died Mar. 15, 2010.

LOWE, MARVIN, artist, educator; b. Bklyn., May 19, 1922; m. Juel Watkins, Apr. 1, 1949; 1 dau., Melissa. Student, Julliard Sch. Music, 1952-54; BA, Bklyn. Coll., 1956; MFA, U. Iowa, 1961. Prof. fine arts Ind. U., Bloomington, 1968-92, prof. emeritus, from 1992. Vis. artist-lectr., 1970-91. Exhibited in 64 one-person shows; over 200 group and invitational exhbns.; participated in U.S. info. exhbns. in Latin Am., Japan, USSR, and most European countries; represented in 84 permanent collections including Phila. Mus. Art, Bklyn. Mus., Smithsonian Instn., Brit. Mus., Japan Print Assn., N.Y.C. Pub. Libr., Calif. Palace Legion of Honor, San Francidso, Boston Pub. Libr., Columbia U., Libr. of Congress, Indpls. Mus. Art, Ringling Mus., Honolulu Acad. Art, Ft. Wayne Mus. Art, Purdue U. Mus. Fine Art, Springfield, Mass, Retrospective exhbn. Ind. U. Art Mus., 1998 Served with USNR, 1942-45. Fellow Nat. Endowment for Arts, 1975; fellow Ford Found., 1979, Ind. Arts Commn., 1987; recipient numerous Purchase awards, 1960—; grantee: Ind. Arts. Commn., 1997, Florsheim, 1997. Home: Tucson, Ariz. Died Apr. 28, 2010.

LOWE, TERRANCE ALEXANDER, food service administrator; b. Detroit, July 28, 1951; s. Theodore Marian and Cecelia Pearl (Matel) Lowe; m. Judy Leo, May 4, 1991; 1 stepchild, Frank Clements; 1 child, Alexander Theodore. BS, Mich. State U., 1973; MBA, Lake Forest Coll., 1983. Asst. food svc. dir. Wishard Meml. Hosp., Indpls., 1974—77; food svc. dir. Altenheim Cmty. Home, Indpls., 1977—78, Ind. Christian Retirement Pk., Zionsville, 1978; food svc. adminstr. & project chmn. Dial-A-Dietitian, Victory Meml. Hosp., Waukegan, Ill., from 1978. Founder Famous Chef's Cuisine Benefit and Program; lectr. Ind. U., Indpls., 1976, Purdue U., 1976; owner Stash's Egg Co., Waukegan, 1982—84; intermediate facilitator Victory Intermediate Care Ctr., 1983—84; food svc. cons. Arlington Pk. Race Track, Ill., from 1988. Actor: (films) Goodnight Sweet Wife A Murder in Boston, Only the Lonely, Warshawski, Curly Sue, Gladiator, The Babe, Folks, Mo Monay, Watch It, Straight Talk, Home Alone 2; contbr. articles to profl. jours. Adv. com., vice chmn. Indpls. Pub. Schs. Indsl. Coop. Edn. and Tng., 1975—78; corp. rep. Sch. Mgmt. Lake Forest Coll., from 1983. Recipient Appreciation award, Purdue U. Indpls., 1975, Indpls. Pub. Schs., 1978, Ctrl. Nine Vocat. Sch. Svcs., 1978, Highest Recognition award, Hosp. Food Svc. Adminstrs., 1992. Fellow: Health Care Food Svc. Adminstrs.; mem.: Internat. Food Svc. Execs. Assn., Am. Soc. Hosp. Food Svcs. Adminstrs., Kappa Sigma. Roman Catholic. Died Feb. 24, 2009.

LOWERY, CLINTON HERSHEY, former naval officer; b. Pitts., Apr. 10, 1929; s. Robert John and Alma May (Hershey) L.; m. Elenore Berenda, July 28, 1956; children: Gregg C., Michael J., Keith D., Kim A., Douglas S. BS, U. Pitts., 1951, MD, 1955. Diplomate: Am. Bd. Surgery. Intern St. John's Gen. Hosp., Pitts., 1955-56; resident Naval Regional Med. Ctr., Portsmouth, Va., 1958-62; commd. capt. USN, 1956, advanced through grades to rear adm., 1979; staff surgeon Naval Regional Med. Ctr., Camp Lejeune, N.C., 1962-66; asst. chief surgery Portsmouth, 1966-72; comdr. 1st Med. Bn. RVN, 1967-68; chief of surgery Camp Pendleton, Calif., 1972-74; dir. clin. services Charleston, S.C., 1974-77; comdr. Camp Pendleton, 1977-79; asst. chief Bur. Medicine and Surgery for Health Care Programs, Washington, 1979-82; fleet surgeon U.S. Pacific Fleet, U.S. Pacific Command, 1982-83; ret., 1983; v.p. risk mgmt. Pa. Hosp. Ins. Co., Camp Hill, 1983-86. Decorated Legion of Merit. Fellow ACS, ACP; mem. Southeastern Surg. Soc., Assn. Mil. Surgeons, Am. Coll. Physician Execs. Home: Valencia, Pa. Died Sept. 9, 2009.

LOZANO, JOHN MANUEL, priest; b. Lora del Rio, Spain, June 18, 1930; came to U.S., 1976; s. Antonio and Rosario (Nieto) L. BA, Licentia in Theology, U. Catholique, Angers, France, 1956; Licentia in Bibl. Scis., Bibl. Inst., Rome, 1958; ThD, Angelicum U., Rome, 1959. Joined Clarentians Soc., 1948; ordained priest Roman Cath. Ch., 1956. Prof. spirituality Claretianum, Rome, 1962-67, dir. studium, 1961-68; prof. theology and history of spirituality Inst. della Vita Religiosa, Lateran U., Rome, from 1971; prof. spirituality Cath. Theol. Union, Chgo., from 1979. Consultor Roman Congregation for Causes of the Saints, 1970—. Author: Mystic and Man of Action, 1977, Discipleship, 1981, 2d edit., 1983, Life as a Parable, 1985; contbg. author: I Mondi dell'Uomo, 1977, Together Before the Lord, 1983, Ency. of Religion, 1985. Mem. Cath. Theol. Soc. Am., Soc. for Sci. Study Religion. Died Apr. 24, 2009.

LUBAR, JEFFREY STUART, journalist, trade association executive; b. Rockville Centre, NY, Apr. 15, 1947; s. Sidney and Rose (Grupsmith) L.; m. Barbara Ruth Bigelman; children: Debra, Adam, Rachel. BA, American U., 1969. Dir. Washington News Bur., Susquehanna Broadcasting Co., 1969-86; v.p. pub. affairs Nat. Assn. Realtors, Washington, 1987-99; dir. comm. Mortgage Ins. Companies of America, 2000—10. Mem. exec. com. of corrs. Radio-TV Assn. (U.S. Congress), 1974-75 Served with AUS, 1969-75. Mem.: Nat. Press Club. Jewish. Home: Fairfax Station, Va. Died July 5, 2010.

LUBETKIN, SEYMOUR ARTHUR, engineer; b. Newark, Mar. 25, 1923; s. William and Dorothy (Kimmel) L.; B.S.M.E., Newark Coll. Engring., 1947, M.E.E., 1950; M.C.E., NYU, 1957; m. Shirley Lowenstein, Dec. 30, 1950; children— Sanford, Richard, Roy. Asst. chief engr. Passaic Valley Sewerage Commrs., 1950-54, chief engr., 1954-78; pres. Environ. Tech., Inc.; v.p. Roy F. Weston, Inc., 1978-84; adviser N.J. Dept. Environ. Protection, U.S. EPA, Water Resources Research Council of Rutgers U., Interstate San. Commn. Bd. mgrs. N.J. Y Camps, 1955-60, 70-73; bd. dirs. NJ. YM&YWHA, 1961-63. Served with U.S. Army, 1943-46. Registered profl. engr., N.J., Ariz., Fla., Ind., Md., N.Mex., N.Y., Ohio, Pa., W.Va. Diplomate Am. Acad. Environ. Engrs. Mem. Water Pollution Control Fedn. (bd. of control 1975-78; Wm. D. Hatfield award 1983), N.J. Water Pollution Control Assn. (exec. bd. 1975-78, chmn. liaison com. 1980-84, Dr. Heukelikian award 1973), Am. Contract Bridge League (life master), Tau Beta Pi. Jewish. Club: Masons. Mem. editorial adv. staff Pollution Engring. mag., 1978-80; contbr. articles to engring. jours. Home: Houston, Tex. Died Dec. 1, 2009.

LUBORSKY, FRED EVERETT, research physicist; b. Phila., May 14, 1923; s. Meyer and Cecelia (Miller) L.; m. Florence R. Glass, Aug. 25, 1946; children— Judith, Mark, Rhoda BS, U. Pa., 1947; PhD, Ill. Inst. Tech., 1952. Teaching-research asst. Ill. Inst. Tech., Chgo., 1947-51; research assoc. Gen. Elec. Co., Schnectady, 1951-52, West Lynn, Mass., 1952-58, research physicist Schenectady, 1958-92. Gen. chmn. 2d Joint Internat. Magnetism and Magnetic Materials Conf., 1979; chmn. adv. com. Conf. on Magnetism and Magnetic Materials, 1980 Editor: Amorphous Metallic Alloys, 1984; mem. editorial bd. Internat. Jour. Rapid Solidification, 1984—; mem. editorial adv. bd. Internat. Jour. Magnetism, 1972—; contbr. articles to profl. jours.; patentee in field Served with USN, 1944-46 Recipient citation achievement in indsl. sci. AAAS, 1956; Brit. Sci. Research Council fellow, 1977; Coolidge fellow in research and devel. Gen. Elec. Corp., 1978 Fellow IEEE (editorial bd. Transactions on Magnetics jour. 1968—, editor-in-chief 1972-75, editorial bd. Spectrum jour. 1972-73, Centennial medal 1984, mem. Fellows com. 1993—), Am. Inst. Chemists, N.Y. Acad. Scis.; mem. Nat. Acad. Engring., Magnetics Soc. of IEEE (pres. 1975-77, named disting. lectr. 1979, achievement award 1981), Am. Chem. Soc., Materials Research Soc. Home: Schenectady, NY. Died Feb. 3, 2010.

LUCAS, ARTHUR MONROE, clergy member; b. Alexandria, Va., Aug. 24, 1947; s. Talbot Paul Lucas and Jean Perry (Giles) Lucas Jenkins; m. Lou Matthews, Aug. 9, 1969; children: Katherine Elizabeth, Martin Brandon. BA, U. Va., 1969; MDiv, Duke U., 1973. Ordained to ministry United. Meth. Ch., 1976. Resident in clin. pastoral edn. Meml. Hosp. System, Houston, 1973-76; dir. pastoral care Meth. Med. Ctr., St. Joseph, Mo., 1976-84; dir. pastoral care and counseling Heartland Health System, St. Joseph, 1984-85, exec. dir. Heartland Health Ministries, 1985-86, adminstr. Heartland Samaritan Ctr., 1986-90; dir. pastoral care Barnes Healthcare System, St. Louis, from 1990; rsch. asst. urban policy study NIMH, Durham, N.C., 1971-72. Presenter pastoral care workshops and profl. confs.; coord. program for pastoral care bd. ordained ministry Mo. West Ann. Conf., United Meth. Ch., 1983-90, chmn. NW dist. com. on superintendency, 1985-90, mem. NW dist. coun. on ministries, 1977-90, rep. to regional prison chaplaincy screening com. United Meth. div. chaplains and related ministries, 1980—. Contbr. articles to various publs. Corr. sec. bd. dirs. Robidoux Resident Theatre, 1988-90. Fellow Coll. Chaplains of Am. Protestant Health Assn.; mem. Assn. Clin. Pastoral Edn. (cert. supr.). Avocations: reading, travel. Home: Saint Louis, Mo. Died Jan. 10, 2009.

LUCAS, JO DESHA, law educator, editor; b. Richmond, Va., Nov. 7, 1921; s. Robert Desha and Hill Miller (Carter) L.; m. Johanna Westley, June 17, 1950; children: Robin Desha, John Carter. AB, Syracuse U., 1947, M.P.A., 1951; LL.B., U. Va., 1951; LL.M., Columbia U., 1952. Bar: Va. 1952. Asst. prof. law U. Chgo., 1953-57, assoc. prof., 1957-61, prof., from 1961, Arnold I. Shure prof. law, from 1982. Chmn. Ill. Supreme Ct. Rules Com., 1974—; reporter Fed. Adv. Com. on Appellate Rules, 1976-78 Author cases on admiralty; co-author: Moore's Federal Practice, 1970—; contbr. articles to legal revs., 1970—. Served with USAAF, 1943-46. Mem. Va. Bar, Chgo. Bar Assn., Order of Coif, Phi Beta Kappa Home: Chicago, Ill. Died May 9, 2010.

LUCAS, REGINALD DEAN, real estate agent, mortgage broker; b. Wilson, NC, Aug. 3, 1951; s. Edward Lucas and Sarah (Weaver) Bostwick; m. Reneé L. Brown, Aug. 12, 1972, Daniel, Todd, Nicholas. AS, Broward Coll., 1975. Cert. real estate brokerage mgr. V.p. Alinco Assoc., Inc., Pembroke Pines, Fla., 1975-77, Prestige Realty, Inc., Hollywood, Fla., 1977, Davie, Fla., 1982-83, Chinelly Real Estate, Inc., Hollywood, 1977-82; pres. Chinelly Real Estate, Inc. #10, Ft. Lauderdale, Fla., from 1983, also bd. dirs.; v.p. South Atlantic Funding, Davie, from 1983, INPRO, Inc., Ft. Lauderdale, from 1984, also bd. dirs. Mem. mgmt. bd. 1st Am. Bank, Ft. Lauderdale, 1985—. Real estate columnist Sun Tattler (newspaper); contbr. articles to profl. jours. Served with USNR, 1969-75. Mem. Fla. Assn. Realtors, Miami Bd. Realtors, Ft. Lauderdale Bd. Realtors, Hollywood Bd. Realtors. Clubs: Broward Commerce (Pembroke Pines). Republican. Avocations: tennis, softball. Home: Pmbk Pines, Fla. Died Jan. 18, 2009.

LUDVIGSON, GAIL ROSENBERG, investment company executive; b. Cambridge, Mass., Dec. 10, 1942; d. Joel and Ida Florence (Berenson) Rosenberg; m. Max Morris Ludvigson, Oct. 24, 1971; children— Laura, Deborah. B.A. in Econs. with honors, Conn. Coll., 1964; M.A. in Econs., Columbia U., 1965. Chartered fin. analyst. Arbitrageur, Smithers & Co., N.Y.C., 1971-72; sr. investment analyst Ticor, Los Angeles, 1972-79, sr. portfolio mgr., 1979-84; asst. v.p. Trust Services Am., Los Angeles, 1984-86, v.p., 1986; v.p. Bankers Trust Co. Calif. N.A., Los Angeles, 1986—. Fellow Fin. Analysts Fedn., Los Angeles Soc. Fin. Analysts; mem. Women's Bus. and Profl. Group of South Bay (membership chmn. 1985-86, program chmn. 1986-87), Los Angeles Assn. Investment Women (pres. 1985-86). Avocation: music. Home: Palos Verdes Peninsula, Calif. Died July 2, 2010.

LUEBKE, NEIL ROBERT, philosophy educator; b. Pierce, Nebr., Sept. 15, 1936; s. Robert Carl and Cinderetta Amelia (Guthmann) L.; m. Phyllis Jean Madsen, June 15, 1957; children: Anne Elizabeth, Karen Marie. BA, Midland Coll., Nebr., 1958; MA, Johns Hopkins U., Balt., 1962, PhD, 1968. Asst., assoc. then prof. philosophy Okla. State U., Stillwater, 1961-98, head philosophy dept., 1979-85, 89-96, Regents Svc. prof., 1997-98, prof. emeritus, from 1998. Dir. Exxon Critical Thinking Project, 1971-74 Contbr. articles to profl. jours. Woodrow Wilson nat. fellow, 1958-59 Mem. Am. Philos. Assn., Soc. Bus. Ethics, Mountain-Plains Philos. Conf. (chmn. 1971-72, 80-81), Southwestern Philos. Soc. (pres. 1981-82), Phi Kappa Phi (nat. pres. 1998-2001). Democrat. Lutheran. Home: Stillwater, Okla. Died June 18, 2009.

LUKENS, DONALD EDGAR (BUZ LUKENS), former United States Representative from Ohio; b. Harveysburg, Ohio, Feb. 11, 1931; s. William A. and Edith (Greene) L.; m. Toshiko Davis (div.) BS, Ohio State U., 1954. Acting minority counsel US House Rules Com., Washington, 1961-63; pres. Washington Young Reps. Com., 1962-63; mem. exec. com. Rep. Nat. Com., Washington, 1963-65; mem. Butler County Rep. Exec. Com., Ohio, 1966-70, US Congress from 24th Ohio Dist., Washington, 1967-71, US Congress from 8th Ohio Dist., Washington, 1987-90; mem. Dist. 4 Ohio State Senate, Columbus, 1971—87. Candidate for nomination Ohio gubernatorial race, 1970. Served to cpt. USAF, 1954-60. Republican. Died May 22, 2010.

LUNDSTEDT, SVEN BERTIL, behavioral and social scientist, educator; b. NYC, May 6, 1926; s. Sven David and Edith Maria L.; m. Jean Elizabeth Sanford, June 16, 1951; children: Margaret, Peter, Janet. AB, U. Chgo., 1952, PhD, 1955; SM, Harvard U., 1960. Lic. in psychology, N.Y., Ohio; cert. Council for Nat. Register of Health Services. Asst. dir. Found. for Research on Human Behavior, 1960-62; asst. prof. Case-Western Res. U., Cleve., 1962-64, assoc. prof., 1964-68; assoc. prof. adminstrv. sci. Ohio State U., Columbus, 1968-69, prof. pub. policy and mgmt., from 1969, Ameritech Research prof., 1987-89, prof. internat. bus. and pub. policy, from 1988, prof. mgmt. and human resources, 1990—2005, prof. emeritus, from 2005, mem. John Glenn Inst. for Pub. Svc. and Pub. Policy, from 1999, emeritus prof. pub. policy and mgmt., from 2004. Affiliate scientist Battelle PNL, from 1974; chmn. Batelle Endowment Program for Tech. and Human Affairs, 1976—80; mem. Univ. Senate, from 2002; dir. project on edn. of CEO Aspen Inst., 1978—80; advisor Task Force on Innovation, US Ho. of Reps., 1983—84; advisor Citizens Network for Fgn. Affairs, from 1988; mem. Am. Com. on US Soviet Rels., from 1985, chair trade and negotiation project; cons. E.I. duPont de Nemours & Co., B.F. Goodrich Co., Bell Tel. Labs., Battelle Meml. Inst., Nat. Fulbright Award Com.; invited spkr. Royal Swedish Acad. Scis., 1989. Author: Higher Education in Social Psychology, 1968; co-author: Managing Innovation, 1982, Managing Innovation and Change, 1989; author, editor: Telecommunications, Values and the Public Interest, 1990; contbr. articles to profl. jours. Pres., Cleve. Mental Health Assn., 1966-68; mem. Ohio Citizen's Task Force on Corrections, 1971-72. Served with U.S. Army, 1944-46 Harvard U. fellow, 1960; grantee Bell Telephone Labs., 1964-65, NSF, 1965-67, Kettering Found., 1978-80, Atlantic Richfield Found., 1980-82, German Marshall Fund of U.S. to conduct internat. ednl. joint ventures on econ. negotiations, Budapest, Hungary, 1990; recipient Ohio Ho. of Reps. award, 1986. Mem.: APA, Internat. Soc. Panetics (mem., sec. bd. govs., founding mem.), Am. Soc. for Pub. Adminstrn. (pres. Central Ohio chpt. 1975—77, founder, chmn. com. on bus. govt. relations 1977—79, editl. bd. Pub. Adminstrn. Rev. 1978—82), Am. Acad. Arts and Scis. (chmn. PIN com. on east/west trade negotiation), Internat. Inst. for Applied Systems Analysis (innovation task force, nat. adv. com. project. internat. negotiation with AAAS, founder, chmn. U.S. Midwest Assn. for IIASA from 1986, sr. social sci. advisor from 1994). Unitarian Universalist. Died Mar. 20, 2009.

LUNSFORD, RUTH MAE, business executive; b. Wolf Creek, Tenn., July 7, 1940; d. Wiley and Gladys Lee (Wiley) L. Student Mercer County Community Coll., 1974-79, St. Joseph U., Phila, 1985—. Cert. purchasing mgr. Stenographer various firms, Vineland, N.J., 1959-63; sec. to mgrs. of purchasing Shieldalloy Corp., Newfield, N.J. and Graphics Systems div. RCA, Dayton, N.J., 1963-69; purchasing asst. Am. Cyanamid Co., Princeton, N.J., 1969-73, buyer 1973-85; purchasing agt. Constrn. Products div. W.R. Grace & Co., Fogelsville, Pa., 1985-90. Mem. Nat. Assn. Purchasing Mgmt., Pub. Relations-Purchasing Mgmt. Assn. Lehigh Valley. Republican. Baptist. Club: Toastmasters (Allentown). Died June 9, 2010.

LUNT, HORACE GRAY, linguist, educator; b. Colorado Springs, Colo., Sept. 12, 1918; s. Horace Fletcher and Irene (Jewett) L.; m. Sally Herman, June 2, 1963; children: Elizabeth, Catherine. AB, Harvard U., 1941; MA, U. Calif., Berkeley, 1942; postgrad., Charles U., Prague, Czechoslovakia, 1946-47; PhD (Rockefeller fellow), Columbia U., 1950. Lectr. in Serbo-Croatian Columbia U., 1948-49; asst. prof. Slavic langs. and lit. Harvard U., 1949-54, assoc. prof., 1954-60, prof., 1960—89, Samuel H. Cross prof. Slavic langs. and lits., 1965-89, Samuel H. Cross prof. Slavic languages & lit. emeritus, 1989—2010, chmn. dept. Slavic langs. and lits., 1959-73, 75-76, 82-83, chmn. Slavic and East European Lang. and Area Ctr., 1983-89; mem. exec. com. Russian Rsch. Ctr., 1970-91, fellow, 1991—2010; mem. exec. com. Harvard Ukrainian Research Inst., 1974-91, fellow, 1991—2010. Author: Grammar of the Macedonian Literary Language, 1952, Old Church Slavonic Grammar, 1955, 7th rev. edit., 2001, Fundamentals of Russian, 1958, 2d rev. ed., 1968, Progressive Palatalization of Common Slavic, 1981, (with M. Taube) The Slavonic Book of Esther: Text, Lexicon, Linguistic Analysis, Problems of Translation, 1998; editor: Harvard Slavic Studies, 1953-70. Served with U.S. Army, 1942-45. Guggenheim fellow, 1960-61 Mem. Macedonian Acad. Arts and Scis. (corr.). Home: Cambridge, Mass. Died Aug. 11, 2010.

LUZA, RADOMIR VACLAV, retired historian, educator; b. Prague, Czechoslovakia, Oct. 17, 1922; s. Vojtech V. and Milada (Vecera) L.; m. Libuse Ladislava Podhrazska, Feb. 5, 1949; children: Radomir V., Sabrina. JuDr, U. Brno, Czechoslovakia, 1948; MA, NYU, 1958, PhD, 1959. Assoc. prof. modern European history La. State U., New Orleans, 1966-67; prof. history Tulane U., New Orleans, 1967—92, prof. history emeritus, from 1992. Scholar-in-residence Rockefeller Found., Bellagio Study Ctr., 1988; prof. gen. history Masaryk U., Brno, 1993—. Author: The Transfer of the Sudeten Germans, 1964, History of the International Socialist Youth Movement, 1970, (with V. Mamatey) A History of the Czechoslovak Republic, 1918-1948, 1973, Austro-German Relations in the Anschluss Era, 1975, Österreich und die Grossdeutsche Idee in der NS-Zeit, 1977, Geschichte der Tschechoslowakischen Republik 1918-1948, 1980, A History of the Resistance in Austria, 1938-1945, 1984, Der Widerstand in Österreich, 1938-1945, 1985, La République Tchécoslovaque 1918-1948, 1987, The Czechoslovak Social Democracy Abroad, 1948-1989, 2001, The Hitler Kiss: A Memoir of the Czech Resistance, 2002, Hitlerovo Objeti Chapters from the Czech Resistance, 2006; Contemporary Austrian Studies. With Czech Resistance, 1939—45, WWII, col. Czech Army, 1995, ret. N, Czech Army. Recipient all Czechoslovak mil. decorations; prize Theodor Körner Found., Vienna, 1965, J. Hlavka Hon. medal Czechoslovak Acad. Scis., 1992, T.G. Masaryk medal Pres. of Czech Rep., 1996, Austrian Cross of Honor Sci. and Art I. Class, 1997, Meml. medal Czech Rep., 2000, 60 Yrs. Victory of Gt. Patriotic War 1941-45 medal, Pres. Russian Fedn. Vladimir Putin, 2005; grantee Social Rsch. Coun., Am. Philos. Soc., Coun. Learned Socs., Fulbright Com., NEH. Mem.: Assn. Historians of Czech Republic (hon.). Died Nov. 24, 2009.

LYNCH, HARRY JAMES, retired biologist; b. Glenfield, Pa., Jan. 18, 1929; s. Harry James and Rachel (McComb) L.; m. Pokum Lee Lynch. BS, Geneva Coll., Beaver Falls, Pa., 1957; PhD, U. Pitts., 1971; postgrad. Bio-Space Tech. Tng. Program, NASA and U. Va., 1970. Clin. chemist West Penn Hosp., Pitts., 1955-56; grad. teaching asst. U. Pitts., 1966-71, sr. teaching fellow, 1971; postdoctoral fellow MIT, Cambridge, 1973-75, rsch. assoc. dept. nutrition, lab. neuroendocrine regulation, 1973-75, lectr., 1976-81, rsch. scientist dept. brain and cognitive sci., 1982-92; ret., 1992. Contbr. more than 60 articles on the pineal gland to profl. jours. and books; patentee on implantable programmed microinfusion apparatus, 1981. With USN, 1950—54. NIH postdoctoral fellow 1971-73. Democrat. Avocation: study of animal behavior. Home: Brookline, Mass. Died Nov. 26, 2009.

LYNCH, JAMES CHARLES, security consultant; b. Newark, Jan. 15, 1919; s. Bernard and Bridget (Fitzsimmons) Lynch; m. Mary Delia Powell, June 29, 1959; 1 child, Brian Joseph 1 stepchild, Maria Nannette. BS in BA, Rutgers U., 1940. Cert. Indsl. Coll. Armed Forces, 1964, protection profl. 1978. Insp. P. Ballantyne & Son, Newark, 1940—42; investigator Retail Credit Co., Newark, 1946; night mgr. Robert Richter Hotel, Miami Beach, 1946—47, night auditor, 1947—48; hotel asst. mgr. Sans Souci Hotel, Miami Beach, Fla., 1948—50; chie Intelligence and Security div. Redstone Arsenal, Ala., 1950—60; security adv. NATO Hawk Prodn. Orgn., Paris, 1960, security program chief, 1964; security specialist US Army Safeguard Systems Command, Huntsville, 1968—72; pres., chmn. bd. Asset Protection Assocs., Inc., Huntsville, Ala., 1973—91; guest lectr. U. Ala., Birmingham, 1979—80, Jefferson State U., Birmingham, 1979—80, U. Fla., Huntsville, 1984—85; cons. intelligence & security Huntsville, from 1991. Contbr. articles to profl. jours. With US Army, 1942—46, ETO. Decorated Silver Star with oak leaf cluster, Bronze Star medal with oak leaf cluster, Purple Heart; recipient, Madison County Hall Heroes, Huntsville, 1987. Mem.: VFW, Security and Intelligence Assn., Am. Legion, Am. Security Coun., Smithsonian Assocs., Assn. US Army, Am. Soc. Indsl. Security (nat. treas. 1984, bd. dirs. 1982—84), Huntsville-Madison County C. of C. (chmn. internat. trade com. 1976—78), KC, Elks, Burning Tree Country, Huntsville Country. Republican. Roman Catholic. Home: Guntersville, Ala. Died Jan. 25, 2009.

LYNCH, RICHARD GREGORY, medical educator; b. Apr. 9, 1934; BA, U. Mo., 1961; MD, U. Rochester, 1966. Resident Washington U., St. Louis, 1966-69, from asst. prof. to assoc. prof. pathology, 1972-80; dir. NIH Tng. Program, 1980-81, 84-87; prof., head dept. pathology U. Iowa, Iowa City, 1981-99, prof. microbiology, 1982-99, Hanson prof. immunology, from 1992. Chmn. pathology B study sect. NIH, 1983-86. Postdoctoral immunology fellow Washington U., St. Louis, 1969-72; recipient Rous-Whipple award, 1997. Died Oct. 12, 2009.

LYNN, RICHARD C., lawyer, consultant; b. Chgo., May 29, 1943; s. Casimir Vincent and Lillian Constance (Habrelewicz) Cwiklinski; m. Karen Ann Parker, Nov. 28, 1970; children: Allison, Brian. BA, Northwestern U., 1965; JD, DePaul U., 1968. Bar: Ill. 1968. Atty. City Products Corp., Des Plaines, Ill., 1969-72, Cotter & Co., Chgo., 1972-75, v.p., gen counsel, from 1978; sole practice Chgo., from 1975. Bd. dirs. YMCA, Chgo., 1984—, Jesse Owens Found., Chgo., 1986—. Mem.: Northwestern U. N. (pres. 1986—, award 1978). Avocations: world history, polit. sci., tennis, golf, running. Home: Oklahoma City, Okla. Died Dec. 5, 2009.

LYONS, JOHN F., lawyer; b. Bloomington, Ind., June 20, 1944; BS, Ind. U., 1966, JD, 1969. Bar: Ind. 1969. Atty. Barrett & McNagny, Fort Wayne, Ind. Fellow Ind. Bar Found.; mem. ABA, Ind. State Bar Assn. (trial lawyers sect.), Allen County Bar Assn., Order of Coif, Beta Gamma Sigma, Phi Alpha Delta. Died Mar. 31, 2009.

LYONS, LAURENCE, securities executive, retired; b. Jersey City, Aug. 11, 1911; s. Louis and Teresa (Serge) L.; m. Gertrude Starr, Sept. 1, 1945 (dec.); 1 son, Jonathan. BS, NYU, 1934, postgrad., 1935. Securities analyst Allen & Co., NYC, 1935-52; with Allen Co., Inc., NYC, from 1952, sr. v.p., 1989-98. Mem. Soc. Security Analysts. Home: Katonah, NY. Died Oct. 8, 2009.

LYONS, PAUL HAROLD, social work educator; b. Newark, Oct. 24, 1942; s. Bernard Israel and Matilda (Waraft) L.; m. Janet Lynn Aruck, July 2, 1966 (dec. Apr. 1971); m. Mary Elizabeth Hardwick, May 21, 1977; 1 child, Max; stepchildren: Jennifer, Nate. BA, Rutgers U., 1964, MA, 1967; PhD, Bryn Mawr Coll., 1980. History instr. Temple U., Phila., 1967-71; history tchr. Miquon Upper Sch., Phila., 1971-80; social worker prof. Stockton Coll., Pomona, N.J., from 1980. Author: Philadelphia Communists, 1936-56, 1982, Class of '66, 1994, New Left, New Right and the Legacy of the Sixties, 1996; adv. bd. Vietnam Generation, New Haven, 1992—. Bd. dirs. The Arc of Atlantic County, Somers Point, N.J., 1993—, Northfield Ednl. Found., 1992-96; mem. Northfield (N.J.) Sch. Bd., 1986-92; v.p. Stockton Fedn. of Tchrs., Pomona, 1993-96; mem. Atlantic County Vol. Ctr., Northfield, 1985-86; staff-asst. dir. Vietnam Summer, Newark, 1967. Mem. Coun. of Social Work Edn. (program coord. 1992-95), Orgn. of Am. Historians. Democrat. Avocations: music, saxophone, running, tennis, travel. Home: Northfield, NJ. Died Jan. 19, 2009.

LYONS, THOMAS NICHOLAS, lawyer; b. Elizabeth, NJ, Mar. 12, 1949; s. John Anthony and Mary Louise (Lestrange) L.; m. Gemma Maria Pellegrino, Aug. 20, 1972; children—Mary Kathryn, Thomas Nicholas III AB, Holy Cross Coll., 1971; JD, Georgetown U., 1975. Bar: N.J. 1975. Legal research asst. Congl. Research Service, Washington, 1972-75; law clk. to judge Superior Ct. Elizabeth, N.J., 1975-76; spl. counsel City of Elizabeth, 1977-78; legal assoc. Mackenzie, Welt, Duane and Lechner, Elizabeth, 1976-78; sr. v.p. and counsel Howard Savings Bank, Livingston, N.J., from 1978. Adj. prof. law Seton Hall U., Newark, 1985— Mcpl. chmn. Mountainside Democratic Com., (N.J.), 1984; mem. N.J. State Dem. Com. Chmn's. and Adv. Bd., Trenton, 1984; trustee Union County Friendly Sons of St. Patrick, Westfield, (N.J.), 1980-84 Mem. Union County Bar Assn., ABA, N.J. State Bar Assn. Roman Catholic. Home: Mountainside, NJ. Died May 8, 2010.

MACARTHUR, JAMES, actor; b. L.A., Dec. 8, 1937; s. Charles MacArthur and Helen Hayes; m. Joyce Bulifant, Nov. 2, 1958 (div. 1967); children: Charles, Mary; m. Melody Patterson, July 12, 1970 (div. 1975); m. Helen Beth Duntz, 1984; children; Juliette, Jamie. Acting debut in The Corn is Green in summer stock, Olney, Md., 1948; appeared on Invitation to a March, 1960; actor: (films) The Young Stranger, 1957, The Light in the Forest, 1958, The Third Man on the Mountain, 1959, Kidnapped, 1960, The Swiss Family Robinson, 1960, The Interns, 1962, Spencer's Mountain, 1963, Battle of the Bulge, 1964-65, The Truth About Spring, 1965, The Bedford Incident, 1965, Ride Beyond Vengeance, 1966, The Love-Ins, 1967, Hang 'Em High, 1967, The Angry Breed, 1968, Alcatraz, 1980, The Night the Bridge Fell Down, 1983; (TV series) Hawaii Five-O, 1968-79; (TV appearances) The Love Boat, 1980 Died Oct. 28, 2010.

MACCORKINDALE, SIMON CHARLES PENDERED, actor; b. Ely, Cambridge, Eng., Feb. 12, 1952; came to U.S., 1981; s. Peter Bernard and Gilliver Mary (Pendered) MacC.; m. Fiona Elizabeth Fullerton, July 10, 1976 (div. Sept. 1983); m. Susan Melody George, Oct. 5, 1984. Student, Haileybury Coll., Hertford, Eng., 1965-70. Producer, dir. Amy Internat. Prodns., Inc., Los Angeles, from 1984, Amy Internat. Prodns., Ltd., Middlesex, Eng., from 1987. Theatre appearances include Journey's End, 1973, Getting On, 1973, Front Page, 1973, Bequest to the Nation, 1973, Back to Methuselah, 1973, Potsdam Quartet, 1973, Happiest Days of Your Life, 1974, Pygmalion, 1974, B-B-Que, 1974, Relatively Speaking, 1974, 77, French Without Tears, 1975, Dark Lady of the Sonnets, 1975, 77, Gayden Chronicles, 1980, Macbeth, 1980, A Merchant of Venice, 1981, A Doll House, 1982, Sleuth, 1982, The Sound of Music, 2008; appeared in one man show The Importance of Being Oscar, 1977, 80, 81, 82, 85; Actor: (films) Juggernaut, 1974, Road to Mandalay, 1977, Death on the Nile, 1977, The Riddle of the Sands, 1978, The Quatermass Conclusion, 1978, Cabo Blanco, 1979, Outpost of Progress, 1981, The Sword & the Sorcerer, 1981, Falcon's Gold, 1982, Jaws 3-D, 1982; (TV mini-series) Time and Again, 1974, Jesus of Nazareth, 1975, Three Weeks, 1976, Out of Battle, 1977, Quartermass, 1978, The Hammer House of Horror, 1980, The Mansions of America, 1980-81, Obsessive Love, 1984, Sincerely, Violet, 1986; (TV series) Hawkeye the Pathfinder, 1973, General Hospital, 1974, Skin Game, 1974, Sutherland's Law, 1975, Hunter's Walk, 1975, I, Claudius, 1976, Will Shakespeare, 1976, Romeo and Juliet, 1976, Baby for Beasts, 1976, Just William, 1977, Within These Walls, 1977, Doomdolt Chase, 1977, This is Your Life, 1977, Dukes of Hazzard, 1979, Scalpels, 1980, Fantasy Island, 1981, Macbeth, 1981, Hart to Hart, 1982, Dynasty, 1982, Manimal, 1983, Matt Houston, 1984, Falcon Crest, 1984-86, Future Probe II, 1985, Casualty, 2002-09 Named Most Promising Newcomer to Motion Pictures, Brit. Standard awards London, 1978. Mem. Acad. Motion Picture Arts and Scis., Brit. Acad. Film and TV Arts, Am. Film Inst., Acad. TV Arts and Scis., Stars Orgn. for Spastics, Screen Actors Guild, Dirs. Guild Am., Brit. Actors Equity. Clubs: St. James (London). Avocations: sports, photography, opera, travel. Died Oct. 14, 2010.

MACDONALD, WILLIAM LLOYD, architectural historian; b. Putnam, Conn., July 12, 1921; s. William Lloyd and Susan Elisabeth (Elrod) MacD.; children: Noel, Nicholas. AB, Harvard U., 1949, AM, 1953, PhD, 1956. Instr. Boston Archtl. Ctr., Mass., 1950-54; from asst. prof. to assoc. prof. Yale U., New Haven, Conn., 1956-65; A.P. Brown prof. Smith Coll., Northampton, Mass., 1965-80; archtl. historian Washington, from 1980. Exec. sec. Byzantine Inst., Boston, 1950-54. Author: Early Christian and Byzantine Architecture, 1962, Northampton Massachusetts Architecture and Buildings, 1976, Piranesi's Carceri: Sources of Invention, 1976, The Pantheon, 1976, Architecture of the Roman Empire I, 1982, II, 1986 (Alice Davis Hitchcock prize, Kevin Lynch award Dept. Urban Studies MIT), (with J.A. Pinto) Villa Adriana: La construzione e il mito da Adriano a Louis Kahn, 1997, Hadrian's Villa and Its Legacy, 1995 (Alice Davis Hitchcock prize, George Wittenborn Meml. award, Book of Yr. award AIA). Lt. USAAF, 1942-45. Emerton, Shaw fellow Harvard U., 1949-50; Vets. Nat. scholar, 1948, J. Paul Getty Ctr. scholar, 1985-86. Fellow Am. Acad. Arts and Scis., Am. Acad. Rome (prize fellow 1954-56); mem. AIA (life), Soc. Archtl. Historians (bd. dirs.), Soc. for Promotion of Roman Studies (life). Home: Washington, DC. Died Mar. 6, 2010.

MACHEMER, ROBERT, ophthalmologist; b. Muenster, Germany, Mar. 16, 1933; came to U.S., 1966, naturalized, 1972; s. Helmut and Erna M.; m. Christine Haller, July 28, 1961; 1 dau., Ruth. Student, univs. Muenster, Freiburg, Germany, Vienna, Austria, 1953-59, med. diploma, 1959; MD, U. Freiburg, 1959; MD (hon.), U. Goettingen, Germany, 1988. Diplomate Am. Bd. Ophthalmology. Rotating intern, Germany, 1960-61; fellow in gen. pathology Univ. Inst. of Pathology, Freiburg, Germany, 1961-62; resident in ophthalmology Augenklinik der Universitaet Goettingen, Germany, 1962-65; sci. asst. U. Goettingen, 1962-68; Akademischer Austauschdienst research fellow Bascom Palmer Eye Inst., U. Miami, Fla., 1966-67, Nat. Council to Combat Blindness research fellow Fla., 1967-68, instr. ophthalmology Fla., 1968-70, asst. prof. ophthalmology Fla., 1970-74, asso. prof. Fla., 1974-78, prof. Fla., 1978; prof., chmn. dept. ophthalmology Duke U. Eye Center, 1978-91, Helena Rubinstein Found. prof., from 1983; mem. staff VA Hosp., Miami, 1969-78, chief sect. ophthalmology, 1969-71, mem. staff Durham, N.C., 1978-80. Mem. policy adv. group, diabetic retinopathy vitrectomy study NIH, 1978-80, mem. study exec. com., 1977-80, mem. data monitoring com. early treatment diabetic retinopathy study, 1980-88, mem. study sect., 1982-84. Author: (with T. Aaberg) Vitrectomy, 1979; mem. editorial bd. Am. Jour. Ophthalmology, 1979—, Graefe's Archive, 1982—; contbr. numerous articles related to retinal detachment and vitreous surgery to med. pubs. Recipient Hermann Wacker award Club Jules Gonin, 1972, Trustees award Rsch. to Prevent Blindness, 1978, von Graefe prize German Ophthal. Soc., 1981, Ernst Jung prize for Medicine Jung Stiftung for Sci. and Rsch., Hamburg, Germany, 1993, Internat. Coun. of Ophthalmology Ganin Medal and prize, 1998; Rsch. to Prevent Blindness Louis B. Mayer scholar, 1971. Mem. Am. Acad. Ophthalmolgy, Pan. Am. Assn. Ophthalmology, Am. Ophthalmol. Soc. (Howe medal 1996, Helen Keller prize for vision rsch. 1997), Retina Soc. (award of merit in retina research 1980), N.C. Med. Soc., Club Jules Gonin (pres. 1986-88), Assn. Research in Vision and Ophthalmology (Proctor medal and lectr. 1988), German Ophthalmol. Soc. Home: Durham, NC. Died Dec. 23, 2009.

MACLAINE, ALLAN HUGH, English language educator; b. Montreal, Can., Oct. 24, 1924; BA, McGill U., 1945; PhD in English, Brown U., 1951. Instr. English McGill U., 1946-47, Brown U., 1947-50, U. Mass., 1951-54; from asst. prof. to prof. Tex. Christian U., 1954-62; prof. English U. R.I., from 1962, also dean div. univ. extension, 1967-71. Author: Student's Comprehensive Guide to the Canterbury Tales, 1964, Robert Fergusson, 1965, Allan Ramsay, 1985, The Christis Kirk Tradition: Scots Poems of Folk Festivity, 1996; also articles. Mem. Coll. English Assn. (pres. 1965, dir. 1961-66), Assn. for Scottish Literary Studies. Home: Charlestown, RI. Died Dec. 17, 2009.

MACMICHAEL, JOSEPH WILLIAM, JR., financial planner; b. Camden, NJ, Feb. 14, 1931; s. Joseph William and Dorothy Idela (Bitting) MacMichael; m. Verna A. MacMichael; children: Joseph W. III, Melissa A., Matthew P. AB, Rutgers U., 1957; MBA, Drexel U., 1961. CLU; CFP, charterd fin. planner. Comml. loan officer Girard Bank, Phila., 1957—61; pres. MacMichael Enterprises, Mt. Laurel, NJ, from 1962, Colonial Pensions Svcs. Inc., from 1984, Haddon Fin. Group Inc., 1985; mng. exec. Integrated Resources Equity Corp., from 1980. Bd. dirs. BCM Internat., LSW Industries. With USMC, 1948—52. Named Young Man of the Yr., Jaycees, 1968, Man of the Yr., Greater Camden Life Underwriters, 1975. Mem.: ChFCs (bd. dirs.), N.J. State Assn. Life Underwriters (past pres.), S. Jersey CLUs (past pres.), S. Jersey Estate Planning Coun. (past pres.), Am. Soc. Pension Actuaries, Am. Acad. Actuaries, Internat. Assn. Fin. Planners, Million Dollar Round Table, Am. Soc. CLUs, Advanced Assn. Life Underwriters, Nat. Assn. Life Underwriters, Tavistock Country Club, Rotary (past pres. Moorestown), Beta Theta Pi. Republican. Died Aug. 11, 2009.

MACMILLAN, ROBERT SMITH, electronics engineer; b. LA, Aug. 28, 1924; s. Andrew James and Moneta (Smith) M.; m. Barbara Macmillan, Aug. 18, 1962; 1 child, Robert G. BS in Physics, Calif. Inst. Tech., 1948, MS in Elec. Engring., 1949, PhD in Elec. Engring./Physics cum laude, 1954. Rsch. engr. Jet Propulsion Lab., Calif. Inst. Tech., Pasadena, 1951-55, asst. prof. elec. engring., 1955-58; assoc. prof. elec. engring. U. So. Calif., LA, 1958-70; mem. sr. tech. staff Litton Sys., Inc., Van Nuys, Calif., 1969-79; dir. sys. engring. Litton Data Command Sys., Agoura Hills, Calif., 1979-89; pres. The Macmillan Group, La Canada Flintridge, Calif., from 1989. Treas., v.p. Video Color Corp., Inglewood, 1965-66; cons. fgn. tech. div. USAF, Wright-Patterson AFB, Ohio, 1957-74, Space Tech. Labs., Glendale, Calif., 1956-60, Space Gen. Corp., El Monte, Calif., 1960-63. With Air Corps US Army, 1943—46. Recipient Nat. Patriot's medal, Nat. Rifle Assn., 2002, Rep. Senatorial medal of freedom, 2004. Mem.: IEEE, Am. Phys. Soc., Am. Inst. Physics, Eta Kappa Nu, Tau Beta Pi, Sigma Xi. Republican. Presbyterian. Achievements include research in ionospheric, radio-wave, propagation; very low frequency radio-transmitting antennas; optical coherence and statistical optics. Home: Long Beach, Calif. Died Sept. 6, 2009.

MADDUX, JAMES FREDERICK, physician; b. Sycamore, Ga., Aug. 17, 1916; s. Creed Taylor and Ida (Nussell) Maddux; m. Agnes Griffin Maddux; children: James Michael, Frederick Taylor, John Stephen, Mary Bernadette. MD, U. Ga., 1941. Diplomate Am. Bd. Psychiatry & Neurology. Intern USPHS Hosp., Balt., 1941—42, resident psychiatry Ft. Worth, 1942—43, Colo. Psychopathic Hosp., Denver, 1946—48; med. officer USPHS, 1942—69; various clin. psychiatry and mental health adminstrv. positions, 1942—62; chief NIMH Clin. Rsch. Ctr., Ft. NIMH Clin. Research Ctr, 1962—69; ret., 1969; prof. psychiatry U. Tex. Health Sci. Ctr., San Antonio, from 1969. Co-author (with D.P. Desmond): Careers of Opiod Users, 1981; contbr. articles to profl. jours. Served to lt. comdr. USCG, 1943—46. Mem.: AMA, Am. Orthopsychiat. Assn. (life), Am. Psychiat. Assn. (life). Democrat. Home: San Antonio, Tex. Died Sept. 29, 2009.

MAHEY, JOHN ANDREW, retired museum director; b. DuBois, Pa., Mar. 30, 1932; s. Manasseh A. and Bernyce (Holdar) M. Student, Columbia U., 1950-52; BA, Pa. State U., 1959, MA, 1962. Asst. dir. Peale Mus., Balt., 1964-69; dir. E.B. Crocker Art Gallery, 1969-72, Cummer Gallery of Art, 1972-75, Meml. Art Gallery of U. Rochester, 1975-79; chief curator Philbrook Art Center, Tulsa, 1979-84; dir. San Antonio Mus. Art, 1984-89, Flint (Mich.) Inst. of Arts, 1989-96; ret., 1996. Contbr. articles on artists to art his. jours.; author exhbn. catalogs. Fulbright scholar, 1962 Mem. Phi Beta Kappa, Phi Alpha Theta. Home: Harrisburg, Pa. Died Mar. 30, 2010.

MAHONEY, EDWARD BRADY PATRICK, philosophy educator; b. Jamaica, NY, Nov. 3, 1932; s. Patrick Joseph and Kathleen Margaret (Brady) M. Student, St. John's U., 1949-51; BA, Cathedral Coll., 1953; MA in Philosophy, St. John's U., 1956; MA in Polit. Sci., Columbia U., 1960, PhD in Philosophy, 1966. Lectr. philosophy Iona Coll., New Rochelle, N.Y., 1956-57; instr. philosophy St. Joseph's Coll., Bklyn., 1957-61; Fulbright Teaching fellow U. Rome, Italy, 1962-63; faculty Columbia U., NYC, 1963-64; asst. prof., then assoc. prof. Duke U., Durham, N.C., 1965-77, prof. philosophy, from 1977. Assoc. Univ. Seminar on Renaissance, Columbia, N.Y.C., 1968— Editor: Philosophy and Humanism, 1976, Studies in the Renaissance, Renaissance Quar.; chmn. editorial bd.: Duke Monographs in Medieval and Renaissance Studies, 1974—. Mem., chmn. Ecumenical Commn. Roman Catholic Diocese of Raleigh, N.C. Guggenheim fellow, 1979-80; Danforth Found. fellow, 1961-62; Fulbright fellow, 1962-63; Younger Humanist fellow Nat. Found. Humanities, 1968-69; Folger Shakespeare Library fellow Washington, 1973 Mem. Internat. Scotist Soc. (council 1976, 81), Renaissance Soc. Am. (exec. bd. 1976—), Soc. Medieval and Renaissance Philosophy (exec. com., pres. 1985—), Am. Philos. Assn., Metaphys. Soc. Am., Societe International pour L'Étude de la Philosophie Médíevale, Medieval Acad. Am., Soc. Ancient Greek Philosophy Democrat. Roman Catholic. Died Jan. 8, 2009.

MAISEL, SHERMAN JOSEPH, economist, educator; b. Buffalo, July 8, 1918; s. Louis and Sophia (Beck) M.; m. Lucy Cowdin, Sept. 26, 1942; children: Lawrence C., Margaret L. AB, Harvard U., Cambridge, Mass., 1939, MPA, 1947, PhD, 1949. Economist, fgn. service officer US Dept. State, 1945-46; teaching fellow Harvard U., 1947-48; asst. prof., assoc. prof., prof. bus. adminstrn. U. Calif. Berkeley, 1948-65, 72-86; mem. bd. govs. Fed. Res. System, 1965-72; sr. economist Nat. Bur. Econ. Research-West, 1973-78; chmn., bd. dirs. Farmers Savings & Loan, 1986-88; pres. Sherman J. Maisel & Associates Inc., 1986—2010. Fellow Fund For Advancement Edn., 1952-53, Inst. Basic Math. with Application to Bus., 1959-60, Center for Advanced Study in Behavioral Scis., 1972; mem. adv. coms. to Bur. Census, FHA, State of Calif., Ford Found., Social Sci. Research Council; mem. bldg. research adv. bd. NRC. Author: Housebuilding in Transition, 1953, Fluctuations, Growth, and Forecasting, 1957, Managing the Dollar, 1973, Real Estate Investment and Finance, 1976, Risk and Capital Adequacy in Commercial Banks, 1981, Macroeconomics: Theories and Policies, 1982, Real Estate Finance, 1987, 2d edit., 1992. Bd. dirs. Berkeley Unified Sch. Dist., 1962-65. Served to capt. AUS, 1941-45. Recipient citation, U. Calif., Berkeley, 1986. Fellow Am. Fin. Assn. (pres. 1973); mem. Am. Econ. Assn. Home: San Francisco, Calif. Died Sept. 29, 2010.

MAJNO, GUIDO, pathologist, educator; b. Milan, Feb. 9, 1922; came to U.S., 1952; s. Edoardo and Elda M.; m. Isabelle Joris; children: Corinne, Lorenzo, Luca. MD, U. Milan, 1947; MA (hon.), Harvard U., 1961; DSc (hon.), U. Mass., 1991. Resident, chief resident in pathology Hosp. Cantonal, Geneva, 1947-52; mem. faculty Harvard Med. Sch., Boston, 1953-68; guest investigator Rockefeller Inst., 1958-59; dir. Inst. Pathology U. Geneva, 1968-73; chmn. pathology dept. U. Mass., Worcester, from 1973. Author: The Healing Hand, 1975. Recipient Sci award Phi Beta Kappa, 1975, Gold-Headed Cane award Am. Soc. Pathologists, 1989. Fellow Am. Acad. Arts and Scis.; mem. Am. Soc. Pathology, Soc. for Cell Biology, Internat. Acad. Pathology, Am. Antiquarian Soc. Died May 27, 2010.

MAKANOFF, LON DAVID, supermarket executive; b. Phila., Feb. 29, 1948; s. Bernard and Dorothy (Frimmel) M.; m. Rebecca Sher, Aug. 30, 1969; children— Jennifer, Eric, Amanda, Aaron BA in Acctg., Phila. Coll. of Textiles and Scis., 1969; postgrad., U. Pa., 1977, NYU, 1977. Ptnr. Deloitte Haskins & Sells, Detroit, 1969-82; sr. v.p. fin., treas. Allied Supermarkets, Inc., Detroit, 1982-85, pres., chief operating officer, 1985-87, also dir.; pres., chief operating officer Meadowdale Foods, Inc., Detroit, from 1987. Audit com. Jewish Welfare Fedn., Detroit, 1982—; chmn. Gen. Foods div. United Found., Detroit, 1984; chmn. Allied Mich. Polit. Action, Detroit, 1983—; trustee Monseigneur Clement Kern Hosp. for Specialized Surgery, 1987—. Mem. Mich. Assn. C.P.A.s, Nat. Assn. Accts., Am. Inst. C.P.A.s, Fin. Execs. Inst., Detroit C. of C., Nat. Assn. Corp. Treasurers, Mich. Mchts. Council (sec., treas.) Clubs: Detroit; Econ., Fairlane (Dearborn, Mich.). Republican. Jewish. Home: West Bloomfield, Mich. Died Apr. 8, 2010.

MAKOWSKI, M. PAUL, electronics research executive; b. Warsaw, Jan. 15, 1922; Arrived in U.S. July 1949. s. Antoni and Stanislawa (Leszowska) M.; m. Eugenia Sawczyn, Dec. 1, 1945; children: Paul, Teresa. BA in Chem., Case Western Reserve U., 1957, MS in Physical Chem., 1961, PhD in Electrochem., 1964. Mgr. Smith Phoenix Co., Cleve., 1950-55; chemist Clevite Research Ctr., Clevite Corp., Cleve., 1955-64; mgr. chemistry Materials Research Lab., Gould Inc., Cleve., 1964-73; assoc. dir. Materials Research Gould Inc., Cleve.; dir. Materials Research Lab., Gould Inc., Cleve., 1976-80; v.p. tech. adminstrn. Gould Inc., Rolling Meadows, Ill., 1980-81, v.p. scientific affairs, 1981-87; pres. TECTRA Cons. Inc., Rolling Meadows, Ill., 1988-93; cons. Rolling Meadows, from 1994. Mem. Frontiers in Chem. Com. Cleve. 1976-80; bd. dirs. Microelectronics and Computer Corp. Austin, Tex. 1986-87. Inventor several patents in electrodeposition and catalysis. Mem. Ill. Gov.'s Commn. on Sci. and Tech. Chgo., 1986-87, Tech. Commercialization Coun. Ill. Dept. Commerce and Community Affairs. Mem. Am. Chem. Soc., Electrochem. Soc. Chgo., Materials Rsch. Avocation: stamp collecting/philately. Home: Palatine, Ill. Died May 17, 2010.

MAKSYMOWYCH, ROMAN, scientist, educator; b. West Ukraine, Oct. 15, 1924; s. Andrew and Eudokia (Stecyna) M.; m. Anna Nadia Holowinsky, Oct. 14, 1951; children: Andrew, Alexandra, Nestor, Maria. Student, U. Innsbruck, Austria, 1949; MS in Botany, U. Pa., 1956, PhD in Botany, 1959. Rsch. asst. U. Pa., Phila., 1952-54, 55-57, teaching asst., 1954-55, asst. instr., 1957-58; asst. prof. Villanova (Pa.) U., 1959-62, assoc. prof., 1962-66, prof. biology, from 1967. Author: Analysis of Leaf Development, 1973, Analysis of Growth and Development of Xanthium, 1990; contbr. articles to profl. publs. NSF grantee, 1959-60. Home: Willow Grove, Pa. Died Apr. 7, 2010.

MALCHON, JEANNE KELLER, retired state legislator; b. Newark, June 17, 1923; d. Leslie Stafford and Edith Katherine (Marcelle) Keller; m. Richard Malchon, 1946 (dec.); 1 child, Richard Jr. AA, Va. Intermont Coll., 1943. Draftsman Curtis-Wright Propeller Divsn., Caldwell, NJ, 1943—44; civilian employee US Army, Hickam Field, Hawaii, 1944—45; merchandising rep. L. Bamberger & Co., Newark, 1946—49; with Office Tech. Assessment Task Force, 1971; mem. Gov.'s Commn. Criminal Justice Standards and Goals, 1981—82, Fla. Jud. Coun., 1972—82; commr. Pinellas County, Fla., 1975—82; mem. Supreme Ct. Dispute Resolution Alternatives Com., Nat. Com. and Nat. Air Quality Commn., 1978—82; mem. Dist. 18 Fla. State Senate, 1982—92; vice chmn. Senate Health and Rehab. Svc. Com., 1985—86; mem. exec. com. American Lung Assn., 1977—85, nat. pres., 1982—84; chmn. Nat. Air Conservation Com., 1978—83. Bd. dirs. Ctr. Govtl. Responsibility. Recipient award, Soroptimists, 1979, Outstanding Equal Opportunity Efforts award, Pinellas County Urban League, 1980, environment award, Fla. Sierra Club, 1984, Disting. Svc. award, Pinellas County Assn. Respiratory Care Mgrs., 1985, Human Svc. award, United Way Pinellas County, 1986; named Most Effective Senator, Fla. Sheriff's Assn., 1983, Outstanding Legislator of Yr., Fla. Nurses Assn., 1985, Legislator of Yr., Fla. Psychol. Assn., 1985, Fla. Consumer Fedn., 1986. Mem.: Nat. Assn. Counties (criminal justice steering com. 1975—80, chmn. law enforcement subcom. 1979—80), State Assn. County Commrs. (dir. 1975—80, chmn. urban affairs com. 1979—80). Democrat. Home: Clearwater, Fla. Died Aug. 23, 2009.

MALEC, THOMAS OLIVER, lawyer; b. Milford, Conn., Aug. 5, 1942; s. John A. and Genevieve (Sledziona) Malec; m. Maureen Dorothy Smith, Aug. 27, 1965; children: Pamela A., Kimberly I. BS in Acctg., Quinnipiac Coll., 1964; JD, Bklyn. Law Sch., 1968. Bar: Conn. 1968, US Dist. Ct. Conn. 1969. Sole practice, West Haven, Conn., from 1968; prof. law orgn. Quinnipiac Coll., 1975—80, bd. dirs., 1972—78; adv. bd. dirs. Am. Nat. Bank, West Haven, Conn., from 1978. Mem.: KC (judge advocate from 1975), Conn. Bar Assn. Democrat. Roman Catholic. Home: Orange, Conn. Died Apr. 17, 2009.

MALISZEWSKI, THADDEUS W., lawyer; b. Hartford, Conn., Jan. 10, 1922; s. Joseph and Apolonia (Hajdasz) Maliszewski; m. Barbara C. Karpienia Maliszewski, Jan. 27, 1951; children: Thaddeus M., Michelle, Lance, Michael, John, Paul. AS, Hillyer Jr. Coll., Hartford, 1942; BA in Econs., Wesleyan U., Middletown, Conn., 1947; JD, U. Conn., 1950. Bar: Conn. 1950, US Dist. Ct. Conn. 1951, US Ct. Mil. Appeals 1957, US Supreme Ct. 1959, US Ct. Appeals (2d cir.) 1961. Sole practice law Hartford & Windsor, Conn., from 1950; sr. judge Windsor Mcpl. Ct., 1955—60; pros. atty. Circuit Ct., Enfield, Conn., 1963. Contbr. articles to legal jours. Vice chmn. Vets. Housing Coun., Hartford, 1949; nat. v.p. Polish-Am. Congress, Chgo., 1977—83; chmn. Dem. Town Com., Windsor, 1976—78. Served as sgt. USAAF, 1943—46, PTO, lt. col. ret. Res., brig. gen., Conn. N.G. Res. Recipient Disting. Svc. award, Polish United Socs., 1974, Polish Army Vets., 1977; scholar, Auerbach Found. Mem.: Polish Legion Am. Vets. (nat. vice comdr. 1952—54), U. Conn. Law Sch. Assn. (trustee 1966—68), Conn. Trial Lawyers Assn. (trustee 1968). Democrat. Roman Catholic. Died Sept. 14, 2009.

MALKOVICH, MARK PAUL, III, musician, performing company executive; b. Eveleth, Minn., July 10, 1930; s. Mark II and Mary Frances (Greben) M.; m. Joan Shewring, Feb. 7, 1959; children: Mark IV, Erik, Kent, Kara. BS in Chemistry, Columbia U., 1952, MS, 1953; studied piano with Dorothy Crost Bourgin, Chgo. Mus. Coll., 1947-50; William Beller ch. Piano Dept., Columbia U., 1951-54; Adele Marcus, Juilliard Sch., 1959-62; MusD (hon.), Salve Regina, 1993; DFA, U. RI, 1994; MusD, Cath. U. Am., 1999. Pres. Chem. Gum Industries, Ltd., NYC, 1964—69. Artistic and gen. dir. Newport Music Festival, 1975-2010; exec. dir. Palm Beach Festival, Fla., 1984-86; guest lectr. TV and radio appearances and adjudicator at music competitions; pres. Chopin Found. of U.S., Miami, Fla., 1985; presented North American debuts of Bella Davidovich, Jean-Philippe Collard, Dmitry Sitkovetsky, Andrei Gavrilov, Mikhail Pletnev, others; founder Sports US*A*SR; negotiator/agt. for USSR leading hockey players Fetisov, Krutov, Larionov, Makarov, 1989. Recipient Individual Achievement award Bus. Vols. for the Arts, RI, 1998; named to RI Heritage Hall of Fame, 2000; named hon. citizen, Tbilisi, Republic of Ga., hon. prof. Tbilisi Conservatoire. Mem. Harvard Mus. Assn., Newport Reading Rm., Newport Hist. Soc., Spouting Rock Beach Assn., Royal Arts Found. (pres.), Clambake Club. Died May 30, 2010.

MALONE, JOHN MICHAEL, JR., academic administrator; b. Detroit, June 12, 1951; s. John Michael and Thereza Mattoso Malone; m. Mary Leslie Malone, Mar. 22, 1981; children: John Michael Malone III, Austin Phillip. BS magna cum laude, John Carroll U., 1973; MD, Wayne State U., 1977. Resident Wayne State U., Detroit, 1973—77, intern, 1981—84, asst. prof., 1986—92, assoc. prof., 1992—2001, prof., chair, from 2001. Assoc. dean. Wayne State U., Sch. Medicine, from 1995; sr. v.p. acad. affairs Detroit Med. Ctr., 1995—2001. Fellow, M.D. Anderson, Houston, 1984—86. Home: Grosse Pointe Park, Mich. Died Jan. 25, 2009.

MALTESE, GEORGE JOHN, mathematics professor; b. Middletown, Conn., June 24, 1931; s. Giorgio and Sebastiana (Morello) M.; m. Marlene Erika Kunz, Apr. 14, 1956; children: Christopher, Michelle. BA, Wesleyan U., Middletown, Conn., 1953; postgrad., U. Frankfurt, Germany, 1953-54; PhD, Yale U., 1960. Instr. MIT, 1961-63; asst. prof. U. Md., College Park, 1963-66, assoc. prof., 1966-69, prof., 1969-73, U. Münster, Fed. Republic Germany, from 1973. Vis. prof. U. Frankfurt, 1966-67, 70-71, U. Palermo, Italy, 1967, 71, 76. U. Pisa, Italy, 1972, U. Kuwait, 1977, U. Bahrain, 1988, U. Oman, 1991. Contbr. articles to profl. jours. Served with AUS, 1954-56. Fulbright fellow, 1953-54; NATO postdoctoral fellow, 1960-61 Mem. Am. Math. Soc., Math. Assn. Am., Unione Matematica Italiana, Deutsche Mathematiker Verein. Home: Middletown, Conn. Died Oct. 27, 2009.

MANDELBROT, BENOIT B., mathematician, research scientist, educator; b. Warsaw, Nov. 20, 1924; arrived in US, 1958, naturalized, 2000; s. Charles and Belle (Lurie) M.; m. Aliette Kagan, Nov. 5, 1955; children: Laurent, Didier. Diploma, Ecole Polytechnique, Paris, 1947; MS in Aeronautics, Calif. Inst. Tech., 1948; PhD in Math., U. Paris, 1952; DSc (hon.), Syracuse U., 1985, Laurentian U., Ont., Can., 1986, Boston U., 1987, SUNY, 1988, U. Bremen, Germany, 1988, U. Guelph, Ont., Can., 1989, Pace U., 1989, U. Dallas, 1992, Union Coll., 1993, U. Buenos Aires, 1993, U. Tel Aviv, 1995, Open U., UK, 1998, Athens U. Bus. and Fin., 1998, U. St. Andrews, Scotland, 1999, Emory U., Atlanta, 2002, Politecnico di Torino, Italy, 2005; DSc, JOhn Hopkins U., 2010; Dr. Medicine and Surgery (hon.), U. Bari, Italy, 2007; AM (hon.), Yale U., 2000. Postdoctoral mem. and Rockefeller scholar Inst. for Advanced Study, Princeton, NJ, 1953—54; jr. prof. math. U. Geneva, 1955-57, U. Lille and Ecole Polytechnique, Paris, 1957-58; rsch. staff mem. IBM Watson Rsch. Ctr., Yorktown Heights, NY, 1958-74, IBM fellow, 1974-93, IBM fellow emeritus, from 1993; vis. prof. engring. Yale U., New Haven, 1970, prof. math. sciences, 1987—99, Sterling prof. math. sciences, 1999—2004, Sterling prof. math. sciences emeritus, 2005—10; Battelle fellow Pacific Northwest Nat. Lab, 2005—07. Vis. prof. econs. Harvard U., 1962-63, applied math., 1963-64, math., 1979-80, 84-87, U. Paris, 1966, physiology Einstein Coll. Medicine, 1970, Coll. France, 1973, Inst. Hautes Etudes Sci. Bures, 1980, Mittag-Leffler Inst., Sweden, 1984, 2001, 02, 04, Max Planck Inst. Math, Bonn, Germany, 1988, Cambridge, 1990, 2005, Oxford U., 1990, Imperial Coll., London, 1991; Hitchcock prof. U. Calif., Berkeley, 1992; visitor MIT, 1953, Inst. lectr., 1964-; spkr. and organizer profl. confs. Author: Logique, langage et théorie de l'information, 1957, Les objets fractals: forme, hasard et dimension, 1975, 4th edit., 1995, Fractals: Form, Chance and Dimension, 1977, The Fractal Geometry of Nature, 1982, La Geometria della Natura, 1987, Fractals and Scaling in Finance: Discontinuity, Concentration, Risk, 1997, Fractales, hasard et finance, 1997, Multifractals and 1/f Noise: Wild Self-Affinity in Physics, 1999, Nel mondo dei frattali, 2001, Gaussian Self-Affinity and Fractals: Globality, The Earth, 1/f Noise and R/S, 2002, (with M.L. Frame) Fractals, Graphics and Mathematics Education, 2002, (with R.L. Hudson) The (Mis)Behavior of Markets: A Fractal View of Risk, Ruin, and Reward, 2004, Fractals and Chaos: The Mandelbrot Set and Beyond, 2004,; contbr. articles to profl. jours. Recipient Franklin medal Franklin Inst., 1986, Alexander von Humboldt Preis, 1987, Caltech disting. svc. award, 1988, Moet-Hennessy Sci. and Art prize, 1988, Harvey prize, 1989, Nev. prize U. Nev. Sys., 1991, Wolf prize for physics, 1993, Honda prize, 1994, Medal of City of Paris, 1996, John Scott award City of Phila., 1999, L.F. Richardson medal European Geophys. Soc., 2000, Sven Berggren prize, Lund, Sweden, 2002, Japan prize for Sci. and Tech., 2003, Fin. Times (Germany) award, 2004, Waclaw Sierpinski prize, 2005 Wladislaw Orlicz medal, 2005, Casimir Funk award Piasa, 2005; Guggenheim fellow, 1968. Fellow AAAS, IEEE (Charles Proteus Steinmetz medal 1988), Am. Acad. Arts and Scis., European Acad. Arts, Scis. and Humanities, Am. Phys. Soc., French Physics Soc. (hon.), Inst. Math. Stats., Econometric Soc., Am. Geophys. Union, Am. Statistic Assn.; mem. NAS U.S.A. (Barnard medal 1985), Am. Philos. Soc., Internat. Statis. Inst. (elected,), Am. Math. Soc., Norwegian Acad. Sci. and Letters (fgn. mem.), Sigma Xi (nat. lectr. 1980-82, Procter prize 2002). Achievements include origination of theory of fractals, a nascent interdisciplinary theory of roughness; many aspects this theory strongly attack young minds provides mathematical conjectures including very difficult ones, and also provides practical tools to handle financial data, mountains, clouds, fractures of metals, dynamic attractors, and all other shapes and phenomena in nature or man's works that are equally irregular or broken-up at all scales; the best known fractal is called Mandelbrot set. Home: Cambridge, Mass. Died Oct. 14, 2010.

MANGUS, MARVIN DALE, geologist; b. Altoona, Pa., Sept. 13, 1924; s. Alfred Ross and Myrna Belle (Truby) Mangus; m. Jane Gray Mangus, Aug. 21, 1926; children: Alfred R., Donald H. BS, Pa. State U., 1945, MS in Geology, 1946. Geologist US Geol. Survey, 1946—58; sr. geologist Atlantic Refining Co., Guatemala, 1958—60, Calgary, Alta., Canada, 1960—62; regional geologist Atlantic Richfield, Anchorage, 1962—70; geologic cons. Fackler, Calderwood, Mangus, 1970—77; geol. cons. Anchorage, from 1977. Fellow: Geol. Soc. America; mem.: Pioneers of Alaska, Geol. Soc. Alaska (pres. 1965—66), Am. Inst. Profl. Geologists, Can. Soc. Petroleum Geologists, Am. Soc. Petroleum Geologists, Petroleum Club, Arts, Landscape Club (Washington);, Explorers Club. Home: Anchorage, Alaska. Died Feb. 20, 2009.

MANKIEWICZ, THOMAS FRANK, screenwriter, director, producer; b. L.A., June 1, 1942; s. Joseph Leo and Rosa M. Student, Phillips Exeter Acad., NH, 1955—59, Yale U., New Haven, 1959—63. Filmmaker-in-residence Dodge Coll. Film and Media Arts, Chapman U., Orange, Calif., 2006. Author: (book, Broadway musical) Georgy!, 1970; screenwriter: (teleplay, musical spl.) Movin' with Nancy, 1967, The Sweet Ride, 1968, (teleplay, musical spl.) The Beat of the Brass, 1968, Diamonds Are Forever, 1971, Live and Let Die, 1973, The Man With with the Golden Gun, 1974, The Eagle Has Landed, 1976, The Cassandra Crossing, 1977, Ladyhawke, 1985; screenwriter, co-prodr.: Mother, Juggs and Speed, 1976; creative cons.: Superman, 1978, Superman II, 1980; dir. (teleplay, tv pilot) Hart to Hart, 1979-80, (screenplay) Dragnet, 1987, Delirious, 1991, (cable tv series) Tales from the Crypt, 1992, (cable tv movie) Taking the Heat, 1993; exec. prodr. Hot Pursuit, 1985. Bd. dirs. William Holden Wildlife Found., L.A., 1995—. Mem. Greater L.A. Zoo Assn. (bd. trustees 1997—, chmn. 2002--), Motion Picture Acad. Arts and Scis. (bd. govs. 1979-81), Thoroughbred Owners Calif. (bd. dirs. 2005). Avocations: wildlife conservation, thoroughbred horse racing and breeding. Home: Los Angeles, Calif. Died July 31, 2010.

MANKILLER, WILMA PEARL, retired tribal leader; b. Stilwell, Okla., Nov. 18, 1945; d. Charley and Clara Irene (Sitton) M.; m. Hector N. Olaya, Nov. 13, 1963 (div. 1975); children: Felicia Marie Olaya, Gina Irene Olaya; m. Charlie Soap, Oct. 13, 1986. Student, Skyline Coll., San Bruno Coll., 1973, San Francisco State Coll., 1973-75; BA in Social Sci., Union Coll., 1977; postgrad., U. Ark., 1979; DHL (hon.), U. New Eng., 1986; PhD in Pub. Svc. (hon.), R.I. Coll., 1989; DHL (hon.), Yale U., 1990; PhD (hon.), Dartmouth Coll., 1991; LLD (hon.), Mills Coll., 1992. Cmty. devel. dir. Cherokee Nation, Tahlequah, Okla., 1977-83, dep. chief, 1983-85, prin. chief, 1985-95; Montgomery fellow Darmouth Coll., 1996. Author: Mankiller: A Chief and Her People, 1993; co-author: (with Vine Deloria Jr. & Gloria Steinem) Every Day Is A Good Day: Reflections By Contemporary Indigenous Women, 2004 co-editor: The Readers Companion to the History of Women in the U.S., 1998. Recipient Donna Nigh First Lady award Okla. Commn. for Status of Women, 1985, Am. Leadership award Harvard U., 1986, Elizabeth Blackwell award, 1996, Dorothy Height Lifetime Achievement award, 1997, Presdl. Medal of Freedom, 1998; inducted Okla. Women's Hall of Fame, 1986. Avocations: reading, writing. Home: Stilwell, Okla. Died Apr. 6, 2010.

MANLEY, CHARLES ARTHUR, advertising executive; b. Phila., June 29, 1930; s. Charles Edward and Dorothy Ruth (Henry) Manley; m. Helen Louise Albee, May 5, 1951; children: Robert Douglas, Nancy Lynn. BSBA, Drexel U., 1958. Mgr. advt. Crane Co., NYC, 1958—65; account exec. Michener Co., Phila., 1965—67; dir. advt. and pub. rels. Singer Co., NYC, 1967—71; dir. mktg. GAF Corp., NYC, 1971—78, Falcon Safety Products, Mountainside, NJ, 1978—79; sr. v.p. account svcs. Kelly Michener Inc., Valley Forge, Pa., 1979—84; v.p. Intermark Advt., Bradenton, Fla., from 1984. Dir. Comm. and Mktg. Inc., Medford, NJ, Am. Telecomm. Co., Lancaster, Pa. Contbr. articles to profl. jours. Lt. US Army, 1952—54, Korea. Republican. Died Aug. 19, 2010.

MANLEY, FRANK, language educator, writer; b. Scranton, Pa., Nov. 13, 1930; s. Aloysius F. and Kathryn L. (Needham) M.; m. Carolyn Mary Holliday, Mar. 14, 1952; children: Evelyn, Mary. BA, Emory U., 1952, MA, 1953; PhD, Johns Hopkins U., 1959. Instr., then asst. prof. Yale U., New Haven, 1959-64; assoc. prof., then prof. dept. English Emory U., Atlanta, 1964-2000, chmn. dept., 1968-70, Candler prof. English, 1982-2000, dir. creative writing program, 1990-2000, retired, 2000. Editor: The Anniversaries (John Donne), 1963, (with R. Sylvester) De Fructu qui ex Doctrina Percipitur Richard Pace, 1967, All Fools (George Chapman), 1968, A Dialogue of Comfort (St. Thomas More), vol. 12, 1977 (with Louis L. Martz) Epistola ad Pomeranum, vol. 7, 1990, Yale edit. More's complete works; author: Resultances, 1980 (Devins award for poetry 1980), Two Masters (co-winner Gt. Am. New Play Contest 9th Ann. Humana Festival New Am. Plays 1985), (with F. Watkins) Some Poems and Some Talk About Poetry, 1985, Within the Ribbons: 9 Stories, 1989, (play) The Trap, 1993, The Cockfighter: a Novel, 1998, Among Prisoners: Stories, 2000, (poems) The Emperors, 2001, True Hope: A Novel, 2002. With US Army, 1953—55. Guggenheim Found. fellow, 1966-67, 78-79; recipient NEH transl. program fellowship, 1981-83, Nat. Endowment Arts Creative Writing Fellowship in Fiction, 1995-97, Disting. Teaching award, 1984, Tchr.-scholar of Yr. award, 1989, Disting. Alumnus award The Marist Sch., 1993, Miller Playmaker award Theater Emory, 2007. Roman Catholic. Home: Decatur, Ga. Died Nov. 11, 2009.

MANSON, LIONEL ARNOLD, immunology educator, researcher; b. Toronto, Ont., Can., Dec. 24, 1923; came to U.S., 1947; naturalized citizen, 1962; s. Max and Florence (Rachlin) M.; m. Rosalie Weisblatt, May 27, 1945; children: Aaron Nachum, Florence Natanya, David Sholom Eliezar. BA, U. Toronto, 1945, MA, 1947; PhD, Washington U., St. Louis, 1949. Rsch. asst. dept. biochemistry U. Toronto, summer 1944, 45; tchg. asst. dept. biol. chemistry Washington U., 1947-48; instr., sr. instr. dept. microbiology Western Res. U., 1950-54; from fellow to prof. Wistar Inst., 1954-89; from rsch. asst. prof. to prof. dept. microbiology U. Pa., Phila., from 1954. Mem. grad. group microbiology U. Pa., 1955—, mem. grad. group molecular biology, 1965—, mem. grad. group immunology, 1971—, chmn. grad. group immunology, 1974-81, mem. grad. group human genetics, 1977—, sr. fellow dept. biology, 1987—; cons. New Eng. Nuclear Corp., Newton, Mass., 1981-83, Creative Biomolecules, Hopkinton, Mass., 1983-85. Editor Jour. Cellular Physiology, 1966-76, Transplantation Procs., 1969—, Hazardous Materials Mgmt. Jour., 1979-81; assoc. editor Jour. Immunology, 1980-82; series editor Biomembranes, 1971—; sr. editor Immunologic Techniques, 1985—; contbr. over 125 articles to profl. jours. Fulbright scholar, France Dept. State, 1963-64; fellow Nat. Cancer Inst., Israel, 1971-72; recipient fellowship NRC Can., 1945-46, 46-47, rsch. fellowship NIH, 1948-49, Postdoctoral award NRC, 1949-50. Mem. AAAS, Am. Assn. Biol. Chemists, Am. Chem. Soc., Am. Soc. Cell Biology, Am. Soc. Microbiology, Am. Acad. Microbiology, European Assn. Biol. Chemists, N.Y. Acad. Scis., Transplantation Soc., Israeli Immunological Soc., Am. Assn. Immunologists, Am. Assn. Cancer Rsch., Sigma Xi. Jewish. Achievements include development of oncotope hypothesis, to explain the progressive growth of tumors in the autochthonous host; a new paradigm for development of immunotherapeutic programs against cancer. Home: Media, Pa. Died Apr. 1, 2009.

MAPLE, MARILYN JEAN, educational media coordinator; b. Turtle Creek, Pa., Jan. 16, 1931; d. Harry Chester and Agnes (Dobbie) Kelley; 1 child, Sandra Maple. BA, U. Fla., 1972, MA, 1975, PhD, 1985. Journalist various newspaper including Mountain Eagle, Jasper, Ala., Boise (Idaho) Statesman, Daytona Beach (Fla.) Jour., Lorain (Ohio) Jour.; account exec. Frederides & Co., NYC; prodr. hist. films Fla. State Mus., Gainesville, 1967-69; writer, dir., prodr. med. and sci. films and TV prodns. for 6 medically related colls. U. Fla., Gainesville, from 1969. Pres. Media Modes, Inc., Gainesville. Author: On the Wings of a Butterfly, The Refuge Two Bunny Tails; columnist Health Care Edn. mag.; contbr. Fla. Hist. Quar. Recipient Blakslee award, 1969, spl. award, 1979; Monsour lectr., 1979. Mem. Health Edn. Media Assn. (bd. dirs., awards 1977, 79), Phi Delta Kappa, Kappa Tau Alpha. Died Aug. 17, 2010.

MARABLE, JAMES ROSE, JR., civil engineer; b. Atlanta, Oct. 5, 1924; s. James Rose and Mary Spotswood (Glinn) Marable; m. Dawn Io Key, Dec. 24, 1946; children: Nancy Marable Livingston, Jane Marable Adams, Anne Marable, James Stephen. BCE, Ga. Inst. Tech., 1949; MS, La. State U., 1950. Registered profl. engr., Ga., Ala., Tex., Okla., Fla., SC, NC, Tenn., Pa., Va., Calif. Hydraulic engr. US C.E. Vicksburg Waterways Expt. Sta., 1950—51; sr. designer Ga. Power Co., Atlanta, 1951—54; structural engr. Kuhlke & Wade Archs., Augusta, Ga., 1954—56, W.Va. Pulp & Paper Co., Charleston, SC, 1956—57; asst. chief, structural sect. Union Bag-Camp Corp., Savannah, Ga., 1957—60; sr. structural engr. Robert & Co. Assos., Atlanta, 1960—66; chief engr., br. office Simons-Eastern Co., Atlanta, Greenville, SC, 1967—72, project mgr., 1972—75; v.p. Archtl. Corp. Atlanta, 1975—77; mgr., civil engring. Simons Eastern Cons. Inc., Decatur, Ga., 1977—89; sr. staff specialist, from 1989. Instr. La. State U., 1949—50. Scoutmaster Boy Scouts America, 1952—54; pres. Columbia Valley Civic Assn., Decatur, 1965—66. With US Army, 1943—46, ETO. Named Engr. of Yr., Engrs. Greater Atlanta, 1974, Ga. Soc. Profl. Engrs., 1974. Fellow: ASCE (life); mem.: Ga. Engring. Found. (life; v.p. 1978, pres. elect 1979, pres. 1980), Mason, Am. Legion (comdr. 1949), Chi Epsilon. Presbyterian. Died Jan. 9, 2009.

MARCINEK, JOYCE E., business executive; b. Nevada, Ohio, July 28, 1930; d. W. Frank and Bernice Marie McCallister; student Newark Coll. Engring., 1952-53, Sinclair Community Coll., 1968-69. With sales, service, public relations depts. Standard Oil Co., Canton and Akron, Ohio, 1957-63; with TRW Supermet, Dayton, Ohio, 1966-70, sales engr., 1972-75; acct. Texaco Inc., Atlanta, 1970-72; asst. to pres. Hot Sam div. Gen. Host, Troy, Mich., 1975-76; accounts rep. Kelly Services, Lexington, Ky., 1976-77, br. mgr., 1977-80; v.p. Career Mgmt., Inc., Lexington, 1980-82; dir. personnel EBS Inc., subs. Traveler's Ins. Co., Lexington, 1982-83; pres. Kelleher Wholesale Div., and Joymar Corp., Orlando, Fla., 1983-86, gen. mgr. Joymar Corp. Temp. Resources, Inc., Southfield, Mich., 1986-87, cons., personnel, 1987—. Active Urban League, Todd Trease Teddy Bear Fund; bd. dirs. Jr. Achievement, program chmn., 1981-82, also contest judge; sponsor, coordinator secretarial scis. Explorer troop Bluegrass council Boy Scouts Am.; team capt. United Way, 1978-81; mem. Better Bus. Bur. Recipient Distributive Edn. award Lexington Edn.-Work Council, 1978; adv. bd. Ken. Jr. Coll., 1982-83. Mem. Sales Mktg. Execs. (dir., coordinator seminar 1979), Adminstrv. Mgmt. Assn. (dir.), Lexington C. of C. (dir., mem. pres.'s council). Club: Zonta (regional dir. public relations). Died July 26, 2010.

MARCUS, JOSEPH, child psychiatrist; b. Cleve., Feb. 27, 1928; s. William and Sarah (Marcus) Schwartz; m. Cilla Furmanovitz, Oct. 3, 1951; children: Oren, Alon. B.Sc., Western Res. U., 1963; MD, Hebrew U., 1958. Intern Tel Hashomer Govt. Hosp., Israel, 1956-57; resident in psychiatry and child psychiatry Ministry of Health, Govt. of Israel, 1958-61; acting head dept. child psychiatry Ness Ziona Rehab. Ctr., 1961-62; sr. psychiatrist Lasker dept. child psychiatry Hadassah U. Hosp., 1962-64; research asso. Israel Inst. Applied Social Research, 1966-69; practice medicine specializing in psychiatry Jerusalem, 1966-72; assoc. dir. devel. neuropsychiatry Jerusalem Infant and Child Devel. Ctr., 1969-70; dept. head Eytanim Hosp., 1970-72; cons. child psychiatrist for Jerusalem Ministry of Health, 1970-72; dir. dept. child psychiatry and devel. Jerusalem Mental Health Ctr., 1972-75; prof. child psychiatry, dir. unit for research in child psychiatry and devel. U. Chgo., 1975-85, prof. emeritus, co-dir. unit for research in child psychiatry and devel., from 1986; vis. research psychiatrist UCLA Dept. Psychiatry, from 1987. Chief editor: Early Child Devel. and Care, 1972-76; mem. editorial bd.: Israel Annals of Psychiatry and Related Disciplines, 1965-70, Internat. Yearbook of Child Psychiatry and Allied Professions, 1968-74; contbr. articles to med. jours. Mem. Am. Acad. Child Psychiatry (com. on research, com. on psychiat. aspects of infancy), Soc. Research in Child Devel., Internat. Assn. Child Psychiatry and Allied Professions (asst. gen. sec. 1966-74), European Union Paedopsychiatry (hon.), World, Israel psychiat. assns., Internat. Coll. Psychosomatic Medicine, Israel Center Psychobiology. Home: Santa Barbara, Calif. Died Feb. 24, 2009.

MARCUVITZ, NATHAN, physicist, educator; b. Bklyn., Dec. 29, 1913; s. Samuel and Rebecca (Feiner) M.; m. Muriel Spanier, June 30, 1946; children— Andrew, Karen. B.E.E., Poly. Inst. Bklyn., 1935, M.E.E., 1941, D.E.E., 1947; Laurea Honoris Causa, Politecnico Di Torino, 1993; D in Engring. (hon.), Polytechnic U., 2000. Engr. RCA Labs., 1936-40; research asso. Radiation Lab., Mass. Inst. Tech., 1941-46; asst. prof. elec. engring. Poly. Inst. Bklyn., 1946-49, asso. prof., 1949-51, prof., 1951-65; dir. Poly. Inst. Bklyn. (Microwave Research Inst.), 1957-61; v.p. research, acting dean Poly. Inst. Bklyn. (Grad. Center), 1961-63, prof. electrophysics, 1961-66, dean research, dean, 1964-65; asst. dir. def. research and engring. Dept. Def., Washington, 1963-64; prof. applied physics N.Y.U., 1966-73; prof. electrophysics Poly. Inst. N.Y., from 1973, prof. emeritus, from 1978. Vis. prof. Harvard U., spring 1971. Author: Waveguide Handbook, Vol. 10, 1951, (with L. Felsen) Radiation and Scattering of Waves, 1973; also numerous articles. Recipient Microwave Career award IEEE Microwave Theory and Techniques Soc., 1985. Fellow IEEE (Heinrich Hertz medal 1989); mem. Nat. Acad. Engring., Am. Phys. Soc., Sigma Xi, Tau Beta Pi, Eta Kappa Nu. Died Feb. 14, 2010.

MARGOLIS, NANCY KROLL, marketing, publishing, and advertising executive; b. N.Y.C., Sept. 12, 1947; d. Herman and Florence (Yondorf) Kroll; m. Paul D. Margolis, Nov. 12, 1972; children: Kara, Seth. Student, Parsons Sch. Design, 1964-65; BA, Ohio State U., 1969. Traffic coord. Wells, Rich, Greene, N.Y.C., 1970-72; asst. producer Nadler & Larimer, N.Y.C., 1972-73; pres. Nancy Britton Agy., Greenwich, Conn., 1973-75; v.p. Joseph Jacobs Orgn., N.Y.C., 1976-84; assoc. pub. advt. dir. Hadassah Mag., N.Y.C., 1984-86, Margolis & Kroll Mktg. Pub., 1986—: The Jewish Traveler, 1987; founder Zero In Promotions, 1989; editor in chief Newlywed mag., 1989-92. Recipient 4 advt. awards The Advt. Club of Westchester. Bd. dirs. N.Y. Jewish Week, Westchester CHADD. Died Apr. 9, 2009.

MARICQ, HILDEGARD RAND, physician, researcher; b. Rakvere, Estonia, Apr. 23, 1925; came to U.S., 1954; d. August and Elvine Rosalie (Vunderlich) Rand; m. John George Maricq, Oct. 9, 1948; children: Michel Matti, Andres Villu, Peter Toivo. Candidate in natural and med. sci., Free U., Brussels, 1946-49, MD, 1953; post-doctoral fellow, Columbia U., 1965-67. Clin. investigator VA Hosp., Lyons, N.J., 1963-65, dir. Schizophrenic Research Sect., 1970-73; fellow biological sci. in relation to mental health Columbia U., NYC, 1965—67, rsch. assoc. Coll. Physicians and Surgeons, 1973-75; assoc. prof. research medicine Med. U. S.C., Charleston, 1975-81, prof. research medicine, 1981—97, prof. emeritus, from 1997. Contbr. articles to sci. jours. Mem. Am. Physiol. Soc., Am. Coll. Rheumatology, European Soc. for Microcirculation, Soc. for Vascular Medicine and Biology, Microcirculatory Soc., Soc. Biol. Psychiatry. Home: Charleston, SC. Died Oct. 25, 2009.

MARINETTI, GUIDO V., biochemistry professor; b. Rochester, NY, June 26, 1918; s. Michael and Nancy (Lippa) M.; m. Antoinette Francione, Sept. 19, 1942; children: Timothy D., Hope L. BS, U. Rochester, 1950, PhD, 1953. Research biochemist Western Regional Lab., Albany, Calif., 1953-54; instr. U. Rochester, NY, 1954-57, asst. prof., 1957-60, assoc. prof., 1960-66, prof. sch. medicine and dentistry, 1966—97; prof. emeritus dept biochemistry and biophysics, from 1997. Cons. Eastman Kodak, 1978, Rochester Gas & Electric, 1979 Author: Disorders of Lipid Metabolism, 1990, I Beat Heart Disease, So Can You, 2006; editor: Lipid Chromatographic Analysis, 3 vols., 1969, 2nd edit., 1976; contbr. over 165 pub. articles in sci. jours. Served with USAAF, 1942-46. Recipient Nat. Infantile Paralysis award, 1952; recipient Glycerine Research award, 1957; NSF grantee, 1953; recipient Lederle Med. Faculty award, 1955, 56 Mem. Am. Soc. Biol. Chemists, Am. Chem. Soc., AAAS, Sigma Xi, Phi Beta Kappa Achievements include research in membrane structure and function, biochemistry of phospholipids, phosphatidylinositiol metabolism in isolated synaptomsomes, membrane hormone receptors. Home: New York, NY. Died Oct. 17, 2009.

MARK, MELVIN, mechanical engineering educator, consultant; b. St. Paul, Nov. 15, 1922; s. Isadore William and Fannye (Abrahamson) M.; m. Elizabeth J. Wyner, Sept. 9, 1951; children: Jonathan S., David W., Peter B. B.M.E., U. Minn., 1943, MS, 1946; Sc.D. (Teaching, Research fellow), Harvard, 1950. Registered profl. engr., Mass., Minn. Instr. N.D. State U., 1943-44, U. Minn., 1945-47; project mgr. Gen. Electric Co., Lynn., Mass., 1950-52; mgr. Raytheon Co., Wayland, Mass., 1952-56; cons. engr., from 1956; prof. Lowell Technol. Inst., 1957-59, dean faculty, 1959-62; prof. mech. engring. Northeastern U., Boston, 1963-84, dean engring., 1968-79, provost, sr. v.p. for acad. affairs, 1979-84. Vis. lectr. Mass. Inst. Tech., 1955, Brandeis U., 1958; vis. prof. U. Mass., 1984-86; mem. Mass. Bd. Registration of Profl. Engrs. and Land Surveyors, 1990-2001. Author: Thermodynamics: An Auto-Instructional Text, 1967, Concepts of Thermodynamics, 1975, Thermodynamics: Principles and Applications, 1979, Engineering Thermodynamics, 1985; contbr. articles to profl. jours. Served with USAAF, 1944-45. Recipient prize Lincoln Arc Welding Found., 1947. Hon. fellow ASME (fellow 1948-50); mem. Am. Soc. Engring. Edn., Sigma Xi, Tau Beta Pi, Pi Tau Sigma, Phi Kappa Phi. Achievements include patents in field. Home: Newton, Mass. Died Oct. 27, 2009.

MARKARIAN, NOUBAR, textile company executive; b. Larnaca, Cyprus, Dec. 15, 1922; s. Paul and Gulenia (Torikian) M.; came to U.S., 1938; student Coll. S. Murat, Sevres, France, 1935-38; B.S., Sch. Engring., Columbia, 1944; m. Judith Armistead Isley, Feb. 23, 1946; children—Judy, Beverly, Linda, Nancy, Amy, Richard. Partner, v.p. Mark Knitting Mills, Bergenfield, N.J., 1945—; v.p. Valette Undergarments, Inc., Fajardo, P.R., 1958-61; sec.-treas. Johnson Corp., Bergenfield, 1961—. Vice chmn. bd. dirs. No. Valley chpt. ARC; v.p. bd. trustees Dwight Sch., Englewood, N.J. Mem. Internat. House Assn. Episcopalian. Clubs: Bay Head (N.J.) Yacht; Englewood (N.J.) Field; Rotary (pres. Bergenfield 1962-63), Columbia Alumni of Bergen County (pres. 1957-58); Columbia of N.Y.; Mantoloking (N.J.) Yacht. Home: Tenafly, NJ. Died May 12, 2009.

MARKER, ROBERT SYDNEY, retired management consultant; b. Nashville, July 27, 1922; s. Forest M. and Lassie (Weatherford) M.; m. Elizabeth Davis, Oct. 27, 1943; children— Christopher, Andrew. BA, Emory U., 1946. Account exec. Griswold-Eshleman, 1949-51; advt. mgr. B.F. Goodrich Co., 1947-49; copy group head Maxon, Inc., 1951-56; sr. v.p., dir. creative services McManus, John & Adams, 1956-63; v.p. McCann-Erickson, Inc., 1963-64, sr. v.p., 1964-67; mgr. McCann-Erickson, Inc. (Detroit office), 1964-68, exec. v.p. NYC, 1967-68, pres., 1968-71, chmn. bd., chief exec. officer, 1971-74, also bd. dirs., mem. exec. com.; chmn. exec. com. Needham, Harper & Steers, Inc., 1975-80; mng. ptnr. Robert S. Marker, Inc., Tequesta, Fla. and NYC, 1980-90. Bd. dirs. Am. Assn. Advt. Agys., Detroit Adcraft Club, 1965, Detroit Advt. Assn., 1965, N.Y. Bd. Trade. Mem. Mayor's Council on Environment. Served with USAAC, 1943-46. Recipient Creative Advt. awards N.Y. Art Dirs. Club, Creative Advt. awards Detroit Advt. Club, Creative Advt. awards Chgo. Copy Club, Creative Advt. awards Alpha Delta Sigma. Mem. Am. Assn. Advt. Agys. (dir., chmn. Eastern region), Alpha Delta Sigma, Sigma Delta Chi. Clubs: Turtle Creek (Fla.); Winged Foot (Mamaroneck, N.Y.). Home: Jupiter, Fla. Died Sept. 20, 2009.

MARKESBERY, WILLIAM R., neurology and pathology educator, physician; b. Florence, Ky., Sept. 30, 1932; s. William M. and Sarah E. (Tanner) M.; m. Barbara A. Abram, Sept. 5, 1958; children— Susanne Hartley, Catherine Kendall, Elizabeth Allison BA, U. Ky., 1960; MD with distinction, U. Ky. Med. Coll., 1964. Diplomate Am. Bd. Neurology and Psychiatry Diplomate Am. Bd. Pathology. Intern U. Hosp., Lexington, KY, 1964-65; resident neurology Presbyn. Hosp., NYC, 1965-67; fellow neuropathology Coll. Physicians and Surgeons, Columbia U., NYC, from 1967; asst. prof. pathology, neurology U. Rochester, N.Y., 1969-72; assoc. prof. pathology, neurology U. Ky., Lexington, 1972-77, prof. neurology, pathology, from 1977, dir. Ctr. on Aging, from 1979, prof. neurology, pathology, dir., from 1977. Mem. pathology study sect. NIH, Washington, 1982-85, nat. adv. coun. NIH, 1990-94; chmn. Med. Sci. Adv. Bd., Chgo., 1989-94, Nat. Alzheimer's Assn., Chgo., 1985-86, adv. panel on dementia U.S. Congress of Tech., Washington, 1985-86; dir. Alzheimer's Disease Research Ctr., 1985—, Alzheimer's Diseases Program Project Grant, 1984—. Mem. multiple editl. bds.; contbr. more than 400 articles to profl. jours. With U.S. Army, 1954-56 Recipient Disting. Achievement award Ky. Research Found., Lexington, 1978; named U. Ky. Disting. Alumni prof., 1985, Disting. Research prof., U. Ky., 1977, Disting. Alumni U. Ky. Coll. Medicine, 1993; inductee U. Ky. Disting Alumni, 1989; prin. investigator NIH, Washington, 1977—, Intellectual Achevement UK Libr. Assocs., 2004, Lifetime Achievement award, 2008, Altech. Disting. Lectr. award, 2008, Zaven Khachaturian award, Zaver award Nat. Alzheimer's Assn., 2009. Mem. Am. Acad. Neurology, Am. Assn. Neuropathologists (exec. com. 1984-86, pres1991—), Soc. Neurosci., Am. Neurol. Assn., Alpha Omega Alpha. Home: Lexington, Ky. Died Jan. 30, 2010.

MARKHAM, CHARLES BUCHANAN, retired lawyer; b. Durham, NC, Sept. 15, 1926; s. Charles Blackwell and Sadie Helen (Hackney) M. AB, Duke U., 1945; postgrad., U. N.C., 1945-46; LL.B., George Washington U., 1951. Bar: D.C. 1951, N.Y. 1961, N.C. 1980, U.S. Ct. Appeals (2d cir.) 1962, U.S. Ct. Appeals (D.C. cir.) 1955, U.S. Supreme Ct. 1964. Reporter Durham Sun, 1945; asst. state editor, editorial writer Charlotte (N.C.) News, 1947-48; dir. publicity and rsch. Young Dem. Clubs Am., Washington, 1948-49, exec. sec., 1949-50; polit. analyst Dem. Senatorial Campaign Com., Washington, 1950-51; spl. atty. IRS, Washington and NYC, 1952-60; assoc. Battle, Fowler, Stokes and Kheel, NYC, 1960-65; dir. rsch. U.S. Equal Employment Opportunity Commn., Washington, 1965-68; dep. asst. sec. U.S. Dept. HUD, Washington, 1969-72; asst. dean Rutgers U. Law Sch., Newark, 1974-76; assoc. prof. law N.C. Central U., Durham, 1976-81, prof. law, 1981-83; mayor City of Durham, 1981-85; ptnr. Markham and Wickham, Durham, 1984-86. Trustee Hist. Preservation Soc. Durham, 1982-86; bd. dirs. Stagville Ctr., 1984-86; mem. Gov.'s Crime Commn., Raleigh, 1985; dep. commr. N.C. Indsl. Commn., Raleigh, 1986-93. Editor: Jobs, Men and Machines: The Problems of Automation, 1964 Mem. Carolina Club, Phi Beta Kappa, Omicron Delta Kappa, Phi Delta Phi, Phi Delta Theta. Republican. Episcopalian. Home: Durham, NC. Died Mar. 22, 2010.

MARKHAM, JESSE WILLIAM, economist, educator; b. Richmond, Va., Apr. 21, 1916; s. John James and Edith (Luttrell) M.; m. Penelope Jane Anton, Oct. 15, 1944; children: Elizabeth Anton Markham McLean, John James, Jesse William. AB, U. Richmond, 1941; postgrad., Johns Hopkins U., 1941-42, U.S. Fgn. Svc. Sch., 1945; MA, Harvard U., 1947, PhD, 1949. Acct. E.I. duPont de Nemours Co., Richmond, 1935-38; tchg. fellow Harvard U., 1946-48; asst. prof. Vanderbilt U., 1948-52, assoc. prof., 1952-53; chief economist FTC, Washington, 1953-55; assoc. prof. Princeton U., 1955-57, prof. econs., 1957-68; prof. Harvard Grad. Sch. Bus. Adminstrn., 1968-72, Charles Edward Wilson prof., 1972-82, prof. emeritus, from 1982; prof. Harvard U. Ext. Svcs., from 1984. Vis. prof. Columbia U., 1958; Ford Found. vis. prof. Harvard Grad. Sch. Bus. ADminstrn., 1965-66; rsch. prof. Law and Econs. Ctr., Emory U., 1982-84; rsch. staff, mem. bd. editors Patent Trademark Copyright Rsch. Inst., George Washington U., 1955-70; econs. editor Houghton Mifflin Co., 1961-71; U.S. del. commn. experts on bus. practices European Productivity Agy., OEEC, 1956, 57, 58, 59, 61; vis. prof. Harvard U., 1961-62; dir. Ford Found. Seminar Region II, 1961; adv. com. mktg. to sec. commerce, 1967-71; mem. Am. Bar Assn. Commn. to study FTC, 1969. Author: Competition in the Rayon Industry, 1952, The Fertilizer Industry: Study of an Imperfect Market, 1958, The American Economy, 1963, (with Charles Fiero and Howard Piquet) The European Common Market: Friend or Competitor, 1964, (with Gustav Papnek) Industrial Organization and Economic Development, 1970, Conglomerate Enterprise and Public Policy, 1973, (with Paul Teplitz) Baseball Economics and Public Policy, 1982; sect. on oligopoly Internat. Ency. Social Scis.; contbr. articles to econ. jours. Del. People to People Diplomacy Mission to USSR, 1989; active Boy Scouts Am.; chmn. Harvard Parents Com., 1969-72. Served as lt. USNR, World War II. Ford Found. rsch. prof., 1958-59. Mem. Am. Econ. Assn., U.S. C. of C. (econ. policy com.), Harvard Club (N.Y.C., Sarasota, Fla.), The Cedars Club, Phi Beta Kappa. Episcopalian. Died June 21, 2009.

MARKOWITZ, DAVID, retired chemical company executive; b. NYC, Oct. 24, 1923; s. George and Mania (Villansky) M.; m. Rosalie Estelle Jaffe, June 29, 1947; children— Joseph Rueben, Laura Susan B.Ch.E., Poly Inst. N.Y., 1943, M.Ch.E., 1947. Registered profl. engr., Mass. With Koppers Co., Pitts., 1943-60; with Foster Grant Corp., Leominster, Mass., 1960-74, pres., 1971-74; sr. exec. v.p., mem. exec. com. Am. Hoechst Corp., Somerville, N.J., 1975-85, now dir. Dir. Goody Products, Inc. Kearny, N.J.; dir. Kinemotive Corp. Farmingdale, N.Y. Fellow Poly. Inst. N.Y. Mem. Soc. Plastics Engrs., Am. Inst. Chem. Engrs. Clubs: Greenacres Country (Lawrenceville, N.J.). Democrat. Jewish. Avocations: reading; golf. Died Nov. 12, 2009.

MARKS, JAMES ALVIN, engineering educator; b. Wisconsin Rapids, Wis., Oct. 9, 1926; s. Alvin John and Selma (Hedin) M.; m. Marilyn Pearl Kaul, July 29, 1949 (dec. 1978); children— Kenneth, Jonathan, David, Robert; m. June Louise Stone, Dec. 2, 1979 BS in Mech. Engring., Purdue U., 1948, MS in Indsl. Engring., 1951. Engr. Consol. Paper Co., Wisconsin Rapids, 1948-49; instr. Purdue U., Lafayette, Ind., 1949-51; engr. Badger Ordnance Co., Baraboo, Wis., 1951-54; instr. U. Wis.-Madison, 1954-56, prof. engring., from 1956, engring. placement dir., from 1956. Author: Job Titles and Definitions for Engineers, 1972, rev. edit., 1981; contbr. articles to profl. jours. Alderman Common Council, City of Madison, 1960-65; supr. Dane County Bd., Madison, 1957-60. Served as seaman USNR, 1944-46 Mem. Midwest Coll. Placement Assn. (pres. 1972-73), Am. Legion Home: Verona, Wis. Died Apr. 13, 2009.

MARKS, JUSTIN DAVIS, JR., minister, guidance counselor; b. Cynthiana, Ky., Oct. 17, 1940; s. Justin Davis and Mary Preston (Butler) Marks; m. Lois Johnson Marks, Sept. 9, 1965; children: Justine Lovell, Justin Davis III. BA in Bible and Christian Edn., Am. Bapt. Coll. Bible, Nashville, 1965; diploma, Sch. Bible Prophecy, Atlanta, 1966; MDiv, Lexington Theol. Sem., 1977; ThD, Bernadean U., 1979. Cert. ordained to ministry Nat. Bapt. Conv. USA, 1967. Pastor Cadiz 2d Bapt. Ch., Ky., 1967—72, 1st Bapt. Ch., Nicholasville, Ky., 1973—77; fellow Bapt. Ch., Evansville, Ind., from 1978; guidance counselor Earle C. Clements Jr. CC, Morganfield, Ky., from 1978; dean, tchr. Cen. Am. U. Extension, Kans. City, Mo., from 1985; dean Marks Caldwell Bible Inst., Evansville, from 1985, Christian Leadership Conf., 1974—75; instr. barbering West Ky. Area Vocat. Tech. Sch., 1966—72; mission mem. State Bapt. Conv., 1963; sr. patrol leader Blue Grass Coun. Boy Scouts Am., Lexington, Ky. Mem. Jessamine County Ministers Assn., Masons. Democrat. Home: Evansville, Ind. Died July 6, 2010.

MARR, ROBERT BRUCE, physicist, researcher; b. Quincy, Mass., Mar. 25, 1932; s. Ralph George and Ethel (Beals) M.; m. Nancy Rosa Parkes, June 12, 1954; children: Richard, Jonathan, Rebecca. BS, MIT, 1953; MA, Harvard U., 1955, PhD, 1959. Research asso. Brookhaven Nat. Lab., Upton, NY, 1959-61, asso. physicist, 1961-64, physicist, 1964-68, sr. physicist, 1968-95, assoc. chmn. applied math. dept., 1974-75, 83-88, chmn., 1975-78; ret., 1995. Adj. assoc. prof. Columbia U., 1969; lectr. SUNY at Stony Brook, 1969-70, vis. prof. dept. computer sci., 1979; guest mathematician U. Colo., 1970; vis. mathematician Lawrence Berkeley Lab., 1978; cons. NSF, NIH, 1969— Contbr. articles to profl. jours. Served with U.S. Army, 1958-59. NSF grantee, 1974 Mem. Soc. for Magnetic Resonance in Medicine (trustee 1982-87, sec.-treas. 1984-86, treas. 1986-87). Home: Patchogue, NY. Died Apr. 26, 2010.

MARR, WARREN QUINCY, II, retired editor; b. Pitts., July 31, 1916; s. Warren Quincy and Cecelia Antoinette (McGee) M. Student Wilberforce U., 1934-37, N.Y. Sch. Interior Decoration, 1948-49, New Sch. for Social Rsch., 1962-63; m. Carmel Dolores Carrington, Apr. 11, 1948; children: Charles Carrington, Warren Quincy III. Linotype operator St. Louis Argus, 1938-39; with The Plaindealer, Kansas City, Kans., 1939-42, asst. editor, 1941-42; impressario Warren Marr, II, Presents, N.Y.C., 1943-48; decorator James Lassiter & Sons, Madison, N.J., 1948-52; pres. Dilworth-Leslie Sponsors, 1949-66; propr. House of Marr, Inc., Bklyn., 1952-56; plant mgr. Nisonger Corp., New Rochelle, N.Y., 1956-60; sec. Am. Missionary Assn. Coll. Centennials, N.Y.C., 1961-68; pub. rels. asst. NAACP, N.Y.C., 1968-74, editor The Crisis mag., 1974-81. Founder, dir. Amistad Awards, 1962—; co-founder Amistad Rsch. Ctr., Tulane U., 1966; founder, vol. exec. dir. Friends of Amistad, 1971-88; pres. art com. Tougaloo (Miss.) Coll., 1966-67, York Coll., N.Y.C., 1984; chmn. bd. dirs. Waltann Sch. Creative Arts, 1963-70; mem. Art Commn. of N.Y.C., 1981-89; bd. dirs. Bklyn. Arts and Culture Assn., Community Council of Medgar Evers Coll., Internat. Art of Jazz, Access. Recipient various awards; named hon. citizen of New Orleans, 1979; awarded key to City of Cin., 1983. Editor: (with Maybelle Ward) Minorities and the American Dream: A Bicentennial Perspective, 1976; (with Harry Ploski) The Negro Almanac, 1976; contbr. articles to various jours. Home: Brooklyn, NY. Died Apr. 20, 2010.

MARRA, MICHAEL, construction executive; b. Providence, Apr. 8, 1924; s. Anthony and Camella (Marotto) Marra; m. Rosemarie DeLuise, Nov. 17, 1960; children: Anthony John, Gerianne, Marianne (twins). Student, Providence Coll., 1942—43; BS, R.I. Coll., 1976, MEd, 1978. Gen. contractor specializeing in heavy earthwork excavations, drilling and blasting rock, Providence, from 1946. Pres. Statewide Freight Svc. Inc., Providence, from 1960; explosive cons., Providence, from 1963; instr. diesel injection, lobbyist R.I. Indsl. Edn. Soc., from 1976; notary pub., from 1976. Rep. candidate R.I. Ho. Reps., 1966; chmn. 5th ward U.S. Senatorial Campaign John H. Chaffee, 1972, Mayoral Campaign. With AUS, 1944—46, ETO, MTO. Recipient Eagle Scout Order of Arrow, Scouters Key, Boy Scouts Am. Mem.: DAV, VFW, Providence Engring. Soc., R.I. Indsl. Arts Club, Am. Indsl Arts Assn., Nat. Security Coun., Internat. Soc. Explosives Specialists, Am. Welding Soc. (ednl. chmn. 1968—73, pres. 1974—75), Holy Name Soc., Mil. Order Cootie, R.I. Coll. Alumni Assn., Elks, Epsilon Pi Tau (province pres. 1977—78). Roman Catholic. Home: Bayville, NY. Died Mar. 31, 2009.

MARSDEN, JERROLD ELDON, mathematician, educator, engineer; b. Ocean Falls, British Columbia, Aug. 17, 1942; married 1965; 1 child. BSc, U. Toronto, Canada, 1965; PhD in Math., Princeton U., 1968. Instr. math. Princeton U., N.J., 1968; lectr. U. Calif., Berkeley, 1968-69, asst. prof., 1969-72, assoc. prof., 1972-77, prof. math., 1977—2010; asst. prof. U. Toronto, Canada, 1970-71; prof. Calif. Inst. Tech., Pasadena, 1995—2010. Recipient Norbert Weiner Applied Math. prize Am. Math. Soc., 1990. Mem. IEEE, Am. Phys. Soc. Achievements include research in mathematical physics, global analysis, hydrodynamics, quantum mechanics, nonlinear Hamiltonian systems. Died Sept. 21, 2010.

MARSH, JOSEPH FRANKLIN, JR., retired academic administrator; b. Charleston, W.Va., Feb. 24, 1925; s. Joseph Franklin and Florence (Keller) M. Student, Concord Coll., 1941-42, W.Va. U., 1942-43; AB, Dartmouth Coll., 1947; student, Nat. Inst. Pub. Affairs, Washington, 1947-48; M.P.A., Harvard U., 1949; LL.D., Davis and Elkins Coll., 1968; L.H.D., Alderson-Broaddus Coll., 1982. Cons. Hoover Commn., Washington, 1948; instr. in gt. issues Dartmouth U., 1952—54, instr. economics, 1953—55, asst. prof., 1955—59; pres. Concord U., Athens, W.Va., 1959—73, pres. emeritus, from 1985; edn. cons., 1973—74; pres. Waynesburg (Pa.) U., 1974—83, pres. emeritus, 1983—2009; v.p. The Armand Hammer United World Coll. of the Am. West, Montezuma, N.Mex., 1984—85; pres. Marsh Edn Cons., Athens, W.Va., 1985—2009. Dir. One Valley Bank of Mercer County, 1987-98, hon. dir., 1998-2000. Contbr. articles to profl. jours. Mem. State Dept. Ednl. Mission to U.A.R., 1965-66, Mercer County (W.Va.) Planning Commn., 1964-74, 83-94, hon., 1994-2009; vice chmn. W.Va. Com. for Constl. Amendments, 1966; mem. regional coun. Internat. Edn. Study Mission to Europe, 1970; bd. dirs. Am. Assn. State Colls. and Univs., 1972-73, Regional Coun. for Internat. Edn., 1973, Hospice Care Mercer County,

W.Va., 1987-91, Faculty Merit Found. W.Va., 1990-2009, Greater Mercer County Charitable Found., Inc., W.Va., 1998-02, exec. com. 2001-02, chmn., pres., 1998-2001; bd. dirs. Charitable Found. of the Virginians, Inc., 2002-05, Pa. Assn. Colls. and Univs., 1974-83, exec. com., 1980-82; bd. dirs. Pa. Commn. for Ind. Colls. and Univs., 1974-83, sec.-treas., 1976-77, vice chmn., 1977-80, chmn., 1980-82; trustee Found. Ind. Colls. Pa., 1974-83, mem. exec. com., 1979-82; bd. visitors Midway Coll., Ky., 1979-93; adv. com. Pa. State Coun. Higher Edn., 1980-82; trustee Concord U. Found., 1986, bd. dirs., 1987—; active Town of Athens Planning Commn., 1986-94, pres. commn. 1987-94; bd. trustees, Princeton (W.Va.) Cmty. Hosp. Found., 1989-98, vice chmn., 1989-97; Gov's. appointee to bd. dirs. State Coll. System W.Va., 1989-96, chmn. adminstrv. com., 1990-91, vice chmn. of bd., 1991-95, chmn., 1995-96; gov.'s appointee to the W.Va. Parkways, Econ. Devel. and Tourism Authority, 1998—2006, asst. sec., 2001-02, sec., 2002-03, vice chmn., 2003-04; gov.'s appointee Edn. Commn. of the States, 1998-2002. Served as gunnery officer USNR, 1943-46. Named Outstanding Young Man, W.Va. Jr. C. of C., 1960; recipient Alumnus of Yr. award Concord U., 1973, Golden Alumnus award, 1992, Outstanding Alumnus award for Career Achievement, 1996; Outstanding Citizen award Athens Woman's Club, 1992, Total Community Involvement Award, Town of Athens, WV, 2001; Rotary fellow Oxford (Eng.) U., 1950-52. Mem. AAUP, Am. Assn. Univ. Adminstrs., Am. Econ. Assn., Royal Inst. Pub. Adminstrn., Oxford Union Debating Soc. (life), Oxford Soc. (life), Pa. Soc., Duquesne Club (Pitts.), Univ. Club (Bluefield), Masons, Rotary (dist. gov. 1992-93), The Guild of Carillonneurs N.Am. (hon.), Phi Beta Kappa, Phi Tau, Phi Delta Pi, Phi Sigma Kappa, Alpha Kappa Psi (hon.). Methodist. Home: Athens, W.Va. Died Dec. 30, 2010.

MARSHALEK, EUGENE RICHARD, retired physics educator, researcher; b. NYC, Jan. 17, 1936; s. Frank M. and Sophie (Weg) M.; m. Sonja E. M. Lennhart, Dec. 8, 1962; children: Thomas, Frank. BS, Queens Coll., 1957; PhD, U. Calif., Berkeley, 1962. NSF postdoctoral fellow Niels Bohr Inst., Copenhagen, 1962-63; rsch. assoc. Brookhaven Nat. Lab., Upton, N.Y., 1963-65; asst. prof. physics U. Notre Dame, Ind., 1965-69, assoc. prof. Ind., 1969-78, prof. Ind., from 1978, prof. emeritus Ind., ret. Ind., from 2002. Contbr. articles to profl. jours. Recipient Alexander von Humboldt sr. scientist award, 1985. Fellow Am. Phys. Soc.; mem. AAAS, Sigma Xi. Home: South Bend, Ind. Died Oct. 19, 2009.

MARSTEN, RICHARD BARRY, scientific organization executive; b. NYC, Oct. 28, 1925; s. Jesse and Rosalind M.; m. Sarah Betty Jaffe, June 26, 1949; children: Michael Frederick, Jessica Claire. BS in Elec. Engring, M.I.T., 1946, MS, 1946, postgrad., 1946-49; PhD, U. Pa., 1951. Registered profl. engr., N.J. With RCA, 1957-69, mgr. radar systems projects Missile and Surface Radar div., 1959-61, mgr. spacecraft electronics, 1961-67, chief engr. Astro Electronics div., 1967-69; dir. communications programs Office of Applications, NASA, Washington, 1969-76; dean Sch. Engring. City U. N.Y., 1975-79, prof. engring., 1979-81; mgr. space program Office of Technology Assessment, U.S. Congress, 1980-81; exec. dir. Bd. on Telecommunications and Computer Applications, Nat. Acad. Engring./NRC, Washington, from 1981. Mem. broadcast panel study space applications Nat. Acad. Scis., 1967, chmn. point-to-point communications panel, 1968; mgr., dir. study on communications for social needs Pres.'s Domestic Council, 1971; mem. panel automation opportunities to health care Fed. Council Sci. and Tech., 1972-73; mem. panel on telecommunications research in U.S. and selected fgn. countries, com. on telecommunications Nat. Acad. Engring., 1973-74; chmn. telecommunications adv. panel Office of Technology Assessment, 1979-80; adv. council Nat. Energy Found.; organizing com. Telecommunications Policy Research Conf., 1987—; bd. dirs. SSE Telecom Inc.; trustee W.F. Albright Inst. Archeol. Research, 1986—; mem. adv. bd. Pub. Service Satellite Consortium, 1987—. Editor: Communications Satellite Systems Technology, 1966. Recipient Exceptional Service medal, also Group Achievement award NASA, 1974; citation White House, 1972; citation Internat. Women's Yr., 1975; NASA/USSR Apollo-Soyuz Space medal, 1976 Assoc. fellow AIAA (chmn. nat. tech. activities com. communications 1967-69, chmn. tech. program 1st Communications Satellite Systems Conf. 1966, chmn. tech. splty. group on info. systems 1970-71); fellow IEEE (com. policy bd. 1972-79, adv. EASCON 1973-75, program chmn. EASCON 1970, bd. govs. com. soc. 1977-80, chmn. com. on telecommunications policy 1978-80, cons. mem. 1980-81, mem. 1981-83, mem. steering com. U.S. Tech. Policy Conf. 1978—, mem. U.S. Tech. Policy Com. 1982-87, bd. govs. aero. and elec. systems soc. 1982-87, v.p. tech. ops. 1985-87, EASCON bd. dirs. 1985—, engring. research and devel. com. 1985—, aerospace research and devel. com. 1986—), N.Y. Acad. Scis. (aerospace research and devel. com. 1986—). Clubs: Cosmos (Washington). Died Mar. 26, 2010.

MARTIN, BETTY, geriatrics nurse; b. Rhinebeck, NY, Nov. 3, 1936; d. Harold Elmer and Loretta Matilda (Tetro) M.; 1 foster child, Dale Marie Fisher Murtagh. Diploma, Capital City Sch. Nursing, Washington, 1958. Cert. in med./surg. nursing, gerontology. Staff nurse D.C. Gen. Hosp., Washington; pvt. duty nurse Dept. Manpower, Labor Dept., Washington; clin. nurse on geriatric team Greater S.E. Community Hosp., Washington. Home: Red Hook, NY. Died Jan. 24, 2010.

MARTIN, GERALD, electronics engineer; b. Bklyn., July 27, 1921; B.S. in Elec. Engring., U. Denver, 1949; M.S. in Engring. Adminstrn., George Washington U., 1960; m. Tillie Sosno, Dec. 26, 1948; children— Judy Lynne, Robert Allan. Head air traffic control and landing research and devel. div. Bur. Ships, Dept. Navy, Washington, 1949-56; tech. staff cons. Nat. Security Agy., Ft. George G. Meade, Md., 1956-59; supervisory engr. research and devel. service FAA, Washington, 1959-61; tech. dir. U.S. Naval Electronic Systems Security Engring. Center, Washington, 1961-81. Served with U.S. Army, 1942-46. Recipient Superior Civilian Service award Dept. Navy. Mem. IEEE (sr.), Nat. Soc. Profl. Engrs., D.C. Soc. Profl. Engrs. Home: Fredericksburg, Va. Died Oct. 28, 2009.

MARTIN, JAMES JOHN, JR., systems analyst, retired research and development company executive; b. Paterson, NJ, Feb. 3, 1936; s. James John and Lillian M.; m. Lydia Elizabeth Bent, June 11, 1954; children: David, Peter, Laura, Daniel, Lucas. BA, U. Wis.-Madison, 1955; postgrad., Div. Sch., Harvard U., 1955-57; MS, Navy Postgrad. Sch., 1963; PhD, MIT, 1965. Commd. ensign USN, 1957, advanced through grades to comdr., 1971, ret., 1977; sector v.p. Sci. Applications Internat. Corp., La Jolla, Calif., 1977-95. Author: Bayesian Decision Problems and Markov Chains, 1967; editor: On Not Confusing Ourselves, 1991; contbr. articles to profl. jours. Decorated Legion of Merit. Mem. Internat. Inst. Strategic Studies, Ops. Research Soc. Am., Mil. Ops. Research Soc. (bd. dirs. 1974-77) Democrat. Avocation: cooking. Home: La Jolla, Calif. Died July 13, 2010.

MARTIN, MICHAEL TOWNSEND, sports association executive, marketing professional, consultant; b. NYC, Nov. 21, 1941; s. Townsend Bradley and Irene (Redmond) M.; m. Jennifer Johnston, Nov. 7, 1964 (div. Jan. 1977); children: Ryan Bradley, Christopher Townsend; m. Jean Kathleen Meyer, Mar. 1, 1980 Grad., The Choate Sch., 1960; student, Rutgers U., 1961-62. Asst. gen. mgr. N.Y. Jets Football Club, NYC, 1968-74; v.p. NAMANCO Prodns., NYC, 1975-76; v.p., gen. mgr. Cosmos Soccer Club, NYC, 1976-77; exec. asst. Warner Communications, NYC, 1978-84; owner, operator Martin Racing Stable, NYC, 1983—2010; pres. Sports Mark, Inc., NYC, 1990—2003. Bd. dirs. Mote Marine Lab., Sarasota, Fla., Animal Rescue Coalition, Coun. of Visitors, Woods Hole Marine Biol. Lab., Nat. Lighthouse Ctr. and Mus., Lemur Conservation Found., Sta. WEDU PBS, Tampa Fla.; bd. mem. Ringling Coll. Bd. Art and Design; program com. Sta. WNET Channel 13; bd. advisors The Pennington Sch., Dir.'s Cir., Scripps Instn. Oceanography Mem. Athletics Congress (life, cert. official 1984—), U.S. Tennis Assn. (life), Internat. Oceanographic Found. (Miami life mem.), Fla. Thoroughbred Breeders Assn., Quogue Field Club, The Union Club. Republican. Episcopalian. Avocation: collecting inuit (eskimo) art. Home: New York, NY. Died Apr. 17, 2010.

MARTIN, RAYMOND ALBERT, theology educator; b. Mt. Carroll, Ill., Nov. 3, 1925; m. Alice Bast, May 29, 1949; children: Bill, Barbara, Mary, Tim. BA, Wartburg Coll., 1947; BD, Wartburg Theol. Sem., 1951; ThM, Princeton Theol. Sem., 1952, PhD, 1957; postdoctoral studies, Harvard Div. Sch., 1963-64. Instr. Greek Wartburg Coll., Waverly, Iowa, 1952-54; reference librarian Princeton (N.J.) Theol. Sem., 1957; missionary to India Luth. Ch., 1957-69; prof. Old Testament and N.T. Gurukul Luth. Theol. Coll., India, 1957-69; treas. Gurukul Sem., 1958-69, librarian, 1962-63; prof. bibl. and intertestmamental studies Wartburg Theol. Sem., Dubuque, from 1969. Vis. prof. bibl. studies United Theol. Coll., Bangalore, India, 1981, Santal Theol. Sem. in Benagaria, Santal Parganas, Bihar, India, 1985, Austin Presbyn. Theology Sem., 1989; co-founder, sec. Soc. Bibl. Studies in India, 1965-69. Author: The Syntax of the Greek of Jeremiah, 1957, India List of Theological Periodicals, 1967, Syntactical Evidence of Semitic Sources in Greek Documents, 1974, Syntactical and Critical Concordance to the Greek Text of Baruch and the Epistle of Jeremiah, Vol. XII of the Computer Bible, 1977, An Introduction to New Testament Greek, 1976, James in Augsburg Commentary on the New Testament, 1982, An Introduction to Biblical Hebrew, 1987, Syntax Criticism of the Synoptic Gospels, 1987, Syntactical Concordance to the Correlated Greek and Hebrew Texts of Ruth, Vol XXX of the Computer Bible, 1988, 89, Syntax Criticism of Johannine Literature, The Catholic Epistles and The Gospel Passion Accounts, 1989; contbr. articles and papers to profl. publs. Home: Dubuque, Iowa. Died Aug. 4, 2009.

MARTIN, ROY ALLAN, consulting electrical and safety engineer; b. Coffee County, Tenn., Mar. 8, 1920; s. Roy and Ella (Barton) Martin; m. Norma Arnell Hixon, May 15, 1942 (div. 1967); children: Linda Christine, Norma Janis; m. Olivia Arlington Traywick, June 13, 1970. BS in Elec. Engring., Ga. Inst. Tech., 1942; MS in Elec. Engring., 1951. Registered profl. engr., Ga., Fla. With constrn. firm, 1935—37, Ga. Power Co., 1937—42, Western Union, 1946; mem. faculty Ga. Inst. Tech., Atlanta, 1946—68; prin. Roy A. Martin Assocs. Inc.; engring. and med. consultation specializing in tech. and personal injury investigations Atlanta, from 1968. Contbr. articles to profl. publs. 1st lt. USAF, 1942—46, Panama, Ecuador. Episcopalian. Avocations: golf, fishing, amateur radio, dance. Home: Atlanta, Ga. Died July 16, 2009.

MARTIN, SAMUEL ELMO, linguistics educator; b. Pittsburg, Kans., Jan. 29, 1924; AB, U. Calif., 1947, AM, 1949; PhD, Yale U., 1950. Instr. to asst. prof. Japanese and Korean Yale U., New Haven, 1950-58, assoc. prof. Far Ea. linguistics, 1958-62, prof., from 1962, chmn. dept. East and South Asian langs., 1963-65, chmn. dept. linguistics, 1966-80. Vis. prof. Georgetown U., 1955, U. Mich., 1956, U. Alta. (Can.), 1959, U. Wash., 1962-63; vis. prof. linguistics and dir. Pacific and Asian Linguistics Inst. U. Hawaii, 1965-66; sec. com. Uralic and Altaic studies Am. Coun. Learned Socs., 1958-64 Author: Korean-English Dictionary, 1968, Beginning Korean, 1969, A Reference Grammar of Japanese, 1975, Advanced Japanese Conversation, 1976; contbr. articles to profl. publs. Mem. Linguistic Soc. Am., Am. Orient Soc., Assn. Asian Studies. Rsch. in phonemics, morphophonemics and hist. phonology of Japanese, Korean and Chinese. Died Nov. 28, 2009.

MARTÍNEZ, TOMÁS ELOY, writer, journalist; b. Tucumán, Argentina, 1934; BA Spanish & Latin Am. Studies, U. Tucumán; MA, U. Paris; doctorates (hon.). Exec. editor Primera Plana, Buenos Aires, Panorama, Buenos Aires; editor La Opinión, Buenos Aires, Página 12, Buenos Aires, El Nacional, Caracas, Argentina; founder, exec. editor El Diario de Caracas; prof. Latin America Lit. U. Maryland, 1984—87; prof. Rutgers U., 1995—2010, dir. Latin America Studies Program, 1995—2010; syndicated columnist, 1995—2010. Dir. Ctr. Hemispheric Studies Rutgers U., 2000—10, writer in residence, 2000—10. Author: (essays) Structures of the Argentine Cinema, 1961, The Poetry of Ramos Sucre, 1981, The Argentine Dream, 1999, Requiem for a Lost Country, 2003, (short stories) The Commonplace Death, 1998, (novels) Sagrado, 1967, The Peron Novel, 1988, The Hand of the Master, 1991, Santa Evita, 1995, The Flight of the Queen, 2002 (Alfaguara Internat. Novel award), The Tango Singer, 2004. Woodrow Wilson Ctr. for Scholars fellowship, 1983, Guggenheim fellowship, 1987. Mem.: Com. to Protect Journalists. Died Jan. 31, 2010.

MARVEL, JOHN THOMAS, chemical company executive; b. Champaign, Ill., Sept. 14, 1938; s. Carl Shipp and Alberta (Hughes) M.; m. Joyce Elizabeth Strand, June 30, 1961 (div. Feb. 1981); children: Scott T., Chris A., Carl R.; m. Mary Anne Hamilton, July 24, 1982. Student, DePauw U., 1955-57; AB, U. Ill., 1959; PhD, MIT, 1964; postgrad., Stanford U., 1977. Instr. U. Ariz., Tucson, 1964-65, asst. prof., 1965-68; sr. rsch. chemist Monsanto, St. Louis, 1968-70, rsch. specialist, 1970-72, from sr. rsch. group leader to mgr., 1972-78, from assoc. dir. rsch. to dir. rsch., 1978-81, gen. mgr., 1981-85; v.p. Hybritech Internat., St. Louis, 1983-85; gen. mgr. Monsanto, Brussels, 1985-87; v.p. R&D Ethyl Corp., Baton Rouge, 1988-94; dir. corp. rels. Magellan U., Tucson, from 1994; v.p. Edn. Mall, Tucson, from 1994. Mem. USDA Nat. Agrl. Rsch. and Extension Users Adv. Bd., Washington, 1988-91, chmn., 1988-89. Recipient USDA Commendation, 1991, Coll. of Basic Scis. Outstanding Svc. award La. State U., 1992. Mem. AAAS, Indsl. Rsch. Inst. (ethyl rep. 1988—), Am. Chem. Soc., N.Y. Acad. Scis., Chem. Soc., Soc. Chem. Industry, Internat. Union Pure and Applied Chemistry, Rotary Club of Baton Rouge, Sigma Xi, Lambda Upsilon. Home: Tucson, Ariz. Died Feb. 27, 2010.

MARYANSKI, FRED J., academic administrator; BA in Math., Providence Coll.; MA in Computer Sci., Stevens Inst. Tech.; PhD in Computer Sci., U. Conn. Affiliate prof. Worcester Poly. Inst.; faculty Kans. State U., U. Conn., Storrs, from 1983, vice chancellor academic adminstrn., interim chancellor, provost U. affairs, 1999—2000, sr. vice provost academic affairs, provost, exec. v.p. academic affairs, 1999—2004; pres. Nev. State Coll., Henderson, 2005—10. With Digital Equipment Corp., 1986—89. Died July 2, 2010.

MASON, BRIAN HAROLD, geologist, curator; b. N.Z., Apr. 18, 1917; came to U.S., 1947, naturalized, 1953; s. George Harold and Catherine (Fairweather) M.; m. Anne Marie Linn (div.); m. Virginia Powell (div.); m. Margarita Babb Mason, 1984 (dec. Feb. 15, 2009) M.Sc., U. New Zealand, 1938; PhD, U. Stockholm, 1943. Lectr. geology Canterbury Coll., N.Z., 1944-47; prof. mineralogy Ind. U., 1947-53; chmn. dept. mineralogy Am.erican Mus. Natural History, NYC, 1953-65. Author: Principles of Geochemistry, 3d edit, 1967, Meteorites, 1962, The Literature of Geology, 1958, (with L. G. Berry) Mineralogy, 1959, (with W.G. Melson) The Lunar Rocks, 1970, Victor Moritz Goldschmidt: Father of Modern Geochemistry, 1992. Recipient Leonard medal, Meteoritical Soc., 1972, Roebling medal, Mineralogical Soc. America, 1993. Fellow Mineral. Soc. Am., Geol. Soc. Am.; mem. Geochem. Soc., Royal Soc. N.Z., Swedish Geol. Soc. Died Dec. 3, 2009.

MASON, EDWARD ARCHIBALD, chemical and nuclear engineer; b. Rochester, NY, Aug. 9, 1924; s. Henry Archibald and Monica (Brayer) M.; m. Barbara Jean Earley, Apr. 15, 1950; children— Thomas E., Kathleen M., Paul D., Mark J., Anne M., Mary Beth. BS, U. Rochester, 1945; MS, Mass. Inst. Tech., 1948, Sc.D., 1950. Asst. prof. chem. engring. Mass. Inst. Tech., Cambridge, 1950-53, assoc. prof. nuclear engring., 1957-63, prof., 1963-77, dept. head, 1971-75; commr. Nuclear Regulatory Commn., Washington, 1975-77; v.p. research Standard Oil Co. (Ind.) (now Amoco Corp.), Chgo., 1977-89, cons., from 1989. Dir. rsch. Ionics, Inc., Cambridge, Mass., 1953-57; sr. designer engr. Oak Ridge Nat. Lab., 1957; mem. adv. com. reactor safeguards AEC, 1972-75; cons. other govt. agys., industry; dir. Cetus Corp., Commonwealth Edison Co., XMR, Inc., Symbollon, Corp. Patentee in field; contbr. articles to profl. jours. Mem. adv. com. M.I.T., U. Chgo., U. Tex., Ga. Inst. Tech., U. Calif., Berkeley; bd. dirs. John Crerar Library. Served with USNR, 1943-46. NSF Sr. Postdoctoral fellow, 1965-66 Fellow AAAS, Am. Inst. Chem. Engrs. (R.E. Wilson award in nuclear chem. engring, 1989), Am. Acad. Arts and Scis. (councillor 1987-91), Am. Nuclear Soc., Am. Inst. Chemists; mem. Nat. Acad. Engring. (councilor 1978-84), N.Y. Acad. Scis., Western Soc. Engrs., Am. Chem. Soc., Phi Beta Kappa, Sigma Xi, Tau Beta Pi, Harbour Ridge Yacht and Country Club. Clubs: Oyster Harbors (Mass.) Golf. Died June 23, 2010.

MASON, RAYMOND E., JR., distributing company executive; b. Columbus, Ohio, Mar. 20, 1920; s. Raymond E. and Lula Estella (Potter) Mason; m. Margaret E. Edwards, Feb. 6, 1942; children: Raymond E. III, Michael D., Bruce R. BS, Ohio State U., 1941; grad., U.S. Command and Gen. Staff, 1962, U.S. Army War Coll., 1965; D of Bus. Sci. (hon.), Ohio State U., 2001; D (hon.), Franklin U., 2004; D of laws (hon.), Cumberland Coll., 2003. Ops. mgr. Suburban Motor Freight, Columbus, 1946-47; pres., gen. mgr. CFL Lines, Columbus, 1947-48; pres., chmn. Columbus Truck & Equipment Co., from 1949. Pres., chmn. REM Realty, Columbus, from 1962, Bode-Finn Co., Cin., 1966—99; chmn. Ford Bros. Inc., Ironton, Ohio, 1975—79; mem. distbr. adv. coun. Mack Trucks; mng. dir. J. D. Ranch, Myakka City, Fla. Active Boy Scouts Am.; former trustee Freedoms Found. Valley Forge, Ohio Hist. Found.; vice-chmn. New Coll. Found.; dir. Mote Marine Lab. Ohio State U. Found.; chmn. bd. trustees emeritus Franklin U. With US Army, 1941—45, maj. gen. USAR. Decorated Bronze Star medal with V for Valor, Legion of Merit, Silver Star; recipient Pres. Unit citation, Truck Dealer of the Yr. award, Time mag., 1972, Good Scout award, Ctrl. Ohio Coun. Boy Scouts Am., Silver Beaver award, Boy Scouts Am., Silver Antelope award, Disting. Citizen of Yr. award, Centennial medal, Ohio State U., Pacesetters award, Coll. Bus. ISU, 1996, Virginia Steckler Internat. Svc. award, ARC, 1998, Lifetime Achievement award, Ohio State U., 1999, Harrison Sayre award, 2001, Philanthropist of the Yr., Columbus Found., 2001; named State of Ohio Vet. Hall of Fame, 1997, Buckeye Boys State Hall of Fame, 1999, Ohio State U. ROTC Hall of Fame, Jr. Achievement Ctrl. Ohio Bus. Hall of Fame, 2000; Baden-Powell fellow, World Scout Found. Mem.: Ohio Truck Assn., Am. Truck Dealers, Ohio State U. Alumni Assn., Army War Coll. Alumni Assn., Armor Assn., U.S. Army Arty. Assn., Columbus Club, Rotary (past dist. gov., Man of Yr., Paul Harris fellow), Masons. Home: Osprey, Fla. Died Aug. 13, 2010.

MASTERS, G(EORGE) MALLARY, humanities educator; b. Savannah, Ga., June 19, 1936; s. George Mallary and Edna Lee (Brabham) M. BS in French, Columbia U., 1960; MA, Johns Hopkins, 1962, PhD, 1964. Instr. Loyola Coll., Balt., 1961-62, asst. prof., U. Mo., Columbia, 1964-66, SUNY, Binghamton, 1966-69, assoc. prof., 1969-70, U. N.C., Chapel Hill, 1970-77, prof., from 1977. Chair S.E. Inst. Medieval and Renaissance Studies, 1978-79, co-chair, 1978-80; editor romance notes U. N.C., 1987-90, dir. grad. studies romance langs., 1988-90. Author: Rebelaisian Dialectic, 1969; author, editor: La Ligneé de Saturne, 1973, Actes du colloque international: Montaigne, 1580-1980, 1983, Medieval and Renaissance Studies 10, 1984, Le Parcours des Essais: Montaigne 1588-1988, 1989. Nat. Humanities fellow, 1968, Am. Coun. Learned Socs. fellow, 1976-77, Pogue Competitive fellow U. N.C., 1991—. Died Feb. 21, 2009.

MASTERSON, JAMES FRANCIS, psychiatrist; b. Phila., Mar. 25, 1926; s. James Francis and Evangeline (O'Boyle) Masterson; m. Patricia Cooke, Jan. 28, 1950; children: James F., Richard K., Nancy. BS, U. Notre Dame, 1947; MD, Jefferson Med. Sch., Phila., 1951. Diplomate Am. Bd. Psychiatry, Am. Bd. Neurology. Intern Phila. Gen. Hosp., 1951—52; resident psychiatry Payne Whitney Clinic, NY Hosp., NYC, 1952—55, chief resident, 1955—56, dir. adolescent OPD, 1956—66, head adolescent program, 1968—75, asst. attending psychiatrist, 1956—60, assoc. attending psychiatrist, 1960—70, attending psychiatrist, 1970—2010; dir. Symptomatic Adolescent Rsch. Project, 1957—67; founder, dir. Masterson Inst Psychoanalytic Psychotherapy & The Masterson Group, P.C., NYC, 1977—2010. Author: Psychotherapy of the Borderline Adolescent, Psychotherapy of the Borderline Adult, Countertransference, Narcissistic Personality Disorder, The Real Self, The Psychiatric Dilemma of Adolescence, The Test of Time: From Borderline Adolescent to Functioning Adult, The Personality Disorders: As Seen Through the Lens of Attachment Theory and Neurobiology Development of the Self, 2005; contbr. articles to profl. jours. Fellow: Am. Coll. Psychoanalysts, Am. Psychiat. Assn.; mem.: AMA, NY County Med. Soc., NY Soc. Adolescent Psychiatry (founder, past pres.), Am. Coll. Psychoanalysis. Home: Rye, NY. Died Apr. 12, 2010.

MATHERS, WILLIAM HARRIS, lawyer; b. Newport, RI, Aug. 27, 1914; s. Howard and Margaret I. (Harris) M.; m. Myra T. Martin, Jan. 17, 1942; children: William Martin, Michael Harris, John Grinnell, Myra Tutt, Ursula Fraser. AB, Dartmouth Coll., 1935; JD, Yale U., 1938. Bar: NY 1940. With Milbank, Tweed & Hope, 1938-48; mem. Milbank, Tweed, Hope & Hadley, 1948-57; v.p., sec., dir. Yale & Towne Mfg. Co., Stamford, Conn., 1957-60; ptnr. Chadbourne & Parke, 1960-75, counsel, from 1983; exec. v.p., gen. counsel, sec., dir. United Brands Co., 1975-82. Mayor, trustee Village of Cove Neck, N.Y., 1950-82; trustee Barnard Coll., 1958-69. Served as pvt. to maj. U.S. Army, 1942-46. Mem. ABA, N.Y. State Bar Assn., Nassau County Bar Assn., Assn. of Bar of City of N.Y., New Eng. Soc. in City of N.Y., Casque and Gauntlet, Corbey Court, Piping Rock Club, Seminole Golf Club, N.Y. Yacht Club, Cold Spring Harbor Beach Club, Phi Beta Kappa, Psi Upsilon. Home: Cheshire, Conn. Died July 27, 2010.

MATHIAS, CHARLES MCCURDY (MAC MATHIAS), lawyer, former United States Senator from Maryland; b. Frederick, Md., July 24, 1922; s. Charles McCurdy and Theresa McElfresh (Trail) M.; m. Ann Hickling Bradford, Nov. 8, 1958; children: Charles Bradford, Robert Fiske. BA, Haverford Coll., 1944; student, Yale U., 1943-44; LL.B., U. Md., 1949. Bar: Md. 1949, U.S. Supreme Ct. 1954. Asst. atty. gen. State of Md., Annapolis, Md., 1953-54; city atty. City of Frederick, Md., 1954-59; mem. Md. House of Delegates, 1958, US Congress from 6th Md. Dist., 1961—69; US Senator from Md., 1969-87; ptnr. Jones Day Reavis and Pogue, Washington, 1987-93. Milton Eisenhower vis. prof. Johns Hopkins U.; mem. Md. Governor's Commn. on State Taxes & Tax Structure, 1989-90, Md. Civil War Heritage Commn., 1992-95 Served from seaman to capt. USNR. Decorated Order of Merit (Federal Republic of Germany), Legion of Honor (France), Order of Orange Nassau (The Netherlands), Order of Brit. Empire (Eng.). Republican. Episcopalian. Home: Chevy Chase, Md. Died Jan. 25, 2010.

MATHISEN, HAROLD CLIFFORD, foundation administrator; b. East Orange, NJ, Apr. 1, 1924; s. Harold and Ottilie Christine (Nordland) Mathisen; m. Dora Elizabeth Bachtel, Sept. 14, 1946; children: Margaret Bennett, Harold, Elizabeth Mathisen Andersen, Barbara Ramsland. AB, Princeton U., 1943; MBA, Harvard U., 1948. Asst. to contr. Kaiser Frazer Corp., Willow Run, Mich., 1948—52; investment analyst Smith Barney & Co., NYC, 1952—61; pres. Alliance Found., NYC, from 1961. Treas. AGF Mgmt. Co., NYC, 1969—85; portfolio mgr. Legg Mason Wood Walker, Inc., NYC, 1967—78, NYC, 1982—2005, Citigroup, NYC, 2005—07. Pres. Alliance Growth Fund, NYC, 1968—78; trustee, pres. McAuley Water St. Mission, NYC, 1967—99; asst. treas., investment mgr. Christian and Missionary Alliance, Nyack, 1978—80; asst. treas. NY Internat. Bible Soc., NYC, 1980—82. Lt. USNR, 1944—46. Mem.: Inst. Chartered Fin. Analysts, NY Soc. Securities Analysts, Sigma Xi, Phi Beta Kappa. Home: Chatham, NJ. Died Feb. 14, 2010.

MATLOCK, KENNETH JEROME, building materials company executive; b. Oak Park, Ill., May 30, 1928; s. Harvey and Lillian (Sivertsen) Samuelson; m. Dorothy Belowski, Nov. 3, 1956; children— Geoffrey, Barbara, Gail, Paul. Student, James Millikin U., 1946-48; BS in Accountancy, U. Ill., 1950; postgrad., Northwestern U. Inst. Mgmt., summer 1963. C.P.A., Ill., Fla. Sr. audit mgr. Price Waterhouse & Co., Chgo., 1950-64; with Celotex Corp., Chgo., 1964-65, v.p. fin. ops. Tampa, Fla., 1965-74; asst. to v.p. Jim Walter Corp., Tampa, 1966-69, controller, 1970-72, v.p., 1972-74, v.p., chief acctg. officer, 1974-88, sr. v.p., CFO, 1987-91; v.p., CFO Walter Industries, Inc., Tampa, 1987-88, exec. v.p., bd. dirs. Tampa, from 1991, exec. v.p., CFO, also bd. dirs. Adviser Jr. Achievement, Chgo., 1958-60; active Heart Fund, United Fund, 1956-58. Served with USNR, 1945-46. Mem. AICPA, Ill. Soc. CPAs. Fla. Soc. CPAs, Fin. Execs. Inst. Home: Saint Petersburg, Fla. Died Dec. 11, 2009.

MATTHAEI, GAY HUMPHREY, interior designer; b. NYC, Mar. 13, 1931; d. Robert Louis and Ethel Gladys Humphrey; m. Konrad Henry Matthaei, Nov. 16, 1956; children: Marcella, Leslie, Konrad. BA, Mt. Holyoke Coll., 1952; MIA, Columbia U., 1954, MA, cert. Russian Inst., 1954; grad., Parsons Sch. Design, 1970. Lectr., cons. NBC, 1956; dir. Radrick Prodns., Where Time Is a River, 1966—67; cons. N.Y.C. Parks Recreation and Cultural Adminstrn., 1970—72; assoc. Pearl R. Mitchell A.S.I.D., 1972—74, owner, 1974—97; owner, mgr. Gay Matthaei Interiors, NYC, 1975—2003. Ptnr. Two Fold Graphics, 1992—96. Restorations include Town Farms Inn, 1978, State Capital of Conn., 1977-78, Pres.'s House, Mt. Holyoke Coll., 1982, Samuel Russell House, Wesleyan Coll., 1984, Courtly Manor, Greenwich, Conn., 1987 Buhl Family Found., 1993; author: The Ledgerbook of Thomas Blue Eagle, 1994, 1995, (CD-Rom) The Journey of Thomas Blue Eagle, 1995, Sketchbook of Thomas Blue Eagle (Best Books for Teenagers NY Pub. Libr. 2002). Trustee Mt. Holyoke Coll.; mem. Commn. on State Capital Preservation and Restoration, Conn., 1997-82, Greenwich Bd. Realtors, Nat. Bd. Realtors; literacy vol., Greenich, Conn., 2005. Recipient Christopher award, 1994, Internat. Readers Assn. award, 1995, EMMA award, best CD-Rom award Multimedia Asia, others. Mem.: Nat. Mus. Am. Indian (charter), Mt. Holyoke Club, Phi Beta Kappa. Home: Stamford, Conn. Died Jan. 1, 2010.

MATTHEWS, LEONARD SARVER, advertising and marketing executive; b. Glendean, Ky., Jan. 6, 1922; s. Clell and Zetta Price (Sarver) M.; m. Dorothy Lucille Fessler; children: Nancy, James, Douglas. BS summa cum laude, Northwestern U., 1948. With Leo Burnett Co., Inc., Chgo., 1948-75, v.p., dir., 1958-59, exec. v.p. charge mktg. services, 1959-61, exec. v.p. client svc., 1961-69, pres., 1970-75; asst. sec. commerce for domestic and internat. bus., 1976; pres., exec. com., dir. Young and Rubicam, 1977-78; pres. Am. Assn. Advt. Agys., 1979-89; co-founder Matthews & Johnston, Stamford, Conn., 1989-92; chmn. Next Century Media, 1992—99. Mem. adv. bd. Scripps Capital, San Diego. Ensign USCGR, 1942-46. Named to Advt. Hall of Fame, 1999. Mem. Advt. Coun. (life bd. dirs.), Sky Club (N.Y.C.), Pine Valley Golf Club (N.J.), Rancho Santa Fe Golf (Calif.), Georgetown Club (Washington), Delta Sigma Pi, Beta Gamma Sigma. Republican. Lutheran. Home: Rancho Santa Fe, Calif. Died May 31, 2009.

MATTHIESEN, LEROY THEODORE, bishop emeritus; b. Olfen, Tex., June 11, 1921; s. Joseph A. and Rosa (Englert) Matthiesen. BA, Josephinum Coll., Columbus, Ohio, 1942; MA, Cath. U., Washington, 1961; LittD, Register Sch. Journalism., Denver, 1962. Ordained priest Diocese of Amarillo, Tex., 1946; prin. Alamo Cath. HS, from 1969; pastor St. Francis Parish, from 1972; ordained bishop, 1980; bishop Diocese of Amarillo, 1980—97, bishop emeritus, 1997—2010. Roman Catholic. Died Mar. 22, 2010.

MATTIS, LOUIS PRICE, pharmaceutical and consumer products company executive; b. Balt., Dec. 12, 1941; s. Louis Wadsworth and Sara Helene (Myers) M.; children: Louis Wadsworth, Deborah Cook Collier. AB in Internat. Affairs, Lafayette Coll., Easton, Pa., 1962; MBA, Tulane U., 1964. V.p., gen. mgr. Warner Lambert Co., Manila, 1971-74, regional dir. Hong Kong, 1974-76, region pres. Sydney, Australia, 1976-79; exec. v.p. Americas-Far East Richardson-Vicks, Inc., 1979-81, pres. Americas-Far East, 1981-84, exec. v.p., 1985-87; group v.p. Sterling Winthrop Inc., NYC, 1987-88, chmn., pres., CEO, 1988-94; dir. Salomon Bros. Fund, 1992—2005. Mem. Snowmass Club. Avocations: skiing, woodworking. Home: Carbondale, Colo. Died July 14, 2010.

MATTSSON, AKE, psychiatrist, physician; b. Stockholm, May 30, 1929; came to U.S., 1956, naturalized, 1964; s. Erik H. and Thyra (Mattsson) M.; m. Margareta Fürst, Jan. 5, 1953; children: Erik, Peter, Nicholas; m. Judith Whitley Powell, Nov. 25, 2000. MB, Karolinska Inst., Stockholm, 1950, MD, 1955. Intern Vanderbilt U. Med. Sch., Nashville, 1955-56; resident in pediat. and child psychiatry Karolinska Hosp., Stockholm, 1958-60; fellow in child devel. Case Western Res. U. Med. Sch., 1957-58, resident in psychiatry and child psychiatry, 1960-64, asst. prof. psychiatry, 1964-70; prof. psychiatry and pediat. U. Va. Med. Sch., 1970-77, U. Pitts Med. Sch., 1977-78; prof. psychiatry and pediat., dir. divsn. child and adolescent psychiatry NYU Med. Sch., 1978-85, rsch. prof. psychiatry, from 1985; prof. psychiatry U. Va. Med. Sch., 1985-91; prof. psychiatry and pediat., dir. divsn. child and adolescent psychiatry Med. Sch., East Carolina U., Greenville, NC, 1991-97; med. dir. divsn. mental health V.I. Dept. Health, St. Thomas, 1997—2003; med. dir. New Dimension, Inc., Washington, from 2005. Clin. prof. psychiatry Med. Sch. George Washington U., from 2004. Contbr. numerous articles to med. jours. Served with Swedish Navy, 1948-59. Fulbright-Hays grantee, 1975. Mem. Am. Psychol. Assn., Am. Acad. Child Adolescent Psychiatry (delegate fellow 2003), N.Y. Acad. Scis., Soc. Biol. Psychiatry, Am. Acad. Psychiatry and the Law. Died Mar. 31, 2009.

MATY, GEORGE ANTHONY, retail executive; b. New England, ND, July 2, 1921; s. Edmund Felix and Eva Barbara (Nikrant) Matychowiak; m. Agatha Ann Holthaus, Apr. 22, 1944; children: Eve Maria, Susan Elizabeth, Mark Arthur, Joseph George, Magdelan Ann. BS in Commerce, St. Louis U., 1941. Acct. GMAC, East St. Louis, Ill., 1941—42, Arthur R. Lindburg Co., St. Louis, 1946—48; gen. mgr. East Side Motors Inc., East St. Louis, 1948—58; mgr. sales Lindburg Cadillac Co., St. Louis, 1958—80, exec. v.p., from 1980. Mem.: Greater St. Louis Auto Dealer Assn., Mo. Auto Dealer Assn., Mo. Athletic Club. Died July 24, 2009.

MATZ, KENNETH H., JR., retired newscaster; b. Phila., Oct. 25, 1945; s. Kenneth H. and Kathryn M.; m. Phyllis Ann Walton, Mar. 9, 1991 (div.); 1 child, Justin T.; m. Deborah Matz BBA, Lebanon Valley Coll., 1969. Radio news anchor WIBG, KYW, Phila., 1969-77; TV news anchor WITI-TV, Milw., 1977-79, KGO-TV/ABC, San Francisco, 1979-81, KTTV-TV/Metromedia, LA, 1981-84, WMAR-TV, Balt., 1984-89, WCIX-TV/CBS, Miami, Fla., 1989-92, WCAU-TV/NBC, Phila., 1992-98. Host Pa. Jr. Miss Program, 1995-96. Vol. host Muscular Dystrophy Assn. Telethon, Milw., 1978-80, Children's Miracle Network Telethon, Balt., 1984-89; hon. bd. dirs. Nazareth Hosp., 1995-96; bd. dirs. Pa. AP Broadcasters Assn., 1975-77. With USAR, 1969-76. Recipient award Am. Heart Assn., March of Dimes, Nat. Kidney Found., Disting. Journalism award Soc. Profl. Journalists, 1988. Mem. NATAS (Emmy award for Investigative Report 1991, for Best Regularly Scheduled Daily News Program 1983, 84, Emmy award nomination for Outstanding News Feature Series, 1992, 94, for Outstanding Pub. Affairs Program, 1994, for Outstanding Individual Achievement, 1995, 97, 98). Avocations: scuba diving, wine, tennis. Home: Sarasota, Fla. Died Jan. 23, 2010.

MAUCK, GARY L., hotel executive, consultant; b. Dayton, Ohio, Feb. 10, 1943; s. John Frederick and Dorothy Mary (McClure) Mauck; m. Diane J. Grossmiller, Sept. 3, 1971. BA, U. Ariz., 1965. Mgr. mktg. meetings-trade shows Motorola Semicondr. Products Sector, Phoenix, 1966—84; pres. Gary Mauck & Assocs., Inc., Phoenix, from 1984; mem. Phoenix and Valley Sun Conv. Bur., from 1984; chmn. Fiesta Bowl Com., Phoenix, from 1980. Mem.: Phoenix Press Box Assn., U. Ariz. Alumni Assn., Internat. Exhibitors Assn., Meeting Planners Internat., Meeting Cons. Club, Phoenix Press Club, Phi Gamma Delta. Republican. Home: Phoenix, Ariz. Died Jan. 2, 2009.

MAUSNER, HOWARD, clinical psychologist; b. NYC, Sept. 28, 1917; s. Max and Anne (Landberg) Mausner; m. Ruth Montner, June 22, 1939; children: Pamela Amy, Jeffrey Neil, Keith Lincoln. Lic. psychologist Colo. BA Bklyn. Coll., 1938; MA Columbia U., 1940; D.Psychology U. Denver, 1983; postgrad. New Sch. Social Rsch., 1940—43; rsch. psychologist VA, NYC, 1947—49; chief psychologist Jewish Vocat. Svcs., Detroit, 1949—55, Nat. Jewish Hosp., Denver, 1955—57; pvt. practice Denver, from 1957; cons. dept. phys. medicine U. Colo. Med. Sch., Denver, 1966—80; rehab. rsch. psychologist, 1966—80; ct. psychologist 18th Jud. Dist. Ct., Littleton, Colo., 1965—76; vocat. cons. Bur. Hearings and Appeals, HEW, from 1965; psychol. cons. Ct. House, Inc., Adolescent Group Home, Littleton, from 1969. With USAAF, 1943—46. Mem.: Am. Assn. Counseling Devel., Am. Psychol. Assn., Nat. Rehab. Assn., Colo. Rehab. Assn., Colo. Soc. Psychologists Pvt. Practice, Internat. Assn. Counseling Svcs. Home: Loveland, Colo. Died Feb. 6, 2009.

MAXNER, JOYCE KAREN, family therapist, author; b. Lynn, Mass., Oct. 23, 1929; d. Arthur Martin Leopold and Mary Grace Meyerson; married, 1951 (div. 1968); children: Daryl, John; m. Joseph Maxner, Mar. 7, 1970 (div. 1976). AA, Centenary Coll. for Women, 1949; BA, Harvard U., 1976; MS, Villanova U., 1979. Copywriter Advt. Agys., Boston, 1949-64, Sta. WLYN, Lynn, 1950-52; advt. exec., writer Unicorn Studio, Marblehead, Mass., 1964-69; mgr. advt., writer Am. Art Guild, NYC, 1972-73; asst. pub. Bergen News, Cliffside Park, N.J., 1974; artists' rep., pub. rels. rep. Ft. Lee, N.J., 1975-76; juvenile probation officer Del. County Juvenile Ct., Media, Pa., 1979-82; family therapist Family Inst. Va., Richmond, 1982-84; pvt. practice Newtown Square, Pa., from 1984. Author: Nicholas Cricket, 1989 (selected for permanent collection Delta Blues Mus., Best Design for Children's Book award N.Y. Bookbinders Guild 1990), Lady Bugatti, 1991. Pres. Women's Am. Ogn. for Rehab. through Tng., Marblehead, 1957-58; troop leader Girl Scouts USA, Marblehead, 1960-61. Mem. AACD, Pen Am. Ctr., Phila. Children's Reading Roundtable, Soc. Children's Book Writers, Harvard Alumni Assn., Author's Guild. Died Mar. 5, 2009.

MAXWELL, CHARLES NEVILLE, mathematics educator; b. Tuscaloosa, Ala., Oct. 27, 1927; s. Joseph Alston and Lucille (DeVere) M.; m. Patsie H. Maxwell, Aug. 2, 1952; children: Bess Devere, Jane Alston, Anna Hale, Mary Neville. BS in Math., U. Chgo., 1949, MS in Math., 1951; PhD in Math., U. Ill., 1955. Instr. math. U. Mich., Ann Arbor, 1955-58; assoc. prof. U. Ala., Tuscaloosa, 1958-63; prof. math. So. Ill. U., Carbondale, from 1963. With USN, 1946-47, PTO. Mem. Am. Math. Soc., Math. Assn. Am., Sigma Xi. Home: Carbondale, Ill. Died June 28, 2010.

MAY, DAVID A., retired dean; b. Buffalo, May 23, 1947; children: Jordan D., Jared R. AAS in Bus. Adminstrn., Niagara County C.C., Sanborn, NY, 1983; BS in Pub. Adminstrn., Empire State Coll., 1988; MA in Orgn. Mgmt., U. Phoenix, 1996; PhD in Mgmt., LaSalle U., 1997. V.p. Simpson Security, Inc., Niagara Falls, NY, 1973—78; lt. Niagara Falls (N.Y.) Police Dept., 1974—98; dean N.Y. Paralegal Sch.; ret., 2002. Bd. dirs. NCCJ, 1984-90, ARC, 1986-89,

Music Sch. of Niagara, 1987-90; bd. dirs. Niagara Falls Little Theatre, chmn., 1994; pres. Niagara Cmty. Ctr., Niagara Falls, 1987, Niagara Falls Sch. Bd., 1984-94, Niagara Falls Meml. Day Assn., 1990, 91, 93; mem. Niagara County Legislature, 1994. Recipient Svc. award Fellowship House Found., Niagara Falls, 1986; named Civic Leader of Yr., Niagara Cmty. Ctr., Niagara Falls, 1990. Mem. Kiwanis Club North Niagara Falls (pres. 1987, state gov. 1989, Kiwanian of the Yr. 1991), Lasalle Am. Legion (vice commdr. 1975), Lasalle Sportsmens Club (fin. sec. 1989). Avocations: playing tennis, golf, amateur historian. Home: Colorado Springs, Colo. Died Jan. 4, 2009.

MAYFIELD, WILLIAM STEPHEN, law educator; b. Gary, Indiana, Mar. 2, 1919; s. William Henry and Elnora Elizabeth (Williams) M.; m. Octavia Smith, Feb. 6, 1949 (dec.); children: Pamela L., William E., Stephanie K. Stokes; m. Mildred G. Harris, May 25, 1991. BA, Detroit Inst. Tech., 1946; JD, Detroit Coll. Law, 1949. Bar: Mich. 1949, U.S. Supreme Ct. 1996. Mem. firm Lewis, Rowlette, Brown, Wanzo and Bell, Detroit, 1949-51; atty. U.S. Office Price Stblzn., Detroit, 1951-53; referee Friend of the Court, Detroit, 1953-72; vis. prof. Law Center, La. State Univ., Baton Rouge, summer, 1979; prof. law So. U., Baton Rouge, from 1972. Mem. com. sci. and tech. in cts. La. Supreme Ct., 1978 Mem. regional bd. Boy Scouts Am., Detroit, 1961-63; Served with U.S. Army, 1942-46. Mem. Am. Bar Assn., Nat. Bar Assn., Wolverine Bar Assn., World Assn. Law Profs., Detroit Coll. Law Alumni Assn., Assn. Henri Capitanti, Comml. Law League Am., Ret. Officers Assn. (pres. Greater Baton Rouge 1985), Am. Legion, Mil. Order of the World Wars, Delta Theta Phi (Outstanding Prof. of Yr. award 1983) Home: Louisville, Ky. Died May 19, 2009.

MAZUR, GERALD, lawyer, educator; b. NYC, July 1, 1925; m. Toby Ann Fuchs, July 1, 1962; children: Kara Susan, Kim Loren. BA, U. Wis., 1947; JD, Cornell U., 1950. Bar: NY 1950, NY (US Dist. Ct. (so. dist.)) 1950. Asst. counsel Nat. Enforcement Commn., Washington, 1952—55; law asst. NY Supreme Ct., NYC, 1955—68, referee, 1968—76, supervising referee, from 1976; lectr. Baruch Coll., NYC, from 1980. Co-author (with Irving L. Levey): Condemnation U.S.A., 1969. With US Army, 1942, ETO. Mem.: Cornell Law Assn., Bronx County Bar Assn. (bd. dirs. 1970—74). Home: Somers, NY. Died May 31, 2010.

MCALLISTER, GENE ROBERT, electronics company executive, electrical engineer; b. La Porte, Ind., Apr. 28, 1930; s. Leonard Leroy and Ethel May (Kellog) McA.; m. Diane Stanton, Jan. 29, 1955; children: Jean Anne, Thomas Michael. BSEE, Purdue U., 1959. Jr. engr. No. Ind. Pub. Service Co., La Porte, 1948-59; engr. Magnavox G&I Electronics Co., Ft. Wayne, Ind., 1959-60, asst. product mgr., 1960-63, product mgr., 1963-68, dir. mktg., 1968-74, v.p., gen. mgr. sensors, 1974-82, also bd. dirs.; v.p., dir. ops. Magnavox Electronic Systems Co., Ft. Wayne, 1982-85, group v.p., 1985-87, exec. v.p., ops. and COO, 1987-91, pres., COO, 1991, pres., CEO, from 1992. Mem. Leadership Ft. Wayne, 1981—; bd. dirs. Jr. Achievement, 1982—; mem. Ft. Wayne Corp. Coun., 1991—, Ft. Wayne Community Found., 1991—. With U.S. Army, 1951-53, Korea. Mem. Nat. Security Indsl. Assn. (bd. dirs., ASW exec. com.), Machinery and Allied Products Inst. (govt. contracts council 1970—), Magnavox Mgmt. Club (bd. dirs. 1984—), Ft. Wayne C. of C. (legis. com. 1982—), Assn. U.S. Army, Navy League, Summit Club, Sycamore Hills Golf Club. Clubs: Pine Valley Country (bd. dirs. 1978-82), Ft. Wayne Racquet, Olympia (bd. dirs 1970-79). Avocations: golf, tennis, bowling, racquetball, water-skiing. Home: Auburn, Ind. Died Oct. 18, 2009.

MCANERNEY, ROBERT MOORE, lawyer; b. Greenwich, Conn., Jan. 29, 1924; BA, Williams Coll., 1947; JD, U. Va., 1953. Bar: Conn. 1954, US Supreme Ct. 1969. Assoc. firm Sullivan & Cromwell, NYC, 1953; assoc. Durey & Pierson, Stamford, Conn., 1953—63, ptnr., 1960—63, McAnerney & Millar, Darien, Conn., from 1963; assoc. dir. Union Trust Co.; dir., mem. exec. com. Conn. Attys. Title Ins. Co. Fellow: Am. Bar Found.; mem.: ABA (del. 1978—81), New Eng. Bar Assn. (dir. 1979—83), Stamford Bar Assn., Conn. Bar Assn. (bd. govs. 1964—67, chmn. family law com. mem. 1967—71, chmn. law office econs. com. 1973—75, chmn. spl. com. legis. liaison 1977—78, pres. assn. 1980—81). Died Feb. 11, 2010.

MCAULIFFE, DANIEL JOSEPH, lawyer; b. NYC, Mar. 27, 1945; s. Daniel Joseph and Ethel Louise (Dierks) McA.; m. J. Wyn Drake, May 20, 1972 (div. Sept. 1977); 1 child, Kelly Elizabeth McAuliffe; m. Shirley J. Wahl, Apr. 8, 2006. BA, Fordham U., 1966; JD, Harvard U., 1969. Bar: DC 1969, Ariz. 1973, Supreme Ct. Ariz., Calif., Nev., Supreme jud. Ct. Mass., US Supreme Ct., US Cts. Appeals (9th & 10th cir.), US Dist. Ct., Dist. Ariz., US Dist. Ct. Dist. Nev. Trial atty. U.S. Dept. Justice, Washington, 1969-71, Dep. Asst. Atty. Gen., 1971-73; atty. Snell & Wilmer, Phoenix, 1973-77, ptnr., from 1977. Mem. Ariz. Commn. on Judicial Qualifications, Task Force Ariz. Commn. on Courts, Ariz. Bar Found. Fellows (vice chmn.). Author/editor: Arizona Legal Forms Vols. 1 and 2, 1988. Chmn. Phoenix Human Rels. Commn., 1974-79; bd. dirs. Phoenix Symphony Assn., 1989—, Phoenix Symphony Coun., 1987—. Mem. ABA, State Bar Calif., Fed. Bar Assn., Am. Judicature Soc., Am. Law Inst., Ariz. State Bar Assn. (chmn. civil practice & procedure com. 1984-91; bd. govs. 1991-1999 & 2002-2003; chmn. professionalism course com. 1994; exec. coun. appellate practice sect. 1995, task force tech. 1995; 2nd v.p. 2004, pres. 2007-08). Avocations: tennis, reading. Home: Phoenix, Ariz. Died Mar. 12, 2010.

MCBARNETTE, LORNA SCOTT, state official; b. N.Y.C., June 13, 1939; d. Malcolm M. and Georgiana (Wilson) Scott; children— Joan, Stanley. A.A.S., N.Y.C. Community Coll., 1961; B.A. in Econs., SUNY-Old Westbury, 1975; postgrad. L.I. U.-C.W. Post Coll., 1975-76; M.S. in Health Policy and Mgmt., Harvard U., 1978. Adminstrv. mgr. Dept. Clin. Labs., Hillside Med. Ctr., Jamaica, N.Y., 1970-76, asst. hosp. adminstr., 1978-79; assoc. exec. dir. Queens Hosp. Ctr. L.I. Jewish Hosp., Jamaica, 1979-81; v.p. clin. and ambulatory services St. Peter's Hosp., Albany, 1981-83; exec. dep. commr. N.Y. State Dept. Health, Albany, 1983—; supr. blood bank and hematology Booth Meml. Hosp., Flushing, N.Y., 1961-65, SUNY Downstate Med. Ctr., Bklyn., 1966-67; supr. dept. clin. labs. L.I. Jewish Hillside Med. Ctr., 1967-70. Contbr. articles to profl. jours. Vice chmn. bd. dirs. L.I. Minority Aliance, Inc., 1978-82; adv. council Hofstra U. Upward Bound program, 1981-82. Recipient Cert. of Merit, County of Nassau, 1975; named Woman of Yr., N.Y. State Women's Advs., 1984; USPHS trainee, 1977-78; Kaiser Found. fellow, 1977-78. Mem. Am. Pub. Health Assn. (governing council 1981-82, leadership cert. of appreciation 1984), Am. Soc. Pub. Adminstrn. (exec. council 1981-82), Am. Assn. Blood Banks (dir. 1976-78), Am. Coll. Hosp. Adminstrs., N.Y. Pub. Health Assn., Ctr. for Women in Govt. (dir.), Health Systems Agy. of Northeastern N.Y. (dir.). Clubs: Altrusa, Black and Hispanic Educators and Adminstrs. of Capital Dist. Home: Hampton Bays, NY. Died Mar. 17, 2009.

MCCABE, RICHARD EDMUND, priest; b. Milw., Sept. 15, 1929; s. John and Margaret Mary (Burke) McC. BS, Regis Coll., 1951; postgrad., St. Mary's Theol. Sch., Houston, 1954-58; MSW, Worden Sch., San Antonio, 1962. Ordained priest Roman Cath. Ch., 1958. Parish priest, St. Louis, Austin (Tex.), 1958-62; chaplain Seton Hosp., Austin, 1962-64, Adoration Convent, Austin, from 1964; founder, pastor Lakeway Ch., Austin, from 1966. Founder, bd. dirs. Cath. Charities, Diocese of Austin, 1962—, cons. nat. disasters, 1965—; founder, bd. dirs. St. Vincent de Paul Soc., Austin, Waco, Tex., Temple, Tex., cons. nat. disasters, 1965—; founder, bd. dirs. Christ Child Soc. Ladies of Charity; pres. Austin Conf. Chs., 1970-71; founder St. Vincent de Paul Stores, Austin, Waco, Temple, Rosebud, Tex., Round Rock, Tex., Taylor, Tex., Lockhart, Tex. Chmn., mem. profl. adv. com. Austin Mental Health and Mental Retardation Ctr., 1971—; founder, bd. dirs. Caritas of Austin, Waco and Temple, Big Bros. of Austin, Gov.'s Retirement Residence, Austin; founder, v.p. Capitol Kidney Found.; pres. Internat. Coops., Austin Rehab. Ctr., Inc., Austin Coun. on Alcoholism; bd. dirs. Project Adopt, Campaign for Human Devel. Recipient Svc. to Juvenile Ct. award, 1962, Svc. to Mankind award, 1972. Mem. Acad. Cert. Social Workers, Nat. Assn. Social Workers, Town and Gown Club, Headliners Club. Home: Austin, Tex. Died Sept. 12, 2009.

MCCAFFREY, ROBERT HENRY, JR., retired manufacturing company executive; b. Syracuse, NY, Jan. 20, 1927; s. Robert Henry and May Ann (McGuire) McC.; m. Dorothy Anne Evers, Sept. 22, 1956; children: Michael Robert, Kathleen Mary. BS, Syracuse U., 1949. Sales asst. Sealright Corp., Fulton, NY, 1949-50; with TEK Hughes div. Johnson & Johnson, Metuchen, NJ, 1950-67, gen. sales mgr., 1958-59, v.p. sales, 1959-62, pres., 1962-67; gen. mgr. med. div. Howmet Corp., NYC, 1967-70; group v.p. Howmedica, Inc., 1970-73, sr. v.p., 1973-74, exec. v.p., also bd. dirs., 1974-76; pres., CEO C.R. Bard, Inc., Murray Hill, NJ, 1976-78, chmn. bd. dirs., CEO, 1978-89, chmn. bd., 1989-91, also bd. dirs., chmn. exec. com., 1991—99. Bd. dirs. Summit and Elizabeth Trust, Summit Bancorp, Thomas & Betts Corp. Trustee Found. for Univ. Medicine and Dentistry N.J., 1987-90, Syracuse U., 1979-04, chmn. corp. adv. council, 1974-75. With AUS, 1945-46. Mem. Orthopedic Surg. Mfrs. Assn., Health Industry Mfrs. Assn. (bd. dir., chmn. 1982-83), N.Y. Sales Execs. Club, Sigma Chi. Republican. Roman Catholic. Avocations: reading, skiing, golf. Home: Shrewsbury, Mass. Died Aug. 21, 2009.

MCCAFFREY, WILLIAM THOMAS, retired financial services company executive; b. NYC, July 7, 1936; s. Daniel and Alice (Dineen) McC.; m. Mary Margaret Timms, June 25, 1960; children: Ann, William E., Christine. BS, NYU, 1970; MS in Bus., Columbia U., 1972. Dir. pub. The Equitable Fin. Cos., NYC, 1968-71, asst. v.p. communications, 1972-74, v.p., office of the pres., 1975-77, v.p. corp. devel., 1977-79, v.p., personnel dir., 1980-84, sr. v.p. pers. and adminstrn., 1984-85, exec. v.p. corp., 1986-87, exec. v.p., chief adminstrv. officer, 1988-96, sr. exec. v.p., COO, from 1996, chmn. benefits com., from 1986. Bd. dirs. Equitable Variable Life Ins. Co., N.Y.C., Equitable Life Assurance Soc. U.S., Innovir, All Faiths Cemetery, AXA Assistance Inc., E.Q. Advisors Trust. Bd. dirs. Equitable Found., 1987—, Bronx-Lebanon Hosp.; project mgr. Grace Commn., Washington, 1982-85; chmn. bd. trustees Xavier U., New Orleans, 1986—; chmn. bd. Outreach, N.Y.C. Sgt. U.S. Army, 1957-58. Mem. West Side Tennis Club (Forest Hills, N.Y.) (gov. 1988—). Avocations: tennis, photography. Home: Long Beach, NY. Died June 18, 2009.

MCCAIN, HUGH BOYD, JR., sociologist, educator; b. Atlanta, July 8, 1945; s. Hugh Boyd and Dorothy Mae (Johnson) McC.; m. Gail Zimmerman, Aug. 14, 1971; 1 child, Carisa Bernadette. BA, Emory U., 1967, MA, 1969, PhD, 1973. Instr. U. Richmond, Va., 1971-73, asst. prof. Va., 1973-75; assoc. prof. Jacksonville (Ala.) State U., 1975-83, prof., from 1984. Bd. dirs. Second Chance, Inc., Anniston, Ala.; lectr. profl. socs. Mem. Nat. Coun. Family Rels., Soc. for Study Social Problems, So. Sociol. Soc. Democrat. Methodist. Home: Jacksonville, Ala. Died Apr. 19, 2010.

MCCALPIN, FRANCIS WILLIAM, lawyer; b. St. Louis, Nov. 8, 1921; s. George Ambrose and Marguerite (Miles) McC.; m. Margaret Wickes, Feb. 27, 1954; children: Martha, William Francis, Katherine McCalpin Winfrey, Lucy McCalpin Hejlek, David Christopher. AB, St. Louis U., 1943; LL.B., Harvard U., 1948. Bar: Mo. 1948, Ill. 1953. Sec., bd. dirs. Hardy Investment Co.; bd. dirs. Color Process Co.; mem. nat. adv. com. to legal services program Office Econ. Opportunity, 1965-73; mem. Mo. Coordinating Bd. Higher Edn., 1974-82, chmn., 1974; dir. Legal Services Corp., 1979-81, 1993-2003 chmn. bd., 1980-81. Trustee, sec. St. Louis Ednl. TV Commn. KETC-TV, 1965-72; trustee Jr. Coll. Dist. St. Louis, 1962-65, St. Louis U., 1972-74; bd. dirs. Family and Children's Svc., St. Louis, 1972-78, 79-85, v.p., 1979-85; bd. dirs. Am. Bar Found., 1976-87, v.p., 1982-84, pres., 1984-86, chmn. fellows, 1976-77, cons. Ford. Found., 1990. Served with USMCR, 1942-46, 50-51. Mem. ABA (chmn. spl. com. on availabilty of legal services 1965-70, chmn. spl. com. on prepaid legal services 1970-73, chmn. standing com. on legal aid and indigent defendants 1973-76, 83-85, asst. sec. 1975-79, sec. 1979-83, vice-chmn. sr. lawyers div., 1989-90, medal 1988), Ill. Bar Assn., Mo. Bar Integrated (gov. 1967-73), Bar Assn. St. Louis (pres. 1961-62), Nat. Conf. Bar Presidents (treas. 1970-71, pres. 1973-74), Nat. Legal Aid & Defenders Assn. (pres.-elect 1987-89, pres., 1989-92). Clubs: Harvard (St. Louis). Republican. Home: Saint Louis, Mo. Died Dec. 9, 2009.

MCCANN, RICHARD STEPHEN, lawyer; b. Wilmington, Del., Dec. 26, 1938; s. Francis E.B. and Naomi H. (Riley) McC.; m. Gloria M. Baum (div. 1973); 1 child, Heather Marie; m. Sharon R. Cannon. BA, Georgetown U., 1960, JD, 1963; MA in City Planning, U. Pa., 1965. Bar: Del. 1964. Alderman City of Newark, Newark, 1964-66, pvt. practice law, from 1970; city planner Dover, Del., 1966-70. Atty. Del. Police Chief's Coun., Dover, 1971—, Del. Police Chief's Found., Dover, 1983—. Atty. Aetna Hose, Hook & Ladder Co., Newark, 1975—. Mem. ABA, Del. Bar Assn. Avocations: skiing, gardening, cannons. Home: Bear, Del. Died Jan. 26, 2009.

MCCARRAGHER, BERNARD JOHN, retired manufacturing company executive; b. Waukesha, Wis., Sept. 17, 1927; s. Bernard J. and Agnes A. (Brennan) McC.; m. Mary J. Horschak, June 20, 1953; 11 children. BS, Marquette U., 1951. CPA, Wis. Sr. acct. Arthur Andersen & Co., Milw., 1951-57; controller Payne Lumber Co., Oshkosh, Wis., 1957-59; budget mgr. Bergstrom Paper Co., Neenah, Wis., 1959-62; various positions Menasha Corp., Neenah, 1962-81, fin. v.p., 1981-84, sr. v.p., 1984-91, also bd. dirs., chmn. bd. dirs., 1994. Served with U.S. Army, 1946-48. Mem. Fin. Execs. Inst. (treas. 1985-87). Lodges: Rotary (bd. dirs. Neenah club). Republican. Roman Catholic. Home: Brookfield, Wis. Died May 21, 2010.

MCCARTHY, KAREN, former United States Representative from Missouri; b. Haverhill, Mass., Mar. 18, 1947; m. Arthur Benson II (div.). BS in English, Biology, U. Kans., 1969, MBA, 1985; MEd in English, U. Mo., Kansas City, 1976. Tchr. Shawnee Mission (Kans.) South High Sch., 1969-75, The Sunset Hill (Kans.) Sch., 1975-76; mem. Mo. House of Reps., Jefferson City, 1977-94; cons. govt. affairs Marion Labs., Kansas City, Mo., 1986-93; mem. US Congress from 5th Mo. Dist., Washington, 1995—2005. Rsch. analyst pub. fin. dept. Stearn Bros. & Co., 1984-85, Kansas City, Mo.; rsch. analyst Midwest Rsch. Inst., econs. and mgmt. scis. dept., Kansas City, 1985-86. Del. Dem. Nat. Conv., 1992, Dem. Nat. Party Conf., 1982, Dem. Nat. Policy Com. Policy Commn., 1985-86 Recipient Outstanding Young Woman Am. award, 1977, Outstanding Woman Mo. award Phi Chi Theta, Woman of Achievement award Mid-Continent Coun. Girl Scouts U.S., 1983, 87, Annie Baxter Leadership award, 1993; named Conservation Legislator of Yr., Conservation Fed. Mo., 1987. Fellow Inst. of Politics; mem. Nat. Inst. of Politics; mem. Nat. Conf. on State Legis. (del. on trade and econ. devel. to Fed. Republic of Germany, Bulgaria, Japan, France and Italy, mem. energy com. 1978-84, fed. taxation, trade and econ. devel. com. 1986, chmn. fed. budget and taxation com. 1987, vice chmn. state fed. assembly 1988, pres.-elect 1993, pres. 1994), Nat. Dem. Inst. for Internat. Affairs (instr. No. Ireland 1988, Baltic Republics 1992, Hungary 1993). Democrat. Roman Catholic. Home: Blue Springs, Mo. Died Oct. 5, 2010.

MCCHESNEY, KATHRYN MARIE, educator; b. Curwensville, Pa., Jan. 14, 1936; d. Orland William and Lillian Irene (Morrison) Spencer. BA, U. Akron, 1962; MLS, Kent State U., 1965, Postgrad., 1971—84. Tchr. English Springfield Local HS, Akron, Ohio, 1962—63, libr., 1963—64, head libr., 1965—68; asst. to dean, instr. Kent State U. Sch. Libr. Sci., 1968—69, asst. dean, 1969—77, asst. prof., from 1969. Co-author: The Library in Society, 1984; contbr. articles to profl. jours. Rep. Uniontown Cmty. Coun., 1964—66. Mem.: AAUP, Ohio Assns. Sch. Libr., Am., Ohio Libr. Assns., Sigma Phi Epsilon, Phi Alpha Theta, Phi Sigma Alpha, Beta Phi Mu. Home: Uniontown, Ohio. Died May 26, 2010.

MCCLANAHAN, RUE (EDDI-RUE MCCLANAHAN), actress; b. Healdton, Okla., Feb. 21, 1934; d. William Edwin and Dreda Rheua-Nell (Medaris) McC.; m. Tom Bish, 1958; 1 child, Mark Thomas Bish; m. Norman Hartweg; m. Peter DeMaio; m. Gus Fisher, 1976; m. Tom Keel, 1984 (div. 1985); m. Morrow Wilson, 1997. BA in German & Theatre Arts cum laude, U. Tulsa, 1956. Stage appearances include Lottice and Lovage, Vienna, 1993, Harvey (London); (Broadway) Jimmy Shine, 1968-69, Who's Happy Now?, 1969, Sticks and Bones, 1972, California Suite, 1977, After-Play, 1995, The Women, 2002, Wicked, 2005; (TV series) Another World, 1970-71, Where the Heart Is, 1971-72, Maude, 1973-78, Apple Pie, 1978, Mama's Family, 1982-84, Golden Girls, 1985-92, Golden Palace, 1992-93, Safe Harbor, 1999, Sordid Lives, 2008; (TV movies) Hogan's Goat, 1971, Having Babies III, 1978, Sgt. Matlowch vs. the U.S. Air Force, 1978, Rainbow, 1978, Topper, 1979, The Great American Traffic Jam, 1980, Word of Honor, 1981, The Day the Bubble Burst, 1982, The Little Match Girl, 1987, Liberace, 1988, Take My Daughters Please, 1988, Let Me Hear You Whisper, 1988, To the Heroes, 1989, After the Shock, 1990, Children of the Bride, 1990, To My Daughter, 1990, The Dreamer of Oz, 1990, Baby of the Bride, 1991, Mother of the Bride, 1993, Danielle Steele's Message from Nam, 1993, Burning Passion: The Margaret Mitchell Story, 1994, Nunsense, 1995, A Holiday to Remember, 1995, Columbo: Ashes to Ashes, 1998, Generation Gap, 2008; (TV appearances) Burke's Law, 1964, Love of Life,

1971, All in the Family, 1972, The ABC Afternoon Playbreak, 1973, Law & Order, 2009, Meet the Browns, 2009; (films) The Grass Eater, 1961, Five Minutes to Love, 1963, How to Succeed with Girls, 1964, Angel's Flight, 1965, Walk the Angry Beach, 1968, The People Next Door, 1970, They Might Be Giants, 1971, The Pursuit of Happiness, 1971, Some of My Best Friends Are, 1971, Modern Love, 1990, This World, Then the Fireworks, 1996, Dear God, 1996, Out to Sea, 1997, Rusty: A Dog's Tale, 1997, Starship Troopers, 1997, Border to Border, 1998, Columbo: Ashes to Ashes, 1998, A Saintly Switch, 1999, The Moving of Sophia Miles, 2000, (off-Broadway prodn.) The Vagina Monologues, 2001, (mini-series) Innocent Victims, 1995; author: (autobiography) My First Five Husbands...And the Ones Who Got Away, 2007 Recipient Obie award for leading off-Broadway role in Who's Happy Now, 1970; Emmy award Best Actress in a comedy, 1987; named Woman of Yr., Pasadena Playhouse, 1986; Spl. scholar Pasadena (Calif.) Playhouse, 1959, Phi Beta Gamma scholar, 1955. Mem. Actors Studio, Actors Equity Assn., AFTRA, Screen Actors Guild. Died June 3, 2010.

MCCLEERY, WINSTON THEODORE, information technology executive; b. Mobile, Ala., Sept. 6, 1935; s. Robert Alton and Theadora K. (Kiebel) McC.; m. Sandra Thoss, Dec. 28, 1958; children: Winston T., Jacqueline McCleery McNeely. BS, Springhill Coll., 1957; postgrad., U. Ala., 1957-58. Logic design engr. Autonetics N.Am. Aviation, Anaheim, Calif., 1960—65; dir. info. sys. Litton Industries, LA, 1965—69; founder, owner Winston T. McCleery, Cons., from 1969; pres., CEO Mgmt. Software Systems, Inc., Mobile, from 1979. Patentee in field. With U.S. Army, 1958-60. Recipient Cert. for Heroism, Boy Scouts Am., 1949, Collifontanum award, Spring Hill Coll., 2006. Mem. Data Processing Mgmt. Assn., Assn. Computer Machinery, Am. Mgmt. Assn., Ind. Computer Cons.'s Assn., Optimists (pres. 1972). Republican. Achievements include contributions to the design and development of the U.S. Army Field Artillery's first digital fire direction computer; member of design team of the centaur missile's guidance system that made the first soft landing on the moon; design and development of seamless, integrated, on-line and instant-time computer application system for main frame class computers; inventor computer power and temperature environment control system, development of automatic documentation system used to document computer programs written in the Cobol language. Home: Mobile, Ala. Died Mar. 26, 2010.

MC CLELLAN, CATHARINE, anthropologist, educator; b. York, Pa., Mar. 1, 1921; d. William Smith and Josephine (Niles) McClellan; m. John Thayer Hitchcock, June 6, 1974. AB magna cum laude in Classical Archaeology, Bryn Mawr Coll., 1942; PhD (Anthropology fellow), U. Calif., Berkeley, 1950. Vis. asst. prof. U. Mo. at Columbia, 1952; asst. prof. anthropology U. Wash., Seattle, 1952-56; anthrop. cons. USPHS, Arctic Health Research Center, Alaska, 1956; asst. prof. anthropology, chmn. dept. anthropology Barnard Coll., Columbia U., 1956-61; asso. prof. anthropology U. Wis. at Madison, 1961-65, prof., 1965-83, prof. emeritus, from 1983, John Bascom prof., 1973. Vis. lectr. Bryn Mawr (Pa.) Coll., 1954; vis. prof. U. Alaska, 1973, 87. Assoc. editor: Arctic Anthropology, 1961; editor, 1975-82; assoc. editor: The Western Canadian Jour. of Anthropology, 1970-73. Served to lt. WAVES, 1942-46. Margaret Snell fellow AAUW, 1950-51; Am. Acad. Arts and Scis. grantee, 1963-64, Nat. Mus. Can. grantee, 1948-74 Fellow Am. Anthrop. Assn., Royal Anthrop. Inst. Gt. Britain and Ireland, AAAS, Arctic Inst. N.Am.; mem. Am. Ethnol. Soc. (sec.-treas. 1958-59, v.p. 1964, pres. 1965), Kroeber Anthrop. Soc., Am. Folklore Soc., Am. Soc. Ethnohistory (exec. com. 1968-71), Sigma Xi. Achievements include research in archaeological and ethnographic field investigations in Alaska and Yukon Territory in Canada. Home: Peterborough, NH. Died Mar. 3, 2009.

MCCLELLAN, EDWIN, literature educator; b. Kobe, Japan, Oct. 24, 1925; came to U.S., 1952; s. Andrew and Teru (Yokobori) McC.; m. Rachel Elizabeth Pott, May 28, 1955; children: Andrew Lockwood, Sarah Rose. MA, U. St. Andrews, Scotland, 1952; PhD, U. Chgo., 1957. Instr. English, U. Chgo., 1957-59, asst. prof. Japanese lang. and lit., 1959-63, assoc. prof., 1963-65, prof., 1965-70, Carl Darling Buck prof., 1970-72, chmn. dept. Far Eastern langs. and civilizations, 1966-72; prof. Japanese lit. Yale U., New Haven, 1972-79, Sumitomo prof. Japanese studies, 1979-98, Sterling prof. Japanese lit., 1998-2000, Sterling prof. emeritus Japanese lit., from 2000, chmn. dept. East Asian langs. and lits. New Haven, 1973-82, 88-91, chmn. council humanities, 1975-77, chmn. council East Asian studies, 1979-82. Vis. lectr. Far Eastern langs. Harvard U., spring 1965; mem. adv. coun. dept. Oriental studies Princeton U., 1966-71; mem. Com. to Visit East Asian Studies, Harvard U., 1982-88; mem. Am. adv. com. Japan Found., 1985-95; mem. bd. Coun. for Internat. Exch. Scholars, 1981-84. Translator: Kokoro (Natsume Soseki), 1957, Grass on the Wayside (Soseki), 1969, A Dark Night's Passing (Naoya Shiga), 1976, Fragments of a Past (Eiji Yoshikawa), 1992; author: Two Japanese Novelists: Soseki and Toson, 1969, Woman in the Crested Kimono, 1985; mem. bd. editors Jour. Japanese Studies, 1986-99; contbr. articles to profl. jours. Liason intelligence officer Royal Air Force, Washington, 1945-47; bd. trustees Society Japanese Studies U. Wash., 1992-99. With Royal Air Force, 1944—48. Recipient Kikuchi Kan prize for contbn. to study of Japanese lit., Tokyo, 1994, Noma Lit. Translation prize, 1995, Order of the Rising Sun, Gold Rays with Neck Ribbon, Japanese Govt., 1998, Dist. Contributions to Asian Studies award Assn. Asian Studies, 2005 Fellow Am. Acad. Arts and Scis. Home: Belmont, Mass. Died Apr. 27, 2009.

MCCLURE, DONALD RAY, city official; b. Erlanger, Ky., Aug. 14, 1931; s. Howard and Anna McC.; m. Rosa Lee, Feb. 28, 1959; 1 child, Lyn BA, U. Ky., 1954; MS in Social Work, U. Tenn., 1956. Exec. dir. Mental Health Ctr., Owensboro, KY., 1960-64; dir. mental retardation Ky. Mental Health, Louisville, 1964; dir. instrl. services Ky. Dept. Child Welfare, Louisville, 1964-68; dir. dept. child services City of Jacksonville, Fla., 1968-71, dir. human resources Fla., 1971-79, chief adminstrv. officer Fla., from 1979. Active Boys Clubs Am.; mem. Gov.'s Task Force on Juvenile Justice and Delinquency Prevention; mem. Jacksonville Criminal Justice Adv. Council; bd. dirs. Child Guidance Clinic. Served to capt. USAF, 1956-59 Recipient medallion Boys Club, Jacksonville, 1977 Mem. Acad. Cert. Social Workers, Nat. Assn. Social Workers (Social Worker of Yr. N.E. Fla. chpt. 1974) Am. Pub. Welfare Assn., Am. Corrections Assn. Clubs: Optimist (v.p. 1969-70). Democrat. Baptist. Home: Jacksonville, Fla. Died June 25, 2009.

MCCLURE, GROVER BENJAMIN, management consultant; b. Houstonia, Mo., Oct. 15, 1918; s. Grover B. and Sue F. (Cook) McC. BA, U. Richmond, 1939. Pres. internat. div. Richardson-Merrell, NYC, 1954-62; pres. Europe and Africa divs. Paris, 1960-81; exec. v.p., dir. Richardson-Vicks, Inc., Wilton, Conn., 1981-85; cons. New Canaan, Conn., from 1985. Bd. dirs., chmn. emeritus Silvermine Art Guild. Served to lt. comdr. USNR, 1941-46. Mem. Silver Springs Club (Ridgefield, Conn.). Republican. Presbyterian. Avocations: tennis, golf, travel, yachting. Home: Redding, Conn. Died June 9, 2009.

MCCLURE, RICHARD FOWLER, furniture company executive; b. Shamokin, Pa., Nov. 8, 1927; s. James Focht and Florence (Fowler) M.C.; m. Dorothy Ann Laity, Jan. 1, 1955; children— Richard Fowler, Thomas Murray. BS in Engring, U. Mich., 1949; MBA, U. Pa., 1951. Mktg. mgr. RCA, 1953-58; v.p. marketing Lewisburg Chair & Furniture Co., 1958-64; pres. Lewisburg div., v.p. Gen. Interior Corp., NYC, 1964-70, pres., chief exec. officer corp., 1970-72; also dir.; pres., chief exec. officer McClure Furniture Industries, Lewisburg, Pa., 1972-81; pres. McClure & Co., Lewisburg, MARC Internat., Balt., 1993. Dir. First Nat. Trust Bank, Sunbury, Pa. Bd. dirs. W.D. Himmelreich Meml. Library, Lewisburg, Pa., 1960—, pres., 1960-66; bd. dirs. Evang. Community Hosp., Lewisburg. Served to 1st lt. USAF, 1951-53. Mem. Nat. Assn. Furniture Mfrs. (v.p. 1970, pres. 1972-73, dir.), Aircraft Owners and Pilots Assn., Tex. Blockhouse Hunting and Fishing Lodge, Sigma Chi. Clubs: Bucknell University Golf. Republican. Presbyterian. Home: Lewisburg, Pa. Died Aug. 19, 2010.

MC CLUSKY, MILDRED B., die casting company consultant; b. Solvay, NY, Sept. 22, 1922; d. Ben and Anna (Rychter) Kazel; m. Benny Mc Clusky, May 2, 1942 (dec. Nov. 1963); 1 child, Adam. Insp. Frazier & Jones, Solvay, NY, 1940—42; head insp. Easy Washer, Syracuse, 1942—45; office mgr. and bookkeeper Syracuse Die Casting & Mfg. Co., Inc., 1950—62, pres. and CEO, 1963—77, cons., from 1977. Mem.: Soc. Die Casting Engrs., Syracuse C. of C. Roman Catholic. Home: Hilton Head Island, SC. Died June 8, 2010.

MCCOLLUM, CLIFFORD GLENN, college dean emeritus; b. South Gifford, Mo., May 12, 1919; s. William Henry and Aultie V. (Westfall) McC.; m. Alice Elizabeth Erickson, Aug. 18, 1940; children: Eric Edward, Lisa Buren. Student, Central Coll., 1935-37; BS, U. Mo., 1939, MA, 1947, EdD, 1949. Tchr. pub. schs., Monett, Mo., 1938-39, Poplar Bluff, Mo., 1939-41, Boonville, Mo., 1941-42; asst. prof. sci. U. No. Iowa, 1949-55, assoc. prof., 1956-59, prof., 1959-84, prof. emeritus, from 1984, head dept. sci., 1957-68; dean U. No. Iowa (Coll. Natural Scis.), 1968-84, dean emeritus, 1984—2010. Prof. State U. N.Y. at Oneonta, 1955-56; Dir., instl. rep. Central States Univs., Inc.; cons. Coronet Instrnl. Films; cons. on sci. curricula to pub. schs. and colls.; speaker in field. Contbr. articles to profl. jours. Served with USAAF, 1943-46. Sci. Bldg. at U. Norther Iowa named in his honor, upon retirement. Fellow AAAS (nat. committeeman 1964-67), Iowa Acad. Sci. (pres. 1979-80); mem. Am. Inst. Biol. Scis., Nat. Assn. Biology Tchrs. (regional dir. 1963-65), Nat. Assn. Research in Sci. Teaching, Nat. Sci. Tchrs. Assn., Sigma Xi, Phi Delta Kappa. Home: Kansas City, Mo. Died May 4, 2010.

MCCOLLUM, JAMES FOUNTAIN, lawyer; b. Reidsville, NC, Mar. 24, 1946; s. James F. and Dell (Frazier) McC.; m. Susan Shasek, Apr. 26, 1969; children: Audra McCollum Bowers, Amy McCollum Sullivan. BS, Fla. Atlantic U., Boca Raton, 1968; JD, Fla. State U., Tallahassee, 1972. Bar: US Ct. Appeals (5th cir.) 1973, Fla. 1972, US Ct. Appeals (11th cir.) 1982, US Supreme Ct. 2006. Assoc. Kennedy & McCollum, 1972-73; prin. McCollum & Rinaldo, PA, 1973-77, McCollum & Oberhausen, PA, 1977-80, McCollum, Oberhausen & Tuck, LLP (and predecessor firm), Sebring, Fla., from 1977. Bd. dirs. Comml. Bancorp, Inc., Comml. Bank Highlands County; pres. Highlands Devel. Concepts, Inc., Sebring, 1982—; sec. Focus Broadcast Comm., Inc., Sebring, 1982-87; mng. ptnr. Highlands Investment Service; pres. Am. Svc. Title & Escrow, Inc., 2001— Treas. Highlands County chpt. ARC, 1973-76; vestryman St. Agnes Episcopal Ch., 1973—, chancellor, 1978—; mem. Fla. Sch. Bd. Atty.'s Assn., 1974-2001, bd. dirs., 1989-97, pres., 1995-96; mem. Com. 100 of Highlands County, 1975-83, bd. dirs., 1985-87, chmn., 1991-92; chmn. Highlands County High Speed Rail Task Force; chmn. bd., treas. Ctrl. Fla. Racing Assn., 1976-78; chmn. Leadership Sebring: life mem., past pres. Highlands Little Theatre, Inc.; bd. dirs. Palms of Sebring Nursing Home, 1988-90, Palms Estate Mobile Home Park, Sebring Airport Authority, 1988-90, treas., 1988, chmn. indsl. com., 1988, vice-chmn., 1989-90, chmn., 1990-91, Highlands County High Speed Rail Task Force, 1986-89, Highlands County Family YMCA, 1985-93, pres. Sebring br., 1992-93, chmn. bldg. com., 1992-94, Good Shepherd Hospice, Inc., v.p., 2000—, chmn. bd. dirs., 2003-05, Primal Connection, Inc., 2006—; commr. Sebring Redevel. Agy., 2006—, chmn. March Dimes Celebrity Chef's Auction, 2010; campaign chmn. Jeb Bush for Gov., Highlands County, 1994, 1998, 2002, George W. Bush for President, 2000, 04. Recipient ARC citation, 1974, Presdl. award of appreciation Fla. Jaycees, 1980-82, 85, Outstanding Svc. award Highlands Coun. of 100, 1988, Most Valuable Player award Highlands Little Theatre, Inc., 1986, Zenon Significant Achievement award, 1991, Best Set award, 2002; named Jaycee of Year, Sebring Jaycees, 1981, Outstanding Local Chpt. Pres., US Jaycees, 1977, Citizen of Yr., United Way Ctrl. Fla., 2004, Highlands Counties Best Lawyer, Highlands Today and News Sun newspapers, 2003, 05, 06, 07, 08, 09, 10 Mem. ABA, ATLA, Comml. Law League Am., Am. Arbitration Assn. (comml. arbitration panel), Nat. Assn. Retail Credit Attys., Fla. Bar (jour. com.), Highlands County Bar Assn. (past chmn. legal aid com.), Fla. Sch. Bd. Attys. Assn. (bd. dirs. 1989-97, v.p. 1993-94, pres. 1994-95), Greater Sebring C. of C. (dir. 1982-89, pres. 1986-87, chmn. transp. com. 1986—, Most Valuable Dir. award 1986-87), Fla. Jaycees (life, internat. senate 1977—), Lions (bd. dirs. 1972-73, v.p. 1994-95, Disting. award 1984). Republican. Episcopalian. Home: Sebring, Fla. Died Aug. 14, 2010.

MCCOLLUM, ROBERT WAYNE, epidemiologist, educator; b. Waco, Tex., Jan. 29, 1925; s. Robert Wayne and Minnie (Brown) McC.; m. Audrey Talmage, Oct. 16, 1954; children: Cynthia, Douglas Scott. AB, Baylor U., 1945; MD, Johns Hopkins, 1948; DPH, London Sch. Hygiene and Tropical Medicine, 1958; MA (hon.), Yale U., 1965, Dartmouth Coll., 1985. Intern in pathology Columbia-Presbyn. Med. Center, NYC, 1948-49; intern in internal medicine Vanderbilt Hosp., Nashville, 1949-50; asst. resident in internal medicine Yale-New Haven Med. Center, 1950-51; faculty Yale Sch. Medicine, 1951-81, prof. epidemiology, 1965-81, chmn. dept. epidemiology and public health, 1969-81; dean Sch. Medicine Dartmouth Coll., Hanover, NH, 1982-90, prof. epidemiology, 1982-95, dean emeritus, 1990—2010, prof. emeritus, 1995—2010. Assoc. physician Yale-New Haven Hosp., 1954-82; v.p. Dartmouth-Hitchcock Med. Ctr., 1983-90, acting v.p. for devel., 1999; cons. WHO, 1962-79 Contbr. articles on epidemiology and control infectious diseases to profl. jours. Bd. sci. advisers Merck Inst., 1981-85; trustee Mary Hitchcock Meml. Hosp., Hanover, 1982-90. Capt. M.C., AUS, 1952-54. Mem. Assn. Tchrs. Preventive Medicine, American Epidemiological Soc., Internat. Epidemiological Assn., Infectious Diseases Soc. America, Conn. Acad. Sci. & Engring., American Coll. Epidemiology Died Sept. 13, 2010.

MCCONNELL, ROB (ROBERT MURRAY GORDON MCCONNELL), jazz musician, composer; b. London, Ont., Can., Feb. 14, 1935; Doctorate (hon.), St. Francis Xavier U., Nova Scotia, Can. Mem. The Boss Brass, 1968—97. Mem. faculty staff, head of the profl. instrumental program Grove Sch. Music, Van Nuys, Calif., from 1988. Recs. All in Good Time (Grammy award for Best Big Band Album of Yr., 1984), Brassy & Sassy, Overtime, Don't Get Around Much Anymore, Mel Tormeé-Rob McConnell and The Boss Brass, Trio Sketches, Our 25th Year, The Brass is Back, Mutual Street, Sabia, 1990, Overtime, 1994, Rob McConnell & The Boss Brass, 1995. Recipient 4 Juno awards, Toronto Musician's award, 1994; named Best Arranger Nat. Assn. Jazz Educators; nominee 7 Juno nominations. Died May 1, 2010.

MCCONNIN, ROBERT ANTHONY, editor; b. Bklyn., May 16, 1931; s. Edward Henry and Gertrude Lucille (Costello) McC. B.S., NYU, 1956, M.A., 1959. Cert. sci. tchr., prin., N.Y. Tchr., Central High Sch. Dist. 3, Merrick, N.Y., 1956-67; salesman John Wiley & Sons, N.Y.C., 1967-71, mktg. mgr., 1971-77, physics editor, 1977—. Producer leading coll. text by Halliday & Resnick. Sec., treas. Nassau Approved Umpires Assn., 1951—. Served with U.S. Army, 1952-58. Mem. Nat. Sci. Tchrs. Assn., N.Y. Acad. Sci., Am. Assn. Physics Tchrs., N.Y. Alumni Fedn. (treas. 1984—). Democrat. Roman Catholic. Avocation: umpire high sch. baseball. Home: Wantagh, NY. Died Sept. 12, 2009.

MC CORMICK, THOMAS FRANCIS, printing company executive; b. Gardner, Mass., Feb. 20, 1929; s. Harold J. and Florence R. (Mailloux) McC.; m. Beverly G. Acey, Nov. 28, 1953; children— Stephen, Harold, Laura, Ann. BS cum laude, Holy Cross Coll., Worcester, Mass., 1950. With Gen. Electric Co., 1953-73, financial analyst, adminstrv. asst. to group v.p. indsl. group NYC, 1965-67; gen. mgr., treas. Maqua Co., Schenectady, 1967-72; mgr. power generation strategy devel. NYC, 1972-73; pub. printer of U.S., Washington, 1973-77; pres. Telegraph Press Inc., Harrisburg, Pa., 1978-85, Crest Litho, Inc., Albany, N.Y., from 1986. Served to lt. (j.g.) USNR, 1950-53. Home: Caroga Lake, NY. Died Mar. 20, 2009.

MCCOY, JOHN GARDNER, retired bank executive; b. Marietta, Ohio, Jan. 30, 1913; s. John Hall and Florence (Buchanan) McC.; m. Jeanne N. Bonnet, Jan. 4, 1941 (dec. 2006); children: John Bonnet, Virginia B. Fickle. AB, Marietta Coll., 1935; MBA, Stanford, 1937; LL.D. (hon.), Kenyon Coll., 1970, Marietta Coll., 1981. With City Nat. Bank & Trust Co. (now Bank One of Columbus), Columbus, 1937-84, v.p., 1946-58, chmn., pres., CEO, 1959-77; pres., vice chmn., CEO Banc One Corp., 1966-84. Trustee Marietta Coll. Recipient Ernest C. Arbuckle award Stanford Bus. Sch., 1986 Mem. Assn. Bank Holding Cos. (past pres.) Clubs: Columbus, Columbus Country, Muirfield Golf, Golf, Wequetonsing (Mich.) Golf, Little Harbor (Harbor Springs, Mich.), Royal Poinciana Golf (Naples, Fla.), Hole In-the-Wall Golf (Naples, Fla.), Naples Yacht (Naples, Fla.). Episcopalian. Home: New Albany, Ohio. Died Apr. 4, 2010.

MCCRARY, EUGENIA LESTER (MRS. DENNIS DAUGHTRY MCCRARY), civic worker, writer; b. Annapolis, Md., Mar. 23, 1929; d. John Campbell and Eugenia (Potts) Lester; m. John Campbell Howard, July 15, 1955 (dec. Sept. 1965); m. Dennis Daughtry McCrary, June 28, 1969; 1 child, Dennis Campbell. AB cum laude, Radcliffe Coll.-Harvard U., 1950; MA, Johns Hopkins U., 1952; postgrad., Harvard U., 1953, Pa. State U., 1953—54, Drew U., 1957—58, Inst. Study of USSR, Munich, 1964. Grad. asst. dept. Romance langs. Pa. State U., 1953—54; tchr. dept. math. The Brearley Sch., NYC, 1954—57; dir. Sch. Langs., Inc., Summit, NJ, 1958—69, trustee, 1960—69. Co-author: Nom de Plume: Eugenia Campbell Lester, (with Allegra Branson) Frontiers Aflame, 1987;

film script adaptation (with John Gallagher) Frontier, 1998. Dist. dir. Ea. Pa. and NJ auditions Met. Opera Nat. Coun., NYC, 1960-66, dist. dir. publicity, 1966-67, nat. vice chmn. publicity, 1967-71, nat. chmn. public rels., 1972-75, hon. nat. chmn. pub. rels., 1976-99; bd. govs., chmn. Van Cortlandt House Mus., 1985-90 Mem. Nat. Soc. Colonial Dames Am. (bd. mgrs. NY 1985-90), Met. Opera Nat. Coun., Soc. Mayflower Descs. (former bd. dirs. NY soc., chmn. house com. 1986-89), Soc. Daus. Holland Dames (bd. dirs. 1982-87, 96—, 3d directress gen. 1987-92, directress gen. 1992-96), L'Eglise du St.-Esprit (vestry 1985-88, sr. warden 1988-90), Huguenot Soc. Am. (governing coun. 1984-90, 2000-03, 2004-05, asst. treas. 1990-91, sec. 1991-95, 2d v.p. 1995-2000), Colonial Dames Am., Daus. of Cin., Colony Club (bd. govs. 1988-96), Causeries du Lundi, The Hereditary Order Descendants of Colonial Govs. Republican. Episcopalian. Home: New York, NY. Died Jan. 8, 2010.

MC CRORY, WALLACE WILLARD, pediatrician, educator; b. Racine, Wis., Jan. 19, 1920; s. Willard L. and Beulah (St. Clair) McC.; m. Sylvia E. Hogben, Feb. 6, 1943; children— Pamela, Michael, Christine. BS, U. Wis., 1941, MD, 1944. Diplomate: Am. Bd. Pediatrics. Rotating intern Phila. Gen. Hosp., 1944-45; resident pediatrics Children's Hosp., Phila., 1945-46, chief resident physician, 1948-49, asso. pediatrician, 1953-55, sr. pediatrician, 1955-58; provisional asst. pediatrician to out-patients, Lewis Cass Ledyard, Jr. fellow pediatrics N.Y. Hosp., 1949-50, pediatrician-in-chief, 1961-80, sr. pediatrician, chief pediatric nephrology, from 1980. Chief pediatric service Univ. Hosp., Iowa City, 1958-61; instr. pathology U. Wis. Med. Sch., 1942-43; instr. pediatrics U. Pa. Sch. Medicine, 1948-49, instr., research fellow pediatrics, 1950-53, asst. prof., 1953-55, asso. prof., 1955-58; prof. pediatrics, chmn. dept. State U. Iowa Coll. Medicine, 1958-61; prof. pediatrics Cornell U. Med. Coll., 1961— Pres. Nat. Kidney Found., 1964-66. Served to capt., M.C. AUS, 1946-48. Fellow N.Y. Acad. Medicine, Royal Soc. Medicine; mem. Am. Pediatric Soc., Am. Acad. Pediatrics, Soc. Pediatric Research, Am. Soc. Nephrology, Am. Soc. Pediatric Nephrology, AAAS, Sigma Xi, Alpha Omega Alpha. Home: Clarksburg, NJ. Died Aug. 20, 2009.

MCCURDY, GILBERT GEIER, retired retail executive; b. Rochester, NY, May 25, 1922; s. Gilbert J.C. and Virginia (Geier) McC.; m. Katherine W. Babcock, Nov. 9, 1946; children— Gilbert Kennedy, Lynda Babcock (Mrs. Hotra). BA, Williams Coll., 1944. With McCurdy & Co., Inc., Rochester, from 1946, controller, asst. treas., 1953-55, v.p., 1956-59, exec. v.p., 1959-62, pres., gen. mgr., 1962-80, chief exec. officer, 1969-80, chmn. bd., chief exec. officer, 1980-92, chmn. exec. com. of bd., from 1993. Chmn. bd. Frederick Atkins, 1968-70. Bd. dirs. Pathway Houses of Rochester, Boys and Girls Club, Rochester; former mem. bd. dirs. United Way of Greater Rochester; life trustee U. Rochester. 1st lt. Signal Corps AUS, 1943—46. Mem. Rochester C. of C. (pres. 1975) Baptist. Home: Pittsford, NY. Died Feb. 16, 2010.

MCDANIEL, JOHN NOBLE, university dean; b. Washington, Jan. 30, 1941; s. Noble Ashby and Emily (Robb) McDaniel; m. Jean Smart, Aug. 26, 1967; children: Scott Noble, Craig Thomas. BA, Hampden-Sydney Coll., 1963; MAT, Johns Hopkins U., 1964; PhD, Fla. State U., 1972. Asst. prof. to prof. Mid. Tenn. State U., Murfreesboro, 1970—84, chmn. dept. English, 1978—84, dean liberal arts, from 1984. Author: The Fiction of Philip Roth, 1974; translator: The History of Folklore in Europe, 1981; contbr. articles to profl. jours. Mem.: Tenn. Coun. Tchrs. English, Tenn. Coun. Arts and Scis. (treas.), Southeastern Conf. Linguistics, South Atlantic Modern Lang. Assn., Tenn. Coll. English Assn. Home: Murfreesboro, Tenn. Died May 3, 2010.

MCDANIEL, MYRA ATWELL, lawyer, former state official; b. Phila., Dec. 13, 1932; d. Eva Lucinda (Yores) Atwell; m. Reuben Roosevelt McDaniel Jr., Feb. 20, 1955; children: Diane Lorraine, Reuben Roosevelt III. BA, U. Pa., 1954; JD, U. Tex., 1975; LLD, Huston-Tillotson Coll., 1984, Jarvis Christian Coll., 1986. Bar: Tex. 1975, U.S. Dist. Ct. (we. dist.) Tex. 1977, U.S. Dist. Ct. (so. and no. dists.) Tex. 1978, U.S. Ct. Appeals (5th cir.) 1978, U.S. Supreme Ct. 1978, U.S. Dist. Ct. (ea. dist.) Tex. 1979. Asst atty. gen. State of Tex., Austin, 1975-81, chief taxation div., 1979-81, gen. counsel to gov., 1983-84, sec. of state, 1984-87; asst. gen. counsel Tex. R.R. Commn., Austin, 1981-82; gen. counsel Wilson Cos., San Antonio and Midland, Tex., 1982; assoc. Bickerstaff, Heath & Smiley, Austin, 1984, ptnr., 1987-96; mng. ptnr. Bickerstaff, Heath, Smiley, Pollan, Kever & McDaniel, Austin, Tex., 1996—2000, of counsel, 2003, Bickerstaff, Heath, Delgado, Acosta LLP, Austin, Tex., 2007. Mem. asset. mgmt. adv. com. State Treasury, Austin, 1984-86; mem. legal affairs com. Criminal Justice Policy Coun., Austin, 1984-8, Inter-State Oil Compact, Oklahoma City, 1984-86; bd. dirs. Austin Cons. Group, 1983-86; mem. Jud. Efficiency Coun., Austin, 1995-96; lectr. in field. Contbr. articles to profl. jours., chpts. to books Del. Tex. Conf. on Librs. and Info. Sci., Austin, 1978, White House Conf. on Librs. and Info. Scis., Washington, 1979; mem. Libr. Svcs. and Constrn. Act Adv. Coun., 1980-84, chmn., 1983-84; mem. long range plan task force Brackenridge Hosp., Austin, 1981; clk. vestry bd. St. James Episcopal Ch., Austin, 1981-83, 89-90; bd. visitors U. Tex. Law Sch., 1983-87, vice chmn., 1983-85; bd. dirs. Friends of Ronald McDonald House Ctrl. Tex., Women's Advocacy, Inc., Capital Area Rehab. Ctr.; trustee Episcopal Found. Tex., 1986-89, St. Edward's U., Austin, 1986—, chmn. acad. com., 1988-2002, vice chair, 2002-04, chmn. 2004-2010; chmn. divsn. capital area campaign United Way, 1986; active nat. adv. bd. Leadership Am.; trustee Episcopal Sem. S.W., 1990-96, Assn. Governing Bds. Univs. and Colls., Leadership Edn. Arts Program, 1995-2004; adv. bd. mem. Women Basketball Coaches Assn., 1996-99; bd. dirs. U.Tex. Law Sch. Found., 1997-98, Wells Fargo Cmty. Bd., Ctrl. Tex., 2000-03; trustee Episcopal Health Charities, 1997-2010. Recipient Tribute to 28 Black Women award Concepts Unltd., 1983; Focus on women honoree Serwa Yetu chpt. Mt. Olive grand chpt. Order of Eastern Star, 1979, Woman of Yr. Longview Metro C. of C., 1985, Woman of Yr. Austin chpt. Internat. Tng. in Communication, 1985, Citizen of Yr. Epsilon Iona chpt. Omega Psi Phi, Lone Star Girl Scout Coun. Women of Distinction, 1997, Profiles in Power Austin Bus. Jour., 1999, Silent Samaritan award Samaritan Counseling Ctr., 2000, Sandra Day O'Connor award Tex. Ctr. Legal Ethics professionalism, 2006. Master Inns of Ct.; mem. ABA, Am. Bar Found., Tex. Bar Found. (trustee 1986-89), Travis County Bar Assn., Travis County Women Lawyers' Assn., Austin Black Lawyers Assn., State Bar Tex. (chmn. Profl. Efficiency & Econ. Rsch. subcom. 1976-84), Golden Key Nat. Honor Soc., Longhorn Assocs. for Excellence in Women's Athletes (adv. coun. 1988-2010), Order of Coif (hon. mem.), Omicron Delta Kappa, Delta Phi Alpha. Democrat. Home: Austin, Tex. Died Feb. 25, 2010.

MCDONALD, FRANCIS JAMES, retired automotive executive; b. Saginaw, Mich., Aug. 3, 1922; s. Francis J. and Mary C. (Fordney) McD.; m. Betty Ann Dettenthaler, Dec. 27, 1944; children: Timothy Joseph, John Thomas, Marybeth McDonald Pallas. BS, Gen. Motors Inst., 1944. With Gen. Motors Corp., Detroit, from 1940, plant mgr. central foundry div., 1955-56, works mgr., Detroit transmission div., 1956-63, gen. mgr. Hydra-Matic div., 1963-65, works mgr. Pontiac Motor div., 1965-68, dir. mfg. ops. Chevrolet Motor div., 1968-69, corp. v.p., gen. mgr. Pontiac Motor div., 1969-72, corp. v.p., gen. mgr. Chevrolet Motor div., 1972-74, exec. v.p. Detroit, 1974-81, pres., COO, 1981-87. Dir., mem. exec. compensation and audit coms. H.J. Heinz Co.; mem.-at-large Oakland County Traffic Improvement Assn. Chmn. Research Inst., William Beaumont Hosp., Royal Oak, Mich., 1973-76, trustee, adv. bd. Troy (Mich.) br.; v.p. Boys Clubs Met. Detrot; bd. dirs. Up with People; chmn. bd. visitors Sch. Econs. and Mgmt., Oakland U., Rochester. Served to lt. (j.g.) USN, 1944-46. Mem. Soc. Automotive Engrs., Engring. Soc. Detroit, Tau Beta Pi. Clubs: Detroit Athletic. Home: Bloomfield Hills, Mich. Died June 13, 2010.

MCDONALD, PATRICIA ANNE, professional society executive; b. Detroit, Mar. 16, 1947; d. William and Esther Carpenter (Rodger) McD. Student, Eastern Mich. U., 1965-68, Wayne State U., 1970-71, U. Mich., 1983. Cert. social worker, Mich. Caseworker State Mich., Detroit, 1968-69; counselor City Detroit Health Dept., 1970-75; psychotherapist The Life Ctr., Ferndale, Mich., 1975-79; field rep. Nat. Multiple Sclerosis Soc., Southfield, Mich., 1979-80, dir. svcs., 1980-83, pres., from 1983. Bd. dirs. Metro Crisis Pregnancy Ctr., Detroit, 1995—, sec., 1999; bd. dirs. Housing Alternatives Inc., Lansing, Mich., 1984-89; svc. cons. Nat. Multiple Sclerosis Soc., N.Y.C., 1981-82, others. Coun. mem. Judson Ctr., Royal Oak, Mich., 1991—. Recipient The Americans with Disabilities Act award, Washington, 1990, Exec. of the Yr. award United Way of Detroit, 1995. Mem. Coun. Exec. Officers (sec. 1988-89). Roman Catholic. Avocations: bicycling, reading, gardening, swimming. Home: Rochester, NY. Died Jan. 4, 2009.

MCDOWELL, CHARLES RICE, retired journalist; b. Danville, Ky., June 24, 1926; s. Charles Rice McDowell & Catherine Frazier (Freland) M.; m. Ann Webb, Apr. 26, 1952. BA, Washington & Lee U., 1948; MS in Journalism, Columbia U., 1949; LHD (hon.), Washington Lee U., 1975; degree (hon.), Centre Coll. With Richmond (Va.) Times-Dispatch, 1949-65, Washington corr., columnist, 1965-98; lectr., freelance writer, moderator Va. Pub. TV, 1998—2010. Panelist PBS Washington Week in Review, 1977-96. Author: One Thing After Another, 1960, What Did You Have in Mind?, 1963, Campaign Fever, 1965; author: (with others) Beyond Reagan, 1986; writer, narrator (documentary) Summer of Judgment, 1983, 84; voices (TV series) The Civil War, 1990, Baseball, 1994; commentator weekly TV series The Lawmakers; contbr. articles to profl. jours. Past chmn. Standing Com. Corrs. Recipient Burkett Miller Presdl. award White-Burkett Miller Ctr. Pub. Affairs at U. Va., 1984, Fourth Estate award for lifetime achievement as a journalist, 1996; named to Soc. Profl. Journalists' Washington Hall of Fame, 1992. Mem. Gridiron Club (past pres.). Died Nov. 5, 2010.

MC DOWELL, JOHN BERNARD, bishop emeritus; b. New Castle, Pa., July 17, 1921; s. Bernard A. and Louise M. (Hannon) Mc Dowell. BA, St. Vincent Coll., 1942, MA, 1944, Catholic U. Am., 1950, PhD, 1952; LittD (hon.), Duquesne U., 1962; grad., St. Vincent Sem., Latrobe, Pa. Ordained priest Diocese of Pitts., 1945; asst. pastor St. Irenaeus Ch., Oakmont, 1945-49; asst. supt. schs. Diocese of Pitts., 1952-55, supt. schs., 1955-70; vicar gen.; pastor Epiphany Parish, Pitts., 1969-96; ordained bishop, 1966; aux. bishop Diocese of Pitts., 1966—96, vicar for edn., 1970-85, aux. bishop emeritus, 1996—2010. Papal chamberlain to Pope Pius XII, 1956, to Pope John XXIII, 1958; domestic prelate to Pope Paul VI, 1964; chmn. ad hoc com. on moral values in our soc. Nat. Conf. Cath. Bishops, from 1973, Bishops Com. for Pastoral on Moral Values, from 1976; mem. Internat. Council for Catechesis, from 1975 Author: Water, Death and Grace: The Life of Hugh C. Boyle, 6th Bishop of Diocese of Pittsburgh, 1999, Catholic Schools, Public Education, and American Culture, 2000, Giants Were On the Earth in Those Days, The Life of John Francis Regis Canevin, 5th Bishop, Diocese of Pittsburgh, 2000, Blessed Are the Poor in Spirit, For Theirs is the Kingdom of Heaven, the Life of Vincent Martin Leonard, the 9th Bishop of Diocese of Pittsburgh, 2001, I Am Going To Tell You A Mystery, the life of the fourth Bishop, Diocese of Pitts., 2002, To Dwell in the House of the Lord All the Days of My Life, the life of Father Charles Bonaventure Maguire, O.F.M., 2003, Reflections on the Life of John Cardinal Wright, S.T.D. Eighth Bishop of Pittsburgh, 2003; co-author: elem. sch. religions series, JHS lit. series, elem. sci. series and elem. reading series; contbr. ednl. articles to various publs.; former editor: Cath. Educator Mag. Bd. dir. Allegheny County Community Coll.; bd. dir. Western Pa. Safety Council, Duquesne U. Named Man of Yr. in Religion Pitts., 1970, 93, Educator of Yr., United Pvt. Acad. Schs. Assn., 1978, Man of Yr., Pitts. chpt. KC, 1989. Mem. Nat. Cath. Ednl. Assn., Cath. Ednl. Assn. Pa., Omicron Delta Kappa Gamma Circle (hon.) Roman Catholic. Home: Allison Park, Pa. Died Feb. 25, 2010.

MCEACHRON, KARL BOYER, JR., retired university official; b. Ada, Ohio, June 27, 1915; s. Karl Boyer and Leila Emily (Honsinger) McEachron; m. Marjorie Blalock, Mar. 20, 1937; children: Norman Bruce, Lawrence Karl, Linda Louise, Donald Lynn. BS in Elec. Engring., Purdue U., 1937. With Gen. Electric Co., 1937—55, project engr., 1952—55; mem. faculty Case Inst. Tech., 1955—57, dean instrn., 1957—64, vice provost, 1964—67; dean Case Inst. Tech. Case Western Res. U., Cleve., 1967—72, dir. admissions and fin. aid, 1972—74, dean undergrad. affairs, 1974—80. Contbr. articles to profl. jours. Named Disting. Alumnus, Purdue U., 1964. Fellow: IEEE (chmn. edn. com. 1959—61, chmn. Cleve. chpt. 1961—62); mem.: Cleve. Soc. Profl. Engrs. (pres. 1975—76), Nat. Soc. Profl. Engrs., Engrs. Coun. Profl. Devel. (com. edn. and accreditation 1956—61, exec. com. 1964—65), Am. Soc. Engring. Edn. (v.p. 1967—69), Eta Kappa Nu, Tau Beta Pi, Sigma Xi. Republican. Methodist. Died Jan. 23, 2010.

MCFARLAND, NORMAN FRANCIS, bishop; b. Martinez, Calif., Feb. 21, 1922; Attended, St. Patrick's Sem. Ordained to ministry Cath. Ch., 1946, consecrated bishop Cath. Ch., 1970. Ordained priest Archdiocese of San Francisco, 1946, aux. bishop, 1970—74; ordained bishop, 1970; apostolic adminstr. Diocese of Reno, 1974—76; bishop Diocese of Reno-Las Vegas, 1976—87, Diocese of Orange, Calif., 1987—98, bishop emeritus, 1998—2010. Roman Catholic. Died Apr. 16, 2010.

MCGAHEY, JOHN PATRICK, lawyer; b. Toledo, Mar. 29, 1941; s. Edwin Patrick and Ann Lillian (Liner) McGahey; m. Kathleen C. Hanley, June 25, 1966; children: Mary K., John P. Jr., Kevin P. AB, Marquette U., 1963; JD, Northwestern U., Ill., 1966. Bar: US Dist. Ct. (no. dist.) Ill. 1967, US Ct. Appeals (7th cir.) 1969. Ptnr. Wilson, Elser, Moskowitz, Edelman & Dicker. Mem.: KC, Northwest Suburban Bar Assn. Chgo. Athletic Assn., Ill. Bar Assn., Chgo. Bar Assn., Plum Grove Club, Oak Park Club. Republican. Roman Catholic. Home: Palatine, Ill. Died Feb. 14, 2010.

MCGARRAHAN, JOHN GOLDEN, lawyer; b. Boston, Feb. 28, 1937; s. Owen Joseph and Ellen Catharine (Golden) McGarrahan; m. Margaret Devon Gatheral, Dec. 29, 1960; children: Sabina, Ellen, Sarah. AB, Harvard U., 1960; LLB cum laude, 1963. Bar: NY, NY (U.S. Dist. Ct. (so. and ea. dists.)), (U.S. Ct. Apls. (2d cir.)), (U.S. Sup. Ct.). Assoc. Casey, Lane & Mittendorf, 1963—67; asst. Mayor City of NY, 1967—70; sole practice NYC, 1970—73; ptnr. McGarrahan & Heard, NYC, from 1973; counsel N.Y. State Senate Com. on Housing and Urban Devel., 1973—76; mem. adv. com. N.Y. State Council on Architecture, 1974—75; mem. Real Estate Bd. NY, from 1981. With US Army, 1956—58. Mem.: ABA, Assn. Bar City N.Y., N.Y. State Bar Assn. Died July 19, 2009.

MCGEE, GEORGE WILLIAM, farmer; b. Logan County, Ill., Apr. 12, 1921; s. William Roy and Maurine Ellen (Lucas) McGee; m. Gloria Faye Lewis, Sept. 7, 1947 (dec. 1982); children: Mark William, Sara Faye. Farmer, Mt. Pulaski, Ill., from 1940; part-owner, operator cash grain farm, from 1953. Dir. 1st Nat. Bank Mt. Pulaski. Active mem. Mt. Pulaski Sch. Bd., 1956—67, Logan County Extension Coun., 1978—80; pres. Mt. Pulaski Sch. Bd., 1965—66. Mem.: Ill. Corn Growers Assn., Land Lincoln Soybean Assn., Logan County Farm Bur. (dir. 1969—78), Shriners Club, Masons Club. Died Feb. 28, 2009.

MCGINN, PETER VINCENT, psychologist, health care executive; b. NYC, July 15, 1948; s. Vincent Edward and Alice Bolton (Mundorff) McG.; m. Marilyn Clare Ricchiuti, Aug. 22, 1970; children: Kathryn Clare, Kerry Elizabeth. BA, Johns Hopkins U., 1970, MA, 1975, PhD, 1976; MS, Pa. State U., 1971. Cons. psychologist RHR Internat., Southfield, Mich., 1980-82, NYC, 1983-85; v.p. human resources United Health Svcs., Binghamton, N.Y., 1985-90, sr. v.p. mgmt. svcs., 1993-95, exec. v.p., from 1995; v.p. human resources Johns Hopkins Health Sys., Balt., 1990-92; pres. Leadership Impact, LLC, from 1999. Home: Vestal, NY. Died Aug. 17, 2009.

MCGOVERN, FRANCIS LEO, III, public safety and risk management administrator, consultant; b. Providence, Feb. 20, 1938; s. Francis L. McGovern III and Margaret Mary (Stewart) McGovern; m. Carole Kettelle, Oct. 24, 1964; children: Kelly Ann, Jamie Lynn. BS, Maine Maritime Acad., 1964. Cert. hazard control mgr., safety exec. Loss prevention engr. Factory Mut., Providence, 1964—71, Mchts. and Businessmens Ins., Harrisburg, Pa., 1971—74; safety and health dir. U. R.I., Kingston, 1974—82; dir. pub. safety, 1982—91; dir. safety and risk mgmt., from 1991. Author: Safety Manual, 1976, A Guide for Architects, 1977. Chmn. Scituate Town Com., RI, 1972—74, Scituate Housing Authority, 1973. Mem.: RI Fire Safety Assn., Nat. Safety Coun., Providence Engring. Soc., Nat. Safety Mgmt. Soc., Am. Soc. Safety Engrs. Avocation: camping. Home: North Scituate, RI. Died Mar. 15, 2010.

MCGOWAN, GEORGE VINCENT, public utility executive; b. Balt., Jan. 30, 1928; s. Joseph H. and Ethna M. (Prahl) McG.; m. Carol Murray, Aug. 6, 1977; children by a previous marriage: Gregg Blair, Bradford Kirby. BS in M.E., U. Md., 1951; LHD (hon.), Villa Julie Coll., 1991, Loyola Coll., Md., 1992; D of Pub. Svc., U. Md., 1997; LHD, U. Balt., 2001. Registered profl. engr., Md. Project engr. nuclear power plant Balt. Gas & Electric Co., 1967-72, chief nuclear engr., 1972-74, pres., chief operating officer, 1980-87, chmn. bd. dirs., CEO, 1988-92, chmn. exec. com., 1993-2000, mgr. corp. staff services, 1974-78, v.p. mgmt. and staff services, 1978-79. Bd. dirs. Orgn. Resources Counselors, Inc., GTS Duratek. Bd. dirs. Coll. Bound Found., Md. Pride of Balt. Recipient Disting. Alumnus award U. Md. Coll. Engring., 1980, U. Md.,

1987, Disting. Marylander award Advt. and Profl. Club Balt., 1992, Disting. Citizen award U. Md., 1991, Disting. Citizen of Yr. award Balt. Coun. Boy Scouts Am., 1991, Disting. Alumnus award Balt. Poly. Inst., 1992, Nat. Multiple Sclerosis Soc. Corp. Honoree, Md. chpt., 1993, Outstanding Vol. Fund Raiser award Nat. Soc. Fund Raising Execs., 1993, Pub. Affairs award Md. Bus. Coun., 1994, United States Energy award, 1995, Jr. Achievement Ctrl. Md. Bus. Hall of Fame, 1996. Mem. ASME (James N. Landis medal 1992), Am. Nuclear Soc., U.S. Energy Assn. of the World Energy Coun., Engrng. Soc. Balt. (Founders Day award 1988), Caves Valley Golf Club, The Ctr. Club (pres. bd. govs.), U. Md. M. Club, Talbot Country Club, Annapolis Yacht Club, Md. Club, Hunters Oak Golf Club. Presbyterian. Home: Queenstown, Md. Died Nov. 5, 2009.

MC GOWAN, THOMAS FRANCIS, manufacturing executive; b. Boston, May 19, 1931; s. Thomas Francis and Catherine Mary (Chisholm) Mc Gowan; m. Mary Lisbeth Dumphy, Apr. 8, 1961; children: Caren Ann, John Timothy. BSBA, Boston Coll., 1952, MBA, 1965. Cert. purchasing mgr. Subcontract mgr. Martin-Marietta Corp., Orlando, Fla., 1959—63; with Rockwell Internat., LA, 1963—75, material mgr., from 1975. Instr. Fullerton Coll., Calif., from 1975, Coast C.C., Costa Mesa, Calif., from 1979. Mem. purchasing mgmt. adv. com. Fullerton Coll., 1975—81, Coastline C.C., 1975—81. Served USN, 1952—59. Mem.: Nat. Assn. Purchasing Mgmt., Purchasing Mgmt. Assn. (pres. 1973—74). Republican. Home: Mesa, Ariz. Died Nov. 12, 2009.

MCGOWN, WAYNE, academic administrator; b. Stevens Point, Wis., Feb. 28, 1929; s. Homer Ernest and Amy Irene (Winkler) McG.; m. Hildy Grevstad, July 1, 1961; children: Carolyn, Ronald, Daniel. BBA, U. Wis., 1950, MS, 1958. State budget dir. State of Wis., Madison, 1963-67, dep. sec, then sec. Dept. Adminstrn., 1967-75, dep. sec. Dept. Transp., 1975-77, dep. sec. Dept. Industry, Labor and Human Rels., 1977-79; spl. asst. to chancellor U. Wis., Madison, 1979-90, dir. univ. rsch. park, from 1984, exec. asst. to chancellor, 1990-94; spl. asst. for health scis., from 1994. Cons. UN Tech. Svcs., Ankara, Turkey, 1979, Coun. State Govts., Lexington, Ky., 1960-68. Bd. dirs. Hist. Sites Found., Baraboo, Wis., 1986—: V.p. State of Wis. Boy Scouts Am., Madison, 1990—, bd. dirs., 1988—. With U.S. Army, 1951-53. Fellow Nat. Acad. Pub. Adminstrn. (Adminstr. of Yr. 1987); mem. Nat. Assn. State Budget Dirs (life, past pres.). Avocations: camping, travel, cross country skiing. Home: Madison, Wis. Died Feb. 10, 2009.

MCGRAW, HAROLD WHITTLESEY, JR., retired publishing executive; b. Bklyn., Jan. 10, 1918; s. Harold Whittlesey and Louise (Higgins) McG.; m. Anne Per-Lee, Nov. 30, 1940 (dec. 2002); children: Suzanne, Harold Whittlesey III, Thomas Per-Lee (dec. 2006), Robert Pearce. AB, Princeton U., 1940. With G.M. Basford (advt. agy.), NYC, 1940-41, Brentano's Bookstores, Inc., 1946; with McGraw-Hill Book Co., Inc., NYC, 1947—88, successively promotion mgr., dir. co. advt. and trade sales, 1947-55, dir., v.p. charge trade book, indsl. and bus. book depts., co. advt., 1955-61, sr. v.p., 1961-68, pres., 1968-74, McGraw-Hill, Inc., 1974-81, CEO, 1975-83, chmn., 1976-88, chmn. emeritus, 1988—2010. Bd. dirs. McGraw Hill, Inc., 1954-88. Founder, pres., bd. dirs. Bus. Council Effective Literacy and Bus. Press Ednl. Found. Served as capt. USAAF, 1941-45. Mem.: Wee Burn Club (Darien, Conn.), Blind Brook Club (Purchase, N.Y.). Home: Darien, Conn. Died Mar. 24, 2010.

MC GREGOR, FRANK HAMILTON, JR., physician; b. New Orleans, Mar. 19, 1938; s. Frank Hamilton and Sarah Louise (Mayo) Mc Gregor; m. Eleanore Ruth Stone, Dec. 16, 1961 (div. 1980); children: Sarah Goodwin, Holly Jane; m. Ava Patricia Carvan, Jan. 3, 1981. BS, Duke U., 1959, MA, 1963, MD, 1965. Diplomate Am. Bd. Surgery. Rsch. assoc. Duke U., Durham, NC, 1959—61, fellow in cardiovasc. surgery, 1965, 1968—69, intern, 1965—66, resident in surgery, 1969—70, Tulane U., New Orleans, 1970—73; practice medicine specializing in surgery Monroe, La., from 1974; mem. staff St. Francis Med. Ctr.; chief surgery, 1979—82; vice chief staff, 1980—81; mem. staff N. Monroe Cmty. Hosp.; chief of staff, 1983—84; chief surgery, 1986. Capt. M.C. AUS, 1966—68, Vietnam. Decorated Bronze Star, Army Commendation medal. Fellow: ACS, Tulane Surg. Soc. (founder, charter mem.), Southeast Surg. Congress, Am. Soc. Abdominal Surgeons; mem.: AMA, Ouchita Parish (v.p. 1980—81), Lions, Alpha Omega Alpha. Republican. Episcopalian. Home: Enid, Miss. Died Jan. 9, 2009.

MCGUIRE, EUGENE P., broadcasting executive; b. NYC, Sept. 3, 1934; s. James Francis and Mary Catherine (Fisher) McG.; m. Jeanette T. Lombardi, May 21, 1955; children: Donna Marie, Eugene Jr., Richard, Anne Marie. Cert. in acctg., Pace U., 1961. Bank clk. Citicorp, NYC, 1952-61; fin. analyst Univac Div.-Sperry Rand, NYC, 1961-64, NBC, Inc., NYC, 1965-68, bus. mgr. Cleve., 1968-74, dir. personnel Washington, 1974-77, v.p. labor relations NYC, 1977-82, exec. v.p. personnel and labor relations, from 1982. Republican. Roman Catholic. Avocations: golf, tennis. Home: Wyckoff, NJ. Died Nov. 29, 2009.

MCGUIRE, RICHARD JOSEPH, retired basketball player; b. Huntington, NY, Jan. 25, 1926; Attended, St. John's U., Dartmouth Coll. Basketball player N.Y. Knicks, 1951-54, head coach, 1965-68; basketball player Detroit Pistons, 1958-60, player, head coach, 1959-63. Head coach Belmont Abbey, 1957-58, 63-64, Marquette U., 1964-65, 76-77. Named to Basketball Hall of Fame, 1993, All- Am. 2d Team Sporting News, 1944, All NBA 2d Team, 1951; recipient Haggarty award, N.Y.C.; selected Helms Found. All-Am. Died Feb. 3, 2010.

MC GURN, BARRETT, communications executive, writer; b. NYC, Aug. 6, 1914; s. William Barrett and Alice (Schneider) McG.; m. Mary Elizabeth Johnson, May 30, 1942 (dec. Feb. 1960); children: William Barrett III, Andrew; m. Janice Ann McLaughlin, June 19, 1962; children: Summers, Martin Barrett, Mark Barrett. AB, Fordham U., 1935, LittD (hon.), 1958. Editor-in-chief Fordham Ram, 1934-35; with N.Y. Herald Tribune, 1935-66, asst. corr. Rome, 1939, bur. chief, 1946-52, 55-62, reporting staff NY, 1935-42, 62-66, bur. chief Paris, 1952—55, acting chief bur. Moscow, 1958; with, assignments in Morocco, Algeria, Tunisia, Hungary (1956 revolution), Egypt, Greece, Yugoslavia, Poland, Cen. Africa, Gaza Strip.; press attache Am. Embassy, Rome, 1966-68, counselor for press affairs Saigon, 1968—69; U.S. consular officer, sec. appointed by Pres., 1969; dir. U.S. Govt. Press Ctr., Vietnam, 1968-69; White House and Pentagon liaison for State Dept. spokesman Washington, 1969-72; World Affairs commentator USIA, 1972-73; dir. pub. info. U.S. Supreme Ct., Washington, 1973-82; dir. communications Cath. Archdiocese of Washington, 1984-87; pres. Carroll Pub. Co. pub. Cath. Standard and El Pregonero, 1987-91; dir. Our Sunday Visitor Pub. Co., 1988-98. Mem. Italian-Am. com. to select Italian fellowship winners for study in U.S., 1950-52; mem. U.S. Nat. Cath. Com. on Comm. Policy, 1970-74, White House Com. on Drug Control Info., 1970-72; interdept. com. on U.S. govt. press info. policy, 1970, interdept. U.S. govt. task force to rescue 100 Ams. kidnapped in Jordan, 1970, one-man U.S. Presdl. mission to Cambodia on media news problems, 1970; archivist John Carroll Soc., Washington, 1990-97. Author: Decade in Europe, 1959, A Reporter Looks at the Vatican, 1962, A Reporter Looks at American Catholicism, 1967, America's Court, The Supreme Court and The People, 1997, The Pilgrim's Guide to Rome, 1999, Yank, Reporting the Greatest Generation, 2004, (one act play) Semper Sistema, Fordham Coll. Stage, 1932; contbg. author: The Best from Yank, 1945, Yank, the GI Story of the War, 1946, Combat, 1950, Highlights from Yank, 1953, Overseas Press Club Cook Book, 1962, I Can Tell it Now, 1964, U.S. Book of Facts, Statistics and Information, 1966, New Catholic Treasury of Wit and Humor, 1967, How I Got that Story, 1967, Heroes for Our Times, 1968, Newsbreak, 1975, Saints for all Seasons, 1978, Informing the People, 1981, The Courage to Grow Old, 1989, Am. Peoples Encyclopedia Yearbook, Close To Glory: Yank Correspondents Untold Stories of World War II, 1992; contbr. articles to profl. jours. Trustee Corrs. Fund, 1965-68; mem. bd. Anglo-Am. Charity Fund in Italy, 1967-68; v.p. Citizens Assn., Westmoreland Hills, Md., 1984-86. Sgt. AUS, 1942-45. Decorated Purple Heart; grand knight Italian Order of Merit; Vietnam Psychol. Warfare medal 1st class; recipient Polk award for outstanding fgn. reporting L.I. U., 1956; named best press corr. abroad Overseas Press Club, 1957; recipient N.Y.C. Fire Dept. Essay Silver Medal, 1924, N.Y. Times Oratorical Contest Bronze Medal, 1930; Christopher award for one of ten most inspiring books of year, 1959; named Man of Year Cath. Inst. Press, 1962, Fordham U. Alumnus of Year in communications, 1963; co-winner ann. Golden Typewriter award N.Y. Newspaper Reporters Assn., 1965, nominated by N.Y. Herald Tribune for Journalism Pulitzer Prize, 1965; outstanding pub. service award N.Y. chpt. Sigma Delta Chi, 1965; recipient Page One award N.Y. Newspaper Guild, 1966, Silurians award, 1966, award N.Y. Newspaper Reporters Assn., 1966, Citation for pub. service N.Y.C. Citizens Budget Commn., 1966, U.S. Govt. medal for civilian svc. in Vietnam, 1969, pres. commendation for Cambodia mission on news problems, 1970, Meritorious Honor award Dept. State, 1972; Lifetime Achievement award Fordham U. Club, Washington, 1986. Mem. Fgn. Press Assn. Italy (v.p. 1951-52, pres. 1961-62), SHAPE Corrs. Assn. Paris (treas. 1955), Authors Guild, Silurians, Am. Fgn. Svc. Assn., Pax Romana Soc. for Cath. Intellectuals, Overseas Press Club (pres. 1963-65), Nat. Press Club, Diplomats and Consular Officers, Ret., Kenwood Club, Cosmos Club, Fordham U. Club Washington (bd. govs. 1980—99). Roman Catholic. Home: Bethesda, Md. Died July 2, 2010.

MCILVEEN, EDWARD E., electrical engineer, association executive; b. Passaic, NJ, Aug. 3, 1911; s. Bert Henry and Rachel (Shephard) McI.; m. Virginia Griffith, Apr. 7, 1934 (div. 1944); 1 dau., Elizabeth Maude; m. Linda Jane Sparnon, July 2, 1944; children: Richard H., Lynne R., Nancy P. B.M.E. cum laude, Poly. Univ. Bklyn., 1943. Engrng. asst. Western Union Telegraph, NYC, 1932-41; research engr. The Okonite Co., Passaic, N.J., 1941-54, asst. mgr. engrng., 1954-63, mgr. cable devel., 1963-68, v.p. engrng. Ramsey, N.J., 1968-78; sec.-treas. Insulated Cable Engrs. Assn., South Yarmouth, Mass., from 1978. Fellow IEEE (insulated conductors com.); mem. Montclair Soc. Engrs. (pres. 1960-61), Bass River Yacht Club (South Yarmouth), Kappa Sigma, Sigma Xi. Home: South Yarmouth, Mass. Died Dec. 26, 2009.

MCINERNY, RALPH MATTHEW, philosopher, educator, writer; b. Mpls., Feb. 24, 1929; s. Austin Clifford and Vivian Gertrude (Rush) McI.; m. Constance Terrill Kunert, Jan. 3, 1953 (dec. May 2001); children: Cathleen, Mary, Anne, David, Elizabeth, Daniel. BA, St. Paul Sem., 1951; MA, U. Minn., 1952; PhD summa cum laude, Laval U., 1954; LittD (hon.), St. Benedict Coll., 1978, U. Steubenville, 1984; DHL (hon.), St. Francis Coll., Joliet, Ill., 1986, St. John Fisher Coll., 1994, St. Anselm's Coll., NH, 1995, Holy Cross Coll., New Orleans, 2001, Assumption Coll., Worcester, Mass., 2007. Instr. Creighton U., 1954-55; prof. U. Notre Dame, Ind., 1955—2009, Michael P. Grace prof. medieval studies Ind., 1988—2009, dir. dept. Ind., 1978-85, dir. Jacques Martin Ctr., 1978—2005. Vis. prof. Cornell U., 1988, Cath. U., 1971, Louvain, 1983, 95; founder Internat. Cath. U.; disting. vis. prof. Truman State U., Mo., 1999; Gifford lectr. Glasgow U., Scotland, 1999-2000, Joseph lectr. Pontifical Gregorian Inst., Rome, 2003; vis. lectr. Pontifical U. of Holy Cross, Rome, 2006, Ctr. of Applied Law, Cath. U. Chile, 2006. Author: The Logic of Analogy, 1961, History of Western Philosophy, vol. 1, 1963, vol. 2, 1968, Thomism in an Age of Renewal, 1966, Studies in Analogy, 1967, New Themes in Christian Philosophy, 1967, St. Thomas Aquinas, 1976, Ethica Thomistica, 1982, History of the Ambrosiana, 1983, Being and Predication, 1986, Miracles, 1986, Art and Prudence, 1988, A First Glance at St. Thomas: Handbook for Peeping Thomists, 1989, Boethius and Aquinas, 1989, Aquinas on Human Action, 1991, The Question of Christian Ethics, 1993, Aquinas Against the Averroists, 1993, The God of Philosophers, 1994, Aquinas and Analogy, 1996, Ethica Thomistica, 1997, Student Guide to Philosophy, 1999, Vernunftgemässes Leben, 2000, Characters in Search of Their Authors, 2001, Conversion of Edith Stein, 2001, John of St. Thomas, Summa Theologiae, 2001, Defamation of Pius XII, 2001, Very Rich Hours of Jacques Maritain, 2003, Aquinas, 2003, Praeambula Fidei, 2005, Nalicanor II: Chi Cosa i andato Shorto?; (novels) Jolly Rogerson, 1967, A Narrow Time, 1969, The Priest, 1973, Gate of Heaven, 1975, Rogerson at Bay, 1976, Her Death of Cold, 1977, The Seventh Station, 1977, Romanesque, 1977, Spinnaker, 1977, Quick as a Dodo, 1978, Bishop as Pawn, 1978, La Cavalcade Romaine, 1979, Lying Three, 1979, Abecedary, 1979, Second Vespers, 1980, Rhyme and Reason, 1981, Thicker than Water, 1981, A Loss of Patients, 1982, The Grass Widow, 1983, Connolly's Life, 1983, Getting Away with Murder, 1984, And Then There Were Nun, 1984, The Noonday Devil, 1985, Sine Qua Nun, 1986, Leave of Absence, 1986, Rest in Pieces, 1985, Cause and Effect, 1987, The Basket Case, 1987, Veil of Ignorance, 1988, Abracadaver, 1989, Body and Soil, 1989, Four on the Floor, 1989, Frigor Mortis, 1989, Savings and Loan, 1990, The Search Committee, 1991, The Nominative Case, 1991, Sister Hood, 1991, Judas Priest, 1991, Easeful Death, 1991, Infra Dig, 1992, Desert Sinner, 1992, Seed of Doubt, 1993, The Basket Case, 1993, Nun Plussed, 1993, Mom and Dead, 1994, The Cardinal Offense, Law and Ardor, 1995, Let's Read Latin, 1995, Aguinas and Analogy, 1996, The Tears of Things, 1995, Half Past Nun, 1997, On This Rockne, 1997, Penguin Classic Aquinas, 1997, The Red Hat, 1998, What Went Wrong With Vatican II, 1998, Lack of the Irish, 1998, Irish Tenure, 1999, Grave Undertakings, 1999, Heirs and Parents, 2000, Shakespearean Variations, 2000, Book of Kills, 2001, Triple Pursuit, 2001, Still Life, 2001, Sub Rosa, 2001, Emerald Aisle, 2001, John of St. Thomas, Summa Theologiae, 2001, Law and Ardor, 2001, As Good as Dead, 2002, Celt and Pepper, 2002, Prodigal Father, 2002, Last Things, 2002, Ablative Case, 2003, Irish Coffee, 2003, Requiem For A Realtor, 2004, Green Thumb, 2004, Blood Ties, 2005, Irish Gilt, 2005, Soul of Wit, 2005, (memoirs) Only I Have Escaped to Tell You, 2006, Prudence of the Flesh, 2006, Perambula Fidei, 2006, The Letter Killeth, 2006, The Widow's Mate, 2007, Irish Alibi, 2007; editor New Scholasticism, 1967-89; editor, pub. Crisis, 1982-96; pub. Catholic Dossier, 1995-2002, Fellowship of Cath. Scholars Quar., 2003—. Exec. dir. Wethersfield Inst., 1989-92; bd. govs. Thomas Aquinas Coll., Santa Paula, Calif., 1993-2001; bd. dirs. Southern Cross Found., 1999—; mem. Pres. Bush's Com. on the Arts and Humanities, 2002—. With USMC, 1946-47. Named to Cath. Edn. Found. Hall of Fame, 2007; recipient Thomas Aquinas medal U. Dallas, 1990, Thomas Aquinas Coll., 1991, St. Thomas Aquinas medal for eminence in philosophy, 1993, Maritain medal Am. Maritain Assn., 1994, P.G. Wodehouse award CRISIS Mag., 1995, Cardinal Journet medal Ave Maria U., Fla., 2007; Fulbright rsch. fellow, Belgium, 1959-60, NEH fellow, 1977-78, NEA fellow, 1983, Catholic Scholars fellow, 1992-95, Oxford fellowship, fellowship, Inst. Psychol. Scis., Blackfriars, Oxford, Eng., 2008; Fulbright scholar, Argentina, 1986, 87, Outstanding Philosophical scholar Delta Epsilon Sigma, 1990; honoree Ralph McInerny Ctr. Thonistic Studies Thomas Internat. U., 2006. Fellow Pontifical Roman Acad. St. Thomas Aquinas; mem. Am. Philos. Assn., Am. Cath. Philos. Assn. (past pres., St. Thomas Aquinas medal 1993), Cath. Acad. Scis., Am. Metaphys. Soc. (pres. 1992), Am. Maritain Assn. (pres. 2004-06), Internat. Soc. for Study Medieval Philosophy, Medieval Acad., Mystery Writers Am. (Lifetime Achievement award 1993), Authors Guild, Fellowship Cath. Scholars (pres. 1992-95, Cardinal Wright award 1996, Premio Roncevalles de Navarre 2002), Christendom Coll., Va. Home: Notre Dame, Ind. Died Jan. 29, 2010.

MC INNES, WILLIAM CHARLES, priest, retired academic administrator; b. Boston, Jan. 20, 1923; s. William Charles and Mary (Byrne) Mc Innes. BS, Boston Coll., 1944, AB, 1950, MA, 1951; STL, Weston Coll., 1958; PhD, NYU, 1955; degree (hon.), U. Bridgeport, Sacred Heart U., Xavier U., Cin., U. Scranton, Loyola U., Chgo., Fairfield U. Joined Soc. of Jesus, 1946; ordained priest Roman Cath. Ch., 1957; prof. mktg. and bus. ethics Sch. Bus. Adminstrn. Boston Coll., 1959-63, assoc. dean Sch. Bus. Adminstrn., 1961-63, dir. honors program, 1963-64, mem. citizens seminar planning com., 1959-63, dir. Nat. Jesuit Honor Soc., 1997—2003; pres. Fairfield (Conn.) U., 1964-73, prof. urban problems, 1969-72; pres. U. San Francisco, 1972-77, Assn. Jesuit Colleges & Universities, 1977-89; campus min. U. Conn., Storrs, 1990-96. Vis. fellow Woodstock Theol. Ctr., 1990—91; adj. prof. bus. ethics Boston (Mass.) Coll., 1996—2009. Life mem. United Cerebral Palsy Assn. Fairfield County; adv. com. Conn. Dept. Social Svcs., 1993—96; priest Chaplain Alumni Assn., emeritus priest; chaplain Boston Coll. Alumni Assn., 1997—2009; past chmn. bd. dirs. ABCD (cmty. action agys.); bd. dirs. Nat. Better Bus. Bur.; past pres. Conn. Assn. Cmty. Action Programs; founder Fairfield County Cmty. Forum Conn. Charter Oak Coll.; vice chmn. Nat. Better Bus. Bur. Found.; chmn. Calif. Coun. Humanities. Served to capt. USAF, 1942—46, CBI. Recipient B.C. Outstanding Alumnus award, 2005, Disting. Svc. award, Carroll Sch., 2008. Mem.: Alpha Epsilon Delta, Phi Kappa Theta, Delta Sigma Pi, Alpha Sigma Nu, Beta Gamma Sigma. Home: Weston, Mass. Died Dec. 9, 2009.

MC INTOSH, JOHN MOHR, retired electric utility executive; b. Savannah, Ga., Jan. 18, 1924; s. Olin Talley and Jane Kirkland (Lawton) McI.; m. Barbara Ann Neff, Mar. 30, 1945; children: Angela, John Mohr, Neff, Olin, Aileen, Barbara. Student, U. Ga., 1941-42. Vice pres. sales Rock Wool Products Corp., Savannah, 1946-49; pres. McIntosh & Co., Savannah, 1949-57; v.p., gen. mgr. Neal-Blun Co., Savannah, 1956-66, pres., 1966-74; chmn. bd., chief exec. officer Savannah Electric & Power Co., 1974-84. Dir. Savannah Foods & Industries, Gt. So. Fed. Savs. & Loan. Chmn. Savannah Port

Authority, 1964-65; gen. chmn. United Way, Savannah, 1972. Served with USAAF, 1942-44. Mem. Southeastern Electric Exchange (dir. 1975—), Edison Electric Inst. (dir. 1981—) Episcopalian. Home: Savannah, Ga. Died Mar. 23, 2010.

MCINTYRE, JOHN WILLIAM, banker; b. Valdosta, Ga., Sept. 14, 1930; s. James A. and Julia (Norton) McI.; m. Joan Pruitt, Oct. 8, 1955; children: Anna, John William, Martha, Michael. BBA, Emory U., 1951; grad. exec. mgmt. program, Stanford U., 1966. With Citizens & So. Nat. Bank, from 1951, gen. v.p. Atlanta, 1977-79, pres., from 1979, chmn., chief exec. officer, from 1990, also bd. dirs.; chmn., chief exec. officer Citizens and So. Ga. Corp., from 1980, also bd. dirs.; chmn. bd. dirs. Citizens and So. Corp. (parent co.), 1986. Bd. dirs. Master Card Internat., Inc., Kaiser Found. Health Plan Ga. Trustee Emory U.; bd. sponsors Atlanta Symphony; trustee Lovett Sch., Atlanta; bd. dirs. City of Atlanta, Fulton County Recreation Authority, Atlanta Exec. Svc. Corps, Bus. Coun. Ga. With USAR, 1952-54. Mem. Assn. Res. City Banks, Ga. C. of C. (dir.) Clubs: Piedmont Driving, Cherokee Town and Country, Commerce. Baptist. Home: Atlanta, Ga. Died July 15, 2009.

MCISAAC, PAUL ROWLEY, electrical engineer, educator; b. Port Washington, NY, Apr. 20, 1926; s. Robert Milton and June Zatella (Barrus) McI.; m. Mary Lou Heldenbrand, Sept. 10, 1949; children— Wendy Lee, Karen Jo, Hugh Paul, Kathleen Anne. B.E.E., Cornell U., 1949; MSE., U. Mich., 1950, PhD, 1954. Research engr. Microwave Tube div. Sperry Gyroscope Co., Great Neck, N.Y., 1954-59; assoc. prof. elec. engring. Cornell U., 1959-65, prof., 1965-2000, assoc. dean engring., 1975-80, prof. emeritus, from 2000. Served with USN, 1944-46. Rotary Found. fellow, 1951-52 Mem. IEEE, AAAS, Sigma Xi. Home: Ithaca, NY. Died Mar. 15, 2010.

MCKAY, KENNETH GARDINER, retired physicist, electronics company executive; b. Montreal, Quebec, Canada, Apr. 8, 1917; came to U.S., 1946, naturalized, 1954; s. James Gardiner and Margaret (Nicholas) McK.; m. Irene C. Smith, July 25, 1942; children— Margaret Craig, Kenneth Gardiner B.Sc., McGill U., 1938, M.Sc., 1939; Sc.D, MIT, 1941; D.Eng. (hon.), Stevens Inst. Tech., 1980. Research engr. Nat. Research Council Can., 1941-46; with Bell Telephone Labs., 1946-66, 73-80, dir. solid state device devel., 1957-59, v.p. systems engring., 1959-62, exec. v.p. systems engring., 1962-66, exec. v.p., 1973-80; v.p. engring AT&T, 1966-73; chmn. bd. Bellcomm Inc., 1966-73, Charles Stark Draper Lab., 1982-87; ret., 1987. Advisor Min. of Transp. and Comms., Republic of China, 1982-95. Trustee Stevens Inst. Tech., 1974-87; bd. govs. McGill U., 1972-77, N.Y. Coll. Osteo. Medicine, 1980-89; mem. vis. com. for engring. Stanford U., 1974-87; mem. sci. and acad. adv. com. U. Calif., 1980-88; mem. Sci. and Tech. Adv. Group, Republic of China, 1982-96. Fellow IEEE, Am. Phys. Soc., N.Y. Acad. Scis.; mem. NAS, NAE (councillor 1970-73), Century Assn. Home: New York, NY. Died Mar. 5, 2010.

MCKEE, KEITH EARL, manufacturing technology executive; b. Chgo., Sept. 9, 1928; s. Charles Richard and Maude Alice (Hamlin) McK.; children: Pamela Ann Houser, Paul Earl. BS, Ill. Inst. Tech., 1950, MS, 1956, PhD, 1962. Engr. Swift & Co., Chgo., 1953-54; rsch. engr. Armour Rsch. Found., Chgo., 1954-62; dir. design and product assurance Andrew Corp., Orland Park, Ill., 1962-67; dir. engring. Rsch. Ctr. Ill. Inst. Tech., Chgo., 1967-80, dir. mfg. prodn. ctr., from 1977. Prof. Ill. Inst. Tech., Chgo., 1979—, dir. indsl. programs, 1994—; coord. Nat. Conf. on Fluid Power, Chgo., 1983-88; mem. com. on materials and processing Dept. Def., Washington, 1986-92. Author: Productivity and Technology, 1988; co-author: Managing Technology Dependence Operation, 2004; editor: Automated Inspection and Process Control, 1987; co-editor: Manufacturing High Technology Handbook, 1987; mng. editor: Manufacturing Competitiveness Frontier, 1977-97. Capt. USMC, 1950-54. Recipient oustanding presentation award Am. Soc. of Quality Control, Milw., 1983. Fellow World Acad. Productivity Scis.; mem. ASCE, Am. Def. Preparedness Assn. (pres. Chgo. chpt. 1972-95), Am. Assn. Engring. Soc. (Washington) (coor. com. on productivity 1978-88), Inst. of Indsl. Engrs., Soc. Mfg. Engrs. (Gold medal 1991), Am. Assn. for Artificial Intelligence, Robotic Industry Assn. (bd. dir. 1978-81), Assn. for Mfg. Excellence, Soc. for Computer Simulation. Democrat. Roman Catholic. Home: Chicago, Ill. Died May 1, 2010.

MCKELL, CYRUS M., retired dean, range plant physiologist, consultant; b. Payson, Utah, Mar. 19, 1926; s. Robert D. and Mary C. (Ellsworth) McK.; m. Betty Johnson; children: Meredith Sue, Brian Marcus, John Cyrus. BS, U. Utah, 1949, MS, 1950; PhD, Oreg. State U., 1956; postgrad., U. Calif., Davis, 1957. Instr. botany Oreg. State U., Corvallis, 1955-56; range rsch. plant physiologist U. Calif. USDA-Agrl. Research Service, Davis, 1956—61; prof., dept. chmn. U. Calif., Riverside, 1961—69; prof. dept. head., dir. Utah State U., Logan, 1969-80; v.p. research NPI, Salt Lake City, 1980-88; dean Coll. of Sci. Weber State U., Ogden, Utah, 1988-94; pres., prin. Applied Ecol. Svcs. Inc., Logan, Utah, 1995—2008. Cons. Ford Found. 1968-72, Rockefeller Found., 1964-70, 89, UN, 1978, 90, NAS, 1980, 89, 91-93, USAID, 1972, UN Devel. Program, 1989; mem. faculty of sci. adv. bd. UAE Nat. U., 2000-02. Editor: Grass Biology and Utilization, 1971, Useful Wildland Shrubs, 1972, Rehabilitation of Western Wildlife Habitat, 1978, Paradoxes of Western Energy Development, 1984, Resource Inventory and Baseline Study Methods for Developing Countries, 1983, Shrub Biology and Utilization, 1989, Wilderness Issues, Arid Lands of the Western United States, 1992; contbr. over 230 articles to profl. jours. Chmn. Cache County Planning Commn., Logan, 1974-79; mem. Utah Energy Conservation and Devel. Coun., 1976-79, Gov.'s Sci. Adv. Coun., 1988-97, chmn., 1990-91, 96-97; mem. Commn. of the Californias, Riverside, 1965-68; mem. Holladay City Planning Commn., 2003-2009. Recipient Utah Gov.'s Sci. and Tech. medal, 1990, Gardner Prize in Sci., awarded by Utah Acad. Scis., Arts and Letters, 1999; Fulbright scholar Spain, 1967-68; World Travel grantee Rockefeller Found., 1964. Fellow: AAAS (com. chmn. 1979—89, sci. exchange to China grantee 1984—85, 1989, sci. panel U.S.-Chile 1987); mem.: Am. Soc. Agronomy, Soc. Range Mgmt. (pres. Calif. sect. 1965, pres. Utah sect. 1982). Mem. Lds Ch. Avocations: travel, photography, history. Home: Holladay, Utah. Died May 14, 2009.

MCKENNA, CHARLES RAYMOND, JR., railroad executive; b. Carnegie, Pa., Feb. 11, 1923; s. Charles Raymond and Marie Elizabeth (McGarry) McK.; m. Patricia Isbella McCullough, Aug. 11, 1948; children— Charles Raymond III, Patricia A., Dennis M., Daniel M. BS, Duquesne U., 1949. Dir. equipment performance Penn Central R.R., Phila., 1972-74, gen. mgr. Northeast region New Haven, 1974-76, Consol. Rail, New Haven, 1976-81; pres. Del. & Hudson R.R. Co., Albany, N.Y., from 1981, also dir.; pres. Boston & Maine R.R., North Billerica, Mass., from 1984, also dir.; pres. Maine Central R.R., Portland, from 1984, also dir.; dir. Napierville Junction R.R., Montreal, Que., Can. Served to 1st sgt. C.E., U.S. Army, 1943-45 Named Man of Yr., Western N.Y. State Transp. Council, 1984 Roman Catholic. Avocations: golf; swimming; reading. Home: Sun City Center, Fla. Died Jan. 30, 2009.

MCKENNA, SIDNEY F., retired technical company executive; b. Detroit, Nov. 27, 1922; s. Michael James and Elizabeth Josephine McK.; m. Helen Mary Spiroff, Sept. 20, 1944; children: Lynne Marie McKenna Hoss, Dennis Michael, Patrick Conlon, Mary Elizabeth McKenna Raimondi, Maureen T. McKenna Anderson, Christopher John. AB, U. Mich., Ann Arbor, 1947; MA, Wayne State U., 1948. With Ward Baking Co., Detroit, 1939-41; prodn. worker Cadillac Motor Co. (div. Gen. Motors Corp.), Detroit, 1941-42; mem. indsl. relations staff Ford Motor Co., Dearborn, Mich., 1942-79, v.p., 1974-79; sr. v.p. United Techs. Corp., Hartford, Conn., 1980-90. Bd. dirs. Schwartz Value Fund. Adv. bd. Providence Hosp., Detroit, 1972-80; bd. dirs. Brighton (Mich.) Hosp., 1976-80, Mercy Coll., Detroit, 1976-80, United Found., 1976-80, St. Francis Hosp., Hartford, Conn., 1983-89, St. Joseph's Coll., 1988-89. Served with USN, 1942-46. Decorated knight St. Gregory. Mem. Labor Policy Assn. (chmn.), Bus. Roundtable, Orgn. Resources Counselors, Nat. Assn. Mfrs. (bd. dirs. 1988-89), Bloomfield Hills Country Club, Birmingham Athletic Club, Mariner Sands Country Club, K.C. Roman Catholic. Died May 23, 2010.

MC KENZIE, HAROLD CANTRELL, JR., retired manufacturing executive; b. Carrollton, Ga., Dec. 25, 1931; s. Harold Cantrell and Sue (Tanner) McK.; m. Katherine Branch, Apr. 11, 1958; children— Ansley, Katherine, Harold Cantrell, III. B of Indsl. Engring., Ga. Inst. Tech., 1953; JD, Emory U., 1955; AMP, Harvard Bus. Sch. Bar: Ga. 1955. Law clk. to judge U.S. Dist. Ct., Atlanta, 1956; ptnr. firm Troutman, Sams, Schroder & Lockerman, Atlanta, 1957-67; exec. v.p., bd. dirs. Ga. Power Co., 1967-81; dir. Intermet Corp., from 1971; pres. So. Electric Internat., Inc., 1981-85; chmn., chief exec. officer Machine Techs., Inc. (doing bus. as MacTech), Martinsville, Va., 1986-89; sr. adv. facilities Atlanta Project of Carter Presdl. Ctr., 1992-96. Mem. Piedmont Driving Club. Episcopalian. Home: Marietta, Ga. Died July 8, 2009.

MC KENZIE, JOHN MAXWELL, physician; b. Glasgow, Scotland, Nov. 13, 1927; arrived in US, 1980; s. Thomas Wilson and Isabell Connor (Spencer) McK.; m. Vieno Laine Kangas, June 29, 1957; children— Ann, Ian, Lesley, Gordon. M.B., Ch.B., U. St. Andrews, Scotland, 1950, MD, 1958. Intern U. St. Andrews, 1950-51, resident, 1953-55, fellow, 1955-56, 57-58; research trainee, fellow Tufts U., 1956-57, 58-59; clin. asst. medicine McGill U., Montreal, Que., Can., 1959-61, asst., then assoc. prof., 1961-68, prof., 1968-80, U. Miami, from 1980, chmn. dept. medicine, 1980-94. Contbr. numerous articles to profl. jours. Served with Royal Army Med. Corps, 1951-53. Recipient Killam award, Can. Coun., 1980. Mem. Am. Thyroid Assn. (Parke-Davis disting. lectr. 1981, pres. 1983-84), Am. Soc. Clin. Investigation, Endocrine Soc. (Ayerst award 1961, Rorer Pharm. Clin. Investigator award 1990), Am. Physiol. Soc., Assn. Am. Physicians, Am. Fedn. Clin. Rsch., AAAS, Internat. Soc. Neuroendocrinology, European Thyroid Assn. (corr.) Home: Miami, Fla. Died Apr. 30, 2009.

MC KENZIE, LIONEL WILFRED, economist, educator; b. Montezuma, Ga., Jan. 26, 1919; s. Lionel Wilfred and Lida (Rushin) McK.; m. Blanche Veron, Jan. 2, 1943 (dec. July 1999); children: Lionel Wilfred (dec.), Gwendolyn Veron (dec.), David Rushin. AB, Duke U., 1939; MA, Princeton U., 1946, PhD, 1956; BLitt, Oxford U., Eng., 1949; postgrad., U. Chgo., 1950-51, LLD (hon.), 1991; D of Econs. (hon.), Keio U., Japan, 1998; DPhil (hon.), Kyoto U., Japan, 2004. Asst. economist WPB, 1942; instr. Mass. Inst. Tech., 1946; from asst. prof. to assoc. prof. Duke, 1948-57; prof. econs. U. Rochester, 1957-64, John Munro prof. economics, 1964-67, Wilson prof. economics, 1967-89, Wilson prof. emeritus, 1989—2010, chmn. dept. economics, 1957-66. Taussig research prof. Harvard U., 1980-81; Mem. math. divsn. NRC, 1960-63, mem. behavioral scis. divsn., 1964-70; mem. math., social scis. bd. Center Advanced Study in Behavioral Scis., Palo Alto, Calif., 1964-70, chmn., 1969-70 Author: Classical General Equilibrium Theory, 2002, Equilibrium Trade & Growth, 2009; assoc. editor Internat. Econs. Rev., 1964-96, Jour. Econ. Theory, 1970-73, Jour. Internat. Econs., 1970-84, Econ. Theory, 1991-95; contbr. articles to profl. jours. Lt. (s.g.) USNR, 1943-45. Recipient Rising Sun award Japan, 1995; Rhodes scholar Oriel Coll. Oxford U., 1939; Guggenheim fellow, 1973-74, fellow Center for Advanced Study in Behavioral Scis., 1973-74. Fellow Econometric Soc. (coun. 1973-78, pres. 1977), Am. Acad. Arts and Scis., Am. Econ. Assn.; mem. NAS, Royal Econ. Soc., Am. Math. Soc., Am. Econ. Assn. (Disting. Fellow 1993), Phi Beta Kappa (chpt. v.p. 1968-70, chpt. pres. 1972-73). Home: Rochester, NY. Died Oct. 12, 2010.

MCKINNEY, BILLY, retired state legislator; b. Feb. 23, 1927; m. Leola Christian; children: James E., Gregory, Cynthia Ann. Student, Clark Coll., 1948. Mem. Ga. House of Reps., Atlanta, 1973—2003. Mem. Health and Ecology Com., Children and Youth Com., Appropriations Com., Atlanta Police Dept., 1948-49; chmn. MARTOC Overview Com.; cons. polit. affairs; chmn. Fulton County Del. With U.S. Army; U.S. Army Corp. Engrs., 1945-46. Mem. Met. Atlanta Rapid Transit Authority Com. Methodist. Home: Atlanta, Ga. Died July 15, 2010.

MCKINNEY, JOSEPH CRESCENT, bishop emeritus; b. Grand Rapids, Mich., Sept. 10, 1928; s. Joseph Crescent and Antoinette (Theisen) McKinney. Attended, Seminaire de Philosophie, Montreal, Can., 1948—50; STL, Collegio di Propaganda Fide, Rome, 1954. Ordained priest Diocese of Grand Rapids, Mich., 1953; high sch. prof. St. Joseph Sem., Grand Rapids, Mich., 1954—62; asst. pastor Sacred Heart parish, Mt. Pleasant, Mich., 1962—65; pastor St. Francis parish, Conklin, Mich., 1965—68, St. Andrew Cathedral, Grand Rapids, 1968—69, St. Stephen parish, Grand Rapids, 1971—77, Sacred Heart parish, Muskegon, 1977, Our Lady Of Consolation parish, Rockford, Mich., 1985—98; asst. chancellor Diocese of Grand Rapids, 1965—68, vicar gen., 1968—2001; ordained bishop, 1968; aux. bishop Diocese of Grand Rapids, 1968—2001, aux. bishop emeritus, 2001—10. Roman Catholic. Died June 9, 2010.

MCKINNEY, VIRGINIA ELAINE ZUCCARO, educational administrator; b. San Francisco, Nov. 18, 1924; d. Salvadore John and Elaine Agnes (Shepard) Zuccaro; children: Joe, Walter Clifton. BA, Calif. State U., LA, 1968; MA, Calif. State U., Northridge, 1969; PhD, Claremont Grad. Sch., 1983. Ofcl ct. reporter LA County Superior Cts., 1948—59; tchr. speech-reading, adult edn. LA Bd. Edn., 1966—71; founder, pres., dir. communication skills program Ctr. Communicative Devel., Inc., LA, 1969—2009; lectr. spl. edn. Calif. State U., LA, 1971—78; lang., reading specialist Marlton Sch. Deaf, LA, 1971—79. Developer, prodr. audiovisual media, 22 films and 4 books, 1963—68, participant (rsch. project) Project Life Devel. Communication Skills Multiply-Handicapped Deaf Adults, 1970, developer, pub. Toe-Hold Literacy Packet, 1973, Linguistics 36, Interactive Computer Lang. Devel. Program, 1986; author: The Picture Plus Dictionary, 1997, (CD) Picture Plus Vocabulary, 2000. Cons. u. and programs hearing-impaired; adv. com. deaf Calif. Dept. Rehab. State Ind. Living Coun., 1979—84, Atty.'s Gen. Commn. Disability, 1987—90; mem. State Ind. Living Coun., 1993—2000. Recipient Leadership award, Nat. Leadership Tng. Program Area Deaf, Calif. State U., Northridge, 1974; grantee, NEA Project Life, 1970, Gallaudet Coll. Ctr. Continuing Edn., 1974. Mem.: Beverly-Hollywood Hearing Soc. (Calif.) (pres. 1967—68), Calif. Assn. Postsecondary Edn. and Disability, Calif. Educators Deaf and Hard Hearing. Republican. Presbyterian. Home: Glendale, Calif. Died Dec. 10, 2009.

MCKNIGHT, WILLIAM EDWIN, minister; b. Grenada, Miss, Mar. 21, 1938; s. Leslie Spurgeon and Lucy Jennings (Sistrunk) McK.; m Sue Belle Roberts, Aug. 5, 1960; children: Susan Michele, William Roberts. BA, Millsaps Coll., 1960; BD, Lexington Theol. Sem., Ky., 1963. Ordained to ministry, 1964. Chaplain intern Grady Hosp., Atlanta, 1963-64; pastor First Christian Ch., Cleveland, Miss., 1964-67, Inverness, Miss., 1964-67, assoc. pastor Jackson, Miss., 1967-70; regional minister Christian Ch. (Disciples of Christ) in Miss., Jackson, 1971—2002. Bd. dir. Nat. City Christian Ch., Washington, DC, Christian Brotherhood Homes, Jackson, So. Christian Svc., Macon, Ga.; mem. Gen. Bd. the Christian Ch., Indpls., 1969—, bd. dir. fin. coun., 1979-82; mem. bd. higher edn., St. Louis, 1979-80. Named one of Outstanding Young Men Am. US Jaycees, 1976. Mem. Miss. Religious Leadership Conf. (pres. 1984-85), Conf. Regional Ministers and Moderators (pres. 1985-86), Coll. of regional Ministers, mem. Mem. Christian Ch. Home: Jackson, Miss. Died Feb. 10, 2009.

MCLAURIN, JOYCE FRANKLIN, customer service executive, fashion consultant; b. New Orleans, Apr. 7, 1944; d. Albert and Ruby M. (Nicholes) Jones; 1 child, Kenneth Franklin. Cert., Dale Carnegie, 1988; student, Southeastern U., Washington, 1989-90, Lee Internat. Sch. Aesthetics, Pikeville, Md., 1993, Inst. Esthederm, Paris, 1993. Lic. esthetician. With offshore drilling Fluor Drilling Svcs., Inc., New Orleans, 1978; work support rep. Xerox Corp., San Diego, 1980-81, credit rep., 1981-85, credit rep. maj. account, 1985-86, coord. maj. account Rosslyn, Va., 1986-89, mgr. customer svc. support mgmt. Springfield, Va., from 1989; fashion cons., owner J.F. McLaurin & Assocs., Rosslyn, from 1975. Coord. fashion show Community Actors Theatre, San Diego, 1980; fashion show coord., producer Corp. Few Nat. Conf., Chgo., 1989-90, Dept. Human Svcs., Washington, 1990; coord. stylist wardrobe Black Entertainment TV-Family Figures, Washington, 1990, Black Entertainment TV-Screen Scene, video, LP, and Teen Summit, Washington, 1990-91. Model coord. Dionne Warwick AIDS Found., Washington, 1988; coord., team capt. corp. sports battle Community Involvement Program, 1988-90. Mem. NAFE, Internat. Alliance Profl. Women Inc., Am. Mgmt. Assn., Blues Alley Music Soc. (bd. dirs.), Xerox Corp. Few (pres., chmn., advisor exec. bd. 1991, Peoples Choice award 1988-89). Died Jan. 28, 2009.

MCLEAN, BRUCE CHARLES, lawyer; b. Waterville, NY, May 11, 1924; s. Charles William and Mary Eloise (Allen) McL.; m. Eleanor May Hart, Aug 30, 1925; children: Gardner Hart, Deborah Allen McLean Hameline, Gregory Bruce, Jennifer Lea. AB, Hamilton Coll., Clinton, NY, 1949; LLB, Cornell U., 1951. Bar: N.Y 1951, U.S. Dist. Ct. (no. dist.) N.Y. Assoc. Kernan and Kernan, Utica, N.Y., 1951-55; sr. v.p., gen. counsel, dir. Mohawk Airlines, Oriskany, N.Y., 1955-72; pres. Horizon Hotel Inc., Oriskany, 1968-72; counsel N.Y. Power Authority, NYC and Albany, 1972-83; corp. counsel Utica Mut. Ins. Co., New Hartford, N.Y., from 1983. Mem. govt. affairs council and ins. council Bus. Council of N.Y. State,

Albany, 1983—; mem. legal adv. bd. Atlantic Legal Found., N.Y.C., 1983—; chmn. screening com. Utica Nat. Group Found., New Hartford, 1989—. Chmn. bd. Mohawk Community Coll. and Found., Utica, 1968-72; pres., bd. dirs. House of Good Shepherd, Utica, 1971, 84-90, Family Svcs. Greater Utica, 1965-69; trustee Oneida County Hist. Soc.; atty. Village of New Hartford, 1962-72; elder, chmn. fin. com. Presbyn. Ch. Mem. N.Y. State Bar Assn., Oneida County Bar Assn., Greater Utica C. of C. (chmn. airport com.), Rotary, Sadaquada Golf Club, Psi Upsilon. Republican. Avocations: skiing, boating, golf. Home: Englewood, Fla. Died Jan. 18, 2009.

MCLEAN, EDWARD BRUCE, biology educator, university administrator, ecology, behavior researcher; b. Washington Ct. House, Ohio, Jan. 10, 1937; s. Richard H. and Nell (Whitmer) McLean; m. Janice Victoria, May 19, 1986; children from previous marriage: Scott Walter, Hillary Beth, Jeremy Ryan. BS, Ohio State U., 1958; MS, 1963, PhD, 1968. Asst. prof. biology So. U., Baton Rouge, 1968—70; asst. prof. to prof. biology John Carroll U., Univ. Heights, Ohio, 1970—81; prof., chmn. dept. biology, from 1981. Contbr. articles to profl. jours. Trustee Shaker Lakes Regional Nature Ctr., Shaker Heights, Ohio, from 1976. With Med. Corps US Army, 1958—60. Grant, So. U. Rsch. Found., 1969, Ohio Biol. Survey, 1980. Fellow: Ohio Acad. Sci.; mem.: Institution Rep. Ohio Biol. Survey, Cooper Ornithological Soc., Wilson Ornithological Soc., Am. Ornithologists' Union. Avocations: birdwatching, camping, fishing, hunting. Home: Cleveland, Ohio. Died June 24, 2009.

MCLEAN, VINCENT RONALD, former manufacturing company financial executive; b. Detroit, June 1, 1931; s. Frederick Ronald and Bernice Mary (Vincent) McL.; m. Joyce Adrienne Koch, July 23, 1960; children— Judith Adrienne, Bruce Ronald BBA, U. Mich., 1954, MBA, 1955. Fin. analyst Ford Motor Co., Detroit, 1954—55, Mobil Oil Corp., NYC, 1958—69; treas. Mobil Chem. Co., NYC, 1966—69; v.p. fin., treas. NL Industries, NYC, 1969—76, exec. v.p. fin. and planning, dir., 1976—82; exec. v.p., CFO, dir. Sperry Corp., NYC, 1982—86; sr. advisor Wertheim Schroder & Co., NYC, 1988—89. Bd. dirs. Legal and Gen. Am., Inc., William Penn Life Ins. Co. NY, Banner Life Ins. Co., Md. Served with U.S. Army, 1955-57 Mem. N.Y. Soc. Security Analysts, Econ. Club N.Y. Home: Westfield, NJ. Died Sept. 7, 2009.

MCMAHON, WILLIAM FRANCIS, lawyer; b. Providence, Nov. 22, 1930; AB, Providence Coll., 1952; JD, Harvard U., 1955. Bar: R.I. 1955, D.C. 1955. Judge of probate, Pawtucket, R.I., 1979-84; ptnr. McMahon & McMahon, Providence. Mem. ABA, New Eng. Bar Assn. (bd. dirs. 1986—), R.I. Bar Assn. (ho. of dels. 1979—, exec. com. 1980—, pres. 1988—), Pawtucket Bar Assn. (pres. 1984). Died Apr. 6, 2009.

MCMANAWAY, CLAYTON E., JR., ambassador; b. Greenville, SC, Mar. 5, 1933; s. Clayton E. and Malinda McM. BS, U. S.C., Columbia, 1955; BA, Am. Inst. Fgn. Trade, Glendale, Ariz., 1959. Dep. asst. sec. Dept. Def., Washington, 1971-73, Dept. State, Washington, 1975-81, Office Sec. of State, Washington, 1981-83, ambassador Port-au-Prince, Haiti, from 1983. Served to lt. (j.g.) USN, 1955-57. Recipient awards Govt. South Vietnam, 1965-70, William A. Jump award U.S. Govt., 1968, Disting. Civilian Service medal U.S. Dept. Def., 1973, Presdl. citation, 1976, Superior Honor award Dept. State, 1978, Exec. Performance award Dept. State, 1983, 84. Died Apr. 6, 2010.

MCMANUS, PATRICK J., mayor, lawyer, accountant; b. Lynn, Mass., July 20, 1954; s. Robert A. and Kathryn M. (Gainey) McM. BA in Govt., Bowdoin Coll., 1976; MBA, Suffolk U., 1981; JD, Boston Coll., 1985. CPA, Mass.; cert. managerial acct., Mass. Tchr. Lynn Pub. H.S.; assoc. prof. bus. and fin. Salem (Mass.) State Coll.; lawyer pvt. practice Lynn; councillor at large City of Lynn, 1986-91, mayor, from 1992. Mem., trustee U.S. Conf. of Mayors, Washington, Brownsfield Task Force, Washington, Urban and Econ. Policy, Washington, Arts, Culture and Recreation, Washington; co-chair Urban Water Coun. Mem. KC, Ancient Order of Hibernians. Democrat. Roman Catholic. Died July 10, 2009.

MCMURRIN, TRUDY ANN, publishing consultant, editor, educator; b. Los Angeles, May 28, 1944; d. Sterling Moss and Natalie (Cotterel) McM.; m. William M. Howard, Mar. 9, 1963 (div. 1967); 1 child, Natalie Roberta Howard; m. Robert Bruce Evans, Sept. 24, 1969 (div. 1971); m. Mick McAllister, June 16, 1982; 1 stepchild, Jeoffrey R. McAllister. BA in History and Philosophy, U. Utah, 1981. Editor U. Utah Press, Salt Lake City, 1967-74, asst. dir., 1974-80, editor-in-chief, 1980-83; dir. So. Meth. U. Press, Dallas, 1983-86; owner Dancing Badger Enterprises, 1986—; adj. prof. dept. communication Weber State U., Ogden, Utah, 1986-88; mem. adv. coun. Gore Sch. Bus., Westminster Coll. of Salt Lake City, 1986—, adj. prof. Coll. Arts and Scis., 1989—, mem. Weldon J. Taylor Exec. Lecture Series Com., 1986—; editorial cons. network Mag., 1989—; cons. and lectr. in field; dir. art, co-designer award-winning books, 1972—. Author (with others), asst. editor: Medicine in the Beehive State, 1940-90, 1992. Mem. adv. bd. Children's Mus. Utah, 1979-81; bd. dirs. Howe Bros. Pub. Co., 1979—; mem. symposium on quality in pre-coll. edn. Rowland Hall-St. Mark's Sch., 1980-81; mem. Coalition to Save Our Sch. Librs., 1983—, Salt Lake City Ballet Guild, Utah Symphony Guild, Utah Opera Guild, Friends of Salt Lake City Libr. Fellow Am. Assn. State and Local History Nat. Endowment for Humanities, 1977, Inst. Am. West, 1981-82; recipient Maud Powell Found. award, 1988. Mem. Assn. Utah Pubs. (pres. 1978-83, bd. dirs. 1987-88), Western Lit. Assn. (mem. exec. council 1987-90, Weber Studies (mem. adv. bd. 1989—), Soc. for Scholarly Pub., Women in Scholarly Pub., Western Writers Am., Medieval Acad. Am., Wasatch Westerners, Intermountain Booksellers Assn., Rocky Mountain Book Pubs. Assn. Home: Salt Lake City, Utah. Died Mar. 14, 2009.

MCMURRY, IDANELLE SAM, educational consultant; b. Morganfield, Ky., Dec. 6, 1924; d. Sam Anderson and Aurelia Marie (Robertson) McM. BA, Vanderbilt U., 1945, MA, 1946. Tchr. English Abbot Acad., Andover, Mass., 1946-50, Hockaday Sch., Dallas, 1951-54, San Jacinto High Sch., Houston, 1954-55; dean of girls Kinkaid Sch., Houston, 1955-63; headmistress Harpeth Hall Sch., Nashville, 1963-79, Hockaday Sch., Dallas, 1979-89; ret.; now pvt. sch. cons. The Edn. Group, Dallas. Bd. dirs. Ednl. Records Bur., 1979-85, trustee, 1980-85. Bd. dirs. Tex. council Girl Scouts U.S., 1980-82, Town North YMCA; trustee Winston Sch., 1979-85, Spl. Care Sch., 1979-81, Asheville Sch., Manzano Day Sch. Mem. Nat. Study Sch. Evaluation (bd. dirs. 1979-83), Headmasters Assn., Nat. Assn. Ind. Schs. (bd. dirs. 1974-84, acad. com. 1974-79, sec. 1978-80, chmn. 1980-84), So. Assn. Ind. Schs. (pres. 1974-75), Tenn. Assn. Ind. Schs. (pres. 1967-68), Mid-South Assn. Ind. Schs. (pres. 1972-73), Ind. Schs. Assn. S.W. (v.p. 1967—), Nat. Assn. Prins. Schs. for Girls (sec. 1970-72, pres. 1975-77, coun. 1970-79), Nat. Assn. Secondary Sch. Prins., Country Day Sch. Headmasters Assn. (exe. com. 1984-87, v.p. 1988-89), So. Assn. Colls. and Schs. (adminstrv. coun. 1974-77, ctrl. reviewing com. 1972-77, vice chmn. secondary commn. 1975-76, chmn. 1976-77, bd. dirs. 1976-81), Ladies Hermitage Assn., Vanderilt Aid Soc. (sec. 1971-73, pres. 1994-96), Ind. Edn. Svcs. (trustee 1980-88, chmn. 1986-88), Susan Komen Found. (adv. bd.), Belle Meade Club, Centennial Club, Phi Beta Kappa, Pi Beta Phi. Democrat. Presbyterian. Home: Nashville, Tenn. Died Oct. 29, 2009.

MCNABOE, JAMES FRANCIS, lawyer; b. Newark, July 24, 1945; s. Frank A. and Eleanor (Baran) McN.; m. Constance G. Ilardi, Nov. 8, 1986. AB, Seton Hall U., 1966; JD, Rutgers U., 1969; student, Northwestern U., Chgo., 1966-67. Bar: N.J. 1969, U.S. Supreme Ct. 1979, N.Y. 1982, U.S. Ct. Appeals (3d cir.) 1982, U.S. Dist. Ct. (ea. dist.) N.Y. 1982, U.S. Dist. Ct. (so. dist.) N.Y. 1997; cert. civil trial atty. N.J., 1982. Law clk. Hoffman & Humphreys, Wayne, NJ, 1969; law clk. Hon. Bertram Polow, Morristown, NJ, 1969—70, Hon. Scott M. Long Jr., 1970—71; assoc. Evans, Hand, Allabough & Amoresano, West Paterson, NJ, 1971—81, Schwartz & Andolino, Livingston, NJ, 1981—85; pvt. practice Hackensack, NJ, 1986—87; assoc. Golden, Rothschild, Spagnola and DiFazio, Somerville, NJ, 1987—88, ptnr., 1989—90; assoc. Sheft & Sheft, Jersey City, 1991—92; trial counsel Caron, Greenberg & Fitzgerald, Rutherford, NJ, 1993—96; mng. atty. Cortner McNaboe Colliau & Elenius, Monmouth Junction, NJ, 1996—2005, sr. litig. atty., from 2005. Mem. ABA, N.J. State Bar Assn., Trial Attys. N.J. Democrat. Roman Catholic. Home: West Orange, NJ. Died May 30, 2010.

MCNALLY, TERRENCE JAMES, business communication educator; b. Cin., Jan. 5, 1937; s. Robert Joseph and Veronica Mary (Lenahan) McNally; m. Joan Eling, Aug. 22, 1964; children: Aileen, Carolyn, Timothy. BA in Philosophy, Duns Scotus Coll., 1960; MA in English, Xavier U., 1963; PhD in English, Loyola U., Chgo., 1968. Asst. prof. English DePaul U., Chgo., 1966—68, Xavier U., Cin., 1968—70; assoc. prof. to prof. English, bus. communication Northern Ky. U., Highland Heights, from 1970; cons. Procter & Gamble Co. and Govt. Agys. Co-author (with Peter Schiff): Contemporary Business Writing, 1968. V.p. Winding Trails Civic Assn., Edgewood, Ky., from 1980. Mem.: Internat. Assn. Bus. Communicators, Assn. Tchrs. Tech. Writing, Am. Bus. Communication Assn. Republican. Avocations: tennis, classical music, history. Home: Covington, Ky. Died May 20, 2010.

MCNAMARA, BARRY THOMAS, lawyer; b. West Haven, Conn., May 15, 1944; s. Joseph T. and Ann McN.; m. Paddy Harris, Aug. 19, 1972. BA in Polit. Philosophy, U. Notre Dame, 1966; JD, Northwestern U., Chgo., 1969. Bar: Ill. 1969, U.S. Dist. Ct. (no. dist.) Ill. 1969, U.S. Ct. Appeals (7th cir.) 1970, U.S. Supreme Ct. 1974, U.S. Dist. Ct. (cen. dist.) Ill. 1979, U.S. Ct. Appeals (2nd, 5th and 9th cirs.) 1980, U.S. Tax Ct. 1982. Assoc. Gardner, Carton & Douglas, Chgo., 1969-75; ptnr. O'Brien, Carey, McNamara, Chgo., 1975-82, D'Ancona & Pflaum, Chgo., 1982-87; adj. prof. sch. law Northwestern U., 1993—2010. Asst. prof. course dir. med. jurisprudence Rush-Presbyn.-St. Luke's Med. Coll., 1973-78; adj. prof. Kent Coll. Law Ill. Inst. Tech., 1987-92; seminar tchr. various profl. and ednl. orgns., 1973-90. Assoc. Rush Presbyn.-St. Luke's Med. Ctr., 1975-80, bd. dirs. Isaac Ray Ctr., 1977-91; chmn. bd. dirs. Chgo. Area Project; bd. dirs. Bethany Hosp., 1977-79, Ill. Citizens for Handgun Control, 1983-90; chmn. Ill. Commn. onDelinquency Prevention, 1978-81; vol. atty. Neighborhood Legal Assistance Ctr., 1970-75, pres., 1972; vice chmn. Ill. Pollution Control Fin. Authority, 1972; mem. jr. governing bd. Chgo. Symphony Orch., 1972-83. Mem. ABA (mem. nat. task force punitive damages litigation sect., antitrust com. litigation sect., civil procedure com. antitrust sect.), Fed. Bar Assn., Seventh Cir. Bar Assn., Ill. State Bar Assn. (chmn. antitrust coun.), Chgo. Bar Assn. (various coms.), Mental Health Assn. Greater Chgo. (bd. dirs. 1980-90, pres. 1985-87), Univ. Club. Democrat. Died June 28, 2010.

MCNAMARA, DANIEL JOSEPH, insurance company executive; b. NYC, Feb. 1, 1928; s. James and Mary (Mulryan) McNamara; m. Patricia Marie Del Balso, Sept. 1, 1951; children: Joseph Michael, Patricia Ann, Daniel John, Jean Marie. BA, Fordham U., 1951, LLD, 1955. Bar: NY 1955. Sec. Nat. Bur. Casualty Underwriters, NYC, 1953—68; asst. gen. mgr. Ins. Rating Bd., NYC, 1968—69; v.p. actuary Chubb & Son, Inc., NYC, 1969—70; pres. Ins. Svcs. Office, NYC, from 1971. Chmn. bd. ISO Telecommunications, Inc., NYC, from 1983. Contbr. articles various profl. jours., chapters to books. Mem. to chmn. Our Lady of Perpetual Help, Parish Coun., Pelham, NY, 1967—75. With USN, 1948—48. Fellow: Casualty Actuarial Soc.; mem.: ABA, State of NY Bar Assn., Internat. Actuarial Assn., Am. Acad. Acturaries, Knights of Malta-Am. Assn., Friendly Sons of St. Patrick, Guild Cath. Lawyers, Downtown Assn., NY Athletic. Home: Greenwich, Conn. Died Jan. 12, 2010.

MC NIVEN, HUGH DONALD, engineering science educator, earthquake engineering researcher; b. Toronto, Ont., Can., Aug. 6, 1922; came to U.S., 1953; s. James and Pearl Mary (Jackson) Mc N.; m. Marion Fitzhugh, Sept. 12, 1959; 1 dau., Carolyn Fitzhugh. BASc., U. Toronto, 1944; M.C.E., Cornell U., 1948; PhD, Columbia U., 1957. Prof. engring. sci. U. Calif.-Berkeley, 1957—91, dir. Earthquake Engring. Research Ctr., 1980-85, prof. emeritus, from 1991. Contbr. articles to profl. jours. Pres. Univ. Art Mus. U. Calif.-Berkeley, 1970-72. Served to capt. Can. Army, 1944-46. Fellow Acoust. Soc. Am.; mem. ASCE, ASME, Earthquake Engring. Research Inst., Seismology Soc. Am. Clubs: Bohemian (San Francisco); Mira Vista Golf (El Cerrito, Calif.); Fox House, American (London). Home: Berkeley, Calif. Died Dec. 7, 2009.

MCPHERSON, LINDA ANNE, medical/surgical nurse; b. Peckville, Pa., June 22, 1946; d. Carl W. and Elizabeth (Wiorkowski) Bliss; children: Nicole Lynn, Deanne Beth. RN, Robert Packer Sch. Nursing, Sayre, Pa., 1967. RN, Pa. Staff nurse Morristown (N.J.) Meml. Hosp., 1967-68; staff nurse Rochester (N.Y.) Gen. Hosp., 1968-70; asst. nurse mgr. Meml. Hosp. Inc., Towanda, Pa., 1986-96, staff nurse, 1970-86 and from 96. Home: Alexandria, Va. Died Jan. 9, 2009.

MCRAE, THOMAS KENNETH, retired investment company executive; b. Richmond, Va., July 7, 1906; s. Christopher Duncan and Sarah Alice (Lawrence) McRae; m. Marion Lanier White, Sept. 11, 1937; children: Thomas Kenneth Jr., John Daniel. BA, U. Richmond, 1927; postgrad., Sch. Banking, Rutgers U., 1936—38. Asst. cashier First Mchts. Nat. Bank, Richmond, 1940—46, asst. v.p., 1946—49, v.p., 1949—63, sr. v.p., 1963—71; v.p. Davenport and Co., Richmond, 1971—85, sr. investment officer, 1985—90. Trustee Va. Supplemental Retirement Sys., 1964—71. Active Va. Mus. Fine Arts. Mem.: Richmond Soc. Fin. Analysts, Country of Va., Rotary, Masons. Republican. Baptist. Avocations: golf, stamp collecting/philately. Home: Richmond, Va. Died Sept. 5, 2009.

MEADOWS, STEPHEN PARRIS, chiropractor; b. Hinton, W.Va., Nov. 26, 1938; s. Clifford Lowe and Mary Catherine (Baker) M.; m. Joan Joyce Montag, Oct. 28, 1961 (div. July 1977); children— Merry Sloan, Marcia Stuart; m. Joyce Leigh Caudle, Oct. 6, 1977 (div. Oct. 1983). Student Marshall U., 1957-61, Winston-Salem State U., 1965-67; D. Chiropractic, Logan Chiropractic Coll., St. Louis, 1964. Practice chiropractic Winston-Salem, N.C., 1964—. Mem. N.Y. Chiropractic Soc., W.Va. Chiropractic Soc., N.C. Chiropractic Assn. (com. chmn. 1977), Am. Chiropractic Assn. Served with U.S. Army, 1959-61. Libertarian. Roman Catholic. Clubs: Trout Unlimited, Mercer's Anglers. Lodge: K.C. Home: Winston Salem, NC. Died Apr. 6, 2010.

MEALING, ISABEL THORPE, retired social worker; b. Oct. 4, 1907; d. Elisha McDonald and Maude (Davis) Thorpe; m. John Pace Mealing, Jr., Aug. 15, 1929 (div. Dec. 1939); children: Elisha Thorpe, Margaret Mae (Mrs. Wayne Frederick Orlowski). AB, Randolph-Macon Woman's Coll., 1928; MSW, Tulane U., 1943; postgrad., U. Va., 1929. High sch. English tchr., Blacksburg, Va., 1928-29; visitor Fulton County Dept. Pub. Welfare, Atlanta, 1937-38; dir. McIntosh County Dept. Pub. Welfare, Darien, Ga., 1938-40; child welfare cons. State of Ga., Atlanta, 1941-44; social worker ARC Lawson Gen. Hosp., Atlanta, 1944-45; asst. field dir. Lawson Gen. Hosp. and Sta. Hosp., Ft. Benning, Ga., 1945-46; chief social work svc. VA Regional Office, Ft. Jackson, S.C., 1947-48; pub. welfare officer Dept. Army, Japan, 1949-51; sr. social worker Valley Forge Army Hosp., 1951; chief social work svc. VA Hosp., Richmond, Va., 1951-52; VA Ctr., Wadsworth, Kans., 1952-68; Dublin, Ga., 1968-77; ret., 1977. Vol. Peace Corps, MOrocco, 1978-80. Author 2 books. Mem. Social Planning Coun., Leavenworth, Kans., 1952-68, v.p., 1955-56, 67-68, pres., 1956-57; bd. dirs. ARC, Leavenworth, 1960-68; bd. govs. United Fund, Leavenworth, 1967-68; bd. dirs. YWCA, Leavenworth, 1962-68, pres., 1964; chmn. welfare com. Mayor's Adv. Com., Leavenworth, 1968; mem. organizational bd. Leavenworth Cmty. Action Program, 1966; adviser Explorer Scouts Am., 1972; bd. dirs. Dublin Mental Health Assn., v.p., 1971-72, pres., 1972-74; pres. Mental Health Assn., Leavenworth, 1964, Darien United Meth. Women, 1987; mem. Midway Mus. Bd., 1982-84; sec. dorcas Soc., 1986—; treas. Lanier of Glyn UDC, 1986-88; vol. Welcome Ctr., Darien, 1987; active Stroll thru History, 1987. Recipient various certs., awards, commendations. Mem. Nat. assn. social Workers (exec. bd. Mo., Kans. chpt. 1954-56, pres. 1971), Am. Assn. Med. Social Workers (pres. Mo-Kans. chpt. 1954-55), Internat. Soc. Poets, Ga. (nominating com. 1945), Confs. on Social Welfare, Hist. Soc. McIntosh County (v.p. 1982-84), Daughters Am. Colonists (regent St. Johns Parish 1982-84, state chmn. vets. affairs), United Daughters Confederacy, DAR (vice regent 1982-84, time keeper 1987-88), Colonial Dames 17th Century (treas. Golden Isles chpt. 1982-84), Magna Charta Dames, dublin Cmty. Resource Forum (pres. 1971-73), First FAmilies of Ga., First Families of S.C., Clan Donald, Dorcas Sewing Soc., Dublin Pilot (charter). Died May 20, 2009.

MEDEIROS, JAMES STEPHEN, aerospace company executive; b. Somerset, Mass., Aug. 20, 1935; s. Frank Veira and Mary (Moniz) M.; m. Virginia Ann Cannon; children— James Stephen, Tracy Ann BA, Providence Coll, 1959; MBA, Pepperdine U., 1971. Group leader Rockwell Internat., Los Angeles, 1962-67, mgr. adminstrn. St. Louis, 1975-80; contracts mgr. McDonnell Douglas, Huntington Beach, Calif., 1967-73; gen. sales adminstr. Cessna Citation, Wichita, Kans., 1973-75; sr. v.p. adminstrn. and strategic planning Gates Learjet Corp., Tucson, from 1980. Lectr. U. Calif.-Irvine, 1971-72 Served to 1st lt. U.S. Army, 1960-62 Mem. Nat. Mgmt. Assn., Nat. Contract Mktg. Assn. Clubs: Old Pueblo Courthouse (Tucson). Republican. Roman Catholic. Home: Tucson, Ariz. Died Mar. 12, 2009.

MEDEIROS, LEONARD LUIZ, guidance counselor; b. New Bedford, Mass., Aug. 9, 1919; s. Luiz Correia and Virginia (Cabral) M.; m. Albertina Grace Silva, Apr. 18, 1948; children: Deborah Virginia, Leonard Jeffrey. BA with Honors, Providence Coll., 1950; MEd with Honors, Boston Coll., 1951; cert. advanced study, Vanderbilt U., 1969. Tchr. Walnut Pk. Country Day Sch., Newton, Mass., 1950-51, Roosevelt Jr. High Sch., New Bedford, 1951-56; sci. tchr. Keith Jr. High Sch., New Bedford, 1956-65; guidance counselor Normandin Jr. High Sch., New Bedford, 1965-84. Part-time tchr. Friends Acad., New Bedford, Acushnet-Westport-Dartmouth Schs. Contbr. articles to profl. jours. Bd. dirs. Lake Arrowhead Estates, Limerick, Maine, 1981-82, 86-89; mem. Dartmouth (Mass.) Sch. Com., 1957-63, Bd. Health, Dartmouth, 1972-75, Charter Commn., 1971-73, Dartmouth Town Meeting, 1953—; trustee Dartmouth Library, 1977—, chmn., 1981-82, vice chair, 1988—. Served with USAAF, 1942-45. Mem. Am. Sch. Counselors Assn. (pres. Mass. chpt. 1980-81, advt. mgr. 1983-85, retirement com. 1987-88), Bristol Plymouth Sch. Counselors Assn. (pres. 1976-78), Mass. Assn. Counseling and Devel. (sec.-treas. 1982-83, pres. 1984-85), New Bedford Educators Assn. (pres. 1969-70), Mass. Tchrs. Assn. (numerous coms. 1954-87, retirement com. 1987-88), Am. Assn. Ret. Persons (v.p. 1987-88, pres. 1988—), Am. Legion. Lodges: KC, Rotary (pres. Dartmouth chpt. 1980-81, pres.-elect 1988—). Democrat. Roman Catholic. Home: Limerick, Maine. Died May 3, 2010.

MEERSON, FELIX ZALMANOVICH, cardiologist; b. Moscow, Aug. 5, 1926; came to U.S., 1993; s. Zalman Moshevich and Minna Iyruhemonna (Ezra) M.; m. Lia Victorovna Shohova, 1953 (div. 1973); children: Nataly, Elena; m. Elena Vorontsova, Oct. 16, 1982; 1 child, Dmitry. MD, Moscow Med. Inst., 1949, PhD, 1952; DSc, Ctrl. Inst. Improving, Moscow, 1958. Sr. rsch. assoc. Inst. Phys. Methods Therapy, Yalta, 1954-55; sr. rsch. assoc. Inst. High Nervous Functioning USSR Acad. Sci., Moscow, 1955-56; assoc. prof. clin. physiology Ctrl. Inst. Improving Physician's Qualifications, 1956-57, prof., 1957-59; prof., head Lab. Exptl. Cardiology Inst. Gen. Pathophysiology Russian Acad. Med. Scis., Moscow, 1960-89, prof., dir. Ctr. Adaptive Medicine, 1990-93, mem. doctorate bd., 1960-93, mem. sci. coun., 1960-93. Sci. cons. Hypoxia Med., Ltd., Moscow, 1990-93, med. insts., Orenburg, Omsk, Irkutsk, Chelyabinsk, Russia, 1970-93; sci. head high mountain expdns. Russian Acad. Med. Scis., Caucasus, Tien Shan, 1980-93. Author: The Myocardium in Hyperfunction, Hypertrophy and Heart Failure, 1969, General Mechanisms of Adaption and Prophylactics, 1973, The Failing Heart: Adaption and Deadaptation, 1983, Adaption, Stress and Prophlaxis, 1984, Physiology of Adaptive Processes, 1986, Adaption to Stressful Situation and Physical Loads, 1988, Adaption to Hypoxia in Therapy and Prophylactics, 1989, Adaptive Protection of the Heart: Protecting Against Stress and Ischemic Damage, 1990, Protective Effects of Adaptation and Prospects of the Development of Adaptive Medicine, 1990, Protective Cross-Effects of Adaptation, 1993, Essentials of Adaptive Medicine: Protective Effects of Adaptation: A Manual, 1994; mem. editl. bd. CV World Report, 1985—, Clin. Cardiology, 1985—, Kardiology, 1985—; contbr. articles to profl. jours. Recipient medal Budapest U., Hungary, 1979, Jan Purkinie medal Prague U., Czechoslavakia, 1970, Laureate of State award USSR Govt., 1978, Hon. Scientist of Russia, Russian Govt., 1988, Gold medal USSR State Exbhn., 1989. Me. Internat. Soc. Adaptive Medicine (pres. 1990-95, founder, life pres. 1995—). Achievements include research in adaption to repeated moderate action of any environmental factor may protect animals and humans from damages impacts of other factors (cross-protective effect of adaptation); develpment of theory of long-term adaptation, a selective increase in expression of certain genes and accumulation of certain structures is the material basis of adaptation; formulation of new discipline Adaptive Medicine which is directed to study fundamental mechanisms of adaptation and use of adaptation for the treatment of diseases. Died Feb. 22, 2010.

MEGGINSON, LEON CASSITY, educator; b. Thomasville, Ala., July 26, 1921; s. William A. and Emma Frances (Cassity) M.; student Samford U., 1938-40; B.S., Miss. Coll., 1947; M.B.A., La. State U., 1949, Ph.D., 1953; m. Joclaire Leslie, June 14, 1985; children— Gayle (Mrs. Thomas A. Ross III), William Leon, William Jay. Factory rep. Hershey Chocolate Co., Birmingham, Ala., 1940-42; instr. bus. La. State U., 1949-50, asst. prof., 1951-54, assoc. prof., 1954-60, prof., 1960-77, prof. emeritus, 1977—, asst. dean Coll. Bus., 1957-60; research prof. mgmt. U. South Ala., 1978-84; J.L. Bedsole prof. bus. Mobile (Ala.) Coll., 1984—; Fulbright research scholar, Spain, 1961-62; resident advisor Ford Found., Karachi, Pakistan, 1968-70; cons. in mgmt. devel. for cos. and tng. instns. Mem. La. Adv. Council for Employment Security, 1956-64, chmn., 1960-64; chmn. East Baton Rouge Parish Family Ct., 1958-60. Trustee, mem. personnel com. Baton Rouge Gen. Hosp., 1957-61, 75-77; pres. W.A. Megginson Edn. Found. Served with AC, AUS, 1942-45. Decorated Air medal with 4 oak leaf clusters; recipient Distinguished Faculty Service award La. State U. Alumni Found., 1971; Phi Kappa Phi scholar U.S. Ala., 1982. Accredited personnel diplomate Am. Soc. Personnel Adminstrn. Mem. Acad. Mgmt. (dir.), So. Mgmt. Assn. (pres. 1972-73), Southwestern Social Sci. Assn. (pres. 1962-63), So. Case Research Assn. (pres. 1971-75). Republican. Baptist. Author: Personnel, 1967, 5th edit., 1985; (Acad. Mgmt. Book award 1967); Human Resources, 1968; (with son Bill Megginson) Successful Small Business Management, 1975, 5th edit., 1988; The Complete Guide to Your Own Business, 1977; (with Kae Chung) Organizational Behavior, 1981; (with Donald Mosley and Paul Pietri) Management Concepts and Applications, 3rd edit., 1989; (with dau. Gayle M. Ross) Business, 1985. Home: Daphne, Ala. Died Feb. 22, 2010.

MEHR, MORTON HENRY, electronic manufacturing executive; b. NYC, Apr. 23, 1927; s. Joseph and Sara (Barden) Mehr; m. Rhoda Irene Sondak, Aug. 30, 1946; children: Ethan, Matthew, Jocelyn. BS in Elec. Engring., Yale U., 1950. Devel. engr. Bradley Labs. Inc., New Haven, 1949—51; engr. C.G.S. Labs., Stamford, Conn., 1951—53; project engr. Stelma Inc., Stamford, 1953—54; engring. group leader Perkin-Elmer, Norwalk, Conn., 1954—60; pres. Measurement Sys. Inc., Norwalk, 1960—86; ret.; bd. dirs.; pvt. practice cons., from 1986. Pres., bd. dirs. Nortech Found. Inc.; regional adviser Norwalk State Tech. Coll. With USN, 1945—46. Mem.: IEEE, Internat. Soc. Optical Engrs., Soc. Info. Display, Ergonomics Soc., Human Factors Soc., Sprite Island Yacht Club. Achievements include patents in field. Home: Norwalk, Conn. Died July 20, 2010.

MEIKLEJOHN, WILLIAM HENRY, physicist; b. Virden, Ill., Jan. 7, 1917; s. John Backus and Ethel (Bone) M.; m. Ella Mae Moore, Nov. 10, 1936 (dec. 1955); children: Jo Ann, William Henry, Anita Louise, Joyce Ellen; m. Arlene Mae Loucks, Mar. 16, 1974. BSEE, U. Ill., 1940; MS in Physics, Union Coll., 1954. Registered profl. engr., Mass. Mgr. GE, Lynn, Mass., 1948-51, scientist Schenectady, N.Y., 1951-84; vis. prof. Carnegie Mellon U., Pitts., 1984-87; with MOVID Info. Tech., Schenectady, N.Y., from 1987. Mem. minerals and metals adv. bd. NAS, Washington, 1952-62. Author publs. in field. Scoutmaster Boy Scouts Am., Lynnfield, Mass., 1945-51, mem. coun., 1948-51; chmn. Redfeather Community Chest, Lynnfield, 1950-51. Mem. IEEE (basic sci. com.), Am. Inst. Physics. Achievements include 14 patents in field. Home: Scotia, NY. Died Jan. 13, 2009.

MEILGAARD, MORTEN CHRISTIAN, food products specialist, international educator; b. Vigerslev, Denmark, Nov. 11, 1928; s. Anton Christian Meilgaard and Ane Maria Elisa Larsen; m. Manon Meadows, Oct. 29, 1962; children: Stephen Paul, Justin Christian. MSChemE, Tech. U. Denmark, 1952, DSc in Food Sci., 1982. Rsch. chemist Carlsberg Breweries, Copenhagen, Denmark, 1947-57; dir. and co-owner Alfred Jorgensen Lab. for Fermentation, Copenhagen, 1957-67; dir. rsch. and devel. Cerveceria Cuauhtemoc, Monterrey, Mex., 1967-73; v.p. rsch. Stroh Brewery Co., Detroit, 1973-89, pres. Strohtech Inc. div., 1986-91; cons., from 1991. Vis. prof. Agrl. U. Denmark, 1994-97. Author: Sensory Evaluation Techniques, 1987, 2d edit., 1991; contbr. articles to profl. jours. Recipient Schwarz award, 1974. Fellow Inst. Brewing; mem. Internat. Med. Advisory Group, European Chemoreception Rsch. Orgn., Assn. Chemoreception Scis., Inst. Food Technologists, Am. Chem. Soc., Dansk Ingeniorforening, Am. Wine Soc., Air Pollution Control Assn., Master Brewers Assn. Am. (chmn. various coms., award of merit 1990), Am. Soc. Brewing Chemists (chmn. various coms.), ASTM (chmn. various coms., award of merit 1992), U.S. Hop Rsch. Coun. (pres. 1978-80, 1982-84, founder). Avocations: theater, music, sailing, skiing. Home: Ann Arbor, Mich. Died Apr. 11, 2009.

MEILMAN, EDWARD, physician; b. Boston, Apr. 6, 1915; s. Harry and Jennie (Sholofsky) M.; m. Rhoeda Berman, Mar. 6, 1946. AB, Harvard U., 1936, MD, 1940. Intern Mt. Sinai Hosp., NYC, 1940-42; resident Beth Israel Hosp., Boston, 1946-48, assoc. in med. and med. research, 1948-53; chmn. dept. medicine L.I. Jewish-Hillside Med. Center, New Hyde Park, NY, 1953-82, chmn. emeritus dept. medicine, from 1982. Prof. medicine SUNY, Stony Brook, 1971— Contbr. articles to profl. jours. Served with USAAF, 1942-46. Fellow N.Y. Acad. Medicine, N.Y. Acad. Scis.; mem. Am. Heart Assn. (fellow council clin. cardiology, council arteriosclerosis), Am. Fedn. Clin. Research, Harvey Soc., Am. Rheumatism Assn., Phi Beta Kappa, Alpha Omega Alpha. Clubs: Harvard (N.Y.C.); Harvard (L.I.). Democrat. Jewish. Home: Great Neck, NY. Died Dec. 3, 2009.

MEINKE, WILLIAM WAYNE, chemist; b. Elyria, Ohio, June 27, 1924; s. William Carl and Marian Ella (McRoberts) M.; m. Marilynn Hope Hayward, July 12, 1947; children— Sue Anne, David William. AB, Oberlin Coll., 1947; PhD, U. Calif., Berkeley, 1950. Mem. faculty U. Mich., 1950-63, prof. chemistry, 1962-63; chief analytical chemistry div. Nat. Bur. Standards, 1963-73; chief Office Standard Reference Materials, 1964-69; head radiation applications KMS Fusion, Inc., Ann Arbor, 1973-76, asst. to chmn., 1976-79; health physicist, radiation protection br. NRC, Washington, from 1980. Chmn. subcom. radiochemistry, com. nuclear sci. NRC, 1958-62; mem. adv. com. to analytical and inorganic chemistry div. Nat. Bur. Standards, 1960-63; adv. com. to analytical div. Oak Ridge Nat. Lab., 1959-63; adv. com. isotopes and radiation devel. AEC, 1961-64; mem. subcom. physiochem. standards Nat. Acad. Scis., NRC, 1963—; rep. Am. Chem. Soc. on Am. Standards Assn. (sect. com. N2 on gen. standards nuclear energy), 1960-68; geochemistry panel Apollo adv. com. NASA, 1963-65; cons. div. internat. affairs AEC and Internat. Atomic Energy Agy., 1961-64; titular mem. commn. on analytical radiochemistry and nuclear materials, 1965-71; commn. on data and standards Internat. Union Pure and Applied Chemistry, 1965-69, mem. U.S. nat. com., 1970—, sec. applied chemistry div., 1971-73; chmn. steering panel on characterization pure materials OECD, 1969-72; mem. sci. adv. bd. Center Radiochemistry and Activation Analysis, U. Pavia, Italy, 1970-73 Editor series monographs on radiochemistry of the elements, 1961; regional editor: The Analyst; adv. bd.: Analytical Chemistry, 1968-71; co-editor: Analytical Chemistry: Key to Progress on National Problems. Served to lt. (j.g.) USNR, 1943-46. Recipient Hevesy medal for radio-analytical chemistry, 1968; Rosa award Nat. Bur. Standards, 1968; Distinguished Service awards Am. Nuclear Soc., 1968; Distinguished Service awards Fed. Exec. Inst., 1968; Gold Medal award U.S. Commerce Dept., 1971 Fellow A.A.A.S.; mem. Soc. Analytical Chemistry (hon.), Am. Chem. Soc. (chmn. nuclear chemistry and technology div. 1968, sec. analytical chemistry div. 1972-73, Fisher award in analytical chemistry 1972), Am. Phys. Soc., Am. Nuclear Soc. (exec. com. isotopes and radiation div. 1963-66), Am. Soc. Testing and Materials, Phi Beta Kappa, Sigma Xi, Gamma Alpha, Phi Lambda Upsilon, Alpha Chi Sigma. Home: Albuquerque, N.Mex. Died Mar. 18, 2009.

MEISLICH, HERBERT, chemistry educator emeritus; b. Bklyn., Mar. 26, 1920; s. Isidore and Bessie (Rose) M.; m. Estelle Kalechstein, July 1, 1951; children— Mindy, Debrah, Susan. AB, Bklyn. Coll., 1940; A.M., Columbia U., 1947, PhD, 1950. With Edgewood Arsenal, Md., 1942-44; asst. prof. chemistry CCNY, 1946-62, assoc. prof., 1963-68, prof., 1969-86, prof. emeritus, from 1986. Author: Introduction to Organic Chemistry, 1960, Fundamentals of Chemistry, 1966, 5th edit., 1980, Introduction to Chemistry, 1968, Schaum's Organic Chemistry, 1977, 2d edit., 1991, Schaum's 3000 Solved Problems in Organic Chemistry, 1993. Mem. New Milford (N.J.) Bd. Edn., 1967-81. Served to lt. (j.g.) USN, 1944-46. Sloan Kettering fellow, 1956 Mem. Am. Chem. Soc. (past chmn. N.Y. sect., councilor) Home: Fort Lee, NJ. Died Mar. 4, 2009.

MELANSON, JAMES, newspaper television editor; b. NYC, Oct. 8, 1946; s. Alfred and Helen (Wirth) M.; m. Maureen McFadden, Oct. 11, 1985. BA in English, Iona Coll., 1968; student, Sch. Visual Arts, NYC, 1970-71. Reporter, editor Billboard mag., NYC, 1972-76; editorial cons., reviewer High Fidelity mag., NYC, 1976-79; home video editor Variety, NYC, 1981-86; TV editor The N.Y. Post, NYC, from 1986; dep. editor Sun. mag. N.Y. Daily News, from 1990; dep. editor daily news Sunday Mag., from 1991. With U.S. Army, 1969-70, Vietnam Avocations: hiking, photography, biking, drawing. Home: Brooklyn, NY. Died Feb. 5, 2009.

MELIAN, JOSEPH THOMAS, construction company executive, consultant; b. N.Y.C., Aug. 14, 1927; s. Joseph Allen and Margaret (Abate) M.; m. Lucille Ann Priani, Jan. 20, 1951; children— Joseph Thomas, Lori Ann Martin, Deborah Marie. Vice pres., treas. Melian Bros. Constrn. Corp., Briarcliff Manor, N.Y., 1954-62; pres. Jaytem Constrn. Corp., Briarcliff Manor, N.Y., 1962-70, J.L.D. Realty Corp., Briarcliff Manor, 1977-84, Briarhill Lanes Inc., Briarcliff Manor, 1984—. Republican. Club: Briarcliff Racquet (pres. 1970-77). Roman Catholic. Avocations: collecting collectables, tennis, bridge. Home: Briarcliff Manor, NY. Died Apr. 28, 2010.

MELLINS, HARRY ZACHARY, radiologist, educator; b. NYC, May 23, 1921; s. David J. and Ray (Hoffman) M.; m. Judith Alice Weiss, Dec. 26, 1950; children— Elizabeth, William, Thomas. AB, Columbia Coll., 1941; MD, L.I. Coll. Medicine, 1944; MS in Radiology, U. Minn., 1951; AM (hon.), Harvard U., 1970. Intern Jewish Hosp., Bklyn., 1944-45, asst. resident in radiology, 1945-46; resident in radiology U. Minn., Mpls., 1948-50, instr. radiology, 1950-52, asst. prof., 1952-53; clin. asst. prof. radiology Wayne State U., Detroit, 1953-56; dir. radiology Sinai Hosp., Detroit, 1953-56; prof., chmn. dept. radiology SUNY, Coll. Medicine, NYC, 1956-69; chief radiology Kings County Hosp. Center, Bklyn., 1956-69; radiologist-in-chief State Univ. Hosp., Bklyn., 1966-69; prof. radiology Harvard Med. Sch., Boston, 1969—87, prof. radiology emeritus, from 1991; dir. diagnostic radiology Peter Bent Brigham Hosp., 1969-79, Brigham and Women's Hosp., 1980-87, dir. edn. and tng., dept. radiology, 1987-94; co-dir. edn. and tng. dept. radiology, 1994-97; chief of radiology Harvard U. Health Svc., 1988-97; radiologist Brigham and Women's Hosp., 1998-99. Nat. cons. in radiology to surgeon gen. U.S. Air Force, 1968-79; mem. radiation study sect. NIH, 1967-71; mem. subcom. for written exam. in diagnostic radiology Am. Bd. Radiology, 1970-75; mem. radiology tng. com. research tng. grants br. Nat. Inst. Gen. Med. Scis.; mem. diagnostic research adv. group div. cancer biology and diagnosis Nat. Cancer Inst., 1975-79; guest examiner Am. Bd. Radiology. Served to capt. M.C. USAAF, 1946-48. Mem. Bklyn. Radiol. Soc. (pres. 1965-66), N.Y. Roentgen Soc. (pres 1966-67), Assn. Univ. Radiologists (pres. 1969-70, Gold medal 1986), Soc. Uroradiology (pres. 1975-76, Gold medal 2000), Am. Roentgen Ray Soc. (pres. 1977-79, Gold medal 1989), Radiol. Soc. N.Am., New Eng. Roentgen Ray Soc. (pres. 1986-87), Soc. Gastrointestinal Radiology, Alpha Omega Alpha (alumnus). Home: Cambridge, Mass. Died Jan. 22, 2009.

MELTZER, JACK, retired dean; b. Bayonne, NJ, Aug. 21, 1921; s. Louis and Debbie (Gold) M.; m. Rae Libin, June 26, 1944; children: Richard, Marc, Ellen. BA, Wayne State U., 1941; MA, U. Chgo., 1947. Dir. planning Michael Reese Hosp., Chgo., 1953-54; S.E. Chgo. Commn. and U. Chgo., 1954-58; propr. Jack Meltzer Assos. (planners), 1958-63; acting dir. Am. Soc. Planning Ofcls., 1967-68; prof., dir. Center Urban Studies, U. Chgo., 1963-71; prof. div. social scis., prof. Sch. Social Service Adminstrn., 1965-83; prof., dean Sch. Social Scis. U. Tex.-Dallas, 1983-86; pvt. practice cons., from 1986. Cons. to govt. and industry, 1945— Author book revs., articles, books. Village trustee, Park Forest, Ill., 1950-52, mem. plan commn., 1949; Served to capt. USAAF, World War II. Mem. AAUP, Am. Soc. Planning Ofcls. (past treas.), Am. Inst. Planners (past v.p. pvt. practice dept.), Nat. Assn. Housing and Renewal Ofcls., Am. Soc. Pub. Adminstrn. Home: Chevy Chase, Md. Died May 5, 2010.

MENCHIN, ROBERT STANLEY, marketing executive; b. Kingston, NY, Oct. 31, 1923; s. Abraham H. and Gertrude (Gorline) M.; m. Marylin Barsky, Dec. 26, 1949; children: Jonathan, Scott. BA, NYU, 1948. Acct. exec. DKG Advt., NYC, 1949-51; dir. spl. porjects Am. Visuals Corp., NYC, 1952-59; dir. advt. and pub. rels Arthur Wiesenberger & Co., NYC, 1959-65; pres. Wall Street Mktg. Commn., Inc., NYC, 1967-77; dir. mktg. comm. Chgo. Bd. Trade, 1977-83, v.p. comm. and member rels., 1983-87; pres. Wall Street Mktg., Chgo., from 1987. Author: The Last Caprice, 1964, Where There's a Will, 1977, The Mature Market: A Strategic Marketing Guide to America's Fastest-Growing Population Segment, 1989, New Work Opportunities for Older Americans, 1993, 101 Classic Jewish Jokes: Jewish Humor from Groucho Marx to Jerry Seinfeld, 1997. With AUS, 1942-45. Mem. Am. Mktg. Assn., Pub. Rels. Soc. Am., Fin. Planners Assn. Home: Chicago, Ill. Died Sept. 9, 2009.

MENK, CARL WILLIAM, executive search company executive; b. Newark, Oct. 19, 1921; s. Carl William and Catherine Regina (Murray) M.; m. Elizabeth Cullum, May 31, 1947; children: Carl, Elizabeth (dec.), Mary, Paul. BSBA, Seton Hall U., 1943; MA, Columbia U., 1950. Sr. v.p. P. Ballantine & Sons, Newark, 1946-69; pres. Boyden Assocs., Inc., NYC, 1969-84; chmn. Canny, Bowen, Inc., NYC, 1984-98, chmn. emeritus, from 1998. Trustee Howard Savs. Bank, 1980—91. 2d lt. pilot USAAF, 1943—46. Mem. Union League NY, Spring Lake Golf Club, John's Island Club, Internat. Exec. Svc. Corps. Republican. Roman Catholic. Died June 10, 2010.

MENKE, SALLY, film editor; b. Mineola, NY, Dec. 17, 1953; d. Warren Wells and Charlotte Menke; m. Aldo Louis Parisot, Aug. 9, 1986; children: Lucas, Isabella. BFA, NYU, 1977. Editor: (films) Cold Feet, 1983, Tom Goes to the Bar, 1986, Teenage Mutant Ninja Turtles, 1990, The Search for Signs of Intelliegent Life in the Universe, 1991, Reservoir Dogs, 1992, Heaven and Earth, 1993, Who Do you Think You're Fooling?, 1994, Pulp Fiction, 1994, Four Rooms (The Man from Hollywood segment), 1995, Mulholland Falls, 1996, Nighwatch, 1997, Jackie Brown, 1997, Joao Mata Sete, 2000, D.C. Smalls, 2001, Daddy and Them, 2001, Kill Bill: Vol. 1, 2002, Kill Bill: Vol. 2, 2004, Grindhouse (Death Proof segment), 2007, Inglorious Basterds, 2009, Peacock, 2010; (TV movies) The Congress, 1986; exec. prodr., editor: (films) All the Prettty Horses, 2000 Died Sept. 27, 2010.

MERKEL, ALFRED WILLIAM, printing executive; b. Lafayette, Ind., Mar. 29, 1929; s. Charles Daniel and Lillian Mae (Bennett) M.; m. Marlowe Marcia Graves, Sept. 2, 1955; children: Jennifer, Todd, Carolyn. BS, Purdue U., 1952. Indsl. engr. R.R. Donnelly, Crawfordsville, Ind., 1952-53; v.p. sch. div. Jostens, Mpls., 1958-72; v.p. Am. Can Co., Indpls., 1972-75; pres. GTE-Directories Press (formerly Times Mirror Press), Los Angeles, from 1975. Area chmn. United Way, Los Angeles, 1983; mem. ALISO-PICO Businessmen's Council, Los Angeles, 1981—. Served to capt. USAF, 1953-58. Mem. Printing Industries So. Calif. (pres. 1980, Man of Yr., 1980), Printing Industries of Am. (vice chmn. 1983—). Clubs: Oakmont (Glendale, Calif.),. Lutheran. Avocations: golf, fishing, gardening. Home: La Canada Flintridge, Calif. Died Feb. 5, 2009.

MEROLA, PATRICK JAMES, pharmaceutical company technician; b. Somerville, NJ, June 6, 1951; s. Patsy Joseph and Mary Catherine (Sala) M.; m. Kathy Ann Strahle, Nov. 11, 1979. Grad. high sch., Middlesex, NJ. Adminstr. office svcs. Union Carbide Corp., Bound Brook, N.J., 1969-74; supr. graphic arts IEEE, NYC, 1974-92; operator scanning electron microscope AgFa-Bayer Corp., Branchburg, N.J., from 1993, mem. Branchburg Employees Safety Team, from 1997. Mem. emergency response team IEEE, Piscataway, N.J., 1988-92. Author: (poetry) The Path Not Taken, 1996 (Critics Choice award 1996), Best Poems of the 90's, 1997 (Editors Choice award 1997), Isle of View, 1997; author, creator The Black Panther; contbr. to books. Mgr. softball team Somerville Area Newcomers, Branchburg, 1997. Named to Nat. Poetry Hall of Fame, 1997. Avocations: music, sports. Home: Middlesex, NJ. Died Jan. 25, 2009.

MERRIFIELD, DONALD PAUL, ministries coordinator, former academic administrator; b. Los Angeles, Nov. 14, 1928; s. Arthur S. and Elizabeth (Baker) M. BS in Physics, Calif. Inst. Tech., 1950; MS, U. Notre Dame, 1951; A.M., Ph.L. in Philosophy, St. Louis U., 1957; PhD, MIT, 1962; S.T.M., U. Santa Clara, Calif., 1966; S.T.D. (hon.), U. So. Calif., 1969; D.H.L. (hon.), U. Judaism, 1984, Hebrew Union Coll.-Jewish Inst. Religion, 1986. Joined Soc. of Jesus, 1951; ordained priest Roman Cath. Ch., 1965; instr. physics Loyola U., Los Angeles, 1961-62; lectr. Engring. Sch., Santa Clara, 1965; cons. theoretical chemistry Jet Propulsion Lab., Calif. Inst. Tech., 1962-69; asst. prof. physics U. San Francisco, 1967-69; pres. Loyola Marymount U., Los Angeles, 1969-84, chancellor, 1984—2002; regent, sr. rsch. fellow Charminade U., Honolulu, 2002—10; mem. religious ministry Catholic Diocese of Hawaii, 2002—10. Contbr. chapters to books. Mem. Sigma Xi. Died Feb. 25, 2010.

MERRILL, GERALD P., state legislator, retired postmaster; b. Pittsburg, NH, Mar. 17, 1926; m. Venessa Merrill; 3 children. Grad., Pittsburg H.S. Ret. postmaster, 1986; mem. N.H. State Ho. of Reps., mem. fin. and appropriations com. Chmn. Pittsburg Sch. Bd. Mem. N.H. Guides Assn. (pres., treas., sec.), Nat. Assn. Postmasters (county dir., N.H. chpt. v.p., pres.), Masons (32d degree). Died May 9, 2009.

MERRILL, HARVIE MARTIN, retired manufacturing executive; b. Detroit, Apr. 26, 1921; s. Harvie and Helen (Nelson) M.; m. Mardelle Merrill; children— Susan, Linda. BS in Chem. Engring, Purdue U., 1942, Bd Che magma cum laude. Devel. engr. Sinclair Refining Co., 1946-47; research and gen. mgr. 3M Co., St. Paul, 1947-65; v.p. fabricated products Plastics div. Stauffer Chem. Co., NYC, 1965-69; with Hexcel Corp., San Francisco, 1969-86, pres., chief exec. officer, 1969-86, chmn. bd., 1976-88. With USAF, 1942-46. Mem.: Interlachen Country Club. Home: Winter Park, Fla. Died Feb. 19, 2010.

MERRILL, LELAND GILBERT, JR., retired environmental science educator; b. Danville, Ill., Oct. 4, 1920; s. Leland Gilbert and May (Babcock) M.; m. Virginia Gilhooley, Sept. 14, 1949; children: Susan Jane, Alison Lee. BS, Mich. State U., 1942; MS, Rutgers U., 1948, PhD, 1949. Research asst. entomology Rutgers U., 1946-49; asst. prof. entomology Mich. State U., 1949-53; mem. faculty Rutgers U., 1953-82, research specialist entomology, 1960-61, dean agr., 1961-71, dir. Inst. Environ. Studies, 1971-76, prof. center coastal and environ. studies, 1976-82; exec. sec. N.J. Acad. Sci., 1984-92. Served to maj. AUS, 1942-46. Medallist, Wrestling XIV Olympiad, 1948. Mem.: Entomol. Soc. Am., AAAS, Epsilon Sigma Phi, Alpha Zeta, Phi Kappa Phi, Alpha Gamma Rho, Sigma Xi. Home: Skillman, NJ. Died July 28, 2009.

MERRILL, LOIS JEAN, dean, nursing educator; b. New Haven, Aug. 3, 1932; d. Robert Warner and Lydia Mabel (Crook) Merrill. BS, U. Conn., 1955; MS, U. Colo., 1960; PhD, U. Nebr., 1978. Nurse Cin. Gen. Hosp., 1955—56; asst. instr. U. Cin., 1956—58; nurse Presbyn. Hosp., Denver, 1959—60; instr. nursing Syracuse U., NY, 1960—63; assoc. prof. U. Ky., Lexington, 1963—69, U. Nebr., Lincoln, 1969—76, assoc. dean, 1969—76; prof., dean nursing U. Evansville, Ind., 1978—86, U. ND, Grand Forks, from 1986. Editor Global Hunger, 1986; mem. editl. bd. Nurse Educator, 1975—84, Jour. Profl. Nursing, 1987—89. Contbr. articles to profl. jours. Mem. adv. bd. Evansville-Vanderburg County Health Occupations Programs, 1978—86; bd. dirs. Vandenburgh City Sch. Practical Nursing, Evansville, 1978—86, Greater Evansville Diabetes Assn., 1985—86. Recipient Mentor award, Eta Lambda/Sigma Theta Tau, 1986. Mem.: United Health Svcs. Corp. Bd., MAIN (bd. dirs. from 1991, chair 1993—94), Midwest Nursing Rsch. Soc., Nat. League Nursing (bd. dirs. 1974—76, accreditation visitor from 1984), ANA (state pres. 1972—74). Home: Grand Forks, ND. Died Dec. 22, 2009.

MERRILL, VINCENT NICHOLS, retired landscape architect; b. Reading, Mass., Apr. 28, 1912; s. Charles Clarkson and Bessie Louise (Nichols) M.; m. Anna Victoria Swanson, Jan. 20, 1943 (dec. Feb. 1996); m. Natalie Ames Prentice, Aug. 16, 1997 (dec. Jan. 2003). AB, Dartmouth Coll., 1933; M in Landscape Architecture, Harvard U., 1937. Office asst. Shurcliff & Shurcliff, Boston, 1937-42, 47-54, ptnr., 1954-58, Shurcliff & Merrill and predecessors Shurcliff, Shurcliff & Merrill, Boston, Mass., 1958-81; prin. Shurcliff & Merrill, Cambridge, Mass., 1981-89; retired, 1998. Founder, bd. dirs., pres. Charles River Watershed Assn., Auburndale, Mass., 1963-75; bd. dirs. Charles Basin Adv. Com., Boston, 1979-82; pres. Hubbard Ednl. Trust, Cambridge, 1981-89, bd. dirs., 1989-95. Capt. U.S. Army, 1942-46, ETO. Recipient Gold medal Mass. Hort. Soc., 1988. Fellow Am. Soc. Landscape Architects; mem. Boston Soc. Landscape Architects (pres. 1961-63), Hort. Club of Boston (hon. mem., pres. 1992-94). Avocation: home landscaping. Home: Plymouth, Mass. Died Jan. 11, 2009.

MERRIN, SEYMOUR, computer company executive; b. Bklyn., Aug. 13, 1931; s. Joseph and Esther Bella (Manelis) M.; m. Elaine Cohen, Sept. 4, 1960 (dec. May 1962); m. Elizabeth Jenifer Slack, Oct. 12, 1963 (dec. Mar. 1995); children: Charles Seymour, Mariamne Jenifer Weights; m. Helene Claire Singer, Sept. 1, 2001 BS, Tufts Coll., 1952; MS, U. Ariz., 1954; PhD, Pa. State U., 1962. Geologist Magma Copper Co., Superior, Ariz., 1954, U.S. Geol. Survey, 1956-58; chemist IBM, Poughkeepsie, NY, 1962-64; mgr. package devel., mgr. reliability and failure analysis Sperry Semiconductor divsn. Sperry Rand, Norwalk, Conn., 1965-68; cons. materials tech. Fairfield, Conn., 1967-69; v.p., dir. Innotech Corp., Norwalk, 1969-74; divsn. mgr. Emdex divsn. Exxon Enterprises, Milford, Conn., 1974-78; chmn., dir. Computerworks, Westport, Conn., 1978-85; v.p., dir. personal computing svc. Gartner Group, Inc., Stamford, Conn., 1984-87; pres. Merrin Resources, Southport, Conn., 1987-89, Merrin Info. Svcs., Inc., Santa Fe, from 1987. Bd. dirs. Micrografx Corp., Allen, Tex.; adv. panel Apple Computer Co., Cupertino, Calif., 1982-83; adv. bd. Compaq Computer Corp., Houston, 1984-85, Computer and Software News, NYC, 1984-89; program adv. bd. Comdex, Boston, 1985—; lectr. in field. Contbr. numerous articles to profl. publs.; patentee in field. Bd. dirs. Futures for Children, Albuquerque, from 2004, Santa Fe Internat. Folk Market, Couse Found., Taos, N.Mex. With US Army, 1954—56. Fellow Geol. Soc. Am., Am. Inst. Chemists; Computing Tech. Industry Assn. (founder, pres. 1981-83, bd. dirs. 1981-84). Died May 12, 2010.

METZNER, CHARLES MILLER, federal judge; b. NYC, Mar. 13, 1912; s. Emanuel and Gertrude (Miller) M.; m. Jeanne Gottlieb, Oct. 6, 1966. AB, Columbia U., 1931, LL.B., 1933. Bar: N.Y. 1933. Pvt. practice, 1934; mem. Jud. Council State N.Y., 1935-41; law clk. to N.Y. supreme ct. justice, 1942-52; exec. asst. to U.S. atty. Gen. Herbert Brownell, Jr., 1953-54; mem. firm Chapman, Walsh & O'Connell, 1954-59; judge U.S. Dist Ct. (so. dist.) N.Y., 1959—77; sr. judge, from 1977. Mem. Law Revision Commn. N.Y. State, 1959; chmn. com. adminstrn. magistrates system U.S. Jud. Conf., 1970-81; chmn. Columbia Coll. Coun., 1965-66. Pres. N.Y. Young Republican Club, 1941; Trustee Columbia U., 1972-84, trustee emeritus, 1984—; bd. dirs. N.Y.C. Ctr. Music and Drama, 1969-74. Recipient Lawyer Div. of Joint Def. Appeal award, 1961, Columbia U. Alumni medal, 1966, Founders award Nat. Coun. U.S. Magistrates, 1989. Mem. ABA, Am. Law Inst., Fed. Bar Coun. (cert. Disting. Jud. Svc. 1989). Home: Sarasota, Fla. Died Nov. 30, 2009.

MEYER, BRUD RICHARD, retired pharmaceutical executive; b. Waukegan, Ill., Feb. 22, 1926; s. Charles Lewis and Mamie Olive (Broom) M.; m. Betty Louise Stine (dec. 1970); children: Linda (Mrs. Gary Stillabower), Louise (Mrs. Donald Knochel), Janet (Mrs. Gerald Cockrell), Jeff, Karen, Blake, Amy; m. Barbara Ann Hamilton, Nov. 26, 1970. BS, Purdue U., 1949. With Eli Lilly & Co., Indpls., 1949-87, indsl. engr., 1949-56, supr. indsl. engr., 1956-59, sr. personnel rep., 1960-64, personnel mgr. Lafayette, Ind., 1964-67, asst. dir., 1967-69, dir. adminstrn., 1969-79, dir. personnel and public relations, 1980-87, ret., 1987. Bd. dirs. Lafayette Home Hosp., 1977—, Hanna Cmty. Ctr., 1983—, Tippecanoe Hist. Corp., 1985—; bd. dirs. United Way Tippecanoe County, 1970-76, pres., 1974; bd. dirs. Legal Aid Soc. Tippecanoe County, 1973—, Jr. Achievement, pres., 1979; bd. dirs. Lilly Credit Union, 1969-75, pres., 1973-74; mem. Citizen's Com. on Alcoholism, 1966-72; bd. dirs. Greater Lafayette Cmty. Ctrs., 1975-79, pres., 1977-78; bd. dirs. Tippecanoe County Child Care, 1990—, pres., 1998-99; mng. dir. Battle Tippecanoe Outdoor Drama Bd. With USAAF, 1943-45. Mem. Pi Tau Sigma, Lambda Chi Alpha, C. of C. Greater Lafayette (bd. dirs., v.p. 1969-73), Battleground Hist. Soc. Methodist. Home: Lafayette, Ind. Died July 3, 2010.

MEYER, CHARLES HILLIARD, hospital executive; b. Bklyn., Nov. 16, 1926; s. Harry and Beatrice (Kessler) M.; m. Miriam Silverman, June 12, 1952 (dec. Sept. 1968); children: Keith, Janice; m. Joan Griffin, Nov. 24, 1980 Student, Mohawk Coll., 1946-47; BA, NYU, 1950; MS, Cornell U., 1952. Labor economist U.S. Bur. Labor Stats., NYC, 1952-53; project engr. Federated Dept. Stores, Bklyn., 1953-55; pers. dir. Jewish Hosp., Bklyn., 1955-60, asst. exec. dir., 1960-62; exec. dir. Bklyn. Womens' Hosp., 1962-69; v.p., chief oper. officer Brookdale Hosp. Med. Ctr., Bklyn., 1969-77, pres., chief exec. officer, from 1977. Lectr. Bklyn. Coll., 1953-68; preceptor Baruch Coll., CUNY, 1971—. Founding mem. community bd. for ambulatory care Brookdale Hosp. Med. Ctr., 1974. With USAF, 1945-46, ATO. Fellow Am. Coll. Healthcare Execs.; mem. Greater N.Y. Hosp. Assn. (immediate past chmn.), League Vol. Hosps. (bd. dirs., past chmn.), Hosp. Assn. N.Y. State (trustee), Phi Beta Kappa, Psi Chi. Home: Delray Beach, Fla. Died Oct. 4, 2009.

MEYER, CHARLES WILLIAM, economics professor; b. Joliet, Ill., Mar. 15, 1932; s. George Frank and Nona (Bargreen) M.; m. Donelle Sedgley, Sept. 4, 1964; 1 child, Eric. BA, U. Ill., 1954, MA, 1955; PhD, Johns Hopkins U., 1961. Asst. prof. econs. Iowa State U., Ames, 1961-64, assoc. prof., 1964-67, prof., 1967—98, prof. emeritus, from 1998. Rsch. coord. Gov.'s Study Iowa Tax System, Des Moines, 1965-66; vis. scholar Social Security Adminstrn., Washington, 1973-74. Author: Social Security Disability Insurance, 1979; co-author: Principles of Public Finance, 1983; co-author: Social Security and Individual Equity, 1993; editor: Social Security, 1987; contbr. articles to profl. jours. 1st lt. U.S. Army, 1955-58. Mem. Am. Econ. Assn., Phi Beta Kappa, Phi Kappa Phi. Home: Ames, Iowa. Died Oct. 21, 2009.

MEYER, JACOB OWEN, minister; b. Myerstown, Pa., Nov. 11, 1934; s. Jacob John and Mary May (Bross) M.; m. Velma Ruth Foreman, June 28, 1935; children— Mary E., Joseph G., Jacob C., Daniel K., Jonathan S., Rachel A., Micah D., Nathaniel A., Solomon E., Sarah A. Student Thomas A. Edison Coll., 1972-73, Evang. Sch. Theology, Myerstown, Pa., 1974-82, Inst. Holy Land Studies, Jerusalem, Israel, 1983, Dropsie Coll., 1984. Founder, pres. Assemblies of Yahweh, Bethel, Pa., 1966—2010, Obadiah Sch. of the Bible, Bethel; ptnr., gen. mgr. Shalom Farm, Bethel; editor Sacred Name Broadcaster mag., Narrow Way mag. Author: Commentary on Galatians, 1983, Memorial Name*Yahweh, 1987; editor Bible transl. The Sacred Scriptures-Bethel edit., 1981. Pres. Tulpehocken PTA, 1975. Home: Bethel, Pa. Died Apr. 9, 2010.

MEYER, MALCOLM HOLT, retired judge; b. Hong Kong, Sept. 28, 1930; s. Clarence E. and Thresa (Heidecke) M.; m. Catherine Dindia, Sept. 2, 1956; children: Christopher M., Holt V. BA, Harvard U., 1952; LLB, Columbia U., 1957. Bar: N.Y. 1958, U.S. Dist. Ct. (so. and ea. dists.) N.Y. 1963. Atty. Webster & Sheffield, NYC, 1959—66; asst. to mayor City of N.Y., 1966—73; judge N.Y. State Family Ct., Staten Island, 1973—95; jud. hearing officer N.Y. State Supreme Ct., Richmond County, 1996—98; ret. Cpl. U.S. Army, 1952-54, Germany. Mem. N.Y. State Family Ct. Judges Assn. (pres. 1990-91), N.Y.C. Family Ct. Judges Asns. (pres. 1985-86). Home: Staten Island, NY. Died Feb. 9, 2009.

MEYER, PETER, college administrator, educator, consultant; b. Bremen, Germany, May 2, 1930; came to U.S., 1937; s. Hans and Marianne M. (Bach) M.; m. Ursula M. Thuemer, July 3, 1951 (div. Feb. 1972); 1 child, David; m. Linda W. Shoulberg, Dec. 31, 1980; 1 stepchild, Amy Shoulberg. BA, Queens Coll., CUNY, 1955; MS, Columbia U., 1957; PhD, NYU, 1963. Asst. dean, counseling supr. Queens Coll., Flushing, N.Y., 1959-69; program assoc. So. Regional Edn. Bd., Atlanta, 1970-72; chmn. social work, prof. Fla. Internat. U., Miami, 1972-76; cons. adult degree programming and mgmt. devel., Burnsville, N.C., 1976-81; exec. dir. Queens Inst. for Lifelong Learning, Charlotte, N.C., 1981-82; dean, prof. social work Pfeiffer Coll., Charlotte, 1982-85; assoc. dir. Ctr. Urban Affairs, assoc. prof. adult and community coll. edn. N.C. State U., Raleigh, 1986—; Served to cpl. U.S. Army, 1951-53. Recipient Founders Day award NYU, 1963; Ford Found. grantee, 1973. Mem. N.C. Adult Edn. Assn. (exec. com.), Council for the Advancement Experiential Learning, Am. Assn. Higher Edn. Author: Awarding College Credit-For Non-College Learning, 1975; contbr. numerous articles on adult edn. and counseling to profl. jours. Home: Raleigh, NC. Died Nov. 5, 2009.

MEYERHOFF, JACK FULTON, corporate financial executive; b. Joliet, Ill, May 15, 1926; s. Charles F. and Helen (Ferguson) M.; m. Mary Margaret Williams, Jan. 2, 1949; children— Keith F., Greg H., Deborah S., Todd C. Postgrad., Ohio Wesleyan U., 1944-45; BS, Miami U., Ohio, 1947. CPA, Ohio, Ill.; cert. Advanced Mgmt. Program, Harvard U., 1968. Mgr. Arthur Andersen & Co., Chgo., Cin., Cleve., 1947-59; treas. MacGregor Sports, Cin., 1959-63; v.p., corp. controller Brunswick Corp., Chgo., 1963-77, CFO, 1972-77; v.p. corp. affairs, 1977-80, v.p. human resources, 1980-81; chmn., CEO MarJac Assocs., Nokomis, Fla., from 1981; pres., dir. Charles Oxford Corp., Nokomis, from 1984. Bd. dirs. Sherwood Med. Industries, Inc., Old Orchard Bank & Trust Co., Tech: Time Inc., Nokomis; organizer, vice chmn. bd. trustees Caldwell Trust Co. and Trust Cos. Am., Venice, Fla., 1993—. Treas., bd. dirs. Cove Sch.; bd. dirs., pres. Skokie Valley Cmty. Hosp., No. Ill. Indsl. Assn.; v.p., bd. dirs. Jr. Achievement; bd. dirs. Chgo. Responsibility Growth, Gulf Area Med. Properties; chmn. bd. Bon Secours-Venice Hosp., HMA Regional Med. Ctr., Venice Hosp. Found.; bd. dirs. J. Clifford MacDonald Handicapped Ctr. of Tampa, Sarasota Com. of 100; bd. dirs., treas. Triangle Econ. Devel. Coun.; bd. dirs., Manatee C.C. Found., Boys and Girls Club of Venice, Pillar

Cmty., Venice, Fla.; mem. adv. coun. Miami U., Georgetown U., U. So. Fla. With USNR, 1944-46. Mem. AICPA, Ohio Soc. CPAs, Ill. Soc. CPAs, Fin. Exec. Inst., Nat. Assn. Acct., Harvard Bus. Sch. Alumni Assn., Miami U. Exec. Alumni Coun. (bd. dirs., treas.), Venice Area C. of C. (bd. dirs., treas.), Sigma Alpha Epsilon, Delta Sigma Pi, Beta Alpha Psi, Beta Gamma Sigma, Venice Yacht Club, Mid Am. Club, Econ. Club, Misty Creek Country Club, Masons, Rotary. Methodist. Died Sept. 14, 2009.

MEYERS, CARLTON ROY, physical education educator; b. Buffalo, Dec. 16, 1922; s. Roy Edward and Helena (Kiphuth) M.; m. Eleanor E. Exner, June 21, 1947; children— Marsha J. Fishbane, JoEllen Schweichler, Pamela J. Butterworth, Suzanne J. Tanbakuchi. B.S., Springfield Coll., 1947; A.M., Tchrs. Coll. Columbia U., 1948, Ed. D., 1949. Asst. prof. health Yale U., New Haven, 1949-54; salesman Meyers Lumber Co., North Tonawanda, N.Y., 1954-57; mem. faculty SUNY, Buffalo, prof. phys. edn. and recreation, 1957—, chmn. dept. instrn., 1968-72. Vis. prof. Didsbury Coll. Edn., Manchester, Eng., 1970-71, Salisbury Coll. Advanced Edn., Adelaide, 1968; hon. teaching fellow Flinders U. South Australia, 1968; mem. sports medicine del. People to People Citizen Ambassador Program, China, 1985. Author: Measurement in Physical Education, 2d edit., 1974; (with Sanford) Swimming and Diving Officiating, 3d edit., 1970; contbr. articles to profl. jours. Bd. dirs. program Erie County Community Coll., Orchard Park, N.Y., 1965-85; mem. mcpl. golf course com. North Tonawanda Recreation Dept., 1975-87; bd. elders Redeemer Lutheran Ch., North Tonawanda, 1958-64, 79-85, pres., 1964-67. Served to lt. USNR, 1943-46; PTO. Schiff nat. scholar Boy Scouts Am., 1941-43; Fulbright sr. lectr. Council Internat. Exchange and Scholars, Iran, 1963-64; recipient Merit award Eastern dist. AAHPERD, 1985. Fellow Am. Coll. Sports Medicine, AAHPERD; mem. AAUP, Am. Ednl. Research Assn., Internat. Soc. Biomechanics. Republican. Avocations: photography; bowling; golf; sailing. Died June 8, 2009.

MEYERSON, STANLEY PHILLIP, retired lawyer; b. Apr. 13, 1916; s. Louis A. and Ella Meyerson; m. Sherry Maxwell, Nov. 30, 1996; children: Marianne Martin, Camilla, Margot Ellis, Stanley P. AB, Duke U., 1937, JD, 1939. Bar: SC 1939, NY 1940, Ga. 1945, US Supreme Ct. Ptnr. Johnson Hatcher & Meyerson, Atlanta, 1945-55, Hatcher, Meyerson, Oxford & Irvin, Atlanta, 1955-78, Westmoreland, Hall, McGee, Oxford & Meyerson, Atlanta, 1978-88, McGee & Oxford, Atlanta, 1988—2006. Former adj. prof. Ga. State U.; dir., officer various corps. Contbr. Co-founder West Paces Ferry Hosp., Atlanta, Annandale at Suwanee for the Handicapped; trustee Hudson Libr., Inc., Highlands, NC, MetroGroup, Atlanta; del. Moscow Conf., Law and Bilateral Econ. Rels., 1990. Lt. comdr. USNR, 1943—45. Mem.: ABA (former professionalism com.), Atlanta Bar Assn. (former sec.), Ga. Bar Assn. (former chmn. tax com.), Georgians for Nixon (chmn. 1960), Duke U. Alumni Assn. (former pres. Atlanta chpt., former sec. N.Y.C. chpt.), Cherokee Town and Country Club (Atlanta), Highlands Country Club, Rotary Club Highlands N.C. Home: Highlands, NC. Died May 23, 2009.

MICHAELS, JAMES EDWARD, bishop emeritus; b. Chgo., Ill., May 30, 1926; Ordained priest Missionary Soc. of St. Columban, Dublin, 1951; ordained bishop, 1966; aux. bishop Archdiocese of Kwangju, Republic of Korea, 1966—73, Diocese of Wheeling-Charleston, W.Va., 1973—87, aux. bishop emeritus, 1987—2010. Roman Catholic. Died Sept. 21, 2010.

MICHALSEN, JAN BJORN, nurse; b. Bklyn., Jan. 26, 1951; s. Reinert and Erna (Vera) Michalsen; m. Lydia Melinda Maida, Jan. 24, 1981. BA, Upsala Coll., 1973; MA, Wagner Coll., 1977. RN, Fla.; cert. Rice Inst. Nursing, 1988. Carpenter Local Union 1456, NYC, 1973-78; computer acctg. CBS Television, LA, 1978-79; broker Noonan, Astley & Pierce, LA, 1980-81. Mem. Cormorant Creek Estates Homeowners, Jacksonville, 1988-89, Mayors Election Com., Jacksonville, 1987—. Mem. Mandarin Community Club. Republican. Lutheran. Avocations: tennis, scuba diving, photography. Home: Jacksonville, Fla. Died Jan. 1, 2009.

MICHEL, WERNER, television company executive; b. Strasbourg, France; s. Erwin and Anna (Haas) M.; m. Rosemary Ashton, Feb. 20, 1969. Ph.D., Sorbonne, Paris, 1933. Dir. broadcast divsn. Voice of Am., 1944-46; assoc. program dir. CBS, 1946-50; prodr. Ford Theatre, 1950-52; exec. prodr. DuMont Network, 1952-56; prodr. Edge of Night - CBS, 1956-57; v.p. broadcasting Reach M. Clinton, N.Y.C., 1957-62, SSC&B Inc., N.Y.C., 1962-75; dir. devel. ABC-TV, Los Angeles, 1975-77; sr. v.p., MGM-TV, Los Angeles, 1977-82; exec. v.p. Guber-Peters Prodns., Los Angeles, 1982-84; sr. ptnr., Bozell Worldwide, N.Y.C., 1984—. Composer of 2 Broadway musicals, 1939, 41. Home: New York, NY. Died Aug. 27, 2010.

MICHELETTO, JOE RAYMOND, food products executive, controller; b. Christopher, Ill., Oct. 19, 1936; s. Steve Pete and Dena (Arro) M.; m. Marlyn Kay Thetford, Jan. 20, 1962; children: Amber, Peter, Joseph. BS in Acctg., So. Ill. U., 1962. Cost acct. Ralston Purina Co., St. Louis, 1962-63, fin. analyst, 1963-66, planning and fin. coordinator Grocery Products div., 1966-69, controller Grocery Products div., 1969-72, v.p. Grocery Products div., 1972-74, v.p., dir. adminstrn. Consumer Products div., 1974-84, corp. v.p., controller, from 1985. Served as sgt. U.S. Army, 1954-58. Mem. Fin. Execs. Inst. Roman Catholic. Home: Edwardsville, Ill. Died May 14, 2010.

MICHELIN, JOSEPH F., state legislator; b. Amesbury, Mass., Jan. 1, 1940; m. Elizabeth Michelin; 3 children. Grad., Amesbury H.S. Mem. bd. selectmen, mem. zoning bd., acting health officer N.H. Ho. of Reps., Sandown, N.H., 1990-94, chair bd. selectmen, 1993-94, mem. labor, indsl. and rehab. svcs.; automobile dealer Sandown. Mem. Timberlane Taxpayers Coalition (founder). Home: Barton, Vt. Died Nov. 28, 2009.

MICKINS, ANDEL WATKINS, retired principal; b. Central, S.C., Oct. 28, 1924; d. Ernest Samuel and Estelle Charlotte (Jamison) Watkins; B.S., Tuskegee Inst., 1946; M.A., Columbia, 1962; postgrad. Iowa State Coll., 1948, U. Miami, m. Isaac C. Mickins, July 11, 1952; 1 son, Isaac Clarence, II. Head home econs. dept. Anderson County Tng. Sr. High Sch., Pendleton, S.C., 1946-52; classroom tchr. Holmes Elem. Sch., Miami, Fla., 1952-62; asst. prin. for curriculum Liberty City Elem. Sch., Miami, 1962-67; prin. R.R. Moton Elem. Sch., Miami, 1967-71, Rainbow Park Elem. Sch., Miami, 1971-81; supervising tchr. U. Miami, summer 1965. Pres., Friendship Garden and Civic Club, 1969-75; 1st v.p. Bapt. Women's Council, 1966—; pres. Ministers Wives and Ministers Widors Council Greater Miami; chmn. exec. bd. Fla. Gen. Bapt. State Conv.; bd. dirs. Black Archives History and Research Found. South Fla. Recipient Sarah Blocker award Fla. Meml. Coll., 1966; plaques Liberty City Elem. Sch., 1967, Rainbow Park Elem. Sch., 1974, Friendship Garden and Civic Club, 1969, Meml. Temple Bapt. Ch., 1965; citation Fla. Gov. Mem. NEA (life), Dade County Admintrs. Assn., Nat. Assn. Elem. Sch. Prins., Alpha Kappa Alpha, Phi Delta Kappa, Kappa Delta Pi, Pi Delta Kappa. Democrat. Clubs: Jack and Jill of Am., Order of Eastern Star. Home: Opa Locka, Fla. Died Sept. 27, 2009.

MIDDLETON, JOHN FRANCIS MARCHMENT, anthropology educator; b. London, May 22, 1921; married; 2 children. BA, U. London, 1941; BSc, U. Oxford, Eng., 1949; DPhil in Anthropology, U. Oxford, 1953. Lectr. anthropology U. London, Eng., 1953-54, 56-63; sr. lectr. U. Cape Town, Republic of South Africa, 1954-56; prof. Northwestern U., Evanston, Ill., 1963-66; prof. anthropology NYU, from 1966, Yale U., New Haven, 1966-72; prof. African anthropology Sch. of Oriental & African Studies London U., 1972-81, Yale U., from 1981; dir. Internat. African Inst., 1973-74, 80-81. Rsch. in anthropology Uganda, 1949-53, Zanzibar, 1958, Nigeria, 1963-64, Ghana, 1976-77, Kenya, 1986; vis. prof. U. Va., Oreg., Lagos, Nigeria, Ecole Pratique des Hautestudes, Paris. Author: Kikuyu of Kenya, 1953, Lugbara Religion, 1960, Land Tenure in Zanzibar, 1961, The Lugbara of Uganda, 1965, others. Mem. Royal Anthrop. Inst. Gt. Brit. and Ireland. Avocations: social anthropology of africa, religion, politics. Home: Guilford, Conn. Died Feb. 27, 2009.

MIEULI, FRANKLIN, professional basketball team executive; b. San Jose, Calif., 1921; s. Giacomo M.; 1 son, Peter. Student, U. Oreg. With family nursery bus.; advt. profl. San Francisco Brewing Co., from 1949; founder, pres. Mieuli & Assocs. Radio and TV Producers; investor in various profl. sports teams including San Francisco Giants and San Francisco 49ers; owner, ptnr. Golden State Warriors, Oakland, Calif., 1962—86. Served with USN, World War II. Died Apr. 25, 2010.

MIGNON, CHARLES WILLIAM, language educator; b. NYC, Dec. 11, 1933; s. Charles William and Dorothy Burgess (Congdon) M.; m. Mary Ann Killian, Dec. 21, 1959; children: Paul Killian, Edward Taylor. AB, Kenyon Coll., 1956; MA, U. Conn., 1959, PhD, 1963. Instr. U. Conn., Storrs, 1962-63; asst. prof. U. Ill., Urbana, 1963-67; asst. prof., assoc. prof. U. Nebr., Lincoln, 1967-73, prof., from 1973. Fulbright lectr. U. Warsaw, Poland, 1972-73. Editor: Upon the Types of the-Ot, 1989, O Pioneers, 1992, My Antonia, 1994. With USAF, 1956-58. Grantee NEH, 1983-84, 86, 94-98. Mem. Modern Lang. Assn., Am. Lit. Assn., Soc. Early Americanists, We. Lit. Assn. Avocation: usta umpire. Home: Lincoln, Nebr. Died Sept. 25, 2009.

MILES, JESSE MC LANE, retired accounting company executive; b. De Funiak Springs, Fla., June 17, 1932; s. Percy Webb and Dora (Pippin) M.; m. Catherine Rita Eugenio, July 18, 1959; children: Jesse Jr., Catherine, Teresa, John, Thomas, Robert BSBA, U. Fla., 1954. CPA NY. Mem. staff, mgr., prin. Arthur Young & Co., NYC, 1954-63, ptnr., 1963-89, dep. chmn.-internat., 1985-89; chmn. Arthur Young Internat., 1985-89; ptnr. Ernst & Young, 1989-92; co-chmn. Ernst & Young Internat., 1989-92; ret., 1992. Mem. AICPA, N.Y. Inst. CPAs, Boca Pointe Country Club. Home: Boca Raton, Fla. Died Sept. 12, 2009.

MILLARD, BETTY M., mental health nurse; b. Covington, Ky., Oct. 31, 1940; d. Lafe (Mickey) and Naomi (Whetzel) Osborne; m. Clark Millard, Aug. 7, 1965 (div.); 1 child, Clark E. Diploma, Jewish Hosp. Sch. of Nursing, Cin., 1961; student, N. Ky. U., from 1990. RN, Ky., Ohio, cert. in pyschiatric nursing. Staff nurse Jewish Hosp., Cin., asst. head nurse; staff nurse St. Elizabeth Med. Ctr., Covington, Ky. Home: Covington, Ky. Died Jan. 15, 2009.

MILLER, ALLEN RICHARD, retired mathematician; b. Bklyn., 1942; BS, Bklyn. Coll., 1965; MA, U. Md., 1971. Mathematician U.S. Naval Rsch. Lab., Washington, 1968-93; prof. George Washington U., Washington, 1992-95. Reviewer: Math. Revs. With U.S. Army, 1965-67. Home: Washington, DC. Died Aug. 15, 2010.

MILLER, CAROLYN WROBEL, indoor air quality consultant, reading researcher; b. Hammond, Ind., Feb. 1, 1943; d. Stanley Jacob and Margaret Caroline (Stupeck) Wrobel; m. Howard Frederick Fodrea, June 17, 1967 (div. Jan. 1987); m. Miller George A., Aug 8, 2003; children: Gregory Kirk, Lynn Renee. BA in Elem. Edn., Purdue U., 1966; MA in Reading and Lang. Devel., U. Chgo., 1973; postgrad., U. Colo., Denver, 1986—87. Cert. elem. tchr., Ind., Ill. Tchr. various schs., Ind., Colo., 1966-87; founder, supr., clinician Reading Clinic, Children's Hosp., Denver, 1969-73; pvt. practice Denver, 1973—87, Deerfield, Ill., from 1973; creator of pilot presch.-kindergarten lang. devel. program Gary, Ind. Diocese Schs., from 1987, therapist lang. and reading disabilities, from 1987; pres. Reading Rsch. Ctr., Arlington Heights, Ill., from 2000; founder Indoor Environ. Health Cons., 2007, dir., 2007. Conducted Lang. Devel. Workshop, Gary, Ind. 1988; Dawson Tech. Sch., 1990, Coll. Lake County, 1991, Prairie State Coll., 1991—, Chgo. City Colls., 1991, R.J. Daley Coll., 1991, Coll. DuPage, 1991—; condr. adult basic edn. workshops for Coll. of DuPage, R.J. Daley Coll., 1992, Ill. Lang. Devel. Literacy Program; tchr. Korean English Lang. Inst., Chgo., 1996, Lang. Devel. Program for Minorities, 2000; dir. pilot study Cabrini Green Tutoring Ctr., Chgo., 2000, Ill. Sch. Dist., 2006; presenter in field. Author: Language Development Program, 1985, Presch. Kindergarten Lang. Devel. Program, 1988, A Multi-Sensory Stimulation Program for the Premature Baby in Its Incubator to Reduce Medical Costs and Academic Failure, 1986, Predicting At-Risk Babies for First Grade Reading Failure Before Birth A 15 Year Study, A Language Development Program, Grades 1 to Adult, 1988, 92, Waukegan Ill. IAQ Study Using an Air Purifier to Reduce Classroom Air Pollutants in a 3rd and 4th Grade Minority Classroom and Improving Student Attention, Physical Health, Performance, and Fine Motor Skills, 2006; editor, pub.: ESL For Native Spanish Speakers, 1996, ESL for Native Korean Speakers, 1996, Environ. Health Rschr. Reporter Environ. News Letter; presentor: Am. Inst. Archs., COTE, Chgo. Chapter, Am. Acad. Environ. Medicine, Greening Am. Schs. Kansas City, Town Meeting, 2006, chair of town meeting. Active Graland Country Day Sch., Denver, 1981-83, N.W. Ind. Children's Chorale, 1988—; Ill. state chair Babies and You com. March of Dimes, 1999—; founder Indoor Environ. Health Consultants, 2007-; mem. Arlington Heights Environ. Control Commn., 2007-. Mem. NEA, IAQ Assn. (Chgo. Chpt, charter mem), Am. Ednl. Rsch. Assn., Internat. Reading Assn., Am. Coun. for Children with Learning Disabilities, Am. Acad. Environ. Medicine (chhmn. pub. rels., mktg. com., chmn. town meeting com. 2005), Assn. for Childhood Edn. Internat., Colo. Assn. for Edn. of Young Children, Infant Stimulation Edn. Assn., Indoor Air Quality Assn., Art Inst. Chgo., U. Chgo. Alumni Club (Denver area ann. fund, Pres. fund com. 1988—, com. mem. Denver area chpt. 1974-87), Arlington Heights, Ill. Environ. Control Commn., Our Lady Wayside Sch. (bd. mem.). Roman Catholic. Avocations: sports, sewing, literature, gardening, antiques, opera. Died July 2, 2010.

MILLER, DAVID LAWRENCE, lawyer; b. Chgo., Dec. 27, 1941; m. Paula Lawson; children: Lawrence, Neal, Allison. Student, Ohio Wesleyan U.; AB, U. Mich., 1964, LLB, 1967. Bar: D.C. 1968, U.S. Tax. Ct. 1969, U.S. Ct. Claims 1972, U.S. Ct. Appeals (D.C. cir.) 1973. Tax atty. chief counsel's office IRS, 1967-71; ptnr. Haynes & Miller, 1971—90, Arter & Hadden, Washington, 1990—2003, Kutak Rock LLP, 2003—10. Mem. ABA (com. on tax-exempt bonds 1977-2010, vice chmn. subcom. on arbitage 1978-79, sect. on taxation), Nat. Assn. Bond Lawyers (steering com. nat. bd. attys. workshop 1983-84, 92, chmn. spl. com. on arbitage rebate 1987-88), D.C. Bar. Died June 15, 2010.

MILLER, DAVID WILLIAM, historian, educator; b. Coudersport, Pa., July 9, 1940; s. Arthur Charles and Kathryn Marie (Long) M.; m. Margaret Vick Richardson, Aug. 22, 1964; 1 child, Roberta Neal. BA, Rice U., 1962; MA, U. Wis., 1963; PhD, U. Chgo., 1968. Instr. history Carnegie Mellon U., Pitts., 1967-68, asst. prof., 1968-73, assoc. prof., 1973-80, prof., from 1980. Adj. prof. religious studies U. Pitts., from 1998. Author: Church, State and Nation in Ireland, 1898-1921, 1973, Queen's Rebels: Ulster Loyalism in Historical Perspective, 1978; editor: Peep o'Day Boys and Defenders: Selected Documents on the Disturbances in County Armagh, 1784-1796, 1990; co-editor: Piety and Power in Ireland, 1760-1960, 2000; assoc. editor: Oxford Dictionary of National Biography, 2004, Encyclopedia of Irish History and Culture, 2004; prin. developer: (interactive atlas) Great American History Machine, 1994. Sr. research fellow Inst. Irish Studies Queen's U., Belfast, Northern Ireland, 1975-76. Democrat. Presbyterian. Avocations: walking, singing. Home: Pittsburgh, Pa. Died Sept. 19, 2009.

MILLER, DONALD ROSS, management consultant; b. Huntington, NY, Aug. 5, 1927; s. George Everett and Ethel May (Ross) M.; m. Constance Higgins, 1948 (div. 1955); children: Donald Ross Jr., Cynthia Lynn, Candace Lee; m. Janet Heyman Behr, Apr. 15, 1965; children: Jeffrey Lawrence, Wendy Lorraine. BS/BEA, MIT, 1950. Cert. mgmt. cons. Inst. of Mgmt. Cons. Staff engr. Stop & Shop, Inc., Boston, 1950-56; v.p., dir. Cresap, McCormick and Paget, Inc., NYC, 1956-76; mng. dir. Donald R. Miller Mgmt. Cons., Palm Desert, Calif., 1977—2005. Pres., CEO Carl Fischer Inc., N.Y.C., 1996; chmn. bd. dirs. Nash Finch Co., Mpls., 1995-2000; bd. dirs. Michael Anthony Jewelers, Inc., Mt. Vernon, N.Y., Western Horizon Resorts, Inc., Gunnison, Colo. Author: Management Practices Manual, 3 vols., 1963, (booklet) Management of Managerial Resources, 1969. Bd. dirs. Queens Mus. Art, Flushing, N.Y., 1982-93, pres., 1988-92; pres. Lexington House, Forest Hills, 1984-2001; mem. MIT Alumni Adv. Coun., Cambridge, Mass., 1955-75; bd. govs. Alumni Ctr. N.Y.C., 1965-75, chmn., 1968-72; bd. dirs. Vol. Cons. Group, N.Y., 1969-79; trustee Queens Theatre in the Park, Flushing Meadow, N.Y., 1976-82; mem. vestry St. Margaret's Episcopal Ch., Palm Desert, Calif., 2003-05, sr. warden, 2004-05; trustee St. Margarets Episc. Sch., 2004-05. With U.S. Maritime Svc., 1945-46, ETO, U.S. Army, 1946-48. Mem. Nat. Assn. Corp. Dirs., Inst. Mgmt. Cons., Sky Club. Episcopal. Avocations: tennis, reading. Died June 8, 2010.

MILLER, DUANE F., service executive; b. Flint, Mich., Dec. 28, 1947; s. Francis N. and Lillian A. (Snider) M.; m. Theresa Miller, Dec. 8, 1975 (div. Dec. 1978). BA, Western Mich. U., 1974. Cert. mech. contractor, Mich. Ptnr. Miller Refrigeration, Flint, 1968-74; mgr. Young Supply, Detroit, 1974-78; service engr. Kroeger Co., Livonia, Mich., 1978-84; owner N.R.G. Services, Walled Lake, Mich., from 1984. Chmn. ERA Walkathon NOW, Detroit, 1976; mgr. Walled Lake Softball League. Served with U.S. Army, 1969-70.

Mem. Pontiac Oakland Refrigeration Assn. (pres. 1982-83), Walled Lake Jaycees (pres. 1979). Avocations: softball, symphony, bowling, hunting. Died Aug. 28, 2009.

MILLER, EDMOND TROWBRIDGE, civil engineer, educator, consultant; b. Pitts., Dec. 9, 1933; s. George Ellsworth and Billie Sue (Watson) M.; m. Nancy Lee Cooper, July 21, 1956; children: Carol Anne, Nancy Ruth, Laura Elizabeth. B.C.E., Ga. Inst. Tech., 1955, MSC.E., 1957; C.E., MIT, 1963; PhD, Tex. A&M U., 1967. Registered profl. engr., Ala., Fla. Asst. prof. civil engring. U. Ala., Tuscaloosa, 1963-64, assoc. prof., 1967-71, prof., 1971-75; v.p. William S. Pollard Cons., Memphis, 1976-77; chmn. dept. civil engring. U. Louisville, 1977-81; prof. U. Ala., Birmingham, 1981-96, chmn. dept. civil engring., 1981-90, interim dean Sch. Engring., 1984; ret., 1996. Instr. civil engring. Tex. A&M U., 1964-67. Served to capt. C.E. AUS, 1956-57. Automotive Safety Found. fellow, 1964-65; recipient Outstanding Achievement in Edn. award Ky. Soc. Profl. Engrs., 1980 Fellow ASCE (dist. 9 council 1978-80), Inst. Transp. Engrs.; mem. Am. Soc. Engring. Edn., Transp. Research Bd., Sigma Xi, Phi Kappa Phi, Tau Beta Pi, Chi Epsilon Christian Scientist. Died May 7, 2010.

MILLER, ELLIOTT CAIRNS, retired bank executive, lawyer; b. Cambridge, Mass., May 4, 1934; s. James Wilkinson and Mary Elliott (Cairns) M.; m. Mary Killion, July 2, 1960; children: Jonathan Vaill, Stephen Killion. AB, Harvard Coll., 1956; JD, U. Mich., 1961; LLM, Boston U., 1970. Bar: Conn. 1962. Assoc. Robinson & Cole, Hartford, Conn., 1961-66, ptnr., 1967-72; v.p., counsel Soc. for Savs., Hartford, Conn., 1972-73, sr. v.p., 1973-78, exec. v.p., 1978, pres., CEO, dir., 1979-90; pres., CEO Soc. for Savs. Bancorp Inc., 1987-90. Bd. dirs. nat. council Savs. Inst., Washington, 1984-88. Trustee, chmn. Kingswood-Oxford Sch., West Hartford, 1977-87; trustee Coordinating Coun. on Founds., 1987-90; bd. dirs. Downtown Coun., Hartford, 1975-90; trustee Greater Hartford Arts Coun., 1980-88; trustee Wadsworth Atheneum, 1990-99; trustee Hartford Stage Co., 1973-85; corporator Hartford Hosp., Inst. of Living; mem. transition com. Conn. State Treas. Denise Nappier, 1998-99. With U.S. Army, 1956-58. Mem. Conn. Bar Assn., 1893 Club (Hartford), Monday Evening Club (Hartford), Dauntless Club (Essex, Conn.), Ferrari Club Am., Bernese Mountain Dog Club. Methodist. Home: Essex, Conn. Died Nov. 2009.

MILLER, EUGENE FERRELL, political science educator; b. Atlanta, Oct. 1, 1935; s. James Douglas and Mary Lou (Ferrell) Miller; m. Eva Jean Fix, June 14, 1958; children: David, Cynthia, Gary, Gregory. BA, Emory U., 1957, MA, 1962; PhD, U. Chgo., 1965. Instr. Davidson Coll., NC, 1962—63; asst. prof. Furman U., Greenville, SC, 1963—67, U. Ga., Athens, 1967—72, assoc. prof., 1972—81, prof. polit. sci., from 1981. Editor: Hume's Essays, 1985; contbr. chapters to books, articles to profl. jours. Co.-dir. conf. series Liberty Fund, Inc., Indpls., from 1982. Recipient Outstanding Tchr. award, U. Ga., 1974, 1979—81, 1983; fellowship, Danforth Found., 1957—62, NEH, 1972—73. Mem.: Am. Polit. Sci. Assn. Methodist. Home: Athens, Ga. Died May 30, 2010.

MILLER, G(ERSON) H(ARRY), science administrator, mathematician, computer scientist, chemist; b. Phila., Mar. 2, 1924; m. Mary Alexa Heath, Jan. 28, 1961; children: Byron, Alexandra. BA, Pomona Coll., 1949; MEd in Counseling and Pers., Temple U., 1951; PhD. in Ednl. Psychology, U. So. Calif., 1957; MS in Math., U. Ill., 1982, postgrad., 1963-65. Jr. high sch. and jr. coll. instr. math. L.A. Sch. Dist., 1953-57; assoc. prof. Western Ill. U., Macomb, 1957-60; prof. Towson State U., Balt., 1960-61; prof. math. and edn. Parsons Coll., Fairfield, Iowa, 1961-65; prof. Tenn. Technol. U., Cookeville, 1966—68; prof. math. and computer sci. Edinboro (Pa.) U., 1968-71, 81-89, asst. dir. Institutional Rsch., 1972-80, emeritus prof., from 1989; dir. Studies On Smoking, Inc. and SOS Stop Smoking Clinic, Edinboro, from 1972. Dir. Nat. Study Math. Requirements for Scientists and Engrs., 1966-73; condr. Nat. Symposium for Am. Inst. Biol. Scis., Am. Chem. Soc. and Am. Soc. Engring. Educators, 1970-75; dir. Math. for Industry Confs.; spkr., presenter in field Contbr. numerous articles to profl. jours. Pres. Edinboro YMCA, 1972-83; bd. dirs. Common Cause, Harrisburg, Pa., 1975-80; Sgt. USAAF, 1943-46, PTO. Grantee U.S. Office Edn., 1968, 70, No Other World, 1973, NAS, 1980, ITT Life Ins. Corp., 1983, Erie County Found., 1987. Fellow Am. Inst. Chemists (cert. profl. chemist), AAAS; mem. APHA, Am. Assn. World Health, Am. Chem. Soc., Am. Soc. Engring. Edn., Internat. Assn. Pure and Applied Chemists, Internat. Soc. for Preventive Oncology, Math. Assn. Am., Am. Diabetes Assn., Sch. Sci. and Math. Assn., N.Y. Acad. Scis. (hon.), Acad. Sr. Profls. (hon.). Died Apr. 21, 2010.

MILLER, HELEN LOUISE, city commissioner; b. Pottstown, Pa., Apr. 23, 1925; d. James E. and Frances Morse; m. Walker Miller (div. 1973); children— Regina Miller, Cotez Rivers, Gail Miller, Alvin, Alvina, Walker (dec.), Dwight (dec.). Commr., City of Opa-Locka (Fla.), 1980-82, 84—, mayor, 1982-84. Mem. Community Devel. Corp., Opa-Locka, 1982—; bd. dirs. Dade League Cities, 1982. Recipient Citizen of Yr. award Zeta Phi Beta; named Outstanding Citizen, Community Action Agy., Miami; Outstanding Black Woman, Miami-Dade Pub. Library; Recognition award as black female mayor Booker T. Found., 1983. Mem. NAACP, Women in Mcpl. Govt., Nat. Conf. Black Mayors, Nat. Orgn. Black Law Enforcement Execs., North Dade Citizens Council, Black Elected Ofcls. of Dade County, Com. 100 Women of Dade County, Com. 100 Women of Fla. Meml. Coll. Democrat. Methodist. Club: Civic (past pres.) (Opa-Locka). Home: Opa Locka, Fla. Died Feb. 8, 2010.

MILLER, HENRY FRANKLIN, lawyer; b. Phila., May 19, 1938; s. Lester and Bessie (Posner) M.; m. Barbara Ann Gendel, June 20, 1964; children: Andrew, Alexa. AB, Lafayette Coll., 1959; JD, U. Pa., 1964. Bar: Pa. 1965. Law clk. U.S. Dist. Ct. Del., Wilmington, 1964-65; assoc. Wolf, Block LLP, Phila., 1965—71, ptnr., 1971—2005; counsel Cozen O Connor, from 2009. Pres. Soc. Hill Synagogue, Phila., 1978-79, Big Brothers/Big Sisters Assn. of Phila., 1980-81, Jewish Family & Children's Agy., Phila., 1986-88. 1st lt. U.S. Army, 1959-60. Mem. Am. Coll. Real Estate Lawyers. Avocations: swimming, hiking, bicycling, reading. Home: Philadelphia, Pa. Died Jan. 28, 2010.

MILLER, HERBERT JOHN, JR., (JACK MILLER), lawyer; b. Mpls., Jan. 11, 1924; s. Herbert John and Catherine (Johnson) M.; m. Carey Kinsolving, Apr. 3, 1948; children: John Kinsolving, William Grady. Student, U. Minn., 1941-43; BA, George Washington U., 1948, LL.B., 1949. Bar: D.C. 1949. Assoc. Kirkland, Fleming, Green, Martin & Ellis, Washington, 1949-58; ptnr. Kirkland, Ellis, Hodson, Chaffetz and Masters, 1958-61; asst. atty. gen., criminal divsn. US Dept. Justice, 1961-65; founding ptnr. Miller, Cassidy, Larroca & Lewin, Washington, 1965—2001; sr. ptnr. Baker & Botts LLP, 2001—09. Chmn. U.S. del. Conferees Attys. Gen. Ams., Mexico City, 1963, Mins. of Govt., Interior and Security of Cen. Am., Panama, and U.S., 1964, 65; chmn. Pres.'s Commn. on D.C. Crime, 1965-67. Capt. AUS, 1943-46. Mem. ABA, Am. Coll. Trial Lawyers, D.C.Bar Assn. (pres. 1970-71), Order of Coif, Phi Delta Phi, Alpha Delta Phi. Clubs: Congressional (Washington). Democrat. Home: Boyds, Md. Died Nov. 14, 2009.

MILLER, JAMES DAVID, banker; b. Reading, Pa., Jan. 21, 1943; s. James Charles and Dorothy Alberta (Weidner) M.; m. Hannah Elizabeth Moore, June 20, 1964; children— Gregory Douglas, Diane Elizabeth. B.S. in Bus. Adminstrn., Lehigh U., 1964, M.B.A., 1967. Chartered fin. analyst, 1971. Investment analyst, portfolio mgr. Am. Bank & Trust, Reading, Pa., 1964-67, Pitts. Nat. Bank, 1967-72; dir. research Moore Leonard & Lynch, Pitts., 1972-75; mgr. personal investment div., chmn. trust investment co. Mellon Bank, Pitts., 1975—; Contbr. articles to co. mag. Mem. Pitts. Soc. Fin. Analysts (sec., treas. 1973-75), Inst. Chartered Fin. Analysts. Republican. Presbyterian. Clubs: St. Clair Country (Pitts.); Pitts. Lehigh (pres. 1978-80). Home: Chicago, Ill. Died Feb. 4, 2009.

MILLER, JAMES HUGH, JR., retired public utility executive; b. New Orleans, Oct. 14, 1922; s. James Hugh and Helen (Piguet) M.; m. Juliet deVilliers, Nov. 22, 1945; children: Juliet Miller Beale, James Hugh, Robert Boyd, Mary Ashley Miller Crosier. BEE, Tulane U., 1943. Jr. engr. Ala. Power Co., Mobile, 1946-58, supr. transmission lines Birmingham, 1958-60, asst. to pres., 1960-62, asst. mgr. elec. ops., 1962-68, sr. v.p., 1968-75; exec. v.p. Ga. Power Co., Atlanta, 1975-82, pres., 1982-87. Home: Atlanta, Ga. Died Oct. 6, 2009.

MILLER, JEAN DIENER, training coordinator; b. Chgo., Feb. 20, 1926; d. Eugene Irl Miller and Marian Roberts (Wentworth) Diener Miller; m. Richard Paul Miller, June 21, 1947; children: Timothy E., Patrick R., Thomas E., Peter D., Leslie Anne. BS, Northwestern U., 1947; MA in Tchg., U. Notre Dame, 1967. Cert. secondary tchr. Ind.; systems profl. Quality analyst asst. Miles Labs., Inc., Elkhart, 1943—47; sec. to chief chemist, 1947—48; tech. writer, 1979—80; tng. coord., from 1980. Sci. tchr. Elkhart Cmty. Schs., 1966—79. Bd. dirs. Elkhart YMCA, 1955—60, Elkhart Family Counseling, 1962—66, Elkhart Mental Health Assn., 1960—62; sec., treas. Trucker's Helper, Inc., from 1979. Nolan scholar, 1946—47. Mem.: Assn. Sys. Mgmt., Delta Zeta (sec. 1946—47), Kappa Kappa Kappa. Republican. Methodist. Avocations: backpacking, music, gardening. Home: Elkhart, Ind. Died Dec. 22, 2009.

MILLER, JESSE EDWARD, savings and loan executive; b. Graceville, Fla., June 24, 1925; s. Jesse Edward and Annie Lou (Knapp) M.; m. Jean Hodo, July 29, 1950; children: Leslie, Mark, Jesse Edward. Student, Emory U., 1943-44; BA in Forestry, Duke U., 1947, M.F., 1948; grad., Sch. Savs. and Loan, Ind. U., 1964. Forester land dept. U.S. Steel Corp., Birmingham, Ala., 1948-51; chief forester U.S. Pipe & Foundry Co., Birmingham, 1951-57, Arthur Brown & Sons, Decatur, Ala., 1957-59; with City Fed. Savs. & Loan Assn., Birmingham, from 1959, pres., 1966-83, chmn. bd., from 1974, chief exec. officer, 1974-85. Dir. So. United Life Ins. Co., Montgomery. Bd. dirs. Birmingham chpt. United Appeal, Birmingham Football Found., Birmingham Better Bus. Bur., Operation New Birmingham, Birmingham adv. bd. Salvation Army, Carraway Meth. Med. Center, Birmingham, Ala. Motorists Assn. Served with USNR, 1944-46. Mem. Ala. Savs. and Loan League (pres. 1968-69), Inst. Fin. Edn., U.S. League Savs. Assns. (dir. 1973) Clubs: Birmingham Country, Mountain Brook, Redstone. Republican. Presbyterian. Home: Birmingham, Ala. Died Mar. 22, 2010.

MILLER, JOHN GRIDER, writer; b. Annapolis, Md., Aug. 23, 1935; s. John Stanley and Ruby Corinne (Young) M.; m. Susan Bradner Bailey, Oct. 26, 1974; children: Kerry, John, Alison. BA, Yale U., 1957. Commd. 2d lt. USMC, 1957, advanced through grades to col., inf./ops. advisor Vietnamese Marine Corps., 1970-71, prin. speechwriter for Commandant Washington, 1971-76, commd. officer Battalion Landing Team, 1977-78, asst. chief of staff ops. and plans III Amphibious Force Okinawa, 1982-83, dep. dir. Marine Corps History Washington, 1983-85, ret., 1985; mng. editor Procs. and Naval History U.S. Naval Inst., Annapolis, Md., 1985-2000. Author: The Battle to Save the Houston, 1985, (Pocket Books edit., 1992, Bluejacket edit., 2000), The Bridge at Dong Ha, 1989, (Dell edit. 1990, Bluejacket edit., 1996, Audiobook edit., 1997), Punching Out: A Guide to Post-Military Transition, 1994, The Co-Vans: U.S. Marine Advisors in Vietnam, 2000; contbf. author: The Marines, 1998, Commandants of the Marine Corps, 2004. Decorated Legion of Merit with gold star, Bronze Star with combat V, Cross of Gallantry, Vietnamese Marine Corps.; recipient Author of Yr. award Naval Inst., 1990, Alfred Thayer Mahan award Navy League of U.S., 2002, Brig. Gen. Robert L. Denig jr. award, Us Marine Corps Combat Correspondents Assn., 2009. Mem. Marine Corps. Hist. Found. (bd. dirs., Gen. Wallace M. Greene Jr. Book award 1989, Disting. Svc. award 1998), Mil. Order of World Wars (past chpt. comdr., chmn. nat. mag. com.), Civitan Internat. (past chpt. pres.), Washington Naval and Maritime Corrs.' Cir., New Providence Club, Annapolis Chorale. Avocations: music, piano, choral singing, boating. Home: Annapolis, Md. Died Aug. 31, 2009; Arlington Nat. Cemetry.

MILLER, JOHN JOHNSTON, pediatric rheumatologist; b. San Francisco, Apr. 9, 1934; s. John Johnston J. Jr. and Florence Irene Ratzell; m. Margaret Anne Robeson, May 30, 1958 (div. Jan. 1990); children; John J., Daniel R., Andrew S. Erich C. BA, Wesleyan U., 1955; MD, U. Rochester, 1960; PhD, U. Melbourne, Australia, 1965. Clin. teaching asst. dept. pediatrics Stanford U., Palo Alto, Calif., 1965-67, asst. prof. dept. pediatrics, 1967-73, clin. assoc. prof. pediatrics, sr. attending physician, 1973-77, assoc. prof. clin. pediatrics, 1977-79, prof. clin. pediatrics, 1979-82, prof. pediatrics, 1982-97, prof. emeritus, from 1997. Vis. investigator Scripps Cline & Rsch. Found., La Jolla, Calif., 1975; dir. Rheumatic Disease Svc., Children's Hosp. Stanford, 1967-96; vis. prof. Hosp. Infanti de Mex, Mexico City, 1997; cons. in field. Editor: Juvenile Rheumatoid Arthritis; co-editor: Adolscent Arthritis, 1999. Comdr. USNR, 1965-67. Fellow Am. Acad. Pediatrics (emeritus), Am. Coll. Rheumatology; mem. Am. Assn. Immunologists. Home: Woodside, Calif. Died July 8, 2009.

MILLER, KENNETH A., vocational education administrator, psychologist; b. NYC, Apr. 22, 1943; s. Irving J. and Mildred (Pickus) M.; m. Nancy Doherty, June 18, 1967; children: Aaron, Stacy. BS, City Coll., 1964; MA, Syracuse U., 1966; EdD, U. Maine, Orono, 1973. Lic. psychologist, Pa. Counselor Sullivan County C.C., Loch Shendrake, N.Y., 1966-69, dean students, 1969-70; dean Delaware County C.C., Media, Pa., 1973-81, v.p., 1981-84; pres. Pa. Inst. Tech., Media, 1984-91; exec. dir. Coun. Private Postsecondary & Vocat. Edn., Sacramento, Calif., from 1991. Fellow Pa. Psychol. Assn.; mem. APA, Am. Assn. Community Colls., Sacramento Leeds, Calif. Postsecondary Edn. Commn., Calif. Occupational Information Coord. Com., Acad. Family Mediators. Home: Sacramento, Calif. Died Jan. 17, 2010.

MILLER, KENNETH MICHAEL, electronics executive, director; b. Chgo., Nov. 20, 1921; s. Matthew and Tillie (Otto) M.; m. Dolores June Miller, Jan. 16, 1943 (dec. Dec. 1968); children: Barbara Anne Reed, Nancy Jeanne Hathaway, Kenneth Michael, Roger Allan; m. Sally J. Ballingham, June 20, 1970 (dec. Apr. 2002). Student, Ill. Inst. Tech., 1940-41, UCLA, 1961. Electronics engr. Rauland Corp., Chgo., 1941-48; gen. mgr. Lear, Inc., Santa Monica, Calif., 1948-59; v.p., gen. mgr. Motorola Aviation Electronics, Inc., Culver City, Calif., 1959-60; v.p., gen. mgr. instrument divsn. Daystrom, Inc., LA, 1961; gen. mgr. metrics divsn. Singer Co., L.A. and Bridgeport, Conn., 1962-65; v.p., gen. mgr. Lear Jet Corp., 1965-66; pres., dir. Infonics, Inc., 1967-68; v.p., gen. mgr. Computer Industries, Inc., 1968-69; dir. ops., tech. products group Am. Std. Corp., McLean, Va.; v.p., gen. mgr. Wilcox Elec. divsn. American Std. Corp., Kansas City, Mo., 1969-71; pres. Wilcox Elec., Inc. subs. Northrop Corp., Kansas City, 1971-72; v.p., dir. World Wide Wilcox, Inc. subs., McLean, 1971-72; pres., CEO, dir. Penril Corp., Rockville, Md., 1973-86; pres. K-M Miller & Associates, Rockville, 1986—2010. Dir. George Mason Bank, NA, Washington, Palmer Nat. Bank, Washington. Mem. adv. bd. Washington Bus. Jour.; contbr. articles to profl. jours. Mem. regional planning coun. Cmty. Mental Health Svcs., Bridgeport, 1964; mem. Bridgeport Capital Fund Com.; trustee Park City Hosp.; vice dir. Montgomery County Arts Coun.; bd. dirs. U. Bridgeport; mem. Md. State Com. High Tech. Recipient Job Makers award Mfrs. Assn. Bridgeport, 1963. Fellow Radio Club Am. (dir., chmn grants-in-aid com.); mem. AIAA, IEEE, Aircraft Owners and Pilots Assn., Am. Mgmt. Assn., Armed Forces Comm. and Electronics Assn. (life), Electronic Industries Assn., Instrument Soc. Am. (life), Nat. Aero. Assn., Soc. Non-Destructive Testing, Soc. Automotive Engrs., Air Force Assn., Am. Radio Relay League (life), Amateur Satellite Corp. (life), Am. Def. Preparedness Assn. (life), Aero. Elec. Soc. (life), Nat. Capital DX Assn. (pres. 1987-88), Assn. Old Crows (life), Mfrs. Assn. Bridgeport (dir.), Bridgeport Engring. Inst., Bridgeport C. of C. (pres. 1964), Quarter Century Wireless Assn. (life, Disting. Svc. award 1994), Soc. Wireless Pioneers, Rolling Hills Country Club (Wichita), Algonquin Club (Bridgeport). Died Mar. 24, 2010.

MILLER, LAWRENCE A., lawyer; b. Cleve., Dec. 3, 1946; BA with highest distinction, Northwestern U., 1969; student, New Coll., Oxford U., Eng., 1969—73; JD, Yale U., 1976. Bar: DC 1992, Ill. 1976, US Ct. Appeals (8th, 10th, 11th & DC cirs.), US Dist. Ct. DC, US Dist. Ct. ND of Ill. Ptnr. Sidley & Austin, Wash., 1976, sr. counsel. Died June 27, 2009.

MILLER, LEROY BENJAMIN, architect; b. Cleve., Dec. 24, 1931; s. Harry Simon and Carol Jane (Goldberg) M.; m. Sue Firestone, July 1, 1956; children: Laurie, Janet, David, Matthew. BArch, U. Mich., 1956. Registered architect, Calif. From assoc. to v.p. Daniel Dworsky & Associates, L.A., 1958-66; prin., pres. Leroy Miller Assocates, L.A., Santa Monica, Calif. Tchr. Calif. State Poly. Coll., Pomona, 1971-72. Exhibited in group shows, 1976, 84, 94. Pres. Leo Baeck Temple, L.A., 1991-93. Cpl. U.S. Army, 1956-58. Recipient Design awards City of Ventura, 1982, City of W. L.A., 1988, City of Pasadena, 1997. Fellow AIA (Design awards L.A. chpt. 1966, 69, 72, 89) Democrat. Jewish. Avocations: writing, music, skiing, racquetball. Home: Santa Monica, Calif. Died Aug. 20, 2010.

MILLER, MELVIN HULL, educator; b. Flushing, Mich., Apr. 19, 1920; s. Melvin Lyle and Dorothy (Hull) M.; m. Shirley Lou Mershon, Sept. 11, 1952; children: Pamela, Mark. AB, Albion Coll., 1942; MA, Mich. State U., 1949; PhD, U. Wis., 1957; postgrad., Oxford U., 1953, U. Birmingham, Eng., 1952. Instr. speech Grinnell (Iowa) Coll., 1949-51; instr.

speech U. Md. Overseas Program, 1951-54, U. Wis.-Milw., 1956-58, asst. prof., 1958-63, assoc. prof., chmn. dept., 1963-66, prof. communication, coordinator grad. studies, from 1966. Author: Syllabus for Public Speaking, 1962, (with W.E. Buys) Creative Speaking, 1974; Contbr. articles to profl. jours. Served to lt. comdr. USNR, 1943-47, PTO. Recipient Andrew T. Weaver award for disting. teaching, 1983 Mem. Speech Communication Assn. (legislative assembly 1967-70), AAUP (chpt. pres. 1968-69), Central States Speech Assn., Wis. Acad. Sci., Arts and Letters. Home: Milwaukee, Wis. Died Mar. 16, 2010.

MILLER, ROBERT CHARLES, retired physicist; b. State College, Pa., Feb. 2, 1925; s. Lawrence P. Miller and Eva Mae (Gross) Wiedemann; m. Virginia Callaghan, Aug. 30, 1952; children: Robin Miller Storey, Jeffrey Lawrence Miller, Lauren Miller Lynch. AB, Columbia U., 1948, MA, 1952, PhD, 1956. Staff mem. Johns-Manville Research Ctr., Finderne, NJ, 1948-49; teaching asst. in physics Columbia U., NYC, 1949-51, lectr. in physics, 1951-53; mem. tech. staff Bell Telephone Labs., Murray Hill, NJ, 1954-63, head solid state spectroscopy research dept., 1963-67; staff mem. Inst. Defense Analyses, Arlington, Va., 1967-68; head optical elec. research dept. Bell Telephone Labs., Murray Hill, 1968-77; mem. tech. staff AT&T Bell Labs., Murray Hill, 1977-84, disting. mem. tech. staff, 1984-88, ret., 1988. Cons. Office of Sec. Def., Arlington, Va., 1968-75. Inventor (with Dr. J.A. Giordmaine) Optical Parametric Oscillator, 1965 (co-recipient R.W. Wood prize, 1986); contbr. articles to profl. jours. Served with U.S. Army, 1943-46, ETO. RCA predoctoral fellow Columbia U., 1953-54. Fellow Am. Phys. Soc.; mem. AAAS, N.Y. Acad. Scis., Sigma Xi. Avocation: sports cars. Home: Cotuit, Mass. Died Feb. 23, 2009.

MILLER, SIEGLINDE F., Small business owner; b. Boeblingen, Baden-Wurttemberg, Baden-Wuerttemberg, Germany, Feb. 20, 1941; Arrived in US 1971. d. Hans Schmidt and Anneliese Franz; m. Garland A. Miller, Apr. 7, 1967. Grad., Handelsschule Tech Coll, Boeblingen, 1958-59. Office clerk Mercedes Benz, Sindelfingen, Fed. Republic of Germany, 1960-65; registrar, translator US Dependent Sch., Boeblingen, 1965-70; adminstr. asst. Hdqrs. VII COSCOM, Boeblingen, 1970-71; sec. Pub. Schs. of Pemberton Twp., Brownsmills, N.J., 1973; sec., translator Hdprs. European Command, Support Command, Stuttgart, Fed. Republic of Germany, 1974-75; gas & oil producer G.A. & S. Miller, Ohio, from 1986. Mem. Assoc. Photographer Internat., UN Assn. of the U.S.A., Nat. Wildlife Fedn. Protestant. Avocations: photography, numismatic, hiking, wildlife. Home: The Plains, Ohio. Died Apr. 19, 2010.

MILLER, THORMUND AUBREY, lawyer; b. Pocatello, Idaho, July 14, 1919; s. Roy Edmund and Lillian (Thordarson) Miller; m. Hannah A. Flansburgh, Feb. 10, 1946 (dec. Jan. 2003); children: Karen Lynette Van Gerpen, Christine Alison Westall; m. Barbara Cornell Singelyn, May 8, 2004. BA, Reed Coll., 1941; LLB, Columbia U., 1948; grad., Advanced Mgmt. Program, Harvard Bus. Sch., 1961. Bar: Calif. 1949, D.C. 1951, U.S. Supreme Ct. 1960. Assoc. McCutchen, Thomas, Matthews, Griffiths & Greene, San Francisco, 1948-50; atty. So. Pacific Transp. Co., Washington, 1950-56, asst. gen. atty., 1956-59, gen. atty., 1959—66, sr. gen. atty. San Francisco, 1966—75, gen. solicitor, 1975—79, gen. commerce counsel, 1979—83, dir., mem. exec. com., 1983—87, v.p., gen. counsel, 1983—89; gen. counsel So. Pacific Comms. Co., San Francisco, 1970—79, dir., 1970—81. Pres. Wood Acres Citizens Assn., Bethesda, Md., 1955-56; exec. com. Holbrook Palmer Recreation Park Found., 1979—, pres., 1982-84; bd. dirs. Atherton Civic Interest League, 1981-2008, pres., 1992-94; mem. Atherton Park and Recreation Commn., 1991-95, Atherton Waste Reduction Commn., 1999-2005, San Mateo Civil Grand Jury, 1997; alumni bd. Reed Coll., 1971-72, trustee, 1987-2002, campaign com., 1995-2000; joint donor Thormund A. Miller/Walter Mintz chair in econ. history; bd. dirs. Assocs. U. Calif. Press, 1994—2006. Lt. USNR, 1942-46. Mem.: ABA, Calif. Bar Assn. Presbyterian. Home: Los Altos, Calif. Died Feb. 2010.

MILLER, TIMOTHY NICHOLAS, public relations executive; b. Evansville, Ind., Dec. 14, 1946; s. Herdis and Mary Ellen (Grant) Miller. BS in Journalism, U. Evansville, Ind., 1980. Prodn. asst. Sta. WTVW-TV, Evansville, 1968—69; gen. mgr. cable TV program origination facilities Telesis Corp., Evansville, 1971—72; exec. dir. graphic products Adfax Agy., Indpls., from 1972; dist. circulation mktg. mgr. Evansville Printing Corp., 1976—77; pub. rels. exec. Ind. Employment Security Divsn., Vets. Employment Svc., Evansville, 1978—81; pub. affairs officer 123D US Army Res. Command Ind. & Mich, Ft. Benjamin Harrison, Ind., from 1981. Project officer Met. Indpls. United Way Campaign; former v.p. Muscular Dystrophy Assn. America; former chmn. Jerry Lewis Labor Day Telethon, Muscular Dystrophy Campaign Fund SW Ind. & Western Ky., Salvation Army Christmas Shopping Tour Underprivileged Children. Prodr. (writer, dir.): Orange Bowl Football Classic, 1970. Served with US Army, 1966—68. Decorated Purple Heart medal, Bronze Star, Vietnamese medals; recipient Fourth Estate award. Mem.: DAV, VFW, Indpls. C. of C. (nat. def. com.), Evansville C. of C. (past bd. dirs., Key Man, Presdl. Honor awards), Assn. US Army (exec. coun. Ind. chpt., Nat. Best Chpt. Newsletter award 1982), Praxis Armed Forces Broadcasters Assn., Pub. Rels. Assn. America, Internat. Assn. Bus. Communicators, U. Evansville Varsity, Press Club Evansville Inc., Indpls. Press Club, Tau Kappa Epsilon. Republican. Roman Catholic. Died Sept. 13, 2009.

MILLER, WALTER JAMES, literature educator, writer; b. McKee City, NJ, Jan. 16, 1918; s. Walter Theodore and Celestia Anna (Simmons) Miller; m. Mary T. Hume; children: Naomi, Jason, Robin, Jared, Elizabeth. BA, CUNY, 1941; MA, Columbia U., 1952. Instr. English Poly. Inst. Bklyn., 1946—53, asst. prof., 1953—55; asst. prof. English and modern langs. Colo. State U., Ft. Collins, 1955—56; assoc. prof. English NYU, 1958—66, prof. English, 1966—84, prof. emeritus, 1984—2010. Dir. Summer Writers Conf. Hofstra U., Hempstead, NY, 1972—79, NYU, NYC, 1983—85. Author: Engineers as Writers, 1953, Making an Angel: Poems, 1977, 1001 Ideas for English Papers, 1994, Love's Mainland: New and Selected Poems, 2001, Joseph in the Pit: A Verse Drama, 2002, Essential Vonnegut: Interviews Conducted by Walter Miller, CDI, 2006; author, translator: Annotated Jules Verne, 1995; editor, translator: Verne's 20,000 Leagues Under the Sea, 1993, The Meteor Hunt, 2006; contbg. editor Simon and Schuster, 1969-97. Pub. relations officer US Infantry, 1943—46. Recipient Spl. award, Engrs. Coun. Profl. Devel., 1966, Charles Angoff award, The Lit. Rev., 1983, Gt. Tchr. award, NYU Alumni Assn., 1980, Fisher Second Harvest award, CUNY Alumni Assn., 1997; fellow, Ruttenberg Found., 1999—2006. Home: Brooklyn, NY. Died June 20, 2010.

MILLER, WILLIAM FRANKLIN, internal medicine educator; b. Stonecreek, Ohio, Jan. 16, 1920; s. Karl Rudolph and Helen Amelia (Miller) M.; m. Laura Deane Barker, Nov. 21, 1942 (dec. 1957); children: Leslie, Karla, Chris, Lisa; m. Jean P. Stevens, Jan. 12, 1958 (div. 1980); 1 child, Katy; m. Rita Gayle Boyd McKemie, Jan. 2, 1981; children: Mary, Frankin; 1 stepchild, Margie McKemie. BA, Wittenberg U., 1942; MD, Case Western Res. U., 1945. Diplomate Am. Bd. Internal Medicine, Am. Bd. Quality Assurance. Intern Met. City Hosp. Cleve., 1945-46; resident in neurology, psychiatry, radiology and medicine VA Hosp., Dayton, Ohio, 1946-48, resident in medicine Dallas, 1948-50, fellow in pulmonary rsch., 1950-51; clin. instr. internal medicine U. Tex. Southwestern Med. Sch., Dallas, 1951-53, asst. prof., 1953-57, assoc. prof., 1957-67, prof., from 1967, dir. postgrad. physician tng. in pulmonary medicine, 1953-82, chief pulmonary div., 1953-82. Chief pulmonary div. Parkland Meml. Hosp., Dallas, 1953-67, Meth. Med. Ctr., Dallas, 1967-82; cons. in pulmonary diseases St. Paul, Presbyn., Meth., Parkland, and VA hosps., 1953—, U.S. Surgeon Gen., Lackland AFB Base, Brooke Army Hosp., San Antonio, 1959-72, NIH, Washington, 1964-80; med. dir. Travelers Health Network Tex., Irving, 1986-90; mem. internat. bd. cons. Hoffmann-La Roche Ltd., Basle, Switzerland, 1971-76. Sr. editor Chest, 1970-76; med. editor Respiratory Care, 1967-90; contbr. over 160 articles on pulmonry physiology and treatment to med. jours., numerous chpts. to books. Bd. dirs. Dallas area Am. Lung Assn., 1969-71, 79-91, Assn. for Clean Air Tex., Dallas, 1985-88, Emphysema Anonymous, Inc., Seminole, Fla., 1973-80; trustee Am. Respiratory Care Found., Dallas, 1979—. Capt. M.C., AUS, 1946-48. Recipient best sci. exhibit of yr. award Tex. Med. Assn., 1976; Forrest M. Bird Achievement award Am. Respiratory Care Assn., 1988, Jimmy A. Young medal, 1979; Pulmonary Rehab. Excellence award Am. Assn. Cardiovascular and Pulmonary Rehab., 1989. Fellow ACP, Am. Coll. Chest Physicians (bd. govs. Tex. 1966-74, Best Med. Movie of Yr. award 1967), Am. Col. Utilization Rev. and Quality Assurance Physicians; mem. AAAS, Am. Fedn. for Clin. Rsch., Am. Thoracic Soc., Cen. Soc. for Clin. Rsch., So. Soc. for Clin Rsch., Dallas Acad. Internal Medicine (pres. 1977-78), Sigma Xi. Lutheran. Avocations: family, sports, photography. Home: Dallas, Tex. Died July 27, 2010.

MILLER, WILLIAM MICHAEL, cosmetics company executive; b. Istanbul, Turkey, Feb. 5, 1923; came to U.S., 1930; s. William Benson and Helen Agnes M.; m. Nevine Sirry, Dec. 21, 1973; children— Patricia, Lane, Peter, Hope. Student, Princeton U., 1943-44; BS in Econs, Wharton Sch., U. Pa., 1947. Buyer L. Bamberger & Co., Newark, 1947-52; v.p. mktg. Brunswick Corp., Chgo., 1952-66; exec. v.p. Elizabeth Arden, Inc., NYC, 1966-76, London, 1976-81. Served with USMC, 1942-46, 50-52. Mem.: N.Y. Yacht; Boca Grande. Republican. Died Apr. 29, 2010.

MILLS, DONALD CALVIN, health care executive; b. Neillsville, Wis., Apr. 3, 1934; s. Calvin B. and Elnora (Uhlman) M.; m. Loretta G. Thorson, Nov. 24, 1954; children: Jan D., Julie D., Jolene D. BBA, U. Minn., 1958, MHA, 1962. Tax acct. First Trust Co., St. Paul, 1958-60; adminstrv. asst. Bethesda Luth. Hosp., St. Paul, 1961-62; adminstr. Moose Lake (Minn.) State Hosp., 1962-68, Mt. Carmel Nursing Home, Milw., 1968-70; v.p. Nat. Health Enterprises, Milw., 1970-72, pres., 1972-74; pres., chief exec. officer Bethesda Luth. Med. Center, St. Paul, from 1974; preceptor program in hosp. and health care adminstrn. U. Minn., from 1975; mem. pediatric task force Health Bd. Met. Council, 1975-76, mem. long term care task force, 1977, task force on econ. impact, 1978. Bd. dir. Health Manpower Mgmt. Inc., 1975-79, pres., 1977-78; bd. dirs. Council Community Hosps., 1974—, mem. policy and issues com., 1979-80; chmn. N.E. Minn. Regional Mental Health Retardation Coordinating Com., 1968; bd. dirs. Bethesda Found., BethCare, Bethesda Luth. Hosp., Bethesda Luth. Infirmary, Inc., Bethesda Community Services, Inc.; mem. Bd. Social Ministry; hosp. bd. rep. Blue Cross/Blue Shield, Minn., 1975—; bd. dirs. Bethesda/Univ. Family physicians, P.A., 1975—; vice chmn. Health East, St. Paul; pres. Health East Found., 1986-89; health care cons., 1989—. Mem. Moose Lake Planning Commn., 1965-68; chmn. St. Paul health facilities United Way, 1977; pres. dist. G-East, St. Paul Assn., 1975-76. With AUS, 1954-56. Fellow Am. Coll. Nursing Home Adminstrs.; mem. Minn. Hosp. Assn. (trustee 1978—, chmn. fin. com. 1977-79, rate rev. adv. subcom. 1978-79, Minn. coalition on health care costs 1979-80) Clubs: Kiwanis. Home: Saint Paul, Minn. Died July 15, 2010.

MILLS, NELLY ELIZABETH, cosmetology educator; b. Concord, Ohio, July 10, 1915; d. Bernardus and Adriana Helena (Van Aartsen de Melker); m. Vane James Mills, Aug. 19, 1939 (dec.); children: Jane Ann Mills Schwab, James Vane. Student, Youngstown Sch. Cosmetology, Kent State U. Beautician Geneva True Temper Corp., Ohio, 1935—39, Marie's House Hair Fashions, Hartsgrove, Ohio, Your Beauty Salon, Ashtabula, Ohio, 1958—70; tchr. Ashtabula County Joint Vocat. Sch., from 1970; advisor Vocat. Indsl. Clubs Am. Mem.: Ohio Vocat. Assn., Am. Vocat. Assn., Eastern Star. Methodist. Home: Geneva, Ohio. Died Jan. 11, 2009.

MILLS, WILLIAM HAROLD, general contractor; b. Feb. 19, 1911; s. Charles W. and Mary (Parker) M.; m. Helen D. Cooper, Nov. 16, 1963; children: William Harold, Susan Ann, Caroline Bridget, Mary Danforth. BS in Civil Engring., MIT, 1934. Ptnr. Clarson & Mills, St. Petersburg, Fla., 1935-46; pres., chief exec. officer Mills & Jones Constrn. Co., St. Petersburg, Fla., from 1946. Dir. Fla. Fed. Savs. and Loan Assn., St. Petersburg, Fla., Gen. Telephone Co., Fla., Founders Life Assurance Co., First Nat. Bank, St. Petersburg, Fla., St. Louis Nat. Baseball Co. (St. Louis Cardinals) Mem. corp. MIT; bd. dirs. St. Petersburg Episcopal Community, Inc.; trustee Fla. Ind. Coll. Found., St. Petersburg Mus. of Fine Arts. Mem. Fla. Council 100, St. Petersburg Com. 100, Tampa Horse Show Assn., Greater St. Petersburg C. of C. (past pres.), Suncoasters, Newcomers Soc., Delta Tau Delta Clubs: MIT of Central Fla, Feather Sound Country, St. Petersburg Yacht, Dragon, Pasadena Golf. Home: Saint Petersburg, Fla. Died June 7, 2009.

MILLSAPS, FRED RAY, investor; b. Blue Ridge, Ga., Apr. 30, 1929; s. Samuel Hunter and Ora Lee (Bradshaw) M.; m. Audrey Margaret Hopkins, June 22, 1957; children: Judith Gail, Stephen Hunter, Walter Scott. AB, Emory U., 1951; postgrad., U. Wis. Sch. Banking, 1955-57, Harvard Bus. Sch., 1962; LLD, Fla. So. Coll., 1991. V.p. Fed. Res. Bank, Atlanta, 1958-64; fin. v.p. Fla. Power & Light Co., 1965-69; chmn., pres. Landmark Banking Corp. of Fla., Ft. Lauderdale, 1969-78. Bd. dirs. Franklin Templeton Mut. Funds, Mut. Shares Funds. Chmn. South Fla. Coordinating Coun., 1976-78, WPBT Cmty. TV Found. of South Fla., 1973-75, Fla. So. Coll., Lakeland, 1976-95, Broward Performing Arts Authority, Honda Classic, Broward Workshop, Holy Cross Health Corp.; mem. Fla. Coun. of 100. Mem. Coral Ridge Country Club. Methodist. Home: Fort Lauderdale, Fla. Died Mar. 24, 2009.

MILSTEIN, PAUL, real estate developer; b. NYC, May 12, 1922; s. Morris Milstein; m. Irma Cameron; children: Howard, Edward, Roslyn, Barbara. Student, NYU Sch. Architecture. Pres. Circle Floor Co. Inc., NYC, 1961; founder, pres. Milstein Properties, NYC. Former chmn. bd. Starrett Corp.; co-chmn. Emigrant Savings Bank. Donates to NY Pub. Library; Cornell U.; life trustee NY Presbyn. Hosp., NYC; trustee Am. Mus. Natural Hist., NYC. Named one of Forbes 400: Richest Americans, from 2006, World's Richest People, Forbes mag., 2007. Died Aug. 9, 2010.

MILTON, WILLIAM HAMMOND, III, trust company executive; b. Schenectady, Mar. 3, 1925; s. William Hammond Jr. and Lois (Preston) M.; m. Maryanna Kennedy, July 26, 1956; children: Alexander, William. Maryanna. BA, Union Coll., Schenectady, 1950; postgrad., Rutgers U., 1961. Statistician Guaranty Trust Co., NYC, 1950-51; trust salesman Schenectady Trust Co., 1953-63, v.p., 1963-74, bd. dirs., sec., from 1972, sr. v.p., 1974-84, exec. v.p., from 1984. Pres. Bank Fiduciary Funds, N.Y.C., 1965-67; bd. dirs., sec. Trustco Bank Corp. N.Y., Schenectady, 1982—. Founder, treas. Schenectady Found., 1966—. Served to lst lt. USAAF, 1943-46, USAF, 1951-53. Avocations: sailing, lotus 1-2-3. Home: Galway, NY. Died Dec. 28, 2009.

MILWID, STEPHEN ANDREW, lawyer; b. Bayonne, NJ, Apr. 13, 1915; s. Felix J. M. and Mary C. (Safner); m. Josephine H. Muldoon, Aug. 17, 1946; children: Mary E., Peter A. AB cum laude, Harvard U., 1937, LL.B., 1940. Bar: N.Y. 1941, Ill. 1946. Assoc. Moot, Sprague, Marcy & Gullick, Buffalo, 1940-41, Lord, Bissell & Kadyk, Chgo., 1946-50; ptnr. Lord, Bissell & Brook, Chgo., from 1951. Editor: Selected Materials on Product Liability Discovery, 1967; contbr. artilces to legal jours. Served to lt. USNR, 1941-46, PTO, ETO. Fellow Am. Coll. Trail Lawyers; mem. Chgo. Bar Assn. (bd. mgrs. 1958-61), Internat. Assn. Ins. Counsel (sec.-treas. 1973-75) Clubs: Union League (Chgo.), Monroe (Chgo.), Law (Chgo.). Republican. Roman Catholic. Home: Chicago, Ill. Died Oct. 10, 2009.

MIMS, ALBERT, safety consultant, executive, educator; b. Keyser, Ky., Feb. 28, 1924; s. Albert and lelia F. Mims; m. margie L. Kolbe, Apr. 12, 1985; children: John Albert, Rebecca Fern. AB, U. N.C., 1953, MS, 1954; MBA, U. Cin., 1962, PhD, 1973. Profl. safet engr.; cert. safety profl., hazard control mgr., safety specialist, safety mgr., safety exec. Safety engr. Procter & Gamble, Cin., 1957-72; assoc. prof. indsl. safety U. Wis., from 1973. Safety cons., CEO, chm. bd. A. Mims Assocs., Madison, Wis., 1972—; active hazardous materials tng. program for compliance officers U.S. Dept. Labor OSHA Tng. Inst., 1973-74; expert witness in field. Mem. editorial bd. Profl. Safety, 1979-84, World Safety jour., 1989—; presented papers to local, nat., and internat. groups on occupational safety; contbr. articles to profl. jours. Active United Appeal/Way, Little League baseball, football, basketball, Dan Beard coun. Boy Scouts Am., 1962-67. With USN Air Corps, 1942-46. Mem. Am. Soc. Safety Engrs. (visitation team mem. for accreditation of colls. and univs.), Am. Indsl. Hygiene Assn., Nat. Safety Mgmt. Soc., Human Factors Soc., System Safety Soc., World Safety Orgn., Nat. Safety Coun. (exec. com., gen. chmn. chem. sect. 1979-80, Disting. Svc. Safety award 1989). Republican. Home: Naples, Fla. Died Apr. 18, 2010.

MINER, THOMAS WESLEY, retired automotive company executive; b. Pontiac, Mich., Feb. 6, 1928; s. Tunis Wesley and Susan (Jessie) M.; m. Jill Craig, Oct. 13, 1951; children: Cathrine C., Thomas Wesley, Lyman C. BA in Econs., Mich. State U., 1951. Various personnel positions Chrysler Corp., Highland Park, Mich., 1955-81, v.p. indsl. relations, 1981-86; indsl. relations cons., from 1986. Served with USN, 1945-46,

51-53, PTO, Korea, Japan. Mem. Labor Policy Assn. Clubs: Detroit Press, Economics. Episcopalian. Home: Bloomfield Hills, Mich. Died Feb. 1, 2010.

MINGLE, JOHN ORVILLE, engineer, educator, lawyer, consultant; b. Oakley, Kans., May 6, 1931; s. John Russell and Beulah Amelia (Johnson) M.; m. Patricia Ruth Schmitt, Aug. 17, 1957; children: Elizabeth Lorene, Stephen Roy. BS, Kans. State U., Manhattan, 1953, MS, 1958; PhD, Northwestern U., 1960; JD, Washburn U., 1980. Bar: Kans., Wyo., U.S. Patent Office; registered profl. engr., Kans. Tng. engr. Gen. Electric Co., Schenectady, 1953-54; mem. faculty Kans. State U., 1956-90, prof. nuclear engring., 1965-90, prof. emeritus, from 1990, Black & Veatch Disting. prof., 1973-78; dir. Inst. Computational Research Engring., 1969-88; exec. v.p., patent counsel Kans. State U. Research Found., 1983-88. Instr. Northwestern U., 1958-59; vis. prof. U. So. Calif., 1967-68; cons. govt. and industry; engring. legal cons. 1990—. Author: The Invarient Imbedding Theory of Nuclear Transport, 1973; also articles. Bd. dirs. Laramie Regional Airport, 1994-97. Officer AUS, 1954—56, lt. US Army, 1954—56. Mem. ABA (chairperson sci. and tech. phys. scis. com. 1982-92), NSPE (sect. exec. com. 1985-87, chmn. 1985-86), Am. Nuclear Soc. (sect. pres. 1976-77), Am. Inst. Chem. Engrs. (profl. devel. com. 1982-95), Am. Soc. Engring. Edn. (chmn. Midwest sect. 1985-86, exec. com. 1984-87), Profl. Engrs. in Edn. (vice chmn. 1978-80, workshop chairperson 1983), Kans. Engring. Soc. (past chpt. pres.), Kans. Bar Assn., Licensing Execs. Soc., Sigma Xi (past chpt. pres., lectr.), Soc. Univ. Patent Adminstrs. (exec. com. 1985-87, v.p. cen. region 1985-87). Home: Laramie, Wyo. Died Oct. 10, 2009.

MINNERLY, ROBERT WARD, retired headmaster; b. Yonkers, NY, Mar. 21, 1935; s. Richard Warren and Margaret Marion (DeBrocky) M.; m. Sandra Overmire, June 12, 1957; children: Scott Ward, John Robert, Sydney Sue. AB, Brown U., Providence, 1957; MAT, U. Tex., Arlington, 1980. Tchr., coach Rumsey Hall Sch., Washington, Conn., 1962—64, Berkshire Sch., Sheffield, Mass., 1964—70, asst. head, 1969—70, headmaster, 1970—76; dir. Salisbury Summer Sch. Reading and English, Conn., 1970; prin. upper sch. Ft. Worth Country Day Sch., 1976—86; headmaster Charles Wright Acad., Tacoma, 1986—96; ednl. cons. The Edn. Group, 1996—2000; interim dir. Harold E. LeMay Mus., 2001—02; exec. dir. R. Merle Palmer Minority Students Scholarship Found., 2004—06. Cons. Tarrant County Coalition on Substance Abuse, 1982-84; mayor's task force Tacoma Edn. Summit, 1991-92; bd. dirs. World Cultural Interaction, Gig Harbor, Wash. Contbr. articles to profl. jours. Bd. dirs. Tacoma/Pierce County Good Will Games Art Coun., 1989, Multicare Found., Tacoma, 2002, Tacoma Baseball Found., 2003—05; mem. exec. com. Am. Leadership Forum, 1991-95; bd. dirs. Broadway Ctr. for Performing Arts, Tacoma, 1988-94, 96-98, mem. exec. com., 1990-93; elected Wash. State Bd. Edn., 1996-2001; bd. dirs. Tacoma Youth Choir, 2000-03. Named Adminstr. of Yr. Wash. Journalism Edn. Assn., 1991; recipient Columbia award, Wash. Fedn. Ind. Schs., 2000. Mem. Pacific N.W. Assn. Ind. Schs. (chmn. long-range planning com. 1989-92, exec. com. 1990-92, 91, v.p. 1994). Presbyterian. Home: Arlington, Tex. Died June 1, 2010.

MINNEY, BRUCE KEVIN, evangelist, refrigeration executive; b. Cleve., Dec. 22, 1958; s. Leonard Clavel Minney and Wilma Catherine (Elliott) Sage; m. Penelope Sue Pertuset, May 20, 1983; 1 child, Joshua Kevin. Student, Cin. Bible Coll., 1977-84. Religious educator Andover (Ohio) Ch. of Christ, 1978, youth worker, 1978; evangelist N. E. Crusaders for Christ, Cin., 1979; emergency med. tech. Milford-Miami (Ohio) Twp. Med. Svcs., 1980-83; youth leader Milford (Ohio) Ch. of Christ, 1984-86, deacon, drama minstry, from 1986; parts dept. mgr. Otis Refrigeration Svc., Inc., Cin., from 1984. Avocations: disc golf, dulcimer, theater. Home: Milford, Ohio. Died Sept. 27, 2009.

MINTZ, SEYMOUR STANLEY, lawyer; b. Newark, Mar. 7, 1912; m. Bettie Mitz; children: John, Jim stepchildren: Alex, Sallie. AB, George Washington U., 1933, JD, 1936. Bar: D.C. 1936. Atty. Office Under Sec. US Dept. Treasury, 1937-38; atty. Office of Chief Counsel, IRS, 1938-42; assoc. Hogan & Hartson LLP, Washington, 1946-49, ptnr., 1949-84, counsel, 1985—2010. Contbr. articles to profl. jours. Fellow Am. Coll. Tax Counsel; mem. ABA, D.C. Bar Assn., Am. Law Inst., Order of Coif. Died Nov. 3, 2010.

MISHKIN, ESAU JACOB, lawyer; b. Morristown, NJ, June 30, 1918; s. Maximilion and Frannie (Ponz) Mishkin; m. Elaine Greenberg, Jan. 26, 1946; children: Eric Marc, Daniel Jed. BA, Drew U., 1939; LLB, Bklyn. Law Sch., 1946. Bar: NY 1946, Dist. Ct. (so. dist.) 1947, US Dist. Ct. (ea. dist.) 1948, US Supreme Ct. 1955, Fla. 1958. Civil trial lawyer in pvt. practice, Garden City, NY, from 1946. Pre-trial master Civil Ct., NYC, 1965—71; atty., bd. dirs. Roslyn Vis. Nurses Assn., 1966—69. Served with US Army, 1941—42, served to lt. AC USN, 1942—46, PTO. Fellow: Roscoe Pound Am. Trial Lawyers Found.; mem.: Assn. Trial Lawyers Am. (assoc. editor jour. 1950), NY State Trial Lawyers Assn., Met. Trial Lawyers Assn. (dir. 1962—65, bd. govs. 1965—69), NY County Lawyers Assn., Nassau Suffolk Trial Lawyers Assn., Nassau County Bar Assn. Home: Longboat Key, Fla. Died Jan. 11, 2010.

MISHKIN, PAUL J., lawyer, educator; b. Trenton, NJ, Jan. 1, 1927; s. Mark Mordecai and Bella (Dworetsky) M.; m. Mildred Brofman Westover; 1 child, Jonathan Mills Westover. AB, Columbia U., 1947, JD, 1950; MA (hon.), U. Pa., 1971. Bar: N.Y. State bar 1950, U.S. Supreme Ct. bar 1958. Mem. faculty Law Sch. U. Pa., Phila., 1950-72; prof. law U. Calif., Berkeley, 1972-75, Emanuel S. Heller prof., 1975—2000, Emanuel S. Heller prof. emeritus, from 2000. Cons. City of Phila., 1953; reporter study div. jurisdiction between state and fed. cts. Am. Law Inst., 1960-65; mem. faculty Salzburg Seminar in Am. Studies, 1974; Charles Inglis Thompson guest prof. U. Colo., 1975; John Randolph Tucker lectr., 1978, Owen J. Roberts Meml. lectr., 1982; vis. fellow Wolfson Coll., Cambridge U., 1984; vis. prof. Duke U. Law Sch., 1989. Author: (with Morris) On Law in Courts, 1965, (with others) Federal Courts and the Federal System, 2d edit, 1973, 3d edit, 1988; contbr. articles to profl. jours. Trustee Jewish Publ. Soc. Am., 1966-75, Ctr. for Law in the Pub. Interest, 2001-04; mem. permanent com. Oliver Wendell Holmes Devise, 1979-87. With USNR 1945-46. Rockefeller Found. rsch. grantee, 1956; Center for Advanced Study in Behavioral Scis. fellow, 1964-65; recipient Russell Prize for Excellence in Teaching, 1996. Fellow Am. Acad. Arts Scis., Am. Bar Found.; mem. Am. Law Inst., Order of Coif, Phi Beta Kappa. Home: Berkeley, Calif. Died June 26, 2009.

MITCHELL, NED ELSWORTH, confectionery company executive; b. Chgo., Sept. 8, 1925; s. Charles Earling and Elsie Edna (Gliot) Mitchell; m. Artemis Diane Safrithis, June 4, 1949; children: Charles John, Mark Dennis, Peter Ned. BSME, Northwestern U., 1947; MBA, U. Chgo., 1957. Factory mgr. E.J. Brach & Sons, Chgo., 1957—67, v.p., 1967—74, sr. v.p., 1974—76, exec. v.p., 1976—77, pres., from 1977. Mem. bd. zoning appeals Village of Deerfield, Ill., 1960—61; mem. sch. bd. Sch. Dist. 110, Lake County, Ill., 1965—69; mem. planning commn. Village of Riverwoods, 1964; chmn. Evang. Health Found., Oakbrook, Ill., 1983—87. Co-editor: Flexography, 1969. 2d lt. US Army, 1944—53. Mem.: Triangle Frat. (trustee), Chocolate Mfg. Assn (bd. dirs. 1980—84, Candy Kettle award 1984), Nat. Confectioners Assn. (sec., treas. 1982—85, 1986—87, v.p. 1985—86), Am. Assn. Candy Technologists, Economics Club (Chgo.), Exec. Program of U. Chgo. Club, Knollwood Club (Lake Forest). Avocations: golf, woodworking, flying. Home: Chicago, Ill. Died Jan. 21, 2009.

MITCHELL, NICHOLAS C., manufacturing company executive; b. McKees Rocks, Pa., July 27, 1930; s. George and Kate (Pateas) M.; m. Grace H. Mitchell; children— Dennis W., Nicholas C., Jr., Max H., Gracelynne, George N. Student Washington and Jefferson Coll., 1948-49, Grove City Coll., 1949-50; B.S. in Bus. Adminstrn., U. Pitts., 1952. Self-employed in restaurants, McKees Rocks & Stowe Twp., 1952-65; pres. Ingot Aid Co., New Castle, Pa., 1965-67, v.p. Pitts. Metals Purifying (acquired Ingot Aid Co.), Saxonburg, Pa., 1967-70; v.p. Diversified Metals, St. Louis, 1970-73; chmn. Mitchell Industries, Pitts., 1973—; pres. Mitchell Fibercon Inc., Pitts. Key Bolt & Forgings, Mitchell Aluminum Products Co.; mem. pub. rels. staff Dem. Com.,Stowe Twp., Pa., 1957; committeeman, McCandless Twp., Pa., 1971-72. Corp. U.S. Army, 1952-54. Mem. Iron and Steel Soc., Am. Concrete Inst., ASTM, Am. Foundry Soc., Smaller Mfr.'s Council. Episcopalian. Clubs: Duquesne (Pitts.), Williams Country; Highland Country (bd. dirs. 1980-83); Rio Pinar Country. Lodges: Masons (32 deg.), Germania, Shriner. Home: Gibsonia, Pa. Died Nov. 11, 2009.

MITCHELL, WILLIAM JOHN, academic administrator, architecture educator; b. Horsham, Australia, Dec. 15, 1944; BArch, U. Melbourne, Victoria, Australia, 1967; M of Environ. Design, Yale U., 1969; MA, U. Cambridge, Eng., 1977. Arch. Yuncken-Freeman Architects, Melbourne, Australia, 1967—68; asst. prof. architecture, urban design UCLA, 1970—74, head architecture, urban design program, 1973—77, assoc. prof. architecture, urban design, 1974—80, prof. architecture, urban design, program head', 1980—86; pres. The Urban Innovations Group, LA, 1973—74; founding ptnr. The Computer-Aided Design Group, Marina Del Rey, Calif., 1978—91; prof. architecture Harvard U., Cambridge, Mass., 1986—89, dir. Master in Design Studies Program, 1986—92, G. Ware and Edythe M. Travelstead prof. architecture, 1989—92; prof. architecture and media arts & sci. MIT, Cambridge, from 1992, dean Sch. of Architecture and Planning, 1992—2003, head media arts and scis. program, 2003—10. Vis. critic Yale U., New Haven, 1970—75, Tulane U., New Orleans, 1981; lectr. dept. architecture U. Cambridge, England, 1978—80; vis. prof. U. Calif., Berkeley, 1982, Carnegie-Mellon U., Pitts., 1979—83, U. Sydney, 1985; disting. vis. scholar U. Adelaide, SA, Australia. Author: Computer-Aided Architecture Design, 1983, The Logic of Architecture: Design, Computation and Cognition, 1990, The Reconfigured Eye: Visual Truth in the Post-Photographic Era, 1992, City of Bits: Space, Pl., and the Infobahn, 1995, Me++: The Cyborg Self and the Networked City, 2003, e-topia: Urban Life Jim But Not as We Know It, 1999, Info. Tech. and Low-Income Communities, 1999; author: (with others) The Art of Computer Graphics Programming, 1987, The Poetics of Gardens, 1988, The Electronic Design Studio: Architectural Knowledge and Media in the Computer Era, 1990, Digital Design Media, 2d edit., 1991; contbr. numerous articles to profl. jour. Fellow: Royal Australian Inst. Architecture. Died June 11, 2010.

MOECK, WALTER F., conductor, music director; b. Milw., Mar. 18, 1922; s. Walter Ernst and Verena Helen (Klein) M.; m. Barbara Conklin; children: Karen, Richard, Stephen. MusB in Trumpet, Eastman Sch. Music, 1947; studies with Pierre Monteux, L'Ecole Monteux, 1951-53; MA in Conducting, U. Iowa, 1955; D in Fine Arts & Music (hon.), London Inst. Applied Rsch., 1993. Instr. brass Univ. Ala., Tuscaloosa, 1947-54, condr. symphony, 1950-54; assoc. condr. Birmingham (Ala.) Symphony, 1948-60; condr. Southeastern Composers Symphony, Tuscaloosa, 1950-54; mus. dir. Birmingham Ballet Co., 1955-62; mus. dir., condr. Ala. Pops Symphony, Birmingham, 1955-73, L.A. Repertoire Orch., 1975-88, San Fernando Valley Theater of Performing Arts, LA, 1977-88, Am. Philharmonia New Project, LA, from 1978. Instr. Birmingham Southern Coll., Samford U., Montevallo U., Indian Springs Sch., 1954-68; cons., judge various mus. orgns., L.A. and Birmingham, 1947—; tchr. writing various groups and individuals, L.A., 1968—; guest condr. New Orleans Philharm., 1980, Burbank (Calif.) Symphony Orch., 1972, Bakersfield (Calif.) Philharm., 1971, Phila. Symphony Orch., 1953; condr., musical dir. Fine Arts Orch. Scottsdale/Phoenix, Sun City Concert Band. Composer: Trumpet Etudes (2 vols.), 1980, various warm-up exercises for all brass instruments, 1980; contbr. articles to Brass Warm-Ups, 1974. Mayor, pres. Town of Hoover, Ala., 1966; pres. Ch. Coun., L.A., 1973-74; mem. Pres. George Bush's Presdl. Task Force, Nat. Rep. Senatorial Com., Nat. Rep. Congrl. Com., Nat. Rep. Com. With U.S. Army, 1943-46. Recipient Key to City of Birmingham, 1986, Merit medal Pres. Bush, 1990, Man of the Yr. award Internat. Biog. Centre of Cambridge, Eng., 1993; Walter Moeck Week proclaimed in his honor musicians of Birmingham, 1986. Fellow Internat. Inst. of Arts and Letters (life); mem. Calif. Symphony Assn. Republican. Roman Catholic. Avocations: golf, reading, hiking. Home: Sun City West, Ariz. Died Jan. 7, 2009.

MOFFITT, JOHN JACOB, television executive; b. Alliance, Ohio, Mar. 10, 1930; s. John Mader and Marguerite Amanda (Ternone) M.; m. John Mae Archer, Aug. 25, 1954 (div. June 1986); children: Debra Lynn, Kimberly Ann, Zaura Jean. BA, Western Res. U., 1952. Exec. producer Sta. WEWS-TV, Cleve., 1947-64; v.p., gen. mgr. Sta. WUAB-TV, Cleve., 1965-85; Sta. WAAM-TV fellow Johns Hopkins U., Balt., 1955-56; v.p., gen. mgr. Sta. KTHT-TV, Houston, 1985-87, Sta. KTVD-TV, Denver, from 1988. Mem. adv. coun. Arbitron, Md., 1980-84; chmn. bd. dirs. Am. Heart Assn., Cleve., 1977-79. Sgt. U.S. Army, 1952-54. Mem. Nat. Assn. Broadcasters (TV bd. dirs. 1990-92), NATAS (pres. Colo. chpt. 1990-91, Bd. of Govs. award 1984). Republican. Avocation: sports. Died Mar. 24, 2010.

MOFFITT, WILLIAM BENJAMIN, lawyer; b. NYC, Jan. 16, 1949; s. William Benjamin and Victoria Lucinda Moffitt; 1 child, Pilar. BA, U. Okla., 1971; JD, Am. U., 1975. Bar: Va. 1976, US Dist. Ct. (ea. dist.) Va. 1976, US Ct. Appeals (4th cir.) 1980, US Ct. Appeals (5th cir.) 1981, US Ct. Appeals (11th cir.) 1982, US Ct. Appeals (6th cir.) 1988, US Ct. Appeals (1st cir.) 1991, US Dist. Ct. Md. 1994, US Ct. Appeals (3rd cir.) 1994. Ptnr. Lowe, Mark & Moffitt, Alexandria, Va., 1976-81, Mark & Moffitt, Alexandria, Va., 1981-85, Moffitt, Keats & Jones, Alexandria, Va., 1985-87, Moffitt & Jones, Alexandria, Va., 1987-89, William B. Moffitt & Assocs., Alexandria, Va., 1989-91, Moffitt, Zwerling & Kemler, Alexandria, Va., 1991-96, Asbill, Junkin & Moffitt, Chartered, Washington, 1996—2004, Asbill Moffitt & Boss (acquired by Cozen O'Connor), Washington, 2004—09. Mem. Legal Svcs. Bd. No. Va., 1982; pres. Va. Coll. Criminal Def. Lawyers, 1983. Contbr. article to profl. jour. Bd. dirs. ACLU, 1981. Named one of Am. Top Black Lawyers, Black Enterprise Mag., 2003. Fellow Am. Bd. Criminal Lawyers; mem. Alexandria Bar Assn., Nat. Assn. Criminal Def. Lawyers (bd. dirs. 1988-2009, strike force chair 1993, nat. sec. 1994, nat. treas. 1995, second v.p. 1996, first v.p. 1997-98, pres.-elect 1998-99, pres. 1999-2000); Internat. Assn. Criminal Def. Lawyers, Va. Assn. Criminal Def. Lawyers. Died Apr. 24, 2009.

MOHN, MELVIN PAUL, anatomist, educator; b. Cleve., June 19, 1926; s. Paul Melvin and Julia (Jacobik) M.; m. Audrey Faye Lonergan, June 28, 1952; children— Shorey Faye, Andrew Paul AB, Marietta Coll., 1950; Sc.M., Brown U., 1952, PhD in Biology, 1955. Instr. SUNY Downstate Med. Ctr., Bklyn., 1955-59, asst. prof., 1959-63; asst. prof. anatomy U. Kans. Sch. Medicine, Kansas City, 1963-65, assoc. prof., 1965-72, prof., 1972-89, prof. emeritus, from 1989. Cons. Nat. Med. Audiovisual Ctr., Atlanta, 1972; vis. lectr. U. Miami Sch. Medicine, Fla., 1966. Bd. dirs. U. Kans. Med. Ctr. Credit Union, 1968-77, Kansas City Youth Symphony, 1972-77; mem. U.S. Pony Club, 1964-71, Med. Arts Symphony, 1965-71, 90—, Spring Hill Chorale, 1990-96, Spring Hill Hist. Soc., 1997—. Served with USN, 1944-46, PTO. McCoy fellow, 1950, Arnold biology fellow, 1954 Fellow AAAS; mem. Am. Soc. Zoologists, Am. Assn. Anatomists, Am. Inst. Biol. Sci., Masons, Lions, Rotary, Ruritan, Olathe Trail Riders, Phi Beta Kappa, Sigma Xi, Beta Beta Beta. Republican. Methodist. Home: Spring Hill, Kans. Died Jan. 2, 2010.

MOIR, DAVID, packaging industry executive; b. NYC, Mar. 12, 1933; s. Robert and Mary (Lee) M.; m. Barbara Donovan, July 6, 1957 (div. May 1985); children: Lori, Sharon, Jennifer, Michelle, Lisa; m. Dominique Lack, Oct. 19, 1986; 1 child, Chelsea. Grad. high sch., Sayville, NY. From pressman to plant mgr. Diamond Nat. Corp., NYC, 1953-69; v.p. ops., pres., chief oper. officer Alford Industries, Ridgefield, N.J., from 1969, also bd. dirs. Patentee cosmetic sampling. Home: Annapolis, Md. Died Oct. 9, 2009.

MOLDENHAUER, WILLIAM CALVIN, soil scientist; b. New Underwood, SD, Oct. 27, 1923; s. Calvin Fred and Ida (Killam) M.; m. Catherine Ann Maher, Nov. 26, 1947; children— Jean Ann, Patricia, Barbara, James, Thomas BS, S.D. State U., 1949; MS, U. Wis., 1951, PhD, 1956. Soil surveyor S.D. State U., Brookings, 1948-54; soil scientist U.S. Dept. Agr., Big Spring, Tex., 1954-57, Ames, Iowa, 1957-72, Morris, Minn., 1972-75; rsch. leader Nat. Soil Erosion Rsch. Lab., Agrl. Rsch. Svc. U.S. Dept. Agr., West Lafayette, Ind., 1975-85; prof. dept. agronomy Purdue U., West Lafayette, 1975-85, prof. emeritus, 1985—2010. Contbr. articles to profl. jours. Served with U.S. Army, 1943-46 Fellow Am. Soc. Agronomy, Soil Sci. Soc., Soil Conservation Soc. Am. (pres. 1979), World Assn. Soil and Water Conservation (pres. 1983-85, exec. sec. 1985-2003, asst. treas. 2003-08). Home: Sioux Falls, SD. Died May 21, 2010.

MOLNAR, JOHN EDGAR, higher education administrator; b. Cin., Sept. 12, 1942; s. John William and Bonnie (Hannaford) M. AB in History with high honors, Coll. of William and Mary, 1964; A.M.L.S., U. Mich., 1965, PhD, 1978; M.Hum., U. Richmond, 1968. Librarian, Kelsey Mus., Ann Arbor, Mich., 1965; asst. librarian Longwood Coll., Farmville, Va., 1965-70; librarian Cleary Coll., Ysilanti, Mich., 1973-75; coord. library planning Coun. of Higher Edn., Richmond, Va., 1975—; co-chmn. Va. Task Force on Computer Sci. Programs, 1982-83; adviser on licensure of fgn. med. sch. grads. Va. Bd. Medicine, 1983—; co-chmn. Va.

Task Force on Fgn. Langs., 1983-85, Va. Fgn. Lang. Council, 1986—. Author: Author-/Title Index to Sabin, 1974. Editor: Assessment of Computer Science Degree Programs in Virginia, 1983; Assessment of the Foreign Language Discipline in Virginia's State-Supported Institutions of Higher Education, 1985, Study of Academic Library Facility Needs in Virginia's Public System of Higher Education, 1986. Mem. Am. Philatelic Soc., SAR, Persons Responsible for Oversight and Approval Nonpub. Degree-granting Instns. Beta Phi Mu. Republican. Anglican. Home: Farmville, Va. Died June 20, 2009.

MONTORO, RAFAEL DE LA TORRE, physician; b. Havana, Cuba, Oct. 14, 1918; came to U.S., 1959, naturalized, 1964; s. Octavio Eliseo and Elisa Isabel (De La Torre y Soublette) M.; M.D., Havana U., 1946; m. Katherine Caragol Sanabria, Mar. 16, 1960 (dec. Apr. 1987); children— Victoria Montoro Zamorano, Rafael, Maria Therese Montoro Gross. Gen. practice medicine, Havana, 1946-52; mem. staff Hijas de Galicia Hosp., 1948-52; mem. Cuban del. WHO, 1952; E.E. and M.P. to Portugal, 1953-56; ambassador to Netherlands, 1956-59; minister to Iceland, 1957-59; adminstr. Profl. Registry Medicaid, N.Y.C., 1966-69; acting dir., physician Psychiat. Hosp., Ponce, P.R., 1970-73; practice gen. medicine, Coral Gables, Fla., 1973—; pres. Delray Med. Group Inc.; mem. staff South Shore Hosp., Miami Beach, Fla. V.p. Count Galvez Hist. Soc.l bd. dirs. Cuban Mus. Arts and Culture, Inst. of Ophthalmology Horacio Ferrer. Decorated grand cross Order Orange Nassau (Netherlands), Order Carlos Manuel de Cespedes (Cuba); grand officer Order Red Cross (Cuba), Order Merit (Chile); comdr. Order Finlay (Cuba); named Marquis de Montoro (Spain). Mem. Fla. Med. Assn., Dade County Med. Assn. Republican. Roman Catholic. Club: Coral Gables Country. Home: Miami, Fla. Died Aug. 17, 2010.

MOODY, DOLORES IRENE, nurse; b. Hazelhurst, Miss., Aug. 14, 1930; d. Med Roy and Lois Louise (Middleton) Ashley; m. Wallace Ross Williams, July 2, 1954 (div. 1963); children— Anthony Ross, Timothy Owen; m. 2d. Jack Wright Moody, May 17, 1974; 1 dau., Nancy E. R.N., Miss. Bapt. Hosp. Sch. Nursing, 1952. Cert. occupational health nurse. Mem. staff surgery Miss. Bapt. Hosp., Jackson, 1952-53; staff nurse Sch. Nursing, Houston, 1953-61; supr. nursing Meml. Hosp., Houston, 1961-64; surg. nurse G.S. Dowdy, M.D., Houston, 1964-69; occupational health nurse Bank of the Southwest, Houston, 1969-75; head nurse Pennzoil Co., Houston, 1975—. Mem. employee edn. com. Am. Cancer Soc., Houston, 1980—; instr. C.P.R. and first aid ARC, Houston, 1980—. Academic scholar Miss. Bapt. Hosp., Jackson, 1949; named Outstanding Employee Meml. Hosp., Houston, 1963; Outstanding Profl. Woman, Houston Assn. Occupational Health Nurses, Houston, 1983. Mem. Houston Assn. Occupational Health Nurses (program co-chmn. 1972-73), Tex. Assn. Occupational Health Nurses (continuing edn. chmn. 1983—), Am. Assn. Occupational Health Nurses. Democrat. Baptist. Home: Montgomery, Tex. Died Jan. 11, 2010.

MOORE, BARBARA C., former ambassador; b. Buffalo, 1951; m. Spencer B. Moore; 1 child, Nicholas. BA, Coll. of New Rochelle, 1973. Tours as info. officer U.S. Info. Agy., Caracas, Venezuela, 1989—93; coun. pub. affairs Santiago, Chile, 1993—97; dep. dir. U.S. Info. Agy. Office of Western Hemisphere Affairs, 1997—98; dep. chief of mission US Embassy, Bogota, Colombia, 1998—2002; US amb. to Rep. of Nicaragua US Dept. State, Managua, 2002—05; fgn. policy adv. US Southern Command (USSOUTHCOMMAND), Miami, 2002. Recipient Superior award, US Dept. State, Meritorious award. Died Mar. 11, 2010.

MOORE, JAMES TICE, history educator; b. Greenville, SC, Aug. 8, 1945; s. William Furman and Aileen Sylvester (Pinion) M.; m. Jessie Louise Roberts, 1965; children: Leslie Anne, Evan Christopher, Sharon Elizabeth. BA in History, U. S.C., 1966; MA in History, U. Va., 1968, PhD in History, 1972. Instr. history Va. Commonwealth U., Richmond, 1970-72, asst. prof. history, 1972-78, assoc. prof. history, 1978-84, acting chmn. dept. history, 1981-82, chmn. dept. history, 1982-86, prof. history, from 1984. Mem. editorial adv. bd. Jour. Southern History, Houston, 1982-85, Va. Mag. History & Biography, Richmond, 1988-91; bd. dirs. Univ. Press of Va., Charlottesville, 1986-89. Co-editor: The Governors of Virginia, 1860-1978, 1982; contbr. articles to books, profl. jours. & encys.; contbr. book revs. to various publs. Apptd. mem. Patrick Henry Meml. State Commn., Richmond, 1985-87. Danforth-Va. tchg. fellow, 1966-67; summer rsch. grantee Va. Commonwealth U., 1977, 92. Mem. Raven Soc. U. Va., Phi Beta Kappa, Phi Kappa Phi. Methodist. Avocations: tennis, jogging, stamp collecting/philately, coin collecting/numismatics. Home: Richmond, Va. Died Apr. 1, 2009.

MOORE, JOHN HAYS, chemistry educator; b. Pitts., Nov. 6, 1941; s. John Hays and Mary (Welfer) M.; m. Judy Ann Williams, Aug. 10, 1963; children: John H. IV, Victoria Inez. BS, Carnegie Tech, 1963; MS, Johns Hopkins U., 1965, PhD, 1967. Rsch. assoc. Johns Hopkins U., Balt., 1967-69; program officer NSF, Washington, 1980-81, 85-86; asst. prof. U. Md., College Park, 1969-73, assoc. prof., 1973-78, prof., from 1978. Author: Building Scientific Apparatus, 1982, 3d edit., 2002; editor-in-chief: Encyclopedia of Chemical Physics and Physical Chemistry, 2001; contbr. 115 publs. to profl. jours. Named Joint Inst. for Lab. Astrophysics fellow, 1975, Am. Phys. Soc. fellow, 1990. Fellow: AAAS. Home: State College, Pa. Died May 2, 2010.

MOORE, ROBERT LEE, JR., coating company executive, dentist; b. Atlanta, Oct. 2, 1929; s. Robert Lee and Eleanor Adelaide (Apperson) M.; m. Alice Jeanne Whitaker, Feb. 13, 1954; children— Alice Helene, June Elizabeth. Student, Emory U., 1947-49; D.D.S., Temple U., 1953, certificate oral pediatrics, 1978. Founder, v.p., chmn. bd. Coatings for Industry, Inc., Souderton, Pa., from 1970; pres. Drs. Moore, Wimberly & Braun Assos. (oral pediatrics), Huntingdon Valley, Pa., from 1955; prof. oral pediatrics Temple U., Phila., from 1955. Mem. staff Temple U., Abington, Shriners, Frankford hosps., St. Christophers Hosp. for Children. Trustee, elder Huntingdon Valley Presbyterian Ch. Served to lt. comdr. USN, 1953-55, Korea. Fellow Internat. Coll. Dentists, Royal Soc. Health; mem. Am. Assn. Hosp. Dentists (pres.), ADA, Acad. Pedodontics, Am. Soc. Dentistry for Children, Pa. Dental Soc. (pres.), Montgomery Bucks Dental Soc., Delta Tau Delta, Psi Omega, Omicron Kappa Upsilon. Clubs: Huntingdon Valley, K.T, Shriners, Rotary. Research in field of high temperature cermet coatings for metals. Died Feb. 28, 2010.

MOORE, SUSAN EVELYN, chemist, biologist; b. Mobile, Ala., July 20, 1954; d. Thurston Theodore and Evelyn (Patty) M. BS magna cum laude, Mobile Coll., 1976; postgrad., U. South Ala. Tech. dir. Ala. Lions Eye Bank, Birmingham, 1979-81; chem. cons. Merck & Co., Inc., Birmingham, 1981-84; indsl. chemist Ashland Co., Huntsville, Ala., 1984-85; electron microscopist U. Ala., Birmingham, 1986-88, supr. Immune Cytopenia Lab., 1988-91, specimen control hosp. labs., 1991-93, lab. mgr. Comprehensive Cancer Ctr., from 1993. Mem. choir 1st Bapt. Ch. of Birmingham, 1980—; offcl. Gulf South Conf. Basketball. U. South Ala. rsch. grantee, 1977-79. Mem. NAFE (charter), Electron Microscopy Soc. Am., Ala. Soc. Electron Microscopists, Nat. Assn. Sports Ofcls. (charter), Nat. Fedn. Interscholastic Ofcls. Assn. (charter), Ala. H.S. Athletic Assn. (basketball and football cert.), Amateur Softball Assn. (umpire), Ala. Jr. Coll. Basketball Assn., SCAC, TAAC (SEC divsn. II, divsn. I softball umpire). Baptist. Avocations: tennis, antique refinishing, softball, basketball. Home: Birmingham, Ala. Died Sept. 8, 2009.

MOORE, THOMAS DAVID, management educator; b. D'Lo, Miss., July 19, 1933; s. Jesse Crawley and Laura Emma (Clark) M.; m. Billie Ruth Armstrong, June 17, 1956; 1 child, Elizabeth Ellen. BBA, U. Miss., 1955, MBA, 1960, PhD, 1964. Indsl. engr. Boeing Airplane Co., Seattle, 1955-59, Fryling Electric Products, Inc., Holly Springs, Miss., 1960-61; assoc. prof. Tenn. Tech. U., Cookeveille, 1964-65; prof. mgmt. U. Ala., Tuscaloosa, from 1965. Contbr. articles to profl. jours.; producer, narrator video tape Econs. for High-Sch., 1969. Exec. dir. Ala. Coun. Econ. Edn., Tuscaloosa, 1967-81; v.p. Ala. Acad. Scis., Tuscaloosa, 1968-70, Tuscaloosa Quarterback Club, 1991-92; bd. dirs. Nat. Assn. Econ. Edn. Dirs., N.Y.C., 1970-74, Indian Hills Country Club, Tuscaloosa, 1975-81, Tuscaloosa C. of C., 1976-79; exec. sec. Allied So. Bus. Assn., Tuscaloosa, 1982-88. Grantee U.S. Small Bus. Adminstrn, 1980-88, Ala. Dept. Econ. and Community Affairs, 1985. Mem. North River Yacht Club, Exch. Club Tuscaloosa (pres. 1970-71), Beta Gamma Sigma. Methodist. Avocations: salt water fishing, hiking, travel. Home: Tuscaloosa, Ala. Died Oct. 9, 2009.

MOORHOUSE, LINDA VIRGINIA, symphony orchestra administrator; b. June 26, 1945; d. William James and Mary Virginia (Wild) M. BA, Pa. State U., 1967. Sec. San Antonio Symphony, Tex., 1970-71, adminstrv. asst. Tex., 1971-75, asst. mgr. Tex., 1975-76; exec. dir. Canton (Ohio) Symphony, from 1977. Mem. Ohio Arts Coun. Music Panel, 1980-82, 87-89, Mich. Arts Coun. Music Panel, 1986. Bd. dirs. Stark County unit Arthritis Fedn., 1986-92, treas., 1989-91; bd. dirs. Canton Palace Theatre Assn., treas., 1994-96, pres., 1998-99; active Cen. Stark County United Way Allocations Panel, 1991-96. Mem. Met. Orch. Mgrs. Assn. (pres. 1983-85), Orgn. Ohio Orchs. (pres. 1985-86), Am. Symphony Orch. League (bd. dirs. 1983-85, nat. 1st ladies' site com. 1997—), Stark County Women's Hall of Fame (charter inductee), Soroptomist (Canton, Ohio, Women of Distinction 1992), Nat. First Ladies Libr. Home: Naples, Fla. Died Dec. 1, 2009.

MORAHAN, THOMAS P., state legislator; b. Oct. 11, 1931; m. Helen Killion; 7 children. Dist. mgr. Bell Atlantic; mem. Rockland County Legislature, 1977—80, 1984—99; mem. Dist. 96 NY State Assembly, 1980—82; mem. Dist. 38 NY State Senate, 1999—2010; cmty. rels. mgr. Orange & Rockland Utilities, 1990—96. Republican. Roman Catholic. Died July 12, 2010.

MORAN, WILLIAM CHARLES, academic administrator; b. Huntington, W.Va., July 12, 1935; s. George Frederick and Caroline (Bischoff) M.; m. Margaret Frances Queen, Aug. 24, 1959; children: Kevin Patrick, Thomas Frederick. AA, St. Charles Coll., Balt., 1955; AB, Marshall U., Huntington, W.Va., 1958; MA, Marshall U., 1959; PhD, U. Tenn., 1965. Tchr. Balt. pub. schs., 1959-60; instr. English Marshall U., Huntington, 1960-61; instr. to asst. prof. English S.E. Mo. State U., Cape Girardeau, 1964-67; prof. and chmn. dept. English Berry Coll., Rome, Ga., 1967-71, assoc. dean, 1969-71, acad. dean, 1971-75; dean Coll. Arts and Scis. Winthrop Univ., Rock Hill, S.C., 1975-78; v.p. acad. affairs, dean Francis Marion Univ., Florence, S.C., 1978-92; pres. Lander Univ., Greenwood, S.C., from 1992. Teaching fellow, Marshall U. 1958-59, U. Tenn., 1961-64. Contbr. articles to profl. jours. Mem. So. Assn. Colls. and Schs. (chair vis. com.), So. Atlantic Assn. Depts. English (founding exec. sec. 1969-71), So. Conf. Deans of Faculties (pres. 1984-85), Phi Kappa Phi, Kappa Delta Pi, Sigma Tau Delta, Eta Sigma Phi, Omicron Delta Kappa, Blue Key, Rotary. Died Mar. 10, 2009.

MORAVCSIK, JULIUS MATTHEW, philosophy educator; b. Budapest, Hungary, Apr. 26, 1931; came to U.S., 1949; s. Julius and Edith (Fleissig) M.; m. Marguerite Germain Truninger, Sept. 14, 1954; children: Adrian Clay, Peter Matthew. BA, Harvard U., 1953, PhD, 1959. Asst. prof. U. Mich., Ann Arbor, 1960-66, assoc. prof., 1966-68; prof. Stanford (Calif.) U., from 1968. Lectr. in 25 countries. Author: Understanding Language, 1975, Thought and Language, 1990, Plato and Platonism, 1992, Meaning, Creativity, and the Partial Inscrutability of the Human Mind, 1998, Was Menschen Verbindet, 2003 The Ties That Bind, 2005. Recipient Sr. Humanist prize Humboldt Found., 1983; fellow Ctr. Advanced Studies Behavioral Scis., 1986-87, Inst. Advanced Studies, 2001-02. Fellow Inst. Advanced Studies Budapest; mem. Am. Philos. Assn. (pres. Pacific divsn. 1987-88), Am. Soc. Aesthetics (trustee 1988-92), Soc. Ancient Greek Philosophy (pres. 1989-91, bd. dirs. Jour. History Philosophy, James Wilbur Award Value Theory 2000), Hungarian Acad. Arts and Scis. (external mem.). Avocations: golf, tennis. Home: Stanford, Calif. Died June 3, 2009.

MOREFIELD, RICHARD HENRY, retired diplomat; b. Los Angeles, Sept. 9, 1929; s. Vincent Randolph and Maria (Torres) M.; m. Dorothea Baker, July 30, 1955; children: Richard Henry (dec. 1976), Elizabeth, Daniel, William, Steven, Kenneth BS, U. San Francisco, 1951; MA, U. Calif.-Berkeley, 1955; Sloan fellow, Stanford U., 1973-74. Joined Fgn. Service US Dept. State, 1956, assigned, 1956-58, 69-70, 74-76, Barranquilla, Colombia, 1958-61, Oslo, 1961-64, Montevideo, Uruguay, 1964-69; mem. US Mission to OAS, 1970-73; consul gen. US Embassy, Bogotá, Colombia, 1976-79, Tehran, Iran, 1979-81, Guadalajara, Mexico, 1984-85; mem. Exec. Seminar on Nat. and Internat. Affairs, Washington, 1981-82; dir. Caribbean affairs US Dept. State, Washington, 1982-84. Contbr. articles to profl. jours. Served to 1st lt. U.S. Army, 1951-53 Recipient Valor award US Dept. State, 1981 Mem. American Fgn. Service Assn., Calif. Hist. Soc., Parents of Murdered Children, Handgun Control Inc. Died Oct. 11, 2010.

MORELAND, DONALD EDWIN, physiologist; b. Enfield, Conn., Oct. 12, 1919; s. Albert Sinclair and Ruth (Cowan) M.; m. Verdie Brown Stallings, Nov. 6, 1954; 1 child, Donna Faye; stepchildren: Frank C., Paul Ziglar. BS in Forestry, N.C. State U., 1949, MS in Plant Physiology, 1950, PhD in Plant Physiology, 1953. Plant physiologist SUNY Coll. Forestry, Syracuse, 1952-53, USDA-Agrl. Rsch. Svc., Raleigh, NC, 1953-71, rsch. leader, 1972-78, sr. exec., 1979-95, collaborator, from 1996; asst. prof. to prof. N.C. State U., Raleigh, 1953-95, prof. emeritus, from 1996. Mem. toxicology study sect. NIH, USPHS, Bethesda, Md., 1963-67. Editor: Biochemical Responses Induced by Herbicides, 1982; mem. editorial bd. Pesticide Biochemistry and Physiology, 1971-97, Pesticide Sci., 1987-96; contbr. articles to profl. jours. 1st lt. U.S. Army, 1941-46. AEC predoctoral fellow, 1950-52. Fellow AAAS, Weed Sci. Soc. Am. (outstanding rsch. award 1973); mem. Am. Chem. Soc., Plant Growth Regulator Soc. Am., Am. Soc. Plant Physiologists, So. Weed Sci. Soc., Sigma Xi. Avocations: woodworking, surf fishing, square dancing. Home: Raleigh, NC. Died Apr. 23, 2010.

MORELLI, CARMEN, lawyer; b. Oct. 30, 1922; s. Joseph and Helen (Carani) Morelli; m. Irene Edna Montminy, June 26, 1943; children: Richard A., Mark D., Carl J. BSBA, Boston U., 1949, JD, 1952. Bar: Conn. 1955, U.S. Dist. Ct. Conn. 1958. Asst. prosecutor Town of Windsor, 1957—58; mem. Conn. Ho. of Reps., 1959—61; atty. Town of Windsor, 1961; rep. Capitol Regional Planning Agy., 1965—72. Mem. Windsor Town Com., 1957—82, chmn., 1964—65, treas., 1960—64, mem. planning and zoning commn., 1965—74, mem. charter revision com., 1963—64; rep. Presdl. Task Force. With USN, 1943—45. Mem.: ABA, Am. Arbitration Assn., Windsor Bar Assn. (pres. 1979), Hartford Bar Assn., conn. Bar Assn., Rotary (sgt. arms, sec. 1989—90, pres. 1990—91), Elks, Windsor C. of C. (v.p. 1978). Roman Catholic. Died Dec. 26, 2009.

MORGAN, GEORGE TAD, retail company executive, credit company executive, lawyer; b. Elgin, Ill., Sept. 25, 1933; s. George N. and Lorona M. (King) M.; m. Celeste Heatherley, Oct. 14, 1967; children— Robert, Mary, Joshua, Gabriel. Student, De Pauw U., 1951-52; BS, Northwestern U., 1955, JD, 1958, postgrad. in Acctg, 1959-63. Bar: Fla., Ill. bars. Assoc. firm. R. S. Lehamnn, Elgin, 1958-64; sr. atty. Montgomery Ward & Co. Inc., Chgo., 1964-65, gen. atty., 1965-70, asst. gen. counsel, 1971-85, assoc. gen. counsel, from 1986, asst. sec., from 1971; atty., asst. sec. Montgomery Ward Credit Corp., Chgo., 1965-70, v.p., sec., gen. counsel, 1971-88. Instr. in taxation and bus. law Elgin Community Coll., 1960-63 Mem. Fla. Bar, Chgo. Bar Assn., Internat. Council Shopping Centers. Episcopalian. Died Jan. 2, 2009.

MORGAN, GLEN BERNARD, judge; b. Cleve., June 25, 1928; s. William E. and Elsie E. (Haversaat) Morgan; m. Marianne Cavas, June 14, 1953; children: Craig, Martha. BBA, Case Western Res. U., 1951; JD, 1954. Bar: Ohio 1954. Ptnr. Nahra & Morgan, Cleve, 1964—69, Zidar Morgan & Tolaro, Cleve, 1969—81; judge Ct. Common Pleas, Akron, Ohio, from 1981; law dir. and prosector City of Macedonia, Ohio, 1962—81. Atty. North Hills Water Dist., Northfield Ctr., Ohio, 1965—78. Mem.: ABA, Cleve. Bar Assn., Akron Bar Assn., Ohio Bar Assn. Republican. Episcopalian. Avocation: golf. Home: Hudson, Ohio. Died Feb. 27, 2009.

MORGAN, HOWARD EDWIN, physiologist; b. Bloomington, Ill., Oct. 8, 1927; s. Lyle V. and Ethel E. (Bailey) Morgan. Student, Ill. Wesleyan U., 1944—45; MD, Johns Hopkins U., 1949. Intern Vanderbilt U., Nashville, 1949—51, resident in ob-gyn., 1951—53, instr., 1953—55, instr. physiology, 1957—59, asst. prof. physiology, 1959—62, assoc. prof., 1962—65, prof. physiology, 1965—67; Evan Pugh prof., chmn. physiology Pa. State U., Hershey, 1967—87; sr. v.p. rsch. Geisinger Clinic, Danville, Pa., 1987—98, mgr. rsch. programs Weis Rsch. Ctr., 1977—79. Sci. adv. panel Cardiovasc. Clin. Rsch. Ctrs. Donald W. Reynolds Found., Las Vegas; mem. Nat. Heart, Lung and Blood Adv. Coun., 1979—83. Editor: Physiol. Revs., 1973—79, Am. Jour. Physiology, Cell Physiology, 1981—84. With US Army, 1955—57. Recipient Carl Wiggers award, 1984; scholar Howard Hughes scholar, 1982. Mem.: Inst. Medicine of NAS, Internat. Soc. Heart Rsch. (Peter Harris award 1995), Biophys. Soc., Biochem. Soc., Am. Soc. Biol. Chemists, Am. Heart Assn. (v.p.

rsch. 1977—79, Disting. Achievement award 1988, Gold Heart award 1994, award of merit 1979), Am. Physiol. Soc. (pres., Daggs award 1992). Home: Lewisburg, Pa. Died Mar. 2, 2009.

MORGAN, LEE LAVERNE, manufacturing executive; b. Aledo, Ill., Jan. 4, 1920; s. L. Laverne and Gladys (Hamilton) M.; m. Mary Harrington, Feb. 14, 1942. BS, U. Ill., 1941. With Caterpillar Tractor Co., Peoria, Ill., 1946-85, mgr. sales devel., 1954-61, v.p. charge engine div., 1961-65, exec. v.p., 1965-72, pres., 1972-77, chmn. bd., 1977-85, also dir. Dir. 3M Co., Boeing Co., Mobil Corp., N.Y. Stock Exch., Waste Mgmt., Inc. Bd. dirs. Monmouth Coll.; trustee Conf. Bd., U.S. Council Internat. Bus., Com. for Econ. Devel. Maj. AUS, 1941-46. Mem. Soc. Automotive Engrs., Bus. Coun., Coun. Fgn. Rels., Peoria Country Club, Tucson Nat. Golf Club, Augusta Nat. Club, Masons. Presbyterian. Home: Peoria, Ill. Died Jan. 21, 2009.

MORGAN, LOUIS NELSON, hospital administrator; b. Newton, N.J., July 6, 1942; s. Louis Marshall and Marie (Gruendyke) M. A.A., Bergen Pines County Hosp. Sch. Radiologic Tech., 1962; cert. Bethesda Naval Hosp. Sch. Nuclear Medicine Tech., 1968; B.S., George Washington U., 1978; M.B.P.A., Southeastern U., 1979; Ph.D., Century U., 1980. Radiologic technologist Hunderton Med. Ctr., Flemmington, N.J., 1963; adminstrv. dept. head nuclear medicine Prince George's Gen. Hosp. and Med. Ctr., Cheverly, Md., 1970—; clin. coordinator, instr. Prince George's Community Coll., Largo, Md., 1974—; site surveyor, insp. Joint Rev. Commn. Allied Health Programs, AMA, 1978—. Served with USAF, 1964-70. Mem. Am. Soc. Radiologic Technologists, Va. Soc. Radiologic Technologists, Am. Soc. Med. Technologists, Soc. Nuclear Medicine, Soc. Nuclear Medicine Technologists (exec. com., program chmn., cert. merit 1976-77, nominations com. 1977-78 Mid-easter chpt.), Am. Coll. Hosp. Adminstrs. (nominee), Am. Hosp. Assn., Hosp. Fin. Mgmt. Assn., Am. Hosp. Radiology Adminstrs., Am. Soc. Pub. Adminstrs. (sect. personnel adminstrn. and labor relations and budget mgmt.), Am. Mktg. Assn., Md. Assn. Nuclear medicine Technologists. Republican. Roman Catholic. Club: Toastmaster's Internat. Home: Arlington, Va. Died May 27, 2009.

MORGAN, RODGER F., manufacturing executive; b. Bklyn., Jan. 21, 1944; s. Rodger F. and Laura (Whalen) M.; m. Connie Lee Heil, 1963 (div. 1968); children: Christine Kelly, Kathleen Dawn; m. Angela, Dec. 5, 1972; children: Rodger Erick, Anthony Joseph, Lynn Marie. Student in graphic arts, N.Y.C. Community Coll. Svc. technician Chemco Photoproducts, Nassau, N.Y., Fabcon, Nassau; ornamental iron worker and supr. IAOBSOIW Local 580, Manhattan, N.Y.; with Ricanlynn Svcs., Inc., Hunter, N.Y. Leader Boy Scouts Am., Lindenhurst, N.Y. Mem. C. of C. Avocations: photography, snowmobiling. Home: East Jewett, NY. Died Jan. 7, 2009.

MORGAN, THEODORE, economist; b. Middletown, Ohio, May 31, 1910; s. Ben and Anna Louella (Knecht) M.; m. Catharine Moomaw, June 30, 1943; children: Stephanie H., Marian DeW., Laura S. AB, Ohio State U., 1930, AM, 1931, BSE, 1931; MA, Harvard U., 1940, PhD, 1941. Asst. prof. Randolph-Macon Women's Coll., Lynchburg, Va., 1941-42; teaching fellow, tutor, instr. Harvard U., Cambridge, Mass., 1940-41, 42-47; advisor, dep. gov. Cen. Bank of Ceylon, Colombo, 1951-53; assoc. prof. to prof. emeritus U. Wis., Madison, 1947—80, prof. emeritus, from 1980. Vis. prof. U. Singapore, 1967-69, Gadjah Mada U., Yogjakarta, Indonesia, 1959-60, Nankai U., Tianjin, China, 1990, U. Manchester, Eng., 1980-82, Sussex U., Brighton, Eng., 1975-76; sr. staff Coun. Econ. Advisors, Washington, 1964-65; advisor Ministry of Econ. Affairs. Govt. Thailand, Bangkok, 1970; rsch. fellow Resource Systems Inst. East-West Ctr., Honolulu, 1985-86. Author: Hawaii, A Century of Economic Change, 1948, Income and Employment, 1947, Introduction to Economics, 1950, 56, Economic Development, 1975, and others. Mem.: Am. Econ. Assn., Royal Econ. Soc. (life). Mem. Unitarian Ch. Avocations: tennis, bicycling, skiing, hiking. Home: Madison, Wis. Died Feb. 8, 2009.

MORGENROTH, WILLIAM MASON, educator; b. Akron, Ohio, May 21, 1915; s. Abraham Lee and Jeanette Elizabeth (Mason) M.; m. Margaret Moellenbrock, Jan. 29, 1959; children— Virginia, Robert, Rebecca, William, Amy, Maria. AB, U. Mich., MBA, 1939; PhD, U. Pitts., 1962. Mgr. indsl. relations Westinghouse Corp., 1951-56; v.p. Mason, Shaver & Rhoades, 1956-58; asst. prof. bus. adminstrn. U. Pitts., 1958-61; asso. prof. Ohio State U., 1961-67; dean Calif. State U., Hayward, 1967-68; prof. Coll. Bus. Adminstrn. U. S.C., Columbia, from 1968. Chmn. C&S Nat. Bank. Lectr., author works in field. Served with USN, 1941-45. Mem. Am. Mgmt. Assn. (pres. Central Ohio chpt. 1966-67), Sales and Mktg. Execs., Nat. Mgmt. Assn. Clubs: Masons. Republican. Lutheran. Home: West Columbia, SC. Died Apr. 5, 2009.

MORIN, ROBERT EDGAR, college dean; b. Chgo., Nov. 8, 1926; s. Aime Louis and Ruth Helen (Swanson) M.; m. Catherine Evaline Myers, Aug. 21, 1949; children— Patricia, Mark. BA, Northwestern U., 1949, MA, 1950; PhD, U. Wis., 1954. Asst. prof. psychology U. Tex. at Austin, 1954-56, 57-61; asst. prof. Iowa State U., Ames, 1956-57; asso. prof. U. Ariz., Tucson, 1961-62, Kent (Ohio) State U., 1962-65, prof., 1965-72, U. No. Iowa, Cedar Falls, from 1972, dean bus. and behavioral scis., 1972-79, dean social and behavioral scis., from 1979. Contbr. profl. jours. Served with USNR, 1945-46. Recipient NSF and NIH grants. Fellow Am. Psychol. Assn.; mem. Psychonomic Soc., Sigma Xi. Clubs: Rotarian. Research on human learning and retention. Home: Cedar Falls, Iowa. Died May 6, 2009.

MORITZ, TIMOTHY BOVIE, psychiatrist; b. Portsmouth, Ohio, July 26, 1936; s. Charles Raymond and Elisabeth Bovie (Morgan) M.; m. Joyce Elizabeth Rasmussen, Oct. 13, 1962 (div. Sept. 1969); children: Elizabeth Wynne, Laura Morgan; m. Antoinette Tanasichuk, Oct. 31, 1981; children: David Michael, Stephanie Lysbeth. BA, Ohio State U., 1959; MD, Cornell U., 1963. Diplomate Am. Bd. Psychiatry and Neurology. Intern in medicine N.Y. Hosp., NYC, 1963-64, resident in psychiatry, 1964-67; spl. asst. to dir. NIMH, Bethesda, Md., 1967-69; dir. Community Mental Health Ctr., Rockland County, NY, 1970-74, Ohio Dept. Mental Health, Columbus, Ohio, 1975-81; med. dir. psychiatry Miami Valley Hosp., Dayton, Ohio, 1981-82; med. dir. N.E. Ga. Community Mental Health Ctr., Athens, Ga., 1982-83, Charter Vista Hosp., Fayetteville, Ark., 1983-87; clin. dir. adult psychiatry Charter Hosp., Las Vegas, Nev., 1987-94; pvt. practice psychiatry Las Vegas, from 1987; med. dir. Problem Gambling Cons., Las Vegas, from 2000. Prof. Wright State U., Dayton, Ohio, 1981-82; asst. prof. Cornell U., N.Y.C., 1970-73; mem. human subjects biomed. scis. rev. com. U. Nev., Las Vegas, 2000-2001; cons. NIMH, Rockville, Md., 1973-83. Author: (chpt.) Rehabilitation Medicine and Psychiatry, 1976; mem. editorial bd. Directions in Psychiatry, 1981-1993. Dir. dept. mental health and mental retardation Gov.'s Cabinet, State of Ohio, Columbus, 1975-81. Recipient Svc. award Ohio Senate, 1981, Svc. Achievement award Ohio Gov., 1981. Fellow Am. Psychiat. Assn. (disting. life, Disting. Svc. award 1981); mem. AMA, Nev. Assn. Psychiat. Physicians, Nev. State Med. Assn., Am. Assn. Chronic Fatigue Syndrome, Clark County Med. Soc., Cornell U. Med. Coll. Alumni Assn., Ohio State U. Alumni Assn. (life). Home: Las Vegas, Nev. Died July 19, 2010.

MORPHEW, DOROTHY RICHARDS-BASSETT, artist, real estate broker; b. Cambridge, Mass., Aug. 4, 1918; d. George and Evangeline Booth Richards; children: Jon Eric Bassett, Marc Alan Bassett, Dana Kimball Bassett. Grad., Boston Art Inst., 1949. Draftsman United Shoe Machinery Co., 1937—42; blueprinter, advt. artist A.C. Lawrence Leather Co., Peabody, Mass., 1949—51; propr. Studio Shop and Studio Potters, Beverly, Mass., 1951—53; tchr. ceramics and art Kingston, NH, from 1953; real estate broker, 1965—81; two-man exhbn. Topsfield (Mass.) Libr., 1960; owner, operator Ceramic Shop, West Stewartstown, NH. With USNR, 1942—44. Recipient Profl. award, New Eng. Ceramic Show, 1975, also numerous certs. in ceramics. Mem.: Englewood (Fla.) Art Guild. Home: Woodstock, Ga. Died Apr. 13, 2010.

MORRIS, EUGENE JEROME, retired lawyer; b. NYC, Oct. 14, 1910; s. Max and Regina (Cohn) M.; m. Terry Lesser, Mar. 28, 1934 (dec. Sept. 1993); 1 child, Richard S.; m. Blanche Bier Funke, June 22, 1994. BSS., CCNY, 1931; LL.B., St. John's U., 1934. Bar: N.Y. 1935. Practiced, NYC, 1935-99; sr. and founding partner firm Demov, Morris & Hammerling, 1946-87; v.p., sr. counsel Ea. region Am. Title Ins. Co., NYC, 1990-93; of counsel Spector & Feldman, 1991-99; ret., 1999. Adj. prof. land use regulation NYU Grad. Sch. Pub. Adminstrn., 1978-81; adj. prof. legal issues in real estate, Real Estate Inst. NYU, 1988—; spl. master Supreme Ct. State of N.Y., 1979-99; arbitrator Civil Ct. N.Y., 1994-99. Editor weekly column N.Y. Law Jour., 1965-87, It's the Law, Real Estate Forum, 1982-87; editor-in-chief N.Y. Practice Guide: Real Estate, 4 vols., 1986, Real Estate Development, 4 vols., 1987; contbr. articles to profl. jours. Mem. N.Y. State Tax Revision Commn., 1977-80, N.Y.C. Rent Guidelines Bd., 1983-85. Served with AUS, 1943-45. Recipient Justice award N.Y. sect. Am. Jewish Congress, 1996. Mem. ABA (chmn. spl. com. housing and urban devel. 1970-73, coun. sect. real property, probate and trust law 1971-74, assoc. editor Real Property, Probate and Trust Jour. 1979-86, editor Real Property, Probate and Property mag., articles editor 1986-94), Am. Judges Assn., Assn. Bar City N.Y. (chmn. com. housing and urban devel. 1971-74, com. on lectures and continuing edn. 1980-83, coun. on jud. adminstrn. 1989-92), N.Y. State Bar Assn. (exec. com. 1980-97, chmn. com. meetings and lectrs. 1982-92, CLE com. 1984-90, ho. of dels. 1986-95, co-editor Real Property Jour. 1995-97, Professionalsim award 2002), Citizens Union, Lambda Alpha (bd. dirs. 1990-98, pres. N.Y. chpt. 1990-93, sec. 1993-95, treas. 1996-97). Died July 24, 2010.

MORRIS, PAUL ROBERT, energy company executive; b. Sykesville, Pa., June 30, 1924; s. John J. and Mary (Skovran) M.; student Ohio State U., 1943-44; B.S.I.E., Pa. State U., 1950; postgrad. Syracuse U., 1964-65, Cornell U., 1965-67; m. Alberta N. Stinson, June 30, 1951; children— Paul Kyler, Barry, Philip Grant. Indsl. engr. Electronic Tube div. Sylvania Corp., Emporium, Pa., Reynoldsville, Pa., Huntington, W. Va., Burlington, Iowa, 1950-53, mfg. dept. mgr., Burlington, 1953-58, indsl. relations supr., Burlington and Seneca Falls, N.Y., 1958-69; mgr. personnel and mfg. services W.M. Chace Co., Detroit, 1969-70; v.p., gen. mgr. Chace Internat. Corp., San Juan, P.R., 1970-75; v.p. new bus. and new facilities devel. GTE Sylvania, Reidsville, N.C., 1975-80; exec. v.p. Reidsville C. of C., 1980-81; sr. project coordinator N.C. Alternative Energy Corp., Research Triangle Park, N.C., 1981-84, waste-to-energy coordinator, Mecklenburg County, 1984—; dir. Chace Internat. Corp., Chace Precision Materials Corp. Mem. Selective Service bd., 1962-63; bd. dirs. Girl Scouts U.S.A., 1950-62; chmn. Boy Scouts Am., 1967-69; bd. dirs. Salvation Army, 1958-64; pres., bd. dirs. U.N.C. Dental Parents Assn. Served with AUS, 1943-46. ETO. Recipient SSS award 1963. Mem. Nat. Foreman's Assn. (pres. 1953), Pa. State U. Alumni Assn., Triangle. Republican. Lutheran. Lodges: Rotary, Mason. Home: Reidsville, NC. Died Nov. 14, 2009.

MORRIS, RALPH WILLIAM, chronopharmacologist; b. Cleveland Heights, Ohio, July 30, 1928; s. Earl Douglas and Viola Minnie (Mau) M.; m. Carmen R. Mueller; children: Christopher Lynn, Kirk Stephen, Timothy Allen and Todd Andrew (twins), Melissa Mary. BA, Ohio U., Athens, 1950, MS, 1953; PhD, U. Iowa, 1955; postgrad., Seabury-Western Theol. Sem., 1979-81, McHenry County Coll., 1986-88. Research fellow in pharmacology, then teaching fellow U. Iowa, 1952-55; instr. dept. pharmacology Coll. Medicine, 1955-56; asst. prof. dept. pharmacognosy and pharmacology Coll. Pharmacy, 1956-62, assoc. prof., 1962-69; prof. Med. Center, U. Ill., Chgo., 1969-98, prof. emeritus, 1998, adj. prof. dept. pharmacodynamics, 1998-2000. Mem. adv. com. 1st aid and safety Midwest chpt. ARC, 1972-83; cons. in drug edn. to Dangerous Drug Commn., Ill. Dept. Pub. Aid, Chgo., Ill. Dept. Profl. Regulataions, Ill. Dept. Corrections and suburban sch. dists.; adj. prof. edn. Coll. Edn., U. Ill., Chgo., 1976-85; vis. scientist San Jose State U., Calif., 1982-83, St. George Med. Sch., Grenada, 1994. Referee and contbr. articles to profl. and sci. jours., lay mags., radio and TV appearances. Trustee Palatine (Ill.) Pub. Libr., 1967-72, pres., 1969-70; trustee North Suburban Libr. System, 1968-72, pres. 1970-72, mem. long-range planning com., 1975-81; chmn. Ill. Libr. Trustees, 1970-72, intellectual freedom com.; mem. Title XX Ill. Citizens Adv. Coun., 1981-83; trusteee McHenry (Ill.) Pub. Libr. Dist., 1987-89, pres., 1987-89; trustee St. Gregory's Abbey, Three Rivers, Mich., 1989-96; bd. dirs. North Suburban Libr. Found., Wheeling, Ill,. 1998-99; bd. dirs. United Campus Ministry U. Ill. at Chgo., 1983-87; pres. R.W. Morris & Assocs., 1988—; v.p. Lake Barrington Shores Condo X Assn., bd. dirs., 1999—; mem. archtl. commn. Lake Barrington Shores Master Bd., 1999—. Recipient Golden Apple Teaching award U. Ill. Coll. Pharmacy, 1966; cert. of merit Town of Palatine, 1972 Mem. AAAS, Am. Assn. Coll. Pharmacists, Internat. Soc. Chronobiology, European Soc. Chronbiology, Am. Soc. Pharmacology and Exptl. Therapeutics, Am. Library Trustee Assn., Ill. Library Trustee Assn. (v.p. 1970-72, dir. 1969-72), Sigma Xi, Rho Chi, Gamma Alpha. Episcopalian. Died Aug. 17, 2010.

MORRIS, ROBERT, reinsurance analyst; b. Cambridge, Mass., Apr. 20, 1923; s. Henry Winthrop and Alice May (Bartlett) M.; m. Sigrid Margarete Henker, June 18, 1948; children: Elaine Antoinette, Susan Jeanette, Steven Walter. Diploma, Dalhousie Comml. Coll., Can., 1942; BA, MA, U. Pa., 1964. CPCU. Enlisted U.S. Army, 1942, advanced through grades to sgt. maj., 1949, ret., 1962; ins. adjustor Ins. Co. N.Am., Phila., 1962-65, asst. underwriter, 1965-71; asst. v.p. Am. Mut. Reinsurance Co., Chgo., 1971-73, v.p. regional sales, 1973-80, v.p. underwriting, 1980-83, sr. v.p. underwriting, 1983-85; v.p. U.S. Reinsurance Corp., Boston, 1985-89; reins. analyst, advisor, from 1989. Instr. Ins. Soc. Phila., 1966-71; reinsurance cons., Chgo., 1985. Contbr. articles to profl. and tech. jours. Dir. Gulph Mills (Pa.) Civic Assn., 1971-76, v.p., 1972-73. Mem. Soc. CPCU (chmn. edn. com. Phila. chpt. 1966-80, mem. reinsurance sect. Boston chpt. 1982-89), Mil. Officers Assn Am. (life), Am. Legion. Clubs: Chgo. Athletic Assn., Princeton of N.Y., Ambassadors (Kansas City, Mo., life). Lodges: Masons, Shriners. Republican. Avocations: world travel, mountain hiking, genealogy, bicycling. Home: Merrimac, Mass. Died Jan. 2, 2009.

MORRISON, MICHAEL P., lawyer; b. Hinsdale, Ill., Feb. 21, 1944; BA with honors, Mich. State U., 1967; JD, U. Tex., 1972. Bar: Ill. 1972. Ptnr. Hopkins & Sutter, Chgo. Mem. ABA, Ill. State Bar Assn., Chgo. Bar Assn. Died July 3, 2010.

MORRISON, WILLARD LANGDON, JR., environmental services executive, consultant; b. Melrose, Mass., Aug. 22, 1918; s. Willard L. and Ruth (Ansell) M.; m. Joy Overall; children: Leland, Marjorie; m. Janis Marshall; 1 child, Phillip. BS, MIT, 1940; diploma, Inst. Design, Chgo., 1946. Dir. product devel. West Bend (Wis.) Co., 1940-47; coord. indsl. design Montgomery & Ward Co., Chgo., 1948-50; sr. tech. advisor aluminum divsn. Olin Mathieson Chem. Co., Chgo., 1951-54; pres. Morrison and Co, Engrs., Lake Forest, Ill., 1955-60; dir. comml. devel. Archer divsn. R.J. Reynolds Industries, Winston-Salem, N.C., 1961-69; pres. Med. Plastics Corp., Greensboro, N.C., 1969-73; dir. rsch. and engring. Washington Group, Inc., Winston-Salem, 1973-75; dir. mkt. devel. Amerimex Corp., Charlotte, N.C., 1976-79; pres. Microban Products Co. divsn. Tultex Corp., Winston-Salem, 1980-84; pres., owner Advanced Environ. Systems, Inc., Winston-Salem, from 1980. Pres. Antimicrobial Products Sales Co., Winston-Salem, 1968—; ptnr. Profl. Execs. Cons., Charlotte, 1970-75. Mem. Delta Kappa Epsilon. Republican. Avocations: philately, piloting. Pioneer in development of antimicrobial polymers, patentee in field. Home: Winston Salem, NC. Died May 28, 2010.

MORRISSEY, ROBERT JOHN, communications executive; b. Manchester, Conn., Apr. 21, 1944; s. Thomas J. and Lillian F. (Bischoff) M. BA, Fairfield U., 1966; postgrad., U. Mo., 1966-67. Mgr. pub. rels. United Techs. Rsch. Ctr., East Hartford, Conn., 1975-77; various pub. rels. positions United Techs. Corp., Conn., 1967-75, dir. employee communications Hartford, Conn., 1977-82, dir. corp. communication svcs., 1982-86, corp. cons., ombudsman, 1986-88, corp. ombudsman, 1988-92, dir. communications planning, from 1992. Bd. dirs. Conn. Radio Info. Sys., 1995. Mem. exec. com. Downtown Coun. Hartford, 1995. Mem. Pub. Rels. Soc. Am., Internat. Assn. Bus. Comm., Comm. Roundtable, Soc. for Preservation and Encouragement Barbershop Quartet Singing in Am. (past pres. Manchester). Avocations: reading, barbershop quartet singing. Died Aug. 15, 2009.

MORSE, ELEANOR REESE, museum administrator; b. Oct. 21, 1912; d. George W. and Elsie (Douds) Reese; m. A. Reynolds Morse, Mar. 20, 1942 (dec. 2000); 1 child, Brad Goodell. BA in Music, Rollins Coll., 1937, PhD (hon.), 1988; MA, Western Res. U., 1970. Pres. Salvador Dali Found., Cleve., St. Petersburg, Fla., from 1972. Author, publisher: over 30 books on Salvador Dali. Named to Order of Isabella Catolica by King of Spain, 1989. Mem. Knights of Malta. Home: Chagrin Falls, Ohio. Died July 1, 2010.

MORTON, RUSSELL H., lawyer; b. Camden, NJ, June 22, 1939; BA, Rutgers U., 1962; JD, U. San Fernando Valley, 1970. Bar: Calif. 1972. Atty. Zonni, Ginocchio and Taylor, P.C., Santa Ana, Calif. Mem. ABA, State Bar Calif., Long Beach Bar Assn., L.A. County Bar Assn., Orange County Bar Assn. Died Aug. 13, 2009.

MOSBACHER, ROBERT ADAM, SR., oil and gas industry executive, former United States Secretary of Commerce; b. Mt. Vernon, NY, Mar. 11, 1927; s. Emil and Gertrude (Schwartz) M.; m. Jane Pennybacker (dec. 1970); children: Diane, Robert Jr., Kathryn, Lisa Mosbacher Mears. m. Sandra Smith Gerry, 1973 (div. 1982); m. Georgette Paulsin, 1989 (div. 1998); m. Michele McCutchen, 2000 BS, Washington and Lee U., 1947, LLD (hon.), 1984; Ph.D (hon.), U. Houston, 1989. Independent oil and gas producer, from 1948; sec. US Dept. Commerce, Washington, 1989-92; gen. chmn. Pres. Bush's re-election campaign, 1992; gen. chmn. fin. Rep. Nat. Com., Washington, 1992; chmn. Mosbacher Energy Co., Houston, Mosbacher Power Group, Houston, from 1995. Author: Going to Windward: A Mosbacher Family Memoir, 2010. Dir. emeritus Aspen Inst., Ctr. for Strategic and Internat. Studies; chmn. bd. visitors M.D. Anderson Hosp.; chmn. Pres. Ford Fin. Com., 1976; mem. Pres. Regan's Task Force on Pvt. Sctor Initiatives, 1981-83; nat. fin. chmn. George Bush for Pres., 1980, 1988; co-chmn. Republican Nat. Fin. Com. Mem. Am. Petroleum Inst. (dir., exec. com.), Nat. Petroleum Coun. (past chmn.), All Am. Wildcatters Assn. (past chmn.), Am. Assn. Petroleum Landmen (past pres.). Republican. Presbyterian. Avocation: sailing. Died Jan. 24, 2010.

MOSEKA, AMINATA See LINCOLN, ABBEY

MOSS, DAVID EARL, food products executive, small business owner; b. Ronceverte, W.Va., June 18, 1952; s. M. Thurman and Nelverna (Lawrence) M.; m. Patricia Elizabeth Ide, June 6, 1978. BS in Bus. Studies, W.Va. U., 1975; student, Bluefield State Coll., 1991. Lic. real estate sales agent. V.p., gen. mgr., salesperson Lewisburg Wholesale Co., Ronceverte, from 1970; pers. asst. Mountaineer Food Stores, Ronceverte, from 1975, mgr., from 1977, mgr. meat dept., 1978-89, produce mgr., 1980-89. State dir. Eastern Greenbrier Jaycees, Ronceverte, 1976, 77, 78; sec. Fairlea (W.Va.) Ruritan Club, 1983. Named Jaycee of the Month, Eastern Greenbrier Jaycees, 1977. Avocations: tours, hunting, fishing, hiking, gardening. Home: Fairlea, W.Va. Died Jan. 6, 2009.

MOULDER, PETER VINCENT, cardiovascular surgeon, educator; b. Jackson, Mich., Jan. 26, 1921; s. Peter Vincent and Marcella (McDonald) M.; m. Jane Eleanor Lyons, Feb. 9, 1946; children: Mary E. Moulder Jaeger, Peter Vincent III, James L., Jane A. Moulder Kauzlarich. BS magna cum laude, U. Notre Dame, 1942; MD with honors, U. Chgo., 1945; MA (hon.), U. Pa., 1971. Diplomate Am. Bd. Surgery, Am. Bd. Thoracic Surgery. Intern U. Chgo., 1945-46, resident in surgery, 1946-52, 52-53, chief resident in gen. surgery, 1953-54, chief resident thoracic surgery, 1954-55, from instr. to prof. dept. surgery, 1952-68; resident in surgery U. Ill. Rsch. and Ednl. Hosp., Chgo., 1952; prof. dept. surgery U. Pa., Phila., 1968-73, U. Fla., Gainesville, 1973-79, Sch. Medicine, Tulane U., New Orleans, 1980-92, adj. prof. dept. biomed. engring., from 1984; emeritus prof. Tulane U., New Orleans, from 1992; clin. prof. La. State U. Sch. Medicine, from 1992; med. dir. Biosouth Rsch. Labs., from 1992; thoracic surgeon New Orleans Vets. Administrn. Hosp., from 1992. Cons. cardiovascular surgery Naval Hosp., Great Lakes, Ill., 1955-68; cons. thoracic surgery Cook County Hosp., Chgo., 1966-68, Naval Hosp., Phila., 1969-73; dir. surgery Pa. Hosp., Phila., 1968-72; chief thoracic and cardiovascular surgery VA Hosp., Gainesville, 1973-79; med. investigator VA, 1973-80; mem. editorial bd. Annals of Thoracic Surgery, 1965-68, Chest, 1968-73. Mem. editorial bd. Annals Thoracic Surgery, 1965-68, Surg. Clinics N.Am. New Operations, 1966, Chest, 1968-73; contbr. some 275 articles to profl. publs. Lt. (j.g.) USNR, 1942-57, active duty, 1943-48. Recipient Alexander Vishnevsky medal USSR, 1966, Centennial Sci. Honor award U. Notre Dame, 1965, Gold medal Law Sci. Acad., 1968, George Bloch award for Excellence in Tchg. Surgery, U. Chgo., 2002, Outstanding Acheivement award, INPEX XVII Inventors, 2001; named to Mil and Hospitaller Order of St. Lazarus, 1990. Fellow Soc. for Vascular Surgery (disting.); mem. AMA, ACS, IEEE, IEEE Soc. Acoustics, Speech and Signal Processing, IEEE Computer Soc., Am. Physiol. Soc., Am. Assn. Thoracic Surgery, Am. Surg. Assn., Am. Soc. Clin. Surgery, Am. Soc. Artificial Internal Organs, Internat. Soc. Artificial Organs, Am. Math. Assn., Am. Coll. Chest Physicians, Am. Coll. Cardiology, Am. Heart Assn., Cen. Surg. Assn., Soc. Clin. Surgery, Soc. Univ. Surgeons, Soc. Thoracic Surgeons, Internat. Cardiovascular Soc., So. Thoracic Surg. Assn., Assn. for Computing Machinery and SigBio, Assn. for Advancement Med. Instrumentation, Soc. Critical Care Medicine, Orleans Parish Med. Soc., La. State Med. Soc., Alton Ochsner Surg. Soc., New Orleans Surg. Soc., Surg. Soc. La., Chgo. Surg. Soc., Tulane Surg. Soc. (founder), Midwest Chest Club, Cardiovascular Surgeons Club, Coll. Physicians Phila., Alpha Omega Alpha. Roman Catholic. Achievements include having 2 patents in field. Home: New Orleans, La. Died May 2010.

MOUNT, JOHN MEREDITH, chemical company executive; b. Dallas, Feb. 27, 1942; s. Almon Howard and Olive Laverne (Breedlove) M.; m. Rosemary Lynch, Nov. 11, 1967; children: John M. Jr., Mary E. BA, Colgate U., 1965; MBA, Xavier U., Cin., 1984. Mgr. mktg. DuBois Indsl., Cin., Amsterdam, 1972-73, sr. mgr. dist. sales Columbia, S.C., 1974; regional mgr. sales DuBois Instnl. div., NYC, 1975-78, v.p. Huntington, Conn., 1979, sr. v.p., asst. dir. sales Cin., 1979-82, exec. v.p., dir. instnl. sales, 1982-86, pres., 1986, DuBois Co., Cin., from 1986; pres., chief exec. officer DuBois Chems. Inc., from 1989. Exec. v.p. Chemed, Cin., 1986—; bd. dirs. Roto-Rooter, Inc., Cin., Omnicare, Nat. Sanitary Supply. Bd. dirs. Nat. Sanitary Supply, 1988, Omnicare, 1988. Capt. USMC, 1967-72, Vietnam. Mem. Queen City Club, Bankers Club. Home: Cincinnati, Ohio. Died May 11, 2010.

MOYARS-JOHNSON, MARY ANNIS, retired academic administrator; b. Lafayette, Ind., July 19, 1938; d. Edward Raymond and Veronica Marie (Quigg) Moyars; m. Raymond Leon Molter, Aug. 1, 1959 (div. 1970); children: Marilyn Eileen Molter Davis, William Raymond Molter Johnson, Ann Marie Molter Guentert; m. Thomas Elmer Johnson, May 25, 1973 (div. 1989); children: Thomas Edward, John Alan, Barbara Suzanne, Johnson Camp BS, Purdue U., 1960; MA, Purdue U., West Lafayette, Ind., 1991, postgrad., from 1985. Grader great issues Purdue U., West Lafayette, 1960-63, writer ednl. films, 1962-65, publicity dir. convocations and lectures, 1969-74, devel. officer Sch. Humanities, 1979-88, asst. to dir. Optoelectronics Rsch. Ctr., 1989-90, mgr. indsl. rels. Sch. Elec. and Computer Engring., 1990—2002, assoc. v.p. for info. tech., for comm., 2002—04; tchr. English and math. Benton Cmty. Schs., Fowler, Ind., 1966-69; pub. rels. dir. Sycamore Girl Scout Coun., Lafayette, Ind., 1974-78; dir. pub. info. Ind. Senate, Majority Caucus, Indpls., 1977-78; sr. script writer Walters & Steinberg, Lafayette, 1988-89; ret., 2004. Adj. faculty Ivy Tech State Univ., 2005. Author: Colonial Potpourri, 1975, Ouiatanon--The French Post Among the Ouia, 2000; co-author: Historic Colonial French Dress, 1982, 2nd edit., 1998; contbr. articles to profl. jours. Bd. govs. Tippecanoe County Hist. Assn., Lafayette, 1981-97. Mem. Women in Comms., Inc. (Pres. award 1983, pres. Lafayette chpt. 2004-05), Ctr. for French Colonial Rsch. (dir. 1986-89, 2006-07, editor 1988-89), Palatines to Am., Ind. History Assn., Ind. Hist. Soc., French Colonial Hist. Soc. Roman Catholic. Avocations: history, genealogy, embroidery. Home: West Lafayette, Ind. Died Oct. 15, 2009.

MOYE, CHARLES ALLEN, JR., federal judge; b. Atlanta, July 13, 1918; s. Charles Allen and Annie Luther (Williamson) M.; m. Sarah Ellen Johnston, Mar. 9, 1945; children: Henry Allen, Lucy Ellen. AB, Emory U., 1939, JD, 1943. Bar: Ga. 1943. Since practiced in, Atlanta; partner firm Gambrell, Russell, Moye & Killorin (and predecessors), 1955-70; chief judge U.S. Dist. Ct. (no. dist.) Ga., 1979-87, judge, 1970-87, sr. judge, from 1988. Chmn. DeKalb County Republican Exec. Com., 1952-56; chmn. Rep. Exec. Com. 5th Congl. Dist. Ga., 1956-64; mem. Ga. Rep. Central Com., 1952-64; Rep. candidate for Congress, 1954; del. Rep. Nat. Conv., 1956, 60, 64; chmn. Rep. Exec. Com. 4th Congl. Dist., 1964, Rep. presdl. elector, 1964. Mem. ABA, Fed. Bar Assn., Atlanta Bar Assn., State Bar Ga., Lawyers Club Atlanta, Am. Judicature Soc., Am. Bar Found., Am. Law Inst., Atlanta Athletic Club, Order of the Coif, Delta Tau Delta. Congregationalist. Home: Atlanta, Ga. Died July 26, 2010.

MOYER, JAMES WALLACE, physicist, retired consultant; b. Syracuse, Aug. 16, 1919; s. Wallace Earl and Viola (Hook) M.; m. Nedra Blake, Sept. 10, 1940; children: Jeffry Mark, Elaine, Virginia, Julia; m. Ruth Pierce Hughes, Jan. 23, 1993. AB, Cornell U., 1938; postgrad., Rutgers U., 1938-41; PhD, U. Rochester, 1948. Insp. ordnance U.S. Army, 1941-42; physicist Radiation Lab. U. Calif., Berkeley, 1942-43; sr. physicist Tenn. Eastman, Oak Ridge, 1943-46; rsch. assoc. Gen. Electric Rsch., Knolls Atomic Power Lab., Schenectady, N.Y., 1948-55; cons. engr. Gen. Electric Microwave Lab., Palo Alto, Calif., 1955-57; mgr. phys. sci. Gen. Electric Tempo, Santa Barbara, Calif., 1957-60; reserach dir. Sperry Rand Research Ctr., 1960-61, Servo Mechanisms, Inc., 1961-63; dir. applied research Autonetics divsn. N.Am. Aviation, Anaheim, Calif., 1963-65; dir. phys. scis. Northrop Space Lab., 1965-67; dir. engring. Northrop Corp., Beverly Hills, Calif., 1967-70; mgr. phys. systems rsch. and devel. So. Calif. Edison, Rosemead, Calif., 1976-84. Cons., 1984—; cons. Nat. Bur. Standards, 1956-62; mem. panel Nat. Acad. Sci., 1967-70, 71. Mem. IEEE (sr.), Am. Phys. Soc., Sigma Xi. Died Dec. 3, 2009.

MOYER, THOMAS J., state supreme court chief justice; b. Sandusky, Ohio, Apr. 18, 1939; s. Clarence and Idamae (Hessler) Moyer; m. Mary Francis Moyer, Dec. 15, 1984; 1 child, Drew stepchildren: Anne, Jack, Alaine. BA, Ohio State U., 1961, JD, 1964. Asst. atty. gen. State of Ohio, Columbus, 1964-66, dep. asst. to Gov., 1969-71, exec. asst. to Gov., 1975-79; pvt. practice law Columbus, 1966-69; assoc. Crabbe, Brown, Jones, Potts & Schmidt, Columbus, 1972-75; judge US Ct. Appeals (10th cir.), Columbus, 1979-86; chief justice Ohio Supreme Ct., Columbus, 1987—2010. Chair Conference of Chief Justices, 1995—96, Nat. Conf. on Ct. Security, 2005. Sec. bd. trustees Franklin U., Columbus, 1986-87; trustee Univ. Club, Columbus, 1986; mem. nat. coun. adv. com. Ohio State U. Coll. Law, Columbus. Recipient Award of Merit, Ohio Legal Ctr. Inst., Am. Judicature Soc. award, Disting. Svc. award, Nat. Ctr. State Cts., 1997, Innovative Program award, Assn. Family & Conciliation Cts., 1998, Better World award, Ohio Mediation Assn., 1999, Whitney North Seymour medal, Am. Arbitration Assn., 2000, James F. Henry award, 2003; named Outstanding Young Man of Columbus, Columbus Jaycees, 1969. Fellow: Ohio State Bar Found. (Ritter award 1996); mem.: Ohio State Bar Assn. (exec. com., council dels., Ohio Bar medal 1991), Columbus Bar Assn. (pres. 1980-81, Liberty Bell award), Critchon Club, Columbus Maennerchor Club Republican. Avocations: sailing, tennis. Home: Columbus, Ohio. Died Apr. 2, 2010.

MUELLER, DAVID LIVINGSTONE, religion educator; b. Buffalo, Oct. 5, 1929; s. William Arthur and Mary Martha (Fink) M.; m. Marilyn T. Mueller, July 25, 1959; children: Charles David, Mary Elizabeth. Student, Colgate U., 1947-49, U. Heidelberg, Germany, 1949-50; BA, Baylor U., 1951; MDiv., So. Bapt. Theol. Sem., 1954; PhD, Duke U., 1957. Asst. then assoc. prof. religion Baylor U., Waco, Tex., 1957-61; assoc. prof. then prof. theology So. Bapt. Theol. Sem., Louisville, from 1961, Joseph Emerson Brown chair theology, from 1991. Author: An Intervention to the Theology of Alfred Ritschel, 1969, Karl Barth, 1972, Foundation Karl Barth's Doctrine and Reconciliation, 1991. Mem. Am. Acad. Religion (participant Euroam. studies seminar), Nat. Assn. Bapt. Profs. Religion. Home: Kerrville, Tex. Died Mar. 26, 2010.

MUGFORD, ALFRED GEORGE, machine company executive; b. Everett, Mass., Sept. 7, 1928; s. James and Emmie (Boone) M.; m. Martha Black, Nov. 25, 1983; children—Holly Anne Montgomery Nye, Edward du Mee Montgomery, III; children by previous marriage— Janet Anne Sprague, Nancy Anne, George Edward. BS, Bentley Coll., 1950. With Jerguson Gage & Valve Co., Burlington, Mass., 1947-64, controller, 1963-64; treas., controller Sarco Co., Inc., Allentown, Pa., 1964-66; v.p. finance Whitin Machine Works, Whitinsville, Mass., 1966-68, v.p., gen. mgr., 1967-68, corp. staff, 1968; with White Consol. Industries, Cleve., 1963-87, v.p., corp. staff, group v.p., 1969-76, exec. v.p., 1976-84, sr. exec. v.p., 1984-87; cons. to mfg. industry Bay Village, Ohio, from 1987. V.p., bd. dirs. Alpha Assocs., Inc., Mpls. Chmn. Burlington Finance Bd., 1958-62, New Bldg. and Capital Fund Raising Com., 1960-63. Mem. Burlington Jr. C. of C. (charter mem., v.p. 1956-58), MAPI. Presbyterian (chmn. bd. trustees 1961-63). Clubs: Avon Oaks Country (fin. com. 1974-75, trustee, pres. 1977-78, bd. dirs. 1986—), Duquesne, Lions. Died Aug. 14, 2010.

MULDER, DONALD WILLIAM, physician, educator; b. Rehobath, N.Mex., June 30, 1917; s. Jacob D. and Gertrude (Hofstra) M.; m. Gertrude Ellens, Feb. 22, 1943. BA, Calvin Coll., 1940; MD, Marquette U., 1943; MS, U. Mich., 1946. Intern Butterworth Hosp., Grand Rapids, Mich., 1943-44; resident U. Hosp., Ann Arbor, Mich., 1944-46, Denver, 1947-49; asst. prof. medicine in neurology U. Colo., 1949-50; prof. neurology Mayo Found. Faculty, from 1964, Mayo Med. Sch., from 1973; cons. neurology Mayo Clinic, Rochester, Minn., from 1950, gov., 1962-69, chmn. dept. neurology, 1966-71, pres. staff, from 1971, Andersen prof. neurology, 1977-83, prof. emeritus, from 1983; sci. advisor ALS. Contbr. articles on neuromuscular disease to sci. jours. Ret. capt. USNR. Recipient Disting. Alumni award Calvin Coll., 1992. Fellow A.C.P., Am. Acad. Neurology; mem. Am. Neurol. Assn. (hon.). Home: Rochester, Minn. Died Aug. 31, 2009.

MULHOLLEN, DAN BYRON, civil engineer, consultant; b. Doniphan, Mo., Sept. 14, 1942; s. Robert W. and Lena (Crafton) Mulhollen; m. Rebecca Jane O'Neal, Jan. 2, 1967 (div. 1975); children: Melissa Gayle, Kristi Jane; m. Catherine Jean Spence, Dec. 8, 1975. BSCE, U. Ark., 1965. Registered profl. engr., land surveyor, Ark. Mo. Asst. resident engr. Ark. Hwy. Dept., Nashville, 1968—70; assoc. Crafton-Tull Engrs., Rogers, Ark., 1970—75; owner, pres. Mulhollen and Assocs. Inc., Jonesboro, Ark., from 1975; pres. Am. Cons. Engrs. Coun. Ark., Little Rock, 1984—85. Pres. Fine Arts Coun., Jonesboro, 1980—82, Exch. Club, Jonesboro, 1983, Jonesboro Band Boosters Club, 1984—85; chmn. Streets and Hwy. Com. Jonesboro, 1985. Recipient Volunteerism award, Exch. Club, 1982; named Exchangite of Yr., 1982. Mem.: ASCE (area dir. 1984), Elks Lodge, Ark. Assn. Land Surveyors, Ark. Soc. Profl. Engrs. (chapt. pres. 1980). Avocations: sports, banjo. Died Nov. 2, 2009.

MULLER, FRANK, mediator, arbitrator; b. Prague, Czechoslovakia, Nov. 24, 1930; m. Louise De Vel, Dec. 14, 1957; children: Robert, William, David. BE in Civil Engring., Yale U., 1952; LLB, Boston Coll., 1959. Bar: N.Y. 1973, Mass. 1959; registered profl. engr., N.Y., N.J., Mass. Field engr., field supt. Raymond Internat., Inc., NYC, 1955-58; project engr. New Eng. Found., Inc., Boston, 1958-59; house counsel, chief project engr. Daniel O'Connell's Sons, Inc., Holyoke, Mass., 1959-64; v.p., dir., sec. Madigan Praeger, Inc., NYC, 1964-76; dir. constrn. mgmt. svcs. and constrn. dept. Parsons Brinckerhoff Quade Douglas, Inc., NYC, 1976-79; sr. v.p. O'Brien-Kreitzberg & Assocs., NYC, 1979-89; pres. Metro Mediation Svcs. Ltd., NYC, from 1989. Industry prof. exec. 21 program Poly. Inst. N.Y., 1999—; adj. asst. prof. Sch. Cont. Edn. NYU, 1989-94; adj. instr. Polytechnic Inst. N.Y., 1975-77, adj. prof. dept. civil engring.; lectr. profl. assns.; pvt. judge The Pvt. Adjudication Ctr., Inc.; arbitrator N.Y. Small Claims Ct.; mediator Community Dispute Settlement Svc., N.Y. State; arbitrator and mediator panel Am. Arbitration Assn.; mem. mediator panels N.Y. Supreme Ct., Superior Ct. N.J., U.S. Dist. Ct. (ea. dist.) N.Y. Co-author: Construction Management: A Professional Approach, 1978; contbr. articles to profl. jours, chpts. to books. Lt. (j.g.) CEC USN, 1952-55. Recipient Constrn. Mgmt. award ASCE. Mem. Nat. Constrn. Industry Dispute Resolution Com. (past chair), Constrn. Mgmt. Assn. Am. (past pres.). Home: Pelham, NY. Died Dec. 11, 2009.

MULLER, HENRY JOHN, real estate developer; b. NYC, July 27, 1919; s. Henry and Anne (Wulf) M.; m. Cecelia M. Ziffer, May 19, 1943; children: Richard, Robert, Ceil Anne, Roger. BS, Bklyn. Poly. Inst., 1949. Engr. GE Co., Bloomfield, NJ, 1948-49, Prudential Ins. Co., Newark, 1949-56; dep. dir. Harvard U., 1956-64; sr. v.p. 1st Nat. City Bank, NYC, 1964-71; chmn. Citicorp. Realty, NYC, 1971-72; sr. v.p. Allied Maintenance Corp., NYC, 1972-74; exec. v.p. Moorings Devel. Co., Vero Beach, Fla., 1974-77; pres. Muller & Assocs. Inc., Vero Beach, 1977-89, Criterion Svcs. Corp., Vero Beach, from 1988, Muller Homes Inc., Vero Beach, from 1998. With AUS, 1941-46. Mem. Tau Beta Pi, Lambda Chi Alpha. Home: Vero Beach, Fla. Died Dec. 1, 2009.

MULLER, JULIAN PERSHING, publishing company executive; b. NYC, July 20, 1918; s. Maurice and Gabrielle (Daub) M.; m. Effie Louise Pickerell, Dec. 3, 1942; children: Michael, Matthew. AB, Columbia, 1939. Editor Good Housekeeping mag., 1946-52; editor-in-chief Vanguard Press, 1952-55; sr. editor, mng. editor, editor-in-chief, v.p. Harcourt Brace Jovanovich, NYC, from 1955. Served to lt. comdr. USNR, 1941-45. Decorated Navy Cross. Died Feb. 19, 2009.

MULLER, MARCEL W(ETTSTEIN), electrical engineering educator; b. Vienna, Nov. 1, 1922; came to U.S., 1940; s. Georg and Josephine (David) M.; m. Esther Ruth Hagler, Feb. 2, 1947; children: Susan, George, Janet. BSEE, Columbia U., 1949, AM in Physics, 1952; PhD, Stanford U., 1957. Sr. scientist Varian Assocs., Palo Alto, Calif., 1952-66; prof. elec. engring. Washington U., St. Louis, 1966-91, prof. emeritus, rsch. prof., from 1991. Vis. lectr. U. Zurich, Switzerland, 1962-63; vis. prof. U. Colo., Boulder, summer 1969; vis. scientist Max Planck Inst., Stuttgart, Fed. Republic of Germany, 1976-77; cons. Hewlett-Packard Labs., Palo Alto,

1985-89, SRI Internat., Menlo Park, Calif., 1986—. Sgt. U.S. Army, 1943-46. Recipient Humboldt prize Alexander von Humboldt Soc., 1976; Fulbright grantee, 1977, grantee NSF, 1967—. Fellow IEEE, Am. Physical Soc. Achievements include development of Maser quantum noise theory; developments in micromagnetism; contributions to magnetic information storage; invention Magneprint security system. Died Jan. 9, 2010.

MÜLLER, RONALD ERNST, economist, writer; b. NYC, July 6, 1939; s. Robert J. and Hilda (Benz) M. BS in Aero. Engring; BA in Econs. and Polit. Sci. with honors, Air Force Acad., 1961; MA in Econs., Ludwig-Maximillian U., Munich, Ger., 1963; PhD in Econs. with distinction, Am. U., 1970. Commd. 2d lt. USAF, 1961, advanced through grades to capt., 1963, resigned, 1967; dir. polit. info. office NATO, Dusseldorf, Germany, 1964-66; ops. officer for govtl. contracted inter-agy. social sci. rsch. U.S. Dept. Def., 1966-67; prof. econs. Am. U., from 1968; pres. REM Assocs. Ltd.; dir. Inter-Am. Devel. Bank/Am. U. grad. program devel. fin. and banking, 1971-73, 79-81; adv. group experts internat. code of conduct Cen. Transnat. Corps., UN, 1976; spl. adviser to pres. Venezuela, 1976-78; spl. cons. advisor U.S. undersec. commerce, 1977-78; sr. adv. to sec. gen. UN, Bangkok, 1978-79; sr. cons. assoc. Analytic Scis. Corp., Boston, 1978-79; sr. adviser to Prime Minister India, 1980, Prime Minister Jamaica, 1981-83; exec. dir. Ctr. Internat. Tech. Coop., 1980-83; chmn., chief exec. officer DSL Capital Corp., Washington, 1983-90; chmn. REM Capital Assocs. Inc., Washington, from 1990. Cons. in field; numerous congl. testimonies. Author: Political Economy of Foreign Investment, 1972, Revitalizing America, 1982 (runner up Robert F. Kennedy award); co-author: Global Reach: The Power of the Multinational Corporations, 1975 (Sidney Hillman Found. award 1975); Contbr. articles to newspapers and mags. Decorated Air Force Commendation medal; recipient 2d pl. Outstanding U.S. Pub. Svc. by a Pvt. Citizen award Am. Inst. Pub. Svc., 1977.; Fed. Republic of GermanyGrad. fellow, 1961-62. Mem. Am. Econs. Assn., Am. Mktg. Assn., Soc. Internat. Devel., Am. Acad. Polit. and Social Sci., Pi Gamma Mu, Omicron Delta Epsilon (past pres.) Died May 21, 2010.

MULLINS, JOHN MADISON, educational consultant; b. NYC, May 2, 1919; s. George W. and Hazel (Provence) M.; m. Alice N. Drury, Aug. 15, 1942; children: John W., Ross H., David D. AB, Columbia U., 1941. Rsch. asst. Coll. Entrance Exam. Bd., Princeton, N.J., 1941; asst. registrar Columbia U., NYC, 1946-50, assoc. registrar, 1950-52, registrar, 1952-56, dir. budget, 1956-61; asst. treas. Coll. Entrance Exam. Bd., NYC, 1961, controller, 1962-63, treas., 1964, v.p., treas., 1964-80; sr. v.p., 1981; ednl. cons. Coll. Entrance Exam. Bd., NYC, 1982—87. Chmn. evaluation teams Middle States Assn. Colls. and Secondary Schs., 1949-90; chmn. spl. com. N.Y. State Dept. Edn., 1955-56; mem. No. Valley Regional High Sch. Dist., N.J. Bd. Edn., 1954-63, pres., 1957; cons. Ford Found., 1965-68 Trustee Am. U. in Paris, 1965-2001, vice-chmn., 1981-2001 trustee emeritus, 2001—; bd. dirs. Am. U. in Paris Found., 1985-2001, treas., sec.; trustee Demarest Libr. Assn., 1966-67; bd. dirs. Enriched Summer Forum No. Valley, N.J., 1966-69. Lt. comdr. USNR, 1941-45. Mem. Soc. Columbia Grads. (bd. dirs. 1980-86), Loomis Village Residents Assn. (v.p., 1996-1997, pres., 1997-1999), Phi Gamma Delta. Independent. Home: South Hadley, Mass. Died July 11, 2009.

MUNDHENK, DENNIS EDGAR, civilian military official; b. Dayton, Ohio, May 13, 1938; s. Harold Robert and Ethel Lucille (Mishler) M.; m. Anita Louise Gruber, July 30, 1960; children: Brian David, Kent Eugene. BS, U. Dayton, 1960; MBA, Auburn U., 1974; grad., Air Command and Staff Coll., Montgomery, Ala., 1974. Cert. profl. contracts mgr. Mail clk. U.S. Postal Svc., Dayton, 1957-61, 64-66; contract specialist Wright Patterson AFB, Dayton, 1966-73; chief policy and compliance div. White Sands Missile Range, N.Mex., 1974-83, chief equipment contracting br. N.Mex., from 1987; dir. purchasing Armed Forces Recreation Ctr., Garmisch, Fed. Republic Germany, 1983-86. Treas. Temple Bapt. Ch., Las Cruces, N.Mex., 1989—, chmn. deacon bd., 1989—. Officer U.S. Army, 1961-64, Fed. Republic Germany. Mem. Nat. Contracts Mgmt. Assn. (sec. 1987, v.p. 1988, pres. 1989, nat. dir. 1990—), Am. Def. Preparedness Assn., Alpha Kappa Psi. Avocations: gardening, travel. Home: Granbury, Tex. Died Apr. 26, 2009.

MUNDINGER, DONALD CHARLES, retired college president; b. Chgo., Sept. 2, 1929; s. George Edward and Bertha (Trelkenberg) M.; m. June Myrtle Grubbe, June 17, 1951; children: Debra Sue, Donald William, Mary Ruth (dec.). Student, U. Ill., 1947-48; BA, Concordia Coll., River Forest, Ill., 1951, LLD (hon.), 1982; MA, Northwestern U., 1952; PhD, Washington U., St. Louis, 1956; DH (hon.), MacMurray Coll., Jacksonville, Ill., 1984, Ritsumeikan U., Kyoto, Japan, 1992; LLD (hon.), Ill. Coll., Jacksonville, 1993; postdoctoral study, Cambridge U.Eng., 1967-68. Asst. prof. polit. sci., chmn. dept. Augustana Coll., Sioux Falls, S.D., 1956-58; asst. prof. govt. Valparaiso (Ind.) U., 1958-61, assoc. prof., 1961-65, prof., 1965-73; dean Valparaiso (Ind.) U. (Coll. Arts and Scis.), 1965-67; dir. Overseas Center, Cambridge, Eng., 1967-68, v.p. acad. affairs, 1968-73; pres. Ill. Coll., Jacksonville, 1973-93; chmn. Fedn. Ind. Ill. Colls. and Univs., 1975-78; chmn. non-public adv. com. Ill. Bd. Higher Edn., 1988-91. Postdoctoral fellow Center Study Higher Edn., U. Mich., 1964-65; chmn. bd. Council Ind. Colls., 1988-90. Contbr. articles to profl. jours. Mem. Ill. State Bar Assn. (com. on fed. judicial and related appointments 1983-89), Nat. Assn. Ind. Colls. and Univs. (commn. on new initiatives, 1988-90), Pi Sigma Alpha, Phi Eta Sigma. Home: Valparaiso, Ind. Died Aug. 23, 2010.

MUNGER, EDWIN STANTON, political geography educator; b. LaGrange, Ill., Nov. 19, 1921; s. Royal Freeman and Mia (Stanton) M.; m. Ann Boyer, May 2, 1970; 1 child, Elizabeth Stanton Gibson. B.Sc., U. Chgo., 1948, M.Sc., 1949, PhD, 1951. Fulbright fellow Makerere U., 1949-50; research fellow U. Chgo.; field assoc. American Universities Field Staff, 1950-60; faculty Calif. Inst. Tech., Pasadena, from 1961, prof. polit. geography, 1960—88, prof. emeritus, 1988—2010. Research fellow Stellenbosch U., 1955-56; vis. prof. U. Warsaw, 1973 Author books including Afrikaner and African Nationalsim, 1968, The Afrikaners, 1979, Touched by Africa: An Autobiography, 1983, Cultures, Chess and Art: A Collector's Odyssey Across Seven Continents, Vol. 1 Sub Saharan Africa, 1996, Vol. 2, Americas, 1997, Pacific Islands and the Asian Rim, Vol. 3, 1999, 10 short stories for kids--L.A. Times on Africa, 2001-02; editor books including Munger Africana Library Notes, 1969-82; contbr. chpts. to books and numerous articles to profl. jours. Evaluator Peace Corps, Uganda, 1966, Botswana, 1967; chmn. State Dept. Evalustion Team South Africa, 1971; trustee African-Am. Inst., 1956-62; acting pres. Pasadena Playhouse, 1966; chmn. bd. trustees Crane Rogers Found., 1979-82, fellow, 1950-54; mem. exec. com. NAACP, Pasadena, 1979-2010, nat. del., 1984, 85; trustee Leakey Found., 1968-2010, pres., 1971-84; pres. Cape of Good Hope Found., 1985-2010; pres. Internat. Vis. Coun., L.A., 1991-93, bd. dirs., 1979-93. Recipient Alumni Citation award for pub. svc. U. Chgo., 1993, Gandhi Martin Luther King-Ikeda award Morehouse U., 2002. Fellow South African Royal Soc., Royal Soc. Arts, African Studies Assn. (founding bd. dirs. 1963-66, Martin L. King Ikeda-Mahatma Gandhi award 2002); mem. PEN USA West (v.p.), Coun. Fgn. Rels., Cosmos Club, Athenaeum Club, Twilight Club, Chess Collectors Internat. (bd. dirs. 1998-2010). Home: Pasadena, Calif. Died June 15, 2010.

MUNGO, MICHAEL J., real estate developer; b. Bethune, SC, Apr. 7, 1928; m. Mary Meech (dec. Apr. 1978); children: Michael Stewart, Steven Whiteford; m. Jennifer Brewer. AB, U. S.C., 1950, postgard., 1952-53. Sales mgr. C.W. Haynes & Co., Columbia, S.C., 1954-55; pres. Michael J. Mungo Co., Columbia, 1955-80, chmn., from 1980. Author, pub. Sounds, 1979. Chmn. bd. trustees U. S.C., 1969-78, 82, bd. dirs. univ. bus. partnership found., mem. ednl. found.; dir. Mary Meech Mungo Found.; sr. warden Ch. of the Good Shepherd, 1985-88, lay reader, 1949—; trustee Haethwood Hall Episcopal Sch., 1961-67; chmn. trustees Episcopal Diocese of Upper S.C.; mem. Mission Now; active YMCA; chmn., founder Lexington Sch. Dist. #45 Edn. Found.; chmn. S.C. chpt. United Negro Coll. Fund, 1969. With USAAC, 1946-47; USAF, 1951-52. Mem. Columbia Home Builders Assn., Nat. Assn. Home Builders, Columbia C. of C., West Columbia/Cayce C. of C., Columbia Country Club, Capital City Club, Coldstream Country Club, Pres.'s Club, Summit Club, Omicron Delta Kappa. Avocations: golf, fishing, horticulture. Home: Columbia, SC. Died Apr. 11, 2010.

MURA, TOSHIO, civil engineering educator; b. Kanazawa, Ishikawa, Japan, Dec. 7, 1925; came to U.S., 1958; s. Shinzo and Chie (Miyamoto) Fujii; m. Sawa Ozaki, May 3, 1952; children: Miyako, Nanako. BS, U. Tokyo, 1949, PhD, 1954. Asst. prof. Meiji U., Tokyo, 1954-58, Northwestern U., Evanston, Ill., 1961-63, assoc. prof., 1963-66, prof. dept. civil engring., from 1966, Walter P. Murphy disting. prof. civil engring., mech. engring., applied math., theoretical and applied math., from 1986. Cons. Argonne Nat. Lab., Ill., 1956-58, 73, Nat. Bur. Standards, Washington, 1969-70, Atomic Energy Rese.rch Establishment, Harwell, Eng., 1973, Inst. Space and Astronautical Sci., Tokyo, 1983. Author: Micromechanics of Defects in Solids, 1982, Variational Methods in Mechanics, 1992; editor: Mathematical Theory of Dislocations, 1969, Mechanics of Fatigue, 1981. Grantee Japanese Govt., 1950-54; grantee NSF, 1961—, Dept. Energy, 1971-73, Army Research Office, 1978— Fellow ASME, Am. Acad. Mechanics; mem. NAE, Japan Inst. Metals (hon.). Home: Wilmette, Ill. Died Aug. 9, 2009.

MURDOCH, LAWRENCE CORLIES, JR., retired bank executive; b. Phila., June 3, 1926; s. Lawrence C. and Barbara (Boyd) M.; children: Lawrence C. III, Anne G.; m. 2d Eleanor M. Egan, June 16, 1970. BS Wharton Sch., U. Pa. in Econs., 1948; MBA, Wharton Sch., U. Pa., 1956. With Fed. Res. Bank Phila., 1954-92; ret., 1992. Bd. dirs. Cliveden Inc., 1981. Contbr. articles to consumer and monetary publs.; producer documentary films; spokesman (radio and TV). Lt. (j.g.) USN, 1948-54. Mem. Soc. Cin. (pres. 1990-93), Little Egg Harbor Yacht Club (Beach Haven, N.J.), Beta Gamma Sigma, Zeta Psi. Home: Philadelphia, Pa. Died Dec. 5, 2009.

MUROGA, SABURO, computer science and electrical engineering educator; b. Numazu, Shizuoka-ken, Japan, Mar. 15, 1925; came to U.S., 1960; s. Teiji and Kenko (Abe) M.; m. Yoko Nakamura, Feb. 5, 1956; children: Eisuke, Edith Rie, David Kenji, Judith Lisa. Gakushi degree, U. Tokyo, 1947, PhD, 1956. Rsch. staff Nat. Railway Pub. Corp., Tokyo, 1947-49; engring. staff Radio Regulatory Commn., Govt. of Japan, Tokyo, 1950-51; rsch. staff Elec. Regulatory Commn. Labs., Nippon Telegraph Telephone Pub. Corp., Tokyo, 1951-60, IBM Rsch. Ctr., Yorktown Heights, N.Y., 1960-64; prof. U. Ill., Urbana, from 1964. Author: Threshold Logic & Its Applications, 1971, Logic Design & Switching Theory, 1979, VLSI System Design, 1982, (with others) Advances in Computers, vol. 32, 1991. Citation Nippon Telegraph Telephone Pub. Corp., 1959. Fellow IEEE; mem. Inst. Elec. Communication Engrs. Japan (Inada award 1955), Info. Processing Soc. Japan (contbn. award 1991), 1958—, Japanese Student Assn. (hon. chmn. 1981—), Assn. Computing Machinery, Sigma Xi. Home: Urbana, Ill. Died Dec. 9, 2009.

MURPHY, BETTY SOUTHARD, lawyer; b. East Orange, NJ, Mar. 1, 1933; d. Floyd Theodore and Thelma (Casto) Southard; m. Cornelius F. Murphy, May 1, 1965; children: Cornelius Francis Jr., Ann Southard Murphy AB, Ohio State U.; student, Alliance Française and U. Sorbonne, Paris; JD, Am. U. Washington Coll. Law, Washington, DC; LLD (hon.), Ea. Mich. U., Ypsilanti, 1975, Capital U., Columbus, Ohio, 1976, Seattle U., 1986; LHD (hon.), Tusculum Coll., Greenville, Tenn., 1987. Bar: D.C. Corr., free lance journalist, Europe and Asia, UPI, Washington; atty. McInnis, Wilson, Munson & Woods (and predecessor firm Roberts & McInnis); dep. asst. sec., adminstr. Wage and Hour Divsn. US Dept. Labor, 1974-75; mem., chmn. NLRB, 1975-79; ptnr. Baker & Hostetler, LLP, 1980—2010. Adj. prof. law American U., 1972-80, 99-2010; mem. adv. com. on rights and responsibilities of women to Sec. US Dept. Health & Human ServicesS; mem. panel conciliators Internat. Ctr. Settlement Investment Disputes, 1974-85; mem. Adminstrv. Conf. U.S., 1976-80, Pub. Svc. Adv. Bd., 1976-79; mem. human resouces com. Nat. Ctr. for Productivity and Quality of Working Life, 1976-80; mem. Presdl. Commn. on Exec. Exch., 1981-85, Ctr. for Study of the Presidency, 1998—02. Trustee Mary Baldwin Coll., Staunton, Va., 1977—85, Am. U., Washington, 1980—99, George Mason U. Found., Inc., Fairfax, Va., 1993—2000, from 2001, Friends of Dept. of Labor, 1984—2007, Friends of Congl. Law Libr., 1992—2008; US Constn. mem. exec com. Commn. on Bicentennial, 1985—92; chmn. internat. adv. com. Commn. on Bicentennial of US Constn., 1985—92; vice chmn. James Madison Meml. Fellowship Found., 1990—96; mediator World Intellectual Property Orgn., from 1996; nat. bd. dirs. Med. Coll. Pa., Phila., bd. corporators, 1976—85; bd. dirs. Ctr. for Women in Medicine, Phila., 1980—86, Meridian Internat. Ctr., 1992—98; bd. mem. Summer Opera Theatre, 2006—08; bd. govs. St. Agnes Sch., Alexandria, Va., 1981—87. Recipient Ohio Gov.'s award, 1980, fellow award, 1981, Outstanding Pub. Service award, U.S. Info. Service, 1987; named Disting. fellow, John Sherman Myers Soc., 1986, 1996; named one of 24 Legends of Law, DC Bar Assn., 2006, Top 20 Lawyers, Washingtonian Mag., 2008; fellow, Nat. Acad. Human Resources, 1998. Mem.: ABA, NAFTA, Internat. Law Sect., Task Force on Legal Outsourcing & Paralegal Outsourcing, US-Mexico Bar Assn. (US chair labor and law com. 2006—07, bd. dirs. from 2007), Am. Inns Ct. (Professionalism award 2006), Nat. Acad. Human Resources, Nat. Assn. Women Lawyers, Women's Bar Assn., Internat Bar Assn., Am. U. Alumni Assn. (Women's Leadership Award 2004), Supreme Ct. Hist. Soc., Union Internat. des Advocats (gov. bd. 1997—2000, from 2003), Rep. Nat. Lawyers Assn. (nat. v.p. 1990—95, nat. vice chmn. 1996—2000, 2001—03, co-chmn. 2003—08, mem. exec. bd. from 2003, Rep. Lawyer of Yr. 2005), Am. Arbitration Assn. (Surrogati Spkr. Gov. Reagon 1980, 1984, bd. dirs. 1985—2000, mem. editl. bd. 1992, mem. exec. com. 1995—2000, mem. internat. arbitration com. 1980,1984 from 1997, steering com. lawyers for Bush 2000, bd. dirs. 2001—04, mem. Lawyers for McCain 2007—08, co chmn. labor com., Ronald Reagan pres.), Bar Assn. D.C., Inter-Am. Bar Assn. (co-chmn. labor law com. 1975—83, editor newsletter, Silver medal), FBA, ABA (chmn. labor law com. 1980—83, chmn. internat. and comparative law adminstrv. law sect. 1983—88, chmn. customs, tariff and trade com. 1988—90, employment law sect. 1990—2004, chmn. internat. com. dispute resolution sect. from 1995, co-chair, task force internat. outsourcing, sect. internat. law from 2008, Sec. Dispute Resolution Spl. Achievement award 1995—2009), World Peace Through Law Ctr., Mortar Bd., Kappa Beta Pi. Republican. Died Oct. 16, 2010.

MURPHY, CHARLES ARNOLD, physician, surgeon; b. Detroit, Dec. 29, 1932; s. Charles L. and Hazel C. (Robinson) M.; m. Mary Lightford, Aug. 1955; m. Judith L. Dennis, Nov. 12, 1966; 1 child, Charles A. III; m. Sandra M. Walker, July 17, 1971. Student, Wayne State U., 1949-53; D.O., Coll. Osteo Medicine and Surgery, Des Moines, 1957. Diplomate Am. Osteo Bd. Gen. Practice. Intern Flint Osteo. Hosp, Mich., 1957-58; gen. practice medicine Detroit, from 1958. Mem. staff Kirkwood Hosp., 1964-66, Martin Place Hosp., 1958-64, Mich. Osteo. Med. Ctr., 1959-87; osteo. physician City of Detroit, 1959-63; sr. police surgeon Detroit Police Dept., 1977-79; assoc. clin. prof. family medicine Coll. Osteo. Medicine, Mich. State U.; bd. dirs., mem. exec. com. Mich. HMO Plans; mem. central peer rev. adv. com. Mich. Dept. Health; mem. coun. med. dirs. Health Care Network Fellow Am. Coll. Osteo. Gen. Practitioners; mem. Am. Osteo. Assn. (ho. of dels. 1981-87), Greater Detroit Area Hosp. Council, Mich. Osteo. Assn. (ho. of dels. 1970—, trustee 1981-89), NAACP (life), Wayne County Osteo. Assn. (pres. 1976, 77), Mich. Assn. Osteo. Physicians (pres. 1986-87), Mich. Assn. Gen. Practitioners in Osteo. Medicine and Surgery, Coll. Osteo. Medicine and Surgery Alumni Assn., Atlas Club, Kappa Alpha Psi, Psi Sigma Alpha Clubs: Detroit Yacht. Methodist. Died Aug. 26, 2009.

MURPHY, DANIEL HAYES, II, lawyer; b. Hartford, Conn., Jan. 8, 1941; s. Robert Henry and Jane Granville (Cook) M.; m. Deann Ellison, June 30, 1962; children—Edward Ellison, Jessica Jane BA, Yale U., 1962; LL.B., Columbia U., 1965. Bar: N.Y. 1965, U.S. Dist. Ct. (so. and ea. dists.) N.Y. 1967, U.S. Ct. Appeals (2d cir.) 1968, Conn. 1978, Calif. 1984, Fla. 1986. Assoc. White & Case, NYC, 1965-70; asst. U.S. atty. So. Dist. N.Y., NYC, 1970-74; pvt. practice law NYC, 1974-76 and from 85; assoc. Mendes & Mount, NYC, 1977-81, jr. ptnr., 1981-85; spl. master Supreme Ct. N.Y. County, from 1981. Chmn. planning commn., Groton Long Point, Conn., 1977-84 Mem. ABA, N.Y. State Bar Assn., N.Y. County Lawyers Assn., Assn. Bar City N.Y., Yale Club N.Y.C., Ocean Reef Key Largo, Fla. Roman Catholic. Died June 21, 2010.

MURPHY, JOHN HENRY, III, retired publishing executive; b. Balt., Mar. 2, 1916; s. Daniel H. and Sarah (Clements) M.; m. Alice Quivers, Dec. 28, 1940 (dec. May 1979); children: Sharon V. Murphy Smith, Daniel H.; m. Camay Calloway, Feb. 16, 1980. BS, Temple U., 1937; postgrad., Am. Press Inst. Columbia, 1952-71. Office mgr. Washington Afro-American, 1937-45, asst. bus. mgr., 1948, bus. mgr., 1956-61; pres. Afro-American Co. of Balt. City, 1961-74, chmn. bd., 1974—86. Mgr. Washington Tribune, 1945-47; dir. Amalgamated Pubs., Inc. Bd. dirs. Council on Equal Bus. Opportunities; trustee Provident Hosp., Balt; mem. Md. Adv. Com. U.S. Civil Rights Commn.; bd. dirs. St. Augustine's Coll. Balt. Mus. Art.; v.p. bd. dirs. Nat. Aquarium, Balt.; bd. overseers Balt. Sch. for Arts; mem. Gov.'s Commn. on Crime Prevention. Mem. Nat. Newspaper Pubs. Assn. (dir.), Sigma Pi Phi, Gamma Boule, Omega Psi Phi. Clubs: Mason. Home: Baltimore, Md. Died Oct. 16, 2010.

MURPHY, SARAJANE LEONARD, printing and mailing company executive; b. St. Petersburg, Fla., Sept. 19, 1924; d. John Lawson and Mabel Lillian (Houser) Leonard; m. Stanley w. Murphy, Sept. 26, 1946; children: Cynthia Louise, Amy Elizabeth, Peggy Leonard, Stanley W., William Stone, Patrick Francis. Student, Jones Coll., 1942. V.p., treas. Stan Murphy Co., Jacksonville, Fla., from 1955; copy writer Conv. Press, 1960—65, Inland Waterway Guide, 1964—65. Sec. local unit, mem. pub. info. com. Fla. divsn. Am. Cancer Soc.; bd. dirs., mem. exec. com. State Cancer Soc.; bd. dirs. Theatre Jacksonville; past pres., v.p., dir. local & dist. bd. United Meth. Ch. Mem.: Garden Jacksonville Club, Belle Meade Hunt Club (Ga.). Died May 6, 2010.

MURPHY, WALTER FRANCIS, retired political scientist; b. Charleston, SC, Nov. 21, 1929; s. Walter Francis and Ruth (Gaffney) M.; m. Mary Therese Dolan, June 28, 1952 (dec. 2006); children: Kelly Ann, Holly Ann; m. Doris Maher, 2010 AB magna cum laude, U. Notre Dame, 1950; AM, George Washington U., 1954; PhD, U. Chgo., 1957; DLitt (hon.), Coll. Charleston, 1989. Fellow govtl. studies Brookings Instn., 1957-58; faculty mem. Princeton U., 1958-95, McCormick prof. jurisprudence, 1968—95, prof. emeritus, 1995—2010; McCosh Faculty fellow Ford Research prof. govtl. affairs, 1965-66, chmn. dept. politics, 1966-69, McCormick prof. jurisprudence, 1968-95. Fulbright lectr., 1981, 88, 89; adv. com. on jud. conduct N.J. Supreme Ct., 1982-95. Author: Congress and the Court, 1962, Elements of Judicial Strategy, 1964, Wiretapping on Trial, 1965, (with C.H. Pritchett) Courts, Judges and Politics, 4th edit., 1987, (with M. Danielson) American Democracy, 1969, (with J. Tanenhaus) Comparative Constitutional Law, 1977, The Vicar of Christ, 1979, (with D. Lockard) Basic Cases in Constitutional Law, 3d edit., 1991, The Roman Enigma, 1981, (with J. Fleming and S.A. Barber) American Constitutional Interpretation, 2d edit., 1995, Upon This Rock, 1987, Constitution Democracy: Creating and Maintaing a Just Political Order, 2006; book rev. editor: World Politics, 1972-78; contbr. numerous articles to profl. jours. Mem. N.J. adv. com. U.S. Commn. Civil Rights, 1961-68, vice chmn., 1964-68; mem. N.J. Civil Rights Commn., 1968-70. Served to capt. USMC, 1950-55; col. Res., ret. Decorated D.S.C., Purple Heart; recipient Merriam-Cobb-Hughes award Am. Acad. Pub. Affairs, 1963, Chgo. Found. for Lit. award, 1980; Guggenheim fellow, 1973-74; Nat. Endowment for Humanities fellow, 1978-79. Fellow Am. Acad. Arts and Scis., Italian Acad. Advanced Study in Am.; mem. Am. Polit. Sci. Assn. (editorial bd. rev. 1966-72, Birkhead award 1958, sec. 1982-83, v.p. 187-88, Lifetime Achievement award 1995), Pi Gamma Mu. Died Apr. 20, 2010.

MURPHY, WILLIAM LEO, retired prosecutor; b. Chgo., June 25, 1944; s. William L. and Anastasia (Keeney) Murphy; m. Kathleen Nora Brushett, Aug. 24, 1968; children: Michele, Jeannine. AB, Fordham Coll., 1966; JD, Harvard U., 1969. Bar: NY 1969, NY (U.S. Dist. Ct. (so. dist.)) 1973. Asst. dist. atty. NY County, NYC, 1969—75; chief asst. dist. atty. Richmond County, Staten Island, 1976—83, dist. atty., 1983—2003. Lectr. Div. Criminal Justice Services, Albany, 1976—2010. Recipient Spl. award, NY State Ct. Officers, 1984; named Democrat of Yr. award, Young Democrats Richmond County, 1983. Mem.: NY State Dist. Attys. Assn. (sec. 1982—83, pres. 1987—88), Nat. Dist. Attys. Assn., Richmond County Bar Assn., NY State Bar Assn. Democrat. Roman Catholic. Home: Staten Island, NY. Died June 4, 2010.

MURRAY, BERTRAM GEORGE, JR., biology educator; b. Elizabeth, NJ, Sept. 24, 1933; s. Bertram George and Laura Estelle Murray; m. Patti Aylward, June 9, 1973. BA, Rutgers U., 1961; MS, U. Mich., 1963, PhD, 1967. Lectr. Cornell U., Ithaca, N.Y., 1967-68; asst. prof. Mich. State U., E. Lansing, 1968-71; asst. prof. biology Rutgers U., New Brunswick, N.J., 1971-74, assoc. prof. biology, 1974-81, prof. biology, 1981-2000. Author: Population Dynamics, 1979; assoc. editor: Am. Midland Naturalist, 1979-84. Airman USN, 1951-52; sgt. USAF, 1954-57. Fellow Am. Ornithologists Union; mem. Brit. Ornithologists' Union, Wilson Ornithol. Soc., Cooper Ornithol. Soc. Avocations: nature photography, scuba diving, bird watching. Home: Somerset, NJ. Died Aug. 8, 2010.

MURRAY, RAYMOND HAROLD, physician; b. Cambridge, Mass., Aug. 17, 1925; s. Raymond Harold and Grace May (Dorr) M.; children— Maureen, Robert, Michael, Margaret, David, Elizabeth, Catherine, Anne. BS, U. Notre Dame, 1946; MD, Harvard U., 1948. Diplomate Am. Bd. Internal Medicine, also Sub-bd. Cardiovascular Disease. Practice medicine, Grand Rapids, Mich., 1955-62; asst. prof. to prof. medicine Ind. U. Sch. Medicine, 1962-77; prof. dept. medicine Coll. Human Medicine Mich. State U., Lansing, 1977-95, chmn. dept. medicine Coll. Human Medicine, 1977-89, emeritus, from 1995. Chmn. aeromed.-bioscis. panel Sci. Adv. Bd., USAF, 1977-81; mem. adv. coun. Office Alternative Medicine/NIH, 1997-99. Contbr. numerous articles to profl. publs. Served with USNR, 1942-45; Served with USPHS, 1950-53. Master: ACP (gov. Mich. chpt. 1994—98); mem.: Am. Fedn. Clin. Rsch., Am. Heart Assn. (fellow coun. clin. cardiology). Home: Sarasota, Fla. Died Oct. 2, 2009.

MURRAY, THOMAS DWIGHT, advertising agency executive; b. Middletown, Ohio, May 1, 1923; s. Charles H. and Rose (Newbrander) M.; m. Barbara Helen Howlett, Oct. 5, 1946; children— Cynthia Helen, Susan Howlett; m. Carol Callaway Muehl, Apr. 13, 1968; children— David Rutherford, Piper Dee. Student, U. Va., 1941-43. Passenger relations agt. United Airlines, NYC, 1946-47; tech. and advt. writer, copy supr. Frigidaire div. Gen. Motors Corp., Dayton, O., 1947-55; with Campbell-Ewald Co., Detroit, 1955-71, sr. v.p., creative dir., 1968-69, dir., mem. exec. com., 1968-71, exec. v.p., creative dir., 1969-71; chmn. bd., creative dir. Thomas Murray & Austin Chaney, Inc., Hudson, Ohio, 1971-80. Lectr. Wayne State U., U. Mich., Mich. State U., U. Ill., Art Center Los Angeles, Kent State U., Cleve. Advt. Sch., others; advt. adv. council Kent State U., 1976 Author: A Child to Change Your Life, 1976, A Look at Tomorrow, 1985, Tire Tracks Back, 1989; sr. editor Car Collector mag.; essayist Wall St. Jour., 1991—; wrote ad on Apollo 11 moonshot which was read into Congl. Record; contbr. articles to profl. jours. Vice pres., pres. local PTA, 1962-64; chmn. advt. com. United Found., 1966; Bd. dirs. Mich. Mental Health Soc., Big Bros. and Sisters of Greater Akron. Served with F.A. AUS, 1943-46, ETO. Recipient numerous advt. awards including Clio, Andy of N.Y., MOTO award, 1984. Mem. Detroit Copy Club (past pres., dir.) Clubs: Recess, Flying, Uptown Athletic Detroit, Birmingham Athletic, Brown's Run Country. Home: Denver, Colo. Died Jan. 7, 2009.

MURTHA, JOHN PATRICK, JR., United States Representative from Pennsylvania; b. New Martinsville, W.Va., June 17, 1932; s. John Patrick and Mary Edna (Ray) Murtha; m. Joyce Bell, June 10, 1955; children: Donna Sue, John, Patrick. BA in Economics, U. Pitts., 1961; postgraduate student, Ind. U. Pa., 1962-65. Mem. Dist. 72 Pa. State House of Reps., 1969-73; mem. US Congress from 12th Pa. dist., 1974—2010; chmn. US House Appropriation Def. Subcommittee, 1989—95, 2007—10. Author (with John Plashall): From Vietnam to 9/11: On the Front Lines of National Security, 2003. Served in USMC, as lt. 1952-55, as maj. 1966-67, USMC Res., 1955-66, 1967-90 Decorated Bronze Star, 2 Purple Hearts, Cross of Gallantry Vietnam; Recipient Pa. Disting. Svc. medal, 1978, Pa. Meritorious Svc. medal, numerous service awards for work during Johnstown flood, 1977, Iron Mike award Marine Corps League, 1988, Disting. Am. award (Nation's Capital chpt.) Air Force Assn., 1989, Outstanding Vet. award Vets. Caucus of Am. Acad. Physician Assts., 1989, Man of Steel award Cold Finished Steel Bar Inst., 1989, Pa. Disting. Svc. medal & Pa. Meritorius Svc. medal, 2000, Spirit of Hope award United Svc. Orgns., Inc., 2000, Funding Hero award Breast Cancer Rsch. Found., 2002, Profile in Courage award John F. Kennedy Libr. Found., 2006; named Man of Yr. Johnstown Jaycees, 1978 Mem.: VFW, Salvation Army, Am. Legion. Democrat. Roman Catholic. Died Feb. 8, 2010.

MUSA, JOHN DAVIS, information technology executive, writer; b. Amityville, NY, June 11, 1933; s. Khan Hussein and Ione Geraldine (Ryan) M.; m. Marilyn Laurene Allred, June 24, 1959. BA, Dartmouth Coll., 1954, MSEE, 1955. With AT&T Bell Labs., Murray Hill, NJ, 1958-96, mem. tech. staff, 1958-63, supr. guidance program devel., 1963-68, supr. command and control program devel., 1968-69, supr. mgmt. control and new software tech., 1969-72, supr. human factors test, 1972-74, supr. computer graphics, 1974-80, supr. computer measurements, 1980-85, supr. software quality, 1985-90, tech. mgr. software reliability engring., 1991-96. Mem. N.J. Coun. R&D; lectr., spkr. in field. Author: Software Reliability: Measurement, Prediction, Application, 1987, Software Reliability Engineering: More Reliable Software, Faster Development and Testing, 1998, Software Reliability Engineering: More Reliable Software Faster and Cheaper, 2004; editor: (book series) Software Quality Institute; contbr. over 100 articles to prof. jours. and books. Lt. USN, 1955-58. Fellow IEEE (Third Millenium medal for outstanding achievements and contbns.); mem. IEEE Computer Soc. (2d v.p. 1986, v.p. publs. 1984-85, v.p. tech. activities 1986, chair tech com. software engring. 1982-84, founding mem. editl. bd. IEEE Software Mag., Disting. lectr. 1980-83, Meritorious Svc. award 1984, 85, 87, Golden Core award, founding officer com. on software reliability engring., mem. editl. bds. Spectrum mag., 1984-86, Proc. of the IEEE 1983-90, Technique et Science Informatiques jour., sr. editor Software Engring. Inst. book series, sr. founding editor Software Quality Inst. book series, chair steering com. Internat. Conf. on Software Engring.), IEEE Reliability Soc. (Engr. of Yr. 2004), Assn. for Computing Machinery. Achievements include internat. leader in software engring. and in creation new tech. software reliability engring.; created two software reliability models; developed concepts and practice of operational profile, software-reliability engineered testing, concept of execution time; reduced operation software (ROS), and operational development; created concept of fault exposure ratio; developed approach for choosing software development strategies to meet different reliability objectives; international leader in reducing software reliability engineering to practice; organized panel and coordinated joint paper on teaching software reliability engineering. Died Apr. 25, 2009.

MUSCATINE, CHARLES SAMUEL, language educator, writer; b. Bklyn., Nov. 28, 1920; m. Doris Corn, July 21, 1945 (dec. 2006); children: Jeffrey, Alison. BA, Yale U., 1941, MA, 1942, PhD, 1948; L.H.D. (hon.), New Sch. for Social Research, 1982; Litt.D., SUNY, 1989, Rosary Coll., 1991. Mem. faculty dept. English U. Calif., Berkeley, 1948—91, prof., 1960-91, prof. emeritus, 1991—2010, dir. Collegiate Seminar Program, 1974-80. Vis. prof. Wesleyan U., 1951-53; Ward Phillips lectr. U. Notre Dame, 1969; mem. com. of selection J.S. Guggenheim Found., 1969-89, chmn. 1985-89. Author: Chaucer and the French Tradition, 1957, The Book of Geoffrey Chaucer, 1963, Poetry and Crisis in the Age of Chaucer, 1972, The Old French Fabliaux, 1986, Medieval Literature, Style, and Culture, 1999; co-author, editor: Education at Berkeley, 1966, (with M. Griffith) The Borzoi College Reader, 1966, 7th edit., 1992, First Person Singular, 1973; co-editor Integrity in the Coll. Curriculum, 1985. Bd. dirs. No. Calif. chpt. ACLU, 1959-62, 63-66, Assn. Am. Colls., 1979-82, Ctr. for the Common Good, 1994-99; bd. dirs. Fedn. State Humanities Couns., 1989-94, chair, 1991-93; mem. Commn. on Humanities, Rockefeller Found., 1978-79, Calif. Coun. Humanities, 1986-94. With USNR, 1942-45. Recipient Navy Commendation ribbon, 1945, Berkeley citation, 1991; Fulbright fellow, 1958, 62, ACLS Rsch. fellow, 1958, Guggenheim fellow, 1962, NEH Sr. fellow, 1968. Fellow Am. Acad. Arts and Scis., Medieval Acad. of Am.; mem. MLA, New Chaucer Soc. (pres. 1980-81), Aircraft Owners and Pilots Assn., Phi Beta Kappa. Home: Berkeley, Calif. Died Mar. 12, 2010.

MUSSER, BENJAMIN G., retired cardiovascular and thoracic surgeon; b. Pa., SC, Apr. 15, 1921; s. Alvin Keller and Clara Weist (Schlosser) M.; m. Vera Blinn Shoop, Aug. 1, 1942; children: Pamela, Lynne, Cynthia. BS in Sci., Elizabethtown Coll., 1941; MD, Hahemann Med. Coll., 1944; DSc (hon.), Elizabethtown Coll., 1965. Diplomate Am. Bd. Surgery, Am. Bd. Thoracic Surgery. Intern Lancaster (Pa.) Gen. Hosp., 1944-45, Riverside Hosp., Toledo, 1945-46; resident gen. surgery Walter Reed Army Hosp., Washington, 1946-48; lt. col. U.S. Army Med. Corps., 1946-53; resident gen. surgery Tripler Army Hosp., Honolulu, 1948-53; resident thoracic surgery Hahnemann Med. Coll., Phila., 1953-56, Deaconess Hosp., Boston, 1953-56; pvt. practice Cardiovascular & Thoracic Surgery, Harrisburg, Pa., 1956-93. Trainee Nat. Heart Inst., Bethesda, Md., 1953-56. Recipient Silver Star decoration 25th divsn. Korea, 1950. Mem. Pa. Thoracic Soc. (pres. 1988), Flying Physicians Assn. Republican. Presbyterian. Avocation: singing in church choir and barber shop quartet. Home: Scottsdale, Ariz. Died June 17, 2010.

MUSTO, DAVID FRANKLIN, medical researcher, educator, historian, consultant; b. Tacoma, Jan. 8, 1936; s. Charles Hiram and Hilda Marie (Hanson) Mustoe; m. Emma Jean Baudendistel, June 2, 1961; children: Jeanne Marie, David Kyle, John Baird, Christopher Edward. BA, U. Wash., 1956, MD, 1963; MA, Yale U., 1961. Lic. physician, Conn., Pa. Clerk Nat. Hosp. for Nervous Disease, London, 1961; intern Pa. Hosp., Phila., 1963-64; resident Yale U. Med. Ctr., New Haven, 1964-67; spl. asst. to dir. NIMH, Bethesda, Md., 1967-69; vis. asst. prof. Johns Hopkins U., 1968-69; asst. prof. Yale U., 1969-73, assoc. prof., 1973-78, sr. rsch. scientist, 1978-81, prof., from 1981, exec. fellow Davenport Coll., 1983-88; mem. adv. editorial com. Yale Edits. Private Papers James Boswell, from 1975; cons. to the Pres. on drug control policy The White House, 1973-75; mem. White House Strategy Coun. on Drug Abuse, 1978-81; mem. panel on alcohol policy NAS, Washington, 1978-82; cons. White House Conf. on Families, 1979-80. Vis. fellow Clare Coll., Cambridge U., 1994; mem. alcohol adv. com. Nat. Assn. Broadcasters, 1994—; DuMez lectr. U. Md.; Walter Reed meml. lectr. Richmond Acad. Medicine; Galdston lectr. N.Y. Acad. Medicine; Sirridge lectr. U. Mo. Med. Sch.; Clendening lectr. U. Kans. Med. Sch. Author: The American Disease: Origins of Narcotic Control, 1973, expanded edit., 1987, 3rd edit., 1999; co-author: (with P. Korsmeyer) The Quest for Drug Control: Politics and Federal Policy in a Period of Increasing Drug Use, 1963-1981, 2002; editor: One Hundred Years of Heroin, 2002, Drugs in America: A Documentary History, 2002. Historian Pres.'s Commn. on Mental Health, 1977-78; adv. U.S. Del. to UN Commn. Narcotic Drugs, Geneva, 1978-79; mem. nat. coun. Smithsonian Instn., Washington, 1981-90, hon. mem., 1991-2010; hist. cons. Presdl. Commn. Human Immuno-deficiency Virus Epidemic, 1988; mem. nat. adv. com. on anti-drug program Robert Wood Johnson Found., 1989-2002; mem. nat. adv. com. on internat. narcotic policy UN Assn. of U.S.A., 1991; mem. adv. com. causes drug abuse Office Tech. Assessment, Congress U.S., 1992-94; commr. Conn. Alcohol and Drug Abuse Commn., 1992-93; bd. dirs. Coll. on Problems of Drug Dependence, 1990-94; trustee Assocs. of Cushing-Whitney Med. Libr., 1994-2010. With USPHS, 1967-69. Fellow: Coll. Problems of Drug Dependence, Am. Psychiat. Assn. (disting.); mem.: Soc. of Cin. in the State of Conn. (pres. 1998—2001), English-Speaking Union (pres. New Haven br. 1995—98), Am. Assn. History of Medicine (William Osler medal 1961), Am. Hist. Assn., Am. Inst. History of Pharmacy (Kraemers award 1974), New Haven County Med. Assn. (chmn. bicentennial com. 1983), Century Assn., Athenaeum Club (London), Cosmos Club. Home: New Haven, Conn. Died Oct. 8, 2010.

MYBECK, JOHN WALTER, foundation administrator, consultant; b. Crown Point, Ind., Sept. 14, 1940; s. Walter Raymond and Genevieve Lucille (Carlsten) Mybeck; m. Mary Louis Topercer, Aug. 14, 1965; children: John, Jeffrey, Kevin, Matthew. BS, Purdue U., 1962, MS, 1965, PhD, 1970. Asst. dean, evening adminstrn. Purdue U. Calumet, Hammond, Ind., 1970—73, dean, cmty. svcs., 1973—77, dir., U. rels., 1977—79, exec. asst. to chancellor, 1980—81; exec. v.p. Calumet Nat. Bank, Hammond, 1979—80; exec. dir. Constrn. Advancement Found., Griffith, Ind., 1981—86, Operation Keystone, Griffith, Ind., 1984—86, Cmty. Found. Inc., from 1986. Editor, proc. Assn. Continuing Higher Edn., 1971; bd. dirs. Munster Med. Rsch. Found., Ind., from 1980. Mem., town bd., Munster, 1976—79; pres. Northwest Ind. Symphony Soc., Gary, 1980; chmn. Lake County Cmty. Devel. Com., Ind., 1981; trustee Sch. Town Munster, from 1982; pres. Babe Ruth League, Munster, 1985—87. Recipient Appreciation award, Munster Dem. Precinct Orgn., 1979, Citizenship award, Purdue U. Alumni Assn., 1983, Disting. Svc. award, Purdue Calumet Alumni Assn., 1984. Mem.: Ind. Sch. Bds. Assn., Nat. Sch. Bds. Assn., John Purdue Club (Lafayette, Ind.), Masons Lodge (Crown Point, Ind.), Elks Lodge (East Chgo., Ind.). Methodist. Avocations: golf, reading, baseball. Home: Dyer, Ind. Died Jan. 6, 2009.

MYERS, HELEN LORETTA, property manager; b. Hammond, Ind., Sept. 22, 1934; d. Leslie Gilbert and Bessie Vickers (Pollard) Coapstick; m. Ivan Oteen Myers, Dec. 2, 1961 (dec. 1978). Student, St. Joseph's Coll., East Chicago, Ind., 1957-59. Sec., State Farm Ins., Griffith, Ind., 1969; owner, operator Myers' Restaurant, Hartford, Ky., 1969-77, Highland Body Shop, Ind., 1977-84; supr. Kelly Services, Merrillville, Ind., 1984-86, resident br. mgr., Chgo., 1985-87; property mgr. Cypress Trace Shipping Ctr., Ft. Myers, Fla., 1987—; mem. adv. com. Daley Coll., Chgo.; mem. Hyde Park C. of C., Automotive Service Councils (sec.-treas. 1977-86). Republican. Club: Scherwood Golf (Schererville, Ind.).

Lodge: Eastern Star (matron 1967-68, state appts., Grand rep. to Ala. 1974-78). Avocations: golf, reading, hand crafts, walking, bicycling. Home: Fort Myers, Fla. Died Apr. 25, 2010.

MYERS, JACK ELLIOTT, English educator, poet; b. Lynn, Mass., Nov. 29, 1941; s. Alvin George and Ruth Libby (Cohen) M.; m. Willa Naomi Robins, Aug. 15, 1981 (div. Oct. 1992); children: Jacob, Jessica; children from previous marriage: Benjamin, Seth; m. Thea Temple, Sept. 25, 1993. BA, U. Mass., 1970; MFA, U. Iowa, 1972. Prof. English So. Meth. U., Dallas, from 1975. Disting. vis. writer U. Idaho, 1993, Wichita State U., 1994, Old Dominion U., 1998. Author: (poetry) The Family War, 1978, I'm Amazed That You're Still Singing, 1981, As Long As You're Happy, 1985 (Nat. Poetry Series selection), Blindsided, 1993, One On One, 1999, The Glowing River: New and Selected Poems, 2001; editor: A Trout in the Milk: on Richard Hugo; co-editor: A Longman Dictionary of Poetic Terms, 1989, A Profile of 20th-Century American Poetry, 1991, New American Poets of the 90's, 1991. Bd. dirs. The Writer's Garret, Dallas, 1993—. NEA fellow, 1983, 86; recipient award in poetry Tex. Inst. Letters, 1978, 94. Mem. PEN, Assoc. Writing Programs (v.p. 1994, cons. 1995), Writer's Garret (bd. dirs. 1993—). Democrat. Avocation: pocket billiards. Home: Mesquite, Tex. Died Nov. 23, 2009.

MYERS, JAMES CLARK, advertising and public relations executive; b. Chgo., Aug. 26, 1941; s. Herbert George Myers and Lenore (Goldberg) Levi; m. Judy Anne Schnitzer, Feb. 9, 1964; children: Jeffrey Stephan, Jeremy H. BA, Washington U., St. Louis, 1964. Acct. exec. Nahas, Blumberg, Zelikow, Houston, 1967-69; mgr. spl. events Houston Post, 1969-73; pres., creative dir. Motivators, Inc., Houston, 1973—2006; dir. cmty. svcs. Brays Oaks Mgmt. Dist., Houston, from 2006. Employment vice-chmn. Internat. Sci. and Engring. Fair Coun., Washington, 1972-73; bd. dirs. Sci. Engring. Fair of Houston, 1969-73; spl. corrs. Navy Times Newspaper; pres. SW Houston 2000, Inc., 1999-05; chmn. US Cong AGreen TX-9 Mil. Acad. Selection Bd. Contbr. articles to newspapers. Chmn. Houston chpt. Boy Scouts Am.; mem. City of Houston Bldgs. and Stds. Commn., 2005-. Served to capt. USNR, 1964-96. Recipient Wood Badge award, Boy Scouts Am., 1979, Shofar award, 1981; named Fondren SW Citizen of Yr., 2002. Mem. Pub. Relations Soc. Am. (accredited, Silver Anvil award 1983, 87, Excalibur 2001), Bus. Adv. Fedn. (cert.) Jewish. Avocations: model railroading, square dancing, photography. Home: Houston, Tex. Died Mar. 15, 2010.

MYERS, OVAL, JR., plant geneticist, educator; b. Roachdale, Ind., July 28, 1933; s. Oval and Ina Opal (Skelton) M.; M. Joyce Marlene Caldwell, June 21, 1959; children; Gerald, Paul. AB, Wabash Coll., 1958; AM, Dartmouth Coll., 1960; PhD, Cornell U., 1963. Instr. U. Ark., Fayetteville, 1963-65, asst. prof., 1965-68; assoc. prof. So. Ill. U., Carbondale, 1968-75, prof., from 1975. Plant breeder So. Ill. U.-Univ. Fed. de Santa Maria (FAO project), Brazil, 1972-74; chief U.S. AID Party to Lusaka, Zambia, 1987-88; dir. internat. agr. So. Ill. U., 1989-91; chief U.S. AID Party to Peshawar, Pakistan, 1991-94. Co-author: An Approach to Problem Solving in Genetics, 1976, 3d edit., 1993; co-inventor Egyptian soybean cultivar, 1984, Pyramid, 1986, Pharaoh, 1989, Nile, 1994. Fellow AAAS; mem. Rotary Internat. Democrat. Mem. Christian Ch. (Disciples Of Christ). Avocations: tennis, golf, camping. Home: Carbondale, Ill. Died Jan. 14, 2010.

MYERS, ROBERT KENNETH, insurance company executive; b. Camden, NJ, Apr. 28, 1954; s. Robert P. and Beverly J. (Dodel) Myers; m. Rebecca S. Myers. AA, Camden County Coll., 1974; BA, Glassboro State Coll., 1976. Sales rep. Met. Ins. Co., Marlton, NJ, 1979—84, sales mgr., 1984—85; pres. Myers Ins. Svcs., Stratford, NJ, from 1985. Mem.: Life Underwriters Polit. Action Com., Nat. Assn. Life Underwriters (NJ). Died May 15, 2010.

MYERS, WARREN POWERS LAIRD, internist, educator; b. Phila., May 2, 1921; s. John Dashiell and Mary Hall (Laird) M.; m. Katharine Van Vechten, July 1, 1944; children: Warren Powers Laird, Jr., Anne Van Vechten Myers Evans, Duncan McNeir, Sara Myers Gormley. Grad., Episcopal Acad., 1939; BS, Yale U., 1943; MD, Columbia U., 1945; MS in Medicine, U. Minn., 1952; postgrad. (Eleanor Roosevelt Found. fellow), U. Cambridge, Eng., 1962-63. Diplomate: Am. Bd. Internal Medicine. Rotating intern Phila. Gen. Hosp., 1945-46; intern medicine Maimonides Hosp., NYC, 1948-49; resident fellow in medicine Mayo Clinic, Rochester, Minn., 1949-52; clin. asst. Meml. Hosp., NYC, 1952-54, asst. attending physician, 1954-58, assoc. attending physician, 1959, attending physician, 1959-90; instr. Cornell U. Med. Coll., 1955-56, asst. prof., 1956-59, asso. prof., 1959-68, prof. medicine, 1968-86, prof. emeritus and from 1986, assoc. dean, 1977-86; chmn. dept. medicine Meml. Sloan-Kettering Cancer Ctr., NYC, 1967-77; v.p. for ednl. affairs Meml. Hosp., 1977-81, Eugene W. Kettering prof., 1979-86; attending physician N.Y. Hosp., NYC, 1968-86; mem. Sloan-Kettering Inst. Cancer Rsch., NYC, 1969-90; mem. emeritus Meml. Sloan-Kettering Cancer Ctr., NYC, from 1990; cons. Rockefeller U. Hosp., NYC, 1977-86. Mem. clin. cancer tng. com. Nat. Cancer Inst., 1970-73, chmn., 1971-73, chmn. clin. cancer edn. com., 1975-78; adj. prof. medicine Dartmouth Med. Sch., 1987-96, prof. medicine emeritus, 1996—; cons. staff Mary Hitchcock Meml. Hosp., Hanover, N.H., 1987-96. Contbr. articles on cancer, bone metabolism, internal medicine, and med. edn. to med. jours. Bd. dirs. Rye (N.Y.) United Fund, 1969-72, chmn. budget com., 1968-69; bd. dirs. Damon Runyon-Walter Winchell Cancer Fund, 1976-86, pres., 1985-86; trustee Hitchcock Clinic, Lebanon, N.H., 1983-96, Dartmouth-Hitchcock Med. Ctr., Lebanon, 1983-95, chmn. exec. com., 1992-95, tchr.'s coll. Columbia U., 1980-86; trustee Friends of Norris Cotton Cancer Ctr., Dartmouth-Hitchcock Med. Ctr., Lebanon, 1997-2000, v.p., 1999-2000—; elder 5th Ave. Presbyn. Ch., 1969-86, Norwich Congregational Ch., deacon, 1998-2002. With M.C., USNR, 1946-47. Recipient Alumni award for research Mayo Clinic, 1952, Margaret Hay Edwards Achievement medal Am. Assn. Cancer Edn., 1993. Fellow ACP, N.Y. Acad. Medicine (v.p. 1983-85); mem. Am. Clin. and Climatological Assn., Am. Assn. Cancer Research, Endocrine Soc., Harvey Soc., Am. Fedn. Clin. Research, Practioners' Soc. of N.Y., AMA, Am. Assn. Cancer Edn. (pres. 1984-85), Am. Soc. Clin. Oncology, Founders and Patriots Pa., Yale Club, Charaka Club, Century Assn. (N.Y.C.), Alpha Omega Alpha. Presbyterian (elder 1969-86). Clubs: Yale, Charaka, Century Assn. (N.Y.C.). Home: Hanover, NH. Died Apr. 1, 2009.

MYERS, WAYNE ALAN, psychiatrist, educator; b. NYC, Dec. 13, 1931; s. Harry and Eve Myers; m. Joanne Jackson, Mar. 23, 1969; children: Tracy Victoria, Blake Andrew. BS with high honors, U. Ark., 1952; MD, Columbia U., 1956. Cert. in psychiatry and psychoanalysis. Intern Bellevue Hosp., NYC, 1956-57; resident Payne Whitney Clinic, N.Y. Hosp., NYC, 1957-59, 61-62; instr. psychiatry Cornell U. Med. Ctr., NYC, 1962-72, clin. asst. prof. psychiatry, 1972-77, clin. assoc. prof. psychiatry, 1977-84, clin. prof. psychiatry, from 1984; tng. and supervising admitting psychoanalyst Columbia U. Ctr. for Psychoanalytic Tng. & Research, NYC, from 1983. Sec. Assn. for Psychoanalytic Medicine, N.Y.C., 1987-89. Author: Dynamic Therapy of the Older Patient, 1984, Shrink Dreams, 1992; editor: New Concepts in Psychoanalytic Psychotherapy, 1987, New Techniques in the Psychotherapy of Older Patients, 1991, The Perverse and the Near Perverse in Clinical Practice, 1991, contbr. articles to profl. jours. Capt. U.S. Army, 1959-61. Dist. life fellow Am. Psychiat. Assn. (life), Am. Psychoanalytic Assn.; mem. Assn. for Psychoanalytic Medicine (sec.), N.Y. State Med. Soc., N.Y. County Med. Soc., PEN, Author's Guild. Avocations: skiing, squash, creative writing. Home: New York, NY. Died Jan. 16, 2009.

MYERS, WILLIAM GEORGE, state senator, physician; b. Kittanning, Pa., Sept. 28, 1930; s. William George and Emma Adeline (Webb) Roberts; m. Carol Anne Edgar, June 15, 154; children: Jacqueline Jolane, William George, Bradley Stephen, Brian Jeffry, Barry Douglas, Jennifer Sue. BS, U. Pitts., 1952, MD, 1956. Intern Southside Hosp., Pitts., 1956-57, resident in internal medicine, 1957-58; practice medicine Pitts., Bethel Park, Whitehall, Pa., 1958-61, Hobe Sound, Fla., from 1962; dir. Palm Beach/Martin County Med. Ctr., 1973-76; columnist Permission to Speak, 1973-83; mem. Fla. Ho. of Reps., 1978-82, Fla. Senate, from 1982, also Republican floor leader. Mem. Republican State Exec. Com., 1968-72, dist. vice chmn., 1964; county commr. Martin County, Stuart, Fla., 1968-72; chmn. Martin County Rep. Exec. Com., 1964-68. Recipient Disting. Svc. award Fla. Soc. Ophthalmology, Fla. Emergency Technicians and Paramedics, Fla. Assn. Bldg. Contractors, Fla. Heart Assn., Stuart C. of C., 1983; named Senator of Yr., Fla. Hosp. Assn., 1983. Mem. AMA, So. Med. Assn., Fla. Med. Assn., Martin County Med. Assn., Hobe Sound C. of C. (pres. 1963-65). Died May 25, 2010.

MYERSON, RALPH MAYER, physician; b. New Britain, Conn., July 21, 1918; s. Benjamin and Idah Sarah (Fineberg) M.; m. Loretta Francis Walsh, Aug. 7, 1943; children: Patricia Ann Huntington, Paul Andrew. BS summa cum laude, Tufts Coll., Medford, Mass., 1938; MD cum laude, Tufts Med. Coll., Boston, 1942. Diplomate Am. Bd. Internal Medicine. Intern Boston City Hosp., 1942-43, resident, 1946-48; staff physician VA Hosp., Wilmington, Del., 1948-53, asst. chief medicine Phila., 1953-58, chief med. svc., 1958-72, chief of staff, 1972-75; group dir. Smithkline & French Labs., Phila., 1975-80, cons., 1980-85; freelance writer Phila., 1985-90; assoc. dean grad. med. edn. Med. Coll. Pa., Phila., 1990-92; v.p. Dickson Rsch. Group, Berwyn, Pa., 1990-94; Medex, Ardmore, Pa., from 1994. Contbr. 150 articles to profl. jours.; author 7 textbooks on medicine. Capt. U.S. Army Med. Corps, 1943-46. Fellow ACP, Am. Gastroenterology Assn., Am. Coll. Gastroenterology; mem. AMA, Pa. Soc. Medicine, Phi Beta Kappa, Alpha Omega Alpha. Avocations: travel, stamp collecting/philately. Died Jan. 31, 2010.

NACHT, DANIEL JOSEPH, architect; b. Chgo., Sept. 22, 1915; s. George Carl and Hattie (Zaylor) N.; m. Mary Alice Belcher, Nov. 19, 1960; 1 dau., Pamela Jean. BS, U. Ill., 1940. Mem. faculty U. Ill., 1940-42; with Skidmore, Owings & Merrill, Chgo., 1946-53; designer Rogers Engring. Co., San Francisco, 1953-55; architect Starks, Jozens & Nacht, Sacramento, 1956-70, Nacht & Lewis, 1970. Prin. works include Consumnes River Coll, Sacramento County Courthouse. Mem. Capitol Bldg. and Planning Commn., 1959-67; mem. Core Area Com., 1962-64; mem. adv. bd. Salvation Army Sacramento area. With USNR, 1942-46. Fellow A.I.A.; mem. Crocker Art Gallery, Alpha Chi Rho. Clubs: Mason (Shriner). Home: Millerton, NY. Died July 7, 2009.

NADEL, MARVIN, retired engineering and management consulting firm executive; b. Passaic, NJ, Aug. 12, 1926; s. Abraham and Minnie (Groudan) N.; m. Jean D. Flax, June 21, 1953; Amy Judith, Joshua Adam. BS in Chem. Engring., W.Va. U., 1949; postgrad., Stevens Inst. Tech., 1951, U. Pa., 1959. Registered profl. engr., Pa. Tech. coordinator Picatinny Arsenal, Dover, N.J., 1950-52; process engr. Day & Zimmermann, Inc., Phila., 1952-56, project mgr., 1956-64, mgr. environ. engring., 1964-67, dir. research and planning, 1969-76, pres. real estate services div., 1972-91, v.p. corp. devel., dir., 1976-91, mem. exec. com., 1976-91. Pres. William Chanoff Co., Phila., 1967-69, Calam Internat., Inc., Phila., 1976-81 Contbr. articles to profl. jours. Bd. dirs. Arts' Bus. Coun.; mem. panel arbitrators Am. Arbitration Assn.; mem. tech. adv. com. Ben Franklin Tech. Ctr. Home: Philadelphia, Pa. Died July 6, 2009.

NAGY, BELA FERENC, biochemist, educator; b. Nagybanhegyes, Hungary, May 15, 1926; arrived in US, 1957, naturalized, 1961; s. Bela and Julianna (Fruehwirth) Nagy; m. Barbara Peyser, Jan. 19, 1958 (div. 1974); children: Andrew, Julianna; m. Henryka Ursula Bialkowska, Nov. 13, 1980. Diploma, U. Budapest, Hungary, 1953; PhD, Brandeis U., 1964. Asst. prof. U. Budapest, 1953—57; rsch. assoc. Rockefeller Inst., NYC, 1957—58, NYU Med Sch., NYC, 1959—60, Boston Biomed. Rsch. Inst., 1964—78; spl. rsch. fellow Brandeis U., Waltham, Mass., 1960—64; prin. assoc. Harvard U. Med. Sch., Boston, 1970—78; assoc. prof. neurology, pharmacology and cell biophysics U. Cin. Med. Coll., from 1978, rsch. dir. neurology dept., from 1978. Contbr. articles to profl. jours. Recipient Career Devel. award, NIH, 1967—72; fellowship, Nat. Acad. Sci., 1957—59, NIH, 1961—64, grant, NSF, Muscular Dystrophy Assn., from 1973. Mem.: AAAS, Soc. Biol. Chemists, Biophys. Soc. Am., Biochem. Soc. London, Am. Chem. Soc., Soaring 7th Flying (pres. 1984—85). Avocation: flying. Home: Harvard, Mass. Died Jan. 17, 2009.

NAHRWOLD, MICHAEL LANGE, anesthesiologist; b. St. Louis, Nov. 23, 1943; s. Elmer William and Magdalen (Lange) Nahrwold; m. Janice Elaine Geitz; children: Stacey Marie, Marny Michelle, Daniel Alan. AB, Ind. U., 1965; MD, 1969. Diplomate Am. Bd. Anesthesiology. Asst. prof. Hershey Med. Ctr., Pa., 1975—77; assoc. prof. U. Mich., Ann Arbor, 1977—81; prof. anesthesiology, 1981—86; prof. chmn. anesthesiology dept. U. Nebr. Med. Ctr., Omaha, from 1986. Editor in chief Anesthesiology Rev., 1984. With USPHS, 1973—75. Mem.: AMA, Assn. Univ. Anaesthetists, Am. Acad. Clin. Anesthesiologists, Am. Physiol. Soc., Internat. Anesthesia Rsch. Soc., Am. Soc. Anesthesiologists. Republican. Lutheran. Avocation: music. Home: Indianapolis, Ind. Died Sept. 18, 2009.

NASON, STANLEY H., judge; b. NYC, May 5, 1919; s. Irving M. and Dorothea (Halprin) Nason; m. Gloria Faber, Jan. 24, 1943; children: Andrea Ruth Kulin, Susan Gail Passaretti. BA, NYU, 1940, JD, 1948, LLM, 1951. Bar: NY 1948, NY (U.S. Dist. Ct. (so. dist.)) 1951, NY (U.S. Dist. Ct. (ea. dist.)) 1952, (U.S. Supreme Ct.) 1956. Ptnr. Nason & Greenstein, NYC, 1950—69; atty. and counsel to ombudsman, acting ombudsman Housing Devel. Adminstrn., NYC, 1969—73; housing judge NYC Civil Ct., 1973—80; civil ct. judge, 1980—82; family ct. judge Family Ct. State of NY, from 1982. Capt. USAF, 1942—45. Jewish. Home: New York, NY. Died Mar. 26, 2010.

NATHAN, PAUL S., retired editor, writer; b. Oakland, Calif., Apr. 2, 1913; s. Alfred Jacobs and Frances (Strause) N.; m. Dorothy Goldeen, July 14, 1935 (dec. Dec. 1966); children: Andrew J., Carl F., Janet D. Souza; m. Ruth Wilk Notkins, May 26, 1972 (dec. 2005). BA, U. Calif., Berkeley, 1934. Reporter Oakland Post-Enquirer, 1929-36; asst. play editor Paramount Pictures, NYC, 1937-48; Hosp. pub. rels. Will, Folsom & Smith, NYC, 1948-61; sci. editor Nat. Cystic Fibrosis Rsch. Found., NYC and Atlanta, 1963—73; columnist Rights and Permissions (subsequently Rights) Pubs. Weekly, NYC, 1946-98. US liaison Jerusalem Internat. Book Fair, 1976-77 Author: (play) Ricochet, 1980 (Edgar Allan Poe award of Mystery Writers Am. for best play of 1980), Texas Collects: Fine Arts, Furniture, Windmills & Whimseys, 1988; co-editor: (anthology) View: Parade of the Avant-Garde, 1991; author: (novels) Protocol for Murder, 1994, No Good Deed, 1995, Count Your Enemies, 1997; columnist Pub. News, London, 1998-2003; contbr. fiction and articles to Story, NY Times mag., Saturday Evening Post, Saturday Rev., others. Mem.: PEN, Mystery Writers Am., Authors League, Authors Guild, Dramatists Guild, Phi Beta Kappa. Died Dec. 12, 2009.

NATHANS, ROBERT, physicist, researcher; b. Wilington, Del., May 27, 1927; s. Samuel and Sarah Leah (Levitan) N.; m. Barbara Lange, Dec. 18, 1949; children: Mark David, Leah Julie, Jessie Ruth, Samuel Paul, Amy Alexandria. Student, CCNY, 1944-45, Syracuse U., 1945; BS, U. Del., 1949; MS, U. Minn., 1950; PhD, U. Pa., 1954. Asso. prof. physics Pa. State U., 1954-58; physicist Lincoln Lab., MIT, 1959-60; sr. physicist Brookhaven Nat. Lab., Upton, NY, 1960-68; prof. physics and engring. SUNY-Stony Brook, from 1968, dean W. Averell Harriman Coll. Urban and Policy Scis., 1975-76, dir. Inst. Energy Research, 1976-83, dir. Inst. Technology Policy in Devel., from 1983. V.p. Internat. Energy Devel. Inc., Port Jefferson, N.Y., 1978— Served as sgt. AUS, 1945-46. Fulbright prof. Osaka (Japan) U., 1958-59 Fellow Am. Phys. Soc. Research in solid state and nuclear physics. Home: Bellport, NY. Died Apr. 27, 2010.

NATKIN, ROBERT, painter; b. Chgo., Nov. 7, 1930; s. Phillip and Betty Natkin; m. Judith Dolnick; children: Joshua, Leda. BA, Art Inst. Chgo., 1952. Exhibited paintings in numerous one-man shows, including Andrè Emmerich Gallery, N.Y.C., Holburne of Menstrie Mus., Bath, Eng., Art Inst. Chgo., Moore Coll. Art, The Reele Galleries, N.Y.C., Phila., Ivory/Kimpton Gallery, San Francisco, Gimpel Fils Gallery, London, Gimpel & Weitzenhoffer Gallery, N.Y.C., A.B.C.D. Gallery, Paris, Tortue Gallery, Santa Monica, Calif., Butler Inst. Am. Art, Ohio, Galerie Brusberg, Hannover, Fed. Republic Germany, Hirshhorn Mus. and Sculpture Garden, Washington, Okla. Art Ctr., Oklahoma City, 1982, Gloria Luria Gallery, Miami, 1984, Klonarides Gallery, Toronto, 1985; group shows include Mus. Art, Pa. State U., 1973, Poindexter Gallery, N.Y.C., 1976; represented in permanent collections, including Art Inst. Chgo., Mus. Modern Art, N.Y.C., Solomon R. Guggenheim Mus., N.Y.C., Whitney Mus. Am. Art, Hirshhorn Mus. and Sculpture Garden, Smithsonian Instn., Washington, Mus. Fine Arts, Houston, Mus. Art, R.I. Sch. Design, San Francisco Mus. Art, Mus. Art, Carnegie Inst., Duke U. Mus. Art, Centre Georges Pompidou (Beaubourg), Paris, Milw. Art Ctr., Fogg Mus. Harvard U., Met. Mus. Art, N.Y.C., Akron (Ohio) Inst., Albright-Knox Art Gallery, N.Y.C., Butler Inst. Am. Art, L.A. County Mus. Art, Mint Mus. Art, N.C., Wadsworth Atheneum, Conn. Home: Redding, Conn. Died Apr. 20, 2010.

NATOW, ANNETTE BAUM, nutritionist, author, consultant; b. NYC, Jan. 30, 1933; d. Edward and Gertrude (Jackerson) Baum; m. Harry Natow, Nov. 30, 1955; children: Allen,

Laura, Steven. BS, CUNY Bklyn. Coll., 1955; MS, SUNY Coll. Plattsburg, 1960; PhD, Tex. Women's U., 1963. Registered dietitian, N.Y. Asst. prof. SUNY Coll. Plattsburg, 1967-69, CUNY Coll. Lehman, NYC, 1969-70; assoc. prof., chmn. dept. SUNY Downstate Med. Ctr., Bklyn., 1970-76; prof., dir. nutrition programs Adelphi U., Garden City, N.Y., 1976-90, prof. emerita, from 1991; intern Montreal Diet Dispensary, March of Dimes, 1980; pres., writer, cons. NRH Nutrition Cons., Inc., Valley Stream, N.Y., from 1980. Author: No-Nonsense Nutrition, 1978, Geriatric Nutrition, 1980, Nutrition for the Prime of Your Life, 1983, No-Nonsense Nutrition for Kids, 1985, Megadoses: Vitamins as Drugs, 1985, Nutritional Care of the Older Adult, 1986, Pocket Encyclopedia of Nutrition, 1986, The Cholesterol Counter, 1989, 1988, 2d edit., 1989, The Fat Counter, 1989, The Fat Attack Plan, 1990, The Diabetes Carbohydrate and Calorie Counter, 1991, The Pregnancy Counter, 1992, The Iron Counter, 1993, The Sodium Counter, 1993, The Antioxidant Vitamin Counter, 1994, The Fast Food Counter, 1994, The Supermarket Nutrition Counter, 1995, The Protein Counter, 1997, Eating Out, 1998, Most Complete Food Counter, 1999, The Carbohydrate, Fiber and Sugar Counter, 1999; editor Jour. Nutrition for Elderly, 1983—; mem. editl. bd. Environ. Nutrition Newsletter, 1985—; mem. editl. adv. bd. Prevention, 1984-86; contbr. numerous articles to profl. jours. United Hosp. Fund grantee, 1978. Mem. Am. Dietetic Assn., N.Y. State Dietetic Assn., N.Y. State Nutrition Coun. (sec. 1973-74). Avocations: square dancing, music. Died July 27, 2009.

NAYLOR, LARRY LEE, anthropologist, educator; b. Corning, NY, Mar. 14, 1940; s. Harry Earnest Naylor, Francis Jennette McGee; m. Alma Diane Bennett. BS Edn., SUNY, 1962, MS Edn., 1968; DPhil Anthropology, So. Ill. U., 1974. Cert. tchr. N.Y., 1962, N.Mex., 1966. Tchr. elem. sch. Newark Pub. Schs., Newark, 1962—63; tchr. high sch. history Grants Mcpl. Sch. Dist., Grants, N.Mex., 1966—67; asst. prof. anthropology U. Alaska, Fairbanks, 1974—78; asst. prof., dir. anthropology North Tex. State U., Denton, 1978—83; assoc. prof., dir. anthropology U. North Tex., 1983—86, assoc. prof. anthropology dept. geography & anthropology, 1986—90, assoc. prof., chair anthropology, 1990—93, assoc. prof., chair Inst. Anthropology and Cultural Sensitivity Tng. & Rsch. Ctr., 1993—97, prof. anthropology, from 1997. Dir. Cultural Sensitivity Tng. & Rsch. Ctr., U. North Tex., Denton, 1994—97; cons. Native affairs Institute of Social, Econ. and Govt. Rsch., U. Alaska, Fairbanks, 1974—78; advisor Native alcohol abuse Alaska Concern Citizens on Alchhol Abuse, 1975—77; cons. criminal justice program U. Alaska, 1975—76; Consultant Alcan Pipeline Company, Anchorage, 1976—77; Consultant - Pipeline Impact on Native Canadians Canadian Government, Canada, 1976—77; Consultant - Alaskan Pipeline Impact Gulf State Engineering, Houston, 1976—78; Consultant Alaska Native Foundation on Culture Change, Anchorage, 1976, on Gas Pipeline Impact - Tanana Development Corporation, Fairbanks, AK, 1978; Consultant and Member of Emergency Management Projects Advisor Board Texas A & M University, TX. Translator: Eskimos, Reindeer and Land, 1981; author: Science and the Future (Anthropology), 1993, Cultural Anthropology, 1993, Science and the Future (Anthropology), 1994, Anthropology: Study Guide, 1994, Science and the Future (Anthropology), 1995, Culture Change: An Introduction, 1996, Science and the Future (Anthropology), 1996, Interative Study Guide for Anthropology, 1996, Culture Diversity in the United States, 1997, Science and the Future (Anthropology), 1997, American Culture: Myth and Reality of a Culture of Diversity, 1998, Issues and Problems of Culture Diversity in the United States, 1999, Anthropology Study Guide (CD-ROM), 2001; co-author: Applied Social Science for Environmental Planners, 1983; contbr. articles to profl. jours. Mayor City of Krugerville, Tex., 1999—2000. Grantee, Arctic Gas Corp., 1976, Nat. Park Svc., 1976, Gulf Interstate Engring. Corp., 1976—77, Berger Commn., Can. Govt., 1976—77, Inst. of Arctic Biology, 1976, Nat. Park Svc., 1977—78, Bur. Indian Affairs, 1977—78, U. North Tex., 1982, U. North Tedx. Internat. Affairs, 1982, U. North Tex. Internat. Program Office, 1983, U.S. Corp Engrs., 1987, City Mgr.'s Office, Dallas, 1985, U. North Tex., 1989, Harcourt Brace Publ., 1992, 1993, Higher Edn. Assistance Fund, U. North Tex., 1993. Fellow: Soc. Applied Anthropology, Am. Anthrop. Assn.; mem.: AAAS, N.Y. Acad. Scis., Tex. Coop. Edn. Assn., Current Anthropology (assoc.), Ctrl. State Anthropology Assn. (assoc.), Alaska Anthropology Assn., Coun. Edn. and Anthropology. Home: Hunt, Tex. Died June 17, 2010.

NEAL, PATRICIA, actress; b. Packard, Ky., Jan. 20, 1926; d. William Burdette and Eura Mildred (Petrey) N.; m. Roald Dahl, July 2, 1953 (div. 1983); children: Olivia Twenty (dec. 1962), Tessa Sophia, Theo Mathew Roald, Ophelia Magdalene, Lucy Neal. Student, Northwestern U., 1943-45; LHD (hon.), Simmons Coll., Rockford Coll., U. Mass., Northwestern U. Appeared in Broadway prodns.: Another Part of the Forest, 1946 (N.Y. Critics, Antoinette Perry, other awards 1946), Children's Hour, 1952, Roomful of Roses, 1955, Suddenly Last Summer, 1958, The Miracle Worker, 1960; (films) The Fountainhead, 1948, The Hasty Heart, 1948, The Breaking Point, 1949, John Loves Mary, 1949, Three Secrets, 1949, Bright Leaf, 1950, Raton Pass, 1951, Operation Pacific, 1951, The Day the Earth Stood Still, 1951, Week-End with Father, 1951, Diplomatic Courier, 1952, Washington Story, 1952, Something for the Birds, 1952, La tua donna, 1954, Immediate Disaster, 1954, A Face in the Crowd, 1956, Breakfast at Tiffany's, 1961, Hud, 1963 (N.Y. Film Critics award 1964, Acad. Award for Best Actress, 1964, Best Fgn. Actress award Brit. Acad. 1964), Psych 59, 1964, In Harm's Way, 1965, The Subject Was Roses, 1968, The Night Digger, 1970, Baxter, 1973, Happy Mother's Day, Love, George, 1973, Widows Nest, 1976, The Passage, 1978, Ghost Story, 1981, An Unremarkable Life, 1989, Cookie's Fortune, 1999, For the Love of May, 2000, Flying By, 2009; (TV movies) Clash by Night, 1959, Strindberg on Love, 1960, Special for Women: Mother and Daughter, 1961, Westinghouse Presents: That's Where the Town Is Going, 1962, The Homecoming, 1972, Things in Their Season, 1974, The American Woman: Portraits of Courage, 1976, Tail Gunner Joe, 1977, A Love Affair: The Eleanor and Lou Gehrig Story, 1978, The Bastard, 1978, All Quiet on the Western Front, 1979, Shattered Vows, 1984, Love Leads the Way: A True Story, 1984, Caroline?, 1989, A Mother's Right: The Elizabeth Morgan Story, 1992, Heidi, 1993; (TV appearances) Goodyear Playhouse, 1954, Studio One in Hollywood (2 episodes), 1954-58, Omnibus, 1955, Matinee Theatre, 1956, Playhouse 90 (2 episodes), 1957-58, Pursuit, 1958, Suspicion, 1958, Rendezvouis, 1959, Play of the Week, 1960, Drama 61-67, 1962, Checkmate, 1962, The Untouchables, 1962, Zero One, 1962, Ben Casey, 1963, Espionage, 1963, The Waltons, 1971, Circle of Fear, 1972, Kung Fu (2 episodes), 1974, Little House on the Prarie (2 episodes), 1975, Movin' On, 1975, Hallmark Hall of Fame (3 episodes), 1975-90, Glitter, 1984, Murder, She Wrote, 1990; author: (autobiography) As I Am, 1988. Com. mem. Internat. Help for Children, Eng.; hon. bd. dirs. Nat. Found. Encephalitis Research; mem. Washington Speakers Bur., 1978; founder Patricia Neal Rehabilitation Ctr. Named Most Outstanding Woman from Tenn. under 40, 1963; recipient Gold medal Nat. Inst. Social Scis., 1983; Patricia Neal Rehabilitation Hosp. named in her honor, Knoxville, Tenn. Mem. Actors Studio, Pi Beta Phi, Phi Beta. Mem. Ch. of England. Died Aug. 8, 2010.

NEAME, RONALD, director, producer; b. Hendon, Middlesex, Eng., Apr. 23, 1911; s. Stuart Elwin and Ivy Lillian (Close) N.; m. Beryl Yolanda Heanly, Oct. 15, 1933; 1 son, Christopher Elwyn; m. Dona Friedberg, Sept. 12, 1993. Student pvt. schs., London and Sussex, Eng. Asst. cameraman Brit. Internat. Pictures, Estree, Eng., 1928-35, chief cameraman, 1935-45. Dir.: photography, prodn. supr. (films) In Which We Serve, 1942, This Happy Breed, 1943, Blithe Spirit, 1944; co-writer, prodr.: (films) Brief Encounter, 1945, Great Expectations, 1946; prodr.: (films) Oliver Twist, 1947; dir.: (films) Take My Life, 1948, Golden Salamander, 1949, The Promoter, 1952, Man with a Million, 1953, The Man Who Never Was, 1954, Windom's Way, 1957, The Horse's Mouth, 1958, Tunes of Glory, 1960, I Could Go On Singing, 1962, The Chalk Garden, 1963, Mr. Moses, 1964, Gambit, 1966, The Prime of Miss Jean Brodie, 1968, Scrooge, 1970, The Poseidon Adventure, 1972, The Odessa File, 1974, Meteor, 1978, Hopscotch, 1979, First Monday in October, 1981, Foreign Body, 1985, The Magic Baloon, 1989; co-founder film co. Cineguild Co., Denham, Eng., 1943-44. Decorated Comdr. of the Order of the Brit. Empire, 1996. Mem. Dirs. Guild Am., Am. Film Inst., Acad. Motion Picture Arts and Scis. (gov. 1977-79), Brit. Acad. Film and TV Arts (London and Los Angeles), Savile Club (London). Home: Hollywood, Calif. Died June 16, 2010.

NEELEY, G. STEVEN, lawyer, educator, psychotherapist; s. G.W. and Mildred Neeley. BS, Xavier Univ., Ohio, 1980; JD, Univ. Cin. Coll.; MA, Univ. Cin., Cin., 1987, PhD, 1989. Law clk. Law Offices of T.D. Shackleford, Ohio, 1982—84; adj. prof. Union Inst., 1989; vis. asst. prof. Xavier Univ., Ohio, 1989—92; atty. pvt. practice, Loretto, Pa., from 1985; adj. prof. Coll. Mt. St. Joseph, 1992—93; asst. prof. philosphy St. Francis Coll., 1993—97, assoc. prof. philosophy, 1997—2003; philol. psychotherapist pvt. practice, Loretto, Pa., from 1997; prof. philosophy St. Francis U., from 2003. Assoc. editor Contemporary Philosophy; mem. Pre law Adv. Bd. St. Francis, 1999; advisor Philosophy Club St. Francis; presenter in field. Author: The Constitutional Right to Suicide, 1994, Schopenhauer: A Consistant Reading, 2003. Recipient Exellence Tchg. award, Am. Philos. Assn., 2014, Beishop Fenwick Tchr. Yr. award, Xavier, 1991. Mem.: A.P.A. Sarte Cir., AMINTAPHIL, Am. Philol. Assn. (Excellence in Tchg. 1998). Home: Colver, Pa. Died Mar. 14, 2010.

NEERIEMER, DEAN HUGH, lawyer; b. Odon, Ind., Oct. 14, 1923; s. William Bracken and Ethel (Swinda) Neeriemer; 1 child, Laura. BS, Butler U., 1948; LLB, Ind. U., 1950. Bar: Ind. 1950, Ind. (U.S. Dist. Ct. (so. dist.)) 1950. Editor Bobbs-Merrill Co., Indpls., 1948—50; sole practice Washington, Ind., from 1950; pros. atty. 49th Jud. Cir., Washington, Ind., 1952—58. Treas. Ind. State Christian Conv., 1983—84. With. US Army, 1943—44. Named Hon. Alumni award, Johnson Bible Coll., Kimberly Heights, Tenn., 1974. Mem.: Ind. Bar Assn., Daviess County Bar Assn., Mason, Elks. Republican. Died July 21, 2010.

NEF, EVELYN STEFANSSON, retired psychotherapist, author, editor, specialist polar regions; b. NYC, July 24, 1913; d. Jeno and Bella (Klein) Schwartz; m. Bil Baird, 1932 (div. 1938); m. Vilhjalmur Stefansson, 1941 (dec. 1962); m. John Ulric Nef, Apr. 21, 1964 (dec. Dec. 1988). Student, Traphagen Art Sch., NYC, summer 1927, Art Student League, 1931, Inst. Study Psychotherapy, NYC, 1974-77, Advanced Psychoanalytic Seminar, 1977-83. Librarian Stefansson Polar Library, NYC, 1941-52; librarian Stefansson collection Baker Library, Dartmouth Coll., 1952-63, also lectr. polar studies program, 1960-61; adminstrv. officer Am. Sociol. Assn., Washington, 1963-64; freelance writer book reviews, newspaper articles N.Y. Times Book Review, also Washington Post, 1942-72; research assoc. dept. dermatology Washington Hosp. Ctr., 1976-95, coordinator psoriasis social adjustment study, 1977-80. Guest worker Inst. Brain Evolution and Behavior, NIHM; guest on radio and TV programs; mem. vis. com. U. Chgo. Libr., 1973-84, vice chmn., 1977-84; mem. vis. com. on social scis. U. Chgo., 1978-83; bd. dirs. MacDowell Colony, fellow, summer 1993. Author: Within the Circle, 1945, Here is the Far North, 1957, Here is Alaska, 4th rev. edit. (with Linda C. Yahn), 1983, also contbg. author other books; editor-in-chief: Beyond the Pillars of Heracles (Rhys Carpenter), 1966, South from the Spanish Main (Earl Hanson), 1967, Silk, Spices and Empire (Owen and Eleanor Lattimore), 1968, West and By North (Louis B. Wright and Elaine Fowler), 1971, The Moving Frontier (Louis B. Wright and Elaine Fowler), 1972; foreward writer for Eleanor Lattimonew's Turkestan Reunion, 1995; editor, contbr.: Polar Notes, 1960-63, Eleanor Holgate Lattimore, 1895-1970, 1970, Jour. of Polar Studies, 1984; contbr. to: A Chronological Bibliography of the Published Works of Vilhjalmur Stefansson, 1978, Vilhjalmur Stefansson and The Development of Arctic Terrestial Science, 1984. Pres. Evelyn S. Nef Found.; trustee Corcoran Gallery Art, Washington, 1974-89; bd. dirs. Reginald S. Lourie Ctr. for Infants and Young Children, 1989-93, Washington Opera, Nat. Symphony, MacDowell Colony, Paget Found.; mem. adv. coun. dept. geriatrics Mt. Sinai Hosp., N.Y.C. Recipient Vol. Activist award, 1978, recognition award Young Audiences, 1992, Women of Achievement award Washington Irving H.S., 1996, Legend of the Corcoran award Corcoran Gallery, 1996. Mem. Washington Acad. Scis., Smithsonian Assocs. (mem. women's com. 1971-74), Soc. Women Geographers (nat. v.p., chmn. Washington chpt. 1969-71, nat. pres. 1972-75), Explorers Club, Sulgrave Club, Cosmos Club. Research on psychosomatic skin diseases, progressive aging. Home: Washington, DC. Died Dec. 10, 2009.

NEFF, FRANCINE IRVING (MRS. EDWARD JOHN NEFF), retired federal official; b. Albuquerque, Dec. 6, 1925; d. Edward Hackett and Georga (Henderson) Irving; m. Edward John Neff, June 7, 1948; children: Sindle, Edward Vann. AA, Cottey Coll., 1946; BA, U. N.Mex., 1948. Divsn. and precinct chmn. Republican Party, Albuquerque, 1966-71; mem. ctrl. com. Bernalillo County (N.Mex.) Republican Party, 1967-74, mem. exec. bd., 1968-70; mem. N.Mex. State ctrl. com. Republican Party, 1968-74, 77-82, mem. exec. bd., 1970-74, 81-83; Rep. nat. committeewoman State of N.Mex., 1970-74; treas. of U.S. US Dept. Treasury, Washington, 1974-77. Nat. dir. U.S. Savs. Bonds, 1974-77; mktg. v.p. Rio Grande Valley Bank, Albuquerque, 1977-81; bd. dirs. La.-Pacific Corp., Portland, Oreg., D.R. Horton, Inc., Arlington, Tex. N.Mex. state adviser Teenage Reps., 1967-68; del. Rep. Nat. Conv., Miami, 1968, 72; campaign coord. Congressman Lujan of N.Mex., 1970; pres. Albuquerque Federated Rep. Women's Club, 1977; Leader Camp Fire Girls, Albuquerque, 1957-64; pres. Inez (N.Mex.) PTA, 1961; den mother Cub Scouts Am., Albuquerque, 1964-65; former mem. exec. bd. United Way of Albuquerque; former mem. adv. coun. Mgmt. Devel. Ctr., Robert O. Anderson Grad. Sch. Bus. and Adminstrv. Scis., U. N.Mex.; former mem. Def. Adv. Com. on Women in the Svcs., 1980-83; trustee Cottey Coll., Nevada, Mo., 1982-89. Recipient Exceptional Svc. award U.S. Dept. Treasury, 1976, Horatio Alger award Horatio Alger Assn. Disting. Americans, Inc., 1976. Mem. P.E.O. (pres. Albuquerque chpt. 1958-59, 63-64), Albuquerque City Panhellenic Assn. (pres. 1959-60), Greater Albuquerque C. of C. (bd. dirs. 1978-81), Alpha Delta Pi, Sigma Alpha Iota, Phi Kappa Phi, Pi Lambda Theta, Phi Theta Kappa. Republican. Episcopalian. Home: Pena Blanca, N.Mex. Died Feb. 9, 2010.

NEITZEL, DONALD CARL, judge; b. Detroit, Dec. 13, 1921; s. Henry Carl and Catherine Josephine (Reid) Neitzel; m. Hortonse Marie Marentette, Oct. 22, 1949; children: MaryAnn Kinziger, Lisa Marie, Donald C., Nicole. BA, Albion Coll., 1943; JD, U. Mich., 1945. Bar: Mich. 1945, Mich. (U.S. Dist. Ct. (ea. dist.)) 1945, (U.S. Supreme Ct.) 1970. Sole practice, Detroit, 1946—47, Wyandotte, Mich., 1947—56, Southgate, Mich., 1956—78; dist. judge Mich. 28th Dist. Ct., Southgate, from 1979; mcpl. judge City of Southgate, 1958—65, 1977—78; city atty., 1965—77. City atty., City of Riverview, Mich., 1959—62; vice-chmn. City Charter Commn., Southgate, 1956—57. Mem.: Mich. Dist. Judges Assn. (treas.), Wayne County Dist. Judges Assn. (v.p.), Downriver Bar Assn. (pres. 1957—59), Lions (pres. 1958), Wyandotte Exchange (pres. 1952). Democrat. Roman Catholic. Home: Southgate, Mich. Died July 19, 2010.

NELSON, FREDERICK CARL, mechanical engineering educator, dean; b. Braintree, Mass., Aug. 8, 1932; s. Carl Edwin and Marjorie May (Miller) N.; m. Delia Ann Dwaresky; children: Jeffrey, Karen, Richard (dec.), Christine. BSME, Tufts U., 1954; MS, Harvard U., 1955, PhD, 1961. Registered profl. engr., Mass. Instr. Tufts U., Medford, Mass., 1955-57, asst. prof. mech. engring., 1957-64; assoc. prof. mech. engring., 1964-71; prof. mech. engring. Tufts U., Medford, from 1971, dean engring., 1980-94. Cons. SAVIAC, from 2003. Translator: Mechanical Vibrations for Engineers, 1983. Recipient Career Achievement award Tufts U. Dept. Mech. Engring., 1996. Fellow ASME (centennial medal award 1980), AAAS, ASA, Nat. Inst. Applied Scis. of Lyon (medal 1988), Korea Advanced Inst. Sci. and Tech. (medal 1988, partnership award 2003), Tufts U. Alumni Assn. (medal 1991), The Vibration Inst. (bd. dirs. 1999—). Home: Reading, Mass. Died Jan. 7, 2009.

NELSON, JOHN C., lawyer; b. Chgo., July 25, 1927; s. John E. and Astrid (Rutberg) N.; m. Barbara Otis, June 19,1955; children: Karen, Diana, John, James, Kristin. BS, Lawrence Coll., 1952; JD, NYU, 1955. Bar: N.Y. 1956. Assoc. Milbank, Tweed, Hadley & McCoy, NYC, 1955-63, ptnr., from 1963. Mem. ABA, N.Y. State Bar Assn., Assn. Bar City N.Y. Episcopalian. Died Apr. 4, 2009.

NELSON, LAWRENCE BARCLAY, chemical executive; b. NYC, Jan. 9, 1931; s. Arthur Palmer and Josephine (Scheller) N.; m. Audrey Winifred Lawson, June 25, 1955; children: Holly Condit, Scott Palmer. BA, NYU, 1951, PhD in Chemistry, 1955. Rsch. assoc. Mobil Oil Corp., NYC, 1956-60; with Witco Corp., NYC, from 1960, asst. to v.p. mfg./ R & D, Sonneborn div., 1960-62, corp. dir. R & D, 1963-76, v.p., tech. dir. Sonneborn div., 1976-81, corp. v.p., 1981-85, group v.p., from 1985. Mem. Indian Trail Club, Ridgewood (N.J.) Country Club. Home: Franklin Lakes, NJ. Died Jan. 4, 2009.

NELSON, WINIFRED HARRISON, singer, actress, computer programmer; b. Oak Park, Ill., Dec. 29, 1924; d. Fred and Florence Harrison; m. Robert Hartley Nelson, May 5, 1945 (dec. Feb. 24, 1994); children: Richard, Wendy, Steven (dec.), Jonathan, Elizabeth. BA, Knox Coll., 1945; MusM, Northwestern U., 1970. Tchr. voice, 1972-78, Chgo., 1976-80; computer programmer U. Ill., Champaign, 1978-82, Tex. A&M U., College Station, 1982-90. Mem. Chgo. Symphony

Chorus, 1972-80. Mem. Briarcrest Country Club. Presbyterian. Avocations: community theater, music, golf. Home: Bryan, Tex. Died Jan. 12, 2009.

NEMERSON, YALE ROY, physician, educator; b. NYC, Dec. 15, 1931; s. Joseph and Cecile (Bandes) N.; m. Andrea Buchman, Feb. 4, 1979; children: Mathew, Andrea, David. BA, Bard Coll., 1953; MD, NYU, 1960. Intern. Lenox Hill Hosp., N.Y.C., 1960-61; resident Bronx VA Hosp., NYC, 1961-62, Montefiore Hosp., NYC, 1962-64; instr. in medicine Yale U., New Haven, 1964-65, asst. prof., 1965-70, assoc. prof., 1970-75, prof., 1975; prof. medicine SUNY-Stony Brook, 1976-77, head div. hematology, 1976-77; Philip J. and Harriet L. Goodhart prof. medicine Mt. Sinai Sch. Medicine, CUNY, NYC, from 1977. Cons. NIH, N.Y. Blood Ctr. Contbr. articles to profl. jours. NIH fellow, 1971-72; fellow Am. Heart Assn., 1967-72 Mem. Assn. Am. Physicians, Am. Soc. Hematology (Damashek prize 1977), Am. Soc. Clin. Investigation, Am. Soc. Biol. Chemists, Internat. Soc. Thrombosis and Hemostasis, Alpha Omega Alpha Home: Great Barrington, Mass. Died Feb. 12, 2009.

NENOW, ROBERT CHARLES, karate educator, forest technician; b. Allentown, Pa., Apr. 2, 1941; s. Herman W. and Lillian G. (Hardner) N. Grad. high sch., Palmerton, Pa. Cert. 2d degree World Tang Soo Do, 7th degree Oriental Defensive Arts Assn., 7th degree Am. Tae Kwon Do Master. Weapons instr. Dynasty, Inc., Palmerton, from 1978, master instr., 1980-85, sr. master instr., from 1985; pres. Dynasty Karate, Inc., Palmerton, from 1974. Author: Thoughts of a Modern Master, 1983. Served with U.S. Army, 1959-62. Presdl. Sports award, 1975; U.S. Nat. Sr. Black Belt Sparring Champion, 1987, 89. Mem. Oriental Defensive Arts Assn. (C. Johnson Meml. award 1978, Robert Shortlidge Jr. Meml. award 1981). Clubs: Am. Legion Pistol (pres. 1970-75), Lehighton Pistol and Rifle (pres. 1970-75). Democrat. Avocations: physical fitness, shooting, travel, flying private aircraft. Died July 2, 2010.

NERAD, RICHARD A., accounting company executive; b. Traverse City, Mich., Sept. 7, 1927; s. Otto S. and Victoria Alice (Hanslovsky) N.; m. Patricia Ann Hayes, Sept. 19, 1953; children: Judith, Rebecca, Dean. BA, Colo. Coll., 1950; MBA, U. Denver, 1951. CPA, Ill. Staff auditor Arthur Andersen and Co., Chgo., 1951-54, sr. cons., 1954-57, mgr. cons., 1957-64, engagement ptnr., 1964-73, mng. dir. info. practice, 1973-77, dir. methodology, 1977-84, mng. ptnr. profl. ednl. div. St. Charles, Ill., 1985-90, ret., from 1990. Dir., treas. Easter Seals DuPage County, Lombard, Ill., 1966-72, Marion Park, Wheaton, Ill., 1972-78. Lt. U.S. Navy, 1945-46. Mem. AICPA, Ill. Soc. CPA's, Am. Soc. Tng. and Devel. Congregationalist. Avocation: sports. Home: Saint Charles, Ill. Died June 26, 2010.

NESBITT, ROSEMARY SINNETT, theatre educator; b. Syracuse, NY, Oct. 12, 1924; d. Matthew A. and Mary Louise (Kane) Sinnett; m. George R. Nesbitt, June 18, 1955 (dec. Nov. 1971); children: Mary, Anne, George R., Elizabeth. BS magna cum laude, Syracuse U., 1947, MS, 1952. Instr. in speech Wells Coll., Aurora, N.Y., 1949-52, Syracuse U., 1952-57; asst. prof. SUNY, Oswego, 1965-68, assoc. prof., 1968-72, prof. theatre, 1972-77, Disting. teaching prof., from 1977, dir. children's theatre, from 1969. Cons., lectr. pub. schs., N.Y. and New Eng., 1965—; lectr. in field. Author: The Great Rope, 1968, Colonel Meacham's Giant Cheese, 1971; (play) The Great Rope, 1975 (George Washington medal Freedom Found. 1975); plays for children. Founding mem. Oswego Heritage Found., 1963; historian City of Oswego, 1973-80, 88—; founder, bd. dirs. H. Lee White Marine Mus., Oswego, 1983—; chmn. bd. dirs. Port of Oswego Authority, 1986-88, bd. dirs., 1978-88. Recipient George R. Arents Disting. Alumnus award Syracuse U., 1975, Jefferson award Jefferson Award Com., 1984, Svc. to Arts award Cultural Resources Coun. Onondaga County, 1985, Franklin award for Disting. Svc. in Transp. Syracuse U. Sch. mgmt., 1989, Amelia Earhart Woman of the Yr. award Zonta Club of Oswego, Monument for Disting. Svc. to Cmty., City of Oswedo, 1999, Disting. Svc. award Nat. Seaway Trail, 2001, Outstanding Leadership award Leadership Oswego County, 2001; named Woman of Yr. in Cultural Devel., Syracuse Post Standard, 1971, Citizen of Yr., City of Oswego, 1974, Disting. Citizen of N.Y. State, 1999. Mem. AAUW, Equestrian Order of Knights and Ladies of the Holy Sepulchre, Alpha Psi Omega. Democrat. Roman Catholic. Avocations: history, reading, travel. Home: Oswego, NY. Died Aug. 2, 2009.

NETZLEY, ROBERT ELMER, retired state legislator; b. Laura, Ohio, Dec. 7, 1922; s. Elmer and Mary (Ingle) N.; m. Marjorie Lyons, July 28, 1944 (dec. July 14, 2009); children: Kathleen, Carol Anne, Robert. Grad. Midshipman Sch., Cornell U., 1944; BS, Miami U., 1947. Mem. Dist. 7 Ohio House of Reps., 1961-82, mem. Dist. 68, 1982—2000. Pres. Miami County Young Reps., Ohio, 1952-54; chmn. Miami County Rep. Ctrl. and Exec. com.; del. Rep. Nat. Conv., 1980, presdl. elector, 1980 Recipient Purple Heart, Am. and Pacific Theaters. Mem. VFW, Miami County Heart Coun., American Legion, AmVets, Grange, Laura Lions; Phi Kappa Tau. Home: Laura, Ohio. Died July 28, 2010.

NEU, MARY VIVIAN, secondary school educator; b. Chgo., Dec. 22, 1946; d. Robert Joseph and Shirley Cressida Turek; m. Michael Charles Neu, Dec. 27, 1969 (div. 1983). BA, Carleton Coll., 1968; MAT in English, U. Ill., 1969. Cert. secondary English tchr. (7-12). English tchr. Case H.S., Racine, Wis., from 1969. Trustee Racine Pub. Libr., 1984-92, Lakeshores Libr. Systems, Racine, 1992—. Fellowship Nat. Endowment for Humanities, Oberlin Coll., 1990. Mem. Friends of the Racine Pub. Libr. (sec., bd. dirs.), Delta Kappa Gamma (treas. 1985-95). Democrat. Roman Catholic. Avocations: books, plants, dogs. Home: Adrian, Mich. Died Jan. 8, 2009.

NEUBERG, HANS W., internist, educator; b. Hannover, Germany, Mar. 26, 1921; came to U.S., 1937, naturalized, 1943. s. Georg and Gertrud (Dux) N.; m. Birgit Aron, Apr. 8, 1949; children: Peter G., Gerald W. BS, Wagner Coll., 1941; MD, Columbia U., 1950. Diplomate Am. Bd. Internal Medicine. Intern Presbyn. Hosp., NYC, 1950-53, asst. resident, NRC fellow in medicine, 1953-54, asst. attending physician, 1966-80, assoc. attending physician, 1980-91, attending physician, from 1992; pvt. practice, 1954-83. Instr. medicine Columbia U. Coll. Phys. and Surg., N.Y.C., 1954-63, assoc. in medicine, 1963-67, asst. prof. clin. medicine, 1967-80, assoc. clin. prof. medicine, 1980-91, clin. prof. medicine, 1992—, mem. Instnl. Rev. Bd. With AUS, 1943-46. Fellow ACP; mem. Alpha Omega Alpha. Mem. Am. Diabetes Assn. Home: Sleepy Hollow, NY. Died Aug. 10, 2009.

NEUHAUS, OTTO WILHELM, biochemistry educator; b. Zweibrucken, Germany, Nov. 18, 1922; came to U.S., 1927, naturalized, 1931; s. Clemens Jakob and Johanna Amalie (Schnorr) N.; m. Dorothy Ellen Rehn, Aug. 30, 1947; children: Thomas William, Carol Alida, Joanne Marie. BS, U. Wis., 1944; MS, U. Mich., 1947, PhD, 1953. Research chemist Huron Milling Co., 1951-54; mem. faculty Wayne State U., Detroit, 1954-66, asso. prof., 1965-66; prof., chmn. dept. biochemistry U. S.D., Vermillion, 1966-76, acting chmn. dept. physiology and pharmacology, 1975-76, 82-83, prof., chmn. div. biochemistry, physiology and pharmacology, 1976-82, prof., 1982-88, chmn. dept. biochemistry, 1982-86, prof. emeritus, from 1988. Acting registrar of collections. W.H. Over Mus., Vermillion, S.D. Author: (with John Halver) Fish in Research, 1969, (with James Orten) Human Biochemistry, 1982; also research articles. NATO Research fellow, 1961-62 Fellow AAAS; mem. Am. Chem. Soc., Am. Soc. Biol. Chemists, Sigma Xi, Phi Sigma, Alpha Chi Sigma, Phi Lambda Upsilon. Lutheran. Home: Vermillion, SD. Died Nov. 14, 2009.

NEUHAUSEN, BENJAMIN SIMON, auditor, accountant; b. Urbana, Ill., Apr. 23, 1950; s. Stanley Edward and Dolores Renee (Epstein) N.; m. Madeline Cohen, Sept. 6, 1987; 3 children. BA, Mich. State U., 1971; MBA, NYU, 1973. CPA, Ill. Staff auditor Arthur Andersen & Co., NYC, 1973-75, sr. auditor, 1975-78, audit mgr., 1978-79, 81-85; audit ptnr. Arthur Andersen LLP, Chgo., from 1985; practice fellow Fin. Acctg. Standards Bd., Stamford, Conn., 1979-81. Contbr. articles to profl. jours. Bd. dirs. The Renaissance Soc., Chgo., 1987-90. Recipient Charles W. Haskins medal N.Y. Soc. CPAs, 1974. Mem. AICPA (acctg. standards exec. com. 1997—), Ill. Soc. CPAs, Chgo. Athletic Assn. Jewish. Home: Highland Park, Ill. Died July 31, 2009.

NEUMEIER, MATTHEW MICHAEL, lawyer, educator; b. Racine, Wis., Sept. 13, 1954; s. Frank Edward and Ruth Irene (Effenberger) N.; m. Annmarie Prine, Jan. 31, 1987; children: Ruthann Marie, Emilie Irene, Matthew Charles. B in Gen. Studies with distinction, U. Mich., 1981; JD magna cum laude, Harvard U., 1984. Bar: NY 1987, Mich. 1988, Ill. 1991, US Dist. Ct. (ea. dist.) Mich. 1988, US Dist. Ct. (ea., no. dists. and trial bar) Ill. 1991, US Ct. Appeals (7th cir.) 1992, US Ct. Appeals (fed. cir.) 1998, US Supreme Ct. 1991. Sec.-treas. Ind. Roofing & Siding Co., Escanaba, Mich., 1973-78; mng. ptnr. Ind. Roofing Co., Menominee, Mich., 1977-78; law clk. to presiding justice US Ct. Appeals (9th cir.), San Diego, 1984-85; law clk. to chief justice Warren E. Burger US Supreme Ct., Washington, 1985-86; spl. asst. to chmn. US Constn. Bicentennial Commn., Washington, 1986; assoc. Cravath, Swaine & Moore, NYC, 1986-88; spl. counsel Burnham & Ritchie, Ann Arbor, Mich., 1988; assoc. Schlussel, Lifton, Simon, Rands, Galvin & Jackier, P.C., Ann Arbor, Mich., 1988-90, Skadden, Arps, Slate, Meagher & Flom, Chgo., 1990-96; ptnr. Jenner & Block, Chgo., 1996—2007, Howrey LLP, Chgo., from 2007. Adj. prof. computer law and high tech. litig. John Marshall Law Sch., Chgo., 1999—2008. Editor: Harvard Law Rev., 1982—84. Pres., bd. dirs. Univ. Cellar Inc., Ann Arbor, 1979-81; bd. dirs. Econ. Devel. Corp., Menominee, 1978-79, Midwestern divsn. Am. Suicide Found., sec., 1992-97, Commonwealth Plaza Condominium Assn., dir., 1999-2009, pres., 2000-07; dir. Harvard Law Soc. Ill., 2003-, sec., 2005-07, treas., 2007-08, 2nd v.p., 2008-; mem. vestry Ch. Our Savior, 1997-2000; bd. dirs. Chgo. Children's Mus., 1999-, sec., 2003-; chmn. Harvard Law Sch. 15 Yr. Reunion Gift Fund, 1999; vice chair Harvard Law Sch. 20 Yr. Reunion Gift Fund, 2003-04. Mem. ABA, State Bar Mich., Assn. of Bar City of NY, Chgo. Bar Assn., Ill. State Bar Assn., Def. Rsch. Inst., Econ. Club Chgo., City Club Chgo. Republican. Avocations: classic automobiles, piano, choir. Home: Chicago, Ill. Died May 17, 2009.

NEW, ROBERT VALENTINE, JR., diversified financial services company executive; b. LA, Oct. 26, 1951; s. Robert V. Sr. and Arline (Smith) N.; m. Pamela Ann Roche, June 26, 1976; 1 child, Robert V. III. BSBA, Trinity U., 1974. Loan officer S.W. Tex. Nat. Bank, San Antonio, 1974-77; asst. v.p. Frost Nat. Bank, San Antonio, 1977-80; with Tex. Commerce Bancshares, 1981-89, pres., CEO N.W. San Antonio, 1987-88, vice chmn.; dist. dir. NCNB Tex., San Antonio, 1989; pres., CEO Green Bank, N.A., 2006—08, F.N.B. Corp., Hermitage, Pa., from 2008. Trustee Marine Mil. Acad., Harlingen, Tex., 1981—; v.p. Trinity U. Nat. Alumni Bd., San Antonio, 1987—; bd. dirs. Tex. Interscholastic League Found., Austin, Tex. Chmn. Am. Cancer Soc., Houston, 1985, 86; chmn., founder Leadership Clear Lake, Houston, 1985, 86. Sgt. USMC, 1971-73. Mem. Jaycees (Outstanding Young Tex. 1986, Outstanding Young Houstonian 1986). Home: San Antonio, Tex. Died Apr. 18, 2010.

NEWCOMB, WILLIAM WILMON, JR., anthropologist; b. Detroit, Oct. 30, 1921; s. William Wilmon and Esther Gladys (Matthews) N.; m. Glendora Estella Thielan, Aug. 24, 1946; children— Mary Elaine, William Andrew. AB, U. Mich., 1943, MA, 1947, PhD, 1953. Instr. U. Tex., Austin, 1947-50, 51-52, lectr. anthropology, 1961-62, prof., 1962-86, prof. emeritus, from 1987; teaching fellow U. Mich., 1950-51, 52-53; vis. asst. prof. anthropology and sociology Colgate U., 1953-54; curator anthropology Tex. Meml. Mus., Austin, 1954-57, dir. mus., 1957-78; dir. Tex. Archeol. Salvage Project, 1965-66. Author: The Indians of Texas, 1961, The Rock Art of Texas Indians, 1967, The People Called Wichita, 1976, North American Indians: An Anthropological Perspective, 1974, German Artist on the Texas Frontier: Friedrich Richard Petri, 1978. Served with inf. AUS, 1943-46. NSF grantee, 1965-66 Fellow Am. Anthrop. Assn., Tex. Hist. Assn.; mem. Tex. Inst. Letters. Home: Austin, Tex. Died Feb. 8, 2010.

NEWCOMBE, DAVID SUGDEN, physician; b. Boston, June 28, 1929; s. Walter White and Catherine Naomi (Sugden) N.; m. Sissel Margrethe Ostgard, June 26, 1965; children: Catherine, Kirsten, Sarah. BA, Amherst Coll., Mass., 1952; MD, McGill U., 1956. Diplomate Am. Bd. Rhematology; lic. physician, Mass. Intern Boston City Hosp., Boston, 1956-57, fellow, 1962-63; resident in medicine Duke U., Durham, N.C., 1959-60; fellow Boston U., Boston, 1960-61; fellow in biochemistry, asst. in medicine Harvard Med. Sch., Boston, 1963-65; mem. med. staff U. Va. Hosp., Charlottesville, 1965-67; assoc. prof. medicine, mem. attending staff, dir. rheumatology unit Med. Ctr. Hosp. Vt., Burlington, 1967-77; assoc. prof. environ. health scis., assoc. prof. medicine Johns Hopkins Med. Instns., Balt., 1977-82, dir. divsn. exptl. pathology and toxicology, 1983-87, prof. medicine, 1983-92; chief phys. medicine and rehab. svcs. Bedford (Mass.) VA Hosp., 1993-95. Cons. and speaker in field. Contbr. chpts. to books and articles to profl. jours. Capt. Med. Corps., 1957-79, Korea. Recipient NIH trainee; fellow New England Rheumatism Soc., NIH, Am. Cancer Soc; named Am. Men of Sci. Fellow Am. Coll. Clin. Pharmacology, Am. Rheumatism Soc. (founder); mem. Sigma Xi. Home: Weston, Mass. Died June 11, 2010.

NEWMAN, EDWIN HAROLD, retired news commentator; b. NYC, Jan. 25, 1919; s. Myron and Rose (Parker) N.; m. Rigel Grell, Aug. 14, 1944; 1 child, Nancy (Mrs. Henry Drucker). BA, U. Wis., 1940; postgrad. (fellow), La. State U., 1940. With Washington bur. Internat. News Svc., 1941, U.P., 1941-42, 45-46, N.Y. Daily PM, 1946-47; ind. Washington news bur., 1947; asst to Eric Sevareid at Washington bur. CBS, 1947-49; freelance writer, broadcaster London, 1949-52; with European Recovery Program, 1951-52, NBC, 1952—56, chief news bur. London, 1956-57, Rome, 1957-58, Paris, 1958-61, news commentator NYC, 1961-83; columnist King Features Syndicate, 1984-89. Moderator 1st Ford-Carter Debate, 1976, 2d Reagan-Mondale debate, 1984 Narrator: TV spls. including Japan: East is West, 1961, Orient Express, 1964, Who Shall Live?, 1965, Politics: The Outer Fringe, 1966, Pensions-The Broken Promise, 1972, Violence in America, 1977, I Want It All Now, 1978, Spying for Uncle Sam, 1978, Oil and American Power, 1979, The Billionaire Hunts, 1981, Congress: We the People, 1983-84, On Television, 1985-86, Freud, 1987, The Borgias, 1988; host Saturday Night Live, 1984; drama critic WNB C-TV, 1965-71 (Emmy awards 1966, 68, 70, 72, 73, 74, 82, Peabody award 1966); author: Strictly Speaking: Will America Be The Death of English?, 1974, A Civil Tongue, 1976, Sunday Punch, 1979, I Must Say, 1988; contbr. articles and revs. to various periodicals, U.S., Can. and Eng.; chmn. usage panel Am. Heritage Dictionary, 1975-80. Served from ensign to lt. USNR, 1942-45. Decorated chevalier Legion of Honor France; recipient awards Overseas Press Club, 1961, awards U. Wis. Sch. Journalism, 1967, awards U. Mo. Sch. Journalism, 1975 Mem. AFTRA, Authors Guild, Screen Actors Guild. Died Sept. 13, 2010.

NEWMAN, MARK LAWRENCE, associate headmaster; b. NYC, Nov. 12, 1949; s. Archie and Frieda (Drobes) N.; m. Nancy Edna Roelich, Feb. 18, 1973. BA, Queens Coll., 1971; MA, Adelphi U., 1974; Profl. Diploma, St. John's U., Jamaica, NY, 1979. Cert. ednl. adminstr., N.Y. Tchr. Dalton Sch., NYC, 1976-80; dir. health, phys. edn., athletics Harvard Sch., North Hollywood, Calif., 1980-86; assoc. headmaster Bel-Air Prep Sch., LA, from 1987. N.Y. State Regents scholar, 1966, Nat. Merit finalist, 1966. Mem. ASCD, Nat. Mid. Sch. Assn., Nat. Assn. Secondary Sch. Prins. Avocations: theater, travel, tennis. Home: Valley Vlg, Calif. Died Jan. 11, 2009.

NEWMAN-GORDON, PAULINE, French language and literature educator; b. NYC, Aug. 5, 1925; d. Bernard and Eva Newman; m. Sydney A. Gordon, Sept. 13, 1959 (dec.); m. Richard Yellin, Feb. 9, 1997. BA, Hunter Coll., 1947; MA, Columbia U., 1948; PhD, Sorbonne U., Paris, 1951. Instr. French Wellesley (Mass.) Coll., 1952-53; mem. faculty Stanford (Calif.) U., from 1953, prof. French lit., 1969-93, prof. emerita, from 1994. Author: Marcel Proust, 1953, Eugene Le Roy, 1957, Corbiere, Laforgue and Apollinaire, 1964, Helen of Troy Myth, 1968, (poetry) Mooring to France, (prose poem) Sydney: editor: Dictionary of Ideas in Marcel Proust, 1968, also articles in field; contbr. articles to profl. jours. Scholar Internat. Inst. Edn., 1948-51, MLA, 1956-57, AAUW, 1962-63, Am. Philos. Soc., 1970-71, NEH, 1989; elected to Hall of Fame, Alumni Assn. Hunter Coll. of CUNY, 1990 Mem. MLA, Am. Assn. Tchrs. French, Soc. Friends Marcel Proust. Died June 1, 2010.

NEWNHAM, ROBERT EVEREST, materials scientist, educator, research director; b. Amsterdam, NY, Mar. 28, 1929; BS, Hartwick Coll., 1950; MS, Colo. State U., 1952; PhD in Physics, Pa. State U., 1956; PhD in Crystallography, Cambridge U., 1960. Assoc. prof. elec. engring. MIT, 1958—66; assoc. prof. solid state sci. Pa State U., University Park, 1966-71, prof., 1971-98, sect. head, 1977-98, prof. solid state sci., assoc. dir. materials rsch. lab., 1996-98, prof. emeritus solid state sci., materials rsch. lab., from 1998, Alcoa prof. ceramic sci. and engring. Recipient Internat. Ceramics prize Acad. Ceramics, 1992, Benjamin Franklin medal in Elec. Engring., Franklin Inst., 2004. Mem. NAE. Am. Crystallography Assn., Albert Victor Bleininger award 1995), Materials Rsch. Soc. (Turnbull lectrs. 1996); fellow Am. Ceramic Soc.

(John Jeppson medal 1991), Mineralogical Soc. Am. Achievements include research in crystal and solid state physics, x-ray crystallography. Died Apr. 16, 2009.

NEWPORT, DOROTHEA DAVISON, librarian; b. Lima, Ohio, Mar. 29, 1926; d. Joseph Homer and Dorothea Young (Richards) D.; m. Albert Byron Newport, June 7, 1947 (div. 1977); children: Dorothea, John, Paul, Martin. BS in Music Edn., W. Chester State Coll., 1949; MLA, U. Pitts., 1973. Libr. asst. Carnegie Mellon U., Pitts., 1969-73; pub. svcs. librarian Robert Morris Coll., Pitts., 1973-78; reference librarian U. Md., Coll. Park, 1978-79; head librarian Coatesville Area Pub. Libr., Pa., 1979—. Mme. Pa. Libr. Assn., S.E. Pa. Libr. Assn., AAUW, YWCA, ALA, Beta Phi Mu. Democrat. Lutheran. Home: West Chester, Pa. Died Sept. 19, 2009.

NICASTRO, MICHELLE, actress, singer; b. Washington, May 31, 1960; d. Norman Joseph and Carole Rose (Guarino) N.; m. Steve Stark; 2 children BFA, Northwestern U., 1982; studies with Bud Beyer, Alice Spivak, NYC. Appeared in (plays) Fiddler on the Roof, Merlin, 1982-83; actress: (film) Body Rock, 1984, Bad Guys, 1986, When Harry Met Sally, 1989, The Swan Princess (voice only), 1994, The Swan Princess: Escape from Castle Mountain (voice only), 1997, The Swan Princess: Sing Along (voice only), 1998, The Swan Princess: Mystery of the Enchanted Kingdom (voice only), 1999; (TV movies) Hart to Hart: Crimes of the Hart, 1994; (TV appearances) Airwolf, 1984, Suzanne Pleshette Is Maggie Briggs, 1984, Cover Up, 1984, Charles in Charge, 1985, Who's the Boss?, 1985, Knight Rider, 1985, Murder, She Wrote, 1986, Simon & Simon, 1987, Full House, 1987, Days of Our Lives, 1987, It's Gary Shandling's Show, 1988, Santa Barbara (3 episodes), 1988-90, A Peaceable Kingdom, 1989, Dragnet, 1989, Beverly Hill, 90210, 1992, Bodies of Evidence, 1992, The Young Indiana Jones Chronicles, 1993, Wings, 1996, Coach, 1996, Johnny Bravo, 1997, The Angry Beavers, 1997, The Tony Danza Show, 1997, Xena Warrior Princess, 1998 Recipient Sarah Siddons award, 1978. Avocations: singing, travel, tennis, cooking, gardening. Home: Los Angeles, Calif. Died Nov. 5, 2010.

NICHOLLS, RICHARD H., lawyer; b. Toronto, Ont., Can., Oct. 27, 1938; s. Richard S. and Roberta T. Nicholls; m. Judy Carter, Apr. 15, 1963; children: Christopher T., Jamie C.; m. Anne Delaney, June 10, 1978. BA cum laude, Amherst Coll., 1960; LLB, Stamford U., 1963; LLM, NYU, 1964. Bar: Calif. 1964, N.Y. 1965, D.C. Assoc. Mudge Rose Guthrie, Alexander & Ferdon and predecessor, NYC, 1964-70, ptnr., 1971-94; of counsel Orrick, Herrington & Sutcliffe, N.Y., from 1995. Mem. ABA, N.Y. State Bar Assn., Nat. Assn. Bond Lawyers, Stamford Yacht Club. Home: Stamford, Conn. Died Mar. 14, 2009.

NICHOLS, HENRY LOUIS, retired lawyer; b. Collin County, Tex., Nov. 7, 1916; s. Jesse Cleveland and Leva (Stiff) N.; m. Elaine Guentherman, May 17, 1949; children: David Michael, Martha Marie. LL.B., So. Meth. U., 1940. Bar: Tex. 1939. Asst. city atty., Dallas, 1946-50; pvt. practice, from 1951. Mem. adv. bd. Ctr. for Legal Mcpl. Studies. Served to lt. col. AUS, 1941-46; col. USAR ret. Rsch. fellow Southwestern Legal Found., 1964. Fellow Am. Bar Found.; mem. ABA, Dallas Bar Assn. (pres. 1963), State Bar Tex., Tex. Bar Found. (charter), Park City Club. Home: Dallas, Tex. Deceased.

NICHOLSON, RICHARD JOSEPH, trust banking executive; b. NYC, Feb. 19, 1932; s. Robert William and Mary Elizabeth (McShane) N.; m. Barbara Helen Malisky, Oct. 15, 1955; 1 child, Richard Jr. BS in Social Sci., Georgetown U., 1952; MBA, NYU, 1957. Asst. cashier Citibank Trust Divsn., NYC, 1952-66; sr. v.p. 1st Fidelity Bank, Newark, 1966-90, ret., 1990. Mem. exec. com. N.J. Bankers Assn. Trust Divsn., Princeton, 1983-85. Bd. dirs. Family Svc. Bur. of Newark, 1976-2001; mem. coun. Newark Mus., 1979-90. Republican. Roman Catholic. Avocations: travel, history. Home: Monroe Twp, NJ. Died Sept. 16, 2009.

NICHOLSON, WILLIAM THOMAS, advertising executive; b. NYC, Oct. 12, 1944; s. John Joseph and Margaret m. (Abdale) N.; m. Amy Bivona (div. July 1983); 1 child, Dina Marie; m. Nancy Musser, Oct. 17, 1987. BS, St. John's U., Jamaica, NY, 1973, MBA, 1976. Dir. corp. acctg. Pan Am World Airways, NYC, 1969-81; controller Seiko Time Corp., NYC, 1981-83; sr. v.p., chief fin. officer Cunningham & Walsh, NYC, 1983-86; exec. v.p., chief ops. officer Kornhauser & Calene Inc., NYC, from 1986; also bd. dirs. Cornhauser & Calene, NYC. Bd. dirs. Sun Coast Airlines, Ft. Lauderdale, Fla. Mem. Fin. Execs. Inst. (chmn. com. 1987). Clubs: Lotos, Doubles. Republican. Episcopalian. Avocations: reading, travel. Home: Tannersville, NY. Died Apr. 24, 2009.

NIELSEN, BRUCE JOHN, construction executive, real estate developer; b. Racine, Wis., Feb. 18, 1948; s. Clayton H. and Irene G. (Chapas) Nielsen; m. Sandra Kay Ridley, Sept. 13, 1975; children: Scott Clayton, Jennifer Lee. BS in Civil Engring., U. Wis.-Madison, 1972, MS in Constrn. Adminstrn., 1972. Registered profl. engr., Wis. Exec. v.p. Nielsen Iron Works, Inc., Racine, 1972—83; pres. Nielsen Bldg. Sys., Inc., from 1983. Owner, prin. Bruce Nielsen, P.E., Racine, from 1972, B.J. Nielsen Real Estate, from 1976; ptnr. NBS Partnership, from 1983, Delta Real Estate Partnership III, from 1986, Delta Ptnrs. II, from 1986; gen. ptnr. Delta Devel. Corp., Wis., from 1986. Bd. dirs. YMCA, Racine, 1982, Cmty. Action Program, 1977, Tri-County Contractors Assn., 1970—82; chmn. Caledonia Econ. Devel. Com.; chmn. adv. bd. Gateway Tech. Inst. Mem.: Racine Area Mfrs. & C. of C., Racine Jaycees (pres. 1976). Home: Racine, Wis. Died June 7, 2010.

NILES, ERNEST ALBERT, safety consultant; b. Gloversville, N.Y., Sept. 7, 1932; s. Albert L. and Iola (Clark) N.; m. Ella M. Duroska, June 24, 1961; children: Deann E., Karen M., Stephanie A., Lynn E. BS in Chem. Engring., U. R.I., 1954; MA in Safety and Health, NYU, 1975. Registered profl. safety engr., Calif.; cert. safety profl., safety exec. Fire protection rep. Factory Ins. Assocs., Hartford, Conn., 1954-59; safety supr. Givaudan Corp., Clifton, N.J., 1959-66; safety svcs. mgr. Rexall Chem. Co., Paramus, N.J., 1966-69; safety cons. Ind. Tech. Assocs., Newark and East Orange, N.J., 1969-73; dir., safety cons. Ernest A. Niles & Assos., Towaco, N.J., 1974—; instr. Hunter Coll., N.Y.C., NYU, Morris County Coll., Middlesex County Coll. Supt. sch. Montville Reformed Ch., 1975—; chmn. Montville Music Boosters Assn.; mem. adv. bd. Pub. Employee OSHA. With AUS, 1955-57. Mem. Am. Soc. Safety Engrs., N.J. Indsl. Safety Com. (chmn.), Nat. Fire Protection Assn., Vets. of Safety. Died Aug. 22, 2010.

NILSON, EDWIN NORMAN, computer graphics consultant; b. Wethersfield, Conn., Feb. 13, 1917; s. Martin and Johanna (Jensen) N.; m. Edith May Tychsen, Aug. 16, 1941; children— Jean N. Ellestad, Richard E., David H. B.S., Trinity Coll., Hartford, Conn., 1937, Sc.D. (hon.), 1963; M.A., Harvard U., 1938, Ph.D., 1941. Instr. math. Harvard U., Cambridge, Mass., 1939-41, U. Md.-College Park, 1941-42; asst. prof. math., Mt. Holyoke Coll., South Hadley, Mass., 1942-44; sr. aerodynamicist United Aircraft Research Lab, East Hartford, Conn., 1946-48; assoc. prof. math. Trinity Coll., Hartford, 1948-56; mgr. engr. computing Pratt & Whitney Aircraft div. United Techs. Corp., East Hartford, 1956-82, cons. parent co., 1982-83; pres. Edwin N. Nilson Assocs. Ltd., Bloomfield, Conn., 1982-86; cons. United Aircraft Research Labs., East Hartford, 1948-56, Pratt & Whitney Aircraft, 1982—. Author: (with J.H. Ahlberg and J.L. Walsh) Theory of Splines and Their Applications, 1967; (with Saunders MacLane) Notes on Algebraic Functions, 1940; contbr. papers to profl. publs. Served to lt. (j.g.) USNR, 1944-46; U.S. Naval Acad. Mary A. Terry fellow, 1937; sr. fellow, Trinity Coll., 1965-70; recipient George J. Mead award United Techs. Corp., 1982. Mem. Math. Assn. Am., Phi Beta Kappa, Sigma Xi. Republican. Congregationalist. Died Aug. 19, 2009.

NIRENBERG, MARSHALL WARREN, biochemist; b. NYC, Apr. 10, 1927; s. Harry Edward and Minerva (Bykowsky) Nirenberg; m. Perola Zaltzman, July 14, 1961 (dec. 2001); m. Myrna Weissman, 2005; 4 stepchildren. BS in Zoology, U. Fla., 1948, MS, 1952; PhD in Biochemistry, U. Mich., 1957. Postdoctoral fellow American Cancer Soc. at NIH, 1957—59; postdoctoral fellow USPHS at NIH, 1959—60; mem. staff NIH, from 1960; rsch. biochemist, chief lab. biochem. genetics Nat. Heart, Lung and Blood Inst., NIH, Bethesda, Md., 1962—2010. Recipient Molecular Biology award, NAS, 1962, award in biol. scis., Washington Acad. Scis., 1962, medal, HEW, 1964, Modern Medicine award, 1963, Harrison Howe award, Am. Chem. Soc., 1964, Nat. Medal Sci., The White House, 1965, Hildebrand award, Am. Chem. Soc., 1966, Research Corp. award, 1966, A.C.P. award, 1967, award merit, Gairdner Found., Can, 1967, Prix Charles Leopold Meyer, French Acad. Scis., 1967, Franklin medal, Franklin Inst., 1968, Albert Lasker Med. Research award, 1968, Priestly award, 1968; co-recipient Louisa Gross Horowitz prize Columbia, 1968, Nobel prize in physiology or medicine, 1968. Fellow: AAAS, NY Acad. Scis.; mem.: NAS, Pontificial Acad. Scis., Leopoldina Deutsche Akademie der Naturforscher, Soc. Devel. Biology, Soc. for Study Devel. and Growth, Washingon Acad. Scis., Harvey Soc. (hon.), Biophys. Soc., Am. Acad. Arts and Scis., Am. Chem. Soc. (Paul Lewis award enzyme chemistry 1964), Am. Soc. Biol. Chemists. Achievements include research in mechanism protein synthesis, genetic code, nucleic acids, regulatory mechanisms in synthesis macromolecules, and neurobiology. Died Jan. 15, 2010.

NISSEL, MARTIN, radiologist, consultant; b. NYC, July 29, 1921; s. Samuel David and Etta Rebecca (Ostrie) N.; m. Beatrice Goldberg, Dec. 26, 1943; children: Philippa Lyn, Jeremy Michael. BA, NYU, 1941; MD, N.Y. Med. Coll., 1944. Diplomate Am. Bd. Radiology. Intern Met. Hosp., NYC, 1944-45, Lincoln Hosp., NYC, 1947-48; resident in radiology Bronx Hosp., 1948-50, attending radiologist, 1952-54; resident in radiotherapy Montefiore Hosp., Bronx, 1950-51, attending radiotherapist, 1954-65; attending radiologist Buffalo (N.Y.) VA Hosp., 1951-52; attending radiotherapist Univ. Hosp. Boston City Hosp., 1965-69. Asst. prof. radiology Boston U. Sch. of Medicine, 1965-69; chief radiotherapist,dir. radiation ctr. Brookside Hosp., San Pablo, Calif., 1969-77; group leader, radiopharm. drugs FDA, Rockville, Md., 1977-86; pvt. cons. radiopharm. drug devel., 1986—. Contbr. articles to profl. jours. Lectr. Am. Cancer Soc., Contra Costa County, Calif., 1973-76. Capt. MC AUS, 1945-47, Korea. Recipient Contra Costa County Speakers Bur. award Am. Cancer Soc., 1973, 76, Responsible Person for Radiol. Health Program for Radiopharm. Drugs award FDA, 1980-86. Mem. Am. Coll. Radiology, Radiol. Soc. N.Am. Avocations: photography, model train building, travel. Home: Eugene, Oreg. Died Jan. 28, 2009.

NITSCHKE, ROBERT ERNEST, manufacturing executive; b. NYC, June 13, 1922; s. Edward Ernest and Inez Marie (Whitson) N.; m. Marilyn E. Giblin, June 24, 1950; children: Robert Eric, William Jay, Joan Marilyn Nitschke Molloy. BME, Pratt Inst., 1944; M Adminstrv. Engring., NYU, 1956. Registered profl. engr., N.Y.; cert. profl. contracts mgr. Design engr. EDO Corp., NYC, 1946-50; engr. Sperry Gyroscope Co., NYC, 1950-65; contracts mgr. EDO Corp., NYC, 1965-70, v.p. adminstrn.-govt. systems div., 1970-85, v.p. adminstrn., from 1985. Mem. Huntington (N.Y.) Hist. Soc. Served with C.E., U.S. Army, 1943-46, ETO. Mem. Nat. Contracts Mgmt. Assn. Republican. Avocations: genealogy, painting. Home: Plainview, NY. Died May 15, 2010.

NIXON, DAVID ARTHUR, steel company product manager; b. Detroit, Feb. 21, 1942; s. Paul Edward and Irene Winifred (Welsh) N.; m. Sandra Lynn Viau, Feb. 4, 1961; children: Jeffrey, John, James. Grad. high sch., Livonia, Mich., 1960. Tool and die maker Chevrolet div. Gen Motors, Livonia, 1960-67; foreman methods engring. Gen. Electric Jet Engine Plant, Evendale, Ohio, 1967-69; process engr. Garrett Airesearch, Torrance, Calif., 1969-70; tech. service engr. LaSalle Steel Co., Hammond, Ind., 1970-80; product mgr. Quanex Corp. div. LaSalle Steel Co., Griffith, Ind., 1980-87; prin. Dānix Corp., Crown Point, Ind., from 1987. Mem. Am. Soc. for Metals (entertainment chmn. 1978), Fluid Power Soc., Soc. Mfg. Engrs. (cert.). Methodist. Avocations: race engine building, woodworking, computers. Home: Crown Point, Ind. Died Jan. 26, 2009.

NOAH, HOPE ELLEN, communications executive, speech educator, broadcaster, writer; b. NYC, Sept. 17, 1943; d. Mortimer and Anne (Forscher) Shaff; m. Lester Noah, Oct. 30, 1969 (div. July, 1985); children: Meredith Ayn, Allison Jane. BS in Speech, Emerson Coll., 1965. Cert. tchr. speech, English, drama, N.Y., N.J. Film producer Rossmore Prodns. and Selling Methods, Inc., NYC, 1965-66; high sch. English tchr. New City, and Mt. Vernon, NY, Fair Lawn, NJ, 1966-73; pvt. teaching practice, profl. speech writer and cons. various locations, from 1972; sales rep. Wordex Corp., Fair Lawn, 1978-80; spl. assignment, summer sch. tchr. Fair Lawn Bd. Edn., 1980-81; writer weekly column A Single Look and spl. feature articles Bergen News, Palisades Park, N.J., 1982-89; producer, programmer, host weekly program "Hope with Singles" Sta. WMCA-Radio, NYC, 1983-84; columnist, cons. Single Times, NYC, 1984-86; editor-in-chief N.J. Singles Mag., Totowa, 1985-86, Single People mag., Dynasty Media Pubs., Englewood Cliff, N.J., 1985-86, Pizzazz, N.Y.C. tri-state entertainment mag., U.S. Pub. Inc., Rutherford, N.J., 1986-87; owner Noah Comm., from 1986. Pvt. practice advt. and pub. relations, small bus. cons., 1982—; dir. creative advt., creator of "Hope" columns, TODAY newspapers, Wayne, N.J., 1982-84; pub. speaker, guest radio and TV shows including The David Letterman program; cons. to industry, hosps.; performer comml. voice-overs; corp. cons. in Speech Communications; trainer foreign born in accent reductions; lectr. in field. Columnist News Pub. Co., 1986—, Spotlight mag., 1987-91; entertainment writer Cross Over the Bridge column, N.Y.C.; assoc. editor Neighborhood Gazette, N.Y.C.; regular contbr. travel writings, book revs., articles and columns to various mags., bus. jours. and other publs. V.p., then pres. Ridgewood (N.J.) B'nai B'rith Women, 1976-78. Named one of Eighty-Five N.J. Residents to Watch N.J. Monthly Mag., 1985. Mem. AFTRA, Emerson Coll. Alumni Assn., Glen Rock (N.J.) C. of C., Am. Soc. Tng. Dirs., Commerce and Industry Assn. No. N.J. Avocations: reading, theater, walking, family activities, travel. Home: Glen Rock, NJ. Died Feb. 6, 2009.

NOBACK, CHARLES ROBERT, anatomist, educator; b. NYC, Feb. 15, 1916; s. Charles Victor and Beatrice (Cerny) N.; m. Eleanor Louise Loomis, Nov. 23, 1938 (dec. Mar. 24, 1981); children: Charles Victor, Margaret Beatrice, Ralph Theodore, Elizabeth Louise. BS, Cornell U., 1936; MS, NYU, 1938; postgrad., Columbia U., 1936-38; PhD, U. Minn., 1942. Asst. prof. anatomy U. Ga., 1941-44; faculty L.I. Coll. Medicine, 1944-49, asso. prof., 1948-49; mem. faculty Columbia Coll. Phys. and Surg., from 1949, assoc. prof. anatomy, 1953-68, prof., 1968-86, prof. emeritus, from 1986, spl. lectr., 1986-92, acting chmn. dept., 1974-75, lectr., from 1996. Author: The Human Nervous System, 1967, 75, 81, Spinal Cord, 1971, The Nervous System Introduction and Review, 1982, 77, 86, 91, (with R. Demarest) Human Anatomy and Physiology, 1990, 2d edit., 1992, 3d edit., 1995, (with R. Demarest) Human Nervous System: Structure and Function, 1967, 6th edit., 2005, The Primate Brain, 1970, Sensory Systems of Primates, 1978; sr. editor: Advances in Primatology: series editor: Contbns. to Primatology; contbr. articles to profl. jours., sects. to Ency. Britannica, McGraw Hill Ency. Sci. and Tech., Collier's Ency. Recipient Columbia U. Coll. Medicine Physicians and Surgeons Disting. Svc. award, 1999. Fellow N.Y. Acad. Scis. (past rec. sec.), AAAS; mem. Am. Assn. Anatomists, Histochem. Soc., Internat. Primatological Soc., Am. Soc. Naturalists, Cajal Club Am. (past pres.), Assn. Phys. Anthropologists, Harvey Soc., Am. Acad. Neurology, Soc. Neurosci., Sigma Xi. Home: Cresskill, NJ. Died Feb. 4, 2009.

NOBLE, JOHN DRUMMOND, real estate broker; b. Skillman, N.J., Nov. 14, 1918; s. Charles John and Agnes Cecelia (Konow) N.; student N.Y.U., 1938; m. Emily Brown Vass, Feb. 27, 1943; children— John Drummond, Amanda Lucy, Melissa Hallie, Michael Covington. With Home Ins. Co., 1939-40; salesman Moss Industries, Bklyn., 1946; co. mgr. A. J. Breckhand Theatrical Prodns., N.Y.C., 1947-49; salesman Clevenger Realty Co., Phoenix, 1949-51; partner John D. Noble & Assos., Phoenix, 1951—; dir. Stewart Title & Trust Co. Chmn., Phoenix Multiple Listing Service, 1962. Served to capt. AUS, 1940-46. Mem. Phoenix Real Estate Bd. (Realtor of Year 1962, pres. 1965—), Ariz. Assn. Realtors (dir. 1962-67, Realtor of Year 1966, pres. 1968-69), Nat. Assn. Realtors, Realtors Nat. Mktg. Inst., Farm and Land Inst. Episcopalian. Home: Paradise Vly, Ariz. Died July 13, 2010.

NOBLES, LORRAINE BIDDLE, dietitian; b. Washington, Apr. 27, 1926; d. Norton William and Lorraine Verna (Tabler) Biddle; m. Stevens Henry Nobles, Dec. 28, 1961 (dec. Apr. 1987). BS, Ohio U., 1952; MSHE, East Carolina U., 1973, MS, 1989. Asst. adminstr. dietitian Emergency Hosp., Washington, 1952-56; asst. supr. sch. lunch program Arlington (Va.) County, 1956-66; chief dietitian Pitt County Meml. Hosp., Greenville, N.C., 1966-91. Adj. prof. East Carolina U., Greenville, 1969-91. Mem. Am. Dietetic Assn., N.C. Dietetic Assn. (chmn. ann. meeting 1982), Ea. N.C. Dist. Dietetic Assn. (pres. elect 1977-78, pres. 1978-79, sec. 1988-90), Am. and Mid-Atlantic Soc. Parenteral and Enteral Nutrition (2d Pl. Pearls session 1988), Tau Delta Epsilon, Phi Omicron Nu, Kappa Delta Pi. Republican. Episcopalian. Avocations: discussion groups, church work, walking. Home: Greenville, NC. Died Jan. 4, 2009.

NOEL, CRAIG, performing company executive; b. Deming, N.Mex., Aug. 25, 1915; LHD (hon.), U. San Diego. Dir. Old Globe Theatre, San Diego, 1947—82, exec. prodr. Instituted Globe Ednl. Tours, 1974, Old Globe's multicultural theater component Teatro Meta, 1983; established Play Discovery Program, Shakespeare Festival; founder Calif. Theatre Coun.; former v.p. Calif. Confedn. Arts.; introduced various playwrights, including Beckett and Ionesco, to San Diego at La Jolla Mus. Contemporary Art, then Falstaff Tavern (renamed Cassius Carter Centre Stage, 1969). Dir. more than 200 works; prodr. 290 works; recent prodns. include Morning's at Seven, Shirley Valentine, The Norman Conquests, 1979, Taking Steps, 1984, Intimate Exchanges, 1987, The Night of the Iguana, 1987, The Boiler Room, 1987, The White Rose, 1991, Mr. A's Amazing Maze Plays, 1994. Named Outstanding Citizen, U. Ariz. Alumni Assn., One of 25 Persons Who Shaped City's History, San Diego Union; Recipient Gov.'s award for Arts, San Diego's Living Treasure award, Conservator Am. Arts award, Am. Conservatory Theatre, Headliner award, San Diego Press Club, San Diego Gentlemen of Distinction award, combined tribute, Pub. Arts Adv. Coun. and San Diego County Bd. Suprs., Nat. Medal Arts, The White House, 2007; Year proclaimed in his honor, Mayor Maureen O'Connor, San Diego, 1987. Died Apr. 3, 2010.

NOLAN, BARRY HANCE, publishing company executive; b. Easton, Pa., Sept. 15, 1942; s. Arthur James Nolan and Marion (Hance) Slater; m. Janet Lynch, Mar. 20, 1971 (dec. Mar. 1981); 1 child, Tracy; m. Catherine McDermott, Feb. 19, 1983; children: Craig, Kelsey. AB in Econs., Princeton U., 1964; MBA, Columbia U., 1966. Account exec. Papert, Koenig, Lois Advt., NYC, 1966-68; group mgr. new bus.'s Butterick div. Am. Can, NYC, 1969-72; dir. mktg. planning Current Inc. subs. Deluxe Check Printers, Colorado Springs, Colo., 1973-77, v.p. mktg., 1977-79, pres., chief exec. officer, 1980-89, ECM, Inc., Colorado Springs, Colo., 1991-96; asst. to pres. Pacific Water Works Supply Co., Seattle, 1979-80. Co-chair Catalog Leaders of Direct Mktg. Assn., 1982-84. Pres. bd. dirs. Pikes Peak br. Cystic Fibrosis Found., Colorado Springs, 1984-89, nat. trustee-at-large, Washington, 1985-92. Mem. Parcel Shippers Assn. (bd. dirs. 1987-89). Clubs: Cheyenne Mountain Country (Colorado Springs); Sahalee Country (Redmond, Wash.), Broadmoor Golf, Garden of the Gods. Republican. Presbyterian. Avocations: golf, landscape architecture, photography. Home: Colorado Springs, Colo. Died July 16, 2009.

NOLAN, LAWRENCE MATTHEW, association executive; b. N.Y.C., June 13, 1947; s. William Robert and Phyllis (Fraughen) N.; m. Patricia Ann Kelly, Nov. 4, 1967; children— Michael, Kevin, Brendan, Brian. B.S., L.I. U., 1972; M.B.A., C.W. Post U., 1974. Acct. Oppenheimer & Co., N.Y.C., 1968-72; controller U.S. Dynamics Corp., Amityville, N.Y., 1972-76; dir. sr. mgmt. program Am. Mgmt. Assn., N.Y.C., 1976-82; mgr. seminar activities Nat. Assn. Purchasing Mgmt., Oradell, N.J., 1982—. Treas. Civic Assn., Setauket, N.Y., 1978; dir. St. Mary's Home Boys, Syosset, N.Y., 1979—; cons. Cath. Charities, Bklyn., 1979—. Mem. Am. Soc. Tng. and Devel., Nat. Assn. Accts. (pres. 1973-74). Republican. Roman Catholic. Home: Congers, NY. Died June 12, 2010.

NOLAND, KENNETH CLIFTON, artist; b. Asheville, NC, Apr. 10, 1924; s. Harry C. and Bessie (Elkins) N.; m. Cornelia Langer (div.); children: Cady, William L., Lyndon; m. Stephanie Gordon, 1967 (div.); m. Peggy Schiffer; children: Samuel Jesse (div.); m. Paige Rense, 1994. Student, Ozzip Zadkine, Paris, 1948-49; studied, Black Mountain Coll., NC, summers, 1950, 51. Tchr. Inst. Contemporary Arts, 1950-52, Cath. U., 1951-60. One man shows include Galerie Creuze, Paris, 1949, Tibor de Nagy Gallery, N.Y.C., 1957, 58, Jefferson Pl. Gallery, 1958, French & Co., N.Y.C., 1959, Bennington Coll., 1961, Andre Emmerich Gallery, N.Y.C., 15 shows from 1960-83, Andre Emmerich Gallery, Zurich, Switzerland, 1973, 76, 79, 82, David Mirvish Gallery, Toronto, Can., 1965, 67, 74, 76, Jewish Mus., 1965, Salander O'Reilly Galleries, N.Y.C., 1989, Leo Castelli Gallery, N.Y., 1995, Gana Art Gallery, Seoul, 1995-96, also other galleries in Milan, Italy, Paris, Zurich, Dusseldorf, Hamburg and Cologne, Fed. Republic Germany, London, Montreal and Toronto, Can.; retrospective show Guggenheim Mus., N.Y.C., 1977; group shows include Kootz Gallery, N.Y.C., 1954, Norman Mackenzie Art Gallery, Regina, Sask., Can., 1963, Corcoran Gallery, Washington, 1956, 59, 63, 64, 67, 70, 75, Corcoran Gallery Biennial in Italy, 1964, Fogg Art Mus., Cambridge, Mass., 1965, 72, Mus. Modern Art, N.Y.C., 1965, 68, Nat. Gallery, Washington, 1968, U.S. Pavilion Expo 67, Montreal, Art Inst. Chgo., 1962, 70, 72, 76, Balt. Mus., 1957, 70, 77, Jewish Mus., 1963, Tate Gallery, London, 1964, 74, Guggenheim Mus., 1961, 66, 70, 73-74, 76-77, L.A. County Mus., 1964, Inst. Contemporary Art, Boston, 1964, 65, 67, Whitney Mus., N.Y.C., 1961-67, 69-73, 76, Met. Mus. N.Y.C., 1968, 70, Mus. Fine Arts, Boston, 1972, Albright-Knox Gallery, Buffalo, 1978, 80, Ameringer Howard Fine Art, NY, 99; Meredith Long Gall., Houston,Tex., 99; Andre Emmerich, CLosing Exhibition of Gall., NY, 99; CHAC-Mool Gall., CA, 99, Ameringer/Howard Gall., N.Y.C, 1999-2001, Farnsworth Mus. Art, Maine, 2002, Naples (Fla.) Mus., 2002; represented in permanent collections Salander O'Reily Galleries, N.Y.C., Mus. of Fine Arts, Houston, 1994, Ft. Lauderdale, 1994; Arte Metro Roma, Rome Colosseum Ctrl. Subway Mosaic Installed, 1995. Trustee Bennington (Vt.) Coll. Recipient 1st prize Premio Nacional Internat., Inst. Torcuato de Tella, Buenos Aires, 1964, Creative Arts award Brandeis U., 1965, 4th prize Corcoran Biennale, 1967; recipient The N.C. Award/medal of arts, 1995. Died Jan. 5, 2010.

NORBERG, RICHARD EDWIN, retired physicist; b. Newark, Dec. 28, 1922; s. Arthur Edwin and Melita (Roefer) N.; m. Patricia Ann Leach, Dec. 27, 1947 (dec. July 1977); children: Karen Elizabeth, Craig Alan, Peter Douglas; m. Jeanne C. O'Brien, Apr. 1, 1978. BA, DePauw U., 1943; MA, U. Ill., 1947, PhD, 1951. Research assoc., control sytems lab. U. Ill., 1951-53, asst. prof., 1953; mem. faculty Washington U., 1955—93, prof. physics, 1958—93, part-time prof., 1993—2003, chmn. dept., 1962-91. Mem. editl. bd. Magnetic Rsch. Rev. Served with USAAF, 1942-46. Co-recipient ISMAR prize, Internat. Soc. Magnetic Resonance, 2004. Fellow Am. Phys. Soc., Internat. Soc. Magnetic Research. Home: Saint Louis, Mo. Died Apr. 20, 2010.

NORRIS, FRANKLIN GRAY, thoracic and cardiovascular surgeon; b. Washington, June 30, 1923; s. Franklin Gray and Ellie Narcissus (Story) N.; m. Sara Kathryn Green, Aug. 12, 1945; children: Gloria Norris Sales, F. Gray III. BS, Duke U., 1947; MD, Harvard U., 1951. Diplomate Am. Bd. Surgery, Am. Bd. Thoracic and Cardiovasc. Surgery, Am. Bd. Gen. Vascular Surgery. Resident Peter Bent Brigham Hosp., Boston, 1951-54, Bowman Gray Sch. Medicine, 1954-57, practice medicine specializing in thoracic and cardiovasculr, from 1957. Prof. anatomy and physiology, Valencia C.C., Orlando, Fla., 1995—; pres. Norris Assocs., Orlando, 1985—; mem. staff Brevard Meml. Hosp., Melbourne, Fla., Waterman Meml. Hosp., Eustis, Fla., West Orange Meml. Hosp., Winter Garden, Fla., Orlando Regional Med. Ctr., Fla. Hosp., Lucerne Hosp., Arnold Palmer Children Hosp., Princeton, Fla. Hosp. N.E. and South (all Orlando). Bd. dirs. Orange County Cancer Soc., 1958-64, Ctrl. Fla. Respiratory Disease Assn., 1958-65. Capt. USAAF, 1943-45. Decorated Air medal with 3 oak leaf clusters. Mem. ACS, Fla. Heart Assn. (dir. 1958—), Orange County Med. Soc. (exec. com. 1964-75, pres. 1971-75), Ctrl. Fla. Hosp. Assn. (bd. dirs. 1980-85), Soc. Thoracic Surgeons, So. Thoracic Surg. Assn., Am. Coll. Chest Physicians, Fla. Soc. Thoracic Surgeons (pres. 1981-82), Am. Coll. Cardiology, So. Assn. Vascular Surgeons, Fla. Vascular Soc., Citrus Club, Orlando Country Club, Phi Kappa Psi. Presbyterian. (elder). Home: Orlando, Fla. Died Aug. 26, 2009.

NORTH, WILLIAM CHARLES, physician, anesthesiologist, educator; b. Chungking, China, Aug. 17, 1925; s. William Robert and Sarah (Shuey) N.; m. Arlene Boss, Sept. 15, 1945 (dec. July 1970); m. Joyce Surratt, Oct. 7, 1971; children—Thomas, Gregg, David, Christopher, Melinda, Preston, Nancy, Karen, Elisa BA, DePauw U., 1945; MS, Northwestern U., 1948, MD, 1950, PhD, 1952. Diplomate Am. Bd. Anesthesiology. Asst. prof. pharmacology Northwestern U. Med. Sch., Chgo., 1954-59; assoc. prof. pharmacology Duke U., Durham, N.C., 1959-65; prof. pharmacology U. Tenn. Ctr. for Health Scis., Memphis, from 1965, prof. anesthesiology, 1965-91, prof. anesthesiology emeritus, from 1992, chmn. dept. anesthesiology, 1965-82, med. dir. Pain Ctr., 1982-88. Anesthesiologist-in-chief City of Memphis Hosp., 1965-82; attending anesthesiologist Reg. Med. Ctr., U. Tenn. Hosp. Author: Anesthesiology and Intensive Care Medicine, 1982, Proceedings First International Post Graduate Practical Course on Pain, 1981; contbr. articles to profl. jours. Served with USN, 1943-46 Mem. Am. Soc. Pharmacology and Exptl. Therapy, Am. Soc. Anesthesiologists, Internat. Anesthesia Research Soc., Am. Pain Soc., AMA, Assn. Univ. Anesthetists Methodist. Home: Buchanan, Tenn. Died Jan. 7, 2010.

NOSEWORTHY, LLOYD MARVIN, archivist, curator, owner historical research library, former railroad official; b. Des Moines, Jan. 27, 1926; s. Heber and Mabel (Barter) N.; m. Mary Blasko, Oct. 8, 1955; children: Scott Anthony, Kelly James. Student Pacific States U., U. Mich., Detroit Inst. Tech. Former R.R. ofcl.; with real estate dept. N.Y.C. R.R., 1949-64; br. mgr. Kendall Ins. Agy., Detroit, 1964-67; with Lehigh Valley R.R. Co., 1967-87, v.p. adminstrv. services, 1975-76, v.p. properties, 1976-87, also dir.; bd. dirs. Niagara Junction Ry., Ironton R.R., Buffalo Creek R.R., United Real Estate Co., Consol. Real Estate Co. Active Friends of Lehigh U. Libraries, Friends of the Pa. Hist. Mus. Commn., Ctr. for Canal History and Technology; bd. trustees South Bethlehem Hist. Soc. With USNR, 1943-45. Mem. Newcomen Soc., Allentown Art Mus., Soo Line Tech. and Hist. Soc. Club: Bethlehem. Home: Bethlehem, Pa. Died July 4, 2010.

NOVACK, TEVOR D., surgeon, consultant; b. Boston, Sept. 6, 1928; MD, Harvard Med. Sch., 1954. Diplomate Am. Bd. Surgery. Intern Beth Israel Hosp., Boston, 1954-55; resident in surgery Beth Isreal Hosp., Boston, 1955-56; resident in gen. surgery Letterman Gen. Hosp., San Francisco, 1957-59; resident in thoracic surgery Walter Reed Gen. Hosp., Washington, 1966-68; staff Meth. Hosps., Gary and Merrillville, Ind., St. Anthony Med. Ctr., Crown Point, Ind.; med. dir. Gary works U.S. Steel, 1979-94; cons. in occupl. medicine, from 1995; clin. asst. prof. surgery N.W. Ctr. for Med. Edn., Ind. U. Med. Sch., from 1982. Col. U.S. Army, 1956-79. Fellow Am. Coll. Surgeons, Am. Coll. Occupl. and Environ. Medicine; mem. AMA. Home: Valparaiso, Ind. Died Mar. 5, 2010.

NOVAK, TERRY LEE, dean, educator; b. Chamberlain, SD, Sept. 1, 1940; s. Warren F. and Elaine M. N.; m. Barbara Hosea, Aug. 29, 1981; 1 child, David. B.Sc., S.D. State U., 1962; postgrad. (Rotary fellow), U. Paris, 1962-63; M.P.A., Colo. U., 1965, PhD, 1970. Asst. city mgr. City of Anchorage, 1966-68; city mgr. City of Hopkins, Minn., 1968-74, City of Columbia, Mo., 1974-78, City of Spokane, Wash., 1978-91; v.p. bus. and fin. Ea. Wash. U., Cheney, 1991—94, prof. public adminstrn., from 1992, dir. grad. program pub. administrn., 1994-95; dir. Spokane Joint Ctr. for Higher Edn., 1995-98; bus. mgr. Riverpoint campus Wash. State U., 1998-99; prof pub. adminstrn. Eastern Wash. U., from 1999. Asst. adj. prof. U. Mo., Columbia, 1975, 77; adj. instr. Gonzaga U., Spokane, 1986-88; mem. nat. adv. coun. on environ. policy and tech. EPA. Author: Special Assessment Financing in American Cities, 1970; contbr. articles to profl. jours. Mem. ASPA, Internat. City Mgrs. Assn. (Acad. Profl. Devel.). Episcopalian. Home: Spokane, Wash. Died Aug. 15, 2009.

NOVAK, THOMAS J., retired lawyer; b. Chgo., July 17, 1940; s. Edward W. and Margaret R. (Rocket) N.; children: Tricia, Amie, Brandi. BBA, Marquette U., 1964; JD, Loyola U., Chgo., 1967. Bar: Ariz. 1968, U.S. Dist. Ct. Ariz. 1968, U.S. Supreme Ct. 1972. Chief adminstrv. dep. Maricopa County, Phoenix, 1968-72; ct. commr. Maricopa County Superior Ct., Phoenix, 1973-77; ptnr. Sullivan & Novak, Phoenix, 1977-79; judge pro tempore Superior Ct. Ariz., from 1978; pvt. practice Phoenix, 1979—2004; ret., 2004. Instr. Glendale (Ariz.) C.C., 1972-79; lectr. Ariz. State Bar, Phoenix, 1973—. Recipient Outstanding Svc. award Boy Scouts Am., 1978, Top Lawyers, Phoenix Mag., 1998. Mem. Ariz. State Bar Assn. (past chmn. family law com. 1972-73), Ariz. Dist. Atty. Assn. (charter pres. 1972-73). Avocation: bowling. Home: Phoenix, Ariz. Died Jan. 5, 2009.

NOVICK, DAVID, civil engineer, educator; b. NYC, May 14, 1926; s. Harry and Charlotte (Menzin) N.; m. Minna Sommer, Aug. 28, 1953; children: Martha, Linda, Emily. BSCE, Columbia U., 1948, MS, 1954. Registered profl. engr., Ill., N.Y.; registered structural engr., Ill. Founds. and soils engr. Tippetts-Abbett-McCarthy-Stratton, NYC, 1948-54; found., structural engr., exec. v.p. Goodkind & O'Dea, Inc., Hamden, Conn., 1954-56, Chgo., 1956-60; pres. Westenhoff & Novick, Inc., Chgo., 1960-77; exec. v.p. Lester B. Knight & Assos., Chgo., 1977-81; sr. v.p. Parsons, Brinckerhoff, Quade & Douglas, Inc., Chgo., 1981-92, cons., 1992-93; assoc. dir. Urban Systems Lab., U. Ill., Chgo., 1977; adj. prof. systems engring. U. Ill., 1977-80; prin. Dana Engring. Corp., from 1993. Mem. Dispute Resolution Bds., Met. Washington, 1995—; lectr. civil engring. Ill. Inst. Tech., 1970-76; mem., sec. Ill. Structural Engr. Exam Com., 1970-75; Crom lectr. U. Fla., 1982; bd. overseers Armour Coll., Ill. Inst. Tech., 1989-94; ATLSS lectr. Lehigh U., 1994. Author: Life Cycle Considerations in Infrastructure Management, FHWA Life Cycle Cost Symposium, 1993. Trustee North Suburban Mass Transit Dist., 1970-74; bd. dirs. Open Lands Project, 1986-95, exec. com., 1989-92; active METRA Commuter Rail System, Citizen's Adv. Bd., 1992—. With AUS, 1944-46. Fellow ASCE (nat. dir. 1977-80, pres. Ill. sect., co-chmn. task com. nat. civil engring. edn. conf. 1979, Washington Award Commn. 1972-78, 91—, chmn. publs. com. 1979-80, task com. on civil engring. edn. 1981-85, chmn. task com. on Civil Engring. Rsch. Found. 1986-88, chmn. com. engring. mgmt. at orgn. level 1987-88, mem. strategic planning com., 1988-90, Ill. sect. Chgo. Civil Engr. of Yr. 1987, Profl. Activities Com. 1991-96), Civil Engr. Rsch. Found. (chmn. implementation task force 1991-92, ASCE practitioner-in-residence program 1992, 93), Am. Cons. Engrs. Coun. (chmn. com. fellows 1992-94, mem. ACEC constrn. liaison com. 1995—); mem. NSPE (life), ASTM, Am. Ry. Engring. Assn., Ill. Soc. Profl. Engrs. (v.p. 1963-64), Cons. Engrs. Coun. Ill. (bd. dirs. 1989-96, v.p. 1991-92, pres.-elect 1993, pres. 1994, nat. dir. 1995-96), Western Soc. Engrs. (trustee 1972-78), Internat. Soc. Bridge and Structural Engrs., Internat. Soc. Soil Mechanics and Found. Engrs., Soc. Am. Mil. Engrs. (Pub. Svc. award Chgo. Post 1981), Am. Arbitration Assn. (panel arbitrators and mediators), Univ. Club (Chgo.), Chi Epsilon (hon.). Home: Chicago, Ill. Died Mar. 10, 2010.

NOWICK, ARTHUR STANLEY, metallurgy and materials science educator; b. NYC, Aug. 29, 1923; s. Hyman and Clara (Sperling) N.; m. Joan Franzblau, Oct. 30, 1949; children: Jonathan, Steven, Alan, James. AB, Bklyn. Coll., 1943; A.M., Columbia U., 1948, PhD, 1950. Physicist NACA, Cleve., 1944-46; instr. U. Chgo., 1949-51; asst. prof., then assoc. prof. metallurgy Yale U., 1951-57; mgr. metallurgy research IBM Corp Research Center, Yorktown Heights, NY, 1957-66; prof. metallurgy Columbia U., 1966-90, Henry Marion Howe prof. metallurgy and materials sci., 1990-95, prof. emeritus, from 1996. Adj. prof. chem. engring. and materials sci. dept. U. Calif., Irvine, 2001; Frank Golick lectr. U. Mo., 1970; vis. prof. Technion, Haifa, Israel, 1973; co-chmn. Internat. Conf. Internal Friction, 1961, 69; cons. in field. Author: Crystal Properties Via Group Theory, 1995; co-author: Anelastic Relaxation in Crystalline Solids, 1972; co-editor: Diffusion in Solids, 1975, Diffusion in Crystalline Solids, 1984; contbr. articles to profl. jours. Named David Turnbull lecturer Materials Rsch. Soc., 1994; gold medalist Internat. Conf. Internal Friction, 1989. Fellow AIME, Am. Phys. Soc.; mem. Materials Rsch. Soc. (Turnbull lectr. 1994), Sigma Xi (pres. Kappa chpt. 1983-85). Home: Newport Beach, Calif. Died July 21, 2010.

NOYES, RICHARD, state legislator; b. Claremont, NH, May 20, 1923; m. Joan Noyes; 6 children. Grad. H.S., Peterborough, NH. Mem. Dist. 26 N.H. Ho. of Reps.; mem. Munic and County Govt. Coms.; editor, pub. Del. N.H. Constl. Conv., 1974, 84; pres. Bd. of Trade, 1977-78; trustee, mem. exec. com. Schalkenbach Found.; chmn. Coun. Georgist Orgns., 1990-94. Home: Salem, NH. Died May 15, 2009.

NYIKOS, MICHAEL STEPHEN, college official; b. South Bend, Ind., Sept. 8, 1933; s. Michael Paul and Elizabeth (Bukovits) N.; m. Doris Louise Hollister, Aug. 16, 1952; children: Michele, Christopher, Stephen, Maureen. BA cum laude, N.Mex. Highlands U., 1957; MA, U. Mich., 1959, PhD, 1970. Tchr., coach Sound Bend Sch. Corp., 1959-61, adminstr., 1962-64; mem. faculty, adminstr. Ft. Lewis Coll., Durango, Colo., 1964-79, dean students, 1970-79; dean student affairs, v.p. external rels. Colo. Sch. Mines, Golden, 1979-89; v.p. instnl. advancement, exec. asst. to pres. Mesa State Coll., Grand Junction, Colo., from 1989. Chmn., bd. dirs. Ctr. for Applied Rsch. in Prevention Abuse, Boulder, Colo., 1987—. Bd. dirs. United Way, Grand Junction, 1989-92; mem. Grand Junction Park Adv. Bd., 1990—, Rep. Presdl. Task Force, Nat. Rep. Senatorial Com. Named hon. col. 115th Engr. Rgts., 1986. Mem. NRA, Club 20 (officer, bd. dirs. 1991—), Rotary (past officer Grand Junction, bd. dirs. 1990-91), Phi Delta Kappa. Republican. Roman Catholic. Avocations: hunting, golf, reading, writing, weightlifting. Home: Grand Junction, Colo. Died Feb. 10, 2010.

NYMAN, ROBERT J., state legislator; b. Malden, Mass., Aug. 20, 1960; m. Rhonda L. Mem. Hanover Sch. Com., 1979—84, Plymouth Co. Charter Com., 1984—87, from 1993; with McDonald Funeral Home, Mass., from 1985; chmn. Hanover Selectmen; adminstrv. asst. to Senator Russell

Cafedon Mass. State Senate, 1995—99; mem. 5th Plymouth Dist. Mass. House of Reps., 1999—2010. Mem.: KofC - Richard Cardinal Cushing Coun., Mass. Assn. Sch. Com., Mass. Munic Assn., Rockland Eagles No 841, Weymouth Lodge Elks. Democrat. Roman Catholic. Died June 25, 2010.

O'BRIEN, JAMES FRANCIS, chemistry educator; b. Phila., July 4, 1941; s. Francis J. and Marie D. (Smith) O'B.; m. Barbara L. Wiley, June 6, 1970; children: Ted, Michael. BS, Villanova U., 1964; PhD, U. Minn., 1968. Postdoctoral fellow Los Alamos (N.Me.) Sci. Lab., 1968-69; disting. prof. of chemistry S.W. Mo. State U., Springfield, from 1969. Home: Springfield, Mo. Died June 14, 2010.

O'BRIEN, ROBERT JOHN, JR., public relations executive, former government official, air force officer; b. Wheeling, W. Va., Apr. 16, 1935; s. Robert John and Martha Virginia (Hunter) O'B.; m. Margaret Eugenia Schultz BS in Journalism, Northwestern U., Evanston, Ill., 1957; MA in Journalism, U. Wis., Madison, 1970; grad., Indsl. Coll. Armed Forces, 1977. Comnd. officer U.S. Air Force, 1957, advanced through grades to col.; dir. pub. affairs N. Am. Air Def. Command, Colorado Springs, Colo., 1977-80, Air Force Systems Command, Camp Springs, Md., 1980-82; dir. def. info. Office Sec. Def., Washington, 1982-83, dep. asst. sec. def., 1983-86; dir. pub. rels., Washington McDonnell Douglas Corp., Arlington, Va., 1986-97; v.p. pub. rels. The Boeing Co., Arlington, Va., 1997-99. Decorated D.S.M., Legion of Merit, Bronze Star, Air medal, Honor medal (Republic Vietnam) Mem. Air Force Assn., Pub. Rels. Soc. Am., Aviation/Space Writers Assn., U.S. Space Found., Ret. Officers Assn., Williamsburg Nat. Golf Club. Republican. Methodist. Avocations: golf, stamp collecting/philately, model railroading. Home: Williamsburg, Va. Died Mar. 20, 2010.

O'BRIEN, THOMAS CLEMENT, college professor; b. NYC, July 10, 1938; s. Thomas Clement and Dorothy (Beers) O'B.; m. Gail Patricia Marshall, July 1, 1961; children: Thomas C. III, Ellen Marie, Virginia Ann. BS, Iona Coll., 1959; MA, Columbia U., 1960; PhD, NYU, 1968. Sr. editor Macmillan Co., NYC, 1961-63; rsch. assoc. Ednl. Rsch. Coun., Cleve., 1963-68; asst. prof. Boston U., 1968-70; assoc. prof. So. Ill. U., Edwardsville, 1970-76, prof., from 1976. Author: (book) Solve it Books, 1978, Tantalizers, 2000, Palm Software, 2004, Sunburst Software, 1992 Democrat. Roman Catholic. Home: Walnut Creek, Calif. Died June 26, 2009.

O'BRIEN, WILLIAM JOHN, ecology researcher; b. Summit, NJ, Nov. 30, 1942; m. Mavion Meier, 1964; children: Connor, Shay, Lia BA, Gettysburg Coll., 1965; postgrad., Cornell U., 1965-69; PhD, Mich. State U., 1970. sch. rsch. assoc. Ctr. Northern Studies, 1977; disting. lectr. Kans. Acad. Sci., 1990. From asst. prof. to prof. aquatic ecology U. Kans., Lawrence, 1971—2000, full prof., from 1982, dir. exptl. and applied ecology program, 1994—99, chair dept. sys. and ecology, 1991—96. Rsch. scientist Ecosys. Ctr. Marine Biol. Lab., from 1986. Grantee NSF, 1975—. Mem.: Internat. Assn. Theoretical and Applied Limnology, Am. Fisheries Soc., Am. Soc. Limnology and Oceanography. Died Aug. 15, 2009.

O'BYRNE, BRYAN JAY, actor, director; b. Plattsburgh, NY, Feb. 6, 1931; s. Elmer Denney and Bessie Mae (Ducatte) O'B.; 1 son, Sean Kevin (dec.). BS, M.F.A., SUNY, Plattsburgh. Appeared: numerous motion pictures, including The Apple Dumpling Gang Rides Again; appeared: numerous motion pictures, including Hero At Large, Love At First Bite, Fluffy, Dead Ringer, One Man's Way, Two for the Seasaw, Who's Minding the Mint, Gunfight at Abilene, Marnie, Million Dollar Duck, The Great White Hope, Gus, The Car; appeared on: Movies of the Week for TV, including Every Man Needs One; Movies of the Week for TV including It Happened One Christmas, Curse of the Black Widow, Sex and the Married Woman, Rich Man, Poor Man, Book One, The Norliss Tapes, The Year of the Big Cat, High Flying Spy, Killer By Night, The Last Day; other TV appearances include Bob Hope Chrysler Special, Baretta, Maude, C.P.O. Sharkey, Phyllis, Joe Forrester, Matt Helm, Wonderful World of Disney, CBS Salutes Lucy-The First 25 Years, McMillan and Wife, The Night Stalker, Happy Days, Sanford and Son, Bob Newhart Show, Diana Rigg Show, Temperatures Rising, The Partridge Family, Barefoot in the Park, The Bill Cosby Show, The Governor and J.J., Love American Style, Alfred Hitchcock, Big Valley, Gunsmoke, The Fugitive; numerous TV and radio commls.; stage plays Sweet Bird of Youth, Sunrise at Campebello, Duel of Angels, The Glass Menagerie, Skin of Our Teeth, The Miracle Worker; dir.: stage plays The Last Pad. Served with AUS, 1954-55. Mem. N.Y. State Tchrs. Assn., Actors Equity Assn., Screen Writers Guild, Catholic Actors Guild, AFTRA, Acad. TV Arts and Scis. Democrat. Roman Catholic. Died Dec. 4, 2009.

O'CONNELL, WILLIAM RAYMOND, JR., educational consultant, retired academic administrator; b. Richmond, Va., Jan. 4, 1933; s. William Raymond and Mary Helen (Wenenger) O'C.; m. Peggy Annette Tucker, June 29, 1957; 1 child, William Raymond III. B of Music Edn., Richmond Profl. Inst., 1955; MA, Columbia U., 1962, EdD, 1969; HLD (hon.), New Eng. Coll., 1995. Asst. to provost Richmond Profl. Inst., Va., 1955-57, dean of men, 1957-59, dean of students, dean of men, 1959-61; asst. to provost, dir. student info. ctr. Tchrs. Coll. Columbia U., NYC, 1962-65, rsch. asst. inst. of higher edn. Tchrs. Coll., 1965-66; rsch. assoc. So. Regional Edn. Bd., Atlanta, 1966-69, dir. spl. programs, 1969-73, project dir., undergrad. edn. reform, 1973-79; dir. curriculum and faculty devel. Assn. Am. Colls., Washington, 1979-80, v.p. for programs, 1980-82, v.p., 1982-85; pres. New Eng. Coll., Henniker, NH, 1985-95, pres. emeritus, 1995—2009; vis. sr. fellow Assn. Am. Colls. and Univs., 1995—97; dir. health edn. and leadership program Nat. Assn. Student Pers. Adminstrs., 1996—2002, 2003—05. Cons. Coun. for Advancement Small Colls., 1975; adv. com. project on instnl. renewal through improvement of tchg. Soc. for Values in Higher Edn., 1975-78; evaluator NH Postsecondary Edn. Commn., 1987-95, vice chmn., 1990-92, chmn., 1992-94; evaluator Nat. Ctr. for Rsch. to Improve Postsecondary Tchg. and Learning, 1987-90, New Eng. Assn. Schs. and Colls., 1988, 91; higher edn. rev. panel awards for pioneering achievements in higher edn. Charles A. Dana Found., 1988, 89. Author, editor: articles to profl. publs. Pres. Richmond Cmty. Amb. Project, 1958-60, bd. dirs., 1960-61; bd. dirs. Alumni Assn. Acad. divsn. Va. Commonwealth U., 1970-73; chmn. fundraising com. Atlanta Boys Choir, Inc., 1976-77, trustee 1978-79; trustee Atlanta Coun. for Internat. Visitors, 1973-76, 78-79; pres. UN Assn., Atlanta, 1976-77; steering com. Nat. Coun. chpt., divsn. pres. UN Assn. US, 1977-79, nat. coun., 1980-90; steering com. Leadership Concord, 1992-95, chmn., 1994-95. Named Cmty. Amb. to Sweden Cmty. Amb. Project of the Experiment in Internat. Living, 1956. Fellow Royal Soc. of the Arts UK (life); mem. NH Coun. on World Affairs (bd. dirs. 1993-95), Williamsburg AIDS Network (bd. dirs., 2006-08), Greater Concord C. of C. (bd. dirs. 1989-93), Coordinating Coun. for Internat. Univs. (bd. dirs. 2001-06), Va. Commonwealth U. Alumni Assn. (bd. dirs. 2006-09), Phi Delta Kappa. Methodist. Avocations: antiques, travel. Home: Williamsburg, Va. Died Oct. 19, 2009.

O'CONNOR, DANIEL BARRY, brokerage house executive; b. NYC, Feb. 23, 1945; s. Joseph A. and Louise G. (Lucht) O'Connor. BA, Yale U., 1966; JD, Columbia U., 1969. Bar: NY 1970. Assoc. Dewey Ballantine Bushby Palmer & Wood, NYC, 1969—76; investment banker Paine Webber, NYC, from 1976. Home: New York, NY. Died May 2, 2010.

O'CONNOR, LEONARD ALBERT, utilities executive; b. Springfield, Mass., Nov. 19, 1926; s. James W. and Eva (Tatro) O'C.; children: Anita M., Charles F., Stephen J., Thomas J. BA, U. Mass., 1950; MA, U. N.C., 1951; JD, U. Conn. Law Sch., 1973. Utilities analyst SEC, Washington, 1951-52; various exec. positions to tax accountant Conn. Light & Power Co., 1952-66; tax mgr. N.E. Utilities, Hartford, Conn., 1966-70, treas., 1970-89; v.p., chief fin. officer Yankee Energy System, Inc., Rocky Hill, Conn., from 1989, now v.p., cons. Meriden, Conn. Bd. dirs. Bay Bank Conn. Served with USNR, World War II. Mem. ABA, Conn. Bar Assn., Am. Econ. Assn., Tax Execs. Inst. Home: Wethersfield, Conn. Died Aug. 6, 2009.

O'DELL, KAROL JOANNE, experimental prototype company executive; b. Lafayette, Colo., Jan. 4, 1936; d. Clarence Willis and Thelma (Stoner) O'D. Student Wayne State U., 1953-56, U. Detroit, 1956-57. Sec. IBM, Detroit, 1957-59; from bookkeeper to office mgr. Jo-Ad Industries, Inc., 1959-84, v.p., 1984—. Treas. Detroit Puppeteers Guild, 1983—; active Salvation Army. Mem. Nat. Assn. Female Execs., Fellowship Christian Magicians, Puppeteers Am., Fellowship Christian Puppeteers, Unima U.S.A., Commerce Alumni Assn. Avocations: puppetry; religious education; reading. Home: Sterling Heights, Mich. Died Jan. 21, 2009.

ODENKIRCHEN, CARL JOSEF, Romance languages and literatures educator; b. Duisburg/Kaldenhausen, Germany, Jan. 28, 1921; came to U.S., 1929, naturalized, 1940; s. Apollinaris and Paula (Orth) O.; m. Stella Esther Goldberg, Sept. 6, 1948; children: David Michael, Susan Elizabeth. AB, Coll. Charleston, SC, 1942; MA, U. Chgo., 1947; PhD, U. N.C., 1951; postdoctoral study, Sorbonne, Paris, 1953-54. Instr. Romance langs. U. N.C., 1947-49; instr. French and Spanish, Tchrs. Coll., SUNY-Albany, 1950-53; asst. prof. classical and modern langs. Lake Forest (Ill.) Coll., 1956-58; asso. prof. Romance langs. and humanities SUNY-Albany, 1958-61, prof. Romance langs. and comparative lit., 1961-76, prof. Romance langs. and lit., 1976-86, prof. emeritus, from 1986, chmn. dept. comparative lit., 1962-71. Vis. prof. Boston U., 1966-68 Author: A Preliminary Chrestomathy of Old Catalan, 1949, The Play of Adam (Ordo Representacionis Ade), 1976, The Life of St. Alexius, 1978. Mem. Albany Symphony Orch., 1958-61. Served with AUS, 1942-45. Fulbright scholar U. Rome, 1950 Home: Raleigh, NC. Died July 9, 2009.

O'DONNELL, CHARLES PATRICK, retired newspaper executive, consultant; b. Cleve., Nov. 14, 1920; s. Charles Richard and Ella (Kilbane) O'D.; m. Mary Rita Monroe, May 17, 1944 (dec.); children: C. Patrick, Mary, Martha, Robert J. BBA, Case Western Res. U., 1942; IA, Harvard U., 1943. Salesman, research exec. IBM, 1946-52; mgmt. cons., partner Robert Heller & Assos., 1952-56, 59-64; pres. Electronic Tabulating Co., 1956-59; asst. controller East Ohio Gas Co., Cleve., 1964-66; v.p. Providence Gravure, Inc., 1966-69, Providence Journal Co., 1969-78, sr. v.p., 1978-85; pres. O'Donnell & Assocs., Providence, from 1985. Bd. dirs. Charlotte Printing Co., Jackson Newspapers, Inc., Sun Coast Media Group, Inc., Manisses Communications Group, Inc. Treas. Pomenade Indsl. Center Assn., 1981; trustee Providence Preservation Soc., 1981—, v.p. 1986-87; trustee R.I. Philharm. Orch., 1979—, 1st v.p., 1985—, pres., 1987—; active R.I. Hist. Soc., 1984-87; vice chmn. Providence Off-Street Parking Commn., 1986—; trustee St. Joseph Hosp., 1973-77, Indsl. Found. R.I., 1973—. Served to lt. USNR, 1943-46. Mem. Providence C. of C. (dir. 1973-77), Am. Newspaper Publishers Assn., New England Newspaper Assn. (pres. 1985), Hope Club, Agawam Hunt Club (Providence), Dunes Club (Narragansett, R.I.), Knights of Malta, Phi Beta Kappa. Roman Catholic. Home: Providence, RI. Died Feb. 20, 2009.

O'FLAHERTY, PAUL BENEDICT, lawyer; b. Chgo., Feb. 11, 1925; s. Benedict Joseph and Margaret Celestine (Harrington) O'F.; m. Catherine Margaret Bigley, Feb. 13, 1954; children: Paul, Michael, Kathleen, Ann, Neil. JD cum laude, Loyola U., Chgo., 1949. Bar: Ill. 1949, U.S. Dist. Ct. (no. dist.) Ill. 1949, U.S. Ct. Appeals (7th cir.) 1956, U.S. Supreme Ct. 1959. Ptnr. Madden, Meccia, O'Flaherty & Freeman, Chgo., 1949-56; ptnr. Groble, O'Flaherty & Hayes, Chgo., 1956-63, Schiff Hardin & Waite, Chgo., from 1963. Mem. adj. faculty Loyola U., 1959-65 Author: (with others) Illinois Estate Administration, 1983; contbr. articles to profl. jours. Bd. advisors Cath. Charities, Chgo., 1979-92; trustee Clarke Coll., Dubuque, Iowa, 1982—. Served to 2d lt. U.S. Army, 1943-46. Fellow Am. Coll. Trust and Estate Counsel; mem. ABA, Ill. Bar Assn. (past chmn. fed. taxation sect. council), Chgo. Bar Assn. (past chmn. trust law com.), Chgo. Estate Planning Council Clubs: Union League, Metropolitan (Chgo.). Died Jan. 8, 2010.

OFSOWITZ, PAULA JOYCE, data processing executive; b. Detroit, Nov. 21, 1942; d. Samuel and Pearl (Bernstein) Ofsowitz. Student, Dade County Jr. Coll., Fla., 1961—62. Programming cert. control data instr. 1971, cert. Inst. Advanced Tech., 1982. Programmer Fla. Comml. Banks, Inc., Miami, 1972—73, First Fed. Savs. and Loan, Miami, 1973—77; contract programmer Computer Dynamics, Inc., Southfield, Mich., 1977—79; tech. team leader, sr. sys. programmer, tech. instr., sys. engr. Four Phaze Sys., Inc., Southfield, 1979—80, Cupertino Calif., from 1981. Mem.: Smithsonian Inst. Assocs. Democrat. Died July 30, 2009.

OGLE, PEGGY ANN, human services consultant; b. Washington, Feb. 3, 1950; d. William Paul and Lurlene (Lazenby) Ogle. A.A., Miami Dade Coll., 1969; B.S., Fla. State U., 1972, M.S., 1976. Cert. tchr., Fla. Spl. educator Jackson County Schs., Marianna, Fla., 1972-73; edn. dir. Sunland-Tallahassee, Fla., 1974-76; program supr. BARA, Tallahassee, 1976-77; program examiner Dept. of H.R.S., Tallahassee, 1977-79; program adminstr. Dept. of H.R.S.-V., St. Petersburg, Fla., 1979; dir. client services PARC Ctr., St. Petersburg, 1979-82; pres. Program Design Inc., St. Petersburg, 1982—, Personal Fitenss by Program Design Inc.; strategic planning cons. Ann Storck Ctr., Ft. Lauderdale, Fla., 1982-86; cons. State of Fla., Tallahassee, 1982-86; staff trainer, cons. ARA DevCon, Tallahassee, 1984-86; researcher, cons. L.R. O'Neall & Assocs., Tallahassee, 1984-86; mgr. quality assurance contract Healthcare and Retirement Corp. Am. Author: Being Human, 1983, Mirador: An Assessment Guide for Persons with Profound Functional Defecits and Complex Health Care Needs; editor: Developmental Nursing, 1985; contbr. articles to profl. jours. Chmn. Pinellas County Housing Coalition, St. Petersburg, 1982-83. State of Fla. grad. fellow, 1975; recipient Citizenship award, DAR, 1972. Mem. Am. Assn. Mental Deficiencies (gen. div. chmn. S.E. affiliate), Assn. for Severly Handicapped, Life Concepts, Inc. Avocations: tennis; swimming; skiing. Home: Saint Petersburg, Fla. Died Dec. 10, 2009.

OH, JOHN KIE-CHIANG, political science professor, academic administrator; b. Seoul, Nov. 1, 1930; came to U.S., 1954, naturalized, 1971; s. Sung-Jun and Duk-Cho (Kim) O.; m. Bonnie Cho, Sept. 5, 1959; children: Jane J., Marie J., James J. BS, Marquette U., 1957; postgrad., Columbia U., 1957-58; PhD, Georgetown U., 1962. Asst. prof. St. Thomas Coll., St. Paul, 1962-66; assoc. prof. polit. sci. Marquette U., Milw., 1967-71, prof., chmn., 1971-77, dean grad. sch., 1977-85; acad. v.p. Cath. U. Am., Washington, 1985-89, Banigan scholar, prof. dept. politics, 1990-2001, prof. emeritus, from 2001. Adviser Republic of Korea Embassy, 2001—03; nat. chmn. Asian Sect. Fulbright Hays Program. Author: Korea: Democracy on Trial, 1968, (with Peter Cheng et al) Emerging Roles of Asian Nations in the 1980's, 1979, Democratization and Economic Development in Korea, 1990, Korean Politics: The Quest for Democratization and Economic Development, 1999, Thai transl., 2004, The Korean Embassy in America, 2003; contbr. articles to profl. jours. Chmn. scholarship com. World Affairs Coun., 1976-78; mem. Wis. Gov.'s Commn. for UN, Madison, 1971-74; chmn. Korean Studies com., Assn. Asian Studies, 1975-76. Grantee Hill Found., 1963, Relm Found., 1968, Social Sci. Rsch Coun., 1973, Am. Coun. Learned Socs., 1973. Mem. Am. Polit. Sci. Assn., Assn. Asian Studies, Internat. Polit. Sci. Assn., Midwest Conf. Asian Affairs (pres. 1970-71), Assn. Cath. Colls. and Univs. (bd. dirs. 1983-87), Indian Spring Country Club (bd. govs. 2000). Roman Catholic. Home: Evanston, Ill. Died May 29, 2010.

OH, TAI KEUN, business educator, consultant; arrived in US, 1958, naturalized, 1969; m. Gretchen Brenneke Oh, Dec. 26, 1964; children: Erica, Elizabeth, Emily. BA, Seijo U., 1957; MA, Northern Ill. U., 1961; MLS, U. Wis., 1965, PhD, 1970. Asst. prof. mgmt. Roosevelt U., Chgo., 1969—73; assoc. prof. Calif. State U., Fullerton, 1973—76, prof. mgmt., 1976—2001, prof. mgmt. emeritus, from 2001; vis. prof. U. Hawaii, 1983—84, U. Nuertingen, Germany, 1996—97, 1999; advisor Pacific Asian Mgmt. Inst., U. Hawaii; internat. referee Asia-Pacific Jour. Mgmt., from 1990; cons. Calty Design Rsch. Inc.; subs. Toyota Motor Corp.; guest lectr. Chiba U. Commerce, Japan; cons., spkr. in field. Editl. bd. Acad. Mgmt. Rev., 1978—81, contbg. author Ency. Profl. Mgmt., 1978, Handbook of Management, 1985; contbr. articles to profl. jours. Recipient award, Calif. State U., 1987; named Outstanding Prof., Bus. Adminstrn. & Economics, Calif. State U., 1976, 1978; grantee, NSF, 1968—69. Mem.: Acad. Mgmt. Achievements include helped over 100 organizations solve complex human resource and management problems over the course of his career. Home: Brea, Calif. Died Mar. 29, 2010.

O'HARA, ROBERT MELVIN, packaging company executive; b. Phila., Sept. 18, 1926; s. Michael James and Helen (Jeffers) O'H.; m. Grace McGrath, Aug. 21, 1961; children: Ann, James; m. Barbara N. Nichols, Sept. 28, 1974. B.E.E., Ga. Tech. U., 1950; A.M.P., Harvard U., 1969; postgrad., Aspen Inst. for Humanities, 1974. Mgr. beverage div. Atlanta Paper Co., 1953-55, asst. dir. packaging, 1955-57; gen. sales mgr. Mead Packaging Co. (merged with Atlanta Paper Co. 1957), Atlanta, 1957-61, dir. mktg., 1961-63, v.p. mktg., 1963-64, pres., 1969-72; v.p. mktg., mktg. dir. Mead Packaging Europe, Paris, 1964-67; v.p., gen. mgr. Beverage Packaging Co., Atlanta, 1967-69; corp. group v.p. Mead Paper Group, Ohio, 1972-74, Mead Advanced Systems Group, Dayton, 1974-80, sr. v.p., 1980-83; chmn., chief exec. officer KO-

MCO, Dayton, 1983-85, OMS Co., Dayton, from 1985. Bd. dirs. Kerr Glass Co., Los Angeles, TBC Corp., Memphis, UNI/CARE Systems, Detroit; bd. chmn. Cognetics, Inc., London, 1986—; chmn. Entretech Internat./Entretech USA, 1987—. Chmn. Dayton Performing Arts Campaign, 1983; vice chmn. Ga. Industry Assn., 1970-72; bd. dirs. Keep America Beautiful, 1968-72; mgr. campaign Com. to Re-Elect Ford, Montgomery County, Ohio, 1975-76. Served to ensign USN, 1946-47, PTO. Mem. Dayton C. of C. Republican. Episcopalian. Home: Dayton, Ohio. Died Nov. 4, 2009.

OHLSON, DOUGLAS DEAN, artist, educator; b. Cherokee, Iowa, Nov. 18, 1936; s. Lloyd E. and Effie O. (Johnson) O. BA, U. Minn., 1961. Prof. art Hunter Coll., NYC, 1964—2001; ret., 2001. One man shows include Fischbach Gallery, N.Y.C., 1964, 66-70, 72, Susan Caldwell Gallery, N.Y.C., 1974, 76, 77, 79, 81, 82, 83, Portland (Oreg.) Ctr. for Visual Arts, 1977, Ruth Siegel Gallery, N.Y.C., 1985, 87, Andre Zarre Gallery, N.Y.C., 1985, 90, 92, 93, 95, 2000, 04, 09, Gallery 99, Nina Freudenheim Gallery, Buffalo, 1986, Jaffe Gallery, Miami, 1989, Elaine Baker Gallery, Boca Raton, 1986, 2003, Doug Ohlson 20 Years of Painting: 1982-2002, Lorel Tracy Galy Red Bank, NJ, 2006, Elaine Baker Galy, Boca Raton, 2007; group shows include Mus. Modern Art, N.Y.C., 1968, Tate Gallery, London, 1969, Whitney Mus., N.Y.C., 1969, 71, Corcoran Gallery, Washington, 1972, 73, UCLA, 1975, Born in Iowa: The Homecoming, 1986-87, Hunter Coll./Times Sq. Gallery, N.Y.C.; invitational Am. Acad. Arts and Letters, 1992, 94, 97, 2002; represented in permanent collections Met. Mus. Art, N.Y.C., Nat. Gallery Art, Washington, Am. Fedn. Art, Mus. Modern Art, Frankfurt, Fed. Republic Germany, Lowe Art Mus., Miami, Fla., Karl Ernst Osthaus Mus., Hagen, Germany, Mus. Contemporary Art, Helsinki, Mpls. Inst. Art, Dallas Mus., Bklyn. Mus., Whitney Mus., N.Y.C., Harvard Art Mus., Cambridge, Mass. Served with USMC, 1955-58. Guggenheim fellow, 1968; Creative Artists Public Service grantee, 1974; Nat. Endowment for Arts grantee, 1976 Home: New York, NY. Died June 29, 2010.

O'KEEFE, LAWRENCE PATRICK, mechanical engineer, consultant; b. Queens, N.Y., Mar. 4, 1937; s. Vincent F. and Frances A. (O'Melia) O'Keefe; m. Helen R. Lavelle, Nov. 4, 1959; children— Lawrence, Heather, Daniel. B.A. in Econs., Queens Coll., 1959; B.S. in Mech. Engring., N.Mex. State U., 1967; M.S. in Mech. Engring., Cooper Union, 1970. Registered profl. engr., Ga., Fla., Va., N.Y. Project engr. Lunar Module Program, Grumman Aerospace Corp., Bethpage, N.Y. and Las Cruces, N.Mex., 1962-72; ptnr. Cashin Bahrenburg McDowell & O'Keefe Arch-Engrs., Mineola, N.Y., 1972-74; tech. agt. NSF Urban Tech. System, Henrico City, Va., 1974-78; project mgr. Battell So. Ops., Atlanta, 1978-81; v.p., dir. ops. Communications/Electronics Co., Atlanta, 1981; owner Applied Engring. Concepts, Atlanta, 1982—; instr. tech. forecasting Golden Gate U., Hampton, Va., 1977-78. Served to 2d. lt. U.S. Army N.G., 1959-64. Mem. Cons. Engrs. Council, Aircrafts Owners and Pilots Assn. Died Apr. 6, 2010.

O'KEEFE, ROBERT JAMES, retired bank executive; b. Boston, Dec. 30, 1926; s. James J. and Irene (Egan) O'K.; m. Mary U. Hughes, Oct. 12, 1951 (dec.); children: Mary F., Robert James; m. Simone A. Charbonneau, Apr. 3, 1976. AB, Boston Coll., 1951; advanced mgmt. program, Harvard Bus. Sch., 1968. Mem. staff Mass. Inst. Tech., Cambridge, 1951-55; cons. Arthur D. Little, Inc., Cambridge, 1955-58; with Chase Manhattan Bank, NYC, 1958-79, v.p., 1964-69, sr. v.p., 1969-79, Am. Security Bank, Washington, 1979-89; exec. v.p. MNC Info. Svcs., Balt., 1989-90, ret. Trustee Boston Coll., 1974-82, trustee assoc., 1982-86; mem. computer sci. and engring. bd. Nat. Acad. Sci., 1971-73. Served with AUS, 1945-46. Recipient Alumni medal Boston Coll., 1970 Mem. Boston Coll. Alumni Assn. (pres. 1973-74), Am. Legion, KC. Home: Denville, NJ. Died June 17, 2009.

OLASZ, RICHARD D., retired state legislator; b. Homestead, Pa., June 14, 1930; m. Marie Dugan. BS, U. Pitts., 1958. State rep. State of Pa., Dist. 38, Harrisburg, 1981-99. Died Apr. 8, 2010.

OLDS, DAVID MARK, retired broadcasting executive and writer; b. NYC, Dec. 29, 1920; s. Samuel and Dora O.; m. Sally Wendkos, Dec. 18, 1955; children: Nancy, Jennifer, Dorri. BA cum laude, Bklyn. Coll., 1941. Announcer, salesman Sta. KOLO, Reno, Nev., Sta. WNLC, New London, Conn., Sta. WIP, Phila.; program dir. Sta. KYW, Phila., Cleve., 1950-59, Sta. WNEW, NYC, 1959-62; gen. mgr. Sta. WINS, NYC, 1962-65, Sta. WMAQ, Chgo., 1965-68, Sta. WWRL, NYC, 1968-89, Sta. WRVR-FM, 1978-86. Adj. prof. Fordham U. Served to capt. U.S. Army, 1942-46. Decorated Purple Heart. Mem. Internat. Radio and TV Soc. Home: Port Washington, NY. Died Oct. 8, 2009.

O'LEARY, THOMAS HOWARD, resources executive; b. NYC, Mar. 19, 1934; s. Arthur J. and Eleanor (Howard) O'L.; m. Cheryl L. Westrum; children: Mark, Timothy, Thomas, Denis, Daniel, Mary Frances. AB, Holy Cross Coll., 1954; postgrad., U. Pa., 1959-61. Asst. cashier First Nat. City Bank, NYC, 1961-65; asst. to chmn. finance com. Mo. Pacific R.R. Co., 1966-70, v.p. finance, 1971-76, dir., 1972-82, chmn. finance com., 1976-82; treas. Mo. Pacific Corp., St. Louis, 1968-71, v.p. finance, 1971-72, exec. v.p., 1972-74, dir., 1972-82, pres., 1974-82; chmn. bd., CEO Mississippi River Transmission Corp., 1974-82; vice chmn. Burlington No., Inc., Seattle, 1982-89; chmn., CEO Burlington Resources, from 1989. Bd. dirs. BF Goodrich, Kroger Co. Served to capt. USMC, 1954-58. Mem. Blind Brook Club (N.Y.C.), Chgo. Club. Died Apr. 28, 2009.

OLER, WILLIAM HENRY, furniture company executive; b. NYC, Oct. 1, 1923; s. Wesley M. and Imogene (Rubel) Oler; m. Jeanne Harold, Dec. 28, 1946; children: William, Peter, Amy, Imogene. BE, Yale U., 1945. V.p. Hauck Mfg. Co., Lebanon, Pa., 1948—60, F.B. Turck & Co., NYC, 1960—63; v.p. sales Okonite Co., Ramsey, NJ, 1963—69; sr. v.p. ops. Gen. Felt Industries, Inc., Saddle Brook, NJ, from 1969; v.p. Knoll Internat., NYC, from 1981. Pres. Yale Sci. and Engring. Soc., New Haven, 1977—79; trustee Trinity Pawling Sch., NY, from 1982, Choruses of the World, NYC, from 1982. Capt. USMC, 1942—46, PTO. Recipient Yale medal, Yale U., 1981. Mem.: Yale Alumni Assn. Greenwich (pres. from 1986), Yale Club NY (NYC), Innis Arden Golf Club (Old Greenwich, Conn.). Home: Darien, Conn. Died Aug. 28, 2009.

OLIVER, WILLIAM JOHN, pediatrician, educator; b. Blackshear, Ga., Mar. 30, 1925; s. John Wesley and Katherine (Schalwig) O.; m. Marguerite Bertoni, May 28, 1949; children: Ralph Scott, Catherine, Susan. Student, Ga. Southwestern Coll., 1942-43, Mercer U., 1943-44; MD cum laude, U. Mich., 1948. Diplomate Am. Bd. Pediatrics (examiner), Subsplty. Bd. Pediatric Nephrology. Intern, resident U. Mich. Med. Center, 1948-53, dir. pediatric labs., 1959-67; pvt. practice medicine specializing in pediatrics Ann Arbor, Mich., from 1953; instr. dept. pediatrics U. Mich., 1953-56, asst. prof., 1956-61, assoc. prof., 1961-65, prof., 1965, chmn. dept. pediatrics, 1967-79; chief pediatric service Wayne County Hosp., 1958-61. Co-chmn. task force on recent advances of coordinating com. on continuing edn. and recertification Am. Bd. Pediats. and Am. Acad. Pediats., 1977-80; mem. task force for pediatric rev. edn. program, 1980-88; mem. com. program for renewal certification in pediat. Am. Bd. Pediat., 1989-91, mem. exam writing com. for cert. pediatric nephrology, 1989-93, PRCP pilot test com., 1993-96; mem. rev. and question writing com. for Pediat. in Rev. Am. Acad. Pediat., 1991-97; cons. U. Riyadh, Saudi Arabia, 1980, Rsch. Rev. Com. on Pediat., 1989; ednl. cons. dept. pediat. Stanford U. Hosps., 1991-98; mem. self-assessment program for Pediat. in Rev., 1990-98; investigator adaptation primitive So. Ams. Indians, 1976-2010, African Pygmies, 1987-2010, worldwide primitive socs., 1997. Author: Primitive Peoples Without Salt, 1998, Amerindian Children: Mortality Study--Human Behavior and Evolution Society, 2005, child abuse study, 2006, Risk to Children of Computed Tomography, 2010; mem. editl. bd. IRCS Jour. Med. Sci., 1975-90. Pres. Mich. Kidney Disease Found., 1969, Washtenaw County br. Mich. Childrens Aid Soc., 1964; trustee Ann Arbor Hands-On Mus., 1983-88; pres. bd. trustees Perry Nursery Sch., Ann Arbor, 1989-90. With USNR, 1950-52. Fellow Am. Acad. Pediatrics (chmn. com. med. edn. 1974-80, chmn. coun. on pediatric edn. 1975-80, chmn. task force oversight of pediatric rev. and edn. program 1984-88, Clifford G. Grulee award 1979); mem. Soc. Pediatric Rsch., Midwest Soc. Pediatric Rsch. (pres. 1968), Am. Soc. Nephrology, Assn. Med. Sch. Pediatric Dept. Chairmen (mem. coun. 1977-79), Soc. for Exptl. Biology and Medicine, Am. Pediatric Soc., Alpha Omega Alpha, Gamma Sigma Epsilon. Home: Ann Arbor, Mich. Died May 11, 2010.

OLNEY, ROBERT C., diversified products manufacturing executive; b. Bklyn., Aug. 19, 1926; s. Herbert Mason and Martha L. (Otten) O.; m. Wanda G. Olney, July 17, 1948 (dec. 1988); children: Robert C. Jr., Thomas J., Douglas P.; m. Ann Waters Bell, Mar. 14, 1992. BA in Econs., Cornell U., 1946. With Chem. Bank, NYC, 1946-48; various mgmt. positions 3M Co., from 1948; v.p., gen. mgr. 3M-Nat. Adv. Co., Bedford Pk., Ill., 1976-80; chmn., mng. dir. 3M UK plc, Bracknell, Eng., 1980-86; dir. Yale-Valor plc, Chiswick, London, Eng., 1986-91; chmn. Nutone Inc., Cin., 1987-91. Cons. Outdoor Consulting Inc., N.Y.C.; bd. dirs. Honeytree Inc., Mich. Mem. Greenville Country Club, Worshipful Co. of Upholders (London), Royal Automobile Club (London). Avocation: skiing. Home: Montchanin, Del. Died Feb. 27, 2009.

OLSEN, CHARLES FRANK, engineering educator; b. Lakewood, NJ, May 19, 1932; s. Clarence Edward and Elizabeth (Warren) Olsen; m. Lee Brutto Olsen, Sept. 6, 1958; 1 child, Kurt Brian. BS, US Naval Acad., 1954; MSE, George Washington U., 1963; DSc, 1972. Commd. ensign USN, 1954, lt., 1965, edn. specialist Norfolk, Va., 1965—66; prof. US Naval Acad., Annapolis, Md., from 1966, dept. chmn., from 1977, chmn. weapons and sys. engring. dept., from 1977. Contbr. articles to profl. jours. Mem.: Am. Soc. Engring. Edn. Republican. Episcopalian. Home: Annapolis, Md. Died Jan. 16, 2009.

OLSEN, DAVID ALEXANDER, retired insurance company executive; b. Bklyn., Nov. 29, 1937; s. Alexander and Meile (Anderson) O.; m. Roberta Ruth Garverick, May 11, 1963; children: Bradford, Amy. With marine dept. Gt. Am. Ins. Co., NYC and Chgo., 1959-62; acct. exec. Johnson & Higgins, San Francisco, 1966-71, v.p., mgr. marine dept. Chgo., 1971-78, exec. v.p. Ill. br., 1978-79, br. mgr., exec. v.p. Houston, 1979-80, chmn., bd. dirs. Tex. br., 1980-85, exec. v.p. NYC, 1985-87, pres., COO, 1987-93, CEO, 1990-97, chmn., 1991—97. Bd. dirs. U.S. Trust Corp. Trustee Bowdoin Coll., South St. Seaport Mus., Salisbury (Conn.) Congl. Ch., Vis. Nurse Assn., Landmark Vols. 1st lt. U.S. Army, 1960-62. Mem. India House, Sharon Country Club, Psi Upsilon. Avocations: art, photography, antiques, scuba diving, tennis, skiing. Home: Salisbury, Conn. Died Nov. 14, 2009.

OLSEN, KENNETH HAROLD, geophysicist, astrophysicist, historian; b. Ogden, Utah, Feb. 20, 1930; s. Harold Reuben and Rose (Hill) O.; m. Barbara Ann Parson, June 15, 1955; children: Susan L., Steven K., Christopher P., Richard S. BS, Idaho State Coll., 1952; MS, Calif. Inst. Tech., 1954, PhD, 1957. Grad. rsch. asst. Calif. Inst. Tech., Mt. Wilson and Palomar Obs., Pasadena, 1952-57; staff mem., group leader Los Alamos (N.Mex.) Nat. Lab., 1957-89, lab. assoc., 1989-95; geophys. cons. Lynnwood, Wash., from 1989. Vis. rsch. fellow Applied Seismol. Group, Swedish Nat. Def. Inst., Stockholm, Sweden, 1983; sr. vis. scientist fellow Norwegian Seismic Array, Oslo, Norway, 1983; vis. scholar Geophysics Program, U. Wash., Seattle, 1989-91. Author, editor: Continental Rifts: Evolution, Structure, Tectonics, 1995; contbr. articles to profl. jours. Mem. Am. Geophys. Union, Geol. Soc. Am., Seismol. Soc. Am., Am. Astron. Soc., Royal Astron. Soc. Home: Lynnwood, Wash. Died Feb. 15, 2010.

OLSEN, MERLIN JAY, sportscaster, retired professional football player; b. Logan, Utah, Sept. 15, 1940; s. Lynn Jay and Merle (Barrus) O.; m. Susan Wakley, Mar. 30, 1962; children: Kelly Lynn, Jill Catherine, Nathan Merlin. BS in Fin., Utah State U., 1962, MS in Economics, 1970. Defensive tackle Los Angeles Rams, 1962-76; with Allied Chem. Corp., 1962-67; owner Merlin Olsen Porsche Audi; motivational cons. Liggett & Myers, 1971-72, Consol. Cigar, 1972-73; pub. relations exec. Combined Communications Corp., 1972-73; TV spokesman Florists' Transworld Delivery; sports analyst NBC Sports, 1977—93. Actor: (films) The Undefeated, 1969, One More Train to Rob, 1971, Something Big, 1971, Mitchell, 1975; (TV series) Little House on the Prairie, 1977-81, Father Murphy, 1981-83, Fathers & Sons, 1986, Aaron's Way, 1988; (TV movies) A Fire in the Sky, 1975, The Golden Moment: An Olympic Love Story, 1980, The Juggler of Notre Dame, 1984, Time Bomb, 1984, Aaron's Way: The Harvest, 1988; (TV guest appearances) Petticoat Junction, 1970, The Brian Keith Show, 1972, Kung Fu, 1973, Walking Tall, 1981; host, narrator: (TV specials) Lifequest, 1987-89, The Sleeping Beauty, 1987, The Nutcracker, 1990, Fantastic Facts, 1991-92 Grand marshall 94th Tournament of Roses Parade; v.p. So. Calif. Multiple Sclerosis Soc. Recipient Outland Trophy, 1961, Bert Bell award, Maxwell Football Club, 1974; named to NFL Pro Bowl Team, 1962-75, The Coll. Football Hall of Fame, 1980, The Pro Football of Fame, 1982, The 75th Anniversary All-NFL Team, 1994, The Calif. Sports Hall of Fame, 2010; named First Team Al-America, 1960, 1961, NFL Rookie of Yr., 1962, NFL All-Pro, 1964, 1966-70, NFL Pro Bowl MVP, 1968 Mem. Sigma Chi, Phi Kappa Phi. Church Of Jesus Christ Of Latter Day Saints. Home: Pasadena, Calif. Died Mar. 11, 2010.

OLSON, HERBERT THEODORE, trade association executive; b. Bridgeport, Conn., Feb. 9, 1929; s. Herbert Theodore and Inez Evelyn (Lindahl) O.; children: Christina, Victoria; m. Kathleen A. Harrison, Dec. 27, 1988. Student, Heidelberg Coll., 1947-49; AB, Ohio U., 1951, postgrad., 1951-52. Asst. to dean of men Ohio U., Athens, 1951-52; with Union Carbide Corp., 1952-71, mgr. employee rels., coord. pub. affairs NYC, 1969-71; exec. v.p. Am. Assn. for Aging, Washington, 1971-75; dir. spl. projects Am. Healthcare Assn., Washington, 1975-79; pres. Promotional Products Assn. Internat., Irving, Tex., 1979-96, pres. emeritus, from 1996. Event coord.-supplier Stars Showcase, 1998-2000; mem. adv. bd. Allied Bank. Mem. nat. exploring com., vice chmn. nat. events com., ann. meetings com., mem.-at-large nat. coun. Boy Scouts Am., from 1980; treas. U.S. Found. for Internat. Scouting, 1988—99, chmn. audit com., 1984—87, mem. internat. com., 1998—2003, mem. direct svc. coun. bd., 1997—2002; mem. long-term care for elderly rsch. rev. and adv. com. Dept. Health, 1972—77; mem. Longterm Care grant rev. com. HEW, 1972—77; mem. planning commn. City of Torrance, Calif., 1962—64, city councilman, 1964—67; chmn. Gov.'s Operation Leegit; mem. adv. bd. Irving Hosp.; chmn. bd. dirs. Irving Cancer Soc., 1997—2002; exec. bd. cir. 10 coun. Boy Scouts Am., from 1979; bd. mem. Irving chpt. Salvation Army, from 2005, adv. coun. Irving, from 2005; mem. exec. bd. Circle 10 Coun., from 1979; mem. Irving Vistors and Cmty Bur., 2004—05; chmn. Irving Sister Cities, from 2006; bd. dirs. Irving Conv. and Visitors Bur., from 2001, chmn., from 2004; bd. dirs. DFW Humane Soc., from 2001. Lord Baden Powell fellow, 1986; recipient Disting. Eagle award Boy Scouts Am., 1974, Silver Beaver award, 1968, Silver Buffalo award, 1998; named person of Yr. in Promotional Products in Counselor Mag., 1995, Hall of Fame Promotional Products Assn. Internat., 1997, Hall of Fame Can. Promo Prod. Assn., 1996. Mem. Meeting Planners Internat. (charter), Am. Soc. Assn., Execs., U.S. C. of C., Washington Soc. Assn. Execs., Nat. Assn. Exhibit Mgrs., Small Bus. Legis. Coun. (chmn. bd. 1993-95), Dallas Ft. Worth Soc. Assn. Execs. (v.p. 1985-87), Irving C. of C. (bd. dirs. 1999-2004), Am. Advt. Fedn., Am. Cancer Soc. (Irving chpt.), Tex. Soc. Assn. Execs., Las Colinas Country Club, Rotary (bd. dirs. 2004—), Internat. Fellowship Scouting Rotarians (world chmn. 2005-06, internat. commr. 06—), Masons, Shriners, Kiwanis (lt. gov.), DFW Humane Soc. Irving (bd. dirs. 2000-). Baptist. Home: Irving, Tex. Died Apr. 28, 2010.

OLSON, LEROY CALVIN, retired educational administration educator; b. Kane, Pa., Mar. 7, 1926; s. Vernon Reinhold and Gertrude Viola Olson; m. Miriam Marie Vogler, June 19, 1954; children— David Lee, Thomas Edward, Steven Andrew. BS, Clarion State Coll., 1949; M.Ed., Pa. State Coll., 1950; Ed.D., Pa. State U., 1962; postgrad., U. Del., Newark, 1964-65. Tchr.-counselor Boiling Springs H.S., Pa., 1950-52, Gordon Jr. H.S., Coatesville, Pa., 1952-54; guidance dir. Ctrl. Dauphin Sch. Dist., Harrisburg, Pa., 1954-57; coordinator pupil personnel services, asst. supt. for instrn. and personnel, acting supt. Alfred I. duPont Sch. Dist., Wilmington, Del., 1957-65; prof. ednl. adminstrn. Temple U., Phila., 1965-92, prof. emeritus, from 1992. Cons. to schs. bds. and dists., also Nat., Wis., Pa. sch. bds. assns. Contbr. articles to profl. jours. Trustee Luth. Ch., 1963-66, chmn. bd., 1976-78, chmn. various coms., discussion groups. Served with USNR, 1944-46, PTO. Recipient Disting. Alumni award, Clarion State Coll., 1972. Mem. Am. Personnel and Guidance Assn., AAUP, Am. Assn. Sch. Personnel Adminstrs., Assn. Supervision and Curriculum Devel., Council Profs. Instrn. Supervision, Nat. Staff Devel. Council, Am. Legion, Phi Delta Kappa, Phi Kappa Phi. Republican. Home: West Grove, Pa. Died Dec. 5, 2009.

OLSON, M(ELVIN) RICHARD, bank executive, director; b. Chgo. Heights, Ill., Dec. 26, 1942; s. Melvin Richard and Gwenyth (Hills) Olson; life ptnr. BA, Blackburn U., 1964; JD, Chgo.-Kent Coll. Law, 1968. Bar: (Ill.) 1968, (US Dist. Ct. (no. dist.)) 1968. Trust officer & sec. Evanston Trust & Savings, Ill., 1966—68; trust officer Milw. Western Bank,

1969—73; with Mich. Nat. Bank Detroit, Troy, from 1973, group v.p., 1978—82, sr. v.p., from 1982; dir. Centrevest REIT, Southfield, Mich., from 1983, Mich. Nat. Investment Corp., Bloomfield Hills, Mich., from 1984. Sec. Planning Commn. Brandon Twp., Ortonville, Mich., from 1980; chmn. planned giving Am. Cancer Soc. Southeast Mich., 1981—83, Crittendon Hosp., Rochester, Mich., 1980—83. Recipient Achievement award, Am. Cancer Soc., Southfield, 1983. Mem.: Troy C. of C., Fiduciary and Estate Coun. (Detroit) (dir. 1980—84). Home: Rochester Hls, Mich. Died July 28, 2009.

OLSON, PAULA CATHERINE, state official; b. Chgo., Aug. 18, 1938; s. Bernard B. and Pauline Fern (Beam) Ledenbach; m. Thomas J. Olson, Feb. 16, 1957 (div. 1976); children: Michael Scott, Carla Marie. Student, American River Coll., 1969—71. Sec. Aerojet-Gen., Sacramento, 1956—59; legis. sec. State of Calif., Sacramento, 1964—68; exec. sec. Senator A. Sieroty, Calif. Senate, Sacramento, 1968—82; com. sec. revenue and tax. com. Calif. Senate, from 1982. Home: Sacramento, Calif. Died May 24, 2009.

OLSON, RONALD WAYNE, lawyer, judge; b. Chgo., Oct. 29, 1931; s. Philip John and Adeline (Hoffmann) O.; m. Sandra Jane Forbes, Sept. 2, 1967; children— Ronald Wayne, Kirsten Ann. Student, U. Ill., 1949-52; BS, Northwestern U., 1953, JD, 1955; LL.M., Georgetown U., 1958. Bar: Ill. bar 1956. Practice in, Chgo., from 1959; atty. Spencer & Crowe, 1959-62; asst. states atty. Cook County, Ill., 1961-62; atty., mem. firm Rhyne & Rhyne, Washington, 1962-63; atty. Bergstrom, Rohde, Dahlgren & Olson, 1963-73; counsel Bergstrom, Davis & Teeple, from 1973. Lectr. pension-profit sharing plans U. Chgo., 1960; faculty John Marshall Sch. Law, Chgo., 1965—; now assoc. judge Cir. Ct. Cook County, Chgo.; asst. dean, dir. gen. practice grad. sch. Conducted study def. of indigent accused in Cook County under auspices of Ill. Pub. Defenders Assn., 1969 Co-author: Antitrust Adviser, 1978, 3d edit., 1985. Candidate Ill. Constl. Conv., 1969. Served to ensign USNR, 1955-59; capt. JAG Corps Res. ret. Mem. Navy League (judge adv. gen. Chgo. chpt.), Theta Xi, Phi Delta Phi. Home: Chicago, Ill. Died Jan. 17, 2010.

OLTARSH, KENNETH S., lawyer; b. NYC, May 21, 1924; s. Abraham L. and Annabelle W. Oltarsh; m. Naomi D. Oltarsh, Aug. 19, 1955; children: Valerie Oltarsh-McCarthy, Frederic D. BA, Ohio State U., Columbus, 1946; JD, Harvard U., Cambridge, Mass., 1949. Bar: NY 1949, US Ct. Appeals (2d cir.), NY 1956. Atty. Leve Hecht Hadfield & McAlpin, NYC, 1950—52, US Atomic Energy Commn., NYC, 1952—54; ptnr. Duncombe, Oltarsh & Schott, NYC, 1955—62, Solinger & Gordon, NYC, 1962—82, Hall Dickler, LLP, NYC, 1982—2003; of counsel Siller Wilk LLP, NYC, from 2003. Dir. 55 E 66th St. Tenants Corp., NYC, 1981—94, 69th Tenants Corp., NYC, 2001—06; trustee Coldbrook South Unit Owners Trust, Lenox, Mass., 1995—98. Air force cadet USAF, 1943, Maine. Mem.: ABA, Assn. Bar NY, Phi Beta Kappa. Avocation: tennis. Died Aug. 5, 2010.

O'MAHONY, THOMAS PATRICK, air force executive; b. Utica, N.Y., Dec. 31, 1933; s. Charles Joseph and Loretta Veronica (Herman) O'M.; m. Judith Gail Peryer, Sept. 6, 1958; children— Jeannine O'Mahony Robbins, Terrance, Lori. Student Utica Coll., 1956-59, Air War Coll., 1971, Fed. Exec. Inst., 1984, Def. Systems Mgmt. Coll., 1977, Harvard U., 1985. Div. chief Radar Systems, Air Force Electronic Systems Div., Hanscom AFB, Mass., 1972-74, asst. dir., dir. Cobra Dane Radar System, 1974-77, dir., Cobra Judy Radar System, 1977-81, asst. dep. Tactical systems, 1981-83, dep. comdr. Intelligence, Countermeasures and Support Systems, 1983-86, dep. comdr. Devel. Plans and Support Systems, 1986-87, dep. comdr. Advanced Decision Systems, 1987—. Mem. Indsl. Planning Commn., Burlington, Mass., 1973-75. Served with USAF, 1951-55, Korea. Recipient Presdl. rank forMeritorious Service, 1987. Mem. Armed Forces Communications Electronics Assn. (pres. 1985), Air Force Assn., Air Lift Assn. Democrat. Roman Catholic. Avocations: physical fitness; reading; public speaking. Home: Burlington, Mass. Died June 16, 2010.

OMAN, SIDNEY MAYNARD, mayor, funeral home executive; b. Trenton, NJ, Feb. 17, 1928; s. John B. and Martha (Smith) O.; m. Lillian Callis, Aug. 1, 1947; children: Robert Maynard, Susan Lynne. BS, U. N.C., 1951; MS, Echols Coll. Mortuary Sci., 1952. Dir. public relations, City of Norfolk, Va., 1959-64; pres. and owner Gay & Oman Funeral Homes, Inc., Va., from 1947; instr. police sci. dept. Old Dominion U., 1970-80; mayor City of Chesapeake, Va., from 1980. Moderator: TV series The Sounding Bd, Sta., WAVY. Served with USMC, 1946-48. Recipient First Citizens award Tidewater VFW, 1968; First Citizen of Chesapeake, 1969 Mem. Chesapeake C. of C. (pres. 1969-70), Va. State Bd. Funeral Dirs. and Embalmers (pres. 1975-80), Tidewater Funeral Dirs. Assn. (pres. 1974-75), Nat. Conf. Funeral Service Exam. Bds. U.S.A., Nat. Funeral Dirs. Assn., Va. Council Alcoholism and Drug Dependence, Greater Hampton Rds. Indsl. Orgn., U.S. Conf. Mayors, Nat. League Cities, DAV. Clubs: Kiwanis (pres.), Chesapeake Better Bus, Deep Creek Rurtan, Masons, Shriners, Elks. Methodist. Home: Chesapeake, Va. Died Apr. 27, 2009.

O'MARA, ETHEL ROSE, writer, former educator; b. N.Y.C., May 31, 1920; d. Adolf and Rose Marie (Kurtz) Leitner; m. William Patrick O'Mara, July 27, 1974; stepchildren— Patricia, Maureen, Susan, William, Michael. AB, Hunter Coll., 1941; MS, Fordham U., 1952. Lab. asst. Bd. Edn., N.Y.C., 1945-56; sci. tchr. Jr. High Sch., Mamaroneck, N.Y., 1956-57, U.S. Army, Berlin, Fed. Republic Germany, 1957-58, Munich, Fed. Republic Germany, 1958-59; sci. tchr., dept. head Edgemont High Sch., Scarsdale, N.Y., 1959-75; freelance writer, 1980-90; ch. flutist, pianist; presenter travelogue slide shows to small grops. Composer: America Belongs to God. Author: Calamity Cruise With Bright Spots, 1985; contbr. articles to mags. Mem. Natural Resources Def. Coun., Nature Consevancy, Friends of Earth, Environ. Def. Fund, Common Cause, Union of Concerned Scientists, Lincolndale Property Owners Assn. Recipient Bronze medal N.Y.C. Jr. High Sch. Competition; NSF grantee Am. U., 1961, CCNY, 1964, Coll. at Middleburg, Conn., 1967. Roman Catholic. Avocations: travel, music, bridge, golf, photography. Home: Canon City, Colo. Died May 18, 2009.

OMINSKY, HARRIS, lawyer; b. Phila., Sept. 14, 1932; s. Joseph and Lillian (Herman) O.; m. Rosalyn Rita Rutenberg; children— Michelle, David. BS in Econs., U. Pa., 1953, LLB cum laude, 1956. Bar: Pa. 1956. Ptnr. Ominsky & Ominsky, Phila., 1958-64; ptnr. Blank, Rome, Comisky & McCauley, Phila., 1964—2003, Blank Rome LLP, 1964—2003; co-chmn. real estate dept. Blank, Rome, Comisky & McCauley, Phila., 1988-93. Lectr. Law Sch., Temple U., Phila., 1969-71, lectr. Real Estate Inst., 1996—. Author: Real Estate Practice: New Perspectives, 1996, Real Estate Practice: Breaking New Ground, 2001, If I'm Still Around, I Can't Be Dead, 2002, Real Estate Lore, 2006; contbr. columns to newspapers and mags.; contbr. numerous articles to profl. jours. Pres. bd. Phila. Singing City Choir, 1984-88; chmn. zoning com. Merion Civic Assn., Pa., 1984-91. Fellow Am. Bar Found.; mem. ABA (Harrison Tweed Spl. Merit award 1988), Pa. Bar Assn. (ho. of dels. 1984—2004), Pa. Bar Inst. (bd. dirs. 1981—, exec. com. 1986-93, v.p. 1988-89, pres. 1989-90, lectr., planner 1969—), Phila. Bar Assn. (chmn. real estate taxes subcom. 1984-85, real property sect. 1991-92, Leon J. Obermayer Edn. award 1989, Good Deed award real property sect. 1999), Am. Coll. Real Estate Lawyers (bd. govs. 1993-95), Order of Coif. Home: Merion Station, Pa. Died Aug. 16, 2010.

O'NEIL, MICHAEL A., lawyer; b. Toledo, June 22, 1940; BS in Edn., U. Mich., 1963; JD, DePaul U., 1967. Bar: Ill. 1967, Tex. 1969. Mem. Gardere & Wynne, Dallas. Mem. ABA, U.S. Trademark Assn., Licensing Execs. Soc., Am. Intellectual Property Law Assn., Sustaining Life Fellow, State Bar Tex., Dallas Jr. Bar assn. (pres. 1974), Dallas Bar Assn. (bd. dirs. 1983-84, 86, sec.-treas. 1985), Phi Eta Sigma, Pi Tau Sigma, Tau Beta Pi, Phi Alpha Delta. Died Aug. 13, 2009.

O'NEILL, JOHN JOSEPH, speech educator; b. De Pere, Wis., Dec. 6, 1920; s. John Joseph and Elizabeth (Murray) O'N.; m. Dorothy Jane Arnold, Dec. 28, 1943; children— Katherine, Thomas, John, Philip. BS, Ohio State U., 1947, PhD, 1951. From instr. to assoc. prof. speech Ohio State U., 1949-59; prof. speech U. Ill. at Champaign, 1959-91, prof. emeritus, from 1991; prof. audiology U. Ill. Coll. Medicine, Chgo., 1965-79, head speech and hearing sci. dept., 1973-79. Research assoc. U.S. Naval Sch. Aviation Medicine, summers 1953, 54; cons. in field. Co-author: Visual Communication, 1961, 81;, Hard of Hearing, 1964, Applied Audiometry, 1966. Pres. Columbus Hearing Soc., 1956-58; Bd. dirs. Champaign County Assn. Crippled-United Cerebral Palsy, 1961-63. Served with inf. AUS, 1942-46. Decorated Purple Heart, Bronze Star with oak leaf cluster, Jubilee of Liberty medal, France, 2000; recipient Disting. Alumnus award dept. speech Ohio State U., 1969, recipient honors, 1979. Fellow Am. Speech and Hearing Assn. (pres. 1969), Ohio Psychol. Assn.; mem. Am. Bd. Examiners Speech Pathology and Audiology (pres. 1967-68), Acad. Rehabilitative Audiology (pres. 1969) Home: Urbana, Ill. Died June 29, 2009.

OPALA, MARIAN PETER, state supreme court justice; b. Lódz, Poland, Jan. 20, 1921; JD, Oklahoma City U., 1953, BSB in Econs., 1957, LLD (hon.), 1981; LLM, NYU, 1968; HHD, Okla. Christian U. Sci. & Arts, 1981. Bar: Okla. 1953, US Supreme Ct. 1970. Asst. county atty., Oklahoma County, 1953—56; practiced law Oklahoma City, 1956—60, 1965—67; referee Okla. Supreme Ct., Oklahoma City, 1960—65; prof. law Oklahoma City U. Sch. Law, 1965—69; asst. to presiding justice Supreme Ct. Okla., 1967—68; administrv. dir. Cts. Okla., 1968—77; presiding judge Okla. State Indsl. Ct., 1977—78; judge Workers Compensation Ct., 1978; justice Okla. Supreme Ct., 1978—2010, chief justice, 1991—92. Adj. prof. law Okla. City U., 1962-2010, U. Okla. Coll. Law, 1969—; prof. law U. Tulsa Law Sch., 1982-2010; mem. permanent faculty Am. Acad. Jud. Edn., 1970-2010; mem. NYU Inst. Jud. Adminstrn.; mem. faculty Nat. Jud. Coll., U. Nev., 1975-2010; chmn. Nat. Conf. State Ct. Adminstrs., 1976-77; mem. Nat. Conf. Commrs. Uniform State Laws, 1982-2010 Co-author: Oklahoma Court Rules for Perfecting a Civil Appeal, 1969 Mem. Adminstrn. Conf. US, 1993-95. Recipient Herbert Harley award, Am. Judicature Soc., 1977, Disting. Alumni award, Oklahoma City U., 1979, Americanism medal, Nat. Soc. DAR, 1984, ABA/Am. Law Inst. Harrison Tweed Spl. Merit award, 1987, Humanitarian award, NCCJ, 1991, Jour. Record award, 1995, Constn. award, Rogers State U., 1996, Jud. Excellence award, Okla. Bar Assn., 1997, Leo H. Whinery Disting. Svc. award, 1999, Lifetime Achievement award, Oklahoma City Univ. Sch. Law, 2000, First Amendment award, FOI Okla., Inc., 2002; inductee Okla. Hall of Fame, 2000. Mem. ABA (edn. com. appellate judges conf. 1984-93), Okla. Bar Assn. (Earl Sneed Continuing Legal Edn. award 1988, Jud. Excellence award 1997), Okla. County Bar Assn., Am. Soc. Legal History, Oklahoma City Title Lawyers Assn., Am. Judicature Soc. (bd. dirs. 1988-92), Am. Law Inst. (elected), Order of Coif, Phi Delta Phi (Oklahoma City Alumni award). Died Oct. 11, 2010.

OPPENBORN, HENRY LUDWIG, JR., judge; b. Miami, Sept. 19, 1924; s. Henry Ludwig and Nelly Bly (Burr) Oppenborn; m. Bobbie Lee Cameron, Feb. 26, 1955; children: Anna Wilhelmine, Henry Ludwig III, James Burr. AB, U. Fla., 1956; JD, U. Miami, 1960. Bar: Fla. 60, Fla. (U.S. Dist. Ct. (so. dist.)) 1961. Assoc. McDonald & McDonald, Miami, 1960—62, Lally, Miller & Hodges, Miami, 1962—67, Coughlin & Oppenborn, North Miami, Fla., 1967—71; asst. county atty. Dade County, Miami, 1972—73; judge County Ct., State of Fla., Miami, from 1973. Dir. Legal Svcs. Greater Miami, Inc., 1967—70. Maj. US Army, 1943—54. Decorated Silver Star medal, Purple Heart. Mem.: Scottish Rite, 82d Airborne Div. Assn. (chmn. S. Fla. Chpt. 1963—64), Mil. Order World Wars (comdr. 1976—77), Mil. Order of Purple Heart (state and Local comdr. 1965—67), Law Alumni U. Miami (dir. from 1981), Dade County Bar Assn. (dir. 1967—70, cert. of merit 1970), Fla. Bar, Masons (33d deg.), Lions (Miami) (pres. 1968—69), Phi Alpha Delta, Fla. Blue Key. Democrat. Episcopalian. Home: Miami, Fla. Died June 9, 2010.

OPPENHEIMER, VALERIE KINCADE, retired sociology professor; b. London, Oct. 25, 1932; d. Forrest James and Sylvia Doris (Blake) Kincade; m. Edward Anthony Oppenheimer, Apr. 11, 1965 (dec. 2005); 1 son, Christopher. BA, Vassar Coll., 1954; MA, U. Calif.-Berkeley, 1962, PhD, 1966. Asst. prof. sociology U. Ariz., Tucson, 1963-66, U. Ill., Chgo., 1967-69; lectr., asst. prof. sociology UCLA, 1968-73, assoc. prof., 1973-80, prof., 1980—94. Cons. NIH, Washington, 1973-75; mem. Census Adv. Com., 1979-82 Author: Female Labor Force in United States, 1970, Work and the Family, 1982; editor: Aging: Social Change, 1982. Recipient sr. service award NIH, 1981-83; Russell Sage Found. grantee, 1970-77 Mem. Population Assn. Am. (dir. 1974-77, 1st v.p. 1983), Am. Sociol. Assn. (council 1986-88) Home: Los Angeles, Calif. Died Nov. 2, 2009.

ORB, JOHN ALEXANDER, retired investment banker; b. Chgo., Feb. 9, 1919; s. John A. and Rowena (Walker) O.; m. Elizabeth Nevins, Feb. 28, 1942 (dec.); children: John Alexander IV, Joan Orb Garrison, Linda Orb Drake; m. Jean G. Tennant, June 23; 1961. BA, Yale U., 1941. Exec. v.p., dir. Merrill Lynch, Pierce, Fenner & Smith Inc., NYC, until 1974; exec. v.p. Smith Barney, Harris Upham & Co. Inc., NYC, 1975-77, pres., from 1977, chief operating officer, from 1977, chmn., 1982-88, chief exec. officer, from 1982, also dir. Bd. dirs. Chgo. Bd. Trade, 1973; bd. govs. Midwest Stock Exchange, 1965-69 Served to lt. col. USAAF, 1941-46. Decorated D.F.C. Mem. Nat. Assn. Securities Dealers (dist. chmn. 1968), Investment Bankers Assn. (past vice chmn. Central states group), Securities Industry Assn. (dir. 1980-85), Bond Club N.Y., Blind Brook Club, Tavern Club (Chgo.), Hyannisposrt (Mass.) Club, Nat. Golf Links of Am. Home: New York, NY. Died June 26, 2010.

O'REILLY, ROBERT FRANCIS, foreign language educator; b. Watertown, NY, Apr. 8, 1939; s. John Haley and Irene Biche O'R. BA, Syracuse U., 1961; MA, U. Wis., 1963, PhD, 1967. Asst. prof. of French Syracuse (N.Y.) U., 1967-75, assoc. prof. of French, from 1975. Contbr. articles to profl. jours./books. Fulbright fellow Syracuse U., 1961-62. Mem. Modern Lang. Assn., Internat. Assn. on Fantastic in Arts, Phi Beta Kappa. Home: Syracuse, NY. Died Jan. 7, 2009.

ORESMAN, ROGER B., lawyer, director; b. NYC, Oct. 26, 1920; s. A. Louis and Gertrude (Bergel) O.; m. Charlotte Stephenson, June 26, 1948 (div. Jan. 1970); m Janice Carlson Fortenbaugh, Mar 20, 1975; stepchildren: Samuel B. Fortenbaugh IV, Cristina C. Fortenbaugh. AB, Harvard U., 1941, MBA, 1943; LL.B., Columbia U., 1952. Bar: N.Y 1952. Indsl. engr. Botany Mills, N.J., 1946-47; mgmt. cons. Aronson & Oresman, NYC, 1947-49; assoc. Milbank, Tweed, Hadley & McCloy, NYC, 1952-58, ptnr., from 1958. Dir. Amerada Hess Corp., Thomas Jefferson Life Ins. Co. Trustee Randolph-Macon Woman's Coll., Lynchburg, Va. Served to lt. USNR, 1943-46. Mem. Assn. Bar City N.Y. (exec. com. 1959-62) Home: New York, NY. Died Apr. 2, 2010.

ORKIN, LOUIS RICHARD, physician, educator; b. NYC, Dec. 23, 1915; s. Samuel David and Rebecca (Rish) O.; m. Florence Fine, Mar. 5, 1938; 1 dau., Rita. BA, U. Wis., 1937; MD, NYU, 1941; AAS in Marine Tech., Kingsborough Coll., 1992. Intern Bellevue Hosp., NYC, 1942, resident anesthesiology, 1946-48; practice medicine specializing in anesthesiology Bronx, NY, 1946—48; dir. anesthesiology Backus Hosp., Norwich, Conn., 1948-50; asst. prof. anesthesiology NYU Coll. Medicine, 1950-55; prof., chmn. dept. anesthesiology Albert Einstein Coll. Medicine, 1955-82, Disting. univ. prof., 1982-86, dist. univ. prof. emeritus, from 1986. Vis. prof. depts. bioengring., anesthesiology U. Calif., San Diego, 1971; Cons. VA, USPHS, USN; mem. com. anesthesiology Nat. Acad. Scis., 1964-69; mem. com. anesthetic drugs FDA, Dept. Health, Edn. and Welfare, 1970— Author: Patient in Shock, 1965, Physiology of Obstetrical Anesthesia, 1969; Contbr. articles to profl. jours. V.p. and trustee Wood Library Mus. Served to capt. M.C. AUS, 1942-45. Decorated Bronze Star; honoree Albert Einstein Coll. Medicine, 2005. Fellow Am. Coll. Chest Physicians, NY Acad. Sci., NY Acad. Medicine, Am. Coll. Anesthesiology (past chmn. bd. govs.); mem. NY State Soc. Anesthesiologists (past pres.; Disting. Svc. award 2000). Home: New York, NY. Died Apr. 16, 2010.

ORNAUER, RICHARD LEWIS, retired educational association administrator; b. Bklyn., Oct. 19, 1922; s. Edwin L. and Emma (Handler) O.; m. Jane Robb, May 15, 1955 (div. Jan. 7, 1976); children: David S., Michael J., SaraJo; m. J. Rexene Ashford, Nov. 24, 1985. BJ, U. Mo., 1947. Wire editor Coastal Georgian, Brunswick, Ga., 1947-48; reporter copy-reader, night editor, city editor Nassau Daily Rev.-Star, Rockville Centre, N.Y., 1948-53; city editor L.I. Press, Jamaica, N.Y., 1953-71; asst. commr. Nassau County Dept. Social Services, Mineola, 1971-74; pub. health info. program officer Nassau County Dept. Health, Mineola, 1974-87; adminstr. Bur. Epidemiology, 1979-84; dir. communications N.Y. State Sch. Bds. Assn., Albany, 1987-89. Instr. Queens Coll., Flushing, N.Y., 1955-59; instr., mentor AARP Driver Safety Program, Dover, Del., 1993—; asst. state coord. Kent County, Del., 1996—, mem. AARP Del. State Leadership Coun., 1996, 1999-2001, exec. bd. Hofstra U. Sch. Bd. Forum, 1969-87; chmn. Merrick Planning Com., 1959-61; mem. publs. com. N.Y. State Sch. Bds. Assn., 1961-64, cons. to com., 1980-81, mem. BOCES com., 1971-74; vice chmn. State Sch. Bd. Leaders Com., 1975-79, cons. to com., 1980, bd. dirs., 1979-87, v.p., 1981, 84, 85, 86, 87, mem. exec. com.,

1981-87, cons. to disting. service com., 1984, 85; cons. cities com., 1986, cons. grants com., 1987; del. L.I. Ednl. Conf. Bd., 1967-86; trustee Merrick Bd. Edn., 1962-87, pres., 1966-71; trustee Bd. Coop. Ednl. Services Nassau County, 1967-87, v.p., 1967-71, pres., 1971-87; mem. exec. com. Nassau-Suffolk Sch. Bds. Assn., 1962-87, v.p., 1974-77, pres., 1977-79; mem. exec. com. Merrick Citizens Com. for Pub. Schs., 1959-87; mem. fed. relations network 4th Congl. dist. Nat. Sch. Bds. Assn., 1973-87, study com. on career edn., 1976-78, sub-chmn. for N.E. region presdl. task force on edn. of handicapped children, 1977-78, presdl. task force on critical viewing of TV by children, 1979-80; del. Northeast Region, Nat. Sch. Bds. Assn., 1980-87, vice chmn., 1985-87, chmn., 1987; adv. com. N.Y. State Senate Standing Com. on Civil Service and Pensions, 1978-79; mem. Instructional Svc. TV Com. WLIW-TV/Channel 21, pres., 1973-82; mem. Com. for Better Schs. of Merrick, 1975-87, Hist. Soc. Merricks, 1976-88; bd. dirs. L.I. Coalition Fair Broadcasting, 1979-82; mem. commr.'s adv. council N.Y. State Edn. Dept., 1980-87; mem. City of Dover Pub. Safety Issues Implementation Studies Commn., 1993—; adv. com. on signage City of Dover, 1999-2000; mem. Dover City Transp. Com., 2001—; comms. officer Dover AFB Mus., 1995-96. Mem. citizens adv. com. Dover/Kent County Met. Planning Orgn., 1993—, chmn. 1995-2001, Project Prioritization Policy com., 2002-03, del. Planned Parenthood, United Way; ptnr. Spl. Olympics, Medic Alert Internat.; active Sta. WHYY, Wilmington-Phila., Del. Hospice, Nat. Wildflower Rsch. Ctr., Am. Farmland Trust, Southern Poverty Law Ctr.; Kent County rep. to the prioritization sys. steering com. Del. Dept. Transp., 1996-98, mem. pub. adv. com. on calming devices, 1999-2000; founding mem. FDR Meml.; mem. steering com. Del. State Scenic and Hist. Hwy., 2003—. With AUS, 1942-45, PTO. Recipient citations N.Y. State Police Conf., 1949, citations Rockville Centre Police Benevolent Assn., 1953, citations Nassau Div. Am. Cancer Soc., 1961, citations Nassau Am. Legion, 1963, citations Nassau Library System, 1964, citations Firemen's Assn. of Nassau County, 1964, citations Nassau County Scholastic Press Assn., 1965, citations United Fund of L.I., 1970, citations Kiwanis Clubs Internat., 1971, citations Jewish War Vets., 1972, citations WLIW-TV, 1982; Educator of Yr. award Hofstra U. chpt. Phi Delta Kappa, 1973; Educator of Yr. award Assn. for the Help of Retarded Children, Nassau County chpt., 1977; Disting. Service award Nassau-Suffolk Sch. Bds. Assn., 1979, 87, Spl. Merit award Nassau-Suffolk Sch. Bds. Assn., 1987; named Educator of Yr. U.S. Congress, 1987, County of Nassau, 1987, Town of Hempstead (N.Y.), 1987, Merrick Bd. Edn., 1987, various depts. Nassau County Bd. Coop. Ednl. Services, 1987, Merrick Sch. Dist. Faculty Assn., 1987; named Man of Yr. L.I. Spl. Edn. Adminstrs. Assn., 1979, Man of Yr. Merrick C. of C., 1980, Man of Yr. N.Y. State Legislature, 1980, 87, Man of Yr. Nassau-L.I. dist. N.Y. State Congress Parents and Tchrs., 1980 Mem. Nat. Sch. Pub. Rels. Assn. (exec. com. N.Y. State chpt., Capital Dist. chpt.), Edn. Writers Assn., Am. Newspaper Guild, Nat. Congress Parents and Tchrs. (life), N.Y. State Congress Parents and Tchrs. (life), N.Y. State Pub. Health Assn., Assn. Emotionally Handicapped Children, Assn. to Help Retarded Children, Assn. Children With Learning Abilities, N.Am. Assn. Environ. Edn., N.Y. Citizens Com. Pub. Schs., Nat. Soc. Autistic Children, Am. Assn. Career Edn., Ad Hoc Planning Com. Mobilized Community Resources, L.I. Sch.-Community Relations Assn., N.Y. Civil Svc. Employees Assn., N.Y. State Outdoor Edn. Assn., Nat. Parks and Conservation Assn., Nat. Arbor Day Found., ARC, Nat. Audubon Soc., Consumers Union, Statue of Liberty-Ellis Island Found. (charter), Habitat for Humanity, U.S. Com. of UNICEF, LWV, World War II Meml. Com. (charter) Nature Conservancy, NatConf. Sch. Bds. Assn. Communicators, Am. Assn. Retired Persons (Greater Dover area chpt., bd. dirs. 1995-2001), Ednl. Press Assn. Am., U. Mo. Alumni Assn., Boise State U. Alumni Assn., Albany Inst. History and Art (charter mem.), N.Y. State Mus. Assocs., Smithsonian Inst. Assocs., Libr. Congress Assocs. (charter), U.S. Holocaust Meml. Mus. Assocs. (charter), Ret. Pub. Employees Assn. N.Y. State, Nat. Geographic Soc., Nat. Wildlife Fedn., Newtonville Neighborhood Assn., Mifflin Rd. Neighborhood Assn. (gov. rels. chmn., exec. com.), Deerfield Civ. Assn., Consumer Union Assocs., Common Cause, Nat. Com. to Preserve Social Security and Medicare, Soc. Profl. Journalists, Sigma Delta Chi (life, Empire State chpt.), Alpha Epsilon Pi (life). Jewish. Home: Dover, Del. Died June 11, 2009.

OROPEZA, JENNY, state legislator; b. Montebello, Calif., Sept. 27, 1957; m. Tom Mullins Oropeza, 1977. BS in Bus. Adminstrn., Calif. State U., Long Beach. Former spl. liaison to ofcl. Foreign visitors Assn. Commn. Structural Challenges Budgeting Calif.; mem. Long Beach Unified Sch. Dist. Bd. Edn., 1988—94, Long Beach City Coun., 1994—2000; mem. Dist. 55 Calif. State Assembly, 2000—06; mem. Dist. 28 Calif. State Senate, 2006—10, chair majority caucus, mem. rules com., bus., professions and econ. devel. com., energy, utilities and comm. com., govtl. orgn. com., transp. and housing com. Trustee Calif. State U. Sys. Recipient Smith-Weiss Environ. Champion award, LA League Conservation Voters, 2006; named Legislator of Yr., League Calif. City's Latino Caucus, 2005. Democrat. Died Oct. 20, 2010.

O'ROURKE, INNIS, JR., concrete company executive, consultant; b. Kings Point, NY, Sept. 22, 1921; s. Innis O'Rourke and Augusta (Linherr) Travers; m. Louise Olympe Fraser, Mar. 4, 1950; children: Innis III, Colleen. BA, Yale u., 1942. Jr. exec. Transit Mix Concrete Corp., NYC, 1946-50; pres. PreCast, Inc., NYC, 1950-78, Concrete Conduit Corp., NYC, 1950-78; chmn. bd. Prefabricated Concrete Inc., NYC, 1969-77; dir. JWP Inc., Purchase, N.Y., from 1985. Adv. bd. MHT Co., N.Y.C., 1962-87; arbitrator N.Y. Stock Exchange, 1965—; trustee Green point Savs. Bank, 1966—. Trustee Upper Brookville Village, N.Y., 1968—. Served to lt. USN, 1942-46, PTO. Mem.: Creek (sec. 1977) (Locust Valley, N.Y.), (bd. govs. 1957—), Yale (N.Y.C.). Avocations: golf, paddle tennis, swimming, shooting. Home: Oyster Bay, NY. Died Apr. 29, 2009.

ORR, ROBERT STRAUB, chemist, educator; b. Phila., Dec. 18, 1937; s. Robert John and Elizabeth (Straub) O.; m. Joanne Weisser, Nov. 25, 1969; children: Jonathan, Rosalynd. AB, U. Pa., 1959; MS, U. Del., 1962, PhD, 1964. Asst. prof. Del. Valley Coll. Sci. and Agriculture, Doylestown, Pa., 1964-68, assoc. prof., 1968-72, prof. of chemistry, from 1972. Head judge Bucks County Sci. Fair, Doylestown, 1987—; dir. Delaware Valley Coll. Honors Program, 1987—, Inst. for Quality Edn. in Scis., Doylestown, 1989—. Recipient Svc. award Alpha Phi Omega, 1992, E. Emmet Reid Undergrad. Teaching award Am. Chem. Soc., 1993. Mem. Am. Chem. Soc., Pa. Sci. Tchrs. Assn., Pa. Sci. Suprs. Assn., Pa. Assn. Coll. Chemistry Tchrs., Sigma Xi. Home: Lansdale, Pa. Died Dec. 25, 2009.

ORSATTI, ALFRED KENDALL (KEN ORSATTI), retired labor union administrator; b. L.A., Jan. 31, 1932; s. Alfredo and Margaret (Hayes) O.; m. Patricia Decker, Sept. 11, 1960; children: Scott, Christopher, Sean. BS, U. So. Calif., 1956. Assoc. prodr., v.p. Sabre Prodns., LA, 1957-58; assoc. prodr. Ror Vic Prodns., LA, 1958-59; bus. rep. AFTRA, LA, 1960-61; Hollywood exec., sec. SAG, LA, 1961-81, nat. exec. dir., 1981—2000. Del. Los Angeles County Fedn. Labor, Los Angeles, Hollywood Film Council, Los Angeles; v.p., mem. exec. Calif. Fedn. Labor; pres. Calif. Theatrical Fedn.; chmn. arts, entertainment and media com. dept. profl. employees AFL-CIO Mem. Mayor's Film Devel. Com., Los Angeles. Mem. Actors and Artists Am. Assn. (1st v.p.) Died Aug. 31, 2010.

ORYSHKEVICH, ROMAN SVIATOSLAV, retired physician, physiatrist, dentist, educator; b. Olesko, Ukraine, Aug. 5, 1928; came to U.S., 1955, naturalized, 1960; s. Simeon and Caroline (Deneszczuk) O.; m. Oksana Lishchynsky, June 16, 1962; children: Marta, Mark, Alexandra. DDS, Ruperto-Carola U., Heidelberg, Ger., 1952, MD, 1953, PhD cum laude, 1955. Cert. Am. Assn. Electromyography and Electrodiagnosis, 1964; diplomate Am. Bd. Phys. Medicine and Rehab., 1966, Am. Bd. Electrodiagnostic Medicine, 1989. Research fellow in cancer Esptl. Cancer Inst., Rupert-Charles U., 1953-55; rotating intern Coney Island Hosp., Bklyn., 1955-56; resident in diagnostic radiology NYU Bellevue Med. Ctr.-Univ. Hosp., 1956-57; resident, fellow in phys. medicine and rehab. Western Res. U. Highland View Hosp., Cleve., 1958-60; orthopedic surgery Met. Gen. Hosp., Cleve., 1959; asst. chief rehab. medicine service VA West Side Med. Ctr., Chgo., 1961-74, acting chief, 1974-75, chief, 1975-99; dir., coord. edn. U. Ill. Integrated Residency Program, Phys. Medicine & Rehab, 1974-89; clin. instr. U. Ill., 1962-65, asst. clin. prof., 1965-70, asst. prof., 1970-75, assoc. clin. prof., 1975-94, clin. prof., 1994-99; ret., 1999. Author, editor: Who and What in U.W.M.M., 1978; contbr. articles to profl. jours; splty. cons. in phys. medicine and rehab. to editl. bd. Chgo. Med. Jours., 1978-89. Founder, pres. Ukrainian World Med. Mus., Chgo., 1977; founder, 1st pres. Am. Mus. Phys. Medicine and Rehab., 1980-91. Fellow AAUP, Am. Acad. Phys. Medicine and Rehab.; mem. AAAS, Assn. Acad. Physiatrists, Am. Assn. Electromyography and Electrodiagnosis, Ill. Soc. Phys. Medicine and Rehab. (pres., dir. 1979-80), Ukrainian Med. Assn. N.Am. (dir., pres. chpt. 1977-79, fin. mgr. 17th med. conv. and congress Chgo. 1977, adminstr. and conv. chmn. 1979), World Fedn. Ukrainian Med. Assns. (co-founder and 1st exec. sec. research and sci. 1977-79), Internat. Rehab. Medicine Assn., Rehab. Internat. U.S.A., Nat. Assn. VA Physicians, Assn. Med. Rehab. Dirs. and Coordinators, Nat. Rehab. Assn., Nat. Assn. Disability Examiners, Am. Med. Writers Assn., Biofeedback Rsch. Soc. Am., Chgo. Soc. Phys. Medicine and Rehab. (pres., founder 1978-79), Ill. Rehab. Assn., Ukrainian Acad. Med. Scis. (founder, pres. 1979-80), Gerontol. Soc., Internat. Soc. Electrophysiol. Kinesiology, Internat. Soc. Prosthetics and Orthotics, Fedn. Am. Scientists. Ukrainian Catholic. Avocations: research in prosthetics, amputations, normal and pathological gaits, bracing orthotics. Home: Elmwood Park, Ill. Died Dec. 26, 2009.

OSACKY, JOHN (BISHOP JOB OF HARTFORD), archbishop; b. Chgo., Mar. 18, 1946; Bishop of Hartford The Orthodox Ch. in America, Cumberland, RI, 1983—93, archbishop Midwest, 1993—2009. Died Dec. 18, 2009.

OSAGHAE, MOSES O., political scientist, educator; b. Benin City, Nigeria, Apr. 17, 1949; arrived in US, 1975; s. Geoffrey Omoghan and Agnes Esengbe (Isibor) Osaghae; m. Esther A. Osakue, Sept. 2, 1972; children: Osariemen Joy, Igbovomwan Timothy. BBA, Ft. Valley State Coll., Ga., 1978; MA, Tex. Tech. U., 1981, PhD, 1985. Civil servant Dept. Edn., Benin City, Nigeria, 1967—75; actor Midwest TV, Benin City, 1973—75; instr. Tex. Tech. U., Lubbock, from 1981; dir. Internat. Inst. Nigerian Devel., Lubbock, from 1983. Recipient Billy Ross award, Dept. Mass Comm., Tex. Tech. U., 1980—81, Best Mgr. award, Internat. Ctr. Arid and Semi-Arid Land Studies, Tex. Tech. U., 1983—84, Lubbock Rotary award, 1984. Mem.: Acad. Polit. Sci. Assn., Am. Polit. Sci. Assn., Nat. Advt. Assn., Pi Sigma Alpha. Democrat. Roman Catholic. Home: Benin City, Nigeria. Died Mar. 3, 2009.

OSMUNDSON, THEODORE OLE, landscape architect; b. Portsmouth, Va., Jan. 29, 1921; s. Theodore Ole and Zylphia Anne (Whitehurst) O.; m. Lorraine Frieda Wiese, Dec. 18, 1943; children— Gordon, Richard, Douglas. Student, Coll. William and Mary, 1939-40, Va. Poly. Inst., Norfolk, 1939-40; BS, Iowa State U., 1943. Landscape draftsman San Diego Park Dept., 1944, Garrett Eckbo Landscape Architect, San Francisco, 1945; landscape supt. Calif. Nursery Co., Niles, 1945; pvt. practice landscape architecture Oakland, Calif., 1946-49, San Francisco, from 1949. Pres. Calif. Bd. Landscape Architects, 1961-69 Designer: Kaiser Center Roof Garden, Oakland, 1956, U. Calif. at Davis Swim Center, 1968, U. Calif., Davis Putah Creek Recreation Area, 1969, Thoreau Hall Roof Garden, U. Calif., Davis, 1987, Los Alamitos Trail, San Jose, Calif., 1988, Tillman Park, Alameda, Calif., 1992. Pres. Kensington (Calif.) Democratic Club; mem. Berkeley (Calif.) Art Commn.; pres. Friends of Frederick Law Olmsted Papers, 1981-86. Recipient award for outstanding service Landscape Architecture Found., 1981; Bradford Williams medal Landscape Architect mag., 1981, Christian Peterson Design award Iowa State U., 1988; U. Hawaii East West Center grantee, 1963; Ednl. Facilities Lab. grantee, 1970-71 Fellow Am. Soc. Landscape Architects (ASLA medal 1986, nat. pres. 1967-69, pres. Found. 1969-71, chmn. jury of fellows 1980-82, U.S. advt. IFLA yearbook 1983-90, del. to Internat. Fedn. Landscape Architects 1980-89, sr. del. to Internat. Fedn. Landscape Architects 1989-90, pres. Internat. Fedn. Landscape Architects 1990-92, Outstanding Landscape Architect award No. Calif. chpt. 1981, Pres.'s medal 1986); mem. Calif. Council Landscape Architects (pres. 1968-69, Honor award 1977, chmn. South Market Parks task force 1986), Sierra Club, Planning and Conservation League, People for Open Space, Lambda Alpha, Pi Kappa Alpha Home: Kensington, Calif. Died Apr. 9, 2009.

OSTEEN, WILLIAM LINDSAY, SR., federal judge; b. Greensboro, NC, July 15, 1930; BA, Guilford Coll., 1953; LLB, U. N.C., 1956. With Law Office of W.H. McElwee, Jr., North Wilkesboro, NC, 1956-58; pvt. practive Greensboro, N.C., 1958-59; with Booth & Osteen, Greensboro, NC, 1959-69; US atty. (mid. dist.) Tenn. US Dept. Justice, Greensboro, NC, 1969-74; ptnr. Osteen, Adams & Osteen LLP, Greensboro, NC, 1974-91; judge US Dist. Ct. (mid. dist.) N.C., Greensboro, NC, 1991—2006, sr. judge, from 2006. With USAR, 1958-51. Recipient Judge John J. Parker Meml. award, 2008. Fellow Am. Coll. Trial Lawyers; mem. ABA, N.C. State Bar, N.C. Bar Assn. (mem. and chair subcom. N.C. sentencing commn.), U. N.C. Law Alumni Assn., Greensboro Bar Assn. (Disting. Svc. award, 2004) Died Aug. 9, 2009.

OSTER, ZVI H., nuclear medicine physician, educator; b. Burdujeni, Romania, Mar. 2, 1932; came to the U.S., 1979; s. Aizik-Edmond Oster and Shifra (Meirovici) Sperber; m. Levana Blanche Marcusohn, July 5, 1950; children: Michal, Ady-Shmuel, Shai. MD, Jerusalem Hebrew U., 1962; degree (hon.), Jerusalem Hebrew U. Med. Sch., 1968. Resident Hadassah U. Hosp., Jerusalem, Israel, 1962-67; assoc. dean Jerusalem Med. Sch., Israel, 1967-73; resident fellow Johns Hopkins Med. Sch., Balt., 1973-75, asst. prof., 1975-76, NYU, NYC, 1976-77; chief nuclear medicine Ch. Shiba Med. Ctr., Tel Hashomer, Israel, 1977-79; prof. SUNY, Stony Brook, from 1979. Died June 10, 2010.

OSTERHOUT, MICHAEL DENNIS, broadcast executive; b. Chgo., Sept. 14, 1948; s. Sidney and Imogene Muriel (Gephart) O.; m. Marsha Jean Cooper, Sept. 30, 1978; 1 child, Sidney Leighton. BA in Biology, Mercer U., 1970; postgrad., Troy State U., 1972; MBA, U. South Fla., 1983. Account exec. Sta. WYZE-FM, Atlanta, 1974-76, Sta. WDAE-FM, Tampa, Fla., 1976-78; local sales mgr. Sta. WRBQ-FM, Tampa, 1978-79, gen. sales mgr., 1979-82; gen. mgr. Sta. WRBQ-AM-FM, Tampa, 1982-83; v.p. Harte Hanks Radio, Tampa, 1983-84, Eden's Broadcasting, Tampa, 1984-86, exec. v.p., chief operating officer, 1986-87, pres., chief operating officer, from 1987; pres., CEO New Spectrum Broadcasting, from 1992, Cmty. Info. TV, from 1995; pres. Spectrum Europe Inc., from 1996. Chmn. Eastman Radio Bd., N.Y.C., 1985-87; bd. dirs. ABC Radio Networks, N.Y.C., 1983—. Chmn. Lowry Park Zoo Assn., 1983-86; trustee Fla. Interam. Scholarship Found., Tampa Bay Performing Arts Ctr., Fla. Orch., Pres.'s Coun. U. Tampa, U. Tampa, U. South Fla., Mercer U.; bd. dirs. S.E.R.V.E., Tampa Boys and Girls Club. Sgt. USAF, 1971-74. Recipient Commendation award Am. Women in Radio and TV, 1985. Mem. Nat. Assn. Broadcasters (bd. dirs. 1988—, mem. internat. com. 1986—, mem. radio futures com./ Radio Advt. Bur.), Fla. Assn. Broadcasters (bd. dirs. 1986—), Pinellas County Com. of 100, Pinellas Suncoast C. of C., St. Petersburg C. of C., Tampa Advt. Fedn., Art Watch, Sigma Nu. Clubs: Boys and Girls of Am. (bd. dirs. 1985—), Tampa, Centre, Temple Terrace (Fla.) Country; Pres.'s (St. Petersburg, Fla.). Republican. Presbyterian. Avocations: golf, reading, travel. Home: Lutz, Fla. Died June 26, 2010.

OSTERHOUT, RICHARD ALFRED, brokerage house executive; b. Montgomery, NY, Feb. 6, 1929; s. Wray and Maude (Miller) Osterhout; m. Barbara Jennings, Dec. 31, 1950; children: Michaels, Jeffrey, Ross, Susan, Richard. Broker Advest, Inc., Hartford, Conn., from 1947. With USNR, 1952—54, Korea. Mem.: NY Stock Exch. Home: East Granby, Conn. Died Apr. 27, 2010.

OSTERN, WILHELM CURT, retired trust company executive; b. Geisenheim am Rhein, Germany, Sept. 29, 1923; came to U.S., 1956, naturalized, 1970; s. Wilhelm A. and Margarete R. (Seul) Ostern; m. Olga Atterbury, Nov. 24, 2001; children from previous marriage: Karen, Ellen, Wilhelm. Grad., Staatliches Realgymnasium, Geisenheim, 1941. With Bayer AG, and predecessor, 1941-88, officer and/or dir. subsidiaries and affiliates, 1956-89; vice chmn., chief fin. officer Mobay Corp., Pitts., 1974-86. Vice chmn. Bayer USA, Inc., Pitts., 1986—88, chmn., 1988—91; bd. dirs., chmn. fin. com. ACE Ltd., 1987—91; bd. dirs. Schott Corp., Inc., Carl Zeiss, Inc. Mem. Carnegie Mus. Sustaining Fund. With German Army, 1942-45. Hon. Consul Fed. Republic of Germany. Mem. Am. Coun. Germany, Soc. Contemporary Crafts Pitts. (bd. dirs.). Clubs: Brook (N.Y.C.); Duquesne (Pitts.). Home: Saint Charles, Ill. Died Aug. 17, 2010.

OSTWALD, MARTIN, retired classicist; b. Dortmund, Germany, Jan. 15, 1922; arrived in U.S., 1946, naturalized, 1956; s. Max and Hedwig (Strauss) Ostwald; m. Lore Ursula Weinberg, Dec. 27, 1948; children: Mark F., David H. BA, U. Toronto, 1946; AM, U. Chgo., 1948; PhD, Columbia U., 1952; D (hon.), Fribourg U., Switzerland, 1995, Dortmund U., Germany, 2001. Instr. classics and humanities Wesleyan U., Middletown, Conn., 1950-51; from lectr. to asst. prof. Greek and Latin Columbia U., 1951-58; mem. faculty Swarthmore Coll., from 1958, prof. classics, 1966-92, prof. emeritus, from 1992; prof. classical studies U. Pa., 1968-92, prof. emeritus, from 1992. Vis. assoc. prof. Princeton (N.J.) U., 1964, mem. Inst. Advanced Study, 1974—75, 1981—82, 1990—91; vis. prof. U. Calif., Berkeley, 1969, Tel-Aviv U., from 1996; vis. fellow Balliol Coll. Oxford (Eng.) U., 1970—71, vis. fellow Wolfson Coll., 1987, 91; dir. fellowships-in-residence classics NEH, 1976—77; dir. d'etudes EHESS, Paris, 1991; mem. Inst. Advanced Studies, Tel Aviv, 1994, 2003. Translator: Nicomachean Ethics (Aristotle), 1962; author: (book) Nomos and the Beginings of the Athenian Democracy, 1969, Autonomia, Its Genesis and Early History, 1982, From Popular Sovereignty to the Sovereignty of Law, 1987, Ananke in Thucydides, 1988, Oligarchia, 2000; author: (with T. G. Rosenmeyer and J. W. Halporn) The Meters of Greek and Latin Poetry, 2d edit., 1980; author: Language & History in Ancient Greek Literature, 2009; mem. editl. bd. Cambridge Ancient History, 1976—94; contbr. articles to profl. jours. Fellow, Am. Coun. Learned Socs., 1965—66, NEH, 1970—71, 1990—91; Fulbright Rsch. fellow, Greece, 1961—62, Guggenheim fellow, 1977—78, Lang. fellow, Swarthmore Coll., 1986—87. Fellow: AAAS; mem.: Soc. Ancient Philosophy, Classical Assn. Atlantic States, Classical Assn. Can., Am. Philol. Assn. (pres. 1986—87), Am. Philos. Soc., Soc. Promotion Hellenic Studies (hon.). Home: Swarthmore, Pa. Died Apr. 10, 2010.

OTIS, JACK, social work educator; b. NYC, Feb. 13, 1923; s. Abraham Osipowitz and Esther (Goldberg) O.; children: Elisabeth H., Erich R., Greta M., Marcus H., Alicia. AB, Bklyn. Coll., 1946; MS in Social Work, U. Ill., 1948, MEd, 1955, PhD, 1957. Social worker Jewish Social Svc. Bur. Dade County, 1948-49; Psychiat. social worker Free Synagogue Social Service, NYU, 1949-50; asso. prof. U. Ill., 1950-61; dep. dir. Office Juvenile Delinquency and Youth Devel., Dept. Health, Edn. and Welfare, 1961-65; dean Grad. Sch. Social Work U. Tex., 1965-77, prof. emeritus, from 1993. Cons. to govt., 1961—; presenter Internat. Coun. on Social Welfare, Inter-Univ. Consortium for Internat. Social Devel., Internat. Assn. Schs. Social Work, 1994; dep. dir. Pres.'s Com. Juvenile Delinquency and Youth Crime, 1961-65; spl. cons. for Am. social work edn. and rsch. European Ctr. for Social Welfare Tng. and Rsch., Vienna, Austria, 1976—; Dean Dan Sanders Meml. lectr. U. Ill., 1999. Author: (with George Barnett) Corporate Society and Education, 1961; contbr. article on child labor to Ency. Social Work, 1995. Bd. overseers Ctr. for Study Violence, Brandeis U., 1966-70; commencement spkr. U. Tex. Sch. Social Work, 2001. With AUS, 1943-46, PTO. Fulbright-Hays rsch.fellow Austria, 1977-78; established annual Dean Jack Otis Social problem and Social Policy Lecture, U. Tex., 2007. Mem. AAUP, Coun. on Social Work Edn. (commn. on accreditation), Philosophy of Edn. Soc., Nat. Assn. Social Workers (chair Calif. Task Force on Child Labor 2001-03), Am. Acad. Polit. and Social Sci., N.Y. Acad. Sci., Johannesburg Child Welfare Soc. (rsch. cons. South Africa chpt. 1990-91), Phi Kappa Phi (pres.). Died Jan. 5, 2010.

OTT, C(LARENCE) H(ENRY_, ambassador, retired accounting professor; b. Richmond, Mich., Jan. 20, 1918; s. Ferdinand and Wilhelmina (Radkte) Ott; m. Helen Louise McKay, Oct. 29, 1942 (dec. Apr. 1994); children: James Richard, Dennis McKay, Richard Darrel, Delene Michelle. BA, Valparaiso U., 1940; MBA, Northwestern U., 1970; PhD, Southeastern U., 1980. CPA N.Y., cert. mgmt. acct., N.Y. Chief acct. G.E. X-Ray Corp., Chgo., 1940—41; pub. auditor Arthur Andersen & Co., Chgo., 1941—43; renegotiator contracts U.S. Army Air Corps, Chgo., 1943—45; internal auditor David Bradley Mfg. (Sears), Bradley, Ill., 1945—48; contr., treas. Manco Mfg. Co., Bradley, 1948—59; owner, operator Yellow-Checker Cab Co., Kankakee, Ill., 1959—70; chmn. acctg., prof. Rochester Inst. Tech., NY, 1970—73, Southwestern Mich. Coll., Dowagiac, 1973—2008; citizen amb. People to People Internat., Kansas City, Mo., 1992—2008. Curriculum advisor Southwestern Mich. Coll., Dowagiac, from 1992. Citizen amb. People to People Internat., Bora Bora, Que., Canada, Cuba, China, Egypt, England, France, Galapagos Island, Greece, Greenland, Iceland, India, Israel, Italy, Japan, Moorea, Morocco, Portugal, Singapore, Tahiti, Turkey, Russia, Spain, Ecuador, Greek Islands, Hong Kong, Jordan; del. to Russia to facilitate their transition to Dem. form of govt.; del. leader Wharton Sch. Fin. U. Pa., Phila., 1992. Mem.: Planning Execs. Inst. (spkr., chmn.), Inst. Cert. Mgmt. Accts., Nat. Assn. Accts., Pi Gamma Mu, Pi Kappa Alpha, Alpha Kappa Psi. Republican. Avocations: travel, golf, bowling, reading, exercise. Home: Dowagiac, Mich. Died Nov. 5, 2009.

OVERBERG, PAUL JOSEPH, life insurance company executive; b. Toledo, Feb. 25, 1926; s. Frank and Frieda (Bohnett) O.; m. Lottie Marie Modlinski, Apr. 3, 1948; children: Cynthia Ann, Debra Denise, David Paul. BBA, U. Toledo, 1948; MA, U. Mich., 1950. Asst. actuary, actuarial student Pan Am. Life Ins. Co., New Orleans, 1950-54; asst. actuary Am. United Life Ins. Co., Indpls., 1954-57; group actuary, then asso. actuary Security Mut. Life Ins. Co., Binghamton, N.Y., 1957-61; with Allstate Life Ins. Co., Northbrook, Ill., 1961-86, chief actuary, 1963-86, sr. v.p., 1974-86; also dir.; v.p. Cross-Country Life Ins. Co., 1961-80; sr. v.p., chief actuary Northbrook Life Ins. Co., 1978-86; chmn., chief exec. officer Am. Chambers Life Ins. Co. and Am. Employers Life Ins. Co. (subs. CEM Assocs.), Naperville, Ill., from 1988. Actuary Allstate Life Ins. Can., 1964-86, valuation actuary, 1977-86; asst. sec. Allstate Ins. Co., 1963-86; dir. ins. ops. United Chambers Adminstrs. and subs. Am. Chambers Life Ins. Co., United Chambers Insured Plans. Served as aviation cadet USAAF, 1944-45. Fellow Soc. Actuaries; mem. Am. Acad. Actuaries, Nat. Assn. Securities Dealers (past gov.), Can. Inst. Actuaries, Chgo. Actuarial Club, Chgo. Execs. Club, Ill. C. of C. Clubs: Lake Forest. Republican. Roman Catholic. Home: Lake Forest, Ill. Died June 4, 2009.

OVERBEY, RICHARD WALKER, advertising agency executive; b. Mobile, Ala., Apr. 20, 1934; s. James Thomas and Frances (Bowden) W.; m. Marion Mitchiner, Mar. 21, 1959; 3 children. B.A., Vanderbilt U., 1956. Tchr., advisor Julius T. Wright Sch., Mobile, 1958-59; prodn. mgr. Howard Barney and Co., Mobile, 1959-62; pub. relations rep. Internat. Paper Co., Mobile, 1962-69; asst. cashier, asst. mgr. travel dept. Amsouth/The Am. Nat. Bank & Trust Co., Mobile, 1969-71, asst. v.p., advt. dir., 1971-75, v.p., asst. mktg. dir., 1975-77, v.p., mgr. internat. dept., 1977-79, v.p., sr. mktg. officer, 1979-81; pres., chief exec. officer Colonial Bank N.A., Mobile, 1981-82; sr. v.p. Barney & Patrick Advt., Inc., Mobile, 1982—. Vice chmn. U.S. Olympic Com. Ala., 1982, mem. ho. of dels., 1982-84; mem. Am. Jr. Miss Judges Com., 1982; chmn. Heart Assn., 1982; Christmas Seal chmn. Am. Lung Assn., 1981; pres. Sr. Citizens Services, 1979-81; pres. Port City Pacer, 1980; sec. YMCA, 1978; pres. Mobile Opera Guild, 1978-79; rep. Ala. U.S. Olympic Torch Relay Team, XIII Olympic Winter Games, Lake Placid, 1980. Served with U.S. Army, 1956-58. Recipient M.O. Beale Scroll of Merit, Mobile Opera, 1978. Mem. Pub. Relations Soc. Am., Pub. Relations Council Ala., Ala. World Trade Assn., Ala. C. of C., Mobile Area C. of C. (chmn. world trade com. 1982), U.M.S. Prep. Sch. Alumni Assn. (pres. 1982). Died Jan. 27, 2010.

OWEN, RAYMOND HAROLD, minister; b. Gleason, Tenn., Apr. 21, 1932; s. Charlie Emerson and Lula (Page) O.; m. Lavell Coburn, Oct. 4, 1952; children: Dana (dec.), Darryl R., Dyton L. BA in Religion, Oklahoma City U., 1964; ThM, So. Meth. U., 1967; MA in Evangelism, Scarritt Coll., Nashville, 1972; DD (hon.), Oklahoma City U., 1979. Ordained to ministry United Meth. Ch., 1967. Pastor 1st United Meth. Ch., Hugo, Okla.; dist. supt. Meth. Ch., Bartlesville Dist., Okla., 1977-82; sr. min. Epworth United Meth. Ch., Oklahoma City, 1971-73, New Haven United Meth. Ch., Tulsa, 1973-77, 1st United Meth. Ch., Bartlesville, Okla., from 1982. Del. Jurisdictional Conf. S.W. United Meth. Ch., 1976, 80, 84, 88—, Gen. Conf., 1980, 84, 88, 90; mem. exec. com. World Meth. Coun. 1986—; bd. dirs. Green Co. Retirement Villa, Bartlesville. Author: Probingins in Prayer, 1975, Seedtime and Harvest, 1980, Questions That Shape Destiny, 1983, Listening To Life, 1987. 2d lt. U.S. Army, 1954-60. Mem. Rotary. Died May 15, 2010.

OWEN, WILLIAM REAGAN, cardiologist, educator; b. Athens, Tex., Oct. 14, 1925; s. Charles Reagan and Gladys (Bishop) O.; m. Margaret Ellen Severin, Mar. 12, 1927; children: Claudia Owen Lummis, Susan Owen Dawson. MD, Harvard Med. Sch., 1949. Diplomate American Bd. Internal Medicine. Intern Mass. Gen. Hosp., Boston, 1949-50, resident in internal medicine, 1950-53; resident in cardiology Nat. Heart Inst., Bethesda, Md., 1953-55, sr. surgeon, 1953-55; prof. clin. medicine U. Tex. Med. Sch., Houston, 1965—2010. Assoc. prof. medicine Baylor Med. Sch., Houston; bd. govts. Univ. Club, Houston, 1983-95. Sr. surgeon USPHS, NIH, 1952-55. Recipient Sr. Svc. award U.S. Tennis Assn., White Plains, N.Y., 1989; named to The Tex. Tennis Hall of Fame, 2006 Fellow Am. Coll. Cardiology; mem. Tex. Tennis Assn. (pres. 1989-91, Caswell award 1992, Julius Zinn Sr. Svc. award 1998). Republican. Unitarian Universalist. Avocations: tennis, photography, sailing. Home: Houston, Tex. Died June 5, 2010.

OWENS, ARTHUR PAUL, accountant; b. Bradford, Ill., Aug. 4, 1927; s. Arthur Paul and Mary Cecelia (Cluskey) O.; m. Geraldine Ann Bushell, Nov. 22, 1956; children— Mary, Julie, John, Catherine, Karen, Colette, Sheila, Ellen. B.S., Notre Dame U., 1950; M.A. in Health Adminstn., U. Iowa, 1963. Asst. v.p. Ind. Blue Cross, Indpls., 1966-71; exec. dir. Health and Hosp. Corp., Indpls., 1971-75; chmn. Provider Reimbursement Review Bd. U.S. Dept. Health Human Services, Balt., 1975-80; dir. nat. reimbursement Coopers Lybrand, Phila., 1980-84; mem. provider reimbursement rev. bd. HHS, 1985—. Contbr. chpts. to books, articles to profl. jours. Served with USAF, 1946-47. Mem. Am. Inst. C.P.A.'s, Am. Coll. Hosp. Adminstrs., Health Care Fin. Mgmt. Assn. Republican. Roman Catholic. Home: Fayetteville, Pa. Died Apr. 18, 2009.

OWENS, LOWELL THOMAS, accountant, educator; b. Carbondale, Pa., Jan. 17, 1944; s. Francis Willard and Inez (Bullock) O.; m. Peggy Sharon Waeiss, June 12, 1965; children: Julie Lynne, David Thomas, Susan Elizabeth. BS, Bob Jones U., 1965; MA, George Washington U., 1980. CPA, Ind. Auditor U.S. Gen. Acctg. Office, Detroit, 1965-73, organizational devel. specialist, 1973-81; prof. Grace Coll., Winona Lake, Ind., from 1981; pvt. practice acctg. Lowell T. Owens, CPA, Warsaw, Ind., from 1983. Cons. Combined Com. Services, Warsaw, 1985—, faculty adv. Circle K, Winona Lake, 1983—. Recipient Dir. (office library) and Cert. Appreciation (organizing and mgmt. planning) awards U.S. Gen. Acctg. Office, 1978, Outstanding Achievement award U.S. Gen. Acctg. Office, 1980. Mem. Am. Inst. CPA's, Ind. Soc. CPA's. Lodges: Kiwanis (local bd. dirs. 1984-85) (Outreach Person of Yr. 1982). Avocations: reading, hunting, gardening. Died Jan. 3, 2009.

OWENS, ROBERT STEPHEN, mechanical engineer, manufacturing company executive; b. Albany, NY, Dec. 21, 1929; s. Paul S. and Mary K. (Grady) O.; m. Joan Ann Mahoney, Oct. 3, 1953; children— Timothy, Susan, Christopher, Gregory, Kerry. B. in Marine Engring, Maritime Coll., 1954; B. Mech. Engring., Rensselaer Polytechnic Inst., 1960. Technician test dept. Gen. Electric Co., Schenectady, 1953, tech. specialist chem. research dept. research and devel. center, 1953-58, mech. engr. chemistry research dept., 1958-65, project engr. research and devel., 1965-66, mech. engr. structures and reactions br., 1966-67, mgr. applied surface chemistry unit, dir. studies in friction, 1967-68, mgr. planning and resources, 1968-70, mgr. materials characterization operation, 1970-73, mgr. uranium enrichment program, 1973-75, mgr. planning and resources Engring. Physics Labs., from 1975. Dir. Pioneer Savs. Bank, Troy, N.Y., 1969—, chmn. bd., 1977—; Forrest O. Rathbun, Jr. lectr. Rensselaer Poly. Inst., Troy, 1968 Co-author: Cutting and Grinding Fluids Selection and Application, 1967; contbr. articles on lubrication in metal processing to profl. jours. Recipient Ralph J. Cordiner award Gen. Electric Co., 1963 Mem. Am. Soc. Lubrication Engrs. (v.p., dir. 1968-69), ASTM (mem. various coms. 1966-69) Holder 10 patents in field. Home: Albany, NY. Died July 3, 2010.

OWENS, WILBUR DAWSON, JR., federal judge; b. Albany, Ga., Feb. 1, 1930; s. Wilbur Dawson and Estelle (McKenzie) O.; m. Mary Elizabeth Glenn, June 21, 1958; children: Lindsey, Wilbur Dawson III, Estelle, John. Student, Emory U., 1947-48; JD, U. Ga., 1952. Bar: Ga. 1952. Mem. firm Smith, Gardner & Owens, Albany, 1954-55; v.p., trust officer Bank of Albany, 1955-59; sec.-treas. Southeastern Mortgage Co., Albany, 1959-65; asst. U.S. atty. Middle Dist. Ga., Macon, 1962-65; assoc., then ptnr. Bloch, Hall, Hawkins & Owens, Macon, 1965-72; judge U.S. Dist. Ct. for Mid. Dist. Ga., Macon, from 1972, now sr. U.S. dist. judge. Served to 1st lt., JAG USAF, 1952-54. Mem. State Bar Ga., Macon Bar Assn., Am. Judicature Soc., Phi Delta Theta, Phi Delta Phi. Clubs: Rotarian, Idle Hour Golf and Country. Republican. Presbyterian. Died Apr. 28, 2010.

PACALA, LEON, retired professional society administrator; b. Indpls., May 3, 1926; s. John and Anna (Ferician) P.; m. Janet Lefforge, Dec. 28, 1947 (dec. July 1987); children: Mark, Stephen, James; m. Virginia Strasenburgh, Mar. 10, 1990. AB, Franklin Coll., Ind., 1949; BD, Colgate Rochester Div. Sch., 1952; PhD, Yale U., 1960; LLD (hon.), Nazareth Coll., 1980; LHD (hon.), Franklin Coll., 1987. Ordained to ministry Baptist Ch., 1952. Asst. prof. philosophy and religion DePauw U., 1956-61; participant study religion undergrad. coll. Lilly Found., 1957-59; assoc. prof. religion Bucknell U., 1961-68, prof., 1968-73, chmn. dept., 1961-64, dean, 1962-73; pres. Colgate Rochester (N.Y.) Div. Sch., pres. emeritus, from 1995; also Bexley Hall, Crozer Theol. Sem., 1973-80; exec. dir. Assn. Theol. Schs. in U.S. and Can., 1980-91. Chair, founding mem. World Coun. Theol. Instns., 1986-2002; cons. acad. adminstrn. Beirut Coll. Women, 1972. Author: The Role of ATS in Theological Education, 1980-90, 1998; contbr. articles to profl. jours. Exec. com. Christian Faith in Higher Edn. Projects, 1965-68; trustee Franklin Coll., 1967-73, 98-2002; bd. dirs. Rohesters Jobs, Inc., 1973-80, Union Theol. Sem., N.Y.C., 1999—; trustee Rochester Area Colls., 1973-80; dir. Nat. Housing Ministries, Am. Bapt. Chs., 1976-80; mem. adv. bd. Colgate Rochester Div. Sch., 1997—. With USAAF, 1944-45. Internat. Rotary scholar, Louvain U., Belgium, 1952-53. Mem. Am. Conf. Acad. Deans (exec. com., treas., chmn., presiding officer 1973-74), Am. Assn. Higher Edn., Assn. Am. Colls. (commn. religion higher edn.), Assn. Theol. Schs. (com. accreditation), Am. Bapt. Assn. Sem. Adminstrs. (chmn 1975-80). Home: Pittsford, NY. Died Sept. 8, 2009.

PACE, STEPHEN SHELL, artist, educator; b. Charleston, Mo., Dec. 12, 1918; s. John C. and Ora K. (Reeves) P.; m. Palmina Natalini, Feb. 26, 1949. Student, Inst. Fine Arts, San Miguel, 1945-46, Art Students League, NYC, 1948-49, Grande Chaumiere, Paris, 1950, Inst. D'Arte Statale, Florence, Italy, 1951, Hans Hofmann Sch., NYC, 1951-52; ArtsD (hon.), U. So. Ind., Evansville, 2002, Maine Coll. Art, Portland, 2003. Artist in residence Washington U., 1959; instr. painting Pratt Inst., NYC, 1961-69; artist in residence Des Moines Art Ctr., 1970; vis. artist U. Calif., 1968; asso. prof. Bard Coll., 1969-71, Am. U., 1975-83; artist in residence U. So. Ind., Evansville, 2005. Artist in residence U. So. Ind., Evansville, 2005. One-man shows include Hendler Gallery, 1953, Artists Gallery, 1954, Poindexter Gallery, 1956, 57, Washington U., St. Louis, 1959, Holland-Goldowsky Gallery, Chgo., 1960, Howard Wise Gallery, Cleve., 1960, N.Y., 1960, 61, 63, 64, Dilexi Gallery, San Francisco, 1960, HCE Gallery, 1956-59, 61-63, 66, Dwan Gallery, L.A., 1961, Hayden Gallery, Cambridge, Mass., 1961, Ridley Gallery, Evansville, Ind., 1966, U. Calif., Berkeley, 1968, Graham Gallery, N.Y.C., 1969, Des Moines Art Ctr., 1970, U. Tex., Austin, 1970, Kansas City Art Inst., 1973, A.M. Sachs Gallery, N.Y.C., 1974, 76, 77, 78, 79, 81, 83, 85, Drew U., 1975, Bard Coll., 1975, Am. U., 1976, Roberto Polo Gallery, Washington, 1976, New Harmony (Ind.) Gallery, 1977, Farm Gallery, Far Hill, N.J., 1978, Barbara Fiedler Gallery, Washington, 1980, Chastenet Gallery, Washington, 1981, Katharina Rich Perlow Gallery, N.Y.C., 1987, 89, 91, 94, 97, 98, 00, 02, 04, 06, Vanderwoude-Tananbaum Gallery, N.Y.C., 1991, U. N.C., Greensboro, 1991, Evansville Mus., 1992, Maine Coast Artists, Rockport, 1994-2006, Bates Coll. Mus., Lewiston, Maine, 1994, Union Coll., Schenectady, NY, 1999, A.J. Buecke Gallery, Northeast Harbor, Maine, 2001, Portland (Maine) Mus. Art, 2004, Farnsworth Mus., 2004; exhibited in group shows in U.S., Europe, Japan, Mid. East, India, Burma, Australia, New Zealand, Hawaii, Ctrl. and S.Am.; represented in permanent collections, Whitney Mus., Chrysler Mus., Norfolk, Va., Provincetown (Mass.) Mus., Evansville Mus., U. So. Ill., Carbondale, Michener Found., Walker Art Ctr., U. Calif., CIBA-Geigy Collection, Hallmark Collection, Bundy Art Gallery, U. N.C., Greensboro, Chase Manhattan Bank, Munson-Williams-Procter Inst., Utica, N.Y., Des Moines Art Ctr., Boston Mus. Fine Arts, Met. Mus., N.Y.C., Phillips Collection, Washington, Am. U., Washington, Corcoran Gallery, Washington, Curie Inst., Paris, Hirshhorn Mus., Washington, Bristol Myers Collection, Indpls. Mus., Portland (Maine) Mus., Bowdoin Coll. Mus., Brown U., Providence, Oberlin (Ohio) Coll. Mus, Farnsworth Art Mus., Rockland, Maine, Bates Coll. Mus., Lewiston, Maine, Nat. Mus. Am. Art, Washington, Columbus Mus. Art, Yale U., New Haven, U. of S. Indiana, Evansville, Union Coll., Schenectady, Newark Art Mus., N.J., U. No. Iowa, Cedar Falls, Colby Coll. Mus., Waterville, Maine, Rutgers U. Mus., NB, NJ, New Orleans Mus. Art, NAD, Baruch Coll., N.Y., U. Maine, Orono, U. Denver, Ogunquit (Maine) Mus., Fryeburg (Maine) Acad., Sweet Briar (Va.) Mus., Yeshiva U., NYC Served with AUS, 1941-45, ETO. Recipient Dolian Lorian award for promising Am. painters, 1954, Hallmark award, 1961, Am. Acad. Arts and Letters prize, 2004; grantee Creative Artists Pub. Svc.

Program, 1973; Guggenheim fellow, 1980. Mem.: NAD (Benjamin Altman prize 1993, Edwin Palmer Marine prize 2001, William A. Paton prize 2005). Died Sept. 23, 2010.

PAINE, JAMES CARRIGER, federal judge; b. Valdosta, Ga., May 20, 1924; s. Leon Alexander and Josie Carriger (Jones) P.; m. Ruth Ellen Bailey, Sept. 8, 1950; children: James Carriger, Jonathan Jones, JoEllen. BS, Columbia U., 1947; LL.B., U. Va., 1950, JD, 1970. Bar: Fla. 1950. Mem. firm Earnest, Lewis, Smith & Jones, West Palm Beach, Fla., 1950-54, Jones Adams Paine & Foster, 1954-60, Jones Paine & Foster, 1960-79; judge U.S. Dist. Ct. (so. dist.) Fla., West Palm Beach, 1979-92, sr. judge, from 1992. Bd. dirs., pres. Children's Home Soc. Fla., 1978-80; mem. bd. Episcopal Diocese S.E. Fla. Served to lt. USNR, 1943-47. Mem. Greater West Palm Beach C. of C. (pres. 1973-74), Palm Beach County Bar Assn. Democrat. Died Mar. 7, 2010.

PAISLEY, JOHN EDWARD, radio station executive; b. Galesburg, Ill., Dec. 24, 1949; s. Charles Bertram and Elsie A. P.; m. Lee Ann Adam, Nov. 27, 1976; childfen: Adam, Erin, Ian. BS, U. Miami, Fla., 1972. Salesman Sta. WQAD-TV, Moline, Ill., 1974-76; advt. salesman Daily Dispatch, Moline, 1976-79; realtor Tucker Swanson Realty, Galesburg, Ill., 1979-81; news and ops. dir. Sta. WAIK, Sta. WGBQ-FM, Galesburg, 1981-85, gen. mgr., from 1985. Commr. City Galesburg Plan Commn.; dir.Cottage Hosp. Lifeline Bd.; mem. Salvation Army Adv. Bd. Mem. Galesburg C. of C. (tourism council). Home: Galesburg, Ill. Died Aug. 24, 2009.

PALMER, DENNIS LEE, association administrator, consultant; b. El Monte, Calif., June 16, 1948; s. Richard Lee Palmer and Edna Mae (Hall) Willett Palmer; m. Candyce Ann Sagall, May 20, 1975 (div. Oct. 1978); m. Diana Sue Falkenstien, Apr. 22, 1978; 1 child, Sean Richard. Student, Mt. San Antonio Jr. Coll., 1966—68, Ark. State U., 1971—72, Calif. Poly. U., 1975—76. Program specialist YMCA, Jonesboro, Ark., 1972—73; health, fitness dir. Pomona, Calif., 1973—76, La Canada, 1976—78; exec. dir. LA, from 1978; cons. Contbr. articles to to profl. jours. Bd. dirs. Airport Marina Cons. Ctr., Westchester, Calif., from 1983; mem. soc. fellows YMCA, 1983. Sgt. US Army, 1969—71. Recipient Physical Edn. Merit award, So. chpt. YMCA, 1974—84; named Dir. of Yr., Pacific Region YMCA, 1979. Mem.: Westchester C. of C. (v.p. 1983—84), Am. Coll. Sports Medicine, Assn. Profl. Dirs., Rotary. Republican. Home: Sunland, Calif. Died May 13, 2010.

PALMER, ROBERT MOFFETT, composer, music instructor; b. Syracuse, NY, June 2, 1915; s. Strange J. and Ethel A. (Richardson) P.; m. Alice Frances Westcott, May 25, 1940; children: Alison, Anne. Bachelor of Music, Eastman Sch. of Music, 1938, Master of Music (under Dr. Howard Hanson), 1939; studied with, Roy Harris, 1939; scholarship with, Aaron Copland, Berkshire Music Center, summer 1940. Mem. faculty dept. of theory Sch. Fine Arts, U. Kans., 1940; mem. faculty Cornell U., Ithaca, N.Y., from 1943, now Given Found. prof. music. George E. Miller prof. U. Ill., 1955-56; vis. prof. composition U. Mich., 1956; mem. MacDowell colony, 1954 Commns. include, Koussevitsky Found., League of Composers, Mpls. Orch., Quincy (Ill.) Soc. Fine Arts, Columbia Broadcasting Co., Dimitri Mitropoulos, Am. Acad. Arts and Letters, Coolidge Found. U. Mich., U. Ill., Nat. Assn. Ednl. Broadcasters, Grinnell Coll., N.Y. Philharmonic Orch., Rochester Philharmonic., String Quartet 1-4, 1939, 47, 54, 59, Piano Sonatas 1, 2, 1938, 48, Sonata for Two Pianos, 1944, Quartet for Piano and Strings, 1947, Variations, Chorale and Fugue, 1947, Chamber Concerto for Violin, Oboe and Strings, 1949, Piano Quintet, 1950, Sonata for Viola and Piano, 1951, Quintet for Winds, 1951, Quintet for Clarinet, Strings and Piano, 1952, Sonata for Piano 4-Hands, 1952, Violin and Piano Sonata, 1956, Of Night and the Sea, Chamber Cantata, 1957, Trio for Violin, Cello and Piano, 1958, Meml. Music for Chamber Orch, 1958, Nabuchodonsor-Dramatic Oratorio, 1964, Overture for Orch, 1965, Symphony 2, 1966, Choric Song and Toccata, for Wind Ensemble, 1969, Concerto for Piano and String Orch, 1969, Sinfonia Concertante, for Nine Instruments, 1972, Sonata for Trumpet and Piano, 1972, Piano Quartet 2, 1974, Organon 2 for String Orch, 1975. Guggenheim fellow, 1952, 60; Fulbright sr. research grantee Italy, 1960 Died July 3, 2010.

PALMER, STANTON DEAN, newspaper editor; b. Evanston, Ill., Sept. 15, 1920; s. Paul Lester and Irma Leafy (Macklin) P.; m. Alice LaNeave Boroughs, May 19, 1951; children: Susan Palmer Pierce, David William. BS in Chemistry, U. Chattanooga, 1941. Civilian ordnance insp. U.S. Army Ordnance Dist., Chattanooga, 1941-42; copy editor Chattanooga Free Press, 1948-66, news editor, from 1966. Trumpet player Chattanooga Symphony Orch., 1938-74, Chattanooga Opera Orch., 1950-77. Lt. (s.g.) USN, 1942-46, PTO. Recipient Dedicated Svc. citation Chattanooga Symphony Orch., 1972. Mem. Am. Fedn. Musicians (hon. life, Chattanooga local chpt.). Baptist. Home: Chattanooga, Tenn. Died May 28, 2010.

PALUMBO, NICHOLAS EUGENE, veterinarian, educator; b. New Haven, May 19, 1928; s. Leonard Joseph and Mildred Catherine (Merrifield) P.; m. Patricia Lee Ashby, Jan. 31, 1959 (div. 1983); children: Charles, Katharyn, David, Nancy, Joseph, Nicholas; m. Mary Suzanne Sylvester, Mar. 21, 1987; 1 child, William. BS, U. Mo., 1952, D.V.M., 1959. Intern, then resident in surgery Angell Meml. Animal Hosp., Boston, 1959-61; fellow in lab. animal medicine Johns Hopkins U., 1967; mem. faculty U. Hawaii Med Sch., now prof. comparative medicine, chmn. dept., from 1977. Contbr. articles to profl. jours. Served to capt. USMCR, 1946-52. NIH Grantee, 1968-71 Mem. AMVA, Am. Assn. Lab. Animal Sci., Am. Assn. Lab. Animal Practitioners, Hawaii Vet. Med. Assn. Clubs: Dole Puppy Classic, Field Trial Hawaii. Democrat. Roman Catholic. Home: Honolulu, Hawaii. Died Jan. 10, 2010.

PANICHAS, GEORGE ANDREW, language educator, critic, editor; b. Springfield, Mass., May 21, 1930; s. Andrew and Fotini (Dracouli) Panichas. BA, Am. Internat. Coll., Springfield, Mass., 1951, LittD (hon.), 1984; AM, Trinity Coll., Conn., 1952; PhD, Nottingham U., Eng., 1962. Instr., English and comparative lit. U. Md., College Park, 1962-63, asst. prof., 1963-66, assoc. prof., 1966-68, prof., 1968-92. Co-chmn. Conf. Irving Babbitt: Fifty Years Later, 1983; mem. Richard M. Weaver fellowship awards com., 1984—88, Ingersoll Prizes Jury Panel, 1986. Author: Adventure in Consciousness: The Meaning of D. H. Lawrence's Religious Quest, 1964, Epicurus, 1967, The Reverent Discipline: Essays in Literary Criticism and Culture, 1974, The Burden of Vision: Dostoevsky's Spiritual Art, 1977, The Courage of Judgment: Essays in Criticism, Culture and Society, 1982, The Critic as Conservator: Essays in Literature, Society, and Culture, 1992, The Critical Legacy of Irving Babbitt: An Appreciation, 1999, Growing Wings to Overcome Gravity: Criticism as the Pursuit of Virtue, 1999, Joseph Conrad: His Moral Vision, 2005, Restoring the Meaning of Conservatism, 2008; editor (with G. R. Hibbard and A. Rodway): Renaissance and Modern Essays: Presented to Vivian de Sola Pinto in Celebration of His Seventieth Birthday, 1966; editor: Mansions of the Spirit: Essays in Literature and Religion, 1967, Promise of Greatness: The War of 1914-1918, 1968, The Politics of Twentieth-Century Novelists, 1971, The Simone Weil Reader, 1977, Irving Babbitt: Representative Writings, 1981, Modern Age: The First Twenty-Five Years. A Selection, 1988, In Continuity: The Last Essays of Austin Warren, 1996, The Essential Russell Kirk. Selected Essays, 2007; editor: (with C. G. Ryn) Irving Babbitt in Our Time, 1986; editl. advisor Modern Age: A Quar. Rev., 1971—77; assoc. editor: Modern Age: A Quar. Rev., 1978—83; editor, 1984—2007; adv. bd. Continuity: A Jour. of History, 1984—88, Humanitas, 1993—2010, Culture and Civilization, 2009—10; contbr. articles and revs. to profl. jours. Mem. Acad. Bd. Nat. Humanities Inst., from 1985; trustee Found. Faith in Search of Understanding, 1987. Recipient Henry Regnery award, 2003; grantee, Earhart Found., 1982. Fellow: Royal Soc. Arts (Eng.). Eastern Orthodox. Died Mar. 17, 2010.

PANKAU, BARBARA ROPES, lawyer; b. Miami, Apr. 4, 1951; d. Paul Chapman Ropes and Inga Ropes Roberts; m. Stephen Lamarr Pankau, May 1, 1976 (dec. Feb. 2001); children: Jonathan Lamarr, Emmy Ingrid; m. Jonathan L. Alpert, Dec. 4, 2003. Student, Sorbonne, Paris, 1970—71; BA cum laude, Tufts U., 1972; JD cum laude, U. Fla., 1975. Cert.: Fla. Bar (health law), bar: US Dist. Ct. (ctrl. dist.), US Ct. Appeals (11th cir.) 1981, US Ct. Appeals (5th cir.) 1976, US Claims Ct. 1979, US Supreme Ct. 1979. Legal writing instr. U. Fla. Coll. Law, Gainesville, 1975; assoc., litig. practice Trenam, Simmons, Kempker, Scharf, Brakin, Frye & O'Neill, Tampa, Fla., 1975—79; shareholder Carlton, Fields, Warrd, Emmanuel, Smith & Cutler, P.A., Tampa, 1979—89, Stearns Weaver Miller Alhadeff & Shierson, P.A., Tampa, 1989—90; lawyer Law Offices Barbara R. Pankau, P.A., Tampa, 1990—94; ptnr. Honigman, Miller, Schwartz and Cohn, Tampa, 1994—97, Shumaker, Loop & Kendrick, L.L.P., Tampa, 1997—2008; gen. counsel Universal Healthcare, St. Petersburg, Russia, from 2008, Pankau Law Firm P.A., from 2008. Lectr. in field of health law. Contbr. articles to profl. jours.; guest editor: health law issue, Fla. Bar Jour., 1998. Past dir. Hospice of Fla. Suncoast; past adv. bd. Burdines; adv. bd. trustees Humana Women's Hosp. Tampa, 1983—93; chmn. Tufts Alumni Admissions Program, Ctrl. Fla., 1986—92; moderator, adv. bd. trustees Humana Hosp., St. Petersburg, Fla., 1990—91, trustee, 1988—91; vice chmn., bd. counselors U. Tampa, 1982—83; adv. bd. Suncoast AIDS Network, 1990—91; adv. com. Tampa Tribune/Health Care Guide, 1989—91. Recipient numerous svc. awards, various profl. assns., svc. distinction awards, Tampa C. of C., Jr. League of Tampa, Big Bros./Big Sisters, others; named an Outstanding Lawyer of Am., 2003. Mem.: ABA (gov. bd. health law forum 1989—92, mem.health law forum, adminstrv. law and regulatory practice, bus. law), Fla. Bar Assn. (chmn. health law com., mem. exec. coun. health law sect. 1988—2003), Athena Soc., Fla. Bar (cert. com. health law sect. 1994—96, mem. health law, adminstrv. law, and bus. law sects.), Suncoast Healthcare Execs., Am. Health Lawyers Assn., Hillsborough County Bar Assn., Fla. Acad. Healthcare Attys. Home: Tampa, Fla. Died Jan. 10, 2009.

PANKEN, SHIRLEY, psychologist; b. NYC, Oct. 11, 1922; d. Harry and Anna; m. Irving Panken, 1946; 1 child, Theodore. MA, NYU, 1947, PhD, 1953. Lic. psychol. assn. N.Y. State. Intern psychologist Bellevue Psychiat. Hosp., NYC, 1946—47; staff psychologist Kings County Psychiat. Hosp., Brookyln, 1947—53; psychotherapist Bleuer Psychotherapy, Queens, 1953—55; psychoanalyst Pvt. Practice, NYC, from 1947. Editor: Psychoanalytic Review; author: Psychoanalytic Theory and Therapy of Masochism, 1973, The Joy of Suffering, 1983, Virginia Woolf and the Lust of Creation: A Psychoanalytic Exploration, 1987; contbr. articles. Mem.: Nat. Psychol. Assn. Psychoanalysis. Avocations: reading, writing. Died Jan. 17, 2009.

PAPES, THEODORE CONSTANTINE, JR., retired computer software company executive; b. Gary, Ind., Jan. 31, 1928; s. Theodore Constantine and Mary E. (DiPaolo) P.; m. Centes Marie Morrill, July 17, 1954; children: Matthew, Thaddeus, Daniel, Karin BA, U. Mich., 1952. With IBM Corp., Armonk, NY, 1952—68, v.p., 1969-72, pres. divsn., 1972-78; dir. gen. IBM Europe, Paris, 1979-82; pres., CEO Prodigy Services Co., White Plains, NY, 1984—92. Mem. vis. com. U. Mich. Bus. Sch., 1980-86; co-chmn. Campaign for Mich., 1983-88. Served with USN, 1946-48 Mem. Phi Beta Kappa Avocations: photography; skiing; golfing; jogging. Home: Mount Kisco, NY. Died Jan. 8, 2010.

PARDO, DAVID, retail executive; b. Cairo, Feb. 15, 1954; came to U.S., 1958; s. Albert and Arlette (Kraiem) P. BA, Bklyn. Coll., 1975. Asst. buyer Crazy Eddie, Inc., Bklyn., 1975-77, head buyer, 1978-81, v.p., 1982-84, exec. v.p. Edison, N.J., from 1985. Fundraiser United Jewish Appeal, N.Y.C., 1981-82, B'nai Brith, 1980-83. Named Executive of the Yr., B'nai Brith, N.Y.C., 1982. Republican. Jewish. Avocations: photography, rare coins, little league coaching. Died Aug. 26, 2010.

PARKER, JOHN EGER, advertising agency executive; b. Burbank, Calif., Nov. 14, 1928; s. John Warren and Mary Neff (Eger) P.; m. Iris Landry, Dec. 31, 1955; children— Brian, Lia. BS, U. Calif. at Los Angeles, 1950. Copy writer Batten Barton Durstin & Osborne (advt.), Los Angeles, 1953-54; account exec. Larry Raymond Co., Los Angeles, 1954-59; pres., account exec. Parker Advt. Inc., Palos Verdes Peninsula, Calif., 1959-77; v.p. Easy Rest, Los Angeles, from 1968, Torrance (Calif.) Datsun, from 1969, United TV Programing Service, Los Angeles, from 1973; pres. Parker Industries, Los Angeles, from 1971, Parker Broadcasting Co., from 1977. Bd. visitors Anderson Grad. Sch. Bus. UCLA. Founder Palos Verdes Community Arts Assn., 1975, Los Angeles Music Center; founder, dir. Del Mar Hist. Soc.; dir. Del Mar Found., 1984-86. Served to 1st lt. AUS, 1951-53, Korea. Named Person of Yr. Del Mar, 1984. Mem. Palos Verdes C. of C. (dir. 1967), Del Mar C. of C. (v.p., dir. 1982-86),Am. Assn. Advt. Agys. (gov. Calif. council 1969-70), San Pedro Fine Arts Assn., Sigma Pi, Alpha Kappa Psi. Clubs: Rotarian (v.p. Los Angeles 1958-65), Old Men's, Lomas Santa Fe Country. Home: Rancho Santa Fe, Calif. Died Apr. 8, 2009.

PARKER, ROBERT BROWN, writer; b. Springfield, Mass., Sept. 17, 1932; s. Carroll Snow and Mary Pauline (Murphy) Parker; m. Joan Hall, Aug. 26, 1956; children: David, Daniel. BA, Colby Coll., Waterville, Maine, 1954; MA in English Lit., Boston U., 1957, PhD in English Lit., 1971; LittD (hon.), Northeastern U., 1987. Various bus./advt. positions, NYC, Boston, 1956-62; lectr. Boston U., 1962-64; mem. faculty Lowell State Coll., Mass., 1964-66, Bridgewater State Coll., Mass., 1966-68; asst. prof. English Northeastern U., Boston, 1968-73, assoc. prof., 1973-76, prof., 1976-79; co-founder Pearl Prodns., Boston. Lectr. Suffolk U., Boston, 1965—66. Author: (novels) (Spenser series) The Godwulf Manuscript, 1973, God Save the Child, 1974, Mortal Stakes, 1975, Promised Land, 1976 (Edgar award for Best Novel, 1977), The Judas Goat, 1978, Looking for Rachel Wallace, 1980, Early Autumn, 1980, A Savage Place, 1981, Ceremony, 1982, The Widening Gyre, 1983, Valediction, 1984, A Catskill Eagle, 1985, Taming a Sea Horse, 1986, Pale Kings and Princes, 1987, Crimson Joy, 1988, Playmates, 1989, Stardust, 1990, Pastime, 1991, Double Deuce, 1992, Paper Doll, 1993, Walking Shadow, 1994, Thin Air, 1995, Chance, 1996, Small Vices, 1997, Sudden Mischief, 1998, Hush Money, 1999, Hugger Mugger, 2000, Potshot, 2001, Widow's Walk, 2002, Back Story, 2003, Bad Business, 2004, Cold Service, 2005, School Days, 2005, Hundred-Dollar Baby, 2006, Now and Then, 2007, Rough Weather, 2008, The Professional, 2009, (Jesse Stone series) Night Passage, 1997, Trouble in Paradise, 1998, Death In Paradise, 2001, Stone Cold: A Jesse Stone Novel, 2003, Sea Change, 2006, High Profile, 2007, Stranger In Paradise, 2008, Night and Day, 2009, (Sunny Randall series) Family Honor, 1999, Perish Twice, 2000, Shrink Rap, 2002, Melancholy Baby, 2004, Blue Screen, 2006, Spare Change, 2007, (Philip Marlowe series) Poodle Springs, 1989, Perchance to Dream, 1991, (Everitt Hitch Westerns) Appaloosa, 2006, Resolution, 2008, (fiction) Wilderness, 1979, Love and Glory, 1980, All Our Yesterdays, 1994, Gunman's Rhapsody, 2001, Double Play, 2004, Edenville Owls, 2007, The Boxer and the Spy, 2008, (non-fiction) Sports Illustrated Training with Weights, 1974, Three Weeks in Spring, 1982, A Year At The Races, 1990, Spenser's Boston, 1994. Served with US Army, Korea. Recipient Gumshoe Lifetime Achievement award, 2008. Mem.: Writers Guild of America (Grand Master award 2002). Avocations: jogging, weightlifting. Died Jan. 18, 2010.

PARKINSON, GEORGINA, ballet mistress; b. Brighton, Eng., Aug. 20, 1938; m. Roy Round; 1 child, Tobias. Studied with Royal Ballet Sch. Mem. Royal Ballet, London, from 1955, soloist, from 1959, prin.; ballet mistress Am. Ballet Theatre, NYC, 1978—2009. Created roles in: La Belle Dame Sans Merci (Andree Howard), The Invitation (Kenneth MacMillan), Romeo and Juliet (Kenneth MacMillan), Mayerling (Kenneth MacMillan), The Concert (Jerome Robbins), Enigma Variations (Sir Frederick Ashton), Daphnis and Chloe (John Cranko), Everlast (Twyla Tharp). Died Dec. 18, 2009.

PARKOS, GREGORY T., diversified industry executive; b. Somerville, Mass., Mar. 11, 1930; s. Theodore K. and Mary (Diomandes) P.; m. Joan McDonough, 1977; children: January, Jaclyn BSBA, Bryant Coll., 1950, DSc in Bus. Adminstrn. (hon.), 1988; MBA, Boston U., 1951. V.p. Rosbro Plastics, Pawtucket, R.I., 1957-65, H-F Livermore Co., Boston, 1965-68; pres. Am. Chem. Corp., Providence, 1968-74, CPL Corp, Providence, 1974-79; exec. v.p. Whittaker Corp., Los Angeles, 1979-86, pres., chief operating officer, 1986-91, cons., from 1991. Bd. trustees, Bryant Coll., Smithfield, R.I. Served as spl. agt. Counter Intelligence Corps, U.S. Army, 1951-53, U.S. Fgn. Svc., 1953-56. Mem.: Masons. Greek Orthodox. Home: Venice, Calif. Died Sept. 2, 2009.

PARKS, DONALD ALFRED, geologist; b. NYC, June 9, 1930; s. Arthur and Marie (Irene) Parks; m. Barbara Anne Lawson, Aug. 25, 1979. BA, Hofstra U., 1955; MS, U. Mass., 1957; PhD, NYU, 1973. Cert. petroleum geologist. Prof. geology U. Mass., Amherst, 1955—57; exploration geologist Mobil Oil, Tripoli, Libya, 1957—61; exploration mgr. Pure Oil, Tripoli, 1961—67; staff geologist Newmont Mining, NYC, 1974—78; exec. v.p. Catawba Corp., NYC, 1978—79; pres. Taconic Petroleum Corp., NYC, 1978—79, Parks Petroleum Co., NYC, Carefree, Ariz., from 1979. Lectr. in field; mem. Hoover Medal Bd., from 1979; mem. deans council of 100 Ariz. State U.; bd. dirs. 187th Airborne Regiment Combat Team, from 1984. Contbr. articles to profl. publs. With US Army, 1846—1952, Korea. Japan. U. Mass. fellow, 1955—57. Fellow: Geol. Soc. America; mem.: AIME, Ind.

Petroleum Assn. America, Assn. Profl. Geol. Scis., Am. Inst. Profl. Geologists, Soc. Petroleum Engrs., Am. Assn. Petroleum Geologists (past pres. NY chpt.), Union League Club (NYC), Mining Club. Republican. Presbyterian. Died Nov. 13, 2009.

PARKS, JOE BENJAMIN, entrepreneur visionary, state legislator; b. McAlester, Okla., Dec. 17, 1915; s. James Allen and Mary Florence (Youngblood) P.; m. Florence M. Evans, Oct. 25, 1941 (dec. 1999); children: Anne, Kathryn. BS in Pub. Adminstrn., Okla. State U., 1939. Divsn. dir. US Veterans Adminstrn. (VA), Washington, 1946—56; spl. asst., cons. US Gen. Services Adminstrn. (GSA), Washington, 1957—58; mgr. dist. EDP divsn. RCA Corp., Washington, 1959—65; mgr. Ea. region Dashew Bus. Machines, Arlington, Va., 1966—68; assoc. adminstr. social and rehab. svc. U.S. Dept. Health, Edn. & Welfare, Washington, 1969—73; dir. mktg. govs. sys. divsn. Booz, Allen & Hamilton, Washington, 1974—75; ptnr. Forbes & Parks, Dover, NH, 1976—2002; pres. PatPar, Inc., from 1990; mem. N.H. State Legislature, Concord, 1984—92, chmn. joint com. on elderly affairs, 1987—92, mem. com. on health, human svcs. and elderly, 1983—90; chmn. subcom. mileage and electronic roll call, 1989—90; vice chmn. legis. adminstrn. com., 1990—91; mem. appropriations com., 1991—92; propr. Portsmouth Athenaeum, Portsmouth, NH, from 1992. Corporator Wentworth Douglas Hosp., Dover, 1980-89; pres. Berr Par, Inc., 1994-2010. Columnist Nat. Antiques Rev., 1975-77, Boston Globe N.H. Weekly 1987-88, Foster's Daily Democrat (Dover, N.H.), 1988-90; freelance writer, 1990-2010. Vice-chmn. NH State Rep. Com., 1987-88; chmn. Strafford County, NH, Reps., 1988; Strafford County campaign mgr. George W. Bush for Pres., 1999-2000; bd. dirs. Coastal Maine Bot. Garden, 2001-05, Rockingham Bot. Garden, 2005-06, Ageless Dreamer, 2007-08. Decorated Bronze Star; recipient Lawmakers award for disting. environ. svc. Sierra Club, 1990, NH State award New England Wildflower Soc., 1998; named Norris Cotton Rep. of Yr., 1993; Paul Harris fellow Rotary Internat. Found., 1998. Mem. Am. Rhododendron Soc. (pres. Mass. chpt. 1995-96, Bronze medal 1992, 2003, Silver medal, 2006, Dover NH Pk. renamed Joe B. Parks River Walk Gardens, 2007. Congregationalist. Avocation: plant breeding. Died Mar. 31, 2010.

PARNELL, GROVER SEFTON, JR., lawyer; b. Greenwood, SC, Aug. 4, 1942; s. Grover S. and Irene (Dipner) Parnell; m. Mary J. Zimmerman, Dec. 7, 1968; children: Grover Sefton III, Elizabeth Jane, Geoffrey McKay. BA, Wofford Coll., 1964; JD, U. SC, 1968. Bar: SC 1968, SC (US Dist. Ct.) 1968, (US Ct. Appeals (4th cir.)) 1974, Mass. 1978, (US Ct. Appeals (1st cir.)) 1978. Asst. pub. defender Defender Corp., Greenville, 1970—73; sr. ptnr. Parnell & Allison, Greenville, 1973—78; enforcement atty. US SEC., Boston, from 1978; dir., treas. Pub. Defender Corp., Greenville, 1976—78; chmn. Democratic Party, Greenville, 1976—78. Bd. dirs. Boys' Clubs, Inc., Greenville, 1974—78. Capt. US Army, 1968—70, Vietnam. Decorated Decorated Bronze Star, Air medal. Mem.: Sigma Alpha Epsilon, Phi Delta Phi, Boston Bar Assn., SC Bar. Episcopalian. Home: Wellesley, Mass. Died Aug. 1, 2009.

PAROLLA, HELEN RAINEY, association executive, writer; b. Eugene, Oreg., Jan. 15, 1925; d. Homer Price and Mildred (Collins) Rainey; m. Curry William Gillmore, Sept. 15, 1945 (div. 1968); children— Homer Rainey Gillmore, Daniel Scott Gillmore, Todd Harrison Gillmore; m. Otmar Beatus Parolla, June 27, 1970. Student Oberlin Coll., 1942-43; B.A., U. Tex., 1946, M.A., 1947; postgrad. McCoy Coll., Johns Hopkins U., 1950-51. Speaker, organizer Homer Rainey's gubernatorial campaign, Austin, Tex., 1946; instr. English, U. Tex., Austin, 1946-47; asst. dir. pub. affairs, nat. bd. YWCA, N.Y.C., 1947-49, program cons., 1975-76, coordinator pub. affairs and pub. policy, 1976—; mgmt. aide Housing Authority, Balt., 1950-52; tchr. English, Holy Name of Mary Sch., Croton-on-Hudson, N.Y., 1971-72; writer, researcher, analyst C. W. Wittman, Inc., Mount Kisco, N.Y., 1972-74; dir. pub. policy nat. bd. dirs. YWCA of the U.S.A., N.Y.C., 1976-87; portraitist; pub. speaker. Author: (novel) The Gates of Strength, 1947; (newsletter) Public Policy Bull., 1976-86; also numerous articles in YWCA Interchange, 1976-86. Editor: Public Policy, a Continuing YWCA Program, 1976-86. Past pres., bd. dirs. Religious Coalition for Abortion Rights, Washington, 1976-86; mem. unit com. div. ch. and society Nat. Council Chs., N.Y.C., 1976-86; supt., tchr. ch. sch. Scarborough Presbyterian Ch., N.Y., 1956-86; elder Presbyn. Ch., U.S.A., 1960—; promoter, organizer Interfaith Adult Edn. Seminars, 1966, 68; del. Synod of N.E., N.Y.C., 1978; mem. council on women and the ch. Presbytery of Hudson River, 1979-86; pres. Handel Choir of Balt., 1950-56; bd. dirs. Ossining Choral Soc., N.Y., 1964-68, Human SERVE, 1970—, Religious Network for Equality for Women, N.Y.C., 1976-86, Mem. ACLU, Union Concerned Scientists, Nat. Com. on Pay Equity, Women's Vote Project, Save our Security Coalition, Full Employment Action Council, Phi Beta Kappa. Democrat. Avocations: singing in choral groups; reading; interpretive dance. Home: Santa Fe, N.Mex. Died Jan. 30, 2009.

PARR, HARRY EDWARD, JR., financial executive; b. Dayton, Ohio, Sept. 2, 1928; s. Harry Edward and Naomi Theresa (Oesbeck) P.; m. Michelle Brooks, Mar. 16, 1996; children from previous marriage: Constance, Cynthia, Claudia, Brian, Patrick. BSBA, U. Dayton, 1951. With Chrysler Corp., Detroit, 1953-66; v.p., controller Diebold, Inc., Canton, Ohio, 1966-78, v.p., treas., 1978-82, sr. v.p. fin., treas., 1982-91, also bd. dirs., ret., 1992. Bd. dirs. Jr. Achievement Stark County, Canton United Way; trustee Walsh Coll., Canton, Canton Cultural Ctr. for Arts; trustee, mem. devel. bd. Stark County; bd. dirs. Aultman Health Found. Served to 1st lt. U.S. Army, 1951-53 Mem. Fin. Execs. Inst., Nat. Assn. Accts., Planning Execs. Inst., Canton C. of C. (former trustee) Clubs: Brookside Country (Canton). Died Jan. 6, 2009.

PARRIS, STANFORD ELMER, former United States Representative from Virginia, lawyer; b. Champaign, Ill., Sept. 9, 1929; s. Verne E. and Edna (Kendall) P. BS, U. Ill., 1950; JD, George Washington U., 1958. Bar: Va. 1958, DC 1976. Pres. Woodbridge (Va.) Lincoln Mercury Corp., 1965-79; mem. Dist. 20 Va. House of Delegates, 1969-72; pres. Flying Circus Aerodrome, Inc, from 1970; atty., ptnr. Swayze, Parris, Tydings & Bryan, Fairfax, 1970—72; mem. US Congress from 8th Va. Dist., 1973—75, 1981—91; sec. of state Commonwealth of Va., 1978; mem. St. Lawrence Seaway Devel. Corp., 1991—95. Mem. Fairfax County (Va.) Bd. Suprs., 1964-67; bd. dirs. Fairfax County YMCA; trustee George Mason U., Fairfax. Served with USAF, 1950-54, Korea. Decorated D.F.C., Air medal, Purple Heart; recipient Watchdog of the Treasury award, 1973-74, 1981-90. Mem. ABA, Va. Bar Assn., DC Bar Assn., Fairfax County C. of C., Am. Legion, Delta Theta Phi. Clubs: Alexandria (Va.); Rotary. Republican. Episcopalian. Died Mar. 27, 2010.

PARRISH, DAVID WALKER, JR., retired legal publishing company executive; b. Bristol, Tenn., Feb. 8, 1923; BA, Emory and Henry Coll., 1948; BS, US Mcht. Marine Acad., 1950; LLD, U. Va., Charlottesville, 1978. Pres. The Michie Co., Charlottesville, Va., 1969-89, vice chmn., 1989-96. Named to Sports Hall of Fame, Emory & Henry Coll. Mem.: ABA, Va. Bar Assn. Home: Charlottesville, Va. Died July 2, 2010.

PARRISH, HENRY HOWARD, JR., electrical engineer; b. Gainesville, Fla., Feb. 6, 1944; s. Henry Howard Parrish and Margaret (Adkins) Parrish Blodgett; student U. Fla., 1961-62, 66-67. With Racal-Milgo, Sunrise, Fla., 1968—, Fellow-Modem Devel., 1980-86, realtor, assoc. Coldwell Banker, Plantation, Fla., 1987-88; realtor The Prudential Wites, Coral Springs, Fla., 1988—; sr. elec. engr. GBI, Hollywood, Fla., 1989—; pres., chief exec. officer Great Southeastern Mortgage Co., Coral Springs, Fla., 1987—; chief operating officer SEC Software, Coral Springs, 1987—. With USN, 1962-66. Mem. IEEE (assoc.), Assn. for Computing Machinery, Fla. Assn. Realtors, Fla. Assn. Mortgage Brokers. Home: Pompano Beach, Fla. Died Jan. 11, 2010.

PARRY, ARTHUR E., management consultant; b. Brockton, Mass., May 25, 1929; s. Harry Edward and Linnea (Hagglund) P.; m. Patricia Sarah Godfrey, Feb. 19, 1955; children: Mark Edward, Linnea Louise, Jennifer Ann, James Arthur, Daniel Alan. BA, Boston U., 1953; MA, Governors State U., 1978; MS, U. Tex., Dallas, 1987; PhD, Clayton U., St. Louis, 1988. CPCU. Sec. Home Ins. Co., NYC, 1959-70; v.p. Meridian Ins. Co., Chgo., 1970-73, Zurich Ins. Co., Chgo., 1973-75, Res. Ins. Co., Chgo., 1976-78; sr. v.p. Great Cen. Ins. Co., Peoria, Ill., 1978-81; mgr., risk mgmt. services The Wyatt Co., Dallas, from 1981. Contbr. 30 articles to profl. jours, Mem. Assn. Computing Machinery (ethics com.). Republican. Baptist. Home: Frisco, Tex. Died Feb. 14, 2010.

PARTON, CLAUDE ALLAN, JR., advertising executive; b. Waterbury, Conn., Sept. 25, 1919; s. Claude Allan and Gertrude (Horrocks) P.; m. Carol Plummer Hagen, June 29, 1942; children— Carol E., Donald, Judy, Richard (dec.), Stephen, Rex, Jeanette, Kenneth, Jerry. B.A., Syracuse U., 1941. Announcer, Sta. WSYR-AM, Syracuse, 1939; sports dir. Sta. WOLF-AM, Syracuse, 1940-59; news dir. Sta. WNDR-AM, Syracuse, 1959-64; pres., gen. mgr. Sta. WPAW-AM, Syracuse, 1965-69; sports dir. Sta. WNYS-TV, Syracuse, 1968-73; tournament mgr. Syracuse Bowls, Sta. WSTM TV, Syracuse, 1977-86; sales rep. Brown & Bigelow, St. Paul, 1975—. Promotion dir. Onondaga County chpt. Easter Seal Soc., 1959-63; pres. Greater Syracuse Sports Hall of Fame, 1996—. Staff sgt. USAAF, 1942-46. Inductee Greater Syracuse Bowling Hall of Fame, 1988, Greater Syracuse Sports Hall of Fame, 1992. Mem. Syracuse Execs. Assn. (pres. 1978-79). Republican. Clubs: Syracuse Press (pres. 1956, 63); Syracuse Bowling Assn. (pres. 1982). Home: Baldwinsville, NY. Died May 5, 2010.

PASTERNAK, PAUL ALLEN, public relations executive; b. Bklyn., Apr. 18, 1948; s. Walter and Marion Bernice (Lass) P.; m. Lois Harriet Rosen, Jan. 3, 1977; children: Dori Kayli, Michael Lucas, Lara Faith. BS, Ohio U., 1969, MS, 1970. Asst. account exec. Burson-Marsteller, N.Y.C., 1972-73, account exec., 1973-74, account supr., 1974-76, v.p., client service mgr., 1979-83, v.p., group mgr., 1983-86, sr. v.p., group mgr. 1986-87, exec. v.p. bus. unit mgr., 1987, sr. v.p., dir. human resources, 1986-87, exec. v.p., asst. gen. mgr., 1987—, mem. U.S. mgmt. bd., 1987—; v.p., gen. mgr. Burson-Marsteller Ltda. & Marsteller Ltda., São Paulo, Brazil, 1976-79, dir., 1977-79. Bd. advisors Inst. for Brazilian-Am. Bus. Studies, 1980-83. Served with USAF, 1970-72. Mem. Sigma Delta Chi, U.S. Figure Skating Assn., Contingue Figure Skating Club, Pi Gamma Mu, Tau Kappa Epsilon. Republican. Jewish. Died June 4, 2009.

PATE, SAMUEL RALPH, engineering corporation executive; b. Thorsby, Ala., Oct. 27, 1937; s. Ralph Elvin and Frances Roberta (Marcus) Pate; children: Lisa, Sherri, Frances. BS in Aero. Engring., Auburn U., 1960; MME, U. Tenn., 1965, PhD, 1977. Registered profl. engr., Tenn. With Sverdrup Tech., Inc., 1960—69, project and rsch. engr. AEDC, 1969—74, mgr. rsch., engring. and testing projects br., 1975—78, dep. dir., Propulsion Wind Tunnel Facility, 1978—83; v.p. and gen. mgr. Tech. Group, Tullahoma, Tenn., 1983, sr. v.p. Tech. and Operational Groups, from 1983; cons., 1984—87; v.p., gen. mgr. AEDC Engring. and Ops. Group, 1987—90, Sverdrup Corp A & E Group, from 1990. Pres. Sverdrup Tech., Inc.; adviser U.S.-German Aero. Data Exchange; guest lectr. U. Tenn. Contbr. articles reports to profl. jours. With NG, 1955—59. Recipient Arch T. Colwell Merit award Soc. Automotive Engrs., 1983. Fellow: AIAA (assoc.; chmn. nat. ground testing com., Gen. H.H. Arnold award Tenn. sect. 1969). Died Dec. 7, 2009.

PATTERSON, GRADY LESLIE, JR., retired state treasurer; b. Abbeville, SC, Jan. 13, 1924; s. Grady Leslie and Claudia (McClain) P.; m. Marjorie Harrison Faucett, Dec. 22, 1951; children: Grady Leslie III, Steven G., M. Lynne, Laura A., Amy S., M. Beth LLB, JD, U. S.C., 1950, BS, 1975, LLD (hon.), 1980, The Citadel, 1985, Lander Coll., 1990, U. Charleston, SC, 1992, Clemson U., 1992. Bar: S.C. 1950. County service officer Abbeville County, S.C., 1950; ops. officer S.C. Air N.G., Columbia, 1952-59; asst. atty. gen. State of S.C., Columbia, 1959-66, state treas., 1967-95, 1998—2007, fin. advisor, 1995-98. Served with USAAF, 1943-46; maj. USAF, 1950-52, 61-61, ret. Maj. Gen. Decorated D.S.M. Mem. S.C. Bar Assn. Democrat. Presbyterian. Avocations: golf, jogging. Home: Columbia, SC. Died Dec. 7, 2009.

PATTERSON, JAMES HOWARD, diversified manufacturing company executive; b. Canton, Ohio, Mar. 15, 1931; s. Howard Aiken and Mary Lynn (Trippeer) P.; m. Barbara Stevens, Jan. 10, 1953; children: Carol Lynn, Linda Karen, Leslie Ann. BS, U. Mass., 1952; MBA, Auburn U., Ala., 1968. Commd. 2d lt. U.S. Army, 1952, advanced through grades to maj. gen., 1979; service in Europe, Korea, Vietnam; dir. battlefield systems integration Hdqrs. Material Devel. and Readiness Command, Alexandria, Va., 1979-80; ret., 1980; pres., chief operating officer Holder Internat. Industries, Inc., Tampa, Fla. Cons. in field. Decorated D.S.C., Bronze Star with V, D.F.C., Air medal (21). Mem. Armor Assn., Assn. U.S. Army, Ret. Officers Assn., Army Aviation Assn. Clubs: Carrollwood Country. Republican. Home: Tampa, Fla. Died Oct. 21, 2009.

PATTERSON, MARY JANE, religious organization administrator; b. Marietta, Ohio; BA in Philosophy and Acctg., Ohio State U., MSW. Ordained elder Presbyn. Ch. U.S.A., 1960. Acct. IRS; fin. dir. Columbus (Ohio) YWCA, asst. dir. for teenage programs, 1964-66; career missionary, cmty. developer, social work cons. Commn. Ecumenical Mission-Rels. Presbyn. Ch. East Africa, Nairobi, Kenya, 1966-68; cmty. organizing specialist and ombudsman Protestant Cmty. Svcs. of L.A. Coun. Chs., 1969-71; assoc. dir. Washington Office United Presbyn. Ch. U.S.A., 1971-76, dir., 1976—89; past pres. World Conf. on Religion and Peace, U.S.A., NYC. Participant crisis im the nation program Nat. Coun. Chs., Chgo., L.A., 1968; participant local, regional, nat. and internat. Presbyn. Ch. and interdenominational and ecumenical couns. Mem. nat. bd. UN Assn., PAX World Svc., Washington Office on Africa, Ams. United for Separation Ch. and State, Internat. Human Rights Internship Program.; former mem. bd. dirs. U.S. sect. Amnesty Internat.; past mem. Pres. Carter's Presdl. Adv. Bd. for Ambassadorial Appointments. Recipient numerous awards for civil and human rights, peace and justice issues. Women of Faith Award, Presbyn. Church U.S.A., 1998. Mem. NASW, Nat. Assn. Black Social Workers. Home: Washington, DC. Died Apr. 8, 2009.

PATTERSON, ROBERT ARTHUR, physician, health care consultant, retired health care company executive, retired air force officer; b. Palestine, Ill., Sept. 3, 1915; s. Robert Bruce and Nera (McColpin) P.; m. Judith Scheirer, May 15, 1961; children: Mary Kay, Elaine Alice Mills, Robert Arthur II, Victoria Patterson Goodrum. Student, U. Ill., 1933-35; MD, U. Louisville, 1939. Diplomate: aerospace medicine Am. Bd. Preventive Medicine. Intern Detroit Receiving Hosp., 1939-40; joined Mich. N.G., 1940; commd. USAAF, 1946; advanced through grades to lt. gen. USAF, 1972; rated chief flight surgeon and command pilot; assigned U.S. and ETO, 1940-45; assigned U.S., Spain, Japan, Philippines, 1945-63; dep. dir. plans and hospitalization Office Surgeon Gen., USAF, Washington, 1963-65, dir. plans and hospitalization, 1965-68; surgeon Hdqrs. USAFE, Lindsey Air Sta., Germany, 1968-71, Hdqrs. SAC, Offutt AFB, 1971-72; surgeon gen. USAF, 1972-75, ret., 1975; health care cons. Arlington, Va., 1975; sr. v.p. sci. affairs Baxter Travenol Labs., Inc., Deerfield, Ill., 1976-86, health care cons., from 1987. Decorated D.S.M. with oak leaf cluster, Legion of Merit with two oak leaf clusters, Air Force Commendation medal; recipient citation of honor Air Force Assn., citation of distinction Fed. Hosp. Execs., citation of distinction Am. Hosp. Assn. Fellow Am. Coll. Preventive Medicine, Aerospace Medicine Assn., Am. Coll. Physician Execs. (founder); mem. Assn. Mil. Surgeons (pres. 1972), AMA, Am. Acad. Med. Dirs., Ret. Officers Assn., Soc. Mil. Cons. to Armed Forces, Soc. Armed Forces Med. Labs. Scis., NIH Alumni, U. Ill. Alumni Assn., Aircraft Owners and Pilots Assn., Order Daedalians, Assn. for Advancement of Med. Instrumentation, Exptl. Aircraft Assn., Deutsch Kurzhaar Verband, N.A. Versatile Hunting Dog Assn., Uniformed Services U. Health Scis. Alumni Assn., Air Safety Found., Mid-America (Chgo.), Cen. Fla. Conservation and Hunt (Lake Wales, Fla.), Yacht and Country (bd. govs., 1993-95, pres., 1996-97, Stuart, Fla.), Sunshine Gun, Yacht (Stuart), Willoughby Golf Club (Stuart). Died June 25, 2010.

PATTERSON, ROBERT EUGENE, insurance company executive; b. Lancaster, Pa., June 13, 1932; s. Blanchard S. and Lydia L. (Wert) P.; m. Dorothy J. Shenk, May 26, 1951; children: Craig Robert, Tracy Ann. BS in Econs. magna cum laude, Franklin and Marshall Coll., 1959; postgrad., Temple U., 1960, Harvard U., 1977. CPA, D.C. With Armstrong World Industries, Lancaster, 1950-69, Hamilton Watch Co., Lancaster, 1969-71; v.p. fin., treas. K-D Mfg. Co., Lancaster, 1971-76, dir., officer and dir. subs., 1972-76; sr. v.p. fin., CFO, Blue Shield, Camp Hill, Pa., 1976-95, sr. v.p. cons., 1996-97; chief investment officer Commonwealth of Pa., from 1997. Vice chmn., sec., corp. sec., bd. dirs. Healthguard of Lancaster, Inc.; bd. dirs. Millerville Univ. Found. Served with U.S. Army, 1952-54. Mem. Fin. Execs. Inst. (chpt. pres., area dir., nat. v.p.), Inst. Mgmt. Accts., AICPAs, Pa. Soc. CPAs, Meadia Heights Country Club, Hamilton Club. Episcopalian. Home: Willow Street, Pa. Died Jan. 20, 2009.

PATTERSON, ROBERT M., environmental engineering educator; b. 1946; m. Meredyth Davies; children: Bradley, Lauren. BA, U. of the South, Sewanee, Tenn., 1968; SM, Harvard U., 1970, ScD, 1974. Cert. in comprehensive practice of indsl. hygiene. Sr. scientist GCA, Bedford, Mass., 1973-77, SRI Internat., Menlo Park, Calif., 1977-81; project mgr. Electric Power Rsch. Inst., Palo Alto, Calif., 1981-87; prof. dept. civil and environ. engring. Temple U., Phila., 1987—2010. Author: Radiofrequency and ELF Electromagnetic Energies: A Hand Book for Health Professionals, 1994. Mem. ACGIH (chmn. phys. agts. TLV com.). Died Mar. 14, 2010.

PATTERSON, WILLIAM MICHAEL, advertising executive; b. Dayton, Ohio, Sept. 28, 1932; s. Charles Craig and Clara Cathelina (Ward) Patterson; m. Evelyn G. Wetja, June 12, 1954 (div. June 1981); children: Zachary Alan, Shawn Eric; m. Rose Mary Roche, July 30, 1982; children: Michael, Mark, Matthew, Julie, Martin. BSBA, Ohio State U., 1954. Cert. bus. communicator. Statis. dir. Dayton Rubber Co., Ohio, 1956—58; mktg. dir. Standard Register Co., Dayton, 1958—60; pres. Patterson & Smith, Inc., Richmond, Ind., from 1960. Bd. dirs. Ricoe, Inc., Richmond. Author: Sea Story, 1984. With (j.g.) USN, 1954—56. Republican. Lutheran. Home: Richmond, Ind. Died Oct. 26, 2009.

PATZ, ARNALL, ophthalmologist; b. Elberton, Ga., June 14, 1920; s. Samuel and Sarah (Berman) P.; m. Ellen B. Levy, Mar. 12, 1950; children: William, Susan, David, Jonathan. BS, Emory U., 1942, MD, 1945; DSc (hon.), U. Pa., 1982, Emory U., 1985, Thomas Jefferson U., 1985; MLA, Johns Hopkins U., 1998, LHD (hon.), 2001. Pvt. practice, Balt., 1951-70; faculty Johns Hopkins Sch. Medicine, from 1955, prof., 1973—2010; William Holland Wilmer prof., chmn. dept. ophthalmology, dir. Wilmer Ophthal. Inst., 1979-89, Disting. svc. prof. ophthalmology, 2001. Mem. Nat. Diabetes Adv. Bd., 1977-80. First recipient Edward Lorenzo Holmes award Inst. Medicine Chgo., 1954, 1st Helen Keller prize Helen Keller Rsch. Found., 1994; Sight-Saving award D.C. Soc. Prevention Blindness, 1954, E. Mead Johnson award Am. Acad. Pediatrics, 1956, Albert Lasker award American Pub. Health Assn., 1956, 1st Seeing Eye Rsch. Prof. Ophthalmology award, 1970, Derrick Vail medal Ill. Soc. Prevention Blindness, 1981, Jules Stein award Rsch. to Prevent Blindness, 1981, David Rumbough Sci. award Juvenile Diabetes Found. Internat., 1983, Merit award Retina Rsch. Found., 1983, 1st Issac C. Michaelson award Israel Acad. Scis. and Humanities, 1986, Paul Henkind lectureship Macula Soc., 1989, Pisart award Lighthouse Internat., 2001, Spl. award for Lifetime Contbn. in Vision Rsch., Prevention of Blindness and Low Vision, Assn. for Edn. and Rehab. of Visually Impaired, 2002, Person of Vision award Md. Soc. for Sight, 2004, Presdl. Medal of Freedom, The White House, 2004; named to Ophthalmology Hall of Fame, American Soc. Cataract and Refractive Surgery, 2002. Mem. AMA (Billings silver medal 1973), American Acad. Ophthalmology (honor award 1973, Sr. Honor award 1981, Edward Jackson Meml. lectr. 1982, pres.-elect 1986, pres. 1987, Life Achievement award 1998, Laureate award 2005), Assn. for Rsch. in Vision and Ophthalmology (Friedenwald Meml. award 1980, Weisenfeld award 1993), Nat. Soc. Prevention of Blindness (v.p., 1st Disting. Scientist award), Am. Ophthal. Soc. (Howe medal 1991), Balt. City Med. Soc., Md. Soc. Prevention Blindness (past pres.), Pan-American Assn. Ophthalmology, Md. Soc. Eye Physicians and Surgeons. Home: Baltimore, Md. Died Mar. 11, 2010.

PAUL, WAKELEY SAMPSON WIJEYAKUMAR, lawyer; b. Colombo, Sri Lanka, Feb. 5, 1930; arrived in US, 1968; s. Milroy Aserappa and Pulmani (Kanagasabi) Paul; m. Diana Keyt-Bierne (div.); 1 child, Galina Paul Crosby; m. Sandra Stiebitz, Aug. 23, 1962; 1 child, Dayan William. BA, Cambridge U., 1953, MA, 1956; LLM, Stanford U., 1962. Bar: Middle Temple Eng. 56, Ceylon 1957, NJ 1972. Crown counsel Dept. Atty. Gen., Colombo, Sri Lanka, 1956—68; lectr. Law Coll, Colombo, 1965; 1st asst. pub. defender Office of Pub. Defender, Hackensack, NJ, from 1972. Mem. Nat. Adv. Coun. for South Asian Affairs, from 1981, vice chairperson, 1984. Mem.: Sri Landa Assn. (NYC) (v.p. 1971—79). Republican. Anglican. Home: New Milford, NJ. Died Mar. 9, 2009.

PAULL, DONALD, lawyer, psychologist; b. Chgo., Nov. 22, 1928; s. William Irwin and Tilva (Cohen) P.; m. Janice Simon, June 29, 1957 (div. 1968); children: Michael, Richard; m. Marva Carol Weisler, Mar. 7, 1976. BS, U. Ill., 1949, AM, 1951; BA, Roosevelt Coll., 1950; PhD, Ill. Inst. Tech., 1954, JD, 1974. Bar: Ill. 1974, U.S. Dist. Ct. (no. dist.) 1974, U.S. Dist. Ct. Trial 1983, U.S. Ct. Appeals (7th cir.), U.S. Supreme Ct. 1979; diplomate in clin. psychology Am. Bd. Profl. Psychology, 1962. Intern West Side and Downey VA Hosps., 1956-57; asst. pub. defender Office of Cook County Pub. Defender, Chgo., 1974-80, chief, mental health law div., 1980-90; assoc. Whitted & Kraning, Chgo., from 1990. Assoc. prof. Loyola U., Maywood, Ill., 1984—, Forest Inst. of Profl. Psychology, Des Plaines, 1982—. Contbr. articles to profl. jours. Mem. gov.'s com. to revise mental health code, 1988. With U.S. Army, 1954-56. Mem. Am. Psychol. Assn., Ill. Psychol. Assn. (pres. 1991—), Ill. State Bar Assn. (chmn. com. mentally disabled 1980-82). Home: Lincolnwood, Ill. Died Jan. 8, 2009.

PAVKOVIC, IVAN, psychiatrist; b. Rakitno, Yugoslavia, June 4, 1927; came to U.S., 1960, naturalized, 1965; s. Stjepan and Kaja (Ivankovic) P.; m. Lily Susnjar, Aug. 27, 1958; 1 son, Andre. MD, U. Zagreb, 1953. Intern Columbus Hosp., Chgo., 1960-61; resident Ill. State Psychiat. Inst., Chgo., 1961-64; with Ill. Dept. Mental Health and Devel. Disabilities, from 1964; regional adminstr. Ill. Dept. Mental Health and Devel. Disabilities (Region IV), 1968-77, asso. dir., 1977-80, acting dir., 1980, dir., 1981-83; chief clin. services Ill. Dept. Mental Health and Devel. Disabilities, 1983—2010; dir. Ill. Mental Health Institute, 1983-85; assoc. clin. prof. psychiatry Abraham Lincoln Sch. Medicine, Chgo., 1981—2010; exec. dir. Chgo. Project on Genocide, Psychiatry & Witnessing U. Ill. Cons. West Side VA Hosp., Chgo.; chmn. Ill. Dangerous Drugs Commn. Recipient Gerty award State of Ill., 1965, 66 Fellow Am. Psychiat. Assn.; mem. Ill. Psychiat. Soc., Internat. Assn. Social Psychiatry. Home: Glenview, Ill. Died June 20, 2010.

PEABODY, JUDITH DUNNINGTON, philanthropist; b. Richmond, Va., May 6, 1930; d. Bradford H. and Elizabeth Taylor (Dunnington) Walker; m. Samuel Parkman Peabody, Mar. 31, 1951; 1 child, Elizabeth Taylor. Student, Bryn Mawr Coll., Columbia U. Bd. dirs. Dance Theatre of Harlem, Fresh Air Fund for Children, N.Y.C., N.Y. Shakespeare Festival; co-founder Reality House, N.Y.C.; vol. worker, fund-raiser Gay Men's Health Crisis. Died July 25, 2010.

PEARCE, PHILLIP EDWARDS, investment banker; b. Columbia, SC, Feb. 18, 1929; s. Thomas Butler and Anne (Tribble) P.; m. Mary Anne Hood, Mar. 27, 1954; children: Mary Hood, Frances Smith, Phillip Edwards, Jr. BS, U. S.C., 1953; postgrad., Grad. Sch. Investment Banking, Wharton Sch., U. Pa., 1962-64. Pres. G.H. Crawford Co., Columbia, 1964-69; exec. ptnr. R.S. Dickson, Powell Kistler, Charlotte, N.C., 1969-73; sr. v.p. E.F. Hutton, NYC, from 1973. Gov. N.Y. Stock Exchange, 1971-72 Contbg. author, editor: The Stock Market Handbook, 1968. Mem. Nat. Assn. Security Dealers (chmn. bd. govs. 1968-69) Clubs: Brook (N.Y.C.). Democrat. Methodist. Home: Charlotte, NC. Died Oct. 22, 2009.

PEARLSTEIN, SEYMOUR, artist; b. Bklyn., Oct. 14, 1923; s. Morris Lazarus and Anna (Bassiur) P.; m. Toby Tessie Rubinstein, Mar. 21, 1943; children: Judith Helene, Lawrence Jonathan. Cert., Pratt Inst., Bklyn., 1950, Art Students League N.Y., 1954; student of Jack Potter. Owner, illustrator, designer Sy Pearlstein Advt. Art Studio, NYC, 1946-71; artist-painter rep. by Far Gallery, NYC, 1969-81; prof. N.Y.C. Tech. Coll., CUNY, Bklyn., 1971-94, prof. emeritus, from 1994, chmn. art and advt. design dept., 1985-88. One-man shows Silvermine Guild of Artists, New Canaan, Conn., 1973, Far Gallery, 1973, 75, 78, Klitgord Ctr., N.Y.C., C.C., 1974, De Mers Gallery, Hilton Head, S.C., 1975, Adelphi U., Garden City, N.Y., 1979, Grace Gallery, N.Y.C. Tech. Coll., 1992; group shows A.M. Sachs Gallery, N.Y.C., 1971, Springfield (Mo.) Art Mus., 1971, Am. Acad. Arts and Letters, N.Y.C., 1975, 76, 77, NAD, N.Y.C., 1986, 87, 89, 91, 92, Butler Inst. Art, Ohio, 1975, Ball State U., Queens Mus., N.Y.C., 1978, 81, Dept. State Art in Embassies Program, N.Y. Hist. Soc., 1981, Colo. Heritage Mus., Denver, 1981, 82, 86, Am. Watercolor Soc., N.Y.C., Ingber Gallery, N.Y.C., 1985, Audubon Artists, N.Y.C., 1990, 92, 97, Allied Artists Am., N.Y.C., 1991, 95, 2002, Nat. Arts Club, N.Y.C., 1989, Grace Gallery, N.Y.C. Tech. Coll., CUNY, 1998, 99, 2000, others; represented in permanent collections Mus. N.Mex., Santa Fe, Mint Mus. Art, Charlotte, N.C., NAD, N.Y.C., Fine Arts Gallery, San Diego, Adelphi U., Queens Mus., N.Y.C., Munson-Williams-Proctor Inst., Utica, N.Y., N.Y.C. Tech. Coll., Bklyn. Served with AUS, 1942-46. Recipient Gold medal Nat. Acad. Design, 1969, Hassam Fund Purchase award Am. Acad. Arts and Letters, 1969, 77, Gold medal of honor Nat. Arts Club, 1970, Ranger Fund Purchase award NAD, 1971, 82, Gold medal Soc. Illustrators, 1972, Nat. Inst.-Am. Acad. Arts and Letters grant, 1975 Mem. NAD (sec. coun.) 1980-84, W.H. Leavin prize 1985), Am. Watercolor Soc. (bd. dirs. 1979-80, Watercolor U.S.A. award 1971), Art Students League of N.Y. (life), Allied Artists Am. (bd. dirs. 1976-79, E. Lowe award 1969, gold medal 1980, George Tweed Meml. award 1989, 92), Audubon Artists (bd. dirs. 1986-89, 91-93, Grumbacher award 1971, Fabri medal 1980), Alliance Figurative Artists (c0chmn. 1976-77), Profl. Staff Congress. Home: Forest Hills, NY. Died Feb. 5, 2010.

PEARSALL, DUANE DARWIN, financial executive, venture capitalist; b. Pontiac, Mich., Mar. 3, 1922; s. Sheldon Lansing and Margery (Kincheloe) Pearsall; m. Marjorie Lee Fewel, July 22, 1944; children: Mark S., Craig A., MaryAnn K., Cynthia L. Diploma, Gen. Motors Inst., 1942; BS in Bus. Adminstrn., U. Denver, 1947. Region constrn. mgr. Honeywell Corp., Denver, 1948—55; pres. Pearsall Co., Denver, 1955—67, Statitrol Corp., Lakewood, Colo., 1963—78, Small Bus. Devel. Corp., Golden, Colo., 1978—83; gen. ptnr. Columbine Venture Fund Ltd., Englewood, Colo., from 1983; dir. Clin. Diagnostics Inc., from 1986. Developer, first home smoke detector, 1970. Mem., nominating commn. Colo. Supreme Ct., Denver, from 1981. Lt. USNR, 1942—45. Named Nat. Small Bus. Person of Yr., SBA, 1976, Citizen of Yr., Sertoma Denver, 1978, Fire Protection Man of Yr., Soc. Fire Protection Engrs., Boston, 1980. Mem.: Colo. Assn. Commerce and Industry (vice chmn. from 1984), Denver C. of C. (exec. com., bd. dirs. 1976—79). Republican. Lutheran. Home: Littleton, Colo. Died Apr. 11, 2010.

PEARSON, HENRY CLYDE, retired judge; b. Ocoonita Lee County, Va., Mar. 12, 1925; s. Henry James and Nancy Elizabeth (Seals) P.; m. Jean Calton, July 26, 1956; children: Elizabeth, Frances, Timothy Clyde. Student, Union Coll., 1947-49; LLB, U. Richmond, 1952. Bar: Va. 1952, U.S. Ct. Appeals (4th cir.) 1957, U.S. Supreme Ct. 1958. Sole practice, Jonesville, Va., 1952-56; asst. U.S. atty. Western Dist. Va., Roanoke, 1956-61; ptnr. Hopkins, Pearson & Engleby, Roanoke, 1961—70; so. states presdl. campaign mgr. Nelson A. Rockefeller, 1964; judge U.S. Bankruptcy Ct. Western Dist. Va., Roanoke, 1970-98; ret., 1998. Adv. com. fed. rules bankruptcy procedure; mem. Va. Ho. of Reps., 1954-56, Va. Senate, 1968-70; Republican nominee Gov. of Va., 1961. Editl. bd. Am. Survey Bankruptcy Law, 1979. With USN, 1943—46, PTO. Mem. Va. State Bar, ABA, Va. Trial Lawyers Assn., Assn. Trial Lawyers Am., Am. Judicature Soc., Am. Judges Assn., Fed. Bar Assn., Delta Theta Phi, Tribune Jefferson Senate, Am. Legion, VFW, Masons, Shriners. Methodist. Home: Salem, Va. Died Mar. 26, 2010.

PEARSON, JACK WILLARD, obstetrics and gynecology educator; b. Joliet, Ill., Jan. 16, 1929; s. John Willard and Ida Mae (Bailey) P.; m. Marilyn Nordin, 1951 (dec. Jan 1958); 1 child, Deborah Lee; m. E. Hope Tillman, June 6, 1958; children: Joan Elizabeth, Jack William, Hope Anne. BS, MD, U. Ill. Diplomate Am. Bd. Ob-Gyn (dir. pro tem 1973—). Commd. 1st lt. U.S. Army, 1953, advanced through grades to col., 1967, ret., 1973; prof. ob-gyn Ind. U., Indpls., 1973-83, U. Ariz., Tucson, from 1983. Cons. to Surgeon Gen. U.S. Army, 1968-73. Contbr. articles to profl. jours., chpts. to books. Decorated Legion of Merit. Fellow Am. Coll. Obstetricians and Gynecologists; mem. AMA, Cen. Assn. Obstetricians and Gynecologists, Assn. Profs. of Ob-Gyn, Soc. Med. Cons. to Armed Forces, Soc. Gynecologic Surgeons. Clubs: Cañada Hills Country. Republican. Avocations: golf, swimming, investments. Home: Tucson, Ariz. Died Apr. 25, 2009.

PEASE, JAMES NORMAN, JR., architect; b. Charlotte, NC, Aug. 29, 1921; s. James Norman and Eddie Kilpatrick (Hunter) P.; m. Mary Carson Jones, Nov. 20, 1943; children: James Norman III, Mary Carson, Edwin Jones. Student, N.C. State Coll., 1940-43; BArch, Auburn U., 1955. Lic. architect, N.C., Ga., Mo., N.J., N.Y., S.C., Tex.; registered planner, N.J. With Ross Schumaker, Architect, Raleigh, N.C., 1941, Dietrick & Olsen, Charlotte, 1942; successively project architect, designer, project designer, dir. design, dir. architecture, exec. v.p. J.N. Pease Assocs., Charlotte, 1947-74, pres., from 1974, chmn. bd., from 1977. Bd. dirs. 1st Union Nat. Bank; part-time instr., vis. lectr., juror Coll. Architecture U. N.C., Charlotte. Prin. works include Home Fin. Co. bldg., Charlotte, 1958, Ea. Airline reservations ctrs., Charlotte, Atlanta, Miami, Woodbridge, N.J., Cen. Piedmont Community Coll., 1963—, Appalachian State U., Govt. Ctr., Charlotte, Revenue bldg., N.C., N.C. Ctr. for Pub. TV. Bd. dirs. N.C. Design Found., N.C. Archtl. Found., Cen. Charlotte Assn., Nature Mus. Cen. YMCA, Univ. Rsch. Pk., Carolinas Internat. Tennis Found.; pres. Mecklenburg coun. Boy Scouts Am., 1975-76. With C.E., U.S. Army, 1942-46, PTO. Recipient Kamphoefner prize, 1988. Fellow AIA (pres. N.C. chpt. 1969); mem. Am. Correctional Assn., Archtl. League N.Y., Charlotte C. of C. (dir.), Soc. for Coll. and Univ. Planning, Charlotte City Club, Charlotte Country Club, Piedmont Club. Presbyterian. Died Jan. 28, 2009.

PECK, BERNARD SIDNEY, lawyer; b. Bridgeport, Conn., July 26, 1915; s. James and Sadie Peck; m. Marjorie Eloise Dean, Apr. 10, 1943; children: Daniel Dean, Constance Lynn. BA, Yale U., 1936, LLB, 1939. Bar: Conn. 1939, Fla. 1979, N.Y. 1982. Pvt. practice, Bridgeport, 1939-84; ptnr. Goldstein and Peck, 1946-84, Peck & Peck, Naples, Fla., 1983-87 and from 97, Porter, Wright, Morris & Arthur, Naples, 1987-90, Peck, Peck & Volpe, Naples, 1990-92, Peck, Volpe & Sullivan, Naples, 1992-94, Peck & Faga, Naples, 1994-97; judge Mcpl. Ct., Westport, Conn., 1951-55; ptnr. Peck & Peck, from 1997. Moderator town meeting, Westport, 1950—51; pres. Westport YMCA, 1957, trustee, 1964—84; pres. endowment bd. YMCA, Naples, 1987—88; mem. Westport Rep. Town Com., 1951—79. Capt. US Army, 1942—46. Fellow: Internat. Acad. Trial Lawyers, Am. Coll. Trial Lawyers; mem.: ABA, Collier County Bar Assn., Royal Poinciana Golf Club (bd. dirs. 1983—90, pres. 1987—89), Park Meadows Country Club (Park City, Utah), Yale Club SW Fla. (trustee from 1985), Phi Beta Kappa. Home: Naples, Fla. Died July 31, 2009.

PEHRSON, GORDON OSCAR, JR., author, lawyer, venture capitalist; b. San Antonio, Feb. 18, 1943; s. Gordon Oscar and Frances (Burns) Pehrson; m. Janice Sue Hagedorn, May 17, 1969; children: Christopher Wells, Ashley Stewart; m. Sharon Ann McNellage, Jan. 1, 1983; m. Maria Terrsesa Silvia Basso del Pont, Mar. 25, 1997. AB, Coll. William and Mary, 1964; JD cum laude, U. Mich., 1967; postgrad., U. London, 1967-68. Bar: Ill. 1968, DC 1969, US Ct. Claims 1968, US Ct. Mil. Appeals 1968, US Ct. Appeals (DC cir.) 1976, US Supreme Ct. 1976, US Ct. Appeals (3d and 5th cirs.) 1979, US Ct. Appeals (fed. cir.) 1982, US Tax Ct. 1990. Assoc. Sutherland, Asbill & Brennan, Washington, 1970-75, ptnr., 1975—97; sr. tax and corp. ptnr. Hopkins & Sutter, Washington, 1997—2000; founder, mng. ptnr. Potomac Capital LLP, Washington, from 2000. Adj. prof. law Georgetown U., Washington, 1977—81; vis. prof. law Coll. Ins., NYC, 1997—98; founder, bd. advisors The Inst. Tax Rev., from 1986. Contbr. articles on tax law to profl. jours.; editor The Ins. Tax Rev., 1986-94. Trustee U.S. Supreme Ct. Hist. Soc., 1993—, Food for Christmas Found., 1992-94; bd. advisors Hartford Inst. Ins. Taxation, 1993—, U.S. Humane Soc., 1994-96, Coll. William and Mary Sch. Bus., 1995-99. Fellow in internat. law U. Mich., 1967 Mem.: FBA, ABA (co-chair investment, fin. and taxation, com. sect. torts and ins. practice 1994—96, chair tax procedure com.,sect. adminstrv. law and regulatory practice from 1994), Boodles (London), Am. Law Inst., DC Bar Assn., Fed. Cir. Bar Assn. (chair tax appeals com. 1994—96), Knickerbocker Club (NYC), Econ. Club Washington, Nat. Press Club (Washington), Met. Club (Washington), Order of Coif. Episcopalian. Home: Rockville, Md. Died Sept. 12, 2009.

PELLA, MILTON ORVILLE, science educator; b. Wilmot, Wis., Feb. 13, 1914; s. Charles August and Ida Marie (Pagel) P.; m. Germaine Marie Reich, Dec. 9, 1944. B.E., Milw. State Tchrs. Coll., 1936; MS, U. Wis., 1940, PhD, 1948. Tchr. sci. and math. Wyler Mil. Acad., 1937-38; tchr. elementary sch. Delavan Pub. Schs., 1938-39; tchr. sci. U. Wis. High Sch., 1939-42; prof. sci. edn. U. Wis., Madison, 1946-80, prof. emeritus, from 1980; With Fgn. Ednl. Service, 1959—81. Author: Physical Science for Progress, 3d edit, 1970, Science Horizons— The Biological World, (with Branley and Urban), 1965-70. Served with AUS, 1942-46. Fellow AAAS; mem. Ctrl. Assn. Sci. and Math. (pres. 1955), Nat. Assn. for Rsch. in Sci. Tchg. (pres. 1966), Nat. Sci. Tchrs. Assn. (dir. 1950, 60), Masons. Died Aug. 21, 2010.

PELLATON, ROGER ALBERT, architect; b. N.Y.C., July 5, 1926; s. Roger A. and Alice Yvonne (Imre) P.; m. Helen Jacqueline Schiltz, Aug. 5, 1950 (div. 1963); children— Roger Imre, Nicole Catherine; m. 2d, Mary Karen Eisin, Sept. 2, 1967; 1 dau., Gretchen Catherine. B.A., Harvard Coll., 1947; B.Arch., Harvard Sch. Design, 1949, M. Arch., 1970. Registered architect, N.Y.C. Project mgr. Eggers & Higgins, N.Y.C., 1949-52, 54; assoc. architect John C. Ehrlich, Geneva, N.Y., 1954-57; pvt. practice architecture, Geneva, 1957-61; ptnr. Valvano, Valvano & Pellaton, Rochester, N.Y., 1961-63; project architect J. Edward Luders, Irvington, N.Y., 1963-64; pvt. practice architecture, Ossining, N.Y., 1964-69, 87—; ptnr. Pellaton & Chapman, Ossining, 1969-87. Important works include: Vatican Pavilion exhibits, N.Y. World's Fair, 1964, St. Thomas of Canterbury (1st honor Soc. Am. Registered Architects 1970), Courts of Glenpointe, 1982. Dist. leader Dem. Com., Ossining, 1967—, chmn., 1969; chmn. Hist. Rev. Commn., Ossining, 1975-82; bd. dirs. Westchester County Med. Ctr., Valhalla, N.Y., 1976-78; councilman Town Bd., Ossining, 1978-81; N.Y. State Dem. committeeman 89th Assembly Dist., 1986; bd. dirs. Interfaith Council for Action, Ossining, 1982. Mem. NAACP (bd. dirs. 1983), Nat. Trust Hist. Preservation, Preservation League of N.Y., Westchester Preservation League, AIA (bd. dirs. Westchester/Mid-Hudson chpt. 1984—, pres. 1987), Am. Planning Assn. Home: Ossining, NY. Died Jan. 7, 2010.

PELOTTE, DONALD EDMOND, Bishop Emeritus; b. Waterville, Maine, Apr. 13, 1945; s. Norris Albert and Margaret Yvonne (LaBrie) P. AA, Eymard Sem. and Jr. Coll., Hyde Park, NY, 1965; BA in Philosophy, John Carroll U., 1969; MA, Fordham U., 1971, PhD in Theology, 1975. Ordained priest Congregation of the Blessed Sacrament, 1972; provincial superior Blessed Sacrament, Cleve., 1978—2008; ordained bishop, 1986; coadjutor bishop Diocese of Gallup, N.Mex., 1986-90, bishop N.Mex., 1990—2008, bishop emeritus, 2009—10. Nat. bd. dirs. Maj. Superiors of Men, Silver Spring, Md., 1981-86, Tekakwitha Conf., Great Falls, Mont., 1981—. Author: John Courtney Murray: Theologian in Conflict, 1976. 1st native Am. bishop. Mem. Cath. Theol. Soc. Am., Am. Cath. Hist. Soc. Roman Catholic. Died Jan. 7, 2010.

PELTONEN, LEENA PÄIVI, human genetics educator; b. Helsinki, Finland, June 16, 1952; d. Simo Jaakko and Maire (Karttunen) P.; m. Aarno Veikko Palotie; children: Laura Maria Aarnontytär, Kristian Veikko Aarnonpoika. Candidate Medicine, U. Oulu, Finland, 1973, MD, 1976, PhD in Biochemistry, 1978, Docent in Cell Biology, 1982; Docent in Molecular Genetics, U. Helsinki, Finland, 1991; MD (hon.), U. Uppsala, 2000. Acting assoc. prof. U. Oulu, 1981-84; sr. scientist Acad. Finland U. Helsinki Recombinant DNA Lab., 1985-87; head lab. Nat. Pub. Health Inst., Helsinki, 1987-91, prof. molecular biology, 1991—94; prof. med. genetics U. Helsinki, 1995—98, 2002—03; chmn., prof. dept. human genetics UCLA, 1998—2002; prof. Acad. of Finland, 2003—07, dir. Centre of Excellence in Complex Disease Genetics, 2000—07; head human genetics Wellcome Trust Sanger Inst., 2007—10. Mem. European Molecular Biology Orgn., Nat. Acad. Scis., Helsinki, Internat. Coun. HUGO, 1994-98; chmn. European Med. Rsch. Coun., 1996-98; bioethics com. UNESCO Contbr. articles to profl. jours. Recipient Antoine Marfan award Nat. Marfan Found., 1992, Anders Jahre prize for young scientist Scandinavian Sci. Prize, Oslo, 1992, Poul Astrup prize Scandinavian Sci. Prize, 1992, Lennox K. Black prize Thomas Jefferson U., 1996, Mauro Bachirotto prize European Soc. Human Genetics, 1997, Gysel prize for Biomedical Rsch., 2006, Eric K. Fernstrom prize; named Academician of Science, 2009 Mem. European Acad. Sci. Avocations: poetry, literature, cooking. Home: Los Angeles, Calif. Died Mar. 11, 2010.

PENA, MODESTA CELEDONIA, retired principal; b. San Diego, Tex., Mar. 3, 1929; d. Encarnacion E. and Teofila (Garcia) P. BA, Tex. State Coll. for Women, 1950, MA, 1953. Cert. sch. supr., prin., supt., Tex. Tchr. English San Diego H.S., 1950-76; asst. supt. curriculum and instrn. San Diego Ind. Sch. Dist., 1976-80; gifted edn. resource tchr. William Adams Jr. H.S., Alice, Tex., 1980-83, asst. prin. for instrn., 1983-88; ret., 1988. Faculty Bee County Coll., 1975-76. V.p. San Diego PTA, 1963; charter mem. Duval County Hist. Commn., 1975—; reporter Duval Co. Hist. Com., 1988—; chmn. Com. to Establish Local Pub. Libr., 1993; trustee Duval County-San Diego Pub. Libr., pres., 1993-98, mem., 1999-2004, ex officio mem., 2005—, dir. Duval County literacy program, 1994—; cmty. rep. site-based dist. mgmt. com. San Diego Ind. Sch. Dist., 1995-97. Newspaper Fund Inc. fellow, 1964; recipient Adolfo Arguijo Day award, 1990; named Outstanding Sr. of Duval County, Grayfest, 1992; named to San Diego Hall of Honor, 1995. Mem. Tex. State Tchrs. Assn. (local unit rec. sec. 1952-53, 63-64, 1st v.p. 1957-58, 66-67, pres. 1961), Delta Kappa Gamma (rec. sec. chpt. 1972-74, 1st v.p. 1974-76, pres. 1976-78, chpt. parliamentarian 1984-88, 2003-08, state com. constn./bylaws 1979-81, state com. Eula Lee Carter Meml. Fund, 1987-89, area coord., 1989-1991, state com. pers. 1991-93, state rec. sec. 1993-95, state com. nominations 1995-97, chmn. 1997-99, state conv. chair 1999-2000, state com. necrology 2001-03, state com. ceremonies 2003-05, State convent cons., 2008-09., Chpt. Achievement award 1985, Internat. Golden Gift award 1994, State Achievement award 1996, Internat. Mem. in Print award 2002), Phi Delta Kappa (treas. chpt. 1978-79, rec. sec. chpt. 1983-84). Home: San Diego, Tex. Died June 22, 2010.

PENDERGRASS, TEDDY (THEODORE DEREESE PENDERGRASS JR.), singer; b. Phila., Mar. 26, 1950; s. Ida Pendergrass; m. Karin Michelle Still, June 20, 1987; children: Tisha, Ladonna, Teddy. Student public schs. Drummer for various groups, 1966-69; singer Harold Melvin & the Blue Notes, 1969-75; solo artist, 1975—2010; pres. Teddy Bear Enterprises, Phila. Squire, Memphis. Singer:(albums with Harold Melvin & the Blue Notes) Harold Melvin and & the Blue Notes, 1972, Black & Blue, 1973, To Be True, 1975; (solo albums) Teddy Pendergrass, 1977, Life Is a Song Worth Singing, 1978, Teddy, 1979, Live! Coast to Coast, 1979, TP, 1980, It's Time for Love, 1981, Teddy Pendergrass, 1982, This One's For You, 1982, Heaven Only Knows, 1983, Greatest Hits, 1984, Love Language, 1984, Workin' It Back, 1985, Joy, 1988, Truly Blessed, 1991, A Little More Magic, 1993, You & I, 1997, The Best of Teddy Pendergrass, 1998, This Christmas I'd Rather Have Love, 1998, Greatest Slow James, 2001, From Teddy with Love, 2002, Love Songs Collection, 2004 Recipient civic and pub. service awards., Image award NAACP, 1973, 80, Black Achievement award Ebony Mag., 1979, award outstanding mus. contbn. Afro-Am. Hist. Mus., 1983, award of merit City of Detroit, 12 gold and 7 platinum albums; recipity Keys to Cities, Lakeland (Fla.), Detroit, Savannah (Ga.), Memphis; named New Artist of 1977 for Top Pop Album Billboard Mag. Died Jan. 13, 2010.

PENDLETON, MILES STEVENS, JR., diplomat; b. Montclair, NJ, Mar. 22, 1939; s. Miles Stevens and Lucille (Bond) P.; m. Elisabeth Morgan, Aug. 13, 1967; children: Constance Morrow, Nathaniel Palmer. BA magna cum laude, Yale U., 1961; MPA, Harvard U., 1967; diploma, Nat. War Coll., 1980. Tchr. Ghana Secondary Sch., Koforidua, 1962-63, Adisadel Coll., Cape Coast, Ghana, 1963-64; vice consul Am. Embassy, Tel Aviv, 1968-70, polit. and econ. officer Bujumbura, Burundi, 1970-72; watch officer Ops. Ctr. Dept. State, Washington, 1972-73, staff officer Secretariat Staff, 1973-74, spl. asst. to Dep. Sec. of State Office Dep. Sec., 1974-76, dep. dir. Office of No. European Affairs, 1980-82, dir. Office of Israel and Arab-Israel Affairs, 1982-83, exec. asst. to under sec. of state for polit. affairs, 1983-85, dir. Office of Ecology and Terrestrial Conservation, 1995-97; polit. officer U.S. Mission to NATO, Brussels, 1976-79; min.-counselor for polit. affairs Am. Embassy, London, 1985-89, min., counselor for polit. affairs Paris, 1989-93; prof. strategy Indsl. Coll. Armed Forces Nat. Def. U., Washington, 1993-95. Mem. Am. Fgn. Svc. Assn., North Haven (Maine) Yacht Club, Met. Club (Washington), Phi Beta Kappa. Avocations: sailing, reading. Home: Washington, DC. Died Dec. 19, 2009.

PENN, ARTHUR HILLER, film director; b. Phila., Sept. 27, 1922; s. Harry and Sonia Penn; m. Peggy Maurer, Jan. 27, 1955; children: Matthew, Molly. Student, Black Mountain Coll., Asheville, NC, U. Perugia, Florence, Italy, Actors Studio, Los Angeles; studied with Michael Chekhov. Worked in TV, 1951-53; dir.: (plays) Two for the Seesaw, 1958, The Miracle Worker, 1959 (Tony award for Best Director, 1960), All The Way Home, 1960, Toys in the Attic, 1960, An Evening with Mike Nichols and Elaine May, 1960, Golden Boy, 1964, Wait Until Dark, 1966, Sly Fox, 1976, Fortune's Fool, 2002; dir: (films) The Left-Handed Gun, 1957, The Miracle Worker, 1962, Mickey One, 1965, The Chase, 1965, Bonnie and Clyde, 1967, Alice's Restaurant, 1969, Little Big Man, 1970, Visions of Eight, 1973, Night Moves, 1975, The Missouri Breaks, 1976, Four Friends, 1981, Target, 1985, Dead of Winter, 1987, Penn & Teller Get Killed, 1989, Lumiere et Compagnie, 1995; dir., prodr.: (films) Mickey One, 1965, Four Friends, 1981, Penn & Teller Get Killed, 1989; (TV films) Flesh and Blood, 1968; dir: (TV films) The Portrait, 1993, Inside, 1996; (TV episodes) The Gulf Playhouse (6 episodes), 1953, Goodyear Playhouse (5 episodes), 1953-54, The Philco-Goodyear Television Playhouse (12 episodes), 1953-55, Justice, 1954, Producers Showcase (2 episodes), 1954-55, Playwrights '56 (5 episodes), 1955-56, Playhouse 90 (5 episodes), 1957-58, 100 Centre Street, 2001; exec. prodr. (TV episodes) ITV Play of the Week, 1963, Law and Order (13 episodes), 2000-01 Served with inf. U.S. Army, World War II. Died Sept. 28, 2010.

PENNEY, CHARLES RAND, lawyer, civic worker; b. Buffalo, July 26, 1923; s. Charles Patterson and Gretchen (Rand) P. BA, Yale U., 1945; JD, U. Va., 1951; DFA (hon.), SUNY, 1995, Niagara U., 2007. Bar: Md. 1952, NY 1958, U.S. Supreme Ct. 1958. Law sec. to US Dist. Ct. Judge W.C. Coleman, Balt., 1951-52; dir. devel. office Children's Hosp., Buffalo, 1952-54; sales mgr. Amherst Mfg. Corp., Williamsville, NY, 1954—56, Delevan Electronics Corp., East Aurora, NY; mem. firm Penney & Penney, Buffalo, 1958-61; pvt. practice Niagara County, NY, from 1961. Exhbns. include Mus. Modern Art, NYC, 1962, Whitney Mus. Am. Art, NYC, 1963, 79, 80, Burchfield-Penney Art Ctr., 1973, 92-2003, Meml. Art Gallery, Rochester, 1976, 78, 83, 88, U. Iowa, 1978, Columbus Gallery Fine Arts, Ohio, 1976, 78. Hon. life trustee Burchfield-Penney Art Ctr.; adv. bd. Found. Study of Arts and Crafts Movement at Roycroft; hon. bd. dirs. Buffalo-Lille/France Assn., Inc. 2d lt. U.S. Army, 1943-46. Recipient Pres.'s Disting. Svc. award Buffalo State Coll., 1991, Disting. Svc. to Culture award Coll. Arts and Scis., SUNY, Potsdam, 1983; named Disting. fellow Cultural Studies of the Burchfield-Penney Art Ctr., 1994, Outstanding Individual Philanthropist, Nat. Soc. Fund Raising Execs. Western NY, 1996, Individual Patron of the Arts award Buffalo and Erie County Arts Coun. and Buffalo C. of C., 1997, Citation for Outstanding Achievements and Svc. to Lockport Cmty., NY State Assembly, 1997; awarded Key to City of Lockport, 1997; named to Lockport Hist. Walk of Fame, 1999. Mem. AARP, YWCA Niagra (life), Albright-Knox Art Gallery Buffalo (life), Buffalo Mus. Sci. (Life), Buffalo and Erie County Hist. Soc. (life, Red Jacket award 2000), Niagara County Hist. Soc. (life), Old Ft. Niagara (life), Buffalo Soc. Artists (hon. trustee), Hist. Lockport (life), Landmark Soc. Western NY (life), Hist. Lewiston (life), Friends of U. Rochester Librs. (life) Meml. Art Gallery U. Rochester (hon. bd. mgrs., hon. life), Winslow Homer Soc. of Dirs. Cir. (hon. life), Smithsonian Instn. (benefactors cir.), Rochester Hist. Soc. (life), Am. Hist. Print Collectors Soc. (life), Burchfield Homestead Soc. (hon. life), Charles E. Burchfield Nature and Art Ctr., Archives Am. Art, Mark Twain Soc. (hon.), U. Rochester's Pres.'s Soc. (hon. life), U. Iowa's Pres.'s Club (hon. life), Va. Law Found., Nat. Geog. Soc. (life), World's Fair Collectors Soc., Hist. Soc. of Tonawandas (life), Pres.'s Cir. Buffalo State Coll. (hon. life), Buffalo State Alumni Assn. (life), Yale Sailing Assocs., Yale Glee Club Assocs., Peanut Pals, Grolier Club, Pan Am. Expo Collectors Soc., Buffalo Indsl. Heritage Com., Roycrofters-at-Large Assn. (life), Arctic Cir. Club, Order of the Alaska Walrus, Automobile Club (Lockport), Niagara County Antiques Club (hon.), Rochester Art Club (hon. life), Fine Arts Mus. San Francisco (patron), De Young & Legion of Honor Museums (patron), U. Cir., SUNY Buffalo, Chi Psi, Phi Alpha Delta. Died Aug. 1, 2010.

PENNINGS, PAUL DAMON, sales executive; b. Iron Mountain, Mich., Mar. 7, 1954; s. Lawrence G. and Alice C. (Brey) Pennings; m. Deborah Beuder Pennings, Sept. 3, 1977. BS, Western Ill. U., 1976; MS, Roosevelt U., Chgo., 1984. Salesman Nationwide Papers, Elk Grove, Ill., 1976—78; mktg. rep. Ludlow Corp., Chgo., 1978—81; cons. Tactics-,Inc., Arlington Heights, Ill., 1981—84; sales exec. Videotex America, Chgo., from 1984; instr. mktg. mgmt. Roosevelt U., Chgo. Mem.: Am. Mktg. Assn. (chmn. chpt. from 1981). Republican. Roman Catholic. Avocations: cooking, gardening. Died Apr. 20, 2010.

PERDUE, CHARLES L., JR., social sciences and language educator; b. Panthersville, Ga., Dec. 1, 1930; s. Charles L. Sr. and Eva Mae (Samples) Perdue; m. Nancy J. Martin; children: Martin Clay, Marc Charles, Kelly Scott, Kevin Barry(dec.). Student, North Ga. Coll., 1948-49, Santa Rosa Jr. Coll., Calif., 1953; AB in Geology, U. Calif., Berkeley, 1958, postgrad., 1958-59; MA in Folklore, U. Pa., 1968, PhD in Folklore, 1971. Engring. writer Convair Astronautics, Vandenberg AFB, Calif., 1959-60; geologist, mineral classification br. U.S. Geol. Survey, Washington, 1960-67; asst. prof. English dept. U. Va., Charlottesville, 1971-72, asst. prof. English, sociology and anthropology depts., 1972-73, from asst. prof. to assoc. prof. English and anthropology depts., 1973—92, prof., from 1992. Cons. in field. Author (with others): (book) Weevils in the Wheat: Interviews with Virginia Ex-Slaves, 1976; author: Outwitting the Devil: Jack Tales from Wise country, Virginia, 1987, Pig's Foot Jelly and Persimmon Beer: Foodways from the Virginia Writers' Project, 1992; author: (with Nancy J. Martin-Perdue) Talk About Trouble: A New Deal Portrait of Virginians in the Great Depression, 1996; contbr. articles to profl. jours. With US Army, 1951—54. Recipient award for Outstanding Book Using Oral History, Nat. Oral History Assn., 1997; Univ. Predoctoral fellow, U. Pa., 1967—71, Wilson Gee Inst. Rsch. grantee, U. Va., 1974, 1975, Rsch. grantee, NEH, 1980—81, 1984. Mem.: Va. Folklore Soc. (archivist, editor 1974—89, archivist 1990—94, archivist, pres. 1995—96, archivist from 1997), Nat. Coun. Traditional Arts (bd. dirs. 1971—87, pres. 1973—79), Mid. Atlantic Folklore Assn. (founding mem., bd. dirs.), Am. Folklore Soc. (exec. bd. 1980—83, book rev. editor jour. 1986—87). Died Feb. 14, 2010.

PERELL, EDWARD ANDREW, lawyer; b. Stamford, Conn., Mar. 30, 1940; s. Sydney C. and Dorothy (Barger) P.; m. Nan Lifflander, Oct. 10, 1959; children: Stephanie Perell, Timothy R. BA, Yale Coll., 1962, LLB, 1965. Bar: N.Y. 1966. Assoc. Debevoise & Plimpton, NYC, 1965-72, former ptnr., 1973-88 and from 93, ptnr. NYC and London, 1989-93. Contbr. numerous articles on securities laws, mergers and acquisitions to profl. publs. Chmn. bd. dirs. Fedn. Protestant Welfare Agys., N.Y.C., 1983-87; pres., bd. dirs. Graham-Windham Family Svcs., N.Y.C., 1970-77. Mem. ABA, Assn. of Bar of City of N.Y. Home: New York, NY. Died May 11, 2009.

PERHAM, JOHN CARGIL, editor; b. Concord, NH, Oct. 14, 1918; s. Harry Leavitt and Mary Florence (Norcross) P.; m. Mary Hull, June 20, 1942 (dec. June 25, 1985). AB, Harvard U., 1940, A.M., 1941. Editorial writer Hartford (Conn.) Courant, 1942-51; assoc. editor, asst. mng. editor Barrons, NYC, 1951-65; sr. editor Dun's Rev. (now Bus. Month, The Goldhirsh Group), Boston, from 1966. Home: Stamford, Conn. Died Dec. 21, 2009.

PERKINS, HOMER GUY, manufacturing executive; b. New Haven, Oct. 23, 1916; s. Frank W. and Emily (Oesting) P.; m. Dorothy C. Stock, Jan. 24, 1942; children: Maribeth Perkins Grant, Homer Guy Jr., Hazel Mary Perkins Adolphson, Dorothy Catherine, Caroline Anne, Faith Elizabeth Perkins Crotteau, Ruth Emily Perkins Sico. BA in Internat. Rels., Yale U., 1938; LLD (hon.), Westfield U., Mass., 1977. With Enesco Group, Inc. (formerly Stanhome, Inc.), Westfield, from 1939, v.p., 1965-66, exec. v.p., 1966-70, pres., CEO, 1970-78, chmn., 1978-81. Bd. dir. Stanley Park of Westfield, 1949-2005, treas., 1955-69; pres. Citizens Scholarship Found., Easthampton, Mass., 1966-67, Easthampton Cmty. Chest, 1960-61; chmn. fin. com., bd. dirs. Western Mass. coun. Girl Scouts U.S., 1966-69; devel. com. Clarke Sch. Deaf, Northampton, 1965-68; fin. com. Town of Easthampton, 1962-70, chmn. fin. com., 1967-68; dir. Frank Stanley Beveridge Found., Westfield, 1956-95, pres., 1966-87; trustee Cooley Dickinson Hosp., Northampton, 1963-70, 84-92, chmn. bd. trustees, 1989-91; pres. bd. trustees Northampton Sch. for Girls, 1964-73; bd. dirs. Porter Phelps Huntington Found., Hadley, Mass., 1960-92, Guild of Holy Child, Westfield, 1969-76; bd. overseers Williston Acad., Easthampton, 1961-64, Old Sturbridge Village, Mass., 1970-76; v.p. bd. trustees Williston-Northampton Sch., 1970-75, pres., 1975-78; dir. Lathrop Communities, 2000-07, chair fin. com., 2001, pres. bd. dirs., 2005. With USAAF, 1942-46. Mem. Direct Selling Assn. (chmn. 1975, bd. dirs., mem. Hall of Fame), Paperweight Collectors Assn. (pres. 1991-95), Lions (past pres. Easthampton club). Home: Easthampton, Mass. Died Apr. 2010.

PERKINS, JAMES L., lawyer; b. Des Moines, Iowa, Oct. 8, 1931; AB, Drake U., 1953, JD, 1954; grad., Northwestern Coll. Law. Bar: Iowa 1954, Ill. 1955. Ptnr. Winston & Strawn, Chgo. Mem. ABA, State Ill. Bar Assn., Chgo. Bar Assn., Order of Coif, Delta Theta Phi. Died Aug. 2, 2010.

PERKINS, JARDINE CARTER, lawyer; b. Lumpkin, Ga., Nov. 4, 1918; s. William Leonard and Jardine Elizabeth (Carter) Perkins; m. Patricia A. Alexander, July 1, 1938; children: Patricia, Susan, J. Carter; m. Kyle Barbara Ellen, May 8, 1976. AB, Vanderbilt U., 1939; JD, Stetson U., 1947, La. State U., 1952. Bar: Fla. 1947, La. 1952, Calif. 1964, DC 1969, US Ct. Appeals (5th and 11th cirs.), DC 1969, US Dist. Ct. (so. dist.) Calif. 1964, US Dist. Ct. (ea. and we. dists.) La. 1952, US Supreme Ct. 1966. Gen. atty. Shell Oil Co., Washington, 1965—78, v.p., 1971—78; pvt. practice Leesburg, Fla., from 1979. Cons. in field. With USN. Mem.: ABA, Lake County Bar Assn. (Fla.), DC Bar Assn., State Bar La., State Bar Calif., State Bar of Fla., Elks, Silver Lake Golf & Country, Burning Tree Golf (Washington). Democrat. Episcopalian. Died Aug. 19, 2010.

PERKINS, ROBERT LOUIS, physician, educator; b. Bradford, Pa., Feb. 20, 1931; s. Robert Marcell and Lola Ruth (Freeman) P.; m. Ruth Caloccia, Sept. 7, 1952 (dec. 1978); children: Cathy Lynn, Robert Louis; m. Penelope Joel Brodgen, Dec. 24, 1983 AB, W.Va. U., 1953, BS, 1954; MD, Johns Hopkins U., 1956; MS in Medicine, Ohio State U., 1962. Diplomate Am. Bd. Internal Medicine. Instr. medicine Ohio State U., Columbus, 1961-65, asst. prof., 1965-69, assoc. prof., 1969-73, prof. medicine, from 1973, prof. med. microbiology, from 1974, Pomerene prof., 1977-82, Saslaw prof., 1982-90, dir. infectious diseases div., 1971-87; dir. med. edn. Grant Med. Ctr., Columbus, from 1990. Contbr. chpts. to books, numerous articles to profl. jours. Served to capt. USAF, 1958-60 NIH fellow, 1960-62 Fellow ACP, Infectious Disease Soc. Am.; mem. Ctrl. Soc. for Clin. Rsch., Am. Fedn. Clin. Rsch. Republican. Methodist. Avocations: model aviation; golf. Home: Columbus, Ohio. Died Dec. 29, 2009.

PERKINS, ROY FRANK, internist, former university official; b. Rock Island, Ill., Aug. 31, 1918; s. Frank and Jennie (Baker) P.; m. Marion Karen Mazursky, Mar. 13, 1942; children: Marc, Nancy, Franklin, John, James. BS, U. Ill., Urbana, 1939; MD, U. Ill., Chgo., 1941; MS, U. Minn., 1949. Diplomate Am. Bd. Internal Medicine. Intern LA County Hosp, 1941-42; fellow Mayo Clinic, Rochester, Minn., 1942-48, staff physician, 1948-49; pvt. practice, Alhambra, Calif., 1949-79; staff physician Scripps Clinic and Rsch. Found., La Jolla, Calif., 1979-87; v.p. for med. affairs Baylor U. Med. Ctr., Dallas, 1988-92; ret., 1992. Dir. health care svcs. AMA, Chgo., 1966-67; sr. mgmt. counsel Booz, Allen & Hamilton, Chgo., 1967-90; clin. prof. medicine U. So. Calif., L.A., 1968-92. Contbg. author: The New Health Care Market, 1985; also articles. Capt. M.C., U.S. Army, 1944-46. Mem. Am. Coll. Physician Execs., Am. Diabetes Assn. (bd. govs. So. Calif. 1955-57), L.A. Diabetes Assn. (pres. 1955, San Gabriel br. 1960-61). Home: Pasadena, Calif. Died Oct. 8, 2009.

PERKINS, WILLIAM H., JR., retired finance company executive; b. Rushville, Ill., Aug. 4, 1921; s. William H. and Sarah Elizabeth (Logsdon) P.; m. Eileen Nelson, Jan. 14, 1949; 1 child, Gary Douglas. Pres. Howlett-Perkins Assos., Chgo. Mem. Ill. AEC, 1963-84, sec., 1970-84; apptd. by Pres. to adv. bd. Nat. Armed Forces Mus., Smithsonian Instn., 1964-82; army aide to Anthony Eden and Lord Halifax of Great Britain, UN Conf., 1945. Sgt.-at-arms Democratic Nat. Conv., 1952, 56, del.-at-large, 1964, 68, 72; spl. asst. to chmn. Dem. Nat. Com., 1960; mem. Presdl. Inaugural Com., 1961, 65, 69, 73, ins. policy agent, 1961. With US Army, 1944-46 Mem. Ill. Ins. Fedn. (pres. 1965-84), Ill. C. of C. (chmn. legis. com. 1971), Chgo. Assn. Commerce and Industry (legis. com., Raoul Wallenberg Humanitarian award 1993), Sangamo Club, Masons, Shriners. Methodist. Home: Utica, Ill. Died Apr. 19, 2009.

PERRET, JOSEPH ALOYSIUS, banker, consultant; b. Phila., Feb. 26, 1929; s. Joseph Henry and Mary Rose (Martin) P.; m. Nancy S. Bott, June 24, 1950; children— Kathlyne, Robert, Susan, Michael. Student, U. Pa., 1953-57, Temple U., 1957-58, Stonier Grad. Sch. Banking, 1966. Head analyst Phila. Nat. Bank, 1953-57; spl. banking rep. Burroughs Corp., Phila., 1957-59; v.p. First Pa. Banking & Trust Co., Phila., 1959-66, Md. Nat. Bank, Balt., 1966-70, sr. v.p., 1970-75, Comml. Credit Co., Balt., 1975-78, Sanwa Bank Calif., Los Angeles, 1978-91; cons., from 1991. Chmn. bd. Star System, Inc., San Diego. Mem. Am. Bankers Assn., Data Processing Mgmt. Assn., Balt.-Washington Regional Clearing House (chmn. 1970), Calif. Bankers Cleanring House Assn. (chmn. 1990). Clubs: Country of Md; Merchants (Balt.); Friendly Hills Country (Whittier, Calif.). Home: Luthvle Timon, Md. Died July 2, 2009.

PERRY, CHARLES AUSTIN, retired seminary president; b. White Plains, NY, Nov. 5, 1928; s. Russell Eleven and Jennie-Belle (Greenidge) P.; m. Clara Joy Jones, June 22, 1951; 2 children. BA, Cornell U., 1950; MDiv, Va. Theol. Sem., 1961. Ordained to ministry The Episc. Ch. as deacon, 1961, as priest, 1962. Priest-in-charge Our Saviour Parish, Montpelier, Va., 1962-63; assoc. St. Paul Parish, Charlottesville, Va., 1963-68; rector Trinity Parish, Bloomington, Ind., 1968-70; exec. officer Washington Diocese, 1971-81; provost Cathedral of St. Peter and Paul, Washington, 1978-90; pres., dean Ch. Divinity Sch. of the Pacific, Berkeley, Calif., 1990—95. Fellow Coll. of Preachers. Died Oct. 24, 2010.

PERRY, J. WARREN, health facility administrator, educator; b. Richmond, Ind., Oct. 25, 1921; s. Charles Thomas and Zona M. (Ohler) Perry. BA, DePauw U., 1944; postgrad., Harvard U., 1948—49; MA, Northwestern U., 1952, PhD, 1955; DSc (hon.), D'Youville Coll., 1990, Med. Coll. Ohio, 1996, DePauw U., 1998. Instr. St. John's Mil. Acad., Delafield, Wis., 1944—47; counselor, asst. prof. psychology U. Ill.-Chgo., 1953—56; dir. prosthetic-orthotic edn., asst. prof. orthopaedic surgery Northwestern U. Med. Sch., 1957—61; lectr. psychology U. Chgo., 1957—61; asst. chief div. tng. Vocat. Rehab. Adminstrn., HEW, 1961—64, dep. asst. commr. research and tng., 1964—66; prof. health scis. adminstrn. SUNY-Buffalo, 1966—95, founding dean Sch. Health Related Professions, 1966—77, dean and prof. emeritus, from 1985. Mary E. Switzer Meml. lectr., Dallas, 1977, Lexington, 91; mem. Task Force for Legislation for Allied Health Professions, 1966—67; com. edn. allied health professions and svcs., coun. med. edn. AMA, 1968—73; nat. adv. com. Am. Dietetic Assn., 1970—75, chmn., 1972—75; nat. rev. com., regional med. programs HEW, 1969—72; mem-.steering com. on manpower policy for primary care bd. health promotion and disease prevention Inst. of Medicine-NAS, 1981—83, sr. advisor com. to study role allied health, com. to study med. manpower in VA, 1988—91; spl. med. adv. com. VA, 1974—77; mem. task force on manpower for prevention Fogarty Internat. Inst., NIH, 1975—76; mem. acad. planning com. Mass. Gen. Hosp. Founding editor Jour. Allied Health, 1972—78, editor emeritus, from 1985; contbr. articles to profl. jours. Mem. Legacy Soc.; charter mem. Cmty. Found. for Greater Buffalo, from 1998; patron of the arts Coun. of Buffalo and Erie County, 2000; bd. dirs., dir. com. opera edn. Lyric Opera Guild, Chgo., 1957—61; chmn. acad. divsn. dr., coun. trustees Buffalo Philharm. Orch., 1987—93; bd. dirs. Goodwill Industries, Buffalo, 1969—76; trustee Cmty. Music Sch. Buffalo, 1977—80; adv. bd., v.p. Sisters of Charity Hosp., Buffalo, 1969—87, pres., 1986—88; bd. visitors U. Pitts., 1977—80; coun. trustees D'youville Coll., Buffalo, 1978—88, trustee emeritus, 1989—95; bd. dirs. Am. Lung Assn. Western N.Y., 1975—92, pres., 1983; bd. dirs. ARC, Buffalo, Artpark State Performing Arts Ctr., Lewiston, NY, 1986—96, Am. Lung Assn. N.Y.State, 1981—85, exec. com., 1989—92; chmn. N.Y. State Coalition Smoking or Health, Albany, NY, 1987—91; trustee Theodore Roosevelt Inaugural Site Found., 1987, pres., 1991—94; bd. advisors Buffalo Coun. on World Affairs, 1987—88; trustee Buffalo Opera Co., 1989—94, chmn. opera adv. coun., 1995—97. Recipient Sustained Superior Svc. award, HEW, 1965, Disting. Svc. award, Am. Orthotics-Prosthetics Assn., 1966, Buffalo Opera Co., 1995, Chancellor's award for adminstrv. svc., SUNY, 1977, 1st Allied Health Leadership award, 1988, Disting. Author award, Jour. Allied Health, 1978, Cert. of Merit, AMA, 1979, Pres. Cir. Pin, Buffalo State Coll., 1993, 50th Anniversary Alumni citation, De Pauw U., 1994, Outstanding Svc. award, Theodore Roosevelt Inaugural Site Found., 1994, Theodore Roosevelt Exemplary Citizenship award, 1997, Brotherhood/Sisterhood award in health, NCCJ Western N.Y., 1995, Christmas Seal Hall of Fame award, ALA N.Y. State, 1995, Disting. Citizenship award, Mayor of Buffalo, 1995, Patron of the Arts award, Arts Coun. of Buffalo and Erie County, 2000, Alumni Achievement award, SUNY-Buffalo, 2000, Wisdom award of honor, 1999, Humanitarian award, Coordinated Care Assn. Buffalo, 2002, Clara Barton award, ARC (Greater Buffalo chpt.), 2004; named Outstanding Individual Philanthropist, Nat. Soc, Fundraising Execs. Western N.Y., 1992, Ky. Col., 1969, Nebr. Admn., 1964, Man of the Yr., Opera Found. Buffalo, Inc., 2000, J. Warren Perry Disting. Author award in his honor, Jour. Allied Health, Perry Scholarship in his honor, U. Buffalo Found., J. Warren Perry Outstanding Vol. Leadership award in his honor, Western N.Y. chpt. ALA, J. Warren Perry Meml. lectr. in his honor, SUNY, Buffalo, Buffalo Philharmonic Chorus, 2003; fellow Wisdom Hall of Fame fellow, Wisdom Soc., 1999; Perry Lecture Hall, D'Youville Coll. named in his honor, 2004. Fellow: Assn. Schs. of Allied Health Professions (pres. 1969—70, Cert. of Merit 1977, Pres.'s award 1978, Honors of Soc. award 1984); mem.: Nat. Rehab. Assn., Am. Pers. and Guidance Assn., Am. Dietetics Assn. (hon.), APA, Phi Beta Kappa, Delta Tau Delta, Phi Delta Kappa (pres. 1955). Home: Buffalo, NY. Died Aug. 5, 2010.

PERRY, MALCOLM OLIVER, vascular surgeon; b. Allen, Tex., Sept. 3, 1929; m. Jeannine Perry; children: Malcolm, Jolene. BA, U. Tex., 1951; MD, U. Tex., Dallas, 1955. Diplomate Am. Bd. Surgery, Am. Bd. Gen. Vascular Surgery. Intern Letterman Army Hosp., San Francisco, 1955-56; resident in surgery Parkland Meml. Hosp., Dallas, 1958-62; fellow in vascular surgery U. Calif., San Francisco, 1962-63; asst. prof. surgery U. Tex., Dallas, 1962-67, assoc. prof. surgery, chief vascular surgery, 1967-71, prof. surgery, chief vascular surgery, 1971-74; prof. surgery U. Wash., Seattle, 1974-77; prof. surgery, chief vascular surgery Cornell U. Med. Coll., NYC, 1978-87, Vanderbilt U. Sch. Medicine, Nashville, 1987-91; chief vascular surgery Tex. Tech U. Health Scis. Ctr., Lubbock, 1991-95; prof. surgery Southwestern Med. Sch., Dallas. Capt. USAF, 1955-58; major Tex. Air N.G., 1960-66. Home: Jacksonville, Tex. Died Dec. 5, 2009.

PESCH, LEROY ALLEN, physician, educator, health and hospital consultant, business executive; b. Mt. Pleasant, Iowa, June 22, 1931; s. Herbert Lindsey and Mary Clarissa (Tyner) P.; children from previous marriage: Christopher Allen, Brian Lindsey, Daniel Ethan; m. Donna J. Stone, Dec. 28, 1975 (dec. Feb. 1985); stepchildren: Christopher Scott Kneifel, Linda Suzanne Kneifel; m. Gerri Ann Cotton, Sept. 27, 1986; 1 child, Tyner Ford. Student, State U. Iowa, 1948—49, Iowa State U., 1950—52; MD cum laude, Washington U., St. Louis, 1956. Intern Barnes Hosp., St. Louis, 1956-57; rsch. assoc. NIH, Bethesda, Md., 1957-59; asst. resident medicine Grace-New Haven Hosp., New Haven, 1959-60; clin. fellow Yale Med. Sch., New Haven, 1960-61, instr. medicine, 1961-62, asst. prof. medicine, 1962-63, asst. dir. liver study unit, 1961-63; assoc. physician Grace-New Haven Hosp., 1961-63; assoc. prof. medicine Rutgers U., New Brunswick, NJ, 1963-64, prof., 1964-66, chmn. dept. medicine, 1965-66; assoc. dean, prof. medicine Stanford Sch. Medicine, 1966-68; mem. gen. medicine study sect. NIH, 1965-70, chmn., 1969-70; dean, dir. univ. hosps. SUNY, Buffalo, 1968-71; dep. asst. sec. manpower HEW, 1970-72, spl. cons. to sec. for health, 1970-75; prof. div. biol. scis. and medicine U. Chgo., 1972-77; prof. pathology Northwestern U., 1977-79; health and hosp. cons.; chmn., chief exec. officer Health Resources Corp. Am., 1981-84; chmn. bd. dirs. Republic Health Corp., 1985-88; chmn., chief exec. officer The Bora Health Group, Seattle, 1987-92; pres. Genus Tech. Corp., from 1987; chmn., chief exec. officer The Pesch Group Cos., Sun Valley, Idaho, from 1989. Contbr. articles on internal medicine to profl. jours. Bd. dirs. Buffalo Med. Found., 1969-72, Health Orgn., Western N.Y., 1968-71, Joffrey Ballet, N.Y.C., 1980—; trustee Michael Reese Hosp. and Med. Ctr., Chgo., 1971-76, pres., CEO, 1971-77; mem. exec. bd. Auditorium Theatre Coun., Chgo.; trustee W. Clement and Jessie V. Stone Found.; mem. adv. com. Congl. Awards; pres. Pesch Found. Sr. asst. surgeon USPHS, 1957-59. Mem.: AAAS, Am. Soc. Biol. Chemists, Am. Assn. for Clin. Rsch., Am. Assn. for Study of Liver Disease. Died June 19, 2010.

PETERSEN, RAYMOND CARL, chemist, researcher; b. Ware, Mass., July 24, 1929; s. Peter and Karen Marie (Thompson) P.; m. Norma Mae Hohn, June 6, 1954; children— Carl, Erica. BA., Amherst Coll., 1951; Ph.D., Brown U., 1956. Sr. research scientist Sprague Electric Co., North Adams, Mass., 1956-70; sr. scientist Martin Marietta, Balt., 1971-72; sr. chemist Taylor Instrument Co., Rochester, N.Y., 1972; lab. dir. City of Balt., 1972-79; chief chemist Solarex Corp., Md., 1979—. Contbr. articles to chemistry and photovolaics jours. Patentee in field. Chmn. Democratic Town Com., Williamstown, Mass., 1962-68. Mem. Am. Chem. Soc. (editor of "The Chesapeake Chemist" 1981—), Electrochem. Soc., AAAS. Congregationalist. Avocation: model trains. Home: Ellicott City, Md. Died Feb. 7, 2009.

PETOK, SAMUEL, retired manufacturing company executive; b. Detroit, Aug. 12, 1922; s. Harry and Jennie (Weingarten) P.; m. Fayne Joyce Myers, June 26, 1952; children— Carol, Seth, Michael. BA in History, Wayne State U., Detroit, 1945; postgrad., Medill Sch. Journalism, Northwestern U., 1946. Reporter Detroit Free Press, 1946-50; account exec. McCann Erickson, 1950-52; pub. relations exec. Chrysler Corp., 1952-70; Vice pres. public relations and advt. White Motor Corp., Cleve., 1971-76; dir. communications automotive ops. Rockwell Internat. Co., Troy, Mich., 1976-77, corp. staff v.p. public relations Pitts., 1977-78, v.p. communications, 1978-82, sr. v.p. communications, mem. mgmt. com., 1982-88; retired. Former trustee Arthur W. Page Soc.; trustee Hist. Soc. Princeton. Recipient Page One award Newspaper Guild Detroit, 1948 Mem. Pub. Rels. Soc. Am. (Silver Anvil award 1964), Internat. Pub. Rels. Assn., Overseas Press Club Am., The Old Guard of Princeton, Nassau Club, Cherry Valley Country Club. Home: Skillman, NJ. Died Apr. 27, 2009.

PETTENGILL, DANIEL WALDRON, retired actuary; b. Cambridge, Mass., Mar. 4, 1916; s. Ray Waldron and Rachel Thayer (Little) P.; m. Jane Barbara Guiney, Dec. 22, 1949; children— Ann Pettengill Shea, Sara Pettengill Petersen BA, Bowdoin Coll., 1937. Actuarial student Aetna Life & Casualty Co., Hartford, Conn., 1937-50, asst. actuary, 1950-54, assoc. actuary, 1954-59, actuary, 1959-64, v.p., 1964-78, ret., 1978. Mem. SSA Medicare Fiscal Intermediary and Carrier Groups, 1966-71; mem. Adv. Council on Health Ins. for Disabled, Washington, 1968; chmn. Health Ins. Council, N.Y.C., 1968-69 Contbr. articles, chpts. to profl. publs. Chmn. North Central Conn. Health Planning Agy., 1976-77; mem. Conn. Health Coordinating Council, 1977-79. Served to 1st lt. AUS, 1942-45; NATOUSA, PTO Recipient Outstanding Service award Council-Employee Benefits, 1965, Harold R. Gordon award Internat. Assn. Health Underwriters, 1973, Extraordinary Service award Health Care Fin. Agy., HEW, 1978, citation CSC, 1978 Fellow Soc. Actuaries (v.p. 1973-75); mem. Am. Acad. Actuaries, Inst. Medicine Republican. Mem. United Ch. of Christ. Clubs: Old Guard (West Hartford, Conn.) Avocation: volunteer work. Home: West Hartford, Conn. Died Nov. 5, 2009.

PETTIT, GHERY DEWITT, retired veterinary medicine educator; b. Oakland, Calif., Sept. 6, 1926; s. Hermon DeWitt Pettit and Marion Esther (St. John) Menzies; m. Frances Marie Seitz, July 5, 1948; children: Ghery St. John, Paul Michael. BS in Animal Sci., U. Calif., Davis, 1948, BS in Vet. Sci., 1951, DVM, 1953. Charter diplomate Am. Coll. Vet. Surgeons. Asst. prof. vet. surgery U. Calif., Davis, 1953-61; prof. vet. surgery Wash. State U., Pullman, 1961-91, prof. emeritus, from 1991. Mem. Wash. State Vet. Bd. Govs., 1981—88, chmn., 1987; vis. fellow Sydney U., Australia, 1977. Author/editor: Intervertebral Disc Protrusion in the Dog, 1966; co-author: Centennial History of the Washington State University College of Veterinary Medicine, 1999; cons. editoral bd. Jour. Small Animal Practice, Eng., 1970-88; mem. editoral bd. Compendium on C.E., Lawrenceville, N.J., 1983-86, editoral rev. bd. Jour. Vet. Surgery, Phila., 1984-86, editor 1987-92; contbr. articles to profl. jours., chpts. to books. Elder Presbyn. Ch., Pullman, from 1967. With USN, 1944—46. Recipient Norden Disting. Tchr. award Wash. State U. Class 1971, Faculty of Yr. award Wash. State U. Student Com., 1985. Mem.: AVMA, Am. Coll. Vet. Surgeons (recorder 1970—77, pres., chmn. bd. dirs. 1978—80), Kiwanis Internat., Am. Legion, Phi Kappa Sigma (chpt. advisor from 1981, internat. 2d v.p. 1993—98, internat. pres. 1998—2000, Alumnus of Yr. award 2006), Phi Zeta, Sigma Xi. Republican. Avocations: camping, sailing. Home: Pullman, Wash. Died May 17, 2009.

PETTY, THOMAS LEE, internist, educator; b. Boulder, Colo., Dec. 24, 1932; s. Roy Stone and and Eleanor Marie (Kudrna) P.; m. Carol Lee Piepho, Aug. 7, 1954; children: Caryn, Thomas, John. BA, U. Colo., 1955, MD, 1958. Intern Phila. Gen. Hosp., 1958-59; resident U. Mich., 1959-60, U. Colo., Denver, 1960-62, pulmonary fellow, 1962-63, chief resident medicine, 1963-64, instr. medicine, 1962-64, asst. prof., 1964-68, assoc. prof., 1968-74, prof. medicine, 1974—2009; pres. Presbyn./St. Luke's Ctr. for Health Scis. Edn., 1989-95; practice medicine, specializing in internal medicine, pulmonary medicine Denver, 1962—2009; prof. medicine Rush Univ., 1992—2009. Cons. Kindred Hosp., 1991-2009. Author: For Those Who Live and Breathe, 1967, 2d edit., 1972, Intensive and Rehabilitative Respiratory Care, 1971, 3d edit., 1982, Chronic Obstructive Pulmonary Disease, 1978, 2d edit., 1985, Principles and Practice of Pulmonary Rehabilitation, 1993, Enjoying Life With COPD, 1995, 3d edit., Pulmonary Disorders of the Elderly, 2007, others;

contbr. articles to profl. jours. NIH and Found. grantee, 1966-88. Master ACP, Am. Coll. Chest Physicians (master, pres. 1982); mem. Assn. Am. Physicians, Assn. of Pulmonary Program Dirs. (founding pres. 1983-84, chmn. nat. lung health edn. program 1995—, co-chmn. 2000-04), Am. Bd. Internal Medicine (bd. govs. 1986-92), Am. Thoracic Soc. (Disting. Achievement award 1995), Phi Beta Kappa, Phi Delta Theta, Alpha Omega Alpha, Phi Rho Sigma (pres. 1976-78). Home: Denver, Colo. Died Dec. 12, 2009.

PFAFFENROTH, SARA BEEKEY, English language educator; b. Reading, Pa., Dec. 2, 1941; d. Cyrus Ezra and Viola Bessie (Sweigart) Beekey; m. Peter Albert Pfaffenroth, June 26, 1966; children: Elizabeth Kilmer, Peter Cyrus, Catherine Genevieve. AB, Bryn Mawr Coll., 1963, MA, Ind. U., 1964. Instr. English, Northwestern Mich. Coll., Traverse City, 1964-66, Middlesex County Coll., Edison, N.J., 1966-88; prof. English, County Coll. of Morris, Randolph, N.J., 1968—; grants cons., 1979-82, coord. internat. studies program County Coll. of Morris, 1988—. Editor: Faces and Voices; an Intercultural Reader, 1990. Bd. dirs. Morris Area Girl Scout Coun., German Lang. Sch. Morris County. Recipient poetry award Bryn Mawr Arts Coun., 1963, Gertrude Saucier Hist. Poetry award, 1970; mid-career fellow Princeton U., 1983-84, 96-97. Mem. N.J. Poetry Soc., MLA, Coll. English Assn., Jane Austen Soc. N.Am., N.J. Collegiate Consortium for Internat./Intercultural Edn. (pres.), N.J. Consortia for Internat./Global Edn. (coun. rep.), Communities Coll. Humanities Assn., Soc. for Internat. Edn., Tng. and Rsch. Editor anthologies: Beyond Tether, 1975, A Palette of Poets, 1976, Endless Waters Welling Up, 1977, From Rim to Rim, 1978, Crystal Cadences, 1980; assoc. editor Jour. N.J. Poets, 1989-97. Lutheran. Home: Chester, NJ. Died Oct. 7, 2009.

PFUND, EDWARD THEODORE, JR., electronics company executive; b. Methuen, Mass., Dec. 10, 1923; s. Edward Theodore and Mary Elizabeth (Banning) Pfund; m. Marga Emmi Andre, Nov. 10, 1954 (div. 1978); children: Angela M., Gloria I., Edward Theodore; m. Ann Lorenne Dille, Jan. 10, 1988. BS magna cum laude, Tufts Coll., 1950; postgrad, U. Southern Calif., 1950, Columbia U., 1953, U. Calif., LA, 1956, postgrad, 1958. Radio engr. WLAW, Lawrence-Boston, 1942—50; fgn. svc. staff officer Voice Am., Tangier, Munich, 1950—54; project. engr. Crusade Freedom, Munich, 1955; project mgr., materials specialist United Electrodynamics Inc., Pasadena, Calif., 1956—59; cons. HI Thompson Fiber Glass Co., LA, 1959, Andrew Corp., Chgo., 1959, Satellite Broadcast Assocs., Encino, Calif., 1982, TRW Inc., Redondo Beach, from 1993; dir. programs devel. Asia-Pacific TRW Space & Tech. Group, Redondo Beach, Calif., 1982, Pacific Telecom. Coun., Honolulu, 1993. Tchg. staff Pasadena City Coll., Calif., 1959; dir. engring., chief engr. Electronics Specialty Co., LA, Thomaston, Conn., 1959—61; with Hughes Aircraft Co., 1955, 1961—89; mgr. Middle East Programs, 1971—89, Far East, L.Am. & African Market Devel., LA, 1971—89; dir. internat. programs devel. Hughes Comm. Internat., 1985—89; mng. dir. ET Satellite Assocs. Internat., 1989, Rolling Hills Estates, 1989. Contbr. articles to profl. jours. With US Army, 1942—46. Mem.: AIAA, Sigma Pi Sigma, Phi Beta Kappa. Died Mar. 7, 2010.

PHARIS, WILLIAM LEONARD, retired educational leadership educator; b. NC, July 23, 1928; s. William L. Pharis; m. Dorothy Stewart, June 7, 1952; children: Stewart, Will. BS, Ga. Tchrs. Coll., 1951; MA, George Peabody Coll., 1952; Ed.D., Tchrs. Coll., Columbia U., 1960. Assoc. prof. ednl. adminstrn. U. Nebr., Lincoln, 1960-66; prof., chmn. dept. ednl. adminstrn. and supervision Auburn U., Ala., 1966-69, prof. ednl. leadership, 1981-85. Exec. dir. Nat. Assn. Elem. Sch. Prins., Arlington, Va., 1969-81 Author: Inservice Education of Elementary School Principals, 1962, The Elementary School Principalship in 1978: A Research Study, 1979; also numerous articles. Served in USCG, 1945-47. Home: Auburn, Ala. Died Feb. 24, 2010.

PHELPS, EDITH BLAKESLEE, organization executive; b. Worcester, Mass., June 23, 1917; d. George Hubbard and Edna (Day) Blakeslee; m. William Griswold Phelps, Sept. 5, 1941 (dec.); children: Judith Phelps Felton, Lisa, Catherine. BA, Smith Coll., 1938; postgrad., Clark U., Worcester, 1938-39; Litt.D. (hon.), Emerson Coll., Boston, 1973. Head history dept. Riverdale (N.Y.) Country Sch. Girls, 1939-43; instr. history cadet tng. detachment USAAF, Coll., Idaho, 1943-44; lectr. Council Fgn. Affairs, Boston, 1946-51; head history dept. Concord (Mass.) Acad., 1958-59, asst. headmistress, 1959-63; prin. Dana Hall Sch., Wellesley, Mass., 1963-73; edn. cons. Nat. Assn. Ind. Schs., 1973-74; nat. exec. dir. Girls Clubs Am., Inc., NYC, 1974-82; dir. Ctr. for Study Girls' Devel. Harvard U. Grad. Sch. Edn., Cambridge, Mass., from 1983. Nat. adv. bd. Center Early Adolescence, 1977—; com. chmn. Smith Coll. Day Sch., 1962-65; vis. com. student affairs M.I.T. Corp., 1965-68; chmn. Commn. Ind. Schs., 1965-68, v.p., 1967-69, exec. com., 1965—, pres., 1969-70; chmn. Nat. Collaboration for Youth, 1977—, pres., 1976-79; trustee Smith Coll., 1974—, Middlesex Sch., 1973-76, 83— Contbr. articles to profl. jours. Recipient Smith Coll. medal, 1971; Aspen Inst. presdl. fellow, 1980 Mem. Nat. Assn. Ind. Schs. (dir. 1965-68), Nat. Assn. Prins. of Schs. for Girls, Headmisstresses Assn. East. Died Apr. 15, 2009.

PHILIPS, GEORGE, publishing company executive; b. NYC, Feb. 1, 1931; s. Phillip and Antonina (Richko) P.; m. Barbara Joan Unger, Nov. 1, 1952; children: Andrea, Gregory, Elisabeth BS in Civil Engring., Cooper Union, 1952; MS in Indsl. Mgmt., MIT, 1954. Pres. Corplan Assocs., Chgo., 1956-66; exec. v.p. Tootsie Roll Industries, Chgo., 1966-69; pres. Foto Fair Internat., Dayton, Ohio, 1969-70; v.p. Cadence Industries, West Caldwell, N.J., 1970-80; sr. v.p. AAMCO, Phila., 1980-81; group v.p. Macmillan Inc., NYC, from 1981; also pres. P.F. Collier Inc., NYC. Author, editor: Economic Impact of Technology Upon Chicago, 1978 Trustee Patterson Gen. Hosp., N.J., 1968, Katherine Gibbs Sch., Mountclair, N.J., 1984. Served with U.S. Army, 1955-56 Home: Ridgewood, NJ. Died Sept. 19, 2009.

PHILIPS, GERALD MYRON, advertising agency executive; b. NYC, Oct. 28, 1926; s. Burt R. and Rose (Zuckerman) P.; children: Mark Reid, Amy Sarah, Julie Evan. BA, NYU, 1949; cert. in fine arts, Cooper Union, 1954. Studio artist Am. Book Co., NYC, 1949-50; book designer Country Life Press, Garden City, N.Y., 1950-52; art dir. L.W. Frohlich, Inc., NYC, 1952-54, William Douglas McAdams, NYC, 1954-62; vice chmn., creative dir. for art Kallir, Philips, Ross, Inc., NYC, from 1962. Served with U.S. Army, 1945-46. Recipient Award of Merit N.Y. Art Dirs. Club; recipient Award of Merit Am. Inst. Graphics, Award of Merit N.J. Art Dirs. Club Mem. N.Y. Art Dirs. Club Democrat. Jewish. Home: New York, NY. Died Sept. 20, 2009.

PHILLIPS, DONNA SUE, education educator, educator; b. Decatur, Ill., Oct. 18, 1942; d. Howard C. and Evelyn (McMillan) P. BS in Edn., Ea. Ill. U., Charleston, 1964; MS in Edn., Western Ill. U., Macomb, 1967; PhD, Ohio State U., 1977. Phys. edn. tchr. Forman High Sch., Manito, Ill., 1964-66; instr. Western Ill. U., Macomb, Ill., 1967-72, coach, 1970-85, asst. prof., 1972-77, assoc. prof., 1977-87, prof., from 1987; teaching asst. Ohio State U., Columbus, 1972-73; chair dept. Phys. Edn. Western Ill. U., Macomb, Ill., 1993. Evaluator N. Ctrl. U. High Sch. Urbana, Ill., 1987, N. Ctrl. Moline (Ill.) High Sch., 1988, N. Ctrl. Macomb (Ill.) High Sch., 1991; cons. Ill. State Bd. Edn., 1985-92; rep. Ill. Curriculum Coun., 1989-92. Author: Manual for Fitness Internship Supervisors, 1984, Curriculum Guide for K-12 Physical Education, 1985, Handbook for Teacher Education Majors, 1990. Recipient Ill. Fitness award Western Dist. Ill. AAHPERD, 1988, Faculty Excellence award Western Ill. U., 1989, 92, 93, Svc. award Ill. Assn. Health, Phys. Edn., Recreation and Dance, 1992; named Tchr. of Yr. Coll. Western Ill. U., 1989, Western Ill. Athletic Hall of Fame, 1990; grantee Faculty Mentor Rsch. Ill. Assn. Health, Phys. Edn., Recreation and Dance, 1992, Coll. Western Ill. U., 1992. Mem. AAHPERD (v.p. 1994—), Ill. Assn. Health, Phys. Edn., Recreation and Dance, Am. Assn. Fitness in Bus. and Industry, Phi Epsilon Sigma, Phi Kappa Phi, Kappa Delta Pi. Home: Colchester, Ill. Died Jan. 10, 2010.

PHILLIPS, HARVEY G., musician, performing arts educator; b. Aurora, Mo., Dec. 2, 1929; s. Jesse E. and Lottie A. (Chapman) P.; m. Carol A. Dorvel, Feb. 22, 1954; children: Jesse E., Harvey G., Thomas A. Student, U. Mo., 1947-48, Juilliard Sch. Music, 1950-54, Manhattan Sch. Music, 1956-58; MusD (hon.), New England Conservatory of Mu, 1971; HHD (hon.), U. Mo., Columbia, 1987. Founder, v.p. Mentor Music, Inc., NYC, 1958—79; v.p. Wilder Music, Inc., NYC, 1964-77, Magellan Music, Inc., NYC, from 1971, Peaslee Music Inc., from 1971; established faculty position Aspen Sch. Music, summer 1962, U. Wis., summer 1963, Hartt Sch. Music, Hartford, Conn., 1962-64, Mannes Sch. Music, NYC, 1964-65; exec. v.p. Orch. USA, NYC, 1962-65; exec. v.p., pers. mgr., tubist Symphony of the Air N.Y.C., 1957-66; v.p. Brass Artists, Inc., NYC, from 1964; adminstrv. asst. to Julius Bloom, Rutgers U., New Brunswick, NJ, 1966-67; v.p. fin. affairs New Eng. Conservatory of Music, Boston, 1967-71; mem. faculty Sch. Music, Ind. U., Bloomington, 1971-94, Disting. prof. music, trustee, 1979—94, disting. prof. emeritus, 1994—2010. Adv. bd. Am. Brass Chamber Music, Inc., from 1971; chmn. bd. Summit Brass/Keystone Brass Inst., 1985—92, Rafael Mendez Brass Inst., from 1993; cons. Margun Music, Inc., from 1977; bd. dirs. Summit Brass. Brass coach Festival at Sandpoint, Idaho, 1986-94; mem. faculty Joven Orch., Spain, 1987-94, Festival Casal Orch., San Juan, P.R., 1964-76; dir. 1st Internat. Tuba Symposium Workshop, Ind. U., 1973, Brass-Wind Music Studios, Carnegie Hall, N.Y.C., 1961-67; tubist, King Bros. Circus Band, 1947, Ringling Bros. & Barnum & Bailey Circus Band, 1948-50, N.Y.C. Ballet Orch., 1951-71, N.Y.C. Opera Orch., 1951-62, Voice of Firestone Orch., 1951-53, Sauter-Finegan Orch., 1952-53, Band of America, 1952-54, NBC Opera Orch., 1956-65, Bell Tel. Hour Orch., 1956-66, Goldman Band, 1957-62; founding mem., tubist N.Y. Brass Quintet, 1954-67; condr., co-prodr. Burke-Phillips All Star Concert Band, 1960-62; co-founder, tubist Matteson-Phillips Tubajazz Consort, 1976-2010; founding mem. TubaShop Quartet, 1996—; rec. artist Crest Records, 1958-78-2010; originator Octubafest, TubaChristmas, Tubasantas, Tubajazz, TubaEaster, Tubacompany, Summertubafest; exec. editor Instrumentalist mag., 1986-96, bd. advisors, 1996-2010 Founder, pres. Harvey Phillips Found., Inc., N.Y.C., 1977-2010; bd. dirs. Mid-Am. Festival of the Arts, 1982-90, Bloomington Area Arts Coun., 1983-90; judge 1st Internt. tuba competition of CIEM Internat. Competition for Musical Performers, Geneva, 1991. Served with U.S. Army Field Band, 1955-56. Recipient Disting. Svc. to Music award Kappa Kappa Psi, 1978, Cmty. Svc. award City of Bloomington, 1978, Nat. Assn. Jazz Educators award, 1977, 78, Nat. Music Conf. award, 1977, T.U.B.A. award, 1978, MI Hummel The Tuba Player award, 1990, Disting. Achievement award Ednl. Press Assn. America, 1991, Mentor Ideal award Assn. Concert Bands, 1994, Lifetime Achievement award United Music Instruments, 1995, Sudler award medal of the Order of Merit Sousa Found., 1995, Summit Brass Outstanding Svc. and Support Internat. Brassfest, 1995, Orpheus award Phi Mu Alpha Sinfonia, 1997, Ind. U. President's medal, 2008; elected to Acad. Wind and Percussion Arts Nat. Band Assn., 1995; recipient Edwin Franko Goldman citation Am. Bandmasters Assn., 1996, Devel. of Mus. Artistry and Opportunities for Future Generations award Colonial Euphonium Tuba Inst., 1998, Lifetime Achievement award Rafael Mendez Brass Inst., 1998, Platinum Piston Lifetime Achievement award, U. Ga., 1999; Legion of Hon., Goldman Meml. Band, 2002; Harvey Phillips Day proclaimed New England Conservatory Music, 1971, Harvey Phillips Day proclaimed Marionville, Mo. Bicentennial, 1976, Harvey Phillips Weekend Gov. of Mo., 1982; named hon. mem. U.S. Army Band Pershings Own, 1984, Highest Pres.'s award, Ind. U., 2008; named to Am. Classical Music Hall of Fame, 2007-08. Mem. American Fedn. Musicians, Tubists Universal Brotherhood Assn. (bd. advs. 1973-2010, pres. 1984-87, hon.), Hoagy Carmichael Jazz Soc. (founder, acting pres. 1983), Tau Beta Sigma, Phi Mu Alpha Sinfonia (Orpheus award 1997), Kappa Gamma Psi. Died Oct. 20, 2010.

PHILLIPS, JAMES EDGAR, lawyer; b. NYC, Aug. 30, 1949; s. Jack Louis Phillips and Jacqueline (Kasper) Ehrman; children: Zachary J., Mark H. BA, Boston U., 1971; JD, Case Western Reserve U., 1975. Bar: Ohio 1975, US Supreme Ct. 1977, US Dist. Ct. (so. dist.) 1978, US Ct. Appeals (6th cir.) 1981, US Dist. Ct. (no. dist.) 1982, US Ct. Appeals (7th cir.) 2001. Asst. prosecutor Franklin County Prosecutor Office, Columbus, Ohio, 1975-77, sr. asst. prosecutor, 1977-79; assoc. Vorys, Sater, Seymour & Pease, Columbus, 1979-84, ptnr., from 1984; spl. prosecutor State of Ohio, from 1993. Gen. counsel Nat. Fraternal Order of Police, Washington, 1987-2002, Conrail Police #1, US Postal Police #2; mem. Bd. Profl. Law Enforcement Certification; mem. Wong Sun Soc., 1997—; adj. prof. Ohio State U. Moritz Sch. Law, 2005—. Author: Civil Recovery in Ohio, 1986, Collective Bargaining in the Pub. Sector, 1988; editor Bar Briefs; contbr. articles Jours., 1987-89. Pres. bd. dir. Ohio Ctr. for Law-Related Edn., 1985—95; bd. dirs. Schottenstein Stores Corp., from 2002, Alvis House, 2005—06. Fellow Ohio Bar Found., Columbus Bar Found., Ohio Bar Assn. (chmn. com. law-related edn. 1982-86), Columbus Bar Assn. (bd. govs. 2008-), Sixth Cir. Jud. Conf. (life); Ohio Assn. Criminal Defense Lawyers (bd. dirs., treas.). Avocations: travel, photography. Home: Columbus, Ohio. Died Aug. 11, 2010.

PHILLIPS, JILL META, writer, critic, astrologer; b. Detroit, Oct. 22, 1952; d. Leyson Kirk and Leona Anna (Rasmussen) P. Student pub. schs., Calif. Lit. counselor Book Builders, Charter Oak, Calif., 1966-77; pres. Moon Dance Astro Graphics, Covina, Calif., from 1994. Author: (with Leona Phillips) A Directory of American Film Scholars, 1975, The Good Morning Cookbook, 1976, G.B. Shaw: A Review of the Literature, 1976, T.E. Lawrence: Portrait of the Artist as Hero, 1977, The Archaeology of the Collective East, 1977, The Occult, 1977, D.H. Lawrence: A Review of the Literature and Biographies, 1978, Film Appreciation: A College Guide Book, 1979, Annus Mirabilis: Europe in the Dark and Middle Centuries, 1979, (with Leona Rasmussen Phillips) The Dark Frame: Occult Cinema, 1979, Misfit: The Films of Montgomery Clift, 1979; The Rain Maiden: A Novel of History, 1987, Walford's Oak: A Novel, 1990, The Fate Weaver: A Novel in Two Centuries, 1991, Birthday Secrets, 1998, Your Luck is in the Stars, 2000; columnist Dell Horoscope Mag., Astrology Your Daily Horoscope Mag., 1998—; contbr. book revs. to New Guard mag., 1974-76; contbr. numerous articles to profl. jours. including Dell Horoscope, Midnight Horoscope, Astrology-Your Daily Horoscope, Am. Astrology. Mem. Young Ams. for Freedom, Am. Conservative Union, Elmer Bernstein's Film Music Collection, Ghost Club London, Count Dracula Soc., Dracula Soc. London, Richard III Soc. Republican. Home: Claremont, Calif. Died Nov. 28, 2009.

PHILLIPS, JO ANN, medical/surgical and critical care nurse; b. Johnson County, Tenn., Feb. 19, 1940; d. Ezra Williams; divorced; children: Carl, Bryan. Diploma in practical nursing, Bristol (Tenn.) Tech. Sch., 1979; grad. in nursing, Walters State Community Coll., Morristown, Tenn., 1990. LPN, Tenn. Practical nurse geriatrics unit Johnson County Health Ctr., Mountain City, Tenn.; practical nurse ICU, emergency room, med.-surg. unit Johnson County Meml. Hosp., Mountain City; office nurse S.D. Wilson Jr., Mountain City; charge nurse med.-surg. and telemetry floor Humana Hosp., Morristown; home health care nurse Appalachian Home Health. Recipient Care award Johnson County Care Com., 1977. Died Jan. 25, 2009.

PHILLIPS, JOHN E., lawyer; b. Italy, Tex., Apr. 10, 1939; BBA, Hardin-Simmons U., 1961; LLB, Baylor U., 1967; LLM, So. Meth. U., 1975. Bar: Tex. 1967. Ptnr. Strasburger & Price L.L.P., Dallas. Mem. ABA, Dallas Bar Assn., Tex. Assn. Def. Counsel. Died Nov. 19, 2009.

PHILLIPS, LAUGHLIN, retired museum director, editor; b. Washington, Oct. 20, 1924; s. Duncan and Marjorie Grant (Acker) P.; m. Elizabeth Hood, 1956 (div. 1975); children: Duncan Vance, Elizabeth Laughlin; m. Jennifer Stats Cafritz, 1975. Student, Yale U., 1942-43; MA, U. Chgo., 1949. Fgn. svc. officer, 1949—64, Hanoi, Vietnam, 1950—53, Tehran, Iran, 1957—59; co-founder Washingtonian mag., 1965, editor, 1965-74, editor-in-chief, 1974-79; pres. Washington Mag., Inc., 1965-79; dir. Phillips Collection, 1972-92, chmn. bd., 1967—2002, chmn. emeritus, 2002—10. Trustee Nat. Com. for an Effective Congress, 1966-2010, MacDowell Colony, 1977-79; bd. dirs. UN Assn. America, 1997-2001. With AUS, 1943-46, PTO. Decorated Bronze Star; comendador Orden de Mayo al Mérito (Argentina); chevalier de l'Ordre de la Couronne (Belgium), knight's cross 1st class Order of Danebrog (Denmark); officier Arts et Lettres (France). Mem.: Rolling Rock Club (Ligonier, Pa.), Met. Club (Washington), Cosmos Club (Washington). Home: Washington, Conn. Died Jan. 24, 2010.

PHILLIPS, MIRIAM ERNESTINE, civic worker; b. Haverhill, Mass., Mar. 11, 1918; d. William B. and Ermina Floride (Coburn) Faulcon; m. Oscar George Dudley Phillips, Dec. 19, 1954; children: Peter Joshua, Miriam Elaine. BA in Edn., U. Mass.-Boston, 1985; MA in English, U. Mass., Boston, 1987. Adminstrv. asst. Am. Bapt. Chs. of Mass., Boston, 1948-58. Contbr. articles to religious publs. Nat. denominational v.p. Church Women United, 1974-77, Northeast regional v.p., 1977-80, other nat. and state offices; mem.-at-large Gen. Council, Am. Bapt. Chs. USA, 1969-71, rep. to gen. bd., 1971-78, Participant study tour to People's Republic of China, 1978; mem. exec. com. Bd. Nat. Ministries; rep. to Nat. Council Chs., 1969-72, del. to World Council Chs., 1968; v.p.

Am. Bapt. Chs. Mass., 1972, 73, 1st v.p., 1987—, chmn. ann. meeting com., mem. personnel com., mem. communications com.; nat. chmn. communications Am. Bapt. Women USA, 1964-68; trustee Mass. Bible Soc.; adj. faculty Andover Newton Theol. Sch., 1977-91; trustee Andover Newton Theol. Sch., 1969-91, hon. trustee, 1991—, sec. bd. dirs., mem. coms.; commr. Medford Housing Authority, Mass., 1972—, chmn., 1974-75, 89—; co-founder Medford br. NAACP, chmn. press and publicity; bd. dirs. Middlesex-Cambridge Lung Assn., Family Service Assn. of Greater Boston, Resthaven Home. Recipient Valiant Woman award Ch. Women United, 1979, Walter Telfer award for Excellence in Supervision Andover Newton Theol. Sch., 1989. Avocation: travel. Home: Winchester, Mass. Died Dec. 22, 2009.

PHILLIPS, THELMA, library administrator; b. York County, S.C., Mar. 27, 1924; d. Adam I. and Maggie (Falls) McDaniel; m. Paul Phillips, Aug. 10, 1947; children— Paula Lorraine, Elaine Freddye, Paul, Janet Yvonne. A.B. in Social Scis. N.C. Coll., Durham, 1945; B.L.S., U. Chgo., 1946; postgrad., Tuskegee (Ala.) Inst., 1947-48, Reference librarian Tuskegee Inst., 1946-50; librarian hosp. VA Hosp., Tuskegee, 1950-52; librarian St. Mary's High Sch., Fredericksburg, Tex., 1964-66; librarian County Gillespie, Fredericksburg, 1966-73; extension coordinator Arlington (Tex.) Pub. Library, 1973-76, assoc. dir., 1977—; workshop presenter Central Tex. Library System, 1984; steering com. Tex. Gov.'s Conf., Austin, 1973; project dir. Library Vol. Program, 1980-81; del. White House Conf. Libraries Info. Services, Washington, 1979; adv. bd. Tex. Library Systems Act., 1969-74. Project dir. City of Arlington City-Wide Vol. Program, 1983-84. Named The Arlington Woman, Biog. Feature, 1974. Mem. Southwest Library Assn. (developed Southwest cultures bibliographies 1975-76), ALA, Tex. Library Assn. (Librarian Yr. 1971, pub. library div. pres. 1973-74, dist. 7 chmn. 1979-80, planning. com. 1980-81), Arlington C. of C., Nat. Assn. Vol. Adminstrn., Nat. Conf. Citizen Involvement. Clubs: Soroptimist (Arlington); Democratic Women (Fredericksburg). Home: Fort Worth, Tex. Died Mar. 18, 2010.

PHILLIPS, WILLIAM H., aeronautical engineer; b. Port Sunlight, Eng., May 31, 1918; BA in Engring., MIT, 1939, MA in Engring., 1940. Head aerospace mech. divsn. NACA, 1940-58, chief Flight Dynamics and Control divsn., 1958-79; disting. rsch. assoc. NASA, Hampton, Va., from 1979. Recipient Mechanics and Contrs. Flight award, 1988. Mem. AIAA (Lawrence Sperry award 1944), Nat Acad. Engrs. Home: Middleton, Mass. Died June 27, 2009.

PHINNEY, BERNARD O., research scientist, educator; b. July 29, 1917; s. Bernard Orrin and Franc Maude (Lawrence) P.; m. Sally Ball Bush; children: Scott, Katcha; m. Isabelle Jean Swift, Dec. 11, 1965; children: Peter, David. BA cum laude, U. Minn., 1940, PhD, 1946; DSc (hon.), U. Bristol, 1991. Teaching and rsch. asst. Dept. Botany U. Minn., Mpls., 1940-46; postdoctoral scholar Calif. Inst. Tech., Pasadena, 1946-48; from instr. to prof. U. Calif., LA, 1947-88, prof. emeritus, from 1988. NSF sr. postdoctoral fellow Copenhagen U., 1959-60; NSF-U.S.-Japan rsch. sci. Internat. Christian U., Mitaka, Tokyo, 1966-67; vis. prof. Dept. Chem. U. Bristol, U.K., 1973, 83. Elected mem. Nat. Acad. Scis., Washington, 1985. Rsch. grantee NSF, Dept. Energy, 1956—. Fellow AAAS; mem. Am. Soc. Plant Physiologists (pres. 1989-90), Am. Inst. Biol. Scis., Am. Chem. Soc., Bot. Soc. Am., Genetics Soc. Am., Japanese Soc. Plant Physiologists, Internat. Soc. Plant Molecular Biologists, Phytochem. Soc. Am. Democrat. Avocations: skiing, hiking, fishing, classical music. Home: El Sobrante, Calif. Died Apr. 22, 2009.

PHIPPS, JOHN RANDOLPH, retired army officer; b. Kansas, Ill, May 16, 1919; s. Charles Winslow and Kelsey Ethel (Torrence) P.; m. Pauline M. Prunty, Feb. 8, 1946; children: Charles W., Kelsey J. Phipps-Selander. BS in Econs. with honors, U. Ill., 1941; M.P.A., Sangamon State U., 1976; A course, Command and Gen. Staff Coll., 1959, nuclear weapons employment course, 1962; course, U.S. Army War Coll., 1973, U.S. Nat. Def. U., 1978. Owner, operator chain shoe stores in, Ill., 1946-70; commd. 2d lt. F.A. U.S. Army, 1941, advanced through grades to capt., 1943; service in Philippines and Japan; discharged as maj., 1946; organizer, comdr. Co. E, 130th Inf., Ill.; N.G., Mattoon, 1947, comdg. officer 2d Bn., 130th Inf., 1951, lt. col. 2d Bn., 130th Inf., 1951; called to fed. service, 1952; adv. (29th Regt., 9th Republic of Korea Div.), 1952-53; comdr. officer 1st Bn., 130th Inf., Ill. N.G., 1954, col., 1959; comdg. officer 2d Brigade, 33d Div., 1963-67; asst. div. comdr. 33d Inf. Div., 1967, brig. gen., 1967; comdr. 33d Inf. Brigade, Chgo., 1967-70, Ill. Emergency Ops. Hdqrs., 1970, asst. adj. gen. Ill., 1970-77, acting adj. gen., 1977-78, adj. gen., 1978, promoted to maj. gen., 1978, now maj. gen. ret. Decorated Silver Star, Bronze Star, Disting. Service medal, Combat Infantry Badge, Army Disting. Service medal Ill., various Philippine and Korean decorations; State of Ill. Long and Honorable Service medal. Mem. VFW, Adj. Gens. Assn. U.S., N.G. Assn. U.S., N.G. Assn. Ill., Am. Legion, Amvets. Home: Mattoon, Ill. Died Dec. 14, 2009.

PHIPPS, WILLIAM EUGENE, religion and philosophy educator; b. Waynesboro, Va., Jan. 28, 1930; s. Charles Henry and Ruth LaVell (Patterson) Phipps; m. Martha Ann Swezey, Dec. 21, 1954; children: Charles, Anna, Ruth. BS, Davidson Coll., 1949; MDiv, Union Theol. Sem., 1952; PhD, U. St. Andrews, Scotland, 1954; MA, U. Hawaii, 1963; MHL (hon.), Davis and Elkins Coll., Elkins, W.Va., 1972. Ordained to ministry Presbyn. Ch., 52. Prof. Bible Peace Coll., Raleigh, 1954—56; prof. religion, philosophy Davis and Elkins Coll., from 1956, pres., faculty assn., 1973—75, 1986—87. Author: Paul Against Supernaturalism, 1986, Death: Confronting the Reality, 1987, Genesis and Gender, 1989, Cremation Concerns, 1989, The Sheppards and Lapsley, 1991. Recipient Scholarly and Creative Accomplishments award, Davis and Elkins Coll., 1980. Mem.: Am. Acad. Religion. Democrat. Home: Elkins, W.Va. Died Mar. 2, 2010.

PIANTINI, CARLOS, conductor; b. Santo Domingo, Dominican Republic, May 9, 1927; s. Alberto and Marina (Espinal) P.; m. Marianne Piantini (div. 1977); children: Susan, Vivian, Albert, Frank; m. Yolanda Trujillo, Dec. 5, 1982. MusB, NYU, 1968. Violinist 1st Recital, Santo Domingo, 1937-44, Mex. Symphony, 1944-47, Juilliard Sch., NYC, 1947-50, N.Y. Philharm. Orch., NYC, 1956-71; condr. Vienna (Austria) Acad. Music, 1971-73; artistic dir. Nat. Theatre, Santo Domingo, 1973-78; condr. Caracas (Venezuela) Philharm., 1979-83, Nat. Symphonic Orch., Santo Domingo, from 1983. Domican amb. to UN; head cultural affairs Dominican Rep. Govt., 1950-56. Contbr. articles to profl. jours. Cons. V Centennial Commemorative, Santo Domingo, 1988. Avocation: stamp collecting/philately. Died Mar. 26, 2010.

PICKETT, ALBERT BERG, field quality engineer; b. Carmel, Ind., Feb. 22, 1918; s. Jasper E. and Christi Ann (Berg) Pickett; m. Phyllis Elaine Risinger, Aug. 1, 1941; children: Harriet Diane Pickett Stover, William Joe. Engaged in aerospace and electronics industry, 1951—71; with Indpls. Dept. Met. Devel., 1971—73; bldg. Commr., Carmel, 1973—76, mayor, 1976—82; field quality engr. FMC Ordnance Plant, San Jose, Calif., from 1982. Pres. Ind. Heartland Coordinating Commn.; vice chmn. policy com. Indpls. Regional Transp. Coun. Mem.: N. Cen. Mayors Roundtable Assn., Ind. Assn. Cities and Towns, Kiwanis Lodge, Shriners Lodge, Masons Lodge, Rotary Lodge. Republican. Mem. Soc. Of Friends. Home: Carmel, Ind. Died Aug. 3, 2009.

PICKETT, OWEN BRADFORD, lawyer, former United States Representative from Virginia; b. Richmond, Va., Aug. 31, 1930; m. Sybil Kelly; children: Laura, Karen, Mary. BS, Va. Poly. Inst., 1952; JD, U. Richmond, Va., 1955. CPA Va.; bar: Va. 1955, D.C. 1962. Pvt. practice, Virginia Beach, Va., 1964—86; mem. Va. House of Delegates, Richmond, 1972—86, US Congress from 2nd Va. Dist., Washington, 1987—2001; of counsel Troutman, Sanders, LLP, Virginia Beach, 2001—10. Chmn. Va. Dem. State Ctrl. Com., 1980—82. Mem.: AICPA, ABA, DC Bar Assn., Va. Bar Assn. Democrat. Baptist. Died Oct. 27, 2010.

PICOZZI, ANTHONY, dentist; b. Bklyn., Dec. 24, 1917; s. Louis and Ida (DeRosa) P.; m. Gloria Margaret Patinella, Feb. 9, 1952; children— Kathryn, Lori BS, Columbia U., 1939; DDS, NYU, 1944. Section chief Lever Bros. Rsch., Edgewater, N.J., 1955-68; prof. dentistry NYU, NYC, 1968-74; adminstr., rschr. Fairleigh Dickinson U., Hackensack, N.J., 1974-89; rsch. cons. Warner Lambert Co., Morris Plains, N.J., 1989-97. Cons. Lever Research, Edgewater, 1968-74, W.R. Grace, Balt., 1979-81 Contbr. articles to profl. jours. Served to lt. col. USAR Mem. ADA (mem. coun. on dental rsch. 1987-91), Am. Assn. Dental Research (councillor 1981, bd. dirs. 1988-90), Am. Assn. Dental Schs. (sect. chmn. 1980-81) Home: Franklin Lakes, NJ. Died Sept. 26, 2009.

PIERCE, JON PAGE, aluminum and chemical company executive, personnel administrator; b. Mobile, Ala., Oct. 26, 1940; s. Edwin Patterson and Teva (Jordan) P.; m. Sherry Kaye Hammack, July 18, 1964; children: Lesley, Julie, Brad. BS in Labor and Personnel Mgmt., U. Ala., 1963. Plant employee relations mgr. Kaiser Aluminum and Chem. Corp., Baton Rouge and Spokane, Wash., 1969-77, mgr. employee relations div. Oakland, Calif., 1977-82, dir. compensation and benefits, 1982-85, personnel director, 1985-88, corp. officer, v.p. human resources, from 1988. Instr. Dale Carnegie, Walnut Creek, Calif., 1979-80; adv. group Sr. Human Resources, San Francisco Bay, 1985-87. Bd. dirs., exec. com. United Crusade, Spokane, 1970-73, Baton Rouge, 1976; bd. dirs., mem. exec. com. Spokane C. of C., 1970-73, Jr. Achievement, 1970-73. Served to 1st lt. U.S. Army, 1963-65. Recipient Outstanding Alumnus award dept. mgmt. U. Ala., 1985. Mem. Western Pension Conf., Am. Mgmt. Assn., Am. Compensation Assn., Council on Employee Benefits, Sigma Chi (pres. 1962, Outstanding Mem. award 1963). Clubs: Sherwood Forest Country; Spokane; Lakeview (Oakland). Republican. Avocations: art, golf, fishing, boating, tennis. Home: Walnut Creek, Calif. Died Jan. 21, 2009.

PIERCE, PHILLIPS CARMER, brokerage house executive; b. Balt., Sept. 28, 1945; s. Walter Bryant, II Pierce and Lucille Phillips-Carmer. Attended, U. Va., 1975. Sales and sales mgmt. Internat. Decor, Bailey's Crossroads, Va., 1967—73; home planning cons. Coles Furniture, Fairfax, Va., 1973—75; account asst. Ferris & Co., Inc., Wash., 1975—76, investment broker, 1975—78, Legg Mason Wood Walker, Inc., Tyson's Corner, Va., 1978—80, br. mgr. fin. planning ctr., 1978—79, dir. mktg. tax incentive investments Balt., 1980—82, v.p. tax incentive investments, 1982—84; investment broker A.G. Edwards & Sons, Inc., Balt., from 1985. Instr. No. Va. Cmty. Coll., Annandale, 1977—80, Wash. YWCA, 1977—78, SBA, 1977—78, Lynchburg Coll., Va., 1977, No.Va. Coll., Manassas, 1976—77. Author: numerous sales and mgmt. articles. Democrat. Roman Catholic. Home: Colonial Beach, Va. Died Sept. 14, 2009.

PIETSCH, PAUL ANDREW, optometrist; b. NYC, Aug. 8, 1929; s. Elwood Paul and Bridget (McDonnell) P.; m. Myrtle Evelyn Miller, Dec. 8, 1950; children: Samuel H., Benjamin E., Mary T., Abigail L. AB, Syracuse U., 1954; PhD, U. Pa., 1960. Lab. instr. anatomy Ohio State U., Columbus, 1954-56; asst. instr. anatomy U. Pa., Phila., 1956-60, instr. physiology sch. nursing, 1959; instr. anatomy Wake Forest U., Winston-Salem, N.C., 1960-61; asst. prof. anatomy SUNY, Buffalo, 1961-64; sr. rsch. molecular biologist Dow Chem. Co., Midland, Mich., 1964-70; assoc. prof. optometry Ind. U., Bloomington, 1970-79, prof., 1979-94, prof. emeritus, 1994—2009, adj. prof. medicine, 1980-94. Author: Shufflebrain, 1981; contbr. articles to profl. jours. Cand. for county clk., Midland, 1968; exec. com. Dem. Ctrl. Com., Midland, 1965-70. Cpl. U.S. Army, 1946-49, 51. Recipient Sci. Journalism award AMA, 1973. Mem. Am. Assn. Anatomists, AFT (treas. local 2254 1971-74m pres. 1974-75). Home: Bloomington, Ind. Died Dec. 26, 2009.

PIGFORD, THOMAS HARRINGTON, nuclear engineering educator; b. Meridian, Miss., Apr. 21, 1922; s. Lamar and Zula Vivian (Harrington) P.; m. Catherine Kennedy Cathey, Dec. 31, 1948 (dec. 1992); children: Cynthia Pigford Naylor, Julie Earnest; m. Elizabeth Hood Weekes, Nov. 12, 1994. BS in Chem. Engring., Ga. Inst. Tech., 1943; S.M. in Chem. Engring., M.I.T., 1948, Sc.D. in Chem. Engring., 1952. Asst. prof. chem. engring., dir. Sch. Engring. Practice, M.I.T., 1950-52, asst. prof. nuclear and chem. engring., 1952-55, assoc. prof., 1955-57; head engring., dir. nuclear reactor projects and asst. dir. research lab. Gen. Atomic Co., La Jolla, Calif., 1957-59; prof. nuclear engring., chmn. dept. nuclear engring. U. Calif., Berkeley, 1959—2010; sr. rsch. scientist Lawrence Berkeley Lab., 1959—2010. Mem. panel Nat. Atomic Safety Licensing Bd. AEC-Nuclear Regulatory Commn., 1963-77; mem. Pres.'s Commn. on accident at 3-Mile Island, 1979; mem. bd. radioactive waste mgmt. and energy engring. bd., NAS-NAE, chmn. waste isolation systems panel, waste isolation pilot plant panel, fusion hybrid panel, separations and transmutations panel, transmutation of military plutonium panel, panel on health standard for radioactive waste disposal, chmn. adv. coun. Inst. Nuclear Power Op.; mem. Sec. of Energy's expert cons. group on Chernobyl accident; chmn. nuclear oversight com. Sacramento Mcpl. Utility Dist.; chmn. nuclear safety com. Gulf States Utilities Co.; mem. expert cons. group Swedish Nuclear Power Inspectorate; mem. peer rev. group for waste isolation pilot plant; mem. corp. rev. com. Oak Ridge Nat. Lab; lectr. Taiwan Nat. Sci. Found., 1990; vis. prof. Kyoto U., 1975, Kuwait U., 1976; cons. in field. Author: (with Manson Benedict) Nuclear Chemical Engineering, 1958, 2d edit., 1981; contbr. numerous articles to profl. jours.; patentee in field. Served with USNR, 1944-46. Recipient John Wesley Powell award U.S. Geol. Survey, 1981; named Outstanding Young Man of Greater Boston, Boston Jaycees, 1955; E. I. DuPont DeNemours rsch. fellow, 1948-50; Berkeley citation U. Calif., 1987; Japan Soc. for Promotion Sci. fellow, 1974-75; grantee NSF, 1960-75, EPA, 1973-78, Dept. Energy, 1979-92, Ford Found., 1974-75, Electric Power Rsch. Inst., 1974-75, Mitsubishi Metals Corp., 1989-90; named to Ga. Tech. Hall of Fame, 1995. Fellow Am. Nuclear Soc. (bd. dirs., Arthur H. Compton award 1971); mem. AIME, NAE, Am. Chem. Soc., Am. Inst. Chem. Engrs. (Robert E. Wilson award 1980, Service to Society award 1985), Atomic Indsl. Forum (dir.), Sigma Xi, Phi Kappa Phi, Tau Beta Pi. Home: Oakland, Calif. Died Feb. 27, 2010.

PIIRMA, IRJA, chemist, educator; b. Tallinn, Estonia, Feb. 4, 1920; came to U.S., 1949; d. Voldemar Juri and Meta Wilhelmine (Lister) Tiits; m. Aleksander Piirma, Mar. 10, 1943; children: Margit Ene, Silvia Ann. Diploma in Chemistry, Tech. U., Darmstadt, Fed. Republic of Germany, 1949; MS, U. Akron, 1957, PhD, 1960. Rsch. chemist U. Akron, Ohio, 1952-67, asst. prof., 1967-76, assoc. prof., 1976-81, prof., 1981-90, prof. emerita, from 1990, dept. head, 1982-85. Author: Polymeric Surfactants, 1992; editor: Emulsion Polymerization, 1982; contbr. articles to profl. jours. Recipient Extra Mural Rsch. award BP Am., Inc., 1989. Mem. Am. Chem. Soc. Avocations: swimming, skiing. Home: Cuyahoga Falls, Ohio. Died Dec. 6, 2009.

PILLSBURY, EDMUND PENNINGTON, JR., art advisor; b. San Francisco, Apr. 28, 1943; s. Edmund Pennington and Priscilla Keator (Giesen) P.; m. Mireille Marie-Christine Bernard, Aug. 30, 1969; children: Christine Bullitt, Edmund Pennington III. BA, Yale U., 1965; MA, U. London, 1967, PhD, 1973; DFA, U. North Tex., 1996. Curator European art Yale U. Art Gallery, New Haven, 1972-76; asst. dir. Yale U. Gallery, New Haven, 1975-76; dir. Yale Ctr. Brit. Art, New Haven, 1976-80; chief exec. officer Paul Mellon Ctr. Studies in Brit. Art, London, 1976-80; dir. Kimbell Art Mus., Ft. Worth, 1980-98; founding chmn. Villa I Tatti Coun., Harvard U., 1979-84; dir. Meadows Mus., 2005—07; chmn. fine arts, dir auction services Heritage Auction Galleries. Adj. prof. Yale U., 1976-80, lectr., 1972-76; internat. adv. bd. State Hermitage Mus. Author: Florence and the Arts, 1971, Sixteenth-Century Italian Drawings: Form and Function, 1974, David Hockney: Travels with Pen, Pencil and Ink, 1978, The Graphic Art of Federico Barocci, 1978. Trustee Ft. Worth Country Day Sch., 1982-87, 88-94, St. Paul's Sch., Concord, N.H., Burlington Mag. Found., London; bd. govs. Yale U. Art Gallery; chmn. art adv. panel indemnity program Nat. Endowment Arts, 1984-87; mem. vis. com. Sherman Fairchild Paintings Conservation Ctr., Met. Mus. Art, N.Y.C.; mem. bd. advisors art dept. U. North Tex., Denton; mem. art adv. panel IRS, 1982-84. Decorated chevalier Ordre des Arts et des Lettres, 1985; David E. Finley fellow Nat. Gallery Art, Washington, 1970, Ford Found. fellow Cleve. Mus. Art, 1970-71, Nat. Endowment Arts rsch. fellow, 1974, Morse fellow Yale U., 1975. Mem. Assn. Art Mus. Dirs. (trustee 1989-90), Master Drawings Assn. (bd. dirs.), Coll. Art Assn., Century Club, Ft. Worth Club, Rivercrest Club, City Club. Episcopalian. Home: Fort Worth, Tex. Died Mar. 25, 2010.

PIMPINELLA, RONALD JOSEPH, retired surgeon; b. Utica, N.Y., Sept. 27, 1935; s. Joseph and Josephine (Payne) P.; B.A. magna cum laude, Syracuse U., 1956; M.D., U. Rochester, 1960; children: Andrea, Giancarlo. Intern, Albany (N.Y.) Med. Center, 1960-61; resident in ear-nose-throat Columbia Presbyn. Med. Ctr., 1962-65; chief ENT, Martin Army Hosp., Ft. Benning, Ga., 1965-67; practice medicine specializing in otolaryngology and facial plastic surgery, Torrington, Conn., 1967-88; ret.; chief otolaryngology Charlotte Hungerford Hosp. Capt. U.S. Army, 1965-67. Fellow Am. Assn. Ophthalmology and Otolaryngology, Am. Acad. Facial Plastic and Reconstructive Surgery, ACS; mem. AMA, Conn. Med. Soc. (pres. otolaryngology sect. 1978-83). Roman Catholic. Contbr. articles to med. jours. Home: Ocala, Fla. Died June 29, 2009.

PIRKLE, EARL CHARNELL, retired geologist; b. nr. Buckhead, Ga., Jan. 8, 1922; s. Early Charnell and Eva Lee (Collins) P.; m. Valda Nell Armistead, July 9, 1942; children: Betty Jean, William A., Fredric L. AB, Emory U., 1943; MS, 1947; postgrad., U. Tenn., 1947-50; PhD, U. Cin., 1956. Certified profl. geologist. Prodn. coordinator, research crystallographer Pan-Electronics Labs., Inc., Atlanta, 1942-45; instr. geology U. Tenn., 1947-50; mem. faculty dept. phys. scis. and geology U. Fla., Gainesville, 1950-93, prof. emeritus, from 1993, prof., from 1963, chmn. dept. phys. scis., 1972-79; dir. Phys. Scis., 1979-82. Cons. in field; vis. prof. geology Emory U., summers 1959-65; rsch. cons. Fla. Dept. Nat. Resources Bur. Geology, 1950-70. Author: Natural Regions of the United States, 1977, 4th edit., 1985; Editor: Physical Science- Our Environment, 1968, Our Physical Environment, 1980; Contbr. articles to profl. jours. Served with AUS, 1945-46. Fellow Geol. Soc. Am., Soc. Econ. Geologists; mem. Am. Assn. Petroleum Geologists, Am. Soc. Mining, Metall. and Petroleum Engrs., Fla. Acad. Scis., Southeastern Geol. Soc., Phi Beta Kappa, Sigma Gamma Epsilon, Gamma Theta Epsilon, Sigma Chi. Democrat. Methodist. Died Jan. 8, 2010.

PISKE, RICHARD A., JR., consulting mechanical engineer; b. New Orleans, May 23, 1924; s. Richard A. and Myrtle L. (Mackenroth) P.; m. Louise Oldert, July 6, 1946; children—Richard, Gregory. B.M.E., Tulane U., 1944. Registered profl. engr., Tenn. Regional engring. mgr. Carrier Corp., Atlanta, 1955-62, programs mgr. Mil. Equipment dept., Syracuse, N.Y., 1962-65; prin. in charge I.C. Thomasson Assoc., Cons. Engrs., Knoxville, Tenn., 1966-81; dir. quality assurance Allen & Hoshall, Inc., Cons. Engrs., Knoxville, 1981—. Mem. Nat. Soc. Profl. Engrs., Am. Cons. Engrs. Council (past nat. dir.), Cons. Engrs. Tenn. (past pres.), Tenn. Soc. Profl. Engrs., ASHRAE, Knoxville Tech. Soc. Lutheran. Home: Knoxville, Tenn. Died May 27, 2010.

PISTOR, MICHAEL THOMAS FRITZ, former ambassador; b. Portland, Oreg., Apr. 29, 1930; s. William Jacob and Virginia Maxine (Pollard) P.; m. Shirley Lowry Scott, June 21, 1957 (dec. 2002); children: William Scott, Julia Pollard. BA in English, U. Ariz., 1952. Mag. editor, NYC, 1956-59; fgn. svc. officer U.S. Info. Agy., Tehran, Kampala, Douala, 1959-64, student affairs officer London, 1964-69, program coord., Office African Affairs Washington, 1969-70, dep. asst. dir., then asst. dir. for Near East-South Asia, 1970-73, dir. congl. and pub. liaison, 1977-80, dir. press and pubs., 1985-86, dir. North Africa, Near East, South Asia, 1986-88, counselor-of-the agy., 1988-91; counselor pub. affairs Am. Embassy, London, 1973-77, minister-counselor pub. affairs New Delhi, 1980-84; Murrow fellow Tufts U., Mass., 1984-85; US amb. to Republic of Malawi US Dept. State, 1991—94. 1st lt. U.S. Army, 1952-54. Recipient Edward R. Murrow award Tufts U., 1984, Presdl. Disting. Svc. award Dept. State, 1991. Mem. Am. Fgn. Svc. Assn. (bd. dirs. 1970-73), Internat. Inst. Strategic Studies, Cosmos Club. Episcopalian. Home: Washington, DC. Died Dec. 24, 2009.

PITTENGER, JOHN CHAPMAN, retired dean; b. Phila., May 23, 1930; s. Nicholas Otto and Cornelia Van der Veer (Chapman) Pittenger; m. Pauline Miller Pittenger, Jan. 10, 1981. AB, Harvard U., 1951, LLB, 1958; LHD, Franklin Marshall Coll., 1981. Bar: Pa. 1958. Assoc. Barley, Snyder, Cooper & Mueller, Lancaster, Pa., 1958—61; mem. Dist. 96 Pa. House of Representatives, 1965—66; sec. edn. State of Pa., Harrisburg, Pa., 1972—77; dean Rutgers State U. Sch. Law, Camden, NJ, 1981—86, prof. law, 1986—94; vis. lectr. Harvard U., 1977—78. Co-author (with Harry Bragdon): The Pursuit of Justice, 1969; author: Politics Ain't Beanbag, 1988. With US Army, 1952—55. Recipient Lancaster Jaycee Good Govt. award, 1967, Spl. Award for Leadership, Pa. State U., 1976, Lifetime Achievement award, Lancaster County Democratic Com., 2003; named B'Nai B'rith Man of the Yr. award, 1968. Democrat. Died Dec. 6, 2009.

PITTI, DONALD ROBERT, financial consultant; b. NYC, Sept. 15, 1929; s. August and Mary (Vitaglione) P.; m. Grace Allen Curtis, Aug. 14, 1954; children: Gail, Robert. BA, NYU, 1959; postgrad., Adelphi U., 1963-65. Asst. v.p. Standard & Poor's Corp., NYC, 1959—65; v.p. Quotron, Inc., NYC, 1965—67; pres. Wiesenberger & Co., NYC, 1967—76; v.p. John Nuveen & Co., Inc., NYC, 1976—87; pres. Monarch Resources, Inc., NYC, 1987—88; chmn., CEO Monarch Fin. Svcs., Inc., NYC, 1988—89; pres., CEO Seligman Fin. Svcs. Inc., NYC, 1989—95; pres. Graydon Consulting Corp., Manhasset, NY, from 1996; dir. Fin. Svcs. Inst. St. John's U., NY, from 1995, adj. prof. fin. NY, from 1995. Chmn. Found. Fin. Planning, Atlanta, 1994-2000 Editor: Handbook of Financial Planning, 1988; contbr. articles to profl. publs. With USN, 1948-49, 50-52. Mem. Internat. Assn. Fin. Planning (pres.), Union League, Manhasset Bay Yacht Club, Met. Opera Club. Avocations: gardening, reading, swimming. Home: Manhasset, NY. Died Dec. 18, 2009.

PLAIN, BELVA, writer; b. NYC, Oct. 9, 1919; d. Oscar and Eleanor Offenberg; m. Irving Plain, June 14, 1941 (dec. 1982); children: Barbara, Nancy, John Grad., Barnard Coll. Author: Evergreen, 1978, Random Winds, 1980, Eden Burning, 1982, Crescent City, 1984, The Golden Cup, 1987, Tapestry, 1988, Blessings, 1989, Harvest, 1990, Treasures, 1992, Whispers, 1993, Daybreak, 1994, The Carousel, 1995, Promises, 1996, Secrecy, 1997, Homecoming, 1997, Legacy of Silence, 1998, Fortune's Hand, 2000, After the Fire, 2000, Looking Back, 2001, Her Father's House, 2002, The Sight of the Stars, 2003, Crossroads, 2004 Died Oct. 12, 2010.

PLAINE, LLOYD LEVA, lawyer; b. Washington, Nov. 3, 1947; d. Marx and Shirley P. Leva; m. James W. Hill. BA, U. Pa., 1969; postgrad., Harvard U.; JD, Georgetown U., 1975. Bar: DC 1975. Legis. asst. to Rep. Sidney Yates US House of Reps., 1971-72; with Sutherland, Asbill & Brennan, Washington, 1975-82, ptnr., 1982—2010. Fellow Am. Bar Found., Am. Coll. Trust and Estate Counsel (past regent), Am. Coll. Tax Counsel; mem. ABA (past chmn. real property, probate and trust law sect., past coun. sect. of taxation). Home: Chevy Chase, Md. Died Feb. 2, 2010.

PLATT, ROBERT FRANCIS, financial executive; b. Providence, Aug. 8, 1960; s. William Irving and Dorothy Marie (Kelly) P. BSBA in Acctg., Bryant Coll., 1982. Mgmt. acct. State St. Bank & Trust Co., Boston, 1982-84; fin. acct. 1st Pacific Advisors, LA, 1984-86; securities compliance examiner U.S. SEC, LA, 1986-93, br. chief, from 1993. Democrat. Roman Catholic. Avocations: reading history/political works, running, biking. Home: Attleboro, Mass. Died Feb. 6, 2009.

PLIMPTON, ROBERT STANLEY, SR., agricultural executive, consultant; b. Cin., July 15, 1925; s. John Alden Sr. and Dale Allison (Gelley) P.; m. Patricia Ann Bacon, July 21, 1931 (dec. Nov. 1980); children: R. Gregory, James L. II, Kingsley B., Robert Stanley Jr., Deborah P., Darcy P., Lynn R., Robin S.; m. Theda Oates. Student, U. Conn., 1942-43, 46-49. Pres. Plimpton Assocs., Storrs, Conn., 1950-53, Plimpton Bldg. Cos., Storrs, 1953-57, Let's Dine Out, Inc., Storrs, 1957-63, Atlantic & Pacific Rsch., Inc., North Palm Beach, Fla., 1963-82; dir. Goug Capital Mgmt., Ft. Lauderdale, Fla., from 1982. Contbr. articles to profl. jours. Pres. Com. for Responsible Citizenship, North Palm Beach, 1984-87; senate dist. coord. Calif. Rep. Assembly, Sacramento, Calif., 1988—; state fin. dir. Evangelicals for Bush-Quayle, Sacramento, 1988. 2d lt. USAF, 1943-46. Mem. IDM Country Club, Hound Club. Avocations: skiing, sailing, flying, landscaping, writing. Home: Tequesta, Fla. Died Mar. 15, 2010.

PLUM, FRED, neurologist; b. Atlantic City, Jan. 10, 1924; s. Fred and Frances (Alexander) Plum; m. Susan Butler, Apr. 23, 1990; children from previous marriage: Michael, Christopher, Carol. BA, Dartmouth Coll., 1944, postgrad., 1944—45; MD, Cornell U., 1947; MD (hon.), Karolinska Inst., Stockholm, 1982; DSc (hon.), L.I. U., 1990. Resident N.Y. Hosp., 1947—50, fellow, 1950—53. Instr. neurology Sch. Medicine Cornell U., 1950—53, Anne Parrish Titzell prof. neurology, 1963—98, univ. prof., 1998—2010, chmn. dept. neurology, 1963—98; head neurology sect. U.S. Naval Hosp., St. Albans, NY, 1951—53; from asst. prof. to prof. neurology Sch. Medicine U. Wash., 1953—63; vis. scientist U. Lund, Sweden, 1970—71; vis. physician Rockefeller U. Hosp., 1975—85; assoc. neurosci. rsch. program MIT and Rockefeller U., 1977—87; mem. neurology study sect. NIH, 1964—68; nat. adv. coun. Nat. Inst. Neurol., Communicative Disorders and Stroke, 1984—86; founding mem. McKnight Endowment Fund for Neurosci., 1986, pres., 1986—90. Author (with J.B. Posner): Diagnosis of Stupor and Coma, 1966; author: 3d edit., 1982, Clinical Management of Seizures, 1976, 2d edit., 1983; author: (with others) Cecil Essentials of Medicine, 1986, 3d edit., 1995; editor, contbg. author: Cecil's Textbook of Medicine, 1968, chief editor neurology sect.: Contemporary Neurology series, 1980—96, founding editor: Vols. 1-40, 1966—93, Brain Dysfunction in Metabolic Disorders, 1974, mem. editl. bd.: Archives Neurology, 1958—68, chief editor:, 1972—76; editor: Annals of Neurology, 1977—85; founding editor:, from 1986; editor: Neurology Alert, from 1981; contbr. articles to sci. and profl. jours. Mem.: NAS, Assn. Am. Physicians, Assn. Rsch. Nervous Mental Diseases (pres. 1973, 1987), Am. Soc. Clin. Investigation, Soc. Neurosci., Am. Acad. Neurology (past mem. coun.), Am. Neurol. Assn. (v.p. 1974—75, pres. 1976—77, Jacoby award 1984), Inst. of Medicine, Am. Acad. Arts and Scis., Can., Brit., French, Itatlian, Swiss neurol. socs. (hon.), Alpha Omega Alpha. Achievements include research in conciousness, coma and stroke. Died June 11, 2010.

POCKELL, LESLIE MARK, publishing company executive; b. Norwalk, Conn., June 19, 1942; s. Abe and Mildred (Shapiro) P.; m. Noriko Maejima, June 23, 1967 AB, Columbia Coll., 1964. Articles editor Avant-Garde Mag., NYC, 1967-70; dir. trade dept. St. Martin's Press, NYC, 1970-84; exec. editor, dir. spl. interest group Doubleday & Co. Inc., NYC, 1984-88; editl. dir. Kodansha Internat., 1988-94; dir. book devel. Book-Of-The-Month Club, Inc., NYC, 1994-99; assoc. pub. Warner Books; v.p., assoc. pub. Grand Central Publishing. Adj. lectr. NYU, 1984-86; mem. adv. com. Small Press Ctr., 1995—. Served with U.S. Army, 1964-67 Died July 26, 2010.

POCKER, YESHAYAU, chemistry and biochemistry educator; b. Kishinev, Romania, Oct. 10, 1928; came to U.S., 1961; naturalized, 1967. s. Benzion Israel and Esther Sarah (Sudit) P.; m. Anna Goldenberg, Aug. 8, 1950; children: Rona, Elon I. MSc, Hebrew U., Jerusalem, 1949; PhD, Univ. Coll., London, Eng., 1953; DSc, U. London, 1960. Rsch. assoc. Weizmann Inst. Sci., Rehovot, Israel, 1949-50; humanitarian trust fellow Univ. Coll., 1951-52, asst. lectr., 1952-54, lectr., 1954-61; vis. assoc. prof. Ind. U., Bloomington, 1960-61; prof. U. Washington, Seattle, from 1961. Bicentennial lectr. Mont. State U., Bozeman, 1976; Horizons in Chemistry lectr. U. N.C., Chapel Hill, 1977, guest lectr. U. Kyoto, Japan, 1984; Edward A. Doisy vis. prof. biochemistry St. Louis U. Med. Sch., 1990; plenary lectr. N.Y. Acad. Sci., 1983, Fast Reactions in Biol. Systems, Kyoto, Japan, 1984, NATO, 1989, Consiglio nat. delle Richerche, U. Bari, Italy, 1989, Sigma Tau, Spoleto, Italy, 1990; Internat. lectr. Purdue U., 1990; cons. NIH, 1984, 86, 88; Spl. Topic lectr. on photosynthesis, Leibniz House, Hanover, Fed. Republic Germany, 1991; enzymology, molecular biology lectr., Dublin, Ireland, 1992; 3M lectr., St. Paul, 1996; enzymology, molecular biology, retinal metabolism lectr., Deadwood, S.D., 1996, fast reactions in solutions and Bronsted symposium lectr., Copenhagen, 1997, self assembly kinetics of Alzheimer beta-amyloid peptides, ultrafast studies of insulin-insulin and insulin-receptor interactions; 1st Bannan invited lectr. Seattle U., spring, 1999; invited Bannan lectr. Seattle U., 2000, Alzheimer and Prion Proteins; internat. conf. Port Townsend, Wash., 2000, lectr. water sensing mechanisms, internat. symposium, Taos, N. Mex., 2000, internat. lectr. enzymology, molecular biology. Mem. editorial adv. bd. Inorganica Chimica Acta-Bioinorganic Chemistry, 1981-89; bd. reviewing editors Sci., 1985-2000; contbr. numerous articles to profl. jours.; pub. over 220 papers and 12 revs. Numerous awards worldwide, 1983-97. Mem. Royal Soc. Chemistry, Am. Chem. Soc. (nat. spkr. 1970, 74, 84, chmn. Pauling award com. 1978, plaque awards 1970, 74, 84, Outstanding Svc. award 1979, chmn. selection com. Pauling award 1996), Soc. Exptl. Biology, Am. Soc. Biol. Chemists, N.Y. Acad. Scis., Sigma Xi (nat. lectr. 1971). Avocations: history, philosophy, poetry. Home: Seattle, Wash. Died Mar. 14, 2010.

PODOS, STEVEN MAURICE, ophthalmologist; b. NYC, Nov. 7, 1937; s. Mark A. and Sophia L. (Landress) P.; m. Salle Garber, June 20, 1959; children: Richard Lance, Lisa Beth. AB, Princeton U., 1958; MD, Harvard U., 1962. Diplomate Am. Bd. Ophthalmology. Intern U. Utah Affiliated Hosp., Salt Lake City, 1962-63; resident in ophthalmology Washington U. Med. Ctr., St. Louis, 1963-67, from asst. prof. to prof., 1969-75; practice medicine specializing in ophthalmology NYC, from 1975; clin. assoc. NIH, 1967-69; prof. ophthalmology, chmn. dept. Mt. Sinai Med. Sch., NYC; also ophthalmologist in chief Mt. Sinai Hosp., NYC, from 1975. Mem. editorial bds. various profl. jours.; contbr. articles to med. jours. Mem. sci. adv. bd. Fight for Sight, 1975—; bd. dirs. Nat. Soc. Prevention Blindness, 1977—. Grantee USPHS, 1975—. Mem. Am. Acad. Ophthalmology and Otolaryngology (award of merit), ACS, Am. Ophthalmol. Soc., AAAS, N.Y. Acad. Medicine, Assn. Research Vision and Ophthalmology (trustee 1977-81) Clubs: Princeton. Jewish. Home: New York, NY. Died Oct. 10, 2009.

POELMAN, KAREN CHRISTINE, psychologist, nurse; b. Highland Pk., Ill., Jan. 13, 1944; d. Dirk Adrian and Diane V. (Liukkonen) Poelman. BS, Ga. State U., 1973, MA, 1977, PhD, 1980. Lic. clin. psychologist; RN Ill. Masonic Hosp. Sch. Nursing, 64, Ga. Nurse Ill. State Psychiat. Inst., Chgo., 1964—66, Peace Corps Vol., Kabul, Afghanistan, 1966, Highland Pk. Hosp. Found., 1967—68, St. Joseph's Hosp., Atlanta, 1969—78; clin. psychologist Fulton County Health Dept., Atlanta, from 1979; pvt. practice clin. psychology Atlanta, 1981; cons. US Svc., Atlanta, 1983, Disability Adjudication Sect., Decatur, Ga., 1985; mem. panel psychologists Ga. Dept. Human Resources, Div. Vocat. Rehab., Atlanta, from 1984. Mem.: Nat. Register Health Svc. Providers Psychology, Ga. Psychol. Assn., Southeastern Psychol. Assn., Am. Psychol. Assn., Psi Chi., Phi Kappa Phi, Alpha Lambda Delta. Died Dec. 14, 2009.

POINSETT, BENJAMIN FRANKLIN, electrical engineer; b. Huntington, N.Y., June 21, 1931; s. Herbert Welsh Evans and Mabel Mary Christena (Moser) P.; m. Doris Jean Post, Aug. 23, 1958. B.S. in Elec. Engring., U. Md., 1965; M.S. in Tech. of Mgmt., Am. U., 1974. Field engr. ACF Industries, Riverdale, Md., 1958-63; sr.engr. Link group Gen. Precision Co., Riverdale, Md., 1965-67; project engr. Electro Mech. Research Co., College Park, Md., 1967-68; assoc. prin. engr. Harris Corp., Govt. Electronic Systems Div., Melbourne, Fla., 1968-78; engr. sr. staff Applied Physics Lab., Johns Hopkins U., Laurel, Md., 1978—. Served with U.S. Army, 1953-55. Mem. Assn. Computing Machinery, Armed Forces Communications and Electronics Assn., Assn. Old Crows. Libertarian. Avocations: flying and gliding; amateur radio. Home: Bethesda, Md. Died Nov. 10, 2009.

POLAK, JACQUES JACOBUS, economist; b. Rotterdam, The Netherlands, Apr. 25, 1914; came to U.S., 1940; s. James and Elisabeth F. Polak; m. Josephine Weening, Dec. 21, 1937; children: H. Joost, Willem L. MA in Econs., U. Amsterdam, 1936, PhD in Econs., 1937; PhD in Econs. (hon.), Erasmus U., Rotterdam, 1972. Economist League of Nations, Geneva, Switzerland and Princeton, N.J., 1937-43, Netherlands Embassy, Washington, 1943-44; advisor UN Relief & Rehab. Adminstrn., Washington, 1943-44; from div. chief, asst. dir. to dir. rsch. dept. IMF, Washington, 1947-80, exec. dir., 1981-86; fin. cons. The World Bank, Washington, 1987-89, Orgn. Econ. Coop. & Devel. (OECD), Paris, 1987-89; pres. Per Jacobsson Found., Washington, 1987-97. Profl. lectr. Johns Hopkins U., Balt., 1949-50, George Washington U., 1950-55. Author: (with J. Tinbergen) The Dynamics of Business Cycles, 1950; author: An International Economic System, 1953, Financial Policies and Development, 1989, Economic Theory and Financial Policy-The Selected Essays of Jacques J. Polak, 1994; contbr. articles to profl. jours. Recipient N.G. Pierson medal in Economics, 1997. Fellow Econometric Soc., Royal Netherlands Acad. Sci. (corr.); mem. Cosmos Club (Washington). Home: Bethesda, Md. Died Feb. 26, 2010.

POLITANO, THOMAS P., lawyer; b. Bklyn., Feb. 11, 1926; s. Vincent and Jennie (Cecere) Politano; m. Carol Ann Cummings, Nov. 7, 1964; children: Thomas V., Paul J., Susan E. BS, NYU, 1950; JD, St. John's U., 1954. Bar: NY 1955, US Dist. Ct. Vt. 1977. Sole practice law, Wilmington, Vt., from 1969; vice-chmn. Rep. Town Com., Wilmington, 1985. With USN, 1943—46. Mem.: C. of C. (treas. 1984), Am. Legion (comdr. Wilmington post 1974), Windham County Bar Assn., Vt. Bar Assn., Lions. Republican. Roman Catholic. Died May 23, 2009.

POLITANO, VICTOR ANTHONY, urology educator, physician; b. Point Marion, Pa., Jan. 13, 1919; s. Anthony and Elizabeth (Parco) P.; m. Aida Mishkin, June 20, 1969; children: Victor, Michael, Rebecca, Betty Frances, Jonathan. BS, Marshall U., 1940; MD, Duke U., 1944. Asso. urologist Mass. Gen. Hosp.; instr. surgery Harvard U., 1955-58; asso. prof. surgery div. urology Duke U., 1958-62; prof., chmn. dept. urology U. Miami, from 1962, chmn. emeritus Dept. Urology, 1992. Served with USN, 1945-47, 53-55. Recipient Disting. Faculty scholar award U. Miami, 1995, Pediat. Urology medal Am. Acad. Pediat., 1995; Victor A. Politano chair in urology established at U. Miami Sch. Medicine, 1982. Mem. Am. Urol. Assn. (pres.-elect 1984-85, pres. 1985-86), Soc. Univ. Urologists (pres.), Pediatric Urol. Soc. (pres.), Fla. Urol. Soc. (pres.), AMA, ACS (internat. relations com.), Am.

Assn. Genito-urinary Surgeons, Clin. Soc. Genito-urinary Surgeons, Internat. Soc. Urology, Confederacion Americana de Urologia (pres. 1986-87), Fla. Med. Assn., Dade County Med. Assn., Greater Miami Urol. Soc. Developed technique for anti-reflux ureteral reimplantation, technique for teflon injection to correct urinary incontinence; developed peri-ureteral Polytef paste injection for vesicoureteral reflux. Home: Miami, Fla. Died Feb. 13, 2010.

POLITE, CARLENE HATCHER, writer, educator; b. Detroit; d. John and Lillian Hatcher; m. James S. Patrick, July 21, 2003; children from previous marriage: Glynda Morton, Lila Ashaki. Student, Martha Graham Sch. Dance, NYC, 1952-56; diploma, Acad. Leonardo da Vinci, Rome, 1980. Dancer, student Martha Graham Sch., NYC, 1952-56; dancer Alvin Ailey Dance Co., NYC, 1957-58, Edith Stephen Co., NYC, 1958; dancer, actress Vanguard Playhouse, Detroit, 1960-62; prof. English SUNY, Buffalo, 1971—2000, chair dept. American Studies, 1981, prof. emerita, 2000—09. Tchr. Golden Dragon Kung Fu Acad., 1974-75, Himalayan Inst. Yoga, 1980-82; panelist NEA, Washington, 1981, N.Y. State Coun. Arts, N.Y.C., 1982, N.Y. Found. Arts, 1983, Seattle Arts in Pub. Places, 1989. Author: The Flagellants, 1966, Paris edit., 1967, N.Y. edit., 1968, also other European edits. (Pulitzer prize nominee, 1967, NEA grant, 1967, Rockefeller grant, 1968), Sister X and The Victims of Foul Play, 1975. Coord. Walk to Freedom with Martin Luther King, Detroit, 1963; del., participant UN-Non-Govtl.Orgns. 4th World Conf. on Women, Beijing, 1995. Recipient numerous nat. and internat. awards as artist and educator; invited 1st Ann. Conf. African Presence, Paris, 1991, Internat. Educators and Writers Oxford U., 1997. Avocation: yoga. Home: Buffalo, NY. Died Dec. 7, 2009.

POLKE, SIGMAR, artist; b. Olesnicka, German Democratic Republic, Feb. 13, 1941; arrived in West Germany, 1953. Student glass painting, Dusseldorf-Kaiserwerth, 1959-60; student painting, Gerald Hoehme, Karl-Otto Goetz Staatliche Kunstakademie, Dusseldorf, 1961-67. Founder with Konrad Fischer-Lueg, Gerhard Richter Capitalist realist painting group, Dusseldorf, 1963; painter Dusseldorf, 1967-70, Willich bei Krefeld, 1971-79, Cologne, 1980—2010. Guest instr. Akademie der bildenden Kunste, Hamburg, Germany, 1970-71, prof. 1977-91 One man shows include Galerie René Block, West Berlin, 1966, 68, 69, Galerie Heiner Friedrich, Munich, 1967, 70, Galerie Rudolph Zwirner, Cologne, Galerie Konrad Fischer, Dusseldorf, 1970, 71, 73, Kabinett fur Aktuelle Kunst, Bremerhaven, West Germany, 1970, Galerie Michel Werner, Cologne, 1971, 75, 83, Galerie Toni Gerber, 1971, 76, 81, Galerie Ernst, Hannover, 1971, Rochus Kowallek, Frankfurt, 1972, Galerie Grafikmeyer, Karlsruhe, 1972, Goethe-Inst., Amsterdam, 1972, Galeria Dorothea Loehr, Frankfurt, 1974, Galerie Klein, Bonn, 1974, 75, 80, 86, Kunsthalle, Kiel, 1975, 76, Kunstverein Kassel, West Germany, 1977, Halle fur Internationale Neue Kunst, Zurich, 1978, Galerie Bama, Paris, 1982, Holly Solomon Gallery, N.Y., 1982, Studio d'Arte Cannaviello, Milan, 1983, Marian Goodman Gallery, N.Y., 1983, Mary Boone Gallery, N.Y., 1985, 86, David Nolan Gallery, N.Y., 1987, others; exhibited in group shows at Kaiserstrasse, Dusseldorf, 1963, Stadtisches Mus., Trier, West Germany, 1965, 69, Whitechapel Art Gallery, London, 1970, Kassel, West Germany, 1972, Sao Paulo, 1975, Wurttembergischer Kunstrverein, Stuttgart, 1982, L.A. County Mus. Art, 1987; represented in permanent collections Stadtisches Kunstmuseum, Bonn, Kunstmuseum der Stadt, Dusseldorf, Kunsthalle, Tubingen, Landesmuseum, Darmstadt, Mus. Boymans-van Beuningen, Rotterdam, Stedelijk, Van Abbemuseum, Eindhoven, Centre Georges pompidou, Paris, Mus. Modern Art, N.Y.C.; author: Hohere Wesen befelhlen, 1968, der ganze Korper fuhlt sich leicht und mochte fliegen, 1969, (with others) Die Grafik der Kapitalistischen Realismus, 1971, Bizarre, 1972, (with Achim Duchow) Original und Falschung, 1973. Recipient painting prize Biennial, Sao Paulo, 1975, Rubens prize, City of Siegen, 2007. Mem.: AAAL (fgn.) (hon.), Am. Acad. Arts and Sciences (fgn.) (hon.). Died June 10, 2010.

POLLIN, ABE, professional sports team owner, construction executive; b. Phila., Dec. 3, 1923; s. Morris and Jennie (Sack) P.; m. Irene S. Kerchek, May 27, 1945; children: Robert Norman, James Edward. BA, George Washington U., 1945; student, U. Md., 1941-44. Engaged in home bldg. bus., 1945—2009; pres. Abe Pollin Inc., Balt., from 1962; chmn. Balt. Bullets Basketball Club, Inc. (now Washington Wizards), 1964-97, Washington Wizards, 1997—2009; chmn. bd., CEO Washington Sports & Entertainment, Washington. Dir. County Fed. Savs. & Loan Assn., Rockville, Md. Bd. dirs. United Jewish Appeal, Nat. Jewish Hosp., Jewish Cmty. Ctr.; bd. dirs., adv. com. John F. Kennedy Cultural Ctr. Recipient Duke Ziebert Capital Achievement award, Disting. Civilian Svc. award, US Army, Robert F. Kennedy-Martin Luther King, Jr. award, Coalition to Stop Gun Violence, 1996, United Cerebral Palsy Achievement award, 1996, Jewish Leadership award, 1997. Mem. Nat. Assn. Home Builders, Assn. Builders and Contractors Md., Washington Bd. Trade. Jewish. Died Nov. 24, 2009; Washington.

POND, THOMAS ALEXANDER, physics professor, academic administrator; b. LA, Dec. 4, 1924; s. Arthur Francis and Florence (Alexander) P.; m. Barbara Eileen Newman, Sept. 6, 1958; children: Arthur Phillip Ward, Florence Alexandra. AB, Princeton U., 1947, AM, 1949, PhD, 1953; DSc, SUNY, Stony Brook, 1998. Instr. physics Princeton U., 1951-53; asst. prof., then assoc. prof. physics Washington U., St. Louis, 1953-62; prof. physics SUNY, Stony Brook, 1962-81, prof. emeritus, 1982—2010, chmn. dept., 1962-68, exec. v.p., 1967-79, acting pres., 1970, 75, 78; prof. physics Rutgers U., New Brunswick, NJ, exec. v.p., chief acad. officer, 1982-91, exec. v.p., chief acad. officer emeritus, 1991—2010, acting pres., 1990, prof., 1991-97, prof. emeritus, 1997—2010; acting sr. v.p. for acad. affairs U. Medicine and Dentistry N.J., New Brunswick, 1998. Bd. dirs. Action Com. for L.I., 1978-80, Tri-State Regional Planning Commn., 1979-82; trustee Univs. Research Assn., 1985-87; bd. dirs. Fermilab, 1987-89. Served to ensign USNR, 1943-46. Fellow AAAS; mem. Am. Phys. Soc., Phi Beta Kappa, Sigma Xi. Home: Arlington, Vt. Died Aug. 29, 2010.

POPE, ALFRED, physician, educator; b. Cleve., Jan. 23, 1915; s. Carlyle and Mary Slade (Kline) P.; m. Maria Lorenz, Aug. 19, 1950. Grad., Milton Acad., 1932; AB, Harvard, 1937, MD, 1941. House officer pathology Children's Hosp., Boston, 1941-42; research asst. medicine Mass. Gen. Hosp., Boston, 1943, research fellow medicine, 1944; teaching fellow biol. chemistry, research fellow medicine Harvard, 1943-44, Austin teaching fellow biol. chemistry, 1944-45, asst. neuropathology, 1946-49, tutor biochem. scis., 1947-49, instr. neuropathology, 1949-51, asso., 1951-52, asst. prof., 1953-56, asso. prof., 1956-63, prof. neuropathology, 1964-83; prof. emeritus, from 1983; fellow med. sci. NRC, Montreal Neur. Inst., Can., 1945-46; research asso. neuropathology McLean Hosp., Belmont, Mass., 1946-55. Asso. neuropathologist McLean Hosp., 1955-56, neuropathologist, 1956-83, sr. neuropathologist, 1983—; mem. neurology field investigations com. Nat. Inst. Neur. Diseases and Blindness, 1957-61; mem. neurology study sect., div. research grants NIH, 1961-65 Editorial bd.: Jour. Neurochemistry, 1955-69, Neurology, 1959-63, Archives of Neurology, 1961-66; Contbr. numerous sci. articles to profl. lit. Mem. research adv. com. United Cerebral Palsy Research and Ednl. Found., Inc., 1963-69; adv. com. on epilepsies USPHS, 1966-69; neurology program project com. Nat. Inst. Neurol. Diseases and Stroke, 1969-73; mem. adv. com. on fundamental research Nat. Multiple Sclerosis Soc., 1968-74; Trustee Longy Sch. Music, Cambridge, 1968-80. Mem. Assn. Research Nervous and Mental Disease, Am. Soc. Biol. Chemists, Am. Assn. Neuropathologists, Am. Acad. Neurology, Am. Neur. Assn., Am. Acad. Arts and Scis., Internat. Brain Research Orgn., Internat. Soc. Neurochemistry, Soc. Neurosc., Am. Soc. Neurochemistry. Died Feb. 13, 2009.

POPKIN, GERALD HERBERT, lawyer, life underwriter; b. Fall River, Mass., July 30, 1929; s. Charles and Pauline (Lepler) Popkin; m. Eve Bearse Robinson, Dec. 24, 1955; children: Linda Popkin Greenberg, James M., David A. BBA, U. Mass., 1951; JD, New Eng. Sch. Law, 1958. Bar: Mass. 1959, (U.S. Dist. Ct. Mass.) 1960, (U.S. Supreme Ct.) 1969. Sole practice, Boston, from 1959. Lt. Inf. US Army, 1952—54. Mem.: Am. Soc. C.L.U.s, Mass. Bar Assn., Masons. Jewish. Home: Chestnut Hill, Mass. Died June 6, 2009.

POPOVICS, SANDOR, civil engineer, educator, researcher; b. Budapest, Hungary, Dec. 24, 1921; came to U.S., 1957; s. Milan and Erzsebet (Droppa) P.; m. Lea M. Virtanen, Aug. 29, 1960; children: John, Lisa. 1st Degree in Civil Engring., Poly. U., Budapest, Hungary, 1944; Advanced Degree in Civil Engring., Poly. U., 1956; PhD, Purdue U., 1961. Registered profl. engr. Ariz., Pa. Rsch. engr. Met. Lab., Budapest, 1944-48; adj. prof. Tech. Coll., Budapest, 1949-52; rsch. engr., mgr. Inst. for Bldg. Scis., Budapest, 1949-56; grad. asst. Purdue U., Lafayette, Ind., 1957-59; prof. engring. Auburn (Ala.) U., 1959-69; prof. civil engring. No. Ariz. U., Flagstaff, 1968-76; prof. engring. King Abdulazziz U., Jeddah, Saudi Arabia, 1977-78; Samuel S. Baxter prof. civil engring. Drexel U., Phila., 1979-92, rsch. prof., from 1992. Pres. Optimum Engring. Rsch. Author: Fundamentals of Portland Cement Concrete, 1982, Concrete Materials, 2d edit., 1992, Strength and Related Properties of Concrete, 1998, over 300 tech. papers. Recipient numerous grants and awards. Fellow ASCE (life), Am. Concrete Inst.; mem. ASTM, Ala. Acad. Scis., Ariz. Acad. Scis., Sigma Xi, Chi Epsilon. Avocations: jogging, music, fine art. Died Jan. 14, 2010.

PORTER, AMY R., lawyer; b. Memphis, Jan. 30, 1944; BA magna cum laude, Memphis State U., 1965; JD, Ariz. State U., 1975. Bar: Ariz. 1975. Ptnr. Lewis and Roca, Phoenix; judge pro tempore Ariz. Ct. Appeals, Phoenix, 1985. Instr. Ariz. State U., 1987-88. Mem. ABA, Air and Waste Mgmt. Assn., Def. Rsch. Inst. Died Apr. 10, 2010.

PORTER, DUDLEY, JR., environmentalist, lawyer; b. Paris, Tenn., May 10, 1915; s. Dudley and Mary (Bolling) P.; m. Mary Rhoda Montague, Oct. 21, 1950. Student, Murray State Coll., Ky., 1933-34; LL.B., Cumberland U., 1936. Bar: Tenn. 1937. Asst. atty. gen., Tenn., 1937-40; mem. firm Tyne, Peebles, Henry & Tyne, Nashville, 1940-49; with law dept. Nat. Life & Accident Ins. Co., Nasvhille, 1940-49, asso. gen. counsel, 1948; with Provident Life & Accident Ins. Co., Chattanooga, from 1949, gen. counsel, 1954-72, sr. v.p., 1958-72, sec., 1965-72, vice chmn., sr. counsel, 1972-76; of counsel Chambliss, Bahner & Stophel, Chattanooga, from 1977. Mem. Hamilton County Juvenile Ct. Commn., 1958-64, chmn., 1964; mem. Tenn. Health Planning Council, 1968-76, Tenn. Hist. Commn., 1976-86; trustee Hermitage Assn., Nashville, 1983-90; an incorporator, mem. bd. Sr. Neighbors Chattanooga, 1960-66; vice chmn., trustee Maclellan Charitable Trust. With AUS, 1942-46; judge adv. 100th Inf. Div. ETO. Mem. Am., Tenn., Chattanooga bar assns., Am. Life Conv. (chmn. legal sect. 1958), Assn. Life Ins. Counsel (exec. com. 1970—, pres. 1974-75), Nature Conservancy (life, co-founder and trustee Tenn. chpt.), Sigma Alpha Epsilon. Clubs: Mountain City (Chattanooga); Belle Meade Country (Nashville). Presbyterian. Home: Chattanooga, Tenn. Died Mar. 10, 2009.

PORTER, JOHN ROBERT, JR., space technology company executive, geochemist; b. Oklahoma City, Feb. 27, 1935; s. John Robert and Margaret Florence (Nicholson) P.; m. Amelie Alexanderson Wallace, June 2, 1963 (div.); children: Jennifer A. Porter Dowling, Amelie M. BA, Dartmouth Coll., 1957; MS, Okla. U., 1964. Cert. petroleum geologist, Am. Assn. Petroleum Geologists. Analyst CIA, Washington, 1962-66; chief Earth Resources Program NASA, Washington, 1966-69; chmn. Earth Satellite Corp., Rockville, Md., 1969—2010. Mem. space applications bd. NRC, Washington, 1983-86, GEOSAT Com., Norman, Okla., 1972-96. Trustee Washington Gallery Modern Art, 1966-67. 1st lt. U.S. Army, 1960-62. Mem. Am. Assn. Petroleum Geologists., Chevy Chase Club. Republican. Presbyterian. Avocation: writing fiction. Home: Washington, DC. Died Apr. 23, 2010.

PORTER, ROBERT MARSTON, education educator; b. North Anson, Maine, Aug. 1, 1915; s. Gould Alexander and Mabel Miller (Marston) P.; m. Mary Carville Walker, Apr. 16, 1955; 1 child, Mary Finley. B.A., Bowdoin Coll., 1937; M.A., U. Pa., 1941; Ed.D., Temple U., 1955. Tchr. Germantown Acad., Phila., 1938-42, 46-50; prof. edn. SUNY-Oneonta, 1955-85. Author: Decade of Seminars for the Able and Ambitious, 1958-68; The Catskill Saturday Seminars: 25 Years of a Good Idea, 1958-83; contbr. articles to profl. jours. Cons. Catskill Area Sch. Study Council, Oneonta. Served with U.S. Army, 1942-46, to lt. M.I., 1950-52. Recipient Chancellor's award for excellence in teaching SUNY-Albany, 1983. Mem. Council for Exceptional Children, N.Y. State Assn. for Retarded Children (bd. govs.). Republican. Presbyterian. Lodges: Lions, Kiwanis. Avocation: travelling. Home: Oneonta, NY. Died Jan. 14, 2009.

PORTERFIELD, JAMES TEMPLE STARKE, retired finance educator; b. Annapolis, Md., July 7, 1920; s. Lewis Broughton and Maud Paxton (Starke) P.; m. Betty Gold, Apr. 23, 1949 (dec. 1985); m. Janet Patricia Gardiner Roggeveen, Oct. 5, 1986. AB, U. Calif., Berkeley, 1942; MBA, Stanford U., 1948, PhD, 1955. From asst. to assoc. prof. Harvard U. Bus. Sch., Boston, 1955—59; prof. fin. Stanford (Calif.) U. Grad. Sch. Bus., 1959-79, James Irvin Miller Prof. fin., 1979-90, prof. emeritus, 1990—2010; prof. IMEDE Mgmt. Devel. Inst., Lausanne, Switzerland, 1962-63. Author: Life Insurance Stocks as Investments, 1955, Investment Decisions and Capital Costs, 1965; co-author: Case Problems in Finance, 1959. Served as lt. USNR, 1941-46. Recipient Salgo Noren award Stanford U., 1966, Richard W. Lyman award Stanford U. Alumni Assn., 1995. Home: Portola Valley, Calif. Died Feb. 28, 2010.

PORTNOY, SARA S., lawyer; b. NYC, Jan. 11, 1926; d. Marcus and Gussie (Raphael) Spiro; m. Alexander Portnoy, Dec. 13, 1959 (dec. 1976); children: William, Lawrence. BA, Radcliffe Coll., 1946; LLB, Columbia U., 1949. Bar: N.Y. 1949, U.S. Dist. Ct. (so. dist.) N.Y. 1952, U.S. Dist. Ct. (ea. dist.) N.Y. 1975, U.S. Ct. Appeals (2d cir.) 1975, U.S. Supreme Ct. 1975. Assoc. Seligsberg, Friedman & Berliner, NYC, 1949-51; atty. AT&T, NYC, 1951-61; vol. atty. Legal Aid Soc. of Westchester, NY, 1966-74; assoc. Proskauer Rose Goetz & Mendelsohn, NYC, 1974-78, ptnr., 1978-94; ret., 1994. Mem. Commn. on Human Rights, White Plains, N.Y., 1973-78; mem. bd. visitors Columbia Law Sch., 1996-02; bd. dirs. Legal Aid Soc. of Westchester County, N.Y., 1975-83, Columbia Law Sch. Assn., 1990-94, Mosholu Montifiore Cmty. Ctr., 1998—; mem. Pres.'s Coun. Yaddo; dir. Muscular Dystrophy Assn., 2000-03. Mem. Assn. Bar City of NY (chair com. legal support staff 1994, mem. com. on homeless, sr. lawyers com., chair Pub. Svc. Network 2003-06), South Fork Country Club (dir. 1997-2006), The Children's Storefront (dir. 1998—), Legal Momentum (bd. legal advisors 2004—). Home: New York, NY. Died Apr. 3, 2009.

POSNICK, ADOLPH, chemical company executive; b. Yellow Creek, Sask., Can., May 3, 1926; came to U.S., 1947; s. Frank and Joanne (Shimko) P.; m. Sarah Anne Briggs, May 16, 1947; children— Joann Elizabeth, Barbara Ellen. BS in Ceramic Engring, U. Sask., 1947. Research engr. Ferro Corp., Cleve., 1947-50; tech. dir. Ferro Enamel-Brazil, Sao Paulo, 1950-56, mng. dir., 1956-65; v.p. internat. ops. Ferro Corp., Cleve., 1965-74, sr. v.p. ops., 1974-75, exec. v.p., 1975-76, pres., chief exec. officer, 1976-88, chmn. bd. dirs., chief exec. officer, from 1988. Bd. dirs. fgn. subsidiaries; mem. Brazil-Am. Bus. Coun. Mem. Am., Brazilian ceramic socs., Cleve. World Trade. Clubs: Clevelander, Mid Day, Chagrin Valley Country, Union, Pepper Pike Country. Home: Longboat Key, Fla. Died Jan. 18, 2010.

POST, EMILY (ELIZABETH LINDLEY POST), author; b. Englewood, NJ, May 7, 1920; d. Allen L. and Elizabeth (Ellsworth) Lindley; m. George E. Cookman, 1941 (dec. 1943); 1 child, Allen C.; m. William G. Post, Aug. 5, 1944; children: William G., Lucinda Post Senning, Peter L. Grad. high sch. Dir. Emily Post Inst., 1965—95. Author: Emily Post's Book of Etiquette for Young People, 1968, Wonderful World of Weddings, 1970, Please Say Please, 1972, Emily Post's Etiquette, 1965, rev. edit. 1992, The Complete Book of Entertaining, 1981, Emily Post's Complete Book of Wedding Etiquette, 1982, rev. edit., 1991, Emily Post Talks with Teens about Manners and Etiquette, 1986, Emily Post on Weddings, 1987, Emily Post on Entertaining, 1987, Emily Post on Etiquette, 1987, Emily Post on Invitations and Letters, 1990, Emily Post on Business Etiquette, 1990, Emily Post on Second Weddings, 1991, Emily Post's Wedding Planner, rev. edit., 1991, Emily Post's Table Manners For Today: Advice For Every Dining Occasion, 1994, Emily Post on Guests and Hosts, 1994; contbg. editor: Good Housekeeping Mag. Republican. Episcopalian. Died Apr. 24, 2010.

POTTER, DOUGLAS E., building materials company executive; b. Ware, Mass., Apr. 6, 1930; s. William Warren Potter and Marim De Ferest (Chetwynd) Jennings; m. Roberta Prescott, Nov. 21, 1958; children: Suzanne L. Kent, Stephen P., Laura P. Scanlan. BS in Chem. Engring., U. Rhode Island, 1952. Engr., supr. E.I. DuPont, Seaford, Del., 1952-56; engr., mgr. Owens Corning Fiberglas, Ashton, R.I., 1956-59, tech. mgr. Aiken, S.C., 1959-63; devel. engr. Polaroid Corp., Waltham, Mass., 1963-65; devel. mgr. Owens Corning Fiberglas, Ashton, 1965-70, tech. mgr. Granville, Ohio, 1970-76; tech. v.p. Certain Teed Corp., Valley Forge, Pa., 1976-80, corp. v.p., group pres., from 1980. Patentee in field. Mem.: Chester Valley Golf (Malvern, Pa.). Republican. Avocations: golf, travel. Home: Berwyn, Pa. Died Jan. 3, 2010.

POTTER, JOHN LEITH, retired mechanical and aerospace engineer, educator, consultant; b. Metz, Mo., Feb. 5, 1923; s. Jay Francis Lee and Pearl Delores (Leeth) P.; m. Dorothy Jean Williams, Dec. 15, 1957; children: Stephen, Anne, Carol. BS in Aerospace Engring., U. Ala., Tuscaloosa, 1944, MS in Engring., 1949; MS in Engring. Mgmt., Vanderbilt U., 1976, PhD in Mech. Engring., 1974. Engr., educator various indsl., ednl. and govt. orgns., 1944-52; chief, flight and aerodyns. lab. Redstone Arsenal, Ala., 1952-56; mgr., div. chief, dep. tech. dir., sr. staff scientist Sverdrup Tech., Inc., Tullahoma, Tenn., 1956-83; research prof. Vanderbilt U., Nashville, 1983-92, prof. emeritus, from 1992; cons. engr. Nashville, from 1983. Convener NATO-AGARD, U.S. and Eng., 1980-82, mem. working group, 1984-88; mem. adv. com. Internat. Symposium on Rarefied Gasdynamics, 1970—; invited lectr. USSR Acad. Scis., 1967; mem. NRC com. on assessment nat. aeronautical wind tunnel facilities, 1987-88; mem. NASA working groups, 1987—; mem. Engring. Accreditation Commn., 1985-90. Editor: Rarefied Gas Dynamics, 1977. Contbr. articles to profl. publs., chpts. to books Chmn. bd. dirs. Coffee County Hist. Soc., Tenn., 1971-72; bd. dirs. Southeastern Amateur Athletic Union, 1972-73; pres. Tullahoma Swim Club, 1972-73. Recipient Outstanding Fellow award U. Ala. Aerospace Engring. Dept., 1987; elected 150th Anniversary Disting. Engring. Fellow U. Ala. Coll. Engring., 1988; USAF Arnold Engring. Devel. Ctr. fellow, 1993. Fellow AIAA (assoc. editor jour. 1970-73, publs. com. 1973-78, assoc. editor Progress in Astronautics and Aeronautics 1981-85, Gen. H.H. Arnold award Tenn. chpt. 1964); mem. U. Ala. Capstone Engring. Soc. (regional bd. dirs. 1972-77), Sigma Xi, Tau Beta Pi, Theta Tau, Pi Tau Sigma, Sigma Gamma Tau. Home: Birmingham, Ala. Deceased.

POTTS, RICHARD ALLEN, chemistry educator; b. Massillon, Ohio, Jan. 2, 1940; s. Henry M. and Lillian (Lehman) P.; m. Carolyn Ann Stubur, Mar. 26, 1965; 1 child, Alan R. AB, Hiram Coll., 1962; PhD, Northwestern U., 1966. Asst. prof. U. Mich., Dearborn, 1966-69, assoc. prof., 1969-73, prof. chemistry, from 1973. Mem. Am. Chem. Soc. (councilor Detroit sect. 1986—). Home: Millersburg, Ohio. Died May 27, 2010.

POUND, ROBERT VIVIAN, physics professor; b. Ridgeway, Ont., Can., May 16, 1919; arrived in U.S., 1923, naturalized, 1932; s. Vivian Ellsworth and Gertrude C. (Prout) Pound; m. Betty Yde Andersen, June 20, 1941; 1 child, John Andrew. BA, U. Buffalo, 1941; AM (hon.), Harvard Coll., 1950; DSc (hon.), SUNY, Buffalo, 1994. Rsch. physicist Submarine Signal Co., 1941—42; staff mem. Radiation Lab. MIT, Cambridge, 1942—46; Soc. Fellows jr. fellow Harvard U., Cambridge, 1945—48; asst. prof. physics Harvard Coll., Cambridge, 1948—50, assoc. prof., 1950—56, prof., 1956—68; chmn. dept. physics, 1968—72; Mallinckrodt prof. physics, 1968—89; emeritus, 1989—2010; dir. Physics Lab. Harvard U., Cambridge, 1975—83. Fulbright rsch. scholar Oxford (Eng.) U., 1951; vis. rsch. fellow Merton Coll., 1980; Fulbright lectr., Paris, 58; vis. prof. Coll. de France, 1973; vis. fellow Joint Inst. Lab. Astrophysics, U. Colo., 1979—80; Zernike vis. prof. U. Groningen, The Netherlands, 1982; vis. sr. scientist Brookhaven Nat. Lab., 1986—87; vis. prof. U. Fla., 1987; W.G. Brickwedde lectr. Johns Hopkins U., Balt., 1992; Julian Mack lectr. U. Wis., 1992. Author, editor Mmicrowave Mixers, 1948; contbr. articles to profl. jours. Associated Univs., Inc., 1976—2010. Recipient B.J. Thompson Meml. award, Inst. Radio Engrs., 1948, Eddington medal, Royal Astron. Soc., 1965, Nat. medal Sci., Pres. U.S., 1990; fellow John Simon Guggenheim, 1957—58, 1972—73. Fellow: AAAS, Am. Acad. Arts and Scis., Am. Phys. Soc.; mem.: NAS, French Phys. Soc. (mem. coun. 1958—61), French Acad. Scis. (assoc.; fgn.), Sigma Xi, Phi Beta Kappa. Died Apr. 12, 2010.

POUPARD, JAMES J., controller; b. Monroe, Mich., Mar. 21, 1932; s. Edmund Lawrence and Ruth Mary (Soleau) P.; m. E. Ruth Gilmer, Aug. 21, 1954; children: Michelle, Brenda, Dennis, Gary. PHB in Econs., U. Detroit, 1964. Systems analyst Mercury div. Ford Motor Co., Detroit, 1956-57; acct., analyst Chrysler Corp., Detroit, 1957-67, internat. controller airtemp div. Dayton, Ohio, 1970-72; div. controller Allis Chalmers Corp., Matteson, Ill., 1972-80; v.p., controller Komatsu Dresser Co., Peoria, Ill., from 1980. Bd. dirs. Heart of Ill. United Way, Peoria, 1981-89; bd. dirs. Peoria YMCA, 1983-84, mem. adv. bd., 1990—; bd. dirs. Tri-County Women Strength, 1990—; chmn. FEMA local bd. Emergency Food and Shelter, 1983-93; past coach Jr. League Football, past football ofcl. With USAF, 1951-55. Mem.: Holiday Boat (Rome, Ill.) (vice commodore 1985-86, commodore 1986-87, bd. dirs. 1988—). Roman Catholic. Avocation: power yachting. Home: Henderson, Nev. Died Dec. 14, 2009.

POURCIAU, LESTER JOHN, JR., retired librarian; b. Baton Rouge, Sept. 6, 1936; s. Lester John and Pearlie M. (Hogan) Pourciau; 1 child, Lester John III. BA, La. State U., 1962, MS, 1964; PhD, Ind. U., 1975. Asst. ref. libr. U. S.C., Columbia, 1963—64; ref. libr. Florence County Pub. Libr., SC, 1964—65; coord. ref. svcs. U. Fla., Gainesville, 1966—67; dir. librs. U. Memphis, 1970—99, assoc. v.p. for acad. affairs, dir. librs., 1987—91. Chmn. coun. of head librarians State Univ. and C.C. System Tenn., 1980, 87, 97; acad. assoc. Atlantic Coun. of U.S., U. Memphis; fgn. expert, vis. lectr. Beijing U. of Posts & Telecomms., Beijing Normal U., Peking U., Renmen U., Qinghua U., Chingqing Inst. Posts & Telcomms., Guizhou Normal U., Republic of China, 1993, Beijing U. Posts and Telecom, 1993, Nanjing U. Posts and Telecom., Anhui Normal U., Beijing U. Posts and Telecom., 1994, People's Republic of China, 1994; cons. prof. Beijing U. Posts and Telecom., 1996—; participant 2d Internat. Conf. Crimea 95, Librs. and Assn. in the Transient World, Republic of Crimea; participant, dep. chair organizing com., 1996—; Peking U. Internat. Conf., Beijing, 1998. Contbr. articles to profl. jours. With USAF, 1955-59. Recipient Adminstrv. Staff award Memphis State U., 1981, Commendation Boy Scouts Am., 1985, Commendation Tenn. Sec. State, 1989, Honor award Tenn. Libr. Assn., 1990, Allen J. Hammond award for Disting. Svc. U. Memphis, 1999, SLIS Disting. Alumni award Ind. U., 1999, TRACES award U. Memphis Assn. Retirees, 2003; named Outstanding Alumnus, La. State U., 1988; named Libr. of Yr., Memphis Libr. Coun., 1989; fellow Higher Edn. Act Ind. U.; named to 30th Ann. Honor Roll. ALA Office Intellectual Freedom and Freedom to Read Found. U. Memphis, 1999. Mem.: ALA, Memphis Old Time Car Club (sec. 1981, pres. 1982, 1989), Mid-Am. Old Time Automobile Assn., Antique Automobile Club Am., Nat. Assn. Watch and Clock Collectors (chpt. pres. 1983, sec.-treas. 1988—89). Home: Memphis, Tenn. Died Nov. 30, 2009.

POWER, ARTHUR JOHN, chemical engineer; b. Waltham, Mass., Apr. 8, 1920; s. William John and Clare (Lally) Power; m. Elizabeth Swint Power, June 12, 1948; children: David H., Elise P., Christopher J., S. Bradford. BS in Chem. Engring., MIT, 1942; MS in Chem. Engring., W.Va. U., 1974. Registered profl. engr., W.Va. Sr. engr. Union Carbide Chems., South Charleston, W.Va., 1946—75; prin. process engr. Olin Chems., Stamford, Conn., 1975—80; sr. process engring. specialist Heyward Robinson Co., NYC, 1980—81; sr. cons. Chem. Systems, Inc., Tarrytown, NY, 1981—83; prin. process engr. Solar Energy Rsch. Inst., Golden, Colo., from 1983. Chmn. ednl. coun. MIT, Fairfield County, Conn., 1975—82. Capt. US Army, 1942—46, NATOUSA, ETO. Recipient George B. Morgan award, MIT Ednl. Coun., 1981. Fellow: Am. Inst. Chem. Engrs. (chmn. Charleston sect. 1974—75, mem. nat. admissions com. 1979—83); mem.: Univ. Musicians Assn., MIT Alumni Colo. (bd. dirs. from 1983). Republican. Roman Catholicrr. Home: Boulder, Colo. Died May 7, 2009.

POWERS, CHARLES HENRI, public relations executive, former federal official; b. NYC, May 7, 1945; s. Percy and Dolly (Davis) P.; m. Rosalind B. Silverstone, Sept. 11, 1973; children: Alexander, Gregory. AB, U. Miami, Fla., 1965; MA, NYU, 1967. Reporter Sta. WTVJ-TV, Miami, Fla., 1964-65; assignment editor Sta. WMAL-TV, Washington, 1974-75; with pub. affairs staff IRS, Phila., 1975-78, Washington, 1980-82; press sec. to Senator Richard Schweiker US Senate, Washington, 1978-80; with pub. affairs staff US Dept. Treasury, Washington, 1982-85, dep. asst. sec. for pub. affairs, 1986-88; sr. account exec. Ogilvy & Mather Pub. Relations, Washington, 1985; sr. v.p. pub. affairs The Tobacco Inst., Washington, 1988-91; dir. Office Pub. Affairs, Fed. Housing Fin. Bd., Washington, 1991—92; dep. asst. for pub. affairs US Dept. Transp., Washington, 1992—93; press. sec. US Senate Fin. Com., 1993—94; sr. v.p. Porter Novelli, 1994—2009; prin. Powers Pub. Affairs, 2009—10. Press counsel Pres.'s Commn. on Aviation Security and Terrorism, 1989-90. Bd. dirs. Old Town Civic Assn., Alexandria, Va., 1983-86, 89-91; mem. Mayor's Parking Task Force, Alexandria, 1984-85, Alexandria-Caen, France Sister City com., 1991—. Served to capt. USAF, 1967-74. Recipient Meritorious Service medal, 1974, Exceptional Svc. award US Dept. Treasury, 1988. Mem. U.S. Senate Press Sec.'s Assn., Soc. Profl. Journalists, Radio-TV News Dirs. Assn., Air Force Assn., NYU Club, Nat. Press Club, Army and Navy Club. Republican. Home: Alexandria, Va. Died Jan. 3, 2010.

POWERS, JOHN AUSTIN, alcoholic beverage company executive; b. NYC, Oct. 24, 1926; s. Francis A. and Meta Marie (Touwsma) P.; m. Eileen Herlihy, Mar. 23, 1962; children: Maribeth, John Austin, Jennifer, Cecilia. BA, St. Peters Coll., 1950; A.M.P., Harvard U., 1980. With McCann-Erickson, Inc., 1957-73, chmn. U.K., 1967-70, pres. Europe, 1967-71, v.p. internat., 1968-70, pres. U.S.A., 1971-73; v.p. Heublein, Inc., Farmington, Conn., 1973-78, group exec. wines group, 1975-78, sr. v.p. alcoholic beverages, 1979-81, pres., chief exec. officer, 1982-86, chmn., chief exec. officer, 1986-87, chmn. bd., from 1987; chmn., chief exec. officer United Vintners, Inc., San Francisco, 1973-78, sr. v.p. alcoholic beverages, 1978-81. Bd. dirs. Hartford Nat. Corp., Hartford Steam Boiler and Inspection Co., The Pillsbury Co.; dep. chmn. Internat Distillers & Vintners, Ltd. Bd. dirs. Hosp.; regent U. Hartford; trustee Hartford Grad. Ctr., Bus. Advisory Council, Skidmore Coll., Saratoga Springs, N.Y.; dir. San Francisco Ballet, 1975-77. Served to 2d lt. U.S. Army, 1944-46. Mem. Conn. Bus. and Industries Assn. (bd. dirs.). Clubs: Meadow (Southampton, N.Y.); Hartford Golf (West Hartford, Conn.). Home: New York, NY. Died May 23, 2009.

PRACHTHAUSER, FRANK JAMES, information systems executive; b. Elizabeth, N.J., May 6, 1938; s. Frank J. and Helen A. (Barry) P.; m. Judith A. Sagarese, Apr. 25, 1980; children— Francis J., Jonathan D., Amy E. B.S. in Mgmt., Fairleigh Dickinson U., 1971. Cert. in data processing. Programmer, analyst Am. Cyanamid, Wayne, N.J., 1961-66; programming supr. CIBA Geigy, Ardsley, N.Y., 1966-71; project mgr. Scudder, Stevens and Clark, N.Y.C., 1971-74; dir. info. systems Pantasote, Inc., Greenwich, Conn., 1974-86; v.p. mgmt. info. systems techs., Paine Webber, Inc., Weehawken, N.J. Served with USN, 1957-61. Mem. Data Processing Mgmt. Assn., Assn. Computing Machinery, Digital Equipment Users Soc., AT&T Intermediate Bus. Panel. Democrat. Roman Catholic. Club: Kellogg (Morristown, N.J.). Avocation: Victorian house restoration. Home: Fernandina, Fla. Died Aug. 6, 2009.

PRAHALAD, C.K. (COIMBATORE KRISHNARAO PRAHALAD), finance educator, corporate strategist; b. Coimbatore, India, Aug. 8, 1941; m. Gayatri Prahalad. BS, U. Madras, 1960. Harvey C. Fruehauf prof. bus. adminstrn. & prof. corp. strategy and internat. bus. Stephen M. Ross Sch. Bus., U. Mich. Co-author (with Gary Hamel): Competing for the Future, 1994; co-author: (with Venkat Ramaswamy) The Future of Competition: Co-Creating Unique Value with Customers, 2004; co-author: (with M.S. Krishnan) The New Age of Innovation: Driving Cocreated Value Through Global Networks, 2008; author: The Fortune at the Bottom of the Pyramid: Eradicating Poverty Through Profits, 2004; contbr. articles to profl. jours. Died Apr. 16, 2010.

PRENTISS, AUGUSTIN MITCHELL, JR., former electrical company executive; b. Ft. Coswell, NC, Sept. 30, 1915; s. Augustin Mitchell and Anne Randolph (Hull) P.; m. Nancy Elizabeth Ludwig, July 23, 1948 (div. 1963); children: Gail Randolph Prentiss Miller, Keith Randolph; m. Corinne Payne Phelps, June 24, 1972. BS, U.S. Mil. Acad., 1937; AMP, Harvard U., 1957; MA, Am. U., Washington, 1965. Commd. 2d lt. USAF, 1937, advanced through grades to col., 1945; capt. to col. 5th Air Force, Far East Air Forces, Australia, New Guinea, Philippines, Japan, 1943-46; with SAC, USAF, Andrews AFB, 1946-48, Office Joint Chiefs Staff, Dept. Def., Washington, 1950-53; chief staff Air Devel. Ctr., Wright Patterson AFB, 1953-55; with Office Sec. Def., Research and Engring., Washington, 1958-60; ret. USAF, 1960; mgr. project liaison Westinghouse Electric Corp., Balt., 1960-65, dir. def. systems Washington, 1965-81. Co-author: Civil Defense in Modern War, 1951. Decorated Legion of Merit. Mem. Air Force Assn., Ret. Officers Assn., Air Force Hist. Soc., Mil. Order Carabao. Clubs: Army Navy, Harvard Bus. Sch. (placement com. 1968-72), U.S. Mil. Acad. Class 1937 (treas. 1966-87)(Washington), Army Navy Country (Arlington, Va.). Republican. Episcopalian. Avocations: tennis, cruising, home computers. Home: Bethesda, Md. Died Jan. 28, 2009.

PRESBY, RICHARD ALLEN, library administrator; b. Manila, Philippines, Nov. 5, 1936; arrived in US, 1940; s. Frank Spencer and Anna Louise (Caldwell) Presbrey; married. BA, Calif. Poly. U., 1968; MA, Fullerton State U., 1969, MLS, 1970. Bibliographer Honnold Libr., Claremont, Calif., 1969—72; asst. libr. Subiaco Libr., Alaska, 1973; libr. JHK Librs., San Francisco, 1974—76, dir., 1976—86; appointed libr. William E. Colby Meml. Libr., from 1986. Coord. Republicans for Kennedy, Calif., 1968. Author: Motorist Aid System Bibliography, 1976, Stray Cats, 1978 (Berkeley award, 1979). With USAF, 1957—61. Mem.: Spl. Librs. Assn. (edn. com. 1978—81). Roman Catholic. Died May 16, 2009.

PRESSLEY, LUCIUS C., psychiatrist; b. Chester, SC, July 19, 1928; s. Lucius Crawford and Mildred Cornell (Cassels) P.; m. Margaret Lindsay Burnside, Oct. 4, 1969; children: Elizabeth, Crawford, John. AB, Duke U., 1949; MD, Med. U. S.C., 1961. Diplomate Am. Bd. Psychiatry & Neurology. Resident U. N.C. Sch. Medicine, Chapel Hill, 1962-65; tchg. psychiatrist Wm. S. Hall Psychiat., Columbia, S.C., from 1966. Clin. assoc. prof. Med. U. S.C., Charleston, 1973—, Med. Coll. Ga., Augusta, 1988—; clin. prof. psychiatry U. S.C. Sch. Medicine, Columbia, 1981—, asst. dean continuing med. edn., 1994; lectr. grad. sch. nursing U. S.C., 1972-73; disting. adj. prof. U. S.C. Coll. Pharmacy, 1978-82; cons. S.C. Dept. Corrections, Columbia, 1985-86, Dorn Veterans Hosp., Columbia, 1986—. Co-editor: Essays in the History of Psychiatry, 1980, A Symposium on Public Psychiatry, 1987. Bd. dirs. Health Resources Found., Columbia, 1972-93, 3 Rivers Health Sys. Agy., Columbia, 1981-87. Served in U.S. Army, 1951-53. Fellow Am. Psychiat. Assn.; mem. SAR. Republican. Episcopal. Avocations: gardening, drama, auctions. Home: West Columbia, SC. Died Feb. 16, 2009.

PRICE, SOL, retired retail company executive; b. Bronx, NY, Jan. 23, 1916; m. Helen (Moskowitz) Price, 1938 (dec. 2008); children: Robert, Larry Grad., San Diego State U., 1934; JD, U. So. Calif. Law Sch., 1938. Atty. Procopa, Price, Cory & Schwartz, 1938-54; pres. Fed-Mart Corp., 1954-75; founder Price Co., San Diego, 1976—93. Bd. trustees The Urban Inst. Democrat. Died Dec. 14, 2009.

PRINCE, MARY RUTH, librarian; b. Edwards, Miss., Feb. 22, 1928; d. James Albert and Sarah (Henderson) Brown; A.B., Tougaloo Coll., 1951; M.A., Central Mich. U., 1969; m. James Richard Prince, Apr. 4, 1964; 1 child, Eldred Rene. Librarian, Lawrence (Miss.) High Sch., 1951-52, Boler High Sch., Decatur, Miss., 1953-59, Rosa A. Temple High Sch., Vicksburg, Miss., 1959-64, Stone St. Elem. Sch., Greenwood, Miss., 1964-66, Vicksburg High Sch., 1966-68; asst. prof. Mississippi Valley State U., Itta Bena, Miss., 1968—. Mem. ALA, NAACP, Internat. Platform Assn., Miss. Library Assn., Southeastern Library Assn. Baptist. Died June 22, 2009.

PRITCHARD, DALTON HAROLD, retired electronics executive; b. Crystal Springs, Miss., Sept. 1, 1921; s. Cecil Harold and Marvie Prudence (Lofton) P.; m. Caroline Ann Hnatuk, Apr. 27, 1947; 1 child, Mary Ann Pritchard Poole (dec.). BSE.E., Miss. State U., 1943; postgrad., Harvard, MIT Radar Sch., 1943-44. Mem. tech. staff RCA Labs., Riverhead, NY, 1946-50, mem. tech. staff Princeton, NJ, 1950-75, fellow tech. staff, 1975-87. Session chmn., mem. program com. Internat. Conf. on Consumer Electronics, Chgo., 1980-85 Contbr. articles to profl. jours.; patentee in field. Mem. N.J. Gov.'s Sci. Adv. Council, Princeton, 1981-85. Served to capt. U.S. Army Signal Corps Decorated Bronze Star; recipient Eduard Rhein prize Edward Rhein Found., Berlin, Fed. Republic of Germany, 1980; Disting. Engring. fellow Miss. State U., 1991. Fellow IEEE (Vladimir Zworykin award 1977, David Sarnoff award 1981), Soc. Info. Display, Nat. Assn. Engrs., Nat. Acad. Engring., Sigma Xi, Tau Beta Pi, Kappa Mu Epsilon Republican. Baptist. Avocations: amateur radio, tennis. Home: Hilton Head Island, SC. Died Apr. 18, 2010.

PRITZ, BENJAMIN LIONEL, manufacturing executive; b. Cin., Dec. 20, 1920; s. Walter Heineman Pritz and Dorothy Stix (Lowman) Pritz Steiner; m. Louise Clarisse Aggiman, Nov. 10, 1948; children: Neil Aggiman, Alan Lowman. V.p. Grandpa Brands Co., Cin., 1948—80, pres., from 1980. With USAAF, 1942—46. Mem.: Asian Art Soc., Asian Soc., Graphic Arts Soc., Internat. Snuff Bottle Soc. Club, Bankers Club, Pan Am. Club, Fencers Club (chmn. bd. 1970—83). Jewish. Died June 6, 2010.

PROBALA, ANDREW EUGENE, designer, artist; b. Cleve., Nov. 16, 1908; s. Andras and Anna (Visoky) Probala; m. Ruth J. Kulish Probala, Nov. 24, 1934; 1 child, Paul A. Student, Cleve. Sch. Art, 1922—30, John Huntington Poly. Cleve., 1927—29. Draftsman, designer Rorimer-Brooks Studio, Cleve., 1927—37; designer Irvin & Gormley Inc., Cleve., 1937—40, Fisher Air Craft, Cleve., 1941, A.E. Probala, Cleve., 1941—65, 1977—90, Cleveland Heights, from 1990, Irvin & Co., Cleve., 1965—77. Mem.: Cleve. Soc. Artists (pres. 1969—72). Republican. Avocations: designing, painting, building. Died Jan. 21, 2009.

PROUNIS, THEODORE OTHON, lawyer; b. NYC, Feb. 13, 1926; s. Othon D. and Amelia O. (Petrides) Prounis; m. Lila D. Jentiles, Feb. 22, 1956; 1 child, Othon A. BS, Columbia U., 1949, MS, 1950; JD, Fordham U., 1963. Bar: NY 1964. Pvt. practice, NYC, from 1964. Investor, Archon Deputatos Ecumenical Patriarch Greek Orthodox Ch., Constantinople, Turkey, 1976; mem. Coun. Archdiocese N.Am. and S.Am., NYC, from 1982; trustee, pres. Cathedral Archdiocese Greek Orthodox Ch., from 1986. With USAF, 1944—46, PTO. Mem.: ABA. Republican. Died May 22, 2010.

PROVENCHER, HENRY DAVID, state employee; b. Dorchester, Mass., Mar. 1, 1921; s. Archille Joseph and Lucy Marie (Hasken) P.; ed. Lowell Tech. Inst., 1938-42, McIntosh Bus. Coll., 1946-49, Boston Indsl. Tech. Sch., 1948-52, Lawrence Indsl. Sch., 1952-55, also Lawrence Indsl. Sch.; m. Veronica Mary King, Feb. 19, 1950; children: Paul, Mary, Samuel, Kathleen, Dorothy. With Commonwealth of Mass., Middleborough, 1951-82, storekeeper, 1952-56, prin. storekeeper, 1956-73, adminstrv. storekeeper, hwy. repair foreman, 1973-74; asst. adminstr. Danvers State Mental Hosp., Hawthorne, Mass., 1973-74; permanent evening custodian Middleborough Sch. Dept., 1957-75. Active various capacities Boy Scouts Am. Served with AUS, 1942-45. Mem. DAV (adj. 1950-79, comdr. 1975-76, trustee 1968-75, dist. 7 adj. 1978-79), Am. Legion (chaplain 1979-80), Am. Fedn. State County & Mcpl. Employees Assn., Mass. Storekeepers Assn., Internat. Aux. Police Assn., Am. Fedn. Trades Council, VFW, Am. Automobile Assn., Middleborough Vets. Council (chaplain 1979-80). Roman Catholic. Democrat. Clubs: Eagles, Elks, Country Pond Fish and Game. Home: Bradenton, Fla. Died Aug. 12, 2009.

PRUETT, BARBARA JEAN, librarian; b. Madison, Ind., May 8, 1942; d. Fred Phillip and Dorothy Jean (Keel) P. B.S., Ind. U., 1966; M.A. in Librarianship, Calif. State U.-San Jose, 1971. Head librarian LaGrange High Sch. (Ind.), 1966-68, Santa Clara Planning Dept., San Jose, Calif., 1969-71; head research info. ctr. United Farm Workers, Keene, Calif., 1973-75; head social sci. library Catholic U., Washington, 1975-79; head tech. services Internat. Trade Commn., Washington, 1979-83, library dir., 1983—. Author country music articles; pub. Clouds Hill Publs. Mem. ALA (council 1979—), Country Music Assn., Acad. Country Music, D.C. Library Assn., Assn. Recorded Sound Collections, D.C. Library Assn., Fed. Library Com. (exec. adv. com. 1984—). Home: Washington, DC. Died Mar. 16, 2010.

PRUITT, KENNETH MELVIN, university administrator, biochemist, educator; b. Winston-Salem, NC, Oct. 3, 1933; s. Dennis Leonard Pruitt and Hallie Zelma (Elledge) Hodge; m. Carolyn Mitchell, Jan. 17, 1956 (div. Sept. 1972); children: Ellise Mayor, Torri Chappel, Corinne Cargnoni, Keith Pruitt; m. Angela June Forbus, Dec. 31, 1985. BS in Chemistry, U. N.C., 1956; BS in Meteorology, Pa. State U., 1957; PhD in Chemistry, Brown U., 1965; D in Odontology (hon.), U. Umea, Sweden, 1988. Prof. dept. biomath. U. Ala., Birmingham, from 1979, prof. dept. biochemistry, from 1979, sr. scientist Cystic Fibrosis Rsch. Ctr., 1981-86, state project dir. Ala. Exptl. Program to Stimulate Rsch., from 1988, assoc. v.p. rsch., 1984-92, assoc. v.p. sponsored programs, 1992-95. Cons. State of La. Edn. Quality Support Fund R&D Program, 1989—. Author, editor: The Lactoperoxidase System: Chemistry and Biological Significance, 1985; contbr. articles to profl. jours. Trustee Birmingham Unitarian Ch., 1991-94; chmn. Jefferson County Resource Recovery Commn., Birmingham, 1980. Capt. USAF, 1956-60. Grantee NSF, 1988—, Nat. Inst. Dental Rsch., 1989-93, Dong Kook Pharm. Co., 1990-91. Mem. AAAS, Am. Soc. Biol. Chemists, Am. Chem. Soc., Am. Meteorol. Soc. Avocations: bird watching, poetry, tuba. Home: Birmingham, Ala. Died Jan. 4, 2009.

PRYOR, ERIC JON, minister, writer; b. Suffern, NY, July 16, 1959; s. Peter Anthony Pryor and Joanne Carol Roefs, Nancy Long (Stepmother) and Walter Little Brown (Stepfather); m. Renee Serpa, July 16, 1997; children: Christopher Borg, Sarah Borg. MFA, N.Y. Ctr. Media Arts, 1986; DDiv (hon.), Earth Star Temple, 1987. Ordained to ministry Jubilee Christian Ctr., 1995. Founder, min. Nefom Temple, Woodstock, NY, 1980—2004, New Earth Temple, San Francisco, 1987—90; founder, CEO Christian Gladiators Ministry, Sparks, Nev., 1991—2004, Peculiar Nation Prodns., Sparks, from 1997. Media cons. Jubilee Christian Ctr., San Jose, Calif., 1990—2004. Author: Book of Pagan Rituals, Crash and Burn, What is a Witch Really, My Testemony From My Own Mouth; The Ruelle Tarot; prodr.: (video) Satan Unvieled, Law Enforcement Guide to Satanic Cults, From Pagan to Pentecost; contbr. video. Spokesperson Pagan Religious Cmty., San Francisco, 1987—90. Conservative. Achievements include first to develop the worlds largest networking temples for the practicing Pagan, and Occultist community. Avocations: fishing, drag racing, horseback riding, scuba diving, skydiving. Died June 7, 2009.

PUGH, DAVID ARTHUR, architect; b. Pitts., Aug. 10, 1926; s. George Arthur and Ellen (Burton) P.; m. Patricia Ann Lawton, Dec. 21, 1948; children— Ellen Burton, Margaret Lawton, David Arthur, Douglas Burton. B.Arch., Yale U., 1947. With SOM & Gardner A. Dailey, 1948-49; designer Gardner A. Dailey & Assos., 1950-51, Skidmore, Owings & Merrill, 1952; all San Francisco; designer Skidmore, Owings & Merrill, Portland, Oreg., 1952-55, participating asso., 1955-59, asso., 1959-63, gen. partner, from 1963. Mem. adv. com. Region 10, GSA, 1968-70; adv. panel West Front of Capitol, AIA, Washington, 1979—; pres. Contemporary Crafts Gallery, 1963-66 Prin. works include Portland Hilton Hotel, 1961, Memorial Coliseum, Portland, 1960, Portland Center, urban renewal, 1967, Ga.-Pacific hdqrs. bldg, Portland, 1970, Pacific Nat. Bank Wash. hdqrs. bldg, Tacoma, 1970, Autzen Stadium,U. Oreg, 1968, Salishan, beach resort, Gleneden Beach, Oreg., 1965, U.S. Nat. Bank Ore. hdqrs, Portland, 1973, Portland Transit Mall, 1978. Bd. dirs. Pacific N.W. Ballet Assn.; finance chmn. Portland State U. Found., 1969-70, pres., 1972-73; chmn. bd. Human Resources Council Oreg., 1971-75; bd. dirs. Portland Symphony Soc., 1973-79, Portland Civic Theater, 1973—. Fellow AIA (nat. v.p. 1973, dir. Portland chpt. 1965-66, chancellor Coll. of Fellows 1978-79); mem. Oreg. Hist. Soc., Portland C. of C., Portland Art Assn. Clubs: Rotarian. Home: Lake Oswego, Oreg. Died May 17, 2010.

PUNT, TERRY LEE, retired state legislator; b. Waynesboro, Pa., Aug. 13, 1949; 2 children. Credit mgr. Am. Fin. Consumer Discount Co., 1970—73, Grove Mfg. Co., 1973—78; mem. Dist. 90 Pa. House of Reps., Pa., 1979—88; mem. Dist. 33 Pa. State Senate, 1989—2009. Served in US Army, 1967—70. Mem.: YMCA (bd. dir. 1974—77), Waynesboro Bi-Centennial Cmty., S. Ctr. Pa. Am. Heart Assn. (founding mem., bd. dir. 1975—78), Franklin County Assn. Retarded Citizens (founding mem., pres. 1975—77), Lions (pres. 1975—76). Republican. Protestant. Died Dec. 27, 2009.

PURPEL, DAVID EDWARD, education educator; b. Cambridge, Mass., June 5, 1932; s. Israel William and Sybil (Bergelson) P.; m. Elaine Ladd, Aug. 28, 1958; children: Mark, Rachel, Nancy. AB, Tufts Coll., 1954; MAT, Harvard U., 1956, EdD, 1961. Tchr. Newton (Mass.) Pub. Schs., 1956-57; assoc. prof., dir. programs in tchg. Harvard U., Cambridge, 1961-72; prof. U. N.C., Greensboro, from 1972, dept. chmn., 1976-81; William Allen prof. Seattle (Wash.) U., 1993-94. Vis. prof. Bristol U., Eng., 1970. Series editor: McCutchan Pub., Berkeley, Calif., 1970—; co-author: Supervision: The Reluctant Profession, 1972, Moral Education and the Hidden Curriculum, 1977, Critical Social Issues in American Education, 1993; author: Moral and Spiritual Crisis in Education, 1989 (Book of Yr. Am. Edn. Studies Assn. 1990); (with Sue Shapiro) Beyond Liberation and Excellence, 1995. Home: Greensboro, NC. Died Apr. 19, 2010.

PURTLE, JOHN INGRAM, lawyer, former state supreme court justice; b. Enola, Ark., Sept. 7, 1923; s. John Wesley and Edna Gertrude (Ingram) P.; m. Marian Ruth White, Dec. 31, 1951 (dec. 1995); children: Jeffrey, Lisa K.; m. Phyllis Kelly Purtle. Student, U. Ctrl. Ark., 1946—47; LLB, U. Ark., 1950. Bar: Ark. 1950, U.S. Dist. Ct. (ea. dist.) Ark. 1950. Pvt. practice, Conway, Ark., 1950-53, Little Rock, 1953—78, from 1990; mem. Ark. State Legislature, 1951-52, 69-70; assoc. justice Ark. Supreme Ct., 1979-90. Tchr., deacon Baptist Ch. Served with U.S. Army, 1940-45. Mem. ABA, Ark. Bar Assn., Am. Judicature Soc., Ark. Jud. Coun. Democrat. Deceased.

PUTNAM, ALLAN RAY, association executive; b. July 16, 1920; s. Carl Eugene and Alice (Atwood) P.; m. Marion S. Witmer, Aug. 8, 1942 (dec. Mar. 1993); children: Judith H., Robert W., Victoria, Christian; m. Ann K. Mossman, Sept. 10, 1994. BS in Econs., U. Pa., 1942. Mem. exec. staff Am. Electroplaters Soc., 1946-49; asst. exec. sec., pub. mag. Tool Engr. Am. Soc. Tool and Mfg. Engrs., 1949-59; mng. dir. ASM Internat., Materials Park, Ohio, 1959-84, sr. mng. dir., 1983-85; sec.-gen. World Materials Congress, from 1986. Prees. Nat. Assn. Exhibit Mgrs., 1955, Coun. Engring. and Sci. Soc. Execs., 1958; mgr. Am. Soc. Metals Found. Edn. and Rsch., 1963-85. Bd. govs., treas. Cape Cod Conservatory Music and Arts; bd. govs., pres. Cape Cod Symphony Orch. Served to capt. USAAF, 1942-46. Mem. ASTM, AAAS, NSTA (life), Am. Soc. Assn. Execs. (past dir.), Cleve. Conv. and Visitors Bur. (past dir.), Pres.'s Assn., Am. Mgmt. Assn., Metal Properties Coun. (past dir.), Franklin Inst., Internat. Iron and Steel Inst., Am. Iron and Steel Inst., S.E. Asia Iron and Steel Inst., Metals Soc. (London, hon.), Am. Assn. Cost Engrs., Associacao Brasileira de Metals, Italian Soc. Metallurgy, Chinese Soc. Metals, German Soc. Metals, Australasian Inst. Metals, Am. Nuclear Soc., Soc. Automotive Engrs., Soc. Mfg. Engrs., Cyrogenic Soc., Soc. for Advancement Materials and Process Engring., Am. Soc. Engring. Edn., Iron and Steel Inst. Japan (hon.), Metall. Soc., Greater Cleve. Growth Assn., Buckeye Trail Assn., Country Club (Pepper Pike, Ohio), Apalachian Mountain Club, Horseshoe Trail Club, Univ. Club (Washington), Orleans Yacht Club (bd. dirs.), Rotary (sec.). Died Oct. 13, 2009.

PUTNAM, PAUL ADIN, federal agency administrator; b. Springfield, Vt., July 12, 1930; s. Horace Adin and Beatrice Nellie (Baldwin) P.; m. Elsie Mae (Ramseyer) June 12, 1956; children: Pamela Ann, Penelope Jayne, Adin Tyler II, Paula Anna. BS, U. Vt., 1952; MS, Wash. State U., 1954; PhD, Cornell U., 1957. Research animal scientist Agrl. Rsch. Svc., USDA, Beltsville, Md., 1957-66, investigation leader beef cattle nutrition, 1966-68, chief beef cattle research br., 1968-72; asst. dir. Beltsville Agrl. Rsch. Ctr., 1972-80, dir., 1980-84; dir. cen. plains area Ames, Iowa, 1984-87; assoc. dir. mid. south area Stoneville, Miss., 1987-88; dir. mid south area, 1988-94; ret., 1994; selectman Town of Springfield, Vt., 1996—2002, 2004—06. Contbr. articles to profl. jours. Recipient Kidder medal U. Vt.; Outstanding Performance awards USDA, also cert. merit; Danforth fellow; Borden fellow; Purina Research fellow. Fellow AAAS (rep. sect. O), Am. Soc. Animal Sci. (pres., North Atlantic sect., chmn. various coms., N.E. sect. Disting. Service award); mem. Am. Dairy Sci. Assn., Orgn. Profl. Employees USDA (pres. Beltsville chpt.), Council for Agrl. Sci. and Tech. Home: Springfield, Vt. Died May 8, 2010.

PUTTER, IRVING, retired French language educator; b. NYC, Dec. 3, 1917; s. Joseph and Anna (Schrank) P.; children— Paul Stephen, Candace Anne Putter. BA, CCNY, 1938; MA, State U. Iowa, 1941; PhD, Yale U., 1949. Mem. faculty U. Calif. at Berkeley, 1947-88, prof. French, 1961-88, chmn. dept., 1968-71, humanities research fellow, 1971-72, 78-79, 84-85; ret., 1988. Author: Leconte de Lisle and His Contemporaries, 1951, The Pessimism of Leconte de Lisle: Sources and Evolution, 1954, The Pessimism of Leconte de Lisle: The Work and The Time, 1961, La Dernière Illusion de Leconte de Lisle: Lettres Inédites a Emilie Leforestier, 1968; also numerous articles.; editor, translator: Chateaubriand: Atala, René, 1952. Guggenheim fellow, 1955-56; Fulbright fellow, 1955-56 Home: Santa Clara, Calif. Died Apr. 24, 2009.

PYLE, DONALD ALAN, music educator, tenor; b. Ridgewood, NJ, Jan. 12, 1933; s. Aime A. and Muriel Ann (Barbour) Pyle; m. Barbara Jean Pyle, July 6, 1961 (dec.); m. Virginia R. Tinker, June 4, 1968. Student, Juilliard Sch. Music, 1956—59; BA in Vocal Performance, U. Southern Fla., 1969; MusM, Fla. State U., MusD, 1972. Tenor soloist John Harms Chorus, NYC, St. Michael's Episcopal Ch., Temple Bethel, Juilliard Opera Theatre, Englewood, NJ, St. Leo Coll., Dade City, Fla., 1956—61; mem. South Shore Music Circus, Cohassett, 1958—59; tchg. asst. Fla. State U., Tallahassee, 1969—71, adj. faculty, 1971—72; instr. U. Mo., Columbia, 1972—76; acting dean Swinney Conservatory Music, Ctrl. Meth. Coll., Fayette, Mo., 1976—77, dean, prof. voice, 1977—90; asst. dean. Sch. Fine Arts, U. Conn., 1990—93, assoc. dean, from 1994; tenor soloist US Colls. and Us., Songs Ark, The Labyrinth, Of Mice and Men. Performer: Strauss's Ariadne Auf Naxos, Bacchus, Verdi Requiem, Otello, Rigoletto, Duke, Bizet's Carmen, Don Jose, Handel's Acis & Galatea, Massanet's Le Cid, Flotow's Martha, Lionel, Purcell's Dido & Aeneas, Puccini's Turandot, Calaf, Rossini's Stabat Mater, Bach's St. Matthew's Passion, Mendelsohn's The Elijah and Les Troyens; recordings, Koch Recordings Internat., RCA. Sgt. USMC, 1951—54. Mem.: Gold Key, Blue Key, Nat. Assn. Schs. Music, Nat. Assn. Tchrs. Singing, Phi Kappa Phi, Pi Kappa Lambda, Phi Mu Alpha, Omicron Delta Kappa, Phi Delta Kappa. Roman Catholic. Home: Singer Island, Fla. Died May 14, 2010.

PYLE, ROBERT EDGAR, retired chemical company executive; b. Parkersburg, W.Va., July 25, 1927; s. Edgar Flemming and Mable Marguerite (Relyea) P.; m. Betty Loraine Ray, May 28, 1949; children— Susan Ann, Paul Thomas, Roberta Rae. BS in Chem. Engring, W.Va. U., 1950, MS (Edward Orton, Jr. fellow 1950-51), 1951, PhD (univ. engring. expt. sta. grantee 1951-53), 1953, D.Sc. (hon.), 1980. With Union Carbide Corp., 1952-86, indsl. chems. div. NYC, 1977-79, pres. performance chems. and polymers div., 1979, corp. v.p. Danbury, Conn., 1979-86. Founder, co-chmn. Larchmont-Mamaroneck (N.Y.) Community Com. Specific Learning Disabilities, 1970-73; bd. dirs. W.Va. U. Found., 1976-86. With USNR, 1945-46. Mem. Am. Inst. Chem. Engrs., Fin. Execs. Inst., Sigma Xi, Tau Beta Pi, Sigma Gamma Epsilon. Clubs: Snee Farm Country (Mount Pleasant). Lodges: Masons. Republican. Methodist. Home: Mount Pleasant, SC. Died Jan. 6, 2009.

PYLE, ROBERT NOBLE, public relations executive; b. Wilmington, Del., Oct. 23, 1926; s. Joseph Lybr and LaVerne Ruth (Noble) Pyle; m. Patricia Carlile Pyle, Jan. 21, 2006; children: Robert Noble Jr., Mark C., Nicholas A., Louis P. Crosier, Sarah P. Moore. BA, Dickinson Coll., 1948; postgrad., Wharton Sch., U. Pa., 1949, U. Minn. Pres. Robert N. Pyle, Inc., Wilmington, 1949-52; adminstrv. asst. to US Congress, Washington, 1952-63; bus. and polit. cons. Robert N. Pyle & Assoc., Washington, 1970—2007, chmn. Sec./treas. Bulgarian Am. Bus. Ctr.; cons. in field. Contbr. numerous articles to profl. jours.; reporter covering Nurnburg Trials, Paris Peace Conf. for, Stars & Stripes, Europe, 1946. Dir. World Affairs Coun.; field man Rep. Nat. Congl. Com., 1959—74. With US Army, 1945—46, ETO. Mem.: Palm Valley Golf Club, Kenwood Country Club, La Quinta Resort and Club. Presbyterian. Home: La Quinta, Calif. Died Mar. 18, 2010.

QUELLO, JAMES HENRY, former federal commissioner; b. Laurium, Mich., Apr. 21, 1914; s. Bartholomew and Mary Katherine (Cochis) Q.; m. Mary Elizabeth Butler, Sept. 14, 1937 (dec. Oct. 25, 1999); children: James Michael, Richard Butler. BA, Mich. State U., 1935, D of Humanities (hon.), 1977; D of Pub. Svc. (hon.), No. Mich. U., 1975. V.p., sta. mgr. Goodwill Stas., Inc., Detroit, 1947-72; v.p. Capital Cities Comm. Corp., 1968; commr. FCC, Washington, 1974—98, acting chmn., 1993; founder, chmn. James H. & Mary B. Quello Ctr. for Telecommunications Mgmt. & Law, Mich. State U., East Lansing, Mich., 1998—2010; pub. policy cons. Wiley Rein LLP, Washington, 2001—10. Comm. cons., Detroit, 1972-74; commr. Detroit Housing and Urban Renewal Commn., 1951-72 Contbr. articles to mags., newspapers; author: My Wars Bd. dirs. Greater Detroit Hosp. Assn.; trustee Mich. Vet. Trust Fund; mem. Gov.'s Spl. Commn. on Urban Problems, Mich., Gov.'s Spl. Study Com. on Legis. Compensation, Mayor's Com. on Human Relations; bd. dirs. Am. Negro Emancipation Centennial; mem. exec. bd. Boy Scouts Am.; TV-radio chmn. United Found. Lt. col. AUS, 1940-45. Decorated Bronze Star with oak leaf cluster, Croix de Guerre (France); recipient Internat. Pres.'s award Nat. Assn. TV Program Execs., 1985, Silver Satellite award Am. Women in Radio and TV, 1988, 93, Sol Taishoff award Washington Area Broadcasters Assn., 1989, 93, Pub. Svc. award Fed. Comm. Bar Assn., 1993, Disting. Svc. award Media Inst., 1993, Golden Eagle Amb. award Pa. Assn. Broadcasters, 1993, Disting. Alumni award Mich. State U., Club Dir. award Detroit Adcraft Club, 1993, L.I. Coalition for Fair Broadcasting award, 1993, Nat. Disting. Svc. award Nat. Assn. Pub. TV, 1993, Obie award Ohio Ednl. TV Stas., 1993, Gold Eagle Leadership award Wireless Cable Assn. Internat., 1993, Pres. award Alaska Broadcasting Assn., 1994, Chmn. award Nat. Religious Broadcasters, 1994, Ga. Broadcasters award Broadcasters of America, 1994, 1st Amendment award Radio & TV News Dirs. Found., 1994; named to the Broadcasting & Cable Hall of Fame, 1995 Mem. Nat. Assn. Broadcaster (gov. liaison com. 1964-72, Keystone award 1990, Disting. Svc. award 1994, Honor award for protecting the technical integrity of radio and TV 1994, Broadcasting Cable Hall of Fame, 1995, Nat. Radio Hall of Fame 1996), Mich. Assn. Broadcasters (pres. 1958, legis. chmn. 1959-72, dir., Outstanding Mich. Citizen 1989, Pioneer award 1994, Ellis Island honor award 1997), Greater Detroit Bd. Commerce, Sigma Alpha Epsilon. Clubs: Adcraft (Detroit); Detroit Athletic, Army and Navy Country; Nat. Press (Washington). Democrat. Home: Alexandria, Va. Died Jan. 24, 2010.

QUIGLEY, HERBERT JOSEPH, JR., pathologist, educator; b. Phila., Mar. 6, 1937; s. Herbert Joseph and Mary Kathleen (Carney) G.; m. Jacqueline Jean Stocksdale, Nov. 28, 1965 (div. 1974); 1 child, Amelia Anne. BS in Chemistry, Franklin and Marshall Coll., 1958; MD, U. Pa., 1962. Diplomate Am. Bd. Pathology. Intern Presbyterias Hosp., NYC, 1962—66, resident, 1962—66; chief pathology Monroe County Hosp., Key West, Fla., 1966-68; from asst. prof. to assoc. prof. pathology Creighton U., Omaha, 1968-72, prof., 1972—2003, prof. emeritus, 2003; chief pathology svc. VA Med. Cr., Omaha, 1968-88. Bd. dirs. Triton-Chito Inc., Omaha. Contbr. articles to profl. jours.; patentee in field. Bd. dirs., former pres., chmn. Nebr. Assn. Earth Sci. Clubs, Omaha, 1972—. Lt. comdr. USNR, 1966-68. Recipient career devel. award NIH, 1962-66, Borden prize for med. rsch. Borden Co., Inc., 1962; fellow NIH, Nat. Cancer Inst., 1958-62. Fellow Coll. Am. Pathologists, Am. Soc. Clin. Pathologists, Am. Inst. Chemists; mem. Nebr. Assn. Pathologists, N.Y. Acad. Scis. Republican. Roman Catholic. Avocations: paleontology, geology. Home: Omaha, Nebr. Died June 7, 2010.

QUINLAN, JOSEPH CHARLES, editor; b. Pitts., Sept. 20, 1930; s. Vincent Francis and Marie Emily (Barbach) Q.; m. Marjorie Louise Lemmon, Aug. 6, 1955; children: Stephen V., Patrick A. BS in Journalism, Marquette U., 1953. Publicity writer Allen-Bradley Co., Milw., 1956-62, Barber-Greene Co., Aurora, Ill., 1962-65; publicity mgr. Parker-hammifin Corp., Cleve., 1965-75; pub. rels. account exec. Dodrill-Vasilakes & Co., Cleve., 1975-79; sr. editor Tooling & Prodn. Mag., Solon, Ohio, 1979-90; editor Quality in Mfg. mag. Huebcore Comms., Solon, Ohio, from 1990. Author: Industrial Publicity, 1983. 1st lt. U.S. Army, 1953-56. Recipient Jesse H. Neal awad Am. Bus. Press, 1981. Mem. Am. Soc. Quality Control. Avocations: photography, travel. Home: South Euclid, Ohio. Died Jan. 11, 2009.

RAAB, HERBERT NORMAN, retail executive; b. NYC, Nov. 7, 1925; s. Jacob and Pauline (Neuwirth) R.; m. Blanche Muriel Levin, Jan. 27, 1952 (dec. Mar. 1981); children: Nancy Renée, James Harris; m. Carmen Sandra Fernandez, Aug. 17, 1986. AB, Harvard U., 1947; postgrad., Harvard U. Bus. Sch., 1947-48, Seton Hall U. Law Sch., 1972-75. V.p. Bamberger Div. R.H. Macy Inc., NYC, 1968-75, v.p., 1975-78; pres. and chief exec. officer W&J Sloane, NYC, 1978-80; pvt. practice cons. NYC, 1980-84; sr. v.p. Wayside Furniture Co., Milford, Conn., 1984-90. Adj. prof. U. Bridgeport (Conn.), 1986-91. Jewish. Home: New York, NY. Died May 11, 2009.

RAABE, WILLIAM WALLACE, foreign language professional, educator; b. Columbus, Ohio, Mar. 23, 1928; s. John Christian Spencer and Chrystal Rae (Limes) R.; m. Karon LeAnne Howard, Sept. 2, 1961; 1 child, William Wallace II. BA, Ohio State U., 1949; MS in Edn., Ea. N. Mex. U., Portales, 1973. Educator Hobbs (N. Mex.) Pub. Schs. System, from 1971. Author: (poetry) Troika (Golden Poet of Year award), 1991, Autumn Fields (Golden Poet of Year award), 1992, Famine, 1989. Rep. Precinct Chmn., Lea County N. Mex., 1975-81; mem. Hobbs Community Players (bd. mem. 1976-78). Lt. U. S. Army, 1951-71. Recipient Purple Heart (2 awards), U. S. Army, Korea, 1971, 72, Air Medal, U. S.Army, Korea, 1972, Letter of Commendation, U. S. Army, Germany, 1970, Army Commendation Medal, Ft. Bliss, Tex., 1971. Mem. NEA-Hobbs (exec. bd. 1974-78), N. Mex. Assn. Class Room Tchrs. (exec. bd. 1974-78). Republican. Russian Orthodox. Avocations: photography, genealogy, stamp collecting/philately, community theater. Home: Hobbs, N.Mex. Died Jan. 26, 2009.

RACHLIN, WILLIAM SELIG, retired surgeon; b. Hartford, Conn., May 13, 1929; s. Irving I. and Rose (Saxe) R.; m. Joy B. Loitman; children: Faye, Margo. AB, Princeton U., 1948; MD, Harvard Med. Sch., 1952. Diplomate Am. Bd. Surgery. Intern in surgery Beth Israel Hosp., Boston, 1952-53, asst. resident in surgery, 1953-54, 58-59, chief resident in surgery, 1959-60; pvt. practice surgery, Brookline, Mass., 1960—99. Capt. USAF, 1954-56. Fellow ACS, Am. Coll. Gastroenterology; mem. Mass. Med. Soc. (trustee 1980—), Norfolk Dist. Med. Soc. (pres. 1977-79). Democrat. Jewish. Home: Chestnut Hill, Mass. Died Apr. 8, 2009.

RADCLIFFE, REDONIA LARAE (DONNIE RADCLIFFE), journalist; b. Republican City, Neb., July 13, 1929; m. Robert C. Radcliffe (dec. 2004); 1 child, M. Donnel Nunes. BA, San Jose State U., Calif., 1951. Reporter, women's editor, county editor The Salinas Californian, 1951-59; free-lance writer Europe, 1959—66; reporter Washington Star, 1967-72; White Ho. reporter, columnist Washington Post, 1972-95. Author: Simply Barbara Bush: A Portrait of America's Candid First Lady, 1989, Hillary Rodham Clinton: A First Lady for Our Time, 1993, reissued as Hillary Rodham Clinton: The Evolution of a First Lady, 1999; contbr.: The Fall of a President, 1974, Guide to Washington, 1989. Trustee Calvert County (Md.) Libr.; bd. dirs. Nat. 1st Ladies' Libr. Home: South Acworth, NH. Died Feb. 19, 2010.

RADER, WILLIAM SHERMAN, lawyer; b. Broken Bow, Okla., Apr. 12, 1921; s. William Sherman Sr. and Florence Elizabeth (Klink) R.; m. Birdie Lane Wright, June 2, 1950; children: Margaret Jane Rader DeBoe, Elizabeth Lane Hennessey. BA, U. Ozarks, 1942; LLB, U. Ark., 1949. Bar: Ark. 1949, Mo. 1959, U.S. Dist. Ct. (ea. dist.) 1959. Assoc. Reid and Roy, Blytheville, Ark., 1949-51; pvt. practice Blytheville, 1951-57; ptnr. Oliver & Oliver, Cape Girardeau, Mo., 1957-64, Rader and Grimm, Cape Girardeau, 1964-73; pvt. practice with various assns. Cape Girardeau, 1973-80; judge cir. ct. State of Mo., Cape Girardeau, 1980-90; counsel Finch, Bradshaw, Strom & Steele, Cape Girardeau, 1991. Bd. dirs. Cape Girardeau County Dem. Com., 1987-88. Mem. Mo. Assn. Probate and Assoc. Cir. Judges (pres. 1987-88), Legis. Steering Com., Cape Girardeau County Bar Assn. (pres.), Lions (southeast Mo., bd. dirs. coun. on arts), C. of C. (v.p.). Home: Cape Girardeau, Mo. Died Aug. 29, 2010.

RAE, MATTHEW SANDERSON, JR., lawyer; b. Pitts., Sept. 12, 1922; s. Matthew Sanderson and Olive (Waite) R.; m. Janet Hettman, May 2, 1953; children: Mary-Anna, Margaret Rae Mallory, Janet S. Rae Dupree. AB, Duke, 1946, LLB, 1947; postgrad., Stanford U., 1951. Bar: Md. 1948, Calif. 1951. Asst. to dean Duke Sch. Law, Durham, NC, 1947-48; assoc. Karl F. Steinmann, Balt., 1948-49, Guthrie, Darling & Shattuck, LA, 1953-54; nat. field rep. Phi Alpha Delta Law Frat., LA, 1949-51; research atty. Calif. Supreme Ct., San Francisco, 1951-52; ptnr. Darling, Hall & Rae (and predecessor firms), LA, from 1955. Mem. Calif. Commn. Uniform State Laws, 1985—, chmn., 1993-94; chmn. drafting com. for revision Uniform Prin. and Income Act of Nat. Conf., 1991-97, Probate and Mental Health Task Force, Jud. Coun. Calif., 1996-2000. Vice pres. L.A. County Rep. Assembly, 1959-64; mem. L.A. County Rep. Ctrl. Com., 1960-64, 77-90, 2000—, exec. com., 1977-90; vice chmn. 17th Congl. Dist., 1960-62, 28th Congl. Dist., 1962-64; chmn. 46th Assy. Dist., 1962-64, 27th Senatorial Dist., 1977-85, 29th Senatorial Dist., 1985-90, sec. 53d Assembly Dist., 2000-; mem. Calif. Rep. State Ctrl. Com., 1966—, exec. com., 1966-67; pres. Calif. Rep. League, 1966-67; trustee Rep. Assocs., 1979-94, pres., 1983-85, chmn. bd. dirs., 1985-87. 2d lt. USAAF, WWII. Fellow Am. Coll. Trust and Estate Counsel; academician Internat. Acad. Estate and Trust Law (exec. coun. 1974-78); mem. ABA, L.A. County Bar Assn. (chmn. probate and trust law com. 1964-66, chmn. legis. com. 1980-86, chmn. program com. 1981-82, chmn. membership retention com. 1982-83, trustee 1983-85, dir. Bar Found., 1987-93, Arthur K. Marshall award probate and trust law sect. 1984, Shattuck-Price Meml. award 1990), South Bay Bar Assn., State Bar of Calif. (chmn. state bar jour. com. 1970-71, probate com. 1974-75; exec. com. estate planning trust and probate law sect. 1977-83, chmn. legis. com. 1977-89; co-chmn. 1991-92; probate law cons. group Calif. Bd. Legal Specialization 1977-88; chmn. conf. dels. resolutions com. 1987, exec. com. conf. dels. 1987-90), Lawyers Club L.A. (bd. govs. 1981-87, 1st v.p. 1982-83), Am. Legion (comdr. Allied post 1969-70), Legion Lex (bd. dirs. 1964-99, pres. 1969-71), Air Force Assn., Aircraft Owners and Pilots Assn., Town Hall (gov. 1970-78, pres. 1975), World Affairs Coun., Internat. Platform Assn., Breakfast Club (law, pres. 1989-90), Commonwealth Club, Chancery Club (pres. 1996-97), Rotary, Phi Beta Kappa (councilor Alpha Assn. 1983—, pres. 1996), Omicron Delta Kappa, Phi Alpha Delta (supreme justice 1972-74, elected to Disting. Svc. chpt. 1978), Sigma Nu. Presbyterian. Home: Manhattan Beach, Calif. Died Aug. 3, 2010.

RAHMLOW, KATHERINE LAVINA, author, toy designer, retired federal employee; b. Viroqua, Wis., Feb. 1, 1912; d. Berent Ole and Tena Julia (Christianson) Dahl; m. Herbert Rahmlow, Sept. 25, 1936 (dec. 1980); children: Bruce Arlan, Bonnie Lynn Rahmlow Dennison. Grad. with honors, La Crosse Tchrs. Coll., 1933; postgrad., U. Wis. Sch. Journalism, 1936. Civilian pers. specialist, adminstrn. US Air Force Def. Intelligence Agy., Washington, 1958—68; freelance artist, author and toy designer Springfield, Va., from 1968. Author: (juvenile) Granny Glee and Whoppity Sock, 1979, Granny Glee and Sockabye Land, 1984; creator Granny Glee Doll, 1983. Recipient Spl. Svc. award, US Air Force, 1961—62, First Place award, US Bear Force, 1982. Mem.: Am. Assn. Ret. Persons. Republican. Episcopalian. Avocations: art, needlecrafts, doll making, writing. Home: Virginia Beach, Va. Died May 9, 2010.

RAINE, MICHAUX, III, lawyer; b. Richmond, Va., Apr. 4, 1936; s. Michaux and Missouri (Woolford) Raine; m. Brenda Dod Raine, Nov. 26, 1960; children: Michaux, Susannah Rochet. Student, Hampden Sydney Coll., 1953—54, student, 1958—60; BA, Elon Coll., 1961; JD, T.C. Williams Law Sch., 1965. Bar: Va. 1965, US Dist. Ct. (we. dist.) Va. 1967, US Ct. Appeals (4th cir.) 1983. Tchr., coach Nansemond County Sch. Bd., Suffol, Va., 1961—62; designer Newport News Shipyard, Va., 1962—63; assoc. Wallestine, Goode, Richmond, 1965—67; ptnr. Davis, Davis & Raine, Rocky Mt., Va., 1967—81; pvt. practice Rocky Mt., from 1981; pres., dir. Rocky Mt. Supply Co., from 1980; dir. Earth Veneer Corp., Rocky Mt., from 1976. Served with USAF, 1954—57. Mem.: ABA, McNeil Law Soc., Franklin County Bar Assn., Va. State Bar Assn., Va. Def. Lawyers Assn., Va. Trial Lawyers Assn. Episcopalian. Home: Penhook, Va. Died July 30, 2010.

RAISZ, LAWRENCE GIDEON, medical educator, consultant; b. NYC, Nov. 13, 1925; s. Erwin Joseph and Marie Georgette (Patai) R.; s. Helen Martin, June 5, 1948; children: Stephen, Matthew, Jonathan, Katherine, Nicholas. Student, Harvard U., 1943, MD, 1947; DOdontology (hon.), U. Umea, Sweden, 1990. Diplomate Am. Bd. Internal Medicine, Nat. Bd. Med. Examiners. Intern Harvard Med. Svc., Boston City Hosp., 1947-48; resident in medicine Cushing VA Hosp., 1950, Boston VA Hosp., 1952-54; asst. and instr. in physiology NYU-Bellevue Med. Ctr., 1948-50; asst. and instr. in medicine sch. medicine Boston U., 1953-56; chief renal sect. Boston VA Hosp., 1954-56; asst. chief radioisotope svc. Syracuse VA Hosp., 1956-57; asst. prof. medicine Coll. Medicine SUNY, Syracuse, 1956-61; assoc. prof. pharmacology and medicine Sch. Medicine U. Rochester, 1961-66, assoc. prof. medicine Sch. Medicine, 1966-68, prof. pharmacology, toxicology, and medicine Sch. Medicine, 1966-74, chief div. of clin. pharmacology Sch. Medicine, 1961-74; from prof. medicine, head of endocrine dept. to program dir. U. Conn., Farmington, 1974-97; program dir. Gen. Clin. Rsch. Ctr. U. Conn Health Ctr., Farmington, from 1993; sr. assoc. physician Strong Meml. Hosp., Rochester, 1961-68, physician, 1968-74. Acting chmn. dept. pharmacology Sch. Medicine, U. Rochester, 1962-63, vis. prof. pharmacology, toxicology and medicine Sch. Medicine and Dentistry, 1974-76; vis. assoc. prof. pharmacology Sch. Medicine Stanford U., 1966; vis. prof. Coll. Medicine U. Lagos, Nigeria, 1973; mem. gen. B study sect. NIH, 1986-88; mem. subspecialty bd. on endocrinology and metabolism Am. Bd. Internal Medicine, 1990—; mem. U.S.-Japan Malnutrition Panel, 1985-91; clin. investigator Syracuse VA Hosp., 1957-60; William N. Creasy Vis. Prof. Clin. Pharmacology Med. Sch. Dartmouth Coll., 1977; chmn. Gordon Conf. on Bones and Teeth, 1980; Edwin B. Astwood lectr. Endocrine Soc., 1983. Mem. numerous editorial bds.; contbr. more than 300 articles to profl. jours. With USNR, 1943-45; capt. AUS, 1950-52. Spl. Rsch. fellow Nat. Inst. Arthritis and Metabolic Disease, Strangeways Rsch. Lab., 1960-61, Nat. Inst. Dental Rsch. NIH, 1971-72; Burroughs-Wellcome scholar in Clin. Pharmacology, 1963-68; recipient Prix Andre Lichtwitz, 1980, Class of 1947 Disting. Prof. award Med. Sch. U. Wis., 1988. Mem. AAAS, Am. Fedn. for Clin. Rsch., Am. Soc. for Clin. Investigation, Am. Soc. for Pharmacology and Exptl. Therapeutics, Endocrine Soc., Assn. Am. Physicians, Conn. Endocrine Soc. (pres. 1976), Am. Soc. for Bone and Mineral Rsch. (pres. 1980-81, William F. Neuman award 1986), Conn. Acad. Sci. and Engring., Sigma Xi. Avocations: travel, skiing, wind surfing. Home: Farmington, Conn. Died Aug. 25, 2010.

RAJE, RAVINDRA RAMCHANDRA, toxicology educator, consulting pharmacist; b. Baroda, Gujarat, India, Feb. 7, 1935; came to U.S., 1975, naturalized, 1981; s. Ramchandra R. and Vimlabai (Pradhan) R.; m. Meena Mohile, May 12, 1965; children— Swati, Revati, Parag. B.S. in Chemistry, Maharaja Sayajirao U., Baroda, 1955; B.S. in Pharmacy, Gujarat U., Ahmebabad, 1957; Dr. rer. nat., Bonn. U., Fed. Republic Germany, 1963, cert. food chemistry, 1964. Registered pharmacist, N.Y.; cert. Am. Bd. Toxicology. Pool officer Govt. India, Bombay, 1965-66; research chemist Chemiequip Pvt. Ltd., Goregaon, India, 1966-67; asst. prof. J. N. Med. Coll., Belgaum, India, 1967-72; prin. Coll. Pharmacy, Ulhasnagar, India, 1972-75; postdoctoral research assoc. U. Tenn.-Memphis, 1975-77; assoc. prof. toxicology L.I. U., Bklyn., 1977—; pharmacist Seventh Ave. Pharmacy, Bklyn., 1983—, Midville Chemist, Westbury, N.Y., 1983—. Contbr. research articles to toxicology jours. Mem. AAAS, AAUP, Soc. Toxicology, Sigma Xi, Rho Chi. Home: Farmingdale, NY. Died Apr. 23, 2009.

RAMER, HAL REED, retired academic administrator; b. Kenton, Tenn., June 8, 1923; s. Claude Orion and Dixie Clayton (Carroll) R. BS, George Peabody Coll., 1947; MSW, U. Tenn., 1952; PhD, Ohio State U., 1963. Asst. dean men Ohio State U., Columbus, 1953-58, dir. internat. house, 1958-60, staff asst. to pres., 1960-62; asst. commr. State Dept. Edn., Nashville, 1963-70; founding pres. Vol. State C.C., Gallatin, Tenn., 1970—2003, pres. emeritus, from 2003; ret. Bd. dirs. Sumner Regional Health Sys., Inc. Com. mem. March of Dimes, Gallatin; trustee Nashville United Way, 1970, Hiwassee Coll., 2001; bd. advisors Aquinas Coll., Nashville, from 1967; former chmn. Tenn. Fulbright-Hays Sch. Commn.; bd. visitors U. Tenn. Sch. Social Work; YMCA. With U.S. Army Air Corps, 1943—45. Recipient Distinctive Svc. award Devel. Coun. Peabody Coll., Nashville, 1960s, Disting. Svc. award Tenn. Dept. Edn., 1970, Outstanding Leader award Vanderbilt U. chpt. Phi Delta Kappa, 1987, Gov.'s Svc. award State of Tenn., 1993, Sertoma Club Svc. to Mankind award, 1995-96, Disting. Alumnus award Peabody Coll., 1996, Disting. Svc. award Tenn. Bd. Regents, 1997, Svc. award Am. Assn. Cmty. Col., 1999, Otis Floyd Jr. award for excellence Tenn. Coll. Pub. Rels. Assn., 1999, Lifetime Achievement award Peabody Coll. of Vanderbilt U., 2003; named Rotarian of the Yr., 1979; Paul Harris fellow Rotary Internat., 1981. Mem. Am. Legion, Coun. Pres. C.Cs. (chmn. state Tenn. 1988-89), Tenn. Coll. Assn. (pres. 1985-86), Nat. Alumni Assn. Peabody Coll. (pres. 1970-71, trustee), Tenn. Acad. Sci., Tenn. and Sumner County Hist. Socs. (bd. dirs.), English Speaking Union Internat. (Nashville chpt.), So. Assn. Colls. and Schs., Univ. Club Nashville, Gallatin and Hendersonville C. of C., St. Thomas Aquinas Soc., Torch Club, Alpha Tau Omega, Kappa Phi Kappa, Alpha Phi Omega, Phi Delta Kappa. Methodist. Avocations: antiques, antique cars, photography. Home: Nashville, Tenn. Died Feb. 14, 2010.

RANDOLPH, DAVID, conductor; b. NYC, Dec. 21, 1914; s. Morris and Elsie (Goodman) R.; m. Mildred Greenberg, July 18, 1948 (dec. 2008) BS, CCNY, 1936; MA, Tchrs. Coll., Columbia U., 1942; LHD (hon.), Saint Peter's Coll., Jersey City, 2006; DFA (hon.), CUNY, 2006. Music specialist OWI, NYC, 1943-47. Adj. prof. music NYU, 1948-85, Mostly Mozart course, 1976-85; lectr. Town Hall, N.Y.C., 1955-60, Columbia U., 1957, Cosmopolitan Club, N.Y.C., 1962-63; pre-concert lectr. N.Y. Philharm., Avery Fisher Hall, 1964-86,Cleve. Orch., 1981, Vienna Symphony Orch., 1988; tchr. conducting Dalcroze Sch., 1948-49; music commentator Little Orch. Soc. Concerts and Broadcasts, 1950-62, Met. Opera Intermission Broadcasts, 1951, 52; intermission commentator Lewisohn Stadium Concert Broadcasts, 1952-58; vis. prof. music SUNY, New Paltz, 1970-72, Fordham U., 1972-73; lectr. New Sch. for Social Rsch., 1973-90, IBM, N.Y.C., 1978-86, Beethoven Soc., 1977, 83; prof. music Montclair State Coll., Upper Montclair, N.J., 1973-87; guest condr. Rockland County (N.Y.) Ann. Choral Festival, 1972, 73; adviser film Music to Live By, mem. N.J. Arts Coun., 1967-70; mem. music com. Gov. N.J.'s Commn. to Study Arts, 1965; honored guest Handel Festival, Halle, Germany, 1991. Condr. Randolph Singers, 1944-62 (appeared on NBC Today, and Tonight Shows), concerts Town Hall, NYC, Carnegie Recital Hall, recs. for Columbia, Concert Hall Soc., Esoteric Records, Vanguard, Westminster Records, The Triumphs of Oriana, 1953, Monteverdi's Lagrime d'amante, Beethoven's Elegischer Gesang, Satie's Mass for the Poor, CRI, 13 Modern American Madrigals composed for the Randolph Singers, condr. United Choral Soc., LI, NY, 1961-

86, Masterwork Chamber Orch., 1982-83, Philharmonia Orch. in Brahms' Requiem, Barbican Ctr., London, 1988, Barge Concert, NYC, 1987, 89, NJ Ballet Orch., 1977, 83, guest condr., Conn. Symphony Orch., 1961; condr. concert tour Spain with Am. choruses and Radio TV Orch. of Moscow, 1992; music annotator, CBS, NYC, 1947-48; choral seminar leader Mohonk Mountain House, 1986-95; music dir., condr. Masterwork Chorus and Orch., 1955-93, St. Cecilia Chorus and Orch., NYC, 1965—; performances at Carnegie Hall, Avery Fisher Hall, Lincoln Ctr., Kennedy Ctr. including Brahms' Requiem, Schicksalslied, Nänie, Gesang der Parzen, Mozart's Requiem, C Minor Mass, Vesperae de Confessore, Beethoven's Missa Solemnis, Symphony No. 3 (Eroica), Symphony No. 9, Mass in C Major, Choral Fantasy, Bach's Mass in B Minor, St. John Passion, St. Matthew Passion, Christmas Oratorio, Magnificat, C.P.E. Bach's Magnificat, Haydn's St. Cecilia Mass, Theresienmesse, Paukenmesse, Lord Nelson Mass, The Creation, Heiligmesse, Schöpfungsmesse, Michael Haydn's Requiem, Bruckner's Mass in E Minor, Requiem, Vaughan Williams' A Sea Symphony, Dona Nobis Pacem, Mass in G Minor, Hodie, Verdi's Requiem, Four Sacred Pieces, Honegger's King David, Elgar's The Music Makers, Corigliano's Fern Hill, Salieri's Mass in D, Purcell's The Fairy Queen, Mendelssohn's Elijah, Die erste Walpurgisnacht, Lobgesang, Lauda Sion, Poulenc's Gloria, Rutter's Gloria, Dvorak's Requiem, Te Deum, Kodaly's Te Deum, Berlioz' Requiem, Messe solennelle, Cherubini's Requiem, Schubert's Masses 5 and 6, Stabat Mater, Vivaldi's Gloria, Dixit Dominus, Zelenka's Missa Dei Patris, Gounod's St. Cecilia Mass, Handel's Solomon, Israel in Egypt, Judas Maccabaeus, Dixit Dominus and 173 complete performances of Handel's Messiah, Orff's Carmina Burana, Saint-Saëns' Requiem, Puccini's Messa di Gloria, Zimmermann's Psalmkonzert, Finzi's For St. Cecilia, In Terra Pax, Rachmaninoff's The Bells, others; broadcaster: David Randolph Concerts, WNYC and radio stas. of Nat. Assn. Ednl. Broadcasters, 1946-79, Young Audience telecasts, CBS-TV, 1958-59, series of candid rehearsals of Bach's Mass in B minor, PBS, 1967; host: weekly broadcasts Lincoln Ctr. Spotlight, Sta. WQXR, NYC, 1966-67; regular guest critic First Hearing program Sta. WQXR, NYC, and 68 other stas., 1986-95; author: This Is Music: A Guide to the Pleasures of Listening, 1964, 98, numerous album jacket notes; A New Music Made with a Machine, Horizon Magazine, 1959; editor: David Randolph Choral Series; writer, narrator: Instruments of the Orchestra, 1958, compact disc 1995, Stereo Review's Guide to Understanding Music, 1973; music critic, High Fidelity Mag., 1952-57; composer: A Song for Humanity, 1968, Andante for Strings, 1937, Edward, 1937, three anti-war choruses, 1937; contbg. author: NY Times Guide to Listening Pleasure, 1968; analyzed Mendelssohn's Symphony No. 3 on records for Book of Month Club. Recipient 1st award for edn. by radio Ohio State Inst., 1948, 50, 51, Sylvania TV award, 1959, Disting. Alumni award Columbia U., 1982, cert. of appreciation Mayor of City of N.Y. at Carnegie Hall, 1991, Townsend Harris medal CCNY, 1996, Lifetime Achievement award Carnegie Hall, MidAmerica Prodns., 2000; St. Cecilia Chorus endowed David Randolph Disting. Artist-in-Residence Program at New Sch. in N.Y., 1996. Home: New York, NY. Died May 12, 2010.

RANNEY, HELEN MARGARET, retired internist, hematologist, educator; b. Summer Hill, NY, Apr. 12, 1920; d. Arthur C. and Alesia (Toolan) Ranney. AB, Barnard Coll., 1941; MD, Columbia U., 1947; ScD, U. S.C., 1979, SUNY, Buffalo, 1996. Diplomate Am. Bd. Internal Medicine. Intern Presbyn. Hosp., NYC, 1947—48, resident, 1948—50, asst. physician, 1954—60; practice medicine specializing in internal medicine, hematology NYC, 1954—70; instr. Coll. Phys. and Surg. Columbia, NYC, 1954—60; from assoc. prof. to prof. medicine Albert Einstein Coll. Medicine, NYC, 1960—70; prof. medicine SUNY, Buffalo, 1970—73, U. Calif., San Diego, 1973—90, chmn. dept. medicine, 1973—86, Disting. physician vet. adminstr., 1986—91, prof. emeritus, 1991—2010; cons. Alliance Pharm. Corp., San Diego, 1991—2004; ret., 2004. Master: ACP; fellow: AAAS; mem.: NAS, Am. Acad. Arts and Scis., Am. Assn. Physicians, Harvey Soc., Am. Soc. Hematology, Am. Soc. for Clin. Investigation, Inst. Medicine, Alpha Omega Alpha, Sigma Xi, Phi Beta Kappa. Home: La Jolla, Calif. Died Apr. 5, 2010.

RASKIN, MICHAEL A., retail executive, director; b. N.J., Feb. 26, 1925; s. Harry and Elizabeth Rose (Furstenberg) R.; m. Mary Bonetta Whalen, June 12, 1948; children: Robin Raskin Crowell, Hillary Raskin Maass, Mary Allison Sullivan. AB, Pa. State Coll., 1947; MBA, Columbia U., 1948. With Abraham & Straus, 1949-65; successively mdse. v.p., dir. stores, sr. v.p. Abercrombie & Fitch, NYC, 1966-68; exec. v.p. Dayton's div. Dayton Hudson Corp.; pres. Jos. Magnin Co., San Francisco, from 1978. Chmn., CEO, bd. dirs. Imnar Corp., San Francisco, Info. Please; chmn. More Investments; chmn. exec. com. Acajoe Internat.; bd. dirs. Fortune Almac, Canterbury Cuisine, Cultural Devel. Assocs., HELP Inc., Express Yourself Through Art, Inc., Munsingwear, Inc., B&B Acceptance Corp. Bd. dirs. Amyotrophic Lateral Sclerosis Assn. Home: Portland, Oreg. Died Aug. 31, 2009.

RASSMANN, JOEL H., corporate financial executive; b. NYC, May 16, 1945; Grad., Bernard Baruch Coll., 1967. CPA, N.Y. Acct. S.D. Leidesdorf & Co., 1967—72; ptnr. Kenneth Leventhal & Co., 1972—84; sr. v.p., treas., CFO Toll Brothers Inc., Horsham, Pa., 1984—2002, exec. v.p., treas., CFO, 2002—10. Bd. dirs. Toll Brothers Inc., 1996—2010. Mem. AICPA, N.Y. State Soc. CPA's. Achievements include appearing frequently as commentator on CNBC, CNN, Fox, Bloomberg TV & Radio. Died Sept. 14, 2010.

RAU, ALFRED, management consultant, retired forging company executive; b. Bamberg, Germany, Dec. 31, 1927; came to U.S., 1960, naturalized, 1965; s. Karl E. and Annie R.; m. Albertine Marie Hooijer, Nov. 6, 1955; children—Annette Caroline, Michel George. Bachiller en Ciencias, Sto. Tomas U., Havana, Cuba. Ptnr. Compania Comercial Olympia (S.A.), Havana, Cuba, 1947-56; co-founder, gen. mgr. Metalurgica Basica Nacional (S.A.), Havana, 1956-60; with Nat. Forge Co., Irvine, Pa., 1960-87, exec. v.p., 1968-79, pres., chief operating officer, 1979-85, vice chmn. bd., 1985-87. Mem. Machinery and Allied Products Inst., Internat. Ops. Council, Bus. Internat. Died Feb. 1, 2010.

RAVETCH, IRVING, screenwriter; b. Newark, Nov. 14, 1920; s. I. Shalom and Sylvia (Shapiro) R.; m. Harriet Frank Jr., Nov. 24, 1946. BA, UCLA, 1941. Screenwriter: (films) (with La Cava) Living in a Big Way, 1947, The Outriders, 1950, Vengeance Valley, 1951; (with Harriet Frank, Jr.) The Long, Hot Summer, 1958, The Sound and the Fury, 1959, Home from the Hill, 1959, The Dark at the Top of the Stairs, 1960, House of Cards, 1969, The Cowboys, 1972, Conrack, 1974, The Spikes Gang, 1974, Norma Rae, 1979 (Academy award nomination for Best Adapted Screenplay 1979), Murphy's Romance, 1985, Stanley and Iris, 1990; writer, prodr.: (with Harriet Frank) Hud, 1963 (Academy award nomination Best Adapted Screenplay 1963, N.Y. Film Critics Circle award for Best Screenplay, 1963), Hombre, 1967, The Reivers, 1969; story: (with Harriet Frank) Ten Wanted Men, 1955. Recipient N.Y. Film Critics award, 1963, Writers' Guild Am. award, 1988; Oscar nomination for Hud, Acad. Motion Picture Arts and Scis., 1963, Norma Rae, 1979. Died Sept. 19, 2010.

RAY, HAROLD TREYNOR, JR., rental housing company executive; b. Chgo., June 12, 1918; s. Harold Treynor and Verena Adele (Kloess) R.; m. Dorothy Glenn Adams, July 25, 1942; children— Harold T., III, Herbert Glen, Beth Adrienne. B.S. in Edn., Tex. A&M U., 1970. Certified Housing Mgmt. Dir. Joined USAC, 1940, advanced through grades to lt. col. USAAF, 1967; command pilot, served with SAC; exec. dir. Brenham Housing Authority, 1968—; instr. Tex. Housing Assn. Seminars, 1976-79; pres., mem. bd. dirs. Northeast Washington County Water Supply Corp., 1983-84. Chmn. Services for Handicapped and Aged Persons, 1969-85; chmn. Home Health-Home Care Adv. Council; mem. Brenham State Sch. Adv. Com. Decorated Air medals with two oak leaves, Commendation medal with one oak leaf, Bronze Stars (2), Silver Star. Recipient award Assn. Retarded Citizens, 1983. Mem. Tex. Housing Assn. (v.p.), Nat. Assn. Housing and Redevel. Orgn. Methodist. Lodge: K.T. Home: Brenham, Tex. Died June 13, 2010.

RAYMER, DONALD GEORGE, utility company executive; b. Jackson, Mich., July 16, 1924; s. Donald Rector and Vivian Alverda (Wolfinger) R.; m. Joan Elizabeth Steck, Oct. 16, 1948; children: Mary Margaret Dorward, Dorothy Elizabeth, Charles George. BSE.E., U. Mich., 1948; MS (Sloan fellow), M.I.T., 1960. Relay engr. Central Ill. Public Service Co., Springfield, 1948-56, mgr. system ops., 1956-65, div. mgr. Mattoon, Ill., 1965-68, v.p. Springfield, 1968-78; exec. v.p. Cen. Ill. Pub. Svc. Co., 1978-80, pres., chief exec. officer, 1980-89, also bd. dirs. Bd. dirs. Bank One Springfield, CIPSCO Inc. Vice chmn. Springfield United Fund Campaign, 1964, asso. chmn., 1974; vice chmn. Mattoon United Welfare Fund, 1967; bd. dirs. Meml. Med. Center; chmn. Meml. Med. Ctr., 1987-89. Served to lt. (j.g.) USNR, 1943-46. Mem. IEEE, Am. Mgmt. Assn., Ill. State C. of C. (dir. 1982-88, vice chmn. 1985-87), Greater Springfield C. of C. (dir. 1968-71, 85-88, vice chmn. 1985-88), Chi Phi, Illini Country Club, Sangamo Club. Republican. Episcopalian. Home: Harvard, Mass. Died Nov. 7, 2009.

RAYMOND, ROBERT FRANCIS, management consulting company executive; b. Escanaba, Mich., Mar. 28, 1932; s. Claude Robert and Mary Rosetta (Globie) R.; m. Joyce Joan Betts, Oct. 16, 1934; children: Stephen, Mark, Michael, David, Paul. BSCE, U. Notre Dame, 1954. Registered profl. engr., Ill. Pilot plant rsch. engr. UOP Process, McCook, Ill., 1957—59, petrochem. process licensing engr. Des Plaines, Ill., 1959—64, mktg. mgr. London, Brussels, Eastern dist. U.S.A., 1964—74; v.p. UOP Mgmt. Svcs., Des Plaines, 1974—80, pres., from 1980; vice chmn. UOP Mgmt. Svcs. Ltd., Jeddah, Saudi Arabia, from 1980; dir. bus. devel. and treating techs. UOP, Inc., Des Plaines, from 1988. Lt. USN, 1954—57, PTO. Mem.: Tech. Transfer Soc. Republican. Roman Catholic. Achievements include patentee in field. Home: Dubuque, Iowa. Died July 23, 2009.

RAZIK, TAHER A., education educator; b. Egypt, May 9, 1924; married, Aug. 4, 1962; children: Ramsey, Dena. MA, Ohio State U., 1960, PhD, 1963. Rsch. asst. Ohio State U., 1957-60, rsch. assoc. Bur. Ednl. Rsch., 1960-63; asst. prof., rsch. assoc. SUNY, Buffalo, 1963-67, dir. Instrnl. Comm. Ctr., 1965-68, assoc. prof., 1967-72, prof. dept. ednl. orgn., adminstrn. & policy Grad. Sch. Edn., 1972-95; sr. v.p. for acad. affairs Sultan Quaboos U., Oman, from 1995. Resident cons. UNESCO Internat. Inst. for Ednl. Planning, Paris, 1969-70; sr. expert edn. sect. high level manpower project Ministry of Planning, Baghdad, Iraq, 1974-75; mem. devel. team. United Arab Emirates U., 1976-77; sr. researcher regional offices UNESCO, Paris, 1977-78; found. com. for establishment of Qaboos U., Sultanate of Oman, 1981-87, exec. advisor to minister of edn. Ministry Edn., Mascut, 1981—; mem. comms. adv. com. SUNY, Buffalo, 1966-68, adminstrv. adv. coun. to pres., 1967-68, com. for instrnl. resource ctrs. ad hoc com. on instrnl. programs in comm., 1968-70, cirriculum com. for devel. instrnl. tech. course for tchrs., 1969-71, com. for distbn. instl. funds. faculty ednl. studies, 1971, exec. com. coun. internat. studies, 1971, exec. com. faculty ednl. studies, 1971-74, 76-78, personnel com. faculty ednl. studies, 1978-81, adv. com. for establishment effective teaching, 1985-86, com. on staff devel. and resources faculty ednl. studies, 1985-86, instl. rev. bd. univ. at large, 1988—; presenter internat. confs. including U. Pitts., 1991, U. Qatar, Doha Qatar, 1992, UNESCO, Paris, 1992, Internat. Inst. for Advanced Studies in Systems Rsch. and Cybernetics, 1992, Conf. on Functional Literacy: State Rsch. and its Perspectives, Petersburg, Russia, 1992; presenter workshop U. Qatar., 1985; cons. Ministry Edn., State of Baharain, 1975-76, United Arab Emirates, 1977, Oman, 1980—, U. Qatar, 1979—, Acad. Ednl. Devel., Washington, 1983-84, others. Author: Instruction and Learning: Re-examining Teacher Education in the Arab Gulf Universities: Faculty of Education Self Study, The Experience of Qatar, 1982, 93, Internal Effectiveness of the Educational System in the Sultanate of Oman: A Study of Educational Wastages, 1984, (with others) Explorations in Creativity, 1967, Swedish edit., 1971, Instruction and Learning: A Systems Approach, 1978, Strategies of Curriculum Planning and Development in the Arab Countries, 1982; guest editor Theory Into Practice, 1965, 71; author monographs, rsch. reports, books revs.; compiler bibliographies; contbr. articles to profl. jours., chpts. to books. Decorated Order of Sultan Qaboos, Oman, 1985; recipient IIAS award Internat. Inst. for Advanced Studies in Systems Rsch. and Cybernetics, 1992; grantee in field. Mem. APA, Am. Ednl. Rsch. Assn., Soc. for Gen. Sys. Theory Rsch., Nat. Soc. for Study of comm., Assn. for Ednl. Comm. and Tech., Nat. Soc. for Study of Edn., Nat. Soc. for Performance and Instrn. Home: Henrietta, NY. Died Feb. 21, 2010.

READ, WILLIAM EDGAR, army officer, engineer; b. Charlotte, NC, May 17, 1927; s. William Edgar and Virginia Clark R.; m. Mary Ann Gregory, Dec. 19, 1953; children: Mary V., Ann K., Sarah C. BS, U.S. Mil. Acad., 1950; MS, U. Ill., 1955; MA, Webster Coll., 1974. Registered profl. engr., N.Y., La., Miss., Ark. Commd. 2d lt., C.E. U.S. Army, 1950, advanced through grades to maj. gen., 1979, comdr. 4th Infantry Div. Support Command and Task Force Ivy Vietnam, 1970-71; dist. engr. Tulsa dist., 1971-72; dir. procurement and prodn. U.S. Army Aviation Systems Command, St. Louis, 1972-75, dep. comdg. gen., 1975-76; div. engr. (U.S. Army Engr. Div., Missouri River), Omaha, 1976-78; asst. chief engrs. Office Chief of Engrs., U.S. Army, Washington, 1978-80; div. engr. Lower Miss. Valley, (U.S. Army Engr. Div.), 1980-84; sr. v.p. Walk, Haydel & Assocs., New Orleans, from 1984. Instr., asst. prof. engring. mechanics U.S. Mil. Acad., 1959-62 Mem. Missouri River Basin Commn., 1975-78; mem. Mississippi River Commn., 1977-78, pres., 1981-84. Decorated Disting. Svc. medal, Legion of Merit with cluster, Bronze star with 2 clusters, air medal with 6 oak leaf clusters, Meritorious Svc. medal, Combat Infantry badge. Fellow Soc. Am. Mil. Engrs. (pres. Omaha post 1977-78, regional v.p. 1981-84); mem. Assn. U.S. Army, ASCE, NSPE. Home: Gulfport, Miss. Died Mar. 4, 2009.

READE, C. WIGHT, physician; b. Toledo, Ohio, Sept. 25, 1923; s. Carleton Wight Reade and Margaret Catherine Bushong Wall; m. Nancy Lou Milroy, Mar. 5, 1949 (div. 1974); children: Susan, Sarah, Mary. MD, U. Mich., 1946. Diplomate Am. Bd. Pediatrics, Am. Bd. Radiology. Solo practice pediatrics, Olympia, Wash., 1950-71; ptnr. Olympia Radiologists, 1974-76; chief radiology USPHS, Seattle, 1976-84; asst. prof. radiology U. Oreg. Med. Sch., Portland, 1984-86; itinerant radiologist various locations, 1986-92. Med. disability cons. Social Security, Olympia, 1955-71, Wash. Tchrs. Retirement, 1965-71. Lt. USNR, 1951-53. Mem. King County Med. Assn. Avocations: boating, flying, motorcycling, carpentry. Home: Seattle, Wash. Died Mar. 13, 2010.

REAGIN, LESLIE DYER, III, retail drug company executive; b. Tampa, Fla., Nov. 8, 1943; s. Archibald T. and Leslie Jeanne (Koons) R.; m. Peggy Elaine Weaver, Feb. 20, 1962; children: James Robert, Sharon Lynn. Student, Tampa U., 1962-63. With Eckerd Drug Co., Clearwater, Fla., from 1961, div. v.p., 1971-74, regional v.p., 1974-78, sr. v.p., 1978-80, exec. v.p., from 1980; v.p. Eckerd Jack Corp. Trustee Webber Coll., Babson Park, Fla., Eckerd Polit. Action Com. Mem. Fla. C. of C. (bd. dirs., exec. com., fin. com.), Nat. Assn. Chain Drug Stores. Clubs: Masons, Shriners. Republican. Methodist. Died Dec. 4, 2009.

REDDEN, JAMES ERSKINE, linguist, educator; b. Louisville, Dec. 28, 1928; s. James Clyde and Leora Mae (Kerr) Redden; m. Patricia Jane Stone, Apr. 7, 1950; children: Deborah, Virginia, Barry, David, Nathan, Alexander; m. Dorothy Louise Eggers Lyons, Aug. 5, 1984. BA in German, U. Louisville, 1950; PhD in Linguistics, Ind. U., 1965. Sci. linguist fgn. svcs. inst. Dept. State, Washington, 1961—65; assoc. prof. linguistics Am. U. Beirut, Lebanon, 1965—67; prof. linguistics So. Ill. U., Carbondale, from 1967; sr. rsch. fellow Fulbright Found., Fed. Republic U. Hamburg, Germany, 1973—74; US office edn. rschr. U. Yaoundea, Cameroon, 1971. Cons. Ford Found. Dakar, Senegal, Abidjan, Ivory Coast and Lagos, 1968—71; US aid various Middle Eastern Countries, 1965—71. Author: (book) Descriptive Grammer of Ewondo, 1979, Twi Basic Course, 1963, Lingla Basic Course, 1963, Morea Basic Course, 1966, Descriptive Grammar of Hualapai, 1986; editor: Ann. Procs. Hokan-Yuman Langs. Workshop. NDEA U.S. Office. Edn. fellowship, Ind. U., 1960—61, Am. Coun. Learned Socs. grant, 1963, 1967, NSF grant, 1979—80, Wenner-Gren grant, 1981. Fellow: Am. Anthropol. Assn.; mem.: Can. Linguistic Assn., Linguistic Assn. Gt. Britain, Tchrs. English to Speakers Other Langs., Australian Linguistic Soc., Societas Linguistica Europaea, Internat. Linguistics Assn., West African Linguistics Assn., Linguistic Soc. Am., Lions, Lions. Mem. Christian Ch. Avocations: bridge, model trains. Home: Manassas, Va. Died Jan. 2, 2009.

REDGRAVE, LYNN, actress; b. London, Mar. 8, 1943; d. Michael Scudemore and Rachel (Kempson) R.; m. John Clark, Apr. 2, 1967 (div. Dec. 22, 2000); children: Benjamin, Kelly, Annabel. Ed., Queensgate Sch., London, Central Sch. Speech and Drama. Stage debut as Helena in Midsummer Night's Dream, 1962; theatrical appearances include The Tulip Tree, Andorra, Hayfever, Much Ado About Nothing, Mother Courage, Love for Love, Zoo, Zoo, Widdershins Zoo, Edinburgh Festival, 1969, The Two of Us, London, 1970, Slag, London, 1971, A Better Place, Dublin, 1972, Born Yesterday, Greenwich, 1973, Hellzapoppin, N.Y., 1976, California Suite, 1977, Twelfth Night, Stratford Conn. Shakespeare Festival, 1978, The King and I, St. Louis, 1983, Les Liaisons Dangereuses, L.A., 1989, The Cherry Orchard, L.A.,

1990, Three Sisters, London, 1990, Notebook of Trigorin, U.S., 1996; Broadway appearances include Black Comedy, 1967, My Fat Friend, 1974, Mrs. Warren's Profession (Tony award nomination), 1975, Knock, Knock, 1976, St. Joan, 1977, Sister Mary Ignatius Explains It All, 1985, Aren't We All?, 1985, Sweet Sue, 1987, A Little Hotel on the Side, 1992, The Masterbuilder, 1992, Shakespeare For My Father (Tony and Drama Desk nominations, Elliot Norton award 1993), 1993, also nat. tour, 1996, West End, 1996, Moon over Buffalo, 1996, The Mandrake Root, 2001, Noises Off, 2001, The Constant Wife, 2005; writer, performer (solo show) Nightingale, 2005, (off-Broadway) Grace, 2008; (films) Tom Jones, Girl With Green Eyes, Georgy Girl (Recipient N.Y. Film Critics award, Golden Globe award, Oscar nomination for best actress 1967), The Deadly Affair, Smashing Time, The Virgin Soldiers, Last of the Mobile Hotshots, Don't Turn the Other Cheek, Every Little Crook and Nanny, Everything You Always Wanted to Know About Sex, The National Health, The Happy Hooker, The Big Bus, Sunday Lovers, Morgan Stuart's Coming Home, Getting It Right, Shine, 1996, Gods and Monsters, 1998 (Recipient Golden Globe award for best performance by an actress in a supporting role in a motion picture 1998), Strike, 1998, The Annihilation of Fish, 1999, The Simian Line, 2000, The Next Best Thing, 2000, How to Kill Your Neighbor's Dog, 2000, My Kingdom, 2001, Unconditional Love, 2001 (voice) The Wild Thornberrys Movie, 2002, Hansel & Gretel, 2002, Anita and Me, 2002, Charlie's War, 2003, Peter Pan, 2003, Kinsey, 2004, The White Countess, 2005, Confessions of a Shopaholic, 2009; (TV appearances) The Turn of the Screw, Centennial, 1978, The Muppets, Gauguin the Savage, Beggarman Thief, The Seduction of Miss Leona, Rehearsal for Murder, 1982, Walking On Air, The Fainthearted Feminist, 1984, My Two Loves, 1986, The Old Reliable, 1988, Jury Duty 1989, Whatever Happened to Baby Jane, 1990, Fighting Back (BBC-TV), 1992, Calling the Shots (Masterpiece Theatre), 1993, Toothless, 1997, Indefensible: The Truth About Edward Brannigan, 1997, Different, 1999, White Lies, 1998, A Season for Miracles, 1999, AFI's 100 Years...100 Stars, 1999, Varian's War, 2000, Lion of Oz and the Badge of Courage (voice), 2000; guest appearances include Carol Burnett Show, Evening at the Improv and Steve Martin's Best show Ever, Circus of the Stars, The Nanny, 1999, Richard & Judy, 2005, The Heaven and Earth Show, 2005; co-host nat. TV syndication Not for Women Only, 1977—79; nat., TV spokesperson Weightwatchers, 1984-92; TV series include House Calls, 1981, Teachers Only, 1982, Chicken Soup, 1989; Rude Awakening, 1998, albums: Make Mine Manhattan, 1978, Cole Porter Revisited, 1979; video: (for children) Meet Your Animal Friends, Off We Go, Off We Go Again: audio book readings include, Pride and Prejudice, The Shell Seekers, The Blue Bedroom, The Anastasia Syndrome, The Women in His Life, Snow In April, Gone With The Wind, 1994, The World of Philosophy, 1996; author: This is Living, 1990, Shakespeare For My Father, 1993; text by: Journal: A Mother and Daughter's Recovery from Breast Cancer. Named Runner-up Actress, All Am. Favorites, Box Office Barometer 1975; recipient Sarah Siddons award as Chgo.'s best stage actress of 1976, 94, Order of Brit. Empire, 2001. Mem. The Players (pres. 1994). Died May 3, 2010.

REED, JOAN SPAHR, human services administrator; b. Phila., July 27, 1930; d. Gustav Ludwig and Sarah (Miles) Spahr; m. John F. Reed, Feb. 6, 1956 (div. Feb. 1980); children: John R., Andrew G., Lisa R. McLeod, Leslie J. Becker, Laurie J. Caiazzo. BA in Communications summa cum laude, U. So. Maine, 1984. Asst. to pres. Eastern Appraisal Co., Inc., Portland, Maine, 1975-79; adminstr. welfare dept. City of Westbrook, from 1979. Adv. mem. CETA Program, Portland, 1981-83; career advisor U. So. Maine, Portland, 1984—. Mem. Am. Pub. Welfare Assn., Am. Soc. Pub. Adminstrs., Maine Welfare Dirs. Assn. (pres. 1982-83). Avocations: travel, art collector, interior decorating. Home: Sebago, Maine. Died Jan. 8, 2009.

REED, JOSEPH RAYMOND, civil engineering educator, academic administrator; b. Pitts., Aug. 15, 1930; s. David Raymond and Mary (O'Neil) R.; m. Mary Morris Leggett, Mar. 19, 1960; children: Michelle Edwards, Stephanie Anne Reed Wilkinson, David Shepard Reed. BS in Civil Engring., Pa. State U., 1952, MS in Civil Engring., 1955; PhD in Civil Engring., Cornell U., 1971. Registered profl. engr., Tex. Asst. engr. George H. McGinness Assocs., Pitts., 1953-55; constrn. liaison officer USAF, Dallas, 1956-59; civil engring. faculty Pa. State U., University Park, 1959-64; rsch. asst. Cornell U., Ithaca, N.Y., 1964-67; prof. civil engring. Pa. State U., 1967-95, prof. emeritus, 1996. Cons. Westvaco, Tyrone, Pa., 1981, Ketron, Inc., Phila., 1982-83, McGraw-Hill Book Co., N.Y.C., 1984-91, MacMillan Pub. Co., N.Y.C., 1987, others; acad. officer dept. civil engring. Pa. State U., 1989-95. Chmn. Stormwater Authority, State College, Pa., 1974-78; coach State Little League, Teener League (All-Star team state championship 1986) and Am. Legion Baseball, State College, 1978-89. Capt. USAF, 1956-59, USAFR, 1959-71. Sci.-Faculty fellow NSF, 1966-67; recipient Adviser Leadership award Tau Beta Pi Assn., 1986. Mem. ASCE, Internat. Assn. Hydraulic Rsch., Elks, Scottish Rite, Sigma Xi, Tau Beta Pi, Chi Epsilon, Phi Sigma Kappa (v.p. 1952). Presbyterian. Avocations: golf, bowling, youth baseball. Home: State College, Pa. Died Feb. 27, 2010.

REEG, CLOYD PRITCHARD, oil company executive, researcher; b. Blissfield, Mich., Apr. 23, 1922; s. Cloyd Martin and Marguerite (Pritchard) R.; 1 child, Cloyd Pritchard Jr.; m. Bea Cheely, Dec. 12, 1970 BS in Chem. Engring. cum laude, Ohio State U., 1948. Registered profl. chem. engr. Devel. engr. research dept. Unocal Corp. of Calif., Brea, 1948-53, sect. leader-process engring. and design, research dept., 1953-59, group leader process research and devel., 1959-64, supr. tech. sales, 1964-68, mgr. refining research, refining and products research div., 1968-73, assoc. dir. research dept., head refining and products div., 1973-78, v.p. sci. and tech. div., head of div.'s refining and products research dept., 1978-80, pres. sci. and tech. div., corp. v.p., 1980-86, pres. sci. and tech. and energy mining divs., corp. v.p., from 1986. Patentee in field Mem. Orange County World Affairs Council, 1981—. Served to capt. USAF, 1942-46 Recipient Benjamin G. Lamme medal Coll. Engring., Ohio State U., 1982 Mem. Am. Petroleum Inst., Nat. Petroleum Refiner's Assn., Am. Inst. Chem. Engring., Soc. Petroleum Engrs., Indsl. Research Inst., Tau Beta Pi, Phi Lambda Upsilon Republican. Home: Fullerton, Calif. Died Jan. 11, 2010.

REESE, ELMER EDWARD, automotive components company executive; b. Wilkes-Barre, Pa., Mar. 17, 1928; BSME, LeHigh U., 1952; postgrad. exec. devel. program, Ohio State U., 1969; postgrad. mktg. for execs. program, Harvard U., 1971; postgrad. sr. exec. program, MIT, 1976. Engr. Delco appliance div. Gen. Motors Corp., Rochester, N.Y., 1952-58, sr. project engr., 1958-65, product mgr., 1965-66, staff engr. Delco products div. Dayton, Ohio, 1966-68, asst. chief engr., 1968-70, chief engr., 1970-73, gen. sales mgr., 1973-76, chief engr. Delco Remy div. Anderson, Ind., 1976-78, gen. mgr., 1978-82, gen. mgr. Packard electric div. Warren, Ohio, from 1982. Patentee in field. Chmn. campaign Trumbull County United Way, Warren, 1983-84, campaign Jr. Achievement Fund Drive, Trumbull County, Ohio, 1985; bd. dirs. Trumbull Meml. Hosp., Warren. Served with USAF, 1946-48. Mem. Soc. Automotive Engrs., Youngstown (Ohio) C. of C., Warren C. of C. (bd. dirs.). Home: Savannah, Ga. Died Aug. 29, 2010.

REESE, ROBERT JENKINS, senator, lawyer; b. Lovell, Wyo., June 2, 1947; s. William David and Elsa Edith (Bluhm) R.; divorced; 1 child, William Derek; m. Mary Lynn Cockriel, Dec. 24, 1986; children: Tyler Eric, Whitney Elsa, Kelley Aldra, Meagan Mary. BA, Harvard U., 1969; JD, U. Wyo., 1978. Bar: Wyo. 1978, U.S. Dist. Ct. Wyo. 1978, U.S. Ct. Appeals (10th cir.) 1984. Tchr. Stratford Jr. High Sch., Arlington, Va., 1971-75; dep. county atty. Sweetwater County, Green River, Wyo., 1978-82; pvt. practice Green River, 1983-86; senator State of Wyo., Cheyenne, 1985-93; ptnr. Reese & Mathey, Green River, from 1986. Dem. chmn. Sweetwater County, Green River, 1983-85; trustee Sweetwater County Sch. Dist. No. Two, 1994—. Mem. Wyo. Trial Lawyers Assn. (bd. dirs. 1985-86), Green River C. of C. (bd. dirs. 1984-86), Sweetwater County Bar Assn. (pres. 1985-86, v.p. 1991-92). Democrat. Home: Green River, Wyo. Died Mar. 4, 2010.

REEVES, BILLY DEAN, obstetrics and gynecology educator emeritus; b. Franklin Park, Ill., Jan. 17, 1927; s. Barney William and Martha Dorcus (Benbrook) R.; m. Phyllis Joan Faber, Aug. 25, 1951; children: Philip, Pamela, Tina, Brian, Timothy. BA, Elmhurst Coll., Ill., 1953; BS, U. Ill., Chgo., 1958, MD, 1960; post grad., UCLA, N.Mex. State U., 1953-54, 75-76. Diplomate Am. Bd. Ob-Gyn. Intern Evanston (Ill.) Hosp., 1960-61, resident ob-gyn., 1961-64; NIH fellow in reproductive endocrinology Karolinska Hosp. and Inst., Stockholm, 1968-69; pvt. practice Evanston, 1964-71, Las Cruces, N.Mex., 1972-77; from instr. to asst. prof. Dept. Ob-gyn. Northwestern U. Med. Sch., 1964-71; assoc. prof. Dept. Ob-gyn. Rush Med. Coll., Chgo., 1971-72; clin. assoc. in ob-gyn. U. N.Mex. Med. Sch., Albuquerque, 1972-77; clin. assoc. U. Ariz. Sch. Medicine, Tucson, 1975-78; from clin. prof. to prof. emeritus Tex. Tech. Med. Sch., El Paso, 1976-91; exec. dir. Mesilla Valley Hospice, 1997-98. Contbr. 70 articles and chpts. to med., profl. jours., 1958-93. Adv. bd. Associated Home Health Svcs., Inc., Las Cruces; adv. com. N.Mex. State U. Nursing Sch.; community adv. com. Meml. Gen. Hosp., Las Cruces; tech. advisor on health edn. N.Mex. Health Systems Agy.; mem. N.Mex. State U. Task Force 88; bd. dirs. Meml. Med. Ctr, Los Cruces, 1989-91, Parenthood Edn. Assn. of El Paso, Inc., Planned Parenthood of South Ctrl. N.Mex. (chmn. med. adv. com.). With USNR, 1945-46, 82-88, U.S. Army, 1946-47. Recipient Elmhurst Coll. Alumni Merit award, 1990, William W. Fry award for profl. excellence Tex. Tech. U. Sch. Medicine, 1979. Mem. AMA, ACS, AAAS, ACOG, Am. Coll. Physician Execs., Am. Assn. Advancement Humanities, Am. Fertility Soc., Assn. Profs. Ob-Gyn., North Am. Ob-Gyn. Soc., Ctrl. Assn. Ob-Gyn., Chgo. Gyn. Soc., Com. for Philosophy in Medicine, Dona Ana County Med. Soc. (assoc.), El Paso County Med. Soc., El Paso Surg. Soc., Endocrine Soc., Inst. Medicine in Chgo., Hasting Ctr., N.Mex. Med. Soc. (assoc.), N.Mex. Ob-Gyn. Soc., Soc. for Health and Human Values, Tex. Med. Assn., Tex. Assn. Ob-Gyn., U.S.-Mexico Border Health Assn. Home: Las Cruces, N.Mex. Died July 23, 2010.

REEVES, GEORGE PAUL, bishop; b. Roanoke, Va., Oct. 14, 1918; s. George Floyd and Harriett Faye (Foster) Reeves; m. Adele Beer Reeves, Dec. 18, 1943; children: Cynthia Reeves Pond, George Floyd II. BA, Randolph-Macon Coll., 1940; BD, Yale U., 1943; DD, U. South, 1970, Nashotah House, 1970. Ordained priest Episcopal Ch., 1948, consecrated bishop, 1969; chaplain US Naval Res., 1943—47, Fla. State U., 1947—50; rector All Saints Ch., Winter Pk., Fla., 1950—59, Ch. of Redeemer, Sarasota, Fla., 1959—65, St. Stephens Ch., Miami, Fla., 1965—69; bishop Savannah, Ga., 1969—85; ret., 1985. Mem.: Phi Beta Kappa. Died Apr. 15, 2010.

REGAZZI, JOHN HENRY, retired electronic distributor executive; b. NYC, Jan. 4, 1921; s. Caesar B. and Jennie (Moruzzi) R.; m. Doris Mary Litzau, Feb. 16, 1946; children: Mark, Dale BBA, Pace Coll., 1951. CPA, N.Y. Mgr. Price Waterhouse, NYC, 1946-62; comptroller ABC, NYC, 1962-70; sr. v.p., CFO Avnet, Inc., NYC, 1970-93; retired, 1993. Contbr. articles to profl. jours. Pres. bd. River Dell Regional High Sch., Oradell, N.J., 1962-65; trustee, treas. Oradell Pub. Library, 1970-79; councilman Borough of Oradell, 1979-88. Served as staff sgt. USAF, 1942-45 Mem. AICPA, Fin. Execs. Internat. Republican. Roman Catholic. Home: Las Vegas, Nev. Died Feb. 11, 2009.

REICH, EDGAR, mathematics professor; b. Vienna, June 7, 1927; arrived in U.S. in 1938, naturalized, 1944. s. Jonas and Luna Sarah (Lunenfeld) Reich; m. Phyllis Masten, June 10, 1949 (dec. 1994); children: Eugene, Frances; m. Julia Henop, Dec. 14, 1998 (dec. Feb. 2006). BEE, Poly. Inst. Bklyn., 1947; MS, MIT, 1949; PhD, UCLA, 1954. Rsch. asst. Servomechanisma Lab. MIT, Cambridge, 1947—49; mathematician Rand Corp., Santa Monica, Calif., 1949—56; mem. Inst. Advanced Study, Princeton, NJ, 1954—55; prof. math. U. Minn., Mpls., 1961—2001, prof. emeritus, from 2001, head Sch. Math., 1969—71; mem. Forschungsinstitut Mathematik Swiss Poly. Inst., Zurich, 1971—72, 1978—79, 1986—87. Vis. prof. Swiss Poly. Inst., 1982-83; Christmas lectr. Bar-Ilan U., Ramat Gan, Israel, 1989, plenary lectr. Nahariya, 2006. Contbr. articles to profl. jours. Fulbright research scholar Denmark, 1960-61; Guggenheim fellow, 1960-61; NSF sr. postdoctoral fellow, 1954-55; recipient Silver plaque Alpine Motoring Contest, 1968, Bronze medal U. Jyväskylä, 1973. Mem. Am. Math. Soc., Finnish Acad. Sci. and Letters (fgn.) Home: Inver Grove Heights, Minn. Died July 6, 2009.

REICH, MURRAY HERBERT, chemical engineer, consultant, researcher; b. Bklyn., May 29, 1922; s. Israel and Rose (Reiter) R.; m. Naomi A. Pollack, Mar. 26, 1949; children: Michael Robin, Leslie Alan, Pamela Nadine. BAChemE, CCNY, 1943; MS, Akron U., 1954; MEd, Trenton Stat U., 1974; EdD, Columbia U., 1982. Rsch. chemist FMC Corp., Princeton, N.J., 1956-62; devel. chemist Princeton Chem Rsch., 1962-75, tech. dir., 1975-77; dir. Premac Assocs., Princeton, 1977-94; counselor Rutgers U., New Brunswick, 1979-82; v.p. Biolan Corp., Princeton, 1989-93. Cons. Savant Assoc., 1989-90, Tyndale Plains-Hunter, Ltd., 1991-93, acting pres., 1993—, pres. Contbr. articles to profl. jours. Pres. Princeton Jewish Ctr., 1966-68; fin. chair Princeton Rsch. Forum, 1987-89, Holistic Health Assn. Princeton, 1985-87; mem. adv. coun. Ret. Sr. Vol. Program, 1986—. With USN, 1943-45; PTO. Mem. Am. Chem. Soc., Soc. Plastics Engrs. Princeton Rsch. Forum. Democrat. Achievements include patents for epoxy resins, solid molded golf balls, compostable plastics, degradable agrl. mulch films and polyolefins; patents pending in wound dressings, gels, high slip coatings, hair styling aids, hydrophilic polymers. Died Jan. 9, 2009.

REICH, ROBERT SIGMUND, landscape architect; b. NYC, Mar. 22, 1913; s. Ulysses S. and Adele G. R.; m. Helen Elizabeth Adams, May, 1945; children: Barbara, Betsy, Bob, Bill. BS, Cornell U., 1934, PhD, 1941; postgrad., U. So. Calif., 1951. Instr. landscape design Cornell U., 1936-39, 40-41; instr. landscape design U. Conn., 1939-40; Inst. Land Design La. State U., 1941-46, asst. prof. landscape architecture, 1946-49, asso. prof., 1949-60, prof., from 1960, Alumni prof., from 1967, head dept. landscape architecture, 1964-79, dir. Sch. Landscape Architecture, 1979-83; prof. Landscape Architecture, from 1992. Instr. Shrivenham (Eng.) Am. U., 1946, Biarritz (France) Am. U., 1947; vis. lectr. Tulane U., 1958-67; judge, instr. Nat. Council Garden Clubs, 1956—; mem. task force on parks, recreation and tourism Goals for La. Program; mem. com. to establish Chicot State Park Arboretum, Ville Plate, La., 1964, mem. steering com., 1964-75; examiner La. Bd. Examination for Landscape Architects, 1957-77 Co-author: Landscape and You, 1953. Mem. com. to establish City/Parish Beautification Commn., 1961-82; mem. area and facilities com. Baton Rouge Recreation and Pk. Commn., 1957-83; bd. dirs. Hubbard Edn. Trust, Weston, Mass., 1967—; adv. com. Friends of Frederick Law Olmsted Papers, 1983-95. With U.S. Army, 1942-45; in charge alter arrangements U. United Meth. Ch., 1945—. Recipient Tchg. award of merit Gamma Sigma Delta, 1963, Baton Rouge Green Individual Honor award, 1996. Fellow Am. Soc. Landscape Architects (trustee 1968-71, 83-86, 3d v.p. 1971-73, Medal 1992); mem. AIA (hon.), S.W. Park and Recreation Tng. Inst. (dir. 1975-77, award of merit 1968), Phi Kappa Phi, Pi Alpha xi, Omicron Delta Kappa, Sigma Lambda Alpha. Home: Baton Rouge, La. Died July 31, 2010.

REICHEL, CHARLES EDWARD, learning consultant, career counselor; b. Shawano, Wis., Oct. 16, 1943; s. Edward Charles and Eleanor Anne (Koenig) R.; m. Sharon Anne Werfelmann, June 14, 1970; children: Cara, Carsten, Carlyn. BA, Concordia Sr. Coll., Fort Wayne, Ind., 1965; MDiv, Concordia Seminary, St. Louis, 1969; MA in Urban Affairs, St. Louis U., 1969; PhD in Ednl. Psychology and Counseling, U. Miss., 1977. Lic. profl. counselor, Ga., cert. clin. mental health counselor, cert. advanced level human effectiveness trainer. Pastor Zion Luth. Ch., Holly Springs, Miss., 1969-74; instr. U. Miss., Oxford, 1974-78; dir. Southeast Luth. Resettlement Ministry, Oxford, 1978-82; pastor, campus min. Peace Luth. Ch., Oxford, 1969-84; dir., cons. New Perspective Human Resource Devel., Rome, Ga., 1984-89; prin., dir., cons. Excel Assist Internat., Rome, from 1989; dir. career devel. Shorter Coll., Rome, 1984-91. Author: Training Manual Leadership Enabling and Development, 1978; developer, pub.: (SAT-1/ACT coaching course) How to High-Five the SAT (and Other Highstakes Tests); contbr. articles to profl. jours. Behavioral sci. cons. Floyd Med. Ctr. Family Practice Residency, Rome, 1985-90; interim pastor St. Peter's Luth. Ch., Gadsden, Ala., 1988—, Trinity Luth. Ch., Scottsboro, Ala., 1992—. Mem. ASCD, ACA, Nat. Employment Counselors Assn., Am. Sch. Counselors Assn., Nat. Career Devel. Assn. Lutheran. Died Apr. 5, 2010.

REICHEL, LEATRICE IDA, banker; b. Erie, Pa., Jan. 31, 1930; d. Jacob Charles and Ida Eva (Bovee) Seib; student pub. schs.; widow. With Security Bank, Erie, 1948—, asst. sec., 1970-75, personnel officer, 1972-84, asst. v.p., 1975-84; personnel officer Pennbank, Titusville, Pa., 1984; personnel officer, affirmative action officer Pennbancorp, Titusville, 1986—. Mem. personnel com. Erie chpt. ARC, 1980—, chmn., 1983-85; mem. Erie Merit Rev. Bd. Mem. Nat. Assn. Bank Women (past chmn. N.W. Pa. group), Am. Soc. Personnel Adminstrn., Personnel Assn. N.W. Pa. (pres. 1981-82). Clubs: Aviation Country, Erie Maennerchor Aux., East Erie Turners, Order Eastern Star. Home: Erie, Pa. Died Nov. 22, 2009.

REICHMANN, EBERHARD, German-American culture and language specialist; b. Stuttgart, Germany, Dec. 8, 1926; came to U.S., 1953; s. August and Maria (Köhler) R.; m. Ruth M. Backmund, Dec. 21, 1956. BA, Pedagogical Inst., Schwäb, Gmünd (Fed. Republic Germany), 1949; MA, U. Cin., 1956, PhD, 1959. Tchr. various schs., Baden Württemberg, 1950-53; prof. Ind. U., Bloomington, 1959-90, editor-in-chief Max Kade German-Am. Ctr. Indpls., from 1990. Author: various books; editor: various German textbooks, Mem. Ind. German Heritage Soc. (co-founder 1984), Soc. German-Am. Studies (v.p. 1987). Avocation: music. Home: Nashville, Ind. Died Oct. 16, 2009.

REID, ROBERT LELON, engineering educator, dean; b. Detroit, May 20, 1942; s. Lelon Reid and Verna Beulah (Custer) Menkes; m. Judy Elaine Nestell, July 21, 1962; children: Robert James, Bonnie Kay, Matthew Lelon. ASE, Mott C.C., Flint, Mich., 1961; BChemE, U. Mich., 1963; MME, So. Meth. U., 1966, PhDME, 1969. Registered profl. engr., Tenn., Tex., Wis. Asst. rsch. engr. Atlantic Richfield Co., Dallas, 1964-65; assoc. staff engr. Linde Divsn., Union Carbide Corp., Tonawanda, NY, 1966-68; from asst. to assoc. prof. U. Tenn., Knoxville, 1969-75; assoc. prof. Cleve. State U., 1975-77; from assoc. to full prof. U. Tenn., Knoxville, 1977-82; prof., chmn. U. Tex., El Paso, 1982-87; dean Coll. Engring., Marquette U., Milw., 1987-98, prof. mech. engring., 1998-2001; dean emeritus, 2001. Summer prof. NASA Marshall Space Ctr., Huntsville, Ala., 1970, EXXON Prodn. Rsch., Houston, 1972, 73, NASA Lewis Space Ctr., Cleve., 1986; cons. Oak Ridge Nat. Lab., 1974-75, TVA, 1978, 79, State of Calif., Sacramento, 1985, Tex. Higher Edn. Coordinating Bd., Austin, 1987. Contbr. articles 100 articles on heat transfer and solar energy. Grantee NSF, DOE, TVA, NASA, DOI, 1976-87; named Engr. of Yr. Engring. Socs. El Paso, 1986. Fellow ASME (Centennial medallion 1980, chmn. cryogenics com. 1977-81, chmn. solar energy divsn. 1983-84, chmn. Rio Grande sect. 1985-87, John Yellott award, 1997, Dedicated Svc. award 1998); mem. ASHRAE, Engrs. and Scientists Milw. (bd. dirs. 1988-93, v.p. 1989-90, pres. 1991-92), Wis. Assn. Rsch. Mgmt. (pres. 1996-97). Lutheran. Avocations: travel, classic car restoration. Home: Knoxville, Tenn. Died Apr. 16, 2009.

REID, TOY FRANKLIN, chemical company executive; b. York County, SC, Jan. 13, 1924; s. Toy Fennell and Nellwyn Marteal (Mulliken) R.; m. Martha Josephine Eggerton, May 31, 1947; children: Martha Josephine, Toy Franklin (dec.), Mark Eggerton. BS, U. S.C., 1943; BSChemE, U. Ill., 1947; MS, Ga. Inst. Tech., 1948. Asst. to plant mgr. Holston Def. Corp., 1962, asst. plant mgr., 1963; supt. cellulose esters div. Carolina Eastman Co., 1965-69; asst. research chem. engr. Tenn. Eastman Co., Kingsport, 1948-50, assoc. research chem. engr., 1950-51, research chem. engr., 1951-52, sr. research chem. engr., 1952-54, 55-60, dept. head pilot plant, 1954-55, cellulose esters div. devel., supt. control dept., 1960-62, with, 1963-65, plant mgr., 1969-74, asst. works mgr., 1969-70, asst. to pres., 1970-72; v.p. to sr. v.p. Eastman Kodak Co., Rochester, from 1972; v.p., asst. gen. mgr. Eastman Chems. div., 1974-79, exec. v.p., gen. mgr., from 1979; supt. cellulose esters div. Tenn. Eastman Co., Kingsport, 1963-65, asst. works mgr., 1969-70, asst. to pres., 1970-72, v.p., 1972-73, sr. v.p., 1973-74; plant mgr. Carolina Eastman Co., 1965-69; 1st v.p. Bays Mountain Constrn. Co., 1969-70; asst. gen. mgr. Eastman Chems. Co. div. Eastman Kodak Co., Kingsport, 1974-79, gen. mgr., from 1979. Bd. dirs., exec. com. Eastman Kodak Co.; bd. dirs. First Am. Corp., Am. Elect. Power Co., Provident Life and Accident Ins. Co. Bd. dirs. Holston Valley Hosp. and Med. Ctr., Kingsport Area Community Chest, Inc., United Way of Greater Kingsport, Jr. Achievement of Kingsport; trustee Holston Conf. Colls. of United Meth. Ch; bd. govs. Emory and Henry Coll., Tenn. State Bd. Edn. Served to capt. USAF, 1943-46. Mem. Am. Inst. Chem. Engrs., Chem. Mfrs. Assn. (bd. dirs.), Soc. Chem. Industry, Am. Indsl. Health Council (bd. dirs.), NSPE, Ridgefield Country Club (Kingsfield). Home: Kingsport, Tenn. Died July 26, 2009.

REIDY, WILLIAM EDWARD, holding company executive; b. Chgo., July 31, 1931; s. Edward William and Kathryn Therese (O'Donnell) R.; m. Barbara Mary Beck, Nov. 30, 1957; children: Kathleen, William Jr., Mary Barbara, Daniel. BSBA, U. Notre Dame, 1953. Sales rep. IBM, Chgo., 1958-65; v.p. systems, mgmt. info. system Kraft, Inc., NYC and Glenview, Ill., 1965-75, exec. v.p. Glenview, 1975-79; sr. v.p. Dart & Kraft Inc., Northbrook, Ill., 1979-83, Beatrice Foods Co., Chgo., 1983-85; pres. William E. Reidy Assocs., Chgo., from 1985; sr. v.p. BCI Holdings Corp., Chgo., from 1986, E-II Holdings Inc., Chgo., from 1987. Bd. dirs. Glenview State Bank. Bd. dirs. St. Francis Hosp., Evanston, Ill., 1978—, Chgo. Boys Club, 1975—. Served to lt. USNR, 1953-58. Mem. Assn. for Corp. Growth. Clubs: Tavern, Mid-Day (Chgo.); North Shore Country (Glenview); Old Marsh (North Palm Beach, Fla.). Republican. Roman Catholic. Home: Lake Forest, Ill. Died Dec. 10, 2009.

REISER, ROBERT FRANK, copying machine company executive; b. Bklyn., Nov. 19, 1931; s. Frank Joseph and Grace Eileen (Boyens) R.; m. Mary Claire Lawless; children: Mark, John, Robert, Mary, Martin, Peter. AB in English, St. Peters Coll., 1954; MBA in Mktg., Harvard U., 1958. Dir. budget Moran Towing, NYC, 1958-60, mgr. sales, 1960-64, Xerox Corp., NYC, 1964-65, br. mgr. Washington, 1965-67, region v.p. Chgo., 1967-73, chief staff officer, 1973-75, v.p. mktg., 1975-79, sr. v.p. strategic planning Stamford, Conn., 1975-83, pres. internat. strategic planning, from 1983. Bd. dirs. Rank Xerox Ltd., London. Trustee St. Peter's Coll., Jersey City, 1984—, McQuaid Jesuit High Sch., Rochester, N.Y., 1874-78; bd. visitors U. Conn., Storrs, 1984—; dir. Boys Hope Halfway Houses, St. Louis, 1978-82, Monroe County Dem. Com., Rochester, 1974-76, Brazilian Cultural Found., 1987. Served to 1st lt. U.S. Army, 1954-56. Mem. Nat. Planning Assn. (exec. com. competitive realities 1985), Council of Ams. Clubs: N.Y. Yacht, Pinehurst (N.C.) Country, New Canaan Field. Roman Catholic. Home: Sag Harbor, NY. Died Apr. 3, 2010.

REISSIG, MERLE HARRIS, manufacturing executive; b. Findlay, Ohio, Aug. 24, 1927; s. Walter Roy and Mabel Garnet (Harris) R.; m. Martha Jean Tilton, June 15, 1950; children: Steven Richard, Diane Elizabeth. BS, Ohio State U., 1950. Various positions Ranco, Inc., Dublin, Ohio, 1950—65, asst. to corp. controller, 1965—68, dir. budgets, 1968—70, asst. treas., 1970—72, treas., asst. sec., from 1972. With USN, 1945—46. Mem. Nat. Assn. Corp. Treas., Ohio Mfrs. Assn. (treas., trustee 1982-), Fin. Execs. Inst. (chpt. pres. 1979), Catawba Island Club (Port Clinton, Ohio), Ohio State U. Faculty Club (Columbus), Masons. Republican. Avocations: sports, boating. Home: Columbus, Ohio. Died Jan. 10, 2010.

REMAK, HENRY H.H., foreign language educator; b. Berlin, July 27, 1916; came to U.S., 1936; s. Hans Ismar and Hedwig (Salz) R.; m. Ingrid Miriam Grünfeld, Aug. 3, 1946; children: Roy Andrew, Steven Bruce, Renée June, Ronald Frank. Licencié-ès-Lettres, U. Montpellier, France, 1936; MA, Ind. U., 1937; PhD, U. Chgo., 1947; D-ès-Lettres (hon.), U. Lille, France, 1973. From instr. to prof. Germanic studies and comparative lit. Ind. U., Bloomington, from 1938, also prof. West. European studies, dir. Inst. for Advanced Study, 1988-94, 97-98, vice chancellor, dean of the faculties, 1969-74. Dir. Middlebury (Vt.) German Summer Sch., 1967-71; dir. Nat. Endowment for Humanities Summer and Year-Long Seminar, Bloomington, 1977-79; vis. prof. U. Hamburg, U. Lille, Middlebury U., U. Pa., U. Wis.; bd. dirs. Ind. Humanities Coun., 1984-90; pres., mem. editorial policy bd. Comparative History of Literatures in European Langs., 1977-83. Author: Novellistische Struktur, 1983, German Novella, 1995; co-editor: Oeuvres de Charles-Michel Campion, 1945; contbr. chpts. to books, numerous articles to profl. jours. Bd. dirs. United Fund, Bloomington, 1970-74; mem. Hosp. Bd., Bloomington, 1971-77. Ensign, U.S. Mcht. Marine, 1944-46. Fulbright vis. prof., 1962-63, 67; Fulbright travel grantee, 1987, 88; Guggenheim fellow, 1967-68; named Sagamore of the Wabash, Gov. Ind., 1993. Jewish. Avocations: running, tennis, outdoor swimming, reading, hiking. Home: Bloomington, Ind. Died Feb. 12, 2009.

REMINE, WILLIAM HERVEY, JR., retired surgeon; b. Richmond, Va., Oct. 11, 1918; s. William Hervey and Mabel Inez (Walthall) ReM.; m. Doris Irene Grumbacher, June 9, 1943; children: William H., Stephen Gordon, Walter James, Gary Craig. BS in Biology, U. Richmond, 1940, D.Sc. (hon.), 1965; MD, Med. Coll. Va., Richmond, 1943; MS in Surgery, U. Minn., Mpls., 1952. Diplomate Am. Bd. Surgery. Intern Doctor's Hosp., Washington, 1944; fellow in surgery Mayo Clinic, Rochester, Minn., 1944-45, 47-52; instr. surgery Mayo Grad. Sch. Medicine, Rochester, Minn., 1954-59, asst. prof. surgery, 1959-65, assoc. prof. surgery, 1965-70, prof. surgery, 1970-83, prof. surgery emeritus, from 1983. Surg. cons. to surgeon gen. U.S. Army, 1965-75; surg. lectr., USSR, 1987, 89, Japan, 1988, 90, Egypt, 1990; lectr. Soviet-Am. seminars, USSR, 1987, 89. Sr. author: Cancer of the Stomach, 1964, Manual of Upper Gastro-intestinal Surgery, 1985; editor: Problems in General Surgery, Surgery of the Biliary Tract, 1986; mem. editorial bd. Rev. Surgery, 1965-75, Jour. Lancet, 1968-77; contbr. 200 articles to profl. jours. Served to capt. U.S. Army, 1945-47 Recipient St. Francis surg. award St. Francis Hosp., Pitts., 1976, Disting. Svc. award Alumni Coun., U. Richmond, 1976, Dist. Alumnus award Mayo Found., Priestley Soc. Mayo Clinic Surg. Alumni Legacy award, 2004; named one of Am. Top Surgeons, 2007. Mem. ACS, AAAS, Am. Assn. History of Medicine, AMA, Am. Med. Writers Assn., Am. Soc. Colon and Rectal Surgeons, Soc. Surgery Alimentary Tract (v.p. 1983-84), Am. Surg. Assn., Assn. Mil. Surgeons U.S., Internat. Soc. Surgery, Digestive Disease Found., Priestley Soc. (pres. 1968-69, Legacy award 2004), Central Assn. Physicians and Dentists (pres. 1972-73), Central Surg. Assn., Soc. Med. Cons. Armed Forces, Mayo Clinic Surg. Soc. (chmn. 1964-66), Soc. Head and Neck Surgeons, Soc. Surg. Oncology, So. Surg. Assn., Western Surg. Assn. (pres. 1979-80), Minn. State Med. Assn., Minn. Surg. Soc. (pres. 1966-67), Zumbro Valley Med. Soc., Sigma Xi; hon. mem. Colombian Coll. Surgeons, St. Paul Surg. Soc., Flint Surg. Soc., Venezuelan Surg. Soc., Colombian Soc. Gastroenterology, Dallas So. Clin. Soc., Ga. Surg. Soc., Soc. Postgrad. Surgeons Los Angeles County, Japanese Surg. Soc., Argentine Surg. Digestive Soc., Bassanese Surg. Assn. (Italy), Tex. Surg. Soc., Mayo Clinic Surg. Alum Assn., Omicron Delta Kappa, Alpha Omega Alpha, Beta Beta Beta, Kappa Sigma (pres. 1939-40). Methodist. Avocations: hunting, fishing, golf, photography, boating, music. Home: Ponte Vedra Beach, Fla. Died July 1, 2009.

REMINGTON, DEBORAH WILLIAMS, artist; b. Haddonfield, NJ, June 25, 1930; d. Malcolm Van Dyke and Hazel Irwin (Stewart) R. BFA, San Francisco Art Inst., 1955. Adj. prof. art Cooper Union, NYC, 1973—97, NYU, 1994—98; tchr. Nat. Acad., NYC, 2003—10. One-woman shows include Dilexi Gallery, San Francisco, 1962, 63, 65, San Francisco Mus. Art, 1964, Bykert Gallery, NYC, 1967, 69, 72, 74, Galerie Darthea Speyer, Paris, 1968, 71, 73, 92, Pyramid Gallery, Washington, 1973, 76, zola-Leiberman Gallery, Chgo., 1976, Hamilton Gallery, NYC, 1977, Portland Ctr. Visual Arts, Oreg., 1977, Michael Berger Gallery, Pitts., 1979, Mary Ryan Gallery, NYC, 1982, Ramon Osuna Gallery, Washington, 1983, Newport Harbor Art Mus., 1983, Oakland Mus., Calif., 1984, Jack Shainman Gallery, NYC, 1987, Shoshana Wayne Gallery, LA, 1988, Mitchell Algus Gallery, NYC, 2001; group shows include Whitney Mus. Am. Art, NYC, 1965, 67, 72, San Francisco Mus. Art, 1956, 60, 61, 63, 64, 65, Lausanne Mus., Switz., 1966, Fondation Maeght, St. Paul de Vence, France, 1968, Smithsonian Am. Art Mus., Washington, 1968, Art. Inst., Chgo., 1974, Inst. Contemporary Art, Boston, 1975, Nat. Gallery Modern Art, Lisbon, Portugal, 1981, Toledo Mus. Art, 1975, The 6 Gallery, 1954-57, Natsoulas Gallery, Davis, Calif., 1990, 1st Trienalle des Ameriques Maubeuge, France, 1993, Tamarind Inst. Retrospective, 2000, Worcester Art Mus., Mass., 2001, San Jose Mus. Art, Calif., 2002, Nat. Acad. Mus. Annuals, NY, 2001, 03, 05, 07, numerous others; represented in permanent collections Whitney Mus. Am. Art, Smithsonian Am. Art Mus., Washington, Art Inst., Chgo., Centre d'Art et de Culture Georges Pompidou, Paris, Carnegie Mus., Pitts. Recipient Hassam and Speicher Purchase award Am. Acad. and Inst. Arts and Letters, 1988; NEA fellow, 1979-80; Tamarind Inst. fellow, 1973; Guggenheim fellow, 1984; Pollock-Krasner Found. grantee, 1999. Mem. NAD (Benjamin Altman prize for painting 178th Ann. Exhbn. 2003). Home: New York, NY. Died Apr. 21, 2010.

RENAKER, JANE ANN, golf course executive; b. Dayton, Ohio, Dec. 3, 1922; d. Herbert Elmer and Luella Carolyn (Burkhardt) Quiggle; m. Allan Frazier Renaker, Jan. 24, 1942 (dec. Mar. 1984); children— Carol Anne, Joyce Lynn, Stephen Allan. Grad. high sch., Dayton, Ohio. Bookkeeper, Delco Products, Dayton, 1941-43; bookkeeper, part owner Al's Super Service & Used Cars, Dayton, 1945-56, Renaker Chevrolet & Oldsmoble, Brookville, Ind., 1956-67; operator, part owner Brook Hill Golf Course, Brookville, 1973-83, sole owner, 1983—. Republican. Methodist. Club: Delta Theta Tau. Lodge: Eastern Star (page 1957). Died Dec. 28, 2009.

RENOUD, DOROTHY IDA, publishing company executive; b. Far Rockaway, N.Y., Aug. 11, 1933; d. Herbert William and Elizabeth (Fischer) Owen; m. David Francis Renoud, Jan. 18, 1958; children— David, Douglas. Sales service mgr. Reinhold Pub., N.Y.C., 1951-61; circulation dir. United Tech. Pub., Garden City, N.Y., 1961-80; v.p. Coastal Communications, N.Y.C., 1980—. Recipient Fraundorf award Long Beach Fire Dept., N.Y., 1979. Mem. Nat. Bus. Circulation Assn. (bd. dirs. 1981—). Avocation: camping. Home: Long Beach, NY. Died Feb. 15, 2009.

REUBEN, ALVIN BERNARD, communications and entertainment executive; b. Harrisburg, Pa., Aug. 11, 1940; s. Maurice and Lillian (Katzef) R.; m. Barbara Ann Harrison, Mar. 18, 1968; 1 dau., Mindee Jill. BS in Commerce, Rider U., 1962. Buyer Pomeroy's div. Allied Stores Corp., Harrisburg, 1962-67; sales rep. Random House, Inc., NYC, 1967-74; dir. mktg. Ballantine Books, Inc. (div. Random House), NYC, 1974-76; v.p. sales Simon & Schuster, NYC, 1976-79, sr. v.p. sales Pocket Books div., 1979-81, sr. v.p. mktg., 1981-82, pres. ref. and promotional pub. group, 1982-83, exec. v.p. electronic pub. div., 1983-85; exec. v.p. Prentice Hall div. Simon & Schuster, 1985-86; sr. v.p. mktg., sales and distbn. Vestron, Inc., 1986-89; sr. v.p. St. Martin's Press, NYC, 1989-91; sr. v.p. sales, mktg. Sony Music Video, NYC, 1991-92; sr. v.p. spl. markets Sony Music, NYC, 1992-95; sr.v.p. video and interactive sales and distbn. BMG Entertainment, 1995-97; pres. BMG Video, 1997-99. Instr. edn. in pub. program, grad. program SUNY, 2004-07; bd. advisors, Coastal Carolina Med. Ctr., Hardeeville, SC, 2005-08. With USAFR, 1963-69. Mem. Tau Kappa Epsilon. Died May 2, 2010.

REUSCHE, FRANK LOUIS, ceramic decorating supply company executive; b. Bklyn., Feb. 17, 1925; s. Frank Louis and Marjorie Theresa (Ryan) R.; grad. Fordham Prep. Sch., 1941; B.S., Bethany Coll., 1944; postgrad. Ohio State U., 1945, Rutgers U., 1947-48; m. Amelia V. Ozimek, Sept. 18, 1949 (dec. Oct. 1972); children— Frank Louis III, Thomas R., Marjorie A., Mary T., Madeline C.; m. 2d, Jane Fabian Verney, Dec. 28, 1975; stepchildren— Bruce, Kim, Kerry and Alison Verney. Grad. chemist So. Acid & Sulfur Co., Columbus O., 1945; chemist research and devel. L. Reusche & Co., Newark, 1947-51, v.p., 1951-66. pres., 1966-88; prin., pres., ceramic decorating cons., 1989—. Served with USAAF, 1945-47. Mem. Soc. Glass and Ceramic Decorators, Stained Glass Assn. Am., Am., N.J. ceramic socs., Sigma Nu. Patentee in field. Died June 28, 2009.

REX, WALTER EDWIN, III, (TED REX), humanities educator; b. Bryn Mawr, Pa., Jan. 31, 1927; s. Walter Edwin Jr. and Barbara (Clayton) R. AB, Harvard U., 1950, AM, 1951, PhD, 1956. Instr. Brown U., Providence, 1956-57, Harvard U., Cambridge, Mass., 1957-60; asst. prof. U. Calif., Berkeley, 1960-65, assoc. prof., 1965-72, prof., 1972-92, prof. emeritus, 1992—2010. Chair James L. Clifford prize com. Am. Soc. 18th Century Studies, 1997—98. Author: Essays on Pierre Bayle and Religious Controversy, 1965, The Attraction of the Contrary, 1987, Diderot's Counterpoints, 1998; collaborator multi-vol. book (7 vols.) Inventory of Diderot's Encyclopédie, 1971-72, 89; mem. editl. bd. Eighteenth-Century Studies, 1979-82, 89-92; asst. editor The French Rev., 1981-86; contbr. to books in field. Grantee Humanities Rsch. Inst., 1966-67, 73-74; Pres.'s fellow U. Calif., 1990-91. Mem. MLA, Am. Soc. 18th Century Studies (Clifford lectr. ann. meeting 2000), Soc. Francaise d'étude du 18 siècle, Arts Club (Berkeley), Kosmos Club (Berkeley). Democrat. Avocation: chamber music. Home: Berkeley, Calif. Died Jan. 22, 2010.

REYES, RUDY SAN PEDRO, real estate development and parking company executive; b. Manila, Nov. 27, 1941; s. Benito and Avelina (San Pedro) Reyes; m. Reyes S.P. Suarez Reyes, Dec. 8, 1961; children: Ferdinand, Rudolf, Vanessa, Regina, Ronald. Ab in Polit. Sci. cum laude, Far Eastern U., Milw., 1965; MBA, U. Philippines, 1965. Exec. asst. to exec. v.p. Air Manila Inc., 1969, gen. mgr. traffic & sales dep , 1970; honesty checker parking ops. Edison Parking Corp. (EPC), Newark, 1970—71; supr. Newark ops., Manhattan, NYC ops., 1972—73; gen. mgr. divsn. B, 1976; asst. to v.p. Denison Parking Inc., Indpls., 1977; pres. & gen. mgr. Pacific Industries Inc., Indpls., from 1978; pres. Econo Car Rent-a-Car Indpls.; owner A-1 Car Care Ctrs. Indpls. Bd. dirs. Indpls. Zool. Soc., from 1982, United Way Greater Ind.; bd. nat. govs. Philippine Heritage Endowment Found. Ind. U.; liaison officer T. Sunggani Dist. Boy Scouts America, Indpls.; mem. Riley Area Revitalization Program, Internat. Ctr. Indpls. Mem.: Nat.

Parking Assn., Parking Assn. Indpls., Barangay Philipino-America (Indpls.) (pres. 1982—83), Optimists (Indpls.) (dir. 1980—84, Cmty. Leadership award 1980—81), Kiwanis (dir. 1982—84). Roman Catholic. Home: Indianapolis, Ind. Died Apr. 11, 2010.

REYNOLDS, THOMAS HEDLEY, academic administrator; b. NYC, Nov. 23, 1920; s. Wallace and Helen (Hedley) R.; m. Jean Fine Lytle, Apr. 24, 1943; children: Thomas Scott, David Hewson, John Hedley, Tay. AB, Williams Coll., 1942, LL.D. (hon.), 1978; MA in History, Columbia U., 1947, PhD in History, 1953; LL.D., U. Maine, 1968, Bowdoin Coll., 1969, Colby Coll., 1969; DHL (hon.), Bates Coll., 1990, Middlebury Coll., 1992. Instr. history Hunter Coll., 1947-48; staff historian ARC, Washington, 1948-49; mem. faculty Middlebury Coll., 1949-67, chmn. dept. history, 1957-67, dean of coll., 1964-67; pres. Bates Coll., Lewiston, Maine, 1967-89, U. New Eng., Biddeford, Maine, 1991-95. Mem. Edn. Commn. of States, 1969-80; mem. Higher Edn. Coun., 1971—, Commn. on Maine's Future, 1975—; dir. New Eng. Bd. Higher Edn., 1976—, mem. exec. com., 1977—; chmn. Gov.'s Commn. on Status of Edn. in Maine, 1983—. Bd. advisors AIDS project; bd. dirs. SALT, Inc.; mem. Vt. Hist. Sites Commn., 1964-66; mem. New Eng. Colls. Fund, pres., 1971-72; chmn. Com. on Jud. Responsibility and Disability, 1982—; trustee WCBB Ednl. TV, 1974—; bd. dirs. Nat. Assn. Ind. Colls. and Univs., 1977. Capt. AUS, 1942-46; col. Res. Mem. Am. Hist. Assn., Am. Antiquarian Soc., AAUP, Maine Hist. Soc., Vt. Hist. Soc., Maine Ptnrs. Alliance for Progress. Home: Newcastle, Maine. Died Sept. 22, 2009.

RICE, JAMES HOWARD, construction executive, consultant; b. Oswego, Ill., Jan. 11, 1926; s. Lawrence W. and Darle D. (Breedlove) R.; m. Margaret Ellen Simpson, Sept. 9, 1950; children: James C., Thomas S., Timothy W. BSME, U. Mich., 1950; MS in Bus. Adminstrn., No. Ill. U., 1972. Sales mgr. Barber-Greene Can. Ltd., Toronto, Ont., 1956—60; mktg. coord. Barber-Greene Co., Aurora, Ill., 1961—66, product mgr., 1967—72, v.p. planning and devel., 1972—76, v.p., gen. mgr. mine and smelter div. Denver, 1976—82, v.p. corp. devel. Aurora and Denver, 1982—84; sec., treas. FGM Equities, Inc.; dir. Altex Oil Corp., Denver; chmn. bd. Colo. Mining Assocs., Denver, 1984—85. 1st lt. inf. US Army, 1944—46. Scholar Douglas Aircraft scholar, U. Mich., 1949—50. Mem.: Denver Petroleum Club, Beta Gamma Sigma, Phi Kappa Phi, Tau Beta Pi. Republican. Methodist. Died Feb. 28, 2010.

RICE, JOHN BERCHMANS, JR., bank executive; b. Dighton, Mass., Apr. 22, 1928; s. John Berchmans and Edith Mae (Cameron) R.; m. Roberta Bush Robinson, May 3, 1958; children: Heather Robinson, Ian Cameron. BBA, Northeastern U., 1956, MBA, 1963; grad., Williams Coll., 1961, Rutgers U., 1966. Teller Arlington 5 cents Savs. Bank, Mass., 1948—54; corr. bank officer Bank of New Eng., Boston, 1954—59; asst. treas. Cape Ann Bank & Trust Co., Gloucester, Mass., 1959—61; v.p., treas., dir. Middleboro Trust Co., Mass., 1961—70; pres., dir., CEO First Nat. Bank of Yarmouth, Yarmouthport, Mass., 1970—78, First & Ocean Nat. Bank of Newburyport, Mass., from 1979. Corporator Newburyport Area Indsl. Devel. Corp., Mass., from 1980. Mem. task force City of Newburyport, from 1984; dir. Newburyport C. of C.; trustee Anna Jacques Hosp., Newburyport, 1980. Staff sgt. USMC, 1951—53. Mem.: Mass. Bankers Assn. (bd. dirs. payment systems 1983, chmn. ins. com.), ABA (adv. dir. from 1983). Republican. Congregationalist. Home: Placida, Fla. Died Jan. 1, 2009.

RICE, JOHN THOMAS, architecture educator; b. New London, Conn., Feb. 4, 1931; s. Clarence Benjamin and Emily (Gudal) R. BS in Engring., U. Conn., 1952; MSME, Newark Coll. Engring., 1954; D.Sc. in Engring., Columbia U., 1962. Registered profl. engr., N.Y. Test equipment designer propeller div. Curitss-Wright Corp., Caldwell, NJ, 1952-54; stress analyst Wright Aeronautical div. Curtiss-Wright Corp., Woodridge, NJ, 1954-59; chief structural mechanics Gen. Dynamics/Electric Boat, Groton, Conn., 1962-64; asst. prof. mech. engring. Pratt Inst., Bklyn., 1964-66, assoc. prof., 1966-74, prof., from 1974, chmn. dept. mech. engring., 1981-90. Mem. ASME (chmn. mech. engring. dept. heads com. region II 1987-89, chmn. profl. devel. region II 1989-93, mem. exec. com. met. sect. 1990—, vice chmn. 1991-92, chmn. 1992-93, sec. region II 1993-96, treas. met. sect. 1999—), Pi Tau Sigma, Tau Beta Pi. Home: Flushing, NY. Died July 29, 2009.

RICE, RICHARD LEE, retired architect; b. Raleigh, NC, May 4, 1919; s. Robert Edward Lee and Grace Lucille (Betts) R.; m. Cora Belle Stegall, Apr. 12, 1946; children— Richard Lee, Westwood Carter, David Sinclair. BS in Archtl. Engring., N.C. State U., 1941; grad., U.S. Army Command and Gen. Staff Coll., 1961. Assoc. Cooper-Shumaker, Architects, Raleigh, 1946-47; prin. Richard L. Rice, Architects, Raleigh, 1947-48; assoc. Cooper, Haskins & Rice and predecessor firm, Raleigh, 1948-52, ptnr., 1953-54, Haskins & Rice, Architects, Raleigh, 1954-85; prin. Haskins, Rice, Savage & Pearce, Architects, 1985-91, pres., 1985-91. V.p. N.C. Design Found., 1973; pres. N.C. Archtl. Found., 1975; mem. Raleigh Arts Commn., 1978-82, Raleigh Hist. Properties Commn., 1990-92, Raleigh Hist. Dists. Commn., 1991-92. Archtl. works include renovations, Raleigh Meml. Auditorium, 1964, 78, 91 (SE Regional AIA award of merit 1964), Auditorium, 4 high schs. and 13 elem. schs., Raleigh Civic Ctr., stack addition Wilson Libr. U. N.C., Chapel Hill, 1977, Reidsville, N.C. Jr. High Sch.; assoc. architect Raleigh Radisson Hotel, 1980, One Hanover Sq. Office Bldg., 1985, Two Hanover Sq. Office Bldg., 1990, additions and renovations to Raleigh Meml. Auditorium, 1989, 3 indsl. plants, 7 bldgs., Wake Tech. C.C., 50 chs. Pres. Wake County (N.C.) Hist. Soc., 1973-74; mem. N.C. Gov.'s Com. for Facilities for Physically Handicapped, 1970-73; arbitrator Am. Arbitration Assn. With inf. and C.E. U.S. Army, 1941-46, ETO; col. USAR; ret. Decorated Silver Star.; Legion of Merit; Bronze Star; Purple Heart. Fellow AIA (pres. N.C. chpt. 1970, Disting. Svc. award N.C. chpt. 1975); mem. Raleigh Council Architects (pres. 1950), Nat. Trust for Hist. Preservation, N.C. State Art Soc., Ret. Officers Assn. U.S. (pres. Triangle chpt. 1983), N.C. State U. Gen. Alumni Assn. (pres., chmn. bd. 1960-61, pres. Class 1941, 1986-91), Carolina Country Club, Lions, Torch Club (pres. 1982-83), Phi Eta Sigma, Phi Kappa Phi. Democrat. Baptist. Died Dec. 8, 2009.

RICH, ALAN, music critic, writer; b. Boston, June 17, 1924; (parents Am. citizens); s. Edward and Helen (Hirshberg) R. AB, Harvard, 1945; MA, U. Calif-Berkeley, 1952. Alfred Hertz Meml. Traveling fellow in music, Vienna, 1952-53; Asst. music critic Boston Herald, 1944-45, N.Y. Sun, 1947-48; contbr. Am. Record Guide, 1947-61, Saturday Rev., 1952-53, Mus. Am., 1955-61, Mus. Quar., 1957-58; tchr. music U. Calif. at Berkeley, 1950-58; program and music dir. Pacifica Found., FM radio, 1953-61; asst. music critic N.Y. Times, 1961-63; chief music critic, editor N.Y. Herald Tribune, 1963-66; music critic, editor N.Y. World Jour. Tribune, 1966-67; contbg. editor Time mag., 1967-68; music and drama critic, arts editor N.Y. mag., 1968-81, contbg. editor, 1981-83; music critic, arts editor Calif. (formerly New West mag.), 1979-83, contbg. editor, 1983-85; gen. editor Newsweek mag., NYC, 1983-87; music critic L.A. Herald Examiner, 1987-89, L.A. Daily News, 1989-92, L.A. Weekly, 1992—2008. Tchr. New Sch. Social Rsch., 1972-75, 77-79, U. So. Calif. Sch. Journalism, 1980-82, Calif. Inst. Art, 1982-94, UCLA, 1990-91; artist-in-residence Davis Ctr. Performing Arts CUNY, 1975-76. Author: Careers and Opportunities in Music, 1964, Music: Mirror of the Arts, 1969, Listeners Guides to Classical Music, Opera, Jazz, 3 vols., 1980, The Lincoln Center Story, 1984, Play-by-Play: Bach, Mozart, Beethoven, Tchaikovsky, 4 vols., 1995, American Pioneers, 1995, So I've Heard: Notes of a Migratory Music Critic, 2006; author: (interactive CD-ROM computer programs): Schubert's Trout Quintet, 1991, So I've Heard: Bach and Before, 1992, So I've Heard: The Classical Ideal, 1993, So I've Heard: Beethoven and Beyond, 1993; contbr. articles to entertainment mags. Recipient Deems Taylor award ASCAP, 1970, 73, 74 Mem. Music Critics Circle N.Y. (sec. 1961-63, chmn. 1963-64), N.Y. Drama Critics Circle, Am. Theatre Critics Assn., Music Critics Assn., PEN. Democrat. Avocations: gardening, cooking. Home: Los Angeles, Calif. Died Apr. 23, 2010.

RICH, SHIRLEY, casting director; b. Chgo., Dec. 10, 1922; d. Meyer David and Hattie (Goldman) R.; m. Lewis M. Krohn, Oct. 26, 1952; children: Steven Krohn, Lisa Krohn. BFA, U. Iowa, 1944; MA, Smith Coll., 1946. Asst. casting dir. Rodgers & Hammerstein, NYC, 1948-51; eastern talent scout MGM, NYC, 1951-54; casting dir. Harold Prince, NYC, 1963-69, Shirley Rich, Inc., NYC, from 1969. Cons., tchr. U. Iowa, Iowa City, Columbia U., N.Y.C., Cornell U., Ithaca, N.Y.; judge Irene Ryan Awards, Washington; Tony award voter Am. Theatre Wing, N.Y.C., 1990. Casting dir. (films) Rachel, Rachel, 1968, Puzzle of a Downfall Child, Diary of a Mad Housewife, Who is Harry Kellerman, Serpico, 1973, The Effect of Gamma Rays, One Summer Love, Three Days of the Condor, 1975, Summer Wishes, Winter Dreams, The Hideaways, Saturday Night Fever, Slow Dancing in the Big City, Tristan and Iseult, Kramer v. Kramer, 1979, Taps, 1981, Teresa, Tender Mercies, Jaws 2, The Formula, W.W. and the Dixie Dance Kings, Bad News Bears, Ballad of the Sad Cafe, 1991; (TV movies) American Playhouse: Andre's Mother, American Playhouse: Ask Me Again, The Belarus Secret, After the Fall, Prince of Central Park, Siege, Doing Life, Studs Lonigan, Kojak: The Marcus Nelson Murder; (plays) The Sign in Sidney Brustein's Window, 1964, Ballroom, Is There Life After High School, Crimes of the Heart, Hide and Seek, Night Watch, God's Favorite, Via Galactica, 70 Girls 70, Not Now Darling, Sly Fox, 1976, Private Lives, 1983, Fiddler on the Roof, 1964, Cabaret, 1966, Zorba, 1968; asst. casting dir. South Pacific, 1949, The King and I, 1951, Burning Bright, The Happy Time, The Heart of the Matter. Rockefeller Found. fellow, 1946-47; recipient Smith medal, Smith Coll., 1983, Dist. Alumni award U. Iowa, 1994. Mem. Casting Soc. Am. (mem. at large bd. dirs 1988-91, Hoyt Bowers award 1991), Acad. Motion Pictures Arts and Scis. Democrat. Jewish. Avocations: cooking, travel. Home: Rye, NY. Died Dec. 28, 2009.

RICHARDS, GLENORA, artist; b. Feb. 18, 1909; d. Tracy Henry and Bertha (Huber) Case; m. Walter DuBois Richards, June 20, 1931 (dec. May 2006); children: Timothy, Henry Tracy(dec.). Student, Cleve. Sch. Art, 1927-30. Exhibited in group shows at Nat. Collection Fine Arts (Smithsonian Inst.), NAD, Portraits, Inc., N.Y.C., Phila., Pa. Soc. Miniature Painters, L.A., Royal Soc. Miniature Painters, Sculptors and Gravers, R.W.S. Galleries, London, 1958, 95, IBM Gallery Arts and Scis., N.Y.C., 1966; represented in permanent collection Phila. Mus. Arts, Smithsonian Inst., Worcester (Mass.) Art Mus., Yale Mus. Fine Arts; contbr. articles to profl. jours.; designer commemorative stamp of Edna St. Vincent Millay, 1981, of Dr. Mary Walker, 1982. Recipient Pa. Soc. prize Pa. Soc. Miniature Painters, 1947. Mem. Am. Soc. Miniature Painters (Levantia White Boardman Meml. medal 1947), Nat. Assn. Women Artists (medal of honor 1953, 74, Aileen O. Webb prize 1971), Miniature Painters, Sculptors and Gravers Soc. Washington (Elizabeth Muhlhoffer award 1956, 57, 61, hon. award for miniature portrait 1969, Levantia White Boardman Meml. prize 1979, 81), Miniature Art Soc. N.J. (Best on Ivory 1974, 77), Miniature Soc. Fla. (Richard B. Baumgardner award 1989). Home: Lancaster, Mass. Died Oct. 21, 2009.

RICHARDSON, JOHN GRISSEN, sociology educator; b. LA, July 4, 1944; s. Joseph Grissen and Erie Louise (Park) Richardson; m. Theresa Rupke, June 22, 1967; children: Genevieve, Anne, Nicole. BA, U. Pacific, 1966; MA, U. Calif., Davis, 1968, PhD, 1976. Lectr. sociology Calif. State U., Hayward, 1970—72; asst. prof. U. Alaska, Fairbanks, 1973—74, Western Wash. U., Bellingham, 1974—79, assoc. prof. sociology, 1979—85, mem. profl. edn. adv. bd., from 1983, prof., from 1985. Editor-in-chief Handbook of Theory and Research in the Sociology of Education, 1985. Mem. Whatcom County Mental Health Bd., Bellingham, 1975—76. Grantee, Nat. Com. Exceptional Children, 1973, Spencer Found., 1985—86. Mem.: Internat. Sociol. Assn., Am. Sociol. Assn. Democrat. Home: Lutz, Fla. Died June 23, 2009.

RICHARDSON, WILLIAM SHAW, retired state supreme court justice; b. Honolulu, Dec. 22, 1919; s. Wilfred Kelelani and Amy Lan Kyau (Wung) Richardson; m. Amy Corinne Ching, June 21, 1947 (dec.); children: Corinne, Barbara, William K. BA, U. Hawaii, 1941; JD, U. Cin., 1943, LLD (hon.), 1967. Bar: Hawaii 1946. Sole practice law, 1946—62; lt. gov. State of Hawaii, Honolulu, 1962—66; chief justice Supreme Ct. Hawaii, 1966—82; trustee Bernice Pauahi Bishop Estate, 1983—2010; chmn. Dem. Party Hawaii, 1956—62. Capt. US Army, 1943—46. Mem.: Hawaii Bar Assn., ABA, Masons. Episcopalian. Home: Honolulu, Hawaii. Died June 21, 2010.

RICHMAN, KEITH STUART, retired state legislator; b. Syracuse, NY, Nov. 21, 1953; married; 2 children. BA, U. Calif., Davis, 1975; MD, UCLA, MA in Pub. Health Adminstrn., 1978. Chair bd. dirs. Lakeside HealthCare, Inc.; mem. 38th Dist. Calif. State Assembly, 2000—06. Commr. City Redevelopment Agy., LA; mem. Sun Valley Rotary Found.; chair task force intercollegiate athletics Calif. State U., Northridge; past chair Valley Cmty. Clinic, adv. bd. Mem.: Am. Diabetes Assn. (chpt. founding pres.), Rotary. Republican. Died July 30, 2010.

RICKARD, CORWIN LLOYD, nuclear engineer; b. Medina, Ohio, Sept. 26, 1926; s. Isaac Howard and Carrie (Sivits) R.; m. Anne Major Hillman, Feb. 1, 1948; children: Cheryl Anne, Howard John. BS, U. Rochester, NYC, 1947, MS, 1949; PhD, Cornell U., 1961. Asst. prof. engring. U. Rochester, 1949-52; instr. Cornell U., Ithaca, N.Y., 1952-54; nuclear engr. Brookhaven Nat. Lab., Upton, N.Y., 1954-56; with Gen. Atomic Co., San Diego, 1956-83, v.p., 1967-77, exec. v.p., 1977-83; with Salk Inst. Biotech./Indsl. Assocs. Inc., San Diego, from 1983. Author; patentee power reactors. With USNR, 1944-46. Fellow Am. Nuclear Soc. (pres. 1981-82); mem. ASME, AAAS, Sigma Xi. Died Aug. 5, 2010.

RICKARDS, DONALD ROLAND, college president; b. West Grove, Pa., Apr. 21, 1929; s. Harry Wesley and Claudia Gertrude (Satterethwaite) R.; m. Margaret L. Van Horn; children: Donald Roland Jr., Valerie Catheryn Easton, Linda Claude Brown, Dale Harry. BS, Columbia Internat. U., 1959; MA, Hartford Sem. Found., 1966, PhD, 1969; DMin, Faith Evang. Luth. Sem., Tacoma, 1981; D Missions, Trinity Evang. Div. Sch., Deerfield, Ill., 1988. Ordained Ind. Fundamental Chs. of Am., 1955. Change agt. Arab World Ministries, Tunisia, Algeria, Morocco, 1950-65; prof. Washington Bible Coll., 1967-69, Dallas Theol. Sem., 1969-71, Ft. Wayne (Ind.) Bible Coll., 1976-79, Liberty U., Lynchburg, Va., 1981-89; pastor Ft. Worth Bible Ch., 1971-76, Grace Bapt. Ch., Bakersfield, Calif., 1979-81; pres. Nashville Bible Coll., from 1990. Author: Jesus in the Quran, Tradition, Comment, 1969, A Religious Topical Index of Quran, 1989; contbg. author: Fundamentalist Jour., Eternity, King's Bus., Seedbed, Good News Broadcaster. Mem. Evang. Theol. Soc., Evang. Profs. Missions. Avocations: reading, model airplanes, languages. Home: Florence, Ky. Died Aug. 3, 2010.

RICKER, JOHN BOYKIN, JR., insurance counselor; b. Augusta, Ga., Nov. 20, 1917; s. John B. and Emily Clark (Denny) R.; m. Jane Duncan Darling, Sept. 30, 1950; children: John, Robb Duncan. BA, Southwestern Coll., 1938. Mgr. Cotton Fire and Marine Underwriters, Memphis, 1955-63; pres., chief exec. officer Marine Office of Am., NYC, 1964-74; chmn. bd., pres., chief exec. officer Continental Corp., NYC, 1976-82; with Internat. Ins. Counselors, Essex Fells, N.J., from 1983. Trustee Rhodes Coll., 1986—. Served with USNR, 1942-46. Decorated Bronze Star. Mem. Am. Inst. Marine Underwriters (past pres.), Essex Fells Country Club. Republican. Episcopalian. Died Dec. 14, 2009.

RICO, PATRICIA, retired sports association administrator; b. NYC, Sept. 25, 1933; m. Heliodoro Rico; one child. Pres. USA Track and Field, 1996—2000. Mem. U.S. Olympic Com.; co-dir. USA/Mobil Indoor Track and Field Championships. Co-founder Track Mirror. Mem. Internat. Amateur Athletic Fedn. (mem. women's com., chair U.S. women's track and field com.). Died May 2, 2010.

RIDOLFI, DOROTHY PORTER BOULDEN, nurse, real estate broker; b. SI, NY, Jan. 24, 1937; d. David Porter and Helen Marie (McCloskey) Boulden; m. Edward Benjamin Ridolfi, Aug. 16, 1958; children: Edward Brian, Judyann Nixon, Jacqueline Ryan. RN, St. Francis Hosp., 1957; student, Seton Hall U., South Orange, NJ, 1958, Mercer C.C., 1974, student, 1984, Thomas Edison Coll., 1979—84. Cert. coronary and critical care nurse; real estate cert. South Jersey Sch. Profl. Bus., 1976, lic. real estate instr. NJ, broker NJ, sales person NJ, cert. residential broker, residential specialist. Owner Stay 'N Play Day Camp, 1963—65; nurse Princeton Med. Ctr., NJ, 1972—73; pres., broker Ridolfi Realty Inc., Trenton, NJ, 1977—91; nurse Hamilton Hosp., NJ, 1982—85; instr. real estate Mercer County CC and Career Devel. Sch. Trustee NJ Assn. Realtors Edn. Found., No. Regional Adv. Bd. Bank Mid Jersey. Corr. sec. Hist. Soc., Hightstown, NJ, 1971—72; bd. dirs. Campfire Girls and Boys, 1984; committeewoman Burlington County Dem. Com., Willingboro, NJ, 1966—67, Mercer County Dem. Com., East Windsor, NJ, 1969—72. Mem.: TREND, Mercer County Multiple Listing, Nat. Assn. Realtors, Nat. Fedn. Ind. Bus. (RPAC chmn. 1989), NJ Assn. Realtors (bd. dirs., v.p. 5th dist. 1989, Make Am. Better award 1982), Mercer County Bd. Realtors (bd. dirs.

1981—83, treas., v.p., pres. from 1988, 1997), Soroptomist Internat. of Am. and NJ, Mercer County C. of C. Roman Catholic. Avocations: genealogy, travel, reading. Died Jan. 23, 2009.

RIEGER, WILLIAM W., retired state legislator; b. Phila., Nov. 2, 1922; s. Charles and Hannah Frances R.; m. Lucy Yacovetti, 1942; children: William J., Patricia Vittorelli. Grad. H.S. Mem. Dist. 179 Pa. House of Reps., 1966—2006. Chmn. profl. licensure com. Pa. House Rep., ranking house mem., co-chmn. Phila. delegation, chmn. house ethics com. Recipient Civic award 43rd Ward Cmty. Assn. Mem. San Antonio Soc., Am. Legion, Frank Delano Roosevelt Club. Home: Philadelphia, Pa. Died Dec. 11, 2009.

RIFMAN, EILEEN, music educator; b. Bklyn., June 10, 1944; m. Samuel Sholom Rifman, Aug. 12, 1972; children: Edward, Aimee. MusB, Manhattan Sch. Music, 1966, M Music Edn., 1967; MusM, Ind. U., 1970; cert., Fontainebleau, France, 1967. Music specialist N.Y.C. Pub. Sch. System, 1966-67; instr. Long Beach (Calif.) City Coll., 1970-72, Immaculate Heart Coll., Hollywood, Calif., 1971-74, U. Judaism, Hollywood, 1973-74; co-coord. Community Sch. Performing Arts, LA, 1974-82, instr., 1973-83; pvt. piano tchr. Manhattan Beach, Calif., from 1963; asst. tchr. aide gifted and talented edn. program GATE, Manhattan Beach, Calif., 1990—91. Tchr. Etz Jacob Hebrew Acad., L.A., 1991-95, Ohr Eliyahu Acad., Culver City, 1995-96; peer counselor Beach Cities Health Dist., 1997-2005. Performer Pratt Inst., Clinton Hill Symphony, N.Y.C., 1962, Sta. WNYC-FM, 1964. Chair Cultural Arts Com., Manhattan Beach, 1985-86; bd. dirs. Hermosa Beach (Calif.) Community Ctr., 1990-91. Mem. Nat. Fedn. Music Clubs (adjudicator 1970). Home: Manhattan Beach, Calif. Died Jan. 17, 2009.

RILEY, HARRIS DEWITT, JR., pediatrician, medical educator; b. Clarksdale, Miss., Nov. 12, 1924; s. Harris DeWitt and Louise (Allen) R.; m. Margaret Barry, Sept. 16, 1950; children: Steven Allen, Mark Barry, Margaret Ruth. BA, Vanderbilt U., 1945, MD, 1948. Intern Balt. City Hosps., Johns Hopkins Hosp., 1948-49; resident in pediatrics Babies and Children's Hosp., Case Western Res. U., Cleve., 1949-50, Vanderbilt U. Hosp., 1950-51; instr., fellow in pediatrics and infectious diseases Vanderbilt U. Med. Sch., 1953-57; prof. pediatrics, chmn. dept. U. Okla. Med. Sch., from 1958; med. dir. Children's Meml. Hosp., from 1972; disting. prof. pediatrics U. Okla., 1976; prof. pediatrics Vanderbilt U. Sch. of Medicine, Nashville, from 1991. Served as capt. M.C. USAF, 1951-53. Died Mar. 26, 2010.

RINGEL, FRED MORTON, lawyer; b. Brunswick, Ga., July 19, 1929; s. Phil S. and Louise (Pfeiffer) R.; m. Toby Markowitz, Mar. 18, 1962; children: Andrew Franklin, Douglas Eric, Michael Stanley, Edrea Janet Piper. AB, U. Ga., 1950; LL.B. magna cum laude, Harvard U., 1955. Bar: Ga. 1951, Fla. 1955, N.Y. 1956. Research asst. Am. Law Inst., NYC, 1955-56; assoc. firm Cravath, Swaine & Moore, NYC, 1956-59; atty. W.R. Grace & Co., NYC, 1959-60; mem. firm Rogers, Towers, Bailey, Jones & Gay, P.A., Jacksonville, Fla., from 1961, also treas. Contbr. articles to legal jours. Bd. govs. Fla. Nature Conservancy, 1962-69. Served with USAF, 1951-53; 1t. Col. Res. Recipient Oak Leaf award Nature Conservancy, 1974 Mem. Am. Bar Assn., Am. Law Inst., Phi Beta Kappa. Home: Jacksonville, Fla. Died June 26, 2010.

RINK, WESLEY WINFRED, retired bank executive; b. Hickory, NC, June 14, 1922; s. Dewey Lee and Mabel E. (Yount) R.; m. Patricia A. Jones, Aug. 19, 2000; children from previous marriage: Rebecca S., Christopher L BS in Accountancy, U. Ill., 1947, MS, 1948. Acct., Glidden Co., Chgo., 1948-58; adminstrv. mgr. Central Soya Co., Chgo., 1958-65; v.p., comptroller State Nat. Bank, Evanston, Ill., 1965-71; exec. v.p., dir. Pioneer Trust & Savs. Bank, Chgo., 1971-76; corp. v.p. Exchange Bancorp., Inc., Tampa, 1977-82; sr. v.p. NCNB Nat. Bank Fla., Tampa, 1982-86; fin cons. Temple Terrace, Fla., 1986-2001; ret., 2001. Served to capt. USAAF, 1942—46. Home: Temple Terrace, Fla. Died Sept. 4, 2009.

RINSLEY, JACQUELINE ANN, nurse; b. Chgo., Apr. 5, 1933; d. John Lancelot and Margaret Elizabeth (Zeilinger) Louk; student Washington U., St. Louis, 1951-52; diploma in nursing St. Luke's Hosp. Sch. Nursing, 1955. Psychiat. nurse Topeka State Hosp., 1955-56, sect. head nurse, 1955-56; gen. and pediatric nurse St. John's Hosp., Springfield, Mo., 1956-57, Burge Hosp., 1957-58; head pediatric nurse Stormont-Vail Hosp., Topeka, 1958-60; psychiat. nurse Kans. Neurol. Inst., Topeka, 1960-70, adminstr., 1970-80, dir. nursing edn., 1980-82; legal sec. Dist. Atty.'s Office, 1984—. Mem. Zeta Tau Alpha. Republican. Lutheran. Home: Carmel, Ind. Died Feb. 1, 2009.

RIOS, EVELYN DEERWESTER, columnist, musician, artist, writer; b. Payne, Ohio, June 25, 1916; d. Jay Russell and Flossie Edith (Fell) Deerwester; m. Edwin Tietjen Rios, Sept. 19, 1942 (dec. Feb. 1987); children: Jane Evelyn, Linda Sue Rios Stahlman. BA with honors, San Jose State U., 1964, MA, 1968. Cert. elem., secondary tchr. Calif. Lectr. in music San Jose (Calif.) State U., 1969-75; from bilingual cons. to assoc. editor Ednl. Factors, Inc., San Jose, 1969-76, mgr. field rsch., 1977-78; writer, editor Calif. MediCorps Program, 1978-85; contbg. editor, illustrator Cmty. Family Mag., Wimberly, Tex., 1983-85; columnist The Springer, Dripping Springs, Tex., 1985-90. Author, illustrator, health instr. textbooks elem. schs., 1980—82. Author: The Best of It Seems To Me, 2002. Chmn. Dripping Springs Planning and Zoning Commn., 1991—93; music dir. Cambrian Park (Calif.) Meth. Ch., 1961—64; choir dir. Bethel Luth. Ch., Cupertino, Calif., 1965—66, 1968—83; dir. music St. Aban's Ch., Bogota, Colombia; organist Holy Spirit Episcopal Ch., Dripping Springs, 1987—94. Mem.: Am. Guild Organists (dean 1963—64), Phi Kappa Phi (pres. San Jose chpt. 1973—74). Avocations: weaving, stitching, painting. Home: Atascadero, Calif. Died Mar. 3, 2010.

RIPLEY, EDWARD FRANKLIN, investment company executive; b. Cohasset, Mass., June 26, 1927; s. Sheldon Nichols Ripley and Marguerite (Albertson) Giles; m. Elizabeth Robertson Tucker, Dec. 19, 1964; children: Peter Hobart, Elizabeth Stockton. BA, Lafayette Coll., 1950; MA, Columbia U., 1953; cert. Sch. of Banking of South, La. State U., 1961. Sr. investment officer Mfrs. Hanover Bank, N.Y.C., 1953-57, Va. Nat. Bank, Norfolk, 1957-61; v.p. Studley, Shupert & Co., Phila., 1961-69; pres. Resource Mgmt. Group, Phila., 1969-72; v.p. First Pa. Bank, Phila., 1972-79; adj. prof. Phila. Coll. Textiles and Sci., 1979-91; v.p. Gruntal & Co./E.W. Smith, Phila., 1979-82, Legg, Mason, Wood, Walker, Inc., Phila., 1982-91; v.p. Walnut Asset Mgmt. Inc., Phila., 1991—; cons. Educator Mut. Life Ins. Co., Lancaster, Pa., 1972—, Cigna Corp., Phila., 1980-82, Oppenheimer Capital Corp., N.Y.C., 1981, Meridian Bancorp., Reading, Pa., 1984-85. Vestryman, St. Martin-in-the-Fields Episcopal Ch., Phila., 1980; treas. Voyage House, Phila., 1983; bd. dirs. All Saints Hosp. and Springfield Retirement Home, Phila., Planned Parenthood of Pa.; convener, Ea. Pa. Episc. Synod of Am. Fellow Fin. Analysts Fedn.; mem. Phila. Securities Assn., Mayflower Soc., Soc. Colonial Wars, Mil. Order Fgn. Wars. Republican. Avocations: tennis; tree farming; hiking. Home: Philadelphia, Pa. Died Mar. 16, 2009.

RISCH, MARTIN DONALD, marketing-management consulting company executive; b. Bklyn., Oct. 7, 1929; s. Rene and Lillian (Grant) R.; m. Joan Nattrass, Dec. 26, 1955; children: Lillian, David. BA, Colgate U., 1951; MBA, Harvard U., 1955. Dir. mktg. devel. Riegel Paper Co., NYC, 1950-60, Fitchburg (N.Y.) Paper Co., 1960-64; dir. planning speciality paper div. Litton Industries, Fitchburg, 1965-69, 70-71, v.p. planning paper printing div., 1971-76; pres. Lincoln Assocs., Lexington, Mass., from 1976. 1st lt. USAF, 1951-53, Korea. Mem. TAPPI, Graphic Arts Tech. Found., Packaging Internat., Harvard Club, Oak Hill Country Club. Home: Port Angeles, Wash. Died June 22, 2009.

RITSCHEL, WOLFGANG ADOLF, medical educator, sculptor, artist; b. Trautenau, Bohemia, Jan. 10, 1933; came to U.S., 1968; s. Karl and Eleonore (Olbert) R.; m. Ingrid M. Wallner, Aug. 5, 1991; children from previous marriage: Alexander, Barbara. Mr.Pharm., U. Innsbruck, Austria, 1955; Dr.Univ., U. Strasbourg, France, 1960; PhD, U. Vienna, Austria, 1965; MD, U. Villarreal, Peru, 1989. Chief pharmacist Girol AG, Zurich, Switzerland, 1958-59; head pharmacy rsch. Biochemie AG, Kundl, Austria, 1959-61; seminar docent Teaching Hosp., Kufstein, Austria, 1959-61; head rsch. Albert David Rsch. Inst., Dacca, Pakistan, 1961-64; prof. Dacca U., 1961-64, U. Basel, Switzerland, 1965-68, U. Cin., 1969-97, prof. emeritus, from 1997. Divsn. head U. Cin., 1985-94; vis. prof. Med. Acad. Krakow, Univ. Clermont-Ferrand, S. Marcos, Lima. Author: The Tablet, 1966, Applied Biopharmaceutics, 1973, Laboratory Manual of Biopharmaceutics and Pharmacokinetics, 1974, Handbook of Basic Pharmacokinetics, 6th revised edit., 2004, Graphic Approach to Clinical Pharmacokinetics, 1993, 2d edit., 1994, Japenese edit., 1998, Antacids and Other Drugs in GI Diseases, 1984, Gerontokinetics, 1988, Japanese edit., 1994, (with Betzien, Kaufmann and Schneider) KINPAK: A Comprehensive Approach to Evaluating Blood Level Curves, 1985, (with Koch) Synopsis der Biopharmazie und Pharmkokinetik, 1986; editor: Clinical Pharmacokinetics: Proceedings of An International Symposium at Salzgitter-Ringelheim, 1977, (with Bauer-Brandl) Die Tablette, 2003, Wolfgang A. Ritschel - The Other Life, 1999; contbr. more than 450 articles to profl. jours., 28 chpts. to books; 23 patents in field; numerous solo and group exhbns. of paintings and sculptures in U.S. and Europe, including Internat. Biennale, Florence, Italy 2005; (travel exhbn.) Learned in Science, Explored in Art, 2009-. Recipient Theodor-Koerner prize Austria Ministry of Edn., 1962, Cross of Honor, Pres. Fedn. Republic Austria, 1975, numerous art awards; named Hon. Prof. U. San Marcos, 1973, U. Cayetano Heredia, 1979; Hon. Senator U. Pisa, 1978; Fulbright sr. scholar, 1993, 1996; named to Internat. Order of Merit, Cambridge, 1993. Fellow Am. Coll. Clin. Pharmacology, Am. Assn. Pharm. Scientists; mem. Acad. Am. Pharm. Assn., Fedn. Internat. Pharm., Royal Acad. Sci. (Spain), Acad. of Sci. (hon.). Roman Catholic. Home: Cincinnati, Ohio. Died Feb. 23, 2010.

RIVKIN, WILLIAM B., medical physicist; b. Latvia, Jan. 6, 1921; arrived in US, 1931; s. Oscar W. and Fannie Mary Rivkin; m. Dolores Yolanda Rivkin; children: Francine, Debra Rivkin Haggarty. BSEE, Ill. Inst. Tech., 1945; postgrad., Northwestern U., Evanston, Ill., 1960—61. V.p., gen. mgr. Health Physics Assoc., Northbrook, Ill., 1959—86, Isotope Measurements Labs., 1969—87, Mobile Imaging, Inc., 1970—93; physicist Vets. Adminstrn. Hosp., Hines, 1961—75; health physicist U. Ill., Chgo., 1970—76; CEO Medx, Inc., Wooddale, 1993—98, Arlington Heights, 2003—07. Field engr. Tracerlab, Inc., Boston, 1953—57; criticality engr. Westinghouse Electric Co., Cheswick, Pa., 1957—58; cons. Imaging Concepts, Inc., Highland Park, Ill., 1980—2003. Contbr. chapters to books. Bd. dirs. Northbrook Symphony Orch., 1980—2003, Am. Nuc. Soc., Washington, 1980—85. With Signal Corps. US Army, 1940—42. Mem.: Am. Assn. Physics in Medicine (com. mem. from 1965), Soc. Nuc. Medicine (com. mem. from 1970), Health Physics Soc. (pres. 1970—74), Rotary. Democrat. Jewish. Avocations: sailing, travel. Died Apr. 16, 2010.

ROBB, JAMES WILLIS, Romance languages educator; b. Jamaica, NY, June 27, 1918; s. Stewart Everts and Clara Johanna (Mohrmann) R.; m. Cecilia Uribe-Noguera, 1972 (dec. 2004) Student, Inst. de Touraine, Sorbonne, 1937-38; BA cum laude, Colgate U., 1939; postgrad., U. Nacional de Mex., 1948; MA, Middlebury Coll., 1950; PhD, Cath. U. Am., 1958. Instr. romance langs. Norwich U., 1946-50; from asst. prof. to prof. romance langs. George Washington U., Washington, 1950-88, prof. emeritus, 1988—2004. Corr. mem. Academia Mexicana de la Lengua, 1998. Author: El Estilo de Alfonso Reyes, 1965, 78, Repertorio Bibliográfico de Alfonso Reyes, 1974, Prosa y Poesía de Alfonso Reyes, 1975, 84, Estudios sobre Alfonso Reyes, 1976, Por los Caminos de Alfonso Reyes, 1981, Imágenes de América en Alfonso Reyes y en Germán Arciniegas, 1990, Más Páginas Sobre Alfonso Reyes, 1996-97; contbr. articles to profl. jours. With USNR, 1942—44, Brazil, with USNR, 1944—46, PTO. Recipient Alfonso Reyes Internat. Lit. prize, 1978; Lit. Diploma of Merit, State of Nuevo León and City of Monterrey, Mex., 1979; OAS grantee, 1964; Am. Philos. Soc. grantee, 1977 Mem. MLA, Internat. Assn. Ibero-Am. Lit., Am. Assn. Tchrs. Spanish and Portuguese, Assn. Colombianistas, Phi Beta Kappa. Home: Washington, DC. Died June 27, 2010.

ROBENALT, JOHN ALTON, lawyer; b. Ottawa, Ohio, May 2, 1922; s. Alton Ray and Kathryn (Straman) R.; m. Margaret Morgan Durbin, Aug. 25, 1951 (dec. July 1990); children: John F., William A., James D., Robert M., Mary K., Margaret E., Thomas D.; m. Nancy Leech Kidder, Sept. 21, 1991. BA, Miami U., 1943; LL.B., JD, Ohio State U., 1948. Bar: Ohio 1948. Asst. atty. gen., Ohio, 1949-51; practice in Lima, Ohio, 1951-59; acting municipal judge Lima Municipal Ct., 1955-59; partner Robenalt, Daley, Balyeat & Balyeat, 1959-82; ptnr. Robenalt, Kendall & Robenalt, 1983-85, Robenalt, Kendall, Rodabaugh & Staley, 1985-92, Robenalt & Robenalt, from 1993. Chmn. Lima March of Dimes, 1957-58; Bd. dirs. Lima Civic Center, pres., 1971-72; bd. dirs. Lima Rotating Fund; trustee Allen County Regional Transit Authority, Lima, pres., 1975—. Served with AUS, 1943-45. Mem. ABA, Ohio Bar Assn., Allen County Bar Assn. (pres. 1969-70), Am. Legion, Lima Automobile Club (bd. dirs., pres. 1975-82), Shawnee Country Club (pres. 1968-70), Ohio Automobile Club (trustee 1982-2002, chmn. 1995-97), Elks (bd. trustees 1991-97), Rotary, Delta Tau Delta, Phi Delta Phi. Home: Lima, Ohio. Died Oct. 5, 2009.

ROBERTS, BOBBY GENE, protective service official; b. Bristol, Va., Sept. 5, 1941; s. Robert Dale and Rowena Mae (Shull) Roberts; m. Patsy Barger, Oct. 22, 1965; 1 child, David Allen. Student, East Tenn. State U., 1963, Va. State Police Acad. Asst. mgr. Inter-Mountain Telephone Co., Abingdon, Va., 1961—63; fireman Bristol Fire Dept., 1963; police lt. Bristol Police Dept., from 1963; v.p. Southeastern Security Inc., Bristol, from 1984. Active mem. Radiol. Emergency Preparedness, Bristol Va. Life Saving Crew, Bristol Crl. Little League Baseball. Recipient Police Officer of Yr. award, Bristol Jaycees, 1972, 1976, Officer Appreciation award, Bristol Police Aux., 1979. Mem.: Va. Assn. Drug Enforcement Officers, Va. Security Assn. (state v.p. 1985—86), Tri State Crime Clinic. Democrat. Presbyterian. Avocation: carpentry. Died May 25, 2009.

ROBERTS, BURTON BENNETT, lawyer, retired judge; b. NYC, July 25, 1922; s. Alfred S. and Cecelia (Schanfein) R.; m. Gerhild Ukryn, 1982 BA, NYU, 1943, LL.M., 1953; LL.B., Cornell U., 1949. Bar: NY 1949. Asst. dist. atty. NY County (Manhattan), 1949-66; chief asst. dist. atty. Bronx County, Bronx, NY, 1966-68, acting dist. atty., 1968-69, dist. atty., 1969-72; justice Supreme Ct. NY, 1973-98, adminstrv. judge criminal br. Bronx County 12th Jud. Dist., 1984-98, adminstrv. judge civil br. Bronx County 12th Dist., 1988-98; ret., 1998; counsel Fischbein, Badillo, Wagner & Harding, 1999—2005, Dreier LLP, 2005—10. Pres. Bronx div. Hebrew Home for Aged, 1967-72. With US Army, 1943-45. Decorated Purple Heart, Bronze Star with oak leaf cluster, Combat Infantry badge Mem. Assn. Bar City NY, Am. Bar Assn., NY Bar Assn., Bronx County Bar Assn., NY State Dist. Attys. Assn. (pres. 1971-72) Jewish (exec. bd. temple). Home: New York, NY. Died Oct. 24, 2010.

ROBERTS, MORRIS HENRY, JR., marine biology educator; b. Mt. Kisco, NY, Jan. 15, 1940; s. Morris Henry and Catherine (Pearsall) R.; m. Beverly Ann Martin, Apr. 22, 1963; 1 child, Jean Marie. BA, Kenyon Coll., 1962; MA, Coll. William & Mary, 1965, PhD, 1969. Asst. prof. Providence Coll., 1969-71; dir. invertebrate studies Aquatic Scis. Inc., Boca Raton, Fla., 1971-73, dir. rsch., 1973; assoc. marine scientist Va. Inst. Marine Sci., Gloucester Point, Va., 1973-80, sr. marine scientist, 1980-87; prof. marine sci. Va. Inst. Marine Sci., Coll. William and Mary Sch. Marine Sci., Gloucester Point, from 1987, chmn. dept. environ. sci., from 1994. Co-editor: Water Chlorination, vol. 5, 1985, Chemistry, Environmental Impact and Health Effects; contbr. articles to profl. jours. Pres. Gloucester Choral Soc., 1979-81; chmn. Bd. of Parish Edn., Emmanuel Lutheran Ch., Hampton, Va., 1986-89. Mem. ASTM (Phila. E47.07 sec. biostatics subcom. 1987—, E47.01 chmn. aquatic toxicology subcom. 1989—, Exceptional Svc. award 1993), Am. Soc. Limnology and Oceanography, Nat. Shellfish Assn., World Aquaculture Soc., Soc. Environ. Toxicol. and Chem. Home: Gloucester Point, Va. Died Nov. 11, 2009.

ROBERTS, PERNELL, actor; b. Waycross, Ga., May 18, 1928; m. Kara Knack; 1 son, Christopher (dec. 1991) Student, U. Md. Appeared in summer stock theater, making profl. debut in The Man Who Came to Dinner, Olney (Md.) Theater; actor, Arena Stage, Washington, 1950; appeared in off-Broadway prodns. including Am. Lyric Theatre, Shakespearewrights Co.; Broadway debut in Tonight in Samarkand, 1953; Broadway appearances include A Clearing in the Woods; appeared in summer tours of The King and I; musical version of Gone with the Wind, Los Angeles Civic Light Opera; toured in: musical version of The Music Man; appeared on TV series Bonanza, 1959-65, Trapper John, M.D, 1979-86; appeared in mini-series Captains and Kings, 1976; film appearances include The Magic of Lassie, Centennial, 1978, The Immigrants, 1978, Night Rider, 1979, Hot Rod, 1979, High Noon: Part II, 1980, Incident at Crest Ridge, 1981, TV film Charlie Cobb: Nice Night for a Hanging, Perry Mason: The Case of the All Star Assassin, 1989; host TV series, FBI: The Untold Stories, 1991. Served with USMR. Recipient Drama Desk award for role in Macbeth 1955. Home: Malibu, Calif. Died Jan. 24, 2010.

ROBERTS, ROBERT RAYMOND, engineering educator; b. Willacoochee, Ga., Jan. 17, 1933; s. Owen Russell and Gladys Merle (Gaskins) R.; m. Gail Elizabeth Woodard, June 17, 1959; children— Lisa Gail, Jennifer Lee. B.C.E., Ga. Tech. Inst., 1956, M.S.C.E., 1963; Ph.D., W.Va. U., 1975. Sr. designer Ga. Hwy. Dept., Tifton, 1956-60; assoc. engr. Wilbur Smith & Assocs., Columbia, S.C., 1962-65; asst. prof. U.S.C., Columbia, 1965-70, assoc. prof., 1973—. Served with U.S. Army, 1958-59. NSF grantee, 1967; UMTA fellow, 1970; Nat. Hwy Inst. grantee, 1980. Mem. Inst. Transp. Engrs., Transp. Research Bd., Soc. Automotive Engrs., Nat. Soc. Profl. Engrs., Nat. Acad. Forensic Engrs., Am. Acad. Forensic Scis., Sigma Xi, Chi Epsilon. Contbr. articles to profl. jours. Home: Columbia, SC. Died July 14, 2010.

ROBERTS, SHEILA VALERIE, literature and language professor; b. Johannesburg, May 25, 1942; d. Gideon Peter Williamson and Clara Matilda Freestone; m. Reynhold Lucius Zammit (div.); m. Arthur Edward James Roberts, Jan. 17, 1963 (dec.); children: Ethelwyn Leonora, Kelly, Sandra. BA, U. S. Africa, 1965, BA (hon.), 1968, MA, 1972; LittD, U. Pretoir, 1977. Asst. prof. English Mich. State U., East Lansing, assoc. prof. English, prof. English, U. Wis., Milw., from 1986. External examiner U. Cape Town, Cape, South Africa, U. Wits, Johannesburg; creative writing coord. UWM; vis. prof. Justus Liebig U., Giessen, Germany, 1989, U. Tsukuba, Ibaraki, Japan, 1994—96. Author: (book) Outside Life's Feast, 1975, Dan Jacobson, 1984, Purple Yams, 2001. Recipient Olive Schreiner award, English Acad. South Africa, 1975, Milw. Arts Coun. Fiction award, Wis., 1991, Wis. Writers Short Fiction award, 1992. Mem.: Modern Lang. Assn., Can. Assn. Commonwealth Studies, African Studies. Democrat. Catholic. Avocation: piano. Home: Edwardsburg, Mich. Died Aug. 11, 2009.

ROBERTS, THOMAS HUMPHREY, JR., agricultural research company executive; b. DeKalb, Ill., May 23, 1924; s. Thomas Humphrey and Eleanor (Townsend) R.; m. Nancy Jean Barker, Mar. 12, 1974; children by previous marriage: Thomas Humphrey III, Catherine Roberts Tosh, Susan Shawn, Michael Joseph BS, Iowa State U., 1949; MBA, Harvard U., 1955. With DeKalb AgResearch, Inc. (name changed to DeKalb Corp.), exec. v.p., 1961-62, pres., 1961-85, chmn. bd., 1967-88, former chief exec. officer, also dir., chmn. exec. com., from 1988. Dir. Internat. Minerals & Chem. Corp., Continental Ill. Nat. Bank & Trust Co. Bd. visitors Harvard U. Bus. Sch.; trustee Rush-Presbyn.-St. Luke's Med. Ctr., other agys. Served with USAAF. Died Sept. 12, 2009.

ROBERTSON, HARRY STEVENS, retired mechanical engineer; b. Pitts., Sept. 12, 1931; s. Harry Stevens and Sherley Eloise (Hurlbut) Robertson; m. Carolyn Margaret Young, Oct. 10, 1976. BS, Purdue U., 1953. Profl. engr., Ohio. Foreman Continental Can Co., Elwood, Ind., 1953-57; mfg. engr. Western Electric Co., Indpls., 1957-66, Globe Industries, Dayton, Ohio, 1966-72, Detroit Aluminum & Brass, Bellefontaine, Ohio, 1972-76; cons. engr. H.A. Williams Assoc., Columbus, Ohio, from 1976. Served in USAF, 1954-56. Mem. Am. Inst. Plant Engrs. (pres. 1985), Masons. Avocations: sailing, radio controlled model boats. Home: Clearwater, Fla. Died Mar. 7, 2009.

ROBINSON, JAMES KENNETH, federal official; b. Grand Rapids, Mich., Nov. 27, 1943; s. Kenneth and Marguerite (Anderson) R.; m. Marietta Sebree; children: Steven James, Renee Elizabeth. BA with honors, Mich. State U., 1965; JD magna cum laude, Wayne State U., 1968. Bar: Mich. 1968, U.S. Dist. Ct. (ea. and we. dists) Mich. 1969, U.S. Ct. Appeals (6th cir.) 1969, U.S. Supreme Ct. 1977. Law clk. to judge U.S. Ct. Appeals (6th cir.), 1968-69; assoc. Miller, Canfield, Paddock & Stone, Detroit, 1969-71; from assoc. to ptnr. Honigman Miller Schwartz and Cohn, Detroit, 1972-77, ptnr., 1981-93, chmn. litigation dept.; U.S. atty. Ea. Dist. Mich., 1977-80; adj. prof. Wayne State U. Law Sch., Detroit, 1973-84, dean, prof., 1993-98, prof., from 2001; asst. atty. gen. criminal divsn. U.S. Dept. Justice, Washington, 1998-2001. Adj. prof. Detroit Coll. Law, 1970-73; mem. evidence test drafting com.-multistate bar exam Nat. Conf. Bar Examiners, 1975—; mem. adv. com. on evidence rules Jud. Conf. U.S., 1993-98; chmn. com. on rules of evidence Mich. Supreme Ct., 1975-78; lectr. Mich. Jud. Inst., 1977-98, Mich. Inst. CLE. Author: (with others) Introducing Evidence-A Practical Guide for Michigan Lawyers, 1988, Scope of Discovery, 1986, Michigan Court Rules Practice-Evidence, 1996, Courtroom Handbook on Michigan Evidence, 1997; contbg. author Emerging Problems Under the Federal Rules of Evidence, 3d edit., 1998; contbr. articles to profl. jours.; editor in chief Wayne Law Rev., 1967-68. Chmn. Gov.'s Commn. on Future Higher Edn. in Mich., 1983-84; pres. State Bar of Mich., 1990-91, commr. 1980-81, 83-91. Recipient Disting. Alumni award Wayne State U. Law Sch., 1979, 1986. Fellow Am. Bar Found., Mich. Bar Found., Am. Coll. Trial Lawyers, Internat. Soc. Barristers, Am. Acad. of Appellate Lawyers; mem. ABA (litigation and criminal justice sects., lectr.), Fed. Bar Assn. (dir. 1975-81), Nat. Assn. Former U.S. Attys. (pres. 1984-85), Am. Law Inst., 6th Cir. Jud. Conf., Wayne U. Law Alumni Assn. (pres. 1975-76), Detroit Athletic Club. Home: Metamora, Mich. Died Aug. 6, 2010.

ROBINSON, JOHN BECKWITH, development management consultant; b. Portland, Oreg., May 23, 1922; s. Jewell King and Arvilla Agnes (Beckwith) R.; m. Dilys Walters, Sept. 8, 1945; children— John Gwilym, David Gwyn. BA, U. Oreg., 1944; postgrad., U. Shrivenham, Eng., 1945, U. Oxford, 1946, Am. U., 1947. Staff U.S. Bur. Budget, 1947—48; sr. program and budget officer UNESCO, 1948—51; mem. staff U.S. Bur. Budget, 1951—52; chief personnel policy Mut. Security Agy., Washington, 1952-54, program officer Guatemala, 1954-59, planning officer, later acting asst. dep. dir. for program and planning AID Washington, 1959-61; dep. U.S. rep. devel. assistance com. OECD, 1961-64, asst. dir. devel. policy Pakistan, 1964-68; dep. dir. North Coast Affairs, AID, State Dept., Washington, 1969-71; dep. mission dir. U.S. Econ. Aid Program, Colombia, 1971-73, mission dir. Dominican Republic, 1973-76, mission dir. Honduras, 1976—79; privatization adviser Gov. of Costa Rica, 1986-88; prin. assoc. J.B. Robinson & Assocs. (devel. mgmt. cons.), from 1979. Mem. faculty, fellow Harvard U., 1968-69; cons. NATO, 1951, UN, 1951. Served to 1st lt., inf. AUS, 1943-46, ETO. Recipient Knight Commdr., Order Morazan, Republic Honduras, 1979. Mem. Oriental Club (London), DACOR BACON House (Washington), Minchinhampton Probus Club (pres. 1983-84). Episcopalian. Died Dec. 2009.

ROBINSON, MARGUERITE STERN, anthropologist, educator, consultant; b. NYC, Oct. 11, 1935; d. Philip Van Doren and Lillian (Diamond) Stern; m. Allan Richard Robinson, June 12, 1955 (dec. Sept. 25, 2009); children: Sarah Penelope, Perrine, Laura Ondine. BA, Radcliffe Coll., 1956; PhD, Harvard U., 1965. Assoc. scholar Radcliffe Inst. for Advanced Studies, Cambridge, Mass., 1964-65; asst. prof. anthology Brandeis U., 1965-72, assoc. prof., 1972-78, prof., 1978-85, dean Coll. Arts and Scis., 1973-75; assoc. fellow Inst. Internat. Devel. Harvard U., Cambridge, 1978—79, fellow Inst. Internat. Devel., 1980-85, inst. fellow Inst. Internat. Devel., 1985-2000, inst. fellow emeritus Inst. Internat. Devel., from 2000; dir. Cultural Survival Inc., 1981-99, Am. Inst. Indian Studies, Chgo., 1977—2000, chmn., 1983-84; faculty mem. Microfinance Tng. Program, Boulder, Colo. and Turin, Italy, 1995—2010. Bd. dirs. MasterCard Found., from 2006, Equity Bank Found., Kenya, from 2006, Boulder Inst. Microfinance, from 2008; coun. advisors Ctr. Fin. Inclusion, Accion Internat.; cons. in field. Author: Political Structure in a Changing Sinhalese Village, 1975, Local Politics: The Law of the Fishes, 1988, Pembiayaan Pertanian Pedesaan, 1993, The Microfinance Revolution, Vol. 1: Sustainable Finance for the Poor, 2001, Vol. 2: Lessons from Indonesia, 2002, Mobilizing Savings from the Public: Basic Principles and Practices, 2005, The Future of the Commercial Microfinance Industry in Asia, 2005, Commercial Microfinance and Employment in Developing Countries, 2005; contbg. author: Cambridge Papers in Social Anthropology 3, 1962, Cambridge Papers in Social Anthropology 5, 1968, Enterprises for the Recycling and Composting of Municipal Solid Waste, 1993, The New World of Microenterprise Finance, 1994, New Perspectives on Financing Small Business in Developing Countries, 1995, Assisting Development in a Changing World, 1997, New World of Microfinance, 1997, Agricultural Development in the Third World, 1998, Strategic Issues in Microfinance, 1998, Microfinance: Conversations with the Experts, 1999, Microbanking: Creating Opportunities for the Poor Through Innovation, 2005, Transforming Microfinance Institutions, 2006; The Mzanzi Bank Account Initiative in South Africa, 2009; contbr. articles to profl. jours. Mem. internat. coun. advisors Calmeadow Found., 1996-2000; pres. Greatest Gift Corp. Fellow NIH, 1964-65; grantee NSF, 1966-70, Ford Found., 1972-74, 79, Calmeadow Found., 1994; fellow Indo-Am. Fellowship Program-Indo-U.S. Subcommn. on Edn. and Culture, 1976-77, Am. Inst. Indian Studies, 1976-77; grantee Calmeadow Found., 1994, Disting. Svc. award, Martindale Ctr. Lehigh U., 2010. Fellow Soc. Bunting Inst. Fellows; mem. Assn. Asian Studies, India Internat. Centre. Died Sept. 25, 2009.

ROCHE, JOHN THOMAS, business executive; b. NYC, June 6, 1932; s. Thomas P. and Helen C. (Paulakovic) R.; m. Claire Ten Eyck, Sept. 12, 1955; children: Bradley, Kevin, Bryan. BBA, St. John's U., 1953. With Kidder, Peabody & Co., Inc., NYC, from 1955, asst. treas., 1965-67, v.p., 1975-82, exec. v.p., chief operating officer, from 1982. Dir. Depository Trust Co. Served with U.S. Army, 1953-55. Mem.: Huntington Country, Huntington Crescent; Westhampton Country (N.Y.). Died Jan. 19, 2009.

RODALE, ARDATH HARTER, retired publishing executive; m. Bob Rodale (dec. 1990); children: Maria, Anthony, Heather, Heidi, Davis(dec.). B in Art Edn., Kutztown U., LLD (hon.), 1995; LHD (hon.), DeSales U., 1994, Lehigh U., 1994; HHD (hon.), New Coll. of Calif., San Francisco, 2006. Chmn. Prevention Mag., Rodale Press, Inc., 1990—2007; owner, CEO Rodale Press Inc., Emmaus, Pa., 1990—2002, chief inspiration officer, 2007—09. Chmn. emeritus on the bd. Rodale Inst. Author: Climbing Toward the Light, 1989, Gifts of the Spirit, 1997, Reflections: Finding, Love, Hope and Joy in Everyday Life, 2002. Mem. internat. adv. com. Harvard AIDS Inst. Recipient Outstanding Alumni award, Kutztown U., 1990, Human Rels. award, Allentown Human Rels. Commn., 1995, Extraordinary Voices award, Mothers' Voices, 1996, Woman of Distinction award, Great Valley Girl Scout Coun., 1998, Friend of Lehigh award, Lehigh U., 2002, Lifetime Cmty. Achievement award, Boys & Girls Club of Allentown, 2002, Shining Star award, St. Luke's Hosp., Allentown, 2003, Life & Breath award, Am. Lung Assn., 2003, Exceptional Woman award, Women in Periodical Pub., 2004, LifePath's Cmty. Svc. award, Pa. Inst. of CPA's, 2004, Cir. of Excellence - Enlightened Media award, Internat. Furnishings & Design Assn., 2005, Lehigh Valley Coalition for Alt. Transp. award, 2006; named a Disting. Daughter of Pa., Gov. Tom Ridge, 1997; named one of 50 Best Women in Bus. in Pa., Ctrl. Pa. Bus. Jour., 1996, Top 50 Women Bus. Owners in the US, Working Woman mag., 1997, 50 Leading Women Entrepreneurs in the World, Star Group, 1999. Died Dec. 18, 2009.

ROENIGK, MARTIN ALLEN, insurance company executive; b. Cleve., Sept. 19, 1942; s. Henry Herman and Irene Lena (Rini) Roenigk; m. Elise Feutz, July 5, 1965. BA, Antioch Coll., 1965; MBA, U. Chgo., 1967. CPA Conn. Staff auditor Arthur Andersen & Co., Cleve., 1968; with Travelers Ins. Co., Hartford, Conn., 1970—80, v.p., from 1980. Editor (pub.): MBS News Bull, from 1976. Pres. Greater Middletown Preservation Trust, Conn., 1981, trustee Conn., from 1978; mem. Rep. Town Com., from 1981. With US Army, 1968—70. Mem.: Am. Inst. CPAs, Musical Box Soc. (trustee). Died June 18, 2009.

ROGERS, BENJAMIN TALBOT, mechanical engineer, consultant; b. Cleve., Oct. 4, 1920; s. Benjamin Talbot and Marie Aline (Miller) Rogers; m. Dale Hays, Sept. 11, 1961 (dec. Nov. 1975); children: Leslie, Phyllis. BSME, U. Wis., 1944. Registered profl. engr., N.Mex, Colo., Ariz., Tex. Mech. engr. Black & Veatch, Kansas City, Mo., 1946-49; staff mem. U. Calif., Los Alamos, N.Mex., 1949-76; cons. engring. Los Alamos, N.Mex., 1949-76, Embudo, N.Mex, 1976-80, 81-2000; ret., 2000. Vis. prof. Ariz. State U., 1980—81, 1984; v.p. Barkmann & Rogers Cons. Engrs., Santa Fe, 1964—70. One-man shows include Millicent Rogers Mus., Taos, N.Mex, 1994, Roller Mill Mus., Cleveland, N.Mex, 1995, Ariz. State U. Coll. Architecture, Tempe, 1996, First State Bank Taos, 1997 (Artist of the Month, 1997), Johnson Gallery, Madrid, N.Mex, 1998—99; contbr. articles to tech. and profl. jours. Commr. Rinconada Cmty. Acequia, Embudo, 1961—70; v.p. adv. bd. Embudo Presbyn. Hosp., 1972; pres. Embudo Valley Health Found., 1974. 1st lt. C.E. US Army, 1942—46. Recipient Solar Design award, HUD, Dept. Energy, Solar Energy Rsch. Inst., 1978, Peter van Dresser award, N.Mex Solar Energy Assn., 1983, Maharishi award, Maharishi Found., 1984; grantee, Graham Found. Advanced Studies Fine Arts, 1992, 1995. Fellow: ASHRAE; mem.: NSPE (life), ASME (life), Nat. Assn. Scholars, Am. Soc. Materials (life), Celtic Confederation (founding sec. 2000—03). Republican. Achievements include patents in field. Home: Highlands Ranch, Colo. Died Apr. 4, 2009.

ROGERS, EUGENE JACK, retired medical educator; b. Vienna, June 13, 1921; came to U.S., 1937; s. Louis and Malvina (Haller) R.; m. Joyce M. Lighter, Feb. 9, 1952; children: Jay A., Robert J. BS, CCNY; M.B., Chgo. Med. Sch., 1946, MD, 1947. Diplomate Am. Bd. Phys. Medicine and Rehab. Intern Our Lady of Mercy Med. Ctr. and Cabrini Meml. Hosps., NYC, 1946-48; resident Madigan Hosp., Tacoma, 1951, Mayo Clinic, Rochester, Minn., 1951, N.Y. Med. Coll. Met. Med. Ctr., 1953-55; USPHS fellow, 1955-56; ship's surgeon U.S. Lines, Grace Lines, NYC, 1948-49; indsl. physician Abraham & Strauss Stores, Bklyn., 1949-51; practice medicine specializing in phys. medicine and rehab. Bklyn., 1956-73; dir. rehab. service, attending physician N.Y. City Hosp. Dept., 1955-73; prof., chmn. dept. rehab. medicine Chgo. Med. Sch., North Chicago, Ill., 1973—2005, prof. emeritus dept. rehab. medicine, from 2005, Rosalind Franklin U. Medicine & Sci., 2005; prof. emeritus Chgo. Med. Sch., 2005; prof. chmn. rehab medicine. Cons. N.Y.C. Mayor's Adv. Com. for Aged, 1957; asst. prof. SUNY Downstate Med. Sch., Bklyn., 1958-73; med. dir. Schwab Rehab. Hosp., Chgo., 1973-75; acting chief rehab. service VA Center, North Chicgo, 1975-77; chmn. Ill. Phys. Therapy Exam. Com., 1977-78; examiner Am. Bd. Phys. Medicine and Rehab., 1983; sec., dir. Microtherapeutics, Inc., 1972 Editor: Total Cancer Care, 1975; contbr. articles to med. jours.; contbg. editor Ill. Med. Jour., 1983-89 Served to capt. US Army, 1951—53. Recipient Bronze medal Am. Congress Rehab. Medicine, 1974 Fellow: ACP, Am. Acad. Phys. Medicine and Rehab. (Cert. Appreciation 1993); mem.: Chgo. Med. Sch. Alumni Assn. (asst. treas. 1983—93, treas. 1993—95, sec. 1995—97, 1st v.p. 1999, pres. 2001—03, exec. com., Disting. Alumnus award 1980, Presdl. plaque Greater N.Y. chpt.), Chgo. Med. Sch. Faculty Assembly (spkr. 1978—80), Ill. Soc. Phys. Medicine and Rehab. (pres. 1983—84), Ill. Med. Soc. (chmn. workmen's compensation com. 1980—83), Odd Fellows (pres. 1961—62), Phi Lambda Kappa (trustee 1980), Alpha Omega Alpha. Home: Chicago, Ill. Died May 28, 2009.

ROGSTAD, MARK ROLAND, secondary school educator; b. Belvidere, Ill., Mar. 1, 1957; s. Ronald Glenn and Mary Ellen (Kugath) R. BS, Ea. Ill. U., 1979, MS, 1981; EdD, U. Wyo., 1992. Grad. asst. Eastern Ill. U., Charleston, 1980-81; electronics instr. Proviso West High Sch., Hillside, Ill., 1981-85; tech. educator U. Wyo., Laramie, 1985-88, Mont. State U., Bozeman, 1988-92, Bozeman High Sch., from 1992. Cons. Wyo. State Dept. Edn., Cheyenne, 1986—, Mont. Office of Pub. Instruction, 1989—. Recipient Faculty Growth award U. Wyo., Laramie, 1987, Prin. Tech. award Wyo. State Dept. Edn., Cheyenne, 1986-87, Applied Communication award Mont. Office Pub. Instrn., Helena, 1990-91. Mem. Internat. Tech. Edn. Assn. (MT Teacher Excellence Award, 1995), Coun. on Tech. Tchr. Edn., Nat. Assn. Indsl. Tech., World Future Soc., Tech. Edn. Assn. Mont., Eastern Ill. U. Alumni Assn., Epsilon Pi Tau, Phi Delta Kappa, Pather Club of Charleston. Lutheran. Avocations: photography, computing, amateur radio. Home: Margate, Fla. Died Mar. 23, 2009.

ROLNICKI, THOMAS EDWARD, journalism executive, educator; b. Wausau, Wis., May 13, 1949; s. Edward James and Pauline Mary (Lewandowski) R. BS, U. Wis., 1972; MS, Iowa State U., 1979. Cert. secondary edn. tchr., Wis., Iowa. Tchr. Marshfield (Wis.) High Sch., 1972-74, Ames (Iowa) High Sch., 1974-77; advisor Iowa State U., Ames, 1977-79, lectr., 1978-79; editor U. Minn., Mpls., 1979-80; exec. dir. Nat. Scholastic Press Assn., Mpls., from 1980. Bd. dirs. Student Press Law Ctr., Washington, Am. Collegiate Network, Santa Monica Calif.; dir. journalism workshop Iowa State U., Ames, 1975-79; lectr. U. Minn., 1981—. Author: Magazine Guidebook, 1987, Scholastic Journalism, 1990; editor jour. Trends in High Sch. Media, 1989—, Trends in Coll. Media, 1989—. Bd. dirs. Citiscape Townhomes Assn., Mpls, 1987-89. Recipient Gold Key Columbia Scholastic Press, 1985, Lifetime Achievement award Okla. Scholastic Press, 1990. Mem. Am. Soc. Assn. Execs., Journalism Edn. Assn. (v.p. 1977-79, Medal of Merit 1979, Carl Towley award 1984), Coll. Media Advisors, Soc. Profl. Journalists, Soc. Newspaper Design. Home: Minneapolis, Minn. Died Dec. 20, 2009.

ROMAGNOLI, ADELMO, data processing executive; b. Wilmington, Del., Dec. 5, 1925; s. Adelmo and Catherine (Niccolucci) R.; m. Eleanor Sulpizi, Feb. 4, 1956; children— Adelmo A., Rita, Lisa, Gina. B.S. in Bus. Adminstrn., U. Del-Newark, 1950. Mgr. data processing E.I. DuPont De Nemours & Co., Inc., Wilmington, Del.; adv. bd. Goldey-

Beacom Coll., Wilmington, 1983—. Served with U.S. Army, 1944-46. Mem. Assn. Systems Mgmt. Democrat. Roman Catholic. Club: Kiwanis (dir.). Died Aug. 8, 2009.

ROMANOFF, MILFORD MARTIN, retired building contractor; b. Cleve., Aug. 21, 1921; s. Barney Sanford and Edythe Stolpher (Bort) R.; m. Marjorie Reinwald, Nov. 6, 1945; children: Bennett S., Lawrence M., Janet Beth (dec.). Student, U. Mich. Coll. Arch., 1939-42; BBA, U. Toledo, 1943. Pres. Glass City Constrn. Co., Toledo, 1951-55, Milford Romanoff, Inc., Toledo, 1956—2003. Co-founder Neighborhood Improvement Found. Toledo, 1960; active Lucas County Econ. Devel. Com., from 1979, Childrens Svcs. Bd. Lucas County, 1981—97, Arthritis Bd. Dirs., Crosby Gardens Bd. Advisors, 1983—96, Toledo Met. Area Govt. Exec. Com., from 1996; citizens adv. bd. Recreation Commn. Toledo, 1973—86; campus adv. com. Med. Coll. Ohio, from 1980; trustee Cummings Treatment Ctr. for Adolescents, from 1981; pres. Toledo B'nai Brith Lodge, 1958—59, Cherry Hill Nursing Home, 1964—85; bd. dirs. Anti-Defamation League, 1955—60, Ohio Hillel Orgns., Lucas County Dept. Human Svcs., Arthritis Assn., from 1995, Comprehensive Addiction Svc. Sys., 1998, Kidney Found. Northwestern Ohio, from 1986, sec., 1989; chmn. Comprehensive Addiction Svc. Sys., 1999, Toledo Amateur Baseball and Softball Com., 1979—81; cons. U.S. Care Corp., from 1985; bd. govs. Toledo Housing for Elderly, 1982—84, sec., 1989, pres. bd. govs., from 1990, pres., from 1991; bd. adv. Ret. Sr. Vol. Program, 1987—89, chmn., 1988—90, from 1993, sec. adv. bd., from 1990, bd. dirs., from 2000; vice chmn. adv. bd. Salvation Army, 1986—87, chmn. adv. bd., 1988—90, ct. apptd. spl. advocate adv., bd. treas., from 1988; chmn. Mental Health Adv. Bd., 1983—84, sec., 1989; bd. dirs. Toledo Urban Forestry Commn., from 1991, pres., 1993, 1995, Lucas County Dept. Human Svcs. Bd.; adv. coun. Renaissance Sr. Apts., 1997, chmn. adv. coun., 1999; adv. bd. Lucas Co. Correctional Facility, from 1999; chmn. Compass Bd., from 2002; bd. dirs. Area Office on Aging of Northwest Ohio, 2001, Lucas County Mental Health, 2001; chair Compass Corp. for Recovery Svcs., from 2002; mem. Lucas County Mental Health Bd., 2002, Juvenile Correction Bd. Lucas County, from 2004; bd. dirs. Mental Health Lucas Co.; mem. Juvenile Correction Bd. Lucas County, from 2003; mem. adv. bd. ACLU, from 2005, from 2005; active Dem. Precinct Com., 1975—78; trustee Temple Brotherhood, 1956—58, bd. dirs., from 1981; pres. Ohio B'nai Brith, 1959—60; bd. mem. ACLU, from 2005. Recipient Toledo-Lucas County Jefferson awards, from 2008. Mem.: Friends Libr. Bd., Mental Health Bd. of Lucas County, U. Mich. Alumni Assn., Juvenile Justice (adv. bd.), Toledo Zool. Soc., Econ. Opportunity Planning Assn. Greater Toledo (adv. bd.), Nat. Coun. on Alcoholism & Drug Dependence, Toledo Mus. Art (assoc.), U. Toledo Alumni Assn., Am. Legion, Hadassah (assoc. Toledo chpt.), Masons (Outstanding Cmty. Svc. award of Lucas County 2001), Zeta Beta Tau. Home: Toledo, Ohio. Died June 21, 2009.

ROMINE, KENNY FLOYD, federal government administrator; b. Memphis, Feb. 1, 1927; s. William Armory and Ollie Nora (King) Romine; m. Dorothy Schmus, Oct. 20, 1952 (div. 1956); m. Toni Toyoko Murata, Dec. 20, 1957; 1 child, Kenneth Wayne. With US Marine Corps., 1945, advanced through grades to gunnery sgt., 1958; ret., 1965; salesman Sears Roebuck Co., Jacksonville, NC, 1965—67; ins. agt. Life and Casualty Ins. Co., Jacksonville, 1967—69; fire prevention insp. US Govt. Employment, Camp Lejuene, NC, 1971—75, occupl. safety and health specialist, from 1975. Mem.: Am. Soc. Safety Engrs. (pres. eastern Carolina chpt. 1984—85, sec. region IX 1984—85). Democrat. Baptist. Home: Raleigh, NC. Died Apr. 27, 2010.

RONCALLO, ANGELO DOMINICK, retired judge, former United States Representative from New York; b. Port Chester, NY, May 28, 1927; s. Anthony Marc and Concetta (Prochilo) R.; m. Priscille Pouliot, May 31, 1952; children: Marc (dec.), Paul, John, Jean, James. BA, Manhattan Coll., 1950; JD, Georgetown U., 1954. Bar: N.Y. Councilman Town of Oyster Bay (N.Y.), 1966-67; comptroller County of Nassau (N.Y.), 1968-72; mem. US Congress from 3rd NY Dist., Washington, 1973—75; justice N.Y. State Supreme Ct. 2d dept., 1978-95. With U.S. Army, 1944-46, ETO. Mem. Nassau County Bar Assn. Republican. Roman Catholic. Home: Massapequa, NY. Died May 4, 2010.

ROOD, DON D, insurance executive; b. Flint, Mich., Apr. 3, 1930; s. William and Ruth R.; m. Rose Lorraine Giguere, Apr. 7, 1951; children: Lorraine Cheryl Rood Burris, Don D BS, Central Mich. U., 1952; postgrad., U. Mich., 1954-65. Agt. State Farm Ins. Co., Flint, 1955-60, agy. mgr., 1960-61, tng. dir. Marshall, Mich, 1961-62, agy. dir., 1962-71, dep. regional v.p. Springfield, Pa., 1971-74, v.p. agy. Bloomington, Ill, 1974-76, agy. v.p., 1976-87, sr. agy. officer, from 1980, sr. agy. v.p., from 1987. Bd. dirs. State Farm Life & Accident Assurance Co., Bloomington, State Farm Internat. Svcs. Inc., State Farm Mut. Automobile Ins. Co., State Farm Life Ins. Co., State Farm Annuity and Life Ins. Co., State Farm Fire and Casualty Ins. Co.; underwriter State Farm Lloyds. Served with U.S. Army, 1952-54, Korea. Mem. Nat. Assn. Life Underwriters, Agy. Officers Round Table, Life Ins. Mktg. and Rsch. Assn. (bd. dirs. 1982-85). Home: Carlock, Ill. Died Feb. 14, 2009.

ROOKE, DAVID LEE, retired chemical company executive; b. San Antonio, Tex., May 2, 1923; s. Henry Levi, Jr. and Annie (Davidson) R.; m. Esthermae Litherland, June 2, 1945; children— Eugene, Mark, Paul, Bruce. BS in Chem. Engring, Rice Inst., Houston, 1944; postgrad., U. Houston. With Dow Chem., Midland, Mich., 1946-88, v.p. ops., 1977-78; pres. Dow U.S.A., 1978-82; v.p. Dow Chem. Corp., 1978-82, exec. v.p., 1982-83, sr. v.p., 1983-86, sr. cons., 1986-88, ret., 1988. Bd. dirs. Dow Corning Corp., James Avery Craftsman, Inc. Nat. exec. bd. Boy Scouts Am., 1979-86; bd. dirs. Meth. Mission Home, San Antonio. Served with USNR, 1944-46. Mem. AICE, United Meth. Reporter Found. (Dallas). Methodist. Home: Kerrville, Tex. Died Aug. 5, 2009.

ROPER, JOHN LONSDALE, III, shipyard executive; b. Norfolk, Va., Jan. 19, 1927; s. John Lonsdale II and Sarah (Dryfoos) R.; m. Jane Preston Harman, Sept. 29, 1951; children: Susan Roper, John Lonsdale IV, Sarah Preston Roper Massey, Jane Harman Roper Van Sciver, Katherine Hayward Roper Stout. BSME, U. Va., Charlottesville, 1949; BS in Naval Architecture and Marine Engring., MIT, 1951. CEO, pres. Norfolk Shipbuilding & Drydock Corp., 1985-91, pres., CEO, 1992-98, also bd. dirs.; mgr. Branbleton, LLC, Norfolk, from 1998. Dir. John L. Roper Corp., Cruise Internat., Inc., The Flagship Group Ltd.; pres., dir. Lonsdale Bldg. Corp. Marepcon Corp.-Internat. With USCG, 1945-46. Mem. Shipbuilders Coun. Am. (bd. dirs.). Episcopalian. Home: Norfolk, Va. Died Mar. 28, 2010.

ROSE, ALAN GEORGE, pathologist, educator; b. Kimberly, South Africa, Aug. 13, 1940; s. Cyril William and Sylvia Grace (Jacobsen) R.; m. Jeanne Buron, May 25, 1974 (div. 1994); children: Penelope Cathryn, Camilla Elizabeth; m. Nuja Baboo, Mar. 18, 1994. MBChB, U. Cape Town, 1964, M of Medicine in Clin. Pathology, 1969; FRC in Pathology, Royal Coll., 1983. Intern Groote Schuur Hosp., Cape Town, South Africa, 1965, resident, 1966-69, lectr., specialist, 1969-71, sr. lectr., sr. specialist, 1972-79, assoc. prof., prin. specialist, 1980-87, prof., chmn., 1988-94, head divsn. pathology, 1990-92; prof. pathology U. Minn., St. Paul, from 1994. Co-dir. Jesse E. Edwards Registry of Cardiovascular Diseases, United Hosps., St. Paul, 1994—. Author: Pathology of Heart Valve Replacement, 1987; mem. editorial bd. several profl. jours., 1985—. Active Westerford High Sch. Com., Cape Town, 1988. Fellow Am. Coll. Cardiology; mem. Fedn. South African Socs. Pathology (councillor 1992—), So. Africa Cardiac Soc., Internat. Acad. Pathology (treas., councillor 1982-85), Soc. for Cardiovascular Pathology (councillor 1987-88). Avocations: photography, wood carving, painting. Died Dec. 31, 2009.

ROSE, CHARLES ALEXANDER, lawyer; b. Louisville, June 14, 1932; s. Hector Edward and Mary (Shepard) R.; m. Moncie Watson; children: Marc, Craig, Lorna, Gordon, Alex, Sara. BA, U. Louisville, 1954, JD, 1960. Bar: Ky. 1960, U.S. Ct. Appeals (6th cir.) 1970, Ind. 1978, U.S. Supreme Ct. 1978. Pvt. practice, Louisville, 1960-63; assoc. Jones, Ewen & McKenzie, Louisville, 1963-65; ptnr. Curtis & Rose, Louisville, 1965-81, Weber & Rose, Louisville, from 1981. Organist Scottish Rite Temple, Louisville. Lt. USAF, 1954-56. Mem. ABA, Ky. Bar Assn., Ind. Bar Assn., Louisville Bar Assn., Am. Soc. Hosp. Attys., Am. Bd. Trial Advocates, Brandeis Soc., Fedn. Ins. Counsel, River Road Country Club, Pendennis Club (Louisville), Jefferson Club. Republican. Episcopalian. Home: Louisville, Ky. Died Apr. 8, 2009.

ROSE, IRWIN WILLIAM, optometrist; b. Chgo., May 9, 1926; s. Jacob Joseph and Dora (Eisenberg) Rosenstein; m. Estelle Klein, June 29, 1952; children: Karen, Steven, Lawrence, Beth. OD, Monroe Coll., 1946; postgrad., Chgo. Coll. Optometry, 1952. Pvt. practice, optometry, Watseka, Ill., from 1960. Pres. bd. dirs. Iroquois Mental Health Ctr., 1979—85. Cpl. US Army, 1946—47, cpl. US Army, 1953—54. Mem.: Optometric Extension Program. Hebrew., Corn Belt Optical Soc., Ill. Optometric Assn. (exec. bd. mem. 1966—67), Am. Optometric Assn., Elks, Lions. Home: Watseka, Ill. Died Dec. 11, 2009.

ROSE, ISRAEL HAROLD, mathematics professor; b. New Britain, Conn., May 17, 1917; s. Abraham and Dora (Dubrow) R.; m. Pearl Nitzberg, Jan. 24, 1942 (div. Feb. 1956); 1 son, Steven Philip; m. Susan Ann Lazarus, Mar. 26, 1961; children: Dora, Eric. Student, CCNY, 1934-36; AB, Bklyn. Coll., 1938, A.M., 1941; PhD, Harvard, 1951. Tutor, instr. Bklyn. Coll., 1938-41; instr. Pa. State Coll., 1942-46; asst. prof. U. Mass., 1948-54, assoc. prof., 1954-60; faculty Hunter Coll., 1960-68, prof. math., 1965-68, chmn. dept., 1966-68; prof. math. Lehman Coll., CUNY, 1968-82, prof. emeritus, from 1983, chmn. dept., 1968-72, 80-82, resident prof., from 1983. Vis. asst. prof. Mt. Holyoke Coll., 1951-52, vis. assoc. prof., 1954-55, 58-59; sci. cons. AID, India, summer 1965 Author: A Modern Introduction to College Mathematics, 1959, Algebra: An Introduction to Finite Mathematics, 1963, Vectors and Analytic Geometry, 1968, Elementary Functions: A Precalculus Primer, 1973, (with Esther R. Phillips) Elementary Functions, 1978. NRC predoctoral fellow Harvard, 1946-48; fellow Fund Advancement Edn., 1952-53 Mem. Am. Math. Soc., Math. Assn. Am. (chmn. Met. N.Y. sect. 1973-75), Nat. Council Tchrs. Math., Assn. Tchrs. Math. New Eng. (pres. Conn. Valley sect. 1956-57), Sigma Xi (pres. Hunter Coll. chpt. 1966-67) Home: Hastings On Hudson, NY. Died Oct. 30, 2009.

ROSE, JAMES C., other: manufacturing; b. Memphis, July 12, 1937; s. Charles C. and Emeline (Buck) R.; m. Marcia Holzapfel, June 22, 1963; children: Laura, James, Julianne. BS, Miami U., Oxford, Ohio, 1959; MBA, Eastern Mich. U., 1970. Systems mgr. Warren-Teed Pharms., Columbus, Ohio, 1959—63; systems analyst Honeywell, Inc., St. Petersburg, Fla., 1963—67; systems mgr. Kelsey Hayes, Inc., Romulus, Mich., 1967—70; group v.p. plastics Key Internat. Mfg. Inc., Southfield, Mich., from 1970; investor, cons., from 1986. Dir. Delta Dental Plan of Mich., Lansing. Mem.: Meadowbrook Country Club (Northville, Mich.). Home: Northville, Mich. Died Jan. 17, 2009.

ROSEBROCK, CHARLES A., lawyer; b. NYC, June 1, 1946; BA, Pa. State U., 1968; JD, Emory U., 1971. Bar: N.Y. 1972, Mass. 1978. Mem. Nutter, McClennen & Fish, Boston. Mem. cirriculum adv. com. Mass. Continuing Legal Edn. Mem. Am. Coll. Trust and Estates Counsel, Boston Bar Assn. (mem. estate planning com., mem. probate com.), Boston Estate Planning Coun., Phi Delta Phi (pres. 1970). Died July 25, 2009.

ROSEN, BERNARD CARL, sociologist, psychologist, educator; b. Phila., July 1, 1922; s. Morris and Sophie Slaviter Rosen; m. Shirley Rosenbluth, Sept. 10, 1950; 1 child, Michele Beth. BA, Temple U., 1948; MA, Columbia U., 1950; PhD, Cornell U., 1952. Instr. Yale U., New Haven, Conn., 1952-53; asst. prof. U. Conn., Storrs, 1953-61; prof. U. Nebr., Lincoln, 1961-66, Cornell U., Ithaca, N.Y., 1966-93, prof. emeritus, from 1993. Vis. prof. U. São Paulo, Brazil, 1960-61, Escola Sociologia-Politica, São Paulo, 1963-64, Harvard U., 1966, London Sch. Econs., 1973-74, U. Padua, Italy, 1983-84; cons. Upjohn Inst. for Employment Rsch., 1965, NSF, 1966-89, USAID, 1990, Hunter Coll. Edn. in Depressed Areas Project, 1963, U. Chgo. Study of Adolescence Project, 1963; organizer Conf. on Socialization of Competence, Social Sci. Rsch. Coun., Puerto Rico, 1965, Conf. on Ednl. Aspirations of Can. Youth, Carleton U., Ottawa, 1970, Symposium on Family Structure and Personality, Soc. Rsch. in Child Deve., 1963, Conf. of Personality Deve. Among H.S. Youth, Social Sci. Rsch. Coun., 1963, Nat. Com. for Vis. Scientists, 1978. Author: The Industrial Connection, 1982, Women, Work and Achievement, 1989, Winners and Losers of the Information Revolution, 1998, Masks and Mirrors: Generation X and the Chameleon Personaltiy, 2001, Adolescence and Religion, 1965; co-author: (with A.M. Rattazzi, A. C. Tajoliand D. Capozza) Aspettative Di Istruzione E Occupazione Nei Giovani, 1988; contbr. articles to profl. jours., chpts. to books; co-editor: Achievement in American Society, 1969;ssoc. editor Sociometry, 1966-79; mem. editl. bd. Luso-Brazilian Rev., 1966-71; reviewer jours. in field. With U.S. Army, 1943-46, WW II. Decorated 2 combat stars; ssch. grantee NSF, 1968-73, NIMH, 1956-57, 58-62, Harvard U. 1957, U. Calif., Berkeley, 1964. Avocations: art collecting, travel, visiting museums. Home: Ithaca, NY. Died Nov. 9, 2009.

ROSEN, JUDAH BEN, computer scientist; b. Phila., May 5, 1922; s. Benjamin and Susan (Hurwich) R.; children: Susan Beth, Lynn Ruth. BSEE, Johns Hopkins U., 1943; PhD in Applied Math., Columbia U., 1952. Rschr. Manhattan (N.Y.) Project, 1944—46, Brookhaven (N.Y.) Nat. Lab., 1946—48; rsch. assoc. Princeton (N.J.) U., 1952-54; head applied math. dept. Shell Devel. Co., 1954-62; vis. prof. computer sci. dept. Stanford (Calif.) U., 1962-64; prof. dept. computer sci. and math. rsch. ctr. U. Wis., Madison, 1964-71; prof., head dept. computer sci. U. Minn., Mpls., 1971-92, fellow Supercomputer Inst., 1985—2007; sr. fellow Supercomputer Ctr., San Diego, 1993—2007; adj. rsch. prof. dept. computer sci. and engrin. U. Calif. San Diego, La Jolla, 1992—2007, bioinformatics grad. program faculty, 2001—07; ret. Fulbright prof. Technion, Israel, 1968-69, Davis vis. prof. 1980; invited lectr. Chinese Acad. Sci., Peking, 1980, Guilin, 1996, Samos, Greece, 2000; lectr., cons. Argonne (Ill.) Nat. Lab.; mem. Nat. Computer Sci. Bd. Author: Topics in Parallel Computing, 1992; editor: Nonlinear Programming, 1970, Supercomputers and Large-Scale Optimization, 1988; assoc. editor Global Optimization, 1990—, Annals of Ops. Rsch., 1984—; contbr. articles to profl. jours. and procs. Grantee, NSF, from 1995, ARPA/NIST, 1994—97. Mem. Assn. Computing Machinery, Soc. Indsl. and Applied Math., Math. Programming Soc., European Acad. Scis. Achievements include research in supercomputers and parallel algorithms for optimization, computation of molecular structure and drug design by energy minimization and homology models, algorithms for structured approximation in signal processing. Died Apr. 28, 2009.

ROSEN, MOISHE, religious organization founder; b. Kansas City, Mo., Apr. 12, 1932; s. Ben and Rose (Baker) R.; m. Ceil Starr, Aug. 27, 1950; children: Lyn Rosen Bond, Ruth. Diploma, Northeastern Bible Coll., 1957; DD, Western Conservative Bapt. Sem., 1986. Ordained to ministry Bapt. Ch., 1957. Missionary Am. Bd. Missions to the Jews, NYC, 1956, minister in charge Beth Sar Shalom Los Angeles, 1957-67, dir. recruiting and tng. NYC, 1967-70; leader Jews for Jesus Movement, San Francisco, 1970-73, exec. dir., 1973-96, founder, 1973—2010. Speaker in field. Author: Sayings of Chairman Moishe, 1972, Jews for Jesus, 1974, Share the New Life with a Jew, 1976, Christ in the Passover, 1977, Y'shua, The Jewish Way to Say Jesus, 1982, Overture to Armageddon, 1991, The Universe is Broken: Who on Earth Can Fix It?, 1991, Demystifying Personal Evangelism, 1992, Witnessing to Jews, 1998. Trustee Western Conservative Bapt. Sem., Portland, Oreg., 1979-85, 86-91, Bibl. Internat. Coun. on Bibl. Inerrancy, Oakland, Calif., 1979-89; bd. dirs. Christian Advs. Serving Evangelism, 1987-91. Named Hero of the Faith, Conservative Bapt. Assn. Am., 1997. Died May 19, 2010.

ROSEN, RALPH J., state legislator; b. Chgo., July 27, 1919; m. Joan McMahon; 3 children. AA, U. Chgo., 1938; MS, AA Mil. Sch., 1951; BA, St. Benedict's Coll., Atchison, Kans., 1969. Former naval officer; ret. U.S. diplomat, 1973; former h.s. tchr.; selectman Laconia, N.H., from 1986; N.H. state rep. Dist. 7; mem. sci., tech. and energy coms. N.H. Ho. of Reps.; substitute tchr. Decorated D.F.C. (3), Air Medal (9). Mem. Am. Fighter Aces Assn. Home: Mc Lean, Va. Died May 11, 2010.

ROSENBERG, ALAN SPENCER, organization development consulting firm executive; b. Staten Island, N.Y., Aug. 24, 1940; s. Milton and Dorothy (Meltzer) R.; B.S. in Bus. Psychology, Pa. State U., 1962; M.Ed. in Adult Edn., Temple U., 1973; M.A. in Indsl. Relations, St. Francis Coll., 1975; m. Marsha Leinhardt, Dec. 3, 1960; children: Louis Robert, Milton David. Nat. employment and recruiting mgr. McCrory Stores div. McCrory Corp., York, Pa., 1969-71; employment and tng. mgr. E.I. DuPont de Nemours & Co., New Cumberland, Pa., 1971-73; dir. human resources Giant Food Stores, Inc., Carlisle, Pa., 1973-76; pres. Alan S. Rosenberg Assos., Inc., York, 1976—; mng. ptnr. Mid Hill Profl. Center, York, 1977—; pres. Spencer Cons., York, 1969-76; mem. adj.

faculty York Coll. Pa., 1974—, Pa. State U., 1975—; jobs dir. NAB, 1968. Adult leader Boy Scouts Am., 1973—; bd. dirs. Ohev Sholom Synagogue, York, 1971-72, Community Progress Council, 1974, Susquehanna Employment and Tng. Corp., 1974-76. Contbr. articles on human resource utilization to profl. jours. Mem. Am. Soc. Tng. and Devel., Am. Soc. Personnel Adminstrn. (accredited personnel diplomate), Assoc. Builders and Contractors, Soc. Advancement of Mgmt., Indsl. Relations Research Assn., York Soc. Personnel Adminstrn. (pres. 1986—), Pa. Retailers Assn., Pa. Petroleum Assn., Republican. Jewish. Contbr. numerous articles to nat. profl. jours.; developer tax recovery system and govt. subsidized tng. cost rebate systems for employers. Home: York, Pa. Died June 18, 2009.

ROSENBERG, BRUCE ALAN, English language educator, author; b. NYC, July 27, 1934; s. Howard Alyne and Audrey (Olenick) R.; m. Ann Harleman, June, 1981; children: Eric Peter, Seth Allan, Bradley Michael, Sarah Stewart. Student, Alfred U., 1952-54; BA, Hofstra U., 1955; MA, Pa. State U., 1962; PhD, Ohio State U., 1965. Mem. faculty U. Calif., Santa Barbara, 1965-67, U. Va., Charlottesville, 1967-69, Pa. State U., State College, 1969-77; prof. English lit. and Am. civilization Brown U., from 1977. Fulbright lectr., Warsaw, Poland, 1981 Author: The Art of the American Folk Preacher, 1970, Custer and the Epic of Defeat, 1976, The Code of the West, 1981, The Spy Story, 1987, Can These Bones Live?, 1988, Ian Fleming, 1989, Folklore and Literature, 1991, The Neutral Ground, 1994; asst. editor Chaucer Rev., 1967-69, Jour. Am. Folklore, 1970-79; contbg. editor Oral Tradition, 1985—. Served with U.S. Army, 1955-57. Recipient James Russell Lowell prize, 1970; Chgo. Folklore prize, 1970, 76; Am. Council Learned Socs. fellow, 1967; Nat. Endowment Humanities fellow, 1976-77; Guggenheim fellow, 1982-83 Mem. Folklore Fellows Internat., Am. Folklore Soc., ALSC. Jewish. Home: Providence, RI. Died May 18, 2010.

ROSENBERG, GERALD ALAN, lawyer; b. NYC, Aug. 5, 1944; s. Irwin H. and Doris (Lowinger) R.; m. Rosalind Navin, Aug. 13, 1971; children: Clifford D., Nicholas D. BA cum laude, Yale U., 1966; JD, Harvard U., 1969. Bar: N.Y. 1970, U.S. Dist. Ct. (so. dist.) N.Y. 1971, U.S. Ct. Appeals (2d cir.) 1974, U.S. Dist. Ct. (we. dist.) N.Y. 1977, U.S. Dist. Ct. (cen. dist.) Calif. 1978, U.S. Supreme Ct. 1979, U.S. Dist. Ct. (ea. dist.) N.Y. 1981, U.S. Tax Ct. 1984. Atty. Legal Aid Soc. San Mateo/VISTA, Redwood, Calif., 1969-70; asst. atty. U.S. Dept. Justice, NYC, 1971-75; assoc. Rosenman & Colin, NYC, 1975-77, ptnr., 1978—2002, mem. mgmt. com., 1991—94; counsel KMZ Rosenman, NYC, 2002—04; chief charities bur. Office of the Atty. Gen., NYC, from 2005. Arbitrator U.S. Dist. Ct. (ea. dist.) NY; faculty Ctr. Internat. Legal Studies, Salzburg, Austria, 1999-2004. Bd. dirs. Non Profit Coord. Com. Inc., NYC, 1983-2004, NY Lawyers for the Pub. Interest Inc., 1988-2004, Parks Coun., 1988—, pres., 1991-95; trustee Central Park Conservancy, 1995-2004. Mem. Am. Law Inst. Home: New York, NY. Died Sept. 2009.

ROSENBLUM, M. EDGAR, theater producer; b. Bklyn., Jan. 8, 1932; s. Jacob and Pauline (Feldman) R.; m. Cornelia Hartmann, May 1, 1960; 1 child, Jessica Alex. Student, Bard Coll., 1951-55. Prodr. Folk Rock Chamber Music Series, Woodstock, N.Y., 1956-72; dir. Polari Gallery, Woodstock, 1959-72; asst. to mgr. Nat. Music League, NYC, 1958-59; stage mgr. Joffrey Ballet Nat. Tour, 1960; prodr. When I Was a Child, 41st St Theatre, NYC, 1960-61, Woodstock Playhouse, 1960-73; stage mgr. Turn of the Screw Nat. Tour, 1961; exec. dir. Hudson Valley Repertory Theatre, Woodstock, 1964-67; exec. prodr. The Shadow Box, NYC, 1977; exec. dir. Long Wharf Theatre, New Haven, 1970-96; exec. prodr. Cir. in the Sq., NYC, 1996-97; cons. Theatre Vision, 1997—2010; exec. dir. Ensemble Studio Theatre, NYC. Prodr. and owner, Woodstock (N.Y.) Playhouse, 1959-73; cons. Fedn. for Ext. and Devel. of Am. Profl. Theatre, N.Y.C., 1970, Arts Couns. of New Haven, R.I., Alaska, Conn., Ohio; bd. trustees Am. Arts Alliance, chmn of bd. 1982-84; vis. lectr. Yale U., New Haven, 1985-91; producing cons. Berkshire Theatre Festival, 1998, 99. With U.S. Army, 1953. Recipient award New Haven Arts Coun., 1994; Ezra Stiles Coll. fellow Yale U., 1973. Mem. Am. Arts Alliance (chmn. 1982-84), League of Resident Theatres (mem. exec., liaison and negotiating coms. 1974, v.p. 1993-96, pres.), Nat. Corp. Theatre Fund (founding pres. 1976), Conn. Advocates for the Arts (bd. dirs. 1978—), Greater New Haven C. of C. (bd. dirs.). Died Apr. 18, 2010.

ROSENFELD, ARTHUR HERBERT, lawyer; b. Bklyn., May 24, 1930; s. Abraham and Sadie (Albert) R.; m. Lois E. Glantz, Apr. 15, 1956; children: Felicia Ann, Carolyn Jane, Sara Ellen. Student, St. Andrew's U., 1950-51; AB, Union Coll., Schenectady, 1952; JD, Harvard U., 1955; postgrad., CCNY, 1962-63. Bar: N.Y. 1955. Pres. Warren, Gorham & Lamont, Inc., NYC, 1970-81, Internat. Thomson Profl. Pub., NYC, 1981-84; chmn. bd. Rosenfeld, Emanuel Inc., Larchmont, NY, 1984-88; pres. Prentice Hall Tax & Profl. Ref., NYC, 1988-89, Maxwell Macmillan Profl. and Bus. Reference Div., Englewood Cliffs, NJ, 1989-92; chmn. Arthur H. Rosenfeld Assocs., from 1991; Civic Rsch. Inst., Inc., from 1992. Mem. ABA, N.Y. State Bar Assn., Am. Assn. Pubs. (exec. coun. 1991), Harvard Club. Democrat. Died July 7, 2009.

ROSENFELD, STEPHEN SAMUEL, retired newspaper editor; b. Pittsfield, Mass., July 26, 1932; s. Jay C. and Elizabeth R.; m. Barbara Bromson, Oct. 28, 1962; children: David, Rebecca, Emmet, James. BA in History, Harvard U., 1953; MA, Columbia U., 1959. Reporter Berkshire Eagle, Pittsfield, 1955-57; successively reporter, fgn. corr., editorial writer, columnist, editor editorial page Washington Post, 1959-2000. Co-author: (with Barbara Rosenfeld) Return from Red Square, 1967; author: The Time of Their Dying, 1977. Served to 1st lt. USMC, 1953-55. Mem. Coun. on Fgn. Rels., Alexandria Lit. Soc. Home: Alexandria, Va. Died May 2, 2010.

ROSENTHAL, ALBERT JOSEPH, retired dean; b. NYC, Mar. 5, 1919; m. Barbara Snowden, June 30, 1953; children: Edward H., Thomas S., William I. BA, U. Pa., 1938; LL.B., Harvard U., 1941. Bar: N.Y. 1942, U.S. Supreme Ct. 1947. Law clk. to judge U.S. Ct. Appeals 1st Circuit, Boston, 1941-42; spl. appellate atty. OPA, Washington, 1946-47; law clk. to Justice Felix Frankfurter US Supreme Ct., Washington, 1947-48; asst. loan officer IBRD, Washington, 1948-50; atty. US Dept. Justice, Washington, 1950-52; gen. counsel Small Def. Plants Adminstrn., Washington, 1952-53; ptnr. Golden Wienshienk & Rosenthal, NYC, 1953-64; prof. law Columbia U., NYC, 1964-89, Maurice T. Moore prof., 1974-89, dean Sch. Law, 1979-84, prof. emeritus, dean emeritus, 1989—2010. Hearing officer N.Y. State Dept. Environ. Conservation, 1975, 77; mem. N.Y. State Law Revision Commn., 1987-97; vis. prof. law St. John's U., 1989-92, disting. prof. 1992—; spl. master U.S. Dist. Ct. N.Y., 1990—. Author: (with H. Korn and S. Lubman) Catastrophic Accidents in Government Programs, 1963, (with F. Grad and G. Rathjens) Environmental Control: Priorities, Policies and the Law, 1971, Federal Regulation of Campaign Finance, 1972, (with F. Grad and others) The Automobile and the Regulation of Its Impact on the Environment, 1975; editor: (with L. Henkin) Constitutionalism and Rights: The Influence of the U.S. Constitution Abroad, 1989; contbr. articles to law jours. Mem. Logan Airport Master Plan Study Team, 1975. Served to capt. U.S. Army Air Corps, 1942-45. Fellow Am. Acad. Arts and Scis., Am. law Inst. Home: Scarsdale, NY. Died Mar. 17, 2010.

ROSENTHAL, DAVID, physician; b. Phila., Sept. 30, 1929; m.; Suzanne Rosenthal; children: Michael, Samuel, Abrielle. Student, Julliard Sch. Music, 1948-49, George Washington U., 1953-54, Temple U., 1954-56; DO, Phila. Coll. Osteopathic Med., 1960. Diplomate Am. Bd. Osteopathic Rehabilitation Medicine. Internship Youngstown (Ohio) Osteopathic Hosp., 1960-61; resident VA Hosp. U. Pa., 1970-73; asst. medical dir. Moss Rehabilitation Hosp., Phila., 1974-77; gen. practice Phila., 1960-70; chmn. div. physical medicine & rehabilitation Suburban Gen. Hosp., Norristown, Pa., 1977-98; medical dir. Medical Ctr. Performing Artists, Norristown, Pa., 1984-98, The Rehab Station, Norristown, Pa., 1988-98, exec. dir., 1994-98; retired, 1998. Asst. instr. in phys. medicine and rehab. U. Pa., 1972-73; asst. prof. Temple U., 1973-77, asst. clin. profl., 1977—; asst. clin. prof. Phila. Coll. Ostopathic Medicine, 1978-81; adj. clin. prof. N.Y. Coll., 1980-84; clin. assoc. prof. Phila. Coll., 1981—; hosp. affiliation Moss Rehab. Hosp., Grad. Hosp. City Ave. and Parkview Divsns., Albert Einstein Med. Ctr., Frankford Hosp., Suburban Gen. Hosp.; chmn. med. audit com. Moss Rehab. Hosp., 1974-77, chmn. med. records com., 1974-77; surveyor Commn. on Accreditation of Rehab. Facilities, 1994—. Contbr. articles to profl. jours. Profl. Standards Review Orgn. Health Systems of South Eastern Pa., 1977-82; cons. to com. Rehabilitation and Spl. Devices Food and Drug Adminstrn., 1979-84, panel mem. com., 1979-84. Mem. Am. Osteopathic Assn., Pa. Osteopathic Medical Assn., Dist. X Pa. Osteopathic Medical Assn., Am. Osteopathic Coll. Rehabilitation Medicine (trustee 1975-79, vice chmn., 1977-78, pres. 1979-80, past pres. 1980-81), Am. Congress Rehabilitation Medicine, Phila. Soc. Physical Medicine and Rehabilitation (sec.-treas. 1975-76, v.p. 1975-77, pres. 1977-78), Am. Geriatrics Soc., Pan-Am. Medical Assn., Am. Coll. Sports Medicine, Am. Osteopathic Acad. Sports Medicine, Am. Acad. Clinical Neurophysiology. Home: Philadelphia, Pa. Died Dec. 1, 2009.

ROSOFF, ARNOLD ZANGWILL, retired advertising agency executive; b. Boston, Oct. 4, 1916; s. Frank and Mary Rosoff; m. Billie Tanner, Aug. 28, 1944; children— Leslie, Lory, Lyn BS, Harvard U., 1939. Treas. Arnold & Co., Boston, 1946-52, pres., 1952-75, chmn., 1975-86, Ross Publs. Inc., Boston, 1986-88. Chmn. Advt. Club Charitable Trust. Trustee Beth Israel Hosp., Combined Jewish Philanthropies; bd. dirs. Freedom Trail, Boston, Greater Boston Conv. and Visitors Bur., Franklin Flaschner Found., Mass. Assn. for Blind, Boston Aid to Blind, Ronald McDonald House. Maj. USAAF, 1942-45, ETO. Decorated D.F.C., Air medal. Mem. N.E. Broadcasters Assn., Advt. Club Greater Boston (pres. 1981-82), Exec. Svc. Corps New Eng. Home: Chestnut Hill, Mass. Died Nov. 20, 2009.

ROSS, ALAN STUART, newspaper copy editor; b. Chgo., Aug. 20, 1932; s. Charles K. and Eleanor Merle (Neville) Ross; m. Marie Esther Sassower Kish, Feb. 15, 1970; stepchildren: Betty Jo, Bobbie Jo, Patricia Ann. Student, U. Ill.-Chgo., 1950—53, U. Mo., 1953—55; BA, Columbia Coll., 1959. Reporter, copy boy Chgo. City News Bur., 1957—58; city editor Centralia Sentinel, Ill., 1959—60; sports editor Seymour Tribune, Ind., 1960—63; night news editor Frankfort Times, Ind., 1963—65; copy editor Indpls Star, from 1965. Contbr. articles to profl. jours. With US Army, 1955—57. Mem.: Indpls. Newspaper Guild, Eagle Creek Sailing Club, Riviera Club. Democrat. Unitarian. Avocations: sailing, trumpet, jazz, tennis, golf. Home: Indianapolis, Ind. Died Dec. 23, 2009.

ROSS, BERNARD HARVEY, retired humanities educator; b. Bklyn., Mar. 29, 1934; s. Leonard Sanford and Netie (Friedman) R.; m. Marlene Feldstein, June, 2, 1963; children: Jeffrey, Joanne, Carolyn. BS in Econ., U. Pa., 1955; MA in Govt., N.Y. Univ., 1966, PhD in Govt., 1971. Asst. merchandise mgr. Lightolier, Inc., Jersey City, N.J., 1957-63; contract sales mgr. Airequipt Inc., New Rochelle, N.Y., 1963-64; prof. govt. & pub. adminstrn. American U., Washington, 1967—2005, chair dept. pub. adminstrn., 1989—98, dir. Ctr. for Local & State Govt., 1974—76, dir. Ctr. for Urban Pub. Policy Analysis, 1978—83. Exec. trainer IBM, Washington, 1973-94; pres. Ross Associates, Inc., Kensington, Md. Author: Urban Politics: Power in Metropolitan America 5th edit., 1996, How Washington Works, 1997, Urban Management, 1979. Pres. White Flint Park Assn., Kensington, Md., 1972-74; v.p. Whitley Park Terrace Condo Assn., Bethesda, Md.; mem. Nat. Resources Coun., Washington, 1997, AID Task Force, Washington, 1995. With USN, 1955-57. Founders Day award N.Y. Univ., 1971. Mem. American Pol. Sci. Assn., Urban Affairs Assn. (pres. 1984-86), American Soc. Pub. Adminstr. (nat. program chair 1991). Avocations: sports, reading, stamp collecting/philately. Home: Bethesda, Md. Died July 31, 2010.

ROSS, JAMES FRANCIS, philosophy educator; b. Providence, Oct. 8, 1931; s. James Joseph and Teresa Marie (Sullivan) R.; m. Kathleen Marie Fallon, Dec. 1, 1956; children: Seamus, Ellen, Richard Fallon, Therese. AB, Cath. U. Am., 1953, MA (Basselin Found. fellow), 1954; PhD, Brown U., 1958; JD, U. Pa., 1974. Bar: Pa. bar 1975. Instr., then asst. prof. philosophy U. Mich., 1959-61; asst. prof. U. Pa., 1962-65, asso. prof., 1965-68, prof., from 1968, prof. philosophy and law, from 1994, chmn. philosophy dept. and grad. group in philosophy, 1966-70, 81-83. Rackham rsch. fellow U. Mich., 1960-61; NEH fellow, mem. Inst. Advanced Study, Princeton, 1975-76; vis. prof. Brown U., summer 1977; assoc. mem. Darwin Coll., Cambridge U. (Eng.), 1982-83. Author: Philosophical Theology, 1969, 2d edit., 1980, Introduction to Philosophy of Religion, 1970, Portraying Analogy, 1981; translator, editor: Suarez on Formal and Universal Unity, 1964; editor: Studies in Medieval Philosophy, 1971. Recipient Christian B. and Mary L. Linbach Found. award for Disting. Teaching, 1966; Disting. Scholarship award Cath. U. Am., 1971; Guggenheim fellow, 1982-83 Fellow Soc. Values in Higher Edn.; mem. Am. Philos. Assn., Am. Cath. Philos. Assn. (pres. 1987-89), Soc. for Medieval and Renaissance Philosophy, Am. Theol. Soc., Soc. Theol. Discussion. Roman Catholic. Home: Little Compton, RI. Died July 12, 2010.

ROSSANO, AUGUST THOMAS, environmental engineering educator; b. NYC, Feb. 1, 1916; s. August Thomas and Rosa (Cosenza) R.; m. Margie Chrisney, Dec. 6, 1944; children: August Thomas III, Marilyn, Pamela, Jeannine, Renee, Christopher, Stephen, Teresa. BS, MIT, 1938; MS, Harvard U., 1941, SD, 1954. Diplomate Am. Acad. Environ. Engrs., Am. Bd. Indsl. Hygiene. Commd. lt. (j.g.) USPHS, 1941, advanced through grades to capt., 1955; assigned Hdqrs. USPHS, 1941, 48, Taft Engring. Ctr., Cin., 1954-59; ret., 1963; prof. air resource engring. U. Wash., Seattle, 1963-81, prof. emeritus, from 1981; pres. Rossano Inc. Environ. Engring. Cons., from 1982. Vis. prof. Calif. Inst. Tech., 1960-63; Mem. expert adv. panel on air pollution WHO, Geneva, 1960—, Pan Am. Health Orgn., 1975—; cons. European office WHO, 1960—, U.S. Dept. HEW, 1962—, U.S. Dept. State, 1962—, U.S. Dept. Commerce, 1962—, State of Wash., 1963—, Puget Sound Air Pollution Control Agy., 1967—; cons. govts. U.S., Can., Greece, Czechoslovakia, Republic of China, Peoples Republic of China, Belgium, Netherlands, Mexico, Syria, Iran, Egypt, Brazil, Peru, Chile, Barbados, P.R., Philippines, Venezuela, Curacao, also; Smithsonian Instn. and World Bank, various other nat. and multinat. corps.; mem. subcom. on hydrogen sulfide NRC.; Bd. dirs. Environ. Resources Assos., Bellevue Montessori Sch., Environ. Sci. Service div. E.R.A., N.W. Environmental Scis. Ltd., Inst. Exec. Research, Nat. Air Conservation Commn.; lectr. applied physics and environment Bellevue Montessori Sch., WAsh., 1981—, Arbor Elem. Sch., Issaquah, Wash., 1993—; lectr. in field; co-founder Internat. Environ. Inst., 1988. Author: (with Hal Cooper) Source Testing for Air Pollution Control, 1971; Editor: Air Pollution Control, 1969; Contbr. 115 articles to tech. jours. Patentee pollution control device. Served with C.E. AUS. Recipient Spl. Svc. award USPHS, 1958, Disting. Achievement award Pacific NW-Internat. sect. Air Pollution Control Assn., Lyman A. Ripperton award Air and Waste Mgmt. Assn., 1993, Disting. Achievement educator, 1993, Spl. Svc. award USPHS, 1958, Fulbright Travel Lectr. award to eight univs. and rsch. instns. Italy, 1987; HEW tng. grantee, 1964-70; EPA grantee, 1971—; cert. achievement for 45 Yrs. Continuous Svc., Am. Indsl. Hygiene Assn., 1995. Mem. Harvard Pub. Health Alumni Assn. (pres.), Sigma Xi, Delta Omega (prize essay, 1951), Tau Beta Pi. Clubs: Bellevue Triangle Pool, Bellevue Athletic, Alderbrook (Wash.) Golf and Yacht, Wapato Point Resort, Elliott Bay Yacht, Columbia Towers. Died Aug. 10, 2009.

ROSSANT, JAMES STEPHEN, architect, artist; b. NYC, Aug. 17, 1928; s. Marcus and Anne (Orbach) R.; m. Colette Solange Palacci, Sept. 7, 1955; children: Marianne, Juliette, Cecile, Thomas B.Arch., U. Fla., 1950; M.City and Regional Planning, Harvard U., 1953. Registered architect, N.Y., Calif., Fla. Architect Mayer & Whittlesey, NYC, 1956-60; assoc. Whittlesey & Conklin, NYC, 1961-65; ptnr. Whittlesey Conklin Rossant, NYC, 1966-67, Conklin Rossant, NYC, 1967-94; prin. James Rossant Architects, NYC, from 1994. Prof. Pratt Inst., Bklyn., 1958-2009, Columbia U., N.Y.C., 1968, NYU, 1976-81, Harvard U., Cambridge, Mass., 1985-89; architect Art Commn. City of N.Y., 1979-83 Prin. works include design of Reston, Va., Dodoma, Tanzania, Butterfield House, Ramaz Sch. at N.Y.C.; one man shows include Gallery of Architecture, N.Y., 1976, John Nichols Gallery, 1990, Gallery Ueda, Tokyo, 1991, Galeria Pecanins, Mexico City, 1993, Galerie Mantoux-Gignac, Paris, 1995, 98. Fellow AIA (medal of honor N.Y. chpt. 1977). Democrat. Died Dec. 15, 2009.

ROSTEN, IRWIN, writer, producer, director; b. Bklyn., Sept. 10, 1924; m. Marilyn Ryan; 1 child, Peter. Writer-producer news, pub. affairs Sta. KNXT-CBS, Los Angeles, 1954-60; dir. news, pub. affairs Sta. KTLA, Los Angeles, 1960-63; writer-producer, dir. Wolper Prodns., Inc., Los Angeles, 1963-67; chief documentary dept. MGM Studios, Culver City, Calif., 1967-72; pres. Ronox Prodns., Inc., Los Angeles, 1970-87. Dir., writer, prodr.: (documentaries) Japan: A New Dawn Over Asia-Japan in the 20th Century, 1965, Korea: The 38th Parallel, 1967, National Geographic Specials: Grizzly, 1967, Kifaru: The Black Rhino, 1970, The Incredible Machine, 1975; (TV episodes) Hollywood and the Stars (2 episodes), 1963-64 dir., prodr. (documentaries) Birds Do It, Bees Do It, 1974; dir., writer (documentaries) Hollywood: The Dream Factory, 1972; prodr., writer: (documentaries) The

Thames, 1982; prodr.: (documentaries) Dear Mr. Gable, 1968, The Wolf Men, 1969, The Enchanted Years, 1971, Wildfire!, 1971 Recipient Emmy award Acad. TV Arts and Scis.; recipient Writers Guild America award, Peabody award, Am. Med. Writers Assn. award, Christophers award, Ohio State U. award, Saturday Rev. award, CINE Golden Eagle award Mem. Writers Guild Am., Dirs. Guild America, Acad. TV Arts and Scis., Internat. Documentary Assn. Died May 23, 2010.

ROSTENKOWSKI, DAN (DANIEL DAVID ROSTENKOWSKI), former United States Representative from Illinois; b. Chgo., Ill., Jan. 2, 1928; s. Joseph P. and Priscilla (Dombrowski) R.; m. LaVerne Pirkins, May 12, 1951; children: Dawn, Kristie, Gayle, Stacy (dec. Dec. 24, 2007) Student, St. John's Mil. Acad., 1942-46, Loyola U., 1948-51. Mem. Ill. House of Reps., 1952, Ill. State Senate, 1954—56, US Congress from 8th Ill. Dist., 1959—95; chmn. US House Ways & Means Com., 1981—94. Del. Dem. Nat. Conv., 1960, 64, 68, 72, 76, 80, 84, 88, 92. Democrat. Died Aug. 11, 2010.

ROTH, NATHAN ROBERT, retired construction company executive; b. Monroe, Wis., Dec. 16, 1922; s. Fred and Esther May (Block) R.; m. Dorothy Marie Schulthess; children: John Mark, Mary Elaine Roth-Graphics. Grad. high sch., Monroe. Owner, mgr. Bruni-Miller Co., Monroe, 1945-90; ret., 1990. Advisor Capstone H.S. Project, Monroe, 1975-85. Bd. dirs. Hist. Cheesemaking Ctr., Mornoe, 1993—; past dbd. dirs. Monroe Arts Ctr.; former advisor in founding Blackhaws Tech. Sch., Beloit-Janesville, Wis. Named Sr. Citizen Man of Yr., Monroe Jaycees, 1974, 99. Mem. United Ch. of Christ. Avocations: mountain climbing, astronomy, photography, wood carving, restoring antiques. Home: Carmel, Ind. Died Jan. 13, 2009.

ROTHMAN, SHEILA, banker, accountant, educator; b. N.Y.C., Oct. 12, 1931; d. Joseph Charles and Henrietta (Horowitz) Handshoe; m. Frank Rothman, Sept. 2, 1956; children— Andrew Steven, Richard Robert. B.B.A., C. Coll. N.Y., 1952, M.B.A., 1959; postgrad., 1959-64. Tchr. L.D. Brandeis High Sch., N.Y.C., 1966-68; controller Goodwill Inds. and Sheltered Workshop Inc., Bridgeport, Conn., 1974-77, Cable Mgmt. Services, Bridgeport, 1978-79, Conn. Community Bank (formerly Conn. Women's Bank), Greenwich, 1983—; sr. acct. Moore Mccormack Bulk Transport, Inc., Stamford, Conn., 1980-83; mem. Selectman's com. to Research Tax Relief for the Elderly, Westport, Conn., 1975; dir., sec. Conn. Research Group, Inc., Westport, 1984—. Exec. com., lobbyist Caucus of Conn. Democrats, Hartford, New Haven, 1968-73; statewide treas. Joseph D. Duffey U.S. Senatorial campaign, Hartford, 1969-71; state coordinator McGovern for Pres., Conn., 1971; mem. Women's Polit. Caucus, Westport, Conn., 1971-74, Westport Democratic Town com., 1971-74; Sunday Sch. tchr., prin. Congregation for Humanistic Judaism, Westport, 1971-75. Mem. Nat. Assn. Accts. Avocations: physical fitness activities, new age holistic health activities. Home: Westport, Conn. Died Aug. 18, 2010.

ROTHZEID, BERNARD, architect; b. Bklyn., Nov. 7, 1925; s. Barnet and Lottie (Skyanier) R.; m. Madge Rhodes, Dec. 18, 1923; children: Mitchell Frances, Alexander Skyanier. BArch, MIT, 1951, MArch, 1953. Registered profl. architect N.Y. Project architect I. M. Pei and Ptnrs., NYC, 1956-63; pres. Rothzeid, Kaiserman, Thomson & Bee, Architects and Planners, NYC, from 1963. Bd. dirs. Meth. Hosp., Bklyn, 1970—, Citizens Housing and Planning Council, N.Y.C., 1980—. Served with U.S. Army, 1944-46, PTO. Recipient Fulbright scholarship, 1954, 55, Chattel Housing grant, 1983, Augustus St. Gaudens award Cooper Union, N.Y.C., 1986. Fellow AIA. Jewish. Avocation: gardening. Home: Brooklyn, NY. Died May 25, 2009.

ROTONDO, JANE, beauty salons executive; b. Momence, Ill., Apr. 9, 1922; d. Lee and Ruth Hazel (Hazlette) Snapp; children— Maria Jane Santos, Charles J. II (dec.). Student Champaign Beauty Sch., 1943. Lic. beautician. Sec., supt. Def. Plant, Elwood, Ill., 1940-43; hairdresser, Champaign, Ill., 1943-45; hairdresser for funeral homes, Champaign, from 1955; owner beauty salons in nursing homes, Essex County, N.J., 1964—; fin. sec. Columbus Hosp., Newark, 1965-67; owner, pres. Caravan of Beauty and Caravan by Jane, Essex County, 1966—. Vice pres. Parents without Partners, Essex, N.J., 1968-73 (Woman of Yr. 1970). Home: Bloomfield, NJ. Died Aug. 25, 2009.

ROUNTREE, ASA, lawyer; b. Birmingham, Ala., Aug. 9, 1927; s. John Asa and Cherokee Jemison (Van de Graaff) Rountree; m. Elizabeth Rhodes Blue, Aug. 11, 1951 (dec.); m. Helen Hill Updike, Oct. 10, 1998. AB, U. Ala., 1949; LLB, Harvard U., 1954. Bar: Ala. 1954, U.S. Dist. Ct. (no. dist.) Ala. 1954, U.S. Ct. Appeals (5th cir.) 1955, N.Y. 1962, U.S. Dist. Ct. (so. dist.) N.Y. 1963, U.S. Ct. Appeals (2d cir.) 1963, U.S. Supreme Ct. 1972. Assoc. Cabaniss & Johnston, Birmingham, Ala., 1954-60, ptnr., 1960-62; assoc. Debevoise & Plimpton, NYC, 1962-63, ptnr., 1963-91; spl. counsel Maynard, Cooper, & Gale, P.C., Birmingham, 1991—2006. Bd. dirs. U. Ala. Law Sch. Found. With US Army, 1945—46, lt. US Army, 1951—53. Mem.: ABA (chmn. litig. sect. 1980—81), Am. Coll. Trial Lawyers, Am. Law Inst., Assn. Bar City of N.Y., N.Y. State Bar Assn., Ala. Bar Assn., Am. Bar Found., Mountain Brook Club (Birmingham), River Club (N.Y.C.). Episcopalian. Home: Birmingham, Ala. Died Feb. 11, 2010.

ROVELSTAD, MATHILDE V(ERNER), retired library and information scientist, educator; b. Germany, 1920; came to U.S., 1951. m. Howard Rovelstad, 1970. PhD, U. Tubingen, 1953; MLS, Cath. U. Am., Washington, DC, 1960. Prof. libr. sci. Cath. U. Am., 1960-90, prof. emeritus, from 1990; ret., 1990. Vis. prof. U. Montreal, 1969 Author: Bibliotheken in den Vereinigten Staaten, 1974; translator Bibliographia, an Inquiry into its Definition and Designations (R. Blum), 1980, Bibliotheken in den Vereinigten Staaten von Amerika und in Kanada, 1988; contbr. articles to profl. jours. Research grantee German Acad. Exch. Svc., 1969, Herzog August Bibliothek Wolfenbüttel, Germany, 1995. Mem. Internat. Fedn. Libr. Assns. and Instns. (standing adv. com. on libr. schs. 1975-81), Assn. for Libr. and Info. Sci. Edn. Home: Seattle, Wash. Died July 2, 2010.

ROVINSKY, JOSEPH JUDAH, obstetrician, gynecologist; b. Phila., Sept. 4, 1927; s. Israel and Sarah (Blackman) R.; m. Judith S. Levin, June 24, 1964; children: Audrey, John, Jill, Michael, Paul, David. BA, U. Pa., 1948, MD, 1952. Diplomate Am. Bd. Ob-Gyn. Intern U. Pa. Hosp., Phila., 1952-53; resident in ob-gyn Mt. Sinai Hosp., NYC, 1953-58; practice medicine specializing in ob-gyn, 1958—2008; chmn. dept. ob-gyn City Hosp. Center, Elmhurst, NY, 1964-74; prof. ob-gyn Mt. Sinai Sch. Medicine, NYC, 1969-74; prof., chmn. dept. ob-gyn Sch. Medicine Health Scis. Center, SUNY, Stony Brook, 1975-79, prof., 1975-89; chmn. dept. ob-gyn L.I. Jewish Med. Center, 1973-92; prof. ob-gyn. Albert Einstein Coll. Medicine, 1989-94; dir. dept. ob/gyn. Sound Shore Med. Ctr. of Westchester, New Rochelle, 1992—2007. Mem. obstetric adv. com. N.Y.C. Dept. Health, 1964-92. Author: Medical, Surgical and Gynecological Complications of Pregnancy, 1961, 2d edit., 1965; editor: Davis' Gynecology and Obstetrics, 1968-73. Served to capt., M.C. USAF, 1964-66. Mem. ACS, Am. Coll. Obstetricians and Gynecologists, Am. Soc. Reproductive Medicine, Am. Uro-Gynecologic Soc., N.Y. Acad. Medicine, N.Y. Obstetrical Soc., N.Y. Gynecol. Assn., Med. Soc. State N.Y. Jewish. Home: New York, NY. Died Jan. 4, 2010.

ROWEN, DANIEL, architect; b. Washington, Oct. 10, 1953; s. Hobart Quentin and Alice Brooks (Stadler) R.; m. Coco Myers, June 26, 1993; childen: Max, Harrison, Jensen BA magna cum laude, Brown U., 1975; MArch, Yale U., 1981. Prin. Daniel Rowen Architects, NYC. Prin. works include Gagosian Gallery, N.Y.C., 1991, 93, Coca-Cola Co. Offices, N.Y.C., 1994, Martha Stewart Living, 1994, 96. Recipient citation N.Y. State Assn. Architects, 1991. Mem. AIA, (citation N.Y.C. chpt. 1990, 91, award 1991), Archtl. League N.Y. Home: East Hampton, NY. Died Nov. 17, 2009.

ROWLEY, ROBERT DEANE, JR., retired bishop; b. Cumberland, Md., July 6, 1941; s. Robert Deane Sr. and Alice Marquerite (Wilson) W.; m. Nancy Ann Roland, June 27, 1964; children: Karen Gordon Rowley Butler, Robert Deane III. BA, U. Pitts., 1962, LLB, 1965; LLM, George Washington U., 1970; MDiv, Episcopal Sem. of S.W., 1977, DD (hon.), 1989. Ordained deacon Episcopal Ch., 1977; priest, 1978; bishop, 1989. Bar: Pa. 1965, U.S. Supreme Ct. 1970. Dean of students St. Andrew's Priory Sch., Honolulu, 1977-80; canon St. Andrew's Cathedral, Honolulu, 1979-81; rector St. Timothy's Episcopal Ch., Aiea, Hawaii, 1981—89; canon to bishop Diocese of Bethlehem (Pa.); bishop Diocese of Northwestern Pa., Erie, 1989—2006; pres. 3rd prov., 1993—2002. Capt. USN, 1966-92. Mem. Erie County Bar Assn., Erie Club, Lake Shore Country Club. Episcopalian. Home: York, Pa. Died Jan. 18, 2010.

ROWLINGS, DONALD GEORGE, international investment banker; b. Boston, Aug. 12, 1929; s. George Brookfield and Margaret Justine (McIlroy) R.; m. Jocelyn Clapp, Mar. 9, 1952; children: Jeffrey Donald, Leigh Carolyn, Judith Sayles. BA, Colgate U., 1951; JD, Harvard U., 1956. Bar: Ohio 1957. Assoc. Taft, Stettinius & Hollister, Cin., 1956-63; v.p. fin. and law Chem. & Indsl. Corp., Cin., 1963-71; v.p. fin. Kaiser Engrs. Inc., Oakland, Calif., 1971-81, sr. v.p., 1983-88; mng. dir. Kaiser Engrs. Ltd., London, 1981-83; pres. Rowlings Capital Group Inc., Oakland, Calif., from 1988. Lectr., presenter fin. and devel. of indsl. projects, 1975-87. Served to 1st lt. USAF, Korea. Mem. ABA, Am. Mining Congress, San Francisco Mus. Modern Art, Oakland Mus. Clubs: Lakeview (Oakland). Republican. Avocations: art collecting, photography. Home: Piedmont, Calif. Died Oct. 8, 2009.

ROY, RUSTUM, citizen scientist; b. Ranchi, India, July 3, 1924; came to U.S., 1945, naturalized, 1961; s. Narendra Kumar and Rajkumari (Mukherjee) R.; m. Della M. Martin, June 8, 1948; children: Neill, Ronnen, Jeremy. BSc with honors, Patna U., India, 1942, MSc, 1944; PhD, Pa. State U., 1948; DSc (hon.), Tokyo Inst. Tech., 1987, Alfred U, 1993. Research asst. Pa. State U., 1948-49, mem. faculty, from 1950, prof. geochemistry, from 1957, prof. solid state, from 1968, chmn. solid state tech. program, 1960-67, chmn. sci. tech. and soc. program, 1977-84, dir., 1984-89, dir. materials research lab., 1962-85, Evan Pugh prof., from 1981, Evan Pugh prof. solid state, geochemistry, sci. tech. & soc. emeritus, 1999; sr. sci. officer Nat. Ceramic Lab., India, 1950; mem. com. mineral sci. tech. Nat. Acad. Scis., 1967-69, com. survey materials sci. tech., 1970-74; exec. com. chem. div. NRC, 1967-70, nat. materials adv. bd., 1970-77, mem. com. radioactive waste mgmt., 1974-80, chmn. panel waste solidification, 1976-80, chmn. com. USSR and Eastern Europe, 1976-81. Mem. com. material sci. and engring. NRC, 1986-89; mem. Pa. Gov.'s Sci. Adv. Com.; chmn. materials adv. panel Gov.'s Sci. Adv. Com., 1965-80; mem. adv. com. on engring. NSF, 1968-72, adv. com. to ethical and human value implications sci. and tech., 1974-76, adv. com. div. materials rsch., 1974-77; Hibbert lectr. tech. and religion U. London, 1979; cons. to industry; mem. adv. com. Coll. Engring., Stanford U., 1984-86; internat. sci. lectr. NRC, 1991-92; rsch. prof. materials Ariz. State U., 1999—; vis. prof. medicine U. Ariz., 1999—. Author: Honest Sex, 1968, Crystal Chemistry of Non-metallic Materials, 1974, Experimenting with Truth, 1981, Radioactive Waste Disposal, Vol. 1, the Waste Package, 1983, Lost at the Frontier, 1985; founding editor-in-chief: Materials Rsch. Bull., 1966—, Jour. Materials Edn., 1980-2000, Bull. Sci. Tech. and Soc, 1981-2000, Materials Rsch. Innovations, 1997—; contbr. over 1000 articles to profl. jours., 25 patents in field. Chmn. bd. Dag Hammarskjold Coll., 1973-75; chmn. ad hoc com. sci., tech. and ch. Nat. Coun. Chs., 1966-68; bd. dirs. Kirkridge Retreat, 1958-80, chmn., 1978-80; founder, chmn. bd. Friends of Health; chmn. bd. Campaign for Better Health. Sci. policy fellow Brookings Instn., 1982-83; recipient Ellis Island medal of hon., 1996; named to Order of the Rising Sun with Gold Rays status in Japanese Emperor's birthday honors list, 2002. Fellow: AAAS (chmn. chemistry sect. 1985), Mineral. Soc. Am. (award 1957), Am. Phys. Soc., Indian Acad. Scis. (hon.), Am. Ceramic Soc. (Sosman lectr. 1975, Orton lectr. 1984, disting. life, Educator of Yr. 1993); mem.: U.S. Nat. Acad. Engring., Materials Rsch. Soc. (pres. 1976, founder & architect from 1967, co-chair 1973), Am. Soc. Engring. Educators (Centennial medal 1993, Hall of Fame 1993), Am. Chem. Soc. (Petroleum Rsch. Fund award 1960, Dupont award for Chem. of Materials 1993), Fine Ceramics Assn. Japan (Internat. award), Ceramic Soc.Japan (hon. Centennial award 1991), Mineral Soc. Am., Fedn. Materials Socs. (Nat. Materials Advancement award 1991), Russian Acad. Scis. (elected fgn.), Engring. Acad. Japan (elected fgn.), Indian Nat. Sci. Acad. (elected fgn.), Royal Swedish Acad. Engring. Scis. (elected fgn.). Home: State College, Pa. Died Aug. 26, 2010.

ROYSTON, JOHN PAUL, government official; b. Bridgeport, Conn., May 1, 1936; s. John Peter and Elizabeth Mylod (McNamara) R.; m. Dolores Ann Seeman, Sept. 21, 1963; children— Timothy, Stephen, Matthew, Maria. B.S., Holy Cross Coll., 1959; M.P.A., U. So. Calif., 1971. Asst. program officer AID, Republic of Panama, 1963-66; planning officer OEO, Washington, 1966-70; chief field ops. OMB, Washington, 1970-80; dir. organizational planning U.S. Dept. Edn., Washington, 1980-82; dir. orgn. and mgmt. systems EEOC, Washington, 1982-83, dir. project research, 1985-86; dir. ops. Pres.'s Commn. on Indsl. Competitiveness, Washington, 1983-85; asst. dir. emergency planning, Office of Sec. of Def., 1986—. Pres., Blessed Sacrament PTA, Washington, 1976; v.p. Holy Cross Alumni (Mid-Atlantic), Washington, 1979; pres. Blessed Sacrament Sch. Bd., 1980. Served to capt. USNR, 1959—. Recipient Spl. Achievement award EEOC, 1983, Sec. Dept. Edn., 1981; Presdl. Commendation, White House, 1972. Mem. Am. Soc. for Pub. Adminstrn., Naval Res. Assn. Democrat. Roman Catholic. Club: Kenwood Golf and Country (Bethesda, Md.). Died Dec. 31, 2009.

RUAN, JOHN, retired trucking company executive; b. Beacon, Iowa, Feb. 11, 1914; s. John Arthur and Rachel Anthony (Llewellyn) R.; m. Rose Duffy, July 10, 1941 (dec. May 1943); 1 child, John III; m. Elizabeth J. Adams, Sept. 6, 1946; children: Elizabeth Jayne Ruan Fletcher (dec. 1992), Thomas Heyliger. Student, Iowa State U., 1931-32. Pres. The Ruan Companies, Des Moines, 1932-86. Mem. Des Moines Devel. Corp.; past pres. Greater Des Moines Com., Iowa State Engring. Coll. Adv. Council; fin. chmn., exec. com. Northwestern U. Transp. Ctr.; bd. govs. Iowa State U. Found.; bd. dirs. Des Moines Area Council on Alcoholism, Living History Farms; trustee Hoover Presidential Library Assns., Inc. Named Des Moines Citizen Yr., Des Moines City Council, 1981, Iowa Bus. Leader of Yr. Des Moines Register, 1991; named to Iowa Bus. Hall of Fame, 1982; recipient Disting. Iowa Citizen award Mid-Iowa Council Boy Scouts Am., 1985, Humanitarian award Variety Club of Iowa, 1986, People With Vision award Iowa Soc. Prevent Blindness, 1986. Mem. Am. Trucking Assns., Inc. (treas., exec. com., chmn. fin. com.), Am. Trucking Assns. Found. (trustee), Iowa Assn. Bus. and Industry (bd. dirs.), Des Moines C. of C. (bd. dirs.). Clubs: Wakonda, Des Moines; Lost Tree, Old Port Yacht (North Palm Beach, Fla.); Rancho LaCosta (Carlsbad, Calif.). Republican. Methodist. Avocations: golf, mushroom hunting. Home: Davenport, Iowa. Died Feb. 14, 2010.

RUBENS, WILLIAM STEWART, broadcast executive; b. Bklyn., Dec. 25, 1927; s. Samuel and Betty (Cooperman) R.; m. Ruth Joan Peltz; 1 child, Steven Roy. BBA, CCNY, 1950; postgrad., NYU, 1953-55. Research analyst Harry B. Cohen Advt., NYC, 1951-53; statistician ABC, NYC, 1953-55; research exec. NBC, NYC, 1955-63, dir. mktg. services, 1963-70, v.p. audience research, 1970-72, v.p. research, mem. pres.' council, 1972-89; pres. The Rubens Group, Inc., from 1989. Bd. dirs. Electronic Media Rsch. Coun., N.Y.C., 1972-88; chmn. Cable TV Com., East Hills, N.Y., 1986—; cons. NBC, ABC, CBS, 1988-92. Co-author: Television and Aggression, 1982; contbr. articles to profl. jours. Chmn. Advt. Research Found., 1980. Served with AUS, 1946-47, Korea. Recipient Beville award Nat. Assn. Broadcasters, Broadcast Edn. Assn., 1989. Mem. Am. Mktg. Assn. (bd. dirs. N.Y. chpt. 1986-92), Radio-TV Rsch. Coun. (pres. 1975), Market Rsch. Coun. (pres. 1987-88), Mktg. Sci. Inst. (trustee 1987-88), North Shore Country Club (bd. dirs., chmn. golf com.), Hunter Pun Country Club, Friars Club. Jewish. Home: Boynton Beach, Fla. Died Jan. 30, 2010.

RUBIN, BENJAMIN ARNOLD, microbiologist, immunologist, medical educator, researcher; b. NYC, Sept. 27, 1917; s. Eli and Helen Sarah (Arenoff) R.; m. Mae Koenig, Aug. 31, 1951. BS, CCNY, 1937; MS, Va. Polytech. Inst. & State U., 1938; PhD, Yale U., 1947. Asst. dir. Circle Analytical Lab., NYC, 1938-40; chief lab. and radiology U.S. Army C.E., Nfld., also Cen. Am., 1940-44; asst. chief microbiologist Scherly Rsch. Lab., Lawrenceburg, Ind., 1944; rsch. asst. Yale U., New Haven, 1944-47; chief microbiologist Broockhaven Nat. Lab., LI, 1947-52, Syntex, Mexico City, 1952-54; prof. pub. health and preventitive medicine Coll. of Medicine Baylor U., Houston, 1954-60; mgr. biol. rsch. Wyeth, Radnar, Pa., 1960-84; rsch. prof. Phila. Coll. Osteo. Medicine, 1984-95; ret. Cons. GE, Valley Forge, Pa., 1972-80, U.S. Congressional com. energy and commerce, 1976-80, biological applications of space. Contbr. over 150 articles to sci. jours. Named to Inventors Hall of Fame, 1992; recipient John Scott award and medal, 1982, Proctor medal Phila. Drug Exchange, 1993; named Inventor of Yr., 1985. Achievements include invention of bifurcated needle in Smallpox eradication program. Home: Bala Cynwyd, Pa. Died Mar. 8, 2010.

RUBINSON, LAURNA, social psychologist, educator; b. NYC, Feb. 9, 1945; d. Fred Yale and Sylvia (Newman) Goldberg. BS, L.I. U., 1966; MS, Southern Conn. U., 1969; PhD, U. Ill., Champaign, 1976. Tchr., supr. Branford (Conn.)

Pub. Schs., 1966-71; instr. Danville (Ill.) Area Coll., 1971-73, U. Ill., Champaign, 1973-76, prof., from 1976. Author: Health Education: Foundations for the Future, 1984, Research Techniques for the Health Sciences, 1987, Contemporary Human Sexuality; mem., chair editl. bd. Jour. Sch. Health Edn., Jour. Sex Edn. and Therapy, Jour. Sex Rsch.; contbr. articles to profl. jours. Fellow Am. Sch. Health Assn. (disting. service award 1986); mem. Am. Pub. Health Assn., Am. Psychological Assn., Assn. for Advancement Health Edn. Avocations: racquetball, reading, cross country skiing. Died Jan. 2, 2010.

RUBLE, ROBERT LEE, police chief; b. St. Louis, Mar. 16, 1933; s. Robert E. Lee and Dolores (Fields) R.; m. Patricia Evelyn Scott (div. 1973); children— Rebecca, Lisa; m. 2d, Sheila Margaret Cooper, Oct. 12, 1974. A.A. in Criminal Justice, Kennesaw Coll., 1983; B.S., Brenau Coll., 1983. Enlisted man U.S. Marine Corps, 1950-61, 65-77; ret., 1977; patrolman Tampa (Fla.) Police Dept., 1961-65; spl. agt. frauds VA, Atlanta, 1977-80; chief of police City of Kennesaw (Ga.), 1980—. Chmn. St. Judes and Nat. Kidney Found., 1980-83. Decorated Navy Commendation medal with combat V. Mem. Nat. Assn. Chiefs of Police (exec. bd. 1980—, state pres. 1980-83), Ga. Assn. Chiefs of Police. Democrat. Episcopalian. Lodges: Shriners. Home: Kennesaw, Ga. Died Apr. 22, 2010.

RUCH, WILLIAM HARVEY, management consultant; b. Sunbury, Pa., July 7, 1928; s. Joseph Isaac and Helen Dorothy (Derr) Ruch; m. Lois Eilene Wildsmith, Sept. 28, 1951; children: Dennis Allen, Michael William. Grad., Pub. Sch., Sunbury. Pecision machinist Am. Safety Razor Co., Staunton, Va., 1962—66, machine shop planner, 1966—67, supr. apprentices, 1967—72, maintenance engr. asst., 1972—77; maintenance planner Merck & Co., Inc., Elkton, Va., 1977—79, mech. tng. supr., from 1979; chmn. apprenticeship adv. com. Massanutten Tech. Ctr., Harrisonburg, Va., from 1983; com. to establish minimun standard apprenticeship for Commonwealth of Va., curriculum cons., from 1981; part-time tchr., from 1981. With USAF, 1946—49. Mem.: Nat. Assn. Primitive Riflemen, Nat. Rifle Assn., Marfan Found., World Future Soc. Republican. Lutheran. Died Apr. 27, 2010.

RUDD, PAUL RYAN, actor; b. Boston, May 15, 1940; s. Frank Stanley and Kathryn Frances (Ryan) R.; m. Joan Mannion, Sept. 5, 1965 (div. Nov. 1982); m. Martha Bannerman, Mar. 4, 1983; children: Graeme, Kathryn, Eliza. BA in Psychology, Fairfield U., 1962. Mem. drama faculty Carnegie Mellon U., Pitts., 1983, 84. Stage debut, 1968; appeared with repertory theatres, N.Y. Shakespeare Festival, Lincoln Ctr. Repertory, Hartford Stage, Arena Stage, Longwharf Theatre, San Diego Shakespeare Festival, 1968-73; Broadway debut in The Changing Room, 1973, The National Health, 1974, Ah! Wilderness, 1975, Glass Menagerie, 1976, Streamers, 1976, Henry V, 1976, Romeo and Juliet, 1977, Flowers for Algernon, 1978; Bosoms and Neglect, 1979; off Broadway appearances include Boys In The Band, 1970; Oliver in DA, 1978, The Lady and the Clarinet, 1983; (TV movies) Beacon Hill, 1975, Johnny We Hardly Knew Ye, 1977, Connecticut Yankee in King Arthur's Court, 1978 The Betsy, 1978, The Last Song, 1980, Family Reunion, 1981, Kung Fu: The Movie, 1986; (TV mini-series) Beulah Land, 1980; (TV appearances) Knots Landing (3 episodes), 1980-81, Hart to Hart (2 episodes), 1983, Quincy, 1983, Murder, She Wrote, 1984, Moonlighting, 1985 Recipient Outer Critics Circle award, 1975-76; named Man of Yr., Fairfield U., 1977. Mem. SAG, AFTRA, Actors Equity Assn. Home: Greenwich, Conn. Died Aug. 12, 2010.

RUDIN, WALTER, retired mathematician; b. Vienna, May 2, 1921; came to U.S., 1945; s. Robert and Natalie (Adlersberg) R.; m. Mary Ellen Estill, Aug. 19, 1953; children: Catherine, Eleanor, Robert J., Charles M. BA, MA, Duke U., 1947, PhD, 1949. Instr. Duke U., Durham, N.C., 1949-50, MIT, Cambridge, Mass., 1950-52; asst. prof. math. U. Rochester, N.Y., 1952-55, assoc. prof. N.Y., 1955-57, prof. N.Y., 1957-59; prof. math. U. Wis.-Madison, 1959—91, prof. emeritus, 1991—2010. Author: Principles of Mathematical Analysis, 1953, 64, 76, Fourier Analysis on Groups, 1962, Real and Complex Analysis, 1966, 74, 87, Function Theory on Polydiscs, 1969, Functional Analysis, 1973, Function Theory on the Unit Ball of Cn, 1980; fgn. lang. edits.; contbr. numerous research articles to profl. jours. Served as petty officer Royal Navy, 1943-45. Mem. Am. Math. Soc., Math. Assn. Am. Home: Madison, Wis. Died May 20, 2010.

RUDNICK, LEWIS G., lawyer; b. May 31, 1935; AB with honors, Univ. Ill., Urbana-Champaign, 1957; MBA, Columbia Univ., 1960; JD, Northwestern Univ., 1964. Bar: Ill. 1964, US Dist. Ct. (no. dist. Ill.) 1964. Of Councel, Franchise & Distribution practice group DLA Piper US LLP, Chgo. Former gen. counsel Internat. Franchise Assn. and Internat. Franchise Assn. Edn. Found.; mem., councel Ill. Franchise Adv. Bd.; mem. gov. com. ABA Forum on Franchising, 1977—84, chmn., 1981—83. Editor: Former Jour. of Internat. Franchising & Distribution Law; contbr. articles to profl. jours. Mem.: ABA, Internat. Franchise Assn. (counsel). Died Jan. 24, 2009.

RUGGIERI, BERNARD J., lawyer; b. Apr. 3, 1926; s. Joseph F. and Mary R.; m. Patricia L. Tenney, Sept. 10, 1969; children— Christina, Kate Grad., Brown U.; JD, Bklyn. Law Sch., 1953. Bar: N.Y. 1953, U.S. Dist. Ct. (so. dist.) N.Y. 1954. U.S. Supreme Ct. 1955. Asst. counsel to Gov. Harriman State of N.Y., 1955-57; asst. to mayor, legis. rep. City of N.Y., 1957-64; ptnr. Shea & Gould, NYC, from 1965. Counsel to minority leader N.Y. State Senate, 1964-74; adj. prof. law N.Y. Law Sch., 1981-82 Chmn., N.Y. Democratic Com., 1971-74; chmn. Daytop Village, 1983-85; trustee St. Vincent's Hosp., New Sch., N.Y.C., 1981-82, N.Y. Sch. 2d lt. U.S. Army, 1948-49 Mem. N.Y. State Bar Assn., Assn. Bar City N.Y., N.Y. Coll. Osteo. Medicine (vice chmn.). Died May 8, 2009.

RUIZ, RAMÓN EDUARDO, history professor; b. Sessions Ranch, Calif., Sept. 9, 1921; s. Ramon and Dolores (Urueta) R.; m. Natalia Marrujo, Oct. 14, 1944 (dec. 2006); children: Olivia, Maura. BA, San Diego State Coll., 1947; MA, Claremont Grad. Sch., 1948; PhD, U. Calif., Berkeley, 1954. Asst. prof. U. Oreg., Eugene, 1955-57, Southern Meth. U., Dallas, 1957-58; prof. Smith Coll., Northampton, Mass., 1958-69; prof. Latin American history U. Calif., 1969-91, prof. emeritus, 1991—2010, chmn. dept. history, 1971-76, chmn. divsn. humanities, 1972-74; mem. project grant com. NEH, 1972-73, 75-77, dir. pub. programs divsn., 1979-80; Ralph Chase lectr. San Angelo State U., 2000. Vis. prof. Facultad de Economia, Univ. de Nuevo Leon, Mexico, 1965-66, Coll. de Sonora, Mexico, summer 1983, Pomona Coll., 1983-84, Coll. de Michoacan, Mexico, summer 1986, 87, Univ. Nacional Autonoma de Mexico, fall 1992; scholar-in-residence Colegio de la Frontero Norte, Mexico, 1994-96; MacArthur Found. nominator, 1981-82; mem. project grant com. Ford Found. Author: Cuba: The Making of A Revolution, 1968 (One of Best History Books, Book World Washington Post 1968), Mexico: The Challenge of Poverty and Illiteracy, 1963, An American in Maximillians's Mexico, 1865-1866, 1959; (with James D. Atwater) Out From Under; Benito Juarez and Mexico's Struggle for Independence, 1969; (with John Tebbel) South by Southwest: The Mexican-American and His Heritage, 1969, Interpreting Latin American History, 1970, Labor and the Ambivalent Revolutionaries: Mexico, 1911-23, 1975, The Mexican War: Was it Manifest Destiny?, 1963, The Great Rebellion: Mexico, 1905-1924, 1980 (Hubert C. Herring prize), The People of Sonora and Yanqui Capitalists, 1988, Triumphs and Tragedy: A History of the Mexican People, 1992 (named One of Five Best History Books 1991-92, L.A. Times, Gold Medal award Commonwealth Club San Francisco 1993, History Book Club selection); (with Olivia Teresa Ruiz) Reflexiones Sobre la Identidad de los Pueblos, 1996, On the Rim of Mexico: Encounters of the Rich and Poor, 1998, Memories of a Hyphenated Man, 2003, Mexico: Why a Few are Rich and the People Poor, 2009. Served to lt. USAAF, 1943-46. William Harrison Mills traveling fellow in internat. rels., 1950; John Hay Whitney Found. fellow, 1950; Fulbright fellow Mex., 1965-66; fellow Ctr. for Advanced Study in Behavioral Scis., 1984-85, Rockefeller Resident, Bellagio Study Ctr., 2003, Ena H. Thompson lectureship, Pomona Coll., 1995; recipient Am. Philos. Soc. grant in aid, 1959, Nat. medal Humanities Pres. U.S., 1998. Mem. American Hist. Assn. (Beveridge prize com. 1974-76), Conf. Latin Am. History, Chicano-Latino Faculty Assn. U. Calif. (pres. 1989-91), Phi Beta Kappa, Sigma Delta Pi. Home: Rancho Santa Fe, Calif. Died July 6, 2010.

RUMLER, ROBERT HOKE, agricultural products executive, consultant, retired trade association administrator; b. Chambersburg, Pa., Apr. 4, 1915; s. Daniel Webster and Jennie (Sellers) R.; m. Frances Jeannette Montgomery, June 7, 1939 (dec. 1983); children: Craig M. (dec. 2006), Karen A. Loden; m. Hazel Miller-Karper, Aug. 23, 1986 (dec. 1998). BS, Pa. State U., 1936. Asst. county agt. U. Mo., 1936-37; county agrl. agt. Pa. State U., 1937-45; asst. mgr., editor agrl. promotion divsn. E. I. duPont de Nemours & Co., Inc., Wilmington, Del., 1945-48; asst. exec. sec., COO, Holstein-Friesian Assn. Am., 1948-53, 53-75, exec. sec., CEO, 1975-81, exec. chmn., 1981-82, chmn. emeritus, from 1982. Pres. Holstein-Assoc. USA, Inc., 1968-81; agribus. cons., 1982—; hon. mem. Holstein-Firesian de Mex. (C.A.); bd. dirs., chmn. Vt. Nat. Bank, Vt. Fin. Svcs., Inc., 1957-88; mem. U.S./USSR Joint Com. Agrl. Cooperation; past chmn. U.S. Agrl. Export Devel. Coun., FAS-USDA; mem. coordinating group Nat. Coop. Dairy Herd Improvement program USDA, 1964-80; mem. agrl. policy adv. com. USTR/USDA Multilateral Trade Negotiations, 1973-87, mem. agrl. tech. adv. com., 1987-95. Contbg. editl. writer Holstein World. Trustee Ea. States Expn., trustee emeritus, 1993—; trustee Assoc. Industries Vt.; past bd. dirs. Internat. Stockmans Ednl. Found.; chmn. adv. bd. Pa. State U., Mont Alto, 1988-98, chmn. 1990-94, emeritus 1998, Centennial fellow, 2004; bd. advisors Pa. State U., Harrisburg, 1990-94. Recipient Disting. award Nat. Dairy Herd Improvement Assn., 1974, Disting. Svc. award Nat. Agrl. Mktg. Orgn., 1977, Cert. of Appreciation, USDA, 1982, Disting. Svc. award Holstein Assn., 1985; named Disting. Alumnus, Pa. State U., 1978, Coll. Agr., 2000, Dairy Industry Man of Yr., World Dairy Expo, 1979, Headliner-of-Yr. Livestock Publs. Coun., 1995, Internat. Person of Yr. World Dairy Expo, 1996, 1st Disting. Alumnus AZ Frat., Pa. State U., 1996; Centennial fellow Pa. State Mont Alto Campus, 20054; named to Internat. Livestock Hall of Fame, 1987; Robert H. Rumler scholarhip founded in his name. Fellow Agr. Adventures; mem. Purebred Dairy Cattle Assn. (dir., exec. com.), Nat. Soc. Livestock Record Assns. (past pres., dir., Disting. Svcs. award 1981), Am. Dairy Sci. Assn. (Disting. Svc. award 1977), Agri-Bus. Found. (All-Time Gt. award 1981), Nat. Dairy Shrine (Dairy Hall of Fame 1976), N.E. Master Farmers Assn. (hon. master farmer 1999, Pa. Farm Bur. Disting. Svc. to Agr. award 1999), U.S. Animal Health Assn., Kiwanis, Masons, Elks, Alpha Zeta (hon. roll 1997), Gamma Sigma Delta. Mem. United Ch. of Christ. Home: Chambersburg, Pa. Died Jan. 11, 2010.

RUOF, RICHARD ALAN, minister, poet, writer; b. Lancaster, Pa., Oct. 11, 1932; s. Robert Jacob and Geneva May (Devers) Ruof; m. Anne Margaret Demos; children: Mark Alan Demos Ruof, Anne Tracy Demos Ruof, Richard James Demos Ruof. AB, Franklin and Marshall Coll., 1954; MDiv, Lancaster Theol. Sem., Pa., Union Theol. Sem., Richmond, Va., 1960; STM, Luth. Theol. Sem., Gettysburg, Pa., 1974; DMin, McCormick Theol. Sem., 1981. Ordained to ministry United Ch. Christ, 1960. Pastor Harrisville (Va.) Charge of United Ch. Christ, 1959-62, Thurmont (Md.) Charge, 1962-67, First Congl. Ch., Cortland, NY, 1967-77, St. Paul's United Ch. Christ of Hamlin, Fredericksburg, Pa., 1977-82, St. John's United Ch. Christ, Egg Harbor City, NJ, 1982-87, Friedensburg, Pa., 1987-94, pastor emeritus, 1994. Author: (spiritual poems) Songs of the Lesser Servants, 2003, Melting World, 2004, Return of the Martyrs, 2005, Days of the Eagle, 2005, Departure of the Blossoms, 2006, Poems of the Bridge, 2008, Whispered Messages, 2008, How Still the Songbird Lies, 2009. Mem. Egg Harbor City Bd. Edn., 1984; registrar-treas. Susquehanna Assn. N.Y. Conf., United Ch. Christ, 1968—74. With USNR, 1954—56. Home: Auburn, Pa. Died Feb. 10, 2010.

RUSH, DAVID HAROLD, electronics company executive; b. Bklyn., Apr. 18, 1921; s. Joseph and Ida (Smith) R.; student Rutgers U., N.Y. U.; m. Miriam Nelson, June 17, 1948; children— Barbara, Joel. Flight engr. Pan Am. World Airways, N.Y.C., 1945-48; pres. Rush Photo, N.Y.C., 1948-60; pres. Chromalloy Electronics Div., N.Y.C., 1957-77, also dir.; group v.p. Chromalloy Am. Corp., N.Y.C., 1967, v.p. electronics group, 1968; pres., chmn. bd., chief exec. officer ACR Electronics, Inc., 1976—, Vexilar, Inc., chmn. bd., chief exec. bd. Aptek Micro Systems Inc., 1982—; 1st Fed. Savs. & Loan Assn. of Broward, 1980-83; dir. Miami br. Fed. Res. Bank of Atlanta, 1980-83, chmn., 1983—; cons. AVCO, RAD, Wilmington, Mass., Gen. Electric Co., Phila. Bd. dirs. Holy Cross Hosp.; trustee Nova U., 1982—. Served with USAAC, 1942-45. Mem. Space and Flight Equipment Assn. (pres. 1965-66), Greater Hollywood C. of C. (chmn. bd. 1978-80). Clubs: Masons, Congressional (charter mem.) (Garden City, N.Y.). Patentee in field. Home: Fort Lauderdale, Fla. Died Feb. 26, 2009.

RUSSELL, HUGH EDWARD, lawyer; b. Oshkosh, Wis., Sept. 13, 1924; s. Harold Hugh and Agnes (Horen) Russell; m. Joyce V. Schultz, Apr. 12, 1953; children: Elizabeth, Jay, Sharon, Sue. BS, U. Wis., LLB, 1952. Bar: Wis. 1952. Assoc. Thompson, Gruenewald & McCarthy, Oshkosh, 1952—54, Lees & Bunge, LaCrosse, 1954—56; hearing examiner Worker's Compensation Div., Madison, Wis., 1956—73; dep. adminstr., from 1973; mem. Fla. Gov.s Adv. Com. on Workers Compensation, 1979; cons. workers compensation DC, from 1980. With AUS, 1943—46. Mem.: Wis. Bar Assn., Dane County Bar Assn., Internat. Assn. Indsl. Accident Bds. & Commns. (vice chmn. adminstrn. and procedure com.; mem. faculty Coll. 1982). Lutheran. Home: Madison, Wis. Died June 14, 2010.

RUSSELL, JAMES BENJAMIN, microbiologist, educator, research scientist; s. Lincoln A. and Mary M. Russell; 1 child, Aaron T. BS, Cornell U., Ithaca, NY, 1973; MS, U. Calif., Davis, 1974, PhD, 1978. Asst. prof. U. Ill., Urbana, 1978—81; rsch. microbiologist Agrl. Rsch. Svc., USDA, Ithaca, from 1981; prof. Cornell U., Ithaca, from 1981. Author: Rumen Microbiology and Its Role in Ruminant Nutrition, 2002; contbr. more than 200 articles, revs. to profl. publs., chpts. to books. Recipient Outstanding Tchr. award, U. Ill., 1981, Am. Feed Industry award, USDA, 1993, 2005; named North Atlantic Area Scientist of Yr., 1993, 2005. Fellow: Am. Acad. Microbiology; mem.: Am. Soc. Animal Sci., Am. Dairy Sci. Assn., Am. Soc. Microbiology. Achievements include patents for rumen fluid for calves to prevent needless diarrhea; patents pending for carbonated cow manure to kill pathogenic bacteria. Avocation: swimming. Home: Ithaca, NY. Died Sept. 20, 2009.

RUSSELL, ROBERT WALTER, editor, publisher, financial planner; b. Jersey City, Jan. 5, 1944; s. Robert Charles and Rose Elizabeth (Molino) R.; m. Barbara Ann Weigner, Oct. 28, 1967; children: Robert John, Matthew David, Daniel Christopher. BS, Gettysburg Coll., 1965; MS, U. So. Calif., 1974. Registered stockbroker, financial planner. Exec. dir. Rota Community Coll., Spain, 1971-75, also recreation dir. Rota Spain Naval Sta.; asst. to pres. Howard Community Coll., Columbia, Md., 1975-79; editor Reston Publ., Va., 1979-81; contbg. editor Stranger Register; pres. R&R Assocs., Inc., Columbia, Md., 1981—. Creator: City Puzzles, Columbia Mag., St. Louis Mag., 1984-85. Bd. dirs. Harper's Choice Community Assn., Columbia, 1981—; rep. Columbia City Council, 1982—; bd. dirs., vice chmn. Assn., 1981—; bd. dirs. Family Life Ctr., Columbia, 1978—; chmn. United Way Community Partnerships, 1984-85; pres. Assn. Community Services, Columbia, 1976-7, bd. dirs., 1983—; pub. fin. newsletter. Recipient Audrey Robbins Humanitarian award Howard County Assn. Community Services, 1985. Democrat. Avocations: racquetball, bicycling. Home: Columbia, Md. Died Aug. 19, 2010.

RUSSELL-WOOD, ANTHONY JOHN R., history professor, department chairman; b. Corbridge-on-Tyne, Northumberland, Eng., Oct. 11, 1939; came to U.S., 1971; s. James and Ethel Kate (Roberts) R.-W.; m. Hannelore Elisabeth Schmidt, May 19, 1972; children: Christopher James Owen, Karsten Anthony Alexander. Diploma in Portuguese studies, Lisbon U., Portugal, 1960; BA with honors, Oxford U., Eng., 1963, MA, DPhil., 1967. Lectr. Portuguese lang. and lit. Oxford U., 1963-64; rsch. fellow St. Antony's Coll., Oxford, 1967-70; vis. assoc. prof. Johns Hopkins U., Balt., 1971-72, assoc. prof., 1972-76, prof., from 1976, chmn. dept. history, 1984-90, 96-99, chmn. dept. Hispanic and Italian studies, 1996-97, Herbert Baxter Adams prof., from 2001. Disting. vis. prof. U. Mass.-Dartmouth, 2000; vis. prof. Portuguese and Brazilian studies and history Brown U., 2001. Author: Manuel Francisco Lisboa: A Craftsman of the Golden Age of Brazil, 1968, Fidalgos and Philanthropists: The Santa Casa da Misericordia of Bahia, 1550-1755, 1968, The Black Man in Slavery and Freedom in Colonial Brazil, 1982, Society and Government in Colonial Brazil, 1500-1822, 1992, A World on the Move: The Portuguese in Africa, Asia and America 1415-1808, 1992, Portugal and the Sea: A World Embraced, 1997, The Portuguese Empire, 1415-1808, 1998; Slavery and Freedom in Colonial Brazil, 2002, Universalidade das Santas Casas--500 anos de cultura Lusofona, 2002, Escravos e Libertos no Brasil Colonial, 2005; co-author: From Colony to Nation: Essays on the Independence of Brazil, 1975; editor: Local Government in European Overseas Empires, 1450-1800, 1999, Government and Governance of Empires, 1415-1800, 2000; sr. editor: The Americas, 2002—; gen. editor: An Expanding World: The European Impact on World History, 1450-1800, 1995-2000. Chmn. CLAH Columbus Quincentennial Com.,

1987-90, Md. State Humanities Coun., 1980-82; mem. Md. Heritage Com., 1982-85, Balt. County Commn. Arts and Scis., 1982-84. Decorated comendador Order of Prince Henry (Portugal), Order of Rio Branco (Brazil); recipient Bolton Meml. prize Conf. Latin Am. Hist., 1969, Whitaker prize Middle-Atlantic Coun. Latin Am. Studies, 1983, Dom João de Castro prize Portuguese Nat. Commn. for Commemoration of Discoveries, 1993, Benemérito, Santa Casa da Misericordia, Bahia, 1999, comdr. Internat. Order of Merit of Misericórdias, 2000. Fellow: European Acad. Scis. & Arts, Royal Hist. Soc., Academia de Letras da Bahia (corr.), Instituto Historico e Geografico Brasileiro (corr.), Royal Geog. Soc. (life), Instituto Geografico e Historico da Bahia (corr.); mem.: Conf. on Latin Am. History. Avocations: hiking, bicycling. Home: Lutherville Timonium, Md. Died Aug. 13, 2010.

RUSSO, LAURA, gallery director; b. Waterbury, Conn., Mar. 7, 1943; d. Lawrence and Lillian A. (Russo) Kaplan; m. John I. Lawrence, May 6, 1962 (div. 1974); children: Maia Giosi, Dylan Russo. Cert., Pacific N.W. Coll. Art, 1975. Art instr. Tucker Maxon Oral Sch., Portland, Oreg., 1970-74, Pacific N.W. Coll. Art, Portland, 1977-78; assoc. dir. Fountain Fine Arts, Seattle, 1981-82; asst. dir. Fountain Gallery of Art, Portland, 1975-86; owner, dir. Laura Russo Gallery, Portland, from 1986. Lectr. Portland State Coll., 1992; juror Oreg. Sch. Design, Portland, 1988, Western Oreg. State Coll. 1992, Beaverton Arts Commn., 1992, Oreg. Hist. Soc., 1990; com. mem. Oreg. Com. for Nat. Mus. Women in Arts, 1988; guest interviewer art dept. Oreg. State Coll., 1996; mem. adv. bd. Sch. Fine and Performing Arts Portland State U., 1998—. Mem. com. awards and grants Met. Arts Commn., Portland, 1988, 89; mem. Pacific Northwest Coll. Art; juror Art in Pub. Schs. Program, 1990; juror ArtQuake, Portland, 1994; juror Corvallis (Oreg.) Art Ctr., 1995. Mem. Alumni Friends, Contemporary Arts Coun. (program chmn., v.p. 1989-91), Portland Art Mus. (search com. 1993-94), Oreg. Art Inst., Friends Print Soc., Oreg. Art Inst., L.A. Mus. Contemporary Art, Seattle Art Mus. (lectr. 1987), Art Table (West Coast br.). Democrat. Home: Portland, Oreg. Died Feb. 11, 2010.

RUTH, FRANKLIN WILLIAM, JR., metals manufacturing company executive; b. Dayton, Ohio, Oct. 14, 1917; s. Frank William and Florence U. (Iobst) R.; m. Pearl Showers, Mar. 23, 1940; children: Betsy Ann (Mrs. Derle M. Snyder), Pamela Jane, Franklin William III. BA, Pa. State Coll., 1939. Supr. bookkeeper Pa. Treasury dept., 1939-42; sr. accountant Main & Co. C.P.A.s, Harrisburg, Pa., 1942-44; chief accounting officer Reiff & Nestor, Co., Lykens, Pa., 1944-46, sec., dir., 1946-83, gen. mgr., 1951-83, treas., 1965-83; sec. dir., gen. mgr. Medco Developing Co. Inc., Lykens, 1955-83, treas., 1965-83; sec., gen. mgr. Medco Process Inc., Lykens, 1957-83, treas., 1965-83, dir., from 1957. Bd. dirs. Miners Bank Lykens, sec. 1962-87, pres. 1987—; treas., bd. dirs. New Eng. Tap Co. Inc., 1967-83; bd. dirs., mem. exec. com. Capital Blue Cross, Harrisburg, vice chmn. bd., 1980-82, chmn. bd., 1982—; bd. dirs. Camp Hill Ins. Co. Trustee Pa. State U., 1956-63; sec., dir. Nestor Charitable Found., 1953-83, treas., 1965-83; sec., dir. Mary Margaret Nestor Found., 1953-83, treas., 1965-83; chmn. Upper Dauphin Area Sch. Authority, 1972-80. Mem. N.A.M., Nat. Soc. Pub. Accountants, Am. Soc. Tool and Mfg. Engrs. Clubs: Mason (Shriner). Methodist. Home: Dauphin, Pa. Died Apr. 11, 2009.

RUTMAN, ROBERT JESSE, bioscience researcher; b. NYC, June 23, 1919; s. Leon and Anna Porringer; m. Julia Zubroff, Dec. 1942 (div. 1969); children: Rose, Randi; m. Geraldine Burwell, Jan. 15, 1980; children: Steven, David, Ellen. BS, Pa. State U., 1940; postgrad., U. Idaho, 1941-42; PhD, U. Calif., Berkeley, 1950; MS, U. Pa., 1976. Asst. prof. biochemistry Thomas Jefferson U., Phila., 1950-54; sr. scientist U. Pa., Phila., 1954-61, assoc. prof. chemistry, 1961-68, prof. biochemistry and molecular biology, 1968-88, chmn. biochemistry, 1971-73, 76-78; ret. Vis. prof. U. Ibadan, Nigeria, 1973—74, U. North, South Africa, 1998. Editor: Women and Cancer, 1999, Nat. Black Leadership Initiative on Cancer, 2001, Women and Cancer Jour., 1999. Founder, v.p. M.L. King Jr. Ctr., Phila., 1984-89; chmn. Ile-Ife Humanitarian Ctr., Phila., 1986-88; fin. dir. Campaign Orgn. Polit. Office, Phila., 1965-86; pres. Home and Sch. Assn., Phila., 1962-63, Citizens Commn. Pub Edn., 1963; bd. dirs. West Park Cultural Ctr.,; bd. dirs., editor newsletter Nat. Black Leadership Initiative on Cancer, 2001-02. Capt. AUS, 1943-46. Named Man of Yr., Phila. Tribune, 1985. Fellow AAAS; mem. Nat. Assn. Environ. Profls., Am. Assn. Cancer Rsch., Chimoniex Tennis Club (bd. dirs.). Achievements include patents for in field, atom model, obesifying drug. Avocations: tennis, swimming, dance, music, poetry. Home: Philadelphia, Pa. Died Sept. 20, 2010.

RUTZ, RICHARD FREDERICK, physicist, researcher; b. Alton, Ill., Feb. 9, 1919; s. Erwin William and Esther Norma (Brooks) R.; m. Mary Lamsom Lambert, June 10, 1945; children— Frederick R., Carl R., William L. BA, Shurtleff Coll., Alton, Ill., 1941; MS, State U. Iowa, 1947. Staff mem. Sandia Corp., Albuquerque, 1948-51; mem. staff, mgr. IBM T.J. Watson Sr. Rsch. Ctr., Yorktown Heights, NY, 1951-87. Contbr. articles to profl. jours.; patentee numerous semicond. devices With U.S. Maritime Svc., 1941-42, USAAF, 1942-46. Fellow IEEE; mem. Am. Phys. Soc. Home: Grand Junction, Colo. Died May 11, 2010.

RUZICKA, JEFFREY F., banker; b. Chgo, Jan. 8, 1942; s. James and Blanca (Friser) R.; m. Pamela Barnard, Apr. 20, 1968; children— Alexa L., Christina F. BA, Colgate U., 1964; postgrad., Columbia U. Grad. Sch. Bus., 1964-65; B.I.M., Am. Grad. Sch. Internat. Mgmt., Phoenix, 1970. Staff No. Trust Co., Chgo., from 1970, v.p. internat. dept., 1976-80, gen. mgr. London br., 1980-84, sr. v.p., head internat. dept. Chgo., 1984-88, head dept. internat. corp. services, from 1988. Mem. Mid-Am. Com., Chgo., 1984—; trustee The Latin Sch. Chgo.; bd. dirs. Chgo. Area Project. Mem. Recording for the Blind Inc. (bd. dirs.), German-Am. C. of C. (bd. dirs.). Clubs: Racquet (Chgo.); Bucks (London). Episcopalian. Avocations: sailing; tennis. Home: Chicago, Ill. Died June 6, 2010.

RYAN, FRANK HARRY (FRANCIS HARRY RYAN), plastic surgeon; b. May 21, 1960; BS, U. Mich., Ann Arbor, 1982; MD, Ohio State U. Coll. Medicine, Columbus, 1986. Surgical residency Cedars-Sinai Med. Ctr., U. Mo. & UCLA Med. Ctr., 1986—94; plastic surgeon priv. practice, Beverly Hills, 1994—2010. Mem. adv. bd. A. Craig Matthias Found. Founder Bony Pony Ranch Found., Malibu. Avocations: boating, fishing, golf, skiing, tennis. Died Aug. 16, 2010.

RYAN, JAMES VINCENT, lawyer; b. NYC, Apr. 7, 1927; s. John James and Harriette (Clarke) R.; m. Anne Marie Murray, Aug. 29, 1951; children: James, Maureen, Emmett, Kevin, Deirdre. BS, Purdue U., 1948; LLB, Fordham U., 1951. Bar: N.Y. 1951. Atty. U.S. Dept. Justice, Washington, 1951; asst. U.S. atty. U.S. Dist. Ct. (so. dist.) N.Y., NYC, 1951-54; assoc. Paul, Weiss, Rifkind, Wharton & Garrison, NYC, 1954-55; from assoc. to ptnr. Lundgren, Lincoln & McDaniel, NYC, 1955-65; ptnr. Webster & Sheffield, NYC, 1965-76, Rogers & Wells, NYC, from 1977. Served to lt. (j.g.) USNR, 1945-50. Fellow Am. Coll. Trial Lawyers. Clubs: Winged Foot Country (Mamaroneck, N.Y.) (sec. 1983—), Sky (N.Y.C.). Republican. Roman Catholic. Home: Rye, NY. Died Nov. 12, 2009.

RYAN, JOHN FRANKLIN, retired multinational company executive; b. Huntington, W.Va., Apr. 10, 1925; s. Oscar F. and Mamie J. (Tyler) R.; m. Renee B. Bourn, June 17, 1948; children— Carolyn, Linda, Elizabeth Student, Emory and Henry Coll., 1943-44; BS, Marshall U., 1948. Data processing sales mgr. IBM, Phila., 1958-60; dir. worldwide integrated data systems ITT, Washington, 1960-62, dept. dir., 1962-72, dir. corp. relations, 1972-87, v.p., 1981-87. Cons., 1987—. Mem. Bus.-Govt. Relations Council, pres. 1978; bd. dirs. Pub. Affairs Council. Served with USNR, 1943-45 Mem.: Carlton (pres. 1982), Burning Tree. Died Dec. 16, 2009.

RYAN, MICHAEL, writer; b. Danville, Va., Dec. 31, 1950; s. Michael and Mary (Fitzpatrick) R.; m. Debora Gilbert, May 7, 1977. AB, Harvard Coll., 1972. Assoc. editor Boston Phoenix, 1972-74, Boston Mag., 1974-75; mng. editor Boston mag., 1978-79; corr. TV Guide, NYC, 1975-77; columnist Boston Herald, 1977-78; sr. editor People mag., NYC, 1979-83, sr. corr., 1983-84; sr. editor mag. devel. group Time Inc., NYC, 1985-86; contbg. editor Parade mag., NYC, from 1986. Author: Climbing, 1980. Recipient Penney award U. Mo., 1979, award of Merit, Am. Coll. Emergency Physicians, 1989. Mem. Harvard Club. Home: New York, NY. Died July 19, 2009.

RYAN, MICHAEL BEECHER, lawyer, retired government agency administrator; b. Chgo., Aug. 20, 1936; s. Walter Joseph and Mary Agnes (Beecher) R.; m. Maria Chantal Wiesman, June 1, 1963; children— Mary, Catherine, Matthew. BS in Labor Relations, Manhattan Coll., 1957; JD, U. Notre Dame, 1964. Bar: N.Y. 1964, Ill. 1991. With NLRB, 1964-91, sr. trial atty. Peoria, Ill. region, 1968-74, dep. officer in charge, 1974-78, regional atty., 1978-91; exec. v.p. NLRB Union, 1968-69, pres., 1969-71; mem. Peoria Planning Commn., 1977-89, chmn., 1979-89. Adj. prof. labor relations Bradley U., 1972-74 Mem. Tri-County Land Use Adv. Com., 1978-82; Pres. Catholic Interracial Council Peoria, 1971-72, North Sterling Homeowners Assn., 1973-77. Served with AUS, 1958-61, Korea. Mem. Regional Attys. Guild (chmn. 1982-88), Wedgewood Country Club. Roman Catholic. Home: Peoria, Ill. Died Apr. 3, 2010.

RYAN, MICHAEL EDMOND, communications company executive, lawyer; b. NYC, May 30, 1938; s. John J. and Mary K. (Mulligan) R.; m. Ellen Todaro, Feb. 10, 1962; children: Michael, Patrick, MaryEllen. BBA, St. John's U., Jamaica, NY, 1963; D Comml. Sci., St. John's U.; JD, Fordham U., 1967; grad., Harvard U., 1982-83. Bar: N.Y. 1967, U.S. Supreme Ct. 1972. With N.Y. Times Co., from 1956, prodn. mgr., 1960-63, asst. controller, 1963-67, corp. atty., 1967-70, asst. sec., 1970-74, sec., corp. counsel, 1974-79, v.p. law, fin., adminstrn., 1979-80, sr. v.p. corp. devel., broadcasting, cable-TV and forest products, 1980-89, sr. v.p. corp. devel., corp. staff legal corp. communications, human resources, forest products group, from 1989. Trustee U. Scranton. With U.S. Army, 1961-62. Recipient Am. Jurisprudence Corps. award Lawyers Coop. Pub. Co., 1967 Mem. ABA, Fed. Bar Assn., Assn. Bar City N.Y. Clubs: Sands Point Golf, Forest Hills, West Side Tennis. Home: Flushing, NY. Died Dec. 18, 2009.

RYAN, MICHAEL JOSEPH, superintendent schools; b. Ft. Wayne, Ind., May 2, 1937; s. Albert F. and Laura H. (Casanova) Ryan. BS in Edn., Bowling Green State U., 1961; MEd, U. Toledo, 1964, EdS, 1971; postgrad. in Edn., U. Ariz. Elem. tchr. Sylvania City Schs., Ohio, 1957—65; elem. prin. Whiteford Agrl. Schs., Ottawa Lake, Mich., 1965—72, Rock Island Pub. Schs., Ill., 1972—73; supt. schs. Rivedale Cmty. Schs. No. 100, Port Byron, Ill., 1973—81, Indian Oasis-Baboquivari Unified Sch. Dist. No. 40, Sells, Ariz., from 1981; alt. rep. Papapa Edn. Coun., Sells, from 1981. Mem.: Assn. Sch. Bus. Ofcls., Ariz. Sch. Adminstrs., Am. Assn. Sch. Adminstrs., Coun. Exceptional Children, Met. Opera Guild, Phi Delta Kappa. Roman Catholic. Home: New Haven, Ind. Died May 7, 2010.

RYAN, ROBERT COLLINS, lawyer; b. Evanston, Ill., Sept. 15, 1953; s. Donald Thomas and Patricia J. (Collins) R.; m. Joanne Kay Holata, Nov. 5, 1983. BA in Econs., U. Ill., 1976, BS in Indsl. Engring. with high honors, 1976; JD, Northwestern U., 1979. Bar: Ill. 1979, Nev. 1999, US Dist. Ct. (no. dist.) Ill. 1980, US Dist. Ct. Nev. 2001, US Ct. Appeals (Fed. cir.) 1982, US Patent Office, 1979, US Supreme Ct. 1984. Assoc. Allegretti, Newitt, Witcoff & McAndrews, Ltd., Chgo., 1979-83, ptnr., 1983-88; founding ptnr. McAndrews, Held & Malloy, Ltd., Chgo., 1988-96, of counsel, 1998—2000; v.p. digital gen. sys., Inc. CNASDAQ DGIT, 2001—03; ptnr. Nath & Assocs. PLLC, Washington and Reno, from 2003. Chief legal and intellectual property officer, exec. v.p. StarGuide Digital Networks, Inc., Reno, 1996-2003; mem. Ian Burns & Assocs., P.C., Reno, 1998-2003; of counsel Pauley, Petersen, Kinne & Fejer, Hoffman Estates, Ill., 1998-2002; lectr. engring. law Northwestern U. Tech. Inst., Evanston, Ill., 1981-85, adj. prof. engring. law, 1985-90; lectr. patent law and appellate practice John Marshall Law Sch., 1991-93, adj. prof. patent law and appellate advocacy, 1993-2000; mem. faculty Nat. Jud. Coll., Reno, Nev., 1998-2000; mem. alumni bd. mech. and indsl. engring. dept. U. Ill., Urbana, 1996—; lectr. U. Nev., Reno, 2003--. Exec. editor Northwestern Jour. Internat. Law & Bus., 1978-79; contbr. articles to profl. jours. Bd. dirs. Washoe Assn. Retarded Citizens, Reno, 1997—, sec., 2001, 1st v.p., 2002-03. James scholar U. Ill., 1976. Mem. ABA, Fed. Cir. Bar Assn., Intellectual Property Law Assn. Chgo., Licensing Execs. Soc., Tau Beta Pi, Phi Eta Sigma, Alpha Pi Mu, Phi Kappa Phi. Home: Reno, Nev. Died Aug. 17, 2010.

RYDZ, JOHN S., educator; b. Milw., May 7, 1925; s. John M. and Victoria A. (Kosse) R.; m. Clare L. Steinke, May 18, 1946; children: John A., Karen E. BS in Physics, MIT, 1952; MS in Physics, U. Pa., 1956; postgrad., Case Western Res. U., 1965-70. Mem. staff of sr. exec. v.p. RCA, NYC, 1952-61; exec. v.p. Nuclear Corp. Am. (NUCOR), Phoenix, 1961-63; dir. research Adressograph/Multigraph, Cleve., 1963-65; v.p. Diebold Inc., Canton, Ohio, 1965-70; v.p., chief tech. officer The Singer Co., NYC, 1970-80; corp. v.p. Emhart Corp., Farmington, Conn., 1980-89; pres. Music Memories Inc., Avon, Conn., from 1989. Vis. prof. U. Conn., 1988—; mem. engring. adv. com. NSF, Washington, 1986—. Author: Managing Innovation and Common Sense Manufacturing Management, 1986; contbr. articles to profl. jours.; patentee in field. Mem. MIT Lab. for Mfg. and Productivity, Cambridge, Mass., 1975—, U. Hartford Engring. Exec. Council, West Hartford, Conn., 1982—, Worcester (Mass.) Poly. Inst. Mech. Engring. Adv. Com., 1980—; chmn. engring adv. com. U. Conn., Storrs, 1986—. Served with USN, 1943-46, WWII. Mem. Soc. Mfg. Engrs., IEEE, Indsl. Research Inst. Avocations: astronomy, swimming. Home: Avon, Conn. Died Dec. 3, 2009.

RYLANDER, HENRY GRADY, JR., mechanical engineering educator; b. Pearsall, Tex., Aug. 23, 1921; married; 4 children. BS, U. Tex., 1943, MS, 1952; PhD in Mech. Engring., Ga. Inst. Tech., 1965. Design engr. Steam Div., Aviation Gas Turbine Div., Westinghouse Elec. Corp., 1943-47; from asst. to assoc. prof. mech. engring. U. Tex., Austin, 1947-68, research scientist, 1950, prof. mech. engring., from 1968, Joe J. King prof. engring., from 1980. Cons. engr. TRACOR, Inc., 1964-69; founding dir. Ctr. for Electromechanics, U. Tex., 1977-85, chmn., mech. engring. dept., 1976-86. Named Disting. Grad. Coll. Engring., U. Tex., Austin, 1989. Fellow ASME (Leonardo da Vinci award 1985); mem. ASME. Deceased.

RYSKAMP, CHARLES ANDREW, museum director, educator; b. East Grand Rapids, Mich., Oct. 21, 1928; s. Henry Jacob and Flora (DeGraaf) R. AB, Calvin Coll., 1950; MA, Yale U., 1951, PhD, 1956; MA, Pembroke Coll., Cambridge U., 1954; Litt.D., Trinity Coll., Hartford, 1975; L.H.D., Union Coll., 1977. Nathan Hale fellow Yale U., 1954-55; instr. English Princeton U., 1955-59, asst. prof., 1959-63, assoc. prof., 1963-69; curator English and American lit. U. Library, 1967-69, prof., 1969—2005; emeritus prof. U. Libr., 2005—10. Procter & Gamble faculty fellow, 1958-59; jr. fellow Coun. of Humanities, 1960-61, John E. Annan preceptor, 1961-64; dir. Pierpont Morgan Libr., N.Y.C., 1969-87, dir. emeritus, fellow (hon.), 1997-2010; dir. Frick Collection, N.Y.C., 1987-97, dir. emeritus, fellow (hon.), 1997-2010; dir. vis. Inst. Advanced Study, Princeton, 1997-99; exhbn. of collection of drawings, Pierpont Morgan Libr., 2001; adv. bd. Skowhegan Sch. Painting and Sculpture, Pvt. Papers of James Boswell, Yale U.; vis. com. dept. drawings and printed books and med. and ren. Pierpont Morgan Libr. Coun. and Libr. Com., Frick Collection; bd. adv. Princeton U. Art Mus. Author: William Cowper of the Inner Temple, Esq: A Study of His Life and Works to the Year 1768, 1959, William Blake, Engraver, 1969; editor: (with F.A. Pottle) Boswell: The Ominous Years, 1963, The Cast-Away, 1963, Wilde and the Nineties, 1966, William Blake: The Pickering Manuscript, 1972, (with J. King) The Letters and Prose Writings of William Cowper, vol. I, 1979, vol. II, 1981, vol. III, 1982, Vol. IV, 1984, Vol. V, 1986, (with R. Wendorf) The Works of William Collins, 1979, (with J. Baird) The Poetical Works of William Cowper, vol. I, 1980, vols. II-III, 1995, (with J. King) William Cowper: Selected Letters, 1989, Report to the Fellows of the Pierpont Morgan Library, vols. 16-21, 1969-89, Charles Ryskamp and Friends, 1999, (with Scott Westrem) The Works of John Chalkhill, 1999, Of Cabbages and Kings, 2004, The Ladies, God Bless Them. Trustee, exec. com. Mus. Broadcasting, 1977-87; trustee John Simon Guggenheim Meml. Found., Libr. of Am.; trustee emeritus Corning Mus. Glass, Amon Carter Mus.; past vis. com. dept. paintings conservation Met. Mus. Art; patron William Blake Trust; bd. mgrs. Lewis Walpole Libr., Yale U.; bd. dirs., v.p. Gerard B. Lambert Found.; past v.p. Frederick R. Koch Found.; trustee Venetian Heritage. Decorated Order St. John of Jerusalem, comdr. Order Orange Nassau, The Netherlands, officer Order Leopold II, Belgium, comdr. Order of Falcon, Iceland; recipient Peter Stuyvesant award Dutch American West-India Co., 1987, Gold medal Holland Soc., 1991; Charles Ryskamp Rsch. fellowship, Am. Coun. Learned Socs. Mem. Am. Philos. Soc., Museums Coun. N.Y.C. (past v.p.), Keats-Shelley Assn. Am. (past v.p.), Master Drawings Assn. (past pres.), Met. Opera Assn. (bd. adv., chmn. art and archives com.), Drawing Soc. (nat. com.), Am. Assocs. Royal Nat. Theatre, Bibliog. Soc. Am., Acad. Am. Poets, Am. Antiquarian Soc., Assn. Art Mus. Dirs. (past pres.), NY Geneal. and Biog. Soc. (spl. corr.), Neuropathy Assn. (nat. adv. coun.), Cowper Soc., Assn. Internat. Bibliophilie (com. of Honor), Found. French Mus.

(adv. bd.), Wordsworth Rydal Mount Trust, Grolier Club, Century Assn., Lotos Club, Knickerbocker Club, Elizabethan Club (New Haven), Roxburghe Club (London) Home: New York, NY. Died Mar. 26, 2010.

SABIN, WILLIAM ALBERT, writer; b. Paterson, NJ, May 29, 1931; s. David and Esther (Goodman) S.; m. Marie Frances Noonan, May 31, 1958; children— Margaret, John, Katherine, Christopher, James BA in English, Yale U., 1952, MA in English, 1956. Pub. bus. and office edn. McGraw Hill Book Co., NYC, 1973-78, editor in chief bus. books, 1979-86, pub. bus. books, 1987-90. Author: The Gregg Referance Manual, 10th edit., 2005, The Gregg Reference Manual Online, 10th edit., 2007; co-author: College English: Grammar and Style, 1967. Served as cpl. U.S. Army, 1952-54, ETO Home: Bristol, Maine. Died Jan. 1, 2009.

SABSAY, DAVID, retired library director; b. Waltham, Mass., Sept. 12, 1931; s. Wiegard Isaac and Ruth (Weinstein) S.; m. Helen Glenna Tolliver, Sept. 24,1 966. AB, Harvard U., 1953; BLS, U. Calif., Berkeley, 1955. Circulation dept. supr. Richmond (Calif.) Pub. Library, 1955-56; city libr. Santa Rosa (Calif.) Pub. Library, 1956-65; dir. Sonoma County Library, Santa Rosa, 1965-92; libr. cons., from 1992. Coordinator North Bay Coop. Library System, Santa Rosa, 1960-64; cons. in field, Sebastopol, Calif., 1968—. Contbr. articles to profl. jours. Commendation, Calif. Assn. Library Trustees and Commrs., 1984. Mem. Calif. Library Assn. (pres. 1971, cert. appreciation 1971, 80), ALA. Clubs: Harvard (San Francisco). Home: Sebastopol, Calif. Died Mar. 20, 2010.

SABY, JOHN SANFORD, physicist, consultant; b. Ithaca, NY, Mar. 21, 1921; s. Rasmus S. and Maude Emily (Sanford) S.; m. Mary Elizabeth Long, June 9, 1945; children: Arthur D., Thomas S., Joseph A., Jean E. BA, Gettysburg Coll., Pa., 1942, Sc.D. (hon.), 1969; MS, Pa. State U., 1944, PhD, 1947. Lab. instr. Gettysburg Coll., 1940-42; instr. Cornell U., 1947-50; with Gen. Electric Co., 1951-82, mgr. semicondr./solid state Syracuse, NY, 1954-56, mgr. lamp phenomena research Cleve., 1956-82; cons., from 1982; mem. vis. com. biol. and phys. scis. Case Western Res. U., chmn., 1969. Co-author: Principles of Transistor Circuits, 1953; patentee in field; guest spkr. 53rd Annual Landscape Design Symposium, Miss. State U., 2008. Fellow: IEEE (past com. officer); mem.: Cleve. Assn. Rsch. Dirs. (pres. 1963—64), Am. Phys. Soc., Nat. Assn. Watch and Clock Collectors, Phi Sigma Kappa, Phi Kappa Phi, Sigma Xi, Phi Beta Kappa. Home: Hendersonville, NC. Died Mar. 7, 2010.

SACHS, BERNICE COHEN (MRS. ALLAN ELI SACHS), physician; b. Passaic, NJ, Sept. 16, 1918; d. Joseph and Rose (Mirelson) Cohen; m. Allan Eli Sachs, Dec. 21, 1941; children: Lee William, Robin Beth. BA with distinction, U. Mich., 1939, MD cum laude, 1942. Diplomate Am. Acad. Pain Mgmt. Intern Michael Reese Hosp., Chgo., 1942-43; resident Inst. Psychosomatic and Psychiat. Research and Tng., 1945-49; practice medicine, specializing in psychiatry and psychosomatic medicine Seattle, from 1949; mem. staff Michael Reese Hosp., 1942-49, Group Health Clinic and Hosp., Seattle, from 1949, St. Francis Xavier Cabrini Hosp. Psychiatry Service; chief mental health service Group Health Co-op. Puget Sound, Seattle; bd. dirs. Group Health Credit Union, Group Health Coop., from 1984; chmn. Alcohol and Drug Abuse Commn. Clin. assoc. prof. psychiatry and behavioral scis. U. Wash. Sch. Medicine; nat. and internat. lectr.; bd. dirs. Health and Welfare Council, Seattle-King County, 1957-60; exec. com., bd. dirs. Seattle-King County Safety Council, 1960-63; cons. Chgo. Bd. Pub. Health, 1965-66, Med. Womanpower, 1966; mem. Wash. Gov.'s Adv. Com. Youth Opportunities, 1962-65; chmn. children's program com. Jewish Community Center, Seattle, 1955-59; bd. dirs. Western div. Jewish Welfare Bd., 1958-59; past Pres.'s Assembly, 1961-62; ex-officio bd. dirs. Women's Med. Coll. Pa., 1965; v.p. women's div. Jewish Fedn. and Council, 1966-67; mem. women's com. Brandeis U.; frequent radio and TV appearances Mem. editorial bd. Stress Medicine, Psychosomatics; contbr. numerous articles to profl. jours. Bd. dirs. Edn. and Research Found., Found. for Group Health, Wash. State Physicians for social Responsibility Recipient Elizabeth Blackwell award, 1979; Mac Coll award for excellence in patient edn.; named Woman of Achievement Theta Sigma Pi, 1965, Med. Woman of Yr. Am. Med. Women's Assn., 1966 Fellow AAAS, Am. Psychiat. Assn. (pres. Seattle chpt. 1976-77, coun. internat. affairs 1978-79, com. on profl. liability ins. 1980—, loss control rev. com.), Soc. Clin. and Exptl. Hypnosis, Acad. Psychosomatic Medicine (exec. coun. 1973-76, 79—, sec. 1976-78, pres. 1982, chmn. publs. and pub. rels., chair awards com.), Am. Group Psychotherapy Assn. (life), Am. Soc. Clin. Hypnosis (various offices, newsletter editor 1978-80), Am. Geriatrics Soc. (emeritus mem., founding fellow West div. 1973), Am. Psychosomatic Soc.; mem. AMA, Internat. Soc. Hypnosis (bd. govs. 1983-86, bd. dirs. 1988—), Internat. Soc. for Investigation of Stress (sec. 1989—), Wash. Med. Soc., King County Med. Soc. (media rels. com. 1964-66, 74-76, mental health com. 1967-73, chmn. alcohol and drug abuse 1980-81, trustee 1982-83, jud. coun. 1984-86), Wash. Acad. Clin. Hypnosis (v.p. 1969-70, pres. 1970-73, 75-77, hon. pres. 1977—), Am. Med. Women's Assn. (past pres., sponsor Bernice C. Sachs jr. br. U. Wash. Med. Sch., Presdl. award 1989), Seattle Med. Women's Assn. (pres. br. 37, 1959-64), Pan Am. Med. Women's Alliance (corr. sec. 1960-62, v.p. of U.S. 1962-64), Med. Women's Internat. Assn., Soc. Clin. and Exptl. Hypnosis, Council Med. Administrs., N.Y. Acad. Scis., Internat. Platform Assn., AAUW, Puget Sound Group Psychotherapy Soc., Am. Soc. Clin. Hypnosis (Presdl. award 1980, fellow research and ednl. found.), Am., Puget Sound group psychotherapy assns., Nat. Council Jewish Women, Wash. State Physicians for Social Responsibility (adv. bd. 1985—), Intercoll. Assn. Women Students (nat. resources personnel bd.), Hadassah (Myrtle Wreath award 1967), Nat. Forensic League (Ruby Eye of Distinction), The Found. for Group Health Coop.; Group Health Coop. of Puget Sound (staff inaugural award for Outstanding Community Service), King County Med. Soc. (Valuable Service award), B'nai B'rith Women, Women's Am. ORT, Mortar Board (hon.), Phi Beta Kappa, Alpha Omega Alpha, Phi Kappa Phi, Iota Sigma Pi, Alpha Lambda Delta. Clubs: Women's University (Seattle), Glendale Country. Lodges: Soroptimist. Home: Gig Harbor, Wash. Died Aug. 21, 2010.

SACKLER, MORTIMER DAVID, retired pharmaceutical executive; b. Bklyn., Dec. 7, 1916; s. Isaac and Sophie Sackler; m. Theresa Sackler; children: Ilene, Kathe, Samantha, Sophie, Mortimer, Michael. BA, Harvard U.; MD, Middlesex U. Sch. Medicine; MBA, NYU. Founder, chmn., co-CEO Purdue Pharma LP; bd. mem. eMagin Corp. Bd. trustees Solomon R. Guggenheim Mus. Avocation: art. Home: New York, NY. Died Mar. 24, 2010.

SACKSTEDER, JOHN DENNIS, architect, naturalist; b. Madrid, Sept. 10, 1926; arrived in US, 1941; s. Frederick H. and Denise (Dorin) Sacksteder; m. Thekla Marion West Sacksteder, May 13, 1950; children: Stephanie, Christopher, Andrew, Anthony. B.Arch., U. Pa., 1948, M.Arch., 1949; postgrad., Drexel U., 1980. Registered architect Pa. Designer Frank Weise Architect, Phila., 1949—50; project mgr. Vincent G. Kling Architect, Phila., 1950—54, EPS & B Architects, Phila., 1954—57; prin. architect Sacksteder/Levine Architects, Phila., 1957—63; assoc. ptnr. Nolen & Swinburne, Phila., 1963—65; dir. constrn. U. Pa., Phila., 1965—69; mgr. architecture RCA Corp., Cherry Hill NJ, 1969—76; dir. project mgmr. Wigton Abbott Corp., Plainfield, NJ, 1976—78; mgr. project control Consolidated Rail Corp., Phila., from 1978. Bd. dirs. Ctr. City Residents Assn., Phila., 1950—52, 1983, Fitler Sq. Improvement Assn., Phila., from 1983; lectr., guide Tinicum Nat. Environ. Ctr., Phila., from 1980; chmn. Schuykill Community Garden, Phila., 1985—88; treas. Rivers Edge Civic Assn. Author: Wildflowers Inventory-Tinicum Nat. Environ. Ctr., 1981, Tree Inventory, 1982. Served to lt. (j.g.) USN, 1944—46. Mem.: AIA (industry com. mem. 1973—76, chmn. zoning com. Phila. chpt. 1964), Pa. Soc. Architects, Tau Sigma Delta, Alpha Chi Rho, Phi Kappa Beta. Died May 1, 2009.

SACKTON, FRANK JOSEPH, public affairs educator; b. Chgo., Aug. 11, 1912; m. June Dorothy Raymond, Sept. 21, 1940. Student, Northwestern U., Evanston, Ill., 1936, Yale U., New Haven, Conn., 1946, U. Md., College Park, 1951—52; BS, U. Md., 1970; grad., Command and Gen. Staff Coll., 1942, Armed Forces Staff Coll., 1949, Nat. War Coll., 1954; MPA, Ariz. State U., 1976, DHL (hon.), 1996. Mem. 131st Inf. Regt., Ill. N.G., 1929-40; commd. 2d lt. U.S. Army, 1934, advanced through grades to lt. gen., 1967; brigade plans and ops. officer (33d Inf. Div.), 1941, PTO, 1943-45; div. signal officer, 1942-43; div. intelligence officer, 1944; div. plans and ops. officer, 1945; sec. to gen. staff for Gen. MacArthur Tokyo, 1947-48; bn. comdr. 30th Inf. Regt., 1949-50; mem. spl. staff Dept. Army, 1951; plans and ops. officer Joint Task Force 132, PTO, 1952; comdr. Joint Task Force 7, Marshall Islands, 1953; mem. gen. staff Dept. Army, 1954-55; with Office Sec. Def., 1956; comdr. 18th Inf. Regt., 1957-58; chief staff 1st Inf. Div., 1959; chief army Mil. Mission to Turkey, 1960-62; comdr. XIV Army Corps, 1963; dep. dir. plans Joint Chiefs Staff, 1964-66; army general staff mil. ops., 1966-67; comptroller of the army, 1967-70; ret., 1970; spl. asst. for fed./state relations Gov. Ariz., 1971-75; chmn. Ariz. Programming and Coordinating Com. for Fed. Programs, 1971-75; lectr. Am. Grad. Sch. Internat. Mgmt., 1973-77; vis. asst. prof., lectr. public affairs Ariz. State U., Tempe, 1976-78; founding dean Ariz. State U. Coll. Public Programs, 1979-80; prof. public affairs Ariz. State U., from 1980, finance educator, v.p. bus. affairs, 1981-83, dep. dir. intercollegiate athletics, 1984-85, dir. strategic planning, 1987-88. Contbr. articles to public affairs and mil. jours. Mem. Ariz. Steering Com. for Restoration of the State Capitol, 1974-75, Ariz. State Personnel Bd., 1978-83, Ariz. Regulatory Coun., 1981-93. Decorated D.S.M., Silver Star, also Legion of Merit with 4 oak leaf clusters, Bronze Star with 2 oak leaf clusters, Air medal, Army Commendation medal with 1 oak leaf cluster, Combat Inf. badge. Mem.: Ariz. Acad. Public Adminstrn., Army-Navy Club (Washington), Arizona Country Club (Phoenix), Pi Alpha Alpha (pres. chpt. 1976—82). Home: Scottsdale, Ariz. Died Feb. 14, 2010.

SAEKS, RICHARD EPHRAIM, engineering executive; b. Chgo., Nov. 30, 1941; s. Morris G. and Elsie E. S. BS, Northwestern U., 1964; MS, Colo. State U., 1965; PhD, Cornell U., 1967. Registered profl. engr., Tex. Elec. engr. Warwick Mfg. Co., Niles, Ill., 1961-63; asst. prof. dept. elec. engring. U. Notre Dame, 1967-71, assoc. prof., 1971-73; assoc. prof. depts. elec. engring., math. Tex. Tech U., Lubbock, 1973-77, prof., 1977-79, Paul Whitfield Horn prof. elec. engring., math. computer sci, 1979-83; prof., chmn. elec. engring. Ariz. State U., 1983-88; dean Armour Coll. Engring. Ill. Inst. Tech., 1988-91, Motorola prof., 1991-92; v.p. engring. Accurate Automation Corp., 1992-2000, chief tech. officer, from 2000. Cons. Research Triangle Inst., 1978-80, Marcel Dekker Inc., 1978-80. Author: Generalized Networks, 1972, Resolution Space Operators and Systems, 1973, Interconnected Dynamical Systems, 1981, System Theory: A Hilbert Space Approach, 1982, Shock Structure Analysis and Aerodynamics in a Weakly Ionized Gas, 2006; Editor: Large-Scale Dynamical Systems, 1976, Rational Fault Analysis, 1977, The World of Large Scale Systems, 1982; contbr. 200 articles to profl. jours. Recipient Disting. Faculty Research award Tex. Tech U., 1978, INC 500 award, 1994, SBA Rolnd Tibbets award, 1996, Joeseph G. Wohl Outstanding Career award, IEEE Systems, Man, and Cybernetics Society, 2004 Fellow: AIAA, IEEE (life), IEEE Systems Men and Cybernetics Soc. (pres. 1998—99). Achievements include patents in field. Home: Chattanooga, Tenn. Died Oct. 12, 2009.

SAFER, EDWARD GEORGE, stockbroker; b. Cambridge, Mass., June 8, 1927; s. George Edward Safer and Margaret (Papaz) Kaljian; m. Norma Shirley Rodgers, Oct. 8, 1949; children: Scott Jeffery (dec.), Lesley Allison. BA in Econs., U. Mass., 1950; BSME, U. Hartford, 1956; MBA, Am. Internat. Coll., 1963. Aero. engr. Pratt and Whitney Aircraft, East Hartford, Conn., 1956-59; mgr. engring. Am. Optical Corp., Brattleboro, Vt., 1959-69; registered rep. Hornblower and Weeks Hemphill Noyes, Springfield, Mass., 1969-74; v.p. Burgess and Leith, Inc., Brattleboro, 1974-84; v.p. Advest Inc. div. Burgess Leith, Brattleboro, from 1984. Treas., bd. dirs. Windham Area ARC, Brattleboro, 1972-74. Served with USN, 1945-46, PTO. Mem. Brattleboro Area C. of C. (bd. dirs. 1967-68), Windham County Humane Soc. (bd. dirs. 1970-72), So. Vt. Health Assn. (investment com. 1979—). Republican. Unitarian Universalist. Avocatins: bridge, sailing. Home: Brattleboro, Vt. Died Jan. 23, 2009.

SAFFEIR, HARVEY JOSEPH, insurance company executive, director; b. NYC, Nov. 17, 1929; s. Harry and Pauline (Fleischman) S.; m. Lois Marshall Allen, Sept. 17, 1959; children: Robin, Jo Daviess. AB, Cornell U., 1951. Sr. v.p. Travelers Corp., Hartford, Conn., from 1974, sr. v.p. numerous subs., from 1974. Fellow Soc. Actuaries, Am. Acad. Actuaries; mem. Inst. Internal Auditors, Hartford Club (dir. 1979-82, 91—), Hartford Golf Club. Home: West Hartford, Conn. Died Apr. 16, 2009.

SAILER, HENRY POWERS, lawyer; b. Peking, China, Jan. 7, 1929; s. Randolph Clothier and Louise (Egbert) S.; divorced; children: Anne, Katherine, Henry Powers, Randolph, Elizabeth. AB, Princeton U., 1951; LL.B., Harvard U., 1956. Bar: D.C. 1957. Law clk. Justice John Marshall Harlan, U.S. Supreme Ct., 1958; assoc. Covington & Burling LLP, Washington, 1956-58, 59-62, ptnr., 1962—2010; dir. Nat. Com. on U.S.-China Relations, 1973-78. Mem.: Metropolitan. Democrat. Home: Washington, DC. Died June 22, 2010.

SALCH, STEVEN CHARLES, lawyer, mediator, arbitrator; b. Palm Beach, Fla., Oct. 25, 1943; s. Charles Henry and Helen Louise (Alverson) S.; m. Mary Ann Prim, Oct. 7, 1967; children: Susan Elizabeth, Stuart Trenton. BBA, So. Meth. U., 1965, JD, 1968. Bar: Tex. 1968, US Tax Ct. 1969, US Dist. Ct. (so. dist.) Tex. 1969, US Dist. Ct. (ea. dist.) Tex. 1972, US Ct. Appeals (5th cir.) 1969, US Ct. Appeals (fed. cir.) 1982, US Ct. Fed. Claims, 1982. Assoc. Fulbright & Jaworski, Houston, 1968-71, participating assoc., 1971-75, ptnr., 1975—2008; sr. dir. taxation Grobstein Horwath & Co. LLC, Sherman Oaks, Calif., 2008. Mem. panel of disting. neutrals CPR Inst. Co-author: Tax Practice Before the IRS, 1994; contbr. articles to legal jours. Pres. Tealwood Owners Assn., 1982—83, Meml. H.S. PTA, 1985—86; hon. life mem. Tex. PTA, from 1986; mem. devel. bd. U. Tex. Med. Br., Galveston, from 2002, mem. health system adv. bd., from 2008; adv. dir. 1894 Grand Opera House Soc., from 2002, co-chmn. adv. bd., 2004—05. Mem.: ABA (coun. dir. 1985—88, vice chair tax sect. 1988—91, chair tax sect. 1996—97), Houston Bar Found., Am. Bar Found., Am. Coll. Tax Counsel (regent 5th cir. 1999—2006, sec.-treas. 2006—08, vice. chmn. from 2008), Am. Law Inst., Fed. Bar Assn., Houston Bar Assn., State Bar Tex. (Outstanding Tex. Tax Lawyer 2008), Theodore Tannenwald Foundation (trustee from 2000), Menard Soc., Colonial Williamsburg Found., Galveston Artillery Club, Pelican Club Galveston, Galveston Country Club, Order of Coif, Phi Delta Phi, Phi Eta Sigma, Beta Alpha Psi. Presbyterian. Home: Galveston, Tex. Died Feb. 28, 2010.

SALINGER, J.D. (JEROME DAVID SALINGER), author; b. NYC, Jan. 1, 1919; s. Sol and Miriam (Jillich) Salinger; m. Claire Douglas, 1953 (div. 1967); children: Margaret Ann, Matthew; m. Colleen O'Neill. Attended, NYU, 1936—37, Ursinus Coll., Collegeville, Pa., 1938, Columbia U., 1939. Author: (books) The Catcher in the Rye, 1965, Nine Stories, 1953, Franny and Zooey, 1961, Raise High the Roof Beam, Carpenters and Seymour: An Introduction, 1963, (published/anthologized stories) Go See Eddie, 1940, The Hang of It, 1941, The Long Debut of Lois Taggett, 1942, A Boy in France, 1945, This Sandwich Has No Mayonnaise, 1945, Slight Rebellion off Madison, 1946, A Girl I Knew, 1948, A Perfect Day for Bananafish, 1948, Uncle Wiggily in Connecticut, 1948, Just Before the War with the Eskimos, 1948, The Laughing Man, 1949, Down at the Dinghy, 1949, For Esmé — with Love and Squalor, 1950, Pretty Mouth and Green My Eyes, 1951, De Daumier-Smith's Blue Period, 1952, Teddy, 1953, (published/unanthologized stories) The Young Folks, 1940, The Heart of a Broken Story, 1941, Personal Notes of an Infantryman, 1942, The Inverted Forest, 1943, The Varioni Brothers, 1943, 1944, Soft Boiled Sergeant, 1944, Last Day of the Last Furlough, 1944, Once a Week Won't Kill You, 1944, Elaine, 1945, The Stranger, 1945, I'm Crazy, 1945, A Young Girl in 1941 with No Waist at All, 1947, Blue Melody, 1948, Hapworth 16, 1924, 1965; contbr. short stories to mags. Sgt. US Army, 1942—46. Home: Cornish, NH. Died Jan. 27, 2010.

SALISBURY, ROBERT HOLT, political science professor; b. Elmhurst, Ill., Apr. 29, 1930; s. Robert Holt and Beulah (Hammer) S.; m. Rose Marie Cipriani, June 19, 1953; children: Susan Marie (dec.), Robert Holt, Matthew Gary. AB, Washington and Lee U., 1951; MA, U. Ill., 1952, PhD, 1955. Mem. faculty Washington U., St. Louis, 1955-65, prof., 1965-97, prof. emeritus, from 1997, chmn. dept. polit. sci., 1966-73, 86-92, dir. Center for Study Pub. Affairs, 1974-77, Sidney W. Souers prof. govt., 1982-97. Vis. prof. SUNY, Buffalo, 1965, So. Ill. U., Edwardsville, 1975; affiliated scholar Am. Bar Found., 1981-95; cons. U.S. Conf. Mayors, 1965, Hartford (Conn.) C. of C., 1964, NSF, 1973. Author: Interest Groups Politics in America, 1970, Governing America, 1973, Citizen Participation in the Public Schools, 1980, Interests and Institutions, 1992, The Hollow Core, 1993; contbr. articles to profl. jours. Mem. St. Louis County Charter Commn., 1967, Gov.'s Commn. on Local Govt., 1968-69. Guggenheim fellow, 1990; Rockefeller Ctr. scholar, 1990. Mem. Mo. Polit. Sci. Assn. (pres. 1964-65), Am. Polit.

Sci. Assn. (exec. council 1969-71, v.p. 1980-81), Midwest Polit. Sci. Assn. (pres. 1977-78), Pi Sigma Alpha. Democrat. Methodist. Home: Saint Louis, Mo. Died Apr. 9, 2010.

SALMON, RUSSELL OWEN, II, Latin American studies educator, administrator; b. Port Jervis, NY, Dec. 10, 1933; s. Fred Dunning and Helen (De Woody) S.; m. Cynthia Mae March, June 17, 1956 (div. Oct. 1982); children: Russell C., Scott D., Sarah D. Jones; m. Catherine C. Wenzel, Aug. 9, 1984. BA, Williams Coll., 1956; MA, Middlebury Coll., 1962; PhD, Columbia U., 1969. Tchr. Holderness (N.H.) Sch., 1956-62; prof. dept. Spanish and Portuguese Ind. U., Bloomington, from 1967; dir. Latin Am. Consortium, Bloomington/Notre Dame, from 1988, Ctr. Latin Am. and Caribbean Studies Ind. U. Editor: Homenaje a Andres Iduarte, 1976, Gaucho Literature, 1990, Golden UFOs, 1992. Chair bd. Bloomington Sister Cities Internat, Inc., 1990-91; mem. PASO and NOC rels. com. PAX/I, Indpls., 1985-87. NDFL Title 6 grantee Dept. Edn., 1962-65; Fgn. Lang. fellow Ford Found., Santiago, Chile, 1965-67; Internat. grantee Ford Foudn, Santiago, 1970. Mem. AAUP, MLA, Midwest MLA, Am. Assn. Tchrs. Spanish and Portuguese, Ind. Fgn. Lang. Tchrs. Assn., Latin Am. Studies Assn., Midwest Assn. Latin Am. Studies. Democrat. Presbyterian. Avocations: swimming, canoeing. Home: Bloomington, Ind. Died May 28, 2009.

SALSBERG, ARTHUR PHILIP, publishing executive; b. Bklyn., Aug. 28, 1929; s. Solomon William and Rae (Miller) S.; m. Rhoda Gelb, Sept. 11, 1960; children: Charles Martin, Solomon William. BBA, CCNY, 1951. Mng. editor Ojibway Press, NYC, 1957-64; advt. and promotion mgr. RCA Corp., Harrison, NJ, 1965-67; editor N.Am. Pub. Co., Phila., 1967-70; v.p., gen. mgr. Lawyers World, Inc., Phila., 1970-72; editorial dir. Ziff-Davis Pub. Co., NYC, 1973-83; editor, assoc. pub. CQ Communications, Inc., Hicksville, NY, from 1984. Mag. and newspaper pub. cons.; electronics instr.; local campaign publicist, speech writer for town mayor, town coun., libr. bd., sch. bd. Author: Complete Book of Video Games, 1977, Collier's Ency. Yearbook, 1977, 78, 79, 80, 81, 82, First Book of Modern Electronics Fun Projects, 1986, Second Book of Modern Electronics Fun Projects, 1986; editor: Audio Mag, 1967-70, Lawyers World, 1970-72, Popular Electronics, 1973-83, Comm. Handbook, 1973-83, Stereo Directory, 1973-83, Tape Recorder Directory, 1973-83, Citizens Band Handbook, 1976-83, Invitation to Electronics, 1972-83, Modern Electronics, 1984-91, Computer Craft, 1992-93, MicroComputer Jour., 1994-96; assoc. pub.: Amateur Radio Equipment Buyers Guide, 1988, 89, 90, 91, 92, Amateur Radio Antenna Buyers Guide, 1989, 90, 91-92. Publicity chmn. Nassau coun. Boy Scouts Am., 1975; mem. adv. com. Bramson OR Tech. Inst., 1975. With AUS, 1951-53, Korea. Recipient Indsl. Mktg. Mag. award, 1959 Home: Delray Beach, Fla. Died June 12, 2009.

SALTZ, JAMES G., utilities company executive; b. Abingdon, Va., Oct. 21, 1932; s. Albert T. and Frances N. (Morrison) S.; m. Shelley Jean Wright, Sept. 10, 1955; 1 child, Bryan. BS in Acctg., Concord Coll., 1958; cert. AEP mgmt. devel. program, U. Mich., 1963; cert. exec. devel. program, Ohio State U., 1981-82. Adminstrv. asst. Am. Electric Power, NYC, 1958-60, auditor, 1960; adminstrv. asst. acctg. Ky. Power Co., Ashland, 1960-63, adminstr. asst. managerial, 1963-64, personnel dir., 1964-78, div. mgr., 1978-80, exec. asst., 1980-82, v.p., from 1982. Bd. dirs. Am. Electric Power Service Corp., Columbus, Ohio, 1984—. Active Boyd & Greenup Counties C. of C., Boyd County chpt. ARC, Salvation Army, Jr. Achievement, Ashland Econ. Devel. Com., bd. dirs. Ashland Child Devel. Ctr., all in Ashland.; Ky. C. of C., Frankfort. Mem.: Rotary. Avocation: golf. Home: Ashland, Ky. Died Nov. 21, 2009.

SAM, JOSEPH, retired university dean; b. Gary, Ind., Aug. 15, 1923; s. Andrew and Flora (Toma) S.; m. Frances Adickes, Sept. 11, 1945; children: Sherrie, Joseph A., Suzanne F. Student, Drake U., 1942-43; BS, U. SC, 1948; PhD, Kans. U., 1951. Sr. research chemist McNeil Labs., Phila., 1951-54; research group leader Bristol Labs., Syracuse, NY, 1955-57; sr. scientist E.I. duPont de Nemours & Co., Inc., 1957-59; faculty U. Miss., 1959-86, prof. pharm. chemistry, 1961-68, chmn. dept., 1963-68, dir. univ. research, 1968-81, asso. vice chancellor research, 1981-86; dean U. Miss. (Grad. Sch.), 1968-86. Fulbright lectr. Cairo U., 1965-66 Mem. Am. Pharm. Assn. (found. research achievement award in pharm. and medicinal chemistry 1968), Rho Chi, Phi Lambda Upsilon, Phi Kappa Phi. Home: University, Miss. Died Oct. 3, 2009.

SAMBORN, ALFRED H., engineering educator, civil engineer, consultant; b. Toledo, Apr. 30, 1917; s. Michael Robert and Minnie (Cousins) Samborn; m. Miriam Esther Mann, Oct. 12, 1947; children: Michael Robert, Randall Arthur. BS in Civil Engring., U. Toledo, 1939; postgrad., Case Sch. Applied Sci., Cleve., 1939—40. Registered profl. engr., Mich., Ohio; diplomate Am. Acad. Environ. Engrs. Jr. engr. Ward Products Corp., Cleve., 1939—40; engr. Builders Structural Steel Co., 1940, Giffels & Vallet, Inc., Detroit, 1940—48; pres. Samborn, Stekette, Otis & Evans, Inc.; cons. engrs. Toledo, 1948—77; chmn. bd., 1977—83; founder, emeritus, chmn. bd., from 1983. Continuing & adult edn. instr., prof. civil engring. U. Toledo, from 1984. Chmn. disaster svc. com. Toledo Area chpt. ARC; bd. dirs. Toledo Area Govtl. Rsch. Assn., Neighborhood Improvement Found. Toledo. Lt., s.g. USNR, 1942—46. Mem.: Old Newsboys Goodfellow Assn. (1st v.p. 1980, pres. 1981—82), Am. Legion, Ohio Assn. Cons. Engrs. (Disting. Cons. award 1979), Toledo Soc. Profl. Engrs. (Outstanding Engr. award 1966), Ohio Soc. Profl. Engrs., Tech. Soc. Toledo (Outstanding Engr. award 1966), Nat. Coun. Engring. Examiners (pres. 1979—80, award merit ctrl. zone 1976, Outstanding award 1981), Ohio Bd. Registration Profl. Engrs. & Surveyors, Nat. Soc. Profl. Engrs., Tau Beta Pi (Eminent Engr. Mem. award 1977), Phi Kappa Phi (hon.). Jewish. Home: Glenview, Ill. Died Mar. 19, 2009.

SAMETZ, ARNOLD WILLIAM, b. Bklyn., Dec. 4, 1919; s. Milton William and Natalie (Holland) Sametz; m. Agnes Baroth, Nov. 23, 1965; children: Margaret Rutherford, Laura. BA, Bklyn. Coll., 1940; MA, Princeton U., 1942, PhD, 1951. Instr. Princeton U., 1948—51, asst. prof. econs., 1951—57; assoc. prof. banking and fin. NYU, NYC, 1957—62; prof. fin. Grad. Sch. Bus. Adminstrn. and Charles Simon and Sidney Homer; dir. Salomon Bros. Ctr. Study Fin. Instns., 1975—90; prof. emeritus; fin. econ. cons.; editor Studies Banking and Fin. Lt. USN, 1942—46. Author: Financial Management, An Analytical Approach, 1967, Financial Development and Economic Growth, 1972, Prospects for Capital Formation and Capital Markets, 1978, Securities Activities of Commercial Banks, 1981, The Emerging Financial Industry, 1984, The Battle for Corporate Control, 1990, Institutional Investors--Challenges & Responsibilities, 1991, Financial Reform and Devel. in China's Economic Reform and Development, 1991, Risk Management in the Securities Industry, 1993, The Role of the Financial Sector in the Reform and Reconstruction of Eastern European Countries, 1993; contbr. articles to profl. jours. Mem.: Royal Econ. Soc., Am. Fin. Assn., Am. Econ. Assn. Died Mar. 19, 2009.

SAMNICK, NORMAN KENNETH, lawyer; b. Bklyn., Dec. 7, 1940; s. Herman and Dorothy (Roller) S.; m. Jacquelyn Diane Leopold, Sept. 3, 1943; children: Jonathan Evan, Karen Beth. BBA, CCNY, 1962; LLB, Bklyn. Law Sch., 1965. Bar: N.Y. 1966, U.S. Dist. Ct. (so. dist.) N.Y. 1970. V.p. Warner Communications, NYC, 1975-80, sr. v.p., 1980-85; ptnr. Stroock, Stroock & Lavan, NYC, from 1985. Mem. character and fitness com. Supreme Ct. 2d Dept. Appellate Div., 1980—. Home: Old Brookville, NY. Died July 30, 2009.

SAMPSON, SAMUEL FRANKLIN, sociology educator; b. Malden, Mass., Sept. 22, 1934; s. Samuel Daniel and Margaret Louise (Grimes) S.; m. Patricia Katherine Driscoll, Apr. 8, 1972. BA, U. Okla., 1960, MA, 1961; PhD, Cornell U., 1968. Asst. prof. dept. sociology SUNY, Binghamton, 1965-66; research assoc. dept. sociology Cornell U., Ithaca, NY, 1966-67; lectr., chmn. bd. tutors and advs. Harvard U., Cambridge, Mass., 1967-72; assoc. prof. dept. urban studies and planning MIT, Cambridge, 1971-72; prof. sociology U. Vt., Burlington, 1972-2000, chmn. dept. sociology, 1972-76, 90-96, prof. emeritus, from 2000. Research and policy cons. Public & Community Agys. and Orgns., 1969— Gen. editor: Bobbs-Merrill Studies in Sociology, 1970-77; contbr. articles to profl. jours. Served with USAF, 1954-58. Mem. AAAS, Internat. Sociol. Assn., Am. Sociol. Assn., Am. Acad. Arts and Scis., Ea. Sociol. Soc., Soc. Study Social Problems, New Eng. Sociol. Assn., Soc. Sci. Study Religion. Died Oct. 7, 2009.

SAMUEL, PAUL, retired cardiologist; b. Janoshaza, Hungary, Feb. 17, 1927; arrived in U.S., 1954, naturalized, 1960; s. Adolf and Magda (Zollner) Samuel; m. Gabriella R. Zeichner, Mar. 27, 1954; children: Robert Mark, Adrianne Jill. Baccalaureat, Kemeny Zsigmond Gymnasium, Budapest, Hungary, 1945; MD, U. Paris, 1953. Intern Queens Hosp. Ctr., NYC, 1954-55; resident LI Jewish Med. Ctr., New Hyde Park, NY, 1959-61; pvt. practice Forest Hills, NY, 1961—2000; adj. prof. Rockefeller U., NYC, 1971-81; adj. prof. medicine Cornell U., NYC, from 1979; ret., 2000. Dir. Arteriosclerosis Rsch. Lab. LI Jewish-Hillside Med. Ctr., New Hyde Park, 1961—2001; chmn. NY Lipid Rsch. Club Rockefeller U., 1977—78; clin. prof. medicine Albert Einstein Coll. Medicine, Bronx, NY, from 1981. Contbr. articles to profl. jours. Fellow: Am. Coll. Cardiology; mem.: ACP, Am. Fedn. Clin. Rsch., Am. Heart Assn. (fellow coun. arteriosclerosis, Disting. Achievement award), Harvey Soc. Home: New York, NY. Died July 2, 2009.

SAMUELSON, PAUL ANTHONY, economist, educator; b. Gary, Ind., May 15, 1915; s. Frank and Ella (Lipton) Samuelson; m. Marion E. Crawford, July 2, 1938 (dec. 1978); children: Jane Kendall, Margaret Wray, William Frank, Robert James, John Crawford, Paul Reid; m. Risha Eckaus, 1981; 1 stepchild, Susan Miller. BA, U. Chgo., 1935; MA, Harvard U., 1936, PhD (David A. Wells prize 1941), 1941; LLD (hon.), U. Chgo., Oberlin Coll., 1961, Boston Coll., 1964, Ind. U., 1966, U. Mich., 1967, Claremont Grad. Sch., 1967, Seton Hall U., 1971, U. N.H., 1971, Keio U., 1971, Widener Coll., 1982, Cath. U. at Riva Aguero U., Lima, Peru, 1980, Harvard, 1972, Gustavus Adolphus Coll., 1974, U. So. Calif., 1975, U. Pa., 1976, U. Rochester, 1976, Emmanuel Coll., 1977, Stonehill Coll., 1978, Indiana U. of Pa., 1993; DLitt (hon.), Ripon Coll., 1962, No. Mich. U., 1973, Valparaiso U., 1987, Columbia U, 1988; LHD (hon.), Williams Coll., 1971; DSc (hon.), U. Mass., 1972, U. R.I., 1972, Tufts U., 1988, East Anglia U., Norwich, Eng., 1966, Rennselaer Poly. Inst., 1998; D (hon.), U. Catholique de Louvain, Belgium, 1976, City U., London, 1980, New U. Lisbon, 1985, Univ. Nat. de Educacion a Distancia, Madrid, 1989, Univ. Politecnica de Valencia, Spain, 1991; D in Social Scis. (hon.), Yale U., 2005. Prof. econs. MIT, 1940—65, inst. prof., 1966, prof. emeritus, 1986—2009; mem. staff Radiation Lab., 1944—45; prof. internat. econ. relations Fletcher Sch. Law & Diplomacy, Tufts U., 1945; cons. Nat. Resources Planning Bd., 1941—43, WPB, 1945, US Dept. Treasury, 1945—52, 1961—74, Bur. Budget, 1952, RAND Corp., 1948—75, Fed. Res. Bd., from 1965; mem. Council Econ. Advisers, Exec. Office of the Pres., 1960—68; econ. adviser to Pres. Kennedy The White House; sr. adviser Brookings Panel on Econ. Activity; mem. spl. commn. on social scis. NSF, 1967—68; cons. Congl. Budget Office, Federal Reserve Bd., 1965—2009; Gordon Y Billard Fellow MIT, Boston, 1986—2009; vis. prof of polit. econ. Ctr. Japan-U.S. Bus. and Econ. Studies, NYU, 1987—2005. Mem. nat. adv. com. Inst. for Rsch. on Poverty; lectr. in field. Author: Foundations of Economic Analysis, 1947, enlarged edit., 1983, Readings in Economics, 1955; author: (with R. Dorfman and R.M. Solow) Linear Programming and Economic Analysis, 1958; author: Collected Scientific Papers, 5 vols., 1966, 1972, 1978, 1986, Economics 1948-1980; co-author (with William Nordhaus): Economics, from 1985; author: numerous other books; columnist Newsweek, 1966—81; assoc. editor: Jour. Pub. Econs., Jour. Internat. Econs., Jour. Fin. Econs., Jour. Nonlinear Analysis, adv. bd.: Challenge Mag.; contbr. articles to profl. jours. Chmn. Pres.'s Task Force Maintaining Am. Prosperity, 1964; mem. Nat. Task Force on Econ. Edn., 1960—61; econ. adviser to Pres. John F. Kennedy, 1959—63; mem. adv. bd. Nat. Commn. Money and Credit, 1958—60. Recipient David A. Wells prize, Harvard U., 1941, John Bates Clark medal, Am. Econ. Assn., 1947, Nobel prize for Economics, Nobel Found., 1970, Medal of Honor, U. Evansville, Ill., 1970, Albert Einstein Commemorative award, 1971, Alumni medal, U. Chgo., 1983, Britannica award, 1989, Gold Scanno prize, Naples, Italy, 1990, Paul A. Samuelson Professorship established in his name, MIT, 1991, Nat. Medal of Sci., Washington, 1996; fellow hon. fellow, London Sch. Econs. and Polit. Sci., Guggenheim, 1948—49, rsch. fellow, Ford Found., 1958—59. Fellow: Econometric Soc. (v.p. 1950, pres. 1951), Am. Philos. Soc., Am. Econ. Assn. (hon.; pres. 1961), Brit. Acad. (corr.); mem.: NAS, AAAS, Nat. Assn. Investment Clubs (Disting. Svc. award in Investment Edn. 1974), Leibniz-Akademie der Wissenschaften und der Literatur (corr.), Internat. Econ. Assn. (pres. 1966—68, hon. pres.), Com. Econ. Devel. (commn. on nat. goals, rsch. adv. bd. 1959—60), Club of Econ. and Mgmt. (medal, hon. Valencia, Spain 1990), Omicron Delta Epsilon (trustee), Phi Beta Kappa. Home: Belmont, Mass. Died Dec. 13, 2009.

SANDEFUR, DANIEL LEE, computer company executive; b. New Orleans, Sept. 16, 1951; s. Kenneth Ray and Evelyn Georgia (Evans) Sandefur; m. Deborah Suanne Thomas, Sept. 16, 1981; 1 child, Jason. BS, Brescia Coll. Quality engr. Gen. Electric Co., Owensboro, Ky., 1978—81; mgr. service logistics Reynolds & Reynolds, Dayton, Ohio, 1981—82; mgr. quality assurance Cin., 1982—83; mgr. field quality Dayton, from 1983. Quality assurance cons. Dan Com Inc., from 1981. Contbr. articles to profl. jours. With USMC, 1969—78. Mem.: Am. Field Svc. Mgrs. Assn., Am. Soc. Quality Control. Democrat. Died June 7, 2010.

SANDEFUR, JOHN EVERETT, real estate company officer; b. Columbus, Ohio, Apr. 20, 1931; s. Everett and Ruth (Montgomery) Sandefur; m. Tana Vaseley Sandefur, June 12, 1954; children: Debra Ann, Jane Ann. BEE, Ohio State U., 1954. Ptnr. E&J Sandefur Builders, Columbus, 1950—60; v.p. Sandefur Builders Inc., Columbus, 1960—67, pres., from 1967, Sandefur Co., from 1977. Mem. Columbus Housing Adv. Bd., 1976; bd. dirs. Godman Guild Assn., 1980. Served to 1st lt. USAF, 1955—57. Mem.: Columbus Home Builders Assn. (pres. 1962), Ohio Home Builders Assn. (pres. 1968), Nat. Rehab. Assn. (pres. 1979), Nat. Apt. Assn. (v.p. 1979), Lions, Shriners, Tau Beta Pi. Methodist. Home: Longboat Key, Fla. Died Sept. 17, 2009.

SANDERSON, FRED HUGO, economist; b. Germany, Apr. 15, 1914; came to U.S., 1937, naturalized, 1944; s. Siegfried and Maria (Schulze) S.; m. Elisabeth Doepfer, Jan. 3, 1938. Lic.Sc.Econ., U. Geneva, Switzerland, 1935; AM, Harvard U., 1942, PhD, 1943. Research asst. Dept. Agr., 1938-42; research asso. com. on research in social scis. Harvard U., 1938-43, teaching fellow, 1942-43; economist OSS, 1943-45; chief Central European econ. sect. div. research for Western Europe Dept. of State, 1946-48, chief Western European econ. br., 1948-52, chief regional econ. staff, 1952-55, asst. chief div., 1955-57, chief div. of research Western Europe, 1957-58; alt. U.S. rep. European Payments Union, 1958-59; dir. finance div. U.S. Mission to OEEC, Paris, 1959-62; chief foodstuffs div. Dept. State, 1963-67; dir. Office Food Policy and Programs, 1967-69, adviser internat. finance, 1970; detailed to Pres.'s Commn. on Internat. Trade and Investment Policy, 1970-71; mem. planning and coordination staff State Dept., 1971-73; fgn. service officer, 1955-73; sr. fellow Brookings Instn., Washington, 1974-83, Resources for Future, Washington, 1983-92, Nat. Ctr. for Food and Agrl. Policy, Washington, from 1992. On leave under Rockefeller Pub. Svc. award to study econ. effects of European coal and steel cmty., 1956-57; cons. to econ. adviser OMGUS, Berlin, 1948; detailed to Pres.'s Materials Policy Commn., 1951; professorial lectr. Sch. Advanced Internat. Studies Johns Hopkins U., 1973-94. Author: Methods of Crop Forecasting, 1954 (David A. Wells prize), Japan's Food Prospects and Policies, 1978, (with S. Roy) Food Trends and Prospects in India, 1979; contbg. author: Resources for Freedom, Vol. III, 1952, The Struggle for Democracy in Germany (G. Almond, editor), 1949, Strains in International Finance and Trade, 1974, The Great Food Fumble, 1975, U.S. Farm Policy in Perspective, 1983, World Food Prospects to the Year 2000, 1984, Agriculture and International Trade, 1988, The GATT Agreement on Agriculture, 1994, Agriculture and Multilateralism, 1994; co-author/editor: Agricultural Protectionism in the Industrialized World, 1990. Mem. Am. Econ. Assn., Am. Agrl. Econ. Assn. Home: Washington, DC. Died July 10, 2010.

SANDLER, MICHAEL I., high tech. company personnel executive; b. NYC, Dec. 5, 1933; m. Elaine Sandler; children: Jeffrey, Steven. Mgr. human resources Honeywell Corp., Framingham, Mass., 1961—67; v.p. human resources Damon Corp., Needham, Mass., 1967—77, GCA Corp., Bedford, Mass., from 1977. Home: Framingham, Mass. Died July 5, 2010.

SANDSTROM, JAMES E., military career officer; b. Minn., Apr. 1, 1949; m. Jeannie; children: Bret, Kelly. BS in Aero. Engring., USAF Acad., Colo. Springs, 1971; M in Aeronautics and Astronautics, Purdue U., W. Lafayette, Ind., 1972; attended, Squadron Officer Sch.; grad., Air Command & Staff Coll., Maxwell AFB, Ala., 1983, Indsl. Coll. Armed Forces, Fort Lesley J. McNair, Wash. DC, 1988; postgrad., Syracuse U., 1997, Johns Hopkins U., 1997. Commd. 2nd lt. USAF, 1971, student, undergraduate pilot tng. Sheppard AFB, Tex., 1972—73, student, F-4 pilot tng., 20th Tactical Fighter Squadron George AFB, Calif., 1973, F-4 pilot and weapons officer, 421st Tactical Fighter Squadron Udorn Royal Thai AFB, Thailand, 1974—75, weapons officerand OV-10 flight comdr., 21st Tactical Air Support Squadron Shaw AFB, SC, 1975—76, F-104 fighter weapons instr. and weapons officer, 69th Tactical Fighter Tng. Squadron Luke AFB, Ariz., 1976—80, F-16 weapons officer and flight comdr., 34th Tactical Fighter Squadron Hill AFB, Utah, 1980—82, project officer, tactics and test directorate, later, chief of standardization and evaluation, 57th fighter weapons wing Nellis AFB, Nev., 1983—85, comdr., 430th Tactial Fighter Squadron, 1985—87, chief current ops. (J31) Hdqrs. US Pacific Command Camp H.M. Smith, Hawaii, 1988-90, dep. comdr. for ops. Tactical Tng. Wing Luke AFB, Ariz., 1990-91, dir. Fighter Tng. and Tactical Hdqrs. Tactical Air Command Langley AFB, Va., 1991-92, comdr. 388th Fighter Wing Hill AFB, Utah, 1992-94, comdr. 23rd Wing Pope AFB, N.C., 1994-95, comdr. 4404th Composite Dhahran, Saudi Arabia, 1994-96, dep. for theater air def., dep. chief plans and ops. hdqrs. Washington, 1996-97, dir. command and control task force, dep. chief staff, 1997, dep. dir. command and control, dep. chief of staff, 1997, dir. command and control, dep. chief of staff air & space, 1997-98, prin. asst. dep. undersec. Air Force for Internat. Affairs, Pentagon, 1998, comdr., 19th Air Force Randolph AFB, Tex., 2002—04, ret., 2004; dir. ops. US Ctrl. Command, MacDill AFB, Fla., 1998—2001, chief of staff, Operation Enduring Freedom, 2001—02; spl. asst. to comdr. Air Edn. anf Tng. Command, Randolph Air Force Base, Tex., 2001—02. Decorated Legion of Merit with oak leaf cluster, Def. Meritorious Svc. medal, Meritorious Svc. medal with oak leaf cluster, Air Force Commendation medal with two oak leaf clusters. Home: Fort Worth, Tex. Died Aug. 18, 2010.

SANFORD, JAMES RICHARD, physicist; b. Zanesville, Ohio, Jan. 29, 1933; s. James C. and Mary W. S.; m. Mary K. Moyer, June 12, 1956; children: Susan, Elizabeth. BA, Oberlin Coll., 1955; MS, Yale U., 1957, PhD, 1961. Physicist Brookhaven Nat. Lab., 1962-69; assoc. dir. Fermi Nat. Accelerator Lab., Batavia, Ill., 1969-76, Brookhaven Nat. Lab., Upton, N.Y., 1976-81, project leader, 1976-81, accelerator dept. head, 1976-83, mem. Super conducting Super Collider design team, from 1983. Cons. Dept. Energy. Mem. Am. Phys. Soc., Sigma Xi. Home: Bellport, NY. Died Feb. 23, 2010.

SANTOS, MARIA ANTONIA, educational administrator; b. Comerio, P.R., July 27, 1921; d. Antonio and Maria Adelaida Santiago; B.A., Hunter Coll., 1953, M.A., 1955; profl. diploma in fgn. langs. NYU, 1962; profl. diploma in supervision and adminstrn. (Ford Found. grantee) Fordham U., 1969, postgrad., 1970; m. Carmelo Santos, July 13, 1940; children— Carmelo J., Rosemary. Tchr. St. Anselm's Catholic Sch., Bronx, N.Y., 1953-54; tchr. Spanish and English as a second lang. Jr. High Sch. 98, Bronx, 1954-59, instr. course for tchrs., 1955-56; tchr. Spanish James Monroe High Sch., Bronx, 1959-68, part-time guidance counselor, 1964-68; dir. bilingual programs and English as a second lang. Dist. 9 N.Y. Bd. Edn., 1969-71; prin. Community Elem. Sch. 114, Dist. 9, 1971—; tchr. adult evening classes Taft High Sch., Bronx, 1956-57; participant tchr. tng. programs in bilingual edn. Lehman Coll., CUNY; participant profl. seminars, courses in field; mem. adv. com. on black and Puerto Rican Studies, State Multiethnic Task Force, 1970-71; cons. Dept. Edn. P.R., 1970. Active edn. com. St. John Vianneys Roman Catholic Ch., 1971. Recipient various grants, workshops and insts., U.S., P.R.; recipient Coalicion de Damas Boricuas Yr. award, 1981, citation from Gov. N.Y., 1981, merit award Council Suprs. and Adminstrs., 1985, ann. award N.Y. Lancers, 1986. Mem. Cath. Tchrs. Assn., Am. Assn. Sch. Adminstrs., Am. Assn. Tchrs. of Spanish and Portuguese, Assn. Sch. and Curriculum Devel., Am. Bilingual Edn. Assn., N.Y. State Bilingual Edn. Assn., Puerto Rican Educators Assn. (co-founder, exec. bd. 1966-67), P.R. Tchrs. Assn. (pres. N.Y.C. chpt. 1977-78), Assn. Tchrs. of English as a Second Lang., Fordham U. Soc. Sch. Adminstrs., Sigma Delta Pi. Club: N.Y. Boringuen Lioness. Co-author: Spanish for Spanish Speaking Students, 1968. Home: Peekskill, NY. Died Oct. 11, 2009.

SARLES, PETER MASON, management consultant; b. NYC, May 29, 1926; s. Van Namee and Ann Edna (McMaster) S.; m. Mary Ann Sheehan, Sept. 13, 1952; children: Scott, Wesley. BA E., Rensselaer Poly. Inst., 1951; S.M. (Sloan fellow), Mass. Inst. Tech., 1961. With Westinghouse Electric Corp., 1951-75, gen. mgr. atomic equipment div. Cheswick, Pa., 1962-69, v.p. mfg. Pitts., 1969-70, exec. v.p. major appliances, 1970-71, v.p. planning and service consumer products, 1971-72, div. gen. mgr. gas turbine systems div., 1972-75; v.p., sr. cons. Soltis Assos., Pocopson, Pa., 1975-76; pres. Sarles & Co., Inc., West Chester, Pa., from 1976; pres., dir. Eta Corp, Montchanin, Del., from 1982. Mng. dir. Gen. Power Corp., Paoli, Pa., 1980-82 Served with USAAF, 1944-46. Mem. Soc. Automotive Engrs. Home: West Chester, Pa. Died Mar. 28, 2009.

SARNOWSKI, THOMAS JOHN, chemist, electronics executive; b. NYC, Oct. 25, 1938; s. Sigmond Francis and Ann Helen (Mikelanis) S.; m. Cathryn Ann Petraglia, Apr. 22, 1972; children: Robert, David. BS in Chemistry, Holy Cross Coll., Worcester, Mass., 1960; MS in Chemistry, Bklyn. Poly. U., 1965. Rsch. chemist CRC Dorp., Glen Cove, N.Y., 1963-69; engr. Photocircuits Corp., Glen Cove, 1969-71, chief engr., 1971-74; gen. mgr. PCK Tech.-Kollmorgen Corp., Glencove, 1974-81, sr. v.p. Melville, N.Y., 1981-84, pres., from 1984. Contbr. 8 articles to profl. publs.; editor: Printed Circuit Book, 1987. Lt. (j.g.) USN, 1958-63. Mem. Inst. for Interconnecting Circuits (pres.'s award 1978). Roman Catholic. Avocations: deep sea fishing, stamp collecting/philately. Home: Oyster Bay, NY. Died Oct. 23, 2009.

SATCHLER, GEORGE RAYMOND, physicist, researcher; b. London, June 14, 1926; came to U.S., 1959; s. George Cecil and Georgina Lillie (Strange) S.; m. Margaret Patricia Gibson, Mar. 27, 1948; children: Patricia Ann, Jacqueline Helen. BA, MA, Oxford U., 1951, D Phil., 1955, DSc, 1989. Rsch. fellow Clarendon Lab., Oxford U., 1954-59, 71; rsch. assoc. physics dept. U. Mich., 1956-57; physicist Oak Ridge (Tenn.) Nat. Lab., 1959-94, assoc. dir. physics div., 1967-74, dir. theoretical physics, 1974-76, mem. disting. rsch. staff, 1976-94; rsch. prof. U. Tenn., from 1994. Author: (with D.M. Brink) Angular Momentum, 1962, Introduction to Nuclear Reactions, 1980, Direct Nuclear Reactions, 1983; contbr. research articles to profl. jours. Served with RAF, 1944-48. Corp. rsch. fellow, 1976-94. Fellow Am. Phys. Soc. (mem. exec. com. nuclear physics div. 1974-75, T.W. Bonner prize 1977) Home: Shelton, Wash. Died Mar. 28, 2010.

SATTEN, NORMA FRANCES, health planner and administrator; b. Bklyn., Nov. 7, 1922; d. Herman and Belle (Lubart) Goldstein; m. Joseph Satten Satten, June 17, 1945; children: Neal, Deborah, Sara. BA, Bklyn. Coll., 1943; MCP, MIT, 1945. Cert. Am. Inst., planners. Planner Kans. Dept. Econ. Devel., Topeka, 1966—68; dir. Kans. Comprehensive Health Planning Program, Topeka, 1968—71; assoc. dir. Bay Area Comprehensive Health Planning, San Francisco, 1971—72; exec. dir. Alameda County Comprehensive Health Planning Coun., Oakland, Calif., 1972—76; pres. Satten-Brusstar-O'Rourke Assocs., Inc., San Francisco, 1976—82; dir. support svcs. Hospice San Francisco, 1983—85; dir. devel. VNA San Francisco, 1985—89; pres. Satten Assocs., San Francisco, from 1990; pres., bd. dirs. North and South Market Adult Day Health Ctr., from 1993; steering com. Topeka Inst. Urban Affairs, Washburn U., 1968—71; cons. continuing edn. health planning HEW, 1970; regional adv. com. Midcontinent Comprehensive Health Planning and Tng. Ctr., U. Okla., Oklahoma City, 1969—71; mem. adv. coun. Kans. Health Manpower Info. Program, 1970—71. Pres. Topeka, 1960—62; bd. dirs. Jewish Childrens and Family Svc., San Francisco, Disabilities Area Bd. V, Oakland, from 1981, LWV Kans., 1962—63. Mem.: Am. Pub. Health Assn. (chmn. coms., chmn. cmty. health planning sect. 1975—77, vice chmn. 1973—75), Am. Acad. Comprehensive Health Planning (sec. 1970—71, Achievement award 1971), Am. Planning Assn. (sec. Gt. Plains chpt. 1959—60). Home: San Francisco, Calif. Died June 14, 2010.

SAUERS, JAMES BYRON, allergist, clinical immunologist; b. Willard, Ohio, Nov. 14, 1930; s. Charles Sylvester Sauers and Margaret Helen (Dungan) Dellinger; m. Ruth Parry Owens, June 28, 1962 (div). BA, Ohio Wesleyan U., 1952; MD, Ohio State U., 1958. Diplomate Am. Bd. Pediatrics. Intern Cleve. Met. Gen. Hosp., 1958-59, resident in pediatrics, 1959-60, Univ. Hosp. Cleve., 1961; fellow in allergies and immunology U. Colo. Med. Ctr., Denver, 1961-63; practice medicine specializing in allergy and clin. immunology Cleve., from 1963; head pediatrics and allergies St. Luke's Hosp., Cleve., from 1963; assoc. clin. prof. pediatrics U. Hosp. Cleve., from 1963, Case Western Res. U., Cleve., from 1963. Served with U.S. Army, 1952-54. Fellow Am. Acad. Pediatrics; mem. Am. Acad. Allergy and Clin. Immunology, AMA, Ohio State Med. Assn., Cleve. Acad. Medicine, Cleve. Allergy Soc. (past pres.). Avocations: antiques, agriculture. Home: Greenwich, Ohio. Died Apr. 15, 2009.

SAUL, THOMAS PATIOUS, reporter; b. Milw., Nov. 5, 1953; s. Thomas Patrick and Elizabeth Ann (Kosek) S.; m. Teresa Rae Jesionowska, Oct. 15, 1983. BA, U. Wis., Milw., 1978. News editor U. Wis. Post, Milw., 1976-78; corr. Milw. Sentinel, 1977-79; editor West Hernando News, Weeki Wachee, Fla., 1979; reporter Daily Sun Jour., Brooksville, Fla., 1980, Citrus County Chronicle, Inverness, Fla., 1980-83, Ocala (Fla.) Star-Banner, 1983-89, sr. reporter, from 1989. Contbr.: The IRE Book 3, 1986. Coach Big Sun Youth Soccer, Ocala, 1985—. Recipient Claudia Ross Meml. award Fla. Press Assn., 1984, 1st Place award for depth reporting Fla. Soc. Newspaper Editors, 1987, Chmn.'s award N.Y. Times, 1986, 87, 89. Mem. Investigative Reporters and Editors, Fla. Press Club. Democrat. Mem. Christian Ch. Avocations: music, guitar, snorkeling. Home: Ithaca, NY. Died Apr. 25, 2009.

SAUNDERS, LELIA BOOTHE, library administrator; b. Roanoke, Va., Oct. 16, 1917; d. John Ferguson and Mabel M. (Zimmerman) S. BA, Roanoke Coll., 1939; B.L.S., Columbia U., 1940. Country librarian Dickinson County Library, Va., 1941-42; circulation librarian Roanoke City Pub. Library, Va., 1942-46; bookmobile librarian Library of Hawaii, 1946-48; army librarian U.S. Armed Services, Germany, 1949-52; br. librarian Enoch Pratt Free Library, Pa., 1952-58; asst. library dir. Arlington County Pub. Library, Va., 1958-79, dir., 1979-86. Chmn., Alexandria Commn. on Status of Women, Va.; sec. Friends of Women Prisoners, Inc., 1984, pres., 1985— Mem. ALA (council mem.), Va. Library Assn. (pres.), COG Library Council (chmn.), Southeastern Library Assn., No. Va. Networking Commn., D.C. Library Assn. (pres. 1985—) Democrat. Presbyterian. Home: Alexandria, Va. Died July 12, 2009.

SAXBE, WILLIAM BART, lawyer, former United States Attorney General, former United States Senator from Ohio; b. Mechanicsburg, Ohio, June 24, 1916; s. Bart Rockwell and Faye Henry (Carey) S.; m. Ardath Louise Kleinhans, Sept. 14, 1940; children: William Bart, Juliet Louise Saxbe Blackburn, Charles Rockwell. AB, Ohio State U., 1940; LLB, 1948; degree (hon.), Central State U., Findlay Coll., Ohio Wesleyan U., Walsh Coll., Capital U., Wilmington Coll., Ohio State U., Bowling Green State U. Bar: Ohio 1948, DC. Practiced in, Mechanicsburg, Ohio, 1948-55; ptnr. Saxbe, Boyd & Prine, 1955-58; mem. Ohio House of Reps., 1947—54, majority leader, 1951-52, speaker, 1953-54; atty. gen. State of Ohio, 1957-58, 63-68; ptnr. Dargusch, Saxbe & Dargusch, 1960-63; US Senator from Ohio, 1969-74; atty. gen. US Dept. Justice, 1974—75; US amb. to India US Dept. State, New Delhi, 1975-77; ptnr. Chester, Saxbe, Hoffman & Wilcox, Columbus, Ohio, 1977-81; of counsel Jones, Day, Reavis & Pogue, Cleve., 1981-84, Pearson, Ball & Dowd (merger Pearson, Ball & Dowd and Reed, Smith & McClay), Washington, 1984-93, Chester Willcox & Saxbe, Columbus, Ohio, 1994—2010; ind. spl. counsel Central States Teamsters Pension Fund, 1982. Author: I've Seen the Elephant: An Autobiography, 2000. Served with 107th Cav. AUS, 1940-42, 107th Cav. USAAF, 1942-45; col. Res. Mem. ABA, Ohio Bar Assn., Am. Judicature Soc., Chi Phi, Phi Delta Phi. Clubs: Mason (Rufus Putnam Disting. Svc. Award), University, Columbus Athletic, Scioto Country, Urbana Country, Burning Tree Country, Bethesda, Md., Country of Fla., Boynton Beach. Republican. Episcopalian. Home: Gulf Stream, Fla. Died Aug. 24, 2010.

SCALAPINO, LESLIE, poet; b. Santa Barbara, Calif., July 25, 1947; d. Robert Anthony and Dee (Jessen) S.; m. Wesley St. John, 1968 (div.); m. Tom White, 1987. BA, Reed Coll.; MA, U. Calif., Berkeley. Co-publisher O Books, 1986-2010 Author: O and Other Poems, 1976, The Woman Who Could Read the Minds of Dogs, 1976, Instead of An Animal, 1978, This Eating and Walking at the Same Time Is Associated All Right, 1979, Considering How Exaggerated Music Is, 1982, That They Were at the Beach, 1985, How Phenomena Appear to Unfold, 1990, The Return of Painting, the Pearl and Orion: A Trilogy, 1991, crowd and Not Evening of Light, 1992, Objects in the Terrifying Tense Longing from Taking Place, 1994, Defoe, 1995, The Front Matter, Dead Souls, 1996, Green and Black: Selected Writings, 1996, R-hu, 2000,Orchid Jetsam, 2001, Dahlia's Iris: Secret Autobiography and Fiction, 2003, Zither and Autobiography, 2003, Floats Horse-Floats or Horse Flows, 2010; editor: I One An Anthology, 1988, O Two An Anthology: What Is the Inside, What is the Outside?, 1991, War: O-Three, 1991, Subliminal Time-O Four, 1993. Nat. Endowment for Arts fellow, 1976, sr. fellow, 1986. Died May 28, 2010.

SCANLON, PETER REDMOND, retired accountant; b. NYC, Feb. 18, 1931; s. John Thomas and Loretta Dolores (Ryan) S.; m. Mary Jane E. Condon, Mar. 7, 1953; children: Peter, Barbara, Mark (dec.), Brian, Janet. BBA in Acctg., Iona Coll., 1952, LLD (hon.), 1992. CPA, N.Y. Mem. profl. staff Coopers & Lybrand, NYC, 1956-66, ptnr., 1966-91, vice chmn., 1976-82, chmn., CEO, 1982-91, ret. chmn., 1991—2009. Hon. ptnr. N.Y.C. Partnership, 1991. Mem. fin. coun. Diocese of Palm Beach, 1995-2002. Lt. USN, 1952-56. Decorated Knight of Malta, Knight Holy Sepulchre; recipient Arthur A. Loftus award Iona Coll., 1974, Trustee award, 1990, Crain's N.Y. All Star award, 1990, Best in Class award Conf. Bd. Youth Edn., 1991. Mem.: AICPA, NY State Soc. CPAs, Jupiter Inlet Beach Club, NY Athletic Club. Roman Catholic. Home: Jupiter, Fla. Died Dec. 3, 2009.

SCHAFFER, MONROE S., grocery company executive; b. NYC, Oct. 24, 1917; s. Samuel and Fannie (Schwartz) Schaffer; children: Barbara, Roberta, Gail. BS, NYU, 1941. V.p. Schaffer Leasing Co., NYC, from 1965; pres. Far Choy Trading Co., NYC, from 1975, S. Schaffer Grocery Corp., NYC, from 1978, Larmon Realty Co., NYC, from 1980, Weyman Assocs., from 1983. V.p. Alyim Grocery Co., Marshall Trading Co. Pres. United Way, New Rochelle, NY, 1980—82. Mem.: Ridgeway Country Club (past pres.). Home: Harrison, NY. Died Mar. 19, 2010.

SCHAFFNER, BERTRAM HENRY, psychiatrist; b. Erie, Pa., Nov. 12, 1912; s. Milton and Gerta (Herzog) S. Student, Harvard U., 1928-29, 32-33; AB, Swarthmore Coll., 1932; MD, Johns Hopkins U., 1937; diploma, William Alanson White Inst., 1953. Diplomate Am. Bd. Psychiatry, Am. Bd. Neurology. Intern Johns Hopkins Hosp., Balt., 1937-38; resident in neurology Mt. Sinai Hosp., NYC, 1938-39; resident in psychiatry Bellevue Hosp., NYC, 1939-40, N.Y. State Psychiat. Inst., NYC, 1946-47; pvt. practice psychiatry and psychoanalysis NYC, from 1947. Lectr. Sch. Nursing Cornell U., N.Y.C., 1950-60; mem. faculty, clin. supr. in psychotherapy William Alanson White Inst. Psychoanalysis, 1960—, med. dir. HIV svc., clin. supr. psychoanalysis, 1993—; cons., editor confs. Josiah Macy Jr. Found., 1949, 50, 51; cons. U.S. Children's Bur., 1946-47, Bur. Mental Health, V.I., 1954-60, World Fedn. Mental Health, 1958-68, others; mem. N.Y. County dist. bd. Com. on Gay and Lesbian Issues; cons. WHO, 1960-67; founder, exec. dir. U.S.-Caribbean Aid to Mental Health, Inc., 1960-68; organizer Biennial Caribbean Confs. for Mental Health, 1959-65; organizer, cons. Caribbean Fedn. for Mental Health, 1959-65; mem. rsch. study Pre-Soviet Russian Family in the Research in Contemporary Cultures, Columbia U., 1949-51. Mem. editl. bd. Jour. of Gay and Lesbian Psychotherapy, 1987—; author: Father Land: A Study of Authoritarianism in the German Family, 1948; contbr. numerous articles to profl. publs. Mem. acquisitions com. The Bklyn. Mus. of Art, 1995—; trustee Bklyn. Mus. of Art. Recipient Adolf Meyer award for Disting. Svc. on Behalf of Improved Care and Treatment of the Mentally Ill in the Caribbean, 1961. Fellow AMA (life), Am. Psychiat. Assn. (chmn. 1983-86, mem. com. on AIDS N.Y. County dist. br. 1989-99, life), Am. Acad. Psychoanalysis (life), Caribbean Psychiat. Assn.; mem. Group for Advancement of Psychiatry (chair internat. rels. com. 1960-65, chair com. on human sexuality 1987-98), Internat. Acad. Sex Rsch. Avocation: collecting asian and indian art. Died Jan. 29, 2010.

SCHANBERG, SAUL MURRAY, pharmacology educator; b. Clinton, Mass., Mar. 22, 1933; m. Rachel Weinbaum, Dec. 18, 1956; children: Laura E., Linda S. BA, Clark U., 1954, MA, 1956; PhD, Yale U., 1961, MD, 1964. Cons. Calif. Dept. Mental Health, 1962-65; intern in pediatrics Albert Einstein Med. Ctr., NYC, 1964-65; rsch. assoc. NIMH, 1965-67; asst. prof. Duke U. Med. Ctr., Durham, N.C., 1967-69, assoc. prof., 1969-73, prof. of pharmacology, from 1973, prof. psychiatry, from 1983; assoc. dean Duke U. Med. Ctr. Sch., 1987-93, chair phamacology, 1987-92. Cons. USPHS, Rockville, Md., 1983-84. NIMH grantee, 1968; NIH grantee, 1967 Fellow Am. Coll. Neuropsychopharmacology Home: Durham, NC. Died May 15, 2009.

SCHANTZ, DOUGLAS N., gas industry company executive; Grad., U. Va.; MBA, U. Chgo. Sr. mgmt. positions Tenneco Energy Co., Transco Energy Co.; exec. v.p., gen. mgr., KM Mktg. LP Kinder-Morgan Inc.; v.p., mktg. bus. & devel. Cinergy Mktg. and Trading; pres., Sequent Energy Mgmt. AGL Resources Inc., 2003—10. Died Mar. 5, 2010.

SCHEEL, NELS EARL, corporate financial executive, accountant; b. Spencer, Wis., Sept. 25, 1925; s. Roland Edward and Louise Ernestine Scheel; m. Elaine Marie Carlisle, Aug. 28, 1949; children: Thomas W., John E., Martha L., Mark A., Mary E. BA, Youngstown Coll., 1949; MBA, U. Pa., 1950. CPA, Ohio. Staff acct. Lybrand Ross Bros., Cleve., 1950-54; asst. controller Century Foods, Youngstown, Ohio, 1954-62; treas., controller The Bailey Co., Cleve., 1962-63, Golden Dawn Foods, Sharon, Pa., 1963-82; v.p., chief fin. officer Peter J. Schmitt Co., Sharon, 1982-89; cons. to industry Columbiana, from 1989. Part-time faculty Youngstown (Ohio) State U., 1954—94; bd. mem. Sovereign Cirs., Inc., North Jackson, Ohio, 1992—2001, bd. chmn., 1995—99, sec.-treas., 1999—2001. Pres. Crestview Bd. Edn., Columbiana, Ohio, 1970-81; trustee Columbiana Cmty. Found., 2002—. Staff sgt. AUS, 1943-46, PTO, hon. discharge. Mem. Am. Inst. CPA's, Ohio Soc. CPA's. Home: Columbiana, Ohio. Died Aug. 4, 2009.

SCHEER, MILTON DAVID, chemical physicist; b. NYC, Dec. 22, 1922; s. Abraham and Lena (Brauner) S.; m. Emily Hirsch, June 23, 1945; children— Jessica, Richard Mark, Julia Rachel. BS, CCNY, 1943; MS, N.Y. U., 1947, PhD, 1951. Chemist Bd. Econ. Warfare, Guatemala, C. Am., 1943-44; research asst. N.Y. U., 1947-50; combustion scientist U.S. Naval Air Rocket Test Sta., Dover, N.J., 1950-52; phys. chemist U.S. Bur. Mines, Pitts., 1952-55; research scientist Gen. Electric Co., Cin., 1955-58; phys. chemist Nat. Bur. Standards, Washington, 1958-68, chief photochemistry sect., 1968-70, chief phys. chemistry div., 1970-77; dir. Center for Thermodynamics and Molecular Sci., Nat. Measurement Lab., 1977-80; research scientist chem. kinetics div. Ctr. for Chem. Physics, Nat. Measurement Lab., 1981-85; ptnr. McNesby & Scheer Research Assocs., 1985-89. Rsch. cons. U.S. Dept. Energy, Germantown, Md., 1990-94; vis. prof. U. Md., 1980-81; Fulbright scholar U. Rome, 1982-83. Contbr. numerous articles to profl. jours. Served with USN, 1944-46. Fellow Am. Inst. Chemists, AAAS; mem. Am. Chem. Soc., Am. Phys. Soc. Home: Silver Spring, Md. Died Dec. 4, 2009.

SCHEETZ, RAYMOND JOHN, SR., retired radiologist; b. Youngstown, Ohio, Sept. 27, 1914; MD, Ohio State U., 1940. Diplomate Am. Bd. Radiology. Intern St. Elizabeth Hosp., Youngstown, Ohio, 1940-41; fellow in radiology Mayo Found., Rochester, Minn., 1941-44; served with U.S. Army Med. Corps, 1945—47; with radiology dept. St. Elizabeth Hosp., 1947—78. Mem. AMA, Am. Coll. Radiology, Am. Roentgen Ray Soc. Home: Kinnelon, NJ. Died Sept. 22, 2009.

SCHENCK, BENJAMIN ROBINSON, insurance consultant; b. NYC, July 21, 1938; s. John T. and Harriet Buffum (Hall) S.; m. Sally V. Sullivan, Aug. 27, 1960; children: Steven T., Elizabeth F., Timothy S. BA, William Coll., Williamstown, Mass, 1960; LL.B., Harvard U., 1963. Bar: N.Y. 1964, Mass. 1978. Asst. counsel to gov. State of N.Y., Albany, 1963-66; assoc. Bond, Schoeneck & King, Syracuse, N.Y., 1966-68; dep. supt., 1st dep. sup. and supt. State of N.Y. Dept. Ins., NYC, 1968-75; sr. v.p. Shearson Hayden Stone Inc., NYC, 1975-77, State Mut. Life Assurance Co. Am., 1977-86, exec. v.p., 1986-89; pres. Worcester Mut. Ins. Co., 1979-83, Cen. Mass. Health Care, Inc., Worcester, 1989-93. Home: Johns Island, SC. Died Jan. 28, 2010.

SCHEURER, EDWIN CHARLES, insurance broker; b. NYC, June 1, 1933; s. Harry I. and Sophie (Rich) Scheurer; m. Edith M. Raabin Scheurer, Nov. 10, 1957; children: Lynne Norma, Andrew Raabin. Student, NYU, 1951—52; BBA, Upsala Coll., 1954. With Frank B. Hall & Co., Inc., NYC, from 1955, sr. v.p., from 1980, dir.; dir., chmn. exec. com. Ins. Fedn. N.Y. Inc. Vice chmn. Greater N.Y. Coun. Boy Scouts Am., 1972—75. Served with AUS, 1956—58. Mem.: City Midday Club, City Athletic Club, Sunningdale Country Club. Republican. Jewish. Home: New York, NY. Died Aug. 14, 2010.

SCHILD, JOYCE ANNA, otolaryngologist, surgeon; b. Chgo., May 26, 1931; d. William Paul and Helen (Kammer) S.; m. John A. Hegber, Dec. 15, 1973. BS, U. Ill., Chgo., 1954, MD, 1956. Diplomate Am. Bd. Otolaryngology. Intern St. Francis Hosp., Peoria, Ill., 1956-57; residency in otolaryngology U. Ill., Chgo., 1958-61, fellow in bronchoesophagology, 1961-62, clin. instr. to assoc. prof. otolaryngology, 1958-82, interim acting head dept. otolaryngology, 1978-79, prof. otolaryngology head and neck surgery Coll. Medicine, from 1982; mem. staff U. Ill. Hosp., Chgo.; otolaryngologist, surgeon Ill. Eye and Ear Infirmary, Chgo. From adj. to assoc. attending otolaryngologist Presbyn. St. Luke's Hosp., Chgo,. 1964-76; acting head bronchoesophagology dept. Children's Meml. Hosp., Chgo., 1972-76, cons. staff, 1976—; mem. staff Michael Reese Hosp., Chgo., 1989—; courtesy staff dept. surgery sect. otolaryngology St. Joseph's Hosp., Chgo., 1961-74; numerous presentations and lectrs. in field. Mem. AMA, Am. Acad. Otolaryngol.-Head-Neck Surgery, Ill. State Med. Soc., Chgo. Med. Soc., Am. Laryngol. Assn., Soc. Univ. Otolaryngologists, Am. Laryngol., Rhinol. and Otol. Soc., Am. Soc. Pediatric Otolaryngology, Chgo. Laryngol. and Otol. Soc. (pres. elect 1983-84, pres. 1984-85, coun. mem. 1985-86), Am. Broncho-Esophagological Assn. (v.p. 1976-77, pres. elect 1978-79, pres. 1979-80, thesis com. 1981-82), Am. Coun. Otolaryngology, Soc. Ear, Nose and Throat Advances in Children, Am. Acad. Pediatrics (com. on accident and poison prevention 1982-85), Pan-Am. Assn. Oto-Rhino-Laryngology, Head and Neck Surgery. Home: Chicago, Ill. Died Apr. 26, 2010.

SCHLAPAK, BENJAMIN RUDOLPH, state official, retired army officer; b. Winsted, Conn., Nov. 14, 1937; s. Rudolph and May Adelaide (Bradford) S.; divorced; children: Eric, Rudy, Sara; m. Helen Ann McCoy, Apr. 25, 1970; children: Tony, Lygia, Nicholas. BSME, Norwich U., 1959; BSCE, Tex. A&M U., 1964, MECE, 1965. Registered profl. engr., Vt., Tex., Hawaii. Commd. 2d lt. U.S. Army, 1959, advanced through grades to col., 1979; asst. div. engr., then dist. engr. U.S. Army Pacific Ocean Div., Ft. Shafter, Hawaii, 1976-80; dir. engring. U.S. Army So. Command, Corozal, Panama, 1980-83; command engr. U.S. Army Western Command, Ft. Shafter, 1983-85, dir., cons. family housing, 1985-89; ret., 1989; project mgr. M & E Pacific Inc., Honolulu, 1989-92; head planning engr. airports div. Hawaii Dept. Transp., Honolulu, from 1992. Contracting officer U.S. Army C.E., Buffalo, 1968-69, Ft. Shafter, 1976-80. Contbr. articles to mil. publs. Mem. Hawaii Gov.'s Com. on Housing, 1988-89; mem. Rapid Transit Sta. Community Adv. Com., Honolulu, 1991-92. Decorated Legion of Merit, Bronze Star with 6 oak leaf clusters; recipient merit award Freedoms Found., 1969. Mem. NSPE, ASCE, Soc. Am. Mil. Engrs., Am. Pub. Works Assn. Home: Honolulu, Hawaii. Died Sept. 6, 2009.

SCHLESINGER, ROBERT JACKSON, business administration educator; b. NY, Dec. 5, 1927; s. Robert B. and Corrine Marie (Jackson) S.; m. Sylvia Barbara Tiersten, Dec. 24, 1980; children: Lisa Roberta, Karen Ann. BSEE, U. Conn., 1953; MS in Ops. Rsch., West Coast U., 1972; PhD, Brunel U., Eng., 1984. Registered profl. engr., Calif. Design engr. GE Co., Syracuse, NY, 1953-55; mem. tech. staff Ramo-Wooldridge, LA, 1955-58; mem. corp. staff Gen. Dynamics Corp., San Diego, 1958-61; v.p. mktg. and systems ITT, Calif., 1961-65, NJ; dir. R&D Packard Bell divsn. Teledyne, Newbury Park, Calif., 1965-68; mem. tech. staff Cal-Tech.'s JPL, Pasadena, Calif., 1968-70; pres., CEO Rho Sigma Inc., LA, 1970-80; prof. info. and decision systems dept. San Diego State U., 1984-97, prof. emeritus, from 1997. Lectr. in field. Author: Principles of Electronic Warfare, 1961; contbr. articles to profl. publs., chpts. to books. Mem. IEEE, Sigma Xi. Avocation: amateur radio. Home: La Mesa, Calif. Died Aug. 5, 2010.

SCHLEY, CHARLES C., printing company executive; b. Bklyn., Apr. 29, 1923; s. Charles A. and Mary E. (Raynis) Schley; m. Mildred Halsey Schley, Apr. 7, 1951; children: C. Halsey, J. Matthew, Joan M., Daniel L., Brian T. BA, Colgate U., 1947. With Sorg Printing Co., NYC, from 1949, sales mgr., from 1978, sr. v.p. sales, from 1978. Lt. USNR, 1942—46. Republican. Roman Catholic. Died Apr. 20, 2010.

SCHMEIDLER, GERTRUDE RAFFEL, psychology educator; b. Long Branch, NJ, June 15, 1912; d. Harry B. and Clare (Holzman) R.; m. Robert Schmeidler, Aug. 27, 1937; children: James, Richard, Emilie, Katherine. BA, Smith Coll., 1932; MA, Clark U., 1933; PhD, Radcliffe/Harvard U., 1935. Instr. Monmouth Coll., Long Branch, N.J., 1935-37; rsch. assoc. Harvard U., Cambridge, Mass., 1942-45; rsch. officer Am. Soc. for Psychical Rsch., NYC, 1946-47; instr. to prof. emeritus CUNY, NYC, from 1947. Author: ESP and Personality Patterns, 1958, Parapsychology and Psychology: Matches and Mismatches, 1988; editor: Extrasensory Perception, 1974, Parapsychology: Its Relation to Physics Psychology, 1976, Research in Parapsychology 1990, 1992. Rep. LWV, Hastings-on-Hudson, 1990. Recipient McDougall award Found. for Rsch. on the Nature of Man, 1964, Disting. Achievement in Parapsychology award So. Calif. Soc. for Psych. Rsch. Inc., 1981. Fellow AAAS, APA, Soc. for Psychol. Study of Social Issues; mem. Am. Soc. for Psychical Rsch. (pres. 1982-84), Parapsychol. Assn. (program chair conv. 1990, pres. 1959, 71, Career award 1988). Home: Whittier, Calif. Died Mar. 9, 2009.

SCHMERLING, ERWIN ROBERT, counselor, retired physicist; b. Vienna, July 28, 1929; came to U.S., 1955, naturalized, 1962; s. Heinrich H. and Lily (Goldsmith) S.; m. Esther M. Schmerling, Apr. 5, 1957; children: Susan D., Elaine M. BA, Cambridge U., 1950, MA, 1954, PhD in Radio Physics, 1958; grad., Advanced Mgmt. Program, Harvard, 1969, Fed. Exec. Inst., 1975. Asst. prof. elec. engring. Pa. State U., University Park, 1955-60, assoc. prof., 1960-62, 63-64; staff scientist NASA-Hdqrs., Washington, 1962-63, program chief ionospheric physics, magnetospheric physics, space plasma physics, 1964-82; asst. dir. space and earth scis. Goddard Space Flight Ctr., NASA, Greenbelt, Md., 1984-86; chief data system scientist Office Space Science and Applications NASA Hdqrs., Washington, 1986-88; SAIS program scientist NASA, Washington, 1988-89; data system scientist solar system exploration div. NASA Hdqrs., Washington, 1989-90, program mgr. astrophysics data systems, 1991-94; counselor Svc. Corps of Retired Execs. (SCORE), 1995—98. Mem. U.S. coms. III and IV Internat. Sci. Radio Union, 1985—, sec. U.S. Com. III, 1966-69, chmn., 1969-72; chmn. subcom. C1 Com. Space Rsch. (COSPAR), 1984-88; mem. Adv. Group Aerospace R&D, NATO, 1978-85; vis. scholar Stanford U., 1983; cons. RCA, Gen. Electric, 1959-62. Contbr. papers to profl. jours. Recipient medal for contbns. to internat. geophys. programs, Soviet Geophys. Soc., 1985. Fellow IEEE (mem. wave propagation standards com.); mem. Am. Geophys. Union, AAAS, Sigma Xi. Home: Wilmington, Del. Died Dec. 12, 2009.

SCHMID, FRANK RICHARD, medical educator; b. NYC, June 25, 1924; s. Frank and Anna (Stimpfle) S.; m. Theresa A. Robey, Oct. 16, 1954; children: Stephen, Margaret, Barbara, Dorothy, John, Jane, Maria, Ann, Christopher. MD, NYU, 1949. Intern Bellevue Hosp., NYC, 1949-50, resident, 1950-51, 52-54; mem. faculty Northwestern U. Med. Sch., Chgo., from 1957, assoc. prof., 1966-69, prof., from 1969, chief sect. arthritis-connective tissue diseases, 1965-89. Home: Glencoe, Ill. Died Aug. 30, 2010.

SCHMIDT, GEORGE, physicist, educator; b. Budapest, Hungary, Aug. 1, 1926; s. Laszlo Schmidt and Katalin Wellisch; m. Katalin Varkonyi, June 26, 1955; children: Franklin R., Ronald W. Diploma in Elec. Engring., Tech. U., Budapest, 1950; PhD in Physics, Hungarian Acad. Scis., Budapest, 1956; M in Engring., Stevens Inst. Tech., 1961. Sr. lectr. Israel Inst. Tech., Haifa, Israel, 1957-58; asst. prof. Stevens Inst. Tech., Hoboken, NJ, 1959-61, assoc. prof., 1961-63, prof. physics, 1963-83, George Meade Bond prof. physics and engring. physics, 1983-92, prof. emeritus, from 1992. Vis. prof. U. Wis., 1965, UCLA, 1972-73; vis. scientist Culham Labs., Culham, Eng., 1965, Ecole Polytechnique, Paris, 1979-80; cons. Sci. Applications Inc., Washington, 1981—, Berkeley Assocs., Washington, 1985. Author: Physics of High Temperature Plasmas, 1966, 2nd rev. edit., 1979; contbr. sci. articles to profl. jours. Recipient Research award Stevens Inst. Tech., 1961. Fellow Am. Phys. Soc.; mem. N.Y. Acad. Scis. Home: Teaneck, NJ. Died Oct. 1, 2009.

SCHMIDT, RUTH ANN, retired academic administrator; b. Mountain Lake, Minn., Sept. 16, 1930; d. Jacob A. and Anna A. (Ewert) S. BA, Augsburg Coll., Mpls., 1952; MA, U. Mo., 1955; PhD, U. Ill., 1962; LLD, Gordon Coll., 1987. Asst. prof. Spanish Mary Baldwin Coll., Staunton, Va., 1955-58, SUNY-Albany, 1962-67, assoc. prof., 1967-78, dean humanities, 1971-76; prof., provost Wheaton Coll., Norton, Mass., 1978-82; pres. Agnes Scott Coll., Decatur, Ga., 1982-94, pres. emerita, 1994—2010. Interim pres. Lyon Coll., 1998; chair Women's Coll. Coalition, 1986-88. Author: Ortega Munilla y sus novelas, 1973, Cartas entre dos amigos del teatro, 1969. Trustee Gordon Coll., Wenham, Mass., 1980-86, Lyon Coll., 1993-2001; bd. dirs. DeKalb C. of C., 1982-85, Atlanta Coll. Art, 1984-94; mem. exec. com. Women's Coll. Coalition, 1983-88; v.p. So. Univ. Conf., 1993. Named Disting. Alumna Augsburg Coll., 1973 Mem. Assn. Am. Colls. (dir. 1979-82, treas. 1982-83), Soc. Values in Higher Edn., Am. Coun. Edn. (commn. on women in higher edn. 1985-88), AAUW, Assn. Pvt. Colls. and Univs. Ga. (pres. 1987-89), Internat. Women's Forum, Young Women's Christian Assn. Acad. Women Achievers, Women's Action for New Directions. Democrat. Presbyterian. Home: Atlanta, Ga. Died May 24, 2010.

SCHMIDT, WILLIAM FREDRIC, utility company executive; b. Cin., Feb. 10, 1928; s. Arthur H. Schmidt and Margaret (Wise) Caseldine; m. Nira P. Pursifull, Oct. 25, 1952; children: Cynthia A., Stephen F., Laurie B. BEE, U. Cin., 1953; MBA, Loyola U., Balt., 1977. Registered profl. engr., N.Y., Ohio. Cost analyst Cin. Gas and Electric Co., 1953-60; cons. engr. Gilbert Assocs., NYC, 1960-64; chief rate cons. Ebasco Services, NYC, 1964-71; v.p. Commonwealth Mgmt. Cons., Washington, 1971-72; dir. rates Potomac Electric Power Co., Washington, 1972-78, v.p. rates, from 1978. Served as sgt. U.S. Army, 1946-47. Fellow Council on Econ. Regulation; mem. IEEE, Edison Elect. Inst. (rate rsch. com.), Assn. Edison Illuminating Cos. (load research com.). Republican. Avocations: sailing, fishing, golf. Home: Longboat Key, Fla. Died Feb. 10, 2009.

SCHNAIBERG, ALLAN, sociology educator; b. Montreal, Que., Can., Aug. 20, 1939; came to U.S., 1964; s. Harry and Belle (Katzoff) S.; m. Edith L. Harshbarger, Sept. 1, 1981; children by previous marriage: Lynn Renee, Jill Ann. BS, McGill U., 1960; MA, U. Mich., 1964, PhD, 1968. Analytical chemist Can. Nat. Rys., Montreal, 1960-61; materials and process engr. Canadair, Ltd., Montreal, 1961-63; asso. dir. West Malaysian Family Survey, Kuala Lumpur, 1966-67; prof. sociology Northwestern U., Evanston, Ill., from 1969, chmn. dept. sociology, 1976-79. Cons. Wissenschaftszentrun, Berlin Author: The Environment: From Surplus to Scarcity, 1992; co-author: Environment and Society: The Enduring Conflict, 1994, Local Environmental Struggles: Citizen Activism in the Treadmill of Production, 1996; co-editor: Distributional Conflicts in Environmental Resource Policy, 1986. Population Council fellow, 1967-68; Nat. Inst. Child Health and Human Devel. research grantee, 1970-72 Mem. Am. Sociol. Assn. (Disting. Contbn. award environ. sociology sect. 1984, chmn. environ. and tech. div. 1991-93), Soc. for Study Social Problems (chmn. environ. problems divsn. 1978-80, mem. C. Wright Mills com. 1979). Home: Chicago, Ill. Died June 6, 2009.

SCHNEIDER, ARTHUR PAUL, retired videotape and film editor, author; b. Rochester, NY, Jan. 26, 1930; s. Mendell Phillip and Frieda (Bl) S.; m. Helen Deloise Thompson, June 5, 1954; children: Robert Paul, Lori Ann. Student, U. So. Calif., 1948. With NBC, 1951-68, film and videotape editor, 1953-60, developer double system method of editing video tape, 1958; pres. Burbank (Calif.) Film Editing, Inc., 1968-72, Electronic Video Industries Inc., 1977-79; supr. video tape editing Consol. Film Industries Inc., Hollywood, Calif., 1972-76, editorial supr., 1980-83; pvt. practice editing, 1983-88. Cons., lectr., author. Film and tape editor all: Bob Hope shows, 1951-67; supr. NBC kinescope and video tape editors (1966-67); video tape editor: Laugh-In Series, 1967-68; video tape editor: Comedy Shop Series, 1977-80; post-prodn. cons. to Video Systems and Broadcast Engring. mag.; video tape editor: TV series Sonny & Cher, 1973, Sonny Comedy Revue, 1974, Tony Orlando and Dawn, 1974, Hudson Bros., summer, 1974, Dean Martin Series, 1975-76, Mickey Mouse Club Series, Walt Disney Prodns., 1976, Redd Foxx Series, 1977; (author: Electronic Post Production and Videotape Editing, 1989 (pub. in Chinese 1995), Electronic Post Production Terms and Concepts, 1990; contbg. author: Association of Cinema and Video Laboratores (ACVL) Handbook, 5th edit., 1995, Focal Guide to Electronic Media CDRom Version, 1998, Jump Cut: Memoirs of a Pioneer Television Editor, 1997, (autobiography) My 50 Years of Television History: Been There, Done That, 2005; oral history interview for Acad. TV Arts and Scis. Found. Archive of Am. TV First 50 Yrs., 2001; contbr. articles to publs. in field. Recipient Broadcast Preceptor award San Francisco State U., 1975; named hon. Ky. Col. Mem. Acad. Television Arts and Scis. (Emmy nominations and Emmy award for video tape editing 1966, 68, 73, 84, gov. 1977-80, sec. 1980-81), Am. Cinema Editors (life, Life Achievement award 1999), Soc. Motion Picture and TV Engrs., Delta Kappa Alpha (life). Home: Port Hueneme, Calif. Died Oct. 1, 2009.

SCHNEIDER, LEONARD RAYMOND, real estate executive; b. NYC, Sept. 3, 1939; s. Cele (Sherman) Schneider; m. Josephine Di Fazio Schneider, June 24, 1962 (div. Jan. 1972); children: Laura, David. BS in Acctg., Brooklyn Coll., 1962; JD, Bklyn. Law Sch., 1965. Atty. J. Leon Israel, NYC,

1965—67; v.p. real estate Parklane Hosiery Co., Inc., Great Neck, NY, 1967—70; sr. v.p. real estate Gordon Jewelry Corp., Houston, from 1970. dir. Home: Houston, Tex. Died July 25, 2009.

SCHNEIDER, STEPHEN HENRY, climatologist, environmental policy analyst, researcher; b. NYC, Feb. 11, 1945; s. Samuel and Doris C. (Swarte) S.; married, 1995; 2 children from previous marriage. BS, Columbia U., 1966, MS, 1967, PhD in Mech. Engring./Plasma Physics, 1971; DSc (hon.), N.J. Inst. Tech., 1990, Monmouth Coll., 1991. NAS, NRC rsch. assoc. Goddard Inst. Space Studies NASA, NYC, 1971-72; fellow advanced study program Nat. Ctr. Atmospheric Research, Boulder, Colo., 1972-73, scientist, dep. head climate project, 1973-78, acting leader climate sensitivity group, 1978-80, head visitors program and dep. dir. advanced study program, 1980-87, sr. scientist, 1980-96, head interdisciplinary climate systems sect., 1987-92; prof. biol. scis. dept., sr. fellow Inst. Internat. Studies Stanford (Calif.) U., 1992—2010, prof. civil and environ. engring. dept. (courtesy). Affiliate prof. U. Corp. Atmospheric Rsch. Lamont-Doherty Geol. Obs., Columbia, U., 1976-83; mem. Carter-Mondale Sci. Policy Task Force, 1976; Clinton-Gore sci. advisor, 1992, 96; sci. advisor, interviewee Nova Sta. WGBH-TV, Planet Earth, Sta. WQED-TV; mem. internat. sci. coms. climatic change, ecology, energy, environ. edn., food and pub. policy; expert witness congl. coms.; mem. Def. Sci. Bd. Task Force on Atmospheric Obscuration; lead author Intergovernmental Panel on Climate Change Working Group I, 1995-96; coord. lead author Working Group II, 1998-2010; mem. core writing team Synthesis Report, 2000-10 Author: (with Lynne E. Mesirow) The Genesis Strategy: Climate and Global Survival, 1976; (with Lynne Morton) The Primordial Bond: Exploring Connections Between Man and Nature Through Humanities and Science, 1981, (with Randi S. Londer) The Coevolution of Climate and Life, 1984, Global Warming: Are We Entering the Greenhouse Century?, 1989; (with W. Bach) Interactions of Food and Climate, 1981; (with R.S. Chen and E. Boulding) Social Science Research and Climate Change: An Interdisciplinary Appraisal, 1983; (with K.C. Land) Forecasting in the Social and Natural Sciences, 1987; (with P. Boston) Scientists on Gaia, 1990, (with Janica Lane) The Patient from Hell: Getting the Best that Modern Medicine Can Offer, 2005; editor-in-chief: The Encyclopedia of Climate and Weather, 1996, Laboratory Earth: The Planetary Experiment We Can't Afford to Lose, 1997; editor: Climatic Change, 1976-2010; contbr. articles on theory of climate, influence of climate on soc., relation of climatic change to world food, population, energy, development and environ. policy issues, environ. aftereffects of nuclear war, carbon dioxide greenhouse effect, pub. understanding sci., environ. edn. Recipient Louis J. Battan Author's award Am. Meteorol. Soc., 1990, Mary B. Ansari Ref. Work award Geosci. Info. Soc., 1997; named one of 100 Outstanding Young Scientists in Am. by Sci. Digest, 1984; MacArthur Found. Prize fellow John D. and Catherine T. MacArthur Found., 1992. Fellow AAAS (Westinghouse award 1991), Scientists Inst. for Pub. Info.; mem. U.S. Assn. Club Rome, Am. Meteorological Soc., Am. Geophysical Union, Fedn. Am. Scientists, Soc. Conservation Biology, Soc. Ecol. Economics., Acad. Europae (fgn.), Ecol. Soc. Am., NAS (elected, 2002). Died July 19, 2010.

SCHNEITER, GEORGE MALAN, professional golfer, real estate developer; b. Ogden, Utah, Aug. 12, 1931; s. George Henery and Bernice Slade (Malan) S.; m. JoAnn Deakin, Jan. 19, 1954; children: George, Gary, Dan, Steve, Elizabeth Ann, Michael. BS in Banking and Fin., U. Utah, 1955. With 5th Army Championship Golf Team, U.S. Army, 1955-56; assoc. golf pro Hidden Valley Golf Club, Salt Lake City, 1957; golf pro Lake Hills Golf Club, Billings, Mont., 1957-90, sec., 1957-61, pres., 1964-90, Schneiter Enterprises, Sandy, Utah, from 1974; developer Schneiter's Golf Course, from 1973, and subdiv., from 1961; player PGA tour, 1958-78, Sr. PGA tour, from 1981. Missionary So. State Mission, LDS Ch., 1951-52. Served with U.S. Army, 1955-56. Named winner, Utah sect. Sr. Championship, Wyo., Open Super Sr. Championshio, Salt Lake City Parks Tournament, Vernal Brigham Payson Open, Yuma Open, Utah Sr. PGA Chamption, Utah Super Sr. Championshio, World Pro Am., Kona, Hawaii, Ft. Carson Golf Championship; fellow Banking & Fin. fellow, First Security Bank Utah, 1953. Mem. PGA, Salt Lake City C. of C., Intermountain Golf Courst Supertaints Assn. Died Feb. 6, 2010.

SCHOCH, RICHARD ALLEN, distillery company executive; b. Chgo., Jan. 13, 1931; s. Harry Hanson and Helen M. (Johnson) Schoch; m. Sally Ann Davis Schoch, July 7, 1962; children: Bret, Bradley, Kari Ann, Brandon. Student, Evanston Jr. Coll., 1950—51, Northwestern U., 1951—52. Asst. state mgr. Mich. Coty Cosmetics, NYC, 1952—56; state mgr. Mich. Tussy Cosmetiques, NYC, 1956—61; sales mgr. Chgo. Jack Daniel Distillery Co., Nashville, 1962—66, Ill. state mgr., 1966—71, regional sales mgr., 1971—82, v.p., from 1982. Pack master Boy Scouts America, Wilmette, Ill., 1975, 1977—78. Presbyterian. Died May 21, 2010.

SCHOENHERR, JOHN CARL, artist, illustrator; b. NYC, July 5, 1935; s. John Ferdinand and Frances (Braun) S.; m. Judith Gray; children: Jennifer L., Ian G. BFA, Pratt Inst., 1956. Painter, illustrator Owl Moon, 1987 (Caldecott medal, 1988); exhibitions include Hiram Blauvelt Art Mus., 1997. Recipient World Sic. Fiction award, World Sci. Fiction Conv., London, 1965, Silver medal, Phila. Acad. Natural Sci., 1984, purchase award, Hiram Blauvelt Art Mus., 1994. Mem.: Soc. Animal Artists (medal 1979, 1985, 2003), Am. Soc. Mammalogists (emeritus). Died Apr. 8, 2010.

SCHÖNEMANN, PETER HANS, psychologist, educator; b. Pethau, Germany, July 15, 1929; arrived in U.S., 1960, naturalized, 2003; s. Max Paul Franz and Hertha Anna (Kahle) S.; m. Roberta Dianne Federbush, Jan. 29, 1962; children: Raoul Dieter, Nicole Deborah. Vordiplom in Psychologie, U. Munich, 1956; Hauptdiplom in Psychologie, U. Goettingen, 1959; PhD, U. Ill., 1964. Thurstone postdoctoral fellow U. N.C., 1965-66; asst. prof., then assoc. prof. Ohio State U., 1966-69; postdoctoral fellow Ednl. Testing Service, Princeton, NJ, 1967-68; vis. prof. Technische Hochschule, Aachen, Fed. Republic Germany, 1981; mem. faculty Purdue U., from 1969, prof. psychology, 1971-2001, emeritus, from 2001. Vis. prof. Univs. Munich, Bielefeld and Braunschweig, 1984-85, Nat. Taiwan U., 1992, 96, 97. Author papers in field. Recipient Found. for the Advancement of Outstanding Scholarship award, Taiwan, 1996. Home: West Lafayette, Ind. Died Apr. 7, 2010.

SCHONK, ROBERT MARTIN, banker; b. Norfolk, Va., May 13, 1925; s. Martin Luther and Marie Elizabeth (Hardee) S.; m. Jean Bolling White, July 17, 1948; children— Robert Martin, Stuart Randolph, John Bolling, Rebecca Meade. BS in Econs, U. Pa., 1949, MBA, 1950; grad., Rutgers U., 1960. Staff accountant Waller & Woodhouse, Norfolk, Va., 1950-52, Paul E. Cofer, Norfolk, 1952; with Va. Nat. Bank, Norfolk, from 1952, sr. v.p., 1961-70, corp. exec. officer, from 1970; treas. Va. Nat. Bankshares, Inc., from 1971; chief fin. officer, treas. Sovran Fin. Corp. Mem. faculty Va.-Md. Bankers Sch., Inst. Mgmt., Old Dominion U., 1965-71 Treas. Feldman Chamber Music Soc., 1962-77; bd. dirs. Hosp. Data Center Va., 1966-74; chmn. rate rev. bd. Va. Hosp. Assn., 1973-75; chmn. bd. Norfolk United Communities Fund, 1976-77, mem. exec. com., 1975-78; bd. dirs. Eastern Va. Health System Agy., 1977—. Served with USAAF, 1943-45. Mem. Bank Adminstrn. Inst., Va. Bankers Assn., Am. Inst. C.P.A.'s. Clubs: Harbor (Norfolk). Episcopalian. Home: Virginia Bch, Va. Died Jan. 20, 2010.

SCHOONER, EDWARD FRANCIS, transportation executive; b. N.Y.C., June 18, 1924; s. Edward Daniel and Anna Sarah (Guss) S.; student Power Meml. Acad., 1942, Acad. Advanced Traffic, 1953; m. Muriel Veronica Allen, July 27, 1946; children: Carol Jeanne Schooner Zieske, Edward Francis. Passenger rep. N.Y. Cen. R.R., 1946-50; passenger rep. Remington Rand, N.Y.C., 1950-52, claims supr., 1952-55, rate auditor, 1955-56, routing mgr., 1956-58; factory traffic mgr. Univac div. Sperry Rand Corp., Ilion, N.Y., 1958-60, gen. traffic mgr., Utica, N.Y., 1960-65, dir. transp. N.Y.C., 1965-68, Bluebell, Pa., 1968-84; v.p. Airfreight Co., 1984-85; mem. shippers adv. bd. Am. Airlines. Sustaining mem. Republican Nat. Fin. Com. Served with AUS, 1942-45. Decorated Bronze Star with oak leaf cluster, Purple Heart with oak leaf cluster, Croix de Guerre with silver palm, Disting. Svc. Cross. Mem. ICC Practitioners, Def. Transp. Assn. (past chpt. pres.), Univac Mgmt. Assn. (past pres.), Nat. Indsl. Traffic League, Transp. Assn. Am., Heritage Found., U.S. Def. Com., Nat. Trust for Historic Preservation, Conservative Caucus, Nat. Transp. Policy Assn. (users panel), DAV (life), Vets. Battle of Bulge, Order Purple Hearts. Home: Eden Prairie, Minn. Died Mar. 23, 2009.

SCHOONHOVEN, RAY JAMES, retired lawyer; b. Elgin, Ill., May 24, 1921; s. Ray Covey and Rosina Madeline (Schram White) S.; m. Marie Theresa Dunn, Dec. 11, 1943; children: Marie Kathleen (Kamie), Ray James, Jr., Pamela Suzanne, John Philip, Rose Lynn. BSc, U. Notre Dame, 1943; JD, Northwestern U., 1948. Bar: Ill. 1949, U.S. Supreme Ct. 1954, D.C. 1973, U.S. Ct. Mil. Appeals 1954. Assoc. Seyfarth, Shaw Fairweather & Geraldson, Chgo., 1949-57; ptnr. Seyfarth, Shaw Fairweather & Geraldson now Seyfarth Shaw, Chgo., 1957-92; ret. Chief rulings and ops. br. Wage Stabilization Bd. Region VII, Chgo., 1951-52. Book rev. editor: Ill. Law Rev., 1948. Served to lt.comdr. USNR, 1942-62. Mem. ABA, Ill. State Bar Assn., Chgo. Bar Assn., D.C. Bar Assn., Chgo. Athletic Assn., Univ. Club. Chgo., Fed. Bar Assn., Order of Coif. Republican. Roman Catholic. Home: Lake Forest, Ill. Died July 10, 2010.

SCHOPPMEYER, MARTIN WILLIAM, education educator; b. Weehawken, NJ, Sept. 15, 1929; s. William G. and Madeleine M. (Haas) S.; m. Marilyn M. Myers, Aug. 9, 1958; children: Susan Ann, Martin William. BS, Fordham U., 1950; EdM, U. Fla., 1955, EdD, 1962. Tchr. Fla. pub. sch., 1955-59; instr., then asst. prof. U. Fla., 1960-63; assoc. prof., then prof. edn. Fla. Atlantic U., Boca Raton, Fla., 1963-68, dir. continuing edn., 1965-67; mem. faculty U. Ark., Fayetteville, Ark., from 1968, prof. edn., 1971-93, Univ. prof., 1993—99, Univ. prof. emeritus, from 1999, program coord. for ednl. adminstrn., 1983-90. Mem. Nat. Adv. Coun. Edn. Professions Devel., 1973-76; exec. sec. Ark. Sch. Study Coun., 1976—; evaluator instructional tng. program Nat. Tng. Fund, 1978; bd. dirs. Women's Ednl. and Devel. Inst., 1977-80, Nat. Sch. Devel. Coun., sec., 1989-90, v.p. 1990, pres., 1990-92; mem. oversight com. South Conway (Ark.) County Sch. Dist.; mem. state commn. to study effect of Amendment 59 to Ark. Constn.; cons. Lake View V. Huckabee, 1994-2002. Author books, monographs, articles in field. Mem. president's coun. Subiaco Acad., 1984-90; chmn. Subiaco Sch. Bd., 1990-93, mem., 1993-97. With U.S. Army, 1951-53, Korea. Recipient numerous fed. grants. Mem. VFW, KC (past grand knight), Ark. Edn. Assn. (past chpt. pres.), Ark. Assn. Ednl. Adminstrs., Am. Legion, Rotary, Kappa Delta Pi, Phi Delta Kappa, Delta Tau Kappa. Roman Catholic. Home: Fayetteville, Ark. Died Jan. 27, 2009.

SCHORR, DANIEL LOUIS, broadcast journalist, author, lecturer; b. NYC, Aug. 31, 1916; s. Louis and Tillie (Godiner) S.; m. Lisbeth Bamberger, 1967; children: Jonathan, Lisa. BSS, CCNY, 1939; doctorate (hon.), Kalamazoo Coll., Columbia Coll., Chgo., Wilkes U., Nebr. Wesleyan U., LI U., Brandeis U., Spartus Coll., Bates Coll., Haverford Coll. Asst. editor Jewish Telegraphic Agy., 1934-41; news editor ANETA (Netherlands) News Agy. in N.Y., 1941-43; freelance corr. N.Y. Times, Christian Sci. Monitor, London Daily Mail, 1948-53; Washington corr. CBS News, also spl. assignments L.Am. and Europe, 1953-55; reopened CBS Moscow Bur., 1955; roving assignments U.S. and Europe, 1958-60; chief CBS News Bur., Germany, 1960-66; Washington corr. CBS, 1966-76; Regents prof. U. Calif., Berkeley, 1977; columnist Des Moines Register-Tribune Syndicate, 1977-80; sr. Washington corr. Cable News Network, 1980-85; sr. news analyst Nat. Pub. Radio, 1985—2010. Author: Don't Get Sick in America!, 1971, Clearing the Air, 1977, Forgive Us Our Press Passes, 1999, Staying Tuned: A Life in Journalism, 2001, Come to Think of It, 2008. With U.S. Army, 1943-46, 47. Decorated officer Orange Nassau (The Netherlands), Grand Cross of Merit (Germany); recipient citations of excellence for radio-TV reporting Soviet Union Overseas Press Club, 1956, Best TV Interpretation of Fgn. News award 1963, ACLU and other awards for pub. suppressed Congsl. intelligence report, Emmy awards for coverage of Watergate, 1972, 73, 74, Peabody award for lifetime of uncompromising reporting of highest integrity, 1992, George Polk award for radio commentary L.I. U., 1994, Disting. Svc. award Am. Soc. Journalism and Mass Comm., 1994, Golden Baton award for lifetime achievement A.I. DuPont Columbia U., 1996; inducted in Hall of Fame Soc. Profl. Journalists, 1991, Comms. Hall of Fame CCNY, 1999. Mem. Am. Acad. Arts and Scis. (elected), Coun. on Fgn. Rels. N.Y.C., Nat. Press Club. Died July 23, 2010.

SCHOTT, BASIL MYRON, archbishop; b. Freeland, Pa., July 21, 1939; s. Michael Schott and Mary. Attended, Immaculate Conception Coll., Troy, NY, St. Mary's Seminary, Norwalk, Conn. Ordained priest Order of Friars Minor, 1965, hegumen, protohegumen, dir. formation, dir. novices, dir. vocations, custodial councilor, custodial treas., spiritual asst. for Secular Franciscans; chaplain Holy Protection Monastery, Byzantine Nuns of St Clare, North Royalton, Ohio, Holy Annunciation Monastery, Byzantine Carmelite Nuns, Sugarloaf, Pa.; hegumen Holy Dormition Monastery, Sybertsville, Pa.; tchr. religious edn. dept. Byzantine Catholic High Sch., Parma, Ohio; syncellus for Priests and Religious Eparchy of Passaic, mem. Presbyteral Coun.; ordained bishop, 1996; bishop Eparchy of Parma (Ruthenian), 1996—2002; archbishop Archeparchy of Pitts. (Ruthenian), Pa., 2002—10. Mem. Gen. Visitation Team, 1988; sec., treas., Episcopal liaison Interparochial Ecumenical, Evangelization and Youth Commissions; liaison Interparochial Religious Edn. Commn.; mem. Consecrated Life and Evangelization Committees US Conf. of Catholic Bishops, chmn. Com. on the Relationship between the Eastern and Latin Churches, mem. adminstrv. bd. Mem.: Eastern Catholic Associates (pres.). Roman Catholic. Died June 10, 2010.

SCHRAMM, JOHN JOSEPH, broadcast executive, consultant; b. Orange, NJ, Jan. 18, 1941; s. Sylvester Anthony and Ruth Monica (Bender) S.; m. Patrice Marie Doran, July 23, 1966; children: Martin William, Margaret Marie. B in Engring., Stevens Inst. of Tech., 1962; MBA, U. Conn., 1968. Dir. corp. devel. Westinghouse Broadcasting, NYC, 1961-1982; exec. v.p. and gen. mgr. Home Theatre Network, Stamford, Conn., 1982-85; exec. v.p. fin. and adminstrn. The People's Choice, Westport, Conn., 1985-86; treas. Satellite Corp. Am., NYC, from 1986. Prin. Southport (Conn.) Devel., 1979—. Editor: Marketing to Education for Profits, 1973. Mem. Assn. for Corporate Growth (pres. N.Y. chpt. 1984-85, asst. treas. 1986-88). Republican. Roman Catholic. Avocations: automobile racing, tennis, golf. Home: Fairfield, Conn. Died Jan. 13, 2009.

SCHREIBER, SIDNEY M., retired state supreme court justice; b. NYC, Nov. 18, 1914; s. Nathan and Estelle (Goldstein) S.; m. Ruth Butt, Dec. 22, 1940; 1 child, Florence. BA summa cum laude, Yale U., 1936, LLB, 1939. Bar: N.J. 1940, U.S. Dist. Ct. N.J. 1940, U.S. Dist. Ct. D.C. 1939, U.S. Ct. Appeals D.C. 1939. Atty. U.S. R.R. Retirement Bd., Washington, 1940, SEC, Phila.; ptnr., atty. McKeown & Schreiber, Newark, Scheiber, Lancaster & Demos, Newark; judge Superior Ct., State of N.J., Jersey City and Elizabeth, 1972-74; assoc. jsutice Supreme Ct., State of N.J., Newark and Trenton, 1975-84; of counsel Riker, Danzig, Scherer, Hyland & Perretti LLP, Morristown, N.J., from 1984. Editor Yale Law Jour., 1938-39; Contbr. articles to legal jours. Mem. Union County (N.J.) Park Commn. 1st lt. Army of U.S. Recipient William J. Brennan award Fed. Bar Assn. N.J., 1984; named Man of Yr., Anti-Defamation League, 1998. Mem. ABA, Union County Bar Assn., Phi Beta Kappa. Died Aug. 5, 2009.

SCHREURS, JAN WILLEM HERMAN, physicist; b. Winterswijk, Netherlands, Feb. 10, 1932; came to U.S., 1962; naturalized, 1968; s. Johan Gerhard and Hendrika Petronella (Harmsen) S.; m. Martha Jantina Bonjernoor, Dec. 17, 1956; children— Jolanda, Marja, Miranda, Peter. B.S., Free U., Amsterdam, 1953, Doctorandus, 1957, Ph.D., 1962. Research asst. Columbia U., N.Y.C., 1957-59; postdoctoral research fellow NRC, Ottawa, Can., 1959-61; research chemist Corning Glass Works, N.Y., 1962-76, research assoc., 1976-85, sr. research assoc., 1985—. Mem. Am. Phys. Soc., N.Y. Acad. Scis. Home: Corning, NY. Died June 1, 2009.

SCHROEDER, AARON HAROLD, songwriter; b. Bklyn., Sept. 7, 1926; s. Max and Pearl (Miller) S. m. Abby Steinberg, Oct. 31, 1967; 1 child, Rachel Amy. Student, music and art high schs., NYC. Contact man Warner Bros. Music, Mills Music; profl. mgr. Charley Barnett; owner A. Schroeder Internat., Ltd. and subs. cos., NYC, 1960; founder, pres. Musicor Records, NYC, 1960-65. Mus. dir. film The Four Musketeers; composer songs for Fund Drives Berkshire United Way, 1986-87, N.Y. State Dept. Agr., Fairview Hosp., 1988, Operation Earth, 1990; composer: (singles) Not as a Stranger, I Got Stung, Mandolins in the Moonlight, Stuck on You, 1960, Twixt Twelve and Twenty, Fools Hall of Fame, Because They're Young, French Foreign Legion, Time and the River, I'm Gonna Knock on Your Door, Rubber Ball, It's Now or Never, 1960, Big Hunk of Love, 1959, Today's Teardrops, Good Luck Charm, 1962, Once She Was Mine; (film themes) Four Musketeers, She Can Put Her Shoes Under My Bed Anytime, If I Could Only Touch Your Life, We're All In the Same Boat; score for motion picture and TV series Lucky

Luke including original songs The Lonesomest Cowboy In the West, Lopin' Along, Lotta Legs' Hotel, Put Your Pistol Back in Your Holster, Cowboy's Lament, numerous others; composer for PBS Pilot "Grover's Corner", 1990, PBS spl. Chanukah at Grover's Corner, 1992 Mem. ASCAP (elections bd.), NARAS (gov. 1962). Home: Great Barrington, Mass. Died Dec. 2, 2009.

SCHROEDER, CHARLES HENRY, corporate treasurer; b. Akron, Ohio, May 25, 1942; s. Charles Henry Sr. and Marion Belle (Buzenberg) S.; m. Marilyn Sue Patterson, Aug. 28, 1965; children— Rebecca Lynn, William Charles BA, Ohio Wesleyan U., 1964; MBA, Case Western Res. U., 1968, Stanford U., 1986. Treas. Ford Corp. subs. Ford Motor Co., South Africa, 1972-75; treas. Ford Microelectronics, Inc., 1980-82, Ford Aerospace Corp., 1978-90; v.p., treas. Loral Aerospace Corp. and Space Systems/Loral, Newport Beach, Calif., from 1990. Mem. Stanford U. Alumni Cons. Team for Orange County non-profit orgns., 1993. Recipient Fin. award for outstanding research Cleve. Soc. Security Analysts, 1967 Mem. L.A. Treas.' Club (pres. 1991—), Case-Western Res. U. Orange County Alumni Assn. (pres. 1990). Republican. Episcopalian. Home: Mission Viejo, Calif. Died Feb. 23, 2009.

SCHROTH, EVELYN MARY, retired language educator; b. Ellington, Wis., Aug. 5, 1919; d. Henry A. and Clara M. (Komp) Schroth. BS, U. Wis., 1940; MS, U. Ill., 1948, AM, 1955; PhD, Pacific Western U., 1979. Tchr. Rhinelander (Wis.) High Sch., 1940-42; chmn. English dept. Waupun (Wis.) High Sch., 1942-44; tchr. Chgo. pub. schs., 1953-63, chmn. dept. English Lindblom High Sch., 1956-62; instr. dept. English U. Ill., Urbana, 1948-50; lectr. Northeastern U., Chgo., 1962-63; assoc. prof., then prof. English, Western Ill. U., Macomb, 1963-87. Program dir. U.S.O., 1946-48. John Hay fellow, 1961. Mem. Linguistic Soc. Am., Nat. Council Tchrs. English, Ill. Tchrs. English, AAUP, Phi Beta, Phi Kappa Phi. Home: Appleton, Wis. Died Nov. 7, 2009.

SCHULTS-BERNDT, ELFIE, music educator; Grad. in Piano Performance, SUNY, Buffalo; PhD in Piano Performance, Music Theory and Lit., Mich. State U. Dir. music Lake Mich. Coll., Benton Harbor. Recipient US Prof. of Yr. award, Carnegie Found. for Advancement of Tchg. and Coun. for Advancement and Support of Edn., 2006. Deceased.

SCHULTZ, FREDERICK HENRY, investor, former government official; b. Jacksonville, Fla., Jan. 16, 1929; s. Clifford G. and Mae (Wangler) S.; m. Nancy Reilly, Aug., 1951; children: Catherine G., Frederick H., Clifford G., John R. BA, Princeton U., 1951; postgrad., U. Fla. Sch. Law, 1954-56. With Barnett Nat. Bank, Jacksonville, 1956-57; owner, operator investment firm, from 1957; mem. Fla. Ho. of Reps., 1963-70, speaker of the house, 1968-70; chmn. bd. Barnett Investment Svcs., Inc.; dir. Barnett Banks Inc., to 1979; vice chmn. bd. govs. Fed. Res. System, Washington, 1979-82; sr. advisor Drexel Burnham Lambert, 1982—90; founder Schultz Ctr. Tchg. & Leadership, from 2002. Served to lt. U.S. Army, 1952-54, Korea Decorated Bronze Star Roman Catholic. Home: Jacksonville, Fla. Died Nov. 23, 2009.

SCHULTZ, ROBERT JOHN, religious institution administrator, pastor; b. Harvey, Ill., Feb. 6, 1945; s. John Schultz and Cora (Lotz) S.; m. Joyce Ann Mahler, June 3, 1967; children: Jeffrey, Michael, Kristin, Rebekah. AA, Concordia Jr. Coll., Milw., 1965; BA, Concordia Sr. Coll., Ft. Wayne, Ind., 1967; MDiv, Concordia Sem., 1971; MS in Urban Edn., U. Nebr., 1978. Assoc. pastor St. Paulus Luth. Ch., San Francisco, 1971-74; pastor Mt. Calvary Luth. Ch., Omaha, 1974-79; assoc. pastor St. Peter Luth. Ch., Hemlock, Mich., 1979-80; pastor St. Mark Luth. Ch., Saginaw, Mich., from 1980; dir. Mich. Luth. Ministries Inst., Saginaw, from 1989. Mem. adv. Bd. Mission Devel., Ann Arbor, Mich., 1984—, Bd. Evangelism and Ch. Growth, Ann Arbor, 1989—; panelist Ask the Pastor-Channel WAQP, Saginaw, 1990—. Speaker Meml. Day activities, Hemlock, 1990. 1st lt. U.S. Army, 1969-75. Home: Freeland, Mich. Died Jan. 16, 2009.

SCHULTZ, ROBERT JORDAN, orthopaedic surgeon, educator; b. Bklyn., June 29, 1930; m. Marcie Schultz. Student, Muhlenberg Coll., 1948-49; BS, Bklyn. Coll., 1952; MD, Chgo. Med. Sch., 1957. Diplomate Am. Bd. Orthopedic Surgery (examiner). Intern Meadowbrook Hosp., Hempstead, NY, 1957-58; resident in surgery Mt. Sinai Hosp., Miami, Fla., 1958-59; resident in orthopaedic surgery Charity Hosp., New Orleans, 1959-62; fellow in hand surgery Columbia Presbyn. Med. Ctr., NYC, 1968; instr. dept. orthopaedic surgery Albert Einstein Coll. Medicine, NYC, 1966-73, asst. prof., 1968-73, assoc. prof., 1973-77; lectr. div. prosthesis and orthotics NYU Postgrad. Med. Sch., from 1968; dir. dept. orthopaedic surgery Albert Einstein Coll. Medicine, NYC, 1969-77; prof. dept. surgery N.Y. Med. Coll., Valhalla, 1988-90, prof. dept. anatomy, 1987-90, dir. sports medicine, dept. orthopaedic surgery, from 1980, dir. Sylvester J. Carter Hand Svc., from 1980, prof., chmn. dept. orthopaedic surgery, from 1977; with U. S. Fal. Med. Ctr., Tampa, from 1990. Dir., attending surgeon dept. orthopaedic surgery Westchester County Med. Ctr., Valhalla, 1977—, dir. sports medicine, 1978—; attending orthopaedic surgeon, Met. Hosp., N.Y.C., 1977—, Lincoln Hosp., Bronx, 1977—, Lenox Hill Hosp., N.Y.C., 1982—, Terence Cardinal Cooke Health Care Ctr., N.Y.C., 1977—, Bronx Mcpl. Hosp. Ctr., 1966-77; dir. and attending orthopaedic surgeon Hosp. of Albert Einstein Coll. Medicine, Bronx, 1969-77; presenter papers, exhibits, invited lectr. to numerous nat. and internat. assns., hosps., med. colls., postgrad. courses; spl. orthopaedic del. to People's Republic of China, 1981, chmn. dels., 1983, 86; med. cons. N.Y. State Athletic Commn., chmn. of med. adv. bd.; adv. coun. USN; vis. prof. Haddasah Hosp. and Med. Sch., Jerusalem, 1972, Browley Bristow Orthopaedic Hosp., Surrey, Eng., 1973, U. Colo., 1977, University Cattolica del Sacro Cuore, Rome, 1984, Michael Reese Hosp. & Med. Ctr., Chgo., 1984, Bethesda Naval Hosp., 1986, U. W.Va. Med. Sch., Morgantown, 1988; adv. com. State of Conn. Higher Edn. Supplemental Loan Authority, 1983—; police surgeon of Westchester County (N.Y.) Police Dept., 1983—, commdg. officer police surgeons, 1984—. Author: The Language of Fractures, 1972; editor Jour. Hand Surgery; mem. editorial bd. Jour. Orthopaedic Surg. Techniques, Surg. Rounds for Orthopaedics; contbr. chpts. to books, articles and abstracts to sci. and med. jours. Mem. grant rev. com. Orthopedic Rsch. and Edn. Found. Career Devel. Awards Com., Fellowsip Grant Com., The Mary and David Hoar Fellowsship Com. N.Y. Acad. Medicine; sr. investigator N.Y. Med. Coll. for Aging and Adult Devel., 1984—. With USN, 1962-66; flight surgeon, 1963-65, capt. USNR, 1980—. Fellow ACS, Am. Acad. Orthopaedic Surgeons, N.Y. Acad. Medicine (sec. sect. orthopaedic surgery 1979-80, chmn. 1980-81); mem. AMA, Am. Orthopaedic Assn., Am. Soc. for Surgery of the Hand, Societe Internationale de Chirurgie Orthopedique et de Traumatologie, Sociedad de Cirugia de la Mano del Caribe (hon.), Amicale Internationale de Chirurgie de la Main (hon.), Soc. Med. Cons. to Armed Forces, Ea. Orthopaedic Assn., Am. Rheumatism Assn., N.Y. Soc. Orthopaedic Surgeons, Westchester Acad. Medicine (chmn. sect. sports medicine, 1979-81), N.Y. Soc. for Surgery of the Hand (sec. 1981-83, v.p. 1983-84, pres. 1985-86). Home: Rye, NY. Died Aug. 8, 2009.

SCHULTZ, WILLIAM LOUIS, former museum director, consultant; b. Manitowoc, Wis., Nov. 25, 1923; s. William G. and Linda (Geisler) S.; m. Grace G. Parrott, Nov. 12, 1949 (dec.); children: William A., Robert L., James R., Timothy P., Thelma A.; m. Carol L. Mosley, Apr. 29, 1988. Student, Cornell U., 1945-46; BS, MS, U. Wis., 1950; postgrad., George Williams Coll., 1951. Dir. phys. edn. Madison YMCA, Wis., 1949-51; exec. dir. Keokuk YMCA, Iowa, 1952-53; dir. Oshkosh YMCA, Wis., 1953-57; met. exec. dir. Madison YMCA, 1957-72; exec. dir. Circus World Mus., Hist. Sites Found., Inc., Baraboo, Wis., 1972-84; cons. athletic and fitness ctrs. 1984-92; ret. Sports cons. D.B. Frampton Co., Columbus, Ohio; circus cons. Genis Book of Records, London; mem. U.S. Marine Corps Boxing and Wrestling Team, Cornell U. Wrestling Team; capt. U. Wis. Gymnastic Team; U.S. rep. World Council of YMCAs on Phys. Edn. Author: The Joy of Remembering. Pres. Inter-Service Club Council of Madison, Phys. Dirs. Soc. Midwestern YMCA's; bd. dirs. Madison and Baraboo Chambers of Commerce; pres. Inter-Agy. Assn. United Way of Madison. Served with USMC, 1943-46. Inducted into Lake Michigan Shore Sports Hall of Fame, 1979; nat. open singles paddleball champion, 1962; nat. open singles racquetball champion, 1968 Mem. Circus Fans of Am., Circus Hist. Soc., Showfolks of Am., YMCA Phys. Dirs. Soc., N.Am. YMCA Profl. Soc. Lodges: Rotary; Elks. Methodist. Died June 7, 2009.

SCHUMACHER, FREDERICK RICHMOND, retired lawyer; b. NYC, Sept. 4, 1930; s. Frederick William and Anna De Rose Elizabeth (Richmond) Schumacher; m. Birte Vestel Schumacher, Dec. 1, 1973; children: Anna Lisa, Ian, Eric. AB, Princeton U., 1952; JD, Cornell U., 1957; postgrad in law. Bar: NY 1957, Calif. 1960; cert. in taxation U. Southern Calif., 1967. Assoc. Law Firm Clark, Carr & Ellis, NYC, 1957—59, Law Firm Thelen, Marrin, Johnson & Bridges, LA, 1960—62, individual practice law, 1963—96; pres. Frederick R. Schumacher Ltd., Newport Beach, Calif., 1982, Colorado Springs, Colo., 1992—96; of counsel Lewis, D'Amato Brisbois & Bisgaard, 1991—92, cons. fed. & nternat. taxes. Author: International Letters of Credit, 1960. Active Rep. Nat. Com., from 1981. Served with USMC, 1952—54. Mem.: Hunting Hall of Fame Found. (charter mem.), Calif. Bar Assn., 1st Marine Divsn. Assn. (life). Died May 29, 2010.

SCHUMAN, EDWIN Z., steel company executive; b. Hartford, Conn., Sept. 3, 1929; s. Leon and Rhea S.; m. Virginia Ruth Stauffer, Aug. 3, 1969; children: Lisa Schuman Gallun, Eric M., Linda J., Karen Schuman Hawkey, Roberta L. Schuman Sheets, Darryl F. B.E. in Civil Engring., Yale U., 1951, M.E. in Structural Engring., 1952. Stress analyst Chance-Vought Aircraft div. United Aircraft, Dallas, 1952-53; field engr. Stone & Webster Engring. Corp., Newark, 1956-57; with Levinson Steel Co., Pitts., 1957-89, exec. v.p., 1967-75, pres., chief operating officer, 1975-87, vice chmn., 1987-89; ptnr. screen printing operation All Ads Up, Pitts., from 1989. Served with Civil Engring. Corps., USN, 1953-56; lt. comdr. Res.; ret. Mem. Steel Service Ctr. Inst. (chpt. pres.), Duquesne Golf Assn., Tau Beta Pi. Home: Pittsburgh, Pa. Died May 3, 2009.

SCHUSSLER, THEODORE, lawyer, physician, educator, consultant; b. July 27, 1934; s. Jack and Fannie (Blank) Schussler; m. Barbara Ann Gordon, June 18, 1961; children: Deborah, Jonathan, Rebecca. BA in Polit. Sci., Bklyn. Coll., 1955; LLB, Bklyn. Law Sch., 1958, JD, 1967; MD, U. Lausanne, Switzerland, 1974. Bar: NY 1959, US Dist. Ct. (so. and ea. dists.) NY 1975, US Tax Ct. 1961, US Ct. Appeals (2nd cir.) 1962, US Supreme Ct. 1975. Clerkship and practice, NYC, 1956, 1958—59; legal editor tax divsn. Prentice-Hall, Inc., Englewood Cliffs, NJ, 1956; vol. criminal law divsn. Legal Aid Soc., NYC, 1959; atty. legal dept. NYC Dept. Welfare, 1959—60; sole practice NYC, from 1960. Sr. staff asst. IBM-Indsl. Medicine Program, 1969—70, 1974—76; intern in medicine St. Vincent's Med. Ctr. of Richmond, SI, NY, 1976—77, resident emergency medicine, 1977—79; resident in gerontology, chief house physician Carmel Richmond Nursing Home, SI, 1978—80; surg. rotation emergency dept. Met. Hosp. Ctr., 1979; house physician dept. medicine Richmond Meml. Hosp. and Health Ctr., 1979—80; gen. practice medicine, from 1980; attending physician, former chief dept. family practice, former chmn. med. care evaluation, med. records and by-laws coms., former physician Cmty. Hosp. Bklyn., 1980—94, advisor emergency dept., former mem. blood transfusion, credential's, emergency dept. coms., 1980—94, mem. med. staff, 1980—94; attending physician Meth. Hosp., Bklyn., 1984—92, supervising emergency dept. physician, dept. ambulatory care, 1980—83; attending physician Kings Hwy. Hosp., 1981—88, coord. emergency dept., 1981; clin. instr. dept. preventive medicine and cmty. health Downstate Med. Ctr. SUNY, Bklyn., 1981—88, clin. asst. prof., 1988—95, SUNY Health Sci. Ctr.; med. dir. divsn. devel. disabilities Mishkon-Jewish Bd. Family & Children's Svc., Bklyn., 1982—2000; primary care physician Jewish Home and Hosp. for Aged, NYC, 1993—94; cons. in gerontology Palm Beach Home for Adults, Bklyn., 1980—92; cons. indsl. medicine IBM, 1990—92; tchr., instr., lectr., prof., 1954—95; med.-legal cons. to professions of medicine and law. Author: Torts, 1961, 1965, 1974, Jurisdiction and Practice in Federal Courts, 1967, Constitutional Law, 1973; contbr. articles to profl. jours. Recipient Pub. and Cmty. Svc. award, United Ind. Dems. 44th Assembly Dist., Bklyn. Fellow: Am. Coll. Legal Medicine; mem.: United Univ. Professions, Assn. Arbitrators of Civil Ct. of NY (small claims divsn., arbitrator), Bklyn. Law Sch. Alumni Assn. (past bd. dirs.), Delta Sigma Rho. Died July 26, 2009.

SCHUTZIUS, LUCY JEAN, retired librarian; b. Cin., Dec. 27, 1938; d. Gregory Girard and Harriet Elsa (Wiggers) Wright; m. Paul Robert Wilson, Aug. 25, 1962 (div. 1968); 1 child, Ellen Field; m. William Carl Schutzius, Dec. 12, 1976; stepchildren: Christopher Matthew, Catharine Alexander, John Benedict, Margaret Elizabeth. BA in French, Middlebury Coll., 1960; MLS, U. Ill., 1963. Tech. libr. Chanute AFB, Rantoul, Ill., 1963-65; libr. Coll. Prep. Sch., Cin., 1969-74; pub. svcs. libr. Raymond Walters Coll., Cin., 1974-79, dir. libr., 1979-92, sr. libr., 1988—2001, sr. libr. emerita, from 2001. Access svcs. libr. U. Cin. Coll. Engring., 1992—2001. Mem.: Friends of Univ. Librarians. Home: Cincinnati, Ohio. Died June 17, 2009.

SCHWAB, JOHN JOSEPH, psychiatrist, educator; b. Cumberland, Md., Feb. 10, 1923; s. Joseph L. and Eleanor (Cadden) S.; m. Ruby Baxter, Aug. 4, 1945; 1 dau., Mary Eleanor. BS, U. Ky., 1946; MD, U. Louisville, 1946; MS in Physiology (Med. fellow), U. Ill., 1949; postgrad., Duke U., 1951-52, U. Fla., 1959-61. Diplomate: Nat. Bd. Med. Examiners. Intern Phila. Gen. Hosp., 1947-48; resident medicine Louisville Gen. Hosp., 1949-50; edn. officer med. coll. U. Yokohama, 1952-54; internist, psychosomaticist Holzer Clinic, Gallipolis, Ohio, 1954-59; resident psychiatry U. Fla. Hosp., 1959-61; NIMH Career tchr. U. Fla., Gainesville, 1962-64, mem. faculty, 1961-73, prof. psychiatry and medicine, 1967-73, dir. cons. liaison program, 1964-67, resident tng. dir., 1965-71; prin. investigator Fla. Health Study, 1969-74; prof., chmn. dept. psychiatry and behavioral scis. Sch. Medicine U. Louisville, 1973-91, prof. psychiatry, 1991-93, prof. emeritus, from 1993, assoc. dir. clin. psychopharm. rsch., from 1991. Chmn. epidemiologic studies rev. com. Ctr. for Epidemiologic Studies, NIMH, 1973-75, cons. psychiatry br., 1975-92; cons. Old Order Amish Study of Depression, 1978—; vol. vis. lectr. Howard U., 1992; ann. vis. lectr. U. Würzburg, Germany, hon. faculty, 1992—; vis. prof. El-Azar U., Cairo, 1991; prin. investigator LSVL Family Health Study, 1982—; dir. U. Fla. Coll. Med. Program: History and Philosophy of Medicine, 1965-72; mem. instn;. rsch. rev. bd. U. Louisville, 2003—. Author: Handbook of Psychiatric Consultation, 1968; also articles; co-author: Sociocultural Roots of Mental Illness: An Epidemiologic Survey, 1978, Social Order and Mental Health, 1979; assoc. editor Psychosomatics, 1965-86; co-editor: Man for Humanity: On Concordance V. Discord in Human Behavior, 1972, Social Psychiatry, vol. 1, 1974, The Psychiatric Examination, 1974, first author Family Mental Health History, Epidem, Clinical Health Issues, 1993, first author Family Functioning: The General Living Systems Research Model, 2000; co-edited 9 books, 11 Monographs, and over 250 articles. Capt. USAMC, 1949-54. Recipient Disting. Mental Health award Mental Health Assn. Ky., 1992. Fellow Am. Coll. Psychiatrists (regent 1977-79), Collegium Internat. Neuro-Psychopharmacologicum, World Assn. Social Psychiatry, AAAS, Am. Psychiat. Assn. (chmn. council research and devel. 1974-75); mem. AMA, Acad. Psychosomatic Medicine (exec. 1965-72, pres. 1970-71), Group for Advancement Psychiatry (bd. dirs. 1985-87), So. Assn., Jefferson County Med. Soc., Ky. Psychiat. Assn., Am. Assn. Social Psychiatry (pres. 1971-73), Alpha Omega Alpha, (Outstanding Performance award for Affirmative Action U. Louisville 1986), World Assn. Soc. Psychiatry (internat. adv. com., Rome, 1991), Psychiatrists for Better Psychiat. (pres. 1990-99), U. of the World (co-chair health, edn. com. 1992-98). Achievements include research on applicability of psychiatric concepts to general medicine, sociocultural aspects of mental illness; establishing guidelines for identification and management of medical patients with illnesses complicated by emotional stress; epidemiology of mental illness; depression and the family; clinical psychopharmacology, historical and epidemiologic perspectives on the family. Home: Woodbridge, Conn. Died June 27, 2010.

SCHWALB, HOWARD RAY, geologist; b. Chgo., Mar. 19, 1924; s. Robert Henry and Ethel Ann (Fick) Schwalb; m. Carol Lee Cathcart, Aug. 15, 1947 (dec. July 1954); m. Phyllis Ann Gentry, Aug. 1, 1957; children: Allen Howard, Steven Ray. BS, U. Ill., 1949; postgrad., U. Colo., 1949—50. Asst. geologist Ill. Geol. Survey, Champaign, 1951—56; acting head oil and gas sect., from 1979. Sr. geologist Phillips Petroleum Co., Evansville, Ind., 1956—61; regional geologist Texota Oil Co., Evansville, 1963—65; cons. geologist, 1965—66; sr. geologist Ky. Geol. Survey, Henderson, 1966—79; lectr. U. Evansville, 1963—76; prin. investigator eastern gas shale project US Dept. Energy, Morgantown, W.Va., 1968—71, New Madrid Study Group NRC, Washington, 1976—81. Contbr. articles to geol. lit. With USAAF, 1943—46. Recipient Rock Hound award, U. Mo.-Rolla, 1981. Mem.: Ill. Acad. Sci., Soc. Econ. Paleontologists & Mineralogists, Interstate Oil Compact Commn., Am. Assn. Petroleum Geologists (pres. eastern sect. 1980—81, A.I. Levorsen award 1983), Sigma Xi. Republican. Home: Green Valley, Ariz. Died July 23, 2010.

SCHWARTZ, BERNARD See CURTIS, TONY

SCHWARTZ, FRANKLIN DAVID, physician, educator, administrator; b. Balt., May 16, 1933; s. George Henry and Anna (Snyder) S.; m. Harriet Joan Mohline, May 25, 1972; children: Michael Howard, Ellen Sue. BS cum laude, U. Md., 1953, MD summa cum laude, 1957. Diplomate: Am. Bd. Internal Medicine, Am. Bd. Nephrology. Intern U. Hosp., Balt., 1957-58, asst. resident in medicine, 1958-60; USPHS research fellow U. Md., 1960-61; practice medicine specializing in nephrology Balt., 1957-60, Washington, 1960-64, Chgo., from 1964; asst. chief renal/metabolism sect. Walter Reed Army Hosp., 1961-64; asst. chief dept. metabolism Walter Reed Army Inst. Research, 1961-64; assoc. dir. sect. nephrology U. Ill. Hosp., Chgo., 1970-71, acting chief, 1971-72, assoc. chief, from 1972, attending physician, from 1972, St. Joseph Hosp., Chgo., from 1971, dir. sect. nephrology, from 1971, chief dept. medicine, 1974-77; pres. med. staff St. Joseph Hosp. and Health Care Ctr., from 1987; adj. physician Rush-Presbyn.-St. Luke's Med. Center, 1964-65, asst. attending physician, 1965-67, assoc. attending physician, 1967-70, dir. hemodialysis unit, 1968-70, cons. physician in medicine, 1970-71; assoc. chief sect. nephrology Columbus-Cuneo Cabrini Med. Center, from 1971; asst. prof. medicine Abraham Lincoln Sch. Medicine, Chgo., 1964-69, assoc. prof., 1969-75, clin. prof., 1975-76, prof. clin. medicine, from 1976, Northwestern U. Sch. Medicine, from 1987; pres., chief exec. officer Dialysis Ctrs. Ltd., United Health Care Ltd., 1972-84. Sec., bd. dirs. Neomedica, Inc., 1984—; pres. Assocs. in Nephrology, S.C., 1972—; cons. staff Ill. Masonic Med. Center, 1970-79, Augustana Hosp., Martha Washington Hosp., Ravenswood Hosp., N.W. Community Hosp., Resurrection Hosp., South Chgo. Community Hosp., Ill. Central Hosp.; mem. renal disease adv. com. Ill. Dept. Pub. Health, 1972-84; mem. sci. adv. bd. Kidney Found. Ill., 1972—; co.-dir. hepatitis project Walter Reed Army Inst. Research, 1962; cons. physician VA West Side Hosp., Chgo., 1972— Contbr. articles to med. jours., chpts. to med. books. Mem. high blood pressure research council Am. Heart Assn.; physician rep. Daus. of Charity Nat. Health System, 1987, 88. Mem. Ill. Med. Soc., Chgo. Med. Soc., Am. Soc. Internal Medicine, Ill. Soc. Internal Medicine (exec. council 1987—), Chgo. Soc. Internal Medicine, World Med. Assn., Pan-Am. Med. Assn., Am. Mgrs. Assn. (pres.'s assn.), Internat. Platform Assn., Am. Soc. Law and Medicine, ACP, Internat. Soc. Nephrology, Am. Soc. Nephrology, Am. Fedn. Clin. Research, AMA, European Dialysis and Transplant Assn., N.Y. Acad. Scis., AAAS, Renal Physicians Assn., Am. Acad. Med. Dirs., Am. Geriatric Soc., Sigma Xi. Died Apr. 24, 2009.

SCHWARTZ, JAMES PETER, real estate broker; b. Bridgeport, Conn., Oct. 30, 1919; s. Joseph and Stephanie (Tischler) S.; m. Natalie Postol, Mar. 12, 1944; 1 child: Joseph William. Reporter Bridgeport Times-Star, 1940-41; reporter, photographer Bridgeport Post, 1942-43, 45-49; pres. Jay James Inc., Fairfield, Conn., 1949-70; owner James P. Schwartz & Assocs., Bridgeport, from 1970. Dir. Lafayette Bank & Trust Co., 1965-85, Lafayette Bancorp, 1985-88, Lafayette Am. Bank & Trust Co., 1992-93. Contbg. editor Photog. Trade News, 1960-70. Treas. Greater Bridgeport Bd. Realtors, 1974-77, sr. v.p., 1978, pres., 1979; pres. Barnum Festival Soc., 1975-76; ringmaster Barnum Festival, 1979; justice of peace, 1970-96; mem. Easton (Conn.) Zoning Bd. Appeals, 1971-76; police commr., Easton, 1976-90, chmn. bd. police commrs., 1986-88; bd. dirs. Bridgeport divsn. Am. Cancer Soc., 1977-94; bd. assocs. U. Bridgeport, 1962-94. With AUS, 1943-45. Named Man of Yr. dept. sociology U. Bridgeport, 1962, Realtor of Yr. award Greater Bridgeport Bd. Realtors, 1979. Mem. Fairfield Bd. Realtors, Nat. Assn. Realtors (bd. dirs.), Conn. Assn. Realtors (treas. 1981-82, pres. 1984-85), Masons, Corinthian Lodge. Home: Bridgeport, Conn. Died Feb. 9, 2010.

SCHWARTZ, WILLIAM B., JR., ambassador; b. Atlanta, Nov. 14, 1921; s. William B. and Ruth (Kuhn) S.; m. Sonia Weinberg, Dec. 3, 1942; children— William B., Arthur Jay, Robert C. BS, U. N.C., 1942. Various positions, then v.p. Nat. Service Industries, Atlanta, 1945-68; pres. Weine Investment Corp., Atlanta, 1969-77; amb. to Bahamas, 1977-81; bd. dirs. Weine Investment Corp., Balco Energy, Phenix Supply, Artex Internat. Mem. pres.'s council Brandeis U., 1966—, chancellor's club U. N.C., Bd. Councillors Carter Ctr., Emory U.; trustee, past chmn. Atlanta chapt. Am. Jewish Com.; chmn. Chatham Valley Found.; bd. dirs. Met. Atlanta Rapid Transit Authority, 1969-76, vice chmn., 1971-73; bd. dirs. Big Bros. Atlanta, Atlanta Jewish Welfare Fedn.; former mem. Pres.'s Council Oglethorp U.; former mem. bd. dirs. Jewish Home for the Aged; chmn. bd. visitors Emory U., 1966-74. Served with USN, 1942-45. Recipient Man of Yr. award Am. Jewish Com., 1972 Mem. Coun. Am. Ambs. Clubs: Standard (Atlanta), Commerce (Atlanta); East Hill (Nassau), Lyford Cay (Nassau); Longboat Key (Fla.); City (Sarasota). Lodges: B'nai Brith, Masons, Shriners. Home: Atlanta, Ga. Died May 18, 2010.

SCHWARZ, CARL A., JR., lawyer; b. NYC, Apr. 27, 1936; s. Carl A. and Genevieve C. Byrne; m. Maryellen McG., Apr. 30, 1966; children: Peter Thomas, Elizabeth Anne. BS, Fordham U., 1957, JD, 1960. Bar: N.Y. 1960, U.S. Dist. Ct. (so., ea., we. and D.C. dists.) N.Y. 1960, U.S. Ct. Appeals (2d cir.) 1960, U.S. Supreme Ct. 1965. Ptnr. Schwarz & DeMarco, Garden City, N.Y. Chmn., bd. trustees N.Y. Sch. Interior Design. Trustee Cath. Charities; Capt. USAF, 1961-65. Mem. Manhasset Bay Yacht Club (vice commodore), Order of Malta. Roman Catholic. Home: Hempstead, NY. Died Mar. 11, 2009.

SCHWARZ, MARTIN, foreign language educator; b. Halle, Germany, June 17, 1931; came to U.S., 1951, naturalized, 1956; s. Edgar and Hilda (Spielberg) S. B.A., U. Louisville, 1955; M.A., Washington U., 1957; PH.D., U. Mich., 1963. Asst. prof. French, U. Mich., Ann Arbor, 1963-69; assoc. prof. French, Rice U., Houston, 1969-71; prof. fgn. langs. U. Tulsa, 1971-81, head fgn. lang. dept., 1971-76; prof. fgn. lang. East Carolina U., Greenville, 1981—, chmn. fgn. lang. dept., 1981-90. Am. Assn. Tchrs. of French, South Atlantic Modern Lang. Assn., MLA. Author: O Mirbeau, Varietes Oeuvre, 1966, Variété de Contes, 1969. Contbr. articles to profl. publs. Died Apr. 8, 2010.

SCHWINN, WILLIAM EDWIN, investment company executive; b. Jersey City, Jan. 11, 1916; s. Peter and Hanna Regina (Frey) Schwinn. Registered rep. Herzfeld Stern, Miami Beach, Fla., 1964, Frances I. DuPont, Coral Gables, 1969. Pres. Cooper Investments Inc., Miami, from 1969. Served with US Army, 1942—46. Mem.: Security Traders Assn. Fla. Lutheran. Home: Miami, Fla. Died Feb. 3, 2010.

SCIALDO, MARY ANN, musician, educator; b. Westchester, NY, Sept. 21, 1942; d. Camille George Scialdo. MusB, Seton Hill Coll., 1963; MusM, Pius XII Inst. Fine Arts, Florence, Italy, 1964; profl. diploma, Manhattan Sch. Music, 1978; postgrad., Peabody Cons. Cert. tchr. NY, Fla. Supr. music Great Barrington (Mass.) Sch. Sys., 1967—68; music, theater prof. Simons Rock Coll., Great Barrington, 1968—70, Cath. U. PR, Ponce, 1971; performing arts instr. Briarcliff Sch. Dist., 1981, Ossining (NY) Sch. Dist., 1982, Albert Leonard Jr. H.S., 1983, Pleasantville (NY) Sch. Dist., 1984; theater and music tchr. Briarcliff Manor Schs., 1984—98; music tchr. Hillsborough County Schs., Tampa, Fla., from 1999. Dir., prodr., mus. and vocal dir., set and costume numerous student prodns. Debut concert: Merkin Hall, N.Y.C., internat. debut concert: Glinka Mus.; performer: (fund raising concert) Chopin Found. NY, (Giannini retrospective) WQXR, WNCN, (CD) Scriabin 24 Preludes, Opus 11, 1998—99. Recipient Outstanding Drama Tchr. award, Emerson Coll., 1st place award, Young Artist Nat. Competition, Nat. Fedn. Music Clubs competition, Disting. Alumna Leadership award, Seton Hill U. Mem.: Sigma Alpha Iota (life). Democrat. Roman Catholic. Died July 1, 2010.

ŠCIBOR-MARCHOCKI, ROMUALD IRENEUS, mathematician, consultant; b. Highland Pk., Mich., Dec. 29, 1926; s. Sigismond August and Sophy L. Scibor-Mar. BS, Wayne State U., 1947; MS, 1948; Postgrad., Calif. Inst. Tech., 1948—49, U. So.uthernCalif., 1955—63. Asst. physics Wayne State U., 1943—47, spl. instr., 1947—48; sr. engr. labs. div. Hoffman Radio Corp., 1949—59; design specialist Rheem Mfg. Co., 1959; scientist Aerojet Gen. Corp. div. Gen. Tire & Rubber Co., 1959—62; sr. scientist Nortonics div. Northrop Corp., 1962—68; mem. tech. staff Jet Propulsion Lab., Pasadena, 1968—72, staff scientist, 1970—72; owner Madchental Kennels, Baldwin Pk., from 1955; with Wells Fargo Security Guard Svcs. div. Baker Protective Svcs., 1973—81; tutor Mt. San Antonio Coll., from 1978, staff math. dept., from 1979; cons. math. & computer sci., from 1980. Contbr. articles to profl. jours. Mem.: AAAS, Nat. Free Lance Photographers Assn., Naturist Soc., Free for All, Nat. Rifle Assn., NY Acad. Sci., Assn. Physics Tchrs., Am. Def. Preparedness Assn., Math. Assn., Acoustical Soc., Calavo Growers Assn., Mensa, Sigma Xi. Home: Baldwin Park, Calif. Died Feb. 24, 2010.

SCOTT, JAMES PALMER, II, air national guard officer; b. Lewes, Del., Jan. 10, 1933; s. James Palmer and Gladys Bertha (Wilkins) S.; m. Joan Marie Pearce, Oct. 8, 1957; children— Pamela, David, Mark. Bus. Assoc., Goldey Beacom Coll., 1952; student aerospace safety mgmt. U. So. Calif., 1966. Dir. ops. 166 Tactical Airlift Group Del. Air N.G. Mem. Air Force Assn., N.G. Assn., Am. Bonanza Soc. (charter), Internat. Swift Assn., Aircraft Owners and Pilots Assn. Home: Wilmington, Del. Died June 27, 2010.

SCOTT, JOHN P., state legislator; b. Wilkes-Barre, Pa., June 12, 1933; m. Betty Colby; children: Michael, Linda, John, Susan. Student, St. Peter's Coll., Montclair State Coll. Senator dist. 36 N.J. State Senate, from 1992. State chmn. Conservative Caucus of N.J.; sales cons. Exec. dir., founder N.J. Found. for Econ. Rsch. Died May 21, 2010.

SCOTT, SHIELDS LAMAR, safety and training executive; b. Meridian, Miss., June 28, 1939; s. Shields Lamar and Mary Evelyn (Parker) Scott; m. Mary Louise Davis, June 28, 1962; 1 child, Shields Lamar III. BS, La. Coll., 1962. Coach and athletic dir. Leakesville High Sch., Miss., 1962—67, Kaplan HS, La., 1967—74; mgr. safety audit Brown & Root, Inc., Houston, 1974—79; fgn. safety Diamond M Co., Houston, 1980—81, mgr. safety, from 1981, mgr. safety and tng., from 1983. Mem.: Am. Soc. Tng. and Devel., Am. Soc. Safety Engrs. Democrat. Baptist. Home: Deer Park, Tex. Died May 22, 2009.

SCOVIL, SAMUEL KINGSTON, mining company executive; b. Cleve., June 15, 1923; s. R. Malcolm and Dorothy Lee (Brown) S.; m. Barbara C. Baker, May 22, 1944; children— Emily, Malcolm (dec.), Samuel, Alexander. BS, Yale U., 1945; grad., Advanced Mgmt. Program, Harvard, 1962. With Republic Steel Corp., 1947-50; with Cleveland Cliffs Inc., from 1950, mgr. sales, 1960-63, v.p. sales, 1963-69, sr. v.p. sales, 1970-72, sr. v.p., 1972-74, pres., 1974-83, chief exec. officer, from 1976, chmn. bd., from 1983, chmn. exec. com. of bd. dirs., from 1988. Bd. dirs. Cleve.-Cliffs, Inc., Holnam Inc. Trustee Univ. Sch., Cleve., Cleve. Clinic Found. Died May 2, 2010.

SCUTT, DER, architect; b. Reading, Pa., Oct. 17, 1934; s. George W. and Hazel (Smith) Scutt; m. Leena Liukkonen Scutt, Feb. 18, 1967; children: Hagen, Kirsti Karina. Student, Wyomissing Poly. Inst., 1952—54, Pa. State U., 1956—58, BArch; MArch, Yale U., 1961. Lectr., contbg. editor Lighting Design and Application, from 1972; design ptnr. Swanke Hayden Connell & Ptnrs., 1981; pvt. practice NYC, 1981—2010; tchr. architecture Barlow Sch., Amenia, NY, 1964—66; vis. critic Yale U., 1982, 1983. Project designer Barlow Sch., Amenia, 1964, Crossroads Office Bldg., Rochester, NY, 1969, One Astor Plaza and Minskoff Theatre, NYC, 1973, Western Union Office Bldg., Upper Saddle River, NJ, 1973, Equitable Life Assurance Data Ctr., Easton, Pa., 1973, Creative Perfumery Ctr., Roure Bertrand DuPont, Teaneck, NJ, 1973, Retrofit, 1982, Hercules Inc. Computer Ctr., Wilmington, Del., 1974, Northwestern Mut. Life Ins. Co., Milw., 1979, Barnes Group Inc. Corp. Hdqrs., Bristol, Conn., 1979, Grand Hyatt Hotel, NYC, 1980, 520 Madison Ave., NYC, 1983, Continental Ctr. Office Tower, NYC, 1983, Trump Tower, NYC, 1983, St. Luke's/Roosevelt Hosp. Hand Surgery Clinic, NYC, 1984, US Hdqrs., Hong Kong Bank, NYC, 1985, Pk. Ave. Office Bldg., NYC, 1986, 100 UN Plaza Tower, NYC, 1986, The Corinthian, NYC, 1988, 625 Madison Ave. Office Bldg., NYC, 1988, Milan, W. 23d St., NYC, 1988, 575 Lexington Ave. Office Bldg., NYC, 1990, Creative Properties, San Diego, 1990, NY Constrn. Industry Hdqs., 1990, Chapin Sch., NY, 1990, KG Land/Nissho, White Plains, NY, 1990, IFF Household Products Hdqrs. Bldg., Hazlet, NJ, 1991, 57 West 57th St., NY, 1991, Sherry French Gallery, NY, 1991, Nat. Maritime Hist. Soc. Hdqs., NY, 1991, 823 UN Plz., NY, 1991, 450 West 33d St., NY, 1991, Golden Gate Bridge, San Francisco, 1992, Kaoping Creek Bridge, Taiwan, 1992, Enhance Reinsurance Corp. Hdqs., NY, 1992, Taiwan West Corridor High-Speed Rail Project, Taipei, Taiwan, 1993, Prin. Mut. Life Ins. Co., White Plains, 1993, IFF World Hdqrs., NYC, 1994, 555 Fifth Ave. Office Bldg., NYC, 1994, Givaudan-Roure Inc., Flavors Hdqs., Clifton, NJ, 1994, Victorian Properties, NY, 1994, CIGNA Ins. Group, White Plains, 1994, Internat. Flavors & Fragrances Corp. Hdqtr., NYC, 1995, ATCO Properties 555 5th Ave Office Bldg. Renovation, 1995, 823 United Nations Plz. Renovation, NYC, 1995, Gateway Office Bldg. Renovations White Palins, NY, 1993. Contbr. articles to profl. jours. Trustee Chapin Sch., 1984—2010, Nat. Maritime Hist. Soc., 1991—2010, Ocean Liner Mus. NY, South St. Seaport Mus., 1994—2010; trustee, hon. mem. NY Geneal. & Biog. Soc. Recipient medal, AIA, 1961, Tucker Award, Bldg. Stone Inst., 1990; Internat. fellowship, Rotary, 1955—56. Fellow: Illuminating Engrs. Soc. (bd. mgrs. NY sect. 1971—72, 1974—75, v.p. 1972—73, pres. 1973—74, Disting. Svc. award 1976); mem.: AIA (sec. NY chpt. 1970—72, fin. com. 1974—78, Brunner scholarship com. 1975—76, chmn. 1976—77, NY chpt. spl. com. proposed zoning modifications 1980, chpt. spl. com. on proposed zoning modifications 1982), US Inst. Theatre Tech. (dir. 1970—72), NY Bldg. Congress (bd. govs., v.p. from 1984, v.p. 1985—87, treas. 1987—88, vice-chmn. from 1988), Archtl. League NY (chmn. scholarships and award com. 1970—72, exec. com. from 1970, v.p. architecture 1972—73). Methodist. Died Mar. 14, 2010.

SEALE, JAMES MILLARD, retired religious organization administrator, minister; b. Middlesboro, Ky., Oct. 4, 1930; s. Albert Tyler and Edith Josephine (Buchanan) S.; m. Mary Dudley Harrod; children: William Alan, Ann Lynn Seale Hazelrigg. BA, Transylvania U., 1952; BD, Lexington Theol. Sem., 1955, MDiv, 1963, D Ministry, 1981. Ordained to ministry Christian Ch. (Disciples of Christ), 1951. Student pastor various Christian Chs., Ky., 1949-54; pastor 1st Christian Ch., Pikeville, Ky., 1954-58, Erlanger (Ky.) Christian Ch., 1958-61; sr. minister 1st Christian Ch., Mt. Sterling, Ky., 1961-70, Paris, Ky., 1978-82; stewardship sec. Gen. Office Christian Ch., Indpls., 1970-74; adminstr. Christian Ch. Home of Louisville, 1974-78; dir. devel. Christian Ch. Homes Ky., Louisville, 1978; pres. Disciples of Christ Hist. Soc., Nashville, 1983-95, pres. emeritus, 1995. Author: A Century of Faith and Caring, 1983, Forward From The Past, 1991; editor: (jour.) Discipliana, 1983—92. Pres. Kiwanis Club, Pikeville, 1957, Mt. Sterling, 1963, lt. gov., Ctrl. Ky., 1965. Mem. Christian Ch. Avocations: writing, photography, golf, fishing. Home: Hopkinsville, Ky. Died June 27, 2010.

SEARLE, LEONARD, astronomer, researcher; b. London, Oct. 23, 1930; m. Eleanor Millard, 1952 (dec. 1999). BS, U. St. Andrews; PhD in Theoretical Physics, Princeton U. Faculty mem. U. Toronto, 1953—60; rsch. fellow Calif. Inst. Tech., 1960—63; faculty mem. Mount Stromblo Observatory, 1963—68; with Carnegie Observatories, 1968—89, dir., 1989—96. Died July 2, 2010.

SEATOR, LYNETTE HUBBARD, freelance writer; b. Chgo., Mar. 23, 1929; d. Alvin Glen and Thelma May (Mulnix) Hubbard; m. Gordon Douglas Seator, June 8, 1949 (dec. 1988); children: Pamela, Penelope, Patricia, Glen. BS, Western Ill. U., 1963; MA, U. Ill., 1965, PhD, 1972. Teaching asst. U. Ill., Champaign-Urbana, 1963-66; instr. Western Ill. U., Macomb, 1966-67; prof. Spanish, Ill. Coll., Jacksonville, 1967-89, Dunbaugh disting. prof., 1976, Pixley prof. humanities, 1988, prof. emeritus, from 1989; columnist Jacksonville Jour.-Courier, 1991-96. Symposium dir. New Understandings of Experience of Women, Moscow, 1991, Jacksonville, 1992, Ill. Coll., 1998; dir. poetry workshop Jacksonville (Ill.) Correctional Facility, 1993-2000; poet in residence MacMurray Coll., 2001. Editor, pub. (poems) Hear Me Out: Poems from Prison, 1996, Speaking Through the Bars: Poems by Women, 1999; author: (poetry) After the Light, 1992, Behind the Wall Poems, 1999; editor: Changing Lives of Russian Women: Conversations and Contentions, 1999; also articles to profl. jours. and newspaper. Pub. rels. dir. Habitat for Humanity, Jacksonville, 1992-96; translator Amnesty Internat., Jacksonville, 1992; bd. dirs. West Ctrl. Ill. Coun. on Fgn. Affairs; pres. Ill. Humanities Coun., Ctrl. Ill. Regional Planning Com., 1999—. Recipient Sears-Roebuck faculty award Ill. Coll., 1988. Mem. MLA, Poets and Writers, Ill. Writers (bd. dirs. 1983-87, 92-95), Midwest L.Am. Studies Assn., Feministas Unidas, Midwest Concerns, Phi Kappa Phi. Democrat. Avocations: travel, swimming, biking, gardening, canoeing. Home: San Miguel de Allende, Mexico. Died Oct. 16, 2009.

SEELEN, RICHARD, protective services official; b. Milw., Sept. 21, 1929; s. Peter Anthony and Marie Margeret (Lehsl) S.; m. Lois Marie St. Onge, Aug. 13, 1949; children: Thomas, Mark, Christine, Robert and David. Grad. high sch., Milw. Firefighter Milw. Fire Dept., 1951-59, lt., 1959-65, capt., 1965-69, battalion chief, 1969-70, dep. chief, 1970-79, asst. chief, 1979-86, chief engr., from 1986. Past pres. Wis. State Ad Hoc Tng. Com.; active various civic orgns. Cpl. USMC, 1946-48. Recipient various mcpl., state awards. Mem. Internat. Assn. Fire Chiefs (metro chpt.), Nat. Fire Protection Assn., Wis. State Fire Chiefs Assn., Milw. County Fire Chiefs Assn., St. Jude League (pres. 1978). Avocation: fishing and golf. Died Jan. 10, 2010.

SEEMANN, ERNEST ALBRIGHT, lawyer; b. Leipzig, Germany, Oct. 18, 1929; came to U.S., 1959, naturalized, 1964; s. Erich Winrich Albrecht and Käte Renate (Wipper) S.; m. Eola Semple Hamlett, Aug. 6, 1965 (dec.); children: Eric Alexander, Ernest Arthur. Grad. in Classical Langs., Sch. St. Thomas, Leipzig, 1945; JD, U. Miami, 1981, LL.M. in Internat. Law, 1982. Editor, corp. exec. Verlagsanstalt Hermann Klemm (book pubs.), Freiburg, Germany, 1955-59; dir. U. Ala. Press, 1962-66, U. Miami (Fla.) Press, 1967-74; pres. E.A. Seemann Pub., Inc., Miami, 1974-82; ptnr. Spencer, Bernstein, Seemann & Klein, Miami, 1982-88; prin. Ernest A. Seeman, Esq., Miami, Fla., 1989-92, Cocoa, Fla., 1993-94, Ernst A. Seeman, Cape Coral, Fla., from 1994. Mem. ABA, Fla. Bar Assn., Deutscher Anwaltverein, Internat. Bar Assn., Schlaraffia Amerika. Episcopalian. Home: Madison, Ala. Died Apr. 19, 2009.

SEGAL, SANFORD LEONARD, mathematics educator; b. Troy, NY, Oct. 11, 1937; s. Joseph and Bessie (Katz) S.; m. Rima Maxwell, Sept. 3, 1959; children: Adam, Joshua, Zoë. BA, Wesleyan U., 1958; PhD, U. Colo., 1963. Instr. U. Rochester, N.Y., 1963-64, asst. prof. N.Y., 1964-70; rsch. fellow U. Vienna, Austria, 1965-66; assoc. prof. U. Rochester, N.Y., 1970-77, assoc. chmn., maths. N.Y., 1969-79; vis. lectr. U. Nottingham, Eng., 1972-73; prof. U. Rochester, N.Y., from 1977, chmn. maths. N.Y., 1979-87. Author: (book) Nine Introductions in Complex Variables, 1981; contbr. numerous articles to profl. jours. Fulbright fellow, Mainz, Germany, 1958-59, Fulbright Rsch. fellow, Vienna, Austria, 1965-66; fellow Inst. Math. Para e Applicada, Brazil, 1982, Alexander Von Humboldt Found., Fed. Rep. Germany, 1988. Mem. Am. Maths. Soc., Math. Assn. Am. (various coms. and chmn.), History Scis. Soc. Democrat. Avocations: gardening, chess, reading. Home: Rochester, NY. Died May 7, 2010.

SEGERSON, JOAN ELIZABETH, financial analyst; b. Rochester, NY, Feb. 26, 1951; d. James Edward and Margaret Isabelle (Crowley) S. BA in Art History, Newton Coll., 1972; MBA in Fin., Boston Coll., 1977. Sec. Inst. of Open Edn., Cambridge, Mass., 1972-73, adminstrv. asst., 1973-74, dir. fin., 1974-76, dir. fin., adminstrn., 1976-78; mgmt. analyst SEC, Washington, 1978-81; budget examiner Office Mgmt. and Budget, Washington, 1981-82; sr. cons. Price Waterhouse, Washington, 1982-83; exec. dir. Nat. Women's Polit. Caucus, Washington, 1983-85; dir. grad. programs Boston Coll. Grad. Sch. Mgmt., 1985-87; fin. programs specialist Dept. Treasury, Washington, 1987-88; sr. budget analyst Agy. Internat. Devel., Washington, from 1988. Dir. pub. rels. No. Va. Spl. Olympics, 1987-88. Recipient Wall St. Jour. award Boston Coll., 1977; named Outstanding Young Woman of 1981, Outstanding MBA Alumnus, Boston Coll., 1986. Roman Catholic. Avocations: travel, reading, gardening, bicycling. Home: Alexandria, Va. Died Mar. 4, 2009.

SEIFTER, SAM, biochemist, educator; b. Cleve., Dec. 1, 1916; s. Jacob and Rose (Rubner) S.; m. Eleanor Charms, Aug. 22, 1943; children— Madeleine, Julian. BS, Ohio State U., 1939; MS, PhD, Western Res. U., 1944. Sr. instr. immunology Western Res. U. Sch. Medicine, Cleve., 1944-45; asst. prof. biochemistry Downstate Med. Sch., SUNY, 1945-48, asso. prof., 1948-53; asso. prof. biochemistry Albert Einstein Coll Medicine, NYC, 1955-60, prof., from 1960, chmn. dept., from 1975. Died Feb. 26, 2009.

SEINUK, YSRAEL ABRAHAM, architectural engineer; b. Havana, Cuba, Dec. 21, 1931; s. Jamie and Sara Seinuk; m. Fanny Seinuk; children: Isaac, Beatrice. Grad. in Civil Engring., U. Havana, 1954. Lic. in 15 states, DC, Puerto Rico, United Kingdom. Founder, CEO Ysrael A. Seinuk P.C., NYC, 1977—2010; co-founder, CEO Cantor Seinuk, NYC; CEO WSP New York, NYC; prof., chmn. structural dept. Irwin S. Chanin Sch. Architecture, Cooper Union, NYC, 1969—2010. Supv. structural design of Trump World Tower, NYC, Bear Stearns World Headquarters, NYC, Time Warner Centre at Columbus Cir., NYC, Riverside So. apartments, NYC, New York Mercantile Exch., Four Times Sq., NYC, 7 World Trade Ctr., NYC, Trump Tower 5th Ave., NYC, Lipstick Bldg., NYC, Arthur Ashe Tennis Stadium, NYC, Torre Mayor, Mexico City. Recipient The 25 Most Influential Hispanics, TIME mag., 2005, Leader of Industry award, Concrete Industry Bd., Urban Visionary award, Cooper Union. Fellow: Inst. Civil Engineers (U.K.), Am. Soc. Civil Engineers, Am. Concrete Inst. Died Sept. 14, 2010.

SEITH, ALEX ROBERT, lawyer; b. Aurora, Ill., July 27, 1934; s. Alex L. and Helen (McKinley) S.; m. Frances Remington, Sept., 1956 (dec. July 1981); children: William, Robert, Kathleen. BA magna cum laude, Yale U., 1956; postgrad., U. Munich, Germany, 1956-57; JD, Harvard U., 1960. Bar: Ill. 1961. Ptnr. Lord, Bissell and Brook, Chgo., 1970-92, Schain, Firsel & Burney, Chgo.; chmn., CEO Great Lakes Networks, Inc. Dir. Paddock Publs. Commentator Sta. WLS-TV, Chgo.; contbr. numerous articles on fgn. affairs, econs. and politics to various newspapers; syndicated weekly newspaper columnist, 1971-84. Mem. Presdl. Adv. Bd. on Ambassadorial Appointments, 1977-81; Democratic candidate for U.S. Senate, Ill., 1978; dep. chmn. Fgn. Affairs Task Force, Dem. Nat. Com., 1974-76; pres. Internat. Visitors Ctr. of Chgo., 1968-70; chmn. Zoning Bd. of Appeals, Cook County, Ill.; chmn. Chgo. Coun. Fgn. Rels., 1968-71, chmn. adv. bd., 1971-73; 1st v.p. Young Dem. Clubs Am., 1967-69. Capt. U.S. Army, 1960; USAR, 1960-68. Decorated Order of Merit, French Legion of Honor, 1974; recipient Superior Pub. Svc. award Cook County, Ill., 1975; Woodrow Wilson scholar; Rotary Internat. fellow, 1956-57 Mem. ABA, Am. Assn. Comparative Study of Law, Am. Fgn. Law Assn., Chgo. Bar Assn., Ill. Bar Assn., Harvard Law Assn. (nat. v.p. 1973-74), Harvard Law Soc. Ill. (pres. 1972-73), Internat. Trade Club Chgo., Société de Droite Comparé. Democrat. Home: Hinsdale, Ill. Died Mar. 23, 2010.

SELDON, JAMES RALPH, economics educator; b. Newmarket, Ont., Can., July 4, 1944; arrived in US, 1981; s. James Menzies and Annie May (Coupland) Seldon; m. Zena Katherine Aronoff, Oct. 19, 1974; 1 child, James D. BA with honours, Carleton U., Ottawa, Ont., 1966; PhD, Duke U., 1969. Asst. prof. U. Man., Winnipeg, Calif., Canada, 1969—76, assoc. prof., 1976—83; assoc. prof. econs. Auburn U., Montgomery, Ala., 1981—83, prof., from 1983. Cons. Hosp. Svcs. Commn., Winnipeg, 1970, Consumer & Corp. Affairs, Winnipeg, 1970—71, Provincial Cabinet Planning Com., Winnipeg, 1972; cons. various law firms, Montgomery, from 1984. Author: Microeconomics and the Canadian Economy, 1973, 2d edit., 1983; contbr. articles to profl jours. Mem.: Can. Health Econs. Rsch. Assn., Southern Econ. Assn., Can. Econs. Assn., Am. Econ. Assn., Bonnie Crest Country Club (Montgomery), Midland Golf and Country Club (Ont.), Omicron Delta Epsilon. Avocations: golf, skiing, stamp collecting/philately. Home: Montgomery, Ala. Died Jan. 2, 2009.

SELF, JOSEPH MORRISON, investment banker; b. Clinton County, Pa., Apr. 23, 1929; s. Luther Esther and Annie (Bettini) S.; m. Anne Gore-Browne Higgins, Oct. 21, 1961; children: John Higgins, Elizabeth Laird, Paul Schoolfield. AB, Duke U., 1953; MBA, Columbia U., 1959. Chartered fin. analyst. Vice pres. Union Svc. Corp., N.Y.C., 1959-69, Morgan Stanley & Co., N.Y.C., 1969-76; mng. dir. Wm Sword & Co., Inc., Princeton, N.J., 1976—; mng. dir. Princeton (N.J.) Capital Mgmt., Inc., 1988—. Mem. investment adv. commn. Diocese of N.J., Trenton, 1981-87; warden St. John on Mountain, Bernardsville, N.J., 1977-79, vestry, 1964-75; trustee Peck Sch., Morristown, N.J., 1973-79; assoc. vestry St. Bartholomew's Ch., N.Y.C., 1963-65; with Cancer Care N.J., Millburn, 1989—. Lt. col., USMCR 1951-73, active duty 1953-57. Mem. Inst. Chartered Fin. Analysts. Republican. Episcopalian. Clubs: Somerset Hills Country (Bernardsville), Univ. (N.Y.C.). Home: Bernardsville, NJ. Died Jan. 20, 2010.

SELOVE, WALTER, physicist; b. Chgo., Sept. 11, 1921; s. Abraham and Rose (Feld) S.; m. Fay Ajzenberg, Dec. 18, 1955. BS, U. Chgo., 1942, PhD, 1949. Staff mem. radiation lab. MIT, Cambridge, 1943-45; staff mem. Argonne Nat. Lab., Lemont, Ill., 1946-49; from instr. to asst. prof. Harvard U., Cambridge, 1950-56; staff mem. Livermore (Calif.) Nat. Lab., 1953-54; assoc. prof. U. Pa., Phila., 1957-60, prof., from 1961. Cons. Congl. Joint Com. on Atomic Energy, Washington, 1957-62. Author: (with others) MIT Radiation Lab. Series, 1945; editor spl. issue Bull. Atomic Scientists, 1958; contbr. articles to profl. jours. Rsch. grantee AEC, ERDA, Dept. Energy, 1957; NRC fellow, 1945, Sr. NSF Postdoctoral fellow, 1956, Guggenheim fellow, 1972. Fellow Am. Phys. Soc. Achievements include patents for radar, first "fast-chopper" neutron spectrometer; discovery of 3d meson resonance; first observation of hadron jets from quarks; development of first 2-dimensional particle calorimeter, of advanced techniques for study of heavy quarks. Home: Wynnewood, Pa. Died Aug. 24, 2010.

SENTER, WILLIAM ROBERT, III, minister, counselor, community leader; b. Chattanooga, Sept. 18, 1935; s. William R. and Virginia (Mack) Senter; m. Linda Anne Howard, Feb. 9, 1963; children: Lydia Elizabeth, Matthew Mack. BS, U. South, 1957; BD, Kenyon Coll., 1961; MDiv, Crozer Theol. Sem., 1973; postgrad., U. Chattanooga, 1955, Vanderbilt Div. Sch., 1971, Southeastern Sch. Alcohol and Drug Studies, Athens, 1976. Ordained to ministry Episcopal Ch., 1961; priest 1962, cert. substance abuse counselor Tenn. Asst. St. James Ch., Knoxville, Tex., 1961—63; priest-in-charge St. Columba's Ch., Bristol, Tenn., 1963—68, Epiphany Episc. Ch., Lebanon, Tenn., 1968—84; rector Grace Episc. Ch., Canton, Miss., from 1984; chaplain Camp Allegheny Girls, Lewisburg, W.Va., 1976; personnel and mgmt. tng. cons. Cracker Barrel Old Country Stores, Lebanon, 1974—76; mem. Gov.'s Commn. Alcohol and Drug Abuse, 1972—77, vice chmn., 1975—77. Bd. dirs. Lebanon YMCA, 1973—78. Mem.: Canton Cmty. Players, Sound and Light Lebanon, Am. Iris Soc., Profl. Alcohol and Drug Counselors Tenn., Am. Assn. Arts and Sci., Nat. Model R.R. Assn., SAR, Alumni Coun. U. South, Tenn. Ornithol. Soc., Delta Tau Delta. Died Feb. 9, 2009.

SENTMAN, LEE H., aerospace engineer, educator; b. Chgo., Jan. 27, 1937; s. Lee H. Jr. and Esther (Dore) S.; m. Janice Gillespie; children: Jeanne, Charles, Christopher, Jessica. BS, U. Ill., 1958; PhD, Stanford U., 1965. Sr. dynamics engr. Lockheed Missiles and Space Co., Sunnyvale, Calif., 1959-65; prof. aero. and astronautical engring. U. Ill., Urbana, 1965—2002, prof. emeritus, from 2002. Cons. to various aerospace cos. Contbr. articles to profl. jours. Fellow: AIAA (Plasmadynamics and Lasers award 1999, Sustained Svc. award 2002); mem.: Optical Soc. Am. Achievements include research in fundamental and overtone HF chemical lasers. Died Mar. 20, 2010.

SENTNER, FRANCES JEAN, utilities executive; b. Cambridge, Mass., July 4, 1923; d. John Joseph and Mildred Veronica (Corbin) McCarthy; m. George Paul Sentner, July 23, 1949; children: Frank, George Jr., Judy, Kathy, Michael. BA in Economics, Rutgers U., 1973, MA, 1976. Clerical staff Fed. Res. Bank, Boston, 1943—44; sec. to cost acct. ITT, Newark, Clifton, NJ, 1944—49; customer svc. dept. Horn-Sales Inc., West Orange, NJ, 1960—73; assoc. acct. Pub. Svc. Electric & Gas Co., Newark, 1973—78, economics staff asst., from 1978. Student adviser Jr. Achievement, Montclair, NJ, 1974—84, project bus. rep., from 1985; group leader United Fund Dr., 1950—60. Den mother Tamarack coun. Cub Scouts America, Nutley, NJ, 1957—60. Mem.: AAUW (life), Cath. Daus. Ams. (regent 1983—85), VFW Aux. (pres. 1981—82, dist. dept. from 1985), Women's Polit. Caucus, Tri-Town Bus. & Profl. Women (pres. from 1985). Roman Catholic. Avocation: singing. Died Jan. 13, 2009.

SERVICE, WILLIS JAMES, engineering company executive; b. Detroit, Oct. 15, 1925; s. Willis James and Martha Lucille (Meno) S.; m. Geraldine Ellen McDowell, Jan. 21, 1947; children— Christine Martha, Ann Marion, Keith Duncan. Ph.B., U. Chgo., 1947; B.S. in Chem. Engring., U. Mich., 1950, M.S. in Chem. Engring., 1951. Registered profl. engr. Tex., La., Md., N.J. Refinery engr., econs. and capital planning, capital budget mgr. Humble Oil & Refining Co. div. Exxon Co. U.S.A., Baytown, Tex., 1951-57; ptnr. Pace Co., 1957-62; sr. v.p. Pace Co. Cons. & Engrs., 1962-85, also dir.; sr. v.p. Pace Cos., also chief tech. officer, sec.-treas., 1972-78; pres. Pace Internat., Inc., 1978-79; sr. v.p. Jacobs Engring. Group Inc., Houston, 1978-85; dir., sr. v.p. Trans Pacific Industries, Inc.; pres. TPI Cons., Inc. mng. dir. Protec (Pty.) Ltd., S. Africa, 1980; dir. N.Am. Resources Corp., Path Corp., Republican precinct chmn. 1952-56; bd. dirs. Water Control and Improvement Dist., Baytown, 1953-57; mem. Pasadena Now, 1981-83. Served to 1st lt. USAAF, 1943-46. U. Chgo. Fellow, 1943-47; U. Mich. Fellow, 1948-51. Mem. Am. Petroleum Inst., Inst. of Petroleum, Am. Inst. Chem. Engrs., Am. Chem. Soc., Can. Soc. Chem. Engring., Chem. Inst. Can., Am. Assn. Cost Engrs., Nat. Assn. Corrosion Engrs., 25-Year Club of Petroleum Industry, Founders Club of Petrochem. Industries, Tau Beta Pi, Phi Lambda Upsilon, Phi Kappa Phi, Phi Gamma Delta. Episcopalian. Clubs: University (Pasadena, Calif.), Houstonian, Petroleum (Houston), Houston City. Researcher thermodynamic properties of freons. Contbr. articles to jours. Patentee petroleum refining. Home: Houston, Tex. Died Aug. 20, 2009.

SETLOW, JANE KELLOCK, biophysicist; b. NYC, Dec. 17, 1919; d. Harold A. and Alberta (Thompson) Kellock; m. Richard Setlow, June 6, 1941; children: Peter, Michael, Katherine, Charles. BA, Swarthmore Coll., 1940; PhD in Biophysics, Yale U., 1959. With dept. radiology Yale U., 1959-60; with biology div. Oak Ridge Nat. Lab., 1960-74; biophysicist Brookhaven Nat. Lab., Upton, N.Y., from 1974. Mem. recombinant DNA molecule program adv. com. NIH, chmn., 1978-2005. Editor: Genetic Engineering, Principles and Methods; mem. editl. bd. various jours.:; contbr. articles to profl. jours. Predoctoral fellow USPHS, 1957-59; postdoctoral fellow, 1960-62 Mem. Biophys. Soc. (pres. 1977-78), Am. Soc. Microbiology. Democrat. Home: Shoreham, NY. Died Mar. 4, 2010.

SEVCENKO, IHOR, history and literature professor; b. Radosc, Poland, Feb. 10, 1922; came to U.S., 1949, naturalized, 1957; s. Ivan and Maria (Cherniatynska) S.; m. Oksana Draj-Xmara, Apr., 1945 (div. 1953); m. Margaret M. Bentley, July 16, 1953 (div. 1966); m. Nancy Patterson, June 18, 1966 (div. 1995); children: Catherine, Elisabeth. Dr.Phil., Charles U., Prague, 1945; Doct. en Phil. et Lettres, U. Louvain, Belgium, 1949; PhD (hon.), U. Cologne, Germany, 1994; D in Hist. Scis. (hon.), U. Warsaw, Poland, 2001; D in Liberal Arts (hon.), Cath. U., Lublin, Poland, 2005. Fellow in Byzantinology Dumbarton Oaks, 1949-50, dir. studies, 1966, prof. Byzantine history and lit., 1965-75, sr. research assoc., 1975—2009; lectr. Byzantine and ancient history U. Calif., Berkeley, 1950-51; fellow Byzantinology and Slavic lit., research program Russia, 1951-52; instr., then asst. prof. Slavic langs. and lit. U. Mich., 1953-57; mem. faculty Columbia U., 1957-72, prof., 1962-65, adj. prof., 1965-72; vis. prof. Harvard U., 1973-74, prof., 1974-92, prof. emeritus, 1992—2009. Vis. fellow All Souls Coll., Oxford U., 1979—80, Wolfson Coll., Oxford U., 1987, 93, Onassis Found., Athens, 2002; vis. mem. Princeton Inst. for Advanced Study, 1956; vis. prof. Munich U., 1969, Coll. de France, 1985, Cologne U., 1992, 96, Ctrl. European U., Budapest, 1995, 97; treas., acting treas., bd. dirs. Am. Rsch. Inst. in Turkey, 1964—66, 1967, from 1975; assoc. dir. Harvard Ukrainian Rsch. Inst., 1973—89, acting dir., 1977, 1985—86; chmn. US Nat. Com. Byzantine Studies, 1966—77; mem. Internat. Com. for Greek Paleography, from 1983; hon. pres. Byzantine studies Ukrainian Nat. Com., from 1993; guest of the rector Collegium Budapest, 1998. Author: Etudes sur la polémique entre Théodore Métochite et Nicéphore Choumnos, 1962, Society and Intellectual Life in Late Byzantium, 1981, Ideology, Letters and Culture in the Byzantine World, 1982, Byzantium and the Slavs in Letters and Culture, 1991, Ukraine Between East and West, 1996; co-author: Der Serbische Psalter, 1978, Life of St. Nicholas of Sion, 1984; contbr. articles to profl. jours. Recipient Hruševs'kyj medal, Sci. Ševcenko Soc., 1996, Antonovych Lit. prize, Kiev, 2000; Guggenheim fellow, 1963, Humboldt-Forschungspreistraeger, 1985. Fellow Mediaeval Acad. Am., Brit. Acad. (corr.); mem. Am. Philos. Soc., Am. Acad. Arts and Scis., Ukrainian Acad. Arts and Scis. US (hon. pres. 2003-09), Sci. Sevcenko Soc., Société des Bollandistes Belgium (adj.), Accademia di Palermo (fgn.), Accademia Nazionale dei Lincei (fgn.), Internat. Assn. Byzantine Studies (v.p. 1976-86, pres. 1986-96, hon. pres. 1996-2009), Christian Archeol. Soc. Athens (hon.), Austrian Acad. Sci. (corr.), Accademia Pontaniana Naples (fgn.), Acad. Humanities Rsch. (Moscow), Polish Acad. Arts and Scis. (fgn.), Cosmos Club (Washington), Harvard Club (NYC), Signet Soc., Phi Beta Kappa (hon.) Home: Cambridge, Mass. Died Dec. 26, 2009.

SEVERS, CHARLES A., III, lawyer; b. NYC, Sept. 16, 1942; s. Charles A. and Gertrude (O'Neill) S.; m. Regina Ferrone, Sept. 4, 1965; children: Charles A. IV, Cornelius Forsythe, Rudyard Pierrepont, Olivia Consuelo Poor. BA, Georgetown U., 1964, JD, 1967. Bar: N.Y. 1968, D.C. 1985. Ptnr. Dewey Ballantine, NYC, 1967-96; gen. counsel, exec. v.p. Nat. Madison Group, NYC, 1996—2007. Lectr. various continuing legal edn. programs. Contbr. articles to profl. jours. Dir., trustee various orgns. Fellow Am. Coll. Trust and Estate Counsel; mem. ABA, N.Y. State Bar Assn., Assn. of Bar of City of N.Y., D.C. Bar Assn., Union Club. Home: New York, NY. Died Jan. 9, 2009.

SEVILLA, STANLEY, lawyer; b. Cin., Apr. 3, 1920; s. Isadore and Dienna (Levy) S.; m. Lois A. Howell, July 25, 1948; children: Stanley, Susan, Donald, Carol, Elizabeth. BA in Econs. with high honors, U. Cin., 1942; JD, Harvard U., 1948. Bar: Calif. 1949. Since practiced in, Los Angeles; assoc. Williamson, Hoge & Curry, 1948-50; mem. firm Axelrod, Sevilla and Ross, 1950-75, Stanley Sevilla (P.C.), from 1975. Gen. counsel La.-Pacific Resources, Inc., 1970-90. Bd. dirs. Caesars World, Inc., 1989-95. With USAAF, 1942-46. Mem. Beverly Hills Bar Assn., Phi Beta Kappa, Tau Kappa Alpha. Home: Pacific Palisades, Calif. Died Jan. 3, 2009.

SEXTON, ROBERT FENIMORE, educational organization executive; b. Cin., Jan. 13, 1942; s. Claude Fenimore and Jane (Wisenall) S.; m. Pam Peyton Papka, Sept. 15, 1985; children: Rebecca, Robert B., Ouita Papka, Paige Papka, Perry Papka. BA, Yale U., 1964; MA in History, U. Wash., Seattle, 1968, PhD in History, 1970; DHL (hon.), Berea Coll., 1990, Georgetown Coll., Ky., 1993, Eastern Ky. U., 2000. Asst. prof. history Murray (Ky.) State U., 1968-70; dir. Office Acad. Programs, Commonwealth of Ky., Frankfort, 1970-73; assoc. dean, exec. dir. Office Exptl. Edn. U. Ky., Lexington, 1973-80; dep. exec. dir. Ky. Coun. Higher Edn., Frankfort, 1980-83; exec. dir. Prichard Com. for Acad. Excellence, Lexington, from 1983; founder, pres. Ky. Ctr. Pub. Issues, Lexington, 1988—94. Vis. scholar Harvard U., Cambridge, Mass., 1992, 94; chair Nat. Ctr. for Internships, Washington, 1973-80, Coalition for Alternatives in Post-Secondary Edn., Washington, 1977-80; bd. dirs. Editl. Projects in Edn., Consortium Policy Rsch. in Edn., Ky. Long Term Policy Rsch. Ctr., Edn. Trust, Trust for Early Edn., 1992-94. Pub. The Ky. Jour., 1988-2001; editor book series: Public Papers of Governors of Kentucky, 1973-86, Mobilizing Citizens for Better Schools, 5 books, 2004; contbr. articles to profl. jours. Co-chmn. Carnegie Ctr. for Literacy, Lexington, 1990-93; mem. Gov.'s Task Force on Health Care, Frankfort, 1992-99; bd. dirs. Ky. Inst. Edn. Rsch. Fund for Improvement in Postsecondary Edn., 1993-2000; chair Bluegrass Edn. Work Coun., Lexington, 1978-80; founder, steering com. Gov.'s Scholars Program, Frankfort, 1983-85. Recipient Charles A. Dana award for pioneering achievement, 1994. Mem. Am. Assn. Higher Edn. (bd. dirs. 1979-83). Democrat. Avocations: fishing, travel. Home: Lexington, Ky. Died Aug. 26, 2010.

SHAFFER, HARRY GEORGE, retired economics professor; b. Vienna, Aug. 28, 1919; arrived in U.S., 1940; s. Max Schaffer and Teofilia (Infeld) Schaffer Weissman; m. Betty Rosenzweig, June 7, 1987; children by previous marriages: Bernard Charles, Ronald Eric, Len Joseph, Tanya Elaine; stepchildren: Rene Carlis, Jamie Paul. BS, NYU, 1947, MA, 1948, PhD, 1958. Instr. Concord Coll., Athens, W.Va., 1948-50, U. Ala., Tuscaloosa, 1950-56; from asst. prof. to prof. U. Kans., Lawrence, 1956-69, prof. econs. and Soviet and East European studies, 1969—90, prof. emeritus, from 1990. Vis. prof. Portland State Coll., Oreg., summer 1963, U. Calif.-Davis, 1973-74. Author: English-Language Periodic Publications on Communism, 1971, Periodicals on the Socialist Countries and on Marxism, 1977, Women in the Two Germanies, 1981, American Capitalism and the Changing Role of Government, 1999; author booklet: The U.S. Conquers the West, 1974; editor: The Soviet Economy, 1963, rev. edit., 1969, The Soviet System in Theory and Practice, 1965, 2d edit., 1984, The Communist World: Marxist and Non-Marxist Views, 1967; (with Jan Prybyla) From Under-Development to Affluence: Western, Soviet and Chinese Views, 1968; editor, contbg. author: The Soviet Treatment of Jews, 1974, Soviet Agriculture, 1977; contbr. articles to profl. jours. Served with M.I., US Army, 1943-44 Mem. Am. Econ. Assn., Assn. Comparative Econ. Studies, AAUP, Ams. for Dem. Action, Common Cause, NAACP, Unity Ch., Beta Gamma Sigma Democrat. Jewish. Home: Lawrence, Kans. Died Nov. 3, 2009.

SHAFFER, RAYMOND C., state legislator; b. Wilkes-Barre, Pa., Dec. 12, 1932; m. Sharon Van Allen; children: Thomas, Robin, Diane, James, Cindy. Grad., Youngstown Coll. Profl. code adminstrn. U.S. Marine Corps; mem. Nev. Senate, Dist. 2, from 1984; majority whip Nev. Senate, 1991. Mem. Western States Water Policy Com. Mem. Disabled Am. War Vets Lions, North Las Vegas Luncheon Optimist Club (pres.), Foot Printers, Internat. Conf. Bldg. Ofcls., Marine Corps League, North Las Vegas Twp. Dem. Club, Nat. Conf. State Legislatures. Democrat. Home: Imperial Beach, Calif. Died Oct. 31, 2009.

SHAHEEN, NASEEB, English literature educator; b. Chgo., June 24, 1931; s. Azeez and Saleemeh (Balluteen) S. BA, Am. Univ. Beirut, Lebanon, 1962; MA, UCLA, 1966, PhD, 1969. Univ. prof. U. Memphis., from 1969. Author: Biblical References in The Faerie Queen, 1976, Ramallah: Its History and Its Genealogies, 1982, Biblical References in Shakespeare's Tragedies, 1987, Biblical References in Shakespeare's History Plays, 1989, Pictorial History of Ramallah, 1992, Biblical References in Shakespeare's Comedies, 1993, Biblical References in Shakespeare's Plays, 1999, reprint, 2002, A Pictorial History of Ramallah, Part II, 2006; contbr. over 45 articles, revs. to profl. jours. Woodrow Wilson Found. fellow, 1968-69. Mem. MLA. Avocation: antiquarian book collection. Died Sept. 26, 2009.

SHAHZADE, ANN MARY, retired speech and language pathologist; b. Arlington, Mass., Jan. 25, 1928; d. Nazar Michael and Mary (Israelian) Skenian; m. Herbert Sarkis Shahzade, Aug. 28, 1955 (div.); children: Joyce, John, David, Edward. AB, Emerson Coll., 1949, MA, 1950; postgrad., Boston U., 1952-72. Speech pathologist Lynn Pub. Schs., Mass., 1949-56, Somerville Sch. Dept., Mass., 1957-58, Cambridge Sch. Dept., Mass., 1969-74; co-founder speech clinic Children's Hosp., Boston, 1952-57; asst. dir. Inst. for Speech Correction, Boston, 1949-59; dir. speech and lang. dept. Cambridge Pub. Schs., 1974-89, ret., 1989. Instr. pub. speaking John Roberts Powers Sch., Boston, 1950-55; speech pathology cons. to pediatricians, Arlington, 1949-60; pvt. practice, Boston, 1957-69. Author: Oral Language Development, 1982, also kindergarten screening test. Mem. NEA, Mass. Tchrs. Assn., Cambridge Tchrs. Assn. (Disting. Svc. award 1989). Democrat. Mem. Armenian Apostolic Ch. Avocations: golf, travel. Home: Falmouth, Mass. Died Oct. 17, 2009.

SHAINESS, NATALIE, psychiatrist, educator; b. NYC, Dec. 2, 1915; d. Jack and Clara (Levy-Hart) S.; div.; children: David Spiegel, Ann Spiegel. BA in Chemistry, NYU, 1936; MD, Va. Commonwealth U., 1939. Diplomate in psychiatry; cert. in psychoanalysis. Pvt. practice, NYC, 1955-98; faculty William Alanson White Inst. Psychiatry, Psychoanalysis, NYC, 1961-81; asst. clin. prof. psychiatry N.Y. Sch. Psychiatry, NYC, 1964-67; faculty med. edn. div. N.Y. Acad. Medicine, 1966-67; lectr. psychiatry Columbia U. Coll. Physicians and Surgeons, NYC, 1966-80; faculty, supervising analyst L.I. Inst. Psychoanalysis, N.Y., from 1980. Invited participant 1st and 2nd Internat. Conf. on Abortion, 1967, 68; research project on menstruation. Editorial bd. Jour. of the Am. Women's Med. Assn., 1985—; author: Sweet Suffering: Woman as Victim, 1984; contbr. over 120 articles to profl. jours. and over 90 profl. book revs. Mem. Physicians for Social Responsibility, Nuclear Freeze, several other antinuclear orgns. Recipient Silver medal Women's Med. Soc. N.Y.C., 1967, 1st Presdl. award Am. Med. Women's Assn., N.Y.C., 1990, Disting. Svc. award Am. Women's Med. Assn., several 1st and 2d pl. awards for poetry APA Arts Assn., honored by Soc. Med. Psychoanalysts, 1993, Am. Med. Women's Assn., 1996. Fellow Am. Acad. Psychoanalysis (past trustee, organizer several panels), Am. Psychiat. Assn. (life mem., organizer several panels), N.Y. Acad. Medicine (hon.), Soc. Med. Psychoanalysts. Avocations: music, the arts. Died Jan. 31, 2009.

SHAMES, IRVING HERMAN, engineering educator; b. Oct. 31, 1923; married; 2 children. BSME, Northeastern U., 1948; MS in Applied Mechanics, Harvard U., 1949; PhD in Applied Mechanics, U. Md., 1953. Instr. U. Md., College Park, 1949-53, asst. prof. mech. engring., 1953-55; asst. prof. Stevens Inst. Tech., Hoboken, N.J., 1955-57; prof., chmn. dept. engring. sci. Pratt Inst., Bklyn., 1957-62, acting chmn. dept. physics, 1960-61; prof., chmn. div. interdisciplinary studies and research Sch. Engring. SUNY, Buffalo, 1962-70, faculty prof. engring., applied sci., 1970-73 and from 79, prof., chmn. dept. engring. scis., aerospace engring. and nuclear engring., 1973-83, disting. teaching prof., from 1980; prof. George Washington U., Washington, from 1995. Lectr. Naval Ordnance Lab, 1952-55; vis. prof. materials dept. Technion, Israel, 1969, mech. engring. dept., 1976; Disting. vis. prof. George Washington U., 1993. Author: Engineering Mechanics: Statics, 1959, 3d rev. edit., 1980, Engineering Mechanics: Dynamics, 1959, 3d rev. edit., 1980, Mechanics of Fluids, 1962, rev. edit., 1982, 3d edit., 1992, Mechanics of Deformable Solids, 1964, (with C. Dym) Solid Mechanics- A Variational Approach, 1973, Introduction to Statics, 1971 Introduction to Solid Mechanics, 1975, (with C. Dym) Energy and Finite Elements in Structural Mechanics, 1985, (with F. Cozzarelli) Elastic and Inelastic Stress Analysis, 1992; editor McGraw-Hill Series in Advanced Engineering; contbr. numerous articles to profl. jours.; several books translated in Portuguese, Spanish, Japanese, Korean, Chinese, Arabic. Mem. Sigma Xi, Tau Beta Pi, Phi Eta Sigma, Pi Tau Sigma, Golden Key. Home: Rye, NY. Died June 30, 2010.

SHAO, OTIS HUNG-I, retired political science professor; b. Shanghai, July 18, 1923; came to U.S., 1949, naturalized, 1956; s. Ming Sun and Hannah (Chen) S.; m. Marie Sheng, Apr. 2, 1955. BA, St. John's U., 1946; MA, U. Colo., 1950; PhD, Brown U., 1957. From instr. to prof. polit. sci. Moravian Coll., Bethlehem, Pa., 1954-62; assoc. prof., then prof. polit. sci. Fla. Presbyn. Coll., St. Petersburg, 1962-68; prof. internat. politics, dean (Grad. Sch., U. Pacific), 1968-74; dir. Pub. Affairs Inst., 1969-74; provost Callison Coll., 1974-76; dean faculty, v.p. Occidental Coll., 1976-78; asso. exec. dir. sr. commn. Western Assn. Schs. and Colls., 1978-80; v.p., dean Hawaii Loa Coll., 1980-85; pres. Sheng Shao Enterprises Calif., 1985-92; CEO, chmn. D.S. Capital Internat., Calif., 1993-94. Mem. grad. students relations com. Council Grad. Schs. U.S., 1970-73; mem. exec. council undergrad. assessment program Ednl. Testing Service, 1978-80. Contbr. articles to profl. jours. Chmn. bd. dirs. Fgn. Policy Assn. Lehigh Valley, 1961-62; bd. dirs. World Affairs Council, San Joaquin County, 1969-77; trustee Inst. Med. Scis., Pacific Med. Center, San Francisco, 1968-72, optical scis. group of Profl. and Pub. Service Found., 1969-72; Resident fellow Harkness House, Brown U., 1953-54, Danforth Asso., 1958-85. Recipient Distinguished Service award Fgn. Policy Assn. Lehigh Valley, 1962 Mem. AAUP (pres. Fla. Presbyn. Coll. chpt. 1965-66), Am. Assn. Higher Edn., Rho Psi, Tau Kappa Epsilon. Democrat. Presbyterian. Home: San Jose, Calif. Died Apr. 16, 2010.

SHAPAZIAN, ROBERT MICHAEL, publishing executive; b. Fresno, Calif., 1942; s. Ara Michael and Margaret (Azhderian) S. BA, U. Calif., 1964; AM, Harvard U., 1965, PhD in Renaissance English and Fine Arts, 1970. Design assoc. Arthur Elrod Associates, LA, 1971-73; v.p. El Mar Corp, Fresno, Calif., 1973-87; dir., art dir. The Lapis Press, Venice, Calif., 1987—2010. Mem. photographic forum San Francisco Mus. Art, 1982-85, Mus. Modern Art, N.Y.C., 1985; mem. photographic com. Met. Mus. Art, N.Y.C., 1994; dir. Gagosian Gallery, L.A. Author: Metaphorics of Artificiality, 1970, Maurice Tabard, 1985; editor: Surrealists Look at Art, 1991 (AIGA award 1991, N.Y. Art Dirs. award 1991), A Witch, 1992 (AIGA award 1992, N.Y. Art Dirs. award 1992, L.A. Art Dirs. award 1992), Pacific Wall (AIGA award 1993), Albucius (We. Art Dirs. award 1993, N.Y. Art Dirs. award 1994), Sam Francis: Saturated Blue, Writings from the Notebooks, 1996. Bd. dirs. Big Brothers/Big Sisters, Fresno, Calif., 1980-82, Film Forum, L.A., 1984-86, Grunwald Ctr. for Graphic Arts, UCLA, 1996—. Recipient Individual Achievement award Lit. Market Pl., N.Y.C., 1992, 23 awards for art direction and design; named Chevalier in Order of Arts and Letters, Govt. of France. Mem. Harvard Club (N.Y.C.). Avocations: twentieth century art, illustrated books, experimental photography. Died June 19, 2010.

SHAPIRA, MICHAEL, advertising agency executive; b. Detroit, Mar. 22, 1942; s. Boris B. and Harriet (Alpert) S.; m. Jeanne O'Leary, Dec. 21, 1978. B. Econs., Wayne State U., Detroit; postgrad. studies, Detroit Coll. Law. Formerly exec. v.p., now pres. W. B. Doner and Co., Southfield, Mich. Died May 24, 2009.

SHAPIRO, ANNA, microbiologist, researcher; b. NYC, Jan. 11, 1910; d. Samuel and Esther (Cohen) Lewis; m. Joseph Shapiro, Feb. 7, 1933 (dec. 1985); children: Joan Elisabeth Brandston (dec.), Joel Elias. BS in Biology and Chemistry, NYU, 1931, MS in Bacteriology, 1934, PhD in Microbiology, 1971. Lab. asst. Bellevue Med. Sch., NYU, 1931-33, instr., 1933-36; lectr. Hofstra U., LI, 1963, Queensborough U., CUNY, Queens, 1964; rsch. asst. Haskins Lab. of Pace Univ., NYC, 1971-80, rsch. assoc., 1980-83. Author: Methods of Enzymology, 1980, The In Vitro Cultivation of Pathogens of Tropical Diseases, 1980; contbr. articles to profl. jours. Mem. AAAS, N.Y. Acad. Sci. (Disting. Svc. award 1992), Sigma Xi. Achievements include rsch. in the conversion of Nitrobacter agilis from a strict autotroph to a heterotroph by using replica plating techniques which can be considered an adaptive mutation; blockade of respiratory systems of parasites by using iron chelators--this work led to further research in pathogenic African trypanosomes. Home: New York, NY. Died Jan. 26, 2009.

SHAPIRO, MAX ANDREW, rabbi; b. Worcester, Mass., Jan. 31, 1917; s. Samuel and Clara (Wolfgang) S.; m. Bernice Clein, Dec. 31, 1944 (dec. Mar. 1984); children: Susan, Steven; m. Abby Lou Evans, Dec. 1989. AB, Clark U., 1939; MEd, Boston Tchrs. Coll., 1940; BHL, Hebrew Union Coll., 1953, MHL, 1955, DD (hon.), 1980; DEd, U. Cin., 1960; LHD (hon.), U. St. Thomas, 1990. Ordained rabbi, 1955. Sr. rabbi Temple Israel, Mpls., 1963-85, rabbi emeritus, from 1985; lectr. dept. religion and philosophy Hamline U., from 1958. Adj. prof. United Theol. Sem., 1975—; bd. govs. Hebrew Union Coll., Jewish Inst. Religion; co-chmn. task force on reform outreach Union Am. Hebrew Congregations, Cen. Conf. Am. Rabbis, 1979-83; dir. Ctr. for Christian-Jewish Learning, U. St. Thomas, St. Paul, 1985—. State commr. against discrimination, 1961-65; bd. dirs. Mt. Sinai Hosp., Mpls., Mpls. United Way, Minn. Coun. on Religion and Race. Rabbi Max A. Shapiro Forest in Israel established in his honor Jewish Nat. Fund., 1976; recipient Humanitarian award Nat. Jewish Hosp., Denver, State of Israel Bonds award, 1972, Internat. Franciscan award, 1989; named Outstanding Citizen, United Way, 1970, City of Mpls., 1966. Mem. Midwest Assn. Reform Rabbis (pres. 1970-71), Rabbinic Alumni Assn. (pres. 1973-74), Cen. Conf. Am. Rabbis (sec.), Minn. Rabbinical Assn. (pres. 1962-64). Home: Hopkins, Minn. Died Oct. 16, 2009.

SHAPIRO, MORRIS, rabbi, psychology educator; b. Goraj, Poland, Mar. 20, 1920; came to U.S., 1948; s. Mendel and Hinda (Harmon) S.; m. Lydia Spiegelman; children: Meyer, Mendel, Hinda; m. Rochelle Ada Berliner, June 23, 1963; children: Jerome, Simcha. BS, U. N.D., 1960, MA, 1959; DD (hon.), Jewish Theol. Sem., 1975. Ordained rabbi, 1939. Rabbi Synagogue, Berlin, N.H., 1952-56, Greenport, N.Y., 1956-57, Grand Forks, N.D., 1957-61, Agudath Jacob Synagogue, Waco, Tex., 1961-64, B'nai Israel Synagogue, Tome River, N.J., 1964-66, South Huntington Jewish Ctr., Melville, N.Y., 1966-88; prof. of psychology SUNY, Farmingdale, from 1974. Pres. Suffolk Bd. Rabbis, Melville, N.Y., 1977-79, mem. Nat. Beth Din, 1988—. Recipient New Life award Israel Bond, 1983, Max Arzt Rabbinical Svc. award, 1990. Mem. Rabbinical Assembly (pres. Nassau-Suffolk chpt. 1975-77, mem. law com. 1983—). Home: Greenlawn, NY. Died Mar. 19, 2010.

SHARP, ALLEN, federal judge; b. Washington, Feb. 11, 1932; s. Robert Lee and Frances Louise (Williams) S.; children: Crystal Catholyn Sharp Bauer, Scarlet Frances Thomas. Student, Ind. State U., 1950-53; AB, George Washington U., 1954; JD, Ind. U., 1957; MA, Butler U., 1986. Bar: Ind. 1957. Practiced in, Williamsport, 1957-68; judge Ct. of Appeals Ind., 1969-73, US Dist. Ct. (no. dist.) Ind., South Bend, 1973—2007, chief judge, 1981—96, sr. judge, 2007—09. Served in JAG USAF, 1957—84, Res. Mem.: Ind. Judges Assn., Phi Delta Kappa, Tau Kappa Alpha, Pi Gamma Mu, Blue Key. Republican. Mem. Christian Ch. Club: Mason. Died July 9, 2009.

SHARP, ROBERT CHARLES, retired corporate executive; b. Clyde, NY, July 5, 1936; s. Robert Napier and Bernice Cyrene (Bower) S.; m. Nancy Dickinson, Sept. 3, 1954; 1 child, Penelope Sharp. BA, BS, U. Rochester, 1960; MS in Mgmt., MIT, 1981. Acct. exec. Eastman Kodak Co., Rochester, N.Y., 1960-63, product specialist mktg. bus. systems, 1963-68, dist. mgr. bus. systems Houston and NYC, 1968-75, regional mgr. bus. systems Atlanta, 1975-79, mgr. distbn. Rochester, 1979-80, mgr. profl. and finishing markets, 1981-83, corp. v.p. gen. mgr. consumer/profl. and finishing markets, 1983-85, corp. v.p., gen. mgr. photofinishing systems div., 1985-89, corp. v.p., gen. mgr. U.S. sales div., 1989-92, corp. v.p., gen. mgr. U.S. and Can. consumer imaging divsn., 1992. Bd. trustees Grad. Sch. Sales and Mktg. Mgmt., Syracuse U. Mem. Photographic Mktg. Assn., Sales Execs. Club, Am. Records Mgmt. Assn. Died Feb. 18, 2009.

SHARP, SHARON BARTS, state official; b. Mishawaka, Ind., Oct. 7, 1939; d. Edwin J. and Gertrude E. (Maculski) Barts; student Holy Cross Central Sch. Nursing, South Bend, Ind., 1957-59; A.A.S., William Rainy Harper Coll., 1975; m. Donald L. Sharp, Sept. 12, 1959; children— Laura Sue, Christopher Barts. Free-lance writer, 1973-77; editor Elk Grove Twp. (Ill.) News, 1975-76; clk. Elk Grove Twp., 1975-79; spl. asst. on women to gov. State of Ill., Chgo., 1979-84; dep. dir. mktg. Ill. Dept. Commerce and Community Affairs, 1984—. Hon. co-chairwoman ERA Ill.; mem. Ill. Displaced Homemaker Adv. Bd.; mem. Cook County Republican Exec. Com., 1975—; co-chmn. Cook County Rep. Central Com., 1975—; Rep. nominee Ill. sec. of state, 1978; pres. Woman's Nat. Rep. Club, 1980—; bd. dirs. Ill. Fedn. Rep. Women; mem. Rep. Women's Task Force of Ill.; mem. Ill. Community Coll. Bd., 1976-79; mem. women's community adv. com. Northwestern U., 1982—; mem. women's bd. William Rainy Harper Coll. Mem. Chgo. Area Public Affairs Group, Women in Mgmt. (recipient Charlotte Danstron Women of Achievement award N.W. Suburban chpt.), Am. Econ. Devel. Council, Mid-Am. Econ. Devel. Council, LWV, Internat. Platform Assn., Ill. Devel. Council. Methodist. Clubs: City, Executive (Chgo.). Died July 5, 2009.

SHARP, WILLIAM LESLIE, retired performing arts educator; b. Chgo., Sept. 3, 1924; s. Arthur Eugene and Alma (Melchior) S.; m. Shirley Vanderwalker, Dec. 27, 1949 (div. 1977); children: Katherine, Arthur, Elizabeth. BA, U. Chgo., 1948, MA, 1949; PhD, Stanford U., 1957. Prof. U. Calif., Riverside, 1957-64, Stanford (Calif.) U., 1964-69, Emerson Coll., Boston, 1969-95, chmn. drama dept., 1969-86; ret., 1995. Author: The Language in Drama, 1970. With U.S. Army, 1943-46, ETO. Died May 29, 2009.

SHARTLE, STANLEY MUSGRAVE, engineering executive, consultant, surveyor; b. Brazil, Ind., Sept. 27, 1922; s. Arthur Tinder and Mildred C. (Musgrave) Shartle; m. Anna Lee Mantle, Apr. 7, 1948; 1 child, Randy. Student, Purdue U., 1947—50. Registered profl. engr., land surveyor. Ind. chief dep. surveyor Hendricks County, Danville, Ind., 1941—42, dep. county surveyor, 1944—50, county engr., surveyor, 1950—54, county hwy. engr., 1975—77; asst. hydrographer Fourteenth Naval Dist., Pearl Harbor, Hawaii, 1942—44; staff engr. Ind. Toll Rd. Commn., Indpls., 1954—61; chief right of way engring. Ind. State Hwy. Commn., Indpls., 1961—75; owner, civil engr. Shartle Engring., Indpls., 1977—89; prin. Parsons Cunningham & Shartle Engrs., Inc., Indpls., from 1990. Right of way engring. cons. Gannett Fleming Transp. Engrs., Inc., Indpls., 1983—88; part-time lectr. Purdue U. Ind. State Hwy. Commn., 1965—67. Author: Shartle Genealogy, 1955, 2d edit., 2005, Musgrave Family History, 1961, 2d edit., 1995, Right of Way Engineering Manual, 1975, (novel) Her Word of Honor, 2001; contbr. articles to profl. jours. Ex-officio mem., charter mem. exec. sec. Hendricks County Planning Commn., 1951—54; mem. citizen adv. com. Hendricks County Subdivision Control Ordinance, from 1988. Recipient Outstanding Contbn. award, Hendricks County Soil and Water Conservation Dist., 1976; named Stanley Shartle Day, Hendricks County, 1997. Mem.: Geog. and Land Info. Soc., Internat. Right of Way Assn. (founder chpt. 10), Ind. Toll Rd. Employees Assn. (pres. 1959—60), Nat. Soc. Profl. Surveyors, Ind. Soc. Profl. Land Surveyors (life; bd. dirs. 1979), Am. Congress Surveying and Mapping (life). Avocations: astronomy, genealogy, geodesy. Home: Brownsburg, Ind. Died Nov. 20, 2009.

SHAW, JO AN, association executive; b. Coshocton, Ohio, Feb. 3, 1929; d. Cleon K. and Daisy L. Shaw; student Bowling Green State U., 1947, 48, Kent State U., 1949-51. Recreational therapist Massillon (Ohio) State Hosp., 1952-60; recreational therapist Sunny Acres Hosp., Cleve., 1960-63; teen program specialist YWCA of Met. Detroit, 1964-69, creative and performing arts dir., 1969-71, public relations dir., 1971—. Coordinator, initiator Believe in Detroit Coalition, 1976-80; mem. community adv. bd. Channel 56, 1978-82. Mem. Detroit Women's Advt. Club (dir.), Detroit Press Club. Methodist. Home: Harrison Township, Mich. Died Mar. 19, 2009.

SHAW, JOHN FREDERICK, retired naval officer; b. Dallas, Oct. 14, 1938; s. John Frederick and Sarah E. (Crouch) S.; m. Janice Muren, July 14, 1962; children: Elizabeth Lee, Suzanne Michele. BS, U.S. Naval Acad., 1960; MS in Mgmt. with distinction, Naval Postgrad. Sch., Monterey, Calif., 1970; grad., Armed Forces Staff Coll., 1971. Commd. ensign USN, 1960, advanced through grades to rear adm., 1983; exec. officer USS Long Beach (CGN 9), 1978-79; comdg. officer USS Bainbridge (CGN 25), 1980-83; dir. guided missile destroyer 51, Arleigh Burke program Comdr. Naval Sea Systems Command, Washington, 1983-85, mgr. AEGIS shipbldg. program, 1985-87; comdr. Cruiser-Destroyer Group One, San Diego, 1987-88; dep. chief staff plans and policy Supreme Allied Comdr., Atlantic, Norfolk, Va., 1988-89, chief staff, 1989-91; ret., 1991; prof. joint mil. ops. Coll. Continuing Edn., Naval War Coll., San Diego, 1992-94. Bd. advisors United Svc. Benefit Assn., Kansas City, Kans., 1987-93; mem. cmty. bd. advisors Sam and Rose Stein Inst. for Rsch. on Aging, 1998-2004; membership chmn., 1999-2000, sec.-treas., 2000-2004, emeritus bd. mem., 2006—; tax. cons. for elderly, AARP, 2000-07,09 Trustee Coronado Libr., 1998—2005, exec. sec., 2001—02, pres., 2002—04. Decorated Def. D.S.M., Legion of Merit with two gold stars, Meritorious Svc. medal with gold star, Navy Commendation medal with gold star, Meritorious Unit Commendation (civilian) USN. Mem. AARP, U.S. Naval Inst. (life), U.S. Naval Acad. Alumni Assn. (life, pres. Washington chpt. 1986, bd. govs. San Diego/Coronado chpt. 1996-99), Surface Navy Assn. (life), San Diego Navy League (dir. 1997-2002), Coronado Men's Golf Club, San Diego Class of 60 Representative. Avocations: golf, reading, economics, travel. Home: Coronado, Calif. Died May 28, 2009.

SHAW, SAMUEL ERVINE, II, retired insurance company executive, consultant; b. Independence, Kans., Apr. 10, 1933; s. Samuel Ervine and Jessie Elizabeth (Guernsey) Shaw; m. Dale Foster Dorman, June 19, 1954; children: Samuel Ervine III, Christopher Atwood, Elizabeth Foster. BA, Harvard U., 1954; JD, Boston Coll., 1965. Bar: Mass., U.S. Supreme Ct. 1971. Enrolled actuary, 1976—93; cons. actuary, 1987; with John Hancock Mut. Life Ins. Co., Boston, 1957—87, group pension and ins. actuary, 2d v.p., 1979—85, v.p., group ins. actuary, 1985—87; dir. Health Reins. Assn. Conn., Hartford, 1980—87. Cons. Internat. Exec. Svc. Corps, Guayaquil, Ecuador, Jakarta, Indonesia, 1988, Perm, Russia, 94, Pension Benefit Guarantee Corp., Washington, 1974—75, Nat. Hosp. Ins. Fund, Nairobi, Kenya, 1990. Mem. Brookline (Mass.) Hist. Commn., 1981—88, Brookline Retirement Bd., 1985—90; chmn. Brookline Com. on Town Orgn. and Structure, 1975—79. Served to maj. USAF, 1954—57. Fellow: Soc. Actuaries; mem.: ABA, Internat. Actuarial Assn., Am. Acad. ACtuaries. Episcopalian. Home: Bedford, Mass. Died May 12, 2009.

SHEA, BERNARD CHARLES, retired pharmaceutical executive; b. Bradford, Pa., Aug. 7, 1929; s. Bernard and Edna Catherine (Green) S.; m. Marilyn Rishell, Apr. 12, 1952; children: David Charles, Melissa Leone. BS in Biology, Holy Cross Coll., Worcester, Mass. Dir. mktg. Upjohn Co., Kalamazoo, 1954-80; pres. pharm. div. Pennwalt Corp., Rochester, NY, 1980-86, v.p. health div. Phila., 1986, sr. v.p. health div., 1987-88, sr. v.p. chemicals, 1988-89; group pres. Atochem N.Am., Inc., Phila., 1989-90, pharm. cons., 1990-93. Served to lt. (j.g.) USN, 1951-54, Korea Home: Zephyrhills, Fla. Died Feb. 19, 2009.

SHEA, WILLIAM FRANCIS, marketing consultant, management executive; b. Manchester, NH, Dec. 28, 1945; s. Robert Edward and Frances Louise (Pickles) S.; m. Deborah Heather Gubner, Apr. 21, 1984 (div. Apr. 1987). BA in History, U. N.H., 1967; MBA in Fin., Roosevelt U., 1977. Ops. mgr. Continental Ill. Nat. Bank and Trust Co., Chgo., 1974-78; sr. rsch. analyst Firestone Tire Co., Akron, Ohio, 1978-79; asst. v.p. First Nat. Bank Chgo., 1979-83; v.p. Cen. Bank Denver, 1983-84; pres. Shea Cons. Group, Denver, Tampa, Miami, and Ft. Lauderdale, Fla., from 1984; mgr. Laventhol & Horwath, Miami, 1987-88; dir. mktg. Inst. Med. Specialities, North Miami Beach, Fla., 1988-89. Lectr., speaker in field. Contbr. numerous articles to profl. jours. Chmn. com. Aventura (Fla.) Mktg. Coun., 1989. Capt. U.S. Army, 1968-74, Vietnam. Decorated Bronze Star, Meritorious Svc. medal, Vietnamese Staff Svc. medal, Army Commendation medal. Mem. Am. Mktg. Assn., The Planning Forum, Acad. for Health Svcs. Mktg., Greater Miami C. of C. (chmn. com. 1988). Republican. Methodist. Avocations: reading, long distance running. Died Jan. 23, 2009.

SHEEHAN, LORRAINE M., state official; b. Manchester, NH, May 2, 1937; Mem. Md. Ho. of Dels., 1974—83; vice-chair Prince George's County del., ways and means com., subcom. on edn. of task force to study state/local fiscal relationships; humane practices commn., chmn. health care subcom., mem. med. assistance program; sec. state State of Md., Annapolis, Md., from 1983. Bd. dirs. Suitland Local Devel. Corp. Trustee Greater S.E. Cmty. Hosp. Found. Recipient Margaret Sanger award, Planned Parenthood Md., 1983, Outstanding State Ofcl. award, Young Democrats of Md., 1984, Disting. Svc. award, Md. Mental Health Assn., 1985. Mem.: PTA, LWV, Greater Southeast Ctr. for Aging., Kettering Civic Fedn., Bus. and Profl. Women's Club (Woman of Yr. award 1984), Marlboro Democratic Club. Died Dec. 19, 2009.

SHEERIN, EDWARD FRANCIS MATTHEW, financial executive; b. Bklyn., Aug. 27, 1946; s. Edward Joseph and Edith Dorothy (Block) Sheerin; m. Marilyn Rita Pittelli, May 1, 1971; children: Matthew Joseph, Janine Anne, Suzanne Rita, Kate Veronica. BA, Queens Coll., 1967; postgrad., Pace U., 1974. With Cowen & Co., NYC, from 1968, bond broker, 1972, mgr. indsl. bond dept., 1974, mgr. corp. bond dept., 1975, gen. ptnr., from 1976. Lectr. in field. Third dep. chief Plandome Volunteer Fire Dept., from 1980. With USN, 1967—68. Mem.: Plandome Country Club, Downtown Athletic Club, Corporate Bond Club. Roman Catholic. Died Dec. 28, 2009.

SHEERIN, JAMES F., hotel company executive; b. Chgo., Aug. 14, 1920; s. Roy F. and Mae T. (Regan) S.; m. Edythe L. Bowman, June 4, 1944; children: Susan, Patricia, James, Kathleen. With Hilton Hotel Corp., Chgo., 1946-60, 69—, v.p. South-S.W. region, 1969-71, sr. v.p., from 1971; with Pick Hotels Corp., Chgo., 1960-69, sr. v.p., gen. mgr., 1966-69. Chmn. Chgo. Conv. and Tourism Bur., 1980-81, Met. Fair and Exposition Authority, Chgo.; apptd. chmn. Adv. Com. on Tourism for State of Ill.; mem. Ill. Devel. Bd. Mem. Chgo. Promotion Council (dir.), Greater Chgo. Hotel and Motel Assn., Am. Hotel and Motel Assn. Clubs: Tavern (N.Y.C.); Irish Fellowship; Hundred of Cook County (Chgo.). Died Jan. 12, 2009.

SHEFFIELD, WILLIAM FREDERICK, land developer, realtor; b. Madison, Fla., June 25, 1925; s. John Henry and Lucille Agnes (Burnett) Sheffield; m. Josephine Suggs Sheffield, Mar. 1944 (div. 1951); children: Pamela Jo, Patricia Ann; m. Rose Marie Younis, Oct. 25, 1958; children: John Howard, Deborah Lucille. Degree, Jones Bus. Coll., 1945. Accredited farm, land broker, sales mgr. Demetree Builders, Jacksonville, 1960—62; prin. Wm. F. Sheffield, Inc., Realtors and Developers, Jacksonville, from 1962. Mem.: Farm and Land Inst. of NAR (Fla. chpt., pres. 1975, regional v.p. 1977), Nat. Assn. Realtors (bd. dirs. 1980—85), Fla. Assn. Realtors (dist. v.p. 1978, chmn. polit. affairs com. 1979, chmn. legis. com. 1985, Kenneth S. Keyes award 1964, George Simon award 1983), Jacksonville Bd. Realtors (pres. 1976, Buck award 1966, named Realtor of Yr. 1978), River Club (Jacksonville), Shriners, Scottish Rite Bodiies, Masons, Royal Order of Jesters, Rotary. Methodist. Home: Jacksonville, Fla. Died Oct. 4, 2009.

SHEIL, WILLIAM BERNARD, retail company executive; b. Chgo., Dec. 10, 1930, s. William L. and Mary A. (Foley) S.; m. Nell Leonard, Dec. 28, 1957; 3 children. B.A. in Journalism, Tulsa U., 1954; M.A. in Journalism, Marquette U., 1961. Sports dir. KWGS and KOTV, 1950-54, WREX-TV, Rockford, Ill., 1957-59, WITI, Milw., 1959-61; with advt./pub. relations dept., Boeing Co., Seattle, 1961-63; with Boeing, Huntsville, Ala., 1963—; pub. relations mgr. Harris Corp., Cleve., 1969-71; dir. N.W. Ayer Internat., 1971-76; dir. corporate fin. relations Harvey Hubbell, Inc., Conn., 1976-79; exec. dir. employee communications program Gordon Jewelry Corp., Houston, 1979—. Pres. Cape Kennedy Pub. Relations Assn.; chmn. Apollo Contractors Information Center; Mem. Greater Houston Convention and Visitors Council. Served to lt. (j.g.) USNR, 1954-56. Mem. Nat. Investor Relations Inst. Died Sept. 21, 2009.

SHELL, LOUIS CALVIN, retired lawyer; b. Dinwiddie County, Va., Dec. 8, 1925; s. Roger LaFayette and Susie Ann (Hill) S.; m. Barbara Marie Pamplin, Aug. 5, 1950; children: Pamela Shell Baskervill, Patricia Shell Caulkins. BA, U. Va., 1946, LLB, 1947. Bar: Va. 1947. Sr. trial atty. Shell, Johnson, Andrews Baskervill & Petersburg. Va. chmn. Petersburg Electoral Bd., 1952, vice mayor city coun., 1957-60; trustee Petersburg Dist. United Meth. Ch. Named Outstanding Young Man, Petersburg Jr. C. of C., 1956. Fellow Am. Coll. Trial Lawyers; mem. Petersburg Bar Assn., Va. State Bar Assn. (coun. 1972-75), Kiwanis. Home: Petersburg, Va. Died Aug. 14, 2009.

SHELLEY, JAMES HERBERT, lawyer, paper company executive; b. Columbia, SC, Oct. 12, 1943; s. William H. and Elizabeth G. (Garner) S.; m. Wayring Patricia Knight, Apr. 1, 1969; children: Joy Patricia, Susan Elizabeth. BA in English, U. S.C., 1965, JD, 1968. Bar: S.C. 1968. With Sonoco Products Co., Hartsville, S.C., from 1969, indsl. devel. coord., 1969-70, indsl. rels. rep., 1970-71, dir. indsl. rels., 1971-78, corp. dir. indsl. rels. and personnel, 1978-86, staff v.p. personnel and indsl. rels., from 1986. Chmn. Sonopal. Bd. dirs. Pee Dee Mental Health, vice chmn. 1977-80; vice chmn. Hartsville YWCA project, 1983-86; bd. trustees S.C. Bus. and Indsl. Polit. Edn. Com. Sgt. USAR, 1968-73. Recipient Outstanding Drill Sgt. award, 1970. Mem. ABA (labor law sect.), S.C. Bar Assn. (sec./treas. employment and labor law sect.), Hartsville Country Club, Prestwood Country Club. Methodist. Home: Hartsville, SC. Died Sept. 1, 2010.

SHELTON, JAMES DOUGLAS, banker; b. Boynton Beach, Fla., Feb. 28, 1939; s. Clarence Wilton and Lou Anna (Ward) S.; m. Claudia Ellen Marshall, Oct. 20, 1973; children: Christopher John, Ryan Marshall. BA, Duke U., 1961; MDiv, Union Sem., 1965; STM, Boston U., 1966; SEP, Stanford U., 1975. Adj. prof. NY Sem., NYC, 1966-68; asst. treas. Bankers Trust Co., NYC, 1968-71; v.p. Chase Manhattan Bank, NYC, 1971-84; sr. v.p. Conn. Bank & Trust, Hartford, Conn., 1984-88; chmn., pres., chief exec. officer First Fed. Savs., East Hartford, Conn., 1988-2001. Bd. dirs. Conn. On-Line Computer Ctr., Avon, chmn., 1989-2001; bd. dirs. Cmty. Bank League of New Eng., Boston, chmn., 1989-96; mem. Conn. Legislature Interstate Banking Task Force, Hartford, 1989-90. Bd. dirs. Jr. Achievement North Ctrl. Conn., Windsor, 1986-90, Sci. Ctr. Conn., West Hartford, 1988-94, Riverfront Recapture, Inc., Hartford, 1994-98, Charter Oak State Coll. Found., New Britain, Conn., 2004—; corporator Am. Sch. for the Deaf, West Hartford, 1986-2001; trustee Noah Webster House, West Hartford Hist. Soc., 2005— Mem. Am. Cmty. Bankers Assn. (bd. dirs. 1995-2001), New Eng. Automated Clearing House Assn. (bd. dir. 1983-98), The Country Club of Farmington, Old Guard of West Hartford. Home: West Hartford, Conn. Died Feb. 6, 2010.

SHELTON, JAMES KENNETH, counselor educator; b. Danville, Va., Apr. 14, 1939; s. James Oliver and Effie Mae Shelton; m. Rose Lee McMullen, Jan. 20, 1960; children— James Kenneth, Angela Lynn. B.S., Appalachian State U., Boone, N.C., 1962; M.S., Radford Coll. (Va.), 1969; Fd.D., Va. Poly. Inst. and State U., Blacksburg, 1974. Tchr., counselor, coach Roanoke County Schs. (Va.), 1962-70; assoc. prof. counselor edn., wrestling coach The Citadel, Charleston, S.C., 1970—; coordinator S.C. Helping Professions Workshop; chmn. support services in instructional devel. Charleston Higher Edn. Consortium; mem. adv. bd. Ednl. Opportunity Ctr. Pub. mem. Palmetto-Low Country Health Systems Agy. Citadel Devel. Found. grantee, 1979—; Gen. Electric Found. grantee, 1979; recipient Pres.'s award S.C. Vocat. Guidance Assn., 1979; Service award State of S.C., 1982. Mem. NEA (life), Am. Assn. for Counseling and Devel., S.C. Personnel and Guidance Assn. (exec. bd.), S.C. Mental Health Assn., S.C. Psychol. Assn., S.C. Vocat. Guidance Assn. Republican. Methodist. Contbr. articles to profl. jours. Died Oct. 30, 2009.

SHER, MICHAEL LEE, lawyer; b. NYC, Oct. 20, 1938; s. David and Mae Phyllis (Tulin) S.; m. JoAnn Veronica Giffuni, Feb. 2, 1970 (div.). AB, Johns Hopkins U., 1961; JD, Fordham U., 1968. Bar: N.Y. 1969, D.C. 1974, U.S. Dist. Ct. (ea., no, so, we. dists.) N.Y., U.S. Cir. Ct. (fed. cir.), U.S. Cir. Ct. (2d cir.), U.S. Supreme Ct. Spl. asst. to dir. pub. affairs Peace Corps, Washington, 1964-65; dep. dir., acting dir. exec. secretariat OEO Office of the Pres., Washington, 1965-66; assoc. Phillips, Nizer, Benjamin, Krim & Ballon, NYC, 1969-70; dir., exec. secretariat, spl. asst., spl. counsel, sec. mgmt. rev. com. N.Y.C. Health and Hosps. Corp., 1971-72; v.p. Wertheim Asst. Mgmt. Svcs., Inc., 1972-76; assoc. Finley, Kumble, Wagner, Heine, Underberg, Manley & Casey, NYC, 1976-79; dep. chmn., exec. dir., spl. counsel State of N.Y. Mortgage Agy., NYC, 1979-82; pvt. practice NYC, from 1982. Lect. Practising Law Inst., U. Nanjing, China; rapporteur Task Force on Internat. Legal Svcs.; founder UNCITRAL Internat. Moot Arbitration Competition, Willem C. Vis Internat. Comml. Arbitration Moot; judge internat. final rounds Jessup Internat. Moot Ct. Competition. Trustee Dalton Sch., N.Y.C., 1962-66, Endl. Alliance, N.Y.C., 1970-88, mem. exec. com., 1974-75; mem. Gov.'s Com. Scholastic Achievement, N.Y.C., 1976-86; aux. mem. housing adv. sounding bd. Young Pres.'s Orgn.; bd. dirs. United Neighborhood Houses of N.Y., N.Y.C., 1983-88; initiator, chmn. Ad Hoc Com. of the Am. Community of Higher Edn.; mem. Nat. Com. on U.S.-China Rels.; aux. mem. sounding bd. young pres's. orgn. Boys Choir of Harlem, 1990—, Fr. Flanagan's Boys Home Boys Town USA, 1990—. Mem. ABA (coord. liaisons internat. law sect., liaison with coun. of Bars of the European union., dispute resolution sect.), Am. Bar Assn. Fellows (life), D.C. Bar Assn., Assn. Bar City N.Y. com. sustaining mem. (mem. coun. on internat. affairs, co-chair UN group, mem. and rapporteur task force on internat. legal svcs., former mem. com. on aeronautics, chmn. sub-com. on econs., founding mem. spl. com. on lawyers in transition and sub-com. on lectrs. and cont. edn., various others), Canadian Bar Assn. hon. mem., Union Internat. des Avocats, dep. sec. gen. Internat. Org., former Am. C. of C. in France 1970-2000. Home: New York, NY. Died Jan. 20, 2010.

SHERMAN, MICHAEL STUART, business research firm executive; b. Norfolk, Va., Dec. 4, 1947; s. Herbert and Helen (Brener) S.; m. Rose Florence Reingold, Aug. 23, 1970; children— David Matthew, Adam Richard BS in Math., Va. Poly. Inst. and State U., 1969; MA in Econs., U. Pitts., 1972, PhD in Econs., 1974. Dir. econ. and market research Nat. Assn. Furniture Mfrs., Washington, 1974-81, exec.v.p., 1981-84; exec. dir. Summer & Casual Furniture Mfrs. Assn., Washington, 1976-84; pres. Assn. Research, Inc., Rockville, Md., from 1984. Mem. Coun. of Am. Survey Rsch. Orgns. Coach Montgomery Soccer, Inc., Rockville, 1982-85; trustee Washington Assn. Research Found., 1987. Mem. Greater Washington Soc. Assn. Execs. (chmn. planning com. 1983, bd. dirs. 1987), Am. Survey Rsch. Orgns. (coun.), Nat. Assn. Bus. Economists, Am. Soc. Assn. Execs. (Idea Fair award 1976, 78, cert. assn. exec.), Am. Econ. Assn., Am. Statis. Assn. Home: North Potomac, Md. Died Aug. 16, 2010.

SHERMAN, ROGER, economics educator; b. Jamestown, NY, Sept. 10, 1930; s. Claire Blanchard and Margaret Gertrude (Burke) S.; m. Charlotte Ann Murphy, Apr. 4, 1953 (div. Feb. 1995); children: Claire Randall, Thomas Allen; m. Geraldine Szott Moohr, May 25, 1996. BS in Math., Grove City Coll., 1952; MBA in Fin., Harvard U., 1959; MS in Econs., Carnegie-Mellon U., 1965, PhD, 1966. Mgr. mfg. control IBM Corp., NYC, 1956-62; asst. prof., assoc. prof., prof. U. Va., Charlottesville, 1965-72, Brown Forman prof. econs., from 1982, chmn. dept. econs., 1982-90. Vis. scholar Oxford U., 1987, Sydney U., 1988. Author: Oligopoly: An Empirical Approach, 1972, The Economics of Industry, 1974, Antitrust Policies and Issues, 1978, The Regulation of Monopoly, 1989; editor: Perspectives on Postal Service Issues, 1980; contbr. articles to profl. jours. Bd. dirs. McGuffey Art Ctr., Charlottesville, 1984-92. Lt. USNR, 1953-62. U. Bristol fellow, 1968-69; Fulbright lectr., Madrid, 1972; Sci. Ctr. Berlinfellow, 1975, 79, 80; Rockefeller Found. Vis. scholar, 1985 Mem. Am. Econ. Assn., Royal Econ. Soc., Econometric Soc. Died Feb. 18, 2010.

SHERMAN, ZACHARY, civil engineer, aerospace engineer, consultant; b. NYC, Oct. 26, 1922; s. Harry and Minnie (Schulsinger) Sherman; m. Bertha Leikin, Mar. 23, 1947; children: Gene Victor, Carol Beth. BCE, CCNY, 1943; MCE, Polytech. U. N.Y., Bklyn., 1953, PhD in Civil Engring. & Mechanics, 1969; MME, Stevens Inst. Tech., 1968. Registered profl. engr., N.Y., N.J. Stress analyst Gen. Dynamics, San Diego, 1943-45; sr. stress analyst Republic Aviation, Farmingdale, NY, 1945-47, 59-62; prof. civil engring. U. Miss., Oxford, 1954-59; lectr. Stevens Inst. Tech., Hoboken, NJ, 1962-67, CUNY, 1967-69; assoc. prof. aerospace engring. Pa. State U., State College, 1969-73; prin. Dr. Zachary Sherman Cons. Engrs., Santa Monica, Calif., from 1973; aerospace engr. FAA, NYC, 1980-86. Designated cons. engr. rep. FAA, from 1986. Contr.: articles to profl. jours. including Jour. of Aircraft AIAA. NSF grantee, 1972. Fellow: ASCE; mem.: AIAA (v.p. Western Conn. chpt. 1977—78), N.Y. Acad. Scis., Sigma Xi. Achievements include development of beam/beam-column deck suspension bridge; solutions to pothole problems; prestressed aircraft wing. Died Nov. 16, 2009.

SHICK, JOHN EARL, retired radiologist; b. Chgo., Feb. 24, 1926; BA, Harvard U., 1947; MD, Northwestern U., 1951. Diplomate Am. Bd. Radiology. Intern St. Luke's Hosp., Chgo., 1951—52; resident in radiology Thomas Jefferson U. Hosp., Phila., 1954—55, Barnes Hosp., St. Louis, 1955—57; pvt. practice Henry Ford Hosp., Detroit, 1957—61, Grossmont Hosp., La Mesa, Calif., 1961—81; ret., 1981. Mem. AMA, Am. Coll. Radiology, Radiol. Soc. N.Am. Home: El Cajon, Calif. Died May 1, 2009.

SHIELDS, ADDIE LAWRENCE, county historian; b. Beekmantown, N.Y., June 24, 1916; d. Howard Clifton and Agnes Elizabeth (Dupee) Lawrence; m. Francis Matthew Shields, Nov. 21, 1940 Ddec. 1964); children— Charlotte Frances, Charles Howard. Lic. Plattsburgh State Normal Sch., 1937; BS in Early Childhood, SUNY-Plattsburgh, 1973. Tchr. Dist. 3 Beekmantown, 1937-41; with family farm, 1940-65, farm operator, 1964-73; asst. dir. Migrant Mexican Day Care Ctr., 1973; historian Clinton County, Plattsburgh, 1978—; chmn. women's com. Farm Bur., mem. State Women's Com.; pres. Clinton County Farm Bur.; sec., treas. NE Local Dairymen's League; chmn. Clinton County's Bicentennial Celebration, 1988. Editor: Landmark in a Passageway-Beekmantown, 1976. Compiler and editor: The Diary of John Jersey McFadden in year 1872, 1982; The John Townsend Addoms Homestead-Underground RR Station, 1981. Compiler: Account Book for the Farmer-1876-Amos Barber (1828-89), 1984. Author preface for M. Benoit Pontbriands Comte Clinton-Marriages a Repertory 1830-80. Dedication by author Morris Glenn-Glenn's History of Adirondacks (Essex County), 1980. Addie Shields Day named in her honor No. N.Y. Am.-Can. Geneal. Soc., 1985. Mem. Clinton County Hist. Assn., N.Y. State Assn. County Historians (sec.), North County Local Historians Assn. (assoc. mem.). Republican. Presbyterian. Died Oct. 31, 2009.

SHIELDS, JACK RICHARD, psychologist, educator; b. Chgo., Feb. 23, 1924; s. Forrest Randolph and Mildred Helen (Swingle) Shields; m. Lillie Owease, Mar. 26, 1965; m. Carol Thompson, July 18, 1979. BS, Stanford U., 1962; MEd, Northeastern U., 1968; PhD, U.S. Internat. U., 1978. Commd. officer U.S. Army Air Force, 1942—62; transferred to U.S. Army, 1962; advanced through grades to lt. col. U.S. Army, 1962—70, ret., 1970; psychologist Alaska Native Hosp., Anchorage, 1970—73, Alaska Psychiat. Inst., Anchorage, 1973—74, G. Pierce Wood Hosp., Arcadia, Fla., 1974—75; psychologist and adult supr. Anchorage Mental Health Clinic, 1975—79; psychologist Alaska Treatment Ctr. for Alcoholism, 1980; cons. Salvation Army, mcpl. agys.; assoc. prof., counselor Alaska Pacific U., Anchorage, from 1980. Contbr.: articles to profl. publs. Mem.: Alaska Psychol. Assn., Soc. for Clin. and Exptl. Hypnosis, Am. Soc. Hypnosis, APA, Lomas Santa Fe Country Club (Solana Beach, Calif.), Masons, Kappa Delta Pi. Died Apr. 12, 2010.

SHINDELL, SIDNEY, preventive medicine physician, educator, department chairman; b. New Haven, May 31, 1923; s. Benjamin Abraham and Freda (Mann) S.; m. Gloria Emhoff, June 17, 1945; children: Barbara, Roger, Lawrence, Judith. BS, Yale U., 1944; MD, L.I. Coll. Medicine, 1946; postgrad., Emory U., 1948-49; LLB, George Washington U., 1951. Diplomate Am. Bd. Preventive Medicine in Occupl. Medicine, Am. Bd. General Preventive Medicine. With USPHS, 1947-52; med. dir. Conn. Commn. on Chronically Ill and Aged, 1952-57, Am. Joint Distbn. Com., 1957-59; asst. prof. preventive medicine U. Pitts., 1960-65; dir. Hosp. Utilization Project Western Pa., 1965-66; prof. dept. preventive medicine Med. Coll. Wis., Milw., 1966-93, chmn. dept., 1966-89, dir. Office Internat. Affairs, 1989-93, prof. emeritus, from 1993; exec. dir. Health Svc. Data of Wis., 1967-73. Mem. bd. sci. advisors Am. Coun. Sci. and Health, 1978—87, from 1992, chmn., 1988—92; mem. Nat. Adv. Com. on Occupl. Safety and Health U.S. Dept. Labor, 1982—84; cons. Caribbean Epidemiology Ctr. Pan Am. Health Orgn./WHO, 1988; field edpiemiology tng. program Ctr. Disease Control, Thailand, 1989; field epidemiology tng. program Nat. Office Occupl. and Environ. Medicine Royal Thai Ministry of Pub Health, 1990; mem. gov.'s white paper com. on health care reform, Wis., 93; acad. cons. Facilities of Medicine Padjadjaran U., Airlangga U., Indonesia, 1993, 94; cons. Project C.U.R.E., from 2002. Author: Statistics, Science and Sense, 1964, A Method of Hospital Utilization Review, 1966, The Law in Medical Practice, 1966, A Coursebook on Health Care Delivery, 1976; contbr. 120 articles to profl. jours. Trustee Med. Coll. Wis., 1996-2002; mem. sch. bd. Fox Point-Bayside (Wis.), Sch. Dist., 1970-71; vice chmn. Citizens' Adv. Com. Met. Problems, 1971-72; bd. dirs. Med. Care Evaluation S.E. Wis., 1973-76; trustee Interfaith Caregivers Alliance, 2001-2002. With AUS, 1943-46. Recipient Frank L. Babbott Meml. award SUNY Health Sci. Ctr., Bklyn., 1996. Fellow Am. Coll. Preventive Medicine (mem. bd. regents 1982-85), APHA, Am. Coll. Occupl. and Environ. Medicine (Pres.'s award 1999), Am. Coll. Legal Medicine; mem. Am. Assn. Health Data Sys. (sec. 1972-73), Assn. Tchrs. Preventive Medicine (dir. 1973-74, pres. 1976-77, spl. recognition award 1992, Duncan Clark award 2002), Assn. Occupl. Health Profls. (pres. 1980-90), Wis. Med. Soc. (mem. coun. on health care financing and delivery, mem. coun. on govt. affairs, mem. ho. of dels., 50 Yr. recognition award 1996, svc. award 2000), Am. Coll. Physician Execs., Internat. Commn. on Occupl. Health, Aircraft Owners and Pilots Assn., Masons, CAP. Died Aug. 31, 2009.

SHIPLEY, LUCIA HELENE, retired chemical company executive; b. Boston, Oct. 26, 1920; d. Harry Jacob and Helen Merrill (Dillingham) Farrington; m. Charles Raymond Shipley, Oct. 11, 1941; children: Helen Merrill, Richard Charles. Student, Smith Coll., 1938-41. Chief exec. officer, treas. Shipley Co. Inc., Newton, Mass., 1957-92, also bd. dirs. Patentee for immersion tin, electroless copper. Recipient Winthrop Sears award Chem. Industry Assn., 1985, Semi award Semicon West, 1990, Dana Hall Sch. Disting. Alumna award. Mem. Garden Club (pres. 1954-56). Republican. Congregationalist. Avocations: gardening, shell collecting, dogs, cage birds. Home: Sanibel, Fla. Died Jan. 22, 2010.

SHIPMAN, PETER HERBERT, financial communications executive; b. London, Ont., Can., Aug. 25, 1934; came to U.S., 1940, naturalized, 1954; s. Gerald Totten and Cora Fern (Foster) S.; m. Joan Chessman, June 16, 1962; children: Julie, James, Jerrold. AB, Dartmouth Coll., 1956; postgrad., Gen. Motors Inst., 1957. With Gen. Motors Corp., Detroit, 1956-57, Merrill, Lynch, Pierce, Fenner & Smith, San Francisco, 1960-65, NYC, 1965-69; sr. v.p., dir. William D. Witter, Inc., NYC, 1969-76; exec. dir. SEC, Washington, 1976-77; sr. v.p., dir. Kuhn Loeb & Co. Inc., from 1977; exec. v.p., dir. Blyth Eastman Dillon & Co., Inc., from 1978; pres., dir. Am. Banker-Bond Buyer Inc., NYC, 1978-85; chmn., chief exec. officer In Finet, Inc. div. Internat. Thomson Orgn., Inc., from 1985. Dir. Newman Communications, Gabelli Group, Inc., Autex Systems, Inc. Served to capt. USMCR, 1957-60. Mem. Psi Upsilon. Clubs: Shenorock Shore (Rye, N.Y.); Bd. Room (N.Y.C.). Presbyterian. Home: Rye, NY. Died May 3, 2009.

SHIRLEY, VIRGINIA LEE, advertising executive; b. Kankakee, Ill., Mar. 24, 1936; d. Glenn Lee and Virginia Helen (Ritter) S. Student, Northwestern U., 1960-61. With prodn. control dept. Armour Pharm., Kankakee, 1954-58; exec. sec. Adolph Richman, Chgo., 1958-61; mgr. media dept. Don Kemper Co., Chgo., 1961-63, 65-69; exec. sec. Playboy mag., Chgo., 1964-65; exec. v.p. SMY Media inc., Chgo., 1969-96, CEO, chmn. bd., 1996-2000, CEO, from 2000. Mem. Tavern Club. Home: Chicago, Ill. Died Dec. 18, 2009.

SHIVELY, JOE E., sales representative; b. Plymouth, Ind., Mar. 3, 1945; s. Claude Russell and Geneva Jane (Baer) Shively; m. Linda Kay Davis, Apr. 13, 1963; children: Mark Allen, Brenda Elaine. BS, Purdue U., 1967, MS, 1968, PhD, 1970. Cert. math. and chemistry tchr. W.Va. Instr. Purdue U., 1970; asst. prof., math. Southern Ill. U., Carbondale, 1970—73; evaluation specialist CEMREL, Carbondale, 1970—73; dir., rsch. and devel. Appalachia Ednl. Lab., Charleston, W.Va., 1973—84; asst. prof., edn. Coll. Grad. Studies Inst., W.Va., 1974; dir., testing W.Va. Dept. Edn., Charleston, 1984—87; evaluation cons. Calif. Test Bur. Subs. McGraw-Hill Corp., Charleston, 1987; sales rep. Riverside Pub., Midlothian, from 1988. Cons. Ala. A&M U., Huntsville, 1978; workshop trainer US V.I. Schs., 1981. Contbr. articles to ednl. jours. Named Ky. Col., 1979, lt. col., a.d.c. to gov., Ala., 1983. Mem.: Am. Evaluation Assn., Internat. Assn. Computing in Edn., Nat. Coun. Measurement in Edn., Am. Psychol. Assn., Am. Ednl. Rsch. Assn., Kanawha Valley Civitan Club (Charleston) (bd. dirs. 1982—83, 1985—87), Phi Delta Kappa, Kappa Delta Pi. Democrat. Avocations: golf, basketball. Died June 20, 2010.

SHOCKNEY, DAVID ALLEN, banker; b. Ft. Wayne, Ind., Apr. 11, 1947; s. James R. and Helen F. (Duncan) Shockney; m. Elizabeth Ann Bair Shockney, June 1, 1974; children: Kristin Elizabeth, Metthew David Kim. BS, Ind. U., 1969; postgrad., Westen State U. Coll. Law, 1974. Audit asst. First Nat. Bank Orange, Calif., 1974—76; auditor First Ctrl. Coast Bank, San Luis Obispo, Calif., 1979—81; controller Presidio Savs. & Loan, Porterville, Calif., 1981—82; v.p. cashier, CFO Ctrl. Sierra Bank, San Andreas, Calif., from 1982; v.p. cashier, CFO, sec. Heritage Oaks Bank, Paso Robles, Calif., 1982—86, exec. v.p., from 1986. Served with USN, 1970—74, PTO. Mem.: Exchange Club (Templeton, Calif.) (treas. 1983—85), Rotary (Templeton) (sec. 1983—85). Republican. Home: Sparks, Nev. Died Mar. 15, 2009.

SHORENSTEIN, WALTER HERBERT, commercial real estate development company executive; b. Glen Cove, NY, Feb. 23, 1915; m. Phyllis J. Finley, Aug. 8, 1945 (dec. 1994); children: Joan (dec. 1985), Carole, Douglas. Student, Pa. State U., 1933-34, U. Pa., 1934-36; D in Econs. (hon.), HanYang U., Seoul, Republic of Korea, 1988. With property sales mgmt. depts. Milton Meyer & Co., San Francisco, 1946-51, ptnr., 1951-60, owner, chmn. bd. dirs., from 1960, Shorenstein Group, San Francisco, Shorenstein Co., San Francisco, 1960—2010. Appt. by Pres. Johnson adv. del. UN Econ. Commn. for Asia and Far East, 1967, Pub. Advisory Com. U.S. Trade Policy; apptd. Pres. Carter Com. for Preservation fo White House; appt. by Pres. Clinton bd. dirs. Corp. Nat. Svc., 1994-96, adv.com. U.S. Commerce Dept. Industry, 1995-96. Past chmn. bd. trustees Hastings Law Ctr., U. Calif., San Francisco; founding mem. exec. adv. com. Hubert H. Humphrey Inst. Pub. Affairs, U. Minn.; bd. visitors; past pres., hon. life bd. dirs. San Francisco Park and Recreation Commn.; chmn. Vietnam Orphans Airlift; bd. dirs. San Francisco Performing Arts Ctr.; trustee Asia Found.; fin. chmn. Dem. Nat. Conv., 1984; founder Joan Shorenstein Ctr. on Press, Politics and Public Policy, Harvard U., 1986; apptd. by Pres. Clinton to Nat. Svc. Commn., 1994, Bd. of Americorp, founding mem. WWII Nat. Monument com., Nat. Endowment Arts, White House Endowment Fund; apptd. by Pres. Carter chair White House Preservation Fund; apptd. by Mayor Frank Jordon chair Save the San Francisco Giants com.; personal advisor Pres. Johnson, Carter, Clinton; chmn. Pacific Rim Econ. Coun., San Francisco; bd. visitors Internat. Studies Bd. Stanford U.; co-founder Orpheum, Curran and Golden Gate Theatres, San Francsico; founder Johnson Presdl. Libr., Carter Ctr.; chmn. San Francisco U. N50 nat. com., 1995, also numerous polit. activities. Maj. USAF, 1940-45. Named Leader of Tomorrow, Time mag., 1953, Calif. Dem. of Yr., 1985; recipient Nat. Brotherhood award NCCJ, 1982, Disting. Svc. award Dem. Nat. Com., 1983, Golden Plate award Am. Acad. Achievement, 1991, Svc. to Youth award Cath. Youth Orgn., 1994, Lifetime Achievement award Dem. Party, 1997; inducted Real Estate Legends Hall of Fame, 1997, Bay Area Coun. Bay Area Bus. Hall of Fame, 1998; Shorenstein award named in his honor Dem. Nat. Com., 1999; named one of Forbes 400: Richest Americans, 2009. Mem. Calif. C. of C. (past bd. dirs.), San Francisco C. of C. (past chmn. bd. dirs., life bd. dirs.). Democrat. Died June 24, 2010.

SHOTZ, FREDERICK ARTHUR, clinical psychotherapist; b. Phila., Jan. 29, 1949; s. Stanley and Suzanne Helen (Wolf) S.; m. Linda Susan Fleischman, Sept. 18, 1973. B.A. in Psychology and Biology, LaSalle Coll., 1971; M.S. summa cum laude in Psychology, Nova U., 1975; Ph.D. in Clin. Psychology, Calif. Coast U., 1983. Founder, trainer, crisis counselor HELP of Phila., 1969-70; crisis counselor Contact Counseling Ctr., Charlotte, N.C., 1971-72; assoc. dir., dir. tng. Miami (Fla.) Crisis Ctr. Switchboard, 1972-73; psychotherapist, clin. dir. Counseling Assocs., Plantation, Fla., 1975—; adj. prof. U. Miami, 1983—; radio commentator. Author: A Comprehensive Training Manual for Telephone Crisis Counselors, 1973. Donor Palm Beach Festival Arts, Broward Art Guild; lectr. Broward Community Coll. Pa. Acad. scholar, 1966-70, Walton Found. scholar, 1966-67; United Methodist Ch. fellow, 1972; recipient Phila. Good Samaritan award, 1968, Internat. Youth in Achievement award, 1981. Mem. Fla. Assn. Psychologists, Psychotheropists and Counselors (exec. sec.), Inst. Creative Art Therapies (bd. dirs.) Fla. Sunset Psychol. Assn. (chmn. bd. dirs.), Am. Personnel and Guidance Assn., Assn. Humanistic Psychology; Am. Assn. Counselor Edn. and Supervision, Sex Edn. and Info. Council U.S. Democrat. Jewish. Died Jan. 23, 2009.

SHREVE, KENNETH HOBART, cardiovascular, thoracic surgical assistant; b. Union City, Pa., Sept. 20, 1954; s. Robert Neil Shreve and Bette Jane (Searle) Shreve Gregor; m. Cheryle Lynn McKinney, Sept. 18, 1975 (div. Aug. 1987); children: Crystal Hope, Kenneth H. II. Student, Pa. State U., 1972-73, Gannon U., 1974-76, postgrad., 1979-80; BS in Allied Health Scis., Hahnemann Med. U., 1978; numerous seminars in field, Fla., Calif., Tex., from 1979. Cert. advanced cardiac life support, Am. Heart Assn., x-ray technician, Fla. Physician's asst. satellite office Office of R.M. Allanigue, MD, Inc., Union City, Pa., 1980-82; asst. Lafayette County Health Ctr. Rural Health div. U. Fla. med. sch., Mayo, 1982-83; asst. in cardiovascular and thoracic surgery St. Augustine (Fla.) Gen. Hosp. and J.P. Magre, MD, from 1983. Team physician Lafayette High Sch. varsity football team, 1982; med. counselor Lafayette County Health Fair, Mayo, 1983; bd. dirs. St. John's Home Med. Supply Corp., also sec. bd. dirs.; lectr. in field. Active Nat. League Families of Prisoners and Missing in Action in SE Asia, legal affairs council Red Badge of Courage Orgn., Vietnam Women's Meml. Project, Ams. for Freedon, Inc., Ams. for a Sound Fgn. Policy. Fellow Am. Acad. Physician Assts.; mem. Am. Assn. Surgeon's Assts. (nat. treas. 1985, chmn. profl. relations com. 1985-88, nat. pres. elect. 1988—, Presdl. award 1987), Assn. Physician Assts. in Cardiovascular Surgery, Fla. Acad. Physician Assts. (mem. profl. and pub. edn. com. 1984, state del. to nat. cong. 1985), Pa. Soc. Physician Assts., Nat. Rifle Assn., Hahnemann Med. U. Alumni Assn., U. Fla. 1853 Soc. Lodges: Masons (32d degree), Shriners. Republican. Baptist. Avocations: swimming, fishing, scuba, guitar, oriental cuisine, holistic health. Home: New Port Richey, Fla. Died Jan. 23, 2009.

SHRIVER, GREGORY B., designer, audio engineer, consultant; b. Norfolk, Va., June 28, 1954; s. Donald Woods and Peggy Ann (Leu) Shriver; m. Bonnie Lynn Klipple, July 3, 1973; children: Joyce Gwendolyn, Nicholas Dimitri. Rsch. asst., dept. anthropology NC State U., 1970, asst. & tech. dir., student drama program, 1971—73; media asst., cultural arts divsn. NC Dept. Pub. Instrn., 1971; various indsl. positions, 1973; designer, audio engr. & constrn. mgr. Stage & Studio Constrn. Svcs., Raleigh, NC, from 1973, CEO; lectr. 61st Audio Engring. Soc. NYC Conv., 1978, New Music Conv., 1982. Designer (audio studios prin. works) The Basement, NYC, The Big Apple, Greene St. Rec. Ltd., (video and film shoots prin. works) The Phillip Glass Ensemble at Sadler's Wells Theatre, London, The Sammy Kahn Spl. Concord Inn, NYC, (concert tours and prodns. prin. works) The Phillip Glass Ensemble, USA and Europe, 1975—82, Harry Belefonte European Tour, 1977, Mike Oldfield Tour Europe, 1979, (opera and dramatic theatre prin. works) E.O.B. at the Met, NYC, 1973, Einstein on the Beach European Tour, 1975, various nightclubs and halls in NYC and Raleigh, (theatre and concert halls prin. works) The Met. Opera, Lincoln Ctr., NYC, The Astoria Theatre, Royal Festival Hall, London, Pavillion de Baltard, Threatre de Champs de Elysees, Paris. Mem.: Audio Engring. Soc. Democrat. Presbyterian. Avocations: gardening, reading, sound systems. Home: Raleigh, NC. Died Nov. 22, 2009.

SHUFFELTON, FRANK CHARLES, language educator; b. St. Marys, Ohio, Mar. 10, 1940; s. Frank B. and Dorothy A. S.; m. Jane Ballou Weiss, Apr. 20, 1963; children: Amy Ballou, George Gordon. AB, Harvard U., 1962; MA, Stanford U., 1968, PhD, 1972. Instr. U. Rochester (N.Y.), 1969-72, asst. prof., 1972-77, assoc. prof., 1977-87, prof., from 1987, dir. coll. writing, 1997—2000, chair, from 2003. Author: Thomas Hooker, 1586-1647, 1977, Thomas Jefferson: A Complete Bibliography, 1983, Thomas Jefferson: 1981-90, 1992; mem. edit. bd. Early Am. Lit., 1984-87, 90-93. Bd. dirs. Jefferson Legacy Found.; mem. adv. bd. Internat. Ctr. Jefferson Studies, 2004-. Lt. USCGR, 1963-67. NEH Sr. fellow, 1988-89; Nat. Merit scholar, 1958-62. Mem. Northeast Am. Soc. 18th Century Studies (pres. 1994-95), Modern Lang. Assn. (chair divsn. Am. lit. to 1800 exec. com. 1996-98), Soc. 18th Century Am. Studies (pres. 1997-99). Home: Rochester, NY. Died Mar. 4, 2010.

SHULMAN, ARNOLD, judge, lawyer; b. Phila., Apr. 12, 1914; s. Edward Nathaniel and Anna (Leshner) S.; m. Mary Frances Johnson, Nov. 26, 1943; children: Diane Shulman Thompson, Warren Scott, Amy Lynn Shulman Haney. Student, Emory U., 1931; JD, U. Ga., 1936. Bar: Ga. 1937. Mem. firm Shulman, Shulman, Bauer & Deitch (and predecessors), Atlanta, to 1977; judge Ga. Ct. Appeals, 1977-84, presiding judge, 1981-83, chief judge, 1983-84; of counsel Troutman, Sanders, Lockerman & Ashmore, Atlanta, 1984-87; appointed sr. appellate ct. judge, from 1987; chief judge settlement conf. div. Ct. Appeals Ga., from 1989; prof. Atlanta Law Sch., 1964-84; adj. prof. Ga. State U. Coll. Law, Atlanta. Author: (with Wiley H. Davis) Georgia Practice and Procedure, 1948, 3d edit., 1968, 4th edit, (with Warren S. Shulman), 1975; contbr. articles to legal jours. Chmn. DeKalb County (Ga.) Sch. Salary Commn., 1960-62, DeKalb County Sch. Study Commn., 1962-64; mem. Fulton County-Atlanta Ct. Study Commn., 1961-62. Served to capt. U.S. Army, 1941-46. Mem. ABA, Atlanta Bar Assn., Ga. State Bar, Lawyers Club (Atlanta). Home: Atlanta, Ga. Died Aug. 4, 2010.

SHUMACKER, HARRIS B., JR., retired surgeon, educator, author; b. Laurel, Miss., May 20, 1908; s. Harris B. and Corinne (Teller) S.; m. Myrtle E. Landau, Dec. 1, 1933 (dec.); children: Peter D., James N.; m. Grace McConnel, Nov. 9, 1998. BS, U. Tenn., Chattanooga, 1927; A.M., Vanderbilt U., 1928; MD, Johns Hopkins U., 1932; D.Sc. (hon.), Ind. U., 1985. Diplomate Am. Bd. Surgery, Am. Bd. Thoracic Surgery. Asst. in surgery Johns Hopkins U., 1932-35, instr., 1938-41, asst. prof., 1941-46; asst. in surgery Yale U., 1936-37, instr., 1937-38, assoc. prof., 1946-48; prof. surgery Ind. U., 1948-70, chmn. dept., 1948-68, Disting. prof., 1970-78, Disting. prof. emeritus, from 1978. Prof., sr. advisor Uniformed Svcs. U. of Health Scis., Bethesda, Md., 1981-87, Disting. prof. surgery, 1988—; pres. Uniformed Svcs U. Assocs., 1987-88; hon. mem. surg. faculties in Peoples Republic of China, 1979-; dir. sect. cardiovascular-thoracic surgery St. Vincent Hosp., 1973-78, sr. surg. cons., 1978-81. Served from capt. to lt. col. M.C., U.S. Army, 1942-46; cons. surgeon gen., 1949-60 Recipient Roswell Park award, 1968, Medal of Honor, Evansville U., 1970, Disting. Alumus award U. Tenn. at Chattanooga, Curtis medal, 1970, Spl. Alumnus award Johns Hopkins U., 1973, Disting. Svc. award Am. Soc. Abdominal Surgery, letter of commendation Surgeon-Gen. USN, 1987, Disting. Svc. medal Uniformed Svc. U. Health Scis., 1988, René Leriche prize Soc. Internat. de Chir., 1993. Fellow Royal Coll. Surgeons Eng. (hon.); mem. Am. Assn. Surgery of Trauma, Am. Surg. Assn. (1st v.p. 1961, sec. 1964-68), So. Surg. Assn., Ctrl. Surg. Assn., Pan-Pacific Surg. Assn. (trustee 1961-64, v.p., 1964-75, pres. 1975-78), AMA (chmn. sect. gen. surgery), Internat. Surg. Soc., Internat. Soc. Cardiovasc. Surgeons (v.p. 1957-59, pres. N.Am. chpt. 1956-58), Soc. Clin. Surgery (pres. 1961-63), ACS (chmn. forum com. 1955-60, chmn. nat. TV com. 1964-68, Disting. Service award 1968), Soc. U. Surgeons (pres. 1951), Soc. for Vascular Surgery (pres. 1958-59, disting. fellow 2003), Am. Thoracic Surg. Assn., Soc. Thoracic Surgeons (hon.), Internat. Surg. Group (v.p. 1974-75, pres. 1975-76), Polish Surg. Assn. (hon.), Sociedad Cubana de Angiologia (hon.), Societa Italiana di Chirurgia (hon.), Internat. Surg. Group (hon.), Phi Beta Kappa, Sigma Xi, Alpha Omega Alpha. Died Nov. 14, 2009.

SHURTLEFF, MALCOLM C., plant pathologist, consultant; b. Fall River, Mass., June 24, 1922; s. Malcolm C. and Florence L. (Jewell) S.; m. Margaret E. Johnson, June 14, 1950; m. Freda L. Nothnagel, Aug. 1, 1998; children: Robert Glen, Janet Lee, Mark Steven. BS in Biology, U. R.I., 1943; MS in Plant Pathology, U. Minn., 1950, PhD in Plant Pathology, 1953. Asst. plant pathologist Conn. Agrl. Expt. Sta., New Haven, 1942, R.I. Agrl. Expt. Sta., Kingston, 1943; asst. extension prof. U. R.I., Kingston, 1950-54; assoc. extension prof. Iowa State U., Ames, 1954-61; prof. plant pathology U. Ill., Champaign-Urbana, 1961-92, prof. emeritus, from 1992; cons., writer Urbana, 1992-98. Adj. prof. Tex. A&M U., College Station, 1998—. Author: How To Control Plant Diseases, 1962, 66 (award Am. Garden Guild 1962, 66), How To Control Lawn Diseases and Pests, 1973, How To Control Tree Diseases and Pests, 1975, Controlling Turfgrass Pests, 1987, 97, 2002, A Glossary of Plant Pathological Terms, 1997, The Plant Disease Clinic and Field Diagnosis of Abiotic Diseases, 1997, Diagnosing Plant Diseases Caused by Nematodes, 2000; editor-in-chief Phytopathology News, 1966-69, Plant Disease, 1969-72; contbr. numerous articles to encys., profl. publs. and mags. Lt. (j.g.) USN, 1943-46, PTO. Recipient Disting. Svc. award USDA, Washington, 1986, E.C. Stakman award U. Minn., 2000. Fellow Am. Phytopathological Soc. (councilor at large 1970-71, Excellence in Extension Plant Pathology award 1991); mem. Internat. Soc. Plant Pathology (chmn. extension com. 1975-80), Am. Phytopathological Soc. (mem. various coms.). Avocation: photography. Home: Pearland, Tex. Died May 29, 2010.

SIDLE, WILLIAM CHRISTOPHER, geologist; b. Montclair, NJ, Aug. 15, 1951; s. Kermit Edward and Helen Marie (O'Gorman) Sidle. BS in Geology, U. Idaho, 1973; MS, Portland State U.. 1979. Cert. geologist Oreg. Mine geologist Bunker Hill Mining Co., Kellogg, Idaho, 1973—77; hydrologist US Geol. Survey, Portland, Oreg., 1978—80; engring. geologist Found. Scis., Inc., Portland, 1980—81; sr. geologist Gulf R & D Co., Houston, 1981—84; tech. mgr. radioactive waste dept. US Dept Energy, Columbus, Ohio, from 1984; cons. Northern Energy Resources Co., Portland, 1977—78. Author: U.S. Geological Survey Resources of Oregon, 1980; contbr. articles to profl. jours. Scout leader Columbia Pacific Coun. Boy Scouts America, 1978—80, Sam Houston Coun., 1981—83. Grant, Ruth Klein Mineralogy Meml. Fund, 1979. Mem.: Am. Inst. Profl. Geologists, Geochem. Soc., Geothermal Resources Coun., Geol. Soc. America, Am. Assn. Petroleum Geologists. Republican. Roman Catholic. Avocations: photography, chess, running, ice skating. Home: Columbus, Ohio. Died Mar. 14, 2010.

SIEFER, ELLIS, physician, surgeon, administrator; b. Detroit, Oct. 22, 1917; s. Harry and Rebecca (Gilter) S.; m. Mary Siefer, Dec. 30, 1940; children: Daniel, James, Miriam. D in Osteopathy, Chgo. Coll. Osteo. Medicine, 1942. Diplomate Am. Bd. Osteo. Surgery. Asst. prof. Chgo. Coll. Osteo. Medicine, 1948-50, assoc. prof., 1950-52; chair dept. surgery Zieger Osteo. Hosp., Detroit, 1952-65; chief of surgery Botsford Gen. Hosp., Farmington Hills, Mich., 1965-82, also bd. dirs.; chmn. Zieger Health Care Corp., Farmington Hills, Mich., from 1985; clin. prof. Mich. State U., Lansing, 1970-83; v.p. med. affairs Botsford Gen. Hosp., Farmington Hills, from 1965. Lectr. in field. Author: The American College of Osteopathic Surgeons: A Proud History, 1993. Recipient Patenge award Mich. State U., 1988, Disting. Svc. award Botsford Gen. Hosp., 1989. Fellow Am. Coll. Osteo. Surgeons (bd. govs. 1965-75, pres. 1971-72, Orel F. Martin award 1989, Disting. Surgeon award 1975), Mich. Assn. for Regional Med. programs (dir. 1968-73); mem. Mich. Osteo. Assn., Am. Osteo. Assn. (life), Oakland County Osteo. Assn., Sigma Sigma Phi. Avocations: hunting, fishing, golf, tennis. Home: Farmington Hills, Mich. Died Jan. 25, 2010.

SIEKEVITZ, PHILIP, biology educator; b. Phila., Feb. 25, 1918; s. Joseph and Tillie (Kaplan) S.; m. Rebecca Burstein, Aug. 7, 1949; children: Ruth, Miriam. BS in Biology, Phila. Coll. Pharmacy and Scis., 1942, PhD (hon.), 1972; PhD in Biochemistry, U. Calif., Berkeley, 1949; PhD (hon.), U. Stockholm, 1974. USPHS fellow Mass. Gen. Hosp., 1949-51; fellow oncology McArdle Lab., U. Wis., 1951-54; mem. faculty Rockefeller U., 1954-88, prof. cell biology, until 1988, ret. Mem. molecular biology panel NSF, 1964-67; panel Internat. Cell Research Orgn., 1963-79; bd. dirs., treas., chmn. Scientists Com. Pub. Information N.Y., 1962-80; bd. dirs. N.Y. Univs. Com., 1965-70; council Am. Fedn. Scientists, 1967-68 Author: (with A. Loewy, J. Menninger, J. Gallant) Cell Structure and Function, 3d edit, 1991; editor: Jour. Cell Biology, 1962-65, Jour. Cellular Physiology, 1970—, Biosci., Jour. Exptl. Zoology, 1969-73, Biochim. Biophysica Acta; mem. editorial bd.: Jour. Cell Sci., Jour. Molecular Brain Rsch. Served with USAAF, 1942-45. Mem. Am. Soc. Biol. Chemists, Am. Soc. Cell Biology (pres. 1966-67), Soc. Neurosci., AAAS, Am. Acad. Arts and Scis., Am. Inst. Biol. Scientists, N.Y. Acad. Scis. (hon. life, governing bd. 1973-79, pres. 1976), Nat. Acad. Scis., Sigma Xi. Home: New York, NY. Died Dec. 5, 2009.

SIEPI, CESARE, opera singer; b. Milan, Feb. 10, 1923; Operatic debut in Rigoletto, Schio, 1941, Il Nabucco, LaScala Opera, Milan, 1946, Don Carlo, Met. Opera, N.Y.C., 1950; soloist debut in, Carnegie Hall, N.Y.C., 1951; sang in Mozart and Verdi requiems, Edinburgh Festival, Albert Hall, London; leading bass at, Salzburg Festival, LaScala, Milan; appeared in: play Bravo Giovanni, 1962; appeared: play Vienna Staatsoper; made many opera recordings for, London Records. (Winner Nat. Singing Competition, Florence 1941, recipient Italy's Orfeo award 1956). Home: Roswell, Ga. Died July 5, 2010.

SIEVERS, JOHN N., telecommunications company executive; b. Aug. 24, 1952; m. Paula Sievers; children: Catelin, Hilary. BA in Econs., Coll. of Wooster, 1974; MBA, Northwestern U., 1979. With B.F. Goodrich, Akron, Ohio, 1978-84; v.p. corp. planning Armtek Corp., New Haven, 1984-89; mng. ptnr. Long Wharf Capital Ptnrs., Inc., New Haven, 1989-91; sr. v.p. mktg. and sales Culbro Corp., NYC, 1991-93; v.p. mktg. and sales So. New Eng. Tel, NYC, 1993, pres. gen. bus. group, 1994-96, pres. consumer and small bus. group, from 1996. Bd. dirs. New Haven-Bridgeport YMCA; vice chmn. 1996 Easter Seals Telethon. Home: New Haven, Conn. Died Dec. 26, 2009.

SILBERMAN, H. LEE, public relations executive, consultant; b. Newark, Apr. 26, 1919; s. Louis and Anna (Horel) S.; m. Ruth Irene Rapp, June 5, 1948; children: Richard Lyle, Gregory Alan, Todd Walter. BA, U. Wis., 1940. Radio continuity writer Radio Sta. WTAQ, Green Bay, Wis., 1940-41; reporter Bayonne Times, NJ, 1941-42; sales exec. War Assets Adminstrn., Chgo., 1946-47; copy editor Acme Newspictures, Chgo., 1947; reporter, editl. writer Wichita Eagle, Kans., 1948-55; reporter Wall St. Jour., NYC, 1955-57, banking editor, 1957-68; 1st v.p., dir. corp. rels. Shearson-Hamill & Co., NYC, 1968-74; N.Y. corr. Economist of London, 1966-72; from contbg. editor to editor in chief Finance mag., 1970-76; from v.p., dir. to exec. v.p. Fin. Svcs. Group, Carl Boyir & Assos., Inc., NYC, 1976-86, exec. v.p., 1981-86; sr. counselor Hill & Knowlton, Inc., NYC, 1986-93, sr. v.p., 1993-96, sr. mng. dir., 1996; pres. LSA Media Cons., from 1997. Cons. in field. Contbr. articles to profl. jours. Capt. C.E. AUS, 1942-46. Recipient Loeb Mag. award U. Conn., 1965; Loeb Achievement award for disting. writing on fin. Gerald M. Loeb Found., 1968 Mem.: Soc. Profl. Journalists, Soc. Silurians, NY. Fin. Writers Assn., Deadline Club NY, Zeta Beta Tau. Republican. Died Nov. 3, 2009.

SILLIMAN, RICHARD GEORGE, retired lawyer, retired manufacturing executive; b. Elgin, Ill., Aug. 11, 1922; s. Charles B. and Mabel Ellen (Winegar) S.; m. Mary L. Yost, June 12, 1945; children— Martha Jane, Charles R. BA in History, Cornell Coll., Mt. Vernon, Iowa, 1946; JD, Northwestern U., 1949. Bar: Ill. 1949. Atty. various US agy., Chgo., 1949-52; atty., asst. sec. Elgin Nat. Watch Co., Ill., 1952-59, sec., gen. atty. Ill., 1959-62; asst. gen. counsel Deere & Co., Moline, Ill., 1962-75, assoc. gen. counsel, 1975-82, sec., assoc. gen. counsel, 1982-87. Mem. editorial bd. Ill. Law Rev., 1948-49. Contbr. articles to profl. jour. Past pres., hon. dir. Quad-City Symphony Orch., Moline and Davenport, Iowa, 1968-87; bd. dir., trustee Upper Rock Island County YMCA, Moline, 1965-87; bd. dir. Police-Fire Commn., Elgin, 1957-61; bd. dir., sec. Elgin YMCA, 1955. Served with USN, 1943-46 Mem. Ill. State Bar Assn. (past chmn. com. on corp. law dept.), Union League (Chgo.). Avocations: golf, music. Home: East Moline, Ill. Died May 9, 2010.

SILVERSTEIN, BENJAMIN, construction and manufacturing company executive; b. Bklyn., June 23, 1923; s. Morris and Pauline (Zwerling) S.; m. Ethel Bold, June 25, 1948; children: Stephen Robert, Harriet Ellen. BBA, CCNY, 1947; MBA, NYU, 1956. Statistician Biller Snyder Inc., NYC, 1947-50; contr. Triangel Sheet Metal Works, Inc., New Hyde Park, N.Y., 1950-54; treas. Triangle Sheet Metal Works, Inc.,

New Hyde Park, N.Y., 1954-65, CEO, v.p., treas., sec., from 1966. Mem. Nat. Assn. Bus. Economists. Republican. Jewish. Avocations: tennis, bicycling, hiking, reading history and biography. Home: New York, NY. Died Jan. 17, 2009.

SIMERAL, WILLIAM GOODRICH, retired chemical company executive; b. Portland, Oreg., May 22, 1926; s. Claire Cornelius and Geneva G. Simeral; m. Elizabeth Louise Ross, June 25, 1949; children: Linda Simeral McGregor, Karen Simeral Schousen, William Goodrich Jr., John David; m. Marion Poore Anderson, Nov. 3, 2001. BS in Physics, Franklin and Marshall Coll., Lancaster, Pa., 1948; PhD in Physics, U. Mich., 1953. With E.I. duPont de Nemours and Co., Inc., 1953-87, v.p., gen. mgr. plastics dept. Wilmington, Del., 1974-76, v.p., gen. mgr. plastic products and resins dept., 1976-77, sr. v.p., dir., mem. exec. com., 1977-81, exec. v.p., dir., mem. exec. com., 1981-87; vice chmn. bd., chief operating officer Conoco Inc., 1984-85. Trustee Franklin and Marshall Coll., 1977—, chmn. bd., 1991-94; trustee, bd. dirs. Wilmington Med. Ctr., 1978-93, chmn. bd., 1982-86; bd. dirs. YMCA Wilmington and New Castle County, 1978-81. Mem. Chem. Mfrs. Assn. (vice chmn. bd. 1980-81, chmn. exec. com. 1981-82, chmn. bd. 1982-83), Am. Phys. Soc., Phi Beta Kappa, Sigma Xi, Wilmington Country Club. Home: Wilmington, Del. Died Oct. 28, 2009.

SIMMONS, ALAN JAY, electrical engineer, consultant; b. NYC, Oct. 14, 1924; s. George and Cherry (Danzig) S.; m. Mary Marcella Bachhuber, April 12, 1947; children, G. David, Peter A., Michael A.; Philip E., Paul I. BS in Physics and Chemistry, Harvard U., 1945; MSEE, MIT, 1948; PhDEE, U. Md., 1957. Electronic scientist Naval Rsch. Lab., Washington, 1948-57; dir. rsch. TRG Inc., Boston, 1957-65; div. mgr. TRG div. Control Data Corp., Boston, 1965-71; group leader MIT Lincoln Lab., Lexington, 1971-87; cons. Winchester, Mass., from 1987. Contbr. articles to profl. jours.; patentee in field. Mem. Town Dem. Com., Winchester, Mass., 1963. Lt. (j.g.) USN, 1943-46. Fellow IEEE (life); mem. AAAS (life), Antennas and Propagation Soc. (pres. 1986). Avocations: gardening, hiking, tennis, travel. Died Feb. 9, 2009.

SIMMONS, JEAN MERILYN, actress; b. London, Jan. 31, 1929; d. Charles and Winifred Ada (Lovel) Simmons; m. Stewart Granger, Dec. 20, 1950 (div. 1960); 1 child, Tracy; m. Richard Brooks, Nov. 1, 1960 (div. 1977); 1 child, Kate. Student, Orange Hill Sch., Burnt Oak, London. Actress appearing in English and American films including Mr. Emmanuel, 1944, Kiss the Bride Goodbye, 1945, Caesar and Cleopatra, 1945, Great Expectations, 1946, Uncle Silas, 1947, The Woman in the Hall, 1947, Black Narcissus, 1947, Hamlet, 1948 (Acad. award nomination), The Blue Lagoon, 1949, Adam and Evelyn, 1949, So Long at the Fair, 1950, The Clouded Yellow, 1951, Androcles and the Lion, 1952, The Actress, 1953, The Robe, 1953, Young Bess, 1953, The Egyptian, 1954, Footsteps in the Fog, 1955, Guys and Dolls, 1956, The Big Country, 1958, Home Before Dark, 1958, This Earth Is Mine, 1959, Spartacus, 1960, Elmer Gantry, 1960, The Grass Is Greener, 1960, All the Way Home, 1963, Life at the Top, 1965, Rough Night in Jericho, 1967, Divorce American Style, 1967, Heidi, 1968, The Happy Ending, 1969 (Acad. award nomination), Say Hello to Yesterday, 1971, Mr. Sycamore, 1975, The Dawning, 1988, How to Make an American Quilt, 1995, numerous others; theatre appearances include A Little Night Music, Phila., 1974; (TV mini-series) The Dain Curse, 1978, A Small Killing, 1981, Valley of the Dolls, 1981, The Thornbirds, 1983 (Emmy award), North and South, 1985, North and South Book II, 1986; (TV movies) December Flower, 1987, The Legend of Lost Loves, 1988, Great Expectations, 1989, One More Mountain, 1994, Daisies in December, 1995; guest TV series Murder She Wrote, 1989, Dark Shadows, 1991, Angel Falls, 1993 In the Heat of the Night, 1993. Died Jan. 22, 2010.

SIMMONS, THOMAS MURRAY, lawyer; b. Chgo., Feb. 25, 1932; s. Roscoe C. and Althea (Merchant) S.; B.S. in Humanities, Loyola U., Chgo., 1953; J.D., Boston Coll., 1956; postgrad. in bus. adminstrn., Suffolk U., Boston; m. Gertrude Lustig, Nov. 30, 1963 (div.); children— Karen, Paul. Admitted to Mass. bar, 1956, also U.S. Supreme Ct. bar; practiced in Boston, 1956—; approved examiner titles Mass. Land Ct. Incorporator, past pres. Adult Edn. Inst. New Eng.; mem. nat. panel arbitrators New Eng. council Am. Arbitration Assn.; mem. adv. gen. bd. spl. classes Boston Pub. Schs., 1968; mem. Bd. Examiners City of Boston, 1969-83; area spl. gifts chmn. Am. Cancer Soc., 1967-68; mem. bd. Greater Boston Council Alcoholism, 1970, treas., 1973; trustee Found. for Coop. Housing, Washington, 1975-82, Carney Hosp., Boston, 1980; bd. dirs. Boston chpt. NAACP, 1971-72, chmn. legal com., counsel to chpt., 1972-73; chmn. commn. promotion parish councils Roman Catholic Archdiocese Boston, 1969-80, chmn. lay caucus, 1970, pres. Council Cath. Men, 1968, now cons., sec. Cath. Alumni Sodality Boston, 1969-76, pres., 1976; mem. bd. Cath. Interraccial Council, 1969-71; mem. bd. Nat. Council Cath. Laity, 1971—, 1st v.p., 1973, pres., 1978; exec. com. Nat. Cath. Community Service, 1971-79; bd. govs. USO, 1973-79; vice chmn. Roxbury Community Coll. Found. Recipient St. Thomas More award Nat. Council Cath. Men, 1970. Hon. mem. Greater Boston C. of C. Past legal editor New Eng. Real Estate Jour. Mem. Mass. Bar Assn., Mass. Trial Lawyers Assn., Blue Key. Democrat. Died Nov. 28, 2009.

SIMMONS, VAUGHAN PIPPEN, medical consultant; b. Balt., Nov. 19, 1922; s. Harry S. and Sarah Jane (Pippen) S.; m. Marguerite Carolyn Massino, Dec. 27, 1947 (dec. 1990); children: Malynda Sarah, Jefferson Vaughan. Student, Ill. Inst. Tech., 1943-44; BS, U. Chgo., 1947, MD, 1949. Diplomate Am. Bd. Life Ins. Medicine. From instr. to asst. prof. Marquette U. Sch. Medicine, Milw., 1950-56; asst. med. dir. Northwestern Mut. Life Ins. Co., Milw., 1956-60; med. dir. Fidelity Mut. Life Ins. Co., Phila., 1961-73, v.p., 1968-73; v.p., med. dir. Colonial Penn Life Ins. Co., Phila., 1973-84. Vis. lectr. ins. medicine Temple U. Sch. Medicine, Phila., 1966-84; asst. prof. anatomy Jefferson Med. Coll., Phila., 1977-88, hon. asst. prof. anatomy, 1988—. Patentee in field (3); contbr. articles to profl. jours. Mem. ofcl. bd. St. Luke United Methodist Ch., Bryn Mawr, Pa., 1963-83, chmn. commn. membership and evangelism, 1963-71, trustee, 1968-83. Served with M.C., U.S. Army, 1943-45, as lt. (j.g.) USNR, 1952-54; Korea Fellow Coll. Physicians Phila. (chmn. pub. health sect. 1967-68, ins. medicine sect. 1970-72, planning com. 1981-82, adv. bd. Francis C. Wood Inst. History of Medicine 1984-88), Milw. Acad. Medicine, Am. Geriatrics Soc., N.Y. Acad. Medicine; mem. Am. Acad. Ins. Medicine (founding editor Ins. Medicine 1969-71, exec. coun. 1970-72, publs. com. 1967-75), Am. Life Ins. Assn. (sec. med. sect. 1974-77), Pa. Hist. Soc., Am. Assn. Automotive Medicine (dir. 1980-83), Am. Legion, Sigma Xi, Alpha Kappa Kappa. Clubs: Union League (bd. dirs. 1982-85, v.p. 1985-86), Sketch (Phila.). Avocations: photography, amateur radio, drawing, painting, medical research and writing. Home: Catonsville, Md. Died Mar. 2, 2009.

SIMON, BARRY PHILIP, lawyer, retired air transportation executive; b. Paterson, NJ, Nov. 22, 1942; s. Alfred Louis and Rhoda (Tapper) S.; m. Hinda Bookstaber, Feb. 9, 1964; children: Alan, John, Eric. BA, Princeton U., NJ, 1964; LLB, Yale U., New Haven, 1967. Bar: NY 1965, Tex. 1986. Assoc. atty. Hughes, Hubbard & Reed, NYC, 1967-69, Sullivan & Cromwell, NYC, 1969-72, Shea & Gould, NYC, 1972-73; v.p., gen. counsel Teleprompter Corp., NYC, 1973-82; v.p., sec., gen. counsel Continental Airlines, LA and Houston, 1982-86, v.p. in-charge internat. divsn. Houston, 1987-90, sr. v.p. legal affairs, gen. counsel, sec., 1990-92, sr. v.p. internat. ops. Houston, 1996—2004; sr. v.p. Tex. Air Corp., 1986-87; sr. v.p. legal affairs, gen. counsel, sec. Ea. Airlines, Miami, Fla., 1987-90; exec. v.p., gen. counsel GAF Corp., Wayne, NJ, 1993-95, N.W. Airlines Corp., Eagan, Minn., 2004—06. Bd. dirs. Amadeus Reservations Sys., Nat. Energy and Gas Transmission. Mem. copyright com. Nat. Cable TV Assn., Washington, 1974-76, mem. utilities com., 1973-82; bd. dirs. Houston Grand Opera, Inprint, Alley Theatre. Recipient Class of 1888 Lit. prize Princeton U., 1961 Died July 14, 2010.

SIMON, MARTIN STANLEY, economist, consultant; b. St. Louis, Sept. 6, 1926; s. Elmer Ellis and Bee Marion (Werner) S.; m. Rita Edith Scheinhorn, June 18, 1950; children: Deborah, Richard. BBA, CCNY, 1949; MA, NYU, 1953. Econ. statistician Indsl. Commodity Corp, NYC, 1949-52; agrl. econ. statistician Dept. Agr., Washington, 1952-58; commodity analyst Connell Rice & Sugar Co., Inc., Westfield, NJ, 1958-62, asst. to pres., 1962-67, v.p., 1967-74; sr. v.p. Connell Rice & Sugar Co., Inc. (now The Connell Co.), Berkeley Heights, NJ, 1974-99; pres. Eureka Group, LLC, Westfield, NJ, from 1999, The Rice Econs. Group, LLC, Westfield, NJ, from 1999; cons. AID, Jamaica, 1963; mem. Rice Insp. Industry Adv. Com., Washington, 1971-72; adv. U.S. Del. to UN FAO Intergovtl. Meetings on Rice, 1981; export dir., bd. dirs. Assn. Administrn. Rice Quotas, Inc., 1997-99. Served with U.S. Army, 1944-46, ETO. Recipient Class of 1920 award for merit in econ. stats. CCNY, 1949 Mem. Am. Econ. Assn., Rice Millers Assn. (chmn. legis. options working group 1984-86, govt. programs com. 1986-87, chmn. PL480 subcom. 1988-90), Nat. Economists Club. Home: Basking Ridge, NJ. Died Jan. 31, 2010.

SIMPSON, JOANNE MALKUS, meteorologist; b. Boston, Mar. 23, 1923; d. Russell and Virginia (Vaughan) Gerould; m. Robert H. Simpson, Jan. 6, 1965; children by previous marriage: David Starr Malkus, Steven Willem Malkus, Karen Elizabeth Malkus. BS, U. Chgo., 1943, MS, 1945, PhD, 1949; DSc (hon.), SUNY, Albany, 1991. Instr. physics and meteorology Ill. Inst. Tech., 1946-49, asst. prof., 1949-51; meteorologist Woods Hole Oceanographic Instn., 1951-61; prof. meteorology UCLA, 1961-65; dir. exptl. meteorology lab. NOAA, Dept. Commerce, Washington, 1965-74; prof. environ. scis. U. Va., Charlottesville, 1974—79, W.W. Corcoran prof. environ. scis., 1974—79; head Severe Storms br. Goddard Lab. Atmospheres, NASA, Greenbelt, Md., 1979—88; chief scientist for meteorology Goddard Space Flight Ctr., NASA, 1988—2004, chief scientist emeritus for meteorology, 2004—10; project scientist tropical rainfall measuring mission, 1986—98. Mem. Bd. on Atmospheric Scis. and Climate, NRC/NAS, 1990-93, 97-2000, Bd. on Geophys. and Environ. Data, 1993-96, com. on climate, ecosystems, infectious diseases and human health, 1998-2000; mem. sr. adv. bd. NOAA, 1998-2003. Author: (with Herbert Riehl) Cloud Structure and Distributions Over the Tropical Pacific Ocean; assoc. editor: Revs. Geophysics and Space Physics, 1964-72, 75-77; contbr. articles to profl. jours. Mem. Fla. Gov.'s Environ. Coordinating Coun., 1971-74. Recipient Disting. Authorship award NOAA, 1969, Silver medal Dept. Commerce, 1967, Gold medal, 1972, Vincent J. Schaefer award Weather Modification Assn., 1979, Cmty. Headliner award Women in Comm., 1973, Profl. Achievement award U. Chgo. Alumni Assn., 1975, 92, Lifetime Achievement award Women in Sci. Engring., 1990, Exceptional Sci. Achievement award NASA, 1982, William Nordberg award NASA, 1994, NASA Medal Outstanding Leadership, 1998, I.M.O. prize World Meteorol. Orgn., 2002, Presdl. Rank award for Civil Svc., 2003, 04; named Woman of Yr., L.A. Times, 1963; Guggenheim fellow, 1954-55, Goddard Sr. fellow, 1988-2004. Fellow Am. Geophys. Union, Am. Meterol. Soc. (mem. coun. 1975-77, 79-81, mem. exec. com. 1977, 79-81, commr. sci. and tech. activities 1982-88, pres.-elect 1988, pres. 1989, publs. commr. 1992-98, hon. mem. 1995, Meisinger award 1962, Rossby Rsch. medal 1983, Charles Franklin Brooks award 1992, Charles E. Anderson award 2001), World Meterol. Orgn. (IMO prize 2002), Explorers Club, Nat. Acad. Engring., Am. Acad. Arts & Sciences; mem. Royal Meteorol. Soc. (hon.), Cosmos Club, Phi Beta Kappa, Sigma Xi. Home: Washington, DC. Died Mar. 4, 2010.

SIMPSON, MIKE, state legislator; b. Dec. 11, 1962; m. Linda Simpson; 3 children. Mem. Dist. 65 Mich. House of Reps., Mich., 2007—09. Democrat. Died Dec. 18, 2009.

SIMPSON, ROBERT SMITH, retired diplomat, writer; b. Arlington County, Va., Nov. 9, 1906; s. Hendree Paine and Edith Lydia (Smith) S.; m. Henriette S. Lanniée, Nov. 7, 1934 (dec. 2006); children: Margaret Lanniée Simpson Maurin-Stunkard, Zélia Tinsley. BS, U. Va., 1927, MS, 1928; LL.B., Cornell U., 1931; postgrad., Columbia U., 1931-32. Spl. labor adviser, exec. NRA, 1933-34; trade. assn. exec., adminstrv. agt. Asphalt, Shingle and Roofing Code Authority, 1934-35; instr., then asst. prof. bus. law U. Pa., 1935-44; spl. adviser Pa. Unemployment Relief and Assistance Commn., co-drafter Pa. Unemployment Compensation Act, 1936; adviser N.J. Civil Service Commn., 1939; adv. unemployment compensation and relief joint Pa. State Commn., 1939-42; asst. dir. fgn. div. recruitment and manning orgn. War Shipping Adminstrn., 1942-43; with US Dept. State, 1943-62, 65-66; fgn. svc. officer, 1944-62; consul gen. Mozambique, 1954-57; adv. US Dept. Labor, 1958-60, dir. office country programs, 1960-61; dep. examiner bd. fgn. service examiners US Dept. State, 1961-62, cons., 1965-66; lectr. Georgetown U., 1973, research prof. diplomacy, 1974-77; del. and/or mem. numerous nat. and internat. meetings; founding mem., bd. dirs. Inst. Study Diplomacy, Georgetown U., Washington, 1978-94, emeritus founding mem., from 1995. Co-drafter UN Charter and Food and Agrl. Orgn. (Rome) Constitution, 1944; co-organizer Divsn. Internat. Labor, Health and Social Affairs Dept. State, and Labor attache program of Fgn. Svc. Author: Anatomy of the State Department, 1967, The Crisis in American Diplomacy, 1980, Some Perspectives on the Study of Diplomacy, 1986, Education in Diplomacy, 1987; editor: Belgium in Transition, 1946, Resources and Needs of American Diplomacy, 1968; Instruction in Diplomacy: The Liberal Arts Approach, 1972. Annual diplomacy debate named in his honor Univ. Va. Mem. Am. Fgn. Svc. Assn., Consular Officers Assn., Assn. for Diplomatic Studies and Tng., Inst. for Study of Diplomacy (Georgetown U., founding mem., bd. dirs.), Jefferson Lit. and Debating Soc. (U. Va. assoc.), Raven Soc., Phi Beta Kappa, Phi Sigma Kappa. Presbyterian. Died Sept. 5, 2010.

SIMPSON, SANFORD L., state agency administrator; b. Chgo., Apr. 7, 1943; s. Sanford L. Simpson and Sarah (Dabe) Rawlinson. BA, Goddard Coll., 1965; BDiv, Tufts U., 1967. Min. edn. First Ch. (Unitarian), Chestnuthill, Mass., 1965-67; dir. neighborhood ctrs. Lynn (Mass.) Economic Opportunity, 1968-69; dir. Malden Ctr. Ea. Middlesex Opportunity, Malden, Mass., 1969-71; dir. elderly programs Cambridge (Mass.) Economic Opportunity, 1971-72; dir. housing counseling Community Inter Faith Housogn, Indpls., 1973-74; dep. dir. ACTION, Inc. of Del. County, Muncie, Ind., 1974-82, exec. dir., from 1982. Cons. Regional Homelessness Task Force, Muncie-Marion, Ind., 1967—, Legal Svcs. Adv. Com., Muncie, 1980—. Chmn. Mayor's Task Force on Self-Sufficiency, Muncie, 1987-88, Emergency Food & Shelter Program Bd., Muncie, 1985-88; mem. Community Concerns Coun., Muncie, 1982-88. Mem. Ind. Community Action Dirs. Assn. (treas. 1984—), Ind. Human Svcs. Coalition, Nat. Assn. Community Action Agys., Muncie C. of C. Home: Muncie, Ind. Died July 12, 2010.

SIMS, JOHN ROGERS, JR., lawyer; b. Red Star, W.Va., Apr. 10, 1924; s. John Rogers and Myrtle (Hutchison) S.; m. Geraldine L. Bucklew, Oct. 8, 1966; children: John Rogers III, Joyce Rebecca. BS in Commerce, U. Va., 1950, LLB, 1952. Assoc. Dow, Lohnes & Albertson, Washington, 1953-57; gen. counsel D.C. Transit Sys., Inc., Washington, 1957-65; individual practice law Washington, 1965-68; ptnr. Wrape and Hernly, Arlington, Va., 1968-71, Sims, Walker & Steinfeld (and predecessor firm), Washington, 1972-95; pvt. practice Nellysford, Va., from 1995. Chmn. bd. dirs. John Sims Assocs., Inc., 1978-2000, Purnell Bros. Transport, Ltd., 1981-91; co-founder, bd. dirs., gen. counsel A Presdl. Classroom for Young Ams., Inc., chmn. bd. dirs., 1979-83; dir., v.p., gen. counsel, sec. SunWorld Internat. Airways, Inc., 1984-88; chmn. corp. bd. adv. Omniplex World Svcs. Corp., 1997—. Vice chmn. Falls Church (Va.) Planning Commn., 1958-64; pres. Falls Church Republican Party, 1961-62; bd. dirs. Heart Assn. No. Va., Inc., pres., 1963-64; bd. dirs., v.p., gen. counsel Commonwealth Doctors Hosp., Fairfax, Va., 1967-74; bd. dirs., vice chmn. Jefferson Area Bd. for Aging. Served with Armed Forces, 1943-45. Mem. ABA, W.Va. Bar Assn., D.C. Bar Assn., Va. State Bar, Motor Carrier Lawyers Assn. (nat. pres. 1971-72), Assn. for Transp. Law, Logistics and Policy, Va. Trial Lawyers Assn., Rotary, Masons (Shriner), Washington Golf and Country Club, Farmington Country Club (Charlottesville, Va.). Presbyterian. Home: Nellysford, Va. Died Aug. 6, 2010.

SINGER, HERBERT J., lawyer; b. Chgo., Apr. 12, 1941; BS in Gen. Engring., U. Ill., 1963; JD, Loyola U., Chgo., 1966. Bar: Ill. 1967, U.S. Patent and Trademark Office 1967, U.S. Supreme Ct. 1970. Ptnr. Silverman, Cass & Singer Ltd. and predecessor firms, Chgo., from 1967. Mem. ABA, Ill. Bar Assn., Chgo. Bar Assn., Am. Arbitration Assn. (arbitrator), Intellectual Property Law Assn. Chgo. (bd. dirs. 1976-79), Lawyers Club Chgo., Internat. Trademark Assn. Home: Northbrook, Ill. Died Jan. 18, 2009.

SINGER, J. DAVID, political science professor; b. Bklyn., Dec. 7, 1925; s. Morris L. and Anne (Newman) S.; m. C. Diane Macaulay, Apr., 1990; children: Kathryn Louise, Eleanor Anne. BA, Duke U., 1946; LLD (hon.), Northwestern U., 1983; PhD, NYU, 1956. Instr. NYU, 1954-55, Vassar Coll., 1955-57; vis. fellow social relations Harvard U., 1957-58; vis. asst. prof. U. Mich., Ann Arbor, 1958-60, sr. scientist Mental Health Research Inst., 1960-82, assoc. prof., 1964-65, prof. polit. sci., 1965—2009, coordinator World Politics Program, 1969-75, 81-90; vis. prof. U. Oslo and Inst. Social

Research, 1963-64, 90, Carnegie Endowment Internat. Peace and Grd. Inst. Internat. Studies, Geneva, 1967-68, Zuma and U. Mannheim (W. Ger.), 1976, Grad. Inst. Internat. Studies, Geneva, 1983-84, U. Groningen, 1991, Nat. Chengchi U., Taiwan, 1998. Author: Financing International Organization: The United Nations Budget Process, 1961, Deterrence, Arms Control and Disarmament: Toward a Synthesis in National Security Policy, 1962, rev. 1984, (with Melvin Small) The Wages of War, 1816-1965: A Statistical Handbook, 1972, (with Susan Jones) Beyond Conjecture in International Politics: Abstracts of Data Based Research, 1972, (with Dorothy La Barr) The Study of International Politics: A Guide to Sources for the Student, Teacher and Researcher, 1976, Correlates of War I and II, 1979, 80, (with Melvin Small) Resort to Arms: International and Civil War, 1816-1980, 1982, Models, Methods, and Progress: A Peace Research Odyssey, 1990, (with Paul Diehl) Measuring the Correlates of War, 1998, (with D. Geller) Nations at War, 1998; monographs; contbr. articles to profl. jours.; mem. editorial bd. ABC: Polit. Sci. and Govt., 1968-84, Polit. Sci. Reviewer, 1971—, Conflict Mgmt. and Peace Sci., 1978—, Etudes Polemologigues, 1978—, Internat. Studies Quar., 1989—, Jour. Conflict Resolution, 1989—, Internat. Interactions, 1989—. With USNR, 1943-66. Ford fellow, 1956; Ford grantee, 1957-58; Phoenix Meml. Fund grantee, 1959, 1981-82; Fulbright scholar, 1963-64; Carnegie Corp. research grantee, 1963-67; NSF grantee, 1967-76, 1986-89, 1992-94; Guggenheim grantee, 1978-79 Mem. Am. Polit. Sci. Assn. (Helen Dwight Reid award com. 1967, 95, chmn. Woodrow Wilson award com., chmn. nominating com. 1970), Internat. Polit. Sci. Assn. (chmn. conflict and peace rsch. com. 1974—), World Assn. Internat. Rels., Internat. Soc. Polit. Psychology, Internat. Soc. Rsch. on Aggression, Social Sci. History Assn., Peace Sci. Soc., Internat. Peace Rsch. Assn. (pres. 1972-73), Consortium on Peace Rsch., Fedn. Am. Scientists (nat. coun. 1991-95), Union Concerned Scientists, Arms Control Assn., Internat. Studies Assn. (pres. 1985-86), Com. Nat. Security, Am. Com. on East-West Accord, World Federalist Assn. Home: Ann Arbor, Mich. Died Dec. 28, 2009.

SISSON, THOMAS EDWIN (PETE), lawyer, development company executive; b. Memphis, Aug. 28, 1927; s. Thomas Andrew and Dora (Butler) Sisson; m. Jewel Omega Hipps Sisson, Oct. 25, 1953; children: Thomas Edwin Jr., Judy Sisson Wimbs, Jerry Allan, Debbie Sisson Dees, Ginger Sisson Hamlet, Larry William, Steve Herbert. BS, Memphis State U., 1950; LLB, U. Memphis, 1961. Bar: Tenn. Commr. Dept. Pub. Works, Memphis, 1964—68; ptnr. Sisson and Sisson, Memphis, from 1968; mem. Shelby County Bd. Commrs., Shelby County, Tenn., from 1976; pres. TESCO Devel., Inc., Memphis, from 1981. Campaign chmn. Girl Scouts USA, Memphis, 1967—68; pres. Memphis Jr. C. of C., 1958—59. Recipient Perry Pipkin Jr. award, Memphis Jr. C. of C., 1957—58; named Boss of Yr., Memphis Chpt. Am. Bus. Women Assn., 1965. Mem.: ABA, Tenn. Bar Assn., Shelby County Bar Assn., Memphis Bar Assn. Republican. Home: Cordova, Tenn. Died Jan. 31, 2009.

SISTRUNK, WILLIAM HICKS, air force officer; b. Utica, Miss., Aug. 11, 1937; s. John David Sr. and Mary Elaine (McCay) S.; m. Sue Carole Dismuke, Oct. 12, 1960; children: William H. Jr., Mark McCay. BS in Geology, U. Miss., Oxford, 1960; M of Pers. Mgmt., Ctrl. Mich. U., 1975. Commd. 2d lt. USAF, 1960, advanced through grades to maj. gen., 1988; student Armed Forces Staff Coll., Norfolk, Va., 1971-72; air ops. officer Mil. Airlift Support Squadron, Tan Son Nhut Air Base, Vietnam, 1972; air ops. officer gen. war and mobilization div. Directorate Plans, Hdqrs. USAF, Washington, 1973-76; ops. officer 6th Mil. Airlift Squadron, McGuire AFB, N.J., 1976-78, comdr., 1978-80; student Nat. War Coll., Ft. McNair, D.C., 1980-81; dep. comdr. for ops. 63d Mil. Airlift Wing, Norton AFB, Calif., 1981-82; comdr. 436th Mil. Airlift Wing, Dover AFB, Del., 1983-85; insp. gen. Mil. Airlift Command, Scott AFB, Ill., 1985-86; vice comdr. 22d Air Force, Travis AFB, Calif., 1986-88; comdr. 322d Airlift Div., Ramstein Air Base, Fed. Republic Germany, 1988-90; chief of staff Mil. Airlift Command, Scott AFB, 1990-92; ret., 1992. Decorated D.S.M. with 1 oak leaf cluster, Legion of Merit, Meritorious Svc. medal with 3 oak leaf clusters. Mem. Air Force Assn., Airlift/Tanker Assn., Order of Daedalians. Methodist. Avocations: golf, fishing, woodworking, computers. Home: Montgomery, Ala. Died June 16, 2009.

SITAR, ANDREW A., food company executive; b. Boston, Dec. 19, 1928; s. Andrew A. and Anne Agnes (Sullivan) S.; m. Lorraine J. Gervais; children: Charmaine, Andrew Jr., Wayne, Kim. BBA, Northeastern U., 1952. Gen. foreman Builders Specialties Inc., Brighton, Mass., 1952-60; dir. distbn. Penn Fruit Co., Phila., 1961-69; v.p. distbn. Pueblo Internat., Brentwood, N.Y., 1969-77, P&C Food Markets, Syracuse, N.Y., from 1977. Bd. dirs. Syracuse Boys Clubs, 1987—. Served to sgt. U.S. Army, 1946-48. Mem. Food Mgmt. Inst. (planning com. 1982-85, speaker, discussion leader various confs.). Clubs: Calvary (Syracuse). Republican. Roman Catholic. Avocations: boating, sailing, swimming. Home: Baldwinsville, NY. Died Sept. 28, 2009.

SITKOFF, THEODORE, public management executive; b. Phila., Jan. 25, 1932; BS in Econs., U. Pa., 1953, Masters of Govt. Adminstr., 1955. Acct. Commonwealth of Pa., 1955-59, comptr. dept. pub. welfare, 1959-61, dir. accounts gov.'s office of adminstrn., 1961-64; mem. hdqs. staff Pub. Adminstrn. Svc., McLean, Va., 1964-69, v.p., 1973-77, pres., from 1977, CEO; fin. dir. Fed. Land Devel. Authority Govt. of Malaysia and UN Exec. Corp., 1970-72. Founder Ctr. Privatization. Died Dec. 15, 2009.

SKADOW, RONALD ROBERT, lawyer; b. Chgo., Mar. 17, 1942; s. Robert H. and Lois R. (Daumke) Skadow; m. Patricia A. Coon, May 24, 1968; 1 child, Peter Coon. BS, Northwestern U., 1963; JD, 1966. Bar: Ill. 1966. Assoc. Chapman, Pennington, Montgomery, Holmes & Sloan, Chgo., 1967—69; asst. gen. counsel Allied Products Corp., Chgo., 1969—75; assoc. gen. counsel Canteen Corp., Chgo., 1975—86, gen. counsel, from 1986, v.p., from 1987. Vestryman St. Michael's Episcopal Ch., Barrington, Ill., 1983—85, jr. warden, 1986—87. With USMC, 1966—72. Mem.: ABA, Chgo. Bar Assn., Barrington (Barrington, Ill.). Republican. Home: Tryon, NC. Died May 20, 2010.

SLAATTÈ, HOWARD ALEXANDER, minister, philosophy educator; b. Evanston, Ill., Oct. 18, 1919; s. Iver T. and Esther (Larsen) S.; m. Mildred Gegenheimer, June 20, 1951; children: Elaine Slaatte, Mark, Paul. AA, Kendall Coll., 1940; BA cum laude, U. ND, 1942; B.D. cum laude, Drew U., 1945, PhD, 1956; Drew fellow, Mansfield Coll., Oxford U., Eng., 1949-50. Ordained to ministry Meth. Ch. as elder, 1943. Pastor Detroit Conf. United Meth. Ch., 1950-65; assoc. prof. systematic theology Temple U., 1956-60; vis. prof., prof. philosophy and religion McMurry Coll. (now named McMurry U.), 1960-65; prof. dept. philosophy Marshall U., Huntington, W.Va., 1965-89, prof. emeritus, from 1989, chmn. dept., 1966-81, mem. grad. council, 1970-73, mem. research bd., 1974-76, mem. acad. standards and policy com., 1975-77, research grantee, 1976, 77; mem. bd. Campus Christian Center, 1973-75; prof. ethics St. Leo (Fla.) Coll., 1993. Lectr. Traverse City (Mich.) State Hosp., 1966-71, Am. Ontoanalytical Assn. internat. conf., Acapulco, Mex., 1970, World Congress Logotherapy, San Diego, 1980, other orgns. Author: Time and Its End, 1962, Fire in the Brand, 1963, The Pertinence of the Paradox, 1968, The Paradox of Existentialist Theology, 1971, Modern Science and the Human Condition, 1974, The Arminian Arm of Theology, 1977, The Dogma of Immaculate Perception, 1979, Discovering Your Real Self, 1980, The Seven Ecumenical Councils, 1980, The Creativity of Consciousness, 1983, Contemporary Philosophies of Religion, 1986, Time, Existence and Destiny, 1988, Critical Survey of Ethics, 1988; co-author: The Philosophy of Martin Heidegger, 1983, Religious Issues in Contemporary Philosophy, 1988, Our Cultural Cancer and Its Cure, 1995, A Re-Appraisal of Kierkegaard, 1995, Plato's Dialogues and Ethics, 1999, A Purview of Wesley's Theology, 2000; contbr. Analecta Frankliana, 1981; gen. editor: (series) Contemporary Existentialism; contbr. to theol. and philos. jours. Mem. W.Va. Conf. United Meth. Ch., 1966-87, ret., 1987; bd. dirs. Inst. for Advanced Philos. Research, 1979-90; chmn. bd. dirs. Salvation Army of Huntington, W. Va.; courtesy prof. U. South Fla., 1993-99. Recipient Outstanding Educators of Am. award, 1975, Profl. Excellence award Faculty Merit Found., State of W.Va., 1986, U. N.D. Found. award, 2000; named to Honorable Order of Ky. Colonels, W.Va. Ambassador of Good Will; named Internat. Man of Yr., 1993; NSF fellow, 1965, Benedum Found. rsch. grantee, 1970, NSF rsch.-grantee, 1965, 71. Mem. W.Va. Philos. Assn. (pres., 1966-67, 83-84), Am. Philos. Assn., AAUP, Am. Acad. Religion. Home: Cary, NC. Died Jan. 23, 2010.

SLATTERY, JAMES JOSEPH (JOE SLATTERY), actor; b. Memphis, Feb. 7, 1922; s. James Joseph and Katie May (Carlin) S.; m. Mary Margaret Costello, May 23, 1944 (dec. Aug. 1987); children: James Joseph, John P., Ann, Mary, Nancy; m. Marilyn Daus, Sept. 16, 1989. AB, Hendrix Coll., Conway, Ark., 1947. Pres. Am. Fedn. TV and Radio Artists, 1976-79. Actor. Served with USAAF, 1942-46; to lt. col. USAF (ret.) Recipient Disting. Grad. award Hendrix Coll., 1986. Mem. Screen Actors Guild. Roman Catholic. Died Oct. 2, 2009.

SLEIGH, SYLVIA, artist, educator; b. Llandudno, North Wales, May 8, 1916; came to U.S., 1961; d. John Harold and Katherine Amy (Miller) S.; m. Lawrence Alloway, June 28, 1954. Student, Sch. Art, Brighton, Sussex, Eng., 1932-36; diploma, U. London Extra-Mural Dept., 1947. Vis. asst. prof. SUNY-Stony Brook, 1978; instr. New Sch. Social Research, NYC, 1974-77, 78-80; Edith Kreeger Wolf disting. prof. Northwestern U., Evanston, Ill., 1977; vis. artist Baldwin Seminar Oberlin Coll., Ohio, 1982, New Sch. Social Rsch., NYC. One person shows include Bennington (Vt.) Coll., 1963, Soho 20 Art Gallery, NYC, 1974, 76, 80, 82, 85, 99, 2004, A.I.R. Gallery, NYC, 1974, 76, 78, Ohio State U., Columbus, 1976, Matrix, Wadsworth Atheneum, Hartford, Conn., 1976, Marianne Deson Gallery, Chgo., 1990, G.W. Einstein, Inc., NYC., 1980, 83, 85, U. Mo., Saint Louis, 1981, Zaks Gallery, Chgo., 1985, 95, Milw. Art Mus., Butler Inst., Youngstown, Ohio, 1990, Stiebel Modern, NYC, 1992, 94, Gallery 609, Denver, Canton (Ohio) Art Inst., Deven Golden Fine Arts, NYC, 1999, Phila. Art Alliance, Phila., 2001, Snug Harbor Cultural Ctr., Newhouse Ctr. Contemporary Art, S.I., NY, 2005, Hudson River Mus., Yonkers, NY, 2006, I-20 Gallery, NYC, 2007; exhibited in group shows Newhouse Gallery, S.I., NY, Stamford (Conn.) Mus., 1985, Albany Inst. Art, Cin. Art Mus., New Orleans Mus. Art, Denver Art Mus., Pa. Acad. Fine Arts, 1989, Carlsten Art Gallery, Stevens Point, Wis., 1993, Stiebel Modern, NYC, 1994, Soho 20, NYC, 1993, 96, Katzen Brown Gallery, NYC, 1989, Zaks Gallery, Chgo., 1986, Steinbaum Krauss Gallery, 1997, Deven Golden Fine Arts, Ltd., NYC, 1997, Rutgers U., New Brunswick, NJ, 1984, 86, RioArriba Gallery, Abiquiu, N.Mex., 1996, Milw. Art Mus., 1996, Steinbaum Krauss Gallery, 1997, NY Mus. exhbn. traveling until 2001, David and Alfred Smart Mus., Chgo., Broome St. Gallery, NYC, Deven Golden Fine Arts, NYC, A.I.R. Gallery, NYC, Apex Art Co., NYC, 1998, McKee Gallery, NYC, 1998, Royal Coll. Art, London, 1998, Heckscher Mus. Art, Huntington, N.Y., 1999, Printworks Gallery, 2000, SoHo 20, NYC, 2004, Mason Gross at Rutgers U., NJ, 2005, Mus. Contemp. Art, LA, 2006, I-20 Gallery, NYC, 2006, A+D Gallery, Chgo., 2007. Panelist Creative Artists Pub. Service Program, NYC, 1976. Nat. Endowment for Arts grantee, 1982, Pollock-Krasner Found. grantee, 1985. Mem. Women's Caucus for Art, Coll. Art Assn. (Lifetime Achievement in Art award, 2007). Home: New York, NY. Died Oct. 24, 2010.

SLITER, JOHN W., management consultant; b. Troy, NY, Sept. 8, 1934; s. Arthur John and Myrtle Irene (Little) S.; m. Jane Ann Wood, Aug. 15, 1953; children— Deborah Ann, John W., Christopher Carl, Rebecca Sue, Herbert Alan BBA, Bryant Coll., 1954. Co-gen. mgr. Sliter's Dairy, Inc., Troy, N.Y., 1954-61; regional merchandising dir. Am. Dairy Assn., Chgo., 1961-66; gen. mgr. Am. Dairy Assn. and Dairy Council of N.Y., Syracuse, 1966-73; chief exec. officer United Dairy Industry Assn., Rosemont, Ill., 1973-85; prin., owner J.W. Sliter Assocs., Wheeling, Ill., from 1985. Adv. trustee Coll. Agr., U. Ill., Champaign, 1983-86. Mem. Internat. Dairy Fedn. (bd. dirs. U.S. nat. com. 1980-85, chmn. 1981-84, pres. 1986-90), Internat. Milk Promotion Group (bd. dirs. 1980-84) Republican. Presbyterian. Avocations: traveling; serving as foster parents. Home: Mount Prospect, Ill. Died Dec. 9, 2009.

SLOAN, MARY JEAN, retired media specialist; b. Lakeland, Fla., Nov. 29, 1927; d. Marion Wilder and Elba (Jinks) Sloan. BS, Peabody Coll., Nashville, 1949; MLS, Atlanta U., 1978, SLS, 1980. Cert. libr. media specialist. Music dir. Pinecrest Sch., Tampa, Fla., 1949-50, Polk County Schs., Bartow, Fla., 1950-54; pvt. music tchr. Lakeland, 1954-58; tchr. Clayton County Schs., Jonesboro, Ga., 1958-59; media specialist Eastualley Sch., Marietta, Ga., 1959-89; ret., 1989. Coord. conf. Ga. Libr. Media Dept., Jekyll Island, 1982-83, sec., Atlanta, 1982-83, com. chmn. ethnic conf., Atlanta, 1978, pres., 1984-85, state pres., 1985-86; program chmn. Ga. Media Orgns. Conf, Jekyll Island, 1988. Contbr. to bibliographies. Recipient Walter Bell award Ga. Assn. Instrnl. Tech., 1988, Disting. Svc. award, 1991. Mem. ALA (del. 1984, 85, 90), NEA, Southeastern Libr. Assn., Am. Assn. Sch. Librs., Soc. for Sch. Librs., Internat., Ga. Assn. Educators (polit. action com. 1983), Beta Phi Mu, Phi Delta Kappa. Republican. Methodist. Died June 26, 2009.

SLOAN, SANDRA LYNN, health care administrator; b. Oak Park, Ill., July 2, 1958; d. David John and Donna Marie (Theis) S.; m. Glenn Eric Hahn, Oct. 5, 1985; children: Cody, Haley. BA, U. Ill., 1981; MS, Rush U., 1991. Realtor C-21 Sloan, Bensenville, Ill., 1981-89; asst. product mgr. Am. Hosp. Assn., Chgo., 1991-92; mgr. contract svcs. Rush Med. Assn., Chgo., 1992-94; dir. contract svcs. SNI Mgmt. Assn., Hinsdale, Ill., from 1994. Republican. Home: Clarendon Hills, Ill. Died Aug. 24, 2010.

SLOAN, WILLIAM PATRICK, printing company executive; b. Oak Park, Ill., Nov. 2, 1934; s. Frank A. and Thyra (Bartell) Sloan; m. Karen Mix Sloan, Jan. 31, 1980. BS, U. Ill., 1957. Mgr. composition R.R. Donnelley & Sons Co., Chgo., 1957—68; group mgr. Electronic Graphics divsn., 1968—73, regional sales mgr., 1973—78; pres., asst. sec., dir. Sorg Printing Co., Calif., from 1979, dir. Ill., from 1979. With US Army, 1956—57. Mem.: Printing Industries Calif., Western Stock Transfer Assn., Am. Soc. Corp. Secs., Printing Industries No. Calif. (dir. from 1980, treas. from 1981, v.p. from 1983), World Trade Club, Bankers Club (San Francisco), Olympic Club, Caxton Club, Commonwealth Club, Rotary, Sigma Iota Epsilon. Home: Belvedere Tiburon, Calif. Died June 10, 2010.

SLUNG, HILTON B., retired surgeon; b. Louisville, May 10, 1950; MD, U. Louisville, 1976. Diplomate Am. Bd. Surgery, Am. Bd. Colon and Rectal Surgery. Intern Georgetown U. Hosp., Washington, 1976-77, resident in gen. surgery, 1977-79, Marshall U. Hosp., Huntington, 1980-82; fellow in colon and rectal surgery Grant Hosp., Columbus, Ohio, 1983-84; mem. staff Jewish Hosp., Louisville, 1984-99, Suburban Hosp., 1984-99. Mem. courtesy staff Bapt. East Hosp., 1984—; clin. instr. surgery U. Louisville. Fellow ACS; mem. Am. Soc. Colon and Rectal Surgery, So. Med. Assn., Jefferson County Med. Soc. Died Apr. 15, 2009.

SMALL, ERWIN, veterinarian, educator; b. Boston, Nov. 28, 1924; Cert., Vt. State Sch. Agr., 1943; BS, U. Ill., 1955, DVM, 1957, MS, 1965. Diplomate: Am. Coll. Vet. Internal Medicine, Am. Coll. Vet. Dermatology. Intern Angell Meml. Animal Hosp., Boston, 1957-58; with U. Ill. Coll. Vet. Medicine, Urbana, 1958-92, prof. vet. clin. medicine, 1968-92, assoc. dean alumni and public affairs, chief of medicine, 1970-84, asst. dept. chmn., 1989-92, prof. emeritus, assoc. dean alumni and pub. affairs Urbana, from 1992. Contbr. articles to profl. jours. Served with USMC, 1944-46, 50-51, PTO. Recipient Nat. Gamma award Ohio State U., 1971, Ill. State VMA Svc. award, 1973, Nat. Zeta award Auburn U., 1974, Bustad Companion Animal Veterinarian award, 1993, Disting. Svc. award U. Ill. Alumni Assn., 1995; named Outstanding Tchr., Nordens Labs., 1967, Outstanding Educator, 1973, Outstanding Faculty Mem., Dad's Assn. U. Ill., 1990, Veterinarian of Yr., Mass. Soc. for Prevention Cruelty to Animals, 1993; recipient recognition for svc. with USMC War Dog Platoon, War Dog Meml., Quantico, Va., 2001, ISUMA Pres. award, 2002. Fellow Am. Coll. Vet. Pharmacology and Therapeutics; mem. AVMA (chmn. coun. edn. 1981-82, chmn. program com. 1983-87, Pres.'s award 1992, AVMA award 1998), Am. Animal Hosp. Assn. (award 1983, Midwest Region Svc. award 1989), Am. Coll. Vet. Dermatology (pres.), Internat. Vet. Symposia (pres.), Am. Assn. Vet. Clinics (pres., Faculty Achievement award 1992), Ill. Vet. Med. Polit. Action Com. (past chmn.), Chgo. Vet. Med. Assn. (lifetime achievement award 1997), Am. Coll. Vet. Internal Medicine (Robert W. Kirk award 1997), Coll. of Vet. Med. Alumni Assn. (Vet. Med. Achievement award 1997), Am. Legion, VFW, Moose, Omega Tau Sigma (pres. 1971-79), Phi Zeta, Gamma Sigma Delta. Republican. Jewish. Home: Champaign, Ill. Died July 1, 2009.

SMITH, BRIAN BETHEA, architect, development coordinator; b. Orangeburg, SC, Dec. 29, 1954; s. Hugh Elmore and Martha Elizabeth (Meares) Smith. BA in Architecture, Clemson U., 1977; MA in Architecture and Real Estate Devel., Ga. Inst. Tech., 1979. Registered architect, Ga. Architect Thompson, Ventulett & Stainback, Atlanta, 1979—81; architect, project mgr. Niles Bolton Assocs. Inc., Atlanta, from 1981. Contbr. Piedmont Arts Festival, from 1983; active Theater League Am., from 1984. Mem.: Sigma Nu, Tau Sigma Delta, Phi Eta Sigma, Urban Land Inst., AIA. Avocations: skiing, sailing, travel. Died Aug. 20, 2010.

SMITH, BRUCE SHERWOOD, retail executive; b. Norfolk, Va., May 26, 1961; s. Richard Ballenger and Carol (Bassett) S.; m. Jacquel Faris, Mar. 19, 1983; 1 child, Dana Jacquel. Student, Va. Poly. Inst., 1979-83. Salesman Nat. TV & Appliance, Blacksburg, Va., 1980-81, asst. mgr., 1981-83, mgr. Waynesboro, Va., 1983-85, Danville, Va., 1983-85, ops. mgr. Salem, Va., 1985-87, owner, pres. Burlington, N.C., from 1987. Episcopalian. Avocations: golf, recreational sports, hunting, fishing. Home: Salem, Va. Died Jan. 27, 2009.

SMITH, CATHERINE SHIRLEY, employment company executive; b. Malden, Mass., Apr. 10, 1930; d. Daniel John and Dolena Mackenzie (MacGinns) Smith. Student, Keene Tchrs. Coll., 1948—49, U. Fla., 1949—51; BS in Psychology, U. NH, 1952. Dept. mgr. John Hancock Co., Boston, 1952—53; office mgr. Am. Std. Co., Denver, 1953—57; owner, pres. Mile-Hi Employment, Inc., from 1958. Mem.: NOW, Colo. Rep. 250 Club, Nature Conservatory, Am. Mus. Natural History, Audubon Soc., Animal Protection Inst. Am., Denver Zool. Assn., Smithsonian Assn., Am. Soc. Profl. Exec. Women, Nat. Assn. Female Execs. Home: Denver, Colo. Died Mar. 1, 2010.

SMITH, DAVID JOSEPH, retired biochemistry educator; b. NYC, Aug. 8, 1921; s. Irving Lester and Jennie (Abelman) S.; m. Sylvia Butensky, Sept. 30, 1944; children: Judith, Lois, Diane. Student, NYU, 1937-40; DDS, Columbia U., 1944, MS in Philosophy, 1974. Lic. dentist. Assoc. research dentist N.Y. State Dept. Health, Albany, 1953-63; from asst. prof. to assoc. prof. biochemistry Columbia U., NYC, 1963-74, assoc prof. oral biology, 1971-74; prof. biochemistry, chmn. dept. Fairleigh-Dickinson U., Hackensack, N.J., 1974-85. Served to capt. U.S. Army, 1944-46, ETO. Fellow U. Coll., London, 1980-81. Mem. Biochem. Soc. Home: Palisades, NY. Died May 24, 2009.

SMITH, DONALD CAMERON, retired preventive medicine physician; b. Peterborough, Ont., Can., Feb. 2, 1922; arrived in U.S., 1952, naturalized, 1960; m. Jean Morningstar, Sept. 11, 1946. MD, Queen's U., 1945; MSc in Medicine, U. Toronto, Ont., 1948, DPH, 1949. Diplomate Am. Bd. Preventive Medicine, Am. Bd. Pediatrics. Intern Victoria Hosp., London, Ont., Canada, 1945-46; fellow in physiology U. Toronto, 1947—49; med. officer health Kent County (Ont.) Health Unit, 1950—52; Commonwealth Fund fellow in pediat. U. Mich. Hosp., 1952-55; prof. maternal and child health Sch. Pub. Health U. Mich., prof. pediat. Med. Sch., chmn. dept. health and human devel., 1961-79; prof. psychiatry and behavioral scis. Northwestern U. Med. Sch., Chgo., 1979-85; ret., 1985. Chmn. Medicaid Adv. Coun., 1969—72; vis. prof. maternal and child health Harvard U., 1969—72; prin. advisor health and med. affairs to gov., Mich., 1972—78; dir. Mich. Dept. Mental Health, 1974—78; chmn. State Pub. Health Adv. Coun., 1982—90; chmn. health care policy bd. Mich. Dept. Corrections, 1986—91; med. dir. Sisters Mercy Health Corp., 1981—91. Surgeon lt. Royal Can. Navy, 1946—47. Died May 17, 2009.

SMITH, DOUGLAS SYDNEY, army officer; b. Madison, Wis., Jan. 29, 1929; s. Sydney W. and Dora E. (Reed) S.; m. Mary Howard Harding, Oct. 4, 1969; children by previous marriage— Michael, Martha, Thomas, Sue, Brian, Stephen. BS in Bus. Adminstrn., St. Benedict's Coll., Atchison, Kans., 1967; MS in Adminstrn, George Washington U., 1972. Enlisted in U.S. Army, 1947, commd. 2d lt., 1954; advanced through grades to brig. gen. U.S. Army (Joint Chiefs of Staff, Pentagon); bn. comdr. 9th inf. div. Vietnam, 1968-69; asst. div. comdr. 24th Inf. Div., Ft. Stewart, Ga., 1981-83; asst. dep. chief staff tng. U.S. Tng. and Doctrine Command, 1983-84; pres. DMS Assocs., Inc., 1984-90; v.p. Sage Assocs., Inc., 1990-93. Active Boy Scouts Am., 1970-78. Decorated D.S.M., Silver Star with one oakleaf cluster, Legion of Merit, D.F.C., Bronze Star with V, Air medal, Purple Heart, numerous others. Mem. Assn. U.S. Army, U.S. Armor Assn., VFW, Mil. Order of Purple Heart. Clubs: Army-Navy. Episcopalian. Died Oct. 23, 2009.

SMITH, DWIGHT L., historian, educator; b. West Elkton, Ohio, Apr. 11, 1918; s. Clarence S. and Mary A. (Barnhart) S.; m. Jane de Leon, May 6, 1955; 1 child, Gregory B. AB, Ind. Ctrl. Coll., Indpls., 1940; AM, Ind. U., 1941, PhD, 1949; LittD, U. Indpls., 1987. Instr. Ind. Ctrl. Coll., Indpls., 1942-43, Ohio State U., Columbus, 1949-53; asst. prof., prof. Miami U., Oxford, Ohio, 1953-84, prof. emeritus, from 1984. Vis. prof. Centre Coll., Danville, Ky., 1952, Columbia U., N.Y.C., 1954-55, Ind. U., Bloomington, 1962-63, U. Alta., Edmonton, 1964, Colo. Coll., Colorado Springs, 1965, U. B.C., Vancouver, 1967, U. N.Mex., Albuquerque, 1968; rsch. historian Ohio Hist. Soc., Columbus, 1950-51; editor, cons. Am. Bibliog. Ctr., Santa Barbara, Calif., 1966-81; fellow Newberry Libr., Chgo., 1952, 64, 67; rsch. fellow Miami U., 1957, 59, 82; fellow Inst. Environ. Scis., Miami U., 1977; Lilly Endowment fellow Clements Libr., Ann Arbor, Mich., 1962; Samuel Foster Haven fellow Am. Antiquarian Soc., Worcester, Mass., 1982; rsch. fellow Huntington Libr., San Marino, Calif., 1983. Author: From Greene Ville to Fallen Timbers, 1952, The Western Journals of John May, 1961, Down the Colorado, 1965, Western Life in the Stirrups, 1965, The Photographer and the River, 1967, John D. Young and the Colorado Gold Rush, 1969 (award The Lakeside Classic 1969), Survival on a Westward Trek, 1989; (with C. Gregory Crampton) The Hoskaninni Papers, 1961, (with C. Gregory Crampton) The Colorado River Survey, 1987; (with Ray Swick) A Journey Through the West, 1997; bibliographer: (with Lloyd W. Garrison) The American Political Process, 1972, America: History and Life, Vol. 0, 1972; Afro-American History, Vol. 1, 1974, Indians of the United States and Canada, vol. 1, 1974 (award Outstanding Acad. Book for 1974 Choice), Era of the American Revolution, 1975, The American and Canadian West, 1979, Afro-American History, vol. 2, 1981, The History of Canada, 1983, Indians of the United States and Canada, vol. 2, 1983, The War of 1812, 1985; editor The Old Northwest, 1974-87; contbr. articles to profl. jours., chpts. to books. Pres. Friends of Librs., Miami U., 1979-80. Staff sgt. USAAF, 1943-46. Recipient rsch. grants Am. Philos. Soc., Phila., 1954, Caxton Club, Chgo., 1964, award of merit Am. Bibliog. Ctr., Santa Barbara, Calif., 1980, grant Nat. Endowment Humanities, 1977, rsch. grant Province of Que., 1981-82. Mem. Soc. Ethnohistory (pres. 1955-56), Assn. Bibliography of History (pres. 1979-80), Oxford Mus. Assn. (pres. 1957-58), Ohio Acad. History (pres. 1978-79, disting. svc. award 1985), Western History Assn. (award of merit 1993). Presbyterian. Home: Oxford, Ohio. Died May 6, 2010.

SMITH, EARL PEARSON, retired art educator; b. Detroit, Sept. 30, 1931; d. Millard E. and Iona M. (Pearson) S.; m. Violet A. Sherfey, Sept. 6, 1952; children: Stephen Earl, William Stewart, Jonathan Andrew. BA, Mich. State U., 1953, MA, 1957; PhD, Syracuse U., 1970. Cert. tchr., Ala., Mich., N.Y. Tchr. art and math. Southfield (Mich.) Pub. Schs., 1957-68; asst. prof. dept. curriculum and instruction U. Va., Charlottesville, Va., 1969-75; assoc. prof. dept. ednl. media Auburn (Ala.) U., 1975-85; prof. dept. art and classics Troy (Ala.) State U., 1985—94; ret., 1994. Guest lectr. Salen-Lindblad Cruising, N.Y.C., 1989; docent trainer Montgomery (Ala.) Mus. Art, 1990; Fulbright lectr. to Ghana, U.S. Info. Agy., Washington, 1987-88. Mem. editorial bd. Art Edn. Mag., Washington, 1988-92; curator (exhibit) Art of West Africa, 1989, dir. US Info. Agency Cultural Exch., Africa, 1993-94; artist (painting) Pastel Portraits. 1st. lt. U.S. Army, 1954-56. Summer Rsch. grantee Troy State U., 1989. Mem. Nat. Art Edn. Assn. (editorial cons. 1988-90, Art Educator of Yr. 1987-88), Ala. Art Edn. Assn. (higher edn. rep. to bd.), African Studies Assn., NEA (life). Presbyterian. Avocation: illustrating historical buildings and sites in the USA. Home: Rochester Hills, Mich. Died Jan. 1, 2009.

SMITH, FREDERICK COE, retired manufacturing executive; b. Ridgewood, NJ, June 3, 1916; s. Frederick Coe and Mary (Steffee) S.; m. Ruth Pfeiffer, Oct. 5, 1940; children: Frederick Coe, Geoffrey, Roger, William, Bart. BS, Cornell U., 1938; MBA, Harvard U., 1940. With Armstrong Cork Co., Lancaster, Pa., 1940-41; with Huffy Corp., Dayton, Ohio, 1946-86, pres., chief exec. officer, 1961-72, chmn., chief exec. officer, 1972-76, chmn., 1976-78, chmn. exec. com., 1979-86. Past chmn. Sinclair C.C. Found.; past chmn. nat. bd. dirs. Planned Parenthoo Fedn.; past dir. Internat. Parenthood Fedn.; past chmn. Dayton Found.; trustee emeritus Alan Gutmacher Inst., Ohio United Way; past chmn. employment and tng. com. Gov.'s Human Investment Coun. Lt. col. USAAF, 1941-46. Decorated Legion of Merit. Home: Dayton, Ohio. Died May 16, 2010.

SMITH, GEORGE EDWIN, physician; b. Lake Odessa, Mich., Apr. 12, 1914; MD, Univ. Mich. Medical Sch., 1939. Diplomate Am. Bd. Ob-Gyn. Intern Grace Hosp., Detroit, 1939-40; resident ob-gyn Detroit Womens Hosp., 1940-42,46-47; staff mem. Beaumont Hosp.; ob-gyn. pvt. practice, Royal Oak, Mich.; retired, 1979. Mem. AMA. Home: Royal Oak, Mich. Died Oct. 12, 2009.

SMITH, GEORGE THORNEWELL, retired state supreme court justice; b. Camilla, Ga., Oct. 15, 1916; s. George C. and Rosa (Gray) S.; m. Eloise Taylor, Sept. 1, 1943 (dec.). Grad., Abraham Baldwin Agrl. Coll., 1940; LLB, U. Ga., 1948. Bar: Ga. 1947. Assoc. Cain & Smith, Cairo, Ga., 1947-71; city atty. Cairo, 1949-58; atty. Grady County, 1950-59; solicitor Cairo City Ct., 1951-59; mem. Ga. House of Reps., 1959-67, speaker of the house, 1963-67; lt. gov. State of Ga., 1967-71; city atty. East Point, Ga., 1973-76; judge Ga. Ct. Appeals, 1976-81; justice Ga. Supreme Ct., Atlanta, 1981-91, presiding justice, 1990-91; of counsel Browning & Smith LLC, Marietta, Ga., from 1992. Past mem. exec. com. Nat. Conf. Appellate Judges; vice chmn. Nat. Conf. Lt. Govs. Trustee Nat. Arthritis Found. Lt. comdr. USN, 1940-45. Only person in the state's history to serve in an elective capacity in all 3 brs. of govt.; recipient Guardian of Justice award, Ga. Trial Lawyers, Regent's Hall of Fame award, U. Ga. Found., 2007, Disting. Svc. award, Abraham Baldwin Agrl. Coll., 2007. Mem. State Bar Ga., Cobb County Bar Assn., Lawyers Club Atlanta, Am. Legion, VFW, Moose, Kiwanis. Avocations: hunting, golf. Home: Marietta, Ga. Died Aug. 23, 2010.

SMITH, GORDON HOWELL, retired lawyer; b. Syracuse, NY, Oct. 26, 1915; s. Lewis P. and Maud (Mixer) S.; m. Eunice Hale, June 28,1947; children: Lewis Peter, Susan S. Rizk, Catherine S. Maxson, Maud S. Daudon. BA, Princeton U., 1932-36; LL.B., Yale U., 1939. Bar: N.Y. 1939, Ill. 1946. Asso. Lord, Day & Lord, NYC, 1939-41, Gardner, Carton & Douglas, Chgo., 1946-51; partner Mackenzie, Smith & Michell, Syracuse, 1951-53, Gardner, Carton & Douglas, 1954-57, 60-85, of counsel, 1986-96. Sec., dir. Smith-Corona, Inc., 1951-54, v.p., Syracuse, 1957-60 Bd. dirs. Rehab. Inst. Chgo., chmn., 1974-78, 83-86; bd. dirs. United Way Met. Chgo., 1962-85. Served to lt. comdr. USNR, 1941-46. Mem. Am. Soc. Corporate Secs., Am., Ill., Chgo. bar assns. Clubs: Comml., Law, Econ., Legal, Chgo., Old Elm (Chgo.). Died Dec. 1, 2009.

SMITH, HAL HORACE, III, stock brokerage executive; b. Detroit, May 25, 1931; s. Hal Horace and Margaret Thompson (Wheeler) S.; m. Kathleen J. Graham, Dec. 1, 1856; children: Hal Horace IV, Graham W., Dean M., Sarah M., Jeffrey Y. Student, Trinity Coll., 1952. Salesman Smith, Hague Noble Co., Detroit, 1954—56; staff rsch. dept. Reynolds & Co., NYC, 1956; ptnr. Smith, Hague & Co., Detroit, 1956—71, pres., from 1971. Chmn. bd. Griswold & Co., Detroit, from 1974; pres., dir. Detroit Stock Exch., 1970—74; gov. Assn. Stock Exch. Firms, 1965—71. With US Army, 1952—54. Mem.: Security Traders Assn. Detroit, Nat. Assn. Security Dealers (past vice-chmn., dir. dist. 8), Detroit Athletic Club, Detroit Club, Country Club, Bond Club Detroit. Episcopalian. Home: Grosse Pointe, Mich. Died Oct. 30, 2009.

SMITH, HOWARD FRANK, economic educator; b. Detroit, June 17, 1918; s. Frank Joseph and Lilian (Musolf) Smith; m. Ann Smith; children: Mark Andrew, Andrea Helen Smith Kingman. AB, Wayne U., 1940; MBA, Harvard U., 1942; MA, Am. U., 1951, PhD, 1963. Economist War Prodn. Bd., Washington, 1942—43, Dept. Army, Tokyo, 1946—50; fgn. svc. officer Dept. State, Washington, 1951—68; prof. econs. Calif. Poly. State U., SanLuis Obispo, from 1968. Contbr. articles to profl. jours. Served to capt. US Army, 1943—46, ETO, PTO. Mem.: Western Econ. Assn., Am. Econ. Assn. Republican. Home: Morro Bay, Calif. Died May 13, 2010.

SMITH, JAMES PERRY, agricultural educator; b. Southwest City, Mo., Aug. 15, 1933; s. Eual Clay and Susan Marie (Perry) Smith; m. Molly Jayne Smith, Aug. 21, 1955; children: James Duston, Rebecca Dawn. BS, Okla. State U., 1960; MS, Ark. U., 1963. Cert. life vocat. agr. tchr. Mo. Instr. animal sci. dept. Okla. State U., Stillwater, 1964—69; sec. Okla. Quarter Horse Assn., 1969—73; vocat. agr. instr. McDonald County HS, Anderson, Mo., 1978—85; technician Eagle-Picher Industries, from 1985; processor Teledyne, Neosho, Mo., 1974—78. Show supt. McDonald County Fair Bd.; mem. McDonald County Extension Coun., Econ. Security Corp.; road commr. Buffalo spl. dist.; bd. dirs. Sunday Sch. supt. Goodman United Meth. Ch. Contbr. articles to profl. jours. Sgt. US Army, 1955—57. Recipient Pres.'s award, 1979. Mem.: Mo. Cattleman's Assn., Mo. Vacat. Assn., Am. Vocat. Assn. Home: Joplin, Mo. Died Mar. 1, 2009.

SMITH, JESSE GRAHAM, JR., dermatologist, educator; b. Winston-Salem, NC, Nov. 22, 1928; s. Jesse Graham and Pauline Field (Griffith) S.; m. Dorothy Jean Butler, Dec. 28, 1950; children: Jesse Graham, Cynthia Lynn, Grant Butler. BSM, Duke U., 1962, MD, 1951. Diplomate: Am. Bd. Dermatology (dir. 1974-83, pres. 1980-81). Intern VA Hosp., Chamblee, Ga., 1951—52; resident in dermatology Duke U., 1954—56, assoc. prof. dermatology, 1960—62, prof., 1962—67; resident U. Miami, 1956—57, asst. prof., 1956—60; prof. dermatology Med. Coll. Ga., 1967—91, chmn. dept. dermatology, 1967—91, acting chmn. dept. pathology, 1973—75, acting v.p. devel., 1984—85; chief staff Talmadge Meml. Hosp., Augusta, Ga., 1970—72; chief divsn. of dermatology U. South Ala., Mobile, 1991—98, prof. dermatology, 1991—99, prof. emeritus, from 1999. Mem. adv. coun. Nat. Inst. Arthritis, 1975-79 Mem. editl. bd. Archives of Dermatology, 1963-72, Jour. Investigative Dermatology, 1966-67, Jour. AMA, 1974-80; mem. editl. bd. So. Med. Jour., 1976-2000, assoc. editor, 1991-92, editor, 1992-2000; editor Jour. Am. Acad. Dermatology, 1978-88; contbr. chpts. to books, articles to profl. jours. Served with USPHS, 1952-54. Recipient Disting. Alumnus award Duke U. 1981 Fellow ACP, Royal Soc. Medicine; mem. Am. Acad. Dermatology (hon., dir. 1971-74, 78-88, pres.-elect 1988-89, pres. 1989-90, master 2003), Can. Dermatol. Assn. (hon.), Am. Dermatol. Assn. (hon. sec. 1976-81, pres. 1981-82), Soc. Investigative Dermatology (dir. 1964-69, pres. 1979-80), S.E. Dermatol. Assn. (sec. 1970-71, pres. 1975-76), Ga. Soc. Dermatology (pres. 1979-80), So. Med. Assn. (chmn. sect. dermatology 1973-74, Disting. Svc. award 2005), Assn. Profs. Dermatology (dir. 1976-77, 80-82, pres. 1984-86), Med. Rsch. Found. Ga. (bd. dir. 1967-91, pres. 1974-75), Alpha Omega Alpha Home: Mobile, Ala. Died May 18, 2010.

SMITH, JOHN EDWIN, philosophy educator; b. Bklyn., May 27, 1921; s. Joseph Robert and Florence Grace (Dunn) S.; m. Marilyn Blanche Schulhof, Aug. 25, 1951 (dec. 2006); children: Robin Dunn, Diana Edwards. AB, Columbia U., 1942, PhD, 1948; BD, Union Theol. Sem., NYC, 1945; MA, Yale U., 1959; LL.D., U. Notre Dame, 1964. Instr. religion and philosophy Vassar Coll., 1945-46; instr., then asst. prof. Barnard Coll., 1946-52; mem. faculty Yale U., from 1952, prof. philosophy, 1959—91, chmn. dept., 1961—91, Clark prof. philosophy, 1972-91, Clark prof. philosophy emeritus, 1991—2009. Vis. prof. Union Theol. Sem., 1959, U. Mich., 1958; guest prof. U. Heidelberg, Germany, 1955-56; Fagothey chair of philosophy U. Santa Clara, 1984, vis. prof. Boston Coll., 1992; Dudleian lectr. Harvard, 1960; lectr. Am. Week, U. Munich, Germany, 1961; Suarez lectr. Fordham U., 1963; pub. lectr. King's College, Univ. London, 1965; Aquinas lectr. Marquette U., 1967; Warfield lectr. Princeton Theol. Sem., 1970; Fulbright lectr. Kyoto U., Japan, 1971; Sprunt lectr. Union Theol. Sem., Va., 1973; Mead-Swing lectr. Oberlin Coll., 1975; H. Richard Niebuhr lectr. Elmhurst Coll., Ill., 1977; Merrick lectr. Ohio Wesleyan U., 1977; Roy Wood Sellars lectr. Bucknell U., 1978; O'Hara lectr. U. Notre Dame, 1984; Winston Churchill lectr. Bristol (Eng.) U., 1985; Hooker disting. vis. prof. Mc Master U., 1985; mem. adv. com. Nat. Humanities Inst., New Haven, 1974, dir., 1977-80; Winston Churchill lectr. Bristol U., Eng., 1985. Author: Royce's Social Infinite, 1950, Value Convictions and Higher Education, 1958, Reason and God, 1961, The Spirit of American Philosophy, 1963, 2d edit., 1983, The Philosophy of Religion, 1965, Religion and Empiricism, 1967, Experience and God, 1968, revised edit., 1995, Themes in American Philosophy, 1970, Contemporary American Philosophy, 1970, The Analogy of Experience, 1973, Purpose and Thought: The Meaning of Pragmatism, 1978, America's Philosophical Vision, 1992, Jonathan Edwards, Puritan, Preacher, Philosopher, 1992, Quasi-Religions: Humanism, Marxism, Nationalism, 1994, Reason, Experience, and God, 1997; translator: (R. Kroner): Kant's Weltanschauung, 1956; editor: (Jonathan

Edwards): Religious Affections, Vol. 2, 1959, An Edwards Reader, 1995; gen. editor, Yale edit.: Works of Jonathan Edwards, 1965-91, gen. editor emeritus, 1992—; Editorial bd.: Monist, 1962-2009, Jour. Religious Studies, Philosophy East and West, Jour. Chinese Philosophy, The Personalist Forum, Jour. Faith and Philosophy, Jour. Speculative Philosophy. Named Hon. Alumnus, Harvard Div. Sch., 1960; recipient Herbert W. Schneider award Soc. for Advancement of Am. Philosophy, 1990, Founder's medal Metaphys. Soc. Am., 1996; Am. Coun. Learned Socs. fellow, 1964-65. Mem. Culinary Inst. Am. (dir. New Haven affiliate), Am. Philos. Assn. (v.p. 1980, pres. 1981), Am. Theol. Soc. (pres. 1967-68), Metaphys. Soc. Am. (pres. 1970-71, founder's medal, 1996), Hegel Soc. Am. (pres. 1971), Charles S. Peirce Soc. (pres. 1992). Home: Hamden, Conn. Died Dec. 7, 2009.

SMITH, LORAN BRADFORD, political science professor; b. Medford, Mass., July 23, 1946; s. Gordon T. and Edith A. S. BA, Salem State Coll., 1968; MA, Okla. State U., 1971; PhD, U. Nebr., 1980. Instr. Black Hills State Coll., Spearfish, S.D., 1971-74, Augustana Coll., Sioux Falls, S.D., 1974-77; asst. prof. Mo. So. State Coll., Joplin, 1980-82, Washburn U., Topeka, Kans., 1982-86, assoc. prof., 1988-92; grad. faculty U. Kans., Lawrence, 1988-89; prof. Washburn U., from 1992. Election analyst KSNT-TV, Topeka, 1984-92, KTKA-TV, Topeka, 2008-. Contbr. articles to profl. jours. Chair pilot task force City of Topeka, 1983-84, mem. charter rev. com., 1999; chair Univ. Coun., 2003-2005; mem. coll. faculty coun., chair CAS curriculum com., social sci. divsn. Mem. Am. Polit. Sci. Assn., Am. Soc. Pub. Adminstrs. (Kans. chpt. v.p. 1985-87, pres. 1987-88), Urban Affairs Assn., Kansas Delta Alumni Corp., Sigma Phi Epsilon (Disting. Alumnus award 1997, vol. Yr. 2008). Home: Hudson, Kans. Died July 24, 2009.

SMITH, MARTIN HENRY, retired pediatrician; b. Gainesville, Ga., Nov. 3, 1921; s. Charles E. and Mamie Mae (Emmett) S.; m. Mary Gillis, Feb. 25, 1950; children: Susan, Margaret, Mary MD, Emory U., 1945. Diplomate Am. Bd. Pediatrics. Intern City Hosp. System, Winston-Salem, NC, 1945-46; fellow in infectious diseases Grady Meml. Hosp., Atlanta, 1948-49; resident Henrietta Egleston Hosp., Atlanta, 1949-50, Children's Hosp., Washington, 1950-51; practice medicine, specializing in pediatrics Gainesville, Ga.; ret., 1988; clin. asst. prof. Emory U. Hosp., Atlanta; chief of staff Hall County Hosp., Gainesville, 1965-66. Mem. Nat. Vaccine Adv. Commn., 1990—, chmn., 1991. Contbr. articles to profl. jours. Chmn. Nat. Vaccine Adv. Com., 1991—. Capt. M.C., U.S. Army, 1946-48 Fellow Am. Acad. Pediatrics (chpt. chmn. 1966-69, dist. chmn. 1977-83, pres.-elect 1984-85, pres. 1985-86); mem. Hall County Med. Soc. (pres. 1960), Ga. Pediatric Soc. (pres. 1965-66), Med. Assn. Ga., AMA, Alpha Omega Alpha Clubs: Chattahoochee Country (Gainesville); Piedmont Driving (Atlanta). Episcopalian. Home: Gainesville, Ga. Died Jan. 18, 2010.

SMITH, NORMAN CLARK, fund raising and non-profit management consultant; b. Hartford, Conn., Jan. 2, 1917; s. Raymond W. and Elinor (Smith) S. AB, Middlebury Coll., 1939; postgrad., Hartford Coll. Law, Trinity Coll. Tchr. Loomis Sch., 1945-50, adminstr., tchr., 1952-53, asst. bus. mgr., 1953-55, bus. mgr., 1955-58, controller, 1958-63; treas. Vassar Coll., 1963-64; v.p. devel., planning Emory U., Atlanta, 1964-76; v.p. univ. devel. U. Del., 1976-79. Bd. dirs., past chmn. bd. Nat. Soc. Fund Raising Execs.; past trustee LoomisInst., Watkinson Sch.; past chmn. Ga. Conservancy; past pres. Mashantucket Land Trust of Southeastern Conn.; trustee emeritus, pas pres. Conn. River Mus., Essex; mem. Conn. State Coun. on Environ. Quality, Naval War Coll. Found. (mem. The Navy League); mem. citizens adv. coun. Project Oceanology; trustee Conn. Antiquarian and Landmarks Soc.; former mem. Nat. Exec. Svc. Corps.; past pres. Groton Edn. Found. Capt. USNR, 1941-45, 50-52; commanding officer Conn. State Naval Militia, 1946-50. Decorated Navy Cross. Mem. Chi Psi, Omicron Delta Kappa. Clubs: Rotary. Home: Mystic, Conn. Died Jan. 17, 2009.

SMITH, NORMAN OBED, retired physical chemist, educator; b. Winnipeg, Man., Can., Jan. 23, 1914; came to U.S., 1950, naturalized, 1958; s. Ernest and Ruth (Kilpatrick) S.; m. Anna Marie O'Connor, July 1, 1944; children: Richard Obed, Graham Michael, Stephen Housley. B.Sc., U. Man., 1935, M.Sc., 1936; PhD, NYU, 1939. Teaching fellow NYU, 1936-39; mem. faculty dept. chemistry U. Man., Winnipeg, 1939-50, asst. prof., 1946-49, assoc. prof., 1949-50, Fordham U., NYC, 1950-65, prof. chemistry, 1965-84, prof. emeritus, from 1984, chmn. dept., 1974-78; ret., 1984. Sr. phys. chemist Arthur D. Little, Inc., Cambridge, Mass., 1957; indsl. cons. Author: (with others) The Phase Rule and Its Applications, 1951, Chemical Thermodynamics, A Problems Approach, 1967, Elementary Statistical Thermodynamics, A Problems Approach, 1982; contbr. to: Ency. Brit, 1974. Fellow Chem. Inst. Can.; mem. Am. Chem. Soc., Asso. Can. Coll. Organists, Am. Guild Organists (dir. chpt. 1964-66, 79-82, 91-92), Sigma Xi, Phi Lambda Upsilon. Home: Arlington Heights, Ill. Died May 29, 2010.

SMITH, PETER, chemist, educator, consultant; b. Ashton-Upon-Mersey, Cheshire, Eng., Sept. 7, 1924; came to U.S., 1951; s. Peter and Winifred Emma (Jenkins) S.; m. Hilary Joan Hewitt Roe, 1951; children: Helen Andrews Winifred, Eric Peter, Richard Harry, Gillian Carol. BA Queens' Coll., Cambridge U., 1946, MA, 1949, PhD, 1953. Jr. sci. officer Royal Aircraft Establishment, Farnborough, Hampshire, Eng., 1943-46; demonstrator chemistry dept. Leeds U., Yorkshire, England, 1950-51; postdoctoral research fellow in chemistry Harvard U., Cambridge, Mass., 1951-54; asst. prof. chemistry Purdue U., West Lafayette, Ind., 1954-59, Duke U., Durham, N.C., 1959-61, assoc. prof., 1961-70, prof., 1970-95, prof. emeritus chemistry, from 1995. Contbg. author: chem. research jours. Fulbright post-doctoral scholar Fulbright Commn., Harvard U., 1951-53 Mem. Am. Chem. Soc., Royal Soc. Chemistry, Am. Phys. Soc., Sigma Xi, Phi Lambda Upsilon, Alpha Chi Sigma Home: Durham, NC. Died Sept. 1, 2009.

SMITH, RICHARD HOWARD, banker; b. Tulare, Calif., Aug. 27, 1927; s. Howard Charles and Sue Elizabeth (Cheyne) Smith; m. Patricia Ann Howery Smith, Mar. 12, 1950 (dec. Sept. 2001); children: Jeffrey Howard, Holly Lee, Gregory Scott, Deborah Elaine; m. Charlene Burruel Smith, Mar. 27, 2004. BA, Principia Coll., 1958; LLB, LaSalle U., 1975; postgrad., Sch. Banking U. Wash., 1972. Prin. Aurora Elementary Sch., Tulare, 1951—53, Desert Sun Sch., Idyllwild, Calif., 1953—55; trust adminstr. trainee Bank Am., San Diego, 1955—58; asst. trust officer Ventura, Redlands, Riverside, LA, 1958—65, Security Pacific Bank, Fresno, Calif., 1965—68, trust officer, 1968—72, v.p., mgr., 1972—88, Security Pacific Bank, Pasadena, 1988—94; v.p. Bank America, LA, 1994—95, ret., 1995; pres. Fiduciary Svcs., Fresno, from 1995; instr. San Bernardino Valley Coll., from 1962, Fresno City Coll., from 1977. With USN, 1945—46. Home: Fresno, Calif. Deceased.

SMITH, RICHARD SCHIEDT, steel company executive; b. Lancaster, Pa., Aug. 25, 1922; s. Howard Persifor and Norma Ruth (Schiedt) S.; m. Mary Elizabeth Allen, Jan. 24, 1948; children: G. S. Wylie, Abby Anne, Laura Elizabeth. AB, Amherst Coll., 1943. With Lionel D. Edie & Co., NYC, 1946-49, Northwestern Mut. Life Ins. Co., Milw., 1949-52; with First Nat. City Bank N.Y., 1952-62, v.p., 1957-62; v.p., treas. M.A. Hanna Co., Cleve., 1962-63; v.p. finance Hanna Mining Co., Cleve., 1963-64; v.p. adminstrn. Nat. Steel Corp., Pitts., 1964-72, group v.p., 1972-77, sr. v.p., 1977-81, exec. v.p., 1981-82, vice chmn., from 1982, also dir. Dir. United Techs. Corp., Hartford Ins. Group, St. John d'el Rey Mining Co. Served with AUS, 1942-45. Decorated Purple Heart.; Bronze Star; Presdl. Unit citation with oak leaf cluster. Mem. Am. Mgmt. Assn. Clubs: Duquesne (Pitts.), Fox Chapel Golf (Pitts.); Laurel Valley Golf (Ligonier, Pa.); Augusta (Ga.) Nat. Golf. Home: Pittsburgh, Pa. Died July 31, 2010.

SMITH, ROBERT CORNELIUS, lawyer; b. Hammond, Ind., Sept. 10, 1925; s. John Decatur and Grace Melvina (Kirtley) Smith; m. Jeannette Vaughn Renegar, Dec. 23, 1944; children: Kirtley, Douglas, Vaughn, Calvin. BBA, Tulane U., 1947, LLB, 1948. Bar: La. 1948, US Dist. Ct. (ea. dist.) La. 1948, US Dist. Ct. (we. dist.) La. 1955, US Ct. Appeals (5th cir.) 1949. Assoc. Milling, Saal, Godchaux, New Orleans, 1948—50; chief atty. crime div. Legal Aid Bur., 1950—53; atty. Amoco Prodn. Co., 1953—63; sr. atty., 1963—79; regional atty., from 1979; mem., chmn. legal com. Offshore Operators Assn., New Orleans, from 1963; mem. com. on exploration & prodn. law Am. Petroleum Inst., Washington, from 1980. Coun. commr. Area Boy Scouts Am., New Orleans, 1968—70; pres. Orleans Parish Sch. Bd., 1970—72, Assn. Retarded Citizens, 1974; mem. Coun. Devel. Disabilities, Baton Rouge, 1970—83; bd. dirs. So. Baptist Hosp., from 1983. Comdr. USNR, 1943—46, PTO. Recipient Silver Beaver award, Boy Scouts Am., New Orleans, 1972, Cert. of Merit, New Orleans, 1982. Mem.: New Orleans Bar Assn., La. Bar Assn., Essex (New Orleans), Bienville (sec. 1982—84). Republican. Baptist. Home: New Orleans, La. Died Jan. 9, 2010.

SMITH, ROBERT MOORS, anesthesiologist; b. Winchester, Mass., Dec. 10, 1912; s. Francis E. and Elsie C. (Davis) S.; m. Margaret Louise Nash, Aug. 7, 1937; children: Jonathan E., Marcia A., Karen E. AB, Dartmouth Coll., 1934; MD, Harvard U., 1938. Diplomate: Am. Bd. Anesthesiology. Rotating intern Faulkner Hosp., Jamaica Plain, Mass., 1938-39, asst. in pathology, 1939; intern in surgery Boston City Hosp., 1939-41; gen. practice medicine Cohasset, Mass., 1941-42; anesthesiologist Children's Hosp. Med. Center, Boston, 1946-81, dir. anesthesiology, 1946-80, pres. staff, 1966-68; assoc. anesthesiologist Peter Bent Brigham Hosp., Boston, 1958-61; asso. anesthesiologist Boston Lying-In Hosp., 1964-70; instr. anesthesia Harvard Med. Sch., Boston, 1948-55, assoc. in anesthesia, 1955, asst. clin. prof. anesthesia, 1963-66, assoc. clin. prof., 1966-81, clin. prof. anesthesia, 1976-81, clin. prof. emeritus, from 1981; chief anesthesiology Kennedy Meml. Children's Hosp., 1981-88; anesthesiologist Franciscan Children's Hosp., 1988-94. Bd. dirs. Minuteman council Boy Scouts Am. Served to maj. U.S. Army, 1941-46. Recipient Disting. Svc. award Am. Soc. Anesthesiologists, 1988. Fellow Am. Coll. Anesthesiologists (gov. 1952-58); mem. AMA, Mass. Med. Soc., New Eng. Soc. Anethesiologists (pres. 1966), Mass. Soc. Anesthesiologists (pres. 1955, dir. 1965-68), New Eng. Pediatric Soc., Assn. Univ. Anesthesiologists, Am. Acad. Pediatrics (chmn. com. pediatric anesthesiology 1963-64, 76-77), Royal Acad. Surgeons (Ireland) (hon.), Pan Am. Med. Soc. Home: Woburn, Mass. Died Nov. 25, 2009.

SMITH, ROBERT WALTER, food company executive; b. Chgo., Nov. 11, 1937; s. Ernest Gilmer and Anna (Reptik) S.; m. Audrey Mavis Segar, Apr. 20, 1962; children: Melissa Ann, Kathleen Diane, Michael Robert. BS, U. Ariz., 1963. Mgmt. trainee Fleming Cos. Inc., Houston, 1963-64, mgr. store planning, 1964-65, Austin, 1965-66, Phila., 1966-72, dir. site selection Topeka, 1972-75, dir. store devel., 1975-83, v.p. store devel. Oklahoma City, from 1983, sr. v.p. retail devel., from 1993. Mem. Nat. Assn. Corp. Real Estate Execs., Internat. Coun. Shopping Ctrs. Republican. Lutheran. Home: Oklahoma City, Okla. Died July 5, 2010.

SMITH, STEVEN JEROME, home building company executive; b. Phila., Sept. 24, 1940; s. Clarence and Margaret (O'Conner) S.; m. Rebecca Reed, 1960; children: Scott, Jennifer. SB in Indsl. Mgmt., MIT, 1962. Various positions with Whirlpool, Benton Harbor, Mich., 1962-70, Engelhard Industries, Murray Hill, N.J., 1970-72, Ryan Homes Inc., Pitts., 1972-84, pres., chief operating officer, 1984-86, pres., chief exec. officer, from 1986. Bd. dirs. NVRyan L.P., McLean, Va., Union Nat. Bank, Pitts. Mem. adv. bd. Salvation Army, Pitts., 1986—; agt. Class of 1962, Cambridge, Mass., 1962—; chmn. bd. trustees D.T. Watson Hosp., Sewickley, Pa., 1983—; bd. dirs. Pitts. Pub. Theater, 1986—. Recipient Corp. Leadership award MIT, 1985. Mem.: Allegheny Country, Edgeworth (Sewickley). Avocations: paddle tennis, golf, puzzles. Home: Sewickley, Pa. Died Apr. 18, 2010.

SMITH, THOMAS EARLE, JR., lawyer, state senator; b. Oxford, NC, July 22, 1938; s. Thomas Earle and Margaret Louise (Osterhout) Smith; m. Elizabeth Eulalia Munn, June 23, 1962; children: Mary Dresden, Amy Louise. AB, Davidson Coll., 1960; JD, USC, 1963. Bar: SC Bar Assn. 1963. Mem. firm James P. Mozingo, 1963—65; ptnr. firm Nettles, Smith, Turbeville and Reddeck, Pamplico, 1973—79; pvt. practice Pamplico, SC, 1965—73, from 1979; ptnr. Smith-Floyd, from 1989. Dir. Pamplico Bank and Trust Co., Johnsonville State Bank, SC; ptnr. Ind. Warehouse, Pamplico, from 1972; mem. SC House of Reps., 1966—72, SC Senate, 1973—88. Recipient Outstanding Legislator award, SC Coun. Exceptional Children, 1976; named Senate of Yr., SC Assn. Retarded Citizens, 1975, Legislator of Yr., SC Young Dems., 1979. Mem.: ABA, SC Bar Assn., Lions Club, Shriners, Masons. Democrat. Methodist. Home: Pamplico, SC. Died Apr. 1, 2010.

SMITH, VIRGINIA BEATRICE, retired academic administrator; b. Seattle, June 24, 1923; d. Frank B. and Myrtle M. (Partridge) S. BA, U. Wash., 1944, JD, 1946, MA in Econs., 1950; postgrad., Columbia U., 1948-49, LHD (hon.), 1957, Hood Coll., 1977, Ottawa U., 1974, Alverno Coll., 1982, De Paul U., 1982, Gettysburg Coll., 1983, Empire State Coll./SUNY, 1986, Seattle Pacific U., 1986; DHL (hon.), R.I. Coll., 1978; DCL (hon.), Bloomfield Coll., 1985; DH (hon.), Alfred U., 1985. Bar: Wash. 1947, Calif. 1958. Price economist Seattle Dist. Office Price Adminstrn., 1944-46; instr. econs. and bus. Coll. of Puget Sound, Tacoma, 1947-48, Seattle Pacific Coll., 1949-50, asst. prof., 1950-51, assoc. prof., 1951-52, chmn. dept. econs. and bus., 1950-52; program coord. Inst. Indls. Rels. U. Calif., Berkeley, 1952-60, adminstrv. asst., 1958-60, asst. to v.p., 1962-65, asst. v.p., 1965-67; assoc. firm Sam Kagel, San Francisco, 1958-67; asst. dir. Carnegie Commn. on Higher Edn., Berkeley, 1967-71, assoc. dir., 1971-73; dir. fund for improvement of postsecondary edn. US Dept. Health Edn. & Welfare (HEW), Washington, 1973-77; pres. Vassar Coll., Poughkeepsie, N.Y., 1977-86; acting pres. Mills Coll., Oakland, Calif., 1990-91. Assoc. counsel to trustee Yuba Consol. Industries, 1963-64; mem. American-USSR Seminar on Higher Edn., 1976; faculty mem. Salzburg (Austria) Seminar in Am. Studies, summer, 1976; mem. Commn. of Scholars, Ill. Bd. Higher Edn., 1975, U.S. Del. to Paris OECD Conf. on Higher Edn., 1973; dir. Marine Midland Banks, 1977-90, Harcourt Brace Jovanovich Contbr. articles on edn. to profl. publs. Chmn. Berkeley Pers. Bd., 1970-73; trustee Ednl. Testing Svc., 1977-81, chmn., 1981; trustee Carnegie Found. for Advancement of Teaching, 1980-83, Culinary Inst. Am., 1980-86; mem. Def. Adv. Com. on Women in the Svcs., 1979-81. Fulbright scholar, 1956-57 Mem. ABA (chmn. commn. nonprofl. legal studies in colls. and univs. 1984-89), Assn. Am. Colls. (bd. dirs. 1977-82, vice chmn. 1981, chmn. 1982), Soc. Values in Higher Edn. (pres. bd. dirs. 1981-86). Died Aug. 27, 2010.

SMITH, WILLIAM T., II, state senator, farmer; b. Corning, NY, Jan. 25, 1916; s. Maynard and Carrie (Shriver) Smith; m. Dorothy Nowak Smith; children: William T. III, Bonnifer, Deborah, Michael, Judith Smith Kelemen(dec.). BA, NY State Coll. Agr., Cornell U., 1938. Owner, mgr. Smithome Farms, Big Flats, NY; mem. NY State Senate, from 1962, dep. majority leader. Mem. Nat. Commn. Against Drunk Driving, Presdl. Commn. Drunk Driving, 1982—83; mem. bd. dir. Students Against Driving Drunk, Chemung County Planning Bd. NY, 1958—62; mem. Big Flats Rep. Town Com., Big Flats Park Commn. Recipient NY State Youth Bur. Disting. Svc. award, 1974, Outstanding Legislator of Yr. award, Nat. Rep. Legislators Assn., 1983, Law Maker of Yr. award, Nat. Child Support Enforcement Assn., 1985. Mem.: Big Flats C. of C. (trustee), Corning Country, Coldbrook, Fin & Feather, Fur, Rotary. Republican. Presbyterian. Home: Big Flats, NY. Died Mar. 30, 2010.

SMITH, WILLIAM TERRY, health care products executive; b. Topeka, June 1, 1942; s. Robert Edward and Elsie Marie (Reilly) S.; m. Marcia B. Baughman, Mar. 28, 1964; children— Amy, Andrew BS in Bus. Adminstrn., Northwestern U. Various mktg. positions Mead Johnson & Co., Evansville, Ind., 1966-75; various mktg. and bus. positions Abbott Labs., Chgo. and Columbus, Ohio, 1975-79, Bausch & Lomb, Rochester, N.Y., 1979-81, exec. v.p. Soflens div., 1981-82, pres. profl. products div., 1982-83, sr. v.p., group pres. profl. eye care products, 1983-85, also dir.; pres., chief exec. officer Bola Optilal, Pztaluma, Calif., 1985-87, Sola Ophthalmics, Phoenix, 1987-89, Intelligent Surg. Lasers, San Diego, from 1990. Bd. dirs. Better Vision Inst., N.Y.C., Roberts Wesleyan Coll., Rochester Republican. Avocations: travel; tennis. Home: Scottsdale, Ariz. Died Aug. 20, 2009.

SMOTRICH, DAVID ISADORE, architect; b. Norwich, Conn., Oct. 6, 1933; s. Max Z. and Ida (Babinsky) S.; m. Bernice D. Strachman, Mar. 25, 1956; children: Ross Lawrence, Maura Faye, Hannah. AB, Harvard Coll., 1955, MArch, 1960. Master planning team, Town of Arad, State of Israel, 1961-62; assoc. Platt Assocs., NYC, 1963-65; gen. ptnr. Smotrich & Platt, NYC, 1965-74, Smotrich Platt & Buttrick, NYC, 1975-76, Smotrich & Platt, NYC, 1976-85, David Smotrich & Ptnrs., NYC, from 1985. Cons. to Jerusalem Master Plan Office, Israel Ministry of Housing, 1967. Planning bd. Town of New Castle, N.Y., 1974-81; exec. bd. Road Rev. League, Bedford, N.Y., 1966-70. With AUS, 1955-57. Recipient Bard award, 1969, 85, Archtl. Record award, 1971, 73-75, 78, Design award HUD, 1980. Mem. AIA (Nat. Honor award 1969, N.Y. State Honor awards 1984, 94, Cmty. Design awards 1991, 93, AIA Coll. of Fellows 1993), Assn. Engrs. and Archs. in Israel, Phi Beta Kappa, Harvard Club (N.Y.C.). Home: Chappaqua, NY. Died June 20, 2010.

SMULLIN, LOUIS DIJOUR, electrical engineer, educator; b. Detroit, Feb. 5, 1916; married; 4 children BSE., U. Mich., 1936; S.M., MIT, 1939. Draftsman Swift Elec. Welder Co., Mich., 1936; engr. Ohio Brass Co., 1936-38, Farnsworth TV Corp., 1939-40, Scintilla Magneto div. Bendix Aviation Corp., 1940-51; sect. head radiation lab. MIT, Cambridge, 1941-46; head microwave tube lab. Fed. Telecommunications Labs. div. Internat. Telephone and Telegraph Corp., N.J., 1946-48; head tube lab. Research Lab. Electronics, 1948-50; div. head Lincoln Lab., 1950-55; from assoc. to prof. MIT, Cambridge, 1955-76, Dugald Caleb Jackson prof. elec. engring., from 1976, chmn. dept. elec. engring., from 1967. Mem. steering com. Kanpur Indo-Am. Program, 1961-65; vis. prof. Indian Inst. Tech., Kanpur, 1965-66; NSF working group sci. and engring. instrn., India; bd. govs. Israel Inst. Tech. Fellow IEEE, Am. Acad. Arts and Scis.; mem. Nat. Acad. Engring. (telecommunications com.), Am. Phys. Soc. Died June 4, 2009.

SMYTH, JOSEPH VINCENT, manufacturing executive; b. Belfast, Ireland, July 18, 1919; s. Joseph Leo and Margaret M. (Murray) S.; m. Marie E. Cripe, Mar. 22, 1941; children: Kevin W., Brian J., Ellen M., Vincent P. BS cum laude, U. Notre Dame, 1941. With Arnolt Corp., Warsaw, Ind., 1946-63, exec. v.p., gen. mgr., until 1963; pres., gen. mgr. Hills-McCanna Co., Carpentersville, Ill., 1963-72; pres. Lunkenheimer Co., Cin., 1972-79; v.p. Condec Flow Control Group, Chgo., 1979-82; cons., from 1982. Mem.: K.C. Home: Orlando, Fla. Died Nov. 10, 2009.

SMYTH, RICHARD ANDREW, philosophy and liberal studies educator; b. Milton, Mass., Dec. 28, 1933; s. Ralston Blackburn and Eleanor Rogers (Greene) S.; m. Luan Lawson, Sept. 15, 1956; children: Nathan, Susan, James. BA, Yale U., 1955; postgrad., Freiburg U., Germany, 1956-57, Princeton U., 1957; MA, Ind. U., 1959, PhD, 1961. Prof. U. N.C., Chapel Hill, from 1961. Author: Forms of Intuition, 1978; contbr. articles to profl. jours. With USMCR, 1957-63. Mem. AAAS (coun. 1963), Am. Philos. Assn., Am. Comparative Lit. Assn., N.C. Philos. Assn. (past pres.). Home: Chapel Hill, NC. Died Jan. 19, 2009.

SNEDEKER, JOHN HAGGNER, university president; b. Plainfield, NJ, May 30, 1925; s. Alfred H. and Anna Marie (Ward) S.; m. Noreen I. Davey, Dec. 30, 1950; children—John D., Philip A., Patrick W. BS cum laude, N.Y. U., 1951, MA, 1951; Ed.D., Ind. U., 1959. Dir. lab. human devel. U. Mont., 1952-56; cons. psychologist research Purdue U., 1955; assoc. prof., dir. bur. research Ball State U., 1956-61; prof. higher edn., research asso. Ind. U., 1958; prof., dean Western Wash. State U., Bellingham, 1961-62; pres. Western N.Mex. U., Silver City, from 1962. Mem. exec. bd. Internat. Coun. Spl. Edn., 1952-56; Rocky Mountain regional rep. APA, 1953-56; mem. Gov. Wash. Com. Licensing Tchr. Edn., 1961, Wash. State Legislature Rsch. Tech. Com., 1961. Author or co-author rating scales, attitude and opinion measurement devices; contbr. jours. Bd. dirs. Nat. Sci. Fair; trustee N.Mex. Health Found. Served with U.S. Army, 1943-48. Fellow AAAS; mem. Midwest Psychol. Assn., Inter-Am. Soc. Psychology, Am. Ednl. Research Assn., Holland Soc. N.Y. Died Aug. 6, 2010.

SNELBECKER, GLENN EUGENE, psychologist, educator; b. Dover, Pa., Sept. 24, 1931; s. William S. and Anna M. Snelbecker; m. Janice C. Fixler, Sept. 23, 1962; children: David M., Karen A., Laura B. BS, Elizabethtown Coll., Pa., 1957; MS, Bucknell U., Lewisburg, Pa., 1958; PhD, Cornell U., 1961. Lic. psychologist, Pa. Clin. psychology postdoctoral intern Brockton (Mass.) VA Hosp. and Boston U., 1961—62; clin. psychologist U.S. VA Hosp., Brockton, 1961—67; prof. Temple U., Phila., 1967—2010. Cons. Mgmt. Assn. Tech. Comm. and Health, Wyndmoor, from 1963; dir. project RAINBOW U.S. Dept. Edn., Phila Sch. Dist., Phila., 1995—2001; co-dir. model program elem., HS tchr.-technologists NSF, Phila., 1985—92; keynote spkr. Fifth Internat. Conf. on Tech. and Christian Edn., Seoul, 2004, Second Internat. Conf. Asia-Pacific Econ. Cooperation Cyber Cmty., Busan, 2004; subject An Interview with Glenn E. Snelbecker. Author: Learning Theory, Instructional Theory, 1985, (online learning book) Functional Relevance, 2008; contbr. chapters to books (Book of Yr. award, 1985, 1988), articles to profl. jours. Sgt. US Army, 1952—55. Fellow APA, Phila. Soc. Clin. Psychologists, Am. Ednl. Rsch. Assn. Avocation: travel. Home: Glenside, Pa. Died Jan. 24, 2010.

SNELL, KATHRYNE ELIZABETH, retired public relations executive; b. Bicknell, Ind., Dec. 16, 1922; d. Homer Hugh and Lima Blanche (Wagstaff) Cargal; grad. Community Leadership Devel. Acad. Lansing Community Coll., 1983; m. Elwyn Snell, Apr. 4, 1944; children— Kathryne Ann Snell Nuveman, Edward Franklin. Cashier/bookkeeper, agt. Indian Trials Bus Line, Owosso, Mich., 1941-45; personnel clk. Universal Electric Co., Owosso, 1947-51, sec. to v.p./dir. indsl. relations, 1951-55, exec. sec. to chmn. bd., 1955-78, dir. pub. rels., 1972-88; rep. J.A. Co., 1981-85. Sec., Washington Sch. P.T.A., 1958-60; sec. Shiawassee dist. exec. bd. Girl Scouts U.S., 1960-61; sec. Mother's Club, troop and Post 85 Boy Scouts Am., 1963-65, co. coord. Post 68, 1982-89; bd. dirs. Com. on Alcohol and Drug Abuse, Shiawassee area, 1974-76; mem. Bicentennial Com., Owosso area, 1976-77; mem. indsl. com., spl. gifts com. Shiawassee Area United Way, 1974-79, campaign chmn., 1988-89, bd. dirs., 1988—, v.p. 1989, pres., 1990-91; mem. Shiawassee dist. Boy Scouts Am., 1976—, mem. exec. bd. Tall Pine council, 1985-90, recipient Silver Beaver award, 1985; mem. Heritage Bridge Com., City of Owosso, 1983-86; chmn. bd. Christian Edn., First Bapt. Ch., 1967-69, ch. trustee, 1979-86 chmn., 1981-86, moderator 1986-90, lic. lay minister, 1987. Mem. Profl. Secretaries Internat. (Sec. of Year Shiawassee Valley chpt. 1969, pres. Mich. div. 1975-77), Pvt. Industry Coun. (chmn. program planning and assessment com. 1984-88), Owosso-Corunna Area C. of C. (hon. life, mem. exec. bd., v.p. Ambs. 1977-80, Internat. Woman of Year in Bus. and Industry 1975, dir. 1973-87, v.p. 1979-80, pres. 1981-83, Curwood Festival Mountie 1985—, Athena award 1988, Mountie of Yr. 1996), NAFE, Shiawassee YWCA. Clubs: Owosso City (bd. govs., sec. 1983-84, v.p. 1984-87), Zonta (dir. 1979-81, pres. 1983-85), Order Ea. Star. Home: Owosso, Mich. Died June 9, 2009.

SNODGRASS, LOUISE VIRGINIA, state legislator, dental assistant; b. Balt., June 28, 1942; d. Peter Francis and Mary Frances (Gelwicks) Kramer; m. Franklin P. Snodgrass III, Sept. 9, 1962; children: Anne, Mark. Cert. dental asst., U. Md., Balt. Lic. dental asst. Dental asst., from 1966; mem. Md. Ho. of Dels. from Dist. 3, from 1995. Mem. Commerce and Govt. Matters Subcom. Md. Ho. of Dels., mem. Subcom. on Procurement, Unfunded Mandates Task Force. Elected liaison Md. State Bd. Dental Examiners; mem. Frederick County (Md.) Ctrl. Com., 1986-94, past vice chair, past sec., 1986-90; bd. dirs. Md. Mayors Assn., 1991-94, hon. mem., 1994; past pres. Frederick County Coun. Govt., 1991, 92, 93; liaison to transp. svcs. adv. com. Md. Mcpl. League, 1990-94, chmn. state conv., 1991, legis. mem., 1991-94, appointed to subcom. on annexation, 1992, legis. chmn., 1993-94, past pres., v.p., sec.-treas. Frederick chpt.; Mayor Middletown, Md., 1986-94; active J. Elmer Harp Med. Ctr., Inc. Assn., Frederick Meml. Hosp. Aux., Frederick County Rep. Men's Club; life mem. Middletown Hist. Soc. Named Outstanding Legislator of Yr., Md. Mcpl. League, 1995, cert. appreciation, 1996. Mem. Md. Dental Assts. Assn. (past pres.), Am. Dental Assts. Assn. (trustee). Died June 12, 2009.

SNYDER, CHARLES ROYCE, sociologist, educator; b. Haverford, Pa., Dec. 28, 1924; BA, Yale U., 1945, MA, 1949, PhD, 1954. Mem. staff Ctr. Alcohol Studies Yale U., 1950-60, asst. prof. sociology, 1956-60; prof. sociology So. Ill. U., Carbondale, 1960-85, chmn. dept., 1964-75, 81-85, prof. emeritus, from 1985. Vis. prof. human genetics Sackler Sch. Medicine, Tel Aviv U., 1980; cons. behavioral scis. tng. com. Nat. Inst. Gen. Med. Scis., NIH, 1962-64; mem. planning com., chmn. program 28th Internat. Congress Alcohol and Alcoholism, 1964. Author: Alcohol and the Jews, 1958; editor: (with D.J. Pittman) Society, Culture and Drinking Patterns, 1962; mem. editl. bd. Quar. Jour. Studies on Alcohol, 1957-83; assoc. editor Sociol. Quar., 1960-63. Mem. theol. commn. United Ch. of Christ, 1964-71; bd. dirs. Ill. Stewardship Alliance, 1990-95. With USNR, WWII. Fellow Am. Sociol. Assn.; mem. Soc. Study Social Problems (v.p. 1963-64, rep. to council Am. Sociol. Assn. 1964-66), Midwest Sociol. Soc. (bd. dirs. 1970-71), Pyrenees Homeowners Assn. (pres. 2009), AAUP. Home: Denver, Colo. Died Sept. 15, 2009.

SNYDER, WILLIAM E., lawyer; b. Evanston, Ill., Nov. 3, 1944; BS, Northwestern U., 1966, JD cum laude, 1969. Bar: Ill. 1969. Law clk. to Hon. Julius J. Hoffman, 1969-71; mem. Michael, Best & Friedrich, Chgo. Articles editor Northwestern U. Law Rev., 1968-69. Named Nat. Coll. Debate champion, 1966. Mem. ABA, Am. Arbitration Assn. Comml. Panel of Arbitrators, Nat. Assn. Securities Dealers (mem. nat. panel arbitrators), Ill. State Bar Assn., Chgo. Bar Assn. Died Jan. 30, 2009.

SOBERMAN, ROBERT KENNETH, astrophysicist; b. NYC, Apr. 8, 1930; s. Julius and Helen (Mile) Soberman; m. Diana Helene Gross, June 6, 1954; children: Ellen M. Novick, June A. Jarema. BS, CCNY, 1950; MS, NYU, 1952, PhD, 1956; MBA, Temple U., Phila., 1972. Physicist AVCO, Wilmington, Mass., 1957—59; assoc. prof. elec. engring. Northeastern U., Boston, 1959—60; br. mgr. meteor physics Air Force Geophysics Lab., Bedford, Mass., 1960—66; mgr. environ. sci. Gen. Electric, Phila., 1966—76; v.p. rsch. U. City Sci., Phila., 1976—78; dir. dept. applied sci. Franklin Rsch. Ctr., Phila., 1978—88. Adj. prof. Drexel U., Phila., 1968—78; lectr. astronomy U. Pa., from 1972. Contbr.: articles to profl. jours. Fellow: Explorers Club; mem.: Internat. Astron. Union, Am. Geophys. Union, Am. Astronom. Soc., AAAS, Sigma Xi. Achievements include patents for electro-optics and electro-mechanics. Home: Philadelphia, Pa. Died Mar. 2, 2009.

SOLES, ADA LEIGH, former state legislator, government advisor; b. Jacksonville, Fla., May 19, 1937; d. Albert Thomas and Dorothy (Winter) Wall; m. James Ralph Soles, 1959; children: Nancy Beth, Catherine. BA, Fla. State U., 1959. Mem. New Castle County Libr. Adv. Bd., 1975-80, 95—, chmn., 1975-77; chmn. Del. State Libr. Adv. Bd., 1975-78; mem. Del. State Ho. Reps., 1980-92; sr. advisor Gov. of Del., 1993-94; mem. U. Del. Libr. Assocs. Bd., 1995—; adminstrv. asst. U. Del. Commn. on Status of Women, 1976-77; acad. advisor U. Del. Coll. Arts and Scis., 1977-92. Mem. LWV (state pres. 1978-80), Phi Beta Kappa, Phi Kappa Phi, Mortar Bd., Alpha Chi Omega. Episcopalian. Home: Newark, Del. Died June 7, 2010.

SOLVAY, JACQUES ERNEST, chemical company executive; b. Ixelles, Brussels, Dec. 4, 1920; s. Ernest John and Marie Helene (Graux) Solvay; m. Marie-Claude Boulin, Feb. 9, 1949; children: Anne-Christine, Marie Noel, Carole, Jean-Marie. Degree in Elec. & Mech., U. Brussels, 1947. With Solvay & Cie, Brussels, from 1955, dir., 1967—71, chmn. bd., from 1971; dir. Soc. Generale de Banque, Brussels; chmn. Soltex Polymer Corp., from 1974, Inst. Edith Cavell-Marie Depage, from 1970. Decorated comdr. Order of Leopold, knight Order Brit. Empire, Legion of Honor (France). Mem.: Belge-Brit. Union (pres.), Fedn. des Industries Chimiques de Belgique (pres.), Inst. Internat. de Physiqie et de Chimie (pres.). Home: La Hulpe, Belgium. Died Apr. 29, 2010.

SOMMER, ELMER CHARLES, oil industry executive; b. Pitts., June 15, 1931; s. Elmer Charles and Edythe Harris (Payne) S.; m. Dorothy Ody, Dec. 28, 1963; children: Sandra, Michelle, Amy. BS in Chem. Engring., U. Pitts., 1954; postgrad., Claremont Grad. Sch., 1980. U.S. sales mgr. Phillips Petroleum Co., Akron, Ohio, 1970—73, worldwide tech. svc. mgr., 1973—75, mgr. corp. budgeting Bartlesville, Okla., 1975—78, mgr. corp. planning, 1978—83, mgr. worldwide licensing, from 1983. Mem.: Am. Chem. Soc., Masons. Republican. Methodist. Home: Bartlesville, Okla. Died Dec. 18, 2009.

SOMMER, JOSEPH THOMAS, manufacturing executive; b. Chgo., Apr. 23, 1941; s. Joseph J. and Solveig E. Sommer; children: Joseph Thomas, Jeffrey Todd. BS, U. Ill., 1964. With Magnetic Coil Mfg. Co., Chgo., from 1964, exec. v.p., 1972—87, pres., from 1987; mgmt. cons. Mem.: Sigma Chi (bd. dirs. chpt.). Home: Palatine, Ill. Died Sept. 13, 2009.

SONIN, AIN A., mechanical engineering educator, consultant; b. Tallinn, Estonia, Dec. 24, 1937; came to U.S., 1965; m. Epp Jurima, July 24, 1961; children: Juhan, Aldo. BA Sc., U. Toronto, Ont., Can., 1960, MA Sc., 1961, PhD, 1965. Rsch. fellow, teaching asst. U. Toronto, 1960-65; asst. prof. MIT, Cambridge, 1965-68, assoc. prof., 1968-74, prof. mech. engring., from 1974. Sr. scientist Thermo Electron Corp., Waltham, Mass., 1981-82; cons. in field. Contbr. over 70 articles to profl. jours. in fluid and thermal sciences. Mem. ASME, AAAS, Am. Phys. Soc. Achievements include 4 patents in field. Home: Lexington, Mass. Died June 27, 2010.

SONNENBERG, BEN, playwright, poet, editor, producer; b. NYC, Dec. 30, 1936; s. Benjamin and Hilda (Caplan) S.; m. Dorothy Gallagher, Mar. 10, 1981; children by previous marriages: Susanna, Emma, Saidee. Literary advisor Oxford (Eng.) Playhouse, 1963-65; lit. mgr. Repertory Theatre of Lincoln Ctr., NYC, 1971-72; lectr. drama ctr. Juilliard Sch., NYC, 1977-78; editor Grand Street, NYC, 1981-90. Author: Jane Street, The Courtship of Rita Hayworth, Mole Wedding, (plays) Poems of Anna Comnena and More Poems, 1990, Lost Property, Memoirs and Confessions of a Bad Boy, 1991; editor: Grand Street Reader, 1986, Performance and Reality: Essays from Grand Street; prodr. Westbeth Growing Up, 1995, Breadman, 1996, Lavender Lake, 1997; contbr. articles to The Nation, London mag., Yale Rev., Raritan, Harper's/Queen (Eng.), The Paris Rev. Fellow Royal Soc. of Lit.; mem. PEN. Home: New York, NY. Died June 24, 2010.

SORENSEN, ROBERT HOLM, diversified technology company executive, retired; b. Racine, Wis., Mar. 14, 1921; s. Viggo Marius and Lydia Marie (Holm) S.; m. Harriet Norma Kruse, Feb. 27, 1944; children: Anitra A., Scott E., Lyle R. BSE.E., Northwestern U., 1947; grad. advanced mgmt. program, Harvard U., 1957; DSc (hon.), Grand View Coll., 1991. Sr. engr. Engring. Research Assocs., Inc., St. Paul, 1947-51; ops. mgr. Sperry Rand Corp. (formerly Remington Rand Inc.), Norwalk, Conn., 1952-59; with Perkin-Elmer Corp., 1959-86, v.p. optical group Norwalk, 1965-66, sr. v.p., 1966-73, pres., chief operating officer, 1973-77, chief exec. officer, 1977-84, chmn. bd., 1980-85; retired, 1986. With USN, 1943-46. Recipient Award of Merit, Northwestern U., 1987. Mem. Tau Beta Pi, Eta Kappa Nu. Clubs: Silver Spring Country (Ridgefield, Conn.). Home: Peterborough, NH. Died Sept. 24, 2009.

SORENSEN, TED (THEODORE CHAIKIN SORENSEN), lawyer, former federal official; b. Lincoln, Nebr., May 8, 1928; s. Christian Abraham and Annis (Chaikin) Sorensen; m. Camilla Palmer, 1949 (div.); children: Eric Kristen, Stephen Edgar, Philip Jon; m. Sara Elbery, 1964 (div.); m. Gillian Martin, June 28, 1969; 1 child, Juliet Suzanne BS in Law, U. Nebr., 1949, LLB, 1951, LLD, 1969, U. Canterbury, 1966, Alfred U., 1969, Temple U., 1969, Fairfield U., 1969, U. Wis., Stout, 1998. Bar: Nebr. 1951, NY 1966, US Supreme Ct. 1966, DC 1971. Atty. Fed. Security Agy., 1951-52; asst. to Senator John F. Kennedy US Senate, 1953-61; sec. New Eng. Senators' Conf., 1953-59; spl. counsel to Pres. John F. Kennedy The White House, 1961-64; sr. counsel Paul, Weiss, Rifkind, Wharton & Garrison, NYC, 1966—2002, of counsel, 2002—10. Mem. Pres.'s Advisory Com. on Trade Negotiations, 1978; chmn. Governor's Panel on NY State Export Credit Agy., 1982. Author: Decision Making in the White House, 1963, Kennedy, 1965, The Kennedy Legacy, 1969, Watchmen in the Night: Presidential Accountability After Watergate, 1975, A Different Kind of Presidency, 1984, Counselor: A Life at the Edge of History, 2008; co-author (with Ralf Dahrendorf): A Widening Atlantic? Domestic Change and Foreign Policy, 1986; editor: Let the Word Go Forth: The Speeches, Statements and Writings of John F. Kennedy, 1988, Why I Am A Democrat, 1996. Dem. candidate for US Senate, 1970; chmn. Dem. Nat. Com. task force on polit. action, 1981-82, mem. task force on fgn. policy, 1986; nat. co-chair Gary Hart's Presdl. Campaign, 1984; mem. Internat. Trade Roundtable, 1985; chmn., 1994-99, dir. Twentieth Century Fund., Coun. on Fgn. Rels., 1993-2004, Ctrl. Asian-Am. Enterprise Fund, 1995-99, Nat. Dem. Inst. for Internat. Affairs, 1993-99; trustee NY Acad. Medicine, 1991-97; advisor Russian-Am. Press and Info. Ctr., pres's Commn. on White House Fellows; chmn. adv. bd. Brandeis Internat. Ctr. Ethics, Justice and Pub. Life; mem. adv. bd. Partnership a Secure America; hon. co-chair ABA Commn. on the Renaissance of Idealism in the Legal Profession. Named one of Ten Outstanding Young Men of Yr., Jr. C. of C., 1961; fellow Inst. Politics, Harvard U. Kennedy Sch. Govt., 2002. Mem. Order of Coif, Phi Beta Kappa. Died Oct. 31, 2010.

SOSOWER, MARK LAWRENCE, educator; b. Teaneck, NJ, Apr. 26, 1949; s. Leon Sosower and Evelyn Malek; m. Mary Julia Linehan, June 15, 1980; children: Deborah Linehan, Robert Linehan. PhD, NYU, 1981. Vis. lectr. NC State U., Raleigh, 1982—85, disting. prof. Author: (monograph) Palatinus Graecus 88 and the Manuscript Tradition of Lysias. Home: Durham, NC. Died Dec. 27, 2009.

SOTER, GEORGE NICHOLAS, advertising executive; b. Chgo., May 16, 1924; s. Nicholas A. and Emily (Damascus) S.; m. Effie Hartocollis, Feb. 7, 1949; children: Nicholas, Thomas, Peter. Student, U. Chgo., 1947-51. Writer McCann-Erickson, Chgo., 1951-53; with Needham, Louis & Brorby, Chgo., 1954-62, v.p., creative dir. NYC, 1958-62; v.p., assoc. creative dir. Lennen & Newell Inc., NYC, 1962-67; v.p., co-dir. creative svcs., mgmt. supr. Kenyon & Eckhardt Inc., NYC, 1968-73; exec. v.p., creative dir. Pampuzac-Soter Assocs. Inc., NYC, 1974-76; sr. writer Marsteller Inc., NYC, 1980-82; v.p., creative Lord, Geller, Federico, Einstein, Inc., NYC, 1982-87; sr. v.p., creative dir. Great Scott Advt. Co. Inc., NYC, 1987-93; dir. Soter Advt. & Mktg. Consulting Svcs., NYC, from 1993; copy editor Am. Mgmt. Assn., NYC, 1995—2006. Founder, pres. Greek Island Ltd., N.Y.C., 1963—86; dir. Interpub. Product Devel. Workshop, N.Y.C., 1967. With U.S. Army, 1943-47, ETO. Home: New York, NY. Died Jan. 8, 2009.

SOUDER, PAUL CLAYTON, banker; b. Greencastle, Ind., Dec. 2, 1920; s. Dewey C. and Julia (Dowell) S.; m. Doris E. Elliott, Sept. 27, 1941; children— Douglas Paul, Julie Jan. AB, DePauw U., 1941; grad., Harvard Grad. Sch. Bus. Adminstrn., 1943, Rutgers U., 1951. Office mgr. Comml. Credit Corp., 1941; credit mgr. Mich. Nat. Bank, 1946, asst. v.p. Saginaw, 1947-52; v.p. Saginaw, 1952-62; sr. v.p., dir., 1961-71; exec. v.p., 1971-72; pres., dir., 1972-80; vice chmn., 1980-85. Chmn. MNC Outstate Banks, 1980; chmn. bd. dirs. Mich. Nat. Bank; bd. dirs. MNB Valley Bank, MNB-West Bank, MNB-Michiana Bank, Mich. Bank-Huron, Mich. Bank-Mid South, Auto-Owners Ins. Co., Auto-Owners Life Ins. Co. Mich. Nat. Bank, Mich. Nat. Corp., Detroit & Mackinac R.R. Co., Jameson Corp., Lake Huron Broadcasting Corp., Homeowners Mut. Ins. Co., Mich. Nat. Bank Midland, Property Owners Ins. Co., Owners Ins. Co., W.F. McNally Co., Inc., Mich. Nat. Bank Detroit, Mich. Nat. bank-Mid Mich.; past chmn. bd. dirs. First Nat. Bank, East Lansing. Author: Financing Oil Production in Michigan, 1951. Past pres. Greater Mich. Found.; trustee Mich. Wildlife Found., Mich. State U. Devel. Fund; bd. dirs., v.p. Frank N. Andersen Found.; bd. dirs. Woldumar Nature Center. Served from ensign to lt. comdr. USNR, 1942-46. Recipient Distinguished Service awards; Saginaw's Outstanding Young Man. Mem. Robert Morris Assos., Am., Mich. bankers assn., Ind. Petroleum Assn., Am., Mich. oil and gas assns., C. of C. (dir.) Clubs: Saginaw (Detroit), Bankers (Detroit), Econ. (Detroit); Otsego Ski. Methodist. Home: Lansing, Mich. Died Nov. 29, 2009.

SOUTHWORTH, WILLIAM DIXON, retired education educator; b. Union City, Tenn., Dec. 28, 1918; s. Thomas and Gertrude (Dyer) S.; m. Violet Kuehn, July 22, 1944 (dec. 2006); 1 child: Linda Jean. PhB, Marquette U., Milw., 1948, MEd, 1950; PhD, NYU, 1961. Tchr., coach La Follette Sch., Milwaukee County, Wis., 1948-51; teaching dist. prin. Grand View Sch., Milwaukee County, 1951-56; supervising dist. prin. Maple Dale Sch., Milwaukee County, 1956-58; bldg. prin. Main St. Sch., Port Washington, NY, 1958-65; asst. supt. for elem. edn. Huntington pub. schs., NY, 1965-67; assoc. prof., acting head dept. adminstrn. and supervision St. John's U., Jamaica, NY, 1967, chmn. dept., 1968-73, prof., 1968-84. Parliamentarian for 35 internat., nat. regional orgns., expert witness, pub. moderator, and workshop leader. Author: Care and Nurture of the Doctoral Candidate, 1968, 74, Q The Story of Captain Quimby Scott, U.S. Navy WWII, 1997, The Art of Successful Meetings, 1997, Murder on the Flagship, 1998, Corpsman!, 1998, Murder Impossible, 2002, The Wonderful World of Words: How to Build and Retain a Superior Vocabulary, 2002, The Sensual Sailor, 2003, Murders in Old Main, 2004; contbr. over 270 articles to ednl. jours., condominium and parliamentary publs. With USN, 1938—44. Lutheran. Home: Saint Petersburg, Fla. Died Oct. 8, 2009.

SOUWEINE, JONATHAN Z., lawyer; b. Bklyn., Mar. 16, 1948; s. William and Harriet S.; m. Judith D.W. Souweine; children: Jesse, Daniel, Isaac. BA cum laude, Columbia U., 1969; JD cum laude, Harvard U., 1972. Bar: Mass. 1972, US Dist. Ct. Mass. 1973. Law clk. to U.S. Dist. Ct. Judge Dist. of Conn., 1972-73; atty., Mass PIRG, 1973—76; asst. atty. gen. Commonwealth of Mass., 1977-78; bd. dirs. Mass. Water Resources Authority, 1985-89; bd. suprs. Eastern Hampshire Regional Solid Waste Dist., 1990-94; bd. dir. Mass PIRG Edn. Fund, 1998—2004; ptnr. Lesser, Newman, Souweine & Nasser, Northampton, Mass. Bd. dir. Conn. River Watershed Coun., 1998—2004, Jewish Cmty. of Amherst, 1998—99; mem. Mass. Highway Conn. River Crossing Study Adv. Grp., 2002—04. Mem. Hampshire County Bar Assn., Franklin County Bar Assn., Mass. Bar Assn., Mass. Acad. Trial Lawyers (bd. govs. 1989-94, 96—), Assn. Trial Lawyers Am. Home: Amherst, Mass. Died Apr. 7, 2009.

SOYER, DAVID, cellist, music educator; b. Phila., Feb. 24, 1923; s. Samson and Esther (Faggin) Soyer; m. Janet Putnam, June 23, 1957; children: Daniel, Jeffrey. Student pub. schs., NYC; DFA (hon.), U. South Fla., 1976, SUNY, 1983. Prof. cello Curtis Inst. Music, 1967; prof. music U. Md.; prof. Manhattan Sch. Music Boston U.; prof. Juilliard Sch. Music, NYC. Musician (cellist): Bach Aria Group, 1948—49, Guilet Quartet, 1949—51, New Music Quartet, 1954—55, Guarneri String Quartet, from 1964 (5 Grammy awards for Guarneri Quartet recs.). With USNR, 1942—46. Mem.: Century Assn. Jewish. Home: New York, NY. Died Feb. 25, 2010.

SPARKS, ALLEN KAY, electronics company executive; b. Chgo., Sept. 26, 1933; s. Allen Kay and Violet Elsie (Lindstrom) Sparks; m. Nina Suzanne Bade, Nov. 5, 1955; 1 child, Alison Claire. AB in Chemistry, Ripon Coll., 1955; PhD in Chemistry, Case Inst. Tech., 1960. Dir. chem. rsch. Signal Co., Des Plaines, Ill., 1972—75, v.p. tech. chem. div. East Rutherford, NJ, 1975—76, v.p. ops. chem. div., 1976—78, v.p., gen. mgr., 1978—80, Norplex Div., LaCrosse, Wis., 1980—85, pres., 1985—86, Eng. Materials Group Crane Co., Manhattan, Ill., from 1986; dir. Norplex Hong Kong, Ltd., Norplex France SARL, Paris, Norplex UK Ltd, Northampton, England. Contbr. articles to profl. jours. Bd. dirs. Elk Grove Twp. Republicans, Ill., 1971—74; bd. advisors Viterbo Coll., LaCrosse, 1982—86; pres. Dist. 59 Bd. Edn., Elk Grove, 1968—74; area chmn. Des Plaines Cmty. Chest, 1964. Allied Corp. fellowship, Case Inst. Tech., 1958—60. Mem.: Sigma Xi. Achievements include patents in field. Avocations: travel, photography, swimming, golf. Home: Manhattan, Ill. Died Jan. 21, 2009.

SPARKS, JOHN EDWARD, lawyer; b. Rochester, Ind., July 3, 1930; s. Russell Leo and Pauline Anna (Whittenberger) S.; m. Margaret Joan Snyder, Sept. 4, 1954; children: Thomas Edward, William Russell, Kathryn Chapman McCarthy. AB, Ind. U., 1952; LL.B., U. Calif., Berkeley, 1957; postgrad., London Sch. Econs., 1957-58. Bar: Calif. 1958, U.S. Supreme Ct., 1968. Assoc. Brobeck, Phleger & Harrison, San Francisco, 1958-66, ptnr., 1967-95, of counsel, 1996—2003; pvt. practice, from 2003. Adj. prof. law U. San Francisco, 1967-69; pres. Legal Aid Soc. San Francisco, 1978-79, dir., 1971-81. Editor U. Calif. Law Rev., 1956-57. Served to 1st lt. Q.M.C. U.S. Army, 1952-54, Korea. Recipient Wheeler Oak Meritorious award U. Calif., Berkeley, 1986. Fellow Am. Bar Found., Am. Coll. Trial Lawyers; mem. ABA, State Bar Calif., Bar Assn. San Francisco (bd. dirs. 1974-75), Boalt Hall Alumni Assn. (pres. 1983-84). Democrat. Died Feb. 25, 2009.

SPAULDING, SUZANNE MARIE, nursing educator; b. Ithaca, NY, Mar. 26, 1939; d. Arthur Kenneth and Edna (Hogan) S. BS in Nursing, Nazareth Coll., Rochester, NY, 1960; MS in Nursing Edn., Syracuse U., 1971, PhD in Counseling, 1980. Sch. nurse, tchr. Webster (N.Y.) Central Schs., 1961-64, North Syracuse (N.Y.) Central Schs., 1965-69; staff nurse Community Gen. Hosp., Syracuse, 1964-65; health mgr. European tour Concordia Wind Ensemble, Boston, 1970-72; instr. U. R.I. Coll. Nursing, Kingston, 1971-73; grad. asst. dept. guidance counseling Syracuse U., 1973-76; nurse practitioner, medicine Crouse Irving Meml. Hosp., Syracuse, 1978-87, v.p. edn. Sch. Nursing, from 1987. Cons. Onadanga Community Coll., Syracuse, 1975-76; speaker in field. Mem. Onondaga County Long-Term Care Profl. Adv. Bd.; chmn. Explorers post in nursing Hiawatha coun. Boy Scouts Am.; cons. N.Y. Edn. Dept. Helene Fuld Health grantee, 1989. Mem. Nat. League Nursing, N.Y. State Coalition Nurse Practitioners, N.Y. State Nursing Assn., Fedn. Accessible Nursing Edn. and Licensure, Nat. League Nursing Coun. (resolutions com.), N.Y. Hosp. Assn. (nursing shortage task force). Avocations: boating, biking, music. Died Jan. 24, 2009.

SPECTOR, ROBERT DONALD, language educator; b. NYC, Sept. 21, 1922; s. Morris and Helen (Spiegel) S.; m. Eleanor Helen Luskin, Aug. 19, 1945; children: Stephen Brett, Eric Charles. BA, L.I. U., 1948, DHL, 1994; MA, NYU, 1949; PhD, Columbia U., 1962. Instr. L.I. U., Bklyn., 1948-59, asst. prof., 1959-62, asso. prof., 1962-65, prof. English, 1965-94, chmn. senate, 1966-67, 69-70, chmn. dept., 1970-75, dir. humanities and comm. arts, 1975-84, coord. div. of humanities and div. of comms. and performing arts, from 1990, dir. humanities, 1984-90, prof. emeritus, from 1993. Editor, cons. Johnson Reprint Corp., 1967-84 Author: English Literary Periodicals, 1966, Tobias George Smollett, 1968, updated edit., 1989, Pär Lagerkvist, 1973, Arthur Murphy, 1979, Tobias Smollett: A Reference Guide, 1980, The English Gothic, 1983, Backgrounds to Restoration and Eighteenth-Century English Literature, 1989, Political Controversy, 1992, Smollett's Women, 1994, Samuel Johnson and the Essay, 1997, Love Poems & Others, 1998, Mélange a Deux, 1999, Nature's Bounty in Brooklyn, 2000, Poems of Love and Laughter, 2003, New Poems, 2003, All About Love: Poems for Eleanor, 2007; editor: Essays on the Eighteenth Century Novel, 1965, Great British Short Novels, 1970, 9 other vols. English and Am. lit., revs., articles, poetry and song lyrics. Trustee L.I. U., 1969-70; chmn. George Polk Award Com., 1977—. Served with USCGR, 1942-46. Recipient L.I. U. Trustee award for scholarly achievement, 1978, Tristram Walker Metcalfe Alumnus of Year, 1981; Swedish Govt. travel and research grantee, 1966; fellow Huntington Library, 1974; fellow Folger Library, 1975; fellow Newberry Library, 1976 Mem. MLA, Am.-Scandinavian Found. (publs. com. 1962-84), P.E.N., Acad. Am. Poets. Home: Brooklyn, NY. Died Feb. 25, 2009.

SPEISER, STUART MARSHALL, lawyer; b. NYC, June 4, 1923; s. Joseph and Anne (Jonath) S.; m. Mary J. McCormick, Feb. 12, 1950 (dec. 1984); 1 son, James Joseph; m. Maxine Sprouse, June 24, 1985 (dec. 2004) Student, U. Pa., 1939-42; LL.B., Columbia U., 1948. Bar: N.Y. 1948. Practiced in, NYC, from 1948; mem. Speiser, Shumate, Geoghan & Krause, 1957-68; mem. firm Speiser, Shumate, Geoghan, Krause & Rheingold, 1968-70, Speiser & Krause (P.C.), 1971-88; of counsel Speiser, Krause & Madole, P.C., NYC, 1989—2010. Chmn. bd. Aerial Application Corp., 1968-71, Hydrophilics Internat., 1971-77; Hon. atty. gen., La., 1958—2010 Author: Preparation Manual for Aviation Negligence Cases, 1958, Death in the Air, 1957, Liability Problems in Airline Crash Cases, 1957, Private Airplane Accidents, 1958, Speiser's Negligence Jury Charges, 1960, Speiser's Aviation Law Guide, 1962, Lawyers Aviation Handbook, 1964, Recovery for Wrongful Death, 3d edit., 1992, Lawyers Economic Handbook, 1970, 4th edit., 1995, Attorney's Fees, 1972, Res Ipsa Loquitur, 1973, A Piece of the Action, 1977, Aviation Tort Law, 1978, Lawsuit, 1980, Superstock, 1982, The American Law of Torts, 1983, How to End the Nuclear Nightmare, 1984, The USOP Handbook, 1986, Mainstreet Capitalism, 1988, Ethical Economics and the Faith Community, 1989, Lawyers and the American Dream, 1993; bd. editors: Jour. Post Keynesian Economics, 1977-2010 Pilot USAAF, 1943-46. Fellow Internat. Soc. Barristers; mem. ABA, ATLA (chmn. aviation law 1955-64), AIAA (assoc.) Home: Scottsdale, Ariz. Died Oct. 4, 2010.

SPENCER, WILLIAM MICAJAH, III, science research company executive; b. Birmingham, Ala., Dec. 10, 1920; s. William Micajah and Margaret Woodward (Evins) Spencer; m. Evalina Sommerville Brown, Sept. 28, 1946; children: Murray Brown Spencer South, Margaret Anne Spencer Smith. BS, U. South, 1941; postgrad., Grad. Sch. Bus. Adminstrn., Harvard U., 1947. V.p. Motion Industries, Inc. (formerly Owen-Richards Co.), Birmingham, 1946—52, pres., 1952—72, chmn. bd., 1972—84; chmn. Molecular Engring. Assocs., Birmingham, from 1984. Dir. Genuine Parts Co., Atlanta, AmSouth Bank, AmSouth Bancorp., Mead Corp., Robertson Banking Co., ALTEC, Inc. Pres. Birmingham C. of C., 1963—64, Birmingham Festival Arts, 1964—65, Bapt. Med. Center Found., Birmingham, Ala. Safety Coun., 1979—80; chmn. Birmingham Mus. Art, 1986. Served to capt. USMC, 1942—46. Decorated Bronze Star. Mem.: Blue Key, Omega Delta Kappa, Phi Beta Kappa. Episcopalian. Home: Birmingham, Ala. Died Mar. 28, 2010.

SPERBER, DANIEL, physicist; b. Vienna, May 8, 1930; came to U.S., 1955, naturalized, 1967; s. Emanuel and Nelly (Lieberman) S.; m. Ora Yuval, Nov. 29, 1963; 1 son, Ron Emanuel. M.Sc., Hebrew U., 1954; PhD, Princeton U., 1960. Tng. and rsch. asst. Israel Inst. Tech., Haifa, 1954-55, Princeton U., 1955-60; sr. scientist, rsch. adviser Ill. Inst. Tech. Rsch. Inst., Chgo., 1960-67; assoc. prof. physics Ill. Inst. Tech., 1964-67, Rensselaer Poly. Inst., Troy, NY, 1967-72, prof., from 1972. Nordita prof. Niels Bohr Inst., Copenhagen, 1973-74, NATO research fellow, vis., prof., 1974-77; vis. prof. G.S.I., Darmstadt, Fed. Republic Germany, 1983; sr. Fulbright research scholar, Saha Inst. Nuclear Physics, Calcutta, India, 1987-88. Contbr. sci. papers to profl. jours. Served to capt. Israeli Army, 1948-51. Fellow Am. Phys. Soc.; mem. Israel Phys. Soc., N.Y. Acad. Scis., Sigma Xi. Jewish. Home: Geneva, NY. Died Aug. 15, 2009.

SPIEGEL, HERBERT, psychiatrist, educator; b. McKeesport, Pa., June 29, 1914; s. Samuel and Lena (Mendlowitz) S.; m. Natalie Shainess, Apr. 24, 1944 (div. Apr. 1965); children: David, Ann; m. Marcia Greenleaf, Jan. 29, 1989. BS, U. Md., 1936, MD, 1939. Diplomate Am. Bd. Psychiatry. Intern St. Francis Hosp., Pitts., 1939-40; resident in psychiatry St. Elizabeth's Hosp., Washington, 1940-42; practice medicine specializing in psychiatry NYC, from 1946; attending psychiatrist Columbia-Presbyn. Hosp., NYC, 1960—2009; faculty psychiatry Columbia U. Coll. Physicians and Surgeons, 1960—2009. Adj. prof. psychology John Jay Coll. Criminal Justice, CUNY, 1983-2009; mem. faculty Sch. Mil. Neuropsychiatry, Mason Gen. Hosp., Brentwood, N.Y., 1944-46. Author: (with A. Kardiner) War Stress and Neurotic Illness, 1947, (with D. Spiegel) Trance and Treatment: Clinical Uses of Hypnosis, 1978, 2d edit., 2004; subject of book: (by Donald S. Connery) The Inner Source: Exploring Hypnosis with Herbert Spiegel, M.D.; mem. edit. bd.: Preventive Medicine, 1972; Contbr. articles to profl. jours. Profl. advisory com. Am. Health Found.; pub. edn. com., smoking and health com. N.Y.C. div. Am. Cancer Soc.; adv. com. Nat. Aid to Visually Handicapped. Served with M.C. AUS, 1942-46. Decorated Purple Heart. Fellow Am. Psychiat. Assn., Am. Coll. Psychiatrists, Am. Soc. Clin. Hypnosis, Am. Acad. Psychoanalysis, Internat. Soc. Clin. and Exptl. Hypnosis, William A. White Psychoanalytic Soc., N.Y. Acad. Medicine, N.Y. Acad. Scis.; mem. Am. Orthopsychiat. Assn., Am. Psychosomatic Soc., AAAS, AMA, N.Y. County Med. Soc. Home: New York, NY. Died Dec. 15, 2009.

SPIEGEL, JEANNE S., economist; b. Merion, Pa., Oct. 23, 1926; d. Stanley R. and Julia (Nusbaum) Sundheim; B.A., Wellesley Coll., 1948; postgrad. U. Pa., 1976-78; m. Walter F. Spiegel, Oct. 8, 1950; children— Walter D., Karen J., James R. Economist, Dept. Labor, Washington, 1949-50; with Walter F. Spiegel, Inc., Cons. Engrs., Jenkintown, Pa., 1963—, office mgr., 1965-78, contract adminstr., 1965-75, energy analyst, chief economist, 1975—, corp. sec., 1967—. Mem. Nat. Assn. Women in Constrn. (chpt. pres.). Home: Silver Spring, Md. Died Jan. 8, 2010.

SPILMAN, ROBERT HENKEL, furniture company executive; b. Knoxville, Tenn., Sept. 27, 1927; s. Robert Redd and Lila (Henkel) S.; m. Jane Bassett, Apr. 2, 1955; children: Robert Henkel Jr., Virginia Perrin, Vance Henkel. BS, N.C. State U., 1950. With Cannon Mills, 1950-57; with Bassett Table Co., Va., 1957-60; dir. Bassett Furniture Industries Inc., 1960—97, exec. v.p., 1966, pres., 1966-89, CEO, 1979—97, chmn., 1982—97, ret., 1997. Adv. bd. Liberty Mut. Ins. Co Trustee Va. Found. Ind. Colls.; bd. dir. Blue Ridge Airport Authority. Lt. U.S. Army, WWII and Korea. Recipient Best CEO Home Furnishing Industry award, Wall Street Transcript, 1981, 1982; named Humanitarian of Yr., City of Hope, 1982; named to Furniture Hall of Fame, 2005. Mem. Am. Furniture Mfrs. Assn. (James T. Ryan award 1984), Nat. Furniture Mfrs. Assn. (bd. dir., past pres.), Furniture Factories Mktg. Assn. (past chmn., bd. dirs.), Va. Mfrs. Assn. (past dir. exec. com.), Bassett Country Club, Commonwealth Club, Kinloch Golf Club, Linville Golf Club, Grandfather Golf and Country Club (Linville, N.C.), The Country Club Va., Olde Farm (Bristol, Va.). Episcopalian. Avocation: fishing. Home: Manakin Sabot, Va. Died Nov. 15, 2009.

SPITZER, WILLIAM GEORGE, physicist, retired dean; b. L.A., Apr. 24, 1927; s. Max and May Lea (Axleband) S.; m. Jeanette Dorothy Navsky, June 23, 1949; children: Matthew Laurence, Margaret Ilene BA, UCLA, 1949; MS, U. So. Calif., 1952; PhD, Purdue U., 1957. Mem. tech. staff Bell Telephone Lab., Murray Hill, N.J., 1957-62; mem. tech. staff Bell & Howell Research Ctr., Pasadena, Calif., 1962-63; prof. material sci. & physics U. So. Calif., Los Angeles, 1963—92, chmn. dept. material sci., 1967-69, chmn. dept. physics, 1969-72, 78-81, vice provost, dean Grad. studies, 1983-85, dean Letters, Arts and Scis., 1985-89, acting provost, 1993. Contbr. chpts. to books, articles to profl. jours. Served with U.S. Army, 1945-46 Hon. DHL awarded by Hebrew Union Coll., Jewish Inst. of Religion, 1992. Fellow Am. Phys. Soc.; mem. IEEE (sr.) Home: Oceanside, Calif. Died Apr. 14, 2010.

SPRINGER, JOHN KELLEY, hospital administrator; b. Salem, Ohio, May 11, 1931; s. Wilbur Johnson and Nellie Marie (Kelley) S.; m. Jane Lee Parsons, Oct. 13, 1956; children: Kelley Lynn, Dana Lee, Susan Elizabeth, Nellie Jane. AB, Dartmouth Coll., 1953; MHA, U. Mich., 1960; LLD (hon.), Briarwood Coll., 1991. Adminstrv. resident Mary Hitchcock Meml. Hosp., Hanover, NH, 1959-60, asst. adminstr., 1960-64, assoc. adminstr., 1964-69, adminstr. for ops., 1969-71; assoc. exec. dir. Hartford (Conn.) Hosp., 1971-73, exec. dir., 1974-76, pres., 1977-87, vice chmn., CEO, 1987-89, vice chmn., 1989—92; pres., CEO Conn. Health Sys., 1986—96. Bd. dirs. Hartford Mut. Fund; pres. Combined Hosps. Alcoholism Program, Inc., 1972—75; chmn. Capital Area Health Consortium, 1987—90; lectr. Sch. Pub. Health Yale U., 1975. Deacon 1st Ch. of Christ Congl., West Hartford, 1975-79; bd. dirs. Urban League Greater Hartford, 1973-76, Hartford Sem. Found., Greater Hartford chpt. ARC, vice-chmn., 1978-80; trustee New London (N.H.) Hosp., 2003, Dartmouth Hitchcock Alliance; bd. visitors Rockefeller Ctr., Dartmouth Coll., pres. Dartmouth Class 1953, 2008-. Capt. USMC, 1953-58; col. USMCR, ret. Mem.: Lake Sunapee Vis. Nurse Assn. (bd. dirs. 2003—04), Greater Hartford C. of C. (bd. dirs. 1980—82), Am. Hosp. Assn. (coun. on fin. 1975—78, del.-at-large 1979—80, chmn. 1981—86, bd. trustees 1992—94, award of honor 1996), Conn. Hosp. Assn. (chmn. bd. trustees 1982—83), New Eng. Hosp. Assembly (pres. 1972), Am. Coll. Healthcare Execs., Harbour Ridge Yacht and Country Club, Lake Sunapee Yacht Club, Lake Sunapee Country Club, Twilight Club, Hartford Golf Club, Hartford Club. Home: Sunapee, NH. Died Feb. 4, 2010.

SPROLE, FRANK ARNOTT, retired pharmaceutical executive, lawyer; b. Bklyn., Sept. 13, 1918; s. Frank Newland and Eleanor Arnott (Greenberg) S.; m. Sarah Louise Knapp, Sept. 23, 1944; children: Wendy Sprole Bangs, Frank J., Anne Sprole Mauk, Jonathan K., Sarah Sprole Obregon. BA, Yale U., 1942; LLB, Columbia U., 1949. Bar: N.Y. 1949. Assoc. firm Winthrop Stimson, Putnam & Roberts, NYC, 1949-50; atty. Bristol-Myers Co., NYC, 1950-52, asst. sec., 1952-55, sec., 1955-67, v.p., 1965-73, sr. v.p., 1973-77, vice-chmn. bd., 1977-84; ret., 1984. Officer Proprietary Assn., Washington, 1978-84; dir., officer Knapp Fund, N.Y.C., 1960-93. Pres. bd. trustees Hotchkiss Sch., Lakeville, Conn., 1980-85; trustee Internat. Inst. Rural Reconstrn., N.Y.C., and Manila, 1983-87. Lt. comdr. USNR, 1942-45, PTO. Mem. Assn. of Bar of City of N.Y., Yale Club of N.Y.C., Wee Burn Country Club, Bohemian Club, John's Island Club, Riomar Country Club, Oak Harbor Club. Republican. Episcopalian. Home: Darien, Conn. Died Aug. 13, 2010.

SPRUNG, ARNOLD, lawyer; b. NYC, Apr. 18, 1926; s. David L. and Anna (Stork) S.; m. Audrey Ann Caire; children: Louise, John, Thomas, Doran, D'Wayne. AB, Darmuth Coll., 1947; JD, Columbia U., 1950. Bar: N.Y. 1950, U.S. Dist. Ct. (so. dist.) N.Y. 1950, U.S. Patent Office 1952, U.S. Dist. Ct. (we. dist.) N.Y. 1954, U.S. Ct. Appeals (2d cir.) 1958, U.S. Ct. Customs and Patent Appeals 1958, U.S. Dist. Ct. (ea. dist.) N.Y. 1962, U.S. Dist. Ct. (no. dist.) Tex. 1971, U.S. Supreme Ct. 1971, and others. Sr. ptnr. Sprung, Kramer, Schaefer & Briscoe, Westchester, N.Y., from 1950. Lt. USN, 1943-46, PTO. Mem. ABA, N.Y. Intellectual Property Assn. Avocations: skiing, wind surfing, racquetball, biking, tennis. Home: Park City, Utah. Died Jan. 3, 2010.

SQUIRE, ALEXANDER, management consultant; b. Dumfrieshire, Scotland, Sept. 29, 1917; s. Frederick John and Lillian (Ferguson) S.; m. Isabelle L. Kerr, June 23, 1945; children: Jonathan, David, Deborah, Stephen, Philip, Martha, Timothy, Rebecca, Elizabeth. BS, MIT, 1939. Research metallurgist Handy and Harman, Fairfield, Conn., 1939-41; devel. metallurgist Sullivan Machinery Co., Michigan City, Ind., 1941-42; head powder metallurgy br. Watertown Arsenal Lab., Mass., 1942-45; mgr. metall. devel. Westinghouse Electric Corp., Pitts., 1945-50; project mgr. Bettis Atomic Power Lab., Pitts., 1950-62; gen. mgr. plant apparatus div. Westinghouse, 1962-69; dir. purchases and traffic Westinghouse Electric Corp., 1969-71; pres. Westinghouse Hanford Co., Richland, Wash., 1971-79; bus. cons. Richland, 1979-80; dep. mng. dir. Wash. Public Power Supply System, 1980-85, cons., from 1985. Mem. Nat. Acad. Engring., Am. Nuclear Soc., Am. Soc. Metals, AIME, Am. Def. Preparedness Assn. Died May 16, 2009.

STABLER, WELLS, former ambassador; b. Boston, Oct. 31, 1919; s. Jordan Herbert and Elizabeth Huidekoper (Wells) S.; m. Emily Elizabeth Atkinson, Aug. 5, 1953; children: Elizabeth Wells, Susan Brooke, Edward Malcolm, Eric Atkinson. A.B. cum laude, Harvard U., 1941. With Fgn. Service, U.S. Dept. State, 1941-78, US amb. to Spain, US Dept. State 1975-78; pvt. practice as internat. cons., 1978—2009; cons. German Marshall fund of U.S., Washington, 1978-83. Trustee Youth for Understanding, Inc., Washington, 1983-87; mem. nat. council Phillips Collection, Washington; Decorated grand officer Order of Star (Jordan); grand officer Order of St. Agata (San Marino); grand officer Order of Merit (Italy); Grand Cross Isabel La Catolica (Spain), others; recipient William J. Carr medal for Disting. Service, U.S. Dept. State, 1978. Episcopalian. Clubs: Met. (Washington); Chevy Chase (Md.). Home: Washington, DC. Died Nov. 13, 2009.

STAGG, EVELYN WHEELER, educator, state legislator; b. Sept. 30, 1916; d. Alton Grover and Edythe (Boyce) Wheeler; m. David Stagg, May 15, 1942; children: Christie Stagg Austin, Bonnie, Carol Stagg Kevan. BA, Middlebury Coll., 1939; MA, U. Vt., 1971. Assoc. prof. Castleton State Coll., Vt., 1966-82; mem. Vt. Ho. of Reps., 1982-90, chmn. house edn. com., 1982-90, vice chmn. health and welfare com., 1985-86, mem. ways and means com., 1989-90. Commn. of the States, 1987-88; cons. communications projects, Bomoseen, Vt., 1982—. Contbr. articles to profl. jours. Chmn. Women's Legis. Caucus, 1984-88; pres., bd. dirs. Rutland Area Vis. Nurse Assn., 1969-75, 89-92; bd. dirs. Rutland Mental Health Assn., 1986-88, Condo Assn., CCI; adv. bd. nursing Castleton State Coll.; vol. LUVS (Naples youth haven) for abused children, 1992—; trustee pub. funds, 1990-96, Castle Libr., 1992-95; bd. civil authority, 1984-93; mem. customer adv. coun. U.S. Postal Svc., Naples. Mem. Women's Caucus, Vt. Women's Polit. Caucus of Collier County, Nat. Women's Polit. Caucus, Inst. for Gen. Semantics, Internat. Soc. for Gen. Semantics, Am. Philatelic Soc., Democratic Women's Club of Collier County, Castleton Hist. Soc. Clubs: Women's, Rutland County Stamp, Collier Co. League of Women Voters. Avocations: stamp and coin collecting, sailing, skiing, travel. Died June 18, 2010.

STALLMEYER, JAMES EDWARD, engineering educator; b. Covington, Ky., Aug. 11, 1926; s. Joseph Julius and Anna Catherine (Scheper) S.; m. Mary Katherine Davenport, Apr. 11, 1953; children: Cynthia Marie, James Duncan, Michael John, Catherine Ann, John Charles, Gregory Edward. BS, U. Ill., 1947, MS, 1949, PhD, 1953. Jr. engr. So. Ry. System, 1947; research asst. U. Ill., Urbana, 1947-49, research asso., 1951-52, asst. prof. civil engring, 1952-57, assoc. prof., 1957-60, prof., 1960-91, prof. emeritus, from 1991. Cons. on structural problems various indsl. and govt. agys. Author: (with E.H. Gaylord Jr.), Design of Steel Structures; editor: (with E.H. Gaylord Jr.) Structural Engineering Handbook; contbr. to Shock and Vibration Handbook. Served with USN, 1944-46. Standard Oil fellow, 1949-51; recipient Adams meml. award, 1964, Everitt award for teaching excellence, 1981 Mem. ASCE, Am. Concrete Inst., Am. Ry. Engring. Assn., ASTM, Am. Welding Soc., Am. Soc. Metals, Soc. Exptl. Stress Analysis, Scabbard and Blade, Sigma Xi, Chi Epsilon, Sigma Tau, Tau Beta Pi, Phi Kappa Phi. Clubs: KC. Republican. Roman Catholic. Home: Champaign, Ill. Died Mar. 5, 2009.

STAMM, WILLIAM, city fire chief; b. Milw., Nov. 7, 1916; s. Jacob Herman and Florence (Buetler) Stamm; m. Etelka Ann Wittmann, June 4, 1938; 1 child, Charlene Anita Stamm Wussow. A in Fire Tech., Milw. Area Tech. Coll., 1964. With Milw. Fire Dept., from 1940, fire lt., 1948—50, fire capt., 1950—59, bn. chief, 1959—62, dep. chief, 1962—70, chief, from 1970. Bd. dirs. ARC, Good Samaritan Hosp., St. Francis Children's Activity and Achievement Ctr. Contbr. articles to profl. jours. Recipient State Firefighter of Yr. award, Schlitz Brewery, 1971, Disting. Svc. award Ptnr. Am., 1973; named Nat. Fire Chief of Yr., Dictograph Co., 1980. Mem.: Joint Coun. Nat. Fire Svc. Orgns. (past chmn.), So. Wis.-No. Ill. Fire Chiefs, Milw. County Fire Chiefs, Internat. Assn. Fire Chiefs (exec. bd. metro com.), Met. Fire Chiefs, Milw. Athletic Club, Shriners Lodge, Masons Lodge, Eagles Lodge (Nat. Firefighter of Yr. award 1972). Died May 15, 2009.

STANASZEK, WALTER F, pharmacy education educator, consultant, writer; b. Chgo., Oct. 23, 1940; s. Walter E. and Blanche (Boots) S.; m. Mary Jane Weisman, May 7, 1966; children: Mary Beth, Jennifer Lynn, Sara Anne. BS, U. Ill., Chgo., 1962, MS, 1966, PhD, 1970. Pharmacist Carson's Pharmacy, Danville, Ill., 1962-64; asst. to dir. U. Ill. Pharmacy Svcs., Chgo., 1967-70; asst./assoc. prof. U. Okla., Okla. City, 1970-85, prof. pharmacy practice, from 1985. Bd. dirs. Alzheimer's Disease and Related Disorders Assn. Co-author: The Inverted Medical Dictionary, 1991, Understanding Medical Terms: A Guide for Pharmacy Practice, 1991; co-editor: Clinical Pharmacy Practice, 1972; contbg. editor: (journal) U.S. Pharmacist, 1976-89; editorial bd. mem. Journal of Geriatric Drug Therapy, 1985—; contbr. articles to profl. jours. Recipient Lyman award Am. Assn. Colls. of Pharmacy, 1973. Fellow Am. Coll. Apothecaries (assoc.); mem. Am. Pharm. Assn., Am. Soc. Hosp. Pharmacists. Roman Catholic. Home: Norman, Okla. Died Sept. 2, 2009.

STANG, ARNOLD, actor, writer, film director; b. NYC, Sept. 28, 1928; s. Harold Louis and Anna (Chest) S.; m. JoAnne Taggart, Sept. 21, 1949; children: David Donald, Deborah Jane Stang-Healy. Ind. actor, dir., writer, NYC, from 1936. Actor: (Broadway prodns.) Front Page, A Funny Thing Happened On the Way to the Forum, Wallflower, All in Favor, (TV shows) Bonanza, Ed Sullivan Show, McHale's Navy, Bewitched, Milton Berle Show, Jack Benny Show, Jackie Gleason Show, Top Cat, Emergency, Robert Klein Show, Playhouse 90, Frank Sinatra Spls., Bob Hope Spls., What's My Line, Bill Cosby Show, Tales From The Dark Side, numerous others, (stock theatrical prodns.) Don't Drink the Water, Death Knocks, Charley's Aunt, Finian's Rainbow, Three Men on a Horse, The Gazebo, Wish You Were Here, Pajama Game, Let 'Em Eat Cake, Anything Goes, Luv, Tobacco Road, Play It Again, Sam, Annie Get Your Gun, (starring film roles) Double for Della, Arnold the Benedict, Honorable Myrtle, The Expectant Father, Dondi, The Wonderful World of the Brothers Grimm, The Aristocats, Hello Down There, Alakazam the Great, The Man With the Golden Arm, The Cottonwood, Hercules in New York, Skidoo, My Sister Eileen, Seven Days Leave, Let's Go Steady, It's A Mad, Mad, Mad World, Dennis the Menace, numerous featured roles; rec. artist numerous albums including Winnie & Baby Pooh, Winnie the Pooh, Peter and the Wolf, Arnold Stang Meets Gus Edwards, Beezy the Sneezy Bee, The Hippy Hippo, Chester the Chimp, Further Adventures of Harry the Horse. Mem. Screen Actors Guild, Acad. Motion Picture Arts and Scis., Actors Equity Assn., AFTRA. Clubs: Players (N.Y.C.). Avocations: gardening, poetry, carpentry, social work. Died Dec. 20, 2009; Newton, Mass.

STANSBERRY, JAMES WESLEY, air force officer; b. Grafton, W.Va., Dec. 29, 1927; s. William Adrian and Phyllis Gay (Robinson) S.; m. Audrey Mildred Heinz, May 7, 1950; children: Nora G., Amy G. Stansberry Goodhand, Lisa Porten. BS, U.S. Mil. Acad., 1949; MBA with hons., Air Force Inst. Tech., 1956. Advanced through grades from pvt. to lt. gen. USAF; chief prodn. (Kawasaki Gifu Contract Facility), Gifu, Japan, 1956-57; dep. asst. to Sec. of Def. for atomic energy Washington, 1970-71; dep. dir. procurement policy U.S. Air Force, 1972-73; dep. chief staff contracting and mfg. (Hdqrs. Air Force Systems Command), Andrews AFB, Md., 1977-81; comdr. Electronic Systems Div. Hanscom AFB, Mass., 1981-84; pres. Stansberry Assocs. Inc., from 1984. Bd. dirs. Griffon Corp., Triton. Decorated DSM with oak leaf cluster, Legion of Merit with oak leaf cluster; named Disting. grad. Lancaster (N.Y.) H.S., award, Wall St. Jour., 1956, Mervin E. Gross award, USAF, 1956. Mem.: AFIT (Alumnus medal 2009), Order of Sword. Methodist. Home: Virginia Beach, Va. Died June 28, 2010.

STANTON, FRED RANDOLPH, lawyer, director; b. Andalusia, Ala., July 17, 1924; s. Ross Homer and Edna (Baisden) Stanton; m. Barbara Wetherell Stanton, June 5, 1948; children: Elaine, Diane, Fred, Edmund. BA, Emory U., 1948; LLB, U. Fla., 1951. Bar: Fla. 1951, US Dist. Ct. (so. dist.) Fla. 1952, US Ct. Appeals (5th cir.) 1970, US Supreme Ct. 1971. Assoc., sr. ptnr. Therrel, Baisden, Stanton, Wood & Setlin, Miami, Fla., from 1952. Past pres. United Cerebral Palsy; bd. dirs. Dade County ARC, Fla., Miami-Dade CC Found. Inc.; pres. Manfred Inter-Faith Retreat Ctr.; active United Way Dade Count; past chmn. legal sect.; mem. citizens bd. U. Miami; mem. com. 100 Miam's for Me; chancellor Episcopal Diocese SE Fla. With USMC, 1943, with USMC, 1951—52, Rep. of Korea. Recipient Humanitarian award, United Cerebral Palsy, 1981, Legion of Honor, Miami Beach Kiwanis Club, 1978. Mem.: ABA, Miami Beach C. of C., Fla. Bar, Dade County Bar Assn., Miami Beach Bar Assn., Miami Beach Kiwanis (past pres., past lt. gov. Fla. dist., pres. Miami Beach scholarship fund), Miami, La Gorce Country, Riviera County. Died Sept. 12, 2009.

STANTON, WILLIAM JOHN, JR., marketing educator, author; b. Chgo., Dec. 15, 1919; s. William John and Winifred (McGann) S.; m. Imma Mair, Sept. 14, 1978; children by previous marriage: Kathleen Louise, William John III. BS, Lewis Inst. (Ill. Inst. Tech.), 1940; MBA, Northwestern U., 1941, PhD, 1948; D (hon.), Cath. U. Santo Domingo, Dominican Republic, 2003. Mgmt. trainee Sears Roebuck & Co., 1940-41; instr. U. Ala., 1941-44; auditor Olan Mills Portrait Studios, Chattanooga, 1944-46; asst. prof., asso. prof. U. Wash., 1948-55; prof. U. Colo., Boulder, 1955-90, prof. emeritus, 1990—2009, head mktg. dept., 1955-71, acting dean, 1963-64; assoc. dean U. Colo. (Sch. Bus.), 1964-67; ret. Author: Economic Aspects of Recreation in Alaska, 1953; author: (with others) Challenge of Business, 1975; author: (with M. Etzel and B. Walker) Marketing, 14th edit., 2007, Marketing, Spanish, Chinese, Portuguese, Indonesian and Korean transl., 2003; author: (with R. Varaldo) Italian edit., 2d edit., 1989; author: (with others) South African edit., 1992; author: (with M.S. Sommers and J.G. Barnes) Canadian edit., Fundamentals of Marketing, 11th edit., 2004; author: (with K. Miller and R. Layton) Australian edit., 4th edit., 2000; author: (with Rosann Spiro and G.A. Rich) Management of a Sales Force, 12th edit., Spanish, Portuguese, Chinese, and Russian transl., 2007; contbr. articles to profl. jour. Mem. Am. Mktg. Assn., Mktg. Educators Assn., Beta Gamma Sigma. Roman Catholic. Home: Boulder, Colo. Died Dec. 28, 2010.

STARR, EDWARD, public relations executive; b. Queens Village, NY, Nov. 30, 1926; s. Daniel Francis and Mary (Glennon) S.; m. Grace Wall, Nov. 13, 1949; children: Edward T., Christopher D., Matthew W. BA, St. John's U., 1954. Sr. writer NBC, NYC, 1947-50, mgr. publs. and communications, 1950-55; account exec. Hill & Knowlton Inc., NYC, 1955-62, v.p., 1962-67, sr. v.p., 1967-71, exec. v.p., from 1971, dir., from 1976. Instr. Pace U., 1965 Author: What You Should Know About Public Relations, 1968. Vice chmn., dir. YMCA, N.Y., 1981—; bd. dirs. The Christophers Inc., N.Y.C., 1979—; mem. Lincoln Ctr. Leadership Com., 1977—; mem. fin bd. TV Ctr. Diocese of Rockville Centre, Uniondale, N.Y., 1979—. Served to 1st lt. U.S. Army, 1945-46, 51-52. Recipient Pietas medal St. John's U., 1974 Mem. Pub. Relations Soc. Am. Clubs: Pinnacle, Cherry Valley. Roman Catholic. Home: Berkeley Heights, NJ. Died June 21, 2009.

STATNIKOV, EFIM SMULEVICH, physicist, researcher; d. Shmuel Moshkovich Statnikov and Liya Boruhovna Chudnovskaya; m. Liubov Dmitrievna Bogdanova, Mar. 10, 1960; children: Mayya Efimovna Kundzich, Itta Efimovna Statnikova. PhD, Tech. U., Brjansk, Russia, 1959. Cert. Physicist in engring., Russian Acoustical Acad., 1982. V.p. Applied Ultrasonics, Irondale, Ala., from 1999. Home: Birmingham, Ala. Died Oct. 9, 2009.

STAUB, JAMES DUNN, corporate executive; b. Stamford, Conn., Mar. 2, 1933; s. Howard Randal and Margaret (Dunn) S.; m. Judith Hazel Flanders, Aug. 14, 1960 (div. 1980); children: Kila, Jonathan, David, Blair. M.Fgn.Trade, Thunderbird Coll., Glendale, Ariz., 1958; BA, Kenyon Coll, Gambier, Ohio, 1956; cert., Sorbonne, Paris, 1965, Stanford U., 1979. Sr. analyst Alexander & Baldwin Inc., Honolulu, 1970-76, treas., from 1982, dir.; asst. treas. Rogers Foods, Idaho Falls,

1976-82, v.p., treas., from 1980, R Foods Inc., Honolulu, from 1980; treas., dir. ABPRI Inc., Honolulu, from 1982; sr. v.p. Atalanta/Sosnoff Capital Corp., NYC, from 1984; mng. dir. Atalanta-Sosnoff Capital Corp., 1988. Assoc. editor Jour. Bus. Research, 1987—. Mem. Fin. Exec. Inst., Treasurers of U.S.A., Honolulu C. of C. Clubs: Oahu Country (Honolulu); Tennis (San Francisco). Democrat. Roman Catholic. Died July 5, 2010.

STAUFER, ALFRED J(OSE), aircraft company executive; b. San Jose, Costa Rica, Feb. 7, 1940; arrived in US, 1958, naturalized, 1968; s. Josef Soelkner and Maria Obermayer (Riederer) Staufer; m. Vicki Ann Schrack, Apr. 15, 1976; children: J. Chris, Eric P. Student, U. Ala., 1959—62; BS in Engring., U. Beverly Hills, 1979. Staff Mooney-Aerostar Aircraft Co., Kerrville, Tex., 1962—70; svc. mgr. N.Am. Rockwell AeroComdr. Divsn., Albany, Ga., 1971—72; project engr. Piper Aircraft Corp., Vero Beach, Fla., 1972—73, super. engring. projects, 1973—74, sr. engr. Lockhaven, Pa., 1974, regional mgr. Western Europe-Latin Am. internat. sales, 1974—79, adminstr. internat. worldwide distbn. and sales, 1979—80, dir. internat. sales, 1981—82, dir. internat. prodn. programs, 1983—87, dir. internat. sales and prodn. programs, from 1988. With Tex. Air NG, 1963—69. Mem.: AIAA, Am. Mgmt. Assn., Soc. Automotive Engrs., Indian River County C. of C., Rotary Internat. Home: Lakeland, Fla. Died Jan. 30, 2009.

STAUP, JOHN GARY, safety engineer; b. Cleve., May 10, 1931; m. Ellsworth Leroy and May Ann (Weisgerber) S.; m. Elizabeth Louise Friemoth, Jan. 10, 1953; children: Michael Steven, Valerie Elysa Staup Gerdemann, Timothy Karl. BA, Dayton U., 1949; student, U. Mich. Design engr. Gramm Trailer, Delphos, Ohio, 1955-57, F.C. Russell Co., Pandora, Ohio, 1957-59, Ins. Svc. Office, Lima, Ohio, 1959-65, Ctrl. Mut. Ins., Van Wert, Ohio, 1965-76, Mid. Am. Tech. Svcs., Delphos, from 1980. Adminstr. safety programs and security programs for various firms. Sgt. USAF, 1951-55. Mem. Am. Single Shot Rifle Assn. (sec.-treas. 1991—), Maumee Valley Soc. Safety Engr., Optimist Club (v.p.). Avocations: gun collecting, civic involvement, public speaking, target shooting, travel. Died Feb. 15, 2010.

STEARNS, CHARLES EDWARD, geology educator; b. Billerica, Mass., Jan. 19, 1920; s. Albert Warren and Frances Mansell (Judkins) S.; m. Helen Louise Hurley Stearns, Dec. 17, 1942 (dec. Oct. 1983); children: Jonathan, Martha Pendleton, Rebecca C., Carola H., Jeremie (dec.), Kate A. AB, Tufts Coll., Medford, Mass., 1939; AM, Harvard U., 1942; PhD, 1950; LLD, U. Mass., N. Dartmouth, Mass., 1962. Asst. in geology Tufts U., 1941-42, instr. in geology, 1942-45, asst. prof. geology, 1945-51, assoc. prof. geology, 1954-57, prof., 1957-87, dean Coll. of Liberal Arts, 1954-67, 68-69; asst. prof. geology Harvard U., 1951-54. Sec. Examiner Club Boston, 1955-84; pres., 1966-68, treas. 1976-78 First Parish Ch. in Billerica; pres. Bennett Pub. Libr. Assn., 1954, Billerica Hist. Soc., 1968-78, 88-90; chmn. Billerica Hist. Commn., 1974-92. Mem. AAAS, Colonial Soc. Mass., Geol. Soc. Am., Inst. Italian Paleontology, Internat. Assn. for Quaternary Rsch., Phi Beta Kappa, Sigma Xi, Delta Upsilon. Home: Las Vegas, Nev. Died June 27, 2010.

STEARNS, CHARLES RICHARD, meteorologist, educator, farmer; b. McKeesport, Pa., May 21, 1925; s. Fenton Verle and Lois Annette (Sellers) S.; children: James, Laura. BS, U. Wis., 1950, MS, 1952, PhD, 1967. Farmer, Princeton, Wis., 1952-55; physicist Winzen Rsch., Mpls., 1955-57; project asst. U. Wis., Madison, 1957-65, asst. prof. meteorology, 1965-70, assoc. prof., 1970-75, prof., 1975-99, prof. emeritus, from 1999. Author, editor: Antarctic Meteorology, 1993. Chair Plan Commn., Oregon, Wis., 1970-85. Served with inf. U.S. Army, 1943-46, PTO. Decorated Bronze Star. Fellow Am. Meteorol. Soc., Mem. AAAS, Am. Geophys. Union. Home: Oregon, Wis. Died June 22, 2010.

STEARNS, WILLIAM ALLEN, lawyer; b. Chgo., Dec. 20, 1937; s. Walter Brockway and Margaret Deborah (Isham) S.; m. Mary Margaret Schubert, Dec. 28, 1963; children: William Isham, Catherine Elizabeth, James Sievers. AB, Harvard U., 1959; JD, Northwestern U., 1965. Bar: Wis. 1965, U.S. Dist. Ct. (ea. dist.) Wis. 1966, U.S. Dist. Ct. (we. dist.) Wis. 1970, U.S. Ct. Appeals (5th cir.) 1980, U.S. Ct. Appeals (7th cir.) 1975. Assoc. Quarles, Herriott & Clemons, Milw., 1965-71; ptnr. Quarles and Brady, Milw., from 1972. With U.S. Army, 1959-62. Mem. ABA, Wis. Bar Assn., Milw. Bar Assn., University Club Milw. Republican. Episcopalian. Avocations: bicycling, photography, outdoor activities. Home: Milwaukee, Wis. Died Apr. 22, 2010.

STEELE, JACK ELLWOOD, physician, medical researcher; b. Lacon, Ill., Jan. 27, 1924; s. Maurice Edgar and Ruth Naomi (Feller) S.; m. Ruth Eleanor (Kelley), Oct. 1, 1955; children: Jill Mayer, Suzy Ruth Ellen Steele. MD, Northwestern U., 1950; MS in Sys. Engring., Wright State U., 1977. Intern Cin. Gen. Hosp., 1949-50; fellow in rsch., tchg. Northwestern U., Chgo., 1950-51; psychiat. ward officer USAF Hosp., Wright Patterson AFB, Ohio, 1951-53; rsch. officer with numerous titles Aerospace Med. Lab., Wright Patterson AFB, Ohio, 1953, rsch. neurologist, flight surgeon, asst. chief math and analysis sect., lab. bionicist, 1971; advanced through grades to col. USAF, 1971; psychiat. physician Dayton (Ohio) Mental Health Ctr., 1973-91; med. dir. BuDa Methadone Clinic, Dayton, 1988, Nova House drug treatment, Dayton, 1988-90; pres. Gen. Bionics Corp., Dayton, from 1977. Editor: Bionics Symposium, 1960; contbr. articles to profl. jours. Recipient Air Force Commendation medal for bionics. Mem. AMA, IEEE, Am. Soc. of Clin. Hypnosis, Soc. Clin. and Exptl. Hypnosis, Swedish Soc. of Clin. Hypnosis, Am. Legion, Loyal Order of Moose. Avocations: photography, travel. Home: Dayton, Ohio. Died Jan. 19, 2009.

STEEN, JOHN GERALD, convention bureau administrator; b. North Adams, Mass., Aug. 10, 1936; s. James Ralph and Doris Ellen (Booth) S.; divorced; children: Kelly, Shawn. V.p. Hertz Corp., Burlingame, Calif., 1962-72; pres. Pacific Car Rental, Burlingame, Calif., 1972-74; exec. dir. San Mateo County Conv. and Vis. Bur., San Francisco, 1974-96. Bd. dirs. Greater San Francisco Bay Area Vacation Coun., Western Symphony, Mariners Island Assn. #1, Phoenix in the Hill, Hibernia Club of San Mateo County, Cow Palace, Easter Seal Soc. of San Mateo County; mem. exec. com. San Mateo Performing Arts Ctr.; mem. exec. bd. Bay Area Super Bowl Task Force; mem. organizing com. Am. Sports, 1996. Mem. Calif. Assn. Meeting. Planners (pres.), No. Calif. Soc. Assn. Execs. (past pres.), Western Assn. Conv. and Vis. Burs. (past pres.), San Mateo County Conv. and Vis. Burs. (exec. dir.), Conquistadors de El Camino Real (exec. dir.), Confrerie De La Chaine Des Rotisseurs (vice conseiller gastronomique), Western Tourism Industry Assn., Sacramento Soc. Assn. Execs., Am. Soc. Assn. Execs., Hotel Sales Mgrs. Assn., U.S. Robotics Soc., Assn. Travel Mktg. Execs., Soc. for Advancement of Travel for the Handicapped, Calif. Travel Industry Assn., Calif. Assn. C. of C. Execs., Nat. Tour Assn., So. Calif. Soc. Assn. Execs., Golden Gate U. Adv. Com., Nat. Assn. Exhibit Mgrs., Wash. Legal Found., Can. Coll. Adv. Com., Internat. Assn. Conv. Vis. Burs. Lodges: Rotary. Republican. Roman Catholic. Home: Newport, Oreg. Died Sept. 24, 2009.

STEFFENS, JEFFREY EDWARD, manufacturing executive; b. Plainfield, NJ, July 15, 1953; s. Howard Leslie and Lenore Ann (Rossbach) S.; m. Ellen Margret Simpson, Nov. 21, 1981 (div. 1988). BA, Union Coll., Cranford, NJ, 1976. Vice pres. Steffens Security Systems, Inc., Elizabeth, N.J., 1974-76, Halsted Corp., Jersey City, 1976-81; chmn., chief exec. officer Superior Bag Mfg. Corp., Linden, N.J., from 1981. Bd. dirs. Northeast Textiles, Inc., Linden, Northeast Vinyl Products, Inc., Linden. Patentee in field. Named Champion, U.S. Combat Shooting Assn., 1987. Mem. Independent Armored Car Operators Assn., Inc., N.J. State Policemen's Benevolent Assn., Woodbridge Racket Club. Avocations: tennis, skiing, target shooting. Home: Edison, NJ. Died Jan. 9, 2009.

STEFFY, PAUL MARTIN, retired judge; b. Balt., Feb. 9, 1923; s. Paul Martin and Gertrude M. (Scharf) S.; m. Kathleen Detsch, May 31, 1948 (dec. Apr. 1972); children: Paul Martin, Anne, Gail, Mark, Thomas, John; m. Evelyn de Rubertis, Dec. 15, 1974. AA, St. Charles Coll., 1942; AB, Loyola Coll., Balt., 1944; JD, Georgetown U., 1948. Bar: Md. 1948, U.S. Dist. Ct. Md. 1948, U.S. Dist. Ct. D.C. 1951, U.S. Dist. Ct. W.Va., 1956, U.S. Ct. Appeals (8th cir.) 1958, U.S. Supreme Ct. 1958, U.S. Ct. Mil. Appeals 1959, U.S. Ct. Appeals (D.C. cir.) 1972. Trial atty. food and drug divsn. Gen. Counsel's Office Fed. Security Agy., HEW, Washington, 1948-59; hearing examiner/adminstrv. law judge HEW, Los Angeles, 1959-78; adj. prof. law Northrop U., Inglewood, Calif., 1982-88. Participant adminstrv. law Nat. Jud. Coll., Reno, 1982. Served to lt. (j.g.) USNR ret., 1944-46; PTO. Republican. Roman Catholic. Home: Chico, Calif. Died Sept. 25, 2009.

STEGGLES, JOHN CHARLES, retired insurance company executive, consultant; b. Larling, Norfolk, Eng., Aug. 21, 1919; came to U.S., Oct. 1950, naturalized, 1959; s. Ernest John and Ann Gayton (Burt) S.; m. Pamela R. Graham, Jan. 22, 1945; children: Christopher J., Angela M. Grad., Brit. Army Staff Coll., Eng., 1941. With Alexander Howden & Co. Ltd., Lloyds of London, 1937-50; v.p. North Star Reins. Co., NYC, 1950-55, Gen. Reins. Corp., NYC, 1956-74, sr. v.p. Hartford, Conn., 1974-83, exec. cons., 1983-89; chmn., pres. John C. Steggles & Assocs., Inc., West Hartford, Conn., from 1980. Served to capt. Royal Arty. and Intelligence Staff, 1939-46. Mem.: John's Insland (Vero Beach, Fla.), Eastward Ho (Chatham, Mass.). Republican. Episcopalian. Home: Vero Beach, Fla. Died Aug. 28, 2009.

STEIL, GLENN, state legislator; b. Aug. 29, 1940; m. Barbara Steil; children: Darlene, Glenn II. Former chmn. Mich. Jobs Commn. & Consumer & Indusl. Svc. Subcom.; former mem. Mich. Capital Com., Appropriations Com.; former chmn. Caucus; mem. Judiciary & Gen. Govt. Subcom., Joint Com. Adminstrn. Rules; chmn. Mich. State Senate; state senator Dist. 30 Mich., 1995—2002; state rep. Dist. 72 Mich., from 2005; chief exec. officer Compatico; Trustee Davenport Coll. Recipient Disting. Alumni award, Davenport Coll., 1988. Mem.: Grand Rapids Youth Commonwealth (pres.). Republican. Died May 7, 2010.

STEIN, JOSEPH, playwright; b. NYC, May 30, 1912; s. Charles and Emma S.; m. Sadie Singer (dec. 1974); children: Daniel, Harry, Joshua; m. Elisa Loti, Feb. 7, 1975; children: John, Jenny Lyn. BSS, CCNY, 1934; MSW, Columbia U., 1937. Psychiat. social worker, NYC, 1938-45. Writer: radio shows, including Raleigh's Room, 1948-49, Henry Morgan Show, 1949-52; TV shows, including Your Show of Shows, 1952-54; Sid Caesar Show, 1954-55; playwright Plain and Fancy, 1955; Mr. Wonderful, 1957, Juno, 1959, Take Me Along, 1959, Enter Laughing, 1963, Fiddler on the Roof, 1964 (American Theatre Wing Tony award for Best Musical, 1965, N.Y. Drama Critics Circle award Best Musical 1965), Zorba, 1968 (Tony nomination), Irene, 1975, King of Hearts, 1978, Carmelina, 1979, The Baker's Wife, 1983, (Olivier award nomination London 1989), Rags, 1986 (Tony nomination); screenplays Enter Laughing, 1970; Fiddler on the Roof, 1972 (Screen Writers Guild award). Recipient Townshend Harris medal, Alumni. Assn. City Coll., 2004, Oscar Hammerstein award in Musical Theatre, York Theatre Co., 2007, Lifetime Achievement award, Dramatists Guild of America, 2008, Encompass New Opera Theatre, 2009, Disting. Achievement award, Writers & Artists for Peace in the Middle East; named to The Theatre Hall of Fame, 2008. Mem. Authors League, Screen Writers Guild (Edwin Forrest award for Outstanding Contbr. to Theatre, 2001), Dramatists Guild Coun. Home: New York, NY. Died Oct. 24, 2010.

STEINBRENNER, GEORGE MICHAEL, III, professional baseball team and shipbuilding company executive; b. Rocky River, Ohio, July 4, 1930; s. Henry G. and Rita (Haley) Steinbrenner; m. Elizabeth Joan Zieg, May 12, 1956; children: Henry George III, Jennifer Lynn, Jessica Joan, Harold Zeig. BA, Williams Coll., 1952; postgrad., Ohio State U., 1954—55. Asst. football coach Northwestern U., 1955, Purdue U., 1956—57; treas. Kinsman Transit Co., Cleve., 1957—63; pres. Kinsman Marine Transit Co., Cleve., 1963—67, dir., 1965; pres., chmn. bd. Am. Ship Bldg. Co., Cleve., 1967—78, chmn. bd., 1978—2010; prin. owner NY Yankees, Bronx, 1973—90, 1993—2008, limited ptnr., 1990—93, chmn., 2008—10; owner Bay Harbor Inn, Tampa, Fla., 1988—2010. Bd. dirs. Gt. Lakes Internat. Corp., Gt. Lakes Assocs., Cin. Sheet Metal & Roofing Co., Nashville Bridge Co., Nederlander-Steinbrenner Prodns. Chmn. Olympic Overview Commn.; v.p. US Olympic Com., 1989; mem. Cleve. Little Hoover Com., group chmn., 1966; chmn. Cleve. Urban Coalition; vice chmn. Greater Cleve. Growth Corp., Greater Cleve. Jr. Olympic Found.; founder Silver Shield Found., NYC. 1st lt. USAF, 1952—54. Recipient Gen. Douglas MacArthur award, US Olympic Com., 2002; named Outstanding Young Man of Yr., Ohio Jr. C. of C., 1960, Cleve. Jr. C. of C., 1960, Chief Town Crier, Cleve., 1968, Man of Yr., Cleve. Press Club, 1968, New Yorker of Yr.; named one of The Most Influential People in the World of Sports, Bus. Week, 2007, 2008, Forbes 400: Richest Americans, 2009. Mem.: Greater Cleve. Growth Assn. (bd. dirs.). Avocation: owns racehorse Bellamy Road trained by Nick Zito. Died July 13, 2010; Tampa, Fla.

STEINER, PETER OTTO, economics educator, dean; b. NYC, July 9, 1922; s. Otto Davidson and Ruth (Wurzburger) S.; m. Ruth E. Riggs, Dec. 20, 1947 (div. 1967); children: Mary Catherine, Alison Ruth, David Denison; m. Patricia F. Owen, June 2, 1968. AB, Oberlin Coll., 1943; MA, Harvard, 1949, PhD, 1950. Instr. U. Calif., Berkeley, 1949-50, asst. prof. economics, 1950-57; assoc. prof. U. Wis., Madison, 1957-59, prof., 1959-68; prof. economics & law U. Mich., Ann Arbor, 1968-91, prof. emeritus, 1991—2010, chmn. dept. economics, 1971-74, dean Coll. Lit., Sci. & Arts, 1981-89. Vis. prof. U. Nairobi, Kenya, 1974—75; cons. U.S. Bur. Budget, 1961—62, Treasury Dept., 1962—63, various pvt. firms, from 1952. Author: An Introduction to the Analysis of Time Series, 1956, (with R. Dorfman) The Economic Status of the Aged, 1957, (with R.G. Lipsey) Economics, 10th edit., 1993, On the Process of Planning, 1968, Public Expenditure Budgeting, 1969, Mergers: Motives, Effects, Policies, 1975, Thursday Night Poker: Understand, Enjoy and Win, 1996; contbr. articles to profl. publs. Served to lt. USNR, 1944-46. Social Sci. Research Council Faculty Research fellow, 1956; Guggenheim fellow, 1960; Ford Faculty Research fellow, 1965 Mem. Am. Econ. Assn., Econometric Soc., AAUP (chmn. com. Z 1970-73, pres. 1976-78) Died June 26, 2010.

STEINFORT, ROY (CHARLES ROY STEINFORT), retired publishing executive; b. Covington, Ky., Oct. 1, 1921; s. Charles Roy and Elsie (Joering) S.; m. Patricia Ann Milton. BA, U. Ky., 1946. Reporter Courier-Jour., 1946-47; dir. sports info. U. Ky., 1948-49; with AP, 1949—51, dep. dir. broadcast services NYC, 1964-74, dir. broadcast services, v.p., 1974-86; media cons., 1986—2010; editor, pub. Aberdeen (Miss.) Examiner, 1951-61. Served with USNR, 1943-45. Inducted into Ky. Journalism Hall of Fame, 1985 Mem. Kappa Sigma. Clubs: N.Y. Athletic, Nat. Press, International. Home: Vienna, Va. Died Mar. 21, 2010.

STEMPLER, JACK LEON, aerospace executive; b. Newark, Oct. 30, 1920; s. Morris and Ida (Friedman) S.; m. J. Adelaide Williams, Oct. 28, 1950; children: Mark N., Sandra J., Carrie B. BA, Montclair State U., NJ, 1943; LL.B., Cornell U., 1948. Bar: NY 1949, DC 1949. Atty. com. uniform code mil. justice Dept. Def., 1948-49, atty. adviser legis. div., 1949-50; asst. counsel Munitions Bd., 1950-53; counsel Armed Forces Housing Agy., 1952-54, Advanced Research Projects Agy., 1958-65; asst. gen. counsel logistics Dept. Def., 1953-65, asst. to sec. def. for legislative affairs, 1965-70; gen. counsel Dept. Air Force, 1970-77; asst. to sec. of def. for legis. affairs, 1977-81; v.p. legis. affairs LTV Aerospace, Washington, 1982-92; ret., 1992. Cons. in field. Served to 1st lt. USMCR, 1942-46, PTO. Recipient Outstanding Civilian Performance award Dept. Def., 1959, Distinguished Civilian Service award, 1965, Distinguished Civilian Service award with palm, 1969, with 2d bronze palm, 1970; Exceptional Civilian Service award USAF, 1973, 75, 77; awarded Presdl. rank of Disting. Exec., 1980; recipient Disting. Public Service award Dept. Def., 1981 Mem. Fed. Bar Assn., D.C. Bar Assn., Cornell Law Sch. Assn. Home: Woodbridge, Va. Died Dec. 22, 2009.

STENVIG, CHARLES S., former mayor; b. Mpls., Jan. 16, 1928; s. Selmer and Myrtle (Lee) S.; m. Audrey Thompson, Aug. 6, 1951; children: Terri, Tracy, Todd, Thomas. BA, Augsburg Coll., 1951. From mem. to dep. chief Mpls. Police Dept., 1956-81; mayor City of Mpls., Mpls., 1969-73, 76-78; pres. Police Officers Fedn. Mpls., 1965-69. Mem. Dir N.G., 1952-53 Served with AUS, 1946-47, PTO. Recipient Law Enforcement commendation S.A.R., 1970, Reverence for Law award Eagles, 1969 Mem. Internat. Conf. Police Assn. (v.p. 1966-69, award 1970), Minn. Police and Peace Officers Assn., VFW (Gold medal of merit 1972, nat. security com.), Sons of Norway, Mil. Order Cootie. Lodges: Masons, Shriners. Methodist. Home: Minneapolis, Minn. Died Feb. 22, 2010.

STEPHAN, ALEXANDER FRIEDRICH, German language and literature educator; b. Lüdenscheid, Fed. Republic Germany, Aug. 16, 1946; arrived in US, 1968; s. Eberhard and

Ingeborg (Hörnig) S.; m. Halina Konopacka, Dec. 15, 1969; 1 child, Michael. MA, U. Mich., 1969; PhD, Princeton U., 1973. Instr. German Princeton (NJ) U., 1972-73; from asst. prof. to prof. German UCLA, 1973-85; prof. German U. Fla., Gainesville, 1985-2000, chmn., 1985-93; prof. German, Ohio Eminent scholar, sr. fellow Mershon Ctr., Ohio State U., from 2000. Author: Christa Wolf, 1976, Die deutsche Exilliteratur, 1979, Christa Wolf (Forschungsbericht), 1981, Max Frisch, 1983, Anna Seghers im Exil, 1993, Im Visier des FBI, 1995, paperback edit. 1998, English transl. Communazis, 2000, Anna Seghers: Das siebte Kreuz. Welt und Wirkung eines Romans, 1997; editor: Peter Weiss: Die Ästhetik des Widerstands, 1983, 3d edit., 1990, Exil. Literatur und die Künste, 1990, Exil-Studien, from 1993, Christa Wolf: The Author's Dimension, 1993, 2d edit., 1995, Themes and Structures, 1997, Uwe Johnson: Speculations about Jakob and Other Writings, 2000, Early 20th Century German Fiction, 2003, Anna Seghers, Die Entscheidung, 2003, Americanism and Anti-Americanism. The German Encounter with American Culture after 1945, 2004, Exile and Otherness: New Approaches to the Experience of the Nazi Refugees, 2005, The Americanization of Europe: Culture, Diplomacy, and Anti-Americanism After 1945, 2006; co-editor: Studies in GDR Culture and Society, 1981—90, Schreiben im Exil, 1985, The New Sufferings of Young Werther and Other Stories from the GDR, 1997, Rot=Braun? Brecht Dialog, 2000, Nationalsozialismus und Stalinismus bei Brecht und Zeitgenossen, 2000, Jeans, Rock und Vietnam. Amerikanische Kultur in der DDR, 2002, Refuge and Reality: Feuchtwanger and the European Emigres in California, 2005, Das Amerika der Autoren von Kafka bis, 2006, America On My Mind, 2006; co-prodr.: (TV films) Im Visier des FBI, 1995, Das FBI und Marlene Dietrich, 2000, Das FBI und Brechts Telephon, 2002, Exilanten und das OSS, 2002, Thomas Mann und der CIA, 2002. Grantee, NEH, 1974, 1984, 1997, Am. Coun. Learned Socs., 1976, 1977, 1984, Am. Philos. Soc., 1979, 1981, 1992, Humboldt Found., 1988, 1994, 1998—99, 2002—03, Guggenheim Found., 1989, German Acad. Exch. Svcs., 1993, 1997, Feuchtwanger Meml. Libr., 1998, Weichmann Stiftung, 1998, Transcoop/AvH, 2002—04; Fulbright Sr. Specialist, from 2005. Mem.: German PEN, German Assn. for Am. Studies, German Studies Assn., Internat. Anna Seghers Soc., Soc. Exile Studies. Home: Columbus, Ohio. Died May 29, 2009.

STEPHANY, JAROMIR, artist, educator; AAS, Rochester Inst. Tech., 1956, BFA, 1958; MFA, Ind. U., 1960. Co-lectr. history of photography Rochester (N.Y.) Inst. Tech., 1961-66; assoc. prof. Md. Inst., Balt., 1966-73, chmn. dept. photography and film, 1968-73; assoc. prof. U. Md., Baltimore County, from 1973, chmn. visual arts dept., 1976-77. Mem. staff George Eastman House (now Internat. Mus. Photography), 1961-66;photographer-in-residence Skidmore Coll., 1969; vis. assoc. prof. U. Del., Newark, 1976; lectr. and cons. in field. Author: The Developing Image, 1979; editor: (newsletter) The Annapolis Power Squadron, 1990—; contbr. articles to profl. jours.; one-man shows include Foto Gallery, N.Y.C., 1975, Greater Reston Art Ctr., Va., 1977; exhibited in group shows at Fells Point Gallery, Balt., 1976, G.H. Dalsheimer Gallery, Balt., 1982, Franklin Inst. Sci. Mus., 1983, IBM Gallery Sci. and Art, N.Y.C., 1984, Rehoboth Art Ctr., 1985, U. Md., Baltimore County, 1988, 90, 92; represented in permanent collection St. Petersburg (Fla.) Mus. of Art. Grantee Union Ind. Art Colls., 1971-72, U. Md., 1982, 91, U.S. Power Squadron, 1993. Mem. Nat. Soc. Photographic Edn. (bd. dirs. 1973-74), Md. Coun. Arts Media (com. 1973), Soc. Photographic Edn. (lectr., nat. conv., 1st chmn. 1974-80, editor newsletter). Home: Severna Park, Md. Died Apr. 14, 2010.

STEPHENS, GEORGE CHRISTOPHER, geology educator; b. Washington, Jan. 20, 1943; s. Russell Montgomery and Christina Haas (Chambers) S.; m. Suzanne W. Nicholson, May 1, 1982; children: Christopher, Sarah. BS, George Washington U., 1967, MS, 1969; PhD, Lehigh U., 1972. Asst. prof. geology LaSalle Coll., Phila., 1972-75, Bryn Mawr (Pa.) Coll., 1975-78, George Washington U., Washington, 1978-82, assoc. prof., 1982-88, prof., 1988—2009, dept. chair, 1989-98. Geologist Alrae Engring., Inc., Vancouver, B.C., Can., 1969-76, U.S. Geol. Survey, Denver, 1980-85. Contbr. 31 articles and 47 abstracts to profl. publs. Recipient Antarctic Svc. medal NSF, 1970. Fellow Geol. Soc. Am.; mem. Am. Geophys. Union, Geol. Assn. Can. Home: Arlington, Va. Died Nov. 2, 2009.

STEPHENS, SIDNEY DEE, human resources specialist, retired chemical manufacturing company executive; b. St. Joseph, Mo., Apr. 26, 1945; s. Lindsay Caldwell and Edith May (Thompson) S.; m. Ellen Marie Boeh, June 15, 1968 (div. 1973); m. Elizabeth Ann Harris, Sept. 22, 1973; 1 child, Laura Nicole. BS, Mo. Western State U., 1971; MA, U. Houston, 1980; advanced cert. employment law, Inst. Applied Mgmt. and Law, 1998. Cert. Stephen Covey programs facilitator, 1997. Assoc. urban planner Met. Planning Commn., St. Joseph, 1967-71; prodn. acctg. assoc. Quaker Oats Co., St. Joseph, 1971-72, office mgr., pers. rep. Rosemont, Ill., 1972-73, employee and cmty. rels. mgr. New Brunswick, NJ, 1973-75, Pasadena, Tex., 1975-80; mgmt. cons., Houston, from 1981; regional mgr. human resources Syngenta Crop Protection Inc., from 2001, ret., from 2004; pvt. advisor fin. adminstrn. Ross Estates Investments, Ltd., Houston, from 2004; pvt. mgmt. cons. Stephens & Stephens Ltd., from 2006. Contbr. articles to profl. jours. With USNR, 1963-65. Mem. ASTD, Nat. Soc. for Human Resources Mgmt., Houston Human Resources Mgmt. Assn. (cmty. and govtl. affairs com. 1984-85, 85-86). Republican. Methodist. Died Sept. 4, 2009.

STEPHENSON, LARRY WAYNE, university administrator, accounting educator; b. Worthington, Ky., Apr. 18, 1940; s. Morris and Lucille (Tackett) Stephenson; m. Kay Wheeler, July 13, 1963; children: Kerry Rae Stephenson Logan, Robert Crayton. AB, Morehead State U., Ky., 1964, AM in Edn., 1968, M in Higher Edn., 1976. Tchr. & coach Augusta Pub. Schs., Ky., 1964—67; dir., housing Morehead State U., 1967—76, dean, students, 1976—80, dir., adminstrv. svcs., from 1980. Mem.: Am. Assn. Counseling and Devel., Nat. Assn. Student Pers. Advs. Democrat. Home: Falmouth, Ky. Died Jan. 24, 2009.

STERN, BARBARA BEA, marketing educator; b. NYC, Dec. 3, 1939; d. Al and Rose (Zipes) Bergenfeld; m. Harry Mark Stern, June 28, 1959 (div. May 1980); children: Leslie, Wendy. BA, Cornell U., 1959; MA, Hunter Coll., 1961; PhD, CUNY, 1965; MBA, Fordham U., 1981. Acad. dean St. Peter's Coll., Englewood Cliffs, N.J., 1976-79; asst. prof. mktg. Montclair (N.J.) State Coll., 1981; assoc. prof. mktg. Kean Coll. of N.J., Union, 1981-86, asst. chmn. dept. mgmt. sci., 1982-86; prof. mktg. Rutgers U., Newark, from 1986, vice-chair dept. mktg. Author: Is Networking for You?, 1981; mem. editl. bds. scholarly jours.; contbr. articles to profl. jours. Recipient Leavey award for Excellence Freedoms Found. Valley Forge, 1984. Mem. Am. Mktg. Assn. (co-chair summer edn. conf. 1995), Am. Acad. Advt. (chmn. pubs. com. 1990-94, award for outstanding contbn. to rsch. 1997), Assn. for Consumer Rsch. (adv. coun.), Soc. for Consumer Psychology, Round Table Scholars, Phi Beta Kappa, Phi Kappa Phi, Omicron Delta Epsilon. Home: San Francisco, Calif. Died Jan. 15, 2009.

STERN, JOSEPH SMITH, JR., former footwear manufacturing company executive; b. Cin., Mar. 31, 1918; s. Joseph S. and Miriam (Haas) S.; m. Mary Stern, June 14, 1942; children: Peter Joseph, William Frederick, Peggy Ann Graeter. AB, Harvard U., 1940, MBA, 1943; HHD (hon.), Xavier U., 1988; DSc (hon.), U. Cin., 1989. With R. H. Macy & Co., NYC, 1940-41; with U.S. Shoe Corp., Cin., 1941-68, v.p., 1951-65, pres., 1965-66, chmn. bd., chief exec. officer, 1966, chmn. exec. com., 1966-68, dir., 1956-70. Prof. bus. policy emeritus U. Cin. Pres. bd. trustees Cin. and Hamilton County Pub. Libr.; chmn. Cin. Bicentennial Com., Greater Cin. Tall Stacks Commn.; trustee Cin. Music Hall Assn., Cin. Hist. Soc., Children's Hosp. Med. Center, Cin. Symphony Orch., Cin Country Day Sch., 1956-72, Family Svc., Cin., 1964-82; trustee, pres. Cin. Mus. Festival Assn.; pres. bd. trustees Children's Convalescent Hosp., Cin., 1972-75; bd. overseers vis. com. univ. libr. Harvard U. Served to lt. USNR, 1943-46. Recipient Disting. Community Svc. award NCCJ, 1986, Great Living Cincinnatian award Cin. C. of C., 1989, Disting. Svc. award U. Cin. Coll. Bus., 1992. Mem. Am. Footwear Industries Assn. (life; dir.) Jewish (past pres. temple). Clubs: Literary (Cin.), Harvard (Cin.) (pres. 1965), Queen City (Cin.), Queen City Optimists, Harvard (N.Y.C.). Home: Cincinnati, Ohio. Died Jan. 2, 2010.

STERNS, HARVEY NELSON, education educator; b. Detroit, Feb. 25, 1924; s. Roy Andrew and Florence Edith (Gross) S.; children: Robin, Holly. BS, Wayne State U., 1950, MEd, 1955; PhD, U. Mich., 1968. Cert. tchr., Mich. Elem. tchr. Dependent Schs., Germany, 1952-57; art tchr. Oak Park (Mich.) Schs., 1957-62; elem. prin. L'Anse Creuse Schs., Mt. Clemens, Mich., 1962-66; asst. supt. Orchard Lake Schs., West Bloomfield, Mich., 1966-69; assoc. prof. Marshall U., Huntington, W.Va., 1969-72; from prof., assoc. dean to prof. edn. Lock Haven (Pa.) U., 1972-90, prof., chair, 1990-92, prof. emeritus, from 1992. Contbr. chpt. to book, articles to profl. jours. With USAF, 1943-46. Mem. AAUP, ASCD, Phi Delta Kappa (historian 1988-90), Phi Kappa Phi. Home: Kingshill,. Died Jan. 15, 2009.

STEVENS, ALVA LEWIS, management consultant; b. Traverse City, Mich., Oct. 15, 1938; s. Jack Jerome and Dorothy Rose (Hunter) Stevens; m. Anna Maria Montano, July 9, 1960; children: Donald, James, Thomas, Robert. BA, Golden Gate U., 1973; diploma, Harvard Grad. Sch. Bus., 1976. Cost acctg. mgr. Optical Coating Lab., Santa Rosa, Calif., 1962—68; v.p. T. & W. Mfg. Co., Santa Rosa, 1968—69, gen. mgr., 1968—69; mgr. materials Prescolite, San Leandro, Calif., 1969—74; v.p. mfg. North Face, Berkeley, Calif., 1974—77; pres. A.L. Stevens, Inc., Diablo, Calif. Contbr. scientific papers. With USN, 1956—59. Mem.: Am. Prodn. and Inventory Control Soc. (pres. Golden Gate chpt. 1975, regional v.p. 1976—77, Personal Achievement award 1976). Republican. Roman Catholic. Home: Alamo, Calif. Died Apr. 24, 2009.

STEVENS, MARILYN RUTH, editor; b. Wooster, Ohio, May 30, 1943; d. Glenn Willard and Gretchen Elizabeth (Ihrig) Amstutz; m. Bryan J. Stevens, Oct. 11, 1969; children: Jennifer Marie, Gretchen Anna. BA, Coll. Wooster, 1965; MAT, Harvard U., 1966; JD, Suffolk U., 1975. Bar: Mass. 1975. Tchr. Lexington (Mass.) Pub. Schs., 1966-69; with Houghton Mifflin Co., Boston, from 1969, editl. dir. sch. depts., 1978-81, editl. dir. math. scies. sch. divsn., 1981-84, mng. editor sch. pub., 1984—2005. Mem.: Cosmopolitan Neighborhood Assn. Home: Boston, Mass. Died July 23, 2009.

STEVENS, TED (THEODORE FULTON STEVENS), former United States Senator from Alaska; b. Indpls., Nov. 18, 1923; s. George A. and Gertrude (Chancellor) S.; m. Ann Mary Cherrington, Mar. 29, 1952 (dec. 1978); children: Susan B., Elizabeth H., Walter C., Theodore Fulton, Ben A.; m. Catherine Chandler, 1980; 1 child, Lily Irene. BA, U. Calif. at Los Angeles, 1947; LL.B., Harvard U., 1950. Bar: Calif., Alaska, D.C., U.S. Supreme Ct. bars. Atty. Northcutt Ely, Washington, 1950—52, Collins & Clasby, Fairbanks, Alaska, 1953; US atty. Dist. Alaska US Dept. Justice, Fairbanks, Alaska, 1953-56; legis. counsel US Dept. Interior, Washington, 1956—57, asst to sec., 1958—59, solicitor, 1960; ptnr. Stevens & Roderick, Anchorage, 1961—63, Stevens & Stringer, Anchorage, 1964, Stevens, Savage, Holland, Erwin & Edwards, Anchorage, 1964—65, Stevens & Holland, Anchorage, 1966—68; mem. Alaska House of Reps., 1965-68, majority leader, speaker pro tem, 1967-68; US Senator from Alaska, 1968—2009; minority whip, 1977—81; majority whip, 1981—85; pres. pro tempore, 2003—07; chmn. US Senate Appropriations Com., 1997—2001, 2003—05, US Senate Commerce, Sci., & Transp. Com., 2005—07, vice chmn., 2007—09. Served in USAF, 1943—46. Decorated Disting. Flying Cross, Air medal with Cluster, Yuan Hai Medal Chinese Nationalist Govt., China-Burma-India Ribbion; recipient Alaska 49'er, Alaska Press Club, 1963, Disting. Svc. Award, UCLA, 1971, Man of Yr. Award, Nat. Fisheries Inst., 1975; named Alaskan of Yr., 1974. Mem. ABA, Alaska Bar Assn., Calif. Bar Assn., D.C. Bar Assn., American Legion, VFW. Lodges: Rotary, Pioneers of Alaska, Igloo #4. Republican. Episcopalian. Died Aug. 10, 2010.

STEVENSON, CHARLES BEMAN, business educator; b. Columbus, Ohio, Oct. 30, 1922; s. Arthur Edwin and Mary Lucille (Beman) S.; BA, George Washington U., 1960, MA, 1962; diploma U.S. Army Command and Gen. Staff Coll., 1962; postgrad. U. Pitts., 1968-74, 80-81; m. Sara DeSalles Gilroy, June 12, 1948. Enlisted in U.S. Army, 1942, commd. 2d lt., 1943, advanced through grades to lt. col., 1963, ret., 1968; prof. mil. sci. Indiana U. Pa., 1965-68, asst. prof. bus. mgmt., 1968-71, assoc. prof., 1972-89, also dir. IUP Econ. Edn. Ctr., prof. emeritus, 1991—, sec., founder IUP Coll. Bus. Adv. Coun., 1978—; founder Coll. Bus. Fgn. Student Intern. Program; v.p. Mgmt. Scis. Resources, 1988-89; pres., mgmt. cons. CBS & Assocs, 1990—; pub. policy expert Heritage Found., 1986—; founder IUP Wash. D.C. Leadership Tgn. Trips, 1987-91; lectr. in field. Mem. edn. com. Pa. C. of C. 1976-83; chmn. Indiana County ARC, 1975-76; trustee Episcopal Diocese of Pitts., 1975-78, 79-80, mem. planning commn., 1975-82; mem. vestry, sr. warden St. Peter's Episc. Ch., 1983-85; mem. Episc. Diocesan Council, 1983-85. Decorated Legion of Merit; recipient Achievement awards, honor certs. Freedoms Found. at Valley Forge, 1986, Pub. Svc. award Dept. Army, 1986; others. Mem. NRA, VFW, Ind. Personnel Assn. (pres. 1981-83) Am. Mgmt. Assn., Ret. Officers Assn., Mil. Order World Wars (comdr., founder chpt. 200), Assn. Pa. U. Bus. and Econ. Faculty (pres. 1985-88). Republican. Club: Army and Navy (Washington). Home: Madison, Conn. Died Mar. 19, 2009.

STEVENSON, NEIL MACGILL, retired military officer, minister; b. Bklyn., Dec. 26, 1930; s. Henry and Margaret (MacGill) S.; m. G. Diane Neal, July 6, 1953; children: Heather Rosecrans, Holly Hankins, Heidi Tanguay BA, Tarkio Coll., 1952, D.D. (hon.), 1983; M.Div., Pitts. Theol. Sem., 1955, M.Th., 1968. Ordained to ministry Presbyterian Ch. U.S.A., 1955. Commd. officer U.S. Navy, advanced through grades to rear adm., command chaplain Naval Air Sta. Glenview, Ill., 1965-67, chaplain III MAF Vietnam, 1968-69, chief chaplain's staff Washington, 1969-72, command chaplain Orlando, Fla., 1973-76, fleet chaplain Pacific Fleet, 1977-80, dep. chief chaplain Washington, 1980-83, chief chaplain, 1983—85. Decorated Legion of Merit with Combat V, Meritorious Service medal, Nat. Def. medal, Armed Forces Expeditionary medal Home: Williamsburg, Va. Died Nov. 21, 2009.

STEVER, HORTON GUYFORD, aerospace scientist, engineer, educator, consultant; b. Corning, NY, Oct. 24, 1916; s. Ralph Raymond and Alma (Matt) Stever; m. Louise Risley Floyd, June 29, 1946 (dec. 2007); children: Horton Guyford, Sarah, Margarette, Roy. AB, Colgate U., 1938, ScD (hon.), 1958; PhD, Calif. Inst. Tech., 1941; LLD, U. Pitts., 1966, Lehigh U., 1967, Allegheny Coll., 1968, Ill. Inst. Tech., 1975; DSc, Northwestern U., 1966, Waynesburg Coll., 1967, U. Mo., 1975, Clark U., 1976, Bates Coll., 1977; DH, Seton Hill Coll., 1968; D.Engring., Washington and Jefferson Coll., 1969, Widener Coll., Poly. Inst. N.Y., 1972, Villanova U., 1973, U. Notre Dame, 1974; DPS, George Washington U., 1981. Staff radiation lab. MIT, Cambridge, Mass., 1941—42, asst. prof., 1946—51, assoc. prof. aero. engring., 1951—56, prof. aero. and astro., 1956—65, head depts. mech. engring., naval architecture, marine engring., 1961—65, assoc. dean engring., 1956—59, exec. officer guided missiles program, 1946—48; chief scientist USAF, 1955—56; pres. Carnegie-Mellon U., Pitts., 1965—72; dir. NSF, Washington, 1972—76; sci. adviser, chmn. Fed. Council Sci. & Tech., 1973—76; sci. & tech. adviser to Pres. Office Sci. & Tech. Policy, 1976—77. Secretariat guided missiles com. Joint Chiefs of Staff, 1945; sci. liaison officer London Mission, OSRD, 1942—45; guided missiles tech. evaluation group Rsch. and Devel. Bd., 1946—48; sci. adv. bd. to chief of staff USAF, 1947—69, chmn., 1962—69; steering com. tech. adv panel on aeros. Dept. Def., 1956—62; chmn. spl. com. space tech. NASA, chmn. rsch. adv. com. missile and spacecraft aerodynamics, 1959—65; mem. Nat. Sci. Bd., 1970—72, ex-officio, chmn. exec. com., 1972—75; mem. Def. Sci. Bd., 1962—68; adv. panel U.S. Ho. Reps. Com. Sci. and Astronautics, 1959—72; mem. Pres.'s Commn. on Patent System, 1965—67; chmn. U.S.-USSR Joint Commn. Sci. and Tech. Cooperation, 1973—77, Fed. Council Arts and Humanities, 1972—76; Pres. com. Nat. Sci. medal, 1973—77. Author: Flight, 1965, In War and Peace: My Life in Science and Technology, 2002; contbr. articles to profl. jours. Past trustee Colgate U., Shady Side Acad., Sarah Mellon Scaife Found., Buckingham Sch; trustee Univ. Rsch Assn., from 1977, pres., 1982—85; trustee Woods Hole Oceanographic Inst., from 1980, Sci. Svc., from 1982, Univ. Corp. for Atmospheric Rsch., 1980—83; bd. dirs. Saudi Arabia Nat. Ctr. for Sci. and Tech., 1978—81; bd. govs. U.S. Israel Binat. Sci. Found., 1972—76, chmn., 1972—73; mem. Carnegie Commn. on Sci., Tech. and Govt., 1988—93. Recipient Pres.'s Cert. of Merit, 1948, Exceptional Civilian Svc. award, USAF, 1956, Scott Gold medal, American Ordinance Assn., 1960, Award, US Dept. Def., 1969, NASA, 1988, Nat. Medal of Sci., The White House, 1991, Vannever Busch award, Nat. Sci. Bd., 1997. Fellow: AAAS, AIAA (hon.; pres. 1960—62), Am. Phys. Soc., Royal Soc. Arts, Am. Philos. Soc., Am. Acad. Arts and Scis., Royal Aero. Soc.; mem.: NAE (chmn. aero. and space engring. bd. 1967—69, fgn. sec. 1984—88), NAS (chmn. assembly engring. 1979—83, chmn. policy divsn. 1995—97), Royal Acad. of Engring. of Great Britain (fgn. mem.), Acad. Engring. of Japan (fgn. mem.), Cosmos Club, Phi Beta Kappa, Tau Beta Pi, Sigma Gamma Tau, Sigma Xi. Episcopalian. Died Apr. 9, 2010.

STEWART, JAMES JOSEPH, pharmacist; b. Bklyn., Mar. 19, 1925; s. James B. and Katherine (Bulmer) S.; m. Eileen Nelson, Aug. 30, 1947 (div.); children: James, Eileen, Margaret, John, Thomas, Donald, Kathleen, Theresa, Keith; m. Elizabeth Farrar, Sept. 29, 1985. B.S. in Pharmacy, St. John's U., 1950. Asst. to med. dir. Am. Export Lines, 1947-48; pharmacy intern Clayton & Edwards Pharmacy, 1948-50; surg. supply salesman Fulton Surg. Co., 1950-52; pharmacist, purchasing agt. Rockefeller U., N.Y.C., 1952—, supt. purchases, 1970—, chief pharmacist, 1965—, dir. purchasing, 1970—. Coach Little League, 1975-77; cub master Cub Scouts, 1960-63; scout master Boy Scouts Am., 1964-66. Served with USNR, 1943-46; PTO. Mem. Nat. Assn. Ednl. Buyers, Am. Soc. Hosp. Pharmacists. Roman Catholic. Avocations: tennis, fishing, gardening. Home: Westwood, NJ. Died May 3, 2009.

STILES, STUART LEE, wholesale company executive; b. Green Bay, Wis., Sept. 14, 1915; s. Walter Stephen and Leela S.; m. Nancy Jean Gochnaver, Feb. 24, 1945; children—Stephen, Wendy, Darcy. Ph.B., U. Wis., Madison, 1940. With Morley Murphy Co., Green Bay, Wis., from 1940, pres., from 1977, vice chmn. bd., from 1978. Mem. adv. bd. Salvation Army; bd. dirs. Nat. R.R. Mus., Green Bay; treas. Bellin Hosp. Bd. Served to lt. USNR, 1940-45. Mem. U. Wis. Green Bay Founders Assn. Clubs: Masons. Congregationalist. Died May 25, 2009.

STINE, RICHARD DENGLER, college administrator; b. Phila., Sept. 9, 1926; s. Harold S. and Alice E. (Dengler) S.; m. Elizabeth White Leiby, May 18, 1968; children: Nancy Bosniak, Catherine Chumley, John Bower II, Elizabeth Deane Leiby Wruck, Jane Leiby Geason. AB, U. Pa., 1947, PhD, 1951; D.Litt., Monmouth Coll., NJ, 1973. Dir. admissions Roanoke Coll., 1951-53, dir. admissions and devel., 1953-54; campaign dir. Tamblyn & Brown, NYC, 1954-56; project dir. devel. U. Pa., 1956-60, dir. med. devel., 1960-67, asst. to v.p. devel. and pub. relations, 1967-68; asso. Heald, Hobson & Assos., NYC, 1968-70; pres. Monmouth (Ill.) Coll., 1970-74; dir. undergrad. programs Wright Inst., Berkeley, Calif., 1974-76; v.p. for devel. Claremont (Calif.) U. Center, 1976-80; v.p. instl. advancement Monmouth (N.J.) Coll., 1980-83; dir. Roberson Ctr. for Arts and Scis., Binghamton, N.Y., 1983-86; mgr. campaign The Cooper Union for Advancement of Sci. and Art, NYC, from 1986. Home: Wheeler, Oreg. Died Apr. 22, 2009.

STINNETT, LEE HOUSTON, newspaper association executive; b. Madisonville, Ky., Jan. 8, 1939; s. James Houston and Eolia Frances (Hutchings) S. BA, U. Ky., 1961, MA, 1963. Reporter Times-Picayune, New Orleans, 1963-64; med. reporter The News, Charlotte, N.C., 1965-66; devel. writer Emory U., Atlanta, 1966-67, univ. editor, 1968-69; assoc. dir. So. Newspaper Pubs. Assn. and Found., Atlanta, 1970-80; project dir. Am. Soc. Newspaper Editors, Washington, 1981-82, exec. dir., from 1983. Contbr. articles to profl. jours. Del. Arlington Civic Fedn.; active civil rights groups and polit. orgns., Washington and No. Va., Whitman-Walker Clinic, Washington; pres. Arlington Gay and Lesbian Alliance, 1989-90. Mem. Newspaper Assn. Mgrs., Four Seasons Garden (pres. 1983), ACLU of No. Va. (bd. dirs. 1992-94). Democrat. Avocations: gardening, swimming, music. Died Nov. 7, 2009.

STINSON, MARY FLORENCE, retired nursing educator; b. Wheeling, W.Va., Feb. 11, 1931; d. Rolland Francis and Mary Angela (Voellinger) Kellogg; m. Charles Walter Stinson, Feb. 12, 1955; children: Kenneth Charles, Karen Marie Wiberg, Kathryn Anne Kartye. BSN, Coll. Mt. St. Joseph, 1953, postgrad., 1983; MEd, Xavier U., Cin., 1967; postgrad., U. Cin., 1981. Staff nurse contagious disease ward Cin. Gen. Hosp., 1953-54, asst. head nurse med. and polio wards, 1955, acting head nurse, clin. instr., 1955-56; instr. St. Francis Hosp. Sch. Practical Nursing, Cin., 1956-57, Good Samaritan Hosp. Sch. Nursing, Cin., 1957—66; instr. refresher courses for nurses Cin. Bd. Edn. and Ohio State Nurses Assn. Dist. 8, 1967—70; coord. sch. health office Coll. Mt. St. Joseph, Ohio, 1969-72, instr. dept. nursing, 1974-79, asst. prof., 1979-89; RN assessor pre-admission screening sys. providing options & resources today Coun. on Aging Southwestern Ohio, 1989-90, quality assurance coord. pre-admission screen sys. providing options & resources today program, 1990-93, quality assurance supr. pre-admission screen sys. providing options & resources today and elderly svcs. programs, 1993-94; quality assurance mgr. Coun. Aging Southwestern Ohio, 1995-2000; ret., 2000. Staff nurse St. Francis/St. George Hosp., Cin., 1988-89; vol. ombudsman Pro Srs. of S.W. Ohio, 2005—. Charter mem. Adoptive Parents Assn. St. Joseph Infant and Maternity Home, 1966—70; women's com. for performing arts series Coll. Mt. St. Joseph; chmn. by-law com. Coll. Mt. St. Joseph Nursing Honor Soc., 1996—98; active St. Antoninus Rosary Altar and Sch. Soc., 1973—84, St. Antoninus Athletic Club, com. chmn., 1969—70; bd. dirs. Coll. Mt. St. Joseph Alumni Assn., 1982—84, sec., 1968—69, v.p., 1969—70, pres., 1970—71, chmn. revision of constn., 1976—77; homecoming chmn. Coll. Mt. St. Joseph, 1970, co-chmn., 1977, co-chair com. to celebrate 75 years of nursing edn., 2001—02; mem. com. to plan 50th ann. of graduation Coll. Mt. St. Joseph Alumni Assn., 2003. Mem. River Squares Club (v.p. 1967), Sigma Theta Tau (charter Omicron Omicron chpt. 1998—), St. Antonious Adult Social Group (pres. 2005-08). Democrat. Roman Catholic. Home: Cincinnati, Ohio. Died May 27, 2010.

STIRM, ROBERT PAUL, lawyer, construction company executive; b. NYC, Mar. 6, 1923; s. Paul and Gertrude Evelyn (Lindemeyer) S.; m. Martha Carolyn Godwin, Nov. 29, 1975; children— Carter L. Vinson, Paul Harter Stirm, Martha Sarah Vinson. BA, N.Y. U., 1946, JD, 1949, LL.M., 1954. Bar: N.Y. bar 1950. Dist. counsel Peter Kiewit Sons' Co., Trenton, N.J., 1951-66; gen. counsel Gulf Reston, Inc., Reston, Va., 1967-68; with Daniel Internat. Corp., Greenville, S.C., from 1968, v.p. law, corp. sec., from 1968. Dir. Applied Engring. Co., Fortis Corp. Served with AUS, 1943-46. Mem. Am. Bar Assn., S.C. Bar Assn., Zeta Psi, Phi Delta Phi. Clubs: Greenville Country (Greenville), Poinsett (Greenville). Methodist. Home: Greenville, SC. Died May 10, 2009.

STIVALA, SALVATORE SILVIO, chemist, educator; b. NYC, June 23, 1923; s. Ambrose and Betty (Latteri) S.; m. Virginia Cincotti, Oct. 14, 1950; children: Victoria, Richard. Student, Columbia U., 1941-43, AB, 1949; MS in Chem. Engring, Stevens Inst. Tech., 1952, MS, 1958, M.Engring. (hon.), 1964; PhD, U. Pa., 1960. Research engr. U.S. Testing Co., Hoboken, N.J., 1949-50; materials engr. Picatinny Arsenal, 1950-51; research asso., instr. Stevens Inst. Tech., Hoboken, 1951-57, asst. prof., 1960-61, asso. prof., 1961-64, prof. chemistry and chem. engring., from 1964, Rene Wasserman prof. chemistry and chem. engring., from 1981. NSF faculty fellow U. Pa., 1957-59; cons. govt. and industry. Co-author: Autoxidation of Hydrocarbons and Polyolefins, 1969, Elements of Polymer Degradation, 1971; co-editor: New Developments in Industrial Polysaccharides, 1985, Industrial Polysaccharides: The Impact of Biotechnology and Advanced Methodologies, 1987; contbr. to books, ency., sci. jours. Served with U.S. Army, 1943-46. Recipient Freygang Tchr. award Stevens Inst. Tech., 1964, Ottens research award, 1968; recipient Honor Scroll N.J. sect. Am. Inst. Chemists, 1977 Mem. Am. Chem. Soc., Soc. Plastics Engrs., ASTM, Sigma Xi, Phi Lambda Upsilon. Home: Englewd Clfs, NJ. Died Mar. 26, 2010.

STOCKER, ARTHUR FREDERICK, classics educator; b. Bethlehem, Pa., Jan. 24, 1914; s. Harry Emilius and Alice (Stratton) S.; m. Marian West, July 16, 1968. AB summa cum laude, Williams Coll., 1934; A.M., Harvard U., 1935, PhD, 1939. Instr. Greek Bates Coll., 1941—42; asst. prof. classics U. Va., 1946—52, assoc. prof. Va., 1952—60, prof. Va., 1960—84, prof. emeritus Va., from 1984, chmn. dept. Va., 1955-63, 68-78, assoc. dean Grad. Sch. Arts and Scis. Va., 1962—66; vis. asst. prof. classics U. Chgo., summer 1951. Editor: (with others) Servianorum in Vergilii Carmina Commentariorum Editio Harvardiana, Vol. II, 1946, Vol. III, 1965; assoc. editor: Classical Outlook. Served with USAAF, 1942-46, with USAAFR and USAFR, 1946-1974, ret. col., USAF. Sheldon Traveling fellow, Harvard U., 1940—41. Mem. Va. Classical Assn. (pres. 1949-52), Mid. West and South Classical Assn. (pres. So. sect. 1960-62, pres. 1970-71), Nat. Huguenot Soc. (pres. gen. 1989-91), Am. Philol. Assn., Mediaeval Acad. Am., Poetry Soc. Va. (pres. 1966-69), Soc. Colonial Wars in the State of Va., SAR (chpt. pres. 1972, 91), Huguenot Soc. Va. (pres. 1981-83), Raven Soc. (Raven award 1977), Phi Beta Kappa, Omicron Delta Kappa, Sons Am. Revolution, Sons Revolution. Republican. Presbyterian (elder). Clubs: Masons, Colonnade (Charlottesville, Va.), Farmington Country (Charlottesville, Va.), Commonwealth (Richmond, Va.), Army and Navy (Washington). Died Jan. 13, 2010.

STODDART, GEORGE ANDERSON, engineering and construction company executive; b. Oyster Bay, NY, Sept. 16, 1933; s. Percival D. and Florence A. (Anderson) S.; m. Gail Miller, Dec. 6, 1958; children: Penelope G., Timothy M. BS, Yale U., 1956; postgrad., NYU, 1960-62. With Scudder Stevens & Clark, NYC, 1960-73, ptnr., 1969-73; v.p. Thomson McKinnon, NYC, 1973-75; asst. v.p. Gulf and Western, Inc., NYC, 1975-77; with McDermott Internat., New Orleans, from 1977, v.p., from 1982. Mem. Chartered Fin. Analysts, N.Y. Soc. Security Analysts, Petroleum Investor Relations Assn., AIME Republican. Episcopalian. Home: Mount Kisco, NY. Died Apr. 6, 2010.

STOLLEY, ALEXANDER, advertising executive; b. Coethen Anhalt, Germany, May 12, 1922; arrived in US, 1923, naturalized, 1929; s. Mihail and Tatiana (Rainich) Stolarevsky; m. Patricia Martin, June 26, 1944 (dec. Aug. 1970); children: Christopher, Peter, Laura Stolley Smith, Annabel Stolley Hetzer, Megan Stolley Berry; m. Bette Scott Vogt, June 15, 1973. ME, U. Cin., 1948. With Cin. Milacron, Inc., 1941-50, dir. employee relations, 1948-50; with Northlich, Stolley, Inc., Cin., 1950-89, exec. v.p., 1959-67, pres., 1967-84; chmn. Northlich, Stolley, LaWarre, Inc. (formerly Northlich, Stolley, Inc.), Cin., 1984-89. Mem. exec. com. Cincinnatus Assn., 1968-73, sec., 1970-71, v.p., 1971-72, pres., 1972-73; mem. Cin. Council on World Affairs, 1969—; chmn. Contemporary Arts Center, Cin., 1966-67; mem. exec. com. Cin. Conv. and Visitors Bur., 1975, chmn. long range planning com., 1983; trustee Cin. Symphony Orch., 1969-75. Served to 1st lt. AUS, 1943-46. Mem. Bus., Profl. Advt. Assn., Greater Cin. C. of C. (exec. com. 1982-83) Clubs: Cin. Country, Literary, Gasparilla Beach, Lemon Bay Golf, Boca Bay Pass. Home: Bellows Falls, Vt. Died Jan. 14, 2010.

STONE, DAVID BARNES, investment advisor; b. Brookline, Mass., Sept. 2, 1927; s. Robert Gregg and Bertha L. (Barnes) S.; m. Sara Cruikshank, June 16, 1951 (div. July 1976); children— David Stevenson, Benjamin Barnes, Peter Cruikshank, Jonathan Fitch, Andrew Hasbrouck; m. Ellen J. Desmond, Feb. 16, 1980 (dec. Dec. 1999); 1 son, Daniel Desmond. AB, Harvard, 1950, MBA, 1952; D.C.S. (hon.), Suffolk U., 1969; LL.D., Northeastern U., 1974; L.H.D., Curry Coll., 1981. Vice pres. Hayden, Stone Inc. (and predecessor), 1962-65, chmn. exec. com., 1965-67; pres. N.Am. Mgmt. Corp., 1968-78, chmn., from 1978. Dir. Mass. Fin. Svcs. Group of Mut. Funds, 1989—; pres. Stonetex Oil Corp., Dallas, trustee, Eastern Enterprises. Pres. bd. trustees New Eng. Aquarium, 1959-70, chmn. bd. trustees, 1970-76; bd. overseers Boys Club Boston, 1956-61, treas., 1961-67; trustee Charles Hayden Found., 1966-92, Wellesley Coll., vice chmn. bd., 1992-95; chmn. Meml. Dr. Trust; mem. Woods Hole Oceanographic Instn. With U.S. Mcht. Marines, 1945-47. Mem. Investment Bankers Assn. (chmn. New Eng. group 1963, bd. govs. 1964-67) Clubs: Kittansett (Marion, Mass.); Country (Brookline, Mass). Home: Marion, Mass. Died Apr. 12, 2010.

STONE, DAVID M., former federal agency administrator, retired career military officer; b. 1952; m. Cynthia Faith Voth, 1977. Diploma, U.S. Naval Acad., 1974; MS in Nat. Security Affairs, U.S. Naval Postgrad. Sch., 1977; MA in Nat. Security/Strategic Studies, U.S. Naval War Coll., 1986; MS in Mgmt., Salve Regina Coll. Commd. ensign USN, 1974, advanced through ranks to rear adm., ret., 2002, various assignments to comdr. Middle East Force and Destroyer Squadron 50, 1994-96; chief of staff U.S. Sixth Fleet, 1996-98; comdr. NATO's Standing Naval Force Mediterranean, 1998-99; deputy director surface warfare USN, 99-00, Nimitz battlegroup comm., 2000-01; dir., environ. protection, safety & occupational health Office of the Chief of Naval Ops., Washington, 2001—02; fed. security dir. L.A. Internat. Airport, 2002—03; dep. chief of staff Transp. Security Adminstrn. (TSA), US Dept. Homeland Security, 2003—04, acting adminstr., 2003—04, asst. sec., adminstr., 2004—05. Decorated Legion of Merit (3 times), Def. Meritorious Svc. medal (2 times), Meritorious Svc. medal (3 times), Navy Commendation medal (3 times), Navy Achievement medal, others. Died Nov. 22, 2009.

STONE, EDWARD DURELL, JR., landscape architect and planner; b. Norwalk, Conn., Aug. 30, 1932; s. Edward Durell and Orlean (Vandiver) S.; m. Jacqueline Marty, Dec. 15, 1954 (div.); children: Edward D. III, Patricia Marty; m. Helen S. Eccelstone, Aug. 5, 1995. BA in Architecture, Yale U., 1954; M.Landscape Architecture, Harvard U., 1959. Pres. Edward D. Stone, Jr., & Assos. (P.A.), Ft. Lauderdale, Fla., 1960-89, chmn., from 1989; vis. critic, lectr. Tex. A&M U., Lawrence Inst. Tech., U. Ga., U. Mich., U. Ill., U. Va., U. Tenn.; adj. prof. landscape architecture U. Miami, Fla.; cons. First Lady's Com. More Beautiful Capital, 1965-68, Fla. Gov.'s. Conf. Environ. Quality, 1968-69; mem. Commn. Fine Arts, Washington, 1971-85; CEO Edward D. Stone & Assocs., Ft. Lauderdale, Fla. Mem. vis. com. Harvard U. Sch. Design; guest lectr. Chautaqua Inst., 1989, Golf Course Europe '89, Wiesbaden, Fed. Republic Germany, 1st Internat. Resort Conf., Tokyo, 1989, Symposium on European Recreational and Leisure Devel., Opio, France, 1989 Landscape archtl. designer: Pepsico World Hdqrs, Purchase, N.Y., 1972, Bal Harbour Shops (Fla.), 1971, El Morro Resort, Puerto La Cruz, Venezuela, 1972—, Profl. Golf Assn. Hdqrs. Master Plan, Palm Beach, Fla., 1978-79, Grand Cypress Resort, Orlando, Fla., 1983, Carambola Beach and Golf Club, St. Croix, V.I., 1988, Ft. Lauderdale (Fla.) Beach Revitalization, 1989, Onagawa, Japan, 1989, Pont Royal, Aix-en-Provence, France, 1989, Treyburn, Durham N.C., 1984, Euro Disney, Marne la Vallee, France, 1990, Riverwalk, Ft. Lauderdale, FL, 1989, El Conquistador, P.R., 1990. V.p. Landscape Architecture Found.; bd. dirs. Fla. Trust for Hist. Preservation, 1985-88. Capt. USAF, 1954-57. Recipient Profl. Landscape Architecture award HUD, 1968, awards Am. Assn. Nurserymen, 1967, 69, 70, 71, 77, 83, 88, 90, 91, Fla. Nurserymen and Growers Assn., 1982, 83, 85, 86, 88, 90, 91, 92, Am. Resort and Residential Devel. Assn., 1984, 85, 88, 89, 90, 91, 92, Interior Landscape Assn., 1984, 85. Fellow Am. Soc. Landscape Architects (13 awards 1963-88, 8 awards Fla. chpt. 1981-89, awards N.C. chpt. 1987, 88, 89, 92, medal 1994). Died July 10, 2009.

STORM, JACLYNN W., mental health and oncological nurse; b. Saginaw, Mich., Oct. 9, 1963; d. Jack Raymond and Rae Joyce (Minnis) S. AAS, Delta Coll., University Center, Mich., 1985, AAS in Nursing, 1988; student, Saginaw Valley U., Saginaw, Mich. Cert. in sign lang., advanced first aid and emergency care, chemotherapy, CPR, BCLS. Camp health dir. Saginaw YMCA-Camp Timbers; staff and charge nurse in oncology St. Marys Hosp., Saginaw; psychiat. staff and charge nurse Saginaw Gen. Hosp. Mem. Delta Coll. Student Nurse Assn. Alumni. Home: Saginaw, Mich. Died Jan. 5, 2009.

STOVER, CARL FREDERICK, foundation executive; b. Pasadena, Calif., Sept. 29, 1930; s. Carl Joseph and Margarete (Müller) S.; m. Catherine Swanson, Sept. 3, 1954 (div.); children: Matthew Joseph, Mary Margaret Stover Marker, Claire Ellen Stover Herrell; m. Jacqueline Kast, Sept. 7, 1973. BA magna cum laude, Stanford U., 1951, MA, 1954. Instr. polit. sci. Stanford U., 1953-55; fiscal mgmt. officer USDA, 1955-57; assoc. dir. conf. program pub. affairs Brookings Instn., 1957-59, sr. staff govtl. studies, 1960; fellow Center Study Democratic Instns., Santa Barbara, Calif., 1960-62; asst. to chmn. bd. editors Ency. Brit., 1960-62; sr. polit. scientist Stanford Research Inst., 1962-64; dir. pub. affairs fellowship program Stanford U., 1962-64; pres. Nat. Inst. Pub. Affairs, Washington, 1964-70, Nat. Com. U.S.-China Relations, 1971-72; pres., dir. Federalism Seventy-Six, Washington, 1972-74; dir. cultural resources devel. Nat. Endowment Arts, 1974-78; pres., dir. Cultural Resources, Inc., Washington, 1978-85; bd. dirs. H.E.A.R. Found., 1976-86, treas., 1976-80, pres., 1980-86. Bd. dirs. Ctr. for World Lit., pres., 1987-90, chmn., 1990-92; pvt. profl. cons., 1970-2010; scholar-in-residence Nat. Acad. Pub. Adminstrn., 1980-82; cons. in field. Author: The Government of Science, 1962, The Technological Order, 1963; Founding editor: Jour. Law and Edn., 1971-73; pub. Delos mag., 1987-92. Treas. Nat. Com. U.S.-China Rels., 1966-71, 82-87, 89-94, bd. dirs., 1966-74, 79-98, dir. emeritus, 1998-2010; bd. dirs. Coord. Coun. Lit. Mags., 1966-68, H.E.A.R. Found., 1976-86, treas., 1976-80;

trustee Inst. of Nations, 1972-76, Nat. Inst. Pub. Affairs, 1967-71, Kinesis Ltd., 1972-78; vol. Nat. Exec. Svc. Corps, 1984-89; mem. Fellowship of Reconciliation Fellow AAAS, Phi Beta Kappa (hon. lectr. 1972-87); mem. Am. Soc. Pub. Adminstrn., Fedn. Am. Scientists, Soc. Internat. Devel., Jordan Soc. (dir. 1982-84), Nat. Acad. Pub. Adminstrn. (hon.), Internat. Soc. Panetics (pres. 1991-95, chmn. 1995-98, chmn. emeritus 1990-2009, bd. govs. 1991—2009, founding mem. 1991-2010). Democrat. Presbyterian. Home: Silver Spring, Md. Died Jan. 19, 2010.

STRAHM, SAMUEL EDWARD, retired veterinarian; b. Fairview, Kans., Feb. 9, 1936; s. Silas Tobias and Martha Mary (Beyer) S.; m. Barbara Jean Wenger, June 1, 1958; children: Gregory Lee, Bryan Scott, Andrea Marie Enloe. BS, DVM, Kansas State U., 1959. Owner Osage Animal Clinic Inc., Pawhuska, Okla., 1959—2007, pres., 1985—2007; ret., 2007. Bd. dirs. 1st Nat. Bank, Pawhuska, Okla.; bd. cons. Profl. Exam Svc., 1990-2000; adv. bd. USDA Users, 1991-95; adv. com. Pew Nat. Health Profession Vet. Medicine, 1991; state adv. coun. Okla. Coop. Extension Svcs., 2000—, chmn.-elect, 2000-01, chmn., 2001-07. Bd. dirs. Okla. Sch. Bd. Assn., 1977-98, 2d v.p., 1993, 1st v.p., 1994, pres., 1996; Okla. All-State Sch. Bd., 1993, Pawhuska Sch. Bd., 1974-98, 2001-06, pres., 2003-06; active Pawhuska Planning Commn., 1965-70, Okla. State U. Centennial Commn., Stillwater, 1986-91; bd. dirs. Nat. Sch. Bd. Assn., 1996-99, exec. com., 1997-99, western reg. chmn., 1996. Recipient Disting. Alumni award Coll. Vet. Medicine Kans. State U., 1994, Fairview HS, 2004, Outstanding Svc. award Nat. Sch. Bds. Assn., 1997, Disting. Svc. award Nat. Bd. Exam. Com., 2000, Friend of Yr. award Okla. Coop. Extension, 2002. Mem.: Acad. Vet. Consultants, AVMA (pres. 1989—90, coun. govt. affair 1992—98, coun. edn. 2003—06, AVMA award 1986), Am. Vet. Med. Found. (chmn. 1995—98, treas. from 2004), Am. Assn. Theriogenealogy, Am. Assn. Bovine Practitioners (Practitioner of Yr. award 2002), Am. Assn. Vet. State Bds., Am. Assn. Vet. Specialty Bd. (rep. coun. on edn.), Am. Assn. Food Hygiene Vets. (bd. dirs. 2000—06), Nat. Bd. Vet. Med. Examiners (Disting. Svc. award 2000), Okla. Vet. Med. Assn. (all offices from 1959, Veterinarian of Yr. 1990, Disting. Svc. award 1998), Kans. Vet. Med. Assn., Okla. Bd. Vet. Med. Examiners (pres.), Pawhuska C. of C. (pres. 1968), Toastmasters Club, Pawhuska Jaycees (all offices 1959—69). Republican. Baptist. Avocations: gardening, fishing, flying. Home: Pawhuska, Okla. Died Dec. 17, 2009.

STRASSBURGER, JOHN ROBERT, retired academic administrator; b. Sheboygan, Wis., Apr. 6, 1942; s. J. Robert and Elizabeth (Mathewson) S.; m. Gertrude Hunter Mackie, Aug. 24, 1968; children: Sarah Electa, Gertrude Hunter. BA, Bates, 1964; Honours degree, Cambridge U., Eng., 1966; PhD, Princeton U., 1976; LHD (hon.), Tohoku Gakuin U., 2002. Faculty Hiram Coll., Ohio, 1970-82; program officer NEH, Washington, 1982-84; prof. history, exec. v.p., dean Coll., Knox Coll., Galesburg, Ill., 1984-94; pres. Ursinus Coll., Collegeville, Pa., 1995—2010, pres. emeritus, 2010, CEO Philip & Muriel Berman Mus. Art. Mem. commn. govt. rels. American Coun. Edn., 1997-2010 Contbr. articles to profl. jours. Bd. trustees Perkiomen Sch., 1997-2010 Mem. American Conf. Acad. Deans (chair 1990-91), Sunday Breakfast Club (Phila.) Coun. Independent Colleges (chmn. bd. 2008-09) Home: Collegeville, Pa. Died Sept. 22, 2010.

STRAUSBAUGH, J(OHN) DEAN, judge; b. Columbus, Ohio, Aug. 27, 1918; s. Harold Dale and Ethel Minerva (Dean) Strausbaugh; m. Mary Elizabeth Smith, Aug. 30, 1949; children: Elizabeth Ann O'Boyl, John Dean Jr. BA, Duke U., 1940; postgrad. in Indsl. Adminstrn., Bus. Sch. Harvard U., 1943; JD, U. Mich., 1947. Bar: Ohio 1948. Pvt. practice, Columbus, Ohio, 1948—54; reading clk. Ohio Ho. of Reps., 1950—54; 1st asst. City Atty's Office, Columbus, 1954—55; judge Franklin County Mcpl. Ct., Columbus, 1955—68, 10th Dist. Ct. Appeals, Columbus, from 1969. Bd. dirs. Mt. Carmel Hosp., Columbus; past pres. Columbus Area Cmmty. Mental Health Ctr.; mem. adv. bd. Franklin County Leukemia Soc., Alcoholism Prevention Bd., Columbus Dept. Health; bd. dirs. Community Agy. for Labor and Mgmt. Mem., past governing bd. 1st Cmty. Ch.; past bd. dirs., v.p. Catholic Social Svc. Served to lt. USN, 1943—46. Recipient Disting. Svc.1955 award, Columbus Jaycees. Mem.: University Club (pres.), Delta Tau Delta., Ohio Mcpl. Judges Assn. (pres. 1966—69), Ohio Cts. of Appeals Assn. (chief justice 1983), Columbus Bar Assn., Ohio State Bar Assn. Home: Columbus, Ohio. Died Mar. 18, 2010.

STRAUSS, PETER J., lawyer; b. Cin., Mar. 18, 1942; s. Carl Albert and Eleanor (Mendelson) S.; m. Katherine Louise Kraft, Aug. 31, 1968; children: Matthew, Anthony, Michael Clinton. BA, Williams Coll., 1963; MA, Columbia U., 1966; JD, Georgetown U., 1969. Bar: Ohio 1969, U.S. Dist. Ct. (so. dist.) Ohio 1969, U.S. Ct. Appeals (6th cir.) 1969. Urban developer City Cin., 1963-64, Office Econ. Opportunity, NYC, 1965-66; ptnr. Graydon, Head & Ritchey, Cin., from 1969. City councilman, Cin., 1981-93; vice mayor City Cin., 1987-93. Recipient Award of Merit Ohio Legal Ctr. Inst., 1985. Mem. ABA, Ohio Bar Assn., Cin. Bar Assn. Democrat. Jewish. Avocations: tennis, skiing, bicycling. Home: Cincinnati, Ohio. Died Feb. 12, 2010.

STREKEL, ROSEMARY TOMCZAK, investment company executive; b. Rochester, NY, Jan. 26, 1947; d. Leonard Victor and Ann Agnes (Kozlowska) Tomczak; m. Lawrence Francis Strekel, Dec. 17, 1966; children: Matthew Lawrence, Alexander Francis. BA in English, Coll. New Rochelle, 1968; MBA in Fin., U. Conn., 1977. Econ. rsch. analyst Sperry & Hutchinson Co., NYC, 1968—69; statistician Phoenix Mut. Life. Ins. Co., Hartford, Conn., 1969—74, securities analyst, 1974—77, mgr. bond investments, 1977—78, investment officer, 1978—82, asst. v.p. bond investments, 1982—84, 2d v.p. bond investments, from 1984. Fellow: CFA's, Life Mgmt. Inst.; mem.: Hartford Soc. Fin. Analysts. Republican. Roman Catholic. Home: Old Lyme, Conn. Died Apr. 24, 2010.

STRELZER, MARTIN, retired religious organization administrator; b. NYC, Oct. 17, 1925; s. Samuel Strelzer and Sadie Rothman; m. Florence Moskowitz, Jan. 30, 1947; children: Stuart, Amy. BBS, NYU, 1953. Pres. Harry D. Spielberg, Inc., NYC, 1967-70, Amstrel Textiles, Inc., NYC, 1970-83, Temple Beth-El, Closter, N.J., 1971-83; pres. N.J. West Hudson Valley region Union of Am. Hebrew Congregations, Paramus, N.J., 1976-80, trustee NYC, 1976-83, mem. exec. com., 1982-83, chmn. new congregations com., 1979-83; N.Am. dir. World Union for Progressive Judaism, NYC, 1984-95. Arbitrator Am. Arbitration Assn., N.Y.C., 1970-83. Chmn. Israel Bonds Campaign, Bergen County, N.J., 1971-72, United Jewish Appeal campaign, No. Valley, N.J., 1973-74, Community Rels. Com., Bergen County, 1980-81. Recipient Circle of Light Israel Bonds Testimonial Closter, N.J., 1980. Democrat. Home: Boynton Beach, Fla. Died Nov. 18, 2009.

STRICKLAND, BUNNY JUMP, caterer, accountant, bridal consultant; b. Athens, Ga., Apr. 12, 1925; d. Claude Arthur and Myrtle Florence (Barnwell) Jump; m. Warren Davis Strickland, Dec. 22, 1945; children— Warren David, Jacque Bonita Niles. A.A., Mercer U., 1969. Bookkeeper Firestone Tires, Jesup, Ga., 1950-61, Rural Electric Assn., Jesup, 1964-67, Jones Ford, Jesup, 1967-69, Wayne TV, Jesup, 1969-82; cosmetologist Laurie's, Jesup, 1961-64; contract caterer ITT-Rayonier, Jesup, 1980—; caterer, food service cons., Jesup, 1982—; bridal cons., floral designer, cake designer, gown seamstress, Jesup, 1962—. Asst. chmn. Bloodmobile Procurement Team, 1958; chmn. fund raising com. PTA, 1958; campaign aide Jones for Ga. Ho. Reps., 1955; hostess Thomas for U.S. Congress, 1982; pres. Band Boosters, 1961; chmn. benevolent com. 1st Bapt. Ch., 1968-75, dir. Sunday Schs., 1956- 68, tchr., 1978—; active Hosp. Aux., Jesup. Winner 1st place in class, Body Building Competition, Dalton, Ga., 1983, 3rd place overall, 1983; placed 2nd Paper Chase Mile Run, 1983. Mem. AAU. Democrat. Club: Jesup Garden (sec. 1974-78, pres. 1977-81). Lodge: Eastern Star. Avocations: oil painting; cooking; sewing; running; body building. Home: Roswell, Ga. Died Apr. 22, 2010.

STRINGER, GRETCHEN ENGSTROM, consulting volunteer administrator; b. Pitts., Feb. 25, 1925; d. Birger and Gertrude Anne (Schuchman) Engstrom; m. Loren F. Stringer, Oct. 3, 1953 (dec. Sept. 1992); children: Lizbeth, Pamela, William E., Frederick E. BA, Oberlin Coll., 1946; Cert. in Teaching, U. Pitts., 1951, SUNY, Buffalo, 1964, M, 1996. Cert. vol. adminstr. Owner, founder, pres. Vol. Cons., Clarence, NY, from 1979; owner, founder, officer Non Profit Mgmt. Ctr., Buffalo, 1995-2000. Founding pres., bd. dirs. Ctrl. Referral Svc. Author: The Board Manual Workbook, 1980, rev., 2004, The Instructors Guide, 1982, A Magical Formula, 1980; co-author: Non Profit Management Education, 1998; contbr. articles to profl. jours. Exec. dir. Vol. Action Ctr., United Way Buffalo and Erie County, 1978-81; founding vice chair Erie County Commn. on Status of Women, 1989-2000; pres. Girl Scout Coun. of Buffalo and Erie County, chair, gen. mgr. cadette encampment; bd. dirs. Clarence Ctrl. Sch. Dist., 1976-86; chair, gen. mgr. Buffalo and Erie County Bicentennial Parade, 1976, Erie County Ski Swap; bd. dirs. Longview Protestant Home for Children Bd., Millard Fillmore Jr. Bd., Prevention is Primary, N.Y. Bd. State Foster Care Youth Ind. Project, others; Cmty. Hero Torch Bearer Summer Olympics, 1996; del. White House Conf. on Small Bus., 1995; vol. steering com. Martin House Restoration Corp., 1988—. Recipient Pinny Wilson Vol. award Buffalo and Erie County, 1981, Continuing Svc. award Mass. Mutual, 1987, Girl Scouts Thanks Badge, 1983, Susan Reid Greene Russell award Jr. League of Buffalo, 1994, Assoc. of Yr. award Am. Bus. Women, 1997, Women Bus. Advocate of Yr. Small Bus. Adminstrn., 1998, Prime Time award Coord. Care, 1999, Woman of Achievement award AAUW, Buffalo chpt., 2001, Woman of Achievement award Every Woman Opportunity Ctr., 2004. Mem. Nat. Assn. Women Bus. Owners (bd. pres. Buffalo chpt. 1998-2000), N.Y. Assn. Vol. Ctrs. (founding exec. bd.), Vol. Admisntrs. Western N.Y. (founding pres. 1980), Buffalo Ambassadors of C. of C. (bd. dirs.), Women's Pavilion Pan Am. Centennial 2001 (founder, pres. bd. dirs. 1999-2001), Jr. League Buffalo, Inc. (sustainer v.p. 1998-2000), Assn. Vol. Adminstrn. (chair, gen. mgr. nat. conf. 1986, nat. trainer, re-cert. chair, subcom. vol. adminstrn. higher edn.). Died Jan. 6, 2009.

STROHMEYER, JOHN, writer, retired editor; b. Cascade, Wis., June 26, 1924; s. Louis A. and Anna Rose (Saladunas) S.; m. Nancy Jordan, Aug. 20, 1949 (dec. 2000); children: Mark, John, Sarah; m. Sylvia Ciernick Broady, Oct. 25, 2003. Student, Moravian Coll., 1941—43; AB, Muhlenberg Coll., 1947; MA in Journalism, Columbia U., 1948; LHD (hon.), Lehigh U., 1983. With Nazareth Item, Pa., 1940—41; night reporter Bethlehem Globe-Times, Pa., 1941—43, 1945—47; investigative reporter Providence Jour.-Bull., 1949—56; editor Bethlehem Globe-Times, 1956—64, v.p., 1961—84, dir., 1963—84. African-Am. journalism tchr. in Nairobi, Freetown, 1964; Atwood prof. journalism U. Alaska, Anchorage, 1987-88, writer-in-residence, 1989-2010; Clendinen Prof., U. S. Fla., 2001. Author: Crisis in Bethlehem: Big Steel's Struggle to Survive, 1986, Extreme Conditions: Big Oil and The Transformation of Alaska, 1993, Historic Anchorage, 2001. Lt. (j.g.) USNR, 1943-45. Pulitzer Traveling fellow, 1948; Nieman fellow, 1952-53; recipient Comenius award Moravian Coll., 1971; Pulitzer prize for editl. writing, 1972; Alicia Patterson Found. fellow, 1984, 85. Mem. Am. Soc. Newspaper Editors, Pa. Soc. Newspaper Editors (pres. 1964-66), Anchorage Racquet Club. Died Mar. 3, 2010.

STRONG, RUSSELL ARTHUR, university administator; b. Kalamazoo, Apr. 20, 1924; s. Walter A. and Dana (Sleeman) Strong; m. June Thomas, Aug. 17, 1946; children: William W., Jonathan T., David R., Christopher C., Timothy B. State editor Kalamazoo Gazette, 1948—51; dir. pub. info. Western Mich. U., Kalamazoo, 1951—63, dir. alumni rels., 1979—84, dir. devel. rsch., from 1984. Dir. news and info. Davidson Coll., NC, 1966—74; editor Mich. State U., East Lansing, 1963—66, Wake Forest U., Winston-Salem, NC, 1974; dir. info. svc. Wright State U., Fairborn, Ohio, 1975—76; dir. coll. rels. St. Andrews Presbyn. Coll., Laurinburg, NC, 1976—79. Author: First Over Germany, Biographical Directory, Command and Staff Officers; contbr. articles to profl. jours., chapters to books. Served to 1st lt. USAF, 1943—45. Decorated D.F.C., air medal with three oak leaf clusters. Mem.: 8th Air Force Meml. Mus. Found., 306th Bomb Group Hist. Assn. (editor, historian, sec.), 8th Air Force Hist. Soc. (v.p. 1983—84), Air Force Assn., Torch Club. Methodist. Died Oct. 2, 2009.

STROOCK, THOMAS FRANK, oil and gas company executive; b. NYC, Oct. 10, 1925; s. Samuel and Dorothy (Frank) S.; m. Marta Freyre de Andrade, June 19, 1949; children: Margaret, Sandra, Elizabeth, Anne. BA in Econs., Yale U., 1948; LLB (hon.), U. Wyo., 1995; PhD (hon.), Universidad del Valle, Guatemala, 2001. Landman Stanolind Oil & Gas Co., Tulsa, 1948-52; pres. Stroock Leasing Corp., Casper, Wyo., 1952-89, Alpha Exploration, Inc., 1980-89; ptnr. Stroock, Rogers & Dymond, Casper, 1960-82; dir. First Wyo. Bank, Casper, 1967-89; mem. Wyo. Senate, 1969-89, chmn. appropriations com., 1983-89, co-chmn. joint appropriations com., 1983-89, mem. mgmt. and audit com., pres., 1988-89; mem. steering com. Edn. Commn. of States; amb. to Guatemala Govt. of U.S., 1989-93; pres. Alpha Devel. Corp., from 1992; prof. pub. diplomacy U. Wyo., Laramie, 1993—2002, chmn. internat. adv. bd., from 2001. Dir. Wyo. Med. Ctr., 1996-2004. Rep. precinct committeeman, 1960-68; pres. Natrona County Sch. Bd., 1966, 69; pres. Wyo. State Sch. Bds. Assn., 1965-66; chmn. Casper Cmty. Recreation, 1955-60; chmn. Natrona County United Fund, 1963-64, Wyo. State Rep. Com., 1975-78, exec. com. 1954-60; del. Rep. Nat. Conv., 1956-76, 92; regional coord. campaign George Bush for pres., 1979-80, 87-88; chmn. Western States Rep. Chmn. Assn., 1977-78; chmn. Wyo. Higher Edn. Commn., 1969-71, Wyo. Health Access Task Force, 2003-04; mem. Nat. Petroleum Coun., 1972-77; chmn. trustees Sierra Madre Found. for Geol. Rsch., New Haven; chmn. Wyo. Nat. Gas Pipline Authority, 1987-88; bd. dirs. Ucross Found., Denver; mem. Nat. Pub. Lands Adv. Coun., 1981-85; trustee Nature Conservancy, 1993-2005; chmn. Wyo. Health Reform Commn., 1993-95, Universidad del Valle Found., Guatemala City, 1995-2000, trustee, 2000-2005. Sgt. USMC, 1943-46. Mem. Rocky Mountain Oil and Gas Assn., Petroleum Assn. Wyo., Kiwanis, Casper Country Club, Casper Petroleum Club, Yale Club N.Y. Republican. Unitarian Universalist. Died Dec. 13, 2009.

STROUPE, HENRY SMITH, university dean; b. Alexis, NC, June 3, 1914; s. Stephen Morris and Augie (Lineberger) S.; m. Mary Elizabeth Denham, June 2, 1942; children— Stephen Denham, David Henry. Student, Mars Hill Jr. Coll., 1931-33; BS, Wake Forest Coll., 1935, MA, 1937; PhD, Duke U., 1942. Faculty Wake Forest U., Winston-Salem, N.C., 1937—, assoc. prof. history, 1949-54, prof., 1954-84, prof. emeritus, from 1984, chmn. dept. history, 1954-68, dir. evening classes, 1957-61, dir. div. grad. studies, 1961-67, dean grad. sch., 1967-84, dean emeritus, from 1984. Vis. prof. history Duke U., 1960. Author: The Religious Press in the South Atlantic States, 1802-1865: An Annotated Bibliography with Historical Introduction and Notes, 1956; Mem. editorial bd.: N.C. Hist. Rev, 1963-69. Mem. N.C. Civil War Centennial Commn., 1959-60. Served from ensign to lt. USNR, 1943-46. Recipient Christopher Crittenden award N.C. Lit. and Hist. Assn., 1982 Mem. NC Hist. Soc. (pres. 1965), NC Lit. and Hist. Assn. (pres. 1974), Phi Beta Kappa, Omicron Delta Kappa. Democrat. Baptist. Died Aug. 20, 2009.

STUART, GLORIA, actress; b. Santa Monica, Calif., July 14, 1910; m. Blair Gordon Newell, June 21, 1930 (div. May 17, 1934); m. Arthur Shekman, July 29, 1934 (dec. Jan. 12, 1978); children: Blair Gordon Newell, Cylvia. Student, U. Calif., Berkeley. Founding mem. SAG. Actress: (films) Streets of Women, 1932, Back Street, 1932, The All-American, 1932, The Old Dark House, 1932, Air Mail, 1932, Laughter in Hell, 1933, Sweepings, 1933, Private Jones, 1933, The Invisible Man, 1933, The Girl in 419, 1933, The Kiss Before the Mirror, 1933, It's Great to Be Alive, 1933, Secret of the Blue Room, 1933, The Invisible Man, 1933, Roman Scandals, 1933, Beloved, 1934, I Like It That Way, 1934, I'll Tell the World, 1934, The Love Captive, 1934, Here Comes the Navy, 1934, Gift of Gab, 1934, Maybe It's Love, 1935, Gold Diggers of 1935, 1935, Laddie, 1935, Professional Soldier, 1935, The Prisoner of Shark Island, 1936, The Crime of Dr. Forbes, 1936, Poor Little Rich Girl, 1936, 36 Hours to Kill, 1936, The Girl on the Front Page, 1936, Wanted: Jane Turner, 1936, Girl Overboard, 1937, The Lady Escapes, 1937, Life Begins in College, 1937, Change of Heart, 1938, Rebecca of Sunnybrook Farm, 1938, Island in the Sky, 1938, Keep Smiling, 1938, Time Out for Murder, 1938, The Lady Objects, 1938, The Three Musketeers, 1939, Winner Take All, 1939, It Could Happen to You, 1939, Here Comes Elmer, 1943, The Whistler, 1944, Enemy of Women, 1944, She Wrote the Book, 1946, My Favorite Year, 1982, Mass Appeal, 1984, Wildcats, 1986, Titanic, 1997 (Acad. Award Nomination for Best Supporting Actress, Saturn award for Best Supporting Actress, Golden Globe award for Best Performance by an Actress in a Supporting Role, SAG award for Outstanding Performance by a Female Actor in a Supporting Role), The Love Letter, 1999, The Million Dollar Hotel, 2000, Land of Plenty, 2004; (TV movies) The Legend of Lizzie Borden, 1975, Adventures of The Queen, 1975, Flood!, 1976, In the Glitter Palace, 1977,

The Incredible Journey of Dr. Meg Laurel, 1979, The Best Place to Be, 1979, The Two Worlds of Jennie Logan, 1979, Fun and Games, 1980, The Violation of Sarah McDavid, 1981, Merlene of the Movies, 1981, There Were Times, Dear, 1985, Shootdown, 1985, She Knows Too Much, 1989, My Mother, the Spy, 2000, Murder, She Wrote: the Last Free Man, 2001; (TV appearances) The Waltons, 1975, Enos, 1980, Manimal, 1983, Murder, She Wrote, 1987, The Invisible Man, 2001, Touched By An Angel, 2001, General Hospital (2 episodes), 2002-03, Miracles, 2003 Avocation: painting. Died Sept. 26, 2010.

STUDWELL, WILLIAM EMMETT, librarian, writer; b. Stamford, Conn., Mar. 18, 1936; s. Alfred Theodore and Mary Alice (Baker) S.; m. Ann Marie Stroia, Aug. 28, 1965 (dec. 2003); 1 child, Laura Ann. BA, U. Conn., 1958, MA, 1959; MLS, Cath. U. Am., 1967. Tech. abstracter Libr. Congress, Washington, 1963-66, asst. editor decimal classification office, 1966-68; head libr. Kirtland C.C., Roscommon, Mich., 1968-70; head/prin. cataloger No. Ill. U., DeKalb, 1970-2000; freelance writer, editor, from 2001. Mem. US Adv. Com. to Chemistry Sects., Universal Decimal Classification, 1968-72; chmn. adv. group Libr. Rsch. Ctr., Urbana, Ill., 1982-84. Author: Chaikovskii, Delibes, Stravinskii, 1977, Christmas Carols, 1985, Adolphe Adam and Leo Delibes, 1987, Ballet Plot Index, 1987 (named one of Outstanding Academic Books, Choice Mag., 1989), Cataloging Books, 1989, Library of Congress Subject Headings, 1990, Opera Plot Index, 1990, Christmas Card Songbook, 1991, Subject Access to Films and Videos, 1992, Popular Song Reader, 1994, Christmas Carol Reader, 1995 (named one of the Best Christmas Books, Pub.'s Weekly Mag., 1995), National and Religious Song Reader, 1996, Americana Song Reader, 1997, Minor Ballet Composers, 1997, State Songs of the United States, 1997 (academic best seller), Publishing Glad Tidings, 1998, College Fight Songs, 1998, Barbershops, Bullets, and Ballads, 1999, Circus Songs, 1999, The End of the Year, 1999, The Classic Rock and Roll Reader, 1999, They Also Wrote, 2000, The Big Band Reader, 2000, The Clandestine Classical Music Reader, 2000, Forward! Forward! Is the Word, 2000, College Fight Songs II, 2001, Lest We Forget, 2001, A Fable, A Fantasy, and a Farewell, 2002, The French Violin School, 2002, Suzannah's Redemption, or The Devil Gets His Due, 2003, The Man Who Invented God and Other Fantastic Tales, 2004, Ten Terrible Tales, 2005, College Fight Songs III, 2005, The Christmas Carol in the New Millennium, 2006, An Easy Guide to Christmas Carols, 2006, Seven Deadly Singles, 2007, Final Flights of Fancy, 2008, The Clandestine Classical Music Reader, 2008, Fabulous Fables and Fantastic Fantasies, 2009, Beautiful Winners Before Beautiful Dreamer, 2009, Agatha's Agony, or, Larry's Last Laugh, 2010; asst. editor Western Assn. of Map Librs. Info. Bull., 1989—94; editor: Music Reference Svcs. Quar., 1991—99, Resources in Music History Book Series, 1999—2008, The Millennia Collection, from 2000; contbg. editor Technicalities, 1996—2004; contbr. articles to profl. jours.; Cons. (films) A Christmas Carol. US expert on Christmas Carols; internat. recognized expert on Am. Coll. fight songs; internat. leader to devel. standardization code for libr. congress subject headings; leading internat. proponent multinat., multicultural and multilingual subject access sys. Named most productive author among librs. in US, Coll. and Rsch. Librs. Mag., 1983-87, 93-97, Outstanding Alumnus, Sch. Libr. and Info. Sci., Cath. U. America, 2003. Mem. Ill. Assn. Coll. and Rsch. Librs. (exec. bd. 1980-85, newsletter editor 1980-85, lifetime achievement award 1992), Ill. Libr. Assn., Librs. for Social Responsibility (editor newsletter 1986-87, bd. dirs. 1986-94). Home: Aurora, Ill. Died Aug. 2, 2010.

SUAREZ, ROBERTO, retired publishing executive; b. Havana, Cuba, Mar. 5, 1928; came to U.S., 1961; m. Pitucha Campuzano, 1950; children: Elena, Roberto, Raul, Teresa, Miriam, Esperanza, Gonzalo, Carlos, Ana, Miguel Student, Colegio de Belén, Cuba; grad., Villanova Coll., 1949. Various postions in real estate, constrn., fin., Havana, 1950-60; from part-time mailer to contr. The Herald's subs., 1962-72; contr. Knight Pub. Co., Charlotte, N.C., 1972-78; v.p., gen. mgr. The Charlotte Observer, 1978-86, pres., 1986—95; pub. El Nuevo Herald, 1986-87; pres. The Miami Herald, 1990-95, pres. emeritus, 1995—2010. Past pres. Art and Sci. Coun., Spirit Sq. Arts Ctr., Charleston; chair Kids Voting/Dade County; bd. dirs. United Way. Recipient Gold medal Knight-Ridder Pub. Co., 1989, Heritage award Hispanic Alliance, 1990, Leadership award ASPIRA, 1991, Mariono Guastella award Asociacion de Publicitarios Latinoamericanos, 1993. Mem. Inter Am. Press Assn. (pres. exec. com.), N.C. Press Assn. (former treas.), Interam. Businessmen Assn. Home: Miami, Fla. Died July 6, 2010.

SUBLETTE, JULIA WRIGHT, music educator, performer, adjudicator; b. Natural Bridge, Va., Sept. 13, 1929; d. Paul Thomas and Annie Belle (Watkins) Wright; m. Richard Ashmore Sublette, Oct. 18, 1952; children: C. Mark, Carey P., Sylvia S. Bennett, Wright D. BA in Music, Furman U., 1951; MusM, Cin. Conservatory, 1954; postgrad., Chautaugua Inst., NYC, 1951-52; PhD, Fla. State U., 1993. Ind. piano tchr., from 1953; instr. music and humanities Okaloosa-Walton C.C., Niceville, Fla., from 1978, U. West Fla., Pensacola. Panelist Music Tchr. Nat. Conv., Milw., 1992; instr. art humanities Troy State U., Ala.; featured performer N.W. Fla. Symphony Orch. Editor Fla. Music Tchr., 1991-99; contbr. articles to profl. music jours. Mem. AAUW, Music Tchrs. Nat. Assn. (cert., chmn. so. divsn. jr. high sch. piano/instrumental contests 1986-88), Fla. State Music Tchrs. Assn., So. Assn. Women Historians, Southeastern Hist. Keyboard Soc., Friday Morning Music Club, Colonial Dames of 17th Century Am., Pi Kappa Lambda. Avocations: reading, travel, folk music, herb gardening. Home: Shalimar, Fla. Died Jan. 27, 2009.

SUBRAMANYA, SHIVA, aerospace systems engineer; b. Hole-Narasipur, India, Apr. 8, 1933; s. S. T. Srikantaiah; m. Lee S. Silva, Mar. 3, 1967; children: Paul Kailas, Kevin Shankar. BSc, Mysore U., Bangalore, India, 1956; MSc, Karnatak U., Dharwar, India, 1962; postgrad., Clark U., 1963; MBA, Calif. State U., Dominguez Hills, 1973; D in Bus. Adminstrn., PhD in Bus. Adminstrn., Nova Southeastern U., 1986. Sr. scientific officer AEC, Bombay, India, 1961-63; chief engr. TEI, Newport, R.I., 1964-67; prin. engr. Gen. Dynamics Corp., San Diego, 1967-73; asst. project mgr. def. and systems group TRW, Colorado Springs, Colo., 1973-87, asst. project mgr. space and def. group Redondo Beach, Calif., 1987-98; cons. aerospace industry Cerritos, Calif., from 1998. Cons. Contbr. articles to profl. jours. Apptd. mem. by Pres. India Atomic Energy Commn.; v.p. Inst. Cultural Rejuvenation, India, VHP Am., Berlin, Conn., 1984—88; pres. IPF Am., Redondo Beach, 1981—86, Indian Profl. Forum. Recipient medal of Merit, US Dept. Def., Meritorious Svc. award, US Dept Def., awards, various orgns. Mem.: Am. Acad. Mgmt., Armed Forces Comm. and Electronics Assn. (v.p.-elect Rocky Mountain chpt. from 1986, Meritorious Svc. award 1985, Merit medal 1990). Hindu. Avocation: social service. Died Jan. 8, 2009.

SUDAN, RAVINDRA NATH, electrical engineer, physicist, educator; b. Chineni, Kashmir, India, June 8, 1931; came to U.S., 1958, naturalized, 1971; s. Brahm Nath and Shanti Devi (Mehta) S.; m. Dipali Ray, July 3, 1959; children: Rajani, Ranjeet. BA with first class honors, U. Punjab, 1948; diploma, Indian Inst. Sci., 1952, Imperial Coll., London, 1953; PhD, U. London, 1955. Engr., Brit. Thomson-Houston Co., Rugby, Eng, 1955-57; Engr. Imperial Chem. Industries, Calcutta, India, 1957-58; research assoc. Cornell U., Ithaca, N.Y., 1958-59, asst. prof. elec. engring., 1959-63, assoc. prof., 1963-68, prof., 1968-75, IBM prof. engring., 1975—2001, IBM prof. engring. emeritus, from 2001, dir. Lab. Plasma Studies, 1975-85, dep. dir. Cornell Theory Ctr., 1985-87, prof., from 1987. Cons. Lawrence Livermore Lab., Los Alamos Sci. Lab., Sci. Applications Inc., Physics Internat. Co.; vis. research asso. Stanford U., summer 1963; cons. U.K. Atomic Energy Authority, Culham Lab., summer 1965; vis. scientist Internat. Center Theoretical Physics, Trieste, Italy, 1965-66, summers 1970, 73, Plasma Physics Lab. Princeton U., 1966-67, spring 1989, Inst. for Advanced Study, Princeton, N.J., spring 1975; head theoretical plasma physics group U.S. Naval Research Lab., 1970-71, sci. adviser to dir., 1974-75; chmn. Ann. Conf. on Theoretical Aspects of Controlled Fusion, 1975, 2d Internat. Conf. on High Power Electron and Ion Beam Research and Tech., 1977 Mem. editl. bd. Physics of Fluids, 1973-76, Comments on Plasma Physics, 1973, Nuclear Fusion, 1976-84, Physics Reports, 1990—; co-editor Handbook of Plasma Physics; contbr. over 220 articles to sci. jours. Recipient Gold medal Acad. Scis. of the Czech Republic, 1993. Fellow IEEE, AAAS, Am. Phys. Soc. (Maxwell prize 1989), Nat. Rsch. Coun. (chmn. Plasma Sci. com. 1993—). Achievements include patents (with S. Humphries, Jr) intense ion beam generator. Home: Ithaca, NY. Deceased.

SUGAR, JOSEPH ROBERT, musician, conductor, educator; b. Worcester, Mass., Dec. 14, 1928; s. Elias George and Emily Angeline (David) Sugar; m. Clara Anne Steele, Dec. 26, 1955; children: Thomas Elias, Robert Albert. AA, Bergen Jr. Coll., Teaneck, NJ, 1948; BA, LI U., 1950; MA, Columbia U., 1955; profl. diploma, 1956. Brass instr. LI U., NY, 1949, prof., advisor to music chmn. for courses music edn. C. W. Post Coll. Greenvale, NY, from 1990, dir. music edn., 1990-2001; asst. bands. Ind. U., Bloomington, Ind., 1950; dir. Instrumental Music, Matawan, NJ, 1954-56; band dir. Upsala Coll., East Orange, NJ, 1956-57; band. dir., instr. music Bethpage Elem. Sch., NY, 1957-66; instr. baton twirling Bethpage HS, 1957-67; band. dir. Hewlett-Woodmere Jr. HS, NY, 1966-78; asst. band dir., instr. baton twirling Hewlett HS, 1967-69, band dir., 1983-84, dir. jazz ensemble, 1983-89; band dir. Dowling Coll., Oakdale, NY, 1977-79; dist. dir. music Hewlett-Woodmere Pub. Schs., 1978-89. Summer band sch. co-dir., Manasquan, NJ, 1955—64; creative music cultural workshop, Bethpage, 1959—62; dir. NY Jazz Ensemble, Hempstead, 1976, Kismet Shrine Temple Band, 1997—2008; clinician numerous music festivals, from 1970; choral dir., instrumentalist Air Force Band of Rockies, 504th Air Force Band, Colorado Springs; band master emeritus Kismet Shrine, from 2009. Performer: Indpls. Symphony Orch., 1950, MATS Hdg. Band Westover AFB, 1950—51, Joe Sugar and the Big Band, 1980—2006; musician (numerous entertainers including): Vic Damone, Diahann Carroll, Al Martino, Jerry Vale, Georgia Gibbs, Toni Arden, Johnny Ray, Eddie Fisher, Cab Calloway, Marilyn Michaels, Frankie Lane, Henny Youngman, Anna Maria Alberghetti, Patti Page, Bobby Rydell, Buddy Greco, Billy Eckstine, Julius La Rosa, The Four Aces, Don Cornell, Connie Francis; musician: (with Audio-Fidelity) (albums) 20th Century Fox, Paramount, MGM, 1958—61; author: Where Are We Headed in Music Education?, 1960, Twirling Tips in 3 Volumes, 1963, Presidents March, 1982; composer, condr.: albums Ten Nights in a Harem, 1963. Mem. Boy Scouts Am.; youth choir dir. Levittown Presbyn. Ch., NY, 1966. With USAF, 1950—52. Recipient Merit award, Music Belongs, 1972, 1st Pl. award, E. Nat. Music Festival, 1977, Apprecation of Outstanding Leadership award, Black Music Caucus, 1982, cert. of Merit award, NY State Senate, 1982, citation, Town of Hempstead, 1982, Oustanding Ret. Band Dirs. award, NY State Band Dirs. Assn., 2007, Disting. Svc. award, Hewlett-Woodmere Pub. Schs., 1989, Ricky Pub. Svc. award, Usdan Music Camp, 2008, Lifetime Achievement award, 2008, Usdan Art Ctr., Adjunct Faculty Recognition award, C.W. Post, 2008, Masonic-Daniel Scouting Bd. award, 2009, Rickie award, Assemblyman Harvey Weisenberg; named Man of the Yr., Wantagh C. of C., 1979; named to Tchr. Hall of Fame, Hewlett-Woodmere Pub. Schs., 1990; grantee, Ford Found., 1962. Mem.: DAV (life), NY State Coun. Music Adminstrs. (Disting. Svc. award 1990), Internat. Trumpet Guild, Nat. Assn. Jazz Educators, Nassau Music Educators Assn. (pres. 1970, mem. adv. bd. 1980—81, Pres. award 1970, Svc. award 1973, 1987), NY State Sch. Music Assn. (pres. 1980—82, Disting. Svc. award 1989), NY State Adminstrs. Music Edn. (pres. 1987—90), Music Educators Nat. Conf. (life; pres. ea. divsn. 1985—87), Wantagh Friends Libr., Jones Beach Power Squadron (sr.), Masonic 60Yr. Pin Damascus Lodge, Kiwanis (past pres., award 1979), Am. Legion (past cmdr., award 1978), Masons (50 Yr. award, 50 Yr. BSA award, Outstanding Adj. award), Wantagh Spiked Shoe (past pres., award 1979), Wantagh Dads and Booster (past pres.), Tri M, Kappa Kappa Psi, Phi Delta Kappa, Phi Mu Alpha (life). Republican. Home: Wantagh, NY. Died Nov. 1, 2009.

SUGARMAN, JULE MEYER, children's services consultant, former public administrator; b. Cin., Sept. 23, 1927; s. Melville Harty and Rachel Wolf (Meyer) S.; m. Sheila Mary Shanley, May 20, 1956 (dec. 1983); children: Christopher (dec. 2002), Maryanne, Jason, James; m. Candace Sullivan, Apr. 2, 1989. Student, Western Res. U., 1945-46; AB with highest distinction, Am. U., 1951. Budget examiner Civil Svc. Commn.; dir. Head Start, 1965-69; adminstr. Human Resources Adminstrn., NYC, 1970-73; chief adminstrv. officer City of Atlanta, 1974-76; vice chmn. CSC, Washington, 1977-78; dep. dir. Office Personnel Mgmt. (OPM), 1979-81; mng. dir. Human Service Info. Ctr., 1981-83; v.p. Hahnemann U., 1983-86; sec. Wash. State Dept. Social and Health Services, 1986-89; exec. dir. Spl. Olympics Internat., Washington, 1989-91. Cons. Delotte & Touch, 1997-98. Program dir. AmeriCorps, Calven County, 2000; vice chmn. Boys and Girls Clubs So. Md., 2000-. Served with U.S. Army, 1946-48. Recipient Meritorious Service award Dept. State, 1963, Alumni Service award Am. U., 1977, Disting. Pub. Svc. award Nat. Acad. Pub. Adminstrn., 1988, Gov.'s Volunteer of Yr. award, 2001. Home: Seattle, Wash. Died Nov. 2, 2010.

SUGG, ROBERT PERKINS, retired judge; b. Eupora, Miss., Feb. 21, 1916; s. Amos Watson and Virgie Christian (Cooper) S.; m. Elizabeth Lorraine Carroll, June 23, 1940; children: Robert Perkins, Charles William, John David. Student, Wood Jr. Coll., 1933—34, Miss. State U., 1935—37, Jackson Sch. Law, 1939—40; LLM (hon.), Miss. Coll. Sch. Law, 2007. Bar: Miss. Practice law, 1940; chancery judge, 1951—71; assoc. justice Miss. Supreme Ct., 1971—83; county pros. atty. Webster County, Miss., 1949—50; spl. chancery judge Hinds, Scott and Jasper counties, Miss., 1989; sr. judge, 1990—2000. Mem. adv. coun. Nat. Ctr. for State Cts., 1973-79. Bd. govs. Miss. Jud. Coll., 1973-80; literacy missions assoc. Home Mission Bd. of So. Bapt. Conv., 1983—; tchr. internat. class First Bapt, Ch., Jackson, Miss., 1980-2004, 08-, tchr. adult Bible class, 1973-2002, mem. fin. com. 1995-98, vision com. 1996-97, legal com. 1998-2001, missions com., 1997-2001. Named Outstanding Citizen, Eupora Jr. C. of C., 1970, Alumnus of Year, Wood Jr. Coll., 1973; recipient Svc. to Humanity award Miss. Coll., 1976, Literacy Missions Svc. award Home Mission Bd. of So. Bapt. Conv., 1995. Mem. Miss. State Bar, CAP (Miss. Wing, squadron comdr. 1974-76), Am. Legion (post comdr. 1950) Democrat. Baptist (chmn. bd. deacons 1964). Home: Ridgeland, Miss. Died Jan. 1, 2010.

SUJANSKY, JOANNE GENOVA, management consultant; b. Freedom, Pa., Mar. 21, 1950; d. John W. and Mary Ellen (Mandarino) Genova; m. R. Charles Sujansky, Jr., Apr. 22, 1977; children— Cara, Justin. B.S., Slippery Rock State Coll. 1972, M.Ed., 1974; Ph.D., U. Pitts., 1980. Grad. asst. Slippery Rock (Pa.) State Coll., 1972-74; dir. tng., employee counselor Presbyn.-Univ. Hosp., Pitts., 1974-78; dir. edn. Mercy Hosp., Pitts., 1978-80; pres. JGS Assocs., Pitts., 1980—. Past bd. dirs. Job Adv. Service of Pitts. Mem. Am. Soc. Tng. and Devel. (Nat. pres.-elect, nat. bd. mem.; past pres. Pitts. chpt., Torch award 1983, Outstanding Leadership award, Pitts. 1980), Pitts. Personnel Assn., Exec. Women's Council. Home: Pittsburgh, Pa. Died Dec. 10, 2009.

SULLIVAN, FREDERICK WILLIAM, retired utility company executive, mechanical engineer; b. Fall River, Mass., Sept. 6, 1928; s. Frederick William and Ruth (Mottershead) S.; m. Bernice Roszkowicz, June 28, 1952; children: Karen L., William F. BSM.E., Northeastern U., 1951. Engr. Fall River Gas Co., Mass., 1947-54; cons. Stone & Webster, NYC, 1954-71, mgmt. cons. Europe, 1964-68; v.p. Consol. Edison, NYC, 1971-75; sr. v.p. Bklyn. Union Gas. Co., 1975-86; chmn., c.e.o. Methane Devel. Corp., Bklyn., 1985-86. Chmn., c.e.o. Gas Energy Inc., Bklyn., Fuel Resources Inc., Bklyn., Del. Valley Propane Co., Moorestown, N.J., 1985-86; pres., c.e.o. Elizabethton Gas Co., 1986-91; bd. dirs. Elizabethtown Gas Co. Mem. Am. Gas Assn. (chmn. operating sect. 1984-85), New Eng. Gas. Assn., ASME, Soc. Gas Lighting, Instn. Gas. Engrs. (Great Britain) Clubs: Plainfield Country. Home: Pinehurst, NC. Died Apr. 6, 2010.

SULLIVAN, JAMES JOSEPH, architect; b. Boston, Aug. 23, 1922; s. Gilbert and Ellen (Flaherty) S.; cert. Sch. Practical Arts, Boston, 1942, Art Students League, N.Y.C., 1947, Boston Archtl. Center, 1950-53; m. Mary Elizabeth Clarkson, Apr. 3, 1948; children: Mary Ellen Armold, Kathleen S. Picard, Michael J., Ann S. Harnett, Joseph C., James Joseph, Jr. Registered architect, Mass., N.Y., Calif., N.Mex., Fla., N.C., N.H. Architect dist. public works U.S. Navy, Boston, 1952-58; asso. Cabot, Cabot & Forbes, Boston, 1958-63; dir. bldg. div. Charles A. Maguire & Assocs., Boston, 1963-66; pres., treas. Sullivan Design Group, Inc., Braintree, Mass., 1966—; instr. house constrn. adult edn. M.I.T., 1952-54; tchr. apprentice tng. program, Boston, 1956-60. Chmn. Bldg. Code Com., Braintree, 1970-72; mem. designer selection bd. Commonwealth of Mass., 1971-76, chmn., 1975-76; commr. Sewer Dept., Braintree, 1979—; pres. Sullivan Design Group, Inc., 1986-87. Served with USCGR, 1942-46. Recipient outstanding accomplishment awards Dept. Public Works, 1st Naval Dist. Hdqrs., Boston, 1957, 58. Mem. AIA, Boston Archtl. Center Alumni Assn., Mus. Fine Arts, Royal Inst.

Architects Ireland. Democrat. Roman Catholic. Clubs: Martha's Vineyard Art Assn., Cochato, Braintree, Chappaquiddick Beach, Quincy Neighborhood, Edgartown Yacht. Author: You and Your Architect, 1969, 73. Home: Braintree, Mass. Died Jan. 30, 2010.

SULLIVAN, JOSEPH A., mathematics educator; b. Boston, June 5, 1923; s. Joseph and Alice C. (O'Brien) S.; m. Mary C. Peterson, Jan. 12, 1947; children: Brian, Paul, James, Gregory. AB, Boston Coll., 1944; MS, MIT, 1947; PhD, Ind. U., 1950. Instr. to assoc. prof. math. U. Notre Dame, Ind., 1950-59; prof. math. Boston Coll., Newton, from 1960. Co-author: Introduction to Analysis, 1959, Intermediate Analysis, 1964, Real Analysis, 1971. Lt. (j.g.) USNR, 1943-46; PTO. Mem. Math. Assn. Am., Am. Math. Soc. Roman Catholic. Avocation: golf. Home: Norwood, Mass. Died Dec. 23, 2009.

SULLIVAN, PHILLIP MANNING, banker; b. Salem, Mass., Feb. 10, 1933; s. William Joseph and Eleanor Regina (Manning) S.; m. Carolyn Florence Ellison, June 23, 1956; children— Phillip Manning, Andrea Jane BS in Edn., Salem State Coll., 1954; MBA, Boston U., 1962. Cert. tchr., Mass. Sr. v.p. First Nat. Bank of Boston, from 1958. Gen. chmn. Somerville United Fund, Mass., 1964; chmn. Task Force on Pub. Fin. of the Arts and Humanities in Mass., Boston, 1978-80; chmn. bd. trustees Mass. Coll. Art, Boston, 1981—. Served to capt. USMC, 1954-58 Named One of 10 Outstanding Young Men, Boston Jaycees, 1969 Mem. Bank Officers Assn. of City of Boston Roman Catholic. Home: South Orleans, Mass. Died May 2, 2010.

SULTAN, LARRY, photographer; b. Bklyn., July 13, 1946; BA in Polit. Sci., U. Calif., San Francisco, 1968; MFA in Photography, San Francisco Art Inst., 1973. Instr. photography San Francisco Art Inst., 1978—88; prof. art Calif. Coll. Arts, 1989—2009, chmn. Photography Dept., 1993—99. One-man shows include Ohio Silver Gallery, L.A., 1972, U. Calif. Gallery, San Francisco, 1974, Ctr. for Creative Photography, Tucson, 1977, Fogg Art Mus., Cambridge, Mass., 1978, Light Gallery, L.A., 1981, Blue Sky Gallery, Portland, Oreg., 1981, Portland (Maine) Sch. Art, 1982, U. Colo. Art Gallery, Boulder, 1982, R.I. Sch. Design, Providence, 1987, Janet Borden, Inc., N.Y.C., 1989, Headlands Ctr. for Arts, Sausalito, Calif., 1989, The Exploratorium, San Francisco, 1990, San Jose (Calif.) Mus. Art, 1992, Stephen Wirtz Gallery, San Francisco, 1992, Mus. Contemporary Art, San Diego, 1994, Chgo. Cultural Ctr., The Corcoran Gallery of Art, Washington, Scottsdale Ctr. Arts, Ariz., Bronx Mus. Art, 1996, Galerie MK, Rotterdam, 2000, Janet Borden Gallery, NY, 2001, 2004, Reflex Modern Art, Amsterdam, 2002, Recontres d'Arles, France, 2002, Isabella Brancolini Art Contemporane Gallery, Italy, 2003, Stephen Wirtz Gallery, San Francisco, 2003, 2004, San Francisco Mus. Art, 2004, Galerie Thomas Zander, Germany, 2004, The Apartment, Athens, Greece, 2004, Musée de l'Elysée, Switzerland, 2005, Photographers' Gallery, London, 2005, Maes & Matthys Gallery, Belgium, 2005; exhibited in group shows at Fogg Art Mus., 1976, La Mamelle Gallery, San Francisco, 1976, San Francisco Mus. Modern Art, 1977, 82, 85, 89, 91, L.A. Inst. of Contemporary Art, 1978, Chgo. Mus. Contemporary Art, 1979, Santa Barbara Mus. Art, 1981, Seibu Mus. Art, Tokyo, 1982, Univ. Art Mus., Berkeley, Calif., 1983, Internat. Ctr. Photography, N.Y.C., 1984, Barbican Art Gallery, London, 1985, Mus. Modern Art, N.Y.C., 1985, 89, 91, U. Colo. Gallery, 1986, Los Angeles County Mus. Art, 1987, Burden Gallery, N.Y.C., 1988, Northlight Gallery, Tempe, Ariz., 1990, Birmingham (Ala.) Mus. Art, 1990, Met. Mus. Art, N.Y.C., 1991, Milw. Art Mus., 1991, Stephen Wirtz Gallery, San Francisco, 1991, 96, Dartmouth Coll. Art Gallery, Hanover, N.H., 1996, List Art Ctr., Providence, 1991, Transamerica Pyramid, San Francisco, Presentation House, Ctr. Visual and Performing Arts, Vancouver, BC, U. Art Mus. Berkeley, Calif., Weatherspoon Art Gallery, Greenville, N.C., 1995, To Keep Her Countenance, Stephen Wirtz Gallery, 1996, Scene of the Crime, Armand Hammer Mus., 1997, Friends and Family, Mus. Contemporary Photography, Chgo., 1997, Matrix: 20 Years, Univ. Art Mus., Berkeley, Calif., 1998, The American Lawn: Surface of Everyday Life, Centre Canadien D'Architecture, 1998, Bay Area Now, Yerba Buena Ctr. for Arts, San Francisco, 1999, Made in California, L.A. Mus. Modern Art, 2000, Immodest Gazes, La Fundacio La Caiza, Barcelona, 2000, Picturing Media: Modern Photographs from the Collections, THe Met. Mus. Art, NY, 2001, Settings and Players: Theatrical Ambiguity in American Photography, White Cube, London, 2001, House Broken, Rena Branstein Gallery, San Francisco, 2002, Visions From America, Whitney Mus. Am. Art, 2002, Turning Corners, Univ. Art Mus., Berkeley, 2003, Family Ties, Peabody Essex Mus., Salem, Mass., 2003, Baja to Vancouver: The West Coast and Contemporary Art, Vancouver Art Gallery, 2004, Culture and Continuity, The Jewish Mus., NY, 2005, About Face, Santa Barbara Mus. Art, 2005, Girls in Film, Zwirner and Wirth Gallery, NY, 2005, Berlin Bienalle, 2006; represented in permanent collections at Art Inst. Chgo., Baltimore Mus. Art, Bibliotheque Nationale, France, Birmingham Mus. Art, Ctr. for Creative Photography, Ariz., Chase Manhattan Bank, Corcoran Mus. Art, Washington DC, Frods Regional D'Art contemporain, France, J. Paul Getty Mus., Calif., The Mus. Modern Art, NY, Milw. Art Mus., The Met. Mus. Art, NY, Whitney Mus. Am. Art, NY, The Nat. Gallery Art, Washington DC, San Francisco Mus. Modern Art, San Jose (Calif.) Mus. Art., U. Ala., U. Colo. Publicatins include How to Read Music in One Evening, 1974, Evidence, 1977, Headlands: The Marin Coast at the Golden Gate, 1989, Pictures from Home, 1992, The Valley, 2004. Bd. trustees Headlands Ctr. for Arts, 1992—98. Recipient Art in Pub. Places grant Nat. Endowment for the Arts, 1976, Photography fellowship Nat. Endowment for the Arts, 1977, 80, 92, Spl. Projects grant Calif. Arts Coun., 1978, Guggenheim fellowship, 1983, Artists fellowship Marin Arts Coun., 1986, Fleishhaker Found. Eureka fellowship Calif. Arts Coun., 1989, Louis Comfort Tiffany fellowship, 1991, Civitella Ranieri Found. fellowship, 2000, Internat. Arts and Lectures grant US State Dept., 2000, Flintridge Found. Artist's fellowship, 2000; Engelhard award Inst. Contemporary Art, 1988, Pub. Arts award Oakland Cultural Arts, 1990, Creative Work Fund award Haas Found., 1996, Award of Merit Soc. Environ. Graphic Design, 1997. Died Dec. 13, 2009.

SUMMERS, CLYDE WILSON, law educator; b. Grass Range, Mont., Nov. 21, 1918; s. Carl Douglas and Anna Lois (Yontz) S.; m. Evelyn Marie Wahlgren, Aug. 30, 1947; children: Mark, Erica, Craig, Lisa. BS, U. Ill., 1939, JD, 1942, LLD, 1998; LLM, Columbia U., 1946, JSD, 1952; LL.D., U. Leuven, Belgium, 1967, U. Stockholm, 1978, U. Ill., 1998. Bar: N.Y. 1951. Mem. law faculty U. Toledo, 1942-49, U. Buffalo, 1949-56; prof. law Yale U., New Haven, 1956-66, Garver prof. law, 1966-75; Jefferson B. Fordham prof. law U. Pa., 1975-90, prof. emeritus, 1990—2010. Hearing examiner Conn. Commn. on Civil Rights, 1963-71 Co-author: Labor Cases and Material, 1968, 1982, Rights of Union Members, 1979, Legal Protection for the Individual Employee, 1989, 1996, 2002; co-editor: Labor Relations and the Law, 1953, Employment Relations and the Law, 1959, Comparative Labor Law Jour., 1984—97. Chmn. Gov.'s Com. on Improper Union Mgmt. Practices N.Y. State, 1957-58; chmn. Conn. Adv. Council on Unemployment Ins. and Employment Service, 1960-72; mem. Conn. Labor Relations Bd., 1966-70, Conn. Bd. Mediation and Arbitration, 1964-72. Guggenheim fellow, 1955-56; Ford fellow, 1963-64; German-Marshall fellow, 1977-78; NEH fellow, 1977-78, Fullbright fellow, 1984-85. Mem. Nat. Acad. Arbitrators, Internat. Soc. Labor Law and Social Legislation (pres.). Congregationalist. Home: Philadelphia, Pa. Died Oct. 30, 2010.

SUMMERTREE, KATONAH See WINDSOR, PATRICIA

SUMNER, BILLY TAYLOR, engineering and architectural planning executive; b. Chgo., July 13, 1923; s. Lawton Taylor and Adele (Shelton) S.; m. Mary Sue Williams, Nov. 23, 1951; children— Kimberly Suell, Shelton Williams. B.E. magna cum laude, Vanderbilt U., 1946. Resident engr. Polk, Powell & Hendon, Nashville, 1946-51; Southeastern engring. rep., mgr. Nashville plant Universal Concrete Pipe Co., Columbus, Ohio, 1951-53; cons. Dixie Poultry Processors, Franklin, Tenn., 1953-54; resident mgr. Nashville office Geo. P. Rice, New Orleans, 1954-55; chmn. emeritus Barge, Waggoner, Sumner & Cannon, Engrs., Architects and Planners, Nashville, Knoxville, Morristown, Tricities, Cookeville, Memphis, Oak, Ridge, Huntsville, Dothan, Montgomery, Ala., Miamisburg, Ohio, Indpls., from 1955. Pres. Tenn. Bot. Gardens and Fine Arts Center, 1967-69; Trustee, v.p. Children's Mus., Nashville. Served with U.S. Army, 1943-46. Mem. ASCE, Am. Water Works Assn., Water Pollution Control Fedn., Am. Pub. Works Assn., Soc. Am. Mil. Engrs., Am. Inst. Cons. Engrs. (councilor 1972-73, v.p. 1973), Am. Cons. Engr. Council (v.p. 1973-74, pres. 1975-76), Nat. Soc. Profl. Engrs. (vice chmn. 1967-69, chmn. 1969-70), Tau Beta Pi, Sigma Nu. Clubs: Rotarian. (Nashville), Belle Meade Country (Nashville), Nashville City (Nashville), Cumberland (Nashville). Presbyterian. Home: Nashville, Tenn. Died Dec. 1, 2009.

SUNSTEIN, CAROLYN RUTH NETTER, antique dealer; b. Phila., Jan. 5, 1922; d. Morton Angelo and Dorothy G. (Goldsmith) Netter; B.S. in Edn., Temple U., Phila., 1942; m. Charles Gerstley Sunstein, Aug. 22, 1941; children— Florence Gertsley Sunstein Begun, Lynn Carol, Charles Gerstley, Jr. Antique miniature collector, 1942—; dealer, show coordinator Phila. Miniature Show, 1972—; lectr., appraiser, 1977—; adv. bd. Warmans Antique Guild, 1981. Sec., Adoption Ctr. Del. Valley, 1982—; bd. dirs. Samuel Paley Day Care Ctr., 1942—, Albert Einstein Med. Ctr., 1975—, Nat. Adoption Ctr., 1980—. Mem. Pa. Antique Assn., Nat. Assn. Miniature Enthusiasts, Internat. Guild Miniature Artisans (pres. 1986-88). Republican. Jewish. Home: Villanova, Pa. Died May 17, 2009.

SUNSTEIN, CHARLES GERSTLEY, stockbroker; b. Phila., Apr. 24, 1917; s. Leon Cleveland and Florence (Gerstley) S.; B.S., U. N.C., 1940; m. Carolyn Ruth Netter, Aug. 22, 1941; children— Florence Sunstein Begun, Lynn C., Charles G. Stockbroker, Gerstley, Sunstein & Co., Phila., 1946-58, partner, 1958-69, pres., 1963-69; partner, 1st v.p. Drexel Burnham Lambert, Phila., 1969-88; prin. Charles G. Sunstein Assn., 1988—. Bd. dirs. Albert Einstein Med. Ctr., Jewish Ys and Ctrs., Fedn. Day Care Services, Fedn. Jewish Agys., Phila. Served with AUS, 1941-46. Clubs: Locust, B'nai B'rith. Home: Southeastern, Pa. Died Mar. 23, 2009.

SUSSKIND, HERBERT, biomedical engineer, educator; b. Ratibor, Germany, Mar. 23, 1929; came to U.S., 1938; s. Alex and Hertha (Loewy) S.; m. E. Suzanne Lieberman, June 18, 1961; children: Helen J., Alex M., David A. BChE cum laude, CCNY, 1950; MChE, NYU, 1961. Engr., sect. supr. Brookhaven Nat. Lab., Upton, N.Y., 1950-77, biomed. engr., 1977-94, asst. to chmn. med. dept., 1989-94, rsch. collaborator, from 1994; assoc. prof. medicine SUNY, Stony Brook, from 1979. Co-inventor 3 patents in field. Co-founder, 1st pres. Huntington Twp. Jewish Forum, Huntington, N.Y., 1970-73; trustee Huntington Hebrew Congregation, 1970-78. Mem. Biomed. Engring. Soc., Soc. Nuclear Medicine, Am. Thoracic Soc., Am. Nuclear Soc. (exec. com., treas. L.I. Sect., 1978-83), Am. Inst. Chem. Engrs., CCNY Alumni Assn. (pres. 1982-84), CCNY Engring. & Architecture Alumni Assn., N.Y.C. (pres. 1963-65). Home: Huntington, NY. Died Dec. 2, 2009.

ŠUTEJ, VJEKOSLAV, conductor; b. Rijeka, Croatia, July 31, 1951; s. Josip and Alemka (Stefanini) Š.; m. Linela Malici; 1 child Alemka. Degree, Music Acad., Zagreb, Croatia, 1975. Music dir. Opera Split, Split, Croatia, 1985-90, La Fenice, Venice, Italy, 1990-93, Orquesta Simfonica de Sevilla, Seville, Spain, 1991—94, Houston Grand Opera, Houston, 1994—98, Zagreb Philharmonic Orch., 2003—09. Home: Houston, Tex. Died Dec. 2, 2009.

SUTER, CARY GRAYSON, neurologist, educator; b. Bridgewater, Va., Oct. 9, 1919; s. David I. and Elizabeth (Dundore) S.; m. Anna Deane Carr, May 3, 1947; children— Cary Carr, Anna Deane. AB, BS, Hampden-Sydney Coll., 1943; MD, U. Va., 1947. Instr. pathology U. Va., Charlottesville, 1947-48, resident in neurology-psychiatry, 1951-54, asst. prof. neurology-psychiatry, 1954-57; intern U. Ala., 1948-49; resident in internal medicine Cleve. Clinic, 1949-51; resident in neurology Mayo Clinic, 1957-59; 1st dir. Va. Epilepsy Clinic for Children, 1954-57; asst. prof. Med. Coll. Va., Va. Commonwealth U., Richmond, 1959-62, assoc. prof., 1962-65, prof., from 1965, dir. EEG Lab. and Epilepsy Clinic, chief staff neurology service coll. hosp., from 1959, chmn. dept. neurology, 1965-84. Cons. VA Hosp., Richmond, Va.; individual practice medicine, Richmond. Fellow Am. Acad. Neurology; mem. AMA, Am. Epilepsy Soc., So. EEG Soc., Am. EEG Soc., Am. Neurol. Assn., Soc. Electromyography and Electrodiagnosis, Phi Beta Kappa, Alpha Omega Alpha. Episcopalian. Home: Richmond, Va. Died Aug. 31, 2009.

SUTHERLAND, DONALD GRAY, retired lawyer; b. Houston, Jan. 19, 1929; s. Robert Gray and Elizabeth (Cunningham) S.; m. Mary Reynolds Moodey, July 23, 1955; children: Stuart Gray, Elizabeth Dana. BS, Purdue U., 1954; LLB, Ind. U., Bloomington, 1954. Bar: Ind. 1954, U.S. Dist. Ct. (so. dist.) Ind. 1954, U.S. Tax Ct. 1956, U.S. Ct. Claims 1957, U.S. Ct. Appeals (7th cir.) 1981, U.S. Ct. Appeals (3d cir.) 1984, U.S. Ct. Internat. Trade 1987, U.S. Supreme Ct. 1987. Assoc. IceMiller, Indpls., 1954-64, ptnr., 1965-98, ret., 1998. Practitioner in residence Ind. U. Sch. of Law, Bloomington, 1987; trustee, pres. Pegasus Funds, Detroit, 1992-99; trustee, chmn. bd. dirs., pres. Bison Money Market Fund., Indpls., 1982-92. Contbr. articles to numerous profl. jours. Bd. dirs., v.p. Japan-Am. Soc. of Ind., Inc., Indpls., 1988-97; bd. dirs. Conner Prairie Inc., Fishers, Ind., 1988-97, v.p., 1989-90, chmn. bd., 1990-93; tennis ceremonies 10th Pan-Am. Games, Indpls., 1987; bd. dirs. The Children's Bur. Indpls., 1962-73, v.p., 1968-70, pres., 1970-72; bd. dirs. Orchard Country Day Sch., Indpls., 1970-73, Episc. Cmty. Svcs., Indpls., 1965-73, v.p., 1968, pres., 1969; trustee United Episc. Charities, Indpls., 1970-71, pres., 1971. With USMC, 1946-48. Mem.: Nat. Jr. Tennis League of Indpls. (bd. dirs. from 2003), Econ. Club (bd. dirs. Ind. chpt. 1988—94), Contemporary Club of Indpls. (pres. 2003—04), Woodstock Club. Republican. Avocations: golf, tennis, opera. Died May 2, 2009.

SUTHERLAND, DAME JOAN ALSTON, retired soprano; b. Sydney, Nov. 7, 1926; d. McDonald S.; m. Richard Bonynge, 1954; one son. Student, Royal Coll. Music, London, 1951; Mus D (hon.), U. Syndey, 1984, Oxford U., 1992. Appeared concert and oratorio performances, Australia; appeared in: opera Judith, Syndey Conservatory of Music; debut Covent Garden in Magic Flute, 1952, Die Zauberflöte, 1952; Italian debut in Handel's Alcina, Teatro la Fenice, Venice, 1960; Bellini's Puritani, Glyndebourne Festival, Sussex, Eng., 1960; Bellini's Beatrice di Tenda, La Scala, 1961, Rossini's Semiramide, La Scala, 1962; Meyerbeer's Les Huguenots, La Scala, 1962, N.Y. debut, Carnegie Hall, 1961; Opera debut Lucia, 1961; opened Sutherland-Williamson Opera Co. tour, Australia, 1965; appeared: Handel's Julius Caesar, Hamburg Opera, 1969; Bellini's Norma, Met. Opera, 1970; opened, Lyric Opera Chgo. with, Semiramide, 1971; San Francisco Opera with, Norma, 1972; San Francisco Opera with Trovatore, 1975; Met. Opera with I Puritani, 1976; Vancouver Opera with Le Roi de Lahore, 1977; premiered new prodn., Met. Opera in Tales of Hoffmann, 1973; first prodn. in Am. in eighty years Esclarmonde, Massenet, San Fancisco Opera, 1974; author: (with Richard Bonynge) The Joan Sutherland Album, 1986; A Prima Donna's Progress, 1997; actress: various films. Decorated Order of Merit, 1991; Dame Comdr. of the Most Excellent Order of the British Empire, 1979; Companion, Order Australia, 1975; recipient Grammy Award best classical vocal soloist, 1981, Kennedy Ctr. Honors, John F. Kennedy Ctr. for the Performing Arts, 2004; Fellow Royal Coll. Music. Died Oct. 10, 2010.

SUTPHEN, HAROLD AMERMAN, JR., retired paper company executive; b. Verona, NJ, Feb. 13, 1926; s. Harold Amerman and Marion Esther (Mason) S.; m. Greta May Peterson, June 24, 1950; children— Judith Amerman, Peter Lehmann, Pamela Torrance. Grad., Phillips Exeter Acad., 1944; BS in Mech. Engring, Princeton, 1950. With Universal Oil Products Co., Chgo., 1950-51, Texaco, Inc., 1951-52; bus. research analyst Arthur D. Little, Inc., 1952-56; asst. div. mgr. adminstrn., fine papers div. W.Va. Pulp and Paper Co. (name now changed to Westvaco Corp.), 1956-60, v.p., 1967-80, sr. v.p., 1980-88, mgr. fine papers div., 1974-88, dir., 1975-88. V.p., treas. U.S. Envelope Co., Springfield, Mass., 1960-62, pres., CEO, 1962-67, chmn. bd., 1967-74; bd. dirs. Assessment Appeals, Fairfield, Conn., 1993-97, chmn., 1996-97. Served with AUS, 1944-46. Mem. Holland Soc. N.Y., Phi Beta Kappa. Clubs: Country of Fairfield (Conn.); Weston (Conn.) Gun. Home: Fairfield, Conn. Died Mar. 28, 2009.

SWADLEY, WILLIAM THOMAS, retail company executive; b. Columbus, Ohio, June 8, 1939; s. William Francis and Mary Loreta (Dow) S.; m. Katherine Ann Walker, Nov. 5, 1965; children: Jennifer, Jonathan. BS in Journalism, Marquette U., 1961. Mgr. Jakes Restaurant, Milwaukee, 1961-63; salesman Gulf Oil Corp., Boston, 1963-65; owner Village Green, Rockford, Ill., from 1965-. Bd. dirs. Rockford Area Crime Stoppers 1980--, Rockford Art Mus. 1981-85. Served as cpl. U.S. Army. Republican. Roman Catholic. Home: Rockford, Ill. Died Jan. 20, 2009.

SWANI, PARVESH, transportation company executive; b. Peshawar, North-West Frontier, Pakistan, Sept. 12, 1937; s. Girdhari Lal and Krishna Kumari (Bagga) S.; m. Sushma Khanna, Aug. 28, 1965; children: Sanjay, Rahul. BS, Allahabad U., India, 1956, MS in Math., 1958; MBA, U. Pitts., 1970. CPA, Fla., CMA. Traffic and operating exec. Indian Railways, various locations, India, 1961-69; traffic planning engr. Pa. Dept. Transp., Harrisburg, 1970-71; sr. cost analyst Seaboard Coastline R.R., Jacksonville, Fla., 1971-74, mgr. econ. analysis, 1974-77; dir. econs. Family Lines Rail System, Jacksonville, 1977-82; asst. v.p. strategic planning and analysis Seaboard System R.R., Jacksonville, 1982-85, v.p. corp. planning and analysis, 1985-86; v.p. joint planning Chessie System R.R., Balt., 1985-86; v.p. fin. and planning Distbn. Services Group CSX Transp., Inc., Balt., from 1986. Bd. dirs. Total Distrn. Services, Inc., Balt. Pres. India Cultural Soc. Jacksonville, 1975-76; mem. Nat. Aquarium Balt., 1987—; nat. assoc. Smithsonian Instn., 1986—. Mem. Am. Inst CPA's, Fla. Soc. CPA's, Am. Mgmt. Assn., Council Logistics Mgmt., Md. Acad. Scis., The Planning Forum, Center Club. Avocations: skiing, fishing, tennis, travel. Home: Baltimore, Md. Died July 19, 2009.

SWANN, BRENDA GAIL, geriatrics nurse; b. Atlanta, May 26, 1956; d. James Albert and Nora Angie (Baker) S. AS, SUNY, Albany, 1986. RN, Ga.; cert. gerontological nurse. Staff nurse HCA Doctors Hosp., Tucker, Ga., 1978-84; office nurse Bi-County Pediatrics, Lilburn, Ga., 1982-84; supr. Janet Hill Personal Care Home, Snellville, Ga., from 1985. Died Jan. 6, 2009.

SWANSON, THOMAS JOSEPH, mortgage company executive; b. Perry, Fla., July 16, 1928; s. Thomas Joseph and Isabelle (Biaza) S.; m. Marylee Young, Apr. 1, 1951. BA in Edn., Fla. State U., 1950; LLB, John Marshall Law Sch., 1957; cert. mortgage banking, Northwestern U., 1968. With claims div. Gen. Accident Fire and Life Assurance Co., Atlanta, 1955-58; v.p. quality control ops., SE regional office Fed. Nat. Mortgage Assn., Atlanta, from 1958. Mem. Atlanta Symphony Orchestra Guild, High Mus. of Art, Ga. Trust Hist. Preservation, Atlanta Steinway Soc. Mem. State Bar Assn. Ga. (real property law sect.), Mortgage Bankers Am., Mortgage Bankers Ga., Atlanta City Club, East Lake Country Club. Republican. Episcopalian. Avocations: piano, golf, animal related activities. Home: Atlanta, Ga. Died May 27, 2009.

SWARTZ, EDWARD MARTIN, lawyer, author; b. Winthrop, Mass., Jan. 17, 1934; s. Jacob W. and Sadie (Bass) S.; m. Linda Katzen, Aug. 1, 1964 (div.); children: James, Joan, Sharron; m. Barbara Marcus BA with honors, U. Mass., 1955; JD magna cum laude, Boston U., 1958; LLM, U. Mich., 1960. Mass. 1958, D.C. 1971. Asst. atty. gen. Commonwealth of Mass., Boston, 1963-65, spl. asst. atty. gen., 1970; ptnr., chief trial counsel Swartz & Swartz, Boston, 1968—2010. Founder World Against Toys Causing Harm, 1985; lectr. law Boston U., 1989-2010; mem. Atty. Gen.'s speakers Bur., chmn. com. on conflict of interest, 1970. Author: Toys That Don't Care, 1971, Hazardous Products Litigation, 1973, Toys That Kill, 1986, Slaughter By Product, 1986. Cook fellow U. Mich., 1960; recipient Disting. Faculty award Mass. Acad. Trial Lawyers, 1987, Ammy award Am. Lawyers Best Personal Injury Performance 1981, Toy Safety award Oreg. Trial Lawyers Assn., 1990. Mem. ABA, Am. Trial Lawyers Assn. (nat. chmn. c.l.e. com. 1968-71), Mass. Bar Assn., Boston Bar Assn., Mass. Trial Lawyer's Assn. (pres. 1974), Mass. Soc. Prevention Blindness (v.p., Man of Vision award 1982). Home: Boston, Mass. Died Sept. 3, 2010.

SWENSON, HARRY WILLIAM, controller; b. Orange, NJ, Aug. 15, 1930; s. Carl Henric and Judit (Igelstrom) S.; m. Grace Ann Leonardis, Dec. 27, 1953; children: Karen, Susan, Harry, Teresa. BBA in Accounting, Upsala Coll., 1952; MBA, Rutgers U., 1958. With Price Waterhouse & Co., 1954-59; treas., asst. sec. Chipman Chem. Co., Bound Brook, N.J., 1959-67; v.p. fin. Pacific Air Lines, San Francisco, 1967-68; asst. v.p. Air West, Inc., San Francisco, 1968-70; treas., controller Hughes Air Corp., San Francisco, 1971-72, v.p. fin., treas., 1973-80, also dir. Sector controller Building Materials Sector, U.S. Industries, Inc., Stamford, Conn., 1980— Bd. dirs. Govtl. Research Council San Mateo County, Calif., 1976-80. Served to sgt. U.S. Army, 1952-54. Mem. N.J., Calif. state socs. C.P.A.s, Am. Inst. C.P.A.s. Died Jan. 4, 2009.

SWIFT, FRANK MEADOR, lawyer; b. NYC, Dec. 27, 1911; s. Frank Meador and Alberta (Rankin) S.; m. Harriet Elizabeth Simpson, May 30, 1944 (dec. Jan. 2003); children: Frank Meador (dec.), Thomas Lamar. Student, Emory U., 1930-32; LL.B., U. Ga., 1935. Bar: Ga. 1935. Partner Swift, Currie, McGhee & Hiers, Atlanta, 1965-82, of counsel, from 1982. Served to comdr. USNR, 1942-46. Mem. Am., Ga. bar assns., Lawyers Club Atlanta, Clubs: Piedmont Driving. Republican. Presbyterian. Home: Saint Simons Island, Ga. Died Mar. 3, 2009.

SWINSKY, MORTON, securities trader; b. NYC, Nov. 21, 1934; s. Frank and Molly (Cohen) Swinsky; children: Karen, Dana. Student, CCNY, NYU Grad. Sch. Bus. Trader C.J. Devine & Co., NYC, 1952—55, head trader, 1954—64; sr. v.p., sr. trader Merrill Lynch Co. Govt. Securities Inc., 1964—79; exec. v.p., mng. dir. William E. Pollock & Co., NYC, from 1979. Mem.: Fed. Agy. Traders Assn. (founder), St. James' (London), Tuxedo (N.Y.). Republican. Jewish. Home: New York, NY. Died June 19, 2010.

SYAL, JANG B., finance company executive; b. Jullunder, North Panjab, India, Apr. 10, 1948; s. Darshan S. and Shanti D. (Chhatwal) S.; m. Mukta Kochhar, Nov. 27, 1978 (div. June 1988); m. Shanta Duggal, Jan. 31, 1992. BS in Engring., Panjab U., Chandigarh, India, 1970; MBA in Mktg., Punjabi U., Patiala, India, 1973; MBA in Acctg. and Fin., No. Ill. U., 1975. Cert. fin. planner. Acctg. specialist Area One Vocat. Tech. Sch., Dubuque, Iowa, 1975-79; asst. prof. acctg. Clarke Coll., Dubuque, 1979-82, U. Wis., Eau Claire, 1982-83; pvt. practice Cherry Hill, N.J., 1983-85; assoc. v.p. investments Dean Witter Reynolds, Inc., Cherry Hill, 1985-94, v.p. investments, from 1994. Fin. cons. AARP, Cherry Hill, 1986—, Guru Nanak Sikh Soc. Delaware Valley, Deptford, N.J., 1985—. Contbr. article to profl. jour. Tax advisor to sr. citizens, 1985—. Mem. Midwest Bus. Adminstrn. Assn., Inst. Cert. Fin Planners, Delaware Valley Soc. Cert. Fin. Planners, Beta Gamma Sigma (life merit cert. 1975, gold medal for acad. excellence in grad. bus. studies). Avocations: reading, travel, tennis, ping pong/table tennis, boating. Home: Sicklerville, NJ. Died Jan. 10, 2009.

SYKES, DAVID TERRENCE, lawyer; b. Phila., Oct. 24, 1937; s. David Malcolm and Hester Lydia (Kliphouse) Sykes; m. Mary Carlisle Ferguson, Nov. 5, 1966; children: David Graham, Matthew Carlisle. BA, Hamilton Coll., 1959; LLB, Temple U. Sch. Law, Phila., 1965. Bar: Pa. 1965, US Dist. Ct. (ea. dist.) Pa. 1965, US Ct. Appeals (3rd cir.) 1965, Supreme Ct. Pa., US Supreme Ct. 1975, cert.: Am. Bd. Certification (bus. bankruptcy specialist). Assoc. Duane Morris LLP, Phila., 1965—71, ptnr., 1972—2004, of counsel, 2004—10, chmn. reorganization & fin. sect., 1972—93, mem. ptnrs. bd., 1981—2004, mng. ptnr., 1994—97, vice chmn., 1998—2004. Law lectr. Temple U. Sch. Law, 1983—88; co-founder, past chair Ea. Dist. Pa. Bankruptcy Conf.; co-founder, pres. bd. dirs. Consumer Bankruptcy Assistance Project. Contbr. articles to profl. jours. Bd. vis. Temple U. Sch. Law; pres. PTA, mem. bd. trustees Chestnut Hill Acad., 1985—87. Active duty USN, 1959—62, U.S.S. Springfield. Recipient Equal Justice award, Cmty. Legal Svcs., 1996; named a SuperLawyer, Phila Mag., 2006; named one of America's Leading Bus. Lawyers, Chambers USA, 2003—10, Corp. Counsel mag.'s Best Lawyers, 2005. Fellow: Am. Coll. Investment Counsel; mem.: ABA (Nat. Pub. Svc. award 1999), Am. Bankruptcy Inst., Assn. Comml. Fin. Attorneys, Internat. Bar Assn., Comml. Law League of America, Am. Coll. Bankruptcy (v.p. 1997—2001, dir. 2001—05, pres. 2005—07, charter fellow, Disting. Svc. award 2008), Phila. Bar Assn. (chmn. bus. law sect. 1983, chmn. banking & fin. institutions com. 1989, First Union Fidelity award 2000), Pa. Bar Assn. Democrat. Episcopalian. Avocations: skiing, golf. Home: Philadelphia, Pa. Died Feb. 1, 2010.

SYLVESTER, CHARLES THOMAS, retired diplomat; b. Annapolis, Md., Apr. 8, 1934; s. John and Ruth (Yarnell) S.; m. Evelyn Elizabeth Kluger, June 20, 1959; children: John A., Thomas Y. BS, U.S. Naval Acad., 1955. Commd. fgn. service officer US Dept. State, 1961; vice consul Bordeaux, France, 1961-63; Chinese lang. Tng., 1963-65; 2d sec. US Embassy, Saigon, Vietnam, 1965-67, Taipei, Taiwan, 1967-70; internat. relations officer US Dept. State, Washington, 1970-74; first sec. US Embassy, Tromso, Norway, 1974-76, polit. counselor Peking, China, 1976-80, consul gen. Bordeaux, France, 1980-83; dir. pub. affairs European bur. US Dept. State, Washington, 1983-85, insp., 1986-87, consul gen. Shanghai, 1987—89. Served to lt. aviator USN, 1955-61. Mem. Am. Fgn. Service Assn. Democrat. Home: Washington, DC. Died Feb. 7, 2010.

SYMCHOWICZ, SAMSON, retired biochemist; b. Krakow, Poland, Mar. 20, 1923; came to U.S., 1954; s. Chiel and Esther M. S.; m. Sarah R. Nussbaum, May 24, 1953; children: Esther, Beatrice, Caren. Chem. engr., Poly. Inst. Prague, Czechoslovakia, 1950; MS in Chemistry, Bklyn. Poly. Inst., 1956; PhD in Biochemistry, Rutgers U., 1960. Asst. biochemist McGill U., Montreal, Que., Can., 1951-54, SUNY, 1954-56; biochemist Schering-Plough Corp., Bloomfield, N.J., 1956-73, assoc. dir. biol. rsch., 1973-80, dir. drug metabolism, 1980-92; ret. Editorial bd. Drug Metabolism and Disposition; contbr. over 90 sci. papers to profl. publs. Mem. Internat. Soc. Study of Xenobiotics, Am. Chem. Soc., N.Y. Acad. Sci., Soc. Pharmacology and Exptl. Therapeutics. Home: Livingston, NJ. Died Jan. 2, 2009.

SZASZ, FERENC M., historian, educator; b. Davenport, Iowa, Feb. 14, 1940; s. Ferenc Paul Szasz and Mary Ineta Plummer; m. Margaret Connell, Aug. 1, 1969; children: Eric, Chris, Maria. BA, Ohio Wesley U., 1962; PhD, U. Rochester, 1969. Vis. instr. to prof. history U. N.Mex., Albuquerque, 1967—2003. Author: The Day The Sun Rose Twice, 1986, Scots in the North American West, 2000, Religion in the Modern American West, 2000; contbr. articles to profl. jours. Democrat. Mem. United Ch. Of Christ. Avocation: travel. Home: Albuquerque, N.Mex. Died June 20, 2010.

SZONNTAGH, EUGENE L., chemical engineer, educator, chemist, historian, archaeometrist, organologist; b. Budapest, Hungary, July 31, 1924; arrived in US, 1957; s. Jenö Szonntag and Anna Vaisz; m. Nora Jenser, July 27, 1950; children: Desi, Thomas. Diploma in Chem. Engring., Tech. U. Budapest, 1948, DTech, 1975, PhD, 1999; postgrad, Tech. U., Austria, 1957, Bryn Mawr Coll., 1970. Registered profl. engr., Pa.; profl. indsl. hygienist. Chem. engr. Hungarian R.R., Budapest, 1948—50; asst. to assoc. prof. Veszprem U., Hungary, 1950—56; from scientist to sr. scientist Leeds and Northrup Co., North Wales, Pa., 1957—72; prin. engr. Honeywell, Inc., Ft. Washington, Pa.; dir. ops. Continuing Edn., Inc., 1972—73; prin. engr. Honeywell, Inc., Clearwater, Fla., 1973—86; assoc. prof. U. South Fla., Tampa, 1987—91, prof., 1991—2007. Author: (book) Atmospheric Sampling and Analysis of Chemical Agents, 2009; Contbr. over 100 articles to profl. jours., 8 chpts. to books; 38 patents in field. Dir. music, organist emeritus St. Alfred's Ch., Palm Harbor, Fla., 1983—93; dir. music, organist Faith Luth. Ch., 1994—95, Holy Spirit Episcopal Ch., Safety Harbor, Fla., 1996—2008. Recipient Indsl. Rsch. 100 award Chromatography, 1964, Star Inventor award Honeywell, 1982. Mem. Am. Chem. Soc., Am. Inst. Archaeology, Am. Musical Instrument Soc., Organ Hist. Soc., Instrument Soc. Am. (historian 1978-82), Am. Guild Organists (acad.; cert. choir master, chpt. dean 1970-72, 84-86). Avocations: collecting musical instruments, travel, archaeology, photography. Home: Bradenton, Fla. Died May 8, 2010.

SZYMONIAK, ELAINE EISFELDER, retired state senator; b. Boscobel, Wis., May 24, 1920; d. Hugo Adolph and Pauline (Vig) Eisfelder; Casimir Donald Szymoniak, Dec. 7, 1943; children: Kathryn, Peter, John, Mary, Thomas. BS, U. Wis., 1941; MS, Iowa State U., 1977. Speech clinician Waukesha (Wis.) Pub. Sch., 1941-43, Rochester (N.Y.) Pub. Sch., 1943-44; rehab. aide U.S. Army, Chickasha, Okla., 1944-46; audiologist U. Wis., Madison, 1946-48; speech clinician Buffalo Pub. Sch., 1948-49, Sch. for Handicapped, Salina, Kans., 1951-52; speech pathologist, audiologist, counselor, resource mgr. Vocat. Rehab. State Iowa, Des Moines, 1956-85; mem. Iowa Senate, Des Moines, 1989—2000; ret., 2000. Bd. dir. On With Life, Terrace Hill Found. Adv. bd. Iowa State Inst. for Social and Behavioral Health; mem. Child Care Resource and Referral Cmty. Empowerment Bd., Greater Des Moines Coun. for Internat. Understanding, United Way, 1987—88, Urban Dreams, Iowa Maternal and Child Health com.; pres. Chrysalis Found., 1997; mem. City-County Study Commn.; Mem. Des Moines City coun., 1978—88; bd. dirs. Nat. League Cities, Washington, 1982—84, Civic Ctr., House of Mercy, Westminster House, Iowa Leadership Consortium, Iowa Comprehensive Health Assn. Named Woman of Achievement, YWCA, 1982, Visionary Woman, 1993, Young Women's Resource Ctr., 1989; named to Iowa Women's Hall of Fame, 1999; named Des Moines Woman of Influence, Bus. Record, 2000. Mem. Am. Speech Lang. and Hearing Assn., Iowa Speech Lang. and Hearing Assn. (pres. 1977-78), Nat. Coun. State Legislators (fed. state com. on health, adv. com. on child protection), Women's Polit. Caucus, Nexus (pres. 1981-82, mem. Supreme Ct. Select Com.), Wellmark Found. (adv. bd.), Des Moines (Iowa) Women's Club (bd. dir. 2003—), Prairie Club. Avocations: reading, travel, swimming, whitewater rafting. Home: Urbandale, Iowa. Died May 20, 2009.

TABER, LYNN SULLIVAN, education educator; b. Warren, Ohio, Feb. 21, 1947; d. James Wesley and Madelyn Jane (Nicholas) Sullivan; m. Robert Clinton Taber, June 12, 1992. BA in Psychology and English, Kent State U., 1968; MA in Coll. Student Pers., U. Colo., 1973; M in Mktg., Northwestern U., 1985; PhD in Ednl. Adminstrn., U. Tex., 1995. Cert. Laubach Literacy Action tutor, 1989. Counselor, instr. Laramie County C.C., Cheyenne, Wyo., 1973-76; dir., asst. dean, assoc. dean Triton Coll., River Grove, Ill., 1976-86; assoc. v.p., v.p. Fla. C.C., Jacksonville, 1986-92; W.K. Kellogg rsch. fellow U. Tex., Austin, 1992-95; adminstrv. intern asst. to pres. C.C. Denver, Colo., 1993; asst. prof. higher edn. adminstrn. U. Ala., Tuscaloosa, from 1996. Mem. Ill. Coun. C.C. Admintrs., 1976-86, sec., 1985; cons. in field. Co-author: The Company We Keep-Collaboration in the Community College, 1995. Study team mem. Jacksonville (Fla.) Cmty. Coun., Inc., 1986-92; 1st v.p., bd. mem. Learn to Read, Inc., Jacksonville, 1988-90; chmn., CEO, bd. mem. Pine Castle, Inc., Jacksonville, 1990-92; co-facilitator INSIGHT-A Cmty. Visioning Process, Jacksonville, 1992. Roueche scholar in C.C. leadership U. Tex., Austin, 1994. Mem. Am. Ednl. Rsch. Assn., Am. Assn. C.C. (presenter 1981—), Phi Kappa Phi, Kappa Delta Phi. Avocations: travel, reading, walking, assisting judges at aerobatic competitions. Home: Sun City Center, Fla. Died Jan. 8, 2009.

TACKET, HALL SANFORD, retired internist; b. Dyer, Tenn., Apr. 12, 1921; s. John Otis and Lucile (Sanford) T.; m. Jeanne Snedecor, Apr. 17, 1925; children: Lynn, Carol, Hall Sanford Jr. BS, U. Tenn., 1943, MD, 1944. Diplomate Am. Bd. Internal Medicine, 1952. Instr. to assoc. prof. medicine U. Tenn. Coll. Medicine, Memphis, 1950-64, clin. prof., 1964-87, prof., 1987-96, emeritus prof., from 1996; internist pvt. practice, Memphis, 1950-86. Chief gen. internal med. Baptist Meml. Hosp., Memphis, 1979-91, dir. med. edn., 1979-91. Contbr. articles to profl. jours. Cpt. U.S. Army, 1945-47. Master ACP (gov. Tenn.); fellow Am. Coll. Cardiology. Home: Chevy Chase, Md. Died Aug. 29, 2009.

TADDEI, GIUSEPPE, baritone; b. Genova, Italy, June 26, 1916; Appeared as Figaro in The Marriage of Figaro, Salzburg, 1948; N.Y. Met. debut as Falstaff in Falstaff, 1985; performances include Vienna Staatsoper; numerous recs. including La Bohème, Ernani, Un Ballo in Maschera, Guillaume Tell, Rigoletto, Falstaff, Don Giovanni, Cosi Fan Tutte, others. Died June 2, 2010.

TADROS, MOHSEN SHOKRY, agriculturist; b. Cairo, Jan. 1, 1930; s. Shokry Tadros Boulos; m. Etedal Lala Tadros; children: Ramez, Karam. MSc, Cairo U., 1960; PhD, Ain Shams U., Cairo, 1965; degree (hon.), Ohio U., Athens, 1978. Cert. sr. ecologist Ecological Soc. Am. Bd. Profl. Certification, 1999. Biology tchr. High Agrl. Inst., Menia, Egypt, 1958-66, lectr. Kafr El Sheikh, Egypt, 1966-67, Tanta U., Kafr El-Sheikh, Egypt, 1968-77, assoc. prof., 1978-81, prof. agrl. zoology, 1982-89, prof. emeritus, from 1990. Cons., New Valley Govt. Kharga, Egypt 1952-55; rsch. supr., Tanta U., 1966—; vis. prof., State U. NJ, 1979-82; prin. investigator Link Project, NJ and Egypt, 1987-91. Author gen. zoology textbooks, 1976, 77. Recipient award, Tanta U., 1999. Mem. Ecol. Soc. Am., Entomol. Soc. US, Zool. Soc. Egypt, Entomology Soc. Egypt, Internat. Assn. Ecology, Acarological Soc. Am. Avocations: swimming, reading, tennis, gardening. Home: Cairo, Egypt. Died Apr. 2, 2009.

TAFT, JOHN AILES, JR., hospital executive; b. Evanston, Ill., Aug. 6, 1927; s. John Ailes and Mildred (Bent) Taft; m. Portia Downs, June 20, 1952; children: Sarah, Peter, Andrew, Mary. BS, Northwestern U., 1947; MHA, 1957; MBA, Dartmouth Coll., 1950. Adminstrv. asst. Chgo. Wesley Meml. Hosp., 1954—57; v.p. Delnor Hosp., St. Charles, Ill.,

1957—61; pres., 1961—86; adminstr., chief exec. officer Grace Hosp., Morganton, NC, 1986—89, Daviess County Hosp., Washington, Ind., from 1989. Bd. dirs. Fox Valley Hospice, 1979—86, Health Sys. Agency, Cary, Ill., 1983—86, Ind. Easter Seals, from 1990. With USNR, 1945—46. Fellow: Am. Coll. Healthcare Execs.; mem.: Chgo. Hosp. Coun. (dir. 1982—86), NC Hosp. Assn. (dir. 1989), Ill. Hosp. Assn. (dir. 1978—82, 1984—86). Home: Madison, Wis. Died May 3, 2010.

TAKASUGI, NAO, retired state legislator, real estate developer; b. Oxnard, Calif., Apr. 5, 1922; s. Shingoro and Yasuye (Hayashi) T.; m. Judith Shigeko Mayeda, Mar. 23, 1952; children: Scott, Russell, Ronald, Tricia, Lea. BS, Temple U., 1945; MBA, U. Pa. Wharton Sch., 1946. Mem. city council City of Oxnard, Calif., 1976-82, mayor Calif., 1982-92; mem. Calif. State Assembly, 1992-98. Bus. developer, cons.; commr. Oxnard Harbor Dist., 2000-08; bd. trustees, Pacific Commr. Bank, 2002-09. Profiled in Tom Brokaw's The Greatest Generation, 1999. Mem. Oxnard Planning Commn., 1974-76; pres. World Trade Ctr. Assn., Oxnard; apptd. (by Calif. gov.) chmn. UN Anniversary; assemblyman Calif. State Assembly 37th Dist.; bd. govs. Japanese Am. Nat. Mus. Decorated Order of Sacred Treasure with Gold Rayette medal Japanese Gov., 1992. Mem. Ventura County Japanese Am. Citizens League, World Trade Ctr. Assn. (pres. Oxnard chpt.), U.S. Conf. Mayors (mem. nat. adv. bd.), Nat. League of Cities (nat. bd. dirs.), Ventura County Transp. Com., League Calif. Cities (bd. dirs.), South Coast Area Bd. Dirs. (chmn. transp. com.), Assn. Ventura County Cities, Oxnard Housing Authoritry (chmn.), Oxnard Redevel. Agy. (chmn.), Optimists Club (Oxnard). Republican. Methodist. Home: Oxnard, Calif. Died Nov. 19, 2009.

TALBOT, PHILLIPS, retired Asian affairs specialist, former ambassador; b. Pitts., June 7, 1915; s. Kenneth Hammet and Gertrude (Phillips) T.; m. Mildred Aleen Fisher, Aug. 18, 1943 (dec. June 20, 2004); children: Susan Talbot Jacox, Nancy, Bruce Kenneth (dec.). BA, U. Ill., 1936, BS in Journalism, 1936; student, London Sch. Oriental Studies, 1938—39, Aligarh Muslim U., India, 1939—40; PhD, U. Chgo., 1954; LLD (hon.), Mills Coll., 1963, Elmhurst Coll., Ill., 2007. Reporter Chgo. Daily News, 1936-38, corr. India and Pakistan, 1946-48, 49-50; assoc. Inst. Current World Affairs, 1938-41, 46-51; instr. U. Chgo., 1948-50, Columbia U., NYC, 1951; exec. dir. American Universities Field Staff, 1951-61; asst. sec. for Near Eastern & S. Asian affairs US Dept. State, 1961-65, US amb. to Greece Athens, 1965-69; pres. Asia Soc., NYC, 1970-81, pres. emeritus, 1981—2010. Phi Beta Kappa vis. scholar, 1973-74. Author: (with S.L. Poplai) India and America, 1958, India in the 1980s, 1983, An American Witness to India's Partition, 2007; editor: South Asia in the World Today, 1950. Life trustee Aspen Inst., US-Japan Found.; counselor United Bd. for Christian Higher Edn. in Asia; elder Presbyn. Ch. 2d lt. cav. Officers Res. Corps, 1936; 1st lt. NG, 1937-38; lt. comdr. USNR, 1941-46. Recipient Padma Shri honors, India, 2002, Bharatiya Shiromani Purskar award, 2006. Mem. Am. Acad. Diplomacy, Coun. Am. Ambs., Coun. Fgn. Rels., Century Assn., Cosmos Club. Died Sept. 1, 2010.

TAMKIN, ALVIN CHASIN, lawyer; b. Boston, June 19, 1924; BS in Bus. Adminstrn., Boston U., 1946, LLB, 1948. Bar: Mass. 1948, US Dist. Ct. Mass. 1949. Pvt. practice, Boston, 1948—63; mem. Mass. House of Reps., 1955—62; govs. councillor Mass., 1960—62; presiding justice Mass. Dist. Ct., Hingham, from 1963; chmn. civil rules com. and edn. com. Dist. Cts. Mass., 1970—76, assoc. justice appelate divsn., 1975—79; mem. civil adv. com. Supreme Jud. Ct., 1970—84. Hon. pres. New Eng. Region Am. Jewish Congress; hon. trustee Combined Jewish Philanthropies. Mem.: ABA, Plymouth County Bar Assn., Mass. Bar Assn., Boston U. Law Sch. Alumni Assn. (past pres.). Home: Needham Hgts, Mass. Died Aug. 10, 2010.

TANFORD, CHARLES, physiology educator; b. Halle, Germany, Dec. 29, 1921; came to U.S., 1939, naturalized, 1947; s. Max and Charlotte (Eisenbruch) T.; m. Lucia Lander Brown, Apr. 3, 1948 (div. Feb. 1969); children— Victoria, James Alexander, Sarah Lander. BA, NYU, 1943; MA, Princeton U., 1944, PhD, 1947. Postdoctoral fellow Harvard U., Cambridge, Mass., 1947-49, vis. prof. chemistry, 1966; asst. prof. chemistry U. Iowa, Iowa City, 1949-54, assoc. prof., 1954-59, prof., 1956-60; prof. biochemistry Duke U., Durham, N.C., 1960-70, James B. Duke prof. biochemistry, 1970-80, James B. Duke prof. physiology, from 1980; George Eastman vis. prof. Oxford (Eng.) U., 1977-78; Walker-Ames prof. U. Wash., Seattle, 1979; Reilly lectr. U. Notre Dame, Ind., 1979. Author: Physical Chemistry of Macromolecules, 1961, The Hydrophobic Effect, 1973, 2d edit., 1980; Contbr. numerous articles to profl. jour. Recipient Alexander von Humboldt prize, 1984; Guggenheim fellow, 1956; Merck Award, Am. Soc. for Biochemistry &Molecular Biology, 1992. Mem. Am. Acad. Arts, Scis., Nat. Acad. Scis. Unitarian (pres. Unitarian-Universalist Fellowship 1968). Died Oct. 1, 2009.

TANNEHILL, NORMAN BRUCE, JR., consultant, educator; b. Pitts., Aug. 22, 1950; s. Norman B. and Maxine (Hart) T.; m. Marianne Witt, Sept. 22, 1979 (div. July 1990); children: Andrea, Norman Bruce III; m. Darcy Anita Bartins, Feb. 14, 1991; 1 child, Courtney. BSBA, Robert Morris U., 1975, MS, 1989. Owner, CEO Tannehill Info. Sys. Ltd., Coraopolis, from 1989. Adj. faculty Robert Morris U., 1989-97, C.C. of Allegheny County, Pitts., 1991—, Waynesburg Coll., 1998—. Mem. IEEE Computer Soc., Assn. for Computing Machinery, Assn. for Ednl. Comms. Tech., Mensa. Home: Mc Donald, Pa. Died Jan. 5, 2009.

TANNENBAUM, ABE ALAN, architect; b. Milw., May 14, 1922; s. Jacob and Rose (Lauwasser) T.; children: Terry, Jodi. BS in Architecture, U. Ill., 1950. Prin. Tannenbaum and Assocs., Architects and Planners, Milw., 1950-92. Bd. dirs. Guaranty Bank. Mem. City of Glendale (Wis.) Plan Commn., Cmty. Devel. Authority. Recipient 4 Gold medals Nat. Phys. Fitness Competitions. Mem. AIA (emeritus), Wis. Architects Assn. (bd. dirs. 1963-64, pres. southeast sect. 1963-64). Avocations: tennis, ballroom dancing. Home: Waukesha, Wis. Died Jan. 20, 2009.

TANNENBAUM, PERCY H., psychology educator; b. Montreal, Que., Can., May 31, 1927; s. Charles and Ronya (Tannenbaum) T.; m. Brocha Kaplan, Sept. 16, 1948; children: Brian Dov, Nili. B.Sc., McGill U., 1948; MS, U. Ill., 1951, PhD, 1953. Reporter, staff writer Montreal Herald, 1947-50; asst. prof. Mich. State U., 1953-54; research asst. prof. U. Ill., 1954-59; prof. psychology and journalism, dir. Mass Communication Research Center, U. Wis., 1959-67; prof. communication and psychology U. Pa., 1967-70; prof. public policy emeritus, rsch. psychologist U. Calif., Berkeley, from 1970. Cons. panel social psychology NSF, NIMH, Nat. Acad. Scis., govt. and industry.; fellow Center Advanced Study Behavioral Scis., 1965-66; fellow Inst. Advanced Studies, Berlin, Fed. Republic Germany, 1984-85. Author: Turned-On TV/Turned-Off Voters, 1983; Author: (with others) The Measurement of Meaning, 1957; Co-editor: (with others) Theories of Cognitive Consistency: A Sourcebook; editor: (with others) Entertainment Functions of Television. Fellow Am. Psychol. Assn., AAAS; mem. AAUP, Am. Assn. Public Opinion Research, Internat. Assn. Mass. Communications Research. Home: Berkeley, Calif. Died Oct. 2, 2009.

TARAKI, SHIRLEE, librarian; b. Chgo., Apr. 25, 1922; d. Frank and Leah (Simon) Heda; m. Mohamed Rasul Taraki, June 3, 1944 (dec. Aug. 1972); children: Lisa, Yosuf. BA in Psychology, U. Chgo., 1943, MA in Edn., 1947. Instr. English, Ministry of Edn., Kabul, Afghanistan, 1947-65, materials technician, 1965-72; libr. asst. Northwestern U., Evanston, Ill., 1973-90; libr. Ctr. for Women's Health St. Francis Hosp., Evanston, 1990-95. Producer slide presentation An American Woman in Afghanistan, 1974—. Vol. Mather Pavilion at Wagner, Evanston, 1993—; mem. Evanston Comm. on Aging, 1999-2003. Mem. NOW (Evanston-North Shore chpt., founder), Circle Pines Ctr., Afghanistan Reconstrn. Support Com. (co-chair), Afghan Women's Task Force (founder, chair), Amnesty Internat., Phi Beta Kappa. Avocations: music, needlecrafts. Home: Evanston, Ill. Died Jan. 23, 2009.

TARBOX, GURDON LUCIUS, JR., retired museum executive; b. Plainfield, NJ, Dec. 25, 1927; s. Gurdon Ludius and Lillie (Hodgson) T.; m. Milver Ann Johnson, Sept. 25, 1952; children: Janet Ellen LeGrand, Joyce Elaine Schumacher, Paul Edward, Lucia Ann Raatma. BS, Mich. State U., 1952; MS, Purdue U., 1954; D Pub. Svc., U. S.C., 1993. Asst. dir. Brookgreen Gardens, Murrells Inlet, S.C., 1954-59, trustee, 1959-94, dir., 1963-94, pres., 1990-94, pres. emeritus, from 1994. Bd. dirs. Bartlett Tree Expert Co. Chmn. Georgetown County Mental Health Commn., 1964-66; mem. exec. coun. Confedn. S.C. Local Hist. Socs., 1976-80; trustee S.C. Hall Fame, 1976, S.C. Heritage Trust, 1981-86, S.C. Mansion Commn., 1986-99. Served with AUS, 1946-48. Recipient Order of Palmetto, State of S.C., 1999, Francis K. Hutchinson medal for svc. to conservation The Garden Club of Am., 1995. Mem. Am. Assn. Bot. Gardens and Arboreta (dir. 1971-74, sec.-treas. 1982, v.p. 1983, pres. 1985-86), Georgetown County Hist. Soc. (pres. 1970-74), Am. Assn. Mus. (coun. 1983), Southeastern Mus. Conf. (dir. 1977-80), S.C. Fedn. Museums (pres. 1974-76), Am. Assn. State and Local History, S.C. Confedn. Local Hist. Socs., Rotary (pres. 1979-80). Episcopalian. Home: Pawleys Island, SC. Died Apr. 21, 2010.

TARDIE, RAYMOND EDWARD, highway surveyor, general contracting company executive; b. Middleboro, Mass., Apr. 26, 1934; s. Raymond Edmund and Esther (Robinson) T. Equipment operator East Bridgewater Sand & Gravel, 1952-60, owner, operator, 1960-70; pres., treas. Tri-Town Contracting Corp., East Bridgewater, Mass., 1970—. Chmn., East Bridgewater Housing Authority, 1979-81, mem., 1971-81; treas. Plymouth County Hwy. Assn., 1982. Mem. South Shore Boat Assn. (past pres., past commodore), Old Colony Power Squadron. Democrat. Roman Catholic. Club: East Bridgewater Commercial. Lodges: Lions, Masons. Home: Stuart, Fla. Died May 15, 2009.

TARSOLY, BALAZS KOLOZSVARY, engineer, economist; b. Komadi, Hungary, Aug. 2, 1923; came to U.S., l956; s. Balazs and Irma (Bujdoso) T.; divorced: l child, Peter Huba. Student, U. Tech. and Econ. Scis., Budapest, Hungary, 1946-56; PhD (hon.), Internat. U. Found., 1985. Adminstr. Indsl. Tng. Inst. Systems, Budapest, 1951-56; owner, mgr. K. Tarsoly Machine Shop and R & D, Amityville, N.Y., from 1957. Inventor vertical cement kiln process, material separator energy apparatus, tool gas motor, vortex motors and gas separation on temperature manipulation. Mem. Soc. Mfg. Engrs., Soc. Am. Inventors, Am. Def. Preparedness Assn., Am. Soc. for Metals, Soc. Broadcast Engrs., U.S. Naval Inst., N.Y. Acad. Scis. Republican. Mem. Hungarian Reformed Ch. Avocations: chess, travel, history, photography, video. Died Jan. 16, 2009.

TASKER, FRED L., physician, educator; b. Gloucester, Mass., May 13, 1931; s. Fred L. and Frances C. (Spiller) Tasker; m. Edna May Taylor, June 27, 1955; children: Gregory Allen, Patricia Ann, Cynthia Ann, Jennifer Sue. BS, Calvin Coll., Grand Rapids, Mich., 1961; MS in Physiology and Pharmacology, U. ND, 1963; MD, U. Kans., Kans. City, 1966. Intern Wesley Med. Ctr., Wichita, 1966—67, resident, surgery, 1967—68; dir. emergency rm. and dept. St. Joseph Hosp., Wichita, 1969—70; resident, ophthalmology Eye & Ear Hosp., Pitts., 1970—73; pvt. practice Sandusky, Ohio, from 1973; clin. asst. prof. surgery Med. Coll. Ohio, Toledo, from 1975; chief staff Good Samaritan Hosp., Sandusky, 1982—83. Cons. ophthalmologist Providence Hosp., Meml. Hosp., Sandusky. Contbr. articles to publs. With USAF, 1950—54. Mem.: AMA, Nat. Wildlife Assn., Internat. Assn. Ophthalmic Surgeons, Am. Acad. Ophthalmology, Erie County Med. Soc., Ohio State Med. Assn., Sigma Xi. Republican. Home: Huron, Ohio. Died Nov. 8, 2009.

TATE, CURTIS E., JR., management educator; b. Trezvant, Tenn., July 5, 1920; s. Curtis E. and Mary Kathryn (Haskins) T.; m. Evelyn Ruth Mann, Apr. 12, 1945 (div. May, 1969); m. Mary Jim Combs, Aug. 28, 1977; children: Curtis Emory, Milton Oglesby. Student, N. Ga. Coll., 1943-44, U. Ga., 1945-46; AB, Bethel Coll., 1946; MS, U. Tenn., 1952. Clk. Family Gen. Grocery, Trezevant, Tenn., 1938-42; clk. purchasing dept. P&G Defense Corp., Milan, Twnn., 1942; plant mgr. Keathley Pie Co., Memphis, 1946-50; instr. Furman U., Greenville, S.C., 1952-53; bus. mgr. Lander Coll., Greenwood, S.C., 1953-56; from asst. to assoc. prof. Coll. of Bus. Adminstrn. U. Ga., Athens, 1956—91; prof. emeritus Terry Coll. of Bus. U. Ga., Athens, from 1991. Bd. dirs. Flexible Products, Inc., Marietta, Ga., 1968-76; asst. to dean fund raising Terry Coll. Bus., 1991-98. Co-author: Successful Small Business Management, 1975, latest rev. edit., 1985, Complete Guide to Your Own Business, 1977, Dow-Jones-Irwin Business Papers, 1977, Bus. Policy: Administrative, Strategic and Constituency Issues, 1983, 92, Managing for Profits, 1984, Small Business Management and Entrepreneurship, 1992. With U.S. Army, 1942-45, ETO. Fellow N. Am. Case Rsch. Assn. (sec., v.p., bd. dirs., pres. so. casewriters, Outstandinc Case Contbr. 1992), Acad. Mgmt., NACRA (past pres. adv. coun. 1998), Kiwanis, Sigma Iota Epsilon, Beta Gamma Sigma. Died May 29, 2010.

TAVERNA, ROSE CHRISTINE, d. Salvatore J. and Mary S. Taverna; student Bergen (N.J.) Jr. Coll., CCNY. With Nat. Wage Stblzn. Bd., Washington, 1948, Standard Brands Inc., N.Y.C., 1949; with Dancer Fitzgerald Sample Inc., N.Y.C., 1950-87, asst. treas., 1965-87, v.p., 1972-81, sr. v.p., 1981-87, sec. of corp., 1977-87; dir. Program Syndication Svcs., Inc. Died June 23, 2009.

TAYLOR, CARL ERNEST, preventive medicine physician, epidemiologist, educator; b. Landour, Mussoorie, India, July 26, 1916; s. John C. and Elizabeth (Siehl) Taylor; m. Mary Daniels, Feb. 14, 1943; children: Daniel, Elizabeth, Henry. BS, Muskingum Coll., 1937, DSc, 1962; MD, Harvard, 1941, MPH, 1951, DPH, 1953; LHD (hon.), Towson U., 1974. Diplomate Am. Bd. Preventive Medicine. Intern, resident pathology, surg. staff, tropical disease rsch. Gorgas Hosp., Panama, 1941—44; charge med. service Marine Hosp., Pitts., 1944—46; supt. Meml. Hosp., Fategarh, India, 1947—50; rsch. assoc. Harvard Sch. Pub. Health, Boston, 1950—52, asst. prof. epidemiology, 1957—59, assoc. prof., 1959-61; prof. preventive and social medicine Christian Med. Coll., Ludhiana, Punjab, India, 1953—56; prof. internat. health, chmn. dept. internat. health Johns Hopkins Sch. Hygiene and Pub. Health, Balt., 1961—83, prof. emeritus, from 1984. Cons. AID, from 1959; UNICEF country rep. in China, 1984—87; expert com. WHO, 1963, 1966—67, 1970—73, 1975; mem. Nat. Adv. Commn. Health Manpower; chmn. Nat. Council for Internat. Health. Contbr. articles to profl. jours. Fellow: Am. Pub. Health Assn., Royal Soc. Tropical Medicine and Hygiene, Royal Coll. Physicians; mem.: Nat. Acad. Medicine, Inst. Medicine, Indian Assn. for Advancement Med. Edn., Am. Soc. Tropical Medicine and Hygiene, Assn. Tchrs. Preventive Medicine. Achievements include research in rural health, population dynamics, nutrition, epidemiology of leprosy. Home: Baltimore, Md. Died Feb. 4, 2010.

TAYLOR, DAVID WYATT AIKEN, retired clergyman; b. Tsingkiangpu, Kiangsu, China, Dec. 13, 1925; s. Hugh Kerr and Fanny Bland (Graham) T.; m. Lillian Ross McCulloch, Aug. 25, 1951; children: Frances Bland, David Wyatt. BA, Vanderbilt U., 1949; B.D. cum laude, Union Theol. Sem. Va., 1952; Th.M., Princeton Theol. Sem., 1953; D.D. (hon.), King Coll., Bristol, Tenn., 1959. Ordained to ministry Presbyn. Ch. U.S., 1952. Pastor chs., Elkton, Va., 1953-55, Bristol, Va., 1955-62; ednl. sec. bd. world missions Presbyn. Ch. U.S., 1962-68, program div. dir., 1968-73, ecumenical officer gen. assembly mission bd. Atlanta, 1973-82; pastor Orange Park Presbyn. Ch., Orange Park, Fla., 1982-86; gen. sec. for strategy and interpretation Consultation on Ch. Union, Princeton, NJ, 1986-88, gen. sec., 1988-93; ret., 1993. Instr. Bible Presbyn. Jr. Coll., Maxton, N.C., 1951; mem. program bd., div. Christian edn. Nat. Council Chs., 1965-69, bd. mgrs., dept. edn. for mission, 1962-68, mem. program bd., div. overseas ministries, 1968-78, mem. governing bd., 1976-80, chmn. governing bd. credentials com., 1978; chmn. Church World Service, Inc., 1973-75; mem. adminstrn. and fin. com. Nat. Council Chs., 1973-75, mem. commn. on faith and order, 1978-93; mem. commn. on interchurch aid World Council Chs., 1973-75; mem. 5th Assembly, 1975; rep. Presbyn. Ch. U.S. to World Alliance Ref. Chs., 1976-82; bd. dirs. Presbyn. Survey mag., 1963-68; mem. Consultation on Ch. Union, 1974-93; chmn. Nat. Ecumenical Officers Assn., 1978-81; exec. coun. NC Coun. Chs., 2003—. Bd. dirs. Abingdon Presbytery's Children's Home, Wytheville, Va., 1958-62. Served with AUS, 1944-46, PTO. Mem. Sigma Chi. Presbyterian. Home: Cary, NC. Died May 23, 2010.

TAYLOR, ELINOR ZIMMERMAN, retired state legislator; b. Norristown, Pa., Apr. 18, 1921; d. Harold I. and Ruth A. (Rahn) Zimmerman; m. William M. Taylor, 1947; 1 child, Barbara. BS, West Chester State Tchrs. Coll., 1943; student, Columbia U., 1944, U. Del., 1955; MEd, Temple U., 1958. Tchr. Ridley Park (Pa.) H.S., 1943-46, West Chester (Pa.) H.S., 1946-50; prof. West Chester State Coll., 1955-68, adminstr., 1968-76; mem. Pa. House of Reps., 1977—2006. Chmn. subcom. on higher edn.; sec. Rep. Caucus; bd. dirs. Pa.

Higher Edn. Assistance Agy.; active Gov. Commn. on Funding Higher Edn., Women; in Politics and Polit. Action Com.; Rep. chmn. Health and Welfare Com.; trustee Charles S. Swope Found.; founding trustee Bd. Chester County Edn. Found. Councilwoman Borough of West Chester, Pa., 1974-77, mem. recreation com., 1974-77. Named West Chester Citizen of Yr., 1985, Legislator of Yr. Pa. Assn. Home Health Agys., 1993; recipent Hon. award Pa. State Assn. for Health, Phys. Edn. and Recreation, 1962, Hon. Umpires award U.S. Field Hockey Assn., 1967, Disting. Alumni award West Chester State Coll., 1977, alumni award Temple U., 1982, Love of Children of Greater West Chester Golden Heart award, Achievement cert. Pa. Fedn. of Bus. and Profl. Women's Club, George Washington Honor award Valley Forge Freedom Found., Guardian of Small Bus. award, 1993-94, cert. of appreciation Am. Legion, 1995, Margaret Hoover Brigham award Chester County Emergency Med. Svc., 1995, Police Athletic League award, 1995; named to Henderson H.S. Hall of Fame, 1994. Mem. AAUW (former pres.), Nat. Assn. Women Legislators, Chester County Art Assn., Pa. Paramedice Assn. (hon.). Republican. Presbyterian. Home: Stuart, Fla. Died July 27, 2010.

TAYLOR, EUGENE FRANCIS, advertising agency executive; b. Hoboken, NJ, May 14, 1924; s. Arleigh and Helen (Fleming) T.; m. Marion Laberdee, Dec. 12, 1952; children: Megan Fleming, Alice Allyn. AB, Fordham U., 1948; postgrad., U. N.C.-Chapel Hill, 1948-51. Exec. v.p. Post Keyes Gardner, Chgo., 1965-69; dir. Hornblow Cox Freeman, London, 1969-72; sr. v.p. Erwin Wasey Inc., Los Angeles, 1972-75; v.p. mktg. Yardley of London, NYC, 1975-77; sr. v.p. Wells Rich Greene Inc., NYC, 1977-81; exec. v.p. for creative services Campbell-Ewald Co., Warren, Mich., from 1981. Mem.: N.Y. Athletic; Detroit Athletic. Democrat. Roman Catholic. Home: Saint Clair Shores, Mich. Died Mar. 21, 2010.

TAYLOR, JAMES A., lawyer; b. Oklahoma City, June 12, 1949; AB cum laude, Dartmouth Coll., 1971; JD with spl. distinction, U. Okla., 1974. Bar: Tex. 1974. Ptnr. Baker & Botts L.L.P., Dallas. Note editor Oklahoma Law Review, 1973. Mem. ABA, Am. Coll. Real Estate Lawyers, State Bar Tex., Dallas Bar Assn., Order Coif. Died Jan. 5, 2009.

TAYLOR, JERRY ALAN, osteopathic physician; b. Detroit, July 12, 1939; s. Harry and Ann (Skolnick) Taylor; m. Laura Dorsey, June 18, 1972; children: Megan, Erin. Student, Wayne State U., 1957—61, U. Detroit, 1960—61, U. Mich., 1960; MD, Coll. Osteo. Medicine and Surgery, Des Moines, 1965. Intern Botsford Gen. Hosp., Farmington, Mich., 1965—66; pvt. practice Garden City, Mich., 1966—67; resident, orthop. surgery Doctors Hosp., Columbus, Ohio, 1969—71, Botsford Gen. Hosp., Farmington, Mich., 1971—73; fellow, hand surgery Grace Hosp., Detroit, 1972—73; pvt. practice Southfield, Mich., from 1973. Mem. staff Botsford Gen. Hosp., Farmington Hills, Mich., Oakland Gen. Hosp., Madison Heights, Mich. Contbr. articles to profl. jours. Served to lt. comdr. USNR, 1967—69. Fellow: Am. Osteo. Coll. Surgeons, Am. Osteo. Acad. Orthop. Surgery; mem.: Detroit Acad. Orthop. Surgeons, Oakland County Osteo. Assn., Mich. Assn. Osteo. Physicians and Surgeons, Mich. Acad. Osteo. Orthop. Surgeons, Am. Assn. Hand Surgery, Am. Osteo. Assn., Am. Osteo. Acad. Orthops. Home: Bloomfield Hills, Mich. Died Jan. 12, 2010.

TAYLOR, MAUREEN EUGENIA, hospital administrator; b. N.Y.C., Feb. 16, 1947; d. Samuel Goodwin and Genevieve (Scott) Taylor; 1 child, Jamal. B.S. in Criminal Justice, Mercy Coll., 1980; M.P.A., NYU, 1984; postgrad. N.Y. Inst. Tech., 1983—. Adminstrv. sec., asst. Mt. Sinai Hosp., N.Y.C., 1973-77; adminstrv. asst. Transit Police Acad., N.Y.C., 1978-79; bus. instr. PRC Metronamics, Corona, N.Y., 1979-80; clerical skills instr. ICD Rehab. Ctr., N.Y.C., 1980-81; adj. instr. Monroe Bus. Inst., N.Y.C., 1981-82; exec. asst. Dept. Juvenile Justice, N.Y.C., 1981-84; hosp. adminstr. Health & Hosp. Corp., 1984—; co-owner, pres. TPC Cons. Services, N.Y.C., 1982—. Recipient Criminal Justice Departmental award Mercy Coll., 1980; Mayor's Grad. scholar N.Y. Inst. Tech., 1983. Mem. Am. Soc. Pub. Adminstrn., Adminstrv. Mgmt. Soc., Am. Correctional Assn., Correctional Edn. Assn., Nat. Assn. Female Execs. Democrat. Roman Catholic. Died Nov. 30, 2009.

TAYLOR, RICHARD TRELORE, retired lawyer; b. Kewanee, Ill., Aug. 5, 1917; s. Earl G. and Lucile (Cully) T.; m. Maureen Hoey, Feb. 9, 1946. BS, U. Ill., 1939, JD, 1946; LL.M., Columbia U., 1947; LHD (hon.), Marlboro Coll., 2001. Bar: Ill. 1946, N.Y. 1947. Assoc. Cadwalader, Wickersham & Taft, NYC, 1947-57, ptnr., 1957-87, presiding ptnr., 1977-87, of counsel, 1988-89. Hon. trustee Marlboro Coll. With US Army, 1941—45. Decorated Bronze Star Mem. Univ. Club (N.Y.C.). Died Dec. 18, 2009.

TAYLOR, ROBERT SUNDLING, language educator, critic; b. Newton, Mass., Jan. 19, 1925; s. Frank Millikan and Elsie (Sundling) T.; m. Brenda K. Slattery, June 20, 1964; children: Gillian, Douglas. AB, Colgate U., 1947; postgrad., Brown U. Art, music, film and theatre critic Boston Herald, 1948-67; editor publs. Inst. Contemporary Art, Boston, 1967; art critic Boston Globe, 1967-90, arts editor, 1973-76, book columnist, from 1978. Prof. English, Wheaton Coll., Norton, Mass., 1961-96; fiction coord. Ea. States Writers Conf., Salem (Mass.) State Coll., 1979-80. Author: (novel) In Red Weather, 1961, Saranac: America's Magic Mountain, 1986, Fred Allen: His Life and Wit, 1989, New England: The Home Front, WWII, 1991; co-author: Treasures of New England, 1976. Trustee, Abbot Public Library, Marblehead, Mass., 1980-83. Served with USN, 1943-46. Mem. Mass. Hist. Soc. Clubs: St. Botolph (Boston). Home: Marblehead, Mass. Died Oct. 25, 2009.

TAYLOR, RUSH WALKER, JR., retired ambassador; b. Little Rock, Nov. 3, 1934; s. Rush Walker and Hallie (Nuckols) T.; m. Joanna Bellows, Jan. 5, 1965; children: Ann, Charlotte, Emily. AB, Harvard U., 1956; LLB, U. Va., 1959; grad., Armed Forces Staff Coll., 1969, Nat. War Coll., 1979. Joined Fgn. Svc., US Dept. State, 1962; vice consul US Embassy, Yaounde, Cameroon, 1962-65, asst. to amb. Rome, 1965-67; staff mem. Bur. European Affairs US Dept. State, Washington, 1967-70, staff asst. to sec., 1970-71, spl. asst. to sec., 1971-72; prin. officer US Embassy, Oporto, Portugal, 1972-75, dep. chief of mission, charge d' affaires Nassau, The Bahamas, 1975-79; staff mem. Office of Inspector Gen., Washington, 1979-81; dir. Office of Press Rels., Washington, 1981-83; exec. dir. U.S. Del. High Frequency World Adminstrn. Radio Conf., Geneva, 1983-84; dep. coord., prin. dep. dir. Bur. Internat. Communications and Info. Policy US Dept. State, Washington, 1984-88, US amb. to Togo Lome, 1988—90. Episcopalian. Home: Arlington, Va. Died Mar. 7, 2010.

TAYLOR, THOMAS HUDSON, JR., import company executive; b. Somerville, Mass., June 8, 1920; s. Thomas Hudson and Virginia Gwendolyn (Wilson) Taylor; m. Mary Jane Potter, Dec. 1, 1943; children: Thomas Hudson III, James R., Jane, John E., Virginia. BS in Econs., Wharton Sch. Fin. and Commerce, U. Pa., 1947. Capt. USAAF, 1941—45. Decorated Air medal. Mem.: Princeton(Gastonia City), Beta Theta Pi. Republican. Methodist. Home: Gastonia, NC. Died Jan. 19, 2009.

TAYLOR, WALTER WALLACE, retired lawyer; b. Newton, Iowa, Sept. 18, 1925; s. Carrol W. and Eva (Greenly) T.; m. Mavis A. Harvey, Oct. 9, 1948; children: Joshua Michael (dec. 1980), Kevin Eileen, Kristin Lisa, Jeremy Walter, Margaret Jane, Melissa E., Amy M. AA, Yuba Coll., 1948, AB, 1950; MA, U. Calif., 1955; JD, McGeorge Coll. Law, 1962. Adminstrv. analyst USAF, Sacramento, 1951-53; personnel, rsch. analyst Calif. Personnel Bd., Sacramento, 1954-56; civil svc., personnel analyst, chief counsel, gen. mgr. Calif. Employees Assn., Sacramento, 1956-75; staff counsel, chief profl. stds. Calif. Commn. Tchr. Credentialing, 1975-88, ret., 1988. Staff counsel State Office Real Estate Appraiser Licensing and Certification, 1992-94, ret.; tchr. discipline civil service, personnel cons. Author: Know Your Rights, 1963-64. Served USCGR, 1943-46. Mem. Calif. State Bar, Am., Sacramento County Bar Assns. Democrat. Home: Sacramento, Calif. Died Jan. 21, 2010.

TEHON, STEPHEN WHITTIER, research engineer; b. Shenandoah, Iowa, Oct. 20, 1920; s. Leo Roy and Mary Viola (Bruner) T.; m. Betty Irene Albright, Oct. 24, 1942; children: Chloe Ann, Susan, Rebecca, Penelope, Candace. BS in Engring. Physics, U. Ill., 1942, MS in Elec. Engring., 1946, PhD, 1958. Sr. engr. Curtiss-Wright, Columbus, Ohio, 1946-47; instr. elec. engring. U. Ill., Urbana, 1947-52; sr. engr., cons. engr. Gen. Electric Electronics Lab., Syracuse, N.Y., 1952-66, cons. engr., sr. staff engr., 1967-80, prin. staff scientist, 1980-87; staff scientist GMK Cons. Svc., Syracuse, N.Y., from 1988. Research engr. Tecumseh Products Research Lab., Ann Arbor, Mich., 1966-67; adj. prof. U. Mich., 1966-67, Syracuse U., 1977—; vis. prof. Clarkson Coll. Tech., Potsdam, N.Y., 1979. Co-author: Electronics Engineers Handbook, 3d edit., 1987, Solid State Magnetic and Dielectric Devices, 1959, Amplifier Handbook, 1966. Served to lt. USNR, 1942-45. Fellow IEEE (life); mem. Sigma Xi, Eta Kappa Nu. Patentee in field. Died Nov. 27, 2009.

TEITELBAUM, BERNARD W(ILLIAM), stockbroker, security analyst; b. N.Y.C., Dec. 14, 1918; s. Aaron and Chaja (Mandelbaum) T.; m. Elizabeth V. Kroo, Aug. 1946 (div. Apr. 1974). Grad. Yeshivah Mokaz Harav, Jerusalem, Palestine, 1939; B.S. in Fin., NYU, 1942. Ordained rabbi, 1939. Dir. Am. Joint Distbn. Com., Fed. Republic Germany, 1946-47; pres. Tamar Foods, N.Y.C., 1947-49; mgr. Am. Eretz Israel Corp., N.Y.C., 1949-54; security analyst, account exec. Ira Haupt & Co., N.Y.C., 1955-63; account exec., portfolio mgr. Hirsch & Co., N.Y.C., 1963-73, Prudential Bache Securities, N.Y.C., 1973—; pres. Fin. Forum NYU, 1939-42. Mem. nat. governing council Am. Jewish Congress, 1960-82, Met. Council, N.Y., 1963-83, v.p. Bklyn. div., 1964-82, v.p. Flatbush, 1955-84; chmn. Flatbush div. Religious Zionists of Am., 1958-82, pres., 1958-70, mem. Greater N.Y. Council, 1958-75; chmn. Flatbush Bible Soc., 1975-77. Served with U.S. Army, 1945-46, ETO. Fellow Fin. Analysts Fedn.; mem. N.Y. Soc. Security Analysts (sr.), Phi Alpha Kappa (pres. fin. 1942-45). Democrat. Avocations: opera; classical music; art collecting; travel; interior design. Home: Brooklyn, NY. Died June 4, 2010.

TELLER, AARON JOSEPH, chemical engineer; b. Bklyn., June 30, 1921; s. David and Mollie (Tascher) T.; m. Sherry R. April, June 30, 1946; 1 son, Richard Eric. B. Chem. Engring., Cooper Union, 1943; M. Chem. Engring., Bklyn. Poly. Inst., 1949; PhD, Case Inst. Tech., 1951. Research engr. Manhattan Project, 1942-44; devel. engr. Publicker Comml. Alcohol Co., 1944-45; prodn. mgr. Martin Labs., 1945-47; chief devel. engr. City Chem. Corp., 1946-47; chmn. chem. engring. and chem. depts. Fenn Coll., 1947-56; research prof., chmn. chem. engring. U. Fla., 1956-60; tech. dir. Mass Transfer, Inc., 1960-62, Colonial Iron Works, Inc., 1960-62, cons. tech. dir., 1962-64; ind. indsl. cons., from 1947; dean Sch. Engring. and Sci., Cooper Union, 1962-70; pres. Teller Environmental Systems, Inc., 1970-86; cons., sr. tech. advisor Rsch. Cottrell, Somerville, N.J., from 1986, v.p. tech., 1989, mem. Office of Pres., 1989-92, sr. v.p. tech., from 1992. Editor: Liquid-Gas Operations (Perry's Chem. Engring. Handbook), 4th edit, 1963; Contbr. articles to profl. jours. Mem. Nat. Adv. Council on Air Pollution. Recipient Bus. Week environ. award, 1972, Valeur award, 1978 Fellow Am. Inst. Chem. Engring. (Sensebaugh award 1991); mem. Nat. Engrs. Commn. on Air Resources (chmn. commn. on resource economy 1972-74), Am. Inst. Chem. Engrs. (chmn. Cleve. and Peninsular Fla. sects. 1953, 58, chmn. pollution control program 1958-61, chmn. air com. 1963-66, 22d Ann. Inst. lectr. 1972) Patentee in mass transfer and air pollution control systems. Home: Palm Beach, Fla. Died June 26, 2010.

TEMPLIN, ROBERT JAMES, automotive executive; b. Toronto, Ont., Can., Dec. 9, 1927; arrived in US, 1934; s. Albert Alexander and Elizabeth Lydia (Zingle) Templin; m. Peggy Ann Wyatt, July 15, 1974; children: Patricia E., Lucie E., R. James. B in Chem.Engring., Rensselaer Poly Inst., 1947. Registered profl. engr., Mich. Asst. chief engr. Cadillac Motor Car Div., Detroit, 1965—69, chief engr., 1973—84. Tech. dir. Gen. Motors Rsch. Lab., Warren, Mich., 1969—70; spl. asst. to pres. Gen. Motors Corp., Detroit, 1970—72; dir. advanced design & process Buick Olds Cadillac Group, Warren, from 1984; mem. Rensselaer Coun., Troy, NY, from 1979; cons. Ordnance Corps, US Army, Yuma, Ariz., 1950—51, Washington-Heidelberg, 1954. Mem.: Soc. Automotive Engrs. Republican. Avocations: amateur radio, photography, scuba diving. Home: Austin, Tex. Died July 22, 2009.

TENNEY, DUDLEY BRADSTREET, retired lawyer; b. NYC, July 13, 1918; s. Parker Gillespie and Josephine (Keeler) T.; m. Margaret Carter, June 13, 1941 (div. Oct. 1977); children: Ann, Janet Greene; m. Dorothy Walsh, Jan. 7, 1978 (dec. Sept. 1982); m. Joyce McPherson, Jan. 4, 1986. AB summa cum laude, Oberlin Coll., 1939; JD magna cum laude, Harvard U., 1942. Bar: N.Y. 1948. Assoc. firm Cahill, Gordon & Reindel, NYC, 1946-54, ptnr., 1955-86. Pres.: Harvard U. Law Rev., 1941-42. Served to maj. AUS, 1942-46, CBI. Mem. ABA, Assn. Bar City of N.Y., World Trade Ctr. Club (N.Y.C.), Manhasset Bay Yacht Club (Port Washington, N.Y.). Home: Sands Point, NY. Died Sept. 18, 2009.

TER HORST, JERALD FRANKLIN, public affairs counselor, former White House press secretary; b. Grand Rapids, Mich., July 11, 1922; s. John Henry and Maude (Van Strien) ter H.; m. Louise Jeffers Roth, Jan. 20, 1945(dec. Mar. 21, 2009); children: Karen Bayens Morris, Margaret Fulton Robinson, Peter Roth, Martha Morgan Lubin. Student, Mich. State U., 1941-42; BA, U. Mich., 1947. Reporter Grand Rapids Press, 1946-51; mem. staff Detroit News, 1953-74, city and state polit. writer, 1953-57, fgn. assignments include Berlin crisis, Vietnam, Israel, Germany, USSR, Latin Am., 1959, Washington corr., 1958-60; chief Detroit News (Washington bur.), 1961-74; press sec. The White House, Washington, 1974; nat. affairs columnist Detroit News/Universal Press Syndicate, 1974-81; dir. nat. pub. affairs Ford Motor Co., 1981-91. Writer North American Newspaper Alliance, 1958-74 Author: Gerald Ford and Future of the Presidency, 1974, The Flying White House: The Story of Air Force One, 1979; contbr. to mags. and TV documentaries. Bd. dirs. Nat. Press Found., 1982-98, WETA-TV (Channel 26), 1988-99, Brady Campaign to Prevent Gun Violence, 1992-2002; chmn. Gridiron Found., 1978-2005, Grad. Sch. Polit. Mgmt., George Washington U., 1985-96. Officer USMCR, 1943-46, 51-52. Recipient Conscience in Media award, Am. Soc. Journalists & Authors, 1975. Mem. Pub. Rels. Soc. Am., Soc. Profl. Journalists, Psi Upsilon. Presbyterian (elder). Clubs: Gridiron, Nat. Press. Overseas Writers. Died Mar. 31, 2010.

TEUBNER, FERDINAND CARY, JR., retired publishing executive; b. Phila., Sept. 22, 1921; s. Ferdinand Cary Teubner and Esther Roslyn (Test) Alperstein; m. Ruth May Hazen, Nov. 1, 1953; 1 child, Janell Caron Teubner Crispyn. Student, U. Pa., 1940-41; grad., Charles Morris Price Sch. Advt. and Journalism, 1949. Rep. W.H. Hoedt Studios, Inc., Phila., 1945-52; account exec. Patterson Prodns., Inc., Phila., 1955-56, v.p., 1956-57; staff exec. Am. Assn. Advt. Agys., NYC, 1957-59; rep. W.H. Martin & Co., Inc., NYC, 1959-62; advt. salesman Editor & Pub. Co., Inc., NYC, 1962-65, advt. mgr., 1965-76, gen. mgr., treas., 1976-78, treas., pub., 1978-95, dir., 1969-95; sec.-treas., dir. E & P Research, Inc., NYC, 1985-95, ret., 1995. Served with USAAF, 1942-45, ETO; served with U.S. Army, 1952-55, Korea, ret. maj. AUS, 1981. Decorated Purple Heart; recipient Silver Shovel award Internat. Newspaper Mktg. Assn., 1993, David Paul Hegg II Lifetime Achievement award Episcopal Diocese Newark, 2003. Mem. Sales Execs. Club N.Y.C., Res. Officer Assn. Clubs: Union League, Lake Valhalla Country. Episcopalian. Home: Montville, NJ. Died Mar. 7, 2009.

THEISS, CLIFFORD ANTHONY, state official; b. Yonkers, NY, Jan. 1, 1941; s. Joseph Bernard and Dorothy Claire (Di Roma) Theiss; m. Mary Margaret Mannen Theiss, Sept. 30, 1972; 1 child, Kristina Marie. BSBA, Georgetown U., 1962; postgrad., Naval Officers Candidate Sch., 1962—63. Asst. buyer J.C. Penney Co., NYC, 1966—68; sr. sales rep. TWA, NYC, 1968—71, supr. tour mktg., 1971—72; mgr. leisure mktg. Hertz, NYC, 1972—76; dir. bus., travel Thomas Cook, NYC, 1976—78; dir. airline mktg. Hertz, 1978—80; dep. commr. NY State Dept. Econ. Devel., NYC, from 1980. Regional dir. United Fund Westchester, Bronxville, NY, 1974—77; v.p. programs Local Parish Mens Club, Bronxville, 1983—84, bd. dirs., 1983—84, team capt. renovation fund raising com., 1983. Lt. jg USN, 1962—66, capt. USNR, 1989. Mem.: Naval Res. Assn. (chpt. v.p. 1980—84), Travel Industry Am. Assn. (NY State rep. 1983). Roman Catholic. Home: Bronxville, NY. Died June 8, 2009.

THOMA, RICHARD WILLIAM, chemical safety and waste management consultant; b. Milw., Dec. 7, 1921; s. Joseph Donath and Margaret Mary (Murphy) T.; m. Ida Mary Scharfschwerdt, Mar. 15, 1952; children: Adele, Richard W., Joseph O., John C. AA, U. Chgo., 1941; BS, U. Wis., Madison, 1947, MS in Biochemistry, 1949, PhD, 1951. R&D fermentation E.R. Squibb & Sons, Inc., New Brunswick, NJ, 1951-82; dir. process devel. New Brunswick Sci. Co., Inc., Edison, 1982-84, cons., from 1984. Safety officer Harbor br.

Oceanographic Inst. St. Lucie County, Fla., 1988—96. Contbr. articles to profl. jours.; patentee microbiol. transformation of steroids. Commr. Somerset County Bd. Elections, 1981-84; mem. Bridgewater Town Coun., 1975-81, Environ. Commn., 1974-75, Sewerage Authority, 1975-76, Police Commn., 1977-81; chmn. Birdgewater Dem. Mcpl. Com., 1980-87; alderman St. Lucie Village, 1996-98. With AUS, 1942-46. Mem. VFW, Am. Chem. Soc., Am. Soc. Microbiology, Am. Acad. Microbiology, Phi Beta Kappa, Sigma Xi, Phi Lambda Upsilon. Home: Fort Pierce, Fla. Died Aug. 5, 2010.

THOMAS, BARBARA DEE STEEN, women's health nurse; b. New Kensington, Pa., Feb. 10, 1963; d. Walter and Idella Lorraine (Mitchell) Steen; m. Steven Douglas Thomas, Sept. 14, 1985; 1 child, Justin Drew. BSN, Indiana U. of Pa., 1985. RN, N.C. Staff nurse John F. Kennedy Med. Ctr.; primary nurse Moses Cone Meml. Hosp., Greensboro, N.C. Mem. Sigma Theta Tau. Home: South Lyon, Mich. Died Feb. 26, 2009.

THOMAS, BROOKS (BENJAMIN BROOKS THOMAS), retired publishing executive; b. Phila., Nov. 28, 1931; s. Walter Horstman and Ruth Sterling (Boomer) Thomas; m. Galen Pinckard Clark, Apr. 15, 1969 (div. 1973); m. Kiono Tucciarone, Oct. 7, 2004. BA, Yale U., 1953, LLB, 1956; grad. Advanced Mgmt. Program, Harvard U., 1973. Bar: Pa. 1957, N.Y. 1960. With law firm Winthrop, Stimson, Putnam & Roberts, NYC, 1960—68; sec., gen. counsel Harper & Row, Pubs., Inc., NYC, 1968—69, v.p., gen. counsel, 1969—73, exec. v.p., 1973—79, COO, 1977—81, pres., 1979—87, CEO, 1981—87, chmn. bd., 1986—87; sterling fellow, 2008. Chmn. bd. dirs. Harper & Row, Ltd., London, 1973—87; bd. dirs. Harper & Row, Pty. Ltd., Australia, Harla S.A. de C.V., Mexico, Harper & Row Pubs. Asia, Pty. Ltd., Singapore. Trustee Outward Bound USA, 1980—2010, vice chmn., 1983—84, chmn., 1984—87; bd. dirs. Nat. Book Awards, 1985—87, chmn., 1986—87; bd. dirs. Outward Bound Internat., 1997—2003, Outward Bound Expenditionary Learning, 2000—10; pres., bd. dirs. Butterfield House, 1968—72; trustee, bd. dirs. RADG, Inc., 1987—89; bd. dirs. Thomason Island Outward Bound Edn. Ctr., 1987—96, Colo. Outward Bound Sch., 1990—96, bd. govs., 1996—2010; bd. dirs. Young Audiences, Inc., 1977—2010, chmn., 1985—2010, Vail Valley Inst., 1989—2010; trustee Episcopal Acad., 2000—10, sec., 2002—10; mem. devel. bd. Yale U., 1985—89, adv. bd. Sch. Orgn. and Mgmt., 1987—96. Lt. (j.g.) USNR, 1956—59. Mem.: ABA, Assn. Am. Pubs. (bd. dirs. 1980—85, chmn. 1983—85), Assn. Bar City of N.Y., Century Assn. (N.Y.C.), Yale U. Alumni Assn. (law sch. rep. 1980—83), Coun. Fgn. Rels., Essex Yacht Club (Conn.), N.Y. Yacht Club (N.Y.C.), Univ. Club (N.Y.C.), Yale Club (N.Y.C.), Merion Cricket Club (Phila.). Home: New York, NY. Died Feb. 5, 2010.

THOMAS, ETHEL COLVIN NICHOLS (MRS. LEWIS VICTOR THOMAS), counselor, educator; b. Cranston, R.I., Mar. 31, 1913; d. Charles Russell and Mabel Maria (Colvin) Nichols; Ph.B., Pembroke Coll. in Brown U., 1934; M.A., Brown U., 1938; Ed.D., Rutgers U., 1979; m. Lewis Victor Thomas, July 26, 1945 (dec. Oct. 1965); 1 child, Glenn Nichols. Tchr. English, Cranston High Sch., 1934-39; social dir. and adviser to freshmen, Fox Hall, Boston U., 1939-40; instr. to asst. prof. English Am. Coll. for Girls, Istanbul, Turkey, 1940-44; dean freshman, dir. admission Women's Coll. of Middlebury, Vt., 1944-45; tchr. English, Robert Coll., Istanbul, 1945-46; instr. English, Rider Coll., Trenton, N.J., 1950-51; tchr. English, Princeton (N.J.) High Sch., 1951-61, counselor, 1960-62, 72-83, coll. counselor, 1962-72, sr. peer counselor, 1986—. Mem. NEA, AAUW, Nat. Assn. Women Deans Adminstrs. and Counselors, Am. Assn. Counseling and Devel., Bus. and Profl. Women's Club (named Woman of Yr., Princeton chpt. 1977), Met. Mus. Art, Phi Delta Kappa, Kappa Delta Pi. Presbyn. Clubs: Brown University (N.Y.C.); Nassau. Home: Kent, Ohio. Died Jan. 26, 2009.

THOMAS, JAMES EDWARD, JR., brokerage house executive; b. Atlanta, Apr. 23, 1950; s. James Edward and Dortha Jean (White) Thomas; m. Leslie Ann Stagmaier, Sept. 6, 1975; children: Steele Stagmaier, Katherine Mills. BA magna cum laude, U. Ga., 1972, JD cum laude, 1975. Mgr. Genuine Parts Co., Atlanta, 1975-77; v.p. Robinson Humphrey Co., Atlanta, 1977-94; ptnr. J.C. Bradford and Co., Atlanta, 1994—2000; mng. dir. Wachovia Securities, Ga., 2000—02; chmn., CEO Stillpoint Advisors, Inc., from 2003. Bd. dirs. Enstar Comm. Corp., The Kinston Group, Inc., Atlanta, Tophat Soccer Club, Atlanta, Hall's Boathouse, Inc., Lakemont, Ga., Vista Environ. Info., Inc., San Diego. Pres. Castlewood Civic Orgn., Inc., Atlanta; mem. Lake Rabun Homeowners Assn., Lakemont, Ga.; mem. bd. advisors U. Ga., Habitat for Humanity. Mem. Internat. Platform Assn., Ga. Bar Assn., La Societe des Tetes Grandes, Capital City Club, U. Ga. LEADS Adv. Bd., Ga Tennis Found. (treas., trustee). Republican. Episcopalian. Avocations: boating, tennis, golf. Home: Atlanta, Ga. Died Mar. 20, 2009.

THOMAS, SIDNEY, fine arts educator, researcher; b. NYC, Dec. 21, 1915; s. Hyman and Rose (Samilowitz) T.; m. Rae Dinkowitz, May 26, 1940; children: David Phillip, Deborah Rose. BA, CCNY, 1935; MA, Columbia U., 1938, PhD, 1943. Tutor in English CCNY, NYC, 1939-43; instr. English Queens Coll., NYC, 1946-54; self-employed as editor, 1954-58; asst. editor Merriam-Webster, Springfield, Mass., 1958-61; assoc. prof. fine arts Syracuse U. (N.Y.), 1961-66, prof., 1966-85, prof. emeritus, from 1985, dir. humanities doctoral program, 1964-72, chmn. dept. fine arts, 1969-73. Bibliographer Shakespeare Assn., N.Y.C., 1949-54 Author: The Antic Hamlet, 1943; co-editor: The Nature of Art, 1964; editor: Images of Man, 1972. Served to sgt., inf. U.S. Army, 1943-45, ETO. Research fellow Folger Shakespeare Library, Washington, 1947-48 Mem.: AAUP (pres. Syracuse U. chpt. 1974), ACLU, MLA (life), Shakespeare Assn. Am., Phi Beta Kappa. Home: Jamesville, NY. Died Nov. 7, 2009.

THOMAS, WILLIAM F., newspaper editor; b. Bay City, Mich., June 11, 1924; s. William F. and Irene Marie (Billette) T.; m. Patricia Ann Wendland, Dec. 28, 1948; children: Michael William, Peter Matthew, Scott Anthony. BS, Northwestern U., 1950, MS cum laude, 1951; LHD (hon.), Pepperdine U., Los Angeles. Asst. chief copy editor Buffalo Evening News, 1950-55; editor Sierra Madre (Calif.) News, 1955-56; reporter, asst. city editor, then city editor Los Angeles Mirror, 1957-62; asst. city editor, then met. editor Los Angeles Times, 1968-71, editor, 1971-72, editor, exec. v.p., from 1972. Served with U.S. Army, 1943-46. Died Feb. 11, 2009.

THOMPSON, BERT ALLEN, retired librarian; b. Bloomington, Ind., Dec. 13, 1930; s. James Albert and Dorothy Fern (Myers) T.; m. Martha Ellen Palmer; children— John Carter II, Anne Palmer, Paul Julian. BS, Ball State Tchrs. Coll., 1953; AM, Ind. U., 1960; certificate in archival adm., U. Denver, 1967. Tchr., libr. Ind. pub. schs., 1953-55; ref. asst. Indpls. Pub. Libr., 1956-59; head ref. svc. Mankato (Minn.) State U., 1959-61; instr. Grad. Libr. Sch. No. Ill. U., Dekalb, 1961-63; dir. libs., asst. prof. ednl. media U. Nebr. at Kearney, 1963-69; dir. libr. svc. Benedictine U., Lisle, Ill., 1969-90, spl. collections libr., 1990-92. Mem. exec. bd. Ill. regional Libr. Coun., 1976-79. Recipient 1st Melvin R. George LIBRAS award for Outstanding Svc. to Libr. Cooperation, 1993. Mem. Ill. (de Lafayette Reid Research scholar 1976), Cath. Libr. Assn. (treas. Ill. chpt. 1973-75, nat. sec.-treas. coll./univ. sect. 1981-85, nat. bd. dirs. 1987-93), Nebr. Libr. Assn, chmn. coll. and univ. sect. 1963-64) Episcopalian. Home: Wheaton, Ill. Died Sept. 27, 2009.

THOMPSON, EARL ALBERT, economics professor; b. L.A., Oct. 15, 1938; s. Hyman Harry and Sue (Field) T.; m. Velma Montoya, June 9, 1961; 1 son, Bret. BA, UCLA, 1959; MA (fellow), Harvard U., 1961, PhD, 1961. Asst. prof. economics Stanford (Calif.) U., 1962-65; asst. prof. UCLA, 1965-68, assoc. prof., 1968-70, prof., 1970—2010. Co-author: Ideology and the Evolution of Vital Institutions, 2001. Grantee NSF, Lily Found., Found. Rsch. in Econs. and Edn. Mem. Am. Econ. Assn. Home: Los Angeles, Calif. Died July 29, 2010.

THOMPSON, ED, epidemiologist, educator, former state agency administrator, public health service officer; m. Marsha Thompson; children: Mark, Matt, Matt 1 stepchild, Morgan. BA, Millsaps Coll.; MD, U. Miss. Sch. Medicine; MPH, Johns Hopkins U. Sch. Hygine and Pub. Health. Lic. Miss. State Bd. Med. Licensure, 1979, cert. in pub. health and gen. preventive medicine Am. Bd. Preventive Medicine, 1991. Clinician, dep. chief disease control Miss. State Dept. Health, 1982—85, state epidemiologist, 1983—93, chief bur. preventative health services, 1985—93, state health officer, 1993—2002, 2007; dep. dir. pub. health services Centers for Disease Control, Atlanta, dir. pub. health practice; prof. medicine U. Miss. Sch. Medicine, Jackson, 2006—09. Mem. exec. com. Coun. State and Territorial Epidemiologists, 1988—93, pres., 1992—93; mem. exec. com. Assn. State and Territorial Health Officials, 1998—2001, pres., 1998—99; mem. Adv. Com. on Immunization Practices; mem. adv. com. to dir. Centers for Disease Control; mem. Sec.'s Adv. Coun. for Pub. Health Preparedness. Mem.: AMA, Miss. Pub. Health Assn., Miss. State Med. Assn., Am. Pub. Health Assn. Died Dec. 1, 2009.

THOMPSON, HUGH WALTER, chemistry professor; b. NYC, Dec. 7, 1936; s. Will S. and Myra M. Thompson; m. Elizabeth Barnes, 1964; 1 child, Victoria. AB, Cornell U., Ithaca, NY, 1958; PhD, MIT, Cambridge, 1963; postgrad., Columbia U., 1962-64. Asst. prof., assoc. prof., prof. chemistry dept. Rutgers U., Newark, from 1964. Contbr. articles to profl. jours. Mem. Am. Chem. Soc., Sigma Xi. Died Feb. 21, 2009.

THOMPSON, JOSEPH B., photography company owner; b. Camden, NJ, Sept. 22, 1937; s. Joseph B. Sr. and Carolyn (Magonigle) T.; m. Joyce C. Gard, Dec. 16, 1960; children: Pam, Joseph B. III. BS, Drexel U., 1964. V.p. Quaker Photo Svcs., Phila., 1958-65; group mfg. mgr. McGraw Hill, Inc., NYC, 1965-70; pres., owner Berry & Homer, Inc., Phila., from 1970, Antonelli Insts., Phila., from 1974. Coun. Pa. Adv. Coun., 1982-85. Trustee Winona, 1983—. Recipient Liberty Bell award Mayor of Phila., 1981, Valley Forge Gold Medal award Freedom Found. of Valley Forge, Pa., Citation, Commonwealth Pa., 1985, Phila. City Coun.; named U.S. Congl. Record, 1988. Mem. Prof. Photographers Am., Nat. Assn. Trade and Tech. Schs. (Outstanding Mem. award 1988), Exhibit Designers and Producers Assn., Pa. Assn. Pvt. Sch. Adminstrs., Inc., Soc. Comml. Photographers of Dela. Valley, Phila. C. of C. Avocations: golf, coins, fishing. Home: Moorestown, NJ. Died Mar. 25, 2009.

THOMPSON, LEONARD CLARK, lawyer, insurance executive; b. Waltham, Mass., Mar. 20, 1921; s. George Jarvis and Ruth Warren (Barnes) T.; m. Margery Scull Taylor, July 27, 1943; children— Esther Hunt, Richard Warren (dec.), Susan Wellington. A.B., Williams Coll., 1943; J.D., Cornell U., 1948. Bar: Mo. 1971. Various mgmt. positions Glens Falls Ins. Co., Phila., Pitts., and Glens Falls, N.Y., 1948-70; br. claims mgr. Continental Ins. Co., Kansas City, Mo., 1970-76, regional rehab. supr., 1976-77; bond claims atty. Reliance Ins. Co., Kansas City, Mo., 1977-79; claims mgr. liability Nat. Dealer Services, Kansas City, Mo., 1979—. Pres. Edgeworth (Pa.) Sch. Bd., 1957-61; v.p. Quaker Valley (Pa.) Joint Bd., 1957-61; bd. dirs. Kansas City Rehab. Inst., 1966—, pres., 1984—. Recipient award of Merit Mo. Dept. Probation and Parole, 1977. Mem. ABA, Mo. Bar Assn. Club: Woodside Racquet (Kansas City, Mo.). Home: El Paso, Tex. Died Feb. 19, 2009.

THOMPSON, MARION ELIZABETH, educator; b. Madison, Wis., June 4, 1921; d. Louis Carl and Pearl Laura Hinkel (Peterson) Gunderson; B.A., U. Wis., 1943, M.A., 1960, Ph.D., 1971; m. George Grinde Thompson, May 30, 1942; children— Diane Flautt, George Thompson, David Thompson. Asst. prof. internat./global broadcasting William Paterson Coll. of N.J., 1972-74; asso. prof. Emerson Coll., Boston, 1976-81, dir. grad. studies dept. mass communications, 1980—; vis. prof. comparative broadcasting systems Boston U., 1977; vis. prof. internat. broadcasting Curry Coll., 1980. Mem. Internat. Inst. Communications, Nat. Acad. TV Arts and Scis., Internat. Communications Assn., Nat. Assn. Ednl. Broadcasters, AAUP, AAUW, Speech Communication Assn., Am.-Scandinavian Assn., Phi Beta. Died June 29, 2009.

THOMPSON, PETER CAMPBELL, investment counselor; b. Newton, Mass., Mar. 18, 1933; m. Joan Jackson, Sept. 8, 1962; children: Christopher, Andrew. AB, Dartmouth Coll., 1955. With Bank of Boston, 1957-66; investment counselor David L. Babson & Co., Cambridge, Mass., 1966-83, pres., investment counselor, from 1983. Mem. The Trustees of Reservations, Beverly, Mass., 1985—. Mem. Boston Security Analysts Soc. Home: Westwood, Mass. Died Jan. 3, 2010.

THOMPSON, PHILIP DOUGLAS, retired federal agency administrator; b. Berea, Ky., Sept. 11, 1923; s. Jamie Campbell and Julia Meta (Hatcher) Thompson; m. Lois Marie Coldiron, Sept. 10, 1949; children: Julia-Anna Thompson Marsden, Philip Douglas Thompson Jr. BA in Philosophy & Psychology, U. Ky., 1954, postgrad., 1954—55. Adminstr. aide U.S. mil. dist. U.S. Army, Lexington, Ky., 1957—58; pers. mgmt. insp. Civil Svc. Commn., Cinn., 1959—60; pers. officer IRS, Washington, 1960—64; dir. tng. Fed. Water Pollution Control, Washington, 1964—67, Dept. Interior, Washington, 1967—68; dir. tng., programs and personnel Fed. Power Commn., Washington, 1968—69; dir. exec. devel. Dept. Energy, Washington, 1979—81. Elder Presbyn. Ch., clk. of session; mem. Jr. C. of C. Sgt. US Army, 1942—45, Scotland. Fellow: Soc. Antiquarians; mem.: DAV, VFW, U. Ky. Alumni Assn. (pres. 1977—78), Jr. C of C, Am. Soc. Tng. & Development, Argyll Ednl. Soc. (pres., chmn. bd.), St. Andrews Soc. (pres. 1996—97, bd. trustees from 1999), Vets. Invasion of France Omaha Beach, Mil. Order of Purple Heart, Vets. Battle of Bulge, Sons of Revolution, Am. Legion, Order of Ky. Col. (hon.). Presbyterican. Avocations: violin, clocks, making furniture. Home: Gainesville, Va. Died Oct. 22, 2009.

THOMPSON, WADE FRANCIS BRUCE, manufacturing executive; b. Wellington, New Zealand, July 23, 1940; came to US, 1961, naturalized, 1990. m. Angela Ellen Barry, Jan. 20, 1967; children: Amanda and Charles (twins). B in Commerce, Cert. Acctg., Victoria U., Wellington, 1961; MSc, NYU, 1963; PhD of Commerce (hon.), Victoria U., 2007. Dir. diversification Sperry & Hutchinson, NYC, 1967-72; v.p. Texstar Corp., NYC, 1972-77; chmn. Hi-Lo Trailer Co., Butler, Ohio, 1977—2003; chmn., pres., CEO Thor Industries Inc., Jackson Center, Ohio, 1980—2009. Trustee Mystic Seaport Mus., Conn., 1984-2009; trustee Wade F.B. Thompson Charitable Found. Inc., 1985-2009, Mcpl. Art Soc., NYC, 1932-2009, Seventh Regiment Armory Conservancy, NYC, 1997-2009; founder The Drive Against Prostate Cancer. Recipient Oliver R. Grace award for Disting. Svc., Cancer Rsch. Inst., 2007, Jacqueline Kennedy Onassis award for Oustanding Contbn. to NYC, Mcpl. Art Soc., 2007, Frederick Law Olmsted award, 2009. Mem. Union Club (NYC). Avocations: tennis, collecting contemporary art. Home: New York, NY. Died Nov. 12, 2009.

THOMSON, JAMES ROBERT, JR., teacher educator; b. Tuscaloosa, Ala., Aug. 9, 1926; s. James Robert and Ruth (Dorman) T.; m. Rebecca Ramsey, Mar. 18, 1948; children: James Robert III, Ollie Ramsey. AB, U. Ala., 1949, MA, 1954, Ed.D., 1960. Tchr. Tuscaloosa County High Sch., Northport, Ala., 1949-56; prin. Hope Elementary Sch., Tuscaloosa County, Ala., 1956-58; asst. prof. gen. edn. Miss. State U., 1960-63, head dept. elementary and secondary edn., 1963-72, dir. student teaching, 1963-69, 72—. Dir. recreation, Northport, 1953-58. Served with AUS, 1945-46. Mem. Assn. Student Teaching, Miss. Assn. Student Teaching (pres. 1968), NEA, Miss. Edn. Assn., Assn. Tchr. Educators, Assn. Miss. Tchr. Educators (pres. 1980-81, 1988-89), Am. Ednl. Research Assn., Mid-South Ednl. Research Assn., Nat. Art Edn. Assn., Southeastern Regional Assn. Tchr. Educators, Miss. Acad. Sci., Miss. Sci. Tchrs. Assn., Phi Delta Kappa, Kappa Delta Pi, Pi Delta Phi. Methodist (chmn. ofcl. bd. 1951-52, chmn. com. edn. 1958-60, 80-81, supt. ch. sch. 1963-67). Home: Huntsville, Ala. Died Apr. 8, 2009.

THOR, DANIEL EINAR, immunologist; b. Davenport, Iowa, Sept. 4, 1938; s. Harry Raymond and Florence Elvira (Berglund) T.; m. Lois Anita Vistain, Jan. 9, 1971; children— Emaly Alida, Carlton George James Vistain. Student, Monmouth Coll., 1956-59; MD, U. Ill., 1963, PhD, 1968. Intern Presbyn.-St. Luke's Hosp., Chgo., 1963-64, resident, 1964-66; instr. surgery, medicine, microbiology U. Ill. Hosps., Chgo., 1966-68; research investigator NIH, Bethesda, Md., 1968-71; asso. prof. microbiology, pathology U. Tex. Health Sci. Center, San Antonio, 1971-76, prof., from 1976. Mem. com. immunodiagnosis Nat. Cancer Inst., NIH, 1973-78; Bd. dirs. Cancer Therapy and Research Found. S. Tex., Asthma and Immunology Found., San Antonio. Contbr. articles to profl. jours. Served to sr. surgeon USPHS, 1968-71. Recipient Landsteiner Centennial award, 1969 Fellow Am. Soc. Clin. Oncology, Am. Soc. Exptl. Biology; mem. Am. Assn. Immunologists, Am. Assn. Cancer Research, AAAS, Reticuloendothelial Soc., AAUP, Gideons Internat. (pres. San Antonio North Camp 1974-76), Am. Soc. Internal Medicine, Sigma Xi. Died Apr. 20, 2010.

THRALL, GORDON FISH, publishing executive; b. Jamestown, NY, July 28, 1923; s. Clyde Lowell and Beulah Mae (Fish) Thrall; m. Betty Jane Roberts Thrall, Sept. 24, 1964 (dec. May 28, 2005); 1 child, Jenifer Jane. AB in History & Polit. Sci., Alfred U., 1949; JD, Baylor U., 1953. Bar: Tex. 1953, US Supreme Ct. 1957, DC 1958, US Ct. Appeals (DC cir.) 1958, US Ct. Mil. Appeals 1958, US Dist. Ct. (ea. dist.) Tex. 1976, US Ct. Appeals (5th cir.) 1986. Law clk. US Dist. Ct. (ea. dist.) Tex., 1953—54; asst. prosecutor Dallas County Dist. Atty., 1954—55; assoc. firm Phinney & Hallman, Dallas, 1955—56; asst. Tex. Atty. Gen., 1957; adviser, examiner ICC, Washington, 1957—59; asst. gen. counsel Tex. State Bar, Austin, 1959—61; county atty. Reagan County, Big Lake, Tex., 1961—72; ptnr. Norman, Thrall, Angle, Guy & Day LLP, Jacksonville, Tex., 1972—2002; v.p. Heflin & Thrall Lang. Publs. Inc., from 2002. Mem. exec. com. Tex. Bapt. Gen. Conv., 1965—70, adminstrv. bd., 1991—95; deacon Southern Bapt. Ch.; chmn. Permian Basin Dist. Concho Valley Coun. Boy Scouts America, Big Lake, 1965—66, Jacksonville United Fund Drive, 1987, pres., 89, Cherokee County Health Facilities Devel. Corp., from 1982; v.p., bd. dirs. Travis Towers Retirement Facility, Jacksonville, 1980—2003; co-trustee Summers A. Norman Found., 1988—2002; mem. Nan Travis Meml. Hosp. Found. Bd., from 1994; pres. bd. visitors Jacksonville Coll., 1998—2003. Mem.: Jacksonville C. of C. (pres. 1979), Big Lake C. of C. (pres. 1963, 1967), Tex. Bar Found., Tex. State Bar (vice chmn. UPL com. 1964), Masons (32 Degree award), Big Lake Lions (pres. 1969), Kiwanis (pres. 1978, lt. gov. divsn. 34 1982), Cherokee Country Club (dir. 1981—83). Republican. Home: Jacksonville, Tex. Died July 3, 2010.

THURSTON, DONALD ALLEN, broadcast executive; b. Gloucester, Mass., Apr. 2, 1930; s. Joseph Allen and Helen Ruth (Leach) T.; m. Oralie Alice Lane, Sept. 9, 1951; children: Corydon Leach, Carolie Lane. Grad., Mass. Radio and Telegraph, 1949; HHD (hon.), North Adams State Coll., Mass., 1977; LHD (hon.), Emerson Coll., 1995. Announcer, engr. Sta. WTWN, St. Johnsbury, Vt., 1949-52; v.p., gen. mgr. Sta. WIKE, Newport, Vt., 1952-60; v.p., treas., gen. mgr. Sta. WMNB, North Adams, 1960-66; pres., treas. Berkshire Broadcasting Co., Inc., North Adams, 1966—2003. Bd. dirs. Broadcast Capital Fund, Inc., 1980-96, chmn. bd., 1981-89; bd. dirs. Broadcast Music, Inc., NYC, 1990-2005, chmn. bd., 1994-97. Pres. No. Berkshire Indsl. Devel. Corp., 1965-67; commr. Mass. Cmty. Antenna TV Commn., 1972-74; trustee Mass. Coll. Liberal Arts, 1991-2001, vice chmn. bd. trustees, 1993-96, chmn., 1996-2001. Recipient Laymen's award Vt. Tchrs. Assn., 1958; Laymen's award Mass. Tchrs. Assn., 1962; Abe Lincoln Merit award So. Baptist Radio and TV Commn., 1975; named Man of Yr. Vt. Assn. Broadcasters, 1978 Mem. North Adams C. of C. (Hayden award 1967, pres. 1964-67), Nat. Assn. Broadcasters (dir. 1965-69, 73-77, chmn. radio 1976-77, chmn. bd., chmn. exec. com. 1977-79, Disting. Svc. award 1980), Mass. Broadcasters Assn. (pres. 1964, Disting. Svc. award 1964, 71, 78), Taconic Golf Club (Williamston, Mass.; bd. dirs. 1975-89). Republican. Methodist. Home: Clarksburg, Mass. Died Oct. 6, 2009.

TICHENOR, CAROLYN JEAN, business development executive; b. Indpls., Sept. 16, 1943; d. Edsel Ralph and Tracy Mae (Byrdsong) Ford; 1 child, DeLynn Michelle Hayes. B.B.A., U. Tex.-Arlington, 1977; postgrad. U. Minn., 1980, U. Wash., 1981, Ind. U.-Purdue U., Indpls., 1984, U. Ill.-Chgo., 1985, Wilberforce U., 1985. Account clk. Civil Rights Commn., Indpls., 1971-74; acctg. asst. U. Tex.-Arlington, 1974-77; fiscal trainee Community Addiction Services Agy., Indpls., 1978; chief acct. Goodwill Industries, 1978-79; bus. devel. cons. Minority Bus. Devel. Ctr., Indpls., 1979—; instr. Lockyear Coll., Indpls., 1985—. Mem. U. Tex.-Arlington Alumni Assn., Flanner House Track and Field Com., Black Adoption Com. Democrat. Mem. Disciples of Christ Ch. Avocations: camping; sewing; reading; music. Home: Indianapolis, Ind. Died Sept. 24, 2009.

TICHENOR, LESLIE MILLS, interior design and retail executive; b. Louisville, Ky., Dec. 10, 1945; d. Arthur Wilbur and Mable Lucille (Davidson) M.; m. Everett Scott Tichenor, Aug. 19, 1967. Student U. Cin., 1964-67, U. Louisville, 1967-78. Ch. organist Suburban Christian Ch., Louisville, Ky., 1962-64; mem. sales staff Stewart Dept. Store, Louisville, 1962-66; life guard, camp counselor Tall Trees Camp, Louisville, 1964-65; archtl. draftsman Design Environment Group Architects, Louisville, 1966-67; owner, sec., treas. ES Tichenor Co., Louisville, 1968—. Com. head ch. art and architecture Diocese of Ky. Episcopal Ch., Louisville, 1972-87; trustee Thomas Edison House, Butchertown House, Louisville, 1980-85. Mem. Delta Delta Delta. Republican. Home: Louisville, Ky. Died Sept. 22, 2009.

TIFT, MARY LOUISE, artist; b. Seattle, Jan. 2, 1913; d. John Howard and Wilhelmina (Pressler) Dreher; m. William Raymond Tift, Dec. 4, 1948. BFA cum laude, U. Wash., 1933; postgrad., Art Ctr. Coll., LA, 1945-48, U. Calif., San Francisco, 1962-63. Art dir. Vaughn Shedd Advt., LA, 1948; asst. prof. design Calif. Coll. Arts & Crafts, Oakland, Calif., 1949-59; coord. design dept. San Francisco Art Inst., 1959-62. Subject of cover story, Am. Artist mag., 1980, studio article, 1987; one-woman shows, Gumps Gallery, San Francisco, 1977, 1986, 90, Diane Gilson Gallery, Seattle, 1978, Oreg. State U., 1981, Univ. House, Seattle, Frye Art Mus., Seattle, 2000; exhibited in group shows including Brit. Biennale, Yorkshire, Eng., 1970, Grenchen Triennale, Switzerland, 1970, Polish Biennale, Crakow, 1972, Nat. Gallery, Washington, 1973, Madrid Biennale, 1980, U.S.-U.K. Impressions, Eng., 1988; represented in permanent collections, Phila. Mus. Art, Bklyn. Mus., Seattle Art Mus., Library Congress, Achenbach Print Collection, San Francisco Palace Legion of Honor, San Diego Mus. Art, U.S. Art in Embassies. Served to lt. USNR, 1943-45. Mem. Print Club Phila., World Print Council, Calif. Soc. Printmakers, Phi Beta Kappa, Lambda Rho. Christian Scientist. Home: Seattle, Wash. Deceased.

TILLERY, JAMES FORREST, educational administrator; b. Winston-Salem, N.C., Dec. 28, 1938; s. Jounest and Annie Y. (Lyons) T.; B.S., A&T State U., Greensboro, N.C., 1963; postgrad. D.C. Tchrs. Coll., 1969, 70; M.S. in Elem. Adminstrn., Bowie State Coll., 1973; m. Betty Lucille Puryear, Dec. 30, 1967; 1 dau., Erika Puryear. Tchr., East End High Sch., Southhill, Va., 1963-67, Crummell Elem. Sch., Washington, 1967-72, Harris Elem. Sch., Washington, 1971-72; tchr. 16th and Butler Elem. Sch., Washington, 1972-74, acting prin., 1974-77; acting asst. prin. Garnet C. Wilkinson Elem. Sch., Washington, 1977-79, asst. prin., 1979-81; acting prin. Birney Elem. Sch., Washington, 1981-82, prin., 1982—; ednl. coord. Clark Elem. Sch., 1990—; mem. com. for planning workshops for adminstrs. D.C. Sch. System and NAACP. Officer, 16th and Butler Elem. Sch. PTA, 1972-76; 2d v.p. Birney Sch. PTA, 1981; mem. exec. bd. D.C. Dept. Recreation; mem. parents adv. bd. Day Care Program; active YMCA, Laurel Boys Club, Met. Police Boys and Girls Clubs, Nat. PTA. Mem. Nat. Assn. Elem. Sch. Prins., D.C. Assn. Elem. Sch. Prins., Council Sch. Officers, Omega Psi Phi. Democrat. Methodist. Home: Laurel, Md. Died Aug. 22, 2009.

TILSON, PHILIP ALAN, engineer; b. NY, Mar. 21, 1930; s. George Henry and Constance Earle (Kilpatrick) T.: m. Marilynne L. Tilson (div. 1971); m. Romana Helen Dumbrique, July 11, 1975; children: Philip A. Jr., Katherine A., Nancy L., James M. BS, U. Md., 1956; BS Mech. Engr., NYU, 1959, MS Indsl. Engr., 1961; MS Human Rels., U. Okla., 1978. Commd. USAF, 1951, advance through grades to col., 1981; mgr. A&I div. MBB, Arlington, Va., 1981-85; pres. Logistics Cons., Alexandria, Va., 1985-87; v.p., gen. mgr. US Tech. Corp., Danielson, Conn., from 1987—. Mem. Plainfield (Conn.) Indsl. Pk. Commn., Rep. party task force, Washington, 1988——. Recipient various mil. awds. Mem. Navy Yacht Club Groton (commodore, 1990), Masonic Orgn. (various leadershippositions). Roman Catholic. Avocations: boating, camping. Home: Stafford, Va. Died Jan. 17, 2009.

TIMM, BARBARA A., critical care nurse; b. Chgo., July 4, 1955; d. Lyle M. and June Barbara (Marbach) Johannsen; m. Robert H. Timm, Dec. 27, 1989; 1 child, Elissa Ann Hoffman. BS in Nursing, No. Ill. U., 1977; cert. in IV therapy, Oakton Community Coll., 1978. RN, La., Tex. Spl. x-ray procedures nurse Baylor U. Med. Ctr., Dallas, clin. nurse post anasthesia recovery unit; cath lab. nurse recovery room Bossier Med. Ctr., Bossier City, La.; staff nurse emergency room Riverside Community Hosp., Bossier City. Capt. USAF, 1978-81, USAFR, 1987-90. Home: Princeton, La. Died Jan. 24, 2009.

TIMMONS, WILLIAM EDWARD, lawyer; b. Stanley, Wis., July 14, 1924; s. William James and Rose (Covy) T.; widowed, 1985; children: Patricia, William, Michael, Ann, Mary, Nancy, Laura. BA, Loras Coll., 1948; JD, Georgetown U., 1950. Bar: Iowa 1951, U.S. Dist. Ct. (no. dist.) Iowa 1952, U.S. Supreme Ct. 1961, U.S. Dist. Ct. (so. dist.) Iowa 1984. 1st asst. atty. Dubuque County, Iowa, 1952-59; ins. commr. State of Iowa, Des Moines, 1959-67; ptnr. Patterson Law Firm, Des Moines, 1967-96. Sgt. U.S. Army, 1942-46. Mem. Iowa Bar Assn., Def. Bar Assn., Nat. Assn. Ins. Commn. (pres. 1964-65), Union League, Des Moines Club. Democrat. Roman Catholic. Home: Des Moines, Iowa. Died Jan. 9, 2009.

TING, WALASSE, artist, poet; b. Shanghai, Oct. 13, 1929; came to U.S., 1957; s. Ho Chang and Ping (Sen) T.; m. Natalie R. Lipton, June 4, 1962; 1 dau., Mia. Self ed. Exhibited one-man shows: Martha Jackson Gallery, N.Y.C., 1959-60, Gallerie Rive Gauche, Paris, 1961, Lefebre Gallery, N.Y.C., 1963, 65, 66, 71, 82, 84; represented permanent collections: Chgo. Art Inst., Detroit Inst. Art, Chrysler Mus., Rockefeller Inst., Mus. Modern Art, Balt. Mus. Stedelejk Mus., Amsterdam, Silkebork Kunstmuseum, Denmark, Israel Nat. Mus., Jerusalem.; Author: poems One Cent Life, 1964, Chinese Moonlight, 1967, Hot and Sour Soup, 1967, Green Banana, 1971. Guggenheim fellow, 1970 Died May 17, 2010.

TINGLEFF, THOMAS ALAN, transportation company executive; b. Elgin, Ill., Sept. 17, 1946; s. Howard Christian and Mary Louise (Burnier) T.; m. Barbara Jean Nelson, Oct. 27, 1979. BS in Acctg., U. Ill.-Urbana, 1969; MBA, U. Chgo., 1979. C.P.A. Asst. v.p. internal audit Chgo. and Northwestern Transp. Co., Chgo., 1976-80, v.p. fin., 1980-89, sr. v.p. fin. and acctg., from 1989. Served to 1st lt. U.S. Army, 1969-71. Home: Wheaton, Ill. Died Mar. 30, 2009.

TINKER, GEORGE HENRY, lawyer; b. Aurora, Ill., Feb. 25, 1926; s. Harold William and Bertha Amelia (Schroeder) T.; m. Barbara Jean Messenger, May 16, 1953 (div.); children— Catherine Jean, John Howard, David Frederick (dec.). Ph.B., U. Chgo., 1945; JD, Tulane U., 1949. Bar: Ill. 1949. Mem. firm Hamper, Atwell, Dolph & Tinker, Aurora, 1949-53; with Kemper Group, Long Grove, Ill., from 1953, gen. counsel, from 1978. Dir. Ill. Ins. Info. Service, 1980— Mem. Am. Bar Assn., Fedn. Ins. counsel. Home: Genoa, Ill. Died Apr. 6, 2010.

TINKHAM, WILLIAM KNIPE, historian, retired educator; b. Dartmouth, Mass., Feb. 22, 1916; s. William Nelson and Mabel Winsor (White) T.; student New Coll., U. Oxford, Eng., 1945-47; AB, Boston U., 1954; AM, Harvard U., 1957; postgrad. Tufts U., 1958-59; m. Caroline Brown, Oct. 23, 1965. Br. mgr. New Bedford (Mass.) Instn. for Savs., 1936-42, 47-50; lectr. history Lasell Jr. Coll., Newton, Mass., 1959-60; instr. history Boston State Coll., 1962-66, asst. prof., 1966-68, assoc. prof., 1968-83, ret., 1983. Mem. nat. coun. Evangelical and Cath. Mission of Episc. Ch.; jr. warden, mem. corp. and vestry Ch. of Advent, Boston, Episc. Synod of Am. With inf. AUS, 1942-45. Decorated European-African-Middle Eastern Service medal with Seven Battle Stars, Belgian Fourragere. Mem. Mediaeval Acad. Am., Am. Friends Pusey House (Oxford), Mass. Soc. Mayflower Descs., Am. Ch. Union (v.p. New Eng. br. 1960-70), English-Speaking Union, Beacon Hill Civic Assn., Am. Hist. Assn., Plimoth Plantation, Old Dartmouth Hist. Soc., Harvard Grad. Soc. Advanced Study and Research, Oxford and Cambridge Soc. New Eng., Boston Athenaeum (life), New Eng. Hist. Geneal. Soc., New Coll. Soc. Oxford, Guild of Friends Winchester Cathedral, Friends of Lambeth Palace Libr. London, Soc. King Charles the Martyr, Prayer Book Soc. of Episc. Ch., Oxford Soc., Am. Legion, Harvard Club (Boston), Wamsutta Club, Phi Alpha Theta. Republican. Contbr. articles to profl. jours. Home: Boston, Mass. Died May 28, 2009.

TISHMAN, ROBERT VALENTINE, real estate and construction company executive; b. NYC, Apr. 7, 1916; s. David and Ann (Valentine) T.; m. Phyllis Gordon (dec. 1985); children: Lynne Tishman Speyer, Nancy Tishman Gonchar. BA, Cornell U., 1937. With Tishman Realty & Constrn. Co., Inc., NYC, from 1938, pres., 1962-78; mng. ptnr. Tishman Speyer Properties, 1978—2010. Chmn. Real Estate Bd. N.Y., 1973-75. Bd. dirs. Citizens Housing and Planning Coun.; trustee Citizens Budget Commn.; chmn. Montefiore Hosp. and Med. Ctr., 1973-79, hon. chmn., 1979-2010; assoc. chmn. Jewish Assn. Svcs. to Aged. Lt. comdr. USNR, World War II. Died Oct. 11, 2010.

TOBIN, WILLIAM JAMES, food company executive; b. NYC, June 3, 1929; s. William James and Rosemary (Dillman) T.; m. Lynn Louise Richards, Apr. 21, 1973; 1 dau., Nicole Louise; 1 dau. by previous marriage, Laura Ann Tobin Smith Student, CCNY, 1952. With Nestle Co., Inc., 1954-70, nat. sales mgr. vending and instl. div., 1968-70; with Nabisco, Inc., from 1970, gen. mgr. food services div. East Hanover, N.J., 1973-75, pres. div., from 1975, corp. v.p., from 1978. Bd. overseers Center Study Foodservice Mgmt., N.Y. U.; trustee Culinary Inst. Author articles in field. Served with USN, 1946-48. Mem. Internat. Foodservice Mfrs. Assn. (1st vice chmn. 1981, chmn. govt. relations com. 1981, chmn. ednl. found.), Nat. Automatic Mdsg. Assn. (dir.), Nat. Inst. Foodservice Industry (bd. dirs.). Clubs: Lake Mohawk. Home: Sparta, NJ. Died May 25, 2010.

TODD, JUDITH F., lawyer; b. Chgo., Jan. 25, 1946; Student, Vassar Coll.; AB, U. Mich., 1968; JD cum laude, U. Miami, 1972. Bar: Fla. 1972, Ill. 1977, Ala. 1981. With Sirote & Permutt PC, Birmingham, Ala., now ptnr. Assoc. editor U. Miami Law Review, 1971-72. Fellow Am. Coll. Trust and Estate Counsel; mem. ABA, Fla. Bar, Ill. State Bar Assn. Died July 14, 2010.

TOMBLINSON, JAMES EDMOND, architect; b. Flint, Mich., Feb. 12, 1927; s. Carl and Edna Ethel (Spears) T.; m. Betsy Kinley, Sept. 26, 1959; children: Amy Lisa, John Timothy (dec.). B.Arch., U. Mich., 1951. Draftsman firms in, Detroit, 1951-53, Flint, 1953-54, 56-57, San Francisco, 1955-56; field engr. Atlas Constructors, Morocco, 1952-53; architect Tomblinson, Harburn, & Assocs., Inc. (and predecessors), Flint, from 1958, pres., 1969-95; chmn. bd. Tomblinson, Harburn & Assocs., Inc. (and predecessors), 1995—2001; chmn. Mich. Bd. Registration Architects, 1975-77; sec. Mundy Twp. Planning Commn., 1974-85, Grand Blanc Planning Commn., City of Mich., from 1985; chmn., from 1988. Pres. Flint Beautification Commn., 1968-69; bd. dirs. Grand Blanc Beautification Commn., 1969-84; founding mem. bd. dirs. Flint YMCA, 1969-75, chmn. camp com., 1971-75; founding mem. bd. dirs. Flint Environ. Action Team, 1971-77, v.p., 1971-73; elder First Presbyn. Ch. Flint, 1983, trustee, 1986-99; exec. com. Tall Pine council Boy Scouts Am., 1975—; bd. dirs. New Paths, 1994-2004, pres., 1985-86, 94—; trustee Grand Blanc Cmty. Found., 1997-2004; mem. vestry St. Christopher's Ch., 2004—. Served with AUS, 1945-46. Recipient various civic service awards. Fellow AIA; mem. Mich. Soc. Architects, Flint Area C. of C. Clubs: Greater Flint Jaycees (dir. 1957-63, v.p. 1963), Flint City, U. Mich. (pres. Flint chpt. 1980—). Lodges: Rotary (pres. 1984-85). Home: Grand Blanc, Mich. Died Aug. 10, 2010.

TOMLINSON, ALEXANDER COOPER, investment banker, consultant; b. Haddonfield, NJ, May 13, 1922; s. Alexander Cooper and Mary (Buzby) T.; m. Elizabeth Anne Brierley, Jan. 10, 1953 (div.); children: William Brierley, Deborah T. Marple, Alexander Cooper III; m. Margaret L. Dickey, Nov. 15, 1986. BS, Haverford Coll., 1943; postgrad., London Sch. Econs. and Polit. Sci., 1947-48; MBA, Harvard U., 1950; LLD (hon.), Haverford Coll., 1995. With Morgan Stanley & Co., NYC, 1950-76, ptnr., 1958-76, mng. dir., 1970-76; dir., pres. Morgan Stanley Can. Ltd. div., Montreal, Que., 1972-76; chmn. exec. com. First Boston, Inc., NYC, 1976-82, dir., 1976-88; pres. Nat. Policy Assn., Washington, 1982-85; exec. dir. Ctr. for Privatization, Washington, 1985-88; pres. Hungarian-Am. Enterprise Fund, Washington, 1990-93; chmn. Fund for Arts and Culture in Ctrl. and Ea. Europe, 1994-97. Mem. U.S. adv. bd. Que. Hydro, 1984-95. Trustee Incorp. Village, Cove Neck, N.Y., 1958-72, 76-82, Cold Spring Harbor Lab., 1976-87, N.Y. Infirmary-Beekman Downtown Hosp., 1968-82, East Woods Sch., Oyster Bay, N.Y., 1962-70, Nature Conservancy, L.I., N.Y., 1970-82, Salisbury Sch., Conn., 1976-87, Carnegie Found. for Advancement Tchg., 1984-90; bd. mgrs. Haverford Coll., 1979-01; bd. dirs. Nat. Bldg. Mus., 1987-94, Nat. Policy Assn., 1982-90, Decatur House Coun., 1990-94; chmn. Am. Friends Can., Inc., 1982-91, Harvard Bus. Sch. Fund, 1981-83. Lt. USNR, 1943-46. Mem. Coun. on Fgn. Rels., Metropolitan Club (Washington), Links (N.Y.). Home: Washington, DC. Died Mar. 14, 2010.

TOMLINSON, GEORGE HERBERT, retired industrial company research executive; b. Fullerton, La., May 2, 1912; emigrated to Can., 1914; s. George Herbert and Irene Loretta (Nourse) T.; m. Frances Fowler, July 17, 1937; children: Peter George, David Lester, Susan Margaret Tomlinson Goff. BA, Bishop's U., 1931; PhD, McGill U., 1935; DCL (hon.), Bishop's U., 1986. Chief chemist Howard Smith Chem. Ltd., Cornwall, Ont., Can., 1936-39; research dir. Howard Smith Paper Mills Ltd., Cornwall, 1939-61, Domtar Ltd., Montreal, Que., 1961-70, v.p. research and environ. tech., 1970-77, sr. sci. adv., 1977-90. Active in forestry problems in Europe and N.Am. Author book; contbr. articles to profl. jours.; patentee in field. Recipient Gov. Gen.'s Gold medal, 1931; Laureate of UN Environ. Programme Global 500, June, 1987. Fellow Royal Soc. Can., Internat. Acad. Wood Sci., Chem. Inst. Can., TAPPI (dir. 1976-79, medal 1969, hon. life mem.); mem. Am. Chem. Soc. (emeritus), Can. Pulp and Paper Assn. (hon. life mem.), Chemists Club (N.Y.). Anglican. Home: Hanover, NH. Died Mar. 16, 2010.

TORACK, RICHARD MAURICE, neuropathologist; b. Passaic, NJ, July 23, 1927; s. Geza J. and Margaret E. (Voros) T.; m. Catherine N. Reagan, Apr. 18, 1953; children: Richard M., James W., Thomas A., Margaret K., William P. MS, Seton Hall U., 1948; MD, Georgetown U., 1952. Asst. pathologist Montefiore Hosp., NYC, 1958-60; asst. prof. pathology Cornell Med. Coll., NYC, 1962-65, assoc. prof. pathology, 1965-68; assoc. attending pathologist N.Y. Hosp., NYC, 1962-68; assoc. prof. pathology Washington U. Sch. Medicine, St. Louis, 1968-70, prof. pathology, from 1970. Author: Pathology Physiology of Dementia,1978, Your Brain Is Younger Than You Think, 1981. Capt. USAF, 1953-55. Mem. Am. Assn. Neuropathology, Am. Soc. Investigative Pathology, Am. Geriatric Soc., N.Y. Acad. Sci. Died Jan. 22, 2009.

TORCH, REUBEN, university administrator; b. Chgo., Dec. 20, 1926; s. Louis and Dora (Rabinowitz) Torch; m. Bernice Laffer Torch, Aug. 14, 1949; children: Deborah, Ellen, Amy. BS, U. Ill.-Urbana, 1947; MS, 1948, PhD, 1953. Asst. prof. to prof., zoology U. Vt., Burlington, 1953—65; prof. biology Oakland U., Rochester, Mich., 1965; asst. to assoc. dean, 1966—73; dean arts & scis., 1973—80; v.p. acad. affairs Calif. State U.-Turlock, from 1980; dir. Moss Landing Marine Lab., Calif., from 1980. Contbr. articles to profl. jours. Trustee Marygrove Coll., Detroit, 1978—80, Drs. Med. Ctr. Found., Modesto, Calif., from 1982; bd. dirs. Modesto Symphony Orch., from 1983, Sierra Vista Children's Home, 1988, United Way, 1988, McHenry Mus., 1990. With USNR, 1944—46. Rsch. fellowship, U. Ill., 1951—52, sci. faculty fellowship, NSF, Duke U. Marine Sta., 1958, Marine Biol. Lab., Woods Hole, Mass., 1959—60, grant, NIH, 1955—56, 1963—66. Mem.: Soc. Protozoologists, Am. Soc. Cell Biology, Sigma Xi. Home: Boca Raton, Fla. Died July 15, 2009.

TOULMIN, STEPHEN EDELSTON, humanities educator; b. London, Mar. 25, 1922; BA in Math. and Physics, King's Coll., Cambridge, Eng., 1942; PhD, King's Coll., 1948; D Tech. (hon.), Royal Inst. Tech., Stockholm, 1991. Lectr. in philosophy of sci. Oxford U., Eng., 1949-55; prof., chmn. dept. of philosophy U. Leeds, Yorkshire, Eng., 1955-59; dir. unit for history of ideas Nuffield Found., London, 1960-65; prof. history of ideas and philosophy Brandeis U., Waltham, Mass., 1965-69; prof. philosophy Mich. State U., East Lansing, 1969-72; prof. humanities U. Calif., Santa Cruz, 1972-73; prof. com. social thought U. Chgo., 1973-86; Avalon prof. humanities Northwestern U., Evanston, Ill., 1986-92, Avalon prof. emeritus, from 1992; prof. U. So. Calif., LA, 1993-2001, 2001—09. Vis. prof. U. Melbourne, Australia, 1954-55, Stanford U., 1959, Columbia U., N.Y.C., 1960, Hebrew U., Jerusalem, 1964, U. South Fla., 1972, Dartmouth Coll., 1979, SUNY, Plattsburgh, 1980, Colo. Coll., 1980, 82, MacMaster U., 1983, Harvard Project Physics Grad. Sch. Edn., Harvard U., 1965; counselor Smithsonian Inst., Washington, 1967-77; cons., staff mem. Nat. Commn. Protection Human Subjects Biomed. Behavioral Rsch., 1975-78; sr. vis. scholar, fellow Inst. Soc. Ethics and Life Scis., Hastings-on-Hudson, N.Y., 1981-2001; regent's lectr. U. Calif. Med. Sch., Davis, 1985; Mary Flexner lectr. Bryn Mawr Coll., 1977; Reyerson lectr. U. Chgo., 1979, John Nuveen lectr., 1980; Tate-Wilson lectr. So. Meth. U., 1980; Or Emet lectr. Osgoode Hall Law Sch., 1981; McDermott lectr. U. Dallas, 1985; lectr. Sigma Xi, 1965-66, Phi Beta Kappa, 1978-79, Phi Beta Kappa-AAAS, 1984, Thomas Jefferson lectr. NEH, Washington, 1997; Tanner lectr. Clare Hall, Cambridge U., 1998; guest prof. social and human scis. Wolfgang Goethe Universitat, Frankfurt, Germany, 1987; vis. fellow Internationales Forschungszentrum Kulturwissenschaften (IFK), Vienna, 1995. Author: The Place of Reason in Ethics, 1949, The Philosophy of Science: An Introduction, 1953, The Uses of Argument, 1958, Foresight and Understanding, 1961, Human Understanding, vol. 1, 1972, Knowing and Acting, 1976, The Return to Cosmology, 1982, Cosmopolis, 1989; (with J. Goodfield) The Fabric of the Heavens, 1961, The Architecture of Matter, 1963, The Discovery of Time, 1965; (with A. Janik) Wittgenstein's Vienna, 1973; (with R. Rieke and A. Janik) An Introduction to Reasoning, 1978; (with A. Jonsen) The Abuse of Casuistry, 1987; (with B. Gustavsen) Beyond Theory, 1996, Return to Reason, 2001; contbr. numerous sci. articles to profl. jours. Recipient Honor Cross 1st class (Austria), 1991; Getty Ctr. for History of Art and Humanities scholar, 1985-86, First Book of the Year prize Am. Soc. Social Philosophy, 1992; Ctr. for Psychosocial Studies fellow, 1974-76. Fellow Am. Acad. Arts and Scis. Died Dec. 4, 2009.

TRAINA, SALVATORE ALBERT, publishing executive; b. Bklyn., Apr. 30, 1927; s. Salvatore and Guilia (LeBarbara) T.; m. Vail Devereux, June 22, 1957; children: Caroline Vail, Robert Brooks. BS, Seton Hall U., 1950; postgrad., Columbia U., 1950-51; MBA, NYU, 1954. Circulation promotion advt. space salesman Fairchild Publs., NYC, 1951-53; Eastern advt. mgr. Modern Bride mag. Ziff-Davis, NYC, 1953-58; advt. mgr. Bride and Home mag. Hearst Mags., NYC, 1958-60, pub. Bride and Home mag., 1960-64; pub. Sports Afield mag., 1964-65, Town and Country mag., 1965-67, Harpers Bazaar mag., 1967-70; pres., chief exec. officer Bartell Media Corp., 1970-74; pres. Ziff-Davis Mag. Network, 1974-76, group v.p., 1976-78; sr. v.p. Ziff-Davis Pub. Co., 1978-81; pres. Ziff-Davis Consumer Mag., 1981-85; exec. v.p. mags. CBS, NYC, 1985; pres. Traina Assocs., NYC, 1985—2000. Mem. Scarsdale Bi-Partisan Com., 1975-78; bd. dirs. Crane Berkeley Assn., 1978-88, pres., 1983-84; mem. nat. bd. dirs., chmn. comms. com., treas. Goodwill Industries of Am., 1979-92, chmn. bd., 1988-92; chmn. bd. trustees Chebeague Island Libr., 1997-2001; pres. bd. dirs. Chebeague Recreation Ctr., 1998-2003; bd. dirs. Chebeague Island Hist. Soc., 2000-08. With USNR, 1945-46. NY State War Svc. scholar, Columbia U. and NYU, 1950. Mem. NYU Grad. Sch. Bus. Adminstrn. Alumni Assn., NYU Alumni Fedn. (comms. com. 1970-73), Union League Club (N.Y.C.). Home: Chebeague Island, Maine. Died Nov. 30, 2009.

TRAUTLEIN, DONALD HENRY, steel company executive; b. Sandusky, Ohio, Aug. 19, 1926; s. Henry Francis and Lillian Amelia (Russell) T.; m. Mary Rankin, Apr. 28, 1956; children: John Russell, James Rankin, Katherine. Student, Bowling Green State U., 1946-47; BS in Bus. Adminstrn. cum laude, Miami U., Oxford, Ohio, 1950. Bus. trainee Gen. Electric Corp., 1950-51; partner Price Waterhouse & Co., NYC, 1951-76; comptroller, sr. v.p. acctg., dir. Bethlehem Steel Corp., Pa., 1977-78, exec. v.p., 1979-80, chmn., chief exec. officer, from 1980. Dir. Chase Manhattan Bank (N.A.), N.Y.C. Chmn. bd. Am. Iron and Steel Inst.; bd. dirs., mem. exec. com. Internat. Iron and Steel Inst. Served with USN, 1945-46. Mem. Conf. Bd., Bus. Council, Bus. Roundtable, Am. Inst. C.P.A.s. Clubs: Univ., Links, Economic (N.Y.C.); Bethlehem, Saucon Valley Country. Episcopalian. Died July 2, 2010.

TREAT, WILLIAM WARDWELL, banker, former judge; b. Boston, May 23, 1918; AB, U. Maine, 1940; MBA, Harvard U., 1947. Bar: Maine 1945, N.H. 1949, U.S. Supreme Ct. 1955. Judge N.H. Probate Ct., Exeter, 1958-83; pres., chmn. bd. Bank Meridian N.A. (formerly Hampton Nat. Bank), 1958-84, chmn., from 1984. Bd. dirs. Exeter & Hampton Electric Co., Unitil Co., Colonial Group, Inc., Amoskeag Bank Shares, Inc.; faculty Nat. Coll. for State Judiciary, Reno, 1975—; chmn. N.H. Jud. Council, 1976-83; adv. bd. Nat. Ctr. for State Cts., 1973-80; pres. Nat. Coll. Probate Judges, 1968-77, pres. emeritus, 1977—; mem. Nat. Fiduciary Acctg. Standards Project, 1975—, Am. Assembly on Death, Taxes and Family Property, 1976—. Author: Treat on Probate, 3 vols., 1968, Local Justice in the Granite State, 1961; contbr. articles to profl. jours.; editor: Probate Court Manual, 1976, Focus on the Bank Director: The Job, 1977. Mem. Rep. Nat. Com., 1954-58, 60-64; mem. U.S. del. to 42d Gen. Assembly of UN; U.S. del. UN Subcommn. on Human Rights, Geneva, Switzerland, 1988—; presdl. elector, sec. U.S. Electoral Coll., 1956, 60; del.-at-large Rep. Nat. Conv., 1960, program chmn., 1964; bd. dirs., v.p. Hundred Club of N.H.; trustee Franklin Pierce Coll., 1985—. Mem. Am. Law Inst., ABA, N.H. Bar Assn., Am. Bankers Assn. (exec. com. community bankers div. 1975-78, chmn. div. communications com. 1976, chmn. task force bank dirs. program 1976-77), N.H. Bankers Assn. (legis. com. 1975-77, fed. legis. com. 1977—), Am. Judicature Soc. (bd. dirs. 1971-77), New Eng. Law Inst. (adv. bd. 1969-76), Soc. Cin., Soc. Mayflower Descendants in State of N.H. Clubs: Harvard, Tavern, Somerset (Boston); Royal Poinciana, Port Royal (Naples, Fla.); Bald Peak Colony (Melvin Village, N.H.). Home: Hampton, NH. Died Jan. 10, 2010.

TREFOUSSE, HANS LOUIS, history professor; b. Frankfurt, Ger., Dec. 18, 1921; came to U.S. 1936; s. George and Elizabeth (Albersheim) T.; m. Rashelle Friedlander, Jan. 26, 1947 (dec. 1999); 1 child, Roger Philip. BA, CCNY, 1942; MA, Columbia U., 1947, PhD, 1950. Instr. Adelphi Coll., Garden City, N.Y., 1949-50; from instr. to disting. prof. Bklyn. Coll., 1950-98, emeritus, from 1998; from assoc. prof. to disting. prof. history Grad. Ctr., CUNY, 1961-98, prof. emeritus, 1998—2010. Author: Andrew Johnson, 1989, Carl Schurz, 1982, Impeachment of a President: Andrew Johnson, the Blacks and Reconstruction, 1975, The Radical Republicans, 1969, Thaddeus Stevens, 1997, Rutherford B. Hayes, 2002, First Among Equals, 2005; editor: Twayne's Statesmen and Leaders of the World, 1967-77; editor Anvil Series, 1994-2005 Lt. col. AUS, 1942-45, USAR, ret. Named Disting. Tchr. Bklyn. Coll., 1960; Guggenheim fellow, 1977; ACLS grant, 1981. Mem. Am. Hist. Assn., Soc. Am. Historians, Orgn. Am. Historians, So. Hist. Assn. Democrat. Jewish. Avocations: swimming, travel. Home: Staten Island, NY. Died Jan. 8, 2010.

TREIRAT, EDUARD, marine engineer; b. Estonia, May 25, 1912; came to U.S., 1949, naturalized, 1955; marine engrng. diploma Marine Coll. Tallinn (Estonia), 1942; student Baltic U., Hamburg, Germany, 1946-47; BS in Engrng., Fairleigh Dickinson U., 1957; postgrad. Stevens Inst. Tech., 1957-59; m. Jenny Eugenia Hendriksson, Dec. 29, 1988. Asst. mgr. planning dept. Revaler Werft Tallinn Estonia, 1942-44; lectr. Nav. and Marine Engrs. Sch., Flensburg, Ger., 1946-49; toolmaker Bergenfield Devel. Co., Dumont, N.J., 1950-52; design engr. Star Kimble Electric Co., Bloomfield, N.J., 1952-56; design engr. Walter Kidde & Co., Belleville, N.J., 1956-61, engrng. supr., 1961-71, chief design engr., 1971-76; sr. staff engr. advanced products devel. Valcor Engrng. Corp., Springfield, N.J., 1976-83; dir. Gen. Valve Co., East Hanover, N.J.; also cons. Served with Estonian Army, 1931-32. Decorated Sharpshooters medal. Mem. Phi Omega Epsilon. Lutheran. Club: EÜS. Patentee in field; also articles. Died Jan. 5, 2009.

TREMBLAY, FRANCIS WILFRED, educational consultant, educator; b. Lebanon, NH, Mar. 10, 1925; s. Albert Napoleon and Mary Ann (Gagnon) Tremblay; m. Eugenia Howson Tremblay, July 21, 1952 (div. Feb. 1973); 1 child, Mary Irene; m. Micheline Francoise Poirier, Nov. 25, 1974; children: Sophie, Annie, Catherine, Paul Gauthier. BA, U. NH, 1949; BE, Wash. State U., 1950, MEd, 1953; EdD, Brigham Young U., 1980. Cert. pub. sch. adminstr. Calif. Tchr. Mullan Pub. Schs., Idaho, 1950—51, Palouse Pub. Schs., Wash., 1951—53; prin. Warm Springs Elem. Sch., Calif., 1954—58; supt. Smith River Union Sch., Calif., 1958—62, Placer Hills Union Sch., Meadow Vista, Calif., 1962—68; cons. Calif. Dept. Edn., Sacramento, 1968—87; adj. prof. Chapman Coll., Orange, Calif., from 1981; mem. Nat. Com. Migrant Student Record Transfer System, 1980. Pres. Del Norte County Tchrs. Assn., Calif., 1963, N. Coast Adminstrs. Assn., Calif., 1963; mem. Common Cause, Sacramento, 1984. With USN, 1943—46, PTO. Nat. Def. Inst. Scholarship, 1965—67. Mem.: Calif. Assn. Compensatory Edn., Calif. Assn. Sch. Adminstrs., Phi Delta Kappa. Democrat. Unitarian Universalist. Died Apr. 15, 2009.

TREPP, LEO, rabbi; b. Mainz, Germany, Mar. 4, 1913; s. Maier Trepp and Selma Hirschberger; m. Miriam de Haas, Apr. 26, 1938 (dec. Dec. 15, 1999); 1 child, Susan Trepp Lachtman; m. Counda Ekert, 2000. PhD, U. Wurzburg, 1935; postgrad., Harvard U., 1944—45; DD, Hebrew Union Coll., 1985; PhD (hon.), U. Wurzburg, 1985, U. Oldenburg, 1989. Ordained rabbi, 1936. Rabbi various temples, various locations, 1940—51; part-time rabbi Santa Rosa, Calif., 1951—61, Eureka, Calif., 1961—90; rabbi emeritus, 1990; Jewish chaplain Vets. Home of Calif., Yountville, Calif., 1954—98; prof. philosophy Napa Valley Coll., 1951—83, prof. emeritus, 1983—2010; prof. Judaic studies U. Mainz, 1983—2010. Guest lectr. Humboldt Univ., Berlin, 2003. Author: Eternal Faith, Eternal People - A Journey into Judaism, 1962, Judaism, Development and Life, 1966, 4th edit., 2000, A History of the Jewish Experience, 1974, 2d edit., 2001, The Complete Book of Jewish Observance, 1980, Judaism and the Religions of Humanity, 1985, What if Shylock were a Marrano, 1985, The Controversy between Samson Raphael Hirsch and Seligmann Baer Bamberger--Halakhical and Societal Implications, 1991, Yamim Nora'im: The Traditional Liturgy and "Gates of Repentance", 1991, numerous books in other langs.; maj. works include Die Juden, 1982, 2d edit., 1998, Jüdische Ethik, 1988, Der jüdische Gottesdienst-Form und Entfaltung, 1991, enlarged edit., 2003, Die Amerikanischen Juden-Profil einer Gemeinschaft, 1991, Jüdisches Denken im 20 Jahrhundant, 1992, (with G. Mayer) Abriss der jüdischen Geschichte, 1992, Geschichte der Deutschen Juden, 1996, Das Vermächtnis der deutschen Juden, 2000, Liturgical Chants of the Synagogue at Mainz, 2004, (CD) Niguney Magenza, 2004, Thy God is My God-Roads to Judaism and the Jewish Community (with Gerda Ekert), 2005; author: Memorial Address on the Victorian Group Nazis at Plenary Session of Parliament of the German State of Rheinland, 2005, Memorial Day of Persecution of German Jews by Pfalz, (essays on) Franz Rosenzweig, 1947, Martin Ruben, 1966, Herman Cohen, 1967, and others; contbr. articles to profl. jours.; author: The Position of Women, 1977, Trialogue: Christians, Muslims, Jews, Talking With the Best, 3 Essays, 1990—91. Mem. Napa Planning Commn., 1964-69. Recipient Great Seal, City of Oldenburg, 1971, George Washington Honor medal, Freedoms Found., 1979; hon. freeman City of Oldenburg, 1990, Hon. Senator, U. Mainz, 1996, Gutenberg Plaquette, City of Mainz, 1993, Cross of Merit 1st class Germany, 1997, Ring of Honor, City of Mainz, 2003, Price Land of Oldenburg, 2003, Symposium in his honor, Univ. of Mainz, 2003; new Jewish chapel named in his honor Vets. Home Calif., 1997; commendation Assembly Calif. Legis., 1998. Mem. Ctrl. Conf. Am. Rabbis, Rabbinical Assembly, Am. Philos. Assn., American Acad. Religion, Northern Calif. Bd. Rabbis. Home: San Francisco, Calif. Died Sept. 2, 2010.

TREZZA, ALPHONSE FIORE, librarian, educator; b. Phila., Dec. 27, 1920; s. Vincent and Amalia (Ferrara) T.; m. Mildred Di Pietro, May 19, 1945; children: Carol Ann Trezza Johnston, Alphonse Fiore. BS, U. Pa., 1948, MS, 1950, postgrad.; LHD (hon.), Rosary Coll., 1997. Cert. libr. Drexel Inst., 1949. Page Free Library, Phila., 1940-41, 45-48, library asst., 1948-49; cataloger, asst. reference librarian Villanova U., 1949-50, instr., 1956-60; head circulation dept. U. Pa. Library, 1950-56; lectr. Drexel Inst. Sch. Library Sci., 1956—60; editor Cath. Library world, 1956-60; exec. sec. Cath. Library Assn., 1956-60; assoc. exec. dir. ALA, exec. sec. library adminstrn. div., 1960-67, assoc. dir. adminstrv. services, 1960—69; dir. Ill. State Library, Springfield, 1969-74; lectr. Grad. Sch. Library and Info. Sci., Cath. U., 1975-82; exec. dir. Nat. Commn. on Libraries and Info. Scis., Washington, 1974-80; dir. intergovt. library Cooperation Project Fed. Library Com./Library of Congress, Washington, 1980-82; assoc. prof. Sch. Library and Info. Studies Fla. State U., Tallahassee, 1982-87, prof., 1987-93, emeritus prof., from 1993. Mem. Ill. Library LSCA TITLE I-II Adv. Commn., 1963-69; mem. network devel. com. Library of Congress, 1977-82; bd. visitors Sch. Library and Info. Sci., U. Pitts., 1977-80; cons. Becker & Hayes, Inc., 1980-84, King Research, Inc., 1981-82; mem. planning com and steering com. Fla. Gov.'s Conf. on Library and Info. Svcs., 1988-91. Nat. chmn. Cath. Book Week, 1954—56; pres. Joliet Diocesan Bd. Edn., 1966—68; auditor Borough of Norwood, Pa., 1958—60; mem. patron's bd. Fla. State U. Sch. Theater, from 2000; bd. mem. Lafayette Oaks Home Assn., from 2002; Dem. committeeman Lombard, Ill., 1961—69; extraordinary min. of Eucharistic Blessed Sacrament Cath. Ch., from 1984, mem. pastoral coun., from 2000. 1st lt. USAF, 1942—45. Decorated Air medal with one cluster; recipient Ofcl. commendation White House Conf. on Libr. and Info. Svc., 1979, citation State Libr. Agys., 1994, Silver award Commn. Libr. Info. Sci., 1996. Mem. ALA (coun. 1973-82, 88-92, mem.

exec. bd. 1974-79, chmn. stats. coordinating com. 1970-74, mem. pub. com. 1975-78, 81-83, 87-89, chmn. adv. com. interface, 1979-83, chmn. membership com. 1983-84, chmn. nominating com. 1988-89, mem. legis. com. 1989-91, adv. bd. ALA Yearbook 1976-91, Assn. Specialized and Coop. Library Agys. legis. com., 1987-89, ad hoc com. White House Conf. on Libr. and Info. Svcs. 1989-91, chmn. awards com. 1990-92, Exceptional Achievement award 1981, J.B. Lippincott award 1989, hon. mem. award, 2007), Cath. Library Assn. (life, adv. coun. 1960—), Ill. Library Assn. (chmn. legis.-library devel. com. 1964-69, mem. exec. bd., libr's. citation 1974), Fla. Library Assn. (bd. dirs. 1987-93, pres. 1991-92, intellectual freedom com., chmn. com. on Fla. Librs. publ., editor, publ. com., planning com., 1991, site com.), Continuing Libr. Edn. Network and Exchange (pres. 1982-83), Internat. Fedn. Library Assns. and Institutions (statistics standing com. 1976-85, planning com.), Coun. Nat. Library Assns. (chmn. 1959-61), Assn. Coll. and Research Librarians (pres. Phila. chpt. 1953-55), Drexel Inst. Library Sch. Alumni Assn. (pres. 1955-56, exec. bd. 1956-60, chmn. chief officers State Library Agys. 1973-74), Chgo. Library Club (pres. 1969), Assn. Library and Info. Sci. Edn. (govt. relation com. 1985-87), Drexel U. Alumni Assn. (Outstanding Alumnus award 1963), Kappa Phi Kappa (chpt. pres. 1948), Beta Phi Mu (hon.). Lodges: K.C. Home: Tallahassee, Fla. Died July 15, 2009.

TRIBBITT, SHERMAN WILLARD, former Governor of Delaware; b. Denton, Md., Nov. 9, 1922; s. Sherman L. and Minnie Thawley Tribbitt; m. Jeanne Webb; children: James, Carol, Sherman Tip. Student, Goldey-Beacom Coll. Mem. Del. House of Reps., 1957—64, 1971—72, speaker, 1959—65, minority leader, 1971—73; lt. gov. State of Del., 1965—69, gov., 1973—77; fed. rep. Del. River Basin Commn., 1977—81. Owner & operator Odessa Supply Co.; dir. Del. Savings & Loan Assn., Del. Mutual Ins. Co.; bd. trustees Goldey Beacom Coll.; v.p. Diamond Group Inc., Arch. & Engrs. Inc.; pres. Odessa Profl. Park Inc., Del. Agr. Mus. Served in USN. Decorated Presdl. Unit citation. Mem.: Friends of Old Drawyers (pres. 1984—2004), Union Lodge 5 (former master). Democrat. Methodist. Home: Rehoboth Beach, Del. Died Aug. 14, 2010.

TRIEBWASSER, MARC A., political science educator, multimedia computing; b. Bklyn., May 16, 1941; s. Emanuel and Belle M. (Cohn) T. BS in Physics, CCNY, 1963, MA in Physics, 1968; MA in Politics, NYU, 1971, PhD in Politics, 1978. Rsch. asst. nuclear reactor lab. Cornell U., Ithaca, N.Y., 1963-65; lectr. physics CCNY, 1966-67; jr. rsch. fellow Ctr./Study Dem. Insts., Santa Barbara, Calif., 1969-70; asst. prof. polit. sci. Pembroke (N.C.) State U., 1973-75; part time instr. politics NYU, NYC, 1975-76, 77-78; instr. govt. St. Lawrence U., Canton, N.Y., 1976-77; asst. prof., head policy sci. concentration Northeast U., Boston, 1978-79; computer cons. Conn. State Dept. Labor, Wethersfield, 1980-81; dir. MicroMedia Inst., prof. polit. sci. Ctrl. Conn. State U., New Britain, from 1979, dir. internet and multimedia studies, from 1979. Prof. polit. sci. Author: (chpt.) Effective Communication, 1992, Mapping Cyberspace, 1997, We Get What We Vote For...Or Do We?, 1999; author, project dir. (video) Am. Govt. Interactive Video Disc, 1994; mem. editl. adv. bd. AE: Readings in Am. Govt., 1974-76, AE: Readings in Econs., 1992—; contbr. articles to profl. jours. Mem. state bd. dirs. Conn. Civil Liberties Union, Hartford, 1996-97. Recipient Apple grant Apple Computer Inc., 1990, Video grant C-SPAN, 1991, 93, Mellon vis. fellowship Yale U., 1983, 94. Mem. AAAS, ACLU, Am. Polit. Sci. Assn. (nat. exec. com. computers and multimedia sect. 1991-93, 95-99, fin. officer 1991-95, Best Instrnl. Software award 1994), Computer Profl. for Social Responsibility, Educators for Social Responsibility. Home: Laguna Beach, Calif. Died Apr. 12, 2009.

TROMBLEY, IRA, state legislator; b. North Hero, Vt., Apr. 16, 1952; m. Lucy Trombley; 3 children. Former mem. Human Resources Investment Coun., Vt.; dir. Grand Isle Sch.; vice chmn. Legislature Info. Tech. Com.; state rep. Grand Isle-Chittenden Dist. 1-1 Vt. House of Reps., Vt., 2003—09. Recipient Mason award, Masons Card Program. Mem.: Pelots Bar Restoration Assn., Mitlon Grange, Champlain Island C. of C. Democrat. Congregational. Died Dec. 20, 2009.

TROUTMAN, DAVID W., protective services official; b. Wooster, Ohio, Feb. 16, 1942; m. Janet; children: Mike, Deanna. Deputy sheriff Summit County, Akron, Ohio, 1966-73; chief probation officer Barberton (Ohio) Mcpl. Ct., 1973-80; elected sheriff Summit county, 1980-84; U.S. marshall No. Dist. Ohio, from 1974. Mem. Am. Jail Assn., Am. Correctional Assn., Nat. Sheriffs Assn. (law & legis. com., united crime reporting commn.), Buckeye State Sheriffs Assn. (pres. 1987). Democrat. Died Oct. 26, 2009.

TRUCE, WILLIAM EVERETT, chemist, educator; b. Chgo., Sept. 30, 1917; s. Stanley C. and Frances (Novak) T.; m. Eloise Joyce McBroom, June 16, 1940; children: Nancy Jane, Roger William. BS, U. Ill., 1939; PhD, Northwestern U., 1943. Mem. faculty Purdue U., 1946-88, prof. chemistry, 1956-88, prof. chemistry emeritus, from 1988, asst. dean Grad. Sch., 1963-66. Com. mem. numerous univ.; chmn. profl. meetings; exec. officer Nat. Organic Symposium, 1961; chmn. Gordon Rsch. Conf. on Organic Reactions and Processes; cons. in field. Co-author book; contbr. articles to profl. jours., chpts. to books. Guggenheim fellow Oxford U., 1957 Mem. Am. Chem. Soc., Phi Beta Kappa (sec. Purdue chpt.), Sigma Xi (pres. Purdue chpt.). Achievements include research in new methods of synthesis, devel. new kinds of compounds and reactions. Died Jan. 6, 2009.

TRZCINSKI, WALTER MICHAEL, chief of police; b. New Britain, Conn., May 19, 1924; s. Alexander Joseph and Anna Rose Trzcinski; m. Elsie Elizabeth Beehdam, Sept. 3, 1944; children— Brenda Ann, Elizabeth Jane, Barbara Lynn. A.S. in Criminal Justice, U. New Haven, 1972. Laborer, Uniroyal, Naugatuck, Conn., 1946-55; security guard Sikorsky's, Bridgeport, Conn., 1955-57; police officer Seymour Police Dept., Conn., 1957—, chief of police, 1981—. Served with U.S. Army, 1943-46. Fellow Conn. Chiefs of Police, So. Central Chiefs of Police, Roman Catholic. Lodges: Am. Legion, V.F.W. Home: Seymour, Conn. Died Apr. 8, 2009.

TSE, CHARLES YUNG CHANG, pharmaceutical executive, lawyer; b. Shanghai, Mar. 22, 1926; s. Kung Chao and Say Ying (Chen) T.; m. Vivian Chang, Apr. 25, 1955; 1 dau., Roberta. BA in Econs, St. John's U., Shanghai, 1949; MS in Acctg, U. Ill., 1950; JD, N.Y. Law Sch., 1990. Asst. to controller Am. Internat. Group, NYC, 1950-54, asst. mgr. Singapore-Malaysia, 1955-57; with Warner-Lambert Co., Morris Plains, NJ, 1957-86, area mgr. S.E. Asia, 1966-68, regional dir. S.E. Asia, 1968-69, v.p. Australasia, 1970-71, pres. Western Hemisphere Group, 1971-72, pres. Pan Am. Mgmt. Center, 1972-76, pres. European Mgmt. Center, 1976-78, pres. Internat. Group, 1979-86, sr. v.p. corp., 1980-83, exec. v.p. corp., 1984-85, vice chmn., 1985-86. Dir. Foster Wheeler Corp., Livingston, N.J., 1984-98, Superior Telecom., Inc., 1996—, Com. of 100; mem. faculty bus. adminstrn. dept. Fairleigh Dickinson U., 1961-64; pres. Cancer Rsch. Inst., Inc., N.Y.C., 1991-92. Bd. visitors CCNY, 1974-78; trustee Morristown Meml. Hosp. (N.J.), 1982-86; bd. dirs. Bus. Council for Internat. Understanding, 1984-87. Mem. NAM (dir. 1984-86), Assn. of the Bar of the City of N.Y. (mem. Asian affairs com. 1991-2001). Home: New York, NY. Died June 19, 2009.

TSUBAKI, ANDREW TAKAHISA, theater director, educator; b. Chiyoda-ku, Tokyo, Japan, Nov. 29, 1931; s. Ken and Yasu (Oyama) T.; m. Lilly Yuri, Aug. 3, 1963; children: Arthur Yuichi, Philip Takeshi. BA in English, Tokyo Gakugei U., Tokyo, Japan, 1954; postgrad. in Drama, U. Saskatchewan, Saskatoon, Canada, 1958-59; MFA in Theatre Arts, Tex. Christian U., 1961; PhD in Speech & Drama, U. Ill., 1967. Tchr. Bunkyo-ku 4th Jr. High Sch., Tokyo, 1954—58; instr., scene designer Bowling Green (Ohio) State U., 1964—68; asst. prof. speech & drama U. Kans., Lawrence, 1968—73, assoc. prof., 1973—79; vis. assoc. prof. Carleton Coll., Northfield, Minn., 1974; lectr. Tsuda U., Tokyo, 1975; vis. assoc. prof. theatre Tel-Aviv (Israel) U., 1975—76; vis. prof. theatre Mo. Repertory Theatre, Kansas City, Mo., 1976, Nat. Sch. Drama, New Delhi, 1983; prof. theatre, film, east Asian Languages and Cultures U. Kans., Lawrence, 1979—2000, prof. emeritus, from 2000. Dir. Internat. Theatre Studies Ctr., U. Kans., Lawrence, 1971-2000, Operation Internat. Classical Theatre, 1988—; Benedict disting. vis. prof. Asian studies Carleton Coll., 1993; area editor Asian Theatre Jour., U. Hawaii, Honolulu, 1982-94; chmn. East Asian Langs. and Cultures, U. Kans., Lawrence, 1983-90; mem. editl. bd. Studies in Am. Drama, Oxford, Miss., 1985-88. Dir. plays Kanjincho, 1973, Rashomon, 1976, 96, King Lear, 1985, Fujito and Shimizu, 1985, Hippolytus, 1990, Busu and the Missing Lamb (Japan) 1992, Suehirogari and Sumidagawa, 1992, 93, Tea, 1995; choreographed Antigone (Greece), 1987, Hamlet (Germany), 1989, The Resistible Rise of Arturo Ui, 1991, Man and the Masses (Germany), 1993, The Children of Fate (Hungary), 1994, The Great Theatre of the World (Germany); editor Theatre Companies of the World, 1986; contbg. author to Indian Theatre: Traditions of Performance, 1990; contbr. 7 entries in Japanese Traditional plays to the Internat. Dictionary of Theatre, vol. 1, 1992, vol. 2, 1994. Recipient citation, Min. Fgn. Affairs Japan, 2003, Statement of Appreciation, Chmn. and Bd. Dirs. Hiratsuka Internat. Exch. Assn., 2004; named to Order of Sacred Treasure, Govt. of Japan, 2006; World Univ. Svc. scholar, U. Saskatchewan, 1958—59, University fellow, U. Ill., 1961—62, Rsch. fellow, The Japan Found., 1974—75, 1990, Rsch. Fulbright grantee, 1983. Fellow Coll. Am. Theatre (elected 2002); mem. Am. Theatre Assn., Asian Theatre Program (chair 1976-79), Assn. for Asian Studies, Assn. Kans. Theatres., Assn. Kans. Theatres U/C Div. (chmn. 1980-82), Assn. for Theatre in Higher Edn., Assn. for Asian Performance. Democrat. Buddhist. Avocations: ki-aikido (5th dan), photography, travel. Home: Lawrence, Kans. Died Dec. 16, 2009.

TUCKER, CHARLES ALBERT, tobacco company executive; b. Geneva, Ill., Dec. 31, 1920; s. Charles Lehman and Mary Louise (Rose) T.; m. Joyce Marie Dunbar, Nov. 18, 1943 (div. 1958); children: James Watson, Jeffrey Charles; m. Sallie Irene Kunz, Dec. 28, 1958; children: Charles Bardley, Julia Irene. AB cum laude, DePauw U., 1943; MBA with distinction, Harvard U., 1947. Dist. sales mgr. Am. Hosp. Supply, Evanston, Ill., 1947-50; gen. sales and advt. mgr. S.O.S. Co., Chgo., 1950-58; pres. Frenchette div. Carter Wallace, NYC, 1958-71; v.p. R.J. Reynolds Foods Inc., N.Y.C., 1972-73; sr. v.p. R.J. Reynolds Tobacco Co., Winston-Salem, N.C., from 1973, also dir. Bd. dirs. Tobacco Inst., Washington; chmn., bd. dirs. Audit Bur. Circulations, Schaumburg, Ill. Served to capt. USAAF, 1943-46. Mem. Internat. Tobacco Mfrs. Assn. (dir.), Am. Advt. Fedn. (dir.) Clubs: N.Y. Yacht. Methodist. Home: Winston Salem, NC. Died Sept. 2, 2009.

TUCKER, JACK RANDOLPH, JR., architectural firm executive; b. Little Rock, Feb. 6, 1939; BArch, BA, U. Ark., 1963. Registered arch., Ark., Tenn.; cert. Nat. Coun. Archtl. Registration Bds. Designer, draftsman, field inspector U. Ark., 1962-64, 66-68; arch., planner Peace Corps, Tunisia, 1964-66; designer, project mgr. Roy P. Harrover and Assocs. Archs., Memphis, 1968-79; prin. Jack. R. Tucker, Jr., Arch., Memphis, 1979-82; prin., owner Jack R. Tucker Jr. and Assocs., Memphis, from 1982. Mem. Shelby County mayor's task force The Econs. of Amenity, 1983; pres. Downtown Neighborhood Assn., 1984, also mem. exec. bd.; mem. exec. bd. Memphis Heritage; mem. selection com., mem. pub. works com. Center City Commn. Policy Com. Downtown Devel. Plan; chmn. Memphis Landmarks Commn.; bd. dirs. Greater Memphis State; mem. profl. adv. bd. U. Ark. Sch. Architecture; active Brooks Meml. Art Gallery, Downtown Transit Task Force, Union Ave. Task Force, Mud Island Found. Support Group. Recipient 30 awards for design. Fellow AIA (past pres. Memphis chpt., Francis Gassner award Memphis chpt. 1994). Home: Memphis, Tenn. Died Apr. 5, 2009.

TUCKER, RICHARD FRANK, petroleum company executive; b. NYC, Dec. 25, 1926; s. Frank W. and Marion (Ohm) T.; m. Genevieve P. Martinson, Oct. 13, 1951. B.Chem. Engring., Cornell U., 1950. With Esso Standard Oil Co., 1950-55; with Caltex Oil Co., 1955-61, Mobil Corp., from 1961, vice chmn. bd., from 1986; pres., chief operating officer Mobil Oil Corp., from 1986. Dir. Nova Pharm. Corp., Perkin Elmer Corp., U.S. Trust, Am. Petroleum Inst. Trustee Cornell U.; mem. bd. overseers Cornell U. Med. Sch. Served with USN, 1945-46. Mem. Nat. Acad. Engring., Council Fgn. Relations. Clubs: Cornell, Sky (N.Y.C.). Died Jan. 31, 2009.

TUCKER, ROBERT DENNARD, health care products executive; b. Tifton, Ga., July 18, 1933; s. Robert Buck and Ethel Margaret (Dennard) T.; m. Peggy Angelyn Smith, June 23, 1957; children: Robert Barron, Jennifer Lee. BBA, Ga. State U., 1958. With sales and sales mgmt. Johnson & Johnson Inc., New Brunswick, NJ, 1958-68; v.p., gen. mgr. ASR Med. Industries, NYC, 1968-72, Howmedica Suture div. Pfizer Inc., NYC, 1972-75; exec. v.p., chief operating officer R. P. Scherer Corp., Detroit, 1976-79; pres., chief operating officer Scherer Sci. Inc., Atlanta, 1980-95, also bd. dirs; chmn., chief exec. officer Scherer Health Care Inc., Atlanta, 1980-95, also bd. dirs. Bd. dirs., pres., CEO Splty. Surgictrs., Inc., Atlanta, 1997—2002; bd. dirs., chmn., CEO Maximum Benefits Co., Atlanta; chmn., CEO Throwleigh Techs., LLC, from 1995; bd. dirs., mem. exec. com. Horizon Med. Products, 2002—05; bd. dirs., chmn compensation com. Averion Internat. Corp., from 2006. Pub: Tuckers of Devon, 1983; author, pub.: Descendants of William Tucker of Throwleigh, Devon. Chmn. bd. Health Industries Mfrs. Assn. polit. action com., Washington, 1983-85; trustee, past pres. Ga. Horse Found., Atlanta; trustee Brenau Coll., Gainesville, Ga., 1985—. Served with Frogmen UDT3 USN, 1951-54, Korea. Decorated Knight of Malta, Imperial Russian Order of St. John; recipient Disting. Service award Brenau Coll., 1987. Mem. Nat. Assn. Mfrs., Health Industries Mfrs. Assn. (bd. dirs. 1979-86, disting. service recognition 1981, 86), Pharm. Mfrs. Assn., Thoroughbred Owners and Breeders Assn. Ky. and Ga. (Man of Yr. 1984). Clubs: Cherokee (Atlanta); Big Canoe (Ga.). Republican. Methodist. Avocations: scuba diving, tennis, genealogy. Home: Monticello, Ga. Died Jan. 22, 2010.

TUFTS, ROBERT L., former state legislator; b. Lewiston, Maine, July 5, 1934; m. Judith Kingsbury, 1960. BS, Farmington State Tchrs. Coll., 1956. Former tchr.; mem. from dist. 112 Maine State Ho. of Reps., 1992-94, mem. from dist. 107, 1994-96. Died Apr. 11, 2010.

TUIA, TUANA'ITAU F., territorial legislator; b. American Samoa, 1920; m. Betty Tuia. Rep. Dist. 8 America Samoa Legislature, 1975—93, house spkr., 1979—92, Senator Tualauta County, 1993—2010. Mem.: American Samoa Bar Assn. Died Jan. 22, 2010.

TULLY, DARROW, newspaper publisher; b. Charleston, W.Va., Feb. 27, 1932; s. William Albert and Dora (McCann) T.; m. Victoria Lynn Werner; children: Bonnie Tully Paul, Michael Andrew. Student, Purdue U., 1951; BA in Journalism, St. Joseph's Coll., 1972; PhD in Journalism (hon.), Calumet Coll., Ind., 1975. V.p., gen. mgr. Stas. WDSM-AM-FM and WDSM-TV, Duluth, Minn., 1956-59; bus. mgr. Duluth Herald & News Tribune, 1960-62; gen. mgr. St. Paul Dispatch & Pioneer Press, 1962-66; pub. Gary (Ind.) Post-Tribune, 1966-73; v.p., pub. Wichita (Kans.) Eagle & Beacon, 1973-75; pres. San Francisco Newspaper Agy., 1975-78; exec. v.p., pub. Ariz. Republic & Phoenix Gazette, 1978-85; editor., pub., chief exec. officer Ojai (Calif.) Valley News, 1987-90; pres., pub., CEO Beacon Comms., Acton, Mass., 1990-92; asst. to pres. newspaper divsn. Chronicle Pub. Co., 1992-94. Author: Minority Representation in the Media, 1968. Trustee Calumet Coll. Recipient Disting. Achievement award Ariz. State U., 1982, Disting. Journalist award No. Ariz. U./AP, 1983, 1st Pl. Editorial Writing award Ariz. Planned Parenthood, 1983. Mem. Am. Soc. Newspaper Editors, Soc. Profl. Journalists. Died June 20, 2010.

TUOHY, WILLIAM, retired news correspondent; b. Chgo., Oct. 1, 1926; s. John Marshall and Lolita (Klaus) T.; m. Mary Ellyn Dufek, 1955 (div.); m. Johanna Iselin, 1964 (div.); 1 child, Cyril Iselin; m. Rose Marie Wheeler, 1998. BS, Northwestern U., 1951. Reporter, night city editor San Francisco Chronicle, 1952-59; assoc. editor, nat. polit. corr., fgn. corr. Newsweek mag., 1959-66; Vietnam corr. L.A. Times, 1966-68, Middle East corr. Beirut, 1969-71, bur. chief Rome, 1971-77, London, 1977-85, Bonn, Fed. Republic Germany, 1985-90, European security corr. London, 1990—95. Author: Dangerous Company, 1987, The Bravest Man: The Story of Richard O'Kane and U.S. Submarines in the Pacific War, 2001, America's Fighting Admirals: Winning the War at Sea in World War II, 2007 Served with USNR, 1944-46. Recipient Nat. Headliner award for Vietnam bur. coverage, 1965, Pulitzer prize internat. reporting (Vietnam), 1969, Overseas Press Club award for best internat. reporting (Middle East), 1970, various others. Died Dec. 31, 2009.

TURNER, EUGENE ANDREW, manufacturing executive; b. Bridgeton, NJ, Aug. 7, 1928; s. Benjamin Homer and Pearl Irene (Wolbert) T.; m. Paula Ann Webb, 1987; children: Mary Ann, John-Reed. BA, Rutgers U., 1956; student, Columbia U., 1980. With Owens Ill., 1950-73, regional mgr. West Coast, 1970-73; v.p. adminstrn. Midland Glass Co., Cliffwood, NJ, 1973-76, pres., chief operating officer, 1981-82, also bd. dirs.;

v.p., gen. mgr. Anchor Hocking Corp., Lancaster, Ohio, 1976-81; dir. ops. Theo Chem. Labs., Tampa, Fla., 1988-90, Profit Counselors Inc, Sarasota, Fla., 1990-94; pres. Profit Sys. Inc., Oklahoma City, from 1994. Mng. cons. 1987-88; trustee Glass Packaging Inst. Mem. Harbor Island Club, Seaview Country Club, Navesink Country Club. Died Aug. 26, 2010.

TURNER, LARRY, state legislator; b. West Memphis, Ark., Jan. 16, 1939; s. Robert Lee and Alleen Bond Turner; m. Johnnie Rodgers Turner, 1965; 1 child, Larry Rodgers. State rep. Dist. 85, Tenn., from 1985; sec. Majority Caucus; vice chmn. Employee & Consumer Affairs, House of Rep., Tenn.; chmn. Shelby County Del., 1987—88, Balck Caucus State Legislature, Tenn., 2001—02; owner Larry Turner & Assoc. Realty Co. Inc., Tenn. Recipient Cert. Outstanding Svc., Dept. Human Svc., 1985, Cert. Appreciation, Memphis Edn. Assn., 1998; named Plaque Outstanding Job as Chmn., Shelby County Legislature Del. C. of C., 1987—88, Tenn. State Most Outstanding Freshman Legislature, 1985. Mem.: KP (bd. mem. from 1975), NAACP, Urban League, Foster Care & Adoption Task Force (pres. from 1982), Friends of Black Children, Damion Lodge. Democrat. Baptist. Died Nov. 27, 2009.

TURNER, WALLACE, retired reporter; b. Titusville, Fla., Mar. 15, 1921; s. Clyde H. and Ina B. (Wallace) T.; m. Pearl Burk, June 12, 1943; chldren: Kathleen Turner, Elizabeth Turner Everett. B.J., U. Mo., 1943; postgrad. (Nieman fellow), Harvard U., 1958-59. Reporter Springfield (Mo.) Daily News, 1943, Portland Oregonian, 1943-59; news dir. Sta. KPTV, Portland, 1959-61; asst. sec. US Dept. Health, Edn. & Welfare (HEW), Washington, 1961-62; reporter The NY Times, San Francisco, 1962—88, San Francisco bur. chief, 1970-85, Seattle bur. chief, 1985-88. Author: Gamblers Money: The New Force in American Life, 1965, The Morman Establishment, 1967. Recipient Heywood Broun award for reporting, 1952, 56; Pulitzer Prize for reporting, 1957 Died Sept. 18, 2010.

TURRENTINE, JAMES DRAKE, lawyer; b. Louisville, Nov. 27, 1942; s. James Lewis and Elizabeth (McNerney) T.; m. JoAnn Butrico, Aug. 17, 1968; children: Elizabeth Ann, Daniel Calhoon, Katherine Drake. BA, U. Pa., 1969; JD, Yale U., 1972. Bar: D.C. 1973, Conn. 1975, U.S. Ct. Appeals (2d cir.) 1975, U.S. Ct. Appeals (D.C. cir.) 1973. Assoc. Leva, Hawes, Symington, Martin & Oppenheimer, Washington, 1972-74, Wiggin & Dana, New Haven, 1974-79, ptnr., 1979—97; chief legal officer, sec. Special Olympics, Inc., 1997—2010. Pres. Saab Systems Inc., Houston, 1988-2010 Contbg. author: Legal Aspects of Doing Business in North America, 1987, 1993; contbr. articles to profl. jours. Bd. dirs. Internat. Ctr. Inc., New Haven, 1977-88, pres., 1981-83; mem. adv. bd. Conn. World Trade Assn., 1987-89, bd. dirs., 1989-93; mem. dist. export coun. US Dept. Commerce, 1987-2010; Sgt. USAF, 1962-66, Vietnam. Mem. ABA, Conn. Bar Assn. (chmn. internat. sect. 1982-84), Internat. Bar Assn., Union Internat. des Avocats, Greater New Haven C. of C. (bd. dirs., chmn. internat. roundtable), Mory's (New Haven), Quinnipiack Club (bd. govs. 1992-2010), Yale Club (N.Y.C.), High Lane Club. Democrat. Home: Washington, DC. Died July 14, 2010.

TYLER, GEORGE THOMAS, lawyer; b. Spartenburg, SC, Dec. 4, 1933; s. George Thomas and Wathen Dallas (Strong) T.; m. Millicent Ann Rosenberg, Mar. 15, 1961; children: Millicent Ann, George Thomas, John Paul. AB, Randolph Macon Coll., 1955; LLB, Georgetown U., 1963. Bar: Md. 1963, D.C. 1978, U.S. Dist. Ct. Md., U.S. Ct. Appeals (4th cir.), U.S. Supreme Ct. Ptnr. Obr Kaler Grimes & Shriver, Balt., from 1968. Lt. USNR, 1956-60. Died May 29, 2010.

UDALL, STEWART LEE, retired lawyer, former United States Secretary of the Interior; b. St. Johns, Ariz., Jan. 31, 1920; s. Levi S. and Louise (Lee) U.; m. Ermalee Webb, Aug. 1, 1947 (dec. 2001); children: Thomas, Scott, Lynn, Lori, Denis, James. LLB, U. Ariz., 1948; LLD, Bates Coll. Bar: Ariz. 1948. Practiced in, Tucson, 1948-54, Washington, 1969; mem. US Congress from 2nd Ariz. Dist., 1955-61; sec. US Dept. Interior, 1961-69; of counsel Hill, Christopher & Phillips (P.C.), Washington. Chmn. bd. Overview Corp.; writer syndicated column Udall on the Environment Author: The Quiet Crisis, 1963, 1976, Agenda for Tommorrow, 1968, America's Natural Treasures, 1971, (with others) The National Parks of America, 1972; co-author: (with others) The Energy Balloon, 1974. Served with USAAF, 1944. Mem. ABA. Mem. Ch. of Jesus Christ of Latter Day Saints. Home: Santa Fe, N.Mex. Died Mar. 20, 2010.

UDVARHELYI, GEORGE BELA, neurosurgery educator emeritus, cultural affairs administrator; b. Budapest, Hungary, May 14, 1920; came to U.S., 1955; s. Bela and Margaret (Bakacs) U.; m. Elspeth Mary Campbell, July 24, 1956; children: Ian Steven, Susan Margaret, Jane Elizabeth. BS, St. Stephen Coll., 1938; MD, U. Budapest, 1944, U. Buenos Aires, 1952; D honoris causa, Semmelweis Med. Sch., Budapest, 1988, Western Md. Coll., 1997. Diplomate Am. Bd. Neurol. Surgery. Intern resident in surgery Red Cross Hosp./11th Mil. Hosp., Budapest, 1942-44; asst. resident Neurol. Univ. Clinic, Budapest, 1944-46; postdoctoral fellow U. Vienna, Austria, 1946-47; fgn. asst. Psychiat. Clinic, U. Berne, Switzerland, 1947-48; asst. resident in neurosurgery Hosp. Espanol, Cordoba, Argentina, 1948-50; resident neurosurgeon Inst. Neurosurgery, U. Buenos Aires, 1950-53; asst. Neurolsurgical Clinic, U. Cologne, Fed. Republic Germany, 1953-54; registrar Royal Infirmary, Edinburgh, Scotland, 1954-55; from fellow to full prof. Johns Hopkins U., Balt., 1955-84, prof. emeritus, dir. cultural affairs, 1984-92, assoc. prof. radiology, 1963-84, Phi Beta Kappa lectr., 1980. Neurosurg. cons. Social Security Adminstrn., Balt., 1962-89, Disability Determination Svc., Balt., 1991-93; vis. prof., guest lectr. U. Va., Charlottesville, 1977, Children's Hosp. Ea. Ont., Ottawa, Can., 1977, U. Salzburg, Austria, 1981, U. Vienna, Austria, 1983, Mayo Clinic, Rochester, Minn., 1983, U. Cape Town, Republic of South Africa, 1984, U. Porto, Portugal, 1985; vis. prof. Temple U., Phila., 1979, U. Vt., Burlington, 1980, Aukland (New Zealand) Gen. Hosp., 1989, George Washington U., 1991, U. Mainz, Fed. Republic Germany, 1991, numerous others; lectr. in field. Contbr. numerous articles to profl. jours., book chpts. Mem. program com. Balt. Symphony Orch., 1972-80, edn. com. Walters Art Gallery, Balt., 1985-88. Recipient Lincoln award Am. Hungarian Found., 1980, Eisenberg award Humanities, 1996; Humanities grantee NEH, 1984-91. Fellow ACS; mem. AAUP, Am. Assn. Neurol. Surgeons (life, Humanitarian award 1991), Congress Neurol. Surgeons (sr.), Am. Assn. Neuropathologists, Pan-Am. Med. Assn., Soc. Brit. Neurol. Surgeons (corr.), Pavlovian Soc. N.Am., German Neurol. Soc. (corr.), Internat. Soc. Pediatric Neurosurgery (founding), Hungarian Neurosurg. Soc. (corr.), Argentine Acad. Sci. (corr.), Am. Soc. for Laser Medicine and Surgery (charter), Johns Hopkins Med. Assn., Johns Hopkins Faculty Club, 14 West Hamilton Club (chair steering com. 1977-83), Cosmos Club (chair program subcom. 1991—), Landsdowne Club (London), Alpha Omega Alpha. Roman Catholic. Avocations: music, literature, travel, chess. Home: Baltimore, Md. Died June 22, 2010.

UGRIN, BÉLA, video producer; b. Endröd, Hungary, July 19, 1928; came to U.S., 1962, naturalized, 1967; s. Gáspár and Regina (Gyuricza) U.; m. Emmanuella Caravageli, Feb. 12, 1964; 1 son, Gregory Alexander. Grad., Inst. Photojournalism, Munich, W. Ger., 1960; BA, U. Houston, 1977; MA, Tex. So. U., 1980; PhD in Edn., Southwest U., 1994. Freelance mag. photographer, Munich, and NYC, 1959-66; chief photographer Westport (Conn.) News, 1967-69; staff photographer Houston Post, 1969-77, chief photographer, 1978-84; pres., exec. producer Belvideo & Mult-Media Inc., from 1992. Producer-dir. Houston Ind. Sch. Dist. Media Svcs. TV, 1988—; pres. Belvideo & MUltimedia Inc., 1992—; lectr. in field. Ind. film producer, 1985—; assoc. dir. Houston ISD Dept. Tech., 1986-88; producer-dir., cultural TV documentary Andre Kertesz: A Poet With the Camera, 1986 (Silver award Houston Internat. Film Festival, 1986); edn. video series including Take Command, 1986-87, Technology and Education Today, 1988; single TV programs including Tomorrow's Teacher, 1989, Visual Literacy, 1989, Top Teachers, 1989, Profession at Risk, 1990, Photo Fence, 1990, Cinco de Mayo, 1990, People Place, 1990, Global Schoolhouse, 1990 (Gold award Pub. Rels. Soc. Am. 1991), Teacher Induction: The Houston Model, 1991, Alternative Certification Program, 1991, Partners in Education, 1991, The Business Connection, 1991, Communities in Schools, 1992, Teachers for America 2000, 1992, Multimedia Instruction, 1992, A New Source for Teachers, 1992, Distance Learning, 1993, Doing Business with Hungary, 1993, School Safety and Violence, 1993, ACP's Growth and Success, 1994, Media Literacy, 1993, Armadillos on the Superhighway, 1994, Foreign Languages, 1994, Dual Language Class, 1995, "PEER"-HISD's Major Checkup, 1995; contbr. articles on video prodns., photography and travel to various publs. Mem. Soc. Profl. Journalists, Internat. TV Assn. Home: Houston, Tex. Died Jan. 9, 2010.

UHL, EDWARD GEORGE, retired manufacturing executive; b. Elizabeth, NJ, Mar. 24, 1918; s. Henry and Mary (Schiller) U.; m. Maurine B. Keleher, July 19, 1942 (dec. 1966); children: Carol Uhl Nordlinger, Kim, Scott, Cynthia Uhl McKitrick; m. Mary Stuart Brugh, Sept. 17, 1966. BS, Lehigh U., 1940, D.Sc. (hon.), 1975. Engr. guided missiles Martin Co., 1946-51, chief project engr., 1951-53, v.p. engring., 1953-55, v.p. ops., 1955-56, v.p., gen. mgr. Orlando div. Fla., 1957-59; v.p. tech. adminstrn. Ryan Aero. Co., 1959-60, v.p., div. mgr., 1961; pres., CEO Fairchild Industries, 1961-76, chmn. bd., CEO, 1976-86. Dir. Md. Nat. Bank, Md. Nat. Corp., Vanguard Technologies Internat., Inc. Trustee Johns Hopkins U.; chmn. bd. trustees Lehigh U.; bd. nominations Aviation Hall Fame. Served from 2d lt. to lt. col. Ordnance Corps AUS, 1941-46. Recipient Hamilton Holt award Rollins Coll., 1965 Fellow AIAA; mem. Air Force Assn., Am. Def. Preparedness Assn. (John C. Jones award 1975), Soc. Automotive Engrs., Phi Beta Kappa, Tau Beta Pi. Clubs: Assembly (Hagerstown); Maryland (Balt.); Talbot Country (Easton); Sky (N.Y.C.). Co-inventor bazooka. Died May 9, 2010.

UHL, HENRY STEPHEN MAGRAW, internist, educator; b. Wilkes-Barre, Pa., July 23, 1921; s. John Hamilton and Rebecca Ursula (Magraw) Uhl; m. Louise Powell Butler, Nov. 30, 1946 (div. 1979); 1 child, Meredith Louise Conley; m. Nancy Hyde Easley, Feb. 16, 1980 (dec. Jan. 29, 1998); m. Bernice Mallard Everett, June 25, 1999. AB, Princeton U., 1943; MD, Harvard U., 1947; MA Adeundem hon., Brown U., 1967. Diplomate: Am. Bd. Internal Medicine. Intern in pathology John Hopkins Hosp., Balt., 1947-48; asst. resident Johns Hopkins Hosp., Balt., 1948, asst. dept. medicine, 1949; asst. in pathology Johns Hopkins Med. Sch., 1947-48, instr. anatomy and pathology, 1948-49; intern med. service Henry Ford Hosp., Detroit, 1949-50; Mich. Heart Assn. research fellow Wayne State U. Coll. Medicine and Detroit Receiving Hosp., 1950-51, sr. asst. resident med. service and asst. in medicine, 1951-52, instr. medicine and research assoc., 1952-53; dir. med. edn. Worcester City Hosp. (Mass.) and Bay State Med. Ctr., Springfield, Mass., 1953-60; mem. faculty, adminstrn. Albany Med. Coll., NY, 1960-66; prof. med. sci. Brown U, Providence, 1966-71; dir., prof. medicine U. NC, Mountain Area Health Edn. Ctr., 1973-78; prof. medicine Creighton U., Omaha, 1978-86, Bowman Gray Sch Medicine, Wake Forest U., Winston-Salem, NC, from 1986; cons. NIH, also hosps., 1960-78. Contbr. articles to profl. jours. Served to ensign M.C. USNR, 1942-45. Recipient Disting. Service award Mountain Area Health Edn. Found., Asheville, NC, 1978 Mem. ACP, Alliance Continuing Med. Edn., Am. Soc. Internal Medicine, Assn. Hosp. Med. Edn. (pres. 1958-60, John C. Leonard Meml. award 1984), Soc. Health and Human Values Clubs: Princeton (NYC); Press (Omaha); Fontenelle Hills Country (Bellevue, Nebr.), Pine Brook Country Club. Achievements include research in Uhl's anomaly. Home: Winston Salem, NC. Died Aug. 28, 2009.

ULRICH, WILLIAM JOHN, history professor; b. Columbus, Ohio, Nov. 1, 1920; s. Fred William and Cornelia (Stephens) Ulrich; m. May Fern Moore, Oct. 5, 1957. BA, Ohio State U., 1942; MA, 1948, PhD, 1959. Instr. John Carroll U., Univ. Heights, Ohio, 1959—61, asst. prof., 1961—68, assoc. prof., 1968—73, prof. history, from 1973, chmn. dept. history, 1965—86. Mem.: Western Res. Hist. Soc., Ohio Acad. History, Southern Hist. Assn., Orgn. Am. Historians, Phi Alpha Theta. Roman Catholic. Avocations: music, stamp collecting/philately. Home: Cleveland, Ohio. Died Apr. 11, 2010.

UMAN, DAVID BEN, management consultant; b. Cambridge, Mass., Apr. 18, 1935; s. Arthur J. and Beatrice (Pollock) Uman; children: Michael A., Jonathan J. Attended, U. Conn., 1953—57; MS in Indsl. Engring., Columbia U., 1965; MBA, CUNY, 1968. Ops. analyst Gen. Foods Corp., Lever Bros. Co., NYC, 1958—68; asst. to pres. Am. Home Products Corp., NYC, 1968—70; v.p. Leasco Corp., NYC, 1970—73; mng. dir. Indsl. Comml. Devel. Ltd., Kingston, Jamaica, 1973—74; v.p. Becton Dickinson & Co., Rutherford, N.J., 1974—76; pres. Mgmt. Adv. Group, Marina del Rey, Calif., from 1976; assoc. prof. strategy Pepperdine Grad. Sch. Bus., LA, from 1986. Author: New Product Programs: Their Planning and Control, 1968, Measurement of Performance in Business, 1977, P3M: A Guide to Productivity Pricing and Profits, 1985; contbr. articles to profl. jours. 1st lt. Signal Corps US Army, 1957—58, 1st lt. Signal Corps US Army, 1963. Mem.: Am. Mgmt. Assn., Planning Execs. Inst., Am. Inst. Indsl. Engrs. (sr.), South Bay Yacht Racing Club. Died Jan. 8, 2010.

UNDERDOWN, DAVID EDWARD, historian, educator; b. Wells, Eng., Aug. 19, 1925; s. John Percival and Ethel Mary (Gell) U. BA, U. Oxford, 1950, MA, 1951, Yale U., 1952; B.Litt., U. Oxford, 1953; D.Litt. hon., U. of South, 1981. Asst. prof. U. of South, Sewanee, Tenn., 1953-58, assoc. prof., 1958-62; then assoc. prof. U. Va., Charlottesville, 1962-68; prof. Brown U., Providence, 1968-85, Munro-Goodwin Wilkinson prof., 1978-85; vis. prof. Yale U., New Haven, 1979, prof., 1986-94, George Burton Adams prof., 1994-96, emeritus, from 1996. Dir. Yale Ctr. Parliamentary History, 1985-96; vis. Mellon prof. Inst. for Advanced Study, 1988-89; vis. fellow All Souls Coll., Oxford, 1992; Ford's lectr. Oxford U., 1992. Author: Royalist Conspiracy in England, 1960, Pride's Purge, 1971, Somerset in the Civil War and Interregnum, 1973, Revel, Riot and Rebellion, 1985, Fire from Heaven, 1992, A Freeborn People, 1996, Start of Play, 2000. Guggenheim fellow, 1964-65, 91-92, fellow Am. Coun. Learned Socs., 1973-74, NEH fellow, 1980-81. Fellow Royal Hist. Soc., Brit. Acad. (corrs.); mem. Am. Hist. Assn. (award for scholarly distinction 2005), Conf. Brit. Studies. Died Sept. 26, 2009.

UNDERWOOD, WILLIAM FLEMING, JR., lawyer; b. Atlanta, Oct. 29, 1944; s. William Fleming and Montine (Smith) Underwood; m. Brenda Marsha Fricks, Jan. 8, 1971; children: Charlotte Ashley, William Fleming III. AA, Ga. Mil. Coll., 1964; ABJ, U. Ga., 1967; LLB, John Marshall Law Sch., 1974. Bar: Ga. 1975, Ga. (U.S. Dist. Ct. (mid. dist.)) 1975, (U.S. Ct. Appeals (5th cir.)) 1975, (U.S. Ct. Appeals (11th cir.)) 1981, (U.S. Supreme Ct.) 1981. Sole practice, Albany, Ga., from 1975; mem. Dougherty County Bd. Commrs., Albany, 1979. 1st lt. US Army, 1967—69. Recipient Disting. Service Life Dynamic Essentials. Dr. Sid Williams, Disting. Service award, Life Dynamic Essentials. Dr. Sid Williams, 1981. Fellow: Ga. Bar Found.; mem.: Assn. Trial Lawyers Am., S.W. Ga. Trial Lawyers Assn., Ga. Trial Lawyers Assn., Ga. Bar Assn., Ga. Assn. Criminal Def. Lawyers, ABA. Democrat. Episcopalian. Died July 22, 2010.

UNGAR, CAROLE WILSON, public relations executive; b. Bklyn., Nov. 7, 1933; d. Morris and Frances (Michaelson) Beckerman; m. Lloyd Diehl Wilson, July 3, 1952 (div. 1965); m. Benjamin Andrew Ungar, Aug. 15, 1972; 1 child, Kimberly Jo Wilson Figueroa. BFA, U. Cin., 1991. Weather girl WNHC-TV, New Haven, 1962-64; actress various orgns., NYC, 1965-72; anchor WLWT-TV, Cin., 1973-86; sr. acct. exec. Judith Bogart Assocs., Cin., 1986-90; pres./owner Carole Wilson Pub. Rels., Inc., Cin., from 1991. Prodr., writer TV documentaries Battered Women, 1979, Women on the Move, 1979; TV program Women USA!, 1980. Bd. dirs. Alice Paul House for Battered Women, Cin., 1980, YWCA, 1978-81; chmn. Career Women of Achievement Project, 1981. Recipient Walter Bartlett award Multimedia Broadcasting, 1989. Mem. Pub. Rels. Soc. Am. (Prism award, Cin. chpt. 1992), Women in Comm. (named Outstanding Woman in Comm., Cin. chpt. 1980). Republican. Avocations: ballet, swimming, theater, symphony, piano. Died Jan. 20, 2009.

UNGER, PAUL A., packaging and international affairs specialist; b. San Diego, Sept. 10, 1914; s. Louis A. and Ray (Seidman) U.; m. Sonja Franz, Jan. 2, 1947; children: Alan, Gerald, Tamara Unger-Hyman. AB, Harvard U., 1936. With pub. rels. dept. Works Progress Adminstrn., Washington, 1936-39; with community rels. Dept. U.S. Housing Authority, Washington, 1939-44; relief adminstr. UN Relief and Rehab. Adminstrn., Egypt and Yugoslavia, 1944-47; deputy asst. sec. U.S. Dept. of Interior, Washington, 1947-50, internat. specialist, 1950-53; devel. mgr. The Unger Co., Cleve., 1953-57, pres., 1957-62, 64-88, chmn., 1988-93; sr. advisor, from 1994, The Unger Co., Cleve., from 1994; dep. adminstr. U.S. Dept. Commerce, Washington, 1962-63. Mem. U.S. com. Internat. .Coun. on Social Welfare; organizer, leader tours to Yugoslavia, Hungary, Austria, Czechoslovakia, East Germany, Poland, USSR, China; leader trade mission to Australia and New Zealand U.S. Dept. of Commerce; mem. U.S. Trade Agreements Com.; U.S. del. GATT Trade Negotiations Confs. Pres. Coun. Internat. Programs; chmn. Cleve. adv. subcom. U.S. Commn. on Civil Rights; chmn. Mayor's Urban Renewal Task Force, Presdl. Campaign Coms. for No. Ohio (chmn.), Gov.'s Internat. Trade Coun.; chmn. Unger Croatia Inst. Pub. Adminstrn. Kennedy Sch. Govt., Harvard U., The Unger Croatia Ctr., Cleve. State U. Recipient Recognition award Rotary, 1974, Neighborhood Ctrs. Assn., 1978, Internat. Exch. award Coun. Internat. Programs, 1985, Outstanding Citizen Achievement award U.S. AID, 2004; inductee Hall of Fame City Club of Cleve., 1995, Cleveland Heights H.S. Hall of Fame, 1997. Mem. City Club (trustee 1972-75, v.p. 1975), Forum Found. (pres. 1988-91), Cleve. Coun. on World Affairs (program chmn., v.p., mem. exec. com.), English Speaking Union (past pres. Cleve. br., nat. v.p.), Cleve. Skating Club, Cleve. Playhouse Club, Cleve. Blue Book. Home: Cleveland, Ohio. Died Jan. 23, 2009.

UNNEWEHR, LEWIS EMORY, electrical engineer; b. Berea, Ohio, Sept. 27, 1925; s. Emory Carl and Ivy May (Lewis) Unnewehr; m. L. Jean Affleck, Aug. 22, 1948; children: David, Laura, Janet, Chris. BSEE, Purdue U., 1946; MSEE, U. Notre Dame, 1952. Assoc. prof. Valparaiso U., Ind., 1949—55; rsch. engr. Franklin Inst., Phila., 1955—57; assoc. prof. Villanova U., Pa., 1957—61; sr. design engr. Garrett Corp., LA, 1961—66; mem. rsch. staff Ford Motor Co., Dearborn, Mich., 1966—81; dir. rsch. and devel. Lima Energy Products, Ohio, 1981—84; dir. advanced electronics dept. Allied Automotive Tech. Ctr., Troy, Mich., 1984—87; mgr. new motor technology Sullair Corp., Mich. City, Ind., from 1987. Co-author (with S.A. Nasar): Electromechanics and Electric Machines, 1979, Electric Vehicle Technology, 1982, Introduction to Electrical Engineering, 1986, Permanent Magnet, Reluctance and Self-Synchronous Motors, 1991; contbr. articles to profl. jours. Fellow: IEEE (vice-chmn. electronics transformer tech. com.); mem.: Optimists Lodge, Elks Lodge, Sigma Xi. Democrat. Presbyterian. Home: Bowie, Md. Died May 19, 2009.

URSICH, DONALD WEAVER, clergyman, marriage and family counselor, drug and alcohol counselor; b. Morgantown, W.Va., Mar. 24, 1939; s. Charles and Freda Marie (Weaver) U.; m. Barbara Christina Neeser, Sept. 22, 1962; children: Christine, Sarena. BA, Southeastern Coll., 1968; MDiv, Interdenominational Theol. Ctr., 1971; MEd, Boston U., 1979; MA in Edn., East Carolina U., 1980. Cert. alcoholism counselor, N.C.; cert. marriage and family therapist, N.C.; registered practicing counselor, N.C. Ordained to ministry United Ch. of Christ, 1981; officer Salvation Army, 1958-81; pvt. practice marriage and family counselor, Fayetteville, N.C., 1979—; drug and alcohol counselor U.S. Army, Ft. Bragg, N.C., 1981—; lectr. and cons. in field. Bd. dirs. Mental Health Assn. Cumberland County (N.C.); asst. dist. commr. Occoneechee council Boy Scouts Am. Served as chaplain U.S. Army, 1971-79. Decorated Commendation medal. Mem. Nat. Alliance for Family Life, Am. Assn. Marriage and Family Therapy, Am. Assn. Counseling and Devel., Nat. Acad. Counselors and Therapists, Am. Group Psychotherapy Assn. Republican. Lodges: Masons, Shriners. Home: Fayetteville, NC. Died Jan. 8, 2009.

USDIN, GENE LEONARD, psychiatrist; b. NYC, Jan. 31, 1922; s. I. L. and Eva (Miller) U.; m. Cecile Weil, Nov. 8, 1947; children: Cecile Catherine Burka, Linda Ann, Steven William, Thomas Michael. Student, U. N.C., 1939—40, U. Fla., 1940—41; BS, Tulane U., 1943, MD, 1946. Diplomate Am. Bd. Psychiatry and Neurology (asst. examiner, 1956-80), Am. Bd. Legal Medicine. Intern Touro Infirmary, New Orleans, 1946—47; resident psychiatry Cin. Gen. Hosp., 1949—51; fellow psychiatry Tulane Sch. Medicine, 1951—52; pvt. practice psychiatry New Orleans, 1952—86; pvt practice psychiatry, from 1996; asst. prof. clin. psychiatry Tulane U., 1959—62, assoc. clin. prof., 1962—67, La. State U., 1967—71, clin. prof., 1971—96, clin. prof. emeritus, from 1996; sr. psychiatrist Ochsner Clinic, 1986-96, sr. psychiatrist emeritus, from 1996; prof. Notre Dame Sem., 1969-75; chief divsn. neurology and psychiatry Touro Infirmary, New Orleans, 1962—66, dir. psychiat. svcs., 1966—71. McLaughlin-Gallie vis. prof. Royal Coll. Physicians and Surgeons of Can., 1983; Robert O. Jones lectr. Atlantic Maritime Provinces Psychiat. Assn. (Can.), 1976; sr. psychiatrist DePaul and Charity Hosps.; sr. psychiat. cons. Ochsner Med. Found., New Orleans, 1980-85, Timberlawn Psychiat. Hosp., Dallas, 1979-93; chmn. psychiat. cons. com. Am. Bar Found., 1970-73; mem. nat. psychiat. adv. bd. Achievement and Guidance Ctrs. Am., Inc., 1991-92. Editor-in-chief Psychiatry Digest, 1964—71, 1975—79, ACP-Psychiat. Update, 1980—94, Psychiatry Digest (Europe), 1981—92, ACP-Psychiat. Update, 1995—96, 2000—04, co-editor, 1994—95; editor: Psychoneurosis and Schizophrenia, 1966, Practical Lectures in Psychiatry for the Medical Practitioner, 1966, Adolescence: Care and Counseling, 1967; editor: (with Peter A. Martin and A.W. Swipe) A Physician in the General Practice of Psychiatry, 1970; editor: Perspectives on Violence, 1972, The Psychiatric Forum, 1973, Psychiatry: Education and Image, 1973, Sleep Research and Clinical Practice, 1973, Overview of the Psychotherapies, 1975, Psychiatric Medicine, 1977, Depression: Clinical, Biological and Psychological Perspectives, 1977, Schizophrenia: Biological and Psychological Perspective, 1978; editor: (with Charles K. Hofling) Aging: The Process and the People, 1978; editor: (with Jerry M. Lewis II) Psychiatry in General Medical Practice, 1979; editor: (with David R. Hawkins) The Office Guide to Sleep Disorders, 1980; editor: Medilex Digest of Psychiatry, 1980—92; editor: (with Jerry M. Lewis) Treatment Planning in Psychiatry, 1982; mem. editl. bd. Clin. Medicine, 1965—71, 1975—88, Med. Digest, 1965—71, Mental Hygiene, 1969—76, Jour. Hosp. and Cmty. Psychiatry, 1975, chmn., 1980—81, mem. editl. bd. Jour. Psychiat. Edn., 1975—89, Psychiatry Bookshelf, 1976—78, Jour. Ottawa Med. Sch., 1976—90, Am. Jour. Family Therapy, 1978—92, Am. Jour. Social Psychiatry, 1981—87, Swiss Med. Digest, Psychiatry, 1981—92, Extracta Medica Practica Psychiatrie, 1981—92, Behavioral Scis. and the Law, 1982—92, Dynamic Psychotherapy, 1982—90, Psychiat. Medicine, 1982—88, 1982—88, Women's Psychiat. Health, 1982—94, Advances in Therapy, 1983—96, Clin. Psychiatry News, 1983—92, Contemporary Psychiatry, 1984—93, The Psychiat. Times, from 1985, book rev. editor, 1988—2002, Health Disease, 1986—93, Clin. Advances in Treatment of Psychiat. Disorders, 1987—93, Acad. Psychiatry, 1989—92, mem. internat. adv. bd. Jour. Psicopatologia, Madrid, 1989—94; contbr. articles to profl. jours. Bd. trustees United Fund Greater New Orleans, 1966-70. Served to lt. (j.g.) USNR, 1947-49. Recipient Physician of Yr. award Orleans Parish Med. Soc., 1984, Outstanding Alumni Lectr. award Tulane U. Sch. Medicine, 1986, Seymour Pollack Disting. Svc. award Am. Acad. Psychiatry and the Law, 1988, Outstanding Contbrn. to Social Psychiatry award Am. Assn. for Social Psychiatry, 1993, Lifetime Achievement awards Tulane Med. Alumni Assn., 1996, Fla. Hosp. Ctr. for Psychiatry, 1996, La. State U. Sch. Medicine Dept. Psychiatry Chmn.'s award, 1998-99, Champion of Pub. Health award Tulane U. Sch. Pub. Health and Tropical Medicine, 2001, Outstanding Contributions award Tulane Univ. Med. Sch., 2005; named Psychiatrist of Yr., La. Psychiat. Med. Assn., 1994, Psychiat. Times, 1997. Fellow Am. Psychiat. Assn. (chmn. com. on psychiatry and law 1964-68, mem. com. on ethics 1970-74, com. on membership 1970-74, com. on evaluation svcs. bd. 1974-77, com. on pub. affairs 1976-78, chmn. ad hoc com. on election procedures, 1980-81, trustee at large 1978-81, coun. on internat. affairs 1986-91, sec. gen. Interamerican Coun. of Psychiat. Orgns. 1988-91, recipient 3d ann. Certificate of Recognition for Excellence in Med. Student Edn. 1993, Warren Williams award, 1995, Spl. Presdl. commendation 1998), So. Psychiat. Assn. (bd. regents 1969-72, chmn. 1971-72, pres. 1973-74), La. Psychiat. Assn. (past pres.), Am. Coll. Psychiatrists (bd. regents 1967-70, pres. 1978-79, E.B. Bowis award for Outstanding Contbns. 1973, Disting. Svc. award for Oustanding Contbns. in Am. Psychiatry 1980), Acad. Psychosomatic Medicine (mem. exec. coun. 1974-76), New Orleans Soc. Psychiatry and Neurology (past pres.), Group Advancement Psychiatry (bd. dirs. 1970-77, treas. 1973-77), Am. Assn. Social Psychiatry (pres. 1986-88), World Assn. for Social Psychiatry (exec. coun. 1988-90); mem. La. Med. Soc. (chmn. com. on mental health 1966-70), Orleans Parish Med. Soc., Nat. Assn. Mental Health (mem. profl. adv. coun. 1968-75), Inst. of Mental Hygiene (pres. 1978-79). Died May 9, 2009.

VACCA, MICHAEL THOMAS, investment company executive; b. Jersey City, Oct. 15, 1925; s. Michael Alphonse and Mary (Petrizzo) V.; m. Filomena Elizabeth Testa, Sept. 28 (dec. May 1, 1974); children: Michael Alphonse, David Michael; m.2nd Kathleen Theresa Ruane, Oct. 31, 1976; children: Patricia Ann, Martin Alphonse. BS in Acctg., NYU, 1954. Acct. Barrow Wade & Guthrie, NYC, 1944-49, Peat Marwick & Mitchell, NYC, 1950-58; with E.F. Hutton& Co., Inc., NYC, from 1959; v.p. E.F. Hutton & Co., Inc., NYC, from 1968. Treas. Cash Res. Mgmt. Co., N.Y.C., 1980—, Mcpl. Cash Res. Mgmt. Co., N.Y.C., 1980—, Hutton Govt. Fund, 1980—, Hutton AMA Fund, 1980— Mem. Middletown Republican Com., N.J., 1983—. Served with U.S. Army, 1949-51. Mem.: Downtown Athletic (N.Y.C.); Italian Am. (Middletown), KC. Republican. Roman Catholic. Home: Middletown, NJ. Died Dec. 6, 2009.

VACHÉ, CLAUDE CHARLES, retired bishop; b. New Bern, NC, Aug. 4, 1926; s. Jean Andre and Edith Virginia (Fitzwilson) V. BA, U. N.C., 1949; M.Div., Seabury-Western Theol. Sem., Evanston, Ill., 1952, D.D. (hon.), 1976, Va. Theol. Sem., 1977, St. Paul's Coll., Lawrenceville, Va., 1977. Ordained to ministry Episcopal Ch. as deacon, 1952, as priest, 1953. Min.-in-charge St. Michael's Ch., Bon Air, Va., 1952-54, rector, 1955-57; chaplain St. Christopher's Sch., Richmond, Va., 1953-56; rector Trinity Ch., Portsmouth, Va., 1957-76; bishop coadjutor Diocese of So. Va., Norfolk, 1976-78, bishop, 1978-91, chmn. ch. deployment bd., 1984-91; mem. com. on pastoral devel., from 1976; mem. standing commn. on ecumenical relations, 1982-85; mem. standing commn. on constns. and canons, 1986-91; chaplain St. George's Coll., Jerusalem, 1992. Home: Portsmouth, Va. Died Nov. 1, 2009.

VAGO, STEVEN, sociology educator, consultant, writer; b. Debrecen, Hungary, June 12, 1937; came to U.S., 1957; s. Joseph and Ibolya (Halasz) V.; m. Kathe Hartley, Feb. 14, 1975. BA, U. Ala., 1961; MA, Wash. U., 1963, PhD, 1967. Prof. St. Louis U., from 1967, dept. chair, 1973-81. Program specialist UNESCO, Paris, 1970-73, cons., 1974—; cons. Hungarian Govt., 1987—, St. Louis, 1980—. Author: Law and Society, 5th edit., 1997, Social Change, 3d edit., 1996. Mem. Am. Sociol. Assn., Am. Population Assn., Internat. Sociol. Assn., Law and Soc. Assn., Am. Acad. Arts and Scis. Republican. Avocations: oenology, chess, swimming long distance. Home: Saint Louis, Mo. Died June 30, 2010.

VALINCY, THOMAS DERRICK, other: manufacturing; b. Cleve., Jan. 17, 1951; BA, Kent State U., 1975. Fin. cons., Cleve., 1970—77; mfg. analyst NCR, Cleve., 1977—79, Sperry Univac, Cleve., 1980—82; strategy analyst Hoover Co., Canton, Ohio, from 1983; pres. Productivity II, Cleve., from 1982, lectr. Author: A Practitioner's Guide to Production and Inventory Control, 1983. Recipient Man of Yr. award, Am. Prodn. and Inventory Control Soc., 1981, 1982. Mem.: Inst. Indsl. Engrs. (dir. from 1982), Am. Prodn. and Inventory Control Soc. (exec. v.p. 1982, pres. 1983—84), Aquamarine Club. Roman Catholic. Home: Willoughby, Ohio. Died Mar. 15, 2010.

VALLEE, BERT LESTER, biochemist, physician, educator; b. Hemer, Westphalia, Germany, June 1, 1919; came to U.S., 1938, naturalized, 1948; s. Joseph and Rosa (Kronenberger) V.; m. Natalie T. Kugris, May 29, 1947. ScB, U. Berne, Switzerland, 1938; MD, NYU, 1943; AM (hon.), Harvard, 1960; MD (hon.), Karolinska Institutet, Stockholm, Sweden, 1987; Prof. (hon.), Tsinghua U., Beijing, 1987; DSc (hon.), Naples, Italy, 1991; PhD in Chemistry (hon.), Ludwig-Maximilians U., Munich, 1995; Prof. (hon.), Stellenbosch U., South Africa, 1995. Rsch. fellow Harvard Med. Sch., Boston, 1946-49, rsch. assoc., 1949-51, assoc., 1951-56, asst. prof. medicine, 1956-60, assoc. prof., 1960-64, prof. biol. chemistry, 1964-65, Paul C. Cabot prof. biol. chemistry, 1965-80, Paul C. Cabot prof. emeritus, biochem. scis., from 1980, Disting. Sr. prof. biochem. scis., 1989-90, Edgar M. Bronfman Disting. sr. prof., from 1990; rsch. assoc. dept. biology MIT, Cambridge, from 1948; physician Peter Bent Brigham Hosp., Boston, 1961-80; biochemist-in-chief Brigham & Women's Hosp., Boston, 1980-89, emeritus, from 1989; prof. (hon.) Shanghai Inst. Biochemistry Chinese Acad. of Scis., 1997. Sci. dir. Biophysics Rsch. Lab., Harvard Med. Sch., Peter Bent Brigham Hosp., 1954-80; head Ctr. for Biochem. and Biophys. Scis. and Medicine, Harvard Med. Sch. and Brigham & Women's Hosp., 1980—; Messenger lectr. Cornell U., 1988. Author 9 books; contbr. articles and chpts. to sci. publs. Founder, trustee Boston Biophysics Research Found., 1957—; founder, pres. Endowment for Research in Human Biology, Inc., 1980—. Recipient Warner-Chilcott award, 1969, Buchman Meml. award Calif. Inst. Tech., 1976; Linderstøm-Lang award and gold medal, 1980; Willard Gibbs Medal award, 1981, William C. Rose award in biochemistry, 1982, Order Andres Bello First Class of Republic of Venezuela, Raulin award, ISTERH, Venezuela, 2002. Fellow NAS, AAAS, Am. Acad. Arts and Scis., N.Y. Acad. Scis.; mem. Am. Soc. Biol. Chemists, Am. Chem. Soc. (Willard Gibbs gold medal 1981), Optical Soc. Am., Biophys. Soc., Swiss Biochem. Soc. (hon. fgn. mem.), Royal Danish Acad. Scis. and Letters, Japan Soc. for Analytical Chemistry (hon.), Alpha Omega Alpha. Home: Boston, Mass. Died May 7, 2010.

VAN BLARCOM, DONALD BOGERT, manufacturing executive; b. Fall River, Mass., Jan. 31, 1929; s. James Smith Payne and Alice Mae (Ainlay) Van B.; m. Loraine Guin, Nov. 21, 1953; children: Karen, Susan, Roger. BS in Adminstrv. Engring., Lafayette Coll., 1952. Sales rep. Ingersoll-Rand Co., Birmingham, Ala., 1952—53; indsl. engr. Reynolds Metals Co., Sheffield, Ala., 1955—59; sales rep. Davidson Equipment Inc., Nashville, 1960—66, v.p. ops., 1971—83; pres., chmn. bd. Armstrong Equipment Co., Birmingham, 1966—67; mgr. Liftruck div. Thompson Tractor Co., Birmingham, 1967—71. Bd. dirs. Middle Tenn. Christian Ctr., Middle Tenn. State U., Murfreesboro, from 1980. With US Army, 1953—55. Mem.: Am. Soc. Profl. Cons., Nashville Equipment Distbrs. Assn. (pres. 1977), Md. Farms Racquet and Country Club (Brentwood, Tenn.). Republican. Ch. Of Christ. Died Nov. 8, 2009.

VANDE HEY, JAMES MICHAEL, retired air force officer; b. Maribel, Wis., Mar. 15, 1916; s. William Henry and Anna (Zimmerman) VandeH.; m. Jean Margretta Schilleman, June 23, 1944; children: James Todd, Dale Michael, Dean Clark. Student, U. Wis., 1947-49; BA, U. Philippines, 1955; post-grad., Air War Coll., Maxwell AFB, Montgomery, Ala., 1956-57. Commd. 2d lt. USAAF, 1941; advanced through grades to brig. gen. USAF, 1967; fighter pilot PTO, 1941-45; including Hawaii, Dec. 7, 1941; duty in command and USAF level including duty in Europe (NATO) and Philippines, 1945-69; dep. chief of staff Hdqrs. USMACV, Saigon, Vietnam, 1969-71; assigned Hdqrs. Tactical Air Command, from 1971; mem. faculty Air War Coll., 1957-59, dep. for acads., dean of faculty, 1959-61; ret., 1971; pres. Vanson Inc., from 1971, Vande Hey Inc., from 1976. Decorated D.S.M., Legion of Merit with two oak leaf clusters, D.F.C. with two oak leaf clusters, Bronze Star, Air medal with 7 oak leaf clusters, decorations from Philippine, Vietnamese and Korean govts. Mem. USAF Hist. Found., Air Force Assn., Pearl Harbor Survivors Assn., Iwo Jima Survivors Assn. Roman Catholic. Home: Schertz, Tex. Died Dec. 21, 2009.

VAN DER MARCK, JAN, art historian; b. Roermond, The Netherlands, Aug. 19, 1929; arrived in U.S., 1957; s. Everard and Anny (Finken) van der Marck; m. Ingeborg Lachmann, Apr. 27, 1961 (dec. 1988); m. Sheila Stamell, May 24, 1990. BA, U. Nijmegen, The Netherlands, 1952, MA, 1954, PhD in Art History, 1956; postgrad., U. Utrecht, The Netherlands, 1956-57, Columbia U., NYC, 1957-59. Curator Gemeentemuseum, Arnhem, Netherlands, 1959-61; asst. dir. fine arts Seattle World's Fair, 1961-62; curator Walker Art Ctr., Mpls., 1963-67; dir. Mus. Contemporary Art, Chgo., 1967-70; assoc. prof. art history U. Wash., Seattle, 1972-74; dir. Dartmouth Coll. Mus. and Galleries, 1974-80, Ctr. for Fine Arts, Miami, 1980-85; curator 20th century art, chief curator Detroit Inst. Arts, 1986-95. Author: (book) Romantische Boekillustratie in Belgie, 1956, Enrico Baj, 1969, Lucio Fontana, 1974, George Segal, 1975, Arman, 1984, Bernar Venet, 1988, The Art of Contemporary Bookbinding, 1997, Art and the American Experience, 1998, Lucio Pozzi, 2001, Jef Bourgeau: A User's Manual, 2007; contbr. articles to art jours., essays to catalogues. Decorated officer Order Arts and Letters, knight Order of Orange Nassau; fellow Netherlands Orgn. Pure Rsch., 1954—55, Rockefeller Found., 1957—59, Aspen Inst., 1974, 1994, Ctr. Advanced Study in Visual Arts, Nat. Gallery, Washington, 1986. Mem.: Les Amis de la Reliure Originale (Paris), Bibliotheca Wittockiana (Brussels). Home: Huntington Woods, Mich. Died Apr. 26, 2010.

VANDER VOORT, DALE GILBERT, textile company executive; b. Paterson, NJ, Feb. 7, 1924; s. Gilbert H. and Lillian (Hatton) Vander V.; m. Florine E. Storey, Aug. 6, 1944 (dec.); children: Lydia Ann, Dale Gilbert, Roy Lee. B.M.E., Clemson U., 1944. Gen. mgr., dir. Stevens Linen Assos.,

Webster, Mass., 1954-56; gen. mgr. Montreal Cottons Ltd., Valleyfield, Que., Canada, 1951-54; supt. Mill 4 Dan River Mills, Danville, Va., 1946-51; sr. v.p. United Merchants & Mfrs. Inc., NYC, 1972-77; chmn. bd. Asso. Textiles Can. Ltd., 1969-77; pres., chief exec. officer Arnold Print Works, Inc., Adams, Mass., 1977-83, Alton Fabrics, Allentown, Pa., 1983-85; pres. Asheville Dye & Finishing, Swannanoa, NC, 1985-87; pres., chief exec. officer River Dyeing and Finishing Co., Asheville, NC, from 1988. Dir. Northwestern Bank, Asheville, N.C., Western Carolina Industries Inc., Brit. Silk Dyeing Co., Valchem Australia, Profile Sports Corp., West Lebanon, N.H. Mem. coun. Luth. Ch., 1962—. Lt. AUS, 1943-46. Decorated Bronze Star, Purple Heart. Mem. ASME, Am. Assn. Textile Chemists and Colorists, Can. Textile Inst. (dir.), Soc. Advancement of Mgmt. (nat. gov. 1961-62), Can. Club (N.Y.), Asheville Country Club. Home: Asheville, NC. Died Sept. 21, 2009.

VAN DYK, JOHN WILLIAM, retired chemist; b. Paterson, N.J., May 2, 1928; s. Andrew and Ida (Zuidema) Van D.; m. Audrey Ann DeVries, May 29, 1951; children— Mark DeVries, Drew Emerson, Dirk Martin. B.A., Rutgers U., 1950; M.A., Columbia U., 1951, Ph.D., 1954. Research chemist E.I. DuPont de Nemours & Co., Wilmington, Del., 1954-66, staff chemist, 1966-82, research assoc., Phila., 1982-85; ret., 1985; cons. to industry. Boese fellow, 1952. Mem. Am. Chem. Soc., Phi Beta Kappa, Sigma Xi. Republican. Presbyterian. Home: Wilmington, Del. Died Jan. 10, 2010.

VAN DYKE, MILTON DENMAN, retired aeronautical engineering educator; b. Chgo., Aug. 1, 1922; s. James Richard and Ruth (Barr) Van D.; m. Sylvia Jean Agard Adams, June 16, 1962; children: Russell B., Eric J., Nina A., Brooke A. and Byron J. and Christopher M. (triplets). BS, Harvard U., 1943; MS, Calif. Inst. Tech., 1947, PhD, 1949. Research engr. NACA, 1943-46, 50-54, 55-58; vis. prof. U. Paris, France, 1958- 59; prof. mechanical engring., aeronautics & astronautics Stanford U., 1959—82, prof. emeritus, 1992—2010. Pres. Parabolic Press. Author: Perturbation Methods in Fluid Mechanics, 1964, An Album of Fluid Motion, 1982; editor: Ann. Rev. Fluid Mechanics, 1969-99. Trustee Soc. For Promotion of Sci. and Scholarship, Inc. Served with USNR, 1944-46. Guggenheim and Fulbright fellow, 1954-55 Mem. Am. Acad. Arts and Scis., Nat. Acad. Engring., Am. Phys. Soc., Phi Beta Kappa, Sigma Xi, Sierra Club. Home: Stanford, Calif. Died May 10, 2010.

VANE, SYLVIA BRAKKE, anthropologist, writer; b. Fillmore County, Minn., Feb. 28, 1918; d. John T. and Hulda Christina Brakke.; m. Arthur Bayard Vane, May 17, 1942; children: Ronald Arthur, Linda, Laura Vane Ames. AA, Rochester Jr. Coll., 1937; BS with distinction, U. Minn., Mpls., 1939; postgrad, Radcliffe Coll., Cambridge, Mass., 1944; MA, Calif. State U., Hayward, 1975. Med. technologist Dr. Frost and Hodapp, Willmar, Minn., 1939-41; head labs. Corvallis Gen. Hosp., Oreg., 1941-42; dir. lab. Cambridge Gen. Hosp., 1942-43; staff Peninsula Clinic, Redwood City, Calif., 1947-49; v.p. Cultural Systems Rsch. Inc., Menlo Park, Calif., from 1978; pres. Ballena Press, 1981—2005. Cons. cultural resource mgmt. So. Calif. Edison Co., Rosemead, 1978-81, San Diego Gas and Elec. Co., 1980-83, Pacific Gas and Elec. Co., San Francisco, 1982-83, Wender, Murase & White, Washington, 1983-87, Yosemite Indians, Mariposa, Calif., 1982-91, San Luis Rey Band of Mission Indians, Escondido, Calif., 1986-89, US Ecology, Newport Beach, Calif., 1986-89, Riverside County Flood Control and Water Conservation Dist., 1985-95, Infotec, Inc., 1989-91, Alexander & Karshmer, Berkeley, Calif., 1989-92, Desert Water Agy., Palm Springs, Calif., 1989-90, Met. Water Dist., 1992-2001, Nat. Park Svc., 1992-2001, Applied Earthworks, Inc., 1997-2001, NW Econ. Assocs., 2002-2004, County of Riverside, 2002-03, Aqua Caliente Cultural Mus., 2005—; bd. dirs. XEI Scientific. Author: (with L.J. Bean), California Indians, Primary Resources, 1977, rev. edit., 1990, The Cahuilla and the Santa Rosa Mountains, 1981, The Cahuilla Landscape, 1991, Ethnology of the Alta California Indians, vol. I Pre Contact, vol. II Post Contact, 1992, Spanish Borderlands Sourcebooks, vols. 3, 4; contbr. chpts. to books. Bd. dir. Sequoia Area coun. Girl Scouts US, 1954-61; bd. dirs., v.p., pres. LWV, South San Mateo County, Calif., 1960-65. Recipient Lifetime Achievement award, Calif. Indian Conf., 2005. Fellow Soc. Applied Anthropology, Am. Anthropology Assn.; mem. Southwestern Anthropology Assn. (prog. chmn. 1976-78, newsletter editor 1976-79), Soc. for Am. Archaeology, Soc. Calif. Archaeology (Martin A. Baumhoff Spl. Achievement award 1998). Mem. United Ch. of Christ. Home: Menlo Park, Calif. Died July 14, 2009.

VAN FOSSEN, LARRY JACK, other: service; b. Sidney, Ohio, Sept. 27, 1937; s. Carl Anderson and Bessie Lena (Laws) Van F.; m. Emily Jane Brockmann, Oct. 14, 1961; children: Elizabeth, William. BBA, U. Cin., 1960; JD summa cum laude, Ohio State U., 1963. Bar: Ohio 1963. Mem. firm Porter, Wright, Morris & Arthur, Columbus, Ohio, 1965—74; chmn., pres., CEO Chem. Lawn Corp., Columbus, 1974—88; pres. Nessoff Corp., Columbus; pres., CEO, bd. dirs. Red Roof Inns Inc.; bd. dirs. Cardinal Distbn. Inc., Famous-Frat. Sportswear, Inc. Trustee Paul G. Duke Found.; mem. nat. coun. Coll. Law, Ohio State U., from 1980. Capt. US Army, 1963—65. Mem.: Ohio Bar Assn., ABA, Worthington Hills Country Club, The Golf Club. Republican. Home: Powell, Ohio. Died May 31, 2009.

VAN TAMELEN, EUGENE EARLE, chemist, educator; b. Zeeland, Mich., July 20, 1925; s. Gerrit and Henrietta (Vanden Bosch) van T.; m. Mary Ruth Houtman, June 16, 1951; children: Jane Elizabeth, Carey Catherine, Peter Gerrit. AB, Hope Coll., 1947, D.Sc., 1970; MS, Harvard, 1949, PhD, 1950; D.Sc., Bucknell U., 1970. Instr. U. Wis., 1950-52, from asst. to asso. prof., 1952-59, prof., 1959-61, Homer Adkins prof. chemistry, 1961-62; prof. chemistry Stanford U., 1962-87, prof. emeritus chemistry, 1987—2009, chmn. chemistry dept., 1974-78. Am.-Swiss Found. lectr., 1964 Mem. editorial adv. bd.: Chem. and Engring. News, 1968-70, Synthesis, 1969-91, Accounts of Chem. Research, 1970-73; editor: Bioorganic Chemistry, 1971-82. Recipient A.T. Godfrey award, 1947; G. Haight traveling fellow, 1957; Guggenheim fellow, 1965, 73; Leo Hendrik Baekeland award, 1965; Prof. Extraordinarius Netherlands, 1967-73 Mem. NAS, Am. Chem. Soc. (Pure Chemistry award 1961, Creative Work in Synthetic Organic Chemistry award 1970), Am. Acad. Arts and Scis., English-Speaking Union (patron 1990-92), Rolls Royce Owners Club (bd. dirs. 1996-2009), Churchill Club (bd. dirs. 1990-92, vice chmn. 1991-92), Los Altos Tomorrow (bd. dirs. 1991-96). Home: Los Altos Hills, Calif. Died Dec. 12, 2009.

VAN VALEN, LEIGH, biologist, educator; b. Albany, NY, Aug. 12, 1935; s. A. Donald and Eleanor (Williams) Van V.; m. Phebe May Hoff, 1959 (div. 1984); children: Katrina, Diana (dec. 1995); m. Virginia C. Maiorana, 1974. BA, Miami U., Ohio, 1956; MA, Columbia U., 1957, PhD, 1961. Boese fellow Columbia U., NYC, 1961-62; NATO and NIH fellow Univ. Coll. London, 1962-63; rsch. fellow Am. Mus. Natural History, NYC, 1963-66; asst. prof. anatomy U. Chgo., 1967-71, assoc. prof. evolutionary biology & conceptual founds. sci., 1971-73, assoc. prof. biology & conceptual founds. of sci., 1973-76, prof. biology and conceptual founds. of sci., 1976-88, prof. ecology, evolution, conceptual founds. sci., 1988—2010; rsch. assoc. dept. geology Field Mus., Chgo., 1971—2010. Author: Deltatheridia, A New Order of Mammals, 1966, Paleocene Dinosaurs or Cretaceous Ungulates in South America?, 1988, The Origin of the Plesiadapid Primates and the Nature of Purgatorius, 1994; editor: Evolutionary Theory, Evolutionary Monographs; mem. editl. bd. Jour. Molecular Evolution, 1970-76, Evolución Biológica; mem. editl. bd. commentators Behavioral and Brain Scis.; assoc. editor Evolution, 1969-71. Nat. adv. bd. Voice of Reason, N.Y. NIH Rsch. Career Devel. award, 1967-72; NSF grantee, 1963-71. Mem. AAUP (pres. U. Chgo. chpt.), Soc. Study Evolution (v.p. 1973, 80), American Soc. Naturalists (v.p. 1974-75), Paleontl. Soc. (councillor 1980-82), Internat. Soc. Cryptozoology (bd. dirs.), Ecol. Soc. Am. Home: Chicago, Ill. Died Oct. 16, 2010.

VAN VYVEN, DALE NULSEN, state legislator; b. Cin., Apr. 20, 1935; s. Richard J. and Vera Nulsen Bennett (Plue) Va V.; m. Anne Saterfield, 1952; children: Pamela S. Van Vyven Seils, Stacey C. Van Vyven Petitt, Margo B. Van Vyven Johnson, Eric; m. Meredith A. Irwin; 1 child, Stuard D. Student, U. Cin., 1953-66. Packaging engr. Avco Corp., Cin., 1955-66; ins. agt. Dale N. Van Vyven, Sharonville, 1967—2004, cons., from 2004; clk. of coun. Sharonville, Ohio, 1964-65; councilman at large, 1966-75; pres. of coun. Sharonville, Ohio, 1975-78; Ohio state rep. Dist. 32, 1978—2000. Del. Rep. Nat. Conv., 1980; chmn. United Conservatives of Ohio, ALEC; mem. Ohio Retirement Study Commn., 1995—, chmn., 1996. Mem. pub. affairs com. March of Dimes, pro sr. bd. trustees. Named Outstanding Legislator Ohio, 1984, 94, Outstanding Am Lgis. Exch. Coun. leader, 1989; recipient Ohio Guardian of Small Bus. award Nat. Fedn. Ind. Bus., 1992. Mem. Sharonville C. of C., Nat. Fedn. Ind. Bus., Kiwanis, Jaycees. Home: Sharonville, Ohio. Died Apr. 12, 2010.

VAN WITSEN, LEO, theatrical costume designer; b. The Hague, Netherlands, July 12, 1912; s. Jacques and Rosa (Blok) Van W. Student Royal Acad. Art, the Hague, 1929-31, Acad. de la Grande Chaumiere, Paris, 1932. Staff costume designer Goldovsky Opera Inst., N.Y.C., 1945-85; faculty designer Juilliard Sch. Music, N.Y.C., 1947-57, Berkshire Music Center, Lenox, Mass., 1946-62; head opera dept. Brooks V. Horn Costume Co., N.Y.C., 1958-78; faculty designer Curtis Inst. Music, Phila., 1977-84. Illustrator book: Bringing Soprano Arias to Life, 1973; author: Costuming for Opera, Vol. I, 1981, Vol. II, 1994 (ALA award); translator (from Dutch) The Agony of Fashion, 1980. Mem. United Scenic Artists. Home: New York, NY. Died Feb. 23, 2009.

VAN ZELST, THEODORE WILLIAM, civil engineer, engineering company executive; b. Chgo., May 11, 1923; s. Theodore Walter and Wilhelmina (Oomens) Van Z.; m. Louann Hurter, Dec. 29, 1951; children: Anne, Jean, David. BS, U. Calif., Berkeley, 1944; BS in Naval Sci., Northwestern U., 1944, BAS., 1945, MS in Civil Engring., 1948. Registered profl. engr., Ill. Pres., Soil Testing Services, Inc., Chgo., 1948-52; pres. Soiltest, Inc., Chgo., 1948-78, chmn. bd., 1978-80; sec., dir. Exploration Data Cons., Inc., 1980-82; exec. v.p. Cenco Inc., Chgo., 1962-77, vice chmn., 1975-77, also dir., 1962-77. Bd. dirs. Minann, Inc., Testing Sci., Inc., Van Zelst, Inc.; chmn. bd. dirs. Envirotech Svcs., Inc., 1983-85; sec., bd. dirs. Van Zelst, Inc. Wadsworth, Ill., 1983—; pres. Geneva-Pacific Corp., 1969-83, Geneva Resources, Inc., 1983-91. Treas. Internat. Road Fedn., 1961-64, sec., 1964-79, dir., 1973-88, vice chmn., 1980-87; pres. Internat. Road Edn. Found., 1978-80, 87-88, hon. life bd. dirs., 1988—; bd. dirs. Chgo. Acad. Scis., 1983-86, v.p., 1985-86, hon. dir., 1986-2007; bd. dirs. Pres.'s Assn., Chgo., 1985-86, Friends of Mitchell Mus., 2003-2004; Asian art coun. Art Inst. Chgo., 2004—. Lt. j.g. USNR, 1944—46. Recipient Service award Northwestern U., 1970, Merit award, 1974, Alumni medal, 1989, Svc. award U. Wis., 1971, La Sallian award, 1975; named Disting. Engring. Alumnus, U. Calif., Berkeley, 2002. Mem. ASCE (Chgo. Civil Engr. of Yr., 1988), Nat. Soc. Profl. Engrs., Western Soc. Engrs., Evanston C. of C. (v.p. 1969-73), Ovid Esbach Soc. (pres. 1968-80), Northwestern U. Alumni Assn., Tau Beta Pi, Sigma Xi. Clubs: Economic, North Shore. Achievements include invention of engring. testing equipment for soil, rock, concrete and asphalt; co-invention of Swing-wing for supersonic aircraft. Home: Glenview, Ill. Died July 6, 2009.

VARN, WILFRED CLAUDE, lawyer; b. DeLand, Fla., Mar. 14, 1919; s. Claude Grady and Marjorie Amelia (Boor) Varn; m. Betty Jean Davenport, Nov. 12, 1949; children: Mary Patricia Varn Moore, Wilfred Claude Jr., George Seward. BSBA, U. Fla, 1947, LLB, (reconferred JD 1967), 1948. Bar: Fla. 1948, U.S. Dist. Ct. (no. dist.) Fla. 1948, U.S. Dist. Ct. (mid. dist. and trial bar so. dist.) Fla. 1956, U.S. Ct. Appeals (5th cir.) 1958, U.S. Supreme Ct. 1959, U.S. Ct. Appeals (5th and 11th cirs.), 1981. Ptnr. Spear and Varn, Panama City, Fla., 1948-54; asst. U.S. Atty. Dept. Justice No. Dist. Fla., 1954-58, U.S. Atty., 1958-61; ptnr. Ervin, Varn, Jacobs & Ervin, Tallahassee, 1961—92; of counsel Ervin, Boyd & Allaman, 1992—2001. Vice chancellor Episcopal Diocese of Fla., Jacksonville, 1994—; Rep. state com. mem. 1961-66. 2d lt. U.S. Army, 1942-46. PTO. Decorated Legion of Merit, U.S. Army, 1972. Fellow Am. Coll. of Trial Lawyers, Am. Bar Found.; mem. Fla. Bar Assn. (50 yr. Membership award 1998), Kiwanis Club (bd. dirs.). Avocations: painting, exercise, travel, hiking, swimming. Home: Tallahassee, Fla. Died May 30, 2009.

VARNERIN, LAWRENCE JOHN, physicist, retired educator; b. Boston, July 10, 1923; s. Lawrence John and Josephine (Nangeroni) V.; m. Marie Elizabeth Hynes, Apr. 19, 1952; children: Melanie Viscelli, Lawrence, Gregory, Sharon Cenci, Suzanne Dahlinger, Bruce, Carol Levandowski, Jeffrey. SB in Physics, MIT, 1947, PhD in Physics, 1949. Supr. TR/ATR microwave tube, electronics divsn. Sylvania corp., Boston, 1949-52; acting mgr. physics dept. Westinghouse Rsch. Labs., Pitts., 1952-57; head heterojunction IC and materials dept. AT&T Bell Labs., Murray Hill, N.J., 1957-86; Chandler-Weaver prof. elec. engring., chmn. elec. engring. computer sci. dept. Lehigh U., Bethlehem, Pa., 1986-92, Chandler-Weaver prof. emeritus, 1992—2009. Assoc. editor Jour. Magnetism and Magnetic Materials, 1973-94. Served with U.S. Army, 1943-46. Fellow IEEE, Am. Phys. Soc.; mem. Magnetics Soc. Roman Catholic. Home: Bethlehem, Pa. Died May 14, 2009.

VAUGHN, CHARLES L., state legislator; b. Springfield, Mass., Feb. 9, 1919; m. Sally J. BA, U. Ariz., 1961; MA, U. N.H., 1969. Mem. N.H. Ho. of Reps. (dist. 35); mem. appropriations and fin. com. N.H. Ho. of Reps. Former dept. head, tchr. Dover (N.H.) H.S.; instr. N.H. Coll.; propr. Portsmouth Atheneum, 1976—. Sch. bd., 1984-92; del. N.H. Constnl. Conv., 1984; exec. com. Rockingham County, 1985-90, mem. Portsmouth charter commn., 1986-87, trustee Portsmouth Libr., 1984—. POW Germany, 1944-45. Mem. Rotary (bd. dirs.), DAV, Am. Legion. Died June 17, 2010.

VAUGHN, JAMES ENGLISH, JR., neurobiologist; b. Kansas City, Mo., Sept. 17, 1939; s. James English and Sue Katherine (Vaughn); m. Christine Singleton, June 18, 1961; children: Stephanie, Stacey. BA, Westminster Coll., 1961; PhD, UCLA, 1965. Postdoctoral rsch. fellow in brain rsch. U. Edinburgh, Scotland, 1965-66; asst. prof. Boston U. Sch. Medicine, 1966-70; head sect. molecular neuromorphology Beckman Rsch. Inst., City of Hope, Duarte, Calif., from 1970, pres. rsch. staff, 1986, chmn. divsn. neurosci., 1987—2001. Editor (assoc. editor): (Jour.) Jour. Neurocytology, 1978—86; contbr. articles to profl. jours.; mem. editl. bd. (Jour.) Synapse, from 1986, reviewer for Jour. Comparative Neurology, from 1974, Brain Research, from 1976. Recipient Alumni Achievement award, Westminster Coll., 2003; grantee, NSF, 1983—87; fellow Neurosci. Rsch. Program, 1969; rsch. grantee, NIH, 1969—99. Mem.: AAAS, N.Y. Acad. Scis., Internat. Brain Rsch. Orgn., Soc. for Neurosci. (chmn. short course 1977), Am. Assn. Anatomists, Am. Soc. Cell Biology, Sigma Xi. Died Mar. 9, 2009.

VAUSE, EDWIN HAMILTON, research foundation administrator; b. Chgo., Mar. 30, 1923; s. Harry Russell and Sylvia Clair (Webster) V.; m. Harriet Evelyn Oestmann, June 30, 1951; children— Karen L., Russell E., Kurt H., Dirk C., Luke E. BS, U. Ill., 1947, MS, 1948; MBA, U. Chgo., 1952; D.Sc. (hon.), U. Evansville, 1977. Registered profl. engr., Ill., Ind. Engr., research dept. Standard Oil Co., Ind., 1948-52, asst. gen. foreman mfg. dept., 1952-57; dir. research adminstrn. Mead Johnson & Co., Evansville, Ind., 1957-60; v.p. Charles F. Kettering Found., Dayton, Ohio, 1960-66, v.p., adminstrn. dir., 1966-67, exec. v.p., 1967-71, v.p. for sci. and tech., 1971-88. Trustee The Found. Center, 1967-73; mem. adv. com. Acad. Forum, Nat. Acad. Scis. Vice-pres. Washington Twp. Bd. Edn., 1963-67; mem. Centerville-Washington Twp. Joint Planning Commn., 1967-68; mem. adv. bd. Center for Students Rights, Dayton, 1966-70; active Boy Scouts Am. Mem. Am. Inst. Chem. Engrs. (past chmn. Chgo. sect.), N.Y. Acad. Scis., Agrl. Research Inst., Nat. Industry State Agrl. Research Council. Clubs: Elks, Kiwanis (past pres.), Masons. Republican. Lutheran. Home: San Diego, Calif. Died Feb. 23, 2009.

VEDAM, KUPPUSWAMY, physics educator; b. Vedharanyam, India, Jan. 15, 1926; s. Tiruvarur Vaidyanathan and Saraswathi (Ramaseshan) K.; m. Nalini Subramanyam, Sept. 14, 1956; children— Saraswathi, Subramanyam. B.Sc. with Honors, Nagpur U., India, 1946, M.Sc., 1947; research student, Indian Inst. Sci., Bangalore, 1948-51; PhD, Saugor U., India, 1953. Lectr. physics U. Saugor, 1947-48, 51-53; sr. research asst. Indian Inst. Sci., 1953-56; asst. prof. physics Pa. State U., 1956-59; sr. research officer Atomic Energy Establishment, Bombay, India, 1960-62; assoc. prof. Pa. State U., University Park, 1962-70, prof. physics, from 1970. Research and numerous publs. on optical properties of materials under high pressure, optical properties of surfaces, thin films and interfaces. Fellow Am. Phys. Soc., Optical Soc. Am.; mem. Materials Research Soc., Sigma Xi. Home: State College, Pa. Died Sept. 4, 2009.

VERGIELS, JOHN M., educator, state legislator; b. Erie, Mich., Nov. 21, 1937; children: Kelly Jean, Jack Lee, Robert Alan. PhD, U. Toledo. Prof. edn. U. Nev.-Las Vegas, chmn. faculty senate, chmn. dept. curriculum and instrn., chmn. dept. secondary, post-secondary and vocat. edn.; Nev. chmn. Western Interstate Comm. on Higher Edn.; mem. Nev. Assembley, from 1973, speaker, from 1983. Mem. Nev. Senate, 1985—, majority leader, 1991, Clark County Democratic Cen. Com.; past pres. Las Vegas Young Dems. Mem. Phi Delta Kappa Home: Las Vegas, Nev. Died Dec. 16, 2009.

VERINK, ELLIS DANIEL, JR., metallurgical engineering educator, consultant; b. Peking, China, Feb. 9, 1920; s. Ellis Daniel and Phoebe Elizabeth (Smith) V.; m. Martha Eulala Owens, July 4, 1942; children: Barbara Ann, Wendy Susan. BS, Purdue U., 1941; MS, Ohio State U., 1963, PhD, 1965. Registered profl. engr., Fla., Pa., Calif. Mgr. chem. sect., sales devel. divsn. Alcoa, New Kensington, Pa., 1946-59, mgr. chem. and petroleum indsl. sales Pitts., 1965—68; prof. materials sci. and engring. U. Fla., Gainesville, from 1968, disting. svc. prof., 1984-91, prof. emeritus, from 1991; pres. Materials Cons., Inc., from 1970. Cons. Aluminum Assn., Washington, 1966-84; mem. U.S. nuclear waste tech. rev. bd., 1989-97. Author: Corrosion Testing Made Easy, The Basics, 1993; editor: Methods of Materials Selections, 1968, Material Stability and Environmental Degradation, 1988; contbr. articles to profl. jours. Pres. Gainesville YMCA, 1977. Recipient Sam Tour award ASTM, 1979, Donald E. Marlowe award Am. Soc. Engring. Edn., 1991; recipient Disting. Alumnus award Ohio State U., 1982, Disting. Faculty award Fla. Blue Key, 1983; named Tchr.-Scholar of Year U. Fla., 1979 Fellow Metall. Soc. of AIME (pres. 1984, Educator of Yr. award 1988), Am. Soc. Materials Internat., Nat. Assn. Corrosion Engrs. Internat. (bd. dirs. 1984-87, Willis Rodney Whitney award; mem. Masons, Shriners, Kiwanis, Sigma Xi, Tau Beta Pi. Republican. Presbyterian. Home: Wesley Chapel, Fla. Died Sept. 28, 2009.

VERLANDER, WILLIAM ASHLEY, insurance company executive; b. Portsmouth, Va., Jan. 23, 1920; (married); 2 children. BS, Ga. Inst. Tech. Accountant W.W. Stribling Co., Atlanta; sr. examiner Ga. Ins. Dept.; partner firm Stribling, Blanton, Rintye & Verlander, Atlanta; co-organizer, exec. v.p., treas. Am. Heritage Life Ins. Co., Jacksonville, Fla., 1956-62, pres., 1962-86, chmn., chief exec. officer, from 1986, also dir. Pres., dir. Am. Heritage Life Investment Corp.; bd. dirs. Barnett Banks, Cain & Bultman, Inc. Past chmn. Downtown Devel. Council of Jacksonville; past pres. Gator Bowl Assn.; mem. nat. advisory bd., then past chmn. Ga. Inst. Tech. Recipient Good Citizens award Jacksonville Jr. C. of C., 1965, C.G. Snead Meml. award as outstanding ins. man in Jacksonville area, 1968, Man of Yr. award Fla. Assn. Life Underwriters, 1970; honored in recognition of outstanding mgmt. accomplishments in commerce and industry Sales and Mktg. Execs. of Jacksonville, 1967; named Outstanding Alumnus Coll. Indsl. Mgmt. Ga. Inst. Tech., 1970 Mem. Jacksonville Area C. of C. (past pres.), Fla. State C. of C. (past pres.) Clubs: River (Jacksonville), San Jose (Jacksonville), Univ. (Jacksonville); Ponte Vedra (Ponte Vedra Beach, Fla.); Capital City (Atlanta). Died June 12, 2009.

VERMILYE, PETER HOAGLAND, banker; b. NYC, Jan. 17, 1920; s. Herbert Noble and Elise Tace (Hillyer) V.; m. Lucy Shaw Mitchell, Oct. 14, 1950; children: Peter H., Dana R., Andrew R., Mary S. AB, Princeton U., 1940. V.p. pension investments J.P. Morgan & Co. and Morgan Guaranty Trust, 1940-64; ptnr. State St. Research & Mgmt., Boston, 1965-69; pres. Alliance Capital Mgmt., NYC, 1970-77; sr. v.p., chief investment officer Citibank, NYC, 1977-84; chmn. Baring Am. Asset Mgmt., Boston, 1984-89; sr. advisor Baring Asset Mgmt., 1990-95, Harbor Capital Mgmt., Boston, 1996—2003, Fortis Investments, from 2004. Chmn. Huntington Theatre, 1989—96; bd. dirs. Engelhard Hanovia, Breadstreet Holdings Corp., 1970—2008. Trustee Boston U., 1970—. Mem.: Brook, Somerset, Myopia. Home: Manchester, Mass. Died Mar. 9, 2009.

VERONIS, PETER, publisher; b. New Brunswick, NJ, June 15, 1923; s. Nicholas M. and Angeliki (Efthemakis) V.; m. Dorothy E. White, Sept. 8, 1947; 1 dau., Judith Anne Veronis Rodgers. Student, Columbia U., 1951-54. Nat. advt. mgr. Springfield (Mass.) Newspapers, 1954-57; v.p., gen. sales mgr. Ridder Johns Co., NYC, 1957-62; corp. exec. Curtis Pub. Co., NYC, 1963-64; assoc. sales mgr. Look mag., 1964-68; v.p., advt. dir. Psychology Today mag., 1968-71; v.p. advt. Saturday Rev., NYC, 1971-73; pub. Book Digest, NYC, 1973-80; pres. PV Pub. Inc., NYC, 1980-81, Conn., from 1988; v.p., founder and dir. CBS Mag. Network, NYC, 1981-85, pres., 1985-87, Diamandis Mag. Network, 1987-88. Served with USN, 1941-51. Home: Stamford, Conn. Died Aug. 20, 2010.

VERRETT, SHIRLEY, soprano; b. New Orleans, May 31, 1931; d. Leon Solomon and Elvira Augustine (Harris) V.; m. Louis Frank LoMonaco, Dec. 10, 1963; 1 dau., Francesca. AA, Ventura Coll., Calif., 1951; diploma in voice (scholarship 1956-61), Juilliard Sch. Music, 1961; MusD (hon.), Coll. Holy Cross, Mass., 1978. CPA, Cert. real estate broker. Faculty mem. U. Mich. Sch. Music, 1996—99, James Earl Jones Disting. univ. prof. voice, 1999—2010. Mem. adv. bd. Opera Ebony. Recital debut Town Hall, N.Y.C., 1958; appeared as Irina in Lost in the Stars, 1958; orchestral debut Phila. Orch., 1960; operatic debut in Carmen, Festival of Two Worlds, Spoleto, Italy, 1962; debuts with Bolshoi Opera, Moscow, 1963, N.Y.C. Opera, 1964, Royal Opera, Covent Garden, 1966, Maggio Fiorentino, Florence, 1967, Met. Opera, 1968, Teatro San Carlos, Naples, 1968, Dallas Civic Opera, 1969, La Scala, 1970, Vienna State Opera, 1970, San Francisco Opera, 1972, Paris Opera, 1973, Opera Co. Boston, 1976, Opera Bastille, Paris, 1990; guest appearances with all major U.S. symphony orchs.; toured Eastern Europe and Greece with La Scala chorus and orch., 1981; TV debut on Ed Sullivan Show, 1963; TV performances include: Great Performances series, live performance of Macbeth at La Scala, Santuzza in Cavalleria Rusticana; film debut Maggio Musicale, 1989, Macbeth, 1986; author: (autobiography) I Never Walked Alone, 2003 Recipient Marian Anderson award, 1955, Nat. Fedn. Music Clubs award, 1961, Walter Naumberg award, 1958, Blanche Thebom award, 1960; named Chevalier Arts and Letters (France), 1970, Commandeur, 1984; John Hay Whitney fellow, 1959; Ford Found. fellow, 1962-63; Martha Baird Rockefeller Aid to Music Fund fellow, 1959-61; grantee William Matteus Sullivan Fund, 1959; grantee Berkshire Music Opera, 1956; recipient Achievement award Ventura Coll., 1963, Achievement award N.Y. chpt. Albert Einstein Coll. Medicine, 1975; 2 plaques Los Angeles Sentinel Newspaper, 1960; plaque Peninsula Music Festival, 1963; Los Angeles Times Woman of Yr. award, 1969 Mem. Mu Phi Epsilon. Died Nov. 5, 2010.

VESTAL, GEORGE ALEXANDER, plastics company executive; b. Fayetteville, NC, Dec. 4, 1927; s. Herman L. and Blanche M. (Martin) V.; m. Lura Janice Williford, Oct. 8, 1950. BS in Bus. Adminstrn, U. N.C., 1956. With Union Carbide Corp., from 1956, gen. mgr. prodn. Cartersville, Ga., 1967-68, engring. prodn. mgr. NYC, 1968-74, gen. mgr. internat. ops., 1974-75, dir. mktg., 1975-79, gen. mgr. home products, 1979-81, v.p., gen. mgr. home products, home and automotive div., 1981-87; exec. v.p. First Brands Corp., Danbury, Conn., 1987; pres. home products div., from 1989. Served with U.S. Navy, 1945-46. Republican. Baptist. Home: Huntersville, NC. Died Feb. 18, 2009.

VETOG, EDWIN JOSEPH, retired gas utility executive; b. NYC, Apr. 7, 1921; s. Lester and Lucy V.; m. Elizabeth Ann Long, July 18, 1942; children: Judith Ann Vetog Ciafone, Victoria Ann Vetog Thode. BBA, CCNY, 1949; MBA, NYU, 1953. With Bklyn. Union Gas Co., 1941-86, various positions, 1941-67, comptroller, 1967-69, v.p., 1969-75, sr. v.p., chief fin. officer, 1975-81, adminstrv. v.p., chief fin. officer, 1981-84, exec. v.p., chief fin. officer, 1984-86. Trustee Ridgewood Savs. Bank, L.I., 1980—; adv. bd. Mfrs. Hanover Trust Co., Bklyn., 1979-86; chmn. Delaware Valley Propane Co., Moorestown, N.J., 1981-86. Pres. Indsl. Home for the Blind, L.I., 1976-85. Served to capt. C.E., U.S. Army, 1942-46. Decorated Bronze Star; decorated medal of Metz (France) Mem. Am. Gas Assn., Fin. Execs. Inst. Clubs: Brooklyn. Lutheran. Home: Setauket, NY. Died Apr. 18, 2009.

VIESSMAN, WARREN, JR., professor emeritus; b. Balt., Nov. 9, 1930; s. Warren and Helen Adair (Berlincke) V.; m. Gloria Marie Scheiner, May 11, 1953 (div. Apr. 1975); children: Wendy, Stephen, Suzanne, Michael, Thomas, Sandra; m. Elizabeth Gertrude Rothe, Aug. 8, 1980; children: Heather, Joshua B in Engring., Johns Hopkins U., 1952, MS in Engring., 1958, DEng, 1961. Registered profl. engr., Md. Engr. W. H. Primrose & Assocs., Towson, Md., 1955-57; project engr. Johns Hopkins U., Balt., 1957-61; from asst. to assoc. prof. N.Mex. State U., Las Cruces, 1961-66; prof. U. Maine, Orono, 1966-68, U. Nebr., Lincoln, 1968-75; sr. specialist Libr. Congress, Washington, 1975-83; prof., chmn. U. Fla., Gainesville, 1983-90, assoc. dean for rsch. and grad. study, 1990-91, assoc. dean for acad. programs, 1991—2003, prof. emeritus environ. engring., from 2003. Vis. scientist Am. Geophys. Union, 1970-71; Maurice Kremer lectr. U. Nebr., 1985, 2001; lectr. Harvard U. Water Policy Seminar, 1988; Wayne S. Nichols Meml. Fund lectr. Ohio State U., 1990; mem. steering com. on groundwater and energy U.S. Dept. Energy, 1979-80; mem. task group on fed. water rsch. U.S. Geol. Survey, 1985-87; mem. com. of water sci. and tech. bd. NAS, 1986-90; mem. water resources working group Nat. Coun. on Pub. Works Improvement, 1987; chmn., chief of engrs. Environ. Adv. Bd., Washington, 1991-93; chmn. solid and hazardous waste mgmt. adv. bd. State U. Sys. Fla. Co-author: Water Management: Technology and Institutions, 1984, Introduction to Hydrology, 2003, Water Supply and Pollution Control, 2005; contbr. over 167 articles to profl. jours. Mem. Water Mgmt. Com., Gainesville, 1983-88, Fla. Environ. Efficiency Study Commn., 1986-88. 1st lt. U.S. Army C.E., 1952-54, Korea. Recipient Comdr.'s award for pub. svc., U.S. Dept. Army, 1993. Diplomate Am. Acad. Water Resources Engrs. (hon. diplomate); fellow ASCE (hon. mem., Julian Hinds award 1989), Am. Water Resources Assn. (nat. pres. 1990, Icko Iben award 1983, Henry P. Caulfield Jr. medal 1996), Univs. Coun. on Water Resources (pres. 1987, Warren A. Hall medal 1994), Sigma Xi, Tau Beta Pi. Democrat. Lutheran. Avocations: scuba diving, woodworking. Home: Gainesville, Fla. Died Apr. 8, 2010.

VILLARREAL, CARLOS CASTAÑEDA, engineering executive; b. Brownsville, Tex., Nov. 9, 1924; s. Jesus Jose and Elisa L. (Castañeda) Villarreal; m. Doris Ann Akers, Sept. 10, 1948 (dec. 1995); children: Timothy Hill, David Akers; m. June Ricchezza McElroy, Oct. 3, 2002. BS, US Naval Acad., 1948; MS, US Navy Postgrad. Sch., 1950; LLD (hon.), St. Mary's U., 1972. Registered profl. engr. Commd. ensign US Navy, 1949, advanced through grades to lt., 1956; comdg. officer U.S.S. Rhea, 1951, U.S.S. Osprey, 1952; comdr. Mine Divsn. 31, 1953; instr. elec. engring. US Naval Acad., 1954—56; resigned, 1956; mgr. marine and indsl. operation Gen. Electric Co., 1956—66; v.p. mktg. and adminstrn. Marquardt Corp., 1966—69; adminstr. Urban Mass Transit Adminstrn., Dept. Transp., Washington, 1969—73; commr. Postal Rate Commn., 1973—79, vice chmn., 1975—79; v.p. Washington ops. Wilbur Smith and Assocs., Fairfax, Va., 1979—84, sr. v.p., 1984—86, exec. v.p., from 1987, also bd. dirs. Lectr. in field; mem. industry sector adv. com. Dept. Commerce; mem. sect. 13 adv. com. Dept. Transp., 1983—86. Contbr. articles to profl. jours. Mem. devel. com. Wolftrap Farm Pk. Performing Arts, 1973—78; bd. edn. St. Elizabeth Sch.; bd. dirs. Assoc. Cath. Charities, 1983—86; chmn. fin. com. Cath. Charities, USA; coun. mem. St. Elizabeth Ch., 1982—86, chmn. fin. com.; active John Carrol Soc. Decorated Knight Sovereign Mil. Hospitaller Order St. John of Jerusalem of Rhodes and Malta, Equestrian Order of Holy Sepulchre of Jerusalem, Knight Comdr.; recipient Outstanding Achievement award, Dept. Transp., 1974. Fellow: ASCE, Am. Cons. Engrs. Coun. (vice chmn. interna. com.); mem.: NSPE (pres. DC soc. 1986—87, bd. dirs. 1988—91), IEEE, Intelligent Transp. Soc. Am. (chmn. fin. com., bd. dirs.), Inst. Traffic Engrs., Inst. World Politics, Internat. Bridge, Tunnel and Turnpike Assn., Washington Soc. Engrs., Transp. Rsch. Bd., Am. Rds. and Transp. Builders Assn. (chmn. pub. transp. adv. coun.), Soc. Am. Mil. Engrs., Soc. Naval Archs. and Marine Engrs., Am. Pub. Transit Assn., Army-Navy Club (pres. 1999—2004), Univ. Club. Republican. Roman Catholic. Home: Rockville, Md. Died Dec. 14, 2009.

VILLELLA, FRED JOSEPH, government executive; b. Punxsutawney, Pa., June 21, 1933; s. Ferdinand and Frances Villella; m. Dona Sugden Lizanetz (div. 1974); children—Mark, Jane, Susan, Paul; m 2d, Edith Speidel, Feb. 18, 1981; stepchildren— Dallas L. Cartright, Tamara L. Cartright. B.A., Gannon U., 1951; postgrad., Command and Staff Coll., 1969; M. Pub. Adminstrn., Ind. U., 1974. Commd. 2d lt., 1955, advanced through grades to lt. col., 1969, ret., 1976; comdr. Law Enforcement Commn., Fort Carson, Colo., 1974-76; instr. Calif. Spl. Tng. Inst., San Luis Obispo, 1976-78, chief acad. div., 1978-80, chief adminstrv. div., 1980-81; assoc. dir. tng. and fire, Fed. Emergency Mgmt. Agy., Washington, 1981—, exec. dep. dir., 1983—. Contbr. articles to profl. publs. Decorated Legion of Merit with oak leaf cluster, Bronze Star with 2 oak leaf clusters; recipient Disting. Civilian Service medal Fed. Emergency Mgmt. Agy., 1983. Republican. Roman Catholic. Home: Arlington, Va. Died July 11, 2010.

VISCHER, HAROLD HARRY, manufacturing executive; b. Toledo, Oct. 17, 1914; s. Harry Philip and Hazel May (Patterson) V.; m. DeNell Meyers, Feb. 18, 1938; children: Harold Harry, Robert P., Michael L. BBA, U. Toledo, 1937. With Ohio Bell Telephone Co., 1937-38; with Firestone Tire & Rubber Co., Toledo, 1948-61, nat. passenger tire sales mgr., 1953-57, dist. mgr., 1957-61; with Bandag Inc., Muscatine, Iowa, 1961-80; exec. v.p., pres. Bandag Inc. (Rubber and Equipment Sales group), 1975-80; also dir.; pres., gen. mgr. Hardline Internat., Inc., Jackson, Mich., 1980-82; chmn. Tred-X Corp., from 1982. Mem. City Council, Muscatine, 1964-76; chmn., mem. Dist. Export Council Iowa, 1964-81; chmn. Muscatine United Way, 1969-70; mem. adv. bd. Engring. Coll. Iowa State U., 1970-81; mem. Muscatine Light & Water Bd., 1979-80. Elected to Nat. Tire Dealers and Retreaders Assn. Hall of Fame, 1988, to Internat. Tire Retreading and Repairing Hall of Fame, 1990. Mem. Nat. Tire and Retreaders Suppliers Group Assn. (chmn. 1979-80, exec. com. 1977-80), Tire Retread Info. Bur. (exec. com. 1974-81), Am. Retreading Assn. (adv. bd. 1970-72), Retreading Industry Assn., Industry Man of Yr. 1979), Christian Business men's Com., Gideons. Republican. Home: Brooklyn, Mich. Died July 17, 2010.

VITTUM, DANIEL WEEKS, JR., lawyer; b. Ky., Feb. 10, 1939; s. Daniel W. and Kathryn Margaret (Jones) Vittum; m. Stephanie Ann Empkie, Aug. 18, 1962 (div. July 1987); children: Daniel W. III, Stephen F.; m. Christine L. Jacobek, Nov. 17, 1990. BS, U. Ill., 1961; JD, U. Mich., 1964. Bar: Ill. 1964, Ill. (US Dist. Ct. (no. dist.)) 1965, US Supreme Ct. 1977, US Ct. Appeals (7th cir.) 1976, US Ct. Appeals (4th cir.) 1982, US Ct. Appeals (9th cir.) 1978, US Ct. Appeals (Fed. cir.) 1982, US Ct. Appeals (6th cir.) 1992. Assoc. Kirkland & Ellis, Chgo., 1964—69, ptnr., from 1970. Pres. Northwestern U. Settlement Assn.; mem. vis. com. U. Mich. Law Sch. Mem.: ABA, Order of Coif, Intellectual Property Law Assn. Chgo., Am. Intellectual Property Assn., Chgo. Yacht Club, Mid-Am. Club, East Bank Club (Chgo.), Phi Beta Kappa. Died May 7, 2009.

VOITLE, ROBERT ALLEN, dean, physiologist; b. Parkersburg, W.Va., May 12, 1938; s. Ray Christian and Ruby Virginia (Hannaman) V.; m. Linda Ellen Loveday, Dec. 5, 1975; children: Robert Allen, Elizabeth Anne, Christian Blair, Vanessa Virginia. BS, W.Va. U., 1962; MS, W.Va., 1965; PhD, U. Tenn., 1969. Asst. in poultry U. Tenn., Knoxville, 1965-69; asst. prof. physiology U. Fla., Gainesville, 1969-75, assoc. prof., 1975-79; prof., head dept. poultry Calif. Poly. State U., San Luis Obispo, 1979-81; dean Coll. Agr., Auburn U., Ala., 1981—2000, prof. poultry sci. Ala., from 2000. Cons. Columbia Bank for Coops., S.C., 1972 Contbr. articles to sci. jours. Pres., other offices Alachua County Fair Assn., Gainesville, 1969-79. Recipient Pub. Service award Alachua County Commn., 1975; recipient Tchr. of Yr. award U. Fla., 1977, Golden Feather award Calif. Poly. Inst., 1982 Mem. Poultry Sci. Assn., So. Poultry Sci. Assn., Gainesville Jaycees (JCI senatorship), Sigma Xi, Gamma Sigma Delta Clubs: Elks. Episcopalian. Home: Auburn, Ala. Died May 21, 2010.

VOLLAND, CAROL TASCHER, financial services executive; b. Morris, Ill., Mar. 23, 1935; d. Murl Elvyn and Helen Marie (Lindquist) Tascher; m. George William Volland, Aug. 12, 1978. Student Monmouth Coll., 1953-55; B.S. in Interior Design, U. Ill., 1957; postgrad. Art Inst. Chgo. Evening Sch., 1959-62. Lic. real estate broker, ins. and securities broker, Colo., Ill. Archtl. and interior designer Peoples Gas Light & Coke Co., Chgo., 1957-65, consumer lectr., corp. architect and interior designer, 1965-70, dir. home planning bur., 1970-74; corp. fashion coord. Ozite Corp. div. Brunswick Corp., Libertyville, Ill., 1974-75, dir. pub. rels., 1975-77, contract sales mgr., 1977-78; pres. Volland & Assocs., Lakewood, Colo., 1982-88; pres. Asset Planning Svcs., Lakewood, 1989—; mem. corp. responsibilities bd. Brunswick Corp. Internat., 1976-77. Author: Creative Moneystretchers for the Home, 1973. Mem. Nat. Home Fashions League (exec. v.p.

1977-78), Am. Soc. Interior Designers, Women in Communications, LWV, Nat. Trust Hist. Preservation, Genesee Found. Republican. Methodist. Home: Golden, Colo. Died Oct. 10, 2009.

VON RAFFLER-ENGEL, WALBURGA (WALBURGA ENGEL), retired language educator; b. Munich, Sept. 25, 1920; came to U.S., 1949, naturalized, 1955; d. Friedrich J. and Gertrud E. (Kiefer) von R.; m. A. Ferdinand Engel, June 2, 1957; children: Lea Maxine, Eric Robert von Raffler. DLitt, U. Turin, Italy, 1947; MS, Columbia U., 1951; PhD, Ind. U., 1953. Free-lance journalist, 1949-58; mem. faculty Bennett Coll., Greensboro, NC, 1953-55, U. Charleston (formerly Morris Harvey Coll.), W.Va., 1955-57, Adelphi U., CUNY, 1957-58, NYU, 1958-59, U. Florence, Italy, 1959-60, Istituto Postuniversitario Orgn. Aziendale, Turin, Italy, 1960-61, Bologna Center of Johns Hopkins U., 1964; assoc. prof. linguistics Vanderbilt U., Nashville, 1965-77, prof. linguistics, 1977-85, prof. emerita, sr. rsch. assoc. Inst. Pub. Policy Studies, 1985—2002, dir. linguistics program, 1978—85; chmn. com. on linguistics Nashville U. Ctr., 1978—85; Italian NSF prof. Psychol. Inst. U. Florence, Italy, 1986-87; prof. NATO Advanced Study Inst., Cortona, Italy, 1988; pres. Kinesics Internat., from 1988, ret. Vis. prof. linguistics Shanxi U., Peoples Republic China, 1988-2002; vis. prof. U. Ottawa, Ont., Can., 1971-72, Lang. Scis. Inst., Internat. Christian U., Tokyo, 1976, U. Paris, Sorbonne, 1965-67, 1978-79; grant evaluator NEH, NSF, Can. Coun.; manuscript reader Ind. U. Press, U. Ill. Press, Prentice-Hall; advisor Trinity U., Simon Frazer U.; dir. internat. seminar Cross-Cultural Comm., 1986-87; mem. Ctr. for Global Media Studies, 1999; State Dept. Italy del. to Congress of the Hague; lectr. in field; specialist in non-verbal comm. Author: Il prelinguaggio infantile, 1964, The Perception of Nonverbal Behavior in the Career Interview, 1983, The Perception of the Unborn Across the Cultures of the World, Japanese edit., 1993, English edit., 1994 (transl. into Chinese), A Traveler's Guide to Cross-Cultural Business Communications, 2000; co-author: Language Intervention Programs, 1960-75; editor, co-editor 12 books; author films and videotape; contbr. of 500 articles to profl. jours. in Engish, Itialian, French, German, Chinese, Japanese. Grantee Am. Coun. Learned Socs., NSF, Can. Coun., Ford Found., Kenan Venture Fund, Japanese Ministry Edn., NATO, UNESCO, Finnish Acad., Meharry Med. Coll., Internat. Sociol. Assn., Internat. Coun. Linguists, Tex. A&M U., Vanderbilt U., others. Mem. AAUP, Internat. Linguistic Assn., Linguistic Soc. Am. (chmn. Golden Anniversary film com. 1974, emerita 1985—), Linguistic Assn. Can. and the U.S., Internat. Assn. for Applied Linguistics (com. on discourse analyses, sessions chmn. 1978), Lang. Origins Soc. (exec. com. 1985-97, chmn. internat. congress, 1987), Internat. Sociol. Assn. (rsch. com. for sociolinguistics, session co-chmn. internat. conf. 1983, session chmn. profl. conf. 1983), Internat. Coun. Psychologists, Internat. Assn. for Intercultural Comms. Studies, Internat. Assn. for Study of Child Lang. (v.p. 1975-78, chmn. internat. conf. Tuscan Acad. Scis., Florence, Italy 1972), Inst. for Nonverbal Comm. Rsch. (workshop leader 1981), Southeastern Conf. on Linguistics, 1980— (hon. mem. 1985—), Semiotic Soc. Am. (organizing com. Internat. Semiotics Inst. 1981), Nat. Assn. Scholars, Tenn. Assn. Scholars (bd. dirs. 1998-99), Internat. Assn. for Intercultural Comms. Studies (panel organizer 1999), United Europe Movement (sect. chmn. 1944-45), Internat. Comm. Assn., Internat. Pragmatics Assn. Achievements include being instrumental in forcing Vanderbilt U. to enroll women on an equal basis with men. Home: San Antonio, Tex. Died Nov. 28, 2009.

VORTMAN, LUKE JEROME, engineer; b. Springfield, Ill., Apr. 18, 1920; s. Luke and Ida Rose (Vogel) Vortman; m. Betty Marjorie Leslie, Dec. 22, 1946. Student, Ill. Coll., 1938—39; BS, U. Ill., 1947, MS, 1949. Tech. staff mem. Sandia Nat. Labs., Albuquerque, 1949—83, disting. mem. tech. staff, from 1983. Contbr. articles to profl. jours. Mem., phys. effects subcom. Adv. Com. Civil Def. Nat. Acad. Scis., mem., subcom. protective structures, 1961—64, chmn., 1965—69, mem., subcom. blast and thermal effects, 1966—73, mem., com. SST Sonic Boom, 1966—71. Served to capt. C.E. US Army, 1942—46. Recipient Disting. Svc. Citation award, Dept. Def. Office Civil Def., 1969. Mem.: AAAS, Am. Nuc. Soc. (chmn., civil explosion application divsn. 1974—75, chmn., membership com. 1981—84, Disting. Svc. award 1984). Home: Albuquerque, N.Mex. Died Dec. 24, 2009.

VOZZA, JOSEPH LOUIS, insurance company executive, director; b. Bergenfield, NJ, Jan. 7, 1930; s. Louis and Gertrude (Watson) V.; m. Evelyn Garifalos Markert, Sept. 17, 1977; children: Carol Powell, David Joseph, Jill Marie Berger. Attended, Pace U., Pohs Inst., N.Y. Sch. Ins. Ins. agt. Buhler Svc. Corp., NYC, 1948—53; pres. Joseph L. Vozza Agy. Inc., Park Ridge, NJ, from 1953. Pres. Pub. Entity Risk Mgmt. Adminstrn., Inc.; exec. dir., adminstr. Mcpl. Excess Liability, NJ; dir. Liberty Nat. Bank, Hillsdale, NJ, 1973—82, chmn., 1978—81; dir. Westwood Savs. and Loan Assn., 1969—78, Valley Nat. Bank, Passaic, NJ, N.J. Valley Nat. Bancorp. Mem. Park Ridge Bd. Edn., 1960-63, pres., 1963; mem. Park Ridge Zoning Bd. Adjustment, 1964-65, Park Ridge Planning Bd., 1965-68, Park Ridge Borough Coun., 1965-68; police commr., Park Ridge, 1966-68; mcpl. chmn. Rep. County Com., Park Ridge, 1971-72; mem. Greater Pascack Valley C. of C., charter, pres. 1967-68. Mem.: Ind. Ins. Agts. Assn., Profl. Ins. Agts., Elks Club (charter, trustee, chmn. Park Ridge), U.S. Power Squadron, Englewood Yacht Club (commodore 1980—81). Home: Nyack, NY. Died June 29, 2010.

WADE, GLEN, electrical engineer, educator; b. Ogden, Utah, Mar. 19, 1921; s. Lester Andrew and Nellie (Vanderwerff) W.; m. LaRee Bailey, Mar. 20, 1945; children: Kathleen Ann, RaLee, Lisa Jean, Mary Sue. BS in Elec. Engring, U. Utah, Salt Lake City, 1948, MS, 1949; PhD, Stanford U., Calif., 1954. Research group leader, asso. prof. elec. engring. Stanford U., 1955-60; asso. dir. engring., microwave and power tube div. Raytheon Co., 1960-61, asst gen. mgr. research div., 1961-63; dir. Sch. Elec. Engring., Cornell U., 1963-66, J.P. Levis prof. engring., 1963-66; prof. elec. engring. U. Calif. at Santa Barbara, from 1966. Indsl. advisor U. RI, 1961-63; vis. lectr. Harvard, 1963; cons. to industry, 1956—; vis. prof. Tokyo U., 1971; Fulbright-Hays lectr., Spain, 1972-73; cons. mem. Dept. Def. Adv. Group Electron Devices, 1966-73; Spl. Chair prof. Nat. Taiwan U., 1980-81, internationally renowned fgn. scholar lectureship, 1988; UN vis. prof. Nanjing Inst. Tech., 1986; UN vis. prof. S.E. U. People's Republic of China, 1989, Nat. Com. Sci. and Tech. vis. prof. U. Guanajuato, Mex., 1994—; elected mem. The Electromagnetics Acad., 1990. Editor: Transactions on Electron Devices, 1961-71, IEEE Jour. Quantum Electronics, 1965-68; series editor: Harcourt Brace Jovanovich, 1964—; contbr. articles to profl. jours. U.S. del. Tech. Cooperation Program internat. meeting, 1970. Served with USNR, 1944-46. Recipient ann. award Nat. Electronics Conf., 1959, Outstanding Teaching award Acad. Senate, U. Calif., Santa Barbara, 1977, Prof. of Yr. award U. Calif. at Santa Barbara Mortar Bd. Sr. Honor Soc., 1988, Hon. Chairmanship award Twentieth Acoustical Imaging, 1992, Disting. Alumnus award Engring. Coll. U. Utah, 1998. Fellow IEEE (life; mem. adminstrv. com. profl. group election devices 1960-71, mem. publs. bd., chmn. info. processing com., mem. exec. com. 1971-72, dir. 1971-72, chmn. ednl. activities bd. 1971-72, editor proc. 1977-80, Centennial award 1984, Millennium medal 2000); mem. Am. Phys. Soc., Phi Kappa Phi, Tau Beta Pi, Sigma Xi, Eta Kappa Nu (Outstanding Young Elec. Engr. award 1955) Home: Santa Barbara, Calif. Died June 9, 2009.

WAGNER, KENNETH A., biologist, educator; b. Union City, Ind., Nov. 30, 1919; AB, DePauw U., 1941, MA, 1946; PhD, U. Mich., 1951. Instr. botany U. Tenn., Knoxville, 1947—49; asst. prof. Fla. State U., Tallahassee, 1949—54; prof., head biology Old Dominion Coll., Norfolk, Va., 1954—59; sci. coord. Powell Labs., Gladstone, Oreg., 1959—66; prof. biology NC Wesleyan Coll., Rocky Mount, 1966—69, Ferris State Coll., Big Rapids, Mich., 1969—84; mem. Sino-Am. Sci. & Tech. Exch., China, 1982. Author (with others): Introduction to Modern Biology, 1972, Under Siege, 1973; contbr. articles to sci. jours. Instr. US Power Squadron, Oreg., 1962—66; del. Alma Coll. Nat. Conf. on Energy, 1971. Home: Greenville, Ohio. Died June 2, 2009.

WAGNER, SHELDON LEON, clinical toxicologist, agricultural chemistry educator; b. Merrill, Wis., Apr. 4, 1929; s. Louis and Frieda (Charne) W.; m. Linda Wessel, May 28, 1960; children: Diane, Deborah. BS, U. Wis., 1954, MD, 1957. Intern Wayne County Hosp., Detroit, 1957-58; resident VA Rsch. Hosp., Chgo., 1958-61; fellow Northwestern U., Chgo., 1961-63; pvt. practice physician Corvallis, Oreg., 1963-70; prof. in agrl. chemistry Oreg. State U., Corvallis, from 1970. Cons. Oreg. Dept. Agrl., Salem, 1970, Oreg. Health Scis. U., Portland, 1978—, EPA, Washington, 1986, Oreg. Health Divsn., Portland, 1979—; adminstr. Nat. Pesticide Med. Monitoring Program, 1986—; assoc. adminstr. Nat. Pesticide Telecom. Network, 1995—. Author: Clinical Toxicology Emergencies, 1984, Acute Health Hazards of Pesticides, 1985, Indoor Air Pollution of Pesticides, 1995; contbr. articles to profl. publs. Mem. curriculum com. Corvallis Sch. Dist., 1968; committeeman Benton County Hospice Program, Corvallis, 1990; chmn. ethics com. Good Samaritan Hosp., Corvallis, 1989. Sgt. USAF, 1946-49. Mem. Am. Coll. Occupational and Environ. Medicine, Soc. Toxicology, Am. Soc. Internat. Medicine, Oreg. Med. Assn., Rotary. Home: Corvallis, Oreg. Died July 19, 2009.

WAINER, ROBERT JOHN, lawyer; b. NYC, June 19, 1929; s. Stanley and Helen (Greason) Wainer; children: Glenn, Mitchell, Robert. BA, Maryville Coll., Tenn., 1951; JD, St. John's U., 1957. Bar: NY 1958, US Dist. Cts. (ea. and so. dists.) NY 1968. Ptnr. Van Horne, Cohn & Wainer, Mineola, NY, 1960—65, Van Horne & Wainer, Garden City, NY, 1965—75; sole practice Woodbury, NY, from 1976. Sec., dir. gen. counsel Support Sys. Assocs., Inc., Northport, NY, from 1975. Past J.P. Village of Northport. Served to capt. USMC, 1951—53, Korea. Mem.: VFW, Nassau Lawyers Assn., Suffolk County Bar Assn., Lions, Mason. Home: Centreville, Va. Died Nov. 2, 2009.

WAINWRIGHT, PAUL EDWARD BLECH, construction company executive; b. Annapolis, Md., Jan. 28, 1917; s. Richard and Alice Sorrel (Blech) W.; m. Helen Mae Rogers, July 10, 1941; children: Richard, Paul Edward Blech, John. BS in Civil Engring, Va. Mil. Inst., 1938. Cost engr. Turner Constrn. Co., NYC, 1938-40, cost engr., asst. supt., 1945-46; cost. engr. for contractors Pacific Naval Air Bases, Honolulu, 1940-42; with Dillingham Corp., Honolulu, 1946-82, asst. v.p., then v.p., 1961-69, group v.p. constrn., 1969-82; cons. constrn. Honolulu, from 1982. Bd. dirs. Hawaii Visitors Bur., 1967, Goodwill Industries Hawaii, 1965-70; pres. Citizens Adminstrn. of Justice Found., 1968, Hawaii Epilepsy Soc., 1975. Served with AUS, 1942-45. Decorated Legion of Merit, Bronze Star, Air medal. Mem. Am. Soc. Mil. Engrs., Beavers, Gen. Contractors Assn. Hawaii (pres. 1966), Hawaii C. of C. (dir. 1964-65), Waikiki Yacht Club, Outrigger Canoe Club. Republican. Episcopalian. Died Apr. 22, 2009.

WAINWRIGHT, STUYVESANT, II, lawyer, former congressman; b. NYC, Mar. 16, 1921; s. Carroll L. and Edith Catherine (Gould) W.; m. Janet Parsons, June 12, 1941; children: Stuyvesant III, Jonathan Mayhew, Janet Snowden Kirby-Smith, Laura Livingston. LLB, Yale U., 1947. Bar: N.Y. 1948. With Satterlee, Warfield & Stephens, NYC, 1947-49; ptnr. Evarts, Balzell, Wainwright & Baker, NYC, 1949-52, Wainwright & Matthews, Huntington, N.Y., 1953-64, Walker, Beale, Wainwright & Wolf, NYC, 1965-70, Battle, Fowler, Lidstone, Jaffin, Pierce & Kheel, NYC, 1970-75; pvt. practice law Wainscott, N.Y., from 1975. Chmn. bd. Miltope Corp., Plainview, N.Y., 1975-79; Authur T. Vanderbilt prof. polit. sci. Rutgers, 1961-62; mem. 83d-86th Congresses, 1st Dist. N.Y.; spl. congl. mission to Far East, 1953. Bd. dirs. Southampton Hosp., N.Y., 1980-86, Guild Hall, East Hampton, N.Y., 1980-86; vestry St. Luke's Ch. of East Hampton; mem. Soc. for Preservation L.I. Antiquities, 1987-90. With OSS, U.S. Army, 1942-45. Mem. Masons, Union Club, Maidstone Club, Cruising Club Am., Phi Delta Phi. Spl. mission to Vietnam with Lt. Gen. James Gavin, 1967. Home: Wainscott, NY. Died Mar. 7, 2010.

WAITE, DENNIS VERNON, brokerage house executive, consultant; b. Chgo., Aug. 26, 1938; s. Vernon George and Marie G. Waite; m. Christine Rene Hibbs; 1 child, Kip Anthony. BA, U. Ill., 1968; MS in Journalism, Northwestern U., 1969. Fin. reporter, columnist Chgo. Sun-Times, Chgo., 1969-76; asst. prof. Northwestern U., Evanston, Ill., 1978-79; assoc. prof. Mich. State U., East Lansing, 1979-82; ptnr. Fin. Rels. Bd., Inc., Chgo., 1982-90, sr. ptnr., 1991-97, sr. counselor, from 1997. Reporter, producer econ. affairs Sta. WTTW-TV, Sta. WBBM-TV, Chgo., 1973-76; adj. faculty English, Coll. of DuPage, 1998—2004. Mem. editorial adv. bd. alumni relations U. Ill., Chgo., 1980-84, 90-94. With USAF, 1956-60, PTO. Rutgers U. fellow, 1972. Mem. Medill Alumni Assn. (bd. dirs. 1989-92). Avocations: reading, writing, history, Tae Kwon Do. Home: Western Springs, Ill. Died May 8, 2010.

WALDMAN, SEYMOUR MORTON, lawyer; b. NYC, Aug. 6, 1926; s. Louis and Bella B. Waldman; m. Lois Citrin, Aug. 5, 1951; children: David, Daniel, Michael, Ellen. BA, Columbia U., 1948, LLB, 1950. Bar: N.Y. 1950, U.S. Ct. Appeals (1st, 2d, 3d, 4th, 5th, 6th and D.C. cirs.), U.S. Dist. Ct. (so. dist.) N.Y., U.S. Dist. Ct. (ea. dist.) N.Y., U.S. Supreme Ct. 1956. From assoc. to ptnr. Waldman & Waldman, NYC, 1950—82; ptnr., of counsel Vladeck, Waldman, Elias & Engelhard, P.C., 1982—2005. Village atty. Village of Croton-on-Hudson, NY, 1972—2005. Chair zoning bd. appeals Village of Croton-on-Hudson, 1963—72; trustee Hosp. Joint Diseases Orthopaedic Inst., 1968—93. With USN, 1944—46. Mem. ABA, N.Y. State Bar Assn., Phi Beta Kappa. Avocation: tennis. Home: Croton On Hudson, NY. Died Jan. 10, 2009.

WALDROP, FRANCIS NEIL, physician; b. Asheville, NC, Oct. 5, 1926; s. Troy Lester and Emma Louise (Ballard) W.; m. Eleanor Dorothy Wickes, June 10, 1950; children: Mark Lester, Barbara Louise. AB, U. Minn., 1946; MD, George Washington U., 1950. Intern George Washington U. Hosp., Washington, 1950-51; resident St. Elizabeth's Hosp., Washington, 1951-54, med. officer, 1951-71; dir. manpower and tng. programs NIMH, Rockville, Md., 1972-75; dep. adminstr. Alcohol, Drug Abuse and Mental Health Adminstrn., HEW, Rockville, 1975-79; ret., 1979. Clin. prof. psychiatry George Washington U. Recipient Superior Service award HEW, 1962, Disting. Service award, 1964. Fellow Am. Psychiat. Assn. (Distinguished life, Vestermark award 1980). Achievements include research, publs. in field. Home: Silver Spring, Md. Died Apr. 12, 2010; Washington.

WALKER, CAROLYN ANN, telephone company official; b. Lynchburg, Va., July 24, 1945; d. Charlie Stencil and Virginia May (Scruggs) W.; student No. Va. Community Coll., 1972—. Long distance operator C & P Telephone, Arlington, Va., 1966-69, employment interviewer, 1969-75, supr. service order typists, 1975-76, govt. liaison, Washington, 1976-78, staff supr., Silver Spring, Md., 1978-82, Washington, 1982-83; staff supr. Bell Atlantic Network Services, Inc., Silver Spring, 1984-89, asst. mgr., Arlington, Va., 1989—. Adv., exec. adv. Jr. Achievement. Mem. Nat. Assn. Female Execs. Home: N Myrtle Bch, SC. Died June 26, 2010.

WALKER, HAROLD EMMETT, accountant; b. Columbus, Ga., Nov. 27, 1932; s. Emmett Boyd and Grace Truman (Wadsworth) W.; m. Janice Carter, June 9, 1956; children: Mark Jackson, Margaret Anne. BBA, U. Tenn., 1954. With audit staff Ernst & Young, Knoxville, Tenn., 1954-66, ptnr. Miami, Fla., 1966-71, mng. ptnr. Ft. Lauderdale, Fla., 1971-76, Ernst & Whinney, Miami, 1976-84, Honolulu, 1984-87, Ernst & Young, San Antonio, 1987-90. Pres. Broward County United Way, Ft. Lauderdale, 1975; pres. Citizens Bd. U. Miami, 1979-80, trustee, 1980-81; mem. exec. com. Miami Citizens Against Crime, 1982-84; vice chmn. Econ. Devel. Corp. of Honolulu. Mem. AICPA (nat. coun. 1977-82), Fla. Inst. CPA's (pres. 1977-78), Nat. Assn. Accts. (pres. Knoxville chpt. 1982), Greater Miami C. of C. (vice chmn. 1981-84), Waialae Country Club, Miami Club (pres. 1981), San Antonio Country Club, The Argyle and Club Girard (San Antonio). Republican. Presbyterian. Died June 16, 2010.

WALKER, JOHN ALVIN, III, pharmacist; b. Rochester, Minn., Apr. 8, 1948; s. John Alvin Walker Jr. and Ione Louise (Kujath) Walker; m. Connie Marie Witt, June 24, 1972 (div. Apr. 1978); m. Teri Jo Ellis, Oct. 13, 1984. BS in Pharmacy, U. Iowa, 1972. Lic. pharmacist Iowa. Intern pharmacy Walgreen's, Racine, Wis., 1972—73; clin. instr. U. Iowa, Iowa City, 1973—81; dir. pharmacy Wayne County Hosp., Corydon, from 1981; cons. Seymour Care Ctr., from 1983. Cons. Seymour Care Ctr., Iowa, from 1983. Contbr. chapters to books, articles to profl. jours. Mem. Focus Drug Abuse Com., Wayne County, from 1983. Mem.: Am. Pharm. Assn. (Chpt. Contbn. award 1982), Am. Soc. Hosp. Pharmacists, Ducks Unltd., Shelby Am. Automobile Club. Republican. Methodist. Avocations: skiing, canoeing, golf. Home: Corydon, Iowa. Died Jan. 1, 2009.

WALKER, ROBERT HARRIS, historian, writer, editor; b. Cin., Mar. 15, 1924; m. Grace Burtt; children: Amy, Rachel, Matthew. BS, Northwestern U., 1945; MA, Columbia U., 1950; PhD, U. Pa., 1955. Edn. specialist U.S. Mil. Govt., Japan, 1946-47; instr. Carnegie Inst. Tech., 1950-51, U. Pa., 1953-54; asst. prof., dir. American Studies U. Wyo., 1955-59;

assoc. prof. George Washington U., 1959-63, prof. American civilization, 1963-94, dir. American studies program, 1959-66, 68-70. First dir. edn. and pub. programs NEH, 1966-68; fellow Woodrow Wilson Internat. Ctr., 1972-73, Rockefeller Rsch. Ctr., 1979, Hoover Instn., Huntington Libr., 1980; specialist grants to Japan, Germany, Thailand, Iran, Greece, Israel, Brazil, China, People's Republic of Korea, Hong Kong, 1964-91; Fulbright lectr., Australia, New Zealand, Philippines, 1971, Sweden, France, West Germany, Norway, all 1987; Am. Coun. Learned Socs. alt. del. UNESCO Gen. Info. Program; co-founder Algonquin Books, 1982. Author: Poet and Gilded Age: Social Themes in Late Nineteenth-Century American Verse, 1963, Everyday Life in the Age of Enterprise, 1865-1900, 1967, American Society, 1981, 2d edit., 1995, Reform in America, 1985, (with R.H. Gabriel) Course of American Democratic Thought, 3d edit., 1986, Cincinnati and the Big Red Machine, 1988, Everyday Life in Victorian America, 1994; editor, compiler: American Studies in the U.S., 1958, American Studies Abroad, 1975, Reform Spirit in America, 1976, 85, American Studies: Topics and Sources, 1976, Friends of Raoul Wallenberg, 1987-1997, 1998; editor: Am. Quar., 1953-54; sr. editor: Am. Studies Internat., 1970-80, Am. studies series for Greenwood Press, over 100 vols. Founding mem. Japan-U.S. Friendship Commn., 1977-80; founding pres. Friends of Raoul Wallenberg Found., 1987-99. With USNR, 1943-46, 50. Mem. Am. Studies Assn. (nat. pres. 1970-71), Cosmos Club, Phi Beta Kappa. Died Jan. 15, 2010.

WALKER, WILLIAM, retired performing company executive; b. Waco, Tex., Oct. 29, 1931; s. William Wallace and Ruby (Barton) W.; m. Marci Martin, May 25, 1957; children: Nancy, David, Thomas, John. MusB, Tex. Christian U., 1956. Baritone Met. Opera, NYC, 1962-80; vis. prof. Tex. Christian U., Ft. Worth, 1980-84, Lamar U., Beaumont, Tex., 1980-85; businessman, 1985-91; gen. dir. Ft. Worth Opera, 1991—2002, gen. dir. emeritus, 2002—10. Bd. vis. sch. fine arts Tex. Christian U., Ft. Worth, 1993 Sgt. U.S. Army, 1952-54, Korea. Recipient Disting. Alumnus award Tex. Christian U., 1970. Mem. Rotary. Avocations: chamber music, travel, golf. Home: Fort Worth, Tex. Died Apr. 10, 2010.

WALKER, WILLIAM E., banker; b. Saxonburg, Pa., Dec. 21, 1926; s. Ira E. and Fanny (Morford) W.; m. Grace Bair, Dec. 27, 1945; children— Holly, Laurie, Scott Grad., Am. Inst. Banking, Pitts., 1963, Rutgers U., 1967. Sr. v.p. Union Nat. Bank, Pitts., 1975-77, exec. v.p., 1977-83, pres., 1983-85, chmn., chief exec. officer, from 1985, also dir. Pres. Union Nat. Life Ins. Co., Pitts.; bd. dirs. Valley Nat. Bank, Freeport, Pa. Served to 1st lt. U.S. Army, 1945-53 Mem. Am. Inst. Banking, Pa. Bankers Assn., Am. Bankers Assn. Home: Sarver, Pa. Died Aug. 3, 2010.

WALL, HELEN KATHARINE, personnel executive; b. Phila., Oct. 15, 1941; d. Milton and Carlyn (Ochs) Epstein; m. C. Robert Reichley, Jr., Aug. 29, 1964 (div. Jan. 1975); m. 2d James L. Wall, May 26, 1979; children— Susanne E., Melissa L. B.S., Temple U., 1963, postgrad., 1976-83. Tchr., Cooke Jr. High Sch., Phila., 1963-65; personnel adminstr. Oxford First Corp., Phila., 1977-78; benefits adminstr. Honeywell, Inc., Ft. Washington, Pa., 1978-79; personnel mgr. Smiths Industries, Inc., Malvern, Pa., 1979-83; employee relations mgr. Thomas & Betts Corp., Montgomeryville, Pa., 1983—. Tutor, classroom aide York Ave. Elem. Sch., Lansdale, Pa., 1971-73; dir. pub. relations LWV, Lansdale, 1972-76; leader jr. troop Girl Scouts U.S.A., North Wales, Pa., 1975-78; recruiter Am. Cancer Soc., North Wales/Lansdale, 1975-76. Phila. Bd. Edn. music scholar, 1959. Mem. Am. Soc. Personnel Adminstrs., North Penn Indsl. Relations Assn., Mfrs. Assn. Delaware Valley, AAUW. Home: Lansdale, Pa. Died June 19, 2009.

WALL, WILLIAM CARTER, JR., engineering and business management consultant, educator, author; b. Huntsville, Ala., June 30, 1930; s. William Carter and Marion Elizabeth (Terry) W.; m. Shirley Lenore Matzet, June 18, 1955; children— William August, Kathleen Mary, Linda Lee, Christie Lynn, Terri Elizabeth, Julie Catherine. B.S. in Mech. Engring., Lafayette Coll., 1953; M.A. in Pub. Adminstrn., U. Okla., 1971, M.B.A., 1975, Ph.D., 1978. Cert. profl. estimator. Engr. Allis-Chalmers, Milw., 1953-55; with Dept. Army, Redstone Arsenal, Ala., 1957-81, chief mgmt. data systems office, Ballistic Missile Def. Systems Command, 1968-76, chief program mgmt. office HAWK Project Office, Missile Materiel Readiness Command, 1976-78, dep. project mgr. ground laser designators project office, Missile Research and Devel. Command, 1978-79, chief def. advanced research projects agy. projects office, Missile Command, 1979-80, dep. project mgr. Tow Project Office, 1980-81; pres. WCW Assocs., Inc., Huntsville, Ala., 1981—; adj. prof. mgmt. Fla. Inst. Tech., Melbourne, 1978—; part time faculty U. Ala., Huntsville, 1979—; prof. mgmt., nat. grad. faculty, dir. Huntsville Ctr., Ctr. for Study of Adminstrn., Nova U., Ft. Lauderdale, Fla., 1981—. Contbr. articles to profl. publs. Active Better Bus. Bur. N.Ala., Nat. Eagle Scout Assn. Served with U.S. Army, 1955-57. Recipient cert. of merit Dept. Army, 1971. Mem. Am. Mgmt. Assn., Assn. U.S. Army, So. Mgmt. Assn., Project Mgmt. Inst., Acad. of Mgmt., Nat. Estimating Soc., Huntsville-Madison County C. of C., Beta Gamma Sigma, Omicron Delta Epsilon. Roman Catholic. Clubs: Redstone Arsenal Officers, K.C. Home: Huntsville, Ala. Died Apr. 25, 2009.

WALLACE, ANDERSON, JR., lawyer, educator; b. Cleve., Sept. 24, 1939; s. Anderson and Agatha Lee (Culpepper) Wallace; m. Kristine Lee Gough; children: Anderson III, Whitney, Nicole Belcher. BA, George Washington U., 1962, JD, 1964, LLM, 1966. Bar: Tex. 68, U.S. Dist. Ct. (no. dist.) Tex. 68, U.S. Ct. Claims 68, U.S. Tax Ct. 68, U.S. Ct. Appeals (5th cir.) 68, U.S. Supreme Ct. 71, U.S. Ct. Appeals (11th cir.) 81. Program mgmt. asst. NASA, Washington, 1962—64; atty. U.S. Dept. Treasury, Washington, 1964—66; tax atty. Price Waterhouse & Co., Atlanta, 1966—67; tax ptnr. Jackson, Walker, Winstead, Cantwell & Miller, Dallas, 1967—84; dir. in charge tax dept. Baker, Mills & Glast, P.C., Dallas, 1984—93; pres. Anderson Wallace, Jr., P.C., Attys., Dallas, from 1993. Instr. Sch. Law So. Meth. U. Trustee S.W. Mus. Sci. and Tech., Dallas, from 1974, Girls Found. Dallas Inc.; chmn. Inst. on Employee Benefits, Southwestern Found., 1976. Mem.: ABA. Died July 21, 2010.

WALLACE, STEWART RAYNOR, consulting exploration and mining geologist; b. Freeport, NY, Mar. 31, 1919; s. Earl Stewart and Marjorie Boynton (Smith) Wallace; m. Alice Isabella Dodge, Sept. 7, 1946 (div. Sept. 1976); children: William Dodge, Margaret Boynton; m. Marjorie Lee Ewer, Apr. 1, 1983. AB, Dartmouth Coll., 1941; MS, U. Mich., 1948, PhD, 1953. Geologist US Geol. Survey, Washington, Denver, 1948—55; chief geologist Molybdenum Co., 1955—69; pres. & dir., exploration Mine Finders Inc., Lakewood, Colo., 1969—76; self-employed cons. geologist Lakewood, from 1976. Contbr. articles to profl. jours. Served to 1st lt. C.E. US Army, 1941—46, ETO. Fellow: Geol. Soc. America; mem.: Soc. Econ. Geologists (v.p. 1978), Assn. Exploration Geochemists, Soc. Mining Engrs. AIME (Jackling award 1974, Disting. mem. 1984). Republican. Home: Littleton, Colo. Died Mar. 12, 2009.

WALSH, EDWARD JOSEPH, food products and cosmetics executive; b. Mt. Vernon, NY, Mar. 18, 1932; s. Edward Aloysius and Charlotte Cecilia (Borup) W.; m. Patricia Ann Farrell, Sept. 16, 1961; children: Edward Joseph, Megan Simpson, John, Robert. BBA, Iona Coll., 1953; MBA, NYU, 1958. Sales rep. M & R Dietetic Labs., Columbus, Ohio, 1955-60; with Armour & Co., 1961-71, Greyhound Corp., 1971-87; v.p. toiletries div. Armour Dial Co., Phoenix, 1973-74, exec. v.p., 1975-77; pres., CEO Armour Internat. Co., Phoenix, 1978-84; pres. The Dial Corp. (formerly Armour-Dial Co.), Phoenix, 1984-87, chief exec. officer, 1984-87; pres., chief exec. officer Purex Corp., 1985; chmn., chief exec. officer The Sparta Group Ltd., Scottsdale, Ariz., 1988—2008. Bd. dirs. Nortrust Holding Corp., Phoenix, Matrixx Initiatives, Inc., Phoenix, 2000—07; mem. bd. advisors Brother to Brother Internat., 1988—2001, bd. dirs., 1988—2004; mem. bd. advisors Universal Tech. Inst., Phoenix, 1996—2004, No. Trust N.A., from 2006. Trustee Scottsdale Meml. Health Found., 1995-98; pres. Mt. Vernon Fire Dept. Mems. Assn., 1960-61. Served with U.S. Army, 1953-55, Germany. Recipient Loftus Lifetime Achievement award, Iona Coll., 2004. Mem. Am. Mgmt. Assn., Nat. Meat Canner Assn. (pres. 1971-72), Cosmetic, Toiletries and Fragrance Assn. (bd. dirs. 1985—87), Nat. Food Processors Assn. (bd. dirs.). Republican. Roman Catholic. Home: Paradise Valley, Ariz. Died Oct. 13, 2009.

WALSH, JAMES ALOYSIUS, rubber company executive; b. Passaic, NJ, Mar. 23, 1921; s. James A. and Mary (Riley) W.; m. Mary Fitzgerald, June 15, 1942 (div. Mar. 1965); children: Michael A., Tyla Ann; m. Sandra Spear, July 1970; children: Diana Lynn, Meaghan E., James F., Patrick O. Grad., Choate Sch., 1939; BS in Indsl. Adminstrn, Yale, 1943. With Armstrong Rubber Co., West Haven, Conn., from 1942, v.p. mfg., 1966-71, pres., 1971-80, chmn., chief exec. officer, 1980-86, also dir. Dir. Copolymer Rubber & Chem. Co., Baton Rouge., Arcowheel, Inc. Mem. bd. visitors Sch. Bus., U. Conn. Mem. Rubber Mfrs. Assn. (bd. dirs.), Newcomen Soc. in N.Am. Clubs: New Haven Country (New Haven), Quinnipack (New Haven), Yale (New Haven); Mory's Assn, Port Royal Country. Died Apr. 20, 2009.

WALSH, JOHN JOSEPH, former federal agency administrator; b. Des Moines, Oct. 9, 1916; s. John Joseph and Hazel (Watrous) W.; m. Vivian Souder, Apr. 12, 1939 (dec. Apr. 1969); children: John J., Jean Evangeline, Thomas Richard; m. 2d Mary Ellen Johnson Casson, Dec. 22, 1970. B.C.S., Southeastern U., Washington, 1940. Spl. agent FBI, 1938-53; project mgr. Bendix Radio Co., Balt., 1953-58; contract adminstr. RCA, Moorestown, N.J., 1958-63; investigator Senate Investigations Subcom., Washington, 1963-76, 77-79; dir. investigations HEW, Washington, 1976-77; dep. asst. sec. US Dept. Labor, Washington, from 1982. Mem.: Manor Country (Rockville, Md.). Roman Catholic. Home: Silver Spring, Md. Died Sept. 2, 2009.

WALSH, PHILIP CORNELIUS, retired mining executive; b. Harrison, NJ, May 23, 1921; s. Philip Cornelius and Frances (Prendergast) Walsh; m. Alexandra Somerville Tuck, May 19, 1945 (dec. Sept. 1993); children: Eugenie Philbin Flaherty, Philip C.C., Frances Cummings, Alexander Tuck, Nicholas Holladay, Elizabeth Lovering; m. Peggy Flanigan McDonnell, Oct. 13, 1996. BA, Yale U., 1943; member of the Class of 1944. With W.R. Grace & Co., Lima, Peru and NYC, 1946-71; v.p. parent co., chief operating officer Latin Am. group, 1961-71, group exec. corp. adminstrv. group, 1970-71; v.p. Cerro Corp., 1972-74, Newmont Mining Corp., 1974-80; chmn. bd. Foote Mineral Co., Exton, Pa., 1979-80; dir. Cyprus Minerals Co., 1980—85; vice chmn. St. Joe Minerals Corp., 1980-85; chmn. bd. Chilean Lithium Co. Ltd., 1980-94; dir. T. Rowe Price Assocs., Inc., 1986—2000; ret., 2000. Past dir. Peabody Coal Co., Piedmont Mining Co.; bd. advisors Fond Elec.; mem. Nat. Strategic Minerals and Metals Program Adv. Commn. Mem. Harding Twp. Bd. Edn., NJ, 1960—66, Harding Twp. Com., 1966—72, police commr., 1966—72; trustee Morristown Meml. Hosp., 1969—79; vis. com. Colo. Sch. Mines, Global Sys. and Cultures. 1st lt. US Army. Decorated Silver Star, Purple Heart. Mem.: AIME (Saunders gold medal 1992, Disting. mem. award 1993), Am. Soc. (hon. dir.), Pan Am. Soc. U.S. (past vice chmn.), Am. Assn. Order of Malta (past chancellor), Fed. Assn. Order of Malta, Edgartown Golf Club, Essex Hunt Club, Edgartown Yacht Club (commodore 1993—95), Racquet and Tennis Club, Somerset Hills Country Club, Sigma Xi, Phi Beta Kappa. Republican. Roman Catholic. Home: Peapack, NJ. Died Mar. 24, 2010.

WALSH, SEMMES GUEST, retired insurance company executive; b. Annapolis, Md., June 15, 1926; m. Annette Hunt Cromwell, Aug. 23, 1952; children: Semmes. G. Jr., Annette T., Marion H., Jacquelyn C. BE, Yale U., 1946; MBA, Harvard U., 1950. Gen. ptnr. Baker, Watts & Co., Balt., 1962-74, mng. ptnr., 1974-80; exec. v.p., chief fin. officer Monumental Corp., Balt., 1980-89, ret., 1989. Bd. dirs. Wm. G. Baker Meml. Fund, Jas. L. Kernan Hosp. Found, Eudowood Found., Anna E. Warfield Meml. Fund., Inc. Lt. (j.g.) USNR, 1943-46. Republican. Episcopalian. Avocations: tennis, golf. Home: Owings Mills, Md. Died Aug. 20, 2010.

WALSH, TOM (THOMAS EDMUND WALSH), retired state legislator; b. Oct. 31, 1942; m. Rita Marie Christenson, 1963; children: Thomas Jr., Christopher. City councilman City of Casper, 1997, Wyo., 1999—2002, Wyo., 2008, mayor Wyo., 2000; mem. Dist. 56 Wyo. House of Reps., Wyo., 2003—08. Republican. Died Jan. 1, 2010.

WALTON, CARMELITA NOREEN, retired nursing administrator; b. Chgo., Nov. 15, 1926; d. Elmo Augusta and Evelyn Mae (Terry) Desobrey; 1 child by previous marriage: Michael Jerome. Student, St. Marys Coll., U. Notre Dame, Ind., 1943—45; grad., Cook County Sch. Nursing, Chgo., 1949; BA Behavioral Social Sci., DePaul U., Chgo., 1993. Cert. nursing adminstr. ANCC; cert. correctional health profl. Head nurse, supr., nurse clinician Cook County Hosp., Chgo., 1951—71; supr. U. Chgo. Hosps. and Clinics, 1963—68; DON Woodlawn Child Health Ctr., Chgo., 1968—69; DON prison health care Cermak Health Svcs., Cook County Jail, Chgo., 1973—93; ret., 1993. Nurse cons. Quality Mgmt., In-Svc. Edn.; med.-surg. staff nurse; cons., surveyor Nat. Commn. on Correctional Health Care, spkr. 13th ann. conv., 1989, apptd. to bd. certification correctional health, 1991— Contbr. articles to profl. jours Recipient Superior Pub. Svc. award City of Chgo., 1984 Mem. APHA, ANA (coun. nursing adminstrn.), Ill. Nurses Assn., Nat. League Nursing, Am. Assn. Diabetes Educators Democrat. Roman Catholic. Home: Chicago, Ill. Died Sept. 28, 2009.

WALTON, HAROLD VINCENT, retired agricultural engineer, academic administrator, educator; b. Christiana, Pa., June 17, 1921; s. Howard King and Alice Lauretta (Kirk) W.; m. Velma Purvis Braun, June 24, 1946; children: H. Richard, Marilyn J. Walton Friedersdorf, Carol A. BS in Agrl. Engring., Pa. State U., 1942, MS in Agrl. Engring., 1950; PhD in Agrl. Engring., Purdue U., 1961. Test engr. Gen. Electric Co., Schenectady, 1943-45; instr. Pa. State U., 1947-50, asst. prof. agrl. engring., 1950-52, assoc. prof., 1952-61, prof., 1961, 76-85, head dept. agrl. engring., 1976-85, ret., 1985; prof., chmn. dept. agrl. engring. U. Mo.-Columbia, 1962-69, chief of party Bhubaneswar, India, 1969-71, prof., 1971-76. Cons. OAS, Trinidad and Tobago, 1980, Ptnrs. of Ams., Brazil, 1984. With US Army, 1945—46. Fulbright scholar, Cyprus, 1989—90. Fellow: Am. Soc. Agrl. Engrs. (bd. dirs. 1967—69, 1985—87). Republican. Home: Kingwood, Tex. Died May 1, 2009.

WALWER, FRANK KURT, dean, legal educator; b. NYC, July 11, 1930; s. Kurt and Beatrice (Ahlert) W.; m. Maryann Pancake, Apr. 15, 1961; 1 child, Gregory F. Assoc. deanm Columbia Univ., 1972-80; dean, prof. U. Tulsa, 1980-91; trustee's prof. law, 1991-94; dean emeritus, prof. Tex. Wesleyan Univ. Law Sch., from 1994. Dean, legal educator; b. 1930; s. Kurt and Beatrice (Ahlert) W.; m. Maryann Pancake, Apr. 15, 1961; 1 child, Gregory F. AB, Columbia U., 1952, LLB, 1956. Bar: N.Y. 1959. Assoc. dean Columbia U., 1972-80; dean, prof. U. Tulsa, 1980-91, trustee's prof. law, 1991-94, dean, prof. Tex. Wesleyan U. Law Sch., 1994—, chmn. Grad. and Profl. Sch. Fin. Aid Svc., 1976-78, pres. Law Sch. Admission Coun., 1983-84; bd. dirs. The Coun. on Postsecondary Accreditation, 1989-92. Mem. Assn. Am. Law Schs. (chmn. sect. econs. of legal edn. 1974-76), ABA (accreditation com. 1988-94, chair legal edn. and bar admissions sect. 1986-87, lawyer competency com. 1986-92, standards rev. com. 1986-94, AALS/ABA commn. on financing), Am. Bar Fellows, Am. Inns of Court. Died Jan. 1, 2010.

WAMPOLD, CHARLES HENRY, JR., lawyer; b. Montgomery, Ala., Oct. 21, 1925; s. Charles Henry and Selma (Manasse) W.; m. Babette Levy, Mar. 14, 1954; children: Jerre Lynn, Carolyn M., Charles Henry III. BA, U. Ala., 1946, LL.B., 1948, JD, 1950. Bar: Ala. 1948. Practice in, Montgomery, from 1949; mem. Capouano, Wampold, Prestwood & Sansone, 1960-83, of counsel, from 1983. Bd. dirs. Griel Meml. Hosp., Mus. Fine Arts, Montgomery Community Council. Mem. ABA, Ala. Bar Assn., Montgomery Area Mental Health Assn., Zeta Beta Tau. Clubs: Lions. Jewish. Home: Montgomery, Ala. Died July 17, 2010.

WARD, JAMES MUNCIE, land developer; b. Nashville, Dec. 28, 1928; s. James Truman and Mary Geneva (Muncie) W.; m. Mary Jane Bolling, Apr. 10, 1953; children— Trudy, Janie. B.E., Vanderbilt U., 1950. With WLAC Radio, Nashville, from 1950, sales dept. staff, 1953-66, gen. mgr., 1966-79; partner Md. Farms Assos., Md. Farms Racquet and Country Club, from 1979. Dir. Nashville City Bank. Pres. Nashville Better Bus. Bur., 1967; pres. Nashville Y.M.C.A., 1970; chmn. Nashville chpt. ARC, 1975; gen. chairperson Leadership Nashville, 1984. Mem. Nashville Advtg. Fedn. (pres. 1969), Am. Advtg. Fedn. (chmn. bd. govs. 1976), Sales and Mktg. Execs. (pres. 1983) Ch. Christ. Clubs: Exchange Club of Nashville (pres. 1975), Nashville City (pres. 1969). Home: Brentwood, Tenn. Died Apr. 7, 2009.

WARD, JAMES THERON, protective services official; b. July 15, 1942; s. Cecil S. and Gerterude (Craig) W.; m. Kathryn Ward; children: Scott, Brian. Grad. high sch., Hollywood, Fla., 1960. Cert. paramedic, Fla. Firefighter Hollywood Fire Dept., 1963-69, driver engr., 1969-73, paramedic lt., 1973-76, capt. fire suppression, 1976-77, chief tng. divsn.,

1977-78, with, 1978-82, chief, from 1982. Initial chmn. Fla. State Emergency Med. Svc. Adv. Coun.; chmn. planning com. Broward Emergency Med. Svc. Coun., Broward County, Fla.; chmn. Broward County Fire Adminstr.'s Emergency Med. Svc. Com. With USAF, 1961-63. Recipient Larry S. Jordon Emergency Med. Svc. Hall of Fame award HRS, 1993; named Emergency Med. Svc. Provider of Yr., Fla. Emergency Med. Svc. Adminstrn., 1994. Mem. Fla. Emergency Med. Svc. Providers Assn. (pres., Al Ridgway award 1989), Fla. Fire Chiefs Assn., Broward County Profl. Fire Chiefs Assn., Internat. Assn. Fire Chiefs, Hollywood Com. of 100, Rotary. Avocations: fishing, scuba diving, photography. Home: Tavernier, Fla. Died Aug. 7, 2010.

WARD, ROBERT EDWARD, retired political science professor, academic administrator; b. San Francisco, Jan. 29, 1916; s. Edward Butler and Claire Catherine (Unger) W.; m. Constance Regina Barnett, Oct. 31, 1942 (dec. Sept. 19, 2007); children: Erica Anne, Katherine Elizabeth (dec.). BA, Stanford U., 1936; MA, U. Calif.-Berkeley, 1938, PhD, 1948. Instr. in polit. sci. U. Mich., 1948-50, asst. prof. polit. sci., 1950-54, assoc. prof., 1954-58, prof., 1958-73, Stanford U., 1973-87, dir. Center for Research in Internat. Studies, 1973-87. Cons. in field; advisor Center for Strategic and Internat. Studies, Washington, 1968-87 Author: Modern Political Systems: Asia, 1963, Political Modernization in Japan and Turkey, 1964. Mem. nat. council Nat. Endowment for Humanities, Washington, 1968-73; mem. Pres.'s Commn. on Fgn. Lang.-Internat. Studies, 1978-79; chmn. Japan-U.S. Friendship Commn., 1980-83; mem. Dept. Def. Univ. Forum, 1982-87. Served to lt. (j.g.) USN, 1942-45. Decorated Legion of Merit, 1945; recipient Japan Found. award Tokyo, 1976, Order of Sacred Treasure (Japan), 1983 Fellow Am. Acad. Arts and Scis.; mem. Am. Polit. Sci. Assn. (pres. 1972-73), Assn. Asian Studies (pres. 1972-73), Social Sci. Research Council (chmn. 1969-71), Am. Philos. Soc. Home: Portola Valley, Calif. Died Dec. 7, 2009.

WARD, THOMAS NELSON, electric utility executive; b. Chambersburg, Pa., July 16, 1923; s. Thomas N. and Mary (Gilbert) W.; m. Jean R. Oyler, June 12, 1948; children: Marilyn J., Thomas G., Barbara B. BS, U. Ill., 1947; student, Rutgers U., 1943-44, U. Mich., 1956-68. C.P.A., N.J., Ohio. Sr. accountant Arthur Andersen & Co. (C.P.A.s), NYC, 1947-54; v.p. adminstrn., sec., treas. Ohio Valley Electric Corp., Piketon, Ohio, from 1954; v.p., sec., treas. Ind.-Ky. Electric Corp., Piketon, from 1954. Served with inf. AUS, 1943-45. Decorated Bronze Star. Mem. Am. Inst. C.P.A.s. Home: Chillicothe, Ohio. Died Apr. 9, 2010.

WARE, GEORGE HENRY, botanist; b. Avery, Okla., Apr. 27, 1924; s. Charles and Mildred (Eshelman) W.; m. June Marie Gleason, Dec. 21, 1955; children: David, Daniel, Patrick, John. BS, U. Okla., 1945, MS, 1948; PhD, U. Wis., 1955. Asst. prof. Northwestern State U. of La., Natchitoches, 1948-56, assoc. prof., 1956-62, prof., 1962-67; dir. Conservation Sect., No. La. Supplementary Edn. Ctr., Natchitoches, 1967-68; dendrologist Morton Arboretum, Lisle, Ill., 1968-92; adminstr. Urban Vegetation Lab., 1986-92, rsch. fellow in dendrology, 1992-94, dendrologist emeritus, rsch. assoc., 1995—2010. Vis. prof. U. Okla., Norman, 1957, 61, 63-64; adj. prof. Western Ill. U., 1972-85; ext. faculty George Williams Coll., Downers Grove, Ill., 1969-76, Nat. Coll. Edn., Evanston, Ill., 1972-76, adj. prof. Aurora U., 2003-10. Trustee nomination caucus Coll. of DuPage, Glen Ellyn, Ill., 1974-78; bd. dirs. Kane-DuPage Soil and Water Conservation Dist., 1969-81, DuPage Environ. Commn., 1992-2010, Openlands Project, 1996-2010; pres. La. Acad. Scis., 1966-67; dir. La. State Sci. Fair, 1966. With USN, 1942-46; hon. dir. Openlands, 2007-10. Recipient Gold Seal award, Nat. Coun. State Garden Clubs, 1991, Am. Forests Urban Forestry Rsch. medal, 1994, Lifetime Svc. award, Nat. Urban and Cmty. Forestry Adv. Coun., 1995, Hutchinson medal, Chgo. Botanic Garden, 1997, Norman J. Colman award, Am. Nursery and Landscape Assn., 1998, award of merit, Am. Pub. Garden Assn., 2000, Liberty Hyde Bailey award, Am. Horticultural Soc., 2002, Conservation Leadership award, Openlands, 2005. Mem.: Am. Forests, Nature Conservancy, Ill. Arborist Assn. (pres. 1987—88), Am. Pub. Garden Assn., Internat. Soc. Arboriculture (Pres. Commendation award 2000, L.C. Chadwick Rsch. award 2008), Southwestern Assn. Naturalists (treas. 1963—69). Home: Batavia, Ill. Died July 4, 2010.

WARE, ROBERT HAYDEN, patent attorney; b. June 7, 1927; BSME, U. Mich., 1947; MSME, Harvard U., 1948, LLB, 1951. Bar: Conn. 1958, Mass., N.Y. Ptnr. Ware, Fressola, Van Der Sluys and Adolphson, Monroe, Conn., 1963—2004; ret., 2004. Past squadron comdr., life mem. and instr. in navigation, sail, weather and pub. boating safety courses, U.S. Power Squadrons; troop com. chmn. and merit badge counselor BSA, 1969-85; mem. Gold award review bd. Housatonic Girl Scout Coun., 1984-87. Mem. ABA, Conn. Bar Assn. (chmn. antitrust sect. 1977-79, client security fund com. 1980-98), Bridgeport Bar Assn., Conn. Patent Law Assn. (pres. 1969-70), Rotary (Paul Harris fellow, pres. Bridgeport club 1982-83). Home: Fairfield, Conn. Died Jan. 23, 2009.

WARGOTZ, HELEN, psychoanalyst; b. N.Y.C., July 17, 1921; d. Louis and Eva (Weinglass) W.; m. Joseph De Marco, July 4, 1942. BA, Hunter Coll., 1942; MSW, Columbia U., 1946. Case worker foster home dept. Jewish Child Care Assn., N.Y.C., 1946-47, psychiat. social worker VA Mental Hygiene Clinic, N.Y.C., 1947-48; 1st case worker mental retardation clinic Flower Hosp. Mental Hygiene Clinic, N.Y.C., 1950-51; psychiat. social worker Youth Bd. Pub. Sch. 140, L.I., 1951-52; family counselor Jewish Family Svc., 1952-55; psychoanalytic psychotherapist L.I. Cons. Ctr., 1955-57; individual and group counselor N.Y. Guild for Jewish Blind, 1957-58; individual and group psychoanalytic psychotherapist, lectr., chmn. speakers' bur. Jamaica Ctr. for Psychotherapy (now Advanced Ctr. for Psychotherapy), 1958-68; psychoanalytic group therapist Mental Health Inst. N.Y.C., 1959-60; chief psychiat. social worker, supr., faculty Children's Clinic, N.Y. Sch. Psychiatry, 1962-63; individual and group counselor Shield David Sch. and Clinic, N.Y.C., 1966-69; chief psychiat. social worker 5th Ave. Ctr. for Counseling and Psychotherapy, N.Y.C., 1968-72; tng. psychoanalyst, faculty, supr., Tng. Inst. for Mental Health Practitioners, 1972-75; cons. N.Y. State Bur. of Disability Determinations, N.Y.C., 1974—; cons. Headstart, 1966; dir. profl. services Allied Teen-Age Guidance and Adult Counseling Service, N.Y.C., 1964—; team mem. evaluating children needing spl. edn. com. Handicapped, 1975—; supr. group therapy T. Reik Clinic, 1956-64; condr. parent edn. course Ft. Lee Adult High Sch., 1966-67; cons. Legal Aid Soc.; cons. on retirement Am. Mgmt. Assn. and various unions; radio and TV panelists. lectr. religious and sch. groups. Columnist: Teen Facts and Parent Strategy, L.I. Graphic Roosevelt Press; contbr. chpts. to book, textbook, articles to publs. Internat. profl. adv. com. Parents Without Partners, 1967—; pres., group discussion leader Club at 92d St., N.Y.C., 1967-68. Workshop fellow N.J. Montclair State Coll., 1966; Inst. for Curriculum in Adminstrn. of Community Mental Health Services fellow, 1971-73. Mem. Council of Psychoanalytic Psychotherapists (charter). Club: City of N.Y. (social welfare, health and hosp. coms. 1958—). Died Jan. 4, 2009.

WARNECKE, JOHN CARL, architect; b. Oakland, Calif., Feb. 24, 1919; s. Carl I. and Margaret (Esterling) W.; children by previous marriage: John Carl, Rodger Cushing, Margaret Esterling, Frederic Pierce. AB, Stanford U., 1941; MA, Harvard U., 1942. Asso. Miller & Warnecke, architects, 1944-46; prin. John Carl Warnecke, AIA, 1947-58; ptnr. Warnecke & Warnecke, 1954-62; pres., dir. design John Carl Warnecke & Assoc., 1958—2010. Works include U.S. Naval Acad. Master Plan, Michelson and Chauvenet Halls, Annapolis, Md., U. Calif. at Santa Cruz Master Plan and Library, Lafayette Sq., Washington, Georgetown U. Library, Washington, Kaiser Center for Tech., Pleasanton, Calif.; bldgs., Stanford U., Hawaii State Capitol, Honolulu, Philip A. Hart Senate office bldg., USSR Embassy, Hennepin Govt. Center, Mpls., J.F. Kennedy Meml. Grave, Arlington Nat. Cemetery, Va., Neiman Marcus and Bergdorf Goodman Stores, Logan Airport, Boston, Am. Hosp, Paris, The Sun Co. Hdqrs, Radnor, Pa., King Abdulaziz U. Med. Center, Jedda, Saudi Arabia, Yanbu Town Ctr. Master Plan, Hilton Hotel & Casino, Atlantic City. Mem. Fine Arts Commn., Washington, 1963-67. Recipient Arnold Brunner prize in architecture Nat. Inst. Arts and Letters, 1957; also 70 nat., regional awards for excellence. Fellow AIA; Mem. NAD (assoc., 1958-94, academician, 1994-2010) Home: San Francisco, Calif. Died Apr. 17, 2010.

WARNER, JAMES DANIEL, clergyman; b. Sheridan, Wyo., May 1, 1924; s. Stephan Daniel and Grace Margaret (Caple) W.; m. Barbara A. Wallgren, Sept. 6, 1952 (dec. 1957); m. Marcy Walk Swan, Feb. 8, 1960; children— Stephen, David, Cheryl, Mark, Kathryn, James, Tammy. BS, Northwestern U., 1950; M in Divinity, Seabury Western Theol. Sem., 1953, DD, 1977. Vicar St. James Ch., Mosinee, Wis., 1953-56; rector St. Paul's Ch., Marmette, Wis., 1956-60; asst. chaplain St. James Ch., U. Wichita, Kans., 1960-62; rector St. Stephen's Ch., Wichita, 1962-70, Trinity Ch., Oshkosh, Wis., 1970-77; bishop Diocese of Nebr., Omaha, from 1977. Pres. St. Com., Diocese of Kans., 1966-68 Pres. Community Planning Council, Wichita, 1965-66, police chaplain several community social agencies. Served in USN, 1942-46, PTO. Episcopalian. Home: Valley, Nebr. Died Sept. 10, 2009.

WARNER, MALLORY REYNOLDS, architect, designer; b. Washington, May 1, 1951; s. Brainard Henry III, and Mildred Keller (Jonathan) W. B.A. in Architecture, Yale U., 1981, M.A. in Architecture, 1983. Designer, draftsman Charles Moore Assocs., Essex, Conn., 1974; project mgr. Studio Castore, Florence, Italy, 1975-78; pvt. practice architecture, Florence, 1976-78; project architect ADD Inc. Architects, Cambridge, Mass., 1978-80; designer Flaherty Giavara Assocs., New Haven, 1981-84; project architect, designer ADD Inc. Architects, Washington, 1984; project architect Arthur Cotton Moore/Assocs., Washington, 1984—88m cofounder Hickok Warner Associates, 1988-2000; Mem. AIA (assoc.). Club: Yale (Washington). Died May 6, 2010.

WARNICK, EDWARD EUGENE, tool manufacturing company executive; b. Rochester, N.Y., Jan. 3, 1927; s. Michael and Anne Helene W.; student Clemson A. and M. Coll., 1944; B.S. in Elec. Engring., Duke U., 1950; postgrad. Johns Hopkins U., 1952, U. Rochester, 1964-67; m. Angela M. Stanziola, Sept. 19, 1975; children— Pamela Lee Moyer, Mark Geoffrey, Phillip Tyler; stepchildren— Michelle Renee Kirstein, Joseph Biagio Mistretta, Chrystie Ann Rakvica. Grad. student engr., electronics design engr. Westinghouse Electric Co., Balt., 1950-53; with Eastman Kodak Co., Rochester, N.Y., 1953-85, sr. design engr., 1953-56, project engr., 1956-58, supervising engr., 1958-64, divisional research lab. mgr., 1964-66, asst. program mgr., 1966-70, program mgr., 1970-74, supt. assembly, 1974-77, asst. mgr. consumer products engring. apparatus div., 1977-79, asst. mgr. copy products, 1979-83, mgr. copy products, 1983-85; pres. Warnico/U.S.A., Inc., 1985-89, Sci. & Tech. Co., Rochester, 1989—. Chmn., Town Planning Bd., 1964-68; mem. Monroe County Planning Council, 1964-68; mem. town-county com. Republican party, 1969. Served with USAAF, 1944-47. Mem. Am. Mgmt. Assn., IEEE, Rochester C. of C., Am. Rose Soc., Am. Soc. Quality Control, Tau Beta Pi, Eta Kappa Nu, Order Red Friars, Omicron Delta Kappa, Order St. Patrick. Clubs: U.S. Power Squadrons, Yacht (Oak Orchard, N.Y.). Patentee in field. Home: Rochester, NY. Died Dec. 14, 2009.

WARREN, RALPH LOUNSBURY, surgery educator; b. Orange, NJ, Sept. 28, 1954; AB, Harvard Coll.; MD, Harvard U., Boston, 1981. Diplomate Am. Bd. Surgery, Am. Bd. Surg. Critical Care. Resident in surgery Mass. Gen. Hosp., Boston, 1981-87, fellow in cardiothoracic surgery, 1987-89, assoc. vis. surgeon, from 1994, asst. chief, clin. dir. trauma svc., from 1992. Lt. col. Air NAt. Guard. Fellow ACS, Internat. Coll. Surgeons, Assn. Mil. Surgeons U.S., Ea. Assn. for Soc. of Trauma, Alliance Air Nat. Guard Flight Surgeons; mem. AMA, Soc. Critical Care Medicine, Aerospace Med. Assn., Soc. Air Force Flight Surgeons, Mass. Med. Soc. Died Dec. 2, 2009.

WARYE, RICHARD JONATHAN, theater arts educator; b. Columbus, Ohio, Mar. 4, 1929; s. John Elton and Alma Barbara (Sanger) W.; m. Verna Elizabeth Beckler, Aug. 21, 1964 (dec. Jan. 1994); 1 stepchild, Pamela Moulton Wilson. BS in Edn., Ohio State U., 1951, MA, 1952, PhD, 1966. Cert. tchr., Mass. Tchr. Claridon Local Sch., Marion County, Ohio, 1953, West High Sch., Columbus, 1957-60; instr., then asst. prof. speech Bates Coll., Lewiston, Maine, 1960-68; prof. theater arts Bridgewater (Mass.) State Coll., 1968-94, prof. emeritus theater arts, from 1994. Dist. dir. Northeast Dist. Unitarian Universalist Ch., Maine, 1962-68; preparer, presenter religious svcs.; bd. mgrs. Universalist-Unitarian Ch., Brockton, Mass. Lt. (j.g.) USNR, 1953-56. Mem. Assn. Theatre in Higher Edn., New Engl. Theatre Conf. Democrat. Home: Bridgewater, Mass. Died Jan. 31, 2009.

WASHINGTON, EDDIE, state legislator; b. St. Louis, June 8, 1953; m. Flor Washington; children: Tikisha, Malik, Kitanda, Albert, Elias, Asian, Racquel. Commr. Waukegan Econ. Devel. Commn.; bd. dirs. Lake City Health Dept. Exec. Bd., 1986—87; trustee, North Shore Sanitation Dist., 1998—2002; precinct commr. 333, 1988—2010; mem. Dist. 60 Ill. House of Reps., 2002—10. Mem.: Lake City Urban League (bd. dir. 1991—93), People Organized & Working for Equal Respect (chmn. 1986—2002), 10th St. Bus. Assn. (v. chmn. 1995—97). Democrat. Died June 4, 2010.

WASSERMAN, ILENE, psychologist; b. Bklyn., Nov. 2, 1950; d. Seymour C. and Shirley O. Wasserman. B.A. magna cum laude with high honors in Psychology, Queens Coll., CUNY, 1972; M.A. in Counseling and Guidance, N.Y. U., 1976; Ph.D. in Ednl. Psychology (scholar), Fordham U., 1981; postdoctoral in psychoanalysis Postgrad. Ctr. for Mental Health, N.Y.C. Cert. Nat. Register Health Service providers in Psychology. Mental hygiene therapy asst. Queens State Sch., Corona, N.Y., 1972-73; research asst. Kingsboro Psychiat. Center Research Found., N.Y. State Dept. Mental Hygiene, Bklyn., 1973-76; asst., Fordham U., N.Y.C., 1977-78, adj. instr. grad. edn., 1979-80; counselor Pace U., N.Y.C., 1979-80, counselor/testing coordinator, 1980-84, adj. asst. prof. pvt. practice, 1983—, dir. tng., 1984-87. Mem. Am. Psychol. Assn., L.I. Inst. Psychoanalysis (faculty), Suffolk County Psychol. Assn., Phi Beta Kappa, Phi Delta Kappa. Died June 21, 2009.

WASSINK, CONSUELO K., scientific writer, technical editor; b. Atlantic City, Aug. 3, 1926; d. John McGill Kuhn and Geraldine Saint Houseworth; m. Harry Wassink, June 20, 1958; 1 child, Melody Diane. AB in Chemistry, Bryn Mawr Coll., 1948; postgrad., U. Colo. Analytical rsch. chemist Merck & Co., Rahway, N.J., 1949-54; tech. writer House of J. Hayden Twiss, NYC, 1954-56; tech. writer, analytical chemist U. Colo. Dept. Chemistry, Boulder, 1957-59; free-lance journalist, 1964-71; tech. report editor US EPA, Denver, 1971-74; pub. affairs specialist U.S. Dept. Interior, Bur. of Land Mgmt., Denver, 1974-75; pub. affairs officer BLM Alaska Outer Continental Shelf Office, Anchorage, 1975-81; tech. and sci. writer, editor Alaska Dept. Nat. Resources, U.S. Fish and Wildlife Svc., 1984-98; with HWW Cons., Anchorage. Fellow Soc. for Tech. Comm. (pres. Alaska chpt. 1984-85, pres. Rocky Mt. chpt. 1972-75, Profl. Performance awrd 1973-74). Avocations: public speaking, computer sci. Died Jan. 28, 2009.

WASWO, MARION MARGARET, association executive, library trustee; b. Bronx, N.Y., Oct. 23, 1917; d. William Joseph and Janette (Matthew) Fanshawe; m. Carl Waswo, Apr. 26, 1941; children— Janette, Nina, Karin, Carl, Rita. Student schs. Mineola, N.Y. Librarian North Bellmore Library (N.Y.), 1946-49, trustee, 1949-74, bd. pres., 1954-74; trustee Nassau Library System, Uniondale, N.Y., 1974-84, bd. pres., 1982-84; trustee N.Y. State Assn. Library Bd., Uniondale, 1980—, pres., 1986. Treas. United Cerebral Palsy Aux., Wantagh, N.Y., 1969-73; v.p. Wantagh Preservation Soc. 1984—. Recipient service awards North Bellmore Library, 1982, North Bellmore Community, 1974, Nassau Library System, 1984; citation, Nassau County Supr., 1974, Town of Hempstead, 1984, 85; Merit award United Cerebral Palsy of Nassau County, 1985. Mem. ALA, N.Y. Library Assn. Republican. Roman Catholic. Home: Bellmore, NY. Died Apr. 12, 2009.

WATANABE, AUGUST MASARU, physician, educator, retired pharmaceutical executive; b. Portland, Oreg., Aug. 17, 1941; s. Frank H. and Mary Y. W.; m. Margaret Whildin Reese, Mar. 14, 1964; children: Nan Reiko, Todd Franklin, Scott Masaru. BS, Wheaton Coll., Ill., 1963; MD, Ind. U., 1967. Diplomate Am. Bd. Internal Medicine. Intern Ind. U. Med. Center, Indpls., 1967-68, resident, 1968-69, 71-72, fellow in cardiology, 1972-74; clin. asso. NIH, 1969-71; clin. instr. medicine Georgetown U. Med. Sch., Washington, 1970-71; mem. faculty Ind. U. Sch. Medicine, Indpls., 1972—2003, prof. medicine and pharmacology, 1978—2003, chmn. dept. medicine, 1983-90; dir. Regenstrief Inst. for Health Care Ind. U. Sch. of Medicine, Indpls., 1984-90; from v.p. to group v.p. rsch. labs. Eli Lilly & Co., Indpls., 1990-94, v.p., pres. Lilly Res labs, 1994—2003; exec. v.p. sci. and tech. Eli Lilly and Co., Indpls., 1996—2003, mem. bd. dirs., 1996—2003; chmn. bd. BioCrossroads, from 2003. Mem. pharmacology study sect. NIH, 1979-81, chmn., 1981-83; cardiovasc.-renal adv. com. FDA, 1982-85; mem. com. A, Nat. Heart, Lung and Blood Inst., 1984-88, chmn., 1986-88; bd. dir. QuatRx,

Endocyte, Kalypsys, Ambrx, Marcadia Biotech; cons. in field. Contbr. articles to profl. jours.; editorial bds. sci. jours. Bd. dir. Ind. U. Found., 1989—, Indpls. Symphony Orch., 1994—, Regenstrief Found., 1995—. NIH grantee, 1972-92. Fellow ACP, Am. Coll. Cardiology, Am. Heart Assn. (councils on clin. cardiology and circulation, research rev. com. Ind. affiliate 1978-82, research and adv. com. North Central region 1978-82, adv. com. cardiovascular drugs 1976-79, chmn. com. 1979-81, chmn. program com. council on basic sci. 1982-84, chmn. com. on sci. sessions programs 1985-88, bd. dirs. 1985-88), Am. Coll. Cardiology (govt. relations com. 1979-81, trustee 1982-87); mem. Am. Fedn. Clin. Research (councilor Midwest sect. 1976-77, chmn.-elect Midwest sect. 1977-78, chmn. sect. 1978-79, chmn. sect. nominating com. 1979-80), Am. Soc. Clin. Investigation, Am. Soc. Clin. Pharmacology and Therapeutics, Am. Soc. Pharmacology and Exptl. Therapeutics (exec. com. div. clin. pharmacology 1978-81), Cardiac Muscle Soc., Central Soc. Clin. Research (councillor 1983-86, pres.-elect 1989, pres. 1990), Internat. Soc. Heart Research, Assn. Am. Physicians, Assn. Profs. of Medicine, Sigma Xi. Home: Indianapolis, Ind. Died June 9, 2009.

WATERLOW, SIMON GORDON, publishing executive; b. Amersham, Buckinghamshire, Eng., June 20, 1941; s. Thoams Gordon and Helen Elizabeth (Robinson) W.; m. Jane Elizabeth Underhill; 1 child, Caroline Elizabeth. MA, Trinity Coll., Cambridge U., Eng., 1963; diploma graphic arts, Heriot Watt, Edinburgh, Scotland, 1964. Prodn. mgr. Readers Digest, Montreal, Que., Can., 1966-71, mgr., 1971-79, v.p., editorial dir., 1979-81; gen. mgr. Torstar Books, Toronto, Ont., Can. and N.Y.C., 1982-86; pres. Ideals Pub. Corp, Nashville, from 1987. Pres. English Speaking Union, Montreal, 1976-77. Mem. Direct Mktg. Assn., Muirfield Club (Scotland), Sloane Club (London). Avocations: outdoor sports, history, travel. Home: Franklin, Tenn. Died Feb. 27, 2009.

WATERS, ZENOBIA PETTUS, retired finance educator; b. Little Rock, Mar. 4, 1927; d. Henry Augustus and Lillie Liddell (Edwards) Pettus; m. Willie Waters, Jr., Jan. 29, 1949 (div. Feb. 1955); children: Pamela E. Reed, Zenobia W. Carter. BA cum laude, Philander Smith Coll., Little Rock, 1964; MEd, U. Wash., 1968. Cert. tchr. Ark., 1966. Office mgr. United Friends of Am., Little Rock, 1946—52; sec. State Dept. Edn., Little Rock, 1958—64; lectr. bus. Philander Smith Coll., Little Rock, 1965—67, asst. prof. bus., 1968—88, assoc. prof. bus. adminstrn., 1988—92, bd. dirs., faculty rep., 1976—80; asst. prof. bus. Ark. Bapt. Coll., Little Rock, 1970—84. Asst. bus. mgr. Philander Smith Coll., Little Rock, 1970—74, dir. summer sessions, 1970—81; spkr. in field. Mem. adv. bd.: Two Centuries of Methodism in Arkansas, 2000; contbr. articles to profl. jours. Dean West Gulf Regional Sch., 1975—77; founder Nat. Campaign Tolerance, Mont, Ala., 2005; vol. Dem. Party, Little Rock, 1986—92; contact person U.S. Presdl. Campaign, Little Rock, 1992; cert. lay spkr. United Meth. Ch., from 1979; pres. so. ctrl. juris United Meth. Women, 1984—88; bd. dirs. Gen. Bd. of Global Ministries, NYC, 1984—88, Aldersgate Camp, Little Rock, 1976—79, St. Paul Sch. Theology, Kansas City, Mo., 1984—88, Mount Sequoyah, Fayetteville, Ark., 1984—88. Recipient Svc. award, Gen. Bd. Global Ministries/Women's Divsn., 1988; named Legend, Union Am. Meth. Ch., 2005; grantee Ford Found. grantee, 1967; fellow, Nissan, 1989. Mem.: AAUW (Edn. Found. award 1983), Nat. Campaign for Tolerance (founding mem.), Nat. Trust for Historic Preservation, United Meth. Women (pres. recognition pins 1963—2004, recognition pins 1963—2005), Phi Delta Phi, Iota Phi Lambda. Methodist. Avocations: reading, walking, writing. Home: Little Rock, Ark. Died Jan. 26, 2009.

WATKINS, WESLEY LEE, accountant; b. Norfolk, Va., Dec. 4, 1953; s. Morrell and Mary Elizabeth (Washington) W. BS, Norfolk State U., 1977. Inventory acct. specialist Norfolk State U. Bookstore (Va.), 1977-79; acct., auditor DMTS, HEW, 1979-80; acct. McClure Lundberry Assocs., 1980-81; contractual acct. Acad. Contemporary Problems, Washington, 1982; fin. cons. Watkins & Watkins, Washington, 1982-86, U.S. Tax Svc., Suffolk, Va., 1987; tax cons., acct. H&R Block, Norfolk, 1988—; tax cons. Watkins & Watkins Fin. Cons., Norfolk, Va., 1987—; cons. Watkins & Watkins Auto Shop, Norfolk, 1983-84. Bd. dirs. Jerusalem Baptist Ch. Credit Union, 1976-96. Named Young Adult of Yr. Jerusalem Bapt. Ch., Norfolk, 1978, 91. Mem. NAACP, Nat. Assn. Accts., Nat. Assn. Tax Practitioners, Nat. Assn. Black Accts., Phi Beta Lambda. Democrat. Home: Norfolk, Va. Died Nov. 29, 2009.

WATNICK, LEWIS, lawyer; b. Detroit, June 27, 1929; s. Sam and Ruth (Wagman) Watnick; m. Sharon Stone, Dec. 20, 1952. AA, LA City Coll., 1949; LLD cum laude, Loyola U., LA, 1952. Bar: Calif. 1952, (U.S. Supreme Ct.) 1957. Staff atty. Sears Roebuck & Co., LA, 1953—54; head dep. dist. atty. LA Dist., from 1954. Author: Search Warrants, 1960—62, Handling a Criminal Case, 1970. Mem.: LA Dist. Attys. Assn., San Fernando Bar Assn. (del.), Criminal Cts. Bar Assn., B'nai B'rith. Republican. Jewish. Home: Thousand Oaks, Calif. Died Mar. 4, 2009.

WATSON, JAMES ELWYN, JR., health physics educator; b. Lumberton, NC, Jan. 10, 1938; s. James E. and Louise (Quantock) W. BS, N.C. State U., 1960, MS, 1962; PhD, U. N.C., 1970. Nuclear engr. U.S. Army, Aberdeen Proving Ground, Md., 1964-67; health physicist Oak Ridge (Tenn.) Nat. Lab., 1967; br. chief TVA, Muscle Shoals, Ala., 1970-74; prof. health physics U. N.C., Chapel Hill, from 1974. Chmn. N.C. Radiation Protection Commn., 1982-83; mem. NAS Panel, 1991-92. 1st lt. Ordnance Corps, U.S. Army, 1962-64. Recipient McGavran Teaching award U. N.C., 1984, Greenberg Alumni award, 1988. Fellow Health Physics Soc. (pres. 1985-86); mem. APHA (chmn. radiological health sect. 1985), U.S. EPA (sci. adv. bd. 1991—), Sigma Xi (nat. lectr. 1991-92), Tau Beta Pi, Sigma Pi Sigma, Phi Kappa Phi. Avocations: outdoor activities, archaeology. Home: Chapel Hill, NC. Died Apr. 2, 2009.

WATTS, DEY WADSWORTH, retired lawyer; b. Chgo., Jan. 8, 1923; s. Amos Holston and Lida Cremora (Hough) W.; m. Faith Whittemore Weis, June 28, 1951; children— William, D. Whittemore, John, Judson, Merideth AB, Princeton U., 1947; LL.B., Harvard U., 1949. Bar: Ill. 1950. Assoc. Chapman and Cutler, Chgo., 1949-63, ptnr., 1963-91, retired, 1991. Gen. counsel Exec. Svc. Corps Chgo., 1996—. Pres. Glencoe Cmty. Chest, Ill., 1959-60; arbitrator Am. Arbitration Assn., Chgo., 1965-91; treas. Little House of Glencoe, 1966-80; chmn. adv. coun. Glencoe Caucus Plan, 1985-87. Capt. AUS, 1943-46, PTO. Fellow Am. Coll. Investment Counsel; mem. ABA, Ill. Bar Assn. (chmn. corp. and securities law com. 1961-62), Chgo. Bar Assn. (chmn. ethics com. 1974-75, chmn. legal econs. com. 1978-79), Legal Club Chgo. (exec. com. 1978-79), Law Club Chgo., Univ. Club, Mid Day Club, Skokie Country Club (sec. 1980-82), Harbour Town Yacht Club (Hilton Head, S.C.). Home: Glenview, Ill. Died Feb. 14, 2009.

WATTS, RAYMOND, marine engineer; b. Norfolk, Va., Feb. 16, 1932; s. John and Lucille (Southall) W.; m. Hatsue Asou Watts, Jan. 6, 1966; 1 child, Kiyosha. B of Marine Engring., SUNY, 1961. With USAF, 1951-54. Mem. Soc. of Naval Architects of Marine Engrs. Avocations: model building, classical music appreciation, computer applications, bicycle riding. Home: Littlestown, Pa. Died Jan. 28, 2009.

WAYBURN, EDGAR, internist, environmentalist; b. Macon, Ga., Sept. 17, 1906; s. Emanuel and Marian (Voorsanger) W.; m. Cornelia Elliott, Sept. 12, 1947; children: Cynthia, William, Diana, Laurie. AB magna cum laude, U. Ga., 1926; MD cum laude, Harvard U., 1930. Hosp. tng. Columbia-Presbyn. Hosp., NYC, 1931-33; assoc. clin. prof. Stanford (Calif.) U., 1933-65, U. Calif., San Francisco, 1960-76; practice medicine specializing in internal medicine San Francisco, 1933-1985; mem. staff Pacific Presbyn. Med. Ctr., San Francisco, 1959-86, chief endocrine clinic, 1959-72, vice chief staff, 1961-63, hon. staff, 1986—2010. Editor: Man Medicine and Ecology, 1970, Your Land and Mine: Evolution of a Conservationist, 2004; contbr. articles to profl. and environ. jours. Mem. Sec. of Interior's Adv. Bd. on Nat. Park System, 1979-83, mem. world commn. on protected areas Internat. Union for Conservation Nature and Natural Resources; leader nat. campaigns Alaska Nat. Interest Lands Conservation Act; trustee Pacific Presbyn. Med. Ctr., 1978-86; bd. dirs. Garden Sullivan Hosp., 1965-80; chmn. People For a Golden Gate Nat. Recreation Area, 1971-2005; mem. citizens' adv. commn. Golden Gate Nat. Recreation Area, San Francisco, 1974-2003, leader nat. campaigns, 1955-90; prin. citizen advocate Redwood Nat. Park, 1968, 78; dir. The Antarctica Project, 1993-2003; mem. adv. bd. Pacific Forest Trust; hon. chmn. Tuolomne River Preservation Trust, 1983-1985; prin. adv. Enlargement of Mt. Tamalpais State Pk.; leader campaign to establish Golden Gate Nat. Recreation Area, 1972. Maj. USAF, 1942-46. Recipient Douglas award Nat. Pk and Conservation Assn., 1987, Leopold award Calif. Nature Conservancy, 1988, Fred Packard award Internat. Union Conservation Nature, 1994, Laureate of Global 500 Roll of Honour award U.N. Environment Programme, 1994, 1st Conservation award Ecotrust, 1994, Albert Schweitzer prize, 1995, Presdl. Medal of Freedom, The White House 1999. Fellow ACP (laureat); mem. AMA, Am. Soc. Internal Medicine, Calif. Med. Assn. (del. 1958-83, Recognition award 1986, Leadership and Quality awards 1986), San Francisco Med. Soc. (pres. 1965, Resolution of Congratulations 1986), Sierra Club (pres. 1961-64, 67-69, John Muir award 1972, hon. pres. 1993-2010), Sierra Club Found. (dir. 1960-87, pres. 1971-78, hon. pres. 1998-2010), Fedn. Western Outdoor Clubs (pres. 1953-55). Avocation: hiking. Died Mar. 5, 2010.

WEARLY, WILLIAM LEVI, retired manufacturing executive; b. Warren, Ind., Dec. 5, 1915; s. Purvis Gardner and Ethel Ada (Jones) W.; m. Mary Jane Riddle, Mar. 8, 1941, Margaret Wearly (Campbell), 1996; children: Patricia Ann, Susan, William Levi, Elizabeth. BS, Purdue U., 1937, Dr Engring. (hon.), 1959. Student career engr. C.A. Dunham Co., Michigan City, Ind., 1936; mem. elec. design staff Joy Mfg. Co., Franklin, Pa., 1937-39, v.p., gen. sales mgr., 1952-56, exec. v.p., 1956-57, pres., dir., 1957-62; v.p., dir. Ingersoll-Rand Co., 1964-66, exec. v.p., 1966-67, chmn., chief exec. officer, 1967-80, chmn. exec. com., 1981-85. Dir. ASA Ltd., Med. Care Am.; trustee LMI; speaker engring. groups. Author tech. publs. relating to mining; patentee in field. Bd. dirs. Boys Clubs Am. Mem. NAE, IEEE, AIME, Nat. Acad. of Engring., C. of C., Sky Club N.Y.C., Blind Brook Golf Club, Desert Forest Golf Club, Minikahda Club, Ariz. Club, Masons, Shriners, Eta Kappa Nu, Tau Beta Pi, Beta Theta Pi. Republican. Methodist. Died Apr. 30, 2010.

WEARY, PEYTON EDWIN, retired medical educator; b. Evanston, Ill., Jan. 10, 1930; s. Leslie Albert and Conway Christian (Fleming) W.; m. Janet Edsall Gregory, Aug. 23, 1952; children: Terry, Conway Christian, Carolyn Fielder. BA, Princeton U., 1970; MD, U. Va., 1955. Diplomate: Am. Bd. Dermatology (dir. 1978-88, pres. 1987-88). Intern, case Western Res. U. Hosps., Cleve., 1955-56; rotating intern Univ. Hosp. Cleve., 1955-56; asst. resident dermatology U. Va., Charlottesville, 1958-60, resident dermatology, 1960-61, instr. dept. dermatology, 1961-62, asst. prof., 1962-65, asso. prof., 1965-70, prof., chmn. dept. dermatology, 1970-93; mem. staff Univ. Hosp., mem. cancer com., 1979—98, ret., 2001, prof. emeritus, from 2001. Univ. Hosp. house staff, 1960-61, clin. staff, 1965-66, pres. clin. staff, 1966-67; co-chair Nat. Coun. on Skin Cancer Prevention, Fed. Coun. on Skin Cancer Prevention, 1997-2001, Ctr. for Disease Control, 1997-2000. Mem. editorial bd. Jour. Am. Acad. Dermatology, 1978-87; editorial adv. bd. Skin and Allergy News, 1978—; contbr. articles to profl. jours. Bd. dirs. Lupus Found. Am., 1980-84; trustee, mem. exec. com. Dermatology Found., 1975-79; pres. Albermarle County unit Am. Cancer Soc., 1967-69. Served from 1st lt. to capt., M.C. U.S. Army, 1956-58. Recipient Walter Reed Disting. Achievement award U. Va. Alumni Assn., 2001 Master: Am. Acad. Dermatology (hon. bd. dir. 1973—76, pres. 1993—95, elected master in dermatology 2000, Gold medal 1990); mem.: Coun. Med. Splty. Socs. (bd. dir. 1989—92, sec. 1992—95), Am. Bd. Med. Spltys. (v.p. 1988, pres.-elect 1989, pres. 1990—92, Disting. Svc. award 1999), Raven Soc., So. Med. Assn., Med. Soc. Va. (Cmty. Svc. award 2001), Albermarie County Med. Soc., Dermatology Found., Am. Dermatol. Assn. (bd. dir. 1987—93, pres. 1992—93), Assn. Profs. Dermatology (sec.-treas. 1976—79), Soc. Investigative Dermatology (bd. dir. 1976—81, v.p. 1985, hon. mem. 1996), Va. Dermatol. Soc. (sec.-treas. 1965—71), Nat. Assn. Physicians Environ. (pres. 1995—97), Alpha Omega Alpha, Sigma Xi. Presbyterian. Home: Charlottesville, Va. Died June 26, 2009.

WEATHERLY, MARK GIVENS, marital and family therapist, educator; b. Alco, La., Mar. 7, 1923; s. Obie Lee and Obie (Givens) Weatherly; m. Katherine Burge Weatherly, Aug. 18, 1951; children: Mark Givens Jr., Susan Weatherly Book, Robert O'Connor. BS, Stetson U., 1949; MEd, U. Va., 1967, EdD, 1970; postgrad., Fla. State U., 1961. Pres., corp. owne Camp Tenn. and Sch., Winchester, 1950—68; instr. Lynchburg Coll., Va., 1965—66; instr., football coach Fork Union Mil. Acad., Va., 1949—53; instr. U. Va. Sch. Gen. Studies, Charlottesville, 1970—71; assoc. prof. edn. Longwood State Coll., Farmville, Va., from 1970; pvt. practice marital and family therapy Farmville, Lynchburg, 1965—81; cons. pub. and pvt. schs. Ctrl. Va., juv. & domestic cts. Author: Readings in Adolescence, 1986. Chmn. Dem. Campaign Senator Harry F. Byrd, Jr., Appomattox County. Served to 2d lt. US Army, 1942—45, PTO. Recipient Mayor's Gold Key, Memphis, 1968, Disting. Svc. medal, Liberty U., Lynchburg, 1985. Mem.: APA, Am. Mental Health Counselors Assn., Am. Assn. Counseling and Devel., Am. Assn. Marital and Family Therapy, Sigma Chi Iota, Phi Delta Kappa. Avocations: gardening, fishing, writing. Died Nov. 12, 2009.

WEAVER, JOHN W., oil company executive; b. York, Pa., Sept. 7, 1924; s. Norman H. and Grace A. (Schaefer) Weaver; m. Patricia Grove Weaver, July 21, 1974; children: LeeAnn, Lorri, Robert, Michael. BSChemE, Drexel U. Successively refinery analyst, tech. asst., sales rep., supply mgr., v.p. supply and distbn. Standard Oil Calif., 1953—75; exec. v.p. adminstrn., ops., supply and distrbn. Standard Oil Co, Ky., 1975—82; exec. v.p. Coral Petroleum; pres. United Refining Co., Ind. Refining Corp., from 1983; cons. US Bankruptcy Ct.; dir. Asphalt Inst. Trustee Drexel U. Mem.: Pendennis Club (Ky.), Am. Petroleum Inst., Nat. Petroleum Refiners Assn. (dir.), Audubon Country Club, Champions Country Club, Desert Island Country Club (Calif.), Indian Wells Country Club (Calif.), Masons Club, Scottish Rite Club, Shriner Club. Died Nov. 18, 2009.

WEAVER, KENNETH NFWCOMER, geologist, state agency administrator; b. Lancaster, Pa., Jan. 16, 1927; s. A. Ross and Cora (Newcomer) W.; m. Mary Elizabeth Hoover, Sept. 9, 1950; children: Wendy Elaine, Matthew Owen. BS, Franklin and Marshall Coll., 1950; MA, Johns Hopkins U., 1952, PhD, 1954. Instr. geology Johns Hopkins, 1953- 54; ops. analyst Ops. Rsch. Office, Washington, 1954-56; chief geologist, then mgr. geology and quarry dept. Medusa Portland Cement Co., Wampum, Pa., 1956-63; dir., state geologist Md. Geol. Survey, Balt., 1963-92; chmn. Md. Land Reclamation Com., 1978-92. Gov.'s rep. Interstate Oil Compact Commn., Interstate Mining Compact Commn.; mem. outer shelf adv. com. U.S. Dept. Interior; chmn. Md. Topographic Mapping Com.; mem. com. on surface mining and reclamation NAS, 1978, vice chmn. com. on disposal of excess spoil, 1980-81, mem. com. on geologic mapping, 1983, liaison mem. bd. earth scis., 1982-88, mem. com. on water resources rsch., 1989-92, chmn. com. on abandoned minelands rsch. priorities, 1987; mem. subcom. on mgmt. of maj. underground constrn. projects Nat. Acad. Engring.; mem. Md. Commn. on Artistic Property, 1988-92. With U.S. Maritime Svc., 1944—46, with AUS, 1954—56. Recipient John Wesley Powell award USGS, 1994; named hdqr. bldg. The Kenneth N. Weaver Bldg. Md. Geol. Survey, 1994. Fellow Geol. Soc. Am. (sec. N.E. sect. 1985-2001), AAAS (sr.); mem. Am. Assn. Petroleum Geologists (Ea. sect., George V. Cohee Pub. Svc. award 1991), Am. Inst. Mining Engrs., Am. Inst. Profl. Geologists (editor 1983-84, Martin Van Couvering Meml. award 1992), Am. Geol. Inst. (governing bd. 1973, exec. com. 1989-90, medal in memory of Ian Campbell 2001), Am. Water Rsch. Assn., Geol. Soc. Washington, Assn. Am. State Geologists (pres. 1973, hon. mem. 1992), Johns Hopkins Club (Balt.). Republican. Presbyterian (elder). Home: Lutherville Timonium, Md. Died July 7, 2010.

WEBB, SHARON LYNN, writer; b. Tampa, Fla., Feb. 29, 1936; d. William Wesley Talbott and Eunice Geraldine Tillman; m. W. Bryan Webb, Feb. 6, 1956; children— Wendy, Jerri, Tracey. Student Fla. So. Coll., 1953-56, U. Miami, 1962; ADN, Miami-Dade Sch. Nursing, 1972. Freelance writer, 1960-66; RN South Miami Hosp., 1972-73, Union Gen. Hosp., Towns County Hosp., Blairsville, Ga., 1973-81. Author: RN, 1981, Earthchild, 1982, Earth Song, 1983, Ram Song, 1984, Adventures of Terra Tarkington, 1985, Pestis 18, 1987, The Halflife, 1989; over 40 short stories. Mem. Author's Guild/League, Sci. Fiction Writers Am. (south/central dir., bd. dirs.). Died Apr. 29, 2010.

WEBER, DAVID JOSEPH, history educator; b. Buffalo, Dec. 20, 1940; s. Theodore Carl and Frances (Maronska) W.; m. Carol Sue Bryant, June 16, 1962; children: Scott David, Amy Carol. BS in Social Sci., SUNY, Fredonia, 1962; MA in

History, U. N.Mex., 1964, PhD in History, 1967. Asst. to full prof. history San Diego State U., 1967-76; prof. history So. Meth. U., Dallas, 1976-79, prof. history and dept. chmn., 1979-86, Robert and Nancy Dedman prof. history, from 1986; dir. Clements Ctr. SW Studies, from 1995. Fulbright-Hays lectr. Universidad de Costa Rica, 1970. Author: The Taos Trappers: The Fur Trade in the Far Southwest, 1540-1846, 1971, The Mexican Frontier, 1821-1846: The American Southwest Under Mexico, 1982 (Ray Billington award 1983), Richard H. Kern: Expeditionary Artist in the Far Southwest, 1848-1853, 1985 (Nat. Cowboy Hall of Fame 1985), The Spanish Frontier in North America, 1992, Barbaros: Spaniards and Their Savages in the Age of Enlightenment, 2005; contbr. articles to profl. jours. Recipient United Meth. U. Scholar/Tchr. of Yr. award, 1986, Spain and America prize Spanish Ministry of Culture, 1993, Real Orden de Isabel la Católica, King of Spain, Juan Carlos. 2003, Orden Mexicana del Aguila Azteca (the Order of the Aztec Eagle), Govt. Mexico, 2005; postdoctoral fellow Am. Philos. Soc., 1975, Huntington Libr., 1975, 2000-01, Am. Coun. Learned Socs., 1980, Ctr. for Adv. Study in Behavioral Scis., Stanford U., 1986-87, NEH, 1974-75, 90-91; Benicke sr. fellow, Yale, 2007-08. Fellow Soc. Am. Historians, Am. Acad. Arts & Scis.; mem. Academia Mexicana de la Historia, Tex. Inst. Letters, Tex. Hist. Assn. (lifetime fellow), Western History Assn. (pres. 1990-91), Mexico-U.S. Historians (pres. 1990), Am. Hist. Assn. (v.p. profl. divsn. 2008-), Orgn. Am. Historians (mem. exec. bd. 2006-09). Democrat. Avocations: running, bicycling, gardening, reading. Home: Dallas, Tex. Died Aug. 20, 2010.

WEBER, HARM ALLEN, college chancellor, former college president; b. Pekin, Ill., Sept. 28, 1926; s. Harm Allen and Hilda (Meyer) W.; m. Arlene Olson, Dec. 18, 1948; children: Jan Christine, Harm Allen III, Matthew Karl. BA, Bethel Coll., St. Paul, 1950; B.D., Bethel Sem., 1954; M.R.E., Christian Theol. Sem., Indpls., 1959; postgrad., Ball State U., Muncie, Ind., 1961-62; D.D., Judson Coll., Elgin, Ill., 1964. Ordained to ministry Baptist Ch., 1953; pastorates at Isle (Minn.) Bapt. Ch., 1950-53, Central Bapt. Ch., Indpls., 1954-60, First Bapt. Ch., Muncie, 1960-64, Covenant Bapt. Ch., Detroit, 1964-69; pres. Judson Coll., Elgin, 1969-91, vice chmn. bd. trustees, chancellor, from 1992. Chmn. Indpls. Fedn. Chs., 1955-59; pres. Delaware County (Ind.) Coun. Chs., 1963-64; chmn. evangelism Detroit Coun. Chs., 1967-69; v.p. Am. Bapt. Home Mission Soc., 1969—; mem. exec. com. Gt. Lakes Coun. on Ministry, 1969—; mem. Ministers and Missionaries Benefit Bd., 1974-75; mem. gen. bd. Am. Bapt. Chs./USA; mem. nat. adv. com. Ednl. Assistance Ltd., 1987—. Mem. Ind. Gov.'s Multiple Sclerosis Bd., 1957-60; bd. dirs. Camp Isongal, Delaware County Crippled Children's Assn.; chmn. bd. dirs. Galloway Meml. Youth Camp, Wahkon, Minn.; mem. state exec. bd. Vols. of Am.-Minn., 1976—; trustee Am. Bapt. Sem. of the West, 1984-86. Mem. Am. Assn. Pres. Ind. Colls. and Univs., Elgin Area C. of C. (dir. 1975-78), Am. Bapt. Assn. Colls. and Univs. (pres. 1986-89). Clubs: Rotary. Home: Bradenton, Fla. Died Apr. 27, 2010.

WEBER, MICHAEL, editor; b. NYC, Sept. 25, 1945; s. David and Dorothy (Silverberg) W. BA in History magna cum laude, CUNY, 1966; postgrad., U. Wis., 1966-67; MA in Am. Civilization, NYU, 1968. Asst. editor in regional studies gen. ency. dept. Macmillan Pub. Co., NYC, 1970-71; assoc. editor in regional studies New Columbia Ency. project Columbia U. Press, NYC, 1971-74; editing supr. coll. divsn. McGraw-Hill Book Co., NYC, 1974-76; assoc. editor in social studies sch. dept. Harcourt Brace Jovanovich, NYC, 1976-79; project editor coll. divsn. St. Martin's Press, NYC, 1979-81, acquisitions editor and devel. editor coll. divsn., 1981-89; exec. editor history and polit. sci. M. E. Sharpe, Inc., Armonk, N.Y., 1989-95. Copyeditor, proofreader, fact-checker for several pubs. house and Met. Mus. of Art. Author: Our National Parks, 1994, Our Congress, 1994, three books on U.S. Presidents; contbr. articles to the New Columbia Ency., 1975, also to other books in field. Mem. Phi Beta Kappa, Phi Alpha Theta. Democrat. Avocations: classical music, wines, hiking, photography. Home: New York, NY. Died Dec. 6, 2009.

WEBSTER, THOMAS GLENN, psychiatrist, educator; b. Topeka, Jan. 23, 1924; s. Guy Welland and Iva Amanda (Keefover) W.; m. Mary Tupper Dooly, June 27, 1948; children— Warnie Louise, Guy Weyman, David Michael AB, Ft. Hays State Coll., 1946; MD, Wayne State U., 1949. Intern Los Angeles County Gen. Hosp., Calif., 1949-50; resident in psychiatry Mass. Mental Health Ctr., Boston, 1953-55, resident in child psychiatry, 1955-56, James Jackson Putnam Children's Ctr., Boston, 1956-58; dir. presch. program for retarded children Greater Boston, 1958-62; coordinator 3d yr. med. student psychiatry clerkship Harvard U. Med. Sch.-Mass. Mental Health Ctr., Boston, 1960-63; practice medicine specializing in psychiatry Boston, 1953-62, Bethesda, Md., 1963-72, Washington, from 1972; tng. specialist psychiatry, then chief continuing edn. br. NIMH, Bethesda, Md., 1963-72; prof. psychiatry George Washington U., Washington, 1972-86, chmn. dept. psychiatry and behavioral scis., 1972-75, prof. emeritus, 1986-96. Vis. prof. Harvard U. Med. Sch., 1980-83, McLean Hosp., 1980-86; U.S.-Poland exchange health scientist, 1981 Pres. Woodhaven Citizens Assn., 1971-72. Served with AUS, 1943-46; as sr. asst. surgeon USPHS, 1951-53 Fellow Am. Coll. Psychiatrists, Am. Coll. Psychoanalysts; mem. Assn. Acad. Psychiatry (pres. 1976-78), Group Advancement Psychiatry Home: Concord, Mass. Died July 2009.

WECHSLER, NANCY FRAENKEL, lawyer; b. NYC, Dec. 12, 1916; d. Osmond Kessler and Helene (Esberg) Fraenkel; m. James A. Wechsler, Oct. 4, 1934; children: Michael (dec.), Holly Wechsler Schwartztol. BA, Barnard Coll., 1937; LL.B. (James Kent scholar), Columbia U., 1940. Bar: N.Y. 1941, U.S. Supreme Ct. 1948. Assoc. firm Hays, St. John, Abramson & Schulman, 1940-41; assoc. Bd. Econ. Welfare, Office Price Adminstrn., Office Econ. Stblzn., Office War Moblzn. and Reconversion and Labor Dept., 1942-48; counsel Pres.'s Com. on Civil Rights, 1946-47; assoc. firm Greenbaum, Wolff & Ernst, NYC, 1955-68, partner, 1968-82; ptnr. Linden & Deutsch, NYC, from 1982. Contbr. articles on lit. property, reproductive freedom to profl. jours.; editorial bd.: Columbia U. Law Rev, 1938-40. Bd. dirs. ACLU, N.Y.C., 1964-67, Nat., 1978—. Recipient Ordronaux prize Columbia U. Law Sch., 1940 Mem. Am. Bar Assn. (governing bd., forum com. on sports and entertainment industries), Assn. Bar City N.Y. (communications law com. 1970-81, 85—, copyright com. 1981-84), Am. Law Inst., Alumni Columbia Law Sch. (assoc., dir. 1980-83), Barnard Coll. Alumnae Assn. (trustee 1971-74), Copyright Soc. U.S.A. (trustee 1973-77), Women's Media Group. Home: New York, NY. Died July 27, 2009.

WEEKS, ARTHUR ANDREW, lawyer, educator; b. Hanceville, Ala., Dec. 2, 1914; s. A.A. and Anna S. (Seibert) W.; m. Carol P. Weeks; children: John David, Carol Christine, Nancy Anna. AB, Samford U., 1936; LL.B., JD, U. Ala., 1939; LL.M., Duke U., 1950; LL.D. (hon.), Widener U., 1980. Bar: Ala. 1939, Tenn. 1948. Sole practice, Birmingham, Ala., 1939-41, 1946-47, 1954-61; dean, prof. law Cumberland U. Sch. Law, 1947-54; dean, prof. Samford U., 1961-72, prof. law, 1972-74, Cumberland Sch. Law, Samford U., from 1984, Del. Sch. Law of Widener U., Wilmington, 1974-82, dean, 1974-80, interim dean, 1982-83, dean emeritus, prof., from 1983; ret. Served to capt. AUS, 1941-46. Mem. ABA, Tenn. Bar Assn., Ala. Bar Assn., Birmingham Bar Assn., Del. Bar Assn. (assoc.), Phi Alpha Delta, Phi Kappa Phi, Delta Theta Phi Home: Birmingham, Ala. Died Aug. 22, 2009.

WEEKS, ROSS LEONARD, JR., museum executive; b. Jamestown, NY, Sept. 11, 1936; s. Ross Leonard and Cecile Forbes (Carrie) W.; m. Patricia Ann Earley, June 10, 1961 (div.); children: Susan Woodall, Ross Leonard III, William Andrew, David James; m. Ndeleshia C. Nanuwa, Oct. 15, 2007. AB, Colgate U., Hamilton, NY, 1958; MS, George Wash. U., Washington, DC, 1971; cert., Fed. Exec. Inst., 1988. Reporter Jamestown Post-Jour., Va., 1958-60, Richmond News Leader, 1960-65; dir. pub. info. Coll. William and Mary, Williamsburg, Va., 1965-71, asst. to exec. v.p., 1971-74, asst. to pres., dir. univ. comms., 1974-81; exec. dir. Jamestown-Yorktown Found., 1981-91, Hist. Crab Orchard Mus., Inc., Tazewell, Va., 1992—2002; ret., 2002; pres. Blue Ridge Concepts, Ltd., from 1999. Editor William and Mary Alumni Gazette, 1966-81; author: Virginia's Tazewell County: A Last Great Place, 2000; editor: 'Cause I'm Colored-The Black Heritage of Tazewell County, 2001; columnist: Clinch Valley News, 1998-2004. Chmn. Williamsburg-James City Bicentennial, 1975-77; treas. Coalfield Regional Tourism Devel. Authority S.W. Va., 1993-97; Va. S.W. Blue Ridge Highlands, Inc., 1993-97, v.p., 1996-97, pres., 1997-99; sec., treas. Frontier Culture Found., 1982-86; exec. dir. Va. Independence Bicentennial Commn., 1981-83; trustee coun. Thirteen Original States, 1982-87; chair Tazewell County Tourism Devel. Commn., 1993-97; mem. regional grant panel Va. Com. on the Arts, 1998—2002; mem. Gov.'s Va. History Initiative, 1995-2002; bus. adminstr. Holy Family Parish, 2003-. Mem. Am. Assn. Mus., Am. Assn. State and Local History, Masons, Rotary (Paul Harris fellow 1987), Clan Ross Assn., SAR (pres. Clinch Mountain Militia chpt. 2001-03), Sigma Delta Chi, Kappa Delta Rho (Ordo Honora 1986). Roman Catholic. Avocations: travel, landscaping, antiques, history. Home: Tazewell, Va. Died Aug. 3, 2010.

WEGMAN, HAROLD HUGH, management consultant; b. Cin., June 29, 1916; s. Clarence H. and Lillian (de Tellem) W.; m. Ruth Ellen Volk, May 1, 1937; children— Susan Ruth (Mrs. Michael Manning), Sally Ann (Mrs. Jerry Fine). BBA, U. Cin., 1941; MBA, Xavier U., 1954. Band leader, studio mgr. Rudolph Wurlitzer Co., 1946-50; Tng. supr., then asst. to v.p. Gruen Watch Co., 1950-55; personnel dir., asst. to pres. Bavarian Brewing Co., Covington, Ky., 1955-59; dir. indsl. relations, asst. to pres. Howard Paper Co., Dayton, Ohio, 1959-62; v.p., gen. mgr. Elano Corp., Xenia, Ohio, 1962-64; v.p., dir. indsl. relations Champion Papers Inc., Hamilton, Ohio, 1964-67; v.p. U.S. Plywood Champion Papers, Inc., 1967-71, Champion Internat., 1971-72; pres. PEP Group, from 1972; dir. Mgmt. Center, Sacred Heart U., from 1974. Contbr. articles to profl. publs. Trustee Foreman Found., 1965-71. Served to lt. (j.g.) USNR, 1944-46. Mem. Am. Soc. Personnel Adminstrs. (bd. dirs. 1969—, treas. 1970), Am. Soc. for Tng. and Devel., NAM, Am. Paper Inst., Am. Mgmt. Assn., Conn. songwriters assn., Lambda Chi Alpha. Home: Ridgefield, Conn. Died June 29, 2010.

WEIBEL, THOMAS MICHAEL, lawyer; b. Milw., June 10, 1951; s. William Joseph and Jeanne F. Weibel; m. Patricia Hawkins, Jan. 26, 1985. BS cum laude, Western Mich. U., 1973; JD, U. Notre Dame, 1976. Bar: Mich., U.S. Dist. Ct. (we. dist.) Mich. Assoc. Smith, Haughey, Rice & Roegge, Grand Rapids, Mich., from 1976. Mem. ABA, Mich. Bar Assn., Fed. Bar Assn., Assn. Trial Lawyers Am., Mich. Trial Lawyers Assn. Home: Grand Rapids, Mich. Died Jan. 31, 2010.

WEINBERG, SIDNEY JAMES, JR., retired investment banker; b. NYC, Mar. 27, 1923; s. Sidney James and Helen (Livingston) W.; m. Elizabeth Houghton, June 30, 1951; children: Elizabeth W. Smith, Sydney Houghton, Peter Amory. BA; in Pub. and Internat. Affairs, Princeton, 1945; MBA, Harvard, 1949. V.p. textile divsn. Owens-Corning Fiberglas Corp., NYC, 1949-65; gen. ptnr. Goldman, Sachs & Co., NYC, 1965—77, head investment banking services dept., 1978—88, ltd. ptnr., 1988—99, sr. dir., 1999—2010. Mem. cons. panel Comptroller Gen. U.S. Trustee Found. Center, 1968-74, Com. Econ. Devel., WNET Ednl. Broadcasting Corp., 1965-79, Carnegie Found. Advancement Teaching, 1965-78, Presbyn. Hosp. City N.Y., Scripps Coll., Claremont, Calif.; trustee Carnegie Instn. Washington, 1983. Served to 1st lt. F.A. AUS, 1944-46, PTO. Mem.: River (N.Y.C.), Recess (N.Y.C.); Century Country (Purchase, N.Y.); Eldorado Country (Indian Wells, Calif.); California (Los Angeles). Died Oct. 4, 2010.

WEINBRENNER, GEORGE RYAN, aeronautical engineer; b. June 10, 1917; s. George Penbrook and Helen Mercedes (Ryan) W.; m. Billie Marjorie Elwood, May 2, 1955. BS, MIT, Cambridge, 1940, MS, 1941; AMP, Harvard U., Cambridge, Mass., 1966; ScD (hon.), Mapua Inst. Tech., Manila, 1994. Commd. 2d lt. USAAF, 1939, advanced through grades to col., 1949; def. attaché Am. Embassy, Prague, Czech Republic, 1958—61; dep. chief staff intelligence Air Force Sys. Command, Washington, 1962—68; comdr. fgn. tech. divsn. USAF, Wright-Patterson AFB, Ohio, 1968—74; comdr. Brooks AFB, Tex., 1974—75; ret., 1975; exec. v.p. B.C. Wills & Co., Inc., Reno, 1975—84; chmn. bd. Hispaño-Technica S.A. Inc., San Antonio, from 1977. Lectr. Sch. Aerospace Medicine Brooks AFB, Tex., 1975-84; adv. dir. Plaza Nat. Bank, San Antonio; cons. Def. Dept., 1981, Dept. Air Force, 1975-84. Decorated D.S.M., Legion of Merit, Bronze Star, Air medal, Purple Heart, Ordre Nat. du Merite, Medaille de la Resistance, Croix de Guerre (France). Fellow AIAA (assoc.); mem. World Affairs Coun., Air Force Assn. (exec. sec. Tex. 1976-94), Assn. Former Intelligence Officers (nat. dir.), Air Force Hist. Found. (dir.), U.S. Strategic Inst., Nat. Mil. Intelligence Assn., Tex. Aerospace & Nat. Def. Tech. Devel. Coun., Am. Astron. Soc., Aerospace Ednl. Foun. (trustee), Disabled Am. Vets. (life), Mil. Order World Wars, Am. Legion, Assn. Old Crows, Army-Navy Club (Washington), Kappa Sigma. Roman Catholic. Home: San Antonio, Tex. Died Mar. 7, 2010.

WEINMAN, JOEL B., optometrist; b. Bklyn., Jan. 8, 1937; s. Frank and Rose (Sobel) W.; m. Gretchen FonDersmith, Sept. 20, 1970; children by previous marriage: Jay, Michael, Richard. Student, U. Pitts., 1954-56; BS, OD, Pa. Coll. Optometry, 1960. Diplomate Nat. Bd. Optometric Examiners, bd. cert. treatment of eye diseases and glaucoma. Pvt. practice optometry, Kutztown, Pa., from 1960; pres. Kutztown Optical, Inc. Instr. Reading Area Community Coll.; cons., lectr. rehab. of partially sighted children Kutztown State Coll.; mem. council sports and vision Bausch & Lomb. Mem. Gov.'s Coun. to Study Health Trends in State of Pa., 1970; mem. opticianary sci. adv. com. Reading Area C.C.; bd. dirs. N.E. chpt. Cystic Fibrosis, 1989—. Fellow Am. Acad. Optometry; mem. APHA, Am. Optometric Assn. (charter mem. sect. contact lenses), Pa. Optometric Assn. (vision screening chmn. 1966-67, chmn. practice mgmt. 1967-68, 73—), Berks County Optometric Soc. (pres. 1968-69), Berkeleigh Optometric Profl. Assn. (pres. 1970—), Vision Conservation Inst., Am. Optometric Found., Assn. Kremer Laser Eye Ctr. Postoperative Mgmt. Surgery, Beta Sigma Kappa. Jewish (dir. temple 1967-69). Clubs: Lions, Rotary. Home: Kutztown, Pa. Died Jan. 15, 2009.

WEIS, ALICE ELIZABETH MICH, geologist; b. Jackson, Mich., Apr. 29, 1933; d. Burt Edwin and Ruth Alice (Jameson) French; m. Paul Lester Weis, Sept. 6, 1969. BS, U. Mich., 1955, MS, 1956. Geologist US Geol. Survey, Washington, 1956—69, Ky. eston, Va., 1973—84. Author: constrn. materials for maps, Nat. Atlas, 1970; contbr. articles to profl. publ. Pres. Presbyn. Ch. choir, Spokane. Mem.: Assoc. Engrs. Spokane, Archaeol. Inst. Am. (social chmn. spokane soc. from 1983), Am. Assn. Petroleum Geologists, Geologic Soc. Am. Home: Spokane, Wash. Died Apr. 27, 2009.

WEISS, JAMES ROBERT, lawyer; b. Munich, Oct. 27, 1949; s. Norman Emanuel and Zelda Jane (Klein) W.; m. Lynn Marcia Levey, June 25, 1972; children: Allana, Tessa. BA, Northwestern U., 1971; JD, Cath. U. Am., 1974. Bar: Pa. 1974, D.C. 1985, Md. 1985. Trial atty. anti-trust div. U.S. Dept. Justice, Washington, 1974-80, asst. chief transp. sect. anti-trust div., 1980-86, chief transp., energy and agr. sect. anti-trust div., 1986-88; ptnr. Preston Gates Ellis & Rouvelas Meeds, Washington, from 1988. Contbr. articles to profl. jours. Mem. ABA (anti-trust sect. rep. to coordinating group on energy law 1988-91), D.C. Bar Assn., Fed. Energy Bar Assn., Md. Bar Assn. Jewish. Avocations: tennis, bicycling, hiking. Home: Rockville, Md. Died June 27, 2010.

WEISS, SHIRLEY F., retired urban and regional planner, economist, educator; b. NYC, Feb. 26, 1921; d. Max and Vera (Hendel) Friedlander; m. Charles M. Weiss, June 7, 1942. BA, Rutgers U., 1942; postgrad., Johns Hopkins U., 1949-50; M in Regional Planning, U. NC, 1958; PhD, Duke U., 1973. Assoc. research dir. Ctr. for Urban and Regional Studies U. N.C., Chapel Hill, 1957-91, lectr. in planning, 1958-62, assoc. prof., 1962-73, prof., 1973-91, prof. emerita, from 1991; joint creator-sponsor Charles and Shirley Weiss Urban Livability Program, U. N.C., Chapel Hill, from 1992; rsch. assoc. Inst. for Rsch. in Social Sci. U. N.C., 1957—73, rsch. prof. Chapel Hill, 1973—91, acting dir. women's studies program Coll. Arts and Scis., 1985, faculty marshal, 1988-91. Grad. edn. advancement bd. U. NC, Chapel Hill, 2001—, tech. com. Water Resources Rsch. Inst., 1976-79; adv. com. on housing for 1980 census Dept. Commerce, 1976-81; cons. Urban Inst., Washington, 1977-80; rev. panel Exptl. Housing Allowance Program, HUD, 1977-80; adv. bd. on built environ. Nat. Acad. Scis.-NRC, 1981-83, program coordinating com. fed. constrn. coun. of adv. bd. on built environ., 1982-83; mem. Planning Accreditation Bd., Site Visitation Pool, Am. Inst. Cert. Planners and Assn. Collegiate Schs. Planning, 1985—; discipline screening com. Fulbright Scholar awards in Architecture and City Planning, Coun. for Internat. Exchange of Scholars, 1985-88; N.Mex. adv. bd. Enterprise Found., Santa Fe, 1997-2002; governing bd. Acad. Freedom Fund, AAUP, 1997-2000. Author: The Central Business District in Transition: Methodological Approaches to CBD Analysis and Forecasting Future Space Requirements, 1957, New Town Development in the United States: Experiment in Private

Entrepreneurship, 1973; co-author: A Probabilistic Model for Residential Growth, 1964, Residential Developer Decisions: A Focused View of the Urban Growth Process, 1966, New Communities U.S.A., 1976; co-author, co-editor: New Community Development: Planning Process, Implementation and Emerging Social Concerns, vols. 1, 2, 1971, City Centers in Transition, 1976, New Communities Research Series, 1976-77; mem. editl. bd.: Jour. Am. Inst. Planners, 1963-68, Rev. of Regional Studies, 1969-74, 82-92, Internat. Regional Sci. Rev., 1975-81. Trustee Friends of Libr., U. N.C., Chapel Hill, 1988-94, Santa Fe Chamber Music Festival, adv. coun., 1990-91, 97-98, trustee, 1991-97, 98-2004, trustee emerita, 2004-; bd. dirs. Triangle Opera, 1986-89, 91-2002, Chamber Orch. of the Triangle, 1997-2005, hon. life mem., 2005-. Recipient Cornelia Phillips Spencer Bell award U. NC, Chapel Hill, 1996, Disting. Alumni award Alumni Assn. Dept. City and Regional Planning, U. NC, Chapel Hill, 1996, Mary Turner Lane award Assn. Women Faculty, 1994, (with Charles M. Weiss) Gifford Phillips award Santa Fe Chamber Music Festival, 2000, Disting. Alumni and Alumnus award U. NC, Chapel Hill, 2003; Adelaide M. Zagoren fellow Douglass Coll., Rutgers U., 1994. Emeritus fellow Urban Land Inst. (sr. fellow, exec. group, cmty. devel. coun. 1978—); mem. Am. Inst. Planners (sec., treas. southeast chpt. 1957-59, v.p. 1960-61), Am. Inst. Cert. Planners, Am. Planning Assn., Am. Econ. Assn., So. Regional Sci. Assn. (pres. 1977-78), Regional Sci. Assn. (councillor 1971-74, v.p. 1976-77), Nat. Assn. Housing and Redevelopment Ofcls., Interamerican Planning Soc., Internat. Fedn. Housing and Planning, Town and Country Planning Assn., Internat. Urban Devel. Assn., Econ. History Assn., Am. Real Estate and Urban Econs. Assn. (regional membership chmn. 1976-82, 84-85, dir. 1977-80), AAUP (chpt. pres. 1976-77, pres. N.C. Conf. 1978-79, mem. nat. coun. 1983-86, William S. Tacey award Assembly of State Confs.), Douglass Soc., Order of Valkyries, Phi Beta Kappa. Home: Chapel Hill, NC. Died Aug. 31, 2010.

WEISS, SUZANNE TERRY, lawyer; b. N.Y.C., Apr. 16, 1946; d. Jerome and Mina Miriam (Stern) W.; m. Joel Jeffrey Margulies, Nov. 17, 1968 (div. 1972). B.F.A., NYU, 1968; J.D., N.Y. Law Sch., 1982. Bar: N.Y. 1983, U.S. Dist. Ct. (ea. and so. dists.) N.Y. 1983. Prodn. asst. sta. WOR-TV, N.Y.C., 1968-69; Asst. prodn. adminstr. Jules Power Prodn., 1969-71; prodn. asst., asst. traffic mgr. WMD Advt., 1971-72; freelance market researcher Research & Forecasts, 1973-76; timetable prodn. mgr., print prodn. asst. TDI/Winston Network, 1977-78; sole practice law, N.Y.C., 1983—. Contbr. editor book and radio series Prophecy for the Year 2000, 1967-72. Recipient Human Rights award N.Y. Law Sch., 1982. Mem. ABA (topics editor Human Rights Jour. 1980-82). Democrat. Jewish. Home: Tucson, Ariz. Died Aug. 24, 2010.

WELCH, DAVID WILLIAM, lawyer; b. St. Louis, Feb. 26, 1941; s. Claude LeRoy Welch and Mary Eleanor (Peggs) Welch; m. Candace Lee Capages, June 5, 1971; children: Joseph Peggs, Heather Elizabeth, Katherine Laura. BSBA, Washington U., St. Louis, 1963; JD, U. Tulsa, 1971. Bar: Okla. 1972, Mo. 1973, U.S. Dist. Ct. (we. dist.) Mo. 1973, U.S. Dist. Ct. (ea. dist.) Mo. 1974, U.S. Ct. Appeals (8th cir.) 1977, U.S. Ct. Appeals (7th cir.) 1991. Contract adminstr. McDonnell Aircraft Corp., St. Louis, 1965-66; bus. analyst Dun & Bradstreet Inc., Los Angeles, 1967-68; atty. U.S. Dept. Labor, Washington, 1972-73; ptnr. Moller Talent, Kuelthau & Welch, St. Louis, 1973-88, Lashly & Baer, St. Louis, 1988-96, Armstrong Teasdale LLP, St. Louis, from 1996. Author: (handbook) Missouri Employment Law, 1988; contbr. book chpts. Missouri Bar Employer-Employee Law, 1985, 87, 89, 92, 94, Missouri Discrimination Law, 1999; co-editor: Occupational Safety and Health Law, 1996. Mem. City of Creve Coeur Ethics Commn., 1987-88, Planning and Zoning Commn., 1988-96; bd. dirs. Camp Wyman, Eureka, Mo., 1982—, sec., 1987-88, 2nd v.p. 1988-89, 1st v.p. 1990-92, pres., 1992-94. Mem. ABA, Fed. Bar Assn., Mo. Bar Assn., Okla. Bar Assn., St. Louis Bar Assn., Kiwanis (bd. dirs. St. Louis 1979—, sec. 1982-83, 93-94, 2003-04, v.p. 1983-84, 88-90, 92-93, 2003-04, Man of Yr. award 1985). Democrat. Mem. Christian Ch. (Disciples Of Christ). Avocations: travel, music. Home: Saint Louis, Mo. Deceased.

WELSH, DONALD EMORY, publishing executive; b. Youngstown, Ohio, Oct. 6, 1943; s. Edward Francis and Clevelle Rose W.; m. Elizabeth Bourne Floyd, June 25, 1966; children: Leah Bourne, Emory Philip. AB, Columbia U., 1965; JD, Cleveland Marshall Sch. Law, 1969. Bar: Ohio 1969. Trust devel. officer Cleve. Trust Co., 1968-70; advt. sales rep. Fortune mag., Time, Inc., NYC, 1970-75; advt. dir. Rolling Stone mag., NYC, 1975-77, v.p., assoc. pub., 1977-78; pub. Muppet mag. and pres. Lorimar Pub. Group (formerly Telepictures Publs., Inc.), 1982-87; pres. Welsh Pub. Group, Inc., 1987-94; exec. v.p. Marvel Comics Group, NYC, 1994-96; chmn. Group XXVII Comms., NYC, 1997-2000; pres. pub. group Digital Convergence Inc., NYC, 2000-2001; chmn. Budget Living Commn., NYC, 2001—05; bus. chmn. DEW LLC, Millerson, NY. Global advisor Outward Bound, U.S.A.; bd. dirs. Cousteau Soc.; former bd. dirs. Big Apple Circus, B.P.A. Consumer Mags. Mem. ABA, Mag. Pubs. Assn. (past bd. dirs.), Century Assn., Sharon Country Club (Conn.), Ocean Reef Club (Fla.), Brook Club (N.Y.C.). Home: Millerton, NY. Died Feb. 6, 2010.

WELSH, PETER CORBETT, museum director, historian; b. Washington, Aug. 28, 1926; s. Arthur Brinkley and Susan Jane (Putney) W.; m. Catherine Beatrice Allen, Nov. 27, 1951 (div. 1969); children— Susan Jane, Peter Corbett; m. Caroline Levert Mastin, Sept. 8, 1970; 1 child, James Munson Corbett. BA, Mt. Union Coll., Alliance, Ohio, 1950; postgrad., U. Va., 1950-51; MA (Hagley fellow), U. Del., 1956. Research asst., fellowship coordinator Eleutherian Mills-Hagley Found., Wilmington, Del., 1956-59; assoc. curator dept. civil history Mus. History and Tech., Smithsonian Instn., 1959-61; curator Growth U.S., 1962-64, curator dept. civil history, 1964-69, asst. dir. gen. mus. of instn., 1969-70, dir. Office Mus. Programs, 1970-71; dir. N.Y. State Hist. Assn., Cooperstown, 1971-74; vis. prof. Cooperstown Grad. Program, N.Y. State Hist. Assn.; dir. Cooperstown Grad. Programs, 1971-74; dir. spl. projects N.Y. State Mus., Albany, 1975-76; dir. Bur. Mus., Pa. Hist. and Mus. Commn., 1976-84; pres. The Welsh Group, 1984-86; curator The Adirondack Mus., Blue Mountain Lake, N.Y., 1986-88, sr. historian, 1988-89; mus. cons., lectr., from 1989. Adj. prof. SUNY; cons. FDR Mus. and Little White House, Warm Springs, Ga., 1968-72; trustee Landon Sch., Bethesda, Md., 1964-70; bd. dirs., mem. exec. com. Ctr. for Conservation of Hist. Art and Artifacts, 1979-83; bd. dirs. Lake Placid Ctr. for the Arts, 1992-96; mem. publs. adv. com. The Adirondack Mus., 2002--. Author: Tanning in the United States: A Brief History, 1964, American Folk Art: The Art and Spirit of the People, 1967, Track and Road: The American Trotting Horse, 1820-1990, 1968, The Art of Enterprise: A Pennsylvania Tradition, 1983, Jacks, Jobbers and Kings: Logging the Adirondacks, 1850-1950, 1996; contbr. articles to profl. publs.; editor Smithsonian Jour. History, 1967-70. Served to 1st lt. AUS, 1951-54. Mem. Am. Hist. Assn., Am. Studies Assn., Am. Assn. Mus., N.Y. State Assn. Mus. (council 1971-75), Am. Assn. State and Local History (publ. com.), Soc. History of Tech., Sigma Nu. Clubs: Country of Harrisburg. Democrat. Roman Catholic. Died Feb. 3, 2010.

WELSHANS, MERLE TALMADGE, retired management consultant; b. Murphysboro, Ill., June 17, 1918; s. Arthur Isaac and Martha Ellen (Blair) W.; m. Mary Katherine Whitenbaugh, June 2, 1942; children: Elizabeth Margaret Van Steenbergh, Arthur Edmund, Janice Ann. BEd, So. Ill. U., 1940; MA, Washington U., St. Louis, 1947, PhD, 1951. Asst. v.p. Merc. Mortgage Co., Olney, Ill., 1940; exec. officer, dept. bus. adminstrn. George Washington U., 1950-54; prof. fin. Grad. Sch. Bus. Adminstrn., Washington U., 1954-69; v.p. fin. Union Electric Co., St. Louis, 1969-83; mgmt. cons., from 1983; ret. Dir. Hotchkis & Wiley Funds, Deaconess Found. Author: (with R.W. Melicher) Finance, 9th edit., 1992; editor Fin. Newsletter, 1965-69. Capt. U.S. Army, 1942-45. Decorated Bronze Star medal. Mem. Fin. Mgmt. Assn. (dir.), Am. Econ. Assn., Am. Fin. Assn., Fin. Analysts Assn. St. Louis (trustee), Beta Gamma Sigma, others. Methodist. Home: Columbia, SC. Died Sept. 26, 2009.

WENDEL, RICHARD FREDERICK, economist, educator, consultant; b. Chgo., Apr. 29, 1930; s. Elmer Carl and Victoria Matilda (Jeffrey) W.; m. Leslie Jane Travis, June 15, 1957; children: John Travis, Andrew Stewart. AB, Augustana Coll., 1951; MBA, U. Pa., 1957, PhD (fellow 1962-64), 1966. Asst. to pres. Flexonics Corp., Maywood, Ill., 1957-59; sales rep., product mgr. Kordite div. Nat. Distillers Corp., Macedon, N.Y., 1959-62; instr. Wharton Sch., U. Pa., 1964-65; asst. prof. mktg. Grad. Sch. Bus. Adminstrn., Washington U., St. Louis, 1965-69; asso. prof. U. Conn., 1969-74, prof., 1974-90, prof. emeritus, 1990. Mem. U.S. Census Field Adv. Commn., 1967-69; mem. acad. adv. commn. Bur. Labor Stats., U.S. Bur. Census Survey of Consumer Expenditures, 1971-76; mem. Conn. Export Devel. Council, Dept. Commerce, 1972-76; dir. Neon Software Inc. Author: (with M.L. Bell) Economic Importance of Highway Advertising, 1966; (with W. Gorman) Selling: Preparation. Persuasion. Strategy., 1983, 88; editor: Readings in Marketing, 1973-74, 75-76, 77-78, 78-79, 79-80, 80-81, (with C.L. Lapp) Add to Your Selling Know-How, 1968; editorial staff: jour. Mktg., 1965-74. Bd. dirs. Roper Center. Served with USAF, 1951-55. Center for Real Estate and Urban Econs. grantee, 1969-70 Mem. Am. Mktg. Assn., N.Y. Acad. Scis. Democrat. Episcopalian. Home: Chestertown, Md. Died Mar. 22, 2010.

WENRICH, JOHN WILLIAM, retired academic administrator; b. York, Pa., June 8, 1937; s. Ralph Chester and Helen Louise (McCollam) W.; m. Linda Larsen, June 23, 1961 (dec. Sept. 1966); 1 child, Thomas Allen; m. Martha Gail Lofberg, Sept. 1, 1967; 1 child, Margaret Ann AB, Princeton U., 1959; MA, U. Mich., 1961, PhD, 1968. Fgn. service officer US Dept. State, Washington, 1962-65; rep. Internat. Devel. Found., NYC, 1965-66; project dir. U. Mich., Ann Arbor, 1966-69; asst. to pres. Coll. San Mateo, Calif., 1969-71; v.p. Ferris State U., Big Rapids, Mich., 1971-75, pres., 1984-88, Canada Coll., Redwood City, Calif., 1975-79, Santa Ana Coll., Calif., 1979-84; chancellor San Diego C.C. Dist., 1988-90, Dallas (Tex.) C.C., 1990—2003, chancellor emeritus, 2003—10. Co-author: Leadership in Administration of Technical and Vocational Education, 1974, Administration of Vocational Education. Recipient Meritorious Service medal Dept. State, 1966; Hinsdale scholar Sch. Edn. U. Mich., 1968 Avocations: bridge, tennis, travel. Home: Dallas, Tex. Died July 6, 2010.

WERMUTH, PAUL CHARLES, retired language educator; b. Phila., Oct. 28, 1925; s. Paul C. and Susan (Manga) W.; m. Barbara Ethel Braun, Aug. 26, 1951; children— Geoffrey Paul, Paul Charles, Alan John, Stephen Mark. AB, MA, Boston U., 1951; PhD, Pa. State U., 1955. Instr. Clarkson Coll., Potsdam, N.Y., 1951-52; part-time instr., grad. asst. Pa. State U., 1952-55; asst. prof. Coll. William and Mary, 1955-57; mem. faculty Central Conn. State Coll., New Britain, 1957-68, asso. prof. English, 1966-68; prof. English Northeastern U., 1968-90, prof. emeritus, from 1990, chmn. dept., 1968-75. Vis. prof. Middlebury Coll., 1963-64 Author: Modern Essays on Writing and Style, 2d edit, 1969, Essays in English, 1967, Bayard Taylor, 1974, Selected Letters of Bayard Taylor, 1997, also articles. Served with USAAF, 1943-46. Danforth summer study grantee, 1961 Mem. Modern Lang. Assn., AAUP, Mensa. Home: Swampscott, Mass. Died Oct. 26, 2009.

WERNER, ROBERT L., lawyer, consultant; b. NYC, Feb. 28, 1913; s. Abraham L. and Elsa (Ludwig) W.; m. Raye Davies, Oct. 13, 1945; children: William, John. AB, Yale U., 1933; LLB, Harvard U., 1936. Bar: N.Y. 1936, U.S. Supreme Ct. 1936, also various fed. cts. and adminstrv. agys. 1936. Spl. asst. to U.S. atty. So. Dist. N.Y., 1936, asst. U.S. atty, 1937-40, confidential asst., 1940-42; dep. asst. atty. gen. U.S. Dept. Justice, Washington, 1946-47; spl. asst. to atty. gen. U.S., 1946-47; mem. law dept. RCA, NYC, 1947, v.p., gen. atty., 1951-62, exec. v.p., gen. atty., 1962-66, exec. v.p., gen. counsel, 1966-78, dir., 1963-79, cons., 1978-83. Mem. adv. bd. Internat. and Comparative Law Ctr. Southwestern Legal Found., Dallas, 1966—, treas., 1970-72, vice chmn., 1972-73, chmn. advisory bd., 1974-76, found. trustee 1976-88, hon. trustee 1988—; lectr. Conf. Bd., Practicing Law Inst., others; mem. nat. adv. council corp. law depts. Practising Law Inst., 1974-78; com. on restrictive bus. practices U.S. council Internat. C. of C., 1973-78; N.Y. Lawyers' Com. for Civil Rights under Law, 1972-78. Trustee Ithaca Coll., N.Y., 1968-88, hon. trustee, 1988—, chmn. bd., 1976-78; trustee Salisbury (Conn.) Sch., 1975-77, N.Y. Chiropractic Coll., 1986-89; bd. dirs. Midtown Arts Common at St. Peter's Ch., 1983-89. Capt. U.S. Army, 1942-44; to lt. col. USAAF, 1944-46, ETO. Recipient Disting. Service award Ithaca Coll., 1988. Fellow Am. Bar Found.; mem. Internat., Fed., Am., N.Y. State, City N.Y., FCC bar assns., IEEE (sr.), Am. Legion, Harvard Law Sch. Assn., Assn. Gen. Counsel (emeritus), U.S. Naval Inst., Internat. Law Assn. (Am. br.), Nat. Legal Aid and Defender Assn. (dir. 1974-79), Am. Judicature Soc., Newcomen Soc., N.Y. County Lawyers' Assn., Am. Soc. Internat. Law, Yale Club, Harvard Club N.Y., Army and Navy Club (Washington), Coral Beach Club (Bermuda). Home: New York, NY. Died May 14, 2010.

WERTZ, ROBERT CHARLES, state legislator; b. Kew Gardens, NY, Aug. 18, 1932; s. Gilbert Charles and Caryll (Lyman) W.; m. Dorothy Ann Nosek, 1959; children: Mary Elizabeth, Donna Elaine, Robert Charles III. BA, Alfred U., 1954; LLB, Albany Law Sch., 1958. Sr. atty. appellate divsn. N.Y. State Supreme Ct., 1965-67; town atty. Smithtown, N.Y., 1967-69; assemblyman dist. 6 N.Y. State Assembly, from 1971. Chair subcom. mental hygiene N.Y. State Assembly, dep. minority leader, health com., mental health com., rules com.; past chmn. Coun. of State Govts.; pvt. practice atty., Smithtown, 1960—. Exec. com. Temporary State Commn. on Southeast Water Resources; bd. dirs. Cleary Sch. Deaf; adv. coun. Maryhaven Sch. for Retarded Children; past pres., trustee Commack Rep. Club; trustee Cleary Sch. for the Deaf, Acad. of St. Joseph; past pres. Coun. of State Govts. Mem. K. of C. Died May 5, 2009.

WEST, BERNIE, producer, writer; b. NYC, May 30, 1918; s. Isidore and Mary (Primakoff) Wessler; m. Miriam (Mimi) Berman, Oct. 26, 1947 (dec. 1947); children: Ellen Paula Wessler Harris, Isabel Lee. BBA, CCNY, 1940. Comedian in vaudeville, then supper clubs, 1941-55; Broadway appearances include Bells Are Ringing, 1956-59, All-American, 1962, The Beauty Part, 1963; indsl. show performer, writer Broadway appearances include, M.C.I. Inc., 1964-71; story editor, then producer: TV series All In The Family, 1971-75; producer, writer: TV series The Jeffersons, 1974-85, Three's Company, 1976-85; exec. producer Threes's a Crowd, 1984-85; cons. What a Country, Sept. 1986; Recipient Emmy award Nat. Acad. TV Arts and Scis. for Bunkers and the Swingers in All in The Family 1973, Emmy honor as story editor All in The Family 1972, NAACP Image award for The Jeffersons, best comedy series 1975, 76). Mem. AFTRA, Screen Actors Guild, Writers Guild West. Democrat. Jewish. Died July 29, 2010.

WESTBY, STEVEN A., lawyer; b. July 2, 1954; BA, Vanderbilt U., 1976; JD, Emory U., 1980. Bar: Ga. 1980. Atty. Hamilton, Westby, Marshall & Antonowich L.L.C., Atlanta. Instr. criminal litigation Nat. Ctr. Paralegal Tng., 1985—. Mem. ABA, State Bar Ga. Died June 3, 2010.

WESTHEIMER, RUTH WELLING, retired management consultant; b. Detroit, May 17, 1922; d. Benjamin Dennis and Elsa (Friedenberg) Welling; m. Robert Irvin BA, U. Wis., 1944. V.p., bd. dirs. Stepping Stones Ctr., Cin., 1976-85; chmn., developer Vol. Action Ctr., Cin., 1979-82; trustee United Way Community Chest, Cin., 1980-88; organizer Cooporate Voluntarism Council, Cin., 1982-85; v.p., exec. com. United Way Community Chest, Cin., 1983-85; chmn. Evaluation Com. United Way, Cin., 1985-88; advisor YWCA Career Women Achievement, Cin., from 1981; bd. dirs. Cancer Family Care, Cin., from 1986; chmn. United Way Agy. Partnership Devel., Cin., from 1988. Treas. Workum Scholarship Found., Cin., 1969-86; chmn. Fine Arts Fund, Trustee Cin. Psychoanalytic Found., 1974-78, Ohio Citizens Coun., Columbus, 1967-70; bd. dirs. Planned Parenthood Assn., Cin., 1991—. Mem. Woman's City Club, League of Women Voters (treas. 1959-68); bd. of trustees, American Classical Music Hall of Fame, Cincinnati. Avocations: tennis, golf, horticulture, travel. Home: Cincinnati, Ohio. Died Apr. 24, 2009.

WESTLUND, BEN (BERNARD JOHN WESTLUND II), state treasurer; b. Long Beach, Calif., Sept. 3, 1949; s. Bernard John and Dorothy W.; m. Libby Westlund; 2 children. BA in History, Whitman Coll., 1972; postgrad, U. Oreg., 1973. Corp. sec. Mgmt. Mktg. Assocs. Inc., 1973—77, Am. Fossil, 1977—78; pres. Westlund Wood, Republic, Wash., 1980; owner Juniper Butte Ranch, Mitchell, Oreg., 1980, High Country Herefords; ptnr. Westlund Investment Co., Lake Oswego, Oreg., 1980; mem. Dist. 53 Oreg. House of Reps., 1997—2003; mem. Dist. 27 Oreg. State Senate, 2003—08; treas. State of Oreg., 2009—10. Mem.: Young Republicans, Multnomah Athletic, Sigma Chi. Club. Democrat. Died Mar. 7, 2010.

WESTON, ARTHUR WALTER, chemist, consultant, retired pharmaceutical executive; b. Smith Falls, Ont., Can., Feb. 13, 1914; came to U.S., 1935, naturalized, 1952; s. Herbert W. and Alice M. (Houghton) W.; m. V. Dawn Thompson, Sept. 10, 1940; children: Roger L., Randall K., Cynthia B. BA, Queen's U., Kingston, Ont., 1934, MA, 1935; PhD, Northwestern U.,

1938. Postdoctoral fellow Northwestern U., Evanston, Ill., 1938-40; with Abbott Labs., North Chgo., Ill., 1940-79, dir. rsch. and devel., 1959-61, v.p. rsch. and devel., 1961-68, dir. company, 1959-68, v.p. sci. affairs, 1968-77, v.p. corp. licensing, 1977-79; v.p., dir. San-Abbott, Japan, 1976-79; cons. Abbott Labs., North Chgo., Ill., 1979-85; pres. Arthur W. Weston & Assocs., Lake Forest, Ill., from 1979. Contbr. chapters to books, articles to profl. jours. Mem. Office Sci. Rsch. and Devel., War Manpower Commn., 1942-45; mem. exec. com. indsl. chemistry, div. chemistry and chem. tech. NRC, 1961-65; mem. indsl. panel on sci. and tech. NSF, 1974-80; mem. ad hoc com. chem. agts. Dept. Def., 1961-65. Mem. Rsch. Dirs. Assn. Chgo. (pres. 1965-66), Am. Chem. Soc. (trustee Chgo. 1965-2004, dir. Chgo. sect. 1952-59, nat. com. corp. assocs. 1967-72), Dirs. Indsl. Rsch., Indsl. Rsch. Inst. (bd. dirs. 1970-73), Phi Beta Kappa, Sigma Xi, Phi Lambda Upsilon. Achievements include patents in field. Died June 26, 2010.

WESTON, JOHN FREDERICK, business educator, consultant; b. Ft. Wayne, Ind., Feb. 6, 1916; s. David Thomas and Bertha W.; children: Kenneth F., Byron L., Ellen J. BA, U. Chgo., 1937, MBA, 1943, PhD, 1948. Instr. U. Chgo. Sch. Bus., 1940-42, asst. prof., 1947-48; prof. The Anderson Sch. UCLA, 1949—86, Cordner prof. The Anderson Sch., 1981-94, prof. emeritus recalled The Anderson Sch., 1986—2009, dir. rsch. program in competition and bus. policy, 1969—86, dir. Ctr. for Managerial Economics & Pub. Policy, 1983-86. Econ. cons. to pres. Am. Bankers Assn., 1945-46; disting. lecture series U. Okla., 1967, U. Utah, 1972, Miss. State U., 1972, Miami State U., 1975. Author: Scope and Methodology of Finance, 1966, International Managerial Finance, 1972, Impact of Large Firms on U.S. Economy, 1973, Financial Theory and Corporate Policy, 1979, 2d edit., 1983, 3d edit., 1988, Mergers, Restructuring and Corporate Control, 1990, Takeovers, Restructuring and Corporate Governance, 3d edit., 2000, Managerial Finance, 9th edit, 1992; assoc. editor: Jour. of Finance, 1948-55; mem. editorial bd., 1957-59; editorial bd. Bus. Econs., Jour. Fin. Rsch., Managerial and Decision Econs.; manuscript referee Am. Econ. Rev., Rev. of Econs. and Statistics, Engring. Economist, Bus. Econs., Fin. Mgmt. Bd. dirs. Bunker Hill Fund. Served with Ordnance Dept. AUS, 1943-45. Recipient UCLA Oustanding Teacher award, 1978, Abramson Scroll award Bus. Econs., 1989-94, Dean's Spl. Award for Outstanding Achievement in Instruction, 1994, UCLA Dickson Emeritus Professorship award, 2009; McKinsey Found. grantee, 1965-68; GE grantee, 1967; Ford Found. Faculty Rsch. fellow, 1961-62. Fellow Nat. Assn. Bus. Economists; mem. Am. Finance Assn. (pres. 1966, adv. bd. 1967-71), Am. Econ. Assn., Western Econ. Assn. (pres. 1962), Econometric Soc., Am. Statis. Assn., Royal Econ. Soc., Fin. Analysts Soc., Fin. Mgmt. Assn. (pres. 1979-80) Died July 20, 2009.

WESTON, WILLIAM ISEDORE, lawyer, law educator; b. Balt., May 11, 1946; s. John and Susie (Baer) W.; m. Ellen Weinberg, Aug. 22, 1971; children: Leah Joy, Kevin Phillip. AB, Loyola Coll., Balt., 1968; JD, U. Md., 1971. Bar: Md. 1972, U.S. Dist. Ct. Md. 1972, D.C. 1980. Asst. dir. pub. rel. Sheppard Pratt Hosp., Towson, Md., 1968-70; asst. exec. dir. Md. State Bar, Balt., 1970-72; pvt. practice, cons., Columbia, Md., from 1972; exec. dir. Bar Assn. Balt. City, 1972-74; asst. dean, asst. prof. law U. Balt., 1974-78, assoc. prof., from 1978; assoc. dean, prof. law Fla. Coastal Sch. of Law, Jacksonville, from 1996. Adminstr. counsel Assn. Reps. Profl. Athletes, 1977-84; cons. health claims arbitration office, State of Md., 1983—, Klaster TV; bd. dirs. Legal Aid, 1974-77; mem., chmn. Bd. Bail Bond Lic. Commrs. City of Balt., 1973-80; speaker, lectr. in field. Columnist The Compleat Lawyer; editor Sports Law Reporter, 1977-80; contbr. articles to profl. publs. Mem. Jacksonville Charter Revision Commn. Mem. ABA (vice chair gen. practice sect. spl. com. law sch. ctrs. 1987-89, com. local rules 1987-89, com. profl. responsibility 1987-89), Bar Assn. Balt. City (exec. council 1974-77), Md. State Bar Assn. (mem. standing com. on unauthorized practice of law 1983—, mem. exec. council gen. practice sect. 1985, chmn. 1988-89, chair gen. practice sect. 1988-89), D.C. Bar Assn., Howard County Bar Assn.; Friends of Jacksonville Aviation (pres.). Home: Hollywood, Fla. Died Feb. 3, 2010.

WETTEREAU, RICHARD BRADWAY, editor; b. NYC, Jan. 21, 1932; s. James Oswald and Elizabeth Seager Bradway Wettereau; m. Cynthia Fairhurst Parks, Oct. 1, 1972; 1 stepchild, Catherine Elston Parks. BA, Columbia U., 1954. Reporter, asst. mng. editor LI Press, 1959—77; LI editor; editor Sunday Edit.; editor, writer Week-in-Rev.; editor-at-large NY Post, from 1977. Editor: Homes of the Signers of the Declaration, 1976, The Pennsy Era on Long Island, 1987; co-author: Victorian Railroad Stations on Long Island, 1988. Active Ctrl. Manhasset Civic Assn. 2d lt. US Army. Decorated Purple Heart. Mem.: N. Hempstead Hist. Soc., Nat. Ry. Hist. Soc., Quaker Club, NY Press Club, LI Press Club, Salurians Club, Sigma Delta Chi. Home: Manhasset, NY. Died Apr. 29, 2010.

WEYAND, FREDERICK CARLTON, retired military officer; b. Arbuckle, Calif., Sept. 15, 1916; s. Frederick C. W. and Velma Semans (Weyand); m. Lora Arline Langhart, Sept. 20, 1940 (dec. May 2001); m. Mary H. Foster, Nov. 17, 2001; children: Carolyn Ann, Robert Carlton, Nancy Diane. AB in Criminology, U. Calif.-Berkeley, 1939; Grad., Command & Gen. Staff Coll., 1942, Armed Forces Staff Coll., 1953; LLD (hon.), U. Akron, 1975. Commd. 2d lt. US Army, 1938, advanced through ranks to gen., 1970, ret., 1976; served with 6th Field Artillery, 1940—42; adjutant Harbor Def. Command, San Francisco, 1942—43; staff mem. Office Chief Intelligence US Dept. War, 1944, asst. chief of staff, 1944—45; staff mem. Mil. Intelligence Svc., 1945—46; chief of staff for intelligence US Army Forces Middle Pacific, 1946—49; comdr. 1st Battalion, 7th Infantry Regiment, asst. chief of staff (G-3) 3rd Infantry Divsn., 1950—51; faculty mem. The Infantry Sch., 1952—53; mil. asst. to asst. sec. for financial mgmt. Dept. Army, US Dept. Def., 1953—54, mil. asst. & exec. to sec., 1954—57, chief legis. liaison, 1961—64; comdr. 3rd Battalion, 6th Infantry Regiment US Army, 1958—59; staff mem. Office US Comdr., Berlin, 1960; chief communication zone US Army Europe, 1960—61; comdr. 25th Infantry Divsn., 1964—67, II Field Force, 1967—68; chief Office Reserve Components US Army, 1968—69; mil. adv. to Amb. Henry Cabot Lodge The Paris Peace Talks, 1969—70; dep. comdr. Mil. Assistance Command Vietnam (MACV), Saigon, 1970—72, comdr., 1972—73, US Army Pacific, 1973; vice chief of staff US Army, 1973—74, chief of staff, 1974—76; sr. v.p. First Hawaiian Bank, Honolulu, 1976-82. Bd. dirs. First Hawaiian, Inc., Ltd., First Hawaiian Bank, First Hawaiian Credit Corp. Chmn. ARC, Honolulu, 1982, Hawaiian Open Golf Tourney, 1981-82. Decorated Disting. Svc. Cross, 1967, Disting. Svc. medal(3), Silver Star, Bronze Star, Legion of Merit Mem. Am. Def. Preparedness Assn., Assn. U.S. Army, U.S. Strategic Inst., USAF Assn. Clubs: Waialae Country. Lodges: Masons. Lutheran. Home: Honolulu, Hawaii. Died Feb. 10, 2010.

WHEATLAND, RICHARD, II, fiduciary services executive, museum executive; b. Boston, Nov. 25, 1923; s. Stephen and Dorothy (Parker) W.; m. Cynthia McAdoo, Feb. 13, 1954; 1 child, Sarah Wheatland Fisher. AB, Harvard U., 1944, postgrad., 1946-47; JD, Columbia U., 1949. Various positions with Marshall Plan adminstrn. Office Spl. Rep. in Europe, Dept. State, Paris, 1950-53; v.p. N.Y. Airways, NYC, 1953-68; pres. Acadia Mgmt. Co., Inc., Boston, 1968-93, chmn., from 1993. Bd. dirs., v.p. Pingree Assocs., Bangor, Maine. Mem. Mayor's Com. Insl. Leaders for Youth, N.Y.C., 1963-66; mem. corp. New Eng. Forestry Found.; mem., former chmn. Fund for Preservation of Wild Life and Natural Areas, Boston, 1980-92, bd. dirs. 1980-91; trustee Penobscot Marine Mus., Searsport, Maine, 1968-90, hon. trustee, 1990—,; bd. dirs. Friends of Pub. Garden, Boston, 1972-89, 90-96, 97—, Beacon Hill Civic Assn., Boston, 1985-89, Boston Natural Areas Fund, 1987—, asst. treas., 1993-94, treas. 1994-96, bd. dirs. 1997, acting chair, 1997—; treas. Frank Hatch for Gov. com., Boston, 1977-78; chmn., bd. trustees & overseers Peabody Essex Mus. (formerly Peabody Mus. of Salem), Salem, Mass., 1992—, trustee, 1972-92, pres., 1983-92. Lt. (j.g.) USN, 1943-46, PTO. Mem. Am. Assn. Mus. (bd. dirs. trustee com. 1976-86, govt. affairs com. 1985-89), Mus. Trustee Assn. (founder, bd. dirs. 1986—, sec. 1986-92), City Club Corp. (former bd. mgrs., former treas.). Avocations: jogging, sailing, travel. Home: Boston, Mass. Died June 2009.

WHEELER, DARRELL DEANE, physiology educator; b. West Liberty, Ky., Feb. 24, 1939; s. Frank and Linnie (Fannin) W.; m. Priscilla A. Rose, Sept. 20, 1963; children: Melissa Lynn, Brian Deane. AB in Chemistry, Transylvania U., 1962; PhD Physiology-Biophysics, U. Ky., 1967, postgrad., 1967-68. Asst. prof. physiology Med. U. S.C., Charleston, 1968-75, assoc. prof., 1975-81, prof., from 1981. Contbr. articles to med. jours. Transylvania U. scholar, 1958-62; NDEA fellow, 1962-63, NIH fellow, 1967-68, also others. Mem. Am. Physiol. Soc., AAAS. Avocation: woodworking. Home: Lexington, SC. Died Jan. 21, 2010.

WHEELER, MARSHALL RALPH, zoologist, educator; b. Carlinville, Ill., Apr. 7, 1917; s. Ralph Adelbert and Hester May (Ward) W.; m. Edna Vivian Cronquist, July 3, 1944; 1 dau., Sandra Wheeler King; m. Linda Carol Lackner, May 10, 1966; children: Karen, Carson. Student, Blackburn Coll., 1935-37; BA, Baylor U., 1939; postgrad., Tex. A&M U., 1939-41; PhD (NRC fellow), U. Tex., 1947. Mem. faculty U. Tex., Austin, from 1947, assoc. prof. zoology, 1955-61, prof., 1961-78, emeritus prof., from 1978. Gosney fellow Calif. Inst. Tech.; former dir. Nat. Drosophila Species Resources Ctr.; mem. Nat. Wildflower Rsch. Ctr. Editor: Studies in Genetics, 1960-72. Served with USN, 1941-45. NSF grantee; NIH grantee. Mem. Entomol. Soc. Am. (editor Annals 1970-75), S.W. Assn. Naturalists (pres. 1961), Southwestern Entomol. Soc. (pres. 1978), Am. Hemerocallis Soc., Wilderness Soc., Nature Conservancy. Home: Austin, Tex. Died Jan. 3, 2010.

WHELPLEY, JAMES DIX, investment company executive; b. Cin., Mar. 16, 1936; s. James Albert and Ruth Francis (Dix) Whelpley; m. Sandra Jo Young, Jan. 17, 1959; children: James Linvill, Tarik Thomas, Tamara Jo. BA, Yale U., 1958; postgrad., N.Y. Grad. Sch. Bus. Adminstrn., 1958—59, Am. U., Beirut, 1961—62. Ofcl. asst. First Nat. City Bank N.Y., NYC, head office overseas divsn., 1958—61, Beirut, 1961—62; salesman Laird, Inc., NYC, 1962—64, mgr. spl. rsch., 1964—68, v.p., dir. rsch., 1968—70; exec. v.p. Bay Securities Corp., San Francisco, 1970; sr. v.p., mgr. investments ISI Corp., San Francisco, 1970—74, pres., investment mgr., from 1970, also bd. dirs.; pres. Whelpley Assocs., Inc., 1975—86, also bd. dirs.; pres. Indego Securities, Inc., from 1987, also bd. dirs. Mem.: Fin. Forum N.Y.C., N.Y. Soc. Security Analysts, Royal Automobile Club (London), World Trade Club, Yale Club, City Midday Club (N.Y.C.), Delta kappa Epsilon. Libertarian. Died June 1, 2010.

WHISTLER, ROY LESTER, chemist, educator, industrialist; b. Morgantown, W.Va., Mar. 31, 1912; s. Park H. and Cloe (Martin) W.; m. Leila Anna Barbara Kaufman, Sept. 6, 1935 (dec. 1994); 1 child, William Harris. BS, Heidelberg Coll., 1934, D.Sc. (hon.), 1957; MS, Ohio State U., 1935; PhD, Iowa State U., 1938; D.Litt. (hon.), St. Thomas Inst., 1982; D.Agr., Purdue U., 1985. Instr. chemistry Iowa State U., 1935-38; research fellow Bur. Standards, 1938-40; sect. leader dept. agr. No. Regional Rsch. Lab., 1940-46; prof. biochemistry Purdue U., 1946-76, Hillenbrand distinguished prof., asst. dept. head, 1974-82, Hillenbrand disting. prof. emeritus Lafayette, Ind., from 1982; chmn. Inst. Agrl. Utilization Research, 1961-75; pres. Lafayette Applied Chemistry Inc., 1980-96. Vis. lectr. U. Witwatersrand, South Africa, 1961, South Africa, 65, South Africa, 77, South Africa, 85, Acad. Sci., France, 1975, Vladivostock Acad. Sci., Russia, 1976, numerous other countries; lectr. Bradley Polytech. Inst., 1941—42; adj. prof. Whistler Ctr. Carbohydrate Chemistry (named by Purdue U. 1984), advisor, bd. dirs.; indsl cons. dir. Pfanstiehl Lab., Inc., 1940—2000, Greenwich Pharm., Inc., 1946—52, Larex, from 1999. Author: Polysaccharide Chemistry, 1953, Industrial Gums, 1959, 2d rev. edit., 1976, 3d rev. edit., 1992; rev. edit.: Methods of Carbohydrate Chemistry, series, 1962—; co-author: Guar, 1979, Carbohydrates for Food Scientists, 1997; editor: Starch-Chemistry and Technology, 2 vols., 1965, 67, rev. edit., 1984, 3d edit. 1999; editl bd. Jour. Carbohydrate Research, 1960-91, Starchs Chemistry and Technology, 1985; bd. advisors: Advances in Carbohydrate Chemistry, 1950-96, Organic Preparations and Procedures Internat., 1970—, Jour. Carbo-Nucleosides-Nucleotides, 1973-77, Stärke, Starch, 1979-99; contbr. numerous articles to profl. jours. Recipient Sigma Xi rsch. award Purdue U., 1953, Medal of Merit, Japanese Starch Tech. Soc., 1967, German Saare medal, 1974, Thomas Burr Osborne award Am. Assn. Cereal Chemists, 1974, Sterling Henricks award USDA, 1991, 93, Nicholas Appert award Inst. Food Technologists, 1994; Roy L. Whistler internat. award in carbohydrates established in his hon., Rsch. bldg. named in his honor Purdue U., 1997; Fred W. Tanner lectr., Chgo., 1994; Named Hillenbrand Disting. prof. Fellow AAAS, Am. Chem. Soc. (chmn. Purdue sect. 1949-50, carbohydrate divsn. 1951, cellular divsn. 1962, nat. councilor 1953-87, bd. dirs. 5th dist. 1955-58, chmn. com. edn. and students, chmn. sub-com. polysaccharide nomenclature, symposium dedicated in his honor 1979, hon. fellow award cellulose divsn. 1983, Hudson award 1960, Anselme Payen award 1967, Carl Lucas Alsburg award 1970, Spencer award 1970, 75, Disting. Svc. award 1983, named one of 10 outstanding chemists Chgo. sect. 1948), Am. Inst. Chemists (pres. 1982-83, Gold medal 1992), Am. Assn. Cereal Chemists (pres. 1978), Internat. Carbohydrate Union (pres. 1972-74); mem. Lafayette Applied Chemistry (pres. 1970-94), Argentine Chem. Soc. (life), Rotary (pres. 1966), Sigma Xi (pres. Purdue sect. 1957-59, nat. exec. com. 1958-62, hon. life mem. 1983—), Phi Lambda Upsilon, Rotary (pres. 1966). Home: West Lafayette, Ind. Died Feb. 7, 2010.

WHITAKER, CHARLES LARIMORE, lawyer; b. Guntersville, Ala., Apr. 20, 1943; s. James G. and Pearl (Hastings) W.; m. Ann Clark, Sept. 2, 1962; children: Paula C., Clark L. BA, Vanderbilt U., 1965; LLB, U. Va., 1968. Assoc. Bradley, Arant, Rose & White, Birmingham, Ala., 1968-74, ptnr., from 1974. Contbr. articles to law revs. Mem. ABA, Birmingham Bar Assn. Avocations: reading, golf. Died Apr. 2, 2009.

WHITE, HARRY EDWARD, JR., retired lawyer; b. Menominee, Mich., Apr. 26, 1939; s. Harry Edward and Verena Charlotte (Leisen) W.; m. Mary P.A. Sheaffer, June 7, 1980. BS in Fgn. Svc., Georgetown U., Washington, 1961; LLB, Columbia U., 1964. Bar: N.Y. 1965, U.S. Supreme Ct. 1970, U.S. Dist. Ct. (so. dist.) N.Y. 1979, U.S. Tax Ct. 1980. Assoc. Milbank, Tweed, Hadley & McCloy, NYC, 1964-65, 67-73, ptnr., 1974—2004. Contbr. chpts. to books, articles to legal jours. Served with M.I., U.S. Army, 1965-66, Vietnam. Decorated Bronze Star. Mem. ABA, N.Y. State Bar Assn. (chmn. taxation com. internat. law practice sect. 1987-90, co-chmn. exempt orgns. com. tax sect. 1987-88), Internat. Law Assn., ssn. Bar City N.Y., Internat. Fiscal Assn., The Players. Republican. Roman Catholic. Home: New York, NY. Died July 23, 2010.

WHITE, HOWARD ALBERICK, telecommunication executive, corporation lawyer; b. NYC, Oct. 6, 1927; s. John Alberick and Maud Lyn (McLenon) W.; m. Evelyn Costela Matthews, Jan 26, 1931. BEE, CCNY, 1949; JD, St. John's U., Jamaica, NY, 1954; MPA, NYU, 1959. Bar: N.Y. 1954, D.C., U.S. Supreme Ct. Assoc. Powsner, Katz & Powsner, Bklyn., 1954-62; gen. atty. FCC, Washington, 1962-63, chief mobile radion br., 1963-64, asst. chief domestic radio div., 1964-65, asst. chief common carrier bur., 1965-66; gen. atty. Communications Satellite Corp., Washington, 1966-68; regulatory counsel ITT World Communications Inc., NYC, 1968-70, v.p., gen. counsel, 1970-73; exec. v.p., gen. counsel ITT Communications and Info. Svcs., Secaucus, N.J., 1973-87; vis. prof. of law St. John's U., from 1988. Bd. dirs. Nat. Pub. Radio, Washington, 1986—; Corp. for Pub. Broadcasting, Washington, 1979-86. With U.S. Army, 1946-47. Mem. ABA, Fed. Communications Bar Assn., N.Y. State Bar Assn., 100 Black Men. Democrat. Episcopalian. Home: Somers, NY. Died Dec. 9, 2009.

WHITE, JAMES LINDSAY, polymer engineering educator; b. Bklyn., Jan. 3, 1938; s. Robert Lindsay and Margaret (Young) W. BS, Poly. Inst. Bklyn., 1959; MS, U. Del., 1962, PhD, 1965. Rsch. engr. Uniroyal Inc., Wayne, N.J., 1963-66, rsch. engr., group leader, 1966-67; assoc. prof. U. Tenn., Knoxville, 1967-70, prof., 1970-76, prof. in charge Polymer Sci. and Engring. Program, 1976-83; dir. Polymer Engring. Ctr. U. Akron, Ohio, 1983-89, dir. Inst. Polymer Engring. Ohio, 1989—2001, head/chmn. dept. polymer engring. Ohio, 1983-97, Harold A. Morton prof. Ohio, from 1997. Author: Principles of Polymer Engineering Rheology, 1990, Twin Screw Extrusion: Technology and Principles, 1990, Rubber Processing: Technology of Materials and Principles, 1995, (with D. Choi) Polyolefins: Processing Structure Development and Properties, 2004; editor-in-chief Internat. Polymer Processing, 1990—; contbr. over 300 articles, papers. Editor (with A.Y. Coran and A. Moet): Polymer Mixing, 2001; editor: (with H Potente) Screw Extrusion, 2003. Recipient Internat. Edn. award Soc. Plastics Engrs., 1987, Internat. Rsch. award, 1992, Extrusion Divsn. Heinz Herrmann Twin Screw Extrusion award, 2004. Mem. Polymer Processing Soc.

(pres. 1985-87, editor 1987-90, editor-in-chief 1990—), Soc. Rheology (editorial bd. 1967-92, Bingham medal 1981), Soc. Rheology Japan (Yuko-sho award 1984). Home: Copley, Ohio. Died Nov. 26, 2009.

WHITE, JOHN IRVING, retired physiology educator; b. Jerseyville, Ill., May 17, 1918; s. John Irving and Florence Lowe White; m. Pauline Cutler, Apr. 20, 1946; children: Barbara White Miyasaki, John Irving IV, Richard Sewall. AA, Blackburn Coll., 1937; BA, U. Ill., 1939; PhD, Rutgers U., 1950. Rsch. assoc. U. Md., Balt., 1950, asst. prof., 1951-54, assoc. prof., 1954-59, prof., 1960-78, prof. emeritus, from 1979. Vol. Meals on Wheels, Venice, Fla., 1995—. Lt. col. U.S. Army, 1941-69. Guggenheim fellow John Simon Guggenheim Found., Heidelberg, Germany and Liege, Belgium, 1958-59. Mem. Am. Physiol. Soc., N.Y. Acad. Sci., Ret. Officers Assn., Ret. Officers Club Sarasota, Venice Elks Club. Avocations: sailing, travel, photography. Home: Sarasota, Fla. Died Mar. 18, 2009.

WHITE, JOHN WILLIAM LOUD, utilities executive; b. Portland, Maine, Aug. 8, 1923; s. Ernest M. and Hilda C. (Loud) W.; m. Marian M. Morton, July 19, 1947; children: Martha White Nichols, Nathaniel, Marian, Benjamin. Student, Dartmouth Coll., 1941-43; BS in Bus. and Engring. Adminstrn., MIT, 1944. Registered profl. engr., Maine, Pa., Mo., N.H. With Consumers Water Co., Portland, from 1946, v.p., 1962-66, pres., from 1966, now vice chmn., also bd. dirs. Past corporator Portland Savs. Bank, Brunswick Savs. Instn.; corporator Maine Med. Ctr.; bd. dirs. Canal Nat. Bank, Canal Corp.; trustee South Freeport (Maine) Water Dist., 1948-69, Freeport Sewer Dist., 1973-77. Mem. Freeport Rep. Town Com. With USN, 1941-45. Mem. Nat. Assn. Water Cos. (pres. 1972-73, exec. com. 1969-76), Am. Water Works Assn., New Eng. Water Works Assn., Maine Water Utilities Assn. Home: Freeport, Maine. Died Apr. 16, 2010.

WHITE, LINDA MARIE, former fraternal organization administrator; b. Cleve., Apr. 21, 1942; BA, Clark Coll., 1963; MA, U. Chgo., 1969. Mgmt analyst HHS, Washington; social security adminstr. Chgo.; area dir. Chgo. East Dist. Office. Bd. dirs. United Negro Coll. Fund. Named one of Most Influential Black Americans, Ebony mag., 2006. Mem.: NAACP (life), Alpha Kappa Alpha Sorority (supreme basileus, internat. pres. 2002—06). Died Feb. 26, 2010.

WHITE, NORRIS SLOANE, physicist, economist; b. NYC, Nov. 30, 1936; s. Henry Leslie Norris and Eunice Laura (Latouche) W. BS in Physics magna cum laude, Bklyn. Coll., 1963; postgrad., Renssalear Polytech. Inst., 1963-64. Nuc. analyst GE, Schenectady, N.Y., 1963-65; advisor Am., British, and French govts., 1975-2000, lordship, from 1995. Advisor Pres. Ford, Reagan, Bush, Clinton. Author: Print and Build, 1968, A New Approach to Terrestrial Magnetism, 1974, Celestial Magnetism, Electricity and Gravity, 2001. Mem. Tour France, 1998. Fellow Royal Soc.; mem. Layman's Club, Alpha Sigma Lambda, Sigma Xi. Republican. Anglican. Avocations: meditation, swimming, walking. Home: New York, NY. Died Jan. 15, 2009.

WHITE, PHILIP LLOYD, educator; b. Akron, Ohio, July 31, 1923; s. Lloyd Putnam and Della (Depew) W.; m. Meda Margaret Miller, Apr. 3, 1958; children: David, Carolyn, Michael, John, Jean. BA in Govt., Baldwin-Wallace Coll., 1947; MA in Econs., Columbia U., 1949, PhD in History, 1954. Lectr. CUNY, 1954-55; asst. prof. U. Tex., Austin, 1955-58; Fulbright lectr. U. Nottingham (England), 1958-59; asst. prof. U. Chgo., 1959-62; assoc. prof. U. Tex., 1962-75, prof., from 1975. Author: Beekmans of New York, 1956, Beekmantown, New York, 1979; co-author: History of the American People, 1970, 75; editor: Beekman Mercantile Papers, 1956. Bd. N.Y. State Ams. for Dem. Action, 1954-55; rsch. asst. Vol. Stevenson, Chgo., 1956; chmn. West Austin Dems., Tex., 1968-73; pres. Tex. Assn. Coll. Tchrs., Austin, 1980-81. Staff sgt. U.S. Army, 1943-46. Fulbright U.S. Dept. State, 1958-59, Charles Warren Ctr. fellow, 1964-65. Mem. World History Assn., Orgn. Am. Hist., Inst. Early Am. history and Culture, Soc. Hist. Early Am. Reps. Home: Austin, Tex. Died Oct. 15, 2009.

WHITE, RALPH DUDLEY, music company executive; b. Buffalo, Aug. 25, 1934; s. Menno Delbert and Hilda White; m. Margaret Jean Chapman, Aug. 18, 1956; 1 child, David Daniel. Student, SUNY, Buffalo, 1952—58, U. Rochester, NYC, 1977, U. Colo., 1978, Harvard U., 1979. Missile test tech. Bell Aero., Buffalo, 1954—58; engring. tech. Sylvania Electric Engring. Rsch. Lab., Buffalo, 1958—69, cons. engr. to purchasing dept., 1964—69, field sales engr., 1969—70, J. D. Ryerson, Rochester, 1969—70; owner, mgr. April Instruments, Batavia, NY, 1970—72; field sales mgr. Nycom, Syracuse, NY, 1973—76; nat. sales mgr. Moog Music, Inc., Cheektowaga, NY, 1976—85; mgr. purchasing Reichert-Jung, Buffalo, 1985—88; mng. cons. Profl. Support, Inc., from 1988. With US Army, 1952—54. Mem.: Purchasing Mgmt. Assn. Buffalo, Nat. Assn. Purshasing Mgrs., Am. Mgmt. Assn. Home: Cape Coral, Fla. Died Mar. 5, 2009.

WHITE, RICHARD NORMAN, civil and environmental engineering educator; b. Chetek, Wis., Dec. 21, 1933; s. Normal Lester and Lorna Elwilda (robinson) W.; m. Margaret Claire Howell, Dec. 28, 1957; children: Barbara Ann, David Charles. BSCE, U. Wis.-Madison, 1956, MS, 1957, PhD, 1961. Registered profl. engr., N.Y. Asst. prof. Cornell U., 1961—65, assoc. prof. civil and environ. engring., 1965-72, prof. structural engring., from 1972, dir. Sch. Civil and Environ. engring., 1978-84, assoc. dean for undergrad. programs, 1987-89, James A. Friend Family prof., 1988—98, prof. emeritus, from 1999; staff assoc. Gulf Gen. Atomic, San Diego, 1967-68. Vis. prof. U. Calif.-Berkeley, 1974-75, U. P.R., Mayaguez, 1982; cons. Def. Nuclear Agy., Washington, 1983-84, Sandia Nat. Lab., Albuquerque, 1981—, Stone & Webster Engring., 1983-87, SRI Internat., Palo Alto, Calif., 1979-83, Bakhtar Assoc., 1988—, Kamtech, 1994-95, numerous others. Author: Structural Engineering, vols. I and II, 1976, vol. III, 1974; Structural Modeling and Experimental Techniques, 1982, Building Structural Design Handbook, 1987; contbr. numerous articles to tech. jours. Served with AUS, 1957. Hon. mem. ASCE (Collingwood prize 1967), Am. Concrete Inst. (hon., Kelly award 1992, Wason medal 1993, Structural Rsch. award 1994, pres. 1997); mem. NAE, Precast/Prestressed Concrete Inst., Sigma Xi, Tau Beta Pi, Chi Epsilon. Presbyterian. Home: Ithaca, NY. Died Oct. 3, 2009.

WHITE, ROBERT EDWARD, think-tank executive; b. Melrose, Mass., Sept. 21, 1926; s. Edward V. and Emily G. (McGuire) W.; m. MaryAnne Cahill, June 4, 1955; children: Christopher, Kevin, Claire, MaryLouise, Laura. BA, St. Michael's Coll., Winooski, Vt., 1952, DHL (hon.), 1978; MA, Tufts U., 1954; DHL (hon.), Simmons Coll., 1985. Joined Fgn. Svc., Dept. State; dir. Latin Am. Peace Corps, Washington, 1968-70; dep. chief mission Am. Embassy, Managua, Nicaragua, 1970-72, Bogota, Colombia, 1972-75; dep. rep. Orgn. Am. States, Washington, 1975-77; US amb. to Paraguay US Dept. State, Asuncion, 1977-79, US amb. to El Salvador San Salvador, 1979-81; sr. assoc. Carnegie Endowment for Internat. Peace, Washington, 1981-83; prof. internat. rels. Simmons Coll., Boston, 1983-85; pres. Ctr. for Internat. Policy, Washington, from 1985. Pres.'s spl. rep. Inter-Am. Conf. on Edn., Sci. and Culture, 1977-79. Contbr. numerous articles to Commonweal, Atlantic, N.Y. Times. With USN, 1944-46; PTO. Fulbright scholar U. Bristol, Eng., 1953. Mem. Fgn. Svc. Assn., Fund for Constl. Govt. (bd. dirs.), Cosmos Club. Home: Alexandria, Va. Died Mar. 19, 2010.

WHITE, THOMAS, JR., city councilman; b. South Jamaica, NY, 1939; m. Marie White; children: Bryan, Lucile. City councilman Dist. 28 NY City Coun., 1992—2001, 2006—10, chair econ. develop. com. Exec. dir. Queens Village Com. Mental Health, 1975—2010. Co-founder, exec. dir. nonprofit agy. J-CAP. Recipient Disting. Svc. award, NY State Black & Puerto Rican Legis. Caucus. Mem.: Queens County Dem. Orgn., United Black Men of Queens, Jamaica Rotary Club Queens, Fred Wilson Dem. Club. Democrat. Home: Jamaica, NY. Died Aug. 27, 2010.

WHITELEY, MARILYNN MAXWELL, education educator; b. Columbus, Ohio, Apr. 17, 1929; d. Marion Wilbur and Thelma (McGrady) Maxwell; children— Kay, Janet, Kenneth. B.S., East Carolina U., 1949; M.Ed., U. Tenn.-Chattanooga, 1975; Ed.D., U. Tenn., 1981. Tchr., Edgecombe County schs., N.C., 1949-51, Hamilton County schs., Tenn., 1966-69, Chattanooga pub. schs., 1969—; adj. prof. edn. U. Tenn., Chattanooga, 1980—. Delta Kappa Gamma scholar, 1974. Mem. Assn. Supervision and Curriculum Devel., Internat. Reading Assn., Nat. Council Tchrs. English, AAUW, United Teaching Profession, Phi Delta Kappa, Delta Kappa Gamma. Methodist. Home: Hixson, Tenn. Died Oct. 19, 2009.

WHITING, WILLIAM E., real estate facilities management executive; b. NYC, Nov. 8, 1933; m. Marie B. Whiting, Aug. 29, 1954; children— Henry, Nadine BA in Arch. Design, pratt Inst. Vice pres. real estate Am. Internat. Group, NYC, from 1973. Bd. dirs. Seamen's Ch., N.Y.C., 1983-85; mem. exec. bd. Juvenile Diabetes Found., N.Y.C., 1984-85. Served with U.S. Army, 1944-46, ETO Mem. Nat. Assn. Corp. Real Estate Execs., Internat. Inst. Valuers (sr. cert. valuer). Republican. Episcopalian. Died Aug. 17, 2009.

WHITNEY, ALAN JOHN, newspaper editor; b. Joliet, Ill., Dec. 18, 1925; s. John Allen and Helen (Kodat) W. Student, U. Chgo., 1946-48; student, Oberlin Coll., 1944, U. Mich., 1943. Mng. editor Chgo. Mag., 1955-56; editor Volitant Pub. Co., NYC, 1957-58; copy editor N.Y. Post, NYC, 1959-70, assoc. mng. editor, from 1970. Served to lt. j.g. USN, 1943-46 Recipient Page One award Chgo. Newspaper Guild, 1951 Mem.: Univ. of Chgo. (pres. 1969). Avocations: painting; sculpture; travel. Home: Evanston, Ill. Died July 14, 2009.

WHITT, RICHARD ERNEST, reporter; b. Greenup County, Ky., Dec. 15, 1944; s. Walter Charles and Irene (Hayes) W.; m. Terri Bellizzi; children: Hayes Chadwick, Emily Catherine, Christen Leigh McCollough. Student, Ashland Community Coll., Ky., 1966-68; BA in Journalism, U. Ky., 1970. Reporter Middlesboro (Ky.) Daily News, 1970-71; asst. state editor Waterloo (Iowa) Courier, 1971-72; city editor Kingsport (Tenn.) Times, 1972-76; No. Ky. bur. chief Courier-Jour., Louisville, 1977, Frankfort bur. chief, 1977-80, spl. projects reporter, 1980-89; investigative reporter Atlanta Jour. & Constn., from 1989. Served with USN, 1962-66. Decorated Air medal; recipient Pulitzer prize for coverage of Beverly Hills Supper Club fire, 1978; named Outstanding Ky. Journalist, 1978; recipient John Hancock award for excellence, 1983; named to U. Ky. Journalism Hall of Fame, 1995. Democrat. Home: Acworth, Ga. Died Jan. 26, 2009.

WHITWORTH, JOHN HARVEY, JR., lawyer; b. Pontotoc, Miss., Aug. 13, 1933; s. John Harvey Sr. and Clara Gladys (Tudor) W. BBA, U. Miss., 1955, JD, 1961; student, U. Delhi, India, 1958-59. Bar: Miss. 1961, N.Y. 1962, U.S. Supreme Ct.1965. Assoc. Dewey Ballantine, NYC, 1961-69, ptnr., 1969-93. Editor in chief U. Miss. Law Jour., 1961. Mem. adv. bd. Nat. Arboretum, Washington, 1986-88; mem. vestry St. Peter's Ch. at Lithgow, Millbrook, N.Y., 1987—. Served with U.S. Army, 1955-57. Mem. Southwestern Legal Found. (trustee 1986—, chmn. Internat. and Comp. Law Ctr. 1984-85). Clubs: Knickerbocker (N.Y.C.), Sandanona Hare Hounds (Millbrook, N.Y.). Republican. Episcopalian. Avocations: landscape gardening, dogs. Home: Millbrook, NY. Died Feb. 19, 2009.

WIEGHART, JAMES GERARD, retired journalist; b. Chgo., Aug. 16, 1933; s. Oscar Frederick and Mary Catherine (Rill) W.; m. Sharon Marie Hulin, Aug. 13, 1955; children: Michelle, Elizabeth, Bridget, Rebecca. BA cum laude, U. Wis., 1958; Litt.D. (hon.), St. Johns U. Reporter Milw. Jour., 1958-62, Milw. Sentinel, 1962-64; press sec. to Senator William Proxmire US Senate, 1965; Washington bur. chief Milw. Sentinel, 1966-69; Washington corr. NY Daily News, 1969, Washington bur. chief, 1975-81, exec. editor, 1981-82, editor, 1982-84; chief polit. corr., columnist Scripps Howard Newspapers, Washington, 1984-86; dep. staff dir., dir. communications to Senator Edward Kennedy US Senate, Washington, 1986-87; pub. info. officer Office Ind. Counsel, Iran/Contra Investigation, Washington, 1987-89; chmn. journalism dept. Ctrl. Mich. U., Mt. Pleasant, 1989—93; cons. Dilenschneider Group, NYC, 1993—2009. Served with AUS, 1951-54. Mem. Sigma Delta Chi. Clubs: Nat. Press (gov. 1970), Gridiron, Century. Democrat. Roman Catholic. Home: Lake, Mich. Died Feb. 21, 2010.

WIEMANN, MARION RUSSELL, JR., (BARON OF CAMSTER), biologist, ambassador general; b. Sept. 7, 1929; s. Marion Russell and Verda (Peek) W.; 1 child from previous marriage, Tamara Lee (Mrs. Donald D. Kelley). BS, Ind. U., 1959; PhD (hon.), World U. Roundtable, 1991; ScD (hon.), The London Inst. Applied Rsch., 1994, ScD (hon.), 1995, World Acad., Germany, 1995. Histo-rsch. technician U. Chgo., 1959, rsch. asst., 1959-62, rsch. technician, 1962-64; tchr. sci. Westchester Twp. Sch., Chesterton, Ind., 1964-66; with U. Chgo., 1965-79, sr. rsch. technician, 1967-70, rsch. technologist, 1970-79; prin. Marion Wiemann & Assocs., cons. R&D, Chesterton, Ind., 1979-89. Advisor Porter County Health Bd., 1989-91; mem. consultive faculty World U., 1991-99, SkyWarn, Nat. Weather Svc., 1993—. Author: Tooth Decay, Its Cause and Prevention Through Controlled Soil Composition and Soil pH, 1985; contbr. articles to profl. jours. and newspapers. Vice-chmn. The Duneland 4th of July Com., 1987-91; v.p. State Microscopical Soc. Ill., 1969-70, pres., 1970-71. With USN, 1951-53. Recipient Disting. Tech. Communicator award Soc. for Tech. Communication, 1974, Internat. Order Merit (Eng.), 1991; ennobled Royal Coll. Heraldry, Australia, 1991, Highland Laird, Scotland, 1995; named Sagamore of the Wabash Gov. Ind., 1985; McCrone Rsch. Inst. scholar, 1968; named Prof. of Sci. Australian Inst. for Co-Ordinated Rsch., Australia, 1995; recipient Scouters Key award Boy Scouts Am., 1968, Arrowhead honor, 1968, Albert Einstein Silver medal, Huguenin, Le Locke, Switzerland, Henri Dunant Silver medal with silver bars, 1995, Henri Dunant Silver medal, 1995, medal of honor, England, 1996. Fellow: Australian Inst. Co-Ordinated Rsch., World Lit. Acad.; mem.: World Explorers Club, Order Internat. Fellowship, World Acad., Assn. Masters Universe, Govs. Club, Order Am. Ambassadors (sovereign ambassador 2006), VFW (post judge adv. 1986—99, apptd. post adj. 1986—99, charter mem., bd. dirs., Cross of Malta 1986). Achievements include demonstration that radiation does not produce dental caries; proved that soil calcium, magnesium, potassium and phosphorous, with soil PH, controls population size and longevity of earthworms and humans and the incidence of dental caries; demonstrated that fluoride neither reduces or prevents dental caries. Home: Rochester, NY. Died Nov. 7, 2009.

WIGAN, GARETH, retired film company executive; b. London, Dec. 2, 1931; m. Patricia Newcomb; 4 children. BA in English Lit., Oxford U., 1952. Agent MCA, London, 1957—60, John Redway & Associates, 1960—61, Gregson & Wigan, 1961—68; co-founder London Internat., 1968—70; independent film prodr., 1970—75; v.p. creative affairs 20th Century Fox, Los Angeles, 1975—76, v.p. production, 1976—83; co-founder W.W. Productions, 1983—87; production consultant Columbia Pictures, 1987—93, exec. v.p., 1993—97; co-vice chair Sony Pictures Entertainment, 1997—98, Columbia Tristar Motion Picture Group, 1998—2008; strategic advisor Sony Pictures Entertainment, 2008—10. Named Visionary of Yr., CineAsia, 2008. Mem.: British Acad. Film & Television Arts, Acad. Motion Picture Arts & Sciences. Home: Santa Monica, Calif. Died Feb. 13, 2010.

WIKSTROM, GUNNAR, JR., academic administrator; b. Quincy, Mass., Apr. 23, 1936; s. Gunnar and Anna Carolina (Nelson) Wikstrom; m. Marilyn Mansfield Wikstrom, May 16, 1959; children: Jeffrey Alan, Daryl Lyn, Milton Curtis, Byron Kent. AB, Tufts U., 1958; BD, Hartford Sem. Found., 1961; MA, U. Ariz., 1967, PhD, 1973. Asst. prof. polit. sci. Northern State Coll., Aberdeen, SD, 1966—68; grad. asst. U. Ariz., Tucson, 1968—71; asst. prof. divsn. social sci., philosophy & religion Buena Vista Coll., Storm Lake, Iowa, 1971—74, assoc. prof., 1974—78, prof., 1978—84, chmn. divsn., 1976—78, 1982—84; dir. Iowa Program Impact, 1976—77; provost, v.p. acad. affairs Coll. Idaho, Caldwell, 1984—88; dir. acad. affairs Inter Faculty Orgn., Minn. State U. Sys., St. Paul, from 1988. Parliamentarian Buena Vista County Dem. Ctrl. Com., 1975—84; councilman Storm Lake City, 1977—84, chmn. fin. com., 1977—84. Author: Municipal Response to Urban Riots, 1974; co-editor: Municipal Government, Politics, and Policy, A Reader, 1982; contbr. revs. to profl. jours. Ordained to ministry Congl. Ch., 1961; min. United Ch. of Christ-Congl. Chs., Minn., Wash., 1961—65. Fellow, Lilly Found., 1978—81, Summer grasntee, Herbert Hoover Libr. Assn., 1983. Mem.: Iowa Assn. Polit. Scientists, Midwest Polit. Sci. Assn., Am. Polit. Sci. Assn., Am. Soc. Pub. Adminstrn. Home: Fridley, Minn. Died May 24, 2009.

WILCH, ROBERT SAMUEL, bishop; b. Jenera, Ohio, May 20, 1923; s. Cora Wilch; m. Sandra Qua, Nov. 23, 1974. BA, Lawrence U., 1947; MDiv, Northwestern Luth. Theol. Sem., St. Paul, 1952; DD (hon.), Northwestern Luth. Theol. Sem., 1975. Asst. to pres. Lawrence U., Appleton, Wis., 1947-49; pastor St. Paul Luth. Ch., Spokane, Wash., 1952-57, St. Peter Luth. Ch., Janesville, Wis., 1957-63; asst. to pres. Wis.-Upper

Mich. Synod, Milw., 1963-74, pres., bishop, from 1974. Exec. bd. dirs. Pacific Northwest Synod, Seattle, 1954-59; shared staff div. for mission in N.Am. Luth. Ch. in Am. N.Y.C., 1972-74, cons. com. on women in ch. and soc., 1980-84. Trustee Carthage Coll., Kenosha, Wis., 1968—, Suomi Coll., Hancock, Mich., 1974—; bd. dirs. Luth. Social Services, Milw., 1974—, St. Luke's Hosp., Milw., 1978-82. Served to lt. (j.g.) USN, 1943-46. Recipient Disting. Service award Project Equality, 1981. Home: Hartland, Wis. Died Jan. 29, 2010.

WILCOX, BENSON REID, cardiothoracic surgeon, educator; b. Charlotte, NC, May 26, 1932; s. James Simpson and Louisa (Reid) W.; m. Lucinda Holderness, July 25, 1959 (div. June 2003); children: Adelaide, Alexandra, Melissa, Reid; m. Harriet H. Davis, Aug. 15, 2005. BA, U. N.C., 1953, MD, 1957. Diplomate Am. Bd. Surgery, Am. Bd. Thoracic Surgery (chmn. 1991-93). Resident Barnes Hosp., St. Louis, 1958—59, N.C. Meml. Hosp., Chapel Hill, 1959—60, 1962—64; clin. assoc. Nat. Heart Inst., Bethesda, Md., 1960—62; instr. U. N.C., Chapel Hill, 1963—65, asst. prof., 1965—68, assoc. prof., 1968—71, chief cardiothoracic surgery divsn., 1969—98, chief emeritus, from 1998, prof. surgery, from 1971. Cons. NIH Grant Com., Bethesda, 1986—89; pres. Atlantic Coast Conf., Greensboro, NC, 1980—81; dir. Am. Bd. Thoracic Surgery, 1983—93, chmn., 1991—93; mem. coun. for grad. edn., 1993—96; bd. dirs. Nat. Residency Matching Program, from 1998, 2007, vice chmn. res. rev. com. for thoracic surgery, 2001—03, pres., 2001—02, sec., treas., 2003—06, rsch. rev. com. thoracic surgery, 2000—06, vice chmn.rsch. rev. com. thoracic surgery, 2004—06. Author (with others): Atlas of the Heart, 1988, Surgical Anatomy of the Heart, 1992, 3d edit., 2004 (BMA Med. Book award 2006); contbr. articles to profl. jours. Recipient Hadassah Myrtle Wreath award, 1979, Disting. Alumnus award Darlington Sch., Rome, Ga., 1997, Samaritan's Purse award, 1999; Markle scholar John and Mary Markle Found., 1967. Mem.: ACS (mem. adv. coun. cardiothoracic surgery from 1992, chmn. 1998—2002), Grad. Med. Edn. (coun. from 1993), Womack Soc. (pres. 1991—93), Thoracic Surgery Dirs. Assn. (pres. 1985—87), So. Surg. Assn., Soc. Univ. Surgeons, Soc. Thoracic Surgeons (treas. 1980—86, pres. 1994—95), Am. Surg. Assn., Am. Assn. Thoracic Surgery, CTS Net Corp. (bd. dirs. 1999—2005). Democrat. Presbyterian. Avocations: medical history, golf, hiking. Home: Pittsboro, NC. Died May 11, 2010.

WILCOX, HARRY HAMMOND, retired anatomist; b. Canton, Ohio, May 31, 1918; s. Harry Hammond and Hattie Estelle (Richner) W.; m. D. June Freed., June 21, 1941; children: Joyce L. Wilcox Graff, Margaret J. (Mrs. Grayson S. Smith), James Hammond. BS, U. Mich., 1939, MS, 1940, PhD, 1948. Asso. prof. biology Morningside Coll., Sioux City, Iowa, 1947-48; asso. in anatomy U. Pa., 1948-52; mem. faculty U. Tenn. Center for Health Scis., 1952-83, Goodman prof. anatomy, 1966-83, emeritus prof. anatomy, from 1983. Assoc. editor: Anat. Record, 1968-83. Docent Memphis Zoo, from 1983, emeritus, 2005. With US Army, 1945—46. Mem.: AAAS, Soc. for Integrative and Comparative Biology, Am.Assn. Anatomists, Sigma Xi. Home: Memphis, Tenn. Died Jan. 22, 2010.

WILCOX, MAUD, editor; b. NYC, Feb. 14, 1923; d. Thor Fredrik and Gerda (Ysberg) Eckert; m. Edward T. Wilcox, Feb. 9, 1944 (dec. 1998); children: Thor(dec.), Bruce, Eric, Karen. AB summa cum laude, Smith Coll., 1944; A.M., Harvard U., 1945. Teaching fellow Harvard U., 1945-46, 48-51; instr. English Smith Coll., Northampton, Mass., 1947-48, Wellesley Coll., Mass., 1951-52; exec. editor Harvard U. Press, 1958-66, humanities editor, 1966-73, editor-in-chief, 1973—89; freelance editorial cons. Cambridge, from 1989; ret. Cons., panelist NEH, Washington, 1974-76, 82-84; cons. Radcliffe Pub. Course, 1991. Mem. MLA (com. scholarly edits. 1982-86), Assn. Am. Univ. Presses (chair com. admissions and standards 1976-77, v.p. 1978-79, chair program com. 1981-82), Phi Beta Kappa. Democrat. Episcopalian. Home: Wellesley Hills, Mass. Died June 25, 2009.

WILD, EARL, musician, composer; b. Pitts., Nov. 26, 1915; Grad., Pitts. Carnegie Tech. (now Carnegie Mellon U.), 1937; DFA, 2007. Performer KDKA Radio, Pitts., 1927—35; pianist Pitts. Symphony Orch., 1924—34; staff pianist NBC Network, 1937—44; staff pianist, conductor, composer ABC Network, 1944—68; composer The Caesar Hour, 1952—56. Musician US Navy; tchr. Ctrl. Conservatory of Music, Beijing, Toho-Gakuen Sch. Music, Tokyo, SunWah Sch., Seoul, Manhattan Sch. Music, Ohio State U.; disting. vis. artist Carnegie Mellon U., Pitts.; founder, artist dir. & pianist Concert Soloists of Wolf Trap, Vienna, 1978—82. With USN, 1942—44. Recipient Alumni Merit award, Carnegie Mellon U., 1996, Disting. Achievement award, 2000, Grammy award, 1997; named Instrumentalist of Yr., Musical Am., 2005. Achievements include becoming first artist to perform a piano recital on US television, 1939; being youngest American piano soloist ever engaged by NBC Symphony; performing for 6 consecutive presidents (Herbert Hoover to Lyndon Johnson). Home: Palm Springs, Calif. Died Jan. 23, 2010.

WILDER, JOHN SHELTON, retired state legislator, former lieutenant governor; b. Fayette City, Tenn., June 3, 1921; s. John Chamblee and Martha (Shelton) W.; m. Marcelle Morton, Dec. 31, 1941 (dec. 2004); children: John Shelton Wilder, II, David Morton. Student, U. Tenn.; LLB, U. Memphis, 1957. Bar: Tenn. 1957. Engaged in farming, Longtown, Tenn., from 1943; supr. mgmt. Longtown Supply Co.; judge Fayette County Ct.; mem. Tenn. State Senate, 1959—60, 1966—2007, spkr., 1971—2007; lt. gov. State of Tenn., 1971—2007. Past pres. Nat. Assn. Soil Conservation Dists., Tenn. Soil Conservation Assn., Tenn. Agrl. Council; exec. com. So. Legis. Conf., Conf. Lt. Govs.; dir. Bank Tenn., Cumberland Bank; chmn. Cumberland BanCorp, Inc. Served with U.S. Army, 1942-43. Mem. Tenn. Cotton Ginners Assn. (past pres.), Shriner, Scottish Rite, Mason, Delta Theta Phi. Clubs: Shriners. Democrat. Methodist. Died Jan. 1, 2010.

WILEY, RICHARD ARTHUR, lawyer; b. Bklyn., July 18, 1928; s. Arthur Ross and Anna Thorsen (Holder) W.; m. Carole Jean Smith, Aug. 13, 1955; children: Kendra Elizabeth, Stewart Alan, Garett Smith. AB, Bowdoin Coll., Brunswick, Maine, 1948, LLD, 1994; BCL, Oxford U., Eng., 1951; LLM, Harvard U., 1959. Bar: Mass. 1954, U.S. Ct. Mil. Appeals 1954, U.S. Dist. Ct. Mass. 1962, U. S. Supreme Ct. 1985. Atty. John Hancock Mut. Life Ins. Co., Boston, 1956-58; from atty. to mng. ptnr. Bingham, Dana & Gould, Boston, 1959-76; gen. counsel, asst. sec. Dept. Def., 1976-77; v.p., counsel First Nat. Bank Boston, 1977-78, exec. v.p., 1978-85, Bank of Boston Corp., 1985; ptnr. Csaplar & Bok, Boston, 1986-90, mem. exec. com., 1987-90, chmn., 1989-90, of counsel, 1990, Gaston & Snow, Boston, 1990-91; dir. Powers and Hall P.C., Boston, 1991-94, of counsel, 1994-95, Hill & Barlow, Boston, 1995—2002, Foley & Hoag LLP, Boston, from 2002. Bd. dirs., chmn. Mass. Higher Edn. Assistance Corp.; bd. dirs. Nomadic Structures, Inc., NP Med., Inc., Nypro, Inc; lectr. Boston U. Law Sch., 1961-64; past vice chmn. New Eng. Conf. on Doing Bus. Abroad; trustee New Eng. Legal Found., chmn., 1980-83; adj. prof. govt. and legal studies Bowdoin Coll., 1995-2002; adj. prof. law Boston Coll. Law Sch., 1998— Author: Cases and Materials on Law of International Trade and Investment, 1961; contbr. articles to profl. jours. Bd. overseers Bowdoin Coll., 1966-81, pres., 1977-80, trustee, 1981-93, trustee emeritus, 1993—; mem. Mass. Edn. Financing Authority, 1986-91, chmn., 1987-91; mem. Wellesley (Mass.) Town Meeting, 1971-75, mem. fin. adv. com., 1973-74; chmn. Mass. Bd. Regents of Higher Edn., 1991; bd. regents Task Force on Student Fin. Aid, 1987; mem. Mass. Higher Edn. Coord. Coun., 1991-95, vice chmn., 1991-93, chmn., 1993-95; chmn. lawyers divsn. United Way Mass. Bay, 1975; mem. devel. com., trustees of donations Episcopal Diocese Mass., 1971-75; trustee, exec. com. North Conway Inst., mem., 1980-92, chmn., 1988-92; bd. trustees Internat. Coun. Trust, Boston; trustee, mem. exec. com., chmn. Mass. Taxpayers Found., 1989-92; chmn. bd. trustees World Peace Found., Boston, 1983-95; corporator Schepens Eye Rsch. Inst., 1991-95; dep. chmn. planning Mass. rep. state com., 1971, vice chmn. fin. com., 1971-72. Officer USAF, 1953-56. Decorated Air Force Commendation medal; recipient Dep. Def. Disting. Pub. Svc. medal, 1977; Rhodes scholar, 1949. Mem.: ABA (vice chmn. fgn. and internat. bus. law com. 1967—69), Boston Bar Assn. (exec. com., antitrust com. 1965—68), Boston Com. on Fgn. Rels. (chmn. 1980—83), Coun. on Fgn. Rels., Phi Beta Kappa. Home: Wellesley, Mass. Died June 12, 2009.

WILKES, JOSEPH ALLEN, architect; b. NYC, Aug. 14, 1919; s. Abraham P. and Rose W.; m. Margaret Wilcoxson, Dec. 7, 1946 (dec. 1990); children: Jeffrey, Roger BA, Dartmouth Coll., 1941; M.Arch., Columbia U., 1949. Registered architect, N.Y., Fla., Md., D.C., Va. Assoc. prof. architecture U. Fla., Gainesville, 1952-59; project dir. Bldg. Research Adv. Bd. Nat. Acad. Sci., Washington, 1959-62; assoc. architect Keyes, Lethbridge & Condon, Washington, 1962-66; ptnr. Wilkes & Faulkner, Washington, 1966-82, Wilkes Faulkner Jenkins & Bass, Washington, 1983-90. Lectr. architecture U. Md., 1971-85 Editor: Ency. of Architecture, 5 vols., 1988-89: chmn. editorial rev. bd.: Architectural Graphic Standards, 7th edit., 1980; archtl. works include: bldgs. Nat. Zool. Park; (bldg. renovation) Fed. Res. Bd. Bldg., Washington. Pres. Nat. Ctr. for a Barrier Free Environment, Washington, 1978; mem. profl. adv. council Nat. Easter Seals Soc. for Crippled Children, 1977-80; mem. Pres. Com. for Employment of Handicapped, Washington, 1976-82. Served to capt. AC U.S. Army, 1942-45; ETO Fellow AIA; mem. Alpha Rho Chi Home: Annapolis, Md. Died Aug. 18, 2010.

WILKINSON, MILTON JAMES, ambassador; b. Lancaster, NH, Dec. 3, 1937; s. Milton Average and Ruth (Russ) W.; m. Ellen Boneparth; children: Pamela, Hilary Anne. Student, Calif. Inst. Tech., 1955-59, Australian Nat. U., Canberra, 1963-64. Various positions abroad Dept. State and U.S. Missions, 1962-79; polit. counselor U.S. Embassy, Bangkok, 1979-83, dep. chief mission Berlin, 1983-85; dep. asst. sec. for European and Can. affairs Dept. State, Washington, 1985-89; amb., dep. U.S. rep. UN Security Coun., NYC, 1989-91; fgn. policy advisor to U.S. comdr. in chief Pacific Command, Hawaii, 1991-93. Co-chmn. bd. dirs. Anglo-Am. Sch., Moscow, 1975-76. Served with U.S. Army, 1959-62. Mem. Am. Fgn. Service Assn. (treas. 1978-79), Siam Soc. Clubs: Royal Bangkok Sports. Avocations: chess, plaster. Home: Santa Rosa, Calif. Died Apr. 1, 2010.

WILKINSON, WILLIAM DURFEE, museum director; b. Utica, NY, Sept. 2, 1924; s. Winfred Durfee and Edith (Lockwood) W.; m. Dorothy May Spencer, Apr. 2, 1966. BS, Harvard U., 1949; postgrad., Munson Inst. Am. Maritime History, Mystic, Conn., 1961-62. Group ins. underwriter Home Life Ins. Co., NYC, 1949-59; adminstr., marine curator Mus. City of New York, 1960-63; registrar Met. Mus. Art, NYC, 1963-71; assoc. dir. Mariners Mus., Newport News, Va., 1971-73, dir., 1973-94, dir. emeritus, from 1994; ret., 1994. Mem. Sec. of Navy Adv. Com. on Naval History, 1986-88, 91-96, chmn. 1991-95; mem. Exec. Coun. Internat. Congress Maritime Mus., 1989-93; bd. dirs. Coun. Am. Maritime Mus., 1975-79, pres., 1978-79; bd. dirs. Mus. Computer Network, Inc., 1972-83, Assn. for Rescue at Sea, Inc., 1977—, Coast Guard Acad. Found., Inc., 1981-87, U.S. Life Saving Svc. Heritage Assn., 1995—. With Corps of Engrs. AUS, 1943-45. Mem. Am. Assn. Mus., Nat. Trust Hist. Preservation (maritime preservation com. 1978-80), Explorers Club. Died Dec. 13, 2009.

WILLARD, DONALD SMITH, retired insurance company executive; b. Hartford, Conn., Mar. 31, 1924; s. Everett C. and Sarah Esther (Northrop) Willard; m. Alison Johnston Rice, Oct. 28, 1944; children: Scott, Malcolm, Laura. Student, U. N.C., 1941—44; MBA, Harvard U., 1947. CLU. Purchasing agt. to comptroller Mt. Holyoke Coll., 1947—54; with Tchrs. Ins. & Annuity Assn. Am., NYC, 1954—87, v.p., 1960—70, exec. v.p., 1970—87, ret., 1987. Mem. faculty U. Nebr., Omaha, 1956—74; cons. Acad. Ednl. Devel., 1964—68. Trustee United Ch. Christ, 1971—74, deacon, 1965—68. Lt. j.g. USNR, 1943—46. Home: Westport, Conn. Died Mar. 18, 2009.

WILLIAMS, CLARENCE LEON, management, sociology and public policy company executive, educator; b. Longview, Tex., Aug. 9, 1937; s. Ruby Marlene (McLemore) W.; m. Kathleen Susan Robbins, June 7, 1975; children: Clarence Leon 2d, Thomas Chatterton. BA, Prairie View A&M U., 1959; MA in Sociology, Calif. State U., 1973; postgrad., U. Oreg., 1973-75. Exec. dir. Galveston County (Tex.) Community Action Coun., 1966-68, San Diego County (Calif.) Econ. Opportunity Commn., 1969-70; from assoc. dep. dir. program and contract dept. to dir. budgeting, planning, rsch. and evaluation dept. Econ. and Youth Opportunities Agy., Inc., LA, 1970-71; dir. Rocky Mtn. Forum Internat. Issues, Denver, 1976-77; cons., adminstr. Regional Ctr. for Health Planning and Rsch. Svcs., Inc., Phila., 1977-78; with Albany (N.Y.) Interracial Coun., Inc., 1978-80; pres. Williams Academic and Pub. Policy Svcs., Fanwood, N.J., from 1981. Vis. asst. prof., assoc. prof. Grad. Sch. Internat. Studies, U. Denver, 1976-77; asst. prof., dir. Black Edn. Program Ea. Wash. State Coll., 1975-76; policy analyst, speaker, guest panelist various colls., univs., instns. nationally and internationally including U. Iowa, U. Krakow, Poland, U. Lodz, Poland, Warsaw (Poland) U., Berlin U., Polish Inst. Sociology, Bergen County Ethical Culture Soc., N.J., 1965-92; policy analyst, mgmt. cons. Nat. Rural Ctr., Washington, 1976-79, Computerland and Computer Showcase Inc., N.J., 1987-88. Policy analyst, adv. mem. numerous task forces, govtl. confs. including Kettering Found. programs and confs. on econ. devel. in Asia, Africa, Latin Am., on trans-national dialog in Senegal, Mali, West Africa, 1976-80, Nat. Alliance of Businessmen, 1973-75, White House Conf. on Aging, 1967, White House Conf. on Hunger, Nutrition, Health and Poverty, 1969, Pres.' Adv. Coun. on Reorganization of OEO, 1971; regional race rels./intergroup rels. officer Home and Housing Fin. Agy., Washington, 1964-66; mem. Citizen Amb. Program, Russia and Ea. Europe, 1992. With USAF, 1961-64. Recipient Das Family Acad. Rsch. award, 1992; rsch. grantee Woodrow Wilson Nat. Found.; fellow Ford Found., Martin Luther King, Jr., Woodrow Wilson Found., U. Oreg., 1973-75; named U.S. Rep. to U.N. Human Rights 30th Anniversary Commemorative Programs, Europe, 1979-80. Mem. Alpha Kappa Delta, Phi Kappa Phi. Died Mar. 21, 2010.

WILLIAMS, FRANK EDWARD, architect; b. Winter Haven, Fla., Dec. 14, 1936; s. John Grover and Addie (Sumerlin) Williams; m. Susan Lewis Williams, Jan. 21, 1968 (div. Dec. 1973); 1 child, David. BArch, U. Calif., Berkeley, 1961; MArch, Harvard U., 1965. Registered architect, NY, Calif. Architect Davis-Brody Architects, NYC, 1968—72, Skidmore Owings & Merrill Architects, San Francisco, 1972—74, Frank Williams & Associates Architects, NYC, 1974—2010; cons. Regional Plan Assn., NYC, 1966—74; prof. Columbia U., NYC, 1968—72. Co-author: Urban Design Manhattan, 1969; prin. works include designs; Architectural League, NYC, 1968, Trianali, Milan, 1970, Smithsonian Instn., Washington, 1972. Mem.: AIA, Archtl. League, Mcpl. Arts Soc., NY State Soc. Architects. Democrat. Home: New York, NY. Died Feb. 25, 2010.

WILLIAMS, GEORGE CHRISTOPHER, biologist, ecology and evolution educator; b. Charlotte, NC, May 12, 1926; s. George Felix and Margaret (Steuart) W.; m. Doris Lee Calhoun, Jan. 25, 1951; children: Jacques, Sibyl, Judith, Phoebe. AB, U. Calif., Berkeley, 1949; PhD in Biology, UCLA, 1955; ScD (hon.), Queen's U., Kingston, Ont., Can., 1995, SUNY, Stony Brook, 2000. Instr. and asst. prof. Mich. State U., East Lansing, 1955-60; assoc. prof. dept. ecology and evolution SUNY, Stony Brook, 1960-66, prof., 1966-90, emeritus prof., 1990—2010. Adj. prof. Queens U., Kingston, Ont., Can., 1980-95. Author: Adaptation and Natural Selection, 1966, Sex and Evolution, 1975, Natural Selection: Domains, Levels and Challenges, 1992, The Pony Fish's Glow, 1997; co-author: (with R.M. Nesse) Why We Get Sick: The New Science of Darwinian Medicine, 1995; co-editor: (with James Paradis) Evolution and Ethics, 1989; editor: Quar. Rev. Biology, SUNY, 1965-98; contbr. article to profl. jours. With U.S. Army, 1944-46. Recipient Eminent Ecologist award Ecol. Soc. Am., 1989, Crafoord prize Royal Swedish Acad., 1999; fellow Ctr. Adv. Study Behavioral Sci., Stanford, 1981-82, Guggenheim Found., 1988-89. Fellow AAAS, NAS (Daniel Giraud Elliot medal 1992), Soc. Study Evolution (v.p. 1973, pres. 1989), Am. Soc. Ichthyologists and Herpetologists, Am. Soc. Naturalists (editor 1974-79), Icelandic Natural History Soc. Home: South Setauket, NY. Died Sept. 8, 2010.

WILLIAMS, HARDY, retired state legislator; b. West Phila., Apr. 14, 1931; Children: Lisa Dawn, Anthony Hardy, Clifford Kelly, Lanna Amia. BS, Pa. State U.; JD, U. Pa. Mem. Pa. House of Reps., 1971—73, 1977—82; mem. Dist. 8 Pa. State Senate, 1983—98. Former rep. State of Pa.; chmn. Senate Pub. Health & Welfare Com.; current mem. Judiciary, Rules & Exec. Nominations, Appropriations, Fin., State Govt. & Vet./Emergency Mgmt. Affairs Coms., State Planning Bd., Gov.'s Adv. Commn. African Am. Affairs. Lt. U.S. Army, 1952-54. Democrat. Baptist. Died Jan. 7, 2010.

WILLIAMS, HAROLD LEROY, utility company executive; b. Lakewood, Ohio, Apr. 15, 1926; s. Harold L. and Bessie H. (Woodall) W.; m. Patricia M. Dixon, Apr. 29, 1950;

children: Kathryn Louise, David James. BSE.E., Tufts U., 1947; MS in Indsl. Engring., Case Inst. Tech., 1952. Registered profl. engr., Ohio. With Cleve. Electric Illuminating Co., 1947-86, mgr. civil and mech. engring., 1961-62, v.p. engring., 1962-74, exec. v.p., 1974-86, Centerior Energy Corp. (parent co. of Cleve. Electric Illuminating), from 1986. Mem. bus. adv. council Baldwin Wallace Coll., 1964—; mem. vis. com. Cleve. State U.-Fenn Coll., 1970—; adv. bd. Salvation Army, Cleve., 1972—; active United Way Services, 1974—. Mem. Cleve. Engring. Soc. (trustee 1976—), Cleve. Soc. Profl. Engrs., Ohio Soc. Profl. Engrs., Nat. soc. Profl. Engrs., IEEE Clubs: Union (Cleve.); Cleve. Yachting. Lodges: Rotary. Republican. Christian Scientist. Home: Cleveland, Ohio. Died Dec. 20, 2009.

WILLIAMS, LUTHER FRANCIS, educator, clergyman; b. Etowah, Tenn., May 14, 1932; s. Frelon Charles and Mattie Lee (Gentry) W.; A.S., Freed Hardeman Coll., 1957; B.S., Tenn. Wesleyan Coll., 1964; M.M. Math., U. S.C., 1967; Ed.D., U. Tenn., 1977; m. Barbara Ann Gibson, July 20, 1950; children— Carol Ann, Patricia Lynn, Barbara Kay. Ordained to ministry Church of Christ, 1951; minister Dublin Ch. of Christ, Ga., 1957-61; tchr. math. Meigs High Sch., Decatur, Tenn., 1961-66; instr. math. Cleveland State Community Coll., Tenn., 1968-74, 75-77, dir. instl. research, 1977-84, asst. dean health and life scis., 1984-87, dir. student info. systems and services, 1987—; minister Central Ch. of Christ, Athens, Tenn., 1969-72, Calhoun, Tenn., 1973-75, Etowah, Tenn., 1976-87. Chmn. bd. dirs. Cleveland State Christian Student Ctr., 1978-82; bd. dirs. Richmond-Tatum Christian Sch., 1979; elder Etowah Ch. of Christ, 1981-87; ednl. dir. Cen. Ch. of Christ, 1988—. Recipient Disting. Service to Edn. award Freed Hardeman Coll., 1984. Mem. E. Tenn. Edn. Assn. (research com. 1985-86), Southeastern Assn. Coll. Researchers, Nat. Council Instructional Adminstrn., Phi Delta Kappa. Republican. Home: Athens, Tenn. Died June 20, 2010.

WILLIAMS, MAURICE JACOUTOT, retired relief organization executive; b. New Brunswick, Can., Nov. 13, 1920; s. Alfred Jacoutot and Yvonne (Theberge) W.; m. Betty Jane Bath, Dec. 18, 1943 (dec. 2006); children: Jon, Peter, Stephen. Student, Northwestern U., 1940-42, U. Manchester, Eng., 1945; MA, U. Chgo., 1949. Research fellow London Sch. Economics, summer 1948; Dir. U.S. student program U. Fribourg, Switzerland, 1946; prin. examiner Chgo. Civil Service Commn., 1949; economist Office Internat. Trade Policy, US Dept. State, Washington, 1950-53; econ. officer US Embassy, London, 1953-55; chief Econ. Def. Coordination, 1955-58; asst. dir. U.S. Operations Mission to Iran, ICA, 1958-60, dep. dir., 1961-63, USAID/Pakistan, 1963-65, dir., 1965-67; chief program div. Near East-South Asia, 1961; asst. adminstr. for Near East-South Asia US Agy. for Internat. Devel. (USAID), 1967-70, dep. adminstr., 1970-74; chmn. Devel. Assistance Com. OECD, Paris, 1974-78; exec. dir. UN World Food Council, 1978-86; sec.-gen., pres. emeritus Soc. Internat. Devel., 1986—2010. Presdl. coordinator Fgn. Disaster Relief, Bangladesh, Peru, Philippines, Managua, Sahel, 1971-74; chief U.S. del. U.S.-N. Vietnam Joint Econ. Commn., 1974— Recipient Nat. Civil Service award, 1971, US Agy. for Internat. Devel. (USAID) Distinguished Honor award, 1974, Rockefeller Pub. Service award, 1974 Mem.: Cosmos. Died May 10, 2010.

WILLIAMS, MINNIE CALDWELL, retired educator; b. Chapel Hill, N.C., Feb. 25, 1917; d. Bruce and Minnie (Stroud) Caldwell; m. Peter Currington Williams Sr., July 25, 1938; children— Peter Jr., Bruce, James, Jacqueline, Charles. B.S. in English, N.C. Central U., 1938, M.A. in Elem. Edn., 1942; postgrad. U. Ill., 1962, U. South Fla., 1965, Fla. State U., 1967. Cert. elem. tchr., N.C.; cert. spl. edn., Fla. Tchr. Weldon pub. schs., N.C., 1940-60, Pinellas County Sch., St. Petersburg, Fla., 1961-80, reading specialist, 1961-80, spl. edn. tchr., 1961-80. Exec. Democratic committeeman, Pinellas County, Fla., 1983-85, local campaign and poll worker; co-chairperson United Way Com; bd. mem. St. Petersburg YWCA. Recipient Ret. Tchrs. award Dixie Hollins High Sch., 1984; Ret. Tchrs. award NAACP, 1980; Panhellenic Service award Greek Orgn., 1980. Mem. Nat. Assn. Ret. Tchrs., Am. Bus. Women Assn., Profl. Bus. Women, Garden Club of St. Petersburg, Delta Sigma Theta (NAACP rep.), Kappa Delta Pi. Baptist. Avocations: Travel; reading; gardening; arts; bowling. Home: Saint Petersburg, Fla. Died Apr. 30, 2010.

WILLIAMS, PHILLIP ADGER, insurance company executive; b. Greensboro, NC, Mar. 31, 1928; s. John Wesley and Lila Lee (Darnell) W.; m. Joan Jeanette Morel, Oct. 26, 1958; children: Paige Leigh, Gail Darnell, Christopher Steven. Student, Guilford Coll., 1946; BA, U. N.C., 1951. V.p. The Travelers Ins. Co., Hartford, Conn., 1967-72; v.p. and actuary The Travelers Corp., Hartford, 1972-84; sr. v.p. and actuary The Travelers Corp., The Travelers Ins. Co. and subs., Hartford, from 1984. Pres. Constn. Plaza Corp., Hartford, 1970-71, pres. Tabco, Inc., Hartford, 1971-76; bd. dirs. Constn. State Ins. Co., Hartford. Editor: Automobile Insurance Ratemaking, 1961. Mem. exec. bd. gov.'s com. on services and expenditures, Hartford, 1971. Served as sgt. U.S. Army, 1946-48. Mem. (fellow) Casualty Actuarial Soc. (pres. 1977-78, bd. dirs. 1972-80), (charter mem.) Am. Acad. Actuaries (pres. 1982-83, bd. dirs. 1975-85), Actuarial Standards Bd. Clubs: Hartford. Republican. Congregationalist. Home: Birmingham, Ala. Died Jan. 17, 2010.

WILLIAMS, RICHARD, JR., animal scientist; b. Centerville, Miss., Jan. 31, 1947; s. Richard Sr. and Effie Etherine Williams; m. Voletta Ann Polk, Mar. 8, 1981; children: Sharon, TeAndrea, Orland, DeVeron. BS, Alcorn State U., 1970; MS, Miss. State U., Starkville, 1976; postgrad., Wayne State U., U. Wash., U. Minn. Cert. tchr. in agrl. edn., math. and sci. Forestry specialist Oreg. State U., Portland, 1966-67; instr., animal scientist Alcorn State U., Lorman, Miss., from 1970, instr. coop. ext., from 1989. Contbr. to Jour. Animal Sci., Miss. Acad. of Sci. Rsch. Symposiums; co-author 6 MAFES publs. Deacon Holly Grove M.B. Ch., 1989—; active Future Farmers Am. Mem. Kiwanis (pres. 1989, v.p. 1993, judging team 4-H club 1991, Outstanding Kiwanian 1991), Omega Psi Phi (pres. 1989-91, Omega Man of Yr. 1991), Alpha Tau Alpha, Gamma Sigma Delta, Masons. Democrat. Baptist. Died Feb. 10, 2010.

WILLIAMS, ROBERT BRICKLEY, lawyer; b. Moon Run, Pa., July 3, 1944; s. David Emanuel and Margaret E. (Brickley) W.; m. Teresa Maria Kutzavitch, Aug. 26, 1967; children: R. Benjamin, Lizabeth A., Matthew M. BA, Swarthmore Coll., 1966; JD, Georgetown U., 1969. Bar: Pa. 1969, U.S. Tax Ct. 1974, U.S. Claims Ct. 1978; accredited estate planner. Sr. ptnr. Eckert Seamans Cherin & Mellott, Pitts., 1969-95, Williams, Coulson, Johnson, Lloyd, Parker & Tedesco, LLC, Pitts., from 1995. Advisor Katz Sch. of Bus. Family Enterprise Ctr., Eberly Coll. of Bus. Ctr. for Family Bus. Trustee Union Cemetery Assn., 1974-97; chmn. Allegheny Tax Soc., Pitts., 1976, Pa. State Tax Conf., 1978, Family Firm Inst., Pitts., 1993, United Way Endowment, Pitts., 1995-97; pres. Union Ch., Gayly, Pa., 1988-92; dir. Estate Planning Coun., Pitts., 1989, Pitts. (Pa.) Presbyn. Found., 1995-98, YMCA Pitts., Cancer Support Network, Neighborhood Elder Care. Fellow Am. Coll. Trusts and Estates Counsel; mem. ABA, Pa. Bar Assn., Allegheny County Bar Assn., Pitts. Rotary (found. chair 1990-96, sec. 1996-98, citation of merit 1993), Pitts. Tax Club. Republican. Avocations: family, travel, charitable and church activities. Home: Mc Kees Rocks, Pa. Died Dec. 15, 2009.

WILLIAMS, ROBERT MICHAEL, manufacturing executive; b. Flint, Mich., Jan. 28, 1941; s. Robert Frank and Selina Athelone (Ballard) Williams; m. Jill Lori Flynn, Sept. 8, 1962; children: Lori Beth, Keri Lee. Student, U. Mich., 1960—62. V.p. Genesee Plumbing & Heating, Flint, 1970—72; pres. Delve, Inc., Davison, Mich., 1966—71, Genova, Inc., Davison, 1971—81, pres., treas., CEO, from 1981. Bd. dirs. Rensselaer Plastics Inc. (Ind.), Wiltic Chem., Inc., Davison Devel., Inc., Charlotte, NC. With US Army, 1961—66. Mem.: Hardware Mktg. Coun. (chmn. indsl. devel. com. Davison/Richfield area), Am. Hardware Mfrs. Assn. (bd. dirs.), Saginaw Bay Yacht Club. Achievements include patents in field. Died Aug. 21, 2009.

WILLIAMS, ROBERT MICHAEL, insurance executive; b. Balt., Mar. 1, 1949; s. Robert E. and Miriam W. Williams; m. Dianne Starr, Apr. 14, 1973. BBA, North Tex. State U., 1971. Constrn. acct. Redman Devel. Co., Dallas, 1971—72; with J.C. Penney Co., Dallas, 1972—74, from 1976, area audit mgr., 1978—80, audit project mgr., 1981—82, supervising sr. auditor J.C. Penney Life Ins. Co., 1982—83, v.p. ops. sales divsn., 1983—86, v.p. adminstrv. svcs., 1987—90, v.p. telemktg., from 1994; sys. and fin. auditor Sanger Harris-Fed. Dept. Stores, Dallas, 1974—76. Chmn. bd. dirs. Plano (Tex.) Balloon Festival, Inc., 1992—94; chmn. career edn. adv. bd. Plano Ind. Sch. Dist., 1992—93; active Jr. Achievement Bus. Tchrs.; bd. dirs. United Way Collin County, 1993, Vol. Ctr. Collin County, from 1995. Home: Garland, Tex. Died Apr. 13, 2010.

WILLIAMS, RUTH YEARSLEY, choral director; b. Phila., Jan. 12, 1927; d. James Raymond and Evelyn Pomeroy (Jarden) Yearsley; m. Lewis Bolton Williams; children: David Randolph, John Raymond, Elaine Pomeroy. MusB, Beaver Coll., 1948; MusM, Westminster Choir Coll., 1950. Tchr. music S.W. Tex. State Coll., San Marcos, 1950-54; choir dir., organist First United Meth. Ch., Victoria, Tex., 1953-83; choir dir. Victoria Coll., from 1954; music dir. Victoria Civic Chorus, from 1980; choir dir., organist First Presbyn. Ch., Victoria, from 1983. Choral clinician various chs., schls., Tex.; reviewer music books Holt, Rinehart and Winston Pubs. Condr. numerous choir tours, Romania, China, N.Y. Worlds Fair, New Orleans Exhbn., Vancouver (B.C., Can.) Worlds Fair, Australia Worlds Fair, 1988. Pres. PTA, Juan Lynn Sch., Victoria, 1968, Victoria Fine Arts Assn., 1969. Mem. Nat. Assn. Tchrs. Singing, Tex. Choral Dirs. Assn., Tex. Music Educators Assn., Delta Kappa Gamma (v.p. 1984). Clubs: Music. Republican. Presbyterian. Avocations: traveling. swimming. Home: Victoria, Tex. Died Jan. 25, 2009.

WILLIAMS, SERELLA HARRIS, health educator; b. Southampton County, Va., Sept. 25, 1928; d. Newit and Annie Beck (Brown) Harris; m. Earl LeGrant Williams, Jr., Feb. 27, 1957; children— N. Wynta, LeGrant Harris. Student Norfolk State Coll., 1947-49; B.S., Morgan State Coll., 1952; M.Edn., Boston U., 1955; postgrad. U. Calif.-Berkeley, U. San Francisco, San Francisco State U. Asst. tumbling coach Norfolk (Va.) State Coll., 1952, women's basketball coach, 1953-60, fencing instr., 1954-60; mem. faculty Hampton (Va.) Inst., now asst. prof. health edn., asst. coordinator health, 1968-70. Vol. ARC; mem. deaconess bd., asst. Sunday sch. tchr. Baptist Ch. Mem. AAHPER and Dance, Morgan Alumni Assn., Boston Alumni Assn., Delta Sigma Theta. Democrat. Home: Norfolk, Va. Died Jan. 21, 2009.

WILLIAMS, STAMIE DUDLEY, farmer; b. Jacksonville, Fla., Mar. 31, 1920; s. Dudley Wake and Effie Lee (O'Glesby) Williams; m. Flora Lee Sauls, June 27, 1948. BSA, U. Fla., 1942. Sanatarian City of Jacksonville, 1948—68; dairy farmer Pine Grove Dairy, Jacksonville, from 1956. Chmn. supervisory com. Farmer Fedn. Jacksonville, from 1965; mem. dairy adv. com. Am. Farm Bur., Jacksonville, from 1982. Mem. mayor's agrl. and recreation com. City of Jacksonville, from 1982. Capt. F.A. US Army, 1942—57. Died Apr. 13, 2010.

WILLIAMS, THOMAS THACKERY, agricultural economics educator; b. N.C., Mar. 13, 1925; s. George and Eliza Williams; BS, Agrl. & Tech. U. N.C., 1948; MS, U. Ill., 1949; PhD (sr. rsch. asst. 1952-54), Ohio State U., 1955; postgrad. Case Inst. Tech., 1957; 2 children. Instr. agrl. econs. Tuskegee (Ala.) Inst., 1949-50, asst. to dean agr., 1950-52; asst. prof., chmn. agrl. econs. So. U., Baton Rouge, 1955-66, prof., chmn. agrl. econs. and dir. R. and D., 1959-66, adminstrv. asst. and prof. agrl. econs., 1969-80, dir. Inst. for Internat. Econ. Devel., 1972-80, prof. and adminstrv. asst. for fed. programs, 1972-80; dir. Human Resources and Devel. Ctr., Tuskegee Inst., Ala., 1980-88; regional dir. region IV U.S. Dept. Health & Human Svcs., 1988—; Title III program coord., 1969-76; cons. in field; mem. selection com. USDA Sec. Agrl. Honor award, 1988—. V.p. Baton Rouge Sister City Internat., 1978, chmn., 1977; mem. Baton Rouge Bd. Christian Giving to Disadvantaged Children, 1976; chmn. Scotlandville Devel. Adv. Coun., 1976; pres. So. Heights Property Owners Assn., 1970, Baton Rouge Human Rels. Com., 1970; mem. Fulbright Selection Com. for Manpower, 1966; La. Manpower Adv. Com., 1969; nat. Fulbright adv. bd. Inst. Internat. Edn., 1970, others. Farm Found. grantee, Russia, 1970, Brazil, 1973; Fulbright Travel grantee, 1967; Ford Found. grantee, 1967-68; AID grantee, 1968; CIES Fulbright Lecture grantee, Tel Aviv, 1967; USOE Fulbright Teaching grantee, Serdang, Malaysia, 1966-67; Fulbright Travel grantee, 1966; Equitable Life Assurance Soc. grantee, 1961; others; recipient So. Agrl. Econs. Lifetime Membership award, 1988. Mem. Am. Assn. Agrl. Econs., Nat. Coun. Social Studies, Acad. Polit. Sci., So. Assn. Profl. Workers, Southeastern Social Sci. Assn., Internat. Devel. Assn. Insts., Nat. Assn. Land Grant Colls. and State Univs., Assn. Black Economists, Assn. U.S. Univ. Dirs. of Internat. Agrl. Programs, Am. Agrl. Econs. Assn., Western Econs. Assn., Am. Assn. Univ. Adminstrs., SE Consortium for Internat. Devel., Omega Psi Phi (Man of Yr., Regional Man of Yr. 1969), Sigma Pi Phi, Kiwanis. Contbr. articles to profl. jours. Died Apr. 8, 2010.

WILLIAMS, TYLER EDWARD, JR., government official; b. Chgo., July 10, 1926; s. Tyler Edward and Anne (Salmon) Williams; m. Frances M. Reif, Aug. 27, 1949; children: Tyler Edward III, Michael, Thomas, Margaret, Gerard, Joseph-(dec.), John, Mary Frances. BS, Ill. Inst. Tech., 1951; MS, 1956; MEd, U. Va., 1972; Postgrad., U. Iowa. Registered profl. engr., Ind. Dept. supr. Oscar Mayer & Co., Chgo., 1949—52; indsl. engr. Am. Gage & Machine Co., Chgo., 1952—54; sr. indsl. engr. Bendix Aviation Corp., Davenport, Iowa, 1954—55; engr., engring. exec. Ordnance Corps, US Army, Rock Island Arsenal, Ill., 1955—63; office sec. Commerce Dept., Washington, 1963—65, Office Comptroller Army, Army Dept., 1965—70, Safeguard System Office, Hdqrs. Army Dept., 1971—73; asst. dir. facilities and logistics Office Dep. Asst. Sec. Def., 1973—75; asst. controller, bd. govs. FRS, 1975—77; office asst. sec. Conservation and Renewable Energy Dept. Energy, Washington, 1977—87; dir. conservation program Designers and Planners, Arlington, Va., from 1987; professorial lectr. George Washington U. Commr., Fairfax County (Va.) Econ. Devel. Authority, 1975—83; capt. USNR, from 1944. Contbr. articles to profl. and tech. jours. Fed. Mid-Career fellowship, U. Va., 1970—71. Mem.: AAAS, Nat. Energy Resources Orgn., Naval Order US, US Naval Inst., Assn. Energy Economists, Am. Soc. Engring. Edn., Am. Soc. Mil. Comptrollers. Home: Fairfax, Va. Died July 17, 2009.

WILLIAMSON, MARILYN LAMMERT, literature educator, academic administrator; b. Chgo., Sept. 6, 1927; d. Raymond Ferdinand and Edith Louise (Eisenbies) Lammert; m. Robert M. Williamson, Oct. 28, 1950 (div. Apr. 1973); 1 child, Timothy L.; m. James H. McKay, Aug. 15, 1974. BA, Vassar Coll., 1949; MA, U. Wis., 1950; PhD, Duke U., 1956. Lectr. Duke U., Durham, NC, 1955-56, 58-59, N.C. State U., Raleigh, 1957-58, 61-62; asst. prof. Oakland U., Rochester, Mich., 1965-68, assoc. prof., 1968-72; prof. English Wayne State U., Detroit, 1972-90, Disting. prof. English, 1990-97, Disting. prof. emerita, from 1997, chmn. dept. English, 1972-74, 81-83, assoc. dean Coll. Liberal Arts, 1974-79, dir. women's studies, 1976-87, dep. provost, 1987-91, sr. v.p. for acad. affairs, provost, 1991-95, 98-200. Pres. Assn. Depts. English, 1976-77. Author: Infinite Variety, 1974, Patriarchy of Shakespeare's Comedies, 1986, British Women Writers 1650-1750, 1990, Tales of Two Dogs, 2005; editor: Renaissance Studies, 1972, Female Poets of Great Britain, 1981, Shakespeare Studies: Middle Comedies, 2003; contbr. articles to profl. jours. Pres. LWV, Rochester, 1963-65. Recipient Detroit Disting. Svc. award, 1986, Faculty Recognition award Bd. Govs., Wayne State U., 1991, 30 Yr. award Mich. Humanities Coun., 2004; Bunting Inst. fellow, 1969-70, AAUW fellow, 1982-83, J.N. Keal fellow, 1985-86. Mem.: MLA (exec. coun. 1977—80, mem. editl. bd. 1992—94), Fed. State Humanities Coun. (bd. dirs. 1994—2001, chair 1997—99), Mich. Coun. Humanities (bd. dirs. 1988—2001, chair 1991—93), Mich. Acad. (pres. 1978—79). Democrat. Home: West Bloomfield, Mich. Died Feb. 19, 2010.

WILLIS, JOHN ALVIN, retired editor; b. Morristown, Tenn., Oct. 16, 1916; s. John Bradford and George Ann (Myers) W.; m. Claire Olivier, Sept. 25, 1960 (div.); m. Marina Sarda, Jan. 26, 1978 (div.) BA cum laude, Milligan Coll., 1938; MA, U. Tenn., 1941; postgrad., Ind U., Harvard U. Asst. editor Theatre World, NYC, 1945-65, editor, 1965—2008; asst. editor Screen World, NYC, 1948-65, editor, 1965—2008; tchr. pub. high schs., NYC, 1950-76; editor Dance World, 1966-80; asst. editor Opera World, 1952-54, Great Stars of American Stage, 1952, Pictorial History of Silent Screen, 1953, Pictorial History of Opera in America, 1959, Pictorial History of the American Theatre, 1950, 60, 70, 80, 85. Mem. Tony Theatre Awards Com. Nat. bd. dirs. U. Tenn. Theatre; mem. com. to select recipients for Mus. Theatre Hall of Fame, NYU. Lt. USNR, 1943-45. Recipient Lucille Lortel Lifetime Achievement award, 1993, Drama Desk Lifetime Achievement award, 1994, Nat. Bd. Rev. Lifetime Achievement Film History award, 1999, Profl. Excellence award Milligan Coll., 1999, Tony Award for Excellence in Theater, 2001; high sch. auditorium renamed John Willis Performing Arts Ctr. in his honor, Morristown, 1993.

Mem. Actors Equity Assn., Broadway Theatre Inst. (Lifetime Achievement award 2003), Nat. Bd. Rev. Motion Pictures (past bd. dirs.). Died June 25, 2010.

WILLKENS, ROBERT F., internist, rheumatologist, educator; b. NYC, July 1, 1927; s. Robert Albert and Christine (Lehreider) Willkens; m. Marjory Elaine Thompson, June 24, 1950; children: Garen, Holly, Rebecca, Matthew. BS in Biology, Antioch Coll., Yellow Springs, Ohio, 1950; MD, U. Rochester, 1954. Diplomate Am. Bd. Internal Medicine, lic. physician Wash. Intern in medicine King County Hosp., Seattle, 1954-55, asst. resident in medicine, 1955-57, chief resident in medicine, 1958-59; rsch. fellow in arthritis Columbia Presbyn. Med. Ctr., NYC, 1957-58; pvt. practice Seattle, 1959—97. Clin. instr. medicine U. Wash., Seattle, 1959—61, clin. asst. prof., 1961—66, clin. assoc. prof., 1966—73, clin. prof., from 1973; pres. med. staff King County Hosp., Seattle, 1964—65; staff Harborview Med. Ctr., Seattle; chmn. Wash. State Bd. Med. Examiners, 1975—77; mem. med. sch. admissions com. U. Wash., 1981—84. Editor: Primary Care Rheumatology, 1990—93; reviewer: Jour. Rheumatology, from 1979, Annals Internal Medicine, from 1980; mem. editl. bd. Rheumatic Therapies, 1983—88, Clin. Aspects Autoimmunity, 1986—88, Arthritis and Rheumatism, 1988—92; contbr. articles to profl. jours. Mem. exec. bd. A Contemporary Theater, 1963—80, pres. exec. bd., 1964—66, mem. adv. coun., from 1980; mem. Gov.'s Coun. Aging, 1968—71; we. Wash. chpt. chmn., bd. dirs. Arthritis Found., 1969—73; bd. dirs. Pike Pl. Mkt. Found., 1982—92; commr. King County Arts Commn., 1984—87, vice chmn., 1982—87; mem. alumni coun. U. Rochester Sch. Medicine and Dentistry, 1982—85. 2d lt. US Army, 1945—47. Recipient Disting. Svc. award, Arthritis Found., 1969, Nat. Vol. Svc. citation, 1986, R. H. Williams Superior Leadership award in medicine, Seattle Acad. Internal Medicine, 1990. Master: Am. Coll. Rheumatology (mem. edn. coun. 1987—90, mem. mktg. and comm. com. 1989—92, mem. program com. 1990, others, Disting. Rheumatologist award 1999); mem.: ACP (Mead Johnson Postgrad. scholar 1958—59), Seattle Arthritis Assn. (pres. 1967—69), King County Med. Soc. (assoc. editor bull. 1963—68, editor 1969—70, chmn. program com. 1969—71), N.W. Rheumatism Assn. (v.p. 1970—71, pres. 1972—74), N. Pacific Soc. Internal Medicine, Am. Rheumatism Assn. (mem. conjoint clinics com. 1969—75, mem. diagnostic and therapeutic com. 1970—71, mem. program com. 1982—85, vice chmn. edn. coun. 1986—88, mem. program com. 1990, Travel grantee 1965, 1967), Am. Fedn. Clin. Rsch. Home: Seattle, Wash. Died Nov. 11, 2009.

WILMOTH, WILLIE HAROLD, financial executive, minister; b. Grayson County, Va., Aug. 3, 1934; s. William Tise and Ila Fay (Baugus) W.; m. Shelba Jean Johnson, June 14, 1966; children— Krystal Dawn, April Denise. A.A., Surry Community Coll., 1969; B.S., East Tenn. State U., 1971. Auditor, Def. Contract Audit Agy., Winston-Salem, N.C., 1971-72 operating acct. Nat. Park Service, Atlanta, 1972-75; systems acct. Dept. Army, Atlanta, 1975-78; fin. mgr. Soil Conservation Service, Raleigh, 1978-83, Richmond, Va., 1984—. Served with USAF, 1961-65. Mem. Orgn. Profl. Employees Dept. Agr. (chpt. pres.). Democrat. Baptist. Clubs: Toastmasters, Woodmen of the World. Home: Lowgap, NC. Died July 2, 2010.

WILSON, ALLAN BYRON, graphics company executive; b. Jackson, Miss., Aug. 19, 1948; s. Allen Bernice Wilson and Mary (Levereault) W.; m. Ines Ghinato, May 19, 1975; 1 child, Lucas Ghinato BS, Rice U., 1970, MS in Elec. Engring., 1971. Systems adminstr. Max Planck Institut für Kohlenforschung, Mülheim Ruhr, Fed. Republic Germany, 1971; systems programmer Digital Equipment Corp., Maynard, Mass., 1972-74, mktg. specialist, 1974-75, mktg. mgr., 1976-79; internat. ops. dir. Intergraph Corp., Huntsville, Ala., 1980-82, v.p. corp. and internat. ops., 1982-83, exec. v.p., 1983-98, San Francisco, from 1998. Contbr. articles to profl. jours. Mem. Assn. for Computing Machinery, IEEE Died Mar. 14, 2010.

WILSON, BRUCE E., insurance company executive; b. Providence, July 5, 1935; s. Richard A. and Marin B. (Waterman) W.; m. Virginia T. Leek, Feb. 18, 1956; children: Bruce Jr., James B., Suzanne L. BS in Acctg., U. R.I., 1957. ARM. Adminstr. Travelers Ins. Co., Hartford, Conn., 1958-65; adminstr. empliyee benefits The Foxboro (Mass.) Co., 1965-69, mgr. corp. risk ins., from 1969. Instr. Bristol Community Coll., Fall River, Mass., 1983—. Contbr. articles to profl. jours. Mem. fin. sch. planning com. Town of Wrentham, Mass., 1967-73, earth removal com., 1965-70. Capt. USAR, 1957-65. Fellow Mass. Risk Ins. Soc. (past pres., bd. dirs. 1979-85), Risk Mgmt. Coun., Machinery and Allied Products Inst., Lions (past pres., bd. dirs. Wrentham chpt. 1980-85). Republican. Avocations: sailing, hiking. Home: Wrentham, Mass. Died Jan. 12, 2009.

WILSON, CHARLIE (CHARLES NESBITT WILSON), lobbyist, former United States Representative from Texas; b. Trinity, Tex., June 1, 1933; s. Charles Edwin and Wilmuth (Nesbitt) Wilson; m. Jerry Wilson (div.); m. Barbara Livshin Alberstadt Zavacky, Feb. 2, 1999. Student, Sam Houston State U., Huntsville, Tex., 1951-52; BS, U.S. Naval Acad., 1956. Commd. ensign U.S. Navy, 1956, advanced through grades to lt.; ret., 1960; mem. Tex. House of Reps., 1960-66, Tex. State Senate, 1966-72, US Congress from 2nd Tex. Dist., 1973—97; ptnr. Hooper, Owen, Gould & Winburn, 1996—2010. Mgr. lumber yard, 1962-72 Democrat. Methodist. Died Jan. 10, 2010; Tex.

WILSON, CONSTANCE M(ARILYN), historian, educator; b. Woonsocket, RI, Oct. 7, 1937; d. Robert William and Eleanor Lee (Nichols) W. BA, Swarthmore Coll., 1959; PhD, Cornell U., 1970. Instr. San Francisco State Coll., 1966-67; from instr. to prof. dept. history No. Ill. U., DeKalb, from 1967. Author: Thailand: A Handbook of Historical Statistics, 1983, The Burma-Thailand Frontier over Sixteen Decades (with others), 1985; contbr. to profl. publs. Fgn. area fellow Am. Coun. Learned Socs., 1961-65, Southeast Asia program fellow Ford Found., 1971-72; grantee Nat. Endowment Humanities, 1973. Mem. Am. Hist. Assn., Assn. Asian Studies, Siam Soc. Mem. Soc. Of Friends. Avocations: ethnomusicology, gardening, travel. Home: Seattle, Wash. Died Feb. 17, 2010.

WILSON, FREDRIC WOODBRIDGE, musicologist, library curator; b. Point Pleasant, NJ, Sept. 8, 1947; s. Fredric Woodbridge and Ruth Elaine (Chapman) Wilson. BA in Music, Lehigh U., 1969; MS in Musicology, NYU, 1978. Conductor Wall Chamber Choir, Wall, NJ, 1969—81, Allaire Singers Spring Lake, NJ, from 1981; curator Gilbert and Sullivan Collection, Pierpont Morgan Libr., from 1981; musician, textural cons. Ky. Opera, from 1987, D'Oyly Ark Opera Co., London, from 1987; chmn. 19th Century Musical Theatre in English Conf., 1985. Editor: Allaire Music Pubs., from 1980; contbr. articles to profl. jours. Mem.: Am. Choral Dirs. Assn., Music Pubs. Assn. (bd. dirs. from 1987), Assn. Profl. Vocal Ensembles, Theatre Library Assn., Music Library Assn., Am. Musicol. Soc., Soc. Textual Scholarship (exec. com. from 1985), NE Assn. Computing in Humanities (pres. from 1985). Home: Manasquan, NJ. Died May 15, 2010.

WILSON, HAROLD WOODROW, chemist; b. Colorado Springs, Colo., July 10, 1917; s. Edwin and Paula (Wolter) W.; student Colo. Sch. Mines, 1935-36, Ind. U., 1938-39; B.Chemistry, U. Mo., 1945. Teaching asst. U. Oreg., 1946-47; lead analytical chemist Sheffield Steel Corp., Kansas City, Mo., 1940-44; sr. organic research chemist Cook Paint & Varnish Co., Kansas City, 1944-45; chief analytical chemist Am. Marietta Corp., Chgo., 1947-53; pres., lab. dir. Wilson Labs., El Paso, Tex., 1953-74, Harmax Labs., Inc., El Paso, 1974—. Served with USNR, World War II; PTO. Fellow Am. Inst. Chemists; mem. Profl. Chemists Assn. (life accreditation), ASTM, Am. Inst. Chemists. Patentee in field. Home: El Paso, Tex. Died Jan. 20, 2009.

WILSON, JAMES HARGROVE, JR., lawyer; b. Oliver, Ga., Nov. 26, 1920; s. James Hargrove and Louise (Sealy) W.; m. Frances Audra Schaffer, Dec. 24, 1942 (dec. Nov. 1990); children: Susan Frances, James Hargrove. AB with honors, Emory U., 1940; LL.B. summa cum laude, Harvard U., 1947. Bar: Ga. 1947, D.C. 1951. Assoc. firm Sutherland, Tuttle & Brennan (now Sutherland, Asbill & Brennan LLP), Atlanta and Washington, 1947-53, ptnr., from 1953. Lectr. Emory U., 1959, chmn. bd. visitors, 1967-68; trustee The Northwestern Mut. Life Ins. Co., Milw., 1972-91; mem. advisory group Commr. of Internal Revenue, 1963-64 Pres.: Harvard Law Review, 1946-47. Chmn. bd. trustees Met. Atlanta Crime Commn., 1970-71; mem. Harvard U. Overseers Com. to Visit Law Sch., 1959-65; trustee Emory U., 1983-90, trustee emeritus, 1990—. Served to lt. comdr. USNR, 1942-46. Fellow Am. Bar Found., Am. Coll. Tax Counsel; mem. ABA, State Bar Ga., D.C. Bar, Atlanta Bar Assn., Am. Law Inst. (coun. 1974—), Lawyers Club Atlanta (pres. 1960-61), Am. Judicature Soc., Harvard Law Sch. Assn. (coun. 1981-85), Emory U. Alumni Assn. (pres. 1966-67), Capital City Club, Piedmont Driving Club, Peachtree Club, Phi Beta Kappa, Omicron Delta Kappa, Kappa Alpha. Methodist. Home: Dallas, Tex. Died Apr. 18, 2009.

WILSON, JOHN PASLEY, retired law educator; b. Newark, Apr. 7, 1933; s. Richard Henry and Susan Agnes (Pasley) Wilson; m. Elizabeth Ann Reed, Sept. 10, 1955 (div.); children: David Cables, John Pasley, Cicely Reed. AB, Princeton U., 1955; LLB, Harvard U., 1962. Bar: US Dist. Ct. NJ 1962, Mass. 1963, US Dist. Ct. Mass. 1963. Budget examiner Exec. Office of Pres., Bur. of Budget, Washington, 1955-56; assoc. Riker, Danzig, Scherer & Brown, Newark, 1962-63; asst. dean Harvard U. Law Sch., Cambridge, Mass., 1963-67; assoc. dean Boston U. Law Sch., 1968-82; dean Golden Gate U. Sch. Law, San Francisco, 1982-88, prof., 1988—2003, prof. emeritus, from 2003, dean emeritus, from 2003. Vis. prof. dept. health policy and mgmt. Harvard U., 1988; cons. Nat. Commn. Protection Human Subjects Biomedical and Behavioral Rsch.; mem. Mass. Gov.'s Commn. Civil and Legal Rights Developmentally disabled; former chmn. adv. com. Ctr. Cmty. Legal Edn., San Francisco. Author: (book) The Rights of Adolescents in the Mental Health System; contbr. chapters to books, articles to profl. jours. Bd. dirs. Greater Boston Legal Svcs., Chewonki Found.; mem. Health Facilities Appeals Bd., Mass.; assoc. mem. Dem. Town Com., Concord; chmn. Bd. Assessors, Concord; bd. overseers Boston Hosp. Women, past chmn. med. affairs com.; past mem. instl. rev. bd. Calif. Pacific Hosp., San Francisco. Served to lt. (j.g.) USNR, 1956—59. NIMH grantee, 1973. Mem.: Nat. Assn. Securities Dealers (arbitrator). Democrat. Home: Greenbrae, Calif. Died Feb. 26, 2010.

WILSON, MINTER LOWTHER, JR., retired officers association executive; b. Morgantown, W.Va., Aug. 19, 1925; s. Minter Lowther and Mary Mildred (Friend) W.; m. Helen Hope Sauerwein, June 18, 1946; children— Mary Florence, Barbara Ann, Karen Lee, Stephen David BS in Mil. Sci. and Engring., U.S. Mil. Acad., 1946; MS in Journalism, U. Wis., Madison, 1963; diploma, NATO Def. Coll., Rome, 1969, U.S. Army War Coll., 1971. Commd. officer U.S. Army, 1946, advanced through grades to col., comdg. officer 1st Brigade, 1st Armored Div., 1968-69; chief of pub. info. Supreme Hdqrs. Allied Powers, Europe, 1969-72; editor Ret. Officer Mag., Alexandria, Va., 1972-88. Dir. communications Ret. Officers Assn., Alexandria, 1972-88. Contbr. articles to profl. jours. Chmn. bd. deacons Ch. of the Covenant, Arlington, 1974-77, elder, 1977-80, 88-93, 98-2003, clk. of session, 1991-94, chmn. bd. trustees, 1982-86; mem. troop com. Boy Scouts Am., 1972-78. Decorated Commendation medal, Legion of Merit (2); recipient George Washington Honor medal Freedoms Found., 1975, 76, 77, George Washington Honor medal encased Freedoms Found., 1979, Honor cert. Freedoms Found., 1973, 74, 78 Mem. West Point Soc. of D.C. (life, bd. govs. 1978-81), Army Distaff Found. (bd. dirs. 1980-83), Assn. U.S. Army, Ret. Officers Assn. (life). Clubs: Army Navy Country. Presbyterian. Avocations: photography, golf, skiing, tennis, racquetball. Home: Dallas, Tex. Died July 5, 2010.

WILSON, THOMAS EDWARD, television executive; b. Lansing, Mich., June 14, 1954; s. Donald Edward and June Elizabeth (Carpenter) W.; m. Julie A. Gruenberg, Sept. 18, 1980; children: Adam, Sarah. BA, Mich. State U., 1976. Sales mgr. Sta. WRBJ Radio, St. Johns, Mich., 1977; promotion mgr. Sta. WEYI-TV, Flint, Mich., 1978-80; promotion dir. Sta. WBRE-TV, Wilkes-Barre, Pa., 1980-86, program mgr., from 1986. Pub. rels. cons. Auto Sports Assocs., Scranton, Pa., 1980-90. Mem. communications com. Red Cross Blood Svcs., Wilkes-Barre, 1985-88; mem. pub. rels. com. Am. Cancer Soc. Duck Derby, Wilkes-Barre, 1990; mem. Wilkes-Barre YMCA, 1980—, pub. rels. cons. Recipient Gold Medallion, Broadcast Promotion/Mktg., L.A., 1988, Silver award, 1982, Gold award Retail Mktg. Group, Louisville, 1982. Avocations: photography, reading. Home: Sarasota, Fla. Died June 8, 2010.

WILSON, WILLIAM ALBERT, former ambassador; b. LA, Nov. 3, 1914; s. William Webster and Adamarian (Smith) Smith; m. Elizabeth Ann Johnson, Feb. 5, 1938; children: Anne Marie Solomone, Marcia Lou Hobbs. Student, Harvard Sch., 1925—32, U. Mex., 1932; AB, Stanford U., 1937; LLD, Barry U., 1984, Pepperdine U., 1985. Draftsman & engr. Web Wilson Oil Tools, Huntington Pk., Calif., 1937—42; pres. Web Wilson Oil Tools, Inc., Gardena, Calif., 1945—60; v.p. Baash-Ross, Compton, Calif., 1960, Smith Dynamics, Gardena, 1960; engring. cons. EB Wiggins Oil Tool, LA, 1937—42; pres. San Vicente Investments, Inc., LA. US amb. to The Holy See US Dept. State, Vatican City, 1981—86; fin. cons. Shearson-Lehman-Hutton. Bd. dirs. St. John's Hosp., Santa Monica, Calif., from 1976; rep. del., 1968, 1972, 1976, 1980. Capt. US Army, 1942—45. Recipient Theodore Roosevelt Meml. award, Navy League, 1982, Gold medal, Italian Red Cross, Rome, 1983, Brotherhood award, NCCJ, 1983. Mem.: Atheletic Club, LA Country Club, Knights Malta. Republican. Roman Catholic. Avocations: hunting, horseback riding. Died Dec. 5, 2009.

WINAHRADSKY, MICHAEL FRANCIS, drug company executive; b. Syracuse, NY, Oct. 21, 1948; s. Frank F. and Genelle M. (Charmley) W.; m. Linda L. Peters, Oct. 10, 1981; children: Kevin M., Kari M. Distbn. ctr. supr. Fay's Inc., Liverpool, N.Y., 1967-76, distbn. ctr. mgr., 1976-81; asst. v.p. distbn. Fay's Drug Co. Inc., Liverpool, N.Y., 1981-82, v.p. distbn., from 1982. Guest speaker Syracuse (N.Y.) U., 1984. Participant Cen. N.Y. chpt. Cystic Fibrosis Bowl for Breath, 1987-93. Mem. Warehouse Edn. and Rsch. Coun., Nat. Fire Protection Assn., Boat Owners U.S., Moose, Elks, Lakeshore Yacht & Country Club, Nat. Assn. Chain Drug Stores (co-chmn. distbn. and logistics com. 1995). Avocations: fishing, cross country skiing, golf. Died Nov. 19, 2009.

WINCHESTER, RICHARD LEE, JR., lawyer; b. Memphis, May 21, 1924; s. Cassius Lee and Harriet Haywood (Bond) Winchester; m. Bette Anne Thompson, July 15, 1944; children: Robin Ann, Richard Lee Jr., John Thompson. LLB, U. Tenn., 1949, JD, 1965. Bar: Tenn. 1949. Sr. ptnr. Winchester Law Firm, Memphis, from 1972; atty. Shelby County, 1961—64; city atty. City of Arlington, Tenn., from 1966. Gen. counsel, bd. chmn. Cmty. Bancshares, Inc.; sec. Beachfront Condos, Inc., N. Fla. Chmn. Germantown Planning Commn., 1958—61; pres., bd. dirs. Mid-South Fair Assn.; bd. dirs. ARC; mem. Gov.'s Commn. on Human Relations, 1962—68; vice chmn., treas. Memphis and Shelby County Dem. Exec. Com., 1958—72; state exec. com., pres. Tenn. Young Dems., 1960—61; del. state and nat. Dem. convs., 1964—68; nat. elector from Tenn., 1960—72; pres. Episc. Planning Commn.; trustee U. Tenn., 1975—84, Episc. Girls Home, Bowld Hosp. Capt. inf. US Army, 1942—46, PTO. Fellow: Tenn. Bar Found. (past pres. jr. sect.); mem.: Omicron Delta Kappa, Phi Kappa Phi, Nat. Assn. Legal Aid and Pub. Defenders, Am. Judicature Soc., Shelby County Bar Assn. (past pres. jr. sect.), Memphis Bar Assn. (past pres.), Tenn. Bar Assn., ABA (past del.), U. Tenn. Alumni Assn. (past bd. govs., 9th dist. rep.), Am. Legion (past post comdr., past state vice comdr.), Kiwanis, Tennessee, 40 and 8, Jesters, VFW (past post vice comdr.), Masons, Shriners, Phi Eta Sigma, Sigma Alpha Epsilon. Episcopalian. Home: Memphis, Tenn. Died Oct. 24, 2009.

WINDFELDER, DONALD HERBERT, banker; b. Milw., Dec. 8, 1921; s. Raymond Andrew and Norma B. W.; m. Carole Weiler, Jan. 29, 1972; children— Andrew, Judith, James, David. Student, U. Notre Dame, 1939-41; BS, U.S. Mcht. Marine Acad., 1944, Babson Coll., 1948. Trader Robert W. Baird & Co., Milw., 1948-54; with Northwestern Mut. Life Ins. Co., Milw., 1954-82, v.p. common stocks, 1973-82; v.p. Nat. Bank of Detroit, from 1982, NBD Trust Co. of Fla., from 1982. Dir. Badger Meter Inc. Pres., bd. dirs. Wis. Humane Soc. Served with USN, 1944-46. Mem.: Town (Milw.); Beach (Palm Beach, Fla.), Palm Beach Yacht (Palm Beach, Fla.), Mayacoo Lakes Country (Palm Beach, Fla.). Republican. Congregationalist. Died Jan. 15, 2010.

WINDMAN, ARNOLD LEWIS, retired mechanical engineer; b. NYC, Oct. 17, 1926; s. Raphael and Anna (Wexler) W.; m. Patricia Foley, Dec. 13, 1967; children— Richard, Marjorie, Kevin, Colleen, Sean, JoAnn, Brian, William. B.M.E., Coll. City N.Y., 1947. Bar: registered profl. engr., N.Y., 13 other states. Project engr. F.E. Sutton, NYC, 1947-50; with Syska & Hennessy, Inc., NYC, 1950-90, pres., 1976-86, vice chmn., 1986-90, also bd. dirs. Pres. Am. Cons. Engrs. Coun., 1985-86; chmn. N.Y. State Bd. Engring. and Land Surveying, 1982-84; bd. dirs., v.p. Sea Pines Plantation,

1997-2000. Bd. dirs. Phelps Meml. Hosp., Tarrytown, N.Y., 1974-82; chmn. planning commn. Hilton Head Island, 2000. Mem. Am. Soc. Heating, Refrigerating and Air Conditioning Engrs., chpt. pres. (1965), N.Y. Assn. Cons. Engrs. (pres. 1981-82, dir. 1977), ASME, Tau Beta Pi, Pi Tau Sigma. Democrat. Jewish. Home: Hilton Head Island, SC. Died June 19, 2010.

WINDSOR, JOHN ROBERT, broadcast journalist, producer; b. NYC; m. Marianne Evkovich; children: Mark, Robin. Student, Yale U., 1958, American U., 1967. Prin. 1st broadcast facility, Martha's Vineyard, Mass., 1971-76; corr., anchor ABC News, NYC, 1976-86; dir. bus. devel. Marcon Mktg., NYC, 1986-88; corr. Fin. News Network, NYC, 1988-89; producer, cons. oral history rsch. Columbia U., NYC, 1989—2010. With USAF, 1957-63. Home: Washington, DC. Died Jan. 25, 2010.

WINDSOR, PATRICIA (KATONAH SUMMERTREE, PERRIN WINTERS, ANNA SEELING), author, educator, lecturer; b. NYC, Sept. 21, 1938; d. Bernhard Edward and Antoinette (Gaus) Seelinger; m. Laurence Charles Windsor, Jr., Apr. 3, 1959 (div. 1978); children: Patience Wells, Laurence Edward; m. Stephen E. Altman, Sept. 21, 1986 (div. 1989). Student, Bennington Coll., 1956—58, Westchester C.C.; AA, NYU. V.p. Windsor-Morehead Assoc., NYC, 1960—63; info. mgr. Family Planning Assn., London, 1974—76; faculty mem. Inst. Children's Lit., Redding Ridge, Conn., 1976—94, from 1999; editor-in-chief AT&T, Washington, 1978—80; instr. U. Md. Writers Inst., Open Univ., Washington, 1980—82; creative developer, faculty mem. Long Ridge Writer's Group, Danbury, Conn., 1988—2000, instr., from 2006; dir. Summertree Studios, Savannah, Ga., from 1992. Dir. Wordspring Lit. Cons., 1989—, Wordworks Writing Cons., 1999—, Born Author Lit. Cons., 2003-; dir. Devel. Writing Workshops, Katonah, NY, 1976-78; judge Internat. Assn. Bus. Communicators, Washington, 1979, 89; lectr. LI U., Jersey City State Coll., Skidmore Coll., others, 1987—; instr. Coastal Ga. Ctr. for Continuing Edn., 1996—, Armstrong Atlantic U. Continuing Edn., 1997-2000, Anne Arundel (Md.) C.C., 2000—, workshop coord., 2000—; dir., founder Born Author.com, 2002—; dir. Windsomethings Art & Crafts, 2004—; owner, designer Tiger Woman Crafts for Meditation, 2005-. Author: The Summer Before, 1973 (ALA Best Book award 1973, transl. 1980 Austrian State prize 1980, also Brit., Norwegian, German edits.), Something's Waiting for You, Baker D, 1974 (starred selection Libr. Jour., Brit., Japanese edits.), Home Is Where Your Feet Are Standing, 1975, Diving for Roses, 1976 (NY Times Outstanding Book for Young Adults award, starred selection Libr. Jour.), Mad Martin, 1976, Killing Time, 1980, Demon Tree, 1983 (pen name Colin Daniel), The Sandman's Eyes, 1985 (Edgar Allan Poe Best Juvenile Mystery award Mystery Writers Am.), How a Weirdo and a Ghost Can Change Your Life, 1986, The Hero, 1988 (highest rating Voice of Youth Advocate), Just Like the Movies, 1990, The Christmas Killer, 1991 (Edgar nominee, Brit., Danish, French edits.), Two Weirdos and a Ghost, 1991, A Weird and Moogly Christmas, 1991, The Blooding, 1996 (YALSA pick for reluctant readers), The House of Death, 1996, Nightwood (nominated Best Book 2006), 2006; columnist The Blood Rev., 1990-92, Savannah Parent, 1990-92; columnist Coastal Senior, 1997-99; also short stories in anthologies and mags.; actress: The Haunting of Hill House, City Lights Theatre Co., 1991; contr. articles Once Upon a Time Mag., 2003, 04, 05. Mem. City Lights Theatre Co., Savannah, Ga., 1991. Mem. Horror Writers Am., Internat. Women's Writing Guild, Children's Book Guild, Authors Guild, Poetry Soc. Ga., Savannah Storytellers. Avocations: skiing, painting, modern dance. Died July 1, 2010.

WINKLER, JOSEPH CONRAD, former recreational products manufacturing executive; b. Newark, May 20, 1916; s. Charles and Mollie (Abrams) W.; m. Geraldine M. Borok, Sept. 20, 1953; children: Charles H., David J. BS, NYU, 1941. Gen. mgr. Indsl. Washing Machine Corp., New Brunswick, NJ, 1941-48; controller Mojud Corp., NYC, 1948-52; controller, asst. treas. Barbizon Corp., NYC, 1952-57; controller Ideal Toy Corp., NYC, 1957-58, McGregor-Doniger, Inc., NYC, 1958-59; dir. fin. and adminstrn. Ideal Toy Corp., NYC, 1960-62, v.p. fin., 1962-68, sr. v.p. fin., 1968-78, exec. v.p., COO, dir., 1978-81, pres., dir., 1981-83; exec. in residence, bus. adv. coun. Sch. Bus. Adminstrn., Montclair (N.J.) State U., 1983-90. Dir. Ideal of Australia Ltd., Melbourne, 1963-82, Ideal of Canada Ltd., Toronto, 1963-82, Ideal of Japan Ltd., Tokyo and Kiowa, 1963-80, Ideal Toy Co. Ltd., High Wycombe and Wokingham, Eng., 1966-82, Arxon Spiel & Freizeit GmbH, Rotgau, Germany, 1968-82, Perfekta Ltd. and Hollis Industries Ltd., Hong Kong, 1970-74, Ideal Loisirs S.A., Paris, 1972-82. Mem. editl. bd. Issues in Internat. Bus., 1985-92. Committeeman, troop treas. Boy Scouts Am., Tenafly, N.J., 1965-71; bd. dirs. N.Y. League Hard of Hearing, 1982-88; active Nat. Roster Sci. and Splized. Pers., War Manpower Commn., 1941-46. Served with Office Statis. Control USAAF, 1945. Mem. Fin. Execs. Inst. Died Apr. 2, 2010.

WINOGRAD, ARTHUR, symphony conductor; b. NYC, Apr. 22, 1920; s. Elias and Mildred (Shapiro) W.; m. Winifred Schaefer, July 4, 1941; 1 son, Nicholas; m. Elizabeth Olsen, May 4, 1950 (dec. 1987); children: Wendy, Peter. Student, New Eng. Conservatory Music, 1937-40, Curtis Inst. Music, 1940-41. Cellist Boston Symphony Orch., 1940, NBC Symphony, 1942-43; founder-mem. Juilliard String Quartet, also mem. chamber music faculty, 1946-55; staff condr. MGM Records, 1954-58, Audio Fidelity Records, 1958-60; condr., music dir. Birmingham (Ala.) Symphony Orch., 1960-64, Hartford Symphony, 1964-85, condr. laureate, 1985—2010. Died Apr. 22, 2010.

WINOKUR, ROBERT M., lawyer; b. NYC, Oct. 28, 1924; s. Harry S. and Katherine S. W.; m. Diane R. Kramer, June 21, 1953; children: Hugh R., Andrew S., Douglas B. BS, CUNY, 1947; SJD, Columbia U., 1949. Bar: Calif., N.Y., U.S. Supreme Ct. Sr. partner firm Winokur, Maier & Zang (and predecessors), San Francisco, 1954-85; of counsel Crosby, Heafey, Roach & May, Oakland, from 1985. Guest lectr. Hastings Coll. Law, U. Calif., NYU Tax Inst., U. So. Calif. Tax Inst., Practising Law Inst.; mem. adv. group to U.S. Commr. Internal Revenue, 1967-68 Contbr. articles to legal jours. Served to lt. U.S. Army, 1943-46. Decorated Bronze Star. Mem. Am., Calif., San Francisco bar assns., Am. Law Inst., San Francisco Tax and City Club. Democrat. Home: San Francisco, Calif. Died Feb. 6, 2010.

WINTER, JERRY ALAN, sociology educator; b. Bronx, July 23, 1937; s. Herman and Rose (Kavkewitz) Winter; m. Gail Doreen Cameron, June 13, 1964; children: Wendy, Miriam. BA, NYU, 1958; MA, U. Mich., 1960, PhD, 1964. Asst. prof. Rutgers U., New Brunswick, N.J., 1965-68; dir. Rsch. on Tng. for Met. Ministry, Washington, 1967-69; asst. prof. sociology Temple U., Phila., 1968-70; assoc. prof. Conn. Coll., New London, 1970-77, prof. sociology, 1977-2000, Lucretia Allyn prof., 2000—02, prof. emeritus, from 2002. Author, editor: Vital Problems for American Society, 1968, Clergy in Action Training, 1971, The Poor, 1971, Continuities in the Sociology of Religion: Creed, Congregation and Community, 1977, Jewish Choices, 1998. Mem. Ethics Com., Waterford, Conn., 1999—2002; chmn. United Way Campaign Com., Conn. Coll., 1987—88. Mem. Assn. for Sociol. Study of Jewry (editor Contemporary Jewry Jour. 1992-97), Phi Beta Kappa, Psi Chi, Alpha Kappa Delta. Democrat. Jewish. Home: Waterford, Conn. Died Mar. 31, 2009.

WINTERS, JOHN DAVID, construction equipment company executive; b. Evansville, Ind., July 21, 1928; s. Frank and Clara Belle (Flentke) W.; m. Marjorie Ruth Schlamp, June 6, 1954; children: Susanna Marie Winters Davis, David Mark. BSME, Rose-Hulman Inst. Tech., 1949, DEng (hon.), 1987. Mgr. sales dept. gen. offices Caterpillar, Inc., Peoria, Ill., 1971-75; plant mgr. Aurora, Ill., 1979-83; v.p., gen. mgr. engine div. Peoria, from 1983; pres. Caterpillar Brasil, S.A., São Paulo, 1975-79. 1st lt. USAF, 1950-55, Korea. Decorated D.F.C., Air medal. Republican. Lutheran. Home: Morris, Ill. Died Nov. 23, 2009.

WIRT, FREDERICK MARSHALL, retired political scientist, educator; b. Radford, Va., July 27, 1924; s. Harry Johnson, Sr. and Goldie (Turpin) W.; m. Elizabeth Cook, Sept. 6, 1947; children: Leslie Lee, Sandra Sue, Wendy Ann. BA, DePauw U., 1948; MA, Ohio State U., 1949, PhD, 1956. Instr. to prof. polit. sci. Denison U., Granville, Ohio, 1952-66; vis. prof., lectr. U. Calif., Berkeley, 1966-68, 69-72; dir. policy scis. grad. program U. Md. Balt. County, 1972-75; prof. polit. sci. U. Ill., Urbana, 1975-2000; ret., 2000. Dir. Inst. for Desegregation Problems, U. Calif.-Berkeley, 1970-72; cons. Motion Picture Assn. Am., Rand Corp., Nat. Inst. Edn., SUNY Sch. Edn. Albany; vis. prof. U. Rochester, Nova U., U. Melbourne; acad. visitor London Sch. Econs. Author: Politics of Southern Equality, 1970 (honorable mention for best book 1972), Power in the City, 1974; (with others) School Desegregation in the North, 1967, The Polity of the School, 1975, Political Science and School Politics, 1977, Education, Recession, and the World Village, 1986, (with others) Culture and Education Policy in the American States, 1992, Ain't What We Was: Civil Rights in the New South, 1997 (Best Book on So. Politics award So. Polit. Sci. Assn., 1998), The Political Dynamics of American Education, 3d edit., 2005. Mem. Granville City Charter Commn., 1964. Grantee Am. Philos. Soc., Denison Rsch. Assn., U. Ill. Rsch. Bd., NEH, Ford Found., Ctr. Advanced Studies; fellow U. Ill., Dept. Edn., Spencer Found.; recipient Lifetime Achievement award Am. Ednl. Rsch. Assn., 1995, Am. Polit. Sci. Assn., 1994. Mem. Am. Polit. Sci. Assn. (nat. council), Midwestern Polit. Sci. Assn., Am. Ednl. Rsch. Assn., Policy Studies Orgn. Home: Coeur D' Alene, Idaho. Died Aug. 21, 2009.

WIRTZ, WILLARD (WILLIAM WILLARD WIRTZ), retired lawyer, former United States Secretary of Labor; b. DeKalb, Ill., Mar. 14, 1912; s. William Wilbur and Alfa Belle (White) W.; m. Mary Jane Quisenberry, Sept. 8, 1936 (dec. 2002); children: Richard, Philip. Student, No. Ill. State Teachers Coll., DeKalb, Ill., 1928-30, U. Calif., Berkeley, 1930-31; AB, Beloit Coll., 1933; LL.B., Harvard, 1937. Instr. Kewanee HS, Ill., 1933-34; asst. prof. U. Iowa Sch. Law, 1937-39, Northwestern U. Sch. Law, 1939-42; asst. gen. counsel Bd. Econ. Warfare, 1942-43; with War Labor Bd., 1943-45, gen. counsel and pub. mem., 1945; chmn. Nat. Wage Stabilization. Bd., 1946; prof. law Northwestern U., 1946-54; pvt. law practice, 1955-61; sec. US Dept. Labor, Washington, 1962-69; ptnr. Wirtz & Gentry, 1970—78, Wirtz & Lapointe, 1979—84, Friedman & Wirtz, 1984—89. Prof. law U. San Diego, 1986-98. Author: Labor and the Public Interest, 1964, The Boundless Resource: A Prospectus for an Education Work Policy, 1975, In the Rearview Mirror: A Collection of Reminiscences & Essays, 2008. Mem. Ill. Liquor Control Commn., 1949-53. Mem. Am., D.C., Ill. Bar Associations, Phi Beta Kappa, Beta Theta Pi, Delta Sigma Rho. Home: Washington, DC. Died Apr. 24, 2010.

WISE, CHARLES DAVIDSON, science educator; b. Huntington, W. Va., June 13, 1926; s. Fred Eugene Wise and Maggie M. Harshbarger; m. Juanita Irene Meadows, Mar. 22, 1947; 1 child, Sandra. AB, MS, W. Va. U., 1950; PhD, U. N.Mex., 1962. Cert. tchr. N.Mex., W. Va., Tex. Tchr. St. Albans (W. Va.) High Sch., 1951-53; lab. assst. Marshall U., 1950-51; grad. fellow U. N.Mex., Albuquerque, 1953-55, grad. asst., 1960-61; rsch. scientist U. Tex., Port Aransas, Tex., 1958-60; prof. Ball State U., Muncie, Ind., 1961-91; rep. Ind. State Legislature, Indpls., 1967-69; senator Ind. State Senate, Indpls., 1969-73. Contbr. articles to profl. jours., 1958—. Bd. dirs. Mental Health Svc. East Cen. Ind., 1974-77; pres. Muncie Bicentennial Festival Com., 1975-77. With U.S. Army, 1944-46. Recipient fellowship U. Ind., 1957, U. Tex., 1957-58, Marshall U. Alumni Community Achievement award, 1993; named Alumnus of Yr., East Bank High Sch., W.Va., 1977. Fellow Ind. Acad. Sci.; mem. Nat. Assn. State Legislators (life mem.), Nat. Audubon Soc., Ind. Audubon Soc. (past pres., conservation award 1977), E. Cen. Ind. Audubon Soc. (pres. 1988-90, conservation award 1984), Sigma Xi Rsch. Soc. (pres. Ball State U. chpt., bd. dir. Hoosier Environ. coun. 1990-93). Republican. Presbyterian. Avocations: birdwatching, travel, languages, genealogy, history. Home: Milton, W.Va. Died July 31, 2009.

WISE, WILLIAM ALLEN, II, academic program director, engineer; b. Essex County, N.J., Jan. 28, 1921; s. Allen Sherwood and Marguerite C. (Hyland) W.; m. Betty Jane Gambrill, Apr. 18, 1942; children— William Allen III, Edmund Gambrill, Jane Sherwood. Student Cornell U., 1939-41; B.C.E., U. Del., 1949; M.S., Stanford U., 1957. Registered profl. engr., Del. Sales, service rep. E.I. duPont de Nemours & Co., Wilmington, Del., 1949; commd. 1st lt. U.S. Army, 1949, advanced through grades to lt. col., 1963; area engr. U.S. C.E., Washington, 1958-60, Heidelberg, Ger., 1962; 64; chief constrn. mgmt. Hdqrs. U.S. Army, Vietnam, 1965-66; dir. services Atlanta Army Depot, 1966-68; ret., 1968; asst. supt. schs. Greece Central Sch. Dist., Rochester, N.Y., 1968-76; dir. facilities and services Delaware County Community Coll., Media, Pa., 1976—; mem. adj. faculty various colls. and univs., 1957-83. Contbr. articles to profl. jours. Served with AUS, 1942-46. Decorated Legion of Merit U.S. Dept. Def., 1966, 68. Mem. Del. Assn. Profl. Engrs., Ret. Officers Assn., Council Ednl. Facility Planners, Assn. Phys. Plant Adminstrs., Nat. Assn. Coll. and Univ. Bus. Officers, Delta Tau Delta. Republican. Methodist. Clubs: Radley Run Country (West Chester, Pa.); Blue and Gold (Newark, Del.). Avocations: investments; golf; travel. Home: Hilton Head Island, SC. Died Feb. 13, 2010.

WISEKAL, FRANK W(ILLIAM), sales and services company executive; b. NYC, Dec. 23, 1934; s. William W. and Anna (Sledge) W.; m. Norma Governale, Jan. 7, 1955; children: Susan, Richard, John, Lee Ann. BA in Indsl. Mgmt., C.W. Post Coll., 1968; grad. mgmt. devel. program, Harvard U., 1972. Bus. mgr. Grumman Aerospace Co., Bethpage, N.Y., 1958-70, dir. contracts, 1970-74; v.p. Grumman Am., Savannah, Ga., 1974-78; sr. v.p., treas. Gulfstream Am. Corp., Savannah, Ga., 1978-79, exec. v.p., 1979-80; sr. v.p., chief fin. officer Dassault Falcon Jet Corp., Teterboro, N.J., 1980-83; pres., chief exec. officer Falcon Jet Corp., Teterboro, N.J., 1983-94; vice-chmn. Dassault Falcon Jet Corp., Teterboro, N.J., from 1995. Served with USN, 1954-57. Roman Catholic. Home: Coral Springs, Fla. Died Mar. 18, 2010.

WISHNICK, WILLIAM, chemical company executive; b. Bklyn., Nov. 9, 1924; s. Robert I. and Freda M. (Frankel) W.; m. Dion Imerman, June 16, 1949 (div. 1969); children: Elizabeth Anne (dec.), Gina I., Amy Jo, Kendall Freda; m. Lisa Fluet, July 12, 1975. Student, Carnegie Inst. Tech., 1942, 45-47; BBA, U. Tex., 1949. With Witco Chem. Co. Inc., NYC, from 1949, v.p., 1954-56, treas., from 1956, exec. v.p., 1957-64, chmn. bd., from 1964, chief exec. officer, from 1971, also dir. Pres., dir. Witco Chem. Co., Can., Ltd., 1958-62, vice chmn. bd., 1962-64, chmn. bd., 1964—; pres. Sonneborn Chem. & Refining Corp.; dir. Witco Chem. Co. Ltd., Eng., Golden Bear Oil Co., Los Angeles, Witco Chem. (France) S.A.R.L. Trustee Mt. Sinai Hosp., N.Y.C.; Carnegie Mellon U. Fellow Poly. Inst. N.Y. Mem. Am. Chem. Soc., Am. Petroleum Inst., Salesmen's Assn. Am. Chem. Industry., N.Y. Paint, Varnish and Lacquer Assn., Tau Delta Phi. Clubs: Chemists (past trustee, jr. v.p.); Harmonie (N.Y.C.); Standard (Chgo.). Republican. Home: New York, NY. Died May 29, 2010.

WITMAN, FRANK MCCONNELL, clergyman, educator; b. Altoona, Pa., Dec. 1, 1931; s. Edwin Henry and Mary Frances (Grose) W.; m. Elsie Ellen McLaughlin, Mar. 28, 1953; children: Mark Allan, Paul David. BA, Calif. State U., LA, 1956; ThM, Sch. Theology at Claremont, Calif., 1959, D Ministry, 1977; cert. supervising pastor, Fuller Theol. Sem., 1983. Ordained elder United Meth. Ch., 1961; cert. L.A. Police Dept. Acad., Advanced Police Chaplain Sch. Assoc. pastor Trinity United Meth. Ch., Pomona, Calif., 1959-62; sr. pastor Rialto (Calif.) United Meth. Ch., 1962-69, United Meth. Ch., Simi Valley, Calif., from 1969. Bd. dirs. United Meth. Fed. Credit Union, Montclair, Calif., chmn. bd., 1976—; mem. adj. faculty Sch. Theology at Claremont, 1992—, trustee, 1966-69; mem. CKW Partnership, adminstrn. and fin. cons., Vista, Calif., 1988—. Co-author: Christian Response in a Hungry World, 1978, Church Administration and Finance, 1995. Chaplain Simi Valley Police Dept., 1978—; guest chaplain U.S. Ho. of Reps., Washington, 1990. Sgt. U.S. Army, 1953-55. Named Young Man of Yr., Rialto Jr. C. of C., 1965, Citizen of Yr., Rialto C. of C., 1969; recipient Disting. Ministry award Sch. Theology at Claremont, 1993, Walter Teagle fellow, 1976-77. Mem. Sch. Theology at Claremont Alumni Assn. (pres. 1965-69), Rotary (bd. dirs. Rialto 1964-65, Simi Valley 1973-74, Paul Harris fellow 1985). Republican. Avocations: camping, leading youth and adult camps, travel. Home: Simi Valley, Calif. Died June 29, 2010.

WITMER, RICHARD CLINTON, advertising executive; b. Rockford, Ill., Aug. 20, 1929; s. Clinton M. and Neva B. (Barnhizer) Witmer; m. Virginia Madden Taylor, Feb. 2, 1952; children: Laura Witmer Brubaker, Nancy Witmer Moore, Marie, Cynthia Witmer Case, Paul. BA, Beloit Coll., 1952. Dir. advt. Warner Electric Corp., Beloit, Wis., 1954—60, G. Leblanc Corp., Kenosha, Wis., 1960—62; dir. advt./sales promotion Childers Mfg. Co., Houston, 1962—65; sr. v.p., treas. Goodwin, Dannenbaum, Littman & Wingfield, Houston, 1965—89, ret., 1989. With US Army, 1948—49. Mem.:

Affiliated Advt. Agencies Internat. (internat. sec., treas. 1982—85), Am. Assn. Advt. Agencies (cmn. S.W. coun. 1978—79), Meml. Bend Club, Univ. Club. Home: Lago Vista, Tex. Died Dec. 2, 2009.

WOBST, FRANK GEORG, banker; b. Dresden, Germany, Nov. 14, 1933; came to U.S., 1958, naturalized, 1963; s. Robert Georg and Marianne (Salewsky) W.; m. Joan Shuey Firkins, Aug. 24, 1957; children: Franck Georg, Ingrid, Andrea. Student, U. Erlangen, 1952-54, U. Goettingen, 1954-58, Rutgers U., 1964. With Fidelity American Bankshares, Inc., Lynchburg, Va., 1958-74, exec. v.p., dir., 1974-85. Chmn., chief exec. officer, dir. Huntington Nat. Bank, 1974-85, chmn. exec. com., 1986—; chmn., chief exec. officer, dir. Huntington Bancshares, Inc., 1974—. Mem. Greater Columbus C. of C., Am. Inst. Banking, Assn. Res. City Bankers, Robert Morris Assos., Newcomen Soc. Clubs: Scioto Country. Home: Columbus, Ohio. Died Dec. 18, 2009.

WOHLFORD, PAUL RAYMOND, JR., lawyer; b. Bristol, Tenn., June 23, 1940; s. Paul Raymond Sr. and Theresa Elizabeth Wohlford; m. Donna Arlene Wohlford, July 24, 1994; children: Jonathan Roberts, Paul R. III. BA, Duke U., 1962; JD, U. Tenn., 1964. Pvt. practice, Bristol, from 1965. Spl. judge City of Bristol Juvenile Ct., 1979-80, judge, 1980—; instr. paralegal program Va. Intermont Coll., 1987-97; mem. Tenn. Commn. on Children and Youth, 1988-91; faculty Nat. Coalition State Juvenile Justice Adv. Groups, 1991-92, Tenn. Jud. Acad., 1996—. Active First Bapt. Ch., Bristol, 1982—; pres. Bristol Family YMCA, 1982-83; mem. ethics com. Bristol Regional Med. Ctr., 1989—; mem. gov.'s select steering com. on edn. Tenn. 2000, 1992; past pres. U. Tenn. Alumni Assn. Bristol chpt., 1990; chmn. Sullivan County Com. on Health, Edn. and Housing, 1998. Recipeint Elizabeth McCain award as outstanding juvenile judge in Tenn., 1987, Disting. Grad. award Nat. Cath. Edn. Assn., 1993. Mem. Nat. Coun. Juvenile and Family Ct. Judges (faculty 1991-92, bd. trustees 1991-96, sec. 1996-97, mem. ct. futures com. 1992-93, jud. edn. com. 1992-93, victims act resource guidelines com. 1992-93, v.p.-treas. 1997-98, v.p. 1998-99, pres. 1999-2000), Tenn. Trial Lawyer's Assn. (bd. govs. 1988-90), Tenn. Bar Assn. (com. on impaired lawyers 1989—), Bristol Bar Assn. (pres. 1986-87), Tenn. Coun. Juvenile and Family Ct. Judges (mem. exec. com. 1983—, v.p. 1985-86, pres. 1986-87), Duke U. Iron Dukes Alumni, Bristol Downtown Optimist Club. Home: Bristol, Tenn. Died Jan. 13, 2010.

WOLBACH, WILLIAM WELLINGTON, SR., retired business executive; b. Boston, May 9, 1915; s. S. Burt and Anna (Wellington) W.; m. Josephine Neilson Harmar, Apr. 15, 1944 (div. Jan. 27, 1982); children: William Wellington, Josephine Harmar Devlin.; m. Emma D. Crispin, Feb. 5, 1982. Student, Milton Acad., 1928-34, Harvard U., 1934-36. Former pres., chief exec. officer, chmn., dir., mem. exec. com. The Boston Co., Boston Safe Deposit & Trust Co.; former dir. Stop & Shop, Inc., Seaboard R.R.; hon. dir. West Point-Pepperell, Inc. Mem. The Country Club (Brookline), Myopia Hunt Club (Hamilton), Essex Country Club (Manchester), Cotton Bay Club (Eleuthera-Bahamas), Harvard Club, Mid-Ocean Club (Bermuda). Home: Manchester, Mass. Died June 23, 2009.

WOLF, ALFRED A., physicist, educator; b. Phila., July 21, 1925; s. Jacob Wolf, Anna Wolf; m. Enid G. Wolf, Nov. 24, 1957 (div. Dec. 1981); children: Marcus M., Laurence J. BSEE, Drexel U., Phila., 1948; MSEE, U. Pa., Phila., 1954, PhD, 1958; ScD, U. Juarez, Mexico, 1977, MD, 1978. Engr.-in-charge Naval Air Devel., Johnsville, Pa., 1949—56; chief scientist Gen. Dynamics, Rochester, NY, 1957—60; dir. rsch. Litton Industries, Silver Spring, Md., 1960—63; disting. prof. elec. engring. Drexel U., Phila., 1963—65; tech. dir. RCA, Burlington, Mass., 1965—67; assoc. tech. dir. Naval Ship R&D Ctr., Annapolis, Md., 1967—78; pres. Prime Rsch. Found., Annapolis, from 1978. Asst. prof. elec. engring. U. Pa., Phila., 1949—59; Pa. scholar, 1952—54; sr. sci. advisor USN, 1971—76; adj. assoc. prof. U. Rochester, 1960—62; adj. prof. U. Md., Annapolis, 1967—69, George Washington U., Washington, 1969—99. Author (prize winning): Biophysics of Wound Healing, 1989; contbr. 105 articles to profl. jours. (14 awards). Cpl. US Army, 1943—46. Recipient Citation of Honor, Drexel U., 1961, Honor citations (8), USN, 1972—83; named Notable Am. of Bicentennial Era, Am. Biog. Inst., 1976; nominee Nobel Prize in Physics, 1972; grantee, NSF, 1956—59; Pa. scholar, 1952—54. Mem.: IEEE (life), Engring. in Medicine and Biology Soc. (chmn. Balt. sect. 1990—95), Sigma Xi. Democrat. Jewish. Achievements include discovery of first high temperature superconductor; 24 patents for electronics devices and systems. Avocation: writing. Died May 30, 2009.

WOLF, EDWARD CHRISTOPHER, music educator; b. Circleville, Ohio, July 21, 1932; s. Edward Christopher and Helen Marie (Groce) Wolf; m. Marjorie Ann Swanson, June 24, 1961; 1 child, Edward Christopher III. MusB, Capital U., 1953; MusM, Northwestern U., 1955; PhD, U. Ill., 1960. Instr. to prof. music Sch. Fine Arts, West Liberty State Coll., from 1960, dir., 1963—75, 1978—79, chair music dept., Concert Series, from 1985. Editor: Music Edn. Mag., from 1976; contbr. articles to profl. jours. Mem.: AAUP, Coll. Music Soc., Sonneck Soc., Luth. Hist. Soc., Pa. German Soc., Music Educators Nat. Conf. (state editor from 1976), W.Va. Music Educators Assn. (pres. 1965—67), Am. Musicol. Soc. Republican. Avocations: photography, travel. Died Jan. 24, 2010.

WOLF, MONICA THERESIA, small business owner, inventor; b. Germany, Apr. 26, 1943; came to U.S., 1953, naturalized, 1959; d. Otto and Hildegard Maria (Heim) Bellemann; children: Clinton, Danielle. BBA, U. Albuquerque, 1986. Developer Word Processing Ctr. Pub. Svc. of N.Mex., Albuquerque, 1971-74, word processing supr., 1974-78, budget coord., 1978-80, lead procedures analyst, 1980-88; owner Monika's Woodworks, 1988-91; founder Monidan Blue, from 1992; ind. dir. Royal Body Care, from 1999. Bd. dirs. Pub. Svc. Co. of N.Mex. Retirees; adv. bd., former student trainer APS Career Enrichment Ctr.; instr. firearm safety and pistol competition. Animal rights activist. Mem.: NAFE, Internat. Word Processing Assn. (founder N.Mex. chpt.), People's Anti-Cruelty Assn. (pres. from 2004), N.Mex. Inventors Club. Democrat. Home: Albuquerque, N.Mex. Died May 11, 2009.

WOLF, RICHARD EDWARD, pediatrician; b. Phila., Jan. 28, 1914; s. Lester and Florence (Leopold) Wolf; m. Margaret Wertheimer, Dec. 22, 1938; children: Richard E. Jr., Susan W. Kaufman, William L. BA, Harvard U., 1935; MD, U. Pa., 1939. Diplomate Am. Bd. Pediat. Intern Phila. Children's Hosp., 1939—41; resident Children's Hosp., 1941—43, dir. pediat. psychiatry Cin., 1948—73; fellow pediat. psychiatry Payne Whitney Clinic, 1946—48; prof. pediat. U. Cin. Coll. Medicine, 1950—84, prof. emeritus, from 1984; med. dir. Babies Milk Fund Assn., 1970—84. Bd. dirs. Radio Reading Svc., Cin., from 1978. Contbr. articles to profl. jours. Mem.: Sigma Xi, Phi Beta Kappa. Home: Cincinnati, Ohio. Died Feb. 23, 2010.

WOLFE, ETHYLE RENEE, academic administrator; b. Burlington, Vt., Mar. 14, 1919; d. Max M. and Rose (Saiger) Wolfe; m. Coleman Hamilton Benedict, Dec. 4, 1954. BA, U. Vt., 1940, MA, 1942; postgrad., Bryn Mawr Coll., 1942—43; PhD, NYU, 1950; LHD (hon.), CUNY, 1989; LittD (hon.), Iona Coll., 1989. Tchg. fellow U. Vt., 1940—42; rsch. fellow Latin Bryn Mawr (Pa.) Coll., 1942—43; instr. classics Bklyn. Coll., 1947—49, instr. classical langs., 1949—54, asst. prof., 1954—59, assoc. prof., 1960—68, prof., from 1968, acting chmn. dept. classics and comparative lit., 1962—63, chmn. dept., 1967—72; dean Bklyn. Coll. Sch. Humanities, 1971—78; exec. officer Bklyn. Coll. Humanities Inst., 1980—89; provost and v.p. for acad. affairs Bklyn. Coll., 1982—88, provost emeritus, 1989. Exec. com., chmn. com. on undergrad. affairs, com. on univ.-wide programs CUNY; study group AAAS, 1987—89, pub., 1987—89; dir. Nat. Core Visitors Programs, 1985—89, Fund for Improvement of Postsecondary Edn.-funded Ctr. for Core Studies, 1987—88; co-chair senate report Chancellor's Coll. Prep. Initiative, 1991; exec. com The Liberal Art of Sci.: Agenda for Action. Mem. editl. bd.: Classical World, 1965—71; co-editor: The Am. Classical Rev., 1971—76; contbr. articles to profl. jours. Recipient Kirby Flower Smith award, 1939, Goethe prize, U. Vt., 1940, Alumni Achievement award, 1985, Nat. Presdl. medal, NEH, Charles Frankel prize, 1990; named Ethyle R. Wolfe Inst. for the Humanities Bklyn. Coll. in her honor, 1989; named to Hall of Honor, U. Vt., 1991, Disting. U. Faculty Sen. Emeritus, CUNY, 1992; grantee, NEH, 1971, 1982—84, Mellon Found., 1982—85, 1986—89, Exxon, 1986—89, Josiah Macy, 1986—90. Mem.: Am. Soc. Papyrologists, Classical Assn. Atlantic States (exec. com.), Vergilian Soc. Am., Archeol. Inst. Am., Am. Philol. Assn., N.Y. Classical Club (past pres., exec. com.), Phi Beta Kappa (pres. 1988—90, past pres. Rho of N.Y. chpt., Spl. Citation of Honor on Sesquicentennial U. Vt. 1998). Home: New York, NY. Died May 6, 2010.

WOLFE, STANLEY, composer, educator; b. NYC, Feb. 7, 1924; s. Bert S. and Dorothy (Sanders) W.; m. Marguerite Wiberg, Aug. 10, 1960; children: Jeffrey, Madeleine. Student, Stetson U., DeLand, Fla., 1946-47, Henry St. Music Sch., 1947-48; BS in Composition, Juilliard Sch. Music, NYC, 1952, MS in Composition, 1955. Faculty Juilliard Sch., NYC, 1955—2005, dir. extension div., 1956-89; adj. prof. music Lincoln Ctr. campus Fordham U., 1969-73; lectr. N.Y. Philharmonic Pre-Concert Series, from 1985. Prin. compositions include King's Heart; dance score, 1956, Canticle for Strings, 1957, Lincoln Square Overture, 1958, Symphony Number 3, 1959, String Quartet, 1961, Symphony Number 4, 1965, Symphony Number 5 (Lincoln Center Commn.), 1970, Symphony Number 6, 1981; Violin Concerto, 1987. Served with AUS, 1943-46. Recipient award Am. Acad. and Inst. Arts and Letters, 1990; Guggenheim fellow in composition, 1957; Nat. Endowment for Arts grantee, 1969, 70, 77 Mem. ASCAP, Am. Music Center, Am. Symphony Orch. League (Alice Ditson award 1961), U.S. Chess Fedn. Home: Yonkers, NY. Died May 29, 2009.

WOLFF, PAUL MARTIN, government official; b. Newcomerstown, Ohio, July 3, 1921; m. Margaret Anne Corbett; children— Jeffrey, Alan, Michael BA, Wittenberg U., 1942; MS in Meterorology, U.S. Navy Postgrad. Sch., 1950; postgrad., U. Chgo. Commd. officer U.S. Navy, 1942, advanced through grades to capt., 1972, founder, comdr. Fleet Numerical Weather Central, 1959-70, ret., 1972; v.p. Ocean Data Systems, 1972-83; pres. Global Weather Dynamics, Monterey, Calif., 1978-83; designer marine weather services for Saudi Arabia and Iran; asst. adminstr. Ocean Services and Coastal Zone Mgmt., NOAA, Washington, from 1983, project mgr. Recipient Oceanographer's award U.S. Navy, 1969; Marine Tech. Soc. award, Solberg Research award Am. Soc. Naval Engrs., 1967 Fellow Am. Meterol. Soc. Died Sept. 16, 2009.

WOLK, JOAN MARCIA, technical writer, consultant; b. Pitts., Dec. 2, 1947; d. Samuel David and Rhoda (Levy) Kopelman; m. Stephen Selis Wolk, Oct. 25, 1970 (div. Sept. 1977); 1 child, Jason. BA in English, Ohio U., 1969; postgrad. in linguistics, Ohio State U., 1970; MA in Linguistics, U. Mass., 1970. Tchr. English, chmn. dept. English Prince George County Bd. Edn., Upper Marlboro, Md., 1970-73; editor, 1977-81; sr. tech. writer Boeing Computer Services, Vienna, Va., 1981-85, systems analyst electronic pub., 1985-87; mgr. tech. writing VM Software, Inc., Reston, Va., 1987-88; mgr., cons. tech. writing Comsys Tech. Svcs., Rockville, Md., 1988—. Democrat. Jewish. Avocations: parapsychology/metaphysics, concerts, theater, opera, walking. Died Mar. 3, 2010.

WOLKEN, JONATHAN, performing company executive; b. Pitts., July 12, 1949; m. JoAnne Wolken; 4 children. BA in Philosophy, Dartmouth Coll., 1971. Co-founder, artistic dir. Pilobolus Dance Theatre, Washington Depot, Conn., 1991, devel. dir., 1991—2010. Artist-in-residence USIS Arts Am. Program, Kuopio, Finland; tchr. Pilobolus Summer Workshop, Maine. Choreographer (Operas) Where the Wild Things Are, Glyndebourne Festival Opera, creator (television feature) Oneiric, Pilobolus/Danish TV. Died June 13, 2010.

WOLMAN, M. GORDON (MARKLEY GORDON WOLMAN), geography educator; b. Balt., Aug. 16, 1924; s. Abel and Anna (Gordon) W.; m. Elaine Mielke, June 20, 1951; children: Elsa Anne, Abel Gordon, Abby Lucille, Fredericka Jeannette. Student, Haverford Coll.; AB in Geology, Johns Hopkins U., 1949; MA in Geology, Harvard U., 1951, PhD in Geology, 1953. Geologist U.S. Geol. Survey, 1951-58, part-time, 1958—2010; assoc. prof. geography Johns Hopkins U., Balt., 1958-62, B. Howell Griswold, Jr. prof., geography and internat. affairs, 1962—2010. Chmn. dept. geography and environ. engring. Johns Hopkins U., 1958—90, interim provost, 1987, 90, prof. environ. health sci., 1998—2010; adv. com. geography U.S. Office Naval Rsch., Oak Ridge Nat. Lab.; exec. com. divsn. earth sci. NRC; internat. environ. programs com., environ. studies bd., com. water, com. mineral resources and environ., chmn. nat. commn. water quality policy NAS; chmn. NRC Com. Adv. U.S. Geol. Survey; chmn. NAS Commn. Geoscis., Environment and Resources, NRC Bd. Sustainability, 1995—2000; chmn. study land use and populationNRC Tri-Acad., China, India; environ. adv. com. Savannah River Tech. ctr.; chmn. U.S. Com. for IIASA, 1999—2003; chmn. adv. com. mgmt. and protection of water resources State. of Md., 2004—08. Author: Fluvial Processes in Geomorphology, 1964; editl. bd.: Science mag. Pres. bd. trustees Park Sch., Balt.; pres. bd. dirs. Sinai Hosp., Balt., Resources for Future, 1980-87; adv. com. Inst. Nuc. Power Ops., 1982-85; active Balt. City Charter Revision Commn., Cmty. Action Com., Balt. With USNR, 1943-46. Recipient Meritorious Contbn. award Assn. Am. Geographers, 1972, Disting. Career award Geomorphology, 1993, D.L. Linton award Brit. Geomorphological Rsch. Group, 1994, Rachel Carson award Chesapeake Appreciation Inc., Ian Campbell medal Am. Geol. Inst., 1997, Nev. Med. Desert Rsch. Inst., Abel Wolman award Chesapeake sect. AWWA, 2003, Lifetime Achievement award Nat. Coun. for Sci. and the Environment, 2004, Outstanding Contbn. to Water Environment award Water Environment Fedn., 2004, Eisenhower medal Johns Hopkins U., 2005, Benjamin Franklin medal in Earth and Environ. Sci., Franklin Inst., 2006, Inaugural Kerk Bryan Lectr. award, Boston, 2007, Olivia Irvine Dodge Conservation award, Irvine Nature Ctr., 2008. Fellow Am. Acad. Arts and Scis., AAAS; mem. ASCE, NAS, NAE, Am. Geophys. Union (chmn. subcom. sedimentation, pres. hydrol. sect., Robert Horton medal 2000), Geol. Soc. Am. (v.p. 1983, pres. 1984, Penrose medal 1999), Am. Philos. Soc., Am. Geog. Soc. (councillor 1965-70, Cullum Geog. medal 1989), Washington Geol. Soc., Agrl. Hist. Soc., Md. Acad. Scis. (exec. com. 1970-75), Am. Geophysical Union, Phi Beta Kappa, Sigma Xi. Home: Baltimore, Md. Died Feb. 24, 2010.

WOLPER, DAVID LLOYD, television producer; b. NYC, Jan. 11, 1928; s. Irving S. and Anna (Fass) W.; m. Margaret Dawn Richard, May 11, 1958 (div.); children: Mark, Michael, Leslie; m. Gloria Diane Hill, July 11, 1974. Student, Drake U., 1946, U. So. Calif., 1948. V.p., treas. Flamingo Films, TV sales co., 1948-50, v.p. West Coast Ops., 1954-58; chmn., pres. Wolper Prodns., LA, from 1958. Cons., exec. producer Warner Bros., Inc., 1976—. Prodr.: (TV specials) Race for Space, 1959, The Rafer Johnson Story, 1961, Hollywood: The Golden Years, 1961, D-Day, 1962, Hollywood: The Fabulous Era, 1962, Americans on Everest, 1963, Hollywood: The Great Stars, 1963, Biography of a Rookie: The Willie Davis Story, 1963, Making of the President 1960, 64, The Incredible World of James, 1965, The Yanks are Coming, Berlin: Kaiser to Khrushchev, December 7: Day of Infamy, The American Woman in the 20th Century, Hollywood and The Stars, March of Time Specials, The Rise and Fall of the Third Reich, The Legend of Marilyn Monroe, Four Days in November, Krebiozen and Cancer, National Geographic, Undersea World of Jacques Cousteau, China: Roots of Madness, The Journey of Robert F. Kennedy, Say Goodbye, George Plimpton, Appointment With Destiny, American Heritage, Smithsonian, They've Killed President Lincoln, Sandburg's Lincoln, Primal Man, The First Woman President; (TV episodes) Chico and the Man, Get Christie Love, Welcome Back, Kotter!, Collison Course; (mini-series) Roots, 1977, The Thorn Birds, 1983; (TV movies) Escape to Freedom, 1963, Victory at Entebbe, Roots: The Next Generations, Moviola, North and South Books I, II, III, Napoleon and Josephine, Alex Haley's Queen, Men Of The Dragon, Unwed Father, The Morning After; (films) If It's Tuesday, This Must Be Belgium, 1969, I Love My Wife, 1970, The Hellstrom Chronicle, 1971, Willy Wonka and The Chocolate Factory, 1971, One Is A Lonely Number, 1972, Devil's Brigade, The Bridge at Remagen, Visions of Eight, This is Elvis, Murder in the First, Surviving Picasso, L.A. Confidential, 1997; live spl. events include Opening and Closing Ceremonies 1984 Olympic Games, Liberty Weekend July 3-6, 1986; author: (autobiography), Producer, 2003 Trustee L.A. County Mus. Art, Am. Film Inst., L.A. Thoracic and Cardiovascular Found., Boys and Girls Clubs Am., U.S. Golf Assn. Found.; bd. dirs. Amateur Athletic Assn. L.A., L.A. Heart Inst., Acad. TV Arts and Scis. Found., So. Calif. Com. for Olympic Games, U. Soc. Calif. Cinema/TV Dept.; bd. govs. Cedars Sinai Med. Ctr.; com. mem. U.S. Olympic Team Benefit; mem. adv. com. Nat. Ctr. Jewish Film. Recipient award for documentaries, San Francisco Internat. Film Festival, 1960, 7 Golden Globe awards, 5 George Foster Peabody awards, Disting. Svc. award, US Jr. C. of C., award, Monte Carlo Internat. Film Festival, 1964, Grand Prix for TV Programs, Cannes Film Festival, 1964, medal of Chevalier, French Nat. Legion of Honor, 1990, Disting. Svc. award, Nat.

Assn. Broadcasters, 2007, David L. Wolper Student Documentary Achievement award named in his honor, Internat. Documentary Assn., David L. Wolper Ctr. for Study of Documentary named in his honor, U. So. Calif.; named one of The 45 People Who Made A Difference, TV Guide, 1998; named to TV Hall of Fame, 1988. Mem.: NATAS (50 Emmy awards, 145 Emmy nominations), Caucus for Prodrs., Writers and Dirs., Prodrs. Guild Am. (David L. Wolper Prodr. of Yr. award named in his honor), Acad. Motion Picture Arts and Scis. (Oscar award, 11 Oscar nominations). Died Aug. 10, 2010.

WOMMACK, W(ILLIAM) W(ALTON), retired manufacturing company executive; b. Winston-Salem, NC, Dec. 12, 1922; s. Sidney LaMar and Ada (Culler) W.; m. Jean Emery, Sept. 14, 1951; children: Judith J., Kent W., Lynne E., Mary E. B.Chem. Engring, N.C. State Coll., 1943; MBA, Harvard U., 1948. Engr. thru div. controller Libbey-Owens-Ford, Toledo, 1948; treas., controller Ottawa River Paper Co., Toledo, 1955-58; asst. gen. mgr. Mead. Corp., Cin., 1958-64, v.p. bd. Dayton, Ohio, 1964-66, group v.p. bd., 1966-69, exec. v.p., 1969-71, vice chmn. bd., 1971-81, also dir., 1968-81. Lt. USNR, 1943-46. Home: Cincinnati, Ohio. Died Apr. 8, 2010.

WOOD, HARRY EUGENE, retired judge; b. Spartanburg, SC, May 31, 1926; s. Boyce Eugene and Jane (Gurley) W.; m. I. Katherine Terrell, Aug. 23, 1947. Student, Wofford Coll., 1942-43; AA, George Washington U., 1949, JD, 1952. Bar: D.C. 1952, U.S. Dist. Ct. D.C. 1952. Law clk. U.S. Ct. Claims, Washington, 1952-54; assoc. Ansell and Ansell, Washington, 1954-57; ptnr. Emery and Wood, Washington, 1958-69; trial judge U.S. Ct. Claims, Washington, 1969-82; judge U.S. Claims Ct., Washington, 1982-86, sr. judge, 1986; ret., 1986. Served with AUS, 1944-46; col. Res. ret. Mem. D.C. Bar Assn., Order of Coif. Home: Staunton, Va. Died Nov. 23, 2009.

WOOD, JAMES NOWELL, foundation administrator, retired museum director; b. Boston, Mar. 20, 1941; s. Charles H. and Helen N. (Nowell) Wood; m. Emese Forizs, Dec. 30, 1966; children: Lenke Hancock, Rebecca Nowell. Diploma, Universita per Stranieri, Perugia, Italy, 1962; BA, Williams Coll., Williamstown, Mass., 1963; MA (Ford Mus. Tng. fellow), NYU, 1966. Asst. to dir. Met. Mus., NYC, 1967-68, asst. curator dept. 20th century art, 1968-70; curator Albright-Knox Art Gallery, Buffalo, 1970-73, assoc. dir., 1973-75; dir. St. Louis Art Mus., 1975-80; pres., dir. Art Inst. Chgo., 1980—2004; pres., CEO J. Paul Getty Trust, LA, 2007—10. Vis. com. visual arts U. Chgo., 1980—94; bd. dirs. Pulitzer Found. Arts, 2005—10, Sterling & Francine Clark Art Inst., NYU Inst. Fine Arts. Mem.: Assn. Art Mus. Dirs., Intermuseum Conservation Assn. (past pres.). Home: Los Angeles, Calif. Died June 11, 2010.

WOOD, ROBERT LEE, transportation executive; b. Ft. Worth, Jan. 26, 1940; s. James A. and Frances (Gilliam) Wood; m. Naomi H. Poore, Mar. 5, 1960; children: Robert Lee, Stephen W., Helen Reena. Student, Draughns Jr. Coll., 1960; BA, Somerset U., 1985. Traffic mgr. H.G. Hill Co., Nashville, 1959—69; terminal mgr. Sears Roebuck Co., Nashville, 1969—74; pres. Rent-A-Driver, Inc., Nashville, from 1974; dir. Maywood Constrn. Co., Nashville, Carriage House Realty and Devel. Co., Wood Group; mem. adv. bd. 1st Bank and Trust. Chmn. recreation com. Nashville Baptist Assn., from 1984; Sunday Sch. dir., 1984—86; trustee Belmont Coll., Nashville, from 1985. With US Army, 1957. Mem.: Donelson-Hermitage C. of C., Nashville C. of C., Nashville HOme Builders Assn., Driver Leasing Council Am. (bd. dirs. 1981—86), Shriners Club, Masons Club, Nat. Commodore Club, Beech Mountain Club, Andrew Jackson Sertoma Club (pres. 1982—83). Republican. Baptist. Avocations: softball, basketball, water and snow skiing, hunting, fishing. Home: Old Hickory, Tenn. Died Mar. 30, 2010.

WOOD, TERRY LEE, mathematics educator; BA, Mich. State U., 1964, MA, 1968, PhD, 1976. Cert. tchr., Mich. Elem. tchr. Lansing (Mich.) Pub. Schs., 1964-65, 66-68; tchr., researcher The Lab. Schs., Chgo., 1979-80; vis. asst. prof. Purdue U., West Lafayette, Ind., 1985-88, asst. prof. math. edn., 1988-93, assoc. prof., 1993-98, prof., from 1998. Co-editor: Transforming Children's Mathematics Education, 1990, Recreating Elementary Mathematics Education: Insights and Issues, 1993, Mathematics Teacher Education International Perspectives, 1999, Beyond Classical Pedagogy: Teaching Elementary School Mathematics, 2001, editor International Handbook of Mathematics Teacher Education, 2008; mem. editl. bd. Ednl. Studies in Math., Jour. Tchr. Edn., Brit. Soc. Learning Math., Math. Tchr. Edn. and Devel. Robert L. Snodgrass scholar. Mem. AAAS, APA, Am. Ednl. Rsch. Assn., Nat. Coun. Tchrs. Math., Psychology Math. Edn. Internat., Psychology Math. Edn. N.Am., Soc. Rsch. in Child Devel. Home: Fort Wayne, Ind. Died Jan. 14, 2010.

WOODBURY, RICHARD BENJAMIN, anthropologist, educator; b. West Lafayette, Ind., May 16, 1917; s. Charles Goodrich and Marion (Benjamin) W.; m. Nathalie Ferris Sampson, Sept. 18, 1948. Student, Oberlin Coll., 1934-36; BS in Anthropology cum laude, Harvard U., 1939, MA, 1942, PhD, 1949; postgrad., Columbia U., 1939-40. Archeol. research, Ariz., 1938, 39, Fla., 1940, Guatemala, 1947-49, El Morro Nat. Monument, N.Mex., 1953-56, Tehuacan, Mex., 1964; archaeologist United Fruit Co. Zaculeu Project, Guatemala, 1947-50; assoc. prof. anthropology U. Ky., 1950-52, Columbia U., 1952-58; rsch. assoc. prof. anthropology interdisciplinary arid lands program U. Ariz., 1959-63; curator archeology and anthropology U.S. Nat. Mus., Smithsonian Instn., Washington, 1963-69, acting. head office anthropology, 1965-66, chmn. office anthropology, 1966-67; prof., chmn. dept. anthropology U. Mass., Amherst, 1969-73, prof., 1973-81, prof. emeritus, from 1981, acting assoc. provost, dean grad. sch., 1973-74. Mem. divsn. anthropology and psychology NRC, 1954-57; bd. dirs. Archaeol. Conservancy, 1979-84, Valley Health Plan, Amherst, 1981-84, Mus. of No. Ariz., 1983-90; liason rep. for Smithsonian Instn., Com. for Recovery of Archeol. Remains, 1965-69; assoc. seminar on ecol. systems and cultural evolution Columbia U., 1964-73; mem. exec. com. bd. dirs. Human Relations Area Files, Inc., New Haven, Conn., 1968-70; cons. Conn. Hist. Commn., 1970-72. Author (with A.S. Trik) The Ruins of Zaculeu, Guatemala, 2 vols., 1953, Prehistoric Stone Implements of Northeastern Arizona, 1954, Alfred V. Kidder, 1973, Sixty Years of Southwestern Archaeology, 1993, (chpt.) (with James A. Neely) The Prehistory of the Tehuacan Valley, Vol. 4, 1972; editor: (with I.A. Sanders) Societies Around the World (2 vols.), 1953, (with others) The Excavation of Hawikuh, 1966, Am. Antiquity, 1954-58, Abstracts of New World Archaeology; editor-in-chief: Am. Anthropologist, 1975-78; mem. editorial bd.: Am. Jour. Archeology, 1957-72. Mem. sch. com., Shutesbury, Mass., 1979—82; chmn. fin. com. Friends of Amherst Stray Animals (Dakin Animal Shelter), 1983—85, trustee, from 1991; mem. Shutesbury Hist. Commn., 1998—2006, sec., 1999—2004. With USAF, 1942—45. Fellow, Mus. No. Ariz., 1985. Fellow AAAS (coun. rep. Am. Anthrop. Assn. 1961-63, com. on desert and arid zones rsch. Southwest and Rocky Mountains divsn. 1958-64, vice-chair 1962-64, com. arid lands 1969-74, sec. 1970-72), Am. Anthrop. Assn. (exec. bd. 1963-66, A.V. Kidder award 1989), Archeol. Inst. Am. (exec. com. 1965-67); mem. Soc. Am. Archeology (treas. 1953-54, pres. 1958-59, chmn. fin. com. 1987-89, Fiftieth Anniversary award 1985, Disting. Svc. award 1988), Ariz. Archeol. and Hist. Soc., Nature Conservancy, Archeol. Conservancy (life). Home: Amherst, Mass. Died Oct. 11, 2009.

WOODEN, JOHN ROBERT, retired men's college basketball coach; b. Martinsville, Ind., Oct. 14, 1910; s. Joshua Hugh and Roxie (Rothrock) W.; m. Nellie C. Riley, Aug. 8, 1932 (dec. March 21, 1985); children: Nancy Anne, James Hugh. BS, Purdue U., 1932; MS, Ind. State U., 1947. Athletic dir., basketball & baseball coach Ind. State Teachers Coll., 1946-48; head basketball coach UCLA, 1948-75. Lectr. to colleges, coaches, bus. Author: Practical Modern Basketball, 1966, They Call Me Coach, 1972; co-author: Wooden: A Lifetime of Reflections and Observations On and Off the Court, 1997, Inch and Miles: Pyramid to Success for Kids, 2004, One on One, 2004, The Wisdom of Wooden: A Century of Family, Faith & Friends (published posthumously), 2010; contbr. articles to profl. jours. Served to lt. USN, 1943—46. Named All-American Basketball Player Purdue U., 1930-32, Coll. Basketball Player of Yr., 1932, Calif. Father of Yr., 1964, 75, Coach of Yr. US Basketball Writers Assn., 1964, 67, 69, 70, 72, 73, Sportsman of Yr. Sports Illus., 1973, GTE Acad. All-American, 1994, Basketball Coach of Century, 2000, Greatest Coach of All-Time, The Sporting News, 2009; named to Helms Athletic Found. All-Time All-American Team, 1943, Nat. Basketball Hall of Fame, Springfield, Mass., (as player) 1960, (as coach) 1970, Ind. State Basketball Hall of Fame, 1962, Nat. Collegiate Basketball Hall of Fame, 2006; recipient Whitney Young award Urban League, 1973, Inaugural Velvet Covered Brick award Layman's Leadership Inst., 1974, Inaugural Dr. James Naismith Peachbasket award, 1974, Medal of Excellence Bellarmine Coll., 1985, Sportslike Pathfinder award to Hoosier with extraordinary svc. on behalf of American youth, 1993, 40 for the Age award Sports Illus., 1994, Inaugural Frank G. Wells Disney award for role model to youth, 1995, Disting. American award Pres. Reagan, 1995, Svc. to Mankind award Lexington Theol. Sem., 1995, NCAA Theodore Roosevelt Sportsman award, 1995, Vince Lombardi award for excellence, 2000, Ind. Legend award, 2000, Presdl. Medal of Freedom, 2003, The White House, Pres. Ford award NCAA, 2006. Coached UCLA to 10 NCAA Championships, 1964, 1965, 1967, 1968, 1969, 1970, 1971, 1972, 1973, 1975, coach UCLA to 4 undefeated seasons, 1964, 1967, 1972, 1973. Died June 4, 2010.

WOODRUFF, BLISS, architect; b. New Haven, Apr. 18, 1922; d. William Watts and Myra Cannon (Kilborn) W.; m. Marian Davis, Sept. 27, 1952; children: Nathaniel Rohde, William Watts II, Davis Miller, Charlotte Bliss. BA, Yale U., 1943, BArch, MArch, Yale U., 1949. Registered architect N.H., Vt., Maine, Mass., Conn., R.I., N.Y., Del. Prin. Bliss Woodruff, Architect, Randolph, N.H. and Hamden, Conn., 1949-54; draftsman Office of Douglas Orr, New Haven, 1954-55; ptnr. John A. Carter, Architect, Nashua, N.H., 1956-57, Carter & Woodruff, Architects, Nashua, 1957-75, Carter, Woodruff & Cheever, Architects, Nashua, 1975-76; prin. Bliss Woodruff, Architecht and Interior Designer, Nashua, from 1976. Prin. works include: (bldgs.) Exeter Clinic, 1963, Bank of N.H., 1971 (award 1971), N.H. Dept. Safety, 1976, (dormitory) Plymouth State Coll., N.H., 1968. Pres. Nashua League of Craftsmen, 1978-85, N.H. Civil Liberties Union, Concord, 1982-84, also bd. dirs., 1982-84. Served to lt. USNR, 1942-46, PTO. Recipient Honor award N.H. chpt. AIA, 1965, First Honor awards N.H. chpt. AIA, 1966, 70, 71. Democrat. Mem. Unitarian Ch. Clubs: Chiltern Mountain (Boston) (treas. 1978-85), Appalachian Mountain (Boston). Avocations: hiking, whitewater canoeing, skiing. Home: Nashua, NH. Died Jan. 28, 2009.

WOODS, ROBERT JOSEPH, government official, information technology executive; b. Nickelsville, Va., Sept. 11, 1946; s. John Thomas and Dorothy Nell (Hartsock) W.; m. Elizabeth Ann Healey, Aug. 24, 1968; children: Mary Beth, Dennis John. BS in Indsl. Engring., Va. Tech., 1969; MS in Adminstrn., George Washington U., 1971; MPA, Harvard U., 1980. Lic. stock broker, Va. Indsl. engr. Naval Facilities Engring. Command, Washington, 1968-71; computer sytems analyst FAA, Washington, 1971-72, indsl. engr., 1972-73, program mgr., exec. staff, 1973-80, mgr. mgmt. engring., 1980-84, mgr. info. resources mgmt., 1984-87; dir. info. resources mgmt. Office of Sec./U.S. Dept. Transp., Washington, from 1987. Sr. assoc. MRF Assocs., Rockville, Md., 1976—; instr. George Mason U., Fairfax, Va., 1982. Contbr. articles to profl. jours. Coach, Sterling Girls Softball, 1979, Vienna Youth Soccer Assn., Va., 1980-86; pres. Tanglewood Community Assn., Vienna, Va., 1983, v.p., 1984; pres., founder Castlewood High Sch. Alumni Scholarship Fund, 1985—; bd. dirs. Interagy. Com. for Info. Resource Mgmt., 1988—. Mem. Fed. Info. Resources Mgmt. Regulations Coun., FEd. Dept. Level Work Group, Am. Inst. Indsl. Engrs. (sr. mem.). Roman Catholic. Avocations: classic car restoration, old house restoration. Home: Vienna, Va. Died Jan. 27, 2009.

WOODWARD, EDWARD, actor; b. Surrey, England, June 1, 1930; s. Edward Oliver and Violet Edith Woodward; m. Venetia Mary Collet, July 30, 1952 (div. Dec. 1, 1986); children: Tim, Peter, Sarah; m. Michele Dotrice, Jan. 17, 1987; 1 child, Emily Student, Kingston Coll., Royal Acad. Dramatic Arts. Mem. Castle Theatre, Farnham, Eng., various repertory cos., Eng. and Scotland. Actor: (stage prodns.) Where There's a Will, 1955, Romeo and Juliet, 1958, Hamlet, 1958, Rattle of a Simple Man, 1962, Two Cities, 1968, Cyrano de Bergerac, 1971, The White Devil, 1971, The Wolf, 1973, Male of the Species, 1975, On Approval, 1976, The Dark Horse Comedy, 1978, Beggar's Opera, 1980, Private Lives, 1980, The Assassin, 1982: (films) Where There's a Will, 1955, Inn For Trouble, 1960, Becket, 1964, The File of the Golden Goose, 1968, Incense for the Damned, 1970, 10 Rillington Place, 1971, Sitting Target, 1972, Young Winston, 1972, Hunted, 1973, The Wicker Man, 1973, Callan, 1974, Three For All, 1975, Stand Up, Virgin Soldiers, 1977, Breaker Morant, 1980, The Appointment, 1981, Who Dares Wins, 1982, Forever Love, 1982, Merlin and the Sword, 1982, Champions, 1983, King David, 1986, Mister Johnson, 1990, (voice only) Aladdin, 1992, Deadly Advice, 1994, The House of Angelo, 1997, Abduction Club, 2002; (TV series) Callan, 1967-72, The Edward Woodward Hour, 1970, Nineteen-Ninety, 1977-78, The Equalizer, 1985-89, Over My Dead Body, 1990-91, Common As Muck, 1994-97, C15: The New Professionals, 1999; (TV films) Saturday, Sunday, Monday, 1978, Blunt Instrument, 1980, Wet Job, 1981, Love Is Forver, 1983, Killer Contract, 1984, A Christmas Carol, 1984, Arthur the King, 1985, Uncle Tom's Cabin, 1986, Memories of Manon, 1988, Codename Kyril, 1988, The Man in the Brown Suit, 1989, Over My Dead Body, 1990, Hands of a Murderer, 1990, Christmas Reunion, 1993, The Shamrock Conspiracy, 1995, Gulliver's Travels, 1996, Harrison: Cry of the City, 1996, Marcie's Dowry, 1999, Messiah, 2001, Night Flight, 2002, (voice only) First Landing, 2007; (TV appearances) Armchair Theatre (2 episodes), 1959-67, Inside Story, 1960, Adventure Story, 1961, Emergency-Ward 10, 1961, Magnolia Street, 1961, You Can't Win, 1961, Sir Francis Drake, 1962, ITV Play of the Week, 1964, The Defenders, 1964, The Troubleshooters, 1965, Thirty-Minute Theatre (2 episodes), 1966-67, Theatre 625 (3 episodes), 1967, The Saint, 1967, Sword of Honor, 1967, The Revenue Men, 1967, The Baron, 1967, Trapped, 1967, Mystery and Imagination, 1968, Sherlock Holmes, 1968, ITV Playhouse (3 episodes), 1968-80, The Bruce Forsyth Show, 1969, Detective (2 episodes), 1968-69, The Root of All Evil?, 1969, BBC Play of the MOonth, 1969-71, Play for Today, 1971, Whodunnit?, 1972, Armchair Cinema, 1975, Nice Work (6 episodes), 1980, Chronicle, 1981, Sunday Night Thriller (2 episodes), 1981, Alfred Hitchcock Presents (2 episodes), 1988, In Suspicious Circustances, 1994, Crusade, 1999, Dark Realm, 2001, La Femme Nikita (4 episodes), 2001, Murder in Suburbia, 2004, Where the Heart Is, 2005, The Bill (2 episodes), 2008, EastEnders (6 episodes), 2009; (TV mini-series) Winston Churchhill: The Wilderness Years, 1981, Five Days, 2007; rec. artist 12 mus. albums, 3 poetry readings, 6 talking book albums. Decorated Officer of the Order of the Brit. Empire (OBE), 1978 Mem.: Garrick, Green Room, Wellington. Avocations: boating, geology. Died Nov. 16, 2009.

WOODWORTH, HAROLD CYRIL, physician; b. Wells, Minn., Sept. 23, 1920; s. Harry Clark and Martha Meta (Wiecking) W.; AB, Dartmouth Coll., 1942; MD, Harvard U., 1944; PhD, Yale U., 1958; m. Evelyn Eileen Mahon, Aug. 17, 1944; children: Richard, Karl. Intern, Mary Hitchcock Hosp., Hanover, N.H., 1944-45; resident internal medicine, White River Junction, Vt., 1947-48; practice family medicine, Bristol, Vt., 1948-52; chief Microbiology Lab., Ctr. Disease Control, USPHS, Atlanta, 1958-68; county health officer Colbert and Lauderdale Counties, Ala., 1968-75; regional health officer N.W. Ala. Regional Health Dept., Tuscumbia, 1975-81; ret., 1981. Served with USN, 1945-46, 52-54. Recipient Physician's Recognition award AMA, 1979-82; Boss of Yr. award Muscle Shoals Bus. and Profl. Women's Assn., 1980; USPHS postdoctoral fellow, 1955-57, Howard Hughes Med. Inst. fellow, 1957-58. Mem. Am. Pub. Health Assn., Ala. Pub. Health Assn., AAAS, Med. Assn. Ala., Lauderdale County Med. Soc. Methodist. Club: Civitan (Florence, Ala.). Home: Florence, Ala. Died Feb. 23, 2009.

WOODY, MARY FLORENCE, nursing educator, academic administrator; b. Chambers County, Ala., Mar. 31, 1926; d. Hugh Ernest and May Lillie (Gilliland) W. Diploma, Charity Hosp. Sch. Nursing, 1947; BS, Columbia U., 1953, MA, 1955. Staff nurse Wheeler Hosp., Lafayette, Ala., 1947-48; polio nurse Willard Parker Hosp., NYC, 1949; staff nurse, supr. VA Hosp., Montgomery, Ala., 1950-53; faculty, field supr. nursing dept. Columbia U. Tchrs. Coll., NYC, 1955-56; asst. dir. nursing Emory U. Hosp., Atlanta, assoc. dir., DON, 1984-93; clin. asst. prof. Emory U. Sch. Nursing, Atlanta, 1956-68, interim dean, 1992-93; asst. dir., DON Grady Meml. Hosp., Atlanta, 1968-79; founding dean, prof. Auburn U. Sch. Nursing, Ala., 1979-84; disting. emeritus prof. Emory U., from 2003. Chair Ga. Statewide Master Planning Com. for Nursing and Nursing Edn., 1971-75; faculty preceptor patient care adminstrn. Sch. Public Health, U. Minn., 1977-79; bd. dirs. Wesley Woods Found. & Long Term Hosp.; chair bd. dirs. Am. Jour. Nursing Co., 1978-83. Recipient Spl. Recognition award 5th Dist. and Ga. Nurses Assn., 1978, 93, Disting. Achievement in Nursing Svc. award Columbia U.

Tchrs. Coll. Alumni Assn., 1992, Jane Van de Vrede Outstanding Svc. to Citizens Ga. award Ga. League Nursing, Cert. Spl. Recognition award Ga. Nurses Assn., 1993, Internat. Founders award Sigma Theta Tau, 1999, The Marie Hippensteel award, 1999, Disting. Prof. award Emeritus Coll. Emory U., 2003; named Ga. Women Pioneer in Health Care, Ga. Commn. on Women and Ga. Womens History Month Com., 1998, Hall of Fame Nursing, Tchrs. Coll., Columbia, U., N.Y Fellow Am. Acad. Nursing (charter, Living Legend 1997); mem. Am. Nurses Assn., Nat. League Nursing, Am. Heart Assn., Emory U. Nell Hodgson Woodruff Sch. Nursing Alumni Assn. (hon.), Sigma Theta Tau (Marie Hippensteel Lingemald award for excellence in nursing 1999); mem. Nursing Tchr.'s Coll. Columbia U. of Hall of Fame (charter). Democrat. Died Apr. 28, 2010.

WOOLRIDGE, ANNA MARIE See LINCOLN, ABBEY

WORBOIS, LOIS EVELYN, writer; b. Mt. Pleasant, Pa., June 30, 1930; d. Edwin Thomas and Louvina Elizabeth (May) Butler; m. Robert John Worbois, Feb. 3, 1951; children: James, Cheryl, John (dec.), Susanne, Allen. BA in English Edn., Seton Hill Coll., Greensburg, Pa., 1988. Free-lance writer Light and Life Press, Winona Lake, Ind., 1969-71; soc. editor News Dispatch, Jeannette, Pa., 1972-75; reporter Standard Observer, Irwin, Pa., 1976-79, woman's editor, 1979-86; free-lance writer, 1986-89; English tchr. Kaohsiung, Taiwan, Republic of China, 1989—. Author: The Thorn, 1977. Mem. adv. bd. Sr. Community Service Projects, Westmoreland County Community Coll., 1976-86; mem. Health and Welfare Council, Westmoreland County, 1980-86. Mem. DAR, Soc. Profl. Journalists. Republican. Methodist. Club: Gideons Internat. Aux. (v.p. 1972, sec. 1979) (Westmoreland County). Home: Irwin, Pa. Died Jan. 25, 2009.

WRAPP, HENRY EDWARD, retired finance educator; b. Paragould, Ark., Mar. 26, 1917; s. Alba Henry and Mildred (Dennis) W.; m. Marguerite Amy Hill, Aug. 19, 1950 (dec. 2001); children: Jennifer, Gregory, Stephen, Amy, Katherine. B.C.S., U. Notre Dame, 1938; MBA, Harvard U., 1948, D.C.S., 1951. With E.I. duPont deNemours & Co., Inc., 1939-43; prof. Harvard U., 1955-62; prof. bus. policy U. Chgo., 1963-83, assoc. dean, 1965-70; faculty St. Vincent De Paul Sem., Boynton Beach, Fla., 1983—90. Served to lt. USNR, 1943-46. Mem.: Delray Dunes Country (Boynton Beach, Fla.). Home: Palm City, Fla. Died Nov. 21, 2009.

WRIGHT, ANDREW, English literature educator; b. Columbus, Ohio, June 28, 1923; s. Francis Joseph and Katharine (Timberman) W.; m. Virginia Rosemary Banks, June 27, 1952; children: Matthew Leslie Francis, Emma Stanbery. AB, Harvard U., 1947; MA, Ohio State U., 1948, PhD, 1951. Prof. English lit. U. Calif., San Diego, from 1963, chmn. dept. lit., 1971-74; dir. U. Calif. Study Center, U.K. and Ireland, 1980-82. Vis. prof. U. Queensland, Australia, 1984, Colegio de la Frontera Norte, San Antonio del Mar, Baja, Calif., 1991-92. Author: Jane Austen's Novels: A Study In Structure, 1953, Joyce Cary: A Preface to His Novels, 1958, Henry Fielding: Mask and Feast, 1965, Blake's Job: A Commentary, 1972, Anthony Trollope: Dream and Art, 1983; Fictional Discourse and Historical Space, 1987; contbg. author numerous books, articles to profl. jours., numerous short stories to lit. mags.; editorial bd. Nineteenth Century Fiction, 1964-86. Bd. dirs. Calif. Coun. Humanities, 1983-87. Guggenheim fellow, 1960, 70; Fulbright Sr. Research fellow, 1960-61 Fellow Royal Soc. Lit.; mem. MLA, Jane Austen Soc., Athenaeum (London), Trollope Soc., Santayana Soc., Phi Beta Kappa. Home: La Jolla, Calif. Died Aug. 3, 2009.

WRIGHT, BARRY BENJAMIN, temporary services executive; b. Greenburg, Pa., Oct. 20, 1933; s. Millard A. and Katherind (Baer) W.; children— Barry, Douglas; m. Melinda Stott, Apr. 20, 1985. B.A., Gettysburg Coll., 1955. Pres. Temporaries, Inc., Washington, 1969-85, chmn., chief exec. officer, 1985—; mem. Met. Washington Bd. Trade, 1969—; dir. Merc. Nat. Bank, Washington, 1986—. Contbr. articles to profl. publs. Founder, chmn. Food for All Seasons Found., Washington, 1974—, D.C. Youth Chorale Assocs., 1980—; v.p. Cultural Alliance Greater Washington, 1978—; bd. dirs. Jr. Achievement Greater Washington, 1981—. Served to lt. (j.g.) USN, 1955-59. Recipient Washingtonian of Yr. award Washington Mag. and Jaycees, 1983, Pres's. medal Catholic U. of Am., 1984, Disting. Alumni award Gettysgurg Coll., 1985; named Man of Yr., Washington Jaycees, 1965. Republican. Presbyterian. Clubs: Columbia Country, Internat.; Jupiter Hills Golf (Fla.). Lodge: Kiwanis. Died May 29, 2010.

WRIGHT, DEIL SPENCER, political science professor; b. Three Rivers, Mich., June 18, 1930; s. William Henry and Gertrude Louise (Buck) W.; m. Patricia Mae Jaffke, Aug. 22, 1953; children: David C., Mark W., Matthew D., Lois L. BA, U. Mich., 1952, M in Pub. Adminstrn., 1954, PhD, 1957. Asst. prof. polit. sci. Wayne State U., Detroit, 1956-59; from asst. to assoc. prof. U. Iowa, Iowa City, 1959-67; assoc. prof. U. Calif., Berkeley, 1965-66; prof. U. N.C., Chapel Hill, 1967-83, alumni disting. prof., from 1983; Carl Hatch vis. prof. U. N.Mex., Albuquerque, 1987. Lectr. USIA, Washington, various dates; cons. Office Mgmt. and Budget, Washington, 1979-80. Author: Understanding Intergovernmental Relations, 3d edit., 1988; editor: Federalism and Intergovernmental Relations, 1984, Globalization and Decentralization, 1996; contbr. over 100 articles to various polit. sci. and pub. adminstrn. jours. Mem. dir's. adv. com. NIH, Bethesda, Md., 1970-74, N.C. Coun. on State Goals and Policies, Raleigh, 1973-77, N.C. State Internship Coun., Raleigh, 1985-93. Internat. Inst. Mgmt. research fellow, Berlin, 1977. Fellow Nat. Acad. Pub. Adminstrn.; mem. AAAS, Am. Polit. Sci. Assn., Am. Soc. Pub. Adminstrn. (Waldo Lifetime Career Achievement award), Midwest Polit. Sci. Assn., Policy Studies Orgn., So. Polit. Sci. Assn. (pres. 1981-82). Lodges: Rotary (bd. dirs. Chapel Hill club 1981, 84, 90, v.p. 2000-01, pres. 2001-02). Republican. Methodist. Home: Chapel Hill, NC. Died June 30, 2009.

WRIGHT, JAMES RICHARD, linguistics educator; b. Cleve., Dec. 15, 1934; s. Richard D. and Opal Carolyn (Wilson) W.; m. Lucinda W. Thomas, Mar. 18, 1961. BA, Northwestern U., 1956; MA, Middlebury Coll., Vt., 1960, Ind. U., 1968, PhD, 1972. Instr. Rollins Coll., Winter Park, Fla., 1960-62; prof. East Carolina U., Greenville, N.C., from 1969. Contbr. articles to profl. jours. With U.S. Army, 1956-58. Danforth grantee, 1960, NDEA fellow, 1965-68. Mem. Linguistic Soc. Am., Phi Sigma Iota. Avocations: electronic music, computer programming. Home: Greenville, NC. Died May 13, 2009.

WRIGHT, JAMES RUSSELL, veterinarian; b. Pontiac, Mich., Aug. 13, 1946; s. Alvin and Alice (Forbes) Wright; m. Janice Mae Bales, Sept. 8, 1967. BS, Mich. State U., 1968, DVM, 1969. Staff orthopedic and neurosurgeon Gasow Vet. Hosp., Birmingham, Mich., from 1969. Contbr. numerous articles to various publs. Evans Scholars scholar, 1966—68. Mem.: Evans Scholars Alumni Assn., Mich. State U. Alumni Assn. (council mem. 1985—89), Oakland County Vet. Med. Assn. (Outstanding Contbn. to Clin. Practice award 1984), Southeastern Mich. Vet. Med. Assn., Mich. Vet. Med. Assn., Am. Vet. Med. Assn., Veterinary Orthopedic Soc. (bd. dirs. 1981—83), Southeastern Vet. Med. Assn. (pres. 1981—82). Republican. Lutheran. Home: Birmingham, Mich. Died June 1, 2010.

WRIGHT, MURRAY BLAIR, JR., architect, consultant, planner; b. Boston, July 22, 1925; s. Murray Blair and Marcella (Buckel) Wright; m. Carolyn Harrington, June 30, 1948; children: David, Marcella, Therese, Mary, John, Elizabeth, Michael, Paul. BS, Ga. Inst. Tech., 1945, BArch, 1947. Registered arch., Ga., Fla. Designer & draftsman Snyder & Nims Archs., Miami, Fla., 1947—48, Alfred B. Parker Archs., Miami, 1948—49; designer & arch. Edwin T. Reeder Assocs. A/E, Miami, 1950—57; pvt. practice Miami, 1958—78, Pensacola, Fla., from 1984. Bd. dirs. HUD Sect. 202 Program; arch. & dir., planning and bldg. Diocese Pensacola-Tallahassee, Fla., 1978—84. Prin. works include Barry Coll. Sci. Ctr., Book and Film Ctr. (City of Miami Bldg. of Month, 1962), Ch. of St. Hugh, Coconut Grove (City of Miami Bldg. of Month, 1963), Primary Centerette Sch. Sch., Liberty City, Miami (US Congress Citation award, 1968). Scoutmaster South Fla. Coun. Boy Scouts America, 1963—64; coach Khoury League, Miami, 1970—73. Served to lt. comdr. USNR, World War II. Recipient Honor medal, Diocese Pensacola-Tallahassee, 1983. Mem.: AIA (various offices 1949—74, chmn., task force 1969, coord., Cmty. Edn. & Environ. Ctr. 1966—67), Soc. Am. Mil. Engrs., Constrn. Specifications Inst. (profl. mem.), Serra Club, KC Lodge, Rotary Lodge. Roman Catholic. Died July 28, 2010.

WRIGHT, ROBERT LEE, retired lawyer, former paper company executive; b. Algood, Tenn., Sept. 3, 1919; s. Denny and Bessie Lela (Phy) W.; m. Lucille V. Hawkins, Aug. 11, 1951; 1 dau., Mary Wright Dorflinger. Student, Tenn. Poly. Inst., 1937-40, 47; LL.B., Vanderbilt U., 1950. Bar: Tenn. 1949. Practice in, Cookeville, 1950; atty. War Claims Commn., Washington, 1951, OPS, 1951-52; atty., real estate project mgr. C.E., 1952-56; with Bowaters So. Paper Corp., Calhoun, Tenn., 1956-86, sec., 1971-86, gen. counsel, 1971-86; also dir.; sec., gen. counsel Bowater Carolina Corp., Catawba, S.C., 1971-86; practice law Cleveland, Tenn., 1986-92. Dir. Terrain Inc., Atlanta, Stonecastle POA Inc., Crossville, Tenn., v.p., 1989—; mem. Tenn. adv. bd. Liberty Mut. Ins. Co., 1976-88; lectr. real estate U. Tenn., 1964-65 Served to 1st lt. AUS, 1944-46. Mem. ABA, Tenn. Bar Assn., Bradley County Bar Assn. (pres. 1968) Clubs: Cleveland Country, Walden, Elks, Cotillion. Home: Knoxville, Tenn. Died Jan. 6, 2009.

WUSSLER, ROBERT JOSEPH, broadcast executive, media consultant; b. Newark, Sept. 8, 1936; s. William and Anna (MacDonald) Wussler; children: Robert Joseph, Rosemary, Sally, Stefanie, Christopher, Jeanne. BA in Comm. Arts, Seton Hall U., South Orange, NJ, 1957, LLD (hon.), 1976, Emerson Coll., Boston, 1976. With CBS News, NYC, 1957-72; v.p., gen. mgr. Sta. WBBM-TV, Chgo., 1972-74; v.p. CBS Sports, NYC, 1974-76, pres., 1977-78, Sta. CBS-TV, NYC, 1976-77, Pyramid Enterprises Ltd., NYC, 1979—80; exec. v.p. Turner Broadcasting System Inc., Atlanta, 1979—89, sr. exec. v.p., 1987—92; pres. Atlanta Sports Teams, Inc., 1981-87; pres., chief exec. officer COMSAT Video Enterprises, Inc., Washington, 1989-92; pres. Wussler Group, 1992—2010. Chmn. bd. dirs. NATAS, 1980—84, 1986—90; co-owner Denver Nuggets, 1989—92; bd. dirs. Atlanta Hawks Ltd., Atlanta Braves Nat. League Baseball Club, Inc. Trustee Marymount Manhattan Coll., 1977—81; bd. regents Seton Hall U., 1978—84. Recipient Emmy awards, numerous other nat. and internat. news and sports awards. Mem.: European Broadcasting Union, Nat. Cable TV Assn. (mem. satellite network com.), Cable Advt. Bur., Ariz. Heart Inst., Internat. Radio and TV Soc., Dirs. Guild Am. Roman Catholic. Died June 5, 2010.

WYETH, JOHN CHURCHILL, II, geologist; b. Chgo., Aug. 13, 1923; s. John Churchill and Frances (Huster) Wyeth; m. Betty Swain, Aug. 8, 1953; children: Terry Richard, Robert Dru, Gregg, Jennette Turjilo, Margaret Reed. BS in Geology, U. Utah, 1950. Geologist, soil sampler Bur. Reclamation, Salt Lake City, 1950—51; petroleum geologist Conoco, Rocky Mts., Gulf Coast, 1952—68; uranium geologist, cons. Conoco, Corpus Christi, 1978—81, dir. geologist, 1969—76, frontier explorer, 1976—78; uranium geologist Corpus Christi, Tex., 1969—78; petroleum geologist, cons., from 1981. Rep. precinct chmn., Roswell, N.Mex., 1964; pres. Reorganized Ch. Jesus Christ Latter-day Saints, Corpus Christi, 1979—83. Mem.: AIME, Corpus Christi Geol. Soc., Am. Assn. Petroleum Geologists. Home: Corpus Christi, Tex. Died Mar. 17, 2009.

WYSCHOGROD, EDITH, philosophy educator; b. NYC; d. Morris and Selma Shurer; m. Michael Wyschogrod, Mar. 6, 1955; children: Daniel, Tamar. AB, Hunter Coll., 1957; PhD, Columbia U., 1970. Prof. philosophy Queens Coll., Flushing, NY, 1967-92; J. Newton Rayzor prof. philosophy and religious thought Rice U., Houston, 1992—2003, emerita, from 2003. Vis. prof. philosophy Villanova U. 2003; Croghan vis. prof. religion Williams Coll. 2004. Author: Emmanuel Levinas: The Problem of Ethical Metaphysics, 1974, 2d edit., 2000, Spirit in Ashes, 1985, Saints and Postmodernism, 1990, An Ethics of Remembering: History, Heterology and the Nameless Others; co-editor: Lacan and Theological Discourse, 1989, The Enigma of Gift and Sacrifice, 2002, The Ethical, 2003, Crossover Queries: Dwelling with Negatives, Embodying Philosophy's Others, 2006. Nat. Humanities Ctr. fellow, 1981, Woodrow Wilson Ctr. fellow, 1987-88, Guggenheim fellow, 1995-96. Fellow Am. Acad. Arts and Scis.; mem. Am. Acad. Religion (pres. 1992-93). Died July 16, 2009.

XIA, JIDING, chemical engineering educator; b. Jiangyin, Jiangsu, China, Mar. 23, 1921; arrived in US, 1993; s. Baogen Xia; m. Ming Yu, Oct. 1, 1958; children: Wei, Men. BS, Zhejiang U., Hangzhou, China, 1945, MS, 1948. Assoc. prof. Haijiang U., Fujian, China, 1949-50, Nanjing Normal U., China, 1953-54; dir. tchg. and rsch. divsn. Southeast U., China, 1954-58; assoc. prof. and dir. teaching/rsch. divsn. So. Yangtze U. (formerly Wuxi U. Light Industry), China, 1958-85, prof. chem. engring., 1985-92; rsch. chemist U. Wis., Madison, 1995-96. Vis. prof. Wayne State U., Detroit, 1993-95; mem. expert group synthetic detergents and fatty acids, Ministry of Light Industry China, 1979-86; vis. prof. The VI Univ. of Paris, 1986;, evaluation com. acad. degree Authorized U., 1980-84, Jiangsu Light Industry Sr. Engrs., 1982-92; project evaluator China Nat. Natural Sci. Found. Surface Chemistry, 1985—; cons. Chemithon Co., Seattle, 1990-93, Aging Toilet Soap Factory, China, 1991—, Tianjin Rsch. Inst. Interface and Colloid Scis., 1993, Stepan Co., Chgo., 1994, Proctor & Gamble Co., Cin., 1994-95, Vista Chem. Co., Houston, 1994—; mem. adv. com. Internat. Symposium on Surfactants in Solution, 1993. Author: Synthetic Detergents, 1976, Chemistry and Technology of Surfactants and Detergents, 1997; author and editor: Protein-Based Surfactants, 2001, Gemini Surfactants-Synthesis Interface Behavior and Applications, 2004; editor: Composite Soaps, 1987; translator: Comprehensive Refining of Sunflower Seed Oil, 1956, Chemistry of Oil and Fats, 1958, Manufacture of Detergents, 1986; mem. editl. bd. Jour. Surfactant Industry, 1982-90, Jour. Petro-Finechemicals, 1982, Chinese Ency. LIght Industry, 1987-91; contbr. more than 120 articles to acad. jours. Recipient award Ministry of Petroleum Industry for EOR Project, 1992, Outstanding Contbn. to Chinese Higher Edn. award State Coun., 1992, Ministry of Light Industry for rsch. on composite soaps, 1983, Remarkable Achievement in Sci. and Tech. Invention and Innovation, UN, 1994; Excellent Advanced Sci. Rsch. fellow Wuxi, 1990, 93. Mem. China Assn. Surfactants and Detergent Industry (hon. dir. 1992, standing dir. 1983-92), Jiangsu Soc. of Daily Chem. Industry (chmn. 1978-85), Am. Chem. Soc. Home: Madison Heights, Mich. Died Dec. 20, 2009.

YAGER, VINCENT COOK, retired bank executive; b. Chgo., June 15, 1928; s. James Vincent and Juanita (Cook) Yager; m. Dorothy Marie Gallagher, Sept. 28, 1957; children: Susan Marie, Sheila Ann. BA, Grinnell Coll., 1951. V.p. comml. loan dept. Madison Bank & Trust, Chgo., 1963-68; v.p. fin. Cor-Plex Internat. Corp., Chgo., 1968-70; pres., CEO, dir. First Nat. Bank Blue Island, Ill., 1970-89; pres., CEO Great Lakes Fin. Resources, Inc., Matteson, Ill., 1982-96, bd. dirs.; ret. With US Army, 1951—53, ETO. Mem.: Econ. Club Chgo., Bankers Club Chgo., Robert Morris Assocs. (pres. chpt. 1981—82), Midlothian Country Club, Rotary. Home: Villa Park, Ill. Died Feb. 14, 2010.

YAMAMOTO, WILLIAM SHIGERU, physiologist, educator; b. Cleve., Sept. 22, 1924; s. Soichi T. and Toyo (Sanada) Y.; m. Mary Ann Stevens, June 19, 1954; children: Kathryn, Polly, Ruth. AB, Park Coll., 1945; MD, U. Pa., 1949, MS (hon.), 1971. Diplomate Nat. Bd. Med. Examiners. Intern Hosp. of U. Pa., Phila., 1951-52; instr. physiology U. Pa. Sch. Medicine, Phila., 1950-51, asst. prof., 1957-62, assoc. prof., 1962-66, prof., 1966-71; prof. biomath. UCLA Sch. Medicine, 1970-71; prof. computer medicine George Washington U., Washington, from 1971, chmn. computer medicine, 1971-89, dir. Robert Wood Johnson clin. scholars Washington, 1975-79. Chmn. Computer Rsch. Study sect., NIH, Bethesda, Md., 1963-67; mem. Nat. Adv. Rsch. Resources Coun. NIH, Bethesda, 1971-75; cons. Am. Coll. Ob-Gyn., Washington, 1989-91. Author: (book) Physiological Control and Regulation, 1962, Ay's Neuroanatomy of Celegans, 1991; contbr. over 50 papers to profl. jours., 1988—. Cons. Nat. Ctr. Health Svcs. Rsch., Arlington, Va., 1969-74; active NAS-NAE com. Health Care Tech., Washington, 1976-77. Capt. U.S. Army Med. Corps, 1953-55. Mem. APA, AAAS, Am. Coll. Preventive Medicine, Assn. Computing Machinery, Am. Coll. Med. Informatics, Biomed. Engring. Soc. (bd. dirs. 1978-81), D.C. Columbia Med. Soc. (parliamentarian 1972). Avocations: construction, instrument making. Home: Arlington, Va. Died Mar. 6, 2009.

YASUNOBU, KERRY T., biochemist, educator; b. Seattle, Nov. 21, 1925; s. Seiji and Chiyono (Kobayashi) Yasunobu; children: Steven, Chrissie. BS, U. Wash., 1950, PhD, 1954. Asst. prof. U. Hawaii, Honolulu, 1958—60, assoc. prof., 1960—64, prof., from 1964. Mem.: Am. Soc. Biol. Chemists, Am. Chem. Soc., Sigma Xi. Home: Honolulu, Hawaii. Died Oct. 4, 2009.

YEAMANS, GEORGE THOMAS, librarian, educator; b. Nov. 7, 1929; s. James Norman and Dolphine Sophia (Manhart) Yeamans; m. Mary Ann Seng, Feb. 1, 1958; children: Debra, Susan, Julia. AB, U. Va., 1950; MLS, U. Ky., 1955; EdD, Ind. U., 1965. Asst. audio-visual dir. Ind. State U., Terre Haute, 1957—58; asst. film libr. Ball State U., Muncie, Ind., 1958—61, film libr., 1961—69, assoc. prof. libr. sci., 1969—72, prof., 1972—95, prof. emeritus, from 1995. Cons. Pendleton (Ind.) Sch. Corp., 1962, 67, Captioned Films for the Deaf Workshop, Muncie, 1963—65, Decatur (Ind.) Sch. Sys., 1978; adjudicator Ind. Media Fair, 1979—93, David Letterman Scholarship Program, 1993. Author: Projectionists' Programmed Primer, 1969, rev. edit., 1982, Mounting and Preserving Pictorial Materials, 1976, Tape Recording, 1978, Transparency Making, 1977, Photographic Principles, 1981, Computer Literacy-A Programmed Primer, 1985, Designing Dynamic Media Presentations, 1996, Robert F. Kennedy Archival Project, 1968—2004, Building Effective Creative Project Teams, 2000, Building Effective Creative Project Teams, rev. ed., 2007; songwriter: Branson Bound, 1996; contbr. articles to profl. jours. Campaign worker Wilson for Mayor, Muncie, 1979. With USMC, 1950—52. Recipient Citations of Achievement, Internat. Biog. Assn., Cambridge, Eng., 1973, Am. Biog. Assn., 1976, Mayor James P. Carey award for achievement for disting. contbns. to Ball State U. and City of Muncie, 1988; Video Info. Sys. grant, Ball State U., 1993. Mem.: ALA, NEA (del. assembly dept. audiovisual instrn. 1967), Audio-Visual Instrn. Dirs. Ind. (exec. bd. 1962—68, pres. 1966—67), Thomas Jefferson Soc. Alumni U. Va., Ind. Pub. Libr. Assn., Ind. Acad. Libr. Assn., Ind. Corp. and Network Libr. Assn., Ind. Libr. Fedn., Assn. Ednl. Comm. and Tech., Autisim Soc. Am., Assn. Ind. Media Educators (chmn. auditing com. 1979—81), Ind. Assn. Ednl. Comms. and Tech. (dist. dir. 1972—76), Am. Assn. Sch. Librs., Phi Delta Kappa. Republican. Unitarian-Universalist. Avocations: photography, stamp collecting/philately, coin collecting/numismatics, genealogy. Died Nov. 6, 2009.

YEN, TEH FU, civil and environmental engineering educator; b. Kun-Ming, China, Jan. 9, 1927; came to U.S., 1949; s. Kwang Pu and Ren (Liu) Y.; m. Shiao-Ping Siao, May 30, 1959 BS, Cen. China U., 1947; MS, W.Va. U., 1953; PhD, Va. Poly. Inst. and State U., 1956; PhD (hon.), Pepperdine U., 1982, Internat. U. Dubna, Russia, 1996, All Russian Petroleum Exploration Inst., St. Petersburg, Russia, 1999. Sr. research chemist Good Yr. Tire & Rubber Co., Akron, 1955-59; fellow Mellon Inst., Pitts., 1959-65; sr. fellow Carnegie-Mellon U., Pitts., 1965-68; assoc. prof. Calif. State U., Los Angeles, 1968-69, U. So. Calif., 1969-80, prof. civil engrng. & environ. engrng., 1980—2010. Hon. prof. Shanghai U. Sci. and Tech., 1986, U. Petroleum, Beijing, 1987, Daqing Petroleum Inst., 1992; cons. Universal Oil Products, 1968-76, Chevron Oil Field Rsch. Co., 1968-75, Finnigan Corp., 1976-77, GE, 1977-80, United Techs., 1978-79, TRW Inc., 1982-83, Exxon, 1981-82, DuPont, 1985-88, Biogas Rsch. Inst.-UN, Chengdu, 1991. Author: numerous tech. books; contbr. articles articles to profl. jours. Recipient Disting. Svc. award Tau Beta Pi, 1974, Imperial Crown Gold medal, Iran, 1976, Achievement award Chinese Engrng. and Sci. Assocs. So. Calif., 1977, award Phi Kappa Phi, 1982, Outstanding Contbn. honor Pi Epsilon Tau, 1984, Svc. award Republic of Honduras, 1989, award in Petroleum Chem. Am. Chem. Soc., 1994, Kapitsa Gold medal Russian Fedn., 1995. Fellow Chem. Soc., Inst. Petroleum, Am. Inst. Chemists; mem. Am. Chem. Soc. (life; bd. dirs. 1993, councillor, founder and chmn. geochemistry divsn. 1979-81, Chinese Acad. Scis. (standing com.), Acad. Scis. Russian Fedn. (academician, fgn. mem.), Assn. Environmental Engrng. and Sci. Profs. Home: Altadena, Calif. Died Jan. 12, 2010.

YEOMANS, GORDON ALLAN, retired education educator; b. Cherry Valley, Ohio, Sept. 30, 1921; s. Ralph Carey Yeomans and Margaret Warner; m. Marjorie Jo Roberts, Feb. 27, 1949; 1 child, Lynne Leigh Yeomans Craver. BA, U. S.W. La., 1951; MA, La. State U., 1952, PhD, 1966. Instr. U. Miss., Oxford, 1952; assoc. prof. Samford U., Birmingham, Ala., 1952-66, U. S.W. La., Lafayette, 1966-67; prof., dept. head Miss. U. for Women, Columbus, 1967-68; prof. U. Tenn., Knoxville, 1968-87, prof. emeritus, 1987. Cons. Andersen Electric Corp., Leeds, Ala., 1958, John Williamson Co., Birmingham, 1960-61, Birmingham (Ala.) Trust Bank, 1962, Union Carbide Corp., Oak Ridge, Tenn., 1969-81, Magnavox Corp., Asheville, N.C., 1975. Author: A Handbook for Speakers, 1969; contbr. author: The Heart of the Valley, 1976, Pamphlets and The American Revolution, 1976; contbr. articles to profl. jours. Program chmn. Knoxville Religious Bicentennial, 1976; adv. coun. Knoxville Alcohol and Drug Rehab. Ctr.; mem. 1st United Meth. Ch., Knoxville, religious drama dir. With USAAF, 1940-45. Tchr. grantee Danforth Found., 1956-57, summer 1963, Rsch. grantee U. Tenn., 1974, 75; named Speech Tchr. of Yr., State of Tenn., 1984. Mem. Speech Communication Assn., So. Speech Communication Assn., East Tenn. Hist. Soc., Knoxville Civil War Roundtable. Democrat. Avocation: antiquarian book dealer and collector. Home: Knoxville, Tenn. Died Apr. 15, 2010.

YERUSHALMI, YOSEF HAYIM, historian, educator; b. NYC, May 20, 1932; s. Leon and Eva (Kaplan) Y.; m. Ophra Pearly, Jan. 4, 1959; 1 child, Ariel. BA, Yeshiva U., 1953; M in Hebrew Lit., Jewish Theol. Sem. Am., 1957; MA, Columbia U., 1961, PhD, 1966; MA (hon.), Harvard, 1970; DHL (hon.), Jewish Theol. Sem. Am., 1987; LHD (hon.), Hebrew Union Coll., 1996; PhD (hon.), U. Haifa, 1997, Ludwig Maximilians U., Munich, 1997; DHL (hon.), Spertus Inst., 2002; PhD (hon.), Ecole Pratique des Hautes Etudes Sorbonne Paris, 2003. Instr. Jewish history Rutgers U., New Brunswick, NJ, 1963-66; asst. prof. Hebrew and Jewish History Harvard U., 1966-70, prof., 1970—80, Jacob E. Safra prof. Jewish history and Sephardic civilization, 1978-80, chmn. dept. near eastern langs. and civilizations, 1978-80, Salo Wittmayer Baron Prof. of Jewish History, Culture, Soc.; dir. Columbia U. Inst. Israel and Jewish Studies, NYC, 1980—2008, Baron prof. emeritus, 2008—09. Author: From Spanish Court to Italian Ghetto: Isaac Cardoso, A Study in Seventeenth-Century Marranism and Jewish Apologetics, 1971, Haggadah and History, 1975, The Lisbon Massacre of 1506, 1976, Zakhor: Jewish History and Jewish Memory, 1982, Freud's Moses: Judaism Terminable and Interminable, 1991, A Field in Anatot: Essays on Jewish History (in German), 1993, Servants of Kings and Not Servants of Servants: Some Aspects of the Political History of the Jews (in German), 1995, Sefardica: Essays on the History of the Jews, Marranos and New Christians of Hispano-Portuguese Origin (in French), 1998; author (in Hebrew): Spinoza on the Survival of the Jews, 1983; contbr. articles to profl. publs. on Spanish and Portuguese Jewry and history of psychoanalysis; chmn. publs. com. Jewish Publ. Soc., 1972-84; pres. Leo Baeck Inst., 1986-91. Bd. dirs. Conf. Jewish Social Studies, Psycho analytic Research and Devel. Fund, Editorial Bd., History and Memory. Recipient Newman medal CUNY, 1975, Nat. Jewish Book award, 1983, 92, Ansley award Columbia U. Press, 1968, Achievement medal Nat. Found. Jewish Culture, 1995, Leopold Lucas prize U. Tübingen, Germany, 2005; Kent fellow, 1963, Nat. Found. Jewish Culture, 1964, NEH, 1976-77, Rockefeller Found., 1983-84, Guggenheim Found., 1989-90, Carl Friedrich von Siemens Stiftung fellow, 1996-97, fellow Inst. Advanced Studies Tel Aviv U., 2004. Fellow Am. Acad. Jewish Research, Am. Acad. Arts and Scis., Acad. Portuguesa da História Lisbon (hon.), Acad. Sci. Lisboa (hon.). Died Dec. 8, 2009.

YLVISAKER, WILLIAM TOWNEND, retired manufacturing executive; b. St. Paul, Feb. 25, 1924; s. Lauritz S. and Winifred Jean (Townend) Y.; children: Laurie Ellen, Elizabeth Maren, Amy Townend, Jon Alastair. Grad., Lawrenceville Sch., 1943; BS, Yale U., 1948. Security analyst Bank N.Y., 1948-49; gen. mgr. Lake Forest Motor Sales, Ill., 1949-52; v.p., gen. mgr. Pheoll Mfg. Co., Chgo., 1952-58; pres. Parker-Kalon div. Gen. Am. Transp. Corp., Clifton, NJ, 1958-61; group v.p., dir. Gen. Am. Transp. Corp., Chgo., 1961-67; chmn., CEO Gould Inc., 1967-86, chmn. exec. com., 1986; pres. Datron Inc., 1988-90. Bd. dirs. Penske Corp., Red Bank, N.J.; bd. govs. Arlington Internat. Racecourse. Bd. dirs. United Republican Fund Ill.; council Grad. Sch. Bus., U. Chgo.; trustee Lawrenceville (N.J.) Sch., Rush-Presbyn.-St. Luke's Med. Sch., Solomon R. Guggenheim Found.; bd. govs. U.S. Polo Assn. Served as ensign USNR, 1943-45. Mem. Conf. Bd., Northwestern U. Assos. Clubs: Links (N.Y.C.); Barrington Hills Country; Racquet (N.Y.C.), Chicago (Chgo.); Palm Beach Polo and Country (West Palm Beach, Fla.); Bath and Tennis (Palm Beach); Meadow (Rolling Meadows, Ill.). Died Feb. 6, 2010.

YOHE, ROBERT L., chemical company executive; b. NYC, May 11, 1936; s. Robert C. and Berdene (Walker) Y. BSChemE, Lafayette Coll., 1958; MBA, Harvard U., 1964. With sales product mgmt. Hooker Chem. Corp., Niagara Falls, N.Y., 1964-68; pres. Chinook Mobilodge, Inc., Yakima, Wash., 1968-71, Environ. Svcs., Inc., Midland Park, N.J., 1971-72; dir. indsl. systems Hooker Chem. Corp., Niagara Falls, 1972-76, v.p., gen. mgr. Durez div., 1976-80, v.p. environ. safety & health, 1980-81; gen. mgr. indsl. chems. Uniroyal Inc., Oxford, Conn., 1981-83; v.p. mergers, acquisitions Olin Corp., Stamford, Conn., 1983-85, pres. chems. group, from 1985, corp. exec. v.p., from 1987. Bd. dirs. Chlorine Inst., Washington, exec. com. 1989; advisors sch. mgmt. SUNY, Buffalo, 1979-80, De Graff Meml. Hosp., North Tonawanda, N.Y., 1979; pres.'s adv. bd. Teikyo Post U., 1990—. Bd. dirs. United Way, North Tonawanda, 1978-79, Southwestern Area Commerce and Industry Assn. of Conn., 1989, Soap and Detergent Assn., 1990; mem. Nat. Lafayette Coun., Easton, Pa., 1987-88. Mem. Soc. Chem. Industry, Bus. Coun. So. Conn. (bd. dirs.), Ambs'. Round Table (forum world affairs 1988—), Highfield Country Club (Middlebury, Conn.), Harvard Club N.Y. Avocations: shooting, golf, tennis, squash, gardening. Home: Middlebury, Conn. Died Oct. 13, 2009.

YORK, JEROME BAILEY (JERRY YORK), private equity firm executive; b. Memphis, June 22, 1938; m. Eilene York; 4 children. BS, U.S. Mil. Acad., 1960; MS, MIT, 1961; MBA, U. Mich., 1966. Various engrng. positions Gen. Motors Corp., Pontiac, Mich., 1962-67; various managerial positions Ford Motor Co., Deerborn, Mich., 1967-70; dir. strategic planning RCA Corp., Hertz Corp. (subs.), 1970-72, v.p., 1972-75; group v.p. Baker Industries, Inc., Parsippany, NJ, 1976-78; pres. Delta Truck Body Co., Inc., Montgomeryville, Pa., 1978-79; asst. contr. Chrysler de Mex. Chrysler Corp., Highland Park, Mich., 1979-82, mng. dir. Chrysler de Mex., 1982-85, v.p., gen. mgr. Dodge divsn., 1986-90, v.p., contr., 1989-90, exec. v.p., CFO, 1990-93; sr. v.p., CFO IBM Corp., Armonk, NY, 1993—95; vice chmn. Tracinda Corp., 1995—99; chmn., pres., CEO Micro Warehouse, Inc., Norwalk, 2000—03; founder, CEO Harwinton Capital LLC, 2000—10. Bd. dirs. MGM Grand, Inc., 1995—2002, Apple Inc. (formerly Apple Computer, Inc.), 1997—2010, Tyco Internat. Ltd., 2002—10, Exide Technologies, 2005—06, Gen. Motors Corp., 2006, Dana Holdings Corp., 2008—10. Home: Oakland, Mich. Died Mar. 18, 2010.

YOST, JAMES EVERETT, retired union official; b. Bluefield, Va., Oct. 16, 1925; s. Lorenzia Wingo and Emma Bell (Smith) Y.; m. Ruth Adkins, Nov. 13, 1946 (div. 1974); children: Conner E., Randel W., Ernest W.; m. Patricia Dickey, July 20, 1974. Grad. high sch. Truck driver State Line Distbg. Co., 1947-51; with Norfolk & Western Ry. Co., Bluefield, W.Va., 1947-56; asst. gen. chmn., sec.-treas. system council 16 Internat. Brotherhood Blacksmiths, Drop Forgers and Helpers (now merged Internat. Brotherhood Boilermakers, Iron Ship Builders, Blacksmiths, Forgers a, 1951-56; asst. to pres. ry. employees dept. AFL-CIO, Chgo., 1956-69, pres., 1969-80, exec. sec.-treas., 1980; internat. rep. Internat. Brotherhood Boilermakers, Iron Ship Builders, Blacksmiths, Forgers and Helpers, 1980-83; carrier mem. Nat. R.R. Adjustment Bd., from 1983; exec. dir. Carrier Mems. Nat. Railroad Adjustment Bd., 1986-93; ret., 1993. Mem. steering com. Nat. Apprenticeship and Tng. Conf., 1970-75; vice chmn. Cooperating Ry. Labor Orgns.; mem. Ry. Labor-Mgmt. Com., 1969-77 Served with AUS, 1944-46, ETO. Democrat. Home: Dania, Fla. Died Feb. 8, 2009.

YOUNATHAN, EZZAT SAAD, retired biochemistry educator; b. Deirut, Egypt, Aug. 25, 1922; came to U.S., 1950; m. Margaret Tims, Aug. 11, 1958; children: Janet Nadya, Carol Miriam. BSc in Chemistry with honors, Cairo U., 1944; MS in Chemistry, Fla. State U., 1953, PhD in Chemistry, 1955. Chemist Govt. Labs., Cairo, 1944-50; postdoctoral rsch. assoc. Coll. Medicine U. Ill., Chgo., 1955-57; asst. prof. Fla. State U., Tallahassee, 1957-59; asst. prof. Sch. Medicine U. Ark., Little Rock, 1959-63, assoc. prof., 1963-68, acting head, 1963-66; prof. biochemistry La. State U., Baton Rouge, 1968—98; ret. Vis. prof. U. Wis., Madison, 1966-67, U. Calif., Berkeley, 1978; chair rsch. grant adv. com. So. U., Baton Rouge, 1993-96. Contbg. author: (book) The Regulation of Carbohydrate Formation and Utilization in Mammals, 1981; contbr. 75 articles to profl. jours. Seagrams Internat. fellow Seagrams Co., Inc., 1950-51, Sr. Rsch. fellow NIH, 1966-67. Mem. AMA, Am. Soc. Biochemistry and Molecular Biology, Am. Chem. Soc., Soc. Exptl. Biol. Medicine. Mem. First Christian Ch. Achievements include discovery of new class of oral hypoglycemic agents; research in metabolism and chemistry of carbohydrates. Home: Baton Rouge, La. Died Feb. 7, 2009.

YOUNG, HOWARD THOMAS, foreign language educator; b. Cumberland, Md., Mar. 24, 1926; s. Samuel Phillip and Sarah Emmaline (Frederick) Y.; m. Carol Osborne, Oct. 5, 1949 (div. 1966); children: Laurie Margaret, Jennifer Anne; m. Edra Lee Airheart, May 23, 1981; 1 child, Timothy Howard. BS summa cum laude, Columbia U., NYC, 1950, MA, 1952, PhD, 1954. Lectr. Columbia U., NYC, 1950-54; asst. prof. Romance langs. Pomona Coll., Claremont, Calif., 1954-60, assoc. prof., 1960-66, Smith prof. Romance langs., 1966-98, prof. emeritus, from 1998. Vis. prof. Middlebury Program in Spain, Madrid, 1986-87, U. Zaragoza, 1967-68, Columbia U., summer 2000; chief reader Spanish AP Ednl. Testing Svc., Princeton, 1975-78, chmn. Spanish lang. devel. commn., 1976-79; mem. fgn. lang. adv. commn. Coll. Bd., NYC, 1980-83; mem. West Coast selection commn. Mellon Fellowships for Humanities, Princeton, 1984-86, European selection com., 1987, 90; trans. cons. Smithsonian Inst. Author: The Victorious Expression, 1964, Juan Ramón Jimènez, 1967, The Line in the Margin, 1980; editor: T.S. Eliot and Hispanic Modernity, 1995; contbr. London Times Higher Edn. Supplement; contbr. numerous articles and book revs. to profl. jours. Dir. NEH summer seminar for Sch. tchrs., 1993. Served with USNR, 1944-46, ETO. Fellow Del Amo Found., 1960-61, NEH, 1975, 89-90; Fulbright fellow; 1967-68; Rockefeller Study Ctr. scholar, 1976. Mem. MLA, Assn. Tchrs. Spanish and Portuguese, Am. Comparative Lit. Assn., Acad. Am. Poets, Assn. Lit. Scholars and Critics. Home: Claremont, Calif. Died Jan. 31, 2009.

YOUNG, JOHN RIPPEY, hotel company executive; b. Stamford, Conn., Aug. 18, 1933; s. Lloyd Van Vleet and Dorothy (Irving) Y.; m. June Higgins, Aug. 20, 1955 (div. Jan. 1972); children— Mark, Cynthia, Pamela; m. Lois Ronk, Aug. 1975 BA, Middlebury Coll, 1957. Asst. v.p. Shawmut Bank, Boston, 1957-67; asst. to chmn. bd. Sheraton Corp., Boston, 1967-72, v.p., 1972-78, sr. v.p., 1978-80, sr. v.p. and treas., from 1980. Served with U.S. Army, 1953-55 Mem. Urban Land Inst., Am. Hotel and Motel Assn., Nat. Assn. Corporate Treas. Clubs: Dedham Country and Polo (Mass.); Groton Long Point Yacht (Conn.). Avocations: skiing; sailing; boating. Home: Dover, Mass. Died Apr. 1, 2010.

YOUNG, MARGARET BUCKNER, civic worker, author; b. Campbellsville, Ky., 1921; d. Frank W. and Eva (Carter) Buckner; m. Whitney M. Young, Jan. 2, 1944 (dec. Mar. 1971); children: Marcia Elaine, Lauren Lee. BA, Ky. State Coll., 1942; MA, U. Minn., 1946. Instr. Ky. State Coll., 1942—44; Ky. State Coll Spelman Coll., Atlanta, 1957—60. Dir. emeritus NY Life Ins. Co.; alt. del. UN Gen. Assembly, 1973; mem. pub. policy com. Advt. Coun.; chmn. Whitney M. Young, Jr. Meml. Found., 1971—92; trustee Met. Mus. Art, 1976—90, Emerita Lincoln Ctr. Performing Arts; bd. govs. UN Assn., 1975—82; bd. visitors US Mil. Acad., 1978—80; dir. Philip Morris Cos., 1972—91. Author: How to Bring Up Your Children Without Prejudice, 1965, The First Book of American Negroes, 1966, The Picture Life of Martin Luther King, Jr., 1968, The Picture Life of Ralph J. Bunche, 1968, Black American Leaders-Watts, 1969, The Picture Life of Thurgood Marshall, 1970. Home: Denver, Colo. Died Dec. 5, 2009.

YOUNG, ROBERT JOHN, animal science educator; b. Calgary, Alta., Canada, Feb. 10, 1923; came to U.S., 1956, naturalized, 1965; s. Harold P. and Kate A. (Thomson) Y.; m. Greta G. Milne, June 16, 1950; children— Kenneth W., Donna E. BSA. with honors, U. B.C., 1950; PhD, Cornell U., 1953. Research asso. dept. med. research Barting & Best, Toronto, Ont., Can., 1953-56; research chemist Internat. Minerals and Chem. Corp., Skokie, Ill., 1956-58, Proctor and Gamble Co., Cin., 1958-60; prof. animal nutrition Cornell U., 1960-83, emeritus prof. animal sci., from 1983, chmn. dept. poultry sci., 1965-76, chmn. dept. animal sci., 1976-83, assoc. dir. research, 1983-84, assoc. dean Coll. Agr. and Life Scis., 1984-85. Author: (with M.L. Scott, M.C. Nesheim) Nutrition of the Chicken, 1976; Contbr. articles in field to profl. jours. Served with RCAF, 1942-45. Mem. Am. Inst. Nutrition, Poultry Sci. Assn., Am. Soc. Animal Sci., Am. Soc. Dairy Sci. Died Apr. 19, 2010.

YOUNG, SHELDON MIKE, lawyer, author; b. Cleve., Aug. 27, 1926; s. Jack and Ray Y.; m. Margery Ann Polster, Dec. 25, 1948 (div. 1988); children: Jeffrey, Martin, Janet; m. Bette Abel Roth, Nov. 11, 1988. BA, Ohio State U., 1948, JD, 1951; LLM, Case Western Res. U., 1962. Bar: Ohio 1951, U.S. Dist. Ct. (no. dist.) Ohio. Gen. counsel Eugene M. Klein & Assoc., Actuaries, Cleve., 1952-72; assoc. Shapiro, Persky & Marken, Cleve., 1972-74; counsel pension tech. svcs. dept. CNA Ins., Chgo., 1974-76; ptnr. Weiss & Young, Cleve., 1976; of counsel Arter & Hadden, Cleve., 1977-85, Squire, Sanders & Dempsey, Cleve., 1985-87; pvt. practice Columbus, 1987-91; of counsel Schwartz, Kelm, Warren & Rubenstein, Columbus, 1991—93, Walter & Haverfield, Columbus, from 1993. Instr. Case Western Res. U. Law Sch., 1962-82, 85, U. Akron Law Sch., 1984, 88. Author: Pension and Profit Sharing Plans, 7 vols., 1977-93, (novel) Toledoth-City of Generations, 2003, rev., 2006; freelance writer for newspapers and mags.; contbr. articles to pension jours. Served with USN, WWII. Recipient award Nathan Burkan Meml. Copyright Competition, 1951. Fellow Am. Coll. Employee Benefits Counsel (charter); mem. ABA, Cleve. Bar Assn., Masons. Jewish. Died Nov. 13, 2009.

YOW, RAYMOND MURRAY, insurance company executive, retired physician; b. Raleigh, NC, Apr. 12, 1924; s. Vernon Spencer and Nell P. Yow; m. M.L. Collins, Feb. 3, 1951 (div. 1988); children: Patricia, Margaret, Norman; m. Cathaleen F. Tawes, Apr. 27, 1988. Student, Va. Mil. Inst., 1941-43, U. Chgo., 1944; BS, U. Ill., 1945, MD, 1948. Diplomate Am. Bd. Urology. Practice medicine specializing in urology., Salisbury, Md., 1955-87; ret., 1987; sr. v.p. Med. Mutual Liability Ins. Soc. Md., Hunt Valley, Md., 1975-83, chief exec. officer, from 1983, also chmn. bd., from 1983. Served to lt. (j.g.) USN, 1949-51 Mem. ACS, Am. Urol. Assn. (pres. mid-Atlantic sect. 1973), Soc. Internat. de Urologie. Republican. Methodist. Avocations: golf, boating. Home: Berlin, Md. Died Nov. 30, 2009.

YU, AITING TOBEY, engineering executive; b. Chekiang, China, Jan. 6, 1921; came to U.S., 1945, naturalized, 1955; s. H.K. and A. (Chow) Y.; m. Natalie Kwok, Nov. 10, 1951; children: Pamela, Leonard T. BS, Nat. Cen. U., Chungking, China, 1943; SM, MIT, 1946; PhD, Lehigh U., 1949; MBA, Columbia U., 1972. Registered profl. engr., Fla. Asst. prof. engring. NYU, 1949-51; design engr. Hewitt-Robins Inc., 1951-54, chief design engr., 1955-58, engring. mgr., 1958-59, dir. systems engring. Totowa, N.J., 1967-68, v.p. ops., 1968-71; tech. dir. West S.Am. Overseas Corp., NYC, 1959-67; prin. A.T. Yu Cons. Engrs., 1971-72; co-founder, chmn. Orba Corp., Mountain Lakes, N.J., from 1972, now chmn. emeritus. Contbr. articles to profl. jours; patentee in field. Recipient nat. outstanding engring. achievement awards by ASCE, NSPE, AIME, ASME; inducted into Nat. Mining Hall of Fame, 1988. Mem. NAE, AIME (chmn. minerals processing div., SME pres. 1986), NSPE, Nat. Acad. Engring., Sigma Xi. Home: Haiku, Hawaii. Died Apr. 8, 2009.

ZABAN, ERWIN, diversified manufacturing company executive; b. Atlanta, Aug. 17, 1921; s. Mandle and Sara Unis (Feidelson) Z.; m. Judy Zaban; children: Carol Zaban Cooper, Laura Zaban Dinerman, Sara Kay Franco. Officer Zep Mfg. Co., 1942-62; exec. v.p. Nat. Service Industries, Atlanta, 1962-66, pres., 1966-79, chief exec. officer, 1972-87, chmn., from 1975, also dir. Bd. dir. Engraph, Inc., Wachovia Corp.; elected mem. bd. visitors Berry Coll. Bd. dirs. Atlanta Symphony Orch., 1982, Jewish Home for the Aged, 1985; trustee Atlanta Hist. Soc., 1985. Named Man of Yr. B'nai B'rith, 1977, Father of Yr. Father's Day Coun.; recipient Disting. Svc. award Atlanta Urban League, 1979, NCCJ, 1988, Human Rels. award Anti-Defamation League, 1981, Bd. Govs. award 11-Alive Community Svc. Awards, 1990; named to Ga. State U. Coll. Bus. Adminstrn. Hall of Fame, 1989. Mem. Standard Club, Commerce Club (bd. dirs.). Home: Atlanta, Ga. Died July 6, 2010.

ZACKHEIM, MARC ALLEN, child psychologist, editor; b. NYC, Oct. 12, 1950; s. Seymour David and Blanche (Kalt) Z.; m. Victoria Fraginals; children: Timonthy, Patrick, David, Marc Jr. AA, U. Fla., 1970, BA with high honors, 1972; MS, Fla. State U., 1974, PhD, 1977. Lic. psychologist Fla., Ill., Ind., Ala. Intern Duke U. Med. Ctr., Durham, N.C., 1976; postdoctoral fellow in psychology Fla. State U., 1978; resident in psychology Rush-Presbyn. St. Luke's Med. Ctr., Chgo., 1979; attending child psychologist Assocs. in Adolescent Psychiatry, Chgo., 1979-85, dir. tng., 1981-85; founder Assocs. in Clin. Psychology and ACP Group Homes, Forest Park, Ill., from 1985; v.p. Westlake Hosp., Orlando, Fla., from 1985, Linden Oaks Hosp., Naperville, Ill., from 1989; faculty Auburn (Ala.) U.; attending childpsychologist Riveredge Hosp., Forest Park, Ill., 1979—2005, Koala Hosp., Plymouth, Ind., 1992—94, Lebanon, Ind., 1993—95. Cons. editor Ednl. and Psychol. Rsch.; contbr. articles to profl. jours., including Readins, A Jour. Am. Orthopsych. Assn. USPHS fellow, 1973-76; apptd. State of Ill. Guardianship and Advocacy Commn. Human Rights Authority, chmn., 1990-94. Fellow Am. Orthopsychiat. Assn.; mem. Am. Psychol. Assn., Ill. Psychol. Assn., Ala. Psychol. Assn., Midwest Psychol. Assn., Fla. Psychol. Assn., S.E. Psychol. Assn. Psychoanalytic Psychology, Acad. Psychosomatic Medicine. Home: Lake Bluff, Ill. Died Nov. 19, 2009.

ZALL, PAUL MAXWELL, language educator, consultant; m. Elisabeth Weisz, June 21, 1948; children: Jonathan, Barnaby, Andrew. BA, Swarthmore Coll., 1948; AM, Harvard U., 1950, PhD, 1951. Teaching fellow Harvard U., 1950-51; instr. Cornell U., 1951-55, U. Oreg., 1955-56; research editor Boeing Co., 1956-57; asst. prof. Calif. State Coll., Los Angeles, 1957-61, asso. prof., 1961-64, prof. English, 1964-86; research scholar, cons. to library docents Huntington Library, San Marino, Calif., 1986-96; acting chmn. dept. Calif. State Coll., 1969-71. Cons. in report writing, proposal preparation and brochures to industry and govt. agys., 1957-99. Author: Elements of Technical Report Writing, 1962, Hundred Merry Tales, 1963, Nest of Ninnies, 1970, Weakly Blast, 1960-85, Literary Criticism of William Wordsworth, 1966, (with John Durham) Plain Style, 1967, Simple Cobler of Aggawam in America, 1969; (with J.R. Trevor) Proverb to Poem, 1970, Selected Satires of Peter Pindar, 1971, Comical Spirit of Seventy Six, 1976, (with Leonard Franco) Practical Writing, 1978, Ben Franklin Laughing, 1980; (with J.A.L. Lemay) Autobiography of Benjamin Franklin, 1981; Norton Critical Edition of Franklin's Autobiography, 1986, Abe Lincoln Laughing, 1983, 95; (with E. Birdsall) Descriptive Sketches, 1984, Mark Twain Laughing, 1985, Being Here, 1987, George Washington Laughing, 1989, Franklin's Autobiography: Model Life, 1989, Founding Mothers, 1991, Becoming American, 1993, 98, Lincoln's Legacy, 1994, Wit and Wisdom of the Founding Fathers, 1996, Blue and Gray Laughing, 1996, Lincoln on Lincoln, 1999, 2003, Dolley Madison, 2001, Franklin on Franklin, 2001, Jefferson on Jefferson, 2002, Washington on Washington, 2003, Adams on Adams, 2004, Benjamin Franklin's Humor, 2005, Lincoln's Legacy of Laughter, 2007. Pres. Friends of South Pasadena Library, 1967-70. Served with USAAF, 1942-45, ETO. Recipient Outstanding Prof. award, 1965; grantee, John Carter Brown Libr., Huntington Libr., 1993; fellow, Am. Philos. Soc., 1964, 1966, Huntington Libr., 1993. Home: South Pasadena, Calif. Died Dec. 16, 2009.

ZAMBIE, ALLAN JOHN, retired lawyer; b. Cleve., June 9, 1935; s. Anton J. and Martha (Adamski) Z.; m. Nancy Hall, Sept. 22, 1973. Student, Ohio U., 1953-54; BA, Denison U., 1957; LL.B., Western Res. U. (now Case Western Res. U.), 1960. Bar: Ohio 1960. Asso. firm Hribar and Conway, Euclid, Ohio, 1961-63; staff atty. The Higbee Co., Cleve., 1963-67, asst. sec., 1967-69, sec., 1969-74, v.p.-sec., 1974-88, gen. counsel, 1978-88; v.p., sec., gen. counsel The Lamson & Sessions Co., Cleve., 1989-94; of counsel Conway, Marken, Wyner, Kurant & Kern Co., LPA, Cleve., 1994—95; v.p.-sec. John P. Murphy Found., Cleve., 2000, exec. v.p., 2008, sr. advisor, sec., 2008—09. V.p. sec. Kulas Found., 2001—06, v.p., sec., treas. Kulas Found., 2006-08. Trustee Cleve. Music Sch. Settlement, pres. bd. trustees, 1980—82, treas., 1996—2001; trustee N.E. Ohio affiliate Am. Heart Assn., 1989—96. With US Army, 1960—61. Mem.: Am. Soc. Corporate Secs. (nat. v.p. 1977), Cleve. Bar Assn., Ohio Bar Assn. Home: Beachwood, Ohio. Died May 11, 2010.

ZARZAR, NAKHLEH PACIFICO, psychiatrist; b. Bethlehem, Palestine, Jan. 21, 1932; came to U.S., 1956; s. Pacifico and Anita Zarzar; m. Doris Azzam, Sept. 22, 1957; children: Michael, Nicholas, David. BA, Am. U. Beirut, 1952, MD, 1956. Diplomate Am. Bd. Psychiatry and Neurology. Clin. dir. family sect. John Umstead Hosp., Butner, N.C., 1959-62, clin. dir., dir. tng., 1962-63, supt., 1964-68; interim supt. Dorothea Dix Hosp., Raleigh, N.C., 1966; regional commr. N.C. Dept. Mental Health, Raleigh, 1966-73, dir., 1973-77; pvt. practice Raleigh, 1971-73 and from 76. Adj. prof. U. N.C., Chapel Hill, 1959—; cons. NIMH, Washington, 1971-77, Vance County Mental Health, Henderson, N.C., 1977-93; lectr. Duke U., Durham, N.C., 1976—. Chmn. Commn. on Mental Health and Human Svcs., So. Regional Edn. Bd., 1977; chair sr. citizens com. Rotary Club West Raleigh, 1991-93. Recipient Spl. award N.C. Mental Health Assn., 1976, N.C. Psychiat. Assn., 1990, Christan Holloman award Raleigh Rotary Club, 1966. Fellow Am. Psychiat. Assn. (life); mem. AMA, N.C. Med. Assn., So. Psychiat. Assn. Avocations: bridge, chess, gardening. Home: Raleigh, NC. Died Aug. 1, 2009.

ZAYEK, FRANCIS MANSOUR, archbishop emeritus; b. Manzanillo, Cuba, Oct. 18, 1920; s. Mansour and Mary (Coury) Zayek. Attended, St. Joseph's Cath. U., Beirut, 1938; DD, PhD, U. Propagation of Faith, 1947; DCL, Pontifical Lateran Univ., 1951. Ordained priest Maronite rite, 1946; rector Maronite Cathedral of Holy Family, Cairo, 1951—56; Oriental sec. to Vatican Apostolic Internunciature; mem. Archdiocesan Tribunal, 1951—56; promoter of justice Sacred Roman Rota, 1956—58; prof. Oriental canon law Internat. Coll. St. Anselm, Rome, 1958—60, Pontifical Lateran Univ., Rome, 1960—61; ordained bishop, 1962; aux. bishop Sao Sebastiano do Rio de Janeiro, Brazil, 1962—66; presided over First Ann. Maronite Conv., Washington, 1964; bishop, exarch Maronite Apostolic Exarchate in the U.S., Detroit, 1966—71; bishop Eparchy of St. Maron of Bklyn., 1971—82; archbishop, bishop Eparchy of St. Maron in Bklyn., 1982—96, archbishop emeritus, 1996—2010. Decorated knight comdr. Equestrian Order of Holy Sepulchre of Jerusalem; recipient medal of merit, Govt. of Republic Italy, 1966. Roman Catholic. Home: Fort Lauderdale, Fla. Died Sept. 14, 2010.

ZEEHANDELAAR, DAVID NICO, lawyer; b. NYC, Sept. 27, 1954; s. Frederik J. and Gertrude B. (Bette) Z.; m. Mona R. Gusoff, June 26, 1977; children: Rachel, Daniel. BA in Polit. Sci., U. Pa., 1976; JD, Villanova U., 1979. Bar: U.S. Ct. Appeals (3d cir.) 1979, N.J. 1982, U.S. Dist. Ct. N.J. 1982, Pa. 1980, U.S. Dist. Ct. (ea. and mid. dists.) Pa. 1982, U.S. Supreme Ct., 1994, U.S. Dist. Ct. (sou. dist.) NY, 1998, U.S. Ct. Appeals (2nd cir.), 2000, U.S. Dist. Ct. (we. dist.) Pa., 2001. Law clk. to presiding justice Ct. Common Pleas, Phila., 1979—80; assoc. Bolger Picker Hankin & Tannenbaum, Phila., 1980—87, ptnr., 1987—96; judge pro tempore Ct. of Common Pleas, Phila., 1996—2010; ptnr., litigation dept. Blank Rome LLP, Phila., 1996—2010. Bar panelist, approved civil arbitrator Superior Ct. of NJ, Law Div., Camden, from 1996. Co-author: Manual for Practice in the Court of Common Pleas, 1983. Mem. ABA, Pa. Bar Assn., N.J. Bar Assn., Phila. Bar Assn., Camden County Bar Assn., Def. Research Inst., Phila. Assn. Def. Counsel, N.J. Assn. Def. Lawyers. Democrat. Jewish. Home: Villanova, Pa. Died Mar. 19, 2010.

ZEITLIN, HERBERT ZAKARY, retired college administrator, educational consultant, writer; b. NYC, Jan. 14; s. Leonard and Martha Josephine (Soff) Zeitlin; m. Eugenia F. Pawlik, July 3, 1949; children: Mark Clyde, Joyce Therese Zeitlin Harris, Ann Victoria, Clare Katherine. BS, NYU, 1947, MA, 1949; EdD, Stanford U., 1956. Tchr. Mepham HS, Bellmore, NY, 1946—47, Nassau County Vocat. Edn. Extension Bd., Mineola, NY; electronics instr., adj. faculty Mephan CC; tchr., counselor, dir. testing Phoenix Union HS and Coll. Dist.; dean eve. coll., prin. high sch. Antelope Valley Union HS and Coll. Dist., Lancaster, Calif.; dean instrn. Southwestern Coll., Chula Vista, Calif.; pres., supt., cons. Triton Coll., River Grove, Ill., 1964—79; dean, pres. West LA Coll., 1976-80; pres. Trident Cons., LA, mgmt. cons., 1976—2010; adj. faculty Ariz. State U., Flagstaff, No. Ill. U., DeKalb, U. Calif., Santa Barbara. Author: Turbulent Birth of Triton College, 2001, Corruption: How to Fight It and Win, 2004, What Makes A Teacher Great?, 2007; editor: in field. Pres. Antelope Valley Breeze & Sage, Bon Vivant Homeowners Assn.; mayor Upper Woodland Hills, Calif. With USAAF, 1942—46. Recipient Spl. commendation, Chgo. Tribune, Richard Ogilvie, former Gov. Ill., Spl. Achievement award for visionary accomplishment, Ill. Sch. Adminstrs. Assn.; named Adminstr. of the Yr., Triton Coll. Faculty Assn., 1974, Most Influential Educator in Ill., Chgo. Sun Times. Mem.: Ariz. State Vocat. Assn. (pres.), Ariz. Vocat. Guidance Assn. (pres.), Maywood Ill. Rotary (pres.), Antelope Valley Rotary (pres.). Home: Woodland Hills, Calif. Died Mar. 2, 2010.

ZELLNER, ARNOLD, economics, econometrics and statistics professor; b. Bklyn., Jan. 2, 1927; s. Israel and Doris (Kleiman) Z.; m. Agnes Marie Sumares, June 20, 1953; children— David S., Philip A., Samuel N., Daniel A., Michael A. AB in Physics, Harvard U., Cambridge, Mass., 1949; PhD in Econs., U. Calif., Berkeley, 1957; D (hon.), U. Autonoma de Madrid, 1986, Tecnia de Lisboa, Portugal, 1991, U. Kiel, Germany, 1998, Erasmus U., Rotterdam, Netherlands, 2006. Asst., then assoc. prof. econs. U. Wash., 1955-60; Fulbright vis. prof. Netherlands Sch. Econs., Rotterdam, 1960-61; assoc. prof., then prof. econs. U. Wis., 1961-66; H.G.B. Alexander disting. service prof. econs. and statistics U. Chgo., 1966-96, prof. emeritus, 1996—2010; dir. H.G.B. Alexander Rsch. Found., 1973—2010. Cons. Battelle Meml. Inst., 1964—71; vis. rsch. prof. U. Calif., Berkeley, 1971, vis. prof., 1997—2007, Am. U., Cairo, 1997, Hebrew U., 1997; trustee Nat. Opinion Rsch. Corp., 1973—80; bd. dirs. Nat. Bur. Econ. Rsch., from 1980; seminar leader NSF-NBER Seminar on Bayesian Inference in Econometrics and Stats., 1970—95. Co-author: Systems Simulation for Regional Analysis, 1969, Estimating the Parameters of the Markov Probability Model, 1970; author: Bayesian Inference in Econometrics, 1971, Basic Issues in Econometrics, 1984, Bayesian Analysis in Econometrics and Statistics: The Zellner View and Papers, 1997, Statistics, Econometrics and Forecasting, 2004; editor: Economic Statistics and Econometrics, 1968, Seasonal Analysis of Economic Time Series, 1978, Simplicity, Inference and Modelling, 2001; assoc. editor: Econometrica, 1962-68; founding co-editor: Jour. Econometrics, 1972—; co-editor Studies in Bayesian Econometrics and Statistics, 1975, The Economics of Marine Resources, 2001, The Structural Econometrics, Time Series Analysis Approach, 2004; founding editor ASA Jour. Bus. and Econ. Stats., 1983; contbr. articles to profl. jours. Pres. Leonard J. Savage Meml. Trust Fund, Chgo., 1977-2000. Fellow AAAS, Am. Acad. Arts and Scis., Am. Econ. Assn., Internat. Inst. Forecasters, Econometric Soc., Am. Statis. Assn. (pres. elect 1990—, pres. 1991—, chmn. bus. and econs. sect. 1980, chmn. Bayesian statis. sci. sect. 1993); mem. Internat. Statis. Inst., Internat. Soc. Bayesian Analysis (co-pres. 1993, pres. 1994-96, Founders award 1998), Soc. Actuaries (trustee, rsch. found., 1994-98). Avocations: golf, tennis, travel, theater, music. Home: Chicago, Ill. Died Aug. 11, 2010.

ZEMPLENYI, TIBOR KAROL, cardiologist, educator; b. Part Lupča, Czechoslovakia, July 16, 1916; came to U.S., 1968, naturalized, 1974; s. David Dezider and Irene (Pollak) Z.; m. Hana Bendová, Aug. 13, 1952; 1 son, Jan. MD, Charles U., Prague, Czechoslovakia, 1946, Docent Habilit., 1966; CSc. (PhD), Czechoslovak Acad. Sci., 1960, DSc., 1964. Clin. asst. with dept medicine Prague Motol Clinic and Charles U., 1946-52; head atherosclerosis rsch. Inst. for Cardiovascular Rsch., Prague, 1952-68; assoc. prof. medicine Charles U., 1966-68, U. So. Calif., LA, 1969-75, prof., 1975-92, prof. emeritus, from 1992. Attending physician L.A. County- U.So. Calif. Med. Ctr. Author: Enzyme Biochemistry of the Arterial Wall, 1968; editl. bd. Atherosclerosis, 1962-75, Cor et Vasa, 1993—; adv. bd. Advances in Lipid Rsch., 1963-66; contbr. articles to numerous profl. jours. WHO fellow for study in Sweden and Gt. Britain, 1959. Fellow Am. Heart Assn., Am. Coll. Cardiology; mem. Western Soc. for Clin. Rsch., Longevity Assn. (mem. sci. bd.), European Atherosclerosis Group, Italian Soc. for Atherosclerosis (hon.). Died Mar. 27, 2010.

ZERMAN, MELVYN BERNARD, retired publishing executive, writer; b. NYC, July 10, 1930; s. Abraham and Ida (Belsky) Zirman; m. Miriam Baron, Jan. 2, 1985 (dec.); children: Andrew, Jared, Lenore. BA, U. Mich., 1952; MA, Columbia U., 1953. With Oxford Book Co., NYC, 1953-55; asst. editor Abelard-Schuman, Pubs., NYC, 1955-57; office mgr., salesman Harper & Row, NYC, 1957-61, sales rep., 1961-69, sales mgr., 1969-79, Random House, Inc., NYC, 1979-83, sales cons., 1983-87; pres., pub. Limelight Edits., NYC, 1983—2004. Mem. exec. com. N.Y. Is Book Country, N.Y.C., 1985-2004. Author: Call the Final Witness, 1977, Beyond a Reasonable Doubt: Inside the American Jury System, 1981 (Freedoms Found. medal 1981), Taking on the Press: Constitutional Rights in Conflict, 1986. Mem.: Phi Beta Kappa. Democrat. Avocations: book collecting, travel. Home: New York, NY. Died Apr. 19, 2010.

ZIEGLER, GREGG, retail executive; b. Elgin, Ill., Mar. 9, 1921; s. Lyle Alvin and Nellie Zell (Gregg) Z.; m. June Marie Anderson; children: Brian Gregg, Mary Lynn Ziegler Schmitendorf. BA in History, Kalamazoo Coll., 1947. Mgr. Lyle A.

Ziegler Hardware Co. dba Ace Hardware, Elgin, 1947-60, sec.-treas., 1960-67, pres., 1967-80, pres., chmn., 1980-85, chmn., from 1985. Vice chmn. Ace Hardware Corp., Oakbrook, Ill., 1985—; bd. dirs. 1st Nat. Bank Elgin; founding dir. The Larkin Bank, Elgin; dir. exec. com. FNW Bancorp Inc., Elgin. Served to capt. USMC, 1942-46, PTO. Mem. Elgin Hist. Soc. Methodist. Home: Elgin, Ill. Died June 22, 2010.

ZIERLER, KENNETH, physiologist, physician, educator; b. Balt., Sept. 5, 1917; s. Joseph and Betsey (Levie) Z.; m. Margery Shapiro, June 8, 1941; children: Peggy Zierler Rosenthal, Linda Zierler Jucovy, Sally, Amy, Michael K. AB, Johns Hopkins U., 1936, postgrad., 1936-37; MD, U. Md., 1941. Intern medicine Sinai Hosp., Balt., 1941-42; asst. resident, resident NYU div. Goldwater Meml. Hosp., NYC, 1942-43; fellow, prof. medicine Johns Hopkins U. Med. Sch., Balt., 1946-72, prof. medicine, 1973—97, prof. physiology, medicine, 1969-72, 73-97, prof. emeritus medicine and physiology, from 1997; assoc. prof. environ. medicine Johns Hopkins Sch. Hygiene and Pub. Health, Balt., 1956-64; asst. physician to physician Johns Hopkins Hosp., Balt., 1946-72, physician-in-charge dept. phys. therapy, 1950-57, chemist-in-charge, 1957-68, physician, from 1973; dir. Inst. for Muscle Disease, NYC, 1972—73. Adj. prof. Rockefeller U., N.Y., 1972-73, Cornell Med. Sch., N.Y., 1972-73; mem. adv. com. on physiology, Office of Naval Rsch., Am. Inst. Biol. Scis., 1964-76, chmn., 1964-72; mem. panel of space biology and medicine Pres.'s Sci. Adv. Com., 1967; cons. task group on tracer kinetics Internat. Commn. on Radiol. Units and Measurements, 1966; mem. cardiovascular B study sect. NIH, 1972-76; co-chmn. rating com. rev. of doctoral programs in biol. scis. N.Y. State Commr. Edn., 1983—. Mem. editl. bd. Johns Hopkins Hosp. bull., 1956-67, Johns Hopkins Med. Jour., 1967-70, Jour. Clin. Investigations, 1959-64, Circulation Rsch., 1962-67, co-editor, 1966, substitute editor, 1968, assoc. editor, 1968-77; mem. editl. com. Ann. Rev. Physiology, 1971-75; assoc. editor Medicine, 1963-72; contbr. over 250 articles to profl. jours.; contbr. chpts. to books. Capt. med. corps U.S. Army, 1943-46, ETO, MTO. Decorated Bronze Star, 3 Battle Stars, Combat Medic Badge; Career scholar Muscular Dystrophy Assn., 1973-91. Mem. Am. Soc. for Clin. Investigations, Assn. Am. Physicians, Endocrine Soc., Am. Diabetes Assn. Home: New Paltz, NY. Died Jan. 18, 2009.

ZILBERBERG, YAKOV MICHAEL, mechanical engineering educator, researcher; b. Odessa, Ukraine, USSR, Oct. 3, 1934; came to U.S., 1977; s. Mikhail Yakovlevich and Polina Davidovna (Belaya) Z.; m. Faina Viner, Dec. 7, 1961; 1 child, Marya. M.S. in Mech. Engring., Technol. Inst., Odessa, 1956, D.Engring., Leningrad, 1970; Ph.D., U. N.H., 1981. Registered profl. engr., Mass., R.I. Chief mechanic, City Cold Store, Odessa, 1956-58; sr. engr. All-Union Rsch. Inst., Odessa, 1958-75; estimator Lutz Engring. Co., Providence, 1977; design/test engr. Megatherm Corp., East Providence, R.I., 1977-78, cons., 1985-87; standard engr. Factory Mut. Rsch. Co., Norwood, Mass., 1979-80; assoc. prof. mech. engring. U. Lowell, Mass., 1980—; cons. Army R&D Ctr., Natick, Mass., 1989—; rsch. fellow Naval Rsch. and Devel. Ctr., Annapolis, Md., 1983; Contbr. articles to profl. jours. Victory fund sponsor Nat. Rep. Congl. Com., Washington, 1984, sustaining mem., 1985, 86, 87. Recipient bronze medals All Union Exhibition of Nat. Economy Achievements, Moscow, 1960, 65, plaque and cert. Naval Rsch. and Devel. Ctr., 1983, cert. of recognition Nat. Rep. Congl. Com., 1984. Mem. ASME, ASHRAE (cert. of recognition 1985, cert. of appreciation 1986), Am. Soc. Engring. Edn., Sigma Xi, Pi Tau Sigma. Jewish. Avocations: playwriting, classical music and literature, soccer, figure skating. Home: Chelmsford, Mass. Died July 24, 2010.

ZIMMERMAN, BEVERLY MAY MCKAY, nursing educator; b. Rochester, N.Y., Mar. 2, 1939; d. James Kenneth and Gertrude Florence (Ritchie) McKay; m. Abraham Abba Zimmerman, Oct. 5, 1968; children— Lisa Marie, Sarah Ritchie. Cert. Pediatric Nurse, Rutgers U., 1975; cert. in Family Therapy, N.J. Ctr. Family Studies, 1983; B.S., Cornell U., 1963; M.Ed., Columbia, 1968, Ed.D., 1980. Instr. N.Y. Hosp., White Plains, 1964-66, Cornell U., N.Y.C., 1968-69; asst. prof. Seton Hall U., South Orange, N.J., 1976-81; assoc. prof. nursing, Fairleigh Dickinson U., Rutherford, N.J., 1981—, assoc. dean Maxwell Becton Coll. Liberal Arts, 1985—. Bd. dirs., treas. New Providence LWV, New Providence, N.J., 1970-76; bd. dirs., pres. Jefferson Sch. PTA, Summit N.J., 1976-81. Computer grantee Fairleigh Dickinson U., 1983, 1984. Mem. Am. Nurses Assn., N.J. State Nurses Assn., Am. Orthopsychiat. Assn., N.J. Soc. Cert. Clin. Specialists Psychiat. Mental Health Nursing. Democrat. Presbyterian. Home: Warren, NJ. Died Jan. 2, 2009.

ZIMMERMAN, WILLIAM JULES, underwriter; b. Phila., Nov. 2, 1924; s. Harry D. and Mathilda T. (Schaeffer) Z.; m. Gloria Clamper, Feb. 26, 1950 (div. Sept. 1977); children— Cynthia Perle, Robin Merle; m. Bette Mae Spielman, Nov. 19, 1977. B.S. in Journalism, Temple U., 1949. C.L.U.; registered health underwriter. With Physicians Drug & Supply Co., Phila., 1949-53; sales rep. John Hancock Life Ins. Co., Phila., 1953-55; sr. sales rep. Paul Revere Cos., Cherry Hill, N.J., 1955—. Author articles in field. Ward leader Republican party, 1964-74. Served with U.S. Army, 1942-45, ETO. Mem. Nat. Assn. Health Underwriters, South Jersey C.L.U. Soc., 999th Signal Service Co. Vets. Assn. (sec. 1965—). Republican. Lodges: Masons (membership chair 1960s), Shriners. Avocations: cryptology; linguistics; languages. Home: Cheltenham, Pa. Died Jan. 1, 2010.

ZINN, HOWARD, historian, educator, playwright; b. NYC, Aug. 24, 1922; s. Edward and Jennie (Rabinowitz) Z.; m. Roslyn Shechter, Oct. 30, 1944 (dec. 2008); children: Myla, Jeff. BA, NYU, 1951; MA, Columbia U., 1952, PhD, 1958. Instr. history, polit. sci. Upsala Coll., 1953-56; lectr. history Bklyn. Coll., 1955-56; chmn. dept. history, social sci., prof. Spelman Coll., Atlanta, 1956-63; fellow Harvard U. Center for East Asian Studies, 1960-61; dir. Non-Western Studies Program Atlanta U. Center, 1961-62; assoc. prof. govt. Boston U., 1964-66, prof. govt., 1966-88, prof. emeritus, 1988—2010. Vis. prof. U. Paris, 1974, 78, 84. Author: LaGuardia in Congress, 1959, SNCC: The New Abolitionists, 1964, The Southern Mystique, 1964, New Deal Thought, 1966, Vietnam: The Logic of Withdrawal, 1967, Disobedience and Democracy: None Fallacies on Law and Order, 1968, The Politics of History, 1970, Post-War America, 1973, Justice in Everyday Life, 1974, A People's History of the United States, 1980, Declarations of Independence: Cross Examining American Ideology, 1990, Failure to Quit: Reflections of an Optimistic Historian, 1993, You Can't Be Neutral on a Moving Train: A Personal History of Our Times, 1994, The Zinn Reader, 1997, Howard Zinn On War, 2001, Howard Zinn On History, 2001, Terrorism and War, 2002, Artists in Times of War and Other Essays, 2003; co-author (with Anthony Arnove) Voices of A People's History of the United States, 2004, (with Mike Konopacki & Paul Buhle) A People's History of American Empire, 2008; (plays) Emma, 1976, Daughter of Venus, 1985, Marx in Soho, 1999; exec. prodr., narrator (documentaries) The People Speak, 2009 Served to 2d lt. USAAF, 1943-45. Decorated Air medal; recipient Albert J. Beveridge prize Am. Hist. Assn., 1958, Thomas Merton award Thomas Merton Ctr., 1991, Olive Br. award Pitts. Writers and Pubs. Alliance for Nuclear Disarmament, 1991, NYU Martin Luther King Jr. Humanitarian award, 2010 Mem. Dramatists Guild, AAUP. Home: Newton, Mass. Died Jan. 27, 2010.

ZINS, WILLIAM ELMER, aerospace consultant; b. Cin., Nov. 29, 1912; s. Matthew and Carolyn (Naegele) Z.; m. Phyllis Marguerite Pengelly, June 29, 1940; children— Jack Robert, Margot Lee, Becky Joy. B.Aerospace Engring., U. Cin., 1937; M.Aerospace Engring., NYU, 1944. Design engr. Consolidated Aircraft, San Diego, 1938-39; commd. 2d lt. U.S. Air Force, 1939, advanced through grades to lt. col., 1951; rated command pilot, 1939-59, ret., 1959; dir. customer service Kaman Aerospace Corp., Bloomfield, Conn., 1959-74; aerospace cons., 1974—. Co-holder world helicopter record for distance in straight line, 1946. Decorated Army Commendation medal. U.S. del. Fedn. Aero. Internat., Nat. Aero. Assn., Washington, 1961-74. Mem. Twirly Birds (founder, pres. 1960-64), Air Force Assn., Am. Helicopter Soc., Assn. U.S. Army. Republican. Presbyterian. Club: Mil. Officers. Home: Enfield, Conn. Died Oct. 27, 2009.

ZODHIATES, SPIROS GEORGE, association executive; b. Cyprus, Mar. 13, 1922; came to U.S., 1946, naturalized, 1949; s. George and Mary (Toumazou) Z.; m. Joan Carol Wassel, Jan. 10, 1948; children: Priscilla Zodhiates Barnes, Lois Zodhiates Jenks, Philip, Mary. Student, Am. U., Cairo, 1941-45; B.Th., Shelton Coll., 1947; MA, N.Y. U., 1951; Th.D., Luther Rice Sem., 1978. Ordained to ministry Gen. Assn. Regular Baptist Chs., 1947; gen. sec., now pres. Am. Mission to Greeks (name changed to AMG Internat. 1974), Chattanooga, N.J., from 1946, pres., from 1965. Author: numerous Bible-study books and booklets including Behavior of Belief, 1959, the Pursuit of Happiness, 1966, To Love is to Live, 1967, Getting the Most Out of Life, 1976, Life After Death, 1977, Hebrew Greek Key Study Bible, 1984, Complete Word Study New Testament, 1991 (Gold Medallion 1993), Complete Word Study Dictionary: New Testament, 1992, Complete Word Study Old Testament, 1994; editor in chief: (Greek) Voice of the Gospel, 1946, Pulpit and Bible Study Helps, 1975—; spkr. New Testament Light radio program. Recipient Gold Cross Greek Red Cross, 1951; decorated Order Brit. Empire Home: Chattanooga, Tenn. Died Oct. 10, 2009.

ZOUARY, MAURICE H., film and television producer; b. July 17, 1921; s. Ellie Louis and Marie Louise Zouary; m. Edith Bruckner, Feb. 3, 1959. Student, N.Y. Sch. Indsl. Art & Design, 1937-39. Gen. asst. Randforce Amusement Theatre, NYC, 1936-39, Translux Theatre Cir., NYC, 1940-42; arts and media Buchanan Advt., NYC, 1944-47; designer Egmont Arens Indsl. Design, NYC, 1947-49; prodr. TV programs for various TV shows NY and Hollywood, Calif., 1949-51; writer of film commls. Grey Advt. Agy., NYC, 1951-54; founder Filmvideo Releasing Corp., NYC, 1957, prodr., from 1957; cons. NBC and CBS, from 1960; pres. TV Nat. Releasing Corp., from 1976; program cons., mng. dir. Movietronics Corp. America, from 2000. Exec. v.p. Movietronics Corp. Am., Inc.; lectr. on history of motion picture sound to various colls., 1968—. Prodr.: (semi-documentary film) Martin Luther*Rebel Priest; author: Kids Eye Views of the News; author, writer, prodr. (documentary) Destruction of a Genius; author: Stories for the Young and Older, DeForest: Father of the Electronic Revolution, The Legend of Marie from Brooklyn; co-author: First Sound of Movies; contbr. articles on pioneering of DeForest's synchronized sound on film, on history of entertainment as relates to communication media; subject of books including The Silent Clowns (Walker Kerr), The Birth of the Talkies (Geduld), Reminiscing with Sissle and Blake (Robert Kimball), The Fleischer Story (Leslie Cabarga). With USNR, 1942-43, C.E., U.S. Army, 1942-44. Named to Hon. Order of Ky. Cols. Fellow Radio Club Am. (life, Lee DeForest award); mem. NATAS, Internat. Radio and TV Soc., Nat. Assn. TV Program Execs., The DeForest Pioneers (award 1976), The Motion Picture Pioneers, Nat. Soc. of Scribes (named Master Calligraphic Artist), Art Students League of N.Y. (life). Republican. Home: Brooklyn, NY. Died June 7, 2010.

ZOWSKI, THADDEUS, mech. engr. b. Ann Arbor, Mich., Mar. 19, 1914; s. Stanislaw Jan and Felicia (Kruszka) Z.; m. Eloise Rhodes Clay, Jan. 15, 1944. BS in Mech. Engring, Poly. Inst., Warsaw, Poland, 1939; MS in Mech. Engring, U. Mich., 1941. Diplomate: Registered profl. engr., Pa., Wash. Mech. engr. S. Morgan Smith Co., York, Pa., 1941-47; with Harza Engring. Co., Chgo., from 1947, chief mech. engr., 1950-79, asso., 1957-68, v.p., mem. sr. profl. staff, from 1968, prin. mech. engr., from 1979. Co-author: Davis' Handbook of Applied Hydraulics, 1969; contbr. articles to tech. mags. and profl. jours. Fellow ASME (life); mem. ASCE, Nat. Soc. Profl. Engrs., Ill. Soc. Profl. Engrs., Iota Alpha. Republican. Home: Wilmette, Ill. Died Apr. 16, 2009.

ZUKOSKI, CHARLES FREDERICK, surgeon, educator; b. St. Louis, Jan. 26, 1926; s. Charles F. Jr. and Bernadine (Edom) Z.; m. Elizabeth Paull Jacob, May 9, 1953; children: Helen, Charles, Robin, Ann. BS, U. N.C., 1947; MD, Harvard U., 1951. Diplomate Am. Bd. Surgery. Intern Roosevelt Hosp., NYC, 1951-52; resident Univ. Hosp., Birmingham, Ala., 1955-58; asst. chief VA Hosp., Birmingham, 1958-59; rschr. Med. Coll. Va., Richmond, 1959-61; asst. prof. Vanderbilt U. Med. Ctr., Nashville, 1961-68; assoc. prof. Coll. Medicine U. N.C., Chapel Hill, 1968-69; prof. surgery Coll. Medicine U. Ariz., Tucson, 1969-95, prof. emeritus dept. surgery Coll. Medicine, from 1995; chief surg. svc. VA Hosp., Tucson, 1990-95. Contbr. 85 articles to profl. publs. Capt. USAF, 1953-55. Fellow NIH, 1959-61, 66-67, Josia Macy Found., 1976-77. Fellow ACS, Am. Surg. Assn.; mem. Soc. Univ. Surgeons, So. Surg. Assn. Achievements include research on immunosuppressive drugs. Home: Tucson, Ariz. Died Aug. 24, 2009.

ZUSPAN, FREDERICK PAUL, obstetrician, gynecologist, educator; b. Richwood, Ohio, Jan. 20, 1922; s. Irl Goff and Kathryn (Speyer) Z.; m. Mary Jane Cox, Nov. 23, 1943; children: Mark Frederick, Kathryn Jane, Bethany Anne. BA, Ohio State U., 1947, MD, 1951. Intern Univ. Hosps., Columbus, Ohio, 1951-52, resident, 1952-54, Western Res. U., Cleve., 1954-56, Oblebay fellow, 1958-60, asst. prof., 1958-60; chmn. dept. ob-gyn. McDowell (Ky.) Meml. Hosp., 1956-58, chief clin. svcs., 1957-58; prof., chmn. dept. ob-gyn. Med. Coll. Ga., Augusta, 1960-66; Joseph Boliver DeLee prof. ob-gyn., chmn. dept. U. Chgo., 1966-75; obstetrician, gynecologist in chief Chgo. Lying-In Hosp., 1966-75; prof., chmn. dept. ob-gyn. Ohio State U., Columbus, 1975-87, R.L. Meiling prof. ob-gyn. Sch. Medicine, 1984-90, prof. emeritus, from 1991. Founding editor Lying In, Jour. Reproductive Medicine; editor-in-chief emeritus Am. Jour. Ob-Gyn. Ob-Gyn. Reports, (with Lindheimer and Katz) Hypertension in Pregnancy, 1976, Current Developments in Perinatology, 1977, (with Quilligan) Operative Obstetrics, 1981, 89, Manual of Practical Obstetrics, 1981, 90, 2000, Clin. and Exptl. Hypertension in Pregnancy, 1979-86; editor: (with Christian) Controversies in Obstetrics and Gynecology, (with Rayburn) Drug Therapy in Ob-Gyn., 1981, 3rd edit., 1992; contbr. articles to med. jours., chpts. to books. Pres. Barren Found., 1974-76. With USNR, 1942-43; 1st lt. USMCR, 1943-45. Decorated DFC, Air medal wth 10 oak leaf clusters. Mem.: Perinatal Rsch. Soc., Soc. Perinatal Obstetrics, Am. Gynecology and Obstetrics Soc. (pres. 1986—87), Internat. Soc. Study of Hypertension in Pregnancy (pres. 1981—83), Soc. Gynecol. Investigation (Pres.'s award 2001), Am. Soc. Clin. Exptl. Hypnosis (exec. sec. 1968, v.p. 1970), Ctrl. Assn. Ob-Gyn. (Cert. of Merit, Rsch. prize 1970), South Atlantic Assn. Ob-Gyn. (Found. prize for rsch. 1962), Assn. Profs. Gynecology and Obstetrics, Am. Coll. Ob-Gyn., Am. Acad. Reproductive Medicine (pres.), Columbus Ob-Gyn. Soc. (pres. 1984—85), Chgo. Gynecol. Soc., Am. Assn. Ob-Gyn., Soc. Gynecol. Investigation, Alpha Omega Alpha, Sigma Xi, Alpha Kappa Kappa. Died June 7, 2009.